CODE OF FEDERAL REGULATIONS

Title 10
Energy

Parts 1 to 50

Revised as of January 1, 2018

Containing a codification of documents
of general applicability and future effect

As of January 1, 2018

Published by the Office of the Federal Register
National Archives and Records Administration
as a Special Edition of the Federal Register

Table of Contents

Cite this Code: CFR

To cite the regulations in this volume use title, part and section number. Thus, 10 CFR 1.1 *refers to title 10, part 1, section 1.*

Explanation

The Code of Federal Regulations is a codification of the general and permanent rules published in the Federal Register by the Executive departments and agencies of the Federal Government. The Code is divided into 50 titles which represent broad areas subject to Federal regulation. Each title is divided into chapters which usually bear the name of the issuing agency. Each chapter is further subdivided into parts covering specific regulatory areas.

Each volume of the Code is revised at least once each calendar year and issued on a quarterly basis approximately as follows:

Title 1 through Title 16 .... as of January 1
Title 17 through Title 27 .... as of April 1
Title 28 through Title 41 .... as of July 1
Title 42 through Title 50 .... as of October 1

The appropriate revision date is printed on the cover of each volume.

LEGAL STATUS

The contents of the Federal Register are required to be judicially noticed (44 U.S.C. 1507). The Code of Federal Regulations is prima facie evidence of the text of the original documents (44 U.S.C. 1510).

HOW TO USE THE CODE OF FEDERAL REGULATIONS

The Code of Federal Regulations is kept up to date by the individual issues of the Federal Register. These two publications must be used together to determine the latest version of any given rule.

To determine whether a Code volume has been amended since its revision date (in this case, January 1, 2018), consult the "List of CFR Sections Affected (LSA)," which is issued monthly, and the "Cumulative List of Parts Affected," which appears in the Reader Aids section of the daily Federal Register. These two lists will identify the Federal Register page number of the latest amendment of any given rule.

EFFECTIVE AND EXPIRATION DATES

Each volume of the Code contains amendments published in the Federal Register since the last revision of that volume of the Code. Source citations for the regulations are referred to by volume number and page number of the Federal Register and date of publication. Publication dates and effective dates are usually not the same and care must be exercised by the user in determining the actual effective date. In instances where the effective date is beyond the cut-off date for the Code a note has been inserted to reflect the future effective date. In those instances where a regulation published in the Federal Register states a date certain for expiration, an appropriate note will be inserted following the text.

OMB CONTROL NUMBERS

The Paperwork Reduction Act of 1980 (Pub. L. 96–511) requires Federal agencies to display an OMB control number with their information collection request.

Many agencies have begun publishing numerous OMB control numbers as amendments to existing regulations in the CFR. These OMB numbers are placed as close as possible to the applicable recordkeeping or reporting requirements.

PAST PROVISIONS OF THE CODE

Provisions of the Code that are no longer in force and effect as of the revision date stated on the cover of each volume are not carried. Code users may find the text of provisions in effect on any given date in the past by using the appropriate List of CFR Sections Affected (LSA). For the convenience of the reader, a "List of CFR Sections Affected" is published at the end of each CFR volume. For changes to the Code prior to the LSA listings at the end of the volume, consult previous annual editions of the LSA. For changes to the Code prior to 2001, consult the List of CFR Sections Affected compilations, published for 1949-1963, 1964-1972, 1973-1985, and 1986-2000.

"[RESERVED]" TERMINOLOGY

The term "[Reserved]" is used as a place holder within the Code of Federal Regulations. An agency may add regulatory information at a "[Reserved]" location at any time. Occasionally "[Reserved]" is used editorially to indicate that a portion of the CFR was left vacant and not accidentally dropped due to a printing or computer error.

INCORPORATION BY REFERENCE

What is incorporation by reference? Incorporation by reference was established by statute and allows Federal agencies to meet the requirement to publish regulations in the Federal Register by referring to materials already published elsewhere. For an incorporation to be valid, the Director of the Federal Register must approve it. The legal effect of incorporation by reference is that the material is treated as if it were published in full in the Federal Register (5 U.S.C. 552(a)). This material, like any other properly issued regulation, has the force of law.

What is a proper incorporation by reference? The Director of the Federal Register will approve an incorporation by reference only when the requirements of 1 CFR part 51 are met. Some of the elements on which approval is based are:

(a) The incorporation will substantially reduce the volume of material published in the Federal Register.

(b) The matter incorporated is in fact available to the extent necessary to afford fairness and uniformity in the administrative process.

(c) The incorporating document is drafted and submitted for publication in accordance with 1 CFR part 51.

What if the material incorporated by reference cannot be found? If you have any problem locating or obtaining a copy of material listed as an approved incorporation by reference, please contact the agency that issued the regulation containing that incorporation. If, after contacting the agency, you find the material is not available, please notify the Director of the Federal Register, National Archives and Records Administration, 8601 Adelphi Road, College Park, MD 20740-6001, or call 202-741-6010.

CFR INDEXES AND TABULAR GUIDES

A subject index to the Code of Federal Regulations is contained in a separate volume, revised annually as of January 1, entitled CFR INDEX AND FINDING AIDS. This volume contains the Parallel Table of Authorities and Rules. A list of CFR titles, chapters, subchapters, and parts and an alphabetical list of agencies publishing in the CFR are also included in this volume.

An index to the text of "Title 3—The President" is carried within that volume.

The Federal Register Index is issued monthly in cumulative form. This index is based on a consolidation of the "Contents" entries in the daily Federal Register.

A List of CFR Sections Affected (LSA) is published monthly, keyed to the revision dates of the 50 CFR titles.

REPUBLICATION OF MATERIAL

There are no restrictions on the republication of material appearing in the Code of Federal Regulations.

INQUIRIES

For a legal interpretation or explanation of any regulation in this volume, contact the issuing agency. The issuing agency's name appears at the top of odd-numbered pages.

For inquiries concerning CFR reference assistance, call 202–741–6000 or write to the Director, Office of the Federal Register, National Archives and Records Administration, 8601 Adelphi Road, College Park, MD 20740-6001 or e-mail *fedreg.info@nara.gov.*

SALES

The Government Publishing Office (GPO) processes all sales and distribution of the CFR. For payment by credit card, call toll-free, 866-512-1800, or DC area, 202-512-1800, M-F 8 a.m. to 4 p.m. e.s.t. or fax your order to 202-512-2104, 24 hours a day. For payment by check, write to: US Government Publishing Office – New Orders, P.O. Box 979050, St. Louis, MO 63197-9000.

ELECTRONIC SERVICES

The full text of the Code of Federal Regulations, the LSA (List of CFR Sections Affected), The United States Government Manual, the Federal Register, Public Laws, Public Papers of the Presidents of the United States, Compilation of Presidential Documents and the Privacy Act Compilation are available in electronic format via *www.ofr.gov.* For more information, contact the GPO Customer Contact Center, U.S. Government Publishing Office. Phone 202-512-1800, or 866-512-1800 (toll-free). E-mail, *ContactCenter@gpo.gov.*

The Office of the Federal Register also offers a free service on the National Archives and Records Administration's (NARA) World Wide Web site for public law numbers, Federal Register finding aids, and related information. Connect to NARA's web site at *www.archives.gov/federal-register.*

The e-CFR is a regularly updated, unofficial editorial compilation of CFR material and Federal Register amendments, produced by the Office of the Federal Register and the Government Publishing Office. It is available at *www.ecfr.gov.*

OLIVER A. POTTS,
Director,
Office of the Federal Register
January 1, 2018

THIS TITLE

Title 10—ENERGY is composed of four volumes. The parts in these volumes are arranged in the following order: parts 1–50, 51–199, 200–499 and part 500–end. The first and second volumes containing parts 1–199 are comprised of chapter I—Nuclear Regulatory Commission. The third and fourth volumes containing part 200–end are comprised of chapters II, III and X—Department of Energy, chapter XIII—Nuclear Waste Technical Review Board, and chapter XVII—Defense Nuclear Facilities Safety Board. The contents of these volumes represent all current regulations codified under this title of the CFR as of January 1, 2018.

For this volume, Susannah C. Hurley was Chief Editor. The Code of Federal Regulations publication program is under the direction of John Hyrum Martinez, assisted by Stephen J. Frattini.

Title 10—Energy

(This book contains parts 1 to 50)

CHAPTER I—NUCLEAR REGULATORY COMMISSION

EDITORIAL NOTE: Nomenclature changes to chapter I appear at 70 FR 69421, Nov. 16, 2005, and at 72 FR 33386, June 18, 2007.

PART 1—STATEMENT OF ORGANIZATION AND GENERAL INFORMATION

AUTHORITY: Atomic Energy Act of 1954, secs. 23, 25, 29, 161, 191 (42 U.S.C. 2033, 2035, 2039, 2201, 2241); Energy Reorganization Act of 1974, secs. 201, 203, 204, 205, 209 (42 U.S.C. 5841, 5843, 5844, 5845, 5849); Administrative Procedure Act (5 U.S.C. 552, 553); Reorganization Plan No. 1 of 1980, 5 U.S.C. Appendix (Reorganization Plans).

SOURCE: 52 FR 31602, Aug. 21, 1987, unless otherwise noted.

EDITORIAL NOTE: Nomenclature changes to part 1 appear at 78 FR 34247, June 7, 2013.

Subpart A—Introduction

§ 1.1 Creation and authority.

(a) The Nuclear Regulatory Commission was established by the Energy Reorganization Act of 1974, as amended, Pub. L. 93–438, 88 Stat. 1233 (42 U.S.C. 5801 *et seq.*). This Act abolished the Atomic Energy Commission and, by section 201, transferred to the Nuclear Regulatory Commission all the licensing and related regulatory functions assigned to the Atomic Energy Commission by the Atomic Energy Act of 1954, as amended, Pub. L. 83–703, 68 Stat. 919 (42 U.S.C. 2011 *et seq.*). These functions included those of the Atomic Safety and Licensing Board Panel. The Energy Reorganization Act became effective January 19, 1975 (E.O. 11834).

(b) As used in this part:

Commission means the five members of the Nuclear Regulatory Commission or a quorum thereof sitting as a body, as provided by section 201 of the Energy Reorganization Act of 1974, as amended.

NRC means the Nuclear Regulatory Commission, the agency established by title II of the Energy Reorganization Act of 1974, as amended, comprising the members of the Commission and all offices, employees, and representatives authorized to act in any case or matter.

[52 FR 31602, Aug. 21, 1987, as amended at 56 FR 29407, June 27, 1991]

§ 1.3 Sources of additional information.

(a) A statement of the NRC's organization, policies, procedures, assignments of responsibility, and delegations of authority is in the Nuclear Regulatory Commission Management Directives System and other NRC issuances, including local directives issued by Regional Offices. Letters and memoranda containing directives, delegations of authority and the like are also issued from time to time and may not yet be incorporated into the Management Directives System, parts of which are revised as necessary. Copies of the Management Directives System and other delegations of authority are available for public inspection and copying for a fee at the NRC Public Document Room, One White Flint North, 11555 Rockville Pike (first floor), Rockville, Maryland 20852–2738, and at each of NRC's Regional Offices. Information may also be obtained from the Office of Public Affairs or from Public Affairs Officers at the Regional Offices.

(b) Commission meetings are open to the public, as provided by the Government in the Sunshine Act, unless they fall within an exemption to the Act's openness requirement and the Commission also has determined that the public interest requires that those particular meetings be closed. Information concerning Commission meetings may be obtained from the Office of the Secretary.

(c) Information regarding the availability of NRC records under the Freedom of Information Act and Privacy Act of 1974 may be obtained from the Office of the Chief Information Officer. NRC's regulations are published in the FEDERAL REGISTER and codified in Title 10, Chapter 1, of the Code of Federal Regulations. They may be viewed electronically at the NRC Web site, *http://www.nrc.gov/reading-rm/doc-collections/cfr/*. Final opinions made in the adjudication of cases are published in "Nuclear Regulatory Commission Issuances," and are available on a subscription basis from the National Technical Information Service, 5301 Shawnee Road, Alexandria, VA 22312.

[52 FR 31602, Aug. 21, 1987, as amended at 53 FR 43419, Oct. 27, 1988; 53 FR 52993, Dec. 30, 1988; 54 FR 53313, Dec. 28, 1989; 57 FR 1639, Jan. 15, 1992; 63 FR 15740, Apr. 1, 1998; 64 FR 48947, Sept. 9, 1999; 67 FR 67097, Nov. 4, 2002; 70 FR 69421, Nov. 16, 2005; 79 FR 75737, Dec. 19, 2014; 80 FR 45842, Aug. 3, 2015; 80 FR 74977, Dec. 1, 2015]

§ 1.5 Location of principal offices and regional offices.

(a) The principal NRC offices are located in the Washington, DC, area. Facilities for the service of process and documents are maintained in the State of Maryland at 11555 Rockville Pike, Rockville, Maryland 20852–2738. The agency's official mailing address is U.S. Nuclear Regulatory Commission, Washington, DC 20555–0001. The locations of NRC offices in the Washington, DC, area are as follows:

(1) One White Flint North Building, 11555 Rockville Pike, Rockville, Maryland 20852–2738.

(2) Two White Flint North Building, 11545 Rockville Pike, Rockville, Maryland 20852–2738.

(3) Three White Flint North Building, 11601 Landsdown Street, North Bethesda, Maryland 20852.

(b) The addresses of the NRC Regional Offices are as follows:

(1) Region I, U.S. NRC, 2100 Renaissance Boulevard, Suite 100, King of Prussia, PA 19406–2713.

(2) Region II, USNRC, 245 Peachtree Center Avenue, NE., Suite 1200, Atlanta, GA 30303–1257.

(3) Region III, USNRC, 2443 Warrenville Road, Suite 210, Lisle, IL 60532–4352.

(4) Region IV, US NRC, 1600 E. Lamar Blvd., Arlington, TX 76011–4511.

[67 FR 67097, Nov. 4, 2002; 67 FR 70835, Nov. 27, 2002, as amended at 67 FR 77652, Dec. 19, 2002; 68 FR 75389, Dec. 31, 2003; 70 FR 69421, Nov. 16, 2005; 71 FR 15007, Mar. 27, 2006; 72 FR 49148, Aug. 28, 2007; 73 FR 5711, Jan. 31, 2008; 73 FR 30457, May 28, 2008; 75 FR 21980, Apr. 27, 2010; 76 FR 72084, Nov. 22, 2011; 77 FR 39903, July 6, 2012; 79 FR 75757, Dec. 19, 2014]

Subpart B—Headquarters

§ 1.11 The Commission.

(a) The Nuclear Regulatory Commission, composed of five members, one of whom is designated by the President as Chairman, is established pursuant to section 201 of the Energy Reorganization Act of 1974, as amended. The Chairman is the principal executive officer of the Commission, and is responsible for the executive and administrative functions with respect to appointment and supervision of personnel, except as otherwise provided by the Energy Reorganization Act of 1974, as amended, and Reorganization Plan No. 1 of 1980 (45 FR 40561); distribution of business; use and expenditures of funds (except that the function of revising budget estimates and purposes is reserved to the Commission); and appointment, subject to approval of the Commission, of heads of major administrative units under the Commission. The Chairman is the official spokesman, as mandated by the Reorganization Plan No. 1 of 1980. The Chairman has ultimate authority for all NRC functions pertaining to an emergency involving an NRC Licensee. The Chairman's actions are governed by the general policies of the Commission.

(b) The Commission is responsible for licensing and regulating nuclear facilities and materials and for conducting research in support of the licensing and regulatory process, as mandated by the Atomic Energy Act of 1954, as amended; the Energy Reorganization Act of 1974, as amended; and the Nuclear Nonproliferation Act of 1978; and in accordance with the National Environmental Policy Act of 1969, as amended, and other applicable statutes. These responsibilities include protecting public health and safety, protecting the environment, protecting and safeguarding nuclear materials and nuclear power plants in the interest of national security, and assuring conformity with antitrust laws. Agency functions are performed through standards setting and rulemaking; technical reviews and studies; conduct of public hearings; issuance of authorizations, permits, and licenses; inspection, investigation, and enforcement; evaluation of operating experience; and confirmatory research. The Commission is composed of five members, appointed by the President and confirmed by the Senate.

(c) The following staff units and officials report directly to the Commission: Atomic Safety and Licensing Board Panel, Office of the General Counsel, Office of the Secretary, Office of Commission Appellate Adjudication, Office of International Programs, and other committees and boards that are authorized or established specifically by the Act. The Advisory Committee on Reactor Safeguards and the Advisory Committee on Nuclear Waste also report directly to the Commission.

(d) The Offices of Congressional Affairs and Public Affairs report directly to the Chairman.

[52 FR 31602, Aug. 21, 1987, as amended at 57 FR 1639, Jan. 15, 1992; 59 FR 63882, Dec. 12, 1994]

INSPECTOR GENERAL

§ 1.12 Office of the Inspector General.

The Office of the Inspector General—

(a) Develops policies and standards that govern NRC's financial and management audit program;

(b) Plans, directs, and executes the long-range, comprehensive audit program;

(c) Conducts and reports on investigations and inquiries, as necessary, to ascertain and verify the facts with regard to the integrity of all NRC programs and operations;

(d) Investigates possible irregularities or alleged misconduct of NRC employees and contractors;

(e) Refers suspected or alleged criminal violations concerning NRC employees or contractors to the Department of Justice;

(f) Reviews existing and proposed legislation and regulations for their impact on economy and efficiency in the administration of NRC's programs and operations;

(g) Keeps the Commission and the Congress fully and currently informed, by means of semiannual and other reports, about fraud, abuse, and other serious deficiencies in NRC's programs and operations; and

(h) Maintains liaison with audit and inspector general organizations and other law enforcement agencies in regard to all matters relating to the promotion of economy and efficiency and the detection of fraud and abuse in programs and operations.

[54 FR 53313, Dec. 28, 1989]

PANELS, BOARDS, AND COMMITTEES

§ 1.13 Advisory Committee on Reactor Safeguards.

The Advisory Committee on Reactor Safeguards (ACRS) was established by section 29 of the Atomic Energy Act of 1954, as amended. Consisting of a maximum of 15 members, it reviews and reports on safety studies and applications for construction permits and facility operating licenses; advises the Commission with regard to hazards of proposed or existing reactor facilities and the adequacy of proposed reactor safety standards; upon request of the Department of Energy (DOE), reviews and advises with regard to the hazards of DOE nuclear activities and facilities; reviews any generic issues or other matters referred to it by the Commission for advice. The Committee, on its own initiative, may conduct reviews of specific generic matters or nuclear facility safety-related items. The ACRS conducts studies of reactor safety research and submits reports thereon to the U.S. Congress and the NRC as appropriate.

§ 1.15 Atomic Safety and Licensing Board Panel.

The Atomic Safety and Licensing Board Panel, established pursuant to section 191 of the Atomic Energy Act of 1954, as amended, conducts hearings for the Commission and such other regulatory functions as the Commission authorizes. The Panel is comprised of any number of Administrative Judges (full-time and part-time), who may be lawyers, physicists, engineers, and environmental scientists; and Administrative Law Judges, who hear antitrust, civil penalty, and other cases and serve as Atomic Safety and Licensing Board Chairmen. The Chief Administrative Judge develops and applies procedures governing the activities of Boards, Administrative Judges, and Administrative Law Judges and makes appropriate recommendations to the Commission concerning the rules governing the conduct of hearings. The Panel conducts all licensing and other hearings as directed by the Commission primarily through individual Atomic Safety and Licensing Boards composed of one or three Administrative Judges. Those boards are appointed by either the Commission or the Chief Administrative Judge.

§ 1.18 [Reserved]

§ 1.19 Other committees, boards, and panels.

Under section 161a. of the Atomic Energy Act of 1954, as amended, the Commission may establish advisory bodies to make recommendations to it. Currently, four committees are in existence.

(a) The Advisory Committee on Medical Uses of Isotopes (ACMUI) was established by the Atomic Energy Commission in July 1958. The ACMUI, composed of physicians and scientists, considers medical questions referred to it by the NRC staff and renders expert opinions regarding medical uses of radioisotopes. The ACMUI also advises the NRC staff, as requested, on matters of policy regarding licensing of medical uses of radioisotopes.

(b) The Licensing Support Network Advisory Review Panel (LSNARP) was established by the Commission on October 3, 1989, pursuant to 10 CFR 2.1011(e) of the Commission's regulations. The LSNARP provides advice to the Commission on the design, development, and operation of the Licensing Support Network (LSN) an electronic information management system for use in the Commission's high-level radioactive waste (HLW) licensing proceeding. Membership consists of those interests that will be affected by the use of the LSN, and selected Federal agencies with expertise in large-scale electronic information systems. The individual representatives of these interests and agencies possess expertise in management information science and in managing records of the Commission's licensing process for the HLW repository.

[52 FR 31602, Aug. 21, 1987, as amended at 54 FR 53314, Dec. 28, 1989; 68 FR 75389, Dec. 31, 2003; 79 FR 75737, Dec. 19, 2014]

COMMISSION STAFF

§ 1.23 Office of the General Counsel.

The Office of the General Counsel, established pursuant to section 25 of the

Atomic Energy Act of 1954, as amended—

(a) Directs matters of law and legal policy, providing opinions, advice, and assistance to the agency with respect to all of its activities;

(b) Reviews and prepares appropriate draft Commission decisions on public petitions seeking direct Commission action and rulemaking proceedings involving hearings, monitors cases pending before presiding officers and reviews draft Commission decisions on Atomic Safety and Licensing Board decisions and rulings;

(c) Provides interpretation of laws, regulations, and other sources of authority;

(d) Reviews the legal form and content of proposed official actions;

(e) As requested, provides the agency with legal advice and opinions on acquisition matters, including agency procurement contracts; placement of work at Department of Energy national laboratories; interagency agreements to acquire supplies and services; and grants and cooperative agreements. Prepares or concurs in all other interagency agreements, delegations of authority, regulations; orders; licenses; and other legal documents and prepares legal interpretations thereof;

(f) Reviews and directs intellectual property (patent) work;

(g) Represents and protects the interests of the NRC in legal matters and in court proceedings, and in relation to other government agencies, administrative bodies, committees of Congress, foreign governments, and members of the public; and

(h) Represents the NRC staff as a party in NRC administrative hearings.

[52 FR 31602, Aug. 21, 1987, as amended at 56 FR 29407, June 27, 1991; 65 FR 59272, Oct. 4, 2000]

§ 1.24 Office of Commission Appellate Adjudication.

The Office of Commission Appellate Adjudication—

(a) Monitors cases pending before presiding officers;

(b) Provides the Commission with an analysis of any adjudicatory matter requiring a Commission decision (e.g., petitions for review, certified questions, stay requests) including available options;

(c) Drafts any necessary decisions pursuant to the Commission's guidance after presentation of options; and

(d) Consults with the Office of the General Counsel in identifying the options to be presented to the Commission and in drafting the final decision to be presented to the Commission.

[56 FR 29407, June 27, 1991]

§ 1.25 Office of the Secretary of the Commission.

The Office of the Secretary of the Commission—

(a) Provides general management services to support the Commission and to implement Commission decisions; and advises and assists the Commission and staff on the planning, scheduling, and conduct of Commission business including preparation of internal procedures;

(b) Prepares the Commission's meeting agenda;

(c) Manages the Commission Staff Paper and COMSECY systems;

(d) Receives, processes, and controls Commission mail, communications, and correspondence;

(e) Maintains the Commission's official records and acts as Freedom of Information administrative coordinator for Commission records;

(f) Codifies Commission decisions in memoranda directing staff action and monitors compliance;

(g) Receives, processes, and controls motions and pleadings filed with the Commission; issues and serves adjudicatory orders on behalf of the Commission; receives and distributes public comments in rulemaking proceedings; issues proposed and final rules on behalf of the Commission; maintains the official adjudicatory and rulemaking dockets of the Commission; and exercises responsibilities delegated to the Secretary in 10 CFR 2.303 and 2.346;

(h) Administers the NRC Historical Program;

(i) Integrates office automation initiatives into the Commission's administrative system;

(j) Functions as the NRC Federal Advisory Committee Management Officer; and

(k) Provides guidance and direction on the use of the NRC seal and flag.

[52 FR 31602, Aug. 21, 1987, as amended at 63 FR 15741, Apr. 1, 1998; 69 FR 2233, Jan. 14, 2004]

§ 1.26 [Reserved]

§ 1.27 Office of Congressional Affairs.

The Office of Congressional Affairs—

(a) Advises the Chairman, the Commission, and NRC staff on all NRC relations with Congress and the views of Congress toward NRC policies, plans and activities;

(b) Maintains liaison with Congressional committees and members of Congress on matters of interest to NRC;

(c) Serves as primary contact point for all NRC communications with Congress;

(d) Coordinates NRC internal activities with Congress;

(e) Plans, develops, and manages NRC's legislative programs; and

(f) Monitors legislative proposals, bills, and hearings.

[57 FR 1639, Jan. 15, 1992]

§ 1.28 Office of Public Affairs.

The Office of Public Affairs—

(a) Develops policies, programs, and procedures for the Chairman's approval for informing the public of NRC activities;

(b) Prepares, clears, and disseminates information to the public and the news media concerning NRC policies, programs, and activities;

(c) Keeps NRC management informed on media coverage of activities of interest to the agency;

(d) Plans, directs, and coordinates the activities of public information staffs located at Regional Offices;

(e) Conducts a cooperative program with schools; and

(f) Carries out assigned activities in the area of consumer affairs.

[57 FR 1639, Jan. 15, 1992]

§ 1.29 Office of International Programs.

The Office of International Programs—

(a) Advises the Chairman, the Commission, and NRC staff on international issues;

(b) Recommends policies concerning nuclear exports and imports, international safeguards, international physical security, nonproliferation matters, and international cooperation and assistance in nuclear safety and radiation protection;

(c) Plans, develops, and manages international nuclear safety information exchange programs and coordinates international research agreements;

(d) Obtains, evaluates, and uses pertinent information from other NRC and U.S. Government offices in processing nuclear export and import license applications;

(e) Establishes and maintains working relationships with individual countries and international nuclear organizations, as well as other involved U.S. Government agencies; and

(f) Assures that all international activities carried out by the Commission and staff are well coordinated internally and Government-wide and are consistent with NRC and U.S. policies.

[57 FR 1639, Jan. 15, 1992]

Chief Financial Officer

§ 1.31 Office of the Chief Financial Officer.

The Office of the Chief Financial Officer—

(a) Oversees all financial management activities relating to NRC's programs and operations and provides advice to the Chairman on financial management matters;

(b) Develops and transmits the NRC's budget estimates to the Office of Management and Budget (OMB) and Congress;

(c) Establishes financial management policy including accounting principles and standards for the agency and provides policy guidance to senior managers on the budget and all other financial management activities;

(d) Provides an agencywide management control program for financial and program managers that establishes internal control processes and provides for timely corrective actions regarding material weaknesses that are disclosed to comply with the Federal Manager's Financial Integrity Act of 1982;

(e) Develops and manages an agencywide planning, budgeting, and performance management process;

(f) Develops and maintains an integrated agency accounting and financial management system, including an accounting system, and financial reporting and internal controls;

(g) Directs, manages, and provides policy guidance and oversight of agency financial management personnel activities and operations;

(h) Prepares and transmits an annual financial management report to the Chairman and the Director, Office of Management and Budget, including an audited financial statement;

(i) Monitors the financial execution of NRC's budget in relation to actual expenditures, controls the use of NRC funds to ensure that they are expended in accordance with applicable laws and financial management principles, and prepares and submits to the Chairman timely cost and performance reports;

(j) Establishes, maintains, and oversees the implementation of license fee polices and regulations; and

(k) Reviews, on a periodic basis, fees and other charges imposed by NRC for services provided and makes recommendations for revising those charges, as appropriate.

[63 FR 15741, Apr. 1, 1998]

EXECUTIVE DIRECTOR FOR OPERATIONS

§ 1.32 Office of the Executive Director for Operations.

(a) The Executive Director for Operations (EDO) reports for all matters to the Chairman, and is subject to the supervision and direction of the Chairman as provided in Reorganization Plan No. 1 of 1980.

(b) The EDO supervises and coordinates policy development and operational activities in the following offices: The Office of Nuclear Reactor Regulation, the Office of New Reactors, the Office of Nuclear Material Safety and Safeguards, the Office of Nuclear Regulatory Research, the Office of Nuclear Security and Incident Response, and the NRC Regional Offices; and the following staff offices: The Office of Enforcement, the Office of Administration, the Office of the Chief Information Officer, the Office of Investigations, the Office of Small Business and Civil Rights, the Office of the Chief Human Capital Officer, and other organizational units as shall be assigned by the Commission. The EDO is also responsible for implementing the Commission's policy directives pertaining to these offices.

(c) The EDO exercises powers and functions delegated to the EDO under the Reorganization Plan No. 1 of 1980, this chapter, or otherwise by the Commission or Chairman, as appropriate. The EDO has the authority to perform any function that may be performed by an office director reporting to the EDO.

[54 FR 53314, Dec. 28, 1989, as amended at 59 FR 63882, Dec. 12, 1994. Redesignated and amended at 63 FR 15741, Apr. 1, 1998; 67 FR 3585, Jan. 25, 2002; 70 FR 69421, Nov. 16, 2005; 73 FR 5711, Jan. 31, 2008; 78 FR 34247, June 7, 2013; 79 FR 75737, Dec. 19, 2014; 80 FR 74978, Dec. 1, 2015]

STAFF OFFICES

§ 1.33 Office of Enforcement.

The Office of Enforcement—

(a) Develops policies and programs for enforcement of NRC requirements;

(b) Manages major enforcement action;

(c) Assesses the effectiveness and uniformity of Regional enforcement actions; and

(d) Manages the NRC allegation program.

[70 FR 69422, Nov. 16, 2005]

§ 1.34 Office of Administration.

The Office of Administration—

(a) Develops and implements agencywide contracting policies and procedures;

(b) Develops policies and procedures and manages the operation and maintenance of NRC offices, facilities, and equipment;

(c) Plans, develops, establishes, and administers policies, standards, and procedures for the overall NRC security program; and

(d) Develops and implements policies and procedures for the review and publication of NRC rulemakings, and ensures compliance with the Regulatory Flexibility Act and the Congressional

Review Act, manages the NRC Management Directives Program, and provides translation services.

[63 FR 15741, Apr. 1, 1998, as amended at 70 FR 69422, Nov. 16, 2005]

§ 1.35 Office of the Chief Information Officer.

The Office of the Chief Information Officer—

(a) Plans, directs, and oversees the NRC's information resources, including technology infrastructure and delivery of information management services, to meet the mission and goals of the agency;

(b) Provides principal advice to the Chairman to ensure that information technology (IT) is acquired and information resources across the agency are managed in a manner consistent with Federal information resources management (IRM) laws and regulations;

(c) Assists senior management in recognizing where information technology can add value while improving NRC operations and service delivery;

(d) Directs the implementation of a sound and integrated IT architecture to achieve NRC's strategic and IRM goals;

(e) Monitors and evaluates the performance of information technology and information management programs based on applicable performance measures and assesses the adequacy of IRM skills of the agency;

(f) Provides guidance and oversight for the selection, control and evaluation of information technology investments;

(g) Provides oversight and quality assurance for the design and operation of the Licensing Support Network (LSN) services and for the completeness and integrity of the LSN database, ensures that the LSN meets the requirements of 10 CFR part 2, subpart J, concerning the use of the LSN in the Commission's high-level waste licensing proceedings, and provides technical oversight of DOE in the design, development, and operation of the LSN; and

(h) Plans, recommends, and oversees the NRC's Information Technology (IT) Security Program consistent with applicable laws, regulations, management initiatives, and policies;

(i) Provides principal advice to the NRC on the infrastructure, as well as the programmatic and administrative aspects of cybersecurity;

(j) Establishes NRC-wide cybersecurity guidelines;

(k) Guides security process maturity, as well as formulating and overseeing the cybersecurity program budget; and

(l) Ensures NRC-wide integration, direction, and coordination of IT security planning and performance within the framework of the NRC IT Security Program.

[70 FR 69422, Nov. 16, 2005, as amended at 80 FR 74978, Dec. 1, 2015]

§ 1.36 Office of Investigations.

The Office of Investigations (OI)—

(a) Conducts investigations of licensees, applicants, their contractors or vendors, including the investigation of all allegations of wrongdoing by other than NRC employees and contractors;

(b) Maintains current awareness of inquiries and inspections by other NRC offices to identify the need for formal investigations;

(c) Makes appropriate referrals to the Department of Justice;

(d) Maintains liaison with other agencies and organizations to ensure the timely exchange of information of mutual interest; and

(e) Issues subpoenas where necessary or appropriate for the conduct of investigations.

[54 FR 53315, Dec. 28, 1989]

§ 1.37 Office of Small Business and Civil Rights.

The Office of Small Business and Civil Rights—

(a) Develops and implements an effective small and disadvantaged business program in accordance with the Small Business Act, as amended, and plans and implements NRC policies and programs relating to equal employment oppportunity and civil rights matters as required by the Equal Employment Opportunity Commission (EEOC) and the Office of Personnel Management (OPM);

(b) Ensures that appropriate consideration is given to Labor Surplus Area firms and Women Business Enterprises, and conducts an outreach program aimed at contractors desiring to do business with NRC;

(c) Maintains liaison with other Government agencies and trade associations;

(d) Coordinates efforts with the Director, Division of Contracts, and Directors of other affected offices;

(e) Develops and recommends for approval by the Executive Director for Operations, NRC policy providing for equal employment opportunity in all aspects of Federal personnel practice;

(f) Develops, monitors, and evaluates the agency's equal employment opportunity efforts and affirmative action programs to ensure compliance with NRC policy;

(g) Serves as the principal contact with local and national public and private organizations to facilitate the NRC equal opportunity program; and

(h) Coordinates all efforts pertaining to small and disadvantaged business utilization and equal employment opportunity with Office Directors and Regional Administrators.

[52 FR 31602, Aug. 21, 1987, as amended at 59 FR 63882, Dec. 12, 1994]

§ 1.38 [Reserved]

§ 1.39 Office of the Chief Human Capital Officer.

The Office of the Chief Human Capital Officer—

(a) Plans and implements NRC policies, programs, and services to provide for the effective organization, utilization, and development of the agency's human resources;

(b) Provides labor relations and personnel policy guidance and supporting services to NRC managers and employees;

(c) Provides training, benefits administration, and counseling services for NRC employees;

(d) Collects, analyzes, and provides data on the characteristics, allocation, utilization, and retention of NRC's workforce;

(e) Provides staffing advice and services to NRC managers and employees; and

(f) Provides executive resources management and organizational and managerial development services to the NRC.

[52 FR 31602, Aug. 21, 1987, as amended at 63 FR 15742, Apr. 1, 1998; 78 FR 34247, June 7, 2013]

§§ 1.40–1.41 [Reserved]

PROGRAM OFFICES

§ 1.42 Office of Nuclear Material Safety and Safeguards.

(a) The Office of Nuclear Material Safety and Safeguards (NMSS) is responsible for regulating activities that provide for the safe and secure production of nuclear fuel used in commercial nuclear reactors; the safe storage, transportation, and disposal of low-level and high-level radioactive waste and spent nuclear fuel; the transportation of radioactive materials regulated under the Atomic Energy Act of 1954, as amended (the Act); and all other medical, industrial, academic, and commercial uses of radioactive isotopes. The NMSS ensures safety and security by implementing a regulatory program involving activities including licensing, inspection, assessment of environmental impacts for all nuclear material facilities and activities, assessment of licensee performance, events analysis, enforcement, and identification and resolution of generic issues. The NMSS is also responsible for developing all new regulations and amending existing regulations for all nuclear material facilities and activities regulated by NMSS.

(b) The Office of Nuclear Material Safety and Safeguards—

(1) Develops and implements NRC policy for the regulation of: Uranium recovery, conversion, and enrichment; fuel fabrication and development; transportation of nuclear materials, including certification of transport containers and reactor spent fuel storage; safe management and disposal of spent fuel and low-level and high-level radioactive waste; and medical, industrial, academic, and commercial uses of radioactive isotopes;

(2) Has lead responsibility within NRC for domestic and international safeguards policy and regulation for fuel cycle facilities, including material control and accountability;

(3) Plans and directs NRC's program of cooperation and liaison with States, local governments, interstate and Indian Tribe organizations; and coordinates liaison with other Federal agencies;

(4) Participates in formulation of policies involving NRC/State cooperation and liaison;

(5) Develops and directs administrative and contractual programs for coordinating and integrating Federal and State regulatory activities;

(6) Maintains liaison between NRC and State, interstate, regional, Tribal, and quasi-governmental organizations on regulatory matters;

(7) Promotes NRC visibility and performs general liaison with other Federal agencies, and keeps NRC management informed of significant developments at other Federal agencies that affect the NRC;

(8) Monitors nuclear-related State legislative activities;

(9) Directs regulatory activities of State Liaison and State Agreement Officers located in Regional Offices;

(10) Participates in policy matters on State Public Utility Commissions (PUCs);

(11) Administers the State Agreements program in a partnership arrangement with the States;

(12) Develops staff policy and procedures and implements State Agreements program under the provisions of Section 274b of the Act;

(13) Provides oversight of the program for reviews of Agreement State programs to determine their adequacy and compatibility as required by Section 274j of the Act and other periodic reviews that may be performed to maintain a current level of knowledge of the status of the Agreement State programs;

(14) Provides training to the States as provided by Section 274i of the Act and also to NRC staff and staff of the U.S. Navy and U.S. Air Force;

(15) Provides technical assistance to Agreement States;

(16) Maintains an exchange of information with the States;

(17) Conducts negotiations with States expressing an interest in seeking a Section 274b Agreement;

(18) Supports, consistent with Commission directives, State efforts to improve regulatory control for radiation safety over radioactive materials not covered by the Act;

(19) Serves as the NRC liaison to the Conference of Radiation Control Program Directors, Inc. (CRCPD) and coordinates NRC technical support of CRCPD committees;

(20) Conducts high-level waste pre-licensing activities, consistent with direction in the Nuclear Waste Policy Act and the Energy Policy Act, to ensure appropriate standards and regulatory guidance are in place, and interacts with the applicant;

(21) Is responsible for regulation and licensing of recycling technologies intended to reduce the amount of waste to be disposed through geologic disposal and to reduce proliferation concerns since the technologies do not produce separated plutonium;

(22) Interacts with the Department of Energy and international experts, in order to develop an appropriate regulatory framework, in recycling during development, demonstration, and deployment of new advanced recycling technologies that recycle nuclear fuel in a manner that does not produce separated plutonium;

(23) Creates and maintains the regulatory infrastructure to support the agency's role in licensing a reprocessing facility and a related fuel fabrication facility and vitrification and/or waste storage facility;

(24) Prepares the NRC to perform its regulatory role for new, expanded, and modified commercial fuel cycle facilities that may include recycling, transmutation, and actinide burning. This includes regulatory processes such as licensing, inspection, assessment of license performance assessment, events analysis, and enforcement that will ensure that this technology can be safely and securely implemented commercially in the United States;

(25) Develops, promulgates, and amends regulations generally associated with the materials regulated by NMSS and for all security-related regulations that will be applied to licensees and holders of certificates of compliance issued by NMSS;

(26) Supports safeguards activities including—

(i) Developing overall agency policy;

(ii) Monitoring and assessing the threat environment, including liaison with intelligence agencies, as appropriate; and

(iii) Conducting licensing and review activities appropriate to deter and protect against threats of radiological sabotage and threats of theft or diversion of nuclear material at regulated facilities and during transport;

(27) Regulates medical, industrial, academic, and commercial uses of radioactive isotopes;

(28) Oversees safe management and disposal of low-level radioactive wastes;

(29) Plans and directs program for financial assurance of NMSS licensees;

(30) Manages the decommissioning of facilities and sites when their licensed functions are over; and

(31) Identifies and takes action for activities under its responsibility, including consulting and coordinating with international, Federal, State, Tribal and local agencies, as appropriate.

[79 FR 75737, Dec. 19, 2014, as amended at 80 FR 74978, Dec. 1, 2015]

§ 1.43 Office of Nuclear Reactor Regulation.

The Office of Nuclear Reactor Regulation—

(a) Develops, promulgates and implements regulations and develops and implements policies, programs, and procedures for all aspects of licensing, inspection, and safeguarding of—

(1) Manufacturing, production, and utilization facilities, except for those concerning fuel reprocessing plants and isotopic enrichment plants;

(2) Receipt, possession, and ownership of source, byproduct, and special nuclear material used or produced at facilities licensed under 10 CFR parts 50, 52, and 54;

(3) Operators of such facilities;

(4) Emergency preparedness at such facilities; and

(5) Contractors and suppliers of such facilities.

(b) Identifies and takes action regarding conditions and licensee performance that may adversely affect public health and safety, the environment, or the safeguarding of nuclear reactor facilities;

(c) Assesses and recommends or takes action regarding incidents or accidents;

(d) Provides special assistance as required in matters involving reactor facilities exempt from licensing;

(e) Provides guidance and implementation direction to Regional Offices on reactor licensing, inspection, and safeguards programs assigned to the Region, and appraises Regional program performance in terms of effectiveness and uniformity;

(f) Performs other functions required for implementation of the reactor licensing, inspection, and safeguard programs; and

(g) Performs review and evaluation related to regulated facilities insurance, indemnity, and antitrust matters.

[70 FR 69422, Nov. 16, 2005, as amended at 72 FR 49470, Aug. 28, 2007]

§ 1.44 Office of New Reactors.

The Office of New Reactors—

(a) Develops, promulgates and implements regulations and develops and implements policies, programs, and procedures for all aspects of licensing, inspection, and safeguarding of—

(1) Manufacturing, production, and utilization facilities licensed under part 52 of this chapter prior to initial commencement of operation;

(2) Receipt, possession, and ownership of source, byproduct, and special nuclear material used or produced at facilities licensed under part 52 of this chapter prior to initial commencement of operation;

(3) Operators of such facilities licensed under part 52 of this chapter prior to initial commencement of operation;

(4) Emergency preparedness at such facilities licensed under part 52 of this chapter prior to initial commencement of operation; and

(5) Contractors and suppliers of such facilities licensed under part 52 of this chapter prior to initial commencement of operation;

(b) Identifies and takes action regarding conditions and licensee performance that may adversely affect public health and safety, the environment, or the safeguarding of nuclear reactor facilities licensed under part 52 of this chapter prior to initial commencement of operation;

(c) Assesses and recommends or takes action regarding incidents or accidents related to facilities licensed under part 52 of this chapter prior to initial commencement of operation;

(d) Provides guidance and implementation direction to Regional Offices on reactor licensing, inspection, and safeguards programs assigned to the Region, and appraises Regional program performance in terms of effectiveness and uniformity, for facilities licensed under 10 CFR part 52 prior to initial commencement of operation;

(e) Performs other functions required for implementation of the reactor licensing, inspection, and safeguard programs for facilities licensed under part 52 of this chapter prior to initial commencement of operation; and

(f) Performs review and evaluation related to regulated facilities insurance and indemnity for facilities licensed under part 52 of this chapter prior to initial commencement of operation.

[73 FR 5712, Jan. 31, 2008]

§ 1.45 Office of Nuclear Regulatory Research.

The Office of Nuclear Regulatory Research—

(a) Plans, recommends, and implements programs of nuclear regulatory research, standards development, and resolution of generic safety issues for nuclear power plants and other facilities regulated by the NRC;

(b) Coordinates research activities within and outside the agency including appointment of staff to committees and conferences; and

(c) Coordinates NRC participation in international standards-related activities and national volunteer standards efforts, including appointment of staff to committees.

[52 FR 31602, Aug. 21, 1987, as amended at 63 FR 69544, Dec. 17, 1998]

§ 1.46 Office of Nuclear Security and Incident Response.

The Office of Nuclear Security and Incident Response—

(a) Develops overall agency policy and provides management direction for evaluation and assessment of technical issues involving security at nuclear facilities, and is the agency safeguards and security interface with the Department of Homeland Security (DHS), the Department of Energy (DOE), other agencies; and the international activities related to the security of radioactive material and nuclear facilities;

(b) Develops, in participation with domestic and international agencies, foreign policy guidance and provides international assistance in nuclear security and safeguards;

(c) Develops emergency preparedness policies, regulations, programs, and guidelines for nuclear facilities;

(d) Provides technical expertise regarding emergency preparedness issues and interpretations; and

(e) Develops and directs the NRC program for response to incidents, and is the agency emergency preparedness and incident response interface with the DHS, the Federal Emergency Management Agency (FEMA) and other Federal agencies.

[70 FR 69422, Nov. 16, 2005, as amended at 72 FR 28450, May 21, 2007]

§ 1.47 NRC Regional Offices.

Each Regional Administrator executes established NRC policies and assigned programs relating to inspection, enforcement, licensing, State agreements, State liaison, and emergency response within Regional boundaries set out in § 1.5(b) of this part.

Subpart C—NRC Seal and Flag

§ 1.51 Description and custody of NRC seal.

(a) Pursuant to section 201(a) of the Energy Reorganization Act of 1974, the Nuclear Regulatory Commission, has adopted an official seal. Its description is as follows: An American bald eagle (similar to that on the Great Seal of the United States of America) of brown and tan with claws and beak of yellow, behind a shield of red, white, and blue, clutching a cluster of thirteen arrows in its left claw and a green olive branch in its right claw, positioned on a field of white, with the words "United States Nuclear Regulatory Commission" in dark blue encircling the eagle. The eagle represents the United States of America and its interests.

(b) The Official Seal of the Nuclear Regulatory Commission is illustrated as follows:

(c) The Secretary of the Commission is responsible for custody of the impression seals and of replica (plaque) seals.

§ 1.53 Use of NRC seal or replicas.

(a) The use of the seal or replicas is restricted to the following:

(1) NRC letterhead stationery;

(2) NRC award certificates and medals;

(3) Security credentials and employee identification cards;

(4) NRC documents, including agreements with States, interagency or governmental agreements, foreign patent applications, certifications, special reports to the President and Congress and, at the discretion of the Secretary of the Commission, such other documents as the Secretary finds appropriate;

(5) Plaques—the design of the seal may be incorporated in plaques for display at NRC facilities in locations such as auditoriums, presentation rooms, lobbies, offices of senior officials, on the fronts of buildings, and other places designated by the Secretary;

(6) The NRC flag (which incorporates the design of the seal);

(7) Official films prepared by or for the NRC, if deemed appropriate by the Director of Governmental and Public Affairs;

(8) Official NRC publications that represent an achievement or mission of NRC as a whole, or that are cosponsored by NRC and other Government departments or agencies; and

(9) Any other uses as the Secretary of the Commission finds appropriate.

(b) Any person who uses the official seal in a manner other than as permitted by this section shall be subject to the provisions of 18 U.S.C. 1017, which provides penalties for the fraudulent or wrongful use of an official seal, and to other provisions of law as applicable.

§ 1.55 Establishment of official NRC flag.

The official flag is based on the design of the NRC seal. It is 50 inches by 66 inches in size with a 38-inch diameter seal incorporated in the center of a dark blue field with a gold fringe.

§ 1.57 Use of NRC flag.

(a) The use of the flag is restricted to the following:

(1) On or in front of NRC installations;

(2) At NRC ceremonies;

(3) At conferences involving official NRC participation (including permanent display in NRC conference rooms);

(4) At Governmental or public appearances of NRC executives;

(5) In private offices of senior officials; or

(6) As the Secretary of the Commission otherwise authorizes.

(b) The NRC flag must only be displayed together with the U.S. flag. When they are both displayed on a speaker's platform, the U.S. flag must occupy the position of honor and be placed at the speaker's right as he or she faces the audience, and the NRC flag must be placed at the speaker's left.

§ 1.59 Report of violations.

In order to ensure adherence to the authorized uses of the NRC seal and flag as provided in this subpart, a report of each suspected violation of this subpart, or any questionable use of the NRC seal or flag, should be submitted to the Secretary of the Commission.

PART 2—AGENCY RULES OF PRACTICE AND PROCEDURE

Subpart D—Additional Procedures Applicable to Proceedings for the Issuance of Licenses To Construct and/or Operate Nuclear Power Plants of Identical Design at Multiple Sites

Subpart E—Additional Procedures Applicable to Proceedings for the Issuance of Licenses To Manufacture Nuclear Power Reactors To Be Operated at Sites Not Identified in the License Application and Related Licensing Proceedings

Subpart F—Additional Procedures Applicable to Early Partial Decisions on Site Suitability Issues in Connection With an Application for a Construction Permit or Combined License To Construct Certain Utilization Facilities; and Advance Issuance of Limited Work Authorizations

EARLY PARTIAL DECISIONS ON SITE SUITABILITY—CONSTRUCTION PERMIT

EARLY PARTIAL DECISIONS ON SITE SUITABILITY—COMBINED LICENSE UNDER 10 CFR PART 52

PHASED APPLICATIONS INVOLVING LIMITED WORK AUTHORIZATIONS

Subpart G—Rules for Formal Adjudications

Subpart H—Rulemaking

Subpart I—Special Procedures Applicable to Adjudicatory Proceedings Involving Restricted Data and/or National Security Information

Subpart J—Procedures Applicable to Proceedings for the Issuance of Licenses for the Receipt of High-Level Radioactive Waste at a Geologic Repository

Subpart K—Hybrid Hearing Procedures for Expansion of Spent Nuclear Fuel Storage Capacity at Civilian Nuclear Power Reactors

Subpart L—Simplified Hearing Procedures for NRC Adjudications

Subpart M—Procedures for Hearings on License Transfer Applications

Subpart N—Expedited Proceedings with Oral Hearings

Subpart O—Legislative Hearings

AUTHORITY: Atomic Energy Act of 1954, secs. 29, 53, 62, 63, 81, 102, 103, 104, 105, 161, 181, 182, 183, 184, 186, 189, 191, 234 (42 U.S.C. 2039, 2073, 2092, 2093, 2111, 2132, 2133, 2134, 2135, 2201, 2231, 2232, 2233, 2234, 2236, 2239, 2241, 2282); Energy Reorganization Act of 1974, secs. 201, 206 (42 U.S.C. 5841, 5846); Nuclear Waste Policy Act of 1982, secs. 114(f), 134, 135, 141 (42 U.S.C. 10134(f), 10154, 10155, 10161); Administrative Procedure Act (5 U.S.C. 552, 553, 554, 557, 558); National Environmental Policy Act of 1969 (42 U.S.C. 4332); 44 U.S.C. 3504 note.

Section 2.205(j) also issued under 28 U.S.C. 2461 note.

Section 2.205(j) also issued under Sec. 31001(s), Pub. L. 104–134, 110 Stat. 1321–373 (28 U.S.C. 2461 note).

SOURCE: 27 FR 377, Jan. 13, 1962, unless otherwise noted.

EDITORIAL NOTE: Nomenclature changes to part 2 appear at 79 FR 75739, Dec. 19, 2014.

§2.1 Scope.

This part governs the conduct of all proceedings, other than export and import licensing proceedings described in part 110, under the Atomic Energy Act of 1954, as amended, and the Energy Reorganization Act of 1974, for—

(a) Granting, suspending, revoking, amending, or taking other action with respect to any license, construction permit, or application to transfer a license;

(b) Issuing orders and demands for information to persons subject to the Commission's jurisdiction, including licensees and persons not licensed by the Commission;

(c) Imposing civil penalties under Section 234 of the Act;

(d) Rulemaking under the Act and the Administrative Procedure Act; and

(e) Standard design approvals under part 52 of this chapter.

[56 FR 40684, Aug. 15, 1991, as amended at 72 FR 49470, Aug. 28, 2007]

§2.2 Subparts.

Each subpart other than subpart C of this part sets forth special rules applicable to the type of proceeding described in the first section of that subpart. Subpart C sets forth general rules applicable to all types of proceedings except rulemaking, and should be read in conjunction with the subpart governing a particular proceeding. Subpart I of this part sets forth special procedures to be followed in proceedings in order to safeguard and prevent disclosure of Restricted Data.

[69 FR 2233, Jan. 14, 2004]

§ 2.3 Resolution of conflict.

(a) In any conflict between a general rule in subpart C of this part and a special rule in another subpart or other part of this chapter applicable to a particular type of proceeding, the special rule governs.

(b) Unless otherwise specifically referenced, the procedures in this part do not apply to hearings in 10 CFR parts 4, 9, 10, 11, 12, 13, 15, 16, and subparts H and I of 10 CFR part 110.

[69 FR 2233, Jan. 14, 2004]

§ 2.4 Definitions.

As used in this part,

ACRS means the Advisory Committee on Reactor Safeguards established by the Act.

Act means the Atomic Energy Act of 1954, as amended (68 Stat. 919).

Adjudication means the process for the formulation of an order for the final disposition of the whole or any part of any proceeding subject to this part, other than rule making.

Administrative Law Judge means an individual appointed pursuant to section 11 of the Administrative Procedure Act to conduct proceedings subject to this part.

Commission means the Commission of five members or a quorum thereof sitting as a body, as provided by section 201 of the Energy Reorganization Act of 1974 (88 Stat. 1242), or any officer to whom has been delegated authority pursuant to section 161n of the Act.

Commission adjudicatory employee means—

(1) The Commissioners and members of their personal staffs;

(2) The employees of the Office of Commission Appellate Adjudication;

(3) The members of the Atomic Safety and Licensing Board Panel and staff assistants to the Panel;

(4) A presiding officer appointed under § 2.313, and staff assistants to a presiding officer;

(5) Special assistants (as defined in § 2.322);

(6) The General Counsel, the Solicitor, the Associate General Counsel for Licensing and Regulation, and employees of the Office of the General Counsel under the supervision of the Solicitor;

(7) The Secretary and employees of the Office of the Secretary; and

(8) Any other Commission officer or employee who is appointed by the Commission, the Secretary, or the General Counsel to participate or advise in the Commission's consideration of an initial or final decision in a proceeding. Any other Commission officer or employee who, as permitted by § 2.348, participates or advises in the Commission's consideration of an initial or final decision in a proceeding must be appointed as a Commission adjudicatory employee under this paragraph and the parties to the proceeding must be given written notice of the appointment.

Contested proceeding means—(1) A proceeding in which there is a controversy between the NRC staff and the applicant for a license or permit concerning the issuance of the license or permit or any of the terms or conditions thereof;

(2) A proceeding in which the NRC is imposing a civil penalty or other enforcement action, and the subject of the civil penalty or enforcement action is an applicant for or holder of a license or permit, or is or was an applicant for a standard design certification under part 52 of this chapter; and

(3) A proceeding in which a petition for leave to intervene in opposition to an application for a license or permit has been granted or is pending before the Commission.

Department means the Department of Energy established by the Department of Energy Organization Act (Pub. L. 95–91, 91 Stat. 565 42 U.S.C. 7101 *et seq.*) to the extent that the Department, or its duly authorized representatives, exercises functions formerly vested in the U.S. Atomic Energy Commission, its Chairman, members, officers and components and transferred to the U.S. Energy Research and Development Administration and to the Administrator thereof pursuant to sections 104 (b), (c) and (d) of the Energy Reorganization Act of 1974 (Pub. L. 93–438, 88 Stat. 1233 at 1237, 42 U.S.C. 5814) and retransferred to the Secretary of Energy pursuant to section 301(a) of the Department of Energy Organization Act (Pub. L. 95–91, 91 Stat. 565 at 577–578, 42 U.S.C. 7151).

Digital ID certificate means a file stored on a participant's computer that contains the participant's name, e-mail address, and participant's digital signature, proves the participant's identity when filing documents and serving participants electronically through the E-Filing system, and contains public keys, which allow for the encryption and decryption of documents so that the documents can be securely transferred over the Internet.

Electric utility means any entity that generates or distributes electricity and which recovers the costs of this electricity, either directly or indirectly through rates established by the entity itself or by a separate regulatory authority. Investor-owned utilities including generation or distribution subsidiaries, public utility districts, municipalities, rural electric cooperatives, and State and Federal agencies, including associations of any of the foregoing, are included within the meaning of "electric utility."

Electronic acknowledgment means a communication transmitted electronically from the E-Filing system to the submitter confirming receipt of electronic filing and service.

Electronic Hearing Docket means the publicly available Web site which houses a visual presentation of the docket and a link to its files.

E-Filing System means an electronic system that receives, stores, and distributes documents filed in proceedings for which an electronic hearing docket has been established.

Ex parte communication means an oral or written communication not on the public record with respect to which reasonable prior notice to all parties is not given.

Facility means a production facility or a utilization facility as defined in §50.2 of this chapter.

Guidance for Electronic Submissions to the NRC means the document issued by the Commission that sets forth the transmission methods and formatting standards for filing and service under E-Filing. The document can be obtained by visiting the NRC's Web site at *http://www.nrc.gov*.

Investigative or litigating function means—

(1) Personal participation in planning, conducting, or supervising an investigation; or

(2) Personal participation in planning, developing, or presenting, or in supervising the planning, development or presentation of testimony, argument, or strategy in a proceeding.

License means a license, including an early site permit, construction permit, operating license, combined license, manufacturing license, or renewed license issued by the Commission.

Licensee means a person who is authorized to conduct activities under a license.

NRC personnel means:

(1) NRC employees;

(2) For the purpose of §§2.702 and 2.709 only, persons acting in the capacity of consultants to the Commission, regardless of the form of the contractual arrangements under which such persons act as consultants to the Commission; and

(3) Members of advisory boards, committees, and panels of the NRC; members of boards designated by the Commission to preside at adjudicatory proceedings; and officers or employees of Government agencies, including military personnel, assigned to duty at the NRC.

NRC Public Document Room means the facility at One White Flint North, 11555 Rockville Pike (first floor), Rockville, Maryland, where certain public records of the NRC that were made available for public inspection in paper or microfiche prior to the implementation of the NRC Agencywide Documents Access and Management System, commonly referred to as ADAMS, will remain available for public inspection. It is also the place where NRC makes computer terminals available to access the Publicly Available Records System (PARS) component of ADAMS on the NRC Web site, *http://www.nrc.gov*, and where copies of publicly available documents can be viewed or ordered for a fee as set forth in §9.35 of this chapter. The facility is staffed with reference librarians to assist the public in identifying and locating documents and in using the NRC Web site and ADAMS. The NRC Public Document Room is open from 7:45 am to 4:15 pm, Monday through Friday, except on Federal holidays. Reference service and access to documents may also be requested by telephone (301–415–4737 or 800–397–4209) between 8:30 am and 4:15 pm, or by e-mail (*PDR@nrc.gov*), facsimile (301–415–3548), or letter (NRC Public Document Room, One White Flint North, 11555 Rockville Pike (first floor), Rockville, Maryland 20852–2738).

NRC records and documents means any book, paper, map, photograph, brochure, punch card, magnetic tape, paper tape, sound recording, pamphlet, slide, motion picture, or other documentary material regardless of form or characteristics, made by, in the possession of, or under the control of the NRC pursuant to Federal law or in connection with the transaction of public business as evidence of NRC organization, functions, policies, decisions, procedures, operations, programs or other activities. "NRC records and documents" do not include objects or articles such as structures, furniture, tangible exhibits or models, or vehicles and equipment.

NRC Web site, http://www.nrc.gov, is the Internet uniform resource locator name for the Internet address of the Web site where NRC will ordinarily make available its public records for inspection.

Optical Storage Media means any physical computer component that meets E-Filing Guidance standards for storing, saving, and accessing electronic documents.

Participant means an individual or organization (including a governmental entity) that has petitioned to intervene in a proceeding or requested a hearing but that has not yet been granted party status by an Atomic Safety and Licensing Board or other presiding officer. Participant also means a party to a proceeding and any interested State, local governmental body, or Federally-recognized Indian Tribe that seeks to participate in a proceeding under § 2.315(c). For the purpose of service of documents, the NRC staff is considered a participant even if not participating as a party.

Person means (1) any individual, corporation, partnership, firm, association, trust, estate, public or private institution, group, government agency other than the Commission or the Department, except that the Department shall be considered a person with respect to those facilities of the Department specified in section 202 of the Energy Reorganization Act of 1974 (88 Stat. 1244), any State or any political subdivision of, or any political entity within a State, any foreign government or nation or any political subdivision of any such government or nation, or other entity; and (2) any legal successor, representative, agent, or agency of the foregoing.

Potential party means any person who has requested, or who may intend to request, a hearing or petition to intervene in a hearing under 10 CFR part 2, other than hearings conducted under Subparts J and M of 10 CFR part 2.

Presiding officer means the Commission, an administrative law judge, an administrative judge, an Atomic Safety and Licensing Board, or other person designated in accordance with the provisions of this part, presiding over the conduct of a hearing conducted under the provisions of this part.

Public Document Room means the place at One White Flint North, 11555 Rockville Pike (first floor), Rockville, Maryland 20852–2738, at which public records of the Commission will ordinarily be made available for inspection.

Safeguards Information means information not classified as National Security Information or Restricted Data which specifically identifies a licensee's or applicant's detailed control and accounting procedures for the physical protection of special nuclear material in quantities determined by the Commission through order or regulation to be significant to the public health and safety or the common defense and security; detailed security measures (including security plans, procedures, and equipment) for the physical protection of source, byproduct, or special nuclear material in quantities determined by the Commission through order or regulation to be significant to the public health and safety or the common defense and security; security measures for the physical protection and location of certain plant equipment vital to the safety of production or utilization facilities; and any other information within the scope of Section 147 of the Atomic Energy Act of 1954, as amended, the unauthorized disclosure of which, as determined by the Commission through order or regulation, could reasonably be expected to have a significant adverse effect on the health and safety of the public or the common defense and security by significantly increasing the likelihood of sabotage or theft or diversion of source, byproduct, or special nuclear material.

Secretary means the Secretary to the Commission.

Except as redefined in this section, words and phrases which are defined in the Act and in this chapter have the same meaning when used in this part.

[27 FR 377, Jan. 13, 1962]

EDITORIAL NOTE: For FEDERAL REGISTER citations affecting §2.4, see the List of CFR Sections Affected, which appears in the Finding Aids section of the printed volume and at *www.fdsys.gov*.

§2.8 Information collection requirements: OMB approval.

This part contains no information collection requirements and therefore is not subject to requirements of the Paperwork Reduction Act (44 U.S.C. 3501 *et seq.*).

[61 FR 43408, Aug. 22, 1996]

Subpart A—Procedure for Issuance, Amendment, Transfer, or Renewal of a License, and Standard Design Approval

§2.100 Scope of subpart.

This subpart prescribes the procedure for issuance of a license; amendment of a license at the request of the licensee; transfer and renewal of a license; and issuance of a standard design approval under subpart E of part 52 of this chapter.

[72 FR 49470, Aug. 28, 2007]

§2.101 Filing of application.

(a)(1) An application for a permit, a license, a license transfer, a license amendment, a license renewal, or a standard design approval, shall be filed with the Director, Office of New Reactors, the Director, Office of Nuclear Reactor Regulation, or the Director, Office of Nuclear Material Safety and Safeguards, as prescribed by the applicable provisions of this chapter. A prospective applicant may confer informally with the NRC staff before filing an application.

(2) Each application for a license for a facility or for receipt of waste radioactive material from other persons for the purpose of commercial disposal by the waste disposal licensee will be assigned a docket number. However, to allow a determination as to whether an application for a limited work authorization, construction permit, operating license, early site permit, standard design approval, combined license, or manufacturing license for a production or utilization facility is complete and acceptable for docketing, it will be initially treated as a tendered application. A copy of the tendered application will be available for public inspection at the NRC Web site, *http://www.nrc.gov*, and/or at the NRC PDR. Generally, the determination on acceptability for docketing will be made within a period of 30 days. However, in selected applications, the Commission may decide to determine acceptability based on the technical adequacy of the application as well as its completeness. In these cases, the Commission, under §2.104(a), will direct that the notice of hearing be issued as soon as practicable after the application has been tendered, and the determination of acceptability will be made generally within a period of 60 days. For docketing and other requirements for applications under part 61 of this chapter, see paragraph (g) of this section.

(3) If the Director, Office of Nuclear Reactor Regulation, Director, Office of New Reactors, or Director, Office of Nuclear Material Safety and Safeguards, as appropriate, determines that a tendered application for a construction permit or operating license for a production or utilization facility, and/or any environmental report required pursuant to subpart A of part 51 of this chapter, or part thereof as provided in paragraphs (a)(5) or (a–1) of this section are complete and acceptable for docketing, a docket number will be assigned to the application or part thereof, and

the applicant will be notified of the determination. With respect to the tendered application and/or environmental report or part thereof that is acceptable for docketing, the applicant will be requested to:

(i) Submit to the Director, Office of Nuclear Reactor Regulation, Director, Office of New Reactors, or Director, Office of Nuclear Material Safety and Safeguards, as appropriate, such additional copies as the regulations in part 50 and subpart A of part 51 of this chapter require;

(ii) Serve a copy on the chief executive of the municipality in which the facility or site which is the subject of an early site permit is to be located or, if the facility or site which is the subject of an early site permit is not to be located within a municipality, on the chief executive of the county, and serve a notice of availability of the application or environmental report on the chief executives of the municipalities or counties which have been identified in the application or environmental report as the location of all or part of the alternative sites, containing as applicable, the docket number of the application; a brief description of the proposed site and facility; the location of the site and facility as primarily proposed and alternatively listed; the name, address, telephone number, and e-mail address (if available) of the applicant's representative who may be contacted for further information; notification that a draft environmental impact statement will be issued by the Commission and will be made available upon request to the Commission; and notification that if a request is received from the appropriate chief executive, the applicant will transmit a copy of the application and environmental report, and any changes to these documents which affect the alternative site location, to the executive who makes the request. In complying with the requirements of this paragraph, the applicant should not make public distribution of those parts of the application subject to § 2.390(d). The applicant shall submit to the Director, Office of New Reactors or Director, Office of Nuclear Reactor Regulation, as appropriate, an affidavit that service of the notice of availability of the application or environmental report has been completed along with a list of names and addresses of those executives upon whom the notice was served; and

(iii) Make direct distribution of additional copies to Federal, State, and local officials in accordance with the requirements of this chapter and written instructions furnished to the applicant by the Director, Office of Nuclear Reactor Regulation, Director, Office of New Reactors, or Director, Office of Nuclear Material Safety and Safeguards, as appropriate. Such written instructions will be furnished as soon as practicable after all or any part of the application, or environmental report, is tendered. The copies submitted to the Director, Office of Nuclear Reactor Regulation, Director, Office of New Reactors, or Director, Office of Nuclear Material Safety and Safeguards, or, as appropriate, and distributed by the applicant shall be completely assembled documents, identified by docket number. Subsequently distributed amendments to applications, however, may include revised pages to previous submittals and, in such cases, the recipients will be responsible for inserting the revised pages.

(4) The tendered application for a construction permit, operating license, early site permit, standard design approval, combined license, or manufacturing license will be formally docketed upon receipt by the Director, Office of New Reactors, Director, Office of Nuclear Reactor Regulation, or Director, Office of Nuclear Material Safety and Safeguards, as appropriate, of the required additional copies. Distribution of the additional copies shall be deemed to be complete as of the time the copies are deposited in the mail or with a carrier prepaid for delivery to the designated addresses. The date of docketing shall be the date when the required copies are received by the Director, Office of New Reactors, Director, Office of Nuclear Reactor Regulation, or Director, Office of Nuclear Material Safety and Safeguards, as appropriate. Within 10 days after docketing, the applicant shall submit to the Director, Office of New Reactors, Director, Office of Nuclear Reactor Regulation, or Director, Office

of Nuclear Material Safety and Safeguards, as appropriate, an affidavit that distribution of the additional copies to Federal, State, and local officials has been completed in accordance with requirements of this chapter and written instructions furnished to the applicant by the Director, Office of New Reactors, Director, Office of Nuclear Reactor Regulation, or Director, Office of Nuclear Material Safety and Safeguards, as appropriate. Amendments to the application and environmental report shall be filed and distributed and an affidavit shall be furnished to the Director, Office of New Reactors, Director, Office of Nuclear Reactor Regulation, or Director, Office of Nuclear Material Safety and Safeguards, as appropriate, in the same manner as for the initial application and environmental report. If it is determined that all or any part of the tendered application and/or environmental report is incomplete and therefore not acceptable for processing, the applicant will be informed of this determination, and the respects in which the document is deficient.

(5) An applicant for a construction permit under part 50 of this chapter or a combined license under part 52 of this chapter for a production or utilization facility which is subject to §51.20(b) of this chapter, and is of the type specified in §50.21(b)(2) or (b)(3) or §50.22 of this chapter or is a testing facility may submit the information required of applicants by part 50 or part 52 of this chapter in two parts. One part shall be accompanied by the information required by §50.30(f) of this chapter, or §52.80(b) of this chapter, as applicable. The other part shall include any information required by §50.34(a) and, if applicable, §50.34a of this chapter, or §§52.79 and 52.80(a), as applicable. One part may precede or follow other parts by no longer than 6 months. If it is determined that either of the parts as described above is incomplete and not acceptable for processing, the Director, Office of Nuclear Reactor Regulation, Director, Office of New Reactors, or Director, Office of Nuclear Material Safety and Safeguards, as appropriate, will inform the applicant of this determination and the respects in which the document is deficient. Such a determination of completeness will generally be made within a period of 30 days. Whichever part is filed first shall also include the fee required by §§50.30(e) and 170.21 of this chapter and the information required by §§50.33, 50.34(a)(1), or 52.79(a)(1), as applicable, and §50.37 of this chapter. The Director, Office of Nuclear Reactor Regulation, Director, Office of New Reactors, or Director, Office of Nuclear Material Safety and Safeguards, as appropriate, will accept for docketing an application for a construction permit under part 52 of this chapter for a production or utilization facility which is subject to §51.20(b) of this chapter, and is of the type specified in §50.21(b)(2) or (b)(3) or §50.22 of this chapter or is a testing facility where one part of the application as described above is complete and conforms to the requirements of part 50 of this chapter. The additional parts will be docketed upon a determination by the Director, Office of Nuclear Reactor Regulation, Director, Office of New Reactors, or Director, Office of Nuclear Material Safety and Safeguards, as appropriate, that it is complete.

(6)–(8) [Reserved]

(9) An applicant for a construction permit for a utilization facility which is subject to §51.20(b) of this chapter and is of the type specified in §50.21(b)(2) or (b)(3) or §50.22 of this chapter, an applicant for or holder of an early site permit under part 52 of this chapter, or an applicant for a combined license under part 52 of this chapter, who seeks to conduct the activities authorized under §50.10(d) of this chapter may submit a complete application under paragraphs (a)(1) through (a)(4) of this section which includes the information required by §50.10(d) of this chapter. Alternatively, the applicant (other than an applicant for or holder of an early site permit) may submit its application in two parts:

(i) Part one must include the information required by §50.33(a) through (f) of this chapter, and the information required by §50.10(d)(2) and (d)(3) of this chapter.

(ii) Part two must include the remaining information required by the Commission's regulations in this chapter which was not submitted in part one, *provided, however*, that this information may be submitted in accordance with the applicable provisions of paragraph (a)(5) of this section, or, for a construction permit applicant, paragraph (a)(1) of this section. Part two of the application must be submitted no later than 18 months after submission of part one.

(a–1) *Early consideration of site suitability issues.* An applicant for a construction permit under part 50 of this chapter or a combined license under part 52 of this chapter for a utilization facility which is subject to § 51.20(b) of this chapter and is of the type specified in § 50.21(b)(2) or (3) or § 50.22 of this chapter or is a testing facility, may request that the Commission conduct an early review and hearing and render an early partial decision in accordance with subpart F of this part on issues of site suitability within the purview of the applicable provisions of parts 50, 51, 52, and 100 of this chapter.

(1) *Construction permit.* The applicant for the construction permit may submit the information required of applicants by the provisions of this chapter in three parts:

(i) Part one shall include or be accompanied by any information required by §§ 50.34(a)(1) and 50.30(f) of this chapter which relates to the issue(s) of site suitability for which an early review, hearing, and partial decision are sought, except that information with respect to operation of the facility at the projected initial power level need not be supplied, and shall include the information required by §§ 50.33(a) through (e) and 50.37 of this chapter. The information submitted shall also include:

(A) Proposed findings on the issues of site suitability on which the applicant has requested review and a statement of the bases or the reasons for those findings,

(B) A range of postulated facility design and operation parameters that is sufficient to enable the Commission to perform the requested review of site suitability issues under the applicable provisions of parts 50, 51, and 100, and

(C) Information concerning the applicant's site selection process and long-range plans for ultimate development of the site required by § 2.603(b)(1).

(ii) Part two shall include or be accompanied by the remaining information required by §§ 50.30(f), 50.33, and 50.34(a)(1) of this chapter.

(iii) Part three shall include the remaining information required by §§ 50.34a and (in the case of a nuclear power reactor) 50.34(a) of this chapter.

(iv) The information required for part two or part three shall be submitted during the period the partial decision on part one is effective. Submittal of the information required for part three may precede by no more than 6 months or follow by no more than 6 months the submittal of the information required for part two.

(2) *Combined license under part 52.* An applicant for a combined license under part 52 of this chapter may submit the information required of applicants by the provisions of this chapter in three parts:

(i) Part one shall include or be accompanied by any information required by §§ 52.79(a)(1) and 50.30(f) of this chapter which relates to the issue(s) of site suitability for which an early review, hearing, and partial decision are sought, except that information with respect to operation of the facility at the projected initial power level need not be supplied, and shall include the information required by §§ 50.33(a) through (e) and 50.37 of this chapter. The information submitted shall also include:

(A) Proposed findings on the issues of site suitability on which the applicant has requested review and a statement of the bases or the reasons for those findings;

(B) A range of postulated facility design and operation parameters that is sufficient to enable the Commission to perform the requested review of site suitability issues under the applicable provisions of parts 50, 51, 52, and 100; and

(C) Information concerning the applicant's site selection process and long-range plans for ultimate development of the site required by § 2.621(b)(1).

(ii) Part two shall include or be accompanied by the remaining information required by §§ 50.30(f), 50.33, and 52.79(a)(1) of this chapter.

(iii) Part three shall include the remaining information required by §§ 52.79 and 52.80 of this chapter.

(iv) The information required for part two or part three shall be submitted during the period the partial decision on part one is effective. Submittal of the information required for part three may precede by no more than 6 months or follow by no more than 6 months the submittal of the information required for part two.

(b) After the application has been docketed, each applicant for a license for receipt of waste radioactive material from other persons for the purpose of commercial disposal by the waste disposal licensee, except applicants under part 61 of this chapter, which must comply with paragraph (f) of this section, shall serve a copy of the application and environmental report, as appropriate, on the chief executive of the municipality in which the activity is to be conducted or, if the activity is not to be conducted within a municipality on the chief executive of the county, and serve a notice of availability of the application or environmental report on the chief executives of the municipalities or counties which have been identified in the application or environmental report as the location of all or part of the alternative sites, containing the docket number of the application; a brief description of the proposed site and facility; the location of the site and facility as primarily proposed and alternatively listed; the name, address, telephone number, and email address (if available) of the applicant's representative who may be contacted for further information; notification that a draft environmental impact statement will be issued by the Commission and will be made available upon request to the Commission; and notification that if a request is received from the appropriate chief executive, the applicant will transmit a copy of the application and environmental report, and any changes to such documents which affect the alternative site location, to the executive who makes the request. In complying with the requirements of this paragraph the applicant should not make public distribution of those parts of the application subject to § 2.390(d). The applicant shall submit to the Director, Office of Nuclear Material Safety and Safeguards or as appropriate, an affidavit that service of the notice of availability of the application or environmental report has been completed along with a list of names and addresses of those executives upon whom the notice was served.

(c) Upon receipt and acceptance for docketing of the required portions of the application dealing with radiological health and safety and environmental matters, notice of receipt will be published in the FEDERAL REGISTER including an appropriate notice of hearing.

(d) The Director, Office of Nuclear Reactor Regulation, Director, Office of New Reactors, or Director, Office of Nuclear Material Safety and Safeguards, as appropriate, will give notice of the docketing of the public health and safety, common defense and security, and environmental parts of an application for a license for a facility or for receipt of waste radioactive material from other persons for the purpose of commercial disposal by the waste disposal licensee, except that for applications pursuant to part 61 of this chapter, paragraph (f) of this section applies to the Governor or other appropriate official of the State in which the facility is to be located or the activity is to be conducted and will publish in the FEDERAL REGISTER a notice of docketing of the application, which states the purpose of the application and specifies the location at which the proposed activity would be conducted.

(e)(1) Each application for construction authorization for a HLW repository at a geologic repository operations area pursuant to parts 60 or 63 of this chapter, and each application for a license to receive and possess high-level radioactive waste at a geologic repository operations area pursuant to parts 60 or 63 of this chapter, and any environmental impact statement required in connection therewith pursuant to subpart A of part 51 of this chapter shall be processed in accordance with the provisions of this paragraph.

(2) To allow a determination as to whether the application is complete and acceptable for docketing, it will be

initially treated as a tendered document, and a copy will be available for public inspection in the Commission's Public Document Room. Twenty copies shall be filed to enable this determination to be made.

(3) If the Director, Office of Nuclear Material Safety and Safeguards or as appropriate, determines that the tendered document is complete and acceptable for docketing, a docket number will be assigned and the applicant will be notified of the determination. If it is determined that all or any part of the tendered document is incomplete and therefore not acceptable for processing, the applicant will be informed of this determination and the respects in which the document is deficient.

(4) [Reserved]

(5) If a tendered document is acceptable for docketing, the applicant will be requested to submit to the Director of Nuclear Material Safety and Safeguards such additional copies of the application and environmental impact statement as the regulations in part 60 or 63 and subpart A of part 51 of this chapter require; serve a copy of such application and environmental impact statement on the chief executive of the municipality in which the geologic repository operations area is to be located, or if the geologic repository operations area is not to be located within a municipality, on the chief executive of the county (or to the Tribal organization, if it is to be located within an Indian reservation); and make direct distribution of additional copies to Federal, State, Indian Tribe, and local officials in accordance with the requirements of this chapter, and written instructions from the Director of Nuclear Material Safety and Safeguards. All such copies shall be completely assembled documents, identified by docket number. Subsequently distributed amendments to the application, however, may include revised pages to previous submittals and, in such cases, the recipients are responsible for inserting the revised pages.

(6) The tendered document will be formally docketed upon receipt by the Director, Office of Nuclear Material Safety and Safeguards as appropriate, of the required additional copies. The date of docketing shall be the date when the required copies are received by the Director, Office of Nuclear Material Safety and Safeguards , as appropriate. Within ten (10) days after docketing, the applicant shall submit to the Director, Office of Nuclear Material Safety and Safeguards as appropriate, a written statement that distribution of the additional copies to Federal, State, Indian Tribe, and local officials has been completed in accordance with requirements of this chapter and written instructions furnished to the applicant by the Director, Office of Nuclear Material Safety and Safeguards , as appropriate. Distribution of the additional copies shall be deemed to be complete as of the time the copies are deposited in the mail or with a carrier prepaid for delivery to the designated addressees.

(7) Amendments to the application and supplements to the environmental impact statement shall be filed and distributed and a written statement shall be furnished to the Director, Office of Nuclear Material Safety and Safeguards , as appropriate, in the same manner as for the initial application and environmental impact statement.

(8) The Director, Office of Nuclear Material Safety and Safeguards as appropriate, will cause to be published in the FEDERAL REGISTER a notice of docketing which identifies the State and location at which the proposed geologic repository operations area would be located and will give notice of docketing to the governor of that State. The notice of docketing will state that the Commission finds that a hearing is required in the public interest, prior to issuance of a construction authorization, and will recite the matters specified in §2.104(a) of this part.

(f) Each application for a license to receive radioactive waste from other persons for disposal under part 61 of this chapter and the accompanying environmental report shall be processed in accordance with the provisions of this paragraph.

(1) To allow a determination as to whether the application or environmental report is complete and acceptable for docketing, it will be initially treated as a tendered document, and a

copy will be available for public inspection in the Commission's Public Document Room, One White Flint North, 11555 Rockville Pike (first floor), Rockville, Maryland 20852–2738. One original and two copies shall be filed to enable this determination to be made.

(i) Upon receipt of a tendered application, the Commission will publish in the FEDERAL REGISTER notice of the filed application and will notify the governors, legislatures and other appropriate State, county, and municipal officials and Tribal governing bodies of the States and areas containing or potentially affected by the activities at the proposed site and the alternative sites. The Commission will inform these officials that the Commission staff will be available for consultation pursuant to §61.71 of this chapter. The FEDERAL REGISTER notice will note the opportunity for interested persons to submit views and comments on the tendered application for consideration by the Commission and applicant. The Commission will also notify the U.S. Bureau of Indian Affairs when Tribal governing bodies are notified.

(ii) The Commission will also post a public notice in a newspaper or newspapers of general circulation in the affected States and areas summarizing information contained in the applicant's tendered application and noting the opportunity to submit views and comments.

(iii) When the Director, Office of Nuclear Material Safety and Safeguards as appropriate, determines that the tendered document is complete and acceptable for docketing, a docket number will be assigned and the applicant will be notified of the determination. If it is determined that all or any part of the tendered document is incomplete and therefore not acceptable for processing, the applicant will be informed of this determination and the aspects in which the document is deficient.

(2)(i) With respect to any tendered document that is acceptable for docketing, the applicant will be requested to:

(A) Submit to the Director, Office of Nuclear Material Safety and Safeguards as appropriate, such additional copies as required by the regulations in part 61 and subpart A of part 51 of this chapter;

(B) Serve a copy on the chief executive of the municipality in which the waste is to be disposed of or, if the waste is not to be disposed of within a municipality, serve a copy on the chief executive of the county in which the waste is to be disposed of;

(C) Make direct distribution of additional copies to Federal, State, Indian Tribal, and local officials in accordance with the requirements of this chapter and written instructions from the Director, Office of Nuclear Material Safety and Safeguards as appropriate; and

(D) Serve a notice of availability of the application and environmental report on the chief executives or governing bodies of the municipalities or counties which have been identified in the application and environmental report as the location of all or part of the alternative sites if copies are not distributed under paragraph (f)(2)(i)(C) of this section to the executives or bodies.

(ii) All distributed copies shall be completely assembled documents identified by docket number. However, subsequently distributed amendments may include revised pages to previous submittals and, in these cases, the recipients will be responsible for inserting the revised pages. In complying with the requirements of paragraph (f) of this section the applicant may not make public distribution of those parts of the application subject to §2.390(d).

(3) The tendered document will be formally docketed upon receipt by the Director, Office of Nuclear Material Safety and Safeguards as appropriate, of the required additional copies. Distribution of the additional copies shall be deemed to be complete as of the time the copies are deposited in the mail or with a carrier prepaid for delivery to the designated addressees. The date of docketing shall be the date when the required copies are received by the Director, Office of Nuclear Material Safety and Safeguards as appropriate. Within ten (10) days after docketing, the applicant shall submit to the Director, Office of Nuclear Material Safety and Safeguards or, as appropriate, a written statement that distribution of the additional copies to Federal, State, Indian Tribal, and local

officials has been completed in accordance with requirements of this section and written instructions furnished to the applicant by the Director, Office of Nuclear Material Safety and Safeguards as appropriate.

(4) Amendments to the application and environmental report shall be filed and distributed and a written statement shall be furnished to the Director, Office of Nuclear Material Safety and Safeguards as appropriate, in the same manner as for the initial application and environmental report.

(5) The Director, Office of Nuclear Material Safety and Safeguards as appropriate, will cause to be published in the FEDERAL REGISTER a notice of docketing which identifies the State and location of the proposed waste disposal facility and will give notice of docketing to the governor of that State and other officials listed in paragraph (f)(3) of this section and will, in a reasonable period thereafter, publish in the FEDERAL REGISTER a notice under § 2.105 offering an opportunity to request a hearing to the applicant and other potentially affected persons.

[41 FR 15833, Apr. 15, 1976]

EDITORIAL NOTE: For FEDERAL REGISTER citations affecting § 2.101, see the List of CFR Sections Affected, which appears in the Finding Aids section of the printed volume and at *www.fdsys.gov*.

§ 2.102 Administrative review of application.

(a) During review of an application by the NRC staff, an applicant may be required to supply additional information. The staff may request any one party to the proceeding to confer with the NRC staff informally. In the case of docketed application for a limited work authorization, construction permit, operating license, early site permit, standard design approval, combined license, or manufacturing license under this chapter, the NRC staff shall establish a schedule for its review of the application, specifying the key intermediate steps from the time of docketing until the completion of its review.

(b) The Director, Office of Nuclear Reactor Regulation, Director, Office of New Reactors, or Director, Office of Nuclear Material Safety and Safeguards, as appropriate, will refer the docketed application to the ACRS as required by law and in such additional cases as he or the Commission may determine to be appropriate. The ACRS will render to the Commission one or more reports as required by law or as requested by the Commission.

(c) The Director, Office of Nuclear Reactor Regulation, Director, Office of New Reactors, or Director, Office of Nuclear Material Safety and Safeguards, as appropriate, will make each report of the ACRS a part of the record of the docketed application, and transmit copies to the appropriate State and local officials.

[27 FR 377, Jan. 13, 1962, as amended at 36 FR 13270, July 17, 1971; 37 FR 15130, July 28, 1972; 47 FR 9986, Mar. 9, 1982; 69 FR 2235, Jan. 14, 2004; 70 FR 61887, Oct. 27, 2005; 72 FR 49472, Aug. 28, 2007; 72 FR 57439, Oct. 9, 2007; 73 FR 5715, Jan. 31, 2008]

§ 2.103 Action on applications for byproduct, source, special nuclear material, facility and operator licenses.

(a) If the Director, Office of Nuclear Reactor Regulation, Director, Office of New Reactors, or Director, Office of Nuclear Material Safety and Safeguards, as appropriate, finds that an application for a byproduct, source, special nuclear material, facility, or operator license complies with the requirements of the Act, the Energy Reorganization Act, and this chapter, he will issue a license. If the license is for a facility, or for receipt of waste radioactive material from other persons for the purpose of commercial disposal by the waste disposal licensee, or for a construction authorization for a HLW repository at a geologic repository operations area under parts 60 or 63 of this chapter, or if it is to receive and possess high-level radioactive waste at a geologic repository operations area under parts 60 or 63 of this chapter, the Director, Office of Nuclear Reactor Regulation, Director, Office of New Reactors, or Director, Office of Nuclear Material Safety and Safeguards, as appropriate, will inform the State, Tribal and local officials specified in § 2.104(c) of the issuance of the license. For notice of issuance requirements for licenses issued under part 61 of this chapter, see § 2.106(d).

(b) If the Director, Office of Nuclear Reactor Regulation, Director, Office of New Reactors, or Director, Office of Nuclear Material Safety and Safeguards, as appropriate, finds that an application does not comply with the requirements of the Act and this chapter he may issue a notice of proposed denial or a notice of denial of the application and inform the applicant in writing of:

(1) The nature of any deficiencies or the reason for the proposed denial or the denial, and

(2) The right of the applicant to demand a hearing within twenty (20) days from the date of the notice or such longer period as may be specified in the notice.

[28 FR 10152, Sept. 17, 1963, as amended at 47 FR 57478, Dec. 27, 1982; 66 FR 55787, Nov. 2, 2001; 69 FR 2235, Jan. 14, 2004; 73 FR 5715, Jan. 31, 2008; 77 FR 46589, Aug. 3, 2012; 79 FR 75739, Dec. 19, 2014]

HEARING ON APPLICATION—HOW INITIATED

§2.104 Notice of hearing.

(a) In the case of an application on which a hearing is required by the Act or this chapter, or in which the Commission finds that a hearing is required in the public interest, the Secretary will issue a notice of hearing to be published in the FEDERAL REGISTER. The notice must be published at least 15 days, and in the case of an application concerning a limited work authorization, construction permit, early site permit, or combined license for a facility of the type described in §§50.21(b) or 50.22 of this chapter or a testing facility, at least 30 days, before the date set for hearing in the notice.[1] In addition, in the case of an application for a limited work authorization, construction permit, early site permit, or combined license for a facility of the type described in §50.22 of this chapter, or a testing facility, the notice must be issued as soon as practicable after the NRC has docketed the application. If the Commission decides, under §2.101(a)(2), to determine the acceptability of the application based on its technical adequacy as well as completeness, the notice must be issued as soon as practicable after the application has been tendered.

(b) The notice of hearing must state:

(1) The nature of the hearing;

(2) The authority under which the hearing is to be held;

(3) The matters of fact and law to be considered;

(4) The date by which requests for hearing or petitions to intervene must be filed;

(5) The presiding officer designated for the hearing, or the procedure that the Commission will use to designate a presiding officer for the hearing.

(c)(1) The Secretary will transmit a notice of hearing on an application for a license for a production or utilization facility, including a limited work authorization, early site permit, combined license, but not for a manufacturing license, for a license for receipt of waste radioactive material from other persons for the purpose of commercial disposal by the waste disposal licensee, for a license under part 61 of this chapter, for a construction authorization for a high-level waste repository at a geologic repository operations area under parts 60 or 63 of this chapter, for a license to receive and possess high-level radioactive waste at a geologic repository operations area under parts 60 or 63 of this chapter, and for a license under part 72 of this chapter to acquire, receive or possess spent fuel for the purpose of storage in an independent spent fuel storage installation (ISFSI) to the governor or other appropriate official of the State and to the chief executive of the municipality in which the facility is to be located or the activity is to be conducted or, if the facility is not to be located or the activity conducted within a municipality, to the chief executive of the

[1] If the notice of hearing concerning an application for a limited work authorization, construction permit, early site permit, or combined license for a facility of the type described in §§50.21(b) or 50.22 of this chapter or a testing facility does not specify the time and place of initial hearing, a subsequent notice will be published in the FEDERAL REGISTER which will provide at least 30 days notice of the time and place of that hearing. After this notice is given, the presiding officer may reschedule the commencement of the initial hearing for a later date or reconvene a recessed hearing without again providing at least 30 days notice.

county (or to the Tribal organization, if it is to be located or conducted within an Indian reservation).

(2) The Secretary will transmit a notice of hearing on an application for a license under part 72 of this chapter to acquire, receive or possess spent fuel, high-level radioactive waste or radioactive material associated with high-level radioactive waste for the purpose of storage in a monitored retrievable storage installation (MRS) to the same persons who received the notice of docketing under § 72.16(e) of this chapter.

[72 FR 49472, Aug. 28, 2007, as amended at 72 FR 57439, Oct. 9, 2007]

§ 2.105 Notice of proposed action.

(a) If a hearing is not required by the Act or this chapter, and if the Commission has not found that a hearing is in the public interest, it will, before acting thereon, publish in the FEDERAL REGISTER, as applicable, or on the NRC's Web site, *http://www.nrc.gov*, or both, at the Commission's discretion, either a notice of intended operation under § 52.103(a) of this chapter and a proposed finding that inspections, tests, analyses, and acceptance criteria for a combined license under subpart C of part 52 have been or will be met, or a notice of proposed action with respect to an application for:

(1) A license for a facility;

(2) A license for receipt of waste radioactive material from other persons for the purpose of commercial disposal by the waste disposal licensee. All licenses issued under part 61 of this chapter shall be so noticed;

(3) An amendment of a license specified in paragraph (a) (1) or (2) of this section and which involves a significant hazards consideration;

(4) An amendment to an operating license, combined license, or manufacturing license for a facility licensed under §§ 50.21(b) or 50.22 of this chapter, or for a testing facility, as follows:

(i) If the Commission determines under § 50.58 of this chapter that the amendment involves no significant hazards consideration, though it will provide notice of opportunity for a hearing pursuant to this section, it may make the amendment immediately effective and grant a hearing thereafter; or

(ii) If the Commission determines under §§ 50.58 and 50.91 of this chapter that an emergency situation exists or that exigent circumstances exist and that the amendment involves no significant hazards consideration, it will provide notice of opportunity for a hearing pursuant to § 2.106 (if a hearing is requested, it will be held after issuance of the amendment);

(5) A license to receive and possess high-level radioactive waste at a geologic repository operations area pursuant to parts 60 or 63 of this chapter, or an amendment thereto, when the license or amendment would authorize actions which may significantly affect the health and safety of the public;

(6) An amendment to a construction authorization for a high-level radioactive waste at a geologic repository operations area pursuant to parts 60 or 63 of this chapter, when such an amendment would authorize actions which may significantly affect the health and safety of the public;

(7) A license under part 72 of this chapter to acquire, receive or possess spent fuel for the purpose of storage in an independent spent fuel storage installation (ISFSI) or to acquire, receive or possess spent fuel, high-level radioactive waste or radioactive material associated with high-level radioactive waste for the purpose of storage in a monitored retrievable storage installation (MRS);

(8) An amendment to a license specified in paragraph (a)(7) of this section when such an amendment presents a genuine issue as to whether the health and safety of the public will be significantly affected; or

(9) Any other license or amendment as to which the Commission determines that an opportunity for a public hearing should be afforded;

(10) In the case of an application for an operating license for a facility of a type described in § 50.21(b) or § 50.22 of this chapter or a testing facility, a notice of opportunity for hearing shall be issued as soon as practicable after the application has been docketed; or

(11) In the case of an application for a license to receive and possess high-level radioactive waste at a geologic

repository operations area, a notice of opportunity for hearing, as required by this paragraph, shall be published prior to Commission action authorizing receipt of such wastes; this requirement is in addition to the procedures set out in §§ 2.101(f)(8) and 2.104 of this part, which provide for a hearing on the application prior to issuance of a construction authorization.

(12) An amendment to an early site permit issued under subpart A of part 52 of this chapter, as follows:

(i) If the early site permit does not provide authority to conduct the activities allowed under § 50.10(e)(1) of this chapter, the amendment will involve no significant hazards consideration, and though the NRC will provide notice of opportunity for a hearing under this section, it may make the amendment immediately effective and grant a hearing thereafter; and

(ii) If the early site permit provides authority to conduct the activities allowed under § 50.10(e)(1) and the Commission determines under §§ 50.58 and 50.91 of this chapter that an emergency situation exists or that exigent circumstances exist and that the amendment involves no significant hazards consideration, it will provide notice of opportunity for a hearing under § 2.106 of this chapter (if a hearing is requested, which will be held after issuance of the amendment).

(13) A manufacturing license under subpart F of part 52 of this chapter.

(b) A notice of proposed action published in the FEDERAL REGISTER will set forth:

(1) The nature of the action proposed;

(2) The manner in which a copy of the safety analysis and of the ACRS report, if any, may be obtained or examined.

(3) For a notice of intended operation under § 52.103(a) of this chapter, the following information:

(i) The identification of the NRC action as making the finding required under § 52.103(g) of this chapter;

(ii) The manner in which the licensee notifications under 10 CFR 52.99(c) which are required to be made available by 10 CFR 52.99(e)(2) may be obtained and examined;

(iii) The manner in which copies of the safety analysis may be obtained and examined; and

(iv) Any conditions, limitations, or restrictions to be placed on the license in connection with the finding under § 52.103(g) of this chapter, and the expiration date or circumstances (if any) under which the conditions, limitations or restrictions will no longer apply.

(c) If an application for a license is complete enough to permit all evaluations, other than completion inspection, necessary for the issuance of a construction permit and operating license, the notice of proposed issuance of a construction permit may provide that on completion of construction and inspection the operating license will be issued without further prior notice.

(d) The notice of proposed action will provide that, within the time period provided under § 2.309(b):

(1) The applicant may file a request for a hearing; and

(2) Any person whose interest may be affected by the proceeding may file a request for a hearing or a petition for leave to intervene if a hearing has already been requested.

(e)(1) If no request for a hearing or petition for leave to intervene is filed within the time prescribed in the notice, the Director, Office of Nuclear Reactor Regulation, Director, Office of New Reactors, or Director, Office of Nuclear Material Safety and Safeguards, as appropriate, may take the proposed action, inform the appropriate State and local officials, and publish in the FEDERAL REGISTER a notice of issuance of the license or other action.

(2) If a request for a hearing or a petition for leave to intervene is filed within the time prescribed in the notice, the presiding officer who shall be an Atomic Safety and Licensing Board established by the Commission or by the Chief Administrative Judge of the Atomic Safety and Licensing Board Panel, will rule on the request and/or petition, and the Secretary or the presiding officer will issue a notice of hearing or an appropriate order.

[27 FR 377, Jan. 13, 1962]

EDITORIAL NOTE: For FEDERAL REGISTER citations affecting § 2.105, see the List of CFR Sections Affected, which appears in the Finding Aids section of the printed volume and at *www.fdsys.gov*.

§ 2.106 Notice of issuance.

(a) The Director, Office of New Reactors, Director, Office of Nuclear Reactor Regulation, or Director, Office of Nuclear Material Safety and Safeguards, as appropriate, will inform the State and local officials specified in § 2.104(c) and publish a document in the FEDERAL REGISTER announcing the issuance of:

(1) A license or an amendment of a license for which a notice of proposed action has been previously published;

(2) An amendment of a license for a facility of the type described in § 50.21(b) or § 50.22 of this chapter, or a testing facility, whether or not a notice of proposed action has been previously published; and

(3) The finding under § 52.103(g) of this chapter.

(b) The notice of issuance will set forth:

(1) In the case of a license or amendment:

(i) The nature of the license or amendment;

(ii) The manner in which copies of the safety analysis, if any, may be obtained and examined; and

(iii) A finding that the application for the license or amendment complies with the requirements of the Act and this chapter.

(2) In the case of a finding under § 52.103(g) of this chapter:

(i) The manner in which copies of the safety analysis, if any, may be obtained and examined; and

(ii) A finding that the prescribed inspections, tests, and analyses have been performed, the prescribed acceptance criteria have been met, and that the license complies with the requirements of the Act and this chapter.

(c) The Director of Nuclear Material Safety and Safeguards will also cause to be published in the FEDERAL REGISTER notice of, and will inform the State, local, and Tribal officials specified in § 2.104(c) of any action with respect to an application for construction authorization for a high-level radioactive waste repository at a geologic repository operations area, a license to receive and possess high-level radioactive waste at a geologic repository operations area pursuant to parts 60 or 63 of this chapter, or an amendment to such license for which a notice of proposed action has been previously published.

(d) The Office of Nuclear Material Safety and Safeguards will also cause to be published in the FEDERAL REGISTER notice of, and will inform the State and local officials or Tribal governing body specified in § 2.104(c) of any licensing action with respect to a license to receive radioactive waste from other persons for disposal under part 61 of this chapter or the amendment of such a license for which a notice of proposed action has been previously published.

[37 FR 15131, July 28, 1972, as amended at 38 FR 9586, Apr. 18, 1973; 46 FR 13978, Feb. 25, 1981; 47 FR 57478, Dec. 27, 1982; 66 FR 55787, Nov. 2, 2001; 69 FR 2235, Jan. 14, 2004; 72 FR 49473, Aug. 28, 2007; 73 FR 5716, Jan. 31, 2008; 77 FR 46590, Aug. 3, 2012]

§ 2.107 Withdrawal of application.

(a) The Commission may permit an applicant to withdraw an application prior to the issuance of a notice of hearing on such terms and conditions as it may prescribe, or may, on receiving a request for withdrawal of an application, deny the application or dismiss it with prejudice. If the application is withdrawn prior to issuance of a notice of hearing, the Commission shall dismiss the proceeding. Withdrawal of an application after the issuance of a notice of hearing shall be on such terms as the presiding officer may prescribe.

(b) The withdrawal of an application does not authorize the removal of any document from the files of the Commission.

(c) The Director, Office of Nuclear Reactor Regulation, Director, Office of New Reactors, or Director, Office of Nuclear Material Safety and Safeguards, as appropriate, will cause to be published in the FEDERAL REGISTER a notice of the withdrawal of an application if notice of receipt of the application has been previously published.

[27 FR 377, Jan. 13, 1962, as amended at 28 FR 10152, Sept. 17, 1963; 69 FR 2236, Jan. 14, 2004; 73 FR 5716, Jan. 31, 2008; 77 FR 46590, Aug. 3, 2012]

§2.108 Denial of application for failure to supply information.

(a) The Director, Office of Nuclear Reactor Regulation, Director, Office of New Reactors, or Director, Office of Nuclear Material Safety and Safeguards, as appropriate, may deny an application if an applicant fails to respond to a request for additional information within thirty (30) days from the date of the request, or within such other time as may be specified.

(b) The Director, Office of Nuclear Reactor Regulation, Director, Office of New Reactors, or Director, Office of Nuclear Material Safety and Safeguards, as appropriate, will cause to be published in the FEDERAL REGISTER a notice of denial when notice of receipt of the application has previously been published, but notice of hearing has not yet been published. The notice of denial will provide that, within thirty (30) days after the date of publication in the FEDERAL REGISTER.

(1) The applicant may demand a hearing, and

(2) Any person whose interest may be affected by the proceeding may file a petition for leave to intervene.

(c) When both a notice of receipt of the application and a notice of hearing have been published, the presiding officer, upon a motion made by the staff under §2.323, will rule whether an application should be denied by the Director, Office of Nuclear Reactor Regulation, Director, Office of New Reactors, or Director, Office of Nuclear Material Safety and Safeguards, as appropriate, under paragraph (a) of this section.

[77 FR 46590, Aug. 3, 2012]

§2.109 Effect of timely renewal application.

(a) Except for the renewal of an operating license for a nuclear power plant under 10 CFR 50.21(b) or 50.22, an early site permit under subpart A of part 52 of this chapter, a manufacturing license under subpart F of part 52 of this chapter, or a combined license under subpart C of part 52 of this chapter, if at least 30 days before the expiration of an existing license authorizing any activity of a continuing nature, the licensee files an application for a renewal or for a new license for the activity so authorized, the existing license will not be deemed to have expired until the application has been finally determined.

(b) If the licensee of a nuclear power plant licensed under 10 CFR 50.21(b) or 50.22 files a sufficient application for renewal of either an operating license or a combined license at least 5 years before the expiration of the existing license, the existing license will not be deemed to have expired until the application has been finally determined.

(c) If the holder of an early site permit licensed under subpart A of part 52 of this chapter files a sufficient application for renewal under §52.29 of this chapter at least 12 months before the expiration of the existing early site permit, the existing permit will not be deemed to have expired until the application has been finally determined.

(d) If the licensee of a manufacturing license under subpart F of part 52 of this chapter files a sufficient application for renewal under §52.177 of this chapter at least 12 months before the expiration of the existing license, the existing license will not be deemed to have expired until the application has been finally determined.

[72 FR 49473, Aug. 28, 2007]

§2.110 Filing and administrative action on submittals for standard design approval or early review of site suitability issues.

(a)(1) A submittal for a standard design approval under subpart E of part 52 of this chapter shall be subject to §§2.101(a) and 2.390 to the same extent as if it were an application for a permit or license.

(2) Except as specifically provided otherwise by the provisions of appendix Q to parts 50 of this chapter, a submittal for early review of site suitability issues under appendix Q to parts 50 of this chapter shall be subject to §§2.101(a)(2) through (4) to the same extent as if it were an application for a permit or license.

(b) Upon initiation of review by the NRC staff of a submittal for an early review of site suitability issues under Appendix Q of part 50 of this chapter, or for a standard design approval under subpart E of part 52 of this chapter, the

Director, Office of New Reactors, or Director, Office of Nuclear Reactor Regulation, as appropriate shall publish in the FEDERAL REGISTER a notice of receipt of the submittal, inviting comments from interested persons within 60 days of publication or other time as may be specified, for consideration by the NRC staff and ACRS in their review.

(c)(1) Upon completion of review by the NRC staff and the ACRS of a submittal for a standard design approval, the Director, Office of New Reactors or Director, Office of Nuclear Reactor Regulation, as appropriate shall publish in the FEDERAL REGISTER a determination as to whether or not the design is acceptable, subject to terms and conditions as may be appropriate, and shall make available at the NRC Web site, *http://www.nrc.gov*, a report that analyzes the design.

(2) Upon completion of review by the NRC staff and, if appropriate by the ACRS, of a submittal for early review of site suitability issues, the NRC staff shall prepare a staff site report which shall identify the location of the site, state the site suitability issues reviewed, explain the nature and scope of the review, state the conclusions of the staff regarding the issues reviewed and state the reasons for those conclusions. Upon issuance of an NRC staff site report, the NRC staff shall publish a notice of the availability of the report in the FEDERAL REGISTER and shall make the report available at the NRC Web site, *http://www.nrc.gov*. The NRC staff shall also send a copy of the report to the Governor or other appropriate official of the State in which the site is located, and to the chief executive of the municipality in which the site is located or, if the site is not located in a municipality, to the chief executive of the county.

[72 FR 49474, Aug. 28, 2007; 73 FR 5716, Jan. 31, 2008]

§2.111 Prohibition of sex discrimination.

No person shall on the grounds of sex be excluded from participation in, be denied a license, standard design approval, or petition for rulemaking (including a design certification), be denied the benefits of, or be subjected to discrimination under any program or activity carried on or receiving Federal assistance under the Act or the Energy Reorganization Act of 1974.

[72 FR 49474, Aug. 28, 2007]

Subpart B—Procedure for Imposing Requirements by Order, or for Modification, Suspension, or Revocation of a License, or for Imposing Civil Penalties

§2.200 Scope of subpart.

(a) This subpart prescribes the procedures in cases initiated by the staff, or upon a request by any person, to impose requirements by order, or to modify, suspend, or revoke a license, or to take other action as may be proper, against any person subject to the jurisdiction of the Commission. However, with regard to the holder of a part 76 certificate of compliance or compliance plan, except for civil penalty procedures in this subpart, the applicable procedures are set forth in §76.70 of this chapter.

(b) This subpart also prescribes the procedures in cases initiated by the staff to impose civil penalties pursuant to section 234 of the Act and section 206 of the Energy Reorganization Act of 1974.

[36 FR 16896, Aug. 26, 1971, as amended at 42 FR 28893, June 6, 1977; 48 FR 44172, Sept. 28, 1983; 62 FR 6668, Feb. 12, 1997]

§2.201 Notice of violation.

(a) In response to an alleged violation of any provision of the Act or this chapter or the conditions of a license or an order issued by the Commission, the Commission may serve on the licensee or other person subject to the jurisdiction of the Commission a written notice of violation; a separate notice may be omitted if an order pursuant to §2.202 or demand for information pursuant to §2.204 is issued that otherwise identifies the apparent violation. The notice of violation will concisely state the alleged violation and may require that the licensee or other person submit, within 20 days of the date of the notice or other specified time, a written explanation or statement in reply if the Commission believes that the licensee has not already addressed all the issues contained in the notice of violation, including:

(1) Corrective steps which have been taken by the licensee or other person and the results achieved;

(2) Corrective steps which will be taken; and

(3) The date when full compliance will be achieved.

(b) The notice may require the licensee or other person subject to the jurisdiction of the Commission to admit or deny the violation and to state the reasons for the violation, if admitted. It may provide that, if an adequate reply is not received within the time specified in the notice, the Commission may issue an order or a demand for information as to why the license should not be modified, suspended or revoked or why such other action as may be proper should not be taken.

[56 FR 40684, Aug. 15, 1991, as amended at 61 FR 43408, Aug. 22, 1996]

§2.202 Orders.

(a) The Commission may institute a proceeding to modify, suspend, or revoke a license or to take such other action as may be proper by serving on the licensee or other person subject to the jurisdiction of the Commission an order that will:

(1) Allege the violations with which the licensee or other person subject to the Commission's jurisdiction is charged, or the potentially hazardous conditions or other facts deemed to be sufficient ground for the proposed action, and specify the action proposed;

(2) Provide that the licensee or other person must file a written answer to the order under oath or affirmation within twenty (20) days of its date, or such other time as may be specified in the order;

(3) Inform the licensee or any other person adversely affected by the order of his or her right, within twenty (20) days of the date of the order, or such other time as may be specified in the order, to demand a hearing on all or part of the order, except in a case where the licensee or other person has consented in writing to the order;

(4) Specify the issues for hearing; and

(5) State the effective date of the order; if the Commission finds that the public health, safety, or interest so requires or that the violation or conduct causing the violation is willful, the order may provide, for stated reasons, that the proposed action be immediately effective pending further order.

(b) A licensee or other person to whom the Commission has issued an order under this section must respond to the order by filing a written answer under oath or affirmation. The answer shall specifically admit or deny each allegation or charge made in the order, and shall set forth the matters of fact and law on which the licensee or other person relies, and, if the order is not consented to, the reasons as to why the order should not have been issued. Except as provided in paragraph (d) of this section, the answer may demand a hearing.

(c) If the answer demands a hearing, the Commission will issue an order designating the time and place of hearing.

(1) If the answer demands a hearing with respect to an immediately effective order, the hearing will be conducted expeditiously, giving due consideration to the rights of the parties.

(2)(i) The licensee or other person to whom the Commission has issued an immediately effective order in accordance with paragraph (a)(5) of this section, may, in addition to demanding a hearing, at the time the answer is filed or sooner, file a motion with the presiding officer to set aside the immediate effectiveness of the order on the ground that the order, including the need for immediate effectiveness, is not based on adequate evidence but on mere suspicion, unfounded allegations, or error. The motion must state with particularity the reasons why the order is not based on adequate evidence and must be accompanied by affidavits or other evidence relied on.

(ii) Any party may file a motion with the presiding officer requesting that the presiding officer order live testimony. Any motion for live testimony must be made in conjunction with the motion to set aside the immediate effectiveness of the order or any party's response thereto. The presiding officer may, on its own motion, order live testimony. The presiding officer's basis for approving any motion for, or ordering on its own motion, live testimony shall be that taking live testimony would assist in its decision on the motion to set aside the immediate effectiveness of the order.

(iii) The NRC staff shall respond in writing within 5 days of the receipt of either a motion to set aside the immediate effectiveness of the order or the presiding officer's order denying a motion for live testimony. In cases in which the presiding officer orders live testimony, the staff may present its response through live testimony rather than a written response.

(iv) The presiding officer shall conduct any live testimony pursuant to its powers in § 2.319 of this part, except that no subpoenas, discovery, or referred rulings or certified questions to the Commission shall be permitted for this purpose.

(v) The presiding officer may, on motion by the staff or any other party to the proceeding, where good cause exists, delay the hearing on the immediately effective order at any time for such periods as are consistent with the due process rights of the licensee or other person and other affected parties.

(vi) The licensee or other person challenging the immediate effectiveness of an order bears the burden of going forward with evidence that the immediately effective order is not based on adequate evidence, but on mere suspicion, unfounded allegations, or error. The NRC staff bears the burden of persuading the presiding officer that adequate evidence supports the grounds for the immediately effective order and immediate effectiveness is warranted.

(vii) The presiding officer shall issue a decision on the motion to set aside the immediate effectiveness of the order expeditiously. During the pendency of the motion to set aside the immediate effectiveness of the order or at any other time, the presiding officer may not stay the immediate effectiveness of the order, either on its own motion, or upon motion of the licensee or other person.

(viii) The presiding officer shall uphold the immediate effectiveness of the order if it finds that there is adequate evidence to support immediate effectiveness. An order upholding immediate effectiveness will constitute the final agency action on immediate effectiveness. The presiding officer will promptly refer an order setting aside immediate effectiveness to the Commission and such order setting aside immediate effectiveness will not be effective pending further order of the Commission.

(d) An answer may consent to the entry of an order in substantially the form proposed in the order with respect to all or some of the actions proposed in the order. The consent, in the answer or other written document, of the licensee or other person to whom the order has been issued to the entry of an order shall constitute a waiver by the licensee or other person of a hearing, findings of fact and conclusions of law, and of all right to seek Commission and judicial review or to contest the validity of the order in any forum as to those matters which have been consented to or agreed to or on which a hearing has not been requested. An order that has been consented to shall have the same force and effect as an order made after hearing by a presiding officer or the Commission, and shall be effective as provided in the order.

(e)(1) If the order involves the modification of a part 50 license and is a backfit, the requirements of § 50.109 of this chapter shall be followed, unless the licensee has consented to the action required.

(2) If the order involves the modification of combined license under subpart C of part 52 of this chapter, the requirements of § 52.98 of this chapter shall be followed unless the licensee has consented to the action required.

(3) If the order involves a change to an early site permit under subpart A of part 52 of this chapter, the requirements of § 52.39 of this chapter must be followed, unless the applicant or licensee has consented to the action required.

(4) If the order involves a change to a standard design certification rule referenced by that plant's application, the requirements, if any, in the referenced design certification rule with respect to changes must be followed, or, in the absence of these requirements, the requirements of § 52.63 of this chapter must be followed, unless the applicant

or licensee has consented to follow the action required.

(5) If the order involves a change to a standard design approval referenced by that plant's application, the requirements of § 52.145 of this chapter must be followed unless the applicant or licensee has consented to follow the action required.

(6) If the order involves a modification of a manufacturing license under subpart F of part 52, the requirements of § 52.171 of this chapter must be followed, unless the applicant or licensee has consented to the action required.

[56 FR 40684, Aug. 15, 1991, as amended at 57 FR 20198, May 12, 1992; 72 FR 49474, Aug. 28, 2007; 80 FR 63419, Oct. 20, 2015]

§ 2.203 Settlement and compromise.

At any time after the issuance of an order designating the time and place of hearing in a proceeding to modify, suspend, or revoke a license or for other action, the staff and a licensee or other person may enter into a stipulation for the settlement of the proceeding or the compromise of a civil penalty. The stipulation or compromise shall be subject to approval by the designated presiding officer or, if none has been designated, by the Chief Administrative Law Judge, according due weight to the position of the staff. The presiding officer, or if none has been designated, the Chief Administrative Law Judge, may order such adjudication of the issues as he may deem to be required in the public interest to dispose of the proceeding. If approved, the terms of the settlement or compromise shall be embodied in a decision or order settling and discontinuing the proceeding.

[36 FR 16896, Aug. 26, 1971]

§ 2.204 Demand for information.

(a) The Commission may issue to a licensee or other person subject to the jurisdiction of the Commission a demand for information for the purpose of determining whether an order under § 2.202 should be issued, or whether other action should be taken, which demand will:

(1) Allege the violations with which the licensee or other person is charged, or the potentially hazardous conditions or other facts deemed to be sufficient ground for issuing the demand; and

(2) Provide that the licensee must, or the other person may, file a written answer to the demand for information under oath or affirmation within twenty (20) days of its date, or such other time as may be specified in the demand for information.

(b) A licensee to whom the Commission has issued a demand for information under this section must respond to the demand by filing a written answer under oath or affirmation; any other person to whom the Commission has issued a demand for information may, in its discretion, respond to the demand by filing a written answer under oath or affirmation. The licensee's answer shall specifically admit or deny each allegation or charge made in the demand for information, and shall set forth the matters of fact and law on which the licensee relies. A person other than a licensee may answer as described above, or by setting forth its reasons why the demand should not have been issued and, if the requested information is not provided, the reasons why it is not provided.

(c) Upon review of the answer filed pursuant to paragraph (a)(2) of this section, or if no answer is filed, the Commission may institute a proceeding pursuant to 10 CFR 2.202 to take such action as may be proper.

(d) An answer may consent to the entry of an order pursuant to § 2.202 in substantially the form proposed in the demand for information. Such consent shall constitute a waiver as provided in § 2.202(d).

[56 FR 40685, Aug. 15, 1991]

§ 2.205 Civil penalties.

(a) Before instituting any proceeding to impose a civil penalty under section 234 of the Act, the Executive Director for Operations or the Executive Director's designee, as appropriate, shall serve a written notice of violation upon the person charged. This notice may be included in a notice issued pursuant to § 2.201 or § 76.70(d) of this chapter. The notice of violation shall specify the date or dates, facts, and the nature of the alleged act or omission with which the person is charged, and shall identify specifically the particular provision or provisions of the law, rule, regulation, license, permit, part 76 certificate of compliance or compliance plan, or cease and desist order involved in the alleged violation and must state the amount of each proposed penalty. The notice of violation shall also advise the person charged that the civil penalty may be paid in the amount specified therein, or the proposed imposition of the civil penalty may be protested in its entirety or in part, by a written answer, either denying the violation or showing extenuating circumstances. The notice of violation shall advise the person charged that upon failure to pay a civil penalty subsequently determined by the Commission, if any, unless compromised, remitted, or mitigated, be collected by civil action, pursuant to Section 234c of the Act.

(b) Within twenty (20) days of the date of a notice of violation or other time specified in the notice, the person charged may either pay the penalty in the amount proposed or answer the notice of violation. The answer to the notice of violation shall state any facts, explanations, and arguments, denying the charges of violation, or demonstrating any extenuating circumstances, error in the notice of violation, or other reason why the penalty should not be imposed and may request remission or mitigation of the penalty.

(c) If the person charged with violation fails to answer within the time specified in paragraph (b) of this section, an order may be issued imposing the civil penalty in the amount set forth in the notice of violation described in paragraph (a) of this section.

(d) If the person charged with violation files an answer to the notice of violation, the Executive Director for Operations or the Executive Director's designee, upon consideration of the answer, will issue an order dismissing the proceeding or imposing, mitigating, or remitting the civil penalty. The person charged may, within twenty (20) days of the date of the order or other time specified in the order, request a hearing.

(e) If the person charged with violation requests a hearing, the Commission will issue an order designating the time and place of hearing.

(f) If a hearing is held, an order will be issued after the hearing by the presiding officer or the Commission dismissing the proceeding or imposing, mitigating, or remitting the civil penalty.

(g) The Executive Director for Operations or the Executive Director's designee, as appropriate may compromise any civil penalty, subject to the provisions of § 2.203.

(h) If the civil penalty is not compromised, or is not remitted by the Executive Director for Operations or the Executive Director's designee, as appropriate, the presiding officer, or the Commission, and if payment is not made within ten (10) days following either the service of the order described in paragraph (c) or (f) of this section, or the expiration of the time for requesting a hearing described in paragraph (d) of this section, the Executive Director for Operations or the Executive Director's designee, as appropriate, may refer the matter to the Attorney General for collection.

(i) Except when payment is made after compromise or mitigation by the Department of Justice or as ordered by a court of the United States, following reference of the matter to the Attorney General for collection, payment of civil penalties imposed under Section 234 of the Act are to be made payable to the U.S. Nuclear Regulatory Commission, in U.S. funds, by check, draft, money order, credit cars, or electronic funds transfer such as Automated Clearing House (ACH) using Electronic Data Interchange (EDI). Federal agencies may also make payment by the On-Line Payment and Collections System (OPAC's). All payments are to be made in accordance with the specific payment instructions provided with Notices of Violation that propose civil penalties and Orders Imposing Civil Monetary Penalties.

(j) *Amount.* A civil monetary penalty imposed under Section 234 of the Atomic Energy Act of 1954, as amended, or any other statute within the jurisdiction of the Commission that provides for the imposition of a civil penalty in an amount equal to the amount set forth in Section 234, may not exceed

$285,057 for each violation. If any violation is a continuing one, each day of such violation shall constitute a separate violation for the purposes of computing the applicable civil penalty.'

[36 FR 16896, Aug. 26, 1971, as amended at 52 FR 31608, Aug. 21, 1987; 54 FR 53315, Dec. 28, 1989; 61 FR 53555, Oct. 11, 1996; 62 FR 6668, Feb. 12, 1997; 63 FR 31850, June 10, 1998; 65 FR 59272, Oct. 4, 2000; 69 FR 62394, Oct. 26, 2004; 73 FR 54673, Sept. 23, 2008; 81 FR 43021, July 1, 2016; 82 FR 8135, Jan. 24, 2017]

§ 2.206 Requests for action under this subpart.

(a) Any person may file a request to institute a proceeding pursuant to § 2.202 to modify, suspend, or revoke a license, or for any other action as may be proper. Requests must be addressed to the Executive Director for Operations and must be filed either by hand delivery to the NRC's Offices at 11555 Rockville Pike, Rockville, Maryland; by mail or telegram addressed to the Executive Director for Operations, U.S. Nuclear Regulatory Commission, Washington, DC 20555–0001; or by electronic submissions, for example, via facsimile, Electronic Information Exchange, e-mail, or CD-ROM. Electronic submissions must be made in a manner that enables the NRC to receive, read, authenticate, distribute, and archive the submission, and process and retrieve it a single page at a time. Detailed guidance on making electronic submissions can be obtained by visiting the NRC's Web site at *http://www.nrc.gov/site-help/e-submittals.html;* by e-mail to *MSHD.Resource@nrc.gov;* or by writing the Office of the Chief Information Officer, U.S. Nuclear Regulatory Commission, Washington, DC 20555–0001. The request must specify the action requested and set forth the facts that constitute the basis for the request. The Executive Director for Operations will refer the request to the Director of the NRC office with responsibility for the subject matter of the request for appropriate action in accordance with paragraph (b) of this section.

(b) Within a reasonable time after a request pursuant to paragraph (a) of this section has been received, the Director of the NRC office with responsibility for the subject matter of the request shall either institute the requested proceeding in accordance with this subpart or shall advise the person who made the request in writing that no proceeding will be instituted in whole or in part, with respect to the request, and the reasons for the decision.

(c)(1) Director's decisions under this section will be filed with the Office of the Secretary. Within twenty-five (25) days after the date of the Director's decision under this section that no proceeding will be instituted or other action taken in whole or in part, the Commission may on its own motion review that decision, in whole or in part, to determine if the Director has abused his discretion. This review power does not limit in any way either the Commission's supervisory power over delegated staff actions or the Commission's power to consult with the staff on a formal or informal basis regarding institution of proceedings under this section.

(2) No petition or other request for Commission review of a Director's decision under this section will be entertained by the Commission.

(3) The Secretary is authorized to extend the time for Commission review on its own motion of a Director's denial under paragraph (c) of this section.

[39 FR 12353, Apr. 5, 1974, as amended at 42 FR 36240, July 14, 1977; 45 FR 73466, Nov. 5, 1980; 52 FR 31608, Aug. 21, 1987; 53 FR 43419, Oct. 27, 1988; 64 FR 48948, Sept. 9, 1999; 68 FR 58799, Oct. 10, 2003; 69 FR 2236, Jan. 14, 2004; 69 FR 41749, July 12, 2004; 74 FR 62679, Dec. 1, 2009; 80 FR 74978, Dec. 1, 2015]

Subpart C—Rules of General Applicability: Hearing Requests, Petitions To Intervene, Availability of Documents, Selection of Specific Hearing Procedures, Presiding Officer Powers, and General Hearing Management for NRC Adjudicatory Hearings

SOURCE: 69 FR 2236, Jan. 14, 2004, unless otherwise noted.

§ 2.300 Scope of subpart C.

The provisions of this subpart apply to all adjudications conducted under the authority of the Atomic Energy

Act of 1954, as amended, the Energy Reorganization Act of 1974, and 10 CFR Part 2, unless specifically stated otherwise in this subpart.

§ 2.301 Exceptions.

Consistent with 5 U.S.C. 554(a)(4) of the Administrative Procedure Act, the Commission may provide alternative procedures in adjudications to the extent that the conduct of military or foreign affairs functions is involved.

§ 2.302 Filing of documents.

(a) Documents filed in Commission adjudicatory proceedings subject to this part shall be electronically transmitted through the E-Filing system, unless the Commission or presiding officer grants an exemption permitting an alternative filing method or unless the filing falls within the scope of paragraph (g)(1) of this section.

(b) Upon an order from the Commission or presiding officer permitting alternative filing methods, or as otherwise set forth in Guidance for Electronic Submissions to the NRC, documents may be filed by:

(1) First-class mail: Office of the Secretary, U.S. Nuclear Regulatory Commission, Washington, DC 20555–0001, Attention: Rulemakings and Adjudications Staff; or

(2) Courier, express mail, and expedited delivery services: Office of the Secretary, Sixteenth Floor, One White Flint North, 11555 Rockville Pike, Rockville, MD 20852, Attention: Rulemakings and Adjudications Staff.

(c) All documents offered for filing must be accompanied by a certificate of service stating the names and addresses of the persons served as well as the manner and date of service.

(d) Filing is considered complete:

(1) By electronic transmission when the filer performs the last act that it must perform to transmit a document, in its entirety, electronically;

(2) By first-class mail as of the time of deposit in the mail;

(3) By courier, express mail, or expedited delivery service upon depositing the document with the provider of the service; or

(4) If a filing must be submitted by two or more methods, such as a filing that the Guidance for Electronic Submission to the NRC indicates should be transmitted electronically as well as physically delivered or mailed on optical storage media, the filing is complete when all methods of filing have been completed.

(e) For filings by electronic transmission, the filer must make a good faith effort to successfully transmit the entire filing. Notwithstanding paragraph (d) of this section, a filing will not be considered complete if the filer knows or has reason to know that the entire filing has not been successfully transmitted.

(f) *Digital ID Certificates.* (1) Through digital ID certificates, the NRC permits participants in the proceeding to access the E-Filing system to file documents, serve other participants, and retrieve documents in the proceeding.

(2) Any participant or participant representative that does not have a digital ID certificate shall request one from the NRC before that participant or representative intends to make its first electronic filing to the E-Filing system. A participant or representative may apply for a digital ID certificate on the NRC Web site at *http://www.nrc.gov/site-help/e-submittals.html.*

(3) Group ID Certificate. A participant wishing to obtain a digital ID certificate valid for several persons may obtain a group digital ID certificate. A Group ID cannot be used to file documents. The Group ID provides access to the E-Filing system for the individuals specifically identified in the group's application to retrieve documents recently received by the system. The Group ID also enables a group of people, all of whom may not have individual digital ID certificates, to be notified when a filing has been made in a particular proceeding.

(g) *Filing Method Requirements*—(1) *Electronic filing.* Unless otherwise provided by order, all filings must be made as electronic submissions in a manner that enables the NRC to receive, read, authenticate, distribute, and archive the submission, and process and retrieve it a single page at a time. Detailed guidance on making electronic submissions may be found in the Guidance for Electronic Submissions to the NRC and on the NRC Web site at *http://www.nrc.gov/site-help/e-submittals.html.*

If a filing contains sections of information or electronic formats that may not be transmitted electronically for security or other reasons, the portions not containing those sections will be transmitted electronically to the E-Filing system. In addition, optical storage media (OSM) containing the entire filing must be physically delivered or mailed. In such cases, the submitter does not need to apply to the Commission or presiding officer for an exemption to deviate from the requirements in paragraph (g)(1) of this section.

(2) *Electronic transmission exemption.* Upon a finding of good cause, the Commission or presiding officer can grant an exemption from electronic transmission requirements found in paragraph (g)(1) of this section to a participant who is filing electronic documents. The exempt participant is permitted to file electronic documents by physically delivering or mailing an OSM containing the documents. A participant granted this exemption would still be required to meet the electronic formatting requirement in paragraph (g)(1) of this section.

(3) *Electronic document exemption.* Upon a finding of good cause, the Commission or presiding officer can exempt a participant from both the electronic (computer file) formatting and electronic transmission requirements in paragraph (g)(1) of this section. A participant granted such an exemption can file paper documents either in person or by courier, express mail, some other expedited delivery service, or first-class mail, as ordered by the Commission or presiding officer.

(4) *Requesting an exemption.* A filer seeking an exemption under paragraphs (g)(2) or (g)(3) of this section must submit the exemption request with its first filing in the proceeding. In the request, a filer must show good cause as to why it cannot file electronically. The filer may not change its formats or delivery methods for filing until a ruling on the exemption request is issued. Exemption requests under paragraphs (g)(2) or (g)(3) of this section sought after the first filing in the proceeding will be granted only if the requestor shows that the interests of fairness so require.

[72 FR 49149, Aug. 28, 2007]

§ 2.303 Docket.

The Secretary shall maintain a docket for each proceeding conducted under this part, commencing with either the initial notice of hearing, notice of proposed action, order, request for hearing or petition for leave to intervene, as appropriate. The Secretary shall maintain all files and records of proceedings, including transcripts and video recordings of testimony, exhibits, and all papers, correspondence, decisions and orders filed or issued. All documents, records, and exhibits filed in any proceeding must be filed with the Secretary as described in §§ 2.302 and 2.304.

§ 2.304 Formal requirements for documents; signatures; acceptance for filing.

(a) *Docket numbers and titles.* Each document filed in an adjudication to which a docket number has been assigned must contain a caption setting forth the docket number and the title of the proceeding and a description of the document (e.g., motion to quash subpoena).

(b) *Paper documents.* In addition to the requirements in this part, paper documents must be stapled or bound on the left side; typewritten, printed, or otherwise reproduced in permanent form on good unglazed paper of standard letterhead size; signed in ink by the participant, its authorized representative, or an attorney having authority with respect to it; and filed with an original and two conforming copies.

(c) *Format.* Each page in a document must begin not less than one inch from the top, with side and bottom margins of not less than one inch. Text must be double-spaced, except that quotations may be single-spaced and indented. The requirements of this paragraph do not apply to original documents, or admissible copies, offered as exhibits, or to specifically prepared exhibits.

(d) *Signatures.* The original of each document must be signed by the participant or its authorized representative, or by an attorney having authority with respect to it. The document must state the capacity of the person signing; his or her address, phone number, and e-mail address; and the date of signature. The signature of a person signing a pleading or other similar document submitted by a participant is a representation that the document has been subscribed in the capacity specified with full authority, that he or she has read it and knows the contents, that to the best of his or her knowledge, information, and belief the statements made in it are true, and that it is not interposed for delay. The signature of a person signing an affidavit or similar document, which should be submitted in accord with the form outlined in 28 U.S.C. 1746, is a representation that, under penalty of perjury, the document is true and correct to the best of that individual's knowledge and belief. If a document is not signed, or is signed with intent to defeat the purpose of this section, it may be struck.

(1) An electronic document must be signed using a participant's or a participant representative's digital ID certificate. Additional signatures can be added to the electronic document, including to any affidavits that accompany the document, by a typed-in designation that indicates the signer understands and acknowledges that he or she is assenting to the representations in paragraph (d) of this section.

(i) When signing an electronic document using a digital ID certificate, the signature page for the electronic document should contain a typed signature block that includes the phrase "Signed (electronically) by" typed onto the signature line; the name and the capacity of the person signing; the person's address, phone number, and e-mail address; and the date of signature.

(ii) If additional individuals need to sign an electronic document, including any affidavits that accompany the document, such individuals must sign by inserting a typed signature block in the electronic document that includes the phrase "Executed in Accord with 10 CFR 2.304(d)" or its equivalent typed on the signature line as well as the name and the capacity of the person signing; the person's address, phone number, and e-mail address; and the date of signature to the extent any of these items are different from the information provided for the digital ID certificate signer.

(2) Paper documents must be signed in ink.

(e) *Designation for service.* The first document filed by any participant in a proceeding must designate the name and address of a person on whom service may be made. This document must also designate the e-mail address, if any, of the person on whom service may be made.

(f) *Acceptance for filing.* Any document that fails to conform to the requirements of this section may be refused acceptance for filing by the Secretary or the presiding officer and may be returned with an indication of the reason for nonacceptance. Any document that is not accepted for filing will not be entered on the Commission's docket.

(g) *Pre-filed written testimony and exhibits.* In any instance in which a participant submits electronically through the E-Filing system written testimony or hearing exhibits in advance of a hearing, the written testimony of each individual witness or witness panel and each individual exhibit shall be submitted as an individual electronic file.

[72 FR 49150, Aug. 28, 2007]

§ 2.305 Service of documents, methods, proof.

(a) *Service of documents by the Commission.* Except for subpoenas, the Commission shall serve all orders, decisions, notices, and other documents to all participants, by the same delivery method those participants use to file and accept service.

(b) *Who may be served.* Any document required to be served upon a participant shall be served upon that person or upon the representative designated by the participant or by law to receive service of documents. When a participant has appeared by attorney, service shall be made upon the attorney of record.

(c) *Method of service accompanying a filing.* Service must be made electronically to the E-Filing system. Upon an order from the Commission or presiding officer permitting alternative filing methods under § 2.302(g)(4), service may be made by personal delivery, courier, expedited delivery service, or by first-class, express, certified or registered mail. As to each participant that cannot serve electronically, the Commission or presiding officer shall require service by the most expeditious means permitted under this paragraph that are available to the participant, unless the Commission or presiding officer finds that this requirement would impose undue burden or expense on the participant.

(1) Unless otherwise provided in this section, a participant will serve documents on the other participants by the same method by which those participants filed.

(2) A participant granted an exemption under § 2.302(g)(2) will serve the presiding officer and the participants in the proceeding that filed electronically by physically delivering or mailing optical storage media containing the electronic document.

(3) A participant granted an exemption under § 2.302(g)(3) will serve the presiding officer and the other participants in the proceeding by physically delivering or mailing a paper copy.

(4) Each document served (as may be required by law, rule, or order of the presiding officer) upon a participant to the proceeding must be accompanied by a signed certificate of service.

(i) If a document is served on participants through only the E-filing system, then the certificate of service must state that the document has been filed through the E-Filing system.

(ii) If a document is served on participants by only a method other than the E-Filing system, then the certificate of service must state the name, address, and method and date of service for all participants served.

(iii) If a document is served on some participants through the E-Filing system and other participants by another method of service, then the certificate of service must include a list of participants served through the E-filing system, and it must state the name, address, and method and date of service for all participants served by the other method of service.

(d) *Method of service not accompanying a filing.* Service of demonstrative evidence, e.g., maps and other physical evidence, may be made by first-class mail in all cases, unless the presiding officer directs otherwise or the participant desires to serve by a faster method. In instances when service of a document, such as a discovery document under § 2.336, will not accompany a filing with the agency, the participant may use any reasonable method of service to which the recipient agrees.

(e) *Service on the Secretary.* (1) All motions, briefs, pleadings, and other documents must be served on the Secretary of the Commission by the same or equivalent method, such as by electronic transmission or first-class mail, that they are served upon the presiding officer, so that the Secretary will receive the filing at approximately the same time that it is received by the presiding officer to which the filing is directed.

(2) When pleadings are personally delivered to a presiding officer conducting proceedings outside the Washington, DC area, service on the Secretary may be accomplished electronically to the E-Filing system, as well as by courier, express mail, or expedited delivery service.

(3) Service of demonstrative evidence (e.g., maps and other physical exhibits) on the Secretary of the Commission may be made by first-class mail in all cases, unless the presiding officer directs otherwise or the participant desires to serve by a faster method. All pre-filed testimony and exhibits shall be served on the Secretary of the Commission by the same or equivalent method that it is served upon the presiding officer to the proceedings, i.e., electronically to the E-Filing system, personal delivery or courier, express mail, or expedited delivery service.

(4) The addresses for the Secretary are:

(i) Internet: The E-Filing system at *http://www.nrc.gov.*

(ii) First-class mail: Office of the Secretary, U.S. Nuclear Regulatory Commission, Washington, DC 20555–0001, Attention: Rulemakings and Adjudications Staff; and

(iii) Courier, express mail, and expedited delivery services: Office of the Secretary, Sixteenth Floor, One White Flint North, 11555 Rockville Pike,

Rockville, Maryland 20852, Attention: Rulemakings and Adjudications Staff.

(f) *When service is complete.* Service upon a participant is complete:

(1) By the E-Filing system, when filing electronically to the E-Filing system is considered complete under § 2.302(d).

(2) By personal delivery, upon handing the document to the person, or leaving it at his or her office with that person's clerk or other person in charge or, if there is no one in charge, leaving it in a conspicuous place in the office, or if the office is closed or the person to be served has no office, leaving it at his or her usual place of residence with some person of suitable age and discretion then residing there;

(3) By mail, upon deposit in the United States mail, properly stamped and addressed;

(4) By expedited service, upon depositing the document with the provider of the expedited service; or

(5) When service cannot be effected by a method provided by paragraphs (f)(1)–(4) of this section, by any other method authorized by law.

(6) When two or more methods of service are required, service is considered complete when service by each method is complete under paragraphs (f)(1)–(4) of this section.

(g) *Service on the NRC staff.* (1) Service shall be made upon the NRC staff of all documents required to be filed with participants and the presiding officer in all proceedings, including those proceedings where the NRC staff informs the presiding officer of its determination not to participate as a party. Service upon the NRC staff shall be by the same or equivalent method as service upon the Office of the Secretary and the presiding officer, e.g., electronically, personal delivery or courier, express mail, or expedited delivery service. If no attorney representing the NRC Staff has filed a notice of appearance in the proceeding and service is not being made through the E-Filing System, service will be made using the following addresses, as applicable: by delivery to the Associate General Counsel for Hearings, Enforcement & Administration, One White Flint North, 11555 Rockville Pike, Rockville MD 20852–0001; by mail addressed to the Associate General Counsel for Hearings, Enforcement & Administration, U.S. Nuclear Regulatory Commission, Washington DC 20555–0001; by email to *OgcMailCenter.Resource@nrc.gov;* or by facsimile to 301–415–3200.

(2) If the NRC staff decides not to participate as a party in a proceeding, it shall, in its notification to the presiding officer and participants of its determination not to participate, designate a person and address for service of documents.

[72 FR 49150, Aug. 28, 2007, as amended at 77 FR 46590, Aug. 3, 2012; 81 FR 86909, Dec. 2, 2016]

§ 2.306 Computation of time.

(a) In computing any period of time, the day of the act, event, or default after which the designated period of time begins to run is not included. The last day of the period so computed is included unless it is a Saturday or Sunday, a Federal legal holiday at the place where the action or event is to occur, or a day upon which, because of an emergency closure of the Federal government in Washington, DC, NRC Headquarters does not open for business, in which event the period runs until the end of the next day that is not a Saturday, Sunday, Federal legal holiday, or emergency closure.

(b) Whenever a participant has the right or is required to do some act within a prescribed period after the service of a notice or other document upon him or her, no additional time is added to the prescribed period except in the following circumstances:

(1) If a notice or document is served upon a participant, by first-class mail only, three (3) calendar days will be added to the prescribed period for all the participants in the proceeding.

(2) If a notice or document is served upon a participant, by express mail or other expedited service only, two (2) calendar days will be added to the prescribed period for all the participants in the proceeding.

(3) If a document is to be served by multiple service methods, such as partially electronic and entirely on optical storage media, the additional number of days is computed according to the service method used to deliver the entire document, excluding courtesy

copies, to all of the other participants in the proceeding. The presiding officer may determine the calculation of additional days when a participant is not entitled to receive an entire filing served by multiple methods.

(4) In mixed service proceedings when all participants are not using the same filing and service method, the number of days for service will be determined by the presiding officer based on considerations of fairness and efficiency.

(c) To be considered timely, a document must be served:

(1) By 5 p.m. Eastern Time for a document served in person or by expedited service; and

(2) By 11:59 p.m. Eastern Time for a document served by the E-Filing system.

[72 FR 49151, Aug. 28, 2007]

§ 2.307 Extension and reduction of time limits; delegated authority to order use of procedures for access by potential parties to certain sensitive unclassified information.

(a) Except as otherwise provided by law, the time fixed or the period of time prescribed for an act that is required or allowed to be done at or within a specified time, may be extended or shortened either by the Commission or the presiding officer for good cause, or by stipulation approved by the Commission or the presiding officer.

(b) If this part does not prescribe a time limit for an action to be taken in the proceeding, the Commission or the presiding officer may set a time limit for the action.

(c) In circumstances where, in order to meet Commission requirements for intervention, potential parties may deem it necessary to obtain access to safeguards information (as defined in § 73.2 of this chapter) or to sensitive unclassified non-safeguards information, the Secretary is delegated authority to issue orders establishing procedures and timelines for submitting and resolving requests for this information.

[69 FR 2236, Jan. 14, 2004, as amended at 73 FR 10980, Feb. 29, 2008]

§ 2.308 Treatment of requests for hearing or petitions for leave to intervene by the Secretary.

Upon receipt of a request for hearing or a petition to intervene, the Secretary will forward the request or petition and/or proffered contentions and any answers and replies either to the Commission for a ruling on the request/petition and/or proffered contentions or to the Chief Administrative Judge of the Atomic Safety and Licensing Board Panel for the designation of a presiding officer under § 2.313(a) to rule on the matter.

§ 2.309 Hearing requests, petitions to intervene, requirements for standing, and contentions.

(a) *General requirements.* Any person whose interest may be affected by a proceeding and who desires to participate as a party must file a written request for hearing and a specification of the contentions which the person seeks to have litigated in the hearing. In a proceeding under 10 CFR 52.103, the Commission, acting as the presiding officer, will grant the request if it determines that the requestor has standing under the provisions of paragraph (d) of this section and has proposed at least one admissible contention that meets the requirements of paragraph (f) of this section. For all other proceedings, except as provided in paragraph (e) of this section, the Commission, presiding officer, or the Atomic Safety and Licensing Board designated to rule on the request for hearing and/or petition for leave to intervene, will grant the request/petition if it determines that the requestor/petitioner has standing under the provisions of paragraph (d) of this section and has proposed at least one admissible contention that meets the requirements of paragraph (f) of this section. In ruling on the request for hearing/petition to intervene submitted by petitioners seeking to intervene in the proceeding on the HLW repository, the Commission, the presiding officer, or the Atomic Safety and Licensing Board shall also consider any failure of the petitioner to participate as a potential party in the pre-license application phase under subpart J of this part in addition to the factors in paragraph (d) of this section. If a request for hearing or petition to intervene is filed in response to any notice of hearing or opportunity for hearing, the applicant/licensee shall be deemed to be a party.

(b) *Timing.* Unless specified elsewhere in this chapter or otherwise provided by the Commission, the request or petition and the list of contentions must be filed as follows:

(1) In proceedings for the direct or indirect transfer of control of an NRC license when the transfer requires prior approval of the NRC under the Commission's regulations, governing statute, or pursuant to a license condition, twenty (20) days from the date of publication of the notice in the FEDERAL REGISTER.

(2) In proceedings for the initial authorization to construct a high-level radioactive waste geologic repository, and the initial licensee to receive and process high level radioactive waste at a geological repository operations area, thirty (30) days from the date of publication of the notice in the FEDERAL REGISTER.

(3) In proceedings for which a FEDERAL REGISTER notice of agency action is published (other than a proceeding covered by paragraphs (b)(1) or (b)(2) of this section), not later than:

(i) The time specified in any notice of hearing or notice of proposed action or as provided by the presiding officer or the Atomic Safety and Licensing Board designated to rule on the request and/or petition, which may not be less than sixty (60) days from the date of publication of the notice in the FEDERAL REGISTER; or

(ii) If no period is specified, sixty (60) days from the date of publication of the notice.

(4) In proceedings for which a FEDERAL REGISTER notice of agency action is not published, not later than the latest of:

(i) Sixty (60) days after publication of notice on the NRC Web site at *http://www.nrc.gov/public-involve/major-actions.html,* or

(ii) Sixty (60) days after the requestor receives actual notice of a pending application, but not more than sixty (60) days after agency action on the application.

(c) *Filings after the deadline; submission of hearing request, intervention petition, or motion for leave to file new or amended contentions*—(1) *Determination by presiding officer.* Hearing requests, intervention petitions, and motions for leave to file new or amended contentions filed after the deadline in paragraph (b) of this section will not be entertained absent a determination by the presiding officer that a participant has demonstrated good cause by showing that:

(i) The information upon which the filing is based was not previously available;

(ii) The information upon which the filing is based is materially different from information previously available; and

(iii) The filing has been submitted in a timely fashion based on the availability of the subsequent information.

(2) *Applicability of §§ 2.307 and 2.323.* (i) Section 2.307 applies to requests to change a filing deadline (requested before or after that deadline has passed) based on reasons not related to the substance of the filing.

(ii) Section 2.323 does not apply to hearing requests, intervention petitions, or motions for leave to file new or amended contentions filed after the deadline in paragraph (b) of this section.

(3) *New petitioner.* A hearing request or intervention petition filed after the deadline in paragraph (b) of this section must include a specification of contentions if the petitioner seeks admission as a party, and must also demonstrate that the petitioner meets the applicable standing and contention admissibility requirements in paragraphs (d) and (f) of this section.

(4) *Party or participant.* A new or amended contention filed by a party or participant to the proceeding must also meet the applicable contention admissibility requirements in paragraph (f) of this section. If the party or participant has already satisfied the requirements for standing under paragraph (d) of this section in the same proceeding in which the new or amended contentions are filed, it does not need to do so again.

(d) *Standing.* (1) General requirements. A request for hearing or petition for leave to intervene must state:

(i) The name, address and telephone number of the requestor or petitioner;

(ii) The nature of the requestor's/petitioner's right under the Act to be made a party to the proceeding;

(iii) The nature and extent of the requestor's/petitioner's property, financial or other interest in the proceeding; and

(iv) The possible effect of any decision or order that may be issued in the proceeding on the requestor's/petitioner's interest.

(2) *Rulings.* In ruling on a request for hearing or petition for leave to intervene, the Commission, the presiding officer, or the Atomic Safety and Licensing Board designated to rule on such requests must determine, among other things, whether the petitioner has an interest affected by the proceeding considering the factors enumerated in paragraph (d)(1) of this section.

(3) *Standing in enforcement proceedings.* In enforcement proceedings, the licensee or other person against whom the action is taken shall have standing.

(e) *Discretionary Intervention.* The presiding officer may consider a request for discretionary intervention when at least one requestor/petitioner has established standing and at least one admissible contention has been admitted so that a hearing will be held. A requestor/petitioner may request that his or her petition be granted as a matter of discretion in the event that the petitioner is determined to lack standing to intervene as a matter of right under paragraph (d)(1) of this section. Accordingly, in addition to addressing the factors in paragraph (d)(1) of this section, a petitioner who wishes to seek intervention as a matter of discretion in the event it is determined that standing as a matter of right is not demonstrated shall address the following factors in his/her initial petition, which the Commission, the presiding officer or the Atomic Safety and Licensing Board will consider and balance:

(1) Factors weighing in favor of allowing intervention—

(i) The extent to which the requestor's/petitioner's participation may reasonably be expected to assist in developing a sound record;

(ii) The nature and extent of the requestor's/petitioner's property, financial or other interests in the proceeding; and

(iii) The possible effect of any decision or order that may be issued in the proceeding on the requestor's/petitioner's interest;

(2) Factors weighing against allowing intervention—

(i) The availability of other means whereby the requestor's/petitioner's interest will be protected;

(ii) The extent to which the requestor's/petitioner's interest will be represented by existing parties; and

(iii) The extent to which the requestor's/petitioner's participation will inappropriately broaden the issues or delay the proceeding.

(f) *Contentions.* (1) A request for hearing or petition for leave to intervene must set forth with particularity the contentions sought to be raised. For each contention, the request or petition must:

(i) Provide a specific statement of the issue of law or fact to be raised or controverted, *provided further*, that the issue of law or fact to be raised in a request for hearing under 10 CFR 52.103(b) must be directed at demonstrating that one or more of the acceptance criteria in the combined license have not been, or will not be met, and that the specific operational consequences of nonconformance would be contrary to providing reasonable assurance of adequate protection of the public health and safety;

(ii) Provide a brief explanation of the basis for the contention;

(iii) Demonstrate that the issue raised in the contention is within the scope of the proceeding;

(iv) Demonstrate that the issue raised in the contention is material to the findings the NRC must make to support the action that is involved in the proceeding;

(v) Provide a concise statement of the alleged facts or expert opinions which support the requestor's/petitioner's position on the issue and on which the petitioner intends to rely at hearing, together with references to the specific sources and documents on which the requestor/petitioner intends to rely to support its position on the issue;

(vi) In a proceeding other than one under 10 CFR 52.103, provide sufficient information to show that a genuine dispute exists with the applicant/licensee on a material issue of law or fact. This information must include references to specific portions of the application (including the applicant's environmental report and safety report) that the petitioner disputes and the supporting reasons for each dispute, or, if the petitioner believes that the application fails to contain information on a relevant matter as required by law, the identification of each failure and the supporting reasons for the petitioner's belief; and

(vii) In a proceeding under 10 CFR 52.103(b), the information must be sufficient, and include supporting information showing, *prima facie*, that one or more of the acceptance criteria in the combined license have not been, or will not be met, and that the specific operational consequences of nonconformance would be contrary to providing reasonable assurance of adequate protection of the public health and safety. This information must include the specific portion of the report required by 10 CFR 52.99(c) which the requestor believes is inaccurate, incorrect, and/or incomplete (*i.e.*, fails to contain the necessary information required by § 52.99(c)). If the requestor identifies a specific portion of the § 52.99(c) report as incomplete and the requestor contends that the incomplete portion prevents the requestor from making the necessary *prima facie* showing, then the requestor must explain why this deficiency prevents the requestor from making the *prima facie* showing.

(2) Contentions must be based on documents or other information available at the time the petition is to be filed, such as the application, supporting safety analysis report, environmental report or other supporting document filed by an applicant or licensee, or otherwise available to a petitioner. On issues arising under the National Environmental Policy Act, participants shall file contentions based on the applicant's environmental report. Participants may file new or amended environmental contentions after the deadline in paragraph (b) of this section (e.g., based on a draft or final NRC environmental impact statement, environmental assessment, or any supplements to these documents) if the contention complies with the requirements in paragraph (c) of this section.

(3) If two or more requestors/petitioners seek to co-sponsor a contention, the requestors/petitioners shall jointly designate a representative who shall have the authority to act for the requestors/petitioners with respect to that contention. If a requestor/petitioner seeks to adopt the contention of another sponsoring requestor/petitioner, the requestor/petitioner who seeks to adopt the contention must either agree that the sponsoring requestor/petitioner shall act as the representative with respect to that contention, or jointly designate with the sponsoring requestor/petitioner a representative who shall have the authority to act for the requestors/petitioners with respect to that contention.

(g) *Selection of hearing procedures.* A request for hearing and/or petition for leave to intervene may, except in a proceeding under 10 CFR 52.103, also address the selection of hearing procedures, taking into account the provisions of § 2.310. If a request/petition relies upon § 2.310(d), the request/petition must demonstrate, by reference to the contention and the bases provided and the specific procedures in subpart G of this part, that resolution of the contention necessitates resolution of material issues of fact which may be best determined through the use of the identified procedures.

(h) *Requirements applicable to States, local governmental bodies, and Federally-recognized Indian Tribes seeking party status.* (1) If a State, local governmental body (county, municipality or other subdivision), or Federally-recognized Indian Tribe seeks to participate as a party in a proceeding, it must submit a request for hearing or a petition to intervene containing at least one admissible contention, and must designate a single representative for the hearing. If a request for hearing or petition to intervene is granted, the Commission, the presiding officer or the Atomic Safety and Licensing Board ruling on the request will admit as a party to the proceeding a single designated representative of the State, a single designated representative for each local governmental body (county, municipality or other subdivision), and a single designated representative for each Federally-recognized Indian Tribe. Where a State's constitution provides that both the Governor and another State official or State governmental body may represent the interests of the State in a proceeding, the Governor and the other State official/government body will be considered separate participants.

(2) If the proceeding pertains to a production or utilization facility (as defined in § 50.2 of this chapter) located within the boundaries of the State, local governmental body, or Federally-recognized Indian Tribe seeking to participate as a party, no further demonstration of standing is required. If the production or utilization facility is not located within the boundaries of the State, local governmental body, or Federally-recognized Indian Tribe seeking to participate as a party, the State, local governmental body, or Federally-recognized Indian Tribe also must demonstrate standing.

(3) In any proceeding on an application for a construction authorization for a high-level radioactive waste repository at a geologic repository operations area under parts 60 or 63 of this chapter, or an application for a license to receive and possess high-level radioactive waste at a geologic repository operations area under parts 60 or 63 of this chapter, the Commission shall permit intervention by the State and local governmental body (county, municipality or other subdivision) in which such an area is located and by any affected Federally-recognized Indian Tribe as defined in parts 60 or 63 of this chapter if the requirements of paragraph (f) of this section are satisfied with respect to at least one contention. All other petitions for intervention in any such proceeding must be reviewed under the provisions of paragraphs (a) through (f) of this section.

(i) *Answers to hearing requests, intervention petitions, and motions for leave to file new or amended contentions filed after the deadline.* Unless otherwise specified by the Commission, the presiding officer, or the Atomic Safety and Licensing Board designated to rule on the request, petition, or motion—

(1) The applicant/licensee, the NRC staff, and other parties to a proceeding may file an answer to a hearing request, intervention petition, or motion for leave to file amended or new contentions filed after the deadline in § 2.309(b) within 25 days after service of the request, petition, or motion. Answers should address, at a minimum, the factors set forth in paragraphs (a) through (h) of this section insofar as these sections apply to the filing that is the subject of the answer.

(2) Except in a proceeding under § 52.103 of this chapter, the participant who filed the hearing request, intervention petition, or motion for leave to file new or amended contentions after the deadline may file a reply to any answer. The reply must be filed within 7 days after service of that answer.

(3) No other written answers or replies will be entertained.

(j) *Decision on request/petition.* (1) In all proceedings other than a proceeding under § 52.103 of this chapter, the presiding officer shall issue a decision on each request for hearing or petition to intervene within 45 days of the conclusion of the initial pre-hearing conference or, if no pre-hearing conference is conducted, within 45 days after the filing of answers and replies under paragraph (i) of this section. With respect to a request to admit amended or new contentions, the presiding officer shall issue a decision on each such request within 45 days of the conclusion of any pre-hearing conference that may be conducted regarding the proposed amended or new contentions or, if no pre-hearing conference is conducted, within 45 days after the filing of answers and replies, if any. In the event the presiding officer cannot issue a decision within 45 days, the presiding officer shall issue a notice advising the Commission and the parties, and the notice shall include the expected date of when the decision will issue.

(2) The Commission, acting as the presiding officer, shall expeditiously grant or deny the request for hearing in a proceeding under § 52.103 of this chapter. The Commission's decision

may not be the subject of any appeal under § 2.311.

[69 FR 2236, Jan. 14, 2004, as amended at 72 FR 49474, Aug. 28, 2007; 73 FR 44620, July 31, 2008; 77 FR 46591, Aug. 3, 2012]

§ 2.310 Selection of hearing procedures.

Upon a determination that a request for hearing/petition to intervene should be granted and a hearing held, the Commission, the presiding officer, or the Atomic Safety and Licensing Board designated to rule on the request/petition will determine and identify the specific hearing procedures to be used for the proceeding as follows—

(a) Except as determined through the application of paragraphs (b) through (h) of this section, proceedings for the grant, renewal, licensee-initiated amendment, or termination of licenses or permits subject to parts 30, 32 through 36, 39, 40, 50, 52, 54, 55, 61, 70 and 72 of this chapter may be conducted under the procedures of subpart L of this part.

(b) Proceedings on enforcement matters must be conducted under the procedures of subpart G of this part, unless all parties agree and jointly request that the proceedings be conducted under the procedures of subpart L or subpart N of this part, as appropriate.

(c) Proceedings on the licensing of the construction and operation of a uranium enrichment facility must be conducted under the procedures of subpart G of this part.

(d) In proceedings for the grant, renewal, licensee-initiated amendment, or termination of licenses or permits for nuclear power reactors, where the presiding officer by order finds that resolution of the contention or contested matter necessitates resolution of issues of material fact relating to the occurrence of a past activity, where the credibility of an eyewitness may reasonably be expected to be at issue, and/or issues of motive or intent of the party or eyewitness material to the resolution of the contested matter, the hearing for resolution of that contention or contested matter will be conducted under subpart G of this part.

(e) Proceedings on applications for a license or license amendment to expand the spent nuclear fuel storage capacity at the site of a civilian nuclear power plant must be conducted under the procedures of subpart L of this part, unless a party requests that the proceeding be conducted under the procedures of subpart K of this part, or if all parties agree and jointly request that the proceeding be conducted under the procedures of subpart N of this part.

(f) Proceedings on an application for initial construction authorization for a high-level radioactive waste repository at a geologic repository operations area noticed pursuant to §§ 2.101(f)(8) or 2.105(a)(5), and proceedings on an initial application for a license to receive and possess high-level radioactive waste at a geologic repository operations area must be conducted under the procedures of subparts G and J of this part. Subsequent amendments to a construction authorization for a high-level radioactive geologic repository, and amendments to a license to receive and possess high level radioactive waste at a high level waste geologic repository may be conducted under the procedures of subpart L of this part, unless all parties agree and jointly request that the proceeding be conducted under the procedures of subpart N of this part.

(g) Proceedings on an application for the direct or indirect transfer of control of an NRC license which transfer requires prior approval of the NRC under the Commission's regulations, governing statutes or pursuant to a license condition shall be conducted under the procedures of subpart M of this part, unless the Commission determines otherwise in a case-specific order.

(h) Except as determined through the application of paragraphs (b) through (g) of this section, proceedings for the grant, renewal, licensee-initiated amendment, or termination of licenses or permits subject to parts 30, 32 through 36, 39, 40, 50, 52, 54, 55, 61, 70 and 72 of this chapter, and proceedings on an application for the direct or indirect transfer of control of an NRC license may be conducted under the procedures of subpart N of this part if—

(1) The hearing itself is expected to take no more than two (2) days to complete; or

(2) All parties to the proceeding agree that it should be conducted under the procedures of subpart N of this part.

(i) In design certification rulemaking proceedings under part 52 of this chapter, any informal hearing held under §52.51 of this chapter must be conducted under the procedures of subpart O of this part.

(j) Proceedings on a Commission finding under 10 CFR 52.103(c) and (g) shall be conducted in accordance with the procedures designated by the Commission in each proceeding.

(k) In proceedings where the Commission grants a petition filed under §2.335(b), the Commission may, in its discretion, conduct a hearing under the procedures of subpart O of this part to assist the Commission in developing a record on the matters raised in the petition.

[69 FR 2236, Jan. 14, 2004, as amended at 72 FR 49475, Aug. 28, 2007]

§2.311 Interlocutory review of rulings on requests for hearings/petitions to intervene, selection of hearing procedures, and requests by potential parties for access to sensitive unclassified non-safeguards information and safeguards information.

(a) An order of the presiding officer, or if a presiding officer has not been designated, of the Chief Administrative Judge, or if he or she is unavailable, of another administrative judge, or of an administrative law judge with jurisdiction under §2.318(a), may be appealed to the Commission with respect to:

(1) A request for hearing;

(2) A petition to intervene; or

(3) A request for access to sensitive unclassified non-safeguards information (SUNSI), including, but not limited to, proprietary, confidential commercial, and security-related information, and Safeguards Information (SGI). An appeal to the Commission may also be taken from an order of an officer designated to rule on information access issues.

(b) These appeals must be made as specified by the provisions of this section, within 25 days after the service of the order. The appeal must be initiated by the filing of a notice of appeal and accompanying supporting brief. Any party who opposes the appeal may file a brief in opposition to the appeal within 25 days after service of the appeal. The supporting brief and any answer must conform to the requirements of §2.341(c)(3). No other appeals from rulings on requests for hearing are allowed.

(c) An order denying a petition to intervene, and/or request for hearing, or a request for access to the information described in paragraph (a) of this section, is appealable by the requestor/petitioner on the question as to whether the request and/or petition should have been granted.

(d) An order granting a petition to intervene, and/or request for hearing, or granting a request for access to the information described in paragraph (a) of this section, is appealable by a party other than the requestor/petitioner on the question as to:

(1) Whether the request for hearing or petition to intervene should have been wholly denied; or

(2) Whether the request for access to the information described in paragraph (a)(3) of this section should have been denied in whole or in part. However, such a question with respect to SGI may only be appealed by the NRC staff, and such a question with respect to SUNSI may be appealed only by the NRC staff or by a party whose interest independent of the proceeding would be harmed by the release of the information.

(e) An order selecting a hearing procedure may be appealed by any party on the question as to whether the selection of the particular hearing procedures was in clear contravention of the criteria set forth in §2.310. The appeal must be filed with the Commission no later than ten (10) days after issuance of the order selecting a hearing procedure.

[73 FR 12631, Mar. 10, 2008, as amended at 77 FR 46592, Aug. 3, 2012; 78 FR 34247, June 7, 2013]

§2.312 Notice of hearing.

(a) In a proceeding in which the terms of a notice of hearing are not otherwise prescribed by this part, the order or notice of hearing will state:

(1) The nature of the hearing and its time and place, or a statement that the time and place will be fixed by subsequent order;

(2) The legal authority and jurisdiction under which the hearing is to be held;

(3) The matters of fact and law asserted or to be considered; and

(4) A statement describing the specific hearing procedures or subpart that will be used for the hearing.

(b) The time and place of hearing will be fixed with due regard for the convenience of the parties or their representatives, the nature of the proceeding and the public interest.

§ 2.313 Designation of presiding officer, disqualification, unavailability, and substitution.

(a) *Designation of presiding officer.* The Commission may provide in the notice of hearing that one or more members of the Commission, an administrative law judge, an administrative judge, an Atomic Safety and Licensing Board, or a named officer who has been delegated final authority in the matter, shall be the presiding officer. The Commission alone shall designate the presiding officer in a hearing conducted under subpart O. If the Commission does not designate the presiding officer for a hearing under subparts G, J, K, L, M, or N of this part, then the Chief Administrative Judge shall issue an order designating:

(1) An Atomic Safety and Licensing Board appointed under Section 191 of the Atomic Energy Act of 1954, as amended, or an administrative law judge appointed pursuant to 5 U.S.C. 3105, for a hearing conducted under subparts G, J, K, L, or N of this part; or

(2) An Atomic Safety and Licensing Board, an administrative law judge, or an administrative judge for a hearing conducted under subpart M of this part.

(b) *Disqualification.* (1) If a designated presiding officer or a designated member of an Atomic Safety and Licensing Board believes that he or she is disqualified to preside or to participate as a board member in the hearing, he or she shall withdraw by notice on the record and shall notify the Commission or the Chief Administrative Judge, as appropriate, of the withdrawal.

(2) If a party believes that a presiding officer or a designated member of an Atomic Safety and Licensing Board should be disqualified, the party may move that the presiding officer or the Licensing Board member disqualify himself or herself. The motion must be supported by affidavits setting forth the alleged grounds for disqualification. If the presiding officer does not grant the motion or the Licensing Board member does not disqualify himself, the motion must be referred to the Commission. The Commission will determine the sufficiency of the grounds alleged.

(c) *Unavailability.* If a presiding officer or a designated member of an Atomic Safety and Licensing Board becomes unavailable during the course of a hearing, the Commission or the Chief Administrative Judge, as appropriate, will designate another presiding officer or Atomic Safety and Licensing Board member. If he or she becomes unavailable after the hearing has been concluded, then:

(1) The Commission may designate another presiding officer;

(2) The Chief Administrative Judge or the Commission, as appropriate, may designate another Atomic Safety and Licensing Board member to participate in the decision;

(3) The Commission may direct that the record be certified to it for decision.

(d) *Substitution.* If a presiding officer or a designated member of an Atomic Safety and Licensing Board is substituted for the one originally designated, any motion predicated upon the substitution must be made within five (5) days after the substitution.

§ 2.314 Appearance and practice before the Commission in adjudicatory proceedings.

(a) *Standards of practice.* In the exercise of their functions under this subpart, the Commission, the Atomic Safety and Licensing Boards, Administrative Law Judges, and Administrative Judges function in a quasi-judicial capacity. Accordingly, parties and their representatives in proceedings subject to this subpart are expected to conduct themselves with honor, dignity, and decorum as they should before a court of law.

(b) *Representation.* A person may appear in an adjudication on his or her own behalf or by an attorney-at-law. A partnership, corporation, or unincorporated association may be represented by a duly authorized member or officer, or by an attorney-at-law. A party may be represented by an attorney-at-law if the attorney is in good standing and has been admitted to practice before any Court of the United States, the District of Columbia, or the highest court of any State, territory, or possession of the United States. Any person appearing in a representative capacity shall file with the Commission a written notice of appearance. The notice must state his or her name, address, telephone number, and facsimile number and email address, if any; the name and address of the person or entity on whose behalf he or she appears; and, in the case of an attorney-at-law, the basis of his or her eligibility as a representative or, in the case of another representative, the basis of his or her authority to act on behalf of the party.

(c) *Reprimand, censure or suspension from the proceeding.* (1) A presiding officer, or the Commission may, if necessary for the orderly conduct of a proceeding, reprimand, censure or suspend from participation in the particular proceeding pending before it any party or representative of a party who refuses to comply with its directions, or who is disorderly, disruptive, or engages in contemptuous conduct.

(2) A reprimand, censure, or a suspension that is ordered to run for one day or less must state the grounds for the action in the record of the proceeding, and must advise the person disciplined of the right to appeal under paragraph (c)(3) of this section. A suspension that is ordered for a longer period must be in writing, state the grounds on which it is based, and advise the person suspended of the right to appeal and to request a stay under paragraphs (c)(3) and (c)(4) of this section. The suspension may be stayed for a reasonable time in order for an affected party to obtain other representation if this would be necessary to prevent injustice.

(3) Anyone disciplined under this section may file an appeal with the Commission within 25 days after issuance of the order. The appeal must be in writing and state concisely, with supporting argument, why the appellant believes the order was erroneous, either as a matter of fact or law. The Commission shall consider each appeal on the merits, including appeals in cases in which the suspension period has already run. If necessary for a full and fair consideration of the facts, the Commission may conduct further evidentiary hearings, or may refer the matter to another presiding officer for development of a record. In the latter event, unless the Commission provides specific directions to the presiding officer, that officer shall determine the procedure to be followed and who shall present evidence, subject to applicable provisions of law. The hearing must begin as soon as possible. In the case of an attorney, if no appeal is taken of a suspension, or, if the suspension is upheld at the conclusion of the appeal, the presiding officer, or the Commission, as appropriate, shall notify the State bar(s) to which the attorney is admitted. The notification must include copies of the order of suspension, and, if an appeal was taken, briefs of the parties, and the decision of the Commission.

(4) A suspension exceeding one (1) day is not effective for seventy-two (72) hours from the date the suspension order is issued. Within this time, a suspended individual may request a stay of the sanction from the appropriate reviewing tribunal pending appeal. No responses to the stay request from other parties will be entertained. If a timely stay request is filed, the suspension must be stayed until the reviewing tribunal rules on the motion. The stay request must be in writing and contain the information specified in §2.342(b). The Commission shall rule on the stay request within ten (10) days after the filing of the motion. The Commission shall consider the factors specified in §2.342(e)(1) and (e)(2) in determining whether to grant or deny a stay application.

[69 FR 2236, Jan. 14, 2004, as amended at 77 FR 46592, Aug. 3, 2012]

§ 2.315 Participation by a person not a party.

(a) A person who is not a party (including persons who are affiliated with or represented by a party) may, in the discretion of the presiding officer, be permitted to make a limited appearance by making an oral or written statement of his or her position on the issues at any session of the hearing or any prehearing conference within the limits and on the conditions fixed by the presiding officer. However, that person may not otherwise participate in the proceeding. Such statements of position shall not be considered evidence in the proceeding.

(b) The Secretary will give notice of a hearing to any person who requests it before the issuance of the notice of hearing, and will furnish a copy of the notice of hearing to any person who requests it thereafter. If a communication bears more than one signature, the Commission will give the notice to the person first signing unless the communication clearly indicates otherwise.

(c) The presiding officer will afford an interested State, local governmental body (county, municipality or other subdivision), and Federally-recognized Indian Tribe that has not been admitted as a party under § 2.309, a reasonable opportunity to participate in a hearing. The participation of any State, local governmental body, or Federally-recognized Indian Tribe shall be limited to unresolved issues and contentions, and issues and contentions that are raised after the State, local governmental body, or Federally-recognized Indian Tribe becomes a participant. Each State, local governmental body, and Federally-recognized Indian Tribe shall, in its request to participate in a hearing, designate a single representative for the hearing. The representative shall be permitted to introduce evidence, interrogate witnesses where cross examination by the parties is permitted, advise the Commission without requiring the representative to take a position with respect to the issue, file proposed findings in those proceedings where findings are permitted, and petition for review by the Commission under § 2.341 with respect to the admitted contentions. The representative shall identify those contentions on which they will participate in advance of any hearing held.

(d) If a matter is taken up by the Commission under § 2.341 or *sua sponte*, a person who is not a party may, in the discretion of the Commission, be permitted to file a brief "*amicus curiae*." Such a person shall submit the amicus brief together with a motion for leave to do so which identifies the interest of the person and states the reasons why a brief is desirable. Unless the Commission provides otherwise, the brief must be filed within the time allowed to the party whose position the brief will support. A motion of a person who is not a party to participate in oral argument before the Commission will be granted at the discretion of the Commission.

[69 FR 2236, Jan. 14, 2004, as amended at 77 FR 46592, Aug. 3, 2012]

§ 2.316 Consolidation of parties.

On motion or on its or his own initiative, the Commission or the presiding officer may order any parties in a proceeding who have substantially the same interest that may be affected by the proceeding and who raise substantially the same questions, to consolidate their presentation of evidence, cross-examination, briefs, proposed findings of fact, and conclusions of law and argument. However, it may not order any consolidation that would prejudice the rights of any party. A consolidation under this section may be for all purposes of the proceeding, all of the issues of the proceeding, or with respect to any one or more issues thereof.

§ 2.317 Separate hearings; consolidation of proceedings.

(a) *Separate hearings.* On motion by the parties or upon request of the presiding officer for good cause shown, or on its own initiative, the Commission may establish separate hearings in a proceeding if it is found that the action will be conducive to the proper dispatch of its business and to the ends of justice and will be conducted in accordance with the other provisions of this subpart.

(b) *Consolidation of proceedings.* On motion and for good cause shown or on its own initiative, the Commission or the presiding officers of each affected proceeding may consolidate for hearing or for other purposes two or more proceedings, or may hold joint hearings with interested States and/or other Federal agencies on matters of concurrent jurisdiction, if it is found that the action will be conducive to the proper dispatch of its business and to the ends of justice and will be conducted in accordance with the other provisions of this subpart.

§2.318 Commencement and termination of jurisdiction of presiding officer.

(a) Unless the Commission orders otherwise, the jurisdiction of the presiding officer designated to conduct a hearing over the proceeding, including motions and procedural matters, commences when the proceeding commences. If a presiding officer has not been designated, the Chief Administrative Judge has jurisdiction or, if he or she is unavailable, another administrative judge or administrative law judge has jurisdiction. A proceeding commences when a notice of hearing or a notice of proposed action under §2.105 is issued. When a notice of hearing provides that the presiding officer is to be an administrative judge or an administrative law judge, the Chief Administrative Judge will designate by order the administrative judge or administrative law judge, as appropriate, who is to preside. The presiding officer's jurisdiction in each proceeding terminates when the period within which the Commission may direct that the record be certified to it for final decision expires, when the Commission renders a final decision, or when the presiding officer withdraws from the case upon considering himself or herself disqualified, whichever is earliest.

(b) The Director, Office of Nuclear Reactor Regulation, Director, Office of New Reactors, or the Director, Office of Nuclear Material Safety and Safeguards, as appropriate, may issue an order and take any otherwise proper administrative action with respect to a licensee who is a party to a pending proceeding. Any order related to the subject matter of the pending proceeding may be modified by the presiding officer as appropriate for the purpose of the proceeding.

[69 FR 2236, Jan. 14, 2004, as amended at 73 FR 5716, Jan. 31, 2008; 77 FR 46592, Aug. 3, 2012]

§2.319 Power of the presiding officer.

A presiding officer has the duty to conduct a fair and impartial hearing according to law, to take appropriate action to control the prehearing and hearing process, to avoid delay and to maintain order. The presiding officer has all the powers necessary to those ends, including the powers to:

(a) Administer oaths and affirmations;

(b) Issue subpoenas authorized by law, including subpoenas requested by a participant for the attendance and testimony of witnesses or the production of evidence upon the requestor's showing of general relevance and reasonable scope of the evidence sought;

(c) Consolidate parties and proceedings in accordance with §§2.316 and 2.317 and/or direct that common interests be represented by a single spokesperson;

(d) Rule on offers of proof and receive evidence. In proceedings under this part, strict rules of evidence do not apply to written submissions. However, the presiding officer may, on motion or on the presiding officer's own initiative, strike any portion of a written presentation or a response to a written question that is irrelevant, immaterial, unreliable, duplicative or cumulative.

(e) Restrict irrelevant, immaterial, unreliable, duplicative or cumulative evidence and/or arguments;

(f) Order depositions to be taken as appropriate;

(g) Regulate the course of the hearing and the conduct of participants;

(h) Dispose of procedural requests or similar matters;

(i) Examine witnesses;

(j) Hold conferences before or during the hearing for settlement, simplification of contentions, or any other proper purpose;

(k) Set reasonable schedules for the conduct of the proceeding and take actions reasonably calculated to maintain overall schedules;

(l) Refer rulings to the Commission under §2.323(f)(1), or certify questions to the Commission for its determination, either in the presiding officer's discretion, or on petition of a party under § 2.323(f)(2), or on direction of the Commission.

(m) Reopen a proceeding for the receipt of further evidence at any time before the initial decision;

(n) Appoint special assistants from the Atomic Safety and Licensing Board Panel under § 2.322;

(o) Issue initial decisions as provided in this part;

(p) Dispose of motions by written order or by oral ruling during the course of a hearing or prehearing conference. The presiding officer should ensure that parties not present for the oral ruling are notified promptly of the ruling;

(q) Issue orders necessary to carry out the presiding officer's duties and responsibilities under this part; and

(r) Establish a schedule for briefs and oral arguments to decide any admitted contentions that, as determined by the presiding officer, constitute pure issues of law.

(s) Take any other action consistent with the Act, this chapter, and 5 U.S.C. 551–558.

[69 FR 2236, Jan. 14, 2004, as amended at 77 FR 46592, Aug. 3, 2012]

§ 2.320 Default.

If a party fails to file an answer or pleading within the time prescribed in this part or as specified in the notice of hearing or pleading, to appear at a hearing or prehearing conference, to comply with any prehearing order entered by the presiding officer, or to comply with any discovery order entered by the presiding officer, the Commission or the presiding officer may make any orders in regard to the failure that are just, including, among others, the following:

(a) Without further notice, find the facts as to the matters regarding which the order was made in accordance with the claim of the party obtaining the order, and enter the order as appropriate; or

(b) Proceed without further notice to take proof on the issues specified.

§ 2.321 Atomic Safety and Licensing Boards.

(a) The Commission or the Chief Administrative Judge may establish one or more Atomic Safety and Licensing Boards, each comprised of three members, one of whom will be qualified in the conduct of administrative proceedings and two of whom have such technical or other qualifications as the Commission or the Chief Administrative Judge determines to be appropriate to the issues to be decided. The members of an Atomic Safety and Licensing Board shall be designated from the Atomic Safety and Licensing Board Panel established by the Commission. In proceedings for granting, suspending, revoking, or amending licenses or authorizations as the Commission may designate, the Atomic Safety and Licensing Board shall perform the adjudicatory functions that the Commission determines are appropriate.

(b) The Commission or the Chief Administrative Judge may designate an alternate qualified in the conduct of administrative proceedings, or an alternate having technical or other qualifications, or both, for an Atomic Safety and Licensing Board established under paragraph (a) of this section. If a member of a board becomes unavailable, the Commission or the Chief Administrative Judge may constitute the alternate qualified in the conduct of administrative proceedings, or the alternate having technical or other qualifications, as appropriate, as a member of the board by notifying the alternate who will, as of the date of the notification, serve as a member of the board. If an alternate is unavailable or no alternates have been designated, and a member of a board becomes unavailable, the Commission or Chief Administrative Judge may appoint a member of the Atomic Safety and Licensing Board Panel who is qualified in the conduct of administrative proceedings or a member having technical or other qualifications, as appropriate, as a member of the Atomic Safety and Licensing Board by notifying the appointee who will, as of the date of the notification, serve as a member of the board.

(c) An Atomic Safety and Licensing Board has the duties and may exercise the powers of a presiding officer as granted by §2.319 and otherwise in this part. Any time when a board is in existence but is not actually in session, any powers which could be exercised by a presiding officer or by the Chief Administrative Judge may be exercised with respect to the proceeding by the chairman of the board having jurisdiction over it. Two members of an Atomic Safety and Licensing Board constitute a quorum if one of those members is the member qualified in the conduct of administrative proceedings.

§2.322 Special assistants to the presiding officer.

(a) In consultation with the Chief Administrative Judge, the presiding officer may, at his or her discretion, appoint personnel from the Atomic Safety and Licensing Board Panel established by the Commission to assist the presiding officer in taking evidence and preparing a suitable record for review. The appointment may occur at any appropriate time during the proceeding but must, at the time of the appointment, be subject to the notice and disqualification provisions as described in §2.313. The special assistants may function as:

(1) Technical interrogators in their individual fields of expertise. The interrogators shall study the written testimony and sit with the presiding officer to hear the presentation and, where permitted in the proceeding, the cross-examination by the parties of all witnesses on the issues of the interrogators' expertise. The interrogators shall take a leading role in examining the witnesses to ensure that the record is as complete as possible;

(2) Upon consent of all the parties, special masters to hear evidentiary presentations by the parties on specific technical matters, and, upon completion of the presentation of evidence, to prepare a report that would become part of the record. Special masters may rule on evidentiary issues brought before them, in accordance with §2.333. Appeals from special masters' rulings may be taken to the presiding officer in accordance with procedures established in the presiding officer's order appointing the special master. Special masters' reports are advisory only; the presiding officer retains final authority with respect to the issues heard by the special master;

(3) Alternate Atomic Safety and Licensing Board members to sit with the presiding officer, to participate in the evidentiary sessions on the issue for which the alternate members were designated by examining witnesses, and to advise the presiding officer of their conclusions through an on-the-record report. This report is advisory only; the presiding officer retains final authority on the issue for which the alternate member was designated; or

(4) Discovery master to rule on the matters specified in §2.1018(a)(2).

(b) The presiding officer may, as a matter of discretion, informally seek the assistance of members of the Atomic Safety and Licensing Board Panel to brief the presiding officer on the general technical background of subjects involving complex issues that the presiding officer might otherwise have difficulty in quickly grasping. These briefings take place before the hearing on the subject involved and supplement the reading and study undertaken by the presiding officer. They are not subject to the procedures described in §2.313.

§2.323 Motions.

(a) *Scope and general requirements*—(1) *Applicability to §2.309(c).* Section 2.309 motions for new or amended contentions filed after the deadline in §2.309(b) are not subject to the requirements of this section. For the purposes of this section the term "all motions" includes any motion *except* §2.309 motions for new or amended contentions filed after the deadline.

(2) *Presentation and disposition.* All motions must be addressed to the Commission or other designated presiding officer. All motions must be made no later than ten (10) days after the occurrence or circumstance from which the motion arises. All written motions must be filed with the Secretary and served on all parties to the proceeding.

(b) *Form and content.* Unless made orally on-the-record during a hearing, or the presiding officer directs otherwise, or under the provisions of subpart

N of this part, a motion must be in writing, state with particularity the grounds and the relief sought, be accompanied by any affidavits or other evidence relied on, and, as appropriate, a proposed form of order. A motion must be rejected if it does not include a certification by the attorney or representative of the moving party that the movant has made a sincere effort to contact other parties in the proceeding and resolve the issue(s) raised in the motion, and that the movant's efforts to resolve the issue(s) have been unsuccessful.

(c) *Answers to motions.* Within ten (10) days after service of a written motion, or other period as determined by the Secretary, the Assistant Secretary, or the presiding officer, a party may file an answer in support of or in opposition to the motion, accompanied by affidavits or other evidence. The moving party has no right to reply, except as permitted by the Secretary, the Assistant Secretary, or the presiding officer. Permission may be granted only in compelling circumstances, such as where the moving party demonstrates that it could not reasonably have anticipated the arguments to which it seeks leave to reply.

(d) *Accuracy in filing.* All parties are obligated, in their filings before the presiding officer and the Commission, to ensure that their arguments and assertions are supported by appropriate and accurate references to legal authority and factual basis, including, as appropriate, citations to the record. Failure to do so may result in appropriate sanctions, including striking a matter from the record or, in extreme circumstances, dismissal of the party.

(e) *Motions for reconsideration.* Motions for reconsideration may not be filed except upon leave of the presiding officer or the Commission, upon a showing of compelling circumstances, such as the existence of a clear and material error in a decision, which could not have reasonably been anticipated, that renders the decision invalid. A motion must be filed within ten (10) days of the action for which reconsideration is requested. The motion and any responses to the motion are limited to ten (10) pages.

(f) *Referral and certifications to the Commission.* (1) If, in the judgment of the presiding officer, the presiding officer's decision raises significant and novel legal or policy issues, or prompt decision by the Commission is necessary to materially advance the orderly disposition of the proceeding, then the presiding officer may promptly refer the ruling to the Commission. This standard also applies to matters certified to the Commission. The presiding officer shall notify the parties of the referral or certification either by announcement on-the-record or by written notice if the hearing is not in session.

(2) A party may petition the presiding officer to certify a question to the Commission for early review. The presiding officer shall apply the criteria in § 2.341(f)(1) in determining whether to grant the petition for certification. No motion for reconsideration of the presiding officer's ruling on a petition for certification will be entertained.

(g) *Effect of filing a motion, petition, or certification of question to the Commission.* Unless otherwise ordered, neither the filing of a motion, the filing of a petition for certification, nor the certification of a question to the Commission stays the proceeding or extends the time for the performance of any act.

(h) *Motions to compel discovery.* Parties may file answers to motions to compel discovery in accordance with paragraph (c) of this section. The presiding officer, in his or her discretion, may order that the answer be given orally during a telephone conference or other prehearing conference, rather than in writing. If responses are given over the telephone, the presiding officer shall issue a written order on the motion summarizing the views presented by the parties. This does not preclude the presiding officer from issuing a prior oral ruling on the matter effective at the time of the ruling, if the terms of the ruling are incorporated in the subsequent written order.

[69 FR 2236, Jan. 14, 2004, as amended at 77 FR 46593, Aug. 3, 2012]

§ 2.324 Order of procedure.

The presiding officer or the Commission will designate the order of procedure at a hearing. The proponent of an order will ordinarily open and close.

§ 2.325 Burden of proof.

Unless the presiding officer otherwise orders, the applicant or the proponent of an order has the burden of proof.

§ 2.326 Motions to reopen.

(a) A motion to reopen a closed record to consider additional evidence will not be granted unless the following criteria are satisfied:

(1) The motion must be timely. However, an exceptionally grave issue may be considered in the discretion of the presiding officer even if untimely presented;

(2) The motion must address a significant safety or environmental issue; and

(3) The motion must demonstrate that a materially different result would be or would have been likely had the newly proffered evidence been considered initially.

(b) The motion must be accompanied by affidavits that set forth the factual and/or technical bases for the movant's claim that the criteria of paragraph (a) of this section have been satisfied. Affidavits must be given by competent individuals with knowledge of the facts alleged, or by experts in the disciplines appropriate to the issues raised. Evidence contained in affidavits must meet the admissibility standards of this subpart. Each of the criteria must be separately addressed, with a specific explanation of why it has been met. When multiple allegations are involved, the movant must identify with particularity each issue it seeks to litigate and specify the factual and/or technical bases which it believes support the claim that this issue meets the criteria in paragraph (a) of this section.

(c) A motion predicated in whole or in part on the allegations of a confidential informant must identify to the presiding officer the source of the allegations and must request the issuance of an appropriate protective order.

(d) A motion to reopen that relates to a contention not previously in controversy among the parties must also satisfy the § 2.309(c) requirements for new or amended contentions filed after the deadline in § 2.309(b).

[69 FR 2236, Jan. 14, 2004, as amended at 77 FR 46593, Aug. 3, 2012]

§ 2.327 Official recording; transcript.

(a) *Recording hearings.* A hearing will be recorded stenographically or by other means under the supervision of the presiding officer. If the hearing is recorded on videotape or some other video medium, before an official transcript is prepared under paragraph (b) of this section, that video recording will be considered to constitute the record of events at the hearing.

(b) *Official transcript.* For each hearing, a transcript will be prepared from the recording made in accordance with paragraph (a) of this section that will be the sole official transcript of the hearing. The transcript will be prepared by an official reporter who may be designated by the Commission or may be a regular employee of the Commission. Except as limited by section 181 of the Act or order of the Commission, the transcript will be available for inspection in the agency's public records system.

(c) *Availability of copies.* Copies of transcripts prepared in accordance with paragraph (b) of this section are available to the parties and to the public from the official reporter on payment of the charges fixed therefor. If a hearing is recorded on videotape or other video medium, copies of the recording of each daily session of the hearing may be made available to the parties and to the public from the presiding officer upon payment of a charge specified by the Chief Administrative Judge.

(d) *Transcript corrections.* Corrections ordered or approved by the presiding officer must be included in the record through the issuance of an order by the presiding officer or the Secretary, as appropriate under the regulations in this part. The order shall reflect the corrections to the transcript through the use of a table, the issuance of a corrected or new transcript, or some other method selected by the presiding officer that will ensure a clear and concise description of the corrections.

[69 FR 2236, Jan. 14, 2004, as amended at 81 FR 47006, July 20, 2016]

§ 2.328 Hearings to be public.

Except as may be requested under section 181 of the Act, all hearings will be public unless otherwise ordered by the Commission.

§ 2.329 Prehearing conference.

(a) *Necessity for prehearing conference; timing.* The Commission or the presiding officer may, and in the case of a proceeding on an application for a construction permit or an operating license for a facility of a type described in §§ 50.21(b) or 50.22 of this chapter or a testing facility, shall direct the parties or their counsel to appear at a specified time and place for a conference or conferences before trial. A prehearing conference in a proceeding involving a construction permit or operating license for a facility of a type described in §§ 50.21(b) or 50.22 of this chapter must be held within sixty (60) days after discovery has been completed or any other time specified by the Commission or the presiding officer.

(b) *Objectives.* The following subjects may be discussed, as directed by the Commission or the presiding officer, at the prehearing conference:

(1) Expediting the disposition of the proceeding;

(2) Establishing early and continuing control so that the proceeding will not be protracted because of lack of management;

(3) Discouraging wasteful prehearing activities;

(4) Improving the quality of the hearing through more thorough preparation, and;

(5) Facilitating the settlement of the proceeding or any portions of it.

(c) *Other matters for consideration.* As appropriate for the particular proceeding, a prehearing conference may be held to consider such matters as:

(1) Simplification, clarification, and specification of the issues;

(2) The necessity or desirability of amending the pleadings;

(3) Obtaining stipulations and admissions of fact and the contents and authenticity of documents to avoid unnecessary proof, and advance rulings from the presiding officer on the admissibility of evidence;

(4) The appropriateness and timing of summary disposition motions under subparts G and L of this part, including appropriate limitations on the page length of motions and responses thereto;

(5) The control and scheduling of discovery, including orders affecting disclosures and discovery under the discovery provisions in subpart G of this part.

(6) Identification of witnesses and documents, and the limitation of the number of expert witnesses, and other steps to expedite the presentation of evidence, including the establishment of reasonable limits on the time allowed for presenting direct and, where permitted, cross-examination evidence;

(7) The disposition of pending motions;

(8) Settlement and the use of special procedures to assist in resolving any issues in the proceeding;

(9) The need to adopt special procedures for managing potentially difficult or protracted proceedings that may involve particularly complex issues, including the establishment of separate hearings with respect to any particular issue in the proceeding;

(10) The setting of a hearing schedule, including any appropriate limitations on the scope and time permitted for cross-examination where cross-examination is permitted; and

(11) Other matters that the Commission or presiding officer determines may aid in the just and orderly disposition of the proceeding.

(d) *Reports.* Prehearing conferences may be reported stenographically or by other means.

(e) *Prehearing conference order.* The presiding officer shall enter an order that recites the action taken at the conference, the amendments allowed to the pleadings and agreements by the parties, and the issues or matters in controversy to be determined in the proceeding. Any objections to the order must be filed by a party within five (5) days after service of the order. Parties may not file replies to the objections unless the presiding officer so directs.

The filing of objections does not stay the decision unless the presiding officer so orders. The presiding officer may revise the order in the light of the objections presented and, as permitted by § 2.319(l), may certify for determination to the Commission any matter raised in the objections the presiding officer finds appropriate. The order controls the subsequent course of the proceeding unless modified for good cause.

§ 2.330 Stipulations.

Apart from any stipulations made during or as a result of a prehearing conference, the parties may stipulate in writing at any stage of the proceeding or orally during the hearing, any relevant fact or the contents or authenticity of any document. These stipulations may be received in evidence. The parties may also stipulate as to the procedure to be followed in the proceeding. These stipulations may, on motion of all parties, be recognized by the presiding officer to govern the conduct of the proceeding.

§ 2.331 Oral argument before the presiding officer.

When, in the opinion of the presiding officer, time permits and the nature of the proceeding and the public interest warrant, the presiding officer may allow, and fix a time for, the presentation of oral argument. The presiding officer will impose appropriate limits of time on the argument. The transcript of the argument is part of the record.

§ 2.332 General case scheduling and management.

(a) *Scheduling order.* The presiding officer shall, as soon as practicable after consulting with the parties by a scheduling conference, telephone, mail, or other suitable means, enter a scheduling order that establishes limits for the time to file motions, conclude discovery, commence the oral phase of the hearing (if applicable), and take other actions in the proceeding. The scheduling order may also include:

(1) Modifications of the times for disclosures under §§ 2.336 and 2.704 and of the extent of discovery to be permitted;

(2) The date or dates for prehearing conferences; and

(3) Any other matters appropriate in the circumstances of the proceeding.

(b) *Model milestones.* In developing the scheduling order under paragraph (a) of this section, the presiding officer shall utilize the applicable model milestones in Appendix B to this part as a starting point. The presiding officer shall make appropriate modifications based upon all relevant information, including but not limited to, the number of contentions admitted, the complexity of the issues presented, relevant considerations which a party may bring to the attention of the presiding officer, the NRC staff's schedule for completion of its safety and environmental evaluations (paragraph (e) of this section), and the NRC's interest in providing a fair and expeditious resolution of the issues sought to be adjudicated by the parties in the proceeding.

(c) *Objectives of scheduling order.* The scheduling order must have as its objectives proper case management purposes such as:

(1) Expediting the disposition of the proceeding;

(2) Establishing early and continuing control so that the proceeding will not be protracted because of lack of management;

(3) Discouraging wasteful prehearing activities;

(4) Improving the quality of the hearing through more thorough preparation; and

(5) Facilitating the settlement of the proceeding or any portions thereof, including the use of Alternative Dispute Resolution, when and if the presiding officer, upon consultation with the parties, determines that these types of efforts should be pursued.

(d) *Effect of NRC staff's schedule on scheduling order.* In establishing a schedule, the presiding officer shall take into consideration the NRC staff's projected schedule for completion of its safety and environmental evaluations to ensure that the hearing schedule does not adversely impact the staff's ability to complete its reviews in a timely manner. Hearings on safety issues may be commenced before publication of the NRC staff's safety evaluation upon a finding by the presiding officer that commencing the hearings at that time would expedite the proceeding. Where an environmental impact statement (EIS) is involved, hearings on environmental issues addressed in the EIS may not commence before the issuance of the final EIS. In addition, discovery against the NRC staff on safety or environmental issues, respectively, should be suspended until the staff has issued the SER or EIS, unless the presiding officer finds that the commencement of discovery against the NRC staff (as otherwise permitted by the provisions of this part) before the publication of the pertinent document will not adversely affect completion of the document and will expedite the hearing.

[69 FR 2236, Jan. 14, 2004, as amended at 70 FR 20461, Apr. 20, 2005]

§ 2.333 Authority of the presiding officer to regulate procedure in a hearing.

To prevent unnecessary delays or an unnecessarily large record, the presiding officer:

(a) May limit the number of witnesses whose testimony may be cumulative;

(b) May strike argumentative, repetitious, cumulative, unreliable, immaterial, or irrelevant evidence;

(c) Shall require each party or participant who requests permission to conduct cross-examination to file a cross-examination plan for each witness or panel of witnesses the party or participant proposes to cross-examine;

(d) Must ensure that each party or participant permitted to conduct cross-examination conducts its cross-examination in conformance with the party's or participant's cross-examination plan filed with the presiding officer;

(e) May take necessary and proper measures to prevent argumentative, repetitious, or cumulative cross-examination; and

(f) May impose such time limitations on arguments as the presiding officer determines appropriate, having regard for the volume of the evidence and the importance and complexity of the issues involved.

§ 2.334 Implementing hearing schedule for proceeding.

(a) Unless the Commission directs otherwise in a particular proceeding, the presiding officer assigned to the proceeding shall, based on information and projections provided by the parties and the NRC staff, take appropriate action to maintain the hearing schedule established by the presiding officer in accordance with 10 CFR 2.332(a) of this part for the completion of the evidentiary record and, as appropriate, the issuance of its initial decision.

(b) *Modification of hearing schedule.* A hearing schedule may not be modified except upon a finding of good cause by the presiding officer or the Commission. In making such a good cause determination, the presiding officer or the Commission should take into account the following factors, among other things:

(1) Whether the requesting party has exercised due diligence to adhere to the schedule;

(2) Whether the requested change is the result of unavoidable circumstances; and

(3) Whether the other parties have agreed to the change and the overall effect of the change on the schedule of the case.

(c) The presiding officer shall provide written notification to the Commission any time during the course of the proceeding when it appears that there will be a delay of more than forty-five (45) days in meeting any of the dates for major activities in the hearing schedule established by the presiding officer under 10 CFR 2.332(a), or that the completion of the record or the issuance of the initial decision will be delayed more than sixty (60) days beyond the time specified in the hearing schedule established under 10 CFR 2.332(a). The notification must include an explanation of the reasons for the projected delay and a description of the actions, if any, that the presiding officer or the Board proposes to take to avoid or mitigate the delay.

[70 FR 20461, Apr. 20, 2005]

§2.335 Consideration of Commission rules and regulations in adjudicatory proceedings.

(a) Except as provided in paragraphs (b), (c), and (d) of this section, no rule or regulation of the Commission, or any provision thereof, concerning the licensing of production and utilization facilities, source material, special nuclear material, or byproduct material, is subject to attack by way of discovery, proof, argument, or other means in any adjudicatory proceeding subject to this part.

(b) A participant to an adjudicatory proceeding subject to this part may petition that the application of a specified Commission rule or regulation or any provision thereof, of the type described in paragraph (a) of this section, be waived or an exception be made for the particular proceeding. The sole ground for petition of waiver or exception is that special circumstances with respect to the subject matter of the particular proceeding are such that the application of the rule or regulation (or a provision of it) would not serve the purposes for which the rule or regulation was adopted. The petition must be accompanied by an affidavit that identifies the specific aspect or aspects of the subject matter of the proceeding as to which the application of the rule or regulation (or provision of it) would not serve the purposes for which the rule or regulation was adopted. The affidavit must state with particularity the special circumstances alleged to justify the waiver or exception requested. Any other participant may file a response by counter-affidavit or otherwise.

(c) If, on the basis of the petition, affidavit, and any response permitted under paragraph (b) of this section, the presiding officer determines that the petitioning participant has not made a *prima facie* showing that the application of the specific Commission rule or regulation (or provision thereof) to a particular aspect or aspects of the subject matter of the proceeding would not serve the purposes for which the rule or regulation was adopted and that application of the rule or regulation should be waived or an exception granted, no evidence may be received on that matter and no discovery, cross examination, or argument directed to the matter will be permitted, and the presiding officer may not further consider the matter.

(d) If, on the basis of the petition, affidavit and any response provided for in paragraph (b) of this section, the presiding officer determines that the *prima facie* showing required by paragraph (b) of this section has been made, the presiding officer shall, before ruling on the petition, certify the matter directly to the Commission (the matter will be certified to the Commission notwithstanding other provisions on certification in this part) for a determination in the matter of whether the application of the Commission rule or regulation or provision thereof to a particular aspect or aspects of the subject matter of the proceeding, in the context of this section, should be waived or an exception made. The Commission may, among other things, on the basis of the petition, affidavits, and any response, determine whether the application of the specified rule or regulation (or provision thereof) should be waived or an exception be made. The Commission may direct further proceedings as it considers appropriate to aid its determination.

(e) Whether or not the procedure in paragraph (b) of this section is available, a participant to an initial or renewal licensing proceeding may file a petition for rulemaking under §2.802.

[69 FR 2236, Jan. 14, 2004, as amended at 77 FR 46593, Aug. 3, 2012]

§2.336 General discovery.

(a) Except for proceedings conducted under subparts G and J of this part or as otherwise ordered by the Commission, the presiding officer or the Atomic Safety and Licensing Board assigned to the proceeding, all parties, other than the NRC staff, to any proceeding subject to this part shall, within thirty (30) days of the issuance of the order granting a request for hearing or petition to intervene and without further order or request from any party, disclose and provide:

(1) The name and, if known, the address and telephone number of any person, including any expert, upon whose opinion the party bases its claims and contentions and may rely upon as a

witness, and a copy of the analysis or other authority upon which that person bases his or her opinion;

(2)(i) A copy, or a description by category and location, of all documents and data compilations in the possession, custody, or control of the party that are relevant to the contentions, provided that if only a description is provided of a document or data compilation, a party shall have the right to request copies of that document and/or data compilation, and

(ii) A copy (for which there is no claim of privilege or protected status), or a description by category and location, of all tangible things (e.g., books, publications and treatises) in the possession, custody or control of the party that are relevant to the contention.

(iii) When any document, data compilation, or other tangible thing that must be disclosed is publicly available from another source, such as at the NRC Web site, *http://www.nrc.gov*, and/or the NRC Public Document Room, a sufficient disclosure would be the location, the title and a page reference to the relevant document, data compilation, or tangible thing.

(3) A list of documents otherwise required to be disclosed for which a claim of privilege or protected status is being made, together with sufficient information for assessing the claim of privilege or protected status of the documents.

(b) Except for proceedings conducted under subparts G and J of this part or as otherwise ordered by the Commission, the presiding officer, or the Atomic Safety and Licensing Board assigned to the proceeding, the NRC staff must, within 30 days of the issuance of the order granting a request for hearing or petition to intervene and without further order or request from any party, disclose or provide to the extent available (but excluding those documents for which there is a claim of privilege or protected status):

(1) The application (if applicable) and applicant or licensee requests that are relevant to the admitted contentions and are associated with the application or proposed action that is the subject of the proceeding;

(2) NRC correspondence with the applicant or licensee that is relevant to the admitted contentions and associated with the application or proposed action that is the subject of the proceeding;

(3) All documents (including documents that provide support for, or opposition to, the application or proposed action) that both support the NRC staff's review of the application or proposed action that is the subject of the proceeding and are relevant to the admitted contentions;

(4) Any NRC staff documents that both represent the NRC staff's determination on the application or proposal that is the subject of the proceeding and are relevant to the admitted contentions; and

(5) A list of all otherwise-discoverable documents for which a claim of privilege or protected status is being made, together with sufficient information for assessing the claim of privilege or protected status of the documents.

(c) Each party and the NRC staff shall make its initial disclosures under paragraphs (a) and (b) of this section, based on the information and documentation then reasonably available to it. A party, including the NRC staff, is not excused from making the required disclosures because it has not fully completed its investigation of the case, it challenges the sufficiency of another entity's disclosures, or that another entity has not yet made its disclosures. All disclosures under this section must be accompanied by a certification (by sworn affidavit) that all relevant materials required by this section have been disclosed, and that the disclosures are accurate and complete as of the date of the certification.

(d) The duty of disclosure under this section is continuing. Parties must update their disclosures every month after initial disclosures on a due date selected by the presiding officer in the order admitting contentions, unless the parties agree upon a different due date or frequency. The disclosure update shall be limited to documents subject to disclosure under this section and does not need to include documents that are developed, obtained, or discovered during the two weeks before the due date. Disclosure updates shall include any documents subject to disclosure that were not included in any previous disclosure update. The duty to update disclosures relevant to an admitted contention ends when the presiding officer issues a decision resolving the contention, or at such other time as may be specified by the presiding officer or the Commission.

(e)(1) The presiding officer may impose sanctions, including dismissal of specific contentions, dismissal of the adjudication, denial or dismissal of the application or proposed action, or the use of the discovery provisions in subpart G of this part against the offending party, for the offending party's continuing unexcused failure to make the disclosures required by this section.

(2) The presiding officer may impose sanctions on a party that fails to provide any document or witness name required to be disclosed under this section, unless the party demonstrates good cause for its failure to make the disclosure required by this section. A sanction that may be imposed by the presiding officer is prohibiting the admission into evidence of documents or testimony of the witness proffered by the offending party in support of its case.

(f)(1) In the event of a dispute over disclosure of documents and records including Safeguards Information referred to in Sections 147 and 181 of the Atomic Energy Act of 1954, as amended, the presiding officer may issue an order requiring disclosure if—

(i) The presiding officer finds that the individual seeking access to Safeguards Information to participate in an NRC adjudication has the requisite "need to know", as defined in 10 CFR 73.2;

(ii) The individual has undergone an FBI criminal history records check, unless exempt under 10 CFR 73.22(b)(3) or 73.23(b)(3), as applicable, by submitting fingerprints to the NRC Office of Administration, Security Processing Unit, Mail Stop T–6E46, U.S. Nuclear Regulatory Commission, Washington, DC 20555–0001, and otherwise following the procedures in 10 CFR 73.57(d) for submitting and processing fingerprints. However, before a final adverse determination by the NRC Office of Administration on an individual's criminal history records check is made, the individual shall be afforded the protections provided by 10 CFR 73.57; and

(iii) The NRC Office of Administration has found, based upon a background check, that the individual is trustworthy and reliable, unless exempt under 10 CFR 73.22(b)(3) or 73.23(b)(3), as applicable. In addition to the protections provided by 10 CFR 73.57 for adverse determinations based on criminal history records checks, the Office of Administration must take the following actions before making a final adverse determination on an individual's background check for trustworthiness and reliability. The Office of Administration will:

(A) For the purpose of assuring correct and complete information, provide to the individual any records, in addition to those required to be provided under 10 CFR 73.57(e)(1), that were considered in the trustworthiness and reliability determination;

(B) Resolve any challenge by the individual to the completeness or accuracy of the records described in §2.336(f)(1)(iii)(A). The individual may make this challenge by submitting information and/or an explanation to the Office of Administration. The challenge must be submitted within 10 days of the distribution of the records described in §2.336(f)(1)(iii)(A), and the Office of Administration must promptly resolve any challenge.

(iv) Individuals seeking access to Safeguards Information to participate in an NRC adjudication for whom the NRC Office of Administration has made a final adverse determination on trustworthiness and reliability may submit a request to the Chief Administrative Judge for review of the adverse determination. Upon receiving such a request, the Chief Administrative Judge shall designate an officer other than the presiding officer of the proceeding to review the adverse determination. For purposes of review, the adverse determination must be in writing and set forth the grounds for the determination. The request for review shall be served on the NRC staff and may include additional information for review by the designated officer. The request must be filed within 15 days after receipt of the adverse determination by the person against whom the adverse determination has been made. Within 10 days of receipt of the request for review and any additional information, the NRC staff will file a response indicating whether the request and additional information has caused the NRC Office of Administration to reverse its adverse determination. The designated officer may reverse the Office of Administration's final adverse determination only if the officer finds, based on all the information submitted, that the adverse determination constitutes an abuse of discretion. The designated officer's decision must be rendered within 15 days after receipt of the staff filing indicating that the request for review and additional information has not changed the NRC Office of Administration's adverse determination.

(2) The presiding officer may include in an order any protective terms and conditions (including affidavits of nondisclosure) as may be necessary and appropriate to prevent the unauthorized disclosure of Safeguards Information.

(3) When Safeguards Information protected from unauthorized disclosure under Section 147 of the Atomic Energy Act of 1954, as amended, is received and possessed by anyone other than the NRC staff, it must also be protected according to the requirements of § 73.21 and the requirements of § 73.22 or § 73.23 of this chapter, as applicable.

(4) The presiding officer may also prescribe additional procedures to effectively safeguard and prevent disclosure of Safeguards Information to unauthorized persons with minimum impairment of the procedural rights which would be available if Safeguards Information were not involved.

(5) In addition to any other sanction that may be imposed by the presiding officer for violation of an order issued pursuant to this paragraph, violation of a provision for the protection of Safeguards Information from unauthorized disclosure that is contained in an order may be subject to a civil penalty imposed under § 2.205.

(6) For the purpose of imposing the criminal penalties contained in Section 223 of the Atomic Energy Act of 1954, as amended, a provision for the protection of Safeguards Information from unauthorized disclosure that is contained in an order issued pursuant to this paragraph is considered to be issued under Section 161b of the Atomic Energy Act of 1954, as amended.

(7) If a presiding officer has yet to be appointed, the authority to take the actions described in paragraphs (f)(1) to (f)(6) of this section resides in the officer with jurisdiction under § 2.318(a).

(g) The disclosures required by this section constitute the sole discovery permitted for NRC proceedings under this part unless there is further provision for discovery under the specific subpart under which the hearing will be conducted or unless the Commission provides otherwise in a specific proceeding.

[69 FR 2236, Jan. 14, 2004, as amended at 73 FR 63567, Oct. 24, 2008, 77 FR 46593, Aug. 3, 2012]

§ 2.337 Evidence at a hearing.

(a) *Admissibility.* Only relevant, material, and reliable evidence which is not unduly repetitious will be admitted. Immaterial or irrelevant parts of an admissible document will be segregated and excluded so far as is practicable.

(b) *Objections.* An objection to evidence must briefly state the grounds of objection. The transcript must include the objection, the grounds, and the ruling. Exception to an adverse ruling is preserved without notation on-the-record.

(c) *Offer of proof.* An offer of proof, made in connection with an objection to a ruling of the presiding officer excluding or rejecting proffered oral testimony, must consist of a statement of the substance of the proffered evidence. If the excluded evidence is in written form, a copy must be marked for identification. Rejected exhibits, adequately marked for identification, must be retained in the record.

(d) *Exhibits.* A written exhibit will not be received in evidence unless the original and two copies are offered and a copy is furnished to each party, or the parties have been previously furnished with copies or the presiding officer directs otherwise. The presiding officer may permit a party to replace with a true copy an original document admitted in evidence.

(e) *Official record.* An official record of a government agency or entry in an official record may be evidenced by an official publication or by a copy attested by the officer having legal custody of the record and accompanied by a certificate of his custody.

(f) *Official notice.* (1) The Commission or the presiding officer may take official notice of any fact of which a court of the United States may take judicial notice or of any technical or scientific fact within the knowledge of the Commission as an expert body. Each fact officially noticed under this paragraph must be specified in the record with sufficient particularity to advise the parties of the matters which have been noticed or brought to the attention of the parties before final decision and each party adversely affected by the decision shall be given opportunity to controvert the fact.

(2) If a decision is stated to rest in whole or in part on official notice of a fact which the parties have not had a prior opportunity to controvert, a party may controvert the fact by filing an appeal from an initial decision or a petition for reconsideration of a final decision. The appeal must clearly and concisely set forth the information relied upon to controvert the fact.

(g) *Proceedings involving applications—*(1) *Facility construction permits.* In a proceeding involving an application for construction permit for a production or utilization facility, the NRC staff shall offer into evidence any report submitted by the ACRS in the proceeding in compliance with section 182(b) of the Act, any safety evaluation prepared by the NRC staff, and any environmental impact statement prepared in the proceeding under subpart A of part 51 of this chapter by the Director, Office of Nuclear Reactor Regulation, Director, Office of New Reactors, or Director, Office of Nuclear Material Safety and Safeguards, as appropriate, or his or her designee.

(2) Other applications where the NRC staff is a party. In a proceeding involving an application for other than a construction permit for a production or utilization facility, the NRC staff shall offer into evidence:

(i) Any report submitted by the ACRS in the proceeding in compliance with section 182(b) of the Act;

(ii) At the discretion of the NRC staff, a safety evaluation prepared by the NRC staff and/or NRC staff testimony and evidence on the contention or contested matter prepared in advance of the completion of the safety evaluation;

(iii) Any NRC staff statement of position on the contention or contested matter provided to the presiding officer under § 2.1202(a); and

(iv) Any environmental impact statement or environmental assessment prepared in the proceeding under subpart A of part 51 of this chapter by the Director, Office of Nuclear Reactor Regulation, Director, Office of New Reactors, or Director, Office of Nuclear Material Safety and Safeguards, as appropriate, or his or her designee if there is any, but only if there are admitted contentions or contested matters with respect to the adequacy of the environmental impact statement or environmental assessment.

(3) Other applications where the NRC staff is not a party. In a proceeding involving an application for other than a construction permit for a production or utilization facility, the NRC staff shall offer into evidence, and (with the exception of an ACRS report) provide one or more sponsoring witnesses, for:

(i) Any report submitted by the ACRS in the proceeding in compliance with section 182(b) of the Act;

(ii) At the discretion of the NRC staff, a safety evaluation prepared by the NRC staff and/or NRC staff testimony and evidence on the contention or contested matter prepared in advance of the completion of the safety evaluation;

(iii) Any NRC staff statement of position on the contention or contested matter under § 2.1202(a); and

(iv) Any environmental impact statement or environmental assessment prepared in the proceeding under subpart A of part 51 of this chapter by the Director, Office of Nuclear Reactor Regulation, Director, Office of New Reactors, or Director, Office of Nuclear Material Safety and Safeguards, as appropriate, or his or her designee if there is any, but only if there are admitted contentions or contested matters with respect to the adequacy of the environmental impact statement or environmental assessment.

[69 FR 2236, Jan. 14, 2004, as amended at 73 FR 5716, Jan. 31, 2008; 77 FR 46594, Aug. 3, 2012]

§ 2.338 Settlement of issues; alternative dispute resolution.

The fair and reasonable settlement and resolution of issues proposed for litigation in proceedings subject to this part is encouraged. Parties are encouraged to employ various methods of alternate dispute resolution to address the issues without the need for litigation in proceedings subject to this part.

(a) *Availability.* The parties shall have the opportunity to submit a proposed settlement of some or all issues to the Commission or presiding officer, as appropriate, or submit a request for alternative dispute resolution under paragraph (b) of this section.

(b) *Settlement judge; alternative dispute resolution.* (1) The presiding officer, upon joint motion of the parties, may request the Chief Administrative Judge to appoint a Settlement Judge to conduct settlement negotiations or remit the proceeding to alternative dispute resolution as the Commission may provide or to which the parties may agree. The order appointing the Settlement Judge may confine the scope of settlement negotiations to specified issues. The order must direct the Settlement Judge to report to the Chief Administrative Judge at specified time periods.

(2) If a Settlement Judge is appointed, the Settlement Judge shall:

(i) Convene and preside over conferences and settlement negotiations between the parties and assess the practicalities of a potential settlement;

(ii) Report to the Chief Administrative Judge describing the status of the settlement negotiations and recommending the termination or continuation of the settlement negotiations; and

(iii) Not discuss the merits of the case with the Chief Administrative Judge or any other person, or appear as a witness in the case.

(3) Settlement negotiations conducted by the Settlement Judge terminate upon the order of the Chief Administrative Judge issued after consultation with the Settlement Judge.

(4) No decision concerning the appointment of a Settlement Judge or the termination of the settlement negotiation is subject to review by, appeal to, or rehearing by the presiding officer or the Commission.

(c) *Availability of parties' attorneys or representatives.* The presiding officer (or Settlement Judge) may require that the attorney or other representative who is expected to try the case for each party be present and that the parties, or agents having full settlement authority, also be present or available by telephone.

(d) *Admissibility in subsequent hearing.* No evidence, statements, or conduct in settlement negotiations under this section will be admissible in any subsequent hearing, except by stipulation of the parties. Documents disclosed may not be used in litigation unless obtained through appropriate discovery or subpoena.

(e) *Imposition of additional requirements.* The presiding officer (or Settlement Judge) may impose on the parties and persons having an interest in the outcome of the adjudication additional requirements as the presiding officer (or Settlement Judge) finds necessary for the fair and efficient resolution of the case.

(f) *Effects of ongoing settlement negotiations.* The conduct of settlement negotiations does not divest the presiding officer of jurisdiction and does not automatically stay the proceeding. A hearing must not be unduly delayed because of the conduct of settlement negotiations.

(g) *Form.* A settlement must be in the form of a proposed settlement agreement, a consent order, and a motion for its entry that includes the reasons why it should be accepted. It must be signed by the consenting parties or their authorized representatives.

(h) *Content of settlement agreement.* The proposed settlement agreement must contain the following:

(1) An admission of all jurisdictional facts;

(2) An express waiver of further procedural steps before the presiding officer, of any right to challenge or contest the validity of the order entered into in accordance with the agreement, and of all rights to seek judicial review or otherwise to contest the validity of the consent order;

(3) A statement that the order has the same force and effect as an order made after full hearing; and

(4) A statement that matters identified in the agreement, required to be adjudicated have been resolved by the proposed settlement agreement and consent order.

(i) *Approval of settlement agreement.* Following issuance of a notice of hearing, a settlement must be approved by the presiding officer or the Commission as appropriate in order to be binding in the proceeding. The presiding officer or Commission may order the adjudication of the issues that the presiding officer or Commission finds is required in the public interest to dispose of the proceeding. In an enforcement proceeding under subpart B of this part, the presiding officer shall accord due weight to the position of the NRC staff when reviewing the settlement. If approved, the terms of the settlement or compromise must be embodied in a decision or order. Settlements approved by a presiding officer are subject to the Commission's review in accordance with § 2.341.

§ 2.339 Expedited decisionmaking procedure.

(a) The presiding officer may determine a proceeding by an order after the conclusion of a hearing without issuing an initial decision, when:

(1) All parties stipulate that the initial decision may be omitted and waive their rights to file a petition for review, to request oral argument, and to seek judicial review;

(2) No unresolved substantial issue of fact, law, or discretion remains, and the record clearly warrants granting the relief requested; and

(3) The presiding officer finds that dispensing with the issuance of the initial decision is in the public interest.

(b) An order entered under paragraph (a) of this section is subject to review by the Commission on its own motion within forty (40) days after its date.

(c) An initial decision may be made effective immediately, subject to review by the Commission on its own motion within thirty (30) days after its date, except as otherwise provided in this chapter, when:

(1) All parties stipulate that the initial decision may be made effective immediately and waive their rights to file a petition for review, to request oral argument, and to seek judicial review;

(2) No unresolved substantial issue of fact, law, or discretion remains and the record clearly warrants granting the relief requested; and

(3) The presiding officer finds that it is in the public interest to make the initial decision effective immediately.

(d) The provisions of this section do not apply to an initial decision directing the issuance of a limited work authorization under 10 CFR 50.10, an early site permit under subpart A of part 52 of this chapter, a construction permit or construction authorization, a combined license under subpart C of part 52 of this chapter, or a manufacturing license under subpart F of part 52.

[69 FR 2236, Jan. 14, 2004, as amended at 72 FR 49475, Aug. 28, 2007]

§ 2.340 Initial decision in certain contested proceedings; immediate effectiveness of initial decisions; issuance of authorizations, permits, and licenses.

(a) *Initial decision—production or utilization facility operating license.* (1) Matters in controversy; presiding officer consideration of matters not put in controversy by parties. In any initial decision in a contested proceeding on an application for an operating license or renewed license (including an amendment to or renewal of an operating license or renewed license) for a production or utilization facility, the presiding officer shall make findings of fact and conclusions of law on the matters put into controversy by the parties and any matter designated by the Commission to be decided by the presiding officer. The presiding officer shall also make findings of fact and conclusions of law on any matter not put into controversy by the parties, but only to the extent that the presiding officer determines that a serious safety, environmental, or common defense and security matter exists, and the Commission approves of an examination of and decision on the matter upon its referral by the presiding officer under, inter alia, the provisions of §§ 2.323 and 2.341.

(2) *Presiding officer initial decision and issuance of permit or license.* (i) In a contested proceeding for the initial issuance or renewal of a construction permit, operating license, or renewed license, or the amendment of an operating or renewed license where the NRC has not made a determination of no significant hazards consideration, the Commission, the Director, Office of Nuclear Reactor Regulation, or the Director, Office of New Reactors, as appropriate, after making the requisite findings, shall issue, deny, or appropriately condition the permit or license in accordance with the presiding officer's initial decision once that decision becomes effective.

(ii) In a contested proceeding for the amendment of a construction permit, operating license, or renewed license where the NRC has made a determination of no significant hazards consideration, the Commission, the Director, Office of Nuclear Reactor Regulation, or the Director, Office of New Reactors, as appropriate (appropriate official), after making the requisite findings and complying with any applicable provisions of § 2.1202(a) or § 2.1403(a), may issue the amendment before the presiding officer's initial decision becomes effective. Once the presiding officer's initial decision becomes effective, the appropriate official shall take action with respect to that amendment in accordance with the initial decision. If the presiding officer's initial decision becomes effective before the appropriate official issues the amendment, then the appropriate official, after making the requisite findings, shall issue, deny, or appropriately condition the amendment in accordance with the presiding officer's initial decision.

(b) *Initial decision—combined license under 10 CFR part 52.* (1) Matters in controversy; presiding officer consideration of matters not put in controversy by parties. In any initial decision in a contested proceeding on an application for a combined license under part 52 of this chapter (including an amendment to or renewal of combined license), the presiding officer shall make findings of fact and conclusions of law on the matters put into controversy by the parties and any matter designated by the Commission to be decided by the presiding officer. The presiding officer shall also make findings of fact and conclusions of law on any matter not put into controversy by the parties, but only to the extent that the presiding officer determines that a serious safety, environmental, or common defense and security matter exists, and the Commission approves of an examination of and decision on the matter upon its referral by the presiding officer under, inter alia, the provisions of §§ 2.323 and 2.341.

(2) *Presiding officer initial decision and issuance of permit or license.* (i) In a contested proceeding for the initial issuance or renewal of a combined license under part 52 of this chapter, or the amendment of a combined license where the NRC has not made a determination of no significant hazards consideration, the Commission, the Director, Office of Nuclear Reactor Regulation, or the Director, Office of New Reactors, as appropriate, after making the requisite findings, shall issue, deny, or appropriately condition the permit or license in accordance with the presiding officer's initial decision once that decision becomes effective.

(ii) In a contested proceeding for the amendment of a combined license under part 52 of this chapter where the NRC has made a determination of no significant hazards consideration, the Commission, the Director, Office of Nuclear Reactor Regulation, or the Director, Office of New Reactors, as appropriate (appropriate official), after making the requisite findings and complying with any applicable provisions of § 2.1202(a) or § 2.1403(a), may issue the amendment before the presiding officer's initial decision becomes effective. Once the presiding officer's initial decision becomes effective, the appropriate official shall take action with respect to that amendment in accordance with the initial decision. If the presiding officer's initial decision becomes effective before the appropriate official issues the amendment, then the appropriate official, after making the requisite findings, shall issue, deny, or appropriately condition the amendment in accordance with the presiding officer's initial decision.

(c) *Initial decision on findings under 10 CFR 52.103 with respect to acceptance criteria in nuclear power reactor combined licenses.* In any initial decision under § 52.103(g) of this chapter with respect to whether acceptance criteria have been or will be met, the presiding officer shall make findings of fact and conclusions of law on the matters put into controversy by the parties, and any matter designated by the Commission to be decided by the presiding officer. Matters not put into controversy by the parties, but identified by the presiding officer as matters requiring further examination, shall be referred to the Commission for its determination; the Commission may, in its discretion, treat any of these referred matters as a request for action under § 2.206 and process the matter in accordance with § 52.103(f) of this chapter.

(d) *Initial decision—manufacturing license under 10 CFR part 52.* (1) Matters in controversy; presiding officer consideration of matters not put in controversy by parties. In any initial decision in a contested proceeding on an application for a manufacturing license under subpart C of part 52 of this chapter (including an amendment to or renewal of a manufacturing license), the presiding officer shall make findings of fact and conclusions of law on the matters put into controversy by the parties and any matter designated by the Commission to be decided by the presiding officer. The presiding officer also shall make findings of fact and conclusions of law on any matter not put into controversy by the parties, but only to the extent that the presiding officer determines that a serious safety, environmental, or common defense and security matter exists, and the Commission approves of an examination of and decision on the matter upon its referral by the presiding officer under, inter alia, the provisions of §§ 2.323 and 2.341.

(2) *Presiding officer initial decision and issuance of permit or license.* (i) In a contested proceeding for the initial issuance or renewal of a manufacturing license under subpart C of part 52 of this chapter, or the amendment of a manufacturing license, the Commission, the Director, Office of Nuclear Reactor Regulation, or the Director, Office of New Reactors, as appropriate, after making the requisite findings, shall issue, deny, or appropriately condition the permit or license in accordance with the presiding officer's initial decision once that decision becomes effective.

(ii) In a contested proceeding for the initial issuance or renewal of a manufacturing license under subpart C of part 52 of this chapter, or the amendment of a manufacturing license, the Commission, the Director, Office of Nuclear Reactor Regulation, or the Director, Office of New Reactors, as appropriate, may issue the license, permit, or license amendment in accordance with § 2.1202(a) or § 2.1403(a) before the presiding officer's initial decision becomes effective. If, however, the presiding officer's initial decision becomes effective before the license, permit, or license amendment is issued under § 2.1202 or § 2.1403, then the Commission, the Director, Office of Nuclear Reactor Regulation, or the Director, Office of New Reactors, as appropriate, shall issue, deny, or appropriately condition the license, permit, or license amendment in accordance with the presiding officer's initial decision.

(e) *Initial decision—other proceedings not involving production or utilization facilities*—(1) *Matters in controversy; presiding officer consideration of matters not put in controversy by parties.* In a proceeding not involving production or utilization facilities, the presiding officer shall make findings of fact and conclusions of law on the matters put into controversy by the parties to the proceeding, and on any matters designated by the Commission to be decided by the presiding officer. Matters not put into controversy by the parties, but identified by the presiding officer as requiring further examination, must be referred to the Director, Office of Nuclear Material Safety and Safeguards, or as appropriate. Depending on the resolution of those matters, the Director, Office of Nuclear Material Safety and Safeguards or as appropriate, after making the requisite findings, shall issue, deny, revoke or appropriately condition the license, or take other action as necessary or appropriate.

(2) *Presiding officer initial decision and issuance of permit or license.* (i) In a contested proceeding under this paragraph (e), the Commissionor the Director, Office of Nuclear Material Safety and Safeguards, or as appropriate, shall issue, deny, or appropriately condition the permit, license, or license amendment in accordance with the presiding officer's initial decision once that decision becomes effective.

(ii) In a contested proceeding under this paragraph (e), the Commission, the Director, Office of Nuclear Material Safety and Safeguards, or as appropriate, may issue the permit, license, or amendment in accordance with §2.1202(a) or §2.1403(a) before the presiding officer's initial decision becomes effective. If, however, the presiding officer's initial decision becomes effective before the permit, license, or amendment is issued under §2.1202 or §2.1403, then the Commission, the Director, Office of Nuclear Material Safety and Safeguards, or as appropriate, shall issue, deny, or appropriately condition the permit, license, or amendment in accordance with the presiding officer's initial decision.

(f) *Immediate effectiveness of certain presiding officer decisions.* A presiding officer's initial decision directing the issuance or amendment of a limited work authorization under §50.10 of this chapter, an early site permit under subpart A of part 52 of this chapter, a construction permit or construction authorization under part 50 of this chapter, an operating license under part 50 of this chapter, a combined license under subpart C of part 52 of this chapter, a manufacturing license under subpart F of part 52 of this chapter, a renewed license under part 54, or a license under part 72 of this chapter to store spent fuel in an independent spent fuel storage facility (ISFSI) or a monitored retrievable storage installation (MRS), an initial decision directing issuance of a license under part 61 of this chapter, or an initial decision under §52.103(g) of this chapter that acceptance criteria in a combined license have been met, is immediately effective upon issuance unless the presiding officer finds that good cause has been shown by a party why the initial decision should not become immediately effective.

(g)–(h) [Reserved]

(i) *Issuance of authorizations, permits, and licenses—production and utilization facilities.* The Commission, the Director, Office of New Reactors, or the Director, Office of Nuclear Reactor Regulation, as appropriate, shall issue a limited work authorization under §50.10 of this chapter, an early site permit under subpart A of part 52 of this chapter, a construction permit or construction authorization under part 50 of this chapter, an operating license under part 50 of this chapter, a combined license under subpart C of part 52 of this chapter, or a manufacturing license under subpart F of part 52 of this chapter within 10 days from the date of issuance of the initial decision:

(1) If the Commission or the appropriate Director has made all findings necessary for issuance of the authorization, permit or license, not within the scope of the initial decision of the presiding officer; and

(2) Notwithstanding the pendency of a petition for reconsideration under §2.345, a petition for review under §2.341, or a motion for stay under §2.342, or the filing of a petition under §2.206.

(j) *Issuance of finding on acceptance criteria under 10 CFR 52.103.* The Commission, the Director of the Office of New Reactors, or the Director of the Office of Nuclear Reactor Regulation, as appropriate, shall make the finding under 10 CFR 52.103(g) that acceptance criteria in a combined license are met within 10 days from the date of the presiding officer's initial decision:

(1) If the Commission or the appropriate director is otherwise able to make the finding under 10 CFR 52.103(g) that the prescribed acceptance criteria are met for those acceptance criteria not within the scope of the initial decision of the presiding officer;

(2) If the presiding officer's initial decision—with respect to contentions that the prescribed acceptance criteria

have not been met—finds that those acceptance criteria have been met, and the Commission or the appropriate director thereafter is able to make the finding that those acceptance criteria are met;

(3) If the presiding officer's initial decision—with respect to contentions that the prescribed acceptance criteria will not be met—finds that those acceptance criteria will be met, and the Commission or the appropriate director thereafter is able to make the finding that those acceptance criteria are met; and

(4) Notwithstanding the pendency of a petition for reconsideration under 10 CFR 2.345, a petition for review under 10 CFR 2.341, or a motion for stay under 10 CFR 2.342, or the filing of a petition under 10 CFR 2.206.

(k) *Issuance of other licenses.* The Commissionor the Director, Office of Nuclear Material Safety and Safeguards, or as appropriate, shall issue a license, including a license under part 72 of this chapter to store spent fuel in either an independent spent fuel storage facility (ISFSI) located away from a reactor site or at a monitored retrievable storage installation (MRS), within 10 days from the date of issuance of the initial decision:

(1) If the Commission or the appropriate Director has made all findings necessary for issuance of the license, not within the scope of the initial decision of the presiding officer; and

(2) Notwithstanding the pendency of a petition for reconsideration under §2.345, a petition for review under §2.341, or a motion for stay under §2.342, or the filing of a petition under §2.206.

[77 FR 46594, Aug. 3, 2012, as amended at 77 FR 51891, Aug. 28, 2012;79 FR 75739, Dec. 19, 2014]

§2.341 Review of decisions and actions of a presiding officer.

(a)(1) Review of decisions and actions of a presiding officer are treated under this section; provided, however, that no party may request further Commission review of a Commission determination to allow a period of interim operation under §52.103(c) of this chapter. This section does not apply to appeals under §2.311 or to appeals in the high-level waste proceeding, which are governed by §2.1015.

(2) Within 120 days after the date of a decision or action by a presiding officer, or within 120 days after a petition for review of the decision or action has been served under paragraph (b) of this section, whichever is greater, the Commission may review the decision or action on its own motion, unless the Commission, in its discretion, extends the time for its review.

(b)(1) Within 25 days after service of a full or partial initial decision by a presiding officer, and within 25 days after service of any other decision or action by a presiding officer with respect to which a petition for review is authorized by this part, a party may file a petition for review with the Commission on the grounds specified in paragraph (b)(4) of this section. Unless otherwise authorized by law, a party to an NRC proceeding must file a petition for Commission review before seeking judicial review of an agency action.

(2) A petition for review under this paragraph may not be longer than twenty-five (25) pages, and must contain the following:

(i) A concise summary of the decision or action of which review is sought;

(ii) A statement (including record citation) where the matters of fact or law raised in the petition for review were previously raised before the presiding officer and, if they were not, why they could not have been raised;

(iii) A concise statement why in the petitioner's view the decision or action is erroneous; and

(iv) A concise statement why Commission review should be exercised.

(3) Any other party to the proceeding may, within 25 days after service of a petition for review, file an answer supporting or opposing Commission review. This answer may not be longer than 25 pages and should concisely address the matters in paragraph (b)(2) of this section to the extent appropriate. The petitioning party may file a reply brief within 10 days of service of any answer. This reply brief may not be longer than 5 pages.

(4) The petition for review may be granted in the discretion of the Commission, giving due weight to the existence of a substantial question with respect to the following considerations:

(i) A finding of material fact is clearly erroneous or in conflict with a finding as to the same fact in a different proceeding;

(ii) A necessary legal conclusion is without governing precedent or is a departure from or contrary to established law;

(iii) A substantial and important question of law, policy, or discretion has been raised;

(iv) The conduct of the proceeding involved a prejudicial procedural error; or

(v) Any other consideration which the Commission may deem to be in the public interest.

(5) A petition for review will not be granted to the extent that it relies on matters that could have been but were not raised before the presiding officer. A matter raised sua sponte by a presiding officer has been raised before the presiding officer for the purpose of this section.

(6) A petition for review will not be granted as to issues raised before the presiding officer on a pending motion for reconsideration.

(c)(1) If within 120 days after the filing of a petition for review the Commission does not grant the petition, in whole or in part, the petition is deemed to be denied, unless the Commission, in its discretion, extends the time for its consideration of the petition and any answers to the petition.

(2) If a petition for review is granted, the Commission may issue an order specifying the issues to be reviewed and designating the parties to the review proceeding. The Commission may, in its discretion, decide the matter on the basis of the petition for review or it may specify whether any briefs may be filed.

(3) Unless the Commission orders otherwise, any briefs on review may not exceed 30 pages in length, exclusive of pages containing the table of contents, table of citations, and any addendum containing appropriate exhibits, statutes, or regulations. A brief in excess of 10 pages must contain a table of contents with page references and a table of cases (alphabetically arranged), cited statutes, regulations, and other authorities, with references to the pages of the brief where they are cited.

(d) Petitions for reconsideration of Commission decisions granting or denying review in whole or in part will not be entertained. A petition for reconsideration of a Commission decision after review may be filed within ten (10) days, but is not necessary for exhaustion of administrative remedies. However, if a petition for reconsideration is filed, the Commission decision is not final until the petition is decided. Any petition for reconsideration will be evaluated against the standard in § 2.323(e).

(e) Neither the filing nor the granting of a petition under this section stays the effect of the decision or action of the presiding officer, unless the Commission orders otherwise.

(f) *Interlocutory review.* (1) A ruling referred or question certified to the Commission under §§ 2.319(l) or 2.323(f) may be reviewed if the certification or referral raises significant and novel legal or policy issues, or resolution of the issues would materially advance the orderly disposition of the proceeding.

(2) The Commission may, in its discretion, grant interlocutory review at the request of a party despite the absence of a referral or certification by the presiding officer. A petition and answer to it must be filed within the times and in the form prescribed in paragraph (b) of this section and must be treated in accordance with the general provisions of this section. The petition for interlocutory review will be granted only if the party demonstrates that the issue for which the party seeks interlocutory review:

(i) Threatens the party adversely affected by it with immediate and serious irreparable impact which, as a practical matter, could not be alleviated through a petition for review of the presiding officer's final decision; or

(ii) Affects the basic structure of the proceeding in a pervasive or unusual manner.

[69 FR 2236, Jan. 14, 2004, as amended at 72 FR 49476, Aug. 28, 2007; 77 FR 46596, Aug. 3, 2012]

§ 2.342 Stays of decisions.

(a) Within ten (10) days after service of a decision or action of a presiding officer, any party to the proceeding may file an application for a stay of the effectiveness of the decision or action pending filing of and a decision on a petition for review. This application may be filed with the Commission or the presiding officer, but not both at the same time.

(b) An application for a stay may be no longer than ten (10) pages, exclusive of affidavits, and must contain the following:

(1) A concise summary of the decision or action which is requested to be stayed;

(2) A concise statement of the grounds for stay, with reference to the factors specified in paragraph (e) of this section; and

(3) To the extent that an application for a stay relies on facts subject to dispute, appropriate references to the record or affidavits by knowledgeable persons.

(c) Service of an application for a stay on the other parties must be by the same method, e.g., electronic or facsimile transmission, mail, as the method for filing the application with the Commission or the presiding officer.

(d) Within ten (10) days after service of an application for a stay under this section, any party may file an answer supporting or opposing the granting of a stay. This answer may not be longer than ten (10) pages, exclusive of affidavits, and should concisely address the matters in paragraph (b) of this section to the extent appropriate. Further replies to answers will not be entertained. Filing of and service of an answer on the other parties must be by the same method, e.g., electronic or facsimile transmission, mail, as the method for filing the application for the stay.

(e) In determining whether to grant or deny an application for a stay, the Commission or presiding officer will consider:

(1) Whether the moving party has made a strong showing that it is likely to prevail on the merits;

(2) Whether the party will be irreparably injured unless a stay is granted;

(3) Whether the granting of a stay would harm other parties; and

(4) Where the public interest lies.

(f) In extraordinary cases, where prompt application is made under this section, the Commission or presiding officer may grant a temporary stay to preserve the status quo without waiting for filing of any answer. The application may be made orally provided the application is promptly confirmed by electronic or facsimile transmission message. Any party applying under this paragraph shall make all reasonable efforts to inform the other parties of the application, orally if made orally.

§ 2.343 Oral argument.

In its discretion, the Commission may allow oral argument upon the request of a party made in a petition for review, brief on review, or upon its own initiative.

§ 2.344 Final decision.

(a) The Commission will ordinarily consider the whole record on review, but may limit the issues to be reviewed to those identified in an order taking review.

(b) The Commission may adopt, modify, or set aside the findings, conclusions and order in the initial decision, and will state the basis of its action. The final decision will be in writing and will include:

(1) A statement of findings and conclusions, with the basis for them on all material issues of fact, law or discretion presented;

(2) All facts officially noticed;

(3) The ruling on each material issue; and

(4) The appropriate ruling, order, or denial of relief, with the effective date.

§ 2.345 Petition for reconsideration.

(a)(1) Any petition for reconsideration of a final decision must be filed by a party within ten (10) days after the date of the decision.

(2) Petitions for reconsideration of Commission decisions are subject to the requirements in § 2.341(d).

(b) A petition for reconsideration must demonstrate a compelling circumstance, such as the existence of a clear and material error in a decision, which could not have been reasonably anticipated, which renders the decision invalid. The petition must state the relief sought. Within ten (10) days after a petition for reconsideration has been served, any other party may file an answer in opposition to or in support of the petition.

(c) Neither the filing nor the granting of the petition stays the decision unless the Commission orders otherwise.

§ 2.346 Authority of the Secretary.

When briefs, motions or other documents are submitted to the Commission itself, as opposed to officers who have been delegated authority to act for the Commission, the Secretary or the Assistant Secretary is authorized to:

(a) Prescribe procedures for the filing of briefs, motions, or other pleadings, when the schedules differ from those prescribed by the rules of this part or when the rules of this part do not prescribe a schedule;

(b) Rule on motions for extensions of time;

(c) Reject motions, briefs, pleadings, and other documents filed with the Commission later then the time prescribed by the Secretary or the Assistant Secretary or established by an order, rule or regulation of the Commission unless good cause is shown for the late filing;

(d) Prescribe all procedural arrangements relating to any oral argument to be held before the Commission;

(e) Extend the time for the Commission to rule on a petition for review under § 2.341;

(f) Extend the time for the Commission to grant review on its own motion under § 2.341;

(g) Direct pleadings improperly filed before the Commission to the appropriate presiding officer for action;

(h) Deny a request for hearings, where the request fails to comply with the Commission's pleading requirements set forth in this part, and fails to set forth an arguable basis for further proceedings;

(i) Refer to the Atomic Safety and Licensing Board Panel or an Administrative Judge, as appropriate requests for hearing not falling under § 2.104, where the requestor is entitled to further proceedings; and

(j) Take action on other minor matters.

[69 FR 2236, Jan. 14, 2004, as amended at 72 FR 49152, Aug. 28, 2007; 77 FR 46597, Aug. 3, 2012; 78 FR 34247, June 7, 2013]

§ 2.347 Ex parte communications.

In any proceeding under this subpart—

(a)(1) Interested persons outside the agency may not make or knowingly cause to be made to any Commission adjudicatory employee, any ex parte communication relevant to the merits of the proceeding.

(2) For purposes of this section, *merits of the proceeding* includes:

(i) A disputed issue;

(ii) A matter which a presiding officer seeks to be referred to the Commission under 10 CFR 2.340(a); and

(iii) A matter for which the Commission has approved examination by the presiding officer under § 2.340(a).

(b) Commission adjudicatory employees may not request or entertain from any interested person outside the agency or make or knowingly cause to be made to any interested person outside the agency, any *ex parte* communication relevant to the merits of the proceeding.

(c) Any Commission adjudicatory employee who receives, makes, or knowingly causes to be made a communication prohibited by this section shall ensure that it, and any responses to the communication, are promptly served on the parties and placed in the public record of the proceeding. In the case of oral communications, a written summary must be served and placed in the public record of the proceeding.

(d) Upon receipt of a communication knowingly made or knowingly caused to be made by a party in violation of this section, the Commission or other adjudicatory employee presiding in a proceeding may, to the extent consistent with the interests of justice and the policy of the underlying statutes, require the party to show cause why its claim or interest in the proceeding should not be dismissed, denied, disregarded, or otherwise adversely affected on account of the violation.

(e)(1) The prohibitions of this section apply—

(i) When a notice of hearing or other comparable order is issued in accordance with §§ 2.104(a), 2.105(e)(2), 2.202(c), 2.205(e), or 2.312; or

(ii) Whenever the interested person or Commission adjudicatory employee responsible for the communication has knowledge that a notice of hearing or other comparable order will be issued in accordance with § 2.104(a), § 2.105(e)(2), § 2.202(c), 2.205(e), or § 2.312.

(2) The prohibitions of this section cease to apply to *ex parte* communications relevant to the merits of a full or partial initial decision when, in accordance with § 2.341, the time has expired for Commission review of the decision.

(f) The prohibitions in this section do not apply to—

(1) Requests for and the provision of status reports;

(2) Communications specifically permitted by statute or regulation;

(3) Communications made to or by Commission adjudicatory employees in the Office of the General Counsel regarding matters pending before a court or another agency; and

(4) Communications regarding generic issues involving public health and safety or other statutory responsibilities of the agency (e.g., rulemakings, congressional hearings on legislation, budgetary planning) not associated with the resolution of any proceeding under this subpart pending before the NRC.

(5) Communications, in contested proceedings and uncontested mandatory proceeding, regarding an undisputed issue.

[69 FR 2236, Jan. 14, 2004, as amended at 72 FR 49476, Aug. 28, 2007; 77 FR 46597, Aug. 3, 2012]

§ 2.348 Separation of functions.

(a) In any proceeding under this part, any NRC officer or employee engaged in the performance of any investigative or litigating function in the proceeding or in a factually related proceeding with respect to a disputed issue in that proceeding, may not participate in or advise a Commission adjudicatory employee about the initial or final decision with respect to that disputed issue, except—

(1) As witness or counsel in the proceeding;

(2) Through a written communication served on all parties and made on-the-record of the proceeding; or

(3) Through an oral communication made both with reasonable prior notice to all parties and with reasonable opportunity for all parties to respond.

(b) The prohibition in paragraph (a) of this section does not apply to—

(1) Communications to or from any Commission adjudicatory employee regarding—

(i) The status of a proceeding;

(ii) Matters for which the communications are specifically permitted by statute or regulation;

(iii) NRC participation in matters pending before a court or another agency; or

(iv) Generic issues involving public health and safety or other statutory responsibilities of the NRC (e.g., rulemakings, congressional hearings on legislation, budgetary planning) not associated with the resolution of any proceeding under this subpart pending before the NRC.

(2) Communications to or from Commissioners, members of their personal staffs, Commission adjudicatory employees in the Office of the General Counsel, and the Secretary and employees of the Office of the Secretary, regarding—

(i) Initiation or direction of an investigation or initiation of an enforcement proceeding;

(ii) Supervision of NRC staff to ensure compliance with the general policies and procedures of the agency;

(iii) NRC staff priorities and schedules or the allocation of agency resources; or

(iv) General regulatory, scientific, or engineering principles that are useful for an understanding of the issues in a proceeding and are not contested in the proceeding.

(3) None of the communications permitted by paragraph (b)(2) (i) through (iii) of this section is to be associated

by the Commission adjudicatory employee or the NRC officer or employee performing investigative or litigating functions with the resolution of any proceeding under this subpart pending before the NRC.

(c) Any Commission adjudicatory employee who receives a communication prohibited under paragraph (a) of this section shall ensure that it, and any responses to the communication, are placed in the public record of the proceeding and served on the parties. In the case of oral communications, a written summary must be served and placed in the public record of the proceeding.

(d)(1) The prohibitions in this section apply—

(i) When a notice of hearing or other comparable order is issued in accordance with §§ 2.104(a), 2.105(e)(2), 2.202(c), 2.205(e), or 2.312; or

(ii) Whenever an NRC officer or employee who is or has reasonable cause to believe he or she will be engaged in the performance of an investigative or litigating function or a Commission adjudicatory employee has knowledge that a notice of hearing or other comparable order will be issued in accordance with §§ 2.104(a), 2.105(e)(2), 2.202(c), 2.205(e), or 2.312.

(iii) A matter which a presiding officer seeks to be referred to the Commission under 10 CFR 2.340(a); and

(iv) A matter for which the Commission has approved examination by the presiding officer under § 2.340(a).

(2) The prohibitions of this section cease to apply to the disputed issues pertinent to a full or partial initial decision when the time has expired for Commission review of the decision in accordance with § 2.341.

(3) Separation of functions does not apply to uncontested proceedings, or to an undisputed issue in contested initial licensing proceedings.

(e) Communications to, from, and between Commission adjudicatory employees not prohibited by this section may not serve as a conduit for a communication that otherwise would be prohibited by this section or for an ex parte communication that otherwise would be prohibited by § 2.347.

(f) If an initial or final decision is stated to rest in whole or in part on fact or opinion obtained as a result of a communication authorized by this section, the substance of the communication must be specified in the record of the proceeding and every party must be afforded an opportunity to controvert the fact or opinion. If the parties have not had an opportunity to controvert the fact or opinion before the decision is filed, a party may controvert the fact or opinion by filing a petition for review of an initial decision, or a petition for reconsideration of a final decision that clearly and concisely sets forth the information or argument relied on to show the contrary. If appropriate, a party may be afforded the opportunity for cross-examination or to present rebuttal evidence.

[69 FR 2236, Jan. 14, 2004, as amended at 72 FR 49477, Aug. 28, 2007; 77 FR 46597, Aug. 3, 2012]

§ 2.390 Public inspections, exemptions, requests for withholding.

(a) Subject to the provisions of paragraphs (b), (d), (e), and (f) of this section, final NRC records and documents, including but not limited to correspondence to and from the NRC regarding the issuance, denial, amendment, transfer, renewal, modification, suspension, revocation, or violation of a license, permit, order, or standard design approval, or regarding a rulemaking proceeding subject to this part shall not, in the absence of an NRC determination of a compelling reason for nondisclosure after a balancing of the interests of the person or agency urging nondisclosure and the public interest in disclosure, be exempt from disclosure and will be made available for inspection and copying at the NRC Web site, *http://www.nrc.gov*, and/or at the NRC Public Document Room, except for matters that are:

(1)(i) Specifically authorized under criteria established by an Executive order to be kept secret in the interest of national defense or foreign policy; and

(ii) Are in fact properly classified under that Executive order;

(2) Related solely to the internal personnel rules and practices of the Commission;

(3) Specifically exempted from disclosure by statute (other than 5 U.S.C.

552(b)), but only if that statute requires that the matters be withheld from the public in such a manner as to leave no discretion on the issue, or establishes particular criteria for withholding or refers to particular types or matters to be withheld.

(4) Trade secrets and commercial or financial information obtained from a person and privileged or confidential;

(5) Interagency or intra-agency memorandums or letters that would not be available by law to a party other than an agency in litigation with the agency, provided that the deliberative process privilege shall not apply to records created 25 years or more before the date on which the records were requested;

(6) Personnel and medical files and similar files, the disclosure of which would constitute a clearly unwarranted invasion of personal privacy;

(7) Records or information compiled for law enforcement purposes, but only to the extent that the production of such law enforcement records or information:

(i) Could reasonably be expected to interfere with enforcement proceedings;

(ii) Would deprive a person of a right to a fair trial or an impartial adjudication;

(iii) Could reasonably be expected to constitute an unwarranted invasion of personal privacy;

(iv) Could reasonably be expected to disclose the identity of a confidential source, including a State, local, or foreign agency or authority, or any private institution which furnished information on a confidential basis, and, in the case of a record or information compiled by a criminal law enforcement authority in the course of a criminal investigation, or by an agency conducting a lawful national security intelligence investigation, information furnished by a confidential source;

(v) Would disclose techniques and procedures for law enforcement investigations or prosecutions, or would disclose guidelines for law enforcement investigations or prosecutions if such disclosure could reasonably be expected to risk circumvention of the law; or

(vi) Could reasonably be expected to endanger the life or physical safety of any individual;

(8) Contained in or related to examination, operating, or condition reports prepared by, on behalf of, or for the use of an agency responsible for the regulation or supervision of financial institutions; or

(9) Geological and geophysical information and data, including maps, concerning wells.

(b) The procedures in this section must be followed by anyone submitting a document to the NRC who seeks to have the document, or a portion of it, withheld from public disclosure because it contains trade secrets, privileged, or confidential commercial or financial information.

(1) The submitter shall request withholding at the time the document is submitted and shall comply with the document marking and affidavit requirements set forth in this paragraph. The NRC has no obligation to review documents not so marked to determine whether they contain information eligible for withholding under paragraph (a) of this section. Any documents not so marked may be made available to the public at the NRC Web site, *http://www.nrc.gov* or at the NRC Public Document Room.

(i) The submitter shall ensure that the document containing information sought to be withheld is marked as follows:

(A) The first page of the document, and each successive page containing such information, must be marked so as to be readily visible, at the top, or by electronic watermark or other suitable marking on the body of the page, with language substantially similar to: "confidential information submitted under 10 CFR 2.390," "withhold from public disclosure under 10 CFR 2.390," or "proprietary," to indicate that it contains information the submitter seeks to have withheld.

(B) Each document or page, as appropriate, containing information sought to be withheld from public disclosure must indicate, adjacent to the information, or as specified in paragraph (b)(1)(i)(A) of this section if the entire page is affected, the basis (*i.e.*, trade secret, personal privacy, etc.) for proposing that the information be withheld from public disclosure under paragraph (a) of this section.

(ii) The Commission may waive the affidavit requirements on request, or on its own initiative, in circumstances the Commission, in its discretion, deems appropriate. Otherwise, except for personal privacy information, which is not subject to the affidavit requirement, the request for withholding must be accompanied by an affidavit that—

(A) Identifies the document or part sought to be withheld;

(B) Identifies the official position of the person making the affidavit;

(C) Declares the basis for proposing the information be withheld, encompassing considerations set forth in § 2.390(a);

(D) Includes a specific statement of the harm that would result if the information sought to be withheld is disclosed to the public; and

(E) Indicates the location(s) in the document of all information sought to be withheld.

(iii) In addition, an affidavit accompanying a withholding request based on paragraph (a)(4) of this section must contain a full statement of the reason for claiming the information should be withheld from public disclosure. This statement must address with specificity the considerations listed in paragraph (b)(4) of this section. In the case of an affidavit submitted by a company, the affidavit shall be executed by an officer or upper-level management official who has been specifically delegated the function of reviewing the information sought to be withheld and authorized to apply for its withholding on behalf of the company. The affidavit shall be executed by the owner of the information, even though the information sought to be withheld is submitted to the Commission by another person. The application and affidavit shall be submitted at the time of filing the information sought to be withheld. The information sought to be withheld shall be incorporated, as far as possible, into a separate document. The affiant must designate with appropriate markings information submitted in the affidavit as a trade secret, or confidential or privileged commercial or financial information within the meaning of § 9.17(a)(4) of this chapter, and such information shall be subject to disclosure only in accordance with the provisions of § 9.19 of this chapter.

(2) A person who submits commercial or financial information believed to be privileged or confidential or a trade secret shall be on notice that it is the policy of the Commission to achieve an effective balance between legitimate concerns for protection of competitive positions and the right of the public to be fully apprised as to the basis for and effects of licensing or rulemaking actions, and that it is within the discretion of the Commission to withhold such information from public disclosure.

(3) The Commission shall determine whether information sought to be withheld from public disclosure under this paragraph:

(i) Is a trade secret or confidential or privileged commercial or financial information; and (ii) If so, should be withheld from public disclosure.

(4) In making the determination required by paragraph (b)(3)(i) of this section, the Commission will consider:

(i) Whether the information has been held in confidence by its owner;

(ii) Whether the information is of a type customarily held in confidence by its owner and, except for voluntarily submitted information, whether there is a rational basis therefor;

(iii) Whether the information was transmitted to and received by the Commission in confidence;

(iv) Whether the information is available in public sources;

(v) Whether public disclosure of the information sought to be withheld is likely to cause substantial harm to the competitive position of the owner of the information, taking into account the value of the information to the owner; the amount of effort or money, if any, expended by the owner in developing the information; and the ease or difficulty with which the information could be properly acquired or duplicated by others.

(5) If the Commission determines, under paragraph (b)(4) of this section, that the record or document contains

trade secrets or privileged or confidential commercial or financial information, the Commission will then determine whether the right of the public to be fully apprised as to the bases for and effects of the proposed action outweighs the demonstrated concern for protection of a competitive position, and whether the information should be withheld from public disclosure under this paragraph. If the record or document for which withholding is sought is deemed by the Commission to be irrelevant or unnecessary to the performance of its functions, it will be returned to the applicant.

(6) Withholding from public inspection does not affect the right, if any, of persons properly and directly concerned to inspect the document. Either before a decision of the Commission on the matter of whether the information should be made publicly available or after a decision has been made that the information should be withheld from public disclosure, the Commission may require information claimed to be a trade secret or privileged or confidential commercial or financial information to be subject to inspection under a protective agreement by contractor personnel or government officials other than NRC officials, by the presiding officer in a proceeding, and under protective order by the parties to a proceeding. *In camera* sessions of hearings may be held when the information sought to be withheld is produced or offered in evidence. If the Commission subsequently determines that the information should be disclosed, the information and the transcript of such *in camera* session will be made publicly available.

(c) The Commission either may grant or deny a request for withholding under this section.

(1) If the request is granted, the Commission will notify the submitter of its determination to withhold the information from public disclosure.

(2) If the Commission denies a request for withholding under this section, it will provide the submitter with a statement of reasons for that determination. This decision will specify the date, which will be a reasonable time thereafter, when the document will be available at the NRC Web site, *http://www.nrc.gov*. The document will not be returned to the submitter.

(3) Whenever a submitter desires to withdraw a document from Commission consideration, it may request return of the document, and the document will be returned unless the information—

(i) Forms part of the basis of an official agency decision, including but not limited to, a rulemaking proceeding or licensing activity;

(ii) Is contained in a document that was made available to or prepared for an NRC advisory committee;

(iii) Was revealed, or relied upon, in an open Commission meeting held in accordance with 10 CFR part 9, subpart C;

(iv) Has been requested in a Freedom of Information Act request; or

(v) Has been obtained during the course of an investigation conducted by the NRC Office of Investigations.

(d) The following information is considered commercial or financial information within the meaning of § 9.17(a)(4) of this chapter and is subject to disclosure only in accordance with the provisions of § 9.19 of this chapter.

(1) Correspondence and reports to or from the NRC which contain information or records concerning a licensee's or applicant's physical protection, classified matter protection, or material control and accounting program for special nuclear material not otherwise designated as Safeguards Information or classified as National Security Information or Restricted Data.

(2) Information submitted in confidence to the Commission by a foreign source.

(e) Submitting information to NRC for consideration in connection with NRC licensing or regulatory activities shall be deemed to constitute authority for the NRC to reproduce and distribute sufficient copies to carry out the Commission's official responsibilities.

(f) The presiding officer, if any, or the Commission may, with reference to the NRC records and documents made available pursuant to this section, issue orders consistent with the provisions of this section and § 2.705(c).

[69 FR 2236, Jan. 14, 2004, as amended at 72 FR 49152, Aug. 28, 2007; 72 FR 49477, Aug. 28, 2007; 75 FR 73937, Nov. 30, 2010; 81 FR 96346, Dec. 30, 2016]

Subpart D—Additional Procedures Applicable to Proceedings for the Issuance of Licenses To Construct and/or Operate Nuclear Power Plants of Identical Design at Multiple Sites

SOURCE: 72 FR 49477, Aug. 28, 2007, unless otherwise noted.

§ 2.400 Scope of subpart.

This subpart describes procedures applicable to licensing proceedings which involve the consideration in hearings of a number of applications, filed by one or more applicants pursuant to appendix N of parts 50 or 52 of this chapter, for licenses to construct and/or operate nuclear power reactors of identical design to be located at multiple sites.

§ 2.401 Notice of hearing on construction permit or combined license applications pursuant to appendix N of 10 CFR parts 50 or 52.

(a) In the case of applications pursuant to appendix N of part 50 of this chapter for construction permits for nuclear power reactors of the type described in § 50.22 of this chapter, or applications pursuant to appendix N of part 52 of this chapter for combined licenses, the Secretary will issue notices of hearing pursuant to § 2.104.

(b) The notice of hearing will also state the time and place of the hearings on any separate phase of the proceeding.

§ 2.402 Separate hearings on separate issues; consolidation of proceedings.

(a) In the case of applications under appendix N of part 50 of this chapter for construction permits for nuclear power reactors of a type described in 10 CFR 50.22, or applications pursuant to appendix N of part 52 of this chapter for combined licenses, the Commission or the presiding officer may order separate hearings on particular phases of the proceeding, such as matters related to the acceptability of the design of the reactor, in the context of the site parameters postulated for the design or environmental matters.

(b) If a separate hearing is held on a particular phase of the proceeding, the Commission or presiding officers of each affected proceeding may, under 10 CFR 2.317, consolidate for hearing on that phase two or more proceedings to consider common issues relating to the applications involved in the proceedings, if it finds that this action will be conducive to the proper dispatch of its business and to the ends of justice. In specifying the place of this consolidated hearing, due regard will be given to the convenience and necessity of the parties, petitioners for leave to intervene, or the attorneys or representatives of such persons, and the public interest.

§ 2.403 Notice of proposed action on applications for operating licenses pursuant to appendix N of 10 CFR part 50.

In the case of applications pursuant to appendix N of part 50 of this chapter for operating licenses for nuclear power reactors, if the Commission has not found that a hearing is in the public interest, the Commission, the Director, Office of New Reactors or Director, Office of Nuclear Reactor Regulation, as appropriate will, prior to acting thereon, cause to be published in the FEDERAL REGISTER, pursuant to § 2.105, a notice of proposed action with respect to each application as soon as practicable after the applications have been docketed.

[73 FR 5717, Jan. 31, 2008]

§ 2.404 Hearings on applications for operating licenses pursuant to appendix N of 10 CFR part 50.

If a request for a hearing and/or petition for leave to intervene is filed within the time prescribed in the notice of proposed action on an application for an operating license pursuant to appendix N of part 50 of this chapter with respect to a specific reactor(s) at a specific site, and the Commission, the Chief Administrative Judge, or a presiding officer has issued a notice of hearing or other appropriate order, then the Commission, the Chief Administrative Judge, or the presiding officer may order separate hearings on particular phases of the proceeding and/or consolidate for hearing two or more proceedings in the manner described in §2.402.

§2.405 Initial decisions in consolidated hearings.

At the conclusion of a hearing held under this subpart, the presiding officer will render a partial initial decision on the common design. The partial initial decision on the common design may be appealed under §2.341. If the proceedings have also been consolidated with respect to matters other than the common design under §2.317(b), the presiding officer may issue a consolidated partial initial decision for those proceedings. No construction permit, full-power operating license, or combined license under part 52 of this chapter will be issued until an initial decision has been issued on all phases of the hearing and all issues under the Act and the National Environmental Policy Act of 1969 appropriate to the proceeding have been resolved.

§2.406 Finality of decisions on separate issues.

Notwithstanding any other provision of this chapter, in a proceeding conducted pursuant to this subpart and appendices N of parts 50 or 52 of this chapter, no matter which has been reserved for consideration in one phase of the hearing shall be considered at another phase of the hearing except on the basis of significant new information that substantially affects the conclusion(s) reached at the other phase or other good cause.

§2.407 Applicability of other sections.

The provisions of subparts A, C, G, L, and N of this part relating to construction permits, operating licenses, and combined licenses apply, respectively, to construction permits, operating licenses, and combined licenses subject to this subpart, except as may be qualified by the provisions of this subpart.

Subpart E—Additional Procedures Applicable to Proceedings for the Issuance of Licenses To Manufacture Nuclear Power Reactors To Be Operated at Sites Not Identified in the License Application and Related Licensing Proceedings

SOURCE: 38 FR 30252, Nov. 2, 1973, unless otherwise noted.

§2.500 Scope of subpart.

This subpart prescribes procedures applicable to licensing proceedings which involve the consideration in separate hearings of an application for a license to manufacture nuclear power reactors under subpart F of part 52 of this chapter.

[72 FR 49478, Aug. 28, 2007]

§2.501 Notice of hearing on application under subpart F of 10 CFR part 52 for a license to manufacture nuclear power reactors.

(a) In the case of an application under subpart F of part 52 of this chapter for a license to manufacture nuclear power reactors of the type described in §50.22 of this chapter to be operated at sites not identified in the license application, the Secretary will issue a notice of hearing to be published in the FEDERAL REGISTER at least 30 days before the date set for hearing in the notice.[1] The notice shall be issued as soon as practicable after the application has been docketed. The notice will state:

(1) The time, place, and nature of the hearing and/or the prehearing conference;

(2) The authority within which the hearing is to be held;

(3) The matters of fact and law to be considered; and

(4) The time within which answers to the notice shall be filed.

(b) The notice of hearing shall comply with the requirements of §2.104(f) of this chapter.

[1] The thirty-day (30) requirement of this paragraph is not applicable to a notice of the time and place of hearing published by the presiding officer after the notice of hearing described in this section has been published.

(c) The place of hearing on an application for a manufacturing license will be Washington, DC, or such other location as the Commission deems appropriate.

[38 FR 30252, Nov. 2, 1973, as amended at 39 FR 26279, July 18, 1974; 39 FR 33202, Sept. 16, 1974; 49 FR 9401, Mar. 12, 1984; 54 FR 15398, Apr. 18, 1989; 54 FR 52342, Dec. 21, 1989; 72 FR 49478, Aug. 28, 2007]

§§ 2.502–2.504 [Reserved]

Subpart F—Additional Procedures Applicable to Early Partial Decisions on Site Suitability Issues in Connection With an Application for a Construction Permit or Combined License To Construct Certain Utilization Facilities; and Advance Issuance of Limited Work Authorizations

SOURCE: 72 FR 49478, Aug. 28, 2007, unless otherwise noted.

§ 2.600 Scope of subpart.

This subpart prescribes procedures applicable to licensing proceedings which involve an early submittal of site suitability information in accordance with § 2.101(a–1), and a hearing and early partial decision on issues of site suitability, in connection with an application for a permit to construct a utilization facility which is subject to § 51.20(b) of this chapter and is of the type specified in § 50.21(b)(2) or (3) or § 50.22 of this chapter or is a testing facility. This subpart also prescribes procedures applicable to proceedings for a construction permit for a utilization facility which is subject to § 51.20(b) of this chapter and is of the type specified in § 50.21(b)(2) or (3) or § 50.22 of this chapter, or proceedings for a combined license under part 52 of this chapter, either of which includes a request to conduct the activities authorized under § 50.10(d) of part 50 of this chapter in advance of issuance of the construction permit or combined license, and submits an application in accordance with § 2.101(a)(9).

(a) The procedures in §§ 2.601 through 2.609 apply to all applications under this subpart.

(b) The procedures in §§ 2.611 through 2.619 apply to applications for a permit to construct a utilization facility which is subject to § 51.20(b) of this chapter and is of the type specified in § 50.21(b)(2) or (3) or § 50.22 of this chapter or is a testing facility.

(c) The procedures in §§ 2.621 through 2.629 apply to applications for combined license under part 52 of this chapter for a nuclear power facility.

(d) The procedures in §§ 2.641 through 2.649 apply to phased applications for construction permits or combined licenses which request limited work authorizations to be issued in advance of issuance of the construction permit or combined license (*i.e.*, a phased application).

[72 FR 49478, Aug. 28, 2007, as amended at 72 FR 57440, Oct. 9, 2007]

§ 2.601 Applicability of other sections.

The provisions of subparts A, C, G, L, and N relating to applications for construction permits and combined licenses, and proceedings thereon apply, respectively, to such applications and proceedings in accordance with this subpart, except as specifically provided otherwise by the provisions of this subpart.

EARLY PARTIAL DECISIONS ON SITE SUITABILITY—CONSTRUCTION PERMIT

§ 2.602 Filing fees.

Each application which contains a request for early review of site suitability issues under the procedures of this subpart shall be accompanied by any fee required by § 50.30(e) and part 170 of this chapter.

§ 2.603 Acceptance and docketing of application for early review of site suitability issues in a construction permit proceeding.

(a) Each part of an application for a construction permit submitted in accordance with § 2.101(a–1) of this part will be initially treated as a tendered application. If it is determined that any one of the parts as described in § 2.101(a–1) is incomplete and not acceptable for processing, the Director of the Office of New Reactors or the Director of the Office of Nuclear Reactor Regulation, as appropriate, will inform the applicant of this determination and the respects in which the document is deficient. Such a determination of completeness will generally be made within a period of 30 days.

(b)(1) The Director of the Office of New Reactors or the Director of the Office of Nuclear Reactor Regulation, as appropriate, will accept for docketing part one of an application for a construction permit for a utilization facility which is subject to § 51.20(b) of this chapter and is of the type specified in § 50.21(b)(2) or (3) or § 50.22 of this chapter, or is a testing facility where part one of the application as described in § 2.101(a–1) is complete. Part one of any application will not be considered complete unless it contains proposed findings as required by § 2.101(a–1)(1)(i) and unless it describes the applicant's site selection process, specifies the extent to which that process involves the consideration of alternative sites, explains the relationship between that process and the application for early review of site suitability issues, and briefly describes the applicant's long-range plans for ultimate development of the site. Upon assignment of a docket number, the procedures in § 2.101(a)(3) and (4) relating to formal docketing and the submission and distribution of additional copies of the application shall be followed.

(2) Additional parts of the application will be docketed upon a determination by the Director of the Office of New Reactors or the Director of the Office of Nuclear Reactor Regulation, as appropriate, that they are complete.

(c) If part one of the application is docketed, the Director of the Office of New Reactors or the Director of the Office of Nuclear Reactor Regulation, as appropriate, will cause to be published in the FEDERAL REGISTER and send to the Governor or other appropriate official of the State in which the site is located, a notice of docketing of the application which states the purpose of the application, states the location of the proposed site, states that a notice of hearing will be published, requests comments within 120 days or such other time as may be specified on the initiation or outcome of an early site review from Federal, State, and local agencies and interested persons.

§ 2.604 Notice of hearing on application for early review of site suitability issues in construction permit proceeding.

(a) Where an applicant for a construction permit requests an early review and hearing and an early partial decision on issues of site suitability pursuant to § 2.101(a–1), the provisions in the notice of hearing setting forth the matters of fact and law to be considered, as required by § 2.104, shall be modified so as to relate only to the site suitability issue or issues under review.

(b) After docketing of part two of the application, as provided in §§ 2.101(a–1) and 2.603, a supplementary notice of hearing will be published under § 2.104 with respect to the remaining unresolved issues in the proceeding within the scope of § 2.104. This supplementary notice of hearing will provide that any person whose interest may be affected by the proceeding and who desires to participate as a party in the resolution of the remaining issues shall file a petition for leave to intervene pursuant to § 2.309 within the time prescribed in the notice. This supplementary notice will also provide appropriate opportunities for participation by a representative of an interested State under § 2.315(c) and for limited appearances under § 2.315(a).

(c) Any person who was permitted to intervene as a party under the initial notice of hearing on site suitability issues and who was not dismissed or did not withdraw as a party may continue to participate as a party to the proceeding with respect to the remaining unresolved issues, provided that within the time prescribed for filing of petitions for leave to intervene in the supplementary notice of hearing, he or she files a notice of his intent to continue as a party, along with a supporting affidavit identifying the specific aspect or aspects of the subject matter of the proceeding as to which he or she wishes to continue to participate as a party and setting forth with particularity the basis for his contentions with regard to each aspect or aspects. A party who files a non-timely notice of intent to continue as a party may be dismissed from the proceeding, absent a determination that the party has made a substantial showing of good cause for failure to file on time, and with particular reference to the factors specified in §§ 2.309(c)(1)(i) through (iv) and 2.309(d). The notice will be ruled upon by the Commission or presiding officer designated to rule on petitions for leave to intervene.

(d) To the maximum extent practicable, the membership of any atomic safety and licensing board designated to preside in the proceeding on the remaining unresolved issues pursuant to the supplemental notice of hearing will be the same as the membership designated to preside in the initial notice of hearing on site suitability issues.

§ 2.605 Additional considerations.

(a) The Commission will not conduct more than one review of site suitability issues with regard to a particular site prior to filing and review of part two of the application described in § 2.101(a–1) of this part.

(b) The Commission, upon its own initiative, or upon the motion of any party to the proceeding filed at least 60 days prior to the date of the commencement of the evidentiary hearing on site suitability issues, may decline to initiate an early hearing or render an early partial decision on any issue or issues of site suitability:

(1) In cases where no partial decision on the relative merits of the proposed site and alternative sites under subpart A of part 51 of this chapter is requested, upon determination that there is a reasonable likelihood that further review would identify one or more preferable alternative sites and the partial decision on one or more site suitability issues would lead to an irreversible and irretrievable commitment of resources prior to the submittal of the remainder of the information required by § 50.30(f) of this chapter that would prejudice the later review and decision on such alternative sites; or

(2) In cases where it appears that an early partial decision on any issue or issues of site suitability would not be in the public interest considering:

(i) The degree of likelihood that any early findings on those issues would retain their validity in later reviews;

(ii) The objections, if any, of cognizant State or local government agencies to the conduct of an early review on those issues; and

(iii) The possible effect on the public interest and the parties of having an early, if not necessarily conclusive, resolution of those issues.

§ 2.606 Partial decision on site suitability issues in construction permit proceeding.

(a) The provisions of §§ 2.331, 2.339, 2.340(b), 2.343, 2.712, and 2.713 apply to any partial initial decision rendered in accordance with this subpart. Section 2.340(c) does not apply to any partial initial decision rendered in accordance with this subpart. No construction permit or combined license may be issued without completion of the full review required by Section 102(2) of the NEPA, as amended, and subpart A of part 51 of this chapter. The authority of the Commission to review such a partial initial decision *sua sponte*, or to raise *sua sponte* an issue that has not been raised by the parties, will be exercised within the same time as in the case of a full decision relating to the issuance of a construction permit or combined license.

(b)(1) A partial decision on one or more site suitability issues pursuant to the applicable provisions of part 50, subpart A of part 51, and part 100 of this chapter issued in accordance with this subpart shall:

(i) Clearly identify the site to which the partial decision applies; and

(ii) Indicate to what extent additional information may be needed and additional review may be required to enable the Commission to determine in accordance with the provisions of the Act and the applicable provisions of the regulations in this chapter whether a construction permit for a facility to be located on the site identified in the partial decision should be issued or denied.

(2) Following either the Commission (acting in the function of a presiding officer) issuance of a partial initial decision, or completion of Commission review of the partial initial decision of the Atomic Safety and Licensing Board, after hearing, on the site suitability issues, the partial decision shall remain in effect either for a period of 5 years or, where the applicant for the

construction permit has made timely submittal of the information required to support the application as provided in § 2.101(a–1), until the proceeding for a permit to construct a facility on the site identified in the partial decision has been concluded,[3] unless the Commission or Atomic Safety and Licensing Board, upon its own initiative or upon motion by a party to the proceeding, finds that there exists significant new information that substantially affects the earlier conclusions and reopens the hearing record on site suitability issues. Upon good cause shown, the Commission may extend the 5-year period during which a partial decision shall remain in effect for a reasonable period of time not to exceed 1 year.

[72 FR 49479, Aug. 28, 2007, as amended at 72 FR 57440, Oct. 9, 2007]

EARLY PARTIAL DECISIONS ON SITE SUITABILITY—COMBINED LICENSE UNDER 10 CFR PART 52

§ 2.621 Acceptance and docketing of application for early review of site suitability issues in a combined license proceeding.

(a) Each part of an application submitted in accordance with § 2.101(a–1) of this part will be initially treated as a tendered application. If it is determined that any one of the parts as described in § 2.101(a–1) is incomplete and not acceptable for processing, the Director of the Office of New Reactors or the Director of the Office of Nuclear Reactor Regulation, as appropriate, will inform the applicant of this determination and the respects in which the document is deficient. Such a determination of completeness will generally be made within a period of 30 days.

(b)(1) The Director of the Office of New Reactors or the Director of the Office of Nuclear Reactor Regulation, as appropriate, will accept for docketing an application for a combined license for a nuclear power facility where part one of the application as described in § 2.101(a–1) is complete. Part one of any application will not be considered complete unless it contains proposed findings as required by § 2.101(a–1)(1)(i) and unless it describes the applicant's site selection process, specifies the extent to which that process involves the consideration of alternative sites, explains the relationship between that process and the application for early review of site suitability issues, and briefly describes the applicant's long-range plans for ultimate development of the site. Upon assignment of a docket number, the procedures in § 2.101(a)(3) and (4) relating to formal docketing and the submission and distribution of additional copies of the application shall be followed.

(2) Additional parts of the application will be docketed upon a determination by the Director of the Office of New Reactors or the Director of the Office of Nuclear Reactor Regulation, as appropriate, that they are complete.

(c) If part one of the application is docketed, the Director of the Office of New Reactors or the Director of the Office of Nuclear Reactor Regulation, as appropriate, will cause to be published in the FEDERAL REGISTER and send to the Governor or other appropriate official of the State in which the site is located, a notice of docketing of the application which states the purpose of the application, states the location of the proposed site, states that a notice of hearing will be published, requests comments within 120 days or such other time as may be specified on the initiation or outcome of an early site review from Federal, State, and local agencies and interested persons.

§ 2.623 Notice of hearing on application for early review of site suitability issues in combined license proceeding.

(a) Where an applicant for a combined license under part 52 of this chapter requests an early review and hearing and an early partial decision on issues of site suitability pursuant to § 2.101(a–2), the provisions in the notice of hearing setting forth the matters of fact and law to be considered, as required by § 2.104, shall be modified so as to relate only to the site suitability issue or issues under review. The notice

[3] The partial decision on site suitability issues shall be incorporated in the decision regarding issuance of the combined license to the extent that it serves as a basis for the decision on a specific site issue.

will provide appropriate opportunities for participation by a representative of an interested State under § 2.315(c) and for limited appearances under § 2.315(a), limited however, to the issues of site suitability for which early review has been requested by the applicant.

(b) After docketing of part two of the application, as provided in §§ 2.101(a–1) and 2.603, a supplementary notice of hearing will be published under § 2.104 with respect to the remaining unresolved issues in the proceeding within the scope of § 2.104. This supplementary notice of hearing will provide that any person whose interest may be affected by the proceeding and who desires to participate as a party in the resolution of the remaining issues shall file a petition for leave to intervene pursuant to § 2.309 within the time prescribed in the notice. This supplementary notice will also provide appropriate opportunities for participation by a representative of an interested State under § 2.315(c) and for limited appearances under § 2.315(a).

(c) Any person who was permitted to intervene as a party under the initial notice of hearing on site suitability issues and who was not dismissed or did not withdraw as a party may continue to participate as a party to the proceeding without having to demonstrate standing under § 2.309(d), *provided, however*, that within the time prescribed for filing of petitions for leave to intervene in the supplementary notice of hearing, the party files a notice of intent to continue as a party. The notice must include the information required by § 2.309(f). A party who files a non-timely notice of intent to continue as a party may be dismissed from the proceeding, absent a determination that the party has made a substantial showing of good cause for failure to file on time, and with particular reference to the factors specified in §§ 2.309(c)(1)(i) through (iv) and 2.309(d). The notice will be ruled upon by the Commission or presiding officer designated to rule on petitions for leave to intervene.

(d) To the maximum extent practicable, the presiding officer (as applicable, the membership of the licensing board) designated to preside in the proceeding on the remaining unresolved issues pursuant to the supplemental notice of hearing will be the same as the presiding officer (as applicable, the membership of the licensing board) designated to preside in the initial notice of hearing on site suitability issues.

§ 2.625 Additional considerations.

(a) The Commission will not conduct more than one review of site suitability issues with regard to a particular site prior to filing and review of part two of the application described in § 2.101(a–1) of this part.

(b) The Commission, upon its own initiative, or upon the motion of any party to the proceeding filed at least 60 days prior to the date of the commencement of the evidentiary hearing on site suitability issues, may decline to initiate an early hearing or render an early partial decision on any issue or issues of site suitability:

(1) In cases where no partial decision on the relative merits of the proposed site and alternative sites under subpart A of part 51 is requested, upon determination that there is a reasonable likelihood that further review would identify one or more preferable alternative sites and the partial decision on one or more site suitability issues would lead to an irreversible and irretrievable commitment of resources prior to the submittal of the remainder of the information required by § 50.30(f) of this chapter that would prejudice the later review and decision on such alternative sites; or

(2) In cases where it appears that an early partial decision on any issue or issues of site suitability would not be in the public interest considering:

(i) The degree of likelihood that any early findings on those issues would retain their validity in later reviews;

(ii) The objections, if any, of cognizant State or local government agencies to the conduct of an early review on those issues; and

(iii) The possible effect on the public interest and the parties of having an early, if not necessarily conclusive, resolution of those issues.

§ 2.627 Partial decision on site suitability issues in combined license proceeding.

(a) The provisions of §§ 2.331, 2.339, 2.340(b), 2.343, 2.712, and 2.713 shall apply to any partial initial decision rendered in accordance with this subpart. Section 2.340(c) shall not apply to any partial initial decision rendered in accordance with this subpart. A limited work authorization may not be issued under 10 CFR 50.10(e) and no construction permit may be issued without completion of the full review required by Section 102(2) of the National Environmental Policy Act of 1969, as amended, and subpart A of part 51 of this chapter. The authority of the Commission to review such a partial initial decision sua sponte, or to raise sua sponte an issue that has not been raised by the parties, will be exercised within the same time period as in the case of a full decision relating to the issuance of a construction permit.

(b)(1) A partial decision on one or more site suitability issues pursuant to the applicable provisions of part 50, subpart A of part 51, and part 100 of this chapter issued in accordance with this subpart shall:

(i) Clearly identify the site to which the partial decision applies; and

(ii) Indicate to what extent additional information may be needed and additional review may be required to enable the Commission to determine in accordance with the provisions of the Act and the applicable provisions of the regulations in this chapter whether a construction permit for a facility to be located on the site identified in the partial decision should be issued or denied.

(2) Following either the Commission (acting in the function of a presiding officer) issuance of a partial initial decision, or completion of Commission review of the partial initial decision of the presiding officer, after hearing, on the site suitability issues, the partial decision shall remain in effect either for a period of 5 years or, where the applicant for the combined license has made timely submittal of the information required to support the application as provided in § 2.101(a–2), until the proceeding for a combined license on the site identified in the partial decision has been concluded, unless the Commission or presiding officer, upon its own initiative or upon motion by a party to the proceeding, finds that there exists significant new information that substantially affects the earlier conclusions and reopens the hearing record on site suitability issues. Upon good cause shown, the Commission may extend the 5-year period during which a partial decision shall remain in effect for a reasonable period of time not to exceed 1 year.

§ 2.629 Finality of partial decision on site suitability issues in a combined license proceeding.

(a) The partial decision on site suitability issues in a combined license proceeding shall be incorporated in the decision regarding issuance of a combined license. Except as provided in 10 CFR 2.758, in making the findings required for issuance of a combined license, the Commission shall treat as resolved those matters resolved in connection with the issuance of the partial decision on site suitability issues. If the Commission reaches an adverse decision, the application shall be denied without prejudice for resubmission, provided, however, that in determining whether the resubmitted application is complete and acceptable for docketing under § 2.101(a)(3), the Director of the Office of New Reactors or the Director of the Office of Nuclear Reactor Regulation, as appropriate, shall determine whether the resubmitted application addresses those matters identified as bases for denial of the original application.

(b) Notwithstanding any provision in 10 CFR 50.109, while a partial decision on site suitability is in effect under § 2.617(b)(2), the Commission may not modify, rescind, or impose new requirements with respect to matters within the scope of the site suitability decision, whether on its own motion, or in response to a request or petition from any person, unless the Commission determines that a modification to the original decision is necessary either for compliance with the Commission's regulations applicable and in effect at the time the partial decision was issued, or to assure adequate protection of the public health and safety or the common defense and security.

PHASED APPLICATIONS INVOLVING LIMITED WORK AUTHORIZATIONS

SOURCE: 72 FR 57440, Oct. 9, 2007, unless otherwise noted.

§ 2.641 Filing fees.

Each application which contains a request for limited work authorization under the procedures of § 2.101(a)(9) and this subpart shall be accompanied by any fee required by § 50.30(e) and part 170 of this chapter.

§ 2.643 Acceptance and docketing of application for limited work authorization.

(a) Each part of an application submitted in accordance with § 2.101(a)(9) will be initially treated as a tendered application. If it is determined that any one of the parts as described in § 2.101(a)(9) is incomplete and not acceptable for processing, the Director of New Reactors or the Director of Nuclear Reactor Regulation will inform the applicant of this determination and the respects in which the document is deficient. A determination of completeness will generally be made within a period of 30 days.

(b) The Director will accept for docketing part one of an application for a construction permit for a utilization facility which is subject to § 51.20(b) of this chapter and is of the type specified in § 50.21(b)(2) or (3) or § 50.22 of this chapter or an application for a combined license where part one of the application as described in § 2.101(a)(9) is complete. Part one will not be considered complete unless it contains the information required by § 50.10(d)(3) of this chapter. Upon assignment of a docket number, the procedures in § 2.101(a)(3) and (4) relating to formal docketing and the submission and distribution of additional copies of the application must be followed.

(c) If part one of the application is docketed, the Director will cause to be published in the FEDERAL REGISTER and send to the Governor or other appropriate official of the State in which the site is located, a notice of docketing of the application which states the purpose of the application, states the location of the proposed site, states that a notice of hearing will be published, and requests comments on the limited work authorization from Federal, State, and local agencies and interested persons. The notice will state that comments must be submitted to the NRC within 60 days or such other time as may be specified in the notice.

(d) Part two of the application will be docketed upon a determination by the Director that it is complete.

(e) If part two of the application is docketed, the Director will cause to be published in the FEDERAL REGISTER and sent to the Governor or other appropriate official of the State in which the site is located, a notice of docketing of part two of the application which states the purpose of the application, states that a notice of hearing will be published, and requests comments on the construction permit or combined license application, as applicable, from Federal, State, and local agencies and interested persons. The notice will state that comments must be submitted to the NRC within 60 days or such other time as may be specified in the notice.

§ 2.645 Notice of hearing.

(a) The notice of hearing on part one of the application must set forth the matters of fact and law to be considered, as required by § 2.104, which will be modified to state that the hearing will relate only to the matters related to § 50.33(a) through (f) of this chapter, and the limited work authorization.

(b) After docketing of part two of the application, as provided in §§ 2.101(a)(9) and 2.643(d), a supplementary notice of hearing will be published under § 2.104 with respect to the remaining unresolved issues in the proceeding within the scope of § 2.104. The supplementary notice of hearing will provide that any person whose interest may be affected by the proceeding and who desires to participate as a party in the resolution of the remaining issues shall, file a petition for leave to intervene within the time prescribed in the notice. The petition to intervene must meet the applicable requirements in subpart C of this part, including § 2.309. This supplementary notice will also provide appropriate opportunities for participation by a representative of an interested State under § 2.315(c) and for limited appearances under § 2.315(a).

(c) Any person who was permitted to intervene under the initial notice of hearing on the limited work authorization and who was not dismissed or did not withdraw as a party, may continue to participate as a party with respect to the remaining unresolved issues only if, within the time prescribed for filing of petitions for leave to intervene in the supplementary notice of hearing, that person files a petition for intervention which meets the applicable requirements in subpart C of this part, including § 2.309, *provided, however,* that the petition need not address § 2.309(d). However, a person who was granted discretionary intervention under § 2.309(e) must address in its petition the factors in § 2.309(e) as they apply to the supplementary hearing.

(d) A party who files a non-timely petition for intervention under paragraph (b) of this section to continue as a party may be dismissed from the proceeding, absent a determination that the party has made a substantial showing of good cause for failure to file on time, and with particular reference to the factors specified in §§ 2.309(c)(1)(i) through (iv) and 2.309(d). The notice will be ruled upon by the Commission or presiding officer designated to rule on petitions for leave to intervene.

(e) To the maximum extent practicable, the membership of the Atomic Safety and Licensing Board, or the individual presiding officer, as applicable, designated to preside in the proceeding on the remaining unresolved issues under the supplemental notice of hearing will be the same as the membership or individual designated to preside in the initial notice of hearing.

§ 2.647 [Reserved]

§ 2.649 Partial decisions on limited work authorization.

The provisions of §§ 2.331, 2.339, 2.340(b), 2.343, 2.712, and 2.713 apply to any partial initial decision rendered in accordance with this subpart. Section 2.340(c) does not apply to any partial initial decision rendered in accordance with this subpart. A limited work authorization may not be issued under 10 CFR 50.10(d) without completion of the review for limited work authorizations required by subpart A of part 51 of this chapter. The authority of the Commission to review such a partial initial decision *sua sponte,* or to raise *sua sponte* an issue that has not been raised by the parties, will be exercised within the same time as in the case of a full decision relating to the issuance of a construction permit or combined license.

Subpart G—Rules for Formal Adjudications

SOURCE: 69 FR 2256, Jan. 14, 2004, unless otherwise noted.

§ 2.700 Scope of subpart G.

The provisions of this subpart apply to and supplement the provisions set forth in subpart C of this part with respect to enforcement proceedings initiated under subpart B of this part unless otherwise agreed to by the parties, proceedings conducted with respect to the initial licensing of a uranium enrichment facility, proceedings for the grant, renewal, licensee-initiated amendment, or termination of licenses or permits for nuclear power reactors, where the presiding officer by order finds that resolution of the contention necessitates resolution of: issues of material fact relating to the occurrence of a past event, where the credibility of an eyewitness may reasonably be expected to be at issue, and/or issues of motive or intent of the party or eyewitness material to the resolution of the contested matter, proceedings for initial applications for construction authorization for high-level radioactive waste repository noticed under §§ 2.101(f)(8) or 2.105(a)(5), proceedings for initial applications for a license to receive and possess high-level radioactive waste at a geologic repository operations area, and any other proceeding as ordered by the Commission. If there is any conflict between the provisions of this subpart and those set forth in subpart C of this part, the provisions of this subpart control.

§ 2.701 Exceptions.

Consistent with 5 U.S.C. 554(a)(4) of the Administrative Procedure Act, the Commission may provide alternative procedures in adjudications to the extent that there is involved the conduct of military or foreign affairs functions.

§ 2.702 Subpoenas.

(a) On application by any party, the designated presiding officer or, if he or she is not available, the Chief Administrative Judge, or other designated officer will issue subpoenas requiring the attendance and testimony of witnesses or the production of evidence. The officer to whom application is made may require a showing of general relevance of the testimony or evidence sought, and may withhold the subpoena if such a showing is not made. However, the officer may not determine the admissibility of evidence.

(b) Every subpoena will bear the name of the Commission, the name and office of the issuing officer and the title of the hearing, and will command the person to whom it is directed to attend and give testimony or produce specified documents or other things at a designated time and place. The subpoena will also advise of the quashing procedure provided in paragraph (f) of this section.

(c) Unless the service of a subpoena is acknowledged on its face by the witness or is served by an officer or employee of the Commission, it must be served by a person who is not a party to the hearing and is not less than eighteen (18) years of age. Service of a subpoena must be made by delivery of a copy of the subpoena to the person named in it and tendering that person the fees for one day's attendance and the mileage allowed by law. When the subpoena is issued on behalf of the Commission, fees and mileage need not be tendered and the subpoena may be served by registered mail.

(d) Witnesses summoned by subpoena must be paid the fees and mileage paid to witnesses in the district courts of the United States by the party at whose instance they appear.

(e) The person serving the subpoena shall make proof of service by filing the subpoena and affidavit or acknowledgment of service with the officer before whom the witness is required to testify or produce evidence or with the Secretary. Failure to make proof of service does not affect the validity of the service.

(f) On motion made promptly, and in any event at or before the time specified in the subpoena for compliance by the person to whom the subpoena is directed, and on notice to the party at whose instance the subpoena was issued, the presiding officer or, if he is unavailable, the Commission may:

(1) Quash or modify the subpoena if it is unreasonable or requires evidence not relevant to any matter in issue, or

(2) Condition denial of the motion on just and reasonable terms.

(g) On application and for good cause shown, the Commission will seek judicial enforcement of a subpoena issued to a party and which has not been quashed.

(h) The provisions of paragraphs (a) through (g) of this section are not applicable to the attendance and testimony of the Commissioners or NRC personnel, or to the production of records or documents in their custody.

§ 2.703 Examination by experts.

(a) A party may request the presiding officer to permit a qualified individual who has scientific or technical training or experience to participate on behalf of that party in the examination and cross-examination of expert witnesses. The presiding officer may permit the individual to participate on behalf of the party in the examination and cross-examination of expert witnesses, upon finding:

(1) That cross-examination by that individual would serve the purpose of furthering the conduct of the proceeding;

(2) That the individual is qualified by scientific or technical training or experience to contribute to the development of an adequate decisional record in the proceeding by the conduct of such examination or cross-examination;

(3) That the individual has read any written testimony on which he intends to examine or cross-examine and any documents to be used or referred to in the course of the examination or cross-examination; and

(4) That the individual has prepared himself to conduct a meaningful and

expeditious examination or cross-examination, and has submitted a cross-examination plan in accordance with § 2.711(c).

(b) Examination or cross-examination conducted under this section must be limited to areas within the expertise of the individual conducting the examination or cross-examination. The party on behalf of whom this examination or cross-examination is conducted and his or her attorney is responsible for the conduct of examination or cross-examination by such individuals.

§ 2.704 Discovery-required disclosures.

(a) *Initial disclosures.* Except to the extent otherwise stipulated or directed by order of the presiding officer or the Commission, a party other than the NRC staff shall, without awaiting a discovery request, provide to other parties:

(1) The name and, if known, the address and telephone number of each individual likely to have discoverable information relevant to disputed issues alleged with particularity in the pleadings, identifying the subjects of the information; and

(2) A copy of, or a description by category and location of, all documents, data compilations, and tangible things in the possession, custody, or control of the party that are relevant to disputed issues alleged with particularity in the pleadings. When any document, data compilation, or other tangible thing that must be disclosed is publicly available from another source, such as at the NRC Web site, *http://www.nrc.gov*, and/or the NRC Public Document Room, a sufficient disclosure would be the location, the title and a page reference to the relevant document, data compilation, or tangible thing;

(3) Unless otherwise stipulated by the parties or directed by order of the presiding officer, these disclosures must be made within 45 days after the issuance of a prehearing conference order following the initial prehearing conference specified in § 2.329. A party must make its initial disclosures based on the information then reasonably available to it. A party is not excused from making its disclosures because it has not fully completed its investigation of the case, because it challenges the sufficiency of another party's disclosures, or because another party has not made its disclosures. The duty of disclosure under this section is continuing. A disclosure update must be made every month after initial disclosures on a due date selected by the presiding officer, unless the parties agree upon a different due date or frequency. The disclosure update shall be limited to documents subject to disclosure under this section and does not need to include documents that are developed, obtained, or discovered during the two weeks before the due date. Disclosure updates shall include any documents subject to disclosure that were not included in any previous disclosure update. The duty to update disclosures relevant to a disputed issue ends when the presiding officer issues a decision resolving that disputed issue, or at such other time as may be specified by the presiding officer or the Commission.

(b) *Disclosure of expert testimony.* (1) In addition to the disclosures required by paragraph (a) of this section, a party other than the NRC staff shall disclose to other parties the identity of any person who may be used at trial to present evidence under § 2.711.

(2) Except in proceedings with prefiled written testimony, or as otherwise stipulated or directed by the presiding officer, this disclosure must be accompanied by a written report prepared and signed by the witness, containing: A complete statement of all opinions to be expressed and the basis and reasons therefor; the data or other information considered by the witness in forming the opinions; any exhibits to be used as a summary of or support for the opinions; the qualifications of the witness, including a list of all publications authored by the witness within the preceding ten years; and a listing of any other cases in which the witness has testified as an expert at trial or by deposition within the preceding four (4) years.

(3) These disclosures must be made at the times and in the sequence directed by the presiding officer. In the absence of other directions from the presiding officer, or stipulation by the parties, the disclosures must be made at least

ninety (90) days before the hearing commencement date or the date the matter is to be presented for hearing. If the evidence is intended solely to contradict or rebut evidence on the same subject matter identified by another party under paragraph (b)(2) of this section, the disclosures must be made within thirty (30) days after the disclosure made by the other party. The parties shall supplement these disclosures when required under paragraph (e) of this section.

(c) *Pretrial disclosures.* (1) In addition to the disclosures required in the preceding paragraphs, a party other than the NRC staff shall provide to other parties the following information regarding the evidence that it may present at trial other than solely for impeachment purposes:

(i) The name and, if not previously provided, the address and telephone number of each witness, separately identifying those whom the party expects to present and those whom the party may call if the need arises;

(ii) The designation of those witnesses whose testimony is expected to be presented by means of a deposition and, when available, a transcript of the pertinent portions of the deposition testimony; and

(iii) An appropriate identification of each document or other exhibit, including summaries of other evidence, separately identifying those which the party expects to offer and those which the party may offer if the need arises.

(2) Unless otherwise directed by the presiding officer or the Commission, these disclosures must be made at least thirty (30) days before commencement of the hearing at which the issue is to be presented.

(3) A party may object to the admissibility of documents identified under paragraph (c) of this section. A list of those objections must be served and filed within fourteen (14) days after service of the disclosures required by paragraphs (c)(1) and (2) of this section, unless a different time is specified by the presiding officer or the Commission. Objections not so disclosed, other than objections as to a document's admissibility under § 2.711(e), are waived unless excused by the presiding officer or Commission for good cause shown.

(d) *Form of disclosures; filing.* Unless otherwise directed by order of the presiding officer or the Commission, all disclosures under paragraphs (a) through (c) of this section must be made in writing, signed, served, and promptly filed with the presiding officer or the Commission.

(e) Supplementation of responses. A party who has made a disclosure under this section is under a duty to supplement or correct the disclosure to include information thereafter acquired if ordered by the presiding officer or in the following circumstances:

(1) When a party learns that in some material respect the information disclosed under paragraph (a) of this section is incomplete or incorrect, and if additional or corrective information has not otherwise been made known to the other parties during the discovery process or in writing, a party shall supplement its disclosures in accordance with the disclosure update schedule in paragraph (a)(3) of this section.

(2) With respect to testimony of an expert from whom a report is required under paragraph (b) of this section, the duty extends both to information contained in the report and to information provided through a deposition of the expert, and any additions or other changes to this information must be disclosed by the time the party's disclosures under § 2.704(c) are due.

(f) Disclosure under this section of documents and records including Safeguards Information referred to in Sections 147 and 181 of the Atomic Energy Act of 1954, as amended, will be according to the provisions in § 2.705(c)(3) through (c)(8).

[69 FR 2256, Jan. 14, 2004, as amended at 73 FR 63567, Oct. 24, 2008; 77 FR 46597, Aug. 3, 2012]

§ 2.705 Discovery-additional methods.

(a) *Discovery methods.* Parties may obtain discovery by one or more of the following methods: depositions upon oral examination or written interrogatories (§ 2.706); interrogatories to parties (§ 2.706); production of documents or things or permission to enter upon land or other property, for inspection and other purposes (§ 2.707); and requests for admission (§ 2.708).

(b) *Scope of discovery.* Unless otherwise limited by order of the presiding officer in accordance with this section, the scope of discovery is as follows:

(1) *In general.* Parties may obtain discovery regarding any matter, not privileged, that is relevant to the subject matter involved in the proceeding, whether it relates to the claim or defense of any other party, including the existence, description, nature, custody, condition, and location of any books, documents, or other tangible things and the identity and location of persons having knowledge of any discoverable matter. When any book, document, or other tangible thing sought is reasonably available from another source, such as at the NRC Web site, *http://www.nrc.gov*, and/or the NRC Public Document Room, sufficient response to an interrogatory on materials would be the location, the title and a page reference to the relevant book, document, or tangible thing. In a proceeding on an application for a construction permit or an operating license for a production or utilization facility, discovery begins only after the prehearing conference and relates only to those matters in controversy which have been identified by the Commission or the presiding officer in the prehearing order entered at the conclusion of that prehearing conference. In such a proceeding, discovery may not take place after the beginning of the prehearing conference held under §2.329 except upon leave of the presiding officer upon good cause shown. It is not a ground for objection that the information sought will be inadmissible at the hearing if the information sought appears reasonably calculated to lead to the discovery of admissible evidence.

(2) *Limitations.* Upon his or her own initiative after reasonable notice or in response to a motion filed under paragraph (c) of this section, the presiding officer may set limits on the number of depositions and interrogatories, and may also limit the length of depositions under §2.706 and the number of requests under §§2.707 and 2.708. The presiding officer shall limit the frequency or extent of use of the discovery methods otherwise permitted under these rules if he or she determines that:

(i) The discovery sought is unreasonably cumulative or duplicative, or is obtainable from some other source that is more convenient, less burdensome, or less expensive;

(ii) The party seeking discovery has had ample opportunity by discovery in the proceeding to obtain the information sought; or

(iii) The burden or expense of the proposed discovery outweighs its likely benefit, taking into account the needs of the proceeding, the parties' resources, the importance of the issue in the proceeding, and the importance of the proposed discovery in resolving the issues.

(3) *Trial preparation materials.* A party may obtain discovery of documents and tangible things otherwise discoverable under paragraph (b)(1) of this section and prepared in anticipation of or for the hearing by or for another party's representative (including his attorney, consultant, surety, indemnitor, insurer, or agent) only upon a showing that the party seeking discovery has substantial need of the materials in the preparation of this case and that he is unable without undue hardship to obtain the substantial equivalent of the materials by other means. In ordering discovery of such materials when the required showing has been made, the presiding officer shall protect against disclosure of the mental impressions, conclusions, opinions, or legal theories of an attorney for a party concerning the proceeding.

(4) *Claims of privilege or protection of trial preparation materials.* When a party withholds information otherwise discoverable under these rules by claiming that it is privileged or subject to protection as trial preparation material, the party shall make the claim expressly and shall describe the nature of the documents, communications, or things not produced or disclosed in a manner that, without revealing information itself privileged or protected, will enable other parties to assess the applicability of the privilege or protection. Identification of these privileged materials must be made within the time provided for disclosure of the materials, unless otherwise extended by order of the presiding officer or the Commission.

(5) *Nature of interrogatories.* Interrogatories may seek to elicit factual information reasonably related to a party's position in the proceeding, including data used, assumptions made, and analyses performed by the party. Interrogatories may not be addressed to, or be construed to require:

(i) Reasons for not using alternative data, assumptions, and analyses where the alternative data, assumptions, and analyses were not relied on in developing the party's position; or

(ii) Performance of additional research or analytical work beyond that which is needed to support the party's position on any particular matter.

(c) *Protective order.* (1) Upon motion by a party or the person from whom discovery is sought, accompanied by a certification that the movant has in good faith conferred or attempted to confer with other affected parties in an effort to resolve the dispute without action by the presiding officer, and for good cause shown, the presiding officer may make any order which justice requires to protect a party or person from annoyance, embarrassment, oppression, or undue burden or expense, including one or more of the following:

(i) That the discovery not be had;

(ii) That the discovery may be had only on specified terms and conditions, including a designation of the time or place;

(iii) That the discovery may be had only by a method of discovery other than that selected by the party seeking discovery;

(iv) That certain matters not be inquired into, or that the scope of discovery be limited to certain matters;

(v) That discovery be conducted with no one present except persons designated by the presiding officer;

(vi) That, subject to the provisions of §§ 2.709 and 2.390, a trade secret or other confidential research, development, or commercial information not be disclosed or be disclosed only in a designated way; or

(vii) That studies and evaluations not be prepared.

(2) If the motion for a protective order is denied in whole or in part, the presiding officer may, on such terms and conditions as are just, order that any party or person provide or permit discovery.

(3) In the case of documents and records including Safeguards Information referred to in Sections 147 and 181 of the Atomic Energy Act of 1954, as amended, the presiding officer may issue an order requiring disclosure if—

(i) The presiding officer finds that the individual seeking access to Safeguards Information in order to participate in an NRC proceeding has the requisite "need to know," as defined in 10 CFR 73.2;

(ii) The individual has undergone an FBI criminal history records check, unless exempt under 10 CFR 73.22(b)(3) or 73.23(b)(3), as applicable, by submitting fingerprints to the NRC Office of Administration, Security Processing Unit, Mail Stop T–6E46, U.S. Nuclear Regulatory Commission, Washington, DC 20555–0001, and otherwise following the procedures in 10 CFR 73.57(d) for submitting and processing fingerprints. However, before a final adverse determination by the NRC Office of Administration on an individual's criminal history records check is made, the individual shall be afforded the protections provided by 10 CFR 73.57; and

(iii) The NRC Office of Administration has found, based upon a background check, that the individual is trustworthy and reliable, unless exempt under 10 CFR 73.22(b)(3) or 73.23(b)(3), as applicable. In addition to the protections provided by 10 CFR 73.57 for adverse determinations based on criminal history records checks, the Office of Administration must take the following actions before making a final adverse determination on an individual's background check for trustworthiness and reliability. The Office of Administration will:

(A) For the purpose of assuring correct and complete information, provide to the individual any records, in addition to those required to be provided under 10 CFR 73.57(e)(1), that were considered in the trustworthiness and reliability determination;

(B) Resolve any challenge by the individual to the completeness or accuracy of the records described in § 2.705(c)(3)(iii)(A). The individual may make this challenge by submitting information and/or an explanation to the

Office of Administration. The challenge must be submitted within 10 days of the distribution of the records described in §2.705(c)(3)(iii)(A), and the Office of Administration must promptly resolve any challenge.

(iv) Individuals seeking access to Safeguards Information to participate in an NRC adjudication for whom the NRC Office of Administration has made a final adverse determination on trustworthiness and reliability may submit a request to the Chief Administrative Judge for review of the adverse determination. Upon receiving such a request, the Chief Administrative Judge shall designate an officer other than the presiding officer of the proceeding to review the adverse determination. For purposes of review, the adverse determination must be in writing and set forth the grounds for the determination. The request for review shall be served on the NRC staff and may include additional information for review by the designated officer. The request must be filed within 15 days after receipt of the adverse determination by the person against whom the adverse determination has been made. Within 10 days of receipt of the request for review and any additional information, the NRC staff will file a response indicating whether the request and additional information has caused the NRC Office of Administration to reverse its adverse determination. The designated officer may reverse the Office of Administration's final adverse determination only if the officer finds, based on all the information submitted, that the adverse determination constitutes an abuse of discretion. The designated officer's decision must be rendered within 15 days after receipt of the staff filing indicating that the request for review and additional information has not changed the NRC Office of Administration's adverse determination.

(4) The presiding officer may include in an order any protective terms and conditions (including affidavits of nondisclosure) as may be necessary and appropriate to prevent the unauthorized disclosure of Safeguards Information.

(5) When Safeguards Information protected from unauthorized disclosure under Section 147 of the Atomic Energy Act of 1954, as amended, is received and possessed by anyone other than the NRC staff, it must also be protected according to the requirements of §73.21 and the requirements of §73.22 or §73.23 of this chapter, as applicable.

(6) The presiding officer may also prescribe additional procedures to effectively safeguard and prevent disclosure of Safeguards Information to unauthorized persons with minimum impairment of the procedural rights which would be available if Safeguards Information were not involved.

(7) In addition to any other sanction that may be imposed by the presiding officer for violation of an order issued pursuant to this paragraph, violation of a provision for the protection of Safeguards Information from unauthorized disclosure that is contained in an order may be subject to a civil penalty imposed under §2.205.

(8) For the purpose of imposing the criminal penalties contained in Section 223 of the Atomic Energy Act of 1954, as amended, a provision for the protection of Safeguards Information from unauthorized disclosure that is contained in an order issued pursuant to this paragraph is considered to be issued under Section 161b of the Atomic Energy Act of 1954, as amended.

(d) *Sequence and timing of discovery.* Except when authorized under these rules or by order of the presiding officer, or agreement of the parties, a party may not seek discovery from any source before the parties have met and conferred as required by paragraph (f) of this section, nor may a party seek discovery after the time limit established in the proceeding for the conclusion of discovery. Unless the presiding officer upon motion, for the convenience of parties and witnesses and in the interests of justice, orders otherwise, methods of discovery may be used in any sequence and the fact that a party is conducting discovery, whether by deposition or otherwise, does not operate to delay any other party's discovery.

(e) *Supplementation of responses.* A party who responded to a request for discovery with a response is under a duty to supplement or correct the response to include information thereafter acquired if ordered by the presiding officer or, with respect to a response to an interrogatory, request for production, or request for admission, within a reasonable time after a party learns that the response is in some material respect incomplete or incorrect, and if the additional or corrective information has not otherwise been made known to the other parties during the discovery process or in writing.

(f) *Meeting of parties; planning for discovery.* Except when otherwise ordered, the parties shall, as soon as practicable and in any event no more than thirty (30) days after the issuance of a prehearing conference order following the initial prehearing conference specified in § 2.329, meet to discuss the nature and basis of their claims and defenses and the possibilities for a prompt settlement or resolution of the proceeding or any portion thereof, to make or arrange for the disclosures required by § 2.704, and to develop a proposed discovery plan.

(1) The plan must indicate the parties' views and proposals concerning:

(i) What changes should be made in the timing, form, or requirement for disclosures under § 2.704, including a statement as to when disclosures under § 2.704(a)(1) were made or will be made;

(ii) The subjects on which discovery may be needed, when discovery should be completed, and whether discovery should be conducted in phases or be limited to or focused upon particular issues;

(iii) What changes should be made in the limitations on discovery imposed under these rules, and what other limitations should be imposed; and

(iv) Any other orders that should be entered by the presiding officer under paragraph (c) of this section.

(2) The attorneys of record and all unrepresented parties that have appeared in the proceeding are jointly responsible for arranging and being present or represented at the meeting, for attempting in good faith to agree on the proposed discovery plan, and for submitting to the presiding officer within ten (10) days after the meeting a written report outlining the plan.

(g) *Signing of disclosures, discovery requests, responses, and objections.* (1) Every disclosure made in accordance with § 2.704 must be signed by at least one attorney of record in the attorney's individual name, whose address must be stated. An unrepresented party shall sign the disclosure and state the party's address. The signature of the attorney or party constitutes a certification that to the best of the signer's knowledge, information, and belief, formed after a reasonable inquiry, the disclosure is complete and correct as of the time it is made.

(2) Every discovery request, response, or objection made by a party represented by an attorney must be signed by at least one attorney of record in the attorney's individual name, whose address must be stated. An unrepresented party shall sign the request, response, or objection and state the party's address. The signature of the attorney or party constitutes a certification that to the best of the signer's knowledge, information, and belief, formed after a reasonable inquiry, the request, response, or objection is:

(i) Consistent with these rules and warranted by existing law or a good faith argument for the extension, modification, or reversal of existing law;

(ii) Not interposed for any improper purpose, such as to harass or to cause unnecessary delay or needless increase in the cost of litigation; and

(iii) Not unreasonable or unduly burdensome or expensive, given the needs of the case, the discovery already had in the case, the amount in controversy, and the importance of the issues at stake in the litigation.

(3) If a request, response, or objection is not signed, it must be stricken unless it is signed promptly after the omission is called to the attention of the party making the request, response, or objection, and a party shall not be obligated to take any action with respect to it until it is signed.

(4) If a certification is made in violation of the rule without substantial justification, the presiding officer, upon motion or upon its own initiative, shall impose upon the person who made the certification, the party on whose

behalf the disclosure, request, response, or objection is made, or both, an appropriate sanction, which may, in appropriate circumstances, include termination of that person's right to participate in the proceeding.

(h) *Motion to compel discovery.* (1) If a deponent or party upon whom a request for production of documents or answers to interrogatories is served fails to respond or objects to the request, or any part thereof, or fails to permit inspection as requested, the deposing party or the party submitting the request may move the presiding officer, within ten (10) days after the date of the response or after failure of a party to respond to the request, for an order compelling a response or inspection in accordance with the request. The motion must set forth the nature of the questions or the request, the response or objection of the party upon whom the request was served, and arguments in support of the motion. The motion must be accompanied by a certification that the movant has in good faith conferred or attempted to confer with other affected parties in an effort to resolve the dispute without action by the presiding officer. Failure to answer or respond may not be excused on the ground that the discovery sought is objectionable unless the person or party failing to answer or respond has applied for a protective order pursuant to paragraph (c) of this section. For purposes of this paragraph, an evasive or incomplete answer or response will be treated as a failure to answer or respond.

(2) In ruling on a motion made under this section, the presiding officer may issue a protective order under paragraph (c) of this section.

(3) This section does not preclude an independent request for issuance of a subpoena directed to a person not a party for production of documents and things. This section does not apply to requests for the testimony or interrogatories of the NRC staff under § 2.709(a), or the production of NRC documents under §§ 2.709(b) or § 2.390, except for paragraphs (c) and (e) of this section.

[69 FR 2256, Jan. 14, 2004, as amended at 73 FR 63568, Oct. 24, 2008; 77 FR 46597, Aug. 3, 2012]

§ 2.706 Depositions upon oral examination and written interrogatories; interrogatories to parties.

(a) *Depositions upon oral examination and written interrogatories.* (1) Any party desiring to take the testimony of any party or other person by deposition on oral examination or written interrogatories shall, without leave of the Commission or the presiding officer, give reasonable notice in writing to every other party, to the person to be examined and to the presiding officer of the proposed time and place of taking the deposition; the name and address of each person to be examined, if known, or if the name is not known, a general description sufficient to identify him or the class or group to which he belongs; the matters upon which each person will be examined and the name or descriptive title and address of the officer before whom the deposition is to be taken.

(2) [Reserved]

(3) Within the United States, a deposition may be taken before any officer authorized to administer oaths by the laws of the United States or of the place where the examination is held. Outside of the United States, a deposition may be taken before a secretary of an embassy or legation, a consul general, vice consul or consular agent of the United States, or a person authorized to administer oaths designated by the Commission.

(4) Before any questioning, the deponent shall either be sworn or affirm the truthfulness of his or her answers. Examination and cross-examination must proceed as at a hearing. Each question propounded must be recorded and the answer taken down in the words of the witness. Objections on questions of evidence must be noted in short form without the arguments. The officer may not decide on the competency, materiality, or relevancy of evidence but must record the evidence subject to objection. Objections on questions of evidence not made before the officer will not be considered waived unless the ground of the objection is one which might have been obviated or removed if presented at that time.

(5) When the testimony is fully transcribed, the deposition must be submitted to the deponent for examination and signature unless he or she is ill, cannot be found, or refuses to sign. The officer shall certify the deposition or, if the deposition is not signed by the deponent, shall certify the reasons for the failure to sign, and shall promptly forward the deposition by registered mail to the Commission.

(6) Where the deposition is to be taken on written interrogatories, the party taking the deposition shall serve a copy of the interrogatories, showing each interrogatory separately and consecutively numbered, on every other party with a notice stating the name and address of the person who is to answer them, and the name, description, title, and address of the officer before whom they are to be taken. Within ten (10) days after service, any other party may serve cross-interrogatories. The interrogatories, cross-interrogatories, and answers must be recorded and signed, and the deposition certified, returned, and filed as in the case of a deposition on oral examination.

(7) A deposition will not become a part of the record in the hearing unless received in evidence. If only part of a deposition is offered in evidence by a party, any other party may introduce any other parts. A party does not make a person his or her own witness for any purpose by taking his deposition.

(8) A deponent whose deposition is taken and the officer taking a deposition are entitled to the same fees as are paid for like services in the district courts of the United States. The fees must be paid by the party at whose instance the deposition is taken.

(9) The witness may be accompanied, represented, and advised by legal counsel.

(10) The provisions of paragraphs (a)(1) through (a)(9) of this section are not applicable to NRC personnel. Testimony of NRC personnel by oral examination and written interrogatories addressed to NRC personnel are subject to the provisions of § 2.709.

(b) *Interrogatories to parties.* (1) Any party may serve upon any other party (other than the NRC staff) written interrogatories to be answered in writing by the party served, or if the party served is a public or private corporation or a partnership or association, by any officer or agent, who shall furnish such information as is available to the party. A copy of the interrogatories, answers, and all related pleadings must be filed with the Secretary of the Commission, and must be served on the presiding officer and all parties to the proceeding.

(2) Each interrogatory must be answered separately and fully in writing under oath or affirmation, unless it is objected to, in which event the reasons for objection must be stated in lieu of an answer. The answers must be signed by the person making them, and the objections by the attorney making them. The party upon whom the interrogatories were served shall serve a copy of the answers and objections upon all parties to the proceeding within fourteen (14) days after service of the interrogatories, or within such shorter or longer period as the presiding officer may allow. Answers may be used in the same manner as depositions (see § 2.706(a)(7)).

§ 2.707 Production of documents and things; entry upon land for inspections and other purposes.

(a) *Request for discovery.* Any party may serve on any other party a request to:

(1) Produce and permit the party making the request, or a person acting on his or her behalf, to inspect and copy any designated documents, or to inspect and copy, test, or sample any tangible things which are within the scope of § 2.704 and which are in the possession, custody, or control of the party upon whom the request is served; or

(2) Permit entry upon designated land or other property in the possession or control of the party upon whom the request is served for the purpose of inspection and measuring, surveying, photographing, testing, or sampling the property or any designated object or operation on the property, within the scope of § 2.704.

(b) *Service.* The request may be served on any party without leave of the Commission or the presiding officer. Except as otherwise provided in § 2.704, the request may be served after the proceeding is set for hearing.

(c) *Contents.* The request must identify the items to be inspected either by individual item or by category, and describe each item and category with reasonable particularity. The request must specify a reasonable time, place, and manner of making the inspection and performing the related acts.

(d) *Response.* The party upon whom the request is served shall serve on the party submitting the request a written response within thirty (30) days after the service of the request. The response must state, with respect to each item or category, that inspection and related activities will be permitted as requested, unless the request is objected to, in which case the reasons for objection must be stated. If objection is made to part of an item or category, the part must be specified.

(e) *NRC records and documents.* The provisions of paragraphs (a) through (d) of this section do not apply to the production for inspection and copying or photographing of NRC records or documents. Production of NRC records or documents is subject to the provisions of §§ 2.709 and 2.390.

§ 2.708 Admissions.

(a) Apart from any admissions made during or as a result of a prehearing conference, at any time after his or her answer has been filed, a party may file a written request for the admission of the genuineness and authenticity of any relevant document described in or attached to the request, or for the admission of the truth of any specified relevant matter of fact. A copy of the document for which an admission of genuineness and authenticity is requested must be delivered with the request unless a copy has already been furnished.

(b)(1) Each requested admission is considered made unless, within a time designated by the presiding officer or the Commission, and not less than ten (10) days after service of the request or such further time as may be allowed on motion, the party to whom the request is directed serves on the requesting party either:

(i) A sworn statement denying specifically the relevant matters of which an admission is requested or setting forth in detail the reasons why he can neither truthfully admit nor deny them; or

(ii) Written objections on the ground that some or all of the matters involved are privileged or irrelevant or that the request is otherwise improper in whole or in part.

(2) Answers on matters to which such objections are made may be deferred until the objections are determined. If written objections are made to only a part of a request, the remainder of the request must be answered within the time designated.

(c) Admissions obtained under the procedure in this section may be used in evidence to the same extent and subject to the same objections as other admissions.

§ 2.709 Discovery against NRC staff.

(a)(1) In a proceeding in which the NRC staff is a party, the NRC staff will make available one or more witnesses, designated by the Executive Director for Operations or a delegee of the Executive Director for Operations, for oral examination at the hearing or on deposition regarding any matter, not privileged, that is relevant to the issues in the proceeding. The attendance and testimony of the Commissioners and named NRC personnel at a hearing or on deposition may not be required by the presiding officer, by subpoena or otherwise. However, the presiding officer may, upon a showing of exceptional circumstances, such as a case in which a particular named NRC employee has direct personal knowledge of a material fact not known to the witnesses made available by the Executive Director for Operations or a delegee of the Executive Director for Operations, require the attendance and testimony of named NRC personnel.

(2) A party may file with the presiding officer written interrogatories to be answered by NRC personnel with knowledge of the facts, as designated by the Executive Director for Operations, or a delegee of the Executive Director for Operations. Upon a finding by the presiding officer that answers to the interrogatories are necessary to a

proper decision in the proceeding and that answers to the interrogatories are not reasonably obtainable from any other source, the presiding officer may require that the NRC staff answer the interrogatories.

(3) A deposition of a particular named NRC employee or answer to interrogatories by NRC personnel under paragraphs (a)(1) and (2) of this section may not be required before the matters in controversy in the proceeding have been identified by order of the Commission or the presiding officer, or after the beginning of the prehearing conference held in accordance with § 2.329, except upon leave of the presiding officer for good cause shown.

(4) The provisions of § 2.704(c) and (e) apply to interrogatories served under this paragraph.

(5) Records or documents in the custody of the Commissioners and NRC personnel are available for inspection and copying or photographing under paragraph (b) of this section and § 2.390.

(6)(i) The NRC staff shall, except to the extent otherwise stipulated or directed by order of the presiding officer or the Commission, provide to the other parties within 45 days after the issuance of a prehearing conference order following the initial prehearing conference specified in § 2.329 and without awaiting a discovery request:

(A) Except for those documents, data compilations, or other tangible things for which there is a claim of privilege or protected status, all NRC staff documents, data compilations, or other tangible things in possession, custody, or control of the NRC staff that are relevant to disputed issues alleged with particularity in the pleadings, including any Office of Investigations report and supporting exhibits, and any Office of Enforcement documents, data compilations, or other tangible things regarding the order. When any document, data compilation, or other tangible thing that must be disclosed is publicly available from another source, such as the NRC Web site, *http://www.nrc.gov*, or the NRC Public Document Room, a sufficient disclosure would be the location, the title, and a page reference to the relevant document, data compilation, or tangible thing; and

(B) A list of all documents, data compilations, or other tangible things otherwise responsive to paragraph (a)(6)(i)(A) of this section for which a claim of privilege or protected status is being made, together with sufficient information for assessing the claim of privilege or protected status of the documents.

(ii) The duty of disclosure under this section is continuing. A disclosure update must be made every month after initial disclosures on a due date selected by the presiding officer, unless the parties agree upon a different due date or frequency. The disclosure update shall be limited to documents subject to disclosure under this section and does not need to include documents that are developed, obtained, or discovered during the two weeks before the due date. Disclosure updates shall include any documents subject to disclosure that were not included in any previous disclosure update. The duty to update disclosures relevant to a disputed issue ends when the presiding officer issues a decision resolving that dispute issue, or at such other time as may be specified by the presiding officer or the Commission.

(7) When any document, data compilation, or other tangible thing that must be disclosed is publicly available from another source, such as at the NRC Web site, *http://www.nrc.gov*, and/or the NRC Public Document Room, a sufficient disclosure would identify the location (including the ADAMS accession number, when available), the title and a page reference to the relevant document, data compilation, or tangible thing.

(b) A request for the production of an NRC record or document not available under § 2.390 by a party to an initial licensing proceeding may be served on the Executive Director for Operations or a delegee of the Executive Director for Operations, without leave of the Commission or the presiding officer. The request must identify the records or documents requested, either by individual item or by category, describe each item or category with reasonable particularity, and state why that record or document is relevant to the proceeding.

(c) If the Executive Director for Operations, or a delegee of the Executive Director for Operations, objects to producing a requested record or document on the ground that it is not relevant or it is exempted from disclosure under §2.390 and the disclosure is not necessary to a proper decision in the proceeding or the document or the information therein is reasonably obtainable from another source, the Executive Director for Operations, or a delegee of the Executive Director for Operations, shall advise the requesting party.

(d) If the Executive Director for Operations, or a delegee of the Executive Director for Operations, objects to producing a record or document, the requesting party may apply to the presiding officer, in writing, to compel production of that record or document. The application must set forth the relevancy of the record or document to the issues in the proceeding. The application will be processed as a motion in accordance with §2.323 (a) through (d). The record or document covered by the application must be produced for the *in camera* inspection of the presiding officer, exclusively, if requested by the presiding officer and only to the extent necessary to determine:

(1) The relevancy of that record or document;

(2) Whether the document is exempt from disclosure under §2.390;

(3) Whether the disclosure is necessary to a proper decision in the proceeding; and

(4) Whether the document or the information therein is reasonably obtainable from another source.

(e) Upon a determination by the presiding officer that the requesting party has demonstrated the relevancy of the record or document and that its production is not exempt from disclosure under §2.390 or that, if exempt, its disclosure is necessary to a proper decision in the proceeding, and the document or the information therein is not reasonably obtainable from another source, the presiding officer shall order the Executive Director for Operations, or a delegee of the Executive Director for Operations, to produce the document.

(f)(1) In the case of requested documents and records including Safeguards Information referred to in Sections 147 and 181 of the Atomic Energy Act of 1954, as amended exempt from disclosure under §2.390, the presiding officer may issue an order requiring disclosure to the Executive Director for Operations or a delegee of the Executive Director for Operations, to produce the documents or records (or any other order issued ordering production of the document or records) if—

(i) The presiding officer finds that the individual seeking access to Safeguards Information to participate in an NRC adjudication has the requisite "need to know," as defined in 10 CFR 73.2;

(ii) The individual has undergone an FBI criminal history records check, unless exempt under 10 CFR 73.22(b)(3) or 73.23(b)(3), as applicable, by submitting fingerprints to the NRC Office of Administration, Security Processing Unit, Mail Stop T–6E46, U.S. Nuclear Regulatory Commission, Washington, DC 20555–0001, and otherwise following the procedures in 10 CFR 73.57(d) for submitting and processing fingerprints. However, before a final adverse determination by the NRC Office of Administration on an individual's criminal history records check is made, the individual shall be afforded the protections provided by 10 CFR 73.57; and

(iii) The NRC Office of Administration has found, based upon a background check, that the individual is trustworthy and reliable, unless exempt under 10 CFR 73.22(b)(3) or 73.23(b)(3), as applicable. In addition to the protections provided by 10 CFR 73.57 for adverse determinations based on criminal history records checks, the Office of Administration must take the following actions before making a final adverse determination on an individual's background check for trustworthiness and reliability. The Office of Administration will:

(A) For the purpose of assuring correct and complete information, provide to the individual any records, in addition to those required to be provided under 10 CFR 73.57(e)(1), that were considered in the trustworthiness and reliability determination;

(B) Resolve any challenge by the individual to the completeness or accuracy of the records described in § 2.709(f)(1)(iii)(A). The individual may make this challenge by submitting information and/or an explanation to the Office of Administration. The challenge must be submitted within 10 days of the distribution of the records described in § 2.709(f)(1)(iii)(A), and the Office of Administration must promptly resolve any challenge.

(iv) Individuals seeking access to Safeguards Information to participate in an NRC adjudication for whom the NRC Office of Administration has made a final adverse determination on trustworthiness and reliability may submit a request to the Chief Administrative Judge for review of the adverse determination. Upon receiving such a request, the Chief Administrative Judge shall designate an officer other than the presiding officer of the proceeding to review the adverse determination. For purposes of review, the adverse determination must be in writing and set forth the grounds for the determination. The request for review shall be served on the NRC staff and may include additional information for review by the designated officer. The request must be filed within 15 days after receipt of the adverse determination by the person against whom the adverse determination has been made. Within 10 days of receipt of the request for review and any additional information, the NRC staff will file a response indicating whether the request and additional information has caused the NRC Office of Administration to reverse its adverse determination. The designated officer may reverse the Office of Administration's final adverse determination only if the officer finds, based on all the information submitted, that the adverse determination constitutes an abuse of discretion. The designated officer's decision must be rendered within 15 days after receipt of the staff filing indicating that the request for review and additional information has not changed the NRC Office of Administration's adverse determination.

(2) The presiding officer may include in an order any protective terms and conditions (including affidavits of nondisclosure) as may be necessary and appropriate to prevent the unauthorized disclosure of Safeguards Information.

(3) When Safeguards Information protected from disclosure under Section 147 of the Atomic Energy Act of 1954, as amended, is received and possessed by anyone other than the NRC staff, it must also be protected according to the requirements of § 73.21 and the requirements of § 73.22 or § 73.23 of this chapter, as applicable.

(4) The presiding officer may also prescribe additional procedures to effectively safeguard and prevent disclosure of Safeguards Information to unauthorized persons with minimum impairment of the procedural rights which would be available if Safeguards Information were not involved.

(5) In addition to any other sanction that may be imposed by the presiding officer for violation of an order issued pursuant to this paragraph, violation of a provision for the protection of Safeguards Information from unauthorized disclosure that is contained in an order may be subject to a civil penalty imposed under § 2.205.

(6) For the purpose of imposing the criminal penalties contained in Section 223 of the Atomic Energy Act of 1954, as amended, a provision for the protection of Safeguards Information from unauthorized disclosure that is contained in an order issued pursuant to this paragraph is considered to be issued under Section 161b of the Atomic Energy Act of 1954, as amended.

(g) A ruling by the presiding officer or the Commission for the production of a record or document will specify the time, place, and manner of production.

(h) A request under this section may not be made or entertained before the matters in controversy have been identified by the Commission or the presiding officer, or after the beginning of the prehearing conference held under § 2.329 except upon leave of the presiding officer for good cause shown.

(i) The provisions of § 2.705 (c) and (e) apply to production of NRC records and documents under this section.

[69 FR 2256, Jan. 14, 2004, as amended at 73 FR 63568, Oct. 24, 2008; 77 FR 46597, Aug. 3, 2012]

§2.710 Motions for summary disposition.

(a) Any party to a proceeding may move, with or without supporting affidavits, for a decision by the presiding officer in that party's favor as to all or any part of the matters involved in the proceeding. Summary disposition motions must be filed no later than 20 days after the close of discovery. The moving party shall attach to the motion a short and concise statement of the material facts as to which the moving party contends that there is no genuine issue to be heard. Any other party may serve an answer supporting or opposing the motion, with or without affidavits, within 20 days after service of the motion. The party shall attach to any answer opposing the motion a short and concise statement of the material facts as to which it is contended there exists a genuine issue to be heard. All material facts set forth in the statement required to be served by the moving party will be considered to be admitted unless controverted by the statement required to be served by the opposing party. The opposing party may, within 10 days after service, respond in writing to new facts and arguments presented in any statement filed in support of the motion. No further supporting statements or responses to the motion will be entertained.

(b) Affidavits must set forth the facts that would be admissible in evidence, and must demonstrate affirmatively that the affiant is competent to testify to the matters stated in the affidavit. The presiding officer may permit affidavits to be supplemented or opposed by depositions, answers to interrogatories or further affidavits. When a motion for summary decision is made and supported as provided in this section, a party opposing the motion may not rest upon the mere allegations or denials of his answer. The answer by affidavits or as otherwise provided in this section must set forth specific facts showing that there is a genuine issue of fact. If no answer is filed, the decision sought, if appropriate, must be rendered.

(c) Should it appear from the affidavits of a party opposing the motion that he or she cannot, for reasons stated, present by affidavit facts essential to justify the party's opposition, the presiding officer may refuse the application for summary decision, order a continuance to permit affidavits to be obtained, or make an order as is appropriate. A determination to that effect must be made a matter of record.

(d)(1) The presiding officer need not consider a motion for summary disposition unless its resolution will serve to expedite the proceeding if the motion is granted. The presiding officer may dismiss summarily or hold in abeyance untimely motions filed shortly before the hearing commences or during the hearing if the other parties or the presiding officer would be required to divert substantial resources from the hearing in order to respond adequately to the motion and thereby extend the proceeding.

(2) The presiding officer shall render the decision sought if the filings in the proceeding, depositions, answers to interrogatories, and admissions on file, together with the statements of the parties and the affidavits, if any, show that there is no genuine issue as to any material fact and that the moving party is entitled to a decision as a matter of law. However, in any proceeding involving a construction permit for a production or utilization facility, the procedure described in this section may be used only for the determination of specific subordinate issues and may not be used to determine the ultimate issue as to whether the permit shall be issued.

(e) The presiding officer shall issue an order no later than forty (40) days after any responses to the summary disposition motion are filed, indicating whether the motion is granted, or denied, and the bases therefore.

[69 FR 2256, Jan. 14, 2004, as amended at 77 FR 46598, Aug. 3, 2012]

§2.711 Evidence.

(a) *General.* Every party to a proceeding has the right to present oral or documentary evidence and rebuttal evidence and to conduct, in accordance with an approved cross-examination plan that contains the information specified in paragraph (c) of this section, any cross-examination required for full and true disclosure of the facts.

(b) *Testimony.* The parties shall submit direct testimony of witnesses in written form, unless otherwise ordered by the presiding officer on the basis of objections presented. In any proceeding in which advance written testimony is to be used, each party shall serve copies of its proposed written testimony on every other party at least fifteen (15) days in advance of the session of the hearing at which its testimony is to be presented. The presiding officer may permit the introduction of written testimony not so served, either with the consent of all parties present or after they have had a reasonable opportunity to examine it. Written testimony must be incorporated into the transcript of the record as if read or, in the discretion of the presiding officer, may be offered and admitted in evidence as an exhibit.

(c) *Cross-examination.* (1) The presiding officer shall require a party seeking an opportunity to cross-examine to request permission to do so in accordance with a schedule established by the presiding officer. A request to conduct cross-examination must be accompanied by a cross-examination plan containing the following information:

(i) A brief description of the issue or issues on which cross-examination will be conducted;

(ii) The objective to be achieved by cross-examination; and

(iii) The proposed line of questions that may logically lead to achieving the objective of the cross-examination.

(2) The cross-examination plan may be submitted only to the presiding officer and must be kept by the presiding officer in confidence until issuance of the initial decision on the issue being litigated. The presiding officer shall then provide each cross-examination plan to the Commission's Secretary for inclusion in the official record of the proceeding.

(d) *Non-applicability to subpart B proceedings.* Paragraphs (b) and (c) of this section do not apply to proceedings initiated under subpart B of this part for modification, suspension, or revocation of a license or to proceedings for imposition of a civil penalty, unless otherwise directed by the presiding officer.

(e) *Admissibility.* Only relevant, material, and reliable evidence which is not unduly repetitious will be admitted. Immaterial or irrelevant parts of an admissible document will be segregated and excluded so far as is practicable.

(f) *Objections.* An objection to evidence must briefly state the grounds of objection. The transcript must include the objection, the grounds, and the ruling. Exception to an adverse ruling is preserved without notation on-the-record.

(g) *Offer of proof.* An offer of proof, made in connection with an objection to a ruling of the presiding officer excluding or rejecting proffered oral testimony, must consist of a statement of the substance of the proffered evidence. If the excluded evidence is in written form, a copy must be marked for identification. Rejected exhibits, adequately marked for identification, must be retained in the record.

(h) *Exhibits.* A written exhibit will not be received in evidence unless the original and two copies are offered and a copy is furnished to each party, or the parties have been previously furnished with copies or the presiding officer directs otherwise. The presiding officer may permit a party to replace with a true copy an original document admitted in evidence.

(i) *Official record.* An official record of a government agency or entry in an official record may be evidenced by an official publication or by a copy attested by the officer having legal custody of the record and accompanied by a certificate of his custody.

(j) *Official notice.* (1) The Commission or the presiding officer may take official notice of any fact of which a court of the United States may take judicial notice or of any technical or scientific fact within the knowledge of the Commission as an expert body. Each fact officially noticed under this paragraph must be specified in the record with sufficient particularity to advise the parties of the matters which have been noticed or brought to the attention of the parties before final decision and each party adversely affected by the decision shall be given opportunity to controvert the fact.

(2) If a decision is stated to rest in whole or in part on official notice of a fact which the parties have not had a prior opportunity to controvert, a

party may controvert the fact by filing an appeal from an initial decision or a petition for reconsideration of a final decision. The appeal must clearly and concisely set forth the information relied upon to controvert the fact.

§ 2.712 Proposed findings and conclusions.

(a) Any party to a proceeding may, or if directed by the presiding officer shall, file proposed findings of fact and conclusions of law, briefs and a proposed form of order or decision within the time provided by this section, except as otherwise ordered by the presiding officer:

(1) The party who has the burden of proof shall, within thirty (30) days after the record is closed, file proposed findings of fact and conclusions of law and briefs, and a proposed form of order or decision.

(2) Other parties may file proposed findings, conclusions of law and briefs within forty (40) days after the record is closed.

(3) A party who has the burden of proof may reply within five (5) days after filing of proposed findings and conclusions of law and briefs by other parties.

(b) Failure to file proposed findings of fact, conclusions of law, or briefs when directed to do so may be considered a default, and an order or initial decision may be entered accordingly.

(c) Proposed findings of fact must be clearly and concisely set forth in numbered paragraphs and must be confined to the material issues of fact presented on-the-record, with exact citations to the transcript of record and exhibits in support of each proposed finding. Proposed conclusions of law must be set forth in numbered paragraphs as to all material issues of law or discretion presented on-the-record. An intervenor's proposed findings of fact and conclusions of law must be confined to issues which that party placed in controversy or sought to place in controversy in the proceeding.

§ 2.713 Initial decision and its effect.

(a) After hearing, the presiding officer will render an initial decision which will constitute the final action of the Commission forty (40) days after its date unless any party petitions for Commission review in accordance with § 2.341 or the Commission takes review sua sponte.

(b) Where the public interest so requires, the Commission may direct that the presiding officer certify the record to it without an initial decision, and may:

(1) Prepare its own decision which will become final unless the Commission grants a petition for reconsideration under § 2.345; or

(2) Omit an initial decision on a finding that due and timely execution of its functions imperatively and unavoidably so requires.

(c) An initial decision will be in writing and will be based on the whole record and supported by reliable, probative, and substantial evidence. The initial decision will include:

(1) Findings, conclusions, and rulings, with the reasons or basis for them, on all material issues of fact, law, or discretion presented on-the-record;

(2) All facts officially noticed and relied on in making the decision;

(3) The appropriate ruling, order, or denial of relief with the effective date;

(4) The time within which a petition for review of the decision may be filed, the time within which answers in support of or in opposition to a petition for review filed by another party may be filed and, in the case of an initial decision which may become final in accordance with paragraph (a) of this section, the date when it may become final.

Subpart H—Rulemaking

§ 2.800 Scope and applicability.

(a) This subpart governs the issuance, amendment, and repeal of regulations in which participation by interested persons is prescribed under Section 553 of title 5 of the U.S. Code.

(b) The procedures in §§ 2.804 through 2.810 apply to all rulemakings.

(c) The procedures in §§ 2.802 through 2.803 apply to all petitions for rulemaking except for initial applications for standard design certification rulemaking under subpart B of part 52 of this chapter, and subsequent petitions for amendment of an existing design certification rule filed by the original applicant for the design certification rule.

(d) The procedures in §§ 2.811 through 2.819, as supplemented by the provisions of subpart B of part 52, apply to standard design certification rulemaking.

[72 FR 49481, Aug. 28, 2007]

§ 2.801 Initiation of rulemaking.

Rulemaking may be initiated by the Commission at its own instance, on the recommendation of another agency of the United States, or on the petition of any other interested person, including an application for design certification under subpart B of part 52 of this chapter.

[72 FR 49482, Aug. 28, 2007]

§ 2.802 Petition for rulemaking—requirements for filing.

(a) *Filing a petition for rulemaking.* Any person may petition the Commission to issue, amend, or rescind any regulation in 10 CFR chapter I. The petition for rulemaking should be addressed to the Secretary, Attention: Rulemakings and Adjudications Staff, and sent by mail addressed to the U.S. Nuclear Regulatory Commission, Washington, DC 20555–0001; by email to *Rulemaking.Comments@nrc.gov;* or by hand delivery to 11555 Rockville Pike, Rockville, Maryland 20852, between 7:30 a.m. and 4:15 p.m. (Eastern time) on Federal workdays.

(b) *Consultation with the NRC.* A petitioner may consult with the NRC staff before and after filing a petition for rulemaking by contacting the Chief, Rules, Announcements, and Directives Branch, Office of Administration, U.S. Nuclear Regulatory Commission, Washington, DC 20555–0001; telephone: 1–800–368–5642.

(1) In any consultation regarding the drafting or amendment of a petition for rulemaking, the assistance that the NRC staff may provide is limited to the following:

(i) Describing the process for filing, docketing, tracking, closing, amending, withdrawing, and resolving a petition for rulemaking;

(ii) Clarifying an existing NRC regulation and the basis for the regulation; and

(iii) Assisting the petitioner to clarify a petition for rulemaking so that the Commission is able to understand the issues of concern to the petitioner.

(2) In any consultation regarding the drafting or amendment of a petition for rulemaking, in providing the assistance permitted in paragraph (b)(1) of this section, the NRC staff will not draft or develop text or alternative approaches to address matters in the petition for rulemaking.

(3) In any consultation regarding a petition for rulemaking, the NRC staff will not advise a petitioner on whether a petition should be amended or withdrawn.

(c) *Content of petition.* (1) Each petition for rulemaking filed under this section must clearly and concisely:

(i) Specify the name of the petitioner, a telephone number, a mailing address, and an email address (if available) that the NRC may use to communicate with the petitioner;

(ii) If the petitioner is an organization, provide additional identifying information (as applicable) including the petitioner's organizational or corporate status, the petitioner's State of incorporation, the petitioner's registered agent, and the name and authority of the individual who signed the petition on behalf of the organizational or corporate petitioner.

(iii) Present the specific problems or issues that the petitioner believes should be addressed through rulemaking, including any specific circumstances in which the NRC's codified requirements are incorrect, incomplete, inadequate, or unnecessarily burdensome;

(iv) Cite, enclose, or reference publicly-available technical, scientific, or other data or information supporting the petitioner's assertion of the problems or issues;

(v) Present the petitioner's proposed solution to the problems or issues raised in the petition for rulemaking (*e.g.*, a proposed solution may include specific regulations or regulatory language to add to, amend in, or delete from 10 CFR chapter I);

(vi) Provide an analysis, discussion, or argument that explains how the petitioner's proposed solution solves the problems or issues identified by the petitioner; and

(vii) Cite, enclose, or reference any other publicly-available data or information supporting the petitioner's proposed solution; and

(viii) If required by 10 CFR 51.68 of this chapter, submit a separate document entitled "Petitioner's Environmental Report," which contains the information specified in 10 CFR 51.45.

(2) To assist the NRC in its evaluation of the petition for rulemaking, the petitioner should clearly and concisely:

(i) Explain why the proposed rulemaking solution is within the authority of the NRC to adopt; and

(ii) Explain why rulemaking is the most favorable approach to address the problem or issue, as opposed to other NRC actions such as licensing, issuance of an order, or referral to another Federal or State agency.

(3) If the petition is signed by multiple petitioners, the petition must designate a lead petitioner who is responsible for disseminating communications received from the NRC to co-petitioners.

(d) [Reserved]

(e) *Request for suspension of an adjudication involving licensing.* The petitioner may request the Commission to suspend all or any part of any licensing proceeding to which the petitioner is a participant pending disposition of the petition for rulemaking.

(f) *Amendment; withdrawal.* If the petitioner wants to amend or withdraw a docketed petition for rulemaking, then the petitioner should include the docket number and the date that the original petition for rulemaking was submitted in a filing addressed to the Secretary, Attention: Rulemakings and Adjudications Staff, and sent by mail addressed to the U.S. Nuclear Regulatory Commission, Washington, DC 20555–0001; or by email to *Rulemaking.Comments@nrc.gov.*

[80 FR 60526, Oct. 7, 2015]

§ 2.803 Petition for rulemaking—NRC action.

(a) *Notification of receipt.* Following receipt of a petition for rulemaking, the NRC will acknowledge its receipt to the petitioner.

(b) *Docketing review.* (1) The NRC will evaluate the petition for rulemaking, including supporting data or information submitted under § 2.802(c), for sufficiency according to the review criteria in § 2.803(b).

(2) If the NRC determines that the petition for rulemaking does not include the information set out in § 2.802(c), that the regulatory change sought by the petitioner is not within the legal authority of the NRC, or that the petition for rulemaking does not raise a potentially valid issue that warrants further consideration, then the NRC will notify the petitioner in writing and explain the deficiencies in the petition for rulemaking.

(3) The petitioner may resubmit the petition for rulemaking without prejudice.

(c) *Docketing.* (1) The NRC will docket a petition for rulemaking and assign a docket number to the petition if the NRC determines the following:

(i) The petition for rulemaking includes the information required by paragraph § 2.802(c),

(ii) The regulatory change sought by the petitioner is within the NRC's legal authority, and

(iii) The petition for rulemaking raises a potentially valid issue that warrants further consideration.

(2) A copy of the docketed petition for rulemaking will be posted in the NRC's Agencywide Documents Access and Management System (ADAMS) and on the Federal rulemaking Web site at: *http://www.regulations.gov.* The NRC will publish a notice of docketing in the FEDERAL REGISTER informing the public that the NRC is reviewing the merits of the petition for rulemaking. The notice of docketing will include the docket number and explain how the public may track the status of the petition for rulemaking.

(d) *NRC communication with petitioners.* If the petition is signed by multiple petitioners, any NRC obligation to inform a petitioner (as may be required under 10 CFR part 2, subpart H) is satisfied, with respect to all petitioners, when the NRC transmits the required notification to the lead petitioner.

(e)–(f) [Reserved]

(g) *Public comment on a petition for rulemaking; hearings.* (1) At its discretion, the NRC may request public comment on a docketed petition for rulemaking.

(2) The NRC will post all comment submissions at *http://www.regulations.gov* and enter the comment submissions into ADAMS, without removing identifying or contact information from comment submissions. Anyone requesting or aggregating comments from other persons for submission to the NRC is responsible for informing those persons not to include identifying or contact information that they do not want to be publicly disclosed in their comment submissions.

(3) No adjudicatory or legislative hearing under the procedures of 10 CFR part 2 will be held on a petition for rulemaking unless the Commission determines to do so, at its discretion.

(h) *Determination on a petition for rulemaking; Closure of docket on a petition for rulemaking.* (1) *Determination.* Following docketing of a petition for rulemaking, the NRC's determination on the petition for rulemaking may be based upon, but is not limited to, the following considerations:

(i) The merits of the petition;

(ii) The immediacy of the safety, environmental, or security concern raised;

(iii) The availability of NRC resources and the priority of the issues raised in relation to other NRC rulemaking issues;

(iv) Whether the problems or issues are already under consideration by the NRC in other NRC processes;

(v) The substance of any public comment received, if comment is requested; and

(vi) The NRC's relevant past decisions and current policies.

(2) *Petition for rulemaking docket closure.* After the NRC determines the appropriate regulatory action in response to the petition for rulemaking, the NRC will administratively close the docket for the petition. The NRC will publish a notice describing that action with any related Docket Identification number (Docket ID), as applicable, in the FEDERAL REGISTER. The NRC may make a determination on a petition for rulemaking and administratively close the docket for the petition for rulemaking by:

(i) Deciding not to undertake a rulemaking to address the issue raised by the petition for rulemaking, and informing the petitioner in writing of the grounds for denial.

(ii) Initiating a rulemaking action (*e.g.*, initiating a new rulemaking, addressing the petition for rulemaking in an ongoing rulemaking, addressing the petition for rulemaking in a planned rulemaking) that considers the issues raised by a petition for rulemaking, and informing the petitioner in writing of this decision and the associated Docket ID of the rulemaking action, if applicable.

(i) *Petition for rulemaking resolution.*—(1) *Petition for rulemaking resolution published in the Federal Register.* The NRC will publish a FEDERAL REGISTER notice informing the public that it has concluded all planned regulatory action with respect to some or all of the issues presented in a petition for rulemaking. This may occur by adoption of a final rule related to the petition for rulemaking, denial by the NRC of the petition for rulemaking at any stage of the regulatory process, or the petitioner's withdrawal of the petition for rulemaking before the NRC has entered the rulemaking process. As applicable, the FEDERAL REGISTER notice will include a discussion of how the regulatory action addresses the issue raised by the petitioner, the NRC's grounds for denial of the petition for rulemaking, or information on the withdrawal. The notice will normally include the NRC's response to any public comment received (if comment is requested), unless the NRC has indicated that it will not be providing a formal written response to each comment received.

(2) *NRC decision not to proceed with rulemaking after closure of a petition for rulemaking docket.* If the NRC closes a petition for rulemaking docket under paragraph (h)(2)(ii) of this section but subsequently decides not to carry out the planned rulemaking to publication of a final rule, the NRC will notify the petitioner in writing of this decision and publish a notice in the FEDERAL REGISTER explaining the basis for its

decision. The decision not to complete the rulemaking action will be documented as denial of the petition for rulemaking in the docket of the closed petition for rulemaking, in the Web sites, in the Government-wide *Unified Agenda of Federal Regulatory and Deregulatory Actions*, online in ADAMS, and at *http://www.regulations.gov* as described in paragraph (j) of this section.

(j) *Status of petitions for rulemaking and rulemakings.* (1) The NRC provides current information on rulemakings and petitions for rulemaking in the NRC Library at *http://www.nrc.gov/about-nrc/regulatory/rulemaking.html.*

(2) The NRC includes a summary of the NRC's planned and ongoing rulemakings in the Government-wide *Unified Agenda of Federal Regulatory and Deregulatory Actions* (the Unified Agenda), published semiannually. This Unified Agenda is available at *http://www.reginfo.gov/public/do/eAgendaMain/.*

(3) All docketed petitions, rulemakings, and public comments are posted online in ADAMS and at *http://www.regulations.gov.*

[80 FR 60526, Oct. 7, 2015]

§ 2.804 Notice of proposed rulemaking.

(a) Except as provided by paragraph (d) of this section, when the Commission proposes to adopt, amend, or repeal a regulation, it will cause to be published in the FEDERAL REGISTER a notice of proposed rulemaking, unless all persons subject to the notice are named and either are personally served or otherwise have actual notice in accordance with law.

(b) The notice will include:

(1) Either the terms or substance of the proposed rule, or a specification of the subjects and issues involved;

(2) The manner and time within which interested members of the public may comment, and a statement that copies of comments may be examined will be made available at the NRC Web site, *http://www.nrc.gov;*

(3) The authority under which the regulation is proposed;

(4) The time, place, and nature of the public hearing, if any;

(5) If a hearing is to be held, designation of the presiding officer and any special directions for the conduct of the hearing; and

(6) Such explanatory statement as the Commission may consider appropriate.

(c) The publication or service of notice will be made not less than fifteen (15) days prior to the time fixed for hearing, if any, unless the Commission for good cause stated in the notice provides otherwise.

(d) The notice and comment provisions contained in paragraphs (a), (b), and (c) of this section will not be required to be applied—

(1) To interpretative rules, general statements of policy, or rules of agency organization, procedure, or practice; or

(2) When the Commission for good cause finds that notice and public comment are impracticable, unnecessary, or contrary to the public interest, and are not required by statute. This finding, and the reasons therefor, will be incorporated into any rule issued without notice and comment for good cause.

(e) The Commission shall provide for a 30-day post-promulgation comment period for—

(1) Any rule adopted without notice and comment under the good cause exception on paragraph (d)(2) of this section where the basis is that notice and comment is "impracticable" or "contrary to the public interest."

(2) Any interpretative rule, or general statement of policy adopted without notice and comment under paragraph (d)(1) of this section, except for those cases for which the Commission finds that such procedures would serve no public interest, or would be so burdensome as to outweigh any foreseeable gain.

(f) For any post-promulgation comments received under paragraph (e) of this section, the Commission shall publish a statement in the FEDERAL REGISTER containing an evaluation of the significant comments and any revisions of the rule or policy statement made as a result of the comments and their evaluation.

[27 FR 377, Jan. 13, 1962, as amended at 50 FR 13010, Apr. 2, 1985; 64 FR 48949, Sept. 9, 1999]

§ 2.805 Participation by interested persons.

(a) In all rulemaking proceedings conducted under the provisions of

§ 2.804(a), the Commission will afford interested persons an opportunity to participate through the submission of statements, information, opinions, and arguments in the manner stated in the notice. The Commission may grant additional reasonable opportunity for the submission of comments.

(b) The Commission may hold informal hearings at which interested persons may be heard, adopting procedures which in its judgment will best serve the purpose of the hearing.

[27 FR 377, Jan. 13, 1962, as amended at 50 FR 13010, Apr. 2, 1985; 50 FR 15865, Apr. 22, 1985]

§ 2.806 Commission action.

The Commission will incorporate in the notice of adoption of a regulation a concise general statement of its basis and purpose, and will cause the notice and regulation to be published in the FEDERAL REGISTER or served upon affected persons.

§ 2.807 Effective date.

The notice of adoption of a regulation will specify the effective date. Publication or service of the notice and regulation, other than one granting or recognizing exemptions or relieving from restrictions, will be made not less than thirty (30) days prior to the effective date unless the Commission directs otherwise on good cause found and published in the notice of rule making.

§ 2.808 Authority of the Secretary to rule on procedural matters.

When briefs, motions or other documents listed herein are submitted to the Commission itself, as opposed to officers who have been delegated authority to act for the Commission, the Secretary or the Assistant Secretary is authorized to:

(a) Prescribe schedules for the filing of statements, information, briefs, motions, responses or other pleadings, where such schedules may differ from those elsewhere prescribed in these rules or where these rules do not prescribe a schedule;

(b) Rule on motions for extensions of time;

(c) Reject motions, briefs, pleadings, and other documents filed with the Commission later than the time prescribed by the Secretary or the Assistant Secretary or established by an order, rule, or regulation of the Commission unless good cause is shown for the late filing; and

(d) Prescribe all procedural arrangements relating to any oral argument to be held before the Commission.

[39 FR 24219, July 1, 1974, as amended at 72 FR 49152, Aug. 28, 2007]

§ 2.809 Participation by the Advisory Committee on Reactor Safeguards.

(a) In its advisory capacity to the Commission, the ACRS may recommend that the Commission initiate rulemaking in a particular area. The Commission will respond to such rulemaking recommendation in writing within 90 days, noting its intent to implement, study, or defer action on the recommendation. In the event the Commission decides not to accept or decides to defer action on the recommendation, it will give its reasons for doing so. Both the ACRS recommendation and the Commission's response will be made available at the NRC Web site, *http://www.nrc.gov*, following transmittal of the Commission's response to the ACRS.

(b) When a rule involving nuclear safety matters within the purview of the ACRS is under development by the NRC Staff, the Staff will ensure that the ACRS is given an opportunity to provide advice at appropriate stages and to identify issues to be considered during rulemaking hearings.

[46 FR 22358, Apr. 17, 1981, as amended at 64 FR 48949, Sept. 9, 1999]

§ 2.810 NRC size standards.

The NRC shall use the size standards contained in this section to determine whether a licensee qualifies as a small entity in its regulatory programs.

(a) A small business is a for-profit concern and is a—

(1) Concern that provides a service or a concern not engaged in manufacturing with average gross receipts of $7.0 million or less over its last 3 completed fiscal years; or

(2) Manufacturing concern with an average number of 500 or fewer employees based upon employment during

each pay period for the preceding 12 calendar months.

(b) A small organization is a not-for-profit organization which is independently owned and operated and has annual gross receipts of $7.0 million or less.

(c) A small governmental jurisdiction is a government of a city, county, town, township, village, school district, or special district with a population of less than 50,000.

(d) A small educational institution is one that is—

(1) Supported by a qualifying small governmental jurisdiction; or

(2) Not state or publicly supported and has 500 or fewer employees.

(e) For the purposes of this section, the NRC shall use the Small Business Administration definition of receipts (13 CFR 121.104). A licensee who is a subsidiary of a large entity does not qualify as a small entity for purposes of this section.

(f) Whenever appropriate in the interest of administering statutes and regulations within its jurisdiction, it is the practice of the NRC to answer inquiries from small entities concerning information on and advice about compliance with the statutes and regulations that affect them. To help small entities obtain information quickly, the NRC has established a toll-free telephone number at 1–800–368–5642.

[60 FR 18346, Apr. 11, 1995, as amended at 62 FR 26220, May 13, 1997; 72 FR 44953, Aug. 10, 2007; 73 FR 42673, July 23, 2008; 77 FR 39387, July 3, 2012; 79 FR 66601, Nov. 10, 2014]

§2.811 Filing of standard design certification application; required copies.

(a) *Serving of applications.* The signed original of an application for a standard design certification, including all amendments to the applications, must be sent either by mail addressed: ATTN: Document Control Desk, U.S. Nuclear Regulatory Commission, Washington, DC 20555–0001; by facsimile; by hand delivery to the NRC's offices at 11555 Rockville Pike, Rockville, Maryland, between the hours of 7:30 a.m. and 4:15 p.m. eastern time; or, where practicable, by electronic submission, for example, via Electronic Information Exchange, e-mail, or CD-ROM. Electronic submissions must be made in a manner that enables the NRC to receive, read, authenticate, distribute, and archive the submission, and process and retrieve it a single page at a time. Detailed guidance on making electronic submissions can be obtained by visiting the NRC's Web site at *http://www.nrc.gov/site-help/e-submittals.html;* by e-mail to *MSHD.Resource@nrc.gov*; or by writing the Office of the Chief Information Officer, U.S. Nuclear Regulatory Commission, Washington, DC 20555–0001. The guidance discusses, among other topics, the formats the NRC can accept, the use of electronic signatures, and the treatment of nonpublic information. If the communication is on paper, the signed original must be sent.

(b) *Form of application.* Each original of an application and an amendment of an application must meet the requirements in §2.813.

(c) *Capability to provide additional copies.* The applicant shall maintain the capability to generate additional copies of the general information and the safety analysis report, or part thereof or amendment thereto, for subsequent distribution in accordance with the written instructions of the Director, Office of New Reactors, the Director, Office of Nuclear Reactor Regulation, or the Director, Office of Nuclear Material Safety and Safeguards, as appropriate.

(d) *Public hearing copy.* In any hearing conducted under subpart O of this part for a design certification rulemaking, the applicant must make a copy of the updated application available at the public hearing for the use of any other parties to the proceeding, and shall certify that the updated copies of the application contain the current contents of the application submitted in accordance with the requirements of this part.

(e) *Pre-application consultation.* A prospective applicant for a standard design certification may consult with NRC staff before filing an application by writing to the Director, Division of New Reactor Licensing, U.S. Nuclear Regulatory Commission, Washington, DC 20555–0001, with respect to the subject matters listed in §2.802(b)(1). A prospective applicant also may telephone the Rules, Announcements, and Directives Branch, toll free on 1–800–368–5642, or send an email to *Rulemaking.Comments@nrc.gov* on these subject matters. In addition, a prospective applicant may confer informally with NRC staff before filing an application for a standard design certification, and the limitations on consultation in § 2.802(b)(2) do not apply.

[72 FR 49482, Aug. 28, 2007, as amended at 74 FR 62679, Dec. 1, 2009; 77 FR 46598, Aug. 3, 2012; 80 FR 60527, Oct. 7, 2015; 80 FR 74978, Dec. 1, 2015]

§ 2.813 Written communications.

(a) *General requirements.* All correspondence, reports, and other written communications from the applicant to the Nuclear Regulatory Commission concerning the regulations in this subpart, and parts 50, 52, and 100 of this chapter must be sent either by mail addressed: ATTN: Document Control Desk, U.S. Nuclear Regulatory Commission, Washington, DC 20555–0001; by hand delivery to the NRC's offices at 11555 Rockville Pike, Rockville, Maryland, between the hours of 7:30 a.m. and 4:15 p.m. eastern time; or, where practicable, by electronic submission, for example, via Electronic Information Exchange, e-mail, or CD-ROM. Electronic submissions must be made in a manner that enables the NRC to receive, read, authenticate, distribute, and archive the submission, and process and retrieve it a single page at a time. Detailed guidance on making electronic submissions can be obtained by visiting the NRC's Web site at *http://www.nrc.gov/site-help/e-submittals.html;* by e-mail to *MSHD.Resource@nrc.gov;* or by writing the Office of the Chief Information Officer, U.S. Nuclear Regulatory Commission, Washington, DC 20555–0001. The guidance discusses, among other topics, the formats the NRC can accept, the use of electronic signatures, and the treatment of nonpublic information. If the communication is on paper, the signed original must be sent. If a submission due date falls on a Saturday, Sunday, or Federal holiday, the next Federal working day becomes the official due date.

(b) *Form of communications.* All paper copies submitted to meet the requirements set forth in paragraph (a) of this section must be typewritten, printed or otherwise reproduced in permanent form on unglazed paper. Exceptions to these requirements imposed on paper submissions may be granted for the submission of micrographic, photographic, or similar forms.

(c) *Regulation governing submission.* An applicant submitting correspondence, reports, and other written communications under the regulations of this chapter is requested but not required to cite whenever practical, in the upper right corner of the first page of the submission, the specific regulation or other basis requiring submission.

[72 FR 49482, Aug. 28, 2007, as amended at 74 FR 62679, Dec. 1, 2009; 80 FR 74978, Dec. 1, 2015]

§ 2.815 Docketing and acceptance review.

(a) Each application for a standard design certification will be assigned a docket number. However, to allow a determination as to whether an application is complete and acceptable for docketing, it will be initially treated as a tendered application. A copy of the tendered application will be available for public inspection at the NRC Web site, *http://www.nrc.gov,* and/or at the NRC Public Document Room. Generally, the determination on acceptability for docketing will be made within a period of 30 days. The Commission may decide to determine acceptability on the basis of the technical adequacy of the application as well as its completeness.

(b) If the Commission determines that a tendered application is complete and acceptable for docketing, a docket number will be assigned to the application or part thereof, and the applicant will be notified of the determination.

[72 FR 49482, Aug. 28, 2007]

§ 2.817 Withdrawal of application.

(a) The Commission may permit an applicant to withdraw an application for a standard design certification before the issuance of a notice of proposed rulemaking on such terms and conditions as the Commission may prescribe, or may, on receiving a request for withdrawal of an application, deny the application or dismiss it without prejudice. The NRC will publish in the FEDERAL REGISTER a document withdrawing the application, if the notice of receipt of the application, an advance notice of proposed rulemaking, or a notice of proposed rulemaking for the standard design certification has been previously published in the FEDERAL REGISTER. If the notice of receipt, advance notice of proposed rulemaking or notice of proposed rulemaking was published on the NRC Web site, then the notice of action on the withdrawal will also be published on the NRC Web site.

(b) The withdrawal of an application does not authorize the removal of any document from the files of the Commission.

[72 FR 49482, Aug. 28, 2007]

§ 2.819 Denial of application for failure to supply information.

(a) The Commission may deny an application for a standard design certification if an applicant fails to respond to a request for additional information within 30 days from the date of the request, or within such other time as may be specified.

(b) If the Commission denies an application because the applicant has failed to respond in a timely fashion to a request for additional information, the NRC will publish in the FEDERAL REGISTER a notice of denial and will notify the applicant with a simple statement of the grounds of denial. If a notice of receipt of application, advance notice of proposed rulemaking, or notice of proposed rulemaking for a standard design certification was published on the NRC Web site, then the notice of action on the denial will also be published on the NRC Web site.

[72 FR 49482, Aug. 28, 2007]

Subpart I—Special Procedures Applicable to Adjudicatory Proceedings Involving Restricted Data and/or National Security Information

SOURCE: 41 FR 53329, Dec. 6, 1976, unless otherwise noted.

§ 2.900 Purpose.

This subpart is issued pursuant to section 181 of the Atomic Energy Act of 1954, as amended, and section 201 of the Energy Reorganization Act of 1974, as amended, to provide such procedures in proceedings subject to this part as will effectively safeguard and prevent disclosure of Restricted Data and National Security Information to unauthorized persons, with minimum impairment of procedural rights.

§ 2.901 Scope of subpart I.

This subpart applies, as applicable, to all proceedings under subparts G, J, K, L, M, and N of this part.

[69 FR 2264, Jan. 14, 2004]

§ 2.902 Definitions.

As used in this subpart:

(a) *Government agency* means any executive department, commission, independent establishment, corporation, wholly or partly owned by the United States of America, which is an instrumentality of the United States, or any board, bureau, division, service, office, officer, authority, administration, or other establishment in the executive branch of the Government.

(b) *Interested party* means a party having an interest in the issue or issues to which particular Restricted Data or National Security Information is relevant. Normally the interest of a party in an issue may be determined by examination of the notice of hearing, the answers and replies.

(c) The phrase *introduced into a proceeding* refers to the introduction or incorporation of testimony or documentary matter into any part of the official record of a proceeding subject to this part.

(d) *National Security Information* means information that has been classified pursuant to Executive Order 12356.

(e) *Party*, in the case of proceedings subject to this subpart includes a person admitted as a party under § 2.309 or an interested State admitted under § 2.315(c).

[41 FR 53329, Dec. 6, 1976, as amended at 47 FR 56314, Dec. 16, 1982; 69 FR 2264, Jan. 14, 2004]

§ 2.903 Protection of restricted data and national security information.

Nothing in this subpart shall relieve any person from safeguarding Restricted Data or National Security Information in accordance with the applicable provisions of laws of the United States and rules, regulations or orders of any Government Agency.

§ 2.904 Classification assistance.

On request of any party to a proceeding or of the presiding officer, the Commission will designate a representative to advise and assist the presiding officer and the parties with respect to security classification of information and the safeguards to be observed.

§ 2.905 Access to restricted data and national security information for parties; security clearances.

(a) *Access to restricted data and national security information introduced into proceedings.* Except as provided in paragraph (h) of this section, restricted data or national security information introduced into a proceeding subject to this part will be made available to any interested party having the required security clearance; to counsel for an interested party provided the counsel has the required security clearance; and to such additional persons having the required security clearance as the Commission or the presiding officer determined are needed by such party for adequate preparation or presentation of his case. Where the interest of such party will not be prejudiced, the Commission or presiding officer may postpone action upon an application for access under this paragraph until after a notice of hearing, answers, and replies have been filed.

(b) *Access to Restricted Data or National Security Information not introduced into proceedings.* (1) On application showing that access to Restricted Data or National Security Information may be required for the preparation of a party's case, and except as provided in paragraph (h) of this section, the Commission or the presiding officer will issue an order granting access to such Restricted Data or National Security Information to the party upon his obtaining the required security clearance, to counsel for the party upon their obtaining the required security clearance, and to such other individuals as may be needed by the party for the preparation and presentation of his case upon their obtaining the required clearance.

(2) Where the interest of the party applying for access will not be prejudiced, the Commission or the presiding officer may postpone action on an application pursuant to this paragraph until after a notice of hearing, answers and replies have been filed.

(c) The Commission will consider requests for appropriate security clearances in reasonable numbers pursuant to this section. A reasonable charge will be made by the Commission for costs of security clearance pursuant to this section.

(d) The presiding officer may certify to the Commission for its consideration and determination any questions relating to access to Restricted Data or National Security Information arising under this section. Any party affected by a determination or order of the presiding officer under this section may appeal forthwith to the Commission from the determination or order. The filing by the staff of an appeal from an order of a presiding officer granting access to Restricted Data or National Security Information shall stay the order pending determination of the appeal by the Commission.

(e) *Application granting access to restricted data or national security information.* (1) An application under this section for orders granting access to restricted data or national security information not received from another Government agency will normally be acted upon by the presiding officer, or if a proceeding is not before a presiding officer, by the Commission.

(2) An application under this section for orders granting access to restricted data or national security information where the information has been received by the Commission from another Government agency will be acted upon by the Commission.

(f) To the extent practicable, an application for an order granting access under this section shall describe the subjects of Restricted Data or National Security Information to which access is desired and the level of classification (confidential, secret or other) of the information; the reasons why access to the information is requested; the names of individuals for whom clearances are requested; and the reasons why security clearances are being requested for those individuals.

(g) On the conclusion of a proceeding, the Commission will terminate all orders issued in the proceeding for access to Restricted Data or National Security Information and all security clearances granted pursuant to them; and may issue such orders requiring the disposal of classified matter received pursuant to them or requiring the observance of other procedures to safeguard such classified matter as it deems necessary to protect Restricted Data or National Security Information.

(h) *Refusal to grant access to restricted data or national security information.* (1) The Commission will not grant access to restricted data or national security information unless it determines that the granting of access will not be inimical to the common defense and security.

(2) Access to Restricted Data or National Security Information which has been received by the Commission from another Government agency will not be granted by the Commission if the originating agency determines in writing that access should not be granted. The Commission will consult the originating agency prior to granting access to such data or information received from another Government agency.

§ 2.906 Obligation of parties to avoid introduction of restricted data or national security information.

It is the obligation of all parties in a proceeding subject to this part to avoid, where practicable, the introduction of Restricted Data or National Security Information into the proceeding. This obligation rests on each party whether or not all other parties have the required security clearance.

§ 2.907 Notice of intent to introduce restricted data or national security information.

(a) If, at the time of publication of a notice of hearing, it appears to the staff that it will be impracticable for it to avoid the introduction of Restricted Data or National Security Information into the proceeding, it will file a notice of intent to introduce Restricted Data or National Security Information.

(b) If, at the time of filing of an answer to the notice of hearing it appears to the party filing that it will be impracticable for the party to avoid the introduction of Restricted Data or National Security Information into the proceeding, the party shall state in the answer a notice of intent to introduce Restricted Data or National Security Information into the proceeding.

(c) If, at any later stage of a proceeding, it appears to any party that it will be impracticable to avoid the introduction of Restricted Data or National Security Information into the proceeding, the party shall give to the other parties prompt written notice of intent to introduce Restricted Data or National Security Information into the proceeding.

(d) Restricted Data or National Security Information shall not be introduced into a proceeding after publication of a notice of hearing unless a notice of intent has been filed in accordance with § 2.908, except as permitted in the discretion of the presiding officer when it is clear that no party or the public interest will be prejudiced.

§ 2.908 Contents of notice of intent to introduce restricted data or other national security information.

(a) A party who intends to introduce Restricted Data or other National Security Information shall file a notice of intent with the Secretary. The notice shall be unclassified and, to the extent consistent with classification requirements, shall include the following:

(1) The subject matter of the Restricted Data or other National Security Information which it is anticipated will be involved;

(2) The highest level of classification of the information (confidential, secret, or other);

(3) The stage of the proceeding at which he anticipates a need to introduce the information; and

(4) The relevance and materiality of the information to the issues on the proceeding.

(b) In the discretion of the presiding officer, such notice, when required by

§ 2.907(c), may be given orally on the record.

§ 2.909 Rearrangement or suspension of proceedings.

In any proceeding subject to this part where a party gives a notice of intent to introduce Restricted Data or other National Security Information, and the presiding officer determines that any other interested party does not have required security clearances, the presiding officer may in his discretion:

(a) Rearrange the normal order of the proceeding in a manner which gives such interested parties an opportunity to obtain required security clearances with minimum delay in the conduct of the proceeding.

(b) Suspend the proceeding or any portion of it until all interested parties have had opportunity to obtain required security clearances. No proceeding shall be suspended for such reasons for more than 100 days except with the consent of all parties or on a determination by the presiding officer that further suspension of the proceeding would not be contrary to the public interest.

(c) Take such other action as he determines to be in the best interest of all parties and the public.

§ 2.910 Unclassified statements required.

(a) Whenever Restricted Data or other National Security Information is introduced into a proceeding, the party offering it shall submit to the presiding officer and to all parties to the proceeding an unclassified statement setting forth the information in the classified matter as accurately and completely as possible.

(b) In accordance with such procedures as may be agreed upon by the parties or prescribed by the presiding officer, and after notice to all parties and opportunity to be heard thereon, the presiding officer shall determine whether the unclassified statement or any portion of it, together with any appropriate modifications suggested by any party, may be substituted for the classified matter or any portion of it without prejudice to the interest of any party or to the public interest.

(c) If the presiding officer determines that the unclassified statement, together with such unclassified modifications as he finds are necessary or appropriate to protect the interest of other parties and the public interest, adequately sets forth information in the classified matter which is relevant and material to the issues in the proceeding, he shall direct that the classified matter be excluded from the record of the proceeding. His determination will be considered by the Commission as a part of the decision in the event of review.

(d) If the presiding officer determines that an unclassified statement does not adequately present the information contained in the classified matter which is relevant and material to the issues in the proceeding, he shall include his reasons in his determination. This determination shall be included as part of the record and will be considered by the Commission in the event of review of the determination.

(e) The presiding officer may postpone all or part of the procedures established in this section until the reception of all other evidence has been completed. Service of the unclassified statement required in paragraph (a) of this section shall not be postponed if any party does not have access to Restricted Data or other National Security Information.

§ 2.911 Admissibility of restricted data or other national security information.

A presiding officer shall not receive any Restricted Data or other National Security Information in evidence unless:

(a) The relevance and materiality of the Restricted Data or other National Security Information to the issues in the preceeding, and its competence, are clearly established; and

(b) The exclusion of the Restricted Data or other National Security Information would prejudice the interests of a party or the public interest.

§ 2.912 Weight to be attached to classified evidence.

In considering the weight and effect of any Restricted Data or other National Security Information received in evidence to which an interested party has not had opportunity to receive access, the presiding officer and the Commission shall give to such evidence such weight as is appropriate under the circumstances, taking into consideration any lack of opportunity to rebut or impeach the evidence.

§ 2.913 Review of Restricted Data or other National Security Information received in evidence.

At the close of the reception of evidence, the presiding officer shall review the record and shall direct that any Restricted Data or other National Security Information be expunged from the record where such expunction would not prejudice the interests of a party or the public interest. Such directions by the presiding officer will be considered by the Commission in the event of review of the determinations of the presiding officer.

Subpart J—Procedures Applicable to Proceedings for the Issuance of Licenses for the Receipt of High-Level Radioactive Waste at a Geologic Repository

SOURCE: 54 FR 14944, Apr. 14, 1989, unless otherwise noted.

§ 2.1000 Scope of subpart J.

The rules in this subpart, together with the rules in subparts C and G of this part, govern the procedure for an application for authorization to construct a high-level radioactive waste repository at a geologic repository operations area noticed under §§ 2.101(f)(8) or 2.105(a)(5), and for an application for a license to receive and possess high level radioactive waste at a geologic repository operations area. The procedures in this subpart take precedence over those in 10 CFR part 2, subpart C, except for the following provisions: §§ 2.301; 2.303; 2.307; 2.309; 2.312; 2.313; 2.314; 2.315; 2.316; 2.317(a); 2.318; 2.319; 2.320; 2.321; 2.322; 2.323; 2.324; 2.325; 2.326; 2.327; 2.328; 2.330; 2.331; 2.333; 2.335; 2.338; 2.339; 2.342; 2.343; 2.344; 2.345; 2.346; 2.348; and 2.390. The procedures in this subpart take precedence over those in 10 CFR part 2, subpart G, except for the following provisions: §§ 2.701, 2.702; 2.703; 2.708; 2.709; 2.710; 2.711; 2.712.

[69 FR 2264, Jan. 14, 2004]

§ 2.1001 Definitions.

Bibliographic header means the minimum series of descriptive fields that a potential party, interested governmental participant, or party must submit with a document or other material.

Circulated draft means a nonfinal document circulated for supervisory concurrence or signature in which the original author or others in the concurrence process have non-concurred. A "circulated draft" meeting the above criterion includes a draft of a document that eventually becomes a final document, and a draft of a document that does not become a final document due to either a decision not to finalize the document or the passage of a substantial period of time in which no action has been taken on the document.

Complex document means a document that consists (entirely or in part) of electronic files having substantial portions that are neither textual nor image in nature, and graphic or other Binary Large Objects that exceed 50 megabytes and cannot logically be divided. For example, specialized submissions may include runtime executable software, viewer or printer executables, dynamic link library (.dll) files, large data sets associated with an executable, and actual software code for analytical programs that a party may intend to introduce into the proceeding.

Document means any written, printed, recorded, magnetic, graphic matter, or other documentary material, regardless of form or characteristic.

Documentary material means:

(1) Any information upon which a party, potential party, or interested governmental participant intends to rely and/or to cite in support of its position in the proceeding for a construction authorization for a high-level radioactive waste repository at a geologic repository operations area pursuant to parts 60 or 63 of this chapter, a license to receive and possess high-level radioactive waste at a geologic repository operations area pursuant to parts 60 or 63 of this chapter;

(2) Any information that is known to, and in the possession of, or developed

by the party that is relevant to, but does not support, that information or that party's position; and

(3) All reports and studies, prepared by or on behalf of the potential party, interested governmental participant, or party, including all related "circulated drafts," relevant to both the license application and the issues set forth in the Topical Guidelines in Regulatory Guide 3.69, regardless of whether they will be relied upon and/or cited by a party. The scope of documentary material shall be guided by the topical guidelines in the applicable NRC Regulatory Guide.

DOE means the U.S. Department of Energy or its duly authorized representatives.

Electronic docket means the NRC information system that receives, distributes, stores, and retrieves the Commission's adjudicatory docket materials.

Image means a visual likeness of a document, presented on a paper copy, microform, or a bit-map on optical or magnetic media.

Interested governmental participant means any person admitted under § 2.315(c) of this part to the proceeding on an application for a construction authorization for a high-level radioactive waste repository at a geologic repository operations area under parts 60 or 63 of this chapter, and an application for a license to receive and possess high level radioactive waste at a geologic repository operations area under parts 60 and 63 of this chapter.

Large document means a document that consists of electronic files that are larger than 50 megabytes.

Licensing Support Network means the combined system that makes documentary material available electronically to parties, potential parties, and interested governmental participants to a proceeding for a construction authorization for a high-level radioactive waste repository at a geologic repository operations area, and an application for a license to receive and possess high level radioactive waste at a geologic repository operations area under parts 60 and 63 of this chapter.

LSN Administrator means the person within the U.S. Nuclear Regulatory Commission responsible for coordinating access to and the integrity of data available on the Licensing Support Network. The LSN Administrator shall not be in any organizational unit that either represents the U.S. Nuclear Regulatory Commission staff as a party to the high-level waste repository licensing proceeding or is a part of the management chain reporting to the Director, Office of Nuclear Material Safety and Safeguards. For the purposes of this subpart, the organizational unit within the NRC selected to be the LSN Administrator shall not be considered to be a party to the proceeding.

Marginalia means handwritten, printed, or other types of notations added to a document excluding underlining and highlighting.

NRC means the U.S. Nuclear Regulatory Commission or its duly authorized representatives.

Party for the purpose of this subpart means the DOE, the NRC staff, the host State, any affected unit of local government as defined in Section 2 of the Nuclear Waste Policy Act of 1982, as amended (42 U.S.C. 10101), any affected Indian Tribe as defined in section 2 of the Nuclear Waste Policy Act of 1982, as amended (42 U.S.C. 10101), and a person admitted under § 2.309 to the proceeding on an application for construction authorization for a high-level radioactive waste repository at a geologic repository operations area under parts 60 or 63 of this chapter, and an application for a license to receive and possess high level radioactive waste at a geologic repository operations area under parts 60 and 63 of this chapter; provided that a host State, affected unit of local government, or affected Indian Tribe files a list of contentions in accordance with the provisions of § 2.309.

Personal record means a document in the possession of an individual associated with a party, interested governmental participant, or potential party that was not required to be created or retained by the party, interested governmental participant, or potential party, and can be retained or discarded at the possessor's sole discretion, or documents of a personal nature that are not associated with any business of the party, interested governmental participant, or potential party.

Potential party means any person who, during the period before the issuance of the first pre-hearing conference order under §2.1021(d), is given access to the Licensing Support Network and who consents to comply with the regulations set forth in subpart J of this part, including the authority of the Pre-License Application Presiding Officer designated pursuant to §2.1010.

Pre-license application electronic docket means the NRC's electronic information system that receives, distributes, stores, and maintains NRC pre-license application docket materials during the pre-license application phase.

Pre-license application phase means the time period before a construction authorization for a high-level radioactive waste repository at a geologic repository operations area under parts 60 or 63 of this chapter is docketed under §2.101(f)(3), and the time period before a license application to receive and possess high-level radioactive waste at a geologic repository operations area under parts 60 or 63 is docketed under §2.101(f)(3).

Pre-License Application Presiding Officer means one or more members of the Commission, or an atomic safety and licensing board, or a named officer who has been delegated final authority in the pre-license application phase with jurisdiction specified at the time of designation.

Preliminary draft means any nonfinal document that is not a circulated draft.

Presiding Officer means one or more members of the Commission, or an atomic safety and licensing board, or a named officer who has been delegated final authority in the matter, designated in the notice of hearing to preside.

Searchable full text means the electronic indexed entry of a document that allows the identification of specific words or groups of words within a text file.

Simple document means a document that consists of electronic files that are 50 megabytes or less.

Topical Guidelines means the set of topics set forth in Regulatory Guide 3.69, Topical Guidelines for the Licensing Support System, which are intended to serve as guidance on the scope of "documentary material".

[54 FR 14944, Apr. 14, 1989, as amended at 56 FR 7795, Feb. 26, 1991; 63 FR 71736, Dec. 30, 1998; 66 FR 29465, May 31, 2001; 66 FR 55788, Nov. 2, 2001; 69 FR 2264, Jan. 14, 2004; 69 FR 32848, June 14, 2004]

§2.1002 [Reserved]

§2.1003 Availability of material.

(a) Subject to the exclusions in §2.1005 and paragraphs (b), (c), and (e) of this section, DOE shall make available, no later than six months in advance of submitting its license application for a geologic repository, the NRC shall make available no later than thirty days after the DOE certification of compliance under §2.1009(b), and each other potential party, interested governmental participant or party shall make available no later than ninety days after the DOE certification of compliance under §2.1009(b)—

(1) An electronic file including bibliographic header for all documentary material (including circulated drafts but excluding preliminary drafts) generated by, or at the direction of, or acquired by, a potential party, interested governmental participant or party; provided, however, that an electronic file need not be provided for acquired documentary material that has already been made available by the potential party, interested governmental participant or party that originally created the documentary material. Concurrent with the production of the electronic files will be an authentication statement for posting on the LSN Web site that indicates where an authenticated image copy of the documents can be obtained.

(2) In electronic image format, subject to the claims of privilege in §2.1006, graphic-oriented documentary material that includes raw data, computer runs, computer programs and codes, field notes, laboratory notes, maps, diagrams and photographs, which have been printed, scripted, or hand written. Text embedded within these documents need not be separately entered in searchable full text.

A bibliographic header must be provided for all graphic-oriented documentary material. Graphic-oriented documents may include—

(i) Calibration procedures, logs, guidelines, data and discrepancies;

(ii) Gauge, meter and computer settings;

(iii) Probe locations;

(iv) Logging intervals and rates;

(v) Data logs in whatever form captured;

(vi) Text data sheets;

(vii) Equations and sampling rates;

(viii) Sensor data and procedures;

(ix) Data Descriptions;

(x) Field and laboratory notebooks;

(xi) Analog computer, meter or other device print-outs;

(xii) Digital computer print-outs;

(xiii) Photographs;

(xiv) Graphs, plots, strip charts, sketches;

(xv) Descriptive material related to the information identified in this paragraph.

(3) In an electronic file, subject to the claims of privilege in § 2.1006, only a bibliographic header for each item of documentary material that is not suitable for image or searchable full text.

(4) An electronic bibliographic header for each documentary material—

(i) For which a claim of privilege is asserted;

(ii) Which constitutes confidential financial or commercial information; or

(iii) Which constitutes Safeguards Information under § 73.21 and the requirements of § 73.22 or § 73.23 of this chapter, as applicable.

(b) Basic licensing documents generated by DOE, such as the Site Characterization Plan, the Environmental Impact Statement, and the license application, or by NRC, such as the Site Characterization Analysis, and the Safety Evaluation Report, shall be made available in electronic form by the respective agency that generated the document.

(c) The participation of the host State in the pre-license application phase shall not affect the State's ability to exercise its disapproval rights under section 116(b)(2) of the Nuclear Waste Policy Act, as amended, 42 U.S.C. 10136(b)(2).

(d) This subpart shall not affect any independent right of a potential party, interested governmental participant or party to receive information.

(e) Each potential party, interested governmental participant or party shall continue to supplement its documentary material made available to other participants via the LSN with any additional material created after the time of its initial certification in accordance with paragraph (a)(1) through (a)(4) of this section until the discovery period in the proceeding has concluded.

[63 FR 71737, Dec. 30, 1998, as amended at 66 FR 29465, May 31, 2001; 69 FR 2264, Jan. 14, 2004; 69 FR 32848, June 14, 2004; 73 FR 63569, Oct. 24, 2008]

§ 2.1004 Amendments and additions.

Any document that has not been provided to other parties in electronic form must be identified in an electronic notice and made available for inspection and copying by the potential party, interested governmental participant, or party responsible for the submission of the document within five days after it has been requested unless some other time is approved by the Pre-License Application Presiding Officer or the Presiding Officer designated for the high-level waste proceeding. The time allowed under this paragraph will be stayed pending Officer action on a motion to extend the time.

[63 FR 71737, Dec. 30, 1998]

§ 2.1005 Exclusions.

The following material is excluded from the requirement to provide electronic access, either pursuant to § 2.1003, or through derivative discovery pursuant to § 2.1019(i)—

(a) Official notice materials;

(b) Reference books and text books;

(c) Material pertaining exclusively to administration, such as material related to budgets, financial management, personnel, office space, general distribution memoranda, or procurement, except for the scope of work on a procurement related to repository siting, construction, or operation, or to the transportation of spent nuclear fuel or high-level waste;

(d) Press clippings and press releases;

(e) Junk mail;

(f) References cited in contractor reports that are readily available;

(g) Classified material subject to subpart I of this part;

(h) Readily available references, such as journal articles and proceedings, which may be subject to copyright.

(i) Correspondence between a potential party, interested governmental participant, or party and the Congress of the United States.

[63 FR 71738, Dec. 30, 1998, as amended at 69 FR 32848, June 14, 2004]

§ 2.1006 Privilege.

(a) Subject to the requirements in § 2.1003(a)(4), the traditional discovery privileges recognized in NRC adjudicatory proceedings and the exceptions from disclosure in § 2.390 may be asserted by potential parties, interested States, local governmental bodies, Federally-recognized Indian Tribes, and parties. In addition to Federal agencies, the deliberative process privilege may also be asserted by States, local governmental bodies, and Federally-recognized Indian Tribes.

(b) Any document for which a claim of privilege is asserted, but is denied in whole or in part by the Pre-License Application Presiding Officer or the Presiding Officer, must be provided in electronic form by the party, interested governmental participant, or potential party that asserted the claim to—

(1) The other participants; or

(2) To the Pre-License Application Presiding Officer or to the Presiding Officer, for entry into a Protective Order file, if the Pre-License Application Presiding Officer or the Presiding Officer so directs under §§ 2.1010(b) or 2.1018(c).

(c) Notwithstanding any availability of the deliberative process privilege under paragraph (a) of this section, circulated drafts not otherwise privileged shall be provided for electronic access pursuant to § 2.1003(a).

[63 FR 71738, Dec. 30, 1998; 64 FR 15920, Apr. 2, 1999, as amended at 69 FR 2265, Jan. 14, 2004]

§ 2.1007 Access.

(a)(1) A system to provide electronic access to the Licensing Support Network shall be provided at the headquarters of DOE, and at all DOE Local Public Document Rooms established in the vicinity of the likely candidate site for a geologic repository, beginning in the pre-license application phase.

(2) A system to provide electronic access to the Licensing Support Network shall be provided at the NRC Web site, *http://www.nrc.gov*, and/or at the NRC Public Document Room beginning in the pre-license application phase.

(3) [Reserved]

(b) Public availability of paper and electronic copies of the records of NRC and DOE, as well as duplication fees, and fee waiver for those records, is governed by the regulations of the respective agencies.

[63 FR 71738, Dec. 30, 1998, as amended at 64 FR 48949, Sept. 9, 1999]

§ 2.1008 [Reserved]

§ 2.1009 Procedures.

(a) Each potential party, interested governmental participant, or party shall—

(1) Designate an official who will be responsible for administration of its responsibility to provide electronic files of documentary material ;

(2) Establish procedures to implement the requirements in § 2.1003;

(3) Provide training to its staff on the procedures for implementation of the responsibility to provide electronic files of documentary material;

(4) Ensure that all documents carry the submitter's unique identification number;

(5) Cooperate with the advisory review process established by the NRC under § 2.1011(d).

(b) The responsible official designated under paragraph (a)(1) of this section shall certify to the Pre-License Application Presiding Officer that the procedures specified in paragraph (a)(2) of this section have been implemented, and that to the best of his or her knowledge, the documentary material specified in § 2.1003 has been identified and made electronically available. The initial certification must be made at the time the participant is required to comply with § 2.1003. The responsible official for the DOE shall also update this certification at the time DOE submits the license application.

[63 FR 71738, Dec. 30, 1998, as amended at 66 FR 29466, May 31, 2001]

§ 2.1010 Pre-License Application Presiding Officer.

(a)(1) The Commission may designate one or more members of the Commission, or an atomic safety and licensing board, or a named officer who has been delegated final authority on the matter to serve as the Pre-License Application Presiding Officer to rule on disputes over the electronic availability of documents during the pre-license application phase, including disputes relating to privilege, and disputes relating to the implementation of the recommendations of the Advisory Review Panel established under § 2.1011(d).

(2) The Pre-License Application Presiding Officer shall be designated at such time during the pre-license application phase as the Commission finds it appropriate, but in any event no later than fifteen days after the DOE certification of initial compliance under § 2.1009(b).

(b) The Pre-License Application Presiding Officer shall rule on any claim of document withholding to determine—

(1) Whether it is documentary material within the scope of this subpart;

(2) Whether the material is excluded under § 2.1005;

(3) Whether the material is privileged or otherwise excepted from disclosure under § 2.1006;

(4) If privileged, whether it is an absolute or qualified privilege;

(5) If qualified, whether the document should be disclosed because it is necessary to a proper decision in the proceeding;

(6) Whether the material should be disclosed under a protective order containing such protective terms and conditions (including affidavits of nondisclosure) as may be necessary and appropriate to limit the disclosure to potential parties, interested governmental participants, and parties in the proceeding, or to their qualified witnesses and counsel.

(i) The Pre-License Application Presiding Officer may issue an order requiring disclosure of Safeguards Information if—

(A) The Pre-License Application Presiding Officer finds that the individual seeking access to Safeguards Information in order to participate in an NRC adjudication has the requisite "need to know," as defined in 10 CFR 73.2;

(B) The individual has undergone an FBI criminal history records check, unless exempt under 10 CFR 73.22(b)(3) or 73.23(b)(3), as applicable, by submitting fingerprints to the NRC Office of Administration, Security Processing Unit, Mail Stop T–6E46, U.S. Nuclear Regulatory Commission, Washington, DC 20555–0001, and otherwise following the procedures in 10 CFR 73.57(d) for submitting and processing fingerprints. However, before a final adverse determination by the NRC Office of Administration on an individual's criminal history records check is made, the individual shall be afforded the protections provided by 10 CFR 73.57; and

(C) The NRC Office of Administration has found, based upon a background check, that the individual is trustworthy and reliable, unless exempt under 10 CFR 73.22(b)(3) or 73.23(b)(3), as applicable. In addition to the protections provided by 10 CFR 73.57 for adverse determinations based on criminal history records checks, the Office of Administration must take the following actions before making a final adverse determination on an individual's background check for trustworthiness and reliability. The Office of Administration will:

(*1*) For the purpose of assuring correct and complete information, provide to the individual any records, in addition to those required to be provided under 10 CFR 73.57(e)(1), that were considered in the trustworthiness and reliability determination;

(*2*) Resolve any challenge by the individual to the completeness or accuracy of the records described in § 2.1010(b)(6)(i)(C)(1). The individual may make this challenge by submitting information and/or an explanation to the Office of Administration. The challenge must be submitted within 10 days of the distribution of the records described in § 2.1010(b)(6)(i)(C)(1), and the Office of Administration must promptly resolve any challenge.

(D) Individuals seeking access to Safeguards Information to participate in an NRC adjudication for whom the NRC Office of Administration has made a final adverse determination on trustworthiness and reliability may submit a request to the Chief Administrative Judge for review of the adverse determination. Upon receiving such a request, the Chief Administrative Judge shall designate an officer other than the Pre-License Application Presiding Officer to review the adverse determination. For purposes of review, the adverse determination must be in writing and set forth the grounds for the determination. The request for review shall be served on the NRC staff and may include additional information for review by the designated officer. The request must be filed within 15 days after receipt of the adverse determination by the person against whom the adverse determination has been made. Within 10 days of receipt of the request for review and any additional information, the NRC staff will file a response indicating whether the request and additional information has caused the NRC Office of Administration to reverse its adverse determination. The designated officer may reverse the Office of Administration's final adverse determination only if the officer finds, based on all the information submitted, that the adverse determination constitutes an abuse of discretion. The designated officer's decision must be rendered within 15 days after receipt of the staff filing indicating that the request for review and additional information has not changed the NRC Office of Administration's adverse determination.

(ii) The Pre-License Application Presiding Officer may include in an order any protective terms and conditions (including affidavits of nondisclosure) as may be necessary and appropriate to prevent the unauthorized disclosure of Safeguards Information.

(iii) When Safeguards Information, protected from disclosure under Section 147 of the Atomic Energy Act of 1954, as amended, is received and possessed by a potential party, interested government participant, or party, other than the NRC staff, it shall also be protected according to the requirements of §73.21 and the requirements of §§73.22 or 73.23 of this chapter, as applicable.

(iv) The Pre-License Application Presiding Officer may also prescribe such additional procedures as will effectively safeguard and prevent disclosure of Safeguards Information to unauthorized persons with minimum impairment of the procedural rights which would be available if Safeguards Information were not involved.

(v) In addition to any other sanction that may be imposed by the Pre-License Application Presiding Officer for violation of a provision for the protection of Safeguards Information from unauthorized disclosure that is contained in an order, the entity in violation may be subject to a civil penalty imposed pursuant to §2.205.

(vi) For the purpose of imposing the criminal penalties contained in Section 223 of the Atomic Energy Act of 1954, as amended, a provision for the protection of Safeguards Information from unauthorized disclosure that is contained in an order issued pursuant to this paragraph is considered to be issued under Section 161b of the Atomic Energy Act of 1954, as amended.

(c) Upon a final determination that the material is relevant, and not privileged, exempt from disclosure, or otherwise exempt from production under §2.1005, the potential party, interested governmental participant, or party who asserted the claim of withholding must make the document available in accordance with the provisions of this subpart within five days.

(d) The service of all pleadings and answers, orders, and decisions during the pre-license application phase shall be made according to the procedures specified in §2.1013(c) and entered into the pre-license application electronic docket.

(e) The Pre-License Application presiding officer possesses all the general powers specified in §§2.319 and 2.321(c).

(f) The Commission, in designating the Pre-License Application Presiding Officer in accordance with paragraphs

(a) (1) and (2) of this section, shall specify the jurisdiction of the Officer.

[63 FR 71738, Dec. 30, 1998, as amended at 66 FR 29466, May 31, 2001; 69 FR 2265, Jan. 14, 2004; 73 FR 63569, Oct. 24, 2008]

§ 2.1011 Management of electronic information.

(a) Electronic document production and the electronic docket are subject to the provisions of this subpart.

(b)(1) The NRC, DOE, parties, and potential parties participating in accordance with the provision of this subpart shall be responsible for obtaining the computer system necessary to comply with the requirements for electronic document production and service.

(2) The NRC, DOE, parties, and potential parties participating in accordance with the provision of this subpart shall comply with the following standards in the design of the computer systems necessary to comply with the requirements for electronic document production and service:

(i) The participants shall make textual (or, where non-text, image) versions of their documents available on a web accessible server which is able to be canvassed by web indexing software (*i.e.*, a "robot", "spider", "crawler") and the participant system must make both data files and log files accessible to this software.

(ii) The participants shall make bibliographic header data available in an HTTP (Hypertext Transfer Protocol) accessible, ODBC (Open Database Connectivity) and SQL (Structured Query Language)-compliant (ANSI IX3.135–1992/ISO 9075–1992) database management system (DBMS). Alternatively, the structured data containing the bibliographic header may be made available in a standard database readable (e.g., XML (Extensible Markup Language *http://www.w3.org/xml/*), comma delimited, or comma separated value (.csv)) file.

(iii) Textual material must be formatted to comply with the ISO/IEC 8859–1 character set and be in one of the following acceptable formats: ASCII, native word processing (Word, WordPerfect), PDF Normal, or HTML.

(iv) Image files must be formatted as TIFF CCITT G4 for bi-tonal images or PNG (Portable Network Graphics) per [*http://www.w3.org/TR/REC-png-multi.html*]) format for grey-scale or color images, or PDF (Portable Document Format—Image). TIFF, PDF, or PNG images will be stored at 300 dpi (dots per inch) or greater, grey scale images at 150 dpi or greater with eight bits of tonal depth, and color images at 150 dpi or greater with 24 bits of color depth. Images found on participant machines will be stored as single image-per-page to facilitate retrieval of no more than a single page, or alternatively, images may be stored in an image-per-document format if software is incorporated in the web server that allows image-per-page representation and delivery.

(v) The participants shall programmatically link, preferably via hyperlink or some other automated process, the bibliographic header record with the text or image file it represents. Each participant's system must afford the LSN software enough information to allow a text or image file to be identified to the bibliographic data that describes it.

(vi) To facilitate data exchange, participants shall adhere to hardware and software standards, including, but not limited to:

(A) Network access must be HTTP/1.1 [*http://www.faqs.org/rfcs/rfc2068.html*] over TCP (Transmission Control Protocol, [*http://www.faqs.org/rfcs/rfc793.html*]) over IP (Internet Protocol, [*http://www.faqs.org/rfcs/rfc791.html*]).

(B) Associating server names with IP addresses must follow the DNS (Domain Name System), [*http://www.faqs.org/rfcs/rfc1034.html*] and [*http://www.faqs.org/rfcs/rfc1035.html*].

(C) Web page construction must be HTML [*http://www.w3.org/TR/REC-html40/*].

(D) Electronic mail (e-mail) exchange between e-mail servers must be SMTP (Simple Mail Transport Protocol, [*http://www.faqs.org/rfcs/rfc821.html*]).

(E) Format of an electronic mail message must be per [*http://www.faqs.org/rfcs/rfc822.html*] optionally extended by MIME (Multipurpose Internet Mail Extensions) per [*http://www.faqs.org/rfcs/rfc2045.html*]) to accommodate multipurpose e-mail.

(c) The Licensing Support Network shall be coordinated by the LSN Administrator, who shall be designated before the start of the pre-license application phase. The LSN Administrator shall have the responsibility to—

(1) Identify technical and policy issues related to implementation of the LSN for LSN Advisory Review Panel and Commission consideration;

(2) Address the consensus advice of the LSN Advisory Review Panel under paragraph (e)(1) of this section that is consistent with the requirements of this subpart;

(3) Identify any problems experienced by participants regarding LSN availability, including the availability of individual participant's data, and provide a recommendation to resolve any such problems to the participant(s) and the Pre-License Application Presiding Officer relative to the resolution of any disputes regarding LSN availability, including disputes on the availability of an individual participant's data;

(4) Identify any problems regarding the integrity of documentary material certified in accordance with §2.1009(b) by the participants to be in the LSN, and provide a recommendation to resolve any such problems to the participant(s) and the Pre-License Application Presiding Officer relative to the resolution of any disputes regarding the integrity of documentary material;

(5) Provide periodic reports to the Commission on the status of LSN functionality and operability.

(6) Evaluate LSN participant compliance with the basic design standards in paragraph (b)(2) of this section, and provide for individual variances from the design standards to accommodate changes in technology or problems identified during initial operability testing of the individual documentary collection websites or the "central LSN site".

(7) Issue guidance for LSN participants on how best to comply with the design standards in paragraph (b)(2) of this section.

(d) The Secretary of the Commission shall reconstitute the LSS Advisory Review Panel as the LSN Advisory Review Panel, composed of the interests currently represented on the LSS Advisory Review Panel. The Secretary of the Commission shall have the authority to appoint additional representatives to the LSN Advisory Review Panel consistent with the requirements of the Federal Advisory Committee Act, 5 U.S.C. app. I, giving particular consideration to potential parties, parties, and interested governmental participants who were not members of the NRC HLW Licensing Support System Advisory Review Panel.

(e)(1) The LSN Advisory Review Panel shall provide advice to—

(i) NRC on the fundamental issues of the type of computer system necessary to access the Licensing Support Network effectively under paragraph (b) of this section; and

(ii) The Secretary of the Commission on the operation and maintenance of the electronic docket established for the HLW geologic repository licensing proceeding under the Commission's Rules of Practice (10 CFR part 2).

(iii) The LSN Administrator on solutions to improve the functioning of the LSN;

(2) The responsibilities of the LSN Advisory Review Panel shall include advice on—

(i) Format standards for providing electronic access to the documentary material certified by each participant to be made available in the LSN to the other parties, interested governmental participants, or potential parties;

(ii) The procedures and standards for the electronic transmission of filings, orders, and decisions during both the pre-license application phase and the high-level waste licensing proceeding;

(iii) Other duties as specified in this subpart or as directed by the Secretary of the Commission.

[63 FR 71739, Dec. 30, 1998, as amended at 66 FR 29466, May 31, 2001]

§2.1012 Compliance.

(a) If the Department of Energy fails to make its initial certification at least six months prior to tendering the application, upon receipt of the tendered application, notwithstanding the provisions of §2.101(f)(3), the Director of the NRC's Office of Nuclear Material Safety and Safeguards will not docket the application until at least six months have elapsed from the time of the certification. The Director may determine that the tendered application is not acceptable for docketing under this subpart if the application is not accompanied by an updated certification pursuant to § 2.1009(b), or if the Secretary of the Commission determines that the application is not submitted on optical storage media in a format consistent with NRC regulations and guidance, or for non-compliance with any other requirements identified in this subpart.

(b)(1) A person, including a potential party given access to the Licensing Support Network under this subpart, may not be granted party status under § 2.309, or status as an interested governmental participant under § 2.315, if it cannot demonstrate substantial and timely compliance with the requirements of § 2.1003 at the time it requests participation in the HLW licensing proceeding under § 2.309 or § 2.315.

(2) A person denied party status or interested governmental participant status under paragraph (b)(1) of this section may request party status or interested governmental participant status upon a showing of subsequent compliance with the requirements of § 2.1003. Admission of such a party or interested governmental participant under §§ 2.309 or 2.315, respectively, is conditioned on accepting the status of the proceeding at the time of admission.

(c) The Presiding Officer shall not make a finding of substantial and timely compliance pursuant to paragraph (b) of this section for any person who is not in compliance with all applicable orders of the Pre-License Application Presiding Officer designated pursuant to § 2.1010.

[54 FR 14944, Apr. 14, 1989, as amended at 56 FR 7796, Feb. 26, 1991; 63 FR 71739, Dec. 30, 1998; 66 FR 29466, May 31, 2001; 69 FR 2265, Jan. 14, 2004; 69 FR 32848, June 14, 2004]

§ 2.1013 Use of the electronic docket during the proceeding.

(a)(1) As specified in § 2.303, the Secretary of the Commission will maintain the official docket of the proceeding on the application for construction authorization for a high-level radioactive waste repository at a geologic repository operations area under parts 60 or 63 of this chapter, and for applications for a license to receive and possess high level radioactive waste at a geologic repository operations area under parts 60 or 63 of this Chapter.

(2) The Secretary of the Commission will establish an electronic docket to contain the official record materials of the high-level radioactive waste repository licensing proceeding in searchable full text, or, for material that is not suitable for entry in searchable full text, by header and image, as appropriate.

(b) Absent good cause, all exhibits tendered during the hearing must have been made available to the parties in electronic form before the commencement of that portion of the hearing in which the exhibit will be offered. The electronic docket will contain a list of all exhibits, showing where in the transcript each was marked for identification and where it was received into evidence or rejected. For any hearing sessions recorded stenographically or by other means, transcripts will be entered into the electronic docket on a daily basis in order to afford next-day availability at the hearing. However, for any hearing sessions recorded on videotape or other video medium, if a copy of the video recording is made available to all parties on a daily basis that affords next-day availability at the hearing, a transcript of the session prepared from the video recording will be entered into the electronic docket within twenty-four (24) hours of the time the transcript is tendered to the electronic docket by the transcription service.

(c)(1) All filings in the adjudicatory proceeding on the application for a high-level radioactive waste geologic repository under part 60 or 63 of this chapter shall be transmitted by the submitter to the Presiding Officer, parties, and Secretary of the Commission, according to the following requirements—

(i) "Simple documents" must be transmitted electronically via EIE;

(ii) "Large documents" must be transmitted electronically in multiple transmissions of 50 megabytes or less each via EIE;

(iii) "Complex documents":

(A) Those portions that can be electronically submitted through the EIE, in 50 MB or less segments, must be transmitted electronically, along with a transmittal letter; and

(B) Those portions that are not capable of being transmitted electronically must be submitted on optical storage media which must also include those portions of the document that had been or will be transmitted electronically.

(iv) Electronic submissions must have the following resolution—

(A) Electronic submissions of files created after January 1, 2004 must have 300 dots per inch (dpi) as the minimum resolution for bi-tonal, color, and grayscale, except in limited circumstances where submitters may need to use an image scanned before January 1, 2004, in a document created after January 1, 2004, or the scanning process for a large, one-page image may not successfully complete at the 300 dpi standard resolution.

(B) Electronic submissions of files created before January 1, 2004, or electronic submissions created after January 1, 2004, which cannot meet the 300 dpi standard for color and grayscale, must meet the standard for documents placed on LSN participant Web sites in §2.1011(b)(2)(iv) of this subpart, which is 150 dpi for color and grayscale documents and 300 dpi for bi-tonal documents.

(v) Electronic submissions must be generated in the appropriate PDF output format by using:

(A) PDF—Formatted Text and Graphics for textual documents converted from native applications;

(B) PDF—Searchable Image (Exact) for textual documents converted from scanned documents; and

(C) PDF—Image Only for graphic-, image-, and forms-oriented documents. In addition, Tagged Image File Format (TIFF) images and the results of spreadsheet applications must to be converted to PDF, except in those rare instances where PDF conversion is not practicable.

(vi) Electronic submissions must not rely on hyperlinks to other documents or Web sites for completeness or access except for hyperlinks that link to material within the same PDF file. If the submittal contains hyperlinks to other documents or Web sites, then it must include a disclaimer to the effect that the hyperlinks may be inoperable or are not essential to the use of the filing. Information contained in hyperlinks to a Web site on the Internet or to another PDF file, that is necessary for the completeness of a filing, must be submitted in its entirety in the filing or as an attachment to the filing.

(vii) All electronic submissions must be free of author-imposed security restrictions.

(2) Filings required to be served shall be served upon either the parties and interested governmental participants, or their designated representatives. When a party or interested governmental participant has appeared by attorney, service must be made upon the attorney of record.

(3) Service upon a party or interested governmental participant is completed when the sender receives electronic acknowledgment ("delivery receipt") that the electronic submission has been placed in the recipient's electronic mailbox.

(4) Proof of service, stating the name and address of the person on whom served and the manner and date of service, shall be shown for each document filed, by—

(i) Electronic acknowledgment ("delivery receipt");

(ii) The affidavit of the person making the service; or

(iii) The certificate of counsel.

(5) All Presiding Officer and Commission issuances and orders will be transmitted electronically to the parties and interested governmental participants.

(d) Online access to the electronic docket, including a Protective Order File if authorized by a Presiding Officer, shall be provided to the Presiding Officer, the representatives of the parties and interested governmental participants, and the witnesses while testifying, for use during the hearing. Use of paper copy and other images will also be permitted at the hearing.

[63 FR 71739, Dec. 30, 1998, as amended at 66 FR 55788, Nov. 2, 2001; 69 FR 2265, Jan. 14, 2004; 69 FR 32849, June 14, 2004]

§ 2.1015 Appeals.

(a) No appeals from any Pre-License Application Presiding Officer or Presiding Officer order or decision issued under this subpart are permitted, except as prescribed in paragraphs (b), (c), and (d) of this section.

(b) A notice of appeal from a Pre-License Application presiding officer order issued under § 2.1010, a presiding officer prehearing conference order issued under § 2.1021, a presiding officer order granting or denying a motion for summary disposition issued in accordance with § 2.1025, or a presiding officer order granting or denying a petition to amend one or more contentions under § 2.309, must be filed with the Commission no later than ten (10) days after service of the order. A supporting brief must accompany the notice of appeal. Any other party, interested governmental participant, or potential party may file a brief in opposition to the appeal no later than ten (10) days after service of the appeal.

(c) Appeals from a Presiding Officer initial decision or partial initial decision must be filed and briefed before the Commission in accordance with the following requirements.

(1) *Notice of appeal.* Within ten (10) days after service of an initial decision, any party may take an appeal to the Commission by filing a notice of appeal. The notice shall specify:

(i) The party taking the appeal; and

(ii) The decision being appealed.

(2) *Filing appellant's brief.* Each appellant shall file a brief supporting its position on appeal within thirty (30) days (40 days if Commission staff is the appellant) after the filing of notice required by paragraph (a) of this section.

(3) *Filing responsive brief.* Any party who is not an appellant may file a brief in support of or in opposition to the appeal within thirty (30) days after the period has expired for the filing and service of the brief of all appellants. Commission staff may file a responsive brief within forty (40) days after the period has expired for the filing and service of the briefs of all appellants. A responding party shall file a single responsive brief regardless of the number of appellants' briefs filed.

(4) *Brief content.* A brief in excess of ten (10) pages must contain a table of contents, with page references, and a table of cases (alphabetically arranged), statutes, regulations, and other authorities cited, with references to the pages of the brief where they are cited.

(i) An appellant's brief must clearly identify the errors of fact or law that are the subject of the appeal. An intervenor-appellant's brief must be confined to issues which the intervenor-appellant placed in controversy or sought to place in controversy in the proceeding. For each issue appealed, the precise portion of the record relied upon in support of the assertion of error must also be provided.

(ii) Each responsive brief must contain a reference to the precise portion of the record which supports each factual assertion made.

(5) *Brief length.* A party shall not file a brief in excess of seventy (70) pages in length, exclusive of pages containing the table of contents, table of citations and any addendum containing statutes, rules, regulations, etc. A party may request an increase of this page limit for good cause. Such a request shall be made by motion submitted at least seven (7) days before the date upon which the brief is due for filing and shall specify the enlargement requested.

(6) *Certificate of service.* All documents filed under this section must be accompanied by a certificate reflecting service upon all other parties to the proceeding.

(7) *Failure to comply.* A brief which in form or content is not in substantial compliance with the provisions of this section may be stricken, either on motion of a party or by the Commission on its own initiative.

(d) When, in the judgment of a Pre-License Application presiding officer or presiding officer, prompt appellate review of an order not immediately appealable under paragraph (b) of this section is necessary to prevent detriment to the public interest or unusual delay or expense, the Pre-License Application presiding officer or presiding officer may refer the ruling promptly to the Commission, and shall provide notice of this referral to the parties, interested governmental participants, or potential parties. The parties, interested governmental participants, or potential parties may also request that the Pre-License Application presiding officer or presiding officer certify under § 2.319 rulings not immediately appealable under paragraph (b) of this section.

(e) Unless otherwise ordered, the filing of an appeal, petition for review, referral, or request for certification of a ruling shall not stay the proceeding or extend the time for the performance of any act.

[56 FR 7797, Feb. 26, 1991, as amended at 56 FR 29410, June 27, 1991; 69 FR 2265, Jan. 14, 2004]

§ 2.1017 Computation of time.

In computing any period of time, the day of the act, event, or default after which the designated period of time begins to run is not included. The last day of the period so computed is included unless it is a Saturday, Sunday, or legal holiday at the place where the action or event is to occur, in which event the period runs until the end of the next day which is neither a Saturday, Sunday, nor holiday. Whenever a party, potential party, or interested governmental participant, has the right or is required to do some act within a prescribed period after the service of a notice or other document upon it, one day shall be added to the prescribed period. If the electronic docket is unavailable for more than four access hours of any day that would be counted in the computation of time, that day will not be counted in the computation of time.

[63 FR 71740, Dec. 30, 1998]

§ 2.1018 Discovery.

(a)(1) Parties, potential parties, and interested governmental participants in the high-level waste licensing proceeding may obtain discovery by one or more of the following methods:

(i) Access to the documentary material made available pursuant to § 2.1003;

(ii) Entry upon land for inspection, access to raw data, or other purposes pursuant to § 2.1020;

(iii) Access to, or the production of, copies of documentary material for which bibliographic headers only have been submitted pursuant to § 2.1003(a);

(iv) Depositions upon oral examination pursuant to § 2.1019;

(v) Requests for admissions pursuant to § 2.708;

(vi) Informal requests for information not made electronically available, such as the names of witnesses and the subjects they plan to address; and

(vii) Interrogatories and depositions upon written questions, as provided in paragraph (a)(2) of this section.

(2) Interrogatories and depositions upon written questions may be authorized by order of the discovery master appointed under paragraph (g) of this section, or if no discovery master has been appointed, by order of the Presiding Officer, in the event that the parties are unable, after informal good faith efforts, to resolve a dispute in a timely fashion concerning the production of information.

(b)(1) Parties, potential parties, and interested governmental participants, pursuant to the methods set forth in paragraph (a) of this section, may obtain discovery regarding any matter, not privileged, which is relevant to the licensing of the likely candidate site for a geologic repository, whether it relates to the claim or defense of the person seeking discovery or to the claim or defense of any other person. Except for discovery pursuant to §§ 2.1018(a)(2) and 2.1019 of this subpart, all other discovery shall begin during the pre-license application phase. Discovery pursuant to §§ 2.1018(a)(2) and 2.1019 of this subpart shall begin after the issuance of the first pre-hearing conference order under § 2.1021 of this subpart, and shall be limited to the issues defined in that order or subsequent amendments to the order. It is not ground for objection that the information sought will be inadmissible at the hearing if the information sought appears reasonably calculated to lead to the discovery of admissible evidence.

(2) A party, potential party, or interested governmental participant may obtain discovery of documentary material otherwise discoverable under paragraph (b)(1) of this section and prepared in anticipation of, or for the

hearing by, or for another party's, potential party's, or interested governmental participant's representative (including its attorney, surety, indemnitor, insurer, or similar agent) only upon a showing that the party, potential party, or interested governmental participant seeking discovery has substantial need of the materials in the preparation of its case and that it is unable without undue hardship to obtain the substantial equivalent of the materials by other means. In ordering discovery of these materials when the required showing has been made, the Presiding Officer shall protect against disclosure of the mental impressions, conclusions, opinions, or legal theories of an attorney or other representative of a party, potential party, or interested governmental participant concerning the proceeding.

(c)(1) Upon motion by a party, potential party, interested governmental participant, or the person from whom discovery is sought, and for good cause shown, the presiding officer may make any order that justice requires to protect a party, potential party, interested governmental participant, or other person from annoyance, embarrassment, oppression, or undue burden, delay, or expense, including one or more of the following:

(i) That the discovery not be had;

(ii) That the discovery may be had only on specified terms and conditions, including a designation of the time or place;

(iii) That the discovery may be had only by a method of discovery other than that selected by the party, potential party, or interested governmental participant seeking discovery;

(iv) That certain matters not be inquired into, or that the scope of discovery be limited to certain matters;

(v) That discovery be conducted with no one present except persons designated by the presiding officer;

(vi) That, subject to the provisions of § 2.390 of this part, a trade secret or other confidential research, development, or commercial information not be disclosed or be disclosed only in a designated way; or

(vii) That studies and evaluations not be prepared.

(2) If the motion for a protective order is denied in whole or in part, the presiding officer may, on such terms and conditions as are just, order that any party, potential party, interested governmental participant or other person provide or permit discovery.

(d) Except as provided in paragraph (b) of this section, and unless the Presiding Officer upon motion, for the convenience of parties, potential parties, interested governmental participants, and witnesses and in the interest of justice, orders otherwise, methods of discovery may be used in any sequence, and the fact that a party, potential party, or interested governmental participant is conducting discovery, whether by deposition or otherwise, shall not operate to delay any other party's, potential party's, or interested governmental participant's discovery.

(e) A party, potential party, or interested governmental participant who has made available in electronic form all material relevant to any discovery request or who has responded to a request for discovery with a response that was complete when made is under no duty to supplement its response to include information thereafter acquired, except as follows:

(1) To the extent that written interrogatories are authorized pursuant to paragraph (a)(2) of this section, a party or interested governmental participant is under a duty to seasonably supplement its response to any question directly addressed to (i) the identity and location of persons having knowledge of discoverable matters, and (ii) the identity of each person expected to be called as an expert witness at the hearing, the subject matter on which the witness is expected to testify, and the substance of the witness' testimony.

(2) A party, potential party, or interested governmental participant is under a duty seasonably to amend a prior response if it obtains information upon the basis of which (i) it knows that the response was incorrect when made, or (ii) it knows that the response though correct when made is no longer true and the circumstances are such that a failure to amend the response is in substance a knowing concealment.

(3) A duty to supplement responses may be imposed by order of the Presiding Officer or agreement of the parties, potential parties, and interested governmental participants.

(f)(1) If a deponent of a party, potential party, or interested governmental participant upon whom a request for discovery is served fails to respond or objects to the request, or any part thereof, the party, potential party, or interested governmental participant submitting the request or taking the deposition may move the Presiding Officer, within five days after the date of the response or after failure to respond to the request, for an order compelling a response in accordance with the request. The motion shall set forth the nature of the questions or the request, the response or objection of the party, potential party, interested governmental participant, or other person upon whom the request was served, and arguments in support of the motion. For purposes of this paragraph, an evasive or incomplete answer or response shall be treated as a failure to answer or respond. Failure to answer or respond shall not be excused on the ground that the discovery sought is objectionable unless the person, party, potential party, or interested governmental participant failing to answer or respond has applied for a protective order pursuant to paragraph (c) of this section.

(2) In ruling on a motion made pursuant to this section, the Presiding Officer may make such a protective order as it is authorized to make on a motion made pursuant to paragraph (c) of this section.

(3) An independent request for issuance of a subpoena may be directed to a nonparty for production of documents. This section does not apply to requests for the testimony of the NRC regulatory staff under § 2.709.

(g) The presiding officer, under § 2.322, may appoint a discovery master to resolve disputes between parties concerning informal requests for information as provided in paragraphs (a)(1) and (a)(2) of this section.

(h) Discovery under this section of documentary material including Safeguards Information referred to in Sections 147 and 181 of the Atomic Energy Act of 1954, as amended, will be according to the provisions in § 2.1010(b)(6)(i) through (b)(6)(vi).

[54 FR 14944, Apr. 14, 1989, as amended at 56 FR 7797, Feb. 26, 1991; 63 FR 71740, Dec. 30, 1998; 69 FR 2266, Jan. 14, 2004; 73 FR 63570, Oct. 24, 2008]

§ 2.1019 Depositions.

(a) Any party or interested governmental participant desiring to take the testimony of any person by deposition on oral examination shall, without leave of the Commission or the Presiding Officer, give reasonable notice in writing to every other party and interested governmental participant, to the person to be examined, and to the Presiding Officer of the proposed time and place of taking the deposition; the name and address of each person to be examined, if known, or if the name is not known, a general description sufficient to identify him or her or the class or group to which he or she belongs, the matters upon which each person will be examined and the name or descriptive title and address of the officer before whom the deposition is to be taken.

(b) Within the United States, a deposition may be taken before any officer authorized to administer oaths by the laws of the United States or of the place where the examination is held. Outside of the United States, a deposition may be taken before a secretary of an embassy or legation, a consul general, vice consul or consular agent of the United States, or a person authorized to administer oaths designated by the Commission. Depositions may be conducted by telephone or by video teleconference at the option of the party or interested governmental participant taking the deposition.

(c) The deponent shall be sworn or shall affirm before any questions are put to him or her. Examination and cross-examination shall proceed as at a hearing. Each question propounded shall be recorded and the answer taken down in the words of the witness. Objections on questions of evidence shall be noted in short form without the arguments. The officer shall not decide on the competency, materiality, or relevancy of evidence but shall record the evidence subject to objection. Objections on questions of evidence not made before the officer shall not be deemed waived unless the ground of the objection is one which might have been obviated or removed if presented at that time.

(d) When the testimony is fully transcribed, the deposition shall be submitted to the deponent for examination and signature unless the deponent is ill or cannot be found or refuses to sign. The officer shall certify the deposition or, if the deposition is not signed by the deponent, shall certify the reasons for the failure to sign, and shall promptly transmit an electronic copy of the deposition to the Secretary of the Commission for entry into the electronic docket.

(e) Where the deposition is to be taken on written questions as authorized under § 2.1018(a)(2), the party or interested governmental participant taking the deposition shall electronically serve a copy of the questions, showing each question separately and consecutively numbered, on every other party and interested governmental participant with a notice stating the name and address of the person who is to answer them, and the name, description, title, and address of the officer before whom they are to be asked. Within ten days after service, any other party or interested governmental participant may serve cross-questions. The questions, cross-questions, and answers shall be recorded and signed, and the deposition certified, returned, and transmitted in electronic form to the Secretary of the Commission for entry into the electronic docket as in the case of a deposition on oral examination.

(f) A deposition will not become a part of the evidentiary record in the hearing unless received in evidence. If only part of a deposition is offered in evidence by a party or interested governmental participant, any other party or interested governmental participant may introduce any other parts. A party or interested governmental participant shall not be deemed to make a person its own witness for any purpose by taking his or her deposition.

(g) A deponent whose deposition is taken and the officer taking a deposition shall be entitled to the same fees as are paid for like services in the district courts of the United States, to be paid by the party or interested governmental participant at whose instance the deposition is taken.

(h) The deponent may be accompanied, represented, and advised by legal counsel.

(i)(1) After receiving written notice of the deposition under paragraph (a) or paragraph (e) of this section, and ten days before the scheduled date of the deposition, the deponent shall submit an electronic index of all documents in his or her possession, relevant to the subject matter of the deposition, including the categories of documents set forth in paragraph (i)(2) of this section, to all parties and interested governmental participants. The index shall identify those records which have already been made available electronically. All documents that are not identical to documents already made available electronically, whether by reason of subsequent modification or by the addition of notations, shall be treated as separate documents.

(2) The following material is excluded from the initial requirements of § 2.1003 to be made available electronically, but is subject to derivative discovery under paragraph (i)(1) of this section—

(i) Personal records;

(ii) Travel vouchers;

(iii) Speeches;

(iv) Preliminary drafts;

(v) Marginalia.

(3) Subject to paragraph (i)(6) of this section, any party or interested governmental participant may request from the deponent a paper copy of any or all of the documents on the index that have not already been provided electronically.

(4) Subject to paragraph (i)(6) of this section, the deponent shall bring a paper copy of all documents on the index that the deposing party or interested governmental participant requests that have not already been provided electronically to an oral deposition conducted pursuant to paragraph (a) of this section, or in the case of a deposition taken on written questions pursuant to paragraph (e) of this section, shall submit such documents with the certified deposition.

(5) Subject to paragraph (i)(6) of this section, a party or interested governmental participant may request that any or all documents on the index that have not already been provided electronically, and on which it intends to rely at hearing, be made electronically available by the deponent.

(6) The deposing party or interested governmental participant shall assume the responsibility for the obligations set forth in paragraphs (i)(1), (i)(3), (i)(4), and (i)(5) of this section when deposing someone other than a party or interested governmental participant.

[54 FR 14944, Apr. 14, 1989, as amended at 56 FR 7797, Feb. 26, 1991; 63 FR 71740, Dec. 30, 1998; 69 FR 2266, Jan. 14, 2004]

§2.1020 Entry upon land for inspection.

(a) Any party, potential party, or interested governmental participant may serve on any other party, potential party, or interested governmental participant a request to permit entry upon designated land or other property in the possession or control of the party, potential party, or interested governmental participant upon whom the request is served for the purpose of access to raw data, inspection and measuring, surveying, photographing, testing, or sampling the property or any designated object or operation thereon, within the scope of §2.1018 of this subpart.

(b) The request may be served on any party, potential party, or interested governmental participant without leave of the Commission or the Presiding Officer.

(c) The request shall describe with reasonable particularity the land or other property to be inspected either by individual item or by category. The request shall specify a reasonable time, place, and manner of making the inspection and performing the related acts.

(d) The party, potential party, or interested governmental participant upon whom the request is served shall serve on the party, potential party, or interested governmental participant submitting the request a written response within ten days after the service of the request. The response shall state, with respect to each item or category, that inspection and related activities will be permitted as requested, unless the request is objected to, in which case the reasons for objection shall be stated. If objection is made to part of an item or category, the part shall be specified.

[54 FR 14944, Apr. 14, 1989, as amended at 56 FR 7797, Feb. 26, 1991]

§2.1021 First prehearing conference.

(a) In any proceeding involving an application for a construction authorization for a HLW repository at a geologic repository operations area under parts 60 or 63 of this chapter, or an application for a license to receive and possess high-level radioactive waste at a geologic repository operations area pursuant to parts 60 or 63 of this chapter, the Commission or the presiding officer will direct the parties, interested governmental participants and any petitioners for intervention, or their counsel, to appear at a specified time and place, within seventy days after the notice of hearing is published, or such other time as the Commission or the presiding officer may deem appropriate, for a conference to:

(1) Permit identification of the key issues in the proceeding;

(2) Take any steps necessary for further identification of the issues;

(3) Consider all intervention petitions to allow the Presiding Officer to make such preliminary or final determination as to the parties and interested governmental participants, as may be appropriate;

(4) Establish a schedule for further actions in the proceeding; and

(5) Establish a discovery schedule for the proceeding taking into account the objective of meeting the three year time schedule specified in section 114(d) of the Nuclear Waste Policy Act of 1982, as amended, 42 U.S.C. 10134(d).

(b) The Presiding Officer may order any further formal and informal conferences among the parties and interested governmental participants including teleconferences, to the extent that it considers that such a conference would expedite the proceeding.

(c) A prehearing conference held pursuant to this section shall be stenographically reported.

(d) The Presiding Officer shall enter an order which recites the action taken at the conference, the schedule for further actions in the proceeding, and any agreements by the parties, and which identifies the key issues in the proceeding, makes a preliminary or final determination as to the parties and interested governmental participants in the proceeding, and provides for the submission of status reports on discovery.

[54 FR 14944, Apr. 14, 1989, as amended at 56 FR 7797, Feb. 26, 1991; 66 FR 55788, Nov. 2, 2001; 69 FR 2266, Jan. 14, 2004]

§ 2.1022 Second prehearing conference.

(a) The Commission or the presiding officer in a proceeding on either an application for construction authorization for a high-level radioactive waste repository at a geologic repository operations area under parts 60 or 63 of this chapter, or an application for a license to receive and possess high-level radioactive waste at a geologic repository operations area under parts 60 or 63 of this chapter, shall direct the parties, interested governmental participants, or their counsel to appear at a specified time and place not later than thirty days after the Safety Evaluation Report is issued by the NRC staff for a conference to consider:

(1) Any amended contentions submitted, which must be reviewed under the criteria in § 2.309(c) of this part;

(2) Simplification, clarification, and specification of the issues;

(3) The obtaining of stipulations and admissions of fact and of the contents and authenticity of documents to avoid unnecessary proof;

(4) Identification of witnesses and the limitation of the number of expert witnesses, and other steps to expedite the presentation of evidence;

(5) The setting of a hearing schedule;

(6) Establishing a discovery schedule for the proceeding taking into account the objective of meeting the three year time schedule specified in section 114(d) of the Nuclear Waste Policy Act of 1982, as amended, 42 U.S.C. 10134(d); and

(7) Such other matters as may aid in the orderly disposition of the proceeding.

(b) A prehearing conference held pursuant to this section shall be stenographically reported.

(c) The Presiding Officer shall enter an order which recites the action taken at the conference and the agreements by the parties, limits the issues or defines the matters in controversy to be determined in the proceeding, sets a discovery schedule, and sets the hearing schedule.

[54 FR 14944, Apr. 14, 1989, as amended at 56 FR 7797, Feb. 26, 1991; 69 FR 2266, Jan. 14, 2004]

§ 2.1023 Immediate effectiveness.

(a) Pending review and final decision by the Commission, an initial decision resolving all issues before the presiding officer in favor of issuance or amendment of either an authorization to construct a high-level radioactive waste repository at a geological repository operations area under parts 60 or 63 of this chapter, or a license to receive and possess high-level radioactive waste at a geologic repository operations area under parts 60 or 63 of this chapter will be immediately effective upon issuance except:

(1) As provided in any order issued in accordance with § 2.342 that stays the effectiveness of an initial decision; or

(2) As otherwise provided by the Commission in special circumstances.

(b) The Director of Nuclear Material Safety and Safeguards, notwithstanding the filing or pendency of an appeal or a petition for review pursuant to § 2.1015 of this subpart, promptly shall issue a construction authorization or a license to receive and possess high-level radioactive waste at a geologic respository operations area, or amendments thereto, following an initial decision resolving all issues before the Presiding Officer in favor of the licensing action, upon making the appropriate licensing findings, except—

(1) As provided in paragraph (c) of this section; or

(2) As provided in any order issued in accordance with § 2.342 of this part that stays the effectiveness of an initial decision; or

(3) As otherwise provided by the Commission in special circumstances.

(c)(1) Before the Director of Nuclear Material Safety and Safeguards may issue a construction authorization or a license to receive and possess waste at a geologic repository operations area in accordance with paragraph (b) of this section, the Commission, in the exercise of its supervisory authority over agency proceedings, shall undertake and complete a supervisory examination of those issues contested in the proceeding before the Presiding Officer to consider whether there is any significant basis for doubting that the facility will be constructed or operated with adequate protection of the public health and safety, and whether the Commission should take action to suspend or to otherwise condition the effectiveness of a Presiding Officer decision that resolves contested issues in a proceeding in favor of issuing a construction authorization or a license to receive and possess high-level radioactive waste at a geologic repository operations area. This supervisory examination is not part of the adjudicatory proceeding. The Commission shall notify the Director in writing when its supervisory examination conducted in accordance with this paragraph has been completed.

(2) Before the Director of Nuclear Material Safety and Safeguards issues a construction authorization or a license to receive and possess high-level radioactive waste at a geologic repository operations area, the Commission shall review those issues that have not been contested in the proceeding before the Presiding Officer but about which the Director must make appropriate findings prior to the issuance of such a license. The Director shall issue a construction authorization or a license to receive and possess high-level radioactive waste at a geologic repository operations area only after written notification from the Commission of its completion of its review under this paragraph and of its determination that it is appropriate for the Director to issue such a construction authorization or license. This Commission review of uncontested issues is not part of the adjudicatory proceeding.

(3) No suspension of the effectiveness of a Presiding Officer's initial decision or postponement of the Director's issuance of a construction authorization or license that results from a Commission supervisory examination of contested issues under paragraph (c)(1) of this section or a review of uncontested issues under paragraph (c)(2) of this section will be entered except in writing with a statement of the reasons. Such suspension or postponement will be limited to such period as is necessary for the Commission to resolve the matters at issue. If the supervisory examination results in a suspension of the effectiveness of the Presiding Officer's initial decision under paragraph (c)(1) of this section, the Commission will take review of the decision sua sponte and further proceedings relative to the contested matters at issue will be in accordance with procedures for participation by the DOE, the NRC staff, or other parties and interested governmental participants to the Presiding Officer proceeding established by the Commission in its written statement of reasons. If a postponement results from a review under paragraph (c)(2) of this section, comments on the uncontested matters at issue may be filed by the DOE within ten days of service of the Commission's written statement.

[54 FR 14944, Apr. 14, 1989, as amended at 56 FR 7797, Feb. 26, 1991; 66 FR 55789, Nov. 2, 2001; 69 FR 2266, Jan. 14, 2004; 79 FR 66601, Nov. 10, 2014]

§ 2.1025 Authority of the Presiding Officer to dispose of certain issues on the pleadings.

(a) Any party may move, with or without supporting affidavits, for a decision by the Presiding Officer in that party's favor as to all or any part of the matters involved in the proceeding. The moving party shall annex to the motion a separate, short, and concise statement of the material facts as to which the moving party contends that there is no genuine issue to be heard. Motions may be filed at any time. Any other party may file an answer supporting or opposing the motion, with or without affidavits, within twenty (20) days after service of the motion. The party shall annex to any answer opposing the motion a separate, short, and concise, statement of the material facts as to which it is contended there exists a genuine issue to be heard. All material facts set forth in the statement to be filed by the moving party will be deemed to be admitted unless controverted by the statement required to be filed by the opposing party. The opposing party may, within ten (10) days after service, respond in writing to new facts and arguments presented in any statement filed in support of the motion. No further supporting statements or responses thereto may be entertained. The Presiding Officer may dismiss summarily or hold in abeyance motions filed shortly before the hearing commences or during the hearing if the other parties or the Presiding Officer would be required to divert substantial resources from the hearing in order to respond adequately to the motion.

(b) Affidavits must set forth those facts that would be admissible in evidence and show affirmatively that the affiant is competent to testify to the matters stated therein. The Presiding Officer may permit affidavits to be supplemented or opposed by further affidavits. When a motion for summary disposition is made and supported as provided in this section, a party opposing the motion may not rest upon the mere allegations or denials of its answer; its answer by affidavits or as otherwise provided in this section must set forth specific facts showing that there is a genuine issue of fact. If no such answer is filed, the decision sought, if appropriate, must be rendered.

(c) The Presiding Officer shall render the decision sought if the filings in the proceeding show that there is no genuine issue as to any material fact and that the moving party is entitled to a decision as a matter of law. However, in any proceeding involving a construction authorization for a geologic repository operations area, the procedure described in this section may be used only for the determination of specific subordinate issues and may not be used to determine the ultimate issue as to whether the authorization must be issued.

[56 FR 7798, Feb. 26, 1991]

§ 2.1026 Schedule.

(a) Subject to paragraphs (b) and (c) of this section, the Presiding Officer shall adhere to the schedule set forth in appendix D of this part.

(b)(1) Pursuant to § 2.307, the presiding officer may approve extensions of no more than fifteen (15) days beyond any required time set forth in this subpart for a filing by a party to the proceeding. Except in the case of exceptional and unforseen circumstances, requests for extensions of more than fifteen (15) days must be filed no later than five (5) days in advance of the required time set forth in this subpart for a filing by a party to the proceeding.

(2) Extensions beyond 15 days must be referred to the Commission. If the Commission does not disapprove the extension within 10 days of receiving the request, the extension will be effective. If the Commission disapproves the extension, the date which was the subject of the extension request will be set for 5 days after the Commission's disapproval action.

(c)(1) The Presiding Officer may delay the issuance of an order up to thirty days beyond the time set forth for the issuance in appendix D.

(2) If the Presiding Officer anticipates that the issuance of an order will not occur until after the thirty day extension specified in paragraph (c)(1) of this section, the Presiding Officer shall notify the Commission at least ten days in advance of the scheduled date for the milestone and provide a justification for the delay.

[56 FR 7798, Feb. 26, 1991, as amended at 69 FR 2266, Jan. 14, 2004]

§ 2.1027 Sua sponte.

In any initial decision in a proceeding on an application for a construction authorization for a high-level radioactive waste repository at a geologic repository operations area under parts 60 or 63 of this chapter, or an application for a license to receive and possess high-level radioactive waste at a geologic repository operations area under parts 60 or 63 of this chapter, the Presiding Officer, other than the Commission, shall make findings of fact and conclusions of law on, and otherwise give consideration to, only those matters put into controversy by the parties and determined to be litigable issues in the proceeding.

[69 FR 2266, Jan. 14, 2004]

Subpart K—Hybrid Hearing Procedures for Expansion of Spent Nuclear Fuel Storage Capacity at Civilian Nuclear Power Reactors

SOURCE: 50 FR 41670, Oct. 15, 1985, unless otherwise noted.

§2.1101 Purpose.

The regulations in this subpart establish hybrid hearing procedures, as authorized by section 134 of the Nuclear Waste Policy Act of 1982 (96 Stat. 2230), to be used at the request of any party in certain contested proceedings on applications for a license or license amendment to expand the spent nuclear fuel storage capacity at the site of a civilian nuclear power plant. These procedures are intended to encourage and expedite onsite expansion of spent nuclear fuel storage capacity.

§2.1103 Scope of subpart K.

The provisions of this subpart, together with subpart C and applicable provisions of subparts G and L of this part, govern all adjudicatory proceedings on applications filed after January 7, 1983, for a license or license amendment under part 50 of this chapter, to expand the spent fuel storage capacity at the site of a civilian nuclear power plant, through the use of high density fuel storage racks, fuel rod compaction, the transshipment of spent nuclear fuel to another civilian nuclear power reactor within the same utility system, the construction of additional spent nuclear fuel pool capacity or dry storage capacity, or by other means. This subpart also applies to proceedings on applications for a license under part 72 of this chapter to store spent nuclear fuel in an independent spent fuel storage installation located at the site of a civilian nuclear power reactor. This subpart shall not apply to the first application for a license or license amendment to expand the spent fuel storage capacity at a particular site through the use of a new technology not previously approved by the Commission for use at any other nuclear power plant. This subpart shall not apply to proceedings on applications for transfer of a license issued under part 72 of this chapter. Subpart M of this part applies to license transfer proceedings.

[69 FR 2266, Jan. 14, 2004]

§2.1105 Definitions.

As used in this part:

(a) *Civilian nuclear power reactor* means a civilian nuclear power plant required to be licensed as a utilization facility under section 103 or 104(b) of the Atomic Energy Act of 1954.

(b) *Spent nuclear fuel* means fuel that has been withdrawn from a nuclear reactor following irradiation, the constituent elements of which have not been separated by reprocessing.

§2.1107 Notice of proposed action.

In connection with each application filed after January 7, 1983, for a license or an amendment to a license to expand the spent nuclear fuel storage capacity at the site of a civilian nuclear power plant, for which the Commission has not found that a hearing is required in the public interest, for which an adjudicatory hearing has not yet been convened, and for which a notice of proposed action has not yet been published as of the effective date of this subpart, the Commission will, prior to acting thereon, cause to be published in the FEDERAL REGISTER a notice of proposed action in accordance with §2.105. The notice of proposed action will identify the availability of the hybrid hearing procedures in this subpart, specify that any party may invoke these procedures by filing a timely request for oral argument under §2.1109, and provide that if a request for oral argument is granted, any hearing held on the application shall be conducted in accordance with the procedures in this subpart.

§2.1109 Requests for oral argument.

(a)(1) In its request for hearing/petition to intervene filed in accordance with §2.309 or in the applicant's or the NRC staff's response to a request for a hearing/petition to intervene, any party may invoke the hybrid hearing procedures in this Subpart by requesting an oral argument. If it is determined that a hearing will be held, the presiding officer shall grant a timely request for oral argument.

(2) The presiding officer may grant an untimely request for oral argument only upon a showing of good cause by the requesting party for failure to file on time and after providing the other parties an opportunity to respond to the untimely request.

(b) The presiding officer shall issue a written order ruling on any requests for oral argument. If the presiding officer grants a request for oral argument, the order shall include a schedule for discovery and subsequent oral argument with respect to the admitted contentions.

(c) If no party to the proceeding requests oral argument, or if all untimely requests for oral argument are denied, the presiding officer shall conduct the proceeding in accordance with the subpart under which the proceeding was initially conducted as determined in accordance with § 2.310.

[50 FR 41670, Oct. 15, 1985, as amended at 69 FR 2267, Jan. 14, 2004]

§ 2.1113 Oral argument.

(a) Twenty-five (25) days prior to the date set for oral argument, each party, including the NRC staff, shall submit to the presiding officer a detailed written summary of all the facts, data, and arguments which are known to the party at such time and on which the party proposes to rely at the oral argument either to support or to refute the existence of a genuine and substantial dispute of fact. Each party shall also submit all supporting facts and data in the form of sworn written testimony or other sworn written submission. Each party's written summary and supporting information shall be simultaneously served on all other parties to the proceeding.

(b) Ten (10) days prior to the date set for oral argument, each party, including the NRC staff, may submit to the presiding officer a reply limited to addressing whether the written summaries, facts, data, and arguments filed under paragraph (a) of this section support or refute the existence of a genuine and substantial dispute of fact. Each party's reply shall be simultaneously served on all other parties to the proceeding.

(c) Only facts and data in the form of sworn written testimony or other sworn written submission may be relied on by the parties during oral argument, and the presiding officer shall consider those facts and data only if they are submitted in that form.

[50 FR 41670, Oct. 15, 1985, as amended at 69 FR 2267, Jan. 14, 2004]

§ 2.1115 Designation of issues for adjudicatory hearing.

(a) After due consideration of the oral presentation and the written facts and data submitted by the parties and relied on at the oral argument, the presiding officer shall promptly by written order:

(1) Designate any disputed issues of fact, together with any remaining issues of law, for resolution in an adjudicatory hearing; and

(2) Dispose of any issues of law or fact not designated for resolution in an adjudicatory hearing.

With regard to each issue designated for resolution in an adjudicatory hearing, the presiding officer shall identify the specific facts that are in genuine and substantial dispute, the reason why the decision of the Commission is likely to depend on the resolution of that dispute, and the reason why an adjudicatory hearing is likely to resolve the dispute. With regard to issues not designated for resolution in an adjudicatory hearing, the presiding officer shall include a brief statement of the reasons for the disposition. If the presiding officer finds that there are no disputed issues of fact or law requiring resolution in an adjudicatory hearing, the presiding officer shall also dismiss the proceeding.

(b) No issue of law or fact shall be designated for resolution in an adjudicatory hearing unless the presiding officer determines that:

(1) There is a genuine and substantial dispute of fact which can only be resolved with sufficient accuracy by the introduction of evidence in an adjudicatory hearing; and

(2) The decision of the Commission is likely to depend in whole or in part on the resolution of that dispute.

(c) In making a determination under paragraph (b) of this section, the presiding officer shall not consider:

(1) Any issue relating to the design, construction, or operation of any civilian nuclear power reactor already licensed to operate at the site, or any civilian nuclear power reactor for which a construction permit has been granted at the site, unless the presiding officer determines that any such issue substantially affects the design, construction, or operation of the facility or activity for which a license application, authorization, or amendment to expand the spent nuclear fuel storage capacity is being considered; or

(2) Any siting or design issue fully considered and decided by the Commission in connection with the issuance of a construction permit or operating license for a civilian nuclear power reactor at that site, unless (i) such issue results from any revision of siting or design criteria by the Commission following such decision; and (ii) the presiding officer determines that such issue substantially affects the design, construction, or operation of the facility or activity for which a license application, authorization, or amendment to expand the spent nuclear fuel storage capacity is being considered.

(d) The provisions of paragraph (c) of this section shall apply only with respect to licenses, authorizations, or amendments to licenses or authorizations applied for under the Atomic Energy Act of 1954, as amended, before December 31, 2005.

(e) Unless the presiding officer disposes of all issues and dismisses the proceeding, appeals from the presiding officer's order disposing of issues and designating one or more issues for resolution in an adjudicatory hearing are interlocutory and must await the end of the proceeding.

[50 FR 41671, Oct. 15, 1985; 50 FR 45398, Oct. 31, 1985]

§2.1117 Burden of proof.

The applicant bears the ultimate burden of proof (risk of non-persuasion) with respect to the contention in the proceeding. The proponent of the request for an adjudicatory hearing bears the burden of demonstrating under §2.1115(b) that an adjudicatory hearing should be held.

[69 FR 2267, Jan. 14, 2004]

§2.1119 Applicability of other sections.

In proceedings subject to this part, the provisions of subparts A, C, and L of this part are also applicable, except where inconsistent with the provisions of this subpart.

[69 FR 2267, Jan. 14, 2004]

Subpart L—Simplified Hearing Procedures for NRC Adjudications

SOURCE: 69 FR 2267, Jan. 14, 2004, unless otherwise noted.

§2.1200 Scope of subpart L.

The provisions of this subpart, together with subpart C of this part, govern all adjudicatory proceedings conducted under the authority of the Atomic Energy Act of 1954, as amended, the Energy Reorganization Act, and 10 CFR part 2, except for proceedings on the licensing of the construction and operation of a uranium enrichment facility, proceedings on an initial application for construction authorization for a high-level radioactive waste geologic repository at a geologic repository operations area noticed under §§2.101(e)(8) or 2.105(a)(5), proceedings on an initial application for a license to receive and possess high-level radioactive waste at a geologic repository operations area, proceedings on enforcement matters unless all parties otherwise agree and request the application of Subpart L procedures, and proceedings for the direct or indirect transfer of control of an NRC license when the transfer requires prior approval of the NRC under the Commission's regulations, governing statutes, or pursuant to a license condition.

[69 FR 2267, Jan. 14, 2004, as amended at 82 FR 52825, Nov. 15, 2017]

§2.1201 Definitions.

The definitions of terms contained in §2.4 apply to this subpart unless a different definition is provided in this subpart.

§ 2.1202 Authority and role of NRC staff.

(a) During the pendency of any hearing under this subpart, consistent with the NRC staff's findings in its review of the application or matter which is the subject of the hearing and as authorized by law, the NRC staff is expected to promptly issue its approval or denial of the application, or take other appropriate action on the underlying regulatory matter for which a hearing was provided. When the NRC staff takes its action, it must notify the presiding officer and the parties to the proceeding of its action. That notice must include the NRC staff's explanation why the public health and safety is protected and why the action is in accord with the common defense and security despite the pendency of the contested matter before the presiding officer. The NRC staff's action on the matter is effective upon issuance by the staff, except in matters involving:

(1) An application to construct and/or operate a production or utilization facility (including an application for a limited work authorization under 10 CFR 50.12, or an application for a combined license under subpart C of 10 CFR part 52);

(2) An application for an early site permit under subpart A of 10 CFR part 52;

(3) An application for a manufacturing license under subpart F of 10 CFR part 52;

(4) An application for an amendment to a construction authorization for a high-level radioactive waste repository at a geologic repository operations area falling under either 10 CFR 60.32(c)(1) or 10 CFR part 63;

(5) An application for the construction and operation of an independent spent fuel storage installation (ISFSI) located at a site other than a reactor site or a monitored retrievable storage installation (MRS) under 10 CFR part 72; and

(6) Production or utilization facility licensing actions that involve significant hazards considerations as defined in 10 CFR 50.92.

(b)(1) The NRC staff is not required to be a party to a proceeding under this subpart, except where:

(i) The proceeding involves an application denied by the NRC staff or an enforcement action proposed by the NRC staff; or

(ii) The presiding officer determines that the resolution of any issue in the proceeding would be aided materially by the NRC staff's participation in the proceeding as a party and orders the staff to participate as a party for the identified issue. In the event that the presiding officer determines that the NRC staff's participation is necessary, the presiding officer shall issue an order identifying the issue(s) on which the staff is to participate as well as setting forth the basis for the determination that staff participation will materially aid in resolution of the issue(s).

(2) Within fifteen (15) days of the issuance of the order granting requests for hearing/petitions to intervene and admitting contentions, the NRC staff shall notify the presiding officer and the parties whether it desires to participate as a party, and identify the contentions on which it wishes to participate as a party. If the NRC staff desires to be a party thereafter, the NRC staff shall notify the presiding officer and the parties, identify the contentions on which it wishes to participate as a party, and make the disclosures required by § 2.336(b)(3) through (5) unless accompanied by an affidavit explaining why the disclosures cannot be provided to the parties with the notice.

(3) Once the NRC staff chooses to participate as a party, it shall have all the rights and responsibilities of a party with respect to the admitted contention/matter in controversy on which the staff chooses to participate.

[69 FR 2267, Jan. 14, 2004, as amended at 72 FR 49483, Aug. 28, 2007; 77 FR 46598, Aug. 3, 2012]

§ 2.1203 Hearing file; prohibition on discovery.

(a)(1) Within thirty (30) days of the issuance of the order granting requests for hearing/petitions to intervene and admitting contentions, the NRC staff shall file in the docket, present to the presiding officer, and make available to the parties to the proceeding a hearing file.

(2) The hearing file must be made available to the parties either by service of hard copies or by making the file available at the NRC Web site, *http://www.nrc.gov.*

(3) The hearing file also must be made available for public inspection and copying at the NRC Web site, *http://www.nrc.gov*, and/or at the NRC Public Document Room.

(b) The hearing file consists of the application, if any, and any amendment to the application, and, when available, any NRC environmental impact statement or assessment and any NRC report related to the proposed action, as well as any correspondence between the applicant/licensee and the NRC that is relevant to the proposed action. Hearing file documents already available at the NRC Web site and/or the NRC Public Document Room when the hearing request/petition to intervene is granted may be incorporated into the hearing file at those locations by a reference indicating where at those locations the documents can be found. The presiding officer shall rule upon any issue regarding the appropriate materials for the hearing file.

(c) The NRC staff has a continuing duty to keep the hearing file up to date with respect to the materials set forth in paragraph (b) of this section and to provide those materials as required in paragraphs (a) and (b) of this section.

(d) Except as otherwise permitted by subpart C of this part, a party may not seek discovery from any other party or the NRC or its personnel, whether by document production, deposition, interrogatories or otherwise.

§2.1204 Motions and requests.

(a) *General requirements.* In proceedings under this subpart, requirements for motions and requests and responses to them are as specified in §2.323.

(b) *Requests for cross-examination by the parties.* (1) In any oral hearing under this subpart, a party may file a motion with the presiding officer to permit cross-examination by the parties on particular admitted contentions or issues. The motion must be accompanied by a cross-examination plan containing the following information:

(i) A brief description of the issue or issues on which cross-examination will be conducted;

(ii) The objective to be achieved by cross-examination; and

(iii) The proposed line of questions that may logically lead to achieving the objective of the cross-examination.

(2) The cross-examination plan may be submitted only to the presiding officer and must be kept by the presiding officer in confidence until issuance of the initial decision on the issue being litigated. The presiding officer shall then provide each cross-examination plan to the Commission's Secretary for inclusion in the official record of the proceeding.

(3) The presiding officer shall allow cross-examination by the parties only if the presiding officer determines that cross-examination by the parties is necessary to ensure the development of an adequate record for decision.

§2.1205 Summary disposition.

(a) Unless the presiding officer or the Commission directs otherwise, motions for summary disposition may be submitted to the presiding officer by any party no later than 45 days before the commencement of hearing. The motions must be in writing and must include a written explanation of the basis of the motion. The moving party must attach a short and concise statement of material facts for which the moving party contends that there is no genuine issue to be heard. Motions for summary disposition must be served on the parties and the Secretary at the same time that they are submitted to the presiding officer.

(b) Any other party may serve an answer supporting or opposing the motion within twenty (20) days after service of the motion.

(c) The presiding officer shall issue a determination on each motion for summary disposition no later than fifteen (15) days before the date scheduled for commencement of hearing. In ruling on motions for summary disposition, the presiding officer shall apply the standards for summary disposition set forth in subpart G of this part.

[69 FR 2267, Jan. 14, 2004, as amended at 77 FR 46598, Aug. 3, 2012]

§ 2.1206 Informal hearings.

Hearings under this subpart will be oral hearings as described in § 2.1207, unless, within fifteen (15) days of the service of the order granting the request for hearing, the parties unanimously agree and file a joint motion requesting a hearing consisting of written submissions. A motion to hold a hearing consisting of written submissions will not be entertained unless there is unanimous consent of the parties.

§ 2.1207 Process and schedule for submissions and presentations in an oral hearing.

(a) Unless otherwise limited by this subpart or by the presiding officer, participants in an oral hearing may submit and sponsor in the hearings:

(1) Initial written statements of position and written testimony with supporting affidavits on the admitted contentions. These materials must be filed on the dates set by the presiding officer.

(2) Written responses and rebuttal testimony with supporting affidavits directed to the initial statements and testimony of other participants. These materials must be filed within twenty (20) days of the service of the materials submitted under paragraph (a)(1) of this section unless the presiding officer directs otherwise.

(3)(i) Proposed questions for the presiding officer to consider for propounding to the persons sponsoring the testimony. Unless the presiding officer directs otherwise, these questions must be received by the presiding officer no later than twenty (20) days after the service of the materials submitted under paragraph (a)(1) of this section, unless that date is less than five (5) days before the scheduled commencement of the oral hearing, in which case the questions must be received by the presiding officer no later than five (5) days before the scheduled commencement of the hearing. Proposed questions need not be filed with any other party.

(ii) Proposed questions directed to rebuttal testimony for the presiding officer to consider for propounding to persons sponsoring the testimony. Unless the presiding officer directs otherwise, these questions must be received by the presiding officer no later than seven (7) days after the service of the rebuttal testimony submitted under paragraph (a)(2) of this section, unless that date is less than five (5) days before the scheduled commencement of the oral hearing, in which case the questions must be received by the presiding officer no later than five (5) days before the scheduled commencement of the hearing. Proposed questions directed to rebuttal need not be filed with any other party.

(iii) Questions submitted under paragraphs (a)(3)(i) and (ii) of this section may be propounded at the discretion of the presiding officer. All questions must be kept by the presiding officer in confidence until they are either propounded by the presiding officer, or until issuance of the initial decision on the issue being litigated. The presiding officer shall then provide all proposed questions to the Commission's Secretary for inclusion in the official record of the proceeding.

(b) *Oral hearing procedures.* (1) The oral hearing must be transcribed.

(2) Written testimony will be received into evidence in exhibit form.

(3) Participants may designate and present their own witnesses to the presiding officer.

(4) Testimony for the NRC staff will be presented only by persons designated by the Executive Director for Operations or his delegee for that purpose.

(5) The presiding officer may accept written testimony from a person unable to appear at the hearing, and may request that person to respond in writing to questions.

(6) Participants and witnesses will be questioned orally or in writing and only by the presiding officer or the presiding officer's designee (e.g., a Special Assistant appointed under § 2.322). The presiding officer will examine the participants and witnesses using questions prepared by the presiding officer or the presiding officer's designee, questions submitted by the participants at the discretion of the presiding officer, or a combination of both. Questions may be addressed to individuals or to panels of participants or witnesses. No party may submit proposed questions to the

presiding officer at the hearing, except upon request by, and in the sole discretion of, the presiding officer.

§2.1208 Process and schedule for a hearing consisting of written presentations.

(a) Unless otherwise limited by this subpart or by the presiding officer, participants in a hearing consisting of written presentations may submit:

(1) Initial written statements of position and written testimony with supporting affidavits on the admitted contentions. These materials must be filed on the dates set by the presiding officer;

(2) Written responses, rebuttal testimony with supporting affidavits directed to the initial statements and testimony of witnesses and other participants, and proposed written questions for the presiding officer to consider for submission to the persons sponsoring testimony under paragraph (a)(1) of this section. These materials must be filed within twenty (20) days of the service of the materials submitted under paragraph (a)(1) of this section unless the presiding officer directs otherwise;

(3) Written questions on the written responses and rebuttal testimony submitted under paragraph (a)(2) of this section, which the presiding officer may, in his or her discretion, require the persons offering the written responses and rebuttal testimony to provide responses. These questions must be filed within seven (7) days of service of the materials submitted under paragraph (a)(2) of this section unless the presiding officer directs otherwise; and

(4) Written concluding statements of position on the contentions. These statements shall be filed within twenty (20) days of the service of written responses to the presiding officer's questions to the participants or, in the absence of questions from the presiding officer, within twenty (20) days of the service of the materials submitted under paragraph (a)(2) of this section unless the presiding officer directs otherwise.

(b) The presiding officer may formulate and submit written questions to the participants that he or she considers appropriate to develop an adequate record.

§2.1209 Findings of fact and conclusions of law.

Each party shall file written post-hearing proposed findings of fact and conclusions of law on the contentions addressed in an oral hearing under §2.1207 or a written hearing under §2.1208 within 30 days of the close of the hearing or at such other time as the presiding officer directs. Proposed findings of fact and conclusions of law must conform to the format requirements in §2.712(c).

[77 FR 46598, Aug. 3, 2012]

§2.1210 Initial decision and its effect.

(a) Unless the Commission directs that the record be certified to it in accordance with paragraph (b) of this section, the presiding officer shall render an initial decision after completion of an informal hearing under this subpart. That initial decision constitutes the final action of the Commission on the contested matter 120 days after the date of issuance, unless:

(1) Any party files a petition for Commission review in accordance with §2.1212;

(2) The Commission, in its discretion, determines that the presiding officer's initial decision is inconsistent with the staff's action as described in the notice required by §2.1202(a) and that the inconsistency warrants Commission review, in which case the Commission will review the initial decision; or

(3) The Commission takes review of the decision sua sponte.

(b) The Commission may direct that the presiding officer certify the record to it without an initial decision and prepare a final decision if the Commission finds that due and timely execution of its functions warrants certification.

(c) An initial decision must be in writing and must be based only upon information in the record or facts officially noticed. The record must include all information submitted in the proceeding with respect to which all parties have been given reasonable prior notice and an opportunity to comment as provided in §§2.1207 or 2.1208. The initial decision must include:

(1) Findings, conclusions, and rulings, with the reasons or basis for them, on all material issues of fact or law admitted as part of the contentions in the proceeding;

(2) The appropriate ruling, order, or grant or denial of relief with its effective date;

(3) The action the NRC staff shall take upon transmittal of the decision to the NRC staff under paragraph (e) of this section, if the initial decision is inconsistent with the NRC staff action as described in the notice required by § 2.1202(a); and

(4) The time within which a petition for Commission review may be filed, the time within which any answers to a petition for review may be filed, and the date when the decision becomes final in the absence of a petition for Commission review or Commission sua sponte review.

(d) Pending review and final decision by the Commission, an initial decision resolving all issues before the presiding officer is immediately effective upon issuance except as otherwise provided by this part (e.g., § 2.340) or by the Commission in special circumstances.

(e) Once an initial decision becomes final, the Secretary shall transmit the decision to the NRC staff for action in accordance with the decision.

[69 FR 2267, Jan. 14, 2004, as amended at 77 FR 46598, Aug. 3, 2012; 79 FR 66601, Nov. 10, 2014]

§ 2.1212 Petitions for Commission review of initial decisions.

Parties may file petitions for review of an initial decision under this subpart in accordance with the procedures set out in § 2.341. Unless otherwise authorized by law, a party to an NRC proceeding must file a petition for Commission review before seeking judicial review of an agency action.

§ 2.1213 Application for a stay.

(a) Any application for a stay of the effectiveness of the NRC staff's action on a matter involved in a hearing under this subpart must be filed with the presiding officer within five (5) days of the issuance of the notice of the NRC staff's action under § 2.1202(a) and must be filed and considered in accordance with paragraphs (b), (c) and (d) of this section.

(b) An application for a stay of the NRC staff's action may not be longer than ten (10) pages, exclusive of affidavits, and must contain:

(1) A concise summary of the action which is requested to be stayed; and

(2) A concise statement of the grounds for a stay, with reference to the factors specified in paragraph (d) of this section.

(c) Within ten (10) days after service of an application for a stay of the NRC staff's action under this section, any party and/or the NRC staff may file an answer supporting or opposing the granting of a stay. Answers may not be longer than ten (10) pages, exclusive of affidavits, and must concisely address the matters in paragraph (b) of this section as appropriate. Further replies to answers will not be entertained.

(d) In determining whether to grant or deny an application for a stay of the NRC staff's action, the following will be considered:

(1) Whether the requestor will be irreparably injured unless a stay is granted;

(2) Whether the requestor has made a strong showing that it is likely to prevail on the merits;

(3) Whether the granting of a stay would harm other participants; and

(4) Where the public interest lies.

(e) Any application for a stay of the effectiveness of the presiding officer's initial decision or action under this subpart shall be filed with the Commission in accordance with § 2.342.

(f) Stays are not available on matters limited to whether a no significant hazards consideration determination was proper in proceedings on power reactor license amendments.

[69 FR 2267, Jan. 14, 2004, as amended at 77 FR 46598, Aug. 3, 2012]

Subpart M—Procedures for Hearings on License Transfer Applications

SOURCE: 63 FR 66730, Dec. 3, 1998, unless otherwise noted.

§ 2.1300 Scope of subpart M.

The provisions of this subpart, together with the generally applicable intervention provisions in subpart C of this part, govern all adjudicatory proceedings on an application for the direct or indirect transfer of control of an NRC license when the transfer requires prior approval of the NRC under the Commission's regulations, governing statutes, or pursuant to a license condition. This subpart provides the only mechanism for requesting hearings on license transfer requests, unless contrary case specific orders are issued by the Commission.

[77 FR 46598, Aug. 3, 2012]

§ 2.1301 Public notice of receipt of a license transfer application.

(a) The Commission will notice the receipt of each application for direct or indirect transfer of a specific NRC license by placing a copy of the application at the NRC Web site, *http://www.nrc.gov*.

(b) The Commission will also publish in the FEDERAL REGISTER a notice of receipt of an application for approval of a license transfer involving 10 CFR part 50 and part 52 licenses, major fuel cycle facility licenses issued under part 70, or part 72 licenses. This notice constitutes the notice required by § 2.105 with respect to all matters related to the application requiring NRC approval.

(c) Periodic lists of applications received may be obtained upon request addressed to the NRC Public Document Room, US Nuclear Regulatory Commission, Washington, DC 20555–0001.

[63 FR 66730, Dec. 3, 1998, as amended at 64 FR 48949, Sept. 9, 1999]

§ 2.1302 Notice of withdrawal of an application.

The Commission will notice the withdrawal of an application by publishing the notice of withdrawal in the same manner as the notice of receipt of the application was published under § 2.1301.

§ 2.1303 Availability of documents.

Unless exempt from disclosure under part 9 of this chapter, the following documents pertaining to each application for a license transfer requiring Commission approval will be placed at the NRC Web site, *http://www.nrc.gov*, when available:

(a) The license transfer application and any associated requests;

(b) Commission correspondence with the applicant or licensee related to the application;

(c) FEDERAL REGISTER notices;

(d) The NRC staff Safety Evaluation Report (SER).

(e) Any NRC staff order which acts on the license transfer application; and

(f) If a hearing is held, the hearing record and decision.

[63 FR 66730, Dec. 3, 1998, as amended at 64 FR 48949, Sept. 9, 1999]

§ 2.1305 Written comments.

(a) As an alternative to requests for hearings and petitions to intervene, persons may submit written comments regarding license transfer applications. The Commission will consider and, if appropriate, respond to these comments, but these comments do not otherwise constitute part of the decisional record.

(b) These comments should be submitted within 30 days after public notice of receipt of the application and addressed to the Secretary, U.S. Nuclear Regulatory Commission, Washington, DC 20555–0001, Attention: Rulemakings and Adjudications Staff.

(c) The Commission will provide the applicant with a copy of the comments. Any response the applicant chooses to make to the comments must be submitted within 10 days of service of the comments on the applicant. Such responses do not constitute part of the decisional record.

§ 2.1308 Oral hearings.

Hearings under this subpart will be oral hearings, unless, within 15 days of the service of the notice or order granting the hearing, the parties unanimously agree and file a joint motion requesting a hearing consisting of written comments. No motion to hold a hearing consisting of written comments will be entertained absent consent of all the parties.

[69 FR 2270, Jan. 14, 2004]

§ 2.1309 Notice of oral hearing.

(a) A notice of oral hearing will—

(1) State the time, place, and issues to be considered;

(2) Provide names and addresses of participants,

(3) Specify the time limit for participants and others to indicate whether they wish to present views;

(4) Specify the schedule for the filing of written testimony, statements of position, proposed questions for the Presiding Officer to consider, and rebuttal testimony consistent with the schedule provisions of § 2.1321.

(5) Specify that the oral hearing shall commence within 15 days of the date for submittal of rebuttal testimony unless otherwise ordered;

(6) State any other instructions the Commission deems appropriate;

(7) If so determined by the NRC staff or otherwise directed by the Commission, direct that the staff participate as a party with respect to some or all issues.

(b) If the Commission is not the Presiding Officer, the notice of oral hearing will also state:

(1) When the jurisdiction of the Presiding Officer commences and terminates;

(2) The powers of the Presiding Officer;

(3) Instructions to the Presiding Officer to certify promptly the completed hearing record to the Commission without a recommended or preliminary decision.

§ 2.1310 Notice of hearing consisting of written comments.

A notice of hearing consisting of written comments will:

(a) State the issues to be considered;

(b) Provide the names and addresses of participants;

(c) Specify the schedule for the filing of written testimony, statements of position, proposed questions for the Presiding Officer to consider for submission to the other parties, and rebuttal testimony, consistent with the schedule provisions of § 2.1321.

(d) State any other instructions the Commission deems appropriate.

§ 2.1311 Conditions in a notice or order.

(a) A notice or order granting a hearing or permitting intervention shall—

(1) Restrict irrelevant or duplicative testimony; and

(2) Require common interests to be represented by a single participant.

(b) If a participant's interests do not extend to all the issues in the hearing, the notice or order may limit her/his participation accordingly.

§ 2.1315 Generic determination regarding license amendments to reflect transfers.

(a) Unless otherwise determined by the Commission with regard to a specific application, the Commission has determined that any amendment to the license of a utilization facility or the license of an Independent Spent Fuel Storage Installation which does no more than conform the license to reflect the transfer action, involves respectively, "no significant hazards consideration," or "no genuine issue as to whether the health and safety of the public will be significantly affected."

(b) Where administrative license amendments are necessary to reflect an approved transfer, such amendments will be included in the order that approves the transfer. Any challenge to the administrative license amendment is limited to the question of whether the license amendment accurately reflects the approved transfer.

[63 FR 66730, Dec. 3, 1998, as amended at 69 FR 2270, Jan. 14, 2004]

§ 2.1316 Authority and role of NRC staff.

(a) During the pendency of any hearing under this subpart, consistent with the NRC staff's findings in its Safety Evaluation Report (SER), the staff is expected to promptly issue approval or denial of license transfer requests. Notice of such action shall be promptly transmitted to the Presiding Officer and parties to the proceeding.

(b) Except as otherwise directed in accordance with § 2.1309(a)(7), the NRC staff is not required to be a party to proceedings under this subpart but will offer into evidence its SER associated with the transfer application and provide one or more sponsoring witnesses.

(c)(1) Within 15 days of the issuance of the order granting requests for hearing/petitions to intervene and admitting contentions, the NRC staff must notify the presiding officer and the parties whether it desires to participate as a party, and identify the contentions on which it wishes to participate as a party. If the NRC staff desires to be a party thereafter, the NRC staff must notify the presiding officer and the parties, and identify the contentions on which it wishes to participate as a party, and make the disclosures required by §2.336(b)(3) through (b)(5) unless accompanied by an affidavit explaining why the disclosures cannot be provided to the parties with the notice.

(2) Once the NRC staff chooses to participate as a party, it will have all the rights and responsibilities of a party with respect to the admitted contention/matter in controversy on which the staff chooses to participate.

[63 FR 66730, Dec. 3, 1998, as amended at 77 FR 46599, Aug. 3, 2012]

§2.1319 Presiding Officer.

(a) The Commission will ordinarily be the Presiding Officer at a hearing under this part. However, the Commission may provide in a hearing notice that one or more Commissioners, or any other person permitted by law, will preside.

(b) A participant may submit a written motion for the disqualification of any person presiding. The motion shall be supported by an affidavit setting forth the alleged grounds for disqualification. If the Presiding Officer does not grant the motion or the person does not disqualify himself and the Presiding Officer or such other person is not the Commission or a Commissioner, the Commission will decide the matter.

(c) If any person presiding deems himself or herself disqualified, he or she shall withdraw by notice on the record after notifying the Commission.

(d) If a Presiding Officer becomes unavailable, the Commission will designate a replacement.

(e) Any motion concerning the designation of a replacement Presiding Officer shall be made within 5 days after the designation.

(f) Unless otherwise ordered by the Commission, the jurisdiction of a Presiding Officer other than the Commission commences as designated in the hearing notice and terminates upon certification of the hearing record to the Commission, or when the Presiding Officer is disqualified.

§2.1320 Responsibility and power of the Presiding Officer in an oral hearing.

(a) The Presiding Officer in any oral hearing shall conduct a fair hearing, develop a record that will contribute to informed decisionmaking, and, within the framework of the Commission's orders, have the power necessary to achieve these ends, including the power to:

(1) Take action to avoid unnecessary delay and maintain order;

(2) Dispose of procedural requests;

(3) Question participants and witnesses, and entertain suggestions as to questions which may be asked of participants and witnesses.

(4) Order consolidation of participants;

(5) Establish the order of presentation;

(6) Hold conferences before or during the hearing;

(7) Establish time limits;

(8) Limit the number of witnesses; and

(9) Strike or reject duplicative, unreliable, immaterial, or irrelevant presentations.

(b) Where the Commission itself does not preside:

(1) The Presiding Officer may certify questions or refer rulings to the Commission for decision;

(2) Any hearing order may be modified by the Commission; and

(3) The Presiding Officer will certify the completed hearing record to the Commission, which may then issue its decision on the hearing or provide that additional testimony be presented.

§2.1321 Participation and schedule for submission in a hearing consisting of written comments.

Unless otherwise limited by this subpart or by the Commission, participants in a hearing consisting of written comments may submit:

(a) Initial written statements of position and written testimony with supporting affidavits on the issues. These materials must be filed on the date set by the Commission or the presiding officer.

(b) Written responses, rebuttal testimony with supporting affidavits directed to the initial statements and testimony of other participants, and proposed written questions for the Presiding Officer to consider for submittal to persons sponsoring testimony submitted under paragraph (a) of this section. These materials shall be filed within 20 days of the filing of the materials submitted under paragraph (a) of this section, unless the Commission or Presiding Officer directs otherwise. Proposed written questions directed to rebuttal testimony for the Presiding Officer to consider for submittal to persons offering such testimony shall be filed within 7 days of the filing of the rebuttal testimony.

(c) Written concluding statements of position on the issues. These materials shall be filed within 20 days of the filing of the materials submitted under paragraph (b) of this section, unless the Commission or the Presiding Officer directs otherwise.

[63 FR 66730, Dec. 3, 1998, as amended at 69 FR 2271, Jan. 14, 2004; 77 FR 46599, Aug. 3, 2012]

§ 2.1322 Participation and schedule for submissions in an oral hearing.

(a) Unless otherwise limited by this subpart or by the Commission, participants in an oral hearing may submit and sponsor in the hearings:

(1) Initial written statements of position and written testimony with supporting affidavits on the issues. These materials must be filed on the date set by the Commission or the presiding officer.

(2)(i) Written responses and rebuttal testimony with supporting affidavits directed to the initial statements and testimony of other participants;

(ii) Proposed questions for the Presiding Officer to consider for propounding to persons sponsoring testimony.

(3) These materials must be filed within 20 days of the filing of the materials submitted under paragraph (a)(1) of this section, unless the Commission or Presiding Officer directs otherwise.

(4) Proposed questions directed to rebuttal testimony for the Presiding Officer to consider for propounding to persons offering such testimony shall be filed within 7 days of the filing of the rebuttal testimony.

(b) The oral hearing should commence within 65 days of the date of the Commission's notice granting a hearing unless the Commission or Presiding Officer directs otherwise. Ordinarily, questioning in the oral hearing will be conducted by the Presiding Officer, using either the Presiding Officer's questions or questions submitted by the participants or a combination of both.

(c) Written post-hearing statements of position on the issues addressed in the oral hearing may be submitted within 20 days of the close of the oral hearing.

(d) The Commission, on its own motion, or in response to a request from a Presiding Officer other than the Commission, may use additional procedures, such as direct and cross-examination, or may convene a formal hearing under subpart G of this part on specific and substantial disputes of fact, necessary for the Commission's decision, that cannot be resolved with sufficient accuracy except in a formal hearing. The staff will be a party in any such formal hearing. Neither the Commission nor the Presiding Officer will entertain motions from the parties that request such special procedures or formal hearings.

[63 FR 66730, Dec. 3, 1998, as amended at 69 FR 2271, Jan. 14, 2004]

§ 2.1323 Presentation of testimony in an oral hearing.

(a) All direct testimony in an oral hearing shall be filed no later than 15 days before the hearing or as otherwise ordered or allowed pursuant to the provisions of § 2.1322.

(b) Written testimony will be received into evidence in exhibit form.

(c) Participants may designate and present their own witnesses to the Presiding Officer.

(d) Testimony for the NRC staff will be presented only by persons designated for that purpose by either the

Executive Director for Operations or a delegee of the Executive Director for Operations.

(e) Participants and witnesses will be questioned orally or in writing and only by the Presiding Officer. Questions may be addressed to individuals or to panels of participants or witnesses.

(f) The Presiding Officer may accept written testimony from a person unable to appear at the hearing, and may request him or her to respond to questions.

(g) No subpoenas will be granted at the request of participants for attendance and testimony of participants or witnesses or the production of evidence.

[63 FR 66730, Dec. 3, 1998, as amended at 69 FR 2271, Jan. 14, 2004]

§2.1324 Appearance in an oral hearing.

(a) A participant may appear in a hearing on her or his own behalf or be represented by an authorized representative.

(b) A person appearing shall file a written notice stating her or his name, address and telephone number, and if an authorized representative, the basis of her or his eligibility and the name and address of the participant on whose behalf she or he appears.

(c) A person may be excluded from a hearing for disorderly, dilatory or contemptuous conduct, provided he or she is informed of the grounds and given an opportunity to respond.

§2.1325 Motions and requests.

(a) Motions and requests shall be addressed to the Presiding Officer, and, if written, also filed with the Secretary and served on other participants.

(b) Other participants may respond to the motion or request. Responses to written motions or requests shall be filed within 5 days after service unless the Commission or Presiding Officer directs otherwise.

(c) The Presiding Officer may entertain motions for extension of time and changes in schedule in accordance with paragraphs (a) and (b) of this section.

(d) When the Commission does not preside, in response to a motion or request, the Presiding Officer may refer a ruling or certify a question to the Commission for decision and notify the participants.

(e) Unless otherwise ordered by the Commission, a motion or request, or the certification of a question or referral of a ruling, shall not stay or extend any aspect of the hearing.

§2.1327 Application for a stay of the effectiveness of NRC staff action on license transfer.

(a) Any application for a stay of the effectiveness of the NRC staff's order on the license transfer application shall be filed with the Commission within 5 days of the issuance of the notice of staff action pursuant to §2.1316(a).

(b) An application for a stay must be no longer than 10 pages, exclusive of affidavits, and must contain:

(1) A concise summary of the action which is requested to be stayed; and

(2) A concise statement of the grounds for a stay, with reference to the factors specified in paragraph (d) of this section.

(c) Within 10 days after service of an application for a stay under this section, any participant may file an answer supporting or opposing the granting of a stay. Answers must be no longer than 10 pages, exclusive of affidavits, and should concisely address the matters in paragraph (b) of this section, as appropriate. No further replies to answers will be entertained.

(d) In determining whether to grant or deny an application for a stay, the Commission will consider:

(1) Whether the requestor will be irreparably injured unless a stay is granted;

(2) Whether the requestor has made a strong showing that it is likely to prevail on the merits;

(3) Whether the granting of a stay would harm other participants; and

(4) Where the public interest lies.

§2.1331 Commission action.

(a) Upon completion of a hearing, the Commission will issue a written opinion including its decision on the license transfer application and the reasons for the decision.

(b) The decision on issues designated for hearing under § 2.309 will be based on the record developed at hearing.

[63 FR 66730, Dec. 3, 1998, as amended at 69 FR 2271, Jan. 14, 2004]

Subpart N—Expedited Proceedings with Oral Hearings

SOURCE: 69 FR 2271, Jan. 14, 2004, unless otherwise noted.

§ 2.1400 Purpose and scope of subpart N.

The purpose of this subpart is to provide simplified procedures for the expeditious resolution of disputes among parties in an informal hearing process. The provisions of this subpart, together with subpart C of this part, govern all adjudicatory proceedings conducted under the authority of the Atomic Energy Act of 1954, as amended, the Energy Reorganization Act of 1974, and 10 CFR part 2 except for proceedings on the licensing of the construction and operation of a uranium enrichment facility, proceedings on an initial application for authorization to construct a high-level radioactive waste repository at a geologic repository operations area noticed under §§ 2.101(f)(8) or 2.105(a)(5), proceedings on an initial application for authorization to receive and possess high-level radioactive waste at a geologic repository operations area, proceedings on an initial application for a license to receive and possess high-level radioactive waste at a geologic repository operations area, proceedings on enforcement matters unless all parties otherwise agree and request the application of subpart N procedures, and proceedings for the direct or indirect control of an NRC license when the transfer requires prior approval of the NRC under the Commission's regulations, governing statutes, or pursuant to a license condition.

§ 2.1401 Definitions.

The definitions of terms in § 2.4 apply to this subpart unless a different definition is provided in this subpart.

§ 2.1402 General procedures and limitations; requests for other procedures.

(a) *Generally-applicable procedures.* For proceedings conducted under this subpart:

(1) Except where provided otherwise in this subpart or specifically requested by the presiding officer or the Commission, written pleadings and briefs (regardless of whether they are in the form of a letter, a formal legal submission, or otherwise) are not permitted;

(2) Requests to schedule a conference to consider oral motions may be in writing and served on the Presiding officer and the parties;

(3) Motions for summary disposition before the hearing has concluded and motions for reconsideration to the presiding officer or the Commission are not permitted;

(4) All motions must be presented and argued orally;

(5) The presiding officer will reflect all rulings on motions and other requests from the parties in a written decision. A verbatim transcript of oral rulings satisfies this requirement;

(6) Except for the information disclosure requirements set forth in subpart C of this part, requests for discovery will not be entertained; and

(7) The presiding officer may issue written orders and rulings necessary for the orderly and effective conduct of the proceeding;

(b) *Other procedures.* If it becomes apparent at any time before a hearing is held that a proceeding selected for adjudication under this subpart is not appropriate for application of this subpart, the presiding officer or the Commission may, on its own motion or at the request of a party, order the proceeding to continue under another appropriate subpart. If a proceeding under this subpart is discontinued because the proceeding is not appropriate for application of this subpart, the presiding officer may issue written orders necessary for the orderly continuation of the hearing process under another subpart.

(c) *Request for cross-examination.* A party may present an oral motion to the presiding officer to permit cross-examination by the parties on particular admitted contentions or issues. The presiding officer may allow cross-examination by the parties if he or she determines that cross-examination by the parties is necessary for the development of an adequate record for decision.

§2.1403 Authority and role of the NRC staff.

(a) During the pendency of any hearing under this subpart, consistent with the NRC staff's findings in its review of the application or matter that is the subject of the hearing and as authorized by law, the NRC staff is expected to promptly issue its approval or denial of the application, or take other appropriate action on the matter that is the subject of the hearing. When the NRC staff takes its action, it must notify the presiding officer and the parties to the proceeding of its action. That notice must include the NRC staff's explanation why the public health and safety is protected and why the action is in accord with the common defense and security despite the pendency of the contested matter before the presiding officer. The NRC staff's action on the matter is effective upon issuance, except in matters involving:

(1) An application to construct and/or operate a production or utilization facility;

(2) An application for the construction and operation of an independent spent fuel storage installation located at a site other than a reactor site or a monitored retrievable storage facility under 10 CFR part 72; or

(3) Production or utilization facility licensing actions that involve significant hazards considerations as defined in 10 CFR 50.92.

(b)(1) The NRC staff is not required to be a party to proceedings under this subpart, except where:

(i) The proceeding involves an application denied by the NRC staff or an enforcement action proposed by the staff; or

(ii) The presiding officer determines that the resolution of any issue in the proceeding would be aided materially by the NRC staff's participation in the proceeding as a party and orders the staff to participate as a party for the identified issue. In the event that the presiding officer determines that the NRC staff's participation is necessary, the presiding officer shall issue an order identifying the issue(s) on which the staff is to participate as well as setting forth the basis for the determination that staff participation will materially aid in resolution of the issue(s).

(2) Within fifteen (15) days of the issuance of the order granting requests for hearing/petitions to intervene and admitting contentions, the NRC staff shall notify the presiding officer and the parties whether it desires to participate as a party, and identify the contentions on which it wishes to participate as a party. If the NRC staff desires to be a party thereafter, the NRC staff shall notify the presiding officer and the parties, identify the contentions on which it wishes to participate as a party, and make the disclosures required by §2.336(b)(3) through (5) unless accompanied by an affidavit explaining why the disclosures cannot be provided to the parties with the notice.

(3) Once the NRC staff chooses to participate as a party, it shall have all the rights and responsibilities of a party with respect to the admitted contention/matter in controversy on which the staff chooses to participate.

[69 FR 2271, Jan. 14, 2004, as amended at 77 FR 46599, Aug. 3, 2012]

§2.1404 Prehearing conference.

(a) No later than forty (40) days after the order granting requests for hearing/petitions to intervene, the presiding officer shall conduct a prehearing conference. At the discretion of the presiding officer, the prehearing conference may be held in person or by telephone or through the use of video conference technology.

(b) At the prehearing conference, each party shall provide the presiding officer and the parties participating in the conference with a statement identifying each witness the party plans to present at the hearing and a written summary of the oral and written testimony of each proposed witness. If the prehearing conference is not held in person, each party shall forward the summaries of the party's witnesses' testimony to the presiding officer and the other parties by such means that will ensure the receipt of the summaries by the commencement of the prehearing conference.

(c) At the prehearing conference, the parties shall describe the results of their efforts to settle their disputes or narrow the contentions that remain for hearing, provide an agreed statement of facts, if any, identify witnesses that they propose to present at hearing, provide questions or question areas that they would propose to have the presiding officer cover with the witnesses at the hearing, and discuss other pertinent matters. At the conclusion of the conference, the presiding officer will issue an order specifying the issues to be addressed at the hearing and setting forth any agreements reached by the parties. The order must include the scheduled date for any hearing that remains to be held, and address any other matters as appropriate.

§ 2.1405 Hearing.

(a) No later than twenty (20) days after the conclusion of the prehearing conference, the presiding officer shall hold a hearing on any contention that remains in dispute. At the beginning of the hearing, the presiding officer shall enter into the record all agreements reached by the parties before the hearing.

(b) A hearing will be recorded stenographically or by other means, under the supervision of the presiding officer. A transcript will be prepared from the recording that will be the sole official transcript of the hearing. The transcript will be prepared by an official reporter who may be designated by the Commission or may be a regular employee of the Commission. Except as limited by section 181 of the Act or order of the Commission, the transcript will be available for inspection in the agency's public records system. Copies of transcripts are available to the parties and to the public from the official reporter on payment of the charges fixed therefor. If a hearing is recorded on videotape or other video medium, copies of the recording of each daily session of the hearing may be made available to the parties and to the public from the presiding officer upon payment of a charge fixed by the Chief Administrative Judge. Parties may purchase copies of the transcript from the reporter.

(c) Hearings will be open to the public, unless portions of the hearings involving proprietary or other protectable information are closed in accordance with the Commission's regulations.

(d) At the hearing, the presiding officer will not receive oral evidence that is irrelevant, immaterial, unreliable or unduly repetitious. Testimony will be under oath or affirmation.

(e) The presiding officer may question witnesses who testify at the hearing, but the parties may not do so.

(f) Each party may present oral argument and a final statement of position at the close of the hearing. Written post-hearing briefs and proposed findings are not permitted unless ordered by the presiding officer.

§ 2.1406 Initial decision—issuance and effectiveness.

(a) Where practicable, the presiding officer will render a decision from the bench. In rendering a decision from the bench, the presiding officer shall state the issues in the proceeding and make clear its findings of fact and conclusions of law on each issue. The presiding officer's decision and order must be reduced to writing and transmitted to the parties as soon as practicable, but not later than twenty (20) days, after the hearing ends. If a decision is not rendered from the bench, a written decision and order will be issued not later than thirty (30) days after the hearing ends. Approval of the Chief Administrative Judge must be obtained for an extension of these time periods, and in no event may a written decision and order be issued later than sixty (60) days after the hearing ends without the express approval of the Commission.

(b) The presiding officer's written decision must be served on the parties and filed with the Commission when issued.

(c) The presiding officer's initial decision is effective and constitutes the final action of the Commission twenty-five (25) days after the date of issuance of the written decision unless any party appeals to the Commission in accordance with §2.1407 or the Commission takes review of the decision sua sponte or the regulations in this part specify other requirements with regard to the effectiveness of decisions on certain applications.

[69 FR 2271, Jan. 14, 2004, as amended at 79 FR 66602, Nov. 10, 2014]

§2.1407 Appeal and Commission review of initial decision.

(a)(1) Within 25 days after service of a written initial decision, a party may file a written appeal seeking the Commission's review on the grounds specified in paragraph (b) of this section. Unless otherwise authorized by law, a party must file an appeal with the Commission before seeking judicial review.

(2) An appeal under this section may not be longer than twenty (20) pages and must contain the following:

(i) A concise statement of the specific rulings and decisions that are being appealed;

(ii) A concise statement (including record citations) where the matters of fact or law raised in the appeal were previously raised before the presiding officer and, if they were not, why they could not have been raised;

(iii) A concise statement why, in the appellant's view, the decision or action is erroneous; and

(iv) A concise statement why the Commission should review the decision or action, with particular reference to the grounds specified in paragraph (b) of this section.

(3) Any other party to the proceeding may, within 25 days after service of the appeal, file an answer supporting or opposing the appeal. The answer may not be longer than 20 pages and should concisely address the matters specified in paragraph (a)(2) of this section. The appellant does not have a right to reply. Unless it directs additional filings or oral arguments, the Commission will decide the appeal on the basis of the filings permitted by this paragraph.

(b) In considering the appeal, the Commission will give due weight to the existence of a substantial question with respect to the following considerations:

(1) A finding of material fact is clearly erroneous or in conflict with a finding as to the same fact in a different proceeding;

(2) A necessary legal conclusion is without governing precedent or is a departure from, or contrary to, established law;

(3) A substantial and important question of law, policy or discretion has been raised by the appeal;

(4) The conduct of the proceeding involved a prejudicial procedural error; or

(5) Any other consideration which the Commission may deem to be in the public interest.

(c) Once a decision becomes final agency action, the Secretary shall transmit the decision to the NRC staff for action in accordance with the decision.

[69 FR 2271, Jan. 14, 2004, as amended at 77 FR 46599, Aug. 3, 2012]

Subpart O—Legislative Hearings

SOURCE: 69 FR 2273, Jan. 14, 2004, unless otherwise noted.

§2.1500 Purpose and scope.

The purpose of this subpart is to provide for simplified, legislative hearing procedures to be used, at the Commission's sole discretion, in:

(a) Any design certification rule making hearings under subpart B of part 52 of this chapter that the Commission may choose to conduct; and

(b) Developing a record to assist the Commission in resolving, under §2.335(d), a petition filed under §2.335(b).

§2.1501 Definitions.

Demonstrative information means physical things, not constituting documentary information.

Documentary information means information, ordinarily contained in documents or electronic files, but may also include photographs and digital audio files.

§2.1502 Commission decision to hold legislative hearing.

(a) The Commission may, in its discretion, hold a legislative hearing in either a design certification rulemaking under § 52.51(b) of this chapter, or a proceeding where a question has been certified to it under § 2.335(d).

(b) *Notice of Commission decision*—(1) *Hearing in design certification rulemakings*. If, at the time a proposed design certification rule is published in the FEDERAL REGISTER under § 52.51(a) of this chapter, the Commission decides that a legislative hearing should be held, the information required by paragraph (c) of this section must be included in the FEDERAL REGISTER notice for the proposed design certification rule. If, following the submission of written public comments submitted on the proposed design certification rule which are submitted in accordance with § 52.51(a) of this chapter, the Commission decides to conduct a legislative hearing, the Commission shall publish a notice in the FEDERAL REGISTER and on the NRC Web site indicating its determination to conduct a legislative hearing. The notice shall contain the information specified in paragraph (c) of this section, and specify whether the Commission or a presiding officer will conduct the legislative hearing.

(2) *Hearings under* § 2.335(d). If, following a certification of a question to the Commission by a Licensing Board under § 2.335(d), the Commission decides to hold a legislative hearing to assist it in resolving the certified question, the Commission shall issue an order containing the information required by paragraph (c) of this section. The Commission shall serve the order on all parties in the proceeding. In addition, if the Commission decides that persons and entities other than those identified in paragraph (c)(2) may request to participate in the legislative hearing, the Commission shall publish a notice of its determination to hold a legislative hearing in the FEDERAL REGISTER and on the NRC Web site. The notice shall contain the information specified in paragraph (c) of this section, and refer to the criteria in § 2.1504 which will be used in determining requests to participate in the legislative hearing.

(c) If the Commission decides to hold a legislative hearing, it shall, in accordance with paragraph (b) of this section:

(1) Identify with specificity the issues on which it wishes to compile a record;

(2) Identify, in a hearing associated with a question certified to the Commission under § 2.335(d), the parties and interested State(s), governmental bodies, and Federally-recognized Indian Tribe under § 2.315(c), who may participate in the legislative hearing;

(3) Identify persons and entities that may, in the discretion of the Commission, be invited to participate in the legislative hearing;

(4) Indicate whether other persons and entities may request, in accordance with § 2.1504, to participate in the legislative hearing, and the criteria that the Commission or presiding officer will use in determining whether to permit such participation;

(5) Indicate whether the Commission or a presiding officer will conduct the legislative hearing;

(6) Specify any special procedures to be used in the legislative hearing;

(7) Set the dates for submission of requests to participate in the legislative hearing, submission of written statements and demonstrative and documentary information, and commencement of the oral hearing; and

(8) Specify the location where the oral hearing is to be held. Ordinarily, oral hearings will be held in the Washington, DC metropolitan area.

§ 2.1503 Authority of presiding officer.

If the Commission appoints a presiding officer to conduct the legislative hearing, the presiding officer shall be responsible for expeditious development of a sufficient record on the Commission-identified issues, consistent with the direction provided by the Commission under § 2.1502(c). The presiding officer has the authority otherwise accorded to it under §§ 2.319(a), (c), (e), (g), (h), and (i), 2.324, and 2.333 to control the course of the proceeding, and may exercise any other authority granted to it by the Commission in accordance with § 2.1502(c)(6).

§ 2.1504 Request to participate in legislative hearing.

(a) Any person or entity who wishes to participate in a legislative hearing noticed under either § 2.1502(b)(1) or (b)(2) shall submit a request to participate by the date specified in the notice. The request must address:

(1) A summary of the person's position on the subject matter of the legislative hearing; and

(2) The specific information, expertise or experience that the person possesses with respect to the subject matter of the legislative hearing.

(b) The Commission or presiding officer shall, within ten (10) days of the date specified for submission of requests to participate, determine whether the person or entity has met the criteria specified by the Commission under § 2.1502(c)(4) for determining requests to participate in the legislative hearing, and issue an order to that person or entity informing them of the presiding officer's decision. A presiding officer's determinations in this regard are final and not subject to any motion for reconsideration or appeal to the Commission; and the Commission's determination in this regard are final and are not subject to a motion for reconsideration.

§ 2.1505 Role of the NRC staff.

The NRC staff shall be available to answer any Commission or presiding officer's questions on staff-prepared documents, provide additional information or documentation that may be available to the staff, and provide other assistance that the Commission or presiding officer may request without requiring the NRC staff to assume the role of an advocate. The NRC staff may request to participate in the legislative hearing by providing notice to the Commission or presiding officer, as applicable, within the time period established for submitting a request to participate; or if no notice is provided under § 2.1502(b)(2), within ten (10) days of the Commission's order announcing its determination to conduct a legislative hearing.

§ 2.1506 Written statements and submission of information.

All participants shall file written statements on the Commission-identified issues, and may submit documentary and demonstrative information. Written statements, copies of documentary information, and a list and short description of any demonstrative information to be submitted must be received by the NRC (and in a hearing on issues stemming from a § 2.335(b) petition, by the parties in the proceeding in which the petition was filed) no later than ten (10) days before the commencement of the oral hearing.

§ 2.1507 Oral hearing.

(a) Not less than five (5) days before the commencement of the oral hearing, the presiding officer shall issue an order setting forth the grouping and order of appearance of the witnesses at the oral hearing. The order shall be filed upon all participants by email or facsimile transmission if possible, otherwise by overnight mail.

(b) The Commission or presiding officer may question witnesses. Neither the Commission nor the presiding officer will ordinarily permit participants to submit recommended questions for the Commission or presiding officer to propound to witnesses. However, if the Commission or presiding officer believe that the conduct of the oral hearing will be expedited and that consideration of such proposed questions will assist in developing a more focused hearing record, the Commission or presiding officer may, in its discretion, permit the participants to submit recommended questions for the Commission or presiding officer's consideration.

(c) The Commission or presiding officer may request, or upon request of a participant may, in the presiding officer's discretion, permit the submission of additional information following the close of the oral hearing. Such information must be submitted no later than five (5) days after the close of the oral hearing and must be served at the same time upon all participants at the oral hearing.

§ 2.1508 Recommendation of presiding officer.

(a) If the Commission is not acting as a presiding officer, the presiding officer shall, within thirty (30) days following the close of the legislative hearing record, certify the record to the Commission on each of the issues identified by the Commission.

(b) The presiding officer's certification for each Commission-identified issue shall contain:

(1) A transcript of the oral phase of the legislative hearing;

(2) A list of all participants;

(3) A list of all witnesses at the oral hearing, and their affiliation with a participant;

(4) A list, and copies of, all documentary information submitted by the participants with ADAMS accession numbers;

(5) All demonstrative information submitted by the participants;

(6) Any written answers submitted by the NRC staff in response to questions posed by the presiding officer with ADAMS accession numbers;

(7) A certification that all documentary information has been entered into ADAMS, and have been placed on the NRC Web site unless otherwise protected from public disclosure;

(8) A certification by the presiding officer that the record contains sufficient information for the Commission to make a reasoned determination on the Commission-identified issue; and

(9) At the option of the presiding officer, a summary of the information in the record and a proposed resolution of the Commission-identified issue with a supporting basis.

§ 2.1509 Ex parte communications and separation of functions.

Section 2.347 applies in a legislative hearing. Section 2.348 applies in a legislative hearing only where the hearing addresses an issue certified to the Commission under § 2.335(d), and then only with respect to the underlying contested matter.

APPENDIX A TO PART 2 [RESERVED]

APPENDIX B TO 10 CFR PART 2—MODEL MILESTONES TO BE USED BY A PRESIDING OFFICER AS A GUIDELINE IN DEVELOPING A HEARING SCHEDULE FOR THE CONDUCT OF AN ADJUDICATORY PROCEEDING IN ACCORDANCE WITH 10 CFR 2.332.

I. MODEL MILESTONES FOR A HEARING ON AN ENFORCEMENT ACTION CONDUCTED UNDER 10 CFR PART 2, SUBPART G

These model milestones would apply to enforcement proceedings conducted under 10 CFR Part 2, Subpart G. As required by 10 CFR 2.332 and 2.334, the presiding officer establishes, by order, a schedule for the conduct of the proceeding. In establishing a schedule, the presiding officer should use these milestones as a starting point, make appropriate modifications to the milestones, and set detailed schedules (e.g., for filings) based upon all relevant information. Such information would include, but not be limited to, the complexity of the issues, any other relevant consideration that a party brings to the attention of the presiding officer, and the NRC's interest in providing a fair and expeditious resolution of the issues to be adjudicated in the proceeding. The model milestones are based on the Commission's Rules of Practice in 10 CFR Part 2, Subparts B, C, and G.

The model milestones are based upon the following assumptions: (i) the issues to be litigated will involve both disputes over fact and issues of compliance with the Commission's regulations and requirements; and (ii) no petitions to intervene are filed pursuant to 10 CFR 2.309(a)–(b). The model milestones reflect electronic filing and service in accordance with 10 CFR 2.305. In some cases, preparation of direct testimony and motions for summary disposition can proceed once initial mandatory disclosures have been made. The time periods set forth in the model milestones reflect these assumptions.

MODEL MILESTONES
[10 CFR Part 2, Subpart G]

• Within 20 days of date of enforcement order:	Person subject to order files answer; if order immediately effective, motion to set aside immediate effectiveness due; requests for hearing due.
• Within 100 days of enforcement order:	Presiding officer issues order on hearing request by person who is subject of enforcement order.
• Within 25 days of presiding officer decision granting hearing:	Presiding officer sets initial schedule for the proceeding.
• Within 145 days of presiding officer decision granting hearing:	Discovery complete.
• Within 155 days of presiding officer decision granting hearing:	Motions for summary disposition due.
• Within 235 days of presiding officer decision granting hearing:	Presiding officer decisions on motions for summary disposition.
• Within 245 days of presiding officer decision granting hearing:	Prehearing conference (optional); presiding officer sets schedule for remainder of proceeding.
• Within 275 days of presiding officer decision granting hearing:	Written testimony filed.
• Within 90 days of end of evidentiary hearing and closing of record:	Presiding officer issues initial decision.

II. MODEL MILESTONES FOR HEARINGS CONDUCTED UNDER 10 CFR PART 2, SUBPART L

These model milestones would apply to proceedings conducted under 10 CFR Part 2, Subpart L, including those on applications for combined licenses (COLs), renewed licenses, and license amendments. While such proceedings differ insofar as the scope and complexity of the NRC staff reviews for the requested actions may vary, such differences will be reflected in the staff's schedule for issuing its review documents in a particular type of action. Because the milestones are keyed to the staff's review schedule, separate milestones are not identified for proceedings on the different types of actions.

As required by 10 CFR 2.332 and 2.334, the presiding officer establishes, by order, a schedule for the conduct of each proceeding. In establishing a schedule, the presiding officer should use these milestones as a starting point, make appropriate modifications to the milestones, and set detailed schedules (e.g., for filings) based upon all relevant information. Such information would include, but not be limited to, the number of contentions admitted, the complexity of the issues, the NRC staff's schedule for completion of its safety and environmental evaluations, any other relevant consideration that a party brings to the attention of the presiding officer, and the NRC's interest in providing a fair and expeditious resolution of the issues sought to be admitted for adjudication in the proceeding. The model milestones are based on the Commission's Rules of Practice in 10 CFR Part 2, Subparts B, C, and L.

The model milestones include only the most significant events in the proceeding and are based upon the following assumptions: (I) the issues to be litigated will involve both disputes over fact and issues of compliance with the Commission's regulations and requirements; (ii) an oral hearing under 10 CFR 2.1207 will be held rather than a written hearing under 10 CFR 2.1208; and (iii) the final Safety Evaluation Report (SER) and final environmental document will be issued simultaneously. The model milestones reflect electronic filing and service in accordance with 10 CFR 2.305.

MODEL MILESTONES

[10 CFR Part 2, Subpart L]

• Within 140 of publication days of notice in FEDERAL REGISTER:	Presiding officer decision on intervention petitions and admission of contentions.
• Within 55 days of presiding officer decision granting intervention and admitting contentions:	Presiding officer to set initial schedule for proceeding, based on staff schedule for issuing draft and final SERs and any necessary NEPA document.
• Within 30 days of issuance of SER and any necessary NEPA document:	Proposed late-filed contentions on SER and necessary NEPA documents filed; motions for summary disposition on previously admitted contentions due.
• Within 85 days of issuance of SER and NEPA document:	Presiding officer decision on admission of proposed late-filed contentions and motions for summary disposition; presiding officer sets schedule for remainder of proceeding.
• Within 14 days after presiding officer decision on amended/late-filed contentions:	All parties complete updates of mandatory disclosures.
• Within 115 days of issuance of SER and NEPA document:	Motions for summary disposition due.
• Within 155 days of issuance of SER and NEPA document:	Written direct testimony filed.
• Within 175 days of issuance of SER and NEPA document:	Evidentiary hearing begins.
• Within 90 days of end of evidentiary hearing and closing of record:	Presiding officer issues initial decision.

III. MODEL MILESTONES FOR A HEARING ON A TRANSFER OF A LICENSE CONDUCTED UNDER 10 CFR PART 2, SUBPART M

These model milestones would apply to proceedings conducted under 10 CFR Part 2, Subpart M on applications for license transfer. As required by 10 CFR 2.332 and 2.334, the presiding officer establishes, by order, a schedule for the conduct of each proceeding. In establishing a schedule, the presiding officer should use these milestones as a starting point, make appropriate modifications to the milestones, and set detailed schedules (e.g., for filings) based upon all relevant information. Such information would include, but not be limited to, the number of contentions admitted, the complexity of the issues, the NRC staff's schedule for completion of its safety and environmental evaluations, any other relevant consideration that a party brings to the attention of the presiding officer, and the NRC's interest in providing a fair and expeditious resolution of the issues sought to be admitted for adjudication in the proceeding. The model milestones are based on the Commission's Rules of Practice in 10 CFR Part 2, Subparts B, C and M.

The model milestones include only the most significant events in the proceeding, and are based upon the following assumptions: (i) The issues to be litigated will involve both disputes over fact and issues of compliance with the Commission's regulations and requirements; (ii) the parties do not file a joint request under 10 CFR 2.1308 for a hearing consisting of written comments; (iii) the final Safety Evaluation Report (SER) is not necessary to resolve the issues to be litigated; (iv) the Commission itself does not serve as the presiding officer; and (v) the Commission does not order further taking of testimony after the presiding officer certifies the record to the Commission under 10 CFR 2.1319(f). The model milestones reflect electronic filing and service in accordance with 10 CFR 2.305.

MODEL MILESTONES

[10 CFR Part 2, Subpart M]

• Within 100 days of publication of FEDERAL REGISTER notice of opportunity for hearing:	Presiding officer decision on intervention petitions and admission of contentions.
• Within 30 days of order granting hearing petitions:	NRC staff and other parties complete mandatory disclosures.
• Within 12 days of completion of mandatory disclosures:	Presiding Officer issues scheduling order to address, inter alia, scheduling of oral hearing, filing of written statements of position, direct testimony, and rebuttal testimony.
• Within 45 days of scheduling order:	Oral hearing commences.
• Within 25 days after hearing ends:	Presiding officer certifies hearing record to the Commission.

IV. MODEL MILESTONES FOR A HEARING ON AN ENFORCEMENT ACTION CONDUCTED UNDER 10 CFR PART 2, SUBPART N

These model milestones would apply to enforcement proceedings conducted under 10 CFR Part 2, Subpart N. As required by 10 CFR 2.332 and 2.334, the presiding officer establishes, by order, a schedule for the conduct of each proceeding. In establishing a schedule, the presiding officer should use these milestones as a starting point, make appropriate modifications to the milestones, and set detailed schedules based upon all relevant information. The model milestones are based on the Commission's Rules of Practice in 10 CFR Part 2, Subparts B, C, and N.

The model milestones are based upon the following assumptions: (i) The issues to be litigated will involve both disputes over fact and issues of compliance with the Commission's regulations and requirements; and (ii) no petitions to intervene are filed pursuant to 10 CFR 2.309(a)–(b). The model milestones reflect electronic filing and service in accordance with 10 CFR 2.305. The only discovery provided is the mandatory disclosure made by each party pursuant to 10 CFR 2.336.

MODEL MILESTONES

[10 CFR Part 2, Subpart N]

• Within 20 of date of enforcement order:	Person subject to order files answer; if order immediately effective, motion to set aside immediate effectiveness due; requests for hearing due, including joint motion to use Subpart N procedures.
• Within 50 days of date of enforcement order:	Presiding officer decision on requests for hearing and confirms use of Subpart N procedures (note: if presiding officer concludes that Subpart N procedures should not be used, the Model Milestone for Enforcement Actions under Subpart G are applicable).
• Within 30 days of presiding officer decision granting hearing:	Mandatory disclosures complete.
• Within 40 days of presiding officer decision granting hearing:	Prehearing conference to specify issues for hearing and set schedules for remaining course of proceeding.
• Within 60 days of presiding officer decision granting hearing:	Evidentiary hearing begins.
• Within 30 days of end of evidentiary hearing and closing of record:	Presiding officer issues initial decision.

[70 FR 20462, Apr. 20, 2005]

APPENDIX C TO PART 2 [RESERVED]

APPENDIX D TO PART 2—SCHEDULE FOR THE PROCEEDING ON CONSIDERATION OF CONSTRUCTION AUTHORIZATION FOR A HIGH-LEVEL WASTE GEOLOGIC REPOSITORY.

Day	Regulation (10 CFR)	Action
0	2.101(f)(8), 2.105(a)(5).	FEDERAL REGISTER Notice of Hearing.
30	2.309(b)(2)	Petition to intervene/request for hearing, w/contentions.
30	2.309(b)(2)	Petition for status as interested government participant.
55	2.315(c)	Answers to intervention & interested government participant Petitions.
62	2.309(h)(1)	Petitioner's response to answers.
70	2.1021	First Prehearing conference.
100	2.309(h)(2)	First Prehearing Conference Order identifying participants in proceeding, admitted contentions, and setting discovery and other schedules.
110	2.1021	Appeals from First Prehearing Conference Order.
120	....	Briefs in opposition to appeals.
150	2.1021, 2.329	Commission ruling on appeals for First Prehearing Conference Order.
548	....	NRC Staff issues SER.
578	2.1022	Second Prehearing Conference.

Day	Regulation (10 CFR)	Action
608	2.1021, 2.1022	Discovery complete; Second Prehearing Conference Order finalizes issues for hearing and sets schedule for prefiled testimony and hearing.
618	2.1015(b)	Appeals from Second Prehearing Conference Order.
628	2.1015(b), *c.f.* 2.710(a).	Briefs in opposition to appeals; last date for filing motions for summary disposition.
648	*c.f.* 2.710(a)	Last date for responses to summary disposition motions.
658	2.710(a)	Commission ruling on appeals from Second Prehearing Conference Order; last date for party opposing summary disposition motion to file response to new facts and arguments in any response supporting summary disposition motion.
698	2.1015(b)	Decision on summary disposition motions (may be determination to dismiss or to hold in abeyance).
720	*c.f.* 2.710(a)	Evidentiary hearing begins.
810	....	Evidentiary hearing ends.
840	2.712(a)(1)	Applicant's proposed findings.
850	2.712(a)(2)	Other parties' proposed findings.
855	2.712(a)(3)	Applicant's reply to other parties' proposed findings.
955	2.713	Initial decision.
965	2.342(a), 2.345(a), 2.1015(c)(1).	Stay motion. Petition for reconsideration, notice of appeal.
975	2.342(d), 2.345(b).	Other parties' responses to stay motion and Petitions for reconsideration.
985	....	Commission ruling on stay motion.
995	2.1015(c)(2)	Appellant's briefs.
1015	2.1015(c)(3)	Appellee's briefs.
1055	2.1023 Supp. Info.	Completion of NMSS and Commission supervisory review; issuance of construction authorization; NWPA 3-year period tolled.
1125	....	Commission decision.

[69 FR 2275, Jan. 14, 2004; 69 FR 25997, May 11, 2004]

PART 4—NONDISCRIMINATION IN FEDERALLY ASSISTED PROGRAMS OR ACTIVITIES RECEIVING FEDERAL FINANCIAL ASSISTANCE FROM THE COMMISSION

AUTHORITY: Atomic Energy Act of 1954, secs. 161, 223, 234, 274 (42 U.S.C. 2201, 2273, 2282, 2021); Energy Reorganization Act of 1974, secs. 201, 401 (42 U.S.C. 5841, 5891); 29 U.S.C. 794; 42 U.S.C. 12101 *et seq.;* 44 U.S.C. 3504 note.

Subpart A also issued under 42 U.S.C. 2000d through d–7.

Subpart B also issued under 29 U.S.C. 706.

Subpart C also issued under 42 U.S.C. 6101 through 6107.

SOURCE: 29 FR 19277, Dec. 31, 1964, unless otherwise noted.

EDITORIAL NOTE: Nomenclature changes to part 4 appear at 77 FR 39904, July 6, 2012.

GENERAL PROVISIONS

§4.1 Purpose and scope.

The regulations in this part implement:

(a) The provisions of title VI of the Civil Rights Act of 1964, Pub. L. 88–352; (78 Stat. 241; 42 U.S.C. 2000a note), and title IV of the Energy Reorganization Act of 1974, Pub. L. 93–438, (88 Stat. 1233; 42 U.S.C. 5801 note), which relate to nondiscrimination with respect to race, color, national origin or sex in any program or activity receiving Federal financial assistance from NRC;

(b) The provisions of section 504 of the Rehabilitation Act of 1973, as amended, Pub. L. 93–112 (87 Stat. 355; 29 U.S.C. 701 note), Pub. L. 95–602 (92 Stat. 2955; 29 U.S.C. 701 note), which relates to nondiscrimination with respect to the disabled in any program or activity receiving Federal financial assistance; and

(c) The provisions of the Age Discrimination Act of 1975, as amended Pub. L. 94–135 (89 Stat. 713; 42 U.S.C. 3001 note), Pub. L. 95–478 (92 Stat. 1513; 42 U.S.C. 3001 note), which relates to nondiscrimination on the basis of age in any program or activity receiving Federal financial assistance.

[52 FR 25357, July 7, 1987]

§4.2 Subparts.

Subpart A sets forth rules applicable to title VI of the Civil Rights Act of 1964 and title IV of the Energy Reorganization Act of 1974. (The Acts are collectively referred to in subpart A as "the Act".) Subpart B sets forth rules applicable specifically to matters pertaining to section 504 of the Rehabilitation Act of 1973, as amended. Subpart C sets forth rules pertaining to the provisions of the Age Discrimination Act of 1975, as amended, Pub. L. 94–135 (89 Stat. 713; 42 U.S.C. 3001 note), Pub. L. 95–478 (92 Stat. 1513; 42 U.S.C. 3001 note), which relates to nondiscrimination on the basis of age in any program or activity receiving Federal financial assistance.

[52 FR 25358, July 7, 1987]

§4.3 Application of this part.

This part applies to any program for which Federal financial assistance is authorized under a law administered by NRC. The types of Federal financial assistance to which this part applies are listed in appendix A of this part; appendix A may be revised from time to time by notice published in the FEDERAL REGISTER. This part applies to money paid, property transferred, or other Federal assistance extended, by way of grant, entitlement, cooperative agreement, loan, contract, or other agreement by NRC, or an authorized contractor or subcontractor of NRC, the terms of which require compliance with this part. If any statutes implemented by this part are otherwise applicable, the failure to list a type of Federal financial assistance in appendix A does not mean a program or activity is not covered by this part. This part does not apply to—

(a) Contracts of insurance or guaranty; or

(b) Procurement contracts; or

(c) Employment practices under any program or activity except as provided in §§4.13, 4.122 and 4.302.

[52 FR 25358, July 7, 1987, as amended at 68 FR 51344, Aug. 26, 2003]

§4.4 Definitions.

(a) *Applicant* means one who submits an application, request, or plan required to be approved by NRC, or by a primary recipient, as a condition to eligibility for Federal financial assistance; "application" means such an application, request, or plan.

(b) *Commission* means the Commission of five members or a quorum thereof sitting as a body; "NRC" means the Nuclear Regulatory Commission and its duly authorized representatives.

(c) *Facility* includes all or any portion of structures, equipment, or other real or personal property or interests therein, and the provisions of facilities includes the construction, expansion, renovation, remodeling, alteration or acquisition of facilities.

(d) *Federal financial assistance* means any grant, entitlement, loan, cooperative agreement, contract (other than a procurement contract or a contract of insurance or guaranty), or any other arrangement by which NRC provides or otherwise makes available assistance in the form of—

(1) Funds;

(2) Services of Federal personnel or other personnel at Federal expense; or

(3) Real and personal property or any interest in or use of property, including—

(i) Transfers or leases of property for less than fair market value or for reduced consideration;

(ii) Proceeds from a subsequent transfer or lease of property if the Federal share of its fair market value is not returned to the Federal Government; and the

(iii) Sale and lease of, and the permission to use (other than on casual or transient basis) Federal property or any interest in such property without consideration or at a nominal consideration, or at a consideration which is reduced for the purpose of assisting the recipient, or in recognition of the public interest to be served by such sale or lease to the recipient.

(e) *Administrative Law Judge* means an individual appointed pursuant to section 11 of the Administrative Procedure Act to conduct proceedings subject to this part.

(f) *Primary recipient* means any recipient which is authorized or required to extend Federal financial assistance to another recipient.

(g) *Program or activity* and *program* mean all of the operations of any entity described in paragraphs (g)(1) through (4) of this section, any part of which is extended Federal financial assistance:

(1)(i) A department, agency, special purpose district, or other instrumentality of a State or of a local government; or

(ii) The entity of such State or local government that distributes such assistance and each such department or agency (and each other State or local government entity) to which the assistance is extended, in the case of assistance to a State or local government;

(2)(i) A college, university or other postsecondary institution, or a public system of higher education; or

(ii) A local educational agency (as defined in 20 U.S.C. 8801), system of vocational education, or other school system;

(3)(i) An entire corporation, partnership, or other private organization, or an entire sole proprietorship—

(A) If assistance is extended to such corporation, partnership, private organization, or sole proprietorship as a whole; or

(B) Which is principally engaged in the business of providing education, health care, housing, social services, or parks and recreation; or

(ii) The entire plant or other comparable, geographically separate facility to which Federal financial assistance is extended, in the case of any other corporation, partnership, private organization, or sole proprietorship; or

(4) Any other entity which is established by two or more of the entities described in paragraph (g)(1), (2), or (3) of this section.

(h) *Recipient* means any State, political subdivision of any State, or instrumentality of any State or political subdivision, any public or private agency, institution, or organization, or other entity, or any individual, in any State, to whom Federal financial assistance is extended, directly or through another recipient, including any successor, assignee, or transferee thereof, but such term does not include any ultimate beneficiary.

(i) *Responsible NRC official* means the Director of the Office of Small Business and Civil Rights or any other officer to whom the Executive Director for Operations has delegated the authority to act.

(j) *United States* means the States of the United States, the District of Columbia, Puerto Rico, the Virgin Islands, American Samoa, Guam, Wake Island, and the territories and possessions of the United States, and the term "State" means any one of the foregoing.

[29 FR 19277, Dec. 31, 1964, as amended at 45 FR 14535, Mar. 6, 1980; 45 FR 18905, Mar. 24, 1980. Redesignated and amended at 52 FR 25358, July 7, 1987; 63 FR 15742, Apr. 1, 1998; 68 FR 51344, Aug. 26, 2003; 68 FR 75389, Dec. 31, 2003]

§ 4.5 Communications and reports.

Except as otherwise indicated, communications and reports relating to this part may be sent to the NRC by mail addressed to the U.S. Nuclear

Regulatory Commission, Washington, DC 20555–0001; by hand delivery to the NRC's offices at 11555 Rockville Pike, Rockville, Maryland; or, where practicable, by electronic submission, for example, via Electronic Information Exchange, or CD-ROM. Electronic submissions must be made in a manner that enables the NRC to receive, read, authenticate, distribute, and archive the submission, and process and retrieve it a single page at a time. Detailed guidance on making electronic submissions can be obtained by visiting the NRC's Web site at *http://www.nrc.gov/site-help/e-submittals.html;* by e-mail to *MSHD.Resource@nrc.gov;* or by writing the Office of the Chief Information Officer, U.S. Nuclear Regulatory Commission, Washington, DC 20555–0001. The guidance discusses, among other topics, the formats the NRC can accept, the use of electronic signatures, and the treatment of nonpublic information.

[68 FR 58799, Oct. 10, 2003, as amended at 74 FR 62679, Dec. 1, 2009; 80 FR 74978, Dec. 1, 2015]

§4.6 Maintenance of records.

Each record required by this part must be legible throughout the retention period specified by each Commission regulation. The record may be the original or a reproduced copy or a microform provided that the copy or microform is authenticated by authorized personnel and that the microform is capable of producing a clear copy throughout the required retention period. The record may also be stored in electronic media with the capability for producing legible, accurate, and complete records during the required retention period. Records such as letters, drawings, specifications, must include all pertinent information such as stamps, initials, and signatures. The licensee shall maintain adequate safeguards against tampering with and loss of records.

[53 FR 19244, May 27, 1988]

§4.8 Information collection requirements: OMB approval.

(a) The Nuclear Regulatory Commission has submitted the information collection requirements contained in this part to the Office of Management and Budget (OMB) for approval as required by the Paperwork Reduction Act (44 U.S.C. 3501 *et seq.*). The NRC may not conduct or sponsor, and a person is not required to respond to, a collection of information unless it displays a currently valid OMB control number. OMB has approved the information collection requirements contained in this part under control number 3150–0053.

(b) The approved information collection requirements contained in this part appear in §§4.32, 4.34, 4.125, 4.127, 4.231, 4.232, 4.322, and 4.324.

[62 FR 52184, Oct. 6, 1997]

Subpart A—Regulations Implementing Title VI of the Civil Rights Act of 1964 and Title IV of the Energy Reorganization Act of 1974

DISCRIMINATION PROHIBITED

§4.11 General prohibition.

No person in the United States shall, on the ground of sex, race, color, or national origin, be excluded from participation in, be denied the benefits of, or be otherwise subjected to discrimination under any program to which this subpart applies.

[29 FR 19277, Dec. 31, 1964, as amended at 40 FR 8778, Mar. 3, 1975]

§4.12 Specific discriminatory actions prohibited.

(a) A recipient to which this subpart applies may not, directly or through contractual or other arrangements, on the ground of sex, race, color, or national origin:

(1) Deny an individual any service, financial aid, or other benefit provided under the program;

(2) Provide any service, financial aid, or other benefit to an individual which is different, or is provided in a different manner, from that provided to others under the program;

(3) Subject an individual to segregation or separate treatment in any matter related to his receipt of any service, financial aid, or other benefit under the program;

(4) Restrict an individual in any way in the enjoyment of any advantage or privilege enjoyed by others receiving any service, financial aid, or other benefit under the program;

(5) Treat an individual differently from others in determining whether he satisfies any admission, enrollment, quota, eligibilty, membership or other requirement or condition which individuals must meet in order to be provided any service, financial aid, or other benefit provided under the program;

(6) Deny an individual an opportunity to participate in the program through the provision of services or otherwise or afford him an opportunity to do so which is different from that afforded others under the program (including the opportunity to participate in the program as an employee but only to the extent set forth in §4.13).

(b) A recipient in determining the types of services, financial aid, or other benefits, or facilities which will be provided under any such program, or the class of individuals to whom, or the situations in which, such services, financial aid, other benefits, or facilities will be provided under any such program, or the class of individuals to be afforded an opportunity to participate in any such program, may not, directly or through contractual or other arrangements, utilize criteria or methods of administration which have the effect of subjecting individuals to discrimination because of their sex, race, color, or national origin, or have the effect of defeating or substantially impairing accomplishment of the objectives of the program as respects individuals of a particular sex, race, color, or national origin.

(c) In determining the site or location of facilities, a recipient or applicant may not make selections with the purpose or effect of excluding individuals from, denying them the benefits of, or subjecting them to discrimination under any program to which this subpart applies, on the grounds of sex, race, color, or national origin; or with the purpose or effect of defeating or substantially impairing the accomplishment of the objectives of the Act or this subpart.

(d) As used in this section the services, financial aid, or other benefits provided under a program receiving Federal financial assistance shall be deemed to include any services, financial aid, or other benefit provided in or through a facility provided with the aid of Federal financial assistance.

(e) The enumeration of specific forms of prohibited discrimination in this section and §4.13 does not limit the generality of the prohibition in §4.11.

(f) This subpart does not prohibit the consideration of sex, race, color, or national origin if the purpose and effect are to remove or overcome the consequences of practices or impediments which have restricted the availability of, or participation in, the program or activity receiving Federal financial assistance, on the grounds of sex, race, color or national origin. Where previous discriminatory practice or usage tends, on the grounds of sex, race, color, or national origin, to exclude individuals from participation in, to deny them the benefits of, or to subject them to discrimination under any program or activity to which this subpart applies, the applicant or recipient has an obligation to take reasonable action to remove or overcome the consequences of the prior discriminatory practice or usage, and to accomplish the purposes of the Act.

[29 FR 19277, Dec. 31, 1964, as amended at 38 FR 17927, July 5, 1973; 40 FR 8778, Mar. 3, 1975; 68 FR 51344, Aug. 26, 2003]

§4.13 Employment practices.

(a) Where a primary objective of the Federal financial assistance to a program to which this subpart applies is to provide employment, a recipient may not, directly or through contractual or other arrangements, subject an individual to discrimination on the ground of sex, race, color, or national origin in its employment practices under such program (including recruitment or recruitment advertising, employment, layoff or termination, upgrading, demotion, or transfer, rates of pay or other forms of compensation, and use of facilities), including programs where a primary objective of the Federal financial assistance to a program is (1) to assist such individuals through employment to meet expenses incident to the commencement or continuation of their education or training, or (2) to provide work experience which contributes to the education or training of such individuals. (Examples of such Federal financial assistance are nuclear training equipment grants, grants and loans of materials for training, and fellowships.) The requirements applicable to construction employment under any such program shall be those specified in or pursuant to part III of Executive Order 11246 or any Executive order which supersedes it.

(b) Where a primary objective of the Federal financial assistance is not to provide employment, but discrimination on the grounds of sex, race, color, or national origin in the employment practices of the recipient or other persons subject to this subpart tends, on the grounds of sex, race, color, or national origin, to exclude individuals from participation in, to deny them the benefits of, or to subject them to discrimination under any program to which this subpart applies, the provisions of paragraph (a) of this section shall apply to the employment practices of the recipient or other persons subject to this subpart to the extent necessary to assure equality of opportunity to, and nondiscriminatory treatment of, beneficiaries.

[38 FR 17927, July 5, 1973, as amended at 40 FR 8778, Mar. 3, 1975; 68 FR 51344, Aug. 26, 2003]

§4.14 Medical emergencies.

A recipient shall not be deemed to have failed to comply with §4.11 if immediate provision of a service or other benefit to an individual is necessary to prevent his death or serious impairment of his health, and such service or other benefit cannot be provided except by or through a medical institution which refuses or fails to comply with §4.11.

ASSURANCES REQUIRED

§4.21 General requirements.

(a) Every grant, loan or contract to which this subpart applies, except an application to which §4.22 applies, shall, as a condition to its approval by NRC, or by the appropriate NRC contractor or subcontractor, and the extension of any Federal financial assistance pursuant thereto, contain or be accompanied by an assurance that the program will be conducted in compliance with all requirements imposed by or pursuant to this subpart. In the case of a grant, loan, or contract involving Federal financial assistance to provide real property or structures thereon, the assurance shall obligate the recipient, or, in the case of a subsequent transfer, the transferee, for the period during which the real property or structures are used for a purpose for which the Federal financial assistance is extended, or for another purpose involving the provision of similar services or benefits. In the case of personal property the assurance shall obligate the recipient for the period during which he retains ownership or possession of the property. In all other cases the assurance shall obligate the recipient for the period during which Federal financial assistance is extended pursuant to the grant, loan or contract. The Commission will specify the form of the foregoing assurances and the extent to which like assurances will be required of subgrantees, contractors and subcontractors, successors in interest, and other participants. Any such assurance shall include provisions which give the United States a right to seek its judicial enforcement.

(b) In the case of real property, structures or improvements thereon, or interests therein, which was acquired with Federal financial assistance, or in the case where Federal financial assistance is provided in the form of a transfer of real property or interest therein from the Federal Government, the instrument effecting or recording the transfer shall contain a covenant running with the land assuring nondiscrimination for the period during which the real property is used for a purpose for which the Federal financial assistance is extended or for another purpose involving the provision of similar services or benefits. Where no transfer of property is involved, but property is improved with Federal financial assistance, the recipient shall agree to include such a covenant in any subsequent transfer of such property. Where the property is obtained from the Federal Government, such covenant may also include a condition coupled with a right to be reserved by the NRC to revert title to the property in the event of a breach of the covenant where, in the discretion of the NRC, such a condition and right of reverter is appropriate to the program and to the nature of the grant and the grantee. In such event if a transferee of real property proposes to mortgage or otherwise encumber the real property as security for financing construction of new, or improvement of existing, facilities on such property for the purposes for which the property was transferred, the NRC may agree, upon request of the transferee and if necessary to accomplish such financing, and upon such conditions as the NRC deems appropriate, to forbear the exercise of such right to revert title for so long as the lien of such mortgage or other encumbrance remains effective.

(c) Transfers of surplus property are subject to regulations issued by the Administrator of General Services (41 CFR 101–6.2).

[29 FR 19277, Dec. 31, 1964, as amended at 38 FR 17927, July 5, 1973; 68 FR 51344, Aug. 26, 2003; 68 FR 75389, Dec. 31, 2003]

§ 4.22 Continuing Federal financial assistance.

Every application by a State or a State agency for continuing Federal financial assistance shall require the submission of and every grant, loan, or contract to or with a State or a State agency for continuing Federal financial assistance to which this subpart applies, shall, as a condition to its approval and the extension of any Federal financial assistance pursuant to the grant, loan or contract, contain or be accompanied by, a statement that the program is (or, in the case of a new program, will be) conducted in compliance with all requirements imposed by or pursuant to this subpart, and shall provide or be accompanied by provisions for such methods of administration for the program as are found by the responsible NRC official to give reasonable assurance that the recipient and all other recipients of Federal financial assistance under such program will comply with all requirements imposed by or pursuant to this subpart.

[38 FR 17928, July 5, 1973, as amended at 68 FR 51344, Aug. 26, 2003]

§ 4.24 Assurances from institutions.

(a) In the case of a grant, loan or contract involving Federal financial assistance to an institution of higher education, the assurance required by § 4.21 shall extend to admission practices and to all other practices relating to the treatment of students.

(b) The assurance required with respect to an institution of higher education, hospital, or any other institution, insofar as the assurance relates to the institution's practices with respect to admission or other treatment of individuals as students, patients, or clients of the institution or to the opportunity to participate in the provision of services or other benefits to such individuals, shall be applicable to the entire institution.

[29 FR 19277, Dec. 31, 1964, as amended at 68 FR 51344, Aug. 26, 2003]

Compliance Information

§ 4.31 Cooperation and assistance.

The responsible NRC official shall to the fullest extent practicable seek the cooperation of recipients in obtaining compliance with this subpart and shall provide assistance and guidance to recipients to help them comply voluntarily with this subpart.

§ 4.32 Compliance reports.

(a) Each recipient shall keep records and submit to the responsible NRC official, timely, complete, and accurate compliance reports at the times and in the form and containing the information that the responsible NRC official may determine to be necessary to enable the official to ascertain whether the recipient has complied or is complying with this subpart.

(b) In the case in which a primary recipient extends Federal financial assistance to any other recipient, the other recipient shall also submit necessary compliance reports to the primary recipient to enable the primary recipient to carry out its obligations under this subpart.

(c) The primary recipient shall retain each record of information needed to complete a compliance report pursuant to paragraph (a) of this section for three years or as long as the primary recipient retains the status of primary recipient as defined in §4.4, whichever is shorter.

[53 FR 19244, May 27, 1988, as amended at 68 FR 51344, Aug. 26, 2003]

§4.33 Access to sources of information.

Each recipient shall permit access by the responsible NRC official during normal business hours to such of its books, records, accounts, and other sources of information, and its facilities as may be pertinent to ascertain compliance with this subpart. Where any information required of a recipient is in the exclusive possession of any other agency, institution or person and that agency, institution or person shall fail or refuse to furnish this information, the recipient shall so certify in its report and shall set forth what efforts it has made to obtain the information.

§4.34 Information to beneficiaries and participants.

Each recipient shall make available to participants, beneficiaries, and other interested persons such information regarding the provisions of this subpart and its applicability to the program for which the recipient receives Federal financial assistance, and make such information available to them in such manner, as the responsible NRC official finds necessary to apprise such persons of the protections against discrimination assured them by the Act and this subpart.

[29 FR 19277, Dec. 31, 1964, as amended at 68 FR 51344, Aug. 26, 2003]

CONDUCT OF INVESTIGATIONS

§4.41 Periodic compliance reviews.

The responsible NRC official shall from time to time review the practices of recipients to determine whether they are complying with this subpart.

§4.42 Complaints.

Any person who believes himself or any specific class of individuals to be subjected to discrimination prohibited by this subpart may by himself or by a representative file with the responsible NRC official a written complaint. A complaint must be filed not later than ninety (90) days from the date of the alleged discrimination, unless the time for filing is extended by the responsible NRC official. A complaint shall be signed by the complainant or his representative.

§4.43 Investigations.

The responsible NRC official will make a prompt investigation whenever a compliance review, report, complaint, or any other information indicates a possible failure to comply with this subpart. The investigation should include, where appropriate, a review of the pertinent practices and policies of the recipient, the circumstances under which the possible noncompliance with this subpart occurred, and other factors relevant to a determination as to whether the recipient has failed to comply with this subpart.

§4.44 Resolution of matters.

(a) If an investigation pursuant to §4.43 indicates a failure to comply with this subpart, the responsible NRC official will so inform the recipient and the matter will be resolved by voluntary means whenever possible. If it has been determined that the matter cannot be resolved by voluntary means, action will be taken as provided for in §§4.46 through 4.49.

(b) If an investigation does not warrant action pursuant to paragraph (a) of this section, the responsible NRC official will so inform the recipient and the complainant, if any, in writing.

§4.45 Intimidatory or retaliatory acts prohibited.

No recipient or other person shall intimidate, threaten, coerce, or discriminate against any individual for the purpose of interfering with any right or privilege secured by the Act or this subpart, or because he has made a complaint, testified, assisted, or participated in any manner in an investigation, proceeding, or hearing under this subpart. The identity of complainants shall be kept confidential, except to the extent necessary to carry out the purposes of this subpart including the conduct of any investigation, hearing, or judicial proceeding arising thereunder.

[29 FR 19277, Dec. 31, 1964, as amended at 40 FR 8778, Mar. 3, 1975]

MEANS OF EFFECTING COMPLIANCE

§ 4.46 Means available.

If there appears to be a failure or threatened failure to comply with any of the provisions of this subpart, and if the noncompliance or threatened concompliance cannot be corrected by informal means, compliance with this subpart may be effected by the suspension or termination of or refusal to grant or to continue Federal financial assistance or by any other means authorized by law. Such other means may include, but are not limited to: (a) A reference to the Department of Justice with a recommendation that appropriate proceedings be brought to enforce any rights of the United States under any law of the United States (including other titles of the Act), or any assurance or other contractual undertaking, and (b) any applicable proceeding under State or local law.

§ 4.47 Noncompliance with § 4.21.

If an applicant fails or refuses to furnish an assurance required under § 4.21 or otherwise fails or refuses to comply with a requirement imposed by or pursuant to that section, Federal financial assistance may be refused in accordance with the procedures of § 4.48.

[45 FR 14535, Mar. 6, 1980]

§ 4.48 Termination of or refusal to grant or to continue Federal financial assistance.

No order suspending, terminating, or refusing to grant or continue Federal financial assistance shall become effective until: (a) The responsible NRC official has advised the applicant or recipient of his failure to comply and has determined that compliance cannot be secured by voluntary means, (b) there has been an express finding on the record, after opportunity for hearing, of a failure by the applicant or recipient to comply with the requirement imposed by or pursuant to this subpart, (c) the action has been approved by the Commission pursuant to § 4.72, and (d) the expiration of thirty (30) days after the Commission has filed with the committee of the House and the committee of the Senate having legislative jurisdiction over the program involved, a full written report of the circumstances and the grounds for such action. Any action to suspend or terminate or to refuse to grant or to continue Federal financial assistance shall be limited to the particular political entity, or part thereof, or other applicant or recipient as to whom such finding has been made and shall be limited in its effect to the particular program, or part thereof, in which such noncompliance has been so found.

§ 4.49 Other means authorized by law.

No action to effect compliance by any other means authorized by law shall be taken until: (a) The responsible NRC official has determined that compliance cannot be secured by voluntary means, (b) the recipient or other person has been notified of its failure to comply and of the action to be taken to effect compliance, and (c) the expiration of at least ten (10) days from the mailing of such notice to the recipient or other person. During this period of at least ten (10) days, additional efforts shall be made to persuade the recipient or other person to comply with this subpart and to take such corrective action as may be appropriate.

[38 FR 17928, July 5, 1973]

OPPORTUNITY FOR HEARING

§ 4.51 Notice of opportunity for hearing.

(a) Whenever an opportunity for hearing is required by § 4.48, the responsible NRC official shall serve on the applicant or recipient, by registered or certified mail, return receipt requested, a notice of opportunity for hearing which will:

(1) Inform the applicant or recipient of his right within twenty (20) days of the date of the notice of opportunity for hearing, or such other period as may be specified in the notice, to request a hearing;

(2) Set forth the alleged item or items of noncompliance with this subpart;

(3) Specify the issues;

(4) State that compliance with this subpart may be effected by an order providing for the termination of or refusal to grant or to continue assistance, as appropriate; and

(5) Provide that the applicant or recipient may file a written answer to the notice of opportunity for hearing under oath or affirmation within twenty (20) days of its date, or such other period as may be specified in the notice.

(b) The applicant or recipient may respond to a notice of opportunity for hearing by filing a written answer under oath or affirmation. The answer shall specifically admit or deny each allegation, or, where the applicant or recipient does not have knowledge or information sufficient to form a belief, the answer may so state and the statements shall have the effect of a denial. Allegations of fact not denied shall be deemed to be admitted. The answer shall separately state and identify matters alleged as affirmative defenses and may also set forth the matters of fact and law on which the applicant or recipient relies. The answer may request a hearing.

(c) If the answer requests a hearing, the Commission will issue a notice of hearing specifying:

(1) The time, place, and nature thereof;

(2) The legal authority and jurisdiction under which the hearing is to be held; and

(3) The matters of fact and law asserted or to be considered. The time and place of hearing will be fixed with due regard for the convenience and necessity of the parties or their representatives and for the public interest. An answer to a notice of hearing is not required.

(d) An applicant or recipient may file an answer, and waive or fail to request a hearing, without waiving the requirement for findings of fact and conclusions of law or the right to seek Commission review in accordance with the provisions of §§4.71 through 4.74. At the time an answer is filed the applicant or recipient may also submit written information or argument for the record if he does not request a hearing.

(e) An answer or stipulation may consent to the entry of an order in substantially the form set forth in the notice of opportunity for hearing; such order may be entered by the responsible Commission official. The consent of the applicant or recipient to the entry of an order shall constitute a waiver by him of a right to: (1) A hearing under the Act and §4.48, (2) findings of fact and conclusions of law, and (3) seek Commission review.

(f) The failure of an applicant or recipient to file an answer within the period prescribed, or, if he requests a hearing, his failure to appear therefor, shall constitute a waiver by him of a right to: (1) A hearing under the Act and §4.48, (2) conclusions of law, and (3) seek Commission review. In the event of such waiver, the responsible NRC official may find the facts on the basis of the record available and enter an order in substantially the form set forth in the notice of opportunity for hearing.

(g) An order entered in accordance with paragraph (e) or (f) of this section shall constitute the final decision of the Commission, unless the Commission, on its own motion, within forty-five (45) days after entry of the order, issues its own decision, which shall then constitute the final decision of the Commission.

(h) A copy of an order entered by the responsible NRC official shall be mailed to the applicant or recipient and to the complainant, if any.

(i) Nothing in this section shall be deemed to place the burden of proof on the applicant or recipient.

[29 FR 19277, Dec. 31, 1964, as amended at 38 FR 17928, July 5, 1973; 40 FR 8778, Mar. 3, 1975; 68 FR 51344, Aug. 26, 2003]

HEARINGS AND FINDINGS

§4.61 Presiding officer.

One or more members of the Commission or one or more administrative law judges appointed pursuant to section 3105 of title 5 of the United States Code shall: (a) Preside at a hearing and (b) make findings of fact and conclusions of law if an applicant or recipient waives a hearing and submits written information or argument for the record in accordance with §4.51(d).

[35 FR 11459, July 17, 1970]

§ 4.62 Right to counsel.

In all proceedings under §§ 4.51–4.81, the applicant or recipient and the responsible NRC official shall have the right to be represented by counsel. A notice of appearance shall be filed by counsel prior to participation in any such proceedings.

§ 4.63 Procedures, evidence, and record.

(a) The hearing, decision, and any administrative review thereof shall be conducted in conformity with 5 U.S.C. 554–557 (sections 5–8 of the Administrative Procedure Act), and in accordance with such procedures as are proper (and not inconsistent with §§ 4.61 through 4.64) relating to the conduct of the hearing, giving of notices subsequent to those provided for in § 4.51, taking of testimony, exhibits, arguments and briefs, requests for finding, and other related matters. Both the responsible NRC official and the applicant or recipient shall be entitled to introduce all relevant evidence on the issues as stated in the notice of hearing or as determined by the presiding officer at the outset of or during the hearing.

(b) Technical rules of evidence shall not apply to hearings conducted pursuant to this subpart, but rules or principles designed to assure production of the most credible evidence available and to subject testimony to test by cross-examination shall be applied where reasonably necessary by the presiding officer. The presiding officer may exclude irrelevant, immaterial, or unduly repetitious evidence. All documents and other evidence offered or taken for the record shall be open to examination by the parties and opportunity shall be given to refute facts and arguments advanced on either side of the issues. A transcript shall be made of the oral evidence except to the extent the substance thereof is stipulated for the record.

(c) Each decision made after a hearing has been held shall be based on the hearing record, and written findings of fact and conclusions of law shall be made.

(d) If an applicant or recipient waives a hearing and submits written information or argument for the record in accordance with § 4.51(d), written findings of fact and conclusions of law shall be made.

[29 FR 19277, Dec. 31, 1964, as amended at 35 FR 11459, July 17, 1970; 38 FR 17928, July 5, 1973]

§ 4.64 Consolidated or joint hearings.

In cases in which the same or related facts are asserted to constitute noncompliance with this subpart with respect to two or more Federal statutes, authorities, or other means by which Federal financial assistance is extended and to which this subpart applies or noncompliance with this subpart and the regulations of one or more other Federal departments or agencies issued under title VI of the Civil Rights Act of 1964, the Commission may, by agreement with such other departments or agencies, where applicable, provide for the conduct of consolidated or joint hearings, and for the application to such hearings of rules of procedure not inconsistent with this subpart. Final decisions in such cases, insofar as this regulation is concerned shall be made in accordance with § 4.72.

[29 FR 19277, Dec. 31, 1964, as amended at 40 FR 8778, Mar. 3, 1975; 68 FR 51344, Aug. 26, 2003]

DECISION AND NOTICE

§ 4.71 Initial decision or certification.

The officer designated:

(a) To preside at a hearing, or,

(b) To make findings of fact and conclusions of law if an applicant or recipient waives a hearing and submits written information or argument for the record in accordance with § 4.51(d), shall render an initial decision on the record, or, if the Commission so directs, shall certify the entire record to the Commission for decision, together with a recommended decision on the record. A copy of such initial decision, or of such certification and recommended decision, shall be mailed to the applicant or recipient.

§ 4.72 Exceptions and final decision.

(a) The applicant or recipient, within thirty (30) days of the mailing of an initial decision or a recommended decision, may file with the Commission his exceptions to such decision, with his reasons therefor.

(b) In the absence of exceptions to an initial decision, the Commission may, on its own motion within forty-five (45) days after the mailing of such initial decision, serve on the applicant or recipient a notice that the Commission will review the decision.

(c) Upon the filing of exceptions to an initial decision or of a notice of review, the Commission shall review such initial decision and issue its own decision on the record with its reasons therefor.

(d) In the absence of either exceptions to an initial decision or of a notice of review, such initial decision shall constitute the final decision of the Commission.

(e) Upon the filing of exceptions to a recommended decision, the Commission shall review such recommended decision and issue its own decision on the record with its reasons therefor.

(f) In the absence of exceptions to a recommended decision, the Commission shall review such recommended decision and issue its own decision on the record with its reasons therefor.

§4.73 Rulings required.

Each decision of a presiding officer or the Commission shall set forth the rulings on each finding, conclusion, or exception presented, and shall identify the requirement or requirements imposed by or pursuant to this subpart with which it is found that the applicant or recipient has failed to comply.

§4.74 Content of orders.

The final decision may provide for suspension or termination of, or refusal to grant or continue Federal financial assistance, in whole or in part, to which this regulation applies, and may contain such terms, conditions, and other provisions as are consistent with and will effectuate the purposes of the Act and this subpart, including provisions designed to assure that no Federal financial assistance to which this regulation applies will thereafter be extended to the applicant or recipient determined by such decision to be in default in its performance of an assurance given by it pursuant to this subpart, or to have otherwise failed to comply with this subpart, unless and until it corrects its noncompliance and satisfies the NRC that it will fully comply with this subpart. A copy of the final decision shall be mailed to the applicant or recipient and the complainant, if any.

[29 FR 19277, Dec. 31, 1964, as amended at 68 FR 51344, Aug. 26, 2003]

§4.75 Post termination proceedings.

(a) An applicant or recipient adversely affected by an order issued under §4.74 shall be restored to full eligibility to receive Federal financial assistance if it satisfies the terms and conditions of that order for such eligibility or if it brings itself into compliance with this subpart and provides reasonable assurance that it will fully comply with this subpart.

(b) Any applicant or recipient adversely affected by an order entered pursuant to §4.74 may at any time request the responsible NRC official to restore fully its eligibility to receive Federal financial assistance. Any such request shall be supported by information showing that the applicant or recipient has met the requirements of paragraph (a) of this section. If the responsible NRC official determines that those requirements have been satisfied, he shall restore such eligibility.

(c) If the responsible NRC official denies any such request, the applicant or recipient may submit a request for a hearing in writing, specifying why it believes such official to have been in error. It shall thereupon be given an expeditious hearing, with the decision on the record, in accordance with rules of procedure issued by the responsible NRC official. The applicant or recipient will be restored to such eligibility if it proves at such a hearing that it satisfied the requirements of paragraph (a) of this section. While proceedings under this section are pending, the sanctions imposed by the order issued under §4.74 shall remain in effect.

[38 FR 17928, July 5, 1973, as amended at 40 FR 8778, Mar. 3, 1975]

JUDICIAL REVIEW

§4.81 Judicial review.

Action taken pursuant to section 602 of the Civil Rights Act of 1964 is subject to judicial review as provided in section 603 of that Act.

[40 FR 8778, Mar. 3, 1975]

EFFECT ON OTHER REGULATIONS; FORMS AND INSTRUCTIONS

§4.91 Effect on other regulations.

All regulations, orders, or like directions heretofore issued by any officer of the NRC which impose requirements designed to prohibit any discrimination against individuals on the grounds of sex, race, color, or national origin under any program to which this subpart applies, and which authorize the suspension or termination of or refusal to grant or to continue Federal financial assistance to any applicant for or recipient of such assistance for failure to comply with such requirements, are hereby superseded to the extent that such discrimination is prohibited by this subpart, except that nothing in this subpart shall be deemed to relieve any person of any obligation assumed or imposed under any such superseded regulation, order, instruction, or like direction prior to the effective date of this subpart. Nothing in this subpart, however, shall be deemed to supersede any of the following (including future amendments thereof):

(a) Executive Orders 10925, 11114, and 11246 and regulations issued thereunder, or

(b) Executive Order 11063 and regulations issued thereunder and any other regulations or instructions insofar as such order, regulations or instructions prohibit discrimination on the grounds of sex, race, color, or national origin in any program or situation to which this subpart is inapplicable, or prohibit discrimination on any other ground.

[29 FR 19277, Dec. 31, 1964, as amended at 38 FR 17928, July 5, 1973; 40 FR 8778, Mar. 3, 1975; 68 FR 51344, Aug. 26, 2003]

§4.92 Forms and instructions.

The responsible NRC official shall issue and promptly make available to interested persons forms and detailed instructions and procedures for effectuating this subpart as applied to programs to which this subpart applies and for which he is responsible.

§4.93 Supervision and coordination.

The Commission may from time to time assign to officials of other departments or agencies of the Government, with the consent of the department or agency involved, responsibilities in connection with the effectuation of the purposes of title VI of the Civil Rights Act of 1964 and this subpart, other than responsibility for final decision as provided in §4.72, including the achievement of effective coordination and maximum uniformity within the NRC and within the Executive Branch of the Government in the application of title VI of the Civil Rights Act and this subpart to similar programs and in similar situations. Any action taken, determination made, or requirement imposed by an official of another department or agency acting pursuant to an assignment of responsibility under this section shall have the same effect as though such action had been taken by the responsible NRC official.

[40 FR 8778, Mar. 3, 1975]

Subpart B—Regulations Implementing Section 504 of the Rehabilitation Act of 1973, as Amended

SOURCE: 45 FR 14535, Mar. 6, 1980, unless otherwise noted.

§4.101 Definitions.

As used in this subpart:

(a) *Disabled person* means any person who has a physical or mental impairment that substantially limits one or more major life activities, has a record of such an impairment, or is regarded as having such an impairment. Such term does not include any individual who is an alcoholic or drug abuser whose current use of alcohol or drugs prevents such individual from performing the duties of the job in question or whose employment, by reason of such current alcohol or drug abuse, would constitute a direct threat to property or the safety of others.

(b) As used in paragraph (a) of this section, the phrase:

(1) *Physical or mental impairment* means: (i) Any physiological disorder or condition, cosmetic disfigurement, or anatomical loss affecting one or more of the following body systems: Neurological; musculoskeletal; special sense organs; respiratory, including speech organs; cardiovascular; reproductive; digestive, genitourinary; hemic and lymphatic; skin; and endocrine; or (ii) any mental or psychological disorder, such as mental retardation, organic brain syndrome, emotional or mental illness, and specific learning disabilities. The term *physical or mental impairment* includes, but is not limited to, such diseases and conditions as orthopedic, visual, speech, and hearing impairments, cerebral palsy, epilepsy, muscular dystrophy, multiple sclerosis, cancer, heart disease, diabetes, mental retardation, and emotional illness.

(2) *Major life activities* means functions such as caring for one's self, performing manual tasks, walking, seeing, hearing, speaking, breathing, learning, and working.

(3) *Has a record of such an impairment* means has a history of, or has been misclassified as having, a mental or physical impairment that substantially limits one or more major life activities.

(4) *Is regarded as having an impairment* means:

(i) Has a physical or mental impairment that does not substantially limit major life activities but is treated by a recipient as constituting such a limitation;

(ii) Has a physical or mental impairment that substantially limits major life activities only as a result of the attitudes of others toward such impairment; or

(iii) Does not have a physical or mental impairment but is treated by a recipient as having such an impairment.

(c) *Qualified disabled person* means: (1) With respect to employment, a disabled person who, with reasonable accommodation, can perform essential functions of the job in question and (2) with respect to services, a disabled person who meets the essential eligibility requirements for the receipt of such services.

(d) *Section 504* means section 504 of the Rehabilitation Act of 1973, Pub. L. 93–112, as amended by the Rehabilitation, Comprehensive Services, and Developmental Disabilities Amendments of 1978, Pub. L. 95–602 (29 U.S.C. 794).

DISCRIMINATORY PRACTICES

§4.121 General prohibitions against discrimination.

(a) No qualified disabled person, shall, on the basis of disability, be excluded from participation in, be denied the benefits of, or otherwise be subject to discrimination under any program or activity that receives Federal financial assistance.

(b)(1) A recipient, in providing any aid, benefit, or service, may not, directly or through contractual, licensing, or other arrangements, on the basis of disability:

(i) Deny a qualified disabled person the opportunity to participate in or benefit from the aid, benefit, or service;

(ii) Afford a qualified disabled person an opportunity to participate in or benefit from the aid, benefit, or service that is not equal to that afforded others;

(iii) Provide a qualified disabled person with an aid, benefit, or service that is not as effective in affording equal opportunity to obtain the same result, to gain the same benefit, or to reach the same level of achievement as that provided to others;

(iv) Provide different or separate aid, benefits, or services to disabled persons or to any class of disabled persons than is provided to others unless such action is necessary to provide qualified disabled persons with aid, benefits, or services that are as effective as those provided to others;

(v) Aid or perpetuate discrimination against a qualified disabled person by providing significant assistance to any agency, organization, or person that discriminates on the basis of disability in providing any aid, benefit, or service to beneficiaries of the recipient's program or activity;

(vi) Deny a qualified disabled person the opportunity to participate as a member of planning or advisory boards; or

(vii) Otherwise limit a qualified disabled person in the enjoyment of any right, privilege, advantage, or opportunity enjoyed by others receiving the aid, benefit, or service.

(2) A recipient may not deny a qualified disabled person the opportunity to participate in aid, benefits, or services that are not separate or different, despite the existence of permissibly separate or different aid, benefits, or services.

(3) A recipient may not directly or through contractual or other arrangements, utilize criteria or methods of administration:

(i) That have the effect of subjecting qualified disabled persons to discrimination on the basis of disability,

(ii) That have the purpose or effect of defeating or substantially impairing accomplishment of the objectives of the recipient's program or activity with respect to disabled persons, or

(iii) That perpetuate the discrimination of another recipient if both recipients are subject to common administrative control or are agencies of the same State.

(4) A recipient may not, in determining the site or location of a facility, make selections:

(i) That have the effect of excluding disabled persons from, denying them the benefits of, or otherwise subjecting them to discrimination under any program or activity that receives Federal financial assistance or

(ii) That have the purpose or effect of defeating or substantially impairing the accomplishment of the objectives of the program or activity with respect to disabled persons.

(c) The exclusion of nondisabled persons from aid, benefits, or services limited by Federal statute or Executive Order to disabled persons or the exclusion of a specific class of disabled persons from aid, benefits, or services limited by Federal statute or Executive Order to a different class of disabled persons is not prohibited by this subpart.

(d) Recipients shall administer programs or activities in the most integrated setting appropriate to the needs of qualified disabled persons.

(e) Recipients shall take appropriate steps to ensure that communications with their applicants, employees, and beneficiaries are available to persons with impaired vision and hearing.

[45 FR 14535, Mar. 6, 1980, as amended at 68 FR 51345, Aug. 26, 2003]

§ 4.122 General prohibitions against employment discrimination.

(a) No qualified disabled person shall, on the basis of disability, be subjected to discrimination in employment under any program or activity that receives Federal financial assistance.

(b) A recipient shall make all decisions concerning employment under any program or activity to which this subpart applies in a manner which ensures that discrimination on the basis of disability does not occur and may not limit, segregate, or classify applicants or employees in any way that adversely affects their opportunities or status because of disability.

(c) The prohibition against discrimination in employment applies to the following activities:

(1) Recruitment, advertising, and the processing of applications for employment;

(2) Hiring, upgrading, promotion, award of tenure, demotion, transfer, layoff, termination, right of return from layoff, and rehiring;

(3) Rates of pay or any other form of compensation and changes in compensation;

(4) Job assignments, job classifications, organizational structures, position descriptions, lines of progression, and seniority lists;

(5) Leaves of absence, sick leave, or any other leave;

(6) Fringe benefits available by virtue of employment, whether or not administered by the recipient;

(7) Selection and financial support for training, including apprenticeship, professional meetings, conferences, and other related activities and selection for leaves of absence to pursue training;

(8) Employer sponsored activities, including those that are social or recreational; and

(9) Any other term, condition, or privilege of employment.

(d) A recipient may not participate in a contractual or other relationship that has the effect of subjecting qualified disabled applicants or employees to discrimination prohibited by this subpart. The relationships referred to in this paragraph include relationships with employment and referral agencies, with labor unions, with organizations providing or administering fringe benefits to employees of the recipient, and with organizations providing training and apprenticeships.

[45 FR 14535, Mar. 6, 1980, as amended at 68 FR 51345, Aug. 26, 2003]

§4.123 Reasonable accommodation.

(a) A recipient shall make reasonable accommodation to the known physical or mental limitations of an otherwise qualified disabled applicant or employee unless the recipient can demonstrate that the accommodation would impose an undue hardship on the operation of its program or activity.

(b) Reasonable accommodation may include: (1) Making facilities used by employees readily accessible to and usable by disabled persons, and (2) job restructuring, part-time or modified work schedules, acquisition or modification of equipment or devices, the provision of readers or interpreters, and other similar actions. This list is neither all-inclusive nor meant to suggest that an employer must follow all the actions listed.

(c) In determining pursuant to paragraph (a) of this section whether an accommodation would impose an undue hardship on the operation of a recipient's program or activity, factors to be considered include:

(1) The overall size of the recipient's program or activity with respect to number of employees, number and type of facilities, and size of budget;

(2) The type of the recipient's operations, including the composition and structure of the recipient's workforce; and

(3) The nature and cost of the accommodation needed.

(d) A recipient may not deny any employment opportunity to a qualified disabled employee or applicant if the basis for denial is the need to make reasonable accommodation to the physical or mental limitations of the employee or applicant.

[45 FR 14535, Mar. 6, 1980, as amended at 68 FR 51345, Aug. 26, 2003]

§4.124 Employment criteria.

(a) A recipient may not make use of any employment test or other selection criterion that screens out or tends to screen out disabled persons or any class of disabled persons unless:

(1) The test score or other selection criterion as used by the recipient is shown to be job-related for the position in question; and

(2) Alternative job-related tests or criteria that do not screen out or tend to screen out as many disabled persons are not available.

(b) A recipient shall select and administer tests concerning employment so as best to ensure that, when administered to an applicant or employee who has a disability that impairs sensory, manual, or speaking skills, the test results accurately reflect the applicant's or employee's job skills, aptitude, or whatever other factor the test purports to measure, rather than reflecting the applicant's or employee's impaired sensory, manual, or speaking skills (except where those skills are the factors that the test purports to measure).

§4.125 Preemployment inquiries.

(a) Except as provided in paragraphs (b) and (c) of this section, a recipient may not conduct a preemployment medical examination or may not make preemployment inquiry of an applicant as to whether the applicant is a disabled person or as to the nature of severity of a disability. A recipient may, however, make preemployment inquiry into an applicant's ability to perform job-related functions.

(b) When a recipient is taking remedial action to correct the effects of past discrimination, or when a recipient is taking voluntary action to overcome the effects of conditions that resulted in limited participation in its federally assisted program or activity, or when a recipient is taking affirmative action pursuant to section 503 of the Rehabilitation Act of 1973, the recipient may invite applicants for employment to indicate whether and to what extent they are disabled: *Provided*, That:

(1) The recipient makes clear to the applicant that the information requested is intended for use solely in connection with its remedial action obligations or its voluntary or affirmative action efforts; and

(2) The recipient makes clear to the applicant that the information is being requested on a voluntary basis, that it will be kept confidential as provided in paragraph (d) of this section, that refusal to provide it will not subject the applicant to any adverse treatment, and that it will be used only in accordance with this subpart.

(c) Nothing in this section shall prohibit a recipient from conditioning an offer of employment on the results of a medical examination conducted prior to the employee's entrance on duty: *Provided*, That:

(1) All entering employees are subjected to such an examination regardless of disability; and

(2) The results of such an examination are used only in accordance with the requirements of this subpart.

(d) Information obtained in accordance with this section as to the medical condition or history of the applicant must be collected on separate forms. The recipient shall retain each form as a record for three years from the date the applicant's employment ends, or, if not hired, from the date of application. Each form must be accorded confidentiality as a medical record, except that:

(1) Supervisors and managers may be informed regarding restrictions on the work or duties that may be assigned to disabled persons and regarding necessary accommodations;

(2) First aid and safety personnel may be informed, where appropriate, if the condition associated with the disability might require emergency treatment; and

(3) Government officials investigating compliance with the Rehabilitation Act of 1973 shall be provided relevant information upon request.

[45 FR 14535, Mar. 6, 1980, as amended at 53 FR 19244, May 27, 1988]

§ 4.126 General requirement concerning accessibility.

No qualified disabled person shall, because a recipient's facilities are inaccessible to or unusable by disabled persons, be denied the benefits of, be excluded from participation in, or otherwise be subjected to discrimination under any program or activity that receives Federal financial assistance.

[45 FR 14535, Mar. 6, 1980, as amended at 68 FR 51345, Aug. 26, 2003]

§ 4.127 Existing facilities.

(a) *Accessibility.* A recipient shall operate each program or activity so that when each part is viewed in its entirety it is readily accessible to and usable by disabled persons. This paragraph does not necessarily require a recipient to make each of its existing facilities or every part of an existing facility accessible to and usable by disabled persons.

(b) *Methods.* A recipient may comply with the requirements of paragraph (a) of this section through such means as redesign of equipment, reassignment of classes or other services to accessible buildings, assignment of aids to beneficiaries, home visits, delivery of health, welfare or other social services at alternate accessible sites, alteration of existing facilities and construction of new facilities in conformance with the requirements of § 4.128 or any other methods that result in making its program or activity accessible to and usable by disabled persons. A recipient is not required to make structural changes in existing facilities where other methods are effective in achieving compliance with paragraph (a) of this section. In choosing among available methods for meeting the requirement of paragraph (a) of this section, a recipient shall give priority to those methods that serve disabled persons in the most integrated setting appropriate.

(c) *Time period.* A recipient shall comply with the requirement of paragraph (a) of this section within 60 days of the effective date of this subpart except that where structural changes in facilities are necessary, the changes are to be made within three years of the effective date of this subpart, but in any event, as expeditiously as possible.

(d) *Transition plan.* In the event that structural changes to facilities are necessary to meet the requirement of paragraph (a) of this section, a recipient shall develop a transition plan setting forth the steps necessary to complete the changes. The plan is to be developed with the assistance of interested persons, including disabled persons, or organizations representing disabled persons, and the plan is to meet with the approval of the NRC. The recipient shall retain a copy of the transition plan as a record until any structural change to a facility is complete. A copy of the transition plan is to be made available for public inspection. At a minimum, the plan is to:

(1) Identify physical obstacles in the recipient's facilities that limit the accessibility and usability of its program or activity to disabled persons;

(2) Describe in detail the methods that will be used to make the facilities accessible to and usable by disabled persons;

(3) Specify the schedule for taking the steps necessary to achieve full accessibility under paragraph (a) of this section and, if the time period or the transition plan is longer than 1 year, identify steps that will be taken during each year of the transition period; and

(4) Indicate the person responsible for implementation of the plan.

(e) *Notice.* The recipient shall adopt and implement procedures to ensure that interested persons, including persons with impaired vision or hearing, can obtain information concerning the existence and location of services, activities, and facilities that are accessible to, and usable by, disabled persons.

[45 FR 14535, Mar. 6, 1980, as amended at 53 FR 19244, May 27, 1988; 68 FR 51345, Aug. 26, 2003]

§4.128 New construction.

(a) *Design, construction, and alteration.* New facilities shall be designed and constructed to be readily accessible to and usable by disabled persons. Alterations to existing facilities shall, to the maximum extent feasible, be designed and constructed to be readily accessible to and usable by disabled persons.

(b) *Conformance with Uniform Federal Accessibility Standards.* (1) Effective as of January 18, 1991, design, construction, or alteration of buildings in conformance with sections 3—8 of the Uniform Federal Accessibility Standards (USAF) (appendix A to 41 CFR subpart 101–19.6) shall be deemed to comply with the requirements of this section with respect to those buildings. Departures from particular technical and scoping requirements of UFAS by the use of other methods are permitted where substantially equivalent or greater access to and usability of the building is provided.

(2) For purposes of this section, section 4.1.6(1)(g) of UFAS shall be interpreted to exempt from the requirements of UFAS only mechanical rooms and other spaces that, because of their intended use, will not require accessibility to the public or beneficiaries or result in the employment or residence therein of persons with physical disabilities.

(3) This section does not require recipients to make building alterations that have little likelihood of being accomplished without removing or altering a load-bearing structural member.

[55 FR 52138, 52139, Dec. 19, 1990]

Enforcement

§4.231 Responsibility of applicants and recipients.

(a) *Assurances.* An applicant for Federal financial assistance to which this subpart applies shall submit an assurance, on a form specified by the responsible NRC official, that the program or activity will be operated in compliance with the subpart. An applicant may incorporate these assurances by reference in subsequent applications to the NRC.

(b) *Duration of obligation.* The assurance will obligate the recipient for the period during which Federal financial assistance is extended.

(c) *Remedial action.* (1) If the responsible NRC official finds that a recipient has discriminated against persons on the basis of disability in violation of section 504 or this subpart, the recipient shall take such remedial action as the responsible NRC official deems necessary to overcome the effect of the discrimination.

(2) Where a recipient is found to have discriminated against persons on the basis of disability in violation of section 504 or this subpart and where another recipient exercises control over the recipient that has discriminated, the responsible NRC official, where appropriate, may require either or both recipients to take remedial action.

(3) The responsible NRC official may, where necessary to overcome the effects of discrimination in violation of section 504 or this subpart, require a recipient to take remedial action: (i) With respect to disabled persons who are no longer participants in the recipient's program or activity but who were participants in the program when such discrimination occurred or (ii) with respect to disabled persons who would have been participants in the program or activity had the discrimination not occurred.

(d) *Voluntary action.* A recipient may take steps, in addition to any action that is required by this subpart, to overcome the effects of conditions that resulted in limited participation in the recipient's program or activity by qualified disabled persons.

(e) *Self-evaluation.* (1) A recipient shall as soon as practicable:

(i) Evaluate, with the assistance of interested persons, including disabled persons or organizations representing disabled persons, its current policies and practices and the effects thereof that do not or may not meet the requirements of this subpart;

(ii) Modify, after consultation with interested persons, including disabled persons or organizations representing disabled persons, any policies and practices that do not meet the requirements of this subpart; and

(iii) Take, after consultation with interested persons, including disabled persons or organizations representing disabled persons, appropriate remedial steps to eliminate the effects of any discrimination that resulted from adherence to those policies and practices.

(2) A recipient shall, for at least three years following completion of the evaluation required under paragraph (e)(1) of this section, maintain on file, make available for public inspection, and provide to the responsible NRC official upon request: (i) A list of the interested persons consulted, (ii) a description of areas examined and any problems identified, and (iii) a description of any modifications made and of any remedial steps taken.

(f) *Designation of responsible employee.* A recipient shall designate at least one person to coordinate its efforts to comply with this subpart.

[45 FR 14535, Mar. 6, 1980, as amended at 68 FR 51345, Aug. 26, 2003]

§ 4.232 Notice.

(a) A recipient shall take appropriate initial and continuing steps to notify participants, beneficiaries, applicants, and employees, including those with impaired vision or hearing, and unions or professional organizations holding collective bargaining or professional agreements with the recipient that it does not discriminate on the basis of disability in violation of section 504 and this subpart. The notification shall state, where appropriate, that the recipient does not discriminate in admission or access to, or treatment or employment in, its programs or activities. The notification shall also include an identification of the responsible employee designated pursuant to § 4.231(f). A present recipient shall make the initial notification required by this paragraph within 90 days of the effective date of this subpart. Methods of initial and continuing notification may include the posting of notices, publication in newspapers and magazines, placement of notices in recipients' publications, and distribution of memoranda or other written communications.

(b) If a recipient publishes or uses recruitment materials or publications containing general information that it makes available to participants, beneficiaries, applicants, or employees, if shall include in those materials or publications a statement of the policy described in paragraph (a) of this section. A recipient may meet the requirement of this paragraph either by including appropriate inserts in existing materials and publications or by revising and reprinting the materials and publications.

[45 FR 14535, Mar. 6, 1980, as amended at 68 FR 51345, Aug. 26, 2003]

§4.233 Enforcement procedures.

The enforcement and hearing procedures set forth in §§4.41 through 4.75 of subpart A with respect to discrimination based on sex, race, color or national origin shall be used for the enforcement of the regulations in subpart B with respect to discrimination based on disability.

Subpart C—Regulations Implementing the Age Discrimination Act of 1975, as Amended

SOURCE: 52 FR 25358, July 7, 1987, unless otherwise noted.

GENERAL

§4.301 Purpose and scope.

The purpose of this subpart is to set forth NRC policies and procedures under the Age Discrimination Act of 1975 which prohibits discrimination on the basis of age in programs or activities receiving Federal financial assistance.

§4.302 Application of this subpart.

(a) The Age Discrimination Act of 1975 and these regulations apply to any program or activity receiving Federal financial assistance from NRC.

(b) The Age Discrimination Act of 1975 and these regulations do not apply to—

(1) An age distinction contained in that part of a Federal, State, or local statute or ordinance adopted by an elected, general purpose legislative body that—

(i) Provides any benefits or assistance to persons based on age; or

(ii) Establishes criteria for participation in age-related terms; or

(iii) Describes intended beneficiaries or target groups in age-related terms.

(2) Any employment practice of any employer, employment agency, labor organization, or any labor-management joint apprenticeship training program, except for any program or activity receiving Federal financial assistance for public service employment under the Comprehensive Employment and Training Act of 1974 (CETA) (29 U.S.C. 801 *et seq.*).

§4.303 Definitions.

As used in this subpart:

(a) *Act* means the Age Discrimination Act of 1975, as amended, (title III of Pub. L. 94–135; 89 Stat. 713; 42 U.S.C. 3001 note).

(b) *Action* means any act, activity, policy, rule, standard, or method of administration; or the use of any policy, rule, standard, or method of administration.

(c) *Age* means how old a person is, or the number of elapsed years from the date of a person's birth.

(d) *Age distinction* means any action using age or an age-related term.

(e) *Age-related term* means a word or words which necessarily imply a particular age or range of ages (for example, "children," "adult," "older persons," but not "student").

(f) *Subrecipient* means any of the entities in the definition of "recipient" to which a recipient extends or passes on Federal financial assistance. A subrecipient is generally regarded as a recipient of Federal financial assistance and has all the duties of a recipient in these regulations.

STANDARDS FOR DETERMINING AGE DISCRIMINATION

§4.311 Rules against age discrimination.

The rules stated in this section are limited by the exceptions contained in §§4.313 and 4.314 of this subpart.

(a) *General rule.* No person in the United States shall, on the basis of age, be excluded from participation in, be denied the benefits of, or be subjected to discrimination under, any program or activity receiving Federal financial assistance.

(b) *Specific rules.* A recipient may not, in any program or activity receiving Federal financial assistance, directly or through contractual, licensing, or other arrangements use age distinctions or take any other actions which have the effect, on the basis of age, of—

(1) Excluding individuals from, denying them the benefits of, or subjecting them to discrimination under, a program or activity receiving Federal financial assistance, or

(2) Denying or limiting individuals in their opportunity to participate in any program or activity receiving Federal financial assistance.

(c) The specific forms of age discrimination listed in paragraph (b) of this section do not necessarily constitute a complete list.

§4.312 Definitions of "normal operation" and "statutory objective".

For purposes of §§4.313 and 4.314, the terms "normal operation" and "statutory objective" have the following meaning:

(a) *Normal operation* means the operation of a program or activity without significant changes that would impair its ability to meet its objectives.

(b) *Statutory objective* means any purposes of a program or activity expressly stated in any Federal statute State statute, or local statute or ordinance adopted by an elected general purpose legislative body.

§4.313 Exceptions to the rules against age discrimination. Normal operation or statutory objective of any program or activity.

A recipient is permitted to take an action, otherwise prohibited by §4.311, if the action reasonably takes into account age as a factor necessary to the normal operation or the achievement of any statutory objective of a program or activity. An action reasonably takes into account age as a factor necessary to the normal operation or the achievement of any statutory objective of a program or activity, if—

(a) Age is used as a measure or approximation of one or more other characteristics; and

(b) The other characteristic(s) must be measured or approximated in order for the normal operation of the program or activity to continue, or to achieve any statutory objective of the program or activity; and

(c) The other characteristic(s) can be reasonably measured or approximated by the use of age; and

(d) The other characteristic(s) are impractical to measure directly on an individual basis.

[52 FR 25358, July 7, 1987, as amended at 68 FR 51345, Aug. 26, 2003]

§4.314 Exceptions to the rule against age discrimination. Reasonable factors other than age.

A recipient is permitted to take an action otherwise prohibited by §4.311 which is based on a factor other than age, even though that action may have a disproportionate effect on persons of different ages. An action may be based on a factor other than age only if the factor bears a direct and substantial relationship to the normal operation of the program or activity or to the achievement of a statutory objective.

§4.315 Burden of proof.

The burden of proving that an age distinction or other action falls within the exceptions outlined in §§4.313 and 4.314 is on the recipient of Federal financial assistance.

Duties of NRC Recipients

§4.321 Assurance of compliance.

Each NRC recipient has primary responsibility to ensure that its programs or activities are in compliance with the Act and these regulations. Each recipient will sign an assurance of compliance that its programs or activities will be conducted in compliance with all the requirements imposed by the Act and these regulations. A recipient also has responsibility to maintain records, provide information, and to afford access to its records to NRC, to the extent required to determine whether it is in compliance with the Act and these regulations.

[52 FR 25358, July 7, 1987, as amended at 68 FR 51345, Aug. 26, 2003]

§4.322 Written notice, technical assistance, and educational materials.

(a) NRC will provide written notice to each recipient of its obligations under the Act and these regulations, including its obligation under paragraph (b) of this section.

(b) Where a recipient makes available Federal financial assistance from NRC to a subrecipient, the recipient shall provide the subrecipient written notice of the subrecipient's obligations under the Act and these regulations.

(c) NRC will provide technical assistance, where necessary, to recipients to aid them in complying with the Act and these regulations.

(d) NRC will make available educational materials which set forth the rights and obligations of recipients and beneficiaries under the Act and these regulations.

§ 4.324 Information requirements.

Each recipient shall:

(a) Make available upon request to NRC information necessary to determine whether the recipient is complying with the Act and these regulations.

(b) Permit reasonable access by NRC to the recipient's books, records, accounts, facilities, and other sources of information to the extent necessary to determine whether the recipient is in compliance with the Act and these regulations.

Investigation, Conciliation, and Enforcement Procedures

§ 4.331 Compliance reviews.

(a) NRC may conduct compliance reviews and preaward reviews of recipients or use other similar procedures that will permit it to investigate and correct violations of the Act and these regulations. NRC may conduct these reviews even in absence of a complaint against a recipient. The review may be as comprehensive as necessary to determine whether a violation of these regulations has occurred.

(b) If a compliance review or preaward review indicates a violation of the Act or these regulations, NRC will attempt to achieve voluntary compliance with the Act. If voluntary compliance cannot be achieved, NRC will arrange for enforcement as described in § 4.336.

§ 4.332 Complaints.

(a) Any person, individually or as a member of a class or on behalf of others, may file a complaint with NRC, alleging discrimination prohibited by the Act or these regulations based on an action occurring on or after July 1, 1979. A complainant shall file a complaint within 180 days from the date the complainant first had knowledge of the alleged act of discrimination. However, for good cause shown, NRC may extend this time limit.

(b) NRC will attempt to facilitate the filing of complaints wherever possible, including taking the following measures:

(1) Accepting a complaint as sufficient for further processing that—

(i) Is made in writing;

(ii) Alleges a violation of the Act;

(iii) Identifies the parties involved and the date the complainant first had knowledge of the alleged violation;

(iv) Describes generally the action or practice complained of; and

(v) Is signed by the complainant.

(2) Freely permitting a complainant to add information to the complaint to meet the requirements of a sufficient complaint.

(3) Notifying the complainant and the recipient of their rights and obligations under the complaint procedure, including the right to have a representative at all stages of the complaint procedures.

(4) Notifying the complainant and the recipient (or their representatives) of their right to contact NRC for information and assistance regarding the complaint resolution process.

(c) Each recipient and complainant shall participate actively in efforts toward speedy resolution of the complaint.

(d) NRC will return to the complainant any complaint outside the jurisdiction of these regulations, and will state the reason(s) why it is outside the jurisdiction of these regulations.

§ 4.333 Mediation.

(a) Referral of complaints for mediation. NRC will refer to a mediation agency designated by the Secretary of the Department of Health and Human Services all complaints that—

(1) Fall within the jurisdiction of the Act and these regulations; and

(2) Contain all information necessary for further processing.

(b) Both the complainant and the recipient shall participate in the mediation process to the extent necessary to reach an agreement or make an informed judgment that an agreement is not possible. There must be at least one meeting with the mediator before NRC will accept a judgment that an agreement is not possible. However, the recipient and the complainant need not meet with the mediator at the same time.

(c) If the complainant and the recipient reach an agreement, the mediator shall prepare a written statement of the agreement and have the complainant and recipient sign it. The mediator shall send a copy of the agreement to NRC. NRC will take no further action on the complaint unless the complainant or recipient fails to comply with the agreement.

(d) The mediator shall protect the confidentiality of all information obtained in the course of the mediation process. No mediator shall testify in any adjudicative proceeding, produce any document, or otherwise disclose any information obtained in the course of the mediation process without prior approval of the head of the agency appointing the mediator.

(e) NRC will use the mediation process for a maximum of 60 days after receiving a complaint. Mediation ends if—

(1) From the time NRC receives the complaint 60 days elapse; or

(2) Prior to the end of that 60-day period, the mediator determines an agreement is reached; or

(3) Prior to the end of that 60-day period, the mediator determines that an agreement cannot be reached.

(f) The mediator shall return unresolved complaints to NRC.

§ 4.334 Investigation.

(a) *Informal investigation.* (1) NRC will investigate complaints that are unresolved after mediation or are reopened because of a violation of a mediation agreement.

(2) As part of the initial investigation, NRC will use informal fact-finding methods, including joint or separate discussions with the complaint and recipient to establish the facts and, if possible, settle the complaint on terms that are mutually agreeable to the parties. NRC may seek the assistance of any involved State agency.

(3) NRC will put any agreement in writing and have it signed by the parties and an authorized official at NRC.

(4) The settlement shall not affect the operation of any other enforcement effort of NRC, including compliance reviews and investigation of other complaints which may involve the recipient.

(5) Settlement of a complaint under this section will not constitute a finding of discrimination by the NRC against a recipient or an admission of discrimination by the recipient.

(b) *Formal investigation.* If NRC cannot resolve the complaint through informal investigation, it will begin to develop formal findings through further investigation of the complaint. If the investigation indicates a violation of these regulations, NRC will attempt to obtain voluntary compliance. If NRC cannot obtain voluntary compliance, it will begin enforcement as described in § 4.336.

[52 FR 25358, July 7, 1987, as amended at 68 FR 51345, Aug. 26, 2003]

§ 4.335 Prohibition against intimidation or retaliation.

A recipient may not engage in acts of intimidation or retaliation against any person who—

(a) Attempts to assert a right protected by the Act or these regulations; or

(b) Cooperates in any mediation, investigation, hearing, or other part of NRC's investigation, conciliation, and enforcement process.

§ 4.336 Compliance procedure.

(a) NRC may enforce the Act and these regulations through—

(1) Termination of a recipient's Federal financial assistance from NRC under the program or activity involved where the recipient has violated the Act or these regulations. The determination of the recipient's violation may be made only after a recipient has had an opportunity for a hearing on the record before an administrative law judge. Therefore, cases that are settled in mediation, or prior to a hearing, will not involve termination of a recipient's Federal fiancial assistance from NRC.

(2) Any other means authorized by law including but not limited to—

(i) Referral to the Department of Justice for proceedings to enforce any rights of the United States or obligations of the recipients created by the Act or these regulations.

(ii) Use of any requirement of or referral to any Federal, State, or local government agency that will have the effect of correcting a violation of the Act or these regulations.

(b) NRC will limit any termination under §4.336(a)(1) to the particular recipient and particular program or activity NRC finds in violation of Act or these regulations. NRC will not base any part of a termination on a finding with respect to any program or activity of the recipient that does not receive Federal financial assistance from NRC.

(c) NRC will take no action under paragraph (a) until—

(1) The Commission, or designee, has advised the recipient of its failure to comply with the Act or these regulations and has determined that voluntary compliance cannot be obtained.

(2) 30 days have elapsed after the Commission, or designee, has sent a written report of the circumstances and grounds of the action to the committees of the Congress having legislative jurisdiction over the program or activity involved. A report will be filed whenever any action is taken under paragraph (a) of this section.

(d) NRC also may defer granting new Federal financial assistance to a recipient when termination proceedings under §4.336(a)(1) are initiated.

(1) New Federal financial assistance includes all assistance for which NRC requires an application or approval, including renewal or continuation of existing activities or authorization of new activities, during the deferral period. New Federal financial assistance does not include increases in funding as a result of change computation of formula awards or assistance approved prior to the beginning of termination proceedings under §4.336(a)(1).

(2) NRC will not begin a deferral until the recipient has received a notice of an opportunity for a hearing under §4.336(a)(1). NRC will not continue a deferral for more than 60 days unless a hearing has begun within that time or the time for beginning the hearings has been extended by mutual consent of the recipient and NRC. NRC will not continue a deferral for more than 30 days after the close of the hearing, unless the hearing results in a finding against the recipient.

[52 FR 25358, July 7, 1987, as amended at 68 FR 51345, Aug. 26, 2003]

§4.337 Hearings, decisions, post-termination proceedings.

Certain NRC procedural provisions applicable to title VI of the Civil Rights Act of 1964 apply to NRC enforcement of these regulations. They are §§4.61 through 4.64 and §§4.71 through 4.75.

§4.338 Remedial and affirmative action by recipients.

(a) Where NRC finds a recipient has discriminated on the basis of age, the recipient shall take any remedial action that NRC may require to overcome the effects of the discrimination. If another recipient exercises control over the recipient that has discriminated, NRC may require both recipients to take remedial action.

(b) Even in the absence of a finding of discrimination, a recipient may take affirmative action to overcome the effects of conditions that resulted in limited participation in the recipient's program or activity on the basis of age.

(c) If a recipient, operating a program that serves the elderly or children in addition to persons of other ages, provides special benefits to the elderly or to children, the provision of those benefits shall be presumed to be voluntary affirmative action provided that it does not have the effect of excluding otherwise eligible persons from participation in the program or activity.

[52 FR 25358, July 7, 1987, as amended at 68 FR 51345, Aug. 26, 2003]

§4.339 Alternate funds disbursal procedure.

(a) When NRC withholds funds from a recipient under these regulations, the Commission, or designee, may disburse the withheld funds directly to an alternate recipient, any public or nonprofit private organization or agency, or State or political subdivision of the State.

(b) Any alternative recipient will be required to demonstrate—

(1) The ability to comply with these regulations; and

(2) The ability to achieve the goals of the Federal statute authorizing the Federal financial assistance.

[52 FR 25358, July 7, 1987, as amended at 68 FR 51345, Aug. 26, 2003]

§ 4.340 Exhaustion of administrative remedies.

(a) A complainant may file a civil action following the exhaustion of administrative remedies under the Act. Administrative remedies are exhausted if—

(1) 180 days have elapsed since the complainant filed the complaint and NRC has made no finding with regard to the complaint; or

(2) NRC issues any finding in favor of the recipient.

(b) If NRC fails to make a finding within 180 days or issues a finding in favor of the recipient, NRC will—

(1) Promptly advise the complainant; and

(2) Advise the complainant of his or her right to bring a civil action under section 305(e) of the Act of injunctive relief that will effect the purposes of the Act; and

(3) Inform the complainant that—

(i) The complainant may bring a civil action only in a United States District Court for the district in which the recipient is found or transacts business;

(ii) A complainant prevailing in a civil action has the right to be awarded the costs of the action, including reasonable attorney's fees, but that the complainant must demand these costs in the complaint;

(iii) That before commencing the action, the complainant shall give 30 days notice by registered mail to the Commission, the Secretary of the Department of Health and Human Services, the Attorney General of the United States, and the recipient;

(iv) The notice must state the relief requested, the court in which the complainant is bringing the action, and whether or not attorney's fees are demanded in the event the complainant prevails; and

(v) The complainant may not bring an action if the same alleged violation of the Act by the same recipient is the subject of pending action in any court of the United States.

§ 4.341 Reports.

The NRC shall submit to the Secretary of Health and Human Services, not later than December 31 of each year, a report which—

(a) Describes in detail the steps taken during the preceding fiscal year to carry out the Act; and

(b) Contains data on the frequency, type, and resolution of complaints and on any compliance reviews, sufficient to permit analysis of the agency's progress in reducing age discrimination in programs or activities receiving Federal financial assistance from NRC; and

(c) Contains data directly relevant to the extent of any pattern or practice of age discrimination which NRC has identified in any programs or activities receiving Federal financial assistance from NRC and to progress toward eliminating it; and

(d) Contains evaluative or interpretative information which NRC determines is useful in analyzing agency progress in reducing age discrimination in programs or activities receiving Federal financial assistance from NRC; and

(e) Contains whatever other data the Secretary of HHS may require.

[52 FR 25358, July 7, 1987, as amended at 68 FR 51345, Aug. 26, 2003]

Subpart D [Reserved]

Subpart E—Enforcement of Nondiscrimination on the Basis of Disability in Programs or Activities Conducted by the U.S. Nuclear Regulatory Commission

SOURCE: 51 FR 22888, 22896, June 23, 1986, unless otherwise noted.

§ 4.501 Purpose.

This part effectuates section 119 of the Rehabilitation, Comprehensive Services, and Developmental Disabilities Amendments of 1978, which amended section 504 of the Rehabilitation Act of 1973 to prohibit discrimination on the basis of disability in programs or activities conducted by Executive agencies or the United States Postal Service.

§4.502 Application.

This part applies to all programs or activities conducted by the agency.

§4.503 Definitions.

For purposes of this part, the term—

Assistant Attorney General means the Assistant Attorney General, Civil Rights Division, United States Department of Justice.

Auxiliary aids means services or devices that enable persons with impaired sensory, manual, or speaking skills to have an equal opportunity to participate in, and enjoy the benefits of, programs or activities conducted by the agency. For example, auxiliary aids useful for persons with impaired vision include readers, brailled materials, audio recordings, telecommunications devices and other similar services and devices. Auxiliary aids useful for persons with impaired hearing include telephone handset amplifiers, telephones compatible with hearing aids, telecommunication devices for deaf persons (TDD's), interpreters, notetakers, written materials, and other similar services and devices.

Complete complaint means a written statement that contains the complainant's name and address and describes the agency's alleged discriminatory action in sufficient detail to inform the agency of the nature and date of the alleged violation of section 504. It shall be signed by the complainant or by someone authorized to do so on his or her behalf. Complaints filed on behalf of classes or third parties shall describe or identify (by name, if possible) the alleged victims of discrimination.

Disabled person means any person who has a physical or mental impairment that substantially limits one or more major life activities, has a record of such an impairment, or is regarded as having such an impairment.

As used in this definition, the phrase:

(1) *Physical or mental impairment* includes—

(i) Any physiological disorder or condition, cosmetic disfigurement, or anatomical loss affecting one or more of the following body systems: Neurological; musculoskeletal; special sense organs; respiratory, including speech organs; cardiovascular; reproductive; digestive; genitourinary; hemic and lymphatic; skin; and endocrine; or

(ii) Any mental or psychological disorder, such as mental retardation, organic brain syndrome, emotional or mental illness, and specific learning disabilities. The term "physical or mental impairment" includes, but is not limited to, such diseases and conditions as orthopedic, visual, speech, and hearing impairments, cerebral palsy, epilepsy, muscular dystrophy, multiple sclerosis, cancer, heart disease, diabetes, mental retardation, emotional illness, and drug addiction and alcoholism.

(2) *Major life activities* includes functions such as caring for one's self, performing manual tasks, walking, seeing, hearing, speaking, breathing, learning, and working.

(3) *Has a record of such an impairment* means has a history of, or has been misclassified as having, a mental or physical impairment that substantially limits one or more major life activities.

(4) *Is regarded as having an impairment* means—

(i) Has a physical or mental impairment that does not substantially limit major life activities but is treated by the agency as constituting such a limitation;

(ii) Has a physical or mental impairment that substantially limits major life activities only as a result of the attitudes of others toward such impairment; or

(iii) Has none of the impairments defined in paragraph (1) of this definition but is treated by the agency as having such an impairment.

Facility means all or any portion of buildings, structures, equipment, roads, walks, parking lots, rolling stock or other conveyances, or other real or personal property.

Historic preservation programs means programs conducted by the agency that have preservation of historic properties as a primary purpose.

Historic properties means those properties that are listed or eligible for listing in the National Register of Historic Places or properties designated as historic under a statute of the appropriate State or local government body.

Qualified disabled person means—

(1) With respect to preschool, elementary, or secondary education services provided by the agency, a disabled person who is a member of a class of persons otherwise entitled by statute, regulation, or agency policy to receive education services from the agency.

(2) With respect to any other agency program or activity under which a person is required to perform services or to achieve a level of accomplishment, a disabled person who meets the essential eligibility requirements and who can achieve the purpose of the program or activity without modifications in the program or activity that the agency can demonstrate would result in a fundamental alteration in its nature;

(3) With respect to any other program or activity, a disabled person who meets the essential eligibility requirements for participation in, or receipt of benefits from, that program or activity; and

(4) *Qualified disabled person* is defined for purposes of employment in 29 CFR 1613.702(f), which is made applicable to this part by § 4.540.

Section 504 means section 504 of the Rehabilitation Act of 1973 (Pub. L. 93–112, 87 Stat. 394 (29 U.S.C. 794)), as amended by the Rehabilitation Act Amendments of 1974 (Pub. L. 93–516, 88 Stat. 1617), and the Rehabilitation, Comprehensive Services, and Developmental Disabilities Amendments of 1978 (Pub. L. 95–602, 92 Stat. 2955). As used in this part, section 504 applies only to programs or activities conducted by Executive agencies and not to federally assisted programs.

Substantial impairment means a significant loss of the integrity of finished materials, design quality, or special character resulting from a permanent alteration.

§§ 4.504–4.509 [Reserved]

§ 4.510 Self-evaluation.

(a) The agency shall, by August 24, 1987, evaluate its current policies and practices, and the effects thereof, that do not or may not meet the requirements of this part, and, to the extent modification of any such policies and practices is required, the agency shall proceed to make the necessary modifications.

(b) The agency shall provide an opportunity to interested persons, including disabled persons or organizations representing disabled persons, to participate in the self-evaluation process by submitting comments (both oral and written).

(c) The agency shall, until three years following the completion of the self-evaluation, maintain on file and make available for public inspection:

(1) A description of areas examined and any problems identified, and

(2) A description of any modifications made.

§ 4.511 Notice.

The agency shall make available to employees, applicants, participants, beneficiaries, and other interested persons such information regarding the provisions of this part and its applicability to the programs or activities conducted by the agency, and make such information available to them in such manner as the head of the agency finds necessary to apprise such persons of the protections against discrimination assured them by section 504 and this regulation.

§§ 4.512–4.529 [Reserved]

§ 4.530 General prohibitions against discrimination.

(a) No qualified disabled person shall, on the basis of disability, be excluded from participation in, be denied the benefits of, or otherwise be subjected to discrimination under any program or activity conducted by the agency.

(b)(1) The agency, in providing any aid, benefit, or service, may not, directly or through contractual, licensing, or other arrangements, on the basis of disability—

(i) Deny a qualified disabled person the opportunity to participate in or benefit from the aid, benefit, or service;

(ii) Afford a qualified disabled person an opportunity to participate in or benefit from the aid, benefit, or service that is not equal to that afforded others;

(iii) Provide a qualified disabled person with an aid, benefit, or service that is not as effective in affording equal opportunity to obtain the same result, to gain the same benefit, or to reach the same level of achievement as that provided to others;

(iv) Provide different or separate aid, benefits, or services to disabled persons or to any class of disabled persons than is provided to others unless such action is necessary to provide qualified disabled persons with aid, benefits, or services that are as effective as those provided to others;

(v) Deny a qualified disabled person the opportunity to participate as a member of planning or advisory boards; or

(vi) Otherwise limit a qualified disabled person in the enjoyment of any right, privilege, advantage, or opportunity enjoyed by others receiving the aid, benefit, or service.

(2) The agency may not deny a qualified disabled person the opportunity to participate in programs or activities that are not separate or different, despite the existence of permissibly separate or different programs or activities.

(3) The agency may not, directly or through contractual or other arrangments, utilize criteria or methods of administration the purpose or effect of which would—

(i) Subject qualified disabled persons to discrimination on the basis of disability; or

(ii) Defeat or substantially impair accomplishment of the objectives of a program or activity with respect to disabled persons.

(4) The agency may not, in determining the site or location of a facility, make selections the purpose or effect of which would—

(i) Exclude disabled persons from, deny them the benefits of, or otherwise subject them to discrimination under any program or activity conducted by the agency; or

(ii) Defeat or substantially impair the accomplishment of the objectives of a program or activity with respect to disabled persons.

(5) The agency, in the selection of procurement contractors, may not use criteria that subject qualified disabled persons to discrimination on the basis of disability.

(6) The agency may not administer a licensing or certification program in a manner that subjects qualified disabled persons to discrimination on the basis of disability, nor may the agency establish requirements for the programs or activities of licensees or certified entities that subject qualified disabled persons to discrimination on the basis of disability. However, the programs or activities of entities that are licensed or certified by the agency are not, themselves, covered by this part.

(c) The exclusion of nondisabled persons from the benefits of a program limited by Federal statute or Executive order to disabled persons or the exclusion of a specific class of disabled persons from a program limited by Federal statute or Executive order to a different class of disabled persons is not prohibited by this part.

(d) The agency shall administer programs and activities in the most integrated setting appropriate to the needs of qualified disabled persons.

§§ 4.531–4.539 [Reserved]

§ 4.540 Employment.

No qualified disabled person shall, on the basis of disability, be subjected to discrimination in employment under any program or activity conducted by the agency. The definitions, requirements, and procedures of section 501 of the Rehabilitation Act of 1973 (29 U.S.C. 791), as established by the Equal Employment Opportunity Commission in 29 CFR part 1613, shall apply to employment in federally conducted programs or activities.

§§ 4.541–4.548 [Reserved]

§ 4.549 Program accessibility: Discrimination prohibited.

Except as otherwise provided in §4.550, no qualified disabled person shall, because the agency's facilities are inaccessible to or unusable by disabled persons, be denied the benefits of, be excluded from participation in, or otherwise be subjected to discrimination under any program or activity conducted by the agency.

§ 4.550 Program accessibility: Existing facilities.

(a) *General.* The agency shall operate each program or activity so that the program or activity, when viewed in its entirety, is readily accessible to and usable by disabled persons. This paragraph does not—

(1) Necessarily require the agency to make each of its existing facilities accessible to and usable by disabled persons;

(2) In the case of historic preservation programs, require the agency to take any action that would result in a substantial impairment of significant historic features of an historic property; or

(3) Require the agency to take any action that it can demonstrate would result in a fundamental alteration in the nature of a program or activity or in undue financial and administrative burdens. In those circumstances where agency personnel believe that the proposed action would fundamentally alter the program or activity or would result in undue financial and administrative burdens, the agency has the burden of proving that compliance with § 4.550(a) would result in such alteration or burdens. The decision that compliance would result in such alteration or burdens must be made by the agency head or his or her designee after considering all agency resources available for use in the funding and operation of the conducted program or activity, and must be accompanied by a written statement of the reasons for reaching that conclusion. If an action would result in such an alteration or such burdens, the agency shall take any other action that would not result in such an alteration or such burdens but would nevertheless ensure that disabled persons receive the benefits and services of the program or activity.

(b) *Methods*—(1) *General.* The agency may comply with the requirements of this section through such means as redesign of equipment, reassignment of services to accessible buildings, assignment of aides to beneficiaries, home visits, delivery of services at alternate accessible sites, alteration of existing facilities and construction of new facilities, use of accessible rolling stock, or any other methods that result in making its programs or activities readily accessible to and usable by disabled persons. The agency is not required to make structural changes in existing facilities where other methods are effective in achieving compliance with this section. The agency, in making alterations to existing buildings, shall meet accessibility requirements to the extent compelled by the Architectural Barriers Act of 1968, as amended (42 U.S.C. 4151–4157), and any regulations implementing it. In choosing among available methods for meeting the requirements of this section, the agency shall give priority to those methods that offer programs and activities to qualified disabled persons in the most integrated setting appropriate.

(2) *Historic preservation programs.* In meeting the requirements of § 4.550(a) in historic preservation programs, the agency shall give priority to methods that provide physical access to disabled persons. In cases where a physical alteration to an historic property is not required because of § 4.550(a)(2) or (a)(3), alternative methods of achieving program accessibility include—

(i) Using audio-visual materials and devices to depict those portions of an historic property that cannot otherwise be made accessible;

(ii) Assigning persons to guide disabled persons into or through portions of historic properties that cannot otherwise be made accessible; or

(iii) Adopting other innovative methods.

(c) *Time period for compliance.* The agency shall comply with the obligations established under this section by October 21, 1986, except that where structural changes in facilities are undertaken, such changes shall be made by August 22, 1989, but in any event as expeditiously as possible.

(d) *Transition plan.* In the event that structural changes to facilities will be undertaken to achieve program accessibility, the agency shall develop, by February 23, 1987 a transition plan setting forth the steps necessary to complete such changes. The agency shall provide an opportunity to interested persons, including disabled persons or organizations representing disabled persons, to participate in the development of the transition plan by submitting comments (both oral and written). A copy of the transition plan shall be made available for public inspection. The plan shall, at a minimum—

(1) Identify physical obstacles in the agency's facilities that limit the accessibility of its programs or activities to disabled persons;

(2) Describe in detail the methods that will be used to make the facilities accessible;

(3) Specify the schedule for taking the steps necessary to achieve compliance with this section and, if the time period of the transition plan is longer than one year, identify steps that will be taken during each year of the transition period; and

(4) Indicate the official responsible for implementation of the plan.

§4.551 Program accessibility: New construction and alterations.

Each building or part of a building that is constructed or altered by, on behalf of, or for the use of the agency shall be designed, constructed, or altered so as to be readily accessible to and usable by disabled persons. The definitions, requirements, and standards of the Architectural Barriers Act (42 U.S.C. 4151–4157), as established in 41 CFR 101–19.600 to 101–19.607, apply to buildings covered by this section.

§§4.552–4.559 [Reserved]

§4.560 Communications.

(a) The agency shall take appropriate steps to ensure effective communication with applicants, participants, personnel of other Federal entities, and members of the public.

(1) The agency shall furnish appropriate auxiliary aids where necessary to afford a disabled person an equal opportunity to participate in, and enjoy the benefits of, a program or activity conducted by the agency.

(i) In determining what type of auxiliary aid is necessary, the agency shall give primary consideration to the requests of the disabled person.

(ii) The agency need not provide individually prescribed devices, readers for personal use or study, or other devices of a personal nature.

(2) Where the agency communicates with applicants and beneficiaries by telephone, telecommunication devices for deaf person (TDD's) or equally effective telecommunication systems shall be used.

(b) The agency shall ensure that interested persons, including persons with impaired vision or hearing, can obtain information as to the existence and location of accessible services, activities, and facilities.

(c) The agency shall provide signage at a primary entrance to each of its inaccessible facilities, directing users to a location at which they can obtain information about accessible facilities. The international symbol for accessibility shall be used at each primary entrance of an accessible facility.

(d) This section does not require the agency to take any action that it can demonstrate would result in a fundamental alteration in the nature of a program or activity or in undue financial and adminstrative burdens. In those circumstances where agency personnel believe that the proposed action would fundamentally alter the program or activity or would result in undue financial and administrative burdens, the agency has the burden of proving that compliance with §4.560 would result in such alteration or burdens. The decision that compliance would result in such alteration or burdens must be made by the agency head or his or her designee after considering all agency resources available for use in the funding and operation of the conducted program or activity, and must be accompanied by a written statement of the reasons for reaching that conclusion. If an action required to comply with this section would result in such an alteration or such burdens, the agency shall take any other action that would not result in such an alteration or such burdens but would nevertheless ensure that, to the maximum extent possible, disabled persons receive the benefits and services of the program or activity.

§§ 4.561–4.569 [Reserved]

§ 4.570 Compliance procedures.

(a) Except as provided in paragraph (b) of this section, this section applies to all allegations of discrimination on the basis of disability in programs or activities conducted by the agency.

(b) The agency shall process complaints alleging violations of section 504 with respect to employment according to the procedures established by the Equal Employment Opportunity Commission in 29 CFR part 1613 pursuant to section 501 of the Rehabilitation Act of 1973 (29 U.S.C. 791).

(c) The Civil Rights Program Manager, Office of Small Business and Civil Rights, shall be responsible for coordinating implementation of this section. Complaints should be sent to the NRC using an appropriate method listed in § 4.5.

(d) The agency shall accept and investigate all complete complaints for which it has jurisdiction. All complete complaints must be filed within 180 days of the alleged act of discrimination. The agency may extend this time period for good cause.

(e) If the agency receives a complaint over which it does not have jurisdiction, it shall promptly notify the complainant and shall make reasonable efforts to refer the complaint to the appropriate government entity.

(f) The agency shall notify the Architectural and Transportation Barriers Compliance Board upon receipt of any complaint alleging that a building or facility that is subject to the Architectural Barriers Act of 1968, as amended (42 U.S.C. 4151–4157), or section 502 of the Rehabilitation Act of 1973, as amended (29 U.S.C. 792), is not readily accessible to and usable by disabled persons.

(g) Within 180 days of the receipt of a complete complaint for which it has jurisdiction, the agency shall notify the complainant of the results of the investigation in a letter containing—

(1) Findings of fact and conclusions of law;

(2) A description of a remedy for each violation found; and

(3) A notice of the right to appeal.

(h) Appeals of the findings of fact and conclusions of law or remedies must be filed by the complainant within 90 days of receipt from the agency of the letter required by § 4.570(g). The agency may extend this time for good cause.

(i) Timely appeals shall be accepted and processed by the head of the agency.

(j) The head of the agency shall notify the complainant of the results of the appeal within 60 days of the receipt of the request. If the head of the agency determines that additional information is needed from the complainant, he or she shall have 60 days from the date of receipt of the additional information to make his or her determination on the appeal.

(k) The time limits cited in paragraphs (g) and (j) of this section may be extended with the permission of the Assistant Attorney General.

(l) The agency may delegate its authority for conducting complaint investigations to other Federal agencies, except that the authority for making the final determination may not be delegated to another agency.

[51 FR 22888, 22896, June 23, 1986, as amended at 68 FR 58799, Oct. 10, 2003]

§§ 4.571–4.999 [Reserved]

Appendix A to Part 4—Federal Financial Assistance to Which This Part Applies[1]

(a) *Conferences on regulatory programs.* Agreements for financial assistance to State officials, without full-cost recovery, for visits to NRC facilities and offices or to other locations to confer on regulatory programs and related matters.

(b) *Orientation and instruction.* Agreements for assistance to State and local officials, without full-cost recovery, to receive orientation and on-the-job instruction at NRC facilities and offices.

(c) *Courses in fundamentals of radiation.* Agreements for the conduct of courses for State and local employees, without full-cost recovery, in fundamentals of radiation and radiation protection.

[1] Categories of assistance may be added to appendix A from time to time by notice published in the FEDERAL REGISTER. This part shall be deemed to apply to all grants, loans or contracts entered into under any such category of assistance on or after the effective date of the inclusion of the category of assistance in appendix A.

(d) *Participation in meetings and conferences.* Agreements for participation, without full-cost recovery, in meetings, conferences, workshops, and symposia to assist scientific, professional or educational institutions or groups.

(e) *Research Support.* Agreements for the financial support of basic and applied scientific research and for the exchange of scientific information.

[29 FR 19277, Dec. 31, 1964, as amended at 38 FR 17929, July 5, 1973; 40 FR 8778, Mar. 3, 1975; 45 FR 14539, Mar. 6, 1980; 52 FR 25361, July 7, 1987]

PART 5—NONDISCRIMINATION ON THE BASIS OF SEX IN EDUCATION PROGRAMS OR ACTIVITIES RECEIVING FEDERAL FINANCIAL ASSISTANCE

Subpart A—Introduction

Subpart B—Coverage

Subpart C—Discrimination on the Basis of Sex in Admission and Recruitment Prohibited

Subpart D—Discrimination on the Basis of Sex in Education Programs or Activities Prohibited

Subpart E—Discrimination on the Basis of Sex in Employment in Education Programs or Activities Prohibited

Subpart F—Procedures

AUTHORITY: 20 U.S.C. 1681, 1682, 1683, 1685, 1686, 1687, 1688.

SOURCE: 65 FR 52865, 52875, Aug. 30, 2000, unless otherwise noted.

Subpart A—Introduction

§5.100 Purpose and effective date.

The purpose of these Title IX regulations is to effectuate Title IX of the Education Amendments of 1972, as amended (except sections 904 and 906 of those Amendments) (20 U.S.C. 1681, 1682, 1683, 1685, 1686, 1687, 1688), which is designed to eliminate (with certain exceptions) discrimination on the basis of sex in any education program or activity receiving Federal financial assistance, whether or not such program or activity is offered or sponsored by an educational institution as defined in these Title IX regulations. The effective date of these Title IX regulations shall be September 29, 2000.

§ 5.105 Definitions.

As used in these Title IX regulations, the term:

Administratively separate unit means a school, department, or college of an educational institution (other than a local educational agency) admission to which is independent of admission to any other component of such institution.

Admission means selection for part-time, full-time, special, associate, transfer, exchange, or any other enrollment, membership, or matriculation in or at an education program or activity operated by a recipient.

Applicant means one who submits an application, request, or plan required to be approved by an official of the Federal agency that awards Federal financial assistance, or by a recipient, as a condition to becoming a recipient.

Designated agency official means Program Manager, Civil Rights Program.

Educational institution means a local educational agency (LEA) as defined by 20 U.S.C. 8801(18), a preschool, a private elementary or secondary school, or an applicant or recipient that is an institution of graduate higher education, an institution of undergraduate higher education, an institution of professional education, or an institution of vocational education, as defined in this section.

Federal financial assistance means any of the following, when authorized or extended under a law administered by the Federal agency that awards such assistance:

(1) A grant or loan of Federal financial assistance, including funds made available for:

(i) The acquisition, construction, renovation, restoration, or repair of a building or facility or any portion thereof; and

(ii) Scholarships, loans, grants, wages, or other funds extended to any entity for payment to or on behalf of students admitted to that entity, or extended directly to such students for payment to that entity.

(2) A grant of Federal real or personal property or any interest therein, including surplus property, and the proceeds of the sale or transfer of such property, if the Federal share of the fair market value of the property is not, upon such sale or transfer, properly accounted for to the Federal Government.

(3) Provision of the services of Federal personnel.

(4) Sale or lease of Federal property or any interest therein at nominal consideration, or at consideration reduced for the purpose of assisting the recipient or in recognition of public interest to be served thereby, or permission to use Federal property or any interest therein without consideration.

(5) Any other contract, agreement, or arrangement that has as one of its purposes the provision of assistance to any education program or activity, except a contract of insurance or guaranty.

Institution of graduate higher education means an institution that:

(1) Offers academic study beyond the bachelor of arts or bachelor of science degree, whether or not leading to a certificate of any higher degree in the liberal arts and sciences;

(2) Awards any degree in a professional field beyond the first professional degree (regardless of whether the first professional degree in such field is awarded by an institution of undergraduate higher education or professional education); or

(3) Awards no degree and offers no further academic study, but operates ordinarily for the purpose of facilitating research by persons who have received the highest graduate degree in any field of study.

Institution of professional education means an institution (except any institution of undergraduate higher education) that offers a program of academic study that leads to a first professional degree in a field for which there is a national specialized accrediting agency recognized by the Secretary of Education.

Institution of undergraduate higher education means:

(1) An institution offering at least two but less than four years of college-level study beyond the high school level, leading to a diploma or an associate degree, or wholly or principally

creditable toward a baccalaureate degree; or

(2) An institution offering academic study leading to a baccalaureate degree; or

(3) An agency or body that certifies credentials or offers degrees, but that may or may not offer academic study.

Institution of vocational education means a school or institution (except an institution of professional or graduate or undergraduate higher education) that has as its primary purpose preparation of students to pursue a technical, skilled, or semiskilled occupation or trade, or to pursue study in a technical field, whether or not the school or institution offers certificates, diplomas, or degrees and whether or not it offers full-time study.

Recipient means any State or political subdivision thereof, or any instrumentality of a State or political subdivision thereof, any public or private agency, institution, or organization, or other entity, or any person, to whom Federal financial assistance is extended directly or through another recipient and that operates an education program or activity that receives such assistance, including any subunit, successor, assignee, or transferee thereof.

Student means a person who has gained admission.

Title IX means Title IX of the Education Amendments of 1972, Public Law 92–318, 86 Stat. 235, 373 (codified as amended at 20 U.S.C. 1681–1688) (except sections 904 and 906 thereof), as amended by section 3 of Public Law 93–568, 88 Stat. 1855, by section 412 of the Education Amendments of 1976, Public Law 94–482, 90 Stat. 2234, and by Section 3 of Public Law 100–259, 102 Stat. 28, 28–29 (20 U.S.C. 1681, 1682, 1683, 1685, 1686, 1687, 1688).

Title IX regulations means the provisions set forth at §§5.100 through 5.605.

Transition plan means a plan subject to the approval of the Secretary of Education pursuant to section 901(a)(2) of the Education Amendments of 1972, 20 U.S.C. 1681(a)(2), under which an educational institution operates in making the transition from being an educational institution that admits only students of one sex to being one that admits students of both sexes without discrimination.

§5.110 Remedial and affirmative action and self-evaluation.

(a) *Remedial action.* If the designated agency official finds that a recipient has discriminated against persons on the basis of sex in an education program or activity, such recipient shall take such remedial action as the designated agency official deems necessary to overcome the effects of such discrimination.

(b) *Affirmative action.* In the absence of a finding of discrimination on the basis of sex in an education program or activity, a recipient may take affirmative action consistent with law to overcome the effects of conditions that resulted in limited participation therein by persons of a particular sex. Nothing in these Title IX regulations shall be interpreted to alter any affirmative action obligations that a recipient may have under Executive Order 11246, 3 CFR, 1964–1965 Comp., p. 339; as amended by Executive Order 11375, 3 CFR, 1966–1970 Comp., p. 684; as amended by Executive Order 11478, 3 CFR, 1966–1970 Comp., p. 803; as amended by Executive Order 12086, 3 CFR, 1978 Comp., p. 230; as amended by Executive Order 12107, 3 CFR, 1978 Comp., p. 264.

(c) *Self-evaluation.* Each recipient education institution shall, within one year of September 29, 2000:

(1) Evaluate, in terms of the requirements of these Title IX regulations, its current policies and practices and the effects thereof concerning admission of students, treatment of students, and employment of both academic and non-academic personnel working in connection with the recipient's education program or activity;

(2) Modify any of these policies and practices that do not or may not meet the requirements of these Title IX regulations; and

(3) Take appropriate remedial steps to eliminate the effects of any discrimination that resulted or may have resulted from adherence to these policies and practices.

(d) *Availability of self-evaluation and related materials.* Recipients shall maintain on file for at least three years following completion of the evaluation required under paragraph (c) of this section, and shall provide to the designated agency official upon request, a description of any modifications made pursuant to paragraph (c)(2) of this section and of any remedial steps taken pursuant to paragraph (c)(3) of this section.

§ 5.115 Assurance required.

(a) *General.* Either at the application stage or the award stage, Federal agencies must ensure that applications for Federal financial assistance or awards of Federal financial assistance contain, be accompanied by, or be covered by a specifically identified assurance from the applicant or recipient, satisfactory to the designated agency official, that each education program or activity operated by the applicant or recipient and to which these Title IX regulations apply will be operated in compliance with these Title IX regulations. An assurance of compliance with these Title IX regulations shall not be satisfactory to the designated agency official if the applicant or recipient to whom such assurance applies fails to commit itself to take whatever remedial action is necessary in accordance with § 5.110(a) to eliminate existing discrimination on the basis of sex or to eliminate the effects of past discrimination whether occurring prior to or subsequent to the submission to the designated agency official of such assurance.

(b) *Duration of obligation.* (1) In the case of Federal financial assistance extended to provide real property or structures thereon, such assurance shall obligate the recipient or, in the case of a subsequent transfer, the transferee, for the period during which the real property or structures are used to provide an education program or activity.

(2) In the case of Federal financial assistance extended to provide personal property, such assurance shall obligate the recipient for the period during which it retains ownership or possession of the property.

(3) In all other cases such assurance shall obligate the recipient for the period during which Federal financial assistance is extended.

(c) *Form.* (1) The assurances required by paragraph (a) of this section, which may be included as part of a document that addresses other assurances or obligations, shall include that the applicant or recipient will comply with all applicable Federal statutes relating to nondiscrimination. These include but are not limited to: Title IX of the Education Amendments of 1972, as amended (20 U.S.C. 1681–1683, 1685–1688).

(2) The designated agency official will specify the extent to which such assurances will be required of the applicant's or recipient's subgrantees, contractors, subcontractors, transferees, or successors in interest.

§ 5.120 Transfers of property.

If a recipient sells or otherwise transfers property financed in whole or in part with Federal financial assistance to a transferee that operates any education program or activity, and the Federal share of the fair market value of the property is not upon such sale or transfer properly accounted for to the Federal Government, both the transferor and the transferee shall be deemed to be recipients, subject to the provisions of §§ 5.205 through 5.235(a).

§ 5.125 Effect of other requirements.

(a) *Effect of other Federal provisions.* The obligations imposed by these Title IX regulations are independent of, and do not alter, obligations not to discriminate on the basis of sex imposed by Executive Order 11246, 3 CFR, 1964–1965 Comp., p. 339; as amended by Executive Order 11375, 3 CFR, 1966–1970 Comp., p. 684; as amended by Executive Order 11478, 3 CFR, 1966–1970 Comp., p. 803; as amended by Executive Order 12087, 3 CFR, 1978 Comp., p. 230; as amended by Executive Order 12107, 3 CFR, 1978 Comp., p. 264; sections 704 and 855 of the Public Health Service Act (42 U.S.C. 295m, 298b-2); Title VII of the Civil Rights Act of 1964 (42 U.S.C. 2000e *et seq.*); the Equal Pay Act of 1963 (29 U.S.C. 206); and any other Act of Congress or Federal regulation.

(b) *Effect of State or local law or other requirements.* The obligation to comply with these Title IX regulations is not obviated or alleviated by any State or local law or other requirement that would render any applicant or student ineligible, or limit the eligibility of any applicant or student, on the basis of sex, to practice any occupation or profession.

(c) *Effect of rules or regulations of private organizations.* The obligation to comply with these Title IX regulations is not obviated or alleviated by any rule or regulation of any organization, club, athletic or other league, or association that would render any applicant or student ineligible to participate or limit the eligibility or participation of any applicant or student, on the basis of sex, in any education program or activity operated by a recipient and that receives Federal financial assistance.

§5.130 Effect of employment opportunities.

The obligation to comply with these Title IX regulations is not obviated or alleviated because employment opportunities in any occupation or profession are or may be more limited for members of one sex than for members of the other sex.

§5.135 Designation of responsible employee and adoption of grievance procedures.

(a) *Designation of responsible employee.* Each recipient shall designate at least one employee to coordinate its efforts to comply with and carry out its responsibilities under these Title IX regulations, including any investigation of any complaint communicated to such recipient alleging its noncompliance with these Title IX regulations or alleging any actions that would be prohibited by these Title IX regulations. The recipient shall notify all its students and employees of the name, office address, and telephone number of the employee or employees appointed pursuant to this paragraph.

(b) *Complaint procedure of recipient.* A recipient shall adopt and publish grievance procedures providing for prompt and equitable resolution of student and employee complaints alleging any action that would be prohibited by these Title IX regulations.

§5.140 Dissemination of policy.

(a) *Notification of policy.* (1) Each recipient shall implement specific and continuing steps to notify applicants for admission and employment, students and parents of elementary and secondary school students, employees, sources of referral of applicants for admission and employment, and all unions or professional organizations holding collective bargaining or professional agreements with the recipient, that it does not discriminate on the basis of sex in the educational programs or activities that it operates, and that it is required by Title IX and these Title IX regulations not to discriminate in such a manner. Such notification shall contain such information, and be made in such manner, as the designated agency official finds necessary to apprise such persons of the protections against discrimination assured them by Title IX and these Title IX regulations, but shall state at least that the requirement not to discriminate in education programs or activities extends to employment therein, and to admission thereto unless §§5.300 through 5.310 do not apply to the recipient, and that inquiries concerning the application of Title IX and these Title IX regulations to such recipient may be referred to the employee designated pursuant to §5.135, or to the designated agency official.

(2) Each recipient shall make the initial notification required by paragraph (a)(1) of this section within 90 days of September 29, 2000 or of the date these Title IX regulations first apply to such recipient, whichever comes later, which notification shall include publication in:

(i) Newspapers and magazines operated by such recipient or by student, alumnae, or alumni groups for or in connection with such recipient; and

(ii) Memoranda or other written communications distributed to every student and employee of such recipient.

(b) *Publications.* (1) Each recipient shall prominently include a statement of the policy described in paragraph (a) of this section in each announcement, bulletin, catalog, or application form that it makes available to any person of a type, described in paragraph (a) of this section, or which is otherwise used in connection with the recruitment of students or employees.

(2) A recipient shall not use or distribute a publication of the type described in paragraph (b)(1) of this section that suggests, by text or illustration, that such recipient treats applicants, students, or employees differently on the basis of sex except as such treatment is permitted by these Title IX regulations.

(c) *Distribution.* Each recipient shall distribute without discrimination on the basis of sex each publication described in paragraph (b)(1) of this section, and shall apprise each of its admission and employment recruitment representatives of the policy of nondiscrimination described in paragraph (a) of this section, and shall require such representatives to adhere to such policy.

Subpart B—Coverage

§ 5.200 Application.

Except as provided in §§ 5.205 through 5.235(a), these Title IX regulations apply to every recipient and to each education program or activity operated by such recipient that receives Federal financial assistance.

§ 5.205 Educational institutions and other entities controlled by religious organizations.

(a) *Exemption.* These Title IX regulations do not apply to any operation of an educational institution or other entity that is controlled by a religious organization to the extent that application of these Title IX regulations would not be consistent with the religious tenets of such organization.

(b) *Exemption claims.* An educational institution or other entity that wishes to claim the exemption set forth in paragraph (a) of this section shall do so by submitting in writing to the designated agency official a statement by the highest-ranking official of the institution, identifying the provisions of these Title IX regulations that conflict with a specific tenet of the religious organization.

§ 5.210 Military and merchant marine educational institutions.

These Title IX regulations do not apply to an educational institution whose primary purpose is the training of individuals for a military service of the United States or for the merchant marine.

§ 5.215 Membership practices of certain organizations.

(a) *Social fraternities and sororities.* These Title IX regulations do not apply to the membership practices of social fraternities and sororities that are exempt from taxation under section 501(a) of the Internal Revenue Code of 1954, 26 U.S.C. 501(a), the active membership of which consists primarily of students in attendance at institutions of higher education.

(b) *YMCA, YWCA, Girl Scouts, Boy Scouts, and Camp Fire Girls.* These Title IX regulations do not apply to the membership practices of the Young Men's Christian Association (YMCA), the Young Women's Christian Association (YWCA), the Girl Scouts, the Boy Scouts, and Camp Fire Girls.

(c) *Voluntary youth service organizations.* These Title IX regulations do not apply to the membership practices of a voluntary youth service organization that is exempt from taxation under section 501(a) of the Internal Revenue Code of 1954, 26 U.S.C. 501(a), and the membership of which has been traditionally limited to members of one sex and principally to persons of less than nineteen years of age.

§ 5.220 Admissions.

(a) Admissions to educational institutions prior to June 24, 1973, are not covered by these Title IX regulations.

(b) *Administratively separate units.* For the purposes only of this section, §§ 5.225 and 5.230, and §§ 5.300 through 5.310, each administratively separate unit shall be deemed to be an educational institution.

(c) *Application of §§ 5.300 through 5.310.* Except as provided in paragraphs (d) and (e) of this section, §§ 5.300 through 5.310 apply to each recipient. A recipient to which §§ 5.300 through 5.310 apply shall not discriminate on the basis of sex in admission or recruitment in violation of §§ 5.300 through 5.310.

(d) *Educational institutions.* Except as provided in paragraph (e) of this section as to recipients that are educational institutions, §§ 5.300 through

5.310 apply only to institutions of vocational education, professional education, graduate higher education, and public institutions of undergraduate higher education.

(e) *Public institutions of undergraduate higher education.* §§ 5.300 through 5.310 do not apply to any public institution of undergraduate higher education that traditionally and continually from its establishment has had a policy of admitting students of only one sex.

§ 5.225 Educational institutions eligible to submit transition plans.

(a) *Application.* This section applies to each educational institution to which §§ 5.300 through 5.310 apply that:

(1) Admitted students of only one sex as regular students as of June 23, 1972; or

(2) Admitted students of only one sex as regular students as of June 23, 1965, but thereafter admitted, as regular students, students of the sex not admitted prior to June 23, 1965.

(b) *Provision for transition plans.* An educational institution to which this section applies shall not discriminate on the basis of sex in admission or recruitment in violation of §§ 5.300 through 5.310.

§ 5.230 Transition plans.

(a) *Submission of plans.* An institution to which § 5.225 applies and that is composed of more than one administratively separate unit may submit either a single transition plan applicable to all such units, or a separate transition plan applicable to each such unit.

(b) *Content of plans.* In order to be approved by the Secretary of Education, a transition plan shall:

(1) State the name, address, and Federal Interagency Committee on Education Code of the educational institution submitting such plan, the administratively separate units to which the plan is applicable, and the name, address, and telephone number of the person to whom questions concerning the plan may be addressed. The person who submits the plan shall be the chief administrator or president of the institution, or another individual legally authorized to bind the institution to all actions set forth in the plan.

(2) State whether the educational institution or administratively separate unit admits students of both sexes as regular students and, if so, when it began to do so.

(3) Identify and describe with respect to the educational institution or administratively separate unit any obstacles to admitting students without discrimination on the basis of sex.

(4) Describe in detail the steps necessary to eliminate as soon as practicable each obstacle so identified and indicate the schedule for taking these steps and the individual directly responsible for their implementation.

(5) Include estimates of the number of students, by sex, expected to apply for, be admitted to, and enter each class during the period covered by the plan.

(c) *Nondiscrimination.* No policy or practice of a recipient to which § 5.225 applies shall result in treatment of applicants to or students of such recipient in violation of §§ 5.300 through 5.310 unless such treatment is necessitated by an obstacle identified in paragraph (b)(3) of this section and a schedule for eliminating that obstacle has been provided as required by paragraph (b)(4) of this section.

(d) *Effects of past exclusion.* To overcome the effects of past exclusion of students on the basis of sex, each educational institution to which § 5.225 applies shall include in its transition plan, and shall implement, specific steps designed to encourage individuals of the previously excluded sex to apply for admission to such institution. Such steps shall include instituting recruitment programs that emphasize the institution's commitment to enrolling students of the sex previously excluded.

§ 5.235 Statutory amendments.

(a) This section, which applies to all provisions of these Title IX regulations, addresses statutory amendments to Title IX.

(b) These Title IX regulations shall not apply to or preclude:

(1) Any program or activity of the American Legion undertaken in connection with the organization or operation of any Boys State conference,

Boys Nation conference, Girls State conference, or Girls Nation conference;

(2) Any program or activity of a secondary school or educational institution specifically for:

(i) The promotion of any Boys State conference, Boys Nation conference, Girls State conference, or Girls Nation conference; or

(ii) The selection of students to attend any such conference;

(3) Father-son or mother-daughter activities at an educational institution or in an education program or activity, but if such activities are provided for students of one sex, opportunities for reasonably comparable activities shall be provided to students of the other sex;

(4) Any scholarship or other financial assistance awarded by an institution of higher education to an individual because such individual has received such award in a single-sex pageant based upon a combination of factors related to the individual's personal appearance, poise, and talent. The pageant, however, must comply with other nondiscrimination provisions of Federal law.

(c) *Program or activity* or *program* means:

(1) All of the operations of any entity described in paragraphs (c)(1)(i) through (iv) of this section, any part of which is extended Federal financial assistance:

(i)(A) A department, agency, special purpose district, or other instrumentality of a State or of a local government; or

(B) The entity of such State or local government that distributes such assistance and each such department or agency (and each other State or local government entity) to which the assistance is extended, in the case of assistance to a State or local government;

(ii)(A) A college, university, or other postsecondary institution, or a public system of higher education; or

(B) A local educational agency (as defined in section 8801 of title 20), system of vocational education, or other school system;

(iii)(A) An entire corporation, partnership, or other private organization, or an entire sole proprietorship—

(*1*) If assistance is extended to such corporation, partnership, private organization, or sole proprietorship as a whole; or

(*2*) Which is principally engaged in the business of providing education, health care, housing, social services, or parks and recreation; or

(B) The entire plant or other comparable, geographically separate facility to which Federal financial assistance is extended, in the case of any other corporation, partnership, private organization, or sole proprietorship; or

(iv) Any other entity that is established by two or more of the entities described in paragraphs (c)(1)(i), (ii), or (iii) of this section.

(2)(i) *Program or activity* does not include any operation of an entity that is controlled by a religious organization if the application of 20 U.S.C. 1681 to such operation would not be consistent with the religious tenets of such organization.

(ii) For example, all of the operations of a college, university, or other postsecondary institution, including but not limited to traditional educational operations, faculty and student housing, campus shuttle bus service, campus restaurants, the bookstore, and other commercial activities are part of a "program or activity" subject to these Title IX regulations if the college, university, or other institution receives Federal financial assistance.

(d)(1) Nothing in these Title IX regulations shall be construed to require or prohibit any person, or public or private entity, to provide or pay for any benefit or service, including the use of facilities, related to an abortion. Medical procedures, benefits, services, and the use of facilities, necessary to save the life of a pregnant woman or to address complications related to an abortion are not subject to this section.

(2) Nothing in this section shall be construed to permit a penalty to be imposed on any person or individual because such person or individual is seeking or has received any benefit or service related to a legal abortion. Accordingly, subject to paragraph (d)(1) of this section, no person shall be excluded from participation in, be denied

the benefits of, or be subjected to discrimination under any academic, extracurricular, research, occupational training, employment, or other educational program or activity operated by a recipient that receives Federal financial assistance because such individual has sought or received, or is seeking, a legal abortion, or any benefit or service related to a legal abortion.

Subpart C—Discrimination on the Basis of Sex in Admission and Recruitment Prohibited

§5.300 Admission.

(a) *General.* No person shall, on the basis of sex, be denied admission, or be subjected to discrimination in admission, by any recipient to which §§5.300 through §§5.310 apply, except as provided in §§5.225 and §§5.230.

(b) *Specific prohibitions.* (1) In determining whether a person satisfies any policy or criterion for admission, or in making any offer of admission, a recipient to which §§5.300 through 5.310 apply shall not:

(i) Give preference to one person over another on the basis of sex, by ranking applicants separately on such basis, or otherwise;

(ii) Apply numerical limitations upon the number or proportion of persons of either sex who may be admitted; or

(iii) Otherwise treat one individual differently from another on the basis of sex.

(2) A recipient shall not administer or operate any test or other criterion for admission that has a disproportionately adverse effect on persons on the basis of sex unless the use of such test or criterion is shown to predict validly success in the education program or activity in question and alternative tests or criteria that do not have such a disproportionately adverse effect are shown to be unavailable.

(c) *Prohibitions relating to marital or parental status.* In determining whether a person satisfies any policy or criterion for admission, or in making any offer of admission, a recipient to which §§5.300 through 5.310 apply:

(1) Shall not apply any rule concerning the actual or potential parental, family, or marital status of a student or applicant that treats persons differently on the basis of sex;

(2) Shall not discriminate against or exclude any person on the basis of pregnancy, childbirth, termination of pregnancy, or recovery therefrom, or establish or follow any rule or practice that so discriminates or excludes;

(3) Subject to §5.235(d), shall treat disabilities related to pregnancy, childbirth, termination of pregnancy, or recovery therefrom in the same manner and under the same policies as any other temporary disability or physical condition; and

(4) Shall not make pre-admission inquiry as to the marital status of an applicant for admission, including whether such applicant is "Miss" or "Mrs." A recipient may make pre-admission inquiry as to the sex of an applicant for admission, but only if such inquiry is made equally of such applicants of both sexes and if the results of such inquiry are not used in connection with discrimination prohibited by these Title IX regulations.

§5.305 Preference in admission.

A recipient to which §§5.300 through 5.310 apply shall not give preference to applicants for admission, on the basis of attendance at any educational institution or other school or entity that admits as students only or predominantly members of one sex, if the giving of such preference has the effect of discriminating on the basis of sex in violation of §§5.300 through 5.310.

§5.310 Recruitment.

(a) *Nondiscriminatory recruitment.* A recipient to which §§5.300 through 5.310 apply shall not discriminate on the basis of sex in the recruitment and admission of students. A recipient may be required to undertake additional recruitment efforts for one sex as remedial action pursuant to §5.110(a), and may choose to undertake such efforts as affirmative action pursuant to §5.110(b).

(b) *Recruitment at certain institutions.* A recipient to which §§5.300 through 5.310 apply shall not recruit primarily or exclusively at educational institutions, schools, or entities that admit as students only or predominantly members of one sex, if such actions have the effect of discriminating on the basis of sex in violation of §§ 5.300 through 5.310.

Subpart D—Discrimination on the Basis of Sex in Education Programs or Activities Prohibited

§ 5.400 Education programs or activities.

(a) *General.* Except as provided elsewhere in these Title IX regulations, no person shall, on the basis of sex, be excluded from participation in, be denied the benefits of, or be subjected to discrimination under any academic, extracurricular, research, occupational training, or other education program or activity operated by a recipient that receives Federal financial assistance. Sections 5.400 through 5.455 do not apply to actions of a recipient in connection with admission of its students to an education program or activity of a recipient to which §§ 5.300 through 5.310 do not apply, or an entity, not a recipient, to which §§ 5.300 through 5.310 would not apply if the entity were a recipient.

(b) *Specific prohibitions.* Except as provided in §§ 5.400 through 5.455, in providing any aid, benefit, or service to a student, a recipient shall not, on the basis of sex:

(1) Treat one person differently from another in determining whether such person satisfies any requirement or condition for the provision of such aid, benefit, or service;

(2) Provide different aid, benefits, or services or provide aid, benefits, or services in a different manner;

(3) Deny any person any such aid, benefit, or service;

(4) Subject any person to separate or different rules of behavior, sanctions, or other treatment;

(5) Apply any rule concerning the domicile or residence of a student or applicant, including eligibility for in-state fees and tuition;

(6) Aid or perpetuate discrimination against any person by providing significant assistance to any agency, organization, or person that discriminates on the basis of sex in providing any aid, benefit, or service to students or employees;

(7) Otherwise limit any person in the enjoyment of any right, privilege, advantage, or opportunity.

(c) *Assistance administered by a recipient educational institution to study at a foreign institution.* A recipient educational institution may administer or assist in the administration of scholarships, fellowships, or other awards established by foreign or domestic wills, trusts, or similar legal instruments, or by acts of foreign governments and restricted to members of one sex, that are designed to provide opportunities to study abroad, and that are awarded to students who are already matriculating at or who are graduates of the recipient institution; *Provided,* that a recipient educational institution that administers or assists in the administration of such scholarships, fellowships, or other awards that are restricted to members of one sex provides, or otherwise makes available, reasonable opportunities for similar studies for members of the other sex. Such opportunities may be derived from either domestic or foreign sources.

(d) *Aids, benefits or services not provided by recipient.* (1) This paragraph (d) applies to any recipient that requires participation by any applicant, student, or employee in any education program or activity not operated wholly by such recipient, or that facilitates, permits, or considers such participation as part of or equivalent to an education program or activity operated by such recipient, including participation in educational consortia and cooperative employment and student-teaching assignments.

(2) Such recipient:

(i) Shall develop and implement a procedure designed to assure itself that the operator or sponsor of such other education program or activity takes no action affecting any applicant, student, or employee of such recipient that these Title IX regulations would prohibit such recipient from taking; and

(ii) Shall not facilitate, require, permit, or consider such participation if such action occurs.

§ 5.405 Housing.

(a) *Generally.* A recipient shall not, on the basis of sex, apply different rules or regulations, impose different fees or requirements, or offer different services or benefits related to housing, except as provided in this section (including housing provided only to married students).

(b) *Housing provided by recipient.* (1) A recipient may provide separate housing on the basis of sex.

(2) Housing provided by a recipient to students of one sex, when compared to that provided to students of the other sex, shall be as a whole:

(i) Proportionate in quantity to the number of students of that sex applying for such housing; and

(ii) Comparable in quality and cost to the student.

(c) *Other housing.* (1) A recipient shall not, on the basis of sex, administer different policies or practices concerning occupancy by its students of housing other than that provided by such recipient.

(2)(i) A recipient which, through solicitation, listing, approval of housing, or otherwise, assists any agency, organization, or person in making housing available to any of its students, shall take such reasonable action as may be necessary to assure itself that such housing as is provided to students of one sex, when compared to that provided to students of the other sex, is as a whole:

(A) Proportionate in quantity; and

(B) Comparable in quality and cost to the student.

(ii) A recipient may render such assistance to any agency, organization, or person that provides all or part of such housing to students of only one sex.

§ 5.410 Comparable facilities.

A recipient may provide separate toilet, locker room, and shower facilities on the basis of sex, but such facilities provided for students of one sex shall be comparable to such facilities provided for students of the other sex.

§ 5.415 Access to course offerings.

(a) A recipient shall not provide any course or otherwise carry out any of its education program or activity separately on the basis of sex, or require or refuse participation therein by any of its students on such basis, including health, physical education, industrial, business, vocational, technical, home economics, music, and adult education courses.

(b)(1) With respect to classes and activities in physical education at the elementary school level, the recipient shall comply fully with this section as expeditiously as possible but in no event later than one year from September 29, 2000. With respect to physical education classes and activities at the secondary and post-secondary levels, the recipient shall comply fully with this section as expeditiously as possible but in no event later than three years from September 29, 2000.

(2) This section does not prohibit grouping of students in physical education classes and activities by ability as assessed by objective standards of individual performance developed and applied without regard to sex.

(3) This section does not prohibit separation of students by sex within physical education classes or activities during participation in wrestling, boxing, rugby, ice hockey, football, basketball, and other sports the purpose or major activity of which involves bodily contact.

(4) Where use of a single standard of measuring skill or progress in a physical education class has an adverse effect on members of one sex, the recipient shall use appropriate standards that do not have such effect.

(5) Portions of classes in elementary and secondary schools, or portions of education programs or activities, that deal exclusively with human sexuality may be conducted in separate sessions for boys and girls.

(6) Recipients may make requirements based on vocal range or quality that may result in a chorus or choruses of one or predominantly one sex.

§ 5.420 Access to schools operated by LEAs.

A recipient that is a local educational agency shall not, on the basis of sex, exclude any person from admission to:

(a) Any institution of vocational education operated by such recipient; or

(b) Any other school or educational unit operated by such recipient, unless such recipient otherwise makes available to such person, pursuant to the same policies and criteria of admission, courses, services, and facilities comparable to each course, service, and facility offered in or through such schools.

§ 5.425 Counseling and use of appraisal and counseling materials.

(a) *Counseling.* A recipient shall not discriminate against any person on the basis of sex in the counseling or guidance of students or applicants for admission.

(b) *Use of appraisal and counseling materials.* A recipient that uses testing or other materials for appraising or counseling students shall not use different materials for students on the basis of their sex or use materials that permit or require different treatment of students on such basis unless such different materials cover the same occupations and interest areas and the use of such different materials is shown to be essential to eliminate sex bias. Recipients shall develop and use internal procedures for ensuring that such materials do not discriminate on the basis of sex. Where the use of a counseling test or other instrument results in a substantially disproportionate number of members of one sex in any particular course of study or classification, the recipient shall take such action as is necessary to assure itself that such disproportion is not the result of discrimination in the instrument or its application.

(c) *Disproportion in classes.* Where a recipient finds that a particular class contains a substantially disproportionate number of individuals of one sex, the recipient shall take such action as is necessary to assure itself that such disproportion is not the result of discrimination on the basis of sex in counseling or appraisal materials or by counselors.

§ 5.430 Financial assistance.

(a) *General.* Except as provided in paragraphs (b) and (c) of this section, in providing financial assistance to any of its students, a recipient shall not:

(1) On the basis of sex, provide different amounts or types of such assistance, limit eligibility for such assistance that is of any particular type or source, apply different criteria, or otherwise discriminate;

(2) Through solicitation, listing, approval, provision of facilities, or other services, assist any foundation, trust, agency, organization, or person that provides assistance to any of such recipient's students in a manner that discriminates on the basis of sex; or

(3) Apply any rule or assist in application of any rule concerning eligibility for such assistance that treats persons of one sex differently from persons of the other sex with regard to marital or parental status.

(b) *Financial aid established by certain legal instruments.* (1) A recipient may administer or assist in the administration of scholarships, fellowships, or other forms of financial assistance established pursuant to domestic or foreign wills, trusts, bequests, or similar legal instruments or by acts of a foreign government that require that awards be made to members of a particular sex specified therein; *Provided,* that the overall effect of the award of such sex-restricted scholarships, fellowships, and other forms of financial assistance does not discriminate on the basis of sex.

(2) To ensure nondiscriminatory awards of assistance as required in paragraph (b)(1) of this section, recipients shall develop and use procedures under which:

(i) Students are selected for award of financial assistance on the basis of nondiscriminatory criteria and not on the basis of availability of funds restricted to members of a particular sex;

(ii) An appropriate sex-restricted scholarship, fellowship, or other form of financial assistance is allocated to each student selected under paragraph (b)(2)(i) of this section; and

(iii) No student is denied the award for which he or she was selected under paragraph (b)(2)(i) of this section because of the absence of a scholarship, fellowship, or other form of financial assistance designated for a member of that student's sex.

(c) *Athletic scholarships.* (1) To the extent that a recipient awards athletic scholarships or grants-in-aid, it must provide reasonable opportunities for such awards for members of each sex in proportion to the number of students of each sex participating in interscholastic or intercollegiate athletics.

(2) A recipient may provide separate athletic scholarships or grants-in-aid for members of each sex as part of separate athletic teams for members of each sex to the extent consistent with this paragraph (c) and § 5.450.

§ 5.435 Employment assistance to students.

(a) *Assistance by recipient in making available outside employment.* A recipient that assists any agency, organization, or person in making employment available to any of its students:

(1) Shall assure itself that such employment is made available without discrimination on the basis of sex; and

(2) Shall not render such services to any agency, organization, or person that discriminates on the basis of sex in its employment practices.

(b) *Employment of students by recipients.* A recipient that employs any of its students shall not do so in a manner that violates §§ 5.500 through 5.550.

§ 5.440 Health and insurance benefits and services.

Subject to § 5.235(d), in providing a medical, hospital, accident, or life insurance benefit, service, policy, or plan to any of its students, a recipient shall not discriminate on the basis of sex, or provide such benefit, service, policy, or plan in a manner that would violate §§ 5.500 through 5.550 if it were provided to employees of the recipient. This section shall not prohibit a recipient from providing any benefit or service that may be used by a different proportion of students of one sex than of the other, including family planning services. However, any recipient that provides full coverage health service shall provide gynecological care.

§ 5.445 Marital or parental status.

(a) *Status generally.* A recipient shall not apply any rule concerning a student's actual or potential parental, family, or marital status that treats students differently on the basis of sex.

(b) *Pregnancy and related conditions.* (1) A recipient shall not discriminate against any student, or exclude any student from its education program or activity, including any class or extracurricular activity, on the basis of such student's pregnancy, childbirth, false pregnancy, termination of pregnancy, or recovery therefrom, unless the student requests voluntarily to participate in a separate portion of the program or activity of the recipient.

(2) A recipient may require such a student to obtain the certification of a physician that the student is physically and emotionally able to continue participation as long as such a certification is required of all students for other physical or emotional conditions requiring the attention of a physician.

(3) A recipient that operates a portion of its education program or activity separately for pregnant students, admittance to which is completely voluntary on the part of the student as provided in paragraph (b)(1) of this section, shall ensure that the separate portion is comparable to that offered to non-pregnant students.

(4) Subject to § 5.235(d), a recipient shall treat pregnancy, childbirth, false pregnancy, termination of pregnancy and recovery therefrom in the same manner and under the same policies as any other temporary disability with respect to any medical or hospital benefit, service, plan, or policy that such recipient administers, operates, offers, or participates in with respect to students admitted to the recipient's educational program or activity.

(5) In the case of a recipient that does not maintain a leave policy for its students, or in the case of a student who does not otherwise qualify for leave under such a policy, a recipient shall treat pregnancy, childbirth, false pregnancy, termination of pregnancy, and recovery therefrom as a justification for a leave of absence for as long a period of time as is deemed medically necessary by the student's physician, at the conclusion of which the student shall be reinstated to the status that she held when the leave began.

§ 5.450 Athletics.

(a) *General.* No person shall, on the basis of sex, be excluded from participation in, be denied the benefits of, be treated differently from another person, or otherwise be discriminated against in any interscholastic, intercollegiate, club, or intramural athletics offered by a recipient, and no recipient shall provide any such athletics separately on such basis.

(b) *Separate teams.* Notwithstanding the requirements of paragraph (a) of this section, a recipient may operate or sponsor separate teams for members of each sex where selection for such teams is based upon competitive skill or the activity involved is a contact sport. However, where a recipient operates or sponsors a team in a particular sport for members of one sex but operates or sponsors no such team for members of the other sex, and athletic opportunities for members of that sex have previously been limited, members of the excluded sex must be allowed to try out for the team offered unless the sport involved is a contact sport. For the purposes of these Title IX regulations, contact sports include boxing, wrestling, rugby, ice hockey, football, basketball, and other sports the purpose or major activity of which involves bodily contact.

(c) *Equal opportunity.* (1) A recipient that operates or sponsors interscholastic, intercollegiate, club, or intramural athletics shall provide equal athletic opportunity for members of both sexes. In determining whether equal opportunities are available, the designated agency official will consider, among other factors:

(i) Whether the selection of sports and levels of competition effectively accommodate the interests and abilities of members of both sexes;

(ii) The provision of equipment and supplies;

(iii) Scheduling of games and practice time;

(iv) Travel and per diem allowance;

(v) Opportunity to receive coaching and academic tutoring;

(vi) Assignment and compensation of coaches and tutors;

(vii) Provision of locker rooms, practice, and competitive facilities;

(viii) Provision of medical and training facilities and services;

(ix) Provision of housing and dining facilities and services;

(x) Publicity.

(2) For purposes of paragraph (c)(1) of this section, unequal aggregate expenditures for members of each sex or unequal expenditures for male and female teams if a recipient operates or sponsors separate teams will not constitute noncompliance with this section, but the designated agency official may consider the failure to provide necessary funds for teams for one sex in assessing equality of opportunity for members of each sex.

(d) *Adjustment period.* A recipient that operates or sponsors interscholastic, intercollegiate, club, or intramural athletics at the elementary school level shall comply fully with this section as expeditiously as possible but in no event later than one year from September 29, 2000. A recipient that operates or sponsors interscholastic, intercollegiate, club, or intramural athletics at the secondary or postsecondary school level shall comply fully with this section as expeditiously as possible but in no event later than three years from September 29, 2000.

§ 5.455 Textbooks and curricular material.

Nothing in these Title IX regulations shall be interpreted as requiring or prohibiting or abridging in any way the use of particular textbooks or curricular materials.

Subpart E—Discrimination on the Basis of Sex in Employment in Education Programs or Activities Prohibited

§ 5.500 Employment.

(a) *General.* (1) No person shall, on the basis of sex, be excluded from participation in, be denied the benefits of, or be subjected to discrimination in employment, or recruitment, consideration, or selection therefor, whether full-time or part-time, under any education program or activity operated by a recipient that receives Federal financial assistance.

(2) A recipient shall make all employment decisions in any education program or activity operated by such recipient in a nondiscriminatory manner and shall not limit, segregate, or classify applicants or employees in any way that could adversely affect any applicant's or employee's employment opportunities or status because of sex.

(3) A recipient shall not enter into any contractual or other relationship which directly or indirectly has the effect of subjecting employees or students to discrimination prohibited by §§5.500 through 5.550, including relationships with employment and referral agencies, with labor unions, and with organizations providing or administering fringe benefits to employees of the recipient.

(4) A recipient shall not grant preferences to applicants for employment on the basis of attendance at any educational institution or entity that admits as students only or predominantly members of one sex, if the giving of such preferences has the effect of discriminating on the basis of sex in violation of these Title IX regulations.

(b) *Application.* The provisions of §§5.500 through 5.550 apply to:

(1) Recruitment, advertising, and the process of application for employment;

(2) Hiring, upgrading, promotion, consideration for and award of tenure, demotion, transfer, layoff, termination, application of nepotism policies, right of return from layoff, and rehiring;

(3) Rates of pay or any other form of compensation, and changes in compensation;

(4) Job assignments, classifications, and structure, including position descriptions, lines of progression, and seniority lists;

(5) The terms of any collective bargaining agreement;

(6) Granting and return from leaves of absence, leave for pregnancy, childbirth, false pregnancy, termination of pregnancy, leave for persons of either sex to care for children or dependents, or any other leave;

(7) Fringe benefits available by virtue of employment, whether or not administered by the recipient;

(8) Selection and financial support for training, including apprenticeship, professional meetings, conferences, and other related activities, selection for tuition assistance, selection for sabbaticals and leaves of absence to pursue training;

(9) Employer-sponsored activities, including social or recreational programs; and

(10) Any other term, condition, or privilege of employment.

§5.505 Employment criteria.

A recipient shall not administer or operate any test or other criterion for any employment opportunity that has a disproportionately adverse effect on persons on the basis of sex unless:

(a) Use of such test or other criterion is shown to predict validly successful performance in the position in question; and

(b) Alternative tests or criteria for such purpose, which do not have such disproportionately adverse effect, are shown to be unavailable.

§5.510 Recruitment.

(a) *Nondiscriminatory recruitment and hiring.* A recipient shall not discriminate on the basis of sex in the recruitment and hiring of employees. Where a recipient has been found to be presently discriminating on the basis of sex in the recruitment or hiring of employees, or has been found to have so discriminated in the past, the recipient shall recruit members of the sex so discriminated against so as to overcome the effects of such past or present discrimination.

(b) *Recruitment patterns.* A recipient shall not recruit primarily or exclusively at entities that furnish as applicants only or predominantly members of one sex if such actions have the effect of discriminating on the basis of sex in violation of §§5.500 through 5.550.

§5.515 Compensation.

A recipient shall not make or enforce any policy or practice that, on the basis of sex:

(a) Makes distinctions in rates of pay or other compensation;

(b) Results in the payment of wages to employees of one sex at a rate less than that paid to employees of the opposite sex for equal work on jobs the performance of which requires equal skill, effort, and responsibility, and that are performed under similar working conditions.

§5.520 Job classification and structure.

A recipient shall not:

(a) Classify a job as being for males or for females;

(b) Maintain or establish separate lines of progression, seniority lists, career ladders, or tenure systems based on sex; or

(c) Maintain or establish separate lines of progression, seniority systems, career ladders, or tenure systems for similar jobs, position descriptions, or job requirements that classify persons on the basis of sex, unless sex is a bona fide occupational qualification for the positions in question as set forth in § 5.550.

§ 5.525 Fringe benefits.

(a) *"Fringe benefits" defined.* For purposes of these Title IX regulations, *fringe benefits* means: Any medical, hospital, accident, life insurance, or retirement benefit, service, policy or plan, any profit-sharing or bonus plan, leave, and any other benefit or service of employment not subject to the provision of § 5.515.

(b) *Prohibitions.* A recipient shall not:

(1) Discriminate on the basis of sex with regard to making fringe benefits available to employees or make fringe benefits available to spouses, families, or dependents of employees differently upon the basis of the employee's sex;

(2) Administer, operate, offer, or participate in a fringe benefit plan that does not provide for equal periodic benefits for members of each sex and for equal contributions to the plan by such recipient for members of each sex; or

(3) Administer, operate, offer, or participate in a pension or retirement plan that establishes different optional or compulsory retirement ages based on sex or that otherwise discriminates in benefits on the basis of sex.

§ 5.530 Marital or parental status.

(a) *General.* A recipient shall not apply any policy or take any employment action:

(1) Concerning the potential marital, parental, or family status of an employee or applicant for employment that treats persons differently on the basis of sex; or

(2) Which is based upon whether an employee or applicant for employment is the head of household or principal wage earner in such employee's or applicant's family unit.

(b) *Pregnancy.* A recipient shall not discriminate against or exclude from employment any employee or applicant for employment on the basis of pregnancy, childbirth, false pregnancy, termination of pregnancy, or recovery therefrom.

(c) *Pregnancy as a temporary disability.* Subject to § 5.235(d), a recipient shall treat pregnancy, childbirth, false pregnancy, termination of pregnancy, recovery therefrom, and any temporary disability resulting therefrom as any other temporary disability for all job-related purposes, including commencement, duration, and extensions of leave, payment of disability income, accrual of seniority and any other benefit or service, and reinstatement, and under any fringe benefit offered to employees by virtue of employment.

(d) *Pregnancy leave.* In the case of a recipient that does not maintain a leave policy for its employees, or in the case of an employee with insufficient leave or accrued employment time to qualify for leave under such a policy, a recipient shall treat pregnancy, childbirth, false pregnancy, termination of pregnancy, and recovery therefrom as a justification for a leave of absence without pay for a reasonable period of time, at the conclusion of which the employee shall be reinstated to the status that she held when the leave began or to a comparable position, without decrease in rate of compensation or loss of promotional opportunities, or any other right or privilege of employment.

§ 5.535 Effect of state or local law or other requirements.

(a) *Prohibitory requirements.* The obligation to comply with §§ 5.500 through 5.550 is not obviated or alleviated by the existence of any State or local law or other requirement that imposes prohibitions or limits upon employment of members of one sex that are not imposed upon members of the other sex.

(b) *Benefits.* A recipient that provides any compensation, service, or benefit to members of one sex pursuant to a State or local law or other requirement shall provide the same compensation, service, or benefit to members of the other sex.

§ 5.540 Advertising.

A recipient shall not in any advertising related to employment indicate preference, limitation, specification, or discrimination based on sex unless sex is a bona fide occupational qualification for the particular job in question.

§ 5.545 Pre-employment inquiries.

(a) *Marital status.* A recipient shall not make pre-employment inquiry as to the marital status of an applicant for employment, including whether such applicant is "Miss" or "Mrs."

(b) *Sex.* A recipient may make pre-employment inquiry as to the sex of an applicant for employment, but only if such inquiry is made equally of such applicants of both sexes and if the results of such inquiry are not used in connection with discrimination prohibited by these Title IX regulations.

§ 5.550 Sex as a bona fide occupational qualification.

A recipient may take action otherwise prohibited by §§ 5.500 through 5.550 provided it is shown that sex is a bona fide occupational qualification for that action, such that consideration of sex with regard to such action is essential to successful operation of the employment function concerned. A recipient shall not take action pursuant to this section that is based upon alleged comparative employment characteristics or stereotyped characterizations of one or the other sex, or upon preference based on sex of the recipient, employees, students, or other persons, but nothing contained in this section shall prevent a recipient from considering an employee's sex in relation to employment in a locker room or toilet facility used only by members of one sex.

Subpart F—Procedures

§ 5.600 Notice of covered programs.

Within 60 days of September 29, 2000, each Federal agency that awards Federal financial assistance shall publish in the FEDERAL REGISTER a notice of the programs covered by these Title IX regulations. Each such Federal agency shall periodically republish the notice of covered programs to reflect changes in covered programs. Copies of this notice also shall be made available upon request to the Federal agency's office that enforces Title IX.

§ 5.605 Enforcement procedures.

The investigative, compliance, and enforcement procedural provisions of Title VI of the Civil Rights Act of 1964 (42 U.S.C. 2000d) ("Title VI") are hereby adopted and applied to these Title IX regulations. These procedures may be found at 10 CFR 4.21 through 4.75.

[65 FR 52875, Aug. 30, 2000]

APPENDIX A TO PART 5—LIST OF FEDERAL FINANCIAL ASSISTANCE ADMINISTERED BY THE NUCLEAR REGULATORY COMMISSION TO WHICH TITLE IX APPLIES

NOTE: All recipients of Federal financial assistance from NRC are subject to Title IX, but Title IX's anti-discrimination prohibitions are limited to the educational components of the recipient's program or activity, if any. Failure to list a type of Federal assistance below shall not mean, if Title IX is otherwise applicable, that a program or activity is not covered by Title IX.

(a) *Conferences on regulatory programs and related matters.* Agreements for financial assistance to State and local officials, without full-cost recovery, to confer on regulatory programs and related matters at NRC facilities and offices, or other locations.

(b) *Orientations and instruction.* Agreements for financial assistance to State and local officials, without full-cost recovery, to receive orientation and on-the-job instruction at NRC facilities and offices, or other locations.

(c) *Technical training courses.* Agreements for financial assistance to State and local officials, without full-cost recovery to attend training on nuclear material licensing, inspection and emergency response regulatory responsibilities to ensure compatibility between NRC and Agreement State regulation.

(d) *Participation in meetings and conferences.* Agreements for participation, without full-cost recovery, in meetings, conferences, workshops, and symposia to assist scientific, professional or educational institutions or groups.

(e) *Research support.* Agreements for the financial support of basic and applied scientific research and for the exchanges of scientific information.

[66 FR 709, Jan. 4, 2001]

PART 7—ADVISORY COMMITTEES

AUTHORITY: Atomic Energy Act of 1954, sec. 161 (42 U.S.C. 2201); Energy Reorganization Act of 1974, sec. 201 (42 U.S.C. 5841); 5 U.S.C. Appendix (Federal Advisory Committee Act).

SOURCE: 54 FR 26948, June 27, 1989, unless otherwise noted.

§ 7.1 Policy.

The regulations in this part define the policies and procedures to be followed by the Nuclear Regulatory Commission in the establishment, utilization, and termination of advisory committees. In general, it is the policy of the Commission that—

(a) Except where there is express legal authority to the contrary, the function of NRC advisory committees shall be advisory only.

(b) Each NRC advisory committee shall function in compliance with the Federal Advisory Committee Act and this part.

(c) The number of NRC advisory committees shall be kept to the minimum necessary, and the number of members of each NRC advisory committee shall be limited to the fewest necessary to accomplish committee objectives.

(d)(1) An NRC advisory committee shall be established only:

(i) When establishment of the committee is required by law;

(ii) When the Commission determines that the committee is essential to the conduct of NRC business; or

(iii) When the information to be obtained is not available through an existing advisory committee or a source within the Federal Government.

(2) Before establishing an advisory committee, the Commission shall consider whether:

(i) Committee deliberations will result in a significant contribution to the creation, amendment, or elimination of regulations, guidelines, or rules affecting NRC business;

(ii) The information to be obtained is available through another source within the Federal Government;

(iii) The committee will make recommendations resulting in significant improvements in service or reductions in cost; or

(iv) The committee's recommendations will provide an important additional perspective or viewpoint relating to NRC's mission. The advice or recommendations of an advisory committee should be the result of the advisory committee's independent judgment.

(e) Except where otherwise required by law, an NRC advisory committee shall be terminated whenever the stated objectives of the committee have been accomplished, the subject matter or work of the committee has become obsolete, the committee's main functions have been assumed by another entity within the Federal Government, or the cost of operating the committee has become excessive in relation to the benefits accruing to the Federal Government from its activities.

(1) An advisory committee not required to be established by statute terminates no later than two years after its establishment or last renewal, unless renewed.

(2) An advisory committee required to be established by statute terminates upon the expiration of the time explicitly specified in the statute or implied by operation of the statute.

(f) NRC advisory committees shall be balanced in their membership in terms of the points of view represented and the functions to be performed.

(g) The Congress shall be kept informed of the number, purpose, membership, activities, and cost of NRC advisory committees.

(h) NRC advisory committee meetings shall be open to the public, except where closure is determined to be justified under §7.15.

(i) The Commission may periodically invite feedback from the public regarding the effectiveness of NRC advisory committees.

[54 FR 26948, June 27, 1989, as amended at 67 FR 79838, Dec. 31, 2002]

§7.2 Definitions.

Act means the Federal Advisory Committee Act, as amended, 5 U.S.C. App.

Administrator means the Administrator of General Services.

Advisory committee means any committee, board, commission, council, conference, panel, task force, or similar group, or any subcommittee or other subgroup thereof, that is established by statute for the purpose of providing advice or recommendations on issues of policy to an official, branch, or agency of the Federal Government, or that is established or utilized by the President or any agency official to obtain advice or recommendations on issues or policies that fall within the scope of his or her responsibilities, except that the term "advisory committee" does not include the following advisory meetings or groups:

(1) Any group composed wholly of full-time officers or employees of the Federal Government;

(2) Any group specifically exempted from the Act or these regulations by an Act of Congress;

(3) Any local civic group whose primary function is that of rendering a public service with respect to a Federal program, or any State or local committee, council, board, commission, or similar group established to advise or make recommendations to any State or local government unit or an official thereof;

(4) Any group that performs primarily operational functions specifically provided by law. Operational functions are those specifically authorized by statute or Presidential directive, such as making or implementing Government decisions or policy, as long as the group does not become primarily advisory in nature;

(5) Any meeting initiated by the President or one or more Federal employees for the purpose of obtaining advice or recommendations from one individual;

(6) Any meeting between an NRC employee with a non-governmental individual or group where advice or recommendations are provided by the attendees on an individual basis and are not sought from the group as a whole;

(7) Any meeting with a committee or group created by a non-Federal entity that is not managed or controlled by the President or a Federal employee;

(8) Any meeting of two or more advisory committee members convened solely to:

(i) Discuss administrative matters relating to the operation of their advisory committee;

(ii) Receive administrative information from a Federal employee;

(iii) Gather information or conduct research for a chartered advisory committee to analyze relevant issues and facts for their advisory committee; or

(iv) Draft proposed position papers for deliberation by their advisory committee;

(9) Any meeting with a group initiated by the President or by one or more Federal employees for the purpose of exchanging facts or information;

(10) Any meeting attended only by full-time or permanent part-time officers or employees of the Federal Government and elected officers of State, local, and Tribal governments (or their

designated employees with authority to act on their own behalf), acting in their official capacities. However, the purpose of the meeting must be solely to exchange views, information, or advice relating to the management or implementation of Federal programs established pursuant to statute, that explicitly or inherently share intergovernmental responsibilities or administration;

(11) Any meeting of an NRC contractor, applicant, or licensee with an NRC employee to discuss specific matters involving the solicitation, issuance, or implementation of a contract or the Commission's effort to ensure compliance with its regulations; and

(12) Any meeting of a subcommittee or other subgroup of an advisory committee where the subgroup's recommendations will be reviewed by its parent advisory committee.

Agency means an agency of the Government of the United States as defined in 5 U.S.C. 551(1).

Commission means the Nuclear Regulatory Commission of five members, or a quorum thereof, sitting as a body, as provided by section 201 of the Energy Reorganization Act of 1974, 42 U.S.C. 5841, (88 Stat. 1242).

Committee Management Secretariat means the organization established within the General Services Administration, pursuant to section 7(a) of the Act, which is responsible for all matters relating to advisory committees, and carries out the responsibilities of the Administrator of the General Services Administration under the Act and Executive Order 12024 (42 FR 61445; December 1, 1977).

Committee meeting means any gathering of advisory committee members (whether in person, by telephone, or through electronic means) held with the approval of an agency for the purpose of deliberating on the substantive matters upon which the advisory committee provides advice or recommendations.

Committee member means an individual who is appointed to serve on an advisory committee and has the full right and obligation to participate in the activities of the committee, including voting on committee recommendations.

Designated Federal Officer means a government employee appointed, pursuant to § 7.11(a), to chair or attend each meeting of an NRC advisory committee to which he or she is assigned.

Discretionary advisory committee means any advisory committee that is established, but not required to be established, under the authority of an agency head, and its establishment or termination is within the legal discretion of an agency head.

GSA means the General Services Administration.

Non-discretionary advisory committee means any advisory committee either required by statute or Presidential directive. A non-discretionary committee required by statute generally is identified specifically in a statute by name, purpose, or functions and its establishment is mandated.

NRC means the agency established by title II of the Energy Reorganization Act of 1974, 42 U.S.C. 5801 (88 Stat. 1233), and known as the Nuclear Regulatory Commission.

NRC Advisory Committee Management Officer means the individual appointed, pursuant to § 7.10(a), to supervise and control the establishment and management of NRC advisory committees.

NRC Public Document Room means the Public Document Room maintained by the NRC at 11555 Rockville Pike, Rockville, Maryland 20852–2738.

Presidential advisory committee means an advisory committee established by statute or directed by the President to advise the President.

Staff member means any individual who serves in a support capacity to an advisory committee.

Subcommittee means a subgroup of an advisory committee, whether or not its members are drawn in whole or in part from the parent advisory committee.

Utilized committee means a committee or group not established by the Federal Government, but whose operations are managed or controlled by a Federal agency.

[67 FR 79839, Dec. 31, 2002, as amended at 80 FR 74978, Dec. 1, 2015]

§7.3 Interpretations.

Except as specifically authorized by the Commission in writing, no interpretation of the meaning of the regulations in this part by an NRC officer or employee, other than a written interpretation by the General Counsel, shall be binding upon the Commission.

§7.4 Establishment of advisory committees.

(a) An NRC advisory committee may be established under this part only if its establishment—

(1) Is specifically directed or authorized by statute or by Executive Order of the President; or

(2) Has been determined by the Commission to be in the public interest and essential to the performance of the duties imposed on the Commission by law.

The determination required by paragraph (a)(2) of this section shall be a matter of formal record, and shall include a statement of a clearly defined purpose for the advisory committee.

§7.5 Consultation with Committee Management Secretariat on establishment of advisory committees; advisory committee charters.

(a) Before establishing a discretionary advisory committee, the NRC shall consult with the Committee Management Secretariat. With a full understanding of the background and purpose behind the proposed advisory committee, the Committee Management Secretariat may share its knowledge and experience with the NRC on how best to make use of the proposed committee, alternate methods of attaining the agency's purpose, or whether a preexisting advisory committee performs similar functions. Such consultation should include the transmittal of the proposed committee charter and the following information:

(1) A request for a review of the proposed charter;

(2) An explanation stating why the committee is essential to the conduct of NRC business and is in the public interest;

(3) An explanation stating why the committee's functions cannot be performed by the NRC, an existing NRC advisory committee, or other means (such as a public hearing); and

(4) A description of NRC's plan to attain balanced membership on the committee. The plan must ensure that, in the selection of members for the advisory committee, the NRC will consider a cross-section of those directly affected, interested, and qualified, as appropriate to the nature and functions of the committee. For purposes of attaining balance in an NRC advisory committee's membership, the Commission shall consider for membership interested persons and groups with professional, technical, or personal qualifications or experience that will contribute to the functions and tasks to be performed.

(b) Each proposed committee charter submitted for review pursuant to paragraph (a) of this section shall contain the following information:

(1) The committee's official designation;

(2) The committee's objectives and the scope of its activity;

(3) The period of time necessary for the committee to carry out its purposes;

(4) The NRC official to whom the committee will report;

(5) The NRC office responsible for providing support for the committee;

(6) A description of the duties that the committee will perform, and if such duties are not solely advisory, a specification of the authority for the functions that are not advisory;

(7) The estimated annual operating costs, in dollars and person years, for the committee;

(8) The estimated number and frequency of committee meetings; and

(9) The committee's termination date, if less than two years from the date of the committee's establishment.

(c) The requirements of this part, including the requirements of paragraphs (a) and (b) of this section, shall apply to any subcommittee that functions independently of the parent advisory committee (such as by making recommendations directly to the agency rather than to the parent advisory committee), regardless of whether the subcommittee's members are drawn in whole or in part from the parent advisory committee.

(d) After the Committee Management Secretariat has notified the Commission of the results of its review of a proposal to establish or utilize an NRC discretionary advisory committee, submitted pursuant to paragraph (a) of this section, the Commission shall notify the Committee Management Secretariat whether the advisory committee is actually being established. Filing of the advisory committee charter pursuant to § 7.8 shall be deemed to fulfill this notification requirement. If the advisory committee is not being established, the Commission shall so advise the Committee Management Secretariat, stating whether NRC intends to take any further action with respect to the proposed advisory committee.

(e) The date of filing of an advisory committee charter pursuant to § 7.8 shall be added to the charter when such filing takes place, shall appear on the face of the charter, and shall constitute the date of establishment, renewal, or reestablishment of the committee.

[67 FR 79840, Dec. 31, 2002]

§ 7.6 Amendment to advisory committee charters.

(a) Final authority for amending the charter of an NRC advisory committee established or utilized by the NRC is vested in the Commission.

(b) Any proposed changes made to a current charter for an NRC advisory committee shall be coordinated with the General Counsel to ensure that they are consistent with applicable legal requirements. When a statute or Executive Order that directed or authorized the establishment of an advisory committee is amended, those sections of the advisory committee's charter affected by the amendments shall also be amended.

(c)(1) The charter of an NRC advisory committee established under general agency authority may be amended when the Commission determines that the existing charter no longer reflects the objectives or functions of the committee. Such changes may be minor (such as revising the name of the advisory committee or modifying the estimated number or frequency of meetings), or they may be major (such as revising the objectives or composition of the committee).

(2) The procedures in paragraph (b) of this section shall be used in the case of charter amendments involving minor changes. A proposed major amendment to the charter of an advisory committee established under general agency authority shall be submitted to the Committee Management Secretariat for review with an explanation of the purpose of the changes and why they are necessary.

(3) A committee charter that has been amended pursuant to this paragraph is subject to the filing requirements set forth in § 7.8.

(4) Amendment of an existing advisory committee charter pursuant to this paragraph does not constitute renewal of the committee for purposes of § 7.7.

[67 FR 79840, Dec. 31, 2002]

§ 7.7 Termination, renewal, and rechartering of advisory committees.

(a) Except as provided in paragraph (b)(1) of this section, each NRC advisory committee shall terminate two years after it is established, reestablished, or renewed, unless—

(1) It has been terminated sooner;

(2) It has been renewed or reestablished before the end of such period in accordance with the procedures set forth in paragraph (b) of this section; or

(3) Its duration has been otherwise designated by law. The NRC Committee Management Officer shall notify the Committee Management Secretariat of the effective date of termination of any advisory committee that has been terminated by the NRC.

(b)(1) An NRC advisory committee that is established by statute shall require rechartering by the filing of a new charter every 2 years after the date of enactment of the statute establishing the committee. If a new charter is not filed, the committee is not terminated, but it may not meet or take any actions.

(2) Any other NRC advisory committee may be renewed, provided that such renewal is carried out in compliance with the procedures set forth in § 7.5, except that an advisory committee established by the President

may be renewed by appropriate action of the President and the filing of a new charter. Renewal of an NRC advisory committee shall not be deemed to terminate the appointment of any committee member who was previously appointed to serve on the committee.

[54 FR 26948, June 27, 1989, as amended at 67 FR 79840, Dec. 31, 2002]

§7.8 Charter filing requirements.

No advisory committee may meet or take any action until a charter has been filed by the Committee Management Officer designated in accordance with §7.10.

(a) To establish, renew, or reestablish a discretionary advisory committee, a charter must be filed with:

(1) The Commission;

(2) The Committee on Environment and Public Works of the United States Senate and the Committee on Energy and Commerce of the United States House of Representatives;

(3) The Library of Congress, Anglo-American Acquisitions Division, Government Documents Section, Federal Advisory Committee Desk, 101 Independence Avenue, S.E., Washington, DC 20540–4172; and

(4) The Committee Management Secretariat, indicating the date the charter was filed with the congressional committees.

(b) Charter filing requirements for non-discretionary advisory committees are the same as those in paragraph (a) of this section, except the date of establishment for a Presidential advisory committee is the date the charter is filed with the Secretariat.

(c) Subcommittees that report directly to a Federal employee or agency must comply with this subpart.

[67 FR 79841, Dec. 31, 2002]

§7.9 Public notice of advisory committee establishment, reestablishment, or renewal.

(a) After the Commission has received notice from the Committee Management Secretariat that its review of a proposal to establish, reestablish, renew, or utilize an NRC discretionary advisory committee has been completed, the Commission shall publish a notice in the FEDERAL REGISTER that the committee is being established, reestablished, renewed, or utilized. In the case of a new committee, the notice shall also describe the nature and purpose of the committee and shall include a statement that the committee is necessary and in the public interest.

(b) Notices required to be published pursuant to paragraph (a) of this section shall be published at least 15 calendar days before the committee charter is filed pursuant to §7.8, except that the Committee Management Secretariat may approve publication for less than 15 days for good cause shown. The 15-day advance notice requirement does not apply to advisory committee renewals, notices of which may be published concurrently with the filing of the charter.

[67 FR 79841, Dec. 31, 2002]

§7.10 The NRC Advisory Committee Management Officer.

(a) The Chairman of the Commission or designee shall appoint an NRC Advisory Committee Management Officer to carry out the functions specified in paragraph (b) of this section.

(b) The NRC Advisory Committee Management Officer shall—

(1) Carry out all responsibilities relating to NRC advisory committees delegated to such officer by the Commission;

(2) Ensure that administrative guidelines and management controls are issued that apply to all NRC advisory committees;

(3) Exercise control and supervision over the establishment, procedures, and accomplishments of NRC advisory committees;

(4) Assemble and maintain the reports, records, and other papers of any such committee during this existence;

(5) Carry out, on behalf of the NRC, the provisions of the Freedom of Information Act (5 U.S.C. 552) and implementing NRC regulations (10 CFR part 9, subpart A) with respect to such reports, records, and other papers;

(6) Ensure that, subject to the Freedom of Information Act and implementing NRC regulations at 10 CFR part 9, subpart A, copies of the records, reports, transcript minutes, appendices, working papers, drafts, studies,

agenda, or other documents that were made available to or prepared for or by each NRC advisory committee are available for public inspection and copying at the NRC Web site, *http://www.nrc.gov*, at the NRC Public Document Room, or both, until the advisory committee ceases to exist;

(7) Ensure that, subject to the Freedom of Information Act and implementing NRC regulations, at least eight copies of each report made by each NRC advisory committee and, where appropriate, background papers prepared by consultants, shall be filed with the Library of Congress;

(8) Ensure that NRC keeps such records as will fully disclose the disposition of any funds that may be at the disposal of NRC advisory committees and the nature and extent of their activities; and

(9) Ensure that NRC keeps such other records and provides such support services as are required by § 7.22.

(c) For purposes of paragraph (b) of this section, the term "records" includes (but is not limited to):

(1) A set of approved charters and membership lists for each NRC advisory committee;

(2) Copies of NRC's portion of the Committee Management Secretariat Annual Comprehensive Review of Federal advisory committees required by section 7(b) of the Act;

(3) NRC guidelines on committee management operations and procedures as maintained and updated; and

(4) NRC determinations to close advisory committee meetings made pursuant to § 7.15.

[54 FR 26948, June 27, 1989; 54 FR 28554, July 6, 1989; 54 FR 31646, Aug. 1, 1989; 64 FR 48949, Sept. 9, 1999; 67 FR 79841, Dec. 31, 2002]

§ 7.11 The Designated Federal Officer.

(a) The Chairman of the Commission or designee shall appoint a Designated Federal Officer or alternate Designated Federal Officer for each NRC advisory committee. The individual holding either position must be employed by the Federal Government on either a full-time or a permanent part-time basis.

(b) All meetings of an NRC advisory committee must be convened or approved by the committee's Designated Federal Officer or alternate, and the agenda for each committee meeting (except a meeting of a Presidential advisory committee) must be approved by that individual.

(c) An NRC advisory committee may not hold a meeting in the absence of its Designated Federal Officer or alternate.

(d) It shall also be the responsibility of the Designated Federal Officer or alternate to:

(1) Attend all meetings of the committee for which he or she has been appointed;

(2) Adjourn the meetings of the committee when such adjournment is in the public interest;

(3) Chair the meetings of the committee when so directed by the Commission;

(4) Ensure compliance with the requirements of § 7.13 regarding minutes of meetings of the committee; and

(5) Make copies of committee documents required to be maintained for public inspection and copying pursuant to § 7.14(b) and ensure their availability at the NRC Web site, *http://www.nrc.gov*, at the NRC Public Document Room, or both.

[67 FR 79841, Dec. 31, 2002]

§ 7.12 Public participation in and public notice of advisory committee meetings.

(a) Each meeting of an NRC advisory committee shall be held at a reasonable time and in a place reasonably accessible to the public, including persons with disabilities. Any advisory committee meeting conducted in whole or part by teleconference, video conference, the Internet, or other electronic medium must comply with this section. The size of the meeting room must be sufficient to accommodate advisory committee members, committee or agency staff, and interested members of the public, except that the provisions of this paragraph relating to the room size shall not apply to any part of an NRC advisory committee meeting that has been closed pursuant to § 7.15.

(b) Any member of the public who wishes to do so shall be permitted to file a written statement with an NRC advisory committee regarding any matter discussed at a meeting of the committee. The committee chairman may also permit members of the public to speak at meetings of the committee in accordance with procedures established by the committee.

(c)(1) Except when the President or designee determines in writing that no notice should be published for reasons of national security, at least 15 days prior to an NRC advisory committee meeting, a notice that includes the following information shall be published in the FEDERAL REGISTER:

(i) The exact name of the advisory committee as chartered;

(ii) The time, date, place, and purpose of the meeting;

(iii) A summary of the agenda of the meeting;

(iv) Whether all or part of the meeting is open to the public; and

(v) The name and telephone number of the Designated Federal Officer, alternate, or other responsible agency employee who may be contacted for additional information concerning the meeting.

(2) If any part of the meeting is closed, the notice shall provide the reasons for the closure, citing the specific matter that has been determined to justify the closure under §7.15. The Commission may publish a single notice announcing multiple meetings; however, a meeting may not be announced so far in advance as to prevent the public from being adequately informed of an NRC advisory committee's schedule.

(d) In exceptional circumstances, less than 15 days notice of an advisory committee meeting may be given, provided that there is as much prior notice as possible and the reasons for the shorter time are included in the committee meeting notice published in the FEDERAL REGISTER.

(e) In addition to notice required by paragraph (c) of this section, the NRC may also use other forms of notice, such as press releases, posting the information on the NRC Web site, *http://www.nrc.gov*, or notice by mail, to inform the public of advisory committee meetings. To that end, the Designated Federal Officer or alternate for each NRC advisory committee will, to the extent practicable, maintain lists of people and organizations interested in that advisory committee and notify them of meetings by mail.

(f) Meetings of a subcommittee whose recommendations will not be reviewed by its parent advisory committee shall be conducted in accordance with all notice and openness requirements contained in this section and in §§7.13, 7.14, and 7.15.

[54 FR 26948, June 27, 1989, as amended at 67 FR 79841, Dec. 31, 2002]

§7.13 Minutes of advisory committee meetings.

(a) Detailed minutes shall be kept of each NRC advisory committee meeting. The minutes shall include the following information:

(1) The time, date, and place of the meeting;

(2) A list of the attendees at the meeting who are advisory committee members or staff, agency employees, or members of the public who presented oral or written statements;

(3) An estimate of the number of other members of the public who were present;

(4) The extent of public participation; and

(5) An accurate description of each matter discussed during the meeting and its resolution, if any, by the committee.

(b) The minutes of an NRC advisory committee meeting shall include a copy of each report or other document received, issued, or approved by the committee in connection with the meeting. If it is impracticable to attach a document to the minutes, the minutes shall describe the document in sufficient detail to permit it to be identified readily.

(c) The chairperson of an NRC advisory committee shall certify the accuracy of the minutes of each of the committee's meetings.

(d) A verbatim transcript of an advisory committee meeting may be substituted for minutes required by this section, providing that the use of such a transcript is in accordance with the requirements of paragraphs (a), (b), and (c) of this section.

[54 FR 26948, June 27, 1989, as amended at 67 FR 79842, Dec. 31, 2002]

§ 7.14 Public information on advisory committees.

(a) The Nuclear Regulatory Commission shall maintain systematic information on the nature, functions, and operations of each NRC advisory committee. A complete set of the charters of NRC advisory committees and copies of the annual reports required by § 7.17(a) will be maintained for public inspection at either the NRC Web site, *http://www.nrc.gov*, at the NRC Public Document Room, or both.

(b) Subject to the provisions of the Freedom of Information Act (5 U.S.C. 552) and NRC's Freedom of Information Act regulations at 10 CFR part 9, subpart A, copies of NRC advisory committees' records, reports, transcripts, minutes, appendices, working papers, drafts, studies, agenda, and other documents shall be maintained for public inspection and copying at the NRC Web site, *http://www.nrc.gov*, at the NRC Public Document Room, or both. To provide the public a meaningful opportunity to comprehend fully the work undertaken by an NRC advisory committee, advisory committee records should be available to the public as soon as practicable. Members of the public or other interested parties may review non-exempt advisory committee records without filing a request for these records under the Freedom of Information Act.

(c) Official records generated by or for an advisory committee must be retained for the duration of the advisory committee. Upon termination of the advisory committee, the records must be processed in accordance with the Federal Records Act (44 U.S.C. Chapters 21, 29–33) and regulations issued by the National Archives and Records Administration (*see* 36 CFR Parts 1220, 1222, 1228, and 1234), or in accordance with the Presidential Records Act (44 U.S.C. Chapter 22).

[67 FR 79842, Dec. 31, 2002]

§ 7.15 Procedures for closing an NRC advisory committee meeting.

(a) To close all or part of a meeting of an NRC advisory committee, the committee shall submit a written request for closure to the General Counsel, citing specific exemptions listed in the Government in the Sunshine Act (5 U.S.C. 552b), as implemented by 10 CFR 9.104, that justify the closure. The request shall provide the General Counsel sufficient time for review in order to make a determination prior to publication of the meeting notice pursuant to § 7.12.

(b) If the General Counsel finds that the request for closure is consistent with the provisions of the Government in the Sunshine Act and this part, a determination shall be issued in writing that all or part of the meeting will be closed. The determination shall include a statement of the reasons for the closing, citing the applicable exemptions in the Government in the Sunshine Act (as implemented by 10 CFR 9.104).

(c) Except when the President or designee determines in writing that no notice should be published for reasons of national security, the Secretary of the Commission shall make a copy of the determination to close all or part of an NRC advisory committee meeting available to the public upon request. If such a determination has been issued, the meeting notice published in the FEDERAL REGISTER should comply with the provisions of § 7.12 applicable to closed meetings.

[67 FR 79842, Dec. 31, 2002]

§ 7.16 Annual comprehensive review.

(a) The Chairman of the Commission shall conduct an annual comprehensive review of the activities and responsibilities of each NRC advisory committee to determine whether the committee—

(1) Is carrying out its purposes or, consistent with the provisions of applicable statutes, its responsibilities should be revised.

(2) Should be merged with another advisory committee.

(3) Should be terminated.

(b) The comprehensive review required by paragraph (a) of this section shall include consideration of such information regarding the committee as is required for the Commission's annual report to the GSA Secretariat pursuant to § 7.17(a) and such other information as may be requested from the Committee by the NRC Advisory Committee Management Officer. The results of such review shall be included in the annual report to the GSA Secretariat.

(c) If, as a result of the review required by this section, the Commission determines that an advisory committee is no longer needed, the committee shall be terminated; except that in the case of an advisory committee established by an Act of Congress or the President, the committee's termination shall be recommended to the President or the Congress, as the case may be.

[54 FR 26948, June 27, 1989, as amended at 67 FR 79842, Dec. 31, 2002]

§7.17 Reports required for advisory committees.

(a) The Commission shall furnish a report on the activities of NRC advisory committees annually to the Committee Management Secretariat on a fiscal year basis. The report must contain information regarding NRC advisory committees consistent with instructions provided by the Committee Management Secretariat. A copy of the report shall be made available at the NRC Web site, *http://www.nrc.gov*, at the NRC Public Document Room, or both. The information provided by the Commission regarding its advisory committees is contained in the Committee Management Secretariat's report which is available on its Web site, *http://www.gsa.gov/committeemanagement*.

(b) Any NRC advisory committee holding closed or partially closed meetings shall issue a report, at least annually, setting forth a summary of its activities consistent with the policy of the Government in the Sunshine Act (5 U.S.C. 552b), as implemented by 10 CFR 9.104. A copy of the report shall be made available at the NRC Web site, *http://www.nrc.gov*, at the NRC Public Document Room, or both.

(c) Subject to the Freedom of Information Act (5 U.S.C. 552) and implementing NRC regulations (10 CFR part 9, subpart A), eight copies of each report made by an advisory committee, including any report on closed meetings pursuant to paragraph (b) of this section, and, where appropriate, background papers prepared by consultants, shall be filed for public inspection and use with the Library of Congress, Anglo-American Acquisitions Division, Government Documents Section, Federal Advisory Committee Desk, 101 Independence Avenue, SE., Washington, DC 20540–4172.

[67 FR 79842, Dec. 31, 2002]

§7.18 Appointment, compensation, and expense reimbursement of advisory committee members, staffs, and consultants.

(a) Unless otherwise provided by law, advisory committee members serve at the pleasure of the Commission and their terms are at the sole discretion of the Commission.

(b) Except where otherwise provided by law, the Commission may accept the gratuitous services of an NRC advisory committee member, staff member, or consultant who agrees in advance to serve without compensation.

(c)(1) Subject to the provisions of paragraph (c)(2) of this section, if the Commission determines that compensation of a member of an NRC advisory committee is appropriate, the amount that will be paid shall be fixed by the Chairman of the Commission at a rate that is the daily equivalent of a rate in NRC's General Grade Salary Schedule, unless the member is appointed as a consultant and compensated at a rate applicable to NRC consultants.

(2) In determining an appropriate rate of pay for a member of an NRC advisory committee, the Chairman of the Commission shall give consideration to the significance, scope, and technical complexity of the matters with which the advisory committee is concerned and the qualifications required of the committee member; provided that the Chairman may not set the rate of pay for an NRC advisory committee member higher than the daily equivalent rate for level IV of the Executive Schedule under 5 U.S.C. 5315, unless a higher rate is expressly allowed by another statute. The Chairman may authorize a rate of basic pay in excess of the maximum rate of basic pay established for NRC's General Grade Salary Schedule. This maximum rate includes an applicable locality payment. The Commission may pay advisory committee members on either an hourly or a daily rate basis. The Commission

may not provide additional compensation in any form, such as bonuses or premium pay. The Chairman may not delegate the responsibility for making a determination that a higher rate of pay than that established by NRC's General Grade Salary Schedule is necessary and justified for an NRC advisory committee member, and such a determination must be reviewed annually.

(d)(1) Each NRC advisory committee staff member may be paid at a rate that is the daily equivalent of a rate in NRC's General Grade Salary Schedule in which the staff member's position would appropriately be placed.

(2) A staff member of an NRC advisory committee may not be paid at a rate higher than the daily equivalent of the maximum rate for a GG–15 under NRC's General Grade Salary Schedule, unless the Chairman of the Commission determines that the staff member's position would appropriately be placed at a grade higher than GG–15, provided that in establishing rates of compensation, the Chairman shall comply with any applicable statutes, regulations, Executive Orders, and administrative guidelines. The Commission may provide advisory committee staff members with additional compensation, such as bonuses or premium pay, as long as the aggregate compensation does not exceed the rate of pay for Executive Schedule level IV.

(3) A Federal employee may serve as a staff member of an NRC advisory committee only with the knowledge of the advisory committee's Designated Federal Officer or alternate and the approval of the employee's direct supervisor. A staff member who is not otherwise a Federal employee shall be appointed in accordance with applicable agency procedures, following consultation with the advisory committee.

(e)(1) Subject to the limitations in paragraph (e)(2) of this section, the following factors shall be considered in determining an appropriate rate of pay for a consultant to an NRC advisory committee:

(i) The qualifications required of the consultant, and

(ii) The significance, scope, and technical complexity of the work for which his services are required;

(2) The rate of pay for an NRC advisory committee consultant may not be higher than the maximum rate of basic pay established by NRC's General Salary Schedule (that is, the GG–15, step 10 rate, excluding locality pay or any other supplement), unless a higher rate is expressly allowed by another statute. The appointment and compensation of NRC experts and consultants must be in conformance with applicable regulations issued by the United States Office of Personnel Management (see 5 CFR part 304).

(f) A member or staff member of an NRC advisory committee engaged in the performance of duties away from his or her home or regular place of business may be allowed travel expenses, including per diem in lieu of subsistence, as authorized by section 5703, title 5, United States Code, for persons employed intermittently in the Government service.

(g) Nothing in this section shall:

(1) Prevent any full-time Federal employee who provides services to an NRC advisory committee from receiving compensation at a rate at which he or she would otherwise be compensated as a full-time Federal employee;

(2) Prevent any individual who provides services to an NRC advisory committee, and who immediately before providing such services was a full-time Federal employee, from receiving compensation at a rate at which he or she was compensated as a full-time Federal employee; or

(3) Affect a rate of pay or a limitation on a rate of pay that is specifically established by law or a rate of pay established under the NRC's General Grade Salary Schedule and evaluation system.

[67 FR 79843, Dec. 31, 2002]

§7.19 Advisory committee members with disabilities.

An NRC advisory committee member who is disabled may be provided services by a personal assistant while performing advisory committee duties, if the member;

(a) Qualifies as disabled under section 501 of the Rehabilitation Act of 1973 (29 U.S.C. 794) ; and

(b) Does not otherwise qualify for assistance under 5 U.S.C. 3102 by reason of being an employee of NRC.

[67 FR 79843, Dec. 31, 2002]

§ 7.20 Conflict of interest reviews of advisory committee members' outside interests.

The Designated Federal Officer or alternate for each NRC advisory committee and the General Counsel or designee shall review the interests and affiliations of each member of the Designated Federal Officer's advisory committee annually, and upon the commencement of the member's appointment to the committee, for the purpose of ensuring that such appointment is consistent with the laws and regulations on conflict of interest applicable to that member.

[67 FR 79843, Dec. 31, 2002]

§ 7.21 Cost of duplication of documents.

Copies of the records, reports, transcripts, minutes, appendices, working papers, drafts, studies, agenda, or other documents that were made available to or prepared for or by an NRC advisory committee shall be made available to any person at the actual cost of duplication prescribed in part 9 of this chapter. (For availability of information on advisory committees, see § 7.14.)

§ 7.22 Fiscal and administrative responsibilities.

(a) The Office of the Chief Financial Officer shall keep such records as will fully disclose the disposition of any funds that may be at the disposal of NRC advisory committees.

(b) The Office of the Chief Information Officer shall keep such records as will fully disclose the nature and extent of activities of NRC advisory committees.

(c) NRC shall provide support services (including staff support and meeting space) for each advisory committee established by or reporting to it unless the establishing authority provides otherwise. Where any such advisory committee reports to another agency in addition to NRC, only one agency shall be responsible for support services at any one time, and the establishing authority shall designate the agency responsible for providing such services.

[54 FR 26948, June 27, 1989, as amended at 63 FR 15742, Apr. 1, 1998; 80 FR 74978, Dec. 1, 2015]

PART 8 [RESERVED]

PART 9—PUBLIC RECORDS

Sec.

Subpart A—Freedom of Information Act Regulations

Subpart B—Privacy Act Regulations

AUTHORITY: Atomic Energy Act of 1954, sec. 161 (42 U.S.C. 2201); Energy Reorganization Act of 1974, sec. 201 (42 U.S.C. 5841); 44 U.S.C. 3504 note.

Subpart A also issued under 31 U.S.C. 9701.

Subpart B also issued under 5 U.S.C. 552a.

Subpart C also issued under 5 U.S.C. 552b.

EDITORIAL NOTE: Nomenclature changes to part 9 appear at 82 FR 52825, Nov. 15, 2017.

§ 9.1 Scope and purpose.

(a) Subpart A implements the provisions of the Freedom of Information Act, 5 U.S.C. 552, concerning the availability to the public of Nuclear Regulatory Commission records for inspection and copying.

(b) Subpart B implements the provisions of the Privacy Act of 1974, 5 U.S.C. 552a, concerning disclosure and availability of certain Nuclear Regulatory Commission records maintained on individuals.

(c) Subpart C implements the provisions of the Government in the Sunshine Act, 5 U.S.C. 552b, concerning the opening of Commission meetings to public observation.

(d) Subpart D describes procedures governing the production of agency records, information, or testimony in response to subpoenas or demands of courts or other judicial or quasi-judicial authorities in State and Federal proceedings.

[52 FR 49355, Dec. 31, 1987]

§ 9.3 Definitions.

As used in this part:

Commission means the Commission of five members or a quorum thereof sitting as a body, as provided by section 201 of the Energy Reorganization Act of 1974.

Government agency means any executive department, military department, Government corporation, Government-controlled corporation, or other establishment in the executive branch of the Government (including the Executive Office of the President), or any independent regulatory agency.

NRC means the Nuclear Regulatory Commission, established by the Energy Reorganization Act of 1974.

NRC personnel means employees, consultants, and members of advisory boards, committees, and panels of the NRC; members of boards designated by the Commission to preside at adjudicatory proceedings; and officers or employees of Government agencies, including military personnel, assigned to duty at the NRC.

Working days mean Monday through Friday, except legal holidays.

[52 FR 49355, Dec. 31, 1987]

§9.5 Interpretations.

Except as specifically authorized by the Commission in writing, no interpretation of the meaning of the regulations in this part by an officer or employee of the Commission other than a written interpretation by the General Counsel will be recognized as binding upon the Commission.

[52 FR 49356, Dec. 31, 1987]

§9.6 Communications.

Except as otherwise indicated, communications relating to this part shall be addressed to the Freedom of Information Act and Privacy Act Officer, may be sent to the NRC by mail addressed to the U.S. Nuclear Regulatory Commission, Washington, DC 20555–0001; by hand delivery to the NRC's offices at 11555 Rockville Pike, Rockville, Maryland; or, where practicable, by electronic submission via facsimile to (301) 415–5130 or e-mail to *foia@nrc.gov.* Electronic submissions must be made in a manner that enables the NRC to receive, read, authenticate, distribute, and archive the submission, and process and retrieve it a single page at a time. Detailed guidance on making electronic submissions can be obtained by visiting the NRC's Web site at *http://www.nrc.gov/site-help/e-submittals.html;* by e-mail to *MSHD.Resource@nrc.gov;* or by writing the Office of the Chief Information Officer, U.S. Nuclear Regulatory Commission, Washington, DC 20555–0001. The guidance discusses, among other topics, the formats the NRC can accept, the use of electronic signatures, and the treatment of nonpublic information.

[68 FR 58799, Oct. 10, 2003, as amended at 74 FR 62680, Dec. 1, 2009; 80 FR 74978, Dec. 1, 2015]

§9.8 Information collection requirements: OMB approval.

(a) The Nuclear Regulatory Commission has submitted the information collection requirements contained in this part to the Office of Management and Budget (OMB) for approval as required by the Paperwork Reduction Act (44 U.S.C. 3501 *et seq.*). The NRC may not conduct or sponsor, and a person is not required to respond to, a collection of information unless it displays a currently valid OMB control number. OMB has approved the information collection requirements contained in this part under control number 3150–0043.

(b) The approved information collection requirements contained in this part appear in §§9.23, 9.25, 9.28, 9.29, 9.40, 9.41, 9.53, 9.54, 9.55, 9.65, 9.66, and 9.67.

[62 FR 52184, Oct. 6, 1997, as amended at 63 FR 2876, Jan. 20, 1998; 70 FR 34306, June 14, 2005]

Subpart A—Freedom of Information Act Regulations

SOURCE: 63 FR 2876, Jan. 20, 1998, unless otherwise noted.

§9.11 Scope of subpart.

This subpart prescribes procedures for making NRC agency records available to the public for inspection and copying pursuant to the provisions of the Freedom of Information Act (5 U.S.C. 552) and provides notice of procedures for obtaining NRC records otherwise publicly available. This subpart does not affect the dissemination or distribution of NRC-originated, or NRC contractor-originated, information to the public under any other NRC public, technical, or other information program or policy.

§ 9.13 Definitions.

Agency record means a record in the possession and control of the NRC that is associated with Government business. Agency record does not include records such as—

(1) Publicly-available books, periodicals, or other publications that are owned or copyrighted by non-Federal sources;

(2) Records solely in the possession and control of NRC contractors;

(3) Personal records in possession of NRC personnel that have not been circulated, were not required to be created or retained by the NRC, and can be retained or discarded at the author's sole discretion, or records of a personal nature that are not associated with any Government business; or

(4) Non-substantive information in logs or schedule books of the Chairman or Commissioners, uncirculated except for typing or recording purposes.

Commercial-use request means a request made under § 9.23(b) for a use or purpose that furthers the commercial, trade, or profit interests of the requester or the person on whose behalf the request is made.

Direct costs mean the expenditures that an agency incurs in searching for and duplicating agency records. For a commercial-use request, direct costs include the expenditures involved in reviewing records to respond to the request. Direct costs include the salary of the employee category performing the work based on that basic rate of pay plus 16 percent of that rate to cover fringe benefits and the cost of operating duplicating machinery.

Duplication means the process of making a copy of a record necessary to respond to a request made under § 9.23. Copies may take the form of paper copy, microform, audio-visual materials, disk, magnetic tape, or machine readable documentation, among others.

Educational institution means an institution that operates a program or programs of scholarly research. Educational institution refers to a preschool, a public or private elementary or secondary school, an institution of graduate higher education, an institution of undergraduate higher education, an institution of professional education, or an institution of vocational education.

Freedom of Information Act and Privacy Act Officer means the NRC official designated to fulfill the responsibilities for implementing and administering the Freedom of Information Act and the Privacy Act as specifically designated under the regulations in this part.

Noncommercial scientific institution means an institution that is not operated on a commercial basis, as the term "commercial" is referred to in the definition of "commercial-use request," and is operated solely for the purpose of conducting scientific research, the results of which are not intended to promote any particular product or industry.

Office, unless otherwise indicated, means all offices, boards, panels, and advisory committees of the NRC.

Record means any information that would be an agency record subject to the requirements of the Freedom of Information Act when maintained by the NRC in any format, including an electronic format. Record also includes a book, paper, map, drawing, diagram, photograph, brochure, punch card, magnetic tape, paper tape, sound recording, pamphlet, slide, motion picture, or other documentary material regardless of form or characteristics. Record does not include an object or article such as a structure, furniture, a tangible exhibit or model, a vehicle, or piece of equipment.

Representative of the news media means any person actively gathering news for an entity that is organized and operated to publish or broadcast news to the public. The term news means information that is about current events or that would be of current interest to the public. Examples of news media entities include television or radio stations broadcasting to the public at large, and publishers of periodicals (but only in those instances when they can qualify as disseminators of "news") who make their products available for purchase or subscriptions by the general public.

Review time means the period devoted to examining records retrieved in response to a request to determine whether they are exempt from disclosure in whole or in part. Review time also includes the period devoted to examining records to determine which Freedom of Information Act exemptions, if any, are applicable and identifying records, or portions thereof, to be disclosed.

Search time means the period devoted to looking for agency records, either manually or by automated means, for the purpose of locating those records that are responsive to a request. This includes a page-by-page or line-by-line identification of responsive information within the records.

Unusual circumstances mean—

(1) The need to search for and collect the requested records from field facilities or other establishments that are separate from the office processing the request;

(2) The need to search for, collect, and appropriately examine a voluminous amount of separate and distinct records demanded in a single request; or

(3) The need for consultation, which will be conducted with all practicable speed, with another agency having a substantial interest in the determination of the request or among two or more components of the NRC having substantial subject-matter interest therein.

[63 FR 2876, Jan. 20, 1998, as amended at 70 FR 34306, June 14, 2005]

§9.15 Availability of records.

The NRC will make available for public inspection and copying any reasonably described agency record in the possession and control of the NRC under the provisions of this subpart, and upon request by any person. Records will be made available in any form or format requested by a person if the record is readily reproducible by NRC in that form or format. NRC will make reasonable efforts to maintain its records in forms or formats that are reproducible. NRC will make reasonable efforts to search for records in electronic form or format when requested, except when these efforts would significantly interfere with the operation of any of the NRC's automated information systems. Records that the NRC routinely makes publicly available are described in §9.21. Procedures and conditions governing requests for records are set forth in §9.23.

§9.17 Agency records exempt from public disclosure.

(a) The following types of agency records are exempt from public disclosure under §9.15:

(1) Records—

(i) That are specifically authorized under criteria established by an Executive Order to be kept secret in the interest of national defense or foreign policy, and

(ii) That are in fact properly classified pursuant to such Executive Order;

(2) Records related solely to the internal personnel rules and practices of the agency;

(3) Records specifically exempted from disclosure by statute (other than 5 U.S.C. 552b), provided that the statute—

(i) Requires that the matters be withheld from the public in a manner that leaves no discretion on the issue; or

(ii) Establishes particular criteria for withholding or refers to particular types of matters to be withheld;

(4) Trade secrets and commercial or financial information obtained from a person that are privileged or confidential;

(5) Interagency or intra-agency memorandums or letters that would not be available by law to a party other than an agency in litigation with the agency, provided that the deliberative process privilege shall not apply to records created 25 years or more before the date on which the records were requested;

(6) Personnel and medical files and similar files, the disclosure of which would constitute a clearly unwarranted invasion of personal privacy;

(7) Records or information compiled for law enforcement purposes, but only to the extent that the production of these law enforcement records or information—

(i) Could reasonably be expected to interfere with enforcement proceedings;

(ii) Would deprive a person of a right to a fair trial or an impartial adjudication;

(iii) Could reasonably be expected to constitute an unwarranted invasion of personal privacy;

(iv) Could reasonably be expected to disclose the identity of a confidential source, including a State, local, or foreign agency or authority, or any private institution which furnished information on a confidential basis, and, in the case of a record or information compiled by a criminal law enforcement authority in the course of a criminal investigation, or by an agency conducting a lawful national security intelligence investigation, or information furnished by a confidential source;

(v) Would disclose techniques and procedures for law enforcement investigations or prosecutions, or would disclose guidelines for law enforcement investigations or prosecutions, if the disclosure could reasonably be expected to risk circumvention of the law; or

(vi) Could reasonably be expected to endanger the life or physical safety of any individual;

(8) Matters contained in or related to examination, operating, or condition reports prepared by, on behalf of, or for the use of any agency responsible for the regulation or supervision of financial institutions; or

(9) Geological and geophysical information and data, including maps, concerning wells.

(b) Nothing in this subpart authorizes withholding of information or limiting the availability of records to the public except as specifically provided in this part, nor is this subpart authority to withhold information from Congress.

(c)(1) The NRC shall withhold information under this subpart only if—

(i) The NRC reasonably foresees that disclosure would harm an interest protected by an exemption described in paragraph (a) of this section; or

(ii) Disclosure is prohibited by law.

(2) Nothing in this subpart requires disclosure of information that is otherwise prohibited from disclosure by law, or otherwise exempted from disclosure under 5 U.S.C. 552(b)(3).

(d) Whenever a request is made that involves access to agency records described in paragraph (a)(7) of this section, the NRC may, during only the time as that circumstance continues, treat the records as not subject to the requirements of this subpart when—

(1) The investigation or proceeding involves a possible violation of criminal law; and

(2) There is reason to believe that—

(i) The subject of the investigation or proceeding is not aware of its pendency; and

(ii) Disclosure of the existence of the records could reasonably be expected to interfere with enforcement proceedings.

[63 FR 2876, Jan. 20, 1998, as amended at 81 FR 96346, Dec. 30, 2016]

§ 9.19 Segregation of exempt information and deletion of identifying details.

(a) For records required to be made available under 5 U.S.C. 552(a)(2), the NRC shall delete information that is exempt under one or more of the exemptions cited in § 9.17. The amount of information deleted will be indicated on the released portion of the record, unless providing this indication would harm an interest protected by the exemption(s) under which the matter has been withheld.

(b) In responding to a request for information submitted under § 9.23, in which it has been determined to withhold exempt information, the NRC shall segregate—

(1) Information that is exempt from public disclosure under § 9.17 from nonexempt information; and

(2) Factual information from advice, opinions, and recommendations in predecisional records unless the information is inextricably intertwined, or is contained in drafts, legal work products, and records covered by the lawyer-client privilege, or is otherwise exempt from disclosure.

(c) In denying a request for records, in whole or in part, NRC will make a reasonable effort to estimate the volume of any information requested that is denied and provide the estimate to the person making the request, unless providing the estimate would harm an interest protected by the exemption(s) under which the information has been denied.

(d) When entire records or portions thereof are denied and deletions are made from parts of the record by computer, the amount of information deleted will be indicated on the released portion of the record, unless providing this indication would harm an interest protected by the exemption(s) under which the matter has been denied.

[63 FR 2876, Jan. 20, 1998, as amended at 81 FR 96346, Dec. 30, 2016]

§ 9.21 Publicly available records.

(a) Single copies of NRC publications in the NUREG series, NRC Regulatory Guides, and Standard Review Plans can be ordered from the National Technical Information Service, 5285 Port Royal Road, Springfield, Virginia, 22161.

(b) For the convenience of persons who may wish to inspect without charge, or purchase copies of a record or a limited category of records for a fee, publicly available records of the NRC's activities described in paragraph (c) of this section are also made available at the NRC Web site, *http://www.nrc.gov*, and/or at the Public Document Room located at One White Flint North, 11555 Rockville Pike (first floor), Rockville, Maryland 20852–2738, between 7:45 am and 4:15 pm on Monday through Friday except Federal holidays.

(c) The following records of NRC activities are available for public inspection in an electronic format:

(1) Final opinions including concurring and dissenting opinions as well as orders of the NRC issued as a result of adjudication of cases;

(2) Statements of policy and interpretations that have been adopted by the NRC and have not been published in the FEDERAL REGISTER;

(3) Nuclear Regulatory Commission rules and regulations;

(4) Nuclear Regulatory Commission Manuals and instructions to NRC personnel that affect any member of the public;

(5) Copies of all records, regardless of form or format—

(i) That have been released to any person under § 9.23; and

(ii)(A) That because of the nature of their subject matter, the NRC determines have become or are likely to become the subject of subsequent requests for substantially the same records; or

(B) That have been requested 3 or more times;

(6) Individual indexes to publicly available records, including those records specified in paragraph (c) of this section, may be created by using the search features of the Agencywide Documents Access and Management System (ADAMS), located at the NRC Web site, *http://www.nrc.gov*. This capability made it unnecessary for the NRC to continue publishing its monthly publication, *Documents Made Publicly Available* (NUREG–0540) after March 1999.

(d) The published versions of the records made publicly available under paragraph (c)(1) of this section are available under the title, Nuclear Regulatory Issuances, NUREG–0750, for purchase through the National Technical Information Service.

[64 FR 48950, Sept. 9, 1999, as amended at 67 FR 67098, Nov. 4, 2002; 70 FR 34306, June 14, 2005; 81 FR 96346, Dec. 30, 2016]

§ 9.23 Requests for records.

(a)(1) A person may request access to records routinely made available by the NRC under § 9.21 in person, by telephone, by e-mail, facsimile, or U.S. mail from the NRC Public Document Room, One White Flint North, 11555 Rockville Pike (first floor), Rockville, Maryland 20852–2738.

(i) Each record requested must be described in sufficient detail to enable the NRC Public Document Room staff to locate the record.

(ii) To obtain copies of records expeditiously, a person may open an account with the NRC Public Document Room reproduction contractor. Payment for reproduction services will be made directly to the contractor.

(2) [Reserved]

(b) A person may request agency records by submitting a request authorized by 5 U.S.C. 552(a)(3) to the Freedom of Information Act and Privacy Act Officer by an appropriate method listed in § 9.6 of this chapter. The request must be in writing and clearly state on the envelope and in the letter that it is a "Freedom of Information Act request." The NRC does not consider a request as received until the date it is actually received by the Freedom of Information Act and Privacy Act Officer.

(1) A Freedom of Information Act request covers only agency records that are in existence on the date the Freedom of Information Act and Privacy Act Officer receives the request. A request does not cover agency records destroyed or discarded before receipt of a request or which are created after the date of the request.

(2) All Freedom of Information Act requests for copies of agency records must reasonably describe the agency records sought in sufficient detail to permit the NRC to identify the requested agency records. Where possible, the requester should provide specific information regarding dates, titles, docket numbers, file designations, and other information which may help identify the agency records. If a requested agency record is not described in sufficient detail to permit its identification, the Freedom of Information Act and Privacy Act Officer will contact the requester within 10 working days after receipt of the request and inform the requester of the additional information or clarification needed to process the request.

(3) Upon receipt of a request made under paragraph (b) of this section, the NRC will provide written notification to the requester that indicates the request has been received, the name and telephone number of the NRC point of contact to find out the status of the request, and other pertinent matters regarding the processing of the request.

(4)(i) The NRC shall advise a requester that fees will be assessed if—

(A) A request involves anticipated costs in excess of the minimum specified in § 9.39; and

(B) Search and duplication is not provided without charge under § 9.39; or

(C) The requester does not specifically state that the cost involved is acceptable or acceptable up to a specified limit.

(ii) The NRC has discretion to discontinue processing a request made under this paragraph until—

(A) A required advance payment has been received;

(B) The requester has agreed to bear the estimated costs;

(C) A determination has been made on a request for waiver or reduction of fees; or

(D) The requester meets the requirements of § 9.39.

(c) If a requested agency record that has been reasonably described is located at a place other than at the NRC Web site, *http://www.nrc.gov*, the NRC Public Document Room, or the NRC headquarters, the NRC may, at its discretion, make the record available for inspection and copying at either of the locations.

(d) Except as provided in § 9.39—

(1) If the record requested under paragraph (b) of this section is a record available through the National Technical Information Service, the NRC shall refer the requester to the National Technical Information Service; and

(2) If the requested record has been placed on the NRC Internet Web site, under § 9.21, the NRC may inform the requester that the record is available at the NRC Web site, *http://www.nrc.gov*, and/or at the NRC Public Document Room, and that the record may be obtained in accordance with the procedures set forth in paragraph (a) of this section.

(e) The Freedom of Information Act and Privacy Act Officer will promptly forward a Freedom of Information Act request made under paragraph (b) of this section for an agency record to the head of the office(s) primarily concerned with the records requested, as appropriate. The responsible office will conduct a search for the agency records responsive to the request and compile those agency records to be reviewed for initial disclosure determination and/or identify those that have already been made publicly available at the NRC Web site, *http://www.nrc.gov*, and/or at the NRC Public Document Room.

[63 FR 2876, Jan. 20, 1998, as amended at 64 FR 48950, Sept. 9, 1999; 67 FR 67098, Nov. 4, 2002; 68 FR 58800, Oct. 10, 2003; 70 FR 34306, June 14, 2005]

§9.25 Initial disclosure determination.

(a) *Time for initial disclosure determination.* The NRC will notify a requester within 20 working days of its determination. If the NRC cannot act upon the request within this period, the NRC will provide the requester with the reasons for the delay and provide a projected response date.

(b) *Extension of time limit in unusual circumstances.* In unusual circumstances, the NRC may extend the time limit prescribed in paragraph (a) of this section by not more than 10 working days. The extension may be made by written or telephonic notice to the person making the request to explain the reasons for the extension and indicate the date on which a determination is expected to be made. "Unusual circumstances" is limited to one or more of the following reasons for delay:

(1) The need to search for and collect the requested records from field facilities or other establishments that are separate from the office processing the request;

(2) The need to search for, collect, and appropriately examine a voluminous amount of separate and distinct records which are demanded in a single request; or

(3) The need for consultation, which will be conducted with all practicable speed, with another agency having a substantial interest in the determination of the request or among two or more components of the NRC having substantial subject-matter interest therein.

(c) *Exceptional circumstances.* A requester may be notified in certain exceptional circumstances, when it appears that a request cannot be completed within the allowable time, and will be provided an opportunity to limit the scope of the request so that it may be processed in the time limit, or to agree to a reasonable alternative time frame for processing. When notifying a requester under this paragraph, the NRC, to aid the requester, shall make available its FOIA Public Liaison to assist in the resolution of any disputes between the requester and the agency and shall notify the requester of the requester's right to seek dispute resolution services from the Office of Government Information Services within the National Archives and Records Administration. For purposes of this paragraph, the term "exceptional circumstances" does not include delays that result from the normal predictable workload of FOIA requests or a failure by the NRC to exercise due diligence in processing the request. A requester's unwillingness to agree to reasonable modification of the request or an alternative time for processing the request may be considered as factors in determining whether exceptional circumstances exist and whether the agency exercised due diligence in responding to the request.

(d) *Multiple-Track processing.* To ensure the most equitable treatment possible of all requesters, the NRC will process requests on a first-in, first-out basis, using multiple tracking systems based upon the estimated time it will take to process the request.

(1) NRC uses a three-track system.

(i) The first track is for requests of simple to moderate complexity that are expected to be completed within 20 working days.

(ii) The second track is for requests involving "unusual circumstances" that are expected to take between 21–30 working days to complete (e.g. requests involving possible records from two or three offices and/or various types of files of moderate volume, of which, some are expected to be exempt)

(iii) The third track is for requests that, because of their unusual volume or other complexity, are expected to take more than 30 working days to complete (e.g. requests involving several offices, regional offices, another agency's records, classified records requiring declassification review, records from businesses that are required to be referred to the submitter for their proprietary review prior to disclosure, records in large volumes which require detailed review because of the sensitive nature of the records such as investigative records or legal opinions and recordings of internal deliberations of agency staff).

(2) Upon receipt of requests, NRC will notify requesters of the track in which the request has been placed for processing and the estimated time for completion. Should subsequent information

substantially change the estimated time to process a request, the requester will be notified telephonically or in writing. A requester may modify the request to allow it to be processed faster or to reduce the cost of processing. Partial responses may be sent to requesters as documents are obtained by the FOIA office from the supplying offices.

(e) *Expedited processing.* (1) NRC may place a person's request at the front of the queue for the appropriate track for that request upon receipt of a written request that clearly demonstrates a compelling need for expedited processing. For purposes of determining whether to grant expedited processing, the term compelling need means—

(i) That a failure to obtain requested records on an expedited basis could reasonably be expected to pose an imminent threat to the life or physical safety of an individual; or

(ii) With respect to a request made by a person primarily engaged in disseminating information, urgency to inform the public concerning actual or alleged Federal Government activity.

(2) A person requesting expedited processing must include a statement certifying the compelling need given to be true and correct to the best of his or her knowledge and belief. The certification requirement may be waived by the NRC as a matter of agency discretion.

(3) The Freedom of Information Act and Privacy Act Officer will make the initial determination whether to grant or deny a request for expedited processing and will notify a requester within 10 calendar days after the request has been received whether expedited processing will be granted.

(f) *Disclosure review.* The head of the responsible office shall review agency records located in a search under § 9.23(b) to determine whether the agency records are exempt from disclosure under § 9.17. If the head of the office determines that, although exempt, the disclosure of the agency records will not be contrary to the public interest and will not affect the rights of any person, the head of the office may authorize disclosure of the agency records. If the head of the office authorizes disclosure of the agency records, the head of the office will furnish the agency records to the Freedom of Information Act and Privacy Act Officer, who will notify the requester of the determination in the manner provided in § 9.27.

(g)(1) *Initial disclosure determination on requests for records originated by, or located in the files of the Office of the Inspector General.* If, as a result of the review specified in paragraph (f) of this section, the Assistant Inspector General for Investigations finds that agency records that are originated by or located in the Office of the Inspector General are exempt from disclosure and should be denied in whole or in part, and disclosure of the records is contrary to the public interest and will adversely affect the rights of any person, the Assistant Inspector General for Investigations will submit that finding to the Freedom of Information Act and Privacy Act Officer who will notify the requester of the determination in the manner provided in § 9.27.

(2) *Initial disclosure determinations on requests for records originated by or transmitted to the Commission, or a Commissioner, or records originated by, or for which the Office of the Secretary or an Advisory Committee has primary responsibility.* If, as a result of the review specified in paragraph (f) of this section, the Executive Assistant to the Secretary of the Commission finds that agency records originated by or transmitted to the Commission or a Commissioner, or records originated by, or for which the Office of the Secretary or an Advisory Committee has primary responsibility, are exempt from disclosure and should be denied in whole or in part, and disclosure of the records is contrary to the public interest and will adversely affect the rights of any person, the Executive Assistant to the Secretary of the Commission will submit that finding to the Freedom of Information Act and Privacy Act Officer who will notify the requester of the determination in the manner provided in § 9.27.

(3) *Initial disclosure determination for records originated by, or for which the Office of the General Counsel has principal responsibility.* If, as a result of the review specified in paragraph (f) of this section, the General Counsel finds that agency records that are originated by,

or for which the Office of the General Counsel has primary responsibility, are exempt from disclosure and should be denied in whole or in part, and disclosure of the records is contrary to the public interest and will adversely affect the rights of any person, the General Counsel will submit that finding to the Freedom of Information Act and Privacy Act Officer who will notify the requester of the determination in the manner provided in §9.27.

(h) *Initial disclosure determinations on requests for records other than those for which the initial disclosure determination is made by the Assistant Inspector General for Investigations, the Executive Assistant to the Secretary of the Commission, or the General Counsel.* If, as a result of the review specified in paragraph (f) of this section, the head of the responsible office finds that agency records other than those described in paragraph (g) of this section, that are originated by, or for which the office has primary responsibility, should be denied in whole or in part, the head of the office will submit that finding to the Freedom of Information Act and Privacy Act Officer, who will, in consultation with the Office of the General Counsel, make an independent determination whether the agency records should be denied in whole or in part. If the Freedom of Information Act and Privacy Act Officer determines that the agency records sought are exempt from disclosure and disclosure of the records is contrary to the public interest and will adversely affect the rights of any person, the Freedom of Information Act and Privacy Act Officer will notify the requester of the determination in the manner provided in §9.27.

(i) *Records and information originated by another Federal agency.* If a requested record is located that was originated or contains information originated by another Federal Government agency, or deals with subject matter over which an agency other than the NRC has exclusive or primary responsibility, the NRC will promptly refer the record to that Federal Government agency for disposition or for guidance regarding disposition.

(j) If the NRC does not respond to a request within the 20 working-day period, or within the extended periods described in paragraph (b) of this section, the requester may treat that delay as a denial of the request and immediately appeal as provided in §9.29(a) or sue in a Federal District Court as noted in §9.29(c).

[63 FR 2876, Jan. 20, 1998, as amended at 70 FR 34306, June 14, 2005; 81 FR 96346, Dec. 30, 2016]

§9.27 Form and content of responses.

(a) When the NRC has located a requested agency record and has determined to disclose the agency record, the Freedom of Information Act and Privacy Act Officer will promptly furnish the agency record or notify the requester where and when the agency record will be available for inspection and copying. The NRC's response will notify the requester of the requester's right to seek assistance from the NRC's FOIA Public Liaison. The NRC will also advise the requester of any applicable fees under §§9.35 and 9.37. The NRC will routinely make copies of non-sensitive records disclosed in response to Freedom of Information Act requests publicly available through the Agencywide Document Access and Management System (ADAMS) located in the NRC Library that can be accessed via the NRC Web site at *http://www.nrc.gov/NRC/reading-rm/adams.html.* Records that contain information personal to the requester, involve matters that are not likely to be of public interest to anyone other than the requester or contain privileged or confidential information that should only be disclosed to the requester will not be made publicly available on the NRC Web site.

(b) When the NRC denies access to a requested agency record or denies a request for expedited processing or for a waiver or reduction of fees, the Freedom of Information Act and Privacy Act Officer will notify the requester in writing. The denial will include as appropriate—

(1) The reason for the denial;

(2) A reference to the specific exemption under the Freedom of Information Act, or other appropriate reason, and the Commission's regulations authorizing the denial;

(3) The name and title or position of each person responsible for the denial

of the request, including the head of the office recommending denial of the record;

(4) A statement stating why the request does not meet the requirements of § 9.41 if the request is for a waiver or reduction of fees; and

(5) A statement that the denial may be appealed within 90 calendar days from the date of the denial to the Executive Director for Operations, to the Secretary of the Commission, or to the Inspector General, as appropriate.

(6) A statement that the requester has a right to seek assistance from the NRC's FOIA Public Liaison; and

(7) A statement that the requester has a right to seek dispute resolution services from the NRC's FOIA Public Liaison or the Office of Government Information Services within the National Archives and Records Administration.

(c) The Freedom of Information Act and Privacy Act Officer will maintain a copy of each letter granting or denying requested agency records, denying a request for expedited processing, or denying a request for a waiver or reduction of fees in accordance with the NRC Comprehensive Records Disposition Schedule.

[63 FR 2876, Jan. 20, 1998, as amended at 70 FR 34307, June 14, 2005; 76 FR 72084, Nov. 22, 2011; 81 FR 96346, Dec. 30, 2016]

§ 9.28 Predisclosure notification procedures for information containing trade secrets or confidential commercial or financial information.

(a) *Notice of opportunity to object to NRC's initial disclosure determination.* Whenever NRC makes an initial determination that information should be disclosed in response to a Freedom of Information Act request or a Freedom of Information Act appeal which has been designated by the submitter as trade secrets or confidential commercial or financial information, or the NRC believes the information contains such trade secrets or confidential commercial or financial information, the NRC will give the submitter of the information written notice of NRC's initial determination, or NRC's need for information on which to base a determination, and an opportunity to object. The notice must describe the business information requested or include copies of the requested records or record portions containing the information.

(b) *Submitter objection to disclosure.* The submitter will be allowed 30 calendar days from date of the notice described in paragraph (a) of this section to object to disclosure, unless the Commission determines that a shorter period of time to respond is necessary in a particular instance. If a submitter has any objection to disclosure, the submitter must provide a detailed written statement. The statement must specify all grounds that support why the information is a trade secret or commercial or financial information that is privileged or confidential. If a submitter fails to respond to the notice within the time specified in the notice, the submitter will be considered to have no objection to disclosure of the information. Information provided by the submitter that is not received until after the date specified for response will not be considered unless that date is extended by the Freedom of Information Act and Privacy Act Officer upon request by the submitter.

(c) *Notice of final decision to disclose.* The NRC shall consider a submitter's written statement and specific grounds for nondisclosure. If the NRC agrees to withhold the information from public disclosure, the NRC will inform the requester in the manner described in § 9.27 of the agency decision to deny access to the requested information. Whenever the NRC denies the submitter's request for nondisclosure and decides to disclose the information, the NRC shall give the submitter written notice, which must include:

(1) A statement of the reason(s) for the determination;

(2) A description of the business information to be disclosed; and

(3) A specified disclosure date, which will be 30 calendar days subsequent to the date of the notice, or less, as provided under paragraph (b) of this section, after which the information will be made available to the public.

(d) *Corresponding notice to requesters.* When the NRC provides a submitter with notice and opportunity to object to disclosure under paragraph (b) of this section, the NRC shall also notify the requester(s). Whenever the NRC notifies a submitter of its final decision to disclose the requested information under paragraph (c) of this section, the NRC shall also notify the requester(s). When a submitter files a lawsuit seeking to prevent the disclosure of trade secrets or confidential commercial or financial information, the NRC shall notify the requester(s).

(e) *Notice to submitter of Freedom of Information Act lawsuit.* Whenever a requester files a lawsuit seeking to compel disclosure of trade secrets or confidential commercial or financial information, the NRC shall promptly notify the submitter.

[70 FR 34307, June 14, 2005]

§ 9.29 Appeal from initial determination.

(a) A requester may appeal a notice of denial of a Freedom of Information Act request for access to agency records, denial of a request for waiver or reduction of fees, or denial of a request for expedited processing under this subpart within 90 calendar days of the date of the NRC's denial.

(b) For agency records to which access is denied by the Assistant Inspector General for Investigations, the appeal must be in writing directed to the Inspector General and sent to the Freedom of Information Act and Privacy Act Officer by an appropriate method listed in § 9.6. The appeal should clearly state on the envelope and in the letter that it is an "Appeal from Initial Freedom of Information Act Decision." The NRC does not consider an appeal received until the date it is actually received by the Freedom of Information Act and Privacy Act Officer. The Inspector General will make the NRC determination on the appeal within 20 working days after the receipt of the appeal. If the Inspector General denies an appeal of access to records, in whole or in part, the Inspector General will notify the requester of the denial, explaining the exemptions relied upon and how the exemptions apply to the agency records withheld. The notice will inform the requester that the denial is a final agency action and that judicial review is available in a district court of the United States in the district in which the requester resides or has a principal place of business, in which the agency records are situated, or in the District of Columbia.

(c) For agency records to which access is denied by the Executive Assistant to the Secretary of the Commission, the General Counsel, or an office director reporting to the Commission, the appeal must be in writing directed to the Secretary of the Commission and sent to the Freedom of Information Act and Privacy Act Officer by an appropriate method listed in § 9.6. The appeal should clearly state on the envelope and in the letter that it is an "Appeal from Initial Freedom of Information Act Decision." The NRC does not consider an appeal received until the date it is actually received by the Freedom of Information Act and Privacy Act Officer. The Secretary of the Commission will make the NRC determination on the appeal within 20 working days after the receipt of the appeal. If the Secretary of the Commission denies an appeal of access to records, in whole or in part, the Secretary of the Commission will notify the requester of the denial, explaining the exemptions relied upon and how the exemptions apply to the agency records withheld. The notice will inform the requester that the denial is a final agency action and that judicial review is available in a district court of the United States in the district in which the requester resides or has a principal place of business, in which the agency records are situated, or in the District of Columbia.

(d) For agency records to which access is denied by agency officials other than the Assistant Inspector General for Investigations, the Executive Assistant to the Secretary of the Commission, the General Counsel, or other office director reporting to the Commission, the appeal must be in writing directed to the Executive Director for Operations and sent to the Freedom of Information Act and Privacy Act Officer by an appropriate method listed in § 9.6. The appeal should clearly state on the envelope and in the letter that it is an "Appeal from Initial FOIA Decision." The NRC does not consider an appeal received until the date it is actually received by the Freedom of Information Act and Privacy Act Officer.

The Executive Director for Operations or a Deputy Executive Director will make the NRC determination on the appeal within 20 working days after the receipt of the appeal. If the Executive Director for Operations or a Deputy Executive Director denies an appeal of access to records, in whole or in part, the Executive Director for Operations or a Deputy Executive Director, will notify the requester of the denial, explaining the exemptions relied upon and how the exemptions apply to the agency records withheld. The notice will inform the requester that the denial is a final agency action and that judicial review is available in a district court of the United States in the district in which the requester resides or has a principal place of business, in which the agency records are situated, or in the District of Columbia.

(e) For the denial of a request for expedited processing the appeal must be in writing directed to the Executive Director for Operations and sent to the Freedom of Information Act and Privacy Act Officer by an appropriate method listed in § 9.6. The appeal should clearly state on the envelope and in the letter that it is an "Appeal from Initial FOIA Decision." The NRC does not consider an appeal received until the date it is actually received by the Freedom of Information Act and Privacy Act Officer. The NRC will make a determination on the appeal within 10 working days after the receipt of the appeal. If the Executive Director for Operations or a Deputy Executive Director denies an appeal for expedited processing, the Executive Director for Operations or a Deputy Executive Director, will notify the person making the request of the decision to sustain the denial, including a statement explaining why the request does not meet the requirements of § 9.25(e)(1) and (2). The notice will inform the requester that the denial is a final agency action and that judicial review is available in a district court of the United States in the district in which the requester resides or has a principal place of business, in which the agency records are situated, or in the District of Columbia.

(f) For denial of a waiver or reduction of fees for locating and reproducing agency records, the appeal must be in writing directed to the Executive Director for Operations and sent to the Freedom of Information Act and Privacy Act Officer by an appropriate method listed in § 9.6. The appeal should clearly state on the envelope and in the letter that it is an "Appeal from Initial FOIA Decision." The NRC does not consider an appeal received until the date it is actually received by the Freedom of Information Act and Privacy Act Officer. The NRC will make a determination on the appeal within 20 working days after the receipt of the appeal. If the Executive Director for Operations or a Deputy Executive Director denies an appeal of a waiver or reduction of fees for locating and reproducing agency records, the Executive Director for Operations or a Deputy Executive Director, will notify the person making the request of the decision to sustain the denial, including a statement explaining why the request does not meet the requirements of § 9.41. The notice will inform the requester that the denial is a final agency action and that judicial review is available in a district court of the United States in the district in which the requester resides or has a principal place of business, in which the agency records are situated, or in the District of Columbia.

(g) The Executive Director for Operations, a Deputy Executive Director, the Secretary of the Commission, or the Inspector General will furnish copies of all appeals and written determinations on appeals to the Freedom of Information Act and Privacy Act Officer.

[70 FR 34307, June 14, 2005, as amended at 81 FR 96346, Dec. 30, 2016]

§ 9.30 Contact for dispute resolution services.

(a) NRC's FOIA Public Liaison:

(1) By mail—11555 Rockville Pike, Rockville, MD 20852;

(2) By facsimile—301–415–5130; and

(3) By email—*FOIA.Resource@nrc.gov*.

(b) Office of Government Information Services within National Archives and Records Administration:

(1) By mail—8601 Adelphi Road-OGIS, College Park, MD 20740;

(2) By facsimile—202–741–5769; and

(3) By email—*ogis@nara.gov.*

[81 FR 96346, Dec. 30, 2016]

§9.31 Extension of time for response.

(a) In unusual circumstances defined in §9.13, the NRC may extend the time limits prescribed in §9.25 or §9.29 by not more than 10 working days. The extension may be made by written notice to the person making the request to explain the reasons for the extension and indicate the date on which a determination is expected to be dispatched.

(b) An extension of the time limits prescribed in §§9.25 and 9.29 may not exceed a combined total of 10 working days per request, unless a requester has agreed to an alternative time frame as described in §9.25 (c).

§9.33 Search, review, and special service fees.

(a) The NRC charges fees for—

(1) Search, duplication, and review, when agency records are requested for commercial use;

(2) Duplication of agency records provided in excess of 100 pages when agency records are not sought for commercial use and the request is made by an educational or noncommercial scientific institution, or a representative of the news media;

(3) Search time that exceeds two hours and duplication of agency records of more than 100 pages for requests from all other categories of requesters not described in paragraphs (a)(1) and (a)(2) of this section;

(4) The direct costs of searching for agency records. The NRC will assess fees even when no agency records are located as a result of the search or when agency records that are located as a result of the search are not disclosed; and

(5) Computer searches which includes the cost of operating the Central Processing Unit for the portion of operating time that is directly attributable to searching for agency records plus the operator/programmer salary apportionable to the search.

(b) The NRC may charge requesters who request the following services for the direct costs of the service:

(1) Certifying that records are true copies;

(2) Sending records by special methods, such as express mail, package delivery service, courier, and other means other than first class mail; or

(3) Producing or converting records to formats specified by a requester other than ordinary copying processes that are readily available in NRC.

§9.34 Assessment of interest and debt collection.

(a) The NRC will assess interest on the fee amount billed starting on the 31st day following the day on which the billing was sent in accordance with NRC's regulations set out in §15.37 of this chapter. The rate of interest is prescribed in 31 U.S.C. 3717.

(b) The NRC will use its debt collection procedures under part 15 of this chapter for any overdue fees.

§9.35 Duplication fees.

(a)(1) The charges by the duplicating service contractor for the duplication of records made available under §9.21 at the NRC Public Document Room (PDR), One White Flint North, 11555 Rockville Pike, Room O–1F23, Rockville, Maryland, may be found on the NRC's Web site at *http://www.nrc.gov/reading-rm/pdr/copy-service.html* or by calling the PDR at 1–800–397–4209 or 301–415–4737, by e-mail *pdr@nrc.gov* and are as follows:

(i) Paper-to-paper reproduction is $0.30 per page for standard size (up to and including 11″ × 14″ reduced). Pages 11″ × 17″ are $0.30 per page. Pages larger than 11″ × 17″, including engineering drawings, are $1.50 per square foot.

(ii) Pages larger than 11″ × 17″ are $1.50 per square foot.

(iii) Microfiche-to-paper reproduction is $0.30 per page. Aperture card blowback to paper is $3.00 per square foot.

(iv) Microfiche card duplication is $5.00 per card; CD-ROM duplication is $10.00 each.

(v) The charges for Electronic Full Text (EFT) (ADAMS documents) copying are as follows:

(A) Electronic Full Text (EFT) copying of ADAMS documents to paper (applies to images, OCR TIFF, and PDF text) is $0.30 per page.

(B) EFT copying of ADAMS documents to CD-ROM is $5.00 per CD plus $0.15 per page.

(C) CD-ROM-to-paper reproduction is $0.30 per page.

(vi) Priority rates (rush processing) are as follows:

(A) The priority rate offered for standard size paper-to-paper reproduction is $0.35, microfiche-to-paper reproduction is $0.40, EFT copying of ADAMS documents to paper and CD-ROM-to-paper production is $0.35 per page.

(B) The priority rate for aperture cards is $3.50 per square foot. The priority rate for copying EFT to CD-ROM is $6.00 per CD-ROM plus $0.20 per page.

(vii) Facsimile charges are $1.00 per page for local calls; $2.00 per page for U.S. long distance calls, and $6.00 per page for foreign long distance calls, plus the regular per page copying charge.

(2) A requester may submit mail-order requests for contractor duplication of NRC records made by writing to the NRC Public Document Room. The charges for mail-order duplication of records are the same as those set out in paragraph (a)(1) of this section, plus mailing or shipping charges.

(3) A requester may open an account with the duplicating service contractor. A requester may obtain the name and address and billing policy of the contractor from the NRC Public Document Room.

(4) Any change in the costs specified in this section will become effective immediately pending completion of the final rulemaking that amends this section to reflect the new charges. The Commission will post the charges that will be in effect for the interim period at the NRC Public Document Room. The Commission will publish a final rule in the FEDERAL REGISTER that includes the new charges within 15 working days from the beginning of the interim period.

(b) The NRC will assess the following charges for copies of records to be duplicated by the NRC at locations other than the NRC Public Document Room located at One White Flint North, 11555 Rockville Pike (first floor), Rockville, Maryland.

(1) Sizes up to 8½ × 14 inches made on office copying machines—$0.20 per page of copy; and

(2) The charge for duplicating records other than those specified in paragraphs (a) and (b) of this section is computed on the basis of NRC's direct costs.

(c) In compliance with the Federal Advisory Committee Act, a requester may purchase copies of transcripts of testimony in NRC Advisory Committee proceedings, which are transcribed by a reporting firm under contract with the NRC directly from the reporting firm at the cost of reproduction as provided for in the contract with the reporting firm. A requester may also purchase transcripts from the NRC at the cost of reproduction as set out in paragraphs (a) and (b) of this section.

(d) Copyrighted material may not be reproduced in violation of the copyright laws. Requesters will be given the citation to any copyrighted publication and advised to contact the NRC Public Document Room to arrange to view the publication.

[63 FR 2876, Jan. 20, 1998, as amended at 64 FR 48951, Sept. 9, 1999; 67 FR 67098, Nov. 4, 2002; 70 FR 34308, June 14, 2005; 71 FR 54571, Sept. 18, 2006]

§ 9.37 Fees for search and review of agency records by NRC personnel.

The NRC will charge the following hourly rates for search and review of agency records by NRC personnel:

(a) Clerical search and review at a salary rate that is equivalent to a GG–7/step 6, plus 16 percent fringe benefits;

(b) Professional/managerial search and review at a salary rate that is equivalent to a GG–13/step 6, plus 16 percent fringe benefits; and

(c) Senior executive or Commissioner search and review at a salary rate that is equivalent to an ES–Maximum, plus 16 percent fringe benefits.

[63 FR 2876, Jan. 20, 1998, as amended at 75 FR 41369, July 16, 2010]

§ 9.39 Search and duplication provided without charge.

(a) The NRC will search for agency records requested under § 9.23(b) without charges when agency records are not sought for commercial use and the records are requested by an educational or noncommercial scientific institution, or a representative of the news media.

(b) The NRC will search for agency records requested under § 9.23(b) without charges for the first two hours of search for any request not sought for commercial use and not covered in paragraph (a) of this section.

(c) The NRC will duplicate agency records requested under § 9.23(b) without charge for the first 100 pages of standard paper copies, or the equivalent cost of 100 pages of standard paper copies when providing the requester copies in microfiche or electronic form such as computer disks, if the requester is not a commercial use requester.

(d) The NRC may not bill any requester for fees if the cost of collecting the fee would be equal to or greater than the fee itself.

(e) The NRC may aggregate requests in determining search and duplication to be provided without charge as provided in paragraphs (a) and (b) of this section, if the NRC finds a requester or group of requesters acting in concert, has filed multiple requests that actually constitute a single request, and that the requests involve clearly-related matters.

(f)(1) Except as described in paragraphs (f)(2), (3), and (4) of this section, if the NRC fails to comply with any time limit under §§ 9.25 or 9.29, it may not charge search fees or, in the case of requests from requesters described in § 9.33(a)(2), may not charge duplication fees.

(2) If the NRC has determined that unusual circumstances, as defined in § 9.13, apply and the NRC provided timely written notice to the requester in accordance with the Freedom of Information Act, a failure to comply with the time limit shall be excused for an additional 10 days.

(3) If the NRC has determined that unusual circumstances, as defined in § 9.13, apply and more than 5,000 pages are necessary to respond to the request, the NRC may charge search fees or, in the case of requests from requesters described in § 9.33(a)(2), may charge duplication fees, if the NRC has provided timely written notice to the requester in accordance with the Freedom of Information Act and the NRC has discussed with the requester via written mail, email, or telephone (or made not less than three good-faith attempts to do so) how the requester could effectively limit the scope of the request in accordance with 5 U.S.C. 552(a)(6)(B)(ii).

(4) If a court has determined that exceptional circumstances exist, as defined by 5 U.S.C. 552(a)(6)(C), a failure to comply with the time limit shall be excused for the length of time provided by the court order.

[63 FR 2876, Jan. 20, 1998, as amended at 81 FR 96346, Dec. 30, 2016]

§ 9.40 Assessment of fees.

(a) If the request is expected to require the NRC to assess fees in excess of $25 for search and/or duplication, the NRC will notify the requester that fees will be assessed unless the requester has indicated in advance his or her willingness to pay fees as high as estimated.

(b) In the notification, the NRC will include the estimated cost of search fees and the nature of the search required and estimated cost of duplicating fees.

(c) The NRC will encourage requesters to discuss with the NRC the possibility of narrowing the scope of the request with the goal of reducing the cost while retaining the requester's original objective.

(d) If the fee is determined to be in excess of $250, the NRC will require an advance payment.

(e) Unless a requester has agreed to pay the estimated fees or, as provided for in paragraph (d) of this section, the requester has paid an estimated fee in excess of $250, the NRC may not begin to process the request.

(f) If the NRC receives a new request and determines that the requester has previously failed to pay a properly charged fee under the Freedom of Information Act to the NRC or other Federal agency within 30 calendar days of receipt of the bill on a previous request, the NRC may refuse to accept the new request for processing until payment is made of the full amount owed on the prior request, plus any applicable interest assessed as provided in §9.34.

(g) Within 10 working days of the receipt of NRC's notice that fees will be assessed, the requester will provide advance payment if required, notify the NRC in writing that the requester agrees to bear the estimated costs, or submit a request for a waiver or reduction of fees pursuant to §9.41.

[63 FR 2876, Jan. 20, 1998, as amended at 70 FR 34308, June 14, 2005]

§9.41 Requests for waiver or reduction of fees.

(a)(1) The NRC will collect fees for searching for, reviewing, and duplicating agency records, except as provided in §9.39, unless a requester submits a request in writing for a waiver or reduction of fees. To ensure that there will be no delay in the processing of Freedom of Information Act requests, the request for a waiver or reduction of fees should be included in the initial Freedom of Information Act request letter.

(2) Each request for a waiver or reduction of fees should be addressed to the Office of the Chief Information Officer, and sent using an appropriate method listed in §9.6.

(b) A person requesting the NRC to waive or reduce search, review, or duplication fees will—

(1) Describe the purpose for which the requester intends to use the requested information;

(2) Explain the extent to which the requester will extract and analyze the substantive content of the agency record;

(3) Describe the nature of the specific activity or research in which the agency records will be used and the specific qualifications the requester possesses to utilize information for the intended use in such a way that it will contribute to public understanding;

(4) Describe the likely impact on the public's understanding of the subject as compared to the level of public understanding of the subject before disclosure;

(5) Describe the size and nature of the public to whose understanding a contribution will be made;

(6) Describe the intended means of dissemination to the general public;

(7) Indicate if public access to information will be provided free of charge or provided for an access fee or publication fee; and

(8) Describe any commercial or private interest the requester or any other party has in the agency records sought.

(c) The NRC will waive or reduce fees, without further specific information from the requester if, from information provided with the request for agency records made under §9.23(b), it can determine that disclosure of the information in the agency records is in the public interest because it is likely to contribute significantly to public understanding of the operations or activities of the Federal Government and is not primarily in the commercial interest of the requester.

(d) In making a determination regarding a request for a waiver or reduction of fees, the NRC will consider the following factors:

(1) How the subject of the requested agency records concerns the operations or activities of the Federal Government;

(2) How the disclosure of the information is likely to contribute significantly to public understanding of Federal Government operations or activities;

(3) The extent to which, the requester has a commercial interest that would be furthered by the disclosure of the requested agency records; and whether that commercial interest exceeds the public interest in disclosure.

(e) The Freedom of Information Act and Privacy Act Officer will make an initial determination whether a request for a waiver or reduction of fees meets the requirements of this section. The Freedom of Information Act and Privacy Act Officer will inform requesters whenever their request for a waiver or reduction of fees is denied and will inform them of their appeal rights under §9.29.

[63 FR 2876, Jan. 20, 1998, as amended at 68 FR 58800, Oct. 10, 2003; 80 FR 74978, Dec. 1, 2015]

§9.43 Processing requests for a waiver or reduction of fees.

(a) Within 20 working days after receipt of a request for access to agency records for which the NRC agrees to waive fees under §9.39 (a) through (d) or §9.41(c), the NRC will respond to the request as provided in §9.25.

(b) In making a request for a waiver or reduction of fees, a requester shall provide the information required by §9.41(b).

(c) After receipt of a request for the waiver or reduction of fees made in accordance with §9.41, the NRC will either waive or reduce the fees and notify the requester of the NRC's intent to provide the agency records promptly or deny the request and provide a statement to the requester explaining why the request does not meet the requirements of §9.41(b).

(d) As provided in §9.29, a requester may appeal a denial of a request to waive or reduce fees to the Executive Director for Operations. The appeal must be submitted within 90 calendar days from the date of the notice.

[63 FR 2876, Jan. 20, 1998, as amended at 70 FR 34308, June 14, 2005; 81 FR 96347, Dec. 30, 2016]

§9.45 Annual report to the Attorney General of the United States and Director of the Office of Government Information Services.

(a) On or before February 1 of each year, the NRC will submit a report covering the preceding fiscal year to the Attorney General of the United States and to the Director of the Office of Government Information Services which shall include the information required by 5 U.S.C. 552(e)(1).

(b) The NRC will make its annual FOIA reports available to the public at the NRC Web site, *http://www.nrc.gov*.

[81 FR 96347, Dec. 30, 2016]

Subpart B—Privacy Act Regulations

SOURCE: 40 FR 44484, Sept. 26, 1975, unless otherwise noted.

§9.50 Scope of subpart.

This subpart implements the provisions of section 3 of the Privacy Act of 1974, Pub. L. 93–579, 5 U.S.C. 552a, with respect to (a) the procedures by which individuals may determine the existence of, seek access to and request correction of NRC records concerning themselves, and (b) the requirements applicable to NRC personnel with respect to the use and dissemination of such records. The regulations in this subpart apply to all records which are retrievable from a system of records under the control of the Nuclear Regulatory Commission by the use of an individual's name or of an identifying number, symbol, or other identifying particular assigned to such individual. Except where specifically provided otherwise, this subpart applies to all NRC records maintained on individuals whether they predate or postdate September 27, 1975.

§9.51 Definitions.

As used in this subpart:

(a) *Individual* means a citizen of the United States or an alien lawfully admitted for permanent residence.

(b) The term *maintain* includes maintain, collect, use or disseminate.

(c) *Record* means any item, collection or grouping of information about an individual that is maintained by the NRC, including, but not limited to, his or her education, financial transactions, medical history, employment history or criminal history, and that contains the individual's name, or the identifying number, symbol or other identifying particular assigned to the individual, such as a finger or voice print or a photograph.

(d) *System manager* means the NRC official responsible for maintaining a system of records.

(e) *Systems of records* means a group of records under the control of the NRC from which information is retrieved by the name of an individual or by an identifying number, symbol, or other identifying particular assigned to an individual.

(f) *Statistical record* means a record in a system of records maintained for statistical research or reporting purposes only and not used in whole or in part in making any determination about an identifiable individual, except as provided by the Census Act, 13 U.S.C. 8.

(g) *Routine use* means, with respect to the disclosure of a record, the use of such record for a purpose which is compatible with the purpose for which it was collected, as described in a notice published in the FEDERAL REGISTER.

PROCEDURES APPLICABLE TO REQUESTS BY INDIVIDUALS FOR INFORMATION, ACCESS OR AMENDMENT OF RECORDS MAINTAINED ABOUT THEM

PRESENTATION OF REQUESTS

§ 9.52 Types of requests.

(a) Individuals may make the following requests respecting records about themselves maintained by NRC in a system of records subject to the provisions of the Privacy Act of 1974:

(1) Request a determination whether a record about the individual is contained in a system of records.

(2) Request access to a record about the individual. Access requests may include requests to review the record and to have a copy made of all or any portion thereof in a form comprehensible to the individual.

(3) Request correction or amendment of a record about the individual.

(b) *Requests for accounting of disclosures.* Individuals may, at any time, request an accounting by NRC of disclosures to any other person or Government agency of any record about themselves contained in a system of records controlled by NRC, except the following: (1) Disclosures made pursuant to the Freedom of Information Act, 5 U.S.C. 552; (2) disclosures made within the Nuclear Regulatory Commission; (3) disclosures made to another Government agency or instrumentality for an authorized law enforcement activity pursuant to 5 U.S.C. 552a(b)(7); (4) disclosures expressly exempted by NRC regulations from the requirements of 5 U.S.C. 552a(c)(3) pursuant to 5 U.S.C. 552a (j)(2) and (k).

[40 FR 44484, Sept. 26, 1975, as amended at 60 FR 63900, Dec. 13, 1995]

§ 9.53 Requests; how and where presented.

(a) Requests may be made in person or in writing. Assistance regarding equests or other matters relating to the Privacy Act of 1974 may be obtained by writing to the Freedom of Information Act and Privacy Act Officer, by an appropriate method listed in § 9.6. Requests relating to records in multiple systems of records should be made to the same Officer. That Officer shall assist the requestor in identifying his or her request more precisely and shall be responsible for forwarding the request to the appropriate system manager.

(b) All written requests must be made to the Freedom of Information Act and Privacy Act Officer, U.S. Nuclear Regulatory Commission, and sent by an appropriate method listed in § 9.6, and should clearly state on the envelope and in the letter, as appropriate: "Privacy Act Request," "Privacy Act Disclosure Accounting Request," "Privacy Act Correction Request." The NRC does not consider a request received until the date it is actually received by the Freedom of Information Act and Privacy Act Officer.

(c) Requests may be made in person during official hours at the U.S. Nuclear Regulatory Commission office where the record is located, as listed in the "Notice of System of Records" for the system in which the record is contained.

[40 FR 44484, Sept. 26, 1975, as amended at 41 FR 20645, May 20, 1976; 52 FR 31609, Aug. 21, 1987; 54 FR 53316, Dec. 28, 1989; 63 FR 15743, Apr. 1, 1998; 68 FR 58800, Oct. 10, 2003; 70 FR 34308, June 14, 2005]

§ 9.54 Verification of identity of individuals making requests.

(a) Identification requirements in paragraphs (a) (1) and (2) of this section are applicable to any individual who makes requests respecting records about himself or herself, except that no verification of identity shall be required if the records requested are available to the public under the provisions of the Freedom of Information Act. With respect to certain sensitive records, additional requirements for verification of identity stated in the appropriate published "Notice of System of Records" may be imposed.

(1) *Written requests.* An individual making a written request respecting a record about himself or herself may establish his or her identity by a signature, address, date of birth, employee

identification number, if any, and one other item of identification such as a copy of a driver's license or other document.

(2) *Requests in person.* An individual making a request in person respecting a record about himself or herself may establish his or her identity by the presentation of a single document bearing a photograph (such as a passport or identification badge) or by the presentation of two items of identification which do not bear a photograph but do bear a name, address and signature (such, as a driver's license or credit card).

(b) *Inability to provide requisite documentation of identity.* An individual making a request in person or in writing respecting a record about himself or herself who cannot provide the necessary documentation of identity may provide a notarized statement, swearing or affirming to his or her identity and to the fact that he or she understands that penalties for false statements may be imposed pursuant to 18 U.S.C. 1001, and that penalties for obtaining a record concerning an individual under false pretenses may be imposed pursuant to 5 U.S.C. 552a(i)(3). Forms for such notarized statements may be obtained on request from the Freedom of Information Act and Privacy Act Officer, and sent by an appropriate method listed in § 9.6.

(c) *Verification of parentage or guardianship.* In addition to establishing the identity of the minor, or other individual he or she represents as required in paragraph (a) of this section, the parent or legal guardian of a minor or of an individual judicially determined to be incompetent shall establish his or her status as parent or guardian by furnishing a copy of a birth certificate of the minor showing parentage or a copy of a court order establishing guardianship.

[40 FR 44484, Sept. 26, 1975, as amended at 52 FR 31609, Aug. 21, 1987; 54 FR 53316, Dec. 28, 1989; 63 FR 15743, Apr. 1, 1998; 68 FR 58800, Oct. 10, 2003; 70 FR 34309, June 14, 2005]

§ 9.55 Specification of records.

(a)(1) Requests relating to records shall, insofar as practicable, specify the nature of the record sought, the approximate dates covered by the record, the system of records in which the record is thought to be included and the system manager having custody of the record system as shown in the annual compilation, "Notices of Records Systems", published by the General Services Administration. Requests shall, in addition, comply with any additional specification requirements contained in the published "Notice of System of Records" for that system.

(2) Requests for correction or amendment of records shall, in addition, specify the particular record involved, state the nature of the correction or amendment sought and furnish justification for the correction or amendment.

(b) Requests which do not contain information sufficient to identify the record requested will be returned promptly to the requestor, with a notice indicating what information is lacking. Individuals making requests in person will be informed of any deficiency in the specification of records at the time the request is made. Individuals making requests in writing will be notified of any such deficiency when their request is acknowledged.

§ 9.56 Accompanying persons.

An individual requesting access to records about himself or herself may be accompanied by another individual of his or her own choosing. Both the individual requesting access and the individual accompanying him or her shall sign the required form indicating that the Nuclear Regulatory Commission is authorized to discuss the contents of the subject record in the presence of both individuals.

NRC PROCEDURES FOR PROCESSING REQUESTS

§ 9.60 Acknowledgement of requests.

(a) Written requests by individuals to verify the existence of, obtain access to or correct or amend records about themselves maintained by NRC in a system of records subject to the provisions of the Privacy Act of 1974, shall be acknowledged in writing by the Freedom of Information Act and Privacy Act Officer within ten working days after date of actual receipt. The acknowledgement shall advise the requestor if any additional information is needed to process the request. Wherever practicable, the acknowledgement shall notify the individual whether his or her request to obtain access to the record or to correct or amend the record has been granted or denied.

(b) When an individual requests access to records or permission to correct or amend records in person, every effort will be made to make an immediate determination as to whether access or correction or amendment should be granted. If an immediate determination cannot be made, the request will be processed in the same manner as a written request. Records will be made available for immediate inspection whenever possible.

[40 FR 44484, Sept. 26, 1975, as amended at 53 FR 17689, May 18, 1988; 54 FR 53316, Dec. 28, 1989; 63 FR 15743, Apr. 1, 1998]

§ 9.61 Procedures for processing requests for records exempt in whole or in part.

(a) When an individual requests information concerning the existence of, or access to, records about himself or herself which have been compiled in reasonable anticipation of a civil action or proceeding in either a court or before an administrative tribunal, the NRC shall advise the individual only that no record available to him or her pursuant to the Privacy Act of 1974 has been identified.

(b) *General exemptions.* Generally, 5 U.S.C. 552a(j)(2) allows the exemption of any system of records within the NRC from any part of section 552a except subsections (b), (c) (1) and (2), (e)(4) (A) through (F), (e) (6), (7), (9), (10), and (11), and (i) of the act if the system of records is maintained by an NRC component that performs as one of its principal functions any activity pertaining to the enforcement of criminal laws, including police efforts to prevent, control, or reduce crimes, or to apprehend criminals, and consists of—

(1) Information compiled for the purpose of identifying individual criminal offenders and alleged offenders and consisting only of identifying data and notations of arrests, the nature and disposition of criminal charges, sentencing, confinement, release and parole, and probation status;

(2) Information compiled for the purpose of a criminal investigation, including reports of informants and investigators, and associated with an identifiable individual; or

(3) Reports identifiable to an individual compiled at any stage of the process of enforcement of the criminal laws from arrest or indictment through release from supervision.

(c) *Specific exemptions under 5 U.S.C. 552a(k).* Individual requests for access to records which have been exempted from access under the provisions of 5 U.S.C. 552a(k) shall be processed as follows:

(1) *Information classified under criteria established by an Executive Order to be kept secret in the interest of national defense or foreign policy, and exempted under 5 U.S.C. 552a(k)(1).* (i) Requested information classified by NRC will be reviewed by the responsible official of the NRC to determine whether it continues to warrant classification under criteria established by an Executive Order to be kept secret in the interest of national defense or foreign policy.

(ii) Information which no longer warrants classification under these criteria shall be declassified and made available to the individual. If the requested information has been classified by another agency, the responsible official of the NRC will request the classifying agency to review the information to ascertain if classification is still warranted. If the information continues to warrant classification, the individual shall be advised that the information sought is classified, that it has been reviewed and continues to warrant classification, and that it has been exempted from access pursuant to 5 U.S.C. 552a(k)(1).

(2) *Investigatory material compiled for law enforcement purposes exempted pursuant to 5 U.S.C. 552a(k)(2).* Requests shall be responded to in the manner provided in paragraph (a) of this section unless a review of the information indicates that the information has been used or is being used to deny the individual any right, privilege or benefit for which he or she is eligible or to which he or she would otherwise be entitled under Federal law. In that event,

the individual shall be advised of the existence of the information and shall be provided the information except to the extent it would reveal the identity of a confidential source. Information that would reveal the identity of a confidential source shall be extracted or summarized in a manner which protects the source and the summary or extract shall be provided to the requesting individual.

(3) *Material within a system of records required by statute to be maintained and used solely as statistical records and exempted pursuant to 5 U.S.C. 552a(k)(4).* The exempted information requested will be reviewed by the responsible official of the NRC to determine whether it continues to warrant exemption. Information which no longer warrants exemption shall be made available to the individual. If the information continues to warrant exemption, the individual shall be advised that the information sought is exempt from disclosure, that it has been reviewed and continues to warrant exemption, and that it has been exempted from access pursuant to 5 U.S.C. 552a(k)(4).

(4) *Investigatory material compiled solely for the purpose of determining suitability, eligibility, or qualifications for Federal civilian employment, Federal contracts, or access to classified information and exempted pursuant to 5 U.S.C. 552a(k)(5).* Information exempted pursuant to 5 U.S.C. 552a(k)(5) shall be made available to an individual upon request except to the extent that the information would reveal the identity of a confidential source. Material that would reveal the identity of a confidential source shall be extracted or summarized in a manner which protects the source and the summary or extract shall be provided to the requesting individual.

(5) *Testing or examination material exempted pursuant to 5 U.S.C. 552a(k)(6).* Testing or examination material used solely to determine individual qualifications for appointment or promotion in the Federal service which has been exempted pursuant to 5 U.S.C. 552a(k)(6) shall not be made available to an individual if disclosure would compromise the objectivity or fairness of the testing or examination process but may be made available if no possibility of such compromise exists.

[40 FR 44484, Sept. 26, 1975, as amended at 44 FR 50804, Aug. 30, 1979; 50 FR 50284, Dec. 10, 1985; 60 FR 63900, Dec. 13, 1995; 70 FR 34309, June 14, 2005]

§ 9.62 Records under control of another Government agency.

Requests received by NRC pertaining to records under the control of another Government agency will be returned to the requester with the name of the controlling Government agency, if known, within ten working days after receipt by the NRC.

[70 FR 34309, June 14, 2005]

DETERMINATIONS AND APPEALS

§ 9.65 Access determinations; appeals.

(a) *Initial determinations.* For agency records located in the Office of the Inspector General, the Assistant Inspector General for Investigations shall determine whether access to the record is available under the Privacy Act. For all other agency records, the Freedom of Information Act and Privacy Act Officer with the advice of the system manager having control of the record to which access is requested, shall determine whether access to the record is available under the Privacy Act. The Freedom of Information Act and Privacy Act Officer shall notify the requesting individual in person or in writing of the determination. Unless the request presents unusual difficulties or involves extensive numbers of records, individuals shall be notified of determinations to grant or deny access within 30 working days after receipt of the request.

(1) Notices granting access shall inform the individual when and where the requested record may be seen, how copies may be obtained, and of any fees or anticipated charges which may be incurred pursuant to § 9.85 of this subpart.

(2) Notices denying access must state the reasons for the denial, and advise the individual that the denial may be appealed to the Inspector General, for agency records located in the Office of Inspector General, or the Executive Director for Operations, for all other

agency records, in accordance with the procedures set forth in this section.

(b) *Appeals from denials of access.* If an individual has been denied access to a record the individual may request a final review and determination of that individual's request by the Inspector General or the Executive Director for Operations, as appropriate. A request for final review of an initial determination must be filed within 60 calendar days of the receipt of the initial determination. For agency records denied by the Assistant Inspector General for Investigations, the appeal must be in writing directed to the Inspector General and sent to the Freedom of Information Act and Privacy Act Officer by an appropriate method listed in §9.6. For agency records denied by the Freedom of Information Act and Privacy Act Officer, the appeal must be in writing directed to the Executive Director for Operations and sent to the Freedom of Information Act and Privacy Act Officer by an appropriate method listed in §9.6. The appeal should clearly state on the envelope and in the letter "Privacy Act Appeal-Denial of Access." The NRC does not consider an appeal received until the date it is actually received by the Freedom of Information Act and Privacy Act Officer.

(c) *Final determinations.* (1) The Inspector General, or the Executive Director for Operations or the EDO's designee, shall make a final determination within 30 working days of the receipt of the request for final review, unless the time is extended for good cause shown such as the need to obtain additional information, the volume of records involved, or the complexity of the issue. The extension of time may not exceed 30 additional working days. The requester shall be advised in advance of any extension of time and of the reasons therefor.

(2) If the Inspector General, or the Executive Director for Operations or the EDO's designee, determines that access was properly denied because the information requested has been exempted from disclosure, the Inspector General, or the Executive Director for Operations or the EDO's designee shall undertake a review of the exemption to determine whether the information should continue to be exempt from disclosure. The Inspector General, or the Executive Director for Operations or the EDO's designee, shall notify the individual in writing of the final agency determination to grant or deny the request for access. Notices denying access must state the reasons therefor and must advise the individual of his/her right to judicial review pursuant to 5 U.S.C. 552a(g).

[40 FR 44484, Sept. 26, 1975, as amended at 41 FR 20645, May 20, 1976; 41 FR 25997, June 24, 1976; 52 FR 31609, Aug. 21, 1987; 54 FR 53316, Dec. 28, 1989; 55 FR 33647, Aug. 17, 1990; 63 FR 15743, Apr. 1, 1998; 68 FR 58800, Oct. 10, 2003; 70 FR 34309, June 14, 2005]

§9.66 Determinations authorizing or denying correction of records; appeals.

(a) *Initial determinations.* (1) For agency records located in the Office of the Inspector General, the Assistant Inspector General for Investigations shall determine whether to authorize or refuse correction or amendment of a record. For all other agency records, the Freedom of Information Act and Privacy Act Officer with the advice of the system manager having control of the record, shall determine whether to authorize or refuse correction or amendment of a record. The Freedom of Information Act and Privacy Act Officer shall notify the requesting individual. Unless the request presents unusual difficulties or involves extensive numbers of records, individuals must be notified of determinations to authorize or refuse correction or amendment of a record within 30 working days after receipt of the request. In making this determination, the NRC official shall be guided by the following standards:

(i) Records shall contain only such information about an individual as is relevant and necessary to accomplish an NRC function required to be accomplished by statute or by executive order of the President;

(ii) Records used by NRC in making any determination about any individual shall be as accurate, relevant, current, and complete as is reasonably necessary to assure fairness to the individual in the determination;

(iii) No record shall describe how any individual has exercised rights guaranteed by the First Amendment unless such record is expressly authorized by statute or by the individual about whom the record is maintained, or is pertinent to and within the scope of an authorized law enforcement activity.

(2) For agency records located in the Office of Inspector General, if correction or amendment of a record is authorized, the Assistant Inspector General for Investigations shall correct or amend the record. For all other agency records, the Freedom of Information Act and Privacy Act Officer shall correct or amend the record. The Freedom of Information Act and Privacy Act Officer shall notify the requesting individual in writing that the correction or amendment has been made and provide the individual with a courtesy copy of the corrected record.

(3) If correction or amendment of a record is refused, the Freedom of Information Act and Privacy Act Officer shall notify the requesting individual in writing of the refusal and the reasons therefor, and shall advise the individual that the refusal may be appealed to the Inspector General or the Executive Director for Operations, as appropriate, in accordance with the procedures set forth in this section.

(b) *Appeals from initial adverse determinations.* If an individual's request to amend or correct a record has been denied, in whole or in part, the individual may appeal that action and request a final review and determination of that individual's request by the Inspector General or the Executive Director for Operations, as appropriate. An appeal of an initial determination must be filed within 60 calendar days of the receipt of the initial determination. For agency records denied by the Assistant Inspector General for Investigations, the appeal must be in writing directed to the Inspector General and sent to the Freedom of Information Act and Privacy Act Officer by an appropriate method listed in § 9.6. For agency records denied by the Freedom of Information Act and Privacy Act Officer the appeal must be in writing directed to the Executive Director for Operations and sent to the Freedom of Information Act and Privacy Act Officer by an appropriate method listed in § 9.6. The appeal should clearly state on the envelope and in the letter "Privacy Act Correction Appeal." The NRC does not consider an appeal received until the date it is actually received by the Freedom of Information Act and Privacy Act Officer. Requests for final review must set forth the specific item of information sought to be corrected or amended and should include, where appropriate, records supporting the correction or amendment.

(c) *Final determinations.* (1) The Inspector General, for agency records located in the Office of the Inspector General, or the Executive Director for Operations or the EDO's designee, for all other agency records, shall make a final agency determination within 30 working days of receipt of the request for final review, unless the time is extended for good cause shown such as the need to obtain additional information, the volume of records involved, or the complexity of the issue. The extension of time may not exceed 30 additional working days. The requester shall be advised in advance of any extension of time and of the reasons therefor.

(2) For agency records located in the Office of the Inspector General, if the Inspector General makes a final determination that an amendment or correction of the record is warranted on the facts, the Inspector General or the IG's designee, shall correct or amend the record pursuant to the procedures in § 9.66(a)(2). For all other agency records, if the Executive Director for Operations, or the EDO's designee, makes a final determination that an amendment or correction of the record is warranted on the facts, the EDO or the EDO's designee, shall notify the Freedom of Information Act and Privacy Act Officer to correct or amend the record to the procedures in § 9.66(a)(2).

(3) If the Inspector General, or the Executive Director for Operations or the EDO's designee, makes a final determination that an amendment or correction of the record is not warranted on the facts, the individual shall be notified in writing of the refusal to authorize correction or amendment of the record in whole or in part,

and of the reasons therefor, and the individual shall be advised of his/her right to provide a "Statement of Disagreement" for the record and of his/her right to judicial review pursuant to 5 U.S.C. 552a(g).

[40 FR 44484, Sept. 26, 1975, as amended at 41 FR 20645, May 20, 1976; 41 FR 25997, June 24, 1976; 52 FR 31609, Aug. 21, 1987; 54 FR 53316, Dec. 28, 1989; 55 FR 33647, Aug. 17, 1990; 63 FR 15743, Apr. 1, 1998; 68 FR 58800, Oct. 10, 2003; 70 FR 34309, June 14, 2005]

§ 9.67 Statements of disagreement.

(a) Written "Statements of Disagreement" may be furnished by the individual within 30 calendar days of the date of receipt of the final adverse determination of the Inspector General or the Executive Director for Operations. "Statements of Disagreement" directed to the Executive Director for Operations must be sent to the Freedom of Information Act and Privacy Act Officer by an appropriate method listed in § 9.6, and should be clearly marked on the statement and on the envelope, "Privacy Act Statement of Disagreement." "Statements of Disagreement" directed to the Inspector General must be sent to the Freedom of Information Act and Privacy Officer by an appropriate method listed in § 9.6, and should be clearly marked on the statement and on the envelope "Privacy Act Statement of Disagreement".

(b) The Inspector General or the Executive Director for Operations, or their designees, as appropriate, are responsible for ensuring that: (1) The "Statement of Disagreement" is included in the system or systems of records in which the disputed item of information is maintained; and (2) the original record is marked to indicate the information disputed, the existence of a "Statement of Disagreement" and the location of the "Statement of Disagreement" within the system of records.

[55 FR 33848, Aug. 17, 1990, as amended at 68 FR 58800, Oct. 10, 2003; 70 FR 34309, June 14, 2005]

§ 9.68 NRC statement of explanation.

The Inspector General, or the Executive Director for Operations or the EDO's designee, may if deemed appropriate, prepare a concise statement of the reasons why the requested amendments or corrections were not made. Any NRC "Statement of Explanation" must be included in the system of records in the same manner as the "Statement of Disagreement". Courtesy copies of the NRC statement and of the notation of the dispute as marked on the original record must be furnished to the individual who requested correction or amendment of the record.

[55 FR 33648, Aug. 17, 1990]

§ 9.69 Notices of correction or dispute.

(a) When a record has been corrected upon request or when a "Statement of Disagreement" has been filed, the Freedom of Information Act and Privacy Act Officer shall, within 30 working days thereof, advise all prior recipients of the affected record whose identity can be determined pursuant to an accounting of disclosures required by the Privacy Act or any other accounting previously made, of the correction or of the filing of the "Statement of Disagreement".

(b) Any disclosure of disputed information occurring after a "Statement of Disagreement" has been filed shall clearly identify the specific information disputed and be accompanied by a copy of the "Statement of Disagreement" and a copy of any NRC "Statement of Explanation".

[40 FR 44484, Sept. 26, 1975, as amended at 52 FR 31609, Aug. 21, 1987; 54 FR 53316, Dec. 28, 1989; 63 FR 15743, Apr. 1, 1998]

DISCLOSURE TO OTHERS OF RECORDS ABOUT INDIVIDUALS

§ 9.80 Disclosure of record to persons other than the individual to whom it pertains.

(a) NRC Commissioners and NRC personnel shall not disclose any record which is contained in a system of records maintained by NRC by any means of communication to any person, or to another Government agency, except pursuant to a written request by, or with the prior written consent of, the individual to whom the record pertains, unless disclosure of the record is:

(1) To NRC Commissioners and NRC personnel who have a need for the

record in the performance of their duties;

(2) Required under 5 U.S.C. 552;

(3) For a routine use published in the FEDERAL REGISTER;

(4) To the Bureau of the Census for purposes of planning or carrying out a census or survey or related activity pursuant to the provisions of Title 13 of the United States Code;

(5) To a recipient who has provided the agency with advance adequate written assurance that the record will be used solely as a statistical research or reporting record and the record is transferred in a form that is not individually identifiable. The advance written statement of assurance shall (i) state the purpose for which the record is requested, and (ii) certify that the record will be used only for statistical purposes. Prior to release for statistical purposes in accordance with the provisions of this paragraph, the record shall be stripped of all personally identifying information and reviewed to ensure that the identity of any individual cannot reasonably be determined by combining two or more statistical records;

(6) To the National Archives and Records Administration as a record that has sufficient historical or other value to warrant its continued preservation by the United States Government, or to the Archivist of the United States or designee for evaluation to determine whether the record has such value;

(7) To another agency or to an instrumentality of any governmental jurisdiction within or under the control of the United States for a civil or criminal law enforcement activity if the activity is authorized by law, and if the head of the agency or instrumentality has made a written request to the NRC specifying the particular portion of the record desired and the law enforcement activity for which the record is sought. A record may be disclosed to a law enforcement agency at the initiative of the NRC if criminal conduct is suspected, provided that such disclosure has been established as a routine use by publication in the FEDERAL REGISTER, and the instance of misconduct is directly related to the purpose for which the record is maintained;

(8) To any person upon a showing of compelling circumstances affecting the health or safety of any individual;

(9) To either House of Congress or, to the extent of matter within its jurisdiction, to any committee or subcommittee thereof or to any joint committee of the Congress or to any subcommittee of such joint committee;

(10) To the Comptroller General, or any authorized representatives, in the course of the performance of the duties of the General Accounting Office;

(11) Pursuant to the order of a court of competent jurisdiction; or

(12) To a consumer reporting agency in accordance with 31 U.S.C. 3711(f).

(b) [Reserved]

[40 FR 44484, Sept. 26, 1975, as amended at 60 FR 63900, Dec. 13, 1995]

§9.81 Notices of subpoenas.

When records concerning an individual are subpoenaed or otherwise disclosed pursuant to court order, the NRC officer or employee served with the subpoena shall be responsible for assuring that the individual is notified of the disclosure within five days after such subpoena or other order becomes a matter of public record. The notice shall be mailed to the last known address of the individual and shall contain the following information: (a) The date the subpoena is returnable; (b) the court in which it is returnable; (c) the name and number of the case or proceeding; and (d) the nature of the information sought.

§9.82 Notices of emergency disclosures.

When information concerning an individual has been disclosed to any person under compelling circumstances affecting health or safety, the NRC officer or employee who made or authorized the disclosure shall notify the individual at his or her last known address within five days of the disclosure. The notice shall contain the following information: (a) The nature of the information disclosed; (b) the person or agency to whom the information was disclosed; (c) the date of the disclosure; and (d) the compelling circumstances justifying the disclosure.

FEES

§ 9.85 Fees.

Fees shall not be charged for search or review of records requested under this subpart or for making copies or extracts of records to make them available for review, although fees may be charged for additional copies. Fees established under 31 U.S.C. 483c and 5 U.S.C. 552a(f)(5) shall be charged according to the schedule contained in § 9.35 for actual copies of records disclosed under the Freedom of Information Act from Privacy Act Systems of Records.

[70 FR 34309, June 14, 2005]

ENFORCEMENT

§ 9.90 Violations.

(a) An injunction or other court order may be obtained pursuant to 5 U.S.C. 552a(g) (1–3) to compel NRC to permit an individual to review, amend or copy a record pertaining to him, or to be accompanied by someone of his or her own choosing when he or she reviews his or her record. A court order may be obtained for the payment of a civil penalty imposed pursuant to 5 U.S.C. 552a(g)(4) if NRC intentionally or willfully fails to maintain a record accurately, or fails to comply with any provision of 5 U.S.C. 552a, or any provision of this subpart, if such failure results in an adverse determination or has an adverse effect on an individual. Court costs and attorney's fees may be awarded in civil actions.

(b) Any officer or employee of NRC who willfully maintains a system of records without meeting the notice requirements of 5 U.S.C. 552a(e)(4), or who willfully discloses information knowing such disclosure to be prohibited by 5 U.S.C. 552a or by any rules or regulations issued thereunder, may be guilty of a criminal misdemeanor and upon conviction may be fined up to $5000. Any person who knowingly and willfully requests or obtains any record concerning an individual from NRC under false pretenses may be convicted of a criminal misdemeanor and upon conviction may be fined up to $5,000.

EXEMPTIONS

§ 9.95 Specific exemptions.

Exemptions applicable to Privacy Act Systems of Records are stated in each Privacy Act System of Records Notice which is published in the FEDERAL REGISTER and is available at the NRC Web site, *http://www.nrc.gov.*

[70 FR 34309, June 14, 2005]

Subpart C—Government in the Sunshine Act Regulations

SOURCE: 42 FR 12877, Mar. 7, 1977, unless otherwise noted.

§ 9.100 Scope of subpart.

This subpart prescribes procedures pursuant to which NRC meetings shall be open to public observation pursuant to the provisions of 5 U.S.C. 552b. This subpart does not affect the procedures pursuant to which NRC records are made available to the public for inspection and copying which remain governed by subpart A, except that the exemptions set forth in § 9.104(a) shall govern in the case of any request made pursuant to § 9.23 to copy or inspect the transcripts, recordings, or minutes described in § 9.108. Access to records considered at NRC meetings shall continue to be governed by subpart A of this part.

[52 FR 49362, Dec. 31, 1987]

§ 9.101 Definitions.

As used in this subpart:

(a) *Commission* means the collegial body of five Commissioners or a quorum thereof as provided by section 201 of the Energy Reorganization Act of 1974, or any subdivision of that collegial body authorized to act on its behalf, and shall not mean any body not composed of members of that collegial body.

(b) *Commissioner* means an individual who is a member of the Commission.

(c) *Meeting* means the deliberations of at least a quorum of Commissioners where such deliberations determine or result in the joint conduct or disposition of official Commission business, that is, where discussions are sufficiently focused on discrete proposals or issues as to cause or to be likely to cause the individual participating members to form reasonably firm positions regarding matters pending or likely to arise before the agency. Deliberations required or permitted by §§9.105, 9.106, or 9.108(c) do not constitute "meetings" within this definition.

(d) *Closed meeting* means a meeting of the Commission closed to public observation as provided by §9.104.

(e) *Open meeting* means a meeting of the Commission open to public observation pursuant to this subpart.

(f) *Secretary* means the Secretary to the Commission.

(g) *General Counsel* means the General Counsel of the commission as provided by section 25(b) of the Atomic Energy Act of 1954 and section 201(f) of the Energy Reorganization Act of 1974, and, until such time as the offices of that officer are in the same location as those of the Commission, any member of his or her office specially designated in writing by him or her pursuant to this subsection to carry out his or her responsibilities under this subpart.

[42 FR 12877, Mar. 7, 1977, as amended at 50 FR 20891, May 21, 1985]

§9.102 General requirement.

Commissioners shall not jointly conduct or dispose of Commission business in Commission meetings other than in accordance with this subpart. Except as provided in §9.104, every portion of every meeting of the Commission shall be open to public observation.

§9.103 General provisions.

The Secretary shall ensure that all open Commission meetings are held in a location such that there is reasonable space and adequate visibility and acoustics, for public observation. No additional right to participate in Commission meetings is granted to any person by this subpart. An open meeting is not part of the formal or informal record of decision of the matters discussed therein except as otherwise required by law. Statements of views or expressions of opinion made by Commissioners or NRC employees at open meetings are not intended to represent final determinations or beliefs. Such statements may not be pleaded, cited, or relied upon before the Commission or in any proceeding under part 2 of these regulations (10 CFR part 2) except as the Commission may direct. Members of the public attending open Commission meetings may use small electronic sound recorders to record the meeting, but the use of other electronic recording equipment and cameras requires the advance written approval of the Secretary.

[42 FR 12877, Mar. 7, 1977, as amended at 43 FR 13055, Mar. 29, 1978; 43 FR 37421, Aug. 23, 1978]

§9.104 Closed meetings.

(a) Except where the Commission finds that the public interest requires otherwise, Commission meetings shall be closed, and the requirements of §§9.105 and 9.107 shall not apply to any information pertaining to such meeting otherwise required by this subpart to be disclosed to the public, where the Commission determines in accordance with the procedures of §9.105 that opening such meetings or portions thereof or disclosing such information, is likely to:

(1) Disclose matters that are (i) specifically authorized under criteria established by an Executive order to be kept secret in the interests of national defense or foreign policy, and (ii) in fact properly classified pursuant to such Executive order;

(2) Relate solely to the internal personnel rules and practices of the Commission;

(3) Disclose matters specifically exempted from disclosure by statute (other than 5 U.S.C. 552) provided that such statute (i) requires that the matters be withheld from the public in such a manner as to leave no discretion on the issue, or (ii) establishes particular criteria for withholding or refers to particular types of matters to be withheld;

(4) Disclose trade secrets and commercial or financial information obtained from a person and privileged or confidential, including such information as defined in §2.790(d) of this title;

(5) Involve accusing any person of a crime, imposing a civil penalty on any person pursuant to 42 U.S.C. 2282 or 42 U.S.C. 5846, or any revocation of any license pursuant to 42 U.S.C. sec. 2236, or formally censuring any person;

(6) Disclose information of a personal nature where such disclosure would constitute a clearly unwarranted invasion of personal privacy;

(7) Disclose investigatory reports compiled for law enforcement purposes, including specifically enforcement of the Atomic Energy Act of 11954, as amended, 42 U.S.C. 2011 *et seq.*, and the Energy Reorganization Act of 1974, as amended, 42 U.S.C. 5801 *et seq.*, or information which if written would be contained in such records, but only to the extent that the production of such records or information would: (i) Interfere with enforcement proceedings, (ii) deprive a person of a right to a fair trial or an impartial adjudication, (iii) constitute an unwarranted invasion of personal privacy, (iv) disclose the identity of a confidential source and, in the case of a record compiled by a criminal law enforcement authority in the course of a criminal investigation, or by an agency conducting a lawful national security intelligence investigation, confidential information furnished only by the confidential source, (v) disclose investigative techniques and procedures, or (vi) endanger the life or physical safety of law enforcement personnel;

(8) [Reserved]

(9) Disclose information the premature disclosure of which would be likely to significantly frustrate implementation of a proposed Commission action, except that this subparagraph shall not apply in any instance where the Commission has already disclosed to the public the content or nature of its proposed action, or where the Commission is required to make such disclosure on its own initative prior to taking final action on such proposal; or

(10) Specifically concern the Commission's issuance of a subpoena, or the Commission's participation in a civil action or proceeding or an action or proceeding before a state or federal administrative agency, an action in a foreign court or international tribunal, or an arbitration, or the initiation, conduct or disposition by the Commission of a particular case of formal agency adjudication pursuant to 5 U.S.C. 554 or otherwise involving a determination on the record after an opportunity for a hearing pursuant to part 2 or similar provisions.

(b) Examples of situations in which Commission action may be deemed to be significantly frustrated are: (1) If opening any Commission meeting or negotiations would be likely to disclose information provided or requests made to the Commission in confidence by persons outside the Commission and which would not have been provided or made otherwise; (2) if opening a meeting or disclosing any information would reveal legal or other policy advice, public knowledge of which could substantially affect the outcome or conduct of pending or reasonably anticipated litigation or negotiations; or (3) if opening any meeting or disclosing any information would reveal information requested by or testimony or proposals to be given to other agencies of government, including the Congress and the Executive Branch before the requesting agency would receive the information, testimony or proposals. The examples in the above sentence are for illustrative purposes only and are not intended to be exhaustive.

§ 9.105 Commission procedures.

(a) Action under § 9.104 shall be taken only when a majority of the entire membership of the Commission votes to take such action. A separate vote of the Commissioners shall be taken with respect to each Commission meeting a portion or portions of which are proposed to be closed to the public pursuant to § 9.104, or which respect to any information which is proposed to be withheld under § 9.105(c). A single vote may be taken with respect to a series of meetings, a portion or portions of which are proposed to be closed to the public, or with respect to any information concerning such series of meetings, so long as each meeting in such series involves the same particular matters and is scheduled to be held no more than thirty days after the initial meeting in such series. The vote of each Commissioner participating in such vote shall be recorded and no proxies shall be allowed.

(b) Within one day of any vote taken pursuant to paragraph (a) of this section, § 9.106(a), or § 9.108(c), the Secretary shall make publicly available at the NRC Web site, *http://www.nrc.gov*, a written copy of such vote reflecting the vote of each member on the question. If a portion of a meeting is to be closed to the public, the Secretary shall, within one day of the vote taken pursuant to paragraph (a) of this section or §9.106(a), make publicly available at the NRC Web site, *http://www.nrc.gov*, a full written explanation of its action closing the portion together with a list of all persons expected to attend the meeting and their affiliation.

(c) The notices and lists required by paragraph (b) of this section to be made public may be withheld from the public to the extent that the Commission determines that such information itself would be protected against disclosure by §9.104(a). Any such determination shall be made independently of the Commission's determination pursuant to paragraph (a) of this section to close a meeting, but in accordance with the procedure of that subsection. Any such determination, including a written explanation for the action and the specific provision or provisions of §9.104(a) relied upon, must be made publicly available to the extent permitted by the circumstances.

[42 FR 12877, Mar. 7, 1977, as amended at 64 FR 48951, Sept. 9, 1999]

§9.106 Persons affected and motions for reconsideration.

(a) Whenever any person whose interests may be directly affected by a portion of a meeting requests that the Commission close such portion to the public for any of the reasons referred to in paragraphs (a) (5), (6), or (7) of §9.104, the Commission, upon request of any one Commissioner, shall vote by recorded vote whether to close such meeting.

(b) Any person may petition the Commission to reconsider its action under §9.105(a) or paragraph (a) of this section by filing a petition for reconsideration with the Commission within seven days after the date of such action and before the meeting in question is held.

(c) A petition for reconsideration filed pursuant to paragraph (b) of this section shall state specifically the grounds on which the Commission action is claimed to be erroneous, and shall set forth, if appropriate, the public interest in the closing or opening of the meeting. The filing of such a petition shall not act to stay the effectiveness of the Commission action or to postpone or delay the meeting in question unless the Commission orders otherwise.

§9.107 Public announcement of Commission meetings.

(a) In the case of each meeting, the Secretary shall make public announcement, at least one week before the meeting, of the time, place, and subject matter of the meeting, whether it is to be open or closed to the public, and the name and phone number of the official designated by the Commission to respond to requests for information about the meeting. Such announcement shall be made unless a majority of the members of the Commission determines by a recorded vote that Commission business requires that such meeting be called at an earlier date, in which case the Secretary shall make public announcement of the time, place and subject matter of such meeting, and whether open or closed to the public, at the earliest practical time.

(b) The time or place of a meeting may be changed following the public announcement required by paragraph (a) of this section only if the Secretary publicly announces such changes at the earliest practicable time. The subject matter of as meeting, or the determination of the Commission to open or close a meeting, or portion of a meeting, to the public, may be changed following the public announcement required by this subsection only if: (1) A majority of the entire membership of the Commission determines by a recorded vote that Commission business so requires and that no earlier announcement of the change was possible, and (2) the Secretary publicly announces such change and the vote of each member upon such change at the earliest practicable time.

(c) Immediately following each public announcement required by this section, notice of the time, place, and subject matter of a meeting, whether the meeting is open or closed, any change in one of the preceding, and the name and phone number of the official designated by the Commission to respond to requests for information about the meeting, shall also be submitted for publication in the FEDERAL REGISTER.

(d) The public announcement required by paragraph (a) of this section shall consist of the Secretary:

(1) Publicly posting a copy of the document at the NRC Web site, *http://www.nrc.gov* and, to the extent appropriate under the circumstances;

(2) Mailing a copy to all persons whose names are on a mailing list maintained for this purpose;

(3) Submitting a copy for possible publication to at least two newspapers of general circulation in the Washington, DC metropolitan area;

(4) Any other means which the Secretary believes will serve to further inform any persons who might be interested.

(e) Action under the second sentence of paragraph (a) or (b) of this section shall be taken only when the Commission finds that the public interest in prompt Commission action or the need to protect the common defense or security or to protect the public health or safety overrides the public interest in having full prior notice of Commission meetings.

[42 FR 12877, Mar. 7, 1977, as amended at 53 FR 43420, Oct. 27, 1988; 64 FR 48951, Sept. 9, 1999]

§ 9.108 Certification, transcripts, recordings and minutes.

(a) For every meeting closed pursuant to paragraphs (a) (1) through (10) of § 9.104 and for every determination pursuant to § 9.105(c), the General Counsel shall publicly certify at the time of the public announcement of the meeting, or if there is no public announcement at the earliest practical time, that, in his or her opinion, the meeting may be closed to the public and shall state each relevant exemptive provision unless the Commission votes pursuant to § 9.105(c) that such certification is protected against disclosure by § 9.104(a). A copy of such certification, together with a statement from the presiding officer of the meeting setting forth the time and place of the meeting, and the persons present, shall be retained by the Commission. The Commission shall maintain a complete transcript or electronic recording adequate to record fully the proceedings of each meeting, or portion of a meeting closed to the public, except that in the case of a meeting, or portion of a meeting, closed to the public pursuant to paragraph (c)(10) of § 9.104, the Commission shall maintain such a transcript, or recording or a set of minutes. Such minutes shall fully and clearly describe all matters discussed and shall provide a full and accurate summary of any actions taken, and the reasons therefor, including a description of each of the views expressed on any item and the record of any rollcall vote (reflecting the vote of each Commissioner on the question). All documents considered in connection with any action shall be identified in such minutes.

(b) The Commission shall make promptly available to the public at the NRC Web site, *http://www.nrc.gov*, the transcript, electronic recording, or minutes (as required by paragraph (a) of this section) of the discussion of any item on the agenda, or of any item of the testimony of any witness received at the meeting, except for such item or items of such discussion or testimony as the Commission determines pursuant to paragraph (c) of this section to contain information which may be withheld under § 9.104 or § 9.105(c). Copies of such transcript, or minutes, or a transcription of such recording disclosing the identity of each speaker, shall be furnished to any person upon payment of the actual cost of duplication or transcription as provided in § 9.14. The Secretary shall maintain a complete verbatim copy of the transcript, a complete copy of the minutes, or a complete electronic recording of each meeting, or portion of a meeting, closed to the public, for a period of at least two years after such meeting, or until one year after the conclusion of any Commission proceeding with respect to which the meeting or portion was held, whichever occurs later.

(c) In the case of any meeting closed pursuant to § 9.104, the Secretary of the Commission, upon the advice of the General Counsel and after consultation with the Commission, shall determine which, if any, portions of the electronic recording, transcript or minutes and which, if any, items of information withheld pursuant to § 9.105(c) contain information which should be withheld pursuant to § 9.104, in the event that a request for the recording, transcript, or minutes is received within the period during which the recording, transcript, or minutes must be retained, under paragraph (b) of this section.

(d) If at some later time the Commission determines that there is no further justification for withholding any transcript, recording or other item of information from the public which has previously been withheld, then such information shall be made available.

[42 FR 12877, Mar. 7, 1977, as amended at 50 FR 20891, May 21, 1985; 64 FR 48951, Sept. 9, 1999]

§ 9.109 Report to Congress.

The Secretary shall annually report to the Congress regarding the Commission's compliance with the Government in the Sunshine Act, including a tabulation of the total number of open meetings, the total number of closed meetings, the reasons for closing such meetings and a description of any litigation brought against the Commission pursuant to the Government in the Sunshine Act, including any cost assessed against the Commission in such litigation (whether or not paid by the Commission).

Subpart D—Production or Disclosure in Response to Subpoenas or Demands of Courts or Other Authorities

SOURCE: 50 FR 37645, Sept. 17, 1985, unless otherwise noted.

§ 9.200 Scope of subpart.

(a) This subpart sets forth the procedures to be followed when a subpoena, order, or other demand (hereinafter referred to as a "demand") for the production of NRC records or disclosure of NRC information, including testimony regarding such records, is issued by a court or other judicial or quasi-judicial authority in a proceeding, excluding Federal grand jury proceedings, to which the NRC is not a party. Information and documents subject to this subpart include:

(1) Any material contained in the files of the NRC;

(2) Any information relating to material contained in the files of the NRC.

(b) For purposes of this subpart, the term "employee of the NRC" includes all NRC personnel as that term is defined in § 9.3 of this part, including NRC contractors.

(c) This subpart is intended to provide instructions regarding the internal operations of the NRC and is not intended, and does not, and may not, be relied upon to create any right or benefit, substantive or procedural, enforceable at law by a party against the NRC.

[50 FR 37645, Sept. 17, 1985, as amended at 52 FR 49362, Dec. 31, 1987]

§ 9.201 Production or disclosure prohibited unless approved by appropriate NRC official.

(a) No employee of the NRC shall, in response to a demand of a court or other judicial or quasi-judicial authority, produce any material contained in the files of the NRC or disclose, through testimony or other means, any information relating to material contained in the files of the NRC, or disclose any information or produce any material acquired as part of the performance of that employee's official duties or official status without prior approval of the appropriate NRC official. When the demand is for material contained in the files of the Office of the Inspector General or for information acquired by an employee of that Office, the Inspector General is the appropriate NRC official. In all other cases, the General Counsel is the appropriate NRC official.

(b) Any NRC response to a demand of a court or other judicial or quasi-judicial authority that requires an employee of the NRC to expend more than 50 hours of official time shall be subject to hourly fees in accordance with 10 CFR 170.12(d).

[81 FR 41185, June 24, 2016]

§ 9.202 Procedure in the event of a demand for production or disclosure.

(a) Prior to or simultaneous with a demand upon an employee of the NRC for the production of material or the disclosure of information described in

§ 9.200, the party seeking production or disclosure shall serve the General Counsel of the NRC with an affidavit or statement as described in paragraphs (b) (1) and (2) of this section. Except for employees in the Office of Inspector General, whenever a demand is made upon an employee of the NRC for the production of material or the disclosure of information described in § 9.200, that employee shall immediately notify the General Counsel. If the demand is made upon a regional NRC employee, that employee shall immediately notify the Regional Counsel who, in turn, shall immediately request instructions from the General Counsel. If the demand is made upon an employee in the Office of Inspector General, that employee shall immediately notify the Inspector General. The Inspector General shall immediately provide a copy of the demand to the General Counsel, and as deemed necessary, consult with the General Counsel.

(b)(1) If oral testimony is sought by the demand, a summary of the testimony desired must be furnished to the General Counsel by a detailed affidavit or, if that is not feasible, a detailed statement by the party seeking the testimony or the party's attorney. This requirement may be waived by the General Counsel in appropriate circumstances.

(2) The General Counsel may request a plan from the party seeking discovery of all demands then reasonably foreseeable, including but not limited to, names of all NRC personnel from whom discovery is or will be sought, areas of inquiry, length of time away from duty involved, and identification of documents to be used in each deposition, where appropriate.

(c) The Inspector General or the General Counsel will notify the employee and such other persons, as circumstances may warrant, of the decision on the matter.

[50 FR 37645, Sept. 17, 1985, as amended at 55 FR 33648, Aug. 17, 1990]

§ 9.203 Procedure where response to demand is required prior to receiving instructions.

If a response to the demand is required before the instructions from the Inspector General or the General Counsel are received, a U.S. attorney or NRC attorney designated for the purpose shall appear with the employee of the NRC upon whom the demand has been made, and shall furnish the court or other authority with a copy of the regulations contained in this subpart and inform the court or other authority that the demand has been, or is being, as the case may be, referred for the prompt consideration of the appropriate NRC official and shall respectfully request the court or authority to stay the demand pending receipt of the requested instructions. In the event that an immediate demand for production or disclosure is made in circumstances which would preclude the proper designation or appearance of a U.S. or NRC attorney on the employee's behalf, the employee shall respectfully request the demanding authority for sufficient time to obtain advice of counsel.

[55 FR 33649, Aug. 17, 1990]

§ 9.204 Procedure in the event of an adverse ruling.

If the court or other judicial or quasi-judicial authority declines to stay the effect of the demand in response to a request made in accordance with § 9.203 pending receipt of instructions, or if the court or other authority rules that the demand must be complied with irrespective of instructions not to produce the material or disclose the information sought, the employee upon whom the demand has been made shall respectfully decline to comply with the demand, citing these regulations and *United States ex rel. Touhy* v. *Ragen*, 340 U.S. 462 (1951).

PART 10—CRITERIA AND PROCEDURES FOR DETERMINING ELIGIBILITY FOR ACCESS TO RESTRICTED DATA OR NATIONAL SECURITY INFORMATION OR AN EMPLOYMENT CLEARANCE

Subpart A—General Provisions

Subpart B—Criteria for Determining Eligibility for Access to Restricted Data or National Security Information or an Employment Clearance

Subpart C—Procedures

Subpart D—Miscellaneous

AUTHORITY: Atomic Energy Act of 1954, secs. 145, 161 (42 U.S.C. 2165, 2201); Energy Reorganization Act of 1974, sec. 201 (42 U.S.C. 5841); E.O. 10450, 18 FR 2489, 3 CFR, 1949–1953 Comp., p. 936, as amended; E.O. 10865, 25 FR 1583, 3 CFR, 1959–1963 Comp., p. 398, as amended; E.O. 12968, 60 FR 40245, 3 CFR, 1995 Comp., p. 391.

SOURCE: 47 FR 38676, Sept. 2, 1982, unless otherwise noted.

EDITORIAL NOTE: Nomenclature changes to part 10 appear at 70 FR 30897, May 31, 2005; 77 FR 39904, July 6, 2012; 81 FR 86909, Dec. 2, 2016.

Subpart A—General Provisions

§ 10.1 Purpose.

(a) This part establishes the criteria, procedures, and methods for resolving questions concerning:

(1) The eligibility of individuals who are employed by or applicants for employment with NRC contractors, agents, and other individuals who are NRC employees or applicants for NRC employment, and other persons designated by the Deputy Executive Director for Materials, Waste, Research, State, Tribal, Compliance, Administration, and Human Capital Programs of the NRC, for access to Restricted Data under the Atomic Energy Act of 1954, as amended, and the Energy Reorganization Act of 1974, or for access to national security information;

(2) The eligibility of NRC employees, or the eligibility of applicants for employment with the NRC, for employment clearance; and

(3) The eligibility of individuals who are employed by or are applicants for employment with NRC licensees, certificate holders, holders of standard design approvals under part 52 of this chapter, applicants for licenses, certificates, and NRC approvals, and others who may require access related to a license, certificate, or NRC approval, or other activities as the Commission may determine, for access to Restricted Data under the Atomic Energy Act of 1954, as amended, and the Energy Reorganization Act of 1974, or for access to national security information.

(b) This part is published to implement the Atomic Energy Act of 1954, as amended, the Energy Reorganization Act of 1974, as amended, Executive Order 10865, 25 FR 1583 (February 24, 1960) Executive Order 10450, 18 FR 2489 (April 27, 1954), and Executive Order 12968, 60 FR 40245 (August 2, 1995).

[64 FR 15641, Apr. 1, 1999, as amended at 72 FR 49483, Aug. 28, 2007]

§ 10.2 Scope.

The criteria and procedures in this part shall be used in determining eligibility for NRC access authorization and/or employment clearance involving:

(a) Employees (including consultants) of contractors and agents of the Nuclear Regulatory Commission and applicants for employment;

(b) NRC licensees, certificate holders and holders of standard design approvals under part 52 of this chapter, applicants for licenses, certificates, and standard design approvals under part 52 of this chapter, and their employees (including consultants) and applicants for employment (including consulting);

(c) NRC employees (including consultants) and applicants for employment; and

(d) Any other person designated by the Deputy Executive Director for Materials, Waste, Research, State, Tribal, Compliance, Administration, and Human Capital Programs of the Nuclear Regulatory Commission.

[47 FR 38676, Sept. 2, 1982, as amended at 64 FR 15641, Apr. 1, 1999; 72 FR 49483, Aug. 28, 2007]

§ 10.3 [Reserved]

§ 10.4 Policy.

It is the policy of the Nuclear Regulatory Commission to carry out its responsibility for the security of the nuclear energy program in a manner consistent with traditional American concepts of justice. To this end, the Commission has established criteria for determining eligibility for access authorization and/or employment clearance and will afford those individuals described in § 10.2 the opportunity for administrative review of questions concerning their eligibility for access authorization and/or employment clearance.

§ 10.5 Definitions.

Access authorization means an administrative determination that an individual (including a consultant) who is employed by or an applicant for employment with the NRC, NRC contractors, agents, and licensees of the NRC, or other person designated by the Deputy Executive Director for Materials, Waste, Research, State, Tribal, Compliance, Administration, and Human Capital Programs, is eligible for a security clearance for access to Restricted Data or National Security Information.

Commission means the Nuclear Regulatory Commission of five members or a quorum thereof sitting as a body, as provided by section 201 of the Energy Reorganization Act of 1974, or its designee.

Eligible or *Eligibility* means both initial eligibility and continued eligibility of an individual for access authorization and/or employment clearance.

Employment Clearance means an administrative determination that an individual (including a consultant) who is an NRC employee or applicant for NRC employment and other persons designated by the Deputy Executive Director for Materials, Waste, Research, State, Tribal, Compliance, Administration, and Human Capital Programs of the NRC is eligible for employment or continued employment pursuant to subsection 145(b) of the Atomic Energy Act of 1954, as amended.

Hearing Counsel means an NRC attorney assigned by the General Counsel to prepare and administer hearings in accordance with this part.

Hearing Examiner means a qualified attorney appointed by the Director, Office of Administration, to conduct a hearing in accordance with this part.

National Security Information means information that has been determined under Executive Order 13526 or any predecessor or successor order to require protection against unauthorized disclosure and that is so designated.

NRC Personnel Security Review Panel means an appeal panel appointed by the Deputy Executive Director for Materials, Waste, Research, State, Tribal, Compliance, Administration, and Human Capital Programs and consisting of three members, two of whom shall be selected from outside the security field. One member of the Panel shall be designated as Chairman.

Personnel Security Review Examiners are persons designated by the Executive Director for Operations to conduct a review of the record in accordance with this part.

Restricted Data means all data concerning design, manufacture, or utilization of atomic weapons, the production of special nuclear material, or the use of special nuclear material in the production of energy, but shall not include data declassified or removed from the Restricted Data category pursuant to section 142 of the Atomic Energy Act of 1954, as amended.

[47 FR 38676, Sept. 2, 1982, as amended at 51 FR 35999, Oct. 8, 1986; 52 FR 31609, Aug. 21, 1987; 54 FR 53316, Dec. 28, 1989; 64 FR 15641, Apr. 1, 1999; 75 FR 73938, Nov. 30, 2010]

Subpart B—Criteria for Determining Eligibility for Access to Restricted Data or National Security Information or an Employment Clearance

§ 10.10 Application of the criteria.

(a) The decision as to access authorization and/or employment clearance is a comprehensive, common-sense judgment, made after consideration of all the information, favorable or unfavorable, relevant to whether the granting of access authorization and/or employment clearance would not endanger the common defense and security and would be clearly consistent with the national interest.

(b) The criteria in § 10.11 set forth a number of the types of derogatory information used to assist in making determinations of eligibility for access authorization and/or employment clearance. These criteria are not exhaustive but contain the principal types of derogatory information which create a question as to the individual's eligibility for access authorization and/or employment clearance. While there must necessarily be adherence to such criteria, the NRC is not limited to them, nor precluded from exercising its judgment that information or facts in a case under its cognizance are derogatory although at variance with, or outside the scope of, the stated categories. These criteria are subject to continuing review and may be revised from time to time as experience and circumstances may make desirable.

(c) When the reports of investigation of an individual contain information reasonably tending to establish the truth of one or more of the items in the criteria, such information shall be regarded as derogatory and shall create a question as to the individual's eligibility for access authorization and/or employment clearance. A question concerning the eligibility of an individual for access authorization and/or employment clearance shall be resolved in accordance with the procedures set forth in § 10.20 *et seq.*

(d) In resolving a question concerning the eligibility or continued eligibility of an individual for access authorization and/or employment clearance, the following principles shall be applied by the Director, Division of Facilities and Security, Hearing Examiners, and the NRC Personnel Security Review Panel:

(1) Information reasonably tending to establish the truth of one or more of the items in the criteria shall be the basis for recommending denial or revocation of access authorization and/or employment clearance unless evidence to support faith in the individual's reliability and trust-worthiness is affirmatively shown.

(2) When deemed material to the deliberations, the extent of the activity, conduct, or condition, the period in which they occurred or existed, the length of time which has since elapsed, and the attitude and convictions of the individual shall be considered in determining whether the recommendation will be adverse or favorable.

[47 FR 38676, Sept. 2, 1982, as amended at 64 FR 15641, Apr. 1, 1999]

§ 10.11 Criteria.

(a) The criteria for determining eligibility for access authorization and/or employment clearance shall relate, but not be limited, to the following where an individual:

(1) Committed, attempted to commit, aided, or abetted another who committed or attempted to commit any act of sabotage, espionage, treason, sedition, or terrorism.

(2) Publicly or privately advocated actions that may be inimical to the interest of the United States, or publicly or privately advocated the use of force or violence to overthrow the Government of the United States or the alteration of the form of government of the United States by unconstitutional means.

(3) Knowingly established or continued a sympathetic association with a saboteur, spy, traitor, seditionist, anarchist, terrorist, or revolutionist, or with an espionage agent or other secret

agent or representative of a foreign nation whose interests may be inimical to the interests of the United States, or with any person who advocates the use of force or violence to overthrow the Government of the United States or the alteration of the form of government of the United States by unconstitutional means.

(4) Joined or engaged in any activity knowingly in sympathy with or in support of any foreign or domestic organization, association, movement, group, or combination of persons which unlawfully advocates or practices the commission of acts of force or violence to prevent others from exercising their rights under the Constitution or laws of the United States or any State or any subdivisions thereof by unlawful means, or which advocate the use of force and violence to overthrow the Government of the United States or the alteration of the form of government of the United States by unconstitutional means. (Ordinarily, criteria (3) and (4) will not include chance or casual meetings or contacts limited to normal business or official relations.)

(5) Deliberately misrepresented, falsified or omitted relevant and material facts from or in a personnel security questionnaire, a personal qualifications statement, a personnel security interview, or any other information submitted pursuant this part.

(6) Willfully violated or disregarded security regulations or was grossly negligent with respect thereto to a degree which could endanger the common defense and security; or by intention or gross carelessness disclosed Restricted Data or national security information to any person not authorized to receive it.

(7) Has any illness or mental condition which in the opinion of competent medical authority may cause significant defect in the judgment or reliability of the individual.

(8) Has been convicted of crimes indicating habitual criminal tendencies.

(9) Has been convicted of a crime, or has a background, where the facts, circumstances, or conduct are of a nature indicating poor judgment, unreliabilty, or untrustworthiness.

(10) Is a user of alcohol habitually and to excess, or has been such without adequate evidence of rehabilitation.

(11) Has been, or is, a user of a drug or other substance listed in the schedules of Controlled Substances established pursuant to the Controlled Substances Act of 1970 (such as amphetamines, barbiturates, narcotics, etc.), except as prescribed or administered by a physician licensed to dispense drugs in the practice of medicine, without adequate evidence of rehabilitation.

(12) Refused, without satisfactory explanation, to answer questions before a congressional committee, Federal or state court, or Federal administrative body including the NRC regarding charges relevant to the individual's eligibility for access authorization and/or employment clearance.

(13) Engaged in any other conduct or is subject to any other circumstances which tend to show that the individual is not reliable or trustworthy, or which furnishes reason to believe that the individual may be subject to coercion, influence, or pressures which may cause the individual to act contrary to the national interest.

§ 10.12 Interview and other investigation.

(a) The Director, Division of Facilities and Security, Office of Administration, may authorize the granting of access authorization and/or employment clearance on the basis of the information in the possession of the NRC or may authorize an interview with the individual, if the individual consents to be interviewed, or other investigation as the Director deems appropriate. On the basis of this interview and/or an investigation, the Director may authorize the granting of access authorization and/or employment clearance.

(b) The individual may elect on constitutional or other grounds not to participate in an interview or other investigation; however, such refusal or failure to furnish or authorize the furnishing of relevant and material information is deemed to be derogatory information pursuant to § 10.11(a) (5) and (12).

(c) If the Director, Division of Facilities and Security, cannot make a favorable finding regarding the eligibility of an individual for access authorization and/or employment clearance, the question of the individual's eligibility must be resolved in accordance with the procedures set forth in § 10.20 *et seq.*

[47 FR 38676, Sept. 2, 1982, as amended at 52 FR 31609, Aug. 21, 1987; 54 FR 53316, Dec. 28, 1989; 64 FR 15642, Apr. 1, 1999]

Subpart C—Procedures

§ 10.20 Purpose of the procedures.

These procedures establish methods for the conduct of hearings and administrative review of questions concerning an individual's eligibility for an access authorization and/or an employment clearance pursuant to the Atomic Energy Act of 1954, as amended, and Executive Orders 10450, 10865, and 12968 when a resolution favorable to the individual cannot be made on the basis of the interview or other investigation.

[64 FR 15642, Apr. 1, 1999]

§ 10.21 Suspension of access authorization and/or employment clearance.

In those cases where information is received which raises a question concerning the continued eligibility of an individual for an access authorization and/or an employment clearance, the Director, Division of Facilities and Security, through the Director, Office of Administration, shall forward to the Deputy Executive Director for Materials, Waste, Research, State, Tribal, Compliance, Administration, and Human Capital Programs or other Deputy Executive Director, his or her recommendation as to whether the individual's access authorization and/or employment clearance should be suspended pending the final determination resulting from the operation of the procedures provided in this part. In making this recommendation the Director, Division of Facilities and Security, shall consider factors such as the seriousness of the derogatory information developed, the degree of access of the individual to classified information, and the individual's opportunity by reason of his or her position to commit acts adversely affecting the national security. An individual's access authorization and/or employment clearance may not be suspended except by the direction of the Executive Director for Operations, Deputy Executive Director for Materials, Waste, Research, State, Tribal, Compliance, Administration, and Human Capital Programs or other Deputy Executive Director.

[64 FR 15642, Apr. 1, 1999]

§ 10.22 Notice to individual.

A notification letter, prepared by the Division of Facilities and Security, approved by the Office of the General Counsel, and signed by the Director, Office of Administration, must be presented to each individual whose eligibility for an access authorization and/or an employment clearance is in question. Where practicable, the letter will be presented to the individual in person. The letter will be accompanied by a copy of this part and must state:

(a) That reliable information in the possession of the NRC has created a substantial doubt concerning the individual's eligibility for an access authorization and/or an employment clearance;

(b) The information that creates a substantial doubt regarding the individual's eligibility for an access authorization and/or an employment clearance, that must be as comprehensive and detailed as the national security interests and other applicable law permit;

(c) That the individual has the right to be represented by counsel or other representative at their own expense;

(d) That the individual may request within 20 days of the date of the notification letter, any documents, records and reports which form the basis for the question of their eligibility for an access authorization and/or an employment clearance. The individual will be provided within 30 days all such documents, records and reports to the extent they are unclassified and do not reveal a confidential source. The individual may also request the entire investigative file, which will be promptly provided, as permitted by the national security interests and other applicable law;

(e) That unless the individual files with the Director, Office of Administration, a written request for a hearing within 20 days of the individual's receipt of the notification letter or 20 days after receipt of the information provided in response to a request made under paragraph (d) of this section, whichever is later, the Director, Division of Facilities and Security, through the Director, Office of Administration, will submit a recommendation as to the final action to the Deputy Executive Director for Materials, Waste, Research, State, Tribal, Compliance, Administration, and Human Capital Programs on the basis of the information in the possession of the NRC;

(f) That if the individual files a written request for a hearing with the Director, Office of Administration, the individual shall file with that request a written answer under oath or affirmation that admits or denies specifically each allegation and each supporting fact contained in the notification letter. A general denial is not sufficient to controvert a specific allegation. If the individual is without knowledge, he or she shall so state and that statement will operate as a denial. The answer must also state any additional facts and information that the individual desires to have considered in explanation or mitigation of allegations in the notification letter. Failure to specifically deny or explain or deny knowledge of any allegation or supporting fact will be deemed an admission that the allegation or fact is true.

(g) That if the individual does not want to exercise his or her right to a hearing, but does want to submit an answer to the allegations in the notification letter, the individual may do so by filing with the Director, Office of Administration, within 20 days of receipt of the notification letter or 20 days after receipt of the information provided in response to a request made under paragraph (d) of this section, whichever is later, a written answer in accordance with the requirements of paragraph (f) of this section;

(h) That the procedures in § 10.24 *et seq.* will apply to any hearing and review.

[64 FR 15642, Apr. 1, 1999]

§ 10.23 Failure of individual to request a hearing.

(a) In the event the individual fails to file a timely written request for a hearing pursuant to § 10.22, a recommendation as to the final action to be taken will be made by the Director, Division of Facilities and Security, through the Director, Office of Administration, to the Deputy Executive Director for Materials, Waste, Research, State, Tribal, Compliance, Administration, and Human Capital Programs on the basis of the information in the possession of the NRC, including any answer filed by the individual.

(b) The Director, Office of Administration, may for good cause shown, at the request of the individual, extend the time for filing a written request for a hearing or for filing a written answer to the matters contained in the notification letter.

[47 FR 38676, Sept. 2, 1982, as amended at 52 FR 31609, Aug. 21, 1987; 54 FR 53316, Dec. 28, 1989; 64 FR 15642, Apr. 1, 1999]

§ 10.24 Procedures for hearing and review.

(a) Upon receipt of a timely filed request for a hearing and answer complying with the requirements set forth in § 10.22, the Director, Office of Administration, shall forthwith appoint a Hearing Examiner, and the General Counsel shall forthwith assign an NRC attorney to act as Hearing Counsel. The Director, Office of Administration, shall promptly notify the individual of the identity of the Hearing Examiner and proposed hearing date, which shall be selected with due regard for the convenience of the parties and their representatives.

(b) Within 72 hours of being notified of the identity of the Hearing Examiner, the individual may request that the Hearing Examiner be disqualified for cause by filing with the Director, Office of Administration, a written statement of the individual's reasons for seeking disqualification. The time for filing the request may be extended by the Director, Office of Administration, for good cause shown. If the Director, Office of Administration, grants the request the procedures of paragraph (a) of this section and this paragraph shall be followed just as though there had been no prior appointment.

(c) The individual shall have the right to appear at the hearing before the Hearing Examiner, to be represented by counsel or other representative, to introduce documentary or other evidence, and to call, examine, and cross-examine witnesses, subject to the provisions and limitations set forth in this part.

[47 FR 38676, Sept. 2, 1982, as amended at 51 FR 35999, Oct. 8, 1986; 52 FR 31609, Aug. 21, 1987; 54 FR 53316, Dec. 28, 1989]

§ 10.25 NRC Hearing Counsel.

(a) Hearing Counsel assigned pursuant to § 10.24 will, before the scheduling of the hearing, review the information in the case and will request the presence of witnesses and the production of documents and other physical evidence relied upon by the Director, Division of Facilities and Security, in making a finding that a question exists regarding the eligibility of the individual for an NRC access authorization and/or an employment clearance in accordance with the provisions of this part. When the presence of a witness and the production of documents and other physical evidence is deemed by the Hearing Counsel to be necessary or desirable for a determination of the issues, the Director, Division of Facilities and Security, will make arrangements for the production of evidence and for witnesses to appear at the hearing by subpoena or otherwise.

(b) Hearing Counsel is authorized to consult directly with individual's counsel or representative or the individual, if the individual is not so represented, for purposes of reaching mutual agreement upon arrangements for expeditious hearing of the case. Such arrangements may include clarification of issues and stipulations with respect to testimony and contents of documents and other physical evidence. Such stipulations when entered into shall be binding upon the individual and the NRC for the purposes of this part. Prior to any consultation with the individual, the Hearing Counsel shall advise the individual of his or her rights under this part, of his or her right to counsel or other representation, and of the possibility that any statement made by the individual to the Hearing Counsel may be used in subsequent proceedings.

(c) The individual is responsible for producing witnesses in his or her own behalf and/or presenting other evidence before the Hearing Examiner to support the individual's answer and defense to the allegations contained in the notification letter. When requested by the individual, however, the Hearing Counsel may assist the individual to the extent practicable and necessary. The Hearing Counsel may at his or her discretion request the Director, Division of Facilities and Security, to arrange for the issuance of subpoenas for witnesses to attend the hearing in the individual's behalf, or for the production of specific documents or other physical evidence, provided a showing of the necessity for assistance has been made.

[47 FR 38676, Sept. 2, 1982, as amended at 64 FR 15643, Apr. 1, 1999]

§ 10.26 Appointment of Hearing Examiner.

The appointment of a Hearing Examiner, pursuant to § 10.24 of this part, shall be from a list of qualified attorneys possessing the highest degree of integrity, ability, and good judgment. To qualify, an attorney shall have an NRC "Q" access authorization and may be an employee of the NRC, its contractors, agents or licensees. However, no employee or consultant of the NRC shall serve as Hearing Examiner hearing the case of an employee (including a consultant) or applicant for employment with the NRC; nor shall any employee or consultant of an NRC contractor, agent or licensee serve as Hearing Examiner hearing the case of an employee (including a consultant) or an applicant for employment of that contractor, agent, or licensee. No Hearing Examiner shall be selected who has knowledge of the case or of any information relevant to the disposition of it, or who for any reason would be unable to issue a fair and unbiased recommendation.

§ 10.27 Prehearing proceedings.

(a) After the appointment of the Hearing Examiner, he or she shall be furnished the record in the case, which shall consist of the letter of notification, the request for hearing and its supporting answer, and the notice of hearing, if it has been issued, and any stipulations agreed to by the individual and the Hearing Counsel.

(b) The Hearing Examiner may on his or her own motion, or on that of either party, convene a prehearing conference with the Hearing Counsel and the individual and his or her counsel or representative, if any, for the purpose of clarifying the issues, identifying witnesses who may be called, identifying documents and other physical evidence that may be offered into evidence, and entering into stipulations of fact.

(c) The parties will be notified by the Hearing Examiner at least ten days in advance of the hearing of the time and place of the hearing. For good cause shown, the Hearing Examiner may order postponements or continuances from time to time. If, after due notice, the individual fails to appear at the hearing, or appears but is not prepared to proceed, the Hearing Examiner shall, unless good cause is shown, return the case to the Director, Division of Facilities and Security, who shall make a recommendation on final action to be taken, through the Director, Office of Administration, to the Deputy Executive Director for Materials, Waste, Research, State, Tribal, Compliance, Administration, and Human Capital Programs on the basis of the information in the possession of the NRC.

[47 FR 38676, Sept. 2, 1982, as amended at 52 FR 31609, Aug. 21, 1987; 54 FR 53316, Dec. 28, 1989; 64 FR 15643, Apr. 1, 1999]

§ 10.28 Conduct of hearing.

(a) The Hearing Examiner shall conduct the hearing in an orderly, impartial and decorous manner. Technical rules of evidence may be relaxed so that a full evidentiary record may be made based on all material and relevant facts. Hearsay evidence may for good cause shown be received at the discretion of the Hearing Examiner and accorded such weight as the circumstances warrant.

(b) The proceedings shall be open only to duly authorized representatives of the staff of the NRC, the individual, his or her counsel or representative, and such persons as may be officially authorized by the Hearing Examiner. Witnesses shall not testify in the presence of other witnesses except that the Hearing Examiner may, at his or her discretion, allow for expert witnesses to be present during testimony relevant to their own testimony.

(c) Witnesses, including the individual, shall be examined under oath or affirmation by the party who called them and may be cross-examined by the other. The Hearing Examiner shall rule on all evidentiary matters, may further examine any witness, and may call for additional witnesses or the production of documentary or other physical evidence if, in the exercise of his or her discretion, such additional evidence is deemed necessary to the resolution of an issue.

(d) If it appears during the hearing that Restricted Data or national security information may be disclosed, the Hearing Examiner shall assure that disclosure is made only to persons authorized to receive it.

(e) The Hearing Examiner may, at any time during the hearing, permit the Hearing Counsel to amend the notification letter to add or modify allegations to be considered. In the event of such an amendment to the notification letter, the individual shall be given an opportunity to answer the amended allegations. If the changes are of such a substantial nature that the individual cannot answer the amended allegations without additional time, the Hearing Examiner shall grant such additional time as he or she deems necessary.

(f) The Hearing Examiner may receive and consider evidence in the form of depositions or responses to interrogatories upon a showing that the witness is not available for good reason such as death, serious illness or similar cause, or in the form of depositions, interrogatories, affidavits or statements with agreement of the parties. The Hearing Examiner may take official notice at any stage of the proceeding, where appropriate, of any fact not subject to reasonable dispute in that it is either (1) generally known within the United States or (2) capable of accurate and ready determination by resort to sources whose accuracy cannot reasonably be questioned. A party is entitled upon timely request to an opportunity to be heard as to the propriety of taking such official notice. In the absence of prior notification the request may be made after notice is taken.

(g) Hearing Counsel shall examine and cross-examine witnesses and otherwise assist the Hearing Examiner in such a manner as to bring out a full and true disclosure of all facts, both favorable and unfavorable, having a bearing on the issues before the Hearing Examiner. In performing these duties, the Hearing Counsel shall avoid the attitude of a prosecutor and shall always bear in mind that the proceeding is an administrative hearing and not a trial.

(h) Hearing Counsel shall not participate in the deliberations of the Hearing Examiner, and shall express no opinion to the Hearing Examiner concerning the merits of the case. Hearing Counsel shall also, during the course of the hearing, advise the individual of his or her rights under these procedures when the individual is not represented by counsel or other representative.

(i) The individual shall be afforded an opportunity to cross-examine persons who have made oral or written statements adverse to the individual relating to a controverted issue except that any such statement may be received and considered by the Hearing Examiner without affording such opportunity in either of the following circumstances:

(1) The head of the department or agency supplying the statement certifies that the person who furnished the information is a confidential informant who has been engaged in obtaining intelligence information for the Government and that disclosure of the informant's identity would substantially harm the national interest or would endanger the well-being of the informant.

(2) The Commission has determined, after considering the information furnished by the investigative agency concerning the reliability of the person who furnished the information and the accuracy of the statement concerned, that the statement appears to be reliable and material, and that failure of the Hearing Examiner to receive and consider such statement would, in view of the fact that access authorization and/or employment clearance is being sought, be substantially harmful to the national security and that the person who furnished the information cannot appear to testify due to death, serious illness, or similar cause.

(j)(1) Whenever the procedure under paragraph (i)(1) of this section is used, the individual shall be given a summary of the information which shall be as comprehensive and detailed as the national security permits.

(2) Whenever the procedure under paragraph (i)(2) is used, the individual shall be provided the identity of the person and the information to be considered.

(3) In both paragraph (i) (1) and (2) procedures, appropriate consideration shall be accorded to the fact that the individual did not have an opportunity to cross-examine such informant or person.

(k) Records provided by investigative agencies that were compiled as a regular or routine procedure by the business or agency from which obtained, or other physical evidence other than investigative reports, may be received and considered subject to rebuttal without authenticating witnesses, provided that the investigative agency furnished such information to the NRC pursuant to its responsibilities in connection with assisting the NRC in determining the individual's eligibility for access authorization and/or employment clearance.

(l) Records compiled in the regular course of business, or other physical evidence other than investigative reports, relating to a controverted issue which, because they are classified, may not be inspected by the individual, may be received and considered provided that:

(1) The Commission has made a determination that such records or other physical evidence appears to be material;

(2) The Commission has made a determination that failure to receive and

consider such records or other physical evidence would, in view of the fact that access authorization and/or employment clearance is being sought, be substantially harmful to the national security; and

(3) To the extent that national security permits, a summary or description of such records or other physical evidence is made available to the individual. In every such case, information as to the authenticity and accuracy of such physical evidence furnished by the investigative agency shall be considered.

(m) If the Hearing Examiner determines that additional investigation of any material information is required, he or she shall request in writing that the Director, Office of Administration, arrange for the investigation and shall specify those issues upon which more evidence is requested and identify, where possible, any persons or sources that might provide the evidence sought.

(n) A written transcript of the entire proceeding must be made by a person possessing appropriate NRC access authorization and/or employment clearance and, except for portions containing Restricted Data or National Security Information, or other lawfully withholdable information, a copy of the transcript will be furnished the individual without cost. The transcript or recording will be made part of the applicant's or employee's personnel security file.

[47 FR 38676, Sept. 2, 1982, as amended at 52 FR 31609, Aug. 21, 1987; 54 FR 53316, Dec. 28, 1989; 64 FR 15643, Apr. 1, 1999]

§ 10.29 Recommendation of the Hearing Examiner.

(a) The Hearing Examiner's findings and recommendation shall be based upon the entire record consisting of the transcript of the hearing, the documentary and other evidence adduced therein, and the letter of notification and answer. The Hearing Examiner shall also consider the circumstances of the receipt of evidence pursuant to § 10.28, the individual's record of past employment, and the nature and sensitivity of the job the individual is or may be expected to perform.

(b) The Hearing Examiner shall make specific findings on each allegation in the notification letter including the reasons for his or her findings, and shall make a recommendation as to the action which should be taken in the case.

(c) The Hearing Examiner's recommendation shall be predicated upon his or her findings. If, after considering all the factors in light of the criteria in this part, the Hearing Examiner is of the opinion that granting or continuing access authorization and/or employment clearance to the individual will not endanger the common defense and security and will be clearly consistent with the national interest, a favorable recommendation shall be made; otherwise, an adverse recommendation shall be made.

(d) The Hearing Examiner shall submit his or her findings and recommendation in a signed report together with the record of the case to the Director, Office Administration, with the least practical delay.

(e) The Hearing Examiner shall not consider the possible impact of the loss of the individual's services upon the NRC program.

[47 FR 38676, Sept. 2, 1982, as amended at 52 FR 31609, Aug. 21, 1987; 54 FR 53316, Dec. 28, 1989]

§ 10.30 New evidence.

After the close of the hearing, in the event the individual discovers new evidence not previously available or known to him or her, the individual may petition the Hearing Examiner if the Hearing Examiner's recommendation has not yet been issued, or thereafter, the Director, Office of Administration, to reopen the record to receive that evidence. If the Hearing Examiner or the Director, respectively, deem it material and appropriate, the record may be reopened to accept the evidence either by stipulation, with the agreement of the Hearing Counsel, or in a reconvened hearing.

[47 FR 38676, Sept. 2, 1982, as amended at 52 FR 31610, Aug. 21, 1987; 54 FR 53316, Dec. 28, 1989]

§ 10.31 Actions on the recommendations.

(a) Upon receipt of the findings and recommendation from the Hearing Examiner, and the record, the Director, Office of Administration, shall forthwith transmit it to the Deputy Executive Director for Materials, Waste, Research, State, Tribal, Compliance, Administration, and Human Capital Programs who has the discretion to return the record to the Director, Office of Administration, for further proceedings by the Hearing Examiner with respect to specific matters designated by theDeputy Executive Director for Materials, Waste, Research, State, Tribal, Compliance, Administration, and Human Capital Programs .

(b)(1) In the event of a recommendation by the Hearing Examiner that an individual's access authorization and/or employment clearance be denied or revoked, the Deputy Executive Director for Materials, Waste, Research, State, Tribal, Compliance, Administration, and Human Capital Programs shall immediately notify the individual in writing of the Hearing Examiner's findings with respect to each allegation contained in the notification letter, and that the individual has a right to request a review of his or her case by the NRC Personnel Security Review Panel and of the right to submit a brief in support of his or her contentions. The request for a review must be submitted to the Deputy Executive Director for Materials, Waste, Research, State, Tribal, Compliance, Administration, and Human Capital Programs within five days after the receipt of the notice. The brief will be forwarded to the , for transmission to the NRC Personnel Security Review Panel not later than 10 days after receipt of the notice.

(2) In the event the individual fails to request a review by the NRC Personnel Security Review Panel of an adverse recommendation within the prescribed time, the Deputy Executive Director for Materials, Waste, Research, State, Tribal, Compliance, Administration, and Human Capital Programs may at his or her discretion request a review of the record of the case by the NRC Personnel Security Review Panel. The request will set forth those matters at issue in the hearing on which the Deputy Executive Director for Materials, Waste, Research, State, Tribal, Compliance, Administration, and Human Capital Programs desires a review by the NRC Personnel Security Review Panel.

(c) Where the Hearing Examiner has made a recommendation favorable to the individual, the Deputy Executive Director for Materials, Waste, Research, State, Tribal, Compliance, Administration, and Human Capital Programs may at his or her discretion request a review of the record of the case by the NRC Personnel Security Review Panel. If this request is made, the Deputy Executive Director for Materials, Waste, Research, State, Tribal, Compliance, Administration, and Human Capital Programs shall immediately cause the individual to be notified of that fact and of those matters at issue in the hearing on which the Deputy Executive Director for Materials, Waste, Research, State, Tribal, Compliance, Administration, and Human Capital Programs desires a review by the NRC Personnel Security Review Panel. The Deputy Executive Director for Materials, Waste, Research, State, Tribal, Compliance, Administration, and Human Capital Programs will further inform the individual that within 10 days of receipt of this notice, the individual may submit a brief concerning those matters at issue for the consideration of the NRC Personnel Security Review Panel. The brief must be forwarded to the Deputy Executive Director for Materials, Waste, Research, State, Tribal, Compliance, Administration, and Human Capital Programs for transmission to the NRC Personnel Security Review Panel.

(d) In the event of a request for a review pursuant to paragraphs (b) and (c) of this section, the Hearing Counsel may file a brief within 10 days of being notified by the Deputy Executive Director for Materials, Waste, Research, State, Tribal, Compliance, Administration, and Human Capital Programs that a review has been requested. The brief will be forwarded to the Deputy Executive Director for Materials, Waste, Research, State, Tribal, Compliance, Administration, and Human Capital Programs for transmission to the NRC Personnel Security Review Panel.

(e) The Hearing Counsel may also request a review of the case by the NRC Personnel Security Review Panel. The request for review, which will set forth those matters at issue in the hearing on which the Hearing Counsel desires a review, will be submitted to the Deputy Director Executive for Management Services within five days after receipt of the Hearing Examiner's findings and recommendation. Within 10 days of the request for review, the Hearing Counsel may file a brief which will be forwarded to the Deputy Executive Director for Materials, Waste, Research, State, Tribal, Compliance, Administration, and Human Capital Programs and Chief for transmission to the NRC Personnel Security Review Panel. A copy of the request for review, and a copy of any brief filed, will be immediately sent to the individual. If the Hearing Counsel's request is for a review of a recommendation favorable to the individual, the individual may, within 10 days of receipt of a copy of the request for review, submit a brief concerning those matters at issue for consideration of the NRC Personnel Security Review Panel. The brief will be forwarded to the Deputy Executive Director for Materials, Waste, Research, State, Tribal, Compliance, Administration, and Human Capital Programs and Chief Information Officer for transmission to the NRC Personnel Security Review Panel and Hearing Counsel. A copy of the brief will be made a part of the applicant's personnel security file.

(f) The time limits imposed by this section for requesting reviews and the filing of briefs may be extended by the Deputy Executive Director for Materials, Waste, Research, State, Tribal, Compliance, Administration, and Human Capital Programs for good cause shown.

(g) In the event a request is made for a review of the record by the NRC Personnel Security Review Panel, the Deputy Executive Director for Materials, Waste, Research, State, Tribal, Compliance, Administration, and Human Capital Programs shall send the record, with all findings and recommendations and any briefs filed by the individual and the Hearing Counsel, to the NRC Personnel Security Review Panel. If neither the individual, the Deputy Executive Director for Materials, Waste, Research, State, Tribal, Compliance, Administration, and Human Capital Programs and, nor the Hearing Counsel requests a review, the final determination will be made by the Deputy Executive Director for Materials, Waste, Research, State, Tribal, Compliance, Administration, and Human Capital Programs on the basis of the record with all findings and recommendations.

[64 FR 15643, Apr. 1, 1999]

§ 10.32 Recommendation of the NRC Personnel Security Review Panel.

(a) The Deputy Executive Director for Materials, Waste, Research, State, Tribal, Compliance, Administration, and Human Capital Programs shall designate an NRC Personnel Security Review Panel to conduct a review of the record of the case. The NRC Personnel Security Review Panel shall be comprised of three members, two of whom shall be selected from outside the security field. To qualify as an NRC Personnel Security Review Panel member, the person designated shall have an NRC "Q" access authorization and may be an employee of the NRC, its contractors, agents, or licensees. However, no employee or consultant of the NRC shall serve as an NRC Personnel Security Review Panel member reviewing the case of an employee (including a consultant) or applicant for employment with the NRC; nor shall any employee or consultant of an NRC contractor, agent or licensee serve as an NRC Personnel Security Review Panel member reviewing the case of an employee (including a consultant) or an applicant for employment of that contractor, agent, or licensee. No NRC Personnel Security Review Panel member shall be selected who has knowledge of the case or of any information relevant to the disposition of it, or who for any reason would be unable to issue a fair and unbiased recommendation.

(b) The NRC Personnel Security Review Panel shall consider the matter under review based upon the record supplemented by any brief submitted by the individual or the Hearing Counsel. The NRC Personnel Security Review Panel may request additional briefs as the Panel deems appropriate. When the NRC Personnel Security Review Panel determines that additional evidence or further proceedings are necessary, the record may be returned to the Deputy Executive Director for Materials, Waste, Research, State, Tribal, Compliance, Administration, and Human Capital Programs with a recommendation that the case be returned to the Director, Office of Administration, for appropriate action, which may include returning the case to the Hearing Examiner and reconvening the hearing to obtain additional testimony. When additional testimony is taken by the Hearing Examiner, a written transcript of the testimony will be made a part of the record and will be taken by a person possessing an appropriate NRC access authorization and/or employment clearance and, except for portions containing Restricted Data or National Security Information, or other lawfully withholdable information, a copy of the transcript will be furnished the individual without cost.

(c) In conducting the review, the NRC Personnel Security Review Panel shall make its findings and recommendations as to the eligibility or continued eligibility of an individual for an access authorization and/or an employment clearance on the record supplemented by additional testimony or briefs, as has been previously determined by the NRC Personnel Security Review Panel as appropriate.

(d) The NRC Personnel Security Review Panel shall not consider the possible impact of the loss of the individual's services upon the NRC program.

(e) If, after considering all the factors in light of the criteria set forth in this part, the NRC Personnel Security Review Panel is of the opinion that granting or continuing an access authorization and/or an employment clearance to the individual will not endanger the common defense and security and will be clearly consistent with the national interest, the NRC Personnel Security Review Panel shall make a favorable recommendation; otherwise, the NRC Personnel Security Review Panel shall make an adverse recommendation. The NRC Personnel Security Review Panel shall prepare a report of its findings and recommendations and submit the report in writing to the Deputy Executive Director for Materials, Waste, Research, State, Tribal, Compliance, Administration, and Human Capital Programs , who shall furnish a copy to the individual. The findings and recommendations must be fully supported by stated reasons.

[64 FR 15644, Apr. 1, 1999]

§ 10.33 Action by the Deputy Executive Director for Materials, Waste, Research, State, Tribal, Compliance, Administration, and Human Capital Programs.

(a) The Deputy Executive Director for Materials, Waste, Research, State, Tribal, Compliance, Administration, and Human Capital Programs, on the basis of the record accompanied by all findings and recommendations, shall make a final determination whether access authorization and/or employment clearance shall be granted, denied, or revoked, except when the provisions of § 10.28 (i), (j), or (l) have been used and the Deputy Executive Director for Materials, Waste, Research, State, Tribal, Compliance, Administration, and Human Capital Programs determination is adverse, the Commission shall make the final agency determination.

(b) In making the determination as to whether an access authorization and/or an employment clearance shall be granted, denied, or revoked, the Deputy Executive Director for Materials, Waste, Research, State, Tribal, Compliance, Administration, and Human Capital Programs or the Commission shall give due recognition to the favorable as well as the unfavorable information concerning the individual and shall take into account the value of the individual's services to the NRC's program and the consequences of denying or revoking access authorization and/or employment clearance.

(c) In the event of an adverse determination, the Deputy Executive Director for Materials, Waste, Research, State, Tribal, Compliance, Administration, and Human Capital Programs shall promptly notify the individual through the Director, Office of Administration, of his or her decision that an access authorization and/or an employment clearance is being denied or revoked and of his or her findings with respect to each allegation contained in the notification letter for transmittal to the individual.

(d) In the event of a favorable determination, the Deputy Executive Director for Materials, Waste, Research, State, Tribal, Compliance, Administration, and Human Capital Programs shall promptly notify the individual through the Director, Office of Administration.

[64 FR 15644, Apr. 1, 1999]

§ 10.34 Action by the Commission.

(a) Whenever, under the provisions of § 10.28(i), (j), or (l) an individual has not been afforded an opportunity to confront and cross-examine witnesses who have furnished information adverse to the individual and an adverse recommendation has been made by the Deputy Executive Director for Materials, Waste, Research, State, Tribal, Compliance, Administration, and Human Capital Programs , the Commission shall review the record and determine whether an access authorization and/or an employment clearance should be granted, denied, or revoked, based upon the record.

(b) When the Commission determines to deny or revoke access authorization and/or employment clearance, the individual shall promptly be notified through the Director, Office of Administration, of its decision that access authorization and/or employment clearance is being denied or revoked and of its findings and conclusions with respect to each allegation contained in the notification letter for transmittal to the individual.

(c) Nothing contained in these procedures shall be deemed to limit or affect the responsibility and powers of the Commission to deny or revoke access to Restricted Data or national security information if the security of the nation so requires. Such authority may not be delegated and may be exercised when the Commission determines that invocation of the procedures prescribed in this part is inconsistent with the national security. Such determination shall be conclusive.

[47 FR 38676, Sept. 2, 1982, as amended at 52 FR 31610, Aug. 21, 1987; 54 FR 53316, Dec. 28, 1989; 64 FR 15645, Apr. 1, 1999]

§ 10.35 Reconsideration of cases.

(a) Where, pursuant to the procedures set forth in §§ 10.20 through 10.34, the Deputy Executive Director for Materials, Waste, Research, State, Tribal, Compliance, Administration, and Human Capital Programs or the Commission has made a determination granting an access authorization and/or an employment clearance to an individual, the individual's eligibility for an access authorization and/or an employment clearance will be reconsidered only when subsequent to the time of that determination, new derogatory information has been received or the scope or sensitivity of the Restricted Data or National Security Information to which the individual has or will have access has significantly increased. All new derogatory information, whether resulting from the NRC's reinvestigation program or other sources, will be evaluated relative to an individual's continued eligibility in accordance with the procedures of this part.

(b) Where, pursuant to these procedures, the Commission or Deputy Executive Director for Materials, Waste, Research, State, Tribal, Compliance, Administration, and Human Capital Programs has made a determination denying or revoking an access authorization and/or an employment clearance to an individual, the individual's eligibility for an access authorization and/or an employment clearance may be reconsidered when there is a bona fide offer of employment and/or a bona fide need for access to Restricted Data or National Security Information and either material and relevant new evidence is presented, which the individual and his or her representatives are without fault in failing to present before, or there is convincing evidence of reformation or rehabilitation. Requests for reconsideration must be submitted in writing to the Deputy Executive Director for Materials, Waste, Research, State, Tribal, Compliance, Administration, and Human Capital Programs through the Director, Office of Administration. Requests must be accompanied by an affidavit setting forth in detail the information referred to above. The Deputy Executive Director for Materials, Waste, Research, State, Tribal, Compliance, Administration, and Human Capital Programs shall cause the individual to be notified as to whether his or her eligibility for an access authorization and/or an employment clearance will be reconsidered and if so, the method by which a reconsideration will be accomplished.

(c) Where an access authorization and/or an employment clearance has been granted to an individual by the Director, Division of Facilities and Security, without recourse to the procedures set forth in §§10.20 through 10.34, the individual's eligibility for an access authorization and/or an employment clearance will be reconsidered only in a case where, subsequent to the granting of the access authorization and/or employment clearance, new derogatory information has been received or the scope or sensitivity of the Restricted Data or National Security Information to which the individual has or will have access has significantly increased. All new derogatory information, whether resulting from the NRC's reinvestigation program or other sources, will be evaluated relative to an individual's continued eligibility in accordance with the procedures of this part.

[64 FR 15645, Apr. 1, 1999]

Subpart D—Miscellaneous

§ 10.36 Terminations.

In the event the individual is no longer an applicant for access authorization and/or employment clearance or no longer requires such, the procedures of this part shall be terminated without a final determination as to the individual's eligibility for access authorization and/or employment clearance.

§ 10.37 Attorney representation.

In the event the individual is represented by an attorney or other representative, the individual shall file with the Director, Office of Administration, a document designating such attorney or representative and authorizing such attorney or representative to receive all correspondence, transcripts, and other documents pertaining to the proceeding under this part.

[47 FR 38676, Sept. 2, 1982, as amended at 52 FR 31610, Aug. 21, 1987; 54 FR 53316, Dec. 28, 1989]

§ 10.38 Certifications.

Whenever information is made a part of the record under the exceptions authorized by § 10.28 (i), (j), or (l), the record shall contain certificates evidencing that the required determinations have been made.

PART 11—CRITERIA AND PROCEDURES FOR DETERMINING ELIGIBILITY FOR ACCESS TO OR CONTROL OVER SPECIAL NUCLEAR MATERIAL

GENERAL PROVISIONS

REQUIREMENTS FOR SPECIAL NUCLEAR MATERIAL ACCESS AUTHORIZATION

CRITERIA FOR DETERMINING ELIGIBILITY FOR ACCESS TO, OR CONTROL OVER, SPECIAL NUCLEAR MATERIAL

VIOLATIONS

AUTHORITY: Atomic Energy Act of 1954, secs. 161, 223 (42 U.S.C. 2201, 2273); Energy Reorganization Act of 1974, sec. 201 (42 U.S.C. 5841); 44 U.S.C. 3504 note.

Section 11.15(e) also issued under 31 U.S.C. 9701; 42 U.S.C. 2214.

SOURCE: 45 FR 76970, Nov. 21, 1980, unless otherwise noted.

GENERAL PROVISIONS

§ 11.1 Purpose.

This part establishes the requirements for special nuclear material access authorization, and the criteria and procedures for resolving questions concerning the eligibility of individuals to receive special nuclear material access authorization for conduct of certain activities, licensed or otherwise, which involve access to or control over special nuclear material.

§ 11.3 Scope.

(a) The requirements, criteria, and procedures of this part apply to the establishment of and eligibility for special nuclear material access authorization for employees, contractors, consultants of, and applicants for employment with licensees or contractors of the Nuclear Regulatory Commission. This employment, contract, service, or consultation may involve any duties or assignments within the criteria of § 11.11 or § 11.13 requiring access to, or control over, formula quantities of special nuclear material (as defined in part 73 of this chapter).

(b) The requirements, criteria, and procedures of this part are in addition to and not in lieu of any requirements, criteria, or procedures for access to or control over classified special nuclear material.

[45 FR 76970, Nov. 21, 1980, as amended at 64 FR 15645, Apr. 1, 1999]

§ 11.5 Policy.

It is the policy of the Nuclear Regulatory Commission to carry out its authority to establish and administer, in a manner consistent with traditional American concepts of justice, a personnel security program in the interests of the common defense and security for the purpose of safeguarding special nuclear material and preventing sabotage which would endanger the public by exposure to radiation. To this end, the Commission has established criteria for determining eligibility for special nuclear material access authorization and will afford affected individuals the opportunity for administrative review of questions concerning their eligibility for special nuclear material access authorization.

§ 11.7 Definitions.

As used in this part:

Terms defined in parts 10, 25, 50, 70, 72, 73, and 95 of this chapter have the same meaning when used in this part.

NRC–"R" special nuclear material access authorization means an administrative determination based upon a national agency check with law and credit investigation that an individual in the course of employment is eligible to work at a job falling within the criterion of § 11.11(a)(2).

NRC–"U" special nuclear material access authorization means an administrative determination based upon a single scope background investigation, normally conducted by the Office of Personnel Management, that an individual in the course of employment is eligible to work at a job falling within the criterion of 11.11(a)(1) or 11.13.

Special nuclear material access authorization means an administrative determination that an individual (including a contractor or consultant) who is employed by or is an applicant for employment with an affected Commission contractor, licensee of the Commission, or contractor of a licensee of the Commission may work at a job which affords access to or control over special nuclear material and that permitting the individual to work at that job would not be inimical to the common defense and security.

[45 FR 76970, Nov. 21, 1980, as amended at 46 FR 58282, Dec. 1, 1981; 50 FR 39077, Sept. 27, 1985; 55 FR 11574, Mar. 29, 1990; 64 FR 15645, Apr. 1, 1999]

§ 11.8 Information collection requirements: OMB approval.

(a) The Nuclear Regulatory Commission has submitted the information collection requirements contained in this part to the Office of Management and Budget (OMB) for approval as required by the Paperwork Reduction

Act (44 U.S.C. *et seq.*). The NRC may not conduct or sponsor, and a person is not required to respond to, a collection of information unless it displays a currently valid OMB control number. OMB has approved the information collection requirements contained in this part under control number 3150–0062.

(b) The approved information collection requirements contained in this part appear in §§11.9, 11.11, 11.13, 11.15, and 11.16.

[62 FR 52185, Oct. 6, 1997]

§11.9 Specific exemptions.

The Commission may, upon application of any interested party, grant an exemption from the requirements of this part. Exemptions will be granted only if they are authorized by law and will not constitute an undue risk to the common defense and security. Documentation related to the request, notification and processing of an exemption shall be maintained for three years beyond the period covered by the exemption.

[45 FR 76970, Nov. 21, 1980, as amended at 53 FR 19245, May 27, 1988]

§11.10 Maintenance of records.

Each record required by this part must be legible throughout the retention period specified by each Commission regulation. The record may be the original or a reproduced copy or a microform provided that the copy or microform is authenticated by authorized personnel and that the microform is capable of producing a clear copy throughout the required retention period. The record may also be stored in electronic media with the capability for producing legible, accurate, and complete records during the required retention period. Records such as letters, drawing, specification, must include all pertinent information such as stamps, initials, and signatures etc. The licensee shall maintain adequate safeguards against tampering with and loss of records.

[53 FR 19245, May 27, 1988]

Requirements for Special Nuclear Material Access Authorization

§11.11 General requirements.

(a) Each licensee who uses, processes, stores, transports, or delivers to a carrier for transport, formula quantities of special nuclear material (as defined in part 73 of this chapter) subject to the physical protection requirements of §§73.20, 73.25, 73.26, 73.45, and 73.46, and each person subject to the general licensing requirements of §70.20a, shall identify at its facility or plant (excluding all non-power reactor facilities and storage of fuel incident thereto and facilities and plants in which the licensee possesses or uses only irradiated special nuclear material subject to the exemption of §73.6(b)), describe, and if not already provided, provide to the Commission, by December 26, 1985 by amendment to its security plan:

(1) All jobs in which an individual could steal or divert special nuclear material, or commit sabotage which would endanger the public by exposure to radiation, by working alone or in cooperation with an individual who does not possess an NRC-U special nuclear material access authorization, or by directing or coercing any individual to assist in the theft, diversion, or sabotage. Such jobs include but are not limited to:

(i) All positions in the licensee's security force,

(ii) Management positions with the authority to:

(A) Direct the actions of members of the security force or alter security procedures, or

(B) Direct routine movements of special nuclear material, or

(C) Direct the routine status of vital equipment.

(iii) All jobs which require unescorted access within onsite alarm stations.

(iv) All jobs which require unescorted access[2] to special nuclear material or within vital areas.

(2) All jobs which require unescorted access within protected areas and

[2] This does not alter the requirement for methods to observe individuals within material access areas as stated in §73.46(e)(9) of this chapter.

which do not fall within the criterion of paragraph (a)(1) of this section.

(b) After 365 days following Commission approval of the amended security plan submitted in accordance with paragraph (a) of this section, no individual may be permitted to work at any job determined by the Commission to fall within the criterion of paragraph (a)(1) of this section without an NRC-U special nuclear material access authorization, and no individual may be permitted unescorted access to any protected area at any site subject to this part without either an NRC-U or NRC-R special nuclear material access authorization. The exceptions to the requirement for an NRC-U and NRC-R special nuclear material access authorization are as follows:

(1) Exceptions to the requirement for an NRC-U special nuclear material access authorization for an individual to work at a job within the criteria of paragraph (a)(1) are provided for:

(i) Any individual employed in such a job on October 28, 1985, who is not yet in receipt of an NRC-U special nuclear material access authorization from the Commission, provided that a complete application has been submitted to and is pending before the NRC for processing for that employee in accordance with § 11.15 (a) and (b); or

(ii) Any individual in possession of an NRC-L or R access authorization or an equivalent active Federal security clearance but not yet in receipt of the NRC-U special nuclear material access authorization, provided that a complete application has been submitted to and is pending before the NRC for processing for that employee in accordance with § 11.15 (a) or (b), or both.

(2) Exceptions to the requirement for an NRC-R special nuclear material access authorization for an individual to have unescorted access to a protected area are provided for:

(i) Any individual employed in such a job on October 28, 1985 who is not yet in receipt of an NRC-R special nuclear material access authorization from the Commission, provided that a complete application has been submitted to and is pending before the NRC for processing for that employee in accordance with § 11.15 (a) and (b); or

(ii) Any individual in possession of an NRC-L access authorization or an equivalent active Federal security clearance, provided that a complete application has been submitted to the NRC for processing for that employee in accordance with § 11.15 (a) or (b), or both.

[45 FR 76970, Nov. 21, 1980, as amended at 46 FR 56599, Nov. 18, 1981; 50 FR 39077, Sept. 27, 1985]

§ 11.13 Special requirements for transportation.

(a) All individuals who, after 365 days following approval of the amended security plan submitted in accordance with § 11.11(a), transport, arrange for transport, drive motor vehicles in road shipments of special nuclear material, pilot aircraft in air shipments of special nuclear material, act as monitors at transfer points, or escort road, rail, sea, or air shipments of special nuclear material subject to the appropriate physical protection requirements of §§ 73.20, 73.25, 73.26, or 73.27 of this chapter, or who are authorized to alter the scheduling and routing of such transport shall have NRC-U special nuclear material access authorization. Exceptions are provided for:

(1) Any individual who is employed in such a job on October 28, 1985 and who is not yet in receipt of an NRC-U special nuclear material access authorization from the Commission, provided that a complete application has been submitted to and is pending before the NRC for processing for that employee in accordance with § 11.15 (a) and (b) or

(2) Any individual in possession of an NRC-L or R access authorization or equivalent active Federal security clearance but not yet in receipt of the NRC-U special nuclear material access authorization, provided that a complete application has been submitted to and is pending before the NRC for processing for that employee in accordance with § 11.15 (a) or (b), or both.

(b) Each licensee who, 365 days after Commission approval of the amended security plan submitted in accordance with § 11.11(a), transports or delivers to a carrier for transport special nuclear material subject to the physical protection requirement of §§ 73.20, 73.25,

73.26, or 73.27 of this chapter shall confirm and record prior to shipment the name and special nuclear material access authorization number of all individuals identified in paragraph (a) of this section assigned to the shipment. The licensee shall retain this record for three years after the last shipment is made. However, the licensee need not confirm and record the special nuclear material access authorization number in the case of any individual for whom an application has been submitted and is pending before the NRC in accordance with paragraph (a) of this section.

[50 FR 39078, Sept. 27, 1985, as amended at 53 FR 19245, May 27, 1988]

§ 11.15 Application for special nuclear material access authorization.

(a)(1) Application for special nuclear material access authorization, renewal, or change in level must be filed by the licensee on behalf of the applicant with the Director, Division of Facilities and Security, Mail Stop T7–D57, either by mail addressed to the U.S. Nuclear Regulatory Commission, Washington, DC 20555–0001; by hand delivery to the NRC's offices at 11555 Rockville Pike, Rockville, Maryland; or, where practicable, by electronic submission, for example, via Electronic Information Exchange, or CD-ROM. Electronic submissions must be made in a manner that enables the NRC to receive, read, authenticate, distribute, and archive the submission, and process and retrieve it a single page at a time. Detailed guidance on making electronic submissions can be obtained by visiting the NRC's Web site at *http://www.nrc.gov/site-help/e-submittals.html;* by e-mail to *MSHD.Resource@nrc.gov;* or by writing the Office of the Chief Information Officer, U.S. Nuclear Regulatory Commission, Washington, DC 20555–0001. The guidance discusses, among other topics, the formats the NRC can accept, the use of electronic signatures, and the treatment of nonpublic information. Applications for affected individuals employed on October 28, 1985, shall be submitted within 60 days of notification of Commission approval of the amended security plan.

(2) Licensees who wish to secure NRC-U or NRC-R special nuclear material access authorizations for individuals in possession of an active NRC Q or L access authorization or other security clearance granted by another Federal agency based on an equivalent investigation shall submit a "Security Acknowledgment" (NRC Form 176) and a "Request for Access Authorization" (NRC Form 237). NRC will process these requests by verifying the data on an NRC-cleared individual, or by contacting the Federal agency that granted the clearance, requesting certification of the security clearance, and determining the investigative basis and level of the clearance. Licensees may directly request the Federal agency that administered the security clearance, if other than NRC, to certify to the NRC that it has on file an active security clearance for an individual and to specify the investigative basis and level of the clearance.

(b) Applications for special nuclear material access authorization for individuals, other than those qualifying under the provisions of § 11.15(a)(2), must be made on forms supplied by the Commission, including:

(1) Questionnaire for National Security Positions (SF–86, Parts 1 and 2);

(2) Two completed standard fingerprint cards (FD–258);

(3) Security Acknowledgment (NRC Form 176);

(4) Other related forms where specified in accompanying instruction (NRC–254); and

(5) A statement by the employer, prospective employer, or contractor identifying the job to be assigned to or assumed by the individual and the level of authorization needed, justified by appropriate reference to the licensee's security plan.

(c)(1) Except as provided in paragraph (c)(2) of this section, NRC-U special nuclear material access authorizations must be renewed every five years from the date of issuance. Except as provided in paragraph (c)(3) of this section, NRC-R special nuclear material access authorizations must be renewed every ten years from the date of issuance. An application for renewal must be submitted at least 120 days before the expiration of the five-year period for NRC-U and ten-year period for NRC-R, respectively, and must include:

(i) A statement by the licensee that at the time of application for renewal the individual's assigned or assumed job requires an NRC-U or an NRC-R special nuclear material access authorization, justified by appropriate reference to the licensee's security plan;

(ii) The Questionnaire for National Security Positions (SF–86, Parts 1 and 2);

(iii) Two completed standard fingerprint cards (FD–258); and

(iv) Other related forms specified in accompanying NRC instructions (NRC Form 254).

(2) An exception to the time for submission of NRC-U special nuclear material access authorization renewal applications and the paperwork required is provided for individuals who have a current and active DOE-Q access authorization and are subject to DOE Reinvestigation Program requirements. For these individuals, the submission to DOE of the SF–86 pursuant to DOE Reinvestigation Program requirements (generally every five years) will satisfy the NRC renewal submission and paperwork requirements even if less than five years has passed since the date of issuance or renewal of the NRC-U access authorization. Any NRC-U special nuclear material access authorization renewed in response to provisions of this paragraph will not be due for renewal until the date set by DOE for the next reinvestigation of the individual pursuant to DOE's Reinvestigation Program.

(3) An exception to the time for submission of NRC-R special nuclear material access authorization renewal applications and the paperwork required is provided for individuals who have a current and active DOE-L or DOE-Q access authorization and are subject to DOE Reinvestigation Program requirements. For these individuals, the submission to DOE of the SF–86 pursuant to DOE Reinvestigation Program requirements will satisfy the NRC renewal submission and paperwork requirements even if less than ten years have passed since the date of issuance or renewal of the NRC-R access authorization. Any NRC-R special nuclear material access authorization renewed pursuant to this paragraph will not be due for renewal until the date set by DOE for the next reinvestigation of the individual pursuant to DOE's Reinvestigation Program.

(4) Notwithstanding the provisions of paragraph (c)(2) of this section, the period of time for the initial and each subsequent NRC-U renewal application to NRC may not exceed seven years.

(5) Notwithstanding the provisions of paragraph (c)(3) of this section, the period of time for the initial and each subsequent NRC-R renewal application to NRC may not exceed twelve years. Any individual who is subject to the DOE Reinvestigation Program requirements but, for administrative or other reasons, does not submit reinvestigation forms to DOE within seven years of the previous submission, for a NRC-U renewal or twelve years of the previous submission for a NRC-R renewal, shall submit a renewal application to NRC using the forms prescribed in paragraph (c)(1) of this section before the expiration of the seven year period for NRC-U or twelve year period for NRC-R renewal.

(d) If at any time, due to new assignment or assumption of duties, a change in a special nuclear material access authorization level from NRC "R" to "U" is required, the individual shall apply for a change of level of special nuclear material access authorization. The application must include a description of the new duties to be assigned or assumed, justified by appropriate reference to the licensee's security plan.

(e) The Office of Personnel Management (OPM) bills the NRC for the cost of each background investigation conducted in support of an application for special nuclear material access authorization (application). The combined cost of the OPM investigation and the NRC's application processing overhead (NRC processing fee) are recovered through a material access authorization fee imposed on applicants for special nuclear material access authorization.

(1) Each application for a special nuclear material access authorization, renewal, or change in level must be accompanied by a remittance, payable to the U.S. Nuclear Regulatory Commission, which is equal to the NRC material access authorization fee. This fee must be determined using the following

formula: the OPM investigation billing rates on the day of NRC receipt of the application + the NRC processing fee = the NRC material access authorization fee. The NRC processing fee is determined by multiplying the OPM investigation billing rate on the day of NRC receipt of the application by 55.8 percent (*i.e.*, OPM rate × 55.8 percent).

(2) Updated OPM investigation billing rates are published periodically in a Federal Investigations Notice (FIN) issued by the OPM's Federal Investigative Services. Copies of the current OPM investigation billing rates schedule can be obtained by contacting the NRC's Personnel Security Branch, Division of Facilities Security, Office of Administration by email to: *Licensee_Access_Authorization_Fee.Resource@nrc.gov.*

(3) The NRC's Material Access Authorization Program (MAAP) is considered reimbursable work representing services provided to an organization for which the NRC is entitled payment. The NRC is authorized to receive and retain fees from licensees for services performed. The NRC's Office of the Chief Financial Officer periodically reviews the fees charged for MAAP and makes recommendations on revising those charges to reflect costs incurred by the NRC in providing those services. The reviews are performed using cost analysis techniques to determine the direct and indirect costs. Based on this review the MAAP fees are adjusted to reflect the current cost for the program. Copies of the current NRC material access authorization fee may be obtained by contacting the NRC's Personnel Security Branch, Division of Facilities Security, Office of Administration by email to: *Licensee_Access_Authorization_Fee.Resource@nrc.gov.* Any change in the NRC's access authorization fees will be applicable to each access authorization request received on or after the effective date of the OPM's most recently published investigation billing rates schedule. Applicants shall calculate the access authorization fee according to the stated formula (*i.e.*, OPM rate × 55.8 percent) and with reference to the following table:

The NRC application fee for an access authorization of type . . .	Is the sum of the current OPM investigation billing rate charged for an investigation of type . . .	Plus the NRC's processing fee (rounded to the nearest dollar), which is equal to the OPM investigation billing rate for the type of investigation referenced multiplied by . . .
i. NRC–R [1]	NACLC—National Agency Check with Law and Credit (Standard Service, Code C).	55.8%
ii. NRC—R Based on Certification of Comparable Investigation [2].	No fee assessed for most applications.	
iii. NRC—R renewal [1]	NACLC—National Agency Check with Law and Credit (Standard Service, Code C).	55.8%
iv. NRC—U requiring single scope investigation.	SSBI—Single Scope Background Investigation (Standard Service, Code C).	55.8%
v. NRC—U requiring single scope investigation (expedited processing).	SSBI—Single Scope Background Investigation (Priority Handling, Code A).	55.8%
vi. NRC—U based on certification of comparable investigation [2].	No fee assessed for most applications.	
vii. NRC—U renewal [2]	SSBI-PR—Periodic Reinvestigation for SSBI (Standard Service, Code C).	55.8%

[1] If the NRC, having reviewed the available data, deems it necessary to perform a single scope investigation, the appropriate NRC–U fee will be assessed before the conduct of the investigation.

[2] If the NRC determines, based on its review of available data, that a single scope investigation is necessary, the appropriate NRC–U fee will be assessed before the conduct of the investigation.

(4) Certain applications from individuals having current Federal access authorizations may be processed expeditiously at no cost to the licensee because the Commission, at its discretion, may decide to accept the certification of access authorizations and investigative data from other Federal government agencies that grant personnel access authorizations.

(f)(1) Any Federal employee, employee of a contractor of a Federal agency, licensee, or other person visiting an affected facility for the purpose of conducting official business, who possesses an active NRC or DOE-Q access authorization or an equivalent Federal security clearance granted by another Federal agency ("Top Secret") based on a comparable single scope background investigation may be permitted, in accordance with § 11.11, the same level of unescorted access that an NRC-U special nuclear material access authorization would afford.

(2) Any Federal employee, employee of a contractor of a Federal agency, licensee, or other person visiting an affected facility for the purpose of conducting official business, who possesses an active NRC or DOE-L access authorization or an equivalent security clearance granted by another Federal agency ("Secret") based on a comparable or greater background investigation consisting of a national agency check with law and credit may be permitted, in accordance with § 11.11, the same level of unescorted access that an NRC-R special nuclear material access authorization would afford. An NRC or DOE-L access authorization or an equivalent security clearance ("Secret"), based on a background investigation or national agency check with credit granted or being processed by another Federal agency before January 1, 1998, is acceptable to meet this requirement.

[64 FR 15645, Apr. 1, 1999, as amended at 68 FR 62511, Nov. 5, 2003; 68 FR 65765, Nov. 21, 2003; 68 FR 58800, Oct. 10, 2003; 72 FR 27410, May 16, 2007; 74 FR 62680, Dec. 1, 2009; 77 FR 26152, May 3, 2012; 77 FR 46257, Aug. 3, 2012; 80 FR 74978, Dec. 1, 2015]

§ 11.16 Cancellation of request for special nuclear material access authorization.

When a request for an individual's access authorization is withdrawn or canceled, the licensee shall notify the Chief, Personnel Security Branch, NRC Division of Facilities and Security immediately, by telephone, so that the investigation may be discontinued. The caller shall provide the full name and date of birth of the individual, the date of request, and the type of access authorization originally requested ("U" or "R"). The licensee shall promptly submit written confirmation of the telephone notification to the Personnel Security Branch, NRC Division of Facilities and Security. A portion of the fee for the "U" special nuclear material access authorization may be refunded depending upon the status of the single scope investigation at the time of withdrawal or cancellation.

[64 FR 15647, Apr. 1, 1999]

CRITERIA FOR DETERMINING ELIGIBILITY FOR ACCESS TO, OR CONTROL OVER, SPECIAL NUCLEAR MATERIAL

§ 11.21 Application of the criteria.

(a) The decision to grant or deny special nuclear material access authorization is a comprehensive, common-sense judgment, made after consideration of all the relevant information, favorable or unfavorable, that to grant or deny special nuclear material access authorization is or is not inimical to the common defense and security and is or is not clearly consistent with the national interest.

(b) To assist in making these determinations, on the basis of all the information in a particular case, there are set forth in § 10.11 of this chapter a number of specific types of derogatory information. These criteria are not exhaustive but contain the principal types of derogatory information which in the opinion of the Commission create a question as to the individual's eligibility for special nuclear material access authorization. These criteria are subject to continuing review and may be revised from time to time as experience and circumstances may make desirable.

(c) When the reports of an investigation of an individual contain information reasonably falling within one or more of the classes of derogatory information listed in § 10.11, it creates a question as to the individual's eligibility for special nuclear material access authorization. In these cases, the application of the criteria must be made in light of and with specific regard to whether the existence of the information supports a reasonable belief that the granting of a special nuclear material access authorization would be inimical to the common defense and security. The Director, Division of Facilities and Security, may authorize the granting of a special nuclear material access authorization on the basis of the information in the case or may authorize the conduct of an interview with the individual and, on the basis of the interview and other investigation as the Director deems appropriate, may authorize the granting of a special nuclear material access authorization. Otherwise, a question concerning the eligibility of an individual for a special nuclear material access authorization must be resolved in accordance with the procedures set forth in §§10.20 through 10.38 of this chapter.

(d) In resolving a question concerning the eligibility or continued eligibility of an individual for a special nuclear material access authorization by action of the Hearing Examiner or a Personnel Security Review Panel,[3] the following principle shall be applied by the Examiner and the Personnel Security Review Panel: Where there are sufficient grounds to establish a reasonable belief as to the truth of the information regarded as substantially derogatory and when the existence of this information supports a reasonable belief that granting access would be inimical to the common defense and security, this will be the basis for a recommendation for denying or revoking special nuclear material access authorization if not satisfactorily rebutted by the individual or shown to be mitigated by circumstance.

[45 FR 76970, Nov. 21, 1980, as amended at 47 FR 38683, Sept. 2, 1982; 64 FR 15647, Apr. 1, 1999]

VIOLATIONS

§ 11.30 Violations.

(a) The Commission may obtain an injunction or other court order to prevent a violation of the provisions of—

(1) The Atomic Energy Act of 1954, as amended;

(2) Title II of the Energy Reorganization Act of 1974, as amended; or

(3) A regulation or order issued pursuant to those Acts.

(b) The Commission may obtain a court order for the payment of a civil penalty imposed under section 234 of the Atomic Energy Act:

(1) For violations of—

(i) Sections 53, 57, 62, 63, 81, 82, 101, 103, 104, 107, or 109 of the Atomic Energy Act of 1954, as amended;

(ii) Section 206 of the Energy Reorganization Act;

(iii) Any rule, regulation, or order issued pursuant to the sections specified in paragraph (b)(1)(i) of this section;

(iv) Any term, condition, or limitation of any license issued under the sections specified in paragraph (b)(1)(i) of this section.

(2) For any violation for which a license may be revoked under section 186 of the Atomic Energy Act of 1954, as amended.

[57 FR 55070, Nov. 24, 1992]

§ 11.32 Criminal penalties.

(a) Section 223 of the Atomic Energy Act of 1954, as amended, provides for criminal sanctions for willful violation of, attempted violation of, or conspiracy to violate, any regulation issued under sections 161b, 161i, or 161o of the Act. For purposes of section 223, all regulations in part 11 are issued under one or more of sections 161b, 161i, or 161o, except for the sections listed in paragraph (b) of this section.

(b) The regulations in part 11 that are not issued under sections 161b, 161i, or 161o for the purposes of section 223 are as follows: §§11.1, 11.3, 11.5, 11.7, 11.8, 11.9, 11.16, 11.21, 11.30, and 11.32.

[57 FR 55070, Nov. 24, 1992]

PART 12—IMPLEMENTATION OF THE EQUAL ACCESS TO JUSTICE ACT IN AGENCY PROCEEDINGS

Subpart A—General Provisions

Sec.

[3] The functions of the Hearing Examiner and the Personnel Security Review Panel are described in part 10 of this chapter.

Subpart B—Information Required From Applicants

Subpart C—Procedures for Considering Applications

AUTHORITY: 5 U.S.C. 504(c)(1).

SOURCE: 59 FR 23121, May 5, 1994, unless otherwise noted.

Subpart A—General Provisions

§ 12.101 Purpose.

The purpose of this part is to state the regulatory requirements for award of attorney fees to eligible individuals and entities in certain administrative proceedings before the Nuclear Regulatory Commission, in implementation of the Equal Access to Justice Act, 5 U.S.C. 504 (EAJA), which provides for the award of attorney fees and other expenses to parties to "adversary adjudications", as defined in 5 U.S.C. 504(b)(1)(C). In general, an "adversary adjudication" is an adjudication that is required by statute to be determined on the record after opportunity for hearing before an agency of the United States and in which the position of the agency, or any component of the agency, is presented by an attorney or other representative who enters an appearance and participates in the proceeding. However, some agency adjudications are expressly excluded from coverage by 5 U.S.C. 504 (e.g., an adjudication for the purpose of granting or renewing a license) even though they fall within this general definition, and certain appeals before an agency board of contract appeals and Program Fraud Civil Remedies Act hearings conducted under 31 U.S.C. ch. 38 are expressly covered.

An eligible party may receive an award in an adversary adjudication when the party prevails over the Commission, unless the Commission's position was substantially justified or special circumstances make an award unjust. The regulations in this part describe the parties eligible for awards and the proceedings that are covered. They also explain how to apply for awards, and the procedures and standards that the Commission will use to make them.

§ 12.102 When the EAJA applies.

The EAJA applies to any covered adversary adjudication pending or commenced before the Commission on or after August 5, 1985.

§ 12.103 Proceedings covered.

(a) The EAJA applies to the following proceedings:

(1) Hearings under the Program Fraud Civil Remedies Act (31 U.S.C. 3801–12);

(2) Any appeal of a decision made pursuant to section 6 of the Contract Disputes Act of 1978 (41 U.S.C. 605) before an agency board of contract appeals as provided in section 8 of that Act (41 U.S.C. 607); and

(3) Adversary adjudications conducted by the Commission pursuant to any other statutory provision that requires a proceeding before the Nuclear Regulatory Commission to be so conducted as to fall within the meaning of "adversary adjudication" under 5 U.S.C. 504(b)(1)(C).

(b) The Commission's failure to identify a type of proceeding as an adversary adjudication shall not preclude the filing of an application by a party who believes the proceeding is covered by the EAJA. Whether the proceeding is covered will then be an issue for resolution in proceedings on the application.

(c) If a proceeding includes both matters covered by the EAJA and matters specifically excluded from coverage, any award made will include only fees and expenses related to covered issues.

§ 12.104 Eligibility of applicants.

(a) To be eligible for an award of attorney fees and other expenses under the EAJA, the applicant must be a party to the adversary adjudication for which it seeks an award. The term "party" is defined in 5 U.S.C. 551(3). The applicant must show that it meets all conditions of eligibility set out in this subpart and in subpart B.

(b) The types of eligible applicants are as follows:

(1) An individual with a net worth of not more than $2 million;

(2) The sole owner of an unincorporated business who has a net worth of not more than $7 million, including both personal and business interests, and not more than 500 employees;

(3) A charitable or other tax-exempt organization described in section 501(c)(3) of the Internal Revenue Code (26 U.S.C. 501(c)(3)) with not more than 500 employees;

(4) A cooperative association as defined in section 15(a) of the Agricultural Marketing Act (12 U.S.C. 1141j(a)) with not more than 500 employees; and

(5) Any other partnership, corporation, association, unit of local government, or organization with a net worth of not more than $7 million and not more than 500 employees.

(c) For the purpose of eligibility, the net worth and number of employees of an applicant shall be determined as of the date the proceeding was initiated.

(d) An applicant who owns an unincorporated business will be considered as an "individual" rather than a "sole owner of an unincorporated business" if the issues on which the applicant prevails are related primarily to personal interests rather than to business interests.

(e) The employees of an applicant include all persons who regularly perform services for remuneration for the applicant, under the applicant's direction and control. Part-time employees shall be included on a proportional basis.

(f) The net worth and number of employees of the applicant and all of its affiliates shall be aggregated to determine eligibility. Any individual, corporation, or other entity that directly or indirectly controls or owns a majority of the voting shares or other interests of the applicant, or any corporation or other entity of which the applicant directly or indirectly owns or controls a majority of the voting shares or other interest, will be considered an affiliate for purposes of this part, unless the adjudicative officer determines that such treatment would be unjust and contrary to the purposes of the Act in light of the actual relationship between the affiliated entities. In addition, the adjudicative officer may determine that financial relationships of the applicant other than those described in this paragraph constitute special circumstances that would make an award unjust.

(g) An applicant that participates in a proceeding primarily on behalf of one or more other persons or entities that would be ineligible is not itself eligible for an award.

§ 12.105 Standards for awards.

(a) A prevailing applicant may receive an award for fees and expenses incurred in connection with a proceeding or a significant and discrete substantive portion of the proceeding, unless the position of the Commission over which the applicant has prevailed was substantially justified. The position of the Commission includes, in addition to the position taken by the Commission in the adversary adjudication, the action or failure to act by the Commission upon which the adversary adjudication is based. The burden of proof that an award should not be made to a prevailing applicant because the Commission's position was substantially justified is on the Commission counsel.

(b) An award will be reduced or denied if the applicant has unduly or unreasonably protracted the proceeding or if special circumstances make the award sought unjust.

§ 12.106 Allowable fees and expenses.

(a) Awards will be based on rates customarily charged by persons engaged in the business of acting as attorneys, agents, and expert witnesses, even if the services were made available without charge or at reduced rate to the applicant.

(b) No award for the fee of an attorney or agent under this part may exceed $75.00 per hour. No award to compensate an expert witness may exceed the highest rate at which the Commission pays expert witnesses. However, an award may also include the reasonable expenses of the attorney, agent, or witness as a separate item, if the attorney, agent, or witness ordinarily charges clients separately for these expenses.

(c) In determining the reasonableness of the fee sought for an attorney, agent, or expert witness, the adjudicative officer shall consider the following:

(1) If the attorney, agent, or witness is in private practice, his or her customary fees for similar services, or, if an employee of the applicant, the fully allocated costs of the services;

(2) The prevailing rate for similar services in the community in which the attorney, agent, or witness ordinarily performs services;

(3) The time actually spent in the representation of the applicant;

(4) The time reasonably spent in light of the difficulty or complexity of the issues in the proceeding; and

(5) Other factors that bear on the value of the services provided.

(d) The reasonable cost of any study, analysis, engineering report, test, project, or similar matter prepared on behalf of a party may be awarded, to the extent that the charge for the services does not exceed the prevailing rate for similar services, and the study or other matter was necessary for preparation of applicant's case.

§ 12.107 Rulemaking on maximum rates for attorney fees.

(a) If warranted by an increase in the cost of living or by special circumstances (such as limited availability of attorneys qualified to handle certain types of proceedings), the Commission may adopt regulations providing that attorney fees may be awarded at a rate higher than $75 per hour in some, or all of the types of proceedings covered by this part. The Commission will conduct any rulemaking proceedings for this purpose under the informal rulemaking procedures of the Administrative Procedure Act.

(b) Any person may file with the Commission a petition for rulemaking to increase the maximum rate for attorney fees, in accordance with the requirements of 10 CFR 2.802. The petition should identify the rate the petitioner believes the Commission should establish and the types of proceedings in which the rate should be used. It should also explain fully the reasons why the higher rate is warranted. Within 90 days after the petition is filed, the Commission will determine whether it will initiate a rulemaking proceeding, deny the petition, or take other appropriate action on the petition. The Commission will act on the petition in accordance with 10 CFR 2.803.

§ 12.108 Awards against other agencies.

If an applicant is entitled to an award because it prevails over another agency of the United States that participates in a proceeding before the Commission and takes a position that is not substantially justified, the award or an appropriate portion of the award shall be made against that agency.

§ 12.109 Decisionmaking authority.

Unless otherwise ordered by the Commission in a particular proceeding, each application under this part shall be assigned for decision to the official or decisionmaking body that entered the decision in the adversary adjudication. That official or decisionmaking body is referred to in this part as the "adjudicative officer."

Subpart B—Information Required From Applicants

§ 12.201 Contents of application.

(a) An application for an award of fees and expenses under the EAJA shall identify the applicant and the proceeding for which an award is sought. The application shall show that the applicant has prevailed and identify the position of the Commission or other agency that the applicant alleges was not substantially justified. Unless the applicant is an individual, the application shall also state the number of employees of the applicant and describe briefly the type and purpose of its organization or business.

(b) The application shall also include a statement that the applicant's net worth does not exceed $2 million (if an individual) or $7 million (for all other applicants, including their affiliates). However, an applicant may omit this statement if:

(1) The applicant attaches a copy of a ruling by the Internal Revenue Service that it qualifies as an organization described in section 501(c)(3) of the Internal Revenue Code (26 U.S.C. 501(c)(3)) or, in the case of a tax-exempt organization not required to obtain a ruling from the Internal Revenue Service on its exempt status, a statement that describes the basis for the applicant's belief that it qualifies under this section; or

(2) The applicant states that it is a cooperative association as defined in section 15(a) of the Agricultural Marketing Act (12 U.S.C. 1141j(a)).

(c) The application shall state the amount of fees and expenses for which an award is sought.

(d) The application may also include any other matters that the applicant wishes the Commission to consider in determining whether, and in what amount, an award should be made.

(e) The application shall be signed by the applicant or an authorized officer or attorney of the applicant. It shall also contain or be accompanied by a written verification under oath or under penalty of perjury that the information provided in the application is true and correct.

§ 12.202 Net worth exhibit.

(a) Each applicant, except a qualified tax-exempt organization or cooperative association must provide with its application a detailed exhibit showing the net worth of the applicant and any affiliates (as defined in § 12.104(f) of this part) when the proceeding was initiated. The exhibit may be in any form convenient to the applicant that provides full disclosure of the applicant's and its affiliates' assets and liabilities and is sufficient to determine whether the applicant qualifies under the standards in this part. The adjudicative officer may require an applicant to file additional information to determine its eligibility for an award.

(b) Ordinarily, the net worth exhibit will be included in the public record of the proceeding. However, an applicant that objects to public disclosure of information in any portion of the exhibit and believes there are legal grounds for withholding it from disclosure may submit that portion of the exhibit directly to the adjudicative officer in a sealed envelope labeled "Confidential Financial Information," accompanied by a motion to withhold the information from public disclosure. The motion shall describe the information sought to be withheld and explain, in detail, why it falls within one or more of the specific exemptions from mandatory disclosure under the Freedom of Information Act, 5 U.S.C. 552(b)(1)–(9), why public disclosure of the information would adversely affect the applicant, and why disclosure is not required in the public interest. The material in question shall be served on counsel representing the agency against which the applicant seeks an award, but need not be served on any other party to the proceeding. If the adjudicative officer finds that the information should not be withheld from disclosure, it shall be placed in the public record of the proceeding. Otherwise, any request to inspect or copy the exhibit shall be disposed of in accordance with the Commission's established procedures under the Freedom of Information Act, 10 CFR part 9, subpart A.

§ 12.203 Documentation of fees and expenses.

The application shall be accompanied by full documentation of the fees and expenses, including the cost of any study, analysis, engineering report, test, project, or similar matter for which an award is sought. A separate itemized statement shall be submitted for each professional firm or individual whose services are covered by the application, showing the hours spent in connection with the proceeding by each individual, a description of the specific services performed, the rates at which each fee has been computed, any expenses for which reimbursement is sought, the total amount claimed, and the total amount paid or payable by the applicant or by any other person or entity for the services provided. The adjudicative officer may require the applicant to provide vouchers, receipts, logs, or other substantiation for any fees or expenses claimed, pursuant to § 12.306 of this part.

§ 12.204 When an application may be filed.

(a) An application may be filed whenever the applicant has prevailed in the proceeding or in a significant and discrete substantive portion of the proceeding, but in no case later than 30 days after the date on which a decision or order disposing of the merits of the proceeding or any other complete resolution of the proceeding, such as a settlement or voluntary dismissal, becomes final and unappealable, both within the NRC and to the courts.

(b) If after the filing of an application for an award, review or reconsideration is sought or taken of a decision as to which an applicant believes it has prevailed, proceedings for the award of fees shall be stayed pending final disposition of the underlying controversy. When the United States appeals the underlying merits of an adversary adjudication to a court, no decision on an application for fees and other expenses in connection with that adversary adjudication shall be made until a final and unreviewable decision is rendered by the court on the appeal or until the underlying merits of the case have been finally determined pursuant to the appeal.

Subpart C—Procedures for Considering Applications

§ 12.301 Filing and service of documents.

Any application for an award or other pleading or document related to an application shall be filed and served on all parties to the proceeding in the same manner as other pleadings in the proceeding, except as provided in § 12.202(b) for confidential financial information.

§ 12.302 Answer to application.

(a) Within 30 days after service of an application, counsel representing the NRC against which an award is sought may file an answer to the application. Unless the NRC counsel requests an extension of time for filing or files a statement of intent to negotiate under paragraph (b) of this section, failure to file an answer within the 30-day period may be treated as a consent to the award requested.

(b) If the NRC counsel and the applicant believe that the issues in the fee application can be settled, they may jointly file a statement of their intent to negotiate a settlement. The filing of this statement shall extend the time for filing an answer for an additional 30 days, and further extensions may be granted by the adjudicative officer upon request by the NRC counsel and the applicant.

(c) The answer shall explain in detail any objections to the award requested and identify the facts relied on in support of the NRC counsel's position. If the answer is based on any alleged facts not already in the record of the proceeding, the NRC counsel shall include with the answer either supporting affidavits or a request for further proceedings under § 12.306.

§ 12.303 Reply.

Within 15 days after service of an answer, the applicant may file a reply. If the reply is based on any alleged facts not already in the record of the proceeding, the applicant shall include with the reply either supporting affidavits or a request for further proceedings under § 12.306.

§ 12.304 Comments by other parties.

Any party to a proceeding other than the applicant and the NRC counsel may file comments on an application within 30 days after it is served, or on an answer within 15 days after it is served. A commenting party may not participate further in proceedings on the application unless the adjudicative officer determines that the public interest requires participation in order to permit full exploration of matters raised in the comments.

§ 12.305 Settlement.

The applicant and the NRC counsel may agree on a proposed settlement of the award before final action on the application, either in connection with a settlement of the underlying proceeding, or after the underlying proceeding has been concluded, in accordance with the NRC's standard settlement procedure. If a prevailing party and the NRC's counsel agree on a proposed settlement of an award before an application has been filed, the application shall be filed with the proposed settlement.

§ 12.306 Further proceedings.

(a) Ordinarily, the determination of an award will be made on the basis of the written record. However, on request of either the applicant or the NRC counsel, or on the adjudicative officer's own initiative, the adjudicative officer may order further proceedings, such as an informal conference, oral argument, additional written submissions or, as to issues other than substantial justification (such as the applicant's eligibility or substantiation of fees and expenses), pertinent discovery or an evidentiary hearing. Further proceedings shall be held only when necessary for full and fair resolution of the issues arising from the application, and shall be conducted as promptly as possible. Whether or not the position of the agency was substantially justified shall be determined on the basis of the administrative record, as a whole, which is made in the adversary adjudication for which fees and other expenses are sought.

(b) A request that the adjudicative officer order further proceedings under this section shall specifically identify the information sought or the disputed issues and shall explain why the additional proceedings are necessary to resolve the issues.

§ 12.307 Decision.

(a) The adjudicative officer shall issue an initial decision on the application within 90 days after completion of proceedings on the application. If the adjudicative officer fails to issue an initial decision within 90 days, he or she shall notify the parties of the reason for the delay and shall set a new deadline.

(b) The initial decision shall include written findings and conclusions on the applicant's eligibility and status as a prevailing party, and an explanation of the reasons for any difference between the amount requested and the amount awarded. The decision shall also include, if at issue, findings on whether the NRC's position was substantially justified, whether the applicant unduly protracted the proceedings, or whether special circumstances make an award unjust. If the applicant has sought an award against more than one agency, the decision shall allocate responsibility for payment of any award made among the agencies, and shall explain the reasons for the allocation made.

§ 12.308 Agency review.

(a) Either the applicant or the NRC counsel may seek review of the initial decision on the fee application, or the Commission may decide to review the decision on its own initiative, in accordance with the Commission's review procedures set out in 10 CFR 2.341. The filing of a petition for review is mandatory for a party to exhaust its administrative remedies before seeking judicial review. If neither the applicant nor NRC counsel seeks review and the Commission does not take review on its own initiative, the initial decision on the application shall become a final decision of the NRC 120 days after it is issued.

(b) Notwithstanding anything to the contrary in any other part of the Commission's regulations, the initial decision shall be inoperative (*i.e.*, the decision shall not be final and any award made shall not be paid) until the later of—

(1) The expiration of the 120 day period provided in paragraph (a) of this section; or

(2) If within the 120 day period provided in paragraph (a) of this section the Commission elects to review the decision, the Commission's issuance of a final decision on review of the initial decision.

(c) Whether to review a decision on its own motion is a matter within the discretion of the Commission. If review is taken, the Commission will issue a final decision on the application or remand the application to the adjudicative officer for further proceedings.

[59 FR 23121, May 5, 1994, as amended at 77 FR 46599, Aug. 3, 2012]

§ 12.309 Judicial review.

Judicial review of final agency decisions on awards may be sought as provided in 5 U.S.C. 504(c)(2).

§ 12.310 Payment of award.

An applicant seeking payment of an award shall submit to the appropriate official of the paying agency a copy of the Commission's final decision granting the award, accompanied by a certification that the applicant will not seek review of the decision in the United States courts. Where the award is granted against the Commission, the applicant shall make the submission to the Director, Division of Accounting and Finance, Office of the Controller, U.S. Nuclear Regulatory Commission, Washington, DC 20555. The NRC will pay the amount awarded to the applicant within 60 days.

PART 13—PROGRAM FRAUD CIVIL REMEDIES

Sec.

AUTHORITY: 31 U.S.C. 3801 through 3812; 44 U.S.C. 3504 note.

Section 13.3 also issued under 28 U.S.C. 2461 note.

Section 13.13 also issued under 31 U.S.C. 3730.

SOURCE: 56 FR 47135, Sept. 18, 1991, unless otherwise noted.

§ 13.1 Basis and purpose.

(a) *Basis.* This part implements the Program Fraud Civil Remedies Act of 1986, Public Law No. 99–509, §§ 6101–6104, 100 Stat. 1874 (October 21, 1986) (31 U.S.C. 3801–3812). 31 U.S.C. 3809 requires each authority head to promulgate regulations necessary to implement the provisions of that Act.

(b) *Purpose.* This part (1) establishes administrative procedures for imposing civil penalties and assessments against persons who make, submit, or present, or cause to be made, submitted, or presented, false, fictitious, or fraudulent claims or written statements to authorities or to their agents, and (2) specifies the hearing and appeal rights of persons subject to allegations of liability for such penalties and assessments.

§ 13.2 Definitions.

As used in this part:

ALJ means an Administrative Law Judge in the authority appointed pursuant to 5 U.S.C. 3105 or detailed to the authority pursuant to 5 U.S.C. 3344.

Authority means the Nuclear Regulatory Commission.

Authority head means the Commission of five members or a quorum thereof sitting as a body, as provided by section 201 of the Energy Reorganization Act of 1974 (88 Stat. 1242).

Benefit means, in the context of "statement", anything of value, including but not limited to any advantage, preference, privilege, license, permit, favorable decision, ruling, status, or loan guarantee.

Claim means any request, demand, or submission—

(a) Made to the authority for property, services, or money (including money representing grants, loans, insurance, or benefits);

(b) Made to a recipient of property, services, or money from the authority or to a party to a contract with the authority—

(1) For property or services if the United States—

(i) Provided such property or services;

(ii) Provided any portion of the funds for the purchase of such property or services; or

(iii) Will reimburse such recipient or party for the purchase of such property or services; or

(2) For the payment of money (including money representing grants, loans, insurance, or benefits) if the United States—

(i) Provided any portion of the money requested or demanded; or

(ii) Will reimburse such recipient or party for any portion of the money paid on such request or demand; or

(c) Made to the authority which has the effect of decreasing an obligation to pay or account for property, services, or money.

Complaint means the administrative complaint served by the reviewing official on the defendant under § 13.7.

Defendant means any person alleged in a complaint under § 13.7 to be liable for a civil penalty or assessment under § 13.3.

Digital ID certificate means a file stored on a participant's computer that contains the participant's name, e-mail address, and participant's digital signature, proves the participant's identity when filing documents and serving participants electronically through the E-Filing system, and contains public keys, which allow for the encryption and decryption of documents so that the documents can be securely transferred over the Internet.

Electronic acknowledgment means a communication transmitted electronically from the E-Filing system to the submitter confirming receipt of electronic filing and service.

Electronic Hearing Docket means the publicly available Web site which houses a visual presentation of the docket and a link to its files.

E-Filing System means an electronic system that receives, stores, and distributes documents filed in proceedings for which an electronic hearing docket has been established.

Government means the United States Government.

Guidance for Electronic Submissions to the NRC means the document issued by the Commission that sets forth the transmission methods and formatting standards for filing and service under E-Filing. The document can be obtained by visiting the NRC's Web site at *http://www.nrc.gov.*

Individual means a natural person.

Initial decision means the written decision of the ALJ required by § 13.10 or § 13.37, and includes a revised initial decision issued following a remand or a motion for reconsideration.

Investigating official means the Inspector General of the Nuclear Regulatory Commission or the Assistant Inspector General for Investigations, Office of the Inspector General.

Knows or has reason to know means that a person, with respect to a claim or statement—

(a) Has actual knowledge that the claim or statement is false, fictitious, or fraudulent;

(b) Acts in deliberate ignorance of the truth or falsity of the claim or statement; or

(c) Acts in reckless disregard of the truth or falsity of the claim or statement.

Makes, wherever it appears, shall include the terms presents, submits, and causes to be made, presented, or submitted. As the context requires, *making* or *made* shall likewise include the corresponding forms of such terms.

Optical Storage Media means any physical computer component that meets E-Filing Guidance standards for storing, saving, and accessing electronic documents.

Participant means an individual or organization that has petitioned to intervene in a proceeding or requested a hearing but that has not yet been granted party status by an Atomic Safety and Licensing Board or other presiding officer. Participant also means a party to a proceeding and any interested State, local governmental body, or affected Federally-recognized Indian Tribe that seeks to participate in a proceeding in accordance with §2.315(c). For the purpose of service of documents, the NRC staff is considered a participant even if not participating as a party.

Person means any individual, partnership, corporation, association, or private organization and includes the plural of that term.

Representative means any person designated by a party in writing.

Reviewing official means the General Counsel of the Nuclear Regulatory Commission or his or her designee who is—

(a) Not subject to supervision by, or required to report to, the investigating official;

(b) Not employed in the organizational unit of the authority in which the investigating official is employed; and

(c) Serving in a position for which the rate of basic pay is not less than the minimum rate of basic pay for grade GS–16 under the General Schedule.

Statement means any representation, certification, affirmation, document, record, or accounting or bookkeeping entry made—

(a) With respect to a claim or to obtain the approval or payment of a claim (including relating to eligibility to make a claim); or

(b) With respect to (including relating to eligibility for)—

(1) A contract with, or a bid or proposal for a contract with, or

(2) A grant, loan, or benefit from,

(i) The authority, or

(ii) Any State, political subdivision of a State, or other party, if the United States government provides any portion of the money or property under such contract or for such grant, loan, or benefit, or if the Government will reimburse such State, political subdivision, or party for any portion of the money or property under such contract or for such grant, loan, or benefit.

[56 FR 47135, Sept. 18, 1991; 56 FR 49945, Oct. 2, 1991, as amended at 62 FR 40427, July 29, 1997; 65 FR 59272, Oct. 4, 2000; 71 FR 15007, Mar. 27, 2006; 72 FR 49152, Aug. 28, 2007; 72 FR 64529, Nov. 16, 2007]

§ 13.3 Basis for civil penalties and assessments.

(a) *Claims.* (1) Any person who makes a claim that the person knows or has reason to know—

(i) Is false, fictitious, or fraudulent;

(ii) Includes or is supported by any written statement which asserts a material fact which is false, fictitious, or fraudulent;

(iii) Includes or is supported by any written statement that—

(A) Omits a material fact;

(B) Is false, fictitious, or fraudulent as a result of such omission; and

(C) Is a statement in which the person making such statement has a duty to include such material fact; or

(iv) Is for payment for the provision of property or services which the person has not provided as claimed, shall be subject, in addition to any other remedy that may be prescribed by law, to a civil penalty of not more than $10,957 for each such claim.

(2) Each voucher, invoice, claim form, or other individual request or demand for property, services, or money constitutes a separate claim.

(3) A claim shall be considered made to the authority, recipient, or party when such claim is actually made to an agent, fiscal intermediary or other entity, including any State or political subdivision thereof, acting for or on behalf of the authority, recipient, or party.

(4) Each claim for property, services, or money is subject to a civil penalty regardless of whether such property, services, or money is actually delivered or paid.

(5) If the Government has made any payment (including transferred property or provided services) on a claim, a person subject to a civil penalty under paragraph (a)(1) of this section shall also be subject to an assessment of not more than twice the amount of such claim or that portion thereof that is

determined to be in violation of paragraph (a)(1) of this section. Such assessment shall be in lieu of damages sustained by the Government because of such claim.

(b) *Statements.* (1) Any person who makes a written statement that—

(i) The person knows or has reason to know—

(A) Asserts a material fact which is false, fictitious, or fraudulent; or

(B) Is false, fictitious, or fraudulent because it omits a material fact that the person making the statement has a duty to include in such statement; and

(ii) Contains or is accompanied by an express certification or affirmation of the truthfulness and accuracy of the contents of the statement, shall be subject, in addition to any other remedy that may be prescribed by law, to a civil penalty of not more than $10,957 for each such statement.

(2) Each written representation, certification, or affirmation constitutes a separate statement.

(3) A statement shall be considered made to the authority when such statement is actually made to an agent, fiscal intermediary, or other entity, including any State or political subdivision thereof, acting for or on behalf of the authority.

(c) No proof of specific intent to defraud is required to establish liability under this section.

(d) In any case in which it is determined that more than one person is liable for making a claim or statement under this section, each such person may be held liable for a civil penalty under this section.

(e) In any case in which it is determined that more than one person is liable for making a claim under this section on which the Government has made payment (including transferred property or provided services), an assessment may be imposed against any such person or jointly and severally against any combination of such persons.

[56 FR 47135, Sept. 18, 1991, as amended at 61 FR 53555, Oct. 11, 1996; 62 FR 59275, Nov. 3, 1997; 65 FR 59273, Oct. 4, 2000; 71 FR 15007, Mar. 27, 2006; 73 FR 54673, Sept. 23, 2008; 81 FR 43021, July 1, 2016; 82 FR 8135, Jan. 24, 2017]

§ 13.4 Investigation.

(a) If an investigating official concludes that a subpoena pursuant to the authority conferred by 31 U.S.C. 3804(a) is warranted—

(1) The subpoena so issued shall notify the person to whom it is addressed of the authority under which the subpoena is issued and shall identify the records or documents sought;

(2) The investigating official may designate a person to act on his or her behalf to receive the documents sought; and

(3) The person receiving such subpoena shall be required to tender to the investigating official or the person designated to receive the documents a certification that the documents sought have been produced, or that such documents are not available and the reasons therefor, or that such documents, suitably identified, have been withheld based upon the assertion of an identified privilege.

(b) If the investigating official concludes that an action under the Program Fraud Civil Remedies Act may be warranted, the investigating official shall submit a report containing the findings and conclusions of such investigation to the reviewing official. To the extent possible, before initiating an investigation or submitting a report involving a licensee false statement to the reviewing official, the investigating official shall consult with the Executive Director for Operations to ascertain whether any other agency action is under consideration, pending, or may be taken with regard to the licensee, and to allow for coordination between any action under this part and other enforcement action.

(c) Nothing in this section shall preclude or limit an investigating official's discretion to refer allegations directly to the Department of Justice for suit under the False Claims Act or other civil relief, or to refer the matter to the Executive Director for Operations for enforcement action under the Atomic Energy Act, or to defer initiating an investigation or postpone a report or referral to the reviewing official to avoid interference with other enforcement action by the Commission or with a criminal investigation or prosecution.

(d) Nothing in this section modifies any responsibility of an investigating official to report violations of criminal law to the Attorney General.

§ 13.5 Review by the reviewing official.

(a) If, based on the report of the investigating official under § 13.4(b), the reviewing official determines that there is adequate evidence to believe that a person is liable under § 13.3 of this part, the reviewing official shall transmit to the Attorney General a written notice of the reviewing official's intention to issue a complaint under § 13.7.

(b) Such notice shall include—

(1) A statement of the reviewing official's reasons for issuing a complaint;

(2) A statement specifying the evidence that supports the allegations of liability;

(3) A description of the claims or statements upon which the allegations of liability are based;

(4) An estimate of the amount of money or the value of property, services, or other benefits requested or demanded in violation of § 13.3 of this part;

(5) A statement of any exculpatory or mitigating circumstances that may relate to the claims or statements known by the reviewing official or the investigating official; and

(6) A statement that there is a reasonable prospect of collecting an appropriate amount of penalties and assessments.

§ 13.6 Prerequisities for issuing a complaint.

(a) The reviewing official may issue a complaint under § 13.7 only if—

(1) The Department of Justice approves the issuance of a complaint in a written statement described in 31 U.S.C. 3803(b)(1), and

(2) In the case of allegations of liability under § 13.3(a) with respect to a claim, the reviewing official determines that, with respect to such claim or a group of related claims submitted at the same time such claim is submitted (as defined in paragraph (b) of this section), the amount of money or the value of property or services demanded or requested in violation of § 13.3(a) does not exceed $150,000.

(b) For the purposes of this section, a related group of claims submitted at the same time shall include only those claims arising from the same transaction (e.g., grant, loan, application, or contract) that are submitted simultaneously as part of a single request, demand, or submission.

(c) Nothing in this section shall be construed to limit the reviewing official's authority to join in a single complaint against a person claims that are unrelated or were not submitted simultaneously, regardless of the amount of money, or the value of property or services, demanded or requested.

[56 FR 47135, Sept. 18, 1991; 56 FR 49945, Oct. 2, 1991]

§ 13.7 Complaint.

(a) On or after the date the Department of Justice approves the issuance of a complaint in accordance with 31 U.S.C. 3803(b)(1), the reviewing official may serve a complaint on the defendant, as provided in § 13.8.

(b) The complaint shall state—

(1) The allegations of liability against the defendant, including the statutory basis for liability, an identification of the claims or statements that are the basis for the alleged liability, and the reasons why liability allegedly arises from such claims or statements;

(2) The maximum amount of penalties and assessments for which the defendant may be held liable;

(3) Instructions for filing an answer to request a hearing, including a specific statement of the defendant's right to request a hearing by filing an answer and to be represented by a representative; and

(4) That failure to file an answer within 30 days of service of the complaint will result in the imposition of the maximum amount of penalties and assessments without right to appeal, as provided in § 13.10.

(c) At the same time the reviewing official serves the complaint, he or she shall serve the defendant with a copy of these regulations.

§ 13.8 Service of complaint.

(a) Service of a complaint must be made by certified or registered mail or by delivery in any manner authorized by Rule 4(d) of the Federal Rules of Civil Procedure. Service is complete upon receipt.

(b) Proof of service, stating the name and address of the person on whom the complaint was served, and the manner and date of service, may be made by—

(1) Affidavit of the individual serving the complaint by delivery;

(2) A United States Postal Service return receipt card acknowledging receipt; or

(3) Written acknowledgment of receipt by the defendant or his or her representative.

[56 FR 47135, Sept. 18, 1991, as amended at 71 FR 15007, Mar. 27, 2006]

§ 13.9 Answer.

(a) The defendant may request a hearing by filing an answer with the reviewing official within thirty (30) days of service of the complaint. Service of an answer shall be made by electronically delivering a copy to the reviewing official in accordance with § 13.26. An answer shall be deemed a request for hearing.

(b) In the answer, the defendant—

(1) Shall admit or deny each of the allegations of liability made in the complaint;

(2) Shall state any defense on which the defendant intends to rely;

(3) May state any reasons why the defendant contends that the penalties and assessments should be less than the statutory maximum; and

(4) Shall state the name, address, and telephone number of the person authorized by the defendant to act as defendant's representative, if any.

(c) If the defendant is unable to file an answer meeting the requirements of paragraph (b) of this section within the time provided, the defendant may, before the expiration of 30 days from service of the complaint, file with the reviewing official a general answer denying liability and requesting a hearing, and a request for an extension of time within which to file an answer meeting the requirements of paragraph (b) of this section. The reviewing official shall file promptly with the ALJ the complaint, the general answer denying liability, and the request for an extension of time as provided in § 13.11. For good cause shown, the ALJ may grant the defendant up to 30 additional days within which to file an answer meeting the requirements of paragraph (b) of this section.

[56 FR 47135, Sept. 18, 1991; 56 FR 64839, Dec. 12, 1991; 72 FR 49152, Aug. 28, 2007]

§ 13.10 Default upon failure to file an answer.

(a) If the defendant does not file an answer within the time prescribed in § 13.9(a), the reviewing official may refer the complaint to the ALJ.

(b) Upon the referral of the complaint, the ALJ shall promptly serve on defendant in the manner prescribed in § 13.8 a notice that an initial decision will be issued under this section.

(c) The ALJ shall assume the facts alleged in the complaint to be true, and, if such facts establish liability under § 13.3, the ALJ shall issue an initial decision imposing the maximum amount of penalties and assessments allowed under the statute.

(d) Except as otherwise provided in this section, by failing to file a timely answer, the defendant waives any right to further review of the penalties and assessments imposed under paragraph (c) of this section and the initial decision shall become final and binding upon the parties 30 days after it is issued.

(e) If, before such an initial decision becomes final, the defendant files a motion with the ALJ seeking to reopen on the grounds that extraordinary circumstances prevented the defendant from filing an answer, the initial decision shall be stayed pending the ALJ's decision on the motion.

(f) If, on such motion, the defendant can demonstrate extraordinary circumstances excusing the failure to file a timely answer, the ALJ shall withdraw the initial decision in paragraph (c) of this section if such a decision has been issued, and shall grant the defendant an opportunity to answer the complaint.

(g) A decision of the ALJ denying a defendant's motion under paragraph (e) of this section is not subject to reconsideration under § 13.38.

(h) The defendant may appeal to the authority head the decision denying a motion to reopen by filing a notice of appeal with the authority head within

15 days after the ALJ denies the motion. The timely filing of a notice of appeal shall stay the initial decision until the authority head decides the issue.

(i) If the defendant files a timely notice of appeal with the authority head, the ALJ shall forward the record of the proceeding to the authority head.

(j) The authority head shall decide expeditiously whether extraordinary circumstances excuse the defendant's failure to file a timely answer based solely on the record before the ALJ.

(k) If the authority head decides that extraordinary circumstances excused the defendant's failure to file a timely answer, the authority head shall remand the case to the ALJ with instructions to grant the defendant an opportunity to answer.

(l) If the authority head decides that the defendant's failure to file a timely answer is not excused, the authority head shall reinstate the initial decision of the ALJ, which shall become final and binding upon the parties 30 days after the authority head issues such decision.

§ 13.11 Referral of complaint and answer to the ALJ.

Upon receipt of an answer, the reviewing official shall file the complaint and answer with the ALJ.

§ 13.12 Notice of hearing.

(a) When the ALJ receives the complaint and answer, the ALJ shall promptly serve a notice of hearing upon the defendant in the manner prescribed by § 13.8. At the same time, the ALJ shall send a copy of such notice to the representative of the authority.

(b) Such notice shall include—

(1) The tentative time and place, and the nature of the hearing;

(2) The legal authority and jurisdiction under which the hearing is to be held;

(3) The matters of fact and law to be asserted;

(4) A description of the procedures for the conduct of the hearing;

(5) The name, address, and telephone number of the representative of the authority and of the defendant, if any; and

(6) Such other matters as the ALJ deems appropriate.

§ 13.13 Parties to the hearing.

(a) The parties to the hearing shall be the defendant and the authority.

(b) Pursuant to 31 U.S.C. 3730(c)(5), a private plaintiff under the False Claims Act may participate in these proceedings to the extent authorized by the provisions of that Act.

§ 13.14 Separation of functions.

(a) The investigating official, the reviewing official, and any employee or agent of the authority who takes part in investigating, preparing, or presenting a particular case may not, in such case or a factually related case—

(1) Participate in the hearing as the ALJ;

(2) Participate or advise in the initial decision or the review of the initial decision by the authority head, except as a witness or a representative in public proceedings; or

(3) Make the collection of penalties and assessments under 31 U.S.C. 3806.

(b) The ALJ shall not be responsible to, or subject to the supervision or direction of, the investigating official or the reviewing official.

(c) Except as provided in paragraph (a) of this section, the representative for the Government may be employed anywhere in the authority, including in the offices of either the investigating official or the reviewing official.

[56 FR 47135, Sept. 18, 1991; 56 FR 64839, Dec. 12, 1991]

§ 13.15 Ex parte contacts.

No party or person (except employees of the ALJ's office) shall communicate in any way with the ALJ on any matter at issue in a case, unless on notice and opportunity for all parties to participate. This provision does not prohibit a person or party from inquiring about the status of a case or asking routine questions concerning administrative functions or procedures.

§ 13.16 Disqualification of reviewing official or ALJ.

(a) A reviewing official or ALJ in a particular case may disqualify himself or herself at any time.

(b) A party may file with the ALJ a motion for disqualification of a reviewing official or an ALJ. Such motion shall be accompanied by an affidavit alleging personal bias or other reason for disqualification.

(c) Such motion and affidavit shall be filed promptly upon the party's discovery of reasons requiring disqualification, or such objections, shall be deemed waived.

(d) Such affidavit shall state specific facts that support the party's belief that personal bias or other reason for disqualification exists and the time and circumstances of the party's discovery of such facts. It shall be accompanied by a certificate of the representative of record that it is made in good faith.

(e) Upon the filing of such a motion and affidavit, the ALJ shall proceed no further in the case until he or she resolves the matter of disqualification in accordance with paragraph (f) of this section.

(f)(1) If the ALJ determines that a reviewing official is disqualified, the ALJ shall dismiss the complaint without prejudice.

(2) If the ALJ disqualifies himself or herself, the case shall be reassigned promptly to another ALJ.

(3) If the ALJ denies a motion to disqualify, the authority head may determine the matter only as part of its review of the initial decision upon appeal, if any.

§ 13.17 Rights of parties.

Except as otherwise limited by this part, all parties may—

(a) Be accompanied, represented, and advised by a representative;

(b) Participate in any conference held by the ALJ;

(c) Conduct discovery;

(d) Agree to stipulation of fact or law, which shall be made part of the record;

(e) Present evidence relevant to the issues at the hearing;

(f) Present and cross-examine witnesses;

(g) Present oral arguments at the hearing as permitted by the ALJ; and

(h) Submit written briefs and proposed findings of fact and conclusions of law after the hearing.

§ 13.18 Authority of the ALJ.

(a) The ALJ shall conduct a fair and impartial hearing, avoid delay, maintain order, and assure that a record of the proceeding is made.

(b) The ALJ has the authority to—

(1) Set and change the date, time, and place of the hearing upon reasonable notice to the parties;

(2) Continue or recess the hearing in whole or in part for a reasonable period of time;

(3) Hold conferences to identify or simplify the issues, or to consider other matters that may aid in the expeditious disposition of the proceeding;

(4) Administer oaths and affirmations;

(5) Issue subpoenas requiring the attendance of witnesses and the production of documents at depositions or at hearings;

(6) Rule on motions and other procedural matters;

(7) Regulate the scope and timing of discovery;

(8) Regulate the course of the hearing and the conduct of representatives and parties;

(9) Examine witnesses;

(10) Receive, rule on, exclude, or limit evidence;

(11) Upon motion of a party, take official notice of facts;

(12) Upon motion of a party, decide cases, in whole or in part, by summary judgment where there is no disputed issue of material fact;

(13) Conduct any conference, argument, or hearing on motions in person or by telephone; and

(14) Exercise such other authority as is necessary to carry out the responsibilities of the ALJ under this part.

(c) The ALJ does not have the authority to find Federal statutes or regulations invalid.

§ 13.19 Prehearing conferences.

(a) The ALJ may schedule prehearing conferences as appropriate.

(b) Upon the motion of any party, the ALJ shall schedule at least one prehearing conference at a reasonable time in advance of the hearing.

(c) The ALJ may use prehearing conferences to discuss the following:

(1) Simplification of the issues;

(2) The necessity or desirability of amendments to the pleadings, including the need for a more definite statement;

(3) Stipulations and admissions of fact or as to the contents and authenticity of documents;

(4) Whether the parties can agree to submission of the case on a stipulated record;

(5) Whether a party chooses to waive appearance at an oral hearing and to submit only documentary evidence (subject to the objection of other parties) and written argument;

(6) Limitation of the number of witnesses;

(7) Scheduling dates for the exchange of witness lists and of proposed exhibits;

(8) Discovery;

(9) The time and place for the hearing; and

(10) Such other matters as may tend to expedite the fair and just disposition of the proceedings.

(d) The ALJ may issue an order containing all matters agreed upon by the parties or ordered by the ALJ at a prehearing conference.

§ 13.20 Disclosure of documents.

(a) Upon written request to the reviewing official, the defendant may review any relevant and material documents, transcripts, records, and other materials that relate to the allegations set out in the complaint and upon which the findings and conclusions of the investigating official under § 13.4(b) are based, unless such documents are subject to a privilege under Federal law. Upon payment of fees for duplication, the defendant may obtain copies of such documents.

(b) Upon written request to the reviewing official, the defendant also may obtain a copy of all exculpatory information in the possession of the reviewing official or investigating official relating to the allegations in the complaint, even if it is contained in a document that would otherwise be privileged. If the document would otherwise be privileged, only that portion containing exculpatory information must be disclosed.

(c) The notice sent to the Attorney General from the reviewing official as described in § 13.5 is not discoverable under any circumstances.

(d) The defendant may file a motion to compel disclosure of the documents subject to the provisions of this section. Such a motion may only be filed with the ALJ following the filing of an answer pursuant to § 13.9.

§ 13.21 Discovery.

(a) The following types of discovery are authorized:

(1) Requests for production of documents for inspection and copying;

(2) Requests for admissions of the authenticity of any relevant document or of the truth of any relevant fact;

(3) Written interrogatories; and

(4) Depositions.

(b) For the purpose of this section and §§ 13.22 and 13.23, the term "documents" includes information, documents, reports, answers, records, accounts, papers, and other data and documentary evidence. Nothing contained herein shall be interpreted to require the creation of a document.

(c) Unless mutually agreed to by the parties, discovery is available only as ordered by the ALJ. The ALJ shall regulate the timing of discovery.

(d) *Motions for discovery.* (1) A party seeking discovery may file a motion with the ALJ. Such a motion shall be accompanied by a copy of the requested discovery, or in the case of depositions, a summary of the scope of the proposed deposition.

(2) Within ten days of service, a party may file an opposition to the motion and/or a motion for protective order as provided in § 13.24.

(3) The ALJ may grant a motion for discovery only if he or she finds that the discovery sought—

(i) Is necessary for the expeditious, fair, and reasonable consideration of the issues;

(ii) Is not unduly costly or burdensome;

(iii) Will not unduly delay the proceeding; and

(iv) Does not seek privileged information.

(4) The burden of showing that discovery should be allowed is on the party seeking discovery.

(5) The ALJ may grant discovery subject to a protective order under § 13.24.

(e) *Depositions*. (1) If a motion for deposition is granted, the ALJ shall issue a subpoena for the deponent, which may require the deponent to produce documents. The subpoena shall specify the time and place at which the deposition will be held.

(2) The party seeking to depose shall serve the subpoena in the manner prescribed in § 13.8.

(3) The deponent may file with the ALJ a motion to quash the subpoena or a motion for a protective order within ten days of service.

(4) The party seeking to depose shall provide for the taking of a verbatim transcript of the deposition, which it shall make available to all other parties for inspection and copying.

(f) Each party shall bear its own costs of discovery.

§ 13.22 Exchange of witness lists, statements, and exhibits.

(a) At least 15 days before the hearing or at such other times as may be ordered by the ALJ, the parties shall exchange witness lists, copies of prior statements of proposed witnesses, and copies of proposed hearing exhibits, including copies of any written statements that the party intends to offer in lieu of live testimony in accordance with § 13.33(b). At the time the above documents are exchanged, any party that intends to rely on the transcript of deposition testimony in lieu of live testimony at the hearing, if permitted by the ALJ, shall provide each party with a copy of the specific pages of the transcript it intends to introduce into evidence.

(b) If a party objects, the ALJ shall not admit into evidence the testimony of any witness whose name does not appear on the witness list or any exhibit not provided to the opposing party as provided above unless the ALJ finds good cause for the failure or that there in no prejudice to the objecting party.

(c) Unless another party objects within the time set by the ALJ, documents exchanged in accordance with paragraph (a) of this section shall be deemed to be authentic for the purpose of admissibility at the hearing.

§ 13.23 Subpoenas for attendance at hearing.

(a) A party wishing to procure the appearance and testimony of any individual at the hearing may request that the ALJ issue a subpoena.

(b) A subpoena requiring the attendance and testimony of an individual may also require the individual to produce documents at the hearing.

(c) A party seeking a subpoena shall file a written request therefor not less than 15 days before the date fixed for the hearing unless otherwise allowed by the ALJ for good cause shown. Such request shall specify any documents to be produced and shall designate the witnesses and describe the address and location thereof with sufficient particularity to permit such witnesses to be found.

(d) The subpoena shall specify the time and place at which the witness is to appear and any documents the witness is to produce.

(e) The party seeking the subpoena shall serve it in the manner prescribed in § 13.8. A subpoena on a party or upon an individual under the control of a party may be served by first class mail.

(f) A party or the individual to whom the subpoena is directed may file with the ALJ a motion to quash the subpoena within ten days after service or on or before the time specified in the subpoena for compliance if it is less than ten days after service.

§ 13.24 Protective order.

(a) A party or a prospective witness or deponent may file a motion for a protective order with respect to discovery sought by an opposing party or with respect to the hearing, seeking to limit the availability or disclosure of evidence.

(b) In issuing a protective order, the ALJ may make any order which justice requires to protect a party or person from annoyance, embarrassment, oppression, or undue burden or expense, including one or more of the following:

(1) That the discovery not be had;

(2) That the discovery may be had only on specified terms and conditions, including a designation of the time or place;

(3) That the discovery may be had only through a method of discovery other than that requested;

(4) That certain matters not be inquired into, or that the scope of discovery be limited to certain matters;

(5) That discovery be conducted with no one present except persons designated by the ALJ;

(6) That the contents of discovery or evidence by sealed;

(7) That a deposition after being sealed be opened only by order of the ALJ;

(8) That a trade secret or other confidential research, development, commercial information, or facts pertaining to any criminal investigation, proceeding, or other administrative investigation not be disclosed or be disclosed only in a designated way; or

(9) That the parties simultaneously file specified documents or information enclosed in sealed envelopes to be opened as directed by the ALJ.

§ 13.25 Fees.

The party requesting a subpoena shall pay the cost of the fees and mileage of any witness subpoenaed in the amounts that would be payable to a witness in a proceeding in United States District Court. A check for witness fees and mileage shall accompany the subpoena when served, except that when a subpoena is issued on behalf of the authority, a check for witness fees and mileage need not accompany the subpoena.

§ 13.26 Filing and service of papers.

(a) *Filing*. (1) Unless otherwise provided by order, all filings must be made as electronic submissions in a manner that enables the NRC to receive, read, authenticate, distribute, and archive the submission, and process and retrieve it a single page at a time. Detailed guidance on making electronic submissions may be found in the E-Filing Guidance and on the NRC Web site at *http://www.nrc.gov/site-help/e-submittals.html*. If a filing contains sections of information or electronic formats that may not be transmitted electronically for security or other reasons, portions not containing those sections will be transmitted electronically to the E-Filing system. In addition, optical storage media (OSM) containing the entire filing must be physically delivered or mailed. In such cases, the submitter does not need to apply to the Commission for an exemption to deviate from the requirements in paragraph (a) of this section.

(2) Electronic transmission exemption. The ALJ may relieve a participant who is filing electronic documents of the transmission requirements in paragraph (a) of this section. Such a participant will file electronic documents by physically delivering or mailing an OSM containing the documents. The electronic formatting requirement in paragraph (a) of this section must be met.

(3) Electronic document exemption. The ALJ may relieve a participant of both the electronic (computer file) formatting and transmission requirements in paragraph (a)(1) of this section. Such a participant will file paper documents physically or by mail to the Secretary, U.S. Nuclear Regulatory Commission, Washington, DC 20555–0001, Attention: Rulemakings and Adjudications Staff. Filing by mail is complete upon deposit in the mail.

(4) Requesting an exemption. A participant seeking an exemption under paragraphs (a)(2) or (a)(3) of this section must submit the exemption request with its first filing in the proceeding. In the request, the requestor must show good cause as to why it cannot file electronically. The filer may not change its formats and delivery methods for filing until a ruling on the exemption request is issued. Exemption requests submitted after the first filing in the proceeding will be granted only if the requestor shows that the interests of fairness so require.

(5) Every pleading and document filed in the proceeding shall contain a caption setting forth the title of the action, the case number assigned by the presiding officer, and a designation of the document (e.g., motion to quash subpoena).

(6) Filing is complete when the filer performs the last act that it must perform to submit a document, such as hitting the send/submit/transmit button for an electronic transmission or depositing the document, in its entirety, in a mailbox.

(b) *Signatures.* The original of each document must be signed by the participant or its authorized representative, or by an attorney having authority with respect to it. The document must state the capacity of the person signing; his or her address, phone number, and e-mail address; and the date of signature. The signature of a person signing a pleading or other similar document submitted by a participant is a representation that the document has been subscribed in the capacity specified with full authority, that he or she has read it and knows the contents, that to the best of his or her knowledge, information, and belief the statements made in it are true, and that it is not interposed for delay. The signature of a person signing an affidavit or similar document, which should be submitted in accord with the form outlined in 28 U.S.C. 1746, is a representation that, under penalty of perjury, the document is true and correct to the best of that individual's knowledge and belief. If a document is not signed, or is signed with intent to defeat the purpose of this section, it may be struck.

(1) An electronic document must be signed using a participant's or a participant representative's digital ID certificate. Additional signatures can be added to the electronic document, including to any affidavits that accompany the document, by a typed-in designation that indicates the signer understands and acknowledges that he or she is assenting to the representations in paragraph (d) of this section.

(i) When signing an electronic document using a digital ID certificate, the signature page for the electronic document should contain a typed signature block that includes the phrase "Signed (electronically) by" typed onto the signature line; the name and the capacity of the person signing; the person's address, phone number, and e-mail address; and the date of signature.

(ii) If additional individuals need to sign an electronic document, including any affidavits that accompany the document, these individuals must sign by inserting a typed signature block in the electronic document that includes the phrase "Executed in Accord with 10 CFR 2.304(d)" or its equivalent typed on the signature line as well as the name and the capacity of the person signing; the person's address, phone number, and e-mail address; and the date of signature to the extent any of these items are different from the information provided for the digital ID certificate signer.

(2) Paper documents must be signed in ink.

(c) *Service.* A participant filing a document with the ALJ shall at the time of filing, serve a copy of such document on every other participant. Service upon any participant of any document other than those required to be served as prescribed in § 13.8 shall be made electronically to the E-Filing system. When a participant is represented by a representative, service shall be made upon such representative in lieu of the actual participant. Upon an order from the ALJ permitting alternative filing methods under paragraphs (a)(2) or (a)(3) of this section, service may be made by physical delivery or mail. As to each participant that cannot serve electronically, the ALJ shall require service by the most expeditious means permitted under this paragraph that are available to the participant, unless the ALJ finds that this requirement would impose undue burden or expense on the participant.

(1) Unless otherwise provided in this paragraph, a participant will serve documents on the other participants by the same method that those participants filed.

(2) A participant granted an exemption under paragraph (a)(2) of this section will serve the participants in the proceeding that filed electronically by physically delivering or mailing an OSM containing the electronic document.

(3) A participant granted an exemption under paragraph (a)(3) will serve the other participants in the proceeding by physically delivering or mailing a paper copy.

(4) A certificate of service stating the names and addresses of the persons served as well as the method and date of service must accompany any paper served upon participants to the proceeding.

(5) Proof of service, which states the name and address of the person served

as well as the method and date of service, may be made as required by law, by rule, or by order of the Commission.

[72 FR 49152, Aug. 28, 2007]

§ 13.27 Computation of time.

(a) In computing any period of time under this part or in an order issued thereunder, the time begins with the day following the act, event, or default, and includes the last day of the period, unless it is a Saturday or Sunday, a Federal legal holiday at the place where the action or event is to occur, or a day on which, because of emergency closure of the federal government in Washington, DC, NRC Headquarters does not open for business, in which event it includes the next day that is not a Saturday, Sunday, holiday or emergency closure.

(b) When the period of time allowed is less than seven (7) days, intermediate Saturdays, Sundays, Federal legal holidays, and emergency closures shall be excluded from the computation.

(c) Whenever an action is required within a prescribed period by a document served pursuant to § 13.26, no additional time is added to the prescribed period except in the following circumstances:

(1) If a notice or document is served upon a participant, by first-class mail only, three (3) calendar days will be added to the prescribed period for all the participants in the proceeding.

(2) If a notice or document is served upon a participant, by express mail or other expedited service only, two (2) calendar days will be added to the prescribed period for all the participants in the proceeding.

(3) If a document is to be served by multiple service methods, such as partially electronic and entirely on an OSM, the additional number of days is computed according to the service method used to deliver the entire document, excluding courtesy copies, to all of the other participants in the proceeding. The presiding officer may determine the calculation of additional days when a participant is not entitled to receive an entire filing served by multiple methods.

(4) In mixed service proceedings where all participants are not using the same filing and service method, the number of days for service will be determined by the presiding officer based on considerations of fairness and efficiency. The same number of additional days will be added to the prescribed period for all the participants in the proceeding with the number of days being determined by the slowest method of service being used in the proceeding.

(d) To be considered timely, a document must be served:

(1) By 5 p.m. Eastern Time for a document served in person or by expedited service; and

(2) By 11:59 p.m. Eastern Time for a document served by the E-Filing system.

[72 FR 49153, Aug. 28, 2007]

§ 13.28 Motions.

(a) Any application to the ALJ for an order or ruling shall be by motion. Motions shall state the relief sought, the authority relied upon, and the facts alleged, and shall be filed with the ALJ and served on all other parties.

(b) Except for motions made during a prehearing conference or at the hearing, all motions shall be in writing. The ALJ may require that oral motions be reduced to writing.

(c) Within 15 days after a written motion is served, or such other time as may be fixed by the ALJ, any party may file a response to such motion.

(d) The ALJ may not grant a written motion before the time for filing responses thereto has expired, except upon consent of the parties or following a hearing on the motion, but may overrule or deny such motion without awaiting a response.

(e) The ALJ shall make a reasonable effort to dispose of all outstanding motions prior to the beginning of the hearing.

§ 13.29 Sanctions.

(a) The ALJ may sanction a person, including any party or representative for—

(1) Failing to comply with an order, rule, or procedure governing the proceeding;

(2) Failing to prosecute or defend an action; or

(3) Engaging in other misconduct that interferes with the speedy, orderly, or fair conduct of the hearing.

(b) Any such sanction, including but not limited to those listed in paragraphs (c), (d), and (e) of this section, shall reasonably relate to the severity and nature of the failure or misconduct.

(c) When a party fails to comply with an order, including an order for taking a deposition, the production of evidence within the party's control, or a request for admission, the ALJ may—

(1) Draw an inference in favor of the requesting party with regard to the information sought;

(2) In the case of requests for admission, deem each matter of which an admission is requested to be admitted;

(3) Prohibit the party failing to comply with such order from introducing evidence concerning, or otherwise relying upon testimony relating to the information sought; and

(4) Strike any part of the pleadings or other submissions of the party failing to comply with such request.

(d) If a party fails to prosecute or defend an action under this part commenced by service of a notice of hearing, the ALJ may dismiss the action or may issue an initial decision imposing penalties and assessments.

(e) The ALJ may refuse to consider any motion, request, response, brief or other document which is not filed in a timely fashion.

§ 13.30 The hearing and burden of proof.

(a) The ALJ shall conduct a hearing on the record in order to determine whether the defendant is liable for a civil penalty or assessment under § 13.3 and, if so, the appropriate amount of any such civil penalty or assessment considering any aggravating or mitigating factors.

(b) The authority shall prove defendant's liability and any aggravating factors by a preponderance of the evidence.

(c) The defendant shall prove any affirmative defenses and any mitigating factors by a preponderance of the evidence.

(d) The hearing shall be open to the public unless otherwise ordered by the ALJ for good cause shown.

§ 13.31 Determining the amount of penalties and assessments.

(a) In determining an appropriate amount of civil penalties and assessments, the ALJ and the authority head, upon appeal, should evaluate any circumstances that mitigate or aggravate the violation and should articulate in their opinions the reasons that support the penalties and assessments they impose. Because of the intangible costs of fraud, the expense of investigating such conduct, and the need to deter others who might be similarly tempted, ordinarily double damages and a significant civil penalty should be imposed.

(b) Although not exhaustive, the following factors are among those that may influence the ALJ and the authority head in determining the amount of penalties and assessments to impose with respect to the misconduct (*i.e.*, the false, fictitious, or fraudulent claims or statements) charged in the complaint:

(1) The number of false, fictitious, or fraudulent claims or statements;

(2) The time period over which such claims or statements were made;

(3) The degree of the defendant's culpability with respect to the misconduct;

(4) The amount of money or the value of the property, services, or benefit falsely claimed;

(5) The value of the Government's actual loss as a result of the misconduct, including foreseeable consequential damages and the costs of investigation;

(6) The relationship of the amount imposed as civil penalties to the amount of the Government's loss;

(7) The potential or actual impact of the misconduct upon national defense, public health or safety, or public confidence in the management of Government programs and operations, including particularly the impact on the intended beneficiaries of such programs;

(8) Whether the defendant has engaged in a pattern of the same or similar misconduct;

(9) Whether the defendant attempted to conceal the misconduct;

(10) The degree to which the defendant has involved others in the misconduct or in concealing it;

(11) Where the misconduct of employees or agents is imputed to the defendant, the extent to which the defendant's practices fostered or attempted to preclude such misconduct;

(12) Whether the defendant cooperated in or obstructed an investigation of the misconduct;

(13) Whether the defendant assisted in identifying and prosecuting other wrongdoers;

(14) The complexity of the program or transaction, and the degree of the defendant's sophistication with respect to it, including the extent of the defendant's prior participation in the program or in similar transactions;

(15) Whether the defendant has been found, in any criminal, civil, or administrative proceeding to have engaged in similar misconduct or to have dealt dishonestly with the Government of the United States or of a State, directly or indirectly; and

(16) The need to deter the defendant and others from engaging in the same or similar misconduct.

(c) Nothing in this section shall be construed to limit the ALJ or the authority head from considering any other factors that in any given case may mitigate or aggravate the offense for which penalties and assessments are imposed.

§ 13.32 Location of hearing.

(a) The hearing may be held—

(1) In any judicial district of the United States in which the defendant resides or transacts business;

(2) In any judicial district of the United States in which the claim or statement in issue was made; or

(3) In such other place as may be agreed upon by the defendant and the ALJ.

(b) Each party shall have the opportunity to present argument with respect to the location of the hearing.

(c) The hearing shall be held at the place and at the time ordered by the ALJ.

§ 13.33 Witnesses.

(a) Except as provided in paragraph (b) of this section, testimony at the hearing shall be given orally by witnesses under oath or affirmation.

(b) At the discretion of the ALJ, testimony may be admitted in the form of a written statement or deposition. Any such written statement must be provided to all other parties along with the last known address of such witness, in a manner which allows sufficient time for other parties to subpoena such witness for cross-examination at the hearing. Prior written statements of witnesses proposed to testify at the hearing and deposition transcripts shall be exchanged as provided in § 13.22(a).

(c) The ALJ shall exercise reasonable control over the mode and order of interrogating witnesses and presenting evidence so as to—

(1) Make the interrogation and presentation effective for the ascertainment of the truth;

(2) Avoid needless consumption of time; and

(3) Protect witnesses from harassment or undue embarrassment.

(d) The ALJ shall permit the parties to conduct such cross-examination as may be required for a full and true disclosure of the facts.

(e) At the discretion of the ALJ, a witness may be cross-examined on matters relevant to the proceeding without regard to the scope of his or her direct examination. To the extent permitted by the ALJ, cross-examination on matters outside the scope of direct examination shall be conducted in the manner of direct examination and may proceed by leading questions only if the witness is a hostile witness, an adverse party, or a witness identified with an adverse party.

(f) Upon motion of any party, the ALJ shall order witnesses excluded so that they cannot hear the testimony of other witnesses. This rule does not authorize exclusion of—

(1) A party who is an individual;

(2) In the case of a party that is not an individual, an officer or employee of the party appearing for the entity pro se or designated by the party's representative; or

(3) An individual whose presence is shown by a party to be essential to the presentation of its case, including an

individual employed by the Government engaged in assisting the representative for the Government.

§ 13.34 Evidence.

(a) The ALJ shall determine the admissibility of evidence.

(b) Except as provided in this part, the ALJ shall not be bound by the Federal Rules of Evidence. However, the ALJ may apply the Federal Rules of Evidence where appropriate, e.g., to exclude unreliable evidence.

(c) The ALJ shall exclude irrelevant and immaterial evidence.

(d) Although relevant, evidence may be excluded if its probative value is substantially outweighed by the danger of unfair prejudice, confusion of the issues, or by considerations of undue delay or needless presentation of cumulative evidence.

(e) Although relevant, evidence may be excluded if it is privileged under Federal law.

(f) Evidence concerning offers of compromise or settlement shall be inadmissible to the extent provided in Rule 408 of the Federal Rules of Evidence.

(g) The ALJ shall permit the parties to introduce rebuttal witnesses and evidence.

(h) All documents and other evidence offered or taken for the record shall be open to examination by all parties, unless otherwise ordered by the ALJ pursuant to § 13.24.

§ 13.35 The record.

(a) The hearing will be recorded and transcribed. Transcripts may be obtained following the hearing from the ALJ at a cost not to exceed the actual cost of duplication.

(b) The transcript of testimony, exhibits and other evidence admitted at the hearing, and all papers and requests filed in the proceeding constitute the record for the decision by the ALJ and the authority head.

(c) The record may be inspected and copied (upon payment of a reasonable fee) by anyone, unless otherwise ordered by the ALJ pursuant to § 13.24.

§ 13.36 Post-hearing briefs.

The ALJ may require the parties to file post-hearing briefs. In any event, any party may file a post-hearing brief. The ALJ shall fix the time for filing such briefs, not to exceed 60 days from the date the parties receive the transcript of the hearing or, if applicable, the stipulated record. Such briefs may be accompanied by proposed findings of fact and conclusions of law. The ALJ may permit the parties to file reply briefs.

§ 13.37 Initial decision.

(a) The ALJ shall issue an initial decision based only on the record, which shall contain findings of fact, conclusions of law, and the amount of any penalties and assessments imposed.

(b) The findings of fact shall include a finding on each of the following issues:

(1) Whether the claims or statements identified in the complaint, or any portions thereof, violate § 13.3; and

(2) If the person is liable for penalties or assessments, the appropriate amount of any such penalties or assessments considering any mitigating or aggravating factors that he or she finds in the case, such as those described in § 13.31.

(c) The ALJ shall promptly serve the initial decision on all parties within 90 days after the time for submission of post-hearing briefs and reply briefs (if permitted) has expired. The ALJ shall at the same time serve all parties with a statement describing the right of any defendant determined to be liable for a civil penalty or assessment to file a motion for reconsideration with the ALJ or a notice of appeal with the authority head. If the ALJ fails to meet the deadline contained in this paragraph, he or she shall notify the parties of the reason for the delay and shall set a new deadline.

(d) Unless the initial decision of the ALJ is timely appealed to the authority head, or a motion for reconsideration of the initial decision is timely filed, the initial decision shall constitute the final decision of the authority head and shall be final and binding on the parties 30 days after it is issued by the ALJ.

§ 13.38 Reconsideration of initial decision.

(a) Except as provided in paragraph (d) of this section, any party may file a motion for reconsideration of the initial decision within 20 days of receipt of the initial decision. If service was made by mail, receipt will be presumed to be five days from the date of mailing in the absence of contrary proof.

(b) Every such motion must set forth the matters claimed to have been erroneously decided and the nature of the alleged errors. Such motion shall be accompanied by a supporting brief.

(c) Responses to such motions shall be allowed only upon request of the ALJ.

(d) No party may file a motion for reconsideration of an initial decision that has been revised in response to a previous motion for reconsideration.

(e) The ALJ may dispose of a motion for reconsideration by denying it or by issuing a revised initial decision.

(f) If the ALJ denies a motion for reconsideration, the initial decision shall constitute the final decision of the authority head and shall be final and binding on the parties 30 days after the ALJ denies the motion, unless the initial decision is timely appealed to the authority head in accordance with § 13.39.

(g) If the ALJ issues a revised initial decision, that decision shall constitute the final decision of the authority head and shall be final and binding on the parties 30 days after it is issued, unless it is timely appealed to the authority head in accordance with § 13.39.

§ 13.39 Appeal to authority head.

(a) Any defendant who has filed a timely answer and who is determined in an initial decision to be liable for a civil penalty or assessment may appeal such decision to the authority head by filing a notice of appeal with the authority head in accordance with this section.

(b)(1) A notice of appeal may be filed at any time within 30 days after the ALJ issues an initial decision. However, if another party files a motion for reconsideration under § 13.38, consideration of the appeal shall be stayed automatically pending resolution of the motion for reconsideration.

(2) If a motion for reconsideration is timely filed, a notice of appeal may be filed within 30 days after the ALJ denies the motion or issues a revised initial decision, whichever applies.

(3) The authority head may extend the initial 30 day period for an additional 30 days if the defendant files with the authority head a request for an extension within the initial 30 day period and shows good cause.

(c) If the defendant files a timely notice of appeal with the authority head and the time for filing motions for reconsideration under § 13.38 has expired, the ALJ shall forward the record of the proceeding to the authority head.

(d) A notice of appeal shall be accompanied by a written brief specifying exceptions to the initial decision and reasons supporting the exceptions.

(e) The representative for the Government may file a brief in opposition to exceptions within 30 days of receiving the notice of appeal and accompanying brief.

(f) There is no right to appear personally before the authority head.

(g) There is no right to appeal any interlocutory ruling by the ALJ.

(h) In reviewing the initial decision, the authority head shall not consider any objection that was not raised before the ALJ unless a demonstration is made of extraordinary circumstances causing the failure to raise the objection.

(i) If any party demonstrates to the satisfaction of the authority head that additional evidence not presented at each hearing is material and that there were reasonable grounds for the failure to present such evidence at such hearing, the authority head shall remand the matter to the ALJ for consideration of such additional evidence.

(j) The authority head may affirm, reduce, reverse, compromise, remand, or settle any penalty or assessment, determined by the ALJ in any initial decision.

(k) The authority head shall promptly serve each party to the appeal with a copy of the decision of the authority head and a statement describing the right of any person determined to be liable for a penalty or assessment to seek judicial review.

(l) Unless a petition for review is filed as provided in 31 U.S.C. 3805 after a defendant has exhausted all administrative remedies under this part and within 60 days after the date on which the authority head serves the defendant with a copy of the authority head's decision, a determination that a defendant is liable under § 13.3 is final and is not subject to judicial review.

§ 13.40 Stays ordered by the Department of Justice.

If at any time the Attorney General or an Assistant Attorney General designated by the Attorney General transmits to the authority head a written finding that continuation of the administrative process described in this part with respect to a claim or statement may adversely affect any pending or potential criminal or civil action related to such claim or statement, the authority head shall stay the process immediately. The authority head may order the process resumed only upon receipt of the written authorization of the Attorney General.

§ 13.41 Stay pending appeal.

(a) An initial decision is stayed automatically pending disposition of a motion for reconsideration or of an appeal to the authority head.

(b) No administrative stay is available following a final decision of the authority head.

§ 13.42 Judicial review.

Section 3805 of title 31, United States Code, authorizes judicial review by an appropriate United States District Court of a final decision of the authority head imposing penalties or assessments under this part and specifies the procedures for such review.

§ 13.43 Collection of civil penalties and assessments.

Sections 3806 and 3808(b) of title 31, United States Code, authorize actions for collection of civil penalties and assessments imposed under this part and specify the procedures for such actions.

§ 13.44 Right to administrative offset.

The amount of any penalty or assessment which has become final, or for which a judgment has been entered under § 13.42 or § 13.43, or any amount agreed upon in a compromise or settlement under § 13.46, may be collected by administrative offset under 31 U.S.C. 3716, except that an administrative offset may not be made under this subsection against a refund of an overpayment of Federal taxes, then or later owing by the United States to the defendant.

§ 13.45 Deposit in Treasury of United States.

All amounts collected pursuant to this part shall be deposited as miscellaneous receipts in the Treasury of the United States, except as provided in 31 U.S.C. 3806(g).

§ 13.46 Compromise or settlement.

(a) Parties may make offers of compromise or settlement at any time.

(b) The reviewing official has the exclusive authority to compromise or settle a case under this part at any time after the date on which the reviewing official is permitted to issue a complaint and before the date on which the ALJ issues an initial decision.

(c) The authority head has exclusive authority to compromise or settle a case under this part at any time after the date on which the ALJ issues an initial decision, except during the pendency of any review under § 13.42 or during the pendancy of any action to collect penalties and assessments under § 13.43.

(d) The Attorney General has exclusive authority to compromise or settle a case under this part during the pendancy of any review under § 13.42 or of any action to recover penalties and assessments under 31 U.S.C. 3806.

(e) The investigating officer may recommend settlement terms to the reviewing official, the authority head, or the Attorney General, as appropriate. The reviewing official may recommend settlement terms to the authority head, or the Attorney General, as appropriate.

(f) Any compromise or settlement must be in writing.

§ 13.47 Limitations.

(a) The notice of hearing with respect to a claim or statement must be served in the manner specified in § 13.8 within 6 years after the date on which such claim or statement is made.

(b) If the defendant fails to serve a timely answer, service of a notice under § 13.10(b) shall be deemed a notice of hearing for purposes of this section.

(c) The statute of limitations may be extended by agreement of the parties.

PART 14—ADMINISTRATIVE CLAIMS UNDER FEDERAL TORT CLAIMS ACT

Subpart A—General

AUTHORITY: 28 U.S.C. 2672, 2679; Atomic Energy Act of 1954, sec. 161 (42 U.S.C. 2201); Energy Reorganization Act of 1974, sec. 201 (42 U.S.C. 5841); 28 CFR 14.11.

SOURCE: 47 FR 8983, Mar. 3, 1982, unless otherwise noted.

Subpart A—General

§ 14.1 Scope of regulations.

(a) The terms "Nuclear Regulatory Commission" and "NRC" as used in this part mean the agency established by section 201(a) of the Energy Reorganization Act of 1974, but do not include any contractor with the Nuclear Regulatory Commission.

(b) The regulations in this part supplement the Department of Justice's regulations in 28 CFR parts 14 and 15.

(c) These regulations apply to administrative claims under the Federal Tort Claims Act, as amended, asserted on or after the effective date of this rule, for money damages against the United States for damage to or loss of property or personal injury or death caused by the negligent or wrongful act or omission of any employee of the NRC while acting within the scope of his or her office or employment, under circumstances where the United States, if a private person, would be liable to the claimant in accordance with the law of the place where the act or omission occurred.

(d) These regulations also set forth the procedures when lawsuits are commenced against an employee of the NRC resulting from the operation of a motor vehicle while acting within the scope of his or her employment.

§ 14.3 Limit on attorney fees; penalty.

(a) An attorney may not charge or receive fees in excess of:

(1) 25 percent of any judgment rendered under 28 U.S.C. 1346(b);

(2) 25 percent of any settlement made under 28 U.S.C. 2677; or

(3) 20 percent of any award, compromise, or settlement made under 28 U.S.C. 2672.

(b) Any attorney who charges or receives any amount in excess of that allowed under this section is subject to a fine of not more than $2,000 or imprisonment for not more than one year, or both. (28 U.S.C. 2678)

Subpart B—Filing Procedures and Requirements

§ 14.11 Who may file a claim.

(a) A claim for damage to or loss of property may be presented by the owner of the property interest which is the subject of the claim, his or her duly authorized agent, or his or her legal representative.

(b) A claim for personal injury may be presented by the injured person, his or her duly authorized agent, or his or her legal representative.

(c) A claim based on death may be presented by the executor or administrator of the decedent's estate, or by any other person legally entitled to assert the claim under applicable State law.

(d) A claim for loss wholly compensated by an insurer with the rights of a subrogee may be presented by the insurer. A claim for loss partially compensated by an insurer with the rights of a subrogee may be presented by the insurer or the insured individually, to the extent of their respective interests, or jointly. Whenever an insurer presents a claim asserting the rights of a subrogee, the insurer shall present with the claim appropriate evidence that the insurer has the rights of a subrogee.

(e) If a claim is presented by an agent or legal representative that person shall:

(1) Present the claim in the name of the claimant;

(2) Sign the claim;

(3) Show the title or legal capacity of the person signing the claim; and

(4) Include with the claim evidence of his or her authority to present a claim on behalf of the claimant as agent, executor, administrator, parent, guardian, or other representative.

§ 14.13 When is a claim presented to NRC.

For purposes of the provisions of 28 U.S.C. 2672, a claim is presented when NRC receives from a claimant, or the claimant's duly authorized agent or legal representative, an executed Standard Form 95 or other written notification of an incident. An executed Standard Form 95 or written notification must be accompanied by a claim for money damages in a sum certain for damage to or loss of property, personal injury, or death alleged to have occurred by reason of the incident.

§ 14.15 Where to present a claim to NRC.

A claimant shall mail or deliver the claim to the office of employment of the NRC employee whose negligent or wrongful act or omission is alleged to have caused the loss or injury. If the office of employment is not known, the claimant shall file the claim with the Office of the General Counsel, U.S. Nuclear Regulatory Commission, Washington, DC 20555.

[47 FR 8983, Mar. 3, 1982, as amended at 51 FR 35999, Oct. 8, 1986]

§ 14.17 A claim must be presented to the appropriate agency.

A claimant shall present the claim to the Federal agency whose activities gave rise to the claim. If a claim is erroneously presented to the NRC, the NRC shall transfer it to the appropriate agency, if the proper agency can be identified from the claim, and shall advise the claimant of the transfer. If transfer is not feasible, the NRC shall return the claim to the claimant. The fact of transfer does not, in itself, preclude further transfer, return of the claim to the claimant, or other appropriate disposition of the claim. A claim shall be presented, as required by 28 U.S.C. 2401(b), as of the date it is received by the appropriate agency.

§ 14.19 When a claim is filed with more than one agency.

(a) If the NRC and one or more other Federal agencies is or may be involved in the events giving rise to the claim, and if the claim is filed with the NRC, the NRC shall contact all other affected agencies in order to designate the single agency which will investigate and decide the merits of the claim.

(1) In the event that an agreed upon designation cannot be made by the affected agencies, the Department of Justice will be consulted and will designate a primary agency to investigate and decide the merits of the claim. If the NRC is designated as the primary agency, it shall notify the claimant that all future correspondence concerning the claim shall be directed to the NRC.

(2) All involved Federal agencies can agree either to conduct their own administrative reviews and to coordinate the results or to have the investigations conducted by the primary agency. In either event, the primary agency is responsible for the final determination of the claim.

(b) A claimant presenting a claim arising from an incident to more than one agency should identify each agency to which the claim is submitted at the time each claim is presented. If a claim arising from an incident is presented to more than one Federal agency without any indication that more than one agency is involved, and any one of the concerned Federal agencies takes final action on that claim, the final action is conclusive on the claims presented to the other agencies in regard to the time required for filing suit set forth in 28 U.S.C. 2401(b). However, if NRC, as a subsequently involved Federal agency, desires to take further action with a view towards settling the claim, the NRC may treat the matter as a request for reconsideration of the final denial under 10 CFR 14.39, unless suit has been filed in the interim, and advise the claimant of the action.

§ 14.21 Filing a claim after an agency final denial.

If, after a final denial by another agency, the claimant files with the NRC a claim arising out of the same incident on which the claim filed with the other agency was based, the submission of the claim to NRC will not toll the requirement of 28 U.S.C. 2401(b) that suit must be filed within six months of the final denial by the other agency, unless the other agency specifically and explicitly treats the submission to NRC as a request for reconsideration under 10 CFR 14.39 and advises the claimant of the action.

§ 14.23 Evidence and information to be submitted.

(a) *Death.* In support of a claim based on death, the claimant may be required to submit the following evidence or information:

(1) An authenticated death certificate or other competent evidence showing cause of death, date of death, and age of decedent.

(2) Decedent's employment or occupation at time of death, including his or her monthly or yearly salary or earnings (if any), and the duration of his or her last employment or occupation.

(3) Full names, addresses, birth dates, kinship, and marital status of the decedent's survivors, including identification of those survivors who were dependent for support upon the decedent at the time of death.

(4) Degree of support afforded by the decedent to each survivor dependent upon him or her for support at the time of death.

(5) Decedent's general physical and mental condition before death.

(6) Itemized bills for medical and burial expenses incurred by reason of the incident causing death, or itemized receipts of payment for these expenses.

(7) If damages for pain and suffering prior to death are claimed, a physician's detailed statement specifying the injuries suffered, duration of pain and suffering, any drugs administered for pain, and the decedent's physical condition in the interval between injury and death.

(8) Any other evidence or information which may have a bearing on either the responsibility of the United States for the death or the amount of damages claimed.

(b) *Personal injury.* In support of a claim for personal injury, including pain and suffering, the claimant may be required to submit the following evidence or information:

(1) A written report by the attending physician or dentist setting forth the nature and extent of the injury, nature and extent of treatment, any degree of temporary or permanent disability and prognosis, period of hospitalization, and any diminished earning capacity. In addition, the claimant may be required to submit to a physical or mental examination by a physician employed by the NRC or another Federal agency. The claimant may request in writing a copy of the report of the examining physician if the claimant has:

(i) Furnished the report referred to in paragraph (a)(1) of this section on request; and

(ii) Made or agrees to make available to the NRC all other reports of the claimant's physical or mental condition which have been or are made by any physician.

(2) Itemized bills for medical, dental, and hospital expenses incurred, or itemized receipts of payment for these expenses.

(3) If the prognosis reveals the necessity for future treatment, a statement of expected expenses for the treatment.

(4) If a claim is made for loss of time from employment, a written statement from his or her employer showing actual time lost from employment, whether he or she is a full- or part-time employee, and wages or salary actually lost.

(5) If a claim is made for loss of income and the claimant is self-employed, documentary evidence showing the amount of earnings actually lost.

(6) Any other evidence or information which may have a bearing on either the responsibility of the United States for the personal injury or the damages claimed.

(c) *Property damage.* In support of a claim for damage to or loss of property, real or personal, the claimant may be required to submit the following evidence or information:

(1) Proof of ownership of the property interest which is the subject of the claim.

(2) A detailed statement of the amount claimed with respect to each item of property.

(3) An itemized receipt of payment for necessary repairs or itemized written estimates of the cost of these repairs.

(4) A statement listing date of purchase, purchase price, and salvage value, where repair is not economical.

(5) Any other evidence or information which may have a bearing on either the responsibility of the United States for the injury to or loss of property or the damages claimed.

§ 14.25 Amending a claim.

The claimant may amend a claim presented in compliance with 10 CFR 14.13 at any time prior to final agency action or prior to the exercise of the claimant's option under 28 U.S.C. 2675(a). The claimant or his or her duly authorized agent or legal representative shall sign each amendment and submit it in writing. Upon the timely filing of an amendment to a pending claim, the agency shall have six months in which to make a final disposition of the claim as amended and the claimant's option under 28 U.S.C. 2675(a) does not accrue until six months after the filing of an amendment.

§ 14.27 Time limit.

The claimant shall furnish evidence and information of the types described in 10 CFR 14.23, to the extent reasonably practicable, when the claim is initially presented. If the claimant fails to furnish sufficient evidence and information within six months after the claim was initially presented to enable NRC to adjust, determine, compromise and settle the claim, NRC may consider the claim a nullity.

Subpart C—Commission Action and Authority

§ 14.31 Investigation.

The NRC may:

(a) Require the claimant to furnish any evidence or information which is relevant to its consideration of the claim;

(b) Examine the claimant; or

(c) Investigate, or request any other Federal agency to investigate, a claim filed under this part.

§ 14.33 Officials authorized to act.

The General Counsel or the General Counsel's designee shall exercise the authority to adjust, determine, compromise and settle a claim under the provisions of 28 U.S.C. 2672.

[51 FR 35999, Oct. 8, 1986]

§ 14.35 Limitation on NRC's authority.

(a) The NRC shall effect an award, compromise, or settlement of a claim hereunder in excess of $25,000 only with the prior written approval of the Attorney General or his designee. For the purposes of this paragraph, a principal claim and any derivative or subrogated claim are treated as a single claim.

(b) The NRC may adjust, determine, compromise, or settle a claim under this part only after consultation with the Department of Justice if, in the opinion of the Office of the General Counsel:

(1) A new precedent or a new point of law is involved;

(2) A question of policy is or may be involved;

(3) The United States is or may be entitled to indemnity or contribution from a third party and the NRC is unable to adjust the third party claim; or

(4) The compromise of a particular claim, as a practical matter, will or may control the disposition of a related claim in which the amount to be paid may exceed $25,000.

(c) The NRC may adjust, determine, compromise, or settle a claim under this part only after consultation with the Department of Justice if the NRC is informed or is otherwise aware that the United States, or an employee, agent, or cost-plus contractor of the United States, is involved in litigation based on a claim arising out of the same incident or transaction.

(d) When Department of Justice approval or consultation is required under this section or the advice of the Department of Justice is otherwise requested, the NRC shall direct the referral or request to the Assistant Attorney General, Civil Division, Department of Justice, in writing. The NRC shall ensure that the referral or request contains:

(1) A short and concise statement of the facts and the reasons for the referral or request;

(2) Copies of relevant portions of NRC's claim file; and

(3) A statement of the recommendations or views of the NRC.

A referral or request to the Department of Justice may be made at any time after presentment of a claim to the NRC.

[47 FR 8983, Mar. 3, 1982, as amended at 51 FR 35999, Oct. 8, 1986]

§ 14.37 Final denial of claim.

The NRC shall send notice of a final denial of a claim in writing to the claimant, his or her attorney or legal representative, by certified or registered mail. The notification of final denial may include a statement of the reasons for the denial. The NRC shall include a statement in the notification of final denial that, if the claimant is dissatisfied with NRC's action, he or she may file suit in an appropriate U.S. District Court not later than 6 months after the date of mailing of the notification.

§ 14.39 Reconsideration of a claim.

Prior to the commencement of suit and prior to the expiration of the 6-month period provided in 28 U.S.C. 2401(b), a claimant, or his or her duly authorized agent, or legal representative, may file a written request with the NRC for reconsideration of a final denial of a claim. Upon the timely filing of a request for reconsideration, the NRC shall have 6 months from the date of filing in which to make a final disposition of the claim, and the claimant's option under 28 U.S.C. 2675(a) does not accrue until 6 months after the filing of a request for reconsideration. Final NRC action on a request for reconsideration shall be effected in accordance with the provisions of 10 CFR 14.37.

§ 14.41 Payment of approved claims.

(a) The NRC shall pay any award, compromise, or settlement in an amount of $2,500 or less made under the provisions of 28 U.S.C. 2672 out of the appropriations available to it. The NRC shall obtain payment of any award, compromise, or settlement in excess of $2,500 from the Department of the Treasury by forwarding Standard Form 1145 to the Payment Branch, Claims Group, General Accounting Office. If an award, compromise, or settlement is in excess of $25,000, Standard Form 1145 must be accompanied by evidence that the award, compromise, or settlement has been approved by the Attorney General or the Attorney General's designee. When the use of Standard Form 1145 is required, it must be executed by the claimant or it must be accompanied by either a claims settlement agreement or a Standard Form 95 executed by the claimant.

(b) If a claimant is represented by an attorney, the voucher for payment must designate both the claimant and his or her attorney as payees, and the check must be delivered to the attorney whose address appears on the voucher.

§ 14.43 Acceptance of payment constitutes release.

Acceptance by the claimant, his agent, or legal representative, of any award, compromise, or settlement made under the provisions of 28 U.S.C.

2672 or 2677, is final and conclusive on the claimant, his or her agent or legal representative and any other person on whose behalf or for whose benefit the claim has been presented. Acceptance constitutes a complete release of any claim against the United States and against any employee of the Government whose act or omission gave rise to the claim.

Subpart D—Employee Drivers

§ 14.51 Procedures when employee drivers are sued.

(a) Any NRC employee against whom a civil action or proceeding is brought for damage to property, or for personal injury or death, on account of the employee's operation of a motor vehicle in the scope of his or her office or employment with the NRC, shall promptly deliver all process and pleadings served upon the employee, or an attested true copy, to the Office of the General Counsel. If the action is brought against an employee's estate, this procedure applies to the employee's personal representative.

(b) In addition, upon the employee's receipt of any process or pleadings, or any prior information regarding the commencement of a civil action or proceeding, the employee shall immediately advise the Office of the General Counsel by telephone or telegraph

[47 FR 8983, Mar. 3, 1982, as amended at 51 FR 35999, Oct. 8, 1986]

§ 14.53 Scope of employment report.

A report containing all data bearing upon the question whether the employee was acting within the scope of his or her office or employment will be furnished by the General Counsel or designee to the United States Attorney for the district encompassing the place where the civil action or proceeding is brought. A copy of the report also will be furnished to the Director of the Torts Branch, Civil Division, Department of Justice, at the earliest possible date, or within the time specified by the United States Attorney.

[51 FR 35999, Oct. 8, 1986]

§ 14.55 Removal of State court proceedings.

Upon a certification by the United States Attorney that the defendant employee was acting within the scope of his or her office or employment at the time of the incident out of which the suit arose, any civil action or proceeding commenced in a State court may be removed to the district court of the United States for the district and division encompassing the place where the action or proceeding is pending in accordance with 28 U.S.C. 2679.

§ 14.57 Suit against United States exclusive remedy.

The remedy against the United States provided by 28 U.S.C. 1346(b) and 2672 for damage to or loss of property or personal injury or death, resulting from the operation by an employee of the Government of any motor vehicle while acting within the scope of his or her office or employment, is exclusive of any other civil action or proceeding by reason of the same subject matter against the employee or his or her estate whose act or omission gave rise to the claim.

PART 15—DEBT COLLECTION PROCEDURES

Subpart A—Application and Coverage

Subpart B—Administrative Collection of Claims

AUTHORITY: Atomic Energy Act of 1954, secs. 161, 186 (42 U.S.C. 2201, 2236); Energy Reorganization Act of 1974, sec. 201 (42 U.S.C. 5841); 5 U.S.C. 5514; 26 U.S.C. 6402; 31 U.S.C. 3701, 3713, 3716, 3719, 3720A; 42 U.S.C. 664; 44 U.S.C. 3504 note; 31 CFR parts 900 through 904; 31 CFR part 285; E.O. 12146, 44 FR 42657, 3 CFR, 1979 Comp., p. 409; E.O. 12988, 61 FR 4729, 3 CFR, 1996 Comp., p. 157.

SOURCE: 47 FR 7616, Feb. 22, 1982, unless otherwise noted.

Subpart A—Application and Coverage

§ 15.1 Application.

(a) This part applies to claims for the payment of debts owed to the United States Government in the form of money or property and; unless a different procedure is specified in a statute, regulation, or contract; prescribes procedures by which the NRC—

(1) Collects, compromises, suspends, offsets, and terminates collection action for claims;

(2) Determines and collects interest and other charges on these claims; and

(3) Refers unpaid claims over 180 days delinquent to Treasury for offset and collection and to the DOJ for litigation.

(b) The following are examples of kinds of debts to which special statutory and administrative procedures apply:

(1) A claim against an employee for erroneous payment of pay and allowances subject to waiver under 5 U.S.C. 5584 are covered by the provisions of 10 CFR part 16.

(2) A claim against an applicant for, or a holder or former holder of, an NRC license involving the payment of civil penalties imposed by the NRC under 10 CFR 2.205.

(3) A claim involved in a case pending before any Federal Contract Appeals Board or Grant Appeals Board. However, nothing in this part prevents negotiation and settlement of a claim pending before a Board.

(c) The NRC is not limited to collection remedies contained in the revised Federal Claims Collection Standards (FCCS). The FCCS is not intended to impair common law remedies.

[47 FR 7616, Feb. 22, 1982, as amended at 55 FR 32377, Aug. 9, 1990; 56 FR 51830, Oct. 16, 1991; 67 FR 30318, May 6, 2002]

§ 15.2 Definitions.

Administrative offset means withholding money payable by the United States Government to, or held by the Government for, a person to satisfy a debt the person owes the United States Government.

Administrative wage garnishment is the process of withholding amounts from an employee's disposable pay and the paying of those amounts to a creditor in satisfaction of a withholding order.

Claim and *debt* are used synonymously to refer to an amount of money, funds, or property that has been determined by an agency official to be owed to the United States from any person, organization, or entity, except another Federal agency. For the purposes of administrative offset under 31 U.S.C. 3716, the terms *claim* and *debt* include an amount of money, funds, or property owed by a person to a State (including past-due support being enforced by a State), the District of Columbia, American Samoa, Guam, the United States Virgin Islands, the Commonwealth of the Northern Mariana Islands, or the Commonwealth of Puerto Rico.

Cross-servicing means that the Treasury or another debt collection center is taking appropriate debt collection action on behalf of one or more Federal agencies or a unit or subagency thereof.

Delinquent. A debt is considered delinquent if it has not been paid by the date specified in the initial written demand for payment or applicable contractual agreement with the NRC unless other satisfactory payment arrangements have been made by that date. If the debtor fails to satisfy obligations under a payment agreement with the NRC after other payment arrangements have been made, the debt becomes a delinquent debt.

Federal agencies include agencies of the executive, legislative, and judicial branches of the Government, including Government corporations.

License means any license, permit, or other approval issued by the Commission.

Payment in full means payment of the total debt due the United States, including any interest, penalty, and administrative costs of collection assessed against the debtor.

Recoupment is a special method for adjusting debts arising under the same transaction or occurrence. For example, obligations arising under the same contract generally are subject to recoupment.

Salary offset means an administrative offset to collect a debt under 5 U.S.C. 5514 by deduction(s) at one or more officially established pay intervals from the current pay account of an employee without his/her consent.

Tax refund offset means withholding or reducing a tax refund payment by an amount necessary to satisfy a debt owed by the payee(s) of a tax refund payment.

Treasury as used in 10 CFR part 15 means the Department of the Treasury.

Withholding order means any order for withholding or garnishment of pay issued by an agency, or judicial or administrative body.

[55 FR 32377, Aug. 9, 1990, as amended at 56 FR 51830, Oct. 16, 1991; 67 FR 30318, May 6, 2002]

§15.3 Communications.

Unless otherwise specified, communications concerning the regulations in this part may be addressed to the Secretary of the Nuclear Regulatory Commission and sent either by mail to the U.S. Nuclear Regulatory Commission, Washington, DC 20555–0001, ATTN: Rulemakings and Adjudications Staff; by hand delivery to the NRC's offices at 11555 Rockville Pike, One White Flint North, Rockville, Maryland; or, where practicable, by electronic submission, for example, via Electronic Information Exchange, or CD-ROM. Electronic submissions must be made in a manner that enables the NRC to receive, read, authenticate, distribute, and archive the submission, and process and retrieve it a single page at a time. Detailed guidance on making electronic submissions can be obtained by visiting the NRC's Web site at *http://www.nrc.gov/site-help/e-submittals.html;* by e-mail to *MSHD.Resource@nrc.gov;* or by writing the Office of the Chief Information Officer, U.S. Nuclear Regulatory Commission, Washington, DC 20555–0001. The guidance discusses, among other topics, the formats the NRC can accept, the use of electronic signatures, and the treatment of nonpublic information.

[68 FR 58801, Oct. 10, 2003, as amended at 74 FR 62680, Dec. 1, 2009; 80 FR 74978, Dec. 1, 2015]

§15.5 Claims that are covered.

(a) These procedures generally apply to any claim for payment of a debt which:

(1) Results from activities of the NRC, including fees imposed under part 170 and part 171; or

(2) Is referred to the NRC for collection.

(b) These procedures do not apply to:

(1) A claim based on a civil monetary penalty for violation of a licensing requirement unless §2.205 of this chapter provides otherwise;

(2) A claim as to which there is an indication of fraud, the presentation of a

false claim, or misrepresentation on the part of the debtor or any other party having an interest in the claim;

(3) A claim based in whole or in part on conduct in violation of the antitrust laws;

(4) A claim under the Internal Revenue Code of 1986.

(5) A claim between Federal agencies. Federal agencies should attempt to resolve interagency claims as referenced in Executive Order 12146 (3 CFR, 1980 Comp., pp. 409–412).

(6) A claim once it becomes subject to salary offset under 5 U.S.C. 5514. These claims are subject to the provisions of 10 CFR part 16.

(7) A claim involving bankruptcy is covered by Title 11 of the United States Code.

[47 FR 7616, Feb. 22, 1982, as amended at 55 FR 32377, Aug. 9, 1990; 56 FR 51830, Oct. 16, 1991; 67 FR 30318, May 6, 2002]

§ 15.7 Monetary limitation on NRC's authority.

The NRC's authority to compromise a claim, or to terminate or suspend collection action on a claim covered by these procedures, is limited by 31 U.S.C. 3711(a) to claims that—

(a) Have not been referred to another Federal Agency for further collection actions; and

(b) Do not exceed $100,000 (exclusive of interest, penalties, and administrative charges) or such higher amount as the Attorney General shall from time to time prescribe for purposes of compromise or suspension or termination of collection activity.

[47 FR 7616, Feb. 22, 1982, as amended at 55 FR 32378, Aug. 9, 1990; 67 FR 30318, May 6, 2002]

§ 15.8 Information collection requirements: OMB approval.

This part contains no information collection requirements, and therefore, is not subject to the requirements of the Paperwork Reduction Act (44 U.S.C. 3501 *et seq.*).

[67 FR 30319, May 6, 2002]

§ 15.9 No private rights created.

(a) The failure of NRC to include in this part any provision of the FCCS, 31 CFR Chapter IX, parts 900–904, does not prevent the NRC from applying these provisions.

(b) A debtor may not use the failure of the NRC to comply with any provision of this part or of the Federal Claims Collections Standards as a defense.

[47 FR 7616, Feb. 22, 1982, as amended at 55 FR 32378, Aug. 9, 1990; 67 FR 30319, May 6, 2002]

§ 15.11 Form of payment.

These procedures are directed primarily to the recovery of money on behalf of the Government. The NRC may demand:

(a) The return of specific property; or

(b) The performance of specific services.

[47 FR 7616, Feb. 22, 1982, as amended at 67 FR 30319, May 6, 2002]

§ 15.13 Subdivision of claims.

The NRC shall consider a debtor's liability arising from a particular transaction or contract as a single claim in determining whether the claim is less than the monetary limitation for the purpose of compromising or suspending or terminating collection action. A claim may not be subdivided to avoid the monetary limitation established by 31 U.S.C. 3711(a)(2) and § 15.7.

[55 FR 32378, Aug. 9, 1990]

Subpart B—Administrative Collection of Claims

§ 15.20 Aggressive agency collection activity.

(a) The NRC shall take aggressive action to collect all debts. These collection activities will be undertaken promptly and follow-up action will be taken as appropriate. These regulations do not require the Department of Justice, Department of the Treasury (Treasury), or any other Treasury-designated collection center to duplicate collection activities previously undertaken by NRC.

(b) Debt referred or transferred to Treasury or to a Treasury-designated debt collection center under the authority of 31 U.S.C. 3711(g) must be serviced, collected, or compromised, or the collection action will be suspended or terminated, in accordance with the statutory requirements and authorities applicable to the collection of the debts.

(c) The NRC shall cooperate with other agencies in their debt collection activities.

(d) The NRC will consider referring debts that are less than 120 days delinquent to Treasury or to a Treasury-designated debt collection center to accomplish efficient, cost-effective debt collection. Referrals to debt collection centers are at the discretion of, and for a time period acceptable to, Treasury.

(e) The NRC shall transfer any debt that has been delinquent for 120 days or more to Treasury so that it may take appropriate action to collect the debt or terminate collection actions. This requirement does not apply to any debt that—

(1) Is in litigation or foreclosure;

(2) Will be disposed of under an approved asset sale program;

(3) Has been referred to a private collection contractor for a period of time acceptable to Treasury;

(4) Is at a debt collection center for a period of time acceptable to Treasury;

(5) Will be collected under internal offset procedures within 3 years after the date the debt first became delinquent; or

(6) Is exempt from this requirement based on a determination by Treasury that exemption for a certain class of debt is in the best interest of the United States.

(f) Agencies operating Treasury-designated debt collection centers are authorized to charge a fee for services rendered regarding referred or transferred debts. The fee may be paid out of amounts collected and may be added to the debt as an administrative cost.

[67 FR 30319, May 6, 2002, as amended at 79 FR 66602, Nov. 10, 2014]

§ 15.21 Written demands for payment.

(a) The NRC shall make appropriate written demands upon the debtor for payment of money or the return of specific property in terms which specify:

(1) The basis of the indebtedness and the right of the debtor to seek review within the NRC;

(2) The amount claimed;

(3) A description of any property which is to be returned by a date certain;

(4) The date on which payment is to be made (which is normally the date the initial written demand letter statement was mailed or hand delivered, unless otherwise specified by contractual agreement, established by Federal statute or regulation, or agreed to under a payment agreement);

(5) The applicable standards for assessing interest, penalties, and administrative costs under 31 CFR 901.9;

(6) The applicable policy for reporting the delinquent debt to consumer reporting agencies; and

(7) The name, address, and phone number of a contact person or office within the NRC will be included with each demand letter.

(b) The NRC shall normally send two demand letters to debtors. The initial demand letter will be followed approximately 30 days later with a second demand letter, unless circumstances indicate that alternative remedies better protect the Government's interest, that the debtor has explicitly refused to pay, or that sending a further demand letter is futile. Depending upon the circumstances, the first and second demand letters may—

(1) Offer or seek to confer with the debtor;

(2) State the amount of the interest and penalties that will be added on a daily basis as well as the administrative costs that will be added to the debt until the debt is paid; and

(3) State that the authorized collection procedures include any procedure authorized in this part including:

(i) Contacts with the debtor's employer when the debtor is employed by the Federal Government or is a member of the military establishment or the Coast Guard;

(ii) The NRC may report debts to credit bureaus, refer debts to debt collection centers and collection agencies for cross-servicing (including wage garnishment), tax refund offset, administrative offset, and litigation. Any eligible debt that is delinquent for 180 days or more will be transferred to the Treasury for collection. Credit bureau reporting for transferred debts will be handled by Treasury or a Treasury-designated center.

(iii) Possible reporting of the delinquent debt to consumer reporting agencies in accordance with the guidance and standards contained in 31 CFR 901.4.

(iv) The suspension or revocation of a license or other remedy under § 15.29;

(v) Installment payments possibly requiring security; and

(vi) The right to refer the claim to DOJ for litigation.

(c) The NRC shall normally send only one written demand to a debtor who is a current NRC employee. The procedure described in § 15.33 and 10 CFR part 16 will be followed if full payment is not received either 30 days from the date the initial written demand was mailed or hand delivered. If the NRC cannot obtain full payment by following the procedures described in § 15.33 and 10 CFR part 16, the NRC may follow other collection procedures described in this subpart.

(d) The failure to state in a letter of demand a matter described in § 15.21 is not a defense for a debtor and does not prevent the NRC from proceeding with respect to that matter.

(e) When the NRC learns that a bankruptcy petition has been filed with respect to a debtor, the NRC will cease collection action immediately unless it has been determined that under 11 U.S.C. 362, the automatic stay has been lifted or is no longer in effect.

[47 FR 7616, Feb. 22, 1982, as amended at 55 FR 32378, Aug. 9, 1990; 56 FR 51830, Oct. 16, 1991; 67 FR 30319, May 6, 2002]

§ 15.23 Telephone or internet inquiries and investigations.

(a) If a debtor has not responded to one or more demands, the NRC shall make reasonable efforts by telephone or internet to determine the debtor's intentions.

(b) The NRC may undertake an investigation to locate a debtor if the whereabouts of a debtor is a problem, or if a debtor cannot be contacted by telephone.

(c) The NRC, under 15 U.S.C. 1681(f), may obtain consumer credit information from private firms, including the name, address, former addresses, place of employment, and former places of employment of a debtor.

[47 FR 7616, Feb. 22, 1982, as amended at 67 FR 30319, May 6, 2002]

§ 15.25 Personal interviews.

(a) The NRC may seek an interview with the debtor at the offices of the NRC when—

(1) A matter involved in the claim needs clarification;

(2) Information is needed concerning the debtor's circumstances; or

(3) An agreement for payment might be negotiated.

(b) The NRC shall grant an interview with a debtor upon the debtor's request. The NRC will not reimburse a debtor's interview expenses.

[47 FR 7616, Feb. 22, 1982, as amended at 55 FR 32378, Aug. 9, 1990]

§ 15.26 Reporting claims.

(a) In addition to assessing interest, penalties, and administrative costs under § 15.37, the NRC may report a debt that has been delinquent for 90 days to a consumer reporting agency if all the conditions of this paragraph are met.

(1) The debtor has not—

(i) Paid or agreed to pay the debt under a written payment plan that has been signed by the debtor and agreed to by the NRC; or

(ii) Filed for review of the debt under § 15.26 (a)(2)(iv).

(2) The NRC has included a notification in the second written demand (see § 15.21(b)) to the individual debtor stating—

(i) That the payment of the debt is delinquent;

(ii) That within not less than 60 days after the date of the notification, the NRC intends to disclose to a consumer reporting agency that the individual debtor is responsible for the debt;

(iii) The specific information to be disclosed to the consumer reporting agency; and

(iv) That the debtor has a right to a complete explanation of the debt (if that has not already been given), to dispute information in NRC records about the debt, and to request reconsideration of the debt by administrative appeal or review of the debt.

(3) The NRC has reconsidered its initial decision on the debt when the debtor has requested a review under paragraph (a)(2)(iv) of this section.

(4) The NRC has taken reasonable action to locate a debtor for whom the NRC does not have a current address to send the notification provided for in paragraph (a)(2) of this section.

(b) If there is a substantial change in the condition or amount of the debt, the NRC shall—

(1) Promptly disclose that fact(s) to each consumer reporting agency to which the original disclosure was made;

(2) Promptly verify or correct information about a debt on request of a consumer reporting agency for verification of information disclosed by the NRC; and,

(3) Obtain assurances from the consumer reporting agency that the agency is complying with all applicable Federal, state and local laws relating to its use of consumer credit information.

(c) The information the NRC discloses to the consumer reporting agency is limited to—

(1) Information necessary to establish the identity of the individual debtor, including name, address, and taxpayer identification number;

(2) The amount, status, and history of the debt; and

(3) The NRC activity under which the debt arose.

[55 FR 32378, Aug. 9, 1990, as amended at 67 FR 30319, May 6, 2002]

§15.27 Contact with debtor's employing agency.

If the debtor is employed by the Federal government or is a member of the military establishment or the Coast Guard, collection by offset must be accomplished in accordance with 5 U.S.C. 5514 and the provisions of 10 CFR part 16.

[56 FR 51830, Oct. 16, 1991]

§15.29 Suspension or revocation of license.

In non-bankruptcy cases, the NRC may suspend or revoke any license, permit, or approval which the NRC has granted to the debtor for any inexcusable, prolonged, or repeated failure of the debtor to pay a delinquent debt. Before suspending or revoking any license, permit, or approval for failure to pay a debt, the NRC shall issue to the debtor (by certified mail) an order or a demand for information as to why the license, permit, or approval should not be suspended or revoked. The NRC shall allow the debtor no more than 30 days to pay the debt in full, including applicable interest, penalties, and administrative costs of collection of the delinquent debt. The NRC may revoke the license, permit, or approval at the end of this period. If a license is revoked under authority of this part, a new application, with appropriate fees, must be made to the NRC. The NRC may not consider an application unless all previous delinquent debts of the debtor to the NRC have been paid in full. The suspension or revocation of a license, permit, or approval is also applicable to Federal programs or activities that are administered by the states on behalf of the Federal Government to the extent that they affect the Federal Government's ability to collect money or funds owed by debtors. In bankruptcy cases, before advising the debtor of NRC's intention to suspend or revoke licenses, permits, or approvals, the NRC will seek legal advice from its Office of the General Counsel concerning the impact of the Bankruptcy Code which may restrict such action.

[67 FR 30320, May 6, 2002]

§15.31 Disputed debts.

(a) A debtor who disputes a debt shall explain why the debt is incorrect in fact or in law within 30 days from the date that the initial demand letter was mailed or hand-delivered. The debtor may support the explanation by affidavits, cancelled checks, or other relevant evidence.

(b) If the debtor's arguments appear to have merit, the NRC may extend the interest waiver period as described in §15.37(j) pending a final determination of the existence or amount of the debt.

(c) The NRC may investigate the facts involved in the dispute and, if it considers it necessary, arrange for a conference at which the debtor may present evidence and any arguments in support of the debtor's position.

[47 FR 76716, Feb. 22, 1982, as amended at 55 FR 32379, Aug. 9, 1990]

§ 15.32 Contracting for collection services.

The NRC may contract for collection services in order to recover delinquent debts only if the debts are not subject to the DCIA requirement to transfer debts to Treasury for debt collection services, e.g. debts that are less than 180 days delinquent. However, the NRC retains the authority to resolve disputes, compromise claims, suspend or terminate collection action, and initiate enforced collection through litigation. When appropriate, the NRC shall contract for collection services in accordance with the guidance and standards contained in 31 CFR chapter IX, parts 900–904.

[67 FR 30320, May 6, 2002]

§ 15.33 Collection by administrative offset.

(a) *Application.* (1) The NRC may administratively undertake collection by centralized offset on each claim which is liquidated or certain in amount in accordance with the guidance and standards in 31 CFR Chapter IX, parts 900–904 and 5 U.S.C. 5514.

(2) This section does not apply to:

(i) Debts arising under the Social Security Act, except as provided in 42 U.S.C. 404;

(ii) Payments made under the Social Security Act, except as provided for in 31 U.S.C. 3716(c) (see 31 CFR 285.4, Federal Benefit Offset);

(iii) Debts arising under, or payments made under, the Internal Revenue Code (see 31 CFR 285.2, Tax Refund Offset) or the tariff laws of the United States;

(iv) Offsets against Federal salaries to the extent these standards are inconsistent with regulations published to implement such offsets under 5 U.S.C. 5514 and 31 U.S.C. 3716 (see 5 CFR part 550, subpart K, and 31 CFR 285.7, Federal Salary Offset);

(v) Offsets under 31 U.S.C. 3728 against a judgment obtained by a debtor against the United States;

(vi) Offsets or recoupments under common law, State law, or Federal statutes specifically prohibiting offsets or recoupments of particular types of debts; or

(vii) Offsets in the course of judicial proceedings, including bankruptcy.

(3) Unless otherwise provided for by contract or law, debts or payments that are not subject to administrative offset under 31 U.S.C. 3716 may be collected by administrative offset under the common law or their applicable statutory authority.

(4) Unless otherwise provided by law, the NRC may not initiate administrative offset of payments under the authority of 31 U.S.C. 3716 to collect a debt more than 10 years after the Government's right to collect the debt first accrued, unless facts material to the Government's right to collect the debt were not known and could not reasonably have been known to the NRC, or collection of "approval" fees has been deferred under 10 CFR part 170. If the collection of "approval" fees has been deferred, the ten-year period begins to run at the end of the deferral period.

(5) In bankruptcy cases, the NRC will seek legal advice from its Office of the General Counsel concerning the impact of the Bankruptcy Code on pending or contemplated collections by offset.

(b) *Mandatory centralized offset.* (1) The NRC is required to refer past due, legally enforceable, nontax debts that are over 120 days delinquent to Treasury for collection by centralized administrative offset. A debt is legally enforceable if there has been a final NRC determination that the debt, in the amount stated, is due and there are no legal bars to collection action. Debts that are less than 120 days delinquent also may be referred to Treasury for this purpose.

(2) The names and taxpayer identifying numbers (TINs) of debtors who owe debts referred to Treasury as described in paragraph (b)(1) of this section must be compared to the names and TINs on payments to be made by Federal disbursing officials. Federal disbursing officials include disbursing officials of Treasury, the Department of Defense, the United States Postal Service, other Government corporations, and disbursing officials of the United States designated by Treasury. When the name and TIN of a debtor

match the name and TIN of a payee and all other requirements for offset have been met, the payment will be offset to satisfy the debt.

(3) Federal disbursing officials will notify the debtor/payee in writing that an offset has occurred to satisfy, in part or in full, a past due, legally enforceable delinquent debt. The notice must include a description of the type and amount of the payment from which the offset was taken, the amount of offset that was taken, the identity of the creditor agency (NRC) requesting the offset, and a contact point within NRC who will respond to questions regarding the offset

(c) *NRC administrative offset.* (1) Before referring a delinquent debt to Treasury for administrative offset, the NRC adopts the following administrative offset procedures:

(i) Offsets may be initiated only after the debtor has been sent written notice of the type and amount of the debt, the intention of the NRC to use administrative offset to collect the debt, and an explanation of the debtor's rights under 31 U.S.C. 3716; and

(ii) The debtor has been given—

(A) The opportunity to inspect and copy NRC records related to the debt;

(B) The opportunity for a review within the NRC of the determination of indebtedness; and

(C) The opportunity to make a written agreement to repay the debt.

(iii) The procedures set forth in paragraph (c)(1)(i) of this section may be omitted when—

(A) The offset is in the nature of a recoupment;

(B) The debt arises under a contract as set forth in Cecile Industries, Inc. v. Cheney, 995 F.2d 1052 (Fed. Cir. 1993) (notice and other procedural protections set forth in 31 U.S.C. 3716(a) do not supplant or restrict established procedures for contractual offsets accommodated by the Contracts Disputes Act); or

(C) The NRC first learns of the existence of the amount owed by the debtor when there is insufficient time before payment would be made to the debtor/payee to allow for prior notice and an opportunity for review. This applies to non-centralized offsets conducted under paragraph (d) of this section. When prior notice and an opportunity for review are omitted, the NRC shall give the debtor notice and an opportunity for review as soon as practicable and shall refund any money ultimately found not to have been owed to the NRC.

(iv) When an agency previously has given a debtor any of the required notice and review opportunities with respect to a particular debt (31 CFR 901.2), the NRC need not duplicate the notice and review opportunities before administrative offset may be initiated.

(2) When referring delinquent debts to Treasury, the NRC shall certify, in a form acceptable to Treasury, that:

(i) The debt is past due and legally enforceable; and

(ii) The NRC has complied with all due process requirements under 31 U.S.C. 3716(a) and the NRC's regulations.

(3) Payments that are prohibited by law from being offset are exempt from centralized administrative offset. The Treasury shall exempt payments under means-tested programs from centralized administrative offset when requested in writing by the head of the payment-certifying or authorizing agency. Also, the Treasury may exempt other classes of payments from centralized offset upon the written request of the head of the payment-certifying or authorizing agency.

(4) Benefit payments made under the Social Security Act (42 U.S.C. 301 *et seq.*), part B of the Black Lung Benefits Act (30 U.S.C. 921 *et seq.*), and any law administered by the Railroad Retirement Board (other than tier 2 benefits), may be offset only in accordance with Treasury regulations, issued in consultation with the Social Security Administration, the Railroad Retirement Board, and the Office of Management and Budget (31 CFR 285.4).

(5) In accordance with 31 U.S.C. 3716(f), the Treasury may waive the provisions of the Computer Matching and Privacy Protection Act of 1988 concerning matching agreements and postmatch notification and verification (5 U.S.C. 552a(o) and (p)) for centralized administrative offset upon receipt of a certification from the NRC that the due process requirements enumerated in 31 U.S.C. 3716(a) have been met. The

certification of a debt in accordance with paragraph (c)(2) of this section will satisfy this requirement. If a waiver is granted, only the Data Integrity Board of the Department of the Treasury is required to oversee any matching activities, in accordance with 31 U.S.C. 3716(g). This waiver authority does not apply to offsets conducted under paragraphs (c) and (d) of this section.

(d) *Non-centralized administrative offset.* (1) Generally, non-centralized administrative offsets are ad hoc case-by-case offsets that NRC would conduct, at its discretion, internally or in cooperation with the agency certifying or authorizing payments to the debtor. Unless otherwise prohibited by law, when centralized administrative offset is not available or appropriate, past due, legally enforceable, nontax delinquent debts may be collected through non-centralized administrative offset. In these cases, the NRC may make a request directly to a payment-authorizing agency to offset a payment due a debtor to collect a delinquent debt. For example, the NRC will request the Office of Personnel Management (OPM) to offset a Federal employee's lump sum payment upon leaving Government service to satisfy an unpaid advance.

(2) Before requesting Treasury to conduct a non-centralized administrative offset, the NRC adopts the following procedures, which provide that such offsets may occur only after:

(i) The debtor has been provided due process as set forth in paragraph (c)(1) of this section; and

(ii) The Treasury has received written certification from NRC that the debtor owes the past due, legally enforceable delinquent debt in the amount stated, and that the NRC has fully complied with its regulations concerning administrative offset.

(3) Treasury shall comply with offset requests by NRC to collect debts owed to the United States, unless the offset would not be in the best interests of the United States with respect to the Treasury's program, or would otherwise be contrary to law. Appropriate use should be made of the cooperative efforts of other agencies in effecting collection by administrative offset.

(4) When collecting multiple debts by non-centralized administrative offset, the NRC will apply the recovered amounts to those debts in accordance with the best interests of the United States, as determined by the facts and circumstances of the particular case, particularly the applicable statute of limitations.

(e) *Requests to OPM to offset a debtor's anticipated or future benefit payment under the Civil Service Retirement and Disability Fund.* Upon providing OPM written certification that a debtor has been afforded the procedures provided in paragraph (c)(1) of this section, the NRC will request OPM to offset a debtor's anticipated or future benefit payments under the Civil Service Retirement and Disability Fund (Fund) in accordance with regulations codified at 5 CFR 831.1801–831.1808. Upon receipt of such a request, OPM will identify and "flag" a debtor's account in anticipation of the time when the debtor requests, or becomes eligible to receive, payments from the Fund. This will satisfy any requirement that offset be initiated prior to the expiration of the time limitations referenced in paragraph (a)(4) of this section.

(f) *Review requirements.* (1) For purposes of this section, whenever the NRC is required to afford a debtor a review within the agency, the NRC shall provide the debtor with a reasonable opportunity for an oral hearing in accordance with 10 CFR 16.9, when the debtor requests reconsideration of the debt, and the NRC determines that the question of the indebtedness cannot be resolved by review of the documentary evidence, for example, when the validity of the debt turns on an issue of credibility or veracity.

(2) Unless otherwise required by law, an oral hearing under this section is not required to be a formal evidentiary hearing, although the NRC should carefully document all significant matters discussed at the hearing.

(3) This section does not require an oral hearing with respect to debt collection systems in which a determination of indebtedness rarely involves issues of credibility or veracity, and the NRC has determined that review of the written record is ordinarily an adequate means to correct prior mistakes.

(4) In those cases in which an oral hearing is not required by this section, the NRC shall accord the debtor a "paper hearing," that is, a determination of the request for reconsideration based upon a review of the written record.

[67 FR 30320, May 6, 2002, as amended at 79 FR 66602, Nov. 10, 2014]

§ 15.35 Payments.

(a) *Payment in full.* The NRC shall make every effort to collect a claim in full before it becomes delinquent. If a claim is paid in one lump sum after it becomes delinquent, the NRC shall impose charges for interest, penalties, and administrative costs as specified in § 15.37.

(b) *Payment by installment.* If a debtor furnishes satisfactory evidence of inability to pay a claim in one lump sum, payment in regular installments may be arranged. Evidence may consist of a financial statement or a signed statement that the debtor's application for a loan to enable the debtor to pay the claim in full was rejected. Except for a claim described in 5 U.S.C. 5514 and codified in 10 CFR part 16, all installment payment arrangements must be in writing and require the payment of interest and administrative charges.

(1) Installment note forms may be used. The written installment agreement must contain a provision accelerating tho dobt payment in the event the debtor defaults. If the debtor's financial statement discloses the ownership of assets which are free and clear of liens or security interests, or assets in which the debtor owns an equity, the debtor may be asked to secure the payment of an installment note by executing a Security Agreement and Financing Statement transferring to the United States a security interest in the asset until the debt is discharged.

(2) If the debtor owes more than one debt, the NRC will apply the payment to the various debts in accordance with the best interests of the United States, as determined by the facts and circumstances of the particular case.

(c) *To whom payment is made.* Payment of a debt is made by check, electronic transfer, draft, credit card, or money order and should be payable to the United States Nuclear Regulatory Commission, License Fee and Accounts Receivable Branch, P.O. Box 954514, St. Louis, MO. 63195–4514, unless payment is—

(1) Made pursuant to arrangements with DOJ;

(2) Ordered by a Court of the United States; or

(3) Otherwise directed in any other part of this chapter.

[47 FR 7616, Feb. 22, 1982, as amended at 52 FR 31610, Aug. 21, 1987; 54 FR 53316, Dec. 28, 1989; 55 FR 32379, Aug. 9, 1990; 56 FR 51830, Oct. 16, 1991; 63 FR 15743, Apr. 1, 1998; 67 FR 30322, May 6, 2002]

§ 15.37 Interest, penalties, and administrative costs.

(a) The NRC shall assess interest, penalties, and administrative costs on debts owed to the United States Government in accordance with the guidance provided under the FCCS, 31 CFR 901.9.

(b) Before assessing any charges on delinquent debt, the NRC shall mail or hand-deliver a written notice to the debtor explaining its requirements concerning these charges under 31 CFR 901.2 and 901.9, except where these charges are included in a contractual or repayment agreement.

(c) Interest begins to accrue from the date on which the initial written demand, advising the debtor of the interest requirements, is first mailed or hand delivered to the debtor unless a different date is specified in a statute, regulation, or contract.

(d) The NRC shall assess interest based upon the rate of the current value of funds to the United States Treasury (the Treasury tax and loan account rate) prescribed for the current quarter and published in the FEDERAL REGISTER and the Treasury Financial Manual Bulletins, unless a different rate is prescribed by statute, regulation, or contract.

(e) Interest is computed only on the principal of the debt and the interest rate remains fixed for the duration of the indebtedness, unless a debtor defaults on a repayment agreement and seeks to enter into a new agreement.

(f) The NRC shall assess against a debtor charges to cover administrative costs incurred as a result of a delinquent debt. Administrative costs may include costs incurred in obtaining a credit report or in using a private debt collector, to the extent they are attributable to the delinquency.

(g) The NRC shall assess a penalty charge of 6 percent a year on any portion of a debt that is delinquent for more than 90 days. The charge accrues retroactively to the date that the debt became delinquent.

(h) Amounts received by the NRC as partial or installment payments are applied first to outstanding penalty and administrative cost charges, second to accrued interest, and third to outstanding principal.

(i) The NRC shall waive collection of interest on the debt or any portion of the debt which is paid in full within 30 days after the date on which interest began to accrue.

(j) The NRC may waive interest during the period a debt disputed under § 15.31 is under investigation or review by the NRC. However, this additional waiver is not automatic and must be requested before the expiration of the initial 30-day waiver period. The NRC may grant the additional waiver only when it finds merit in the explanation the debtor has submitted under § 15.31.

(k) The NRC may waive the collection of interest, penalties, and administrative costs if it finds that one or more of the following conditions exist:

(1) The debtor is unable to pay any significant sum toward the debt within a reasonable period of time;

(2) Collection of interest, penalties, and administrative costs will jeopardize collection of the principal of the debt;

(3) The NRC is unable to enforce collection in full within a reasonable time by enforced collection proceedings; or

(4) Collection would be against equity and good conscience or not in the best interests of the United States, including the situation in which an administrative offset or installment payment agreement is in effect.

(l) The NRC is authorized to impose interest and related charges on debts not subject to 31 U.S.C. 3717, in accordance with common law.

[55 FR 32380, Aug. 9, 1990, as amended at 67 FR 30322, May 6, 2002]

§ 15.38 Use of credit reports.

The NRC may institute a credit investigation of the debtor at any time following receipt of knowledge of the debt in order to aid NRC in making appropriate determinations as to:

(a) The collection and compromise of a debt;

(b) The collection of interest, penalties, and administrative costs;

(c) The use of administrative offset;

(d) The use of other collection methods; and

(e) The likelihood of collecting the debt.

[55 FR 32380, Aug. 9, 1990]

§ 15.39 Bankruptcy claims.

When the NRC learns that a bankruptcy petition has been filed with respect to a debtor, before proceeding with further collection action, the NRC will immediately seek legal advice from its Office of the General Counsel concerning the impact of the Bankruptcy Code on any pending or contemplated collection activities. Unless the NRC determines that the automatic stay imposed at the time of filing pursuant to 11 U.S.C. 362 has been lifted or is no longer in effect, collection activity against the debtor will in most cases stop immediately.

(a) After seeking legal advice from its Office of the General Counsel, a proof of claim usually will be filed with the bankruptcy court or the Trustee.

(b) If the NRC is a secured creditor, it may seek relief from the automatic stay regarding its security, subject to the provisions and requirements of 11 U.S.C. 362.

(c) Offset is stayed in most cases by the automatic stay. However, the NRC will seek legal advice from its Office of the General Counsel to determine whether its payments to the debtor and payments of other agencies available for offset may be frozen by the agency until relief from the automatic stay can be obtained from the bankruptcy court. The NRC will seek legal advice from its Office of the General Counsel to determine if recoupment is available.

[67 FR 30322, May 6, 2002]

Subpart C—Compromise of a Claim

§ 15.41 When a claim may be compromised.

(a) The NRC may compromise a claim not in excess of the monetary limitation if it has not been referred to DOJ for litigation.

(b) Unless otherwise provided by law, when the principal balance of a debt, exclusive of interest, penalties, and administrative costs, exceeds $100,000 or any higher amount authorized by the Attorney General, the authority to accept the compromise rests with the DOJ. The NRC will evaluate the compromise offer, using the factors set forth in this part. If an offer to compromise any debt in excess of $100,000 is acceptable to the NRC, the NRC shall refer the debt to the Civil Division or other appropriate litigating division in the DOJ using a CCLR. The referral must include appropriate financial information and a recommendation for the acceptance of the compromise offer. DOJ approval is not required if the compromise offer is rejected by NRC.

[67 FR 30322, May 6, 2002]

§ 15.43 Reasons for compromising a claim.

A claim may be compromised for one or more of the reasons set forth below:

(a) The full amount cannot be collected because:

(1) The debtor is unable to pay the full amount within a reasonable time; or

(2) The debtor refuses to pay the claim in full and the Government is unable to enforce collection in full within a reasonable time by enforced collection proceedings.

(b) There is a real doubt concerning the Government's ability to prove its case in Court for the full amount claimed, either because of the legal issues involved or a bona fide dispute as to the facts.

(c) The cost of collecting the claim does not justify the enforced collection of the full amount. The NRC shall apply this reason for compromise in accordance with the guidance in 31 CFR 902.2.

(d) The NRC shall determine the debtor's inability to pay, the Government's ability to enforce collection, and the amounts that are acceptable in compromise in accordance with the FCCS, 31 CFR part 902.

(e) Compromises payable in installments are discouraged, but, if necessary, must be in the form of a legally enforceable agreement for the reinstatement of the prior indebtedness less sums paid thereon. The agreement also must provide that in the event of default—

(1) The entire balance of the debt becomes immediately due and payable; and

(2) The Government has the right to enforce any security interest.

[47 FR 7616, Feb. 22, 1982, as amended at 55 FR 32380, Aug. 9, 1990; 67 FR 30322, May 6, 2002]

§ 15.45 Consideration of tax consequences to the Government.

(a) The NRC may accept a percentage of a debtor's profits or stock in a debtor corporation in compromise of a claim. In negotiating a compromise with a business concern, the NRC should consider requiring a waiver of tax-loss-carry-forward and tax-loss-carry-back rights of the debtor. For information on reporting requirements, see § 15.60.

(b) When two or more debtors are jointly and severally liable, the NRC will pursue collection activity against all debtors, as appropriate. The NRC will not attempt to allocate the burden of payment between the debtors but will proceed to liquidate the indebtedness as quickly as possible. The NRC will ensure that a compromise agreement with one debtor does not release the NRC's claim against the remaining debtors. The amount of a compromise with one debtor shall not be considered a precedent or binding in determining the amount that will be required from other debtors jointly and severally liable on the claim.

[67 FR 30322, May 6, 2002]

§ 15.47 Finality of a compromise.

An offer of compromise must be in writing and signed by the debtor. An offer of compromise which is accepted by the NRC is final and conclusive on the debtor and on all officials, agencies, and courts of the United States, unless obtained by fraud, misrepresentation, the presentation of a false claim, or mutual mistake of fact.

§ 15.49 Mutual releases of the debtor and the Government.

(a) In all appropriate instances, a compromise that is accepted by NRC should be implemented by means of a mutual release.

(1) The debtor is released from further non-tax liability on the compromised debt in consideration of payment in full of the compromised amount.

(2) The Government and its officials, past and present, are released and discharged from any and all claims and causes of action arising from the same transaction held by the debtor.

(b) If a mutual release is not executed when a debt is compromised, unless prohibited by law, the debtor is still deemed to have waived any and all claims and causes of action against the Government and its officials related to the transaction giving rise to the compromised debt.

[67 FR 30322, May 6, 2002]

Subpart D—Suspension or Termination of Collection Action

§ 15.51 When collection action may be suspended or terminated.

The NRC may suspend or terminate collection action on a claim not in excess of the monetary limitation of $100,000 or such other amount as the Attorney General may direct, exclusive of interest, penalties, and administrative costs, after deducting the amount of partial payments or collections, if any of the debt has not been referred to the DOJ for litigation. If, after deducting the amount of any partial payments or collections, the principal amount of a debt exceeds $100,000, or such other amount as the Attorney General may direct, exclusive of interest, penalties, and administrative costs, the authority to suspend or terminate rests solely with the DOJ. If the NRC believes that suspension or termination of any debt in excess of $100,000 may be appropriate, the NRC shall refer the debt to the Civil Division or other appropriate litigating division in the DOJ, using the CCLR. The referral should specify the reasons for the NRC's recommendation. If, prior to referral to the DOJ, the NRC determines that a debt is plainly erroneous or clearly without legal merit, the NRC may terminate collection activity, regardless of the amount involved, without obtaining DOJ concurrence.

[67 FR 30323, May 6, 2002]

§ 15.53 Reasons for suspending collection action.

The NRC may suspend collection activity when:

(a) The NRC cannot locate the debtor;

(b) The debtor's financial condition is not expected to improve; or

(c) The debtor has requested a waiver or review of the debt.

(d) Based on the current financial condition of the debtor, the NRC may suspend collection activity on a debt when the debtor's future prospects justify retention of the debt for periodic review and collection activity and:

(1) The applicable statute of limitations has not expired; or

(2) Future collection can be effected by administrative offset, notwithstanding the expiration of the applicable statute of limitations for litigation of claims, with due regard to the 10-year limitation for administrative offset prescribed by 31 U.S.C. 3716(e)(1); or

(3) The debtor agrees to pay interest on the amount of the debt on which collection will be suspended, and such suspension is likely to enhance the debtor's ability to pay the full amount of the principal of the debt with interest at a later date.

(e)(1) The NRC shall suspend collection activity during the time required for consideration of the debtor's request for waiver or administrative review of the debt, if the statute under which the request is sought prohibits the NRC from collecting the debt during that time.

(2) If the statute under which the request is sought does not prohibit collection activity pending consideration

of the request, the NRC may use discretion, on a case-by-case basis, to suspend collection. Further, the NRC ordinarily should suspend collection action upon a request for waiver or review, if the NRC is prohibited by statute or regulation from issuing a refund of amounts collected prior to NRC consideration of the debtor's request. However, the NRC should not suspend collection when the NRC determines that the request for waiver or review is frivolous or was made primarily to delay collection.

(f) When the NRC learns that a bankruptcy petition has been filed with respect to a debtor, in most cases, the collection activity on a debt must be suspended, pursuant to the provisions of 11 U.S.C. 362, 1201, and 1301, unless the NRC can clearly establish that the automatic stay has been lifted or is no longer in effect. The NRC should seek legal advice immediately from its Office of the General Counsel and, if legally permitted, take the necessary steps to ensure that no funds or money are paid by the NRC to the debtor until relief from the automatic stay is obtained.

[67 FR 30323, May 6, 2002]

§ 15.55 Reasons for terminating collection action.

The NRC may terminate collection activity when:

(a) The NRC is unable to collect any substantial amount through its own efforts or through the efforts of others;

(b) The NRC is unable to locate the debtor;

(c) Costs of collection are anticipated to exceed the amount recoverable,

(d) The debt is legally without merit or enforcement of the debt is barred by any applicable statute of limitations;

(e) The debt cannot be substantiated; or

(f) The debt against the debtor has been discharged in bankruptcy.

[67 FR 30323, May 6, 2002]

§ 15.57 Termination of collection action.

(a) Before terminating collection activity, the NRC should have pursued all appropriate means of collection and determined, based upon the results of the collection activity, that the debt is uncollectible. Termination of collection activity ceases active collection of the debt. The termination of collection activity does not preclude the NRC from retaining a record of the account for purposes of:

(1) Selling the debt, if the Treasury determines that such sale is in the best interests of the United States;

(2) Pursuing collection at a subsequent date in the event there is a change in the debtor's status or a new collection tool becomes available;

(3) Offsetting against future income or assets not available at the time of termination of collection activity; or

(4) Screening future applicants for prior indebtedness.

(b) Generally, the NRC will terminate collection activity on a debt that has been discharged in bankruptcy, regardless of the amount. However, the NRC may continue collection activity, subject to the provisions of the Bankruptcy Code, for any payments provided under a plan of reorganization.

[67 FR 30323, May 6, 2002]

§ 15.59 Exception to termination.

When a significant enforcement policy is involved, or recovery of a judgment is a prerequisite to the imposition of administrative sanctions, the NRC may refer debts for litigation, although termination of collection activity may be appropriate.

[67 FR 30323, May 6, 2002]

§ 15.60 Discharge of indebtedness; reporting requirements.

(a) Before discharging a delinquent debt (also referred to as a close out of the debt), the NRC shall take all appropriate steps to collect the debt in accordance with 31 U.S.C. 3711(g), including, as applicable, administrative offset; tax refund offset; Federal salary offset; referral to Treasury, Treasury-designated debt collection centers, or private collection contractors; credit bureau reporting; wage garnishment; litigation; and foreclosure. Discharge of indebtedness is distinct from termination or suspension of collection activity under 10 CFR 15.55 and 15.57 and is governed by the Internal Revenue Code. When collection action on a debt is suspended or terminated, the debt remains delinquent, and further collection action may be pursued at a later date. When the NRC discharges a debt in full or in part, further collection action is prohibited. Therefore, the NRC will make the determination that collection action is no longer warranted before discharging a debt. Before discharging a debt, the NRC must terminate debt collection action.

(b) Section 3711(i), title 31, United States Code, requires agencies to sell a delinquent nontax debt upon termination of collection action if Treasury determines such a sale is in the best interests of the United States. Since the discharge of a debt precludes any further collection action (including the sale of a delinquent debt), the NRC may not discharge a debt until the requirements of 31 U.S.C. 3711(i) have been met.

(c) Upon discharge of an indebtedness, the NRC shall report the discharge to the IRS in accordance with the requirements of 26 U.S.C. 6050P and 26 CFR 1.6050P–1. The NRC may request Treasury or a Treasury-designated debt collection center to file a discharge report to the IRS on the NRC's behalf.

(d) When discharging a debt, the NRC shall request that litigation counsel release any liens of record securing the debt.

[67 FR 30323, May 6, 2002]

Subpart E—Referral of a Claim

§ 15.61 Prompt referral.

(a) The NRC shall promptly refer debts that are subject to aggressive collection activity (as described in subpart B of this part) and that cannot be compromised, or debts on which collection activity cannot be suspended or terminated, to DOJ for litigation. Debts for which the principal amount exceeds $1,000,000, or such other amount as the Attorney General may direct, exclusive of interest and penalties, must be referred to the Civil Division or other division responsible for litigating such debts at DOJ, Washington, DC. Debts for which the principal amount is $1,000,000 or less, or such other amount as the Attorney General may direct, exclusive of interest or penalties, must be referred to the DOJ's Nationwide Central Intake Facility, as required by the CCLR instructions. Debts will be referred as early as possible, consistent with the NRC's aggressive collection activity and well within the one year of the NRC's final determination of the fact and the amount of the debt.

(b) DOJ has exclusive jurisdiction over the debts referred to in paragraph (a) of this section. The NRC shall terminate the use of any administrative collection activities to collect a debt when the debt is referred to DOJ. The NRC shall advise the DOJ of the collection activities it used and the results. The NRC shall refrain from having any contact with the debtor and shall direct all inquiries to DOJ. The NRC shall immediately notify DOJ of any payments credited to the debtor's account after the account has been referred to DOJ. DOJ shall notify NRC in a timely manner of any payments it receives from the debtor.

[67 FR 30324, May 6, 2002]

§ 15.65 Referral of a compromise offer.

The NRC may refer a debtor's firm written offer of compromise, which is substantial in amount, to the Civil Division or other appropriate litigating division in DOJ using a CCLR accompanied by supporting data and particulars concerning the debt.

[67 FR 30324, May 6, 2002]

§ 15.67 Referral to the Department of Justice.

(a) Unless excepted by DOJ, the NRC shall complete the CCLR accompanied by a Certificate of Indebtedness, to refer all administratively uncollectible claims to the DOJ for litigation.

(b) The NRC shall indicate the actions it wishes DOJ to take regarding the referred claim on the CCLR.

(c) Before referring a debt to DOJ for litigation, the NRC shall notify each person determined to be liable for the debt that, unless the debt can be collected administratively, litigation may be initiated. This notification must comply with Executive Order 12988 (3 CFR, 1996 Comp., pp 157–163) and may be given as part of a demand letter or as a separate document.

(d) The NRC shall preserve all files and records that DOJ may need to prove the claim in court.

(e) The NRC may ordinarily not refer for litigation claims of less than $2,500, exclusive of interest, penalties, and administrative charges, or such other amount as the Attorney General shall from time to time prescribe.

(f) The NRC may not refer claims of less than the minimum amount unless:

(1) Litigation to collect a smaller claim is important to ensure compliance with NRC's policies and programs;

(2) The claim is being referred solely to secure a judgment against the debtor, which will be filed as a lien against the debtor's property under 28 U.S.C. 3201 and returned to the NRC for enforcement, or

(3) The debtor has the clear ability to pay the claim, and the Government effectively can enforce payment, with due regard for the exemptions available to the debtor under state and Federal law and the judicial remedies available to the Government.

[67 FR 30324, May 6, 2002]

PART 16—SALARY OFFSET PROCEDURES FOR COLLECTING DEBTS OWED BY FEDERAL EMPLOYEES TO THE FEDERAL GOVERNMENT

Sec.

AUTHORITY: Atomic Energy Act of 1954, sec. 161 (42 U.S.C. 2201), Energy Reorganization Act of 1974, sec. 201 (42 U.S.C. 5841); 31 U.S.C. 3711, 3716, 3717, 3718; 5 U.S.C. 5514; Pub. L. 97–365, 96 Stat. 1749; 4 CFR parts 101 through 105; 5 CFR 550.1101 through 550.1108.

SOURCE: 56 FR 51830, Oct. 16, 1991, unless otherwise noted.

§16.1 Purpose and scope.

(a) This part provides procedures for the collection by administrative offset of a Federal employee's salary without his/her consent to satisfy certain debts owed to the Federal Government. This part applies to all Federal employees who owe debts to the Nuclear Regulatory Commission (NRC) and to current employees of the NRC who owe debts to other Federal agencies. This part does not apply when the employee consents to recovery from his/her current pay account.

(b) These procedures do not apply to debts or claims arising under:

(1) The Internal Revenue Code of 1954, as amended, 26 U.S.C. 1 *et seq.;*

(2) The tariff laws of the United States; or

(3) Any case where a collection of a debt by salary offset is explicitly provided for or prohibited by another statute.

(c) These procedures do not apply to any adjustment to pay arising out of an employee's selection of coverage or a change in coverage under a Federal benefits program requiring periodic deductions from pay if the amount to be recovered was accumulated over four pay periods or less.

(d) These procedures do not preclude the compromise, suspension, or termination of collection action where appropriate under the standards implementing the revised Federal Claims Collection Standards (FCCS), 31 U.S.C. 3711 *et seq.*, 31 CFR chapter IX, parts 900 through 904.

(e) This part does not preclude an employee from requesting waiver of an overpayment under 5 U.S.C. 5584, 10 U.S.C. 2774, or 32 U.S.C. 716 or in any way questioning the amount or validity of the debt by submitting a subsequent claim to the NRC. This part does not preclude an employee from requesting a waiver pursuant to other statutory provisions applicable to the particular debt being collected.

(f) The NRC is not limited to collection remedies contained in the revised FCCS. The FCCS is not intended to impair common law remedies.

[56 FR 51830, Oct. 16, 1991, as amended at 63 FR 15743, Apr. 1, 1998; 67 FR 57507, Sept. 11, 2002]

§ 16.3 Definitions.

For the purposes of this part, the following definitions apply:

Administrative charges are those amounts assessed by NRC to cover the costs of processing and handling delinquent debts due the Government.

Administrative offset means withholding money payable by the United States Government to, or held by the Government for, a person to satisfy a debt the person owes the United States Government.

Agency means any agency of the executive, legislative, and judicial branches of the Federal Government, including Government corporations.

Centralized salary offset computer matching describes the computerized process used to match delinquent debt records with Federal salary payment records when the purpose of the match is to identify Federal employees who owe debt to the Federal Government.

Creditor agency means the agency to which the debt is owed, including a debt collection center when acting in behalf of a creditor agency in matters pertaining to the collection of a debt.

Debt and *claim* are used synonymously to refer to an amount of money, funds, or property that has been determined by an agency official to be owed to the United States from any person, organization, or entity, except another Federal agency. For the purposes of administrative offset under 31 U.S.C. 3716, the terms *debt* and *claim* include an amount of money, funds, or property owed by a person to a State (including past-due support being enforced by a State), the District of Columbia, American Samoa, Guam, the United States Virgin Islands, the Commonwealth of the Northern Mariana Islands, or the Commonwealth of Puerto Rico.

Debt collection center means the Department of the Treasury or other Government agency or division designated by the Secretary of the Treasury with authority to collect debts on behalf of creditor agencies.

Delinquent debt record refers to the information about a debt that an agency submits to Treasury when the agency refers the debt for collection by offset in accordance with the provision of 31 U.S.C. 3716.

Disbursing official means an official who has authority to disburse Federal salary payments pursuant to 31 U.S.C. 3321 or another law.

Disposable pay means that part of current basic pay, special pay, incentive pay, retired pay, retainer pay, or in the case of an employee not entitled to basic pay, other authorized pay remaining after the deduction of:

(1) Any amount required by law to be withheld;

(2) Amounts properly withheld for Federal, state or local income tax purposes;

(3) Amounts deducted as health insurance premiums;

(4) Amounts deducted as normal retirement contributions, not including amounts deducted for supplementary coverage; and

(5) Amounts deducted as normal life insurance premiums not including amounts deducted for supplementary coverage.

Employee is any individual employed by any agency of the executive, legislative, and judicial branches of the Federal Government, including Government corporations.

FCCS means the Federal Claims Collection Standards jointly published by the Department of the Treasury and the Department of Justice at 31 CFR Chapter IX, Parts 900 through 904.

Hearing official means an individual responsible for conducting any hearing with respect to the existence or amount of a debt claimed or the repayment schedule if not established by written agreement between the employee and the NRC, and who renders a decision on the basis of this hearing.

Paying agency means the agency that employs the individual who owes the debt and authorizes the payment of his/her current pay.

Salary offset means an administrative offset to collect a debt under 5 U.S.C. 5514 by deduction(s) at one or more officially established pay intervals from the current pay account of an employee without his or her consent.

Treasury as used in 10 CFR part 16 means the Department of the Treasury.

Waiver means the cancellation, remission, forgiveness, or non-recovery of a debt allegedly owed by an employee to an agency as permitted or required by 5 U.S.C. 5584, 10 U.S.C. 2774, 32 U.S.C. 716, 5 U.S.C. 8346(b), or any other law.

[56 FR 51830, Oct. 16, 1991, as amended at 67 FR 57507, Sept. 11, 2002]

§ 16.5 Application.

The regulations in this part are to be followed when:

(a) The NRC is owed a debt by an individual currently employed by another Federal agency;

(b) The NRC is owed a debt by an individual who is a current employee of the NRC; or

(c) The NRC employs an individual who owes a debt to another Federal agency.

§ 16.7 Notice requirements.

(a) If the NRC is the creditor agency, deductions will not be made unless the NRC provides the employee with a signed written notice of the debt at least 30 days before salary offset commences. The notice will be delivered in person or by certified or registered mail, return receipt requested, with receipt returned as proof of delivery.

(b) The written notice must contain:

(1) A statement that the debt is owed and an explanation of its origin, nature, and amount;

(2) The NRC's intention to collect the debt by deducting from the employee's current disposable pay account;

(3) The amount and frequency of the intended deduction (stated as a fixed dollar amount or as a percentage of pay, not to exceed 15 percent of disposable pay) and the intention to continue the deduction until the debt is paid in full or otherwise resolved.

(4) An explanation of interest, penalties, and administrative charges, including a statement that these charges will be assessed unless excused in accordance with the Federal Claims Collection Standards at 4 CFR parts 101–105;

(5) The employee's right to inspect and copy government records pertaining to the debt or, if the employee or his or her representative cannot personally inspect the records, to request and receive a copy of these records;

(6) If not previously provided, the opportunity (under terms agreeable to the NRC) to establish a schedule for the voluntary repayment of the debt or to enter into a written agreement to establish a schedule for repayment of the debt in lieu of offset (31 CFR Chapter IX, 901.2). The agreement must be in writing, signed by the employee and the NRC, and documented in the NRC's files.

(7) The employee's right to a hearing conducted by an official arranged for by the NRC (an administrative law judge, or alternatively, a hearing official not under the control of the head of the agency) if a petition is filed as prescribed in § 16.9;

(8) The methods and time period for petitioning for hearings;

(9) A statement that the timely filing of a petition for a hearing will stay the commencement of collection proceedings;

(10) A statement that a final decision on the hearing will be issued not later than 60 days after the filing of the petition requesting the hearing unless the employee requests and the hearing official grants a delay in the proceedings;

(11) A statement that knowingly false or frivolous statements, representations, or evidence may subject the employee to appropriate disciplinary procedures under chapter 75 of title 5, United States Code and 5 CFR part 752, penalties under the False Claims Act, sections 3729–3731 of title 31, United States Code or other applicable statutory authority, or criminal penalties under section 286, 287, 1001 and 1002 of title 18, United States Code or any other applicable statutory authority;

(12) A statement of other rights and remedies available to the employee under statutes or regulations governing the program for which the collection is being made; and

(13) Unless there are contractual or statutory provisions to the contrary, a statement that amounts paid on or deducted for the debt which are later waived or found not owed to the United States will be promptly refunded to the employee.

[56 FR 51830, Oct. 16, 1991, as amended at 67 FR 57508, Sept. 11, 2002]

§ 16.8 Information collection requirements: OMB approval.

This part contains no information collection requirements, and, therefore, is not subject to the requirements of the Paperwork Reduction Act (44 U.S.C. 3501 *et. seq.*).

[67 FR 57508, Sept. 11, 2002]

§ 16.9 Hearing.

(a) *Request for hearing.* (1) An employee shall file a petition for a hearing in accordance with the instructions outlined in the creditor agency's notice of offset.

(2) If the NRC is the creditor agency, a hearing may be requested by filing a written petition stating why the employee disputes the existence or amount of the debt or the repayment schedule if it was not established by written agreement between the employee and the NRC. The employee shall sign the petition and fully identify and explain with reasonable specificity all the facts, evidence, and witnesses, if any, which the employee believes support his or her position. The petition for a hearing must be received no later than fifteen (15) calendar days after receipt of the notice of offset unless the employee can show that the delay in meeting the deadline date was because of circumstances beyond his or her control or because of failure to receive notice of the time limit (unless otherwise aware of it).

(b) *Hearing procedures.* (1) The hearing will be presided over by a hearing official arranged by NRC (an administrative law judge or, alternatively, a hearing official not under the supervision or control of the head of the agency.)

(2) The hearing must conform to procedures contained in the revised FCCS, 31 CFR Chapter IX, 901.3(e). The burden is on the employee to demonstrate either that the existence or the amount of the debt is in error or that the terms of the repayment schedule would result in undue financial hardship or would be against equity and good conscience.

(3) An employee is entitled to representation of his or her choice at any stage of the proceeding. NRC attorneys may not be provided as representatives for the debtor. The NRC will not compensate the debtor for representation expenses, including hourly fees for attorneys, travel expenses, and costs for reproducing documents.

[56 FR 51830, Oct. 16, 1991, as amended at 67 FR 57508, Sept. 11, 2002]

§ 16.11 Written decision.

(a) The hearing official will issue a written opinion no later than 60 days after the hearing.

(b) The written opinion must include:

(1) A statement of the facts presented to demonstrate the nature and origin of the alleged debt;

(2) The hearing official's analysis, findings, and conclusions;

(3) The amount and validity of the debt; and

(4) The repayment schedule, where appropriate.

§ 16.13 Procedures for centralized administrative offset.

(a) The NRC must notify Treasury of all debts that are delinquent as defined in the FCCS (over 180 days old) so that recovery may be made by centralized administrative offset. This includes those debts the NRC seeks to recover from the pay account of an employee of another agency via salary offset. The Treasury and other Federal disbursing officials will match payments, including Federal salary payments, against such debts. When a match occurs, and all the requirements for offset have been met, the payments will be offset to collect the debt. Prior to offset of the pay account of an employee, the NRC must comply with the requirements of 5 U.S.C. 5514, 5 CFR part 550, and 10 CFR part 15. Procedures for notifying Treasury of a debt for purposes of collection by centralized administrative offset are contained in 31 CFR part 285 and 10 CFR 15.33. Procedures for internal salary offset are contained in § 16.15 of this chapter.

(b) When the NRC determines that an employee of another Federal agency owes a delinquent debt to the NRC, the NRC will, as appropriate:

(1) Arrange for a hearing upon the proper petitioning by the employee;

(2) Provide the Federal employee with a notice and an opportunity to dispute the debt as contained in 5 U.S.C. 5514 and 10 CFR 15.26.

(3) Submit the debt to Treasury for centralized administrative offset and certify in writing that the debtor has been afforded the legally required due process notification.

(4) If collection must be made in installments, the NRC must advise the paying agency of the amount or percentage of disposable pay to be collected in each installment.

(c) *Offset amount.* (1) The amount offset from a salary payment under this section shall be the lesser of:

(i) The amount of the debt, including any interest, penalties, and administrative costs; or

(ii) An amount up to 15 percent of the debtor's disposable pay.

(2) Alternatively, the amount offset may be an amount agreed upon, in writing, by the debtor and the NRC.

(3) Offsets will continue until the debt, including any interest, penalties, and administrative costs, is paid in full or otherwise resolved to the satisfaction of the NRC.

(d) *Priorities.* (1) A levy pursuant to the Internal Revenue Code of 1986 shall take precedence over other deductions under this section.

(2) When a salary payment may be reduced to collect more than one debt, amounts offset under this section will be applied to a debt only after amounts offset have been applied to satisfy past due child support debt assigned to a State pursuant 26 U.S.C. 6402(c) and 31 CFR 205.7(h)(2).

(e) *Notice.* (1) Before offsetting a salary payment, the disbursing official, or the paying agency on behalf of the disbursing official, shall notify the Federal employee in writing of the date that deductions from salary will commence and of the amount of such deductions.

(2)(i) When an offset occurs under this section, the disbursing official, or the paying agency on behalf of the disbursing official, shall notify the Federal employee in writing that an offset has occurred including:

(A) A description of the payment and the amount of the offset taken;

(B) Identification of NRC as the agency requesting the offset; and,

(C) A contact point within the NRC that will handle concerns regarding the offset.

(ii) The information described in paragraphs (e)(2)(i)(B) and (e)(2)(i)(C) of this section does not need to be provided to the Federal employee when the offset occurs if such information was included in a prior notice from the disbursing official or paying agency.

(3) The disbursing official will advise the NRC of the names, mailing addresses, and taxpayer identifying numbers of the debtors from whom amounts of past-due, legally enforceable debt were collected and of the amounts collected from each debtor. The disbursing official will not advise the NRC of the source of payment from which such amounts were collected.

(f) *Fees.* Agencies that perform centralized salary offset computer matching services may charge a fee sufficient to cover the full cost of such services. In addition, Treasury or a paying agency acting on behalf of Treasury, may charge a fee sufficient to cover the full cost of implementing the administrative offset program. Treasury may deduct the fees from amounts collected by offset or may bill the NRC. Fees charged for offset shall be based on actual administrative offsets completed.

(g) *Disposition of amounts collected.* The disbursing official conducting the offset will transmit amounts collected for debts, less fees charged under paragraph (f) of this section, to NRC. If an erroneous offset payment is made to the NRC, the disbursing official will notify the NRC that an erroneous offset payment has been made. The disbursing official may deduct the amount of the erroneous offset payment from future amounts payable to the NRC. Alternatively, upon the disbursing official's request, the NRC shall return promptly to the disbursing official or the affected payee an amount equal to the amount of the erroneous payment (without regard to whether any other amounts payable to the agency have been paid). The disbursing official and the NRC shall adjust the debtor records appropriately.

[67 FR 57508, Sept. 11, 2002]

§ 16.15 Procedures for internal salary offset.

(a) Deductions to liquidate an employee's debt will be by the method and in the amount stated in the NRC's notice of intention to offset as provided in § 16.7. Debts will be collected in one lump sum where possible. If the employee is financially unable to pay in one lump sum, collection must be made in installments.

(b) Debts will be collected by deduction at officially established pay intervals from an employee's current pay account unless alternative arrangements for repayment are made.

(c) Installment deductions will be made over a period not greater than the anticipated period of employment. The size of installment deductions must bear a reasonable relationship to the size of the debt and the employee's ability to pay. The deduction for the pay intervals for any period may not exceed 15% of disposable pay unless the employee has agreed in writing to a deduction of a greater amount.

(d) Offset against any subsequent payment due an employee who retires or resigns or whose employment or period of active duty ends before collection of the debt is completed is provided for in accordance with 31 U.S.C. 3716. These payments include but are not limited to final salary payment or lump-sum leave due the employee from the paying agency as of the date of separation to the extent necessary to liquidate the debt.

§ 16.17 Refunds.

(a) The NRC will refund promptly any amounts deducted to satisfy debts owed to the NRC when the debt is waived, found not owed to the NRC, or when directed by an administrative or Judicial order.

(b) The creditor agency will promptly return any amounts deducted by NRC to satisfy debts owed to the creditor agency when the debt is waived, found not owed, or when directed by an administrative or judicial order.

(c) Unless required or permitted by law or contract, refunds under this section may not bear interest.

§ 16.19 Statute of limitations.

If a debt has been outstanding for more than 10 years after the agency's right to collect the debt first accrued, the agency may not collect by salary offset unless facts material to the Government's right to collect were not known and could not reasonably have been known by the NRC official or officials who were charged with the responsibility for discovery and collection of the debts.

§ 16.21 Non-waiver of rights.

An employee's involuntary payment of all or any part of a debt collected under these regulations will not be construed as a waiver of any rights that the employee may have under 5 U.S.C. 5514 or any other provision of contract or law, unless there are statutes or contract(s) to the contrary.

§ 16.23 Interest, penalties, and administrative charges.

Charges may be assessed for interest, penalties, and administrative charges in accordance with the FCCS, 31 CFR Chapter IX, 901.9.

[67 FR 57509, Sept. 11, 2002]

PART 19—NOTICES, INSTRUCTIONS AND REPORTS TO WORKERS: INSPECTION AND INVESTIGATIONS

Sec.

AUTHORITY: Atomic Energy Act of 1954, secs. 53, 63, 81, 103, 104, 161, 223, 234, 1701 (42 U.S.C. 2073, 2093, 2111, 2133, 2134, 2201, 2273, 2282, 2297f); Energy Reorganization Act of

1974, secs. 201, 211, 401 (42 U.S.C. 5841, 5851, 5891); 44 U.S.C. 3504 note.

SOURCE: 38 FR 22217, Aug. 17, 1973, unless otherwise noted.

§ 19.1 Purpose.

The regulations in this part establish requirements for notices, instructions, and reports by licensees and regulated entities to individuals participating in NRC-licensed and regulated activities and options available to these individuals in connection with Commission inspections of licensees and regulated entities, and to ascertain compliance with the provisions of the Atomic Energy Act of 1954, as amended, titles II and IV of the Energy Reorganization Act of 1974, and regulations, orders, and licenses thereunder. The regulations in this part also establish the rights and responsibilities of the Commission and individuals during interviews compelled by subpoena as part of agency inspections or investigations under Section 161c of the Atomic Energy Act of 1954, as amended, on any matter within the Commission's jurisdiction.

[72 FR 49483, Aug. 28, 2007]

§ 19.2 Scope.

(a) The regulations in this part apply to:

(1) All persons who receive, possess, use, or transfer material licensed by the NRC under the regulations in parts 30 through 36, 39, 40, 60, 61, 63, 70, or 72 of this chapter, including persons licensed to operate a production or utilization facility under parts 50 or 52 of this chapter, persons licensed to possess power reactor spent fuel in an independent spent fuel storage installation (ISFSI) under part 72 of this chapter, and in accordance with 10 CFR 76.60 to persons required to obtain a certificate of compliance or an approved compliance plan under part 76 of this chapter;

(2) All applicants for and holders of licenses (including construction permits and early site permits) under parts 50, 52, and 54 of this chapter;

(3) All applicants for and holders of a standard design approval under subpart E of part 52 of this chapter; and

(4) All applicants for a standard design certification under subpart B of part 52 of this chapter, and those (former) applicants whose designs have been certified under that subpart.

(b) The regulations in this part regarding interviews of individuals under subpoena apply to all investigations and inspections within the jurisdiction of the NRC other than those involving NRC employees or NRC contractors. The regulations in this part do not apply to subpoenas issued under 10 CFR 2.702.

[72 FR 49484, Aug. 28, 2007]

§ 19.3 Definitions.

As used in this part:

Act means the Atomic Energy Act of 1954, (68 Stat. 919) including any amendments thereto.

Commission means the United States Nuclear Regulatory Commission.

Exclusion means the removal of counsel representing multiple interests from an interview whenever the NRC official conducting the interview has concrete evidence that the presence of the counsel would obstruct and impede the particular investigation or inspection.

License means a license issued under the regulations in parts 30 through 36, 39, 40, 60, 61, 63, 70, or 72 of this chapter, including licenses to manufacture, construct and/or operate a production or utilization facility under parts 50, 52, or 54 of this chapter.

Licensee means the holder of such a license.

Regulated activities means any activity carried on which is under the jurisdiction of the NRC under the Atomic Energy Act of 1954, as amended, or any title of the Energy Reorganization Act of 1972, as amended.

Regulated entities means any individual, person, organization, or corporation that is subject to the regulatory jurisdiction of the NRC, including (but not limited to) an applicant for or holder of a standard design approval under subpart E of part 52 of this chapter or a standard design certification under subpart B of part 52 of this chapter.

Restricted area means an area, access to which is limited by the licensee for the purpose of protecting individuals against undue risks from exposure to radiation and radioactive materials. Restricted area does not include areas used as residential quarters, but separate rooms in a residential building may be set apart as a restricted area.

Sequestration means the separation or isolation of witnesses and their attorneys from other witnesses and their attorneys during an interview conducted as part of an investigation, inspection, or other inquiry.

Worker means an individual engaged in activities licensed or regulated by the Commission and controlled by a licensee or regulated entity, but does not include the licensee or regulated entity.

[38 FR 22217, Aug. 17, 1973, as amended at 40 FR 8783, Mar. 3, 1975; 53 FR 31680, Aug. 19, 1988; 55 FR 247, Jan. 4, 1990; 56 FR 23470, May 21, 1991; 56 FR 65948, Dec. 19, 1991; 57 FR 61785, Dec. 29, 1992; 58 FR 7736, Feb. 9, 1993; 66 FR 55789, Nov. 2, 2001; 69 FR 76600, Dec. 22, 2004; 72 FR 49484, Aug. 28, 2007]

§ 19.4 Interpretations.

Except as specifically authorized by the Commission in writing, no interpretation of the meaning of the regulations in this part by any officer or employee of the Commission other than a written interpretation by the General Counsel will be recognized to be binding upon the Commission.

§ 19.5 Communications.

Except where otherwise specified in this part, all communications and reports concerning the regulations in this part should be addressed to the Regional Administrator of the appropriate U.S. Nuclear Regulatory Commission Regional Office listed in Appendix D of part 20 of this chapter. Communications, reports, and applications may be delivered in person at the Commission's offices at One White Flint North, 11555 Rockville Pike (first floor), Rockville, Maryland.

[67 FR 67098, Nov. 4, 2002]

§ 19.8 Information collection requirements: OMB approval.

(a) The Nuclear Regulatory Commission has submitted the information collection requirements contained in this part to the Office of Management and Budget (OMB) for approval as required by the Paperwork Reduction Act (44 U.S.C. 3501 *et seq.*). The NRC may not conduct or sponsor, and a person is not required to respond to, a collection of information unless it displays a currently valid OMB control number. OMB has approved the information collection requirements contained in this part under control number 3150–0044.

(b) The approved information collection requirements contained in this part appear in §§ 19.13 and 19.16.

[62 FR 52185, Oct. 6, 1997]

§ 19.11 Posting of notices to workers.

(a) Each licensee (except for a holder of an early site permit under subpart A of part 52 of this chapter, or a holder of a manufacturing license under subpart F of part 52 of this chapter) shall post current copies of the following documents:

(1) The regulations in this part and in part 20 of this chapter;

(2) The license, license conditions, or documents incorporated into a license by reference, and amendments thereto;

(3) The operating procedures applicable to licensed activities;

(4) Any notice of violation involving radiological working conditions, proposed imposition of civil penalty, or order issued pursuant to subpart B of part 2 of this chapter, and any response from the licensee.

(b) Each applicant for and holder of a standard design approval under subpart E of part 52 of this chapter, each applicant for an early site permit under subpart A of part 52 of this chapter, each applicant for a standard design certification under subpart B of part 52 of this chapter, and each applicant for and holder of a manufacturing license under subpart F of part 52 of this chapter shall post:

(1) The regulations in this part;

(2) The operating procedures applicable to the activities regulated by the NRC which are being conducted by the applicant or holder; and

(3) Any notice of violation, proposed imposition of civil penalty, or order issued under subpart B of part 2 of this chapter, and any response from the applicant or holder.

(c) [Reserved]

(d) If posting of a document specified in paragraphs (a)(1), (2) or (3), or (b)(1) or (2) of this section is not practicable, the licensee or regulated entity may post a notice which describes the document and states where it may be examined.

(e)(1) Each licensee, each applicant for a specific license, each applicant for or holder of a standard design approval under subpart E of part 52 of this chapter, each applicant for an early site permit under subpart A of part 52 of this chapter, and each applicant for a standard design certification under subpart B of part 52 of this chapter shall prominently post NRC Form 3, "Notice to Employees," dated August 1997. Later versions of NRC Form 3 that supersede the August 1997 version shall replace the previously posted version within 30 days of receiving the revised NRC Form 3 from the Commission.

(2) Additional copies of NRC Form 3 may be obtained by writing to the Regional Administrator of the appropriate U.S. Nuclear Regulatory Commission Regional Office listed in appendix D to part 20 of this chapter, via email to *FORMS.Resource@nrc.gov*, or by visiting the NRC's online library at *http://www.nrc.gov/reading-rm/doc-collections/forms/*.

(f) Documents, notices, or forms posted under this section shall appear in a sufficient number of places to permit individuals engaged in NRC-licensed or regulated activities to observe them on the way to or from any particular licensed or regulated activity location to which the document applies, shall be conspicuous, and shall be replaced if defaced or altered.

(g) Commission documents posted under paragraphs (a)(4) or (b)(3) of this section shall be posted within 2 working days after receipt of the documents from the Commission; the licensee's or regulated entity's response, if any, shall be posted within 2 working days after dispatch by the licensee or regulated entity. These documents shall remain posted for a minimum of 5 working days or until action correcting the violation has been completed, whichever is later.

[38 FR 22217, Aug. 17, 1973, as amended at 40 FR 8783, Mar. 3, 1975; 47 FR 30454, July 14, 1982; 58 FR 52408, Oct. 8, 1993; 60 FR 24551, May 9, 1995; 61 FR 6764, Feb. 22, 1996; 62 FR 48166, Sept. 15, 1997; 68 FR 58801, Oct. 10, 2003; 72 FR 49484, Aug. 28, 2007; 73 FR 30457, May 28, 2008; 79 FR 66602, Nov. 10, 2014]

§ 19.12 Instruction to workers.

(a) All individuals who in the course of employment are likely to receive in a year an occupational dose in excess of 100 mrem (1 mSv) shall be—

(1) Kept informed of the storage, transfer, or use of radiation and/or radioactive material;

(2) Instructed in the health protection problems associated with exposure to radiation and/or radioactive material, in precautions or procedures to minimize exposure, and in the purposes and functions of protective devices employed;

(3) Instructed in, and required to observe, to the extent within the workers control, the applicable provisions of Commission regulations and licenses for the protection of personnel from exposure to radiation and/or radioactive material;

(4) Instructed of their responsibility to report promptly to the licensee any condition which may lead to or cause a violation of Commission regulations and licenses or unnecessary exposure to radiation and/or radioactive material;

(5) Instructed in the appropriate response to warnings made in the event of any unusual occurrence or malfunction that may involve exposure to radiation and/or radioactive material; and

(6) Advised as to the radiation exposure reports which workers may request pursuant to § 19.13.

(b) In determining those individuals subject to the requirements of paragraph (a) of this section, licensees must take into consideration assigned activities during normal and abnormal situations involving exposure to radiation and/or radioactive material which can reasonably be expected to occur during the life of a licensed facility. The extent of these instructions must be commensurate with potential radiological health protection problems present in the work place.

[60 FR 36043, July 13, 1995]

§ 19.13 Notifications and reports to individuals.

(a) Radiation exposure data for an individual, and the results of any measurements, analyses, and calculations of radioactive material deposited or retained in the body of an individual, shall be reported to the individual as specified in this section. The information reported shall include data and results obtained pursuant to Commission regulations, orders or license conditions, as shown in records maintained by the licensee pursuant to Commission regulations. Each notification and report shall: be in writing; include appropriate identifying data such as the name of the licensee, the name of the individual, the individual's social security number; include the individual's exposure information; and contain the following statement:

This report is furnished to you under the provisions of the Nuclear Regulatory Commission regulation 10 CFR part 19. You should preserve this report for further reference.

(b) Each licensee shall make dose information available to workers as shown in records maintained by the licensee under the provisions of 10 CFR 20.2106. The licensee shall provide an annual report to each individual monitored under 10 CFR 20.1502 of the dose received in that monitoring year if:

(1) The individual's occupational dose exceeds 1 mSv (100 mrem) TEDE or 1 mSv (100 mrem) to any individual organ or tissue; or

(2) The individual requests his or her annual dose report.

(c)(1) At the request of a worker formerly engaged in licensed activities controlled by the licensee, each licensee shall furnish to the worker a report of the worker's exposure to radiation and/or to radioactive material:

(i) As shown in records maintained by the licensee pursuant to § 20.2106 for each year the worker was required to be monitored under the provisions of § 20.1502; and

(ii) For each year the worker was required to be monitored under the monitoring requirements in effect prior to January 1, 1994.

(2) This report must be furnished within 30 days from the time the request is made or within 30 days after the exposure of the individual has been determined by the licensee, whichever is later. This report must cover the period of time that the worker's activities involved exposure to radiation from radioactive material licensed by the Commission and must include the dates and locations of licensed activities in which the worker participated during this period.

(d) When a licensee is required by §§ 20.2202, 20.2203 or 20.2204 of this chapter to report to the Commission any exposure of an individual to radiation or radioactive material, the licensee shall also provide the individual a report on his or her exposure data included in the report to the Commission. This report must be transmitted no later than the transmittal to the Commission.

(e) At the request of a worker who is terminating employment with the licensee that involved exposure to radiation or radioactive materials, during the current calendar quarter or the current year, each licensee shall provide at termination to each worker, or to the worker's designee, a written report regarding the radiation dose received by that worker from operations of the licensee during the current year or fraction thereof. If the most recent individual monitoring results are not available at that time, a written estimate of the dose must be provided together with a clear indication that this is an estimate.

[38 FR 22217, Aug. 17, 1973, as amended at 40 FR 8783, Mar. 3, 1975; 44 FR 32352, June 6, 1979; 58 FR 67658, Dec. 22, 1993; 59 FR 41642, Aug. 15, 1994; 72 FR 68058, Dec. 4, 2007]

§ 19.14 Presence of representatives of licensees and regulated entities, and workers during inspections.

(a) Each licensee, applicant for a license, applicant for or holder of a standard design approval under subpart E of part 52 of this chapter, applicant for an early site permit under subpart A of part 52 of this chapter, and applicant for a standard design certification under subpart B of part 52 of this chapter shall afford to the Commission at all reasonable times opportunity to inspect materials, activities, facilities, premises, and records under the regulations in this chapter.

(b) During an inspection, Commission inspectors may consult privately with workers as specified in §19.15. The licensee, regulated entity, or the licensee's or regulated entity's representative may accompany Commission inspectors during other phases of an inspection.

(c) If, at the time of inspection, an individual has been authorized by the workers to represent them during Commission inspections, the licensee or regulated entity shall notify the inspectors of such authorization and shall give the workers' representative an opportunity to accompany the inspectors during the inspection of physical working conditions.

(d) Each workers' representative shall be routinely engaged in NRC-licensed or regulated activities under control of the licensee or regulated entity, and shall have received instructions as specified in §19.12.

(e) Different representatives of licensees or regulated entities, and workers may accompany the inspectors during different phases of an inspection if there is no resulting interference with the conduct of the inspection. However, only one workers' representative at a time may accompany the inspectors.

(f) With the approval of the licensee or regulated entity, and the workers' representative an individual who is not routinely engaged in licensed or regulated activities under control of the license or regulated entity (for example, a consultant to the licensee, the regulated entity, or the workers' representative), shall be afforded the opportunity to accompany Commission inspectors during the inspection of physical working conditions.

(g) Notwithstanding the other provisions of this section, Commission inspectors are authorized to refuse to permit accompaniment by any individual who deliberately interferes with a fair and orderly inspection. With regard to areas containing information classified by an agency of the U.S. Government in the interest of national security, an individual who accompanies an inspector may have access to such information only if authorized to do so. With regard to any area containing proprietary information, the workers' representative for that area shall be an individual previously authorized by the licensee or regulated entity to enter that area.

[72 FR 49484, Aug. 28, 2007, as amended at 76 FR 72084, Nov. 22, 2011]

§19.15 Consultation with workers during inspections.

(a) Commission inspectors may consult privately with workers concerning matters of occupational radiation protection and other matters related to applicable provisions of Commission regulations and licenses to the extent the inspectors deem necessary for the conduct of an effective and thorough inspection.

(b) During the course of an inspection any worker may bring privately to the attention of the inspectors, either orally or in writing, any past or present condition which he has reason to believe may have contributed to or caused any violation of the act, the regulations in this chapter, or license condition, or any unnecessary exposure of an individual to radiation from licensed radioactive material under the licensee's control. Any such notice in writing shall comply with the requirements of §19.16(a).

(c) The provisions of paragraph (b) of this section shall not be interpreted as authorization to disregard instructions pursuant to §19.12.

§19.16 Requests by workers for inspections.

(a) Any worker or representative of workers who believes that a violation of the Act, the regulations in this chapter, or license conditions exists or has occurred in license activities with regard to radiological working conditions in which the worker is engaged, may request an inspection by giving notice of the alleged violation to the Administrator of the appropriate Commission Regional Office, or to Commission inspectors. Any such notice shall be in writing, shall set forth the specific grounds for the notice, and shall be signed by the worker or representative of workers. A copy shall be provided the licensee by the Regional Office Administrator, or the inspector no later than at the time of inspection except that, upon the request of the worker giving such notice, his name and the name of individuals referred to therein shall not appear in such copy or on any record published, released or made available by the Commission, except for good cause shown.

(b) If, upon receipt of such notice, the Regional Office Administrator determines that the complaint meets the requirements set forth in paragraph (a) of this section, and that there are reasonable grounds to believe that the alleged violation exists or has occurred, he shall cause an inspection to be made as soon as practicable, to determine if such alleged violation exists or has occurred. Inspections pursuant to this section need not be limited to matters referred to in the complaint.

[38 FR 22217, Aug. 17, 1973, as amended at 40 FR 8783, Mar. 3, 1975; 47 FR 30454, July 14, 1982; 52 FR 31610, Aug. 21, 1987]

§ 19.17 Inspections not warranted; informal review.

(a) If the Administrator of the appropriate Regional Office determines, with respect to a complaint under § 19.16, that an inspection is not warranted because there are no reasonable grounds to believe that a violation exists or has occurred, he shall notify the complainant in writing of such determination. The complainant may obtain review of this determination by submitting a written statement of position to the Executive Director for Operations, either by mail to the U.S. Nuclear Regulatory Commission, Washington, DC 20555–0001; by hand delivery to the NRC's offices at 11555 Rockville Pike, Rockville, Maryland; or, where practicable, by electronic submission, for example, via Electronic Information Exchange, or CD-ROM. Electronic submissions must be made in a manner that enables the NRC to receive, read, authenticate, distribute, and archive the submission, and process and retrieve it a single page at a time. Detailed guidance on making electronic submissions can be obtained by visiting the NRC's Web site at *http://www.nrc.gov/site-help/e-submittals.html;* by e-mail to *MSHD.Resource@nrc.gov;* or by writing the Office of the Chief Information Officer, U.S. Nuclear Regulatory Commission, Washington, DC 20555–0001. The guidance discusses, among other topics, the formats the NRC can accept, the use of electronic signatures, and the treatment of nonpublic information. The Executive Director for Operations will provide the licensee with a copy of such statement by certified mail, excluding, at the request of the complainant, the name of the complainant. The licensee may submit an opposing written statement of position with the Executive Director for Operations who will provide the complainant with a copy of such statement by certified mail. Upon the request of the complainant, the Executive Director for Operations or his designee may hold an informal conference in which the complainant and the licensee may orally present their views. An informal conference may also be held at the request of the licensee, but disclosure of the identity of the complainant will be made only following receipt of written authorization from the complainant. After considering all written and oral views presented, the Executive Director for Operations shall affirm, modify, or reverse the determination of the Administrator of the appropriate Regional Office and furnish the complainant and the licensee a written notification of his decision and the reason therefor.

(b) If the Administrator of the appropriate Regional Office determines that an inspection is not warranted because the requirements of § 19.16(a) have not been met, he shall notify the complainant in writing of such determination. Such determination shall be without prejudice to the filing of a new complaint meeting the requirements of § 19.16(a).

[38 FR 22217, Aug. 17, 1973, as amended at 40 FR 8783, Mar. 3, 1975; 52 FR 31610, Aug. 21, 1987; 67 FR 77652, Dec. 19, 2002; 68 FR 58801, Oct. 10, 2003; 74 FR 62680, Dec. 1, 2009; 80 FR 74978, Dec. 1, 2015]

§ 19.18 Sequestration of witnesses and exclusion of counsel in interviews conducted under subpoena.

(a) All witnesses compelled by subpoena to submit to agency interviews shall be sequestered unless the official conducting the interviews permits otherwise.

(b) Any witness compelled by subpoena to appear at an interview during an agency inquiry may be accompanied, represented, and advised by counsel of his or her choice. However, when the agency official conducting the inquiry determines, after consultation with the Office of the General Counsel, that the agency has concrete evidence that the presence of an attorney representing multiple interests would obstruct and impede the investigation or inspection, the agency official may prohibit that counsel from being present during the interview.

(c) The interviewing official is to provide a witness whose counsel has been excluded under paragraph (b) of this section and the witness's counsel a written statement of the reasons supporting the decision to exclude. This statement, which must be provided no later than five working days after exclusion, must explain the basis for the counsel's exclusion. This statement must also advise the witness of the witness' right to appeal the exclusion decision and obtain an automatic stay of the effectiveness of the subpoena by filing a motion to quash the subpoena with the Commission within five days of receipt of this written statement.

(d) Within five days after receipt of the written notification required in paragraph (c) of this section, a witness whose counsel has been excluded may appeal the exclusion decision by filing a motion to quash the subpoena with the Commission. The filing of the motion to quash will stay the effectiveness of the subpoena pending the Commission's decision on the motion.

(e) If a witness' counsel is excluded under paragraph (b) of this section, the interview may, at the witness' request, either proceed without counsel or be delayed for a reasonable period of time to permit the retention of new counsel. The interview may also be rescheduled to a subsequent date established by the NRC, although the interview shall not be rescheduled by the NRC to a date that precedes the expiration of the time provided under § 19.18(d) for appeal of the exclusion of counsel, unless the witness consents to an earlier date.

[55 FR 247, Jan. 4, 1990, as amended at 56 FR 65948, Dec. 19, 1991; 57 FR 61785, Dec. 29, 1992]

§ 19.20 Employee protection.

Employment discrimination by a licensee, a holder of a certificate of compliance issued under part 76 of this chapter or regulated entity subject to the requirements in this part as delineated in § 19.2(a), or a contractor or subcontractor of a licensee, a holder of a certificate of compliance issued under part 76 of this chapter, or regulated entity subject to the requirements in this part as delineated in § 19.2(a), against an employee for engaging in protected activities under this part or parts 30, 40, 50, 52, 54, 60, 61, 63, 70, 72, 76, or 150 of this chapter is prohibited.

[72 FR 49485, Aug. 28, 2007]

§ 19.30 Violations.

(a) The Commission may obtain an injunction or other court order to prevent a violation of the provisions of—

(1) The Atomic Energy Act of 1954, as amended;

(2) Title II of the Energy Reorganization Act of 1974, as amended; or

(3) A regulation or order issued pursuant to those Acts.

(b) The Commission may obtain a court order for the payment of a civil penalty imposed under section 234 of the Atomic Energy Act:

(1) For violations of—

(i) Sections 53, 57, 62, 63, 81, 82, 101, 103, 104, 107, or 109 of the Atomic Energy Act of 1954, as amended;

(ii) Section 206 of the Energy Reorganization Act;

(iii) Any rule, regulation, or order issued pursuant to the sections specified in paragraph (b)(1)(i) of this section;

(iv) Any term, condition, or limitation of any license issued under the sections specified in paragraph (b)(1)(i) of this section.

(2) For any violation for which a license may be revoked under section 186

of the Atomic Energy Act of 1954, as amended.

[57 FR 55071, Nov. 24, 1992]

§ 19.31 Application for exemptions.

The Commission may, upon application by any interested person or upon its own initiative, grant such exemptions from the requirements of the regulations in this part as it determines are authorized by law, will not result in undue hazard to life and property.

[72 FR 49485, Aug. 28, 2007]

§ 19.32 Discrimination prohibited.

No person shall on the grounds of sex be excluded from participation in, be denied a license, be denied the benefit of, or be subjected to discrimination under any program or activity carried on which is under the jurisdiction of the NRC under the Atomic Energy Act of 1954, as amended, or under any title of the Energy Reorganization Act of 1974, as amended. This provision will be enforced through agency provisions and regulations similar to those already established, with respect to racial and other discrimination, under Title VI of the Civil Rights Act of 1964. This remedy is not exclusive, however, and will not prejudice or cut off any other legal remedies available to a discriminatee.

[72 FR 49485, Aug. 28, 2007]

§ 19.40 Criminal penalties.

(a) Section 223 of the Atomic Energy Act of 1954, as amended, provides for criminal sanctions for willful violation of, attempted violation of, or conspiracy to violate, any regulation issued under sections 161b, 161i, or 161o of the Act. For purposes of section 223, all the regulations in part 19 are issued under one or more of sections 161b, 161i, or 161o, except for the sections listed in paragraph (b) of this section.

(b) The regulations in part 19 that are not issued under sections 161b, 161i, or 161o for the purposes of section 223 are as follows: §§ 19.1, 19.2, 19.3, 19.4, 19.5, 19.8, 19.16, 19.17, 19.18, 19.30, 19.31, and 19.40.

[57 FR 55071, Nov. 24, 1992]

PART 20—STANDARDS FOR PROTECTION AGAINST RADIATION

Subpart A—General Provisions

Sec.

Subpart B—Radiation Protection Programs

Subpart C—Occupational Dose Limits

Subpart D—Radiation Dose Limits for Individual Members of the Public

Subpart E—Radiological Criteria for License Termination.

Subpart F—Surveys and Monitoring

AUTHORITY: Atomic Energy Act of 1954, secs. 11, 53, 63, 65, 81, 103, 104, 161, 170H, 182, 186, 223, 234, 274, 1701 (42 U.S.C. 2014, 2073, 2093, 2095, 2111, 2133, 2134, 2201, 2210h, 2232, 2236, 2273, 2282, 2021, 2297f); Energy Reorganization Act of 1974, secs. 201, 202 (42 U.S.C. 5841, 5842); Low-Level Radioactive Waste Policy Amendments Act of 1985, sec. 2 (42 U.S.C. 2021b); 44 U.S.C. 3504 note.

Subpart A—General Provisions

SOURCE: 56 FR 23391, May 21, 1991, unless otherwise noted.

§ 20.1001 Purpose.

(a) The regulations in this part establish standards for protection against ionizing radiation resulting from activities conducted under licenses issued by the Nuclear Regulatory Commission. These regulations are issued under the Atomic Energy Act of 1954, as amended, and the Energy Reorganization Act of 1974, as amended.

(b) It is the purpose of the regulations in this part to control the receipt, possession, use, transfer, and disposal of licensed material by any licensee in such a manner that the total dose to an individual (including doses resulting from licensed and unlicensed radioactive material and from radiation sources other than background radiation) does not exceed the standards for protection against radiation prescribed in the regulations in this part. However, nothing in this part shall be construed as limiting actions that may be necessary to protect health and safety.

§ 20.1002 Scope.

The regulations in this part apply to persons licensed by the Commission to receive, possess, use, transfer, or dispose of byproduct, source, or special nuclear material or to operate a production or utilization facility under parts 30 through 36, 39, 40, 50, 52, 60, 61, 63, 70, or 72 of this chapter, and in accordance with 10 CFR 76.60 to persons required to obtain a certificate of compliance or an approved compliance plan under part 76 of this chapter. The limits in this part do not apply to doses due to background radiation, to exposure of patients to radiation for the purpose of medical diagnosis or therapy, to exposure from individuals administered radioactive material and released under § 35.75, or to exposure from voluntary participation in medical research programs.

[72 FR 49485, Aug. 28, 2007]

§ 20.1003 Definitions.

As used in this part:

Absorbed dose means the energy imparted by ionizing radiation per unit mass of irradiated material. The units of absorbed dose are the rad and the gray (Gy).

Accelerator-produced radioactive material means any material made radioactive by a particle accelerator.

Act means the Atomic Energy Act of 1954 (42 U.S.C. 2011 *et seq.*), as amended.

Activity is the rate of disintegration (transformation) or decay of radioactive material. The units of activity are the curie (Ci) and the becquerel (Bq).

Adult means an individual 18 or more years of age.

Airborne radioactive material means radioactive material dispersed in the air in the form of dusts, fumes, particulates, mists, vapors, or gases.

Airborne radioactivity area means a room, enclosure, or area in which airborne radioactive materials, composed wholly or partly of licensed material, exist in concentrations—

(1) In excess of the derived air concentrations (DACs) specified in appendix B, to §§ 20.1001–20.2401, or

(2) To such a degree that an individual present in the area without respiratory protective equipment could exceed, during the hours an individual is present in a week, an intake of 0.6 percent of the annual limit on intake (ALI) or 12 DAC-hours.

Air-purifying respirator means a respirator with an air-purifying filter, cartridge, or canister that removes specific air contaminants by passing ambient air through the air-purifying element.

ALARA (acronym for "as low as is reasonably achievable") means making every reasonable effort to maintain exposures to radiation as far below the dose limits in this part as is practical consistent with the purpose for which the licensed activity is undertaken, taking into account the state of technology, the economics of improvements in relation to state of technology, the economics of improvements in relation to benefits to the public health and safety, and other societal and socioeconomic considerations, and in relation to utilization of nuclear energy and licensed materials in the public interest.

Annual limit on intake (ALI) means the derived limit for the amount of radioactive material taken into the body of an adult worker by inhalation or ingestion in a year. ALI is the smaller value of intake of a given radionuclide in a year by the reference man that would result in a committed effective dose equivalent of 5 rems (0.05 Sv) or a committed dose equivalent of 50 rems (0.5 Sv) to any individual organ or tissue. (ALI values for intake by ingestion and by inhalation of selected radionuclides are given in table 1, columns 1 and 2, of appendix B to §§ 20.1001–20.2401).

Assigned protection factor (APF) means the expected workplace level of respiratory protection that would be provided by a properly functioning respirator or a class of respirators to properly fitted and trained users. Operationally, the inhaled concentration can be estimated by dividing the ambient airborne concentration by the APF.

Atmosphere-supplying respirator means a respirator that supplies the respirator user with breathing air from a source independent of the ambient atmosphere, and includes supplied-air respirators (SARs) and self-contained breathing apparatus (SCBA) units.

Background radiation means radiation from cosmic sources; naturally occurring radioactive material, including radon (except as a decay product of source or special nuclear material); and global fallout as it exists in the environment from the testing of nuclear explosive devices or from past nuclear accidents such as Chernobyl that contribute to background radiation and are not under the control of the licensee. "*Background radiation*" does not include radiation from source, byproduct, or special nuclear materials regulated by the Commission.

Bioassay (radiobioassay) means the determination of kinds, quantities or concentrations, and, in some cases, the locations of radioactive material in the human body, whether by direct measurement (in vivo counting) or by analysis and evaluation of materials excreted or removed from the human body.

Byproduct material means—

(1) Any radioactive material (except special nuclear material) yielded in, or made radioactive by, exposure to the radiation incident to the process of producing or using special nuclear material;

(2) The tailings or wastes produced by the extraction or concentration of uranium or thorium from ore processed primarily for its source material content, including discrete surface wastes resulting from uranium solution extraction processes. Underground ore bodies depleted by these solution extraction operations do not constitute "byproduct material" within this definition;

(3)(i) Any discrete source of radium-226 that is produced, extracted, or converted after extraction, before, on, or after August 8, 2005, for use for a commercial, medical, or research activity; or

(ii) Any material that—

(A) Has been made radioactive by use of a particle accelerator; and

(B) Is produced, extracted, or converted after extraction, before, on, or after August 8, 2005, for use for a commercial, medical, or research activity; and

(4) Any discrete source of naturally occurring radioactive material, other than source material, that—

(i) The Commission, in consultation with the Administrator of the Environmental Protection Agency, the Secretary of Energy, the Secretary of Homeland Security, and the head of any other appropriate Federal agency, determines would pose a threat similar to the threat posed by a discrete source of radium-226 to the public health and safety or the common defense and security; and

(ii) Before, on, or after August 8, 2005, is extracted or converted after extraction for use in a commercial, medical, or research activity.

Class (or *lung class* or *inhalation class*) means a classification scheme for inhaled material according to its rate of clearance from the pulmonary region of the lung. Materials are classified as D, W, or Y, which applies to a range of clearance half-times: for Class D (Days) of less than 10 days, for Class W (Weeks) from 10 to 100 days, and for

Class Y (Years) of greater than 100 days.

Collective dose is the sum of the individual doses received in a given period of time by a specified population from exposure to a specified source of radiation.

Commission means the Nuclear Regulatory Commission or its duly authorized representatives.

Committed dose equivalent ($H_{T,50}$) means the dose equivalent to organs or tissues of reference (T) that will be received from an intake of radioactive material by an individual during the 50-year period following the intake.

Committed effective dose equivalent ($H_{E,50}$) is the sum of the products of the weighting factors applicable to each of the body organs or tissues that are irradiated and the committed dose equivalent to these organs or tissues ($H_{E,50} = \Sigma\ w_T\ H_{T,50}$).

Constraint (dose constraint) means a value above which specified licensee actions are required.

Controlled area means an area, outside of a restricted area but inside the site boundary, access to which can be limited by the licensee for any reason.

Critical Group means the group of individuals reasonably expected to receive the greatest exposure to residual radioactivity for any applicable set of circumstances.

Declared pregnant woman means a woman who has voluntarily informed the licensee, in writing, of her pregnancy and the estimated date of conception. The declaration remains in effect until the declared pregnant woman withdraws the declaration in writing or is no longer pregnant.

Decommission means to remove a facility or site safely from service and reduce residual radioactivity to a level that permits—

(1) Release of the property for unrestricted use and termination of the license; or

(2) Release of the property under restricted conditions and the termination of the license.

Deep-dose equivalent (H_d), which applies to external whole-body exposure, is the dose equivalent at a tissue depth of 1 cm (1000 mg/cm^2).

Demand respirator means an atmosphere-supplying respirator that admits breathing air to the facepiece only when a negative pressure is created inside the facepiece by inhalation.

Department means the Department of Energy established by the Department of Energy Organization Act (Pub. L. 95–91, 91 Stat. 565, 42 U.S.C. 7101 *et seq.*) to the extent that the Department, or its duly authorized representatives, exercises functions formerly vested in the U.S. Atomic Energy Commission, its Chairman, members, officers, and components and transferred to the U.S. Energy Research and Development Administration and to the Administrator thereof pursuant to sections 104 (b), (c), and (d) of the Energy Reorganization Act of 1974 (Pub. L. 93–438, 88 Stat. 1233 at 1237, 42 U.S.C. 5814) and retransferred to the Secretary of Energy pursuant to section 301(a) of the Department of Energy Organization Act (Pub. L. 95–91, 91 Stat 565 at 577–578, 42 U.S.C. 7151).

Derived air concentration (DAC) means the concentration of a given radionuclide in air which, if breathed by the reference man for a working year of 2,000 hours under conditions of light work (inhalation rate 1.2 cubic meters of air per hour), results in an intake of one ALI. DAC values are given in table 1, column 3, of appendix B to §§ 20.1001–20.2401.

Derived air concentration-hour (DAC-hour) is the product of the concentration of radioactive material in air (expressed as a fraction or multiple of the derived air concentration for each radionuclide) and the time of exposure to that radionuclide, in hours. A licensee may take 2,000 DAC-hours to represent one ALI, equivalent to a committed effective dose equivalent of 5 rems (0.05 Sv).

Discrete source means a radionuclide that has been processed so that its concentration within a material has been purposely increased for use for commercial, medical, or research activities.

Disposable respirator means a respirator for which maintenance is not intended and that is designed to be discarded after excessive breathing resistance, sorbent exhaustion, physical damage, or end-of-service-life renders it unsuitable for use. Examples of this type of respirator are a disposable half-mask respirator or a disposable escape-only self-contained breathing apparatus (SCBA).

Distinguishable from background means that the detectable concentration of a radionuclide is statistically different from the background concentration of that radionuclide in the vicinity of the site or, in the case of structures, in similar materials using adequate measurement technology, survey, and statistical techniques.

Dose or *radiation dose* is a generic term that means absorbed dose, dose equivalent, effective dose equivalent, committed dose equivalent, committed effective dose equivalent, or total effective dose equivalent, as defined in other paragraphs of this section.

Dose equivalent (H_T) means the product of the absorbed dose in tissue, quality factor, and all other necessary modifying factors at the location of interest. The units of dose equivalent are the rem and sievert (Sv).

Dosimetry processor means an individual or organization that processes and evaluates individual monitoring equipment in order to determine the radiation dose delivered to the equipment.

Effective dose equivalent (H_E) is the sum of the products of the dose equivalent to the organ or tissue (H_T) and the weighting factors (w_T) applicable to each of the body organs or tissues that are irradiated ($H_E = \Sigma w_T H_T$).

Embryo/fetus means the developing human organism from conception until the time of birth.

Entrance or access point means any location through which an individual could gain access to radiation areas or to radioactive materials. This includes entry or exit portals of sufficient size to permit human entry, irrespective of their intended use.

Exposure means being exposed to ionizing radiation or to radioactive material.

External dose means that portion of the dose equivalent received from radiation sources outside the body.

Extremity means hand, elbow, arm below the elbow, foot, knee, or leg below the knee.

Filtering facepiece (dust mask) means a negative pressure particulate respirator with a filter as an integral part of the facepiece or with the entire facepiece composed of the filtering medium, not equipped with elastomeric sealing surfaces and adjustable straps.

Fit factor means a quantitative estimate of the fit of a particular respirator to a specific individual, and typically estimates the ratio of the concentration of a substance in ambient air to its concentration inside the respirator when worn.

Fit test means the use of a protocol to qualitatively or quantitatively evaluate the fit of a respirator on an individual.

Generally applicable environmental radiation standards means standards issued by the Environmental Protection Agency (EPA) under the authority of the Atomic Energy Act of 1954, as amended, that impose limits on radiation exposures or levels, or concentrations or quantities of radioactive material, in the general environment outside the boundaries of locations under the control of persons possessing or using radioactive material.

Government agency means any executive department, commission, independent establishment, corporation wholly or partly owned by the United States of America, which is an instrumentality of the United States, or any board, bureau, division, service, office, officer, authority, administration, or other establishment in the executive branch of the Government.

Gray [See § 20.1004].

Helmet means a rigid respiratory inlet covering that also provides head protection against impact and penetration.

High radiation area means an area, accessible to individuals, in which radiation levels from radiation sources external to the body could result in an individual receiving a dose equivalent in excess of 0.1 rem (1 mSv) in 1 hour at 30 centimeters from the radiation source or 30 centimeters from any surface that the radiation penetrates.

Hood means a respiratory inlet covering that completely covers the head and neck and may also cover portions of the shoulders and torso.

Individual means any human being.

Individual monitoring means—

(1) The assessment of dose equivalent by the use of devices designed to be worn by an individual;

(2) The assessment of committed effective dose equivalent by bioassay (see *Bioassay*) or by determination of the time-weighted air concentrations to which an individual has been exposed, i.e., DAC-hours; or

(3) The assessment of dose equivalent by the use of survey data.

Individual monitoring devices (individual monitoring equipment) means devices designed to be worn by a single individual for the assessment of dose equivalent such as film badges, thermoluminescence dosimeters (TLDs), pocket ionization chambers, and personal ("lapel") air sampling devices.

Internal dose means that portion of the dose equivalent received from radioactive material taken into the body.

Lens dose equivalent (LDE) applies to the external exposure of the lens of the eye and is taken as the dose equivalent at a tissue depth of 0.3 centimeter (300 mg/cm^2).

License means a license issued under the regulations in parts 30 through 36, 39, 40, 50, 60, 61, 63, 70, or 72 of this chapter.

Licensed material means source material, special nuclear material, or byproduct material received, possessed, used, transferred or disposed of under a general or specific license issued by the Commission.

Licensee means the holder of a license.

Limits (dose limits) means the permissible upper bounds of radiation doses.

Loose-fitting facepiece means a respiratory inlet covering that is designed to form a partial seal with the face.

Lost or missing licensed material means licensed material whose location is unknown. It includes material that has been shipped but has not reached its destination and whose location cannot be readily traced in the transportation system.

Member of the public means any individual except when that individual is receiving an occupational dose.

Minor means an individual less than 18 years of age.

Monitoring (radiation monitoring, radiation protection monitoring) means the measurement of radiation levels, concentrations, surface area concentrations or quantities of radioactive material and the use of the results of these measurements to evaluate potential exposures and doses.

Nationally tracked source is a sealed source containing a quantity equal to or greater than Category 1 or Category 2 levels of any radioactive material listed in Appendix E of this part. In this context a sealed source is defined as radioactive material that is sealed in a capsule or closely bonded, in a solid form and which is not exempt from regulatory control. It does not mean material encapsulated solely for disposal, or nuclear material contained in any fuel assembly, subassembly, fuel rod, or fuel pellet. Category 1 nationally tracked sources are those containing radioactive material at a quantity equal to or greater than the Category 1 threshold. Category 2 nationally tracked sources are those containing radioactive material at a quantity equal to or greater than the Category 2 threshold but less than the Category 1 threshold.

Negative pressure respirator (tight fitting) means a respirator in which the air pressure inside the facepiece is negative during inhalation with respect to the ambient air pressure outside the respirator.

Nonstochastic effect means health effects, the severity of which varies with the dose and for which a threshold is believed to exist. Radiation-induced cataract formation is an example of a nonstochastic effect (also called a deterministic effect).

NRC means the Nuclear Regulatory Commission or its duly authorized representatives.

Occupational dose means the dose received by an individual in the course of employment in which the individual's assigned duties involve exposure to radiation or to radioactive material from licensed and unlicensed sources of radiation, whether in the possession of the licensee or other person. Occupational dose does not include doses received from background radiation, from any medical administration the individual has received, from exposure to individuals administered radioactive material and released under § 35.75, from voluntary participation in medical research programs, or as a member of the public.

Particle accelerator means any machine capable of accelerating electrons, protons, deuterons, or other charged particles in a vacuum and of discharging the resultant particulate or other radiation into a medium at energies usually in excess of 1 megaelectron volt. For purposes of this definition, "accelerator" is an equivalent term.

Person means—

(1) Any individual, corporation, partnership, firm, association, trust, estate, public or private institution, group, Government agency other than the Commission or the Department of Energy (except that the Department shall be considered a person within the meaning of the regulations in 10 CFR chapter I to the extent that its facilities and activities are subject to the licensing and related regulatory authority of the Commission under section 202 of the Energy Reorganization Act of 1974 (88 Stat. 1244), the Uranium Mill Tailings Radiation Control Act of 1978 (92 Stat. 3021), the Nuclear Waste Policy Act of 1982 (96 Stat. 2201), and section 3(b)(2) of the Low-Level Radioactive Waste Policy Amendments Act of 1985 (99 Stat. 1842)), any State or any political subdivision of or any political entity within a State, any foreign government or nation or any political subdivision of any such government or nation, or other entity; and

(2) Any legal successor, representative, agent, or agency of the foregoing.

Planned special exposure means an infrequent exposure to radiation, separate from and in addition to the annual dose limits.

Positive pressure respirator means a respirator in which the pressure inside the respiratory inlet covering exceeds the ambient air pressure outside the respirator.

Powered air-purifying respirator (PAPR) means an air-purifying respirator that uses a blower to force the ambient air through air-purifying elements to the inlet covering.

Pressure demand respirator means a positive pressure atmosphere-supplying respirator that admits breathing air to the facepiece when the positive pressure is reduced inside the facepiece by inhalation.

Public dose means the dose received by a member of the public from exposure to radiation or to radioactive material released by a licensee, or to any other source of radiation under the control of a licensee. Public dose does not include occupational dose or doses received from background radiation, from any medical administration the individual has received, from exposure to individuals administered radioactive material and released under § 35.75, or from voluntary participation in medical research programs.

Qualitative fit test (QLFT) means a pass/fail fit test to assess the adequacy of respirator fit that relies on the individual's response to the test agent.

Quality Factor (Q) means the modifying factor (listed in tables 1004(b).1 and 1004(b).2 of § 20.1004) that is used to derive dose equivalent from absorbed dose.

Quantitative fit test (QNFT) means an assessment of the adequacy of respirator fit by numerically measuring the amount of leakage into the respirator.

Quarter means a period of time equal to one-fourth of the year observed by the licensee (approximately 13 consective weeks), providing that the beginning of the first quarter in a year coincides with the starting date of the year and that no day is omitted or duplicated in consecutive quarters.

Rad (See § 20.1004).

Radiation (ionizing radiation) means alpha particles, beta particles, gamma rays, x-rays, neutrons, high-speed electrons, high-speed protons, and other particles capable of producing ions. Radiation, as used in this part, does not include non-ionizing radiation, such as radio- or microwaves, or visible, infrared, or ultraviolet light.

Radiation area means an area, accessible to individuals, in which radiation levels could result in an individual receiving a dose equivalent in excess of 0.005 rem (0.05 mSv) in 1 hour at 30 centimeters from the radiation source or from any surface that the radiation penetrates.

Reference man means a hypothetical aggregation of human physical and physiological characteristics arrived at by international consensus. These characteristics may be used by researchers and public health workers to standardize results of experiments and to relate biological insult to a common base.

Rem (See § 20.1004).

Residual radioactivity means radioactivity in structures, materials, soils, groundwater, and other media at a site resulting from activities under the licensee's control. This includes radioactivity from all licensed and unlicensed sources used by the licensee, but excludes background radiation. It also includes radioactive materials remaining at the site as a result of routine or accidental releases of radioactive material at the site and previous burials at the site, even if those burials were made in accordance with the provisions of 10 CFR part 20.

Respiratory protective device means an apparatus, such as a respirator, used to reduce the individual's intake of airborne radioactive materials.

Restricted area means an area, access to which is limited by the licensee for the purpose of protecting individuals against undue risks from exposure to radiation and radioactive materials. Restricted area does not include areas used as residential quarters, but separate rooms in a residential building may be set apart as a restricted area.

Sanitary sewerage means a system of public sewers for carrying off waste water and refuse, but excluding sewage treatment facilities, septic tanks, and leach fields owned or operated by the licensee.

Self-contained breathing apparatus (SCBA) means an atmosphere-supplying respirator for which the breathing air source is designed to be carried by the user.

Shallow-dose equivalent (H_s), which applies to the external exposure of the skin of the whole body or the skin of an extremity, is taken as the dose equivalent at a tissue depth of 0.007 centimeter (7 mg/cm^2).

Site boundary means that line beyond which the land or property is not owned, leased, or otherwise controlled by the licensee.

Source material means—

(1) Uranium or thorium or any combination of uranium and thorium in any physical or chemical form; or

(2) Ores that contain, by weight, one-twentieth of 1 percent (0.05 percent), or more, of uranium, thorium, or any combination of uranium and thorium. Source material does not include special nuclear material.

Special nuclear material means—

(1) Plutonium, uranium-233, uranium enriched in the isotope 233 or in the isotope 235, and any other material that the Commission, pursuant to the provisions of section 51 of the Act, determines to be special nuclear material, but does not include source material; or

(2) Any material artificially enriched by any of the foregoing but does not include source material.

Stochastic effects means health effects that occur randomly and for which the probability of the effect occurring, rather than its severity, is assumed to be a linear function of dose without threshold. Hereditary effects and cancer incidence are examples of stochastic effects.

Supplied-air respirator (SAR) or *airline respirator* means an atmosphere-supplying respirator for which the source of breathing air is not designed to be carried by the user.

Survey means an evaluation of the radiological conditions and potential hazards incident to the production, use, transfer, release, disposal, or presence of radioactive material or other sources of radiation. When appropriate, such an evaluation includes a physical survey of the location of radioactive material and measurements or calculations of levels of radiation, or concentrations or quantities of radioactive material present.

Tight-fitting facepiece means a respiratory inlet covering that forms a complete seal with the face.

Total Effective Dose Equivalent (TEDE) means the sum of the effective dose equivalent (for external exposures) and the committed effective dose equivalent (for internal exposures).

Unrestricted area means an area, access to which is neither limited nor controlled by the licensee.

Uranium fuel cycle means the operations of milling of uranium ore, chemical conversion of uranium, isotopic enrichment of uranium, fabrication of uranium fuel, generation of electricity by a light-water-cooled nuclear power plant using uranium fuel, and reprocessing of spent uranium fuel to the extent that these activities directly support the production of electrical power for public use. Uranium fuel cycle does not include mining operations, operations at waste disposal sites, transportation of radioactive material in support of these operations, and the reuse of recovered non-uranium special nuclear and byproduct materials from the cycle.

User seal check (fit check) means an action conducted by the respirator user to determine if the respirator is properly seated to the face. Examples include negative pressure check, positive pressure check, irritant smoke check, or isoamyl acetate check.

Very high radiation area means an area, accessible to individuals, in which radiation levels from radiation sources external to the body could result in an individual receiving an absorbed dose in excess of 500 rads (5 grays) in 1 hour at 1 meter from a radiation source or 1 meter from any surface that the radiation penetrates.

NOTE: At very high doses received at high dose rates, units of absorbed dose (e.g., rads and grays) are appropriate, rather than units of dose equivalent (e.g., rems and sieverts)).

Waste means those low-level radioactive wastes containing source, special nuclear, or byproduct material that are acceptable for disposal in a land disposal facility. For the purposes of this definition, low-level radioactive waste means radioactive waste not classified as high-level radioactive waste, transuranic waste, spent nuclear fuel, or byproduct material as defined in paragraphs (2), (3), and (4) of the definition of Byproduct material set forth in this section.

Week means 7 consecutive days starting on Sunday.

Weighting factor w_T, for an organ or tissue (T) is the proportion of the risk of stochastic effects resulting from irradiation of that organ or tissue to the total risk of stochastic effects when the whole body is irradiated uniformly. For calculating the effective dose equivalent, the values of w_T are:

ORGAN DOSE WEIGHTING FACTORS

Organ or tissue	w_T
Gonads	0.25
Breast	0.15
Red bone marrow	0.12
Lung	0.12
Thyroid	0.03
Bone surfaces	0.03
Remainder	[1] 0.30
Whole Body	[2] 1.00

[1] 0.30 results from 0.06 for each of 5 "remainder" organs (excluding the skin and the lens of the eye) that receive the highest doses.

[2] For the purpose of weighting the external whole body dose (for adding it to the internal dose), a single weighting factor, w_T = 1.0, has been specified. The use of other weighting factors for external exposure will be approved on a case-by-case basis until such time as specific guidance is issued.

Whole body means, for purposes of external exposure, head, trunk (including male gonads), arms above the elbow, or legs above the knee.

Working level (WL) is any combination of short-lived radon daughters (for radon-222: polonium-218, lead-214, bismuth-214, and polonium-214; and for radon-220: polonium-216, lead-212, bismuth-212, and polonium-212) in 1 liter of air that will result in the ultimate emission of 1.3×10^5 MeV of potential alpha particle energy.

Working level month (WLM) means an exposure to 1 working level for 170 hours (2,000 working hours per year/12 months per year = approximately 170 hours per month).

Year means the period of time beginning in January used to determine compliance with the provisions of this part. The licensee may change the starting date of the year used to determine compliance by the licensee provided that the change is made at the beginning of the year and that no day is omitted or duplicated in consecutive years.

[56 FR 23391, May 21, 1991, as amended at 57 FR 57878, Dec. 8, 1992; 58 FR 7736, Feb. 9, 1993; 60 FR 36043, July 13, 1995; 60 FR 48625, Sept. 20, 1995; 61 FR 65127, Dec. 10, 1996; 62 FR 4133, Jan. 29, 1997; 62 FR 39087, July 21, 1997; 63 FR 39481, July 23, 1998; 64 FR 54556, Oct. 7, 1999; 66 FR 55789, Nov. 2, 2001; 67 FR 16304, Apr. 5, 2002; 67 FR 20370, Apr. 24, 2002; 67 FR 62872, Oct. 9, 2002; 71 FR 65707, Nov. 8, 2006; 72 FR 55921, Oct. 1, 2007; 72 FR 68058, Dec. 4, 2007; 74 FR 62680, Dec. 1, 2009]

§ 20.1004 Units of radiation dose.

(a) *Definitions*. As used in this part, the units of radiation dose are:

Gray (Gy) is the SI unit of absorbed dose. One gray is equal to an absorbed dose of 1 Joule/kilogram (100 rads).

Rad is the special unit of absorbed dose. One rad is equal to an absorbed dose of 100 ergs/gram or 0.01 joule/kilogram (0.01 gray).

Rem is the special unit of any of the quantities expressed as dose equivalent. The dose equivalent in rems is equal to the absorbed dose in rads multiplied by the quality factor (1 rem = 0.01 sievert).

Sievert is the SI unit of any of the quantities expressed as dose equivalent. The dose equivalent in sieverts is equal to the absorbed dose in grays multiplied by the quality factor (1 Sv = 100 rems).

(b) As used in this part, the quality factors for converting absorbed dose to dose equivalent are shown in table 1004(b).1.

TABLE 1004(b).1—QUALITY FACTORS AND ABSORBED DOSE EQUIVALENCIES

Type of radiation	Quality factor (Q)	Absorbed dose equal to a unit dose equivalent[a]
X-, gamma, or beta radiation	1	1
Alpha particles, multiple-charged particles, fission fragments and heavy particles of unknown charge	20	0.05
Neutrons of unknown energy	10	0.1
High-energy protons	10	0.1

[a] Absorbed dose in rad equal to 1 rem or the absorbed dose in gray equal to 1 sievert.

(c) If it is more convenient to measure the neutron fluence rate than to determine the neutron dose equivalent rate in rems per hour or sieverts per hour, as provided in paragraph (b) of this section, 1 rem (0.01 Sv) of neutron radiation of unknown energies may, for purposes of the regulations in this part, be assumed to result from a total fluence of 25 million neutrons per square centimeter incident upon the body. If sufficient information exists to estimate the approximate energy distribution of the neutrons, the licensee may use the fluence rate per unit dose equivalent or the appropriate Q value from table 1004(b).2 to convert a measured tissue dose in rads to dose equivalent in rems.

TABLE 1004(b).2—MEAN QUALITY FACTORS, Q, AND FLUENCE PER UNIT DOSE EQUIVALENT FOR MONOENERGETIC NEUTRONS

	Neutron energy (MeV)	Quality factor[a] (Q)	Fluence per unit dose equivalent[b] (neutrons cm^{-2} rem^{-1})
(thermal)	2.5×10^{-8}	2	980×10^6
	1×10^{-7}	2	980×10^6
	1×10^{-6}	2	810×10^6
	1×10^{-5}	2	810×10^6
	1×10^{-4}	2	840×10^6
	1×10^{-3}	2	980×10^6
	1×10^{-2}	2.5	1010×10^6
	1×10^{-1}	7.5	170×10^6
	5×10^{-1}	11	39×10^6
	1	11	27×10^6
	2.5	9	29×10^6
	5	8	23×10^6
	7	7	24×10^6
	10	6.5	24×10^6
	14	7.5	17×10^6
	20	8	16×10^6
	40	7	14×10^6
	60	5.5	16×10^6
	1×10^2	4	20×10^6
	2×10^2	3.5	19×10^6
	3×10^2	3.5	16×10^6
	4×10^2	3.5	14×10^6

[a] Value of quality factor (Q) at the point where the dose equivalent is maximum in a 30-cm diameter cylinder tissue-equivalent phantom.

[b] Monoenergetic neutrons incident normally on a 30-cm diameter cylinder tissue-equivalent phantom.

§ 20.1005 Units of radioactivity.

For the purposes of this part, activity is expressed in the special unit of curies (Ci) or in the SI unit of becquerels (Bq), or their multiples, or disintegrations (transformations) per unit of time.

(a) One becquerel = 1 disintegration per second (s^{-1}).

(b) One curie = 3.7×10^{10} disintegrations per second = 3.7×10^{10} becquerels = 2.22×10^{12} disintegrations per minute.

[56 FR 23391, May 21, 1991; 56 FR 61352, Dec. 3, 1991]

§ 20.1006 Interpretations.

Except as specifically authorized by the Commission in writing, no interpretation of the meaning of the regulations in this part by an officer or employee of the Commission other than a written interpretation by the General Counsel will be recognized to be binding upon the Commission.

§ 20.1007 Communications.

Unless otherwise specified, communications or reports concerning the regulations in this part should be addressed to the Executive Director for Operations (EDO), and sent either by mail to the U.S. Nuclear Regulatory Commission, Washington, DC 20555–0001; by hand delivery to the NRC's offices at 11555 Rockville Pike, Rockville, Maryland; or, where practicable, by electronic submission, for example, via Electronic Information Exchange, or CD-ROM. Electronic submissions must be made in a manner that enables the NRC to receive, read, authenticate, distribute, and archive the submission, and process and retrieve it a single page at a time. Detailed guidance on making electronic submissions can be obtained by visiting the NRC's Web site at *http://www.nrc.gov/site-help/e-submittals.html;* by e-mail to *MSHD.Resource@nrc.gov;* or by writing the Office of the Chief Information Officer, U.S. Nuclear Regulatory Commission, Washington, DC 20555–0001. The guidance discusses, among other topics, the formats the NRC can accept, the use of electronic signatures, and the treatment of nonpublic information.

[68 FR 58801, Oct. 10, 2003, as amended at 74 FR 62680, Dec. 1, 2009; 80 FR 74979, Dec. 1, 2015]

§ 20.1008 Implementation.

(a) [Reserved]

(b) The applicable section of §§ 20.1001–20.2402 must be used in lieu of requirements in the standards for protection against radiation in effect prior to January 1, 1994[1] that are cited in license conditions or technical specifications, except as specified in paragraphs (c), (d), and (e) of this section. If the requirements of this part are more restrictive than the existing license condition, then the licensee shall comply with this part unless exempted by paragraph (d) of this section.

(c) Any existing license condition or technical specification that is more restrictive than a requirement in §§ 20.1001–20.2402 remains in force until there is a technical specification change, license amendment, or license renewal.

(d) If a license condition or technical specification exempted a licensee from a requirement in the standards for protection against radiation in effect prior to January 1, 1994,[1] it continues to exempt a licensee from the corresponding provision of §§ 20.1001–20.2402.

(e) If a license condition cites provisions in requirements in the standards for protection against radiation in effect prior to January 1, 1994[1] and there are no corresponding provisions in §§ 20.1001–20.2402, then the license condition remains in force until there is a technical specification change, license amendment, or license renewal that modifies or removes this condition.

[59 FR 41643, Aug. 15, 1994]

§ 20.1009 Information collection requirements: OMB approval.

(a) The Nuclear Regulatory Commission has submitted the information collection requirements contained in this part to the Office of Management and Budget (OMB) for approval as required by the Paperwork Reduction Act (44 U.S.C. 3501 *et seq.*). The NRC may not conduct or sponsor, and a person is not required to respond to, a collection of information unless it displays a currently valid OMB control number. OMB has approved the information collection requirements contained in this part under control number 3150–0014.

(b) The approved information collection requirements contained in this part appear in §§ 20.1003, 20.1101, 20.1202, 20.1203, 20.1204, 20.1206, 20.1208, 20.1301, 20.1302, 20.1403, 20.1404, 20.1406, 20.1501, 20.1601, 20.1703, 20.1901, 20.1904, 20.1905, 20.1906, 20.2002, 20.2004, 20.2005, 20.2006, 20.2102, 20.2103, 20.2104, 20.2105, 20.2106, 20.2107, 20.2108, 20.2110, 20.2201, 20.2202, 20.2203, 20.2204, 20.2205, 20.2206, 20.2207, 20.2301, and appendix G to this part.

(c) This part contains information collection requirements in addition to those approved under the control number specified in paragraph (a) of this section. These information collection requirements and the control numbers under which they are approved are as follows:

[1] See §§ 20.1–20.602 codified as of January 1, 1993.

(1) In § 20.2104, NRC Form 4 is approved under control number 3150–0005.

(2) In §§ 20.2106 and 20.2206, NRC Form 5 is approved under control number 3150–0006.

(3) In § 20.2006 and appendix G to 10 CFR part 20, NRC Form 540 and 540A is approved under control number 3150–0164.

(4) In § 20.2006 and appendix G to 10 CFR part 20, NRC Form 541 and 541A is approved under control number 3150–0166.

(5) In § 20.2006 and appendix G to 10 CFR part 20, NRC Form 542 and 542A is approved under control number 3150–0165.

(6) In § 20.2207, NRC Form 748 is approved under control number 3150–0202.

[63 FR 50128, Sept. 21, 1998, as amended at 67 FR 67099, Nov. 4, 2002; 71 FR 65707, Nov. 8, 2006; 72 FR 55922, Oct. 1, 2007; 77 FR 39905, July 6, 2012]

Subpart B—Radiation Protection Programs

SOURCE: 56 FR 23396, May 21, 1991, unless otherwise noted.

§ 20.1101 Radiation protection programs.

(a) Each licensee shall develop, document, and implement a radiation protection program commensurate with the scope and extent of licensed activities and sufficient to ensure compliance with the provisions of this part. (See § 20.2102 for recordkeeping requirements relating to these programs.)

(b) The licensee shall use, to the extent practical, procedures and engineering controls based upon sound radiation protection principles to achieve occupational doses and doses to members of the public that are as low as is reasonably achievable (ALARA).

(c) The licensee shall periodically (at least annually) review the radiation protection program content and implementation.

(d) To implement the ALARA requirements of § 20.1101 (b), and notwithstanding the requirements in § 20.1301 of this part, a constraint on air emissions of radioactive material to the environment, excluding Radon-222 and its daughters, shall be established by licensees other than those subject to § 50.34a, such that the individual member of the public likely to receive the highest dose will not be expected to receive a total effective dose equivalent in excess of 10 mrem (0.1 mSv) per year from these emissions. If a licensee subject to this requirement exceeds this dose constraint, the licensee shall report the exceedance as provided in § 20.2203 and promptly take appropriate corrective action to ensure against recurrence.

[56 FR 23396, May 21, 1991, as amended at 61 FR 65127, Dec. 10, 1996; 63 FR 39482, July 23, 1998]

Subpart C—Occupational Dose Limits

SOURCE: 56 FR 23396, May 21, 1991, unless otherwise noted.

§ 20.1201 Occupational dose limits for adults.

(a) The licensee shall control the occupational dose to individual adults, except for planned special exposures under § 20.1206, to the following dose limits.

(1) An annual limit, which is the more limiting of—

(i) The total effective dose equivalent being equal to 5 rems (0.05 Sv); or

(ii) The sum of the deep-dose equivalent and the committed dose equivalent to any individual organ or tissue other than the lens of the eye being equal to 50 rems (0.5 Sv).

(2) The annual limits to the lens of the eye, to the skin of the whole body, and to the skin of the extremities, which are:

(i) A lens dose equivalent of 15 rems (0.15 Sv), and

(ii) A shallow-dose equivalent of 50 rem (0.5 Sv) to the skin of the whole body or to the skin of any extremity.

(b) Doses received in excess of the annual limits, including doses received during accidents, emergencies, and planned special exposures, must be subtracted from the limits for planned special exposures that the individual may receive during the current year (see § 20.1206(e)(1)) and during the individual's lifetime (see § 20.1206(e)(2)).

(c) When the external exposure is determined by measurement with an external personal monitoring device, the deep-dose equivalent must be used in place of the effective dose equivalent, unless the effective dose equivalent is determined by a dosimetry method approved by the NRC. The assigned deep-dose equivalent must be for the part of the body receiving the highest exposure. The assigned shallow-dose equivalent must be the dose averaged over the contiguous 10 square centimeters of skin receiving the highest exposure. The deep-dose equivalent, lens-dose equivalent, and shallow-dose equivalent may be assessed from surveys or other radiation measurements for the purpose of demonstrating compliance with the occupational dose limits, if the individual monitoring device was not in the region of highest potential exposure, or the results of individual monitoring are unavailable.

(d) Derived air concentration (DAC) and annual limit on intake (ALI) values are presented in table 1 of appendix B to part 20 and may be used to determine the individual's dose (see § 20.2106) and to demonstrate compliance with the occupational dose limits.

(e) In addition to the annual dose limits, the licensee shall limit the soluble uranium intake by an individual to 10 milligrams in a week in consideration of chemical toxicity (see footnote 3 of appendix B to part 20).

(f) The licensee shall reduce the dose that an individual may be allowed to receive in the current year by the amount of occupational dose received while employed by any other person (see § 20.2104(e)).

[56 FR 23396, May 21, 1991, as amended at 60 FR 20185, Apr. 25, 1995; 63 FR 39482, July 23, 1998; 67 FR 16304, Apr. 5, 2002; 72 FR 68059, Dec. 4, 2007]

§ 20.1202 Compliance with requirements for summation of external and internal doses.

(a) If the licensee is required to monitor under both §§ 20.1502 (a) and (b), the licensee shall demonstrate compliance with the dose limits by summing external and internal doses. If the licensee is required to monitor only under § 20.1502(a) or only under § 20.1502(b), then summation is not required to demonstrate compliance with the dose limits. The licensee may demonstrate compliance with the requirements for summation of external and internal doses by meeting one of the conditions specified in paragraph (b) of this section and the conditions in paragraphs (c) and (d) of this section.

(NOTE: The dose equivalents for the lens of the eye, the skin, and the extremities are not included in the summation, but are subject to separate limits.)

(b) *Intake by inhalation.* If the only intake of radionuclides is by inhalation, the total effective dose equivalent limit is not exceeded if the sum of the deep-dose equivalent divided by the total effective dose equivalent limit, and one of the following, does not exceed unity:

(1) The sum of the fractions of the inhalation ALI for each radionuclide, or

(2) The total number of derived air concentration-hours (DAC-hours) for all radionuclides divided by 2,000, or

(3) The sum of the calculated committed effective dose equivalents to all significantly irradiated[1] organs or tissues (T) calculated from bioassay data using appropriate biological models and expressed as a fraction of the annual limit.

(c) *Intake by oral ingestion.* If the occupationally exposed individual also receives an intake of radionuclides by oral ingestion greater than 10 percent of the applicable oral ALI, the licensee shall account for this intake and include it in demonstrating compliance with the limits.

(d) *Intake through wounds or absorption through skin.* The licensee shall evaluate and, to the extent practical, account for intakes through wounds or skin absorption.

NOTE: The intake through intact skin has been included in the calculation of DAC for hydrogen-3 and does not need to be further evaluated.

[56 FR 23396, May 21, 1991, as amended at 57 FR 57878, Dec. 8, 1992]

[1] An organ or tissue is deemed to be significantly irradiated if, for that organ or tissue, the product of the weighting factor, w_T, and the committed dose equivalent, $H_{T,50}$, per unit intake is greater than 10 percent of the maximum weighted value of $H_{T,50}$, (*i.e.*, $W_T H_{T,50}$) per unit intake for any organ or tissue.

§ 20.1203 Determination of external dose from airborne radioactive material.

Licensees shall, when determining the dose from airborne radioactive material, include the contribution to the deep-dose equivalent, lens dose equivalent, and shallow-dose equivalent from external exposure to the radioactive cloud (see appendix B to part 20, footnotes 1 and 2).

NOTE: Airborne radioactivity measurements and DAC values should not be used as the primary means to assess the deep-dose equivalent when the airborne radioactive material includes radionuclides other than noble gases or if the cloud of airborne radioactive material is not relatively uniform. The determination of the deep-dose equivalent to an individual should be based upon measurements using instruments or individual monitoring devices.

[56 FR 23396, May 21, 1991, as amended at 60 FR 20185, Apr. 25, 1995; 63 FR 39482, July 23, 1998]

§ 20.1204 Determination of internal exposure.

(a) For purposes of assessing dose used to determine compliance with occupational dose equivalent limits, the licensee shall, when required under § 20.1502, take suitable and timely measurements of—

(1) Concentrations of radioactive materials in air in work areas; or

(2) Quantities of radionuclides in the body; or

(3) Quantities of radionuclides excreted from the body; or

(4) Combinations of these measurements.

(b) Unless respiratory protective equipment is used, as provided in § 20.1703, or the assessment of intake is based on bioassays, the licensee shall assume that an individual inhales radioactive material at the airborne concentration in which the individual is present.

(c) When specific information on the physical and biochemical properties of the radionuclides taken into the body or the behavior or the material in an individual is known, the licensee may—

(1) Use that information to calculate the committed effective dose equivalent, and, if used, the licensee shall document that information in the individual's record; and

(2) Upon prior approval of the Commission, adjust the DAC or ALI values to reflect the actual physical and chemical characteristics of airborne radioactive material (e.g., aerosol size distribution or density); and

(3) Separately assess the contribution of fractional intakes of Class D, W, or Y compounds of a given radionuclide (see appendix B to part 20) to the committed effective dose equivalent.

(d) If the licensee chooses to assess intakes of Class Y material using the measurements given in § 20.1204(a)(2) or (3), the licensee may delay the recording and reporting of the assessments for periods up to 7 months, unless otherwise required by §§ 20.2202 or 20.2203, in order to permit the licensee to make additional measurements basic to the assessments.

(e) If the identity and concentration of each radionuclide in a mixture are known, the fraction of the DAC applicable to the mixture for use in calculating DAC-hours must be either—

(1) The sum of the ratios of the concentration to the appropriate DAC value (e.g., D, W, Y) from appendix B to part 20 for each radio-nuclide in the mixture; or

(2) The ratio of the total concentration for all radionuclides in the mixture to the most restrictive DAC value for any radionuclide in the mixture.

(f) If the identity of each radionuclide in a mixture is known, but the concentration of one or more of the radionuclides in the mixture is not known, the DAC for the mixture must be the most restrictive DAC of any radionuclide in the mixture.

(g) When a mixture of radionuclides in air exists, licensees may disregard certain radionuclides in the mixture if—

(1) The licensee uses the total activity of the mixture in demonstrating compliance with the dose limits in § 20.1201 and in complying with the monitoring requirements in § 20.1502(b), and

(2) The concentration of any radionuclide disregarded is less than 10 percent of its DAC, and

(3) The sum of these percentages for all of the radionuclides disregarded in the mixture does not exceed 30 percent.

(h)(1) In order to calculate the committed effective dose equivalent, the licensee may assume that the inhalation of one ALI, or an exposure of 2,000 DAC-hours, results in a committed effective dose equivalent of 5 rems (0.05 Sv) for radionuclides that have their ALIs or DACs based on the committed effective dose equivalent.

(2) When the ALI (and the associated DAC) is determined by the nonstochastic organ dose limit of 50 rems (0.5 Sv), the intake of radionuclides that would result in a committed effective dose equivalent of 5 rems (0.05 Sv) (the stochastic ALI) is listed in parentheses in table 1 of appendix B to part 20. In this case, the licensee may, as a simplifying assumption, use the stochastic ALIs to determine committed effective dose equivalent. However, if the licensee uses the stochastic ALIs, the licensee must also demonstrate that the limit in § 20.1201(a)(1)(ii) is met.

[56 FR 23396, May 21, 1991, as amended at 60 FR 20185, Apr. 25, 1995]

§ 20.1205 [Reserved]

§ 20.1206 Planned special exposures.

A licensee may authorize an adult worker to receive doses in addition to and accounted for separately from the doses received under the limits specified in § 20.1201 provided that each of the following conditions is satisfied—

(a) The licensee authorizes a planned special exposure only in an exceptional situation when alternatives that might avoid the dose estimated to result from the planned special exposure are unavailable or impractical.

(b) The licensee (and employer if the employer is not the licensee) specifically authorizes the planned special exposure, in writing, before the exposure occurs.

(c) Before a planned special exposure, the licensee ensures that the individuals involved are—

(1) Informed of the purpose of the planned operation;

(2) Informed of the estimated doses and associated potential risks and specific radiation levels or other conditions that might be involved in performing the task; and

(3) Instructed in the measures to be taken to keep the dose ALARA considering other risks that may be present.

(d) Prior to permitting an individual to participate in a planned special exposure, the licensee ascertains prior doses as required by § 20.2104(b) during the lifetime of the individual for each individual involved.

(e) Subject to § 20.1201(b), the licensee does not authorize a planned special exposure that would cause an individual to receive a dose from all planned special exposures and all doses in excess of the limits to exceed—

(1) The numerical values of any of the dose limits in § 20.1201(a) in any year; and

(2) Five times the annual dose limits in § 20.1201(a) during the individual's lifetime.

(f) The licensee maintains records of the conduct of a planned special exposure in accordance with § 20.2105 and submits a written report in accordance with § 20.2204.

(g) The licensee records the best estimate of the dose resulting from the planned special exposure in the individual's record and informs the individual, in writing, of the dose within 30 days from the date of the planned special exposure. The dose from planned special exposures is not to be considered in controlling future occupational dose of the individual under § 20.1201(a) but is to be included in evaluations required by § 20.1206 (d) and (e).

[56 FR 23396, May 21, 1991, as amended at 63 FR 39482, July 23, 1998]

§ 20.1207 Occupational dose limits for minors.

The annual occupational dose limits for minors are 10 percent of the annual dose limits specified for adult workers in § 20.1201.

§ 20.1208 Dose equivalent to an embryo/fetus.

(a) The licensee shall ensure that the dose equivalent to the embryo/fetus during the entire pregnancy, due to the occupational exposure of a declared pregnant woman, does not exceed 0.5 rem (5 mSv). (For recordkeeping requirements, see § 20.2106.)

(b) The licensee shall make efforts to avoid substantial variation above a uniform monthly exposure rate to a declared pregnant woman so as to satisfy the limit in paragraph (a) of this section.

(c) The dose equivalent to the embryo/fetus is the sum of—

(1) The deep-dose equivalent to the declared pregnant woman; and

(2) The dose equivalent to the embryo/fetus resulting from radionuclides in the embryo/fetus and radionuclides in the declared pregnant woman.

(d) If the dose equivalent to the embryo/fetus is found to have exceeded 0.5 rem (5 mSv), or is within 0.05 rem (0.5 mSv) of this dose, by the time the woman declares the pregnancy to the licensee, the licensee shall be deemed to be in compliance with paragraph (a) of this section if the additional dose equivalent to the embryo/fetus does not exceed 0.05 rem (0.5 mSv) during the remainder of the pregnancy.

[56 FR 23396, May 21, 1991, as amended at 63 FR 39482, July 23, 1998]

Subpart D—Radiation Dose Limits for Individual Members of the Public

SOURCE: 56 FR 23398, May 21, 1991, unless otherwise noted.

§ 20.1301 Dose limits for individual members of the public.

(a) Each licensee shall conduct operations so that—

(1) The total effective dose equivalent to individual members of the public from the licensed operation does not exceed 0.1 rem (1 mSv) in a year, exclusive of the dose contributions from background radiation, from any medical administration the individual has received, from exposure to individuals administered radioactive material and released under § 35.75, from voluntary participation in medical research programs, and from the licensee's disposal of radioactive material into sanitary sewerage in accordance with § 20.2003, and

(2) The dose in any unrestricted area from external sources, exclusive of the dose contributions from patients administered radioactive material and released in accordance with § 35.75, does not exceed 0.002 rem (0.02 millisievert) in any one hour.

(b) If the licensee permits members of the public to have access to controlled areas, the limits for members of the public continue to apply to those individuals.

(c) Notwithstanding paragraph (a)(1) of this section, a licensee may permit visitors to an individual who cannot be released, under § 35.75, to receive a radiation dose greater than 0.1 rem (1 mSv) if—

(1) The radiation dose received does not exceed 0.5 rem (5 mSv); and

(2) The authorized user, as defined in 10 CFR Part 35, has determined before the visit that it is appropriate.

(d) A licensee or license applicant may apply for prior NRC authorization to operate up to an annual dose limit for an individual member of the public of 0.5 rem (5 mSv). The licensee or license applicant shall include the following information in this application:

(1) Demonstration of the need for and the expected duration of operations in excess of the limit in paragraph (a) of this section;

(2) The licensee's program to assess and control dose within the 0.5 rem (5 mSv) annual limit; and

(3) The procedures to be followed to maintain the dose as low as is reasonably achievable.

(e) In addition to the requirements of this part, a licensee subject to the provisions of EPA's generally applicable environmental radiation standards in 40 CFR part 190 shall comply with those standards.

(f) The Commission may impose additional restrictions on radiation levels in unrestricted areas and on the total quantity of radionuclides that a licensee may release in effluents in order to restrict the collective dose.

[56 FR 23398, May 21, 1991, as amended at 60 FR 48625, Sept. 20, 1995; 62 FR 4133, Jan. 29, 1997; 67 FR 20370, Apr. 24, 2002; 67 FR 62872, Oct. 9, 2002]

§ 20.1302 Compliance with dose limits for individual members of the public.

(a) The licensee shall make or cause to be made, as appropriate, surveys of radiation levels in unrestricted and controlled areas and radioactive materials in effluents released to unrestricted and controlled areas to demonstrate compliance with the dose limits for individual members of the public in §20.1301.

(b) A licensee shall show compliance with the annual dose limit in §20.1301 by—

(1) Demonstrating by measurement or calculation that the total effective dose equivalent to the individual likely to receive the highest dose from the licensed operation does not exceed the annual dose limit; or

(2) Demonstrating that—

(i) The annual average concentrations of radioactive material released in gaseous and liquid effluents at the boundary of the unrestricted area do not exceed the values specified in table 2 of appendix B to part 20; and

(ii) If an individual were continuously present in an unrestricted area, the dose from external sources would not exceed 0.002 rem (0.02 mSv) in an hour and 0.05 rem (0.5 mSv) in a year.

(c) Upon approval from the Commission, the licensee may adjust the effluent concentration values in appendix B to part 20, table 2, for members of the public, to take into account the actual physical and chemical characteristics of the effluents (e.g., aerosol size distribution, solubility, density, radioactive decay equilibrium, chemical form).

[56 FR 23398, May 21, 1991; 56 FR 61352, Dec. 3, 1991, as amended at 57 FR 57878, Dec. 8, 1992; 60 FR 20185, Apr. 25, 1995]

Subpart E—Radiological Criteria for License Termination

SOURCE: 62 FR 39088, July 21, 1997, unless otherwise noted.

§20.1401 General provisions and scope.

(a) The criteria in this subpart apply to the decommissioning of facilities licensed under parts 30, 40, 50, 52, 60, 61, 63, 70, and 72 of this chapter, and release of part of a facility or site for unrestricted use in accordance with §50.83 of this chapter, as well as other facilities subject to the Commission's jurisdiction under the Atomic Energy Act of 1954, as amended, and the Energy Reorganization Act of 1974, as amended. For high-level and low-level waste disposal facilities (10 CFR parts 60, 61, and 63), the criteria apply only to ancillary surface facilities that support radioactive waste disposal activities. The criteria do not apply to uranium and thorium recovery facilities already subject to appendix A to 10 CFR part 40 or the uranium solution extraction facilities.

(b) The criteria in this subpart do not apply to sites which:

(1) Have been decommissioned prior to the effective date of the rule in accordance with criteria identified in the Site Decommissioning Management Plan (SDMP) Action Plan of April 16, 1992 (57 FR 13389);

(2) Have previously submitted and received Commission approval on a license termination plan (LTP) or decommissioning plan that is compatible with the SDMP Action Plan criteria; or

(3) Submit a sufficient LTP or decommissioning plan before August 20, 1998 and such LTP or decommissioning plan is approved by the Commission before August 20, 1999 and in accordance with the criteria identified in the SDMP Action Plan, except that if an EIS is required in the submittal, there will be a provision for day-for-day extension.

(c) After a site has been decommissioned and the license terminated in accordance with the criteria in this subpart, or after part of a facility or site has been released for unrestricted use in accordance with §50.83 of this chapter and in accordance with the criteria in this subpart, the Commission will require additional cleanup only, if based on new information, it determines that the criteria of this subpart were not met and residual radioactivity remaining at the site could result in significant threat to public health and safety.

(d) When calculating TEDE to the average member of the critical group the licensee shall determine the peak annual TEDE dose expected within the first 1000 years after decommissioning.

[62 FR 39088, July 21, 1997, as amended at 66 FR 55789, Nov. 2, 2001; 68 FR 19726, Apr. 22, 2003; 72 FR 49485, Aug. 28, 2007]

§ 20.1402 Radiological criteria for unrestricted use.

A site will be considered acceptable for unrestricted use if the residual radioactivity that is distinguishable from background radiation results in a TEDE to an average member of the critical group that does not exceed 25 mrem (0.25 mSv) per year, including that from groundwater sources of drinking water, and that the residual radioactivity has been reduced to levels that are as low as reasonably achievable (ALARA). Determination of the levels which are ALARA must take into account consideration of any detriments, such as deaths from transportation accidents, expected to potentially result from decontamination and waste disposal.

§ 20.1403 Criteria for license termination under restricted conditions.

A site will be considered acceptable for license termination under restricted conditions if:

(a) The licensee can demonstrate that further reductions in residual radioactivity necessary to comply with the provisions of § 20.1402 would result in net public or environmental harm or were not being made because the residual levels associated with restricted conditions are ALARA. Determination of the levels which are ALARA must take into account consideration of any detriments, such as traffic accidents, expected to potentially result from decontamination and waste disposal;

(b) The licensee has made provisions for legally enforceable institutional controls that provide reasonable assurance that the TEDE from residual radioactivity distinguishable from background to the average member of the critical group will not exceed 25 mrem (0.25 mSv) per year;

(c) The licensee has provided sufficient financial assurance to enable an independent third party, including a governmental custodian of a site, to assume and carry out responsibilities for any necessary control and maintenance of the site. Acceptable financial assurance mechanisms are—

(1) Funds placed into a trust segregated from the licensee's assets and outside the licensee's administrative control, and in which the adequacy of the trust funds is to be assessed based on an assumed annual 1 percent real rate of return on investment;

(2) A statement of intent in the case of Federal, State, or local Government licensees, as described in § 30.35(f)(4) of this chapter; or

(3) When a government entity is assuming custody and ownership of a site, an arrangement that is deemed acceptable by such governmental entity.

(d) The licensee has submitted a decommissioning plan or License Termination Plan (LTP) to the Commission indicating the licensee's intent to decommission in accordance with §§ 30.36(d), 40.42(d), 50.82 (a) and (b), 70.38(d), or 72.54 of this chapter, and specifying that the licensee intends to decommission by restricting use of the site. The licensee shall document in the LTP or decommissioning plan how the advice of individuals and institutions in the community who may be affected by the decommissioning has been sought and incorporated, as appropriate, following analysis of that advice.

(1) Licensees proposing to decommission by restricting use of the site shall seek advice from such affected parties regarding the following matters concerning the proposed decommissioning—

(i) Whether provisions for institutional controls proposed by the licensee:

(A) Will provide reasonable assurance that the TEDE from residual radioactivity distinguishable from background to the average member of the critical group will not exceed 25 mrem (0.25 mSv) TEDE per year;

(B) Will be enforceable; and

(C) Will not impose undue burdens on the local community or other affected parties.

(ii) Whether the licensee has provided sufficient financial assurance to enable an independent third party, including a governmental custodian of a site, to assume and carry out responsibilities for any necessary control and maintenance of the site;

(2) In seeking advice on the issues identified in § 20.1403(d)(1), the licensee shall provide for:

(i) Participation by representatives of a broad cross section of community interests who may be affected by the decommissioning;

(ii) An opportunity for a comprehensive, collective discussion on the issues by the participants represented; and

(iii) A publicly available summary of the results of all such discussions, including a description of the individual viewpoints of the participants on the issues and the extent of agreement or disagreement among the participants on the issues; and

(e) Residual radioactivity at the site has been reduced so that if the institutional controls were no longer in effect, there is reasonable assurance that the TEDE from residual radioactivity distinguishable from background to the average member of the critical group is as low as reasonably achievable and would not exceed either—

(1) 100 mrem (1 mSv) per year; or

(2) 500 mrem (5 mSv) per year provided that the licensee—

(i) Demonstrates that further reductions in residual radioactivity necessary to comply with the 100 mrem/y (1 mSv/y) value of paragraph (e)(1) of this section are not technically achievable, would be prohibitively expensive, or would result in net public or environmental harm;

(ii) Makes provisions for durable institutional controls;

(iii) Provides sufficient financial assurance to enable a responsible government entity or independent third party, including a governmental custodian of a site, both to carry out periodic rechecks of the site no less frequently than every 5 years to assure that the institutional controls remain in place as necessary to meet the criteria of § 20.1403(b) and to assume and carry out responsibilities for any necessary control and maintenance of those controls. Acceptable financial assurance mechanisms are those in paragraph (c) of this section.

[62 FR 39088, July 21, 1997, as amended at 76 FR 35564, July 17, 2011]

§ 20.1404 Alternate criteria for license termination.

(a) The Commission may terminate a license using alternate criteria greater than the dose criterion of §§ 20.1402, 20.1403(b), and 20.1403(d)(1)(i)(A), if the licensee—

(1) Provides assurance that public health and safety would continue to be protected, and that it is unlikely that the dose from all man-made sources combined, other than medical, would be more than the 1 mSv/y (100 mrem/y) limit of subpart D, by submitting an analysis of possible sources of exposure;

(2) Has employed to the extent practical restrictions on site use according to the provisions of § 20.1403 in minimizing exposures at the site; and

(3) Reduces doses to ALARA levels, taking into consideration any detriments such as traffic accidents expected to potentially result from decontamination and waste disposal.

(4) Has submitted a decommissioning plan or License Termination Plan (LTP) to the Commission indicating the licensee's intent to decommission in accordance with §§ 30.36(d), 40.42(d), 50.82 (a) and (b), 70.38(d), or 72.54 of this chapter, and specifying that the licensee proposes to decommission by use of alternate criteria. The licensee shall document in the decommissioning plan or LTP how the advice of individuals and institutions in the community who may be affected by the decommissioning has been sought and addressed, as appropriate, following analysis of that advice. In seeking such advice, the licensee shall provide for:

(i) Participation by representatives of a broad cross section of community interests who may be affected by the decommissioning;

(ii) An opportunity for a comprehensive, collective discussion on the issues by the participants represented; and

(iii) A publicly available summary of the results of all such discussions, including a description of the individual viewpoints of the participants on the issues and the extent of agreement and disagreement on the issues.

(5) Has provided sufficient financial assurance in the form of a trust fund to enable an independent third party, including a governmental custodian of a site, to assume and carry out responsibilities for any necessary control and maintenance of the site.

(b) The use of alternate criteria to terminate a license requires the approval of the Commission after consideration of the NRC staff's recommendations that will address any comments provided by the Environmental Protection Agency and any public comments submitted pursuant to § 20.1405.

[62 FR 39088, July 21, 1997, as amended at 76 FR 35564, July 17, 2011]

§ 20.1405 Public notification and public participation.

Upon the receipt of an LTP or decommissioning plan from the licensee, or a proposal by the licensee for release of a site pursuant to §§ 20.1403 or 20.1404, or whenever the Commission deems such notice to be in the public interest, the Commission shall:

(a) Notify and solicit comments from:

(1) Local and State governments in the vicinity of the site and any Indian Nation or other indigenous people that have treaty or statutory rights that could be affected by the decommissioning; and

(2) The Environmental Protection Agency for cases where the licensee proposes to release a site pursuant to § 20.1404.

(b) Publish a notice in the FEDERAL REGISTER and in a forum. such as local newspapers, letters to State of local organizations, or other appropriate forum, that is readily accessible to individuals in the vicinity of the site, and solicit comments from affected parties.

§ 20.1406 Minimization of contamination.

(a) Applicants for licenses, other than early site permits and manufacturing licenses under part 52 of this chapter and renewals, whose applications are submitted after August 20, 1997, shall describe in the application how facility design and procedures for operation will minimize, to the extent practicable, contamination of the facility and the environment, facilitate eventual decommissioning, and minimize, to the extent practicable, the generation of radioactive waste.

(b) Applicants for standard design certifications, standard design approvals, and manufacturing licenses under part 52 of this chapter, whose applications are submitted after August 20, 1997, shall describe in the application how facility design will minimize, to the extent practicable, contamination of the facility and the environment, facilitate eventual decommissioning, and minimize, to the extent practicable, the generation of radioactive waste.

(c) Licensees shall, to the extent practical, conduct operations to minimize the introduction of residual radioactivity into the site, including the subsurface, in accordance with the existing radiation protection requirements in subpart B and radiological criteria for license termination in subpart E of this part.

[72 FR 49485, Aug. 28, 2007, as amended at 76 FR 35564, June 17, 2011]

Subpart F—Surveys and Monitoring

SOURCE: 56 FR 23398, May 21, 1991, unless otherwise noted.

§ 20.1501 General.

(a) Each licensee shall make or cause to be made, surveys of areas, including the subsurface, that—

(1) May be necessary for the licensee to comply with the regulations in this part; and

(2) Are reasonable under the circumstances to evaluate—

(i) The magnitude and extent of radiation levels; and

(ii) Concentrations or quantities of residual radioactivity; and

(iii) The potential radiological hazards of the radiation levels and residual radioactivity detected.

(b) Notwithstanding § 20.2103(a) of this part, records from surveys describing the location and amount of subsurface residual radioactivity identified at the site must be kept with records important for decommissioning, and such records must be retained in accordance with §§ 30.35(g), 40.36(f), 50.75(g), 70.25(g), or 72.30(d), as applicable.

(c) The licensee shall ensure that instruments and equipment used for quantitative radiation measurements (e.g., dose rate and effluent monitoring) are calibrated periodically for the radiation measured.

(d) All personnel dosimeters (except for direct and indirect reading pocket ionization chambers and those dosimeters used to measure the dose to the extremities) that require processing to determine the radiation dose and that are used by licensees to comply with § 20.1201, with other applicable provisions of this chapter, or with conditions specified in a license must be processed and evaluated by a dosimetry processor—

(1) Holding current personnel dosimetry accreditation from the National Voluntary Laboratory Accreditation Program (NVLAP) of the National Institute of Standards and Technology; and

(2) Approved in this accreditation process for the type of radiation or radiations included in the NVLAP program that most closely approximates the type of radiation or radiations for which the individual wearing the dosimeter is monitored.

[56 FR 23398, May 21, 1991, as amended at 63 FR 39482, July 23, 1998; 76 FR 35564, June 17, 2011]

§ 20.1502 Conditions requiring individual monitoring of external and internal occupational dose.

Each licensee shall monitor exposures to radiation and radioactive material at levels sufficient to demonstrate compliance with the occupational dose limits of this part. As a minimum—

(a) Each licensee shall monitor occupational exposure to radiation from licensed and unlicensed radiation sources under the control of the licensee and shall supply and require the use of individual monitoring devices by—

(1) Adults likely to receive, in 1 year from sources external to the body, a dose in excess of 10 percent of the limits in § 20.1201(a),

(2) Minors likely to receive, in 1 year, from radiation sources external to the body, a deep dose equivalent in excess of 0.1 rem (1 mSv), a lens dose equivalent in excess of 0.15 rem (1.5 mSv), or a shallow dose equivalent to the skin or to the extremities in excess of 0.5 rem (5 mSv);

(3) Declared pregnant women likely to receive during the entire pregnancy, from radiation sources external to the body, a deep dose equivalent in excess of 0.1 rem (1 mSv); [2] and

(4) Individuals entering a high or very high radiation area.

(b) Each licensee shall monitor (see § 20.1204) the occupational intake of radioactive material by and assess the committed effective dose equivalent to—

(1) Adults likely to receive, in 1 year, an intake in excess of 10 percent of the applicable ALI(s) in table 1, columns 1 and 2, of appendix B to §§ 20.1001–20.2402;

(2) Minors likely to receive, in 1 year, a committed effective dose equivalent in excess of 0.1 rem (1 mSv); and

(3) Declared pregnant women likely to receive, during the entire pregnancy, a committed effective dose equivalent in excess of 0.1 rem (1 mSv).

[56 FR 23398, May 21, 1991, as amended at 60 FR 20185, Apr. 25, 1995; 63 FR 39482, July 23, 1998]

Subpart G—Control of Exposure From External Sources in Restricted Areas

SOURCE: 56 FR 23398, May 21, 1991, unless otherwise noted.

§ 20.1601 Control of access to high radiation areas.

(a) The licensee shall ensure that each entrance or access point to a high radiation area has one or more of the following features—

(1) A control device that, upon entry into the area, causes the level of radiation to be reduced below that level at which an individual might receive a deep-dose equivalent of 0.1 rem (1 mSv) in 1 hour at 30 centimeters from the radiation source or from any surface that the radiation penetrates;

(2) A control device that energizes a conspicuous visible or audible alarm signal so that the individual entering the high radiation area and the supervisor of the activity are made aware of the entry; or

(3) Entryways that are locked, except during periods when access to the areas

[2] All of the occupational doses in § 20.1201 continue to be applicable to the declared pregnant worker as long as the embryo/fetus dose limit is not exceeded.

is required, with positive control over each individual entry.

(b) In place of the controls required by paragraph (a) of this section for a high radiation area, the licensee may substitute continuous direct or electronic surveillance that is capable of preventing unauthorized entry.

(c) A licensee may apply to the Commission for approval of alternative methods for controlling access to high radiation areas.

(d) The licensee shall establish the controls required by paragraphs (a) and (c) of this section in a way that does not prevent individuals from leaving a high radiation area.

(e) Control is not required for each entrance or access point to a room or other area that is a high radiation area solely because of the presence of radioactive materials prepared for transport and packaged and labeled in accordance with the regulations of the Department of Transportation provided that—

(1) The packages do not remain in the area longer than 3 days; and

(2) The dose rate at 1 meter from the external surface of any package does not exceed 0.01 rem (0.1 mSv) per hour.

(f) Control of entrance or access to rooms or other areas in hospitals is not required solely because of the presence of patients containing radioactive material, provided that there are personnel in attendance who will take the necessary precautions to prevent the exposure of individuals to radiation or radioactive material in excess of the limits established in this part and to operate within the ALARA provisions of the licensee's radiation protection program.

§ 20.1602 Control of access to very high radiation areas.

In addition to the requirements in § 20.1601, the licensee shall institute additional measures to ensure that an individual is not able to gain unauthorized or inadvertent access to areas in which radiation levels could be encountered at 500 rads (5 grays) or more in 1 hour at 1 meter from a radiation source or any surface through which the radiation penetrates.

Subpart H—Respiratory Protection and Controls To Restrict Internal Exposure in Restricted Areas

SOURCE: 56 FR 23400, May 21, 1991, unless otherwise noted.

§ 20.1701 Use of process or other engineering controls.

The licensee shall use, to the extent practical, process or other engineering controls (e.g., containment, decontamination, or ventilation) to control the concentration of radioactive material in air.

[64 FR 54556, Oct. 7, 1999]

§ 20.1702 Use of other controls.

(a) When it is not practical to apply process or other engineering controls to control the concentrations of radioactive material in the air to values below those that define an airborne radioactivity area, the licensee shall, consistent with maintaining the total effective dose equivalent ALARA, increase monitoring and limit intakes by one or more of the following means—

(1) Control of access;

(2) Limitation of exposure times;

(3) Use of respiratory protection equipment; or

(4) Other controls.

(b) If the licensee performs an ALARA analysis to determine whether or not respirators should be used, the licensee may consider safety factors other than radiological factors. The licensee should also consider the impact of respirator use on workers' industrial health and safety.

[64 FR 54556, Oct. 7, 1999]

§ 20.1703 Use of individual respiratory protection equipment.

If the licensee assigns or permits the use of respiratory protection equipment to limit the intake of radioactive material,

(a) The licensee shall use only respiratory protection equipment that is tested and certified by the National Institute for Occupational Safety and Health (NIOSH) except as otherwise noted in this part.

(b) If the licensee wishes to use equipment that has not been tested or certified by NIOSH, or for which there is no schedule for testing or certification, the licensee shall submit an application to the NRC for authorized use of this equipment except as provided in this part. The application must include evidence that the material and performance characteristics of the equipment are capable of providing the proposed degree of protection under anticipated conditions of use. This must be demonstrated either by licensee testing or on the basis of reliable test information.

(c) The licensee shall implement and maintain a respiratory protection program that includes:

(1) Air sampling sufficient to identify the potential hazard, permit proper equipment selection, and estimate doses;

(2) Surveys and bioassays, as necessary, to evaluate actual intakes;

(3) Testing of respirators for operability (user seal check for face sealing devices and functional check for others) immediately prior to each use;

(4) Written procedures regarding—

(i) Monitoring, including air sampling and bioassays;

(ii) Supervision and training of respirator users;

(iii) Fit testing;

(iv) Respirator selection;

(v) Breathing air quality;

(vi) Inventory and control;

(vii) Storage, issuance, maintenance, repair, testing, and quality assurance of respiratory protection equipment;

(viii) Recordkeeping; and

(ix) Limitations on periods of respirator use and relief from respirator use;

(5) Determination by a physician that the individual user is medically fit to use respiratory protection equipment:

(i) Before the initial fitting of a face sealing respirator;

(ii) Before the first field use of non-face sealing respirators, and

(iii) Either every 12 months thereafter, or periodically at a frequency determined by a physician.

(6) Fit testing, with fit factor ≥10 times the APF for negative pressure devices, and a fit factor ≥500 for any positive pressure, continuous flow, and pressure-demand devices, before the first field use of tight fitting, face-sealing respirators and periodically thereafter at a frequency not to exceed 1 year. Fit testing must be performed with the facepiece operating in the negative pressure mode.

(d) The licensee shall advise each respirator user that the user may leave the area at any time for relief from respirator use in the event of equipment malfunction, physical or psychological distress, procedural or communication failure, significant deterioration of operating conditions, or any other conditions that might require such relief.

(e) The licensee shall also consider limitations appropriate to the type and mode of use. When selecting respiratory devices the licensee shall provide for vision correction, adequate communication, low temperature work environments, and the concurrent use of other safety or radiological protection equipment. The licensee shall use equipment in such a way as not to interfere with the proper operation of the respirator.

(f) Standby rescue persons are required whenever one-piece atmosphere-supplying suits, or any combination of supplied air respiratory protection device and personnel protective equipment are used from which an unaided individual would have difficulty extricating himself or herself. The standby persons must be equipped with respiratory protection devices or other apparatus appropriate for the potential hazards. The standby rescue persons shall observe or otherwise maintain continuous communication with the workers (visual, voice, signal line, telephone, radio, or other suitable means), and be immediately available to assist them in case of a failure of the air supply or for any other reason that requires relief from distress. A sufficient number of standby rescue persons must be immediately available to assist all users of this type of equipment and to provide effective emergency rescue if needed.

(g) Atmosphere-supplying respirators must be supplied with respirable air of grade D quality or better as defined by the Compressed Gas Association in publication G–7.1, "Commodity Specification for Air," 1997 and included in the regulations of the Occupational

Safety and Health Administration (29 CFR 1910.134(i)(1)(ii)(A) through (E)). Grade D quality air criteria include—

(1) Oxygen content (v/v) of 19.5–23.5%;

(2) Hydrocarbon (condensed) content of 5 milligrams per cubic meter of air or less;

(3) Carbon monoxide (CO) content of 10 ppm or less;

(4) Carbon dioxide content of 1,000 ppm or less; and

(5) Lack of noticeable odor.

(h) The licensee shall ensure that no objects, materials or substances, such as facial hair, or any conditions that interfere with the face—facepiece seal or valve function, and that are under the control of the respirator wearer, are present between the skin of the wearer's face and the sealing surface of a tight-fitting respirator facepiece.

(i) In estimating the dose to individuals from intake of airborne radioactive materials, the concentration of radioactive material in the air that is inhaled when respirators are worn is initially assumed to be the ambient concentration in air without respiratory protection, divided by the assigned protection factor. If the dose is later found to be greater than the estimated dose, the corrected value must be used. If the dose is later found to be less than the estimated dose, the corrected value may be used.

[64 FR 54557, Oct. 7, 1999, as amended at 67 FR 77652, Dec. 19, 2002]

§ 20.1704 Further restrictions on the use of respiratory protection equipment.

The Commission may impose restrictions in addition to the provisions of §§ 20.1702, 20.1703, and Appendix A to Part 20, in order to:

(a) Ensure that the respiratory protection program of the licensee is adequate to limit doses to individuals from intakes of airborne radioactive materials consistent with maintaining total effective dose equivalent ALARA; and

(b) Limit the extent to which a licensee may use respiratory protection equipment instead of process or other engineering controls.

[64 FR 54557, Oct. 7, 1999]

§ 20.1705 Application for use of higher assigned protection factors.

The licensee shall obtain authorization from the Commission before using assigned protection factors in excess of those specified in Appendix A to part 20. The Commission may authorize a licensee to use higher assigned protection factors on receipt of an application that—

(a) Describes the situation for which a need exists for higher protection factors; and

(b) Demonstrates that the respiratory protection equipment provides these higher protection factors under the proposed conditions of use.

[64 FR 54557, Oct. 7, 1999]

Subpart I—Storage and Control of Licensed Material

SOURCE: 56 FR 23401, May 21, 1991, unless otherwise noted.

§ 20.1801 Security of stored material.

The licensee shall secure from unauthorized removal or access licensed materials that are stored in controlled or unrestricted areas.

§ 20.1802 Control of material not in storage.

The licensee shall control and maintain constant surveillance of licensed material that is in a controlled or unrestricted area and that is not in storage.

Subpart J—Precautionary Procedures

SOURCE: 56 FR 23401, May 21, 1991, unless otherwise noted.

§ 20.1901 Caution signs.

(a) *Standard radiation symbol.* Unless otherwise authorized by the Commission, the symbol prescribed by this part shall use the colors magenta, or purple, or black on yellow background. The symbol prescribed by this part is the three-bladed design:

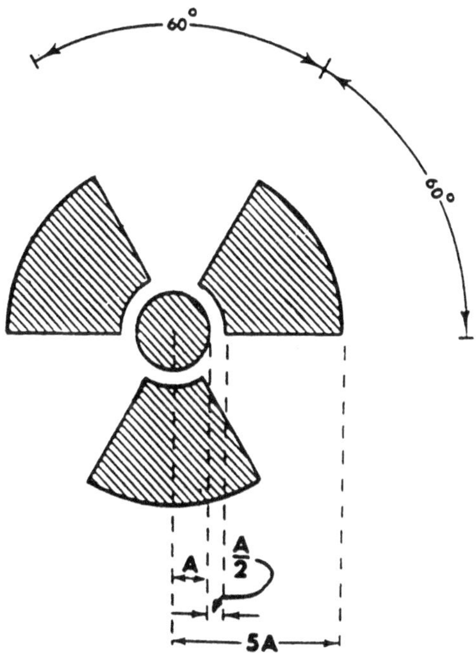

RADIATION SYMBOL

(1) Cross-hatched area is to be magenta, or purple, or black, and

(2) The background is to be yellow.

(b) *Exception to color requirements for standard radiation symbol.* Notwithstanding the requirements of paragraph (a) of this section, licensees are authorized to label sources, source holders, or device components containing sources of licensed materials that are subjected to high temperatures, with conspicuously etched or stamped radiation caution symbols and without a color requirement.

(c) *Additional information on signs and labels.* In addition to the contents of signs and labels prescribed in this part, the licensee may provide, on or near the required signs and labels, additional information, as appropriate, to make individuals aware of potential radiation exposures and to minimize the exposures.

§ 20.1902 Posting requirements.

(a) *Posting of radiation areas.* The licensee shall post each radiation area with a conspicuous sign or signs bearing the radiation symbol and the words "CAUTION, RADIATION AREA."

(b) *Posting of high radiation areas.* The licensee shall post each high radiation area with a conspicuous sign or signs bearing the radiation symbol and the words "CAUTION, HIGH RADIATION AREA" or "DANGER, HIGH RADIATION AREA."

(c) *Posting of very high radiation areas.* The licensee shall post each very high radiation area with a conspicuous sign or signs bearing the radiation symbol and words "GRAVE DANGER, VERY HIGH RADIATION AREA."

(d) *Posting of airborne radioactivity areas.* The licensee shall post each airborne radioactivity area with a conspicuous sign or signs bearing the radiation symbol and the words "CAUTION, AIRBORNE RADIOACTIVITY AREA" or "DANGER, AIRBORNE RADIOACTIVITY AREA."

(e) *Posting of areas or rooms in which licensed material is used or stored.* The licensee shall post each area or room in which there is used or stored an amount of licensed material exceeding 10 times the quantity of such material specified in appendix C to part 20 with a conspicuous sign or signs bearing the radiation symbol and the words "CAUTION, RADIOACTIVE MATERIAL(S)" or "DANGER, RADIOACTIVE MATERIAL(S)."

[56 FR 23401, May 21, 1991, as amended at 60 FR 20185, Apr. 25, 1995]

§ 20.1903 Exceptions to posting requirements.

(a) A licensee is not required to post caution signs in areas or rooms containing radioactive materials for periods of less than 8 hours, if each of the following conditions is met:

(1) The materials are constantly attended during these periods by an individual who takes the precautions necessary to prevent the exposure of individuals to radiation or radioactive materials in excess of the limits established in this part; and

(2) The area or room is subject to the licensee's control.

(b) Rooms or other areas in hospitals that are occupied by patients are not required to be posted with caution signs pursuant to § 20.1902 provided that the patient could be released from licensee control pursuant to § 35.75 of this chapter.

(c) A room or area is not required to be posted with a caution sign because of the presence of a sealed source provided the radiation level at 30 centimeters from the surface of the source container or housing does not exceed 0.005 rem (0.05 mSv) per hour.

(d) Rooms in hospitals or clinics that are used for teletherapy are exempt from the requirement to post caution signs under § 20.1902 if—

(1) Access to the room is controlled pursuant to 10 CFR 35.615; and

(2) Personnel in attendance take necessary precautions to prevent the inadvertent exposure of workers, other patients, and members of the public to radiation in excess of the limits established in this part.

[56 FR 23401, May 21, 1991, as amended at 57 FR 39357, Aug. 31, 1992; 62 FR 4133, Jan. 29, 1997; 63 FR 39482, July 23, 1998]

§ 20.1904 Labeling containers.

(a) The licensee shall ensure that each container of licensed material bears a durable, clearly visible label bearing the radiation symbol and the words "CAUTION, RADIOACTIVE MATERIAL" or "DANGER, RADIOACTIVE MATERIAL." The label must also provide sufficient information (such as the radionuclide(s) present, an estimate of the quantity of radioactivity, the date for which the activity is estimated, radiation levels, kinds of materials, and mass enrichment) to permit individuals handling or using the containers, or working in the vicinity of the containers, to take precautions to avoid or minimize exposures.

(b) Each licensee shall, prior to removal or disposal of empty uncontaminated containers to unrestricted areas, remove or deface the radioactive material label or otherwise clearly indicate that the container no longer contains radioactive materials.

§ 20.1905 Exemptions to labeling requirements.

A licensee is not required to label—

(a) Containers holding licensed material in quantities less than the quantities listed in appendix C to part 20; or

(b) Containers holding licensed material in concentrations less than those specified in table 3 of appendix B to part 20; or

(c) Containers attended by an individual who takes the precautions necessary to prevent the exposure of individuals in excess of the limits established by this part; or

(d) Containers when they are in transport and packaged and labeled in accordance with the regulations of the Department of Transportation,[3] or

(e) Containers that are accessible only to individuals authorized to handle or use them, or to work in the vicinity of the containers, if the contents are identified to these individuals by a readily available written record (examples of containers of this type are containers in locations such as water-filled canals, storage vaults, or hot cells). The record must be retained as long as the containers are in use for the purpose indicated on the record; or

(f) Installed manufacturing or process equipment, such as reactor components, piping, and tanks; or

(g) Containers holding licensed material (other than sealed sources that are either specifically or generally licensed) at a facility licensed under Parts 50 or 52 of this chapter, not including non-power reactors, that are within an area posted under the requirements in § 20.1902 if the containers are:

(1) Conspicuously marked (such as by providing a system of color coding of containers) commensurate with the radiological hazard;

(2) Accessible only to individuals who have sufficient instruction to minimize radiation exposure while handling or working in the vicinity of the containers; and

(3) Subject to plant procedures to ensure they are appropriately labeled, as specified at § 20.1904 before being removed from the posted area.

[56 FR 23401, May 21, 1991, as amended at 60 FR 20185, Apr. 25, 1995; 72 FR 68059, Dec. 4, 2007]

§ 20.1906 Procedures for receiving and opening packages.

(a) Each licensee who expects to receive a package containing quantities of radioactive material in excess of a Type A quantity, as defined in § 71.4 and appendix A to part 71 of this chapter, shall make arrangements to receive—

(1) The package when the carrier offers it for delivery; or

(2) Notification of the arrival of the package at the carrier's terminal and to take possession of the package expeditiously.

(b) Each licensee shall—

(1) Monitor the external surfaces of a labeled[3a] package for radioactive contamination unless the package contains only radioactive material in the form of a gas or in special form as defined in 10 CFR 71.4;

(2) Monitor the external surfaces of a labeled[3a] package for radiation levels unless the package contains quantities of radioactive material that are less than or equal to the Type A quantity, as defined in § 71.4 and appendix A to part 71 of this chapter; and

(3) Monitor all packages known to contain radioactive material for radioactive contamination and radiation levels if there is evidence of degradation of package integrity, such as packages that are crushed, wet, or damaged.

(c) The licensee shall perform the monitoring required by paragraph (b) of this section as soon as practical after receipt of the package, but not later than 3 hours after the package is received at the licensee's facility if it is received during the licensee's normal working hours, or not later than 3 hours from the beginning of the next working day if it is received after working hours.

(d) The licensee shall immediately notify the final delivery carrier and the NRC Operations Center (301–816–5100), by telephone, when—

(1) Removable radioactive surface contamination exceeds the limits of § 71.87(i) of this chapter; or

(2) External radiation levels exceed the limits of § 71.47 of this chapter.

(e) Each licensee shall—

(1) Establish, maintain, and retain written procedures for safely opening packages in which radioactive material is received; and

(2) Ensure that the procedures are followed and that due consideration is

[3] Labeling of packages containing radioactive materials is required by the Department of Transportation (DOT) if the amount and type of radioactive material exceeds the limits for an excepted quantity or article as defined and limited by DOT regulations 49 CFR 173.403 (m) and (w) and 173.421–424.

[3a] Labeled with a Radioactive White I, Yellow II, or Yellow III label as specified in U.S. Department of Transportation regulations, 49 CFR 172.403 and 172.436–440.

given to special instructions for the type of package being opened.

(f) Licensees transferring special form sources in licensee-owned or licensee-operated vehicles to and from a work site are exempt from the contamination monitoring requirements of paragraph (b) of this section, but are not exempt from the survey requirement in paragraph (b) of this section for measuring radiation levels that is required to ensure that the source is still properly lodged in its shield.

[56 FR 23401, May 21, 1991, as amended at 57 FR 39357, Aug. 31, 1992; 60 FR 20185, Apr. 25, 1995; 63 FR 39482, July 23, 1998]

Subpart K—Waste Disposal

SOURCE: 56 FR 23403, May 21, 1991, unless otherwise noted.

§ 20.2001 General requirements.

(a) A licensee shall dispose of licensed material only—

(1) By transfer to an authorized recipient as provided in § 20.2006 or in the regulations in parts 30, 40, 60, 61, 63, 70, and 72 of this chapter;

(2) By decay in storage; or

(3) By release in effluents within the limits in § 20.1301; or

(4) As authorized under §§ 20.2002, 20.2003, 20.2004, 20.2005, or 20.2008.

(b) A person must be specifically licensed to receive waste containing licensed material from other persons for:

(1) Treatment prior to disposal; or

(2) Treatment or disposal by incineration; or

(3) Decay in storage; or

(4) Disposal at a land disposal facility licensed under part 61 of this chapter; or

(5) Disposal at a geologic repository under part 60 or part 63 of this chapter.

[56 FR 23403, May 21, 1991, as amended at 66 FR 55789, Nov. 2, 2001; 72 FR 55922, Oct. 1, 2007]

§ 20.2002 Method for obtaining approval of proposed disposal procedures.

A licensee or applicant for a license may apply to the Commission for approval of proposed procedures, not otherwise authorized in the regulations in this chapter, to dispose of licensed material generated in the licensee's activities. Each application shall include:

(a) A description of the waste containing licensed material to be disposed of, including the physical and chemical properties important to risk evaluation, and the proposed manner and conditions of waste disposal; and

(b) An analysis and evaluation of pertinent information on the nature of the environment; and

(c) The nature and location of other potentially affected licensed and unlicensed facilities; and

(d) Analyses and procedures to ensure that doses are maintained ALARA and within the dose limits in this part.

§ 20.2003 Disposal by release into sanitary sewerage.

(a) A licensee may discharge licensed material into sanitary sewerage if each of the following conditions is satisfied:

(1) The material is readily soluble (or is readily dispersible biological material) in water; and

(2) The quantity of licensed or other radioactive material that the licensee releases into the sewer in 1 month divided by the average monthly volume of water released into the sewer by the licensee does not exceed the concentration listed in table 3 of appendix B to part 20; and

(3) If more than one radionuclide is released, the following conditions must also be satisfied:

(i) The licensee shall determine the fraction of the limit in table 3 of appendix B to part 20 represented by discharges into sanitary sewerage by dividing the actual monthly average concentration of each radionuclide released by the licensee into the sewer by the concentration of that radionuclide listed in table 3 of appendix B to part 20; and

(ii) The sum of the fractions for each radionuclide required by paragraph (a)(3)(i) of this section does not exceed unity; and

(4) The total quantity of licensed and other radioactive material that the licensee releases into the sanitary sewerage system in a year does not exceed 5 curies (185 GBq) of hydrogen-3, 1 curie (37 GBq) of carbon-14, and 1 curie (37 GBq) of all other radioactive materials combined.

(b) Excreta from individuals undergoing medical diagnosis or therapy with radioactive material are not subject to the limitations contained in paragraph (a) of this section.

[56 FR 23403, May 21, 1991, as amended at 60 FR 20185, Apr. 25, 1995]

§ 20.2004 Treatment or disposal by incineration.

(a) A licensee may treat or dispose of licensed material by incineration only:

(1) As authorized by paragraph (b) of this section; or

(2) If the material is in a form and concentration specified in § 20.2005; or

(3) As specifically approved by the Commission pursuant to § 20.2002.

(b)(1) Waste oils (petroleum derived or synthetic oils used principally as lubricants, coolants, hydraulic or insulating fluids, or metalworking oils) that have been radioactively contaminated in the course of the operation or maintenance of a nuclear power reactor licensed under part 50 of this chapter may be incinerated on the site where generated provided that the total radioactive effluents from the facility, including the effluents from such incineration, conform to the requirements of appendix I to part 50 of this chapter and the effluent release limits contained in applicable license conditions other than effluent limits specifically related to incineration of waste oil. The licensee shall report any changes or additions to the information supplied under §§ 50.34 and 50.34a of this chapter associated with this incineration pursuant to § 50.71 of this chapter, as appropriate. The licensee shall also follow the procedures of § 50.59 of this chapter with respect to such changes to the facility or procedures.

(2) Solid residues produced in the process of incinerating waste oils must be disposed of as provided by § 20.2001.

(3) The provisions of this section authorize onsite waste oil incineration under the terms of this section and supersede any provision in an individual plant license or technical specification that may be inconsistent.

[57 FR 57656, Dec. 7, 1992]

§ 20.2005 Disposal of specific wastes.

(a) A licensee may dispose of the following licensed material as if it were not radioactive:

(1) 0.05 microcurie (1.85 kBq), or less, of hydrogen-3 or carbon-14 per gram of medium used for liquid scintillation counting; and

(2) 0.05 microcurie (1.85 kBq), or less, of hydrogen-3 or carbon-14 per gram of animal tissue, averaged over the weight of the entire animal.

(b) A licensee may not dispose of tissue under paragraph (a)(2) of this section in a manner that would permit its use either as food for humans or as animal feed.

(c) The licensee shall maintain records in accordance with § 20.2108.

§ 20.2006 Transfer for disposal and manifests.

(a) The requirements of this section and appendix G to 10 CFR part 20 are designed to—

(1) Control transfers of low-level radioactive waste by any waste generator, waste collector, or waste processor licensee, as defined in this part, who ships low-level waste either directly, or indirectly through a waste collector or waste processor, to a licensed low-level waste land disposal facility (as defined in part 61 of this chapter);

(2) Establish a manifest tracking system; and

(3) Supplement existing requirements concerning transfers and recordkeeping for those wastes.

(b) Any licensee shipping radioactive waste intended for ultimate disposal at a licensed land disposal facility must document the information required on NRC's Uniform Low-Level Radioactive Waste Manifest and transfer this recorded manifest information to the intended consignee in accordance with appendix G to 10 CFR part 20.

(c) Each shipment manifest must include a certification by the waste generator as specified in section II of appendix G to 10 CFR part 20.

(d) Each person involved in the transfer for disposal and disposal of waste, including the waste generator, waste collector, waste processor, and disposal facility operator, shall comply with the requirements specified in section III of appendix G to 10 CFR part 20.

(e) Any licensee shipping byproduct material as defined in paragraphs (3) and (4) of the definition of *Byproduct material* set forth in § 20.1003 intended for ultimate disposal at a land disposal facility licensed under part 61 of this chapter must document the information required on the NRC's Uniform Low-Level Radioactive Waste Manifest and transfer this recorded manifest information to the intended consignee in accordance with appendix G to this part.

[63 FR 50128, Sept. 21, 1998, as amended at 72 FR 55922, Oct. 1, 2007]

§ 20.2007 Compliance with environmental and health protection regulations.

Nothing in this subpart relieves the licensee from complying with other applicable Federal, State, and local regulations governing any other toxic or hazardous properties of materials that may be disposed of under this subpart.

§ 20.2008 Disposal of certain byproduct material.

(a) Licensed material as defined in paragraphs (3) and (4) of the definition of *Byproduct material* set forth in § 20.1003 may be disposed of in accordance with part 61 of this chapter, even though it is not defined as low-level radioactive waste. Therefore, any licensed byproduct material being disposed of at a facility, or transferred for ultimate disposal at a facility licensed under part 61 of this chapter, must meet the requirements of § 20.2006.

(b) A licensee may dispose of byproduct material, as defined in paragraphs (3) and (4) of the definition of *Byproduct material* set forth in § 20.1003, at a disposal facility authorized to dispose of such material in accordance with any Federal or State solid or hazardous waste law, including the Solid Waste Disposal Act, as authorized under the Energy Policy Act of 2005.

[72 FR 55922, Oct. 1, 2007]

Subpart L—Records

SOURCE: 56 FR 23404, May 21, 1991, unless otherwise noted.

§ 20.2101 General provisions.

(a) Each licensee shall use the units: curie, rad, rem, including multiples and subdivisions, and shall clearly indicate the units of all quantities on records required by this part.

(b) In the records required by this part, the licensee may record quantities in SI units in parentheses following each of the units specified in paragraph (a) of this section. However, all quantities must be recorded as stated in paragraph (a) of this section.

(c) Not withstanding the requirements of paragraph (a) of this section, when recording information on shipment manifests, as required in § 20.2006(b), information must be recorded in the International System of Units (SI) or in SI and units as specified in paragraph (a) of this section.

(d) The licensee shall make a clear distinction among the quantities entered on the records required by this part (e.g., total effective dose equivalent, shallow-dose equivalent, lens dose equivalent, deep-dose equivalent, committed effective dose equivalent).

[56 FR 23404, May 21, 1991, as amended at 60 FR 15663, Mar. 27, 1995; 63 FR 39483, July 23, 1998]

§ 20.2102 Records of radiation protection programs.

(a) Each licensee shall maintain records of the radiation protection program, including:

(1) The provisions of the program; and

(2) Audits and other reviews of program content and implementation.

(b) The licensee shall retain the records required by paragraph (a)(1) of this section until the Commission terminates each pertinent license requiring the record. The licensee shall retain the records required by paragraph (a)(2) of this section for 3 years after the record is made.

§ 20.2103 Records of surveys.

(a) Each licensee shall maintain records showing the results of surveys and calibrations required by §§ 20.1501 and 20.1906(b). The licensee shall retain these records for 3 years after the record is made.

(b) The licensee shall retain each of the following records until the Commission terminates each pertinent license requiring the record:

(1) Records of the results of surveys to determine the dose from external sources and used, in the absence of or in combination with individual monitoring data, in the assessment of individual dose equivalents. This includes those records of results of surveys to determine the dose from external sources and used, in the absence of or in combination with individual monitoring data, in the assessment of individual dose equivalents required under the standards for protection against radiation in effect prior to January 1, 1994; and

(2) Records of the results of measurements and calculations used to determine individual intakes of radioactive material and used in the assessment of internal dose. This includes those records of the results of measurements and calculations used to determine individual intakes of radioactive material and used in the assessment of internal dose required under the standards for protection against radiation in effect prior to January 1, 1994; and

(3) Records showing the results of air sampling, surveys, and bioassays required pursuant to § 20.1703(c)(1) and (2). This includes those records showing the results of air sampling, surveys, and bioassays required under the standards for protection against radiation in effect prior to January 1, 1994; and

(4) Records of the results of measurements and calculations used to evaluate the release of radioactive effluents to the environment. This includes those records of the results of measurements and calculations used to evaluate the release of radioactive effluents to the environment required under the standards for protection against radiation in effect prior to January 1, 1994.

[56 FR 23404, May 21, 1991, as amended at 60 FR 20185, Apr. 25, 1995; 66 FR 64737, Dec. 14, 2001]

§ 20.2104 Determination of prior occupational dose.

(a) For each individual who is likely to receive an annual occupational dose requiring monitoring under § 20.1502, the licensee shall determine the occupational radiation dose received during the current year.

(b) Prior to permitting an individual to participate in a planned special exposure, the licensee shall determine—

(1) The internal and external doses from all previous planned special exposures; and

(2) All doses in excess of the limits (including doses received during accidents and emergencies) received during the lifetime of the individual.

(c) In complying with the requirements of paragraphs (a) or (b) of this section, a licensee may—

(1) Accept, as a record of the occupational dose that the individual received during the current year, a written signed statement from the individual, or from the individual's most recent employer for work involving radiation exposure, that discloses the nature and the amount of any occupational dose that the individual may have received during the current year;

(2) Accept, as the record of cumulative radiation dose, an up-to-date NRC Form 4, or equivalent, signed by the individual and countersigned by an appropriate official of the most recent employer for work involving radiation exposure, or the individual's current employer (if the individual is not employed by the licensee); and

(3) Obtain reports of the individual's dose equivalent(s) from the most recent employer for work involving radiation exposure, or the individual's current employer (if the individual is not employed by the licensee) by telephone, telegram, electronic media, or letter. The licensee shall request a written verification of the dose data if the authenticity of the transmitted report cannot be established.

(d) The licensee shall record the exposure history of each individual, as required by paragraphs (a) or (b) of this section, on NRC Form 4, or other clear and legible record, including all of the information required by NRC Form 4.[4]

[4] Licensees are not required to partition historical dose between external dose equivalent(s) and internal committed dose equivalent(s). Further, occupational exposure histories obtained and recorded on NRC Form 4

Continued

The form or record must show each period in which the individual received occupational exposure to radiation or radioactive material and must be signed by the individual who received the exposure. For each period for which the licensee obtains reports, the licensee shall use the dose shown in the report in preparing the NRC Form 4. For any period in which the licensee does not obtain a report, the licensee shall place a notation on the NRC Form 4 indicating the periods of time for which data are not available.

(e) If the licensee is unable to obtain a complete record of an individual's current and previously accumulated occupational dose, the licensee shall assume—

(1) In establishing administrative controls under § 20.1201(f) for the current year, that the allowable dose limit for the individual is reduced by 1.25 rems (12.5 mSv) for each quarter for which records were unavailable and the individual was engaged in activities that could have resulted in occupational radiation exposure; and

(2) That the individual is not available for planned special exposures.

(f) The licensee shall retain the records on NRC Form 4 or equivalent until the Commission terminates each pertinent license requiring this record. The licensee shall retain records used in preparing NRC Form 4 for 3 years after the record is made. This includes records required under the standards for protection against radiation in effect prior to January 1, 1994.

[56 FR 23404, May 21, 1991, as amended at 57 FR 57878, Dec. 8, 1992; 60 FR 20186, Apr. 25, 1995; 60 FR 36043, July 13, 1995; 72 FR 68059, Dec. 4, 2007]

§ 20.2105 Records of planned special exposures.

(a) For each use of the provisions of § 20.1206 for planned special exposures, the licensee shall maintain records that describe—

(1) The exceptional circumstances requiring the use of a planned special exposure; and

(2) The name of the management official who authorized the planned special exposure and a copy of the signed authorization; and

(3) What actions were necessary; and

(4) Why the actions were necessary; and

(5) How doses were maintained ALARA; and

(6) What individual and collective doses were expected to result, and the doses actually received in the planned special exposure.

(b) The licensee shall retain the records until the Commission terminates each pertinent license requiring these records.

§ 20.2106 Records of individual monitoring results.

(a) *Recordkeeping requirement.* Each licensee shall maintain records of doses received by all individuals for whom monitoring was required pursuant to § 20.1502, and records of doses received during planned special exposures, accidents, and emergency conditions. These records[5] must include, when applicable—

(1) The deep-dose equivalent to the whole body, lens dose equivalent, shallow-dose equivalent to the skin, and shallow-dose equivalent to the extremities;

(2) The estimated intake of radionuclides (see § 20.1202);

(3) The committed effective dose equivalent assigned to the intake of radionuclides;

(4) The specific information used to assess the committed effective dose equivalent pursuant to § 20.1204 (a) and (c), and when required by § 20.1502;

(5) The total effective dose equivalent when required by § 20.1202; and

(6) The total of the deep-dose equivalent and the committed dose to the organ receiving the highest total dose.

(b) *Recordkeeping frequency.* The licensee shall make entries of the records specified in paragraph (a) of this section at least annually.

---

before January 1, 1994, might not have included effective dose equivalent, but may be used in the absence of specific information on the intake of radionuclides by the individual.

[5] Assessments of dose equivalent and records made using units in effect before the licensee's adoption of this part need not be changed.

(c) *Recordkeeping format.* The licensee shall maintain the records specified in paragraph (a) of this section on NRC Form 5, in accordance with the instructions for NRC Form 5, or in clear and legible records containing all the information required by NRC Form 5.

(d) *Privacy protection.* The records required under this section should be protected from public disclosure because of their personal privacy nature. These records are protected by most State privacy laws and, when transferred to the NRC, are protected by the Privacy Act of 1974, Public Law 93–579, 5 U.S.C. 552a, and the Commission's regulations in 10 CFR part 9.

(e) The licensee shall maintain the records of dose to an embryo/fetus with the records of dose to the declared pregnant woman. The declaration of pregnancy shall also be kept on file, but may be maintained separately from the dose records.

(f) The licensee shall retain the required form or record until the Commission terminates each pertinent license requiring this record. This includes records required under the standards for protection against radiation in effect prior to January 1, 1994.

[56 FR 23404, May 21, 1991, as amended at 60 FR 20186, Apr. 25, 1995; 63 FR 39483, July 23, 1998]

§ 20.2107 Records of dose to individual members of the public.

(a) Each licensee shall maintain records sufficient to demonstrate compliance with the dose limit for individual members of the public (see § 20.1301).

(b) The licensee shall retain the records required by paragraph (a) of this section until the Commission terminates each pertinent license requiring the record.

§ 20.2108 Records of waste disposal.

(a) Each licensee shall maintain records of the disposal of licensed materials made under §§ 20.2002, 20.2003, 20.2004, 20.2005, 10 CFR part 61 and disposal by burial in soil, including burials authorized before January 28, 1981.[6]

(b) The licensee shall retain the records required by paragraph (a) of this section until the Commission terminates each pertinent license requiring the record. Requirements for disposition of these records, prior to license termination, are located in §§ 30.51, 40.61, 70.51, and 72.80 for activities licensed under these parts.

[56 FR 23404, May 21, 1991, as amended at 60 FR 20186, Apr. 25, 1995; 61 FR 24673, May 16, 1996]

§ 20.2109 [Reserved]

§ 20.2110 Form of records.

Each record required by this part must be legible throughout the specified retention period. The record may be the original or a reproduced copy or a microform provided that the copy or microform is authenticated by authorized personnel and that the microform is capable of producing a clear copy throughout the required retention period. The record may also be stored in electronic media with the capability for producing legible, accurate, and complete records during the required retention period. Records, such as letters, drawings, and specifications, must include all pertinent information, such as stamps, initials, and signatures. The licensee shall maintain adequate safeguards against tampering with and loss of records.

Subpart M—Reports

SOURCE: 56 FR 23406, May 21, 1991, unless otherwise noted.

§ 20.2201 Reports of theft or loss of licensed material.

(a) *Telephone reports.* (1) Each licensee shall report by telephone as follows:

(i) Immediately after its occurrence becomes known to the licensee, any lost, stolen, or missing licensed material in an aggregate quantity equal to or greater than 1,000 times the quantity specified in appendix C to part 20 under such circumstances that it appears to the licensee that an exposure

[6] A previous § 20.304 permitted burial of small quantities of licensed materials in soil before January 28, 1981, without specific Commission authorization.

could result to persons in unrestricted areas; or

(ii) Within 30 days after the occurrence of any lost, stolen, or missing licensed material becomes known to the licensee, all licensed material in a quantity greater than 10 times the quantity specified in appendix C to part 20 that is still missing at this time.

(2) Reports must be made as follows:

(i) Licensees having an installed Emergency Notification System shall make the reports to the NRC Operations Center in accordance with § 50.72 of this chapter, and

(ii) All other licensees shall make reports by telephone to the NRC Operations Center (301–816–5100).

(b) *Written reports.* (1) Each licensee required to make a report under paragraph (a) of this section shall, within 30 days after making the telephone report, make a written report setting forth the following information:

(i) A description of the licensed material involved, including kind, quantity, and chemical and physical form; and

(ii) A description of the circumstances under which the loss or theft occurred; and

(iii) A statement of disposition, or probable disposition, of the licensed material involved; and

(iv) Exposures of individuals to radiation, circumstances under which the exposures occurred, and the possible total effective dose equivalent to persons in unrestricted areas; and

(v) Actions that have been taken, or will be taken, to recover the material; and

(vi) Procedures or measures that have been, or will be, adopted to ensure against a recurrence of the loss or theft of licensed material.

(2) Reports must be made as follows:

(i) For holders of an operating license for a nuclear power plant, the events included in paragraph (b) of this section must be reported in accordance with the procedures described in § 50.73(b), (c), (d), (e), and (g) of this chapter and must include the information required in paragraph (b)(1) of this section, and

(ii) All other licensees shall make reports to the Administrator of the appropriate NRC Regional Office listed in appendix D to part 20.

(c) A duplicate report is not required under paragraph (b) of this section if the licensee is also required to submit a report pursuant to §§ 30.55(c), 37.57, 37.81, 40.64(c), 50.72, 50.73, 70.52, 73.27(b), 73.67(e)(3)(vii), 73.67(g)(3)(iii), 73.71, or 150.19(c) of this chapter.

(d) Subsequent to filing the written report, the licensee shall also report any additional substantive information on the loss or theft within 30 days after the licensee learns of such information.

(e) The licensee shall prepare any report filed with the Commission pursuant to this section so that names of individuals who may have received exposure to radiation are stated in a separate and detachable part of the report.

[56 FR 23406, May 21, 1991, as amended at 58 FR 69220, Dec. 30, 1993; 60 FR 20186, Apr. 25, 1995; 66 FR 64738, Dec. 14, 2001; 67 FR 3585, Jan. 25, 2002; 78 FR 17006, Mar. 19, 2013]

§ 20.2202 Notification of incidents.

(a) Immediate notification. Notwithstanding any other requirements for notification, each licensee shall immediately report any event involving byproduct, source, or special nuclear material possessed by the licensee that may have caused or threatens to cause any of the following conditions—

(1) An individual to receive—

(i) A total effective dose equivalent of 25 rems (0.25 Sv) or more; or

(ii) A lens dose equivalent of 75 rems (0.75 Sv) or more; or

(iii) A shallow-dose equivalent to the skin or extremities of 250 rads (2.5 Gy) or more; or

(2) The release of radioactive material, inside or outside of a restricted area, so that, had an individual been present for 24 hours, the individual could have received an intake five times the annual limit on intake (the provisions of this paragraph do not apply to locations where personnel are not normally stationed during routine operations, such as hot-cells or process enclosures).

(b) Twenty-four hour notification. Each licensee shall, within 24 hours of discovery of the event, report any event involving loss of control of licensed material possessed by the licensee that may have caused, or threatens to cause, any of the following conditions:

(1) An individual to receive, in a period of 24 hours—

(i) A total effective dose equivalent exceeding 5 rems (0.05 Sv); or

(ii) A lens dose equivalent exceeding 15 rems (0.15 Sv); or

(iii) A shallow-dose equivalent to the skin or extremities exceeding 50 rems (0.5 Sv); or

(2) The release of radioactive material, inside or outside of a restricted area, so that, had an individual been present for 24 hours, the individual could have received an intake in excess of one occupational annual limit on intake (the provisions of this paragraph do not apply to locations where personnel are not normally stationed during routine operations, such as hot-cells or process enclosures).

(c) The licensee shall prepare any report filed with the Commission pursuant to this section so that names of individuals who have received exposure to radiation or radioactive material are stated in a separate and detachable part of the report.

(d) Reports made by licensees in response to the requirements of this section must be made as follows:

(1) Licensees having an installed Emergency Notification System shall make the reports required by paragraphs (a) and (b) of this section to the NRC Operations Center in accordance with 10 CFR 50.72; and

(2) All other licensees shall make the reports required by paragraphs (a) and (b) of this section by telephone to the NRC Operations Center (301) 816–5100.

(e) The provisions of this section do not include doses that result from planned special exposures, that are within the limits for planned special exposures, and that are reported under § 20.2204.

[56 FR 23406, May 21, 1991, as amended at 56 FR 40766, Aug. 16, 1991; 57 FR 57879, Dec. 8, 1992; 59 FR 14086, Mar. 25, 1994; 63 FR 39483, July 23, 1998]

§ 20.2203 Reports of exposures, radiation levels, and concentrations of radioactive material exceeding the constraints or limits.

(a) *Reportable events.* In addition to the notification required by § 20.2202, each licensee shall submit a written report within 30 days after learning of any of the following occurrences:

(1) Any incident for which notification is required by § 20.2202; or

(2) Doses in excess of any of the following:

(i) The occupational dose limits for adults in § 20.1201; or

(ii) The occupational dose limits for a minor in § 20.1207; or

(iii) The limits for an embryo/fetus of a declared pregnant woman in § 20.1208; or

(iv) The limits for an individual member of the public in § 20.1301; or

(v) Any applicable limit in the license; or

(vi) The ALARA constraints for air emissions established under § 20.1101(d); or

(3) Levels of radiation or concentrations of radioactive material in—

(i) A restricted area in excess of any applicable limit in the license; or

(ii) An unrestricted area in excess of 10 times any applicable limit set forth in this part or in the license (whether or not involving exposure of any individual in excess of the limits in § 20.1301); or

(4) For licensees subject to the provisions of EPA's generally applicable environmental radiation standards in 40 CFR part 190, levels of radiation or releases of radioactive material in excess of those standards, or of license conditions related to those standards.

(b) *Contents of reports.* (1) Each report required by paragraph (a) of this section must describe the extent of exposure of individuals to radiation and radioactive material, including, as appropriate:

(i) Estimates of each individual's dose; and

(ii) The levels of radiation and concentrations of radioactive material involved; and

(iii) The cause of the elevated exposures, dose rates, or concentrations; and

(iv) Corrective steps taken or planned to ensure against a recurrence, including the schedule for achieving conformance with applicable limits, ALARA constraints, generally applicable environmental standards, and associated license conditions.

(2) Each report filed pursuant to paragraph (a) of this section must include for each occupationally overexposed[1] individual: the name, Social Security account number, and date of birth. The report must be prepared so that this information is stated in a separate and detachable part of the report and must be clearly labeled "Privacy Act Information: Not for Public Disclosure."

(c) For holders of an operating license or a combined license for a nuclear power plant, the occurrences included in paragraph (a) of this section must be reported in accordance with the procedures described in §§ 50.73(b), (c), (d), (e), and (g) of this chapter, and must include the information required by paragraph (b) of this section. Occurrences reported in accordance with § 50.73 of this chapter need not be reported by a duplicate report under paragraph (a) of this section.

(d) All licensees, other than those holding an operating license or a combined license for a nuclear power plant, who make reports under paragraph (a) of this section shall submit the report in writing either by mail addressed to the U.S. Nuclear Regulatory Commission, ATTN: Document Control Desk, Washington, DC 20555–0001; by hand delivery to the NRC's offices at 11555 Rockville Pike, Rockville, Maryland; or, where practicable, by electronic submission, for example, Electronic Information Exchange, or CD-ROM. Electronic submissions must be made in a manner that enables the NRC to receive, read, authenticate, distribute, and archive the submission, and process and retrieve it a single page at a time. Detailed guidance on making electronic submissions can be obtained by visiting the NRC's Web site at *http://www.nrc.gov/site-help/e-submittals.html;* by e-mail to *MSHD.Resource@nrc.gov;* or by writing the Office of the Chief Information Officer, U.S. Nuclear Regulatory Commission, Washington, DC 20555–0001. A copy should be sent to the appropriate NRC Regional Office listed in appendix D to this part.

[56 FR 23406, May 21, 1991, as amended at 60 FR 20186, Apr. 25, 1995; 61 FR 65127, Dec. 10, 1996; 68 FR 14308, Mar. 25, 2003; 68 FR 58801, Oct. 10, 2003; 72 FR 49486, Aug. 28, 2007; 74 FR 62680, Dec. 1, 2009; 80 FR 74979, Dec. 1, 2015]

§ 20.2204 Reports of planned special exposures.

The licensee shall submit a written report to the Administrator of the appropriate NRC Regional Office listed in appendix D to part 20 within 30 days following any planned special exposure conducted in accordance with § 20.1206, informing the Commission that a planned special exposure was conducted and indicating the date the planned special exposure occurred and the information required by § 20.2105.

[56 FR 23406, May 21, 1991, as amended at 60 FR 20186, Apr. 25, 1995]

§ 20.2205 Reports to individuals of exceeding dose limits.

When a licensee is required by §§ 20.2203 or 20.2204 to report to the Commission any exposure of an identified occupationally exposed individual, or an identified member of the public, to radiation or radioactive material, the licensee shall also provide the individual a report on his or her exposure data included in the report to Commission. This report must be transmitted no later than the transmittal to the Commission.

[72 FR 68059, Dec. 4, 2007]

§ 20.2206 Reports of individual monitoring.

(a) This section applies to each person licensed by the Commission to—

(1) Operate a nuclear reactor designed to produce electrical or heat energy pursuant to § 50.21(b) or § 50.22 of this chapter or a testing facility as defined in § 50.2 of this chapter; or

(2) Possess or use byproduct material for purposes of radiography pursuant to parts 30 and 34 of this chapter; or

(3) Possess or use at any one time, for purposes of fuel processing, fabricating, or reprocessing, special nuclear material in a quantity exceeding 5,000 grams of contained uranium-235, uranium-233, or plutonium, or any combination

[1] With respect to the limit for the embryo/fetus (§ 20.1208), the identifiers should be those of the declared pregnant woman.

thereof pursuant to part 70 of this chapter; or

(4) Possess high-level radioactive waste at a geologic repository operations area pursuant to part 60 or 63 of this chapter; or

(5) Possess spent fuel in an independent spent fuel storage installation (ISFSI) pursuant to part 72 of this chapter; or

(6) Receive radioactive waste from other persons for disposal under part 61 of this chapter; or

(7) Possess or use at any time, for processing or manufacturing for distribution pursuant to parts 30, 32, 33 or 35 of this chapter, byproduct material in quantities exceeding any one of the following quantitites:

Radionuclide	Quantity of radionuclide [1] in curies
Cesium-137	1
Cobalt-60	1
Gold-198	100
Iodine-131	1
Iridium-192	10
Krypton-85	1,000
Promethium-147	10
Techetium-99m	1,000

[1] The Commission may require as a license condition, or by rule, regulation, or order pursuant to § 20.2302, reports from licensees who are licensed to use radionuclides not on this list, in quantities sufficient to cause comparable radiation levels.

(b) Each licensee in a category listed in paragraph (a) of this section shall submit an annual report of the results of individual monitoring carried out by the licensee for each individual for whom monitoring was required by § 20.1502 during that year. The licensee may include additional data for individuals for whom monitoring was provided but not required. The licensee shall use Form NRC 5 or electronic media containing all the information required by Form NRC 5.

(c) The licensee shall file the report required by § 20.2206(b), covering the preceding year, on or before April 30 of each year. The licensee shall submit the report to the REIRS Project Manager by an appropriate method listed in § 20.1007 or via the REIRS Web site at *http://www.reirs.com.*

[56 FR 23406, May 21, 1991, as amended at 56 FR 32072, July 15, 1991; 66 FR 55789, Nov. 2, 2001; 68 FR 58802, Oct. 10, 2003]

§ 20.2207 Reports of transactions involving nationally tracked sources.

Each licensee who manufactures, transfers, receives, disassembles, or disposes of a nationally tracked source shall complete and submit a National Source Tracking Transaction Report as specified in paragraphs (a) through (e) of this section for each type of transaction.

(a) Each licensee who manufactures a nationally tracked source shall complete and submit a National Source Tracking Transaction Report. The report must include the following information:

(1) The name, address, and license number of the reporting licensee;

(2) The name of the individual preparing the report;

(3) The manufacturer, model, and serial number of the source;

(4) The radioactive material in the source;

(5) The initial source strength in becquerels (curies) at the time of manufacture; and

(6) The manufacture date of the source.

(b) Each licensee that transfers a nationally tracked source to another person shall complete and submit a National Source Tracking Transaction Report. The report must include the following information:

(1) The name, address, and license number of the reporting licensee;

(2) The name of the individual preparing the report;

(3) The name and license number of the recipient facility and the shipping address;

(4) The manufacturer, model, and serial number of the source or, if not available, other information to uniquely identify the source;

(5) The radioactive material in the source;

(6) The initial or current source strength in becquerels (curies);

(7) The date for which the source strength is reported;

(8) The shipping date;

(9) The estimated arrival date; and

(10) For nationally tracked sources transferred as waste under a Uniform Low-Level Radioactive Waste Manifest, the waste manifest number and

the container identification of the container with the nationally tracked source.

(c) Each licensee that receives a nationally tracked source shall complete and submit a National Source Tracking Transaction Report. The report must include the following information:

(1) The name, address, and license number of the reporting licensee;

(2) The name of the individual preparing the report;

(3) The name, address, and license number of the person that provided the source;

(4) The manufacturer, model, and serial number of the source or, if not available, other information to uniquely identify the source;

(5) The radioactive material in the source;

(6) The initial or current source strength in becquerels (curies);

(7) The date for which the source strength is reported;

(8) The date of receipt; and

(9) For material received under a Uniform Low-Level Radioactive Waste Manifest, the waste manifest number and the container identification with the nationally tracked source.

(d) Each licensee that disassembles a nationally tracked source shall complete and submit a National Source Tracking Transaction Report. The report must include the following information:

(1) The name, address, and license number of the reporting licensee;

(2) The name of the individual preparing the report;

(3) The manufacturer, model, and serial number of the source or, if not available, other information to uniquely identify the source;

(4) The radioactive material in the source;

(5) The initial or current source strength in becquerels (curies);

(6) The date for which the source strength is reported;

(7) The disassemble date of the source.

(e) Each licensee who disposes of a nationally tracked source shall complete and submit a National Source Tracking Transaction Report. The report must include the following information:

(1) The name, address, and license number of the reporting licensee;

(2) The name of the individual preparing the report;

(3) The waste manifest number;

(4) The container identification with the nationally tracked source.

(5) The date of disposal; and

(6) The method of disposal.

(f) The reports discussed in paragraphs (a) through (e) of this section must be submitted by the close of the next business day after the transaction. A single report may be submitted for multiple sources and transactions. The reports must be submitted to the National Source Tracking System by using:

(1) The on-line National Source Tracking System;

(2) Electronically using a computer-readable format;

(3) By facsimile;

(4) By mail to the address on the National Source Tracking Transaction Report Form (NRC Form 748); or

(5) By telephone with followup by facsimile or mail.

(g) Each licensee shall correct any error in previously filed reports or file a new report for any missed transaction within 5 business days of the discovery of the error or missed transaction. Such errors may be detected by a variety of methods such as administrative reviews or by physical inventories required by regulation. In addition, each licensee shall reconcile the inventory of nationally tracked sources possessed by the licensee against that licensee's data in the National Source Tracking System. The reconciliation must be conducted during the month of January in each year. The reconciliation process must include resolving any discrepancies between the National Source Tracking System and the actual inventory by filing the reports identified by paragraphs (a) through (e) of this section. By January 31 of each year, each licensee must submit to the National Source Tracking System confirmation that the data in the National Source Tracking System is correct.

(h) Each licensee that possesses Category 1 nationally tracked sources shall report its initial inventory of Category 1 nationally tracked sources to the National Source Tracking System by January 31, 2009. Each licensee that possesses Category 2 nationally tracked sources shall report its initial inventory of Category 2 nationally tracked sources to the National Source Tracking System by January 31, 2009. The information may be submitted by using any of the methods identified by paragraph (f)(1) through (f)(4) of this section. The initial inventory report must include the following information:

(1) The name, address, and license number of the reporting licensee;

(2) The name of the individual preparing the report;

(3) The manufacturer, model, and serial number of each nationally tracked source or, if not available, other information to uniquely identify the source;

(4) The radioactive material in the sealed source;

(5) The initial or current source strength in becquerels (curies); and

(6) The date for which the source strength is reported.

[71 FR 65707, Nov. 8, 2006, as amended at 72 FR 59163, Oct. 19, 2007]

Subpart N—Exemptions and Additional Requirements

SOURCE: 56 FR 23408, May 21, 1991, unless otherwise noted.

§ 20.2301 Applications for exemptions.

The Commission may, upon application by a licensee or upon its own initiative, grant an exemption from the requirements of the regulations in this part if it determines the exemption is authorized by law and would not result in undue hazard to life or property.

§ 20.2302 Additional requirements.

The Commission may, by rule, regulation, or order, impose requirements on a licensee, in addition to those established in the regulations in this part, as it deems appropriate or necessary to protect health or to minimize danger to life or property.

Subpart O—Enforcement

§ 20.2401 Violations.

(a) The Commission may obtain an injunction or other court order to prevent a violation of the provisions of—

(1) The Atomic Energy Act of 1954, as amended;

(2) Title II of the Energy Reorganization Act of 1974, as amended; or

(3) A regulation or order issued pursuant to those Acts.

(b) The Commission may obtain a court order for the payment of a civil penalty imposed under section 234 of the Atomic Energy Act:

(1) For violations of—

(i) Sections 53, 57, 62, 63, 81, 82, 101, 103, 104, 107 or 109 of the Atomic Energy Act of 1954, as amended;

(ii) Section 206 of the Energy Reorganization Act;

(iii) Any rule, regulation, or order issued pursuant to the sections specified in paragraph (b)(1)(i) of this section; and

(iv) Any term, condition, or limitation of any license issued under the sections specified in paragraph (b)(1)(i) of this section.

(2) For any violation for which a license may be revoked under Section 186 of the Atomic Energy Act of 1954, as amended.

[56 FR 23408, May 21, 1991; 56 FR 61352, Dec. 3, 1991, as amended at 57 FR 55071, Nov. 24, 1992]

§ 20.2402 Criminal penalties.

(a) Section 223 of the Atomic Energy Act of 1954, as amended, provides for criminal sanctions for willful violation of, attempted violation of, or conspiracy to violate, any regulation issued under sections 161b, 161i, or 161o of the Act. For purposes of section 223, all the regulations in §§ 20.1001 through 20.2402 are issued under one or more of sections 161b, 161i, or 161o, except for the sections listed in paragraph (b) this section.

(b) The regulations in §§ 20.1001 through 20.2402 that are not issued under Sections 161b, 161i, or 161o for the purposes of Section 223 are as follows: §§ 20.1001, 20.1002, 20.1003, 20.1004, 20.1005, 20.1006, 20.1007, 20.1008, 20.1009, 20.1405,

20.1704, 20.1903, 20.1905, 20.2002, 20.2007, 20.2301, 20.2302, 20.2401, and 20.2402.

[57 FR 55071, Nov. 24, 1992, as amended at 62 FR 39089, July 21, 1997]

APPENDIX A TO PART 20—ASSIGNED PROTECTION FACTORS FOR RESPIRATORS [A]

	Operating mode	Assigned Protection Factors
I. Air Purifying Respirators [Particulate [b] only] [c]:		
Filtering facepiece disposable [d].	Negative Pressure	([d])
Facepiece, half [e]	Negative Pressure	10
Facepiece, full	Negative Pressure	100
Facepiece, half	Powered air-purifying respirators.	50
Facepiece, full	Powered air-purifying respirators.	1000
Helmet/hood	Powered air-purifying respirators.	1000
Facepiece, loose-fitting.	Powered air-purifying respirators.	25
II. Atmosphere supplying respirators [particulate, gases and vapors [f]]:		
1. Air-line respirator:		
Facepiece, half	Demand	10
Facepiece, half	Continuous Flow	50
Facepiece, half	Pressure Demand	50
Facepiece, full	Demand	100
Facepiece, full	Continuous Flow	1000
Facepiece, full	Pressure Demand	1000
Helmet/hood	Continuous Flow	1000
Facepiece, loose-fitting.	Continuous Flow	25
Suit	Continuous Flow	([g])
2. Self-contained breathing Apparatus (SCBA):		
Facepiece, full	Demand	[h] 100
Facepiece, full	Pressure Demand	[i] 10,000
Facepiece, full	Demand, Recirculating.	[h] 100
Facepiece, full	Positive Pressure Recirculating.	[i] 10,000
III. Combination Respirators:		
Any combination of air-purifying and atmosphere-supplying respirators.	Assigned protection factor for type and mode of operation as listed above.	

[a] These assigned protection factors apply only in a respiratory protection program that meets the requirements of this Part. They are applicable only to airborne radiological hazards and may not be appropriate to circumstances when chemical or other respiratory hazards exist instead of, or in addition to, radioactive hazards. Selection and use of respirators for such circumstances must also comply with Department of Labor regulations.

Radioactive contaminants for which the concentration values in Table 1, Column 3 of Appendix B to Part 20 are based on internal dose due to inhalation may, in addition, present external exposure hazards at higher concentrations. Under these circumstances, limitations on occupancy may have to be governed by external dose limits.

[b] Air purifying respirators with APF <100 must be equipped with particulate filters that are at least 95 percent efficient. Air purifying respirators with APF = 100 must be equipped with particulate filters that are at least 99 percent efficient. Air purifying respirators with APFs >100 must be equipped with particulate filters that are at least 99.97 percent efficient.

[c] The licensee may apply to the Commission for the use of an APF greater than 1 for sorbent cartridges as protection against airborne radioactive gases and vapors (e.g., radioiodine).

[d] Licensees may permit individuals to use this type of respirator who have not been medically screened or fit tested on the device provided that no credit be taken for their use in estimating intake or dose. It is also recognized that it is difficult to perform an effective positive or negative pressure pre-use user seal check on this type of device. All other respiratory protection program requirements listed in § 20.1703 apply. An assigned protection factor has not been assigned for these devices. However, an APF equal to 10 may be used if the licensee can demonstrate a fit factor of at least 100 by use of a validated or evaluated, qualitative or quantitative fit test.

[e] Under-chin type only. No distinction is made in this Appendix between elastomeric half-masks with replaceable cartridges and those designed with the filter medium as an integral part of the facepiece (e.g., disposable or reusable disposable). Both types are acceptable so long as the seal area of the latter contains some substantial type of seal-enhancing material such as rubber or plastic, the two or more suspension straps are adjustable, the filter medium is at least 95 percent efficient and all other requirements of this Part are met.

[f] The assigned protection factors for gases and vapors are not applicable to radioactive contaminants that present an absorption or submersion hazard. For tritium oxide vapor, approximately one-third of the intake occurs by absorption through the skin so that an overall protection factor of 3 is appropriate when atmosphere-supplying respirators are used to protect against tritium oxide. Exposure to radioactive noble gases is not considered a significant respiratory hazard, and protective actions for these contaminants should be based on external (submersion) dose considerations.

[g] No NIOSH approval schedule is currently available for atmosphere supplying suits. This equipment may be used in an acceptable respiratory protection program as long as all the other minimum program requirements, with the exception of fit testing, are met (*i.e.*, § 20.1703).

[h] The licensee should implement institutional controls to assure that these devices are not used in areas immediately dangerous to life or health (IDLH).

[i] This type of respirator may be used as an emergency device in unknown concentrations for protection against inhalation hazards. External radiation hazards and other limitations to permitted exposure such as skin absorption shall be taken into account in these circumstances. This device may not be used by any individual who experiences perceptible outward leakage of breathing gas while wearing the device.

[64 FR 54558, Oct. 7, 1999; 64 FR 55524, Oct. 13, 1999]

APPENDIX B TO PART 20—ANNUAL LIMITS ON INTAKE (ALIS) AND DERIVED AIR CONCENTRATIONS (DACS) OF RADIONUCLIDES FOR OCCUPATIONAL EXPOSURE; EFFLUENT CONCENTRATIONS; CONCENTRATIONS FOR RELEASE TO SEWERAGE

INTRODUCTION

For each radionuclide table 1 indicates the chemical form which is to be used for selecting the appropriate ALI or DAC value. The ALIs and DACs for inhalation are given for an aerosol with an activity median aerodynamic diameter (AMAD) of 1 μm and for three classes (D,W,Y) of radioactive material, which refer to their retention (approximately days, weeks or years) in the pulmonary region of the lung. This classification applies to a range of clearance half-times of less than 10 days for D, for W from 10 to 100 days, and for Y greater than 100 days. The class (D, W, or Y) given in the column headed "Class" applies only to the inhalation ALIs and DACs given in table 1, columns 2 and 3. Table 2 provides concentration limits for airborne and liquid effluents released to the general environment. Table 3 provides concentration limits for discharges to sanitary sewer systems.

NOTATION

The values in tables 1, 2, and 3 are presented in the computer "E" notation. In this notation a value of 6E−02 represents a value of 6×10^{-2} or 0.06, 6E + 2 represents 6×10^{2} or 600, and 6E + 0 represents 6×10^{0} or 6.

TABLE 1 "OCCUPATIONAL"

Note that the columns in table 1, of this appendix captioned "Oral Ingestion ALI," "Inhalation ALI," and "DAC," are applicable to occupational exposure to radioactive material.

The ALIs in this appendix are the annual intakes of a given radionuclide by "Reference Man" which would result in either (1) a committed effective dose equivalent of 5 rems (stochastic ALI) or (2) a committed dose equivalent of 50 rems to an organ or tissue (non-stochastic ALI). The stochastic ALIs were derived to result in a risk, due to irradiation of organs and tissues, comparable to the risk associated with deep dose equivalent to the whole body of 5 rems. The derivation includes multiplying the committed dose equivalent to an organ or tissue by a weighting factor, w_T. This weighting factor is the proportion of the risk of stochastic effects resulting from irradiation of the organ or tissue, T, to the total risk of stochastic effects when the whole body is irradiated uniformly. The values of w_T are listed under the definition of weighting factor in § 20.1003. The non-stochastic ALIs were derived to avoid non-stochastic effects, such as prompt damage to tissue or reduction in organ function.

A value of $w_T = 0.06$ is applicable to each of the five organs or tissues in the "remainder" category receiving the highest dose equivalents, and the dose equivalents of all other remaining tissues may be disregarded. The following parts of the GI tract—stomach, small intestine, upper large intestine, and lower large intestine—are to be treated as four separate organs.

Note that the dose equivalents for extremities (hands and forearms, feet and lower legs), skin, and lens of the eye are not considered in computing the committed effective dose equivalent, but are subject to limits that must be met separately.

When an ALI is defined by the stochastic dose limit, this value alone, is given. When an ALI is determined by the non-stochastic dose limit to an organ, the organ or tissue to which the limit applies is shown, and the ALI for the stochastic limit is shown in parentheses. (Abbreviated organ or tissue designations are used: LLI wall = lower large intestine wall; St. wall = stomach wall; Blad wall = bladder wall; and Bone surf = bone surface.)

The use of the ALIs listed first, the more limiting of the stochastic and non-stochastic ALIs, will ensure that non-stochastic effects are avoided and that the risk of stochastic effects is limited to an acceptably low value. If, in a particular situation involving a radionuclide for which the non-stochastic ALI is limiting, use of that non-stochastic ALI is considered unduly conservative, the licensee may use the stochastic ALI to determine the committed effective dose equivalent. However, the licensee shall also ensure that the 50-rem dose equivalent limit for any organ or tissue is not exceeded by the sum of the external deep dose equivalent plus the internal committed dose to that organ (not the effective dose). For the case where there is no external dose contribution, this would be demonstrated if the sum of the fractions of the nonstochastic ALIs (ALI_{ns}) that contribute to the committed dose equivalent to the organ receiving the highest dose does not exceed unity (*i.e.*, Σ (intake (in µCi) of each radionuclide/ALI_{ns}) <1.0). If there is an external deep dose equivalent contribution of H_d then this sum must be less than $1-(H_d/50)$ instead of being <1.0.

The derived air concentration (DAC) values are derived limits intended to control chronic occupational exposures. The relationship between the DAC and the ALI is given by: DAC = ALI(in µCi)/(2000 hours per working year × 60 minutes/hour × 2 × 10^4 ml per minute) = [ALI/2.4 × 10^9] µCi/ml, where 2 × 10^4 ml is the volume of air breathed per minute at work by "Reference Man" under working conditions of "light work."

The DAC values relate to one of two modes of exposure: either external submersion or the internal committed dose equivalents resulting from inhalation of radioactive materials. Derived air concentrations based upon submersion are for immersion in a semi-infinite cloud of uniform concentration and apply to each radionuclide separately.

The ALI and DAC values relate to exposure to the single radionuclide named, but also include contributions from the in-growth of any daughter radionuclide produced in the body by the decay of the parent. However, intakes that include both the parent and daughter radionuclides should be treated by the general method appropriate for mixtures.

The value of ALI and DAC do not apply directly when the individual both ingests and inhales a radionuclide, when the individual is exposed to a mixture of radionuclides by either inhalation or ingestion or both, or when the individual is exposed to both internal and external radiation (see § 20.1202). When an individual is exposed to radioactive materials which fall under several of the translocation classifications (*i.e.*, Class D, Class W, or Class Y) of the same radionuclide, the exposure may be evaluated as if it were a mixture of different radionuclides.

It should be noted that the classification of a compound as Class D, W, or Y is based on the chemical form of the compound and does not take into account the radiological half-life of different radioisotopes. For this reason, values are given for Class D, W, and Y compounds, even for very short-lived radionuclides.

TABLE 2

The columns in table 2 of this appendix captioned "Effluents," "Air," and "Water," are applicable to the assessment and control of dose to the public, particularly in the implementation of the provisions of § 20.1302. The concentration values given in columns 1 and 2 of table 2 are equivalent to the radionuclide concentrations which, if inhaled or ingested continuously over the course of a year, would produce a total effective dose equivalent of 0.05 rem (50 millirem or 0.5 millisieverts).

Consideration of non-stochastic limits has not been included in deriving the air and water effluent concentration limits because non-stochastic effects are presumed not to occur at the dose levels established for individual members of the public. For radionuclides, where the non-stochastic limit was governing in deriving the occupational DAC, the stochastic ALI was used in deriving the corresponding airborne effluent limit in table 2. For this reason, the DAC and airborne effluent limits are not always proportional as was the case in appendix B to §§ 20.1–20.601.

The air concentration values listed in table 2, column 1, were derived by one of two methods. For those radionuclides for which the stochastic limit is governing, the occupational stochastic inhalation ALI was divided by 2.4×10^9 ml, relating the inhalation ALI to the DAC, as explained above, and then divided by a factor of 300. The factor of 300 includes the following components: a factor of 50 to relate the 5-rem annual occupational dose limit to the 0.1-rem limit for members of the public, a factor of 3 to adjust for the difference in exposure time and the inhalation rate for a worker and that for members of the public; and a factor of 2 to adjust the occupational values (derived for adults) so that they are applicable to other age groups.

For those radionuclides for which submersion (external dose) is limiting, the occupational DAC in table 1, column 3, was divided by 219. The factor of 219 is composed of a factor of 50, as described above, and a factor of 4.38 relating occupational exposure for 2,000 hours per year to full-time exposure (8,760 hours per year). Note that an additional factor of 2 for age considerations is not warranted in the submersion case.

The water concentrations were derived by taking the most restrictive occupational stochastic oral ingestion ALI and dividing by 7.3×10^7. The factor of 7.3×10^7 (ml) includes the following components: the factors of 50 and 2 described above and a factor of 7.3×10^5 (ml) which is the annual water intake of "Reference Man."

Note 2 of this appendix provides groupings of radionuclides which are applicable to unknown mixtures of radionuclides. These groupings (including occupational inhalation ALIs and DACs, air and water effluent concentrations and sewerage) require demonstrating that the most limiting radionuclides in successive classes are absent. The limit for the unknown mixture is defined when the presence of one of the listed radionuclides cannot be definitely excluded either from knowledge of the radionuclide composition of the source or from actual measurements.

TABLE 3 "SEWER DISPOSAL"

The monthly average concentrations for release to sanitary sewers are applicable to the provisions in § 20.2003. The concentration values were derived by taking the most restrictive occupational stochastic oral ingestion ALI and dividing by 7.3×10^6 (ml). The factor of 7.3×10^6 (ml) is composed of a factor of 7.3×10^5 (ml), the annual water intake by "Reference Man," and a factor of 10, such that the concentrations, if the sewage released by the licensee were the only source of water ingested by a reference man during a year, would result in a committed effective dose equivalent of 0.5 rem.

LIST OF ELEMENTS

Name	Atomic	
	Symbol	No.
Actinium	Ac	89
Aluminum	Al	13
Americium	Am	95
Antimony	Sb	51
Argon	Ar	18
Arsenic	As	33
Astatine	At	85
Barium	Ba	56
Berkelium	Bk	97
Beryllium	Be	4
Bismuth	Bi	83
Bromine	Br	35
Cadmium	Cd	48
Calcium	Ca	20
Californium	Cf	98
Carbon	C	6
Cerium	Ce	58
Cesium	Cs	55
Chlorine	Cl	17
Chromium	Cr	24

LIST OF ELEMENTS—Continued

Name	Atomic	
	Symbol	No.
Cobalt	Co	27
Copper	Cu	29
Curium	Cm	96
Dysprosium	Dy	66
Einsteinium	Es	99
Erbium	Er	68
Europium	Eu	63
Fermium	Fm	100
Fluorine	F	9
Francium	Fr	87
Gadolinium	Gd	64
Gallium	Ga	31
Germanium	Ge	32
Gold	Au	79
Hafnium	Hf	72
Holmium	Ho	67
Hydrogen	H	1
Indium	In	49
Iodine	I	53
Iridium	Ir	77
Iron	Fe	26
Krypton	Kr	36
Lanthanum	La	57
Lead	Pb	82
Lutetium	Lu	71
Magnesium	Mg	12
Manganese	Mn	25
Mendelevium	Md	101
Mercury	Hg	80
Molybdenum	Mo	42
Neodymium	Nd	60
Neptunium	Np	93
Nickel	Ni	28
Niobium	Nb	41
Nitrogen	N	7
Osmium	Os	76
Oxygen	O	8
Palladium	Pd	46
Phosphorus	P	15

LIST OF ELEMENTS—Continued

Name	Atomic	
	Symbol	No.
Platinum	Pt	78
Plutonium	Pu	94
Polonium	Po	84
Potassium	K	19
Praseodymium	Pr	59
Promethium	Pm	61
Protactinium	Pa	91
Radium	Ra	88
Radon	Rn	86
Rhenium	Re	75
Rhodium	Rh	45
Rubidium	Rb	37
Ruthenium	Ru	44
Samarium	Sm	62
Scandium	Sc	21
Selenium	Se	34
Silicon	Si	14
Silver	Ag	47
Sodium	Na	11
Strontium	Sr	38
Sulfur	S	16
Tantalum	Ta	73
Technetium	Tc	43
Tellurium	Te	52
Terbium	Tb	65
Thallium	Tl	81
Thorium	Th	90
Thulium	Tm	69
Tin	Sn	50
Titanium	Ti	22
Tungsten	W	74
Uranium	U	92
Vanadium	V	23
Xenon	Xe	54
Ytterbium	Yb	70
Yttrium	Y	39
Zinc	Zn	30
Zirconium	Zr	40

			Table 1 Occupational Values			Table 2 Effluent Concentration		Table 3 Releases to Sewers
			Col. 1	Col. 2	Col. 3	Col. 1	Col.2	
			Oral Ingestion	Inhalation				Monthly Average Concentration (μCi/ml)
Atomic No.	Radionuclide	Class	ALI (μCi)	ALI (μCi)	DAC (μCi/ml)	Air (μCi/ml)	Water (μCi/ml)	
1	Hydrogen-3	Water, DAC includes skin absorption	8E+4	8E+4	2E-5	1E-7	1E-3	1E-2
		Gas (HT or T_2) Submersion[1]: Use above values as HT and T_2 oxidize in air and in the body to HTO						
4	Beryllium-7	W, all compounds except those given for Y	4E+4	2E+4	9E-6	3E-8	6E-4	6E-3
		Y, oxides, halides, and nitrates	-	2E+4	8E-6	3E-8	-	-
4	Beryllium-10	W, see 7Be	1E+3 LLI wall	2E+2	6E-8	2E-10	-	-
			(1E+3)	-	-	-	2E-5	2E-4
		Y, see 7Be	-	1E+1	6E-9	2E-11	-	-
6	Carbon-11[2]	Monoxide	-	1E+6	5E-4	2E-6	-	-
		Dioxide	-	6E+5	3E-4	9E-7	-	-
		Compounds	4E+5	4E+5	2E-4	6E-7	6E-3	6E-2
6	Carbon-14	Monoxide	-	2E+6	7E-4	2E-6	-	-
		Dioxide	-	2E+5	9E-5	3E-7	-	-
		Compounds	2E+3	2E+3	1E-6	3E-9	3E-5	3E-4

Atomic No.	Radionuclide	Class	Table 1 Occupational Values Col. 1 Oral Ingestion ALI (μCi)	Table 1 Col. 2 Inhalation ALI (μCi)	Table 1 Col. 3 Inhalation DAC (μCi/ml)	Table 2 Effluent Concentration Col. 1 Air (μCi/ml)	Table 2 Col. 2 Water (μCi/ml)	Table 3 Releases to Sewers Monthly Average Concentration (μCi/ml)
7	Nitrogen-13 [2]	Submersion[1]	-	4E-6	2E-8	-	-	-
8	Oxygen-15[2]	Submersion[1]	-	4E-6	2E-8	-	-	-
9	Fluorine-18[2]	D, fluorides of H, Li, Na, K, Rb, Cs, and Fr	5e+4	7E+4	3E-5	1E-7	-	-
			St wall (5E+4)	-	-	-	7E-4	7E3
		W, fluorides of Be, Mg Ca, Sr, Ba, Ra, Al, Ga, In, Ti, As, Sb, Bi, Fe, Ru, Os, Co, Ni, Pd, Pt, Cu, Ag, Au, Zn, Cd, Hg, Sc, Y, Ti, Zr, V, Nb, Ta, Nm, Tc, and Re	-	9e+4	4e-5	1e-7	-	-
		y, LANTHANUM FLUORIDE	-	8e+4	3e-5	1e-7	-	-
11	Sodium-22	D, all compounds	4E+2	6E+2	3E-7	9E-10	6E-6	6E-5
11	Sodium-24	D, all compounds	4E+3	5E+3	2E-6	7E-9	5E-5	5E-4
12	Magnesium-28	D, all compounds except those given for W	7E+2	2E+3	7E-7	2E-9	9E-6	9E-5
		W, oxides, hydroxides, carbides, halides, and nitrates		1E+3	6E-7	2E-9	-	-
13	Aluminum-26	D, all compounds except those given for W	4E+2	6E+1	3E-8	9E-11	6E-6	6E-5
		W, oxides, hydroxides, carbides, halides, and nitrates	-	9E+1	4E-8	1E-10	-	-

			Table 1 Occupational Values			Table 2 Effluent Concentrations		Table 3 Releases to Sewers
			Col. 1	Col. 2	Col. 3	Col. 1	Col. 2	
			Oral Ingestion	Inhalation				Monthly Average
Atomic No.	Radionuclide	Class	ALI (μCi)	ALI (μCi)	DAC (μCi/ml)	Air (μCi/ml)	Water (μCi/ml)	Concentration (μCi/ml)
14	Silicon-31	D, all compounds except those given for W and Y	9E+3	3E+4	1E-5	4E-8	1E-4	1E-3
		W, oxides, hydroxides, carbides, and nitrates	-	3E+4	1E-5	5E-8	-	-
		Y, aluminosilicate glass	-	3E+4	1E-5	4E-8	-	-
14	Silicon-32	D, see ^{31}Si	2E+3	2E+2	1E-7	3E-10	-	-
			LLI wall (3E+3)	-	-	-	4E-5	4E-4
		W, see ^{31}Si	-	1E+2	5E-8	2E-10	-	-
		Y, see ^{31}Si	-	5E+0	2E-9	7E-12	-	-
15	Phosphorus-32	D, all compounds except phosphates given for W	6E+2	9E+2	4E-7	1E-9	9E-6	9E-5
		W, phosphates of Zn^{2+}, S^{3+}, Mg^{2+}, Fe^{3+}, Bi^{3+}, and lanthanides	-	4E+2	2E-7	5E-10	-	-
15	Phosphorus-33	D, see ^{32}P	6E+3	8E+3	4E-6	1E-8	8E-5	8E-4
		W, see ^{32}P	-	3E+3	1E-6	4E-9	-	-
16	Sulfur-35	Vapor	-	1E+4	6E-6	2E-8	-	-
		D, sulfides and sulfates except those given for W	1E+4	2E+4	7E-6	2E-8	-	-
			LLI wall (8E+3)	-	-	-	1E-4	1E-3
		W, elemental sulfur, sulfides of Sr, Ba, Ge, Sn, Pb, As, Sb, Bi, Cu, Ag, Au, Zn, Cd, Hg, W, and Mo. Sulfates of Ca, Sr, Ba, Ra, As, Sb, and Bi	6E+3					
			-	2E+3	9E-7	3E-9	-	-
17	Chlorine-36	D, chlorides of H, Li, Na, K, Rb, Cs, and Fr	2E+3	2E+3	1E-6	3E-9	2E-5	2E-4
		W, chlorides of lanthanides, Be, Mg, Ca, Sr, Ba, Ra, Al, Ga, In, Tl, Ge, Sn, Pb, As, Sb, Bi, Fe, Ru, Os, Co, Rh, Ir, Ni, Pd, Pt, Cu, Ag, Au, Zn, Cd, Hg, Sc, Y, Ti, Zr, Hf, V, Nb, Ta, Cr, Mo, W, Mn, Tc, and Re	-	2E+2	1E-7	3E-10	-	-

Atomic No.	Radionuclide	Class	Table 1 Occupational Values Col. 1 Oral Ingestion ALI (μCi)	Table 1 Col. 2 Inhalation ALI (μCi)	Table 1 Col. 3 Inhalation DAC (μCi/ml)	Table 2 Effluent Concentrations Col. 1 Air (μCi/ml)	Table 2 Col. 2 Water (μCi/ml)	Table 3 Releases to Sewers Monthly Average Concentration (μCi/ml)
17	Chlorine-38[2]	D, see ^{36}Cl	2E+4	4E+4	2E-5	6E-8	-	-
			St. wall (3E+4)	-	-	-	3E-4	3E-3
		W, see ^{36}Cl	-	5E+4	2E-5	6E-8	-	-
17	Chlorine-39[2]	D, see ^{36}Cl	2E+4	5E+4	2E-5	7E-8	-	-
			St. wall (4E+4)	-	-	-	5E-4	5E-3
		W, see ^{36}Cl	-	6E+4	2E-5	8E-8	-	-
18	Argon-37	Submersion[1]	-	-	1E+0	6E-3	-	-
18	Argon-39	Submersion[1]	-	-	2E-4	8E-7	-	-
18	Argon-41	Submersion[1]	-	-	3E-6	1E-8	-	-
19	Potassium-40	D, all compounds	3E+2	4E+2	2E-7	6E-10	4E-6	4E-5
19	Potassium-42	D, all compounds	5E+3	5E+3	2E-6	7E-9	6E-5	6E-4
19	Potassium-43	D, all compounds	6E+3	9E+3	4E-6	1E-8	9E-5	9E-4
19	Potassium-44[2]	D, all compounds	2E+4	7E+4	3E-5	9E-8	-	-
			St. wall (4E+4)	-	-	-	5E-4	5E-3
19	Potassium-45[2]	D, all compounds	3E+4	1E+5	5E-5	2E-7	-	-
			St. wall (5E+4)	-	-	-	7E-4	7E-3
20	Calcium-41	W, all compounds	3E+3	4E+3	2E-6	-	-	-
			Bone surf (4E+3)	Bone surf (4E+3)	-	5E-9	6E-5	6E-4
20	Calcium-45	W, all compounds	2E+3	8E+2	4E-7	1E-9	2E-5	2E-4
20	Calcium-47	W, all compounds	8E+2	9E+2	4E-7	1E-9	1E-5	1E-4
21	Scandium-43	Y, all compounds	7E+3	2E+4	9E-6	3E-8	1E-4	1E-3
21	Scandium-44m	Y, all compounds	5E+2	7E+2	3E-7	1E-9	7E-6	7E-5
21	Scandium-44	Y, all compounds	4E+3	1E+4	5E-6	2E-8	5E-5	5E-4
21	Scandium-46	Y, all compounds	9E+2	2E+2	1E-7	3E-10	1E-5	1E-4
21	Scandium-47	Y, all compounds	2E+3	3E+3	1E-6	4E-9	-	-
			LLI wall (3E+3)	-	-	-	4E-5	4E-4
21	Scandium-48	Y, all compounds	8E+2	1E+3	6E-7	2E-9	1E-5	1E-4
21	Scandium-49[2]	Y, all compounds	2E+4	5E+4	2E-5	8E-8	3E-4	3E-3
22	Titanium-44	D, all compounds except those given for W and Y	3E+2	1E+1	5E-9	2E-11	4E-6	4E-5
		W, oxides, hydroxides, carbides, halides, and nitrates	-	3E+1	1E-8	4E-11	-	-
		Y, $SrTiO_3$	-	6E+0	2E-9	8E-12	-	-

Atomic No.	Radionuclide	Class	Table 1 Occupational Values			Table 2 Effluent Concentrations		Table 3 Releases to Sewers
			Col. 1 Oral Ingestion ALI (μCi)	Col. 2 Inhalation ALI (μCi)	Col. 3 Inhalation DAC (μCi/ml)	Col. 1 Air (μCi/ml)	Col. 2 Water (μCi/ml)	Monthly Average Concentration (μCi/ml)
22	Titanium-45	D, see ^{44}Ti	9E+3	3E+4	1E-5	3E-8	1E-4	1E-3
		W, see ^{44}Ti	-	4E+4	1E-5	5E-8	-	-
		Y, see ^{44}Ti	-	3E+4	1E-5	4E-8	-	-
23	Vanadium-47[2]	D, all compounds except those given for W	3E+4	8E+4	3E-5	1E-7	-	-
			St. wall (3E+4)	-	-	-	4E-4	4E-3
		W, oxides, hydroxides, carbides, and halides	-	1E+5	4E-5	1E-7	-	-
23	Vanadium-48	D, see ^{47}V	6E+2	1E+3	5E-7	2E-9	9E-6	9E-5
		W, see ^{47}V	-	6E+2	3E-7	9E-10	-	-
23	Vanadium-49	D, see ^{47}V	7E+4	3E+4	1E-5	-	-	-
			LLI wall (9E+4)	Bone surf (3E+4)	-	5E-8	1E-3	1E-2
		W, see ^{47}V	-	2E+4	8E-6	2E-8	-	-
24	Chromium-48	D, all compounds except those given for W and Y	6E+3	1E+4	5E-6	2E-8	8E-5	8E-4
		W, halides and nitrates	-	7E+3	3E-6	1E-8	-	-
		Y, oxides and hydroxides	-	7E+3	3E-6	1E-8	-	-
24	Chromium-49[2]	D, see ^{48}Cr	3E+4	8E+4	4E-5	1E-7	4E-4	4E-3
		W, see ^{48}Cr	-	1E+5	4E-5	1E-7	-	-
		Y, see ^{48}Cr	-	9E+4	4E-5	1E-7	-	-
24	Chromium-51	D, see ^{48}Cr	4E+4	5E+4	2E-5	6E-8	5E-4	5E-3
		W, see ^{48}Cr	-	2E+4	1E-5	3E-8	-	-
		Y, see ^{48}Cr	-	2E+4	8E-6	3E-8	-	-
25	Manganese-51[2]	D, all compounds except those given for W	2E+4	5E+4	2E-5	7E-8	3E-4	3E-3
		W, oxides, hydroxides, halides, and nitrates	-	6E+4	3E-5	8E-8	-	-
25	Manganese-52m[2]	D, see ^{51}Mn	3E+4	9E+4	4E-5	1E-7	-	-
			St. wall (4E+4)	-	-	-	5E-4	5E-3
		W, see ^{51}Mn	-	1E+5	4E-5	1E-7	-	-
25	Manganese-52	D, see ^{51}Mn	7E+2	1E+3	5E-7	2E-9	1E-5	1E-4
		W, see ^{51}Mn	-	9E+2	4E-7	1E-9	-	-
25	Manganese-53	D, see ^{51}Mn	5E+4	1E+4	5E-6	-	7E-4	7E-3
			-	Bone surf (2E+4)	-	3E-8	-	-
		W, see ^{51}Mn	-	1E+4	5E-6	2E-8	-	-
25	Manganese-54	D, see ^{51}Mn	2E+3	9E+2	4E-7	1E-9	3E-5	3E-4
		W, see ^{51}Mn	-	8E+2	3E-7	1E-9	-	-
25	Manganese-56	D, see ^{51}Mn	5E+3	2E+4	6E-6	2E-8	7E-5	7E-4
		W, see ^{51}Mn	-	2E+4	9E-6	3E-8	-	-

Atomic No.	Radionuclide	Class	Table 1 Occupational Values Col. 1 Oral Ingestion ALI (μCi)	Table 1 Col. 2 Inhalation ALI (μCi)	Table 1 Col. 3 Inhalation DAC (μCi/ml)	Table 2 Effluent Concentrations Col. 1 Air (μCi/ml)	Table 2 Col. 2 Water (μCi/ml)	Table 3 Releases to Sewers Monthly Average Concentration (μCi/ml)
26	Iron-52	D, all compounds except those given for W	9E+2	3E+3	1E-6	4E-9	1E-5	1E-4
		W, oxides, hydroxides, and halides	-	2E+3	1E-6	3E-9	-	-
26	Iron-55	D, see ^{52}Fe	9E+3	2E+3	8E-7	3E-9	1E-4	1E-3
		W, see ^{52}Fe	-	4E+3	2E-6	6E-9	-	-
26	Iron-59	D, see ^{52}Fe	8E+2	3E+2	1E-7	5E-10	1E-5	1E-4
		W, see ^{52}Fe	-	5E+2	2E-7	7E-10	-	-
26	Iron-60	D, see ^{52}Fe	3E+1	6E+0	3E-9	9E-12	4E-7	4E-6
		W, see ^{52}Fe	-	2E+1	8E-9	3E-11	-	-
27	Cobalt-55	W, all compounds except those given for Y	1E+3	3E+3	1E-6	4E-9	2E-5	2E-4
		Y, oxides, hydroxides, halides, and nitrates	-	3E+3	1E-6	4E-9	-	-
27	Cobalt-56	W, see ^{55}Co	5E+2	3E+2	1E-7	4E-10	6E-6	6E-5
		Y, see ^{55}Co	4E+2	2E+2	8E-8	3E-10	-	-
27	Cobalt-57	W, see ^{55}Co	8E+3	3E+3	1E-6	4E-9	6E-5	6E-4
		Y, see ^{55}Co	4E+3	7E+2	3E-7	9E-10	-	-
27	Cobalt-58m	W, see ^{55}Co	6E+4	9E+4	4E-5	1E-7	8E-4	8E-3
		Y, see ^{55}Co	-	6E+4	3E-5	9E-8	-	-
27	Cobalt-58	W, see ^{55}Co	2E+3	1E+3	5E-7	2E-9	2E-5	2E-4
		Y, see ^{55}Co	1E+3	7E+2	3E-7	1E-9	-	-
27	Cobalt-60m[2]	W, see ^{55}Co	1E+6	4E+6	2E-3	6E-6	-	-
			St. wall (1E+6)	-	-	-	2E-2	2E-1
		Y, see ^{55}Co	-	3E+6	1E-3	4E-6	-	-
27	Cobalt-60	W, see ^{55}Co	5E+2	2E+2	7E-8	2E-10	3E-6	3E-5
		Y, see ^{55}Co	2E+2	3E+1	1E-8	5E-11	-	-
27	Cobalt-61[2]	W, see ^{55}Co	2E+4	6E+4	3E-5	9E-8	3E-4	3E-3
		Y, see ^{55}Co	2E+4	6E+4	2E-5	8E-8	-	-
27	Cobalt-62m[2]	W, see ^{55}Co	4E+4	2E+5	7E-5	2E-7	-	-
			St. wall (5E+4)	-	-	-	7E-4	7E-3
		Y, see ^{55}Co	-	2E+5	6E-5	2E-7	-	-
28	Nickel-56	D, all compounds except those given for W	1E+3	2E+3	8E-7	3E-9	2E-5	2E-4
		W, oxides, hydroxides, and carbides	-	1E+3	5E-7	2E-9	-	-
		Vapor	-	1E+3	5E-7	2E-9	-	-
28	Nickel-57	D, see ^{56}Ni	2E+3	5E+3	2E-6	7E-9	2E-5	2E-4
		W, see ^{56}Ni	-	3E+3	1E-6	4E-9	-	-
		Vapor	-	6E+3	3E-6	9E-9	-	-

Atomic No.	Radionuclide	Class	Table 1 Occupational Values Col. 1 Oral Ingestion ALI (μCi)	Table 1 Col. 2 Inhalation ALI (μCi)	Table 1 Col. 3 Inhalation DAC (μCi/ml)	Table 2 Effluent Concentrations Col. 1 Air (μCi/ml)	Table 2 Col. 2 Water (μCi/ml)	Table 3 Releases to Sewers Monthly Average Concentration (μCi/ml)
28	Nickel-59	D, see ^{56}Ni	2E+4	4E+3	2E-6	5E-9	3E-4	3E-3
		W, see ^{56}Ni	-	7E+3	3E-6	1E-8	-	-
		Vapor	-	2E+3	8E-7	3E-9	-	-
28	Nickel-63	D, see ^{56}Ni	9E+3	2E+3	7E-7	2E-9	1E-4	1E-3
		W, see ^{56}Ni	-	3E+3	1E-6	4E-9	-	-
		Vapor	-	8E+2	3E-7	1E-9	-	-
28	Nickel-65	D, see ^{56}Ni	8E+3	2E+4	1E-5	3E-8	1E-4	1E-3
		W, see ^{56}Ni	-	3E+4	1E-5	4E-8	-	-
		Vapor	-	2E+4	7E-6	2E-8	-	-
28	Nickel-66	D, see ^{56}Ni	4E+2	2E+3	7E-7	2E-9	-	-
			LLI wall (5E+2)	-	-	-	6E-6	6E-5
		W, see ^{56}Ni	-	6E+2	3E-7	9E-10	-	-
		Vapor	-	3E+3	1E-6	4E-9	-	-
29	Copper-60[2]	D, all compounds except those given for W and Y	3E+4	9E+4	4E-5	1E-7	-	-
			St. wall (3E+4)	-	-	-	4E-4	4E-3
		W, sulfides, halides, and nitrates	-	1E+5	5E-5	2E-7	-	-
		Y, oxides and hydroxides	-	1E+5	4E-5	1E-7	-	-
29	Copper-61	D, see ^{60}Cu	1E+4	3E+4	1E-5	4E-8	2E-4	2E-3
		W, see ^{60}Cu	-	4E+4	2E-5	6E-8	-	-
		Y, see ^{60}Cu	-	4E+4	1E-5	5E-8	-	-
29	Copper-64	D, see ^{60}Cu	1E+4	3E+4	1E-5	4E-8	2E-4	2E-3
		W, see ^{60}Cu	-	2E+4	1E-5	3E-8	-	-
		Y, see ^{60}Cu	-	2E+4	9E-6	3E-8	-	-
29	Copper-67	D, see ^{60}Cu	5E+3	8E+3	3E-6	1E-8	6E-5	6E-4
		W, see ^{60}Cu	-	5E+3	2E-6	7E-9	-	-
		Y, see ^{60}Cu	-	5E+3	2E-6	6E-9	-	-
30	Zinc-62	Y, all compounds	1E+3	3E+3	1E-6	4E-9	2E-5	2E-4
30	Zinc-63[2]	Y, all compounds	2E+4	7E+4	3E-5	9E-8	-	-
			St. wall (3E+4)	-	-	-	3E-4	3E-3
30	Zinc-65	Y, all compounds	4E+2	3E+2	1E-7	4E-10	5E-6	5E-5
30	Zinc-69m	Y, all compounds	4E+3	7E+3	3E-6	1E-8	6E-5	6E-4
30	Zinc-69[2]	Y, all compounds	6E+4	1E+5	6E-5	2E-7	8E-4	8E-3
30	Zinc-71m	Y, all compounds	6E+3	2E+4	7E-6	2E-8	8E-5	8E-4
30	Zinc-72	Y, all compounds	1E+3	1E+3	5E-7	2E-9	1E-5	1E-4
31	Gallium-65[2]	D, all compounds except those given for W	5E+4	2E+5	7E-5	2E-7	-	-
			St. wall (6E+4)	-	-	-	9E-4	9E-3
		W, oxides, hydroxides, carbides, halides, and nitrates	-	2E+5	8E-5	3E-7	-	-

Atomic No.	Radionuclide	Class	Table 1 Occupational Values Col. 1 Oral Ingestion ALI (μCi)	Table 1 Col. 2 Inhalation ALI (μCi)	Table 1 Col. 3 Inhalation DAC (μCi/ml)	Table 2 Effluent Concentrations Col. 1 Air (μCi/ml)	Table 2 Col. 2 Water (μCi/ml)	Table 3 Releases to Sewers Monthly Average Concentration (μCi/ml)
31	Gallium-66	D, see ^{65}Ga	1E+3	4E+3	1E-6	5E-9	1E-5	1E-4
		W, see ^{65}Ga	-	3E+3	1E-6	4E-9	-	-
31	Gallium-67	D, see ^{65}Ga	7E+3	1E+4	6E-6	2E-8	1E-4	1E-3
		W, see ^{65}Ga	-	1E+4	4E-6	1E-8	-	-
31	Gallium-68[2]	D, see ^{65}Ga	2E+4	4E+4	2E-5	6E-8	2E-4	2E-3
		W, see ^{65}Ga	-	5E+4	2E-5	7E-8	-	-
31	Gallium-70[2]	D, see ^{65}Ga	5E+4	2E+5	7E-5	2E-7	-	-
			St. wall (7E+4)	-	-	-	1E-3	1E-2
		W, see ^{65}Ga	-	2E+5	8E-5	3E-7	-	-
31	Gallium-72	D, see ^{65}Ga	1E+3	4E+3	1E-6	5E-9	2E-5	2E-4
		W, see ^{65}Ga	-	3E+3	1E-6	4E-9	-	-
31	Gallium-73	D, see ^{65}Ga	5E+3	2E+4	6E-6	2E-8	7E-5	7E-4
		W, see ^{65}Ga	-	2E+4	6E-6	2E-8	-	-
32	Germanium-66	D, all compounds except those given for W	2E+4	3E+4	1E-5	4E-8	3E-4	3E-3
		W, oxides, sulfides, and halides	-	2E+4	8E-6	3E-8	-	-
32	Germanium-67[2]	D, see ^{66}Ge	3E+4	9E+4	4E-5	1E-7	-	-
			St. wall (4E+4)	-	-	-	6E-4	6E-3
		W, see ^{66}Ge	-	1E+5	4E-5	1E-7	-	-
32	Germanium-68	D, see ^{66}Ge	5E+3	4E+3	2E-6	5E-9	6E-5	6E-4
		W, see ^{66}Ge	-	1E+2	4E-8	1E-10	-	-
32	Germanium-69	D, see ^{66}Ge	1E+4	2E+4	6E-6	2E-8	2E-4	2E-3
		W, see ^{66}Ge	-	8E+3	3E-6	1E-8	-	-
32	Germanium-71	D, see ^{66}Ge	5E+5	4E+5	2E-4	6E-7	7E-3	7E-2
		W, see ^{66}Ge	-	4E+4	2E-5	6E-8	-	-
32	Germanium-75[2]	D, see ^{66}Ge	4E+4	8E+4	3E-5	1E-7	-	-
			St. wall (7E+4)	-	-	-	9E-4	9E-3
		W, see ^{66}Ge	-	8E+4	4E-5	1E-7	-	-
32	Germanium-77	D, see ^{66}Ge	9E+3	1E+4	4E-6	1E-8	1E-4	1E-3
		W, see ^{66}Ge	-	6E+3	2E-6	8E-9	-	-
32	Germanium-78[2]	D, see ^{66}Ge	2E+4	2E+4	9E-6	3E-8	-	-
			St. wall (2E+4)	-	-	-	3E-4	3E-3
		W, see ^{66}Ge	-	2E+4	9E-6	3E-8	-	-

Atomic No.	Radionuclide	Class	Table 1 Occupational Values Col. 1 Oral Ingestion ALI (μCi)	Table 1 Col. 2 Inhalation ALI (μCi)	Table 1 Col. 3 Inhalation DAC (μCi/ml)	Table 2 Effluent Concentrations Col. 1 Air (μCi/ml)	Table 2 Col. 2 Water (μCi/ml)	Table 3 Releases to Sewers Monthly Average Concentration (μCi/ml)
33	Arsenic-69[2]	W, all compounds	3E+4	1E+5	5E-5	2E-7	-	-
			St. wall (4E+4)	-	-	-	6E-4	6E-3
33	Arsenic-70[2]	W, all compounds	1E+4	5E+4	2E-5	7E-8	2E-4	2E-3
33	Arsenic-71	W, all compounds	4E+3	5E+3	2E-6	6E-9	5E-5	5E-4
33	Arsenic-72	W, all compounds	9E+2	1E+3	6E-7	2E-9	1E-5	1E-4
33	Arsenic-73	W, all compounds	8E+3	2E+3	7E-7	2E-9	1E-4	1E-3
33	Arsenic-74	W, all compounds	1E+3	8E+2	3E-7	1E-9	2E-5	2E-4
33	Arsenic-76	W, all compounds	1E+3	1E+3	6E-7	2E-9	1E-5	1E-4
33	Arsenic-77	W, all compounds	4E+3	5E+3	2E-6	7E-9	-	-
			LLI wall (5E+3)	-	-	-	6E-5	6E-4
33	Arsenic-78[2]	W, all compounds	8E+3	2E+4	9E-6	3E-8	1E-4	1E-3
34	Selenium-70[2]	D, all compounds except those given for W	2E+4	4E+4	2E-5	5E-8	1E-4	1E-3
		W, oxides, hydroxides, carbides, and elemental Se	1E+4	4E+4	2E-5	6E-8	-	-
34	Selenium-73m[2]	D, see ^{70}Se	6E+4	2E+5	6E-5	2E-7	4E-4	4E-3
		W, see ^{70}Se	3E+4	1E+5	6E-5	2E-7	-	-
34	Selenium-73	D, see ^{70}Se	3E+3	1E+4	5E-6	2E-8	4E-5	4E-4
		W, see ^{70}Se	-	2E+4	7E-6	2E-8	-	-
34	Selenium-75	D, see ^{70}Se	5E+2	7E+2	3E-7	1E-9	7E-6	7E-5
		W, see ^{70}Se	-	6E+2	3E-7	8E-10	-	-
34	Selenium-79	D, see ^{70}Se	6E+2	8E+2	3E-7	1E-9	8E-6	8E-5
		W, see ^{70}Se	-	6E+2	2E-7	8E-10	-	-
34	Selenium-81m[2]	D, see ^{70}Se	4E+4	7E+4	3E-5	9E-8	3E-4	3E-3
		W, see ^{70}Se	2E+4	7E+4	3E-5	1E-7	-	-
34	Selenium-81[2]	D, see ^{70}Se	6E+4	2E+5	9E-5	3E-7	-	-
			St. wall (8E+4)	-	-	-	1E-3	1E-2
		W, see ^{70}Se	-	2E+5	1E-4	3E-7	-	-
34	Selenium-83[2]	D, see ^{70}Se	4E+4	1E+5	5E-5	2E-7	4E-4	4E-3
		W, see ^{70}Se	3E+4	1E+5	5E-5	2E-7	-	-

Atomic No.	Radionuclide	Class	Table 1 Occupational Values Col. 1 Oral Ingestion ALI (μCi)	Table 1 Col. 2 Inhalation ALI (μCi)	Table 1 Col. 3 Inhalation DAC (μCi/ml)	Table 2 Effluent Concentrations Col. 1 Air (μCi/ml)	Table 2 Col. 2 Water (μCi/ml)	Table 3 Releases to Sewers Monthly Average Concentration (μCi/ml)
35	Bromine-74m[2]	D, bromides of H, Li, Na, K, Rb, Cs, and Fr	1E+4	4E+4	2E-5	5E-8	-	-
			St. wall (2E+4)	-	-	-	3E-4	3E-3
		W, bromides of lanthanides, Be, Mg, Ca, Sr, Ba, Ra, Al, Ga, In, Tl, Ge, Sn, Pb, As, Sb, Bi, Fe, Ru, Os, Co, Rh, Ir, Ni, Pd, Pt, Cu, Ag, Au, Zn, Cd, Hg, Sc, Y, Ti, Zr, Hf, V, Nb, Ta, Mn, Tc, and Re	-	4E+4	2E-5	6E-8	-	-
35	Bromine-74[2]	D, see ^{74m}Br	2E+4	7E+4	3E-5	1E-7	-	-
			St. wall (4E+4)	-	-	-	5E-4	5E-3
		W, see ^{74m}Br	-	8E+4	4E-5	1E-7	-	-
35	Bromine-75[2]	D, see ^{74m}Br	3E+4	5E+4	2E-5	7E-8	-	-
			St. wall (4E+4)	-	-	-	5E-4	5E-3
		W, see ^{74m}Br	-	5E+4	2E-5	7E-8	-	-
35	Bromine-76	D, see ^{74m}Br	4E+3	5E+3	2E-6	7E-9	5E-5	5E-4
		W, see ^{74m}Br	-	4E+3	2E-6	6E-9	-	-
35	Bromine-77	D, see ^{74m}Br	2E+4	2E+4	1E-5	3E-8	2E-4	2E-3
		W, see ^{74m}Br	-	2E+4	8E-6	3E-8	-	-
35	Bromine-80m	D, see ^{74m}Br	2E+4	2E+4	7E-6	2E-8	3E-4	3E-3
		W, see ^{74m}Br	-	1E+4	6E-6	2E-8	-	-
35	Bromine-80[2]	D, see ^{74m}Br	5E+4	2E+5	8E-5	3E-7	-	-
			St. wall (9E+4)	-	-	-	1E-3	1E-2
		W, see ^{74m}Br	-	2E+5	9E-5	3E-7	-	-
35	Bromine-82	D, see ^{74m}Br	3E+3	4E+3	2E-6	6E-9	4E-5	4E-4
		W, see ^{74m}Br	-	4E+3	2E-6	5E-9	-	-
35	Bromine-83	D, see ^{74m}Br	5E+4	6E+4	3E-5	9E-8	-	-
			St. wall (7E+4)	-	-	-	9E-4	9E-3
		W, see ^{74m}Br	-	6E+4	3E-5	9E-8	-	-
35	Bromine-84[2]	D, see ^{74m}Br	2E+4	6E+4	2E-5	8E-8	-	-
			St. wall (3E+4)	-	-	-	4E-4	4E-3
		W, see ^{74m}Br	-	6E+4	3E-5	9E-8	-	-
36	Krypton-74[2]	Submersion[1]	-	-	3E-6	1E-8	-	-
36	Krypton-76	Submersion[1]	-	-	9E-6	4E-8	-	-
36	Krypton-77[2]	Submersion[1]	-	-	4E-6	2E-8	-	-
36	Krypton-79	Submersion[1]	-	-	2E-5	7E-8	-	-
36	Krypton-81	Submersion[1]	-	-	7E-4	3E-6	-	-

Atomic No.	Radionuclide	Class	Table 1 Occupational Values: Col. 1 Oral Ingestion ALI (μCi)	Table 1: Col. 2 Inhalation ALI (μCi)	Table 1: Col. 3 Inhalation DAC (μCi/ml)	Table 2 Effluent Concentrations: Col. 1 Air (μCi/ml)	Table 2: Col. 2 Water (μCi/ml)	Table 3 Releases to Sewers: Monthly Average Concentration (μCi/ml)
36	Krypton-83m[2]	Submersion[1]			1E-2	5E-5	-	
36	Krypton-85m	Submersion[1]	-	-	2E-5	1E-7	-	
36	Krypton-85	Submersion[1]	-	-	1E-4	7E-7	-	-
36	Krypton-87[2]	Submersion[1]	-	-	5E-6	2E-8	-	-
36	Krypton-88	Submersion[1]	-	-	2E-6	9E-9	-	-
37	Rubidium-79[2]	D, all compounds	4E+4	1E+5	5E-5	2E-7	-	-
			St. wall (6E+4)	-	-	-	8E-4	8E-3
37	Rubidium-81m[2]	D, all compounds	2E+5	3E+5	1E-4	5E-7	-	-
			St. wall (3E+5)	-	-	-	4E-3	4E-2
37	Rubidium-81	D, all compounds	4E+4	5E+4	2E-5	7E-8	5E-4	5E-3
37	Rubidium-82m	D, all compounds	1E+4	2E+4	7E-6	2E-8	2E-4	2E-3
37	Rubidium-83	D, all compounds	6E+2	1E+3	4E-7	1E-9	9E-6	9E-5
37	Rubidium-84	D, all compounds	5E+2	8E+2	3E-7	1E-9	7E-6	7E-5
37	Rubidium-86	D, all compounds	5E+2	8E+2	3E-7	1E-9	7E-6	7E-5
37	Rubidium-87	D, all compounds	1E+3	2E+3	6E-7	2E-9	1E-5	1E-4
37	Rubidium-88[2]	D, all compounds	2E+4	6E+4	3E-5	9E-8	-	-
			St. wall (3E+4)	-	-	-	4E-4	4E-3
37	Rubidium-89[2]	D, all compounds	4E+4	1E+5	6E-5	2E-7	-	-
			St. wall (6E+4)	-	-	-	9E-4	9E-3
38	Strontium-80[2]	D, all soluble compounds except $SrTiO_3$	4E+3	1E+4	5E-6	2E-8	6E-5	6E-4
		Y, all insoluble compounds and $SrTiO_3$	-	1E+4	5E-6	2E-8	-	-
38	Strontium-81[2]	D, see ^{80}Sr	3E+4	8E+4	3E-5	1E-7	3E-4	3E-3
		Y, see ^{80}Sr	2E+4	8E+4	3E-5	1E-7	-	-
38	Strontium-82	D, see ^{80}Sr	3E+2	4E+2	2E-7	6E-10	-	-
			LLI wall (2E+2)	-	-	-	3E-6	3E-5
		Y, see ^{80}Sr	2E+2	9E+1	4E-8	1E-10	-	-
38	Strontium-83	D, see ^{80}Sr	3E+3	7E+3	3E-6	1E-8	3E-5	3E-4
		Y, see ^{80}Sr	2E+3	4E+3	1E-6	5E-9	-	-
38	Strontium-85m[2]	D, see ^{80}Sr	2E+5	6E+5	3E-4	9E-7	3E-3	3E-2
		Y, see ^{80}Sr	-	8E+5	4E-4	1E-6	-	-
38	Strontium-85	D, see ^{80}Sr	3E+3	3E+3	1E-6	4E-9	4E-5	4E-4
		Y, see ^{80}Sr	-	2E+3	6E-7	2E-9	-	-
38	Strontium-87m	D, see ^{80}Sr	5E+4	1E+5	5E-5	2E-7	6E-4	6E-3
		Y, see ^{80}Sr	4E+4	2E+5	6E-5	2E-7	-	-

Atomic No.	Radionuclide	Class	Table 1 Occupational Values Col. 1 Oral Ingestion ALI (μCi)	Table 1 Col. 2 Inhalation ALI (μCi)	Table 1 Col. 3 Inhalation DAC (μCi/ml)	Table 2 Effluent Concentrations Col. 1 Air (μCi/ml)	Table 2 Col. 2 Water (μCi/ml)	Table 3 Releases to Sewers Monthly Average Concentration (μCi/ml)
38	Strontium-89	D, see ^{80}Sr	6E+2	8E+2	4E-7	1E-9	-	-
			LLI wall					
			(6E+2)	-	-	-	8E-6	8E-5
		Y, see ^{80}Sr	5E+2	1E+2	6E-8	2E-10	-	-
38	Strontium-90	D, see ^{80}Sr	3E+1	2E+1	8E-9	-	-	-
			Bone surf	Bone surf				
			(4E+1)	(2E+1)	-	3E-11	5E-7	5E-6
		Y, see ^{80}Sr	-	4E+0	2E-9	6E-12	-	-
38	Strontium-91	D, see ^{80}Sr	2E+3	6E+3	2E-6	8E-9	2E-5	2E-4
		Y, see ^{80}Sr	-	4E+3	1E-6	5E-9	-	-
38	Strontium-92	D, see ^{80}Sr	3E+3	9E+3	4E-6	1E-8	4E-5	4E-4
		Y, see ^{80}Sr	-	7E+3	3E-6	9E-9	-	-
39	Yttrium-86m[2]	W, all compounds except those given for Y	2E+4	6E+4	2E-5	8E-8	3E-4	3E-3
		Y, oxides and hydroxides	-	5E+4	2E-5	8E-8	-	-
39	Yttrium-86	W, see ^{86m}Y	1E+3	3E+3	1E-6	5E-9	2E-5	2E-4
		Y, see ^{86m}Y	-	3E+3	1E-6	5E-9	-	-
39	Yttrium-87	W, see ^{86m}Y	2E+3	3E+3	1E-6	5E-9	3E-5	3E-4
		Y, see ^{86m}Y	-	3E+3	1E-6	5E-9	-	-
39	Yttrium-88	W, see ^{86m}Y	1E+3	3E+2	1E-7	3E-10	1E-5	1E-4
		Y, see ^{86m}Y	-	2E+2	1E-7	3E-10	-	-
39	Yttrium-90m	W, see ^{86m}Y	8E+3	1E+4	5E-6	2E-8	1E-4	1E-3
		Y, see ^{86m}Y	-	1E+4	5E-6	2E-8	-	-
39	Yttrium-90	W, see ^{86m}Y	4E+2	7E+2	3E-7	9E-10	-	-
			LLI wall					
			(5E+2)	-	-	-	7E-6	7E-5
		Y, see ^{86m}Y	-	6E+2	3E-7	9E-10	-	-
39	Yttrium-91m[2]	W, see ^{86m}Y	1E+5	2E+5	1E-4	3E-7	2E-3	2E-2
		Y, see ^{86m}Y	-	2E+5	7E-5	2E-7	-	-
39	Yttrium-91	W, see ^{86m}Y	5E+2	2E+2	7E-8	2E-10	-	-
			LLI wall					
			(6E+2)	-	-	-	8E-6	8E-5
		Y, see ^{86m}Y	-	1E+2	5E-8	2E-10	-	-
39	Yttrium-92	W, see ^{86m}Y	3E+3	9E+3	4E-6	1E-8	4E-5	4E-4
		Y, see ^{86m}Y	-	8E+3	3E-6	1E-8	-	-
39	Yttrium-93	W, see ^{86m}Y	1E+3	3E+3	1E-6	4E-9	2E-5	2E-4
		Y, see ^{86m}Y	-	2E+3	1E-6	3E-9	-	-
39	Yttrium-94[2]	W, see ^{86m}Y	2E+4	8E+4	3E-5	1E-7	-	-
			St. wall					
			(3E+4)	-	-	-	4E-4	4E-3
		Y, see ^{86m}Y	-	8E+4	3E-5	1E-7	-	-
39	Yttrium-95[2]	W, see ^{86m}Y	4E+4	2E+5	6E-5	2E-7	-	-
			St. wall					
			(5E+4)	-	-	-	7E-4	7E-3
		Y, see ^{86m}Y	-	1E+5	6E-5	2E-7	-	-

Atomic No.	Radionuclide	Class	Table 1 Occupational Values Col. 1 Oral Ingestion ALI (μCi)	Table 1 Col. 2 Inhalation ALI (μCi)	Table 1 Col. 3 Inhalation DAC (μCi/ml)	Table 2 Effluent Concentrations Col. 1 Air (μCi/ml)	Table 2 Col. 2 Water (μCi/ml)	Table 3 Releases to Sewers Monthly Average Concentration (μCi/ml)
40	Zirconium-86	D, all compounds except those given for W and Y	1E+3	4E+3	2E-6	6E-9	2E-5	2E-4
		W, oxides, hydroxides, halides, and nitrates	-	3E+3	1E-6	4E-9	-	-
		Y, carbide	-	2E+3	1E-6	3E-9	-	-
40	Zirconium-88	D, see ^{86}Zr	4E+3	2E+2	9E-8	3E-10	5E-5	5E-4
		W, see ^{86}Zr	-	5E+2	2E-7	7E-10	-	-
		Y, see ^{86}Zr	-	3E+2	1E-7	4E-10	-	-
40	Zirconium-89	D, see ^{86}Zr	2E+3	4E+3	1E-6	5E-9	2E-5	2E-4
		W, see ^{86}Zr	-	2E+3	1E-6	3E-9	-	-
		Y, see ^{86}Zr	-	2E+3	1E-6	3E-9	-	-
40	Zirconium-93	D, see ^{86}Zr	1E+3	6E+0	3E-9	-	-	-
			Bone surf (3E+3)	Bone surf (2E+1)	-	2E-11	4E-5	4E-4
		W, see ^{86}Zr	-	2E+1	1E-8	-	-	-
			-	Bone surf (6E+1)	-	9E-11	-	-
		Y, see ^{86}Zr	-	6E+1	2E-8	-	-	-
			-	Bone surf (7E+1)	-	9E-11	-	-
40	Zirconium-95	D, see ^{86}Zr	1E+3	1E+2	5E-8	-	2E-5	2E-4
			-	Bone surf (3E+2)	-	4E-10	-	-
		W, see ^{86}Zr	-	4E+2	2E-7	5E-10	-	-
		Y, see ^{86}Zr	-	3E+2	1E-7	4E-10	-	-
40	Zirconium-97	D, see ^{86}Zr	6E+2	2E+3	8E-7	3E-9	9E-6	9E-5
		W, see ^{86}Zr	-	1E+3	6E-7	2E-9	-	-
		Y, see ^{86}Zr	-	1E+3	5E-7	2E-9	-	-
41	Niobium-88[2]	W, all compounds except those given for Y	5E+4	2E+5	9E-5	3E-7	-	-
			St. wall (7E+4)	-	-	-	1E-3	1E-2
		Y, oxides and hydroxides	-	2E+5	9E-5	3E-7	-	-
41	Niobium-89m[2] (66 min)	W, see ^{88}Nb	1E+4	4E+4	2E-5	6E-8	1E-4	1E-3
		Y, see ^{88}Nb	-	4E+4	2E-5	5E-8	-	-
41	Niobium-89 (122 min)	W, see ^{88}Nb	5E+3	2E+4	8E-6	3E-8	7E-5	7E-4
		Y, see ^{88}Nb	-	2E+4	6E-6	2E-8	-	-
41	Niobium-90	W, see ^{88}Nb	1E+3	3E+3	1E-6	4E-9	1E-5	1E-4
		Y, see ^{88}Nb	-	2E+3	1E-6	3E-9	-	-
41	Niobium-93m	W, see ^{88}Nb	9E+3	2E+3	8E-7	3E-9	-	-
			LLI wall (1E+4)	-	-	-	2E-4	2E-3
		Y, see ^{88}Nb	-	2E+2	7E-8	2E-10	-	-
41	Niobium-94	W, see ^{88}Nb	9E+2	2E+2	8E-8	3E-10	1E-5	1E-4
		Y, see ^{88}Nb	-	2E+1	6E-9	2E-11	-	-
41	Niobium-95m	W, see ^{88}Nb	2E+3	3E+3	1E-6	4E-9	-	-
			LLI wall (2E+3)	-	-	-	3E-5	3E-4
		Y, see ^{88}Nb	-	2E+3	9E-7	3E-9	-	-

Atomic No.	Radionuclide	Class	Table 1 Occupational Values Col. 1 Oral Ingestion ALI (μCi)	Table 1 Col. 2 Inhalation ALI (μCi)	Table 1 Col. 3 Inhalation DAC (μCi/ml)	Table 2 Effluent Concentrations Col. 1 Air (μCi/ml)	Table 2 Col. 2 Water (μCi/ml)	Table 3 Releases to Sewers Monthly Average Concentration (μCi/ml)
41	Niobium-95	W, see ^{88}Nb	2E+3	1E+3	5E-7	2E-9	3E-5	3E-4
		Y, see ^{88}Nb	-	1E+3	5E-7	2E-9	-	-
41	Niobium-96	W, see ^{88}Nb	1E+3	3E+3	1E-6	4E-9	2E-5	2E-4
		Y, see ^{88}Nb	-	2E+3	1E-6	3E-9	-	-
41	Niobium-97[2]	W, see ^{88}Nb	2E+4	8E+4	3E-5	1E-7	3E-4	3E-3
		Y, see ^{88}Nb	-	7E+4	3E-5	1E-7	-	-
41	Niobium-98[2]	W, see ^{88}Nb	1E+4	5E+4	2E-5	8E-8	2E-4	2E-3
		Y, see ^{88}Nb	-	5E+4	2E-5	7E-8	-	-
42	Molybdenum-90	D, all compounds except those given for Y	4E+3	7E+3	3E-6	1E-8	3E-5	3E-4
		Y, oxides, hydroxides, and MoS_2	2E+3	5E+3	2E-6	6E-9	-	-
42	Molybdenum-93m	D, see ^{90}Mo	9E+3	2E+4	7E-6	2E-8	6E-5	6E-4
		Y, see ^{90}Mo	4E+3	1E+4	6E-6	2E-8	-	-
42	Molybdenum-93	D, see ^{90}Mo	4E+3	5E+3	2E-6	8E-9	5E-5	5E-4
		Y, see ^{90}Mo	2E+4	2E+2	8E-8	2E-10	-	-
42	Molybdenum-99	D, see ^{90}Mo	2E+3	3E+3	1E-6	4E-9	-	-
			LLI wall (1E+3)	-	-	-	2E-5	2E-4
		Y, see ^{90}Mo	1E+3	1E+3	6E-7	2E-9	-	-
42	Molybdenum-101[2]	D, see ^{90}Mo	4E+4	1E+5	6E-5	2E-7	-	-
			St. wall (5E+4)	-	-	-	7E-4	7E-3
		Y, see ^{90}Mo	-	1E+5	6E-5	2E-7	-	-
43	Technetium-93m[2]	D, all compounds except those given for W	7E+4	2E+5	6E-5	2E-7	1E-3	1E-2
		W, oxides, hydroxides, halides, and nitrates	-	3E+5	1E-4	4E-7	-	-
43	Technetium-93	D, see ^{93m}Tc	3E+4	7E+4	3E-5	1E-7	4E-4	4E-3
		W, see ^{93m}Tc	-	1E+5	4E-5	1E-7	-	-
43	Technetium-94m[2]	D, see ^{93m}Tc	2E+4	4E+4	2E-5	6E-8	3E-4	3E-3
		W, see ^{93m}Tc	-	6E+4	2E-5	8E-8	-	-
43	Technetium-94	D, see ^{93m}Tc	9E+3	2E+4	8E-6	3E-8	1E-4	1E-3
		W, see ^{93m}Tc	-	2E+4	1E-5	3E-8	-	-
43	Technetium-95m	D, see ^{93m}Tc	4E+3	5E+3	2E-6	8E-9	5E-5	5E-4
		W, see ^{93m}Tc	-	2E+3	8E-7	3E-9	-	-
43	Technetium-95	D, see ^{93m}Tc	1E+4	2E+4	9E-6	3E-8	1E-4	1E-3
		W, see ^{93m}Tc	-	2E+4	8E-6	3E-8	-	-
43	Technetium-96m[2]	D, see ^{93m}Tc	2E+5	3E+5	1E-4	4E-7	2E-3	2E-2
		W, see ^{93m}Tc	-	2E+5	1E-4	3E-7	-	-
43	Technetium-96	D, see ^{93m}Tc	2E+3	3E+3	1E-6	5E-9	3E-5	3E-4
		W, see ^{93m}Tc	-	2E+3	9E-7	3E-9	-	-
43	Technetium-97m	D, see ^{93m}Tc	5E+3	7E+3	3E-6	-	6E-5	6E-4
			-	St. wall (7E+3)	-	1E-8	-	-
		W, see ^{93m}Tc	-	1E+3	5E-7	2E-9	-	-

Atomic No.	Radionuclide	Class	Table 1 Occupational Values Col. 1 Oral Ingestion ALI (μCi)	Table 1 Col. 2 Inhalation ALI (μCi)	Table 1 Col. 3 Inhalation DAC (μCi/ml)	Table 2 Effluent Concentrations Col. 1 Air (μCi/ml)	Table 2 Col. 2 Water (μCi/ml)	Table 3 Releases to Sewers Monthly Average Concentration (μCi/ml)
43	Technetium-97	D, see ^{93m}Tc	4E+4	5E+4	2E-5	7E-8	5E-4	5E-3
		W, see ^{93m}Tc	-	6E+3	2E-6	8E-9	-	-
43	Technetium-98	D, see ^{93m}Tc	1E+3	2E+3	7E-7	2E-9	1E-5	1E-4
		W, see ^{93m}Tc	-	3E+2	1E-7	4E-10	-	-
43	Technetium-99m	D, see ^{93m}Tc	8E+4	2E+5	6E-5	2E-7	1E-3	1E-2
		W, see ^{93m}Tc	-	2E+5	1E-4	3E-7	-	-
43	Technetium-99	D, see ^{93m}Tc	4E+3	5E+3	2E-6	-	6E-5	6E-4
			-	St. wall (6E+3)	-	8E-9	-	-
		W, see ^{93m}Tc	-	7E+2	3E-7	9E-10	-	-
43	Technetium-101[2]	D, see ^{93m}Tc	9E+4	3E+5	1E-4	5E-7	-	-
			St. wall (1E+5)	-	-	-	2E-3	2E-2
		W, see ^{93m}Tc	-	4E+5	2E-4	5E-7	-	-
43	Technetium-104[2]	D, see ^{93m}Tc	2E+4	7E+4	3E-5	1E-7	-	-
			St. wall (3E+4)	-	-	-	4E-4	4E-3
		W, see ^{93m}Tc	-	9E+4	4E-5	1E-7	-	-
44	Ruthenium-94[2]	D, all compounds except those given for W and Y	2E+4	4E+4	2E-5	6E-8	2E-4	2E-3
		W, halides	-	6E+4	3E-5	9E-8	-	-
		Y, oxides and hydroxides	-	6E+4	2E-5	8E-8	-	-
44	Ruthenium-97	D, see ^{94}Ru	8E+3	2E+4	8E-6	3E-8	1E-4	1E-3
		W, see ^{94}Ru	-	1E+4	5E-6	2E-8	-	-
		Y, see ^{94}Ru	-	1E+4	5E-6	2E-8	-	-
44	Ruthenium-103	D, see ^{94}Ru	2E+3	2E+3	7E-7	2E-9	3E-5	3E-4
		W, see ^{94}Ru	-	1E+3	4E-7	1E-9	-	-
		Y, see ^{94}Ru	-	6E+2	3E-7	9E-10	-	-
44	Ruthenium-105	D, see ^{94}Ru	5E+3	1E+4	6E-6	2E-8	7E-5	7E-4
		W, see ^{94}Ru	-	1E+4	6E-6	2E-8	-	-
		Y, see ^{94}Ru	-	1E+4	5E-6	2E-8	-	-
44	Ruthenium-106	D, see ^{94}Ru	2E+2	9E+1	4E-8	1E-10	-	-
			LLI wall (2E+2)	-	-	-	3E-6	3E-5
		W, see ^{94}Ru	-	5E+1	2E-8	8E-11	-	-
		Y, see ^{94}Ru	-	1E+1	5E-9	2E-11	-	-
45	Rhodium-99m	D, all compounds except those given for W and Y	2E+4	6E+4	2E-5	8E-8	2E-4	2E-3
		W, halides	-	8E+4	3E-5	1E-7	-	-
		Y, oxides and hydroxides	-	7E+4	3E-5	9E-8	-	-
45	Rhodium-99	D, see ^{99m}Rh	2E+3	3E+3	1E-6	4E-9	3E-5	3E-4
		W, see ^{99m}Rh	-	2E+3	9E-7	3E-9	-	-
		Y, see ^{99m}Rh	-	2E+3	8E-7	3E-9	-	-

			Table 1 Occupational Values			Table 2 Effluent Concentrations		Table 3 Releases to Sewers
			Col. 1	Col. 2	Col. 3	Col. 1	Col. 2	
			Oral Ingestion	Inhalation				Monthly Average
Atomic No.	Radionuclide	Class	ALI (μCi)	ALI (μCi)	DAC (μCi/ml)	Air (μCi/ml)	Water (μCi/ml)	Concentration (μCi/ml)
45	Rhodium-100	D, see ^{99m}Rh	2E+3	5E+3	2E-6	7E-9	2E-5	2E-4
		W, see ^{99m}Rh	-	4E+3	2E-6	6E-9	-	-
		Y, see ^{99m}Rh	-	4E+3	2E-6	5E-9	-	-
45	Rhodium-101m	D, see ^{99m}Rh	6E+3	1E+4	5E-6	2E-8	8E-5	8E-4
		W, see ^{99m}Rh	-	8E+3	4E-6	1E-8	-	-
		Y, see ^{99m}Rh	-	8E+3	3E-6	1E-8	-	-
45	Rhodium-101	D, see ^{99m}Rh	2E+3	5E+2	2E-7	7E-10	3E-5	3E-4
		W, see ^{99m}Rh	-	8E+2	3E-7	1E-9	-	-
		Y, see ^{99m}Rh	-	2E+2	6E-8	2E-10	-	-
45	Rhodium-102m	D, see ^{99m}Rh	1E+3	5E+2	2E-7	7E-10	-	-
			LLI wall					
			(1E+3)	-	-	-	2E-5	2E-4
		W, see ^{99m}Rh	-	4E+2	2E-7	5E-10	-	-
		Y, see ^{99m}Rh	-	1E+2	5E-8	2E-10	-	-
45	Rhodium-102	D, see ^{99m}Rh	6E+2	9E+1	4E-8	1E-10	8E-6	8E-5
		W, see ^{99m}Rh	-	2E+2	7E-8	2E-10	-	-
		Y, see ^{99m}Rh	-	6E+1	2E-8	8E-11	-	-
45	Rhodium-103m[2]	D, see ^{99m}Rh	4E+5	1E+6	5E-4	2E-6	6E-3	6E-2
		W, see ^{99m}Rh	-	1E+6	5E-4	2E-6	-	-
		Y, see ^{99m}Rh	-	1E+6	5E-4	2E-6	-	-
45	Rhodium-105	D, see ^{99m}Rh	4E+3	1E+4	5E-6	2E-8	-	-
			LLI wall					
			(4E+3)	-	-	-	5E-5	5E-4
		W, see ^{99m}Rh	-	6E+3	3E-6	9E-9	-	-
		Y, see ^{99m}Rh	-	6E+3	2E-6	8E-9	-	-
45	Rhodium-106m	D, see ^{99m}Rh	8E+3	3E+4	1E-5	4E-8	1E-4	1E-3
		W, see ^{99m}Rh	-	4E+4	2E-5	5E-8	-	-
		Y, see ^{99m}Rh	-	4E+4	1E-5	5E-8	-	-
45	Rhodium-107[2]	D, see ^{99m}Rh	7E+4	2E+5	1E-4	3E-7	-	-
			St. wall					
			(9E+4)	-	-	-	1E-3	1E-2
		W, see ^{99m}Rh	-	3E+5	1E-4	4E-7	-	-
		Y, see ^{99m}Rh	-	3E+5	1E-4	3E-7	-	-
46	Palladium-100	D, all compounds except those given for W and Y	1E+3	1E+3	6E-7	2E-9	2E-5	2E-4
		W, nitrates	-	1E+3	5E-7	2E-9	-	-
		Y, oxides and hydroxides	-	1E+3	6E-7	2E-9	-	-
46	Palladium-101	D, see ^{100}Pd	1E+4	3E+4	1E-5	5E-8	2E-4	2E-3
		W, see ^{100}Pd	-	3E+4	1E-5	5E-8	-	-
		Y, see ^{100}Pd		3E+4	1E-5	4E-8	-	-
46	Palladium-103	D, see ^{100}Pd	6E+3	6E+3	3E-6	9E-9	-	-
			LLI wall					
			(7E+3)	-	-	-	1E-4	1E-3
		W, see ^{100}Pd	-	4E+3	2E-6	6E-9	-	-
		Y, see ^{100}Pd	-	4E+3	1E-6	5E-9	-	-
46	Palladium-107	D, see ^{100}Pd	3E+4	2E+4	9E-6	-	-	-
			LLI wall	Kidneys				
			(4E+4)	(2E+4)	-	3E-8	5E-4	5E-3
		W, see ^{100}Pd	-	7E+3	3E-6	1E-8	-	-
		Y, see ^{100}Pd	-	4E+2	2E-7	6E-10	-	-

Atomic No.	Radionuclide	Class	Table 1 Occupational Values			Table 2 Effluent Concentrations		Table 3 Releases to Sewers
			Col. 1	Col. 2	Col. 3	Col. 1	Col. 2	
			Oral Ingestion	Inhalation				Monthly Average
			ALI (μCi)	ALI (μCi)	DAC (μCi/ml)	Air (μCi/ml)	Water (μCi/ml)	Concentration (μCi/ml)
46	Palladium-109	D, see ^{100}Pd	2E+3	6E+3	3E-6	9E-9	3E-5	3E-4
		W, see ^{100}Pd	-	5E+3	2E-6	8E-9	-	-
		Y, see ^{100}Pd	-	5E+3	2E-6	6E-9	-	-
47	Silver-102[2]	D, all compounds except those given for W and Y	5E+4	2E+5	8E-5	2E-7	-	-
			St. wall (6E+4)	-	-	-	9E-4	9E-3
		W, nitrates and sulfides	-	2E+5	9E-5	3E-7	-	-
		Y, oxides and hydroxides	-	2E+5	8E-5	3E-7	-	-
47	Silver-103[2]	D, see ^{102}Ag	4E+4	1E+5	4E-5	1E-7	5E-4	5E-3
		W, see ^{102}Ag	-	1E+5	5E-5	2E-7	-	-
		Y, see ^{102}Ag	-	1E+5	5E-5	2E-7	-	-
47	Silver-104m[2]	D, see ^{102}Ag	3E+4	9E+4	4E-5	1E-7	4E-4	4E-3
		W, see ^{102}Ag	-	1E+5	5E-5	2E-7	-	-
		Y, see ^{102}Ag	-	1E+5	5E-5	2E-7	-	-
47	Silver-104[2]	D, see ^{102}Ag	2E+4	7E+4	3E-5	1E-7	3E-4	3E-3
		W, see ^{102}Ag	-	1E+5	6E-5	2E-7	-	-
		Y, see ^{102}Ag	-	1E+5	6E-5	2E-7	-	-
47	Silver-105	D, see ^{102}Ag	3E+3	1E+3	4E-7	1E-9	4E-5	4E-4
		W, see ^{102}Ag	-	2E+3	7E-7	2E-9	-	-
		Y, see ^{102}Ag	-	2E+3	7E-7	2E-9	-	-
47	Silver-106m	D, see ^{102}Ag	8E+2	7E+2	3E-7	1E-9	1E-5	1E-4
		W, see ^{102}Ag	-	9E+2	4E-7	1E-9	-	-
		Y, see ^{102}Ag	-	9E+2	4E-7	1E-9	-	-
47	Silver-106[2]	D, see ^{102}Ag	6E+4	2E+5	8E-5	3E-7	-	-
			St. wall (6E+4)	-	-	-	9E-4	9E-3
		W, see ^{102}Ag	-	2E+5	9E-5	3E-7	-	-
		Y, see ^{102}Ag	-	2E+5	8E-5	3E-7	-	-
47	Silver-108m	D, see ^{102}Ag	6E+2	2E+2	8E-8	3E-10	9E-6	9E-5
		W, see ^{102}Ag	-	3E+2	1E-7	4E-10	-	-
		Y, see ^{102}Ag	-	2E+1	1E-8	3E-11	-	-
47	Silver-110m	D, see ^{102}Ag	5E+2	1E+2	5E-8	2E-10	6E-6	6E-5
		W, see ^{102}Ag	-	2E+2	8E-8	3E-10	-	-
		Y, see ^{102}Ag	-	9E+1	4E-8	1E-10	-	-
47	Silver-111	D, see ^{102}Ag	9E+2	2E+3	6E-7	-	-	-
			LLI wall (1E+3)	Liver (2E+3)	-	2E-9	2E-5	2E-4
		W, see ^{102}Ag	-	9E+2	4E-7	1E-9	-	-
		Y, see ^{102}Ag	-	9E+2	4E-7	1E-9	-	-
47	Silver-112	D, see ^{102}Ag	3E+3	8E+3	3E-6	1E-8	4E-5	4E-4
		W, see ^{102}Ag	-	1E+4	4E-6	1E-8	-	-
		Y, see ^{102}Ag	-	9E+3	4E-6	1E-8	-	-

Atomic No.	Radionuclide	Class	Table 1 Occupational Values Col. 1 Oral Ingestion ALI (μCi)	Table 1 Col. 2 Inhalation ALI (μCi)	Table 1 Col. 3 Inhalation DAC (μCi/ml)	Table 2 Effluent Concentrations Col. 1 Air (μCi/ml)	Table 2 Col. 2 Water (μCi/ml)	Table 3 Releases to Sewers Monthly Average Concentration (μCi/ml)
47	Silver-115[2]	D, see ^{102}Ag	3E+4	9E+4	4E-5	1E-7	-	-
			St. wall					
			(3E+4)	-	-	-	4E-4	4E-3
		W, see ^{102}Ag	-	9E+4	4E-5	1E-7	-	-
		Y, see ^{102}Ag	-	8E+4	3E-5	1E-7	-	-
48	Cadmium-104[2]	D, all compounds except those given for W and Y	2E+4	7E+4	3E-5	9E-8	3E-4	3E-3
		W, sulfides, halides, and nitrates	-	1E+5	5E-5	2E-7	-	-
		Y, oxides and hydroxides	-	1E+5	5E-5	2E-7	-	-
48	Cadmium-107	D, see ^{104}Cd	2E+4	5E+4	2E-5	8E-8	3E-4	3E-3
		W, see ^{104}Cd	-	6E+4	2E-5	8E-8	-	-
		Y, see ^{104}Cd	-	5E+4	2E-5	7E-8	-	-
48	Cadmium-109	D, see ^{104}Cd	3E+2	4E+1	1E-8	-	-	-
			Kidneys	Kidneys				
			(4E+2)	(5E+1)	-	7E-11	6E-6	6E-5
		W, see ^{104}Cd	-	1E+2	5E-8	-	-	-
				Kidneys				
			-	(1E+2)	-	2E-10	-	-
		Y, see ^{104}Cd	-	1E+2	5E-8	2E-10	-	-
48	Cadmium-113m	D, see ^{104}Cd	2E+1	2E+0	1E-9	-	-	-
			Kidneys	Kidneys				
			(4E+1)	(4E+0)	-	5E-12	5E-7	5E-6
		W, see ^{104}Cd	-	8E+0	4E-9	-	-	-
				Kidneys				
			-	(1E+1)	-	2E-11	-	-
		Y, see ^{104}Cd	-	1E+1	5E-9	2E-11	-	-
48	Cadmium-113	D, see ^{104}Cd	2E+1	2E+0	9E-10	-	-	-
			Kidneys	Kidneys				
			(3E+1)	(3E+0)	-	5E-12	4E-7	4E-6
		W, see ^{104}Cd	-	8E+0	3E-9	-	-	-
				Kidneys				
			-	(1E+1)	-	2E-11	-	-
		Y, see ^{104}Cd	-	1E+1	6E-9	2E-11	-	-
48	Cadmium-115m	D, see ^{104}Cd	3E+2	5E+1	2E-8	-	4E-6	4E-5
				Kidneys				
			-	(8E+1)	-	1E-10	-	-
		W, see ^{104}Cd	-	1E+2	5E-8	2E-10	-	-
		Y, see ^{104}Cd	-	1E+2	6E-8	2E-10	-	-
48	Cadmium-115	D, see ^{104}Cd	9E+2	1E+3	6E-7	2E-9	-	-
			LLI wall					
			(1E+3)	-	-	-	1E-5	1E-4
		W, see ^{104}Cd	-	1E+3	5E-7	2E-9	-	-
		Y, see ^{104}Cd	-	1E+3	6E-7	2E-9	-	-
48	Cadmium-117m	D, see ^{104}Cd	5E+3	1E+4	5E-6	2E-8	6E-5	6E-4
		W, see ^{104}Cd	-	2E+4	7E-6	2E-8	-	-
		Y, see ^{104}Cd	-	1E+4	6E-6	2E-8	-	-

Atomic No.	Radionuclide	Class	Table 1 Occupational Values			Table 2 Effluent Concentrations		Table 3 Releases to Sewers
			Col. 1	Col. 2	Col. 3	Col. 1	Col. 2	
			Oral Ingestion	Inhalation				Monthly Average
			ALI (μCi)	ALI (μCi)	DAC (μCi/ml)	Air (μCi/ml)	Water (μCi/ml)	Concentration (μCi/ml)
48	Cadmium-117	D, see ^{104}Cd	5E+3	1E+4	5E-6	2E-8	6E-5	6E-4
		W, see ^{104}Cd	-	2E+4	7E-6	2E-8	-	-
		Y, see ^{104}Cd	-	1E+4	6E-6	2E-8	-	-
49	Indium-109	D, all compounds except those given for W	2E+4	4E+4	2E-5	6E-8	3E-4	3E-3
		W, oxides, hydroxides, halides, and nitrates	-	6E+4	3E-5	9E-8	-	-
49	Indium-110[2] (69.1 min)	D, see ^{109}In	2E+4	4E+4	2E-5	6E-8	2E-4	2E-3
		W, see ^{109}In	-	6E+4	2E-5	8E-8	-	-
49	Indium-110 (4.9 h)	D, see ^{109}In	5E+3	2E+4	7E-6	2E-8	7E-5	7E-4
		W, see ^{109}In	-	2E+4	8E-6	3E-8	-	-
49	Indium-111	D, see ^{109}In	4E+3	6E+3	3E-6	9E-9	6E-5	6E-4
		W, see ^{109}In	-	6E+3	3E-6	9E-9	-	-
49	Indium-112[2]	D, see ^{109}In	2E+5	6E+5	3E-4	9E-7	2E-3	2E-2
		W, see ^{109}In	-	7E+5	3E-4	1E-6	-	-
49	Indium-113m[2]	D, see ^{109}In	5E+4	1E+5	6E-5	2E-7	7E-4	7E-3
		W, see ^{109}In	-	2E+5	8E-5	3E-7	-	-
49	Indium-114m	D, see ^{109}In	3E+2	6E+1	3E-8	9E-11	-	-
			LLI wall (4E+2)	-	-	-	5E-6	5E-5
		W, see ^{109}In	-	1E+2	4E-8	1E-10	-	-
49	Indium-115m	D, see ^{109}In	1E+4	4E+4	2E-5	6E-8	2E-4	2E-3
		W, see ^{109}In	-	5E+4	2E-5	7E-8	-	-
49	Indium-115	D, see ^{109}In	4E+1	1E+0	6E-10	2E-12	5E-7	5E-6
		W, see ^{109}In	-	5E+0	2E-9	8E-12	-	-
49	Indium-116m[2]	D, see ^{109}In	2E+4	8E+4	3E-5	1E-7	3E-4	3E-3
		W, see ^{109}In	-	1E+5	5E-5	2E-7	-	-
49	Indium-117m[2]	D, see ^{109}In	1E+4	3E+4	1E-5	5E-8	2E-4	2E-3
		W, see ^{109}In	-	4E+4	2E-5	6E-8	-	-
49	Indium-117[2]	D, see ^{109}In	6E+4	2E+5	7E-5	2E-7	8E-4	8E-3
		W, see ^{109}In	-	2E+5	9E-5	3E-7	-	-
49	Indium-119m[2]	D, see ^{109}In	4E+4	1E+5	5E-5	2E-7	-	-
			St. wall (5E+4)	-	-	-	7E-4	7E-3
		W, see ^{109}In	-	1E+5	6E-5	2E-7	-	-
50	Tin-110	D, all compounds except those given for W	4E+3	1E+4	5E-6	2E-8	5E-5	5E-4
		W, sulfides, oxides, hydroxides, halides, nitrates, and stannic phosphate	-	1E+4	5E-6	2E-8	-	-
50	Tin-111[2]	D, see ^{110}Sn	7E+4	2E+5	9E-5	3E-7	1E-3	1E-2
		W, see ^{110}Sn	-	3E+5	1E-4	4E-7	-	-

			Table 1 Occupational Values			Table 2 Effluent Concentrations		Table 3 Releases to Sewers
			Col. 1	Col. 2	Col. 3	Col. 1	Col. 2	
			Oral Ingestion	Inhalation				Monthly Average
Atomic No.	Radionuclide	Class	ALI (μCi)	ALI (μCi)	DAC (μCi/ml)	Air (μCi/ml)	Water (μCi/ml)	Concentration (μCi/ml)
50	Tin-113	D, see ^{110}Sn	2E+3	1E+3	5E-7	2E-9	-	-
			LLI wall					
			(2E+3)	-	-	-	3E-5	3E-4
		W, see ^{110}Sn	-	5E+2	2E-7	8E-10	-	-
50	Tin-117m	D, see ^{110}Sn	2E+3	1E+3	5E-7	-	-	-
			LLI wall	Bone surf				
			(2E+3)	(2E+3)	-	3E-9	3E-5	3E-4
		W, see ^{110}Sn	-	1E+3	6E-7	2E-9	-	-
50	Tin-119m	D, see ^{110}Sn	3E+3	2E+3	1E-6	3E-9	-	-
			LLI wall					
			(4E+3)	-	-	-	6E-5	6E-4
		W, see ^{110}Sn	-	1E+3	4E-7	1E-9	-	-
50	Tin-121m	D, see ^{110}Sn	3E+3	9E+2	4E-7	1E-9	-	-
			LLI wall					
			(4E+3)	-	-	-	5E-5	5E-4
		W, see ^{110}Sn	-	5E+2	2E-7	8E-10	-	-
50	Tin-121	D, see ^{110}Sn	6E+3	2E+4	6E-6	2E-8	-	-
			LLI wall					
			(6E+3)	-	-	-	8E-5	8E-4
		W, see ^{110}Sn	-	1E+4	5E-6	2E-8	-	-
50	Tin-123m[2]	D, see ^{110}Sn	5E+4	1E+5	5E-5	2E-7	7E-4	7E-3
		W, see ^{110}Sn	-	1E+5	6E-5	2E-7	-	-
50	Tin-123	D, see ^{110}Sn	5E+2	6E+2	3E-7	9E-10	-	-
			LLI wall					
			(6E+2)	-	-	-	9E-6	9E-5
		W, see ^{110}Sn	-	2E+2	7E-8	2E-10	-	-
50	Tin-125	D, see ^{110}Sn	4E+2	9E+2	4E-7	1E-9	-	-
			LLI wall					
			(5E+2)	-	-	-	6E-6	6E-5
		W, see ^{110}Sn	-	4E+2	1E-7	5E-10	-	-
50	Tin-126	D, see ^{110}Sn	3E+2	6E+1	2E-8	8E-11	4E-6	4E-5
		W, see ^{110}Sn	-	7E+1	3E-8	9E-11	-	-
50	Tin-127	D, see ^{110}Sn	7E+3	2E+4	8E-6	3E-8	9E-5	9E-4
		W, see ^{110}Sn	-	2E+4	8E-6	3E-8	-	-
50	Tin-128[2]	D, see ^{110}Sn	9E+3	3E+4	1E-5	4E-8	1E-4	1E-3
		W, see ^{110}Sn	-	4E+4	1E-5	5E-8	-	-
51	Antimony-115[2]	D, all compounds except those given for W	8E+4	2E+5	1E-4	3E-7	1E-3	1E-2
		W, oxides, hydroxides, halides, sulfides, sulfates, and nitrates	-	3E+5	1E-4	4E-7	-	-
51	Antimony-116m[2]	D, see ^{115}Sb	2E+4	7E+4	3E-5	1E-7	3E-4	3E-3
		W, see ^{115}Sb	-	1E+5	6E-5	2E-7	-	-
51	Antimony-116[2]	D, see ^{115}Sb	7E+4	3E+5	1E-4	4E-7	-	-
			St. wall					
			(9E+4)	-	-	-	1E-3	1E-2
		W, see ^{115}Sb	-	3E+5	1E-4	5E-7	-	-
51	Antimony-117	D, see ^{115}Sb	7E+4	2E+5	9E-5	3E-7	9E-4	9E-3
		W, see ^{115}Sb	-	3E+5	1E-4	4E-7	-	-

			Table 1 Occupational Values			Table 2 Effluent Concentrations		Table 3 Releases to Sewers
			Col. 1	Col. 2	Col. 3	Col. 1	Col. 2	
			Oral Ingestion	Inhalation				Monthly Average
Atomic No.	Radionuclide	Class	ALI (μCi)	ALI (μCi)	DAC (μCi/ml)	Air (μCi/ml)	Water (μCi/ml)	Concentration (μCi/ml)
51	Antimony-118m	D, see ^{115}Sb	6E+3	2E+4	8E-6	3E-8	7E-5	7E-4
		W, see ^{115}Sb	5E+3	2E+4	9E-6	3E-8	-	-
51	Antimony-119	D, see ^{115}Sb	2E+4	5E+4	2E-5	6E-8	2E-4	2E-3
		W, see ^{115}Sb	2E+4	3E+4	1E-5	4E-8	-	-
51	Antimony-120 (16 min)	D, see ^{115}Sb	1E+5	4E+5	2E-4	6E-7	-	-
			St. wall (2E+5)	-	-	-	2E-3	2E-2
		W, see ^{115}Sb	-	5E+5	2E-4	7E-7	-	-
51	Antimony-120 (5.76 d)	D, see ^{115}Sb	1E+3	2E+3	9E-7	3E-9	1E-5	1E-4
		W, see ^{115}Sb	9E+2	1E+3	5E-7	2E-9	-	-
51	Antimony-122	D, see ^{115}Sb	8E+2	2E+3	1E-6	3E-9	-	-
			LLI wall (8E+2)	-	-	-	1E-5	1E-4
		W, see ^{115}Sb	7E+2	1E+3	4E-7	2E-9	-	-
51	Antimony-124m[2]	D, see ^{115}Sb	3E+5	8E+5	4E-4	1E-6	3E-3	3E-2
		W, see ^{115}Sb	2E+5	6E+5	2E-4	8E-7	-	-
51	Antimony-124	D, see ^{115}Sb	6E+2	9E+2	4E-7	1E-9	7E-6	7E-5
		W, see ^{115}Sb	5E+2	2E+2	1E-7	3E-10	-	-
51	Antimony-125	D, see ^{115}Sb	2E+3	2E+3	1E-6	3E-9	3E-5	3E-4
		W, see ^{115}Sb	-	5E+2	2E-7	7E-10	-	-
51	Antimony-126m[2]	D, see ^{115}Sb	5E+4	2E+5	8E-5	3E-7	-	-
			St. wall (7E+4)	-	-	-	9E-4	9E-3
		W, see ^{115}Sb	-	2E+5	8E-5	3E-7	-	-
51	Antimony-126	D, see ^{115}Sb	6E+2	1E+3	5E-7	2E-9	7E-6	7E-5
		W, see ^{115}Sb	5E+2	5E+2	2E-7	7E-10	-	-
51	Antimony-127	D, see ^{115}Sb	8E+2	2E+3	9E-7	3E-9	-	-
			LLI wall (8E+2)	-	-	-	1E-5	1E-4
		W, see ^{115}Sb	7E+2	9E+2	4E-7	1E-9	-	-
51	Antimony-128[2] (10.4 min)	D, see ^{115}Sb	8E+4	4E+5	2E-4	5E-7	-	-
			St. wall (1E+5)	-	-	-	1E-3	1E-2
		W, see ^{115}Sb	-	4E+5	2E-4	6E-7	-	-
51	Antimony-128 (9.01 h)	D, see ^{115}Sb	1E+3	4E+3	2E-6	6E-9	2E-5	2E-4
		W, see ^{115}Sb	-	3E+3	1E-6	5E-9	-	-
51	Antimony-129	D, see ^{115}Sb	3E+3	9E+3	4E-6	1E-8	4E-5	4E-4
		W, see ^{115}Sb	-	9E+3	4E-6	1E-8	-	-
51	Antimony-130[2]	D, see ^{115}Sb	2E+4	6E+4	3E-5	9E-8	3E-4	3E-3
		W, see ^{115}Sb	-	8E+4	3E-5	1E-7	-	-
51	Antimony-131[2]	D, see ^{115}Sb	1E+4	2E+4	1E-5	-	-	-
			Thyroid (2E+4)	Thyroid (4E+4)	-	6E-8	2E-4	2E-3
		W, see ^{115}Sb	-	2E+4	1E-5		-	-
			-	Thyroid (4E+4)	-	6E-8	-	-

Atomic No.	Radionuclide	Class	Table 1 Occupational Values Col. 1 Oral Ingestion ALI (µCi)	Table 1 Col. 2 Inhalation ALI (µCi)	Table 1 Col. 3 Inhalation DAC (µCi/ml)	Table 2 Effluent Concentrations Col. 1 Air (µCi/ml)	Table 2 Col. 2 Water (µCi/ml)	Table 3 Releases to Sewers Monthly Average Concentration (µCi/ml)
52	Tellurium-116	D, all compounds except those given for W	8E+3	2E+4	9E-6	3E-8	1E-4	1E-3
		W, oxides, hydroxides, and nitrates	-	3E+4	1E-5	4E-8	-	-
52	Tellurium-121m	D, see ^{116}Te	5E+2	2E+2	8E-8	-	-	-
			Bone surf	Bone surf				
			(7E+2)	(4E+2)	-	5E-10	1E-5	1E-4
		W, see ^{116}Te	-	4E+2	2E-7	6E-10	-	-
52	Tellurium-121	D, see ^{116}Te	3E+3	4E+3	2E-6	6E-9	4E-5	4E-4
		W, see ^{116}Te	-	3E+3	1E-6	4E-9	-	-
52	Tellurium-123m	D, see ^{116}Te	6E+2	2E+2	9E-8	-	-	-
			Bone surf	Bone surf				
			(1E+3)	(5E+2)	-	8E-10	1E-5	1E-4
		W, see ^{116}Te	-	5E+2	2E-7	8E-10	-	-
52	Tellurium-123	D, see ^{116}Te	5E+2	2E+2	8E-8	-	-	-
			Bone surf	Bone surf				
			(1E+3)	(5E+2)	-	7E-10	2E-5	2E-4
		W, see ^{116}Te	-	4E+2	2E-7	-	-	-
				Bone surf				
			-	(1E+3)	-	2E-9	-	-
52	Tellurium-125m	D, see ^{116}Te	1E+3	4E+2	2E-7	-	-	-
			Bone surf	Bone surf				
			(1E+3)	(1E+3)	-	1E-9	2E-5	2E-4
		W, see ^{116}Te	-	7E+2	3E-7	1E-9	-	-
52	Tellurium-127m	D, see ^{116}Te	6E+2	3E+2	1E-7	-	9E-6	9E-5
				Bone surf				
			-	(4E+2)	-	6E-10	-	-
		W, see ^{116}Te	-	3E+2	1E-7	4E-10	-	-
52	Tellurium-127	D, see ^{116}Te	7E+3	2E+4	9E-6	3E-8	1E-4	1E-3
		W, see ^{116}Te	-	2E+4	7E-6	2E-8	-	-
52	Tellurium-129m	D, see ^{116}Te	5E+2	6E+2	3E-7	9E-10	7E-6	7E-5
		W, see ^{116}Te	-	2E+2	1E-7	3E-10	-	-
52	Tellurium-129[2]	D, see ^{116}Te	3E+4	6E+4	3E-5	9E-8	4E-4	4E-3
		W, see ^{116}Te	-	7E+4	3E-5	1E-7	-	-
52	Tellurium-131m	D, see ^{116}Te	3E+2	4E+2	2E-7	-	-	-
			Thyroid	Thyroid				
			(6E+2)	(1E+3)	-	2E-9	8E-6	8E-5
		W, see ^{116}Te	-	4E+2	2E-7	-	-	-
				Thyroid				
			-	(9E+2)	-	1E-9	-	
52	Tellurium-131[2]	D, see ^{116}Te	3E+3	5E+3	2E-6	-	-	-
			Thyroid	Thyroid				
			(6E+3)	(1E+4)	-	2E-8	8E-5	8E-4
		W, see ^{116}Te	-	5E+3	2E-6	-	-	-
				Thyroid				
			-	(1E+4)	-	2E-8	-	-

Atomic No.	Radionuclide	Class	Table 1 Occupational Values Col. 1 Oral Ingestion ALI (μCi)	Table 1 Col. 2 Inhalation ALI (μCi)	Table 1 Col. 3 Inhalation DAC (μCi/ml)	Table 2 Effluent Concentrations Col. 1 Air (μCi/ml)	Table 2 Col. 2 Water (μCi/ml)	Table 3 Releases to Sewers Monthly Average Concentration (μCi/ml)
52	Tellurium-132	D, see ^{116}Te	2E+2	2E+2	9E-8	-	-	-
			Thyroid	Thyroid				
			(7E+2)	(8E+2)	-	1E-9	9E-6	9E-5
		W, see ^{116}Te	-	2E+2	9E-8	-	-	-
				Thyroid				
			-	(6E+2)	-	9E-10	-	-
52	Tellurium-133m[2]	D, see ^{116}Te	3E+3	5E+3	2E-6	-	-	-
			Thyroid	Thyroid				
			(6E+3)	(1E+4)	-	2E-8	9E-5	9E-4
		W, see ^{116}Te	-	5E+3	2E-6	-	-	-
				Thyroid				
			-	(1E+4)	-	2E-8	-	-
52	Tellurium-133[2]	D, see ^{116}Te	1E+4	2E+4	9E-6	-	-	-
			Thyroid	Thyroid				
			(3E+4)	(6E+4)	-	8E-8	4E-4	4E-3
		W, see ^{116}Te	-	2E+4	9E-6	-	-	-
				Thyroid				
			-	(6E+4)	-	8E-8	-	-
52	Tellurium-134[2]	D, see ^{116}Te	2E+4	2E+4	1E-5	-	-	-
			Thyroid	Thyroid				
			(2E+4)	(5E+4)	-	7E-8	3E-4	3E-3
		W, see ^{116}Te	-	2E+4	1E-5	-	-	-
				Thyroid				
			-	(5E+4)	-	7E-8	-	-
53	Iodine-120m[2]	D, all compounds	1E+4	2E+4	9E-6	3E-8	-	-
			Thyroid					
			(1E+4)	-	-	-	2E-4	2E-3
53	Iodine-120[2]	D, all compounds	4E+3	9E+3	4E-6	-	-	-
			Thyroid	Thyroid				
			(8E+3)	(1E+4)	-	2E-8	1E-4	1E-3
53	Iodine-121	D, all compounds	1E+4	2E+4	8E-6	-	-	-
			Thyroid	Thyroid				
			(3E+4)	(5E+4)	-	7E-8	4E-4	4E-3
53	Iodine-123	D, all compounds	3E+3	6E+3	3E-6	-	-	-
			Thyroid	Thyroid				
			(1E+4)	(2E+4)	-	2E-8	1E-4	1E-3
53	Iodine-124	D, all compounds	5E+1	8E+1	3E-8	-	-	-
			Thyroid	Thyroid				
			(2E+2)	(3E+2)	-	4E-10	2E-6	2E-5
53	Iodine-125	D, all compounds	4E+1	6E+1	3E-8	-	-	-
			Thyroid	Thyroid				
			(1E+2)	(2E+2)	-	3E-10	2E-6	2E-5
53	Iodine-126	D, all compounds	2E+1	4E+1	1E-8	-	-	-
			Thyroid	Thyroid				
			(7E+1)	(1E+2)	-	2E-10	1E-6	1E-5
53	Iodine-128[2]	D, all compounds	4E+4	1E+5	5E-5	2E-7	-	-
			St. wall					
			(6E+4)	-	-	-	8E-4	8E-3
53	Iodine-129	D, all compounds	5E+0	9E+0	4E-9	-	-	-
			Thyroid	Thyroid				
			(2E+1)	(3E+1)	-	4E-11	2E-7	2E-6

			Table 1 Occupational Values			Table 2 Effluent Concentrations		Table 3 Releases to Sewers
			Col. 1	Col. 2	Col. 3	Col. 1	Col. 2	
			Oral Ingestion	Inhalation				Monthly Average
Atomic No.	Radionuclide	Class	ALI (µCi)	ALI (µCi)	DAC (µCi/ml)	Air (µCi/ml)	Water (µCi/ml)	Concentration (µCi/ml)
53	Iodine-130	D, all compounds	4E+2	7E+2	3E-7	-	-	-
			Thyroid	Thyroid				
			(1E+3)	(2E+3)	-	3E-9	2E-5	2E-4
53	Iodine-131	D, all compounds	3E+1	5E+1	2E-8	-	-	-
			Thyroid	Thyroid				
			(9E+1)	(2E+2)	-	2E-10	1E-6	1E-5
53	Iodine-132m[2]	D, all compounds	4E+3	8E+3	4E-6	-	-	-
			Thyroid	Thyroid				
			(1E+4)	(2E+4)	-	3E-8	1E-4	1E-3
53	Iodine-132	D, all compounds	4E+3	8E+3	3E-6	-	-	-
			Thyroid	Thyroid				
			(9E+3)	(1E+4)	-	2E-8	1E-4	1E-3
53	Iodine-133	D, all compounds	1E+2	3E+2	1E-7	-	-	-
			Thyroid	Thyroid				
			(5E+2)	(9E+2)	-	1E-9	7E-6	7E-5
53	Iodine-134[2]	D, all compounds	2E+4	5E+4	2E-5	6E-8	-	-
			Thyroid					
			(3E+4)	-	-	-	4E-4	4E-3
53	Iodine-135	D, all compounds	8E+2	2E+3	7E-7	-	-	-
			Thyroid	Thyroid				
			(3E+3)	(4E+3)	-	6E-9	3E-5	3E-4
54	Xenon-120[2]	Submersion[1]	-	-	1E-5	4E-8	-	-
54	Xenon-121[2]	Submersion[1]	-	-	2E-6	1E-8	-	-
54	Xenon-122	Submersion[1]	-	-	7E-5	3E-7	-	-
54	Xenon-123	Submersion[1]	-	-	6E-6	3E-8	-	-
54	Xenon-125	Submersion[1]	-	-	2E-5	7E-8	-	-
54	Xenon-127	Submersion[1]	-	-	1E-5	6E-8	-	-
54	Xenon-129m	Submersion[1]	-	-	2E-4	9E-7	-	-
54	Xenon-131m	Submersion[1]	-	-	4E-4	2E-6	-	-
54	Xenon-133m	Submersion[1]	-	-	1E-4	6E-7	-	-
54	Xenon-133	Submersion[1]	-	-	1E-4	5E-7	-	-
54	Xenon-135m[2]	Submersion[1]	-	-	9E-6	4E-8	-	-
54	Xenon-135	Submersion[1]	-	-	1E-5	7E-8	-	-
54	Xenon-138[2]	Submersion[1]	-	-	4E-6	2E-8	-	-
55	Cesium-125[2]	D, all compounds	5E+4	1E+5	6E-5	2E-7	-	-
			St. wall					
			(9E+4)	-	-	-	1E-3	1E-2
55	Cesium-127	D, all compounds	6E+4	9E+4	4E-5	1E-7	9E-4	9E-3

			Table 1 Occupational Values			Table 2 Effluent Concentrations		Table 3 Releases to Sewers
			Col. 1	Col. 2	Col. 3	Col. 1	Col. 2	
			Oral Ingestion	Inhalation				Monthly Average
Atomic No.	Radionuclide	Class	ALI (μCi)	ALI (μCi)	DAC (μCi/ml)	Air (μCi/ml)	Water (μCi/ml)	Concentration (μCi/ml)
55	Cesium-129	D, all compounds	2E+4	3E+4	1E-5	5E-8	3E-4	3E-3
55	Cesium-130[2]	D, all compounds	6E+4	2E+5	8E-5	3E-7	-	-
			St. wall (1E+5)	-	-	-	1E-3	1E-2
55	Cesium-131	D, all compounds	2E+4	3E+4	1E-5	4E-8	3E-4	3E-3
55	Cesium-132	D, all compounds	3E+3	4E+3	2E-6	6E-9	4E-5	4E-4
55	Cesium-134m	D, all compounds	1E+5	1E+5	6E-5	2E-7	-	-
			St. wall (1E+5)	-	-	-	2E-3	2E-2
55	Cesium-134	D, all compounds	7E+1	1E+2	4E-8	2E-10	9E-7	9E-6
55	Cesium-135m[2]	D, all compounds	1E+5	2E+5	8E-5	3E-7	1E-3	1E-2
55	Cesium-135	D, all compounds	7E+2	1E+3	5E-7	2E-9	1E-5	1E-4
55	Cesium-136	D, all compounds	4E+2	7E+2	3E-7	9E-10	6E-6	6E-5
55	Cesium-137	D, all compounds	1E+2	2E+2	6E-8	2E-10	1E-6	1E-5
55	Cesium-138[2]	D, all compounds	2E+4	6E+4	2E-5	8E-8	-	-
			St. wall (3E+4)	-	-	-	4E-4	4E-3
56	Barium-126[2]	D, all compounds	6E+3	2E+4	6E-6	2E-8	8E-5	8E-4
56	Barium-128	D, all compounds	5E+2	2E+3	7E-7	2E-9	7E-6	7E-5
56	Barium-131m[2]	D, all compounds	4E+5	1E+6	6E-4	2E-6	-	-
			St. wall (5E+5)	-	-	-	7E-3	7E-2
56	Barium-131	D, all compounds	3E+3	8E+3	3E-6	1E-8	4E-5	4E-4
56	Barium-133m	D, all compounds	2E+3	9E+3	4E-6	1E-8	-	-
			LLI wall (3E+3)	-	-	-	4E-5	4E-4
56	Barium-133	D, all compounds	2E+3	7E+2	3E-7	9E-10	2E-5	2E-4
56	Barium-135m	D, all compounds	3E+3	1E+4	5E-6	2E-8	4E-5	4E-4
56	Barium-139[2]	D, all compounds	1E+4	3E+4	1E-5	4E-8	2E-4	2E-3
56	Barium-140	D, all compounds	5E+2	1E+3	6E-7	2E-9	-	-
			LLI wall (6E+2)	-	-	-	8E-6	8E-5
56	Barium-141[2]	D, all compounds	2E+4	7E+4	3E-5	1E-7	3E-4	3E-3
56	Barium-142[2]	D, all compounds	5E+4	1E+5	6E-5	2E-7	7E-4	7E-3
57	Lanthanum-131[2]	D, all compounds except those given for W	5E+4 [4]	1E+5	5E-5	2E-7	6E-4	6E-3
		W, oxides and hydroxides	-	2E+5	7E-5	2E-7	-	-

Atomic No.	Radionuclide	Class	Table 1 Occupational Values Col. 1 Oral Ingestion ALI (μCi)	Table 1 Col. 2 Inhalation ALI (μCi)	Table 1 Col. 3 Inhalation DAC (μCi/ml)	Table 2 Effluent Concentrations Col. 1 Air (μCi/ml)	Table 2 Col. 2 Water (μCi/ml)	Table 3 Releases to Sewers Monthly Average Concentration (μCi/ml)
57	Lanthanum-132	D, see ^{131}La	3E+3	1E+4	4E-6	1E-8	4E-5	4E-4
		W, see ^{131}La	-	1E+4	5E-6	2E-8	-	-
57	Lanthanum-135	D, see ^{131}La	4E+4	1E+5	4E-5	1E-7	5E-4	5E-3
		W, see ^{131}La	-	9E+4	4E-5	1E-7	-	-
57	Lanthanum-137	D, see ^{131}La	1E+4	6E+1	3E-8	-	2E-4	2E-3
				Liver				
			-	(7E+1)	-	1E-10	-	-
		W, see ^{131}La	-	3E+2	1E-7	-	-	-
				Liver				
			-	(3E+2)	-	4E-10	-	-
57	Lanthanum-138	D, see ^{131}La	9E+2	4E+0	1E-9	5E-12	1E-5	1E-4
		W, see ^{131}La	-	1E+1	6E-9	2E-11	-	-
57	Lanthanum-140	D, see ^{131}La	6E+2	1E+3	6E-7	2E-9	9E-6	9E-5
		W, see ^{131}La	-	1E+3	5E-7	2E-9	-	-
57	Lanthanum-141	D, see ^{131}La	4E+3	9E+3	4E-6	1E-8	5E-5	5E-4
		W, see ^{131}La	-	1E+4	5E-6	2E-8	-	-
57	Lanthanum-142[2]	D, see ^{131}La	8E+3	2E+4	9E-6	3E-8	1E-4	1E-3
		W, see ^{131}La	-	3E+4	1E-5	5E-8	-	-
57	Lanthanum-143[2]	D, see ^{131}La	4E+4	1E+5	4E-5	1E-7	-	-
			St. wall					
			(4E+4)	-	-	-	5E-4	5E-3
		W, see ^{131}La	-	9E+4	4E-5	1E-7	-	-
58	Cerium-134	W, all compounds except those given for Y	5E+2	7E+2	3E-7	1E-9	-	-
			LLI wall					
			(6E+2)	-	-	-	8E-6	8E-5
		Y, oxides, hydroxides, and fluorides	-	7E+2	3E-7	9E-10	-	-
58	Cerium-135	W, see ^{134}Ce	2E+3	4E+3	2E-6	5E-9	2E-5	2E-4
		Y, see ^{134}Ce	-	4E+3	1E-6	5E-9	-	-
58	Cerium-137m	W, see ^{134}Ce	2E+3	4E+3	2E-6	6E-9	-	-
			LLI wall					
			(2E+3)	-	-	-	3E-5	3E-4
		Y, see ^{134}Ce	-	4E+3	2E-6	5E-9	-	-
58	Cerium-137	W, see ^{134}Ce	5E+4	1E+5	6E-5	2E-7	7E-4	7E-3
		Y, see ^{134}Ce	-	1E+5	5E-5	2E-7	-	-
58	Cerium-139	W, see ^{134}Ce	5E+3	8E+2	3E-7	1E-9	7E-5	7E-4
		Y, see ^{134}Ce	-	7E+2	3E-7	9E-10	-	-
58	Cerium-141	W, see ^{134}Ce	2E+3	7E+2	3E-7	1E-9	-	-
			LLI wall					
			(2E+3)	-	-	-	3E-5	3E-4
		Y, see ^{134}Ce	-	6E+2	2E-7	8E-10	-	-
58	Cerium-143	W, see ^{134}Ce	1E+3	2E+3	8E-7	3E-9	-	-
			LLI wall					
			(1E+3)	-	-	-	2E-5	2E-4
		Y, see ^{134}Ce	-	2E+3	7E-7	2E-9	-	-

Atomic No.	Radionuclide	Class	Table 1 Occupational Values			Table 2 Effluent Concentrations		Table 3 Releases to Sewers
			Col. 1 Oral Ingestion ALI (μCi)	Col. 2 Inhalation ALI (μCi)	Col. 3 Inhalation DAC (μCi/ml)	Col. 1 Air (μCi/ml)	Col. 2 Water (μCi/ml)	Monthly Average Concentration (μCi/ml)
58	Cerium-144	W, see ^{134}Ce	2E+2	3E+1	1E-8	4E-11	-	-
			LLI wall (3E+2)	-	-	-	3E-6	3E-5
		Y, see ^{134}Ce	-	1E+1	6E-9	2E-11	-	-
59	Praseodymium-136[2]	W, all compounds except those given for Y	5E+4	2E+5	1E-4	3E-7	-	-
			St. wall (7E+4)	-	-	-	1E-3	1E-2
		Y, oxides, hydroxides, carbides, and fluorides	-	2E+5	9E-5	3E-7	-	-
59	Praseodymium-137[2]	W, see ^{136}Pr	4E+4	2E+5	6E-5	2E-7	5E-4	5E-3
		Y, see ^{136}Pr	-	1E+5	6E-5	2E-7	-	-
59	Praseodymium-138m	W, see ^{136}Pr	1E+4	5E+4	2E-5	8E-8	1E-4	1E-3
		Y, see ^{136}Pr	-	4E+4	2E-5	6E-8	-	-
59	Praseodymium-139	W, see ^{136}Pr	4E+4	1E+5	5E-5	2E-7	6E-4	6E-3
		Y, see ^{136}Pr	-	1E+5	5E-5	2E-7	-	-
59	Praseodymium-142m[2]	W, see ^{136}Pr	8E+4	2E+5	7E-5	2E-7	1E-3	1E-2
		Y, see ^{136}Pr	-	1E+5	6E-5	2E-7	-	-
59	Praseodymium-142	W, see ^{136}Pr	1E+3	2E+3	9E-7	3E-9	1E-5	1E-4
		Y, see ^{136}Pr	-	2E+3	8E-7	3E-9	-	-
59	Praseodymium-143	W, see ^{136}Pr	9E+2	8E+2	3E-7	1E-9	-	-
			LLI wall (1E+3)	-	-	-	2E-5	2E-4
		Y, see ^{136}Pr	-	7E+2	3E-7	9E-10	-	-
59	Praseodymium-144[2]	W, see ^{136}Pr	3E+4	1E+5	5E-5	2E-7	-	-
			St. wall (4E+4)	-	-	-	6E-4	6E-3
		Y, see ^{136}Pr	-	1E+5	5E-5	2E-7	-	-
59	Praseodymium-145	W, see ^{136}Pr	3E+3	9E+3	4E-6	1E-8	4E-5	4E-4
		Y, see ^{136}Pr	-	8E+3	3E-6	1E-8	-	-
59	Praseodymium-147[2]	W, see ^{136}Pr	5E+4	2E+5	8E-5	3E-7	-	-
			St. wall (8E+4)	-	-	-	1E-3	1E-2
		Y, see ^{136}Pr	-	2E+5	8E-5	3E-7	-	-
60	Neodymium-136[2]	W, all compounds except those given for Y	1E+4	6E+4	2E-5	8E-8	2E-4	2E-3
		Y, oxides, hydroxides, carbides, and fluorides	-	5E+4	2E-5	8E-8	-	-
60	Neodymium-138	W, see ^{136}Nd	2E+3	6E+3	3E-6	9E-9	3E-5	3E-4
		Y, see ^{136}Nd	-	5E+3	2E-6	7E-9	-	-
60	Neodymium-139m	W, see ^{136}Nd	5E+3	2E+4	7E-6	2E-8	7E-5	7E-4
		Y, see ^{136}Nd	-	1E+4	6E-6	2E-8	-	-

			Table 1 Occupational Values			Table 2 Effluent Concentrations		Table 3 Releases to Sewers
			Col. 1	Col. 2	Col. 3	Col. 1	Col. 2	
			Oral Ingestion	Inhalation				Monthly Average
Atomic No.	Radionuclide	Class	ALI (µCi)	ALI (µCi)	DAC (µCi/ml)	Air (µCi/ml)	Water (µCi/ml)	Concentration (µCi/ml)
60	Neodymium-139[2]	W, see ^{136}Nd	9E+4	3E+5	1E-4	5E-7	1E-3	1E-2
		Y, see ^{136}Nd	-	3E+5	1E-4	4E-7	-	-
60	Neodymium-141	W, see ^{136}Nd	2E+5	7E+5	3E-4	1E-6	2E-3	2E-2
		Y, see ^{136}Nd	-	6E+5	3E-4	9E-7	-	-
60	Neodymium-147	W, see ^{136}Nd	1E+3	9E+2	4E-7	1E-9	-	-
			LLI wall					
			(1E+3)	-	-	-	2E-5	2E-4
		Y, see ^{136}Nd	-	8E+2	4E-7	1E-9	-	-
60	Neodymium-149[2]	W, see ^{136}Nd	1E+4	3E+4	1E-5	4E-8	1E-4	1E-3
		Y, see ^{136}Nd	-	2E+4	1E-5	3E-8	-	-
60	Neodymium-151[2]	W, see ^{136}Nd	7E+4	2E+5	8E-5	3E-7	9E-4	9E-3
		Y, see ^{136}Nd	-	2E+5	8E-5	3E-7	-	-
61	Promethium-141[2]	W, all compounds except those given for Y	5E+4	2E+5	8E-5	3E-7	-	-
			St. wall					
			(6E+4)	-	-	-	8E-4	8E-3
		Y, oxides, hydroxides, carbides, and fluorides	-	2E+5	7E-5	2E-7	-	-
61	Promethium-143	W, see ^{141}Pm	5E+3	6E+2	2E-7	8E-10	7E-5	7E-4
		Y, see ^{141}Pm	-	7E+2	3E-7	1E-9	-	-
61	Promethium-144	W, see ^{141}Pm	1E+3	1E+2	5E-8	2E-10	2E-5	2E-4
		Y, see ^{141}Pm	-	1E+2	5E-8	2E-10	-	-
61	Promethium-145	W, see ^{141}Pm	1E+4	2E+2	7E-8	-	1E-4	1E-3
				Bone surf				
			-	(2E+2)	-	3E-10	-	-
		Y, see ^{141}Pm	-	2E+2	8E-8	3E-10	-	-
61	Promethium-146	W, see ^{141}Pm	2E+3	5E+1	2E-8	7E-11	2E-5	2E-4
		Y, see ^{141}Pm	-	4E+1	2E-8	6E-11	-	-
61	Promethium-147	W, see ^{141}Pm	4E+3	1E+2	5E-8	-	-	-
			LLI wall	Bone surf				
			(5E+3)	(2E+2)	-	3E-10	7E-5	7E-4
		Y, see ^{141}Pm	-	1E+2	6E-8	2E-10	-	-
61	Promethium-148m	W, see ^{141}Pm	7E+2	3E+2	1E-7	4E-10	1E-5	1E-4
		Y, see ^{141}Pm	-	3E+2	1E-7	5E-10	-	-
61	Promethium-148	W, see ^{141}Pm	4E+2	5E+2	2E-7	8E-10	-	-
			LLI wall					
			(5E+2)	-	-	-	7E-6	7E-5
		Y, see ^{141}Pm	-	5E+2	2E-7	7E-10	-	-
61	Promethium-149	W, see ^{141}Pm	1E+3	2E+3	8E-7	3E-9	-	-
			LLI wall					
			(1E+3)	-	-	-	2E-5	2E-4
		Y, see ^{141}Pm	-	2E+3	8E-7	2E-9	-	-
61	Promethium-150	W, see ^{141}Pm	5E+3	2E+4	8E-6	3E-8	7E-5	7E-4
		Y, see ^{141}Pm	-	2E+4	7E-6	2E-8	-	-
61	Promethium-151	W, see ^{141}Pm	2E+3	4E+3	1E-6	5E-9	2E-5	2E-4
		Y, see ^{141}Pm	-	3E+3	1E-6	4E-9	-	-

Atomic No.	Radionuclide	Class	Table 1 Occupational Values Col. 1 Oral Ingestion ALI (µCi)	Table 1 Col. 2 Inhalation ALI (µCi)	Table 1 Col. 3 Inhalation DAC (µCi/ml)	Table 2 Effluent Concentrations Col. 1 Air (µCi/ml)	Table 2 Col. 2 Water (µCi/ml)	Table 3 Releases to Sewers Monthly Average Concentration (µCi/ml)
62	Samarium-141m[2]	W, all compounds	3E+4	1E+5	4E-5	1E-7	4E-4	4E-3
62	Samarium-141[2]	W, all compounds	5E+4	2E+5	8E-5	2E-7	-	-
			St. wall (6E+4)	-		-	8E-4	8E-3
62	Samarium-142[2]	W, all compounds	8E+3	3E+4	1E-5	4E-8	1E-4	1E-3
62	Samarium-145	W, all compounds	6E+3	5E+2	2E-7	7E-10	8E-5	8E-4
62	Samarium-146	W, all compounds	1E+1	4E-2	1E-11	-	-	-
			Bone surf (3E+1)	Bone surf (6E-2)	-	9E-14	3E-7	3E-6
62	Samarium-147	W, all compounds	2E+1	4E-2	2E-11	-	-	-
			Bone surf (3E+1)	Bone surf (7E-2)	-	1E-13	4E-7	4E-6
62	Samarium-151	W, all compounds	1E+4	1E+2	4E-8	-	-	-
			LLI wall (1E+4)	Bone surf (2E+2)	-	2E-10	2E-4	2E-3
62	Samarium-153	W, all compounds	2E+3	3E+3	1E-6	4E-9	-	-
			LLI wall (2E+3)	-	-	-	3E-5	3E-4
62	Samarium-155[2]	W, all compounds	6E+4	2E+5	9E-5	3E-7	-	-
			St. wall (8E+4)	-	-	-	1E-3	1E-2
62	Samarium-156	W, all compounds	5E+3	9E+3	4E-6	1E-8	7E-5	7E-4
63	Europium-145	W, all compounds	2E+3	2E+3	8E-7	3E-9	2E-5	2E-4
63	Europium-146	W, all compounds	1E+3	1E+3	5E-7	2E-9	1E-5	1E-4
63	Europium-147	W, all compounds	3E+3	2E+3	7E-7	2E-9	4E-5	4E-4
63	Europium-148	W, all compounds	1E+3	4E+2	1E-7	5E-10	1E-5	1E-4
63	Europium-149	W, all compounds	1E+4	3E+3	1E-6	4E-9	2E-4	2E-3
63	Europium-150 (12.62 h)	W, all compounds	3E+3	8E+3	4E-6	1E-8	4E-5	4E-4
63	Europium-150 (34.2 y)	W, all compounds	8E+2	2E+1	8E-9	3E-11	1E-5	1E-4
63	Europium-152m	W, all compounds	3E+3	6E+3	3E-6	9E-9	4E-5	4E-4
63	Europium-152	W, all compounds	8E+2	2E+1	1E-8	3E-11	1E-5	1E-4
63	Europium-154	W, all compounds	5E+2	2E+1	8E-9	3E-11	7E-6	7E-5
63	Europium-155	W, all compounds	4E+3	9E+1	4E-8	-	5E-5	5E-4
			-	Bone surf (1E+2)	-	2E-10	-	-
63	Europium-156	W, all compounds	6E+2	5E+2	2E-7	6E-10	8E-6	8E-5

Atomic No.	Radionuclide	Class	Table 1 Occupational Values Col. 1 Oral Ingestion ALI (µCi)	Table 1 Col. 2 Inhalation ALI (µCi)	Table 1 Col. 3 Inhalation DAC (µCi/ml)	Table 2 Effluent Concentrations Col. 1 Air (µCi/ml)	Table 2 Col. 2 Water (µCi/ml)	Table 3 Releases to Sewers Monthly Average Concentration (µCi/ml)
63	Europium-157	W, all compounds	2E+3	5E+3	2E-6	7E-9	3E-5	3E-4
63	Europium-158[2]	W, all compounds	2E+4	6E+4	2E-5	8E-8	3E-4	3E-3
64	Gadolinium-145[2]	D, all compounds except those given for W	5E+4	2E+5	6E-5	2E-7	-	-
			St. wall (5E+4)	-	-	-	6E-4	6E-3
		W, oxides, hydroxides, and fluorides	-	2E+5	7E-5	2E-7	-	-
64	Gadolinium-146	D, see ^{145}Gd	1E+3	1E+2	5E-8	2E-10	2E-5	2E-4
		W, see ^{145}Gd	-	3E+2	1E-7	4E-10	-	-
64	Gadolinium-147	D, see ^{145}Gd	2E+3	4E+3	2E-6	6E-9	3E-5	3E-4
		W, see ^{145}Gd	-	4E+3	1E-6	5E-9	-	-
64	Gadolinium-148	D, see ^{145}Gd	1E+1	8E-3	3E-12	-	-	-
			Bone surf (2E+1)	Bone surf (2E-2)	-	2E-14	3E-7	3E-6
		W, see ^{145}Gd	-	3E-2	1E-11	-	-	-
			-	Bone surf (6E-2)	-	8E-14	-	-
64	Gadolinium-149	D, see ^{145}Gd	3E+3	2E+3	9E-7	3E-9	4E-5	4E-4
		W, see ^{145}Gd	-	2E+3	1E-6	3E-9	-	-
64	Gadolinium-151	D, see ^{145}Gd	6E+3	4E+2	2E-7	-	9E-5	9E-4
			-	Bone surf (6E+2)	-	9E-10	-	-
		W, see ^{145}Gd	-	1E+3	5E-7	2E-9	-	-
64	Gadolinium-152	D, see ^{145}Gd	2E+1	1E-2	4E-12	-	-	-
			Bone surf (3E+1)	Bone surf (2E-2)	-	3E-14	4E-7	4E-6
		W, see ^{145}Gd	-	4E-2	2E-11	-	-	-
			-	Bone surf (8E-2)	-	1E-13	-	-
64	Gadolinium-153	D, see ^{145}Gd	5E+3	1E+2	6E-8	-	6E-5	6E-4
			-	Bone surf (2E+2)	-	3E-10	-	-
		W, see ^{145}Gd	-	6E+2	2E-7	8E-10	-	-
64	Gadolinium-159	D, see ^{145}Gd	3E+3	8E+3	3E-6	1E-8	4E-5	4E-4
		W, see ^{145}Gd	-	6E+3	2E-6	8E-9	-	-
65	Terbium-147[2]	W, all compounds	9E+3	3E+4	1E-5	5E-8	2E-4	1E-3
65	Terbium-149	W, all compounds	5E+3	7E+2	3E-7	1E-9	7E-5	7E-4
65	Terbium-150	W, all compounds	5E+3	2E+4	9E-6	3E-8	7E-5	7E-4
65	Terbium-151	W, all compounds	4E+3	9E+3	4E-6	1E-8	5E-5	5E-4
65	Terbium-153	W, all compounds	5E+3	7E+3	3E-6	1E-8	7E-5	7E-4
65	Terbium-154	W, all compounds	2E+3	4E+3	2E-6	6E-9	2E-5	2E-4
65	T[illegible]m-155	W, all compounds	6E+3	8E+3	3E-6	1E-8	8E-5	8E-4
65	T[illegible]m-156m (5.0 h)	W, all compounds	2E+4	3E+4	1E-5	4E-8	2E-4	2E-3

Atomic No.	Radionuclide	Class	Table 1 Occupational Values Col. 1 Oral Ingestion ALI (μCi)	Table 1 Occupational Values Col. 2 Inhalation ALI (μCi)	Table 1 Occupational Values Col. 3 Inhalation DAC (μCi/ml)	Table 2 Effluent Concentrations Col. 1 Air (μCi/ml)	Table 2 Effluent Concentrations Col. 2 Water (μCi/ml)	Table 3 Releases to Sewers Monthly Average Concentration (μCi/ml)
65	Terbium-156m (24.4 h)	W, all compounds	7E+3	8E+3	3E-6	1E-8	1E-4	1E-3
65	Terbium-156	W, all compounds	1E+3	1E+3	6E-7	2E-9	1E-5	1E-4
65	Terbium-157	W, all compounds	5E+4 LLI wall	3E+2 Bone surf	1E-7	-	-	-
			(5E+4)	(6E+2)	-	8E-10	7E-4	7E-3
65	Terbium-158	W, all compounds	1E+3	2E+1	8E-9	3E-11	2E-5	2E-4
65	Terbium-160	W, all compounds	8E+2	2E+2	9E-8	3E-10	1E-5	1E-4
65	Terbium-161	W, all compounds	2E+3 LLI wall	2E+3	7E-7	2E-9	-	-
			(2E+3)	-	-	-	3E-5	3E-4
66	Dysprosium-155	W, all compounds	9E+3	3E+4	1E-5	4E-8	1E-4	1E-3
66	Dysprosium-157	W, all compounds	2E+4	6E+4	3E-5	9E-8	3E-4	3E-3
66	Dysprosium-159	W, all compounds	1E+4	2E+3	1E-6	3E-9	2E-4	2E-3
66	Dysprosium-165	W, all compounds	1E+4	5E+4	2E-5	6E-8	2E-4	2E-3
66	Dysprosium-166	W, all compounds	6E+2 LLI wall	7E+2	3E-7	1E-9	-	-
			(8E+2)	-	-	-	1E-5	1E-4
67	Holmium-155[2]	W, all compounds	4E+4	2E+5	6E-5	2E-7	6E-4	6E-3
67	Holmium-157[2]	W, all compounds	3E+5	1E+6	6E-4	2E-6	4E-3	4E-2
67	Holmium-159[2]	W, all compounds	2E+5	1E+6	4E-4	1E-6	3E-3	3E-2
67	Holmium-161	W, all compounds	1E+5	4E+5	2E-4	6E-7	1E-3	1E-2
67	Holmium-162m[2]	W, all compounds	5E+4	3E+5	1E-4	4E-7	7E-4	7E-3
67	Holmium-162[2]	W, all compounds	5E+5 St. wall	2E+6	1E-3	3E-6	-	-
			(8E+5)	-	-	-	1E-2	1E-1
67	Holmium-164m[2]	W, all compounds	1E+5	3E+5	1E-4	4E-7	1E-3	1E-2
67	Holmium-164[2]	W, all compounds	2E+5 St. wall	6E+5	3E-4	9E-7	-	-
			(2E+5)	-	-	-	3E-3	3E-2
67	Holmium-166m	W, all compounds	6E+2	7E+0	3E-9	9E-12	9E-6	9E-5
67	Holmium-166	W, all compounds	9E+2 LLI wall	2E+3	7E-7	2E-9	-	-
			(9E+2)	-	-	-	1E-5	1E-4
67	Holmium-167	W, all compounds	2E+4	6E+4	2E-5	8E-8	2E-4	2E-3
68	Erbium-161	W, all compounds	2E+4	6E+4	3E-5	9E-8	2E-4	2E-3
68	Erbium-165	W, all compounds	6E+4	2E+5	8E-5	3E-7	9E-4	9E-3

			Table 1 Occupational Values			Table 2 Effluent Concentrations		Table 3 Releases to Sewers
			Col. 1	Col. 2	Col. 3	Col. 1	Col. 2	
			Oral Ingestion	Inhalation				Monthly Average
Atomic No.	Radionuclide	Class	ALI (μCi)	ALI (μCi)	DAC (μCi/ml)	Air (μCi/ml)	Water (μCi/ml)	Concentration (μCi/ml)
68	Erbium-169	W, all compounds	3E+3	3E+3	1E-6	4E-9	-	-
			LLI wall					
			(4E+3)	-	-	-	5E-5	5E-4
68	Erbium-171	W, all compounds	4E+3	1E+4	4E-6	1E-8	5E-5	5E-4
68	Erbium-172	W, all compounds	1E+3	1E+3	6E-7	2E-9	-	-
			LLI wall					
			(1E+3)	-	-	-	2E-5	2E-4
69	Thulium-162[2]	W, all compounds	7E+4	3E+5	1E-4	4E-7	-	-
			St. wall					
			(7E+4)	-	-	-	1E-3	1E-2
69	Thulium-166	W, all compounds	4E+3	1E+4	6E-6	2E-8	6E-5	6E-4
69	Thulium-167	W, all compounds	2E+3	2E+3	8E-7	3E-9	-	-
			LLI wall					
			(2E+3)	-	-	-	3E-5	3E-4
69	Thulium-170	W, all compounds	8E+2	2E+2	9E-8	3E-10	-	-
			LLI wall					
			(1E+3)	-	-	-	1E-5	1E-4
69	Thulium-171	W, all compounds	1E+4	3E+2	1E-7	-	-	-
			LLI wall	Bone surf				
			(1E+4)	(6E+2)	-	8E-10	2E-4	2E-3
69	Thulium-172	W, all compounds	7E+2	1E+3	5E-7	2E-9	-	-
			LLI wall					
			(8E+2)	-	-	-	1E-5	1E-4
69	Thulium-173	W, all compounds	4E+3	1E+4	5E-6	2E-8	6E-5	6E-4
69	Thulium-175[2]	W, all compounds	7E+4	3E+5	1E-4	4E-7	-	-
			St. wall					
			(9E+4)	-	-	-	1E-3	1E-2
70	Ytterbium-162[2]	W, all compounds except those given for Y	7E+4	3E+5	1E-4	4E-7	1E-3	1E-2
		Y, oxides, hydroxides, and fluorides	-	3E+5	1E-4	4E-7	-	-
70	Ytterbium-166	W, see ^{162}Yb	1E+3	2E+3	8E-7	3E-9	2E-5	2E-4
		Y, see ^{162}Yb	-	2E+3	8E-7	3E-9	-	-
70	Ytterbium-167[2]	W, see ^{162}Yb	3E+5	8E+5	3E-4	1E-6	4E-3	4E-2
		Y, see ^{162}Yb	-	7E+5	3E-4	1E-6	-	-
70	Ytterbium-169	W, see ^{162}Yb	2E+3	8E+2	4E-7	1E-9	2E-5	2E-4
		Y, see ^{162}Yb	-	7E+2	3E-7	1E-9	-	-
70	Ytterbium-175	W, see ^{162}Yb	3E+3	4E+3	1E-6	5E-9	-	-
			LLI wall					
			(3E+3)	-	-	-	4E-5	4E-4
		Y, see ^{162}Yb	-	3E+3	1E-6	5E-9	-	-
70	Ytterbium-177[2]	W, see ^{162}Yb	2E+4	5E+4	2E-5	7E-8	2E-4	2E-3
		Y, see ^{162}Yb	-	5E+4	2E-5	6E-8	-	-
70	Ytterbium-178[2]	W, see ^{162}Yb	1E+4	4E+4	2E-5	6E-8	2E-4	2E-3
		Y, see ^{162}Yb	-	4E+4	2E-5	5E-8	-	-

Atomic No.	Radionuclide	Class	Table 1 Occupational Values Col. 1 Oral Ingestion ALI (μCi)	Table 1 Col. 2 Inhalation ALI (μCi)	Table 1 Col. 3 Inhalation DAC (μCi/ml)	Table 2 Effluent Concentrations Col. 1 Air (μCi/ml)	Table 2 Col. 2 Water (μCi/ml)	Table 3 Releases to Sewers Monthly Average Concentration (μCi/ml)
71	Lutetium-169	W, all compounds except those given for Y	3E+3	4E+3	2E-6	6E-9	3E-5	3E-4
		Y, oxides, hydroxides, and fluorides	-	4E+3	2E-6	6E-9	-	-
71	Lutetium-170	W, see ^{169}Lu	1E+3	2E+3	9E-7	3E-9	2E-5	2E-4
		Y, see ^{169}Lu	-	2E+3	8E-7	3E-9	-	-
71	Lutetium-171	W, see ^{169}Lu	2E+3	2E+3	8E-7	3E-9	3E-5	3E-4
		Y, see ^{169}Lu	-	2E+3	8E-7	3E-9	-	-
71	Lutetium-172	W, see ^{169}Lu	1E+3	1E+3	5E-7	2E-9	1E-5	1E-4
		Y, see ^{169}Lu	-	1E+3	5E-7	2E-9	-	-
71	Lutetium-173	W, see ^{169}Lu	5E+3	3E+2	1E-7	-	7E-5	7E-4
			-	Bone surf (5E+2)	-	6E-10	-	-
		Y, see ^{169}Lu	-	3E+2	1E-7	4E-10	-	-
71	Lutetium-174m	W, see ^{169}Lu	2E+3	2E+2	1E-7	-	-	-
			LLI wall (3E+3)	Bone surf (3E+2)	-	5E-10	4E-5	4E-4
		Y, see ^{169}Lu	-	2E+2	9E-8	3E-10	-	-
71	Lutetium-174	W, see ^{169}Lu	5E+3	1E+2	5E-8	-	7E-5	7E-4
			-	Bone surf (2E+2)	-	3E-10	-	-
		Y, see ^{169}Lu	-	2E+2	6E-8	2E-10	-	-
71	Lutetium-176m	W, see ^{169}Lu	8E+3	3E+4	1E-5	3E-8	1E-4	1E-3
		Y, see ^{169}Lu	-	2E+4	9E-6	3E-8	-	-
71	Lutetium-176	W, see ^{169}Lu	7E+2	5E+0	2E-9	-	1E-5	1E-4
			-	Bone surf (1E+1)	-	2E-11	-	-
		Y, see ^{169}Lu	-	8E+0	3E-9	1E-11	-	-
71	Lutetium-177m	W, see ^{169}Lu	7E+2	1E+2	5E-8	-	1E-5	1E-4
			-	Bone surf (1E+2)	-	2E-10	-	-
		Y, see ^{169}Lu	-	8E+1	3E-8	1E-10	-	-
71	Lutetium-177	W, see ^{169}Lu	2E+3	2E+3	9E-7	3E-9	-	-
			LLI wall (3E+3)	-	-	-	4E-5	4E-4
		Y, see ^{169}Lu	-	2E+3	9E-7	3E-9	-	-
71	Lutetium-178m[2]	W, see ^{169}Lu	5E+4	2E+5	8E-5	3E-7	-	-
			St wall (6E+4)	-	-	-	8E-4	8E-3
		Y, see ^{169}Lu	-	2E+5	7E-5	2E-7	-	-
71	Lutetium-178[2]	W, see ^{169}Lu	4E+4	1E+5	5E-5	2E-7	-	-
			St. wall (4E+4)	-	-	-	6E-4	6E-3
		Y, see ^{169}Lu	-	1E+5	5E-5	2E-7	-	-
71	Lutetium-179	W, see ^{169}Lu	6E+3	2E+4	8E-6	3E-8	9E-5	9E-4
		Y, see ^{169}Lu	-	2E+4	6E-6	3E-8	-	-

			Table 1 Occupational Values			Table 2 Effluent Concentrations		Table 3 Releases to Sewers
			Col. 1	Col. 2	Col. 3	Col. 1	Col. 2	
			Oral Ingestion	Inhalation				Monthly Average
Atomic No.	Radionuclide	Class	ALI (μCi)	ALI (μCi)	DAC (μCi/ml)	Air (μCi/ml)	Water (μCi/ml)	Concentration (μCi/ml)
72	Hafnium-170	D, all compounds except those given for W	3E+3	6E+3	2E-6	8E-9	4E-5	4E-4
		W, oxides, hydroxides, carbides, and nitrates	-	5E+3	2E-6	6E-9	-	-
72	Hafnium-172	D, see ^{170}Hf	1E+3	9E+0	4E-9	-	2E-5	2E-4
			-	Bone surf (2E+1)	-	3E-11	-	-
		W, see ^{170}Hf	-	4E+1	2E-8	-	-	-
			-	Bone surf (6E+1)	-	8E-11	-	-
72	Hafnium-173	D, see ^{170}Hf	5E+3	1E+4	5E-6	2E-8	7E-5	7E-4
		W, see ^{170}Hf	-	1E+4	5E-6	2E-8	-	-
72	Hafnium-175	D, see ^{170}Hf	3E+3	9E+2	4E-7	-	4E-5	4E-4
			-	Bone surf (1E+3)	-	1E-9	-	-
		W, see ^{170}Hf	-	1E+3	5E-7	2E-9	-	-
72	Hafnium-177m[2]	D, see ^{170}Hf	2E+4	6E+4	2E-5	8E-8	3E-4	3E-3
		W, see ^{170}Hf	-	9E+4	4E-5	1E-7	-	-
72	Hafnium-178m	D, see ^{170}Hf	3E+2	1E+0	5E-10	-	3E-6	3E-5
			-	Bone surf (2E+0)	-	3E-12	-	-
		W, see ^{170}Hf	-	5E+0	2E-9	-	-	-
			-	Bone surf (9E+0)	-	1E-11	-	-
72	Hafnium-179m	D, see ^{170}Hf	1E+3	3E+2	1E-7	-	1E-5	1E-4
			-	Bone surf (6E+2)	-	8E-10	-	-
		W, see ^{170}Hf	-	6E+2	3E-7	8E-10	-	-
72	Hafnium-180m	D, see ^{170}Hf	7E+3	2E+4	9E-6	3E-8	1E-4	1E-3
		W, see ^{170}Hf	-	3E+4	1E-5	4E-8	-	-
72	Hafnium-181	D, see ^{170}Hf	1E+3	2E+2	7E-8	-	2E-5	2E-4
			-	Bone surf (4E+2)	-	6E-10	-	-
		W, see ^{170}Hf	-	4E+2	2E-7	6E-10	-	-
72	Hafnium-182m[2]	D, see ^{170}Hf	4E+4	9E+4	4E-5	1E-7	5E-4	5E-3
		W, see ^{170}Hf	-	1E+5	6E-5	2E-7	-	-
72	Hafnium-182	D, see ^{170}Hf	2E+2	8E-1	3E-10	-	-	-
			Bone surf (4E+2)	Bone surf (2E+0)	-	2E-12	5E-6	5E-5
		W, see ^{170}Hf	-	3E+0	1E-9	-	-	-
			-	Bone surf (7E+0)	-	1E-11	-	-
72	Hafnium-183[2]	D, see ^{170}Hf	2E+4	5E+4	2E-5	6E-8	3E-4	3E-3
		W, see ^{170}Hf	-	6E+4	2E-5	8E-8	-	-
72	Hafnium-184	D, see ^{170}Hf	2E+3	8E+3	3E-6	1E-8	3E-5	3E-4
		W, see ^{170}Hf	-	6E+3	3E-6	9E-9	-	-

Atomic No.	Radionuclide	Class	Table 1 Occupational Values			Table 2 Effluent Concentrations		Table 3 Releases to Sewers
			Col. 1	Col. 2	Col. 3	Col. 1	Col. 2	
			Oral Ingestion	Inhalation				Monthly Average
			ALI (μCi)	ALI (μCi)	DAC (μCi/ml)	Air (μCi/ml)	Water (μCi/ml)	Concentration (μCi/ml)
73	Tantalum-172[2]	W, all compounds except those given for Y	4E+4	1E+5	5E-5	2E-7	5E-4	5E-3
		Y, elemental Ta, oxides, hydroxides, halides, carbides, nitrates, and nitrides	-	1E+5	4E-5	1E-7	-	-
73	Tantalum-173	W, see ^{172}Ta	7E+3	2E+4	8E-6	3E-8	9E-5	9E-4
		Y, see ^{172}Ta	-	2E+4	7E-6	2E-8	-	-
73	Tantalum-174[2]	W, see ^{172}Ta	3E+4	1E+5	4E-5	1E-7	4E-4	4E-3
		Y, see ^{172}Ta	-	9E+4	4E-5	1E-7	-	-
73	Tantalum-175	W, see ^{172}Ta	6E+3	2E+4	7E-6	2E-8	8E-5	8E-4
		Y, see ^{172}Ta	-	1E+4	6E-6	2E-8	-	-
73	Tantalum-176	W, see ^{172}Ta	4E+3	1E+4	5E-6	2E-8	5E-5	5E-4
		Y, see ^{172}Ta	-	1E+4	5E-6	2E-8	-	-
73	Tantalum-177	W, see ^{172}Ta	1E+4	2E+4	8E-6	3E-8	2E-4	2E-3
		Y, see ^{172}Ta	-	2E+4	7E-6	2E-8	-	-
73	Tantalum-178	W, see ^{172}Ta	2E+4	9E+4	4E-5	1E-7	2E-4	2E-3
		Y, see ^{172}Ta	-	7E+4	3E-5	1E-7	-	-
73	Tantalum-179	W, see ^{172}Ta	2E+4	5E+3	2E-6	8E-9	3E-4	3E-3
		Y, see ^{172}Ta	-	9E+2	4E-7	1E-9	-	-
73	Tantalum-180m	W, see ^{172}Ta	2E+4	7E+4	3E-5	9E-8	3E-4	3E-3
		Y, see ^{172}Ta	-	6E+4	2E-5	8E-8	-	-
73	Tantalum-180	W, see ^{172}Ta	1E+3	4E+2	2E-7	6E-10	2E-5	2E-4
		Y, see ^{172}Ta	-	2E+1	1E-8	3E-11	-	-
73	Tantalum-182m[2]	W, see ^{172}Ta	2E+5	5E+5	2E-4	8E-7	-	-
			St. wall (2E+5)	-	-	-	3E-3	3E-2
		Y, see ^{172}Ta	-	4E+5	2E-4	6E-7	-	-
73	Tantalum-182	W, see ^{172}Ta	8E+2	3E+2	1E-7	5E-10	1E-5	1E-4
		Y, see ^{172}Ta	-	1E+2	6E-8	2E-10	-	-
73	Tantalum-183	W, see ^{172}Ta	9E+2	1E+3	5E-7	2E-9	-	-
			LLI wall (1E+3)	-	-	-	2E-5	2E-4
		Y, see ^{172}Ta	-	1E+3	4E-7	1E-9	-	-
73	Tantalum-184	W, see ^{172}Ta	2E+3	5E+3	2E-6	8E-9	3E-5	3E-4
		Y, see ^{172}Ta	-	5E+3	2E-6	7E-9	-	-
73	Tantalum-185[2]	W, see ^{172}Ta	3E+4	7E+4	3E-5	1E-7	4E-4	4E-3
		Y, see ^{172}Ta	-	6E+4	3E-5	9E-8	-	-
73	Tantalum-186[2]	W, see ^{172}Ta	5E+4	2E+5	1E-4	3E-7	-	
			St. wall (7E+4)	-	-	-	1E-3	1E-2
		Y, see ^{172}Ta	-	2E+5	9E-5	3E-7	-	-
74	Tungsten-176	D, all compounds	1E+4	5E+4	2E-5	7E-8	1E-4	1E-3
74	Tungsten-177	D, all compounds	2E+4	9E+4	4E-5	1E-7	3E-4	3E-3

Atomic No.	Radionuclide	Class	Table 1 Occupational Values: Col. 1 Oral Ingestion ALI (µCi)	Table 1 Occupational Values: Col. 2 Inhalation ALI (µCi)	Table 1 Occupational Values: Col. 3 Inhalation DAC (µCi/ml)	Table 2 Effluent Concentrations: Col. 1 Air (µCi/ml)	Table 2 Effluent Concentrations: Col. 2 Water (µCi/ml)	Table 3 Releases to Sewers: Monthly Average Concentration (µCi/ml)
74	Tungsten-178	D, all compounds	5E+3	2E+4	8E-6	3E-8	7E-5	7E-4
74	Tungsten-179[2]	D, all compounds	5E+5	2E+6	7E-4	2E-6	7E-3	7E-2
74	Tungsten-181	D, all compounds	2E+4	3E+4	1E-5	5E-8	2E-4	2E-3
74	Tungsten-185	D, all compounds	2E+3	7E+3	3E-6	9E-9	-	-
			LLI wall (3E+3)	-	-	-	4E-5	4E-4
74	Tungsten-187	D, all compounds	2E+3	9E+3	4E-6	1E-8	3E-5	3E-4
74	Tungsten-188	D, all compounds	4E+2	1E+3	5E-7	2E-9	-	-
			LLI wall (5E+2)	-	-	-	7E-6	7E-5
75	Rhenium-177[2]	D, all compounds except those given for W	9E+4	3E+5	1E-4	4E-7	-	-
			St. wall (1E+5)	-	-	-	2E-3	2E-2
		W, oxides, hydroxides, and nitrates	-	4E+5	1E-4	5E-7	-	-
75	Rhenium-178[2]	D, see ^{177}Re	7E+4	3E+5	1E-4	4E-7	-	-
			St. wall (1E+5)	-	-	-	1E-3	1E-2
		W, see ^{177}Re	-	3E+5	1E-4	4E-7	-	-
75	Rhenium-181	D, see ^{177}Re	5E+3	9E+3	4E-6	1E-8	7E-5	7E-4
		W, see ^{177}Re	-	8E+3	4E-6	1E-8	-	-
75	Rhenium-182 (12.7 h)	D, see ^{177}Re	7E+3	1E+4	5E-6	2E-8	9E-5	9E-4
		W, see ^{177}Re	-	2E+4	6E-6	2E-8	-	-
75	Rhenium-182 (64.0 h)	D, see ^{177}Re	1E+3	2E+3	1E-6	3E-9	2E-5	2E-4
		W, see ^{177}Re	-	2E+3	9E-7	3E-9	-	-
75	Rhenium-184m	D, see ^{177}Re	2E+3	3E+3	1E-6	4E-9	3E-5	3E-4
		W, see ^{177}Re	-	4E+2	2E-7	6E-10	-	-
75	Rhenium-184	D, see ^{177}Re	2E+3	4E+3	1E-6	5E-9	3E-5	3E-4
		W, see ^{177}Re	-	1E+3	6E-7	2E-9	-	-
75	Rhenium-186m	D, see ^{177}Re	1E+3	2E+3	7E-7	-	-	-
			St. wall (2E+3)	St. wall (2E+3)	-	3E-9	2E-5	2E-4
		W, see ^{177}Re	-	2E+2	6E-8	2E-10	-	-
75	Rhenium-186	D, see ^{177}Re	2E+3	3E+3	1E-6	4E-9	3E-5	3E-4
		W, see ^{177}Re	-	2E+3	7E-7	2E-9	-	-
75	Rhenium-187	D, see ^{177}Re	6E+5	8E+5	4E-4	-	8E-3	8E-2
			-	St. wall (9E+5)	-	1E-6	-	-
		W, see ^{177}Re	-	1E+5	4E-5	1E-7	-	-
75	Rhenium-188m[2]	D, see ^{177}Re	8E+4	1E+5	6E-5	2E-7	1E-3	1E-2
		W, see ^{177}Re	-	1E+5	6E-5	2E-7	-	-
75	Rhenium-188	D, see ^{177}Re	2E+3	3E+3	1E-6	4E-9	2E-5	2E-4
		W, see ^{177}Re	-	3E+3	1E-6	4E-9	-	-

Atomic No.	Radionuclide	Class	Table 1 Occupational Values Col. 1 Oral Ingestion ALI (μCi)	Table 1 Col. 2 Inhalation ALI (μCi)	Table 1 Col. 3 Inhalation DAC (μCi/ml)	Table 2 Effluent Concentrations Col. 1 Air (μCi/ml)	Table 2 Col. 2 Water (μCi/ml)	Table 3 Releases to Sewers Monthly Average Concentration (μCi/ml)
75	Rhenium-189	D, see ^{177}Re	3E+3	5E+3	2E-6	7E-9	4E-5	4E-4
		W, see ^{177}Re	-	4E+3	2E-6	6E-9	-	-
76	Osmium-180[2]	D, all compounds except those given for W and Y	1E+5	4E+5	2E-4	5E-7	1E-3	1E-2
		W, halides and nitrates	-	5E+5	2E-4	7E-7	-	-
		Y, oxides and hydroxides	-	5E+5	2E-4	6E-7	-	-
76	Osmium-181[2]	D, see ^{180}Os	1E+4	4E+4	2E-5	6E-8	2E-4	2E-3
		W, see ^{180}Os	-	5E+4	2E-5	6E-8	-	-
		Y, see ^{180}Os	-	4E+4	2E-5	6E-8	-	-
76	Osmium-182	D, see ^{180}Os	2E+3	6E+3	2E-6	8E-9	3E-5	3E-4
		W, see ^{180}Os	-	4E+3	2E-6	6E-9	-	-
		Y, see ^{180}Os	-	4E+3	2E-6	6E-9	-	-
76	Osmium-185	D, see ^{180}Os	2E+3	5E+2	2E-7	7E-10	3E-5	3E-4
		W, see ^{180}Os	-	8E+2	3E-7	1E-9	-	-
		Y, see ^{180}Os	-	8E+2	3E-7	1E-9	-	-
76	Osmium-189m	D, see ^{180}Os	8E+4	2E+5	1E-4	3E-7	1E-3	1E-2
		W, see ^{180}Os	-	2E+5	9E-5	3E-7	-	-
		Y, see ^{180}Os	-	2E+5	7E-5	2E-7	-	-
76	Osmium-191m	D, see ^{180}Os	1E+4	3E+4	1E-5	4E-8	2E-4	2E-3
		W, see ^{180}Os	-	2E+4	8E-6	3E-8	-	-
		Y, see ^{180}Os	-	2E+4	7E-6	2E-8	-	-
76	Osmium-191	D, see ^{180}Os	2E+3	2E+3	9E-7	3E-9	-	-
			LLI wall (3E+3)	-	-	-	3E-5	3E-4
		W, see ^{180}Os	-	2E+3	7E-7	2E-9	-	-
		Y, see ^{180}Os	-	1E+3	6E-7	2E-9	-	-
76	Osmium-193	D, see ^{180}Os	2E+3	5E+3	2E-6	6E-9	-	-
			LLI wall (2E+3)	-	-	-	2E-5	2E-4
		W, see ^{180}Os	-	3E+3	1E-6	4E-9	-	-
		Y, see ^{180}Os	-	3E+3	1E-6	4E-9	-	-
76	Osmium-194	D, see ^{180}Os	4E+2	4E+1	2E-8	6E-11	-	-
			LLI wall (6E+2)	-	-	-	8E-6	8E-5
		W, see ^{180}Os	-	6E+1	2E-8	8E-11	-	-
		Y, see ^{180}Os	-	8E+0	3E-9	1E-11	-	-
77	Iridium-182[2]	D, all compounds except those given for W and Y	4E+4	1E+5	6E-5	2E-7	-	-
			St. wall (4E+4)	-	-	-	6E-4	6E-3
		W, halides, nitrates, and metallic iridium	-	2E+5	6E-5	2E-7	-	-
		Y, oxides and hydroxides	-	1E+5	5E-5	2E-7	-	-
77	Iridium-184	D, see ^{182}Ir	8E+3	2E+4	1E-5	3E-8	1E-4	1E-3
		W, see ^{182}Ir	-	3E+4	1E-5	5E-8	-	-
		Y, see ^{182}Ir	-	3E+4	1E-5	4E-8	-	-

			Table 1 Occupational Values			Table 2 Effluent Concentrations		Table 3 Releases to Sewers
			Col. 1	Col. 2	Col. 3	Col. 1	Col. 2	
			Oral Ingestion	Inhalation				Monthly
Atomic No.	Radionuclide	Class	ALI (μCi)	ALI (μCi)	DAC (μCi/ml)	Air (μCi/ml)	Water (μCi/ml)	Average Concentration (μCi/ml)
77	Iridium-185	D, see ^{182}Ir	5E+3	1E+4	5E-6	2E-8	7E-5	7E-4
		W, see ^{182}Ir	-	1E+4	5E-6	2E-8	-	-
		Y, see ^{182}Ir	-	1E+4	4E-6	1E-8	-	-
77	Iridium-186	D, see ^{182}Ir	2E+3	8E+3	3E-6	1E-8	3E-5	3E-4
		W, see ^{182}Ir	-	6E+3	3E-6	9E-9	-	-
		Y, see ^{182}Ir	-	6E+3	2E-6	8E-9	-	-
77	Iridium-187	D, see ^{182}Ir	1E+4	3E+4	1E-5	5E-8	1E-4	1E-3
		W, see ^{182}Ir	-	3E+4	1E-5	4E-8	-	-
		Y, see ^{182}Ir	-	3E+4	1E-5	4E-8	-	-
77	Iridium-188	D, see ^{182}Ir	2E+3	5E+3	2E-6	6E-9	3E-5	3E-4
		W, see ^{182}Ir	-	4E+3	1E-6	5E-9	-	-
		Y, see ^{182}Ir	-	3E+3	1E-6	5E-9	-	-
77	Iridium-189	D, see ^{182}Ir	5E+3	5E+3	2E-6	7E-9	-	-
			LLI wall (5E+3)	-	-	-	7E-5	7E-4
		W, see ^{182}Ir	-	4E+3	2E-6	5E-9	-	-
		Y, see ^{182}Ir	-	4E+3	1E-6	5E-9	-	-
77	Iridium-190m[2]	D, see ^{182}Ir	2E+5	2E+5	8E-5	3E-7	2E-3	2E-2
		W, see ^{182}Ir	-	2E+5	9E-5	3E-7	-	-
		Y, see ^{182}Ir	-	2E+5	8E-5	3E-7	-	-
77	Iridium-190	D, see ^{182}Ir	1E+3	9E+2	4E-7	1E-9	1E-5	1E-4
		W, see ^{182}Ir	-	1E+3	4E-7	1E-9	-	-
		Y, see ^{182}Ir	-	9E+2	4E-7	1E-9	-	-
77	Iridium-192m	D, see ^{182}Ir	3E+3	9E+1	4E-8	1E-10	4E-5	4E-4
		W, see ^{182}Ir	-	2E+2	9E-8	3E-10	-	-
		Y, see ^{182}Ir	-	2E+1	6E-9	2E-11	-	-
77	Iridium-192	D, see ^{182}Ir	9E+2	3E+2	1E-7	4E-10	1E-5	1E-4
		W, see ^{182}Ir	-	4E+2	2E-7	6E-10	-	-
		Y, see ^{182}Ir	-	2E+2	9E-8	3E-10	-	-
77	Iridium-194m	D, see ^{182}Ir	6E+2	9E+1	4E-8	1E-10	9E-6	9E-5
		W, see ^{182}Ir	-	2E+2	7E-8	2E-10	-	-
		Y, see ^{182}Ir	-	1E+2	4E-8	1E-10	-	-
77	Iridium-194	D, see ^{182}Ir	1E+3	3E+3	1E-6	4E-9	1E-5	1E-4
		W, see ^{182}Ir	-	2E+3	9E-7	3E-9	-	-
		Y, see ^{182}Ir	-	2E+3	8E-7	3E-9	-	-
77	Iridium-195m	D, see ^{182}Ir	8E+3	2E+4	1E-5	3E-8	1E-4	1E-3
		W, see ^{182}Ir	-	3E+4	1E-5	4E-8	-	-
		Y, see ^{182}Ir	-	2E+4	9E-6	3E-8	-	-
77	Iridium-195	D, see ^{182}Ir	1E+4	4E+4	2E-5	6E-8	2E-4	2E-3
		W, see ^{182}Ir	-	5E+4	2E-5	7E-8	-	-
		Y, see ^{182}Ir	-	4E+4	2E-5	6E-8	-	-
78	Platinum-186	D, all compounds	1E+4	4E+4	2E-5	5E-8	2E-4	2E-3
78	Platinum-188	D, all compounds	2E+3	2E+3	7E-7	2E-9	2E-5	2E-4
78	Platinum-189	D, all compounds	1E+4	3E+4	1E-5	4E-8	1E-4	1E-3
78	Platinum-191	D, all compounds	4E+3	8E+3	4E-6	1E-8	5E-5	5E-4

Atomic No.	Radionuclide	Class	Table 1 Occupational Values: Col. 1 Oral Ingestion ALI (μCi)	Table 1 Occupational Values: Col. 2 Inhalation ALI (μCi)	Table 1 Occupational Values: Col. 3 Inhalation DAC (μCi/ml)	Table 2 Effluent Concentrations: Col. 1 Air (μCi/ml)	Table 2 Effluent Concentrations: Col. 2 Water (μCi/ml)	Table 3 Releases to Sewers: Monthly Average Concentration (μCi/ml)
78	Platinum-193m	D, all compounds	3E+3	6E+3	3E-6	8E-9	-	-
			LLI wall (3E+4)	-	-	-	4E-5	4E-4
78	Platinum-193	D, all compounds	4E+4	2E+4	1E-5	3E-8	-	-
			LLI wall (5E+4)	-	-	-	6E-4	6E-3
78	Platinum-195m	D, all compounds	2E+3	4E+3	2E-6	6E-9	-	-
			LLI wall (2E+3)	-	-	-	3E-5	3E-4
78	Platinum-197m[2]	D, all compounds	2E+4	4E+4	2E-5	6E-8	2E-4	2E-3
78	Platinum-197	D, all compounds	3E+3	1E+4	4E-6	1E-8	4E-5	4E-4
78	Platinum-199[2]	D, all compounds	5E+4	1E+5	6E-5	2E-7	7E-4	7E-3
78	Platinum-200	D, all compounds	1E+3	3E+3	1E-6	5E-9	2E-5	2E-4
79	Gold-193	D, all compounds except those given for W and Y	9E+3	3E+4	1E-5	4E-8	1E-4	1E-3
		W, halides and nitrates	-	2E+4	9E-6	3E-8	-	-
		Y, oxides and hydroxides	-	2E+4	8E-6	3E-8	-	-
79	Gold-194	D, see ^{193}Au	3E+3	8E+3	3E-6	1E-8	4E-5	4E-4
		W, see ^{193}Au	-	5E+3	2E-6	8E-9	-	-
		Y, see ^{193}Au	-	5E+3	2E-6	7E-9	-	-
79	Gold-195	D, see ^{193}Au	5E+3	1E+4	5E-6	2E-8	7E-5	7E-4
		W, see ^{193}Au	-	1E+3	6E-7	2E-9	-	-
		Y, see ^{193}Au	-	4E+2	2E-7	6E-10	-	-
79	Gold-198m	D, see ^{193}Au	1E+3	3E+3	1E-6	4E-9	1E-5	1E-4
		W, see ^{193}Au	-	1E+3	5E-7	2E-9	-	-
		Y, see ^{193}Au	-	1E+3	5E-7	2E-9	-	-
79	Gold-198	D, see ^{193}Au	1E+3	4E+3	2E-6	5E-9	2E-5	2E-4
		W, see ^{193}Au	-	2E+3	8E-7	3E-9	-	-
		Y, see ^{193}Au	-	2E+3	7E-7	2E-9	-	-
79	Gold-199	D, see ^{193}Au	3E+3	9E+3	4E-6	1E-8	-	-
			LLI wall (3E+3)	-	-	-	4E-5	4E-4
		W, see ^{193}Au	-	4E+3	2E-6	6E-9	-	-
		Y, see ^{193}Au	-	4E+3	2E-6	5E-9	-	-
79	Gold-200m	D, see ^{193}Au	1E+3	4E+3	1E-6	5E-9	2E-5	2E-4
		W, see ^{193}Au	-	3E+3	1E-6	4E-9	-	-
		Y, see ^{193}Au	-	2E+4	1E-6	3E-9	-	-
79	Gold-200[2]	D, see ^{193}Au	3E+4	6E+4	3E-5	9E-8	4E-4	4E-3
		W, see ^{193}Au	-	8E+4	3E-5	1E-7	-	-
		Y, see ^{193}Au	-	7E+4	3E-5	1E-7	-	-
79	Gold-201[2]	D, see ^{193}Au	7E+4	2E+5	9E-5	3E-7	-	-
			St. wall (9E+4)	-	-	-	1E-3	1E-2
		W, see ^{193}Au	-	2E+5	1E-4	3E-7	-	-
		Y, see ^{193}Au	-	2E+5	9E-5	3E-7	-	-

Atomic No.	Radionuclide	Class	Table 1 Occupational Values Col. 1 Oral Ingestion ALI (μCi)	Table 1 Col. 2 Inhalation ALI (μCi)	Table 1 Col. 3 Inhalation DAC (μCi/ml)	Table 2 Effluent Concentrations Col. 1 Air (μCi/ml)	Table 2 Col. 2 Water (μCi/ml)	Table 3 Releases to Sewers Monthly Average Concentration (μCi/ml)
80	Mercury-193m	Vapor	-	8E+3	4E-6	1E-8	-	-
		Organic D	4E+3	1E+4	5E-6	2E-8	6E-5	6E-4
		D, sulfates	3E+3	9E+3	4E-6	1E-8	4E-5	4E-4
		W, oxides, hydroxides, halides, nitrates, and sulfides	-	8E+3	3E-6	1E-8	-	-
80	Mercury-193	Vapor	-	3E+4	1E-5	4E-8	-	-
		Organic D	2E+4	6E+4	3E-5	9E-8	3E-4	3E-3
		D, see ^{193m}Hg	2E+4	4E+4	2E-5	6E-8	2E-4	2E-3
		W, see ^{193m}Hg	-	4E+4	2E-5	6E-8	-	-
80	Mercury-194	Vapor	-	3E+1	1E-8	4E-11	-	-
		Organic D	2E+1	3E+1	1E-8	4E-11	2E-7	2E-6
		D, see ^{193m}Hg	8E+2	4E+1	2E-8	6E-11	1E-5	1E-4
		W, see ^{193m}Hg	-	1E+2	5E-8	2E-10	-	-
80	Mercury-195m	Vapor	-	4E+3	2E-6	6E-9	-	-
		Organic D	3E+3	6E+3	3E-6	8E-9	4E-5	4E-4
		D, see ^{193m}Hg	2E+3	5E+3	2E-6	7E-9	3E-5	3E-4
		W, see ^{193m}Hg	-	4E+3	2E-6	5E-9	-	-
80	Mercury-195	Vapor	-	3E+4	1E-5	4E-8	-	-
		Organic D	2E+4	5E+4	2E-5	6E-8	2E-4	2E-3
		D, see ^{193m}Hg	1E+4	4E+4	1E-5	5E-8	2E-4	2E-3
		W, see ^{193m}Hg	-	3E+4	1E-5	5E-8	-	-
80	Mercury-197m	Vapor	-	5E+3	2E-6	7E-9	-	-
		Organic D	4E+3	9E+3	4E-6	1E-8	5E-5	5E-4
		D, see ^{193m}Hg	3E+3	7E+3	3E-6	1E-8	4E-5	4E-4
		W, see ^{193m}Hg	-	5E+3	2E-6	7E-9	-	-
80	Mercury-197	Vapor	-	8E+3	4E-6	1E-8	-	-
		Organic D	7E+3	1E+4	6E-6	2E-8	9E-5	9E-4
		D, see ^{193m}Hg	6E+3	1E+4	5E-6	2E-8	8E-5	8E-4
		W, see ^{193m}Hg	-	9E+3	4E-6	1E-8	-	-
80	Mercury-199m[2]	Vapor	-	8E+4	3E-5	1E-7	-	-
		Organic D	6E+4	2E+5	7E-5	2E-7	-	-
			St. wall (1E+5)	-	-	-	1E-3	1E-2
		D, see ^{193m}Hg	6E+4	1E+5	6E-5	2E-7	8E-4	8E-3
		W, see ^{193m}Hg	-	2E+5	7E-5	2E-7	-	-
80	Mercury-203	Vapor	-	8E+2	4E-7	1E-9	-	-
		Organic D	5E+2	8E+2	3E-7	1E-9	7E-6	7E-5
		D, see ^{193m}Hg	2E+3	1E+3	5E-7	2E-9	3E-5	3E-4
		W, see ^{193m}Hg	-	1E+3	5E-7	2E-9	-	-
81	Thallium-194m[2]	D, all compounds	5E+4	2E+5	6E-5	2E-7	-	-
			St. wall (7E+4)	-	-	-	1E-3	1E-2

Atomic No.	Radionuclide	Class	Table 1 Occupational Values Col. 1 Oral Ingestion ALI (μCi)	Table 1 Col. 2 Inhalation ALI (μCi)	Table 1 Col. 3 Inhalation DAC (μCi/ml)	Table 2 Effluent Concentrations Col. 1 Air (μCi/ml)	Table 2 Col. 2 Water (μCi/ml)	Table 3 Releases to Sewers Monthly Average Concentration (μCi/ml)
81	Thallium-194[2]	D, all compounds	3E+5	6E+5	2E-4	8E-7	-	-
			St. wall (3E+5)	-	-	-	4E-3	4E-2
81	Thallium-195[2]	D, all compounds	6E+4	1E+5	5E-5	2E-7	9E-4	9E-3
81	Thallium-197	D, all compounds	7E+4	1E+5	5E-5	2E-7	1E-3	1E-2
81	Thallium-198m[2]	D, all compounds	3E+4	5E+4	2E-5	8E-8	4E-4	4E-3
81	Thallium-198	D, all compounds	2E+4	3E+4	1E-5	5E-8	3E-4	3E-3
81	Thallium-199	D, all compounds	6E+4	8E+4	4E-5	1E-7	9E-4	9E-3
81	Thallium-200	D, all compounds	8E+3	1E+4	5E-6	2E-8	1E-4	1E-3
81	Thallium-201	D, all compounds	2E+4	2E+4	9E-6	3E-8	2E-4	2E-3
81	Thallium-202	D, all compounds	4E+3	5E+3	2E-6	7E-9	5E-5	5E-4
81	Thallium-204	D, all compounds	2E+3	2E+3	9E-7	3E-9	2E-5	2E-4
82	Lead-195m[2]	D, all compounds	6E+4	2E+5	8E-5	3E-7	8E-4	8E-3
82	Lead-198	D, all compounds	3E+4	6E+4	3E-5	9E-8	4E-4	4E-3
82	Lead-199[2]	D, all compounds	2E+4	7E+4	3E-5	1E-7	3E-4	3E-3
82	Lead-200	D, all compounds	3E+3	6E+3	3E-6	9E-9	4E-5	4E-4
82	Lead-201	D, all compounds	7E+3	2E+4	8E-6	3E-8	1E-4	1E-3
82	Lead-202m	D, all compounds	9E+3	3E+4	1E-5	4E-8	1E-4	1E-3
82	Lead-202	D, all compounds	1E+2	5E+1	2E-8	7E-11	2E-6	2E-5
82	Lead-203	D, all compounds	5E+3	9E+3	4E-6	1E-8	7E-5	7E-4
82	Lead-205	D, all compounds	4E+3	1E+3	6E-7	2E-9	5E-5	5E-4
82	Lead-209	D, all compounds	2E+4	6E+4	2E-5	8E-8	3E-4	3E-3
82	Lead-210	D, all compounds	6E-1	2E-1	1E-10	-	-	-
			Bone surf (1E+0)	Bone surf (4E-1)	-	6E-13	1E-8	1E-7
82	Lead-211[2]	D, all compounds	1E+4	6E+2	3E-7	9E-10	2E-4	2E-3
82	Lead-212	D, all compounds	8E+1	3E+1	1E-8	5E-11	-	-
			Bone surf (1E+2)	-	-	-	2E-6	2E-5
82	Lead-214[2]	D, all compounds	9E+3	8E+2	3E-7	1E-9	1E-4	1E-3
83	Bismuth-200[2]	D, nitrates	3E+4	8E+4	4E-5	1E-7	4E-4	4E-3
		W, all other compounds	-	1E+5	4E-5	1E-7	-	-
83	Bismuth-201[2]	D, see ^{200}Bi	1E+4	3E+4	1E-5	4E-8	2E-4	2E-3
		W, see ^{200}Bi	-	4E+4	2E-5	5E-8	-	-
83	Bismuth-202[2]	D, see ^{200}Bi	1E+4	4E+4	2E-5	6E-8	2E-4	2E-3
		W, see ^{200}Bi	-	8E+4	3E-5	1E-7	-	-

Atomic No.	Radionuclide	Class	Table 1 Occupational Values, Col. 1 Oral Ingestion ALI (μCi)	Table 1, Col. 2 Inhalation ALI (μCi)	Table 1, Col. 3 Inhalation DAC (μCi/ml)	Table 2 Effluent Concentrations, Col. 1 Air (μCi/ml)	Table 2, Col. 2 Water (μCi/ml)	Table 3 Releases to Sewers, Monthly Average Concentration (μCi/ml)
83	Bismuth-203	D, see ^{200}Bi	2E+3	7E+3	3E-6	9E-9	3E-5	3E-4
		W, see ^{200}Bi	-	6E+3	3E-6	9E-9	-	-
83	Bismuth-205	D, see ^{200}Bi	1E+3	3E+3	1E-6	3E-9	2E-5	2E-4
		W, see ^{200}Bi	-	1E+3	5E-7	2E-9	-	-
83	Bismuth-206	D, see ^{200}Bi	6E+2	1E+3	6E-7	2E-9	9E-6	9E-5
		W, see ^{200}Bi	-	9E+2	4E-7	1E-9	-	-
83	Bismuth-207	D, see ^{200}Bi	1E+3	2E+3	7E-7	2E-9	1E-5	1E-4
		W, see ^{200}Bi	-	4E+2	1E-7	5E-10	-	-
83	Bismuth-210m	D, see ^{200}Bi	4E+1	5E+0	2E-9	-	-	-
			Kidneys (6E+1)	Kidneys (6E+0)	-	9E-12	8E-7	8E-6
		W, see ^{200}Bi	-	7E-1	3E-10	9E-13	-	-
83	Bismuth-210	D, see ^{200}Bi	8E+2	2E+2	1E-7	-	1E-5	1E-4
			-	Kidneys (4E+2)	-	5E-10	-	-
		W, see ^{200}Bi	-	3E+1	1E-8	4E-11	-	-
83	Bismuth-212[2]	D, see ^{200}Bi	5E+3	2E+2	1E-7	3E-10	7E-5	7E-4
		W, see ^{200}Bi	-	3E+2	1E-7	4E-10	-	-
83	Bismuth-213[2]	D, see ^{200}Bi	7E+3	3E+2	1E-7	4E-10	1E-4	1E-3
		W, see ^{200}Bi	-	4E+2	1E-7	5E-10	-	-
83	Bismuth-214[2]	D, see ^{200}Bi	2E+4	8E+2	3E-7	1E-9	-	-
			St. wall (2E+4)	-	-	-	3E-4	3E-3
		W, see ^{200}Bi	-	9E-2	4E-7	1E-9	-	-
84	Polonium-203[2]	D, all compounds except those given for W	3E+4	6E+4	3E-5	9E-8	3E-4	3E-3
		W, oxides, hydroxides, and nitrates	-	9E+4	4E-5	1E-7	-	-
84	Polonium-205[2]	D, see ^{203}Po	2E+4	4E+4	2E-5	5E-8	3E-4	3E-3
		W, see ^{203}Po	-	7E+4	3E-5	1E-7	-	-
84	Polonium-207	D, see ^{203}Po	8E+3	3E+4	1E-5	3E-8	1E-4	1E-3
		W, see ^{203}Po	-	3E+4	1E-5	4E-8	-	-
84	Polonium-210	D, see ^{203}Po	3E+0	6E-1	3E-10	9E-13	4E-8	4E-7
		W, see ^{203}Po	-	6E-1	3E-10	9E-13	-	-
85	Astatine-207[2]	D, halides	6E+3	3E+3	1E-6	4E-9	8E-5	8E-4
		W	-	2E+3	9E-7	3E-9	-	-
85	Astatine-211	D, halides	1E+2	8E+1	3E-8	1E-10	2E-6	2E-5
		W	-	5E+1	2E-8	8E-11	-	-
86	Radon-220	With daughters removed	-	2E+4	7E-6	2E-8	-	-
		With daughters present	-	2E+1 (or 12 working level months)	9E-9 (or 1.0 working level)	3E-11	-	-

Atomic No.	Radionuclide	Class	Table 1 Occupational Values: Col. 1 Oral Ingestion ALI (μCi)	Table 1: Col. 2 Inhalation ALI (μCi)	Table 1: Col. 3 Inhalation DAC (μCi/ml)	Table 2 Effluent Concentrations: Col. 1 Air (μCi/ml)	Table 2: Col. 2 Water (μCi/ml)	Table 3 Releases to Sewers: Monthly Average Concentration (μCi/ml)
86	Radon-222	With daughters removed	-	1E+4	4E-6	1E-8	-	-
		With daughters present	-	1E+2 (or 4 working level months)	3E-8 (or 0.33 working level)	1E-10	-	-
87	Francium-222[2]	D, all compounds	2E+3	5E+2	2E-7	6E-10	3E-5	3E-4
87	Francium-223[2]	D, all compounds	6E+2	8E+2	3E-7	1E-9	8E-6	8E-5
88	Radium-223	W, all compounds	5E+0	7E-1	3E-10	9E-13	-	-
			Bone surf (9E+0)	-	-	-	1E-7	1E-6
88	Radium-224	W, all compounds	8E+0	2E+0	7E-10	2E-12	-	-
			Bone surf (2E+1)	-	-	-	2E-7	2E-6
88	Radium-225	W, all compounds	8E+0	7E-1	3E-10	9E-13	-	-
			Bone surf (2E+1)	-	-	-	2E-7	2E-6
88	Radium-226	W, all compounds	2E+0	6E-1	3E-10	9E-13	-	-
			Bone surf (5E+0)	-	-	-	6E-8	6E-7
88	Radium-227[2]	W, all compounds	2E+4	1E+4	6E-6	-	-	-
			Bone surf (2E+4)	Bone surf (2E+4)	-	3E-8	3E-4	3E-3
8	Radium-228	W, all compounds	2E+0	1E+0	5E-10	2E-12	-	-
			Bone surf (4E+0)	-	-	-	6E-8	6E-7
89	Actinium-224	D, all compounds except those given for W and Y	2E+3	3E+1	1E-8	-	-	-
			LLI wall (2E+3)	Bone surf (4E+1)	-	5E-11	3E-5	3E-4
		W, halides and nitrates	-	5E+1	2E-8	7E-11	-	-
		Y, oxides and hydroxides	-	5E+1	2E-8	6E-11	-	-
89	Actinium-225	D, see ^{224}Ac	5E+1	3E-1	1E-10	-	-	-
			LLI wall (5E+1)	Bone surf (5E-1)	-	7E-13	7E-7	7E-6
		W, see ^{224}Ac	-	6E-1	3E-10	9E-13	-	-
		Y, see ^{224}Ac	-	6E-1	3E-10	9E-13	-	-
89	Actinium-226	D, see ^{224}Ac	1E+2	3E+0	1E-9	-	-	-
			LLI wall (1E+2)	Bone surf (4E+0)	-	5E-12	2E-6	2E-5
		W, see ^{224}Ac	-	5E+0	2E-9	7E-12	-	-
		Y, see ^{224}Ac	-	5E+0	2E-9	6E-12	-	-
89	Actinium-227	D, see ^{224}Ac	2E-1	4E-4	2E-13	-	-	-
			Bone surf (4E-1)	Bone surf (8E-4)	-	1E-15	5E-9	5E-8
		W, see ^{224}Ac	-	2E-3	7E-13	-	-	-
			-	Bone surf (3E-3)	-	4E-15	-	-
		Y, see ^{224}Ac	-	4E-3	2E-12	6E-15	-	-

			Table 1 Occupational Values			Table 2 Effluent Concentrations		Table 3 Releases to Sewers
			Col. 1	Col. 2	Col. 3	Col. 1	Col. 2	
			Oral Ingestion	Inhalation				Monthly Average
Atomic No.	Radionuclide	Class	ALI (μCi)	ALI (μCi)	DAC (μCi/ml)	Air (μCi/ml)	Water (μCi/ml)	Concentration (μCi/ml)
89	Actinium-228	D, see ^{224}Ac	2E+3	9E+0	4E-9	-	3E-5	3E-4
				Bone surf				
			-	(2E+1)	-	2E-11	-	-
		W, see ^{224}Ac	-	4E+1	2E-8	-	-	-
				Bone surf				
			-	(6E+1)	-	8E-11	-	-
		Y, see ^{224}Ac	-	4E+1	2E-8	6E-11	-	-
90	Thorium-226[2]	W, all compounds except those given for Y	5E+3	2E+2	6E-8	2E-10	-	-
			St. wall					
			(5E+3)	-	-	-	7E-5	7E-4
		Y, oxides and hydroxides	-	1E+2	6E-8	2E-10	-	-
90	Thorium-227	W, see ^{226}Th	1E+2	3E-1	1E-10	5E-13	2E-6	2E-5
		Y, see ^{226}Th	-	3E-1	1E-10	5E-13	-	-
90	Thorium-228	W, see ^{226}Th	6E+0	1E-2	4E-12	-	-	-
			Bone surf	Bone surf				
			(1E+1)	(2E-2)	-	3E-14	2E-7	2E-6
		Y, see ^{226}Th	-	2E-2	7E-12	2E-14	-	-
90	Thorium-229	W, see ^{226}Th	6E-1	9E-4	4E-13	-	-	-
			Bone surf	Bone surf				
			(1E+0)	(2E-3)	-	3E-15	2E-8	2E-7
		Y, see ^{226}Th	-	2E-3	1E-12	-	-	-
				Bone surf				
			-	(3E-3)	-	4E-15	-	-
90	Thorium-230	W, see ^{226}Th	4E+0	6E-3	3E-12	-	-	-
			Bone surf	Bone surf				
			(9E+0)	(2E-2)	-	2E-14	1E-7	1E-6
		Y, see ^{226}Th	-	2E-2	6E-12	-	-	-
				Bone surf				
			-	(2E-2)	-	3E-14	-	-
90	Thorium-231	W, see ^{226}Th	4E+3	6E+3	3E-6	9E-9	5E-5	5E-4
		Y, see ^{226}Th	-	6E+3	3E-6	9E-9	-	-
90	Thorium-232	W, see ^{226}Th	7E-1	1E-3	5E-13	-	-	-
			Bone surf	Bone surf				
			(2E+0)	(3E-3)	-	4E-15	3E-8	3E-7
		Y, see ^{226}Th	-	3E-3	1E-12	-	-	-
				Bone surf				
			-	(4E-3)	-	6E-15	-	-
90	Thorium-234	W, see ^{226}Th	3E+2	2E+2	8E-8	3E-10	-	-
			LLI wall					
			(4E+2)	-	-	-	5E-6	5E-5
		Y, see ^{226}Th	-	2E+2	6E-8	2E-10	-	-
91	Protactinium-227[2]	W, all compounds except those given for Y	4E+3	1E+2	5E-8	2E-10	5E-5	5E-4
		Y, oxides and hydroxides	-	1E+2	4E-8	1E-10	-	-
91	Protactinium-228	W, see ^{227}Pa	1E+3	1E+1	5E-9	-	2E-5	2E-4
				Bone surf				
			-	(2E+1)	-	3E-11	-	-
		Y, see ^{226}Pa	-	1E+1	5E-9	2E-11	-	-

Atomic No.	Radionuclide	Class	Table 1 Occupational Values Col. 1 Oral Ingestion ALI (μCi)	Table 1 Col. 2 Inhalation ALI (μCi)	Table 1 Col. 3 Inhalation DAC (μCi/ml)	Table 2 Effluent Concentrations Col. 1 Air (μCi/ml)	Table 2 Col. 2 Water (μCi/ml)	Table 3 Releases to Sewers Monthly Average Concentration (μCi/ml)
91	Protactinium-230	W, see ^{227}Pa	6E+2	5E+0	2E-9	7E-12	-	-
			Bone surf					
			(9E+2)	-	-	-	1E-5	1E-4
		Y, see ^{227}Pa	-	4E+0	1E-9	5E-12	-	-
91	Protactinium-231	W, see ^{227}Pa	2E-1	2E-3	6E-13	-	-	-
			Bone surf	Bone surf				
			(5E-1)	(4E-3)	-	6E-15	6E-9	6E-8
		Y, see ^{226}Pa	-	4E-3	2E-12	-	-	-
				Bone surf				
			-	(6E-3)	-	8E-15	-	-
91	Protactinium-232	W, see ^{227}Pa	1E+3	2E+1	9E-9	-	2E-5	2E-4
				Bone surf				
			-	(6E+1)	-	8E-11	-	-
		Y, see ^{227}Pa	-	6E+1	2E-8	-	-	-
				Bone surf				
			-	(7E+1)	-	1E-10	-	-
91	Protactinium-233	W, see ^{227}Pa	1E+3	7E+2	3E-7	1E-9	-	-
			LLI wall					
			(2E+3)	-	-	-	2E-5	2E-4
		Y, see ^{227}Pa	-	6E+2	2E-7	8E-10	-	-
91	Protactinium-234	W, see ^{227}Pa	2E+3	8E+3	3E-6	1E-8	3E-5	3E-4
		Y, see ^{227}Pa	-	7E+3	3E-6	9E-9	-	-
92	Uranium-230	D, UF_6, UO_2F_2, $UO_2(NO_3)_2$	4E+0	4E-1	2E-10	-	-	-
			Bone surf	Bone surf				
			(6E+0)	(6E-1)	-	8E-13	8E-8	8E-7
		W, UO_3, UF_4, UCl_4	-	4E-1	1E-10	5E-13	-	-
		Y, UO_2, U_3O_8	-	3E-1	1E-10	4E-13	-	-
92	Uranium-231	D, see ^{230}U	5E+3	8E+3	3E-6	1E-8	-	-
			LLI wall					
			(4E+3)	-	-	-	6E-5	6E-4
		W, see ^{230}U	-	6E+3	2E-6	8E-9	-	-
		Y, see ^{230}U	-	5E+3	2E-6	6E-9	-	-
92	Uranium-232	D, see ^{230}U	2E+0	2E-1	9E-11	-	-	-
			Bone surf	Bone surf				
			(4E+0)	(4E-1)	-	6E-13	6E-8	6E-7
		W, see ^{230}U	-	4E-1	2E-10	5E-13	-	-
		Y, see ^{230}U	-	8E-3	3E-12	1E-14	-	-
92	Uranium-233	D, see ^{230}U	1E+1	1E+0	5E-10	-	-	-
			Bone surf	Bone surf				
			(2E+1)	(2E+0)	-	3E-12	3E-7	3E-6
		W, see ^{230}U	-	7E-1	3E-10	1E-12	-	-
		Y, see ^{230}U	-	4E-2	2E-11	5E-14	-	-
92	Uranium-234[3]	D, see ^{230}U	1E+1	1E+0	5E-10	-	-	-
			Bone surf	Bone surf				
			(2E+1)	(2E+0)	-	3E-12	3E-7	3E-6
		W, see ^{230}U	-	7E-1	3E-10	1E-12	-	-
		Y, see ^{230}U	-	4E-2	2E-11	5E-14	-	-

			Table 1 Occupational Values			Table 2 Effluent Concentrations		Table 3 Releases to Sewers
			Col. 1	Col. 2	Col. 3	Col. 1	Col. 2	
			Oral Ingestion	Inhalation				Monthly Average
Atomic No.	Radionuclide	Class	ALI (μCi)	ALI (μCi)	DAC (μCi/ml)	Air (μCi/ml)	Water (μCi/ml)	Concentration (μCi/ml)
92	Uranium-235[3]	D, see ^{230}U	1E+1	1E+0	6E-10	-	-	-
			Bone surf	Bone surf				
			(2E+1)	(2E+0)	-	3E-12	3E-7	3E-6
		W, see ^{230}U	-	8E-1	3E-10	1E-12	-	-
		Y, see ^{230}U	-	4E-2	2E-11	6E-14	-	-
92	Uranium-236	D, see ^{230}U	1E+1	1E+0	5E-10	-	-	-
			Bone surf	Bone surf				
			(2E+1)	(2E+0)	-	3E-12	3E-7	3E-6
		W, see ^{230}U	-	8E-1	3E-10	1E-12	-	-
		Y, see ^{230}U	-	4E-2	2E-11	6E-14	-	-
92	Uranium-237	D, see ^{230}U	2E+3	3E+3	1E-6	4E-9	-	-
			LLI wall					
			(2E+3)	-	-	-	3E-5	3E-4
		W, see ^{230}U	-	2E+3	7E-7	2E-9	-	-
		Y, see ^{230}U	-	2E+3	6E-7	2E-9	-	-
92	Uranium-238[3]	D, see ^{230}U	1E+1	1E+0	6E-10	-	-	-
			Bone surf	Bone surf				
			(2E+1)	(2E+0)	-	3E-12	3E-7	3E-6
		W, see ^{230}U	-	8E-1	3E-10	1E-12	-	-
		Y, see ^{230}U	-	4E-2	2E-11	6E-14	-	-
92	Uranium-239[2]	D, see ^{230}U	7E+4	2E+5	8E-5	3E-7	9E-4	9E-3
		W, see ^{230}U	-	2E+5	7E-5	2E-7	-	-
		Y, see ^{230}U	-	2E+5	6E-5	2E-7	-	-
92	Uranium-240	D, see ^{230}U	1E+3	4E+3	2E-6	5E-9	2E-5	2E-4
		W, see ^{230}U	-	3E+3	1E-6	4E-9	-	-
		Y, see ^{230}U	-	2E+3	1E-6	3E-9	-	-
92	Uranium-natural[3]	D, see ^{230}U	1E+1	1E+0	5E-10	-	-	-
			Bone surf	Bone surf				
			(2E+1)	(2E+0)	-	3E-12	3E-7	3E-6
		W, see ^{230}U	-	8E-1	3E-10	9E-13	-	-
		Y, see ^{230}U	-	5E-2	2E-11	9E-14	-	-
93	Neptunium-232[2]	W, all compounds	1E+5	2E+3	7E-7	-	2E-3	2E-2
				Bone surf				
			-	(5E+2)	-	6E-9	-	-
93	Neptunium-233[2]	W, all compounds	8E+5	3E+6	1E-3	4E-6	1E-2	1E-1
93	Neptunium-234	W, all compounds	2E+3	3E+3	1E-6	4E-9	3E-5	3E-4
93	Neptunium-235	W, all compounds	2E+4	8E+2	3E-7	-	-	-
			LLI wall	Bone surf				
			(2E+4)	(1E+3)		2E-9	3E-4	3E-3
93	Neptunium-236 (1.15E+5 y)	W, all compounds	3E+0	2E-2	9E-12	-	-	-
			Bone surf	Bone surf				
			(6E+0)	(5E-2)	-	8E-14	9E-8	9E-7
93	Neptunium-236m (22.5 h)	W, all compounds	3E+3	3E+1	1E-8	-	-	-
			Bone surf	Bone surf				
			(4E+3)	(7E+1)	-	1E-10	5E-5	5E-4
93	Neptunium-237	W, all compounds	5E-1	4E-3	2E-12	-	-	-
			Bone surf	Bone surf				
			(1E+0)	(1E-2)	-	1E-14	2E-8	2E-7

Atomic No.	Radionuclide	Class	Table 1 Occupational Values Col. 1 Oral Ingestion ALI (μCi)	Table 1 Occupational Values Col. 2 Inhalation ALI (μCi)	Table 1 Occupational Values Col. 3 Inhalation DAC (μCi/ml)	Table 2 Effluent Concentrations Col. 1 Air (μCi/ml)	Table 2 Effluent Concentrations Col. 2 Water (μCi/ml)	Table 3 Releases to Sewers Monthly Average Concentration (μCi/ml)
93	Neptunium-238	W, all compounds	1E+3	6E+1	3E-8	-	2E-5	2E-4
			-	Bone surf (2E+2)	-	2E-10	-	-
93	Neptunium-239	W, all compounds	2E+3	2E+3	9E-7	3E-9	-	-
			LLI wall (2E+3)	-	-	-	2E-5	2E-4
93	Neptunium-240[2]	W, all compounds	2E+4	8E+4	3E-5	1E-7	3E-4	3E-3
94	Plutonium-234	W, all compounds except PuO_2	8E+3	2E+2	9E-8	3E-10	1E-4	1E-3
		Y, PuO_2	-	2E+2	8E-8	3E-10	-	-
94	Plutonium-235[2]	W, see ^{234}Pu	9E+5	3E+6	1E-3	4E-6	1E-2	1E-1
		Y, see ^{234}Pu	-	3E+6	1E-3	3E-6	-	-
94	Plutonium-236	W, see ^{234}Pu	2E+0	2E-2	8E-12	-	-	-
			Bone surf (4E+0)	Bone surf (4E-2)	-	5E-14	6E-8	6E-7
		Y, see ^{234}Pu	-	4E-2	2E-11	6E-14	-	-
94	Plutonium-237	W, see ^{234}Pu	1E+4	3E+3	1E-6	5E-9	2E-4	2E-3
		Y, see ^{234}Pu	-	3E+3	1E-6	4E-9	-	-
94	Plutonium-238	W, see ^{234}Pu	9E-1	7E-3	3E-12	-	-	-
			Bone surf (2E+0)	Bone surf (1E-2)	-	2E-14	2E-8	2E-7
		Y, see ^{234}Pu	-	2E-2	8E-12	2E-14	-	-
94	Plutonium-239	W, see ^{234}Pu	8E-1	6E-3	3E-12	-	-	-
			Bone surf (1E+0)	Bone surf (1E-2)	-	2E-14	2E-8	2E-7
		Y, see ^{234}Pu	-	2E-2	7E-12	-	-	-
			-	Bone surf (2E-2)	-	2E-14	-	-
94	Plutonium-240	W, see ^{234}Pu	8E-1	6E-3	3E-12	-	-	-
			Bone surf (1E+0)	Bone surf (1E-2)	-	2E-14	2E-8	2E-7
		Y, see ^{234}Pu	-	2E-2	7E-12	-	-	-
			-	Bone surf (2E-2)	-	2E-14	-	-
94	Plutonium-241	W, see ^{234}Pu	4E+1	3E-1	1E-10	-	-	-
			Bone surf (7E+1)	Bone surf (6E-1)	-	8E-13	1E-6	1E-5
		Y, see ^{234}Pu	-	8E-1	3E-10	-	-	-
			-	Bone surf (1E+0)	-	1E-12	-	-

Atomic No.	Radionuclide	Class	Table 1 Occupational Values Col. 1 Oral Ingestion ALI (μCi)	Table 1 Col. 2 Inhalation ALI (μCi)	Table 1 Col. 3 Inhalation DAC (μCi/ml)	Table 2 Effluent Concentrations Col. 1 Air (μCi/ml)	Table 2 Col. 2 Water (μCi/ml)	Table 3 Releases to Sewers Monthly Average Concentration (μCi/ml)
94	Plutonium-242	W, see ^{234}Pu	8E-1	7E-3	3E-12	-	-	-
			Bone surf	Bone surf				
			(1E+0)	(1E-2)	-	2E-14	2E-8	2E-7
		Y, see ^{234}Pu	-	2E-2	7E-12	-	-	-
				Bone surf				
			-	(2E-2)	-	2E-14	-	-
94	Plutonium-243	W, see ^{234}Pu	2E+4	4E+4	2E-5	5E-8	2E-4	2E-3
		Y, see ^{234}Pu	-	4E+4	2E-5	5E-8	-	-
94	Plutonium-244	W, see ^{234}Pu	8E-1	7E-3	3E-12	-	-	-
			Bone surf	Bone surf				
			(2E+0)	(1E-2)	-	2E-14	2E-8	2E-7
		Y, see ^{234}Pu	-	2E-2	7E-12	-	-	-
				Bone surf				
			-	(2E-2)	-	2E-14	-	-
94	Plutonium-245	W, see ^{234}Pu	2E+3	5E+3	2E-6	6E-9	3E-5	3E-4
		Y, see ^{234}Pu	-	4E+3	2E-6	6E-9	-	-
94	Plutonium-246	W, see ^{234}Pu	4E+2	3E+2	1E-7	4E-10	-	-
			LLI wall					
			(4E+2)	-	-	-	6E-6	6E-5
		Y, see ^{234}Pu	-	3E+2	1E-7	4E-10	-	-
95	Americium-237[2]	W, all compounds	8E+4	3E+5	1E-4	4E-7	1E-3	1E-2
95	Americium-238[2]	W, all compounds	4E+4	3E+3	1E-6	-	5E-4	5E-3
				Bone surf				
			-	(6E+3)	-	9E-9	-	-
95	Americium-239	W, all compounds	5E+3	1E+4	5E-6	2E-8	7E-5	7E-4
95	Americium-240	W, all compounds	2E+3	3E+3	1E-6	4E-9	3E-5	3E-4
95	Americium-241	W, all compounds	8E-1	6E-3	3E-12	-	-	-
			Bone surf	Bone surf				
			(1E+0)	(1E-2)	-	2E-14	2E-8	2E-7
95	Americium-242m	W, all compounds	8E-1	6E-3	3E-12	-	-	-
			Bone surf	Bone surf				
			(1E+0)	(1E-2)	-	2E-14	2E-8	2E-7
95	Americium-242	W, all compounds	4E+3	8E+1	4E-8	-	5E-5	5E-4
				Bone surf				
			-	(9E+1)	-	1E-10	-	-
95	Americium-243	W, all compounds	8E-1	6E-3	3E-12	-	-	-
			Bone surf	Bone surf				
			(1E+0)	(1E-2)	-	2E-14	2E-8	2E-7
95	Americium-244m[2]	W, all compounds	6E+4	4E+3	2E-6	-	-	-
			St. wall	Bone surf				
			(8E+4)	(7E+3)	-	1E-8	1E-3	1E-2
95	Americium-244	W, all compounds	3E+3	2E+2	8E-8	-	4E-5	4E-4
				Bone surf				
			-	(3E+2)	-	4E-10	-	-
95	Americium-245	W, all compounds	3E+4	8E+4	3E-5	1E-7	4E-4	4E-3

			Table 1 Occupational Values			Table 2 Effluent Concentrations		Table 3 Releases to Sewers
			Col. 1	Col. 2	Col. 3	Col. 1	Col. 2	
			Oral Ingestion	Inhalation				Monthly Average
Atomic No.	Radionuclide	Class	ALI (μCi)	ALI (μCi)	DAC (μCi/ml)	Air (μCi/ml)	Water (μCi/ml)	Concentration (μCi/ml)
95	Americium-246m[2]	W, all compounds	5E+4	2E+5	8E-5	3E-7	-	-
			St. wall (6E+4)	-	-	-	8E-4	8E-3
95	Americium-246[2]	W, all compounds	3E+4	1E+5	4E-5	1E-7	4E-4	4E-3
96	Curium-238	W, all compounds	2E+4	1E+3	5E-7	2E-9	2E-4	2E-3
96	Curium-240	W, all compounds	6E+1	6E-1	2E-10	-	-	-
			Bone surf (8E+1)	Bone surf (6E-1)	-	9E-13	1E-6	1E-5
96	Curium-241	W, all compounds	1E+3	3E+1	1E-8	-	2E-5	2E-4
			-	Bone surf (4E+1)	-	5E-11	-	-
96	Curium-242	W, all compounds	3E+1	3E-1	1E-10	-	-	-
			Bone surf (5E+1)	Bone surf (3E-1)	-	4E-13	7E-7	7E-6
96	Curium-243	W, all compounds	1E+0	9E-3	4E-12	-	-	-
			Bone surf (2E+0)	Bone surf (2E-2)	-	2E-14	3E-8	3E-7
96	Curium-244	W, all compounds	1E+0	1E-2	5E-12	-	-	-
			Bone surf (3E+0)	Bone surf (2E-2)	-	3E-14	3E-8	3E-7
96	Curium-245	W, all compounds	7E-1	6E-3	3E-12	-	-	-
			Bone surf (1E+0)	Bone surf (1E-2)	-	2E-14	2E-8	2E-7
96	Curium-246	W, all compounds	7E-1	6E-3	3E-12	-	-	-
			Bone surf (1E+0)	Bone surf (1E-2)	-	2E-14	2E-8	2E-7
96	Curium-247	W, all compounds	8E-1	6E-3	3E-12	-	-	-
			Bone surf (1E+0)	Bone surf (1E-2)	-	2E-14	2E-8	2E-7
96	Curium-248	W, all compounds	2E-1	2E-3	7E-13	-	-	-
			Bone surf (4E-1)	Bone surf (3E-3)	-	4E-15	5E-9	5E-8
96	Curium-249[2]	W, all compounds	5E+4	2E+4	7E-6	-	7E-4	7E-3
			-	Bone surf (3E+4)	-	4E-8	-	-
96	Curium-250	W, all compounds	4E-2	3E-4	1E-13	-	-	-
			Bone surf (6E-2)	Bone surf (5E-4)	-	8E-16	9E-10	9E-9
97	Berkelium-245	W, all compounds	2E+3	1E+3	5E-7	2E-9	3E-5	3E-4
97	Berkelium-246	W, all compounds	3E+3	3E+3	1E-6	4E-9	4E-5	4E-4
97	Berkelium-247	W, all compounds	5E-1	4E-3	2E-12	-	-	-
			Bone surf (1E+0)	Bone surf (9E-3)	-	1E-14	2E-8	2E-7
97	Berkelium-249	W, all compounds	2E+2	2E+0	7E-10	-	-	-
			Bone surf (5E+2)	Bone surf (4E+0)	-	5E-12	6E-6	6E-5

Atomic No.	Radionuclide	Class	Table 1 Occupational Values Col. 1 Oral Ingestion ALI (μCi)	Table 1 Col. 2 Inhalation ALI (μCi)	Table 1 Col. 3 Inhalation DAC (μCi/ml)	Table 2 Effluent Concentrations Col. 1 Air (μCi/ml)	Table 2 Col. 2 Water (μCi/ml)	Table 3 Releases to Sewers Monthly Average Concentration (μCi/ml)
97	Berkelium-250	W, all compounds	9E+3	3E+2	1E-7	-	1E-4	1E-3
			-	Bone surf (7E+2)	-	1E-9	-	-
98	Californium-244[2]	W, all compounds except those given for Y	3E+4	6E+2	2E-7	8E-10	-	-
			St. wall (3E+4)	-	-	-	4E-4	4E-3
		Y, oxides and hydroxides	-	6E+2	2E-7	8E-10	-	-
98	Californium-246	W, see ^{244}Cf	4E+2	9E+0	4E-9	1E-11	5E-6	5E-5
		Y, see ^{244}Cf	-	9E+0	4E-9	2E-11	-	-
98	Californium-248	W, see ^{244}Cf	8E+0	6E-2	3E-11	-	-	-
			Bone surf (2E+1)	Bone surf (1E-1)	-	2E-13	2E-7	2E-6
		Y, see ^{244}Cf	-	1E-1	4E-11	1E-13	-	-
98	Californium-249	W, see ^{244}Cf	5E-1	4E-3	2E-12	-	-	-
			Bone surf (1E+0)	Bone surf (9E-3)	-	1E-14	2E-8	2E-7
		Y, see ^{244}Cf	-	1E-2	4E-12	-	-	-
			-	Bone surf (1E-2)	-	2E-14	-	-
98	Californium-250	W, see ^{244}Cf	1E+0	9E-3	4E-12	-	-	-
			Bone surf (2E+0)	Bone surf (2E-2)	-	3E-14	3E-8	3E-7
		Y, see ^{244}Cf	-	3E-2	1E-11	4E-14	-	-
98	Californium-251	W, see ^{244}Cf	5E-1	4E-3	2E-12	-	-	-
			Bone surf (1E+0)	Bone surf (9E-3)	-	1E-14	2E-8	2E-7
		Y, see ^{244}Cf	-	1E-2	4E-12	-	-	-
			-	Bone surf (1E-2)	-	2E-14	-	-
98	Californium-252	W, see ^{244}Cf	2E+0	2E-2	8E-12	-	-	-
			Bone surf (5E+0)	Bone surf (4E-2)	-	5E-14	7E-8	7E-7
		Y, see ^{244}Cf	-	3E-2	1E-11	5E-14	-	-
98	Californium-253	W, see ^{244}Cf	2E+2	2E+0	8E-10	3E-12	-	-
			Bone surf (4E+2)	-	-	-	5E-6	5E-5
		Y, see ^{244}Cf	-	2E+0	7E-10	2E-12	-	-
98	Californium-254	W, see ^{244}Cf	2E+0	2E-2	9E-12	3E-14	3E-8	3E-7
		Y, see ^{244}Cf	-	2E-2	7E-12	2E-14	-	-
99	Einsteinium-250	W, all compounds	4E+4	5E+2	2E-7	-	6E-4	6E-3
			-	Bone surf (1E+3)	-	2E-9	-	-
99	Einsteinium-251	W, all compounds	7E+3	9E+2	4E-7	-	1E-4	1E-3
			-	Bone surf (1E+3)	-	2E-9	-	-
99	Einsteinium-253	W, all compounds	2E+2	1E+0	6E-10	2E-12	2E-6	2E-5

Atomic No.	Radionuclide	Class	Table 1 Occupational Values Col. 1 Oral Ingestion ALI (μCi)	Table 1 Col. 2 Inhalation ALI (μCi)	Table 1 Col. 3 Inhalation DAC (μCi/ml)	Table 2 Effluent Concentrations Col. 1 Air (μCi/ml)	Table 2 Col. 2 Water (μCi/ml)	Table 3 Releases to Sewers Monthly Average Concentration (μCi/ml)
99	Einsteinium-254m	W, all compounds	3E+2	1E+1	4E-9	1E-11	-	-
			LLI wall (3E+2)	-	-	-	4E-6	4E-5
99	Einsteinium-254	W, all compounds	8E+0	7E-2	3E-11	-	-	-
			Bone surf (2E+1)	Bone surf (1E-1)	-	2E-13	2E-7	2E-6
100	Fermium-252	W, all compounds	5E+2	1E+1	5E-9	2E-11	6E-6	6E-5
100	Fermium-253	W, all compounds	1E+3	1E+1	4E-9	1E-11	1E-5	1E-4
100	Fermium-254	W, all compounds	3E+3	9E+1	4E-8	1E-10	4E-5	4E-4
100	Fermium-255	W, all compounds	5E+2	2E+1	9E-9	3E-11	7E-6	7E-5
100	Fermium-257	W, all compounds	2E+1	2E-1	7E-11	-	-	-
			Bone surf (4E+1)	Bone surf (2E-1)	-	3E-13	5E-7	5E-6
101	Mendelevium-257	W, all compounds	7E+3	8E+1	4E-8	-	1E-4	1E-3
			-	Bone surf (9E+1)	-	1E-10	-	-
101	Mendelevium-258	W, all compounds	3E+1	2E-1	1E-10	-	-	-
			Bone surf (5E+1)	Bone surf (3E-1)	-	5E-13	6E-7	6E-6
-	Any single radionuclide not listed above with decay mode other than alpha emission or spontaneous fission and with radioactive half-life less than 2 hours	Submersion[1]	-	2E+2	1E-7	1E-9	-	-
-	Any single radionuclide not listed above with decay mode other than alpha emission or spontaneous fission and with radioactive half-life greater than 2 hours		-	2E-1	1E-10	1E-12	1E-8	1E-7
-	Any single radionuclide not listed above that decays by alpha emission or spontaneous fission, or any mixture for which either the identity or the concentration of any radionuclide in the mixture is not known		-	4E-4	2E-13	1E-15	2E-9	2E-8

FOOTNOTES:

[1]"Submersion" means that values given are for submersion in a hemispherical semi-infinite cloud of airborne material.

[2]These radionuclides have radiological half-lives of less than 2 hours. The total effective dose equivalent received during operations with these radionuclides might include a significant contribution from external exposure. The DAC values for all radionuclides, other than those designated Class "Submersion," are based upon the committed effective dose equivalent due to the intake of the radionuclide into the body and do NOT include potentially significant contributions to dose equivalent from external exposures. The licensee may substitute 1E-7 μCi/ml for the listed DAC to account for the submersion dose prospectively, but should use individual monitoring devices or other radiation measuring instruments that measure external exposure to demonstrate compliance with the limits. (See § 20.1203.)

[3]For soluble mixtures of U-238, U-234, and U-235 in air, chemical toxicity may be the limiting factor (see § 20.1201(e)). If the percent by weight (enrichment) of U-235 is not greater than 5, the concentration value for a 40-hour workweek is 0.2 milligrams uranium per cubic meter of air average. For any enrichment, the product of the average concentration and time of exposure during a 40-hour workweek shall not exceed 8E-3 (SA) μCi-hr/ml, where SA is the specific activity of the uranium inhaled. The specific activity for natural uranium is 6.77E-7 curies per gram U. The specific activity for other mixtures of U-238, U-235, and U-234, if not known, shall be:

SA = 3.6E-7 curies/gram U U-depleted

SA = $[0.4 + 0.38 \text{ (enrichment)} + 0.0034 \text{ (enrichment)}^2]$ E-6 , enrichment $\geq$ 0.72

where enrichment is the percentage by weight of U-235, expressed as percent.

NOTE:

1. If the identity of each radionuclide in a mixture is known but the concentration of one or more of the radionuclides in the mixture is not known, the DAC for the mixture shall be the most restrictive DAC of any radionuclide in the mixture.

2. If the identity of each radionuclide in the mixture is not known, but it is known that certain radionuclides specified in this appendix are not present in the mixture, the inhalation ALI, DAC, and effluent and sewage concentrations for the mixture are the lowest values specified in this appendix for any radionuclide that is not known to be absent from the mixture; or

	Table 1 Occupational Values			Table 2 Effluent Concentrations		Table 3 Releases to Sewers
	Col. 1	Col. 2	Col. 3	Col. 1	Col. 2	
	Oral Ingestion	Inhalation				Monthly Average
Radionuclide	ALI (μCi)	ALI (μCi)	DAC (μCi/ml)	Air (μCi/ml)	Water (μCi/ml)	Concentration (μCi/ml)
If it is known that Ac-227-D and Cm-250-W are not present	-	7E-4	3E-13	-	-	-
If, in addition, it is known that Ac-227-W,Y, Th-229-W,Y, Th-230-W, Th-232-W,Y, Pa-231-W,Y, Np-237-W, Pu-239-W, Pu-240-W, Pu-242-W, Am-241-W, Am-242m-W, Am-243-W, Cm-245-W, Cm-246-W, Cm-247-W, Cm-248-W, Bk-247-W, Cf-249-W, and Cf-251-W are not present	-	7E-3	3E-12	-	-	-
If, in addition, it is known that Sm-146-W, Sm-147-W, Gd-148-D,W, Gd-152-D,W, Th-228-W,Y, Th-230-Y, U-232-Y, U-233-Y, U-234-Y, U-235-Y, U-236-Y, U-238-Y, Np-236-W, Pu-236-W,Y, Pu-238-W,Y, Pu-239-Y, Pu-240-Y, Pu-242-Y, Pu-244-W,Y, Cm-243-W, Cm-244-W, Cf-248-W, Cf-249-Y, Cf-250-W,Y, Cf-251-Y, Cf-252-W,Y, and Cf-254-W,Y are not present	-	7E-2	3E-11	-	-	-
If, in addition, it is known that Pb-210-D, Bi-210m-W, Po-210-D,W, Ra-223-W, Ra-225-W, Ra-226-W, Ac-225-D,W,Y, Th-227-W,Y, U-230-D,W,Y, U-232-D,W, Pu-241-W, Cm-240-W, Cm-242-W, Cf-248-Y, Es-254-W, Fm-257-W, and Md-258-W are not present	-	7E-1	3E-10	-	-	-

Radionuclide	Table 1 Occupational Values			Table 2 Effluent Concentrations		Table 3 Releases to Sewers
	Col. 1	Col. 2	Col. 3	Col. 1	Col. 2	
	Oral Ingestion ALI (μCi)	Inhalation ALI (μCi)	Inhalation DAC (μCi/ml)	Air (μCi/ml)	Water (μCi/ml)	Monthly Average Concentration (μCi/ml)
If, in addition, it is known that Si-32-Y, Ti-44-Y, Fe-60-D, Sr-90-Y, Zr-93-D, Cd-113m-D, Cd-113-D, In-115-D,W, La-138-D, Lu-176-W, Hf-178m-D,W, Hf-182-D,W, Bi-210m-D, Ra-224-W, Ra-228-W, Ac-226-D,W,Y, Pa-230-W,Y, U-233-D,W, U-234-D,W, U-235-D,W, U-236-D,W, U-238-D,W, Pu-241-Y, Bk-249-W, Cf-253-W,Y, and Es-253-W are not present	-	7E+0	3E-9	-	-	-
If it is known that Ac-227-D,W,Y, Th-229-W,Y, Th-232-W,Y, Pa-231-W,Y, Cm-248-W, and Cm-250-W are not present -	-	-		1E-14	-	-
If, in addition, it is known that Sm-146-W, Gd-148-D,W, Gd-152-D, Th-228-W,Y, Th-230-W,Y, U-232-Y, U-233-Y, U-234-Y, U-235-Y, U-236-Y, U-238-Y, U-Nat-Y, Np-236-W, Np-237-W, Pu-236-W,Y, Pu-238-W,Y, Pu-239-W,Y, Pu-240-W,Y, Pu-242-W,Y, Pu-244-W,Y, Am-241-W, Am-242m-W, Am-243-W, Cm-243-W, Cm-244-W, Cm-245-W, Cm-246-W, Cm-247-W, Bk-247-W, Cf-249-W,Y, Cf-250-W,Y, Cf-251-W,Y, Cf-252-W,Y, and Cf-254-W,Y are not present			-	1E-13	-	-
If, in addition, it is known that Sm-147-W, Gd-152-W, Pb-210-D, Bi-210m-W, Po-210-D,W, Ra-223-W, Ra-225-W, Ra-226-W, Ac-225-D,W,Y, Th-227-W,Y, U-230-D,W,Y, U-232-D,W, U-Nat-W, Pu-241-W, Cm-240-W, Cm-242-W, Cf-248-W,Y, Es-254-W, Fm-257-W, and Md-258-W are not present			-	1E-12	-	-
If, in addition it is known that Fe-60, Sr-90, Cd-113m, Cd-113, In-115, I-129, Cs-134, Sm-145, Sm-147, Gd-148, Gd-152, Hg-194 (organic), Bi-210m, Ra-223, Ra-224, Ra-225, Ac-225, Th-228, Th-230, U-233, U-234, U-235, U-236, U-238, U-Nat, Cm-242, Cf-248, Es-254, Fm-257, and Md-258 are not present	-	-	-	-	1E-6	1E-5

3 If a mixture of radionuclides consists of uranium and its daughters in ore dust (10 μm AMAD particle distribution assumed) prior to chemical separation of the uranium from the ore, the following values may be used for the DAC of the mixture: 6E-11 μCi of gross alpha activity from uranium-238, uranium-234, thorium-230, and radium-226 per milliliter of air; 3E-11 μCi of natural uranium per milliliter of air; or 45 micrograms of natural uranium per cubic meter of air.

4 If the identity and concentration of each radionuclide in a mixture are known, the limiting values should be derived as follows: determine, for each radionuclide in the mixture, the ratio between the concentration present in the mixture and the concentration otherwise established in Appendix B for the specific radionuclide when not in a mixture. The sum of such ratios for all of the radionuclides in the mixture may not exceed "1" (i.e., "unity").

Example: If radionuclides "A," "B," and "C" are present in concentrations C_A, C_B, and C_C, and if the applicable DACs are DAC_A, DAC_B, and DAC_C, respectively, then the concentrations shall be limited so that the following relationship exists:

$$\frac{C_A}{DAC_A} + \frac{C_B}{DAC_B} + \frac{C_C}{DAC_C} < 1$$

[56 FR 23409, May 21, 1991; 56 FR 61352, Dec. 3, 1991, as amended at 57 FR 57879, Dec. 8, 1992. Redesignated at 58 FR 67659, Dec. 22, 1993, as amended at 71 FR 15007, Mar. 27, 2006; 72 FR 55922, Oct. 1, 2007; 75 FR 73938, Nov. 30, 2010]

Appendix C to Part 20—Quantities[1] of Licensed Material Requiring Labeling

Radionuclide	Quantity (µCi)
Hydrogen-3	1,000
Beryllium-7	1,000
Beryllium-10	1
Carbon-11	1,000
Carbon-14	100
Fluorine-18	1,000
Sodium-22	10
Sodium-24	100
Magnesium-28	100
Aluminum-26	10
Silicon-31	1,000
Silicon-32	1
Phosphorus-32	10
Phosphorus-33	100
Sulfur-35	100
Chlorine-36	10
Chlorine-38	1,000
Chlorine-39	1,000
Argon-39	1,000
Argon-41	1,000
Potassium-40	100
Potassium-42	1,000
Potassium-43	1,000
Potassium-44	1,000
Potassium-45	1,000
Calcium-41	100
Calcium-45	100
Calcium-47	100
Scandium-43	1,000
Scandium-44m	100
Scandium-44	100
Scandium-46	10
Scandium-47	100
Scandium-48	100
Scandium-49	1,000
Titanium-44	1
Titanium-45	1,000
Vanadium-47	1,000
Vanadium-48	100
Vanadium-49	1,000
Chromium-48	1,000
Chromium-49	1,000
Chromium-51	1,000
Manganese-51	1,000
Manganese-52m	1,000
Manganese-52	100
Manganese-53	1,000
Manganese-54	100
Manganese-56	1,000
Iron-52	100
Iron-55	100
Iron-59	10
Iron-60	1
Cobalt-55	100
Cobalt-56	10
Cobalt-57	100
Cobalt-58m	1,000
Cobalt-58	100
Cobalt-60m	1,000
Cobalt-60	1
Cobalt-61	1,000
Cobalt-62m	1,000
Nickel-56	100
Nickel-57	100
Nickel-59	100
Nickel-63	100
Nickel-65	1,000
Nickel-66	10
Copper-60	1,000
Copper-61	1,000
Copper-64	1,000
Copper-67	1,000
Zinc-62	100
Zinc-63	1,000
Zinc-65	10
Zinc-69m	100
Zinc-69	1,000
Zinc-71m	1,000
Zinc-72	100
Gallium-65	1,000
Gallium-66	100
Gallium-67	1,000
Gallium-68	1,000
Gallium-70	1,000
Gallium-72	100
Gallium-73	1,000
Germanium-66	1,000
Germanium-67	1,000
Germanium-68	10
Germanium-69	1,000
Germanium-71	1,000
Germanium-75	1,000
Germanium-77	1,000
Germanium-78	1,000
Arsenic-69	1,000
Arsenic-70	1,000
Arsenic-71	100
Arsenic-72	100
Arsenic-73	100
Arsenic-74	100
Arsenic-76	100
Arsenic-77	100
Arsenic-78	1,000
Selenium-70	1,000
Selenium-73m	1,000
Selenium-73	100
Selenium-75	100
Selenium-79	100
Selenium-81m	1,000
Selenium-81	1,000
Selenium-83	1,000
Bromine-74m	1,000
Bromine-74	1,000
Bromine-75	1,000
Bromine-76	100
Bromine-77	1,000
Bromine-80m	1,000
Bromine-80	1,000
Bromine-82	100
Bromine-83	1,000
Bromine-84	1,000
Krypton-74	1,000
Krypton-76	1,000
Krypton-77	1,000
Krypton-79	1,000
Krypton-81	1,000
Krypton-83m	1,000
Krypton-85m	1,000
Krypton-85	1,000
Krypton-87	1,000
Krypton-88	1,000
Rubidium-79	1,000
Rubidium-81m	1,000
Rubidium-81	1,000
Rubidium-82m	1,000
Rubidium-83	100
Rubidium-84	100
Rubidium-86	100
Rubidium-87	100
Rubidium-88	1,000
Rubidium-89	1,000
Strontium-80	100

Radionuclide	Quantity (μCi)
Strontium-81	1,000
Strontium-83	100
Strontium-85m	1,000
Strontium-85	100
Strontium-87m	1,000
Strontium-89	10
Strontium-90	0.1
Strontium-91	100
Strontium-92	100
Yttrium-86m	1,000
Yttrium-86	100
Yttrium-87	100
Yttrium-88	10
Yttrium-90m	1,000
Yttrium-90	10
Yttrium-91m	1,000
Yttrium-91	10
Yttrium-92	100
Yttrium-93	100
Yttrium-94	1,000
Yttrium-95	1,000
Zirconium-86	100
Zirconium-88	10
Zirconium-89	100
Zirconium-93	1
Zirconium-95	10
Zirconium-97	100
Niobium-88	1,000
Niobium-89m (66 min)	1,000
Niobium-89 (122 min)	1,000
Niobium-90	100
Niobium-93m	10
Niobium-94	1
Niobium-95m	100
Niobium-95	100
Niobium-96	100
Niobium-97	1,000
Niobium-98	1,000
Molybdenum-90	100
Molybdenum-93m	100
Molybdenum-93	10
Molybdenum-99	100
Molybdenum-101	1,000
Technetium-93m	1,000
Technetium-93	1,000
Technetium-94m	1,000
Technetium-94	1,000
Technetium-96m	1,000
Technetium-96	100
Technetium-97m	100
Technetium-97	1,000
Technetium-98	10
Technetium-99m	1,000
Technetium-99	100
Technetium-101	1,000
Technetium-104	1,000
Ruthenium-94	1,000
Ruthenium-97	1,000
Ruthenium-103	100
Ruthenium-105	1,000
Ruthenium-106	1
Rhodium-99m	1,000
Rhodium-99	100
Rhodium-100	100
Rhodium-101m	1,000
Rhodium-101	10
Rhodium-102m	10
Rhodium-102	10
Rhodium-103m	1,000
Rhodium-105	100
Rhodium-106m	1,000
Rhodium-107	1,000
Palladium-100	100

Radionuclide	Quantity (μCi)
Palladium-101	1,000
Palladium-103	100
Palladium-107	10
Palladium-109	100
Silver-102	1,000
Silver-103	1,000
Silver-104m	1,000
Silver-104	1,000
Silver-105	100
Silver-106m	100
Silver-106	1,000
Silver-108m	1
Silver-110m	10
Silver-111	100
Silver-112	100
Silver-115	1,000
Cadmium-104	1,000
Cadmium-107	1,000
Cadmium-109	1
Cadmium-113m	0.1
Cadmium-113	100
Cadmium-115m	10
Cadmium-115	100
Cadmium-117m	1,000
Cadmium-117	1,000
Indium-109	1,000
Indium-110 (69.1min.)	1,000
Indium-110 (4.9h)	1,000
Indium-111	100
Indium-112	1,000
Indium-113m	1,000
Indium-114m	10
Indium-115m	1,000
Indium-115	100
Indium-116m	1,000
Indium-117m	1,000
Indium-117	1,000
Indium-119m	1,000
Tin-110	100
Tin-111	1,000
Tin-113	100
Tin-117m	100
Tin-119m	100
Tin-121m	100
Tin-121	1,000
Tin-123m	1,000
Tin-123	10
Tin-125	10
Tin-126	10
Tin-127	1,000
Tin-128	1,000
Antimony-115	1,000
Antimony-116m	1,000
Antimony-116	1,000
Antimony-117	1,000
Antimony-118m	1,000
Antimony-119	1,000
Antimony-120 (16min.)	1,000
Antimony-120 (5.76d)	100
Antimony-122	100
Antimony-124m	1,000
Antimony-124	10
Antimony-125	100
Antimony-126m	1,000
Antimony-126	100
Antimony-127	100
Antimony-128 (10.4min.)	1,000
Antimony-128 (9.01h)	100
Antimony-129	100
Antimony-130	1,000
Antimony-131	1,000
Tellurium-116	1,000

Radionuclide	Quantity (μCi)
Tellurium-121m	10
Tellurium-121	100
Tellurium-123m	10
Tellurium-123	100
Tellurium-125m	10
Tellurium-127m	10
Tellurium-127	1,000
Tellurium-129m	10
Tellurium-129	1,000
Tellurium-131m	10
Tellurium-131	100
Tellurium-132	10
Tellurium-133m	100
Tellurium-133	1,000
Tellurium-134	1,000
Iodine-120m	1,000
Iodine-120	100
Iodine-121	1,000
Iodine-123	100
Iodine-124	10
Iodine-125	1
Iodine-126	1
Iodine-128	1,000
Iodine-129	1
Iodine-130	10
Iodine-131	1
Iodine-132m	100
Iodine-132	100
Iodine-133	10
Iodine-134	1,000
Iodine-135	100
Xenon-120	1,000
Xenon-121	1,000
Xenon-122	1,000
Xenon-123	1,000
Xenon-125	1,000
Xenon-127	1,000
Xenon-129m	1,000
Xenon-131m	1,000
Xenon-133m	1,000
Xenon-133	1,000
Xenon-135m	1,000
Xenon-135	1,000
Xenon-138	1,000
Cesium-125	1,000
Cesium-127	1,000
Cesium-129	1,000
Cesium-130	1,000
Cesium-131	1,000
Cesium-132	100
Cesium-134m	1,000
Cesium-134	10
Cesium-135m	1,000
Cesium-135	100
Cesium-136	10
Cesium-137	10
Cesium-138	1,000
Barium-126	1,000
Barium-128	100
Barium-131m	1,000
Barium-131	100
Barium-133m	100
Barium-133	100
Barium-135m	100
Barium-139	1,000
Barium-140	100
Barium-141	1,000
Barium-142	1,000
Lanthanum-131	1,000
Lanthanum-132	100
Lanthanum-135	1,000
Lanthanum-137	10
Lanthanum-138	100
Lanthanum-140	100
Lanthanum-141	100
Lanthanum-142	1,000
Lanthanum-143	1,000
Cerium-134	100
Cerium-135	100
Cerium-137m	100
Cerium-137	1,000
Cerium-139	100
Cerium-141	100
Cerium-143	100
Cerium-144	1
Praseodymium-136	1,000
Praseodymium-137	1,000
Praseodymium-138m	1,000
Praseodymium-139	1,000
Praseodymium-142m	1,000
Praseodymium-142	100
Praseodymium-143	100
Praseodymium-144	1,000
Praseodymium-145	100
Praseodymium-147	1,000
Neodymium-136	1,000
Neodymium-138	100
Neodymium-139m	1,000
Neodymium-139	1,000
Neodymium-141	1,000
Neodymium-147	100
Neodymium-149	1,000
Neodymium-151	1,000
Promethium-141	1,000
Promethium-143	100
Promethium-144	10
Promethium-145	10
Promethium-146	1
Promethium-147	10
Promethium-148m	10
Promethium-148	10
Promethium-149	100
Promethium-150	1,000
Promethium-151	100
Samarium-141m	1,000
Samarium-141	1,000
Samarium-142	1,000
Samarium-145	100
Samarium-146	1
Samarium-147	100
Samarium-151	10
Samarium-153	100
Samarium-155	1,000
Samarium-156	1,000
Europium-145	100
Europium-146	100
Europium-147	100
Europium-148	10
Europium-149	100
Europium-150 (12.62h)	100
Europium-150 (34.2y)	1
Europium-152m	100
Europium-152	1
Europium-154	1
Europium-155	10
Europium-156	100
Europium-157	100
Europium-158	1,000
Gadolinium-145	1,000
Gadolinium-146	10
Gadolinium-147	100
Gadolinium-148	0.001
Gadolinium-149	100
Gadolinium-151	10
Gadolinium-152	100
Gadolinium-153	10

Radionuclide	Quantity (μCi)
Gadolinium-159	100
Terbium-147	1,000
Terbium-149	100
Terbium-150	1,000
Terbium-151	100
Terbium-153	1,000
Terbium-154	100
Terbium-155	1,000
Terbium-156m (5.0h)	1,000
Terbium-156m (24.4h)	1,000
Terbium-156	100
Terbium-157	10
Terbium-158	1
Terbium-160	10
Terbium-161	100
Dysprosium-155	1,000
Dysprosium-157	1,000
Dysprosium-159	100
Dysprosium-165	1,000
Dysprosium-166	100
Holmium-155	1,000
Holmium-157	1,000
Holmium-159	1,000
Holmium-161	1,000
Holmium-162m	1,000
Holmium-162	1,000
Holmium-164m	1,000
Holmium-164	1,000
Holmium-166m	1
Holmium-166	100
Holmium-167	1,000
Erbium-161	1,000
Erbium-165	1,000
Erbium-169	100
Erbium-171	100
Erbium-172	100
Thulium-162	1,000
Thulium-166	100
Thulium-167	100
Thulium-170	10
Thulium-171	10
Thulium-172	100
Thulium-173	100
Thulium-175	1,000
Ytterbium-162	1,000
Ytterbium-166	100
Ytterbium-167	1,000
Ytterbium-169	100
Ytterbium-175	100
Ytterbium-177	1,000
Ytterbium-178	1,000
Lutetium-169	100
Lutetium-170	100
Lutetium-171	100
Lutetium-172	100
Lutetium-173	10
Lutetium-174m	10
Lutetium-174	10
Lutetium-176m	1,000
Lutetium-176	100
Lutetium-177m	10
Lutetium-177	100
Lutetium-178m	1,000
Lutetium-178	1,000
Lutetium-179	1,000
Hafnium-170	100
Hafnium-172	1
Hafnium-173	1,000
Hafnium-175	100
Hafnium-177m	1,000
Hafnium-178m	0.1
Hafnium-179m	10
Hafnium-180m	1,000
Hafnium-181	10
Hafnium-182m	1,000
Hafnium-182	0.1
Hafnium-183	1,000
Hafnium-184	100
Tantalum-172	1,000
Tantalum-173	1,000
Tantalum-174	1,000
Tantalum-175	1,000
Tantalum-176	100
Tantalum-177	1,000
Tantalum-178	1,000
Tantalum-179	100
Tantalum-180m	1,000
Tantalum-180	100
Tantalum-182m	1,000
Tantalum-182	10
Tantalum-183	100
Tantalum-184	100
Tantalum-185	1,000
Tantalum-186	1,000
Tungsten-176	1,000
Tungsten-177	1,000
Tungsten-178	1,000
Tungsten-179	1,000
Tungsten-181	1,000
Tungsten-185	100
Tungsten-187	100
Tungsten-188	10
Rhenium-177	1,000
Rhenium-178	1,000
Rhenium-181	1,000
Rhenium-182 (12.7h)	1,000
Rhenium-182 (64.0h)	100
Rhenium-184m	10
Rhenium-184	100
Rhenium-186m	10
Rhenium-186	100
Rhenium-187	1,000
Rhenium-188m	1,000
Rhenium-188	100
Rhenium-189	100
Osmium-180	1,000
Osmium-181	1,000
Osmium-182	100
Osmium-185	100
Osmium-189m	1,000
Osmium-191m	1,000
Osmium-191	100
Osmium-193	100
Osmium-194	1
Iridium-182	1,000
Iridium-184	1,000
Iridium-185	1,000
Iridium-186	100
Iridium-187	1,000
Iridium-188	100
Iridium-189	100
Iridium-190m	1,000
Iridium-190	100
Iridium-192 (73.8d)	1
Iridium-192m (1.4min.)	10
Iridium-194m	10
Iridium-194	100
Iridium-195m	1,000
Iridium-195	1,000
Platinum-186	1,000
Platinum-188	100
Platinum-189	1,000
Platinum-191	100
Platinum-193m	100
Platinum-193	1,000
Platinum-195m	100

Radionuclide	Quantity (μCi)
Platinum-197m	1,000
Platinum-197	100
Platinum-199	1,000
Platinum-200	100
Gold-193	1,000
Gold-194	100
Gold-195	10
Gold-198m	100
Gold-198	100
Gold-199	100
Gold-200m	100
Gold-200	1,000
Gold-201	1,000
Mercury-193m	100
Mercury-193	1,000
Mercury-194	1
Mercury-195m	100
Mercury-195	1,000
Mercury-197m	100
Mercury-197	1,000
Mercury-199m	1,000
Mercury-203	100
Thallium-194m	1,000
Thallium-194	1,000
Thallium-195	1,000
Thallium-197	1,000
Thallium-198m	1,000
Thallium-198	1,000
Thallium-199	1,000
Thallium-200	1,000
Thallium-201	1,000
Thallium-202	100
Thallium-204	100
Lead-195m	1,000
Lead-198	1,000
Lead-199	1,000
Lead-200	100
Lead-201	1,000
Lead-202m	1,000
Lead-202	10
Lead-203	1,000
Lead-205	100
Lead-209	1,000
Lead-210	0.01
Lead-211	100
Lead-212	1
Lead-214	100
Bismuth-200	1,000
Bismuth-201	1,000
Bismuth-202	1,000
Bismuth-203	100
Bismuth-205	100
Bismuth-206	100
Bismuth-207	10
Bismuth-210m	0.1
Bismuth-210	1
Bismuth-212	10
Bismuth-213	10
Bismuth-214	100
Polonium-203	1,000
Polonium-205	1,000
Polonium-207	1,000
Polonium-210	0.1
Astatine-207	100
Astatine-211	10
Radon-220	1
Radon-222	1
Francium-222	100
Francium-223	100
Radium-223	0.1
Radium-224	0.1
Radium-225	0.1
Radium-226	0.1

Radionuclide	Quantity (μCi)
Radium-227	1,000
Radium-228	0.1
Actinium-224	1
Actinium-225	0.01
Actinium-226	0.1
Actinium-227	0.001
Actinium-228	1
Thorium-226	10
Thorium-227	0.01
Thorium-228	0.001
Thorium-229	0.001
Thorium-230	0.001
Thorium-231	100
Thorium-232	100
Thorium-234	10
Thorium-natural	100
Protactinium-227	10
Protactinium-228	1
Protactinium-230	0.1
Protactinium-231	0.001
Protactinium-232	1
Protactinium-233	100
Protactinium-234	100
Uranium-230	0.01
Uranium-231	100
Uranium-232	0.001
Uranium-233	0.001
Uranium-234	0.001
Uranium-235	0.001
Uranium-236	0.001
Uranium-237	100
Uranium-238	100
Uranium-239	1,000
Uranium-240	100
Uranium-natural	100
Neptunium-232	100
Neptunium-233	1,000
Neptunium-234	100
Neptunium-235	100
Neptunium-236 (1.15×10^5 y)	0.001
Neptunium-236 (22.5h)	1
Neptunium-237	0.001
Neptunium-238	10
Neptunium-239	100
Neptunium-240	1,000
Plutonium-234	10
Plutonium-235	1,000
Plutonium-236	0.001
Plutonium-237	100
Plutonium-238	0.001
Plutonium-239	0.001
Plutonium-240	0.001
Plutonium-241	0.01
Plutonium-242	0.001
Plutonium-243	1,000
Plutonium-244	0.001
Plutonium-245	100
Americium-237	1,000
Americium-238	100
Americium-239	1,000
Americium-240	100
Americium-241	0.001
Americium-242m	0.001
Americium-242	10
Americium-243	0.001
Americium-244m	100
Americium-244	10
Americium-245	1,000
Americium-246m	1,000
Americium-246	1,000
Curium-238	100
Curium-240	0.1
Curium-241	1

Radionuclide	Quantity (μCi)
Curium-242	0.01
Curium-243	0.001
Curium-244	0.001
Curium-245	0.001
Curium-246	0.001
Curium-247	0.001
Curium-248	0.001
Curium-249	1,000
Berkelium-245	100
Berkelium-246	100
Berkelium-247	0.001
Berkelium-249	0.1
Berkelium-250	10
Californium-244	100
Californium-246	1
Californium-248	0.01
Californium-249	0.001
Californium-250	0.001
Californium-251	0.001
Californium-252	0.001
Californium-253	0.1
Californium-254	0.001
Any alpha emitting radionuclide not listed above or mixtures of alpha emitters of unknown composition	0.001
Einsteinium-250	100
Einsteinium-251	100
Einsteinium-253	0.1
Einsteinium-254m	1
Einsteinium-254	0.01
Fermium-252	1
Fermium-253	1
Fermium-254	10
Fermium-255	1
Fermium-257	0.01
Mendelevium-257	10
Mendelevium-258	0.01
Any radionuclide other than alpha emitting radionuclides not listed above, or mixtures of beta emitters of unknown composition	0.01

[1] The quantities listed above were derived by taking 1/10th of the most restrictive ALI listed in table 1, columns 1 and 2, of appendix B to §§20.1001–20.2401 of this part, rounding to the nearest factor of 10, and arbitrarily constraining the values listed between 0.001 and 1,000 μCi. Values of 100 μCi have been assigned for radionuclides having a radioactive half-life in excess of 10^9 years (except rhenium, 1000 μCi) to take into account their low specific activity.

NOTE: For purposes of §§20.1902(e), 20.1905(a), and 20.2201(a) where there is involved a combination of radionuclides in known amounts, the limit for the combination should be derived as follows: determine, for each radionuclide in the combination, the ratio between the quantity present in the combination and the limit otherwise established for the specific radionuclide when not in combination. The sum of such ratios for all radionuclides in the combination may not exceed "1" (*i.e.*, "unity").

[56 FR 23465, May 21, 1991; 56 FR 61352, Dec. 3, 1991. Redesignated and amended at 58 FR 67659, Dec. 22, 1993; 60 FR 20186, Apr. 25, 1995]

Appendix D to Part 20—United States Nuclear Regulatory Commission Regional Offices

	Address	Telephone (24 hour)	E-Mail
NRC Headquarters Operations Center	USNRC, Division of Incident Response Operations, Washington, DC 20555–0001.	(301) 816–5100 (301) 951–0550 (301) 816–5151 (fax)	*H001@nrc.gov*
Region I: Connecticut, Delaware, District of Columbia, Maine, Maryland, Massachusetts, New Hampshire, New Jersey, New York, Pennsylvania, Rhode Island, and Vermont.	USNRC, Region I, 2100 Renaissance Boulevard, Suite 100, King of Prussia, PA 19406–2713.	(610) 337–5000, (800) 432–1156 TDD: (301) 415–5575.	*RidsRgn1MailCenter@nrc.gov*
Region II: Alabama, Florida, Georgia, Kentucky, North Carolina, Puerto Rico, South Carolina, Tennessee, Virginia, Virgin Islands, and West Virginia.	USNRC, Region II, 245 Peachtree Center Avenue, NE., Suite 1200, Atlanta, GA 30303–1257..	(404) 997–4000 (800) 877–8510 TDD: (301) 415–5575	*RidsRgn2MailCenter@nrc.gov*
Region III: Illinois, Indiana, Iowa, Michigan, Minnesota, Missouri, Ohio and Wisconsin.	USNRC, Region III, 2443 Warrenville Road, Suite 210, Lisle, IL 60532–4352.	(630) 829–9500 (800) 522–3025 TDD: (301) 415–5575	*RidsRgn3MailCenter@nrc.gov*
Region IV: Alaska, Arizona, Arkansas, California, Colorado, Hawaii, Idaho, Kansas, Louisiana, Mississippi, Montana, Nebraska, Nevada, New Mexico, North Dakota, Oklahoma, Oregon, South Dakota, Texas, Utah, Washington, Wyoming, and the U.S. territories and possessions in the Pacific.	US NRC, Region IV, 1600 E. Lamar Blvd., Arlington, TX 76011–4511..	(817) 860–8100 (800) 952–9677 TDD: (301) 415–5575	*RidsRgn4MailCenter@nrc.gov*

[68 FR 58802, Oct. 10, 2003, as amended at 71 FR 15007, Mar. 27, 2006; 73 FR 30457, May 28, 2008; 75 FR 21980, Apr. 27, 2010; 76 FR 72084, Nov. 22, 2011; 77 FR 39905, July 6, 2012; 79 FR 66602, Nov. 10, 2014]

APPENDIX E TO PART 20— NATIONALLY TRACKED SOURCE THRESHOLDS

The Terabecquerel (TBq) values are the regulatory standard. The curie (Ci) values specified are obtained by converting from the TBq value. The curie values are provided for practical usefulness only and are rounded after conversion.

Radioactive material	Category 1 (TBq)	Category 1 (Ci)	Category 2 (TBq)	Category 2 (Ci)
Actinium-227	20	540	0.2	5.4
Americium-241	60	1,600	0.6	16
Americium-241/Be	60	1,600	0.6	16
Californium-252	20	540	0.2	5.4
Cobalt-60	30	810	0.3	8.1
Curium-244	50	1,400	0.5	14
Cesium-137	100	2,700	1	27
Gadolinium-153	1,000	27,000	10	270
Iridium-192	80	2,200	0.8	22
Plutonium-238	60	1,600	0.6	16
Plutonium-239/Be	60	1,600	0.6	16
Polonium-210	60	1,600	0.6	16
Promethium-147	40,000	1,100,000	400	11,000
Radium-226	40	1,100	0.4	11
Selenium-75	200	5,400	2	54
Strontium-90	1,000	27,000	10	270
Thorium-228	20	540	0.2	5.4
Thorium-229	20	540	0.2	5.4
Thulium-170	20,000	540,000	200	5,400
Ytterbium-169	300	8,100	3	81

[71 FR 65708, Nov. 8, 2006]

APPENDIX F TO PART 20 [RESERVED]

APPENDIX G TO PART 20—REQUIREMENTS FOR TRANSFERS OF LOW-LEVEL RADIOACTIVE WASTE INTENDED FOR DISPOSAL AT LICENSED LAND DISPOSAL FACILITIES AND MANIFESTS

I. MANIFEST

A waste generator, collector, or processor who transports, or offers for transportation, low-level radioactive waste intended for ultimate disposal at a licensed low-level radioactive waste land disposal facility must prepare a Manifest (OMB Control Numbers 3150–0164, –0165, and –0166) reflecting information requested on applicable NRC Forms 540 (Uniform Low-Level Radioactive Waste Manifest (Shipping Paper)) and 541 (Uniform Low-Level Radioactive Waste Manifest (Container and Waste Description)) and, if necessary, on an applicable NRC Form 542 (Uniform Low-Level Radioactive Waste Manifest (Manifest Index and Regional Compact Tabulation)). NRC Forms 540 and 540A must be completed and must physically accompany the pertinent low-level waste shipment. Upon agreement between shipper and consignee, NRC Forms 541 and 541A and 542 and 542A may be completed, transmitted, and stored in electronic media with the capability for producing legible, accurate, and complete records on the respective forms. Licensees are not required by NRC to comply with the manifesting requirements of this part when they ship:

(a) LLW for processing and expect its return (*i.e.*, for storage under their license) prior to disposal at a licensed land disposal facility;

(b) LLW that is being returned to the licensee who is the "waste generator" or "generator," as defined in this part; or

(c) Radioactively contaminated material to a "waste processor" that becomes the processor's "residual waste."

For guidance in completing these forms, refer to the instructions that accompany the forms. Copies of manifests required by this appendix may be legible carbon copies, photocopies, or computer printouts that reproduce the data in the format of the uniform manifest.

NRC Forms 540, 540A, 541, 541A, 542 and 542A, and the accompanying instructions, in hard copy, may be obtained by writing or calling the Office of the Chief Information Officer, U.S. Nuclear Regulatory Commission, Washington, DC 20555–0001, telephone (301) 415–7232, or by visiting the NRC's Web site at *http://www.nrc.gov* and selecting forms from the index found on the home page.

This appendix includes information requirements of the Department of Transportation, as codified in 49 CFR part 172. Information on hazardous, medical, or other waste, required to meet Environmental Protection Agency regulations, as codified in 40 CFR parts 259, 261 or elsewhere, is not addressed in this section, and must be provided on the required EPA forms. However, the required EPA forms must accompany the Uniform Low-Level Radioactive Waste Manifest required by this chapter.

As used in this appendix, the following definitions apply:

Chelating agent has the same meaning as that given in §61.2 of this chapter.

Chemical description means a description of the principal chemical characteristics of a low-level radioactive waste.

Computer-readable medium means that the regulatory agency's computer can transfer the information from the medium into its memory.

Consignee means the designated receiver of the shipment of low-level radioactive waste.

Decontamination facility means a facility operating under a Commission or Agreement State license whose principal purpose is decontamination of equipment or materials to accomplish recycle, reuse, or other waste management objectives, and, for purposes of this part, is not considered to be a consignee for LLW shipments.

Disposal container means a container principally used to confine low-level radioactive waste during disposal operations at a land disposal facility (also see "high integrity container"). Note that for some shipments, the disposal container may be the transport package.

EPA identification number means the number received by a transporter following application to the Administrator of EPA as required by 40 CFR part 263.

Generator means a licensee operating under a Commission or Agreement State license who (1) is a waste generator as defined in this part, or (2) is the licensee to whom waste can be attributed within the context of the Low-Level Radioactive Waste Policy Amendments Act of 1985 (e.g., waste generated as a result of decontamination or recycle activities).

High integrity container (HIC) means a container commonly designed to meet the structural stability requirements of §61.56 of this chapter, and to meet Department of Transportation requirements for a Type A package.

Land disposal facility has the same meaning as that given in §61.2 of this chapter.

NRC Forms 540, 540A, 541, 541A, 542, and 542A are official NRC Forms referenced in this appendix. Licensees need not use originals of these NRC Forms as long as any substitute forms are equivalent to the original documentation in respect to content, clarity, size, and location of information. Upon agreement between the shipper and consignee, NRC Forms 541 (and 541A) and NRC Forms 542 (and 542A) may be completed, transmitted, and stored in electronic media. The electronic media must have the capability for producing legible, accurate, and complete records in the format of the uniform manifest.

Package means the assembly of components necessary to ensure compliance with the packaging requirements of DOT regulations, together with its radioactive contents, as presented for transport.

Physical description means the items called for on NRC Form 541 to describe a low-level radioactive waste.

Residual waste means low-level radioactive waste resulting from processing or decontamination activities that cannot be easily separated into distinct batches attributable to specific waste generators. This waste is attributable to the processor or decontamination facility, as applicable.

Shipper means the licensed entity (*i.e.*, the waste generator, waste collector, or waste processor) who offers low-level radioactive waste for transportation, typically consigning this type of waste to a licensed waste collector, waste processor, or land disposal facility operator.

Shipping paper means NRC Form 540 and, if required, NRC Form 540A which includes the information required by DOT in 49 CFR part 172.

Source material has the same meaning as that given in §40.4 of this chapter.

Special nuclear material has the same meaning as that given in §70.4 of this chapter.

Uniform Low-Level Radioactive Waste Manifest or *uniform manifest* means the combination of NRC Forms 540, 541, and, if necessary, 542, and their respective continuation sheets as needed, or equivalent.

Waste collector means an entity, operating under a Commission or Agreement State license, whose principal purpose is to collect and consolidate waste generated by others, and to transfer this waste, without processing or repackaging the collected waste, to another licensed waste collector, licensed waste processor, or licensed land disposal facility.

Waste description means the physical, chemical and radiological description of a low-level radioactive waste as called for on NRC Form 541.

Waste generator means an entity, operating under a Commission or Agreement State license, who (1) possesses any material or component that contains radioactivity or is radioactively contaminated for which the licensee foresees no further use, and (2) transfers this material or component to a licensed land disposal facility or to a licensed waste collector or processor for handling or treatment prior to disposal. A licensee performing processing or decontamination services may be a "waste generator" if the transfer of low-level radioactive waste from its facility is defined as "residual waste."

Waste processor means an entity, operating under a Commission or Agreement State license, whose principal purpose is to process, repackage, or otherwise treat low-level radioactive material or waste generated by others prior to eventual transfer of waste to a licensed low-level radioactive waste land disposal facility.

Waste type means a waste within a disposal container having a unique physical description (*i.e.*, a specific waste descriptor code or description; or a waste sorbed on or solidified in a specifically defined media).

Information Requirements

A. General Information

The shipper of the radioactive waste, shall provide the following information on the uniform manifest:

1. The name, facility address, and telephone number of the licensee shipping the waste;
2. An explicit declaration indicating whether the shipper is acting as a waste generator, collector, processor, or a combination of these identifiers for purposes of the manifested shipment; and
3. The name, address, and telephone number, or the name and EPA identification number for the carrier transporting the waste.

B. Shipment Information

The shipper of the radioactive waste shall provide the following information regarding the waste shipment on the uniform manifest:

1. The date of the waste shipment;
2. The total number of packages/disposal containers;
3. The total disposal volume and disposal weight in the shipment;
4. The total radionuclide activity in the shipment;
5. The activity of each of the radionuclides H-3, C-14, Tc-99, and I-129 contained in the shipment; and
6. The total masses of U-233, U-235, and plutonium in special nuclear material, and the total mass of uranium and thorium in source material.

C. Disposal Container and Waste Information

The shipper of the radioactive waste shall provide the following information on the uniform manifest regarding the waste and each disposal container of waste in the shipment:

1. An alphabetic or numeric identification that uniquely identifies each disposal container in the shipment;
2. A physical description of the disposal container, including the manufacturer and model of any high integrity container;
3. The volume displaced by the disposal container;
4. The gross weight of the disposal container, including the waste;
5. For waste consigned to a disposal facility, the maximum radiation level at the surface of each disposal container;
6. A physical and chemical description of the waste;
7. The total weight percentage of chelating agent for any waste containing more than 0.1% chelating agent by weight, plus the identity of the principal chelating agent;
8. The approximate volume of waste within a container;
9. The sorbing or solidification media, if any, and the identity of the solidification media vendor and brand name;
10. The identities and activities of individual radionuclides contained in each container, the masses of U-233, U-235, and plutonium in special nuclear material, and the masses of uranium and thorium in source material. For discrete waste types (*i.e.*, activated materials, contaminated equipment, mechanical filters, sealed source/devices, and wastes in solidification/stabilization media), the identities and activities of individual radionuclides associated with or contained on these waste types within a disposal container shall be reported;
11. The total radioactivity within each container; and
12. For wastes consigned to a disposal facility, the classification of the waste pursuant to § 61.55 of this chapter. Waste not meeting the structural stability requirements of § 61.56(b) of this chapter must be identified.

D. Uncontainerized Waste Information

The shipper of the radioactive waste shall provide the following information on the uniform manifest regarding a waste shipment delivered without a disposal container:

1. The approximate volume and weight of the waste;
2. A physical and chemical description of the waste;
3. The total weight percentage of chelating agent if the chelating agent exceeds 0.1% by weight, plus the identity of the principal chelating agent;
4. For waste consigned to a disposal facility, the classification of the waste pursuant to § 61.55 of this chapter. Waste not meeting the structural stability requirements of § 61.56(b) of this chapter must be identified;
5. The identities and activities of individual radionuclides contained in the waste, the masses of U-233, U-235, and plutonium in special nuclear material, and the masses of uranium and thorium in source material; and
6. For wastes consigned to a disposal facility, the maximum radiation levels at the surface of the waste.

E. Multi-Generator Disposal Container Information

This section applies to disposal containers enclosing mixtures of waste originating from different generators. (Note: The origin of the LLW resulting from a processor's activities may be attributable to one or more "generators" (including "waste generators") as defined in this part). It also applies to mixtures of wastes shipped in an uncontainerized form, for which portions of the mixture within the shipment originate from different generators.

1. For homogeneous mixtures of waste, such as incinerator ash, provide the waste description applicable to the mixture and the volume of the waste attributed to each generator.

2. For heterogeneous mixtures of waste, such as the combined products from a large compactor, identify each generator contributing waste to the disposal container, and, for discrete waste types (*i.e.*, activated materials, contaminated equipment, mechanical filters, sealed source/devices, and wastes in solidification/stabilization media), the identities and activities of individual radionuclides contained on these waste types within the disposal container. For each generator, provide the following:

(a) The volume of waste within the disposal container;

(b) A physical and chemical description of the waste, including the solidification agent, if any;

(c) The total weight percentage of chelating agents for any disposal container containing more than 0.1% chelating agent by weight, plus the identity of the principal chelating agent;

(d) The sorbing or solidification media, if any, and the identity of the solidification media vendor and brand name if the media is claimed to meet stability requirements in 10 CFR 61.56(b); and

(e) Radionuclide identities and activities contained in the waste, the masses of U–233, U–235, and plutonium in special nuclear material, and the masses of uranium and thorium in source material if contained in the waste.

II. CERTIFICATION

An authorized representative of the waste generator, processor, or collector shall certify by signing and dating the shipment manifest that the transported materials are properly classified, described, packaged, marked, and labeled and are in proper condition for transportation according to the applicable regulations of the Department of Transportation and the Commission. A collector in signing the certification is certifying that nothing has been done to the collected waste which would invalidate the waste generator's certification.

III. CONTROL AND TRACKING

A. Any licensee who transfers radioactive waste to a land disposal facility or a licensed waste collector shall comply with the requirements in paragraphs A.1 through 9 of this section. Any licensee who transfers waste to a licensed waste processor for waste treatment or repackaging shall comply with the requirements of paragraphs A.4 through 9 of this section. A licensee shall:

1. Prepare all wastes so that the waste is classified according to § 61.55 and meets the waste characteristics requirements in § 61.56 of this chapter;

2. Label each disposal container (or transport package if potential radiation hazards preclude labeling of the individual disposal container) of waste to identify whether it is Class A waste, Class B waste, Class C waste, or greater then Class C waste, in accordance with § 61.55 of this chapter;

3. Conduct a quality assurance program to assure compliance with §§ 61.55 and 61.56 of this chapter (the program must include management evaluation of audits);

4. Prepare the NRC Uniform Low-Level Radioactive Waste Manifest as required by this appendix;

5. Forward a copy or electronically transfer the Uniform Low-Level Radioactive Waste Manifest to the intended consignee so that either (i) receipt of the manifest precedes the LLW shipment or (ii) the manifest is delivered to the consignee with the waste at the time the waste is transferred to the consignee. Using both (i) and (ii) is also acceptable;

6. Include NRC Form 540 (and NRC Form 540A, if required) with the shipment regardless of the option chosen in paragraph A.5 of this section;

7. Receive acknowledgement of the receipt of the shipment in the form of a signed copy of NRC Form 540;

8. Retain a copy of or electronically store the Uniform Low-Level Radioactive Waste Manifest and documentation of acknowledgement of receipt as the record of transfer of licensed material as required by 10 CFR parts 30, 40, and 70 of this chapter; and

9. For any shipments or any part of a shipment for which acknowledgement of receipt has not been received within the times set forth in this appendix, conduct an investigation in accordance with paragraph E of this appendix.

B. Any waste collector licensee who handles only prepackaged waste shall:

1. Acknowledge receipt of the waste from the shipper within one week of receipt by returning a signed copy of NRC Form 540;

2. Prepare a new manifest to reflect consolidated shipments that meet the requirements of this appendix. The waste collector shall ensure that, for each container of waste

in the shipment, the manifest identifies the generator of that container of waste;

3. Forward a copy or electronically transfer the Uniform Low-Level Radioactive Waste Manifest to the intended consignee so that either: (i) Receipt of the manifest precedes the LLW shipment or (ii) the manifest is delivered to the consignee with the waste at the time the waste is transferred to the consignee. Using both (i) and (ii) is also acceptable;

4. Include NRC Form 540 (and NRC Form 540A, if required) with the shipment regardless of the option chosen in paragraph B.3 of this section;

5. Receive acknowledgement of the receipt of the shipment in the form of a signed copy of NRC Form 540;

6. Retain a copy of or electronically store the Uniform Low-Level Radioactive Waste Manifest and documentation of acknowledgement of receipt as the record of transfer of licensed material as required by 10 CFR parts 30, 40, and 70 of this chapter;

7. For any shipments or any part of a shipment for which acknowledgement of receipt has not been received within the times set forth in this appendix, conduct an investigation in accordance with paragraph E of this appendix; and

8. Notify the shipper and the Administrator of the nearest Commission Regional Office listed in appendix D of this part when any shipment, or part of a shipment, has not arrived within 60 days after receipt of an advance manifest, unless notified by the shipper that the shipment has been cancelled.

C. Any licensed waste processor who treats or repackages waste shall:

1. Acknowledge receipt of the waste from the shipper within one week of receipt by returning a signed copy of NRC Form 540;

2. Prepare a new manifest that meets the requirements of this appendix. Preparation of the new manifest reflects that the processor is responsible for meeting these requirements. For each container of waste in the shipment, the manifest shall identify the waste generators, the preprocessed waste volume, and the other information as required in paragraph I.E. of this appendix;

3. Prepare all wastes so that the waste is classified according to §61.55 of this chapter and meets the waste characteristics requirements in §61.56 of this chapter;

4. Label each package of waste to identify whether it is Class A waste, Class B waste, or Class C waste, in accordance with §§61.55 and 61.57 of this chapter;

5. Conduct a quality assurance program to assure compliance with §§61.55 and 61.56 of this chapter (the program shall include management evaluation of audits);

6. Forward a copy or electronically transfer the Uniform Low-Level Radioactive Waste Manifest to the intended consignee so that either: (i) Receipt of the manifest precedes the LLW shipment or (ii) the manifest is delivered to the consignee with the waste at the time the waste is transferred to the consignee. Using both (i) and (ii) is also acceptable;

7. Include NRC Form 540 (and NRC Form 540A, if required) with the shipment regardless of the option chosen in paragraph C.6 of this section;

8. Receive acknowledgement of the receipt of the shipment in the form of a signed copy of NRC Form 540;

9. Retain a copy of or electronically store the Uniform Low-Level Radioactive Waste Manifest and documentation of acknowledgement of receipt as the record of transfer of licensed material as required by 10 CFR parts 30, 40, and 70 of this chapter;

10. For any shipment or any part of a shipment for which acknowledgement of receipt has not been received within the times set forth in this appendix, conduct an investigation in accordance with paragraph E of this appendix; and

11. Notify the shipper and the Administrator of the nearest Commission Regional Office listed in appendix D of this part when any shipment, or part of a shipment, has not arrived within 60 days after receipt of an advance manifest, unless notified by the shipper that the shipment has been cancelled.

D. The land disposal facility operator shall:

1. Acknowledge receipt of the waste within one week of receipt by returning, as a minimum, a signed copy of NRC Form 540 to the shipper. The shipper to be notified is the licensee who last possessed the waste and transferred the waste to the operator. If any discrepancy exists between materials listed on the Uniform Low-Level Radioactive Waste Manifest and materials received, copies or electronic transfer of the affected forms must be returned indicating the discrepancy;

2. Maintain copies of all completed manifests and electronically store the information required by 10 CFR 61.80(l) until the Commission terminates the license; and

3. Notify the shipper and the Administrator of the nearest Commission Regional Office listed in appendix D of this part when any shipment, or part of a shipment, has not arrived within 60 days after receipt of an advance manifest, unless notified by the shipper that the shipment has been cancelled.

E. Any shipment or part of a shipment for which acknowledgement is not received within the times set forth in this section must:

1. Be investigated by the shipper if the shipper has not received notification or receipt within 20 days after transfer; and

2. Be traced and reported. The investigation shall include tracing the shipment and filing a report with the nearest Commission Regional Office listed in appendix D to this

part. Each licensee who conducts a trace investigation shall file a written report with the appropriate NRC Regional Office within 2 weeks of completion of the investigation.

[60 FR 15664, Mar. 27, 1995, as amended at 60 FR 25983, May 16, 1995; 68 FR 58802, Oct. 10, 2003; 73 FR 30457, May 28, 2008; 80 FR 74979, Dec. 1, 2015]

PART 21—REPORTING OF DEFECTS AND NONCOMPLIANCE

AUTHORITY: Atomic Energy Act of 1954, secs. 53, 63, 81, 103, 104, 161, 223, 234, 1701 (42 U.S.C. 2073, 2093, 2111, 2133, 2134, 2201, 2273, 2282, 2297f); Energy Reorganization Act of 1974, secs. 201, 206 (42 U.S.C. 5841, 5846); Nuclear Waste Policy Act of 1982, secs. 135, 141 (42 U.S.C. 10155, 10161); 44 U.S.C. 3504 note.

SOURCE: 42 FR 28893, June 6, 1977, unless otherwise noted.

GENERAL PROVISIONS

§ 21.1 Purpose.

The regulations in this part establish procedures and requirements for implementation of section 206 of the Energy Reorganization Act of 1974. That section requires any individual director or responsible officer of a firm constructing, owning, operating or supplying the components of any facility or activity which is licensed or otherwise regulated pursuant to the Atomic Energy Act of 1954, as amended, or the Energy Reorganization Act of 1974, who obtains information reasonably indicating: (a) That the facility, activity or basic component supplied to such facility or activity fails to comply with the Atomic Energy Act of 1954, as amended, or any applicable rule, regulation, order, or license of the Commission relating to substantial safety hazards or (b) that the facility, activity, or basic component supplied to such facility or activity contains defects, which could create a substantial safety hazard, to immediately notify the Commission of such failure to comply or such defect, unless he has actual knowledge that the Commission has been adequately informed of such defect or failure to comply.

§ 21.2 Scope.

(a) The regulations in this part apply, except as specifically provided otherwise in parts 31, 34, 35, 39, 40, 60, 61, 63, 70, or part 72 of this chapter, to:

(1) Each individual, partnership, corporation, or other entity applying for or holding a license or permit under the regulations in this chapter to possess, use, or transfer within the United States source material, byproduct material, special nuclear material, and/or spent fuel and high-level radioactive waste, or to construct, manufacture, possess, own, operate, or transfer within the United States, any production or utilization facility or independent spent fuel storage installation (ISFSI) or monitored retrievable storage installation (MRS); and each director and responsible officer of such a licensee;

(2) Each individual, corporation, partnership, or other entity doing business within the United States, and each director and responsible officer of such an organization, that constructs a production or utilization facility licensed for manufacture, construction, or operation under parts 50 or 52 of this chapter, an ISFSI for the storage of spent fuel licensed under part 72 of this chapter, an MRS for the storage of spent fuel or high-level radioactive waste under part 72 of this chapter, or a geologic repository for the disposal of high-level radioactive waste under part 60 or 63 of this chapter; or supplies

basic components for a facility or activity licensed, other than for export, under parts 30, 40, 50, 52, 60, 61, 63, 70, 71, or part 72 of this chapter;

(3) Each individual, corporation, partnership, or other entity doing business within the United States, and each director and responsible officer of such an organization, applying for a design certification rule under part 52 of this chapter; or supplying basic components with respect to that design certification, and each individual, corporation, partnership, or other entity doing business within the United States, and each director and responsible officer of such an organization, whose application for design certification has been granted under part 52 of this chapter, or who has supplied or is supplying basic components with respect to that design certification;

(4) Each individual, corporation, partnership, or other entity doing business within the United States, and each director and responsible officer of such an organization, applying for or holding a standard design approval under part 52 of this chapter; or supplying basic components with respect to a standard design approval under part 52 of this chapter;

(b) For persons licensed to construct a facility under either a construction permit issued under §50.23 of this chapter or a combined license under part 52 of this chapter (for the period of construction until the date that the Commission makes the finding under §52.103(g) of this chapter), or to manufacture a facility under part 52 of this chapter, evaluation of potential defects and failures to comply and reporting of defects and failures to comply under §50.55(e) of this chapter satisfies each person's evaluation, notification, and reporting obligation to report defects and failures to comply under this part and the responsibility of individual directors and responsible officers of these licensees to report defects under Section 206 of the Energy Reorganization Act of 1974.

(c) For persons licensed to operate a nuclear power plant under part 50 or part 52 of this chapter, evaluation of potential defects and appropriate reporting of defects under §§50.72, 50.73, or §73.71 of this chapter, satisfies each person's evaluation, notification, and reporting obligation to report defects under this part, and the responsibility of individual directors and responsible officers of these licensees to report defects under Section 206 of the Energy Reorganization Act of 1974.

(d) Nothing in these regulations should be deemed to preclude either an individual, a manufacturer, or a supplier of a commercial grade item (as defined in §21.3) not subject to the regulations in this part from reporting to the Commission, a known or suspected defect or failure to comply and, as authorized by law, the identity of anyone so reporting will be withheld from disclosure. NRC regional offices and headquarters will accept collect telephone calls from individuals who wish to speak to NRC representatives concerning nuclear safety-related problems. The location and telephone numbers of the four regions (answered during regular working hours), are listed in appendix D to part 20 of this chapter. The telephone number of the NRC Operations Center (answered 24 hours a day—including holidays) is (301) 816–5100.

(e) The regulations in this part apply in accordance with 10 CFR 76.60 to each individual, partnership, corporation, or other entity required to obtain a certificate of compliance or an approved compliance plan under part 76 of this chapter.

[56 FR 36089, July 31, 1991, as amended at 59 FR 14086, Mar. 25, 1994; 59 FR 48959, Sept. 23, 1994; 60 FR 48373, Sept. 19, 1995; 66 FR 55790, Nov. 2, 2001; 72 FR 49486, Aug. 28, 2007]

§21.3 Definitions.

As used in this part:

Basic component. (1)(i) When applied to nuclear power plants licensed under 10 CFR part 50 or part 52 of this chapter, basic component means a structure, system, or component, or part thereof that affects its safety function necessary to assure:

(A) The integrity of the reactor coolant pressure boundary;

(B) The capability to shut down the reactor and maintain it in a safe-shutdown condition; or

(C) The capability to prevent or mitigate the consequences of accidents which could result in potential offsite exposures comparable to those referred to in §§ 50.34(a)(1), 50.67(b)(2), or 100.11 of this chapter, as applicable.

(ii) Basic components are items designed and manufactured under a quality assurance program complying with appendix B to part 50 of this chapter, or commercial grade items which have successfully completed the dedication process.

(2) When applied to standard design certifications under subpart C of part 52 of this chapter and standard design approvals under part 52 of this chapter, basic component means the design or procurement information approved or to be approved within the scope of the design certification or approval for a structure, system, or component, or part thereof, that affects its safety function necessary to assure:

(i) The integrity of the reactor coolant pressure boundary;

(ii) The capability to shut down the reactor and maintain it in a safe-shutdown condition; or

(iii) The capability to prevent or mitigate the consequences of accidents which could result in potential offsite exposures comparable to those referred to in §§ 50.34(a)(1), 50.67(b)(2), or 100.11 of this chapter, as applicable.

(3) When applied to other facilities and other activities licensed under 10 CFR parts 30, 40, 50 (other than nuclear power plants), 60, 61, 63, 70, 71, or 72 of this chapter, basic component means a structure, system, or component, or part thereof, that affects their safety function, that is directly procured by the licensee of a facility or activity subject to the regulations in this part and in which a defect or failure to comply with any applicable regulation in this chapter, order, or license issued by the Commission could create a substantial safety hazard.

(4) In all cases, basic component includes safety-related design, analysis, inspection, testing, fabrication, replacement of parts, or consulting services that are associated with the component hardware, design certification, design approval, or information in support of an early site permit application under part 52 of this chapter, whether these services are performed by the component supplier or others.

Commercial grade item. (1) When applied to nuclear power plants licensed pursuant to 10 CFR part 50, commercial grade item means a structure, system, or component, or part thereof that affects its safety function, that was not designed and manufactured as a basic component. Commercial grade items do not include items where the design and manufacturing process require in-process inspections and verifications to ensure that defects or failures to comply are identified and corrected (*i.e.*, one or more critical characteristics of the item cannot be verified).

(2) When applied to facilities and activities licensed pursuant to 10 CFR parts 30, 40, 50 (other than nuclear power plants), 60, 61, 63, 70, 71, or 72, commercial grade item means an item that is:

(i) Not subject to design or specification requirements that are unique to those facilities or activities;

(ii) Used in applications other than those facilities or activities; and

(iii) To be ordered from the manufacturer/supplier on the basis of specifications set forth in the manufacturer's published product description (for example, a catalog).

Commission means the Nuclear Regulatory Commission or its duly authorized representatives.

Constructing or *construction* means the analysis, design, manufacture, fabrication, placement, erection, installation, modification, inspection, or testing of a facility or activity which is subject to the regulations in this part and consulting services related to the facility or activity that are safety related.

Critical characteristics. When applied to nuclear power plants licensed pursuant to 10 CFR part 50, critical characteristics are those important design, material, and performance characteristics of a commercial grade item that, once verified, will provide reasonable assurance that the item will perform its intended safety function.

Dedicating entity. When applied to nuclear power plants licensed pursuant to 10 CFR part 50, dedicating entity means the organization that performs the dedication process. Dedication may be performed by the manufacturer of the item, a third-party dedicating entity, or the licensee itself. The dedicating entity, pursuant to § 21.21(c) of this part, is responsible for identifying and evaluating deviations, reporting defects and failures to comply for the dedicated item, and maintaining auditable records of the dedication process.

Dedication. (1) When applied to nuclear power plants licensed pursuant to 10 CFR part 50, dedication is an acceptance process undertaken to provide reasonable assurance that a commercial grade item to be used as a basic component will perform its intended safety function and, in this respect, is deemed equivalent to an item designed and manufactured under a 10 CFR part 50, appendix B, quality assurance program. This assurance is achieved by identifying the critical characteristics of the item and verifying their acceptability by inspections, tests, or analyses performed by the purchaser or third-party dedicating entity after delivery, supplemented as necessary by one or more of the following: commercial grade surveys; product inspections or witness at holdpoints at the manufacturer's facility, and analysis of historical records for acceptable performance. In all cases, the dedication process must be conducted in accordance with the applicable provisions of 10 CFR part 50, appendix B. The process is considered complete when the item is designated for use as a basic component.

(2) When applied to facilities and activities licensed pursuant to 10 CFR parts 30, 40, 50 (other than nuclear power plants), 60, 61, 63, 70, 71, or 72, dedication occurs after receipt when that item is designated for use as a basic component.

Defect means:

(1) A deviation in a basic component delivered to a purchaser for use in a facility or an activity subject to the regulations in this part if, on the basis of an evaluation, the deviation could create a substantial safety hazard;

(2) The installation, use, or operation of a basic component containing a defect as defined in this section;

(3) A deviation in a portion of a facility subject to the early site permit, standard design certification, standard design approval, construction permit, combined license or manufacturing licensing requirements of part 50 or part 52 of this chapter, provided the deviation could, on the basis of an evaluation, create a substantial safety hazard and the portion of the facility containing the deviation has been offered to the purchaser for acceptance;

(4) A condition or circumstance involving a basic component that could contribute to the exceeding of a safety limit, as defined in the technical specifications of a license for operation issued under part 50 or part 52 of this chapter; or

(5) An error, omission or other circumstance in a design certification, or standard design approval that, on the basis of an evaluation, could create a substantial safety hazard.

Deviation means a departure from the technical requirements included in a procurement document, or specified in early site permit information, a standard design certification or standard design approval.

Director means an individual, appointed or elected according to law, who is authorized to manage and direct the affairs of a corporation, partnership or other entity. In the case of an individual proprietorship, *director* means the individual.

Discovery means the completion of the documentation first identifying the existence of a deviation or failure to comply potentially associated with a substantial safety hazard within the evaluation procedures discussed in § 21.21(a).

Evaluation means the process of determining whether a particular deviation could create a substantial hazard or determining whether a failure to comply is associated with a substantial safety hazard.

Notification means the telephonic communication to the NRC Operations Center or written transmittal of information to the NRC Document Control Desk.

Operating or operation means the operation of a facility or the conduct of a licensed activity which is subject to the regulations in this part and consulting services related to operations that are safety related.

Procurement document means a contract that defines the requirements which facilities or basic components must meet in order to be considered acceptable by the purchaser.

Responsible officer means the president, vice-president or other individual in the organization of a corporation, partnership, or other entity who is vested with executive authority over activities subject to this part.

Substantial safety hazard means a loss of safety function to the extent that there is a major reduction in the degree of protection provided to public health and safety for any facility or activity licensed or otherwise approved or regulated by the NRC, other than for export, under parts 30, 40, 50, 52, 60, 61, 63, 70, 71, or 72 of this chapter.

Supplying or *supplies* means contractually responsible for a basic component used or to be used in a facility or activity which is subject to the regulations in this part.

[42 FR 28893, June 6, 1977; 42 FR 36803, July 18, 1977, as amended at 43 FR 48622, Oct. 19, 1978; 46 FR 58283, Dec. 1, 1981; 47 FR 57480, Dec. 27, 1982; 56 FR 36089, July 31, 1991; 59 FR 5519, Feb. 7, 1994; 60 FR 48373, Sept. 19, 1995; 61 FR 65171, Dec. 11, 1996; 64 FR 72000, Dec. 23, 1999; 66 FR 55790, Nov. 2, 2001; 72 FR 49486, Aug. 28, 2007]

§21.4 Interpretations.

Except as specifically authorized by the Commission in writing, no interpretation of the meaning of the regulations in this part by any officer or employee of the Commission other than a written interpretation by the General Counsel will be recognized to be binding upon the Commission.

§21.5 Communications.

Except where otherwise specified in this part, written communications and reports concerning the regulations in this part must be addressed to the NRC's Document Control Desk, and sent by mail to the U.S. Nuclear Regulatory Commission, Washington, DC 20555–0001; by hand delivery to the NRC's offices at 11555 Rockville Pike, Rockville, Maryland; or, where practicable, by electronic submission, for example, Electronic Information Exchange, or CD-ROM. Electronic submissions must be made in a manner that enables the NRC to receive, read, authenticate, distribute, and archive the submission, and process and retrieve it a single page at a time. Detailed guidance on making electronic submissions can be obtained by visiting the NRC's Web site at *http://www.nrc.gov/site-help/e-submittals.html;* by e-mail to *MSHD.Resource@nrc.gov;* or by writing the Office of the Chief Information Officer, U.S. Nuclear Regulatory Commission, Washington, DC 20555–0001. The guidance discusses, among other topics, the formats the NRC can accept, the use of electronic signatures, and the treatment of nonpublic information. In the case of a licensee or permit holder, a copy of the communication must also be sent to the appropriate Regional Administrator at the address specified in appendix D to part 20 of this chapter.

[72 FR 49487, Aug. 28, 2007, as amended at 74 FR 62680, Dec. 1, 2009; 80 FR 74979, Dec. 1, 2015]

§21.6 Posting requirements.

(a)(1) Each individual, partnership, corporation, dedicating entity, or other entity subject to the regulations in this part shall post current copies of—

(i) The regulations in this part;

(ii) Section 206 of the Energy Reorganization Act of 1974; and

(iii) Procedures adopted pursuant to the regulations in this part.

(2) These documents must be posted in a conspicuous position on any premises within the United States where the activities subject to this part are conducted.

(b) If posting of the regulations in this part or the procedures adopted pursuant to the regulations in this part is not practicable, the licensee or firm subject to the regulations in this part may, in addition to posting section 206, post a notice which describes the regulations/procedures, including the name of the individual to whom reports may be made, and states where they may be examined.

(c) The effective date of this section has been deferred until January 6, 1978.

[42 FR 28893, June 6, 1977, as amended at 60 FR 48374, Sept. 19, 1995]

§ 21.7 Exemptions.

The Commission may, upon application of any interested person or upon its own initiative, grant such exemptions from the requirements of the regulations in this part as it determines are authorized by law and will not endanger life or property or the common defense and security and are otherwise in the public interest. Suppliers of commercial grade items are exempt from the provisions of this part to the extent that they supply commercial grade items.

[42 FR 28893, June 6, 1977, as amended at 43 FR 48622, Oct. 19, 1978]

§ 21.8 Information collection requirements: OMB approval.

(a) The Nuclear Regulatory Commission has submitted the information collection requirements contained in this part to the Office of Management and Budget (OMB) for approval as required by the Paperwork Reduction Act (44 U.S.C. 3501 *et seq.*). The NRC may not conduct or sponsor, and a person is not required to respond to, a collection of information unless it displays a currently valid OMB control number. OMB has approved the information collection requirements contained in this part under control number 3150–0035.

(b) The approved information collection requirements contained in this part appear in §§ 21.7, 21.21 and 21.51.

[62 FR 52185, Oct. 6, 1997]

NOTIFICATION

§ 21.21 Notification of failure to comply or existence of a defect and its evaluation.

(a) Each individual, corporation, partnership, dedicating entity, or other entity subject to the regulations in this part shall adopt appropriate procedures to—

(1) Evaluate deviations and failures to comply to identify defects and failures to comply associated with substantial safety hazards as soon as practicable, and, except as provided in paragraph (a)(2) of this section, in all cases within 60 days of discovery, in order to identify a reportable defect or failure to comply that could create a substantial safety hazard, were it to remain uncorrected, and

(2) Ensure that if an evaluation of an identified deviation or failure to comply potentially associated with a substantial safety hazard cannot be completed within 60 days from discovery of the deviation or failure to comply, an interim report is prepared and submitted to the Commission through a director or responsible officer or designated person as discussed in § 21.21(d)(5). The interim report should describe the deviation or failure to comply that is being evaluated and should also state when the evaluation will be completed. This interim report must be submitted in writing within 60 days of discovery of the deviation or failure to comply.

(3) Ensure that a director or responsible officer subject to the regulations of this part is informed as soon as practicable, and, in all cases, within the 5 working days after completion of the evaluation described in paragraphs (a)(1) or (a)(2) of this section if the manufacture, construction, or operation of a facility or activity, a basic component supplied for such facility or activity, or the design certification or design approval under part 52 of this chapter—

(i) Fails to comply with the Atomic Energy Act of 1954, as amended, or any applicable rule, regulation, order, or license of the Commission or standard design approval under part 52 of this chapter, relating to a substantial safety hazard, or

(ii) Contains a defect.

(b) If the deviation or failure to comply is discovered by a supplier of basic components, or services associated with basic components, and the supplier determines that it does not have the capability to perform the evaluation to determine if a defect exists, then the supplier must inform the purchasers or affected licensees within five working days of this determination so that the purchasers or affected licensees may evaluate the deviation or failure to comply, pursuant to § 21.21(a).

(c) A dedicating entity is responsible for—

(1) Identifying and evaluating deviations and reporting defects and failures to comply associated with substantial safety hazards for dedicated items; and

(2) Maintaining auditable records for the dedication process.

(d)(1) A director or responsible officer subject to the regulations of this part or a person designated under § 21.21(d)(5) must notify the Commission when he or she obtains information reasonably indicating a failure to comply or a defect affecting—

(i) The manufacture, construction or operation of a facility or an activity within the United States that is subject to the licensing requirements under parts 30, 40, 50, 52, 60, 61, 63, 70, 71, or 72 of this chapter and that is within his or her organization's responsibility; or

(ii) A basic component that is within his or her organization's responsibility and is supplied for a facility or an activity within the United States that is subject to the licensing, design certification, or approval requirements under parts 30, 40, 50, 52, 60, 61, 63, 70, 71, or 72 of this chapter.

(2) The notification to NRC of a failure to comply or of a defect under paragraph (d)(1) of this section and the evaluation of a failure to comply or a defect under paragraphs (a)(1) and (a)(2) of this section, are not required if the director or responsible officer has actual knowledge that the Commission has been notified in writing of the defect or the failure to comply.

(3) Notification required by paragraph (d)(1) of this section must be made as follows—

(i) Initial notification by facsimile, which is the preferred method of notification, to the NRC Operations Center at (301) 816–5151 or by telephone at (301) 816–5100 within two days following receipt of information by the director or responsible corporate officer under paragraph (a)(1) of this section, on the identification of a defect or a failure to comply. Verification that the facsimile has been received should be made by calling the NRC Operations Center. This paragraph does not apply to interim reports described in § 21.21(a)(2).

(ii) Written notification to the NRC at the address specified in § 21.5 within 30 days following receipt of information by the director or responsible corporate officer under paragraph (a)(3) of this section, on the identification of a defect or a failure to comply.

(4) The written report required by this paragraph shall include, but need not be limited to, the following information, to the extent known:

(i) Name and address of the individual or individuals informing the Commission.

(ii) Identification of the facility, the activity, or the basic component supplied for such facility or such activity within the United States which fails to comply or contains a defect.

(iii) Identification of the firm constructing the facility or supplying the basic component which fails to comply or contains a defect.

(iv) Nature of the defect or failure to comply and the safety hazard which is created or could be created by such defect or failure to comply.

(v) The date on which the information of such defect or failure to comply was obtained.

(vi) In the case of a basic component which contains a defect or fails to comply, the number and location of these components in use at, supplied for, being supplied for, or may be supplied for, manufactured, or being manufactured for one or more facilities or activities subject to the regulations in this part.

(vii) The corrective action which has been, is being, or will be taken; the name of the individual or organization responsible for the action; and the length of time that has been or will be taken to complete the action.

(viii) Any advice related to the defect or failure to comply about the facility, activity, or basic component that has been, is being, or will be given to purchasers or licensees.

(ix) In the case of an early site permit, the entities to whom an early site permit was transferred.

(5) The director or responsible officer may authorize an individual to provide the notification required by this paragraph, provided that, this shall not relieve the director or responsible officer of his or her responsibility under this paragraph.

(e) Individuals subject to this part may be required by the Commission to supply additional information related to a defect or failure to comply. Commission action to obtain additional information may be based on reports of defects from other reporting entities.

[42 FR 28893, June 6, 1977, as amended at 46 FR 58283, Dec. 1, 1981; 47 FR 57480, Dec. 27, 1982; 52 FR 31611, Aug. 21, 1987; 56 FR 36089, July 31, 1991; 59 FR 14086, Mar. 25, 1994; 60 FR 48374, Sept. 19, 1995; 66 FR 55790, Nov. 2, 2001; 67 FR 77652, Dec. 19, 2002; 72 FR 49487, Aug. 28, 2007]

PROCUREMENT DOCUMENTS

§21.31 Procurement documents.

Each individual, corporation, partnership, dedicating entity, or other entity subject to the regulations in this part shall ensure that each procurement document for a facility, or a basic component issued by him, her or it on or after January 6, 1978, specifies, when applicable, that the provisions of 10 CFR part 21 apply.

[60 FR 48374, Sept. 19, 1995]

INSPECTIONS, RECORDS

§21.41 Inspections.

Each individual, corporation, partnership, dedicating entity, or other entity subject to the regulations in this part shall permit the Commission to inspect records, premises, activities, and basic components as necessary to accomplish the purposes of this part.

[60 FR 48374, Sept. 19, 1995]

§21.51 Maintenance and inspection of records.

(a) Each individual, corporation, partnership, dedicating entity, or other entity subject to the regulations in this part shall prepare and maintain records necessary to accomplish the purposes of this part, specifically—

(1) Retain evaluations of all deviations and failures to comply for a minimum of five years after the date of the evaluation;

(2) Suppliers of basic components must retain any notifications sent to purchasers and affected licensees for a minimum of five years after the date of the notification.

(3) Suppliers of basic components must retain a record of the purchasers of basic components for 10 years after delivery of the basic component or service associated with a basic component.

(4) Applicants for standard design certification under subpart B of part 52 of this chapter and others providing a design which is the subject of a design certification, during and following Commission adoption of a final design certification rule for that design, shall retain any notifications sent to purchasers and affected licensees for a minimum of 5 years after the date of the notification, and retain a record of the purchasers for 15 years after delivery of design which is the subject of the design certification rule or service associated with the design.

(5) Applicants for or holders of a standard design approval under subpart E of part 52 of this chapter and others providing a design which is the subject of a design approval shall retain any notifications sent to purchasers and affected licensees for a minimum of 5 years after the date of the notification, and retain a record of the purchasers for 15 years after delivery of the design which is the subject of the design approval or service associated with the design.

(b) Each individual, corporation, partnership, dedicating entity, or other entity subject to the regulations in this part shall permit the Commission the opportunity to inspect records pertaining to basic components that relate to the identification and evaluation of deviations, and the reporting of defects and failures to comply, including (but not limited to) any advice given to purchasers or licensees on the placement, erection, installation, operation, maintenance, modification, or inspection of a basic component.

[56 FR 36090, July 31, 1991, as amended at 60 FR 48374, Sept. 19, 1995; 72 FR 49488, Aug. 28, 2007]

ENFORCEMENT

§21.61 Failure to notify.

(a) Any director or responsible officer of an entity (including dedicating entity) that is not otherwise subject to the deliberate misconduct provisions of this chapter but is subject to the regulations in this part who knowingly and consciously fails to provide the notice required as by § 21.21 shall be subject to a civil penalty equal to the amount provided by section 234 of the Atomic Energy Act of 1954, as amended.

(b) Any NRC licensee or applicant for a license (including an applicant for, or holder of, a permit), applicant for a design certification under part 52 of this chapter during the pendency of its application, applicant for a design certification after Commission adoption of a final design certification rule for that design, or applicant for or holder of a standard design approval under part 52 of this chapter subject to the regulations in this part who fails to provide the notice required by § 21.21, or otherwise fails to comply with the applicable requirements of this part shall be subject to a civil penalty as provided by Section 234 of the Atomic Energy Act of 1954, as amended.

(c) The dedicating entity, pursuant to § 21.21(c) of this part, is responsible for identifying and evaluating deviations, reporting defects and failures to comply for the dedicated item, and maintaining auditable records of the dedication process. NRC enforcement action can be taken for failure to identify and evaluate deviations, failure to report defects and failures to comply, or failure to maintain auditable records.

[60 FR 48374, Sept. 19, 1995, as amended at 72 FR 49488, Aug. 28, 2007]

§ 21.62 Criminal penalties.

(a) Section 223 of the Atomic Energy Act of 1954, as amended, provides for criminal sanctions for willful violation of, attempted violation of, or conspiracy to violate, any regulation issued under sections 161b, 161i, or 161o of the Act. For purposes of section 223, all the regulations in part 21 are issued under one or more of sections 161b, 161i, or 161o, except for the sections listed in paragraph (b) of this section.

(b) The regulations in part 21 that are not issued under sections 161b, 161i, or 161o for the purposes of section 223 are as follows: §§ 21.1, 21.2, 21.3, 21.4 21.5, 21.7, 21.8, 21.61, and 21.62.

[57 FR 55071, Nov. 24, 1992]

PART 25—ACCESS AUTHORIZATION

AUTHORITY: Atomic Energy Act of 1954, secs. 145, 161, 223, 234 (42 U.S.C. 2165, 2201, 2273, 2282); Energy Reorganization Act of 1974, sec. 201 (42 U.S.C. 5841); 44 U.S.C. 3504 note; E.O. 10865, 25 FR 1583, as amended, 3 CFR, 1959–1963 Comp., p. 398; E.O. 12829, 58 FR 3479, 3 CFR, 1993 Comp., p. 570; E.O. 13526, 75 FR 707, 3 CFR, 2009 Comp., p. 298; E.O. 12968, 60 FR 40245, 3 CFR, 1995 Comp., p. 391.

Section 25.17(f) and Appendix A also issued under 31 U.S.C. 9701; 42 U.S.C. 2214.

SOURCE: 45 FR 14481, Mar. 5, 1980, unless otherwise noted.

GENERAL PROVISIONS

§ 25.1 Purpose.

The regulations in this part establish procedures for granting, reinstating, extending, transferring, and terminating access authorizations of licensee personnel, licensee contractors or agents, and other persons (e.g., individuals involved in adjudicatory procedures as set forth in 10 CFR part 2, subpart I) who may require access to classified information.

[62 FR 17687, Apr. 11, 1997]

§ 25.3 Scope.

The regulations in this part apply to licensees, certificate holders, and others who may require access to classified information related to a license, certificate, an application for a license or certificate, or other activities as the Commission may determine.

[70 FR 32227, June 2, 2005]

§ 25.5 Definitions.

Access authorization means an administrative determination that an individual (including a consultant) who is employed by or an applicant for employment with the NRC, NRC contractors, agents, licensees and certificate holders, or other person designated by the Executive Director for Operations, is eligible for a security clearance for access to classified information.

Act means the Atomic Energy Act of 1954 (68 Stat. 919), as amended.

Certificate holder means a facility operating under the provisions of parts 71 or 76 of this chapter.

Classified information means either classified National Security Information, Restricted Data, or Formerly Restricted Data or any one of them. It is the generic term for information requiring protection in the interest of National Security whether classified under an Executive Order or the Atomic Energy Act.

Classified National Security Information means information that has been determined under E.O. 13526, as amended, or any predecessor or successor order to require protection against unauthorized disclosure and that is so designated.

Cognizant Security Agency (CSA) means agencies of the Executive Branch that have been authorized by E.O. 12829 to establish an industrial security program for the purpose of safeguarding classified information under the jurisdiction of those agencies when disclosed or released to U.S. industry. These agencies are the Department of Defense, the Department of Energy, the Central Intelligence Agency, and the Nuclear Regulatory Commission. A facility has a single CSA which exercises primary authority for the protection of classified information at the facility. The CSA for the facility provides security representation for other government agencies with security interests at the facility. The Secretary of Defense has been designated as Executive Agent for the National Industrial Security Program.

Commission means the Nuclear Regulatory Commission or its duly authorized representatives.

"L" access authorization means an access authorization granted by the Commission that is normally based on a national agency check with a law and credit investigation (NACLC) or an access national agency check and inquiries investigation (ANACI) conducted by the Office of Personnel Management.

License means a license issued pursuant to 10 CFR parts 50, 52, 60, 63, 70, or 72.

Matter means documents or material.

National Security Information means information that has been determined pursuant to Executive Order 12958, as amended, or any predecessor order to require protection against unauthorized disclosure and that is so designated.

Need-to-know means a determination made by an authorized holder of classified information that a prospective recipient requires access to a specific classified information to perform or assist in a lawful and authorized governmental function under the cognizance of the Commission.

Person means (1) any individual, corporation, partnership, firm, association, trust, estate, public or private institution, group, government agency other than the Commission or the Department of Energy (DOE), except that the DOE shall be considered a person to the extent that its facilities are subject to the licensing and related regulatory authority of the Commission pursuant to section 202 of the Energy Reorganization Act of 1974 and sections 104, 105 and 202 of the Uranium Mill

Tailings Radiation Control Act of 1978, any State or any political subdivision of, or any political entity within a State, any foreign government or nation or any political subdivision of any such government or nation, or other entity; and (2) any legal successor, representative, agent, or agency of the foregoing.

"Q" access authorization means an access authorization granted by the Commission normally based on a single scope background investigation conducted by the Office of Personnel Management, the Federal Bureau of Investigation, or other U.S. Government agency which conducts personnel security investigations.

Restricted Data means all data concerning design, manufacture or utilization of atomic weapons, the production of special nuclear material, or the use of special nuclear material in the production of energy, but shall not include data declassified or removed from the Restricted Data category pursuant to section 142 of the Act.

Visit authorization letters (VAL) means a letter, generated by a licensee, certificate holder or other organization under the requirements of 10 CFR parts 25 and/or 95, verifying the need-to-know and access authorization of an individual from that organization who needs to visit another authorized facility for the purpose of exchanging or acquiring classified information related to the license.

[45 FR 14481, Mar. 5, 1980, as amended at 46 FR 58283, Dec. 1, 1981; 47 FR 38683, Sept. 2, 1982; 48 FR 24320, June 1, 1983; 50 FR 36984, Sept. 11, 1985; 55 FR 11574, Mar. 29, 1990; 62 FR 17687, Apr. 11, 1997; 64 FR 15647, Apr. 1, 1999; 70 FR 32227, June 2, 2005; 75 FR 73941, Nov. 30, 2010]

§ 25.7 Interpretations.

Except as specifically authorized by the Commission in writing, no interpretation of the meaning of the regulations in this part by any officer or employee of the Commission other than a written interpretation by the General Counsel will be recognized to be binding upon the Commission.

§ 25.8 Information collection requirements: OMB approval.

(a) The Nuclear Regulatory Commission has submitted the information collection requirements contained in this part to the Office of Management and Budget (OMB) for approval as required by the Paperwork Reduction Act (44 U.S.C. 3501 *et seq.*). The NRC may not conduct or sponsor and a person is not required to respond to, a collection of information unless it displays a currently valid OMB control number. OMB has approved the information collection requirements contained in this part under control number 3150–0046.

(b) The approved information collection requirements contained in this part appear in §§ 25.11, 25.17, 25.21, 25.23, 25.25, 25.27, 25.29, 25.31, 25.33, and 25.35.

(c) This part contains information collection requirements in addition to those approved under the control number specified in paragraph (a) of this section. These information collection requirements and the control numbers under which they are approved are as follows:

(1) In §§ 25.17(b), 25.21(c), 25.27(a), 25.29, and 25.31, NRC Form 237 is approved under control number 3150–0050.

(2) In §§ 25.17(c), 25.21(c), 25.27(b), 25.29, and 25.31, SF–86 is approved under control number 3206–0007.

(3) In § 25.21(b), NRC Form 354 is approved under control number 3150–0026.

(4) In § 25.33, NRC Form 136 is approved under control number 3150–0049.

(5) In § 25.35, NRC Form 277 is approved under control number 3150–0051.

[49 FR 19624, May 9, 1984, as amended at 57 FR 3720, Jan. 31, 1992; 62 FR 17687, Apr. 11, 1997; 62 FR 52185, Oct. 6, 1997]

§ 25.9 Communications.

Except where otherwise specified, communications and reports concerning the regulations in this part should be addressed to the Director, Division of Facilities and Security, Mail Stop T7–D57, and sent either by mail to the U.S. Nuclear Regulatory Commission, Washington, DC 20555–0001; by hand delivery to the NRC's offices at 11555 Rockville Pike, Rockville, Maryland; or, where practicable, by electronic submission, for example, Electronic Information Exchange, or CD-

ROM. Electronic submissions must be made in a manner that enables the NRC to receive, read, authenticate, distribute, and archive the submission, and process and retrieve it a single page at a time. Detailed guidance on making electronic submissions can be obtained by visiting the NRC's Web site at *http://www.nrc.gov/site-help/e-submittals.html;* by e-mail to *MSHD.Resource@nrc.gov;* or by writing the Office of the Chief Information Officer, U.S. Nuclear Regulatory Commission, Washington, DC 20555–0001. The guidance discusses, among other topics, the formats the NRC can accept, the use of electronic signatures, and the treatment of nonpublic information.

[68 FR 58803, Oct. 10, 2003, as amended at 74 FR 62681, Dec. 1, 2009; 80 FR 74979, Dec. 1, 2015]

§ 25.11 Specific exemptions.

The NRC may, upon application by any interested person or upon its own initiative, grant exemptions from the requirements of the regulations of this part, that are—

(a) Authorized by law, will not present an undue risk to the public health and safety, and are consistent with the common defense and security; or

(b) Coincidental with one or more of the following:

(1) An application of the regulation in the particular circumstances conflicts with other NRC rules or requirements;

(2) An application of the regulation in the particular circumstances would not serve the underlying purpose of the rule or is not necessary to achieve the underlying purpose of the rule;

(3) When compliance would result in undue hardship or other costs that significantly exceed those contemplated when the regulation was adopted, or that significantly exceed those incurred by others similarly situated;

(4) When the exemption would result in benefit to the common defense and security that compensates for any decrease in the security that may result from the grant of the exemption;

(5) When the exemption would provide only temporary relief from the applicable regulation and the licensee or applicant has made good faith efforts to comply with the regulation;

(6) When there is any other material circumstance present that was not considered when the regulation was adopted that would be in the public interest to grant an exemption. If this condition is relied on exclusively for satisfying paragraph (b) of this section, the exemption may not be granted until the Executive Director for Operations has consulted with the Commission.

[64 FR 15647, Apr. 1, 1999]

§ 25.13 Maintenance of records.

(a) Each licensee or organization employing individuals approved for personnel security access authorization under this part, shall maintain records as prescribed within the part. These records are subject to review and inspection by CSA representatives during security reviews.

(b) Each record required by this part must be legible throughout the retention period specified by each Commission regulation. The record may be the original or a reproduced copy or a microform provided that the copy or microform is authenticated by authorized personnel and that the microform is capable of producing a clear copy throughout the required retention period. The record may also be stored in electronic media with the capability for producing legible, accurate, and complete records during the required retention period. Records such as letters, drawings, specifications, must include all pertinent information such as stamps, initials, and signatures. The licensee shall maintain adequate safeguards against tampering with and loss of records.

[45 FR 14481, Mar. 5, 1980, as amended at 53 FR 19245, May 27, 1988; 62 FR 17687, Apr. 11, 1997]

Access Authorizations

§ 25.15 Access permitted under "Q" or "L" access authorization.

(a) A "Q" access authorization permits an individual access on a need-to-know basis to (1) Secret and Confidential Restricted Data and (2) Secret and

Confidential National Security Information including intelligence information, CRYPTO (*i.e.*, cryptographic information) or other classified communications security (COMSEC) information.

(b) An "L" access authorization permits an individual access on a need-to-know basis to Confidential Restricted Data and Secret and Confidential National Security Information other than the categories specifically included in paragraph (a) of this section. In addition, access to certain Confidential COMSEC information is permitted as authorized by a National Communications Security Committee waiver dated February 14, 1985.

(c) Each employee of the Commission is processed for one of the two levels of access authorization. Licensees and other persons will furnish National Security Information and/or Restricted Data to a Commission employee on official business when the employee has the appropriate level of NRC access authorization and need-to-know. Some individuals are permitted to begin NRC employment without an access authorization. However, no NRC employee shall be permitted access to any classified information until the appropriate level of access authorization has been granted to that employee by NRC.

[45 FR 14481, Mar. 5, 1980, as amended at 47 FR 9195, Mar. 4, 1982; 50 FR 36984, Sept. 11, 1985]

§25.17 Approval for processing applicants for access authorization.

(a) Access authorizations must be requested for licensee employees or other persons (e.g., 10 CFR part 2, subpart I) who need access to classified information in connection with activities under 10 CFR parts 50, 52, 54, 60, 63, 70, 72, or 76.

(b) The request must be submitted to the facility CSA. If the NRC is the CSA, the procedures in §25.17 (c) and (d) will be followed. If the NRC is not the CSA, the request will be submitted to the CSA in accordance with procedures established by the CSA. The NRC will be notified of the request by a letter that includes the name, Social Security number and level of access authorization.

(c) The request must include a completed personnel security packet (see §25.17(d)) and request form (NRC Form 237) signed by a licensee, licensee contractor official, or other authorized person.

(d)(1) Each personnel security packet submitted must include the following completed forms:

(i) Questionnaire for National Security Positions (SF–86, Parts 1 and 2) (Part 2 is to be completed by the applicant and placed in a sealed envelope which is to be forwarded to NRC unopened. No licensee, licensee contractor official, or other person at a facility is permitted to review Part 2 information);

(ii) Two standard fingerprint cards (FD–258);

(iii) Security Acknowledgment (NRC Form 176); and

(iv) Other related forms where specified in accompanying instructions (NRC Form 254).

(2) Only a Security Acknowledgment (NRC Form 176) need be completed by any person possessing an active access authorization, or who is being processed for an access authorization, by another Federal agency. The active or pending access authorization must be at an equivalent level to that required by the NRC and be based on an adequate investigation of not more than five years old.

(e) To avoid delays in processing requests for access authorizations, each security packet should be reviewed for completeness and correctness (including legibility of response on the forms) before submittal.

(f) The Office of Personnel Management (OPM) bills the NRC for the cost of each background investigation conducted in support of an application for access authorization (application). The combined cost of the OPM investigation and the NRC's application processing overhead (NRC processing fee) are recovered through an access authorization fee imposed on applicants for access authorization.

(1) Each application for access authorization, renewal, or change in level must be accompanied by a remittance, payable to the U.S. Nuclear Regulatory Commission, which is equal to the NRC access authorization fee. This fee must

be determined using the following formula: the OPM investigation billing rates on the day of NRC receipt of the application + the NRC processing fee = the NRC access authorization fee. The NRC processing fee is determined by multiplying the OPM investigation billing rate on the day of NRC receipt of the application by 55.8 percent (*i.e.*, OPM rate × 55.8 percent).

(2) Updated OPM investigation billing rates are published periodically in a Federal Investigations Notice (FIN) issued by the OPM's Federal Investigative Services. Copies of the current OPM investigation billing rates schedule can be obtained by contacting the NRC's Personnel Security Branch, Division of Facilities Security, Office of Administration by email to *Licensee_Access_Authorization_Fee.Resource@nrc.gov*

(3) The NRC's Information Access Authority Program (IAAP) is considered reimbursable work representing services provided to an organization for which the NRC is entitled payment. The NRC is authorized to receive and retain fees from licensees for services performed. The NRC's Office of the Chief Financial Officer periodically reviews the fees charged for IAAP and makes recommendations on revising those charges to reflect costs incurred by the NRC in providing those services. The reviews are performed using cost analysis techniques to determine the direct and indirect costs. Based on this review the IAAP fees are adjusted to reflect the current cost for the program. Copies of the current NRC access authorization fee may be obtained by contacting the NRC's Personnel Security Branch, Division of Facilities Security, Office of Administration by email to: *Licensee_Access_Authorization_Fee.Resource@nrc.gov.* Any change in the NRC's access authorization fee will be applicable to each access authorization request received on or after the effective date of the OPM's most recently published investigation billing rates schedule.

(4) Certain applications from individuals having current Federal access authorizations may be processed more expeditiously and at less cost, because the Commission, at its discretion, may decide to accept the certification of access authorization and investigative data from other Federal Government agencies that grant personnel access authorizations.

[62 FR 17687, Apr. 11, 1997, as amended at 68 FR 62512, Nov. 5, 2003; 70 FR 32227, June 2, 2005; 72 FR 27411, May 16, 2007; 77 FR 26153, May 3, 2012; 77 FR 46258, Aug. 3, 2012]

§ 25.19 Processing applications.

Each application for an access authorization or access authorization renewal must be submitted to the CSA. If the NRC is the CSA, the application and its accompanying fee must be submitted to the NRC Division of Facilities and Security. If necessary, the NRC Division of Facilities and Security may obtain approval from the appropriate Commission office exercising licensing or regulatory authority before processing the access authorization or access authorization renewal request. If the applicant is disapproved for processing, the NRC Division of Facilities and Security shall notify the submitter in writing and return the original application (security packet) and its accompanying fee.

[64 FR 15648, Apr. 1, 1999]

§ 25.21 Determination of initial and continued eligibility for access authorization.

(a) Following receipt by the CSA of the reports of the personnel security investigations, the record will be reviewed to determine that granting an access authorization or renewal of access authorization will not endanger the common defense and security and is clearly consistent with the national interest. If this determination is made, access authorization will be granted or renewed. If the NRC is the CSA, questions as to initial or continued eligibility will be determined in accordance with part 10 of chapter I. If another agency is the CSA, that agency will, under the requirements of the NISPOM, have established procedures at the facility to resolve questions as to initial or continued eligibility for access authorization. These questions will be determined in accordance with established CSA procedures already in effect for the facility.

(b) The CSA must be promptly notified of developments that bear on continued eligibility for access authorization throughout the period for which the authorization is active (e.g., persons who marry subsequent to the completion of a personnel security packet must report this change by submitting a completed NRC Form 354, "Data Report on Spouse" or equivalent CSA form).

(c)(1) Except as provided in paragraph (c)(2) of this section, an NRC "Q" access authorization must be renewed every five years from the date of issuance. Except as provided in paragraph (c)(2) of this section, an NRC "L" access authorization must be renewed every ten years from the date of issuance. An application for renewal must be submitted at least 120 days before the expiration of the five-year period for a "Q" access authorization and the ten-year period for an "L" access authorization, and must include:

(i) A statement by the licensee or other person that the individual continues to require access to classified National Security Information or Restricted Data; and

(ii) A personnel security packet as described in § 25.17(d).

(2) Renewal applications and the required paperwork are not required for individuals who have a current and active access authorization from another Federal agency and who are subject to a reinvestigation program by that agency that is determined by the NRC to meet the NRC's requirements. (The DOE Reinvestigation Program has been determined to meet the NRC's requirements.) For these individuals, the submission of the SF–86 by the licensee or other person to the other Government agency pursuant to their reinvestigation requirements will satisfy the NRC's renewal submission and paperwork requirements, even if less than five years have passed since the date of issuance or renewal of the NRC "Q" access authorization, or if less than 10 years have passed since the date of issuance or renewal of the NRC "L" access authorization. Any NRC access authorization continued in response to the provisions of this paragraph will, thereafter, not be due for renewal until the date set by the other Government agency for the next reinvestigation of the individual pursuant to the other agency's reinvestigation program. However, the period of time for the initial and each subsequent NRC "Q" renewal application to the NRC may not exceed seven years or, in the case of an NRC "L" renewal application, twelve years. Any individual who is subject to the reinvestigation program requirements of another Federal agency but, for administrative or other reasons, does not submit reinvestigation forms to that agency within seven years for a "Q" renewal or twelve years for an "L" renewal of the previous submission, shall submit a renewal application to the NRC using the forms prescribed in § 25.17(d) before the expiration of the seven-year period for a "Q" renewal or twelve-year period for an "L" renewal.

(3) If the NRC is not the CSA, reinvestigation program procedures and requirements will be set by the CSA.

[62 FR 17688, Apr. 11, 1997, as amended at 64 FR 15648, Apr. 1, 1999]

§ 25.23 Notification of grant of access authorization.

The determination to grant or renew access authorization will be furnished in writing to the licensee or organization that initiated the request. Upon receipt of the notification of original grant of access authorization, the licensee or organization shall obtain, as a condition for grant of access authorization and access to classified information, an executed "Classified Information Nondisclosure Agreement" (SF–312) from the affected individual. The SF–312 is an agreement between the United States and an individual who is cleared for access to classified information. An employee issued an initial access authorization shall execute a SF–312 before being granted access to classified information. The licensee or other organization shall forward the executed SF–312 to the CSA for retention. If the employee refuses to execute the SF–312, the licensee or other organization shall deny the employee access to classified information and submit a report to the CSA. The SF–312 must be signed and dated by the employee and witnessed. The employee's and witness' signatures must bear the same date. The individual shall also be given a security orientation briefing in accordance with § 95.33 of this chapter. Records of access authorization grant and renewal notification must be maintained by the licensee or other organization for three years after the access authorization has been terminated by the CSA. This information may also be furnished to other representatives of the Commission, to licensees, contractors, or other Federal agencies. Notifications of access authorization will not be given in writing to the affected individual except:

(a) In those cases when the determination was made as a result of a Personnel Security Hearing or by a Personnel Security Review Panel ; or

(b) When the individual also is the official designated by the licensee or other organization to whom written NRC notifications are forwarded.

[62 FR 17688, Apr. 11, 1997, as amended at 64 FR 15648, Apr. 1, 1999]

§ 25.25 Cancellation of requests for access authorization.

When a request for an individual's access authorization or renewal of an access authorization is withdrawn or canceled, the requestor shall notify the CSA immediately by telephone so that the single scope background investigation, national agency check with law and credit investigation, or other personnel security action may be discontinued. The requestor shall identify the full name and date of birth of the individual, the date of request, and the type of access authorization or access authorization renewal requested. The requestor shall confirm each telephone notification promptly in writing.

[64 FR 15648, Apr. 1, 1999]

§ 25.27 Reopening of cases in which requests for access authorizations are canceled.

(a) In conjunction with a new request for access authorization (NRC Form 237 or CSA equivalent) for individuals whose cases were previously canceled, new fingerprint cards (FD–257) in duplicate and a new Security Acknowledgment (NRC Form 176), or CSA equivalent, must be furnished to the CSA along with the request.

(b) Additionally, if 90 days or more have elapsed since the date of the last Questionnaire for National Security Positions (SF–86), or CSA equivalent, the individual must complete a personnel security packet (see § 25.17(d)). The CSA, based on investigative or other needs, may require a complete personnel security packet in other cases as well. A fee, equal to the amount paid for an initial request, will be charged only if a new or updating investigation by the NRC is required.

[62 FR 17689, Apr. 11, 1997, as amended at 64 FR 15648, Apr. 1, 1999]

§ 25.29 Reinstatement of access authorization.

(a) An access authorization can be reinstated provided that:

(1) No more than 24 months has lapsed since the date of termination of the clearance;

(2) There has been no break in employment with the employer since the date of termination of the clearance;

(3) There is no known adverse information;

(4) The most recent investigation must not exceed 5 years (Top Secret, Q) or 10 years (Secret, L); and

(5) The most recent investigation must meet or exceed the scope of the investigation required for the level of access authorization that is to be reinstated or granted.

(b) An access authorization can be reinstated at the same, or lower, level by submission of a CSA-designated form to the CSA. The employee may not have access to classified information until receipt of written confirmation of reinstatement and an up-to-date personnel security packet will be furnished with the request for reinstatement of an access authorization. A new Security Acknowledgement will be obtained in all cases. Where personnel security packets are not required, a request for reinstatement must state the level of access authorization to be reinstated and the full name and date of birth of the individual to establish positive identification. A fee, equal to the amount paid for an initial request, will be charged only if a new or updating investigation by the NRC is required.

[62 FR 17689, Apr. 11, 1997]

§ 25.31 Extensions and transfers of access authorizations.

(a) The NRC Division of Facilities and Security may, on request, extend the authorization of an individual who possesses an access authorization in connection with a particular employer or activity to permit access to classified information in connection with an assignment with another employer or activity.

(b) The NRC Division of Facilities and Security may, on request, transfer an access authorization when an individual's access authorization under one employer or activity is terminated, simultaneously with the individual being granted an access authorization for another employer or activity.

(c) Requests for an extension or transfer of an access authorization must state the full name of the person, date of birth, and level of access authorization. The Director, Division of Facilities and Security, may require a new personnel security packet (see § 25.17(c)) to be completed by the applicant. A fee, equal to the amount paid for an initial request, will be charged only if a new or updating investigation by the NRC is required.

(d) The date of an extension or transfer of access authorization may not be used to determine when a request for renewal of access authorization is required. Access authorization renewal requests must be timely submitted, in accordance with § 25.21(c).

[45 FR 14481, Mar. 5, 1980, as amended at 48 FR 24320, June 1, 1983; 57 FR 3721, Jan. 31, 1992; 62 FR 17689, Apr. 11, 1997; 64 FR 15648, Apr. 1, 1999]

§ 25.33 Termination of access authorizations.

(a) Access authorizations will be terminated when:

(1) An access authorization is no longer required;

(2) An individual is separated from the employment or the activity for which he or she obtained an access authorization for a period of 90 days or more; or

(3) An individual, pursuant to 10 CFR part 10 or other CSA-approved adjudicatory standards, is no longer eligible for an access authorization.

(b) A representative of the licensee or other organization that employs the individual whose access authorization will be terminated shall immediately notify the CSA when the circumstances noted in paragraph (a)(1) or (a)(2) of this section exist; inform the individual that his or her access authorization is being terminated, and the reason; and that he or she will be considered for reinstatement of an access authorization if he or she resumes work requiring the authorization.

(c) When an access authorization is to be terminated, a representative of the licensee or other organization shall conduct a security termination briefing of the individual involved, explain the Security Termination Statement (NRC Form 136 or CSA approved form) and have the individual complete the form. The representative shall promptly forward the original copy of the completed Security Termination Statement to CSA.

[62 FR 17689, Apr. 11, 1997, as amended at 64 FR 15649, Apr. 1, 1999]

CLASSIFIED VISITS

§ 25.35 Classified visits.

(a) The number of classified visits must be held to a minimum. The licensee, certificate holder, applicant for a standard design certification under part 52 of this chapter (including an applicant after the Commission has adopted a final standard design certification rule under part 52 of this chapter), or other facility, or an applicant for or holder of a standard design approval under part 52 of this chapter shall determine that the visit is necessary and that the purpose of the visit cannot be achieved without access to, or disclosure of, classified information. All classified visits require advance notification to, and approval of, the organization to be visited. In urgent cases, visit information may be furnished by telephone and confirmed in writing.

(b) Representatives of the Federal Government, when acting in their official capacities as inspectors, investigators, or auditors, may visit a licensee, certificate holder, or other facility without furnishing advanced notification, provided these representatives present appropriate Government credentials upon arrival. Normally, however, Federal representatives will provide advance notification in the form of an NRC Form 277, "Request for Visit or Access Approval," with the "need-to-know" certified by the appropriate NRC office exercising licensing or regulatory authority and verification of an NRC access authorization by the Division of Facilities and Security.

(c) The licensee, certificate holder, or others shall include the following information on all Visit Authorization Letters (VAL) which they prepare.

(1) Visitor's name, address, and telephone number and certification of the level of the facility security clearance;

(2) Name, date and place of birth, and citizenship of the individual intending to visit;

(3) Certification of the proposed visitor's personnel clearance and any special access authorizations required for the visit;

(4) Name of person(s) to be visited;

(5) Purpose and sufficient justification for the visit to allow for a determination of the necessity of the visit; and

(6) Date or period during which the VAL is to be valid.

(d) Classified visits may be arranged for a 12 month period. The requesting facility shall notify all places honoring these visit arrangements of any change in the individual's status that will cause the visit request to be canceled before its normal termination date.

(e) The responsibility for determining need-to-know in connection with a classified visit rests with the individual who will disclose classified information during the visit. The licensee, certificate holder or other facility shall establish procedures to ensure positive identification of visitors before the disclosure of any classified information.

[62 FR 17689, Apr. 11, 1997, as amended at 64 FR 15649, Apr. 1, 1999; 72 FR 49488, Aug. 28, 2007]

VIOLATIONS

§25.37 Violations.

(a) An injunction or other court order may be obtained to prohibit a violation of any provision of:

(1) The Atomic Energy Act of 1954, as amended;

(2) Title II of the Energy Reorganization Act of 1974, as amended; or

(3) Any regulation or order issued under these Acts.

(b) National Security Information is protected under the requirements and sanctions of Executive Order 13526, as amended, or any predecessor or successor orders.

[48 FR 24320, June 1, 1983, as amended at 57 FR 55072, Nov. 24, 1992; 64 FR 15649, Apr. 1, 1999; 70 FR 32227, June 2, 2005; 75 FR 73941, Nov. 30, 2010]

§25.39 Criminal penalties.

(a) Section 223 of the Atomic Energy Act of 1954, as amended, provides for criminal sanctions for willful violation of, attempted violation of, or conspiracy to violate, any regulation issued under sections 161b, 161i, or 161o of the Act. For purposes of section 223, all the regulations in part 25 are issued under one or more of sections 161b, 161i, or 161o, except for the sections listed in paragraph (b) of this section.

(b) The regulations in part 25 that are not issued under sections 161b, 161i, or 161o for the purposes of section 223 are as follows: §§25.1, 25.3, 25.5, 25.7, 25.8, 25.9, 25.11, 25.19, 25.25, 25.27, 25.29, 25.31, 25.37, and 25.39.

[57 FR 55072, Nov. 24, 1992]

APPENDIX A TO PART 25—FEES FOR NRC ACCESS AUTHORIZATION

The NRC application fee for an access authorization of type . . .	Is the sum of the current OPM investigation billing rate charged for an investigation of type . . .	Plus the NRC's processing fee (rounded to the nearest dollar), which is equal to the OPM investigation billing rate for the type of investigation referenced multiplied by . . .
Initial "L" access authorization [1]	ANACI—Access National Agency Check with Inquiries (Standard Service, Code C).	55.8%
Reinstatement of "L" access authorization [2].	No fee assessed for most applications.	
Renewal of "L" access authorization [1]	NACLC—National Agency Check with Law and Credit (Standard Service, Code C).	55.8%.
Initial "Q" access authorization	SSBI—Single Scope Background Investigation (Standard Service, Code C).	55.8%
Initial "Q" access authorization (expedited processing).	SSBI—Single Scope Background Investigation (Priority Handling, Code A).	55.8%
Reinstatement of "Q" access authorization [2].	No fee assessed for most applications.	
Renewal of "Q" access authorization [1]	SSBI-PR—Periodic Reinvestigation for SSBI (Standard Service, Code C).	55.8%

[1] If the NRC determines, based on its review of available data, that a single scope investigation is necessary, the appropriate fee for an Initial "Q" access authorization will be assessed before the conduct of investigation.
[2] Full fee will only be charged if an investigation is required.

[77 FR 26153, May 3, 2012, as amended at 77 FR 46258, Aug. 3, 2012]

PART 26—FITNESS FOR DUTY PROGRAMS

Subpart A—Administrative Provisions

Subpart B—Program Elements

Subpart C—Granting and Maintaining Authorization

Subpart D—Management Actions and Sanctions To Be Imposed

Subpart E—Collecting Specimens for Testing

Subpart F—Licensee Testing Facilities

Subpart G—Laboratories Certified by the Department of Health and Human Services

Subpart H—Determining Fitness-for-Duty Policy Violations and Determining Fitness

Subpart I—Managing Fatigue.

Subpart J [Reserved]

Subpart K—FFD Programs for Construction

Subparts L–M [Reserved]

Subpart N—Recordkeeping and Reporting Requirements

Subpart O—Inspections, Violations, and Penalties

AUTHORITY: Atomic Energy Act of 1954, secs. 53, 103, 104, 107, 161, 223, 234, 1701 (42 U.S.C. 2073, 2133, 2134, 2137, 2201, 2273, 2282, 2297f); Energy Reorganization Act of 1974, secs. 201, 202 (42 U.S.C. 5841, 5842); 44 U.S.C. 3504 note.

SOURCE: 73 FR 17176, Mar. 31, 2008, unless otherwise noted.

Subpart A—Administrative Provisions

§26.1 Purpose.

This part prescribes requirements and standards for the establishment, implementation, and maintenance of fitness-for-duty (FFD) programs.

§ 26.3 Scope.

(a) Licensees who are authorized to operate a nuclear power reactor under 10 CFR 50.57, and holders of a combined license under 10 CFR Part 52 after the Commission has made the finding under 10 CFR 52.103(g) shall comply with the requirements of this part, except for subpart K of this part. Licensees who receive their authorization to operate a nuclear power reactor under 10 CFR 50.57 after the date of publication of this final rule in the FEDERAL REGISTER and holders of a combined license under 10 CFR Part 52 after the Commission has made the finding under 10 CFR 52.103(g) shall implement the FFD program before the receipt of special nuclear material in the form of fuel assemblies.

(b) Licensees who are authorized to possess, use, or transport formula quantities of strategic special nuclear material (SSNM) under Part 70 of this chapter, and any corporation, firm, partnership, limited liability company, association, or other organization who obtains a certificate of compliance or an approved compliance plan under Part 76 of this chapter, only if the entity elects to engage in activities involving formula quantities of SSNM shall comply with the requirements of this part, except for subparts I and K of this part.

(c) Before the receipt of special nuclear material in the form of fuel assemblies, the following licensees and other entities shall comply with the requirements of this part, except for subpart I of this part; and, no later than the receipt of special nuclear material in the form of fuel assemblies, the following licensees and other entities shall comply with the requirements of this part:

(1) Combined license applicants (under Part 52 of this chapter) who have been issued a limited work authorization under § 50.10(e), if the limited work authorization authorizes the applicant to install the foundations, including the placement of concrete, for safety- and security-related structures, systems, and components (SSCs) under the limited work authorization;

(2) Combined license holders (under Part 52 of this chapter) before the Commission has made the finding under § 52.103(g);

(3) Construction permit applicants (under Part 50 of this chapter) who have been issued a limited work authorization under § 50.10(e), if the limited work authorization authorizes the applicant to install the foundations, including the placement of concrete, for safety- and security-related SSCs under the limited work authorization;

(4) Construction permit holders (under Part 50 of this chapter); and

(5) Early site permit holders who have been issued a limited work authorization under § 50.10(e), if the limited work authorization authorizes the early site permit holder to install the foundations, including the placement of concrete, for safety- and security-related SSCs under the limited work authorization.

(d) Contractor/vendors (C/Vs) who implement FFD programs or program elements, to the extent that the licensees and other entities specified in paragraphs (a) through (c) of this section rely on those C/V FFD programs or program elements to meet the requirements of this part, shall comply with the requirements of this part.

(e) This part does not apply to either spent fuel storage facility licensees or non-power reactor licensees who possess, use, or transport formula quantities of irradiated SSNM.

§ 26.4 FFD program applicability to categories of individuals.

(a) All persons who are granted unescorted access to nuclear power reactor protected areas by the licensees in § 26.3(a) and, as applicable, (c) and perform the following duties shall be subject to an FFD program that meets all of the requirements of this part, except subpart K of this part:

(1) Operating or onsite directing of the operation of systems and components that a risk-informed evaluation process has shown to be significant to public health and safety;

(2) Performing health physics or chemistry duties required as a member of the onsite emergency response organization minimum shift complement;

(3) Performing the duties of a fire brigade member who is responsible for understanding the effects of fire and fire

suppressants on safe shutdown capability;

(4) Performing maintenance or onsite directing of the maintenance of SSCs that a risk-informed evaluation process has shown to be significant to public health and safety; and

(5) Performing security duties as an armed security force officer, alarm station operator, response team leader, or watchman, hereinafter referred to as security personnel.

(b) All persons who are granted unescorted access to nuclear power reactor protected areas by the licensees in § 26.3(a) and, as applicable, (c) and who do not perform the duties described in paragraph (a) of this section shall be subject to an FFD program that meets all of the requirements of this part, except §§ 26.205 through 26.209 and subpart K of this part.

(c) All persons who are required by a licensee in § 26.3(a) and, as applicable, (c) to physically report to the licensee's Technical Support Center or Emergency Operations Facility by licensee emergency plans and procedures shall be subject to an FFD program that meets all of the requirement of this part, except §§ 26.205 through 26.209 and subpart K of this part.

(d) Any individual whose duties for the licensees and other entities in § 26.3(b) require him or her to have the following types of access or perform the following activities shall be subject to an FFD program that meets all of the requirements of this part, except subparts I and K of this part:

(1) All persons who are granted unescorted access to Category IA material;

(2) All persons who create or have access to procedures or records for safeguarding SSNM;

(3) All persons who measure Category IA material;

(4) All persons who transport or escort Category IA material; and

(5) All persons who guard Category IA material.

(e) When construction activities begin, any individual whose duties for the licensees and other entities in § 26.3(c) require him or her to have the following types of access or perform the following activities at the location where the nuclear power plant will be constructed and operated shall be subject to an FFD program that meets all of the requirements of this part, except subparts I and K of this part:

(1) Serves as security personnel required by the NRC, until the licensees or other entities receive special nuclear material in the form of fuel assemblies, at which time individuals who serve as security personnel required by the NRC must meet the requirements applicable to security personnel in paragraph (a)(5) of this section;

(2) Performs quality assurance, quality control, or quality verification activities related to safety- or security-related construction activities;

(3) Based on a designation under § 26.406 by a licensee or other entity, monitors the fitness of the individuals specified in paragraph (f) of this section;

(4) Witnesses or determines inspections, tests, and analyses certification required under Part 52 of this chapter;

(5) Supervises or manages the construction of safety- or security-related SSCs; or

(6) Directs, as defined in § 26.5, or implements the access authorization program, including—

(i) Having access to the information used by the licensee or other entity to make access authorization determinations, including information stored in electronic format;

(ii) Making access authorization determinations;

(iii) Issuing entry-control picture badges in accordance with access authorization determinations;

(iv) Conducting background investigations or psychological assessments used by the licensee or other entity to make access authorization determinations, except that he or she shall be subject to behavioral observation only when he or she is present at the location where the nuclear power plant will be constructed and operated, and licensees and other entities may rely on a local hospital or other organization that meets the requirements of 49 CFR Part 40, "Procedures for Department of Transportation Workplace Drug and Alcohol Testing Programs" (65 FR 41944; August 9, 2001) to collect his or her specimens for drug and alcohol testing;

(v) Adjudicating reviews or appeals of access authorization determinations;

(vi) Auditing the access authorization program; or

(vii) Performing any of the activities or having any of the duties listed in paragraph (e)(6) of this section for any C/V upon whom the licensee's or other entity's access authorization program will rely.

(f) Any individual who is constructing or directing the construction of safety- or security-related SSCs shall be subject to an FFD program that meets the requirements of subpart K of this part, unless the licensee or other entity subjects these individuals to an FFD program that meets all of the requirements of this part, except for subparts I and K of this part.

(g) All FFD program personnel who are involved in the day-to-day operations of the program, as defined by the procedures of the licensees and other entities in § 26.3(a) through (c), and, as applicable, (d), and whose duties require them to have the following types of access or perform the following activities shall be subject to an FFD program that meets all of the requirements of this part, except subparts I and K of this part, and, at the licensee's or other entity's discretion, subpart C of this part:

(1) All persons who can link test results with the individual who was tested before an FFD policy violation determination is made, including, but not limited to the MRO;

(2) All persons who make determinations of fitness;

(3) All persons who make authorization decisions;

(4) All persons involved in selecting or notifying individuals for testing; and

(5) All persons involved in the collection or onsite testing of specimens.

(h) Individuals who have applied for authorization to have the types of access or perform the activities described in paragraphs (a) through (d) of this section shall be subject to §§ 26.31(c)(1), 26.35(b), 26.37, 26.39, and the applicable requirements of subparts C, and E through H of this part.

(i) The following individuals are not subject to an FFD program under this part:

(1) Individuals who are not employed by a licensee or other entity in this part, who do not routinely provide FFD program services to a licensee or other entity in this part, and whose normal workplace is not at the licensee's or other entity's facility, but who may be called on to provide an FFD program service, including, but not limited to, collecting specimens for drug and alcohol testing, performing behavioral observation, or providing input to a determination of fitness. Such individuals may include, but are not limited to, hospital, employee assistance program (EAP) or substance abuse treatment facility personnel, or other medical professionals;

(2) NRC employees, law enforcement personnel, or offsite emergency fire and medical response personnel while responding on site;

(3) SSNM transporter personnel who are subject to U.S. Department of Transportation drug and alcohol FFD programs that require random testing for drugs and alcohol; and

(4) The FFD program personnel of a program that is regulated by another Federal agency or State on which a licensee or other entity relies to meet the requirements of this part, as permitted under §§ 26.4(j), 26.31(b)(2), and 26.405(e), if the FFD program personnel are not employed by the licensee or other entity and their normal workplace is not at the licensee's or other entity's facility.

(j) Individuals who are subject to this part and who are also subject to a program regulated by another Federal agency or State need be covered by only those elements of an FFD program that are not included in the Federal agency or State program, as long as all of the following conditions are met:

(1) The individuals are subject to pre-access (or pre-employment), random, for-cause, and post-event testing for the drugs and drug metabolites specified in § 26.31(d)(1) at or below the cutoff levels specified in § 26.163(a)(1) for initial drug testing and in § 26.163(b)(1) for confirmatory drug testing;

(2) The individuals are subject to pre-access (or pre-employment), random, for-cause, and post-event testing for alcohol at or below the cutoff levels specified in § 26.103(a) and breath specimens are subject to confirmatory testing, if required, with an EBT that meets the requirements specified in § 26.91;

(3) Urine specimens are tested for validity and the presence of drugs and drug metabolites at a laboratory certified by the Department of Health and Human Services (HHS);

(4) Training is provided to address the knowledge and abilities (KAs) listed in § 26.29(a)(1) through (a)(10); and

(5) Provisions are made to ensure that the testing agency or organization notifies the licensee or other entity granting authorization of any FFD policy violation.

[73 FR 17176, Mar. 31, 2008, as amended at 75 FR 73941, Nov. 30, 2010]

§ 26.5 Definitions.

Acute fatigue means fatigue from causes (e.g., restricted sleep, sustained wakefulness, task demands) occurring within the past 24 hours.

Adulterated specimen means a urine specimen that has been altered, as evidenced by test results showing either a substance that is not a normal constituent of urine or showing an abnormal concentration of an endogenous substance.

Alertness means the ability to remain awake and sustain attention.

Aliquot means a portion of a specimen that is used for testing. It is taken as a sample representing the whole specimen.

Analytical run means the process of testing a group of urine specimens for validity or for the presence of drugs and/or drug metabolites. For the purposes of defining the periods within which performance testing must be conducted by any licensee testing facility or HHS-certified laboratory that continuously processes specimens, an analytical run is defined as no more than an 8-hour period. For a facility that analyzes specimens in batches, an analytical run is defined as a group of specimens that are handled and tested together.

Authorization means that a licensee or other entity in § 26.3 has determined that an individual has met the requirements of this part to be granted or maintain the types of access or perform the duties specified in § 26.4(a) through (e), and, at the licensee's or other entity's discretion, § 26.4(f) or (g).

Best effort means documented actions that a licensee or other entity who is subject to subpart C of this part takes to obtain suitable inquiry and employment information in order to determine whether an individual may be granted authorization, when the primary source of information refuses or indicates an inability or unwillingness to provide the information within 3 business days of the request and the licensee or other entity relies on a secondary source to meet the requirement.

Blood alcohol concentration (BAC) means the mass of alcohol in a volume of blood.

Calibrator means a solution of known concentration which is used to define expected outcomes of a measurement procedure or to compare the response obtained with the response of a test specimen/sample. The concentration of the analyte of interest in the calibrator is known within limits ascertained during its preparation. Calibrators may be used to establish a cutoff concentration and/or a calibration curve over a range of interest.

Category IA material means SSNM that is directly usable in the manufacture of a nuclear explosive device, except if the material meets any of the following criteria:

(1) The dimensions are large enough (at least 2 meters in one dimension, greater than 1 meter in each of two dimensions, or greater than 25 centimeters in each of three dimensions) to preclude hiding the item on an individual;

(2) The total weight of an encapsulated item of SSNM is such that it cannot be carried inconspicuously by one person (*i.e.*, at least 50 kilograms gross weight); or

(3) The quantity of SSNM (less than 0.05 formula kilograms) in each container requires protracted diversions to accumulate 5 formula kilograms.

Chain of custody means procedures to account for the integrity of each specimen or aliquot by tracking its handling and storage from the point of specimen collection to final disposition of the specimen and its aliquots. "Chain of custody" and "custody and control" are synonymous and may be used interchangeably.

Circadian variation in alertness and performance means the increases and decreases in alertness and cognitive/motor functioning caused by human physiological processes (e.g., body temperature, release of hormones) that vary on an approximately 24-hour cycle.

Collection site means a designated place where individuals present themselves for the purpose of providing a specimen of their urine, oral fluids, and/or breath to be analyzed for the presence of drugs or alcohol.

Collector means a person who is trained in the collection procedures of subpart E, instructs and assists a specimen donor at a collection site, and receives and makes an initial examination of the specimen(s) provided by the donor.

Commission means the U.S. Nuclear Regulatory Commission (NRC) or its duly authorized representatives.

Confirmatory drug or alcohol test means a second analytical procedure to identify the presence of alcohol or a specific drug or drug metabolite in a specimen. The purpose of a confirmatory test is to ensure the reliability and accuracy of an initial test result.

Confirmatory validity test means a second test performed on a different aliquot of the original urine specimen to further support a validity test result.

Confirmed test result means a test result that demonstrates that an individual has used drugs and/or alcohol in violation of the requirements of this part or has attempted to subvert the testing process by submitting an adulterated or substituted urine specimen. For drugs, adulterants, and substituted specimens, a confirmed test result is determined by the Medical Review Officer (MRO), after discussion with the donor subsequent to the MRO's receipt of a positive confirmatory drug test result from the HHS-certified laboratory and/or a confirmatory substituted or adulterated validity test result from the HHS-certified laboratory for that donor. For alcohol, a confirmed test result is based on a positive confirmatory alcohol test result from an evidential breath testing device (EBT) without MRO review of the test result.

Constructing or construction activities mean, for the purposes of this part, the tasks involved in building a nuclear power plant that are performed at the location where the nuclear power plant will be constructed and operated. These tasks include fabricating, erecting, integrating, and testing safety- and security-related SSCs, and the installation of their foundations, including the placement of concrete.

Contractor/vendor (C/V) means any company, or any individual not employed by a licensee or other entity specified in § 26.3(a) through (c), who is providing work or services to a licensee or other entity covered in § 26.3(a) through (c), either by contract, purchase order, oral agreement, or other arrangement.

Control means a sample used to monitor the status of an analysis to maintain its performance within predefined limits.

Cumulative fatigue means the increase in fatigue over consecutive sleep-wake periods resulting from inadequate rest.

Cutoff level means the concentration or decision criteria established for designating and reporting a test result as positive, of questionable validity (referring to validity screening or initial validity test results from a licensee testing facility), or adulterated, substituted, dilute, or invalid (referring to initial or confirmatory test results from an HHS-certified laboratory).

Dilute specimen means a urine specimen with creatinine and specific gravity concentrations that are lower than expected for human urine.

Directing means the exercise of control over a work activity by an individual who is directly involved in the execution of the work activity, and either makes technical decisions for that activity without subsequent technical review, or is ultimately responsible for the correct performance of that work activity.

Donor means the individual from whom a specimen is collected.

Eight (8)-hour shift schedule means a schedule that averages not more than 9 hours per workday over the entire shift cycle.

Employment action means a change in job responsibilities or removal from a job, or the employer-mandated implementation of a plan for substance abuse treatment in order to avoid a change in or removal from a job, because of the individual's use of drugs or alcohol.

Fatigue means the degradation in an individual's cognitive and motor functioning resulting from inadequate rest.

Formula quantity means SSNM in any combination in a quantity of 5000 grams or more computed by the formula, grams = (grams contained U–235) + 2.5 (grams U–233 + grams plutonium). This class of material is sometimes referred to as a Category I quantity of material.

HHS-certified laboratory means a laboratory that is certified to perform urine drug testing under the Department of Health and Human Services Mandatory Guidelines for Federal Workplace Drug Testing Programs (the HHS Guidelines), which were published in the FEDERAL REGISTER on April 11, 1988 (53 FR 11970), and as amended, June 9, 1994 (59 FR 29908), November 13, 1998 (63 FR 63483), and April 13, 2004 (69 FR 19643).

Illegal drug means, for the purposes of this regulation, any drug that is included in Schedules I to V of section 202 of the Controlled Substances Act [21 U.S.C. 812], but not when used pursuant to a valid prescription or when used as otherwise authorized by law.

Increased threat condition means an increase in the protective measure level, relative to the lowest protective measure level applicable to the site during the previous 60 days, as promulgated by an NRC Advisory.

Initial drug test means a test to differentiate "negative" specimens from those that require confirmatory drug testing.

Initial validity test means a first test used to determine whether a specimen is adulterated, dilute, substituted, or invalid, and may require confirmatory validity testing.

Invalid result means the result reported by an HHS-certified laboratory for a specimen that contains an unidentified adulterant, contains an unidentified interfering substance, has an abnormal physical characteristic, contains inconsistent physiological constituents, or has an endogenous substance at an abnormal concentration that prevents the laboratory from completing testing or obtaining a valid drug test result.

Legal action means a formal action taken by a law enforcement authority or court of law, including an arrest, an indictment, the filing of charges, a conviction, or the mandated implementation of a plan for substance abuse treatment in order to avoid a permanent record of an arrest or conviction, in response to any of the following activities:

(1) The use, sale, or possession of illegal drugs;

(2) The abuse of legal drugs or alcohol; or

(3) The refusal to take a drug or alcohol test.

Licensee testing facility means a drug and specimen validity testing facility that is operated by a licensee or other entity who is subject to this part to perform tests of urine specimens.

Limit of detection (LOD) means the lowest concentration of an analyte that an analytical procedure can reliably detect, which could be significantly lower than the established cutoff levels.

Limit of quantitation (LOQ) means the lowest concentration of an analyte at which the concentration of the analyte can be accurately determined under defined conditions.

Maintenance means, for the purposes of § 26.4(a)(4), the following onsite maintenance activities: Modification, surveillance, post-maintenance testing, and corrective and preventive maintenance.

Medical Review Officer (MRO) means a licensed physician who is responsible for receiving laboratory results generated by a Part 26 drug testing program and who has the appropriate medical training to properly interpret and evaluate an individual's drug and validity test results together with his or her medical history and any other relevant biomedical information.

Nominal means the limited flexibility that is permitted in meeting a scheduled due date for completing a recurrent activity that is required under this part, such as the nominal 12-month frequency required for FFD refresher training in § 26.29(c)(2) and the nominal 12-month frequency required for certain audits in § 26.41(c)(1). Completing a recurrent activity at a nominal frequency means that the activity may be completed within a period that is 25 percent longer or shorter than the period required in this part. The next scheduled due date would be no later than the current scheduled due date plus the required frequency for completing the activity.

Other entity means any corporation, firm, partnership, limited liability company, association, C/V, or other organization who is subject to this part under § 26.3(a) through (c), but is not licensed by the NRC.

Oxidizing adulterant means a substance that acts alone or in combination with other substances to oxidize drugs or drug metabolites to prevent the detection of the drugs or drug metabolites, or a substance that affects the reagents in either the initial or confirmatory drug test. Examples of these agents include, but are not limited to, nitrites, pyridinium chlorochromate, chromium (VI), bleach, iodine/iodide, halogens, peroxidase, and peroxide.

Positive result means, for drug testing, the result reported by a licensee testing facility or HHS-certified laboratory when a specimen contains a drug or drug metabolite equal to or greater than the cutoff concentration. A result reported by an HHS-certified laboratory that a specimen contains a drug or drug metabolite below the cutoff concentration is also a positive result when the laboratory has conducted the special analysis permitted in § 26.163(a)(2). For alcohol testing, a positive result means the result reported by a collection site when the BAC indicated by testing a specimen exceeds the cutoff concentrations established in this part.

Potentially disqualifying FFD information means information demonstrating that an individual has—

(1) Violated a licensee's or other entity's FFD policy;

(2) Had authorization denied or terminated unfavorably under §§ 26.35(c)(2), 26.53(i), 26.63(d), 26.65(g), 26.67(c), 26.69(f), or 26.75(b) through (e);

(3) Used, sold, or possessed illegal drugs;

(4) Abused legal drugs or alcohol;

(5) Subverted or attempted to subvert a drug or alcohol testing program;

(6) Refused to take a drug or alcohol test;

(7) Been subjected to a plan for substance abuse treatment (except for self-referral); or

(8) Had legal action or employment action, as defined in this section, taken for alcohol or drug use.

Protected area has the same meaning as in § 73.2(g) of this chapter: An area encompassed by physical barriers and to which access is controlled.

Quality control sample means a sample used to evaluate whether an analytical procedure is operating within predefined tolerance limits. Calibrators, controls, negative samples, and blind performance test samples are collectively referred to as "quality control samples" and each is individually referred to as a "sample."

Questionable validity means the results of validity screening or initial validity tests at a licensee testing facility indicating that a urine specimen may be adulterated, substituted, dilute, or invalid.

Reviewing official means an employee of a licensee or other entity specified in § 26.3(a) through (c), who is designated by the licensee or other entity to be responsible for reviewing and evaluating any potentially disqualifying FFD information about an individual, including, but not limited to, the results of a determination of fitness, as defined in § 26.189, in order to determine whether the individual may be granted or maintain authorization.

Safety-related structures, systems, and components (SSCs) mean, for the purposes of this part, those structures, systems, and components that are relied on to remain functional during and following design basis events to ensure the integrity of the reactor coolant pressure boundary, the capability to shut down the reactor and maintain it in a safe shutdown condition, or the capability to prevent or mitigate the consequences of accidents that could result in potential offsite exposure comparable to the guidelines in 10 CFR 50.34(a)(1).

Security-related SSCs mean, for the purposes of this part, those structures, systems, and components that the licensee will rely on to implement the licensee's physical security and safeguards contingency plans that either are required under Part 73 of this chapter if the licensee is a construction permit applicant or holder or an early site permit holder, as described in § 26.3(c)(3) through (c)(5), respectively, or are included in the licensee's application if the licensee is a combined license applicant or holder, as described in § 26.3(c)(1) and (c)(2), respectively.

Shift cycle means a series of consecutive work shifts and days off that is planned by the licensee or other entity to repeat regularly, thereby constituting a continuous shift schedule.

Standard means a reference material of known purity or a solution containing a reference material at a known concentration.

Strategic special nuclear material (SSNM) means uranium-235 (contained in uranium enriched to 20 percent or more in the uranium-235 isotope), uranium-233, or plutonium.

Substance abuse means the use, sale, or possession of illegal drugs, or the abuse of prescription and over-the-counter drugs, or the abuse of alcohol.

Substituted specimen means a specimen with creatinine and specific gravity values that are so diminished or so divergent that they are not consistent with normal human physiology.

Subversion and subvert the testing process mean a willful act to avoid being tested or to bring about an inaccurate drug or alcohol test result for oneself or others at any stage of the testing process (including selection and notification of individuals for testing, specimen collection, specimen analysis, and test result reporting), and adulterating, substituting, or otherwise causing a specimen to provide an inaccurate test result.

Supervises or manages means the exercise of control over a work activity by an individual who is not directly involved in the execution of the work activity, but who either makes technical decisions for that activity without subsequent technical review, or is ultimately responsible for the correct performance of that work activity.

Ten (10)-hour shift schedule means a schedule that averages more than 9 hours, but not more than 11 hours, per workday over the entire shift cycle.

Transporter means a general licensee, under 10 CFR 70.20(a), who is authorized to possess formula quantities of SSNM, in the regular course of carriage for another or storage incident thereto, and includes the driver or operator of any conveyance, and the accompanying guards or escorts.

Twelve (12)-hour shift schedule means a schedule that averages more than 11 hours, but not more than 12 hours, per workday over the entire shift cycle.

Unit outage means, for the purposes of this part, that the reactor unit is disconnected from the electrical grid.

Validity screening test means a test to determine the need for initial validity testing of a urine specimen, using a non-instrumented test in which the endpoint result is obtained by visual evaluation (read by the human eye), or a test that is instrumented to the extent that results are machine-read.

Validity screening test lot means a group of validity screening tests that were made from the same starting material.

[73 FR 17176, Mar. 31, 2008, as amended at 81 FR 86909, Dec. 2, 2016]

§ 26.7 Interpretations.

Except as specifically authorized by the Commission in writing, no interpretation of the meaning of the regulations in this part by any officer or employee of the Commission other than a written interpretation by the General Counsel will be recognized to be binding on the Commission.

§ 26.8 Information collection requirements: OMB approval.

(a) The NRC has submitted the information collection requirements contained in this part for approval by the Office of Management and Budget (OMB), as required by the Paperwork Reduction Act (44 U.S.C. 3501 *et seq.*). The NRC may not conduct or sponsor, and a person is not required to respond to, a collection of information unless it displays a currently valid OMB control number. OMB has approved the information collection requirements contained in this part under control number 3150–0146.

(b) The approved information collection requirements contained in this part appear in §§ 26.9, 26.27, 26.29, 26.31, 26.33, 26.35, 26.37, 26.39, 26.41, 26.53, 26.55, 26.57, 26.59, 26.61, 26.63, 26.65, 26.67, 26.69, 26.75, 26.77, 26.85, 26.87, 26.89, 26.91, 26.93, 26.95, 26.97, 26.99, 26.101, 26.103, 26.107, 26.109, 26.111, 26.113, 26.115, 26.117, 26.119, 26.125, 26.127, 26.129, 26.135, 26.137, 26.139, 26.153, 26.155, 26.157, 26.159, 26.163, 26.165, 26.167, 26.168, 26.169, 26.183, 26.185, 26.187, 26.189, 26.203, 26.205, 26.207, 26.211, 26.401, 26.403, 26.405, 26.406, 26.407, 26.411, 26.413, 26.415, 26.417, 26.711, 26.713, 26.715, 26.717, 26.719, and 26.821.

§ 26.9 Specific exemptions.

Upon application of any interested person or on its own initiative, the Commission may grant such exemptions from the requirements of the regulations in this part as it determines are authorized by law and will not endanger life or property or the common defense and security, and are otherwise in the public interest.

§ 26.11 Communications.

Except where otherwise specified in this part, all communications, applications, and reports concerning the regulations in this part must be sent either by mail addressed to ATTN: NRC Document Control Desk, U.S. Nuclear Regulatory Commission, Washington, DC 20555–0001; by hand delivery to the NRC's offices at 11555 Rockville Pike, Rockville, Maryland, between the hours of 8:15 a.m. and 4 p.m. eastern time; or, where practicable, by electronic submission, for example, via Electronic Information Exchange, e-mail, or CD-ROM. Electronic submissions must be made in a manner that enables the NRC to receive, read, authenticate, distribute, and archive the submission, and process and retrieve it a single page at a time. Detailed guidance on making electronic submissions can be obtained by visiting the NRC's Web site at *http://www.nrc.gov/site-help/e-submittals.html;* by e-mail to *MSHD.Resource@nrc.gov;* or by writing the Office of the Chief Information Officer, U.S. Nuclear Regulatory Commission, Washington, DC 20555–0001. The guidance discusses, among other topics, the formats the NRC can accept, the use of electronic signatures, and the treatment of nonpublic information. Copies of all communications must be sent to the appropriate regional office and resident inspector (addresses for the NRC Regional Offices are listed in Appendix D to Part 20 of this chapter).

[73 FR 17176, Mar. 31, 2008, as amended at 74 FR 62681, Dec. 1, 2009; 80 FR 74979, Dec. 1, 2015]

Subpart B—Program Elements

§ 26.21 Fitness-for-duty program.

The licensees and other entities specified in § 26.3(a) through (c) shall establish, implement, and maintain FFD programs that, at a minimum, comprise the program elements contained in this subpart. The individuals specified in § 26.4(a) through (e) and (g), and, at the licensee's or other entity's discretion, § 26.4(f), and, if necessary, § 26.4(j) shall be subject to these FFD programs. Licensees and other entities may rely on the FFD program or program elements of a C/V, as defined in § 26.5, if the C/V's FFD program or program elements meet the applicable requirements of this part.

§ 26.23 Performance objectives.

Fitness-for-duty programs must—

(a) Provide reasonable assurance that individuals are trustworthy and reliable as demonstrated by the avoidance of substance abuse;

(b) Provide reasonable assurance that individuals are not under the influence of any substance, legal or illegal, or mentally or physically impaired from any cause, which in any way adversely affects their ability to safely and competently perform their duties;

(c) Provide reasonable measures for the early detection of individuals who are not fit to perform the duties that require them to be subject to the FFD program;

(d) Provide reasonable assurance that the workplaces subject to this part are free from the presence and effects of illegal drugs and alcohol; and

(e) Provide reasonable assurance that the effects of fatigue and degraded alertness on individuals' abilities to safely and competently perform their duties are managed commensurate with maintaining public health and safety.

§ 26.25 [Reserved]

§ 26.27 Written policy and procedures.

(a) *General.* Each licensee and other entity shall establish, implement, and maintain written policies and procedures to meet the general performance objectives and applicable requirements of this part.

(b) *Policy.* The FFD policy statement must be clear, concise, and readily available, in its most current form, to all individuals who are subject to the policy. Methods of making the statement readily available include, but are not limited to, posting the policy in multiple work areas, providing individuals with brochures, or allowing individuals to print the policy from a computer. The policy statement must be written in sufficient detail to provide affected individuals with information on what is expected of them and what consequences may result from a lack of adherence to the policy. At a minimum, the written policy statement must—

(1) Describe the consequences of the following actions:

(i) The use, sale, or possession of illegal drugs on or off site;

(ii) The abuse of legal drugs and alcohol; and

(iii) The misuse of prescription and over-the-counter drugs;

(2) Describe the requirement that individuals who are notified that they have been selected for random testing must report to the collection site within the time period specified by the licensee or other entity;

(3) Describe the actions that constitute a refusal to provide a specimen for testing, the consequences of a refusal to test, as well as the consequences of subverting or attempting to subvert the testing process;

(4) Prohibit the consumption of alcohol, at a minimum—

(i) Within an abstinence period of 5 hours preceding the individual's arrival at the licensee's or other entity's facility, except as permitted in § 26.27(c)(3); and

(ii) During the period of any tour of duty;

(5) Convey that abstinence from alcohol for the 5 hours preceding any scheduled tour of duty is considered to be a minimum that is necessary, but may not be sufficient, to ensure that the individual is fit for duty;

(6) Address other factors that could affect FFD, such as mental stress, fatigue, or illness, and the use of prescription and over-the-counter medications that could cause impairment;

(7) Provide a description of any program that is available to individuals who are seeking assistance in dealing with drug, alcohol, fatigue, or other problems that could adversely affect an individual's ability to safely and competently perform the duties that require an individual to be subject to this subpart;

(8) Describe the consequences of violating the policy;

(9) Describe the individual's responsibility to report legal actions, as defined in § 26.5;

(10) Describe the responsibilities of managers, supervisors, and escorts to report FFD concerns; and

(11) Describe the individual's responsibility to report FFD concerns.

(c) *Procedures.* Each licensee and other entity shall prepare, implement, and maintain written procedures that describe the methods to be used in implementing the FFD policy and the requirements of this part. The procedures must—

(1) Describe the methods and techniques to be used in testing for drugs and alcohol, including procedures for protecting the privacy and other rights (including due process) of an individual who provides a specimen, procedures for protecting the integrity of the specimen, and procedures used to ensure that the test results are valid and attributable to the correct individual;

(2) Describe immediate and followup actions that will be taken, and the procedures to be used, in those cases in which individuals are determined to have—

(i) Been involved in the use, sale, or possession of illegal drugs;

(ii) Consumed alcohol to excess before the mandatory pre-work abstinence period, or consumed any alcohol during the mandatory pre-work abstinence period or while on duty, as determined by a test that measures BAC;

(iii) Attempted to subvert the testing process by adulterating or diluting specimens (in vivo or in vitro), substituting specimens, or by any other means;

(iv) Refused to provide a specimen for analysis; or

(v) Had legal action taken relating to drug or alcohol use, as defined in § 26.5;

(3) Describe the process that the licensee or other entity will use to ensure that individuals who are called in to perform an unscheduled working tour are fit for duty. At a minimum—

(i) The procedure must require the individual who is called in to state whether the individual considers himself or herself fit for duty and whether he or she has consumed alcohol within the pre-duty abstinence period stated in the policy;

(ii) If the individual has consumed alcohol within this period and the individual is called in for an unscheduled working tour, including an unscheduled working tour to respond to an emergency, the procedure must—

(A) Require a determination of fitness by breath alcohol analysis or other means;

(B) Permit the licensee or other entity to assign the individual to duties that require him or her to be subject to this subpart, if the results of the determination of fitness indicate that the individual is fit to safely and competently perform his or her duties;

(C) Prohibit the licensee or other entity from assigning the individual to duties that require him or her to be subject to this subpart, if the individual is not required to respond to an emergency and the results of the determination of fitness indicate that the individual may be impaired;

(D) State that consumption of alcohol during the 5-hour abstinence period required in paragraph (b)(4)(i) of this section may not by itself preclude a licensee or other entity from using individuals who are needed to respond to an emergency. However, if the determination of fitness indicates that an individual who has been called in for an unscheduled working tour to respond to an emergency may be impaired, the procedure must require the establishment of controls and conditions under which the individual who has been called in can perform work, if necessary; and

(E) State that no sanctions may be imposed on an individual who is called in to perform any unscheduled working tour for having consumed alcohol within the pre-duty abstinence period stated in the policy.

(iii) If the individual reports that he or she considers himself or herself to be unfit for duty for other reasons, including illness, fatigue, or other potentially impairing conditions, and the individual is called in, the procedure must require the establishment of controls and conditions under which the individual can perform work, if necessary;

(4) Describe the process to be followed if an individual's behavior raises a concern regarding the possible use, sale, or possession of illegal drugs on or off site; the possible possession or consumption of alcohol on site; or impairment from any cause which in any way could adversely affect the individual's ability to safely and competently perform his or her duties. The procedure must require that individuals who have an FFD concern about another individual's behavior shall contact the personnel designated in the procedures to report the concern.

(d) *Review.* The NRC may, at any time, review the written policy and procedures to assure that they meet the performance objectives and requirements of this part.

§ 26.29 Training.

(a) *Training content.* Licensees and other entities shall ensure that the individuals who are subject to this subpart have the following KAs:

(1) Knowledge of the policy and procedures that apply to the individual, the methods that will be used to implement them, and the consequences of violating the policy and procedures;

(2) Knowledge of the individual's role and responsibilities under the FFD program;

(3) Knowledge of the roles and responsibilities of others, such as the MRO and the human resources, FFD, and EAP staffs;

(4) Knowledge of the EAP services available to the individual;

(5) Knowledge of the personal and public health and safety hazards associated with abuse of illegal and legal drugs and alcohol;

(6) Knowledge of the potential adverse effects on job performance of prescription and over-the-counter drugs, alcohol, dietary factors, illness, mental stress, and fatigue;

(7) Knowledge of the prescription and over-the-counter drugs and dietary factors that have the potential to affect drug and alcohol test results;

(8) Ability to recognize illegal drugs and indications of the illegal use, sale, or possession of drugs;

(9) Ability to observe and detect performance degradation, indications of impairment, or behavioral changes; and

(10) Knowledge of the individual's responsibility to report an FFD concern and the ability to initiate appropriate actions, including referrals to the EAP and person(s) designated by the licensee or other entity to receive FFD concerns.

(b) *Comprehensive examination.* Individuals who are subject to this subpart shall demonstrate the successful completion of training by passing a comprehensive examination that addresses the KAs in paragraph (a) of this section. The examination must include a comprehensive random sampling of all KAs with questions that test each KA, including at least one question for each KA. The minimum passing score required must be 80 percent. Remedial training and testing are required for individuals who fail to answer correctly at least 80 percent of the test questions. The examination may be administered using a variety of media, including, but not limited to, hardcopy test booklets with separate answer sheets or computer-based questions.

(c) *Training administration.* Licensees and other entities shall ensure that individuals who are subject to this subpart are trained, as follows:

(1) Training must be completed before the licensee or other entity grants initial authorization, as defined in §26.55, and must be current before the licensee or other entity grants an authorization update, as defined in §26.57, or authorization reinstatement, as defined in §26.59;

(2) Individuals shall complete refresher training on a nominal 12-month frequency, or more frequently where the need is indicated. Indications of the need for more frequent training include, but are not limited to, an individual's failure to properly implement FFD program procedures and the frequency, nature, or severity of problems discovered through audits or the administration of the program. Individuals who pass a comprehensive annual examination that meets the requirements in paragraph (b) of this section may forgo the refresher training; and

(3) Initial and refresher training may be delivered using a variety of media (including, but not limited to, classroom lectures, required reading, video, or computer-based training systems). The licensee or other entity shall monitor the completion of training and provide a qualified instructor or designated subject matter expert to answer questions during the course of training.

(d) *Acceptance of training.* Licensees and other entities may accept training of individuals who have been subject to another training program that meets the requirements of this section and who have, within the past 12 months, either had initial or refresher training, or have successfully passed a comprehensive examination that meets the requirements in paragraph (b) of this section.

§26.31 Drug and alcohol testing.

(a) *General.* To provide a means to deter and detect substance abuse, licensees and other entities who are subject to this part shall implement drug and alcohol testing programs for individuals who are subject to this subpart.

(b) *Assuring the honesty and integrity of FFD program personnel.* (1) Licensees and other entities who are subject to this subpart shall carefully select and monitor FFD program personnel, as defined in § 26.4(g), based on the highest standards of honesty and integrity, and shall implement measures to ensure that these standards are maintained. The measures must ensure that the honesty and integrity of these individuals are not compromised and that FFD program personnel are not subject to influence attempts attributable to personal relationships with any individuals who are subject to testing, an undetected or untreated substance abuse problem, or other factors. At a minimum, these measures must include the following considerations:

(i) Licensees and other entities shall complete appropriate background investigations, credit and criminal history checks, and psychological assessments of FFD program personnel before assignment to tasks directly associated with administration of the FFD program. The background investigations, credit and criminal history checks, and psychological assessments that are conducted to grant unescorted access authorization to individuals under a nuclear power plant licensee's access authorization program are acceptable to meet the requirements of this paragraph. The credit and criminal history checks and psychological assessments must be updated nominally every 5 years;

(ii) Individuals who have personal relationships with a donor may not perform any assessment or evaluation procedures, including, but not limited to, determinations of fitness. These personal relationships may include, but are not limited to, supervisors, coworkers within the same work group, and relatives of the donor;

(iii) Except if a directly observed collection is required, a collector who has a personal relationship with the donor may collect specimens from the donor only if the integrity of specimen collections in these instances is assured through the following means:

(A) The collection must be monitored by an individual who does not have a personal relationship with the donor and who is designated by the licensee or other entity for this purpose, including, but not limited to, security force or quality assurance personnel; and

(B) Individuals who are designated to monitor collections in these instances shall be trained to monitor specimen collections and the preparation of specimens for transfer or shipping under the requirements of this part;

(iv) If a specimen must be collected under direct observation, the collector or an individual who serves as the observer, as permitted under § 26.115(e), may not have a personal relationship with the donor; and

(v) FFD program personnel shall be subject to a behavioral observation program designed to assure that they continue to meet the highest standards of honesty and integrity. When an MRO and MRO staff are on site at a licensee's or other entity's facility, the MRO and MRO staff shall be subject to behavioral observation.

(2) Licensees and other entities may rely on a local hospital or other organization that meets the requirements of 49 CFR Part 40, "Procedures for Department of Transportation Workplace Drug and Alcohol Testing Programs" (65 FR 41944; August 9, 2001) to collect specimens for drug and alcohol testing from the FFD program personnel listed in § 26.4(g).

(c) *Conditions for testing.* Licensees and other entities shall administer drug and alcohol tests to the individuals who are subject to this subpart under the following conditions:

(1) *Pre-access.* In order to grant initial, updated, or reinstated authorization to an individual, as specified in subpart C of this part;

(2) *For cause.* In response to an individual's observed behavior or physical condition indicating possible substance abuse or after receiving credible information that an individual is engaging in substance abuse, as defined in § 26.5;

(3) *Post-event.* As soon as practical after an event involving a human error that was committed by an individual who is subject to this subpart, where the human error may have caused or contributed to the event. The licensee or other entity shall test the individual(s) who committed the error(s), and need not test individuals who were affected by the event whose actions likely did not cause or contribute to

the event. The individual(s) who committed the human error(s) shall be tested if the event resulted in—

(i) A significant illness or personal injury to the individual to be tested or another individual, which within 4 hours after the event is recordable under the Department of Labor standards contained in 29 CFR 1904.7, "General Recording Criteria," and subsequent amendments thereto, and results in death, days away from work, restricted work, transfer to another job, medical treatment beyond first aid, loss of consciousness, or other significant illness or injury as diagnosed by a physician or other licensed health care professional, even if it does not result in death, days away from work, restricted work or job transfer, medical treatment beyond first aid, or loss of consciousness;

(ii) A radiation exposure or release of radioactivity in excess of regulatory limits; or

(iii) Actual or potential substantial degradations of the level of safety of the plant;

(4) *Follow-up.* As part of a follow-up plan to verify an individual's continued abstinence from substance abuse; and

(5) *Random.* On a statistically random and unannounced basis, so that all individuals in the population subject to testing have an equal probability of being selected and tested.

(d) *General requirements for drug and alcohol testing*—(1) *Substances tested.* At a minimum, licensees and other entities shall test for marijuana metabolite, cocaine metabolite, opiates (codeine, morphine, 6-acetylmorphine), amphetamines (amphetamine, methamphetamine), phencyclidine, adulterants, and alcohol.

(i) In addition, licensees and other entities may consult with local law enforcement authorities, hospitals, and drug counseling services to determine whether other drugs with abuse potential are being used in the geographical locale of the facility and by the local workforce that may not be detected in the panel of drugs and drug metabolites specified in paragraph (d)(1) of this section.

(A) When appropriate, the licensee or other entity may add other drugs identified under paragraph (d)(1)(i) of this section to the panel of substances for testing, but only if the additional drugs are listed in Schedules I through V of section 202 of the Controlled Substances Act [21 U.S.C. 812].

(B) The licensee or other entity shall establish appropriate cutoff limits for these substances.

(C) The licensee or other entity shall establish rigorous testing procedures for these substances that are consistent with the intent of this part, so that the MRO can evaluate the use of these substances.

(D) The licensee or other entity may not conduct an analysis for any drug or drug metabolites except those identified in paragraph (d)(1) of this section unless the assay and cutoff levels to be used are certified in writing as scientifically sound and legally defensible by an independent, qualified forensic toxicologist who has no relationships with manufacturers of the assays or instruments to be used or the HHS-certified laboratory that will conduct the testing for the licensee or other entity, which could be construed as a potential conflict of interest. The forensic toxicologist may not be an employee of the licensee or entity, and shall either be a Diplomate of the American Board of Forensic Toxicology or currently holds, has held, or is eligible to hold, the position of Responsible Person at an HHS-certified laboratory, as specified in § 26.155(a). All new assays and cutoff levels must be properly validated consistent with established forensic toxicological standards before implementation. Certification of the assay and cutoff levels is not required if the HHS Guidelines are revised to authorize use of the assay in testing for the additional drug or drug metabolites and the licensee or other entity uses the cutoff levels established in the HHS Guidelines for the drug or drug metabolites, or if the licensee or other entity received written approval of the NRC to test for the additional drug or drug metabolites before April 30, 2008.

(ii) When conducting post-event, followup, and for-cause testing, as defined in § 26.31(c), licensees and other entities may test for any drugs listed on Schedules I through V of section 202 of the Controlled Substances Act [21 U.S.C. 812] that an individual is suspected of having abused, and may consider any drugs or metabolites so detected when determining appropriate action under subpart D of this part. If the drug or metabolites for which testing will be performed under this paragraph are not included in the FFD program's drug panel, the assay and cutoff levels to be used in testing for the additional drugs must be certified by a forensic toxicologist under paragraph (d)(1)(i)(D) of this section. Test results that fall below the established cutoff levels may not be considered when determining appropriate action under subpart D of this part, except if the specimen is dilute and the licensee or other entity has requested the HHS-certified laboratory to evaluate the specimen under §§ 26.163(a)(2) or 26.185(g)(3).

(iii) The licensee or other entity shall document the additional drug(s) for which testing will be performed in written policies and procedures in which the substances for which testing will be performed are described.

(2) *Random testing.* Random testing must—

(i) Be administered in a manner that provides reasonable assurance that individuals are unable to predict the time periods during which specimens will be collected. At a minimum, the FFD program shall—

(A) Take reasonable steps to either conceal from the workforce that collections will be performed during a scheduled collection period or create the appearance that specimens are being collected during a portion of each day on at least 4 days in each calendar week at each site. In the latter instance, the portions of each day and the days of the week must vary in a manner that cannot be predicted by donors; and

(B) Collect specimens on an unpredictable schedule, including weekends, backshifts, and holidays, and at various times during a shift;

(ii) At a minimum, be administered by the FFD program on a nominal weekly frequency;

(iii) Require individuals who are selected for random testing to report to the collection site as soon as reasonably practicable after notification, within the time period specified in the FFD program policy;

(iv) Ensure that all individuals in the population subject to testing have an equal probability of being selected and tested;

(v) Require that individuals who are off site when selected for testing, or who are on site and are not reasonably available for testing when selected, shall be tested at the earliest reasonable and practical opportunity when both the donor and collectors are available to collect specimens for testing and without prior notification to the individual that he or she has been selected for testing;

(vi) Provide that an individual completing a test is immediately eligible for another unannounced test; and

(vii) Ensure that the sampling process used to select individuals for random testing provides that the number of random tests performed annually is equal to at least 50 percent of the population that is subject to the FFD program.

(3) *Drug testing.* (i) Testing of urine specimens for drugs and validity, except validity screening and initial drug and validity tests performed by licensee testing facilities under paragraph (d)(3)(ii) of this section, must be performed in a laboratory that is certified by HHS for that purpose, consistent with its standards and procedures for certification. Specimens sent to HHS-certified laboratories must be subject to initial validity and initial drug testing by the laboratory. Specimens that yield positive initial drug test results or are determined by initial validity testing to be of questionable validity must be subject to confirmatory testing by the laboratory, except for invalid specimens that cannot be tested. Licensees and other entities shall ensure that laboratories report results for all specimens sent for testing, including blind performance test samples.

(ii) Licensees and other entities may conduct validity screening, initial validity, and initial drug tests of urine aliquots to determine which specimens are valid and negative and need no further testing, provided that the licensee's or other entity's staff possesses the necessary training and skills for the tasks assigned, the staff's qualifications are documented, and adequate quality controls for the testing are implemented.

(iii) At a minimum, licensees and other entities shall apply the cutoff levels specified in § 26.163(a)(1) for initial drug testing at either the licensee testing facility or HHS-certified laboratory, and in § 26.163(b)(1) for confirmatory drug testing at the HHS-certified laboratory. At their discretion, licensees and other entities may implement programs with lower cutoff levels in testing for drugs and drug metabolites.

(A) If a licensee or other entity implements lower cutoff levels, and the MRO determines that an individual has violated the FFD policy using the licensee's or other entity's more stringent cutoff levels, the individual shall be subject to all management actions and sanctions required by the licensee's or other entity's FFD policy and this part, as if the individual had a confirmed positive drug test result using the cutoff levels specified in this subpart. The licensee or other entity shall document the more stringent cutoff levels in any written policies and procedures in which cutoff levels for drug testing are described.

(B) The licensee or other entity shall uniformly apply the cutoff levels listed in § 26.163(a)(1) for initial drug testing and in § 26.163(b)(1) for confirmatory drug testing, or any more stringent cutoff levels implemented by the FFD program, to all tests performed under this part and equally to all individuals who are tested under this part, except as permitted in §§ 26.31(d)(1)(ii), 26.163(a)(2), and 26.165(c)(2).

(C) In addition, the scientific and technical suitability of any more stringent cutoff levels must be evaluated and certified, in writing, by a forensic toxicologist who meets the requirements set forth in § 26.31(d)(1)(i)(D). Certification of the more stringent cutoff levels is not required if the HHS Guidelines are revised to lower the cutoff levels for the drug or drug metabolites in Federal workplace drug testing programs and the licensee or other entity implements the cutoff levels published in the HHS Guidelines, or if the licensee or other entity received written approval of the NRC to test for lower cutoff levels before April 30, 2008.

(4) *Alcohol testing.* Initial tests for alcohol must be administered by breath or oral fluids analysis using alcohol analysis devices that meet the requirements of § 26.91(a). If the initial test shows a BAC of 0.02 percent or greater, a confirmatory test for alcohol must be performed. The confirmatory test must be performed with an EBT that meets the requirements of § 26.91(b).

(5) *Medical conditions.* (i) If an individual has a medical condition that makes collection of breath, oral fluids, or urine specimens difficult or hazardous, the MRO may authorize an alternative evaluation process, tailored to the individual case, to meet the requirements of this part for drug and alcohol testing. The alternative process must include measures to prevent subversion and achieve results that are comparable to those produced by urinalysis for drugs and breath analysis for alcohol.

(ii) If an individual requires medical attention, including, but not limited to, an injured worker in an emergency medical facility who is required to have a post-event test, treatment may not be delayed to conduct drug and alcohol testing.

(6) *Limitations of testing.* Specimens collected under NRC regulations may only be designated or approved for testing as described in this part and may not be used to conduct any other analysis or test without the written permission of the donor. Analyses and tests that may not be conducted include, but are not limited to, DNA testing, serological typing, or any other medical or genetic test used for diagnostic or specimen identification purposes.

[73 FR 17176, Mar. 31, 2008, as amended at 74 FR 38327, Aug. 3, 2009]

§ 26.33 Behavioral observation.

Licensees and other entities shall ensure that the individuals who are subject to this subpart are subject to behavioral observation. Behavioral observation must be performed by individuals who are trained under § 26.29 to detect behaviors that may indicate possible use, sale, or possession of illegal drugs; use or possession of alcohol on site or while on duty; or impairment from fatigue or any cause that, if left unattended, may constitute a risk to public health and safety or the common defense and security. Individuals who are subject to this subpart shall report any FFD concerns about other individuals to the personnel designated in the FFD policy.

§ 26.35 Employee assistance programs.

(a) Each licensee and other entity who is subject to this part shall maintain an EAP to strengthen the FFD program by offering confidential assessment, short-term counseling, referral services, and treatment monitoring to individuals who have problems that could adversely affect the individuals' abilities to safely and competently perform their duties. Employee assistance programs must be designed to achieve early intervention and provide for confidential assistance.

(b) Licensees and other entities need not provide EAP services to a C/V's employees, including those whose work location is a licensee's or other entity's facility, or to individuals who have applied for, but have not yet been granted, authorization under subpart C of this part.

(c) The EAP staff shall protect the identity and privacy of any individual (including those who have self-referred) seeking assistance from the EAP, except if the individual waives the right to privacy in writing or a determination is made that the individual's condition or actions pose or have posed an immediate hazard to himself or herself or others.

(1) Licensees and other entities may not require the EAP to routinely report the names of individuals who self-refer to the EAP or the nature of the assistance the individuals sought.

(2) If EAP personnel determine that an individual poses or has posed an immediate hazard to himself or herself or others, EAP personnel shall so inform FFD program management, and need not obtain a written waiver of the right to privacy from the individual. The individual conditions or actions that EAP personnel shall report to FFD program management include, but are not limited to, substantive reasons to believe that the individual—

(i) Is likely to commit self-harm or harm to others;

(ii) Has been impaired from using drugs or alcohol while in a work status and has a continuing substance abuse disorder that makes it likely he or she will be impaired while in a work status in the future; or

(iii) Has ever engaged in any acts that would be reportable under § 26.719(b)(1) through (b)(3).

(3) If a licensee or other entity receives a report from EAP personnel under paragraph (c)(2) of this section, the licensee or other entity shall ensure that the requirements of §§ 26.69(d) and 26.77(b) are implemented, as applicable.

§ 26.37 Protection of information.

(a) Each licensee or other entity who is subject to this subpart who collects personal information about an individual for the purpose of complying with this part, shall establish, use, and maintain a system of files and procedures that protects the individual's privacy.

(b) Licensees and other entities shall obtain a signed consent that authorizes the disclosure of the personal information collected and maintained under this part before disclosing the personal information, except for disclosures to the following individuals:

(1) The subject individual or his or her representative, when the individual has designated the representative in writing for specified FFD matters;

(2) Assigned MROs and MRO staff;

(3) NRC representatives;

(4) Appropriate law enforcement officials under court order;

(5) A licensee's or other entity's representatives who have a need to have access to the information to perform their assigned duties under the FFD program, including determinations of fitness, FFD program audits, or some human resources functions;

(6) The presiding officer in a judicial or administrative proceeding that is initiated by the subject individual;

(7) Persons deciding matters under review in § 26.39; and

(8) Other persons pursuant to court order.

(c) Personal information that is collected under this subpart must be disclosed to other licensees and entities, including C/Vs, or their authorized representatives, who are legitimately seeking the information for authorization decisions as required by this part and who have obtained a signed release from the subject individual.

(d) Upon receipt of a written request by the subject individual or his or her designated representative, the FFD program, including but not limited to, the collection site, HHS-certified laboratory, substance abuse expert (SAE), or MRO, possessing such records shall promptly provide copies of all FFD records pertaining to the individual, including, but not limited to, records pertaining to a determination that the individual has violated the FFD policy, drug and alcohol test results, MRO reviews, determinations of fitness, and management actions pertaining to the subject individual. The licensee or other entity shall obtain records related to the results of any relevant laboratory certification, review, or revocation-of-certification proceedings from the HHS-certified laboratory and provide them to the subject individual on request.

(e) A licensee's or other entity's contracts with HHS-certified laboratories and C/Vs providing specimen collection services, and licensee testing facility procedures, must require test records to be maintained in confidence, except as provided in paragraphs (b), (c), and (d) of this section.

(f) This section does not authorize the licensee or other entity to withhold evidence of criminal conduct from law enforcement officials.

§26.39 Review process for fitness-for-duty policy violations.

(a) Each licensee and other entity who is subject to this subpart shall establish procedures for the review of a determination that an individual who they employ or who has applied for authorization has violated the FFD policy. The review procedure must provide for an objective and impartial review of the facts related to the determination that the individual has violated the FFD policy.

(b) The review procedure must provide notice to the individual of the grounds for the determination that the individual has violated the FFD policy, and must provide an opportunity for the individual to respond and submit additional relevant information.

(c) The review procedure must ensure that the individual who conducts the review is not associated with the administration of the FFD program [*see* the description of FFD program personnel in §26.4(g)]. Individuals who conduct the review may be management personnel.

(d) If the review finds in favor of the individual, the licensee or other entity shall update the relevant records to reflect the outcome of the review and delete or correct all information the review found to be inaccurate.

(e) When a C/V is administering an FFD program on which licensees and other entities rely, and the C/V determines that its employee, subcontractor, or applicant has violated its FFD policy, the C/V shall ensure that the review procedure required in this section is provided to the individual. Licensees and other entities who rely on a C/V's FFD program need not provide the review procedure required in this section to a C/V's employee, subcontractor, or applicant when the C/V is administering its own FFD program and the FFD policy violation was determined under the C/V's program.

[75 FR 73941, Nov. 30, 2010]

§26.41 Audits and corrective action.

(a) *General.* Each licensee and other entity who is subject to this subpart is responsible for the continuing effectiveness of the FFD program, including FFD program elements that are provided by C/Vs, the FFD programs of any C/Vs that are accepted by the licensee or other entity, any FFD program services that are provided to the C/V by a subcontractor, and the programs of the HHS-certified laboratories on whom the licensee or other entity and its C/Vs rely. Each licensee and other entity shall ensure that these programs are audited and that corrective actions are taken to resolve any problems identified.

(b) *FFD program.* Each licensee and other entity who is subject to this subpart shall ensure that the entire FFD program is audited as needed, but no less frequently than nominally every 24 months. Licensees and other entities are responsible for determining the appropriate frequency, scope, and depth of additional auditing activities within the nominal 24-month period based on the review of FFD program performance, including, but not limited to, the frequency, nature, and severity of discovered problems, testing errors, personnel or procedural changes, and previous audit findings.

(c) *C/Vs and HHS-certified laboratories.* (1) FFD services that are provided to a licensee or other entity by C/V personnel who are off site or are not under the direct daily supervision or observation of the licensee's or other entity's personnel and HHS-certified laboratories must be audited on a nominal 12-month frequency.

(2) Audits of HHS-certified laboratories that are conducted for licensees and other entities who are subject to this subpart need not duplicate areas inspected in the most recent HHS certification inspection. However, the licensee and other entity shall review the HHS certification inspection records and reports to identify any areas in which the licensee or other entity uses services that the HHS certification inspection did not address. The licensee or other entity shall ensure that any such areas are audited on a nominal 12-month frequency. Licensees and other entities need not audit organizations and professionals who may provide an FFD program service to the licensee or other entity, but who are not routinely involved in providing services to a licensee's or other entity's FFD program, as specified in § 26.4(i)(1).

(d) *Contracts.* (1) The contracts of licensees and other entities with C/Vs and HHS-certified laboratories must reserve the right to audit the C/V, the C/V's subcontractors providing FFD program services, and the HHS-certified laboratories at any time, including at unannounced times, as well as to review all information and documentation that is reasonably relevant to the audits.

(2) Licensees' and other entities' contracts with C/Vs and HHS-certified laboratories must also permit the licensee or other entity to obtain copies of and take away any documents, including reviews and inspections pertaining to a laboratory's certification by HHS, and any other data that may be needed to assure that the C/V, its subcontractors, or the HHS-certified laboratory are performing their functions properly and that staff and procedures meet applicable requirements. In a contract with a licensee or other entity who is subject to this subpart, an HHS-certified laboratory may reasonably limit the use and dissemination of any documents copied or taken away by the licensee's or other entity's auditors in order to ensure the protection of proprietary information and donors' privacy.

(3) In addition, before awarding a contract, the licensee or other entity shall ensure completion of pre-award inspections and/or audits of the procedural aspects of the HHS-certified laboratory's drug-testing operations, except as provided in paragraph (g)(5) of this section.

(e) *Conduct of audits.* Audits must focus on the effectiveness of the FFD program or program element(s), as appropriate, and must be conducted by individuals who are qualified in the subject(s) being audited. The individuals performing the audit of the FFD program or program element(s) shall be independent from both the subject FFD program's management and from personnel who are directly responsible for implementing the FFD program.

(f) *Audit results.* The result of the audits, along with any recommendations, must be documented and reported to senior corporate and site management. Each audit report must identify conditions that are adverse to the proper performance of the FFD program, the cause of the condition(s), and recommended corrective actions. The licensee or other entity shall review the audit findings and take corrective actions, including re-auditing of the deficient areas where indicated, to preclude, within reason, repetition of the condition. The resolution of the audit findings and corrective actions must be documented.

(g) *Sharing of audits.* Licensees and other entities may jointly conduct audits, or may accept audits of C/Vs and HHS-certified laboratories that were conducted by other licensees and entities who are subject to this subpart, if the audit addresses the services obtained from the C/V or HHS-certified laboratory by each of the sharing licensees and other entities.

(1) Licensees and other entities shall review audit records and reports to identify any areas that were not covered by the shared or accepted audit.

(2) Licensees and other entities shall ensure that FFD program elements and services on which the licensee or entity relies are audited, if the program elements and services were not addressed in the shared audit.

(3) Sharing licensees and other entities need not re-audit the same C/V or HHS-certified laboratory for the same period of time.

(4) Each sharing licensee and other entity shall maintain a copy of the shared audit and HHS certification inspection records and reports, including findings, recommendations, and corrective actions.

(5) If an HHS-certified laboratory loses its certification, in whole or in part, a licensee or other entity is permitted to immediately use another HHS-certified laboratory that has been audited within the previous 12 months by another NRC licensee or entity who is subject to this subpart. Within 3 months after the change, the licensee or other entity shall ensure that an audit is completed of any areas that have not been audited by another licensee or entity who is subject to this subpart within the past 12 months.

[73 FR 17176, Mar. 31, 2008, as amended at 74 FR 38327, Aug. 3, 2009]

Subpart C—Granting and Maintaining Authorization

§ 26.51 Applicability.

The requirements in this subpart apply to the licensees and other entities identified in § 26.3(a), (b), and, as applicable, (c) for the categories of individuals in § 26.4(a) through (d), and, at the licensee's or other entity's discretion, in § 26.4(g) and, if necessary, § 26.4(j). The requirements in this subpart also apply to the licensees and other entities specified in § 26.3(c), as applicable, for the categories of individuals in § 26.4(e). At the discretion of a licensee or other entity in § 26.3(c), the requirements of this subpart also may be applied to the categories of individuals identified in § 26.4(f). In addition, the requirements in this subpart apply to the entities in § 26.3(d) to the extent that a licensee or other entity relies on the C/V to meet the requirements of this subpart. Certain requirements in this subpart also apply to the individuals specified in § 26.4(h).

§ 26.53 General provisions.

(a) In order to grant authorization to an individual, a licensee or other entity shall ensure that the requirements in this subpart have been met for either initial authorization, authorization update, authorization reinstatement, or authorization with potentially disqualifying FFD information, as applicable.

(b) For individuals who have previously held authorization under this part but whose authorization has since been favorably terminated, the licensee or other entity shall implement the requirements for either initial authorization, authorization update, or authorization reinstatement, based on the total number of days that the individual's authorization is interrupted, to include the day after the individual's last period of authorization was terminated and the intervening days until the day on which the licensee or other entity grants authorization to the individual. If potentially disqualifying FFD information is disclosed or discovered about an individual, licensees and other entities shall implement the applicable requirements in § 26.69 in order to grant or maintain an individual's authorization.

(c) The licensee or other entity shall ensure that an individual has met the applicable FFD training requirements in §§ 26.29 and 26.203(c) before granting authorization to the individual.

(d) Licensees and other entities who are seeking to grant authorization to an individual who is maintaining authorization under another FFD program that is implemented by a licensee or entity who is subject to this subpart may rely on the transferring FFD program to satisfy the requirements of this subpart. The individual may maintain his or her authorization if he or she continues to be subject to either the receiving FFD program or the transferring FFD program, or a combination of elements from both programs that collectively satisfy the applicable requirements of this part. The receiving FFD program shall ensure that the program elements to which the individual is subject under the transferring FFD program remain current.

(e) Licensees and other entities in § 26.3(a) through (c) may also rely on a C/V's FFD program or program elements when granting or maintaining the authorization of an individual who is or has been subject to the C/V's FFD program, if the C/V's program or program elements meet the applicable requirements of this part.

(1) A C/V's FFD program may grant and maintain an individual's authorization, as defined in § 26.5, under the C/V's FFD program. However, only a licensee or other entity in § 26.3(a) through (c) may grant or maintain an individual's authorization to have the types of access or perform the duties specified in § 26.4(a) through (e) and (g), and, at the licensee's or other entity's discretion, § 26.4(f).

(2) If a C/V's FFD program denies or unfavorably terminates an individual's authorization, and the individual is performing any duties for a licensee or other entity that are specified in § 26.4(a) through (e) and (g), or, at the licensee's or other entity's discretion, § 26.4(f), then the C/V shall inform the affected licensee or other entity of the denial or unfavorable termination. The licensee or other entity shall deny or unfavorably terminate the individual's authorization to perform those duties on the day that the licensee or other entity receives the information from the C/V, or implement the applicable process in § 26.69 to maintain the individual's authorization.

(3) If an individual is maintaining authorization under a C/V's FFD program, a licensee or other entity in § 26.3(a) through (c) may grant authorization to the individual to have the types of access and perform the duties specified in § 26.4(a) through (e) and (g), and, at the licensee's or other entity's discretion, § 26.4(f), and maintain his or her authorization, if the individual continues to be subject to either the receiving FFD program or a combination of elements from the receiving FFD program and the C/V's program that collectively satisfy the applicable requirements of this part. The receiving licensee's or other entity's FFD program shall ensure that the program elements to which the individual is subject under the C/V's FFD program remain current.

(f) Licensees and other entities who are seeking to grant authorization to an individual who has been subject to an FFD program under subpart K may not rely on that program or its program elements to meet the requirements of this subpart, except if the program or program element(s) of the FFD program for construction satisfy the applicable requirements of this part.

(g) The licensees and other entities specified in § 26.3(a) and, as applicable, (c) and (d), shall identify any violation of any requirement of this part to any licensee who has relied on or intends to rely on the FFD program element that is determined to be in violation of this part.

(h) The licensees and other entities specified in § 26.3(a) and, as applicable, (c) and (d), may not initiate any actions under this subpart without the knowledge and written consent of the subject individual. The individual may withdraw his or her consent at any time. If an individual withdraws his or her consent, the licensee or other entity may not initiate any elements of the authorization process specified in this subpart that were not in progress at the time the individual withdrew his or her consent, but shall complete and document any elements that are in progress at the time consent is withdrawn. The licensee or other entity shall record the individual's application for authorization; his or her withdrawal of consent; the reason given by the individual for the withdrawal, if any; and any pertinent information gathered from the elements that were completed (e.g., the results of pre-access drug tests, information obtained from the suitable inquiry). The licensee or other entity to whom the individual has applied for authorization shall inform the individual that—

(1) Withdrawal of his or her consent will withdraw the individual's current application for authorization under the licensee's or other entity's FFD program; and

(2) Other licensees and entities will have access to information documenting the withdrawal as a result of the information sharing that is required under this part.

(i) The licensees and other entities specified in § 26.3(a) and, as applicable, (c) and(d), shall inform, in writing, any individual who is applying for authorization that the following actions related to providing and sharing the personal information required under this subpart are sufficient cause for denial or unfavorable termination of authorization:

(1) Refusal to provide written consent for the suitable inquiry;

(2) Refusal to provide or the falsification of any personal information required under this part, including, but not limited to, the failure to report any previous denial or unfavorable termination of authorization;

(3) Refusal to provide written consent for the sharing of personal information with other licensees or other entities required under this part; and

(4) Failure to report any legal actions, as defined in § 26.5.

§ 26.55 Initial authorization.

(a) Before granting authorization to an individual who has never held authorization under this part or whose authorization has been interrupted for a period of 3 years or more and whose last period of authorization was terminated favorably, the licensee or other entity shall ensure that—

(1) A self-disclosure has been obtained and reviewed under the applicable requirements of § 26.61;

(2) A suitable inquiry has been completed under the applicable requirements of § 26.63;

(3) The individual has been subject to pre-access drug and alcohol testing under the applicable requirements of § 26.65; and

(4) The individual is subject to random drug and alcohol testing under the applicable requirements of § 26.67.

(b) If potentially disqualifying FFD information is disclosed or discovered, the licensee or other entity may not grant authorization to the individual, except under § 26.69.

§ 26.57 Authorization update.

(a) Before granting authorization to an individual whose authorization has been interrupted for more than 365 days but less than 3 years and whose last period of authorization was terminated favorably, the licensee or other entity shall ensure that—

(1) A self-disclosure has been obtained and reviewed under the applicable requirements of § 26.61;

(2) A suitable inquiry has been completed under the applicable requirements of § 26.63;

(3) The individual has been subject to pre-access drug and alcohol testing under the applicable requirements of § 26.65; and

(4) The individual is subject to random drug and alcohol testing under the applicable requirements of § 26.67.

(b) If potentially disqualifying FFD information is disclosed or discovered, the licensee or other entity may not grant authorization to the individual, except under § 26.69.

§ 26.59 Authorization reinstatement.

(a) In order to grant authorization to an individual whose authorization has been interrupted for a period of more than 30 days but no more than 365 days and whose last period of authorization was terminated favorably, the licensee or other entity shall ensure that—

(1) A self-disclosure has been obtained and reviewed under the applicable requirements of § 26.61;

(2) A suitable inquiry has been completed under the requirements of § 26.63 within 5 business days of reinstating authorization. If the suitable inquiry is not completed within 5 business days due to circumstances that are outside of the licensee's or other entity's control and the licensee or other entity is

not aware of any potentially disqualifying information regarding the individual within the past 5 years, the licensee or other entity may maintain the individual's authorization for an additional 5 business days. If the suitable inquiry is not completed within 10 business days of reinstating authorization, the licensee or other entity shall administratively withdraw the individual's authorization until the suitable inquiry is completed;

(3) The individual has been subject to pre-access drug and alcohol testing under the applicable requirements of § 26.65; and

(4) The individual is subject to random drug and alcohol testing under the applicable requirements of § 26.67.

(b) If a licensee or other entity administratively withdraws an individual's authorization under paragraph (a)(2) of this section, and until the suitable inquiry is completed, the licensee or other entity may not record the administrative action to withdraw authorization as an unfavorable termination and may not disclose it in response to a suitable inquiry conducted under the provisions of § 26.63, a background investigation conducted under the provisions of this chapter, or any other inquiry or investigation. The individual may not be required to disclose the administrative action in response to requests for self-disclosure of potentially disqualifying FFD information, except if the individual's authorization was subsequently denied or terminated unfavorably by the licensee or other entity.

(c) Before granting authorization to an individual whose authorization has been interrupted for a period of no more than 30 days and whose last period of authorization was terminated favorably, the licensee or other entity shall ensure that—

(1) A self-disclosure has been obtained and reviewed under the applicable requirements of § 26.61;

(2) The individual has been subject to pre-access drug and alcohol testing under the applicable requirements of § 26.65, if the individual's authorization was interrupted for more than 5 days; and

(3) The individual is subject to random drug and alcohol testing under the applicable requirements of § 26.67.

(d) If potentially disqualifying FFD information is disclosed or discovered, the licensee or other entity may not grant authorization to the individual, except under § 26.69.

§ 26.61 Self-disclosure and employment history.

(a) Before granting authorization, the licensee or other entity shall ensure that a written self-disclosure and employment history has been obtained from the individual who is applying for authorization, except as follows:

(1) If an individual previously held authorization under this part, and the licensee or other entity has verified that the individual's last period of authorization was terminated favorably, and the individual has been subject to a behavioral observation program that includes arrest reporting, which meets the requirements of this part, throughout the period since the individual's last authorization was terminated, the granting licensee or other entity need not obtain the self-disclosure or employment history in order to grant authorization; and

(2) If the individual's last period of authorization was terminated favorably within the past 30 days, the licensee or other entity need not obtain the employment history.

(b) The written self-disclosure must—

(1) State whether the individual has—

(i) Violated a licensee's or other entity's FFD policy;

(ii) Had authorization denied or terminated unfavorably under §§ 26.35(c)(2), 26.53(i), 26.63(d), 26.65(g), 26.67(c), 26.69(f), or 26.75(b) through (e);

(iii) Used, sold, or possessed illegal drugs;

(iv) Abused legal drugs or alcohol;

(v) Subverted or attempted to subvert a drug or alcohol testing program;

(vi) Refused to take a drug or alcohol test;

(vii) Been subject to a plan for substance abuse treatment (except for self-referral); or

(viii) Had legal action or employment action, as defined in § 26.5, taken for alcohol or drug use;

(2) Address the specific type, duration, and resolution of any matter disclosed, including, but not limited to, the reason(s) for any unfavorable termination or denial of authorization; and

(3) Address the shortest of the following periods:

(i) The past 5 years;

(ii) Since the individual's eighteenth birthday; or

(iii) Since the individual's last period of authorization was terminated, if authorization was terminated favorably within the past 3 years.

(c) The individual shall provide a list of all employers, including the employer by whom the individual claims to have been employed on the day before he or she completes the employment history, if any, with dates of employment, for the shortest of the following periods:

(1) The past 3 years;

(2) Since the individual's eighteenth birthday; or

(3) Since authorization was last terminated, if authorization was terminated favorably within the past 3 years.

§ 26.63 Suitable inquiry.

(a) In order to grant authorization, licensees and other entities shall ensure that a suitable inquiry has been conducted, on a best effort basis, to verify the individual's self-disclosed information and determine whether any potentially disqualifying FFD information is available, except if all of the following conditions are met:

(1) The individual previously held authorization under this part;

(2) The licensee or other entity has verified that the individual's last period of authorization was terminated favorably; and

(3) The individual has been subject to a behavioral observation program that includes arrest reporting, which meets the requirements of this part, throughout the period of interruption.

(b) To meet the suitable inquiry requirement, licensees and other entities may rely on the information that other licensees and entities who are subject to this subpart have gathered for previous periods of authorization. Licensees and other entities may also rely on those licensees' and entities' determinations of fitness that were conducted under § 26.189, as well as their reviews and resolutions of potentially disqualifying FFD information, for previous periods of authorization.

(c) The licensee or other entity shall ensure that the suitable inquiry has been conducted, on a best effort basis, by questioning former employers, and the employer by whom the individual claims to have been employed on the day before he or she completes the employment history, if an employment history is required under § 26.61.

(1) For the claimed employment period, the suitable inquiry must ascertain the reason for termination, eligibility for rehire, and other information that could reflect on the individual's fitness to be granted authorization.

(2) If the claimed employment was military service, the licensee or other entity who is conducting the suitable inquiry shall request a characterization of service, reason for separation, and any disciplinary actions related to potentially disqualifying FFD information. If the individual's last duty station cannot provide this information, the licensee or other entity may accept a hand-carried copy of the DD 214 presented by the individual which on face value appears to be legitimate. The licensee or other entity may also accept a copy of a DD 214 provided by the custodian of military records.

(3) If a company, previous employer, or educational institution to whom the licensee or other entity has directed a request for information refuses to provide information or indicates an inability or unwillingness to provide information within 3 business days of the request, the licensee or other entity shall document this refusal, inability, or unwillingness in the licensee's or other entity's record of the investigation, and obtain a confirmation of employment or educational enrollment and attendance from at least one alternate source, with suitable inquiry questions answered to the best of the alternate source's ability. This alternate source may not have been previously used by the licensee or other entity to obtain information about the individual's character. If the licensee or other entity uses an alternate

source because employer information is not forthcoming within 3 business days of the request, the licensee or other entity need not delay granting authorization to wait for any employer response, but shall evaluate and document the response if it is received.

(d) When any licensee or other entity in § 26.3(a) through (d) is legitimately seeking the information required for an authorization decision under this subpart and has obtained a signed release from the subject individual authorizing the disclosure of information, any licensee or other entity who is subject to this part shall disclose whether the subject individual's authorization was denied or terminated unfavorably as a result of a violation of an FFD policy and shall make available the information on which the denial or unfavorable termination of authorization was based, including, but not limited to, drug or alcohol test results, treatment and followup testing requirements or other results from a determination of fitness, and any other information that is relevant to an authorization decision.

(e) In conducting a suitable inquiry, a licensee or other entity may obtain information and documents by electronic means, including, but not limited to, telephone, facsimile, or e-mail. The licensee or other entity shall make a record of the contents of the telephone call and shall retain that record, and any documents or electronic files obtained electronically, under §§ 26.711 and 26.713(a), (b), and (c), as applicable.

(f) For individuals about whom no potentially disqualifying FFD information is known (or about whom potentially disqualifying FFD information is known, but it has been resolved by a licensee or other entity who is subject to this subpart) at the time at which the suitable inquiry is initiated, the licensee or other entity shall ensure that a suitable inquiry has been conducted as follows:

(1) Initial authorization. The period of the suitable inquiry must be the past 3 years or since the individual's eighteenth birthday, whichever is shorter. For the 1-year period immediately preceding the date on which the individual applies for authorization, the licensee or other entity shall ensure that the suitable inquiry has been conducted with every employer, regardless of the length of employment. For the remaining 2-year period, the licensee or other entity shall ensure that the suitable inquiry has been conducted with the employer by whom the individual claims to have been employed the longest within each calendar month, if the individual claims employment during the given calendar month.

(2) Authorization update. The period of the suitable inquiry must be the period since authorization was terminated. For the 1-year period immediately preceding the date on which the individual applies for authorization, the licensee or other entity shall ensure that the suitable inquiry has been conducted with every employer, regardless of the length of employment. For the remaining period since authorization was terminated, the licensee or other entity shall ensure that the suitable inquiry has been conducted with the employer by whom the individual claims to have been employed the longest within each calendar month, if the individual claims employment during the given calendar month.

(3) Authorization reinstatement after an interruption of more than 30 days. The period of the suitable inquiry must be the period since authorization was terminated. The licensee or other entity shall ensure that the suitable inquiry has been conducted with the employer by whom the individual claims to have been employed the longest within the calendar month, if the individual claims employment during the given calendar month.

§ 26.65 Pre-access drug and alcohol testing.

(a) *Purpose.* This section contains pre-access testing requirements for granting authorization to an individual who either has never held authorization or whose last period of authorization was terminated favorably and about whom no potentially disqualifying FFD information has been discovered or disclosed that was not previously reviewed and resolved by a licensee or other entity under the requirements of this subpart.

(b) *Accepting tests conducted within the past 30 days.* If an individual has negative results from drug and alcohol tests that were conducted under the requirements of this part before the individual applied for authorization from the licensee or other entity, and the specimens for such testing were collected within the 30-day period preceding the day on which the licensee or other entity grants authorization to the individual, the licensee or other entity may rely on the results of those drug and alcohol tests to meet the requirements for pre-access testing in this section.

(c) *Initial authorization and authorization update.* Before granting authorization to an individual who has never held authorization or whose authorization has been interrupted for a period of more than 365 days, the licensee or other entity shall verify that the results of pre-access drug and alcohol tests, which must be performed within the 30-day period preceding the day the licensee or other entity grants authorization to the individual, are negative. The licensee or other entity need not conduct pre-access testing if—

(1) The individual previously held authorization under this part and has been subject to a drug and alcohol testing program that includes random testing and a behavioral observation program that includes arrest reporting, which both meet the requirements of this part, from the date the individual's last authorization was terminated through the date the individual is granted authorization; or

(2) The licensee or other entity relies on negative results from drug and alcohol tests that were conducted under the requirements of this part at any time before the individual applied for authorization, and the individual has remained subject to a drug and alcohol testing program that includes random testing and a behavioral observation program that includes arrest reporting, which both meet the requirements of this part, beginning on the date the drug and alcohol testing was conducted through the date the individual is granted authorization and thereafter.

(d) *Authorization reinstatement after an interruption of more than 30 days.* (1) To reinstate authorization for an individual whose authorization has been interrupted for a period of more than 30 days but no more than 365 days, except as permitted in paragraph (d)(2) of this section, the licensee or other entity shall—

(i) Verify that the individual has negative results from alcohol testing and collect a specimen for drug testing within the 30-day period preceding the day the licensee reinstates the individual's authorization; and

(ii) Verify that the drug test results are negative within 5 business days of specimen collection or administratively withdraw authorization until the drug test results are received.

(2) The licensee or other entity need not conduct pre-access testing of these individuals if—

(i) The individual previously held authorization under this part and has been subject to a drug and alcohol testing program that includes random testing and a behavioral observation program that includes arrest reporting, which both meet the requirements of this part, beginning on the date the individual's last authorization was terminated through the date the individual is granted authorization; or

(ii) The licensee or other entity relies on negative results from drug and alcohol tests that were conducted under the requirements of this part at any time before the individual applied for authorization, and the individual remains subject to a drug and alcohol testing program that includes random testing and a behavioral observation program that includes arrest reporting, which both meet the requirements of this part, beginning on the date the drug and alcohol testing was conducted through the date the individual is granted authorization.

(e) *Authorization reinstatement after an interruption of 30 or fewer days.* (1) The licensee or other entity need not conduct pre-access testing before granting authorization to an individual whose authorization has been interrupted for 5 or fewer days. In addition, the licensee or other entity need not conduct pre-access testing if the individual has been subject to a drug and alcohol testing program that includes random testing and a behavioral observation program that includes arrest reporting, which both meet the requirements of this part, from the date the individual's last authorization was terminated through the date the individual is granted authorization.

(2) In order to reinstate authorization for an individual whose authorization has been interrupted for a period of more than 5 days but not more than 30 days, except as permitted in paragraph (e)(1) of this section, the licensee or other entity shall take the following actions:

(i) The licensee or other entity shall subject the individual to random selection for pre-access drug and alcohol testing at a one-time probability that is equal to or greater than the normal testing rate specified in § 26.31(d)(2)(vii) calculated for a 30-day period;

(ii) If the individual is not selected for pre-access testing under paragraph (e)(2)(i) of this section, the licensee or other entity need not perform pre-access drug and alcohol tests; or

(iii) If the individual is selected for pre-access testing under this paragraph, the licensee or other entity shall—

(A) Verify that the individual has negative results from alcohol testing and collect a specimen for drug testing before reinstating authorization; and

(B) Verify that the drug test results are negative within 5 business days of specimen collection or administratively withdraw authorization until negative drug test results are received.

(f) *Administrative withdrawal of authorization.* If a licensee or other entity administratively withdraws an individual's authorization under paragraphs (d)(1)(ii) or (e)(2)(iii)(B) of this section, and until the drug test results are known, the licensee or other entity may not record the administrative action to withdraw authorization as an unfavorable termination. The individual may not be required to disclose the administrative action in response to requests for self-disclosure of potentially disqualifying FFD information, except if the individual's authorization was subsequently denied or terminated unfavorably by a licensee or entity. Immediately on receipt of negative test results, the licensee or other entity shall ensure that any matter that could link the individual to the temporary administrative action is eliminated from the donor's personnel record and other records.

(g) *Sanctions.* If an individual has confirmed positive, adulterated, or substituted test results from any drug, validity, or alcohol tests that may be required in this section, the licensee or other entity shall, at a minimum and as appropriate—

(1) Deny authorization to the individual, as required by § 26.75(b), (d), (e)(2), or (g);

(2) Terminate the individual's authorization, if it has been reinstated, under § 26.75(e)(1) or (f); or

(3) Grant authorization to the individual under § 26.69.

§ 26.67 Random drug and alcohol testing of individuals who have applied for authorization.

(a) When the licensee or other entity collects specimens from an individual for any pre-access testing that may be required under §§ 26.65 or 26.69, and thereafter, the licensee or other entity shall subject the individual to random testing under § 26.31(d)(2), except if—

(1) The licensee or other entity does not grant authorization to the individual; or

(2) The licensee or other entity relies on drug and alcohol tests that were conducted before the individual applied for authorization to meet the applicable requirements for pre-access testing. If the licensee or other entity relies on drug and alcohol tests that were conducted before the individual applied for authorization, the licensee or other entity shall subject the individual to random testing when the individual arrives at a licensee's or other entity's facility for in-processing and thereafter.

(b) If an individual is selected for one or more random tests after any applicable requirement for pre-access testing in §§ 26.65 or 26.69 has been met, the licensee or other entity may grant authorization before random testing is completed, if the individual has met all other applicable requirements for authorization.

(c) If an individual has confirmed positive, adulterated, or substituted test results from any drug, validity, or alcohol test required in this section, the licensee or other entity shall, at a minimum and as appropriate—

(1) Deny authorization to the individual, as required by § 26.75(b), (d), (e)(2), or (g);

(2) Terminate the individual's authorization, if it has been granted, as required by § 26.75(e)(1) or (f); or

(3) Grant authorization to the individual under § 26.69.

§ 26.69 Authorization with potentially disqualifying fitness-for-duty information.

(a) *Purpose.* This section defines the management actions that licensees and other entities who are subject to this subpart shall take to grant or maintain, at the licensee's or other entity's discretion, the authorization of an individual who is in the following circumstances:

(1) Potentially disqualifying FFD information within the past 5 years has been disclosed or discovered about the individual by any means, including, but not limited to, the individual's self-disclosure, the suitable inquiry, drug and alcohol testing, the administration of any FFD program under this part, a self-report of a legal action, behavioral observation, or other sources of information, including, but not limited to, any background investigation or credit and criminal history check conducted under the requirements of this chapter; and

(2) The potentially disqualifying FFD information has not been reviewed and favorably resolved by a previous licensee or other entity under this section.

(b) *Authorization after a first confirmed positive drug or alcohol test result or a 5-year denial of authorization.* The requirements in this paragraph apply to individuals whose authorization was denied or terminated unfavorably for a first violation of an FFD policy involving a confirmed positive drug or alcohol test result and individuals whose authorization was denied for 5 years under § 26.75(c), (d), (e)(2), or (f). To grant, and subsequently maintain, the individual's authorization, the licensee or other entity shall—

(1) Obtain and review a self-disclosure and employment history from the individual that addresses the shorter period of either the past 5 years or since the individual's last period of authorization was terminated, and verify that the self-disclosure does not contain any previously undisclosed potentially disqualifying FFD information before granting authorization;

(2) Complete a suitable inquiry with every employer by whom the individual claims to have been employed during the period addressed in the employment history obtained under paragraph (b)(1) of this section, and obtain and review any records that other licensees or entities who are subject to this part may have developed related to the unfavorable termination or denial of authorization;

(3) If the individual was subject to a 5-year denial of authorization under this part, verify that he or she has abstained from substance abuse for at least the past 5 years;

(4) Ensure that an SAE has conducted a determination of fitness and concluded that the individual is fit to safely and competently perform his or her duties.

(i) If the individual's authorization was denied or terminated unfavorably for a first confirmed positive drug or alcohol test result, ensure that clinically appropriate treatment and followup testing plans have been developed by an SAE before granting authorization;

(ii) If the individual was subject to a 5-year denial of authorization, ensure that any recommendations for treatment and followup testing from an SAE's determination of fitness are initiated before granting authorization; and

(iii) Verify that the individual is in compliance with, and successfully completes, any followup testing and treatment plans.

(5) Within 10 business days before granting authorization, perform a pre-access alcohol test, collect a specimen for drug testing under direct observation, and ensure that the individual is subject to random testing thereafter. Verify that the pre-access drug and alcohol test results are negative before granting authorization.

(6) If the individual's authorization was denied or terminated unfavorably for a first confirmed positive drug or alcohol test result and a licensee or other entity grants authorization to the individual, ensure that the individual is subject to unannounced testing at least quarterly for 3 calendar years after the date the individual is granted authorization. Both random and followup tests, as defined in § 26.31(c), satisfy this requirement. Verify that the individual has negative test results from a minimum of 15 tests distributed over the 3-year period, except as follows:

(i) If the individual does not continuously hold authorization during the 3-year period, the licensee or other entity shall ensure that at least one unannounced test is conducted in any quarter during which the individual holds authorization;

(ii) If the 15 tests are not completed within the 3-year period specified in this paragraph due to periods during which the individual does not hold authorization, the followup testing program may be extended up to 5 calendar years to complete the 15 tests;

(iii) If the individual does not hold authorization during the 5-year period a sufficient number of times or for sufficient periods of time to complete the 15 tests required in this paragraph, the licensee or other entity shall ensure that an SAE conducts a determination of fitness to assess whether further followup testing is required and implement the SAE's recommendations; and

(7) Verify that any drug and alcohol tests required in this paragraph, and any other drug and alcohol tests that are conducted under this part since authorization was terminated or denied, yield results indicating no further drug abuse, as determined by the MRO after review, or alcohol abuse, as determined by the result of confirmatory alcohol testing.

(c) *Granting authorization with other potentially disqualifying FFD information.* The requirements in this paragraph apply to an individual who has applied for authorization, and about whom potentially disqualifying FFD information has been discovered or disclosed that is not a first confirmed positive drug or alcohol test result or a 5-year denial of authorization. If potentially disqualifying FFD information is obtained about an individual by any means, including, but not limited to, the individual's self-disclosure, the suitable inquiry, the administration of any FFD program under this part, a self-report of a legal action, behavioral observation, or other sources of information, including, but not limited to, any background investigation or credit and criminal history check conducted under the requirements of this chapter, before granting authorization to the individual, the licensee or other entity shall—

(1) Obtain and review a self-disclosure and employment history that addresses the shortest of the following periods:

(i) The past 5 years;

(ii) Since the individual's eighteenth birthday; or

(iii) Since the individual's last period of authorization was terminated;

(2) Complete a suitable inquiry with every employer by whom the individual claims to have been employed during the period addressed in the employment history required under paragraph (c)(1) of this section. If the individual held authorization within the past 5 years, obtain and review any records that other licensees or entities who are subject to this part may have developed with regard to potentially disqualifying FFD information about the individual from the past 5 years;

(3) If the designated reviewing official determines that a determination of fitness is required, verify that a professional with the appropriate qualifications, as specified in § 26.189(a), has indicated that the individual is fit to safely and competently perform his or her duties;

(4) Ensure that the individual is in compliance with, or has completed, any plans for treatment and drug and alcohol testing from the determination of fitness, which may include the collection of a urine specimen under direct observation; and

(5) Verify that the results of pre-access drug and alcohol tests are negative before granting authorization, and that the individual is subject to random testing after the specimens have

been collected for pre-access testing and thereafter.

(d) *Maintaining authorization with other potentially disqualifying FFD information.* If an individual is authorized when other potentially disqualifying FFD information is disclosed or discovered, in order to maintain the individual's authorization, the licensee or other entity shall—

(1) Ensure that the licensee's or other entity's designated reviewing official completes a review of the circumstances associated with the information;

(2) If the designated reviewing official concludes that a determination of fitness is required, verify that a professional with the appropriate qualifications, as specified in § 26.189(a), has indicated that the individual is fit to safely and competently perform his or her duties; and

(3) If the reviewing official determines that maintaining the individual's authorization is warranted, implement any recommendations for treatment and followup drug and alcohol testing from the determination of fitness, which may include the collection of urine specimens under direct observation, and ensure that the individual complies with and successfully completes the treatment plans.

(e) *Accepting followup testing and treatment plans from another FFD program.* Licensees and other entities may rely on followup testing, treatment plans, and determinations of fitness that meet the requirements of § 26.189 and were conducted under the FFD program of another licensee or entity who is subject to this subpart.

(1) If an individual leaves the FFD program in which a treatment and/or followup testing plan was required under paragraphs (b), (c), or (d) of this section, the licensee or other entity who imposed the treatment and/or followup testing plan shall ensure that information documenting the treatment and/or followup testing plan is identified to any subsequent licensee or other entity who seeks to grant authorization to the individual. If the individual is granted authorization by the same or another licensee or entity, the licensee or other entity who grants authorization to the individual shall ensure that any followup testing requirements are met and that the individual complies with any treatment plan, with accountability assumed by the granting licensee or other entity. If it is impractical for the individual to comply with a treatment plan that was developed under another FFD program because of circumstances that are outside of the individual's or licensee's or other entity's control (e.g., geographical distance, closure of a treatment facility), then the granting FFD program shall ensure that an SAE develops a comparable treatment plan, with accountability for monitoring the individual's compliance with the plan assumed by the granting licensee or other entity.

(2) If the previous licensee or other entity determined that the individual successfully completed any required treatment and followup testing, and the individual's last period of authorization was terminated favorably, the receiving licensee or entity may rely on the previous determination of fitness and no further review or followup is required.

(f) *Sanctions.* If an individual has confirmed positive, adulterated, or substituted test results from any drug, validity, or alcohol test required in this section, the licensee or other entity shall, at a minimum and as appropriate—

(1) Deny authorization to the individual, as required by § 26.75(b), (d), (e)(2), or (g); or

(2) Terminate the individual's authorization, if it has been granted, as required by § 26.75(e)(1) or (f).

[73 FR 17176, Mar. 31, 2008, as amended at 74 FR 38328, Aug. 3, 2009]

§ 26.71 Maintaining authorization.

(a) Individuals may maintain authorization under the following conditions:

(1) The individual complies with the licensee's or other entity's FFD policies and procedures, as described in § 26.27, including the responsibility to report any legal actions, as defined in § 26.5;

(2) The individual remains subject to a drug and alcohol testing program that meets the requirements of § 26.31, including random testing;

(3) The individual remains subject to a behavioral observation program that meets the requirements of § 26.33; and

(4) The individual successfully completes required FFD training on the schedule specified in § 26.29(c).

(b) If an authorized individual is not subject to an FFD program that meets the requirements of this section for more than 30 continuous days, then the licensee or other entity shall terminate the individual's authorization and the individual shall meet the requirements in this subpart, as applicable, to regain authorization.

Subpart D—Management Actions and Sanctions To Be Imposed

§ 26.73 Applicability.

The requirements in this subpart apply to the licensees and other entities identified in § 26.3(a), (b), and, as applicable, (c) for the categories of individuals specified in § 26.4(a) through (d) and (g). The requirements in this subpart also apply to the licensees and other entities specified in § 26.3(c), as applicable, for the categories of individuals in § 26.4(e). At the discretion of a licensee or other entity in § 26.3(c), the requirements of this subpart also may be applied to the categories of individuals identified in § 26.4(f). In addition, the requirements in this subpart apply to the entities in § 26.3(d) to the extent that a licensee or other entity relies on the C/V to meet the requirements of this subpart. The regulations in this subpart also apply to the individuals specified in § 26.4(h) and (j), as appropriate.

§ 26.75 Sanctions.

(a) This section defines the minimum sanctions that licensees and other entities shall impose when an individual has violated the drug and alcohol provisions of an FFD policy. A licensee or other entity may impose more stringent sanctions, except as specified in paragraph (h) of this section.

(b) Any act or attempted act to subvert the testing process, including, but not limited to, refusing to provide a specimen and providing or attempting to provide a substituted or adulterated specimen, for any test required under § 26.31(c) must result in the immediate unfavorable termination of the individual's authorization and permanent denial of authorization thereafter.

(c) Any individual who is determined to have been involved in the sale, use, or possession of illegal drugs or the consumption of alcohol within a protected area of any nuclear power plant, within a facility that is licensed to possess or use formula quantities of SSNM, within a transporter's facility or vehicle, or while performing the duties that require the individual to be subject to this subpart shall immediately have his or her authorization unfavorably terminated and denied for a minimum of 5 years from the date of the unfavorable termination of authorization.

(d) Any individual who resigns or withdraws his or her application for authorization before authorization is terminated or denied for a first violation of the FFD policy involving a confirmed positive drug or alcohol test result shall immediately have his or her authorization denied for a minimum of 5 years from the date of termination or denial. If an individual resigns or withdraws his or her application for authorization before his or her authorization is terminated or denied for any violation of the FFD policy, the licensee or other entity shall record the resignation or withdrawal, the nature of the violation, and the minimum sanction that would have been required under this section had the individual not resigned or withdrawn his or her application for authorization.

(e) Lacking any other evidence to indicate the use, sale, or possession of illegal drugs or consumption of alcohol on site, a confirmed positive drug or alcohol test result must be presumed to be an indication of offsite drug or alcohol use in violation of the FFD policy.

(1) The first violation of the FFD policy involving a confirmed positive drug or alcohol test result must, at a minimum, result in the immediate unfavorable termination of the individual's authorization for at least 14 days from the date of the unfavorable termination.

(2) Any subsequent confirmed positive drug or alcohol test result, including during an assessment or treatment

period, must result in the denial of authorization for a minimum of 5 years from the date of denial.

(f) Paragraph (e) of this section does not apply to the misuse of prescription and over-the-counter drugs, except if the MRO determines that misuse of the prescription or over-the-counter drug represents substance abuse. Sanctions for misuse of prescription and over-the-counter drugs must be sufficient to deter misuse of those substances.

(g) For individuals whose authorization was denied for 5 years under paragraphs (c), (d), (e)(2), or (f) of this section, any subsequent violation of the drug and alcohol provisions of an FFD policy must immediately result in permanent denial of authorization.

(h) A licensee or other entity may not terminate an individual's authorization and may not subject the individual to other administrative action based solely on a positive test result from any initial drug test, other than positive initial test results for marijuana or cocaine metabolites from a specimen that is reported to be valid on the basis of either validity screening or initial validity testing performed at a licensee testing facility, unless other evidence, including information obtained under the process set forth in §26.189, indicates that the individual is impaired or might otherwise pose a safety hazard. The licensee or other entity may not terminate an individual's authorization or subject an individual to any other administrative action under this section based on the results of validity screening or initial validity testing performed at a licensee testing facility indicating that a specimen is of questionable validity.

(i) With respect to positive initial drug test results from a licensee testing facility for marijuana and cocaine metabolites from a valid specimen, licensee testing facility personnel may inform licensee or other entity management of the positive initial drug test result and the specific drugs or metabolites identified, and licensees or other entities may administratively withdraw the donor's authorization or take lesser administrative actions against the donor, provided that the licensee or other entity complies with the following conditions:

(1) For the drug for which action will be taken, at least 85 percent of the specimens that were determined to be positive as a result of initial drug tests at the licensee testing facility during the past 12-month data reporting period submitted to the NRC under §26.717 were subsequently reported as positive by the HHS-certified laboratory as the result of confirmatory testing;

(2) There is no loss of compensation or benefits to the donor during the period of temporary administrative action;

(3) Immediately on receipt of a negative report from the HHS-certified laboratory or MRO, any matter that could link the donor to the temporary administrative action is eliminated from the donor's personnel record and other records; and

(4) Licensees and other entities may not disclose the temporary administrative action against an individual whose initial drug test result is not subsequently confirmed by the MRO as a violation of the FFD policy in response to a suitable inquiry conducted under the provisions of §26.63, a background investigation conducted under the provisions of this chapter, or to any other inquiry or investigation.

(i) To ensure that no records are retained, access to the system of files and records must be provided to personnel who are conducting reviews, inquiries into allegations, or audits under the provisions of §26.41, and to NRC inspectors.

(ii) The licensee or other entity shall provide the donor with a written statement that the records specified in §§26.713 and 26.715 have not been retained with respect to the temporary administrative action and shall inform the donor in writing that the temporary administrative action that was taken will not be disclosed and need not be disclosed by the individual in response to requests for self-disclosure of potentially disqualifying FFD information.

§ 26.77 Management actions regarding possible impairment.

(a) This section defines management actions that licensees and other entities who are subject to this subpart must take when an individual who is subject to this subpart shows indications that he or she may not be fit to safely and competently perform his or her duties.

(b) If an individual appears to be impaired or the individual's fitness is questionable, except as permitted under §§ 26.27(c)(3), 26.207, and 26.209, the licensee or other entity shall take immediate action to prevent the individual from performing the duties that require him or her to be subject to this subpart.

(1) If an observed behavior or physical condition creates a reasonable suspicion of possible substance abuse, the licensee or other entity shall perform drug and alcohol testing. The results must be negative before the individual returns to performing the duties that require the individual to be subject to this subpart. However, if the physical condition is the smell of alcohol with no other behavioral or physical indications of impairment, then only an alcohol test is required and the results must be negative before the individual returns to performing his or her duties.

(2) If a licensee or C/V who is subject to subpart I of this part is certain that the observed behavior or physical condition is the result solely of fatigue, the licensee or C/V shall ensure that a fatigue assessment is conducted under § 26.211. If the results of the fatigue assessment confirm that the observed behavior or physical condition is the result solely of fatigue, the licensee or C/V need not perform drug and alcohol tests or implement the determination of fitness process otherwise required by § 26.189.

(3) For other indications of possible impairment that do not create a reasonable suspicion of substance abuse (or fatigue, in the case of licensees and C/Vs who are subject to subpart I of this part), the licensee or other entity may permit the individual to return to performing his or her duties only after the impairing or questionable conditions are resolved and a determination of fitness indicates that the individual is fit to safely and competently perform his or her duties.

(c) If a licensee or other entity has a reasonable belief that an NRC employee or NRC contractor may be under the influence of any substance, or is otherwise unfit for duty, the licensee or other entity may not deny access but shall escort the individual. In any such instance, the licensee or other entity shall immediately notify the appropriate Regional Administrator by telephone, followed by written notification (e.g., e-mail or fax) to document the oral notification. If the Regional Administrator cannot be reached, the licensee or other entity shall notify the NRC Operations Center.

Subpart E—Collecting Specimens for Testing

§ 26.81 Purpose and applicability.

This subpart contains requirements for collecting specimens for drug testing and conducting alcohol tests by or on behalf of the licensees and other entities in § 26.3(a) through (d) for the categories of individuals specified in § 26.4(a) through (d) and (g). At the discretion of a licensee or other entity in § 26.3(c), specimen collections and alcohol tests must be conducted either under this subpart for the individuals specified in § 26.4(e) and (f) or the licensee or other entity may rely on specimen collections and alcohol tests conducted under the requirements of 49 CFR Part 40 for the individuals specified in § 26.4(e) and (f). The requirements of this subpart do not apply to specimen collections and alcohol tests that are conducted under the requirements of 49 CFR Part 40, as permitted in this paragraph and under §§ 26.4(j) and 26.31(b)(2) and Subpart K.

§ 26.83 Specimens to be collected.

Except as permitted under § 26.31(d)(5), licensees and other entities who are subject to this subpart shall—

(a) Collect either breath or oral fluids for initial tests for alcohol. Breath must be collected for confirmatory tests for alcohol; and

(b) Collect only urine specimens for both initial and confirmatory tests for drugs.

§ 26.85 Collector qualifications and responsibilities.

(a) *Urine collector qualifications.* Urine collectors shall be knowledgeable of the requirements of this part and the FFD policy and procedures of the licensee or other entity for whom collections are performed, and shall keep current on any changes to urine collection procedures. Collectors shall receive qualification training that meets the requirements of this paragraph and demonstrate proficiency in applying the requirements of this paragraph before serving as a collector. At a minimum, qualification training must provide instruction on the following subjects:

(1) All steps necessary to complete a collection correctly and the proper completion and transmission of the custody-and-control form;

(2) Methods to address "problem" collections, including, but not limited to, collections involving "shy bladder" and attempts to tamper with a specimen;

(3) How to correct problems in collections; and

(4) The collector's responsibility for maintaining the integrity of the specimen collection and transfer process, carefully ensuring the modesty and privacy of the donor, and avoiding any conduct or remarks that might be construed as accusatorial or otherwise offensive or inappropriate.

(b) *Alcohol collector qualifications.* Alcohol collectors shall be knowledgeable of the requirements of this part and the FFD policy and procedures of the licensee or other entity for whom collections are performed, and shall keep current on any changes to alcohol collection procedures. Collectors shall receive qualification training meeting the requirements of this paragraph and demonstrate proficiency in applying the requirements of this paragraph before serving as a collector. At a minimum, qualification training must provide instruction on the following subjects:

(1) The alcohol testing requirements of this part;

(2) Operation of the particular alcohol testing device(s) [i.e., the alcohol screening devices (ASDs) or EBTs] to be used, consistent with the most recent version of the manufacturers' instructions;

(3) Methods to address "problem" collections, including, but not limited to, collections involving "shy lung" and attempts to tamper with a specimen;

(4) How to correct problems in collections; and

(5) The collector's responsibility for maintaining the integrity of the specimen collection process, carefully ensuring the privacy of the donor, and avoiding any conduct or remarks that might be construed as accusatorial or otherwise offensive or inappropriate.

(c) *Alternative collectors.* A medical professional, technologist, or technician may serve as a collector without meeting the collector qualification requirements in paragraphs (a) or (b) of this section, as applicable, only if all of the following conditions are met:

(1) A collector who meets the requirements of paragraphs (a) or (b) of this section cannot reasonably be made available at the time the collection must occur;

(2) The individual is not employed by the licensee's or other entity's FFD program and his or her normal workplace is not at the licensee's or other entity's facility;

(3) The individual does not routinely provide FFD program services to the licensee or other entity;

(4) The individual is licensed or otherwise approved to practice in the jurisdiction in which the collection occurs; and

(5) The individual is provided with detailed, clearly-illustrated, written instructions for collecting specimens under this subpart and follows those instructions.

(d) *Personnel available to testify at proceedings.* The licensee or other entity shall ensure that qualified collection site personnel, when required, are available to testify in an administrative or disciplinary proceeding against an individual when that proceeding is based on positive drug or alcohol test results or adulterated or substituted test results from specimens collected by or under contract to the licensee or other entity.

(e) *Files.* Collection site personnel files must include each individual's resume of training and experience; certification or license, if any; references;

job descriptions; records of performance evaluations and advancement; incident reports, if any; results of tests to establish employee competency for the position he or she holds, including, but not limited to, certification that collectors are proficient in administering alcohol tests consistent with the most recent manufacturer's instructions for the instruments and devices used; and appropriate data to support determinations of honesty and integrity conducted under § 26.31(b).

§ 26.87 Collection sites.

(a) Each FFD program must have one or more designated collection sites that have all necessary personnel, materials, equipment, facilities, and supervision to collect specimens for drug testing and to perform alcohol testing. Each collection site must provide for the collection, security, temporary storage, and shipping or transportation of urine specimens to a drug testing laboratory; the collection of oral fluids or breath specimens; and the security of alcohol testing devices and test results. A properly equipped mobile facility that meets the requirements of this section is an acceptable collection site.

(b) The collection site must provide for the donor's visual privacy while the donor and collector are viewing the results of an alcohol test, and for individual privacy while the donor is submitting a urine specimen, except if a directly observed urine specimen collection is required. Unauthorized personnel may not be present for the specimen collection.

(c) Contracts for collection site services must permit representatives of the NRC, licensee, or other entity to conduct unannounced inspections and audits and to obtain all information and documentation that is reasonably relevant to the inspections and audits.

(d) Licensees and other entities shall take the following measures to prevent unauthorized access to the collection site that could compromise the integrity of the collection process or the specimens.

(1) Unauthorized personnel may not be permitted in any part of the designated collection site where specimens are collected or stored;

(2) A designated collection site must be secure. If a collection site is dedicated solely to specimen collection, it must be secure at all times. Methods of assuring security may include, but are not limited to, physical measures to control access, such as locked doors, alarms, or visual monitoring of the collection site when it is not occupied; and

(3) If a collection site cannot be dedicated solely to collecting specimens, the portion of the facility that is used for specimen collection must be secured and, during the time period during which a specimen is being collected, a sign must be posted to indicate that access is permitted only for authorized personnel.

(e) The following steps must be taken to deter the dilution and adulteration of urine specimens at the collection site:

(1) Agents that color any source of standing water in the stall or room in which the donor will provide a specimen, including, but not limited to, the toilet bowl or tank, must be placed in the source of standing water, so that the reservoirs of water are neither yellow nor colorless;

(2) There must be no other source of water (e.g., no shower or sink) in the enclosure where urination occurs, or the source of water must be rendered unusable; and

(3) Chemicals or products that could be used to contaminate or otherwise alter the specimen must be removed from the collection site or secured. The collector shall inspect the enclosure in which urination will occur before each collection to ensure that no materials are available that could be used to subvert the testing process.

(f) In the exceptional event that a designated collection site is inaccessible and there is an immediate requirement to collect a urine specimen, including, but not limited to, an event investigation, then the licensee or other entity may use a public rest room, onsite rest room, or hospital examining room according to the following procedures:

(1) The facility must be secured by visual inspection to ensure that no unauthorized persons are present, and that undetected access (e.g., through a

rear door not in the view of the collector) is impossible. Security during the collection may be maintained by restricting access to collection materials and specimens. In the case of a public rest room, a sign must be posted or an individual assigned to ensure that no unauthorized personnel are present during the entire collection procedure to avoid embarrassment of the donor and distraction of the collector.

(2) If practical, a water coloring agent that meets the requirements of §26.87(e)(1) must be placed in the toilet bowl to be used by the donor and in any other accessible source of standing water, including, but not limited to, the toilet tank. The collector shall instruct the donor not to flush the toilet.

(3) A collector of the same gender as the donor shall accompany the donor into the area that will be used for specimen collection, but remain outside of the stall, if it is a multi-stalled rest room, or outside of the door to the room, if it is a single rest room, in which the donor will provide the specimen. If a collector of the same gender is not available, the collector shall select a same-gender person to accompany the donor. This person shall be instructed on the collection procedures specified in this subpart and his or her identity must be documented on the custody-and-control form.

(4) After the collector has possession of the specimen, the collector shall inspect the toilet bowl and area to ensure that there is no evidence of a subversion attempt and shall then flush the toilet. The collector shall instruct the donor to participate with the collector in completing the chain-of-custody procedures.

(5) If it is impractical to maintain continuous physical security of a collection site from the time a urine specimen is presented until the sealed container is transferred for shipment, the specimen must remain under the direct control of an individual who is authorized by the licensee or other entity until the specimen is prepared for transfer, storage, or shipping, as required by §26.117. The authorized individual shall be instructed on his or her responsibilities for maintaining custody and control of the specimen and his or her custody of the specimen must be documented on the custody-and-control form.

§26.89 Preparing to collect specimens for testing.

(a) When an individual has been notified of a requirement for testing and does not appear at the collection site within the time period specified by FFD program procedures, the collector shall inform FFD program management that the individual has not reported for testing. FFD program management shall ensure that the necessary steps are taken to determine whether the individual's undue tardiness or failure to appear for testing constitutes a violation of the licensee's or other entity's FFD policy. If FFD program management determines that the undue tardiness or failure to report for testing represents an attempt to subvert the testing process, the licensee or other entity shall impose on the individual the sanctions in §26.75(b). If FFD program management determines that the undue tardiness or failure to report does not represent a subversion attempt, the licensee or other entity may not impose sanctions but shall ensure that the individual is tested at the earliest reasonable and practical opportunity after locating the individual.

(b) Donors shall provide acceptable identification before testing.

(1) Acceptable identification includes photo-identification issued by a licensee or other entity who is subject to this part, or by the Federal, State, or local government. Licensees and other entities may not accept faxes or photocopies of identification.

(2) If the donor cannot produce acceptable identification before any testing that is required under this part other than pre-access testing, the collector shall proceed with the test and immediately inform FFD program management that the donor did not present acceptable identification. When so informed, FFD program management shall contact the individual's supervisor to verify in-person the individual's identity, or, if the supervisor is not available, take other steps to establish the individual's identity and

determine whether the lack of identification was an attempt to subvert the testing process. The donor may not leave the collection site except under supervision until his or her identity has been established.

(3) If the donor is scheduled for pre-access testing and cannot produce acceptable identification, the collector may not proceed with the collection, and shall inform FFD program management that the individual did not present acceptable identification. When so informed, FFD program management will take the necessary steps to determine whether the lack of identification was an attempt to subvert the testing process.

(4) The collector shall explain the testing procedure to the donor, show the donor the form(s) to be used, and ask the donor to sign a consent-to-testing form. The donor may not be required to list prescription medications or over-the-counter preparations that he or she has recently used.

(c) The collector shall inform the donor that, if the donor refuses to cooperate in the specimen collection process (including, but not limited to, behaving in a confrontational manner that disrupts the testing process; admitting to the collector that he or she adulterated, diluted, or adulterated the specimen; is found to have a device, such as a prosthetic appliance, the purpose of which is to interfere with providing an actual urine specimen; or leaving the collection site before all of the collection procedures are completed), it will be considered a refusal to test, and sanctions for subverting the testing process will be imposed under § 26.75(b). If the donor refuses to cooperate in the collection procedures, the collector shall inform FFD program management to obtain guidance on the actions to be taken.

(d) In order to promote the security of specimens, avoid distraction of the collector, and ensure against any confusion in the identification of specimens, a collector shall conduct only one collection procedure at any given time. For this purpose, a urine collection procedure is complete when the urine specimen container has been sealed and initialed, the chain-of-custody form has been executed, and the donor has departed the collection site.

§ 26.91 Acceptable devices for conducting initial and confirmatory tests for alcohol and methods of use.

(a) *Acceptable alcohol screening devices.* Alcohol screening devices (ASDs), including devices that test specimens of oral fluids or breath, must be approved by the National Highway Traffic Safety Administration (NHTSA) and listed in the most current version of NHTSA's Conforming Products List (CPL) for such devices. An ASD that is listed in the NHTSA CPL may be used only for initial tests for alcohol, and may not be used for confirmatory tests.

(b) *Acceptable evidential breath testing devices.* Evidential breath testing devices listed in the NHTSA CPL for evidential devices that meet the requirements of paragraph (c) of this section must be used to conduct confirmatory alcohol tests, and may be used to conduct initial alcohol tests. Note that, among the devices listed in the CPL for EBTs, only those devices listed without an asterisk (*) may be used for confirmatory alcohol testing under this subpart.

(c) *EBT capabilities.* An EBT that is listed in the NHTSA CPL for evidential devices that has the following capabilities may be used for conducting initial alcohol tests and must be used for confirmatory alcohol tests under this subpart:

(1) Provides a printed result of each breath test;

(2) Assigns a unique number to each completed test, which the collector and donor can read before each test and which is printed on each copy of the test result;

(3) Prints, on each copy of the test result, the manufacturer's name for the device, its serial number, and the time of the test;

(4) Distinguishes alcohol from acetone at the 0.02 alcohol concentration level;

(5) Tests an air blank; and

(6) Permits performance of an external calibration check.

(d) *Quality assurance and quality control of ASDs.* (1) Licensees and other entities shall implement the most recent version of the quality assurance plan submitted to NHTSA for any ASD that is used for initial alcohol testing.

(2) Licensees and other entities may not use an ASD that fails the specified quality control checks or that has passed its expiration date.

(3) For ASDs that test breath specimens and meet EBT requirements for confirmatory testing, licensees and other entities shall also follow the device use and care requirements specified in paragraph (e) of this section.

(e) *Quality assurance and quality control of EBTs.* (1) Licensees and other entities shall implement the most recent version of the manufacturer's instructions for the use and care of the EBT consistently with the quality assurance plan submitted to NHTSA for the EBT, including performing external calibration checks no less frequently than at the intervals specified in the manufacturer's instructions.

(2) When conducting external calibration checks, licensees and other entities shall use only calibration devices appearing on NHTSA's CPL for "Calibrating Units for Breath Alcohol Tests."

(3) If an EBT fails an external check of calibration, the licensee or other entity shall take the EBT out of service. The EBT may not be used again for alcohol testing under this subpart until it is repaired and passes an external calibration check.

(4) In order to ensure that confirmed positive alcohol test results are derived from an EBT that is calibrated, the licensee or other entity shall implement one of the following procedures:

(i) If an EBT fails any external check of calibration, cancel every confirmed positive test result that was obtained using the EBT from any tests that were conducted after the EBT passed the last external calibration check; or

(ii) After every confirmed positive test result obtained from using an EBT, conduct an external check of calibration of the EBT in the presence of the donor. If the EBT fails the external calibration check, cancel the donor's test result and conduct another initial and confirmatory test on a different EBT as soon as practicable.

(5) Inspection, maintenance, and calibration of the EBT must be performed by its manufacturer or a maintenance representative or other individual who is certified either by the manufacturer or by a State health agency or other appropriate State agency.

§ 26.93 Preparing for alcohol testing.

(a) Immediately before collecting a specimen for alcohol testing, the collector shall—

(1) Ask the donor whether he or she, in the past 15 minutes, has had anything to eat or drink, belched, or put anything into his or her mouth (including, but not limited to, a cigarette, breath mint, or chewing gum), and instruct the donor that he or she should avoid these activities during the collection process;

(2) If the donor states that he or she has not engaged in the activities listed in paragraph (a)(1) of this section, alcohol testing may proceed;

(3) If the donor states that he or she has engaged in any of the activities listed in paragraph (a)(1) of this section, inform the donor that a 15-minute waiting period is necessary to prevent an accumulation of mouth alcohol from leading to an artificially high reading;

(4) Explain that it is to the donor's benefit to avoid the activities listed in paragraph (a)(1) of this section during the collection process;

(5) Explain that the initial and confirmatory tests, if a confirmatory test is necessary, will be conducted at the end of the waiting period, even if the donor has not followed the instructions; and

(6) Document that the instructions were communicated to the donor.

(b) With the exception of the 15-minute waiting period, if necessary, the collector shall begin for-cause alcohol and/or drug testing as soon as reasonably practical after the decision is made that for-cause testing is required. When for-cause alcohol testing is required, alcohol testing may not be delayed by collecting a specimen for drug testing.

§ 26.95 Conducting an initial test for alcohol using a breath specimen.

(a) The collector shall perform the initial breath test as soon as practical after the donor indicates that he or she has not engaged in the activities listed in § 26.93(a)(1) or after the 15-minute waiting period has elapsed, if required.

(b) To perform the initial test, the collector shall—

(1) Select, or allow the donor to select, an individually wrapped or sealed mouthpiece from the testing materials;

(2) Open the individually wrapped or sealed mouthpiece in view of the donor and insert it into the device as required by the manufacturer's instructions;

(3) Instruct the donor to blow steadily and forcefully into the mouthpiece for at least 6 seconds or until the device indicates that an adequate amount of breath has been obtained;

(4) Show the donor the displayed or printed test result; and

(5) Ensure that the test result record can be associated with the donor and is maintained secure.

(c) Unless problems in administering the breath test require an additional collection, only one breath specimen may be collected for the initial test. If an additional collection(s) is required, the collector shall rely on the test result from the first successful collection to determine the need for confirmatory testing.

§ 26.97 Conducting an initial test for alcohol using a specimen of oral fluids.

(a) To perform the initial test, the collector shall—

(1) Check the expiration date on the device and show it to the donor (the device may not be used after its expiration date);

(2) Open an individually wrapped or sealed package containing the device in the presence of the donor;

(3) Offer the donor the choice of using the device or having the collector use it. If the donor chooses to use it, instruct the donor to insert the device into his or her mouth and use it in the manner described by the device's manufacturer;

(4) If the donor chooses not to use the device, or in all cases when a new test is necessary because the device failed to activate, insert the device into the donor's mouth, and gather oral fluids in the manner described by the device's manufacturer (wear single-use examination or similar gloves while doing so and change them following each test); and

(5) When the device is removed from the donor's mouth, follow the manufacturer's instructions regarding necessary next steps to ensure that the device has activated.

(b) If the steps in paragraph (a) of this section could not be completed successfully (e.g., the device breaks, the device is dropped on the floor, the device fails to activate), the collector shall—

(1) Discard the device and conduct a new test using a new device. The new device must be one that has been under the collector's control before the test;

(2) Record the reason for the new test;

(3) Offer the donor the choice of using the device or having the collector use it unless the donor, in the opinion of the collector, was responsible for the new test needing to be conducted. If the collector concludes that the donor was responsible, then the collector shall use the device to conduct the test; and

(4) Repeat the procedures in paragraph (a) of this section.

(c) If the second collection attempt in paragraph (b) of this section could not be completed, the collector shall—

(1) End the collection of oral fluids and document the reason(s) that the collection could not be completed; and

(2) Immediately conduct another initial test using an EBT.

(d) The collector shall read the result displayed on the device no sooner than the device's manufacturer instructs. In all cases, the collector shall read the result within 15 minutes of the test. The collector shall then show the device and its reading to the donor, record the result, and record that an ASD was used.

(e) Devices, swabs, gloves, and other materials used in collecting oral fluids may not be re-used.

§ 26.99 Determining the need for a confirmatory test for alcohol.

(a) If the initial test result is less than 0.02 percent BAC, the collector shall declare the test result as negative.

(b) If the initial test result is 0.02 percent BAC or higher, the collector shall ensure that the time at which the test was concluded (*i.e.*, the time at which the test result was known) is recorded and inform the donor that a confirmatory test for alcohol is required.

§ 26.101 Conducting a confirmatory test for alcohol.

(a) The confirmatory test must begin as soon as possible, but no more than 30 minutes after the conclusion of the initial test.

(b) To complete the confirmatory test, the collector shall—

(1) In the presence of the donor, conduct an air blank on the EBT before beginning the confirmatory test and show the result to the donor;

(2) Verify that the reading is 0.00. If the reading is 0.00, the test may proceed. If not, then conduct another air blank;

(3) If the reading on the second air blank is 0.00, the test may proceed. If the reading is greater than 0.00, take the EBT out of service and proceed with the test using another EBT. If an EBT is taken out of service for this reason, the EBT may not be used for further testing until it is found to be within tolerance limits on an external check of calibration;

(4) Open an individually wrapped or sealed mouthpiece in view of the donor and insert it into the device as required by the manufacturer's instructions;

(5) Read the unique test number displayed on the EBT, and ensure that the donor reads the same number;

(6) Instruct the donor to blow steadily and forcefully into the mouthpiece for at least 6 seconds or until the device indicates that an adequate amount of breath has been obtained; and

(7) Show the donor the result displayed on or printed by the EBT, record the result, and document the time at which the confirmatory test result was known.

(c) Unless there are problems in administering the breath test that require an additional collection, the collector shall collect only one breath specimen for the confirmatory test. If an additional collection(s) is required because of problems in administering the breath test, the collector shall rely on the breath specimen from the first successful collection to determine the confirmatory test result. Collection procedures may not require collectors to calculate an average or otherwise combine results from two or more breath specimens to determine the confirmatory test result.

(d) If an EBT that meets the requirements of § 26.91(b) and (c) was used for the initial alcohol test, the same EBT may be used for confirmatory testing.

§ 26.103 Determining a confirmed positive test result for alcohol.

(a) A confirmed positive test result for alcohol must be declared under any of the following conditions:

(1) When the result of the confirmatory test for alcohol is 0.04 percent BAC or higher;

(2) When the result of the confirmatory test for alcohol is 0.03 percent BAC or higher and the donor had been in a work status for at least 1 hour at the time the initial test was concluded (including any breaks for rest, lunch, dental/doctor appointments, etc.); or

(3) When the result of the confirmatory test for alcohol is 0.02 percent BAC or higher and the donor had been in a work status for at least 2 hours at the time the initial test was concluded (including any breaks for rest, lunch, dental/doctor appointments, etc.).

(b) When the result of the confirmatory test for alcohol is equal to or greater than 0.01 percent BAC but less than 0.02 percent BAC and the donor has been in a work status for 3 hours or more at the time the initial test was concluded (including any breaks for rest, lunch, dental/doctor appointments, etc.), the collector shall declare the test result as negative and inform FFD program management. The licensee or other entity shall prohibit the donor from performing any duties that require the individual to be subject to this subpart and may not return the individual to performing such duties until a determination of fitness indicates that the donor is fit to safely and competently perform his or her duties.

§ 26.105 Preparing for urine collection.

(a) The collector shall ask the donor to remove any unnecessary outer garments, such as a coat or jacket, which might conceal items or substances that the donor could use to tamper with or adulterate his or her urine specimen. The collector shall ensure that all personal belongings such as a purse or briefcase remain with the outer garments outside of the room or stall in which the urine specimen is collected. The donor may retain his or her wallet.

(b) The collector shall also ask the donor to empty his or her pockets and display the items in them to enable the collector to identify items that the donor could use to adulterate or substitute his or her urine specimen. The donor shall permit the collector to make this observation. If the donor refuses to show the collector the items in his or her pockets, this is considered a refusal to test. If an item is found that appears to have been brought to the collection site with the intent to adulterate or substitute the specimen, the collector shall contact the MRO or FFD program manager to determine whether a directly observed collection is required. If the item appears to have been inadvertently brought to the collection site, the collector shall secure the item and continue with the normal collection procedure. If the collector identifies nothing that the donor could use to adulterate or substitute the specimen, the donor may place the items back into his or her pockets.

(c) The collector shall instruct the donor to wash and dry his or her hands before urinating.

(d) After washing his or her hands, the donor shall remain in the presence of the collector and may not have access to any water fountain, faucet, soap dispenser, cleaning agent, or other materials that he or she could use to adulterate the urine specimen.

(e) The collector may select, or allow the donor to select, an individually wrapped or sealed collection container from the collection kit materials. Either the collector or the donor, with both present, shall unwrap or break the seal of the collection container. With the exception of the collection container, the donor may not take anything from the collection kit into the room or stall used for urination.

§ 26.107 Collecting a urine specimen.

(a) The collector shall direct the donor to go into the room or stall used for urination, provide a specimen of the quantity that has been predetermined by the licensee or other entity, as defined in § 26.109(a), not flush the toilet, and return with the specimen as soon as the donor has completed the void.

(1) The donor shall provide his or her urine specimen in the privacy of a room, stall, or otherwise partitioned area (private area) that allows for individual privacy, except if a directly observed collection is required, as described in § 26.115;

(2) Except in the case of a directly observed collection, no one may go with the donor into the room or stall in which the donor will provide his or her specimen; and

(3) The collector may set a reasonable time limit for voiding.

(b) The collector shall pay careful attention to the donor during the entire collection process to note any conduct that clearly indicates an attempt to tamper with a specimen (e.g., substitute urine is in plain view or an attempt to bring an adulterant or urine substitute into the private area used for urination). If any such conduct is detected, the collector shall document the conduct on the custody-and-control form and contact FFD program management to determine whether a directly observed collection is required, as described in § 26.115.

(c) After the donor has provided the urine specimen and submitted it to the collector, the donor shall be permitted to wash his or her hands. The collector shall inspect the toilet bowl and room or stall in which the donor voided to identify any evidence of a subversion attempt, and then flush the toilet.

§ 26.109 Urine specimen quantity.

(a) Licensees and other entities who are subject to this subpart shall establish a predetermined quantity of urine that donors are requested to provide when submitting a specimen. At a minimum, the predetermined quantity must include 30 milliliters (mL) to ensure that a sufficient quantity of urine is available for initial and confirmatory validity and drug tests at an HHS-certified laboratory, and for retesting of an aliquot of the specimen if requested by the donor under § 26.165(b). The licensee's or other entity's predetermined quantity may include more than 30 mL, if the testing program follows split specimen procedures, tests for additional drugs, or performs initial testing at a licensee testing facility. Where collected specimens are to be split under the provisions of this subpart, the predetermined quantity must include an additional 15 mL.

(b) If the quantity of urine in the first specimen provided by the donor is less than 30 mL, the collector shall take the following steps:

(1) The collector shall encourage the donor to drink a reasonable amount of liquid (normally, 8 ounces of water every 30 minutes, but not to exceed a maximum of 40 ounces over 3 hours) until the donor provides a specimen containing at least 30 mL. The collector shall provide the donor with a separate collection container for each successive specimen;

(2) Once the donor provides a specimen of at least 30 mL, the collection must end. If the specimen quantity is at least 30 mL but is less than the licensee's or other entity's predetermined quantity, the licensee or other entity may not require the donor to provide additional specimens and may not impose any sanctions on the donor. If the donor provides a specimen of 30 mL or more, but the specimen quantity is less than the predetermined quantity, the collector shall forward the specimen to the HHS-certified laboratory for testing. If the donor provides a specimen of at least the predetermined quantity, the specimen may be processed under the FFD program's usual testing procedures;

(3) If the donor has not provided a specimen of at least 30 mL within 3 hours of the first unsuccessful attempt to provide a specimen of the predetermined quantity, the collector shall discontinue the collection and notify the FFD program manager or MRO to initiate the "shy bladder" procedures in § 26.119; and

(4) Neither the donor nor the collector may combine specimens. The collector shall discard specimens of less than 30 mL, except if there is reason to believe that the donor has diluted, adulterated, substituted, or otherwise tampered with the specimen, based on the collector's observations of the donor's behavior during the collection process or the specimen's characteristics, as specified in § 26.111. If the collector has a reason to believe that a specimen that is 15 mL or more, but less than 30 mL, has been diluted, adulterated, substituted, or altered, the collector shall prepare the suspect specimen for shipping to the HHS-certified laboratory and contact FFD program management to determine whether a directly observed collection is required, as described in § 26.115.

§ 26.111 Checking the acceptability of the urine specimen.

(a) Immediately after the donor provides the urine specimen to the collector, including specimens of less than 30 mL but greater than 15 mL, the collector shall measure the temperature of the specimen. The temperature-measuring device used must accurately reflect the temperature of the specimen and not contaminate the specimen. The time from urination to temperature measurement may not exceed 4 minutes. If the temperature of a urine specimen is outside the range of 90 °F to 100 °F (32 °C to 38 °C), that is a reason to believe the donor may have altered or substituted the specimen.

(b) Immediately after the donor provides a urine specimen, including specimens of less than 30 mL but equal to or greater than 15 mL, the collector shall also inspect the specimen to determine its color and clarity and look for any signs of contaminants or adulteration. The collector shall note any unusual findings on the custody-and-control form.

(c) If there is reason to believe that the donor may have attempted to dilute, substitute, or adulterate the specimen based on specimen temperature or other observations made during the collection, the collector shall contact the designated FFD program manager, who may consult with the MRO, to determine whether the donor has attempted to subvert the testing process or whether other circumstances may explain the observations. The FFD program manager or MRO may require the donor to provide a second specimen as soon as possible under direct observation. In addition, the collector shall inform the donor that he or she may volunteer to submit a second specimen under direct observation to counter the reason to believe the donor may have altered or substituted the specimen.

(d) Any specimen of 15 mL or more that the collector suspects has been diluted, substituted, or adulterated, and any specimen of 15 mL or more that has been collected under direct observation under paragraph (c) of this section, must be sent directly to the HHS-certified laboratory for initial and, if required, confirmatory testing, and may not be subject to initial testing at a licensee testing facility.

(e) As much of the suspect specimen as possible must be preserved.

(f) An acceptable specimen is free of any apparent contaminants, meets the required basic quantity of at least 30 mL, and is within the acceptable temperature range.

§ 26.113 Splitting the urine specimen.

(a) Licensees and other entities may, but are not required to, use split-specimen methods of collection.

(b) If the urine specimen is to be split into two specimen bottles, hereinafter referred to as Bottle A and Bottle B, the collector shall take the following steps:

(1) The collector shall instruct the donor to urinate into a specimen container;

(2) The collector, in the presence of the donor and after determining specimen temperature as described in § 26.111(a), shall split the urine specimen. The collector shall pour 30 mL of urine into Bottle A and a minimum of 15 mL of urine into Bottle B. If the quantity of urine available for Bottle B is less than 15 mL, the collector shall pour the remaining urine into Bottle B and forward the specimens in Bottles A and B to the HHS-certified laboratory for drug and validity testing; and

(3) The collector shall ask the donor to observe the splitting of the urine specimen and to maintain visual contact with both specimen bottles until the custody-and-control form(s) for both specimens are completed, the specimens are sealed, and the specimens and form(s) are prepared for secure storage or shipping.

(c) Licensees and other entities may use aliquots of the specimen collected for validity screening and initial validity and drug testing at the licensee testing facility, as permitted under § 26.31(d)(3)(ii), or to test for additional drugs, as permitted under § 26.31(d)(1)(i)(A), but only if sufficient urine is available for this testing after the specimen has been split into Bottle A and Bottle B.

§ 26.115 Collecting a urine specimen under direct observation.

(a) Procedures for collecting urine specimens must provide for the donor's privacy unless directed by this subpart or the MRO or FFD program manager determines that a directly observed collection is warranted. The following circumstances constitute the exclusive grounds for performing a directly observed collection:

(1) The donor has presented, at this or a previous collection, a urine specimen that the HHS-certified laboratory reported as being substituted, adulterated, or invalid to the MRO and the MRO reported to the licensee or other entity that there is no adequate medical explanation for the result;

(2) The donor has presented, at this collection, a urine specimen that falls outside the required temperature range;

(3) The collector observes conduct clearly and unequivocally indicating an attempt to dilute, substitute, or adulterate the specimen; and

(4) A directly observed collection is required under § 26.69.

(b) Before collecting a urine specimen under direct observation, the collector shall obtain the agreement of the FFD program manager or MRO to obtain a urine specimen under direct observation. After obtaining agreement, the collector shall ensure that a specimen is collected under direct observation as soon as reasonably practicable.

(c) The collector shall explain to the donor the reason for direct observation of the collection under paragraph (a) of this section.

(d) The collector shall complete a new custody-and-control form for the specimen that is obtained from the directly observed collection. The collector shall record that the collection was observed and the reason(s) for the directly observed collection on the form.

(e) The collector shall ensure that the observer is the same gender as the individual. A person of the opposite gender may not act as the observer under any conditions. The observer may be a different person from the collector and need not be a qualified collector.

(f) If someone other than the collector is to observe the collection, the collector shall instruct the observer to follow the procedures in this paragraph. The individual who observes the collection shall follow these procedures:

(1) The observer shall instruct the donor to adjust his or her clothing to ensure that the area of the donor's body between the waist and knees is exposed;

(2) The observer shall watch the donor urinate into the collection container. Specifically, the observer shall watch the urine go from the donor's body into the collection container;

(3) If the observer is not the collector, the observer may not take the collection container from the donor, but shall observe the specimen as the donor takes it to the collector; and

(4) If the observer is not the collector, the collector shall record the observer's name on the custody-and-control form.

(g) If a donor declines to allow a directly observed collection that is required or permitted under this section, the donor's refusal constitutes an act to subvert the testing process.

(h) If a collector learns that a directly observed collection should have been performed but was not, the collector shall inform the FFD program manager, or his or her designee. The FFD program manager or designee shall ensure that a directly observed collection is immediately performed.

§26.117 Preparing urine specimens for storage and shipping.

(a) Both the donor and the collector shall keep the donor's urine specimen(s) in view at all times before the specimen(s) are sealed and labeled. If any specimen or aliquot is transferred to another container, the collector shall ask the donor to observe the transfer and sealing of the container with a tamper-evident seal.

(b) Both the collector and the donor shall be present (at the same time) during the procedures outlined in this section.

(c) The collector shall place an identification label securely on each container. The label must contain the date, the donor's specimen number, and any other identifying information provided or required by the FFD program. The collector shall also apply a tamper-evident seal on each container if it is separate from the label. The specimen bottle must be securely sealed to prevent undetected tampering.

(d) The donor shall initial the identification label(s) on the specimen bottle(s) for the purpose of certifying that the specimen was collected from him or her. The collector shall also ask the donor to read and sign a statement on the custody-and-control form certifying that the specimen(s) identified as having been collected from the donor is, in fact, the specimen(s) that he or she provided.

(e) The collector shall complete the custody-and-control form(s) and shall certify proper completion of the collection.

(f) The specimens and chain-of-custody forms must be packaged for transfer to the HHS-certified laboratory or the licensee's testing facility. If the specimens are not immediately prepared for transfer, they must be appropriately safeguarded during temporary storage.

(g) While any part of the chain-of-custody procedures is being performed, the specimens and custody documents must be under the control of the involved collector. The collector may not leave the collection site during the interval between presentation of the specimen by the donor and securing of the specimens with identifying labels bearing the donor's specimen identification numbers and seals initialed by the donor. If the involved collector momentarily leaves his or her workstation, the sealed specimens and custody-and-control forms must be secured or taken with him or her. If the collector is leaving for an extended period of time, the specimens must be packaged for transfer to the HHS-certified laboratory or the licensee testing facility and secured before the collector leaves the collection site.

(h) The specimen(s) sealed in a shipping container must be immediately transferred, appropriately safeguarded during temporary storage, or kept under the personal control of an authorized individual until transferred. These minimum procedures apply to the transfer of specimens to licensee testing facilities from collection sites (except where co-located) as well as to the shipping of specimens to HHS-certified laboratories. As an option, licensees and other entities may ship several specimens via courier in a locked or sealed shipping container.

(i) Collection site personnel shall ensure that a custody-and-control form is packaged with its associated urine specimen bottle. Unless a collection site and a licensee testing facility are co-located, the sealed and labeled specimen bottles, with their associated custody-and-control forms that are being transferred from the collection site to the drug testing laboratory must be placed in a second, tamper-evident shipping container. The second container must be designed to minimize the possibility of damage to the specimen during shipment (e.g., specimen boxes, shipping bags, padded mailers, or bulk insulated shipping containers with that capability), so that the contents of the shipping containers are no longer accessible without breaking a tamper-evident seal.

(j) Collection site personnel shall arrange to transfer the collected specimens to the HHS-certified laboratory or the licensee testing facility. Licensees and other entities shall take appropriate and prudent actions to minimize false negative results from specimen degradation. Specimens that have not been shipped to the HHS-certified laboratory or the licensee testing facility within 24 hours of collection and any specimen that is suspected of having been substituted, adulterated, or tampered with in any way must be maintained cooled to not more than 6 °C (42.8 °F) until they are shipped to the HHS-certified laboratory. Specimens must be shipped from the collection site to the HHS-certified laboratory or the licensee testing facility as soon as reasonably practical but, except under unusual circumstances, the time between specimen shipment and receipt of the specimen at the licensee testing facility or HHS-certified laboratory should not exceed 2 business days.

(k) Couriers, express carriers, and postal service personnel do not have direct access to the custody-and-control forms or the specimen bottles. Therefore, there is no requirement that such personnel document chain of custody on the custody-and-control forms during transit. Custody accountability of the shipping containers during shipment must be maintained by a tracking system provided by the courier, express carrier, or postal service.

§ 26.119 Determining "shy" bladder.

(a) When a donor has not provided a specimen of at least 30 mL within the 3 hours permitted for urine collection, FFD program personnel shall direct the donor to obtain, within 5 business days, an evaluation from a licensed physician who is acceptable to the MRO and has expertise in the medical issues raised by the donor's failure to provide a sufficient specimen. The MRO may perform this evaluation if the MRO has the appropriate expertise.

(b) If another physician will perform the evaluation, the MRO shall provide the other physician with the following information and instructions:

(1) The donor was required to take a drug test, but was unable to provide a sufficient quantity of urine to complete the test;

(2) The potential consequences of refusing to take the required drug test; and

(3) The physician must agree to follow the requirements of paragraphs (c) through (f) of this section.

(c) The physician who conducts this evaluation shall make one of the following determinations:

(1) A medical condition has, or with a high degree of probability could have, precluded the donor from providing a sufficient amount of urine; or

(2) There is an inadequate basis for determining that a medical condition has, or with a high degree of probability could have, precluded the donor from providing a sufficient quantity of urine.

(d) For purposes of this section, a medical condition includes an ascertainable physiological condition (e.g., a urinary system dysfunction) or a medically documented pre-existing psychological disorder, but does not include unsupported assertions of "situational anxiety" or dehydration.

(e) The physician who conducts this evaluation shall provide a written statement of his or her determination and the basis for it to the MRO. This statement may not include detailed information on the donor's medical condition beyond what is necessary to explain the determination.

(f) If the physician who conducts this evaluation determines that the donor's medical condition is a serious and permanent or long-term disability that is highly likely to prevent the donor from providing a sufficient amount of urine for a very long or indefinite period of time, the physician shall set forth this determination and the reasons for it in the written statement to the MRO.

(g) The MRO shall seriously consider and assess the information provided by the physician in deciding whether the donor has a medical condition that has, or with a high degree of probability could have, precluded the donor from providing a sufficient amount of urine, as follows:

(1) If the MRO concurs with the physician's determination, then the MRO shall declare that the donor has not violated the FFD policy and the licensee or other entity shall take no further action with respect to the donor;

(2) If the MRO determines that the medical condition has not, or with a high degree of probability could not have, precluded the donor from providing a sufficient amount of urine, then the MRO shall declare that there has been a refusal to test; or

(3) If the MRO determines that the medical condition is highly likely to prevent the donor from providing a sufficient amount of urine for a very long or indefinite period of time, then the MRO shall authorize an alternative evaluation process, tailored to the individual case, for drug testing.

Subpart F—Licensee Testing Facilities

§26.121 Purpose.

This subpart contains requirements for facilities that are operated by licensees and other entities who are subject to this part to perform initial tests of urine specimens for validity, drugs, and drug metabolites.

§26.123 Testing facility capabilities.

Each licensee testing facility shall have the capability, at the same premises, to perform either validity screening tests or initial validity tests or both, and initial drug tests for each drug and drug metabolite for which testing is conducted.

§26.125 Licensee testing facility personnel.

(a) Each licensee testing facility shall have one or more individuals who are responsible for day-to-day operations and supervision of the testing technicians. The designated individual(s) shall have at least a bachelor's degree in the chemical or biological sciences, medical technology, or equivalent. He or she shall also have training and experience in the theory and practice of the procedures used in the licensee testing facility, and a thorough understanding of quality control practices and procedures, the review, interpretation, and reporting of test results, and proper remedial actions to be taken in response to detection of abnormal test or quality control results.

(b) Other technicians or non-technical staff shall have the necessary training and skills for their assigned tasks. Technicians who perform urine specimen testing shall have documented proficiency in operating the testing instruments and devices used at the licensee testing facility.

(c) Licensee testing facility personnel files must include each individual's resume of training and experience; certification or license, if any; references; job descriptions; records of performance evaluations and advancement; incident reports, if any; results of tests that establish employee competency for the position he or she holds, including, but not limited to, certification that personnel are proficient in conducting testing in accordance with manufacturer's most recent instructions for the instruments and devices used and tests for color blindness; and appropriate data to support determinations of honesty and integrity required by this part.

§ 26.127 Procedures.

(a) Licensee testing facilities shall develop, implement, and maintain clear and well-documented procedures for accession, shipment, and testing of urine specimens.

(b) Written chain-of-custody procedures must describe the methods to be used to maintain control and accountability of specimens from receipt through completion of testing and reporting of results, during storage and shipping to the HHS-certified laboratory, and continuing until final disposition of the specimens.

(c) Licensee testing facilities shall develop, implement, and maintain written standard operating procedures for each assay performed for drug and specimen validity testing. If a licensee testing facility performs validity screening tests, the licensee testing facility shall develop, implement, and maintain written standard operating procedures for each test. The procedures must include, but are not limited to, detailed descriptions of—

(1) The principles of each test;

(2) Preparation of reagents, standards, and controls;

(3) Calibration procedures;

(4) Derivation of results;

(5) Linearity of the methods;

(6) Sensitivity of the methods;

(7) Cutoff values;

(8) Mechanisms for reporting results;

(9) Controls;

(10) Criteria for unacceptable specimens and results;

(11) Reagents and expiration dates; and

(12) References.

(d) Licensee testing facilities shall develop, implement, and maintain written procedures for instrument and test setup and normal operation, including the following:

(1) A schedule for checking critical operating characteristics for all instruments and validity screening tests;

(2) Tolerance limits for acceptable function checks; and

(3) Instructions for major troubleshooting and repair.

(e) Licensee testing facilities shall develop, implement, and maintain written procedures for remedial actions to be taken when systems, and instrumented and non-instrumented tests are out of acceptable limits or errors are detected. Each facility shall maintain documentation that these procedures are followed and that all necessary corrective actions are taken. In addition, each facility shall have systems in place to verify all stages of testing and reporting and to document the verification.

§ 26.129 Assuring specimen security, chain of custody, and preservation.

(a) Each licensee testing facility must be secure at all times. Each licensee or other entity shall have sufficient security measures in place to control access to the licensee testing facility and to ensure that no unauthorized personnel handle specimens or gain access to the licensee testing facility's processes or areas where records are stored. Access to these secured areas must be limited to specifically authorized individuals whose authorization is documented. All authorized visitors and maintenance and service personnel shall be escorted at all times while in the licensee testing facility.

(b) When specimens are received, licensee testing facility personnel shall inspect each package for evidence of possible tampering and shall compare information on the specimen containers within each package to the information on the accompanying custody-and-control forms. Licensee testing facility personnel shall attempt to resolve any discrepancies identified in the information on specimen bottles or on the accompanying custody-and-control forms. When resolving any discrepancies, licensee testing facility personnel shall obtain a memorandum for the record from the specimen collector involved in the discrepancy to document correction of the discrepancy. This memorandum must accompany the specimen(s) and custody-and-control forms to the HHS-certified laboratory if the specimen(s) must be transferred.

(1) Indications of tampering with specimens in transit from the collection site, or at a licensee testing facility, must be reported to senior licensee or other entity management as soon as practical and no later than 8 hours after the indications are identified. In response to a report, licensee or other entity management personnel shall initiate an investigation to determine whether tampering has occurred.

(i) If the investigation determines that tampering has occurred, licensee or other entity management shall ensure that corrective actions are taken.

(ii) If there is reason to believe that the integrity or identity of a specimen is in question (as a result of tampering or discrepancies between the information on the specimen bottle and on the accompanying custody-and-control forms that cannot be resolved), the specimen may not be tested and the licensee or other entity shall ensure that another collection occurs as soon as reasonably practical, except if a split specimen collection was performed, either the Bottle A or Bottle B seal remains intact, and the intact specimen contains at least 15 mL of urine. In this instance, the licensee testing facility shall forward the intact specimen for testing to the HHS-certified laboratory and may not conduct any testing at the licensee testing facility.

(2) The following are exclusive grounds requiring the MRO to cancel the testing of a donor's urine specimen:

(i) The custody-and-control form does not contain information to identify the specimen collector and the collection site cannot provide conclusive evidence of the collector's identity;

(ii) The identification numbers on the specimen bottle seal(s) do not match the identification numbers on the custody-and-control form;

(iii) A specimen bottle seal is broken or shows evidence of tampering and an intact specimen, as specified in paragraph (b)(1)(ii) of this section, does not exist;

(iv) The specimen appears to have leaked out of its sealed bottle and there is less than 15 mL remaining, and an intact specimen, as specified in paragraph (b)(1)(ii) of this section, does not exist; or

(v) As required under § 26.165(f)(2).

(c) The licensee testing facility shall retain specimen containers within the testing facility's accession area until all analyses have been completed. Testing facility personnel shall use aliquots of the specimen and licensee testing facility chain-of-custody forms, or other appropriate methods of tracking aliquot custody and control, when conducting validity screening and initial validity and drug tests. The original specimen bottles and the original custody-and-control forms must remain in secure storage. Licensee testing facility personnel may discard specimens and aliquots as soon as practical after validity screening or initial validity tests have demonstrated that the specimen appears valid and initial test results for drugs and drug metabolites are negative.

(d) The licensee testing facility's procedure for tracking custody and control of specimens and aliquots must protect the identity of the donor, and provide documentation of the testing process and transfers of custody of the specimen and aliquots. Each time a specimen or aliquot is handled or transferred within the licensee testing facility, testing facility personnel shall document the date and purpose and every individual in the chain of custody must be identified.

(e) Urine specimens identified as positive or of questionable validity at a licensee testing facility must be shipped to an HHS-certified laboratory for testing as soon as reasonably practical.

(f) Licensee testing facility personnel shall take appropriate and prudent actions to minimize false negative results from specimen degradation. If validity screening or initial validity testing indicate that the specimen is of questionable validity, or initial drug test results are positive, or if a specimen has not been tested within 24 hours of receipt at the licensee testing facility, then the facility shall maintain the specimen cooled to not more than 6 °C (42.8 °F) until it is forwarded to the HHS-certified laboratory for further testing, if required. Split specimens in Bottle B that are associated with positive specimens or specimens of questionable validity in Bottle A must also be maintained cooled (as previously specified) until test results from the HHS-certified laboratory are known to be negative for Bottle A; until the MRO informs the licensee testing facility that Bottle B must be forwarded to an HHS-certified laboratory for testing; or until the specimen is moved to long-term, frozen storage, under § 26.135(c).

(g) Licensee testing facility personnel shall ensure that the original custody-and-control form is packaged with its associated urine specimen bottle. Sealed and labeled specimen bottles, with their associated custody-and-control forms, being transferred from the licensee testing facility to the HHS-certified laboratory must be placed in a second, tamper-evident shipping container designed to minimize the possibility of damage to the specimen during shipment (e.g., specimen boxes, padded mailers, or bulk insulated shipping containers with that capability) so that the contents of the shipping containers are no longer accessible without breaking a tamper-evident seal.

(h) Couriers, express carriers, and postal service personnel do not have direct access to the custody-and-control forms or the specimen bottles. Therefore, such personnel are not required to document chain of custody on the custody-and-control forms during transit. Custody accountability of the shipping containers during shipment must be maintained by a tracking system provided by the courier, express carrier, or postal service.

§ 26.131 Cutoff levels for validity screening and initial validity tests.

(a) Each validity test result from the licensee testing facility must be based on performing either a validity screening test or an initial validity test, or both, on one or more aliquots of a urine specimen. The licensee testing facility shall forward any specimen that yields a questionable validity screening or initial validity test result to the HHS-certified laboratory for further testing. Licensee testing facilities need not perform validity screening tests before conducting initial validity tests of a specimen.

(b) At a minimum, the licensee testing facility shall test each urine specimen for creatinine, pH, and one or more oxidizing adulterants. Licensees and other entities may not specify more stringent cutoff levels for validity screening and initial validity tests than those specified in this section. If tests or observations indicate one or more of the following from either a validity screening test or an initial validity test, the licensee testing facility shall forward the specimen to the HHS-certified laboratory for additional testing:

(1) Creatinine is less than 20 milligrams (mg) per deciliter (dL);

(2) The pH of the specimen is either less than 4.5 or equal to or greater than 9, using either a colorimetric pH test with a dynamic range of 2 to 12 or pH meter that is capable of measuring pH to one decimal place (for initial validity tests), or colorimetric pH tests, dipsticks, and pH paper (for pH validity screening tests) that have a narrow dynamic range;

(3) Nitrite or other oxidant concentration is equal to or greater than 200 micrograms (mcg) per mL or equal to or greater than 200 mcg/mL nitrite-equivalents using either a nitrite colorimetric test or a general oxidant colorimetric test;

(4) The possible presence of an oxidizing adulterant (e.g., chromium (VI), pyridine (pyridinium chlorochromate)) is determined using either a general oxidant colorimetric test (with a cutoff equal to or greater than 50 mcg/mL chromium (VI)-equivalents) or a chromium (VI) colorimetric test (chromium

(VI) concentration equal to or greater than 50 mcg/mL);

(5) The possible presence of halogen (e.g., bleach, iodine, fluoride) is determined using a general oxidant colorimetric test (with a cutoff equal to or greater than 200 mcg/mL nitrite-equivalents or equal to or greater than 50 mcg/mL chromium (VI)-equivalents), a halogen colorimetric test (halogen concentration equal to or greater than the limit of detection (LOD)), or the odor of the specimen;

(6) The possible presence of glutaraldehyde is determined using either an aldehyde test (aldehyde present) or the characteristic immunoassay response is observed on one or more drug immunoassay tests;

(7) The possible presence of a surfactant is determined by using a surfactant colorimetric test with a cutoff equal to or greater than 100 mcg/mL dodecylbenzene sulfonate-equivalent or a foam/shake test; or

(8) The specimen shows evidence of adulterants, including, but not limited to, the following:

(i) Abnormal physical characteristics;

(ii) Reactions or responses characteristic of an adulterant obtained during the validity screening or initial test; or

(iii) A possible unidentified interfering substance or adulterant, demonstrated by interference occurring on the immunoassay drug tests on two separate aliquots (*i.e.*, valid immunoassay drug test results cannot be obtained).

§ 26.133 Cutoff levels for drugs and drug metabolites.

Subject to the provisions of § 26.31(d)(3)(iii), licensees and other entities may specify more stringent cutoff levels for drugs and drug metabolites than those in the table below and, in such cases, may report initial test results for only the more stringent cutoff levels. Otherwise, the following cutoff levels must be used for initial testing of urine specimens to determine whether they are negative for the indicated drugs and drug metabolites:

INITIAL TEST CUTOFF LEVELS FOR DRUGS AND DRUG METABOLITES

Drug or metabolites	Cutoff level [nanograms (ng)/mL]
Marijuana metabolites	50
Cocaine metabolites	300
Opiate metabolites	2000
Phencyclidine (PCP)	25
Amphetamines	1000

§ 26.135 Split specimens.

(a) If the FFD program follows split-specimen procedures, as described in § 26.113, the licensee testing facility shall analyze aliquots of the specimen for the licensee's or other entity's purposes as described in this part. Except as provided in paragraph (b) in this section, the licensee testing facility shall store Bottles A and B of the specimen in a secure manner until the facility has finished testing. If the initial validity and drug test results are negative and the specimen in Bottle A will not be forwarded to the HHS-certified laboratory, the licensee testing facility may discard both Bottle A and Bottle B. If any test results are positive or indicate that the specimen is of questionable validity, the licensee testing facility shall forward Bottle A to the HHS-certified laboratory for testing and shall retain Bottle B in secure storage, under the requirements of § 26.159(i), or may forward it to the HHS-certified laboratory for storage.

(b) If the MRO confirms any positive, adulterated, or substituted result for a specimen in Bottle A, based on the results of confirmatory testing at an HHS-certified laboratory, and the licensee testing facility has elected to retain Bottle B of the specimen, and the donor requests testing of the specimen in Bottle B, as permitted under § 26.165(b), the MRO shall ensure that Bottle B is forwarded to an HHS-certified laboratory other than the laboratory that tested the specimen in Bottle A, under the procedures specified in § 26.165(b).

(c) If the MRO confirms that the specimen in Bottle A is positive, adulterated, substituted, or invalid and the donor does not request that Bottle B be tested, the licensee or other entity shall ensure that Bottle B is maintained in long-term frozen storage (−20

°C (−4 °F) or less) for a minimum of 1 year. If a licensee testing facility elects to retain the specimen in Bottle B, rather than forwarding it to the HHS-certified laboratory with Bottle A, the licensee testing facility shall ensure proper storage conditions in the event of a prolonged power failure. After the end of 1 year, the licensee or other entity may discard Bottle B, with the exception that the licensee testing facility shall retain any specimens under legal challenge, or as requested by the NRC, until the specimen is no longer needed.

[73 FR 17176, Mar. 31, 2008, as amended at 79 FR 66602, Nov. 10, 2014]

§ 26.137 Quality assurance and quality control.

(a) *Quality assurance program.* Each licensee testing facility shall have a quality assurance program that encompasses all aspects of the testing process including, but not limited to, specimen acquisition, chain of custody, security and reporting of results, validity screening (if validity screening tests are performed), initial validity and drug testing, and validation of analytical procedures. Quality assurance procedures must be designed, implemented, and reviewed to monitor the conduct of each step of the process of validity testing and testing for drugs and drug metabolites.

(b) *Performance testing and quality control requirements for validity screening tests.* (1) Licensee testing facilities may rely on validity screening tests to determine the need for initial tests of specimen validity either at the licensee testing facility or HHS-certified laboratory. Licensees and other entities shall ensure that the HHS-certified laboratory is capable of conducting confirmatory testing for any adulterant for which the licensee testing facility conducts validity screening tests. Licensee testing facilities shall use only validity screening tests that meet the following criteria:

(i) Either the test, by lot number, has been placed on the Substance Abuse and Mental Health Services Administration (SAMHSA) list of point-of-collection tests that are approved for use in the Federal Workplace Drug Testing Program; or

(ii) Before using the test, the licensee or other entity has ensured that the validity screening test, by lot number, effectively identifies specimens of questionable validity by meeting the following performance testing and quality control requirements:

(A) The creatinine validity screening test must use a 20 mg/dL cutoff concentration;

(B) A pH specimen validity screening test must be able to determine if pH is less than 4.5 and if pH is equal to or greater than 9; and

(C) An oxidant validity screening test must be able to determine if an oxidant concentration is equal to or greater than a 200 mcg/mL nitrite-equivalent cutoff, and/or a chromium screening test must be able to determine concentrations equal to or greater than a 50 mcg/mL chromium(VI)-equivalent cutoff, and/or a halogen screening test must be able to determine the halogen concentration is equal to or greater than the LOD. Licensees and other entities who use validity screening tests for additional adulterants shall establish performance testing requirements to challenge the licensee testing facility and the HHS-certified laboratory for the additional validity screening test(s);

(D) The manufacturer has conducted validation studies to document the validity screening test's performance characteristics around each applicable cutoff specified in this section, using performance testing samples that have been formulated to challenge the validity screening test around the applicable cutoffs. These validation studies must demonstrate the validity screening test's ability to differentiate valid samples from those of questionable validity and the performance of the validity screening test(s) around the applicable cutoffs specified in this section; and

(E) The licensee testing facility shall submit three consecutive sets of performance testing samples to the manufacturer, using performance testing samples that have been formulated to challenge the validity screening test around the applicable cutoffs specified in this paragraph and whose formulation levels have been confirmed by an HHS-certified laboratory. For example, one set of performance testing samples used to challenge a creatinine validity screening test must include at least six samples formulated at different concentrations ranging from 0 to 20 mg/dL. A set of performance testing samples used to challenge a pH validity screening test must include at least six samples formulated with different pH levels that are equal to or less than 4.5, and six samples formulated with different pH levels that are equal to or greater than 9. And, a set of performance testing samples used to challenge an oxidizing adulterant validity screening test must include at least six samples to challenge each validity screening test used. The performance testing samples for oxidizing adulterants must contain nitrite and other oxidizing adulterant concentrations in a range of less than or equal to a 200 mcg/mL nitrite-equivalent cutoff to a 500 mcg/mL nitrite-equivalent cutoff; chromium samples formulated in a range less than or equal to a 50 mcg/mL chromium(VI)-equivalent cutoff to 100 mcg/mL chromium(VI)-equivalent cutoff; or halogen samples formulated in a concentration at or near the LOD and 25 percent above the LOD. The results of analyzing the three consecutive sets of performance test samples for each validity screening test (*i.e.*, creatinine, pH, nitrite and general oxidants, chromium, or halogen) must demonstrate that the validity screening test, by lot number, correctly identified at least 90 percent of the total validity performance test challenges on each of three sets of performance testing samples, and, for each individual specimen validity screening test, the test, by lot number, correctly identified at least 90 percent of the validity performance test challenges on each of three sets of performance testing samples; and

(iii) After the licensee testing facility has placed a validity screening test in service, the licensee or other entity shall verify that the test, by lot number, remains on the SAMHSA-approved list. Or, if the SAMHSA-approved list is unavailable, the licensee or other entity shall ensure that the test continues to identify specimens of questionable validity, as demonstrated by documentation from the manufacturer that a set of validity screening tests from each lot in use by the licensee testing facility correctly identified at least 90 percent of the total validity test challenges on a set of performance testing samples, and, for each individual specimen validity screening test, that the test, by lot number, correctly identified at least 90 percent of the validity test challenges. This performance testing must be performed at a nominal annual frequency after the date on which the manufacturer completed the initial validation studies required under paragraph (b)(1)(ii)(D) of this section. The performance testing samples used must be formulated to challenge the validity screening test around the applicable cutoffs of this subpart.

(2) In addition, licensee testing facility personnel who perform the validity screening tests shall conduct quality control testing of validity screening tests as follows:

(i) At the beginning of any 8-hour period during which the licensee testing facility will perform validity screening tests, licensee testing facility personnel shall test a minimum of one quality control sample that is negative for each specific validity test to be performed (e.g., creatinine, pH, nitrites, chromium) during the 8-hour period, and one quality control sample that is formulated to challenge the validity screening test(s) around the cutoffs specified in this subpart for each specific validity test to be performed during the 8-hour period. The results of these quality control tests must be correct before any donor specimens may be tested.

(ii) After screening every ten donor specimens during the 8-hour period, licensee testing facility personnel shall also challenge each validity screening test with at least one quality control sample that is formulated to challenge the validity screening test(s) around the cutoffs specified in this subpart. If fewer than ten donor specimens were screened during the 8-hour period or the number of donor specimens tested exceeds a multiple of ten but is less than the next multiple of ten (e.g., 24 donor specimens, 48 donor specimens), licensee testing facility personnel shall challenge each validity screening test at the end of the 8-hour period during which the validity screening tests were performed.

(3) The licensee testing facility shall also submit at least one specimen out of every ten donor specimens that test negative using each validity screening test that the licensee testing facility uses to an HHS-certified laboratory as part of the licensee testing facility's quality assurance program.

(4) Licensee testing facilities shall store specimen validity tests as specified by the manufacturer's instructions and may not use such tests after the manufacturer's expiration date.

(c) *Validity screening test results.* If the results of a validity screening test indicate that the specimen is of questionable validity, the licensee testing facility may either perform initial validity testing or shall forward the specimen to the HHS-certified laboratory for further testing.

(d) *Quality control requirements for performing initial validity tests.* Licensees and other entities shall ensure that the HHS-certified laboratory is capable of conducting confirmatory testing for any adulterant for which the licensee testing facility conducts initial validity tests.

(1) Creatinine. Creatinine concentration must be measured to 1 decimal place. The initial creatinine test must have a control in the range of 3 to 20 mg/dL and a control in the range of 21 to 25 mg/dL.

(2) Requirements for performing initial pH tests are as follows:

(i) Colorimetric pH tests must have a dynamic range of 2 to 12 and pH meters must be capable of measuring pH to one decimal place.

(ii) An initial colorimetric pH test must have the following calibrators and controls:

(A) One calibrator at 3;

(B) One calibrator at 11;

(C) One control in the range of 2 to 2.8;

(D) One control in the range of 3.2 to 4;

(E) One control in the range of 4.5 to 9;

(F) One control in the range of 10 to 10.8; and

(G) One control in the range of 11.2 to 12.

(iii) If a pH screening test is not used, an initial pH meter test must have the following calibrators and controls:

(A) One calibrator at 4;

(B) One calibrator at 7;

(C) One calibrator at 10;

(D) One control in the range of 2 to 2.8;

(E) One control in the range of 3.2 to 4;

(F) One control in the range of 10 to 10.8; and

(G) One control in the range of 11.2 to 12.

(iv) If a pH screening test is used, an initial pH meter test must have the following calibrators and controls when the screening result indicates that the pH is below the lower decision point in use:

(A) One calibrator at 4;

(B) One calibrator at 7;

(C) One control in the range of 2 to 2.8; and

(D) One control in the range of 3.2 to 4.

(v) If a pH screening test is used, an initial pH meter test must have the following calibrators and controls when the screening test result indicates that the pH is above the upper decision point in use:

(A) One calibrator at 7;

(B) One calibrator at 10;

(C) One control in the range of 10 to 10.8; and

(D) One control in the range of 11.2 to 12.

(3) Oxidizing adulterants. Initial tests for oxidizing adulterants must include a calibrator at the appropriate cutoff concentration for the compound of interest, a control without the compound of interest (*i.e.*, a certified negative control), and a control with at least one of the compounds of interest at a measurable concentration. For nitrite, the licensee testing facility shall have one control in the range of 200 to 400 mcg/mL, one control in the range of 500 to 625 mcg/mL, and a control without nitrite (*i.e.*, a certified negative control).

(4) Other adulterants. Initial tests for other adulterants must include an appropriate calibrator, a control without the compound of interest (*i.e.*, a certified negative control), and a control

with the compound of interest at a measurable concentration.

(5) Each analytical run performed to conduct initial validity testing shall include at least one quality control sample that appears to be a donor specimen to the licensee testing facility technicians.

(6) The licensee testing facility shall also submit at least one specimen out of every 10 donor specimens that test negative on the initial validity tests performed by the licensee testing facility to an HHS-certified laboratory as part of the licensee testing facility's quality assurance program.

(e) *Quality control requirements for initial drug tests.* (1) Any initial drug test performed by a licensee testing facility must use an immunoassay that meets the requirements of the Food and Drug Administration for commercial distribution. Licensee testing facilities may not use non-instrumented immunoassay testing devices that are pending HHS/SAMHSA review and approval for initial drug testing under this part. In addition, licensees and other entities may not take management actions on the basis of any drug test results obtained from non-instrumented devices that may be used for validity screening tests.

(2) Licensee testing facilities shall discard negative specimens or may pool them for use in the licensee testing facility's internal quality control program after certification by an HHS-certified laboratory that the specimens are negative and valid. Licensee testing facilities may not retain any information linking donors to specimens that are pooled for use in the internal quality control program.

(3) Licensee testing facilities may perform multiple initial drug tests for the same drug or drug class, provided that all tests meet the cutoffs and quality control requirements of this part. For example, a licensee testing facility may use immunoassay technique "A" for all drugs using the licensee's or other entity's cutoff levels, but specimens testing positive for amphetamines may also be tested using immunoassay technique "B" to eliminate any possible positives due to structural analogues; or, a valid analytical result cannot be obtained using immunoassay technique "A" and immunoassay technique "B" is used in an attempt to obtain a valid analytical result.

(4) Licensee testing facilities need not assess their false positive testing rates for drugs, because all specimens that test as positive on the initial tests for drugs and drug metabolites must be forwarded to an HHS-certified laboratory for initial and confirmatory testing.

(5) To ensure that the rate of false negative drug tests is kept to the minimum that the immunoassay technology supports, licensee testing facilities shall submit to the HHS-certified laboratory a minimum of 5 percent (or at least one) of the donor specimens screened as negative from every analytical run.

(6) A minimum of 10 percent of all specimens in each analytical run of specimens to be initially tested for drugs by the licensee testing facility must be quality control samples, which the licensee testing facility shall use for internal quality control purposes. (These samples are not forwarded to the HHS-certified laboratory for further testing, other than for performance testing of the samples.) Licensee testing facilities shall ensure that quality control samples that are positive for each drug and metabolite for which the FFD program conducts testing are included in at least one analytical run each calendar quarter. The quality control samples for each analytical run must include—

(i) Sample(s) certified by an HHS-certified laboratory to contain no drugs or drug metabolites (*i.e.*, negative urine samples);

(ii) At least one positive control with drug(s) or drug metabolite(s) targeted at 25 percent above the cutoff;

(iii) At least one positive control with drug(s) or drug metabolite(s) targeted at 25 percent below the cutoff;

(iv) A sufficient number of calibrators to ensure and document the linearity of the assay method over time in the concentration area of the cutoff (after acceptable values are obtained for the known calibrators, those values will be used to calculate sample data); and

(v) At least one positive control, certified to be positive by an HHS-certified laboratory, which appears to be a donor specimen to the licensee testing facility technicians.

(7) Licensee testing facilities shall document the implementation of procedures to ensure that carryover does not contaminate the testing of a donor's specimen.

(f) *Errors in testing.* Each licensee testing facility shall investigate any testing errors or unsatisfactory performance discovered in the testing of quality control samples, in the testing of actual specimens, or through the processing of management reviews and/or MRO reviews, as well as any other errors or matters that could adversely reflect on the licensee testing facility's testing process.

(1) Whenever possible, the investigation must determine relevant facts and identify the root cause(s) of the testing or process error.

(2) The licensee testing facility shall take action to correct the cause(s) of any errors or unsatisfactory performance that are within the licensee testing facility's control.

(3) If false negative results are obtained in any analytical run from testing the quality control samples specified in paragraphs (b), (d), and (e) of this section at the licensee testing facility, the licensee testing facility shall forward all donor specimens from that analytical run to the HHS-certified laboratory for additional testing and implement corrective actions before resuming testing of donor specimens for the drug(s), drug metabolite(s), adulterant(s), or other specimen characteristics (*i.e.*, creatinine, pH) associated with the quality control sample that yielded the false negative result(s).

(4) If a donor specimen that yielded negative validity or drug test results at the licensee testing facility yields positive, substituted, adulterated, or invalid results after confirmatory testing by the HHS-certified laboratory under paragraphs (b)(3), (d)(6), or (e)(5) of this section, the licensee or other entity shall implement corrective actions before resuming testing of donor specimens for the drug(s), drug metabolite(s), adulterant(s), or other specimen characteristics (*i.e.*, creatinine, pH) associated with the donor specimen that yielded the false negative result(s). In addition to resolving any technical, methodological, or administrative errors in the licensee testing facility's testing process, the licensee or other entity may re-collect and test specimens from any donor whose test results from the licensee testing facility may have been inaccurate.

(5) A record of the investigative findings and the corrective actions taken, where applicable, must be dated and signed by the individuals who are responsible for the day-to-day management of the licensee testing facility and reported to appropriate levels of management.

(g) *Accuracy.* Volumetric pipettes and measuring devices must be certified for accuracy or be checked by gravimetric, colorimetric, or other verification procedure. Automatic pipettes and dilutors must be checked for accuracy and reproducibility before being placed in service, and periodically thereafter.

(h) *Calibrators and controls.* Calibrators and controls must be prepared using pure drug reference materials, stock standard solutions obtained from other laboratories, or standard solutions that are obtained from commercial manufacturers and are properly labeled as to content and concentration. Calibrators and controls may not be prepared from the same stock solution. The standards and controls must be labeled with the following dates: when received; when prepared or opened; when placed in service; and when scheduled for expiration.

[73 FR 17176, Mar. 31, 2008, as amended at 74 FR 38328, Aug. 3, 2009]

§ 26.139 Reporting initial validity and drug test results.

(a) The licensee testing facility shall report as negative all specimens that are valid on the basis of validity screening or initial validity tests, or both, and are negative on the initial tests for drugs and drug metabolites. Except as permitted under § 26.75(h), positive test results from initial drug tests at the licensee testing facility may not be reported to licensee or other entity management. In addition, the licensee testing facility may not report results from validity screening or initial validity testing indicating that a specimen is of questionable validity or positive initial drug test results from specimens that are of questionable validity.

(b) Except as provided in §§ 26.37 and 26.75(h), access to the results of initial tests must be limited to the licensee testing facility's staff, the MRO and MRO staff, the FFD program manager, and, when appropriate, EAP staff and the SAE.

(c) The licensee testing facility shall provide qualified personnel, when required, to testify in an administrative or disciplinary proceeding against an individual when that proceeding is based on urinalysis results reported by the licensee testing facility.

(d) The licensee testing facility shall prepare the information required for the annual report to the NRC, as required in § 26.717.

(e) The data in the annual report to the NRC must be presented for either the cutoff levels specified in this part, or for more stringent cutoff levels, if the FFD program uses more stringent cutoff levels for drugs and drug metabolites. If the FFD program tests for drugs and drug metabolites that are not specified in § 26.31(d)(1), the summary must also include the number of positive test results and the cutoff levels used for those drugs and drug metabolites.

(f) The designated FFD program official shall use the available information from the licensee testing facility's validity and drug test results, the results of quality control testing performed at the licensee testing facility, and the results from testing the quality control samples that the licensee testing facility submits to the HHS-certified laboratory to evaluate continued testing program effectiveness and detect any local trends in drugs of abuse that may require management action or FFD program adjustments. FFD program adjustments may include, but are not limited to, training enhancements, procedure changes, the expansion of the FFD program's drug panel to include additional drugs to be tested, or changes in the types of assays, validity screening tests, or instruments used.

Subpart G—Laboratories Certified by the Department of Health and Human Services

§ 26.151 Purpose.

This subpart contains requirements for the HHS-certified laboratories that licensees and other entities who are subject to this part use for testing urine specimens for validity and the presence of drugs and drug metabolites.

§ 26.153 Using certified laboratories for testing urine specimens.

(a) Licensees and other entities who are subject to this part shall use only laboratories certified under the Department of Health and Human Services (HHS) Mandatory Guidelines for Federal Workplace Drug Testing Programs [published in the FEDERAL REGISTER on April 11, 1988 (53 FR 11970), and as amended, June 9, 1994 (59 FR 29908), November 13,1998 (63 FR 63483), and April 13, 2004 (69 FR 19643)] for specimen validity and drug testing, except as permitted under § 26.31(d)(3)(ii). Information concerning the current certification status of laboratories is available from the Division of Workplace Programs, Center for Substance Abuse Prevention, Substance Abuse and Mental Health Services Administration, Room 815, 5600 Fishers Lane, Rockwall 2 Bldg., Rockville, Maryland 20857.

(b) HHS-certified laboratories shall have the capability, at the same premises, to perform both initial and confirmatory tests for specimen validity and for each drug and drug metabolite for which the HHS-certified laboratory provides services to the licensee or other entity.

(c) An HHS-certified laboratory may not subcontract and shall perform all work with its own personnel and equipment unless otherwise authorized by the licensee or other entity.

(d) Licensees and other entities shall use only HHS-certified laboratories that agree to follow the same rigorous specimen testing, quality control, and chain-of-custody procedures when testing for more stringent cutoff levels as may be specified by licensees and other entities for the classes of drugs identified in this part, and for any other substances included in the licensees' or other entities' panels.

(e) Before awarding a contract to an HHS-certified laboratory, the licensee or other entity shall ensure that qualified personnel conduct a pre-award inspection and evaluation of the procedural aspects of the laboratory's drug testing operations. However, if an HHS-certified laboratory loses its certification, in whole or in part, a licensee or other entity may immediately begin using another HHS-certified laboratory that is being used by another licensee or entity who is subject to this part, as permitted by § 26.41(g)(5).

(f) All contracts between licensees or other entities who are subject to this part and HHS-certified laboratories must require the laboratory to implement all applicable requirements of this part. At a minimum, licensees' and other entities' contracts with HHS-certified laboratories must include the following requirements:

(1) Laboratory facilities shall comply with the applicable provisions of any State licensor requirements;

(2) The laboratory shall make available qualified personnel to testify in an administrative or disciplinary proceeding against an individual when that proceeding is based on urinalysis results reported by the HHS-certified laboratory;

(3) The laboratory shall maintain test records in confidence, consistent with the requirements of § 26.37, and use them with the highest regard for individual privacy.

(4) Consistent with the principles established in section 503 of Public Law 100–71, any employee of a licensee or other entity who is the subject of a drug test (or his or her representative designated under § 26.37(d)) shall, on written request, have access to the laboratory's records related to his or her validity and drug test and any records related to the results of any relevant certification, review, or revocation-of-certification proceedings;

(5) The laboratory may not enter into any relationship with the licensee's or other entity's MRO(s) that may be construed as a potential conflict of interest, including, but not limited to, the relationships described in § 26.183(b), and may not derive any financial benefit by having a licensee or other entity use a specific MRO; and

(6) The laboratory shall permit representatives of the NRC and any licensee or other entity using the laboratory's services to inspect the laboratory at any time, including unannounced inspections.

(g) If licensees or other entities use a form other than the current Federal custody-and-control form, licensees and other entities shall provide a memorandum to the laboratory explaining why a non-Federal form was used, but must ensure, at a minimum, that the form used contains all the required information on the Federal custody-and-control form.

[73 FR 17176, Mar. 31, 2008, as amended at 74 FR 38328, Aug. 3, 2009]

§ 26.155 Laboratory personnel.

(a) *Day-to-day management of the HHS-certified laboratory.* HHS-certified laboratories shall have a responsible person to assume professional, organizational, educational, and administrative responsibility for the laboratory's drug testing facilities.

(1) This individual shall have documented scientific qualifications in analytical forensic toxicology. Minimum qualifications are as follows:

(i) Certification by the appropriate State as a laboratory director in forensic or clinical laboratory toxicology; or

(ii) A PhD in one of the natural sciences with an adequate undergraduate and graduate education in biology, chemistry, and pharmacology or toxicology; or

(iii) Training and experience comparable to a Ph.D. in one of the natural sciences, such as a medical or scientific degree with additional training and laboratory/research experience in biology, chemistry, and pharmacology or toxicology; and

(iv) In addition to the requirements in paragraphs (a)(1)(i) through (a)(1)(iii) of this section, the responsible person shall also have the following minimum qualifications:

(A) Appropriate experience in analytical forensic toxicology including experience with the analysis of biological material for drugs of abuse; and

(B) Appropriate training and/or experience in forensic applications of analytical toxicology (e.g., publications, court testimony, research concerning analytical toxicology of drugs of abuse, or other factors that qualify the individual as an expert witness in forensic toxicology).

(2) This individual shall be engaged in and responsible for the day-to-day management of the testing laboratory, even if another individual has overall responsibility for an entire multi-specialty laboratory.

(3) This individual shall be responsible for ensuring that there are enough personnel with adequate training and experience to supervise and conduct the work of the drug testing laboratory. He or she shall ensure the continued competency of laboratory personnel by documenting their in-service training, reviewing their work performance, and verifying their skills.

(4) This individual shall be responsible for ensuring that the laboratory has a manual of standard operating procedures that are complete, up-to-date, available for personnel performing tests, and followed by those personnel. The procedures must be reviewed, signed, and dated by this responsible person whenever the procedures are first placed into use or changed or when a new individual assumes responsibility for management of the laboratory. This individual shall ensure that copies of all procedures and records of the dates on which they are in effect are maintained. (Specific contents of the procedures are described in §26.157.)

(5) This individual shall be responsible for maintaining a quality assurance program to assure the proper performance and reporting of all test results; maintaining acceptable analytical performance for all controls and standards; maintaining quality control testing; and assuring and documenting the validity, reliability, accuracy, precision, and performance characteristics of each test and test system.

(6) This individual shall be responsible for taking all remedial actions that may be necessary to maintain satisfactory operation and performance of the laboratory in response to quality control systems not being within performance specifications, including errors in result reporting or in the analysis of performance testing results. This individual shall ensure that test results are not reported until all corrective actions have been taken and he or she can assure that the test results provided are accurate and reliable.

(b) *Certifying scientist.* (1) HHS-certified laboratories shall have one or more certifying scientists who review all pertinent data and quality control results to certify the laboratory's test results.

(2) A certifying scientist shall be an individual with at least a bachelor's degree in the chemical or biological sciences, medical technology, or an equivalent field who reviews all pertinent data and quality control results. The individual shall have training and experience in the theory and practice of all methods and procedures used in the laboratory, including a thorough understanding of chain-of-custody procedures, quality control practices, and analytical procedures relevant to the results that the individual certifies. Relevant training and experience must also include the review, interpretation, and reporting of test results; maintenance of chain of custody; and proper remedial action to be taken in response to aberrant test or quality control results, or a determination that test systems are out of control limits.

(3) A laboratory may designate certifying scientists who only certify results that are reported negative and certifying scientists who certify results that are reported both negative and adulterated, substituted, dilute, or invalid.

(c) *Day-to-day operations and supervision of analysts.* HHS-certified laboratories shall assign one or more individuals who are responsible for day-to-day operations and supervision of the technical analysts. The designated individual(s) shall have at least a bachelor's degree in the chemical or biological sciences, medical technology, or an equivalent field. The individual(s) shall also have training and experience in the theory and practice of the procedures used in the laboratory, resulting in his or her thorough understanding of quality control practices and procedures; review, interpretation, and reporting of test results; maintenance of the chain of custody; and proper remedial actions to be taken in response to aberrant test or quality control results, or the finding that test systems are out of control limits.

(d) *Other personnel.* Other technicians or nontechnical staff shall have the necessary training and skills for their assigned tasks.

(e) *Training.* HHS-certified laboratories shall make available continuing education programs to meet the needs of laboratory personnel.

(f) *Files.* At a minimum, each laboratory personnel file must include a résumé, any professional certification(s) or license(s), a job description, and documentation to show that the individual has been properly trained to perform his or her job.

§ 26.157 Procedures.

(a) HHS-certified laboratories shall develop, implement, and maintain clear and well-documented procedures for accession, receipt, shipment, and testing of urine specimens.

(b) Written chain-of-custody procedures must describe the methods to be used to maintain control and accountability of specimens from receipt through completion of testing and reporting of results, during storage and shipping to another HHS-certified laboratory, if required, and continuing until final disposition of specimens.

(c) HHS-certified laboratories shall develop, implement, and maintain a written manual of standard operating procedures for each assay performed for licensees and other entities for drug and specimen validity testing. The procedures must include, but are not limited to, detailed descriptions of—

(1) The principles of each test;

(2) Preparation of reagents, standards, and controls;

(3) Calibration procedures;

(4) Derivation of results;

(5) Linearity of methods;

(6) Sensitivity of the methods;

(7) Cutoff values;

(8) Mechanisms for reporting results;

(9) Controls;

(10) Criteria for unacceptable specimens and results;

(11) Reagents and expiration dates; and

(12) References.

(d) HHS-certified laboratories shall develop, implement, and maintain written procedures for instrument setup and normal operation, including the following:

(1) A schedule for checking critical operating characteristics for all instruments;

(2) Tolerance limits for acceptable function checks; and

(3) Instructions for major troubleshooting and repair.

(e) HHS-certified laboratories shall develop, implement, and maintain written procedures for remedial actions to be taken when errors are detected or systems are out of acceptable limits.

The laboratory shall maintain documentation that its personnel follow these procedures and take all necessary corrective actions. In addition, the laboratory shall have systems in place to verify all stages of testing and reporting and to document the verification.

§ 26.159 Assuring specimen security, chain of custody, and preservation.

(a) The HHS-certified laboratories performing services for licensees and other entities under this part shall be secure at all times. Each laboratory shall have in place sufficient security measures to control access to the premises and to ensure that no unauthorized personnel handle specimens or gain access to the laboratory processes or areas where records are stored. Access to these secured areas must be limited to specially authorized individuals whose authorization is documented. All authorized visitors, and maintenance and service personnel, shall be escorted at all times in the laboratory, except personnel who are authorized to conduct inspections and audits on behalf of licensees, other entities, the NRC, or the HHS Secretary, and emergency personnel (including but not limited to firefighters and medical rescue teams).

(b) When a shipment of specimens is received, laboratory personnel shall inspect each package for evidence of possible tampering and shall compare information on specimen bottles within each package to the information on the accompanying custody-and-control forms.

(1) Any direct evidence of tampering or discrepancies in the information on the specimen bottles and the custody-and-control forms attached to the shipment must be reported to the licensee or other entity within 24 hours of the discovery and must be noted on the custody-and-control forms for each specimen contained in the package. When notified, the licensee or other entity shall ensure that an investigation is initiated to determine whether tampering has occurred.

(i) If the investigation determines that tampering has occurred, the licensee or other entity shall ensure that corrective actions are taken.

(ii) If the licensee or other entity has reason to question the integrity and identity of the specimens, the specimens may not be tested and the licensee or other entity shall ensure that another collection occurs as soon as reasonably practical, except if a split specimen collection was performed, either the Bottle A or Bottle B seal remains intact, and the intact specimen contains at least 15 mL of urine. In this instance, if the licensee testing facility has retained the specimen in Bottle B, the licensee testing facility shall forward the intact specimen for testing to the HHS-certified laboratory and may not conduct any testing at the licensee testing facility.

(2) The following are exclusive grounds requiring the MRO to cancel the testing of a donor's urine specimen:

(i) The custody-and-control form does not contain information to identify the specimen collector and the collection site cannot provide conclusive evidence of the collector's identity;

(ii) The identification numbers on the specimen bottle seal(s) do not match the identification numbers on the custody-and-control form;

(iii) A specimen bottle seal is broken or shows evidence of tampering and an intact specimen, as specified in paragraph (b)(1)(ii) of this section, does not exist;

(iv) The specimen appears to have leaked out of its sealed bottle and there is less than 15 mL remaining, and an intact specimen, as specified in paragraph (b)(1)(ii) of this section, does not exist; or

(v) As required under § 26.165(f)(2).

(c) The HHS-certified laboratory shall retain specimen bottles within the laboratory's accession area until all analyses have been completed. Laboratory personnel shall use aliquots and laboratory internal custody-and-control forms when conducting initial and confirmatory tests. The original specimen and the original custody-and-control form must remain in secure storage.

(d) The laboratory's internal custody-and-control form must allow for identification of the donor, and documentation of the testing process and transfers of custody of the specimen.

(e) Each time a specimen is handled or transferred within the laboratory, laboratory personnel shall document the date and purpose on the custody-and-control form and every individual in the chain shall be identified. Authorized technicians are responsible for each urine specimen or aliquot in their possession and shall sign and complete custody-and-control forms for those specimens or aliquots as they are received.

(f) If a specimen is to be transferred to a second HHS-certified laboratory, laboratory personnel shall ensure that a copy of the custody-and-control form is packaged with the aliquot of a single specimen or Bottle B of a split specimen, as appropriate. Sealed and labeled specimen bottles and aliquots, with their associated custody-and-control forms, being transferred from one laboratory to another must be placed in a second, tamper-evident shipping container designed to minimize the possibility of damage to the specimen during shipment (e.g., specimen boxes, padded mailers, or bulk insulated shipping containers with that capability) so that the contents of the shipping containers are inaccessible without breaking a tamper-evident seal.

(g) Couriers, express carriers, and postal service personnel do not have direct access to the custody-and-control forms or the specimen bottles. Therefore, such personnel are not required to document chain of custody on the custody-and-control forms during transit. Custody accountability of the shipping containers during shipment must be maintained by a tracking system provided by the courier, express carrier, or postal service.

(h) Specimens that do not receive an initial test within 7 days of arrival at the laboratory must be placed in secure refrigeration units for short-term storage. Temperatures may not exceed 6 °C (42.8 °F). The laboratory shall ensure proper storage conditions in the event of a prolonged power failure.

(i) Long-term frozen storage at a temperature of −20 °C (−4 °F) or less ensures that positive, adulterated, substituted, and invalid urine specimens and Bottle B of a split specimen will be available for any necessary retests. Unless otherwise authorized in writing by the licensee or other entity, laboratories shall retain and place in properly secured long-term frozen storage all specimens reported as positive, adulterated, substituted, or invalid. At a minimum, such specimens must be stored for 1 year. Within this 1-year period, a licensee, other entity, or the NRC may ask the laboratory to retain the specimen for an additional period of time. If no retention request is received, the laboratory may discard the specimen at the end of 1 year. However, the laboratory shall retain any specimens under review or legal challenge until they are no longer needed.

(j) The laboratory shall discard a valid specimen that tests negative on initial or confirmatory drug tests or may pool such specimens for use in the laboratory's internal quality control program after certifying that the specimens are negative and valid. The laboratory may not retain any information linking donors to specimens that are pooled for use in the internal quality control program.

[73 FR 17176, Mar. 31, 2008, as amended at 79 FR 66602, Nov. 10, 2014]

§ 26.161 Cutoff levels for validity testing.

(a) *Validity test results.* Each validity test result for a specimen that the HHS-certified laboratory reports to the MRO as adulterated, substituted, dilute, or invalid must be based on performing an initial validity test on one aliquot and a confirmatory validity test on a second aliquot. Licensees and other entities shall ensure that the HHS-certified laboratory is capable of conducting, and conducts, confirmatory testing for at least one oxidizing adulterant and any other adulterants specified by the licensee's or other entity's testing program. If initial validity test results indicate that the specimen is valid under the criteria in paragraphs (c) through (f) of this section, the HHS-certified laboratory need not perform confirmatory validity testing of the specimen.

(b) *Initial validity testing.* The HHS-certified laboratory shall perform initial validity testing of each specimen as follows:

(1) Determine the creatinine concentration;

(2) Determine the specific gravity of every specimen for which the creatinine concentration is less than 20 mg/dL;

(3) Determine the pH;

(4) Perform one or more initial validity tests for oxidizing adulterants; and

(5) Perform additional validity tests, the choice of which depends on the observed indicators or characteristics below, when the following conditions are observed:

(i) Abnormal physical characteristics;

(ii) Reactions or responses characteristic of an adulterant obtained during initial or confirmatory drug tests (e.g., non-recovery of internal standards, unusual response); or

(iii) Possible unidentified interfering substance or adulterant.

(c) *Results indicating an adulterated specimen.* The laboratory shall report a specimen as adulterated when the specimen yields any one or more of the following validity testing results:

(1) The pH is less than 3, or equal to or greater than 11, using either a pH meter or a colorimetric pH test for the initial test on the first aliquot and a

pH meter for the confirmatory test on the second aliquot;

(2) The nitrite concentration is equal to or greater than 500 mcg/mL using either a nitrite colorimetric test or a general oxidant colorimetric test for the initial test on the first aliquot and a different confirmatory test (e.g., multi-wavelength spectrophotometry, ion chromatography, capillary electrophoresis) on the second aliquot;

(3) The presence of chromium (VI) is verified using either a general oxidant colorimetric test (with a cutoff equal to or greater than 50 mcg/mL chromium (VI)-equivalents) or a chromium (VI) colorimetric test (chromium (VI) concentration equal to or greater than 50 mcg/mL) for the initial test on the first aliquot and a different confirmatory test (e.g., multi-wavelength spectrophotometry, ion chromatography, atomic absorption spectrophotometry, capillary electrophoresis, inductively coupled plasma-mass spectrometry) with the chromium (VI) concentration equal to or greater than the LOD of the confirmatory test on the second aliquot;

(4) The presence of halogen (e.g., bleach, iodine, fluoride) is verified using either a general oxidant colorimetric test (with a cutoff equal to or greater than 200 mcg/mL nitrite-equivalents or a cutoff equal to or greater than 50 mcg/mL chromium (VI)-equivalents) or a halogen colorimetric test (halogen concentration equal to or greater than the LOD) for the initial test on the first aliquot and a different confirmatory test (e.g., multi-wavelength spectrophotometry, ion chromatography, inductively coupled plasma-mass spectrometry) with a specific halogen concentration equal to or greater than the LOD of the confirmatory test on the second aliquot;

(5) The presence of glutaraldehyde is verified using either an aldehyde test (aldehyde present) or the specimen yields the characteristic immunoassay response on one or more drug immunoassay tests for the initial test on the first aliquot and gas chromatography/mass spectrometry (GC/MS) for the confirmatory test with the glutaraldehyde concentration equal to or greater than the LOD of the analysis on the second aliquot;

(6) The presence of pyridine (pyridinium chlorochromate) is verified using either a general oxidant colorimetric test (with a cutoff equal to or greater than 200 mcg/mL nitrite-equivalents or a cutoff equal to or greater than 50 mcg/mL chromium (VI)-equivalents) or a chromium (VI) colorimetric test (chromium (VI) concentration equal to or greater than 50 mcg/mL) for the initial test on the first aliquot and GC/MS for the confirmatory test with the pyridine concentration equal to or greater than the LOD of the analysis on the second aliquot;

(7) The presence of a surfactant is verified by using a surfactant colorimetric test with a cutoff equal to or greater than 100 mcg/mL dodecylbenzene sulfonate-equivalent for the initial test on the first aliquot and a different confirmatory test (e.g., multi-wavelength spectrophotometry) with a cutoff equal to or greater than 100 mcg/mL dodecylbenzene sulfonate equivalent on the second aliquot; or

(8) The presence of any other adulterant not specified in paragraphs (c)(3) through (c)(7) of this section is verified using an initial test on the first aliquot and a different confirmatory test on the second aliquot.

(d) *Results indicating a substituted specimen.* The laboratory shall report a specimen as substituted when the specimen's creatinine concentration is less than 2 mg/dL and its specific gravity is less than or equal to 1.0010, or equal to or greater than 1.0200, on both the initial and confirmatory creatinine tests (*i.e.*, the same colorimetric test may be used to test both aliquots) and on both the initial and confirmatory specific gravity tests (*i.e.*, a refractometer is used to test both aliquots) on two separate aliquots.

(e) *Results indicating a dilute specimen.* The laboratory shall report a specimen as dilute when the specimen's creatinine concentration is equal to or greater than 2 mg/dL but less than 20 mg/dL and its specific gravity is greater than 1.0010 but less than 1.0030 on a single aliquot.

(f) *Results indicating an invalid specimen.* The laboratory shall report a specimen as invalid when the laboratory obtains any one or more of the following validity testing results:

(1) Inconsistent creatinine concentration and specific gravity results are obtained (*i.e.*, the creatinine concentration is less than 2 mg/dL on both the initial and confirmatory creatinine tests and the specific gravity is greater than 1.0010 but less than 1.0200 on the initial and/or confirmatory specific gravity test, the specific gravity is less than or equal to 1.0010 on both the initial and confirmatory specific gravity tests and the creatinine concentration is equal to or greater than 2 mg/dL on either or both the initial or confirmatory creatinine tests);

(2) The pH is equal to or greater than 3 and less than 4.5, or equal to or greater than 9 and less than 11, using either a colorimetric pH test or pH meter for the initial test and a pH meter for the confirmatory test on two separate aliquots;

(3) The nitrite concentration is equal to or greater than 200 mcg/mL using a nitrite colorimetric test, or equal to or greater than the equivalent of 200 mcg/mL nitrite using a general oxidant colorimetric test for both the initial test and the confirmatory test, or, using either initial test, the nitrite concentration is equal to or greater than 200 mcg/mL but less than 500 mcg/mL using a different confirmatory test (e.g., multi-wavelength spectrophotometry, ion chromatography, capillary electrophoresis) on two separate aliquots;

(4) The possible presence of chromium (VI) is determined using the same chromium (VI) colorimetric test with a cutoff equal to or greater than 50 mcg/mL chromium (VI) for both the initial test and the confirmatory test on two separate aliquots;

(5) The possible presence of a halogen (e.g., bleach, iodine, fluoride) is determined using the same halogen colorimetric test with a cutoff equal to or greater than the LOD for both the initial test and the confirmatory test on two separate aliquots or relying on the odor of the specimen as the initial test;

(6) The possible presence of glutaraldehyde is determined using the same aldehyde test (aldehyde present) or the characteristic immunoassay response is observed on one or more drug immunoassay tests for both the initial test and the confirmatory test on two separate aliquots;

(7) The possible presence of an oxidizing adulterant is determined by using the same general oxidant colorimetric test (with cutoffs equal to or greater than 200 mcg/mL nitrite-equivalents, equal to or greater than 50 mcg/mL chromium (VI)-equivalents, or a halogen concentration equal to or greater than the LOD) for both the initial test and the confirmatory test on two separate aliquots;

(8) The possible presence of a surfactant is determined using the same surfactant colorimetric test with a cutoff equal to or greater than 100 mcg/mL dodecylbenzene sulfonate-equivalent for both the initial test and the confirmatory test on two separate aliquots or a foam/shake test for the initial test;

(9) Interference occurs on the immunoassay drug tests on two separate aliquots (*i.e.*, valid immunoassay drug test results cannot be obtained);

(10) Interference with the drug confirmation assay occurs on at least two separate aliquots of the specimen, and the laboratory is unable to identify the interfering substance;

(11) The physical appearance of the specimen indicates that testing may damage the laboratory's equipment; or

(12) The physical appearances of Bottles A and B (when a split specimen collection is used) are clearly different, and either the test result for Bottle A indicated it is an invalid specimen or the specimen in Bottle A was screened negative for drugs, or both.

(g) *Additional testing by a second laboratory.* If the presence of an interfering substance/adulterant is suspected that could make a test result invalid, but it cannot be identified (e.g., a new adulterant), laboratory personnel shall consult with the licensee's or other entity's MRO and, with the MRO's agreement, shall send the specimen to another HHS-certified laboratory that has the capability to identify the suspected substance.

(h) *More stringent validity test cutoff levels are prohibited.* Licensees and other entities may not specify more stringent cutoff levels for validity tests than those specified in this section.

§26.163 Cutoff levels for drugs and drug metabolites.

(a) *Initial drug testing.* (1) HHS-certified laboratories shall apply the following cutoff levels for initial testing of specimens to determine whether they are negative for the indicated drugs and drug metabolites, except if validity testing indicates that the specimen is dilute or the licensee or other entity has established more stringent cutoff levels:

INITIAL TEST CUTOFF LEVELS FOR DRUGS AND DRUG METABOLITES

Drug or metabolites	Cutoff level [nanograms (ng)/mL]
Marijuana metabolites	50
Cocaine metabolites	300
Opiate metabolites	2000
Phencyclidine (PCP)	25
Amphetamines	1000

(2) At the licensee's or other entity's discretion, as documented in the FFD program policies and procedures, the licensee or other entity may require the HHS-certified laboratory to conduct special analyses of dilute specimens as follows:

(i) If initial validity testing indicates that a specimen is dilute, the HHS-certified laboratory shall compare the responses of the dilute specimen to the cutoff calibrator in each of the drug classes;

(ii) If any response is equal to or greater than 50 percent of the cutoff, the HHS-certified laboratory shall conduct confirmatory testing of the specimen down to the LOD for those drugs and/or drug metabolites; and

(iii) The laboratory shall report the numerical values obtained from this special analysis to the MRO.

(b) *Confirmatory drug testing.* (1) A specimen that is identified as positive on an initial drug test must be subject to confirmatory testing for the class(es) of drugs for which the specimen initially tested positive. The HHS-certified laboratory shall apply the confirmatory cutoff levels specified in this paragraph, except if the licensee or other entity requires the special analysis of dilute specimens permitted in paragraph (a)(2) of this section or the licensee or other entity has established more stringent cutoff levels.

CONFIRMATORY TEST CUTOFF LEVELS FOR DRUGS AND DRUG METABOLITES

Drug or metabolites	Cutoff level (ng/mL)
Marijuana metabolite [1]	15
Cocaine metabolite [2]	150
Opiates:	
Morphine	2000
Codeine	2000
6-acetylmorphine [3]	10
Phencyclidine (PCP)	25
Amphetamines:	
Amphetamine	500
Methamphetamine [4]	500

[1] As delta-9-tetrahydrocannabinol-9-carboxylic acid.
[2] As benzoylecgonine.
[3] Test for 6–AM when the confirmatory test shows a morphine concentration exceeding 2,000 ng/mL.
[4] Specimen must also contain amphetamine at a concentration equal to or greater than 200 ng/mL.

(2) Each confirmatory drug test must provide a quantitative result. When the concentration of a drug or metabolite exceeds the linear range of the standard curve, the laboratory may record the result as "exceeds the linear range of the test" or as "equal to or greater than <insert the value for the upper limit of the linear range>," or may dilute an aliquot of the specimen to obtain an accurate quantitative result when the concentration is above the upper limit of the linear range.

§26.165 Testing split specimens and retesting single specimens.

(a) *Testing split specimens.* (1) If a specimen has been split into Bottle A and Bottle B at the collection site, and the specimen was not initially tested at a licensee testing facility, then the HHS-certified laboratory shall perform initial and confirmatory validity and drug testing, if required, of the specimen in Bottle A.

(2) If a specimen was initially tested at a licensee testing facility and positive or questionable validity test results were obtained, then the HHS-certified laboratory shall perform initial and confirmatory testing, if required, of the specimen in Bottle A.

(3) At the licensee's or other entity's discretion, Bottle B must either be forwarded to the HHS-certified laboratory or maintained in secure storage at the licensee testing facility, as required by §26.135(a) and (c), as applicable. If the specimen in Bottle A is free of any evidence of drugs or drug metabolites, and is a valid specimen, then the licensee

testing facility or HHS-certified laboratory may discard the specimens in Bottles A and B.

(b) *Donor request to MRO for a retest of a single specimen or testing Bottle B of a split specimen.* (1) For a confirmed positive, adulterated, or substituted result reported on a single specimen of 30 mL or more, or a specimen in Bottle A of a split specimen which the donor submitted to the licensee or other entity, a donor may request (through the MRO) that an aliquot from the single specimen or the split (Bottle B) specimen be tested by a second HHS-certified laboratory to verify the result reported by the first laboratory. For an invalid test result, a donor may not request that an aliquot from the single specimen or the split specimen in Bottle B be tested by a second HHS-certified laboratory.

(2) The MRO shall inform the donor that he or she may, within 3 business days of notification by the MRO of the confirmed positive, adulterated, or substituted test result, request the retesting of an aliquot of the single specimen or the testing of the Bottle B split specimen. The MRO shall provide the donor with specific instructions for making this request (*i.e.*, providing telephone numbers or other contact information). The MRO shall have the ability to receive the donor's calls at all times during the 3-day period (e.g., by use of an answering machine with a "time stamp" feature when there is no one in the MRO's office to answer the phone). The donor's request may be oral or in writing.

(3) The donor shall provide his or her permission for retesting an aliquot of the single specimen or the testing of Bottle B. Neither the licensee, MRO, NRC, nor any other entity may order retesting of the single specimen or testing of the specimen in Bottle B without the donor's written permission, except as permitted in § 26.185(l).

(4) If the donor has not requested a retest of an aliquot of a single specimen or a test of the split specimen (Bottle B) within 3 business days, the donor may present to the MRO information documenting that serious injury, illness, lack of actual notice of the confirmed test result, inability to contact the MRO (e.g., there was no one in the MRO's office and the answering machine was not working), or other circumstances unavoidably prevented the donor from making a timely request. If the MRO concludes from the donor's information that there was a legitimate reason for the donor's failure to contact the MRO within the 3 business days permitted, the MRO shall direct the retesting of an aliquot of the single specimen or the test of the split specimen (Bottle B) take place, as if the donor had made a timely request.

(5) As soon as reasonably practical and not more than 1 business day following the day of the donor's request, as permitted in paragraph (b)(3) or (b)(4) of this section, the MRO shall ensure that the HHS-certified laboratory forwards an aliquot of a single specimen, or that the HHS-certified laboratory (or licensee testing facility, as appropriate) forwards Bottle B of a split specimen, to a second HHS-certified laboratory that did not test the specimen in Bottle A.

(6) The HHS-certified laboratory that retests an aliquot of a single specimen or tests the specimen in Bottle B shall provide quantitative test results to the MRO and the MRO shall provide them to the donor.

(c) *Retesting a specimen for drugs.* (1) The second laboratory shall use its confirmatory drug test when retesting an aliquot of a single specimen or testing Bottle B of a split specimen for the drug(s) or drug metabolite(s) for which the first laboratory reported a positive result(s), including retesting specimens that have been subject to the special analysis permitted in § 26.163(a)(2).

(2) Because some drugs or drug metabolites may deteriorate during storage, the retest by the second laboratory is not subject to a specific drug cutoff level, but must provide data sufficient to reconfirm the presence of the drug(s) or drug metabolite(s) down to the assay's LOD.

(3) If the second laboratory fails to reconfirm the presence of the drug(s) or drug metabolite(s) for which the first laboratory reported a positive result(s), the second laboratory shall attempt to determine the reason for not reconfirming the first laboratory's findings by conducting specimen validity tests. The second laboratory shall conduct

the same specimen validity tests it would conduct on a single specimen or the specimen in Bottle A of a split specimen.

(4) The second laboratory shall report all results to the licensee's or other entity's MRO.

(d) *Retesting a specimen for adulterants.* A second laboratory shall use the required confirmatory validity test and criteria in § 26.161(c) to reconfirm an adulterant result when retesting an aliquot from a single specimen or when testing Bottle B of a split specimen. The second laboratory may only conduct the confirmatory validity test needed to reconfirm the adulterant result reported by the first laboratory.

(e) *Retesting a specimen for substitution.* A second laboratory shall use its confirmatory creatinine and confirmatory specific gravity tests, when retesting an aliquot of a single specimen or testing Bottle B of a split specimen, to reconfirm that the creatinine concentration was less than 2 mg/dL and the specific gravity was less than or equal to 1.0010 or equal to or greater than 1.0200. The second laboratory may only conduct the confirmatory creatinine and specific gravity tests to reconfirm the substitution result reported by the first laboratory.

(f) *Management actions and sanctions.* (1) If the MRO confirms a positive, adulterated, or substituted test result(s) from the first HHS-certified laboratory and the donor requests testing of Bottle B of a split specimen or retesting of an aliquot from a single specimen, the licensee or other entity shall administratively withdraw the individual's authorization on the basis of the first confirmed positive, adulterated, or substituted test result until the results of testing Bottle B or retesting an aliquot of the single specimen are available and have been reviewed by the MRO. If the MRO reports that the results of testing Bottle B or retesting the aliquot of a single specimen reconfirm any of the original positive, adulterated, or substituted test result(s), the licensee or other entity shall impose the appropriate sanctions specified in subpart D. If the results of testing Bottle B or retesting the aliquot of a single specimen are negative, the licensee or other entity—

(i) May not impose any sanctions on the individual;

(ii) Shall eliminate from the donor's personnel file and other records any matter that could link the individual to the temporary administrative action;

(iii) May not disclose the temporary administrative action in response to a suitable inquiry conducted under the provisions of § 26.63 or to any other inquiry or investigation required in this chapter. To ensure that no records have been retained, access to the system of files and records must be provided to personnel conducting reviews, inquiries into allegations, or audits under the provisions of § 26.41, or to NRC inspectors; and

(iv) Shall provide the tested individual with a written statement that the records specified in §§ 26.713 and 26.715 have not been retained and shall inform the individual in writing that the temporary administrative action that was taken will not be disclosed and need not be disclosed by the individual in response to requests for self-disclosure of potentially disqualifying FFD information.

(2) If a donor requests that Bottle B be tested or that an aliquot of a single specimen be retested, and either Bottle B or the single specimen are not available due to circumstances outside of the donor's control (including, but not limited to, circumstances in which there is an insufficient quantity of the single specimen or the specimen in Bottle B to permit retesting, either Bottle B or the original single specimen is lost in transit to the second HHS-certified laboratory, or Bottle B has been lost at the HHS-certified laboratory or licensee testing facility), the MRO shall cancel the test and inform the licensee or other entity that another collection is required under direct observation as soon as reasonably practical. The licensee or other entity shall eliminate from the donor's personnel and other records any matter that could link the donor to the original positive, adulterated, or substituted test result(s) and any temporary administrative action, and may not impose any sanctions on the donor for a cancelled test. If test results from

the second specimen collected are positive, adulterated, or substituted and the MRO determines that the donor has violated the FFD policy, the licensee or other entity shall impose the appropriate sanctions specified in subpart D of this part, but may not consider the original confirmed positive, adulterated, or substituted test result in determining the appropriate sanctions.

§ 26.167 Quality assurance and quality control.

(a) *Quality assurance program.* Each HHS-certified laboratory shall have a quality assurance program that encompasses all aspects of the testing process, including, but not limited to, specimen accessioning, chain of custody, security and reporting of results, initial and confirmatory testing, certification of calibrators and controls, and validation of analytical procedures. The performance characteristics (e.g., accuracy, precision, LOD, limit of quantitation (LOQ), specificity) of each test must be validated and documented for each test. Validation of procedures must document that carryover does not affect the donor's specimen results. Periodic re-verification of analytical procedures is required. Quality assurance procedures must be designed, implemented, and reviewed to monitor the conduct of each step of the testing process.

(b) *Calibrators and controls required.* Each analytical run of specimens for which an initial or confirmatory validity test, or an initial or confirmatory drug test, is being performed must include the appropriate calibrators and controls.

(c) *Quality control requirements for performing initial and confirmatory validity tests.* (1) Requirements for performing creatinine tests:

(i) The creatinine concentration must be measured to one decimal place on both the initial and the confirmatory creatinine tests;

(ii) The initial creatinine test must have a calibrator at 2 mg/dL;

(iii) The initial creatinine test must have a control in the range of 1 to 1.5 mg/dL, a control in the range of 3 to 20 mg/dL, and a control in the range of 21 to 25 mg/dL; and

(iv) The confirmatory creatinine test (performed on those specimens with a creatinine concentration less than 2 mg/dL on the initial test) must have a calibrator at 2 mg/dL, a control in the range of 1.0 to 1.5 mg/dL, and a control in the range of 3 to 4 mg/dL.

(2) Requirements for performing specific gravity tests:

(i) The refractometer must report and display the specific gravity to four decimal places, and must be interfaced with a laboratory information management system, or computer, and/or generate a hard copy or digital electronic display to document the numerical result;

(ii) The initial and confirmatory specific gravity tests must have a calibrator or control at 1.0000; and

(iii) The initial and confirmatory specific gravity tests must have the following controls:

(A) One control targeted at 1.0020;

(B) One control in the range of 1.0040 to 1.0180; and

(C) One control equal to or greater than 1.0200 but not greater than 1.0250.

(3) Requirements for performing pH tests:

(i) Colorimetric pH tests that have the dynamic range of 2 to 12 to support the 3 and 11 pH cutoffs and pH meters must be capable of measuring pH to one decimal place. Dipsticks, colorimetric pH tests, and pH paper that have a narrow dynamic range and do not support the 2 to 12 pH cutoffs may be used only to determine whether initial validity tests must be performed;

(ii) At a minimum, pH screening tests must have the following controls:

(A) One control below the lower decision point in use;

(B) One control between the decision points in use; and

(C) One control above the upper decision point in use;

(iii) If a pH screening test is not used, an initial pH meter test must have the following calibrators and controls:

(A) One calibrator at 4;

(B) One calibrator at 7;

(C) One calibrator at 10;

(D) One control in the range of 2 to 2.8;

(E) One control in the range of 3.2 to 4;

(F) One control in the range of 10 to 10.8; and

(G) One control in the range of 11.2 to 12;

(iv) If a pH screening test is used, an initial or confirmatory pH meter test must have the following calibrators and controls when the screening result indicates that the pH is below the lower decision point in use:

(A) One calibrator at 4;

(B) One calibrator at 7;

(C) One control in the range of 2 to 2.8; and

(D) One control in the range of 3.2 to 4;

(v) If a pH screening test is used, an initial or confirmatory pH meter test must have the following calibrators and controls when the screening result indicates that the pH is above the upper decision point in use:

(A) One calibrator at 7;

(B) One calibrator at 10;

(C) One control in the range of 10 to 10.8; and

(D) One control in the range of 11.2 to 12; and

(vi) An initial colorimetric pH test must have the following calibrators and controls:

(A) One calibrator at 3;

(B) One calibrator at 11;

(C) One control in the range of 2 to 2.8;

(D) One control in the range of 3.2 to 4;

(E) One control in the range of 4.5 to 9;

(F) One control in the range of 10 to 10.8;

(G) One control in the range of 11.2 to 12.

(4) Requirements for performing oxidizing adulterant tests:

(i) Initial tests for oxidizing adulterants must include a calibrator at the appropriate cutoff concentration for the compound of interest as specified in § 26.161(c) and (f), a control without the compound of interest (*i.e.*, a certified negative control), and at least one control with one of the compounds of interest at a measurable concentration; and

(ii) A confirmatory test for a specific oxidizing adulterant must use a different analytical method than that used for the initial test. Each confirmatory analytical run must include a calibrator at the appropriate cutoff concentration for the compound of interest as specified in § 26.161(c) and (f), a control without the compound of interest (*i.e.*, a certified negative control), and a control with the compound of interest at a measurable concentration.

(5) Requirements for performing nitrite tests: The initial and confirmatory nitrite tests must have a calibrator at the cutoff concentration, a control without nitrite (*i.e.*, certified negative urine specimen), one control in the range of 200 to 400 mcg/mL, and one control in the range of 500 to 625 mcg/mL.

(6) Requirements for performing "other" adulterant tests:

(i) The initial and confirmatory tests for any "other" adulterant that may be identified in the future must satisfy the requirements in § 26.161(a);

(ii) The confirmatory test for "other" adulterants must use a different analytical principle or chemical reaction than that used for the initial test; and

(iii) The initial and confirmatory tests for "other" adulterants must include an appropriate calibrator, a control without the compound of interest (*i.e.*, a certified negative control), and a control with the compound of interest at a measurable concentration.

(d) *Quality control requirements for performing initial drug tests.* (1) Any initial drug test performed by an HHS-certified laboratory must use an immunoassay that meets the requirements of the Food and Drug Administration for commercial distribution. Non-instrumented immunoassay testing devices that are pending HHS/SAMHSA review and approval may not be used for initial drug testing under this part.

(2) HHS-certified laboratories may perform multiple initial drug tests for the same drug or drug class, provided that all tests meet the cutoffs and quality control requirements of this part. For example, an HHS-certified laboratory may use immunoassay technique "A" for all drugs using the licensee's or other entity's cutoff levels, but specimens testing positive for amphetamines may also be tested using

immunoassay technique "B" to eliminate any possible positives due to structural analogues; or, a valid analytical result cannot be obtained using immunoassay technique "A" and immunoassay technique "B" is used in an attempt to obtain a valid analytical result.

(3) Quality control samples for each analytical run of specimens for initial testing must include—

(i) Sample(s) certified to contain no drugs or drug metabolites (*i.e.*, negative urine samples);

(ii) At least one positive control with a drug(s) or drug metabolite(s) targeted at 25 percent above the cutoff;

(iii) At least one positive control with a drug(s) or drug metabolite(s) targeted at 25 percent below the cutoff;

(iv) A sufficient number of calibrators to ensure and document the linearity of the assay method over time in the concentration area of the cutoff (after acceptable values are obtained for the known calibrators, those values will be used to calculate sample data); and

(v) At least one control that appears to be a donor specimen to the laboratory analysts.

(4) A minimum of 10 percent of the total specimens in each analytical run must be quality control samples, as defined by paragraphs (d)(3)(i) through (iv) of this section.

(e) *Quality control requirements for performing confirmatory drug tests.* (1) Confirmatory tests for drugs and drug metabolites must be performed using gas chromatography/mass spectrometry (GC/MS) or other confirmatory test methodologies that HHS-certified laboratories are permitted to use in Federal workplace drug testing programs for this purpose.

(2) At least 10 percent of the samples in each analytical run of specimens must be calibrators and controls.

(3) Each analytical run of specimens that are subjected to confirmatory testing must include—

(i) Sample(s) certified to contain no drug (*i.e.*, negative urine samples);

(ii) Positive calibrator(s) and control(s) with a drug(s) or drug metabolite(s);

(iii) At least one positive control with a drug(s) or drug metabolite(s) targeted at 25 percent above the cutoff; and

(iv) At least one calibrator or control that is targeted at or below 40 percent of the cutoff.

(f) *Errors in testing.* The licensee or other entity shall ensure that the HHS-certified laboratory investigates any testing errors or unsatisfactory performance discovered in blind performance testing, as required under § 26.168, in the testing of actual specimens, or through the processing of reviews, as well as any other errors or matters that could adversely reflect on the testing process.

(1) Whenever possible, the investigation must determine relevant facts and identify the root cause(s) of the testing or process error. The licensee or other entity, and the HHS-certified laboratory, shall take action to correct the causes of any errors or unsatisfactory performance that are within each entity's control. Sufficient records shall be maintained to furnish evidence of activities affecting quality. The licensee or other entity shall assure that the cause of the condition is determined and that corrective action is taken to preclude repetition. The identification of the significant condition, the cause of the condition, and the corrective action taken shall be documented and reported to appropriate levels of management.

(2) If a false positive error occurs on a blind performance test sample or on a regular specimen, the licensee or other entity shall require the laboratory to take corrective action to minimize the occurrence of the particular error in the future. If there is reason to believe that the error could have been systematic, the licensee or other entity may also require review and re-analysis of previously run specimens.

(3) If a false positive error occurs on a blind performance test sample and the error is determined to be technical or methodological, the licensee or other entity shall instruct the laboratory to provide all quality control data from the batch or analytical run of specimens that included a false positive sample. In addition, the licensee or other entity shall require the laboratory to retest all specimens that analyzed as positive for that drug or

metabolite, or as adulterated, substituted, dilute, or invalid in validity testing, from the time of final resolution of the error back to the time of the last satisfactory performance test cycle. This retesting must be documented by a statement signed by the laboratory's responsible person. The licensee or other entity and the NRC also may require an onsite review of the laboratory, which may be conducted unannounced during any hours of operation of the laboratory.

(g) *Accuracy.* Volumetric pipettes and measuring devices must be certified for accuracy or be checked by gravimetric, colorimetric, or other verification procedures. Automatic pipettes and dilutors must be checked for accuracy and reproducibility both before being placed in service and periodically thereafter.

(h) *Calibrators and controls.* Laboratory calibrators and controls must be prepared using pure drug reference materials, stock standard solutions obtained from other laboratories, or standard solutions that are obtained from commercial manufacturers and are properly labeled as to content and concentration. Calibrators and controls may not be prepared from the same stock solution. The standards and controls must be labeled with the following dates: when received; when prepared or opened; when placed in service; and when scheduled for expiration.

§26.168 Blind performance testing.

(a) Each licensee and other entity shall submit blind performance test samples to the HHS-certified laboratory.

(1) During the initial 90-day period of any contract with an HHS-certified laboratory (not including rewritten or renewed contracts), each licensee or other entity shall submit blind performance test samples to each HHS-certified laboratory with whom it contracts in the amount of at least 20 percent of the total number of specimens submitted (up to a maximum of 100 blind performance test samples) or 30 blind performance test samples, whichever is greater.

(2) Following the initial 90-day period, the number of blind performance test samples submitted per quarter must be a minimum of one percent of all specimens (up to a maximum of 100) or ten blind performance test samples, whichever is greater.

(3) Both during the initial 90-day period and quarterly thereafter, licensees and other entities should attempt to submit blind performance test samples at a frequency that corresponds to the submission frequency for other specimens.

(b) Approximately 60 percent of the blind performance test samples submitted to the laboratory must be positive for one or more drugs or drug metabolites per sample and submitted so that all of the drugs for which the FFD program is testing are included at least once each calendar quarter, except as follows:

(1) Licensees and other entities shall submit blind performance test samples that are positive for marijuana metabolite at least two times each quarter; and

(2) In at least two quarters each year, licensees and other entities shall submit an additional blind performance test sample that is positive for cocaine instead of the required sample that is positive for PCP.

(c) The positive blind performance test samples must be positive for only those drugs for which the FFD program is testing and formulated at concentrations established in paragraph (g)(2) of this section.

(d) To challenge the HHS-certified laboratory's ability to limit false negatives, approximately 10 percent of the blind performance test samples submitted to the laboratory each quarter must be formulated at the concentrations established in paragraph (g)(3) of this section.

(e) To challenge the HHS-certified laboratory's ability to determine specimen validity, the licensee or other entity shall submit blind performance test samples each quarter that are appropriately adulterated, diluted, or substituted, in the amount of 20 percent of the specimens submitted that quarter or at least three samples per quarter (one each that is adulterated, diluted, or substituted), whichever is greater. These samples must be formulated at the concentrations established in paragraphs (g)(4) through (g)(6) of this section.

(f) Approximately 10 percent of the blind performance test samples submitted to the laboratory each quarter must be negative, as specified in paragraph (g)(1) of this section.

(g) Licensees and other entities shall use only blind performance test samples that have been certified by the supplier to be—

(1) Negative. A negative blind performance test sample may not contain a measurable amount of a target drug analyte and must be certified by immunoassay and confirmatory testing;

(2) Drug positive. These samples must contain a measurable amount of the target drug or analyte in concentrations ranging between 150 and 200 percent of the initial cutoff values and be certified by immunoassay and confirmatory testing to contain one or more drug(s) or drug metabolite(s);

(3) A false negative challenge. This blind performance test sample must contain a measurable amount of the target drug or analyte in concentrations ranging between 130 and 155 percent of the initial cutoff values;

(4) Adulterated. The adulterated blind performance test sample must have a pH of less than or equal to 2, or greater than or equal to 12, or a nitrite or other oxidant concentration equal to or greater than 500 mcg/mL, equal to or greater than 50 mcg/mL chromium (VI)-equivalents, or a halogen concentration equal to or greater than the LOD. Blind performance test samples for other adulterants must have adulterant concentrations equal to or greater than (or equal to or less than, as appropriate) the initial cutoff levels used by the licensee's or other entity's HHS-certified laboratory;

(5) Dilute. The dilute blind performance test sample must contain a creatinine concentration that is equal to or greater than 5 mg/dL but less than 20 mg/dL, and the specific gravity must be greater than 1.0010 but less than 1.0030; or

(6) Substituted. The substituted blind performance test sample must contain less than 2 mg/dL of creatinine, and the specific gravity must be less than or equal to 1.0010, or equal to or greater than 1.0200.

(h) In order to ensure that blind performance test samples continue to meet the criteria set forth in paragraph (g) of this section, licensees and other entities shall—

(1) Ensure that all blind performance test sample lots are placed in service by the supplier only after confirmation by an HHS-certified laboratory, and for no more than 6 months;

(2) Ensure that the supplier provides the expiration date for each blind performance test sample to ensure that each sample will have the expected value when it is submitted to and tested by a laboratory; and

(3) At a minimum, require the supplier to check each open lot bi-monthly (*i.e.*, every two months) to ensure that samples remaining in the lot do not fall below 130 percent of the initial cutoff test concentration established by the assay manufacturer. Thus, for example, a lot that was certified by an HHS-certified laboratory at 155 percent of the manufacturer's assay cutoff level, and was reported by the licensee's or other entity's HHS-certified laboratory to be at or above 130 percent of that standard is acceptable. A test that indicated a result below 130 percent of that standard would be unacceptable. Licensees and other entities shall discard blind performance test samples from any lot that is outside of these parameters and may not use any further samples from that lot.

(i) Licensees and other entities shall ensure that each blind performance test sample is indistinguishable to laboratory personnel from a donor's specimen, as follows:

(1) The licensee or other entity shall submit blind performance test samples to the laboratory using the same channels (*i.e.*, from the licensee's or other entity's collection site or licensee testing facility, as appropriate) through which donors' specimens are sent to the laboratory;

(2) The collector and licensee testing facility personnel, as appropriate, shall use a custody-and-control form, place fictional initials on the specimen bottles' labels/seals, and indicate for the

MRO on the MRO's copy that the specimen is a blind performance test sample; and

(3) The licensee or other entity shall ensure that all blind performance test samples include split samples, when the FFD program includes split specimen procedures.

[73 FR 17176, Mar. 31, 2008, as amended at 81 FR 86909, Dec. 2, 2016]

§ 26.169 Reporting Results.

(a) The HHS-certified laboratory shall report test results to the licensee's or other entity's MRO within 5 business days after receiving the specimen from the licensee or other entity. Before reporting any test result to the MRO, the laboratory's certifying scientist shall certify the result as correct. The report must identify the substances for which testing was performed; the results of the validity and drug tests; the cutoff levels for each; any indications of tampering, adulteration, or substitution that may be present; the specimen identification number assigned by the licensee or other entity; and the specimen identification number assigned by the laboratory.

(b) If licensees or other entities specify cutoff levels for drugs or drug metabolites that are more stringent than those specified in this part, the laboratory need only conduct the more stringent tests and shall report the results of the initial and confirmatory tests only for the more stringent cutoff levels.

(c) The HHS-certified laboratory shall report as negative all specimens that are negative on the initial or confirmatory drug and validity tests. Specimens that test as positive, adulterated, substituted, dilute, or invalid on the confirmatory analysis must be reported to the MRO as positive for a specific drug(s) or drug metabolite(s), or as meeting the criteria for an adulterated, substituted, dilute, or invalid specimen.

(1) The laboratory shall report all positive, adulterated, substituted, dilute, and invalid test results for each specimen to the MRO. For example, a specimen may be both adulterated and positive for one or more specific drugs.

(2) For a specimen that has a positive test result, the laboratory shall provide numerical values if the MRO requests such information. The MRO's request for positive confirmatory test results may be either a general request covering all such results or a specific case-by-case request. The laboratory shall routinely provide quantitative values for confirmatory opiate test results for morphine or codeine that are greater than or equal to 15,000 ng/mL, even if the MRO has not requested quantitative values for the test result.

(3) For a specimen that has an adulterated or substituted test result, the laboratory shall provide the MRO with the numerical values that support the reported result. The MRO may not disclose the numerical values to the licensee or other entity, except as permitted in § 26.37(b). If the numerical values for creatinine are below the LOD, the laboratory shall report to the MRO "creatinine: none detected" (*i.e.*, substituted) along with the numerical values of the specific gravity test.

(4) For a specimen that has an invalid result, the laboratory shall contact the MRO and both will decide whether testing by another certified laboratory would be useful in being able to report a positive or adulterated result. This contact may occur through any secure electronic means (e.g., telephone, fax, e-mail). If no further testing is necessary, the laboratory shall report the invalid result to the MRO.

(5) When the concentration of a drug, metabolite, or adulterant exceeds the linear range of the standard curve, the laboratory may report to the MRO that the quantitative value "exceeds the linear range of the test," that the quantitative value is "equal to or greater than <insert the value for the upper limit of the linear range>," or may report an accurate quantitative value above the upper limit of the linear range that was obtained by diluting an aliquot of the specimen.

(d) The MRO and MRO staff may not disclose quantitative test results to a licensee or other entity, but shall report only whether the specimen was positive (and for which analyte), adulterated, substituted, dilute, invalid, or negative, except as permitted under

§ 26.37(b). This paragraph does not preclude either the HHS-certified laboratory or the MRO from providing program performance data, as required under § 26.717.

(e) The laboratory may transmit results to the MRO by various electronic means (e.g., teleprinters, facsimile, or computer) in a manner designed to ensure the confidentiality of the information. The laboratory may not provide results orally by telephone. The licensee or other entity, directly or through the HHS-certified laboratory, shall ensure the security of the data transmission and ensure only authorized access to any data transmission, storage, and retrieval system.

(f) For negative test results, the HHS-certified laboratory may fax, courier, mail, or electronically transmit a computer-generated electronic report and/or a legible image or copy of the completed custody-and-control form to the MRO. However, for positive, adulterated, substituted, dilute, and invalid results, the laboratory shall fax, courier, mail, or electronically transmit a legible image or copy of the completed custody-and-control form to the MRO.

(g) For a specimen that has a positive, adulterated, substituted, dilute, or invalid result, the laboratory shall retain the original custody-and-control form and transmit to the MRO a copy of the original custody-and-control form signed by a certifying scientist.

(h) The HHS-certified laboratory shall provide to the licensee's or other entity's official responsible for coordination of the FFD program an annual statistical summary of urinalysis testing, which may not include any personal identifying information. To avoid sending data from which it is likely that information about a donor's test result can be readily inferred, the laboratory may not send a summary report if the licensee or other entity has fewer than 10 specimen test results in a 1-year period. The summary report must include test results that were reported within the year period. The laboratory shall send the summary report to the licensee or other entity within 14 calendar days after the end of the 1-year period covered by the report. The statistics must be presented either for the cutoff levels specified in this part or for any more stringent cutoff levels that the licensee or other entity may specify. The HHS-certified laboratory shall make available quantitative results for all specimens tested when requested by the NRC, licensee, or other entity for whom the laboratory is performing drug-testing services. If the FFD program tests for additional drugs beyond those listed in § 26.31(d), the summary must include drug test results for the additional drugs. The summary report must contain the following information:

(1) Total number of specimens received;

(2) Number of specimens reported as—

(i) Negative, and

(ii) Negative and dilute;

(3) Number of specimens reported as positive on confirmatory tests by drug or drug metabolite for which testing is conducted, including, but not limited to—

(i) Marijuana metabolite;

(ii) Cocaine metabolite;

(iii) Opiates (total);

(A) Codeine;

(B) Morphine; and

(C) 6-AM;

(iv) Phencyclidine;

(v) Amphetamines (total);

(A) Amphetamine; and

(B) Methamphetamine;

(4) Total number of specimens reported as adulterated;

(5) Total number of specimens reported as substituted;

(6) Total number of specimens reported as positive and dilute [including an indication as to whether the specimen was subject to the special analysis permitted in § 26.163(a)(2)];

(7) Total number of specimens reported as invalid; and

(8) Number of specimens reported as rejected for testing and the reason for the rejection.

Subpart H—Determining Fitness-for-Duty Policy Violations and Determining Fitness

§ 26.181 Purpose.

This subpart contains requirements for determining whether a donor has violated the FFD policy and for making a determination of fitness.

§26.183 Medical review officer.

(a) *Qualifications.* The MRO shall be knowledgeable of this part and of the FFD policies of the licensees and other entities for whom the MRO provides services. The MRO shall be a physician holding either a Doctor of Medicine or Doctor of Osteopathy degree who is licensed to practice medicine by any State or Territory of the United States, the District of Columbia, or the Commonwealth of Puerto Rico. By March 31, 2010, the MRO shall have passed an examination administered by a nationally-recognized MRO certification board or subspecialty board for medical practitioners in the field of medical review of Federally mandated drug tests.

(b) *Relationships.* The MRO may be an employee of the licensee or other entity or a contractor. However, the MRO may not be an employee or agent of, or have any financial interest in, an HHS-certified laboratory or a contracted operator of a licensee testing facility for whom the MRO reviews drug test results. Additionally, the MRO may not derive any financial benefit by having the licensee or other entity use a specific drug testing laboratory or licensee testing facility operating contractor and may not have any agreement with such parties that may be construed as a potential conflict of interest. Examples of relationships between laboratories and MROs that create conflicts of interest, or the appearance of such conflicts, include, but are not limited to—

(1) The laboratory employs an MRO who reviews test results produced by the laboratory;

(2) The laboratory has a contract or retainer with the MRO for the review of test results produced by the laboratory;

(3) The laboratory designates which MRO the licensee or other entity is to use, gives the licensee or other entity a slate of MROs from which to choose, or recommends certain MROs;

(4) The laboratory gives the licensee or other entity a discount or other incentive to use a particular MRO;

(5) The laboratory has its place of business co-located with that of an MRO or MRO staff who review test results produced by the laboratory; or

(6) The laboratory permits an MRO, or an MRO's organization, to have a financial interest in the laboratory.

(c) *Responsibilities.* The primary role of the MRO is to review and interpret positive, adulterated, substituted, invalid, and at the licensee's or other entity's discretion, dilute test results obtained through the licensee's or other entity's testing program and to identify any evidence of subversion of the testing process. The MRO is also responsible for identifying any issues associated with collecting and testing specimens, and for advising and assisting FFD program management in planning and overseeing the overall FFD program.

(1) In carrying out these responsibilities, the MRO shall examine alternate medical explanations for any positive, adulterated, substituted, invalid, or, at the licensee's or other entity's discretion, dilute test result. This action may include, but is not limited to, conducting a medical interview with the donor, reviewing the donor's medical history, or reviewing any other relevant biomedical factors. The MRO shall review all medical records that the donor may make available when a positive, adulterated, substituted, invalid, or dilute test result could have resulted from responsible use of legally prescribed medication, a documented condition or disease state, or the demonstrated physiology of the donor.

(2) The MRO may only consider the results of tests of specimens that are collected and processed under this part, including the results of testing split specimens, in making his or her determination, as long as those split specimens have been stored and tested under the procedures described in this part.

(d) *MRO staff.* Individuals who provide administrative support to the MRO may be employees of a licensee or other entity, employees of the MRO, or employees of an organization with whom a licensee or other entity contracts for MRO services. Employees of a licensee or other entity who serve MRO staff functions may also perform other duties for the licensee or other entity and need not be under the direction of the MRO while performing those other duties.

(1) Direction of MRO staff activities. MROs shall be directly responsible for all administrative, technical, and professional activities of individuals who are serving MRO staff functions while they are performing those functions, and those functions must be under the MRO's direction.

(i) The duties of MRO staff must be maintained independent from any other activity or interest of a licensee or other entity, in order to protect the integrity of the MRO function and donors' privacy.

(ii) An MRO's responsibilities for directing MRO staff must include, but are not limited to, ensuring that—

(A) The procedures being performed by MRO staff meet NRC regulations and HHS' and professional standards of practice;

(B) Records and other donor personal information are maintained confidential by MRO staff and are not released to other individuals or entities, except as permitted under this part;

(C) Data transmission is secure; and

(D) Drug test results are reported to the licensee's or other entity's designated reviewing official only as required by this part.

(iii) The MRO may not delegate any of his or her responsibilities for directing MRO staff to any other individual or entity, except another MRO.

(2) MRO staff responsibilities. MRO staff may perform routine administrative support functions, including receiving test results, reviewing negative test results, and scheduling interviews for the MRO.

(i) The staff under the direction of the MRO may receive, review, and report negative test results to the licensee's or other entity's designated representative.

(ii) The staff reviews of positive, adulterated, substituted, invalid, and, at the licensee's or other entity's discretion, dilute test results must be limited to reviewing the custody-and-control form to determine whether it contains any errors that may require corrective action and to ensure that it is consistent with the information on the MRO's copy. The staff may resolve errors in custody-and-control forms that require corrective action(s), but shall forward the custody-and-control forms to the MRO for review and approval of the resolution.

(iii) The staff may not conduct interviews with donors to discuss positive, adulterated, substituted, invalid, or dilute test results nor request medical information from a donor. Only the MRO may request and review medical information related to a positive, adulterated, substituted, or invalid test result or other matter from a donor.

(iv) Staff may not report nor discuss with any individuals other than the MRO and other MRO staff any positive, adulterated, substituted, invalid, or dilute test results received from the HHS-certified laboratory before those results have been reviewed and confirmed by the MRO. Any MRO staff discussions of confirmed positive, adulterated, substituted, invalid, or dilute test results must be limited to discussions only with the licensee's or other entity's FFD program personnel and may not reveal quantitative test results or any personal medical information about the donor that the MRO may have obtained in the course of reviewing confirmatory test results from the HHS-certified laboratory.

§ 26.185 Determining a fitness-for-duty policy violation.

(a) *MRO review required.* A positive, adulterated, substituted, dilute, or invalid drug test result does not automatically identify an individual as having used drugs in violation of the NRC's regulations, or the licensee's or other entity's FFD policy, or as having attempted to subvert the testing process. An individual who has a detailed knowledge of possible alternate medical explanations is essential to the review of the results. The MRO shall review all positive, adulterated, substituted, and invalid test results from the HHS-certified laboratory to determine whether the donor has violated the FFD policy before reporting the results to the licensee's or other entity's designated representative.

(b) *Reporting of initial test results prohibited.* Neither the MRO nor MRO staff may report positive, adulterated, substituted, dilute, or invalid initial test results that are received from the HHS-certified laboratory to the licensee or other entity.

(c) *Discussion with the donor.* Before determining that a positive, adulterated, substituted, dilute, or invalid test result or other occurrence is an FFD policy violation and reporting it to the licensee or other entity, the MRO shall give the donor an opportunity to discuss the test result or other occurrence with the MRO, except as described in paragraph (d) of this section. After this discussion, if the MRO determines that a positive, adulterated, substituted, dilute, or invalid test result or other occurrence is an FFD policy violation, the MRO shall immediately notify the licensee's or other entity's designated representative.

(d) *Donor unavailability.* The MRO may determine that a positive, adulterated, substituted, dilute, or invalid test result or other occurrence is an FFD policy violation without having discussed the test result or other occurrence directly with the donor in the following three circumstances:

(1) The MRO has made and documented contact with the donor and the donor expressly declined the opportunity to discuss the test result or other occurrence that may constitute an FFD policy violation;

(2) A representative of the licensee or other entity, or an MRO staff member, has successfully made and documented contact with the donor and has instructed him or her to contact the MRO, and more than 1 business day has elapsed since the date on which the licensee's representative or MRO's staff member successfully contacted the donor; or

(3) The MRO, after making all reasonable efforts and documenting the dates and time of those efforts, has been unable to contact the donor. Reasonable efforts include, at a minimum, three attempts, spaced reasonably over a 24-hour period, to reach the donor at the day and evening telephone numbers listed on the custody-and-control form.

(e) *Additional opportunity for discussion.* If the MRO determines that the donor has violated the FFD policy without having discussed the positive, adulterated, substituted, dilute, or invalid test result or other occurrence directly with the donor, the donor may, on subsequent notification of the MRO determination and within 30 days of that notification, present to the MRO information documenting the circumstances, including, but not limited to, serious illness or injury, which unavoidably prevented the donor from being contacted by the MRO or a representative of the licensee or other entity, or from contacting the MRO in a timely manner. On the basis of this information, the MRO may reopen the procedure for determining whether the donor's test result or other occurrence is an FFD policy violation and permit the individual to present information related to the issue. The MRO may modify the initial determination based on an evaluation of the information provided.

(f) *Review of invalid specimens.* (1) If the HHS-certified laboratory reports an invalid result, the MRO shall consult with the laboratory to determine whether additional testing by another HHS-certified laboratory may be useful in determining and reporting a positive or adulterated test result. If the MRO and the laboratory agree that further testing would be useful, the HHS-certified laboratory shall forward the specimen to a second laboratory for additional testing.

(2) If the MRO and the laboratory agree that further testing would not be useful and there is no technical explanation for the result, the MRO shall contact the donor and determine whether there is an acceptable medical explanation for the invalid result. If there is an acceptable medical explanation, the MRO shall report to the licensee or other entity that the test result is not an FFD policy violation, but that a negative test result was not obtained. If the medical reason for the invalid result is, in the opinion of the MRO, a temporary condition, the licensee or other entity shall collect a second urine specimen from the donor as soon as reasonably practical and rely on the MRO's review of the test results from the second collection. The second specimen collected for the purposes of this paragraph may not be collected under direct observation. If the medical reason for the invalid result would similarly affect the testing of another urine specimen, the MRO may authorize an alternative method for

drug testing. Licensees and other entities may not impose sanctions for an invalid test result due to a medical condition.

(3) If the MRO and the laboratory agree that further testing would not be useful and there is no legitimate technical or medical explanation for the invalid test result, the MRO shall require that a second collection take place as soon as practical under direct observation. The licensee or other entity shall rely on the MRO's review of the test results from the directly observed collection.

(g) *Review of dilute specimens.* (1) If the HHS-certified laboratory reports that a specimen is dilute and that drugs or drug metabolites were detected in the specimen at or above the cutoff levels specified in this part or the licensee's or other entity's more stringent cutoff levels, and the MRO determines that there is no legitimate medical explanation for the presence of the drugs or drug metabolites in the specimen, and a clinical examination, if required under paragraph (g)(4) of this section, has been conducted, the MRO shall determine that the drug test results are positive and that the donor has violated the FFD policy.

(2) If the licensee or other entity requires the HHS-certified laboratory to conduct the special analysis of dilute specimens permitted in § 26.163(a)(2), the results of the special analysis are positive, the MRO determines that there is no legitimate medical explanation for the presence of the drug(s) or drug metabolite(s) in the specimen, and a clinical examination, if required under paragraph (g)(4) of this section, has been conducted under paragraph (j) of this section, the MRO shall determine whether the positive and dilute specimen is a refusal to test. If the MRO does not have sufficient reason to believe that the positive and dilute specimen is a subversion attempt, he or she shall determine that the drug test results are positive and that the donor has violated the FFD policy. When determining whether the donor has diluted the specimen in a subversion attempt, the MRO shall also consider the following circumstances, if applicable:

(i) The donor has presented, at this or a previous collection, a urine specimen that the HHS-certified laboratory reported as being substituted, adulterated, or invalid to the MRO and the MRO determined that there is no adequate technical or medical explanation for the result;

(ii) The donor has presented a urine specimen of 30 mL or more that falls outside the required temperature range, even if a subsequent directly observed collection was performed; or

(iii) The collector observed conduct clearly and unequivocally indicating an attempt to dilute the specimen.

(3) If a dilute specimen was collected under direct observation, the MRO may require the laboratory to conduct confirmatory testing at the LOD for any drugs or drug metabolites, as long as each drug class is evaluated as required by § 26.31(d)(1)(ii).

(4) If the drugs detected in a dilute specimen are any opium, opiate, or opium derivative (e.g., morphine/codeine), or if the drugs or metabolites detected indicate the use of prescription or over-the-counter medications, before determining that the donor has violated the FFD policy under paragraph (a) of this section, the MRO or his/her designee, who shall also be a licensed physician with knowledge of the clinical signs of drug abuse, shall conduct the clinical examination for abuse of these substances that is required in paragraph (j) of this section. An evaluation for clinical evidence of abuse is not required if the laboratory confirms the presence of 6–AM (*i.e.*, the presence of this metabolite is proof of heroin use) in the dilute specimen.

(5) An MRO review is not required for specimens that the HHS-certified laboratory reports as negative and dilute. The licensee or other entity may not take any administrative actions or impose any sanctions on a donor who submits a negative and dilute specimen.

(h) *Review of substituted specimens.* (1) If the HHS-certified laboratory reports a specimen as substituted (*i.e.*, the creatinine concentration is less than 2 mg/dL and the specific gravity is less than or equal to 1.0010 or equal to or greater than 1.0200), the MRO shall contact the donor and offer the donor an opportunity to provide a legitimate medical explanation for the substituted result. The burden of proof resides solely with the donor, who must provide legitimate medical evidence within 5 business days that he or she produced the specimen for which the HHS-certified laboratory reported a substituted result. Any medical evidence must be submitted through a physician who is experienced and qualified in the medical issues involved, as verified by the MRO. Claims of excessive hydration, or claims based on unsubstantiated personal characteristics, including, but not limited to, race, gender, diet, and body weight, are not acceptable evidence without medical studies which demonstrate that the donor did produce the laboratory result.

(2) If the MRO determines that there is no legitimate medical explanation for the substituted test result, the MRO shall report to the licensee or other entity that the specimen was substituted.

(3) If the MRO determines that there is a legitimate medical explanation for the substituted test result and no drugs or drug metabolites were detected in the specimen, the MRO shall report to the licensee or other entity that no FFD policy violation has occurred.

(i) *Review of adulterated specimens.* (1) If the HHS-certified laboratory reports a specimen as adulterated with a specific substance, the MRO shall contact the donor and offer the donor an opportunity to provide a legitimate medical explanation for the adulterated result. The burden of proof resides solely with the donor, who must provide legitimate medical evidence within 5 business days that he or she produced the adulterated result. Any medical evidence must be submitted through a physician experienced and qualified in the medical issues involved, as verified by the MRO.

(2) If the MRO determines there is no legitimate medical explanation for the adulterated test result, the MRO shall report to the licensee or other entity that the specimen is adulterated.

(3) If the MRO determines that there is a legitimate medical explanation for the adulterated test result and no drugs or drug metabolites were detected in the specimen, the MRO shall report to the licensee or other entity that no FFD policy violation has occurred.

(j) *Review for opiates, prescription and over-the-counter medications.* (1) If the MRO determines that there is no legitimate medical explanation for a positive confirmatory test result for opiates and before the MRO determines that the test result is a violation of the FFD policy, the MRO or his/her designee, who shall also be a licensed physician with knowledge of the clinical signs of drug abuse, shall determine that there is clinical evidence, in addition to the positive confirmatory test result, that the donor has illegally used opium, an opiate, or an opium derivative (e.g., morphine/codeine). This requirement does not apply if the laboratory confirms the presence of 6-AM (*i.e.*, the presence of this metabolite is proof of heroin use), or the morphine or codeine concentration is equal to or greater than 15,000 ng/mL and the donor does not present a legitimate medical explanation for the presence of morphine or codeine at or above this concentration. The MRO may not determine that the consumption of food products is a legitimate medical explanation for the presence of morphine or codeine at or above this concentration.

(2) If the MRO determines that there is no legitimate medical explanation for a positive confirmatory test result for drugs other than opiates that are commonly prescribed or included in over-the-counter preparations (e.g., benzodiazepines in the first case, barbiturates in the second) and are listed in the licensee's or other entity's panel of substances to be tested, the MRO shall determine whether there is clinical evidence, in addition to the positive confirmatory test result, of abuse of any of these substances or their derivatives.

(3) If the MRO determines that the donor has used another individual's prescription medication, including a medication containing opiates, and no clinical evidence of drug abuse is found, the MRO shall report to the licensee or other entity that the donor has misused a prescription medication. If the MRO determines that the donor has used another individual's prescription medication and clinical evidence of drug abuse is found, the MRO shall report to the licensee that the donor has violated the FFD policy.

(4) In determining whether a legitimate medical explanation exists for a positive confirmatory test result for opiates or prescription or over-the-counter medications, the MRO may consider the use of a medication from a foreign country. The MRO shall exercise professional judgment consistently with the following principles:

(i) There can be a legitimate medical explanation only with respect to a drug that is obtained legally in a foreign country;

(ii) There can be a legitimate medical explanation only with respect to a drug that has a legitimate medical use. Use of a drug of abuse (e.g., heroin, PCP) or any other substance that cannot be viewed as having a legitimate medical use can never be the basis for a legitimate medical explanation, even if the drug is obtained legally in a foreign country; and

(iii) Use of the drug can form the basis of a legitimate medical explanation only if it is used consistently with its proper and intended medical purpose.

(5) The MRO may not consider consumption of food products, supplements, or other preparations containing substances that may result in a positive confirmatory drug test result, including, but not limited to supplements containing hemp products or coca leaf tea, as a legitimate medical explanation for the presence of drugs or drug metabolites in the urine specimen above the cutoff levels specified in § 26.163 or a licensee's or other entity's more stringent cutoff levels.

(6) The MRO may not consider the use of any drug contained in Schedule I of section 202 of the Controlled Substances Act [21 U.S.C. 812] as a legitimate medical explanation for a positive confirmatory drug test result, even if the drug may be legally prescribed and used under State law.

(k) *Results consistent with legitimate drug use.* If the MRO determines that there is a legitimate medical explanation for a positive confirmatory drug test result, and that the use of a drug identified through testing was in the manner and at the dosage prescribed, and the results do not reflect a lack of reliability or trustworthiness, then the donor has not violated the licensee's or other entity's FFD policy. The MRO shall report to the licensee or other entity that no FFD policy violation has occurred. The MRO shall further evaluate the positive confirmatory test result and medical explanation to determine whether use of the drug and/or the medical condition poses a potential risk to public health and safety as a result of the individual being impaired while on duty. If the MRO determines that such a risk exists, he or she shall ensure that a determination of fitness is performed.

(l) *Retesting authorized.* Should the MRO question the accuracy or scientific validity of a positive, adulterated, substituted, or invalid test result, only the MRO is authorized to order retesting of an aliquot of the original specimen or the analysis of any split specimen (Bottle B) in order to determine whether the FFD policy has been violated. Retesting must be performed by a second HHS-certified laboratory. The MRO is also the only individual who may authorize a reanalysis of an aliquot of the original specimen or an analysis of any split specimen (Bottle B) in response to a request from the donor tested.

(m) *Result scientifically insufficient.* Based on the review of inspection and audit reports, quality control data, multiple specimens, and other pertinent results, the MRO may determine that a positive, adulterated, substituted or invalid test result is scientifically insufficient for further action and may declare that a drug or validity test result is not an FFD policy violation, but that a negative test result was not obtained. In this situation, the MRO may request retesting of the original specimen before making this decision. The MRO is neither expected nor required to request such retesting, unless in the sole opinion of the MRO, such retesting is warranted. The MRO may request that the reanalysis be performed by the same laboratory, or that an aliquot of the original specimen be sent for reanalysis to another HHS-certified laboratory. The licensee testing facility and the HHS-certified laboratory shall assist in this review process, as requested by the MRO, by making available the individual(s) responsible for day-to-day management of the licensee testing facility or the HHS-certified laboratory, or other individuals who are forensic toxicologists or who have equivalent forensic experience in urine drug testing, to provide specific consultation as required by the MRO.

(n) *Evaluating results from a second laboratory.* After a second laboratory tests an aliquot of a single specimen or the split (Bottle B) specimen, the MRO shall take the following actions if the second laboratory reports the following results:

(1) If the second laboratory reconfirms any positive test results, the MRO may report an FFD policy violation to the licensee or other entity;

(2) If the second laboratory reconfirms any adulterated, substituted, or invalid validity test results, the MRO may report an FFD policy violation to the licensee or other entity;

(3) If the second laboratory does not reconfirm the positive test results, the MRO shall report that no FFD policy violation has occurred; or

(4) If the second laboratory does not reconfirm the adulterated, substituted, or invalid validity test results, the MRO shall report that no FFD policy violation has occurred.

(o) *Re-authorization after a first violation for a positive test result.* The MRO is responsible for reviewing drug test results from an individual whose authorization was terminated or denied for a first violation of the FFD policy involving a confirmed positive drug test result and who is being considered for re-authorization. In order to determine whether subsequent positive confirmatory drug test results represent new drug use or remaining metabolites from the drug use that initially resulted in the FFD policy violation, the MRO shall request from the HHS-certified laboratory, and the laboratory shall provide, quantitation of the test results and other information necessary to make the determination. If the drug for which the individual first tested positive was marijuana and the confirmatory assay for delta-9-tetrahydrocannabinol-9-carboxylic acid yields a positive result, the MRO shall determine whether the confirmatory test result indicates further marijuana use since the first positive test result, or whether the test result is consistent with the level of delta-9-tetrahydrocannabinol-9-carboxylic acid that would be expected if no further marijuana use had occurred. If the test result indicates that no further marijuana use has occurred since the first positive test result, then the MRO shall declare the drug test result as negative.

(p) *Time to complete MRO review.* The MRO shall complete his or her review of positive, adulterated, substituted, and invalid test results and, in instances when the MRO determines that there is no legitimate medical explanation for the test result(s), notify the licensee's or other entity's designated representative within 10 business days of an initial positive, adulterated, substituted, or invalid test result. The MRO shall notify the licensee or other entity of the results of his or her review in writing and in a manner designed to ensure the confidentiality of the information.

§ 26.187 Substance abuse expert.

(a) *Implementation.* By March 31, 2010, any SAEs on whom licensees and other entities rely to make determinations of fitness under this part shall meet the requirements of this section. An MRO who meets the requirements of this section may serve as both an MRO and as an SAE.

(b) *Credentials.* An SAE shall have at least one of the following credentials:

(1) A licensed physician;

(2) A licensed or certified social worker;

(3) A licensed or certified psychologist;

(4) A licensed or certified employee assistance professional; or

(5) An alcohol and drug abuse counselor certified by the National Association of Alcoholism and Drug Abuse Counselors Certification Commission or by the International Certification Reciprocity Consortium/Alcohol and Other Drug Abuse.

(c) *Basic knowledge.* An SAE shall be knowledgeable in the following areas:

(1) Demonstrated knowledge of and clinical experience in the diagnosis and treatment of alcohol and controlled-substance abuse disorders;

(2) Knowledge of the SAE function as it relates to the public's interests in the duties performed by the individuals who are subject to this subpart; and

(3) Knowledge of this part and any changes thereto.

(d) *Qualification training*. SAEs shall receive qualification training on the following subjects:

(1) Background, rationale, and scope of this part;

(2) Key drug testing requirements of this part, including specimen collection, laboratory testing, MRO review, and problems in drug testing;

(3) Key alcohol testing requirements of this part, including specimen collection, the testing process, and problems in alcohol tests;

(4) SAE qualifications and prohibitions;

(5) The role of the SAE in making determinations of fitness and the return-to-duty process, including the initial evaluation, referrals for education and/or treatment, the followup evaluation, continuing treatment recommendations, and the followup testing plan;

(6) Procedures for SAE consultation and communication with licensees or other entities, MROs, and treatment providers;

(7) Reporting and recordkeeping requirements of this part; and

(8) Issues that SAEs confront in carrying out their duties under this part.

(e) *Continuing education*. During each 3-year period following completion of initial qualification training, the SAE shall complete continuing education consisting of at least 12 continuing professional education hours relevant to performing SAE functions.

(1) This continuing education must include material concerning new technologies, interpretations, recent guidance, rule changes, and other information about developments in SAE practice pertaining to this part, since the time the SAE met the qualification training requirements of this section.

(2) Continuing education activities must include documented assessment tools to assist in determining that the SAE has learned the material.

(f) *Documentation*. The SAE shall maintain documentation showing that he or she currently meets all requirements of this section. The SAE shall provide this documentation on request to NRC representatives, licensees, or other entities who are relying on or contemplating relying on the SAE's services, and to other individuals and entities, as required by § 26.37.

(g) *Responsibilities and prohibitions*. The SAE shall evaluate individuals who have violated the substance abuse provisions of an FFD policy and make recommendations concerning education, treatment, return to duty, followup drug and alcohol testing, and aftercare. The SAE is not an advocate for the licensee or other entity, or the individual. The SAE's function is to protect public health and safety and the common defense and security by professionally evaluating the individual and recommending appropriate education/treatment, follow-up tests, and aftercare.

(1) The SAE is authorized to make determinations of fitness in at least the following three circumstances:

(i) When potentially disqualifying FFD information has been identified regarding an individual who has applied for authorization under this part;

(ii) When an individual has violated the substance abuse provisions of a licensee's or other entity's FFD policy; and

(iii) When an individual may be impaired by alcohol, prescription or over-the-counter medications, or illegal drugs.

(2) After determining the best recommendation for assisting the individual, the SAE shall serve as a referral source to assist the individual's entry into an education and/or treatment program.

(i) To prevent the appearance of a conflict of interest, the SAE may not refer an individual requiring assistance to his or her private practice or to a person or organization from whom the SAE receives payment or in which the SAE has a financial interest. The SAE is precluded from making referrals to entities with whom the SAE is financially associated.

(ii) There are four exceptions to the prohibitions contained in the preceding paragraph. The SAE may refer an individual to any of the following providers of assistance, regardless of his or her relationship with them:

(A) A public agency (e.g., treatment facility) operated by a state, county, or municipality;

(B) A person or organization under contract to the licensee or other entity to provide alcohol or drug treatment and/or education services (e.g., the licensee's or other entity's contracted treatment provider);

(C) The sole source of therapeutically appropriate treatment under the individual's health insurance program (e.g., the single substance abuse in-patient treatment program made available by the individual's insurance coverage plan); or

(D) The sole source of therapeutically appropriate treatment reasonably available to the individual (e.g., the only treatment facility or education program reasonably located within the general commuting area).

§26.189 Determination of fitness.

(a) A determination of fitness is the process entered when there are indications that an individual specified in §26.4(a) through (e), and at the licensee's or other entity's discretion as specified in §26.4(f) and (g), may be in violation of the licensee's or other entity's FFD policy or is otherwise unable to safely and competently perform his or her duties. A determination of fitness must be made by a licensed or certified professional who is appropriately qualified and has the necessary clinical expertise, as verified by the licensee or other entity, to evaluate the specific fitness issues presented by the individual. A professional called on by the licensee or other entity may not perform a determination of fitness regarding fitness issues that are outside of his or her specific areas of expertise. The types of professionals and the fitness issues for which they are qualified to make determinations of fitness include, but are not limited to, the following:

(1) An SAE who meets the requirements of §26.187 may determine the fitness of an individual who may have engaged in substance abuse and shall determine an individual's fitness to be granted authorization following an unfavorable termination or denial of authorization under this part, but may not be qualified to assess the fitness of an individual who may have experienced mental illness, significant emotional stress, or other mental or physical conditions that may cause impairment but are unrelated to substance abuse, unless the SAE has additional qualifications for addressing those fitness issues;

(2) A clinical psychologist may determine the fitness of an individual who may have experienced mental illness, significant emotional stress, or cognitive or psychological impairment from causes unrelated to substance abuse, but may not be qualified to assess the fitness of an individual who may have a substance abuse disorder, unless the psychologist is also an SAE;

(3) A psychiatrist may determine the fitness of an individual who is taking psychoactive medications consistently with one or more valid prescription(s), but may not be qualified to assess potential impairment attributable to substance abuse, unless the psychiatrist has had specific training to diagnose and treat substance abuse disorders;

(4) A physician may determine the fitness of an individual who may be ill, injured, fatigued, taking medications in accordance with one or more valid prescriptions, or using over-the-counter medications, but may not be qualified to assess the fitness of an individual who may have a substance abuse disorder, unless the physician is also an SAE; and

(5) As a physician with specialized training, the MRO may determine the fitness of an individual who may have engaged in substance abuse or may be ill, injured, fatigued, taking medications under one or more valid prescriptions, and/or using over-the-counter medications, but may not be qualified to assess an individual's fitness to be granted authorization following an unfavorable termination or denial of authorization under this part, unless the MRO is also an SAE.

(b) A determination of fitness must be made in at least the following circumstances:

(1) When there is an acceptable medical explanation for a positive, adulterated, substituted, or invalid test result, but there is a basis for believing that the individual could be impaired while on duty;

(2) Before making return-to-duty recommendations after an individual's authorization has been terminated unfavorably or denied under a licensee's or other entity's FFD policy;

(3) Before an individual is granted authorization when potentially disqualifying FFD information is identified that has not previously been evaluated by another licensee or entity who is subject to this subpart; and

(4) When potentially disqualifying FFD information is otherwise identified and the licensee's or other entity's reviewing official concludes that a determination of fitness is warranted under § 26.69.

(c) A determination of fitness that is conducted for cause (*i.e.*, because of observed behavior or a physical condition) must be conducted through face-to-face interaction between the subject individual and the professional making the determination. Electronic means of communication may not be used.

(1) If there is neither conclusive evidence of an FFD policy violation nor a significant basis for concern that the individual may be impaired while on duty, then the individual must be determined to be fit for duty.

(2) If there is no conclusive evidence of an FFD policy violation but there is a significant basis for concern that the individual may be impaired while on duty, then the subject individual must be determined to be unfit for duty. This result does not constitute a violation of this part nor of the licensee's or other entity's FFD policy, and no sanctions may be imposed. However, the professional who made the determination of fitness shall consult with the licensee's or other entity's management personnel to identify the actions required to ensure that any possible limiting condition does not represent a threat to workplace or public health and safety. Licensee or other entity management personnel shall implement the required actions. When appropriate, the subject individual may also be referred to the EAP.

(d) Neither the individual nor licensees and other entities may seek a second determination of fitness if a determination of fitness under this part has already been performed by a qualified professional employed by or under contract to the licensee or other entity. After the initial determination of fitness has been made, the professional may modify his or her evaluation and recommendations based on new or additional information from other sources including, but not limited to, the subject individual, another licensee or entity, or staff of an education or treatment program. Unless the professional who made the initial determination of fitness is no longer employed by or under contract to the licensee or other entity, only that professional is authorized to modify the evaluation and recommendations. When reasonably practicable, licensees and other entities shall assist in arranging for consultation between the new professional and the professional who is no longer employed by or under contract to the licensee or other entity, to ensure continuity and consistency in the recommendations and their implementation.

Subpart I—Managing Fatigue

§ 26.201 Applicability.

The requirements in this subpart apply to the licensees and other entities identified in § 26.3(a), and, if applicable, (c) and (d). The requirements in §§ 26.203 and 26.211 apply to the individuals identified in § 26.4 (a) through (c). In addition, the requirements in § 26.205 through § 26.209 apply to the individuals identified in § 26.4(a).

§ 26.203 General provisions.

(a) *Policy.* Licensees shall establish a policy for the management of fatigue for all individuals who are subject to the licensee's FFD program and incorporate it into the written policy required in § 26.27(b).

(b) *Procedures.* In addition to the procedures required in § 26.27(c), licensees shall develop, implement, and maintain procedures that—

(1) Describe the process to be followed when any individual identified in § 26.4(a) through (c) makes a self-declaration that he or she is not fit to safely and competently perform his or her duties for any part of a working tour as a result of fatigue. The procedure must—

(i) Describe the individual's and licensee's rights and responsibilities related to self-declaration;

(ii) Describe requirements for establishing controls and conditions under which an individual may be permitted or required to perform work after that individual declares that he or she is not fit due to fatigue; and

(iii) Describe the process to be followed if the individual disagrees with the results of a fatigue assessment that is required under § 26.211(a)(2);

(2) Describe the process for implementing the controls required under § 26.205 for the individuals who are performing the duties listed in § 26.4(a);

(3) Describe the process to be followed in conducting fatigue assessments under § 26.211; and

(4) Describe the disciplinary actions that the licensee may impose on an individual following a fatigue assessment, and the conditions and considerations for taking those disciplinary actions.

(c) *Training and examinations.* Licensees shall add the following KAs to the content of the training that is required in § 26.29(a) and the comprehensive examination required in § 26.29(b):

(1) Knowledge of the contributors to worker fatigue, circadian variations in alertness and performance, indications and risk factors for common sleep disorders, shiftwork strategies for obtaining adequate rest, and the effective use of fatigue countermeasures; and

(2) Ability to identify symptoms of worker fatigue and contributors to decreased alertness in the workplace.

(d) *Recordkeeping.* Licensees shall retain the following records for at least 3 years or until the completion of all related legal proceedings, whichever is later:

(1) Records of work hours for individuals who are subject to the work hour controls in § 26.205;

(2) For licensees implementing the requirements of § 26.205(d)(3), records of shift schedules and shift cycles, or, for licensees implementing the requirements of § 26.205(d)(7), records of shift schedules and records showing the beginning and end times and dates of all averaging periods, of individuals who are subject to the work hour controls in § 26.205;

(3) The documentation of waivers that is required in § 26.207(a)(4), including the bases for granting the waivers;

(4) The documentation of work hour reviews that is required in § 26.205(e)(3) and (e)(4); and

(5) The documentation of fatigue assessments that is required in § 26.211(g).

(e) *Reporting.* Licensees shall include the following information in a standard format in the annual FFD program performance report required under § 26.717:

(1) A summary for each nuclear power plant site of all instances during the previous calendar year when the licensee waived one or more of the work hour controls specified in § 26.205(d)(1) through (d)(5)(i) and (d)(7) for individuals described in § 26.4(a). The summary must include only those waivers under which work was performed. If it was necessary to waive more than one work hour control during any single extended work period, the summary of instances must include each of the work hour controls that were waived during the period. For each category of individuals specified in § 26.4(a), the licensee shall report:

(i) The number of instances when each applicable work hour control specified in § 26.205(d)(1)(i) through (d)(1)(iii), (d)(2)(i) and (d)(2)(ii), (d)(3)(i) through (d)(3)(v), and (d)(7) was waived for individuals not working on outage activities;

(ii) The number of instances when each applicable work hour control specified in § 26.205(d)(1)(i) through (d)(1)(iii), (d)(2)(i) and (d)(2)(ii), (d)(3)(i) through (d)(3)(v), (d)(4) and (d)(5)(i), and (d)(7) was waived for individuals working on outage activities; and

(iii) A summary that shows the distribution of waiver use among the individuals within each category of individuals identified in § 26.4(a) (e.g., a table that shows the number of individuals who received only one waiver during the reporting period, the number of individuals who received a total of two waivers during the reporting period).

(2) A summary of corrective actions, if any, resulting from the analyses of these data, including fatigue assessments.

(f) *Audits.* Licensees shall audit the management of worker fatigue as required by § 26.41.

[73 FR 17176, Mar. 31, 2008, as amended at 76 FR 43548, July 21, 2011]

§ 26.205 Work hours.

(a) *Individuals subject to work hour controls.* Any individual who performs duties identified in § 26.4(a)(1) through (a)(5) shall be subject to the requirements of this section.

(b) *Calculating work hours.* For the purposes of this section, a licensee shall calculate the work hours of individuals who are subject to this section as the amount of time the individuals perform duties for the licensee. Except as permitted by paragraphs (b)(1) through (b)(5) of this section, the calculated work hours must include all time performing duties for the licensee, including all within-shift break times and rest periods during which there are no reasonable opportunities or accommodations appropriate for restorative sleep.

(1) Shift turnover. Licensees may exclude shift turnover from the calculation of an individual's work hours. Shift turnover includes only those activities that are necessary to safely transfer information and responsibilities between two or more individuals between shifts. Shift turnover activities may include, but are not limited to, discussions of the status of plant equipment, and the status of ongoing activities, such as extended tests of safety systems and components. Licensees may not exclude work hours worked during turnovers between individuals within a shift period due to rotations or relief within a shift. Activities that licensees may not exclude from work hours calculations also include, but are not limited to, shift holdovers to cover for late arrivals of incoming shift members; early arrivals of individuals for meetings, training, or pre-shift briefings for special evolutions; and holdovers for interviews needed for event investigations.

(2) Within-shift break and rest periods. Licensees may exclude from the calculation of an individual's work hours only that portion of a break or rest period during which there is a reasonable opportunity and accommodations for restorative sleep (e.g., a nap).

(3) Beginning or resuming duties subject to work hour controls. If an individual begins or resumes performing for the licensee any of the duties listed in § 26.4(a) during the calculation period, the licensee shall include in the calculation of the individual's work hours all work hours worked for the licensee, including hours worked performing duties that are not listed in § 26.4(a), and control the individual's work hours under the requirements of paragraph (d) of this section.

(4) Unannounced emergency preparedness exercises and drills. Licensees may exclude from the calculation of an individual's work hours the time the individual works unscheduled work hours for the purpose of participating in the actual conduct of an unannounced emergency preparedness exercise or drill.

(5) Incidental duties performed off site. Licensees may exclude from the calculation of an individual's work hours unscheduled work performed off site (e.g., technical assistance provided by telephone from an individual's home), provided the total duration of the work does not exceed a nominal 30 minutes during any single break period. For the purposes of compliance with the minimum break requirements of § 26.205(d)(2), and the minimum days off requirements of § 26.205(d)(3) through (d)(5) or the maximum average work hours requirements of § 26.205(d)(7), such duties do not constitute work periods, work shifts, or hours worked.

(c) *Work hours scheduling.* Licensees shall schedule the work hours of individuals who are subject to this section consistent with the objective of preventing impairment from fatigue due to the duration, frequency, or sequencing of successive shifts.

(d) *Work hour controls.* Licensees shall control the work hours of individuals who are subject to this section.

(1) Except as permitted in § 26.207, licensees shall ensure that any individual's work hours do not exceed the following limits:

(i) 16 work hours in any 24-hour period;

(ii) 26 work hours in any 48-hour period; and

(iii) 72 work hours in any 7-day period.

(2) Licensees shall ensure that individuals have, at a minimum, the rest breaks specified in this paragraph. For the purposes of this subpart, a break is defined as an interval of time that falls between successive work periods, during which the individual does not perform any duties for the licensee other than one period of shift turnover at either the beginning or end of a shift but not both. Except as permitted in § 26.207, licensees shall ensure that individuals have, at a minimum—

(i) A 10-hour break between successive work periods or an 8-hour break between successive work periods when a break of less than 10 hours is necessary to accommodate a crew's scheduled transition between work schedules or shifts; and

(ii) A 34-hour break in any 9-day period.

(3) Licensees shall either ensure that individuals have, at a minimum, the number of days off specified in this paragraph, or comply with the requirements for maximum average workhours in § 26.205(d)(7). For the purposes of this section, a day off is defined as a calendar day during which an individual does not start a work shift. For the purposes of calculating the average number of days off required in this paragraph, the duration of the shift cycle may not exceed 6 weeks.

(i) Individuals who are working 8-hour shift schedules shall have at least 1 day off per week, averaged over the shift cycle;

(ii) Individuals who are working 10-hour shift schedules shall have at least 2 days off per week, averaged over the shift cycle;

(iii) Individuals who are working 12-hour shift schedules while performing the duties described in § 26.4(a)(1) through (a)(3) shall have at least 2.5 days off per week, averaged over the shift cycle;

(iv) Individuals who are working 12-hour shift schedules while performing the duties described in § 26.4(a)(4) shall have at least 2 days off per week, averaged over the shift cycle; and

(v) Individuals who are working 12-hour shift schedules while performing the duties described in § 26.4(a)(5) shall have at least 3 days off per week, averaged over the shift cycle.

(4) During the first 60 days of a unit outage, licensees need not meet the requirements of § 26.205(d)(3) or (d)(7) for individuals specified in § 26.4(a)(1) through (a)(4), while those individuals are working on outage activities. However, the licensee shall ensure that the individuals specified in § 26.4(a)(1) through (a)(3) have at least 3 days off in each successive (*i.e.*, non-rolling) 15-day period and that the individuals specified in § 26.4(a)(4) have at least 1 day off in any 7-day period;

(5) During the first 60 days of a unit outage, security system outage, or increased threat condition, licensees shall control the hours worked by individuals specified in § 26.4(a)(5) as follows:

(i) During the first 60 days of a unit outage or a planned security system outage, licensees need not meet the requirements of § 26.205(d)(3) or (d)(7). However, licensees shall ensure that these individuals have at least 4 days off in each successive (*i.e.*, non-rolling) 15-day period; and

(ii) During the first 60 days of an unplanned security system outage or increased threat condition, licensees need not meet the requirements of § 26.205(d)(3), (d)(5)(i), or (d)(7).

(6) The 60-day periods in paragraphs (d)(4) and (d)(5) of this section may be extended for each individual in 7-day increments for each non-overlapping 7-day period the individual has worked not more than 48 hours during the unit or security system outage or increased threat condition, as applicable.

(7) Licensees may, as an alternative to complying with the minimum days off requirements in § 26.205(d)(3), comply with the requirements for maximum average work hours in this paragraph.

(i) Individuals may not work more than a weekly average of 54 hours, calculated using an averaging period of up to six (6) weeks, which advances by 7 consecutive calendar days at the finish of every averaging period.

(ii) For purposes of this section, when an individual's work shift starts at the end of a calendar day and concludes during the next calendar day, the licensee shall either consider the hours worked during that entire shift as if they were all worked on the day the shift started, or attribute the hours to the calendar days on which the hours were actually worked.

(iii) Each licensee shall state, in its FFD policy and procedures required by § 26.27 and § 26.203(a) and (b), the work hour counting system in § 26.205(d)(7)(ii) the licensee is using.

(8) Each licensee shall state, in its FFD policy and procedures required by § 26.27 and § 26.203(a) and (b), the requirements with which the licensee is complying: the minimum days off requirements in § 26.205(d)(3) or maximum average work hours requirements in § 26.205(d)(7).

(e) *Reviews.* Licensees shall evaluate the effectiveness of their control of work hours of individuals who are subject to this section. Licensees shall conduct the reviews once per calendar year. If any plant or security system outages or increased threat conditions occurred since the licensee completed the most recent review, the licensee shall include in the review an evaluation of the control of work hours during the outages or increased threat conditions. Licensees shall complete the review within 30 days of the end of the review period. Licensees shall—

(1) Review the actual work hours and performance of individuals who are subject to this section for consistency with the requirements of § 26.205(c). At a minimum, this review must address—

(i) Individuals whose actual hours worked during the review period exceeded an average of 54 hours per week in any shift cycle while the individuals' work hours are subject to the requirements of § 26.205(d)(3) or in any averaging period of up to 6 weeks, using the same averaging period durations that the licensee uses to control the individuals' work hours, while the individuals' work hours are subject to the requirements of § 26.205(d)(7);

(ii) Individuals who were granted more than one waiver during the review period; and

(iii) Individuals who were assessed for fatigue under § 26.211 during the review period.

(2) Review individuals' hours worked and the waivers under which work was performed to evaluate staffing adequacy for all jobs subject to the work hour controls of this section;

(3) Document the methods used to conduct the review and the results of the review; and

(4) Record, trend, and correct, under the licensee's corrective action program, any problems identified in maintaining control of work hours consistent with the specific requirements and performance objectives of this part.

[73 FR 17176, Mar. 31, 2008, as amended at 76 FR 43548, July 21, 2011]

§ 26.207 Waivers and exceptions.

(a) *Waivers.* Licensees may grant a waiver of one or more of the work hour controls in § 26.205(d)(1) through (d)(5)(i) and (d)(7), as follows:

(1) To grant a waiver, the licensee shall meet both of the following requirements:

(i) An operations shift manager determines that the waiver is necessary to mitigate or prevent a condition adverse to safety, or a security shift manager determines that the waiver is necessary to maintain site security, or a site senior-level manager with requisite signature authority makes either determination; and

(ii) A supervisor assesses the individual face to face and determines that there is reasonable assurance that the individual will be able to safely and competently perform his or her duties during the additional work period for which the waiver will be granted. The supervisor performing the assessment shall be trained as required by §§ 26.29 and 26.203(c) and shall be qualified to direct the work to be performed by the individual. If there is no supervisor on site who is qualified to direct the work, the assessment may be performed by a supervisor who is qualified to provide oversight of the work to be performed by the individual. At a minimum, the assessment must address the potential for acute and cumulative fatigue considering the individual's work history for at least the past 14 days, the potential for circadian degradations in alertness and performance considering the time of day for which the waiver will be granted, the potential for fatigue-related degradations in alertness and performance to affect risk-significant functions, and whether any controls and conditions must be established under which the individual will be permitted to perform work.

(2) To the extent practicable, licensees shall rely on the granting of waivers only to address circumstances that could not have been reasonably controlled;

(3) Licensees shall ensure that the timing of the face-to-face supervisory assessment that is required by paragraph (a)(1)(ii) of this section supports a valid assessment of the potential for worker fatigue during the time the individual will be performing work under the waiver. Licensees may not perform the face-to-face assessment more than 4 hours before the individual begins performing any work under the waiver; and

(4) Licensees shall document the bases for individual waivers. The documented basis for a waiver must include a description of the circumstances that necessitate the waiver, a statement of the scope of work and time period for which the waiver is approved, and the bases for the determinations required in paragraphs (a)(1)(i) and (ii) of this section.

(b) *Force-on-force tactical exercises.* For the purposes of compliance with the minimum days off requirements of §26.205(d)(3) or the maximum average work hours requirements of §26.205(d)(7), licensees may exclude shifts worked by security personnel during the actual conduct of NRC-evaluated force-on-force tactical exercises when calculating the individual's number of days off or hours worked, as applicable.

(c) *Common defense and security.* When informed in writing by the NRC that the requirements of §26.205, or any subset thereof, are waived for security personnel to ensure the common defense and security, licensees need not meet the specified requirements of §26.205 for the duration of the period defined by the NRC.

(d) *Plant emergencies.* Licensees need not meet the requirements of §26.205(c) and (d) during declared emergencies, as defined in the licensee's emergency plan.

[73 FR 17176, Mar. 31, 2008, as amended at 76 FR 43549, July 21, 2011]

§26.209 Self-declarations.

(a) If an individual is performing, or being assessed for, work under a waiver of one or more of the requirements contained in §26.205(d)(1) through (d)(5)(i) and (d)(7) and declares that, due to fatigue, he or she is unable to safely and competently perform his or her duties, the licensee shall immediately stop the individual from performing any duties listed in §26.4(a), except if the individual is required to continue performing those duties under other requirements of this chapter. If the subject individual must continue performing the duties listed in §26.4(a) until relieved, the licensee shall immediately take action to relieve the individual.

(b) Following a self-declaration, as described in paragraph (a) of this section, the licensee—

(1) May reassign the individual to duties other than those listed in §26.4(a), but only if the results of a fatigue assessment, conducted under the requirements of §26.211, indicate that the individual is fit to safely and competently perform those other duties; and

(2) Shall permit or require the individual to take a break of at least 10 hours before the individual returns to performing any duties listed in §26.4(a).

[73 FR 17176, Mar. 31, 2008, as amended at 76 FR 43549, July 21, 2011]

§26.211 Fatigue assessments.

(a) Licensees shall ensure that fatigue assessments are conducted under the following conditions:

(1) For cause. In addition to any other test or determination of fitness that may be required under §§26.31(c) and 26.77, a fatigue assessment must be conducted in response to an observed condition of impaired individual alertness creating a reasonable suspicion that an individual is not fit to safely and competently perform his or her duties, except if the condition is observed during an individual's break period. If the observed condition is impaired alertness with no other behaviors or

physical conditions creating a reasonable suspicion of possible substance abuse, then the licensee need only conduct a fatigue assessment. If the licensee has reason to believe that the observed condition is not due to fatigue, the licensee need not conduct a fatigue assessment;

(2) Self-declaration. A fatigue assessment must be conducted in response to an individual's self-declaration to his or her supervisor that he or she is not fit to safely and competently perform his or her duties for any part of a working tour because of fatigue, except if, following the self-declaration, the licensee permits or requires the individual to take a rest break of at least 10 hours before the individual returns to duty;

(3) Post-event. A fatigue assessment must be conducted in response to events requiring post-event drug and alcohol testing as specified in § 26.31(c). Licensees may not delay necessary medical treatment in order to conduct a fatigue assessment; and

(4) Followup. If a fatigue assessment was conducted for cause or in response to a self-declaration, and the licensee returns the individual to duty following a break of less than 10 hours in duration, the licensee shall reassess the individual for fatigue as well as the need to implement controls and conditions before permitting the individual to resume performing any duties.

(b) Only supervisors and FFD program personnel who are trained under §§ 26.29 and 26.203(c) may conduct a fatigue assessment. The fatigue assessment must be conducted face to face with the individual whose alertness may be impaired.

(1) In the case of a fatigue assessment conducted for cause, the individual who observed the condition of impaired alertness may not conduct the fatigue assessment.

(2) In the case of a post-event fatigue assessment, the individual who conducts the fatigue assessment may not have—

(i) Performed or directed (on site) the work activities during which the event occurred;

(ii) Performed, within 24 hours before the event occurred, a fatigue assessment of the individuals who were performing or directing (on site) the work activities during which the event occurred; and

(iii) Evaluated or approved a waiver of one or more of the limits specified in § 26.205(d)(1) through (d)(5)(i) and (d)(7) for any of the individuals who were performing or directing (on site) the work activities during which the event occurred, if the event occurred while such individuals were performing work under that waiver.

(c) A fatigue assessment must provide the information necessary for management decisions and actions in response to the circumstance that initiated the assessment.

(1) At a minimum, the fatigue assessment must address the following factors:

(i) Acute fatigue;

(ii) Cumulative fatigue; and

(iii) Circadian variations in alertness and performance.

(2) Individuals shall provide complete and accurate information that may be required by the licensee to address the factors listed in paragraph (c)(1) of this section. Licensees shall limit any inquiries to obtaining from the subject individual only the personal information that may be necessary to assess the factors listed in paragraph (c)(1) of this section.

(d) The licensee may not conclude that fatigue has not or will not degrade the individual's ability to safely and competently perform his or her duties solely on the basis that the individual's work hours have not exceeded any of the limits specified in § 26.205(d)(1), the individual has had the minimum breaks required in § 26.205(d)(2) or minimum days off required in § 26.205(d)(3) through (d)(5), as applicable, or the individual's hours worked have not exceeded the maximum average number of hours worked in § 26.205(d)(7).

(e) Following a fatigue assessment, the licensee shall determine and implement the controls and conditions, if any, that are necessary to permit the individual to resume performing duties for the licensee, including the need for a break.

(f) Licensees shall document the results of any fatigue assessments conducted, the circumstances that necessitated the fatigue assessment, and any controls and conditions that were implemented.

(g) Licensees shall also prepare an annual summary for each nuclear power plant site of instances of fatigue assessments that were conducted during the previous calendar year for any individual identified in § 26.4(a) through (c). Each summary must include—

(1) The conditions under which each fatigue assessment was conducted (*i.e.*, self-declaration, for cause, post-event, followup);

(2) A statement of whether or not the individual was working on outage activities at the time of the self-declaration or condition resulting in the fatigue assessment;

(3) The category of duties the individual was performing, if the individual was performing the duties described in § 26.4(a)(1) through (a)(5) at the time of the self-declaration or condition resulting in the fatigue assessment; and

(4) The management actions, if any, resulting from each fatigue assessment.

[73 FR 17176, Mar. 31, 2008, as amended at 76 FR 43549, July 21, 2011]

Subpart J [Reserved]

Subpart K—FFD Program for Construction

§ 26.401 General.

(a) At the licensee's or other entity's discretion, a licensee or other entity in § 26.3(c) may establish, implement, and maintain an FFD program that meets the requirements of this subpart to apply to the individuals specified in § 26.4(f). If a licensee or other entity in § 26.3(c) does not elect to implement an FFD program that meets the requirements of this subpart, the individuals specified in § 26.4(f) shall be subject to an FFD program that meets the requirements of subparts A through H, N, and O of this part.

(b) Entities who intend to implement an FFD program under this subpart shall submit a description of the FFD program and its implementation as part of the license, permit, or limited work authorization application.

(c) Nothing in this subpart prohibits the licensees and other entities in § 26.3(c) from subjecting the individuals in § 26.4(f) to an FFD program that meets all of the requirements of this part or FFD program elements that meet all of the applicable requirements of this part.

§ 26.403 Written policy and procedures.

(a) Licensees and other entities who implement an FFD program under this subpart shall ensure that a clear, concise, written FFD policy statement is provided to individuals who are subject to the program. The policy statement must be written in sufficient detail to provide affected individuals with information on what is expected of them and what consequences may result from a lack of adherence to the policy.

(b) Licensees and other entities shall develop, implement, and maintain written procedures that address the following topics:

(1) The methods and techniques to be used in testing for drugs and alcohol, including procedures for protecting the privacy of an individual who provides a specimen, procedures for protecting the integrity of the specimen, and procedures used to ensure that the test results are valid and attributable to the correct individual;

(2) The immediate and followup actions that will be taken, and the procedures to be used, in those cases in which individuals who are subject to the FFD program are determined to have—

(i) Been involved in the use, sale, or possession of illegal drugs;

(ii) Consumed alcohol to excess before or while constructing or directing the construction of safety- or security-related SSCs, as determined by a test that accurately measures BAC;

(iii) Attempted to subvert the testing process by adulterating or diluting specimens (in vivo or in vitro), substituting specimens, or by any other means;

(iv) Refused to provide a specimen for analysis; or

(v) Had legal action taken relating to drug or alcohol use.

(3) The process to be followed if an individual's behavior or condition

raises a concern regarding the possible use, sale, or possession of illegal drugs on or off site; the possible use or possession of alcohol while constructing or directing the construction of safety- or security-related SSCs; or impairment from any cause which in any way could adversely affect the individual's ability to safely and competently perform his or her duties.

[73 FR 17176, Mar. 31, 2008, as amended at 75 FR 73941, Nov. 30, 2010]

§ 26.405 Drug and alcohol testing.

(a) To provide means to deter and detect substance abuse, licensees and other entities who implement an FFD program under this subpart shall perform drug and alcohol testing that complies with the requirements of this section.

(b) If the licensee or other entity elects to impose random testing for drugs and alcohol on the individuals identified in § 26.4(f), random testing must—

(1) Be administered in a manner that provides reasonable assurance that individuals are unable to predict the time periods during which specimens will be collected;

(2) Require individuals who are selected for random testing to report to the collection site as soon as reasonably practicable after notification, within the time period specified in the FFD program policy;

(3) Ensure that all individuals in the population that is subject to random testing on a given day have an equal probability of being selected and tested; and

(4) Provide that an individual completing a test is immediately eligible for another random test.

(c) Individuals identified in § 26.4(f) shall be subject to drug and alcohol testing under the following conditions:

(1) Pre-assignment. Before assignment to construct or direct the construction of safety- or security-related SSCs;

(2) For-cause. In response to an individual's observed behavior or physical condition indicating possible substance abuse or after receiving credible information that an individual is engaging in substance abuse, as defined in § 26.5;

(3) Post-accident. As soon as practical after an event involving a human error that was committed by an individual specified in § 26.4(f), where the human error may have caused or contributed to the accident. The licensee or other entity shall test the individual(s) who committed the error(s), and need not test individuals who were affected by the event but whose actions likely did not cause or contribute to the event. The individual(s) who committed the human error(s) shall be tested if the event resulted in—

(i) A significant illness or personal injury to the individual to be tested or another individual, which within 4 hours after the event is recordable under the Department of Labor standards contained in 29 CFR 1904.7, and subsequent amendments thereto, and results in death, days away from work, restricted work, transfer to another job, medical treatment beyond first aid, loss of consciousness, or other significant illness or injury as diagnosed by a physician or other licensed health care professional, even if it does not result in death, days away from work, restricted work or job transfer, medical treatment beyond first aid, or loss of consciousness; or

(ii) Significant damage, during construction, to any safety-or security-related SSC; and

(4) Followup. As part of a followup plan to verify an individual's continued abstinence from substance abuse.

(d) At a minimum, licensees and other entities shall test specimens for marijuana metabolite, cocaine metabolite, opiates (codeine, morphine, 6-acetylmorphine), amphetamines (amphetamine, methamphetamine), phencyclidine, adulterants, and alcohol at the cutoff levels specified in this part, or comparable cutoff levels if specimens other than urine are collected for drug testing. Urine specimens collected for drug testing must be subject to validity testing.

(e) The specimen collection and drug and alcohol testing procedures of FFD programs under this subpart must protect the donor's privacy and the integrity of the specimen, and implement stringent quality controls to ensure that test results are valid and attributable to the correct individual. At the licensee's or other entity's discretion, specimen collections and alcohol testing may be conducted at a local hospital or other facility under the specimen collection and alcohol testing requirements of 49 CFR Part 40 and subsequent amendments thereto.

(f) Testing of urine specimens for drugs and validity, except validity screening and initial drug and validity tests that may be performed by licensee testing facilities, must be performed in a laboratory that is certified by HHS for that purpose, consistent with its standards and procedures for certification. Any initial drug test performed by a licensee or other entity subject to this subpart must use an immunoassay that meets the requirements of the Food and Drug Administration for commercial distribution. Urine specimens that yield positive, adulterated, substituted, or invalid initial validity or drug test results must be subject to confirmatory testing by the HHS-certified laboratory, except for invalid specimens that cannot be tested. Other specimens that yield positive initial drug test results must be subject to confirmatory testing by a laboratory that meets stringent quality control requirements that are comparable to those required for certification by the HHS.

(g) Licensees and other entities shall provide for an MRO review of positive, adulterated, substituted, and invalid confirmatory drug and validity test results to determine whether the donor has violated the FFD policy, before reporting the results to the individual designated by the licensee or other entity to perform the suitability and fitness evaluations required under § 26.419.

[73 FR 17176, Mar. 31, 2008, as amended at 75 FR 73941, Nov. 30, 2010]

§ 26.406 Fitness monitoring.

(a) The requirements in this section apply only if a licensee or other entity does not elect to subject the individuals specified in § 26.4(f) to random testing for drugs and alcohol under § 26.405(b).

(b) Licensees and other entities shall implement a fitness monitoring program to deter substance abuse and detect indications of possible use, sale, or possession of illegal drugs; use or possession of alcohol while constructing or directing the construction of safety- or security-related SSCs; or impairment from any cause that if left unattended may result in a risk to public health and safety or the common defense and security.

(c) Licensees and other entities shall establish procedures that monitors shall follow in response to the indications and actions specified in paragraph (b) of this section and train the monitors to implement the program.

(d) Licensees and other entities shall ensure that the fitness of individuals specified in § 26.4(f) is monitored effectively while the individuals are constructing or directing the construction of safety- and security-related SSCs, commensurate with the potential risk to public health and safety and the common defense and security imposed by the construction activity. To achieve this objective, licensees and other entities shall consider the number and placement of monitors required, the necessary ratio of monitors to individuals specified in § 26.4(f), and the frequency with which the individuals specified in § 26.4(f) shall be monitored while constructing or directing the construction of each safety- or security-related SSC.

[73 FR 17176, Mar. 31, 2008, as amended at 75 FR 73941, Nov. 30, 2010]

§ 26.407 Behavioral observation.

While the individuals specified in § 26.4(f) are constructing or directing the construction of safety- or security-related SSCs, licensees and other entities shall ensure that these individuals are subject to behavioral observation, except if the licensee or other entity has implemented a fitness monitoring program under § 26.406.

[75 FR 73941, Nov. 30, 2010]

§ 26.409 Sanctions.

Licensees and other entities who implement an FFD program under this subpart shall establish sanctions for FFD policy violations that, at a minimum, prohibit the individuals specified in § 26.4(f) from being assigned to construct or direct the construction of safety- or security-related SSCs unless or until the licensee or other entity determines that the individual's condition or behavior does not pose a potential risk to public health and safety or the common defense and security.

[75 FR 73941, Nov. 30, 2010]

§ 26.411 Protection of information.

(a) Licensees and other entities who collect personal information about an individual for the purpose of complying with this subpart shall establish and maintain a system of files and procedures to protect the personal information. FFD programs must maintain and use such records with the highest regard for individual privacy.

(b) Licensees and other entities shall obtain a signed consent that authorizes the disclosure of the personal information collected and maintained under this subpart before disclosing the personal information, except for disclosures to the individuals and entities specified in § 26.37(b)(1) through (b)(6), (b)(8), and persons deciding matters under review in § 26.413.

§ 26.413 Review process.

Licensees and other entities who implement an FFD program under this subpart shall establish and implement procedures for the review of a determination that an individual in § 26.4(f) has violated the FFD policy. The procedure must provide for an objective and impartial review of the facts related to the determination that the individual has violated the FFD policy.

§ 26.415 Audits.

(a) Licensees and other entities who implement an FFD program under this subpart shall ensure that audits are performed to assure the continuing effectiveness of the FFD program, including FFD program elements that are provided by C/Vs, and the FFD programs of C/Vs that are accepted by the licensee or other entity.

(b) Each licensee and other entity shall ensure that these programs are audited at a frequency that assures their continuing effectiveness and that corrective actions are taken to resolve any problems identified. Licensees and entities may conduct joint audits, or accept audits of C/Vs conducted by others, so long as the audit addresses the relevant C/Vs' services.

(c) Licensees and other entities need not audit HHS-certified laboratories or the specimen collection and alcohol testing services that meet the requirements of 49 CFR Part 40, "Procedures for Department of Transportation Workplace Drug and Alcohol Testing Programs" (65 FR 41944; August 9, 2001), on which licensees and other entities may rely to meet the drug and alcohol testing requirements of this subpart.

§ 26.417 Recordkeeping and reporting.

(a) Licensees and other entities who implement FFD programs under this subpart shall ensure that records pertaining to the administration of the program, which may be stored and archived electronically, are maintained so that they are available for NRC inspection purposes and for any legal proceedings resulting from the administration of the program.

(b) Licensees and other entities shall make the following reports:

(1) Reports to the NRC Operations Center by telephone within 24 hours after the licensee or other entity discovers any intentional act that casts doubt on the integrity of the FFD program and any programmatic failure, degradation, or discovered vulnerability of the FFD program that may permit undetected drug or alcohol use or abuse by individuals who are subject to this subpart. These events must be reported under this subpart, rather than under the provisions of 10 CFR 73.71; and

(2) Annual program performance reports for the FFD program.

§ 26.419 Suitability and fitness evaluations.

Licensees and other entities who implement FFD programs under this subpart shall develop, implement, and maintain procedures for evaluating whether to assign individuals to construct safety- and security-related SSCs. These procedures must provide reasonable assurance that the individuals are fit to safely and competently perform their duties, and are trustworthy and reliable, as demonstrated by the avoidance of substance abuse.

Subparts L–M [Reserved]

Subpart N—Recordkeeping and Reporting Requirements

§26.709 Applicability.

The requirements of this subpart apply to the FFD programs of licensees and other entities specified in §26.3, except for FFD programs that are implemented under subpart K of this part.

§26.711 General provisions.

(a) Each licensee and other entity shall maintain records and submit certain reports to the NRC. Records that are required by the regulations in this part must be retained for the period specified by the appropriate regulation. If a retention period is not otherwise specified, these records must be retained until the Commission terminates the facility's license, certificate, or other regulatory approval.

(b) All records may be stored and archived electronically, provided that the method used to create the electronic records meets the following criteria:

(1) Provides an accurate representation of the original records;

(2) Prevents the alteration of any archived information and/or data once it has been committed to storage; and

(3) Permits easy retrieval and re-creation of the original records.

(c) The licensees and other entities specified in §26.3(a) and, as applicable, (c) and (d), shall inform each individual of his or her right to review information about the individual that is collected and maintained under this part to assure its accuracy. Licensees and other entities shall provide the individual with an opportunity to correct any inaccurate or incomplete information that is documented by licensees and other entities about the individual.

(d) Licensees and other entities shall ensure that only correct and complete information about individuals is retained and shared with other licensees and entities. If, for any reason, the shared information used for determining an individual's eligibility for authorization under this part changes or new information is developed about the individual, licensees and other entities shall correct or augment the shared information contained in the records. If the changed or developed information has implications for adversely affecting an individual's eligibility for authorization, a licensee and other entity specified in §26.3(a) and, as applicable, (c) and (d), who has discovered the incorrect information, or develops new information, shall inform the reviewing official of any FFD program under which the individual is maintaining authorization of the updated information on the day of discovery. The reviewing official shall evaluate the information and take appropriate actions, which may include denial or unfavorable termination of the individual's authorization.

§26.713 Recordkeeping requirements for licensees and other entities.

(a) Each licensee and other entity who is subject to this subpart shall retain the following records for at least 5 years after the licensee or other entity terminates or denies an individual's authorization or until the completion of all related legal proceedings, whichever is later:

(1) Records of self-disclosures, employment histories, and suitable inquiries that are required under §§26.55, 26.57, 26.59, and 26.69 that result in the granting of authorization;

(2) Records pertaining to the determination of a violation of the FFD policy and related management actions;

(3) Documentation of the granting and termination of authorization; and

(4) Records of any determinations of fitness conducted under §26.189, including any recommendations for treatment and followup testing plans.

(b) Each licensee and other entity who is subject to this subpart shall retain the following records for at least 3 years or until the completion of all related legal proceedings, whichever is later:

(1) Records of FFD training and examinations conducted under §26.29; and

(2) Records of audits, audit findings, and corrective actions taken under §26.41.

(c) Licensees and other entities shall ensure the retention and availability of records pertaining to any 5-year denial of authorization under §26.75(c), (d), or (e)(2) and any permanent denial of authorization under § 26.75(b) and (g) for at least 40 years or until, on application, the NRC determines that the records are no longer needed.

(d) Licensees and other entities shall retain any superseded versions of the written FFD policy and procedures required under §§ 26.27, 26.39, and 26.203(b) for at least 5 years or until completion of all legal proceedings related to an FFD violation that may have occurred under the policy and procedures, whichever is later.

(e) Licensees and other entities shall retain written agreements for the provision of services under this part for the life of the agreement or until completion of all legal proceedings related to an FFD policy violation that involved those services, whichever is later.

(f) Licensees and other entities shall retain records of the background investigations, credit and criminal history checks, and psychological assessments of FFD program personnel, conducted under § 26.31(b)(1)(i), for the length of the individual's employment by or contractual relationship with the licensee or other entity, or until the completion of all related legal proceedings, whichever is later.

(g) If a licensee's or other entity's FFD program includes tests for drugs in addition to those specified in this part, as permitted under § 26.31(d)(1), or uses more stringent cutoff levels than those specified in this part, as permitted under § 26.31(d)(3), the licensee or other entity shall retain documentation certifying the scientific and technical suitability of the assays and cutoff levels used, as required under § 26.31(d)(1)(i) and (d)(3)(iii)(C), respectively, for the time the FFD program follows these practices or until the completion of all related legal proceedings, whichever is later.

§ 26.715 Recordkeeping requirements for collection sites, licensee testing facilities, and laboratories certified by the Department of Health and Human Services.

(a) Collection sites providing services to licensees and other entities who are subject to this subpart, licensee testing facilities, and HHS-certified laboratories shall maintain and make available documentation of all aspects of the testing process for at least 2 years or until the completion of all legal proceedings related to a determination of an FFD violation, whichever is later. This 2-year period may be extended on written notification by the NRC or by any licensee or other entity for whom services are being provided.

(b) Documentation that must be retained includes, but is not limited to, the following:

(1) Personnel files, including training records, for all individuals who have been authorized to have access to specimens, but are no longer under contract to or employed by the collection site, licensee testing facility, or HHS-certified laboratory;

(2) Chain-of-custody documents (other than forms recording specimens with negative test results and no FFD violations or anomalies, which may be destroyed after appropriate summary information has been recorded for program administration purposes);

(3) Quality assurance and quality control records;

(4) Superseded procedures;

(5) All test data (including calibration curves and any calculations used in determining test results);

(6) Test reports;

(7) Records pertaining to performance testing;

(8) Records pertaining to the investigation of testing errors or unsatisfactory performance discovered in quality control or blind performance testing, in the testing of actual specimens, or through the processing of appeals and MRO reviews, as well as any other errors or matters that could adversely reflect on the integrity of the testing process, investigation findings, and corrective actions taken, where applicable;

(9) Performance records on certification inspections;

(10) Records of preventative maintenance on licensee testing facility instruments;

(11) Records that summarize any test results that the MRO determined to be scientifically insufficient for further action;

(12) Either printed or electronic copies of computer-generated data;

(13) Records that document the dates, times of entry and exit, escorts, and purposes of entry of authorized visitors, maintenance personnel, and service personnel who have accessed secured areas of licensee testing facilities and HHS-certified laboratories; and

(14) Records of the inspection, maintenance, and calibration of EBTs.

§26.717 Fitness-for-duty program performance data.

(a) Licensees and other entities shall collect and compile FFD program performance data for each FFD program that is subject to this subpart.

(b) The FFD program performance data must include the following information:

(1) The random testing rate;

(2) Drugs for which testing is conducted and cutoff levels, including results of tests using lower cutoff levels, tests for drugs not included in the HHS panel, and any special analyses of dilute specimens permitted under §26.163(a)(2);

(3) Populations tested (*i.e.*, individuals in applicant status, permanent licensee employees, C/Vs);

(4) Number of tests administered and results of those tests sorted by population tested (*i.e.*, individuals in applicant status, permanent licensee employees, C/Vs);

(5) Conditions under which the tests were performed, as defined in §26.31(c);

(6) Substances identified;

(7) Number of subversion attempts by type;

(8) Summary of management actions; and

(9) The information required under §26.203(e)(1) and (e)(2).

(c) Licensees and other entities who have a licensee-approved FFD program shall analyze the data at least annually and take appropriate actions to correct any identified program weaknesses. Records of the data, analyses, and corrective actions taken must be retained for at least 3 years or until the completion of any related legal proceedings, whichever is later.

(d) Any licensee or other entity who terminates an individual's authorization or takes administrative action on the basis of the results of a positive initial drug test for marijuana or cocaine shall also report these test results in the annual summary by processing stage (*i.e.*, initial testing at the licensee testing facility, testing at the HHS-certified laboratory, and MRO determinations). The report must also include the number of terminations and administrative actions taken against individuals for the reporting period.

(e) Licensees and other entities shall submit the FFD program performance data (for January through December) to the NRC annually, before March 1 of the following year.

(f) Licensees and other entities may submit the FFD program performance data in a consolidated report, as long as the report presents the data separately for each site.

(g) Each C/V who maintains a licensee-approved drug and alcohol testing program is subject to the reporting requirements of this section and shall submit the required information either directly to the NRC or through the licensees or other entities to whom the C/V provided services during the year. Licensees, other entities, and C/Vs shall share information to ensure that the information is reported completely and is not duplicated in reports submitted to the NRC.

[73 FR 17176, Mar. 31, 2008, as amended at 79 FR 66603, Nov. 10, 2014]

§26.719 Reporting requirements.

(a) *Required reports.* Each licensee and entity who is subject to this subpart shall inform the NRC of significant violations of the FFD policy, significant FFD program failures, and errors in drug and alcohol testing. These events must be reported under this section, rather than under the provisions of 10 CFR 73.71.

(b) *Significant FFD policy violations or programmatic failures.* The following significant FFD policy violations and programmatic failures must be reported to the NRC Operations Center by telephone within 24 hours after the licensee or other entity discovers the violation:

(1) The use, sale, distribution, possession, or presence of illegal drugs, or the consumption or presence of alcohol within a protected area;

(2) Any acts by any person licensed under 10 CFR part 55 to operate a power reactor, as well as any acts by SSNM transporters, FFD program personnel, or any supervisory personnel who are authorized under this part, if such acts—

(i) Involve the use, sale, or possession of a controlled substance;

(ii) Result in a determination that the individual has violated the licensee's or other entity's FFD policy (including subversion as defined in § 26.5); or

(iii) Involve the consumption of alcohol within a protected area or while performing the duties that require the individual to be subject to the FFD program;

(3) Any intentional act that casts doubt on the integrity of the FFD program; and

(4) Any programmatic failure, degradation, or discovered vulnerability of the FFD program that may permit undetected drug or alcohol use or abuse by individuals within a protected area, or by individuals who are assigned to perform duties that require them to be subject to the FFD program.

(c) *Drug and alcohol testing errors.* (1) Within 30 days of completing an investigation of any testing errors or unsatisfactory performance discovered in performance testing at either a licensee testing facility or an HHS-certified laboratory, in the testing of quality control or actual specimens, or through the processing of reviews under § 26.39 and MRO reviews under § 26.185, as well as any other errors or matters that could adversely reflect on the integrity of the random selection or testing process, the licensee or other entity shall submit to the NRC a report of the incident and corrective actions taken or planned. If the error involves an HHS-certified laboratory, the NRC shall ensure that HHS is notified of the finding.

(2) If a false positive error occurs on a blind performance test sample submitted to an HHS-certified laboratory, the licensee or other entity shall notify the NRC within 24 hours after discovery of the error.

(3) If a false negative error occurs on a quality assurance check of validity screening tests, as required in § 26.137(b), the licensee or other entity shall notify the NRC within 24 hours after discovery of the error.

(d) *Indicators of programmatic weaknesses.* Licensees and other entities shall document, trend, and correct non-reportable indicators of FFD programmatic weaknesses under the licensee's or other entity's corrective action program, but may not track or trend drug and alcohol test results in a manner that would permit the identification of any individuals.

[73 FR 17176, Mar. 31, 2008, as amended at 75 FR 73942, Nov. 30, 2010]

Subpart O—Inspections, Violations, and Penalties

§ 26.821 Inspections.

(a) Each licensee and other entity who is subject to this part shall permit duly authorized NRC representatives to inspect, copy, or take away copies of its records and to inspect its premises, activities, and personnel as may be necessary to accomplish the purposes of this part.

(b) Written agreements between licensees or other entities and their C/Vs must clearly show that—

(1) The licensee or other entity is responsible to the NRC for maintaining an effective FFD program under this part; and

(2) Duly authorized NRC representatives may inspect, copy, or take away copies of any licensee's, other entity's, or C/V's documents, records, and reports related to implementation of the licensee's or other entity's FFD program under the scope of the contracted activities.

§ 26.823 Violations.

(a) An injunction or other court order may be obtained to prohibit a violation of any provision of—

(1) The Atomic Energy Act of 1954, as amended;

(2) Title II of the Energy Reorganization Act of 1974; or

(3) Any regulation or order issued under these Acts.

(b) A court order may be obtained for the payment of a civil penalty imposed under section 234 of the Atomic Energy Act of 1954, for violations of—

(1) Section 53, 57, 62, 63, 81, 82, 101, 103, 104, 107, or 109 of the Act;

(2) Section 206 of the Energy Reorganization Act of 1974;

(3) Any rule, regulation, or order issued under these sections;

(4) Any term, condition, or limitation of any license issued under these sections; or

(5) Any provisions for which a license may be revoked under section 186 of the Atomic Energy Act of 1954.

§ 26.825 Criminal penalties.

(a) Section 223 of the Atomic Energy Act of 1954, as amended, provides for criminal sanctions for willful violation of, attempted violation of, or conspiracy to violate, any regulation issued under sections 161b, 161i, or 161o of the Act. For the purposes of section 223, all of the regulations in Part 26 are issued under one or more of sections 161b, 161i, or 161o, except for the sections listed in paragraph (b) of this section.

(b) The regulations in Part 26 that are not issued under sections 161b, 161i, or 161o for the purposes of section 223 are as follows: §§ 26.1, 26.3, 26.5, 26.7, 26.8, 26.9, 26.11, 26.51, 26.81, 26.121, 26.151, 26.181, 26.201, 26.823, and 26.825.

PART 30—RULES OF GENERAL APPLICABILITY TO DOMESTIC LICENSING OF BYPRODUCT MATERIAL

GENERAL PROVISIONS

EXEMPTIONS

LICENSES

RECORDS, INSPECTIONS, TESTS, AND REPORTS

ENFORCEMENT

SCHEDULES

AUTHORITY: Atomic Energy Act of 1954, secs. 11, 81, 161, 181, 182, 183, 184, 186, 187, 223, 234, 274 (42 U.S.C. 2014, 2111, 2201, 2231, 2232, 2233, 2234, 2236, 2237, 2273, 2282, 2021); Energy Reorganization Act of 1974, secs. 201, 202, 206, 211 (42 U.S.C. 5841, 5842, 5846, 5851); 44 U.S.C. 3504 note.

EDITORIAL NOTE: Nomenclature changes to part 30 appear at 79 FR 75739, Dec. 19, 2014.

GENERAL PROVISIONS

§ 30.1 Scope.

This part prescribes rules applicable to all persons in the United States governing domestic licensing of byproduct material under the Atomic Energy Act of 1954, as amended (68 Stat. 919), and under title II of the Energy Reorganization Act of 1974 (88 Stat. 1242), and exemptions from the domestic licensing requirements permitted by Section 81 of the Act. This part also gives notice to all persons who knowingly provide to any licensee, applicant, certificate of registration holder, contractor, or subcontractor, components, equipment, materials, or other goods or services, that relate to a licensee's, applicant's or certificate of registration holder's activities subject to this part, that they may be individually subject to NRC enforcement action for violation of § 30.10.

[63 FR 1895, Jan. 13, 1998]

§ 30.2 Resolution of conflict.

The requirements of this part are in addition to, and not in substitution for, other requirements of this chapter. In any conflict between the requirements in this part and a specific requirement in another part of the regulations in this chapter, the specific requirement governs.

[30 FR 8185, June 26, 1965]

§ 30.3 Activities requiring license.

(a) Except as provided in paragraphs (b)(2), (b)(3), (c)(2), and (c)(3) of this section and for persons exempt as provided in this part and part 150 of this chapter, no person shall manufacture, produce, transfer, receive, acquire, own, possess, or use byproduct material except as authorized in a specific or general license issued in accordance with the regulations in this chapter.

(b)(1) The requirements, including provisions that are specific to licensees, in this part and parts 19, 20, 21, and 71 of this chapter, as well as the additional requirements for specific broad scope, industrial radiography, irradiator, or well logging uses in 10 CFR parts 33, 34, 36, or 39, respectively, shall apply to Government agencies or Federally recognized Indian Tribes on November 30, 2007, when conducting activities under the authority provided by paragraphs (b)(2) and (b)(3) of this section.

(2) A specifically licensed Government agency or Federally recognized Indian Tribe that possesses and uses accelerator-produced radioactive material or discrete sources of radium-226 for which a license amendment is required to authorize the activities in paragraph (a) of this section, may continue to use these materials for uses permitted under this part until the date of the NRC's final licensing determination, provided that the licensee submits an amendment application on or before June 2, 2008.

(3) A Government agency or Federally recognized Indian Tribe that possesses and uses accelerator-produced radioactive material or discrete sources of radium-226 for which a specific license is required in paragraph (a) of this section, may continue to use such material for uses permitted under this part until the date of the NRC's final licensing determination provided that the agency or Indian Tribe submits an application for a license authorizing activities involving these materials on or before December 1, 2008.

(c)(1) The requirements, including provisions that are specific to licensees in this part and parts 19, 20, 21, and 71 of this chapter, as well as the additional requirements for specific broad scope, industrial radiography, irradiator, or well logging uses in 10 CFR parts 33, 34, 36, or 39, respectively, shall apply to all persons, other than those included in paragraph (b)(1) of this section, on August 8, 2009, or earlier as noticed by the NRC, when conducting activities under the authority provided by paragraphs (c)(2) and (c)(3) of this section.

(2) Except as provided in paragraph (b)(2) of this section, all other licensees, who possess and use accelerator-produced radioactive material or discrete sources of radium-226 for which a license amendment is required to authorize the activities in paragraph (a) of this section, may continue to use these materials for uses permitted under this part until the date of the NRC's final licensing determination, provided that the person submits an amendment application within 6 months from the waiver expiration date of August 7, 2009 or within 6 months from the date of an earlier termination of the waiver as noticed by the NRC, whichever date is earlier.

(3) Except as provided in paragraph (b)(3) of this section, all other persons, who possess and use accelerator-produced radioactive material or discrete sources of radium-226 for which a specific license is required in paragraph (a) of this section, may continue to use such material for uses permitted under this part until the date of the NRC's final licensing determination, provided that the person submits a license application within 12 months from the waiver expiration date of August 7, 2009 or within 12 months from the date of an earlier termination of the waiver as noticed by the NRC, whichever date is earlier.

(d) If a person or licensee is required to file an application for a license or amendment in accordance with paragraphs (b)(2), (b)(3), (c)(2), and (c)(3) of this section, but does not file for the license or amendment within the required time, the authority provided by paragraphs (b)(2), (b)(3), (c)(2), and (c)(3) of this section to receive or use the accelerator-produced radioactive material or discrete sources of radium-226 shall expire with respect to the person's or licensee's authority to receive and use such byproduct material. This authority shall not expire with respect to the responsibility of the person or licensee regarding the possession of such byproduct material, the decommissioning (including financial assurance) of facilities, or the disposal of such byproduct material.

[72 FR 55924, Oct. 1, 2007]

§ 30.4 Definitions.

Accelerator-produced radioactive material means any material made radioactive by a particle accelerator.

Act means the Atomic Energy Act of 1954 (68 Stat. 919), including any amendments thereto;

Agreement State means any state with which the Atomic Energy Commission or the Nuclear Regulatory Commission has entered into an effective agreement under subsection 274b. of the Act. *Non-agreement State* means any other State;

Alert means events may occur, are in progress, or have occurred that could lead to a release of radioactive material but that the release is not expected to require a response by offsite response organizations to protect persons offsite.

Byproduct material means—

(1) Any radioactive material (except special nuclear material) yielded in, or made radioactive by, exposure to the radiation incident to the process of producing or using special nuclear material;

(2)(i) Any discrete source of radium-226 that is produced, extracted, or converted after extraction, before, on, or after August 8, 2005, for use for a commercial, medical, or research activity; or

(ii) Any material that—

(A) Has been made radioactive by use of a particle accelerator; and

(B) Is produced, extracted, or converted after extraction, before, on, or after August 8, 2005, for use for a commercial, medical, or research activity; and

(3) Any discrete source of naturally occurring radioactive material, other than source material, that—

(i) The Commission, in consultation with the Administrator of the Environmental Protection Agency, the Secretary of Energy, the Secretary of Homeland Security, and the head of any other appropriate Federal agency, determines would pose a threat similar to the threat posed by a discrete source of radium-226 to the public health and safety or the common defense and security; and

(ii) Before, on, or after August 8, 2005, is extracted or converted after extraction for use in a commercial, medical, or research activity.

Commencement of construction means taking any action defined as "construction" or any other activity at the site of a facility subject to the regulations in this part that has a reasonable nexus to:

(1) Radiological health and safety; or

(2) Common defense and security.

Commission means the Nuclear Regulatory Commission and its duly authorized representatives;

Consortium means an association of medical use licensees and a PET radionuclide production facility in the same geographical area that jointly own or share in the operation and maintenance cost of the PET radionuclide production facility that produces PET radionuclides for use in producing radioactive drugs within the consortium for noncommercial distributions among its associated members for medical use. The PET radionuclide production facility within the consortium must be located at an educational institution or a Federal facility or a medical facility.

Construction means the installation of foundations, or in-place assembly, erection, fabrication, or testing for any structure, system, or component of a facility or activity subject to the regulations in this part that are related to radiological safety or security. The term "construction" does not include:

(1) Changes for temporary use of the land for public recreational purposes;

(2) Site exploration, including necessary borings to determine foundation conditions or other preconstruction monitoring to establish background information related to the suitability of the site, the environmental impacts of construction or operation, or the protection of environmental values;

(3) Preparation of the site for construction of the facility, including clearing of the site, grading, installation of drainage, erosion and other environmental mitigation measures, and construction of temporary roads and borrow areas;

(4) Erection of fences and other access control measures that are not related to the safe use of, or security of, radiological materials subject to this part;

(5) Excavation;

(6) Erection of support buildings (e.g., construction equipment storage sheds, warehouse and shop facilities, utilities, concrete mixing plants, docking and unloading facilities, and office buildings) for use in connection with the construction of the facility;

(7) Building of service facilities (e.g., paved roads, parking lots, railroad spurs, exterior utility and lighting systems, potable water systems, sanitary sewerage treatment facilities, and transmission lines);

(8) Procurement or fabrication of components or portions of the proposed facility occurring at other than the final, in-place location at the facility; or

(9) Taking any other action that has no reasonable nexus to:

(i) Radiological health and safety, or

(ii) Common defense and security.

Curie means that amount of radioactive material which disintegrates at the rate of 37 billion atoms per second;

Cyclotron means a particle accelerator in which the charged particles travel in an outward spiral or circular path. A cyclotron accelerates charged particles at energies usually in excess of 10 megaelectron volts and is commonly used for production of short half-life radionuclides for medical use.

Decommission means to remove a facility or site safely from service and reduce residual radioactivity to a level that permits—

(1) Release of the property for unrestricted use and termination of the license; or

(2) Release of the property under restricted conditions and termination of the license.

Dentist means an individual licensed by a State or Territory of the United States, the District of Columbia, or the Commonwealth of Puerto Rico to practice dentistry.

Department and *Department of Energy* means the Department of Energy established by the Department of Energy Organization Act (Pub. L. 95–91, 91 Stat. 565, 42 U.S.C. 7101 *et seq.*) to the extent that the Department, or its duly authorized representatives, exercises functions formerly vested in the U.S. Atomic Energy Commission, its Chairman, members, officers and components and transferred to the U.S. Energy Research and Development Administration and to the Administrator thereof pursuant to sections 104 (b), (c) and (d) of the Energy Reorganization Act of 1974 (Pub. L. 93–438, 88 Stat. 1233 at 1237, 42 U.S.C. 5814) and retransferred to the Secretary of Energy pursuant to section 301(a) of the Department of Energy Organization Act (Pub. L. 95–91, 91 Stat. 565 at 577–578, 42 U.S.C. 7151).

Discrete source means a radionuclide that has been processed so that its concentration within a material has been purposely increased for use for commercial, medical, or research activities.

Effective dose equivalent means the sum of the products of the dose equivalent to the organ or tissue and the weighting factors applicable to each of the body organs or tissues that are irradiated. Weighting factors are: 0.25 for gonads, 0.15 for breast, 0.12 for red bone marrow, 0.12 for lungs, 0.03 for thyroid, 0.03 for bone surface, and 0.06 for each of the other five organs receiving the highest dose equivalent.

Government agency means any executive department, commission, independent establishment, corporation, wholly or partly owned by the United States of America which is an instrumentality of the United States, or any board, bureau, division, service, office, officer, authority, administration, or other establishment in the executive branch of the Government;

License, except where otherwise specified means a license for by-product material issued pursuant to the regulations in this part and parts 31 through 36 and 39 of this chapter;

Medical use means the intentional internal or external administration of byproduct material or the radiation therefrom to patients or human research subjects under the supervision of an authorized user as defined in 10 CFR part 35.

Microcurie means that amount of radioactive material which disintegrates at the rate of 37 thousand atoms per second;

Millicurie means that amount of radioactive material which disintegrates at the rate of 37 million atoms per second;

Particle accelerator means any machine capable of accelerating electrons, protons, deuterons, or other charged particles in a vacuum and of discharging the resultant particulate or other radiation into a medium at energies usually in excess of 1 megaelectron volt. For purposes of this definition, accelerator is an equivalent term.

Person means: (1) Any individual, corporation, partnership, firm, association, trust, estate, public or private institution, group, Government agency other than the Commission or the Department, except that the Department shall be considered a person within the meaning of the regulations in this part to the extent that its facilities and activities are subject to the licensing and related regulatory authority of the Commission pursuant to section 202 of the Energy Reorganization Act of 1974 (88 Stat. 1244), any State or any political subdivision of or any political entity within a State, any foreign government or nation or any political subdivision of any such government or nation, or other entity; and (2) any legal successor, representative, agent, or agency of the foregoing;

Physician means a medical doctor or doctor of osteopathy licensed by a State or Territory of the United States, the District of Columbia, or the Commonwealth of Puerto Rico to prescribe drugs in the practice of medicine;

Podiatrist means an individual licensed by a State or Territory of the United States, the District of Columbia, or the Commonwealth of Puerto Rico to practice podiatry.

Principal activities, as used in this part, means activities authorized by the license which are essential to achieving the purpose(s) for which the license was issued or amended. Storage during which no licensed material is accessed for use or disposal and activities incidental to decontamination or decommissioning are not principal activities.

Production facility means production facility as defined in the regulations contained in part 50 of this chapter;

Research and development means: (1) Theoretical analysis, exploration, or experimentation; or (2) the extension of investigative findings and theories of a scientific or technical nature into practical application for experimental and demonstration purposes, including the experimental production and testing of models, devices, equipment, materials and processes. "Research and development" as used in this part and parts 31 through 35 does not include the internal or external administration of byproduct material, or the radiation therefrom, to human beings;

Sealed source means any byproduct material that is encased in a capsule designed to prevent leakage or escape of the byproduct material;

Site area emergency means events may occur, are in progress, or have occurred that could lead to a significant release of radioactive material and that could require a response by offsite response organizations to protect persons offsite.

Source material means source material as defined in the regulations contained in part 40 of this chapter;

Special nuclear material means special nuclear material as defined in the regulations contained in part 70 of this chapter;

United States, when used in a geographical sense, includes Puerto Rico and all territories and possessions of the United States;

Utilization facility means a utilization facility as defined in the regulations contained in part 50 of this chapter;

[30 FR 8185, June 26, 1965]

EDITORIAL NOTE: For FEDERAL REGISTER citations affecting § 30.4, see the List of CFR Sections Affected, which appears in the Finding Aids section of the printed volume and at *www.fdsys.gov*.

§ 30.5 Interpretations.

Except as specifically authorized by the Commission in writing, no interpretation of the meaning of the regulations in this part and parts 31 through 36 and 39 by any officer or employee of the Commission other than a written interpretation by the General Counsel will be recognized to be binding upon the Commission.

[30 FR 8185, June 26, 1965, as amended at 43 FR 6921, Feb. 17, 1978; 52 FR 8241, Mar. 17, 1987; 58 FR 7736, Feb. 9, 1993]

§ 30.6 Communications.

(a) Unless otherwise specified or covered under the regional licensing program as provided in paragraph (b) of this section, any communication or report concerning the regulations in parts 30 through 37 and 39 of this chapter and any application filed under these regulations may be submitted to the Commission as follows:

(1) By mail addressed: ATTN: Document Control Desk, Director, Office of Nuclear Material Safety and Safeguards U.S. Nuclear Regulatory Commission, Washington, DC 20555–0001.

(2) By hand delivery to the NRC's offices at 11555 Rockville Pike, Rockville, Maryland.

(3) Where practicable, by electronic submission, for example, via Electronic Information Exchange, or CD-ROM. Electronic submissions must be made in a manner that enables the NRC to receive, read, authenticate, distribute, and archive the submission, and process and retrieve it a single page at a time. Detailed guidance on making electronic submissions can be obtained by visiting the NRC's Web site at *http://www.nrc.gov/site-help/e-submittals.html;* by e-mail to *MSHD.Resource@nrc.gov;* or by writing the Office of the Chief Information Officer, U.S. Nuclear Regulatory Commission, Washington, DC 20555–0001. The guidance discusses, among other topics, the formats the NRC can accept, the use of electronic signatures, and the treatment of nonpublic information.

(b) The Commission has delegated to the four Regional Administrators licensing authority for selected parts of its decentralized licensing program for nuclear materials as described in paragraph (b)(1) of this section. Any communication, report, or application covered under this licensing program must be submitted to the appropriate Regional Administrator. The Administrators' jurisdictions and mailing addresses are listed in paragraph (b)(2) of this section.

(1) The delegated licensing program includes authority to issue, renew, amend, cancel, modify, suspend, or revoke licenses for nuclear materials issued pursuant to 10 CFR parts 30 through 36, 39, 40, and 70 to all persons for academic, medical, and industrial uses, with the following exceptions:

(i) Activities in the fuel cycle and special nuclear material in quantities sufficient to constitute a critical mass in any room or area. This exception does not apply to license modifications relating to termination of special nuclear material licenses that authorize possession of larger quantities when the case is referred for action from NRC's Headquarters to the Regional Administrators.

(ii) Health and safety design review of sealed sources and devices and approval, for licensing purposes, of sealed sources and devices.

(iii) Processing of source material for extracting of metallic compounds (including Zirconium, Hafnium, Tantalum, Titanium, Niobium, etc.).

(iv) Distribution of products containing radioactive material under §§ 32.11 through 32.30 and 40.52 of this chapter to persons exempt from licensing requirements.

(v) New uses or techniques for use of byproducts, source, or special nuclear material.

(2) *Submissions.* (i) *Region I.* The regional licensing program involves all Federal facilities in the region and non-Federal licensees in the following Region I non-Agreement States and the District of Columbia: Connecticut, Delaware, and Vermont. All mailed or hand-delivered inquiries, communications, and applications for a new license or an amendment, renewal, or termination request of an existing license specified in paragraph (b)(1) of this section must use the following address: U.S. Nuclear Regulatory Commission, Region I, Nuclear Material Section B, Region I, 2100 Renaissance Boulevard, Suite 100, King of Prussia, PA 19406–2713; where email is appropriate it should be addressed to *RidsRgn1MailCenter.Resource@nrc.gov.*

(ii) *Region II.* The regional licensing program involves all Federal facilities in the region and non-Federal licensees in the following Region II non-Agreement States and territories: West Virginia, Puerto Rico, and the Virgin Islands. All mailed or hand-delivered inquiries, communications, and applications for a new license or an amendment, renewal, or termination request of an existing license specified in paragraph (b)(1) of this section must use the following address: U.S. Nuclear Regulatory Commission, Region I, Nuclear Material Section B, Region I, 2100 Renaissance Boulevard, Suite 100, King of Prussia, PA 19406–2713; where email is appropriate it should be addressed to *RidsRgn1MailCenter.Resource@nrc.gov.*

(iii) *Region III.* (A) The regional licensing program for mining and milling involves all Federal facilities in the region, and non-Federal licensees in the Region III non-Agreement States of Indiana, Michigan, Missouri and the Region III Agreement States of Minnesota, Wisconsin, and Iowa. All mailed or hand-delivered inquiries, communications, and applications for a new license or an amendment, renewal, or termination request of an existing license specified in paragraph (b)(1) of this section must use the following address: U.S. Nuclear Regulatory Commission, Region III, Material Licensing Section, 2443 Warrenville Road, Suite 210, Lisle, IL 60532–4352; where e-mail is appropriate it should be addressed to *RidsRgn3MailCenter.Resource@nrc.gov.*

(B) Otherwise, the regional licensing program involves all Federal facilities in the region and non-Federal licensees in the Region III non-Agreement States of Indiana, Michigan, and Missouri. All mailed or hand-delivered inquiries, communications, and applications for a new license or an amendment, renewal, or termination request of an existing license specified in paragraph (b)(1) of this section must use the following address: U.S. Nuclear Regulatory Commission, Region III, Material Licensing Section, 2443 Warrenville Road, Suite 210, Lisle, IL 60532–4352; where e-mail is appropriate it should be addressed to *RidsRgn3MailCenter.Resource@nrc.gov.*

(iv) *Region IV.* (A) The regional licensing program for mining and milling involves all Federal facilities in the region, and non-Federal licensees in the Region IV non-Agreement States and territory of Alaska, Hawaii, Idaho, Montana, South Dakota, Wyoming and Guam and Region IV Agreement States of Oregon, California, Nevada, New Mexico, Louisiana, Mississippi, Arkansas, Oklahoma, Kansas, Nebraska, and North Dakota. All mailed or hand-delivered inquiries, communications, and applications for a new license or an amendment, renewal, or termination request of an existing license specified in paragraph (b)(1) of this section must use the following address: U.S. Nuclear Regulatory Commission, Region IV, Division of Nuclear Materials Safety, 1600 E. Lamar Blvd., Arlington, TX 76011–4511; where email is appropriate, it should be addressed to *RidsRgn4MailCenter@nrc.gov.*

(B) Otherwise, the regional licensing program involves all Federal facilities in the region and non-Federal licensees in the following Region IV non-Agreement States and territory: Alaska, Hawaii, Idaho, Montana, South Dakota, Wyoming, and Guam. All mailed or hand-delivered inquiries, communications, and applications for a new license or an amendment, renewal, or termination request of an existing license specified in paragraph (b)(1) of this section must use the following address: U.S. Nuclear Regulatory Commission, Region IV, Division of Nuclear Materials Safety, 1600 E. Lamar Blvd., Arlington, TX 76011–4511; where email is appropriate, it should be addressed to *RidsRgn4MailCenter@nrc.gov.*

EDITORIAL NOTE: For FEDERAL REGISTER citations affecting § 30.6, see the List of CFR Sections Affected, which appears in the Finding Aids section of the printed volume and at *www.fdsys.gov.*

§ 30.7 Employee protection.

(a) Discrimination by a Commission licensee, an applicant for a Commission license, or a contractor or subcontractor of a Commission licensee or applicant against an employee for engaging in certain protected activities is prohibited. Discrimination includes discharge and other actions that relate to compensation, terms, conditions, or privileges of employment. The protected activities are established in section 211 of the Energy Reorganization Act of 1974, as amended, and in general are related to the administration or enforcement of a requirement imposed under the Atomic Energy Act or the Energy Reorganization Act.

(1) The protected activities include but are not limited to:

(i) Providing the Commission or his or her employer information about alleged violations of either of the statutes named in paragraph (a) introductory text of this section or possible violations of requirements imposed under either of those statutes;

(ii) Refusing to engage in any practice made unlawful under either of the statutes named in paragraph (a) introductory text or under these requirements if the employee has identified the alleged illegality to the employer;

(iii) Requesting the Commission to institute action against his or her employer for the administration or enforcement of these requirements;

(iv) Testifying in any Commission proceeding, or before Congress, or at any Federal or State proceeding regarding any provision (or proposed provision) of either of the statutes named in paragraph (a) introductory text.

(v) Assisting or participating in, or is about to assist or participate in, these activities.

(2) These activities are protected even if no formal proceeding is actually initiated as a result of the employee assistance or participation.

(3) This section has no application to any employee alleging discrimination prohibited by this section who, acting without direction from his or her employer (or the employer's agent), deliberately causes a violation of any requirement of the Energy Reorganization Act of 1974, as amended, or the Atomic Energy Act of 1954, as amended.

(b) Any employee who believes that he or she has been discharged or otherwise discriminated against by any person for engaging in protected activities specified in paragraph (a)(1) of this section may seek a remedy for the discharge or discrimination through an administrative proceeding in the Department of Labor. The administrative proceeding must be initiated within 180 days after an alleged violation occurs. The employee may do this by filing a complaint alleging the violation with the Department of Labor, Employment Standards Administration, Wage and Hour Division. The Department of Labor may order reinstatement, back pay, and compensatory damages.

(c) A violation of paragraphs (a), (e), or (f) of this section by a Commission licensee, an applicant for a Commission license, or a contractor or subcontractor of a Commission licensee or applicant may be grounds for—

(1) Denial, revocation, or suspension of the license.

(2) Imposition of a civil penalty on the licensee, applicant, or a contractor or subcontractor of the licensee or applicant.

(3) Other enforcement action.

(d) Actions taken by an employer, or others, which adversely affect an employee may be predicated upon nondiscriminatory grounds. The prohibition applies when the adverse action occurs because the employee has engaged in protected activities. An employee's engagement in protected activities does not automatically render him or her immune from discharge or discipline for legitimate reasons or from adverse action dictated by nonprohibited considerations.

(e)(1) Each specific licensee, each applicant for a specific license, and each general licensee subject to part 19 shall prominently post the revision of NRC Form 3, "Notice to Employees," referenced in 10 CFR 19.11(c).

(2) The posting of NRC Form 3 must be at locations sufficient to permit employees protected by this section to observe a copy on the way to or from their place of work. Premises must be posted not later than 30 days after an application is docketed and remain posted while the application is pending before the Commission, during the term of the license, and for 30 days following license termination.

(3) Copies of NRC Form 3 may be obtained by writing to the Regional Administrator of the appropriate U.S. Nuclear Regulatory Commission Regional Office listed in appendix D to part 20 of this chapter, via email to *Forms.Resource@nrc.gov*, or by visiting the NRC's online library at *http://www.nrc.gov/reading-rm/doc-collections/forms/*.

(f) No agreement affecting the compensation, terms, conditions, or privileges of employment, including an agreement to settle a complaint filed by an employee with the Department of Labor pursuant to section 211 of the Energy Reorganization Act of 1974, as amended, may contain any provision which would prohibit, restrict, or otherwise discourage an employee from participating in protected activity as defined in paragraph (a)(1) of this section including, but not limited to, providing information to the NRC or to his or her employer on potential violations or other matters within NRC's regulatory responsibilities.

[58 FR 52408, Oct. 8, 1993, as amended at 60 FR 24551, May 9, 1995; 61 FR 6764, Feb. 22, 1996; 68 FR 58803, Oct. 10, 2003; 72 FR 63973, Nov. 14, 2007; 73 FR 30458, May 28, 2008; 79 FR 66603, Nov. 10, 2014]

§ 30.8 Information collection requirements: OMB approval.

(a) The Nuclear Regulatory Commission has submitted the information collection requirements contained in this part to the Office of Management and Budget (OMB) for approval as required by the Paperwork Reduction Act (44 U.S.C. 3501 *et seq.*). The NRC may not conduct or sponsor, and a person is not required to respond to, a collection of information unless it displays a currently valid OMB control number. OMB has approved the information collection requirements contained in this part under control number 3150–0017.

(b) The approved information collection requirements contained in this part appear in §§ 30.9, 30.11, 30.15, 30.19, 30.20, 30.32, 30.34, 30.35, 30.36, 30.37, 30.38, 30.41, 30.50, 30.51, 30.55, and appendices A, C, D, and E to this part.

(c) This part contains information collection requirements in addition to those approved under the control number specified in paragraph (a) of this section. These information collection requirements and the control numbers under which they are approved are as follows:

(1) In §§ 30.32 and 30.37, NRC Form 313 is approved under control number 3150–0120.

(2) In § 30.36, NRC Form 314 is approved under control number 3150–0028.

(3) In § 30.34, DOC/NRC Forms AP–1, AP–A, and associated forms are approved under control number 0694–0135.

[49 FR 19625, May 9, 1984, as amended at 59 FR 61780, Dec. 2, 1994; 62 FR 52186, Oct. 6, 1997; 62 FR 63639, Dec. 2, 1997; 63 FR 29541, June 1, 1998; 67 FR 67099, Nov. 4, 2002; 73 FR 78604, Dec. 23, 2008; 77 FR 43689, July 25, 2012]

§ 30.9 Completeness and accuracy of information.

(a) Information provided to the Commission by an applicant for a license or by a licensee or information required by statute or by the Commission's regulations, orders, or license conditions to be maintained by the applicant or the licensee shall be complete and accurate in all material respects.

(b) Each applicant or licensee shall notify the Commission of information identified by the applicant or licensee as having for the regulated activity a significant implication for public health and safety or common defense and security. An applicant or licensee violates this paragraph only if the applicant or licensee fails to notify the Commission of information that the applicant or licensee has identified as having a significant implication for public health and safety or common defense and security. Notification shall be provided to the Administrator of the appropriate Regional Office within two working days of identifying the information. This requirement is not applicable to information which is already required to be provided to the Commission by other reporting or updating requirements.

[52 FR 49371, Dec. 31, 1987]

§ 30.10 Deliberate misconduct.

(a) Any licensee, certificate of registration holder, applicant for a license or certificate of registration, employee of a licensee, certificate of registration holder or applicant; or any contractor (including a supplier or consultant), subcontractor, employee of a contractor or subcontractor of any licensee or certificate of registration holder or applicant for a license or certificate of registration, who knowingly provides to any licensee, applicant, certificate holder, contractor, or subcontractor, any components, equipment, materials, or other goods or services that relate to a licensee's, certificate holder's or applicant's activities in this part, may not:

(1) Engage in deliberate misconduct that causes or would have caused, if not detected, a licensee, certificate of registration holder, or applicant to be in violation of any rule, regulation, or order; or any term, condition, or limitation of any license issued by the Commission; or

(2) Deliberately submit to the NRC, a licensee, certificate of registration holder, an applicant, or a licensee's, certificate holder's or applicant's, contractor or subcontractor, information that the person submitting the information knows to be incomplete or inaccurate in some respect material to the NRC.

(b) A person who violates paragraph (a)(1) or (a)(2) of this section may be subject to enforcement action in accordance with the procedures in 10 CFR part 2, subpart B.

(c) For the purposes of paragraph (a)(1) of this section, deliberate misconduct by a person means an intentional act or omission that the person knows:

(1) Would cause a licensee, certificate of registration holder or applicant to be in violation of any rule, regulation, or order; or any term, condition, or limitation, of any license issued by the Commission; or

(2) Constitutes a violation of a requirement, procedure, instruction, contract, purchase order, or policy of a licensee, certificate of registration holder, applicant, contractor, or subcontractor.

[63 FR 1896, Jan. 13, 1998]

EXEMPTIONS

§ 30.11 Specific exemptions.

(a) The Commission may, upon application of any interested person or upon its own initiative, grant such exemptions from the requirements of the regulations in this part and parts 31 through 36 and 39 of this chapter as it determines are authorized by law and will not endanger life or property or the common defense and security and are otherwise in the public interest.

(b) Any licensee's activities are exempt from the requirements of this part to the extent that its activities are licensed under the requirements of part 72 of this chapter.

(c) The Department of Energy is exempt from the requirements of this part to the extent that its activities are subject to the requirements of part 60 or 63 of this chapter.

(d) Except as specifically provided in part 61 of this chapter, any licensee is exempt from the requirements of this part to the extent that its activities are subject to the requirements of part 61 of this chapter.

[37 FR 5746, Mar. 21, 1972, as amended at 39 FR 26279, July 18, 1974; 40 FR 8784, Mar. 3, 1975; 43 FR 6921, Feb. 21, 1978; 45 FR 65530, Oct. 3, 1980; 46 FR 13979, Feb. 25, 1981; 47 FR 57480, Dec. 27, 1982; 52 FR 8241, Mar. 17, 1987; 58 FR 7736, Feb. 9, 1993; 66 FR 51838, Oct. 11, 2001; 66 FR 55790, Nov. 2, 2001]

§30.12 Persons using byproduct material under certain Department of Energy and Nuclear Regulatory Commission contracts.

Except to the extent that Department facilities or activities of the types subject to licensing pursuant to section 202 of the Energy Reorganization Act of 1974 are involved, any prime contractor of the Department is exempt from the requirements for a license set forth in sections 81 and 82 of the Act and from the regulations in this part to the extent that such contractor, under his prime contract with the Department manufactures, produces, transfers, receives, acquires, owns, possesses, or uses byproduct material for:

(a) The performance of work for the Department at a United States Government-owned or controlled site, including the transportation of byproduct material to or from such site and the performance of contract services during temporary interruptions of such transportation;

(b) Research in, or development, manufacture, storage, testing or transportation of, atomic weapons or components thereof; or

(c) The use or operation of nuclear reactors or other nuclear devices in a United States Government-owned vehicle or vessel.

In addition to the foregoing exemptions and subject to the requirement for licensing of Department facilities and activities pursuant to section 202 of the Energy Reorganization Act of 1974, any prime contractor or subcontractor of the Department or the Commission is exempt from the requirements for a license set forth in sections 81 and 82 of the Act and from the regulations in this part to the extent that such prime contractor or subcontractor manufacturers, produces, transfers, receives, acquires, owns, possesses, or uses byproduct material under his prime contract or subcontract when the Commission determines that the exemption of the prime contractor or subcontractor is authorized by law; and that, under the terms of the contract or subcontract, there is adequate assurance that the work thereunder can be accomplished without undue risk to the public health and safety.

[40 FR 8784, Mar. 3, 1975, as amended at 43 FR 6921, Feb. 17, 1978]

§30.13 Carriers.

Common and contract carriers, freight forwarders, warehousemen, and the U.S. Postal Service are exempt from the regulations in this part and parts 31 through 37 and 39 of this chapter and the requirements for a license set forth in section 81 of the Act to the extent that they transport or store byproduct material in the regular course of carriage for another or storage incident thereto.

[78 FR 17006, Mar. 19, 2013]

§30.14 Exempt concentrations.

(a) Except as provided in paragraphs (c) and (d) of this section, any person is exempt from the requirements for a license set forth in section 81 of the Act and from the regulations in this part and parts 31 through 36 and 39 of this chapter to the extent that such person receives, possesses, uses, transfers, owns or acquires products or materials containing byproduct material in concentrations not in excess of those listed in §30.70.

(b) This section shall not be deemed to authorize the import of byproduct material or products containing byproduct material.

(c) A manufacturer, processor, or producer of a product or material is exempt from the requirements for a license set forth in section 81 of the Act and from the regulations in this part and parts 31 through 36 and 39 of this chapter to the extent that this person transfers byproduct material contained in a product or material in concentrations not in excess of those specified in § 30.70 and introduced into the product or material by a licensee holding a specific license issued by the Commission expressly authorizing such introduction. This exemption does not apply to the transfer of byproduct material contained in any food, beverage, cosmetic, drug, or other commodity or product designed for ingestion or inhalation by, or application to, a human being.

(d) No person may introduce byproduct material into a product or material knowing or having reason to believe that it will be transferred to persons exempt under this section or equivalent regulations of an Agreement State, except in accordance with a license issued under § 32.11 of this chapter.

[30 FR 8185, June 26, 1965, as amended at 40 FR 8785, Mar. 3, 1975; 43 FR 6921, Feb. 17, 1978; 52 FR 8241, Mar. 17, 1987; 58 FR 7736, Feb. 9, 1993; 72 FR 58486, Oct. 16, 2007]

§ 30.15 Certain items containing byproduct material.

(a) Except for persons who apply byproduct material to, or persons who incorporate byproduct material into, the following products, or persons who initially transfer for sale or distribution the following products containing byproduct material, any person is exempt from the requirements for a license set forth in section 81 of the Act and from the regulations in parts 20 and 30 through 36 and 39 of this chapter to the extent that such person receives, possesses, uses, transfers, owns, or acquires the following products:

(1) Timepieces or hands or dials containing not more than the following specified quantities of byproduct material and not exceeding the following specified levels of radiation:

(i) 25 millicuries of tritium per timepiece,

(ii) 5 millicuries of tritium per hand,

(iii) 15 millicuries of tritium per dial (bezels when used shall be considered as part of the dial),

(iv) 100 microcuries of promethium 147 per watch or 200 microcuries of promethium 147 per any other timepiece,

(v) 20 microcuries of promethium 147 per watch hand or 40 microcuries of promethium 147 per other timepiece hand,

(vi) 60 microcuries of promethium 147 per watch dial or 120 microcuries of promethium 147 per other timepiece dial (bezels when used shall be considered as part of the dial),

(vii) The levels of radiation from hands and dials containing promethium 147 will not exceed, when measured through 50 milligrams per square centimeter of absorber:

(A) For wrist watches, 0.1 millirad per hour at 10 centimeters from any surface,

(B) For pocket watches, 0.1 millirad per hour at 1 centimeter from any surface,

(C) For any other timepiece, 0.2 millirad per hour at 10 centimeters from any surface.

(viii) 0.037 megabecquerel (1 microcurie) of radium-226 per timepiece in intact timepieces manufactured prior to November 30, 2007.

(2)(i) Static elimination devices which contain, as a sealed source or sources, byproduct material consisting of a total of not more than 18.5 MBq (500 μCi) of polonium-210 per device.

(ii) Ion generating tubes designed for ionization of air that contain, as a sealed source or sources, byproduct material consisting of a total of not more than 18.5 MBq (500 μCi) of polonium-210 per device or of a total of not more than 1.85 GBq (50 mCi) of hydrogen-3 (tritium) per device.

(iii) Such devices authorized before October 23, 2012 for use under the general license then provided in § 31.3 and equivalent regulations of Agreement States and manufactured, tested, and labeled by the manufacturer in accordance with the specifications contained in a specific license issued by the Commission.

(3) Balances of precision containing not more than 1 millicurie of tritium

per balance or not more than 0.5 millicurie of tritium per balance part manufactured before December 17, 2007.

(4) [Reserved]

(5) Marine compasses containing not more than 750 millicuries of tritium gas and other marine navigational instruments containing not more than 250 millicuries of tritium gas manufactured before December 17, 2007.

(6) [Reserved]

(7) Ionization chamber smoke detectors containing not more than 1 microcurie (μCi) of americium-241 per detector in the form of a foil and designed to protect life and property from fires.

(8) Electron tubes: *Provided*, That each tube does not contain more than one of the following specified quantities of byproduct material:

(i) 150 millicuries of tritium per microwave receiver protector tube or 10 millicuries of tritium per any other electron tube;

(ii) 1 microcurie of cobalt-60;

(iii) 5 microcuries of nickel-63;

(iv) 30 microcuries of krypton-85;

(v) 5 microcuries of cesium-137;

(vi) 30 microcuries of promethium-147;

And provided further, That the levels of radiation from each electron tube containing byproduct material do not exceed 1 millirad per hour at 1 centimeter from any surface when measured through 7 milligrams per square centimeter of absorber.[1]

(9) Ionizing radiation measuring instruments containing, for purposes of internal calibration or standardization, one or more sources of byproduct material: *Provided*, That;

(i) Each source contains no more than one exempt quantity set forth in § 30.71, Schedule B, and

(ii) Each instrument contains no more than 10 exempt quantities. For purposes of this paragraph (a)(9), an instrument's source(s) may contain either one type or different types of radionuclides and an individual exempt quantity may be composed of fractional parts of one or more of the exempt quantities in § 30.71, Schedule B, provided that the sum of such fractions shall not exceed unity.

(iii) For purposes of this paragraph (a)(9), 0.05 microcurie of americium-241 is considered an exempt quantity under § 30.71, Schedule B.

(10) [Reserved]

(b) Any person who desires to apply byproduct material to, or to incorporate byproduct material into, the products exempted in paragraph (a) of this section, or who desires to initially transfer for sale or distribution such products containing byproduct material, should apply for a specific license pursuant to § 32.14 of this chapter, which license states that the product may be distributed by the licensee to persons exempt from the regulations pursuant to paragraph (a) of this section.

[31 FR 5316, Apr. 2, 1966]

EDITORIAL NOTE: For FEDERAL REGISTER citations affecting § 30.15, see the List of CFR Sections Affected, which appears in the Finding Aids section of the printed volume and at *www.fdsys.gov*.

§ 30.18 Exempt quantities.

(a) Except as provided in paragraphs (c) through (e) of this section, any person is exempt from the requirements for a license set forth in section 81 of the Act and from the regulations in parts 30 through 34, 36, and 39 of this chapter to the extent that such person receives, possesses, uses, transfers, owns, or acquires byproduct material in individual quantities, each of which does not exceed the applicable quantity set forth in § 30.71, Schedule B.

(b) Any person, who possesses byproduct material received or acquired before September 25, 1971, under the general license then provided in § 31.4 of this chapter or similar general license of a State, is exempt from the requirements for a license set forth in section 81 of the Act and from the regulations in parts 30 through 34, 36 and 39 of this chapter to the extent that this person possesses, uses, transfers, or owns byproduct material.

[1] For purposes of this paragraph "electron tubes" include spark gap tubes, power tubes, gas tubes including glow lamps, receiving tubes, microwave tubes, indicator tubes, pickup tubes, radiation detection tubes, and any other completely sealed tube that is designed to conduct or control electrical currents.

(c) This section does not authorize for purposes of commercial distribution the production, packaging, repackaging, or transfer of byproduct material or the incorporation of byproduct material into products intended for commercial distribution.

(d) No person may, for purposes of commercial distribution, transfer byproduct material in the individual quantities set forth in § 30.71 Schedule B, knowing or having reason to believe that such quantities of byproduct material will be transferred to persons exempt under this section or equivalent regulations of an Agreement State, except in accordance with a license issued under § 32.18 of this chapter, which license states that the byproduct material may be transferred by the licensee to persons exempt under this section or the equivalent regulations of an Agreement State.

(e) No person may, for purposes of producing an increased radiation level, combine quantities of byproduct material covered by this exemption so that the aggregate quantity exceeds the limits set forth in § 30.71, Schedule B, except for byproduct material combined within a device placed in use before May 3, 1999, or as otherwise permitted by the regulations in this part.

[35 FR 6427, Apr. 22, 1970, as amended at 36 FR 16898, Aug. 26, 1971; 43 FR 6921, Feb. 17, 1978; 52 FR 8241, Mar. 17, 1987; 58 FR 7736, Feb. 9, 1993; 72 FR 55925, Oct. 1, 2007; 72 FR 58486, Oct. 16, 2007]

§ 30.19 Self-luminous products containing tritium, krypton-85, or promethium-147.

(a) Except for persons who manufacture, process, produce, or initially transfer for sale or distribution self-luminous products containing tritium, krypton-85, or promethium-147, and except as provided in paragraph (c) of this section, any person is exempt from the requirements for a license set forth in section 81 of the Act and from the regulations in parts 20 and 30 through 36 and 39 of this chapter to the extent that such person receives, possesses, uses, transfers, owns, or acquires tritium, krypton-85, or promethium-147 in self-luminous products manufactured, processed, produced, or initially transferred in accordance with a specific license issued pursuant to § 32.22 of this chapter, which license authorizes the initial transfer of the product for use under this section.

(b) Any person who desires to manufacture, process, or produce, or initially transfer for sale or distribution self-luminous products containing tritium, krypton-85, or promethium-147 for use under paragraph (a) of this section, should apply for a license under § 32.22 of this chapter and for a certificate of registration in accordance with § 32.210 of this chapter.

(c) The exemption in paragraph (a) of this section does not apply to tritium, krypton-85, or promethium-147 used in products primarily for frivolous purposes or in toys or adornments.

[34 FR 9026, June 6, 1969, as amended at 40 FR 8785, Mar. 3, 1975; 43 FR 6921, Feb. 17, 1978; 52 FR 8241, Mar. 17, 1987; 58 FR 7736, Feb. 9, 1993; 77 FR 43689, July 25, 2012]

§ 30.20 Gas and aerosol detectors containing byproduct material.

(a) Except for persons who manufacture, process, produce, or initially transfer for sale or distribution gas and aerosol detectors containing byproduct material, any person is exempt from the requirements for a license set forth in section 81 of the Act and from the regulations in parts 19, 20, 21, and 30 through 36 and 39 of this chapter to the extent that such person receives, possesses, uses, transfers, owns, or acquires byproduct material in gas and aerosol detectors designed to protect health, safety, or property, and manufactured, processed, produced, or initially transferred in accordance with a specific license issued under § 32.26 of this chapter, which license authorizes the initial transfer of the product for use under this section. This exemption also covers gas and aerosol detectors manufactured or distributed before November 30, 2007, in accordance with a specific license issued by a State under comparable provisions to § 32.26 of this chapter authorizing distribution to persons exempt from regulatory requirements.

(b) Any person who desires to manufacture, process, or produce gas and aerosol detectors containing byproduct material, or to initially transfer such products for use under paragraph (a) of this section, should apply for a license under § 32.26 of this chapter and for a certificate of registration in accordance with § 32.210 of this chapter.

[77 FR 43689, July 25, 2012]

§ 30.21 Radioactive drug: Capsules containing carbon-14 urea for "in vivo" diagnostic use for humans.

(a) Except as provided in paragraphs (b) and (c) of this section, any person is exempt from the requirements for a license set forth in Section 81 of the Act and from the regulations in this part and part 35 of this chapter provided that such person receives, possesses, uses, transfers, owns, or acquires capsules containing 37 kBq (1 μCi) carbon-14 urea (allowing for nominal variation that may occur during the manufacturing process) each, for "in vivo" diagnostic use for humans.

(b) Any person who desires to use the capsules for research involving human subjects shall apply for and receive a specific license pursuant to part 35 of this chapter.

(c) Any person who desires to manufacture, prepare, process, produce, package, repackage, or transfer for commercial distribution such capsules shall apply for and receive a specific license pursuant to § 32.21 of this chapter.

(d) Nothing in this section relieves persons from complying with applicable FDA, other Federal, and State requirements governing receipt, administration, and use of drugs.

[62 FR 63640, Dec. 2, 1997]

§ 30.22 Certain industrial devices.

(a) Except for persons who manufacture, process, produce, or initially transfer for sale or distribution industrial devices containing byproduct material designed and manufactured for the purpose of detecting, measuring, gauging or controlling thickness, density, level, interface location, radiation, leakage, or qualitative or quantitative chemical composition, or for producing an ionized atmosphere, any person is exempt from the requirements for a license set forth in section 81 of the Act and from the regulations in parts 19, 20, 21, 30 through 36, and 39 of this chapter to the extent that such person receives, possesses, uses, transfers, owns, or acquires byproduct material, in these certain detecting, measuring, gauging, or controlling devices and certain devices for producing an ionized atmosphere, and manufactured, processed, produced, or initially transferred in accordance with a specific license issued under § 32.30 of this chapter, which license authorizes the initial transfer of the device for use under this section. This exemption does not cover sources not incorporated into a device, such as calibration and reference sources.

(b) Any person who desires to manufacture, process, produce, or initially transfer for sale or distribution industrial devices containing byproduct material for use under paragraph (a) of this section, should apply for a license under § 32.30 of this chapter and for a certificate of registration in accordance with § 32.210 of this chapter.

[77 FR 43689, July 25, 2012]

LICENSES

§ 30.31 Types of licenses.

Licenses for byproduct material are of two types: General and specific.

(a) The Commission issues a specific license to a named person who has filed an application for the license under the provisions of this part and parts 32 through 36, and 39.

(b) A general license is provided by regulation, grants authority to a person for certain activities involving byproduct material, and is effective without the filing of an application with the Commission or the issuance of a licensing document to a particular person. However, registration with the Commission may be required by the particular general license.

[65 FR 79187, Dec. 18, 2000]

§ 30.32 Application for specific licenses.

(a) A person may file an application on NRC Form 313, "Application for Material License," in accordance with the instructions in § 30.6 of this chapter. Information contained in previous applications, statements or reports filed with the Commission or the Atomic

Energy Commission may be incorporated by reference, provided that the reference is clear and specific.

(b) The Commission may at any time after the filing of the original application, and before the expiration of the license, require further statements in order to enable the Commission to determine whether the application should be granted or denied or whether a license should be modified or revoked.

(c) Each application shall be signed by the applicant or licensee or a person duly authorized to act for and on his behalf.

(d) An application for license filed pursuant to the regulations in this part and parts 32 through 35 of this chapter will be considered also as an application for licenses authorizing other activities for which licenses are required by the Act, provided that the application specifies the additional activities for which licenses are requested and complies with regulations of the Commission as to applications for such licenses.

(e) Each application for a byproduct material license, other than a license exempted from part 170 of this chapter, shall be accompanied by the fee prescribed in § 170.31 of this chapter. No fee will be required to accompany an application for renewal or amendment of a license, except as provided in § 170.31 of this chapter.

(f) An application for a license to receive and possess byproduct material for the conduct of any activity which the Commission has determined pursuant to subpart A of part 51 of this chapter will significantly affect the quality of the environment shall be filed at least 9 months prior to commencement of construction of the plant or facility in which the activity will be conducted and shall be accompanied by any Environmental Report required pursuant to subpart A of part 51 of this chapter.

(g)(1) Except as provided in paragraphs (g)(2), (3), and (4) of this section, an application for a specific license to use byproduct material in the form of a sealed source or in a device that contains the sealed source must either—

(i) Identify the source or device by manufacturer and model number as registered with the Commission under § 32.210 of this chapter, with an Agreement State, or for a source or a device containing radium-226 or accelerator-produced radioactive material with a State under provisions comparable to § 32.210 of this chapter; or

(ii) Contain the information identified in § 32.210(c) of this chapter.

(2) For sources or devices manufactured before October 23, 2012 that are not registered with the Commission under § 32.210 of this chapter or with an Agreement State, and for which the applicant is unable to provide all categories of information specified in § 32.210(c) of this chapter, the application must include:

(i) All available information identified in § 32.210(c) of this chapter concerning the source, and, if applicable, the device; and

(ii) Sufficient additional information to demonstrate that there is reasonable assurance that the radiation safety properties of the source or device are adequate to protect health and minimize danger to life and property. Such information must include a description of the source or device, a description of radiation safety features, the intended use and associated operating experience, and the results of a recent leak test.

(3) For sealed sources and devices allowed to be distributed without registration of safety information in accordance with § 32.210(g)(1) of this chapter, the applicant may supply only the manufacturer, model number, and radionuclide and quantity.

(4) If it is not feasible to identify each sealed source and device individually, the applicant may propose constraints on the number and type of sealed sources and devices to be used and the conditions under which they will be used, in lieu of identifying each sealed source and device.

(h) As provided by § 30.35, certain applications for specific licenses filed under this part and parts 32 through 35 of this chapter must contain a proposed decommissioning funding plan or a certification of financial assurance for decommissioning. In the case of renewal applications submitted before July 27, 1990, this submittal may follow the renewal application but must be submitted on or before July 27, 1990.

(i)(1) Each application to possess radioactive materials in unsealed form, on foils or plated sources, or sealed in glass in excess of the quantities in § 30.72, "Schedule C—Quantities of Radioactive Materials Requiring Consideration of the Need for an Emergency Plan for Responding to a Release," must contain either:

(i) An evaluation showing that the maximum dose to a person offsite due to a release of radioactive materials would not exceed 1 rem effective dose equivalent or 5 rems to the thyroid; or

(ii) An emergency plan for responding to a release of radioactive material.

(2) One or more of the following factors may be used to support an evaluation submitted under paragraph (i)(1)(i) of this section:

(i) The radioactive material is physically separated so that only a portion could be involved in an accident;

(ii) All or part of the radioactive material is not subject to release during an accident because of the way it is stored or packaged;

(iii) The release fraction in the respirable size range would be lower than the release fraction shown § 30.72 due to the chemical or physical form of the material;

(iv) The solubility of the radioactive material would reduce the dose received;

(v) Facility design or engineered safety features in the facility would cause the release fraction to be lower than shown in § 30.72;

(vi) Operating restrictions or procedures would prevent a release fraction as large as that shown in § 30.72; or

(vii) Other factors appropriate for the specific facility.

(3) An emergency plan for responding to a release of radioactive material submitted under paragraph (i)(1)(ii) of this section must include the following information:

(i) *Facility description.* A brief description of the licensee's facility and area near the site.

(ii) *Types of accidents.* An identification of each type of radio-active materials accident for which protective actions may be needed.

(iii) *Classification of accidents.* A classification system for classifying accidents as alerts or site area emergencies.

(iv) *Detection of accidents.* Identification of the means of detecting each type of accident in a timely manner.

(v) *Mitigation of consequences.* A brief description of the means and equipment for mitigating the consequences of each type of accident, including those provided to protect workers onsite, and a description of the program for maintaining the equipment.

(vi) *Assessment of releases.* A brief description of the methods and equipment to assess releases of radioactive materials.

(vii) *Responsibilities.* A brief description of the responsibilities of licensee personnel should an accident occur, including identification of personnel responsible for promptly notifying offsite response organizations and the NRC; also responsibilities for developing, maintaining, and updating the plan.

(viii) *Notification and coordination.* A commitment to and a brief description of the means to promptly notify offsite response organizations and request offsite assistance, including medical assistance for the treatment of contaminated injured onsite workers when appropriate. A control point must be established. The notification and coordination must be planned so that unavailability of some personnel, parts of the facility, and some equipment will not prevent the notification and coordination. The licensee shall also commit to notify the NRC operations center immediately after notification of the appropriate offsite response organizations and not later than one hour after the licensee declares an emergency.[1]

(ix) *Information to be communicated.* A brief description of the types of information on facility status, radioactive releases, and recommended protective actions, if necessary, to be given to offsite response organizations and to the NRC.

(x) *Training.* A brief description of the frequency, performance objectives

[1] These reporting requirements do not superceed or release licensees of complying with the requirements under the Emergency Planning and Community Right-to-Know Act of 1986, Title III, Pub. L. 99–499 or other state or federal reporting requirements.

and plans for the training that the licensee will provide workers on how to respond to an emergency including any special instructions and orientation tours the licensee would offer to fire, police, medical and other emergency personnel. The training shall familiarize personnel with site-specific emergency procedures. Also, the training shall thoroughly prepare site personnel for their responsibilities in the event of accident scenarios postulated as most probable for the specific site, including the use of team training for such scenarios.

(xi) *Safe shutdown.* A brief description of the means of restoring the facility to a safe condition after an accident.

(xii) *Exercises.* Provisions for conducting quarterly communications checks with offsite response organizations and biennial onsite exercises to test response to simulated emergencies. Quarterly communications checks with offsite response organizations must include the check and update of all necessary telephone numbers. The licensee shall invite offsite response organizations to participate in the biennial exercises. Participation of offsite response organizations in biennial exercises although recommended is not required. Exercises must use accident scenarios postulated as most probable for the specific site and the scenarios shall not be known to most exercise participants. The licensee shall critique each exercise using individuals not having direct implementation responsibility for the plan. Critiques of exercises must evaluate the appropriateness of the plan, emergency procedures, facilities, equipment, training of personnel, and overall effectiveness of the response. Deficiencies found by the critiques must be corrected.

(xiii) *Hazardous chemicals.* A certification that the applicant has met its responsibilities under the Emergency Planning and Community Right-to-Know Act of 1986, title III, Pub. L. 99–499, if applicable to the applicant's activities at the proposed place of use of the byproduct material.

(4) The licensee shall allow the offsite response organizations expected to respond in case of an accident 60 days to comment on the licensee's emergency plan before submitting it to NRC. The licensee shall provide any comments received within the 60 days to the NRC with the emergency plan.

(j) An application from a medical facility, educational institution, or Federal facility to produce Positron Emission Tomography (PET) radioactive drugs for noncommercial transfer to licensees in its consortium authorized for medical use under part 35 of this chapter or equivalent Agreement State requirements shall include:

(1) A request for authorization for the production of PET radionuclides or evidence of an existing license issued under part 30 of this chapter or Agreement State requirements for a PET radionuclide production facility within its consortium from which it receives PET radionuclides.

(2) Evidence that the applicant is qualified to produce radioactive drugs for medical use by meeting one of the criteria in § 32.72(a)(2) of this chapter.

(3) Identification of individual(s) authorized to prepare the PET radioactive drugs if the applicant is a pharmacy, and documentation that each individual meets the requirements of an authorized nuclear pharmacist as specified in § 32.72(b)(2) of this chapter.

(4) Information identified in § 32.72(a)(3) of this chapter on the PET drugs to be noncommercially transferred to members of its consortium.

[30 FR 8185, June 26, 1965, as amended at 36 FR 145, Jan. 6, 1971; 37 FR 5747, Mar. 21, 1972; 43 FR 6922, Feb. 17, 1978; 49 FR 9403, Mar. 12, 1984; 49 FR 27924, July 9, 1984; 52 FR 27786, July 24, 1987; 53 FR 24044, June 27, 1988; 54 FR 14060, Apr. 7, 1989; 68 FR 58004, Oct. 10, 2003; 72 FR 55925, Oct. 1, 2007; 73 FR 63570, Oct. 24, 2008; 77 FR 43689, July 25, 2012; 79 FR 58671, Sept. 30, 2014]

§ 30.33 General requirements for issuance of specific licenses.

(a) An application for a specific license will be approved if:

(1) The application is for a purpose authorized by the Act;

(2) The applicant's proposed equipment and facilities are adequate to protect health and minimize danger to life or property;

(3) The applicant is qualified by training and experience to use the material for the purpose requested in such

manner as to protect health and minimize danger to life or property;

(4) The applicant satisfies any special requirements contained in parts 32 through 37 and 39 of this chapter; and

(5) In the case of an application for a license to receive and possess byproduct material for the conduct of any activity which the NRC determines will significantly affect the quality of the environment, the Director, Office of Nuclear Material Safety and Safeguards or his/her designee, before commencement of construction of the plant or facility in which the activity will be conducted, on the basis of information filed and evaluations made pursuant to subpart A of part 51 of this chapter, has concluded, after weighing the environmental, economic, technical, and other benefits against environmental costs and considering available alternatives, that the action called for is the issuance of the proposed license, with any appropriate conditions to protect environmental values. Commencement of construction prior to such conclusion shall be grounds for denial of a license to receive and possess byproduct material in such plant or facility. Commencement of construction as defined in § 30.4 may include non-construction activities if the activity has a reasonable nexus to radiological safety and security.

(b) Upon a determination that an application meets the requirements of the Act, and the regulations of the Commission, the Commission will issue a specific license authorizing the possession and use of byproduct material (Form NRC 374, "Byproduct Material License").

[30 FR 8185, June 26, 1965, as amended at 36 FR 12731, July 7, 1971; 37 FR 5747, Mar. 21, 1972; 39 FR 26279, July 18, 1974; 43 FR 6922, Feb. 17, 1978; 49 FR 9403, Mar. 12, 1984; 52 FR 8241, Mar. 17, 1987; 58 FR 7736, Feb. 9, 1993; 73 FR 5717, Jan. 31, 2008; 76 FR 56962, Sept. 15, 2011; 78 FR 17006, Mar. 19, 2013]

§ 30.34 Terms and conditions of licenses.

(a) Each license issued pursuant to the regulations in this part and the regulations in parts 31 through 36 and 39 of this chapter shall be subject to all the provisions of the Act, now or hereafter in effect, and to all valid rules, regulations and orders of the Commission.

(b)(1) No license issued or granted pursuant to the regulations in this part and parts 31 through 36, and 39 nor any right under a license shall be transferred, assigned or in any manner disposed of, either voluntarily or involuntarily, directly or indirectly, through transfer of control of any license to any person, unless the Commission shall, after securing full information, find that the transfer is in accordance with the provisions of the Act and shall give its consent in writing.

(2) An application for transfer of license must include:

(i) The identity, technical and financial qualifications of the proposed transferee; and

(ii) Financial assurance for decommissioning information required by § 30.35.

(c) Each person licensed by the Commission pursuant to the regulations in this part and parts 31 through 36 and 39 shall confine his possession and use of the byproduct material to the locations and purposes authorized in the license. Except as otherwise provided in the license, a license issued pursuant to the regulations in this part and parts 31 through 36 and 39 of this chapter shall carry with it the right to receive, acquire, own, and possess byproduct material. Preparation for shipment and transport of byproduct material shall be in accordance with the provisions of part 71 of this chapter.

(d) Each license issued pursuant to the regulations in this part and parts 31 through 36 and 39 shall be deemed to contain the provisions set forth in section 183b.–d., inclusive, of the Act, whether or not these provisions are expressly set forth in the license.

(e) The Commission may incorporate, in any license issued pursuant to the regulations in this part and parts 31 through 36 and 39, at the time of issuance, or thereafter by appropriate rule, regulation or order, such additional requirements and conditions with respect to the licensee's receipt, possession, use and transfer of byproduct material as it deems appropriate or necessary in order to:

(1) Promote the common defense and security;

(2) Protect health or to minimize danger to life or property;

(3) Protect restricted data;

(4) Require such reports and the keeping of such records, and to provide for such inspections of activities under the license as may be necessary or appropriate to effectuate the purposes of the Act and regulations thereunder.

(f) Licensees required to submit emergency plans by § 30.32(i) shall follow the emergency plan approved by the Commission. The licensee may change the approved without Commission approval only if the changes do not decrease the effectiveness of the plan. The licensee shall furnish the change to the appropriate NRC Regional Office specified in § 30.6 and to affected offsite response organizations within six months after the change is made. Proposed changes that decrease, or potentially decrease, the effectiveness of the approved emergency plan may not be implemented without prior application to and prior approval by the Commission.

(g) Each licensee preparing technetium-99m radiopharmaceuticals from molybdenum-99/technetium-99m generators or rubidium-82 from strontium-82/rubidium-82 generators shall test the generator eluates for molybdenum-99 breakthrough or strontium-82 and strontium-85 contamination, respectively, in accordance with § 35.204 of this chapter. The licensee shall record the results of each test and retain each record for 3 years after the record is made.

(h)(1) Each general licensee that is required to register by § 31.5(c)(13) of this chapter and each specific licensee shall notify the appropriate NRC Regional Administrator, in writing, immediately following the filing of a voluntary or involuntary petition for bankruptcy under any chapter of title 11 (Bankruptcy) of the United States Code by or against:

(i) The licensee;

(ii) An entity (as that term is defined in 11 U.S.C. 101(15) controlling the licensee or listing the license or licensee as property of the estate; or

(iii) An affiliate (as that term is defined in 11 U.S.C. 101(2)) of the licensee.

(2) This notification must indicate:

(i) The bankruptcy court in which the petition for bankruptcy was filed; and

(ii) The date of the filing of the petition.

(i) *Security requirements for portable gauges.* Each portable gauge licensee shall use a minimum of two independent physical controls that form tangible barriers to secure portable gauges from unauthorized removal, whenever portable gauges are not under the control and constant surveillance of the licensee.

(j)(1) Authorization under § 30.32(j) to produce Positron Emission Tomography (PET) radioactive drugs for noncommercial transfer to medical use licensees in its consortium does not relieve the licensee from complying with applicable FDA, other Federal, and State requirements governing radioactive drugs.

(2) Each licensee authorized under § 30.32(j) to produce PET radioactive drugs for noncommercial transfer to medical use licensees in its consortium shall:

(i) Satisfy the labeling requirements in § 32.72(a)(4) of this chapter for each PET radioactive drug transport radiation shield and each syringe, vial, or other container used to hold a PET radioactive drug intended for noncommercial distribution to members of its consortium.

(ii) Possess and use instrumentation to measure the radioactivity of the PET radioactive drugs intended for noncommercial distribution to members of its consortium and meet the procedural, radioactivity measurement, instrument test, instrument check, and instrument adjustment requirements in § 32.72(c) of this chapter.

(3) A licensee that is a pharmacy authorized under § 30.32(j) to produce PET radioactive drugs for noncommercial transfer to medical use licensees in its consortium shall require that any individual that prepares PET radioactive drugs shall be:

(i) an authorized nuclear pharmacist that meets the requirements in § 32.72(b)(2) of this chapter, or

(ii) an individual under the supervision of an authorized nuclear pharmacist as specified in § 35.27 of this chapter.

(4) A pharmacy, authorized under § 30.32(j) to produce PET radioactive drugs for noncommercial transfer to medical use licensees in its consortium that allows an individual to work as an authorized nuclear pharmacist, shall meet the requirements of § 32.72(b)(5) of this chapter.

(k) As required by the Additional Protocol, each specific licensee authorized to possess and use byproduct material shall file with the Commission location information described in § 75.11 of this chapter on DOC/NRC Forms AP–1 and associated forms. The licensee shall also permit verification of this information by the International Atomic Energy Agency (IAEA) and shall take other action as may be necessary to implement the US/IAEA Safeguards Agreement, as described in part 75 of this chapter.

[30 FR 8185, June 26, 1965, as amended at 38 FR 33969, Dec. 10, 1973; 43 FR 6922, Feb. 17, 1978; 48 FR 32328, July 15, 1983; 52 FR 1295, Jan. 12, 1987; 52 FR 8241, Mar. 17, 1987; 53 FR 19245, May 27, 1988; 53 FR 23383, June 22, 1988; 54 FR 14061, Apr. 7, 1989; 58 FR 7736, Feb. 9, 1993; 59 FR 61780, Dec. 2, 1994; 65 FR 79187, Dec. 18, 2000; 70 FR 2009, Jan. 12, 2005; 72 FR 55926, Oct. 1, 2007; 73 FR 63570, Oct. 24, 2008; 73 FR 78604, Dec. 23, 2008; 74 FR 7785, Feb. 20, 2009; 76 FR 35564, June 17, 2011; 77 FR 39905, July 6, 2012; 79 FR 58671, Sept. 30, 2014]

§ 30.35 Financial assurance and recordkeeping for decommissioning.

(a)(1) Each applicant for a specific license authorizing the possession and use of unsealed byproduct material of half-life greater than 120 days and in quantities exceeding 10^5 times the applicable quantities set forth in appendix B to part 30 shall submit a decommissioning funding plan as described in paragraph (e) of this section. The decommissioning funding plan must also be submitted when a combination of isotopes is involved if R divided by 10^5 is greater than 1 (unity rule), where R is defined here as the sum of the ratios of the quantity of each isotope to the applicable value in appendix B to part 30.

(2) Each holder of, or applicant for, any specific license authorizing the possession and use of sealed sources or plated foils of half-life greater than 120 days and in quantities exceeding 10^{12} times the applicable quantities set forth in appendix B to part 30 (or when a combination of isotopes is involved if R, as defined in § 30.35(a)(1), divided by 10^{12} is greater than 1), shall submit a decommissioning funding plan as described in paragraph (e) of this section. The decommissioning funding plan must be submitted to NRC by December 2, 2005.

(b) Each applicant for a specific license authorizing possession and use of byproduct material of half-life greater than 120 days and in quantities specified in paragraph (d) of this section shall either—

(1) Submit a decommissioning funding plan as described in paragraph (e) of this section; or

(2) Submit a certification that financial assurance for decommissioning has been provided in the amount prescribed by paragraph (d) of this section using one of the methods described in paragraph (f) of this section. For an applicant, this certification may state that the appropriate assurance will be obtained after the application has been approved and the license issued but before the receipt of licensed material. If the applicant defers execution of the financial instrument until after the license has been issued, a signed original of the financial instrument obtained to satisfy the requirements of paragraph (f) of this section must be submitted to NRC before receipt of licensed material. If the applicant does not defer execution of the financial instrument, the applicant shall submit to NRC, as part of the certification, a signed original of the financial instrument obtained to satisfy the requirements of paragraph (f) of this section.

(c)(1) Each holder of a specific license issued on or after July 27, 1990, which is of a type described in paragraph (a) or (b) of this section, shall provide financial assurance for decommissioning in accordance with the criteria set forth in this section.

(2) Each holder of a specific license issued before July 27, 1990, and of a type described in paragraph (a) of this section shall submit a decommissioning funding plan as described in

paragraph (e) of this section or a certification of financial assurance for decommissioning in an amount at least equal to $1,125,000 in accordance with the criteria set forth in this section. If the licensee submits the certification of financial assurance rather than a decommissioning funding plan, the licensee shall include a decommissioning funding plan in any application for license renewal.

(3) Each holder of a specific license issued before July 27, 1990, and of a type described in paragraph (b) of this section shall submit, on or before July 27, 1990, a decommissioning funding plan as described, in paragraph (e) of this section, or a certification of financial assurance for decommissioning in accordance with the criteria set forth in this section.

(4) Any licensee who has submitted an application before July 27, 1990, for renewal of license in accordance with § 30.37 shall provide financial assurance for decommissioning in accordance with paragraphs (a) and (b) of this section. This assurance must be submitted when this rule becomes effective November 24, 1995.

(5) Waste collectors and waste processors, as defined in 10 CFR part 20, Appendix G, must provide financial assurance in an amount based on a decommissioning funding plan as described in paragraph (e) of this section. The decommissioning funding plan must include the cost of disposal of the maximum amount (curies) of radioactive material permitted by license, and the cost of disposal of the maximum quantity, by volume, of radioactive material which could be present at the licensee's facility at any time, in addition to the cost to remediate the licensee's site to meet the license termination criteria of 10 CFR part 20. The decommissioning funding plan must be submitted by December 2, 2005.

(6) If, in surveys made under 10 CFR 20.1501(a), residual radioactivity in the facility and environment, including the subsurface, is detected at levels that would, if left uncorrected, prevent the site from meeting the 10 CFR 20.1402 criteria for unrestricted use, the licensee must submit a decommissioning funding plan within one year of when the survey is completed.

(d) Table of required amounts of financial assurance for decommissioning by quantity of material. Licensees required to submit the $1,125,000 amount must do so by December 2, 2004. Licensees required to submit the $113,000 or $225,000 amount must do so by June 2, 2005. Licensees having possession limits exceeding the upper bounds of this table must base financial assurance on a decommissioning funding plan.

Greater than 10^4 but less than or equal to 10^5 times the applicable quantities of appendix B to part 30 in unsealed form. (For a combination of isotopes, if R, as defined in § 30.35(a)(1), divided by 10^4 is greater than 1 but R divided by 10^5 is less than or equal to 1)	$1,125,000
Greater than 10^3 but less than or equal to 10^4 times the applicable quantities of appendix B to part 30 in unsealed form. (For a combination of isotopes, if R, as defined in § 30.35(a)(1), divided by 10^3 is greater than 1 but R divided by 10^4 is less than or equal to 1)	225,000
Greater than 10^{10} but less than or equal to 10^{12} times the applicable quantities of appendix B to part 30 in sealed sources or plated foils. (For a combination of isotopes, if R, as defined in § 30.35(a)(1), divided by 10^{10} is greater than, 1, but R divided by 10^{12} is less than or equal to 1)	113,000

(e)(1) Each decommissioning funding plan must be submitted for review and approval and must contain —

(i) A detailed cost estimate for decommissioning, in an amount reflecting:

(A) The cost of an independent contractor to perform all decommissioning activities;

(B) The cost of meeting the 10 CFR 20.1402 criteria for unrestricted use, provided that, if the applicant or licensee can demonstrate its ability to meet the provisions of 10 CFR 20.1403, the cost estimate may be based on meeting the 10 CFR 20.1403 criteria;

(C) The volume of onsite subsurface material containing residual radioactivity that will require remediation to meet the criteria for license termination; and

(D) An adequate contingency factor.

(ii) Identification of and justification for using the key assumptions contained in the DCE;

(iii) A description of the method of assuring funds for decommissioning from paragraph (f) of this section, including means for adjusting cost estimates and associated funding levels periodically over the life of the facility;

(iv) A certification by the licensee that financial assurance for decommissioning has been provided in the amount of the cost estimate for decommissioning; and

(v) A signed original of the financial instrument obtained to satisfy the requirements of paragraph (f) of this section (unless a previously submitted and accepted financial instrument continues to cover the cost estimate for decommissioning).

(2) At the time of license renewal and at intervals not to exceed 3 years, the decommissioning funding plan must be resubmitted with adjustments as necessary to account for changes in costs and the extent of contamination. If the amount of financial assurance will be adjusted downward, this can not be done until the updated decommissioning funding plan is approved. The decommissioning funding plan must update the information submitted with the original or prior approved plan, and must specifically consider the effect of the following events on decommissioning costs:

(i) Spills of radioactive material producing additional residual radioactivity in onsite subsurface material;

(ii) Waste inventory increasing above the amount previously estimated;

(iii) Waste disposal costs increasing above the amount previously estimated;

(iv) Facility modifications;

(v) Changes in authorized possession limits;

(vi) Actual remediation costs that exceed the previous cost estimate;

(vii) Onsite disposal; and

(viii) Use of a settling pond.

(f) The financial instrument must include the licensee's name, license number, and docket number, and the name, address, and other contact information of the issuer, and, if a trust is used, the trustee. When any of the foregoing information changes, the licensee must, within 30 days, submit financial instruments reflecting such changes. The financial instrument submitted must be a signed original or signed original duplicate, except where a copy of the signed original is specifically permitted. Financial assurance for decommissioning must be provided by one or more of the following methods:

(1) *Prepayment.* Prepayment is the deposit before the start of operation into an account segregated from licensee assets and outside the licensee's administrative control of cash or liquid assets such that the amount of funds would be sufficient to pay decommissioning costs. Prepayment must be made into a trust account, and the trustee and the trust must be acceptable to the Commission.

(2) *A surety method, insurance, or other guarantee method.* These methods guarantee that decommissioning costs will be paid. A surety method may be in the form of a surety bond, or letter of credit. A parent company guarantee of funds for decommissioning costs based on a financial test may be used if the guarantee and test are as contained in Appendix A to this part. For commercial corporations that issue bonds, a guarantee of funds by the applicant or licensee for decommissioning costs based on a financial test may be used if the guarantee and test are as contained in Appendix C to this part. For commercial companies that do not issue bonds, a guarantee of funds by the applicant or licensee for decommissioning costs may be used if the guarantee and test are as contained in Appendix D to this part. For nonprofit entities, such as colleges, universities, and nonprofit hospitals, a guarantee of funds by the applicant or licensee may be used if the guarantee and test are as contained in Appendix E to this part. Except for an external sinking fund, a parent company guarantee or a guarantee by the applicant or licensee may not be used in combination with any other financial methods used to satisfy the requirements of this section. A guarantee by the applicant or licensee may not be used in any situation where the applicant or licensee has a parent company holding majority control of the voting stock of the company. Any surety method or insurance used to

provide financial assurance for decommissioning must contain the following conditions:

(i) The surety method or insurance must be open-ended or, if written for a specified term, such as five years, must be renewed automatically unless 90 days or more prior to the renewal date, the issuer notifies the Commission, the beneficiary, and the licensee of its intention not to renew. The surety method or insurance must also provide that the full face amount be paid to the beneficiary automatically prior to the expiration without proof of forfeiture if the licensee fails to provide a replacement acceptable to the Commission within 30 days after receipt of notification of cancellation.

(ii) The surety method or insurance must be payable to a trust established for decommissioning costs. The trustee and trust must be acceptable to the Commission. An acceptable trustee includes an appropriate State or Federal government agency or an entity which has the authority to act as a trustee and whose trust operations are regulated and examined by a Federal or State agency.

(iii) The surety method or insurance must remain in effect until the Commission has terminated the license.

(3) *An external sinking fund in which deposits are made at least annually, coupled with a surety method, insurance, or other guarantee method, the value of which may decrease by the amount being accumulated in the sinking fund.* An external sinking fund is a fund established and maintained by setting aside funds periodically in an account segregated from licensee assets and outside the licensee's administrative control in which the total amount of funds would be sufficient to pay decommissioning costs at the time termination of operation is expected. An external sinking fund must be in the form of a trust. If the other guarantee method is used, no surety or insurance may be combined with the external sinking fund. The surety, insurance, or other guarantee provisions must be as stated in paragraph (f)(2) of this section.

(4) In the case of Federal, State, or local government licensees, a statement of intent containing a cost estimate for decommissioning or an amount based on the table in paragraph (d) of this section, and indicating that funds for decommissioning will be obtained when necessary.

(5) When a government entity is assuming custody and ownership of a site, an arrangement that is deemed acceptable by such government entity.

(g) Each person licensed under this part or parts 32 through 36 and 39 of this chapter shall keep records of information important to the decommissioning of a facility in an identified location until the site is released for unrestricted use. Before licensed activities are transferred or assigned in accordance with § 30.34(b), licensees shall transfer all records described in this paragraph to the new licensee. In this case, the new licensee will be responsible for maintaining these records until the license is terminated. If records important to the decommissioning of a facility are kept for other purposes, reference to these records and their locations may be used. Information the Commission considers important to decommissioning consists of—

(1) Records of spills or other unusual occurrences involving the spread of contamination in and around the facility, equipment, or site. These records may be limited to instances when contamination remains after any cleanup procedures or when there is reasonable likelihood that contaminants may have spread to inaccessible areas as in the case of possible seepage into porous materials such as concrete. These records must include any known information on identification of involved nuclides, quantities, forms, and concentrations.

(2) As-built drawings and modifications of structures and equipment in restricted areas where radioactive materials are used and/or stored, and of locations of possible inaccessible contamination such as buried pipes which may be subject to contamination. If required drawings are referenced, each relevant document need not be indexed individually. If drawings are not available, the licensee shall substitute appropriate records of available information concerning these areas and locations.

(3) Except for areas containing only sealed sources (provided the sources have not leaked or no contamination remains after any leak) or byproduct materials having only half-lives of less than 65 days, a list contained in a single document and updated every 2 years, of the following:

(i) All areas designated and formerly designated restricted areas as defined in 10 CFR 20.1003 (For requirements prior to January 1, 1994, see 10 CFR 20.3 as contained in the CFR edition revised as of January 1, 1993.);

(ii) All areas outside of restricted areas that require documentation under § 30.35(g)(1).

(iii) All areas outside of restricted areas where current and previous wastes have been buried as documented under 10 CFR 20.2108; and

(iv) All areas outside of restricted areas that contain material such that, if the license expired, the licensee would be required to either decontaminate the area to meet the criteria for decommissioning in 10 CFR part 20, subpart E, or apply for approval for disposal under 10 CFR 20.2002.

(4) Records of the cost estimate performed for the decommissioning funding plan or of the amount certified for decommissioning, and records of the funding method used for assuring funds if either a funding plan or certification is used.

(h) In providing financial assurance under this section, each licensee must use the financial assurance funds only for decommissioning activities and each licensee must monitor the balance of funds held to account for market variations. The licensee must replenish the funds, and report such actions to the NRC, as follows:

(1) If, at the end of a calendar quarter, the fund balance is below the amount necessary to cover the cost of decommissioning, but is not below 75 percent of the cost, the licensee must increase the balance to cover the cost, and must do so within 30 days after the end of the calendar quarter.

(2) If, at any time, the fund balance falls below 75 percent of the amount necessary to cover the cost of decommissioning, the licensee must increase the balance to cover the cost, and must do so within 30 days of the occurrence.

(3) Within 30 days of taking the actions required by paragraph (h)(1) or (h)(2) of this section, the licensee must provide a written report of such actions to the Director, Office of Nuclear Material Safety and Safeguards , and state the new balance of the fund.

[53 FR 24044, June 27, 1988, as amended at 56 FR 23471, May 21, 1991; 58 FR 39633, July 26, 1993; 58 FR 67659, Dec. 22, 1993; 58 FR 68730, Dec. 29, 1993; 59 FR 1618, Jan. 12, 1994; 60 FR 38238, July 26, 1995; 61 FR 24673, May 16, 1996; 62 FR 39090, July 21, 1997; 63 FR 29541, June 1, 1998; 68 FR 57335, Oct. 3, 2003; 76 FR 35564, June 17, 2011]

§ 30.36 Expiration and termination of licenses and decommissioning of sites and separate buildings or outdoor areas.

(a) Each specific license expires at the end of the day on the expiration date stated in the license, unless the licensee has filed an application for renewal under § 30.37 not less than 30 days before the expiration date stated in the existing license. If an application for renewal has been filed at least 30 days before the expiration date stated in the existing license, the existing license expires at the end of the day on which the Commission makes a final determination to deny the renewal application or, if the determination states an expiration date, the expiration date stated in the determination.

(b) Each specific license revoked by the Commission expires at the end of the day on the date of the Commission's final determination to revoke the license, or on the expiration date stated in the determination, or as otherwise provided by Commission Order.

(c) Each specific license continues in effect, beyond the expiration date if necessary, with respect to possession of byproduct material until the Commission notifies the licensee in writing that the license is terminated. During this time, the licensee shall—

(1) Limit actions involving byproduct material to those related to decommissioning; and

(2) Continue to control entry to restricted areas until they are suitable for release in accordance with NRC requirements.

(d) Within 60 days of the occurrence of any of the following, consistent with the administrative directions in § 30.6, each licensee shall provide notification to the NRC in writing of such occurrence, and either begin decommissioning its site, or any separate building or outdoor area that contains residual radioactivity so that the building or outdoor area is suitable for release in accordance with NRC requirements, or submit within 12 months of notification a decommissioning plan, if required by paragraph (g)(1) of this section, and begin decommissioning upon approval of that plan if—

(1) The license has expired pursuant to paragraph (a) or (b) of this section; or

(2) The licensee has decided to permanently cease principal activities, as defined in this part, at the entire site or in any separate building or outdoor area that contains residual radioactivity such that the building or outdoor area is unsuitable for release in accordance with NRC requirements; or

(3) No principal activities under the license have been conducted for a period of 24 months; or

(4) No principal activities have been conducted for a period of 24 months in any separate building or outdoor area that contains residual radioactivity such that the building or outdoor area is unsuitable for release in accordance with NRC requirements.

(e) Coincident with the notification required by paragraph (d) of this section, the licensee shall maintain in effect all decommissioning financial assurances established by the licensee pursuant to § 30.35 in conjunction with a license issuance or renewal or as required by this section. The amount of the financial assurance must be increased, or may be decreased, as appropriate, to cover the detailed cost estimate for decommissioning established pursuant to paragraph (g)(4)(v) of this section.

(1) Any licensee who has not provided financial assurance to cover the detailed cost estimate submitted with the decommissioning plan shall do so when this rule becomes effective November 24, 1995.

(2) Following approval of the decommissioning plan, a licensee may reduce the amount of the financial assurance as decommissioning proceeds and radiological contamination is reduced at the site with the approval of the Commission.

(f) The Commission may grant a request to extend the time periods established in paragraph (d) if the Commission determines that this relief is not detrimental to the public health and safety and is otherwise in the public interest. The request must be submitted no later than 30 days before notification pursuant to paragraph (d) of this section. The schedule for decommissioning set forth in paragraph (d) of this section may not commence until the Commission has made a determination on the request.

(g)(1) A decommissioning plan must be submitted if required by license condition or if the procedures and activities necessary to carry out decommissioning of the site or separate building or outdoor area have not been previously approved by the Commission and these procedures could increase potential health and safety impacts to workers or to the public, such as in any of the following cases:

(i) Procedures would involve techniques not applied routinely during cleanup or maintenance operations;

(ii) Workers would be entering areas not normally occupied where surface contamination and radiation levels are significantly higher than routinely encountered during operation;

(iii) Procedures could result in significantly greater airborne concentrations of radioactive materials than are present during operation; or

(iv) Procedures could result in significantly greater releases of radioactive material to the environment than those associated with operation.

(2) The Commission may approve an alternate schedule for submittal of a decommissioning plan required pursuant to paragraph (d) of this section if the Commission determines that the alternative schedule is necessary to the effective conduct of decommissioning operations and presents no undue risk from radiation to the public health and safety and is otherwise in the public interest.

(3) Procedures such as those listed in paragraph (g)(1) of this section with potential health and safety impacts may not be carried out prior to approval of the decommissioning plan.

(4) The proposed decommissioning plan for the site or separate building or outdoor area must include:

(i) A description of the conditions of the site or separate building or outdoor area sufficient to evaluate the acceptability of the plan;

(ii) A description of planned decommissioning activities;

(iii) A description of methods used to ensure protection of workers and the environment against radiation hazards during decommissioning;

(iv) A description of the planned final radiation survey; and

(v) An updated detailed cost estimate for decommissioning, comparison of that estimate with present funds set aside for decommissioning, and a plan for assuring the availability of adequate funds for completion of decommissioning.

(vi) For decommissioning plans calling for completion of decommissioning later than 24 months after plan approval, the plan shall include a justification for the delay based on the criteria in paragraph (i) of this section.

(5) The proposed decommissioning plan will be approved by the Commission if the information therein demonstrates that the decommissioning will be completed as soon as practicable and that the health and safety of workers and the public will be adequately protected.

(h)(1) Except as provided in paragraph (i) of this section, licensees shall complete decommissioning of the site or separate building or outdoor area as soon as practicable but no later than 24 months following the initiation of decommissioning.

(2) Except as provided in paragraph (i) of this section, when decommissioning involves the entire site, the licensee shall request license termination as soon as practicable but no later than 24 months following the initiation of decommissioning.

(i) The Commission may approve a request for an alternative schedule for completion of decommissioning of the site or separate building or outdoor area, and license termination if appropriate, if the Commission determines that the alternative is warranted by consideration of the following:

(1) Whether it is technically feasible to complete decommissioning within the allotted 24-month period;

(2) Whether sufficient waste disposal capacity is available to allow completion of decommissioning within the allotted 24-month period;

(3) Whether a significant volume reduction in wastes requiring disposal will be achieved by allowing short-lived radionuclides to decay;

(4) Whether a significant reduction in radiation exposure to workers can be achieved by allowing short-lived radionuclides to decay; and

(5) Other site-specific factors which the Commission may consider appropriate on a case-by-case basis, such as the regulatory requirements of other government agencies, lawsuits, groundwater treatment activities, monitored natural groundwater restoration, actions that could result in more environmental harm than deferred cleanup, and other factors beyond the control of the licensee.

(j) As the final step in decommissioning, the licensee shall—

(1) Certify the disposition of all licensed material, including accumulated wastes, by submitting a completed NRC Form 314 or equivalent information; and

(2) Conduct a radiation survey of the premises where the licensed activities were carried out and submit a report of the results of this survey, unless the licensee demonstrates in some other manner that the premises are suitable for release in accordance with the criteria for decommissioning in 10 CFR part 20, subpart E. The licensee shall, as appropriate—

(i) Report levels of gamma radiation in units of millisieverts (microroentgen) per hour at one meter from surfaces, and report levels of radioactivity, including alpha and beta, in units of megabecquerels (disintegrations per minute or microcuries) per 100 square centimeters—removable and fixed—for surfaces, megabecquerels (microcuries) per milliliter for water, and becquerels (picocuries) per gram for solids such as soils or concrete; and

(ii) Specify the survey instrument(s) used and certify that each instrument is properly calibrated and tested.

(k) Specific licenses, including expired licenses, will be terminated by written notice to the licensee when the Commission determines that:

(1) Byproduct material has been properly disposed;

(2) Reasonable effort has been made to eliminate residual radioactive contamination, if present; and

(3)(i) A radiation survey has been performed which demonstrates that the premises are suitable for release in accordance with the criteria for decommissioning in 10 CFR part 20, subpart E; or

(ii) Other information submitted by the licensee is sufficient to demonstrate that the premises are suitable for release in accordance with the criteria for decommissioning in 10 CFR part 20, subpart E.

(4) Records required by § 30.51 (d) and (f) have been received.

[59 FR 36034, July 15, 1994, as amended at 60 FR 38238, July 26, 1995; 61 FR 1114, Jan. 16, 1996; 61 FR 24673, May 16, 1996; 61 FR 29637, June 12, 1996; 62 FR 39090, July 21, 1997; 73 FR 42673, July 23, 2008; 81 FR 86909, Dec. 2, 2016]

§ 30.37 Application for renewal of licenses.

Application for renewal of a specific license must be filed on NRC Form 313 and in accordance with § 30.32.

[75 FR 73942, Nov. 30, 2010]

§ 30.38 Application for amendment of licenses and registration certificates.

Applications for amendment of a license must be filed in accordance with § 30.32 and must specify the respects in which the licensee desires its license to be amended and the grounds for the amendment. Applications for amendment of sealed source and device registration certificates must be filed in accordance with § 32.210 of this chapter and any other applicable provisions and must specify the respects in which the certificate holder desires its certificate to be amended and the grounds for the amendment.

[77 FR 43690, July 25, 2012]

§ 30.39 Commission action on applications to renew or amend.

In considering an application to renew or amend a license or to amend a sealed source or device registration certificate, the Commission will apply the applicable criteria set forth in § 30.33 and parts 32 through 36 and 39 of this chapter.

[77 FR 43690, July 25, 2012]

§ 30.41 Transfer of byproduct material.

(a) No licensee shall transfer byproduct material except as authorized pursuant to this section.

(b) Except as otherwise provided in his license and subject to the provisions of paragraphs (c) and (d) of this section, any licensee may transfer byproduct material:

(1) To the Department;

(2) To the agency in any Agreement State which regulates radioactive material pursuant to an agreement under section 274 of the Act;

(3) To any person exempt from the licensing requirements of the Act and regulations in this part, to the extent permitted under such exemption;

(4) To any person in an Agreement State, subject to the jurisdiction of that State, who has been exempted from the licensing requirements and regulations of that State, to the extent permitted under such exemption;

(5) To any person authorized to receive such byproduct material under terms of a specific license or a general license or their equivalents issued by the Atomic Energy Commission, the Commission, or an Agreement State;

(6) To a person abroad pursuant to an export license issued under part 110 of this chapter; or

(7) As otherwise authorized by the Commission in writing.

(c) Before transferring byproduct material to a specific licensee of the Commission or an Agreement State or to a general licensee who is required to register with the Commission or with an Agreement State prior to receipt of the byproduct material, the licensee transferring the material shall verify that the transferee's license authorizes the receipt of the type, form, and quantity of byproduct material to be transferred.

(d) The following methods for the verification required by paragraph (c) of this section are acceptable:

(1) The transferor may have in his possession, and read, a current copy of the transferee's specific license or registration certificate;

(2) The transferor may have in his possession a written certification by the transferee that he is authorized by license or registration certificate to receive the type, form, and quantity of byproduct material to be transferred, specifying the license or registration certificate number, issuing agency and expiration date;

(3) For emergency shipments the transferor may accept oral certification by the transferee that he is authorized by license or registration certificate to receive the type, form, and quantity of byproduct material to be transferred, specifying the license or registration certificate number, issuing agency and expiration date: *Provided*, That the oral certification is confirmed in writing within 10 days;

(4) The transferor may obtain other sources of information compiled by a reporting service from official records of the Commission or the licensing agency of an Agreement State as to the identity of licensees and the scope and expiration dates of licenses and registration; or

(5) When none of the methods of verification described in paragraphs (d)(1) to (4) of this section are readily available or when a transferor desires to verify that information received by one of such methods is correct or up-to-date, the transferor may obtain and record confirmation from the Commission or the licensing agency of an Agreement State that the transferee is licensed to receive the byproduct material.

[38 FR 33969, Dec. 10, 1973, as amended at 40 FR 8785, Mar. 3, 1975; 43 FR 6922, Feb. 17, 1978]

RECORDS, INSPECTIONS, TESTS, AND REPORTS

§ 30.50 Reporting requirements.

(a) *Immediate report.* Each licensee shall notify the NRC as soon as possible but not later than 4 hours after the discovery of an event that prevents immediate protective actions necessary to avoid exposures to radiation or radioactive materials that could exceed regulatory limits or releases of licensed material that could exceed regulatory limits (events may include fires, explosions, toxic gas releases, etc.).

(b) *Twenty-four hour report.* Each licensee shall notify the NRC within 24 hours after the discovery of any of the following events involving licensed material:

(1) An unplanned contamination event that:

(i) Requires access to the contaminated area, by workers or the public, to be restricted for more than 24 hours by imposing additional radiological controls or by prohibiting entry into the area;

(ii) Involves a quantity of material greater than five times the lowest annual limit on intake specified in appendix B of §§ 20.1001–20.2401 of 10 CFR part 20 for the material; and

(iii) Has access to the area restricted for a reason other than to allow isotopes with a half-life of less than 24 hours to decay prior to decontamination.

(2) An event in which equipment is disabled or fails to function as designed when:

(i) The equipment is required by regulation or license condition to prevent releases exceeding regulatory limits, to prevent exposures to radiation and radioactive materials exceeding regulatory limits, or to mitigate the consequences of an accident;

(ii) The equipment is required to be available and operable when it is disabled or fails to function; and

(iii) No redundant equipment is available and operable to perform the required safety function.

(3) An event that requires unplanned medical treatment at a medical facility of an individual with spreadable radioactive contamination on the individual's clothing or body.

(4) An unplanned fire or explosion damaging any licensed material or any device, container, or equipment containing licensed material when:

(i) The quantity of material involved is greater than five times the lowest annual limit on intake specified in appendix B of §§ 20.1001–20.2401 of 10 CFR part 20 for the material; and

(ii) The damage affects the integrity of the licensed material or its container.

(c) Preparation and submission of reports. Reports made by licensees in response to the requirements of this section must be made as follows:

(1) Licensees shall make reports required by paragraphs (a) and (b) of this section by telephone to the NRC Operations Center.[1] To the extent that the information is available at the time of notification, the information provided in these reports must include:

(i) The caller's name and call back telephone number;

(ii) A description of the event, including date and time;

(iii) The exact location of the event;

(iv) The isotopes, quantities, and chemical and physical form of the licensed material involved; and

(v) Any personnel radiation exposure data available.

(2) Written report. Each licensee who makes a report required by paragraph (a) or (b) of this section shall submit a written follow-up report within 30 days of the initial report. Written reports prepared pursuant to other regulations may be submitted to fulfill this requirement if the reports contain all of the necessary information and the appropriate distribution is made. These written reports must be sent to the NRC using an appropriate method listed in § 30.6(a); and a copy must be sent to the appropriate NRC Regional office listed in appendix D to part 20 of this chapter. The reports must include the following:

(i) A description of the event, including the probable cause and the manufacturer and model number (if applicable) of any equipment that failed or malfunctioned;

(ii) The exact location of the event;

(iii) The isotopes, quantities, and chemical and physical form of the licensed material involved;

(iv) Date and time of the event;

(v) Corrective actions taken or planned and the results of any evaluations or assessments; and

(vi) The extent of exposure of individuals to radiation or to radioactive materials without identification of individuals by name.

(3) The provisions of § 30.50 do not apply to licensees subject to the notification requirements in § 50.72. They do apply to those part 50 licensees possessing material licensed under part 30, who are not subject to the notification requirements in § 50.72.

[56 FR 40767, Aug. 16, 1991, as amended at 59 FR 14086, Mar. 25, 1994; 68 FR 58804, Oct. 10, 2003]

§ 30.51 Records.

(a) Each person who receives byproduct material pursuant to a license issued pursuant to the regulations in this part and parts 31 through 36 of this chapter shall keep records showing the receipt, transfer, and disposal of the byproduct material as follows:

(1) The licensee shall retain each record of receipt of byproduct material as long as the material is possessed and for three years following transfer or disposal of the material.

(2) The licensee who transferred the material shall retain each record of transfer for three years after each transfer unless a specific requirement in another part of the regulations in this chapter dictates otherwise.

(3) The licensee who disposed of the material shall retain each record of disposal of byproduct material until the Commission terminates each license that authorizes disposal of the material.

(b) The licensee shall retain each record that is required by the regulations in this part and parts 31 through 36 of this chapter or by license condition for the period specified by the appropriate regulation or license condition. If a retention period is not otherwise specified by regulation or license condition, the record must be retained until the Commission terminates each license that authorizes the activity that is subject to the recordkeeping requirement.

(c)(1) Records which must be maintained pursuant to this part and parts 31 through 36 of this chapter may be

[1] The commercial telephone number for the NRC Operations Center is (301) 816–5100.

the original or a reproduced copy or microform if such reproduced copy or microform is duly authenticated by authorized personnel and the microform is capable of producing a clear and legible copy after storage for the period specified by Commission regulations. The record may also be stored in electronic media with the capability for producing legible, accurate, and complete records during the required retention period. Records such as letters, drawings, specifications, must include all pertinent information such as stamps, initials, and signatures. The licensee shall maintain adequate safeguards against tampering with and loss of records.

(2) If there is a conflict between the Commission's regulations in this part and parts 31 through 36 and 39 of this chapter, license condition, or other written Commission approval or authorization pertaining to the retention period for the same type of record, the retention period specified in the regulations in this part and parts 31 through 36 and 39 of this chapter for such records shall apply unless the Commission, pursuant to § 30.11, has granted a specific exemption from the record retention requirements specified in the regulations in this part or parts 31 through 36 and 39 of this chapter.

(d) Prior to license termination, each licensee authorized to possess radioactive material with a half-life greater than 120 days, in an unsealed form, shall forward the following records to the appropriate NRC Regional Office:

(1) Records of disposal of licensed material made under §§ 20.2002 (including burials authorized before January 28, 1981[1]), 20.2003, 20.2004, 20.2005; and

(2) Records required by § 20.2103(b)(4).

(e) If licensed activities are transferred or assigned in accordance with § 30.34(b), each licensee authorized to possess radioactive material, with a half-life greater than 120 days, in an unsealed form, shall transfer the following records to the new licensee and the new licensee will be responsible for maintaining these records until the license is terminated:

(1) Records of disposal of licensed material made under §§ 20.2002 (including burials authorized before January 28, 1981[1]), 20.2003, 20.2004, 20.2005; and

(2) Records required by § 20.2103(b)(4).

(f) Prior to license termination, each licensee shall forward the records required by § 30.35(g) to the appropriate NRC Regional Office.

[41 FR 18301, May 5, 1976, as amended at 43 FR 6922, Feb. 17, 1978; 52 FR 8241, Mar. 17, 1987; 53 FR 19245, May 27, 1988; 58 FR 7736, Feb. 9, 1993; 61 FR 24673, May 16, 1996]

§ 30.52 Inspections.

(a) Each licensee shall afford to the Commission at all reasonable times opportunity to inspect byproduct material and the premises and facilities wherein byproduct material is used or stored.

(b) Each licensee shall make available to the Commission for inspection, upon reasonable notice, records kept by him pursuant to the regulations in this chapter.

[30 FR 8185, June 26, 1965]

§ 30.53 Tests.

Each licensee shall perform, or permit the Commission to perform, such tests as the Commission deems appropriate or necessary for the administration of the regulations in this part and parts 31 through 36 and 39 of this chapter, including tests of:

(a) Byproduct material;

(b) Facilities wherein byproduct material is utilized or stored;

(c) Radiation detection and monitoring instruments; and

(d) Other equipment and devices used in connection with the utilization or storage of byproduct material.

[30 FR 8185, June 26, 1965, as amended at 43 FR 6922, Feb. 17, 1978; 52 FR 8241, Mar. 17, 1987; 58 FR 7736, Feb. 9, 1993]

§ 30.55 Tritium reports.

(a)–(b) [Reserved]

(c) Except as specified in paragraph (d) of this section, each licensee who is authorized to possess tritium shall report promptly to the appropriate NRC Regional Office listed in appendix D of part 20 of this chapter by telephone and

[1] A previous § 20.304 permitted burial of small quantities of licensed materials in soil before January 28, 1981, without specific Commission authorization. See § 20.304 contained in the 10 CFR, parts 0 to 199, edition revised as of January 1, 1981.

telegraph, mailgram, or facsimile any incident in which an attempt has been made or is believed to have been made to commit a theft or unlawful diversion of more than 10 curies of such material at any one time or more than 100 curies of such material in any one calendar year. The initial report shall be followed within a period of fifteen (15) days by a written report submitted to the appropriate NRC Regional Office which sets forth the details of the incident and its consequences. Copies of such written report shall be sent to the Director, Office of Nuclear Material Safety and Safeguards , using an appropriate method listed in § 30.6(a). Subsequent to the submission of the written report required by this paragraph, the licensee shall promptly inform the Office of Nuclear Material Safety and Safeguards by means of a written report of any substantive additional information, which becomes available to the licensee, concerning an attempted or apparent theft or unlawful diversion of tritium.

(d) The reports described in this section are not required for tritium possessed pursuant to a general license provided in part 31 of this chapter or for tritium contained in spent fuel.

[37 FR 9208, May 6, 1972, as amended at 38 FR 1271, Jan. 11, 1973; 38 FR 2330, Jan. 24, 1973; 41 FR 16446, Apr. 19, 1976; 43 FR 6922, Feb. 17, 1978; 46 FR 55085, Nov. 6, 1981; 49 FR 24707, June 15, 1984; 52 FR 31611, Aug. 21, 1987; 68 FR 58804, Oct. 10, 2003; 73 FR 5718, Jan. 31, 2008]

ENFORCEMENT

§ 30.61 Modification and revocation of licenses and registration certificates.

(a) The terms and conditions of each license and registration certificate issued under the regulations in this part and parts 31 through 36 and 39 of this chapter shall be subject to amendment, revision, or modification by reason of amendments to the Act, or by reason of rules, regulations, and orders issued in accordance with the terms of the Act.

(b) Any license or registration certificate may be revoked, suspended, or modified, in whole or in part, for any material false statement in the application or in any statement of fact required under section 182 of the Act, or because of conditions revealed by such application or statement of fact or any report, record, or inspection or other means that would warrant the Commission to refuse to grant a license or registration certificate on an original application, or for violation of, or failure to observe any of the terms and provisions of the Act or of any rule, regulation, or order of the Commission.

(c) Except in cases of willfulness or those in which the public health, interest, or safety requires otherwise, no license or registration certificate shall be modified, suspended, or revoked unless, before the institution of proceedings therefor, facts or conduct that may warrant such action shall have been called to the attention of the licensee or certificate holder in writing and the licensee or certificate holder shall have been given an opportunity to demonstrate or achieve compliance with all lawful requirements.

[77 FR 43690, July 25, 2012]

§ 30.62 Right to cause the withholding or recall of byproduct material.

The Commission may cause the withholding or recall of byproduct material from any licensee who is not equipped to observe or fails to observe such safety standards to protect health as may be established by the Commission, or who uses such materials in violation of law or regulation of the Commission, or in a manner other than as disclosed in the application therefor or approved by the Commission.

[30 FR 8185, June 26, 1965, as amended at 40 FR 8785, Mar. 3, 1975]

§ 30.63 Violations.

(a) The Commission may obtain an injunction or other court order to prevent a violation of the provisions of—

(1) The Atomic Energy Act of 1954, as amended;

(2) Title II of the Energy Reorganization Act of 1974, as amended; or

(3) A regulation or order issued pursuant to those Acts.

(b) The Commission may obtain a court order for the payment of a civil penalty imposed under section 234 of the Atomic Energy Act:

(1) For violations of—

(i) Sections 53, 57, 62, 63, 81, 82, 101, 103, 104, 107, or 109 of the Atomic Energy Act of 1954, as amended;

(ii) Section 206 of the Energy Reorganization Act;

(iii) Any rule, regulation, or order issued pursuant to the sections specified in paragraph (b)(1)(i) of this section;

(iv) Any term, condition, or limitation of any license issued under the sections specified in paragraph (b)(1)(i) of this section.

(2) For any violation for which a license may be revoked under section 186 of the Atomic Energy Act of 1954, as amended.

[57 FR 55072, Nov. 24, 1992]

§ 30.64 Criminal penalties.

(a) Section 223 of the Atomic Energy Act of 1954, as amended, provides for criminal sanctions for willful violation of, attempted violation of, or conspiracy to violate, any regulation issued under sections 161b, 161i, or 161o of the Act. For purposes of section 223, all the regulations in part 30 are issued under one or more of sections 161b, 161i, or 161o, except for the sections listed in paragraph (b) of this section.

(b) The regulations in part 30 that are not issued under sections 161b, 161i, or 161o for the purposes of section 223 are as follows: §§ 30.1, 30.2, 30.4, 30.5, 30.6, 30.8, 30.11, 30.12, 30.13, 30.15, 30.31, 30.32, 30.33, 30.37, 30.38, 30.39, 30.61, 30.62, 30.63, 30.64, 30.70, 30.71, and 30.72.

[57 FR 55072, Nov. 24, 1992, as amended at 73 FR 42673, July 23, 2008]

SCHEDULES

§ 30.70 Schedule A—Exempt concentrations.

[See footnotes at end of this table]

Element (atomic number)	Isotope	Col. I Gas concentration μCi/ml[1]	Col. II Liquid and solid concentration μCi/ml[2]
Antimony (51)	Sb 122		3×10^{-4}
	Sb 124		2×10^{-4}
	Sb 125		1×10^{-3}
Argon (18)	A 37	1×10^{-3}.	
	A 41	4×10^{-7}.	
Arsenic (33)	As 73		5×10^{-3}
	As 74		5×10^{-4}
	As 76		2×10^{-4}
	As 77		8×10^{-4}
Barium (56)	Ba 131		2×10^{-3}
	Ba 140		3×10^{-4}
Beryllium (4)	Be 7		2×10^{-2}
Bismuth (83)	Bi 206		4×10^{-4}
Bromine (35)	Br 82	4×10^{-7}	3×10^{-3}
Cadmium (48)	Cd 109		2×10^{-3}
	Cd 115m		3×10^{-4}
	Cd 115		3×10^{-4}
Calcium (20)	Ca 45		9×10^{-5}
	Ca 47		5×10^{-4}
Carbon (6)	C 14	1×10^{-6}	8×10^{-3}
Cerium (58)	Ce 141		9×10^{-4}
	Ce 143		4×10^{-4}
	Ce 144		1×10^{-4}
Cesium (55)	Cs 131		2×10^{-2}
	Cs 134m		6×10^{-2}
	Cs 134		9×10^{-5}
Chlorine (17)	Cl 38	9×10^{-7}	4×10^{-3}
Chromium (24)	Cr 51		2×10^{-2}
Cobalt (27)	Co 57		5×10^{-3}
	Co 58		1×10^{-3}
	Co 60		5×10^{-4}
Copper (29)	Cu 64		3×10^{-3}
Dysprosium (66)	Dy 165		4×10^{-3}
	Dy 166		4×10^{-4}
Erbium (68)	Er 169		9×10^{-4}

[See footnotes at end of this table]

Element (atomic number)	Isotope	Col. I Gas concentration μCi/ml [1]	Col. II Liquid and solid concentration μCi/ml [2]
	Er 171		1×10^{-3}
Europium (63)	Eu 152 (T/2 = 9.2 Hrs).		6×10^{-4}
	Eu 155		2×10^{-3}
Fluorine (9)	F 18	2×10^{-6}	8×10^{-3}
Gadolinium (64)	Gd 153		2×10^{-3}
	Gd 159		8×10^{-4}
Gallium (31)	Ga 72		4×10^{-4}
Germanium (32)	Ge 71		2×10^{-2}
Gold (79)	Au 196		2×10^{-3}
	Au 198		5×10^{-4}
	Au 199		2×10^{-3}
Hafnium (72)	Hf 181		7×10^{-4}
Hydrogen (1)	H 3	5×10^{-6}	3×10^{-2}
Indium (49)	In 113m		1×10^{-2}
	In 114m		2×10^{-4}
Iodine (53)	I 126	3×10^{-9}	2×10^{-5}
	I 131	3×10^{-9}	2×10^{-5}
	I 132	8×10^{-8}	6×10^{-4}
	I 133	1×10^{-8}	7×10^{-5}
	I 134	2×10^{-7}	1×10^{-3}
Iridium (77)	Ir 190		2×10^{-3}
	Ir 192		4×10^{-4}
	Ir 194		3×10^{-4}
Iron (26)	Fe 55		8×10^{-3}
	Fe 59		6×10^{-4}
Krypton (36)	Kr 85m	1×10^{-6}.	
	Kr 85	3×10^{-6}.	
Lanthanum (57)	La 140		2×10^{-4}
Lead (82)	Pb 203		4×10^{-3}
Lutetium (71)	Lu 177		1×10^{-3}
Manganese (25)	Mn 52		3×10^{-4}
	Mn 54		1×10^{-3}
	Mn 56		1×10^{-3}
Mercury (80)	Hg 197m		2×10^{-3}
	Hg 197		3×10^{-3}
	Hg 203		2×10^{-4}
Molybdenum (42)	Mo 99		2×10^{-3}
Neodymium (60)	Nd 147		6×10^{-4}
	Nd 149		3×10^{-3}
Nickel (28)	Ni 65		1×10^{-3}
Niobium (Columbium) (41)	Nb 95		1×10^{-3}
	Nb 97		9×10^{-3}
Osmium (76)	Os 185		7×10^{-4}
	Os 191m		3×10^{-2}
	Os 191		2×10^{-3}
	Os 193		6×10^{-4}
Palladium (46)	Pd 103		3×10^{-3}
	Pd 109		9×10^{-4}
Phosphorus (15)	P 32		2×10^{-4}
Platinum (78)	Pt 191		1×10^{-3}
	Pt 193m		1×10^{-2}
	Pt 197m		1×10^{-2}
	Pt 197		1×10^{-3}
Potassium (19)	K 42		3×10^{-3}
Praseodymium (59)	Pr 142		3×10^{-4}
	Pr 143		5×10^{-4}
Promethium (61)	Pm 147		2×10^{-3}
	Pm 149		4×10^{-4}
Rhenium (75)	Re 183		6×10^{-3}
	Re 186		9×10^{-4}
	Re 188		6×10^{-4}
Rhodium (45)	Rh 103m		1×10^{-1}
	Rh 105		1×10^{-3}
Rubidium (37)	Rb 86		7×10^{-4}
Ruthenium (44)	Ru 97		4×10^{-4}
	Ru 103		8×10^{-4}
	Ru 105		1×10^{-3}
	Ru 106		1×10^{-4}

[See footnotes at end of this table]

Element (atomic number)	Isotope	Col. I Gas concentration μCi/ml [1]	Col. II Liquid and solid concentration μCi/ml [2]
Samarium (62)	Sm 153		8×10^{-4}
Scandium (21)	Sc 46		4×10^{-4}
	Sc 47		9×10^{-4}
	Sc 48		3×10^{-4}
Selenium (34)	Se 75		3×10^{-3}
Silicon (14)	Si 31		9×10^{-3}
Silver (47)	Ag 105		1×10^{-3}
	Ag 110m		3×10^{-4}
	Ag 111		4×10^{-4}
Sodium (11)	Na 24		2×10^{-3}
Strontium (38)	Sr 85		1×10^{-4}
	Sr 89		1×10^{-4}
	Sr 91		7×10^{-4}
	Sr 92		7×10^{-4}
Sulfur (16)	S 35	9×10^{-8}	6×10^{-4}
Tantalum (73)	Ta 182		4×10^{-4}
Technetium (43)	Tc 96m		1×10^{-1}
	Tc 96		1×10^{-3}
Tellurium (52)	Te 125m		2×10^{-3}
	Te 127m		6×10^{-4}
	Te 127		3×10^{-3}
	Te 129m		3×10^{-4}
	Te 131m		6×10^{-4}
	Te 132		3×10^{-4}
Terbium (65)	Tb 160		4×10^{-4}
Thallium (81)	Tl 200		4×10^{-3}
	Tl 201		3×10^{-3}
	Tl 202		1×10^{-3}
	Tl 204		1×10^{-3}
Thulium (69)	Tm 170		5×10^{-4}
	Tm 171		5×10^{-3}
Tin (50)	Sn 113		9×10^{-4}
	Sn 125		2×10^{-4}
Tungsten (Wolfram) (74)	W 181		4×10^{-3}
	W 187		7×10^{-4}
Vanadium (23)	V 48		3×10^{-4}
Xenon (54)	Xe 131m	4×10^{-6}.	
	Xe 133	3×10^{-6}.	
	Xe 135	1×10^{-6}.	
Ytterbium (70)	Yb 175		1×10^{-3}
Yttrium (39)	Y 90		2×10^{-4}
	Y 91m		3×10^{-2}
	Y 91		3×10^{-4}
	Y 92		6×10^{-4}
	Y 93		3×10^{-4}
Zinc (30)	Zn 65		1×10^{-3}
	Zn 69m		7×10^{-4}
	Zn 69		2×10^{-2}
Zirconium (40)	Zr 95		6×10^{-4}
	Zr 97		2×10^{-4}
Beta and/or gamma emitting byproduct material not listed above with half-life less than 3 years.		1×10^{-10}	1×10^{-6}

Footnotes to Schedule A:

[1] Values are given only for those materials normally used as gases.

[2] μCi/gm for solids.

Note 1: Many radioisotopes disintegrate into isotopes which are also radioactive. In expressing the concentrations in Schedule A, the activity stated is that of the parent isotope and takes into account the daughters.

Note 2: For purposes of § 30.14 where there is involved a combination of isotopes, the limit for the combination should be derived as follows:

Determine for each isotope in the product the ratio between the concentration present in the product and the exempt concentration established in Schedule A for the specific isotope when not in combination. The sum of such ratios may not exceed "1" (*i.e.*, unity).

Example:

$$\frac{\text{Concentration of Isotope A in Product}}{\text{Exempt concentration of Isotope A}} + \frac{\text{Concentration of Isotope B in Product}}{\text{Exempt concentration of Isotope B}} \leq 1$$

[30 FR 8185, June 26, 1965, as amended at 35 FR 3982, Mar. 3, 1970; 38 FR 29314, Oct. 24, 1973; 59 FR 5520, Feb. 7, 1994]

§ 30.71 Schedule B.

Byproduct material	Microcuries
Antimony 122 (Sb 122)	100
Antimony 124 (Sb 124)	10
Antimony 125 (Sb 125)	10
Arsenic 73 (As 73)	100
Arsenic 74 (As 74)	10
Arsenic 76 (As 76)	10
Arsenic 77 (As 77)	100
Barium 131 (Ba 131)	10
Barium 133 (Ba 133)	10
Barium 140 (Ba 140)	10
Bismuth 210 (Bi 210)	1
Bromine 82 (Br 82)	10
Cadmium 109 (Cd 109)	10
Cadmium 115m (Cd 115m)	10
Cadmium 115 (Cd 115)	100
Calcium 45 (Ca 45)	10
Calcium 47 (Ca 47)	10
Carbon 14 (C 14)	100
Cerium 141 (Ce 141)	100
Cerium 143 (Ce 143)	100
Cerium 144 (Ce 144)	1
Cesium 129 (Cs 129)	100
Cesium 131 (Cs 131)	1,000
Cesium 134m (Cs 134m)	100
Cesium 134 (Cs 134)	1
Cesium 135 (Cs 135)	10
Cesium 136 (Cs 136)	10
Cesium 137 (Cs 137)	10
Chlorine 36 (C1 36)	10
Chlorine 38 (Cl 38)	10
Chromium 51 (Cr 51)	1,000
Cobalt 57 (Co 57)	100
Cobalt 58m (Co 58m)	10
Cobalt 58 (Co 58)	10
Cobalt 60 (Co 60)	1
Copper 64 (Cu 64)	100
Dysprosium 165 (Dy 165)	10
Dysprosium 166 (Dy 166)	100
Erbium 169 (Er 169)	100
Erbium 171 (Er 171)	100
Europium 152 9.2 h (Eu 152 9.2 h)	100
Europium 152 13 yr (Eu 152 13 yr)	1
Europium 154 (Eu 154)	1
Europium 155 (Eu 155)	10
Fluorine 18 (F 18)	1,000
Gadolinium 153 (Gd 153)	10
Gadolinium 159 (Gd 159)	100
Gallium 67 (Ga 67)	100
Gallium 72 (Ga 72)	10
Germanium 68 (Ge 68)	10
Germanium 71 (Ge 71)	100
Gold 195 (Au 195)	10
Gold 198 (Au 198)	100
Gold 199 (Au 199)	100
Hafnium 181 (Hf 181)	10
Holmium 166 (Ho 166)	100
Hydrogen 3 (H 3)	1,000
Indium 111 (In 111)	100
Indium 113m (In 113m)	100
Indium 114m (In 114m)	10
Indium 115m (In 115m)	100
Indium 115 (In 115)	10
Iodine 123 (I 123)	100
Iodine 125 (I 125)	1
Iodine 126 (I 126)	1
Iodine 129 (I 129)	0.1
Iodine 131 (I 131)	1
Iodine 132 (I 132)	10
Iodine 133 (I 133)	1
Iodine 134 (I 134)	10
Iodine 135 (I 135)	10
Iridium 192 (Ir 192)	10
Iridium 194 (Ir 194)	100
Iron 52 (Fe 52)	10
Iron 55 (Fe 55)	100
Iron 59 (Fe 59)	10
Krypton 85 (Kr 85)	100
Krypton 87 (Kr 87)	10
Lanthanum 140 (La 140)	10
Lutetium 177 (Lu 177)	100
Manganese 52 (Mn 52)	10
Manganese 54 (Mn 54)	10
Manganese 56 (Mn 56)	10
Mercury 197m (Hg 197m)	100
Mercury 197 (Hg 197)	100
Mercury 203 (Hg 203)	10
Molybdenum 99 (Mo 99)	100
Neodymium 147 (Nd 147)	100
Neodymium 149 (Nd 149)	100
Nickel 59 (Ni 59)	100
Nickel 63 (Ni 63)	10
Nickel 65 (Ni 65)	100
Niobium 93m (Nb 93m)	10
Niobium 95 (Nb 95)	10
Niobium 97 (Nb 97)	10
Osmium 185 (Os 185)	10
Osmium 191m (Os 191m)	100
Osmium 191 (Os 191)	100
Osmium 193 (Os 193)	100
Palladium 103 (Pd 103)	100
Palladium 109 (Pd 109)	100
Phosphorus 32 (P 32)	10
Platinum 191 (Pt 191)	100
Platinum 193m (Pt 193m)	100
Platinum 193 (Pt 193)	100
Platinum 197m (Pt 197m)	100
Platinum 197 (Pt 197)	100
Polonium 210 (Po 210)	0.1
Potassium 42 (K 42)	10
Potassium 43 (K 43)	10
Praseodymium 142 (Pr 142)	100
Praseodymium 143 (Pr 143)	100
Promethium 147 (Pm 147)	10
Promethium 149 (Pm 149)	10
Rhenium 186 (Re 186)	100
Rhenium 188 (Re 188)	100
Rhodium 103m (Rh 103m)	100
Rhodium 105 (Rh 105)	100
Rubidium 81 (Rb 81)	10
Rubidium 86 (Rb 86)	10
Rubidium 87 (Rb 87)	10
Ruthenium 97 (Ru 97)	100
Ruthenium 103 (Ru 103)	10
Ruthenium 105 (Ru 105)	10
Ruthenium 106 (Ru 106)	1
Samarium 151 (Sm 151)	10
Samarium 153 (Sm 153)	100
Scandium 46 (Sc 46)	10
Scandium 47 (Sc 47)	100
Scandium 48 (Sc 48)	10
Selenium 75 (Se 75)	10
Silicon 31 (Si 31)	100
Silver 105 (Ag 105)	10
Silver 110m (Ag 110m)	1
Silver 111 (Ag 111)	100
Sodium 22 (Na 22)	10
Sodium 24 (Na 24)	10
Strontium 85 (Sr 85)	10
Strontium 89 (Sr 89)	1
Strontium 90 (Sr 90)	0.1
Strontium 91 (Sr 91)	10
Strontium 92 (Sr 92)	10
Sulphur 35 (S 35)	100
Tantalum 182 (Ta 182)	10
Technetium 96 (Tc 96)	10
Technetium 97m (Tc 97m)	100

Byproduct material	Microcuries
Technetium 97 (Tc 97)	100
Technetium 99m (Tc 99m)	100
Technetium 99 (Tc 99)	10
Tellurium 125m (Te 125m)	10
Tellurium 127m (Te 127m)	10
Tellurium 127 (Te 127)	100
Tellurium 129m (Te 129m)	10
Tellurium 129 (Te 129)	100
Tellurium 131m (Te 131m)	10
Tellurium 132 (Te 132)	10
Terbium 160 (Tb 160)	10
Thallium 200 (Tl 200)	100
Thallium 201 (Tl 201)	100
Thallium 202 (Tl 202)	100
Thallium 204 (Tl 204)	10
Thulium 170 (Tm 170)	10
Thulium 171 (Tm 171)	10
Tin 113 (Sn 113)	10
Tin 125 (Sn 125)	10
Tungsten 181 (W 181)	10
Tungsten 185 (W 185)	10
Tungsten 187 (W 187)	100
Vanadium 48 (V 48)	10
Xenon 131m (Xe 131m)	1,000
Xenon 133 (Xe 133)	100
Xenon 135 (Xe 135)	100
Ytterbium 175 (Yb 175)	100
Yttrium 87 (Y 87)	10
Yttrium 88 (Y 88)	10
Yttrium 90 (Y 90)	10
Yttrium 91 (Y 91)	10
Yttrium 92 (Y 92)	100
Yttrium 93 (Y 93)	100
Zinc 65 (Zn 65)	10
Zinc 69m (Zn 69m)	100
Zinc 69 (Zn 69)	1,000
Zirconium 93 (Zr 93)	10
Zirconium 95 (Zr 95)	10
Zirconium 97 (Zr 97)	10
Any byproduct material not listed above other than alpha emitting byproduct material	0.1

[35 FR 6427, Apr. 22, 1970, as amended at 36 FR 16898, Aug. 26, 1971; 59 FR 5519, Feb. 7, 1994; 72 FR 55926, Oct. 1, 2007]

§ 30.72 Schedule C—Quantities of radioactive materials requiring consideration of the need for an emergency plan for responding to a release.

Radioactive material [1]	Release fraction	Quantity (curies)
Actinium-228	0.001	4,000
Americium-241	.001	2
Americium-242	.001	2
Americium-243	.001	2
Antimony-124	.01	4,000
Antimony-126	.01	6,000
Barium-133	.01	10,000
Barium-140	.01	30,000
Bismuth-207	.01	5,000
Bismuth-210	.01	600
Cadmium-109	.01	1,000
Cadmium-113	.01	80
Calcium-45	.01	20,000
Californium-252	.001	9 (20 mg)
Carbon-14 (non-carbon dioxide)	.01	50,000
Cerium-141	.01	10,000
Cerium-144	.01	300
Cesium-134	.01	2,000
Cesium-137	.01	3,000
Chlorine-36	.5	100
Chromium-51	.01	300,000
Cobalt-60	.001	5,000
Copper-64	.01	200,000
Curium-242	.001	60
Curium-243	.001	3
Curium-244	.001	4
Curium-245	.001	2
Europium-152	.01	500
Europium-154	.01	400
Europium-155	.01	3,000
Germanium-68	.01	2,000
Gadolinium-153	.01	5,000
Gold-198	.01	30,000
Hafnium-172	.01	400
Hafnium-181	.01	7,000
Holmium-166m	.01	100
Hydrogen-3	.5	20,000
Iodine-125	.5	10
Iodine-131	.5	10
Indium-114m	.01	1,000
Iridium-192	.001	40,000
Iron-55	.01	40,000
Iron-59	.01	7,000
Krypton-85	1.0	6,000,000
Lead-210	.01	8
Manganese-56	.01	60,000
Mercury-203	.01	10,000
Molybdenum-99	.01	30,000
Neptunium-237	.001	2
Nickel-63	.01	20,000
Niobium-94	.01	300
Phosphorus-32	.5	100
Phosphorus-33	.5	1,000
Polonium-210	.01	10
Potassium-42	.01	9,000
Promethium-145	.01	4,000
Promethium-147	.01	4,000
Radium-226	0.001	100
Ruthenium-106	.01	200
Samarium-151	.01	4,000
Scandium-46	.01	3,000
Selenium-75	.01	10,000
Silver-110m	.01	1,000
Sodium-22	.01	9,000
Sodium-24	.01	10,000
Strontium-89	.01	3,000
Strontium-90	.01	90
Sulfur-35	.5	900
Technitium-99	.01	10,000
Technitium-99m	.01	400,000
Tellurium-127m	.01	5,000
Tellurium-129m	.01	5,000
Terbium-160	.01	4,000
Thulium-170	.01	4,000
Tin-113	.01	10,000
Tin-123	.01	3,000
Tin-126	.01	1,000
Titanium-44	.01	100
Vanadium-48	.01	7,000
Xenon-133	1.0	900,000
Yttrium-91	.01	2,000
Zinc-65	.01	5,000
Zirconium-93	.01	400
Zirconium-95	.01	5,000
Any other beta-gamma emitter	.01	10,000
Mixed fission products	.01	1,000
Mixed corrosion products	.01	10,000
Contaminated equipment beta-gamma	.001	10,000
Irradiated material, any form other than solid noncombustible	.01	1,000

Radioactive material [1]	Release fraction	Quantity (curies)
Irradiated material, solid noncombustible	.001	10,000
Mixed radioactive waste, beta-gamma	.01	1,000
Packaged mixed waste, beta-gamma [4]	.001	10,000
Any other alpha emitter	.001	2
Contaminated equipment, alpha	.0001	20
Packaged waste, alpha [4]	.0001	20
Combinations of radioactive materials listed above [1]	....	....

[1] For combinations of radioactive materials, consideration of the need for an emergency plan is required if the sum of the ratios of the quantity of each radioactive material authorized to the quantity listed for that material in Schedule C exceeds one.

[2] Waste packaged in Type B containers does not require an emergency plan.

[54 FR 14061, Apr. 7, 1989, as amended at 61 FR 9902, Mar. 12, 1996; 72 FR 55926, Oct. 1, 2007]

Appendix A to Part 30—Criteria Relating to Use of Financial Tests and Parent Company Guarantees for Providing Reasonable Assurance of Funds for Decommissioning

I. Introduction

An applicant or licensee may provide reasonable assurance of the availability of funds for decommissioning based on obtaining a parent company guarantee that funds will be available for decommissioning costs and on a demonstration that the parent company passes a financial test. This appendix establishes criteria for passing the financial test and for obtaining the parent company guarantee.

II. Financial Test

A. To pass the financial test, the parent company must meet the criteria of either paragraph A.1 or A.2 of this section. For purposes of applying the Appendix A criteria, tangible net worth must be calculated to exclude all intangible assets and the net book value of the nuclear facility and site, and total net worth, which may include intangible assets, must be calculated to exclude the net book value and goodwill of the nuclear facility and site.

1. The parent company must have:

(i) Two of the following three ratios: A ratio of total liabilities to total net worth less than 2.0; a ratio of the sum of net income plus depreciation, depletion, and amortization to total liabilities greater than 0.1; and a ratio of current assets to current liabilities greater than 1.5; and

(ii) Net working capital and tangible net worth each at least six times the amount of decommissioning funds being assured by a parent company guarantee for the total of all nuclear facilities or parts thereof (or prescribed amount if a certification is used); and

(iii) Tangible net worth of at least $21 million; and

(iv) Assets located in the United States amounting to at least 90 percent of the total assets or at least six times the current decommissioning cost estimates for the total of all facilities or parts thereof (or prescribed amount if a certification is used), or, for a power reactor licensee, at least six times the amount of decommissioning funds being assured by a parent company guarantee for the total of all reactor units or parts thereof.

2. The parent company must have:

(i) A current rating for its most recent uninsured, uncollateralized, and unencumbered bond issuance of AAA, AA, A, or BBB (including adjustments of + and −) as issued by Standard and Poor's or Aaa, Aa, A, or Baa (including adjustment of 1, 2, or 3) as issued by Moody's; and

(ii) Total net worth at least six times the amount of decommissioning funds being assured by a parent company guarantee for the total of all nuclear facilities or parts thereof (or prescribed amount if a certification is used); and

(iii) Tangible net worth of at least $21 million; and

(iv) Assets located in the United States amounting to at least 90 percent of the total assets or at least six times the current decommissioning cost estimates for the total of all facilities or parts thereof (or prescribed amount if a certification is used), or, for a power reactor licensee, at least six times the amount of decommissioning funds being assured by a parent company guarantee for the total of all reactor units or parts thereof.

B. The parent company's independent certified public accountant must compare the data used by the parent company in the financial test, which is derived from the independently audited, year-end financial statements for the latest fiscal year, with the amounts in such financial statement. The accountant must evaluate the parent company's off-balance sheet transactions and provide an opinion on whether those transactions could materially adversely affect the parent company's ability to pay for decommissioning costs. The accountant must verify that a bond rating, if used to demonstrate passage of the financial test, meets the requirements of paragraph A of this section. In connection with the auditing procedure, the licensee must inform the NRC within 90 days of any matters coming to the auditor's attention which cause the auditor to believe that the data specified in the financial test should be adjusted and that the company no longer passes the test.

C.1. After the initial financial test, the parent company must annually pass the test and provide documentation of its continued eligibility to use the parent company guarantee to the Commission within 90 days after the close of each succeeding fiscal year.

2. If the parent company no longer meets the requirements of paragraph A of this section, the licensee must send notice to the Commission of intent to establish alternate financial assurance as specified in the Commission's regulations. The notice must be sent by certified mail within 90 days after the end of the fiscal year for which the year end financial data show that the parent company no longer meets the financial test requirements. The licensee must provide alternate financial assurance within 120 days after the end of such fiscal year.

III. PARENT COMPANY GUARANTEE

The terms of a parent company guarantee which an applicant or licensee obtains must provide that:

A. The parent company guarantee will remain in force unless the guarantor sends notice of cancellation by certified mail to the licensee and the Commission. Cancellation may not occur, however, during the 120 days beginning on the date of receipt of the notice of cancellation by both the licensee and the Commission, as evidenced by the return receipts.

B. If the licensee fails to provide alternate financial assurance as specified in the Commission's regulations within 90 days after receipt by the licensee and Commission of a notice of cancellation of the parent company guarantee from the guarantor, the guarantor will provide alternative financial assurance that meets the provisions of the Commission's regulations in the name of the licensee.

C. The parent company guarantee and financial test provisions must remain in effect until the Commission has terminated the license, accepted in writing the parent company's alternate financial assurances, or accepted in writing the licensee's financial assurances.

D. A standby trust to protect public health and safety and the environment must be established for decommissioning costs before the parent company guarantee agreement is submitted. The trustee and trust must be acceptable to the Commission. An acceptable trustee includes an appropriate State or Federal Government agency or an entity which has the authority to act as a trustee, whose trust operations are regulated and examined by a Federal or State agency. The Commission has the right to change the trustee. An acceptable trust will meet the regulatory criteria established in these regulations that govern the issuance of the license for which the guarantor has accepted the obligation to pay for decommissioning costs.

E. The guarantor must agree that it would be subject to Commission orders to make payments under the guarantee agreement.

F. The guarantor must agree that if the guarantor admits in writing its inability to pay its debts generally, or makes a general assignment for the benefit of creditors, or any proceeding is instituted by or against the guarantor seeking to adjudicate it as bankrupt or insolvent, or seeking dissolution, liquidation, winding-up, reorganization, arrangement, adjustment, protection, relief or composition of it or its debts under any law relating to bankruptcy, insolvency, or reorganization or relief of debtors, or seeking the entry of an order for relief or the appointment of a receiver, trustee, custodian, or other similar official for the guarantor or for any substantial part of its property, or the guarantor takes any action to authorize or effect any of the actions stated in this paragraph, then the Commission may:

1. Declare that the financial assurance guaranteed by the parent company guarantee agreement is immediately due and payable to the standby trust set up to protect the public health and safety and the environment, without diligence, presentment, demand, protest or any other notice of any kind, all of which are expressly waived by guarantor; and

2. Exercise any and all of its other rights under applicable law.

G. 1. The guarantor must agree to notify the NRC, in writing, immediately following the filing of a voluntary or involuntary petition for bankruptcy under any chapter of title 11 (Bankruptcy) of the United States Code, or the occurrence of any other event listed in paragraph F of this Appendix, by or against:

(i) The guarantor;

(ii) The licensee;

(iii) An entity (as that term is defined in 11 U.S.C. 101(14)) controlling the licensee or listing the license or licensee as property of the estate; or

(iv) An affiliate (as that term is defined in 11 U.S.C. 101(2)) of the licensee.

2. This notification must include:

(i) A description of the event, including major creditors, the amounts involved, and the actions taken to assure that the amount of funds guaranteed by the parent company guarantee for decommissioning will be transferred to the standby trust as soon as possible;

(ii) If a petition of bankruptcy was filed, the identity of the bankruptcy court in which the petition for bankruptcy was filed; and

(iii) The date of filing of any petitions.

[53 FR 24046, June 27, 1988, as amended at 63 FR 50479, Sept. 22, 1998; 76 FR 35565, June 17, 2011]

APPENDIX B TO PART 30—QUANTITIES[1] OF LICENSED MATERIAL REQUIRING LABELING

Material	Micro-curies
Americium-241	.01
Antimony-122	100
Antimony-124	10
Antimony-125	10
Arsenic-73	100
Arsenic-74	10
Arsenic-76	10
Arsenic-77	100
Barium-131	10
Barium-133	10
Barium-140	10
Bismuth-210	1
Bromine-82	10
Cadmium-109	10
Cadmium-115m	10
Cadmium-115	100
Calcium-45	10
Calcium-47	10
Carbon-14	100
Cerium-141	100
Cerium-143	100
Cerium-144	1
Cesium-131	1,000
Cesium-134m	100
Cesium-134	1
Cesium-135	10
Cesium-136	10
Cesium-137	10
Chlorine-36	10
Chlorine-38	10
Chromium-51	1,000
Cobalt-58m	10
Cobalt-58	10
Cobalt-60	1
Copper-64	100
Dysprosium-165	10
Dysprosium-166	100
Erbium-169	100
Erbium-171	100
Europium-152 9.2 h	100
Europium-152 13 yr	1
Europium-154	1
Europium-155	10
Fluorine-18	1,000
Gadolinium-153	10
Gadolinium-159	100
Gallium-72	10
Germanium-71	100
Gold-198	100
Gold-199	100
Hafnium-181	10
Holmium-166	100
Hydrogen-3	1,000
Indium-113m	100
Indium-114m	10
Indium-115m	100
Indium-115	10
Iodine-125	1
Iodine-126	1
Iodine-129	0.1
Iodine-131	1
Iodine-132	10
Iodine-133	1
Iodine-134	10
Iodine-135	10
Iridium-192	10
Iridium-194	100
Iron-55	100
Iron-59	10
Krypton-85	100
Krypton-87	10
Lanthanum-140	10
Lutetium-177	100
Manganese-52	10
Manganese-54	10
Manganese-56	10
Mercury-197m	100
Mercury-197	100
Mercury-203	10
Molybdenum-99	100
Neodymium-147	100
Neodymium-149	100
Nickel-59	100
Nickel-63	10
Nickel-65	100
Niobium-93m	10
Niobium-95	10
Niobium-97	10
Osmium-185	10
Osmium-191m	100
Osmium-191	100
Osmium-193	100
Palladium-103	100
Palladium-109	100
Phosphorus-32	10
Platinum-191	100
Platinum-193m	100
Platinum-193	100
Platinum-197m	100
Platinum-197	100
Plutonium-239	.01
Polonium-210	0.1
Potassium-42	10
Praseodymium-142	100
Praseodymium-143	100
Promethium-147	10
Promethium-149	10
Radium-226	.01
Rhenium-186	100
Rhenium-188	100
Rhodium-103m	100
Rhodium-105	100
Rubidium-86	10
Rubidium-87	10
Ruthenium-97	100
Ruthenium-103	10
Ruthenium-105	10
Ruthenium-106	1
Samarium-151	10
Samarium-153	100
Scandium-46	10
Scandium-47	100
Scandium-48	10
Selenium-75	10
Silicon-31	100
Silver-105	10
Silver-110m	1
Silver-111	100
Sodium-24	10
Strontium-85	10
Strontium-89	1
Strontium-90	0.1
Strontium-91	10
Strontium-92	10
Sulphur-35	100
Tantalum-182	10
Technetium-96	10
Technetium-97m	100
Technetium-97	100
Technetium-99m	100
Technetium-99	10
Tellurium-125m	10

Material	Micro-curies
Tellurium-127m	10
Tellurium-127	100
Tellurium-129m	10
Tellurium-129	100
Tellurium-131m	10
Tellurium-132	10
Terbium-160	10
Thallium-200	100
Thallium-201	100
Thallium-202	100
Thallium-204	10
Thorium (natural) [1]	100
Thulium-170	10
Thulium-171	10
Tin-113	10
Tin-125	10
Tungsten-181	10
Tungsten-185	10
Tungsten-187	100
Uranium (natural) [2]	100
Uranium-233	.01
Uranium-234—Uranium-235	.01
Vanadium-48	10
Xenon-131m	1,000
Xenon-133	100
Xenon-135	100
Ytterbium-175	100
Yttrium-90	10
Yttrium-91	10
Yttrium-92	100
Yttrium-93	100
Zinc-65	10
Zinc-69m	100
Zinc-69	1,000
Zirconium-93	10
Zirconium-95	10
Zirconium-97	10
Any alpha emitting radionuclide not listed above or mixtures of alpha emitters of unknown composition	.01
Any radionuclide other than alpha emitting radionuclides, not listed above or mixtures of beta emitters of unknown composition	.1

[1] Based on alpha disintegration rate of Th-232, Th-230 and their daughter products.

[2] Based on alpha disintegration rate of U-238, U-234, and U-235.

NOTE: For purposes of § 20.303, where there is involved a combination of isotopes in known amounts, the limit for the combination should be derived as follows: Determine, for each isotope in the combination, the ratio between the quantity present in the combination and the limit otherwise established for the specific isotope when not in combination. The sum of such ratios for all the isotopes in the combination may not exceed "1" (*i.e.*, "unity").

[35 FR 6425, Apr. 22, 1970, as amended at 36 FR 16898, Aug. 26, 1971; 38 FR 29314, Oct. 24, 1973; 39 FR 23991, June 28, 1974; 45 FR 71763, Oct. 30, 1980. Redesignated at 56 FR 23391, May 21, 1991, and further redesignated at 58 FR 67659, Dec. 22, 1993]

APPENDIX C TO PART 30—CRITERIA RELATING TO USE OF FINANCIAL TESTS AND SELF GUARANTEES FOR PROVIDING REASONABLE ASSURANCE OF FUNDS FOR DECOMMISSIONING

I. INTRODUCTION

An applicant or licensee may provide reasonable assurance of the availability of funds for decommissioning based on furnishing its own guarantee that funds will be available for decommissioning costs and on a demonstration that the company passes the financial test of Section II of this appendix. The terms of the self-guarantee are in Section III of this appendix. This appendix establishes criteria for passing the financial test for the self guarantee and establishes the terms for a self-guarantee.

II. FINANCIAL TEST

A. To pass the financial test a company must meet all of the criteria set forth in this section. For purposes of applying the Appendix C criteria, tangible net worth must be calculated to exclude all intangible assets and the net book value of the nuclear facility and site, and total net worth, which may include intangible assets, must be calculated to exclude the net book value and goodwill of the nuclear facility and site. These criteria include:

(1) Tangible net worth of at least $21 million, and total net worth at least 10 times the amount of decommissioning funds being assured by a self-guarantee for all decommissioning activities for which the company is responsible as self-guaranteeing licensee and as parent-guarantor for the total of all nuclear facilities or parts thereof (or the current amount required if certification is used).

(2) Assets located in the United States amounting to at least 90 percent of total assets or at least 10 times the amount of decommissioning funds being assured by a self-guarantee, for all decommissioning activities for which the company is responsible as self-guaranteeing licensee and as parent-guarantor for the total of all nuclear facilities or parts thereof (or the current amount required if certification is used).

(3) A current rating for its most recent uninsured, uncollateralized, and unencumbered bond issuance of AAA, AA, or A (including adjustments of + and −) as issued by Standard and Poor's, or Aaa, Aa, or A (including adjustments of 1, 2, or 3) as issued by Moody's.

B. To pass the financial test, a company must meet all of the following additional requirements:

(1) The company must have at least one class of equity securities registered under the Securities Exchange Act of 1934.

(2) The company's independent certified public accountant must compare the data used by the company in the financial test, which is derived from the independently audited, year-end financial statements for the latest fiscal year, with the amounts in such financial statement. The accountant must evaluate the company's off-balance sheet transactions and provide an opinion on whether those transactions could materially adversely affect the company's ability to pay for decommissioning costs. The accountant must verify that a bond rating, if used to demonstrate passage of the financial test, meets the requirements of Section II, paragraph A of this appendix. In connection with the auditing procedure, the licensee must inform the NRC within 90 days of any matters coming to the auditor's attention which cause the auditor to believe that the data specified in the financial test should be adjusted and that the company no longer passes the test.

(3) After the initial financial test, the company must annually pass the test and provide documentation of its continued eligibility to use the self-guarantee to the Commission within 90 days after the close of each succeeding fiscal year.

C. If the licensee no longer meets the requirements of Section II.A. of this appendix, the licensee must send immediate notice to the Commission of its intent to establish alternate financial assurance as specified in the Commission's regulations within 120 days of such notice.

III. Company Self-Guarantee

The terms of a self-guarantee which an applicant or licensee furnishes must provide that:

A. The guarantee will remain in force unless the licensee sends notice of cancellation by certified mail to the Commission. Cancellation may not occur, however, during the 120 days beginning on the date of receipt of the notice of cancellation by the Commission, as evidenced by the return receipt.

B. The licensee shall provide alternative financial assurance as specified in the Commission's regulations within 90 days following receipt by the Commission of a notice of cancellation of the guarantee.

C. The guarantee and financial test provisions must remain in effect until the Commission has terminated the license or until another financial assurance method acceptable to the Commission has been put in effect by the licensee.

D. The licensee will promptly forward to the Commission and the licensee's independent auditor all reports covering the latest fiscal year filed by the licensee with the Securities and Exchange Commission pursuant to the requirements of section 13 of the Securities and Exchange Act of 1934.

E. (1) If, at any time, the licensee's most recent bond issuance ceases to be rated in any category of "A−" and above by Standard and Poor's or in any category of "A3" and above by Moody's, the licensee will notify the Commission in writing within 20 days after publication of the change by the rating service.

(2) If the licensee's most recent bond issuance ceases to be rated in any category of A or above by both Standard and Poor's and Moody's, the licensee no longer meets the requirements of Section II.A. of this appendix.

F. The applicant or licensee must provide to the Commission a written guarantee (a written commitment by a corporate officer) which states that the licensee will fund and carry out the required decommissioning activities or, upon issuance of an order by the Commission, the licensee will fund the standby trust in the amount guaranteed by the self-guarantee agreement.

G. (1) A standby trust to protect public health and safety and the environment must be established for decommissioning costs before the self-guarantee agreement is submitted.

(2) The trustee and trust must be acceptable to the Commission. An acceptable trustee includes an appropriate State or Federal Government agency or an entity which has the authority to act as a trustee and whose trust operations are regulated and examined by a Federal or State agency. The Commission has the right to change the trustee. An acceptable trust will meet the regulatory criteria established in these regulations that govern the issuance of the license for which the guarantor has accepted the obligation to pay for decommissioning costs.

H. The guarantor must agree that if the guarantor admits in writing its inability to pay its debts generally, or makes a general assignment for the benefit of creditors, or any proceeding is instituted by or against the guarantor seeking to adjudicate it as bankrupt or insolvent, or seeking dissolution, liquidation, winding-up, reorganization, arrangement, adjustment, protection, relief or composition of it or its debts under any law relating to bankruptcy, insolvency, or reorganization or relief of debtors, or seeking the entry of an order for relief or the appointment of a receiver, trustee, custodian, or other similar official for the guarantor or for any substantial part of its property, or the guarantor takes any action to authorize or effect any of the actions stated in this paragraph, then the Commission may:

(1) Declare that the financial assurance guaranteed by the self-guarantee agreement is immediately due and payable to the standby trust set up to protect the public health and safety and the environment, without diligence, presentment, demand, protest or

any other notice of any kind, all of which are expressly waived by guarantor; and

(2) Exercise any and all of its other rights under applicable law.

I. The guarantor must notify the NRC, in writing, immediately following the occurrence of any event listed in paragraph H of this appendix, and must include a description of the event, including major creditors, the amounts involved, and the actions taken to assure that the amount of funds guaranteed by the self-guarantee agreement for decommissioning will be transferred to the standby trust as soon as possible.

[58 FR 68730, Dec. 29, 1993; 59 FR 1618, Jan. 12, 1994, as amended at 63 FR 50479, Sept. 22, 1998; 76 FR 35566, June 17, 2011]

APPENDIX D TO PART 30—CRITERIA RELATING TO USE OF FINANCIAL TESTS AND SELF-GUARANTEE FOR PROVIDING REASONABLE ASSURANCE OF FUNDS FOR DECOMMISSIONING BY COMMERCIAL COMPANIES THAT HAVE NO OUTSTANDING RATED BONDS

I. INTRODUCTION

An applicant or licensee may provide reasonable assurance of the availability of funds for decommissioning based on furnishing its own guarantee that funds will be available for decommissioning costs and on a demonstration that the company passes the financial test of Section II of this appendix. The terms of the self-guarantee are in Section III of this appendix. This appendix establishes criteria for passing the financial test for the self-guarantee and establishes the terms for a self-guarantee.

II. FINANCIAL TEST

A. To pass the financial test a company must meet all of the criteria set forth in this section. For purposes of applying the Appendix D criteria, tangible net worth must be calculated to exclude all intangible assets and the net book value of the nuclear facility and site, and total net worth, which may include intangible assets, must be calculated to exclude the net book value and goodwill of the nuclear facility and site. These criteria include:

(1) Tangible net worth of at least $21 million, and total net worth of at least 10 times the amount of decommissioning funds being assured by a self-guarantee for all decommissioning activities for which the company is responsible as self-guaranteeing licensee and as parent-guarantor for the total of all nuclear facilities or parts thereof (or the current amount required if certification is used).

(2) Assets located in the United States amounting to at least 90 percent of total assets or at least 10 times the total current decommissioning cost estimate (or the current amount required if certification is used) for all decommissioning activities for which the company is responsible as self-guaranteeing licensee and as parent-guarantor.

(3) A ratio of cash flow divided by total liabilities greater than 0.15 and a ratio of total liabilities divided by total net worth less than 1.5.

B. In addition, to pass the financial test, a company must meet all of the following requirements:

(1) The company's independent certified public accountant must compare the data used by the company in the financial test, which is derived from the independently audited, year-end financial statements for the latest fiscal year, with the amounts in such financial statement. The accountant must evaluate the company's off-balance sheet transactions and provide an opinion on whether those transactions could materially adversely affect the company's ability to pay for decommissioning costs. In connection with the auditing procedure, the licensee must inform the NRC within 90 days of any matters coming to the auditor's attention which cause the auditor to believe that the data specified in the financial test should be adjusted and that the company no longer passes the test.

(2) After the initial financial test, the company must annually pass the test and provide documentation of its continued eligibility to use the self-guarantee to the Commission within 90 days after the close of each succeeding fiscal year.

(3) If the licensee no longer meets the requirements of paragraph II.A of this appendix, the licensee must send notice to the NRC of intent to establish alternative financial assurance as specified in NRC regulations. The notice must be sent by certified mail, return receipt requested, within 90 days after the end of the fiscal year for which the year end financial data show that the licensee no longer meets the financial test requirements. The licensee must provide alternative financial assurance within 120 days after the end of such fiscal year.

III. COMPANY SELF-GUARANTEE

The terms of a self-guarantee which an applicant or licensee furnishes must provide that:

A. The guarantee shall remain in force unless the licensee sends notice of cancellation by certified mail, return receipt requested, to the NRC. Cancellation may not occur until an alternative financial assurance mechanism is in place.

B. The licensee shall provide alternative financial assurance as specified in the regulations within 90 days following receipt by the NRC of a notice of cancellation of the guarantee.

C. The guarantee and financial test provisions must remain in effect until the Commission has terminated the license or until another financial assurance method acceptable to the Commission has been put in effect by the licensee.

D. The applicant or licensee must provide to the Commission a written guarantee (a written commitment by a corporate officer) which states that the licensee will fund and carry out the required decommissioning activities or, upon issuance of an order by the Commission, the licensee will fund the standby trust in the amount of the current cost estimates for decommissioning.

E. A standby trust to protect public health and safety and the environment must be established for decommissioning costs before the self-guarantee agreement is submitted. The trustee and trust must be acceptable to the Commission. An acceptable trustee includes an appropriate State or Federal Government agency or an entity which has the authority to act as a trustee and whose trust operations are regulated and examined by a Federal or State agency. The Commission will have the right to change the trustee. An acceptable trust will meet the regulatory criteria established in the part of these regulations that governs the issuance of the license for which the guarantor has accepted the obligation to pay for decommissioning costs.

F. The guarantor must agree that if the guarantor admits in writing its inability to pay its debts generally, or makes a general assignment for the benefit of creditors, or any proceeding is instituted by or against the guarantor seeking to adjudicate it as bankrupt or insolvent, or seeking dissolution, liquidation, winding-up, reorganization, arrangement, adjustment, protection, relief or composition of it or its debts under any law relating to bankruptcy, insolvency, or reorganization or relief of debtors, or seeking the entry of an order for relief or the appointment of a receiver, trustee, custodian, or other similar official for the guarantor or for any substantial part of its property, or the guarantor takes any action to authorize or effect any of the actions stated in this paragraph, then the Commission may:

(1) Declare that the financial assurance guaranteed by the self-guarantee agreement is immediately due and payable to the standby trust set up to protect the public health and safety and the environment, without diligence, presentment, demand, protest or any other notice of any kind, all of which are expressly waived by guarantor; and

(2) Exercise any and all of its other rights under applicable law.

G. The guarantor must notify the NRC, in writing, immediately following the occurrence of any event listed in paragraph F of this appendix, and must include a description of the event, including major creditors, the amounts involved, and the actions taken to assure that the amount of funds guaranteed by the self-guarantee agreement for decommissioning will be transferred to the standby trust as soon as possible.

[63 FR 29542, June 1, 1998, as amended at 76 FR 35567, June 17, 2011]

Appendix E to Part 30—Criteria Relating to Use of Financial Tests and Self-Guarantee For Providing Reasonable Assurance of Funds For Decommissioning by Nonprofit Colleges, Universities, and Hospitals

I. Introduction

An applicant or licensee may provide reasonable assurance of the availability of funds for decommissioning based on furnishing its own guarantee that funds will be available for decommissioning costs and on a demonstration that the applicant or licensee passes the financial test of Section II of this appendix. The terms of the self-guarantee are in Section III of this appendix. This appendix establishes criteria for passing the financial test for the self-guarantee and establishes the terms for a self-guarantee.

II. Financial Test

A. For colleges and universities, to pass the financial test a college or university must meet either the criteria in Paragraph II.A.(1) or the criteria in Paragraph II.A.(2) of this appendix.

(1) For applicants or licensees that issue bonds, a current rating for its most recent uninsured, uncollateralized, and unencumbered bond issuance of AAA, AA, or A (including adjustments of + or −) as issued by Standard and Poor's (S&P) or Aaa, Aa, or A (including adjustments of 1, 2, or 3) as issued by Moody's.

(2) For applicants or licensees that do not issue bonds, unrestricted endowment consisting of assets located in the United States of at least $50 million, or at least 30 times the total current decommissioning cost estimate (or the current amount required if certification is used), whichever is greater, for all decommissioning activities for which the college or university is responsible as a self-guaranteeing licensee.

B. For hospitals, to pass the financial test a hospital must meet either the criteria in Paragraph II.B.(1) or the criteria in Paragraph II.B.(2) of this appendix:

(1) For applicants or licensees that issue bonds, a current rating for its most recent uninsured, uncollateralized, and unencumbered bond issuance of AAA, AA, or A (including adjustments of + or −) as issued

by Standard and Poor's or Aaa, Aa, or A (including adjustments of 1, 2, or 3) as issued by Moody's.

(2) For applicants or licensees that do not issue bonds, all the following tests must be met:

(a) (Total Revenues less total expenditures) divided by total revenues must be equal to or greater than 0.04.

(b) Long term debt divided by net fixed assets must be less than or equal to 0.67.

(c) (Current assets and depreciation fund) divided by current liabilities must be greater than or equal to 2.55.

(d) Operating revenues must be at least 100 times the total current decommissioning cost estimate (or the current amount required if certification is used) for all decommissioning activities for which the hospital is responsible as a self-guaranteeing license.

C. In addition, to pass the financial test, a licensee must meet all the following requirements:

(1) The licensee's independent certified public accountant must compare the data used by the licensee in the financial test, which is derived from the independently audited, year-end financial statements for the latest fiscal year, with the amounts in such financial statement. The accountant must evaluate the licensee's off-balance sheet transactions and provide an opinion on whether those transactions could materially adversely affect the licensee's ability to pay for decommissioning costs. The accountant must verify that a bond rating, if used to demonstrate passage of the financial test, meets the requirements of Section II of this appendix. In connection with the auditing procedure, the licensee must inform the NRC within 90 days of any matters coming to the auditor's attention which cause the auditor to believe that the data specified in the financial test should be adjusted and that the licensee no longer passes the test.

(2) After the initial financial test, the licensee must repeat passage of the test and provide documentation of its continued eligibility to use the self-guarantee to the Commission within 90 days after the close of each succeeding fiscal year.

(3) If the licensee no longer meets the requirements of Section I of this appendix, the licensee must send notice to the NRC of its intent to establish alternative financial assurance as specified in NRC regulations. The notice must be sent by certified mail, return receipt requested, within 90 days after the end of the fiscal year for which the year end financial data show that the licensee no longer meets the financial test requirements. The licensee must provide alternate financial assurance within 120 days after the end of such fiscal year.

III. SELF-GUARANTEE

The terms of a self-guarantee which an applicant or licensee furnishes must provide that—

A. The guarantee shall remain in force unless the licensee sends notice of cancellation by certified mail, and/or return receipt requested, to the Commission. Cancellation may not occur unless an alternative financial assurance mechanism is in place.

B. The licensee shall provide alternative financial assurance as specified in the Commission's regulations within 90 days following receipt by the Commission of a notice of cancellation of the guarantee.

C. The guarantee and financial test provisions must remain in effect until the Commission has terminated the license or until another financial assurance method acceptable to the Commission has been put in effect by the licensee.

D. The applicant or licensee must provide to the Commission a written guarantee (a written commitment by a corporate officer or officer of the institution) which states that the licensee will fund and carry out the required decommissioning activities or, upon issuance of an order by the Commission, the licensee will fund the standby trust in the amount of the current cost estimates for decommissioning.

E. (1) If, at any time, the licensee's most recent bond issuance ceases to be rated in any category of "A" or above by either Standard and Poor's or Moody's, the licensee shall notify the Commission in writing within 20 days after publication of the change by the rating service.

(2) If the licensee's most recent bond issuance ceases to be rated in any category of "A−" and above by Standard and Poor's or in any category of "A3" and above by Moody's, the licensee no longer meets the requirements of Section II.A. of this appendix.

F. (1) A standby trust to protect public health and safety and the environment must be established for decommissioning costs before the self-guarantee agreement is submitted.

(2) The trustee and trust must be acceptable to the Commission. An acceptable trustee includes an appropriate State or Federal Government agency or an entity which has the authority to act as a trustee and whose trust operations are regulated and examined by a Federal or State agency. The Commission has the right to change the trustee. An acceptable trust will meet the regulatory criteria established in the part of these regulations that governs the issuance of the license for which the guarantor has accepted the obligation to pay for decommissioning costs.

G. The guarantor must agree that if the guarantor admits in writing its inability to pay its debts generally, or makes a general assignment for the benefit of creditors, or any proceeding is instituted by or against the guarantor seeking to adjudicate it as bankrupt or insolvent, or seeking dissolution, liquidation, winding-up, reorganization, arrangement, adjustment, protection, relief or composition of it or its debts under any law relating to bankruptcy, insolvency, or reorganization or relief of debtors, or seeking the entry of an order for relief or the appointment of a receiver, trustee, custodian, or other similar official for guarantor or for any substantial part of its property, or the guarantor takes any action to authorize or effect any of the actions stated in this paragraph, then the Commission may:

(1) Declare that the financial assurance guaranteed by the self-guarantee agreement is immediately due and payable to the standby trust set up to protect the public health and safety and the environment, without diligence, presentment, demand, protest or any other notice of any kind, all of which are expressly waived by guarantor; and

(2) Exercise any and all of its other rights under applicable law.

H. The guarantor must notify the NRC, in writing, immediately following the occurrence of any event listed in paragraph G of this appendix, and must include a description of the event, including major creditors, the amounts involved, and the actions taken to assure that the amount of funds guaranteed by the self-guarantee agreement for decommissioning will be transferred to the standby trust as soon as possible.

[63 FR 29542, June 1, 1998, as amended at 76 FR 35568, June 17, 2011]

PART 31—GENERAL DOMESTIC LICENSES FOR BYPRODUCT MATERIAL

Sec.

AUTHORITY: Atomic Energy Act of 1954, secs. 81, 161, 183, 223, 234, 274 (42 U.S.C. 2111, 2201, 2233, 2273, 2282, 2021); Energy Reorganization Act of 1974, secs. 201, 202, 206 (42 U.S.C. 5841, 5842, 5846); 44 U.S.C. 3504 note.

EDITORIAL NOTE: Nomenclature changes to part 31 appear at 79 FR 75739, Dec. 19, 2014.

§ 31.1 Purpose and scope.

This part establishes general licenses for the possession and use of byproduct material and a general license for ownership of byproduct material. Specific provisions of 10 CFR Part 30 are applicable to general licenses established by this part. These provisions are specified in §31.2 or in the particular general license.

[65 FR 79187, Dec. 18, 2000]

§ 31.2 Terms and conditions.

The general licenses provided in this part are subject to the general provisions of Part 30 of this chapter (§§30.1 through 30.10), the provisions of §§30.14(d), 30.34(a) to (e), 30.41, 30.50 to 30.53, 30.61 to 30.63, and Parts 19, 20, and 21, of this chapter[1] unless indicated otherwise in the specific provision of the general license.

[65 FR 79187, Dec. 18, 2000]

§ 31.3 [Reserved]

§ 31.4 Information collection requirements: OMB approval.

(a) The Nuclear Regulatory Commission has submitted the information collection requirements contained in this part to the Office of Management and Budget (OMB) for approval as required by the Paperwork Reduction Act (44 U.S.C. 3501 *et seq.*). The NRC

[1] Attention is directed particularly to the provisions of Part 20 of this chapter concerning labeling of containers.

may not conduct or sponsor, and a person is not required to respond to, a collection of information unless it displays a currently valid OMB control number. OMB has approved the information collection requirements contained in this part under control number 3150–0016.

(b) The approved information collection requirements contained in this part appear in §§31.5, 31.8, 31.11, and 31.12.

(c) This part contains information collection requirements in addition to those approved under the control number specified in paragraph (a) of this section. These information collection requirements and the control numbers under which they are approved are as follows:

(1) In §31.11. NRC Form 483 is approved under control number 3150–0038.

(2) [Reserved]

[62 FR 52186, Oct. 6, 1997, as amended at 67 FR 67099, Nov. 4, 2002; 72 FR 55926, Oct. 1, 2007]

§31.5 Certain detecting, measuring, gauging, or controlling devices and certain devices for producing light or an ionized atmosphere.[2]

(a) A general license is hereby issued to commercial and industrial firms and research, educational and medical institutions, individuals in the conduct of their business, and Federal, State or local government agencies to acquire, receive, possess, use or transfer, in accordance with the provisions of paragraphs (b), (c) and (d) of this section, byproduct material contained in devices designed and manufactured for the purpose of detecting, measuring, gauging or controlling thickness, density, level, interface location, radiation, leakage, or qualitative or quantitative chemical composition, or for producing light or an ionized atmosphere.

(b)(1) The general license in paragraph (a) of this section applies only to byproduct material contained in devices which have been manufactured or initially transferred and labeled in accordance with the specifications contained in—

(i) A specific license issued under §32.51 of this chapter; or

(ii) An equivalent specific license issued by an Agreement State; or

(iii) An equivalent specific license issued by a State with provisions comparable to §32.51 of this chapter.

(2) The devices must have been received from one of the specific licensees described in paragraph (b)(1) of this section or through a transfer made under paragraph (c)(9) of this section.

(c) Any person who acquires, receives, possesses, uses or transfers byproduct material in a device pursuant to the general license in paragraph (a) of this section:

(1) Shall assure that all labels affixed to the device at the time of receipt and bearing a statement that removal of the label is prohibited are maintained thereon and shall comply with all instructions and precautions provided by such labels;

(2) Shall assure that the device is tested for leakage of radioactive material and proper operation of the on-off mechanism and indicator, if any, at no longer than six-month intervals or at such other intervals as are specified in the label; however:

(i) Devices containing only krypton need not be tested for leakage of radioactive material, and

(ii) Devices containing only tritium or not more than 100 microcuries of other beta and/or gamma emitting material or 10 microcuries of alpha emitting material and devices held in storage in the original shipping container prior to initial installation need not be tested for any purpose;

(3) Shall assure that the tests required by paragraph (c)(2) of this section and other testing, installation, servicing, and removal from installation involving the radioactive materials, its shielding or containment, are performed:

(i) In accordance with the instructions provided by the labels; or

(ii) By a person holding a specific license pursuant to parts 30 and 32 of this chapter or from an Agreement State to perform such activities;

(4) Shall maintain records showing compliance with the requirements of

[2] Persons possessing byproduct material in devices under a general license in §31.5 before January 15, 1975, may continue to possess, use, or transfer that material in accordance with the labeling requirements of §31.5 in effect on January 14, 1975.

paragraphs (c)(2) and (c)(3) of this section. The records must show the results of tests. The records also must show the dates of performance of, and the names of persons performing, testing, installing, servicing, and removing from the installation radioactive material and its shielding or containment. The licensee shall retain these records as follows:

(i) Each record of a test for leakage or radioactive material required by paragraph (c)(2) of this section must be retained for three years after the next required leak test is performed or until the sealed source is transferred or disposed of.

(ii) Each record of a test of the on-off mechanism and indicator required by paragraph (c)(2) of this section must be retained for three years after the next required test of the on-off mechanism and indicator is performed or until the sealed source is transferred or disposed of.

(iii) Each record that is required by paragraph (c)(3) of this section must be retained for three years from the date of the recorded event or until the device is transferred or disposed of.

(5) Shall immediately suspend operation of the device if there is a failure of, or damage to, or any indication of a possible failure of or damage to, the shielding of the radioactive material or the on-off mechanism or indicator, or upon the detection of 185 bequerel (0.005 microcurie) or more removable radioactive material. The device may not be operated until it has been repaired by the manufacturer or other person holding a specific license to repair such devices that was issued under parts 30 and 32 of this chapter or by an Agreement State. The device and any radioactive material from the device may only be disposed of by transfer to a person authorized by a specific license to receive the byproduct material in the device or as otherwise approved by the Commission. A report containing a brief description of the event and the remedial action taken; and, in the case of detection of 0.005 microcurie or more removable radioactive material or failure of or damage to a source likely to result in contamination of the premises or the environs, a plan for ensuring that the premises and environs are acceptable for unrestricted use, must be furnished to the Director, Office of Nuclear Material Safety and Safeguards, ATTN: GLTS, U.S. Nuclear Regulatory Commission, Washington, DC 20555–0001 within 30 days. Under these circumstances, the criteria set out in § 20.1402 of this chapter, "Radiological criteria for unrestricted use," may be applicable, as determined by the Commission on a case-by-case basis;

(6) Shall not abandon the device containing byproduct material;

(7) Shall not export the device containing byproduct material except in accordance with part 110 of this chapter;

(8)(i) Shall transfer or dispose of the device containing byproduct material only by export as provided by paragraph (c)(7) of this section, by transfer to another general licensee as authorized in paragraph (c)(9) of this section, or to a person authorized to receive the device by a specific license issued under parts 30 and 32 of this chapter, or part 30 of this chapter that authorizes waste collection, or equivalent regulations of an Agreement State, or as otherwise approved under paragraph (c)(8)(iii) of this section.

(ii) Shall, within 30 days after the transfer of a device to a specific licensee or export, furnish a report to the Director, Office of Nuclear Material Safety and Safeguards , ATTN: Document Control Desk/GLTS, using an appropriate method listed in § 30.6(a) of this chapter. The report must contain—

(A) The identification of the device by manufacturer's (or initial transferor's) name, model number, and serial number;

(B) The name, address, and license number of the person receiving the device (license number not applicable if exported); and

(C) The date of the transfer.

(iii) Shall obtain written NRC approval before transferring the device to any other specific licensee not specifically identified in paragraph (c)(8)(i) of this section; however, a holder of a specific license may transfer a device for possession and use under its own specific license without prior approval, if, the holder:

(A) Verifies that the specific license authorizes the possession and use, or applies for and obtains an amendment to the license authorizing the possession and use;

(B) Removes, alters, covers, or clearly and unambiguously augments the existing label (otherwise required by paragraph (c)(1) of this section) so that the device is labeled in compliance with §20.1904 of this chapter; however the manufacturer, model number, and serial number must be retained;

(C) Obtains the manufacturer's or initial transferor's information concerning maintenance that would be applicable under the specific license (such as leak testing procedures); and

(D) Reports the transfer under paragraph (c)(8)(ii) of this section.

(9) Shall transfer the device to another general licensee only if—

(i) The device remains in use at a particular location. In this case, the transferor shall give the transferee a copy of this section, a copy of §31.2, 30.51, 20.2201, and 20.2202 of this chapter, and any safety documents identified in the label of the device. Within 30 days of the transfer, the transferor shall report to the Director, Office of Nuclear Material Safety and Safeguards , ATTN: Document Control Desk/GLTS, using an appropriate method listed in §30.6(a) of this chapter—

(A) The manufacturer's (or initial transferor's) name;

(B) The model number and the serial number of the device transferred;

(C) The transferee's name and mailing address for the location of use; and

(D) The name, title, and phone number of the responsible individual identified by the transferee in accordance with paragraph (c)(12) of this section to have knowledge of and authority to take actions to ensure compliance with the appropriate regulations and requirements; or

(ii) The device is held in storage by an intermediate person in the original shipping container at its intended location of use prior to initial use by a general licensee.

(10) Shall comply with the provisions of §§20.2201, and 20.2202 of this chapter for reporting radiation incidents, theft or loss of licensed material, but shall be exempt from the other requirements of parts 19, 20, and 21, of this chapter.

(11) Shall respond to written requests from the Nuclear Regulatory Commission to provide information relating to the general license within 30 calendar days of the date of the request, or other time specified in the request. If the general licensee cannot provide the requested information within the allotted time, it shall, within that same time period, request a longer period to supply the information by providing the Director, Office of Nuclear Material Safety and Safeguards , by an appropriate method listed in §30.6(a) of this chapter, a written justification for the request.

(12) Shall appoint an individual responsible for having knowledge of the appropriate regulations and requirements and the authority for taking required actions to comply with appropriate regulations and requirements. The general licensee, through this individual, shall ensure the day-to-day compliance with appropriate regulations and requirements. This appointment does not relieve the general licensee of any of its responsibility in this regard.

(13)(i) Shall register, in accordance with paragraphs (c)(13)(ii) and (iii) of this section, devices containing at least 370 megabecquerels (10 millicuries) of cesium-137, 3.7 megabecquerels (0.1 millicurie) of strontium-90, 37 megabecquerels (1 millicurie) of cobalt-60, 3.7 megabecquerels (0.1 millicurie) of radium-226, or 37 megabecquerels (1 millicurie) of americium-241 or any other transuranic (*i.e.*, element with atomic number greater than uranium (92)), based on the activity indicated on the label. Each address for a location of use, as described under paragraph (c)(13)(iii)(D) of this section, represents a separate general licensee and requires a separate registration and fee.

(ii) If in possession of a device meeting the criteria of paragraph (c)(13)(i) of this section, shall register these devices annually with the Commission and shall pay the fee required by §170.31 of this chapter. Registration must be done by verifying, correcting, and/or adding to the information provided in a request for registration received from the Commission. The registration information must be submitted to the NRC within 30 days of the date of the request for registration or as otherwise indicated in the request. In addition, a general licensee holding devices meeting the criteria of paragraph (c)(13)(i) of this section is subject to the bankruptcy notification requirement in § 30.34(h) of this chapter.

(iii) In registering devices, the general licensee shall furnish the following information and any other information specifically requested by the Commission—

(A) Name and mailing address of the general licensee.

(B) Information about each device: the manufacturer (or initial transferor), model number, serial number, the radioisotope and activity (as indicated on the label).

(C) Name, title, and telephone number of the responsible person designated as a representative of the general licensee under paragraph (c)(12) of this section.

(D) Address or location at which the device(s) are used and/or stored. For portable devices, the address of the primary place of storage.

(E) Certification by the responsible representative of the general licensee that the information concerning the device(s) has been verified through a physical inventory and checking of label information.

(F) Certification by the responsible representative of the general licensee that they are aware of the requirements of the general license.

(iv) Persons generally licensed by an Agreement State with respect to devices meeting the criteria in paragraph (c)(13)(i) of this section are not subject to registration requirements if the devices are used in areas subject to NRC jurisdiction for a period less than 180 days in any calendar year. The Commission will not request registration information from such licensees.

(14) Shall report changes to the mailing address for the location of use (including change in name of general licensee) to the Director, Office of Nuclear Material Safety and Safeguards, ATTN: GLTS, U.S. Nuclear Regulatory Commission, Washington, DC 20555–0001 within 30 days of the effective date of the change. For a portable device, a report of address change is only required for a change in the device's primary place of storage.

(15) May not hold devices that are not in use for longer than 2 years. If devices with shutters are not being used, the shutter must be locked in the closed position. The testing required by paragraph (c)(2) of this section need not be performed during the period of storage only. However, when devices are put back into service or transferred to another person, and have not been tested within the required test interval, they must be tested for leakage before use or transfer and the shutter tested before use. Devices kept in standby for future use are excluded from the two-year time limit if the general licensee performs quarterly physical inventories of these devices while they are in standby.

(d) The general license in paragraph (a) of this section does not authorize the manufacture or import of devices containing byproduct material.

[39 FR 43532, Dec. 16, 1974, as amended at 40 FR 8785, Mar. 3, 1975; 40 FR 14085, Mar. 28, 1975; 42 FR 25721, May 19, 1977; 42 FR 28896, June 6, 1977; 43 FR 6922, Feb. 17, 1978; 53 FR 19246, May 27, 1988; 56 FR 23471, May 21, 1991; 56 FR 61352, Dec. 3, 1991; 58 FR 67659, Dec. 22, 1993; 64 FR 42275, Aug. 4, 1999; 65 FR 79188, Dec. 18, 2000; 68 FR 58804, Oct. 10, 2003; 72 FR 55926, Oct. 1, 2007; 72 FR 58486, Oct. 16, 2007; 73 FR 5718, Jan. 31, 2008; 73 FR 42673, July 23, 2008]

§ 31.6 General license to install devices generally licensed in § 31.5.

Any person who holds a specific license issued by an Agreement State authorizing the holder to manufacture, install, or service a device described in § 31.5 within such Agreement State is hereby granted a general license to install and service such device in any non-Agreement State and a general license to install and service such device in offshore waters, as defined in § 150.3(f) of this chapter: *Provided*, That:

(a) [Reserved]

(b) The device has been manufactured, labeled, installed, and serviced in accordance with applicable provisions of the specific license issued to such person by the Agreement State.

(c) Such person assures that any labels required to be affixed to the device under regulations of the Agreement State which licensed manufacture of the device bear a statement that removal of the label is prohibited.

[30 FR 8189, June 26, 1965, as amended at 30 FR 10947, Aug. 24, 1965; 39 FR 43533, Dec. 16, 1974; 46 FR 44151, Sept. 3, 1981]

§31.7 Luminous safety devices for use in aircraft.

(a) A general license is hereby issued to own, receive, acquire, possess, and use tritium or promethium-147 contained in luminous safety devices for use in aircraft, provided each device contains not more than 10 curies of tritium or 300 millicuries of promethium-147 and that each device has been manufactured, assembled or initially transferred in accordance with a license issued under the provisions of §32.53 of this chapter or manufactured or assembled in accordance with a specific license issued by an Agreement State which authorizes manufacture or assembly of the device for distribution to persons generally licensed by the Agreement State.

(b) Persons who own, receive, acquire, possess or use luminous safety devices pursuant to the general license in this section are exempt from the requirements of parts 19, 20, and 21, of this chapter, except that they shall comply with the provisions of §§20.2201, and 20.2202 of this chapter.

(c) This general license does not authorize the manufacture, assembly, repair or import of luminous safety devices containing tritium or promethium-147.

(d) This general license does not authorize the export of luminous safety devices containing tritium or promethium-147.

(e) This general license does not authorize the ownership, receipt, acquisition, possession or use of promethium-147 contained in instrument dials.

[30 FR 8189, June 26, 1965, as amended at 33 FR 6463, Apr. 27, 1968; 38 FR 22220, Aug. 17, 1973; 42 FR 28896, June 6, 1977; 43 FR 6922, Feb. 17, 1978; 56 FR 23471, May 21, 1991; 56 FR 61352, Dec. 3, 1991; 58 FR 67659, Dec. 22, 1993]

§31.8 Americium-241 and radium-226 in the form of calibration or reference sources.

(a) A general license is issued to those persons listed in this section to own, receive, acquire, possess, use, and transfer, in accordance with the provisions of paragraphs (b) and (c) of this section, americium-241 or radium-226 in the form of calibration or reference sources:

(1) Any person in a non-Agreement State who holds a specific license issued under this chapter which authorizes receipt, possession, use, and transfer of byproduct material, source material, or special nuclear material; and

(2) Any Government agency, as defined in §30.4 of this chapter, which holds a specific license issued under this chapter which authorizes it to receive, possess, use, and transfer byproduct material, source material, or special nuclear material.

(b) The general license in paragraph (a) of this section applies only to calibration or reference sources which have been manufactured or initially transferred in accordance with the specifications contained in a specific license issued under §32.57 of this chapter or in accordance with the specifications contained in a specific license issued to the manufacturer by an Agreement State which authorizes manufacture of the sources for distribution to persons generally licensed by the Agreement State, or in accordance with a specific license issued by a State with comparable provisions to §32.57.

(c) The general license in paragraph (a) of this section is subject to the provisions of §§30.14(d), 30.34 (a) to (e), and 30.50 to 30.63 of this chapter, and to the provisions of parts 19, 20, and 21, of this chapter. In addition, persons who own, receive, acquire, possess, use, and transfer one or more calibration or reference sources under this general license:

(1) Shall not possess at any one time, at any one location of storage or use, more than 0.185 megabecquerel (5 microcuries) of americium-241 or 0.185 megabecquerel (5 microcuries) of radium-226 in such sources;

(2) Shall not receive, possess, use, or transfer a source unless the source, or the storage container, bears a label which includes the following statement or a substantially similar statement which contains the information called for in the following statement:[1]

The receipt, possession, use, and transfer of this source, Model XX, Serial No. XX, are subject to a general license and the regulations of the United States Nuclear Regulatory Commission or of a State with which the Commission has entered into an agreement for the exercise of regulatory authority. Do not remove this label.

CAUTION—RADIOACTIVE MATERIAL—THIS SOURCE CONTAINS AMERICIUM-241 [or RADIUM-226, as appropriate]. DO NOT TOUCH RADIOACTIVE PORTION OF THIS SOURCE.

(Name of manufacturer or initial transferor)

(3) Shall not transfer, abandon, or dispose of a source except by transfer to a person authorized by a license issued under this chapter or by an Agreement State to receive the source.

(4) Shall store a source, except when the source is being used, in a closed container adequately designed and constructed to contain americium-241 or radium-226 which might otherwise escape during storage.

(5) Shall not use a source for any purpose other than the calibration of radiation detectors or the standardization of other sources.

(d) This general license does not authorize the manufacture or import of calibration or reference sources containing americium-241 or radium-226.

(e) This general license does not authorize the export of calibration or reference sources containing americium-241 or radium-226.

[72 FR 55927, Oct. 1, 2007]

[1] Sources generally licensed under this section before January 19, 1975, may bear labels authorized by the regulations in effect on January 1, 1975. Sources containing radium-226 generally licensed under this section and manufactured before November 30, 2007 shall be labeled in accordance with the applicable State regulations at the time of manufacture or import.

§ 31.9 General license to own byproduct material.

A general license is hereby issued to own byproduct material without regard to quantity. Notwithstanding any other provision of this chapter, a general licensee under this paragraph is not authorized to manufacture, produce, transfer, receive, possess, use, import or export byproduct material, except as authorized in a specific license.

[30 FR 8189, June 26, 1965]

§ 31.10 General license for strontium 90 in ice detection devices.

(a) A general license is hereby issued to own, receive, acquire, possess, use, and transfer strontium 90 contained in ice detection devices, provided each device contains not more than fifty microcuries of strontium 90 and each device has been manufactured or initially transferred in accordance with the specifications contained in a license issued pursuant to § 32.61 of this chapter or in accordance with the specifications contained in a specific license issued to the manufacturer by an Agreement State which authorizes manufacture of the ice detection devices for distribution to persons generally licensed by the Agreement State.

(b) Persons who own, receive, acquire, possess, use, or transfer strontium 90 contained in ice detection devices pursuant to the general license in paragraph (a) of this section:

(1) Shall, upon occurrence of visually observable damage, such as a bend or crack or discoloration from overheating, to the device, discontinue use of the device until it has been inspected, tested for leakage and repaired by a person holding a specific license pursuant to part 30 or 32 of this chapter or from an Agreement State to manufacture or service such devices; or shall dispose of the device pursuant to the provisions of § 20.2001.

(2) Shall assure that all labels affixed to the device at the time of receipt, and which bear a statement which prohibits removal of the labels, are maintained thereon;

(3) Are exempt from the requirements of parts 19, 20, and 21, of this chapter

except that such persons shall comply with the provisions of §§20.2001, 20.2201, and 20.2202 of this chapter.

(c) The general license does not authorize the manufacture, assembly, disassembly, repair, or import of strontium 90 in ice detection devices.

[30 FR 9905, Aug. 10, 1965, as amended at 38 FR 22220, Aug. 17, 1973; 40 FR 8785, Mar. 3, 1975; 42 FR 28896, June 6, 1977; 43 FR 6922, Feb. 17, 1978; 56 FR 23471, May 21, 1991; 56 FR 61352, Dec. 3, 1991; 58 FR 67659, Dec. 22, 1993]

§31.11 General license for use of byproduct material for certain in vitro clinical or laboratory testing.

(a) A general license is hereby issued to any physician, veterinarian in the practice of veterinary medicine, clinical laboratory or hospital to receive, acquire, possess, transfer, or use, for any of the following stated tests, in accordance with the provisions of paragraphs (b), (c), (d), (e), and (f) of this section, the following byproduct materials in prepackaged units:

(1) Iodine-125, in units not exceeding 10 microcuries each for use in in vitro clinical or laboratory tests not involving internal or external administration of byproduct material, or the radiation therefrom, to human beings or animals.

(2) Iodine-131, in units not exceeding 10 microcuries each for use in in vitro clinical or laboratory tests not involving internal or external administration of byproduct material, or the radiation therefrom, to human beings or animals.

(3) Carbon-14, in units not exceeding 10 microcuries each for use in in vitro clinical or laboratory tests not involving internal or external administration of byproduct material, or the radiation therefrom, to human beings or animals.

(4) Hydrogen-3 (tritium), in units not exceeding 50 microcuries each for use in in vitro clinical or laboratory tests not involving internal or external administration of byproduct material, or the radiation therefrom, to human beings or animals.

(5) Iron-59, in units not exceeding 20 microcuries each for use in in vitro clinical or laboratory tests not involving internal or external administration of byproduct material, or the radiation therefrom, to human beings, or animals.

(6) Selenium-75, in units not exceeding 10 microcuries each for use in in vitro clinical or laboratory tests not involving internal or external administration of byproduct material, or the radiation therefrom, to human beings or animals.

(7) Mock Iodine-125 reference or calibration sources, in units not exceeding 0.05 microcurie of iodine-129 and 0.005 microcurie of americium-241 each for use in in vitro clinical or laboratory tests not involving internal or external administration of byproduct material, or the radiation therefrom, to human beings or animals.

(8) Cobalt-57, in units not exceeding 0.37 megabecquerel (10 microcuries) each for use in in vitro clinical or laboratory tests not involving internal or external administration of byproduct material, or the radiation therefrom, to human beings or animals.

(b) A person shall not receive, acquire, possess, use, or transfer byproduct material under the general license established by paragraph (a) of this section unless that person:

(1) Has filed NRC Form 483, "Registration Certificate—In Vitro Testing with Byproduct Material Under General License," with the Director, Office of Nuclear Material Safety and Safeguards , by an appropriate method listed in §30.6(a) of this chapter, and has received from the Commission a validated copy of NRC Form 483 with a registration number assigned; or

(2) Has a license that authorizes the medical use of byproduct material that was issued under part 35 of this chapter.

(c) A person who receives, acquires, possesses, or uses byproduct material pursuant to the general license established by paragraph (a) of this section shall comply with the following:

(1) The general licensee shall not possess at any one time, under the general license in paragraph (a) of this section, at any one location of storage or use, a total amount of iodine-125, iodine-131, selenium-75, cobalt-57 and/or iron-59 in excess of 7.4 megabecquerels (200 microcuries).

(2) The general licensee shall store the byproduct material, until used, in

the original shipping container or in a container providing equivalent radiation protection.

(3) The general licensee shall use the byproduct material only for the uses authorized by paragraph (a) of this section.

(4) The general licensee shall not transfer the byproduct material except by transfer to a person authorized to receive it by a license pursuant to this chapter or from an Agreement State, nor transfer the byproduct material in any manner other than in the unopened, labeled shipping container as received from the supplier.

(5) The general licensee shall dispose of the Mock Iodine-125 reference or calibration sources described in paragraph (a)(7) of this section as required by §20.2001.

(d) The general licensee shall not receive, acquire, possess, or use byproduct material pursuant to paragraph (a) of this section:

(1) Except as prepackaged units which are labeled in accordance with the provisions of a specific license issued under the provisions of §32.71 of this chapter or in accordance with the provisions of a specific license issued by an Agreement State, or before November 30, 2007, and the provisions of a specific license issued by a State with comparable provisions to §32.71 that authorize manufacture and distribution of iodine-125, iodine-131, carbon-14, hydrogen-3 (tritium), selenium-75, iron-59, cobalt-57, or Mock Iodine-125 for distribution to persons generally licensed by the Agreement State or the State with comparable provisions to §32.71.

(2) Unless the following statement, or a substantially similar statement which contains the information called for in the following statement, appears on a label affixed to each prepackaged unit or appears in a leaflet or brochure which accompanies the package:[1]

This radioactive material may be received, acquired, possessed, and used only by physicians, veterinarians in the practice of veterinary medicine, clinical laboratories or hospitals and only for in vitro clinical or laboratory tests not involving internal or external administration of the material, or the radiation therefrom, to human beings or animals. Its receipt, acquisition, possession, use, and transfer are subject to the regulations and a general license of the U.S. Nuclear Regulatory Commission or of a State with which the Commission has entered into an agreement for the exercise of regulatory authority.

(Name of Manufacturer)

(e) The registrant possessing or using byproduct materials under the general license of paragraph (a) of this section shall report in writing to the Director, Office of Nuclear Material Safety and Safeguards , any changes in the information furnished by him in the "Registration Certificate—In Vitro Testing With Byproduct Material Under General License." Form NRC–483. The report shall be furnished within 30 days after the effective date of such change.

(f) Any person using byproduct material pursuant to the general license of paragraph (a) of this section is exempt from the requirements of parts 19, 20, and 21, of this chapter with respect to byproduct materials covered by that general license, except that such persons using the Mock Iodine-125 described in paragraph (a)(7) of this section shall comply with the provisions of §§20.2001, 20.2201, and 20.2202.

[33 FR 16553, Nov. 14, 1968]

EDITORIAL NOTE: For FEDERAL REGISTER citations affecting §31.11, see the List of CFR Sections Affected, which appears in the Finding Aids section of the printed volume and at *www.fdsys.gov*.

§31.12 General license for certain items and self-luminous products containing radium-226.

(a) A general license is hereby issued to any person to acquire, receive, possess, use, or transfer, in accordance with the provisions of paragraphs (b), (c), and (d) of this section, radium-226 contained in the following products manufactured prior to November 30, 2007.

(1) Antiquities originally intended for use by the general public. For the purposes of this paragraph, antiquities mean products originally intended for use by the general public and distributed in the late 19th and early 20th centuries, such as radium emanator jars, revigators, radium water jars,

[1] Labels authorized by the regulations in effect on September 26, 1979, may be used until one year from September 27, 1979.

radon generators, refrigerator cards, radium bath salts, and healing pads.

(2) Intact timepieces containing greater than 0.037 megabecquerel (1 microcurie), nonintact timepieces, and timepiece hands and dials no longer installed in timepieces.

(3) Luminous items installed in air, marine, or land vehicles.

(4) All other luminous products, provided that no more than 100 items are used or stored at the same location at any one time.

(5) Small radium sources containing no more than 0.037 megabecquerel (1 microcurie) of radium-226. For the purposes of this paragraph, "small radium sources" means discrete survey instrument check sources, sources contained in radiation measuring instruments, sources used in educational demonstrations (such as cloud chambers and spinthariscopes), electron tubes, lightning rods, ionization sources, static eliminators, or as designated by the NRC.

(b) Persons who acquire, receive, possess, use, or transfer byproduct material under the general license issued in paragraph (a) of this section are exempt from the provisions of 10 CFR parts 19, 20, and 21, and §30.50 and 30.51 of this chapter, to the extent that the receipt, possession, use, or transfer of byproduct material is within the terms of the general license; provided, however, that this exemption shall not be deemed to apply to any such person specifically licensed under this chapter.

(c) Any person who acquires, receives, possesses, uses, or transfers byproduct material in accordance with the general license in paragraph (a) of this section:

(1) Shall notify the NRC should there be any indication of possible damage to the product so that it appears it could result in a loss of the radioactive material. A report containing a brief description of the event, and the remedial action taken, must be furnished to the Director of the Office of Nuclear Material Safety and Safeguards, U.S. Nuclear Regulatory Commission, Washington, DC 20555–0001 within 30 days.

(2) Shall not abandon products containing radium-226. The product, and any radioactive material from the product, may only be disposed of according to §20.2008 of this chapter or by transfer to a person authorized by a specific license to receive the radium-226 in the product or as otherwise approved by the NRC.

(3) Shall not export products containing radium-226 except in accordance with part 110 of this chapter.

(4) Shall dispose of products containing radium-226 at a disposal facility authorized to dispose of radioactive material in accordance with any Federal or State solid or hazardous waste law, including the Solid Waste Disposal Act, as authorized under the Energy Policy Act of 2005, by transfer to a person authorized to receive radium-226 by a specific license issued under part 30 of this chapter, or equivalent regulations of an Agreement State, or as otherwise approved by the NRC.

(5) Shall respond to written requests from the NRC to provide information relating to the general license within 30 calendar days of the date of the request, or other time specified in the request. If the general licensee cannot provide the requested information within the allotted time, it shall, within that same time period, request a longer period to supply the information by providing the Director of the Office of Nuclear Material Safety and Safeguards, by an appropriate method listed in §30.6(a) of this chapter, a written justification for the request.

(d) The general license in paragraph (a) of this section does not authorize the manufacture, assembly, disassembly, repair, or import of products containing radium-226, except that timepieces may be disassembled and repaired.

[72 FR 55927, Oct. 1, 2007]

§§31.13–31.20 [Reserved]

§31.21 Maintenance of records.

Each record required by this part must be legible throughout the retention period specified by each Commission regulation. The record may be the original or a reproduced copy or a microform provided that the copy or microform is authenticated by authorized personnel and that the microform is capable of producing a clear copy throughout the required retention period. The record may also be stored in electronic media with the capability for producing legible, accurate, and complete records during the required retention period. Records such as letters, drawings, specifications, must include all pertinent information such as letters, stamps, initials, and signatures. The licensee shall maintain adequate safeguards against tampering with and loss of records.

[53 FR 19246, May 27, 1988. Redesignated at 72 FR 55927, Oct. 1, 2007]

§ 31.22 Violations.

(a) The Commission may obtain an injunction or other court order to prevent a violation of the provisions of—

(1) The Atomic Energy Act of 1954, as amended;

(2) Title II of the Energy Reorganization Act of 1974, as amended; or

(3) A regulation or order issued pursuant to those Acts.

(b) The Commission may obtain a court order for the payment of a civil penalty imposed under section 234 of the Atomic Energy Act:

(1) For violations of—

(i) Sections 53, 57, 62, 63, 81, 82, 101, 103, 104, 107, or 109 of the Atomic Energy Act of 1954, as amended;

(ii) Section 206 of the Energy Reorganization Act;

(iii) Any rule, regulation, or order issued pursuant to the sections specified in paragraph (b)(1)(i) of this section;

(iv) Any term, condition, or limitation of any license issued under the sections specified in paragraph (b)(1)(i) of this section.

(2) For any violation for which a license may be revoked under section 186 of the Atomic Energy Act of 1954, as amended.

[57 FR 55072, Nov. 24, 1992. Redesignated at 72 FR 55927, Oct. 1, 2007]

§ 31.23 Criminal penalties.

(a) Section 223 of the Atomic Energy Act of 1954, as amended, provides for criminal sanctions for willful violation of, attempted violation of, or conspiracy to violate, any regulation issued under sections 161b, 161i, or 161o of the Act. For purposes of section 223, all the regulations in part 31 are issued under one or more of sections 161b, 161i, or 161o, except for the sections listed in paragraph (b) of this section.

(b) The regulations in part 31 that are not issued under sections 161b, 161i, or 161o for the purposes of section 223 are as follows: §§ 31.1, 31.2, 31.4, 31.9, 31.22, and 31.23.

[57 FR 55073, Nov. 24, 1992. Redesignated at 72 FR 55927, Oct. 1, 2007, and amended at 77 FR 43690, July 25, 2012]

PART 32—SPECIFIC DOMESTIC LICENSES TO MANUFACTURE OR TRANSFER CERTAIN ITEMS CONTAINING BYPRODUCT MATERIAL

Subpart B—Generally Licensed Items

Subpart C—Specifically Licensed Items

Subpart D—Sealed Source and Device Registration

Subpart E—Violations

AUTHORITY: Atomic Energy Act of 1954, secs. 81, 161, 170H, 181, 182, 183, 223, 234, 274 (42 U.S.C. 2111, 2201, 2210h, 2231, 2232, 2233, 2273, 2282, 2021); Energy Reorganization Act of 1974, sec. 201 (42 U.S.C. 5841); 44 U.S.C. 3504 note.

EDITORIAL NOTE: Nomenclature changes to part 32 appear at 79 FR 75739, Dec. 19, 2014.

§32.1 Purpose and scope.

(a)(1) This part prescribes requirements for the issuance of specific licenses to persons who manufacture or initially transfer items containing byproduct material for sale or distribution to:

(i) Persons exempted from the licensing requirements of part 30 of this chapter, or equivalent regulations of an Agreement State, or

(ii) Persons generally licensed under part 31 of this chapter or equivalent regulations of an Agreement State.

(iii) Persons licensed under part 35 of this chapter.

(2) This part prescribes requirements for the issuance of specific licenses to persons who introduce byproduct material into a product or material owned by or in the possession of a licensee or another, and regulations governing holders of such licenses.

(3) This part prescribes certain requirements governing holders of licenses to manufacture or distribute items containing byproduct material.

(4) This part describes procedures and prescribes requirements for the issuance of certificates of registration (covering radiation safety information about a product) to manufacturers or initial transferors of sealed sources or devices containing sealed sources.

(b) The provisions and requirements of this part are in addition to, and not in substitution for, other requirements of this chapter. In particular, the provisions of part 30 of this chapter apply to applications, licenses and certificates of registration subject to this part, and the provisions of part 37 of this chapter apply to applications and licenses subject to this part.

(c)(1) The requirements in this part, including provisions that are specific to licensees, shall apply to Government agencies and Federally recognized Indian Tribes with respect to accelerator-produced radioactive material or discrete sources of radium-226 on November 30, 2007 except that the agency or Tribe may continue to manufacture or initially transfer items containing accelerator-produced radioactive material or discrete sources of radium-226 for sale or distribution to persons exempted from the licensing requirements of part 30 of this chapter, and to persons generally licensed under part 31 of this chapter, and radioactive drugs and sources and devices to medical use licensees, until the date of the NRC's final licensing determination, provided that the agency or Tribe submits a new license application for these activities on or before December 1, 2008 or an amendment application for these activities on or before June 2, 2008.

(2) The requirements in this part, including provisions that are specific to licensees, shall apply to all persons other than those included in paragraph (c)(1) of this section with respect to accelerator-produced radioactive material or discrete sources of radium-226 on August 8, 2009, or earlier as noticed by the NRC, except that these persons may continue to manufacture or initially transfer items containing accelerator-produced radioactive material or discrete sources of radium-226 for sale or distribution to persons exempted from the licensing requirements of part 30 of this chapter, and to persons generally licensed under part 31 of this chapter, and to sell or manufacture radioactive drugs and sources and devices to medical use licensees until the date of the NRC's final licensing determination, provided that the person submits a license application within 12 months from the waiver expiration date of August 7, 2009 or within 12 months from the date of an earlier termination of the waiver as noticed by the NRC, whichever is earlier; or that the person submits an amendment request within 6 months from the waiver expiration date of August 7, 2009 or within 6 months from the date of an earlier termination of the waiver as noticed by the NRC, whichever date is earlier.

[30 FR 8192, June 26, 1965, as amended at 52 FR 27786, July 24, 1987; 63 FR 1896, Jan. 13, 1998; 72 FR 55928, Oct. 1, 2007; 77 FR 43690, July 25, 2012; 78 FR 17006, Mar. 19, 2013; 80 FR 74979, Dec. 1, 2015]

§ 32.2 Definitions.

As used in this part:

Committed dose for the purposes of this part means the radiation dose that will accumulate over time as a result of retention in the body of radioactive material. Committed dose is a generic term for internal dose and must be calculated by summing the projected dose over the 50 years after intake for all irradiated organs or tissues multiplying the doses to individual organs and tissues by applicable tissue weighting factors.

Dose commitment means the total radiation dose to a part of the body that will result from retention in the body of radioactive material. For purposes of estimating the dose commitment, it is assumed that from the time of intake the period of exposure to retained material will not exceed 50 years.

Lot Tolerance Percent Defective means, expressed in percent defective, the poorest quality in an individual inspection lot that should be accepted.

Nationally tracked source is a sealed source containing a quantity equal to or greater than Category 1 or Category 2 levels of any radioactive material listed in Appendix E to part 20 of this Chapter. In this context a sealed source is defined as radioactive material that is sealed in a capsule or closely bonded, in a solid form and which is not exempt from regulatory control. It does not mean material encapsulated solely for disposal, or nuclear material contained in any fuel assembly, subassembly, fuel rod, or fuel pellet. Category 1 nationally tracked sources are those containing radioactive material at a quantity equal to or greater than the Category 1 threshold. Category 2 nationally tracked sources are those containing radioactive material at a quantity equal to or greater than the Category 2 threshold but less than the Category 1 threshold.

Sealed Source and Device Registry means the national registry that contains all the registration certificates, generated by both the NRC and the Agreement States, that summarize the radiation safety information for the sealed sources and devices and describe the licensing and use conditions approved for the product.

[34 FR 6653, Apr. 18, 1969, as amended at 39 FR 22129, June 20, 1974; 71 FR 65708, Nov. 8, 2006; 77 FR 43690, July 25, 2012]

§ 32.3 Maintenance of records.

Each record required by this part must be legible throughout the retention period specified by each Commission regulation. The record may be the original or a reproduced copy of a microform provided that the copy or microform is authenticated by authorized personnel and that the microform is capable of producing a clear copy throughout the required retention period. The record may also be stored in electronic media with the capability for producing legible, accurate, and complete records during the required retention period. Records such as letters, drawings, specifications, must include all pertinent information such as stamps, initials, and signatures. The licensee shall maintain adequate safeguards against tampering with and loss of records.

[53 FR 19246, May 27, 1988]

§ 32.8 Information collection requirements: OMB approval.

(a) The Nuclear Regulatory Commission has submitted the information collection requirements contained in this part to the Office of Management and Budget (OMB) for approval as required by the Paperwork Reduction Act (44 U.S.C. 3501 *et seq.*). The NRC may not conduct or sponsor, and a person is not required to respond to, a collection of information unless it displays a currently valid OMB control number. OMB has approved the information collection requirements contained in this part under control number 3150–0001.

(b) The approved information collection requirements contained in this part appear in §§ 32.11, 32.12, 32.14, 32.15, 32.16, 32.18, 32.19, 32.20, 32.21, 32.21a, 32.22, 32.23, 32.25, 32.26, 32.27, 32.29, 32.30, 32.31, 32.32, 32.51, 32.51a, 32.52, 32.53, 32.54, 32.55, 32.56, 32.57, 32.58, 32.61, 32.62, 32.71, 32.72, 32.74, 32.201, 32.210, and 32.211.

(c) This part contains information collection requirements in addition to those approved under the control number specified in paragraph (a) of this section. These information collection requirements and the control numbers under which they are approved are as follows:

(1) In § 32.11, NRC Form 313 is approved under control number 3150–0120.

(2) [Reserved]

[49 FR 19625, May 9, 1984, as amended at 59 FR 61780, Dec. 2, 1994; 62 FR 52186, Oct. 6, 1997; 62 FR 63640, Dec. 2, 1997; 71 FR 65708, Nov. 8, 2006; 72 FR 58486, Oct. 16, 2007; 77 FR 43691, July 25, 2012]

Subpart A—Exempt Concentrations and Items

§ 32.11 Introduction of byproduct material in exempt concentrations into products or materials, and transfer of ownership or possession: Requirements for license.

An application for a specific license on Form NRC–313 authorizing the introduction of byproduct material into a product or material owned by or in the possession of the licensee or another and the transfer of ownership or possession of the product or material containing the byproduct material will be approved if the applicant:

(a) Satisfies the general requirements specified in § 30.33 of this chapter; *provided, however*, that the requirements of § 30.33(a)(2) and (3) do not apply to an application for a license to introduce byproduct material into a product or material owned by or in the possession of the licensee or another and the transfer of ownership or possession of the product or material containing the byproduct material, if the possession and use of the byproduct material to be introduced is authorized by a license issued by an Agreement State;

(b) Provides a description of the product or material into which the byproduct material will be introduced, intended use of the byproduct material and the product or material into which it is introduced, method of introduction, initial concentration of the byproduct material in the product or material, control methods to assure that no more than the specified concentration is introduced into the product or material, estimated time interval between introduction and transfer of the product or material, and estimated concentration of the radioisotopes in the product or material at the time of transfer; and

(c) Provides reasonable assurance that the concentrations of byproduct material at the time of transfer will not exceed the concentrations in § 30.70 of this chapter, that reconcentration of the byproduct material in concentrations exceeding those in § 30.70 is not likely, that use of lower concentrations is not feasible, and that the product or material is not likely to be incorporated in any food, beverage, cosmetic, drug or other commodity or product designed for ingestion or inhalation by, or application to, a human being.

[30 FR 8192, June 26, 1965, as amended at 49 FR 19625, May 9, 1984; 72 FR 58487, Oct. 16, 2007]

§ 32.12 Same: Records and material transfer reports.

(a) Each person licensed under § 32.11 shall maintain records of transfer of byproduct material and file a report with the Director of the Office of Nuclear Material Safety and Safeguards by an appropriate method listed in § 30.6(a) of this chapter, including in the address: ATTN: Document Control Desk/Exempt Distribution.

(1) The report must clearly identify the specific licensee submitting the report and include the license number of the specific licensee.

(2) The report must indicate that the byproduct material is transferred for use under § 30.14 of this chapter or equivalent regulations of an Agreement State.

(b) The report must identify the:

(1) Type and quantity of each product or material into which byproduct material has been introduced during the reporting period;

(2) Name and address of the person who owned or possessed the product or material, into which byproduct material has been introduced, at the time of introduction;

(3) The type and quantity of radionuclide introduced into each product or material; and

(4) The initial concentrations of the radionuclide in the product or material at time of transfer of the byproduct material by the licensee.

(c)(1) The licensee shall file the report, covering the preceding calendar year, on or before January 31 of each year. In its first report after December 17, 2007, the licensee shall separately include data for transfers in prior years not previously reported to the Commission or to an Agreement State.

(2) Licensees who permanently discontinue activities authorized by the license issued under § 32.11 shall file a report for the current calendar year within 30 days after ceasing distribution.

(d) If no transfers of byproduct material have been made under § 32.11 during the reporting period, the report must so indicate.

(e) The licensee shall maintain the record of a transfer for one year after the transfer is included in a report to the Commission.

[72 FR 58487, Oct. 16, 2007, as amended at 73 FR 5719, Jan. 31, 2008; 73 FR 42673, July 23, 2008]

§ 32.13 Same: Prohibition of introduction.

No person may introduce byproduct material into a product or material knowing or having reason to believe that it will be transferred to persons exempt under § 30.14 of this chapter or equivalent regulations of an Agreement State, except in accordance with a license issued under § 32.11.

[72 FR 58487, Oct. 16, 2007]

§ 32.14 Certain items containing byproduct material; requirements for license to apply or initially transfer.

An application for a specific license to apply byproduct material to, or to incorporate byproduct material into, the products specified in § 30.15 of this chapter or to initially transfer for sale or distribution such products containing byproduct material for use pursuant to § 30.15 of this chapter will be approved if:

(a) The applicant satisfies the general requirements specified in §30.33 of this chapter;

(b) The applicant submits sufficient information regarding the product pertinent to evaluation of the potential radiation exposure, including:

(1) Chemical and physical form and maximum quantity of byproduct material in each product;

(2) Details of construction and design of each product;

(3) The method of containment or binding of the byproduct material in the product;

(4) Except for electron tubes and ionization chamber smoke detectors and timepieces containing promethium-147 or tritium in the form of gaseous tritium light sources, procedures for and results of prototype testing to demonstrate that the byproduct material will not become detached from the product and that the byproduct material will not be released to the environment under the most severe conditions likely to be encountered in normal use of the product;

(5) In the case of ionizing radiation measuring instruments and timepieces containing tritium in the form of paint, quality control procedures to be followed in the fabrication of production lots of the product and the quality control standards the product will be required to meet;

(6) The proposed method of labeling or marking each unit, except timepieces or hands or dials containing tritium or promethium-147, and its container with the identification of the manufacturer or initial transferor of the product and the byproduct material in the product;

(7) For products for which limits on levels of radiation are specified in §30.15 of this chapter, the radiation level and the method of measurement;

(8) Any additional information, including experimental studies and tests, required by the Commission to facilitate a determination of the safety of the product.

(c) Each product will contain no more than the quantity of byproduct material specified for that product in §30.15 of this chapter. The levels of radiation from each product containing byproduct material will not exceed the limits specified for that product in §30.15 of this chapter.

(d) The Commission determines that the byproduct material is properly contained in the product under the most severe conditions that are likely to be encountered in normal use and handling.

[31 FR 5316, Apr. 2, 1966, as amended at 34 FR 6652, Apr. 18, 1969; 43 FR 6922, Feb. 17, 1978; 63 FR 32971, June 17, 1998; 72 FR 58487, Oct. 16, 2007; 77 FR 43691, July 25, 2012]

§32.15 Same: Quality assurance, prohibition of transfer, and labeling.

(a) Each person licensed under §32.14 for products for which quality control procedures are required shall:

(1) Maintain quality assurance systems in the manufacture of the part or product, or the installation of the part into the product, in a manner sufficient to provide reasonable assurance that the safety-related components of the distributed products are capable of performing their intended functions;

(2) Subject inspection lots to acceptance sampling procedures, by procedures specified in the license issued under §32.14, to provide at least 95 percent confidence that the Lot Tolerance Percent Defective of 5.0 percent will not be exceeded; and

(3) Visually inspect each unit in inspection lots. Any unit which has an observable physical defect that could adversely affect containment of the byproduct material must be considered a defective unit.

(b) No person licensed under §32.14 shall transfer to other persons for use under §30.15 of this chapter or equivalent regulations of an Agreement State:

(1) Any part or product tested and found defective under the criteria and procedures specified in the license issued under §32.14, unless the defective part or product has been repaired or reworked, retested, and found by an independent inspector to meet the applicable acceptance criteria; or

(2) Any part or product contained within any lot that has been sampled and rejected as a result of the procedures in paragraph (a)(2) of this section, unless:

(i) A procedure for defining sub-lot size, independence, and additional testing procedures is contained in the license issued under §32.14; and

(ii) Each individual sub-lot is sampled, tested, and accepted in accordance with the procedures specified in paragraphs (a)(2) and (b)(2)(i) of this section and any other criteria that may be required as a condition of the license issued under §32.14.

(c) [Reserved]

(d)(1) Label or mark each unit, except timepieces or hands or dials containing tritium or promethium-147, and its container so that the manufacturer or initial transferor of the product and the byproduct material in the product can be identified.

(2) For ionization chamber smoke detectors, label or mark each detector and its point-of-sale package so that:

(i) Each detector has a durable, legible, readily visible label or marking on the external surface of the detector containing:

(A) The following statement: "CONTAINS RADIOACTIVE MATERIAL";

(B) The name of the radionuclide ("americium-241" or "Am-241") and the quantity of activity; and

(C) An identification of the person licensed under §32.14 to transfer the detector for use under §30.15(a)(7) of this chapter or equivalent regulations of an Agreement State.

(ii) The labeling or marking specified in paragraph (d)(2)(i) of this section is located where it will be readily visible when the detector is removed from its mounting.

(iii) The external surface of the point-of-sale package has a legible, readily visible label or marking containing:

(A) The name of the radionuclide and quantity of activity;

(B) An identification of the person licensed under §32.14 to transfer the detector for use under §30.15(a)(7) or equivalent regulations of an Agreement State; and

(C) The following or a substantially similar statement: "THIS DETECTOR CONTAINS RADIOACTIVE MATERIAL. THE PURCHASER IS EXEMPT FROM ANY REGULATORY REQUIREMENTS."

(iv) Each detector and point-of-sale package is provided with such other information as may be required by the Commission.

[31 FR 5317, Apr. 2, 1966, as amended at 34 FR 6652, Apr. 18, 1969; 39 FR 22129, June 20, 1974; 43 FR 6922, Feb. 17, 1978; 72 FR 58487, Oct. 16, 2007; 73 FR 42673, July 23, 2008; 77 FR 43691, July 25, 2012]

§32.16 Certain items containing byproduct material: Records and reports of transfer.

(a) Each person licensed under §32.14 shall maintain records of all transfers of byproduct material and file a report with the Director of the Office of Nuclear Material Safety and Safeguards by an appropriate method listed in §30.6(a) of this chapter, including in the address: ATTN: Document Control Desk/Exempt Distribution.

(1) The report must clearly identify the specific licensee submitting the report and include the license number of the specific licensee.

(2) The report must indicate that the products are transferred for use under §30.15 of this chapter, giving the specific paragraph designation, or equivalent regulations of an Agreement State.

(b) The report must include the following information on products transferred to other persons for use under §30.15 or equivalent regulations of an Agreement State:

(1) A description or identification of the type of each product and the model number(s), if applicable;

(2) For each radionuclide in each type of product and each model number, if applicable, the total quantity of the radionuclide; and

(3) The number of units of each type of product transferred during the reporting period by model number, if applicable.

(c)(1) The licensee shall file the report, covering the preceding calendar year, on or before January 31 of each year. In its first report after December 17, 2007, the licensee shall separately include data for transfers in prior years not previously reported to the Commission.

(2) Licensees who permanently discontinue activities authorized by the license issued under §32.14 shall file a

report for the current calendar year within 30 days after ceasing distribution.

(d) If no transfers of byproduct material have been made under §32.14 during the reporting period, the report must so indicate.

(e) The licensee shall maintain the record of a transfer for one year after the transfer is included in a report to the Commission.

[72 FR 58487, Oct. 16, 2007, as amended at 73 FR 5719, Jan. 31, 2008; 73 FR 42673, July 23, 2008]

§32.18 Manufacture, distribution and transfer of exempt quantities of byproduct material: Requirements for license.

An application for a specific license to manufacture, process, produce, package, repackage, or transfer quantities of byproduct material for commercial distribution to persons exempt pursuant to §30.18 of this chapter or the equivalent regulations of an Agreement State will be approved if:

(a) The applicant satisfies the general requirements specified in §30.33 of this chapter: *Provided, however*, That the requirements of §30.33(a) (2) and (3) of this chapter do not apply to an application for a license to transfer byproduct material manufactured, processed, produced, packaged, or repackaged pursuant to a license issued by an Agreement State;

(b) The byproduct material is not contained in any food, beverage, cosmetic, drug, or other commodity designed for ingestion or inhalation by, or application to, a human being;

(c) The byproduct material is in the form of processed chemical elements, compounds, or mixtures, tissue samples, bioassay samples, counting standards, plated or encapsulated sources, or similar substances, identified as radioactive and to be used for its radioactive properties, but is not incorporated into any manufactured or assembled commodity, product, or device intended for commercial distribution; and

(d) The applicant submits copies of prototype labels and brochures and the Commission approves such labels and brochures.

[35 FR 6428, Apr. 22, 1970, as amended at 43 FR 6922, Feb. 17, 1978]

§32.19 Same: Conditions of licenses.

Each license issued under §32.18 is subject to the following conditions:

(a) No more than 10 exempt quantities set forth in §30.71, Schedule B of this chapter shall be sold or transferred in any single transaction. For purposes of this requirement, an individual exempt quantity may be composed of fractional parts of one or more of the exempt quantities in §30.71, Schedule B of this chapter, provided that the sum of such fractions shall not exceed unity.

(b) Each quantity of byproduct material set forth in §30.71, Schedule B of this chapter shall be separately and individually packaged. No more than 10 such packaged exempt quantities shall be contained in any outer package for transfer to persons exempt pursuant to §30.18 of this chapter. The outer package shall be such that the dose rate at the external surface of the package does not exceed 0.5 millirem per hour.

(c) The immediate container of each quantity or separately packaged fractional quantity of byproduct material shall bear a durable, legible label which (1) identifies the radioisotope and the quantity of radioactivity, and (2) bears the words "Radioactive Material."

(d) In addition to the labeling information required by paragraph (c) of this section, the label affixed to the immediate container, or an accompanying brochure, shall also (1) state that the contents are exempt from NRC or Agreement State licensing requirements; (2) bear the words "Radioactive Material—Not for Human Use—Introduction Into Foods, Beverages, Cosmetics, Drugs, or Medicinals, or Into Products Manufactured for Commercial Distribution is Prohibited—Exempt Quantities Should Not be Combined"; and (3) set forth appropriate additional radiation safety precautions and instructions relating to the handling, use, storage, and disposal of the radioactive material.

[35 FR 6428, Apr. 22, 1970]

§32.20 Same: Records and material transfer reports.

(a) Each person licensed under §32.18 shall maintain records of transfer of material identifying, by name and address, each person to whom byproduct material is transferred for use under § 30.18 of this chapter or the equivalent regulations of an Agreement State and stating the kinds, quantities, and physical form of byproduct material transferred.

(b) The licensee shall file a summary report with the Director of the Office of Nuclear Material Safety and Safeguards by an appropriate method listed in § 30.6(a) of this chapter, including in the address: ATTN: Document Control Desk/Exempt Distribution.

(1) The report must clearly identify the specific licensee submitting the report and include the license number of the specific licensee.

(2) The report must indicate that the materials are transferred for use under § 30.18 or equivalent regulations of an Agreement State.

(c) For each radionuclide in each physical form, the report shall indicate the total quantity of each radionuclide and the physical form, transferred under the specific license.

(d)(1) The licensee shall file the report, covering the preceding calendar year, on or before January 31 of each year. In its first report after December 17, 2007, the licensee shall separately include the total quantity of each radionuclide transferred for transfers in prior years not previously reported to the Commission.

(2) Licensees who permanently discontinue activities authorized by the license issued under § 32.18 shall file a report for the current calendar year within 30 days after ceasing distribution.

(e) If no transfers of byproduct material have been made under § 32.18 during the reporting period, the report must so indicate.

(f) The licensee shall maintain the record of a transfer for one year after the transfer is included in a summary report to the Commission.

[72 FR 58488, Oct. 16, 2007, as amended at 73 FR 5719, Jan. 31, 2008; 73 FR 42673, July 23, 2008]

§ 32.21 Radioactive drug: Manufacture, preparation, or transfer for commercial distribution of capsules containing carbon-14 urea each for "in vivo" diagnostic use for humans to persons exempt from licensing; Requirements for a license.

(a) An application for a specific license to manufacture, prepare, process, produce, package, repackage, or transfer for commercial distribution capsules containing 37 kBq (1 μCi) carbon-14 urea (allowing for nominal variation that may occur during the manufacturing process) each for "in vivo" diagnostic use, to persons exempt from licensing under § 30.21 of this chapter or the equivalent regulations of an Agreement State will be approved if:

(1) The applicant satisfies the general requirements specified in § 30.33 of this chapter, provided that the requirements of § 30.33(a) (2) and (3) of this chapter do not apply to an application for a license to transfer byproduct material manufactured, prepared, processed, produced, packaged, or repackaged pursuant to a license issued by an Agreement State;

(2) The applicant meets the requirements under § 32.72(a)(2) of this part;

(3) The applicant provides evidence that each capsule contains 37 kBq (1 μCi) carbon-14 urea (allowing for nominal variation that may occur during the manufacturing process);

(4) The carbon-14 urea is not contained in any food, beverage, cosmetic, drug (except as described in this section) or other commodity designed for ingestion or inhalation by, or topical application to, a human being;

(5) The carbon-14 urea is in the form of a capsule, identified as radioactive, and to be used for its radioactive properties, but is not incorporated into any manufactured or assembled commodity, product, or device intended for commercial distribution; and

(6) The applicant submits copies of prototype labels and brochures and the NRC approves these labels and brochures.

(b) Nothing in this section relieves the licensee from complying with applicable FDA, other Federal, and State requirements governing drugs.

[62 FR 63640, Dec. 2, 1997, as amended at 66 FR 64738, Dec. 14, 2001]

§ 32.21a Same: Conditions of license.

Each license issued under § 32.21 of this part is subject to the following conditions:

(a) The immediate container of the capsule(s) must bear a durable, legible label which:

(1) Identifies the radioisotope, the physical and chemical form, the quantity of radioactivity of each capsule at a specific date; and

(2) Bears the words "Radioactive Material."

(b) In addition to the labeling information required by paragraph (a) of this section, the label affixed to the immediate container, or an accompanying brochure also must:

(1) State that the contents are exempt from NRC or Agreement State licensing requirements; and

(2) Bears the words "Radioactive Material. For "In Vivo" Diagnostic Use Only. This Material Is Not To Be Used for Research Involving Human Subjects and Must Not Be Introduced into Foods, Beverages, Cosmetics, or Other Drugs or Medicinals, or into Products Manufactured for Commercial Distribution. This Material May Be Disposed of in Ordinary Trash."

[62 FR 63640, Dec. 2, 1997]

§ 32.22 Self-luminous products containing tritium, krypton-85 or promethium-147: Requirements for license to manufacture, process, produce, or initially transfer.

(a) An application for a specific license to manufacture, process, or produce self-luminous products containing tritium, krypton-85, or promethium-147, or to initially transfer such products for use pursuant to § 30.19 of this chapter or equivalent regulations of an Agreement State, will be approved if:

(1) The applicant satisfies the general requirements specified in § 30.33 of this chapter: *Provided, however*, That the requirements of § 30.33(a) (2) and (3) do not apply to an application for a license to transfer tritium, krypton-85, or promethium-147 in self-luminous products manufactured, processed, or produced pursuant to a license issued by an Agreement State.

(2) The applicant submits sufficient information relating to the design, manufacture, prototype testing, quality control procedures, labeling or marking, and conditions of handling, storage, use, and disposal of the self-luminous product to demonstrate that the product will meet the safety criteria set forth in § 32.23. The information should include:

(i) A description of the product and its intended use or uses.

(ii) The type and quantity of byproduct material in each unit.

(iii) Chemical and physical form of the byproduct material in the product and changes in chemical and physical form that may occur during the useful life of the product.

(iv) Solubility in water and body fluids of the forms of the byproduct material identified in paragraphs (a)(2)(iii) and (xii) of this section.

(v) Details of construction and design of the product as related to containment and shielding of the byproduct material and other safety features under normal and severe conditions of handling, storage, use, and disposal of the product.

(vi) Maximum external radiation levels at 5 and 25 centimeters from any external surface of the product, averaged over an area not to exceed 10 square centimeters, and the method of measurement.

(vii) Degree of access of human beings to the product during normal handling and use.

(viii) Total quantity of byproduct material expected to be distributed in the product annually.

(ix) The expected useful life of the product.

(x) The proposed method of labeling or marking each unit with identification of the manufacturer or initial transferor of the product and the byproduct material in the product.

(xi) Procedures for prototype testing of the product to demonstrate the effectiveness of the containment, shielding, and other safety features under both normal and severe conditions of handling, storage, use, and disposal of the product.

(xii) Results of the prototype testing of the product, including any change in the form of the byproduct material contained in the product, the extent to which the byproduct material may be released to the environment, any increase in external radiation levels, and any other changes in safety features.

(xiii) The estimated external radiation doses and dose commitments relevant to the safety criteria in § 32.23 and the basis for such estimates.

(xiv) A determination that the probabilities with respect to the doses referred to in § 32.23(d) meet the criteria of that paragraph.

(xv) Quality control procedures to be followed in the fabrication of production lots of the product and the quality control standards the product will be required to meet.

(xvi) Any additional information, including experimental studies and tests, required by the Commission.

(3)(i) The Commission determines that the product meets the safety criteria in § 32.23; and

(ii) The product has been evaluated by the NRC and registered in the Sealed Source and Device Registry.

(b) Notwithstanding the provisions of paragraph (a) of this section, the Commission may deny an application for a specific license under this section if the end uses of the product cannot be reasonably foreseen.

[34 FR 9026, June 6, 1969, as amended at 43 FR 6923, Feb. 17, 1978; 77 FR 43691, July 25, 2012]

§ 32.23 Same: Safety criteria.

An applicant for a license under § 32.22 shall demonstrate that the product is designed and will be manufactured so that:

(a) In normal use and disposal of a single exempt unit, it is unlikely that the external radiation dose in any one year, or the dose commitment resulting from the intake of radioactive material in any one year, to a suitable sample of the group of individuals expected to be most highly exposed to radiation or radioactive material from the product will exceed the dose to the appropriate organ as specified in Column I of the table in § 32.24 of this part.

(b) In normal handling and storage of the quantities of exempt units likely to accumulate in one location during marketing, distribution, installation, and servicing of the product, it is unlikely that the external radiation dose in any one year, or the dose commitment resulting from the intake of radioactive material in any one year, to a suitable sample of the group of individuals expected to be most highly exposed to radiation or radioactive material from the product will exceed the dose to the appropriate organ as specified in Column II of the table in § 32.24.

(c) It is unlikely that there will be a significant reduction in the effectiveness of the containment, shielding, or other safety features of the product from wear and abuse likely to occur in normal handling and use of the product during its useful life.

(d)[1] In use and disposal of a single exempt unit, or in handling and storage of the quantities of exempt units likely to accumulate in one location during marketing, distribution, installation, and servicing of the product, the probability is low that the containment, shielding, or other safety features of the product would fail under such circumstances that a person would receive an external radiation dose or dose commitment in excess of the dose to the appropriate organ as specified in Column III of the table in § 32.24, and the probability is negligible that a person would receive an external radiation dose or dose commitment in excess of the dose to the appropriate organ as specified in Column IV of the table in § 32.24.

[34 FR 9027, June 6, 1969]

[1] It is the intent of this paragraph that as the magnitude of the potential dose increases above that permitted under normal conditions, the probability that any individual will receive such a dose must decrease. The probabilities have been expressed in general terms to emphasize the approximate nature of the estimates which are to be made. The following values may be used as guides in estimating compliance with the criteria:

Low—not more than one such failure per year for each 10,000 exempt units distributed.

Negligible—not more than one such failure per year for each 1 million exempt units distributed.

§ 32.24 Same: Table of organ doses.

Part of body	Column I (rem)	Column II (rem)	Column III (rem)	Column IV (rem)
Whole body; head and trunk: active blood-forming organs; gonads: or lens of eye	0.001	0.01	0.5	15
Hands and forearms; feet and ankles; localized areas of skin averaged over areas no larger than 1 square centimeter	0.015	0.15	7.5	200
Other organs	0.003	0.03	1.5	50

[34 FR 9329, June 13, 1969]

§ 32.25 Conditions of licenses issued under § 32.22: Quality control, labeling, and reports of transfer.

Each person licensed under § 32.22 shall:

(a) Carry out adequate control procedures in the manufacture of the product to assure that each production lot meets the quality control standards approved by the Commission;

(b) Label or mark each unit so that the manufacturer, processor, producer, or initial transferor of the product and the byproduct material in the product can be identified; and

(c) Maintain records of all transfers and file a report with the Director of the Office of Nuclear Material Safety and Safeguards by an appropriate method listed in § 30.6(a) of this chapter, including in the address: ATTN: Document Control Desk/Exempt Distribution.

(1) The report must clearly identify the specific licensee submitting the report and include the license number of the specific licensee.

(2) The report must indicate that the products are transferred for use under § 30.19 of this chapter or equivalent regulations of an Agreement State.

(3) The report must include the following information on products transferred to other persons for use under § 30.19 or equivalent regulations of an Agreement State:

(i) A description or identification of the type of each product and the model number(s);

(ii) For each radionuclide in each type of product and each model number, the total quantity of the radionuclide;

(iii) The number of units of each type of product transferred during the reporting period by model number.

(4)(i) The licensee shall file the report, covering the preceding calendar year, on or before January 31 of each year. In its first report after December 17, 2007, the licensee shall separately include data for transfers in prior years not previously reported to the Commission.

(ii) Licensees who permanently discontinue activities authorized by the license issued under § 32.22 shall file a report for the current calendar year within 30 days after ceasing distribution.

(5) If no transfers of byproduct material have been made under § 32.22 during the reporting period, the report must so indicate.

(6) The licensee shall maintain the record of a transfer for one year after the transfer is included in a report to the Commission.

[34 FR 9027, June 6, 1969, as amended at 43 FR 6923, Feb. 17, 1978; 48 FR 12334, Mar. 24, 1983; 68 FR 58804, Oct. 10, 2003; 72 FR 58488, Oct. 16, 2007; 73 FR 5719, Jan. 31, 2008; 73 FR 42673, July 23, 2008]

§ 32.26 Gas and aerosol detectors containing byproduct material: Requirements for license to manufacture, process, produce, or initially transfer.

An application for a specific license to manufacture, process, or produce gas and aerosol detectors containing byproduct material and designed to protect health, safety, or property, or to initially transfer such products for use under § 30.20 of this chapter or equivalent regulations of an Agreement State, will be approved if:

(a) The applicant satisfies the general requirements specified in § 30.33 of this chapter: *Provided, however*, That the requirements of § 30.33(a) (2) and (3) do not apply to an application for a license to transfer byproduct material in gas and aerosol detectors manufactured, processed or produced pursuant to a license issued by an Agreement State.

(b) The applicant submits sufficient information relating to the design, manufacture, prototype testing, quality control procedures, labeling or marking, and conditions of handling, storage, use, and disposal of the gas and aerosol detector to demonstrate that the product will meet the safety criteria set forth in § 32.27. The information should include:

(1) A description of the product and its intended use or uses;

(2) The type and quantity of byproduct material in each unit;

(3) Chemical and physical form of the byproduct material in the product and changes in chemical and physical form that may occur during the useful life of the product;

(4) Solubility in water and body fluids of the forms of the byproduct material identified in paragraphs (b) (3) and (12) of this section;

(5) Details of construction and design of the product as related to containment and shielding of the byproduct material and other safety features under normal and severe conditions of handling, storage, use, and disposal of the product;

(6) Maximum external radiation levels at 5 and 25 centimeters from any external surface of the product, averaged over an area not to exceed 10 square centimeters, and the method of measurement;

(7) Degree of access of human beings to the product during normal handling and use;

(8) Total quantity of byproduct material expected to be distributed in the product annually;

(9) The expected useful life of the product;

(10) The proposed methods of labeling or marking the detector and its point-of-sale package to satisfy the requirements of § 32.29(b);

(11) Procedures for prototype testing of the product to demonstrate the effectiveness of the containment, shielding, and other safety features under both normal and severe conditions of handling, storage, use, and disposal of the product;

(12) Results of the prototype testing of the product, including any change in the form of the byproduct material contained in the product, the extent to which the byproduct material may be released to the environment, any increase in external radiation levels, and any other changes in safety features;

(13) The estimated external radiation doses and dose commitments relevant to the safety criteria in § 32.27 and the basis for such estimates;

(14) A determination that the probabilities with respect to the doses referred to in § 32.27(c) meet the criteria of that paragraph;

(15) Quality control procedures to be followed in the fabrication of production lots of the product and the quality control standards the product will be required to meet; and

(16) Any additional information, including experimental studies and tests, required by the Commission.

(c)(1) The Commission determines that the product meets the safety criteria in § 32.27; and

(2) The product has been evaluated by the NRC and registered in the Sealed Source and Device Registry.

[34 FR 6653, Apr. 18, 1969, as amended at 43 FR 6923, Feb. 17, 1978; 45 FR 38342, June 9, 1980; 77 FR 43691, July 25, 2012]

§ 32.27 Same: Safety criteria.

An applicant for a license under § 32.26 shall demonstrate that the product is designed and will be manufactured so that:

(a) In normal use and disposal of a single exempt unit, and in normal handling and storage of the quantities of exempt units likely to accumulate in one location during marketing, distribution, installation, and servicing of the product, it is unlikely that the external radiation dose in any one year, or the dose commitment resulting from the intake of radioactive material in any one year, to a suitable sample of the group of individuals expected to be most highly exposed to radiation or radioactive material from the product will exceed the dose to the appropriate organ as specified in Column I of the table in § 32.28.

(b) It is unlikely that there will be a significant reduction in the effectiveness of the containment, shielding, or other safety features of the product from wear and abuse likely to occur in normal handling and use of the product during its useful life.

(c) In use and disposal of a single exempt unit and in handling and storage of the quantities of exempt units likely to accumulate in one location during marketing, distribution, installation, and servicing of the product, the probability is low that the containment, shielding, or other safety features of the product would fail under such circumstances that a person would receive an external radiation dose or dose commitment in excess of the dose to the appropriate organ as specified in Column II of the table in § 32.28, and the probability is negligible that a person would receive an external radiation dose or dose commitment in excess of the dose to the appropriate organ as specified in Column III of the table in § 32.28.[1]

[34 FR 6654, Apr. 18, 1969]

§ 32.28 Same: Table of organ doses.

Part of body	Column I (rem)	Column II (rem)	Column III (rem)
Whole body; head and trunk; active blood-forming organs; gonads; or lens of eye	0.005	0.5	15
Hands and forearms; feet and ankles; localized areas of skin averaged over areas no larger than 1 square centimeter	0.075	7.5	200
Other organs	0.015	1.5	50

[34 FR 6654, Apr. 18, 1969]

§ 32.29 Conditions of licenses issued under § 32.26: Quality control, labeling, and reports of transfer.

Each person licensed under § 32.26 shall:

(a) Carry out adequate control procedures in the manufacture of the product to assure that each production lot meets the quality control standards approved by the Commission;

(b) Label or mark each detector and its point-of-sale package so that:

(1) Each detector has a durable, legible, readily visible label or marking on the external surface of the detector containing:

(i) The following statement: "CONTAINS RADIOACTIVE MATERIAL";

(ii) The name of the radionuclide and quantity of activity; and

(iii) An identification of the person licensed under § 32.26 to transfer the detector for use pursuant to § 30.20 of this chapter or equivalent regulations of an Agreement State.

(2) The labeling or marking specified in paragraph (b)(1) of this section is located where its will be readily visible when the detector is removed from its mounting.

(3) The external surface of the point-of-sale package has a legible, readily visible label or marking containing:

(i) The name of the radionuclide and quantity of activity;

(ii) An identification of the person licensed under § 32.26 to transfer the detector for use pursuant to § 30.20 of this chapter or equivalent regulations of an Agreement State; and

(iii) The following or a substantially similar statement:

THIS DETECTOR CONTAINS RADIOACTIVE MATERIAL AND HAS BEEN MANUFACTURED IN COMPLIANCE WITH U.S. NRC SAFETY CRITERIA IN 10 CFR 32.27. THE PURCHASER IS EXEMPT FROM ANY REGULATORY REQUIREMENTS.

(4) Each detector and point-of-sale package is provided with such other information as may be required by the Commission; and

(c) Maintain records of all transfers and file a report with the Director of the Office of Nuclear Material Safety and Safeguards by an appropriate method listed in § 30.6(a) of this chapter, including in the address: ATTN: Document Control Desk/Exempt Distribution.

(1) The report must clearly identify the specific licensee submitting the report and include the license number of the specific licensee.

(2) The report must indicate that the products are transferred for use under § 30.20 of this chapter or equivalent regulations of an Agreement State.

(3) The report must include the following information on products transferred to other persons for use under

---

[1] It is the intent of this paragraph that as the magnitude of the potential dose increases above that permitted under normal conditions, the probability that any individual will receive such a dose must decrease. The probabilities have been expressed in general terms to emphasize the approximate nature of the estimates which are to be made. The following values may be used as guides in estimating compliance with the criteria:

Low—not more than one such failure per year for each 10,000 exempt units distributed.

Negligible—not more than one such failure per year for each one million exempt units distributed.

§ 30.20 or equivalent regulations of an Agreement State:

(i) A description or identification of the type of each product and the model number(s);

(ii) For each radionuclide in each type of product and each model number, the total quantity of the radionuclide;

(iii) The number of units of each type of product transferred during the reporting period by model number.

(4)(i) The licensee shall file the report, covering the preceding calendar year, on or before January 31 of each year. In its first report after December 17, 2007, the licensee shall separately include data for transfers in prior years not previously reported to the Commission.

(ii) Licensees who permanently discontinue activities authorized by the license issued under § 32.26 shall file a report for the current calendar year within 30 days after ceasing distribution.

(5) If no transfers of byproduct material have been made under § 32.26 during the reporting period, the report must so indicate.

(6) The licensee shall maintain the record of a transfer for one year after the transfer is included in a report to the Commission.

[34 FR 6654, Apr. 18, 1969, as amended at 43 FR 6923, Feb. 17, 1978; 45 FR 38342, June 9, 1980; 48 FR 12334, Mar. 24, 1983; 72 FR 58488, Oct. 16, 2007; 73 FR 5719, Jan. 31, 2008; 73 FR 42673, July 23, 2008]

§ 32.30 Certain industrial devices containing byproduct material: Requirements for license to manufacture, process, produce, or initially transfer.

An application for a specific license to manufacture, process, produce, or initially transfer for sale or distribution devices containing byproduct material for use under § 30.22 of this chapter or equivalent regulations of an Agreement State will be approved if:

(a) The applicant satisfies the general requirements of § 30.33 of this chapter: However, the requirements of § 30.33(a)(2) and (3) do not apply to an application for a license to transfer byproduct material in such industrial devices manufactured, processed, or produced under a license issued by an Agreement State;

(b) The applicant submits sufficient information relating to the design, manufacture, prototype testing, quality control procedures, labeling or marking, and conditions of handling, storage, use, and disposal of the industrial devices to demonstrate that the device will meet the safety criteria set forth in § 32.31. The information should include:

(1) A description of the device and its intended use or uses;

(2) The type and quantity of byproduct material in each unit;

(3) Chemical and physical form of the byproduct material in the device and changes in chemical and physical form that may occur during the useful life of the device;

(4) Solubility in water and body fluids of the forms of the byproduct material identified in paragraphs (b)(3) and (b)(12) of this section;

(5) Details of construction and design of the device as related to containment and shielding of the byproduct material and other safety features under normal and severe conditions of handling, storage, use, and disposal of the device;

(6) Maximum external radiation levels at 5 and 30 centimeters from any external surface of the device, averaged over an area not to exceed 10 square centimeters, and the method of measurement;

(7) Degree of access of human beings to the device during normal handling and use;

(8) Total quantity of byproduct material expected to be distributed in the devices annually;

(9) The expected useful life of the device;

(10) The proposed methods of labeling or marking the device and its point-of-sale package to satisfy the requirements of § 32.32(b);

(11) Procedures for prototype testing of the device to demonstrate the effectiveness of the containment, shielding, and other safety features under both normal and severe conditions of handling, storage, use, and disposal of the device;

(12) Results of the prototype testing of the device, including any change in

the form of the byproduct material contained in the device, the extent to which the byproduct material may be released to the environment, any increase in external radiation levels, and any other changes in safety features;

(13) The estimated external radiation doses and committed doses resulting from the intake of byproduct material in any one year relevant to the safety criteria in § 32.31 and the basis for these estimates;

(14) A determination that the probabilities with respect to the doses referred to in § 32.31(a)(4) meet the criteria of that paragraph;

(15) Quality control procedures to be followed in the fabrication of production lots of the devices and the quality control standards the devices will be required to meet; and

(16) Any additional information, including experimental studies and tests, required by the Commission.

(c)(1) The Commission determines that the device meets the safety criteria in § 32.31.

(2) The device is unlikely to be routinely used by members of the general public in a non-occupational environment.

(3) The device has been registered in the Sealed Source and Device Registry.

[77 FR 43691, July 25, 2012]

§ 32.31 Certain industrial devices containing byproduct material: Safety criteria.

(a) An applicant for a license under § 32.30 shall demonstrate that the device is designed and will be manufactured so that:

(1) In normal use, handling, and storage of the quantities of exempt units likely to accumulate in one location, including during marketing, distribution, installation, and servicing of the device, it is unlikely that the external radiation dose in any one year, or the committed dose resulting from the intake of radioactive material in any one year, to a suitable sample of the group of individuals expected to be most highly exposed to radiation or radioactive material from the device will exceed 200 μSv (20 mrem).

(2) It is unlikely that the external radiation dose in any one year, or the committed dose resulting from the intake of radioactive material in any one year, to a suitable sample of the group of individuals expected to be most highly exposed to radiation or radioactive material from disposal of the quantities of units likely to accumulate in the same disposal site will exceed 10 μSv (1 mrem).

(3) It is unlikely that there will be a significant reduction in the effectiveness of the containment, shielding, or other safety features of the device from wear and abuse likely to occur in normal handling and use of the device during its useful life.

(4) In use, handling, storage, and disposal of the quantities of exempt units likely to accumulate in one location, including during marketing, distribution, installation, and servicing of the device, the probability is low that the containment, shielding, or other safety features of the device would fail under such circumstances that a person would receive an external radiation dose or committed dose in excess of 5 mSv (500 mrem), and the probability is negligible that a person would receive an external radiation dose or committed dose of 100 mSv (10 rem) or greater.[1]

(b) An applicant for a license under § 32.30 shall demonstrate that, even in unlikely scenarios of misuse, including those resulting in direct exposure to the unshielded source removed from the device for 1,000 hours at an average distance of 1 meter and those resulting in dispersal and subsequent intake of 10^{-4} of the quantity of byproduct material (or in the case of tritium, an intake of 10 percent), a person will not receive an external radiation dose or committed dose in excess of 100 mSv (10 rem), and, if the unshielded source is

[1] It is the intent of this paragraph that as the magnitude of the potential dose increases above that permitted under normal conditions, the probability that any individual will receive such a dose must decrease. The probabilities have been expressed in general terms to emphasize the approximate nature of the estimates that are to be made. The following values may be used as guides in estimating compliance with the criteria: Low—not more than one such failure/incident per year for each 10,000 exempt units distributed. Negligible—not more than one such failure/incident per year for each one million exempt units distributed.

small enough to fit in a pocket, that the dose to localized areas of skin averaged over areas no larger than 1 square centimeter from carrying the unshielded source in a pocket for 80 hours will not exceed 2 Sv (200 rem).

[77 FR 43692, July 25, 2012]

§ 32.32 Conditions of licenses issued under § 32.30: Quality control, labeling, and reports of transfer.

Each person licensed under § 32.30 shall:

(a) Carry out adequate control procedures in the manufacture of the device to ensure that each production lot meets the quality control standards approved by the Commission;

(b) Label or mark each device and its point-of-sale package so that:

(1) Each item has a durable, legible, readily visible label or marking on the external surface of the device containing:

(i) The following statement: "CONTAINS RADIOACTIVE MATERIAL";

(ii) The name of the radionuclide(s) and quantity(ies) of activity;

(iii) An identification of the person licensed under § 32.30 to transfer the device for use under § 30.22 of this chapter or equivalent regulations of an Agreement State; and

(iv) Instructions and precautions necessary to assure safe installation, operation, and servicing of the device (documents such as operating and service manuals may be identified in the label and used to provide this information).

(2) The external surface of the point-of-sale package has a legible, readily visible label or marking containing:

(i) The name of the radionuclide and quantity of activity;

(ii) An identification of the person licensed under § 32.30 to transfer the device for use under § 30.22 of this chapter or equivalent regulations of an Agreement State; and

(iii) The following or a substantially similar statement: "THIS DEVICE CONTAINS RADIOACTIVE MATERIAL AND HAS BEEN MANUFACTURED IN COMPLIANCE WITH U.S. NUCLEAR REGULATORY COMMISSION SAFETY CRITERIA IN 10 CFR 32.31. THE PURCHASER IS EXEMPT FROM ANY REGULATORY REQUIREMENTS."

(3) Each device and point-of-sale package contains such other information as may be required by the Commission; and

(c) Maintain records of all transfers and file a report with the Director of the Office of Nuclear Material Safety and Safeguards by an appropriate method listed in § 30.6(a) of this chapter, including in the address: ATTN: Document Control Desk/Exempt Distribution.

(1) The report must clearly identify the specific licensee submitting the report and include the license number of the specific licensee.

(2) The report must indicate that the devices are transferred for use under § 30.22 of this chapter or equivalent regulations of an Agreement State.

(3) The report must include the following information on devices transferred to other persons for use under § 30.22 or equivalent regulations of an Agreement State:

(i) A description or identification of the type of each device and the model number(s);

(ii) For each radionuclide in each type of device and each model number, the total quantity of the radionuclide; and

(iii) The number of units of each type of device transferred during the reporting period by model number.

(4)(i) The licensee shall file the report, covering the preceding calendar year, on or before January 31 of each year.

(ii) Licensees who permanently discontinue activities authorized by the license issued under § 32.30 shall file a report for the current calendar year within 30 days after ceasing distribution.

(5) If no transfers of byproduct material have been made under § 32.30 during the reporting period, the report must so indicate.

(6) The licensee shall maintain the record of a transfer for a period of one year after the transfer is included in a report to the Commission.

[77 FR 43692, July 25, 2012]

Subpart B—Generally Licensed Items

§32.51 Byproduct material contained in devices for use under §31.5; requirements for license to manufacture, or initially transfer.

(a) An application for a specific license to manufacture, or initially transfer devices containing byproduct material to persons generally licensed under §31.5 of this chapter or equivalent regulations of an Agreement State will be approved if:

(1) The applicant satisfies the general requirements of §30.33 of this chapter;

(2) The applicant submits sufficient information relating to the design, manufacture, prototype testing, quality control, labels, proposed uses, installation, servicing, leak testing, operating and safety instructions, and potential hazards of the device to provide reasonable assurance that:

(i) The device can be safely operated by persons not having training in radiological protection;

(ii) Under ordinary conditions of handling, storage, and use of the device, the byproduct material contained in the device will not be released or inadvertently removed from the device, and it is unlikely that any person will receive in 1 year a dose in excess of 10 percent of the annual limits specified in §20.1201(a) of this chapter; and

(iii) Under accident conditions (such as fire and explosion) associated with handling, storage and use of the device, it is unlikely that any person would receive an external radiation dose or dose commitment in excess of the dose to the appropriate organ as specified in Column IV of the table in §32.24.

(3) Each device bears a durable, legible, clearly visible label or labels approved by the Commission which contain in a clearly identified and separate statement:

(i) Instructions and precautions necessary to assure safe installation, operation, and servicing of the device (documents such as operating and service manuals may be identified in the label and used to provide this information);

(ii) The requirements, or lack of requirement, for leak testing, or for testing any on-off mechanism and indicator, including the maximum time interval for such testing, and the identification of radioactive material by isotope, quantity of radioactivity, and date of determination of the quantity; and

(iii) The information called for in the following statement in the same or substantially similar form:[1]

> The receipt, possession, use, and transfer of this device Model ______[2], Serial No. _____[2], are subject to a general license or the equivalent and the regulations of the U.S. NRC or of a State with which the NRC has entered into an agreement for the exercise of regulatory authority. This label shall be maintained on the device in a legible condition. Removal of this label is prohibited.
>
> CAUTION—RADIOACTIVE MATERIAL
>
> ________________________
>
> (Name of manufacturer, or initial transferor)[2]

(4) Each device having a separable source housing that provides the primary shielding for the source also bears, on the source housing, a durable label containing the device model number and serial number, the isotope and quantity, the words, "Caution-Radioactive Material," the radiation symbol described in §20.1901 of this chapter, and the name of the manufacturer or initial distributor.

(5) Each device meeting the criteria of §31.5(c)(13)(i) of this chapter, bears a permanent (e.g., embossed, etched, stamped, or engraved) label affixed to the source housing if separable, or the device if the source housing is not separable, that includes the words, "Caution-Radioactive Material," and, if practicable, the radiation symbol described in §20.1901 of this chapter.

(6) The device has been registered in the Sealed Source and Device Registry.

(b) In the event the applicant desires that the device be required to be tested at intervals longer than six months, either for proper operation of the on-off mechanism and indicator, if any, or for leakage of radioactive material or for

[1] Devices licensed under §32.51 prior to January 19, 1975 may bear labels authorized by the regulations in effect on January 1, 1975.

[2] The model, serial number, and the name of the manufacturer, or initial transferor may be omitted from this label provided the information is elsewhere specified in labeling affixed to the device.

both, he shall include in this application sufficient information to demonstrate that such longer interval is justified by performance characteristics of the device or similar devices, and by design features which have a significant bearing on the probability or consequences of leakage of radioactive material from the device or failure of the on-off mechanism and indicator. In determining the acceptable interval for the test for leakage of radioactive material, the Commission will consider information which includes, but is not limited to:

(1) Primary containment (source capsule);

(2) Protection of primary containment;

(3) Method of sealing containment;

(4) Containment construction materials;

(5) Form of contained radioactive material;

(6) Maximum temperature withstood during prototype tests;

(7) Maximum pressure withstood during prototype tests;

(8) Maximum quantity of contained radioactive material;

(9) Radiotoxicity of contained radioactive material; and

(10) Operating experience with identical devices or similarly designed and constructed devices.

(c) In the event the applicant desires that the general licensee under § 31.5 of this chapter, or under equivalent regulations of an Agreement State, be authorized to install the device, collect the sample to be analyzed by a specific licensee for leakage of radioactive material, service the device, test the on-off mechanism and indicator, or remove the device from installation, the applicant shall include in the application written instructions to be followed by the general licensee, estimated calendar quarter doses associated with such activity or activities, and the bases for these estimates. The submitted information must demonstrate that performance of this activity or activities by an individual untrained in radiological protection, in addition to other handling, storage, and use of devices under the general license, is unlikely to cause that individual to receive a dose in excess of 10 percent of the annual limits specified in § 20.1201(a) of this chapter.

[39 FR 43533, Dec. 16, 1974, as amended at 40 FR 8785, Mar. 3, 1975; 42 FR 25721, May 19, 1977; 43 FR 6923, Feb. 17, 1978; 58 FR 67660, Dec. 22, 1993; 59 FR 5520, Feb. 7, 1994; 65 FR 79189, Dec. 18, 2000; 77 FR 43693, July 25, 2012]

§ 32.51a Same: Conditions of licenses.

(a) If a device containing byproduct material is to be transferred for use under the general license contained in § 31.5 of this chapter, each person that is licensed under § 32.51 shall provide the information specified in this paragraph to each person to whom a device is to be transferred. This information must be provided before the device may be transferred. In the case of a transfer through an intermediate person, the information must also be provided to the intended user prior to initial transfer to the intermediate person. The required information includes—

(1) A copy of the general license contained in § 31.5 of this chapter; if paragraphs (c)(2) through (4) or (c)(13) of § 31.5 do not apply to the particular device, those paragraphs may be omitted.

(2) A copy of §§ 31.2, 30.51, 20.2201, and 20.2202 of this chapter;

(3) A list of the services that can only be performed by a specific licensee;

(4) Information on acceptable disposal options including estimated costs of disposal; and

(5) An indication that NRC's policy is to issue high civil penalties for improper disposal.

(b) If byproduct material is to be transferred in a device for use under an equivalent general license of an Agreement State, each person that is licensed under § 32.51 shall provide the information specified in this paragraph to each person to whom a device is to be transferred. This information must be provided before the device may be transferred. In the case of a transfer through an intermediate person, the information must also be provided to the intended user prior to initial transfer to the intermediate person. The required information includes—

(1) A copy of the Agreement State's regulations equivalent to §§ 31.5, 31.2, 30.51, 20.2201, and 20.2202 of this chapter or a copy of §§ 31.5, 31.2, 30.51, 20.2201, and 20.2202 of this chapter. If a copy of

the NRC regulations is provided to a prospective general licensee in lieu of the Agreement State's regulations, it shall be accompanied by a note explaining that use of the device is regulated by the Agreement State; if certain paragraphs of the regulations do not apply to the particular device, those paragraphs may be omitted.

(2) A list of the services that can only be performed by a specific licensee;

(3) Information on acceptable disposal options including estimated costs of disposal; and

(4) The name or title, address, and phone number of the contact at the Agreement State regulatory agency from which additional information may be obtained.

(c) An alternative approach to informing customers may be proposed by the licensee for approval by the Commission.

(d) Each device that is transferred after February 19, 2002 must meet the labeling requirements in §32.51(a)(3) through (5).

(e) If a notification of bankruptcy has been made under §30.34(h) or the license is to be terminated, each person licensed under §32.51 shall provide, upon request, to the NRC and to any appropriate Agreement State, records of final disposition required under §32.52(c).

[65 FR 79189, Dec. 18, 2000; 65 FR 80991, Dec. 22, 2000]

§32.52 Same: material transfer reports and records.

Each person licensed under §32.51 to initially transfer devices to generally licensed persons shall comply with the requirements of this section.

(a) The person shall report to the Director, Office of Nuclear Material Safety and Safeguards , ATTN: GLTS, by an appropriate method listed in §30.6(a) of this chapter, all transfers of such devices to persons for use under the general license in §31.5 of this chapter and all receipts of devices from persons licensed under §31.5 of this chapter. The report must be submitted on a quarterly basis on NRC Form 653—"Transfers of Industrial Devices Report" or in a clear and legible report containing all of the data required by the form.

(1) The required information for transfers to general licensees includes—

(i) The identity of each general licensee by name and mailing address for the location of use; if there is no mailing address for the location of use, an alternate address for the general licensee shall be submitted along with information on the actual location of use.

(ii) The name, title, and phone number of the person identified by the general licensee as having knowledge of and authority to take required actions to ensure compliance with the appropriate regulations and requirements;

(iii) The date of transfer;

(iv) The type, model number, and serial number of the device transferred; and

(v) The quantity and type of byproduct material contained in the device.

(2) If one or more intermediate persons will temporarily possess the device at the intended place of use before its possession by the user, the report must include the same information for both the intended user and each intermediate person, and clearly designate the intermediate person(s).

(3) For devices received from a §31.5 general licensee, the report must include the identity of the general licensee by name and address, the type, model number, and serial number of the device received, the date of receipt, and, in the case of devices not initially transferred by the reporting licensee, the name of the manufacturer or initial transferor.

(4) If the licensee makes changes to a device possessed by a §31.5 general licensee, such that the label must be changed to update required information, the report must identify the general licensee, the device, and the changes to information on the device label.

(5) The report must cover each calendar quarter, must be filed within 30 days of the end of the calendar quarter, and must clearly indicate the period covered by the report.

(6) The report must clearly identify the specific licensee submitting the report and include the license number of the specific licensee.

(7) If no transfers have been made to or from persons generally licensed under § 31.5 of this chapter during the reporting period, the report must so indicate.

(b) The person shall report all transfers of devices to persons for use under a general license in an Agreement State's regulations that are equivalent to § 31.5 of this chapter and all receipts of devices from general licensees in the Agreement State's jurisdiction to the responsible Agreement State agency. The report must be submitted on Form 653—"Transfers of Industrial Devices Report" or in a clear and legible report containing all of the data required by the form.

(1) The required information for transfers to general licensees includes—

(i) The identity of each general licensee by name and mailing address for the location of use; if there is no mailing address for the location of use, an alternate address for the general licensee shall be submitted along with information on the actual location of use.

(ii) The name, title, and phone number of the person identified by the general licensee as having knowledge of and authority to take required actions to ensure compliance with the appropriate regulations and requirements;

(iii) The date of transfer;

(iv) The type, model number, and serial number of the device transferred; and

(v) The quantity and type of byproduct material contained in the device.

(2) If one or more intermediate persons will temporarily possess the device at the intended place of use before its possession by the user, the report must include the same information for both the intended user and each intermediate person, and clearly designate the intermediate person(s).

(3) For devices received from a general licensee, the report must include the identity of the general licensee by name and address, the type, model number, and serial number of the device received, the date of receipt, and, in the case of devices not initially transferred by the reporting licensee, the name of the manufacturer or initial transferor.

(4) If the licensee makes changes to a device possessed by a general licensee, such that the label must be changed to update required information, the report must identify the general licensee, the device, and the changes to information on the device label.

(5) The report must cover each calendar quarter, must be filed within 30 days of the end of the calendar quarter, and must clearly indicate the period covered by the report.

(6) The report must clearly identify the specific licensee submitting the report and must include the license number of the specific licensee.

(7) If no transfers have been made to or from a particular Agreement State during the reporting period, this information shall be reported to the responsible Agreement State agency upon request of the agency.

(c) The person shall maintain all information concerning transfers and receipts of devices that supports the reports required by this section. Records required by this paragraph must be maintained for a period of 3 years following the date of the recorded event.

[65 FR 79189, Dec. 18, 2000, as amended at 68 FR 58805, Oct. 10, 2003; 73 FR 5719, Jan. 31, 2008]

§ 32.53 Luminous safety devices for use in aircraft: Requirements for license to manufacture, assemble, repair or initially transfer.

An application for a specific license to manufacture, assemble, repair or initially transfer luminous safety devices containing tritium or promethium-147 for use in aircraft, for distribution to persons generally licensed under § 31.7 of this chapter, will be approved if:

(a) The applicant satisfies the general requirements specified in § 30.33 of this chapter;

(b) The applicant submits sufficient information regarding each device pertinent to evaluation of the potential radiation exposure, including:

(1) Chemical and physical form and maximum quantity of tritium or promethium-147 in each device;

(2) Details of construction and design;

(3) Details of the method of binding or containing the tritium or promethium-147;

(4) Procedures for and results of prototype testing to demonstrate that the tritium or promethium-147 will not be released to the environment under the most severe conditions likely to be encountered in normal use;

(5) Quality assurance procedures to be followed that are sufficient to ensure compliance with § 32.55;

(6) Any additional information, including experimental studies and tests, required by the Commission to facilitate a determination of the safety of the device.

(c) Each device will contain no more than 10 curies of tritium or 300 millicuries of promethium-147. The levels of radiation from each device containing promethium-147 will not exceed 0.5 millirad per hour at 10 centimeters from any surface when measured through 50 milligrams per square centimeter of absorber.

(d) The Commission determines that:

(1) The method of incorporation and binding of the tritium or promethium-147 in the device is such that the tritium or promethium-147 will not be released under the most severe conditions which are likely to be encountered in normal use and handling of the device;

(2) The tritium or promethium-147 is incorporated or enclosed so as to preclude direct physical contact by any person with it;

(3) The device is so designed that it cannot easily be disassembled; and

(4) Prototypes of the device have been subjected to and have satisfactorily passed the tests required by paragraph (e) of this section.

(e) The applicant shall subject at least five prototypes of the device to tests as follows:

(1) The devices are subjected to tests that adequately take into account the individual, aggregate, and cumulative effects of environmental conditions expected in service that could adversely affect the effective containment of tritium or promethium-147, such as temperature, moisture, absolute pressure, water immersion, vibration, shock, and weathering.

(2) The devices are inspected for evidence of physical damage and for loss of tritium or promethium-147, after each stage of testing, using methods of inspection adequate for determining compliance with the criteria in paragraph (e)(3) of this section.

(3) Device designs are rejected for which the following has been detected for any unit:

(i) A leak resulting in a loss of 0.1 percent or more of the original amount of tritium or promethium-147 from the device; or

(ii) Surface contamination of tritium or promethium-147 on the device of more than 2,200 disintegrations per minute per 100 square centimeters of surface area; or

(iii) Any other evidence of physical damage.

(f) The device has been registered in the Sealed Source and Device Registry.

[30 FR 8192, June 26, 1965, as amended at 33 FR 6463, Apr. 27, 1968; 43 FR 6923, Feb. 17, 1978; 77 FR 43693, July 25, 2012]

§ 32.54 Same: Labeling of devices.

(a) A person licensed under § 32.53 to manufacture, assemble, or initially transfer devices containing tritium or promethium-147 for distribution to persons generally licensed under § 31.7 of this chapter shall, except as provided in paragraph (b) of this section, affix to each device a label containing the radiation symbol prescribed by § 20.1901 of this chapter, such other information as may be required by the Commission including disposal instructions when appropriate, and the following or a substantially similar statement which contains the information called for in the following statement: [1]

The receipt, possession, use, and transfer of this device, Model* ________, Serial No.* ____, containing ________ (Identity and quantity of radioactive material) are subject to a general license or the equivalent and the regulations of the U.S. NRC or of a State with which the NRC has entered into an agreement for the exercise of regulatory authority. Do not remove this label.

CAUTION—RADIOACTIVE MATERIAL

____

[1] Devices licensed under § 32.53 prior to January 19, 1975 may bear labels authorized by the regulations in effect on January 1, 1975.

(Name of manufacturer, assembler, or initial transferor.)*

*The model, serial number, and name of manufacturer, assembler, or initial transferor may be omitted from this label provided they are elsewhere specified in labeling affixed to the device.

(b) If the Commission determines that it is not feasible to affix a label to the device containing all the information called for in paragraph (a) of this section, it may waive the requirements of that paragraph and require in lieu thereof that:

(1) A label be affixed to the device identifying:

(i) The manufacturer, assembler, or initial transferor; and

(ii) The type of radioactive material; and

(2) A leaflet bearing the following information be enclosed in or accompany the container in which the device is shipped:

(i) The name of the manufacturer, assembler, or initial transferor,

(ii) The type and quantity of radioactive material,

(iii) The model number,

(iv) A statement that the receipt, possession, use, and transfer of the device are subject to a general license or the equivalent and the regulations of the U.S. NRC or of an Agreement State, and

(v) Such other information as may be required by the Commission, including disposal instructions when appropriate.

[33 FR 16331, Nov. 7, 1968, as amended at 40 FR 8785, Mar. 3, 1975; 43 FR 6923, Feb. 17, 1978; 63 FR 39483, July 23, 1998]

§ 32.55 Same: Quality assurance, prohibition of transfer.

(a) Each person licensed under § 32.53 shall visually inspect each device and shall reject any that has an observable physical defect that could adversely affect containment of the tritium or promethium-147.

(b) Each person licensed under § 32.53 shall:

(1) Maintain quality assurance systems in the manufacture of the luminous safety device in a manner sufficient to provide reasonable assurance that the safety-related components of the distributed devices are capable of performing their intended functions; and

(2) Subject inspection lots to acceptance sampling procedures, by procedures specified in paragraph (c) of this section and in the license issued under § 32.53, to provide at least 95 percent confidence that the Lot Tolerance Percent Defective of 5.0 percent will not be exceeded.

(c) The licensee shall subject each inspection lot to:

(1) Tests that adequately take into account the individual, aggregate, and cumulative effects of environmental conditions expected in service that could adversely affect the effective containment of tritium or promethium-147, such as absolute pressure and water immersion.

(2) Inspection for evidence of physical damage, containment failure, or for loss of tritium or promethium-147 after each stage of testing, using methods of inspection adequate for applying the following criteria for defective:

(i) A leak resulting in a loss of 0.1 percent or more of the original amount of tritium or promethium-147 from the device;

(ii) Levels of radiation in excess of 5 microgray (0.5 millirad) per hour at 10 centimeters from any surface when measured through 50 milligrams per square centimeter of absorber, if the device contains promethium-147; and

(iii) Any other criteria specified in the license issued under § 32.53.

(d) No person licensed under § 32.53 shall transfer to persons generally licensed under § 31.7 of this chapter, or under an equivalent general license of an Agreement State:

(1) Any luminous safety device tested and found defective under any condition of a license issued under § 32.53, or paragraph (b) of this section, unless the defective luminous safety device has been repaired or reworked, retested, and determined by an independent inspector to meet the applicable acceptance criteria; or

(2) Any luminous safety device contained within any lot that has been sampled and rejected as a result of the procedures in paragraph (b)(2) of this section, unless:

(i) A procedure for defining sub-lot size, independence, and additional testing procedures is contained in the license issued under § 32.53; and

(ii) Each individual sub-lot is sampled, tested, and accepted in accordance with paragraphs (b)(2) and (d)(2)(i) of this section and any other criteria that may be required as a condition of the license issued under § 32.53.

[77 FR 43693, July 25, 2012]

§ 32.56 Same: Material transfer reports.

(a) Each person licensed under § 32.53 shall file an annual report with the Director, Office of Nuclear Material Safety and Safeguards , ATTN: Document Control Desk/GLTS, by an appropriate method listed in § 30.6(a) of this chapter, which must state the total quantity of tritium or promethium-147 transferred to persons generally licensed under § 31.7 of this chapter. The report must identify each general licensee by name, state the kinds and numbers of luminous devices transferred, and specify the quantity of tritium or promethium-147 in each kind of device. Each report must cover the year ending June 30 and must be filed within thirty (30) days thereafter. If no transfers have been made to persons generally licensed under § 31.7 of this chapter during the reporting period, the report must so indicate.

(b) Each person licensed under § 32.53 shall report annually all transfers of devices to persons for use under a general license in an Agreement State's regulations that are equivalent to § 31.7 of this chapter to the responsible Agreement State agency. The report must state the total quantity of tritium or promethium-147 transferred, identify each general licensee by name, state the kinds and numbers of luminous devices transferred, and specify the quantity of tritium or promethium-147 in each kind of device. If no transfers have been made to a particular Agreement State during the reporting period, this information must be reported to the responsible Agreement State agency upon request of the agency.

[77 FR 43694, July 25, 2012]

§ 32.57 Calibration or reference sources containing americium-241 or radium-226: Requirements for license to manufacture or initially transfer.

An application for a specific license to manufacture or initially transfer calibration or reference sources containing americium-241 or radium-226, for distribution to persons generally licensed under § 31.8 of this chapter, will be approved if:

(a) The applicant satisfies the general requirements of § 30.33 of this chapter;

(b) The applicant submits sufficient information regarding each type of calibration or reference source pertinent to evaluation of the potential radiation exposure, including:

(1) Chemical and physical form and maximum quantity of americium 241 or radium-226 in the source;

(2) Details of construction and design;

(3) Details of the method of incorporation and binding of the americium-241 or radium-226 in the source;

(4) Procedures for and results of prototype testing of sources, which are designed to contain more than 0.005 microcurie of americium-241 or radium-226, to demonstrate that the americium-241 or radium-226 contained in each source will not be released or be removed from the source under normal conditions of use;

(5) Details of quality control procedures to be followed in manufacture of the source;

(6) Description of labeling to be affixed to the source or the storage container for the source;

(7) Any additional information, including experimental studies and tests, required by the Commission to facilitate a determination of the safety of the source.

(c) Each source will contain no more than 5 microcuries of americium-241 or radium-226.

(d) The Commission determines, with respect to any type of source containing more than 0.005 microcurie of americium-241 or radium-226, that:

(1) The method of incorporation and binding of the americium-241 or radium-226 in the source is such that the americium-241 or radium-226 will not

be released or be removed from the source under normal conditions of use and handling of the source; and

(2) The source has been subjected to and has satisfactorily passed appropriate tests required by paragraph (e) of this section.

(e) The applicant shall subject at least five prototypes of each source that is designed to contain more than 0.185 kilobecquerel (0.005 microcurie) of americium-241 or radium-226 to tests as follows:

(1) The initial quantity of radioactive material deposited on each source is measured by direct counting of the source.

(2) The sources are subjected to tests that adequately take into account the individual, aggregate, and cumulative effects of environmental conditions expected in service that could adversely affect the effective containment or binding of americium-241 or radium-226, such as physical handling, moisture, and water immersion.

(3) The sources are inspected for evidence of physical damage and for loss of americium-241 or radium-226, after each stage of testing, using methods of inspection adequate for determining compliance with the criteria in paragraph (e)(4) of this section.

(4) Source designs are rejected for which the following has been detected for any unit: Removal of more than 0.185 kilobecquerel (0.005 microcurie) of americium-241 or radium-226 from the source or any other evidence of physical damage.

[30 FR 8192, June 26, 1965, as amended at 43 FR 6923, Feb. 17, 1978; 72 FR 55928, Oct. 1, 2007; 73 FR 42674, July 23, 2008; 77 FR 43694, July 25, 2012]

§32.58 Same: Labeling of devices.

Each person licensed under §32.57 shall affix to each source, or storage container for the source, a label which shall contain sufficient information relative to safe use and storage of the source and shall include the following statement or a substantially similar statement which contains the information called for in the following statement:[1]

The receipt, possession, use, and transfer of this source, Model, Serial No., are subject to a general license and the regulations of the United States Nuclear Regulatory Commission or of a State with which the Commission has entered into an agreement for the exercise of regulatory authority. Do not remove this label.

CAUTION-RADIOACTIVE MATERIAL–THIS SOURCE CONTAINS AMERICIUM-241 (or RADIUM-226). DO NOT TOUCH RADIOACTIVE PORTION OF THIS SOURCE

(Name of manufacturer or initial transferor)

[72 FR 55929, Oct. 1, 2007]

§32.59 Same: Leak testing of each source.

Each person licensed under §32.57 shall perform a dry wipe test upon each source containing more than 3.7 kilobecquerels (0.1 microcurie) of americium-241 or radium-226 before transferring the source to a general licensee under §31.8 of this chapter or under equivalent regulations of an Agreement State. This test must be performed by wiping the entire radioactive surface of the source with a filter paper with the application of moderate finger pressure. The radioactivity on the filter paper must be measured using methods capable of detecting 0.185 kilobecquerel (0.005 microcurie) of americium-241 or radium-226. If a source has been shown to be leaking or losing more than 0.185 kilobecquerel (0.005 microcurie) of americium-241 or radium-226 by the methods described in this section, the source must be rejected and must not be transferred to a general licensee under §31.8 of this chapter, or equivalent regulations of an Agreement State.

[77 FR 43694, July 25, 2012]

[1] Sources licensed under §32.57 before January 19, 1975, may bear labels authorized by the regulations in effect on January 1, 1975.

§ 32.60 [Reserved]

§ 32.61 Ice detection devices containing strontium-90; requirements for license to manufacture or initially transfer.

An application for a specific license to manufacture or initially transfer ice detection devices containing strontium-90 for distribution to persons generally licensed under § 31.10 of this chapter will be approved if:

(a) The applicant satisfies the general requirements specified in § 30.33 of this chapter;

(b) The applicant submits sufficient information regarding each type of device pertinent to evaluation of the potential radiation exposure, including:

(1) Chemical and physical form and maximum quantity of strontium-90 in the device;

(2) Details of construction and design of the source of radiation and its shielding;

(3) Radiation profile of a prototype device;

(4) Procedures for and results of prototype testing of devices to demonstrate that the strontium-90 contained in each device will not be released or be removed from the device under the most severe conditions likely to be encountered in normal handling and use;

(5) Details of quality control procedures to be followed in manufacture of the device;

(6) Description of labeling to be affixed to the device;

(7) Instructions for handling and installation of the device;

(8) Any additional information, including experimental studies and tests, required by the Commission to facilitate a determination of the safety of the device;

(c) Each device will contain no more than 50 microcuries of strontium-90 in an insoluble form;

(d) Each device will bear durable, legible labeling which includes the radiation caution symbol prescribed by § 20.1901(a) of this chapter, a statement that the device contains strontium-90 and the quantity thereof, instructions for disposal and statements that the device may be possessed pursuant to a general license, that the manufacturer or civil authorities should be notified if the device is found, that removal of the labeling is prohibited and that disassembly and repair of the device may be performed only by a person holding a specific license to manufacture or service such devices;

(e) The Commission determines that:

(1) The method of incorporation and binding of the strontium-90 in the device is such that the strontium-90 will not be released from the device under the most severe conditions which are likely to be encountered in normal use and handling of the device;

(2) The strontium-90 is incorporated or enclosed so as to preclude direct physical contact by any individual with it and is shielded so that no individual will receive a radiation exposure to a major portion of his body in excess of 0.5 rem in a year under ordinary circumstances of use;

(3) The device is so designed that it cannot be easily disassembled;

(4) Prototypes of the device have been subjected to and have satisfactorily passed the tests required by paragraph (f) of this section.

(5) Quality control procedures have been established to satisfy the requirements of § 32.62.

(f) The applicant shall subject at least five prototypes of the device to tests as follows:

(1) The devices are subjected to tests that adequately take into account the individual, aggregate, and cumulative effects of environmental conditions expected in service that could adversely affect the effective containment of strontium-90, such as temperature, moisture, absolute pressure, water immersion, vibration, shock, and weathering.

(2) The devices are inspected for evidence of physical damage and for loss of strontium-90 after each stage of testing, using methods of inspection adequate for determining compliance with the criteria in paragraph (f)(3) of this section.

(3) Device designs are rejected for which the following has been detected for any unit:

(i) A leak resulting in a loss of 0.1 percent or more of the original amount of strontium-90 from the device; or

(ii) Surface contamination of strontium-90 on the device of more than 2,200 disintegrations per minute per 100 square centimeters of surface area; or

(iii) Any other evidence of physical damage.

(g) The device has been registered in the Sealed Source and Device Registry.

[30 FR 9905, Aug. 10, 1965, as amended at 43 FR 6923, Feb. 17, 1978; 56 FR 23472, May 21, 1991; 58 FR 67660, Dec. 22, 1993; 77 FR 43694, July 25, 2012]

§ 32.62 Same: Quality assurance; prohibition of transfer.

(a) Each person licensed under § 32.61 shall visually inspect each device and shall reject any which has an observable physical defect that could affect containment of the strontium-90.

(b) Each person licensed under § 32.61 shall test each device for possible loss of strontium-90 or for contamination by wiping with filter paper an area of at least 100 square centimeters on the outside surface of the device, or by wiping the entire surface area if it is less than 100 square centimeters. The detection on the filter paper of more than 2,200 disintegrations per minute of radioactive material per 100 square centimeters of surface wiped shall be cause for rejection of the tested device.

(c) Each person licensed under § 32.61 shall:

(1) Maintain quality assurance systems in the manufacture of the ice detection device containing strontium-90 in a manner sufficient to provide reasonable assurance that the safety-related components of the distributed devices are capable of performing their intended functions; and

(2) Subject inspection lots to acceptance sampling procedures, by procedures specified in paragraph (d) of this section and in the license issued under § 32.61, to provide at least 95 percent confidence that the Lot Tolerance Percent Defective of 5.0 percent will not be exceeded.

(d) Each person licensed under § 32.61 shall subject each inspection lot to:

(1) Tests that adequately take into account the individual, aggregate, and cumulative effects of environmental conditions expected in service that could possibly affect the effective containment of strontium-90, such as absolute pressure and water immersion.

(2) Inspection for evidence of physical damage, containment failure, or for loss of strontium-90 after each stage of testing, using methods of inspection adequate to determine compliance with the following criteria for defective: A leak resulting in a loss of 0.1 percent or more of the original amount of strontium-90 from the device and any other criteria specified in the license issued under § 32.61.

(e) No person licensed under § 32.61 shall transfer to persons generally licensed under § 31.10 of this chapter, or under an equivalent general license of an Agreement State:

(1) Any ice detection device containing strontium-90 tested and found defective under the criteria specified in a license issued under § 32.61, unless the defective ice detection device has been repaired or reworked, retested, and determined by an independent inspector to meet the applicable acceptance criteria; or

(2) Any ice detection device containing strontium-90 contained within any lot that has been sampled and rejected as a result of the procedures in paragraph (c)(2) of this section, unless:

(i) A procedure for defining sub-lot size, independence, and additional testing procedures is contained in the license issued under § 32.61; and

(ii) Each individual sub-lot is sampled, tested, and accepted in accordance with paragraphs (c)(2) and (e)(2)(i) of this section and any other criteria as may be required as a condition of the license issued under § 32.61.

[30 FR 9905, Aug. 10, 1965, as amended at 39 FR 22130, June 20, 1974; 39 FR 26397, July 19, 1974; 43 FR 6923, Feb. 17, 1978; 77 FR 43694, July 25, 2012]

§ 32.71 Manufacture and distribution of byproduct material for certain in vitro clinical or laboratory testing under general license.

An application for a specific license to manufacturer or distribute byproduct material for use under the general license of § 31.11 of this chapter will be approved if:

(a) The applicant satisfies the general requirements specified in § 30.33 of this chapter.

(b) The byproduct material is to be prepared for distribution in prepackaged units of:

(1) Iodine-125 in units not exceeding 10 microcuries each.

(2) Iodine-131 in units not exceeding 10 microcuries each.

(3) Carbon-14 in units not exceeding 10 microcuries each.

(4) Hydrogen-3 (tritium) in units not exceeding 50 microcuries each.

(5) Iron-59 in units not exceeding 20 microcuries each.

(6) Selenium-75 in units not exceeding 10 microcuries each.

(7) Mock Iodine-125 in units not exceeding 0.05 microcurie of iodine-129 and 0.005 microcurie of americium-241 each.

(8) Cobalt-57 in units not exceeding 0.37 megabecquerel (10 microcuries) each.

(c) Each prepackaged unit bears a durable, clearly visible label:

(1) Identifying the radioactive contents as to chemical form and radionuclide, and indicating that the amount of radioactivity does not exceed 0.37 megabecquerel (10 microcuries) of iodine-131, iodine-125, selenium-75, or carbon-14; 1.85 megabecquerels (50 microcuries) of hydrogen-3 (tritium); or 0.74 megabecquerel (20 microcuries) of iron-59; or Mock Iodine-125 in units not exceeding 1.85 kilobecquerels (0.05 microcurie) of iodine-129 and 0.185 kilobecquerel (0.005 microcurie) of americium-241 each; or cobalt-57 in units not exceeding 0.37 megabecquerel (10 microcuries); and

(2) Displaying the radiation caution symbol described in § 20.1901(a) of this chapter and the words, "Caution, Radioactive Material", and "Not for Internal or External Use in Humans or Animals."

(d) The following statement, or a substantially similar statement which contains the information called for in the following statement, appears on a label affixed to each prepackaged unit or appears in a leaflet or brochure which accompanies the package:[1]

The radioactive material may be received, acquired, possessed, and used only by physicians, veterinarians in the practice of veterinary medicine, clinical laboratories or hospitals and only for in vitro clinical or laboratory tests not involving internal or external administration of the material, or the radiation therefrom, to human beings or animals. Its receipt, acquisition, possession, use, and transfer are subject to the regulations and a general license of the U.S. Nuclear Regulatory Commission or of a State with which the Commission has entered into an agreement for the exercise of regulatory authority.

____
(Name of Manufacturer)

(e) The label affixed to the unit, or the leaflet or brochure which accompanies the package, contains adequate information as to the precautions to be observed in handling and storing such byproduct material. In the case of the Mock Iodine-125 reference or calibration source, the information accompanying the source must also contain directions to the licensee regarding the waste disposal requirements set out in § 20.2001.

[33 FR 16553, Nov. 14, 1968, as amended at 38 FR 34110, Dec. 11, 1973; 39 FR 26148, July 17, 1974; 40 FR 8786, Mar. 3, 1975; 42 FR 21604, Apr. 28, 1977; 42 FR 26987, May 26, 1977; 44 FR 50325, Aug. 28, 1979; 56 FR 23472, May 21, 1991; 58 FR 67660, Dec. 22, 1993; 72 FR 55929, Oct. 1, 2007]

Subpart C—Specifically Licensed Items

§ 32.72 Manufacture, preparation, or transfer for commercial distribution of radioactive drugs containing byproduct material for medical use under part 35.

(a) An application for a specific license to manufacture, prepare, or transfer for commercial distribution radioactive drugs containing byproduct material for use by persons authorized pursuant to part 35 of this chapter will be approved if:

(1) The applicant satisfies the general requirements specified in 10 CFR 30.33;

(2) The applicant submits evidence that the applicant is at least one of the following:

(i) Registered with the U.S. Food and Drug Administration (FDA) as the owner or operator of a drug establishment that engages in the manufacture, preparation, propagation,

[1] Labels authorized by the regulations in effect on September 26, 1979, may be used until one year from September 27, 1979.

compounding, or processing of a drug under 21 CFR 207.20(a);

(ii) Registered or licensed with a state agency as a drug manufacturer;

(iii) Licensed as a pharmacy by a State Board of Pharmacy;

(iv) Operating as a nuclear pharmacy within a Federal medical institution; or

(v) A Positron Emission Tomography (PET) drug production facility registered with a State agency.

(3) The applicant submits information on the radionuclide; the chemical and physical form; the maximum activity per vial, syringe, generator, or other container of the radioactive drug; and the shielding provided by the packaging to show it is appropriate for the safe handling and storage of the radioactive drugs by medical use licensees; and

(4) The applicant satisfies the following labeling requirements:

(i) A label is affixed to each transport radiation shield, whether it is constructed of lead, glass, plastic, or other material, of a radioactive drug to be transferred for commercial distribution. The label must include the radiation symbol and the words "CAUTION, RADIOACTIVE MATERIAL" or "DANGER, RADIOACTIVE MATERIAL"; the name of the radioactive drug or its abbreviation; and the quantity of radioactivity at a specified date and time. For radioactive drugs with a half life greater than 100 days, the time may be omitted.

(ii) A label is affixed to each syringe, vial, or other container used to hold a radioactive drug to be transferred for commercial distribution. The label must include the radiation symbol and the words "CAUTION, RADIOACTIVE MATERIAL" or "DANGER, RADIOACTIVE MATERIAL" and an identifier that ensures that the syringe, vial, or other container can be correlated with the information on the transport radiation shield label.

(b) A licensee described by paragraph (a)(2)(iii) or (iv) of this section:

(1) May prepare radioactive drugs for medical use, as defined in 10 CFR 35.2, provided that the radioactive drug is prepared by either an authorized nuclear pharmacist, as specified in paragraphs (b)(2) and (b)(4) of this section, or an individual under the supervision of an authorized nuclear pharmacist as specified in 10 CFR 35.27.

(2) May allow a pharmacist to work as an authorized nuclear pharmacist if:

(i) This individual qualifies as an authorized nuclear pharmacist as defined in 10 CFR 35.2,

(ii) This individual meets the requirements specified in § 35.55(b) and 35.59 of this chapter, and the licensee has received an approved license amendment identifying this individual as an authorized nuclear pharmacist; or

(iii) This individual is designated as an authorized nuclear pharmacist in accordance with paragraph (b)(4) of this section.

(3) The actions authorized in paragraphs (b)(1) and (b)(2) of this section are permitted in spite of more restrictive language in license conditions.

(4) May designate a pharmacist (as defined in § 35.2 of this chapter) as an authorized nuclear pharmacist if:

(i) The individual was a nuclear pharmacist preparing only radioactive drugs containing accelerator-produced radioactive material, and

(ii) The individual practiced at a pharmacy at a Government agency or Federally recognized Indian Tribe before November 30, 2007 or at all other pharmacies before August 8, 2009, or an earlier date as noticed by the NRC.

(5) Shall provide to the Commission:

(i) A copy of each individual's certification by a specialty board whose certification process has been recognized by the Commission or an Agreement State as specified in § 35.55(a) of this chapter with the written attestation signed by a preceptor as required by § 35.55(b)(2) of this chapter; or

(ii) The Commission or Agreement State license, or

(iii) Commission master materials licensee permit, or

(iv) The permit issued by a licensee or Commission master materials permittee of broad scope or the authorization from a commercial nuclear pharmacy authorized to list its own authorized nuclear pharmacist, or

(v) Documentation that only accelerator-produced radioactive materials were used in the practice of nuclear pharmacy at a Government agency or

Federally recognized Indian Tribe before November 30, 2007 or at all other locations of use before August 8, 2009, or an earlier date as noticed by the NRC; and

(vi) A copy of the State pharmacy licensure or registration, no later than 30 days after the date that the licensee allows, under paragraphs (b)(2)(i) and (b)(2)(iii) of this section, the individual to work as an authorized nuclear pharmacist.

(c) A licensee shall possess and use instrumentation to measure the radioactivity of radioactive drugs. The licensee shall have procedures for use of the instrumentation. The licensee shall measure, by direct measurement or by combination of measurements and calculations, the amount of radioactivity in dosages of alpha-, beta-, or photon-emitting radioactive drugs prior to transfer for commercial distribution. In addition, the licensee shall:

(1) Perform tests before initial use, periodically, and following repair, on each instrument for accuracy, linearity, and geometry dependence, as appropriate for the use of the instrument; and make adjustments when necessary; and

(2) Check each instrument for constancy and proper operation at the beginning of each day of use.

(d) Nothing in this section relieves the licensee from complying with applicable FDA, other Federal, and State requirements governing radioactive drugs.

[59 FR 61780, Dec. 2, 1994; 59 FR 65244, Dec. 19, 1994, as amended at 60 FR 324, Jan. 4, 1995; 67 FR 20370, Apr. 24, 2002; 67 FR 62872, Oct. 9, 2002; 67 FR 77652, Dec. 19, 2002; 71 FR 15007, Mar. 27, 2006; 72 FR 45150, Aug. 13, 2007; 72 FR 55929, Oct. 1, 2007]

§ 32.74 Manufacture and distribution of sources or devices containing byproduct material for medical use.

(a) An application for a specific license to manufacture and distribute sources and devices containing byproduct material to persons licensed under part 35 of this chapter for use as a calibration, transmission, or reference source or for the uses listed in §§ 35.400, 35.500, 35.600, and 35.1000 of this chapter will be approved if:

(1) The applicant satisfies the general requirements in § 30.33 of this chapter;

(2) The applicant submits sufficient information regarding each type of source or device pertinent to an evaluation of its radiation safety, including:

(i) The byproduct material contained, its chemical and physical form, and amount;

(ii) Details of design and construction of the source or device;

(iii) Procedures for, and results of, prototype tests to demonstrate that the source or device will maintain its integrity under stresses likely to be encountered in normal use and accidents;

(iv) For devices containing byproduct material, the radiation profile of a prototype device;

(v) Details of quality control procedures to assure that production sources and devices meet the standards of the design and prototype tests;

(vi) Procedures and standards for calibrating sources and devices;

(vii) Legend and methods for labeling sources and devices as to their radioactive content;

(viii) Instructions for handling and storing the source or device from the radiation safety standpoint; these instructions are to be included on a durable label attached to the source or device or attached to a permanent storage container for the source or device: *Provided*, That instructions which are too lengthy for such label may be summarized on the label and printed in detail on a brochure which is referenced on the label;

(3) The label affixed to the source or device, or to the permanent storage container for the source or device, contains information on the radionuclide, quantity and date of assay, and a statement that the U.S. Nuclear Regulatory Commission has approved distribution of the (name of source or device) to persons licensed to use byproduct material identified in §§ 35.65, 35.400, 35.500, and 35.600 as appropriate, and to persons who hold an equivalent license issued by an Agreement State. However, labels worded in accordance with requirements that were in place on March 30, 1987 may be used until March 30, 1989.

(4) The source or device has been registered in the Sealed Source and Device Registry.

(b)(1) In the event the applicant desires that the source or device be required to be tested for leakage of radioactive material at intervals longer than six months, he shall include in his application sufficient information to demonstrate that such longer interval is justified by performance characteristics of the source or device or similar sources or devices and by design features that have a significant bearing on the probability or consequences of leakage of radioactive material from the source.

(2) In determining the acceptable interval for test of leakage of radioactive material, the Commission will consider information that includes, but is not limited to:

(i) Primary containment (source capsule);

(ii) Protection of primary containment;

(iii) Method of sealing containment;

(iv) Containment construction materials;

(v) Form of contained radioactive material;

(vi) Maximum temperature withstood during prototype tests;

(vii) Maximum pressure withstood during prototype tests;

(viii) Maximum quantity of contained radioactive material;

(ix) Radiotoxicity of contained radioactive material;

(x) Operating experience with identical sources or devices or similarly designed and constructed sources or devices.

(c) If an application is filed pursuant to paragraph (a) of this section on or before October 15, 1974, for a license to manufacture and distribute a source or device that was distributed commercially on or before August 16, 1974, the applicant may continue the distribution of such source or device to group licensees until the Commission issues the license or notifies the applicant otherwise.

[39 FR 26149, July 17, 1974, as amended at 51 FR 36967, Oct. 16, 1986; 62 FR 59276, Nov. 3, 1997; 67 FR 20370, Apr. 24, 2002; 71 FR 15008, Mar. 27, 2006; 72 FR 45150, Aug. 13, 2007; 77 FR 43695, July 25, 2012]

§ 32.201 Serialization of nationally tracked sources.

Each licensee who manufactures a nationally tracked source after February 6, 2007 shall assign a unique serial number to each nationally tracked source. Serial numbers must be composed only of alpha-numeric characters.

[71 FR 65709, Nov. 8, 2006]

Subpart D—Sealed Source and Device Registration

§ 32.210 Registration of product information.

(a) Any manufacturer or initial distributor of a sealed source or device containing a sealed source may submit a request to the NRC for evaluation of radiation safety information about its product and for its registration.

(b) The request for review must be sent to the NRC's Office of Nuclear Material Safety and Safeguards, ATTN: SSDR by an appropriate method listed in § 30.6(a) of this chapter.

(c) The request for review of a sealed source or a device must include sufficient information about the design, manufacture, prototype testing, quality control program, labeling, proposed uses and leak testing and, for a device, the request must also include sufficient information about installation, service and maintenance, operating and safety instructions, and its potential hazards, to provide reasonable assurance that the radiation safety properties of the source or device are adequate to protect health and minimize danger to life and property.

(d) The NRC normally evaluates a sealed source or a device using radiation safety criteria in accepted industry standards. If these standards and criteria do not readily apply to a particular case, the NRC formulates reasonable standards and criteria with the help of the manufacturer or distributor. The NRC shall use criteria and standards sufficient to ensure that the radiation safety properties of the device or sealed source are adequate to protect health and minimize danger to life and property. Subpart A of this part includes specific criteria that apply to certain exempt products and subpart B includes specific criteria applicable to certain generally licensed devices. Subpart C includes specific provisions that apply to certain specifically licensed items.

(e) After completion of the evaluation, the Commission issues a certificate of registration to the person making the request. The certificate of registration acknowledges the availability of the submitted information for inclusion in an application for a specific license proposing use of the product, or concerning use under an exemption from licensing or general license as applicable for the category of certificate.

(f) The person submitting the request for evaluation and registration of safety information about the product shall manufacture and distribute the product in accordance with—

(1) The statements and representations, including quality control program, contained in the request; and

(2) The provisions of the registration certificate.

(g) Authority to manufacture or initially distribute a sealed source or device to specific licensees may be provided in the license without the issuance of a certificate of registration in the following cases:

(1) Calibration and reference sources containing no more than:

(i) 37 MBq (1 mCi), for beta and/or gamma emitting radionuclides; or

(ii) 0.37 MBq (10 μCi), for alpha emitting radionuclides; or

(2) The intended recipients are qualified by training and experience and have sufficient facilities and equipment to safely use and handle the requested quantity of radioactive material in any form in the case of unregistered sources or, for registered sealed sources contained in unregistered devices, are qualified by training and experience and have sufficient facilities and equipment to safely use and handle the requested quantity of radioactive material in unshielded form, as specified in their licenses; and

(i) The intended recipients are licensed under part 33 of this chapter or comparable provisions of an Agreement State; or

(ii) The recipients are authorized for research and development; or

(iii) The sources and devices are to be built to the unique specifications of the particular recipient and contain no more than 740 GBq (20 Ci) of tritium or 7.4 GBq (200 mCi) of any other radionuclide.

(h) After the certificate is issued, the Commission may conduct an additional review as it determines is necessary to ensure compliance with current regulatory standards. In conducting its review, the Commission will complete its evaluation in accordance with criteria specified in this section. The Commission may request such additional information as it considers necessary to conduct its review and the certificate holder shall provide the information as requested.

[52 FR 27786, July 24, 1987, as amended at 60 FR 24551, May 9, 1995; 68 FR 58805, Oct. 10, 2003; 73 FR 5719, Jan. 31, 2008; 77 FR 43695, July 25, 2012]

§32.211 Inactivation of certificates of registration of sealed sources and devices.

(a) A certificate holder who no longer manufactures or initially transfers any of the sealed source(s) or device(s) covered by a particular certificate issued by the Commission shall request inactivation of the registration certificate. Such a request must be made to the NRC's Office of Nuclear Material Safety and Safeguards, ATTN: SSDR by an appropriate method listed in §30.6(a) of this chapter and must normally be made no later than two years after initial distribution of all of the source(s) or device(s) covered by the certificate has ceased. However, if the certificate holder determines that an initial transfer was in fact the last initial transfer more than two years after that transfer, the certificate holder shall request inactivation of the certificate within 90 days of this determination and briefly describe the circumstances of the delay.

(b) If a distribution license is to be terminated in accordance with §30.36 of this chapter, the licensee shall request inactivation of its registration certificates associated with that distribution license before the Commission will terminate the license. Such a request for inactivation of certificate(s) must indicate that the license is being terminated and include the associated specific license number.

(c) A specific license to manufacture or initially transfer a source or device covered only by an inactivated certificate no longer authorizes the licensee to initially transfer such sources or devices for use. Servicing of devices must be in accordance with any conditions in the certificate, including in the case of an inactive certificate.

[77 FR 43695, July 25, 2012]

Subpart E—Violations

§ 32.301 Violations.

(a) The Commission may obtain an injunction or other court order to prevent a violation of the provisions of—

(1) The Atomic Energy Act of 1954, as amended;

(2) Title II of the Energy Reorganization Act of 1974, as amended; or

(3) A regulation or order issued pursuant to those Acts.

(b) The Commission may obtain a court order for the payment of a civil penalty imposed under section 234 of the Atomic Energy Act:

(1) For violations of—

(i) Sections 53, 57, 62, 63, 81, 82, 101, 103, 104, 107, or 109 of the Atomic Energy Act of 1954, as amended;

(ii) Section 206 of the Energy Reorganization Act;

(iii) Any rule, regulation, or order issued pursuant to the sections specified in paragraph (b)(1)(i) of this section;

(iv) Any term, condition, or limitation of any license issued under the sections specified in paragraph (b)(1)(i) of this section.

(2) For any violation for which a license may be revoked under section 186 of the Atomic Energy Act of 1954, as amended.

[57 FR 55073, Nov. 24, 1992]

§ 32.303 Criminal penalties.

(a) Section 223 of the Atomic Energy Act of 1954, as amended, provides for criminal sanctions for willful violation of, attempted violation of, or conspiracy to violate, any regulation issued under sections 161b, 161i, or 161o of the Act. For purposes of section 223, all the regulations in part 32 are issued under one or more of sections 161b, 161i, or 161o, except for the sections listed in paragraph (b) of this section.

(b) The regulations in part 32 that are not issued under subsections 161b, 161i, or 161o for the purposes of section 223 are as follows: §§ 32.1, 32.2, 32.8, 32.11, 32.14, 32.18, 32.21, 32.22, 32.23, 32.24, 32.26, 32.27, 32.28, 32.30, 32.31, 32.51, 32.53, 32.57, 32.61, 32.71, 32.72, 32.74, 32.301, and 32.303.

[57 FR 55073, Nov. 24, 1992, as amended at 59 FR 61781, Dec. 2, 1994; 73 FR 42674, July 23, 2008; 77 FR 43696, July 25, 2012]

PART 33—SPECIFIC DOMESTIC LICENSES OF BROAD SCOPE FOR BYPRODUCT MATERIAL

Sec.

AUTHORITY: Atomic Energy Act of 1954, secs. 81, 161, 181, 182, 183, 223, 234, 274 (42 U.S.C. 2111, 2201, 2231, 2232, 2233, 2273, 2282, 2021); Energy Reorganization Act of 1974, sec. 201 (42 U.S.C. 5841); 44 U.S.C. 3504 note.

SOURCE: 33 FR 14579, Sept. 28, 1968, unless otherwise noted.

§ 33.1 Purpose and scope.

This part prescribes requirements for the issuance of specific licenses of broad scope for byproduct material ("broad licenses") and certain regulations governing holders of such licenses. The provisions and requirements of this part are in addition to, and not in substitution for, other requirements of this chapter. In particular, the provisions of parts 30 and 37 of this chapter apply to applications and licenses subject to this part.

[78 FR 17006, Mar. 19, 2013]

§ 33.8 Information collection requirements: OMB approval.

(a) The Nuclear Regulatory Commission has submitted the information collection requirements contained in this part to the Office of Management and Budget (OMB) for approval as required by the Paperwork Reduction Act (44 U.S.C. 3501 *et seq.*). The NRC may not conduct or sponsor, and a person is not required to respond to, a collection of information unless it displays a currently valid OMB control number. OMB has approved the information collection requirements contained in this part under control number 3150–0015.

(b) The approved information collection requirements contained in this part appear in §§ 33.12, 33.13, 33.14 and 33.15.

(c) This part contains information collection requirements in addition to those approved under the control number specified in paragraph (a) of this section. These information collection requirements and the control numbers under which they are approved are as follows:

(1) In § 33.12, NRC Form 313 is approved under control number 3150–0120.

(2) [Reserved]

[49 FR 19625, May 9, 1984, as amended at 62 FR 52186, Oct. 6, 1997; 67 FR 67099, Nov. 4, 2002]

SPECIFIC LICENSES OF BROAD SCOPE

§ 33.11 Types of specific licenses of broad scope.

(a) A "Type A specific license of broad scope" is a specific license authorizing receipt, acquisition, ownership, possession, use, and transfer of any chemical or physical form of the byproduct material specified in the license, but not exceeding quantities specified in the license, for purposes authorized by the Act. The quantities specified are usually in the multicurie range.

(b) A "Type B specific license of broad scope" is a specific license authorizing receipt, acquisition, ownership, possession, use, and transfer of any chemical or physical form of byproduct material specified in § 33.100, Schedule A, of this part for purposes authorized by the Act. The possession limit for a Type B broad license, if only one radionuclide is possessed thereunder, is the quantity specified for that radionuclide in § 33.100, Schedule A, Column I. If two or more radionuclides are possessed thereunder, the possession limit for each is determined as follows: For each radionuclide, determine the ratio of the quantity possessed to the applicable quantity specified in § 33.100, Schedule A, Column I, for that radionuclide. The sum of the ratios for all radionuclides possessed under the license shall not exceed unity.

(c) A "Type C specific license of broad scope" is a specific license authorizing receipt, acquisition, ownership, possession, use, and transfer of any chemical or physical form of byproduct material specified in § 33.100, Schedule A, for purposes authorized by the Act. The possession limit for a Type C broad license, if only one radionuclide is possessed thereunder, is the quantity specified for that radionuclide in § 33.100, Schedule A, Column II. If two or more radionuclides are possessed thereunder, the possession limit is determined for each as follows: For each radionuclide determine the ratio of the quantity possessed to the applicable quantity specified in § 33.100, Schedule A, Column II, for that radionuclide. The sum of the ratios for all radionuclides possessed under the license shall not exceed unity.

(Sec. 161, as amended, Pub. L. 83–703, 68 Stat. 948 (42 U.S.C. 2201); sec. 201, as amended, Pub. L. 93–438, 88 Stat. 1243 (42 U.S.C. 5841))

[33 FR 14579, Sept. 28, 1968, as amended at 43 FR 6923, Feb. 17, 1978]

§ 33.12 Applications for specific licenses of broad scope.

A person may file an application for specific license of broad scope on NRC

Form 313, "Application for Material License," in accordance with the provisions of § 30.32 of this chapter.

[68 FR 58805, Oct. 10, 2003]

§ 33.13 Requirements for the issuance of a Type A specific license of broad scope.

An application for a Type A specific license of broad scope will be approved if:

(a) The applicant satisfies the general requirements specified in § 30.33 of this chapter;

(b) The applicant has engaged in a reasonable number of activities involving the use of byproduct material; and

(c) The applicant has established administrative controls and provisions relating to organization and management, procedures, record keeping, material control, and accounting and management review that are necessary to assure safe operations, including:

(1) The establishment of a radiation safety committee composed of such persons as a radiological safety officer, a representative of management, and persons trained and experienced in the safe use of radioactive materials;

(2) The appointment of a radiological safety officer who is qualified by training and experience in radiation protection, and who is available for advice and assistance on radiological safety matters; and

(3) The establishment of appropriate administrative procedures to assure:

(i) Control of procurement and use of byproduct material;

(ii) Completion of safety evaluations of proposed uses of byproduct material which take into consideration such matters as the adequacy of facilities and equipment, training and experience of the user, and the operating or handling procedures; and

(iii) Review, approval, and recording by the radiation safety committee of safety evaluations of proposed uses prepared in accordance with paragraph (c)(3)(ii) of this section prior to use of the byproduct material.

§ 33.14 Requirements for the issuance of a Type B specific license of broad scope.

An application for a Type B specific license of broad scope will be approved if:

(a) The applicant satisfies the general requirements specified in § 30.33 of this chapter; and

(b) The applicant has established administrative controls and provisions relating to organization and management, procedures, record keeping, material control and accounting, and management review that are necessary to assure safe operations, including:

(1) The appointment of a radiological safety officer who is qualified by training and experience in radiation protection, and who is available for advice and assistance on radiological safety matters; and

(2) The establishment of appropriate administrative procedures to assure:

(i) Control of procurement and use of byproduct material;

(ii) Completion of safety evaluations of proposed uses of byproduct material which take into consideration such matters as the adequacy of facilities and equipment, training and experience of the user, and the operating or handling procedures; and

(iii) Review, approval, and recording by the radiological safety officer of safety evaluations of proposed uses prepared in accordance with paragraph (b)(2)(ii) of this section prior to use of the byproduct material.

§ 33.15 Requirements for the issuance of a Type C specific license of broad scope.

An application for a Type C specific license of broad scope will be approved if:

(a) The applicant satisfies the general requirements specified in § 30.33 of this chapter; and

(b) The applicant submits a statement that byproduct material will be used only by, or under the direct supervision of, individuals who have received:

(1) A college degree at the bachelor level, or equivalent training and experience, in the physical or biological sciences or in engineering; and

(2) At least 40 hours of training and experience in the safe handling of radioactive materials, and in the characteristics of ionizing radiation, units of radiation dose and quantities, radiation detection instrumentation, and biological hazards of exposure to radiation appropriate to the type and forms of byproduct material to be used; and

(c) The applicant has established administrative controls and provisions relating to procurement of byproduct material, procedures, record keeping, material control and accounting, and management review necessary to assure safe operations.

§ 33.16 Application for other specific licenses.

An application filed pursuant to part 30 of this chapter for a specific license other than one of broad scope will be considered by the Commission as an application for a specific license of broad scope under this part if the requirements of the applicable sections of this part are satisfied.

§ 33.17 Conditions of specific licenses of broad scope.

(a) Unless specifically authorized pursuant to other parts of this chapter, persons licensed under this part shall not:

(1) Conduct tracer studies in the environment involving direct release of byproduct material;

(2) Receive, acquire, own, possess, use, transfer, or import devices containing 100,000 curies or more of byproduct material in sealed sources used for irradiation of materials;

(3) Conduct activities for which a specific license issued by the Commission under part 32, 34, or 35 of this chapter is required; or

(4) Add or cause the addition of byproduct material to any food, beverage, cosmetic, drug, or other product designed for ingestion or inhalation by, or application to, a human being.

(b) Each Type A specific license of broad scope issued under this part shall be subject to the condition that byproduct material possessed under the license may only be used by, or under the direct supervision of, individuals approved by the licensee's radiation safety committee.

(c) Each Type B specific license of broad scope issued under this part shall be subject to the condition that byproduct material possessed under the license may only be used by, or under the direct supervision of, individuals approved by the licensee's radiological safety officer.

(d) Each Type C specific license of broad scope issued under this part shall be subject to the condition that byproduct material possessed under the license may only be used by, or under the direct supervision of, individuals who satisfy the requirements of § 33.15 of this part.

VIOLATIONS

§ 33.21 Violations.

(a) The Commission may obtain an injunction or other court order to prevent a violation of the provisions of—

(1) The Atomic Energy Act of 1954, as amended;

(2) Title II of the Energy Reorganization Act of 1974, as amended; or

(3) A regulation or order issued pursuant to those Acts.

(b) The Commission may obtain a court order for the payment of a civil penalty imposed under section 234 of the Atomic Energy Act:

(1) For violations of—

(i) Sections 53, 57, 62, 63, 81, 82, 101, 103, 104, 107, or 109 of the Atomic Energy Act of 1954, as amended;

(ii) Section 206 of the Energy Reorganization Act;

(iii) Any rule, regulation, or order issued pursuant to the sections specified in paragraph (b)(1)(i) of this section;

(iv) Any term, condition, or limitation of any license issued under the sections specified in paragraph (b)(1)(i) of this section.

(2) For any violation for which a license may be revoked under section 186 of the Atomic Energy Act of 1954, as amended.

[57 FR 55073, Nov. 24, 1992]

§ 33.23 Criminal penalties.

(a) Section 223 of the Atomic Energy Act of 1954, as amended, provides for criminal sanctions for willful violation of, attempted violation of, or conspiracy to violate, any regulation issued under sections 161b, 161i, or 161o of the Act. For purposes of section 223, all the regulations in part 33 are issued under one or more of sections 161b, 161i, or 161o, except for the sections listed in paragraph (b) of this section.

(b) The regulations in part 33 that are not issued under sections 161b, 161i, or 161o for the purposes of section 223 are as follows: §§ 33.1, 33.8, 33.11, 33.12, 33.13, 33.14, 33.15, 33.16, 33.21, 33.23 and 33.100.

[57 FR 55073, Nov. 24, 1992]

SCHEDULES

§ 33.100 Schedule A.

Byproduct material	Col. I curies	Col. II curies
Antimony-122	1	0.01
Antimony-124	1	.01
Antimony-125	1	.01
Arsenic-73	10	.1
Arsenic-74	1	.01
Arsenic-76	1	.01
Arsenic-77	10	.1
Barium-131	10	.1
Barium-140	1	.01
Beryllium-7	10	0.1
Bismuth-210	.1	.001
Bromine-82	10	.1
Cadmium-109	1	.01
Cadmium-115m	1	.01
Cadmium-115	10	.1
Calcium-45	1	.01
Calcium-47	10	.1
Carbon-14	100	1.
Cerium-141	10	.1
Cerium-143	10	.1
Cerium-144	.1	.001
Cesium-131	100	1.
Cesium-134m	100	1.
Cesium-134	.1	.001
Cesium-135	1	.01
Cesium-136	10	.1
Cesium-137	.1	.001
Chlorine-36	1	.01
Chlorine-38	100	1.
Chromium-51	100	1.
Cobalt-57	10	0.1
Cobalt-58m	100	1.
Cobalt-58	1	.01
Cobalt-60	.1	.001
Copper-64	10	.1
Dysprosium-165	100	1.
Dysprosium-166	10	.1
Erbium-169	10	.1
Erbium-171	10	.1
Europium-152 9.2 h	10	.1
Europium-152 13 y	.1	.001
Europium-154	.1	.001
Europium-155	1	.01
Fluorine-18	100	1.
Gadolinium-153	1	.01
Gadolinium-159	10	.1
Gallium-72	10	.1
Germanium-71	100	1
Gold-198	10	.1
Gold-199	10	.1
Hafnium-181	1	.01
Holmium-166	10	.1
Hydrogen-3	100	1
Indium-113m	100	1
Indium-114m	1	.01
Indium-115m	100	1
Indium-115	1	.01
Iodine-125	.1	.001
Iodine-126	.1	.001
Iodine-129	.1	.01
Iodine-131	.1	.001
Iodine-132	10	.1
Iodine-133	1	.01
Iodine-134	10	.1
Iodine-135	1	.01
Iridium-192	1	.01
Iridium-194	10	.1
Iron-55	10	.1
Iron-59	1	.01
Krypton-85	100	1
Krypton-87	10	.1
Lanthanum-140	1	.01
Lutetium-177	10	.1
Manganese-52	1	.01
Manganese-54	1	.01
Manganese-56	10	.1
Mercury-197m	10	.1
Mercury-197	10	.1
Mercury-203	1	.01
Molybdenum-99	10	.1
Neodymium-147	10	.1
Neodymium-149	10	.1
Nickel-59	10	.1
Nickel-63	1	.01
Nickel-65	10	.1
Niobium-93m	1	.01
Niobium-95	1	.01
Niobium-97	100	1.
Osmium-185	1	.01
Osmium-191m	100	1.
Osmium-191	10	.1
Osmium-193	10	.1
Palladium-103	10	.1
Palladium-109	10	.1
Phosphorus-32	1	.01
Platinum-191	10	.1
Platinum-193m	100	1.
Platinum-193	10	.1
Platinum-197m	100	1
Platinum-197	10	.1
Polonium-210	.01	.0001
Potassium-42	1	.01
Praseodymium-142	10	.1
Praseodymium-143	10	.1
Promethium-147	1	.01
Promethium-149	10	.1
Radium-226	0.01	0.0001
Rhenium-186	10	.1
Rhenium-188	10	.1
Rhodium-103m	1,000	10.
Rhodium-105	10	.1
Rubidium-86	1	.01
Rubidium-87	1	.01
Ruthenium-97	100	1.
Ruthenium-103	1	.01
Ruthenium-105	10	.1
Ruthenium-106	.1	.001
Samarium-151	1	.01
Samarium-153	10	.1
Scandium-46	1	.01
Scandium-47	10	.1

Byproduct material	Col. I curies	Col. II curies
Scandium-48	1	.01
Selenium-75	1	.01
Silicon-31	10	.1
Silver-105	1	.01
Silver-110m	.1	.001
Silver-111	10	.1
Sodium-22	0.1	0.001
Sodium-24	1	.01
Strontium-85m	1,000	10.
Strontium-85	1	.01
Strontium-89	1	.01
Strontium-90	.01	.0001
Strontium-91	10	.1
Strontium-92	10	.1
Sulphur-35	10	.1
Tantalum-182	1	.01
Technetium-96	10	.1
Technetium-97m	10	.1
Technetium-97	10	.1
Technetium-99m	100	1.
Technetium-99	1	.01
Tellurium-125m	1	.01
Tellurium-127m	1	.01
Tellurium-127	10	.1
Tellurium-129m	1	.01
Tellurium-129	100	1
Tellurium-131m	10	.1
Tellurium-132	1	.01
Terbium-160	1	.01
Thallium-200	10	.1
Thallium-201	10	.1
Thallium-202	10	.1
Thallium-204	1	.01
Thulium-170	1	.01
Thulium-171	1	.01
Tin-113	1	.01
Tin-125	1	.01
Tungsten-181	1	.01
Tungsten-185	1	.01
Tungsten-187	10	.1
Vanadium-48	1	.01
Xenon-131m	1,000	10.
Xenon-133	100	1.
Xenon-135	100	1
Ytterbium-175	10	.1
Yttrium-90	1	.01
Yttrium-91	1	.01
Yttrium-92	10	.1
Yttrium-93	1	.01
Zinc-65	1	.01
Zinc-69m	10	.1
Zinc-69	100	1.
Zirconium-93	1	.01
Zirconium-95	1	.01
Zirconium-97	1	.01
Any byproduct material other than alpha emitting byproduct material not listed above	.1	.001

(Sec. 201, Pub. L. 93–438; 88 Stat. 1242 (42 U.S.C. 5841))

[33 FR 14579, Sept. 28, 1968, as amended at 72 FR 55930, Oct. 1, 2007]

PART 34—LICENSES FOR INDUSTRIAL RADIOGRAPHY AND RADIATION SAFETY REQUIREMENTS FOR INDUSTRIAL RADIOGRAPHIC OPERATIONS

Subpart A—General Provisions

Subpart B—Specific Licensing Provisions

Subpart C—Equipment

Subpart D—Radiation Safety Requirements

Subpart E—Recordkeeping Requirements

AUTHORITY: Atomic Energy Act of 1954, secs. 81, 161, 181, 182, 183, 223, 234, 274 (42 U.S.C. 2111, 2201, 2231, 2232, 2233, 2273, 2282, 2021); Energy Reorganization Act of 1974, secs. 201, 206 (42 U.S.C. 5841, 5846); 44 U.S.C. 3504 note.

SOURCE: 62 FR 28963, May 28, 1997, unless otherwise noted.

EDITORIAL NOTE: Nomenclature changes to part 34 appear at 79 FR 75739, Dec. 19, 2014.

Subpart A—General Provisions

§ 34.1 Purpose and scope.

This part prescribes requirements for the issuance of licenses for the use of sealed sources containing byproduct material and radiation safety requirements for persons using these sealed sources in industrial radiography. The provisions and requirements of this part are in addition to, and not in substitution for, other requirements of this chapter. In particular, the requirements and provisions of parts 19, 20, 21, 30, 37, 71, 150, 170, and 171 of this chapter apply to applications and licenses subject to this part. This rule does not apply to medical uses of byproduct material.

[78 FR 17006, Mar. 19, 2013]

§ 34.3 Definitions.

ALARA (acronym for "as low as is reasonably achievable") means making every reasonable effort to maintain exposures to radiation as far below the dose limits specified in 10 CFR part 20 as is practical consistent with the purpose for which the licensed activity is undertaken, taking into account the state of technology, the economics of improvements in relation to state of technology, the economics of improvements in relation to benefits to the public health and safety, and other societal and socioeconomic considerations, and in relation to utilization of nuclear energy and licensed materials in the public interest.

Annual refresher safety training means a review conducted or provided by the licensee for its employees on radiation safety aspects of industrial radiography. The review may include, as appropriate, the results of internal inspections, new procedures or equipment, new or revised regulations, accidents or errors that have been observed, and should also provide opportunities for employees to ask safety questions.

Associated equipment means equipment that is used in conjunction with a radiographic exposure device to make radiographic exposures that drives, guides, or comes in contact with the source, (e.g., guide tube, control tube, control (drive) cable, removable source stop, "J" tube and collimator when it is used as an exposure head.

Becquerel (Bq) means one disintegration per second.

Certifying Entity means an independent certifying organization meeting the requirements in appendix A of this part or an Agreement State meeting the requirements in appendix A, parts II and III of this part.

Collimator means a radiation shield that is placed on the end of the guide tube or directly onto a radiographic exposure device to restrict the size of the radiation beam when the sealed source is cranked into position to make a radiographic exposure.

Control (drive) cable means the cable that is connected to the source assembly and used to drive the source to and from the exposure location.

Control drive mechanism means a device that enables the source assembly to be moved to and from the exposure device.

Control tube means a protective sheath for guiding the control cable. The control tube connects the control drive mechanism to the radiographic exposure device.

Exposure head means a device that locates the gamma radiography sealed source in the selected working position. (An exposure head is also known as a source stop.)

Field station means a facility where licensed material may be stored or used and from which equipment is dispatched.

Gray means the SI unit of absorbed dose. One gray is equal to an absorbed dose of 1 Joule/kilogram. It is also equal to 100 rads.

Guide tube (Projection sheath) means a flexible or rigid tube (*i.e.*, "J" tube) for guiding the source assembly and the attached control cable from the exposure device to the exposure head. The guide tube may also include the connections necessary for attachment to the exposure device and to the exposure head.

Hands-on experience means experience in all of those areas considered to be directly involved in the radiography process.

Independent certifying organization means an independent organization that meets all of the criteria of appendix A to this part.

Industrial radiography (radiography) means an examination of the structure of materials by nondestructive methods, utilizing ionizing radiation to make radiographic images.

Lay-barge radiography means industrial radiography performed on any water vessel used for laying pipe.

Offshore platform radiography means industrial radiography conducted from a platform over a body of water.

Permanent radiographic installation means an enclosed shielded room, cell, or vault, not located at a temporary jobsite, in which radiography is performed.

Practical Examination means a demonstration through practical application of the safety rules and principles in industrial radiography including use of all appropriate equipment and procedures.

Radiation Safety Officer for industrial radiography means an individual with the responsibility for the overall radiation safety program on behalf of the licensee and who meets the requirements of §34.42.

Radiographer means any individual who performs or who, in attendance at the site where the sealed source or sources are being used, personally supervises industrial radiographic operations and who is responsible to the licensee for assuring compliance with the requirements of the Commission's regulations and the conditions of the license.

Radiographer certification means written approval received from a certifying entity stating that an individual has satisfactorily met certain established radiation safety, testing, and experience criteria.

Radiographer's assistant means any individual who under the direct supervision of a radiographer, uses radiographic exposure devices, sealed sources or related handling tools, or radiation survey instruments in industrial radiography.

Radiographic exposure device (also called a camera, or a projector) means any instrument containing a sealed source fastened or contained therein, in which the sealed source or shielding thereof may be moved, or otherwise changed, from a shielded to unshielded position for purposes of making a radiographic exposure.

Radiographic operations means all activities associated with the presence of radioactive sources in a radiographic exposure device during use of the device or transport (except when being transported by a common or contract transport), to include surveys to confirm the adequacy of boundaries, setting up equipment and any activity inside restricted area boundaries.

S-tube means a tube through which the radioactive source travels when inside a radiographic exposure device.

Sealed source means any byproduct material that is encased in a capsule designed to prevent leakage or escape of the byproduct material.

Shielded position means the location within the radiographic exposure device or source changer where the sealed source is secured and restricted from movement.

Sievert means the SI unit of any of the quantities expressed as dose equivalent. The dose equivalent in sieverts is equal to the absorbed dose in grays multiplied by the quality factor (1 Sv = 100 rems).

Source assembly means an assembly that consists of the sealed source and a connector that attaches the source to the control cable. The source assembly may also include a stop ball used to secure the source in the shielded position.

Source changer means a device designed and used for replacement of sealed sources in radiographic exposure devices, including those also used for transporting and storage of sealed sources.

Storage area means any location, facility, or vehicle which is used to store or to secure a radiographic exposure device, a storage container, or a sealed source when it is not in use and which is locked or has a physical barrier to prevent accidental exposure, tampering with, or unauthorized removal of the device, container, or source.

Storage container means a container in which sealed sources are secured and stored.

Temporary jobsite means a location where radiographic operations are conducted and where licensed material may be stored other than those location(s) of use authorized on the license.

Underwater radiography means industrial radiography performed when the radiographic exposure device and/or related equipment are beneath the surface of the water.

§ 34.5 Interpretations.

Except as specifically authorized by the Commission in writing, no interpretation of the meaning of the regulations in this part by any officer or employee of the Commission, other than a written interpretation by the General Counsel, will be recognized to be binding upon the Commission.

§ 34.8 Information collection requirements: OMB approval.

(a) The Nuclear Regulatory Commission has submitted the information collection requirements contained in this part to the Office of Management and Budget (OMB) for approval as required by the Paperwork Reduction Act (44 U.S.C. 3501 *et seq.*). The NRC may nor conduct or sponsor, and a person is not required to respond to, a collection of information unless it displays a currently valid OMB control number. OMB has approved the information collection requirements contained in this part under control number 3150–0007.

(b) The approved information collection requirements contained in this part appear in §§ 34.13, 34.20, 34.25, 34.27, 34.29, 34.31, 34.33, 34.35, 34.41, 34.42, 34.43, 34.45, 34.47, 34.49, 34.61, 34.63, 34.65, 34.67, 34.69, 34.71, 34.73, 34.75, 34.79, 34.81, 34.83, 34.85, 34.87, 34.89, 34.101, and appendix A.

(c) This part contains information collection requirements in addition to those approved under the control number specified in paragraph (a) of this section. The information collection requirements and the control numbers under which it is approved are as follows:

(1) In § 34.11, NRC Form 313 is approved under control number 3150–0120.

(2) [Reserved]

[62 FR 52186, Oct. 6, 1997, as amended at 75 FR 73942, Nov. 30, 2010]

Subpart B—Specific Licensing Provisions

§ 34.11 Application for a specific license.

A person may file an application for specific license for use of sealed sources in industrial radiography on NRC Form 313, "Application for Material License," in accordance with the provisions of § 30.32 of this chapter.

[68 FR 58805, Oct. 10, 2003]

§ 34.13 Specific license for industrial radiography.

An application for a specific license for the use of licensed material in industrial radiography will be approved if the applicant meets the following requirements:

(a) The applicant satisfies the general requirements specified in § 30.33 of this chapter for byproduct material, as appropriate, and any special requirements contained in this part.

(b) The applicant submits an adequate program for training radiographers and radiographers' assistants that meets the requirements of § 34.43.

(1) After May 28, 1999, a license applicant need not describe its initial training and examination program for radiographers in the subjects outlined in § 34.43(g).

(2) From June 27, 1997 to May 28, 1999 a license applicant may affirm that all individuals acting as industrial radiographers will be certified in radiation safety by a certifying entity before commencing duty as radiographers. This affirmation substitutes for a description of its initial training and examination program for radiographers in the subjects outlined in § 34.43(g).

(c) The applicant submits procedures for verifying and documenting the certification status of radiographers and for ensuring that the certification of individuals acting as radiographers remains valid.

(d) The applicant submits written operating and emergency procedures as described in § 34.45.

(e) The applicant submits a description of a program for inspections of the job performance of each radiographer and radiographers' assistant at intervals not to exceed 6 months as described in § 34.43(e).

(f) The applicant submits a description of the applicant's overall organizational structure as it applies to the radiation safety responsibilities in industrial radiography, including specified delegation of authority and responsibility.

(g) The applicant identifies and lists the qualifications of the individual(s) designated as the RSO (§ 34.42) and potential designees responsible for ensuring that the licensee's radiation safety program is implemented in accordance with approved procedures.

(h) If an applicant intends to perform leak testing of sealed sources or exposure devices containing depleted uranium (DU) shielding, the applicant must describe the procedures for performing and the qualifications of the person(s) authorized to do the leak testing. If the applicant intends to analyze its own wipe samples, the application must include a description of the procedures to be followed. The description must include the—

(1) Instruments to be used;

(2) Methods of performing the analysis; and

(3) Pertinent experience of the person who will analyze the wipe samples.

(i) If the applicant intends to perform "in-house" calibrations of survey instruments the applicant must describe methods to be used and the relevant experience of the person(s) who will perform the calibrations. All calibrations must be performed according to the procedures described and at the intervals prescribed in § 34.25.

(j) The applicant identifies and describes the location(s) of all field stations and permanent radiographic installations.

(k) The applicant identifies the locations where all records required by this part and other parts of this chapter will be maintained.

Subpart C—Equipment

§ 34.20 Performance requirements for industrial radiography equipment.

Equipment used in industrial radiographic operations must meet the following minimum criteria:

(a)(1) Each radiographic exposure device, source assembly or sealed source, and all associated equipment must meet the requirements specified in American National Standards Institute, N432–1980 "Radiological Safety for the Design and Construction of Apparatus for Gamma Radiography," (published as NBS Handbook 136, issued January 1981). This publication has been approved for incorporation by reference by the Director of the Federal Register in accordance with 5 U.S.C. 552(a)and 1 CFR part 51. This publication may be purchased from the American National Standards Institute, Inc., 25 West 43rd Street, New York, New York 10036; Telephone: (212) 642–4900. Copies of the document are available for inspection at the Nuclear Regulatory Commission Library, 11545

Rockville Pike, Rockville, Maryland 20852. A copy of the document is also on file at the National Archives and Records Administration (NARA). For information on the availability of this material at NARA, call 202–741–6030, or go to: *http://www.archives.gov/federal_register/code_of_federal_regulations/ibr_locations.html.*

(2) Engineering analysis may be submitted by an applicant or licensee to demonstrate the applicability of previously performed testing on similar individual radiography equipment components. Upon review, the Commission may find this an acceptable alternative to actual testing of the component pursuant to the above referenced standard.

(b) In addition to the requirements specified in paragraph (a) of this section, the following requirements apply to radiographic exposure devices, source changers, source assemblies and sealed sources.

(1) The licensee shall ensure that each radiographic exposure device has attached to it a durable, legible, clearly visible label bearing the—

(i) Chemical symbol and mass number of the radionuclide in the device;

(ii) Activity and the date on which this activity was last measured;

(iii) Model (or product code) and serial number of the sealed source;

(iv) Manufacturer's identity of the sealed source; and

(v) Licensee's name, address, and telephone number.

(2) Radiographic exposure devices intended for use as Type B transport containers must meet the applicable requirements of 10 CFR part 71.

(3) Modification of radiographic exposure devices, source changers, and source assemblies and associated equipment is prohibited, unless the design of any replacement component,including source holder, source assembly, controls or guide tubes would not compromise the design safety features of the system.

(c) In addition to the requirements specified in paragraphs (a) and (b) of this section, the following requirements apply to radiographic exposure devices, source assemblies, and associated equipment that allow the source to be moved out of the device for radiographic operations or to source changers.

(1) The coupling between the source assembly and the control cable must be designed in such a manner that the source assembly will not become disconnected if cranked outside the guide tube. The coupling must be such that it cannot be unintentionally disconnected under normal and reasonably foreseeable abnormal conditions.

(2) The device must automatically secure the source assembly when it is cranked back into the fully shielded position within the device. This securing system may only be released by means of a deliberate operation on the exposure device.

(3) The outlet fittings, lock box, and drive cable fittings on each radiographic exposure device must be equipped with safety plugs or covers which must be installed during storage and transportation to protect the source assembly from water, mud, sand or other foreign matter.

(4)(i) Each sealed source or source assembly must have attached to it or engraved on it, a durable, legible, visible label with the words: "DANGER—RADIOACTIVE."

(ii) The label may not interfere with the safe operation of the exposure device or associated equipment.

(5) The guide tube must be able to withstand a crushing test that closely approximates the crushing forces that are likely to be encountered during use, and be able to withstand a kinking resistance test that closely approximates the kinking forces that are likely to be encountered during use.

(6) Guide tubes must be used when moving the source out of the device.

(7) An exposure head or similar device designed to prevent the source assembly from passing out of the end of the guide tube must be attached to the outermost end of the guide tube during industrial radiography operations.

(8) The guide tube exposure head connection must be able to withstand the tensile test for control units specified in ANSI N432–1980.

(9) Source changers must provide a system for ensuring that the source will not be accidentally withdrawn from the changer when connecting or

disconnecting the drive cable to or from a source assembly.

(d) All radiographic exposure devices and associated equipment in use after January 10, 1996, must comply with the requirements of this section.

(e) Notwithstanding paragraph (a)(1) of this section, equipment used in industrial radiographic operations need not comply with § 8.9.2(c) of the Endurance Test in American National Standards Institute N432–1980, if the prototype equipment has been tested using a torque value representative of the torque that an individual using the radiography equipment can realistically exert on the lever or crankshaft of the drive mechanism.

[62 FR 28963, May 28, 1997, as amended at 69 FR 18803, Apr. 9, 2004; 77 FR 39906, July 6, 2012]

§ 34.21 Limits on external radiation levels from storage containers and source changers.

The maximum exposure rate limits for storage containers and source changers are 2 millisieverts (200 millirem) per hour at any exterior surface, and 0.1 millisieverts (10 millirem) per hour at 1 meter from any exterior surface with the sealed source in the shielded position.

§ 34.23 Locking of radiographic exposure devices, storage containers and source changers.

(a) Each radiographic exposure device must have a lock or outer locked container designed to prevent unauthorized or accidental removal of the sealed source from its shielded position. The exposure device and/or its container must be kept locked (and if a keyed-lock, with the key removed at all times) when not under the direct surveillance of a radiographer or a radiographer's assistant except at permanent radiographic installations as stated in § 34.51. In addition, during radiographic operations the sealed source assembly must be secured in the shielded position each time the source is returned to that position.

(b) Each sealed source storage container and source changer must have a lock or outer locked container designed to prevent unauthorized or accidental removal of the sealed source from its shielded position. Storage containers and source changers must be kept locked (and if a keyed-lock, with the key removed at all times) when containing sealed sources except when under the direct surveillance of a radiographer or a radiographer's assistant.

§ 34.25 Radiation survey instruments.

(a) The licensee shall keep sufficient calibrated and operable radiation survey instruments at each location where radioactive material is present to make the radiation surveys required by this part and by 10 CFR part 20 of this chapter. Instrumentation required by this section must be capable of measuring a range from 0.02 millisieverts (2 millirems) per hour through 0.01 sievert (1 rem) per hour.

(b) The licensee shall have each radiation survey instrument required under paragraph (a) of this section calibrated—

(1) At intervals not to exceed 6 months and after instrument servicing, except for battery changes;

(2) For linear scale instruments, at two points located approximately one-third and two-thirds of full-scale on each scale; for logarithmic scale instruments, at mid-range of each decade, and at two points of at least one decade; and for digital instruments, at 3 points between 0.02 and 10 millisieverts (2 and 1000 millirems) per hour; and

(3) So that an accuracy within plus or minus 20 percent of the calibration source can be demonstrated at each point checked.

(c) The licensee shall maintain records of the results of the instrument calibrations in accordance with § 34.65.

§ 34.27 Leak testing and replacement of sealed sources.

(a) The replacement of any sealed source fastened to or contained in a radiographic exposure device and leak testing of any sealed source must be performed by persons authorized to do so by the NRC or an Agreement State.

(b) The opening, repair, or modification of any sealed source must be performed by persons specifically authorized to do so by the Commission or an Agreement State.

(c) *Testing and recordkeeping requirements.* (1) Each licensee who uses a sealed source shall have the source tested for leakage at intervals not to exceed 6 months. The leak testing of the source must be performed using a method approved by the Commission or by an Agreement State. The wipe sample should be taken from the nearest accessible point to the sealed source where contamination might accumulate. The wipe sample must be analyzed for radioactive contamination. The analysis must be capable of detecting the presence of 185 Bq (0.005 microcurie) of radioactive material on the test sample and must be performed by a person specifically authorized by the Commission or an Agreement State to perform the analysis.

(2) The licensee shall maintain records of the leak tests in accordance with § 34.67.

(3) Unless a sealed source is accompanied by a certificate from the transferor that shows that it has been leak tested within 6 months before the transfer, it may not be used by the licensee until tested for leakage. Sealed sources that are in storage and not in use do not require leak testing, but must be tested before use or transfer to another person if the interval of storage exceeds 6 months.

(d) Any test conducted pursuant to paragraph (c) of this section which reveals the presence of 185 Bq (0.005 microcurie) or more of removable radioactive material must be considered evidence that the sealed source is leaking. The licensee shall immediately withdraw the equipment involved from use and shall have it decontaminated and repaired or disposed of in accordance with Commission regulations. A report must be filed with the Director, Office of Nuclear Material Safety and Safeguards , by an appropriate method listed in § 30.6(a) of this chapter, the report to be filed within 5 days of any test with results that exceed the threshold in this paragraph (d), and to describe the equipment involved, the test results, and the corrective action taken. A copy of the report must be sent to the Administrator of the appropriate Nuclear Regulatory Commission's Regional Office listed in appendix D of 10 CFR part 20 of this chapter "Standards for Protection Against Radiation."

(e) Each exposure device using depleted uranium (DU) shielding and an "S" tube configuration must be tested for DU contamination at intervals not to exceed 12 months. The analysis must be capable of detecting the presence of 185 Bq (0.005 microcuries) of radioactive material on the test sample and must be performed by a person specifically authorized by the Commission or an Agreement State to perform the analysis. Should such testing reveal the presence of 185 Bq (0.005 microcuries) or more of removable DU contamination, the exposure device must be removed from use until an evaluation of the wear on the S-tube has been made. Should the evaluation reveal that the S-tube is worn through, the device may not be used again. DU shielded devices do not have to be tested for DU contamination while in storage and not in use. Before using or transferring such a device however, the device must be tested for DU contamination if the interval of storage exceeded 12 months. A record of the DU leak-test must be made in accordance with § 34.67. Licensees will have until June 27, 1998, to comply with the DU leak-testing requirements of this paragraph.

[62 FR 28963, May 28, 1997, as amended at 63 FR 37061, July 9, 1998; 67 FR 77652, Dec. 19, 2002; 68 FR 58805, Oct. 10, 2003; 73 FR 5719, Jan. 31, 2008]

§ 34.29 Quarterly inventory.

(a) Each licensee shall conduct a quarterly physical inventory to account for all sealed sources and for devices containing depleted uranium received and possessed under this license.

(b) The licensee shall maintain records of the quarterly inventory in accordance with § 34.69.

§ 34.31 Inspection and maintenance of radiographic exposure devices, transport and storage containers, associated equipment, source changers, and survey instruments.

(a) The licensee shall perform visual and operability checks on survey meters, radiographic exposure devices, transport and storage containers, associated equipment and source changers before use on each day the equipment is to be used to ensure that the equipment is in good working condition, that the sources are adequately shielded, and that required labeling is present. Survey instrument operability must be performed using check sources or other appropriate means. If equipment problems are found, the equipment must be removed from service until repaired.

(b) Each licensee shall have written procedures for:

(1) Inspection and routine maintenance of radiographic exposure devices, source changers, associated equipment, transport and storage containers, and survey instruments at intervals not to exceed 3 months or before the first use thereafter to ensure the proper functioning of components important to safety. Replacement components shall meet design specifications. If equipment problems are found, the equipment must be removed from service until repaired.

(2) Inspection and maintenance necessary to maintain the Type B packaging used to transport radioactive materials. The inspection and maintenance program must include procedures to assure that Type B packages are shipped and maintained in accordance with the certificate of compliance or other approval.

(c) Records of equipment problems and of any maintenance performed under paragraphs (a) and (b) of this section must be made in accordance with § 34.73.

§ 34.33 Permanent radiographic installations.

(a) Each entrance that is used for personnel access to the high radiation area in a permanent radiographic installation must have either:

(1) An entrance control of the type described in § 20.1601(a)(1) of this chapter that reduces the radiation level upon entry into the area, or

(2) Both conspicuous visible and audible warning signals to warn of the presence of radiation. The visible signal must be actuated by radiation whenever the source is exposed. The audible signal must be actuated when an attempt is made to enter the installation while the source is exposed.

(b) The alarm system must be tested for proper operation with a radiation source each day before the installation is used for radiographic operations. The test must include a check of both the visible and audible signals. Entrance control devices that reduce the radiation level upon entry (designated in paragraph (a)(1) of this section) must be tested monthly. If an entrance control device or an alarm is operating improperly, it must be immediately labeled as defective and repaired within 7 calendar days. The facility may continue to be used during this 7-day period, provided the licensee implements the continuous surveillance requirements of § 34.51 and uses an alarming ratemeter. Test records for entrance controls and audible and visual alarm must be maintained in accordance with § 34.75.

§ 34.35 Labeling, storage, and transportation.

(a) The licensee may not use a source changer or a container to store licensed material unless the source changer or the storage container has securely attached to it a durable, legible, and clearly visible label bearing the standard trefoil radiation caution symbol conventional colors, *i.e.*, magenta, purple or black on a yellow background, having a minimum diameter of 25 mm, and the wording

CAUTION*
RADIOACTIVE MATERIAL
NOTIFY CIVIL AUTHORITIES (or "NAME OF COMPANY")
*______ or "DANGER"

(b) The licensee may not transport licensed material unless the material is packaged, and the package is labeled, marked, and accompanied with appropriate shipping papers in accordance with regulations set out in 10 CFR part 71.

(c) Locked radiographic exposure devices and storage containers must be physically secured to prevent tampering or removal by unauthorized personnel. The licensee shall store licensed material in a manner which will minimize danger from explosion or fire.

(d) The licensee shall lock and physically secure the transport package containing licensed material in the transporting vehicle to prevent accidental loss, tampering, or unauthorized removal of the licensed material from the vehicle.

Subpart D—Radiation Safety Requirements

§ 34.41 Conducting industrial radiographic operations.

(a) Whenever radiography is performed at a location other than a permanent radiographic installation, the radiographer must be accompanied by at least one other qualified radiographer or an individual who has at a minimum met the requirements of § 34.43(c). The additional qualified individual shall observe the operations and be capable of providing immediate assistance to prevent unauthorized entry. Radiography may not be performed if only one qualified individual is present.

(b) All radiographic operations conducted at locations of use authorized on the license must be conducted in a permanent radiographic installation, unless specifically authorized by the Commission.

(c) A licensee may conduct lay-barge, offshore platform, or underwater radiography only if procedures have been approved by the Commission or by an Agreement State.

(d) Licensees will have until June 27, 1998, to meet the requirements for having two qualified individuals present at locations other than a permanent radiographic installation as specified in paragraph (a) of this section.

[62 FR 28963, May 28, 1997, as amended at 63 FR 37061, July 9, 1998]

§ 34.42 Radiation Safety Officer for industrial radiography.

The RSO shall ensure that radiation safety activities are being performed in accordance with approved procedures and regulatory requirements in the daily operation of the licensee's program.

(a) The minimum qualifications, training, and experience for RSOs for industrial radiography are as follows:

(1) Completion of the training and testing requirements of § 34.43(a);

(2) 2000 hours of hands-on experience as a qualified radiographer in industrial radiographic operations; and

(3) Formal training in the establishment and maintenance of a radiation protection program.

(b) The Commission will consider alternatives when the RSO has appropriate training and/or experience in the field of ionizing radiation, and in addition, has adequate formal training with respect to the establishment and maintenance of a radiation safety protection program.

(c) The specific duties and authorities of the RSO include, but are not limited to:

(1) Establishing and overseeing all operating, emergency, and ALARA procedures as required by 10 CFR part 20 of this chapter, and reviewing them regularly to ensure that the procedures in use conform to current 10 CFR part 20 procedures, conform to other NRC regulations and to the license conditions.

(2) Overseeing and approving all phases of the training program for radiographic personnel, ensuring that appropriate and effective radiation protection practices are taught;

(3) Ensuring that required radiation surveys and leak tests are performed and documented in accordance with the regulations, including any corrective measures when levels of radiation exceed established limits;

(4) Ensuring that personnel monitoring devices are calibrated and used properly by occupationally-exposed personnel, that records are kept of the monitoring results, and that timely notifications are made as required by § 20.2203 of this chapter; and

(5) Ensuring that operations are conducted safely and to assume control for instituting corrective actions including stopping of operations when necessary.

(d) Licensees will have until June 27, 1999, to meet the requirements of paragraph (a) or (b) of this section.

[62 FR 28963, May 28, 1997, as amended at 63 FR 37061, July 9, 1998]

§ 34.43 Training.

(a) The licensee may not permit any individual to act as a radiographer until the individual—

(1) Has received training in the subjects in paragraph (g) of this section, in addition to a minimum of 2 months of on-the-job training, and is certified through a radiographer certification program by a certifying entity in accordance with the criteria specified in appendix A of this part. (An independent organization that would like to be recognized as a certifying entity shall submit its request to the Director, Office of Nuclear Material Safety and Safeguards, by an appropriate method listed in § 30.6(a) of this chapter.); or

(2) The licensee may, until June 27, 1999, allow an individual who has not met the requirements of paragraph (a)(1) of this section, to act as a radiographer after the individual has received training in the subjects outlined in paragraph (g) of this section and demonstrated an understanding of these subjects by successful completion of a written examination that was previously submitted to and approved by the Commission.

(b) In addition, the licensee may not permit any individual to act as a radiographer until the individual—

(1) Has received copies of and instruction in the requirements described in NRC regulations contained in this part; in §§ 30.7, 30.9, and 30.10 of this chapter; in the applicable sections of 10 CFR parts 19 and 20, of this chapter, in applicable DOT regulations as referenced in 10 CFR part 71, in the NRC license(s) under which the radiographer will perform industrial radiography, and the licensee's operating and emergency procedures;

(2) Has demonstrated understanding of the licensee's license and operating and emergency procedures by successful completion of a written or oral examination covering this material.

(3) Has received training in the use of the licensee's radiographic exposure devices, sealed sources, in the daily inspection of devices and associated equipment, and in the use of radiation survey instruments.

(4) Has demonstrated understanding of the use of radiographic exposure devices, sources, survey instruments and associated equipment described in paragraphs (b)(1) and (b)(3) of this section by successful completion of a practical examination covering this material.

(c) The licensee may not permit any individual to act as a radiographer's assistant until the individual—

(1) Has received copies of and instruction in the requirements described in NRC regulations contained in this part, in §§ 30.7, 30.9, and 30.10 of this chapter, in the applicable sections of 10 CFR parts 19 and 20 of this chapter, in applicable DOT regulations as referenced in 10 CFR part 71, in the NRC license(s) under which the radiographer's assistant will perform industrial radiography, and the licensee's operating and emergency procedures;

(2) Has developed competence to use, under the personal supervision of the radiographer, the radiographic exposure devices, sealed sources, associated equipment, and radiation survey instruments that the assistant will use; and

(3) Has demonstrated understanding of the instructions provided under (c)(1) of this section by successfully completing a written test on the subjects covered and has demonstrated competence in the use of hardware described in (c)(2) of this section by successful completion of a practical examination on the use of such hardware.

(d) The licensee shall provide annual refresher safety training for each radiographer and radiographer's assistant at intervals not to exceed 12 months.

(e) Except as provided in paragraph (e)(4), the RSO or designee shall conduct an inspection program of the job performance of each radiographer and radiographer's assistant to ensure that the Commission's regulations, license requirements, and the applicant's operating and emergency procedures are followed. The inspection program must:

(1) Include observation of the performance of each radiographer and radiographer's assistant during an actual industrial radiographic operation, at intervals not to exceed 6 months; and

(2) Provide that, if a radiographer or a radiographer's assistant has not participated in an industrial radiographic operation for more than 6 months since the last inspection, the radiographer

must demonstrate knowledge of the training requirements of § 34.43(b)(3) and the radiographer's assistant must re-demonstrate knowledge of the training requirements of § 34.43(c)(2) by a practical examination before these individuals can next participate in a radiographic operation.

(3) The Commission may consider alternatives in those situations where the individual serves as both radiographer and RSO.

(4) In those operations where a single individual serves as both radiographer and RSO, and performs all radiography operations, an inspection program is not required.

(f) The licensee shall maintain records of the above training to include certification documents, written and practical examinations, refresher safety training and inspections of job performance in accordance with § 34.79.

(g) The licensee shall include the following subjects required in paragraph (a) of this section:

(1) Fundamentals of radiation safety including—

(i) Characteristics of gamma radiation;

(ii) Units of radiation dose and quantity of radioactivity;

(iii) Hazards of exposure to radiation;

(iv) Levels of radiation from licensed material; and

(v) Methods of controlling radiation dose (time, distance, and shielding);

(2) Radiation detection instruments including—

(i) Use, operation, calibration, and limitations of radiation survey instruments;

(ii) Survey techniques; and

(iii) Use of personnel monitoring equipment;

(3) Equipment to be used including—

(i) Operation and control of radiographic exposure equipment, remote handling equipment, and storage containers, including pictures or models of source assemblies (pigtails).

(ii) Storage, control, and disposal of licensed material; and

(iii) Inspection and maintenance of equipment.

(4) The requirements of pertinent Federal regulations; and

(5) Case histories of accidents in radiography.

(h) Licensees will have until June 27, 1998, to comply with the additional training requirements specified in paragraphs (b)(1) and (c)(1) of this section.

(i) Licensees will have until June 27, 1999 to comply with the certification requirements specified in paragraph (a)(1) of this section. Records of radiographer certification maintained in accordance with § 34.79(a) provide appropriate affirmation of certification requirements specified in paragraph (a)(1) of this section.

[62 FR 28963, May 28, 1997, as amended at 63 FR 37061, July 9, 1998; 68 FR 58805, Oct. 10, 2003, 73 FR 5720, Jan. 31, 2008]

§ 34.45 Operating and emergency procedures.

(a) Operating and emergency procedures must include, as a minimum, instructions in the following:

(1) Appropriate handling and use of licensed sealed sources and radiographic exposure devices so that no person is likely to be exposed to radiation doses in excess of the limits established in 10 CFR part 20 of this chapter "Standards for Protection Against Radiation";

(2) Methods and occasions for conducting radiation surveys;

(3) Methods for controlling access to radiographic areas;

(4) Methods and occasions for locking and securing radiographic exposure devices, transport and storage containers and sealed sources;

(5) Personnel monitoring and the use of personnel monitoring equipment;

(6) Transporting sealed sources to field locations, including packing of radiographic exposure devices and storage containers in the vehicles, placarding of vehicles when needed, and control of the sealed sources during transportation (refer to 49 CFR parts 171–173);

(7) The inspection, maintenance, and operability checks of radiographic exposure devices, survey instruments, transport containers, and storage containers;

(8) Steps that must be taken immediately by radiography personnel in the event a pocket dosimeter is found to be off-scale or an alarm ratemeter alarms unexpectedly.

(9) The procedure(s) for identifying and reporting defects and noncompliance, as required by 10 CFR part 21 of this chapter;

(10) The procedure for notifying proper persons in the event of an accident;

(11) Minimizing exposure of persons in the event of an accident;

(12) Source recovery procedure if licensee will perform source recovery;

(13) Maintenance of records.

(b) The licensee shall maintain copies of current operating and emergency procedures in accordance with §§ 34.81 and 34.89.

§ 34.46 Supervision of radiographers' assistants.

Whenever a radiographer's assistant uses radiographic exposure devices, associated equipment or sealed sources or conducts radiation surveys required by § 34.49(b) to determine that the sealed source has returned to the shielded position after an exposure, the assistant shall be under the personal supervision of a radiographer. The personal supervision must include:

(a) The radiographer's physical presence at the site where the sealed sources are being used;

(b) The availability of the radiographer to give immediate assistance if required; and

(c) The radiographer's direct observation of the assistant's performance of the operations referred to in this section.

§ 34.47 Personnel monitoring.

(a) The licensee may not permit any individual to act as a radiographer or a radiographer's assistant unless, at all times during radiographic operations, each individual wears, on the trunk of the body, a direct reading dosimeter, an operating alarm ratemeter, and a personnel dosimeter that is processed and evaluated by an accredited National Voluntary Laboratory Accreditation Program (NVLAP) processor. At permanent radiography installations where other appropriate alarming or warning devices are in routine use, the wearing of an alarming ratemeter is not required.

(1) Pocket dosimeters must have a range from zero to 2 millisieverts (200 millirems) and must be recharged at the start of each shift. Electronic personal dosimeters may only be used in place of ion-chamber pocket dosimeters.

(2) Each personnel dosimeter must be assigned to and worn only by one individual.

(3) Film badges must be replaced at periods not to exceed one month and other personnel dosimeters processed and evaluated by an accredited NVLAP processor must be replaced at periods not to exceed three months.

(4) After replacement, each personnel dosimeter must be processed as soon as possible.

(b) Direct reading dosimeters such as pocket dosimeters or electronic personal dosimeters, must be read and the exposures recorded at the beginning and end of each shift, and records must be maintained in accordance with § 34.83.

(c) Pocket dosimeters, or electronic personal dosimeters, must be checked at periods not to exceed 12 months for correct response to radiation, and records must be maintained in accordance with § 34.83. Acceptable dosimeters must read within plus or minus 20 percent of the true radiation exposure.

(d) If an individual's pocket chamber is found to be off-scale, or if his or her electronic personal dosimeter reads greater than 2 millisieverts (200 millirems), and the possibility of radiation exposure cannot be ruled out as the cause, the individual's personnel dosimeter must be sent for processing within 24 hours. In addition, the individual may not resume work associated with licensed material use until a determination of the individual's radiation exposure has been made. This determination must be made by the RSO or the RSO's designee. The results of this determination must be included in the records maintained in accordance with § 34.83.

(e) If the personnel dosimeter that is required by paragraph (a) of this section is lost or damaged, the worker shall cease work immediately until a replacement personnel dosimeter meeting the requirements in paragraph (a) is provided and the exposure is calculated for the time period from issuance to loss or damage of the personnel dosimeter. The results of the calculated exposure and the time period for which the personnel dosimeter was lost or damaged must be included in the records maintained in accordance with § 34.83.

(f) Dosimetry reports received from the accredited NVLAP personnel dosimeter processor must be retained in accordance with § 34.83.

(g) Each alarm ratemeter must—

(1) Be checked to ensure that the alarm functions properly (sounds) before using at the start of each shift;

(2) Be set to give an alarm signal at a preset dose rate of 5 mSv/hr (500 mrem/hr); with an accuracy of plus or minus 20 percent of the true radiation dose rate;

(3) Require special means to change the preset alarm function; and

(4) Be calibrated at periods not to exceed 12 months for correct response to radiation. The licensee shall maintain records of alarm ratemeter calibrations in accordance with § 34.83.

[62 FR 28963, May 28, 1997, as amended at 65 FR 63751, Oct. 24, 2000]

§ 34.49 Radiation surveys.

The licensee shall:

(a) Conduct surveys with a calibrated and operable radiation survey instrument that meets the requirements of § 34.25.

(b) Using a survey instrument meeting the requirements of paragraph (a) of this section, conduct a survey of the radiographic exposure device and the guide tube after each exposure when approaching the device or the guide tube. The survey must determine that the sealed source has returned to its shielded position before exchanging films, repositioning the exposure head, or dismantling equipment.

(c) Conduct a survey of the radiographic exposure device with a calibrated radiation survey instrument any time the source is exchanged and whenever a radiographic exposure device is placed in a storage area (as defined in § 34.3), to ensure that the sealed source is in its shielded position.

(d) Maintain records in accordance with § 34.85.

§ 34.51 Surveillance.

During each radiographic operation the radiographer, or the other individual present, as required by § 34.41, shall maintain continuous direct visual surveillance of the operation to protect against unauthorized entry into a high radiation area, as defined in 10 CFR part 20 of this chapter, except at permanent radiographic installations where all entryways are locked and the requirements of § 34.33 are met.

§ 34.53 Posting.

All areas in which industrial radiography is being performed must be conspicuously posted as required by § 20.1902(a) and (b) of this chapter. Exceptions listed in § 20.1903 of this chapter do not apply to industrial radiographic operations.

[62 FR 28963, May 28, 1997, as amended at 66 FR 64738, Dec. 14, 2001]

Subpart E—Recordkeeping Requirements

§ 34.61 Records of the specific license for industrial radiography.

Each licensee shall maintain a copy of its license, license conditions, documents incorporated by reference, and amendments to each of these items until superseded by new documents approved by the Commission, or until the Commission terminates the license.

§ 34.63 Records of receipt and transfer of sealed sources.

(a) Each licensee shall maintain records showing the receipts and transfers of sealed sources and devices using DU for shielding and retain each record for 3 years after it is made.

(b) These records must include the date, the name of the individual making the record, radionuclide, number of becquerels (curies) or mass (for DU), and manufacturer, model, and serial number of each sealed source and/or device, as appropriate.

§ 34.65 Records of radiation survey instruments.

Each licensee shall maintain records of the calibrations of its radiation survey instruments that are required under § 34.25 and retain each record for 3 years after it is made.

§ 34.67 Records of leak testing of sealed sources and devices containing depleted uranium.

Each licensee shall maintain records of leak test results for sealed sources and for devices containing DU. The results must be stated in units of becquerels (microcuries). The licensee shall retain each record for 3 years after it is made or until the source in storage is removed.

§ 34.69 Records of quarterly inventory.

(a) Each licensee shall maintain records of the quarterly inventory of sealed sources and of devices containing depleted uranium as required by § 34.29 and retain each record for 3 years after it is made.

(b) The record must include the date of the inventory, name of the individual conducting the inventory, radionuclide, number of becquerels (curies) or mass (for DU) in each device, location of sealed source and/or devices, and manufacturer, model, and serial number of each sealed source and/or device, as appropriate.

§ 34.71 Utilization logs.

(a) Each licensee shall maintain utilization logs showing for each sealed source the following information:

(1) A description, including the make, model, and serial number of the radiographic exposure device or transport or storage container in which the sealed source is located;

(2) The identity and signature of the radiographer to whom assigned; and

(3) The plant or site where used and dates of use, including the dates removed and returned to storage.

(b) The licensee shall retain the logs required by paragraph (a) of this section for 3 years after the log is made.

§ 34.73 Records of inspection and maintenance of radiographic exposure devices, transport and storage containers, associated equipment, source changers, and survey instruments.

(a) Each licensee shall maintain records specified in § 34.31 of equipment problems found in daily checks and quarterly inspections of radiographic exposure devices, transport and storage containers, associated equipment, source changers, and survey instruments; and retain each record for 3 years after it is made.

(b) The record must include the date of check or inspection, name of inspector, equipment involved, any problems found, and what repair and/or maintenance, if any, was done.

§ 34.75 Records of alarm system and entrance control checks at permanent radiographic installations.

Each licensee shall maintain records of alarm system and entrance control device tests required under § 34.33 and retain each record for 3 years after it is made.

§ 34.79 Records of training and certification.

Each licensee shall maintain the following records (of training and certification) for 3 years after the record is made:

(a) Records of training of each radiographer and each radiographer's assistant. The record must include radiographer certification documents and verification of certification status, copies of written tests, dates of oral and practical examinations, and names of individuals conducting and receiving the oral and practical examinations; and

(b) Records of annual refresher safety training and semi-annual inspections of job performance for each radiographer and each radiographer's assistant. The records must list the topics discussed during the refresher safety training, the dates the annual refresher safety training was conducted, and names of the instructors and attendees. For inspections of job performance, the records must also include a list showing the items checked and any non-compliances observed by the RSO.

§ 34.81 Copies of operating and emergency procedures.

Each licensee shall maintain a copy of current operating and emergency procedures until the Commission terminates the license. Superseded material must be retained for 3 years after the change is made.

§ 34.83 Records of personnel monitoring procedures.

Each licensee shall maintain the following exposure records specified in § 34.47:

(a) Direct reading dosimeter readings and yearly operability checks required by § 34.47 (b) and (c) for 3 years after the record is made.

(b) Records of alarm ratemeter calibrations for 3 years after the record is made.

(c) Personnel dosimeter results received from the accredited NVLAP processor until the Commission terminates the license.

(d) Records of estimates of exposures as a result of: off-scale personal direct reading dosimeters, or lost or damaged personnel dosimeters until the Commission terminates the license.

[62 FR 28963, May 28, 1997, as amended at 65 FR 63752, Oct. 24, 2000]

§ 34.85 Records of radiation surveys.

Each licensee shall maintain a record of each exposure device survey conducted before the device is placed in storage as specified in § 34.49(c), if that survey is the last one performed in the workday. Each record must be maintained for 3 years after it is made.

§ 34.87 Form of records.

Each record required by this part must be legible throughout the specified retention period. The record may be the original or a reproduced copy or a microform provided that the copy or microform is authenticated by authorized personnel and that the microform is capable of reproducing a clear copy throughout the required retention period. The record may also be stored in electronic media with the capability for producing legible, accurate, and complete records during the required retention period. Records, such as letters, drawings, and specifications, must include all pertinent information, such as stamps, initials, and signatures. The licensee shall maintain adequate safeguards against tampering with and loss of records.

§ 34.89 Location of documents and records.

(a) Each licensee shall maintain copies of records required by this part and other applicable parts of this chapter at the location specified in § 34.13(k).

(b) Each licensee shall also maintain copies of the following documents and records sufficient to demonstrate compliance at each applicable field station and each temporary jobsite;

(1) The license authorizing the use of licensed material;

(2) A copy of 10 CFR parts 19, 20, and 34 of NRC regulations;

(3) Utilization records for each radiographic exposure device dispatched from that location as required by § 34.71.

(4) Records of equipment problems identified in daily checks of equipment as required by § 34.73(a);

(5) Records of alarm system and entrance control checks required by § 34.75, if applicable;

(6) Records of direct reading dosimeters such as pocket dosimeter and/or electronic personal dosimeters readings as required by § 34.83;

(7) Operating and emergency procedures required by § 34.81;

(8) Evidence of the latest calibration of the radiation survey instruments in use at the site, as required by § 34.65;

(9) Evidence of the latest calibrations of alarm ratemeters and operability checks of pocket dosimeters and/or electronic personal dosimeters as required by § 34.83;

(10) Latest survey records required by § 34.85;

(11) The shipping papers for the transportation of radioactive materials required by § 71.5 of this chapter; and

(12) When operating under reciprocity pursuant to § 150.20 of this chapter, a copy of the Agreement State license authorizing the use of licensed materials.

Subpart F—Notifications

§ 34.101 Notifications.

(a) In addition to the reporting requirements specified in § 30.50 and under other sections of this chapter, such as § 21.21, each licensee shall send a written report to the NRC's Office of

Nuclear Material Safety and Safeguards, by an appropriate method listed in §30.6(a) of this chapter, within 30 days of the occurrence of any of the following incidents involving radiographic equipment:

(1) Unintentional disconnection of the source assembly from the control cable;

(2) Inability to retract the source assembly to its fully shielded position and secure it in this position; or

(3) Failure of any component (critical to safe operation of the device) to properly perform its intended function;

(b) The licensee shall include the following information in each report submitted under paragraph (a) of this section, and in each report of overexposure submitted under 10 CFR 20.2203 which involves failure of safety components of radiography equipment:

(1) A description of the equipment problem;

(2) Cause of each incident, if known;

(3) Name of the manufacturer and model number of equipment involved in the incident;

(4) Place, date, and time of the incident;

(5) Actions taken to establish normal operations;

(6) Corrective actions taken or planned to prevent recurrence; and

(7) Qualifications of personnel involved in the incident.

(c) Any licensee conducting radiographic operations or storing radioactive material at any location not listed on the license for a period in excess of 180 days in a calendar year, shall notify the appropriate NRC regional office listed in §30.6(a)(2) of this chapter prior to exceeding the 180 days.

[62 FR 28963, May 28, 1997, as amended at 67 FR 3585, Jan. 25, 2002; 68 FR 58805, Oct. 10, 2003; 73 FR 5720, Jan. 31, 2008]

Subpart G—Exemptions

§ 34.111 Applications for exemptions.

The Commission may, upon application of any interested person or upon its own initiative, grant an exemption from the requirements of the regulations in this part if it determines the exemption is authorized by law and would not endanger life or property or the common defense and security and is otherwise in the public interest.

Subpart H—Violations

§ 34.121 Violations.

(a) The Commission may obtain an injunction or other court order to prevent a violation of the provisions of—

(1) The Atomic Energy Act of 1954, as amended;

(2) Title II of the Energy Reorganization Act of 1974, as amended; or

(3) A regulation or order issued pursuant to these Acts.

(b) The Commission may obtain a court order for the payment of a civil penalty imposed under Section 234 of the Atomic Energy Act;

(1) For violations of—

(i) Sections 53, 57, 62, 63, 81, 82, 101, 103, 104, 107, or 109 of the Atomic Energy Act of 1954, as amended;

(ii) Section 206 of the Energy Reorganization Act;

(iii) Any rule, regulation, or order issued pursuant to the sections specified in paragraph (b)(1)(i) of this section.

(iv) Any term, condition, or limitation of any license issued under the sections specified in paragraph (b)(1)(i) of this section.

(2) For any violation for which a license may be revoked under section 186 of the Atomic Energy Act of 1954, as amended.

§ 34.123 Criminal penalties.

(a) Section 223 of the Atomic Energy Act of 1952, as amended, provides for criminal sanctions for willful violation of, attempted violation of, or conspiracy to violate, any regulation issued under one or more of §§161b, 161i, or 161o of the Act. For purposes of Section 223, all the regulations in 10 CFR part 34 are issued under one or more of §§161b, 161i, or 161o, except for the sections listed in paragraph (b) of this section.

(b) The regulations in 10 CFR part 34 that are not issued under sections 161b, 161i, or 161o for the purposes of Section 223 are as follows: §§34.1, 34.3, 34.5, 34.8, 34.11, 34.13, 34.111, 34.121, 34.123.

APPENDIX A TO PART 34—RADIOGRAPHER CERTIFICATION

I. REQUIREMENTS FOR AN INDEPENDENT CERTIFYING ORGANIZATION

An independent certifying organization shall:

1. Be an organization such as a society or association, whose members participate in, or have an interest in, the fields of industrial radiography;

2. Make its membership available to the general public nationwide that is not restricted because of race, color, religion, sex, age, national origin or disability;

3. Have a certification program open to nonmembers, as well as members;

4. Be an incorporated, nationally recognized organization, that is involved in setting national standards of practice within its fields of expertise;

5. Have an adequate staff, a viable system for financing its operations, and a policy-and decision-making review board;

6. Have a set of written organizational by-laws and policies that provide adequate assurance of lack of conflict of interest and a system for monitoring and enforcing those by-laws and policies;

7. Have a committee, whose members can carry out their responsibilities impartially, to review and approve the certification guidelines and procedures, and to advise the organization's staff in implementing the certification program;

8. Have a committee, whose members can carry out their responsibilities impartially, to review complaints against certified individuals and to determine appropriate sanctions;

9. Have written procedures describing all aspects of its certification program, maintain records of the current status of each individual's certification and the administration of its certification program;

10. Have procedures to ensure that certified individuals are provided due process with respect to the administration of its certification program, including the process of becoming certified and any sanctions imposed against certified individuals;

11. Have procedures for proctoring examinations, including qualifications for proctors. These procedures must ensure that the individuals proctoring each examination are not employed by the same company or corporation (or a wholly-owned subsidiary of such company or corporation) as any of the examinees;

12. Exchange information about certified individuals with the Commission and other independent certifying organizations and/or Agreement States and allow periodic review of its certification program and related records; and

13. Provide a description to the Commission of its procedures for choosing examination sites and for providing an appropriate examination environment.

II. REQUIREMENTS FOR CERTIFICATION PROGRAMS

All certification programs must:

1. Require applicants for certification to (a) receive training in the topics set forth in §34.43(g) or equivalent Agreement State regulations, and (b) satisfactorily complete a written examination covering these topics;

2. Require applicants for certification to provide documentation that demonstrates that the applicant has: (a) received training in the topics set forth in §34.43(g) or equivalent Agreement State regulations; (b) satisfactorily completed a minimum period of on-the-job training; and (c) has received verification by an Agreement State or a NRC licensee that the applicant has demonstrated the capability of independently working as a radiographer;

3. Include procedures to ensure that all examination questions are protected from disclosure;

4. Include procedures for denying an application, revoking, suspending, and reinstating a certificate;

5. Provide a certification period of not less than 3 years nor more than 5 years;

6. Include procedures for renewing certifications and, if the procedures allow renewals without examination, require evidence of recent full-time employment and annual refresher training.

7. Provide a timely response to inquiries, by telephone or letter, from members of the public, about an individual's certification status.

III. REQUIREMENTS FOR WRITTEN EXAMINATIONS

All examinations must be:

1. Designed to test an individual's knowledge and understanding of the topics listed in §34.43(g) or equivalent Agreement State requirements;

2. Written in a multiple-choice format;

3. Have test items drawn from a question bank containing psychometrically valid questions based on the material in §34.43(g).

PART 35—MEDICAL USE OF BYPRODUCT MATERIAL

Subpart A—General Information

Subpart B—General Administrative Requirements

Subpart C—General Technical Requirements

Subpart D—Unsealed Byproduct Material—Written Directive Not Required

Subpart E—Unsealed Byproduct Material—Written Directive Required

Subpart F—Manual Brachytherapy

Subpart G—Sealed Sources for Diagnosis

Subpart H—Photon Emitting Remote Afterloader Units, Teletherapy Units, and Gamma Stereotactic Radiosurgery Units

Subparts I–J [Reserved]

Subpart K—Other Medical Uses of Byproduct Material or Radiation From Byproduct Material

Subpart L—Records

Subpart M—Reports

Subpart N—Enforcement

AUTHORITY: Atomic Energy Act of 1954, secs. 81, 161, 181, 182, 183, 223, 234, 274 (42 U.S.C. 2111, 2201, 2231, 2232, 2233, 2273, 2282, 2021); Energy Reorganization Act of 1974, secs. 201, 206 (42 U.S.C. 5841, 5846); 44 U.S.C. 3504 note.

SOURCE: 67 FR 20370, Apr. 24, 2002, unless otherwise noted.

EDITORIAL NOTE: Nomenclature changes to part 35 appear at 79 FR 75739, Dec. 19, 2014.

Subpart A—General Information

§ 35.1 Purpose and scope.

This part contains the requirements and provisions for the medical use of byproduct material and for issuance of specific licenses authorizing the medical use of this material. These requirements and provisions provide for the radiation safety of workers, the general public, patients, and human research subjects. The requirements and provisions of this part are in addition to, and not in substitution for, others in this chapter. The requirements and provisions of parts 19, 20, 21, 30, 37, 71, 170, and 171 of this chapter apply to applicants and licensees subject to this part unless specifically exempted.

[78 FR 17006, Mar. 19, 2013]

§ 35.2 Definitions.

Address of use means the building or buildings that are identified on the license and where byproduct material may be received, prepared, used, or stored.

Agreement State means any State with which the Commission or the Atomic Energy Commission has entered into an effective agreement under subsection 274b of the Atomic Energy Act of 1954, as amended.

Area of use means a portion of an address of use that has been set aside for the purpose of receiving, preparing, using, or storing byproduct material.

Authorized medical physicist means an individual who—

(1) Meets the requirements in §§ 35.51(a) and 35.59; or

(2) Is identified as an authorized medical physicist or teletherapy physicist on—

(i) A specific medical use license issued by the Commission or Agreement State;

(ii) A medical use permit issued by a Commission master material licensee;

(iii) A permit issued by a Commission or Agreement State broad scope medical use licensee; or

(iv) A permit issued by a Commission master material license broad scope medical use permittee.

Authorized nuclear pharmacist means a pharmacist who—

(1) Meets the requirements in §§ 35.55(a) and 35.59; or

(2) Is identified as an authorized nuclear pharmacist on—

(i) A specific license issued by the Commission or Agreement State that authorizes medical use or the practice of nuclear pharmacy;

(ii) A permit issued by a Commission master material licensee that authorizes medical use or the practice of nuclear pharmacy;

(iii) A permit issued by a Commission or Agreement State broad scope medical use licensee that authorizes medical use or the practice of nuclear pharmacy; or

(iv) A permit issued by a Commission master material license broad scope medical use permittee that authorizes medical use or the practice of nuclear pharmacy; or

(3) Is identified as an authorized nuclear pharmacist by a commercial nuclear pharmacy that has been authorized to identify authorized nuclear pharmacists; or

(4) Is designated as an authorized nuclear pharmacist in accordance with § 32.72(b)(4).

Authorized user means a physician, dentist, or podiatrist who—

(1) Meets the requirements in §§ 35.59 and 35.190(a), 35.290(a), 35.390(a), 35.392(a), 35.394(a), 35.490(a), 35.590(a), or 35.690(a); or

(2) Is identified as an authorized user on—

(i) A Commission or Agreement State license that authorizes the medical use of byproduct material;

(ii) A permit issued by a Commission master material licensee that is authorized to permit the medical use of byproduct material;

(iii) A permit issued by a Commission or Agreement State specific licensee of broad scope that is authorized to permit the medical use of byproduct material; or

(iv) A permit issued by a Commission master material license broad scope permittee that is authorized to permit the medical use of byproduct material.

Brachytherapy means a method of radiation therapy in which sources are used to deliver a radiation dose at a distance of up to a few centimeters by surface, intracavitary, intraluminal, or interstitial application.

Brachytherapy source means a radioactive source or a manufacturer-assembled source train or a combination of these sources that is designed to deliver a therapeutic dose within a distance of a few centimeters.

Client's address means the area of use or a temporary job site for the purpose of providing mobile medical service in accordance with § 35.80.

Cyclotron means a particle accelerator in which the charged particles travel in an outward spiral or circular path. A cyclotron accelerates charged particles at energies usually in excess of 10 megaelectron volts and is commonly used for production of short half-life radionuclides for medical use.

Dedicated check source means a radioactive source that is used to assure the constant operation of a radiation detection or measurement device over several months or years.

Dentist means an individual licensed by a State or Territory of the United States, the District of Columbia, or the Commonwealth of Puerto Rico to practice dentistry.

High dose-rate remote afterloader, as used in this part, means a brachytherapy device that remotely delivers a dose rate in excess of 12 gray (1200 rads) per hour at the point or surface where the dose is prescribed.

Low dose-rate remote afterloader, as used in this part, means a brachytherapy device that remotely delivers a dose rate of less than or equal to 2 gray (200 rads) per hour at the point or surface where the dose is prescribed.

Management means the chief executive officer or other individual having the authority to manage, direct, or administer the licensee's activities, or those persons' delegate or delegates.

Manual brachytherapy, as used in this part, means a type of brachytherapy in which the brachytherapy sources (e.g., seeds, ribbons) are manually placed topically on or inserted either into the body cavities that are in close proximity to a treatment site or directly into the tissue volume.

Medical event means an event that meets the criteria in § 35.3045(a) or (b).

Medical institution means an organization in which more than one medical discipline is practiced.

Medical use means the intentional internal or external administration of byproduct material or the radiation from byproduct material to patients or human research subjects under the supervision of an authorized user.

Medium dose-rate remote afterloader, as used in this part, means a brachytherapy device that remotely delivers a dose rate of greater than 2 gray (200 rads) per hour, but less than or equal to 12 gray (1200 rads) per hour at the point or surface where the dose is prescribed.

Mobile medical service means the transportation of byproduct material to and its medical use at the client's address.

Output means the exposure rate, dose rate, or a quantity related in a known manner to these rates from a brachytherapy source or a teletherapy, remote afterloader, or gamma stereotactic radiosurgery unit for a specified set of exposure conditions.

Patient intervention means actions by the patient or human research subject, whether intentional or unintentional, such as dislodging or removing treatment devices or prematurely terminating the administration.

Pharmacist means an individual licensed by a State or Territory of the United States, the District of Columbia, or the Commonwealth of Puerto Rico to practice pharmacy.

Physician means a medical doctor or doctor of osteopathy licensed by a State or Territory of the United States, the District of Columbia, or the Commonwealth of Puerto Rico to prescribe drugs in the practice of medicine.

Podiatrist means an individual licensed by a State or Territory of the United States, the District of Columbia, or the Commonwealth of Puerto Rico to practice podiatry.

Positron Emission Tomography (PET) radionuclide production facility is defined as a facility operating a cyclotron or accelerator for the purpose of producing PET radionuclides.

Preceptor means an individual who provides, directs, or verifies training and experience required for an individual to become an authorized user, an authorized medical physicist, an authorized nuclear pharmacist, or a Radiation Safety Officer.

Prescribed dosage means the specified activity or range of activity of unsealed byproduct material as documented—

(1) In a written directive; or

(2) In accordance with the directions of the authorized user for procedures performed pursuant to §§ 35.100 and 35.200.

Prescribed dose means—

(1) For gamma stereotactic radiosurgery, the total dose as documented in the written directive;

(2) For teletherapy, the total dose and dose per fraction as documented in the written directive;

(3) For manual brachytherapy, either the total source strength and exposure time or the total dose, as documented in the written directive; or

(4) For remote brachytherapy afterloaders, the total dose and dose per fraction as documented in the written directive.

Pulsed dose-rate remote afterloader, as used in this part, means a special type of remote afterloading brachytherapy device that uses a single source capable of delivering dose rates in the "high dose-rate" range, but—

(1) Is approximately one-tenth of the activity of typical high dose-rate remote afterloader sources; and

(2) Is used to simulate the radiobiology of a low dose-rate treatment by inserting the source for a given fraction of each hour.

Radiation Safety Officer means an individual who—

(1) Meets the requirements in §§ 35.50(a) or (c)(1) and 35.59; or

(2) Is identified as a Radiation Safety Officer on—

(i) A specific medical use license issued by the Commission or Agreement State; or

(ii) A medical use permit issued by a Commission master material licensee.

Sealed source means any byproduct material that is encased in a capsule designed to prevent leakage or escape of the byproduct material.

Sealed Source and Device Registry means the national registry that contains all the registration certificates, generated by both NRC and the Agreement States, that summarize the radiation safety information for the sealed sources and devices and describe the licensing and use conditions approved for the product.

Stereotactic radiosurgery means the use of external radiation in conjunction with a stereotactic guidance device to very precisely deliver a therapeutic dose to a tissue volume.

Structured educational program means an educational program designed to impart particular knowledge and practical education through interrelated studies and supervised training.

Teletherapy, as used in this part, means a method of radiation therapy in which collimated gamma rays are delivered at a distance from the patient or human research subject.

Temporary job site means a location where mobile medical services are conducted other than those location(s) of use authorized on the license.

Therapeutic dosage means a dosage of unsealed byproduct material that is intended to deliver a radiation dose to a patient or human research subject for palliative or curative treatment.

Therapeutic dose means a radiation dose delivered from a source containing byproduct material to a patient or human research subject for palliative or curative treatment.

Treatment site means the anatomical description of the tissue intended to receive a radiation dose, as described in a written directive.

Type of use means use of byproduct material under §§ 35.100, 35.200, 35.300, 35.400, 35.500, 35.600, or 35.1000.

Unit dosage means a dosage prepared for medical use for administration as a single dosage to a patient or human research subject without any further manipulation of the dosage after it is initially prepared.

Written directive means an authorized user's written order for the administration of byproduct material or radiation from byproduct material to a specific patient or human research subject, as specified in § 35.40.

[67 FR 20370, Apr. 24, 2002, as amended at 68 FR 19324, Apr. 21, 2003; 69 FR 55737, Sept. 16, 2004; 70 FR 16361, Mar. 30, 2005; 71 FR 15008, Mar. 27, 2006; 72 FR 45151, Aug. 13, 2007; 72 FR 55930, Oct. 1, 2007]

§ 35.5 Maintenance of records.

Each record required by this part must be legible throughout the specified retention period. The record may be the original, a reproduced copy, or a microform if the copy or microform is authenticated by authorized personnel and the microform is capable of producing a clear copy throughout the required retention period. The record may also be stored in electronic media with the capability for producing legible, accurate, and complete records during the required retention period. Records such as letters, drawings, and specifications must include all pertinent information such as stamps, initials, and signatures. The licensee shall maintain adequate safeguards against tampering with and loss of records.

§ 35.6 Provisions for the protection of human research subjects.

(a) A licensee may conduct research involving human research subjects only if it uses the byproduct materials specified on its license for the uses authorized on its license.

(b) If the research is conducted, funded, supported, or regulated by another Federal agency that has implemented the Federal Policy for the Protection of Human Subjects (Federal Policy), the licensee shall, before conducting research—

(1) Obtain review and approval of the research from an "Institutional Review Board," as defined and described in the Federal Policy; and

(2) Obtain "informed consent," as defined and described in the Federal Policy, from the human research subject.

(c) If the research will not be conducted, funded, supported, or regulated by another Federal agency that has implemented the Federal Policy, the licensee shall, before conducting research, apply for and receive a specific amendment to its NRC medical use license. The amendment request must include a written commitment that the licensee will, before conducting research—

(1) Obtain review and approval of the research from an "Institutional Review Board," as defined and described in the Federal Policy; and

(2) Obtain "informed consent", as defined and described in the Federal Policy, from the human research subject.

(d) Nothing in this section relieves licensees from complying with the other requirements in this part.

[67 FR 20370, Apr. 24, 2002; 67 FR 62872, Oct. 9, 2002]

§ 35.7 FDA, other Federal, and State requirements.

Nothing in this part relieves the licensee from complying with applicable FDA, other Federal, and State requirements governing radioactive drugs or devices.

§ 35.8 Information collection requirements: OMB approval.

(a) The Commission has submitted the information collection requirements contained in this part to the Office of Management and Budget (OMB) for approval as required by the Paperwork Reduction Act (44 U.S.C. 3501*et seq.*). The NRC may not conduct or sponsor, and a person is not required to respond to, a collection of information unless it displays a currently valid OMB control number. OMB has approved the information collection requirements in this part under control number 3150–0010.

(b) The approved information collection requirements contained in this part appear in §§ 35.6, 35.12, 35.13, 35.14, 35.19, 35.24, 35.26, 35.27, 35.40, 35.41, 35.50, 35.51, 35.55, 35.60, 35.61, 35.63, 35.67, 35.69, 35.70, 35.75, 35.80, 35.92, 35.190, 35.204, 35.290, 35.310, 35.315, 35.390, 35.392, 35.394, 35.396, 35.404, 35.406, 35.410, 35.415, 35.432, 35.433, 35.490, 35.491, 35.590, 35.604, 35.605, 35.610, 35.615, 35.630, 35.632, 35.633, 35.635, 35.642, 35.643, 35.645, 35.647, 35.652, 35.655, 35.690, 35.1000, 35.2024, 35.2026, 35.2040, 35.2041, 35.2060, 35.2061, 35.2063, 35.2067, 35.2070, 35.2075, 35.2080, 35.2092, 35.2204, 35.2310, 35.2404, 35.2406, 35.2432, 35.2433, 35.2605, 35.2610, 35.2630, 35.2632, 35.2642, 35.2643, 35.2645, 35.2647, 35.2652, 35.2655, 35.3045, 35.3047 and 35.3067.

(c) This part contains information collection requirements in addition to those approved under the control number specified in paragraph (a) of this section. These information collection requirements and the control numbers under which they are approved are as follows:

(1) In §35.12, NRC Form 313, including NRC Form 313A, which licensees may use to provide supplemental information, is approved under control number 3150–0120.

(2) [Reserved]

[67 FR 20370, Apr. 24, 2002, as amended at 71 FR 15008, Mar. 27, 2006]

§35.10 Implementation.

(a) A Government agency or a Federally recognized Indian Tribe that possesses and uses accelerator-produced radioactive material or discrete sources of radium-226 for which a specific medical use license is required by the Atomic Energy Act of 1954, as amended, must comply with the requirements of this part, including provisions that are specific to licensees, on November 30, 2007. All other persons who possess and use accelerator-produced radioactive material or discrete sources of radium-226 for which a specific medical use license is required, must comply with the requirements of this part, including provisions that are specific to licensees, on August 8, 2009, or earlier as noticed by the NRC.

(b)–(c) [Reserved]

(d) If a license condition exempted a licensee from a provision of Part 35 on October 24, 2002, then the license condition continues to exempt the licensee from the requirements in the corresponding provision of §§35.1–35.4002.

(e) When a requirement in this part differs from the requirement in an existing license condition, the requirement in this part shall govern.

(f) A licensee shall continue to comply with any license condition that requires it to implement procedures required by §§35.610, 35.642, 35.643, and 35.645 until there is a license amendment or renewal that modifies the license condition.

[67 FR 20370, Apr. 24, 2002, as amended at 71 FR 15008, Mar. 27, 2006; 72 FR 55930, Oct. 1, 2007]

§35.11 License required.

(a) A person may manufacture, produce, acquire, receive, possess, prepare, use, or transfer byproduct material for medical use only in accordance with a specific license issued by the Commission or an Agreement State, or as allowed in paragraph (b) or (c) of this section.

(b) A specific license is not needed for an individual who—

(1) Receives, possesses, uses, or transfers byproduct material in accordance with the regulations in this chapter under the supervision of an authorized user as provided in §35.27, unless prohibited by license condition; or

(2) Prepares unsealed byproduct material for medical use in accordance with the regulations in this chapter under the supervision of an authorized nuclear pharmacist or authorized user as provided in §35.27, unless prohibited by license condition.

(c)(1) A Government agency or a Federally recognized Indian Tribe, that possesses and uses accelerator-produced radioactive material or discrete sources of radium-226 for which a specific medical use license is required in paragraph (a) of this section, may continue to use such materials for medical uses until the date of the NRC's final licensing determination, provided that the person submits a medical use license application on or before December 1, 2008.

(2) Except as provided in paragraph (c)(1) of this section, all other persons, who possess and use accelerator-produced radioactive material or discrete sources of radium-226 for which a specific medical use license is required in paragraph (a) of this section, may continue to use this type of material for medical uses permitted under this part until the date of the NRC's final licensing determination, provided that the person submits a medical use license application within 12 months from the waiver expiration date of August 7, 2009 or within 12 months from the date of an earlier termination of the waiver as noticed by the NRC, whichever date is earlier.

[67 FR 20370, Apr. 24, 2002, as amended at 72 FR 55930, Oct. 1, 2006]

§ 35.12 Application for license, amendment, or renewal.

(a) An application must be signed by the applicant's or licensee's management.

(b) An application for a license for medical use of byproduct material as described in §§ 35.100, 35.200, 35.300, 35.400, 35.500, 35.600, and 35.1000 must be made by—

(1) Filing an original and one copy of NRC Form 313, "Application for Material License," that includes the facility diagram, equipment, and training and experience qualifications of the Radiation Safety Officer, authorized user(s), authorized medical physicist(s), and authorized nuclear pharmacist(s); and

(2) Submitting procedures required by §§ 35.610, 35.642, 35.643, and 35.645, as applicable.

(c) A request for a license amendment or renewal must be made by—

(1) Submitting an original and one copy of either—

(i) NRC Form 313, "Application for Material License"; or

(ii) A letter requesting the amendment or renewal; and

(2) Submitting procedures required by §§ 35.610, 35.642, 35.643, and 35.645, as applicable.

(d) In addition to the requirements in paragraphs (b) and (c) of this section, an application for a license or amendment for medical use of byproduct material as described in § 35.1000 must also include information regarding any radiation safety aspects of the medical use of the material that is not addressed in Subparts A through C of this part.

(1) The applicant shall also provide specific information on—

(i) Radiation safety precautions and instructions;

(ii) Methodology for measurement of dosages or doses to be administered to patients or human research subjects; and

(iii) Calibration, maintenance, and repair of instruments and equipment necessary for radiation safety.

(2) The applicant or licensee shall also provide any other information requested by the Commission in its review of the application.

(e) An applicant that satisfies the requirements specified in § 33.13 of this chapter may apply for a Type A specific license of broad scope.

[67 FR 20370, Apr. 24, 2002; 67 FR 62872, Oct. 9, 2002]

§ 35.13 License amendments.

A licensee shall apply for and must receive a license amendment—

(a) Before it receives, prepares, or uses byproduct material for a type of use that is permitted under this part, but is not authorized on the licensee's current license issued under this part; except that—

(1) A Government agency or a Federally recognized Indian Tribe licensee who possesses and uses accelerator-produced radioactive material or discrete sources of radium-226 may continue to use such material for medical uses permitted under this part until the date of the NRC's final licensing determination, provided that the licensee submits an amendment application on or before June 2, 2008.

(2) Except as provided in paragraph (a)(1) of this section, all other licensees who possess and use accelerator-produced radioactive material or discrete sources of radium-226 may continue to use those materials for medical uses permitted under this part until the date of the NRC's final licensing determination, provided that the person submits a medical use license amendment request within 6 months from the waiver expiration date of August 7, 2009 or within 6 months from the date of an earlier termination of the waiver as noticed by the NRC, whichever date is earlier.

(b) Before it permits anyone to work as an authorized user, authorized nuclear pharmacist, or authorized medical physicist under the license, except—

(1) For an authorized user, an individual who meets the requirements in §§ 35.59 and 35.190(a), 35.290(a), 35.390(a), 35.392(a), 35.394(a), 35.490(a), 35.590(a), and 35.690(a);

(2) For an authorized nuclear pharmacist, an individual who meets the requirements in §§ 35.55(a) and 35.59;

(3) For an authorized medical physicist, an individual who meets the requirements in §§35.51(a) and (c) and 35.59;

(4) An individual who is identified as an authorized user, an authorized nuclear pharmacist, or authorized medical physicist—

(i) On a Commission or Agreement State license or other equivalent permit or license recognized by NRC that authorizes the use of byproduct material in medical use or in the practice of nuclear pharmacy;

(ii) On a permit issued by a Commission or Agreement State specific license of broad scope that is authorized to permit the use of byproduct material in medical use or in the practice of nuclear pharmacy;

(iii) On a permit issued by a Commission master material licensee that is authorized to permit the use of byproduct material in medical use or in the practice of nuclear pharmacy; or

(iv) By a commercial nuclear pharmacy that has been authorized to identify authorized nuclear pharmacists.

(5) A physician, podiatrist, or dentist who used only accelerator-produced radioactive materials, discrete sources of radium-226, or both, for medical uses or a nuclear pharmacist who used only accelerator-produced radioactive materials in the practice of nuclear pharmacy at a Government agency or Federally recognized Indian Tribe before November 30, 2007 or at all other locations of use before August 8, 2009, or an earlier date as noticed by the NRC, and for only those materials and uses performed before these dates.

(c) Before it changes Radiation Safety Officers, except as provided in §35.24(c);

(d) Before it receives byproduct material in excess of the amount or in a different form, or receives a different radionuclide than is authorized on the license;

(e) Before it adds to or changes the areas of use identified in the application or on the license, including areas used in accordance with either §35.100 or §35.200 if the change includes addition or relocation of either an area where PET radionuclides are produced or a PET radioactive drug delivery line from the PET radionuclide/PET radioactive drug production area. Other areas of use where byproduct material is used only in accordance with either §35.100 or §35.200 are exempt;

(f) Before it changes the address(es) of use identified in the application or on the license; and

(g) Before it revises procedures required by §§35.610, 35.642, 35.643, and 35.645, as applicable, where such revision reduces radiation safety.

[67 FR 20370, Apr. 24, 2002, as amended at 71 FR 15008, Mar. 27, 2006; 72 FR 55930, Oct. 1, 2007]

§35.14 Notifications.

(a) A licensee shall provide the Commission a copy of the board certification and the written attestation(s), signed by a preceptor, the Commission or Agreement State license, the permit issued by a Commission master material licensee, the permit issued by a Commission or Agreement State licensee of broad scope, the permit issued by a Commission master material license broad scope permittee, or documentation that only accelerator-produced radioactive materials, discrete sources of radium-226, or both, were used for medical use or in the practice of nuclear pharmacy at a Government agency or Federally recognized Indian Tribe before November 30, 2007 or at all other locations of use before August 8, 2009, or an earlier date as noticed by the NRC, and for each individual no later than 30 days after the date that the licensee permits the individual to work as an authorized user, an authorized nuclear pharmacist, or an authorized medical physicist, under §35.13(b). For individuals permitted to work under §35.13(b)(4), within the same 30-day time frame, the licensee shall also provide, as appropriate, verification of completion of;

(1) Any additional case experience required in §35.390(b)(1)(ii)(G) for an authorized user under §35.300;

(2) Any additional training required in §35.690(c) for an authorized user under §35.600; and

(3) Any additional training required in §35.51(c) for an authorized medical physicist.

(b) A licensee shall notify the Commission no later than 30 days after:

(1) An authorized user, an authorized nuclear pharmacist, a Radiation Safety Officer, or an authorized medical physicist permanently discontinues performance of duties under the license or has a name change;

(2) The licensee permits an authorized user or an individual qualified to be a Radiation Safety Officer, under §§ 35.50 and 35.59, to function as a temporary Radiation Safety Officer and to perform the functions of a Radiation Safety Officer in accordance with § 35.24(c).

(3) The licensee's mailing address changes;

(4) The licensee's name changes, but the name change does not constitute a transfer of control of the license as described in § 30.34(b) of this chapter; or

(5) The licensee has added to or changed the areas of use identified in the application or on the license where byproduct material is used in accordance with either § 35.100 or § 35.200 if the change does not include addition or relocation of either an area where PET radionuclides are produced or a PET radioactive drug delivery line from the PET radionuclide/PET radioactive drug production area.

(c) The licensee shall send the documents required in this section to the appropriate address identified in § 30.6 of this chapter.

[67 FR 20370, Apr. 24, 2002, as amended at 68 FR 58805, Oct. 10, 2003; 70 FR 16361, Mar. 30, 2005; 71 FR 15008, Mar. 27, 2006; 72 FR 55931, Oct. 1, 2007]

§ 35.15 Exemptions regarding Type A specific licenses of broad scope.

A licensee possessing a Type A specific license of broad scope for medical use, issued under Part 33 of this chapter, is exempt from—

(a) The provisions of § 35.12(d) regarding the need to file an amendment to the license for medical use of byproduct material, as described in § 35.1000;

(b) The provisions of § 35.13(b);

(c) The provisions of § 35.13(e) regarding additions to or changes in the areas of use at the addresses identified in the application or on the license;

(d) The provisions of § 35.14(a);

(e) The provisions of § 35.14(b)(1) for an authorized user, an authorized nuclear pharmacist, or an authorized medical physicist;

(f) The provisions of § 35.14(b)(5).

(g) The provisions of § 35.49(a).

[67 FR 20370, Apr. 24, 2002, as amended at 72 FR 55931, Oct. 1, 2007]

§ 35.18 License issuance.

(a) The Commission shall issue a license for the medical use of byproduct material if—

(1) The applicant has filed NRC Form 313 "Application for Material License" in accordance with the instructions in § 35.12;

(2) The applicant has paid any applicable fee as provided in Part 170 of this chapter;

(3) The Commission finds the applicant equipped and committed to observe the safety standards established by the Commission in this Chapter for the protection of the public health and safety; and

(4) The applicant meets the requirements of Part 30 of this chapter.

(b) The Commission shall issue a license for mobile medical service if the applicant:

(1) Meets the requirements in paragraph (a) of this section; and

(2) Assures that individuals or human research subjects to whom unsealed byproduct material or radiation from implants containing byproduct material will be administered may be released following treatment in accordance with § 35.75.

§ 35.19 Specific exemptions.

The Commission may, upon application of any interested person or upon its own initiative, grant exemptions from the regulations in this part that it determines are authorized by law and will not endanger life or property or the common defense and security and are otherwise in the public interest.

Subpart B—General Administrative Requirements

§ 35.24 Authority and responsibilities for the radiation protection program.

(a) In addition to the radiation protection program requirements of

§20.1101 of this chapter, a licensee's management shall approve in writing—

(1) Requests for a license application, renewal, or amendment before submittal to the Commission;

(2) Any individual before allowing that individual to work as an authorized user, authorized nuclear pharmacist, or authorized medical physicist; and

(3) Radiation protection program changes that do not require a license amendment and are permitted under §35.26;

(b) A licensee's management shall appoint a Radiation Safety Officer, who agrees, in writing, to be responsible for implementing the radiation protection program. The licensee, through the Radiation Safety Officer, shall ensure that radiation safety activities are being performed in accordance with licensee-approved procedures and regulatory requirements.

(c) For up to 60 days each year, a licensee may permit an authorized user or an individual qualified to be a Radiation Safety Officer, under §§35.50 and 35.59, to function as a temporary Radiation Safety Officer and to perform the functions of a Radiation Safety Officer, as provided in paragraph (g) of this section, if the licensee takes the actions required in paragraphs (b), (e), (g), and (h) of this section and notifies the Commission in accordance with §35.14(b).

(d) A licensee may simultaneously appoint more than one temporary Radiation Safety Officer in accordance with paragraph (c) of this section, if needed to ensure that the licensee has a temporary Radiation Safety Officer that satisfies the requirements to be a Radiation Safety Officer for each of the different types of uses of byproduct material permitted by the license.

(e) A licensee shall establish the authority, duties, and responsibilities of the Radiation Safety Officer in writing.

(f) Licensees that are authorized for two or more different types of uses of byproduct material under Subparts E, F, and H of this part, or two or more types of units under Subpart H of this part, shall establish a Radiation Safety Committee to oversee all uses of byproduct material permitted by the license. The Committee must include an authorized user of each type of use permitted by the license, the Radiation Safety Officer, a representative of the nursing service, and a representative of management who is neither an authorized user nor a Radiation Safety Officer. The Committee may include other members the licensee considers appropriate.

(g) A licensee shall provide the Radiation Safety Officer sufficient authority, organizational freedom, time, resources, and management prerogative, to—

(1) Identify radiation safety problems;

(2) Initiate, recommend, or provide corrective actions;

(3) Stop unsafe operations; and,

(4) Verify implementation of corrective actions.

(h) A licensee shall retain a record of actions taken under paragraphs (a), (b), and (e) of this section in accordance with §35.2024.

§35.26 Radiation protection program changes.

(a) A licensee may revise its radiation protection program without Commission approval if—

(1) The revision does not require a license amendment under §35.13;

(2) The revision is in compliance with the regulations and the license ;

(3) The revision has been reviewed and approved by the Radiation Safety Officer and licensee management; and

(4) The affected individuals are instructed on the revised program before the changes are implemented.

(b) A licensee shall retain a record of each change in accordance with §35.2026.

§35.27 Supervision.

(a) A licensee that permits the receipt, possession, use, or transfer of byproduct material by an individual under the supervision of an authorized user, as allowed by §35.11(b)(1), shall—

(1) In addition to the requirements in §19.12 of this chapter, instruct the supervised individual in the licensee's written radiation protection procedures, written directive procedures, regulations of this chapter, and license conditions with respect to the use of byproduct material; and

(2) Require the supervised individual to follow the instructions of the supervising authorized user for medical uses of byproduct material, written radiation protection procedures established by the licensee, written directive procedures, regulations of this chapter, and license conditions with respect to the medical use of byproduct material.

(b) A licensee that permits the preparation of byproduct material for medical use by an individual under the supervision of an authorized nuclear pharmacist or physician who is an authorized user, as allowed by § 35.11(b)(2), shall—

(1) In addition to the requirements in § 19.12 of this chapter, instruct the supervised individual in the preparation of byproduct material for medical use, as appropriate to that individual's involvement with byproduct material; and

(2) Require the supervised individual to follow the instructions of the supervising authorized user or authorized nuclear pharmacist regarding the preparation of byproduct material for medical use, written radiation protection procedures established by the licensee, the regulations of this chapter, and license conditions.

(c) A licensee that permits supervised activities under paragraphs (a) and (b) of this section is responsible for the acts and omissions of the supervised individual.

§ 35.40 Written directives.

(a) A written directive must be dated and signed by an authorized user before the administration of I-131 sodium iodide greater than 1.11 megabecquerels (MBq) (30 microcuries (μCi)), any therapeutic dosage of unsealed byproduct material or any therapeutic dose of radiation from byproduct material.

(1) If, because of the emergent nature of the patient's condition, a delay in order to provide a written directive would jeopardize the patient's health, an oral directive is acceptable. The information contained in the oral directive must be documented as soon as possible in writing in the patient's record. A written directive must be prepared within 48 hours of the oral directive.

(b) The written directive must contain the patient or human research subject's name and the following information—

(1) For any administration of quantities greater than 1.11 MBq (30 μCi) of sodium iodide I-131: the dosage;

(2) For an administration of a therapeutic dosage of unsealed byproduct material other than sodium iodide I-131: the radioactive drug, dosage, and route of administration;

(3) For gamma stereotactic radiosurgery: the total dose, treatment site, and values for the target coordinate settings per treatment for each anatomically distinct treatment site;

(4) For teletherapy: the total dose, dose per fraction, number of fractions, and treatment site;

(5) For high dose-rate remote afterloading brachytherapy: the radionuclide, treatment site, dose per fraction, number of fractions, and total dose; or

(6) For all other brachytherapy, including low, medium, and pulsed dose rate remote afterloaders:

(i) Before implantation: treatment site, the radionuclide, and dose; and

(ii) After implantation but before completion of the procedure: the radionuclide, treatment site, number of sources, and total source strength and exposure time (or the total dose).

(c) A written revision to an existing written directive may be made if the revision is dated and signed by an authorized user before the administration of the dosage of unsealed byproduct material, the brachytherapy dose, the gamma stereotactic radiosurgery dose, the teletherapy dose, or the next fractional dose.

(1) If, because of the patient's condition, a delay in order to provide a written revision to an existing written directive would jeopardize the patient's health, an oral revision to an existing written directive is acceptable. The oral revision must be documented as soon as possible in the patient's record. A revised written directive must be signed by the authorized user within 48 hours of the oral revision.

(d) The licensee shall retain a copy of the written directive in accordance with § 35.2040.

[67 FR 20370, Apr. 24, 2002; 67 FR 62872, Oct. 9, 2002; 68 FR 75389, Dec. 31, 2003]

§ 35.41 Procedures for administrations requiring a written directive.

(a) For any administration requiring a written directive, the licensee shall develop, implement, and maintain written procedures to provide high confidence that:

(1) The patient's or human research subject's identity is verified before each administration; and

(2) Each administration is in accordance with the written directive.

(b) At a minimum, the procedures required by paragraph (a) of this section must address the following items that are applicable to the licensee's use of byproduct material—

(1) Verifying the identity of the patient or human research subject;

(2) Verifying that the administration is in accordance with the treatment plan, if applicable, and the written directive;

(3) Checking both manual and computer-generated dose calculations; and

(4) Verifying that any computer-generated dose calculations are correctly transferred into the consoles of therapeutic medical units authorized by §§ 35.600 or 35.1000.

(c) A licensee shall retain a copy of the procedures required under paragraph (a) in accordance with § 35.2041.

[67 FR 20370, Apr. 24, 2002, as amended at 72 FR 45151, Aug. 13, 2007]

§ 35.49 Suppliers for sealed sources or devices for medical use.

For medical use, a licensee may only use—

(a) Sealed sources or devices manufactured, labeled, packaged, and distributed in accordance with a license issued under 10 CFR Part 30 and 10 CFR 32.74 of this chapter or equivalent requirements of an Agreement State;

(b) Sealed sources or devices noncommercially transferred from a Part 35 licensee or an Agreement State medical use licensee.

(c) Teletherapy sources manufactured and distributed in accordance with a license issued under 10 CFR Part 30 or the equivalent requirements of an Agreement State.

[67 FR 20370, Apr. 24, 2002, as amended at 71 FR 15008, Mar. 27, 2006]

§ 35.50 Training for Radiation Safety Officer.

Except as provided in § 35.57, the licensee shall require an individual fulfilling the responsibilities of the Radiation Safety Officer as provided in § 35.24 to be an individual who—

(a) Is certified by a specialty board whose certification process has been recognized by the Commission or an Agreement State and who meets the requirements in paragraphs (d) and (e) of this section. (The names of board certifications which have been recognized by the Commission or an Agreement State will be posted on the NRC's Web page.) To have its certification process recognized, a specialty board shall require all candidates for certification to:

(1)(i) Hold a bachelor's or graduate degree from an accredited college or university in physical science or engineering or biological science with a minimum of 20 college credits in physical science;

(ii) Have 5 or more years of professional experience in health physics (graduate training may be substituted for no more than 2 years of the required experience) including at least 3 years in applied health physics; and

(iii) Pass an examination administered by diplomates of the specialty board, which evaluates knowledge and competence in radiation physics and instrumentation, radiation protection, mathematics pertaining to the use and measurement of radioactivity, radiation biology, and radiation dosimetry; or

(2)(i) Hold a master's or doctor's degree in physics, medical physics, other physical science, engineering, or applied mathematics from an accredited college or university;

(ii) Have 2 years of full-time practical training and/or supervised experience in medical physics—

(A) Under the supervision of a medical physicist who is certified in medical physics by a specialty board recognized by the Commission or an Agreement State; or

(B) In clinical nuclear medicine facilities providing diagnostic and/or therapeutic services under the direction of physicians who meet the requirements for authorized users in §§ 35.57, 35.290, or 35.390; and

(iii) Pass an examination, administered by diplomates of the specialty board, that assesses knowledge and competence in clinical diagnostic radiological or nuclear medicine physics and in radiation safety; or

(b)(1) Has completed a structured educational program consisting of both:

(i) 200 hours of classroom and laboratory training in the following areas—

(A) Radiation physics and instrumentation;

(B) Radiation protection;

(C) Mathematics pertaining to the use and measurement of radioactivity;

(D) Radiation biology; and

(E) Radiation dosimetry; and

(ii) One year of full-time radiation safety experience under the supervision of the individual identified as the Radiation Safety Officer on a Commission or Agreement State license or permit issued by a Commission master material licensee that authorizes similar type(s) of use(s) of byproduct material involving the following—

(A) Shipping, receiving, and performing related radiation surveys;

(B) Using and performing checks for proper operation of instruments used to determine the activity of dosages, survey meters, and instruments used to measure radionuclides;

(C) Securing and controlling byproduct material;

(D) Using administrative controls to avoid mistakes in the administration of byproduct material;

(E) Using procedures to prevent or minimize radioactive contamination and using proper decontamination procedures;

(F) Using emergency procedures to control byproduct material; and

(G) Disposing of byproduct material; or

(2) [Reserved]

(c)(1) Is a medical physicist who has been certified by a specialty board whose certification process has been recognized by the Commission or an Agreement State under § 35.51(a) and has experience in radiation safety for similar types of use of byproduct material for which the licensee is seeking the approval of the individual as Radiation Safety Officer and who meets the requirements in paragraphs (d) and (e) of this section; or

(2) Is an authorized user, authorized medical physicist, or authorized nuclear pharmacist identified on the licensee's license and has experience with the radiation safety aspects of similar types of use of byproduct material for which the individual has Radiation Safety Officer responsibilities; and,

(d) Has obtained written attestation, signed by a preceptor Radiation Safety Officer, that the individual has satisfactorily completed the requirements in paragraph (e) and in paragraphs (a)(1)(i) and (a)(1)(ii) or (a)(2)(i) and (a)(2)(ii) or (b)(1) or (c)(1) or (c)(2) of this section, and has achieved a level of radiation safety knowledge sufficient to function independently as a Radiation Safety Officer for a medical use licensee; and

(e) Has training in the radiation safety, regulatory issues, and emergency procedures for the types of use for which a licensee seeks approval. This training requirement may be satisfied by completing training that is supervised by a Radiation Safety Officer, authorized medical physicist, authorized nuclear pharmacist, or authorized user, as appropriate, who is authorized for the type(s) of use for which the licensee is seeking approval.

[67 FR 20370, Apr. 24, 2002, as amended at 70 FR 16361, Mar. 30, 2005; 71 FR 1926, Jan. 12, 2006; 71 FR 15008, Mar. 27, 2006; 74 FR 33904, July 14, 2009; 76 FR 72085, Nov. 22, 2011]

§ 35.51 Training for an authorized medical physicist.

Except as provided in § 35.57, the licensee shall require the authorized medical physicist to be an individual who—

(a) Is certified by a specialty board whose certification process has been recognized by the Commission or an Agreement State and who meets the requirements in paragraphs (b)(2) and (c) of this section. (The names of board certifications which have been recognized by the Commission or an Agreement State will be posted on the NRC's Web page.) To have its certification process recognized, a specialty board shall require all candidates for certification to:

(1) Hold a master's or doctor's degree in physics, medical physics, other physical science, engineering, or applied mathematics from an accredited college or university;

(2) Have 2 years of full-time practical training and/or supervised experience in medical physics—

(i) Under the supervision of a medical physicist who is certified in medical physics by a specialty board recognized by the Commission or an Agreement State; or

(ii) In clinical radiation facilities providing high-energy, external beam therapy (photons and electrons with energies greater than or equal to 1 million electron volts) and brachytherapy services under the direction of physicians who meet the requirements in §35.57, 35.490, or 35.690; and

(3) Pass an examination, administered by diplomates of the specialty board, that assesses knowledge and competence in clinical radiation therapy, radiation safety, calibration, quality assurance, and treatment planning for external beam therapy, brachytherapy, and stereotactic radiosurgery; or

(b)(1) Holds a master's or doctor's degree in physics, medical physics, other physical science, engineering, or applied mathematics from an accredited college or university; and has completed 1 year of full-time training in medical physics and an additional year of full-time work experience under the supervision of an individual who meets the requirements for an authorized medical physicist for the type(s) of use for which the individual is seeking authorization. This training and work experience must be conducted in clinical radiation facilities that provide high-energy, external beam therapy (photons and electrons with energies greater than or equal to 1 million electron volts) and brachytherapy services and must include:

(i) Performing sealed source leak tests and inventories;

(ii) Performing decay corrections;

(iii) Performing full calibration and periodic spot checks of external beam treatment units, stereotactic radiosurgery units, and remote afterloading units as applicable; and

(iv) Conducting radiation surveys around external beam treatment units, stereotactic radiosurgery units, and remote afterloading units as applicable; and

(2) Has obtained written attestation that the individual has satisfactorily completed the requirements in paragraphs (c) and (a)(1) and (a)(2), or (b)(1) and (c) of this section, and has achieved a level of competency sufficient to function independently as an authorized medical physicist for each type of therapeutic medical unit for which the individual is requesting authorized medical physicist status. The written attestation must be signed by a preceptor authorized medical physicist who meets the requirements in §§35.51, 35.57, or equivalent Agreement State requirements for an authorized medical physicist for each type of therapeutic medical unit for which the individual is requesting authorized medical physicist status; and

(c) Has training for the type(s) of use for which authorization is sought that includes hands-on device operation, safety procedures, clinical use, and the operation of a treatment planning system. This training requirement may be satisfied by satisfactorily completing either a training program provided by the vendor or by training supervised by an authorized medical physicist authorized for the type(s) of use for which the individual is seeking authorization.

[67 FR 20370, Apr. 24, 2002; 67 FR 62872, Oct. 9, 2002, as amended at 70 FR 16362, Mar. 30, 2005; 71 FR 15008, Mar. 27, 2006; 74 FR 33904, July 14, 2009]

§ 35.55 Training for an authorized nuclear pharmacist.

Except as provided in §35.57, the licensee shall require the authorized nuclear pharmacist to be a pharmacist who—

(a) Is certified by a specialty board whose certification process has been recognized by the Commission or an Agreement State and who meets the requirements in paragraph (b)(2) of this section. (The names of board certifications which have been recognized by the Commission or an Agreement State will be posted on the NRC's Web page.) To have its certification process recognized, a specialty board shall require all candidates for certification to:

(1) Have graduated from a pharmacy program accredited by the American Council on Pharmaceutical Education (ACPE) or have passed the Foreign Pharmacy Graduate Examination Committee (FPGEC) examination;

(2) Hold a current, active license to practice pharmacy;

(3) Provide evidence of having acquired at least 4000 hours of training/experience in nuclear pharmacy practice. Academic training may be substituted for no more than 2000 hours of the required training and experience; and

(4) Pass an examination in nuclear pharmacy administered by diplomates of the specialty board, that assesses knowledge and competency in procurement, compounding, quality assurance, dispensing, distribution, health and safety, radiation safety, provision of information and consultation, monitoring patient outcomes, research and development; or

(b)(1) Has completed 700 hours in a structured educational program consisting of both:

(i) 200 hours of classroom and laboratory training in the following areas—

(A) Radiation physics and instrumentation;

(B) Radiation protection;

(C) Mathematics pertaining to the use and measurement of radioactivity;

(D) Chemistry of byproduct material for medical use; and

(E) Radiation biology; and

(ii) Supervised practical experience in a nuclear pharmacy involving—

(A) Shipping, receiving, and performing related radiation surveys;

(B) Using and performing checks for proper operation of instruments used to determine the activity of dosages, survey meters, and, if appropriate, instruments used to measure alpha- or beta-emitting radionuclides;

(C) Calculating, assaying, and safely preparing dosages for patients or human research subjects;

(D) Using administrative controls to avoid medical events in the administration of byproduct material; and

(E) Using procedures to prevent or minimize radioactive contamination and using proper decontamination procedures; and

(2) Has obtained written attestation, signed by a preceptor authorized nuclear pharmacist, that the individual has satisfactorily completed the requirements in paragraphs (a)(1), (a)(2), and (a)(3) or (b)(1) of this section and has achieved a level of competency sufficient to function independently as an authorized nuclear pharmacist.

[67 FR 20370, Apr. 24, 2002, as amended at 70 FR 16362, Mar. 30, 2005]

§ 35.57 Training for experienced Radiation Safety Officer, teletherapy or medical physicist, authorized medical physicist, authorized user, nuclear pharmacist, and authorized nuclear pharmacist.

(a)(1) An individual identified as a Radiation Safety Officer, a teletherapy or medical physicist, or a nuclear pharmacist on a Commission or Agreement State license or a permit issued by a Commission or Agreement State broad scope licensee or master material license permit or by a master material license permittee of broad scope before October 24, 2002, need not comply with the training requirements of §§ 35.50, 35.51, or 35.55, respectively.

(2) An individual identified as a Radiation Safety Officer, an authorized medical physicist, or an authorized nuclear pharmacist on a Commission or Agreement State license or a permit issued by a Commission or Agreement State broad scope licensee or master material license permit or by a master material license permittee of broad scope between October 24, 2002 and April 29, 2005 need not comply with the training requirements of §§ 35.50, 35.51, or 35.55, respectively.

(3) A Radiation Safety Officer, a medical physicist, or a nuclear pharmacist, who used only accelerator-produced radioactive materials, discrete sources of radium-226, or both, for medical uses or in the practice of nuclear pharmacy at a Government agency or Federally recognized Indian Tribe before November 30, 2007 or at all other locations of use

before August 8, 2009, or an earlier date as noticed by the NRC, need not comply with the training requirements of § 35.50, § 35.51 or § 35.55, respectively, when performing the same uses. A nuclear pharmacist, who prepared only radioactive drugs containing accelerator-produced radioactive materials, or a medical physicist, who used only accelerator-produced radioactive materials, at the locations and time period identified in this paragraph, qualifies as an authorized nuclear pharmacist or an authorized medical physicist, respectively, for those materials and uses performed before these dates, for purposes of this chapter.

(b)(1) Physicians, dentists, or podiatrists identified as authorized users for the medical use of byproduct material on a license issued by the Commission or Agreement State, a permit issued by a Commission master material licensee, a permit issued by a Commission or Agreement State broad scope licensee, or a permit issued by a Commission master material license broad scope permittee before October 24, 2002, who perform only those medical uses for which they were authorized on that date need not comply with the training requirements of Subparts D through H of this part.

(2) Physicians, dentists, or podiatrists identified as authorized users for the medical use of byproduct material on a license issued by the Commission or Agreement State, a permit issued by a Commission master material licensee, a permit issued by a Commission or Agreement State broad scope licensee, or a permit issued by a Commission master material license broad scope permittee who perform only those medical uses for which they were authorized between October 24, 2002 and April 29, 2005, need not comply with the training requirements of Subparts D through H of this part.

(3) Physicians, dentists, or podiatrists who used only accelerator-produced radioactive materials, discrete sources of radium-226, or both, for medical uses performed at a Government agency or Federally recognized Indian Tribe before November 30, 2007 or at all other locations of use before August 8, 2009, or an earlier date as noticed by the NRC, need not comply with the training requirements of subparts D through H of this part when performing the same medical uses. A physician, dentist, or podiatrist, who used only accelerator-produced radioactive materials, discrete sources of radium-226, or both, for medical uses at the locations and time period identified in this paragraph, qualifies as an authorized user for those materials and uses performed before these dates, for purposes of this chapter.

(c) Individuals who need not comply with training requirements as described in this section may serve as preceptors for, and supervisors of, applicants seeking authorization on NRC licenses for the same uses for which these individuals are authorized.

[70 FR 16363, Mar. 30, 2005, as amended at 72 FR 55931, Oct. 1, 2007; 74 FR 33905, July 14, 2009]

§ 35.59 Recentness of training.

The training and experience specified in Subparts B, D, E, F, G, and H of this part must have been obtained within the 7 years preceding the date of application or the individual must have had related continuing education and experience since the required training and experience was completed.

[71 FR 15008, Mar. 27, 2006]

Subpart C—General Technical Requirements

§ 35.60 Possession, use, and calibration of instruments used to measure the activity of unsealed byproduct material.

(a) For direct measurements performed in accordance with § 35.63, a licensee shall possess and use instrumentation to measure the activity of unsealed byproduct material before it is administered to each patient or human research subject.

(b) A licensee shall calibrate the instrumentation required in paragraph (a) of this section in accordance with nationally recognized standards or the manufacturer's instructions.

(c) A licensee shall retain a record of each instrument calibration required by this section in accordance with § 35.2060.

§ 35.61 Calibration of survey instruments.

(a) A licensee shall calibrate the survey instruments used to show compliance with this part and 10 CFR Part 20 before first use, annually, and following a repair that affects the calibration. A licensee shall—

(1) Calibrate all scales with readings up to 10 mSv (1000 mrem) per hour with a radiation source;

(2) Calibrate two separated readings on each scale or decade that will be used to show compliance; and

(3) Conspicuously note on the instrument the date of calibration.

(b) A licensee may not use survey instruments if the difference between the indicated exposure rate and the calculated exposure rate is more than 20 percent.

(c) A licensee shall retain a record of each survey instrument calibration in accordance with § 35.2061.

§ 35.63 Determination of dosages of unsealed byproduct material for medical use.

(a) A licensee shall determine and record the activity of each dosage before medical use.

(b) For a unit dosage, this determination must be made by—

(1) Direct measurement of radioactivity; or

(2) A decay correction, based on the activity or activity concentration determined by—

(i) A manufacturer or preparer licensed under § 32.72 of this chapter or equivalent Agreement State requirements; or

(ii) An NRC or Agreement State licensee for use in research in accordance with a Radioactive Drug Research Committee-approved protocol or an Investigational New Drug (IND) protocol accepted by FDA; or

(iii) A PET radioactive drug producer licensed under § 30.32(j) of this chapter or equivalent Agreement State requirements.

(c) For other than unit dosages, this determination must be made by—

(1) Direct measurement of radioactivity;

(2) Combination of measurement of radioactivity and mathematical calculations; or

(3) Combination of volumetric measurements and mathematical calculations, based on the measurement made by:

(i) A manufacturer or preparer licensed under § 32.72 of this chapter or equivalent Agreement State requirements; or

(ii) A PET radioactive drug producer licensed under § 30.32(j) of this chapter or equivalent Agreement State requirements.

(d) Unless otherwise directed by the authorized user, a licensee may not use a dosage if the dosage does not fall within the prescribed dosage range or if the dosage differs from the prescribed dosage by more than 20 percent.

(e) A licensee shall retain a record of the dosage determination required by this section in accordance with § 35.2063.

[67 FR 20370, Apr. 24, 2002, as amended at 72 FR 55931, Oct. 1, 2007]

§ 35.65 Authorization for calibration, transmission, and reference sources.

Any person authorized by § 35.11 for medical use of byproduct material may receive, possess, and use any of the following byproduct material for check, calibration, transmission, and reference use.

(a) Sealed sources, not exceeding 1.11 GBq (30 mCi) each, manufactured and distributed by a person licensed under § 32.74 of this chapter or equivalent Agreement State regulations.

(b) Sealed sources, not exceeding 1.11 GBq (30 mCi) each, redistributed by a licensee authorized to redistribute the sealed sources manufactured and distributed by a person licensed under § 32.74 of this chapter or equivalent Agreement State regulations, providing the redistributed sealed sources are in the original packaging and shielding and are accompanied by the manufacturer's approved instructions.

(c) Any byproduct material with a half-life not longer than 120 days in individual amounts not to exceed 0.56 GBq (15 mCi).

(d) Any byproduct material with a half-life longer than 120 days in individual amounts not to exceed the smaller of 7.4 MBq (200 μCi) or 1000 times the quantities in Appendix B of Part 30 of this chapter.

(e) Technetium-99m in amounts as needed.

[67 FR 20370, Apr. 24, 2002, as amended at 71 FR 15009, Mar. 27, 2006]

§ 35.67 Requirements for possession of sealed sources and brachytherapy sources.

(a) A licensee in possession of any sealed source or brachytherapy source shall follow the radiation safety and handling instructions supplied by the manufacturer.

(b) A licensee in possession of a sealed source shall—

(1) Test the source for leakage before its first use unless the licensee has a certificate from the supplier indicating that the source was tested within 6 months before transfer to the licensee; and

(2) Test the source for leakage at intervals not to exceed 6 months or at other intervals approved by the Commission or an Agreement State in the Sealed Source and Device Registry.

(c) To satisfy the leak test requirements of this section, the licensee shall measure the sample so that the leak test can detect the presence of 185 Bq (0.005 μCi) of radioactive material in the sample.

(d) A licensee shall retain leak test records in accordance with § 35.2067(a).

(e) If the leak test reveals the presence of 185 Bq (0.005 μCi) or more of removable contamination, the licensee shall—

(1) Immediately withdraw the sealed source from use and store, dispose, or cause it to be repaired in accordance with the requirements in parts 20 and 30 of this chapter; and

(2) File a report within 5 days of the leak test in accordance with § 35.3067.

(f) A licensee need not perform a leak test on the following sources:

(1) Sources containing only byproduct material with a half-life of less than 30 days;

(2) Sources containing only byproduct material as a gas;

(3) Sources containing 3.7 MBq (100 μCi) or less of beta or gamma-emitting material or 0.37 MBq (10 μCi) or less of alpha-emitting material;

(4) Seeds of iridium-192 encased in nylon ribbon; and

(5) Sources stored and not being used. However, the licensee shall test each such source for leakage before any use or transfer unless it has been leak tested within 6 months before the date of use or transfer.

(g) A licensee in possession of sealed sources or brachytherapy sources, except for gamma stereotactic radiosurgery sources, shall conduct a semi-annual physical inventory of all such sources in its possession. The licensee shall retain each inventory record in accordance with § 35.2067(b).

§ 35.69 Labeling of vials and syringes.

Each syringe and vial that contains unsealed byproduct material must be labeled to identify the radioactive drug. Each syringe shield and vial shield must also be labeled unless the label on the syringe or vial is visible when shielded.

§ 35.70 Surveys of ambient radiation exposure rate.

(a) In addition to the surveys required by Part 20 of this chapter, a licensee shall survey with a radiation detection survey instrument at the end of each day of use. A licensee shall survey all areas where unsealed byproduct material requiring a written directive was prepared for use or administered.

(b) A licensee does not need to perform the surveys required by paragraph (a) of this section in an area(s) where patients or human research subjects are confined when they cannot be released under § 35.75.

(c) A licensee shall retain a record of each survey in accordance with § 35.2070.

§ 35.75 Release of individuals containing unsealed byproduct material or implants containing byproduct material.

(a) A licensee may authorize the release from its control of any individual who has been administered unsealed byproduct material or implants containing byproduct material if the total effective dose equivalent to any other individual from exposure to the released individual is not likely to exceed 5 mSv (0.5 rem).[1]

(b) A licensee shall provide the released individual, or the individual's parent or guardian, with instructions, including written instructions, on actions recommended to maintain doses to other individuals as low as is reasonably achievable if the total effective dose equivalent to any other individual is likely to exceed 1 mSv (0.1 rem). If the total effective dose equivalent to a nursing infant or child could exceed 1 mSv (0.1 rem) assuming there were no interruption of breast-feeding, the instructions must also include—

(1) Guidance on the interruption or discontinuation of breast-feeding; and

(2) Information on the potential consequences, if any, of failure to follow the guidance.

(c) A licensee shall maintain a record of the basis for authorizing the release of an individual in accordance with §35.2075(a).

(d) The licensee shall maintain a record of instructions provided to a breast-feeding female in accordance with §35.2075(b).

[67 FR 20370, Apr. 24, 2002, as amended at 70 FR 16363, Mar. 30, 2005; 72 FR 45151, Aug. 13, 2007]

§35.80 Provision of mobile medical service.

(a) A licensee providing mobile medical service shall—

(1) Obtain a letter signed by the management of each client for which services are rendered that permits the use of byproduct material at the client's address and clearly delineates the authority and responsibility of the licensee and the client;

(2) Check instruments used to measure the activity of unsealed byproduct material for proper function before medical use at each client's address or on each day of use, whichever is more frequent. At a minimum, the check for proper function required by this paragraph must include a constancy check;

(3) Check survey instruments for proper operation with a dedicated check source before use at each client's address; and

(4) Before leaving a client's address, survey all areas of use to ensure compliance with the requirements in Part 20 of this chapter.

(b) A mobile medical service may not have byproduct material delivered from the manufacturer or the distributor to the client unless the client has a license allowing possession of the byproduct material. Byproduct material delivered to the client must be received and handled in conformance with the client's license.

(c) A licensee providing mobile medical services shall retain the letter required in paragraph (a)(1) and the record of each survey required in paragraph (a)(4) of this section in accordance with §35.2080(a) and (b), respectively.

§35.92 Decay-in-storage.

(a) A licensee may hold byproduct material with a physical half-life of less than or equal to 120 days for decay-in-storage before disposal without regard to its radioactivity if it—

(1) Monitors byproduct material at the surface before disposal and determines that its radioactivity cannot be distinguished from the background radiation level with an appropriate radiation detection survey meter set on its most sensitive scale and with no interposed shielding; and

(2) Removes or obliterates all radiation labels, except for radiation labels on materials that are within containers and that will be managed as biomedical waste after they have been released from the licensee.

(b) A licensee shall retain a record of each disposal permitted under paragraph (a) of this section in accordance with §35.2092.

[67 FR 20370, Apr. 24, 2002, as amended at 72 FR 45151, Aug. 13, 2007]

[1] The current revision of NUREG–1556, Vol. 9, "Consolidated Guidance About Materials Licenses: Program-Specific Guidance About Medical Licenses" describes methods for calculating doses to other individuals and contains tables of activities not likely to cause doses exceeding 5 mSv (0.5 rem).

Subpart D—Unsealed Byproduct Material—Written Directive Not Required

§ 35.100 Use of unsealed byproduct material for uptake, dilution, and excretion studies for which a written directive is not required.

Except for quantities that require a written directive under § 35.40(b), a licensee may use any unsealed byproduct material prepared for medical use for uptake, dilution, or excretion studies that is—

(a) Obtained from:

(1) A manufacturer or preparer licensed under § 32.72 of this chapter or equivalent Agreement State requirements; or

(2) A PET radioactive drug producer licensed under § 30.32(j) of this chapter or equivalent Agreement State requirements; or

(b) Excluding production of PET radionuclides, prepared by:

(1) An authorized nuclear pharmacist;

(2) A physician who is an authorized user and who meets the requirements specified in §§ 35.290, or 35.390 and 35.290(c)(1)(ii)(G); or

(3) An individual under the supervision, as specified in § 35.27, of the authorized nuclear pharmacist in paragraph (b)(1) of this section or the physician who is an authorized user in paragraph (b)(2) of this section; or

(c) Obtained from and prepared by an NRC or Agreement State licensee for use in research in accordance with a Radioactive Drug Research Committee-approved protocol or an Investigational New Drug (IND) protocol accepted by FDA; or

(d) Prepared by the licensee for use in research in accordance with a Radioactive Drug Research Committee-approved application or an Investigational New Drug (IND) protocol accepted by FDA.

[67 FR 20370, Apr. 24, 2002, as amended at 68 FR 19324, Apr. 21, 2003; 71 FR 15009, Mar. 27, 2006; 72 FR 55931, Oct. 1, 2007]

§ 35.190 Training for uptake, dilution, and excretion studies.

Except as provided in § 35.57, the licensee shall require an authorized user of unsealed byproduct material for the uses authorized under § 35.100 to be a physician who—

(a) Is certified by a medical specialty board whose certification process has been recognized by the Commission or an Agreement State and who meets the requirements in paragraph (c)(2) of this section. (The names of board certifications which have been recognized by the Commission or an Agreement State will be posted on the NRC's Web page.) To have its certification process recognized, a specialty board shall require all candidates for certification to:

(1) Complete 60 hours of training and experience in basic radionuclide handling techniques and radiation safety applicable to the medical use of unsealed byproduct material for uptake, dilution, and excretion studies as described in paragraphs (c)(1)(i) through (c)(1)(ii)(F) of this section; and

(2) Pass an examination, administered by diplomates of the specialty board, that assesses knowledge and competence in radiation safety, radionuclide handling, and quality control; or

(b) Is an authorized user under §§ 35.290, 35.390, or equivalent Agreement State requirements; or

(c)(1) Has completed 60 hours of training and experience, including a minimum of 8 hours of classroom and laboratory training, in basic radionuclide handling techniques applicable to the medical use of unsealed byproduct material for uptake, dilution, and excretion studies. The training and experience must include—

(i) Classroom and laboratory training in the following areas—

(A) Radiation physics and instrumentation;

(B) Radiation protection;

(C) Mathematics pertaining to the use and measurement of radioactivity;

(D) Chemistry of byproduct material for medical use; and

(E) Radiation biology; and

(ii) Work experience, under the supervision of an authorized user who meets the requirements in §§ 35.57, 35.190, 35.290, 35.390, or equivalent Agreement State requirements, involving—

(A) Ordering, receiving, and unpacking radioactive materials safely and performing the related radiation surveys;

(B) Performing quality control procedures on instruments used to determine the activity of dosages and performing checks for proper operation of survey meters;

(C) Calculating, measuring, and safely preparing patient or human research subject dosages;

(D) Using administrative controls to prevent a medical event involving the use of unsealed byproduct material;

(E) Using procedures to contain spilled byproduct material safely and using proper decontamination procedures; and

(F) Administering dosages of radioactive drugs to patients or human research subjects; and

(2) Has obtained written attestation, signed by a preceptor authorized user who meets the requirements in §§ 35.57, 35.190, 35.290, or 35.390, or equivalent Agreement State requirements, that the individual has satisfactorily completed the requirements in paragraph (a)(1) or (c)(1) of this section and has achieved a level of competency sufficient to function independently as an authorized user for the medical uses authorized under § 35.100.

[67 FR 20370, Apr. 24, 2002, as amended at 68 FR 19324, Apr. 21, 2003; 69 FR 55738, Sept. 16, 2004; 70 FR 16363, Mar. 30, 2005; 71 FR 15009, Mar. 27, 2006; 72 FR 45151, Aug. 13, 2007; 74 FR 33905, July 14, 2009]

§ 35.200 Use of unsealed byproduct material for imaging and localization studies for which a written directive is not required.

Except for quantities that require a written directive under § 35.40(b), a licensee may use any unsealed byproduct material prepared for medical use for imaging and localization studies that is—

(a) Obtained from:

(1) A manufacturer or preparer licensed under § 32.72 of this chapter or equivalent Agreement State requirements; or

(2) A PET radioactive drug producer licensed under § 30.32(j) of this chapter or equivalent Agreement State requirements; or

(b) Excluding production of PET radionuclides, prepared by:

(1) An authorized nuclear pharmacist;

(2) A physician who is an authorized user and who meets the requirements specified in § 35.290, or 35.390 and 35.290(c)(1)(ii)(G); or

(3) An individual under the supervision, as specified in § 35.27, of the authorized nuclear pharmacist in paragraph (b)(1) of this section or the physician who is an authorized user in paragraph (b)(2) of this section;

(c) Obtained from and prepared by an NRC or Agreement State licensee for use in research in accordance with a Radioactive Drug Research Committee-approved protocol or an Investigational New Drug (IND) protocol accepted by FDA; or

(d) Prepared by the licensee for use in research in accordance with a Radioactive Drug Research Committee-approved application or an Investigational New Drug (IND) protocol accepted by FDA.

[67 FR 20370, Apr. 24, 2002, as amended at 68 FR 19324, Apr. 21, 2003; 71 FR 15009, Mar. 27, 2006; 72 FR 55932, Oct. 1, 2007]

§ 35.204 Permissible molybdenum-99, strontium-82, and strontium-85 concentrations.

(a) A licensee may not administer to humans a radiopharmaceutical that contains:

(1) More than 0.15 kilobecquerel of molybdenum-99 per megabecquerel of technetium-99m (0.15 microcurie of molybdenum-99 per millicurie of technetium-99m); or

(2) More than 0.02 kilobecquerel of strontium-82 per megabecquerel of rubidium-82 chloride injection (0.02 microcurie of strontium-82 per millicurie of rubidium-82 chloride); or more than 0.2 kilobecquerel of strontium-85 per megabecquerel of rubidium-82 chloride injection (0.2 microcurie of strontium-85 per millicurie of rubidium-82).

(b) A licensee that uses molybdenum-99/technetium-99m generators for preparing a technetium-99m radiopharmaceutical shall measure the molybdenum-99 concentration of the first eluate after receipt of a generator to demonstrate compliance with paragraph (a) of this section.

(c) A licensee that uses a strontium-82/rubidium-82 generator for preparing a rubidium-82 radiopharmaceutical shall, before the first patient use of the day, measure the concentration of radionuclides strontium-82 and strontium-85 to demonstrate compliance with paragraph (a) of this section.

(d) If a licensee is required to measure the molybdenum-99 concentration or strontium-82 and strontium-85 concentrations, the licensee shall retain a record of each measurement in accordance with § 35.2204.

[67 FR 20370, Apr. 24, 2002, as amended at 72 FR 55932, Oct. 1, 2007]

§ 35.290 Training for imaging and localization studies.

Except as provided in § 35.57, the licensee shall require an authorized user of unsealed byproduct material for the uses authorized under § 35.200 to be a physician who—

(a) Is certified by a medical specialty board whose certification process has been recognized by the Commission or an Agreement State and who meets the requirements in paragraph (c)(2) of this section. (The names of board certifications which have been recognized by the Commission or an Agreement State will be posted on the NRC's Web page.) To have its certification process recognized, a specialty board shall require all candidates for certification to:

(1) Complete 700 hours of training and experience in basic radionuclide handling techniques and radiation safety applicable to the medical use of unsealed byproduct material for imaging and localization studies as described in paragraphs (c)(1)(i) through (c)(1)(ii)(G) of this section; and

(2) Pass an examination, administered by diplomates of the specialty board, which assesses knowledge and competence in radiation safety, radionuclide handling, and quality control; or

(b) Is an authorized user under § 35.390 and meets the requirements in § 35.290(c)(1)(ii)(G), or equivalent Agreement State requirements; or

(c)(1) Has completed 700 hours of training and experience, including a minimum of 80 hours of classroom and laboratory training, in basic radionuclide handling techniques applicable to the medical use of unsealed byproduct material for imaging and localization studies. The training and experience must include, at a minimum—

(i) Classroom and laboratory training in the following areas—

(A) Radiation physics and instrumentation;

(B) Radiation protection;

(C) Mathematics pertaining to the use and measurement of radioactivity;

(D) Chemistry of byproduct material for medical use;

(E) Radiation biology; and

(ii) Work experience, under the supervision of an authorized user who meets the requirements in §§ 35.57, 35.290, or 35.390 and 35.290(c)(1)(ii)(G), or equivalent Agreement State requirements, involving—

(A) Ordering, receiving, and unpacking radioactive materials safely and performing the related radiation surveys;

(B) Performing quality control procedures on instruments used to determine the activity of dosages and performing checks for proper operation of survey meters;

(C) Calculating, measuring, and safely preparing patient or human research subject dosages;

(D) Using administrative controls to prevent a medical event involving the use of unsealed byproduct material;

(E) Using procedures to safely contain spilled radioactive material and using proper decontamination procedures;

(F) Administering dosages of radioactive drugs to patients or human research subjects; and

(G) Eluting generator systems appropriate for preparation of radioactive drugs for imaging and localization studies, measuring and testing the eluate for radionuclidic purity, and processing the eluate with reagent kits to prepare labeled radioactive drugs; and

(2) Has obtained written attestation, signed by a preceptor authorized user who meets the requirements in §§ 35.57, 35.290, or 35.390 and 35.290(c)(1)(ii)(G), or equivalent Agreement State requirements, that the individual has satisfactorily completed the requirements in paragraph (a)(1) or (c)(1) of this section and has achieved a level of competency sufficient to function independently as

an authorized user for the medical uses authorized under §§ 35.100 and 35.200.

[67 FR 20370, Apr. 24, 2002, as amended at 70 FR 16364, Mar. 30, 2005; 71 FR 15009, Mar. 27, 2006; 72 FR 45151, Aug. 13, 2007; 74 FR 33905, July 14, 2009]

Subpart E—Unsealed Byproduct Material—Written Directive Required

§ 35.300 Use of unsealed byproduct material for which a written directive is required.

A licensee may use any unsealed byproduct material prepared for medical use and for which a written directive is required that is—

(a) Obtained from:

(1) A manufacturer or preparer licensed under § 32.72 of this chapter or equivalent Agreement State requirements; or

(2) A PET radioactive drug producer licensed under § 30.32(j) of this chapter or equivalent Agreement State requirements; or

(b) Excluding production of PET radionuclides, prepared by:

(1) An authorized nuclear pharmacist;

(2) A physician who is an authorized user and who meets the requirements specified in §§ 35.290, 35.390, or

(3) An individual under the supervision, as specified in § 35.27, of the authorized nuclear pharmacist in paragraph (b)(1) of this section or the physician who is an authorized user in paragraph (b)(2) of this section; or

(c) Obtained from and prepared by an NRC or Agreement State licensee for use in research in accordance with an Investigational New Drug (IND) protocol accepted by FDA; or

(d) Prepared by the licensee for use in research in accordance with an Investigational New Drug (IND) protocol accepted by FDA.

[67 FR 20370, Apr. 24, 2002, as amended at 68 FR 19324, Apr. 21, 2003; 71 FR 15009, Mar. 27, 2006; 72 FR 55932, Oct. 1, 2007]

§ 35.310 Safety instruction.

In addition to the requirements of § 19.12 of this chapter,

(a) A licensee shall provide radiation safety instruction, initially and at least annually, to personnel caring for patients or human research subjects who cannot be released under § 35.75. To satisfy this requirement, the instruction must be commensurate with the duties of the personnel and include—

(1) Patient or human research subject control;

(2) Visitor control, including—

(i) Routine visitation to hospitalized individuals in accordance with § 20.1301(a)(1) of this chapter; and

(ii) Visitation authorized in accordance with § 20.1301(c) of this chapter;

(3) Contamination control;

(4) Waste control; and

(5) Notification of the Radiation Safety Officer, or his or her designee, and an authorized user if the patient or the human research subject has a medical emergency or dies.

(b) A licensee shall retain a record of individuals receiving instruction in accordance with § 35.2310.

[67 FR 20370, Apr. 24, 2002, as amended at 68 FR 19324, Apr. 21, 2003]

§ 35.315 Safety precautions.

(a) For each patient or human research subject who cannot be released under § 35.75, a licensee shall—

(1) Quarter the patient or the human research subject either in—

(i) A private room with a private sanitary facility; or

(ii) A room, with a private sanitary facility, with another individual who also has received therapy with unsealed byproduct material and who also cannot be released under § 35.75;

(2) Visibly post the patient's or the human research subject's room with a "Radioactive Materials" sign.

(3) Note on the door or in the patient's or human research subject's chart where and how long visitors may stay in the patient's or the human research subject's room; and

(4) Either monitor material and items removed from the patient's or the human research subject's room to determine that their radioactivity cannot be distinguished from the natural background radiation level with a radiation detection survey instrument set on its most sensitive scale and with no interposed shielding, or handle the material and items as radioactive waste.

(b) A licensee shall notify the Radiation Safety Officer, or his or her designee, and an authorized user as soon as possible if the patient or human research subject has a medical emergency or dies.

[67 FR 20370, Apr. 24, 2002, as amended at 68 FR 19325, Apr. 21, 2003]

§ 35.390 Training for use of unsealed byproduct material for which a written directive is required.

Except as provided in § 35.57, the licensee shall require an authorized user of unsealed byproduct material for the uses authorized under § 35.300 to be a physician who—

(a) Is certified by a medical specialty board whose certification process has been recognized by the Commission or an Agreement State and who meets the requirements in paragraphs (b)(1)(ii)(G) and (b)(2) of this section. (Specialty boards whose certification processes have been recognized by the Commission or an Agreement State will be posted on the NRC's Web page.) To be recognized, a specialty board shall require all candidates for certification to:

(1) Successfully complete residency training in a radiation therapy or nuclear medicine training program or a program in a related medical specialty. These residency training programs must include 700 hours of training and experience as described in paragraphs (b)(1)(i) through (b)(1)(ii)(E) of this section. Eligible training programs must be approved by the Residency Review Committee of the Accreditation Council for Graduate Medical Education, the Royal College of Physicians and Surgeons of Canada, or the Committee on Post-Graduate Training of the American Osteopathic Association; and

(2) Pass an examination, administered by diplomates of the specialty board, which tests knowledge and competence in radiation safety, radionuclide handling, quality assurance, and clinical use of unsealed byproduct material for which a written directive is required; or

(b)(1) Has completed 700 hours of training and experience, including a minimum of 200 hours of classroom and laboratory training, in basic radionuclide handling techniques applicable to the medical use of unsealed byproduct material requiring a written directive. The training and experience must include—

(i) Classroom and laboratory training in the following areas—

(A) Radiation physics and instrumentation;

(B) Radiation protection;

(C) Mathematics pertaining to the use and measurement of radioactivity;

(D) Chemistry of byproduct material for medical use; and

(E) Radiation biology; and

(ii) Work experience, under the supervision of an authorized user who meets the requirements in §§ 35.57, 35.390, or equivalent Agreement State requirements. A supervising authorized user, who meets the requirements in § 35.390(b), must also have experience in administering dosages in the same dosage category or categories (*i.e.*, § 35.390(b)(1)(ii)(G)) as the individual requesting authorized user status. The work experience must involve—

(A) Ordering, receiving, and unpacking radioactive materials safely and performing the related radiation surveys;

(B) Performing quality control procedures on instruments used to determine the activity of dosages, and performing checks for proper operation of survey meters;

(C) Calculating, measuring, and safely preparing patient or human research subject dosages;

(D) Using administrative controls to prevent a medical event involving the use of unsealed byproduct material;

(E) Using procedures to contain spilled byproduct material safely and using proper decontamination procedures;

(F) [Reserved]

(G) Administering dosages of radioactive drugs to patients or human research subjects involving a minimum of three cases in each of the following categories for which the individual is requesting authorized user status—

(*1*) Oral administration of less than or equal to 1.22 gigabecquerels (33 millicuries) of sodium iodide I–131, for which a written directive is required;

(*2*) Oral administration of greater than 1.22 gigabecquerels (33 millicuries) of sodium iodide I-131[2];

(*3*) Parenteral administration of any beta emitter, or a photon-emitting radionuclide with a photon energy less than 150 keV, for which a written directive is required; and/or

(*4*) Parenteral administration of any other radionuclide, for which a written directive is required; and

(2) Has obtained written attestation that the individual has satisfactorily completed the requirements in paragraphs (a)(1) and (b)(1)(ii)(G) or (b)(1) of this section, and has achieved a level of competency sufficient to function independently as an authorized user for the medical uses authorized under § 35.300. The written attestation must be signed by a preceptor authorized user who meets the requirements in §§ 35.57, 35.390, or equivalent Agreement State requirements. The preceptor authorized user, who meets the requirements in § 35.390(b) must have experience in administering dosages in the same dosage category or categories (*i.e.*, § 35.390(b)(1)(ii)(G)) as the individual requesting authorized user status.

[67 FR 20370, Apr. 24, 2002, as amended at 68 FR 75389, Dec. 31, 2003; 70 FR 16364, Mar. 30, 2005; 71 FR 15009, Mar. 27, 2006; 74 FR 33905, July 14, 2009]

§ 35.392 Training for the oral administration of sodium iodide I-131 requiring a written directive in quantities less than or equal to 1.22 gigabecquerels (33 millicuries).

Except as provided in § 35.57, the licensee shall require an authorized user for the oral administration of sodium iodide I-131 requiring a written directive in quantities less than or equal to 1.22 Gigabecquerels (33 millicuries), to be a physician who—

(a) Is certified by a medical specialty board whose certification process includes all of the requirements in paragraphs (c)(1) and (c)(2) of this section and whose certification process has been recognized by the Commission or an Agreement State and who meets the requirements in paragraph (c)(3) of this section. (The names of board certifications which have been recognized by the Commission or an Agreement State will be posted on the NRC's Web page.); or

(b) Is an authorized user under § 35.390 for uses listed in § 35.390(b)(1)(ii)(G)(*1*) or (*2*), § 35.394, or equivalent Agreement State requirements; or

(c)(1) Has successfully completed 80 hours of classroom and laboratory training, applicable to the medical use of sodium iodide I-131 for procedures requiring a written directive. The training must include—

(i) Radiation physics and instrumentation;

(ii) Radiation protection;

(iii) Mathematics pertaining to the use and measurement of radioactivity;

(iv) Chemistry of byproduct material for medical use; and

(v) Radiation biology; and

(2) Has work experience, under the supervision of an authorized user who meets the requirements in §§ 35.57, 35.390, 35.392, 35.394, or equivalent Agreement State requirements. A supervising authorized user who meets the requirements in § 35.390(b) must also have experience in administering dosages as specified in §§ 35.390(b)(1)(ii)(G)(1) or 35.390(b)(1)(ii)(G)(2). The work experience must involve—

(i) Ordering, receiving, and unpacking radioactive materials safely and performing the related radiation surveys;

(ii) Performing quality control procedures on instruments used to determine the activity of dosages and performing checks for proper operation of survey meters;

(iii) Calculating, measuring, and safely preparing patient or human research subject dosages;

(iv) Using administrative controls to prevent a medical event involving the use of byproduct material;

(v) Using procedures to contain spilled byproduct material safely and using proper decontamination procedures; and

(vi) Administering dosages to patients or human research subjects, that includes at least 3 cases involving the oral administration of less than or equal to 1.22 gigabecquerels (33 millicuries) of sodium iodide I-131; and

[2] Experience with at least 3 cases in Category (G)(*2*) also satisfies the requirement in Category (G)(*1*).

(3) Has obtained written attestation that the individual has satisfactorily completed the requirements in paragraphs (c)(1) and (c)(2) of this section, and has achieved a level of competency sufficient to function independently as an authorized user for medical uses authorized under § 35.300. The written attestation must be signed by a preceptor authorized user who meets the requirements in §§ 35.57, 35.390, 35.392, 35.394, or equivalent Agreement State requirements. A preceptor authorized user, who meets the requirement in § 35.390(b), must also have experience in administering dosages as specified in §§ 35.390(b)(1)(ii)(G)(*1*) or 35.390(b)(1)(ii)(G)(*2*).

[67 FR 20370, Apr. 24, 2002, as amended at 68 FR 75389, Dec. 31, 2003; 70 FR 16364, Mar. 30, 2005; 71 FR 15009, Mar. 27, 2006; 74 FR 33905, July 14, 2009]

§ 35.394 Training for the oral administration of sodium iodide I–131 requiring a written directive in quantities greater than 1.22 gigabecquerels (33 millicuries).

Except as provided in § 35.57, the licensee shall require an authorized user for the oral administration of sodium iodide I-131 requiring a written directive in quantities greater than 1.22 Gigabecquerels (33 millicuries), to be a physician who—

(a) Is certified by a medical specialty board whose certification process includes all of the requirements in paragraphs (c)(1) and (c)(2) of this section, and whose certification has been recognized by the Commission or an Agreement State, and who meets the requirements in paragraph (c)(3) of this section. (The names of board certifications which have been recognized by the Commission or an Agreement State will be posted on the NRC's Web page.); or

(b) Is an authorized user under § 35.390 for uses listed in § 35.390(b)(1)(ii)(G)(*2*) or equivalent Agreement State requirements; or

(c)(1) Has successfully completed 80 hours of classroom and laboratory training, applicable to the medical use of sodium iodide I–131 for procedures requiring a written directive. The training must include—

(i) Radiation physics and instrumentation;

(ii) Radiation protection;

(iii) Mathematics pertaining to the use and measurement of radioactivity;

(iv) Chemistry of byproduct material for medical use; and

(v) Radiation biology; and

(2) Has work experience, under the supervision of an authorized user who meets the requirements in §§ 35.57, 35.390, 35.394, or equivalent Agreement State requirements. A supervising authorized user, who meets the requirements in § 35.390(b), must also have experience in administering dosages as specified in § 35.390(b)(1)(ii)(G)(*2*). The work experience must involve—

(i) Ordering, receiving, and unpacking radioactive materials safely and performing the related radiation surveys;

(ii) Performing quality control procedures on instruments used to determine the activity of dosages and performing checks for proper operation of survey meters;

(iii) Calculating, measuring, and safely preparing patient or human research subject dosages;

(iv) Using administrative controls to prevent a medical event involving the use of byproduct material;

(v) Using procedures to contain spilled byproduct material safely and using proper decontamination procedures; and

(vi) Administering dosages to patients or human research subjects, that includes at least 3 cases involving the oral administration of greater than 1.22 gigabecquerels (33 millicuries) of sodium iodide I-131; and

(3) Has obtained written attestation that the individual has satisfactorily completed the requirements in paragraphs (c)(1) and (c)(2) of this section, and has achieved a level of competency sufficient to function independently as an authorized user for medical uses authorized under § 35.300. The written attestation must be signed by a preceptor authorized user who meets the requirements in §§ 35.57, 35.390, 35.394, or equivalent Agreement State requirements. A preceptor authorized user, who meets the requirements in § 35.390(b), must also have experience in administering

dosages as specified in § 35.390(b)(1)(ii)(G)(*2*).

[67 FR 20370, Apr. 24, 2002, as amended at 68 FR 75389, Dec. 31, 2003; 70 FR 16365, Mar. 30, 2005; 71 FR 15010, Mar. 27, 2006; 74 FR 33905, July 14, 2009]

§ 35.396 Training for the parenteral administration of unsealed byproduct material requiring a written directive.

Except as provided in § 35.57, the licensee shall require an authorized user for the parenteral administration requiring a written directive, to be a physician who—

(a) Is an authorized user under § 35.390 for uses listed in §§ 35.390(b)(1)(ii)(G)(*3*) or 35.390(b)(1)(ii)(G)(*4*), or equivalent Agreement State requirements; or

(b) Is an authorized user under §§ 35.490, 35.690, or equivalent Agreement State requirements and who meets the requirements in paragraph (d) of this section; or

(c) Is certified by a medical specialty board whose certification process has been recognized by the Commission or an Agreement State under §§ 35.490 or 35.690, and who meets the requirements in paragraph (d) of this section.

(d)(1) Has successfully completed 80 hours of classroom and laboratory training, applicable to parenteral administrations, for which a written directive is required, of any beta emitter, or any photon-emitting radionuclide with a photon energy less than 150 keV, and/or parenteral administration of any other radionuclide for which a written directive is required. The training must include—

(i) Radiation physics and instrumentation;

(ii) Radiation protection;

(iii) Mathematics pertaining to the use and measurement of radioactivity;

(iv) Chemistry of byproduct material for medical use; and

(v) Radiation biology; and

(2) Has work experience, under the supervision of an authorized user who meets the requirements in §§ 35.57, 35.390, 35.396, or equivalent Agreement State requirements, in the parenteral administration, for which a written directive is required, of any beta emitter, or any photon-emitting radionuclide with a photon energy less than 150 keV, and/or parenteral administration of any other radionuclide for which a written directive is required. A supervising authorized user who meets the requirements in § 35.390 must have experience in administering dosages as specified in §§ 35.390(b)(1)(ii)(G)(3) and/or 35.390(b)(1)(ii)(G)(4). The work experience must involve—

(i) Ordering, receiving, and unpacking radioactive materials safely, and performing the related radiation surveys;

(ii) Performing quality control procedures on instruments used to determine the activity of dosages, and performing checks for proper operation of survey meters;

(iii) Calculating, measuring, and safely preparing patient or human research subject dosages;

(iv) Using administrative controls to prevent a medical event involving the use of unsealed byproduct material;

(v) Using procedures to contain spilled byproduct material safely, and using proper decontamination procedures; and

(vi) Administering dosages to patients or human research subjects, that include at least 3 cases involving the parenteral administration, for which a written directive is required, of any beta emitter, or any photon-emitting radionuclide with a photon energy less than 150 keV and/or at least 3 cases involving the parenteral administration of any other radionuclide, for which a written directive is required; and

(3) Has obtained written attestation that the individual has satisfactorily completed the requirements in paragraph (b) or (c) of this section, and has achieved a level of competency sufficient to function independently as an authorized user for the parenteral administration of unsealed byproduct material requiring a written directive. The written attestation must be signed by a preceptor authorized user who meets the requirements in §§ 35.57, 35.390, 35.396, or equivalent Agreement State requirements. A preceptor authorized user, who meets the requirements in § 35.390, must have experience in administering dosages as specified in

§§ 35.390(b)(1)(ii)(G)(*3*) and/or 35.390(b)(1)(ii)(G)(*4*).

[70 FR 16365, Mar. 30, 2005, as amended at 71 FR 15010, Mar. 27, 2006; 74 FR 33906, July 14, 2009]

Subpart F—Manual Brachytherapy

§ 35.400 Use of sources for manual brachytherapy.

A licensee shall use only brachytherapy sources for therapeutic medical uses:

(a) As approved in the Sealed Source and Device Registry; or

(b) In research in accordance with an active Investigational Device Exemption (IDE) application accepted by the FDA provided the requirements of § 35.49(a) are met.

§ 35.404 Surveys after source implant and removal.

(a) Immediately after implanting sources in a patient or a human research subject, the licensee shall make a survey to locate and account for all sources that have not been implanted.

(b) Immediately after removing the last temporary implant source from a patient or a human research subject, the licensee shall make a survey of the patient or the human research subject with a radiation detection survey instrument to confirm that all sources have been removed.

(c) A licensee shall retain a record of the surveys required by paragraphs (a) and (b) of this section in accordance with § 35.2404.

§ 35.406 Brachytherapy sources accountability.

(a) A licensee shall maintain accountability at all times for all brachytherapy sources in storage or use.

(b) As soon as possible after removing sources from a patient or a human research subject, a licensee shall return brachytherapy sources to a secure storage area.

(c) A licensee shall maintain a record of the brachytherapy source accountability in accordance with § 35.2406.

§ 35.410 Safety instruction.

In addition to the requirements of § 19.12 of this chapter,

(a) The licensee shall provide radiation safety instruction, initially and at least annually, to personnel caring for patients or human research subjects who are receiving brachytherapy and cannot be released under § 35.75. To satisfy this requirement, the instruction must be commensurate with the duties of the personnel and include the—

(1) Size and appearance of the brachytherapy sources;

(2) Safe handling and shielding instructions;

(3) Patient or human research subject control;

(4) Visitor control, including both:

(i) Routine visitation of hospitalized individuals in accordance with § 20.1301(a)(1) of this chapter; and

(ii) Visitation authorized in accordance with § 20.1301(c) of this chapter; and

(5) Notification of the Radiation Safety Officer, or his or her designee, and an authorized user if the patient or the human research subject has a medical emergency or dies.

(b) A licensee shall retain a record of individuals receiving instruction in accordance with § 35.2310.

§ 35.415 Safety precautions.

(a) For each patient or human research subject who is receiving brachytherapy and cannot be released under § 35.75, a licensee shall—

(1) Not quarter the patient or the human research subject in the same room as an individual who is not receiving brachytherapy;

(2) Visibly post the patient's or human research subject's room with a "Radioactive Materials" sign; and

(3) Note on the door or in the patient's or human research subject's chart where and how long visitors may stay in the patient's or human research subject's room.

(b) A licensee shall have applicable emergency response equipment available near each treatment room to respond to a source—

(1) Dislodged from the patient; and

(2) Lodged within the patient following removal of the source applicators.

(c) A licensee shall notify the Radiation Safety Officer, or his or her designee, and an authorized user as soon as possible if the patient or human research subject has a medical emergency or dies.

§ 35.432 Calibration measurements of brachytherapy sources.

(a) Before the first medical use of a brachytherapy source on or after October 24, 2002, a licensee shall have—

(1) Determined the source output or activity using a dosimetry system that meets the requirements of § 35.630(a);

(2) Determined source positioning accuracy within applicators; and

(3) Used published protocols currently accepted by nationally recognized bodies to meet the requirements of paragraphs (a)(1) and (a)(2) of this section.

(b) Instead of a licensee making its own measurements as required in paragraph (a) of this section, the licensee may use measurements provided by the source manufacturer or by a calibration laboratory accredited by the American Association of Physicists in Medicine that are made in accordance with paragraph (a) of this section.

(c) A licensee shall mathematically correct the outputs or activities determined in paragraph (a) of this section for physical decay at intervals consistent with 1 percent physical decay.

(d) A licensee shall retain a record of each calibration in accordance with § 35.2432.

[67 FR 20370, Apr. 24, 2002, as amended at 68 FR 19325, Apr. 21, 2003]

§ 35.433 Decay of strontium-90 sources for ophthalmic treatments.

(a) Only an authorized medical physicist shall calculate the activity of each strontium-90 source that is used to determine the treatment times for ophthalmic treatments. The decay must be based on the activity determined under § 35.432.

(b) A licensee shall retain a record of the activity of each strontium-90 source in accordance with § 35.2433.

§ 35.457 Therapy-related computer systems.

The licensee shall perform acceptance testing on the treatment planning system of therapy-related computer systems in accordance with published protocols accepted by nationally recognized bodies. At a minimum, the acceptance testing must include, as applicable, verification of:

(a) The source-specific input parameters required by the dose calculation algorithm;

(b) The accuracy of dose, dwell time, and treatment time calculations at representative points;

(c) The accuracy of isodose plots and graphic displays; and

(d) The accuracy of the software used to determine sealed source positions from radiographic images.

§ 35.490 Training for use of manual brachytherapy sources.

Except as provided in § 35.57, the licensee shall require an authorized user of a manual brachytherapy source for the uses authorized under § 35.400 to be a physician who—

(a) Is certified by a medical specialty board whose certification process has been recognized by the Commission or an Agreement State, and who meets the requirements in paragraph (b)(3) of this section. (The names of board certifications which have been recognized by the Commission or an Agreement State will be posted on the NRC's Web page.) To have its certification process recognized, a specialty board shall require all candidates for certification to:

(1) Successfully complete a minimum of 3 years of residency training in a radiation oncology program approved by the Residency Review Committee of the Accreditation Council for Graduate Medical Education or the Royal College of Physicians and Surgeons of Canada or the Committee on Post-Graduate Training of the American Osteopathic Association; and

(2) Pass an examination, administered by diplomates of the specialty board, that tests knowledge and competence in radiation safety, radionuclide handling, treatment planning, quality assurance, and clinical use of manual brachytherapy; or

(b)(1) Has completed a structured educational program in basic radionuclide handling techniques applicable to the use of manual brachytherapy sources that includes—

(i) 200 hours of classroom and laboratory training in the following areas—

(A) Radiation physics and instrumentation;

(B) Radiation protection;

(C) Mathematics pertaining to the use and measurement of radioactivity; and

(D) Radiation biology; and

(ii) 500 hours of work experience, under the supervision of an authorized user who meets the requirements in §§35.57, 35.490, or equivalent Agreement State requirements at a medical institution, involving—

(A) Ordering, receiving, and unpacking radioactive materials safely and performing the related radiation surveys;

(B) Checking survey meters for proper operation;

(C) Preparing, implanting, and removing brachytherapy sources;

(D) Maintaining running inventories of material on hand;

(E) Using administrative controls to prevent a medical event involving the use of byproduct material;

(F) Using emergency procedures to control byproduct material; and

(2) Has completed 3 years of supervised clinical experience in radiation oncology, under an authorized user who meets the requirements in §§35.57, 35.490, or equivalent Agreement State requirements, as part of a formal training program approved by the Residency Review Committee for Radiation Oncology of the Accreditation Council for Graduate Medical Education or the Royal College of Physicians and Surgeons of Canada or the Committee on Postdoctoral Training of the American Osteopathic Association. This experience may be obtained concurrently with the supervised work experience required by paragraph (b)(1)(ii) of this section; and

(3) Has obtained written attestation, signed by a preceptor authorized user who meets the requirements in §§35.57, 35.490, or equivalent Agreement State requirements, that the individual has satisfactorily completed the requirements in paragraph (a)(1), or paragraphs (b)(1) and (b)(2), of this section and has achieved a level of competency sufficient to function independently as an authorized user of manual brachytherapy sources for the medical uses authorized under §35.400.

[67 FR 20370, Apr. 24, 2002, as amended at 70 FR 16366, Mar. 30, 2005; 71 FR 15010, Mar. 27, 2006; 74 FR 33906, July 14, 2009]

§35.491 Training for ophthalmic use of strontium-90.

Except as provided in §35.57, the licensee shall require the authorized user of strontium-90 for ophthalmic radiotherapy to be a physician who—

(a) Is an authorized user under §35.490 or equivalent Agreement State requirements; or

(b)(1) Has completed 24 hours of classroom and laboratory training applicable to the medical use of strontium-90 for ophthalmic radiotherapy. The training must include—

(i) Radiation physics and instrumentation;

(ii) Radiation protection;

(iii) Mathematics pertaining to the use and measurement of radioactivity; and

(iv) Radiation biology; and

(2) Supervised clinical training in ophthalmic radiotherapy under the supervision of an authorized user at a medical institution, clinic, or private practice that includes the use of strontium-90 for the ophthalmic treatment of five individuals. This supervised clinical training must involve—

(i) Examination of each individual to be treated;

(ii) Calculation of the dose to be administered;

(iii) Administration of the dose; and

(iv) Follow up and review of each individual's case history; and

(3) Has obtained written attestation, signed by a preceptor authorized user who meets the requirements in §§35.57, 35.490, 35.491, or equivalent Agreement State requirements, that the individual has satisfactorily completed the requirements in paragraph (b) of this section and has achieved a level of competency sufficient to function independently as an authorized user of strontium-90 for ophthalmic use.

[67 FR 20370, Apr. 24, 2002, as amended at 68 FR 19326, Apr. 21, 2003; 71 FR 15011, Mar. 27, 2006; 74 FR 33906, July 14, 2009]

Subpart G—Sealed Sources for Diagnosis

§ 35.500 Use of sealed sources for diagnosis.

A licensee shall use only sealed sources for diagnostic medical uses as approved in the Sealed Source and Device Registry.

§ 35.590 Training for use of sealed sources for diagnosis.

Except as provided in § 35.57, the licensee shall require the authorized user of a diagnostic sealed source for use in a device authorized under § 35.500 to be a physician, dentist, or podiatrist who—

(a) Is certified by a specialty board whose certification process includes all of the requirements in paragraphs (b) and (c) of this section and whose certification has been recognized by the Commission or an Agreement State. (The names of board certifications which have been recognized by the Commission or an Agreement State will be posted on the NRC's Web page.); or

(b) Has completed 8 hours of classroom and laboratory training in basic radionuclide handling techniques specifically applicable to the use of the device. The training must include—

(1) Radiation physics and instrumentation;

(2) Radiation protection;

(3) Mathematics pertaining to the use and measurement of radioactivity; and

(4) Radiation biology; and

(c) Has completed training in the use of the device for the uses requested.

[67 FR 20370, Apr. 24, 2002, as amended at 70 FR 16366, Mar. 30, 2005]

Subpart H—Photon Emitting Remote Afterloader Units, Teletherapy Units, and Gamma Stereotactic Radiosurgery Units

§ 35.600 Use of a sealed source in a remote afterloader unit, teletherapy unit, or gamma stereotactic radiosurgery unit.

A licensee shall use sealed sources in photon emitting remote afterloader units, teletherapy units, or gamma stereotactic radiosurgery units for therapeutic medical uses:

(a) As approved in the Sealed Source and Device Registry; or

(b) In research in accordance with an active Investigational Device Exemption (IDE) application accepted by the FDA provided the requirements of § 35.49(a) are met.

§ 35.604 Surveys of patients and human research subjects treated with a remote afterloader unit.

(a) Before releasing a patient or a human research subject from licensee control, a licensee shall survey the patient or the human research subject and the remote afterloader unit with a portable radiation detection survey instrument to confirm that the source(s) has been removed from the patient or human research subject and returned to the safe shielded position.

(b) A licensee shall retain a record of these surveys in accordance with § 35.2404.

§ 35.605 Installation, maintenance, adjustment, and repair.

(a) Only a person specifically licensed by the Commission or an Agreement State shall install, maintain, adjust, or repair a remote afterloader unit, teletherapy unit, or gamma stereotactic radiosurgery unit that involves work on the source(s) shielding, the source(s) driving unit, or other electronic or mechanical component that could expose the source(s), reduce the shielding around the source(s), or compromise the radiation safety of the unit or the source(s).

(b) Except for low dose-rate remote afterloader units, only a person specifically licensed by the Commission or an Agreement State shall install, replace, relocate, or remove a sealed source or source contained in other remote afterloader units, teletherapy units, or gamma stereotactic radiosurgery units.

(c) For a low dose-rate remote afterloader unit, only a person specifically licensed by the Commission or an Agreement State or an authorized medical physicist shall install, replace, relocate, or remove a sealed source(s) contained in the unit.

(d) A licensee shall retain a record of the installation, maintenance, adjustment, and repair of remote afterloader units, teletherapy units, and gamma stereotactic radiosurgery units in accordance with § 35.2605.

§ 35.610 Safety procedures and instructions for remote afterloader units, teletherapy units, and gamma stereotactic radiosurgery units.

(a) A licensee shall—

(1) Secure the unit, the console, the console keys, and the treatment room when not in use or unattended;

(2) Permit only individuals approved by the authorized user, Radiation Safety Officer, or authorized medical physicist to be present in the treatment room during treatment with the source(s);

(3) Prevent dual operation of more than one radiation producing device in a treatment room if applicable; and

(4) Develop, implement, and maintain written procedures for responding to an abnormal situation when the operator is unable to place the source(s) in the shielded position, or remove the patient or human research subject from the radiation field with controls from outside the treatment room. These procedures must include—

(i) Instructions for responding to equipment failures and the names of the individuals responsible for implementing corrective actions;

(ii) The process for restricting access to and posting of the treatment area to minimize the risk of inadvertent exposure; and

(iii) The names and telephone numbers of the authorized users, the authorized medical physicist, and the Radiation Safety Officer to be contacted if the unit or console operates abnormally.

(b) A copy of the procedures required by paragraph (a)(4) of this section must be physically located at the unit console.

(c) A licensee shall post instructions at the unit console to inform the operator of—

(1) The location of the procedures required by paragraph (a)(4) of this section; and

(2) The names and telephone numbers of the authorized users, the authorized medical physicist, and the Radiation Safety Officer to be contacted if the unit or console operates abnormally.

(d) A licensee shall provide instruction, initially and at least annually, to all individuals who operate the unit, as appropriate to the individual's assigned duties, in—

(1) The procedures identified in paragraph (a)(4) of this section; and

(2) The operating procedures for the unit.

(e) A licensee shall ensure that operators, authorized medical physicists, and authorized users participate in drills of the emergency procedures, initially and at least annually.

(f) A licensee shall retain a record of individuals receiving instruction required by paragraph (d) of this section, in accordance with § 35.2310.

(g) A licensee shall retain a copy of the procedures required by §§ 35.610(a)(4) and (d)(2) in accordance with § 35.2610.

§ 35.615 Safety precautions for remote afterloader units, teletherapy units, and gamma stereotactic radiosurgery units.

(a) A licensee shall control access to the treatment room by a door at each entrance.

(b) A licensee shall equip each entrance to the treatment room with an electrical interlock system that will—

(1) Prevent the operator from initiating the treatment cycle unless each treatment room entrance door is closed;

(2) Cause the source(s) to be shielded when an entrance door is opened; and

(3) Prevent the source(s) from being exposed following an interlock interruption until all treatment room entrance doors are closed and the source(s) on-off control is reset at the console.

(c) A licensee shall require any individual entering the treatment room to assure, through the use of appropriate radiation monitors, that radiation levels have returned to ambient levels.

(d) Except for low-dose remote afterloader units, a licensee shall construct or equip each treatment room with viewing and intercom systems to permit continuous observation of the patient or the human research subject from the treatment console during irradiation.

(e) For licensed activities where sources are placed within the patient's or human research subject's body, a licensee shall only conduct treatments which allow for expeditious removal of a decoupled or jammed source.

(f) In addition to the requirements specified in paragraphs (a) through (e) of this section, a licensee shall—

(1) For medium dose-rate and pulsed dose-rate remote afterloader units, require—

(i) An authorized medical physicist and either an authorized user or a physician, under the supervision of an authorized user, who has been trained in the operation and emergency response for the unit to be physically present during the initiation of all patient treatments involving the unit; and

(ii) An authorized medical physicist and either an authorized user or an individual, under the supervision of an authorized user, who has been trained to remove the source applicator(s) in the event of an emergency involving the unit, to be immediately available during continuation of all patient treatments involving the unit.

(2) For high dose-rate remote afterloader units, require—

(i) An authorized user and an authorized medical physicist to be physically present during the initiation of all patient treatments involving the unit; and

(ii) An authorized medical physicist and either an authorized user or a physician, under the supervision of an authorized user, who has been trained in the operation and emergency response for the unit, to be physically present during continuation of all patient treatments involving the unit.

(3) For gamma stereotactic radiosurgery units, require an authorized user and an authorized medical physicist to be physically present throughout all patient treatments involving the unit.

(4) Notify the Radiation Safety Officer, or his/her designee, and an authorized user as soon as possible if the patient or human research subject has a medical emergency or dies.

(g) A licensee shall have applicable emergency response equipment available near each treatment room to respond to a source—

(1) Remaining in the unshielded position; or

(2) Lodged within the patient following completion of the treatment.

§ 35.630 Dosimetry equipment.

(a) Except for low dose-rate remote afterloader sources where the source output or activity is determined by the manufacturer, a licensee shall have a calibrated dosimetry system available for use. To satisfy this requirement, one of the following two conditions must be met.

(1) The system must have been calibrated using a system or source traceable to the National Institute of Standards and Technology (NIST) and published protocols accepted by nationally recognized bodies; or by a calibration laboratory accredited by the American Association of Physicists in Medicine (AAPM). The calibration must have been performed within the previous 2 years and after any servicing that may have affected system calibration; or

(2) The system must have been calibrated within the previous 4 years. Eighteen to thirty months after that calibration, the system must have been intercompared with another dosimetry system that was calibrated within the past 24 months by NIST or by a calibration laboratory accredited by the AAPM. The results of the intercomparison must indicate that the calibration factor of the licensee's system had not changed by more than 2 percent. The licensee may not use the intercomparison result to change the calibration factor. When intercomparing dosimetry systems to be used for calibrating sealed sources for therapeutic units, the licensee shall use a comparable unit with beam attenuators or collimators, as applicable, and sources of the same radionuclide as the source used at the licensee's facility.

(b) The licensee shall have a dosimetry system available for use for spot-check output measurements, if applicable. To satisfy this requirement, the system may be compared with a system that has been calibrated in accordance with paragraph (a) of this section. This comparison must have been performed within the previous year and after each servicing that may have affected system calibration. The spot-check system may be the same system used to meet the requirement in paragraph (a) of this section.

(c) The licensee shall retain a record of each calibration, intercomparison, and comparison in accordance with § 35.2630.

[67 FR 20370, Apr. 24, 2002, as amended at 68 FR 19326, Apr. 21, 2003]

§ 35.632 Full calibration measurements on teletherapy units.

(a) A licensee authorized to use a teletherapy unit for medical use shall perform full calibration measurements on each teletherapy unit—

(1) Before the first medical use of the unit; and

(2) Before medical use under the following conditions:

(i) Whenever spot-check measurements indicate that the output differs by more than 5 percent from the output obtained at the last full calibration corrected mathematically for radioactive decay;

(ii) Following replacement of the source or following reinstallation of the teletherapy unit in a new location;

(iii) Following any repair of the teletherapy unit that includes removal of the source or major repair of the components associated with the source exposure assembly; and

(3) At intervals not exceeding 1 year.

(b) To satisfy the requirement of paragraph (a) of this section, full calibration measurements must include determination of—

(1) The output within ±3 percent for the range of field sizes and for the distance or range of distances used for medical use;

(2) The coincidence of the radiation field and the field indicated by the light beam localizing device;

(3) The uniformity of the radiation field and its dependence on the orientation of the useful beam;

(4) Timer accuracy and linearity over the range of use;

(5) On-off error; and

(6) The accuracy of all distance measuring and localization devices in medical use.

(c) A licensee shall use the dosimetry system described in § 35.630(a) to measure the output for one set of exposure conditions. The remaining radiation measurements required in paragraph (b)(1) of this section may be made using a dosimetry system that indicates relative dose rates.

(d) A licensee shall make full calibration measurements required by paragraph (a) of this section in accordance with published protocols accepted by nationally recognized bodies.

(e) A licensee shall mathematically correct the outputs determined in paragraph (b)(1) of this section for physical decay for intervals not exceeding 1 month for cobalt-60, 6 months for cesium-137, or at intervals consistent with 1 percent decay for all other nuclides.

(f) Full calibration measurements required by paragraph (a) of this section and physical decay corrections required by paragraph (e) of this section must be performed by the authorized medical physicist.

(g) A licensee shall retain a record of each calibration in accordance with § 35.2632.

§ 35.633 Full calibration measurements on remote afterloader units.

(a) A licensee authorized to use a remote afterloader unit for medical use shall perform full calibration measurements on each unit—

(1) Before the first medical use of the unit;

(2) Before medical use under the following conditions:

(i) Following replacement of the source or following reinstallation of the unit in a new location outside the facility; and

(ii) Following any repair of the unit that includes removal of the source or major repair of the components associated with the source exposure assembly; and

(3) At intervals not exceeding 1 quarter for high dose-rate, medium dose-rate, and pulsed dose-rate remote afterloader units with sources whose half-life exceeds 75 days; and

(4) At intervals not exceeding 1 year for low dose-rate remote afterloader units.

(b) To satisfy the requirement of paragraph (a) of this section, full calibration measurements must include, as applicable, determination of:

(1) The output within ±5 percent;

(2) Source positioning accuracy to within ±1 millimeter;

(3) Source retraction with backup battery upon power failure;

(4) Length of the source transfer tubes;

(5) Timer accuracy and linearity over the typical range of use;

(6) Length of the applicators; and

(7) Function of the source transfer tubes, applicators, and transfer tube-applicator interfaces.

(c) A licensee shall use the dosimetry system described in § 35.630(a) to measure the output.

(d) A licensee shall make full calibration measurements required by paragraph (a) of this section in accordance with published protocols accepted by nationally recognized bodies.

(e) In addition to the requirements for full calibrations for low dose-rate remote afterloader units in paragraph (b) of this section, a licensee shall perform an autoradiograph of the source(s) to verify inventory and source(s) arrangement at intervals not exceeding 1 quarter.

(f) For low dose-rate remote afterloader units, a licensee may use measurements provided by the source manufacturer that are made in accordance with paragraphs (a) through (e) of this section.

(g) A licensee shall mathematically correct the outputs determined in paragraph (b)(1) of this section for physical decay at intervals consistent with 1 percent physical decay.

(h) Full calibration measurements required by paragraph (a) of this section and physical decay corrections required by paragraph (g) of this section must be performed by the authorized medical physicist.

(i) A licensee shall retain a record of each calibration in accordance with § 35.2632.

§ 35.635 Full calibration measurements on gamma stereotactic radiosurgery units.

(a) A licensee authorized to use a gamma stereotactic radiosurgery unit for medical use shall perform full calibration measurements on each unit—

(1) Before the first medical use of the unit;

(2) Before medical use under the following conditions—

(i) Whenever spot-check measurements indicate that the output differs by more than 5 percent from the output obtained at the last full calibration corrected mathematically for radioactive decay;

(ii) Following replacement of the sources or following reinstallation of the gamma stereotactic radiosurgery unit in a new location; and

(iii) Following any repair of the gamma stereotactic radiosurgery unit that includes removal of the sources or major repair of the components associated with the source assembly; and

(3) At intervals not exceeding 1 year, with the exception that relative helmet factors need only be determined before the first medical use of a helmet and following any damage to a helmet.

(b) To satisfy the requirement of paragraph (a) of this section, full calibration measurements must include determination of—

(1) The output within ±3 percent;

(2) Relative helmet factors;

(3) Isocenter coincidence;

(4) Timer accuracy and linearity over the range of use;

(5) On-off error;

(6) Trunnion centricity;

(7) Treatment table retraction mechanism, using backup battery power or hydraulic backups with the unit off;

(8) Helmet microswitches;

(9) Emergency timing circuits; and

(10) Stereotactic frames and localizing devices (trunnions).

(c) A licensee shall use the dosimetry system described in § 35.630(a) to measure the output for one set of exposure conditions. The remaining radiation measurements required in paragraph (b)(1) of this section may be made using a dosimetry system that indicates relative dose rates.

(d) A licensee shall make full calibration measurements required by paragraph (a) of this section in accordance with published protocols accepted by nationally recognized bodies.

(e) A licensee shall mathematically correct the outputs determined in paragraph (b)(1) of this section at intervals not exceeding 1 month for cobalt-60 and at intervals consistent with

1 percent physical decay for all other radionuclides.

(f) Full calibration measurements required by paragraph (a) of this section and physical decay corrections required by paragraph (e) of this section must be performed by the authorized medical physicist.

(g) A licensee shall retain a record of each calibration in accordance with § 35.2632.

§ 35.642 Periodic spot-checks for teletherapy units.

(a) A licensee authorized to use teletherapy units for medical use shall perform output spot-checks on each teletherapy unit once in each calendar month that include determination of—

(1) Timer accuracy, and timer linearity over the range of use;

(2) On-off error;

(3) The coincidence of the radiation field and the field indicated by the light beam localizing device;

(4) The accuracy of all distance measuring and localization devices used for medical use;

(5) The output for one typical set of operating conditions measured with the dosimetry system described in § 35.630(b); and

(6) The difference between the measurement made in paragraph (a)(5) of this section and the anticipated output, expressed as a percentage of the anticipated output (*i.e.*, the value obtained at last full calibration corrected mathematically for physical decay).

(b) A licensee shall perform measurements required by paragraph (a) of this section in accordance with written procedures established by the authorized medical physicist. That individual need not actually perform the spot-check measurements.

(c) A licensee shall have the authorized medical physicist review the results of each spot-check within 15 days. The authorized medical physicist shall notify the licensee as soon as possible in writing of the results of each spot-check.

(d) A licensee authorized to use a teletherapy unit for medical use shall perform safety spot-checks of each teletherapy facility once in each calendar month and after each source installation to assure proper operation of—

(1) Electrical interlocks at each teletherapy room entrance;

(2) Electrical or mechanical stops installed for the purpose of limiting use of the primary beam of radiation (restriction of source housing angulation or elevation, carriage or stand travel and operation of the beam on-off mechanism);

(3) Source exposure indicator lights on the teletherapy unit, on the control console, and in the facility;

(4) Viewing and intercom systems;

(5) Treatment room doors from inside and outside the treatment room; and

(6) Electrically assisted treatment room doors with the teletherapy unit electrical power turned off.

(e) If the results of the checks required in paragraph (d) of this section indicate the malfunction of any system, a licensee shall lock the control console in the off position and not use the unit except as may be necessary to repair, replace, or check the malfunctioning system.

(f) A licensee shall retain a record of each spot-check required by paragraphs (a) and (d) of this section, and a copy of the procedures required by paragraph (b), in accordance with § 35.2642.

§ 35.643 Periodic spot-checks for remote afterloader units.

(a) A licensee authorized to use a remote afterloader unit for medical use shall perform spot-checks of each remote afterloader facility and on each unit—

(1) Before the first use of a high dose-rate, medium dose-rate, or pulsed dose rate remote afterloader unit on a given day;

(2) Before each patient treatment with a low dose-rate remote afterloader unit; and

(3) After each source installation.

(b) A licensee shall perform the measurements required by paragraph (a) of this section in accordance with written procedures established by the authorized medical physicist. That individual need not actually perform the spot check measurements.

(c) A licensee shall have the authorized medical physicist review the results of each spot-check within 15 days. The authorized medical physicist shall notify the licensee as soon as possible in writing of the results of each spot-check.

(d) To satisfy the requirements of paragraph (a) of this section, spot-checks must, at a minimum, assure proper operation of—

(1) Electrical interlocks at each remote afterloader unit room entrance;

(2) Source exposure indicator lights on the remote afterloader unit, on the control console, and in the facility;

(3) Viewing and intercom systems in each high dose-rate, medium dose-rate, and pulsed dose-rate remote afterloader facility;

(4) Emergency response equipment;

(5) Radiation monitors used to indicate the source position;

(6) Timer accuracy;

(7) Clock (date and time) in the unit's computer; and

(8) Decayed source(s) activity in the unit's computer.

(e) If the results of the checks required in paragraph (d) of this section indicate the malfunction of any system, a licensee shall lock the control console in the off position and not use the unit except as may be necessary to repair, replace, or check the malfunctioning system.

(f) A licensee shall retain a record of each check required by paragraph (d) of this section and a copy of the procedures required by paragraph (b) of this section in accordance with § 35.2643.

§ 35.645 Periodic spot-checks for gamma stereotactic radiosurgery units.

(a) A licensee authorized to use a gamma stereotactic radiosurgery unit for medical use shall perform spot-checks of each gamma stereotactic radiosurgery facility and on each unit—

(1) Monthly;

(2) Before the first use of the unit on a given day; and

(3) After each source installation.

(b) A licensee shall—

(1) Perform the measurements required by paragraph (a) of this section in accordance with written procedures established by the authorized medical physicist. That individual need not actually perform the spot check measurements.

(2) Have the authorized medical physicist review the results of each spot-check within 15 days. The authorized medical physicist shall notify the licensee as soon as possible in writing of the results of each spot-check.

(c) To satisfy the requirements of paragraph (a)(1) of this section, spot-checks must, at a minimum—

(1) Assure proper operation of—

(i) Treatment table retraction mechanism, using backup battery power or hydraulic backups with the unit off;

(ii) Helmet microswitches;

(iii) Emergency timing circuits; and

(iv) Stereotactic frames and localizing devices (trunnions).

(2) Determine—

(i) The output for one typical set of operating conditions measured with the dosimetry system described in § 35.630(b);

(ii) The difference between the measurement made in paragraph (c)(2)(i) of this section and the anticipated output, expressed as a percentage of the anticipated output (*i.e.*, the value obtained at last full calibration corrected mathematically for physical decay);

(iii) Source output against computer calculation;

(iv) Timer accuracy and linearity over the range of use;

(v) On-off error; and

(vi) Trunnion centricity.

(d) To satisfy the requirements of paragraphs (a)(2) and (a)(3) of this section, spot-checks must assure proper operation of—

(1) Electrical interlocks at each gamma stereotactic radiosurgery room entrance;

(2) Source exposure indicator lights on the gamma stereotactic radiosurgery unit, on the control console, and in the facility;

(3) Viewing and intercom systems;

(4) Timer termination;

(5) Radiation monitors used to indicate room exposures; and

(6) Emergency off buttons.

(e) A licensee shall arrange for the repair of any system identified in paragraph (c) of this section that is not operating properly as soon as possible.

(f) If the results of the checks required in paragraph (d) of this section indicate the malfunction of any system, a licensee shall lock the control console in the off position and not use the unit except as may be necessary to repair, replace, or check the malfunctioning system.

(g) A licensee shall retain a record of each check required by paragraphs (c) and (d) and a copy of the procedures required by paragraph (b) of this section in accordance with § 35.2645.

§ 35.647 Additional technical requirements for mobile remote afterloader units.

(a) A licensee providing mobile remote afterloader service shall—

(1) Check survey instruments before medical use at each address of use or on each day of use, whichever is more frequent; and

(2) Account for all sources before departure from a client's address of use.

(b) In addition to the periodic spot-checks required by § 35.643, a licensee authorized to use mobile afterloaders for medical use shall perform checks on each remote afterloader unit before use at each address of use. At a minimum, checks must be made to verify the operation of—

(1) Electrical interlocks on treatment area access points;

(2) Source exposure indicator lights on the remote afterloader unit, on the control console, and in the facility;

(3) Viewing and intercom systems;

(4) Applicators, source transfer tubes, and transfer tube-applicator interfaces;

(5) Radiation monitors used to indicate room exposures;

(6) Source positioning (accuracy); and

(7) Radiation monitors used to indicate whether the source has returned to a safe shielded position.

(c) In addition to the requirements for checks in paragraph (b) of this section, a licensee shall ensure overall proper operation of the remote afterloader unit by conducting a simulated cycle of treatment before use at each address of use.

(d) If the results of the checks required in paragraph (b) of this section indicate the malfunction of any system, a licensee shall lock the control console in the off position and not use the unit except as may be necessary to repair, replace, or check the malfunctioning system.

(e) A licensee shall retain a record of each check required by paragraph (b) of this section in accordance with § 35.2647.

§ 35.652 Radiation surveys.

(a) In addition to the survey requirement in § 20.1501 of this chapter, a person licensed under this subpart shall make surveys to ensure that the maximum radiation levels and average radiation levels from the surface of the main source safe with the source(s) in the shielded position do not exceed the levels stated in the Sealed Source and Device Registry.

(b) The licensee shall make the survey required by paragraph (a) of this section at installation of a new source and following repairs to the source(s) shielding, the source(s) driving unit, or other electronic or mechanical component that could expose the source, reduce the shielding around the source(s), or compromise the radiation safety of the unit or the source(s).

(c) A licensee shall retain a record of the radiation surveys required by paragraph (a) of this section in accordance with § 35.2652.

§ 35.655 Five-year inspection for teletherapy and gamma stereotactic radiosurgery units.

(a) A licensee shall have each teletherapy unit and gamma stereotactic radiosurgery unit fully inspected and serviced during source replacement or at intervals not to exceed 5 years, whichever comes first, to assure proper functioning of the source exposure mechanism.

(b) This inspection and servicing may only be performed by persons specifically licensed to do so by the Commission or an Agreement State.

(c) A licensee shall keep a record of the inspection and servicing in accordance with § 35.2655.

§ 35.657 Therapy-related computer systems.

The licensee shall perform acceptance testing on the treatment planning system of therapy-related computer systems in accordance with published protocols accepted by nationally recognized bodies. At a minimum, the acceptance testing must include, as applicable, verification of:

(a) The source-specific input parameters required by the dose calculation algorithm;

(b) The accuracy of dose, dwell time, and treatment time calculations at representative points;

(c) The accuracy of isodose plots and graphic displays;

(d) The accuracy of the software used to determine sealed source positions from radiographic images; and

(e) The accuracy of electronic transfer of the treatment delivery parameters to the treatment delivery unit from the treatment planning system.

§ 35.690 Training for use of remote afterloader units, teletherapy units, and gamma stereotactic radiosurgery units.

Except as provided in § 35.57, the licensee shall require an authorized user of a sealed source for a use authorized under § 35.600 to be a physician who—

(a) Is certified by a medical specialty board whose certification process has been recognized by the Commission or an Agreement State and who meets the requirements in paragraphs (b)(3) and (c) of this section. (The names of board certifications which have been recognized by the Commission or an Agreement State will be posted on the NRC's web page.) To have its certification process recognized, a specialty board shall require all candidates for certification to:

(1) Successfully complete a minimum of 3 years of residency training in a radiation therapy program approved by the Residency Review Committee of the Accreditation Council for Graduate Medical Education or the Royal College of Physicians and Surgeons of Canada or the Committee on Post-Graduate Training of the American Osteopathic Association; and

(2) Pass an examination, administered by diplomates of the specialty board, which tests knowledge and competence in radiation safety, radionuclide handling, treatment planning, quality assurance, and clinical use of stereotactic radiosurgery, remote afterloaders and external beam therapy; or

(b)(1) Has completed a structured educational program in basic radionuclide techniques applicable to the use of a sealed source in a therapeutic medical unit that includes—

(i) 200 hours of classroom and laboratory training in the following areas—

(A) Radiation physics and instrumentation;

(B) Radiation protection;

(C) Mathematics pertaining to the use and measurement of radioactivity; and

(D) Radiation biology; and

(ii) 500 hours of work experience, under the supervision of an authorized user who meets the requirements in §§ 35.57, 35.690, or equivalent Agreement State requirements at a medical institution, involving—

(A) Reviewing full calibration measurements and periodic spot-checks;

(B) Preparing treatment plans and calculating treatment doses and times;

(C) Using administrative controls to prevent a medical event involving the use of byproduct material;

(D) Implementing emergency procedures to be followed in the event of the abnormal operation of the medical unit or console;

(E) Checking and using survey meters; and

(F) Selecting the proper dose and how it is to be administered; and

(2) Has completed 3 years of supervised clinical experience in radiation therapy, under an authorized user who meets the requirements in §§ 35.57, 35.690, or equivalent Agreement State requirements, as part of a formal training program approved by the Residency Review Committee for Radiation Oncology of the Accreditation Council for Graduate Medical Education or the Royal College of Physicians and Surgeons of Canada or the Committee on Postdoctoral Training of the American Osteopathic Association. This experience may be obtained concurrently with the supervised work experience required by paragraph (b)(1)(ii) of this section; and

(3) Has obtained written attestation that the individual has satisfactorily completed the requirements in paragraph (a)(1) or paragraphs (b)(1) and

(b)(2), and paragraph (c), of this section, and has achieved a level of competency sufficient to function independently as an authorized user of each type of therapeutic medical unit for which the individual is requesting authorized user status. The written attestation must be signed by a preceptor authorized user who meets the requirements in §§ 35.57, 35.690, or equivalent Agreement State requirements for an authorized user for each type of therapeutic medical unit for which the individual is requesting authorized user status; and

(c) Has received training in device operation, safety procedures, and clinical use for the type(s) of use for which authorization is sought. This training requirement may be satisfied by satisfactory completion of a training program provided by the vendor for new users or by receiving training supervised by an authorized user or authorized medical physicist, as appropriate, who is authorized for the type(s) of use for which the individual is seeking authorization.

[67 FR 20370, Apr. 24, 2002, as amended at 70 FR 16366, Mar. 30, 2005; 71 FR 15011, Mar. 27, 2006; 74 FR 33906, July 14, 2009]

Subparts I–J [Reserved]

Subpart K—Other Medical Uses of Byproduct Material or Radiation From Byproduct Material

§ 35.1000 Other medical uses of byproduct material or radiation from byproduct material.

A licensee may use byproduct material or a radiation source approved for medical use which is not specifically addressed in subparts D through H of this part if—

(a) The applicant or licensee has submitted the information required by § 35.12(b) through (d); and

(b) The applicant or licensee has received written approval from the Commission in a license or license amendment and uses the material in accordance with the regulations and specific conditions the Commission considers necessary for the medical use of the material.

Subpart L—Records

§ 35.2024 Records of authority and responsibilities for radiation protection programs.

(a) A licensee shall retain a record of actions taken by the licensee's management in accordance with § 35.24(a) for 5 years. The record must include a summary of the actions taken and a signature of licensee management.

(b) The licensee shall retain a copy of both authority, duties, and responsibilities of the Radiation Safety Officer as required by § 35.24(e), and a signed copy of each Radiation Safety Officer's agreement to be responsible for implementing the radiation safety program, as required by § 35.24(b), for the duration of the license. The records must include the signature of the Radiation Safety Officer and licensee management.

§ 35.2026 Records of radiation protection program changes.

A licensee shall retain a record of each radiation protection program change made in accordance with § 35.26(a) for 5 years. The record must include a copy of the old and new procedures; the effective date of the change; and the signature of the licensee management that reviewed and approved the change.

§ 35.2040 Records of written directives.

A licensee shall retain a copy of each written directive as required by § 35.40 for 3 years.

§ 35.2041 Records for procedures for administrations requiring a written directive

A licensee shall retain a copy of the procedures required by § 35.41(a) for the duration of the license.

§ 35.2060 Records of calibrations of instruments used to measure the activity of unsealed byproduct material.

A licensee shall maintain a record of instrument calibrations required by § 35.60 for 3 years. The records must include the model and serial number of the instrument, the date of the calibration, the results of the calibration, and the name of the individual who performed the calibration.

§ 35.2061 Records of radiation survey instrument calibrations.

A licensee shall maintain a record of radiation survey instrument calibrations required by § 35.61 for 3 years. The record must include the model and serial number of the instrument, the date of the calibration, the results of the calibration, and the name of the individual who performed the calibration.

§ 35.2063 Records of dosages of unsealed byproduct material for medical use.

(a) A licensee shall maintain a record of dosage determinations required by § 35.63 for 3 years.

(b) The record must contain—

(1) The radiopharmaceutical;

(2) The patient's or human research subject's name, or identification number if one has been assigned;

(3) The prescribed dosage, the determined dosage, or a notation that the total activity is less than 1.1 MBq (30 μCi);

(4) The date and time of the dosage determination; and

(5) The name of the individual who determined the dosage.

§ 35.2067 Records of leaks tests and inventory of sealed sources and brachytherapy sources.

(a) A licensee shall retain records of leak tests required by § 35.67(b) for 3 years. The records must include the model number, and serial number if one has been assigned, of each source tested; the identity of each source by radionuclide and its estimated activity; the results of the test; the date of the test; and the name of the individual who performed the test.

(b) A licensee shall retain records of the semi-annual physical inventory of sealed sources and brachytherapy sources required by § 35.67(g) for 3 years. The inventory records must contain the model number of each source, and serial number if one has been assigned, the identity of each source by radionuclide and its nominal activity, the location of each source, and the name of the individual who performed the inventory.

§ 35.2070 Records of surveys for ambient radiation exposure rate.

A licensee shall retain a record of each survey required by § 35.70 for 3 years. The record must include the date of the survey, the results of the survey, the instrument used to make the survey, and the name of the individual who performed the survey.

§ 35.2075 Records of the release of individuals containing unsealed byproduct material or implants containing byproduct material.

(a) A licensee shall retain a record of the basis for authorizing the release of an individual in accordance with § 35.75, if the total effective dose equivalent is calculated by—

(1) Using the retained activity rather than the activity administered;

(2) Using an occupancy factor less than 0.25 at 1 meter;

(3) Using the biological or effective half-life; or

(4) Considering the shielding by tissue.

(b) A licensee shall retain a record that the instructions required by § 35.75(b) were provided to a breast-feeding female if the radiation dose to the infant or child from continued breast-feeding could result in a total effective dose equivalent exceeding 5 mSv (0.5 rem).

(c) The records required by paragraphs (a) and (b) of this section must be retained for 3 years after the date of release of the individual.

§ 35.2080 Records of mobile medical services.

(a) A licensee shall retain a copy of each letter that permits the use of byproduct material at a client's address, as required by § 35.80(a)(1). Each letter must clearly delineate the authority and responsibility of the licensee and the client and must be retained for 3 years after the last provision of service.

(b) A licensee shall retain the record of each survey required by § 35.80(a)(4) for 3 years. The record must include the date of the survey, the results of the survey, the instrument used to make the survey, and the name of the individual who performed the survey.

§ 35.2092 Records of decay-in-storage.

A licensee shall maintain records of the disposal of licensed materials, as required by § 35.92, for 3 years. The record must include the date of the disposal, the survey instrument used, the background radiation level, the radiation level measured at the surface of each waste container, and the name of the individual who performed the survey.

§ 35.2204 Records of molybdenum-99, strontium-82, and strontium-85 concentrations.

A licensee shall maintain a record of the molybdenum-99 concentration or strontium-82 and strontium-85 concentration tests required by § 35.204(b) and (c) for 3 years. The record must include:

(a) For each measured elution of technetium-99m, the ratio of the measures expressed as kilobecquerel of molybdenum-99 per megabecquerel of technetium-99m (or microcuries of molybdenum per millicurie of technetium), the time and date of the measurement, and the name of the individual who made the measurement; or

(b) For each measured elution of rubidium-82, the ratio of the measures expressed as kilobecquerel of strontium-82 per megabecquerel of rubidium-82 (or microcuries of strontium-82 per millicurie of rubidium), kilobecquerel of strontium-85 per megabecquerel of rubidium-82 (or microcuries of strontium-85 per millicurie of rubidium), the time and date of the measurement, and the name of the individual who made the measurement.

[72 FR 55932, Oct. 1, 2007]

§ 35.2310 Records of safety instruction.

A licensee shall maintain a record of safety instructions required by §§ 35.310, 35.410, and 35.610 for 3 years. The record must include a list of the topics covered, the date of the instruction, the name(s) of the attendee(s), and the name(s) of the individual(s) who provided the instruction.

§ 35.2404 Records of surveys after source implant and removal.

A licensee shall maintain a record of the surveys required by §§ 35.404 and 35.604 for 3 years. Each record must include the date and results of the survey, the survey instrument used, and the name of the individual who made the survey.

§ 35.2406 Records of brachytherapy source accountability.

(a) A licensee shall maintain a record of brachytherapy source accountability required by § 35.406 for 3 years.

(b) For temporary implants, the record must include—

(1) The number and activity of sources removed from storage, the time and date they were removed from storage, the name of the individual who removed them from storage, and the location of use; and

(2) The number and activity of sources returned to storage, the time and date they were returned to storage, and the name of the individual who returned them to storage.

(c) For permanent implants, the record must include—

(1) The number and activity of sources removed from storage, the date they were removed from storage, and the name of the individual who removed them from storage;

(2) The number and activity of sources not implanted, the date they were returned to storage, and the name of the individual who returned them to storage; and

(3) The number and activity of sources permanently implanted in the patient or human research subject.

§ 35.2432 Records of calibration measurements of brachytherapy sources.

(a) A licensee shall maintain a record of the calibrations of brachytherapy sources required by § 35.432 for 3 years after the last use of the source.

(b) The record must include—

(1) The date of the calibration;

(2) The manufacturer's name, model number, and serial number for the source and the instruments used to calibrate the source;

(3) The source output or activity;

(4) The source positioning accuracy within the applicators; and

(5) The name of the individual, the source manufacturer, or the calibration laboratory that performed the calibration.

[67 FR 20370, Apr. 24, 2002, as amended at 68 FR 19326, Apr. 21, 2003]

§ 35.2433 Records of decay of strontium-90 sources for ophthalmic treatments.

(a) A licensee shall maintain a record of the activity of a strontium-90 source required by § 35.433 for the life of the source.

(b) The record must include—

(1) The date and initial activity of the source as determined under § 35.432; and

(2) For each decay calculation, the date and the source activity as determined under § 35.433.

§ 35.2605 Records of installation, maintenance, adjustment, and repair of remote afterloader units, teletherapy units, and gamma stereotactic radiosurgery units.

A licensee shall retain a record of the installation, maintenance, adjustment, and repair of remote afterloader units, teletherapy units, and gamma stereotactic radiosurgery units as required by § 35.605 for 3 years. For each installation, maintenance, adjustment and repair, the record must include the date, description of the service, and name(s) of the individual(s) who performed the work.

§ 35.2610 Records of safety procedures.

A licensee shall retain a copy of the procedures required by §§ 35.610(a)(4) and (d)(2) until the licensee no longer possesses the remote afterloader, teletherapy unit, or gamma stereotactic radiosurgery unit.

§ 35.2630 Records of dosimetry equipment used with remote afterloader units, teletherapy units, and gamma stereotactic radiosurgery units.

(a) A licensee shall retain a record of the calibration, intercomparison, and comparisons of its dosimetry equipment done in accordance with § 35.630 for the duration of the license.

(b) For each calibration, intercomparison, or comparison, the record must include—

(1) The date;

(2) The manufacturer's name, model numbers and serial numbers of the instruments that were calibrated, intercompared, or compared as required by paragraphs (a) and (b) of § 35.630;

(3) The correction factor that was determined from the calibration or comparison or the apparent correction factor that was determined from an intercomparison; and

(4) The names of the individuals who performed the calibration, intercomparison, or comparison.

§ 35.2632 Records of teletherapy, remote afterloader, and gamma stereotactic radiosurgery full calibrations.

(a) A licensee shall maintain a record of the teletherapy unit, remote afterloader unit, and gamma stereotactic radiosurgery unit full calibrations required by §§ 35.632, 35.633, and 35.635 for 3 years.

(b) The record must include—

(1) The date of the calibration;

(2) The manufacturer's name, model number, and serial number of the teletherapy, remote afterloader, and gamma stereotactic radiosurgery unit(s), the source(s), and the instruments used to calibrate the unit(s);

(3) The results and an assessment of the full calibrations;

(4) The results of the autoradiograph required for low dose-rate remote afterloader units; and

(5) The signature of the authorized medical physicist who performed the full calibration.

§ 35.2642 Records of periodic spot-checks for teletherapy units.

(a) A licensee shall retain a record of each periodic spot-check for teletherapy units required by § 35.642 for 3 years.

(b) The record must include—

(1) The date of the spot-check;

(2) The manufacturer's name, model number, and serial number of the teletherapy unit, source and instrument used to measure the output of the teletherapy unit;

(3) An assessment of timer linearity and constancy;

(4) The calculated on-off error;

(5) A determination of the coincidence of the radiation field and the

field indicated by the light beam localizing device;

(6) The determined accuracy of each distance measuring and localization device;

(7) The difference between the anticipated output and the measured output;

(8) Notations indicating the operability of each entrance door electrical interlock, each electrical or mechanical stop, each source exposure indicator light, and the viewing and intercom system and doors; and

(9) The name of the individual who performed the periodic spot-check and the signature of the authorized medical physicist who reviewed the record of the spot-check.

(c) A licensee shall retain a copy of the procedures required by § 35.642(b) until the licensee no longer possesses the teletherapy unit.

§ 35.2643 Records of periodic spot-checks for remote afterloader units.

(a) A licensee shall retain a record of each spot-check for remote afterloader units required by § 35.643 for 3 years.

(b) The record must include, as applicable—

(1) The date of the spot-check;

(2) The manufacturer's name, model number, and serial number for the remote afterloader unit and source;

(3) An assessment of timer accuracy;

(4) Notations indicating the operability of each entrance door electrical interlock, radiation monitors, source exposure indicator lights, viewing and intercom systems, and clock and decayed source activity in the unit's computer; and

(5) The name of the individual who performed the periodic spot-check and the signature of the authorized medical physicist who reviewed the record of the spot-check.

(c) A licensee shall retain a copy of the procedures required by § 35.643(b) until the licensee no longer possesses the remote afterloader unit.

§ 35.2645 Records of periodic spot-checks for gamma stereotactic radiosurgery units.

(a) A licensee shall retain a record of each spot-check for gamma stereotactic radiosurgery units required by § 35.645 for 3 years.

(b) The record must include—

(1) The date of the spot-check;

(2) The manufacturer's name, model number, and serial number for the gamma stereotactic radiosurgery unit and the instrument used to measure the output of the unit;

(3) An assessment of timer linearity and accuracy;

(4) The calculated on-off error;

(5) A determination of trunnion centricity;

(6) The difference between the anticipated output and the measured output;

(7) An assessment of source output against computer calculations;

(8) Notations indicating the operability of radiation monitors, helmet microswitches, emergency timing circuits, emergency off buttons, electrical interlocks, source exposure indicator lights, viewing and intercom systems, timer termination, treatment table retraction mechanism, and stereotactic frames and localizing devices (trunnions); and

(9) The name of the individual who performed the periodic spot-check and the signature of the authorized medical physicist who reviewed the record of the spot-check.

(c) A licensee shall retain a copy of the procedures required by § 35.645(b) until the licensee no longer possesses the gamma stereotactic radiosurgery unit.

§ 35.2647 Records of additional technical requirements for mobile remote afterloader units.

(a) A licensee shall retain a record of each check for mobile remote afterloader units required by § 35.647 for 3 years.

(b) The record must include—

(1) The date of the check;

(2) The manufacturer's name, model number, and serial number of the remote afterloader unit;

(3) Notations accounting for all sources before the licensee departs from a facility;

(4) Notations indicating the operability of each entrance door electrical interlock, radiation monitors, source exposure indicator lights, viewing and intercom system, applicators, source

transfer tubes, and transfer tube applicator interfaces, and source positioning accuracy; and

(5) The signature of the individual who performed the check.

§ 35.2652 Records of surveys of therapeutic treatment units.

(a) A licensee shall maintain a record of radiation surveys of treatment units made in accordance with § 35.652 for the duration of use of the unit.

(b) The record must include—

(1) The date of the measurements;

(2) The manufacturer's name, model number and serial number of the treatment unit, source, and instrument used to measure radiation levels;

(3) Each dose rate measured around the source while the unit is in the off position and the average of all measurements; and

(4) The signature of the individual who performed the test.

§ 35.2655 Records of 5-year inspection for teletherapy and gamma stereotactic radiosurgery units.

(a) A licensee shall maintain a record of the 5-year inspections for teletherapy and gamma stereotactic radiosurgery units required by § 35.655 for the duration of use of the unit.

(b) The record must contain—

(1) The inspector's radioactive materials license number;

(2) The date of inspection;

(3) The manufacturer's name and model number and serial number of both the treatment unit and source;

(4) A list of components inspected and serviced, and the type of service; and

(5) The signature of the inspector.

Subpart M—Reports

§ 35.3045 Report and notification of a medical event.

(a) A licensee shall report any event, except for an event that results from patient intervention, in which the administration of byproduct material or radiation from byproduct material results in—

(1) A dose that differs from the prescribed dose or dose that would have resulted from the prescribed dosage by more than 0.05 Sv (5 rem) effective dose equivalent, 0.5 Sv (50 rem) to an organ or tissue, or 0.5 Sv (50 rem) shallow dose equivalent to the skin; and

(i) The total dose delivered differs from the prescribed dose by 20 percent or more;

(ii) The total dosage delivered differs from the prescribed dosage by 20 percent or more or falls outside the prescribed dosage range; or

(iii) The fractionated dose delivered differs from the prescribed dose, for a single fraction, by 50 percent or more.

(2) A dose that exceeds 0.05 Sv (5 rem) effective dose equivalent, 0.5 Sv (50 rem) to an organ or tissue, or 0.5 Sv (50 rem) shallow dose equivalent to the skin from any of the following—

(i) An administration of a wrong radioactive drug containing byproduct material;

(ii) An administration of a radioactive drug containing byproduct material by the wrong route of administration;

(iii) An administration of a dose or dosage to the wrong individual or human research subject;

(iv) An administration of a dose or dosage delivered by the wrong mode of treatment; or

(v) A leaking sealed source.

(3) A dose to the skin or an organ or tissue other than the treatment site that exceeds by 0.5 Sv (50 rem) to an organ or tissue and 50 percent or more of the dose expected from the administration defined in the written directive (excluding, for permanent implants, seeds that were implanted in the correct site but migrated outside the treatment site).

(b) A licensee shall report any event resulting from intervention of a patient or human research subject in which the administration of byproduct material or radiation from byproduct material results or will result in unintended permanent functional damage to an organ or a physiological system, as determined by a physician.

(c) The licensee shall notify by telephone the NRC Operations Center[3] no later than the next calendar day after discovery of the medical event.

---

[3] The commercial telephone number of the NRC Operations Center is (301) 816–5100.

(d) By an appropriate method listed in § 30.6(a) of this chapter, the licensee shall submit a written report to the appropriate NRC Regional Office listed in § 30.6 of this chapter within 15 days after discovery of the medical event.

(1) The written report must include—

(i) The licensee's name;

(ii) The name of the prescribing physician;

(iii) A brief description of the event;

(iv) Why the event occurred;

(v) The effect, if any, on the individual(s) who received the administration;

(vi) What actions, if any, have been taken or are planned to prevent recurrence; and

(vii) Certification that the licensee notified the individual (or the individual's responsible relative or guardian), and if not, why not.

(2) The report may not contain the individual's name or any other information that could lead to identification of the individual.

(e) The licensee shall provide notification of the event to the referring physician and also notify the individual who is the subject of the medical event no later than 24 hours after its discovery, unless the referring physician personally informs the licensee either that he or she will inform the individual or that, based on medical judgment, telling the individual would be harmful. The licensee is not required to notify the individual without first consulting the referring physician. If the referring physician or the affected individual cannot be reached within 24 hours, the licensee shall notify the individual as soon as possible thereafter. The licensee may not delay any appropriate medical care for the individual, including any necessary remedial care as a result of the medical event, because of any delay in notification. To meet the requirements of this paragraph, the notification of the individual who is the subject of the medical event may be made instead to that individual's responsible relative or guardian. If a verbal notification is made, the licensee shall inform the individual, or appropriate responsible relative or guardian, that a written description of the event can be obtained from the licensee upon request. The licensee shall provide such a written description if requested.

(f) Aside from the notification requirement, nothing in this section affects any rights or duties of licensees and physicians in relation to each other, to individuals affected by the medical event, or to that individual's responsible relatives or guardians.

(g) A licensee shall:

(1) Annotate a copy of the report provided to the NRC with the:

(i) Name of the individual who is the subject of the event; and

(ii) Social security number or other identification number, if one has been assigned, of the individual who is the subject of the event; and

(2) Provide a copy of the annotated report to the referring physician, if other than the licensee, no later than 15 days after the discovery of the event.

[67 FR 20370, Apr. 24, 2002, as amended at 68 FR 58805, Oct. 10, 2003; 76 FR 72085, Nov. 22, 2011]

§ 35.3047 Report and notification of a dose to an embryo/fetus or a nursing child.

(a) A licensee shall report any dose to an embryo/fetus that is greater than 50 mSv (5 rem) dose equivalent that is a result of an administration of byproduct material or radiation from byproduct material to a pregnant individual unless the dose to the embryo/fetus was specifically approved, in advance, by the authorized user.

(b) A licensee shall report any dose to a nursing child that is a result of an administration of byproduct material to a breast-feeding individual that—

(1) Is greater than 50 mSv (5 rem) total effective dose equivalent; or

(2) Has resulted in unintended permanent functional damage to an organ or a physiological system of the child, as determined by a physician.

(c) The licensee shall notify by telephone the NRC Operations Center no later than the next calendar day after discovery of a dose to the embryo/fetus or nursing child that requires a report in paragraphs (a) or (b) in this section.

(d) By an appropriate method listed in § 30.6(a) of this chapter, the licensee shall submit a written report to the appropriate NRC Regional Office listed in

§ 30.6 of this chapter within 15 days after discovery of a dose to the embryo/fetus or nursing child that requires a report in paragraphs (a) or (b) in this section.

(1) The written report must include—

(i) The licensee's name;

(ii) The name of the prescribing physician;

(iii) A brief description of the event;

(iv) Why the event occurred;

(v) The effect, if any, on the embryo/fetus or the nursing child;

(vi) What actions, if any, have been taken or are planned to prevent recurrence; and

(vii) Certification that the licensee notified the pregnant individual or mother (or the mother's or child's responsible relative or guardian), and if not, why not.

(2) The report must not contain the individual's or child's name or any other information that could lead to identification of the individual or child.

(e) The licensee shall provide notification of the event to the referring physician and also notify the pregnant individual or mother, both hereafter referred to as the mother, no later than 24 hours after discovery of an event that would require reporting under paragraph (a) or (b) of this section, unless the referring physician personally informs the licensee either that he or she will inform the mother or that, based on medical judgment, telling the mother would be harmful. The licensee is not required to notify the mother without first consulting with the referring physician. If the referring physician or mother cannot be reached within 24 hours, the licensee shall make the appropriate notifications as soon as possible thereafter. The licensee may not delay any appropriate medical care for the embryo/fetus or for the nursing child, including any necessary remedial care as a result of the event, because of any delay in notification. To meet the requirements of this paragraph, the notification may be made to the mother's or child's responsible relative or guardian instead of the mother. If a verbal notification is made, the licensee shall inform the mother, or the mother's or child's responsible relative or guardian, that a written description of the event can be obtained from the licensee upon request. The licensee shall provide such a written description if requested.

(f) A licensee shall:

(1) Annotate a copy of the report provided to the NRC with the:

(i) Name of the pregnant individual or the nursing child who is the subject of the event; and

(ii) Social security number or other identification number, if one has been assigned, of the pregnant individual or the nursing child who is the subject of the event; and

(2) Provide a copy of the annotated report to the referring physician, if other than the licensee, no later than 15 days after the discovery of the event.

[67 FR 20370, Apr. 24, 2002, as amended at 68 FR 58805, Oct. 10, 2003]

§ 35.3067 Report of a leaking source.

A licensee shall file a report within 5 days if a leak test required by § 35.67 reveals the presence of 185 Bq (0.005 μCi) or more of removable contamination. The report must be filed with the appropriate NRC Regional Office listed in § 30.6 of this chapter, by an appropriate method listed in § 30.6(a) of this chapter, with a copy to the Director, Office of Nuclear Material Safety and Safeguards. The written report must include the model number and serial number, if assigned, of the leaking source; the radionuclide and its estimated activity; the results of the test; the date of the test; and the action taken.

[73 FR 5720, Jan. 31, 2008]

Subpart N—Enforcement

§ 35.4001 Violations.

(a) The Commission may obtain an injunction or other court order to prevent a violation of the provisions of—

(1) The Atomic Energy Act of 1954, as amended;

(2) Title II of the Energy Reorganization Act of 1974, as amended; or

(3) A regulation or order issued under those Acts.

(b) The Commission may obtain a court order for the payment of a civil penalty imposed under Section 234 of the Atomic Energy Act:

(1) For violations of—

(i) Sections 53, 57, 62, 63, 81, 82, 101, 103, 104, 107, or 109 of the Atomic Energy Act of 1954, as amended;

(ii) Section 206 of the Energy Reorganization Act;

(iii) Any rule, regulation, or order issued under the sections specified in paragraph (b)(1)(i) of this section;

(iv) Any term, condition, or limitation of any license issued under the sections specified in paragraph (b)(1)(i) of this section.

(2) For any violation for which a license may be revoked under Section 186 of the Atomic Energy Act of 1954, as amended.

§ 35.4002 Criminal penalties.

(a) Section 223 of the Atomic Energy Act of 1954, as amended, provides for criminal sanctions for willful violation of, attempted violation of, or conspiracy to violate, any regulation issued under sections 161b, 161i, or 161o of the Act. For purposes of Section 223, all the regulations in 10 CFR part 35 are issued under one or more of sections 161b, 161i, or 161o, except for the sections listed in paragraph (b) of this section.

(b) The regulations in 10 CFR part 35 that are not issued under subsections 161b, 161i, or 161o for the purposes of Section 223 are as follows: §§ 35.1, 35.2, 35.7, 35.8, 35.12, 35.15, 35.18, 35.19, 35.65, 35.100, 35.200, 35.300, 35.4001, and 35.4002.

PART 36—LICENSES AND RADIATION SAFETY REQUIREMENTS FOR IRRADIATORS

AUTHORITY: Atomic Energy Act of 1954, secs. 81, 161, 181, 182, 183, 223, 234, 274 (42 U.S.C. 2111, 2112, 2201, 2231, 2233, 2273, 2282, 2021); Energy Reorganization Act of 1974, secs. 201, 206 (42 U.S.C. 5841, 5846); 44 U.S.C. 3504 note.

SOURCE: 58 FR 7728, Feb. 9, 1993, unless otherwise noted.

Subpart A—General Provisions

§ 36.1 Purpose and scope.

(a) This part contains requirements for the issuance of a license authorizing the use of sealed sources containing radioactive materials in irradiators used to irradiate objects or materials using gamma radiation. This part also contains radiation safety requirements for operating irradiators. The requirements of this part are in addition to other requirements of this chapter. In particular, the provisions of parts 19, 20, 21, 30, 37, 71, 170, and 171 of this chapter apply to applications and licenses subject to this part. Nothing in this part relieves the licensee from complying with other applicable Federal, State and local regulations governing the siting, zoning, land use, and building code requirements for industrial facilities.

(b) The regulations in this part apply to panoramic irradiators that have either dry or wet storage of the radioactive sealed sources and to underwater irradiators in which both the source and the product being irradiated are under water. Irradiators whose dose rates exceed 5 grays (500 rads) per hour at 1 meter from the radioactive sealed sources in air or in water, as applicable for the irradiator type, are covered by this part.

(c) The regulations in this part do not apply to self-contained dry-source-storage irradiators (those in which both the source and the area subject to irradiation are contained within a device and are not accessible by personnel), medical radiology or teletherapy, radiography (the irradiation of materials for nondestructive testing purposes), gauging, or open-field (agricultural) irradiations.

[58 FR 7728, Feb. 9, 1993, as amended at 78 FR 17007, Mar. 19, 2013]

§ 36.2 Definitions.

Annually means either (1) at intervals not to exceed 1 year or (2) once per year, at about the same time each year (plus or minus 1 month).

Commencement of construction means taking any action defined as "construction" or any other activity at the site of a facility subject to the regulations in this part that has a reasonable nexus to:

(1) Radiological health and safety; or

(2) Common defense and security.

Construction means the installation of foundations, or in-place assembly, erection, fabrication, or testing for any structure, system, or component of a facility or activity subject to the regulations in this part that are related to radiological safety or security. The term "construction" does not include:

(1) Changes for temporary use of the land for public recreational purposes;

(2) Site exploration, including necessary borings to determine foundation conditions or other preconstruction monitoring to establish background information related to the suitability of the site, the environmental impacts of construction or operation, or the protection of environmental values;

(3) Preparation of the site for construction of the facility, including clearing of the site, grading, installation of drainage, erosion and other environmental mitigation measures, and construction of temporary roads and borrow areas;

(4) Erection of fences and other access control measures that are not related to the safe use of, or security of, radiological materials subject to this part;

(5) Excavation;

(6) Erection of support buildings (e.g., construction equipment storage sheds, warehouse and shop facilities, utilities, concrete mixing plants, docking and unloading facilities, and office buildings) for use in connection with the construction of the facility;

(7) Building of service facilities (e.g., paved roads, parking lots, railroad spurs, exterior utility and lighting systems, potable water systems, sanitary sewerage treatment facilities, and transmission lines);

(8) Procurement or fabrication of components or portions of the proposed facility occurring at other than the final, in-place location at the facility; or

(9) Taking any other action that has no reasonable nexus to:

(i) Radiological health and safety, or

(ii) Common defense and security.

Doubly encapsulated sealed source means a sealed source in which the radioactive material is sealed within a capsule and that capsule is sealed within another capsule.

Irradiator means a facility that uses radioactive sealed sources for the irradiation of objects or materials and in which radiation dose rates exceeding 5 grays (500 rads) per hour exist at 1 meter from the sealed radioactive sources in air or water, as applicable for the irradiator type, but does not include irradiators in which both the sealed source and the area subject to irradiation are contained within a device and are not accessible to personnel.

Irradiator operator means an individual who has successfully completed the training and testing described in § 36.51 and is authorized by the terms of the license to operate the irradiator without a supervisor present.

Panoramic dry-source-storage irradiator means an irradiator in which the irradiations occur in air in areas potentially accessible to personnel and in which the sources are stored in shields made of solid materials. The term includes beam-type dry-source-storage irradiators in which only a narrow beam of radiation is produced for performing irradiations.

Panoramic irradiator means an irradiator in which the irradiations are done in air in areas potentially accessible to personnel. The term includes beam-type irradiators.

Panoramic wet-source-storage irradiator means an irradiator in which the irradiations occur in air in areas potentially accessible to personnel and in which the sources are stored under water in a storage pool.

Pool irradiator means any irradiator at which the sources are stored or used in a pool of water including panoramic wet-source-storage irradiators and underwater irradiators.

Product conveyor system means a system for moving the product to be irradiated to, from, and within the area where irradiation takes place.

Radiation room means a shielded room in which irradiations take place. Underwater irradiators do not have radiation rooms.

Radiation safety officer means an individual with responsibility for the overall radiation safety program at the facility.

Sealed source means any byproduct material that is used as a source of radiation and is encased in a capsule designed to prevent leakage or escape of the byproduct material.

Seismic area means any area where the probability of a horizontal acceleration in rock of more than 0.3 times the acceleration of gravity in 250 years is greater than 10 percent, as designated by the U.S. Geological Survey.

Underwater irradiator means an irradiator in which the sources always remain shielded under water and humans do not have access to the sealed sources or the space subject to irradiation without entering the pool.

[58 FR 7728, Feb. 9, 1993, as amended at 76 FR 56963, Sept. 15, 2011]

§ 36.5 Interpretations.

Except as specifically authorized by the Commission in writing, no interpretation of the meaning of the regulations in this part by any officer or employee of the Commission, other than a written interpretation by the General Counsel, will be recognized to be binding upon the Commission.

§ 36.8 Information collection requirements: OMB approval.

(a) The Nuclear Regulatory Commission has submitted the information collection requirements contained in this part to the Office of Management and Budget (OMB) for approval as required by the Paperwork Reduction Act (44 U.S.C. 3501*et seq.*). The NRC may not conduct or sponsor, and a person is not required to respond to, a collection of information unless it displays a currently valid OMB control number. OMB has approved the information collection requirements contained in this part under control number 3150–0158.

(b) The approved information collection requirements contained in this part appear in §§ 36.11, 36.13, 36.17, 36.19, 36.21, 36.53, 36.69, 36.81, and 36.83.

(c) This part contains information collection requirements in addition to those approved under the control number specified in paragraph (a) of this section. These information collection requirements and the control numbers under which they are approved are as follows:

(1) In § 36.11, NRC Form 313 is approved under control number 3150–0120.

(2) [Reserved]

[58 FR 7728, Feb. 9, 1993, as amended at 62 FR 52187, Oct. 6, 1997]

Subpart B—Specific Licensing Requirements

§ 36.11 Application for a specific license.

A person, as defined in § 30.4 of this chapter, may file an application for a specific license authorizing the use of sealed sources in an irradiator on Form NRC 313, "Application for Material License." Each application for a license, other than a license exempted from part 170 of this chapter, must be accompanied by the fee prescribed in § 170.31 of this chapter. The application and one copy must be sent to the appropriate NRC Regional Office listed in appendix D to part 20 of this chapter.

§ 36.13 Specific licenses for irradiators.

The Commission will approve an application for a specific license for the use of licensed material in an irradiator if the applicant meets the requirements contained in this section.

(a) The applicant shall satisfy the general requirements specified in §§ 30.33(a)(1)–(4) and 30.33(b) of this chapter and the requirements contained in this part.

(b) The application must describe the training provided to irradiator operators including—

(1) Classroom training;

(2) On-the-job or simulator training;

(3) Safety reviews;

(4) Means employed by the applicant to test each operator's understanding of the Commission's regulations and licensing requirements and the irradiator operating and emergency procedures; and

(5) Minimum training and experience of personnel who may provide training.

(c) The application must include an outline of the written operating and emergency procedures listed in § 36.53 that describes the radiation safety aspects of the procedures.

(d) The application must describe the organizational structure for managing the irradiator, specifically the radiation safety responsibilities and authorities of the radiation safety officer and those management personnel who have important radiation safety responsibilities or authorities. In particular, the application must specify who, within the management structure, has the authority to stop unsafe operations. The application must also describe the training and experience required for the position of radiation safety officer.

(e) The application must include a description of the access control systems required by § 36.23, the radiation monitors required by § 36.29, the method of detecting leaking sources required by § 36.59 including the sensitivity of the method, and a diagram of the facility that shows the locations of all required interlocks and radiation monitors.

(f) If the applicant intends to perform leak testing of dry-source-storage sealed sources, the applicant shall establish procedures for leak testing and submit a description of these procedures to the Commission. The description must include the—

(1) Instruments to be used;

(2) Methods of performing the analysis; and

(3) Pertinent experience of the individual who analyzes the samples.

(g) If licensee personnel are to load or unload sources, the applicant shall describe the qualifications and training of the personnel and the procedures to be used. If the applicant intends to contract for source loading or unloading at its facility, the loading or unloading must be done by an organization specifically authorized by the Commission or an Agreement State to load or unload irradiator sources.

(h) The applicant shall describe the inspection and maintenance checks, including the frequency of the checks required by § 36.61.

[58 FR 7728, Feb. 9, 1993, as amended at 76 FR 56963, Sept. 15, 2011]

§ 36.15 Commencement of construction.

Commencement of construction of a new irradiator may not occur prior to the submission to the NRC of both an application for a license for the irradiator and the fee required by § 170.31 of this chapter. Any activities undertaken prior to the issuance of a license are entirely at the risk of the applicant and have no bearing on the issuance of a license with respect to the requirements of the Atomic Energy

Act of 1954 (Act), as amended, and rules, regulations, and orders issued under the Act. Commencement of construction as defined in § 36.2 may include non-construction activities if the activity has a reasonable nexus to radiological safety and security.

[76 FR 56963, Sept. 15, 2011]

§ 36.17 Applications for exemptions.

(a) The Commission may, upon application of any interested person or upon its own initiative, grant any exemptions from the requirements in this part that it determines are authorized by law and will not endanger life or property or the common defense and security and are otherwise in the public interest.

(b) Any application for a license or for amendment of a license authorizing use of a teletherapy-type unit for irradiation of materials or objects may include proposed alternatives for the requirements of this part. The Commission will approve the proposed alternatives if the applicant provides adequate rationale for the proposed alternatives and demonstrates that they are likely to provide an adequate level of safety for workers and the public.

§ 36.19 Request for written statements.

(a) After the filing of the original application, the Commission may request further information necessary to enable the Commission to determine whether the application should be granted or denied.

(b) Each license is issued with the condition that the licensee will, at any time before expiration of the license, upon the Commission's request, submit written statements to enable the Commission to determine whether the license should be modified, suspended, or revoked.

Subpart C—Design and Performance Requirements for Irradiators

§ 36.21 Performance criteria for sealed sources.

(a) *Requirements.* Sealed sources installed after July 1, 1993:

(1) Must have a certificate of registration issued under 10 CFR 32.210;

(2) Must be doubly encapsulated;

(3) Must use radioactive material that is as nondispersible as practical and that is as insoluble as practical if the source is used in a wet-source-storage or wet-source-change irradiator;

(4) Must be encapsulated in a material resistant to general corrosion and to localized corrosion, such as 316L stainless steel or other material with equivalent resistance if the sources are for use in irradiator pools; and

(5) In prototype testing of the sealed source, must have been leak tested and found leak-free after each of the tests described in paragraphs (b) through (g) of this section.

(b) *Temperature.* The test source must be held at −40 °C for 20 minutes, 600 °C for 1 hour, and then be subjected to a thermal shock test with a temperature drop from 600 °C to 20 °C within 15 seconds.

(c) *Pressure.* The test source must be twice subjected for at least 5 minutes to an external pressure (absolute) of 2 million newtons per square meter.

(d) *Impact.* A 2-kilogram steel weight, 2.5 centimeters in diameter, must be dropped from a height of 1 meter onto the test source.

(e) *Vibration.* The test source must be subjected 3 times for 10 minutes each to vibrations sweeping from 25 hertz to 500 hertz with a peak amplitude of 5 times the acceleration of gravity. In addition, each test source must be vibratod for 30 minutes at each resonant frequency found.

(f) *Puncture.* A 50-gram weight and pin, 0.3-centimotor pin diameter, must be dropped from a height of 1 meter onto the test source.

(g) *Bend.* If the length of the source is more than 15 times larger than the minimum cross-sectional dimension, the test source must be subjected to a force of 2000 newtons at its center equidistant from two support cylinders, the distance between which is 10 times the minimum cross-sectional dimension of the source.

§ 36.23 Access control.

(a) Each entrance to a radiation room at a panoramic irradiator must have a door or other physical barrier to prevent inadvertent entry of personnel if the sources are not in the shielded position. Product conveyor systems may serve as barriers as long as they reliably and consistently function as a barrier. It must not be possible to move the sources out of their shielded position if the door or barrier is open. Opening the door or barrier while the sources are exposed must cause the sources to return promptly to their shielded position. The personnel entrance door or barrier must have a lock that is operated by the same key used to move the sources. The doors and barriers must not prevent any individual in the radiation room from leaving.

(b) In addition, each entrance to a radiation room at a panoramic irradiator must have an independent backup access control to detect personnel entry while the sources are exposed. Detection of entry while the sources are exposed must cause the sources to return to their fully shielded position and must also activate a visible and audible alarm to make the individual entering the room aware of the hazard. The alarm must also alert at least one other individual who is onsite of the entry. That individual shall be trained on how to respond to the alarm and prepared to promptly render or summon assistance.

(c) A radiation monitor must be provided to detect the presence of high radiation levels in the radiation room of a panoramic irradiator before personnel entry. The monitor must be integrated with personnel access door locks to prevent room access when radiation levels are high. Attempted personnel entry while the monitor measures high radiation levels, must activate the alarm described in paragraph (b) of this section. The monitor may be located in the entrance (normally referred to as the maze) but not in the direct radiation beam.

(d) Before the sources move from their shielded position in a panoramic irradiator, the source control must automatically activate conspicuous visible and audible alarms to alert people in the radiation room that the sources will be moved from their shielded position. The alarms must give individuals enough time to leave the room before the sources leave the shielded position.

(e) Each radiation room at a panoramic irradiator must have a clearly visible and readily accessible control that would allow an individual in the room to make the sources return to their fully shielded position.

(f) Each radiation room of a panoramic irradiator must contain a control that prevents the sources from moving from the shielded position unless the control has been activated and the door or barrier to the radiation room has been closed within a preset time after activation of the control.

(g) Each entrance to the radiation room of a panoramic irradiator and each entrance to the area within the personnel access barrier of an underwater irradiator must be posted as required by 10 CFR 20.1902. Radiation postings for panoramic irradiators must comply with the posting requirements of 10 CFR 20.1902, except that signs may be removed, covered, or otherwise made inoperative when the sources are fully shielded.

(h) If the radiation room of a panoramic irradiator has roof plugs or other movable shielding, it must not be possible to operate the irradiator unless the shielding is in its proper location. This requirement may be met by interlocks that prevent operation if shielding is not placed properly or by an operating procedure requiring inspection of shielding before operating.

(i) Underwater irradiators must have a personnel access barrier around the pool which must be locked to prevent access when the irradiator is not attended. Only operators and facility management may have access to keys to the personnel access barrier. There must be an intrusion alarm to detect unauthorized entry when the personnel access barrier is locked. Activation of the intrusion alarm must alert an individual (not necessarily onsite) who is prepared to respond or summon assistance.

[58 FR 7728, Feb. 9, 1993, as amended at 63 FR 39483, July 23, 1998]

§ 36.25 Shielding.

(a) The radiation dose rate in areas that are normally occupied during operation of a panoramic irradiator may not exceed 0.02 millisievert (2 millirems) per hour at any location 30 centimeters or more from the wall of the room when the sources are exposed. The dose rate must be averaged over an area not to exceed 100 square centimeters having no linear dimension greater than 20 cm. Areas where the radiation dose rate exceeds 0.02 millisievert (2 millirems) per hour must be locked, roped off, or posted.

(b) The radiation dose at 30 centimeters over the edge of the pool of a pool irradiator may not exceed 0.02 millisievert (2 millirems) per hour when the sources are in the fully shielded position.

(c) The radiation dose rate at 1 meter from the shield of a dry-source-storage panoramic irradiator when the source is shielded may not exceed 0.02 millisievert (2 millirems) per hour and at 5 centimeters from the shield may not exceed 0.2 millisievert (20 millirems) per hour.

§ 36.27 Fire protection.

(a) The radiation room at a panoramic irradiator must have heat and smoke detectors. The detectors must activate an audible alarm. The alarm must be capable of alerting a person who is prepared to summon assistance promptly. The sources must automatically become fully shielded if a fire is detected.

(b) The radiation room at a panoramic irradiator must be equipped with a fire extinguishing system capable of extinguishing a fire without the entry of personnel into the room. The system for the radiation room must have a shut-off valve to control flooding into unrestricted areas.

§ 36.29 Radiation monitors.

(a) Irradiators with automatic product conveyor systems must have a radiation monitor with an audible alarm located to detect loose radioactive sources that are carried toward the product exit. If the monitor detects a source, an alarm must sound and product conveyors must stop automatically. The alarm must be capable of alerting an individual in the facility who is prepared to summon assistance. Underwater irradiators in which the product moves within an enclosed stationary tube are exempt from the requirements of this paragraph.

(b) Underwater irradiators that are not in a shielded radiation room must have a radiation monitor over the pool to detect abnormal radiation levels. The monitor must have an audible alarm and a visible indicator at entrances to the personnel access barrier around the pool. The audible alarm may have a manual shut-off. The alarm must be capable of alerting an individual who is prepared to respond promptly.

§ 36.31 Control of source movement.

(a) The mechanism that moves the sources of a panoramic irradiator must require a key to actuate. Actuation of the mechanism must cause an audible signal to indicate that the sources are leaving the shielded position. Only one key may be in use at any time, and only operators or facility management may possess it. The key must be attached to a portable radiation survey meter by a chain or cable. The lock for source control must be designed so that the key may not be removed if the sources are in an unshielded position. The door to the radiation room must require the same key.

(b) The console of a panoramic irradiator must have a source position indicator that indicates when the sources are in the fully shielded position, when they are in transit, and when the sources are exposed.

(c) The control console of a panoramic irradiator must have a control that promptly returns the sources to the shielded position.

(d) Each control for a panoramic irradiator must be clearly marked as to its function.

§ 36.33 Irradiator pools.

(a) For licenses initially issued after July 1, 1993, irradiator pools must either:

(1) Have a water-tight stainless steel liner or a liner metallurgically compatible with other components in the pool; or

(2) Be constructed so that there is a low likelihood of substantial leakage and have a surface designed to facilitate decontamination. In either case, the licensee shall have a method to safely store the sources during repairs of the pool.

(b) For licenses initially issued after July 1, 1993, irradiator pools must have no outlets more than 0.5 meter below the normal low water level that could allow water to drain out of the pool. Pipes that have intakes more than 0.5 meter below the normal low water level and that could act as siphons must have siphon breakers to prevent the siphoning of pool water.

(c) A means must be provided to replenish water losses from the pool.

(d) A visible indicator must be provided in a clearly visible location to indicate if the pool water level is below the normal low water level or above the normal high water level.

(e) Irradiator pools must be equipped with a purification system designed to be capable of maintaining the water during normal operation at a conductivity of 20 microsiemens per centimeter or less and with a clarity so that the sources can be seen clearly.

(f) A physical barrier, such as a railing or cover, must be used around or over irradiator pools during normal operation to prevent personnel from accidentally falling into the pool. The barrier may be removed during maintenance, inspection, and service operations.

(g) If long-handled tools or poles are used in irradiator pools, the radiation dose rate on the handling areas of the tools may not exceed 0.02 millisievert (2 millirems) per hour.

§ 36.35 Source rack protection.

If the product to be irradiated moves on a product conveyor system, the source rack and the mechanism that moves the rack must be protected by a barrier or guides to prevent products and product carriers from hitting or touching the rack or mechanism.

§ 36.37 Power failures.

(a) If electrical power at a panoramic irradiator is lost for longer than 10 seconds, the sources must automatically return to the shielded position.

(b) The lock on the door of the radiation room of a panoramic irradiator may not be deactivated by a power failure.

(c) During a power failure, the area of any irradiator where sources are located may be entered only when using an operable and calibrated radiation survey meter.

§ 36.39 Design requirements.

Irradiators whose construction begins after July 1, 1993, must meet the design requirements of this section.

(a) *Shielding.* For panoramic irradiators, the licensee shall design shielding walls to meet generally accepted building code requirements for reinforced concrete and design the walls, wall penetrations, and entranceways to meet the radiation shielding requirements of § 36.25. If the irradiator will use more than 2×10^{17} becquerels (5 million curies) of activity, the licensee shall evaluate the effects of heating of the shielding walls by the irradiator sources.

(b) *Foundations.* For panoramic irradiators, the licensee shall design the foundation, with consideration given to soil characteristics, to ensure it is adequate to support the weight of the facility shield walls.

(c) *Pool integrity.* For pool irradiators, the licensee shall design the pool to assure that it is leak resistant, that it is strong enough to bear the weight of the pool water and shipping casks, that a dropped cask would not fall on sealed sources, that all outlets or pipes meet the requirements of § 36.33(b), and that metal components are metallurgically compatible with other components in the pool.

(d) *Water handling system.* For pool irradiators, the licensee shall verify that the design of the water purification system is adequate to meet the requirements of § 36.33(e). The system must be designed so that water leaking from the system does not drain to unrestricted areas without being monitored.

(e) *Radiation monitors.* For all irradiators, the licensee shall evaluate the location and sensitivity of the monitor to detect sources carried by the product conveyor system as required by § 36.29(a). The licensee shall verify that the product conveyor is designed to stop before a source on the product conveyor would cause a radiation overexposure to any person. For pool irradiators, if the licensee uses radiation monitors to detect contamination under § 36.59(b), the licensee shall verify that the design of radiation monitoring systems to detect pool contamination includes sensitive detectors located close to where contamination is likely to concentrate.

(f) *Source rack.* For pool irradiators, the licensee shall verify that there are no crevices on the source or between the source and source holder that would promote corrosion on a critical area of the source. For panoramic irradiators, the licensee shall determine that source rack drops due to loss of power will not damage the source rack and that source rack drops due to failure of cables (or alternate means of support) will not cause loss of integrity of sealed sources. For panoramic irradiators, the licensee shall review the design of the mechanism that moves the sources to assure that the likelihood of a stuck source is low and that, if the rack sticks, a means exists to free it with minimal risk to personnel.

(g) *Access control.* For panoramic irradiators, the licensee shall verify from the design and logic diagram that the access control system will meet the requirements of §36.23.

(h) *Fire protection.* For panoramic irradiators, the licensee shall verify that the number, location, and spacing of the smoke and heat detectors are appropriate to detect fires and that the detectors are protected from mechanical and radiation damage. The licensee shall verify that the design of the fire extinguishing system provides the necessary discharge patterns, densities, and flow characteristics for complete coverage of the radiation room and that the system is protected from mechanical and radiation damage.

(i) *Source return.* For panoramic irradiators, the licensee shall verify that the source rack will automatically return to the fully shielded position if offsite power is lost for more than 10 seconds.

(j) *Seismic.* For panoramic irradiators to be built in seismic areas, the licensee shall design the reinforced concrete radiation shields to retain their integrity in the event of an earthquake by designing to the seismic requirements of an appropriate source such as American Concrete Institute Standard ACI 318–89, "Building Code Requirements for Reinforced Concrete," Chapter 21, "Special Provisions for Seismic Design," or local building codes, if current.

(k) *Wiring.* For panoramic irradiators, the licensee shall verify that electrical wiring and electrical equipment in the radiation room are selected to minimize failures due to prolonged exposure to radiation.

§36.41 Construction monitoring and acceptance testing.

The requirements of this section must be met for irradiators whose construction begins after July 1, 1993. The requirements must be met prior to loading sources.

(a) *Shielding.* For panoramic irradiators, the licensee shall monitor the construction of the shielding to verify that its construction meets design specifications and generally accepted building code requirements for reinforced concrete.

(b) *Foundations.* For panoramic irradiators, the licensee shall monitor the construction of the foundations to verify that their construction meets design specifications.

(c) *Pool integrity.* For pool irradiators, the licensee shall verify that the pool meets design specifications and shall test the integrity of the pool. The licensee shall verify that outlets and pipes meet the requirements of §36.33(b).

(d) *Water handling system.* For pool irradiators, the licensee shall verify that the water purification system, the conductivity meter, and the water level indicators operate properly.

(e) *Radiation monitors.* For all irradiators, the licensee shall verify the proper operation of the monitor to detect sources carried on the product conveyor system and the related alarms and interlocks required by §36.29(a). For pool irradiators, the licensee shall verify the proper operation of the radiation monitors and the related alarm if used to meet §36.59(b). For underwater irradiators, the licensee shall verify the proper operation of the over-the-pool monitor, alarms, and interlocks required by §36.29(b).

(f) *Source rack.* For panoramic irradiators, the licensee shall test the movement of the source racks for proper operation prior to source loading; testing must include source rack lowering due to simulated loss of power. For all irradiators with product conveyor systems, the licensee shall observe and test the operation of the conveyor system to assure that the requirements in § 36.35 are met for protection of the source rack and the mechanism that moves the rack; testing must include tests of any limit switches and interlocks used to protect the source rack and mechanism that moves the rack from moving product carriers.

(g) *Access control.* For panoramic irradiators, the licensee shall test the completed access control system to assure that it functions as designed and that all alarms, controls, and interlocks work properly.

(h) *Fire protection.* For panoramic irradiators, the licensee shall test the ability of the heat and smoke detectors to detect a fire, to activate alarms, and to cause the source rack to automatically become fully shielded. The licensee shall test the operability of the fire extinguishing system.

(i) *Source return.* For panoramic irradiators, the licensee shall demonstrate that the source racks can be returned to their fully shielded positions without offsite power.

(j) *Computer systems.* For panoramic irradiators that use a computer system to control the access control system, the licensee shall verify that the access control system will operate properly if offsite power is lost and shall verify that the computer has security features that prevent an irradiator operator from commanding the computer to override the access control system when it is required to be operable.

(k) *Wiring.* For panoramic irradiators, the licensee shall verify that the electrical wiring and electrical equipment that were installed meet the design specifications.

Subpart D—Operation of Irradiators

§ 36.51 Training.

(a) Before an individual is permitted to operate an irradiator without a supervisor present, the individual must be instructed in:

(1) The fundamentals of radiation protection applied to irradiators (including the differences between external radiation and radioactive contamination, units of radiation dose, NRC dose limits, why large radiation doses must be avoided, how shielding and access controls prevent large doses, how an irradiator is designed to prevent contamination, the proper use of survey meters and personnel dosimeters, other radiation safety features of an irradiator, and the basic function of the irradiator);

(2) The requirements of parts 19 and 36 of NRC regulations that are relevant to the irradiator;

(3) The operation of the irradiator;

(4) Those operating and emergency procedures listed in § 36.53 that the individual is responsible for performing; and

(5) Case histories of accidents or problems involving irradiators.

(b) Before an individual is permitted to operate an irradiator without a supervisor present, the individual shall pass a written test on the instruction received consisting primarily of questions based on the licensee's operating and emergency procedures that the individual is responsible for performing and other operations necessary to safely operate the irradiator without supervision.

(c) Before an individual is permitted to operate an irradiator without a supervisor present, the individual must have received on-the-job training or simulator training in the use of the irradiator as described in the license application. The individual shall also demonstrate the ability to perform those portions of the operating and emergency procedures that he or she is to perform.

(d) The licensee shall conduct safety reviews for irradiator operators at least annually. The licensee shall give each operator a brief written test on the information. Each safety review must include, to the extent appropriate, each of the following—

(1) Changes in operating and emergency procedures since the last review, if any;

(2) Changes in regulations and license conditions since the last review, if any;

(3) Reports on recent accidents, mistakes, or problems that have occurred at irradiators, if any;

(4) Relevant results of inspections of operator safety performance;

(5) Relevant results of the facility's inspection and maintenance checks; and

(6) A drill to practice an emergency or abnormal event procedure.

(e) The licensee shall evaluate the safety performance of each irradiator operator at least annually to ensure that regulations, license conditions, and operating and emergency procedures are followed. The licensee shall discuss the results of the evaluation with the operator and shall instruct the operator on how to correct any mistakes or deficiencies observed.

(f) Individuals who will be permitted unescorted access to the radiation room of the irradiator or the area around the pool of an underwater irradiator, but who have not received the training required for operators and the radiation safety officer, shall be instructed and tested in any precautions they should take to avoid radiation exposure, any procedures or parts of procedures listed in §36.53 that they are expected to perform or comply with, and their proper response to alarms required in this part. Tests may be oral.

(g) Individuals who must be prepared to respond to alarms required by §§36.23(b), 36.23(i), 36.27(a), 36.29(a), 36.29(b), and 36.59(b) shall be trained and tested on how to respond. Each individual shall be retested at least once a year. Tests may be oral.

§36.53 Operating and emergency procedures.

(a) The licensee shall have and follow written operating procedures for—

(1) Operation of the irradiator, including entering and leaving the radiation room;

(2) Use of personnel dosimeters;

(3) Surveying the shielding of panoramic irradiators;

(4) Monitoring pool water for contamination while the water is in the pool and before release of pool water to unrestricted areas;

(5) Leak testing of sources;

(6) Inspection and maintenance checks required by §36.61;

(7) Loading, unloading, and repositioning sources, if the operations will be performed by the licensee; and

(8) Inspection of movable shielding required by §36.23(h), if applicable.

(b) The licensee shall have and follow emergency or abnormal event procedures, appropriate for the irradiator type, for—

(1) Sources stuck in the unshielded position;

(2) Personnel overexposures;

(3) A radiation alarm from the product exit portal monitor or pool monitor;

(4) Detection of leaking sources, pool contamination, or alarm caused by contamination of pool water;

(5) A low or high water level indicator, an abnormal water loss, or leakage from the source storage pool;

(6) A prolonged loss of electrical power;

(7) A fire alarm or explosion in the radiation room;

(8) An alarm indicating unauthorized entry into the radiation room, area around pool, or another alarmed area;

(9) Natural phenomena, including an earthquake, a tornado, flooding, or other phenomena as appropriate for the geographical location of the facility; and

(10) The jamming of automatic conveyor systems.

(c) The licensee may revise operating and emergency procedures without Commission approval only if all of the following conditions are met:

(1) The revisions do not reduce the safety of the facility,

(2) The revisions are consistent with the outline or summary of procedures submitted with the license application,

(3) The revisions have been reviewed and approved by the radiation safety officer, and

(4) The users or operators are instructed and tested on the revised procedures before they are put into use.

§36.55 Personnel monitoring.

(a) Irradiator operators shall wear a personnel dosimeter that is processed and evaluated by an accredited National Voluntary Laboratory Accreditation Program (NVLAP) processor while operating a panoramic irradiator or while in the area around the pool of an underwater irradiator. The personnel dosimeter processor must be accredited for high energy photons in the normal and accident dose ranges (see 10 CFR 20.1501(c)). Each personnel dosimeter must be assigned to and worn by only one individual. Film badges must be processed at least monthly, and other personnel dosimeters must be processed at least quarterly.

(b) Other individuals who enter the radiation room of a panoramic irradiator shall wear a dosimeter, which may be a pocket dosimeter. For groups of visitors, only two people who enter the radiation room are required to wear dosimeters. If pocket dosimeters are used to meet the requirements of this paragraph, a check of their response to radiation must be done at least annually. Acceptable dosimeters must read within plus or minus 30 percent of the true radiation dose.

[58 FR 7728, Feb. 9, 1993, as amended at 65 FR 63752, Oct. 24, 2000]

§ 36.57 Radiation surveys.

(a) A radiation survey of the area outside the shielding of the radiation room of a panoramic irradiator must be conducted with the sources in the exposed position before the facility starts to operate. A radiation survey of the area above the pool of pool irradiators must be conducted after the sources are loaded but before the facility starts to operate. Additional radiation surveys of the shielding must be performed at intervals not to exceed 3 years and before resuming operation after addition of new sources or any modification to the radiation room shielding or structure that might increase dose rates.

(b) If the radiation levels specified in § 36.25 are exceeded, the facility must be modified to comply with the requirements in § 36.25.

(c) Portable radiation survey meters must be calibrated at least annually to an accuracy of ±20 percent for the gamma energy of the sources in use. The calibration must be done at two points on each scale or, for digital instruments, at one point per decade over the range that will be used. Portable radiation survey meters must be of a type that does not saturate and read zero at high radiation dose rates.

(d) Water from the irradiator pool, other potentially contaminated liquids, and sediments from pool vacuuming must be monitored for radioactive contamination before release to unrestricted areas. Radioactive concentrations must not exceed those specified in 10 CFR part 20, table 2, column 2 or table 3 of appendix B, "Annual Limits on Intake (ALIs) and Derived Air Concentrations (DACs) of Radionuclides for Occupational Exposure; Effluent Concentrations; Concentrations for Release to Sewerage."

(e) Before releasing resins for unrestricted use, they must be monitored before release in an area with a background level less than 0.5 microsievert (0.05 millirem) per hour. The resins may be released only if the survey does not detect radiation levels above background radiation levels. The survey meter used must be capable of detecting radiation levels of 0.5 microsievert (0.05 millirem) per hour.

§ 36.59 Detection of leaking sources.

(a) Each dry-source-storage sealed source must be tested for leakage at intervals not to exceed 6 months using a leak test kit or method approved by the Commission or an Agreement State. In the absence of a certificate from a transferor that a test has been made within the 6 months before the transfer, the sealed source may not be used until tested. The test must be capable of detecting the presence of 200 becquerels (0.005 microcurie) of radioactive material and must be performed by a person approved by the Commission or an Agreement State to perform the test.

(b) For pool irradiators, sources may not be put into the pool unless the licensee tests the sources for leaks or has a certificate from a transferor that leak test has been done within the 6 months before the transfer. Water from the pool must be checked for contamination each day the irradiator operates. The check may be done either by using a radiation monitor on a pool water circulating system or by analysis of a sample of pool water. If a check for contamination is done by analysis of a sample of pool water, the results of the analysis must be available within 24 hours. If the licensee uses a radiation monitor on a pool water circulating system, the detection of above normal radiation levels must activate an alarm. The alarm set-point must be set as low as practical, but high enough to avoid false alarms. The licensee may reset the alarm set-point to a higher level if necessary to operate the pool water purification system to clean up contamination in the pool if specifically provided for in written emergency procedures.

(c) If a leaking source is detected, the licensee shall arrange to remove the leaking source from service and have it decontaminated, repaired, or disposed of by an NRC or Agreement State licensee that is authorized to perform these functions. The licensee shall promptly check its personnel, equipment, facilities, and irradiated product for radioactive contamination. No product may be shipped until the product has been checked and found free of contamination. If a product has been shipped that may have been inadvertently contaminated, the licensee shall arrange to locate and survey that product for contamination. If any personnel are found to be contaminated, decontamination must be performed promptly. If contaminated equipment, facilities, or products are found, the licensee shall arrange to have them decontaminated or disposed of by an NRC or Agreement State licensee that is authorized to perform these functions. If a pool is contaminated, the licensee shall arrange to clean the pool until the contamination levels do not exceed the appropriate concentration in table 2, column 2, appendix B to part 20. (See 10 CFR 30.50 for reporting requirements.)

[58 FR 7728, Feb. 9, 1993, as amended at 58 FR 67660, Dec. 22, 1993]

§36.61 Inspection and maintenance.

(a) The licensee shall perform inspection and maintenance checks that include, as a minimum, each of the following at the frequency specified in the license or license application:

(1) Operability of each aspect of the access control system required by §36.23.

(2) Functioning of the source position indicator required by §36.31(b).

(3) Operability of the radiation monitor for radioactive contamination in pool water required by §36.59(b) using a radiation check source, if applicable.

(4) Operability of the over-pool radiation monitor at underwater irradiators as required by §36.29(b).

(5) Operability of the product exit monitor required by §36.29(a).

(6) Operability of the emergency source return control required by §36.31(c).

(7) Leak-tightness of systems through which pool water circulates (visual inspection).

(8) Operability of the heat and smoke detectors and extinguisher system required by §36.27 (but without turning extinguishers on).

(9) Operability of the means of pool water replenishment required by §36.33(c).

(10) Operability of the indicators of high and low pool water levels required by §36.33(d).

(11) Operability of the intrusion alarm required by §36.23(i), if applicable.

(12) Functioning and wear of the system, mechanisms, and cables used to raise and lower sources.

(13) Condition of the barrier to prevent products from hitting the sources or source mechanism as required by §36.35.

(14) Amount of water added to the pool to determine if the pool is leaking.

(15) Electrical wiring on required safety systems for radiation damage.

(16) Pool water conductivity measurements and analysis as required by §36.63(b).

(b) Malfunctions and defects found during inspection and maintenance checks must be repaired without undue delay.

§36.63 Pool water purity.

(a) Pool water purification system must be run sufficiently to maintain the conductivity of the pool water below 20 microsiemens per centimeter under normal circumstances. If pool water conductivity rises above 20 microsiemens per centimeter, the licensee shall take prompt actions to lower the pool water conductivity and shall take corrective actions to prevent future recurrences.

(b) The licensee shall measure the pool water conductivity frequently enough, but no less than weekly, to assure that the conductivity remains below 20 microsiemens per centimeter. Conductivity meters must be calibrated at least annually.

§ 36.65 Attendance during operation.

(a) Both an irradiator operator and at least one other individual, who is trained on how to respond and prepared to promptly render or summon assistance if the access control alarm sounds, shall be present onsite:

(1) Whenever the irradiator is operated using an automatic product conveyor system; and

(2) Whenever the product is moved into or out of the radiation room when the irradiator is operated in a batch mode.

(b) At a panoramic irradiator at which static irradiations (no movement of the product) are occurring, a person who has received the training on how to respond to alarms described in § 36.51(g) must be onsite.

(c) At an underwater irradiator, an irradiator operator must be present at the facility whenever the product is moved into or out of the pool. Individuals who move the product into or out of the pool of an underwater irradiator need not be qualified as irradiator operators; however, they must have received the training described in § 36.51 (f) and (g). Static irradiations may be performed without a person present at the facility.

§ 36.67 Entering and leaving the radiation room.

(a) Upon first entering the radiation room of a panoramic irradiator after an irradiation, the irradiator operator shall use a survey meter to determine that the source has returned to its fully shielded position. The operator shall check the functioning of the survey meter with a radiation check source prior to entry.

(b) Before exiting from and locking the door to the radiation room of a panoramic irradiator prior to a planned irradiation, the irradiator operator shall:

(1) Visually inspect the entire radiation room to verify that no one else is in it; and

(2) Activate a control in the radiation room that permits the sources to be moved from the shielded position only if the door to the radiation room is locked within a preset time after setting the control.

(c) During a power failure, the area around the pool of an underwater irradiator may not be entered without using an operable and calibrated radiation survey meter unless the over-the-pool monitor required by § 36.29(b) is operating with backup power.

§ 36.69 Irradiation of explosive or flammable materials.

(a) Irradiation of explosive material is prohibited unless the licensee has received prior written authorization from the Commission. Authorization will not be granted unless the licensee can demonstrate that detonation of the explosive would not rupture the sealed sources, injure personnel, damage safety systems, or cause radiation overexposures of personnel.

(b) Irradiation of more than small quantities of flammable material (flash point below 140 °F) is prohibited in panoramic irradiators unless the licensee has received prior written authorization from the Commission. Authorization will not be granted unless the licensee can demonstrate that a fire in the radiation room could be controlled without damage to sealed sources or safety systems and without radiation overexposures of personnel.

Subpart E—Records

§ 36.81 Records and retention periods.

The licensee shall maintain the following records at the irradiator for the periods specified.

(a) A copy of the license, license conditions, documents incorporated into a license by reference, and amendments thereto until superseded by new documents or until the Commission terminates the license for documents not superseded.

(b) Records of each individual's training, tests, and safety reviews provided to meet the requirements of § 36.51 (a), (b), (c), (d), (f), and (g) until 3 years after the individual terminates work.

(c) Records of the annual evaluations of the safety performance of irradiator operators required by § 36.51(e) for 3 years after the evaluation.

(d) A copy of the current operating and emergency procedures required by § 36.53 until superseded or the Commission terminates the license. Records of the radiation safety officer's review and approval of changes in procedures as required by § 36.53(c)(3) retained for 3 years from the date of the change.

(e) Evaluations of personnel dosimeters required by § 36.55 until the Commission terminates the license.

(f) Records of radiation surveys required by § 36.57 for 3 years from the date of the survey.

(g) Records of radiation survey meter calibrations required by § 36.57 and pool water conductivity meter calibrations required by § 36.63(b) until 3 years from the date of calibration.

(h) Records of the results of leak tests required by § 36.59(a) and the results of contamination checks required by § 36.59(b) for 3 years from the date of each test.

(i) Records of inspection and maintenance checks required by § 36.61 for 3 years.

(j) Records of major malfunctions, significant defects, operating difficulties or irregularities, and major operating problems that involve required radiation safety equipment for 3 years after repairs are completed.

(k) Records of the receipt, transfer and disposal, of all licensed sealed sources as required by §§ 30.51 and 30.41.

(l) Records on the design checks required by § 36.39 and the construction control checks as required by § 36.41 until the license is terminated. The records must be signed and dated. The title or qualification of the person signing must be included.

(m) Records related to decommissioning of the irradiator as required by § 30.35(g).

[58 FR 7728, Feb. 9, 1993, as amended at 65 FR 63752, Oct. 24, 2000]

§ 36.83 Reports.

(a) In addition to the reporting requirements in other parts of NRC regulations, the licensee shall report the following events if not reported under other parts of NRC regulations:

(1) Source stuck in an unshielded position.

(2) Any fire or explosion in a radiation room.

(3) Damage to the source racks.

(4) Failure of the cable or drive mechanism used to move the source racks.

(5) Inoperability of the access control system.

(6) Detection of radiation source by the product exit monitor.

(7) Detection of radioactive contamination attributable to licensed radioactive material.

(8) Structural damage to the pool liner or walls.

(9) Abnormal water loss or leakage from the source storage pool.

(10) Pool water conductivity exceeding 100 microsiemens per centimeter.

(b) The report must include a telephone report within 24 hours as described in § 30.50(c)(1), and a written report within 30 days as described in § 30.50(c)(2).

Subpart F—Enforcement

§ 36.91 Violations.

(a) The Commission may obtain an injunction or other court order to prevent a violation of the provisions of—

(1) The Atomic Energy Act of 1954, as amended;

(2) Title II of the Energy Reorganization Act of 1974, as amended; or

(3) A regulation or order issued pursuant to those Acts.

(b) The Commission may obtain a court order for the payment of a civil penalty imposed under section 234 of the Atomic Energy Act:

(1) For violations of—

(i) Sections 53, 57, 62, 63, 81, 82, 101, 103, 104, 107, or 109 of the Atomic Energy Act of 1954, as amended;

(ii) Section 206 of the Energy Reorganization Act;

(iii) Any rule, regulation, or order issued pursuant to the sections specified in paragraph (b)(1)(i) of this section;

(iv) Any term, condition, or limitation of any license issued under the sections specified in paragraph (b)(1)(i) of this section.

(2) For any violation for which a license may be revoked under section 186 of the Atomic Energy Act of 1954, as amended.

§ 36.93 Criminal penalties.

(a) Section 223 of the Atomic Energy Act of 1954, as amended, provides for criminal sanctions for willful violation of, attempted violation of, or conspiracy to violate, any regulation issued under sections 161b, 161i, or 161o of the Act. For purposes of section 223, all the regulations in part 36 are issued under one or more of sections 161b, 161i, or 161o, except for the sections listed in paragraph (b) of this section.

(b) The regulations in part 36 that are not issued under sections 161b, 161i, or 161o for the purposes of section 223 are as follows: §§ 36.1, 36.2, 36.5, 36.8, 36.11, 36.13, 36.17, 36.19, 36.91, and 36.93.

PART 37—PHYSICAL PROTECTION OF CATEGORY 1 AND CATEGORY 2 QUANTITIES OF RADIOACTIVE MATERIAL

Subpart A—General Provisions

Sec.

Subpart B—Background Investigations and Access Control Program

Subpart C—Physical Protection Requirements During Use

Subpart D—Physical Protection in Transit

Subpart E [Reserved]

Subpart F—Records

Subpart G—Enforcement

AUTHORITY: Atomic Energy Act of 1954, secs. 11, 53, 81, 103, 104, 147, 148, 149, 161, 182, 183, 223, 234, 274 (42 U.S.C. 2014, 2073, 2111, 2133, 2134, 2167, 2168, 2169, 2201, 2232, 2233, 2273, 2282, 2021); Energy Reorganization Act of 1974, secs. 201, 202 (42 U.S.C. 5841, 5842); 44 U.S.C. 3504 note.

SOURCE: 78 FR 17007, Mar. 19, 2013, unless otherwise noted.

EDITORIAL NOTE: Nomenclature changes to part 37 appear at 79 FR 75739, Dec. 19, 2014.

Subpart A—General Provisions

§ 37.1 Purpose.

This part has been established to provide the requirements for the physical protection program for any licensee that possesses an aggregated category 1 or category 2 quantity of radioactive material listed in Appendix A to this part. These requirements provide reasonable assurance of the security of category 1 or category 2 quantities of radioactive material by protecting these materials from theft or diversion. Specific requirements for access to material, use of material, transfer of material, and transport of material are included. No provision of this part authorizes possession of licensed material.

§ 37.3 Scope.

(a) Subparts B and C of this part apply to any person who, under the regulations in this chapter, possesses or uses at any site, an aggregated category 1 or category 2 quantity of radioactive material.

(b) Subpart D of this part applies to any person who, under the regulations of this chapter:

(1) Transports or delivers to a carrier for transport in a single shipment, a category 1 or category 2 quantity of radioactive material; or

(2) Imports or exports a category 1 or category 2 quantity of radioactive material; the provisions only apply to the domestic portion of the transport.

§ 37.5 Definitions.

As used in this part:

Access control means a system for allowing only approved individuals to have unescorted access to the security zone and for ensuring that all other individuals are subject to escorted access.

Act means the Atomic Energy Act of 1954 (68 Stat. 919), including any amendments thereto.

Aggregated means accessible by the breach of a single physical barrier that would allow access to radioactive material in any form, including any devices that contain the radioactive material, when the total activity equals or exceeds a category 2 quantity of radioactive material.

Agreement State means any state with which the Atomic Energy Commission or the U.S. Nuclear Regulatory Commission has entered into an effective agreement under subsection 274b. of the Act. *Non-agreement State* means any other State.

Approved individual means an individual whom the licensee has determined to be trustworthy and reliable for unescorted access in accordance with subpart B of this part and who has completed the training required by § 37.43(c).

Background investigation means the investigation conducted by a licensee or applicant to support the determination of trustworthiness and reliability.

Becquerel (Bq) means one disintegration per second.

Byproduct material means—

(1) Any radioactive material (except special nuclear material) yielded in, or made radioactive by, exposure to the radiation incident to the process of producing or using special nuclear material;

(2) The tailings or wastes produced by the extraction or concentration of uranium or thorium from ore processed primarily for its source material content, including discrete surface wastes resulting from uranium solution extraction processes. Underground ore bodies depleted by these solution extraction operations do not constitute "byproduct material" within this definition;

(3)(i) Any discrete source of radium-226 that is produced, extracted, or converted after extraction, before, on, or after August 8, 2005, for use for a commercial, medical, or research activity; or

(ii) Any material that—

(A) Has been made radioactive by use of a particle accelerator; and

(B) Is produced, extracted, or converted after extraction, before, on, or after August 8, 2005, for use for a commercial, medical, or research activity; and

(4) Any discrete source of naturally occurring radioactive material, other than source material, that—

(i) The Commission, in consultation with the Administrator of the Environmental Protection Agency, the Secretary of Energy, the Secretary of

Homeland Security, and the head of any other appropriate Federal agency, determines would pose a threat similar to the threat posed by a discrete source of radium-226 to the public health and safety or the common defense and security; and

(ii) Before, on, or after August 8, 2005, is extracted or converted after extraction for use in a commercial, medical, or research activity.

Carrier means a person engaged in the transportation of passengers or property by land or water as a common, contract, or private carrier, or by civil aircraft.

Category 1 quantity of radioactive material means a quantity of radioactive material meeting or exceeding the category 1 threshold in Table 1 of Appendix A to this part. This is determined by calculating the ratio of the total activity of each radionuclide to the category 1 threshold for that radionuclide and adding the ratios together. If the sum is equal to or exceeds 1, the quantity would be considered a category 1 quantity. Category 1 quantities of radioactive material do not include the radioactive material contained in any fuel assembly, subassembly, fuel rod, or fuel pellet.

Category 2 quantity of radioactive material means a quantity of radioactive material meeting or exceeding the category 2 threshold but less than the category 1 threshold in Table 1 of Appendix A to this part. This is determined by calculating the ratio of the total activity of each radionuclide to the category 2 threshold for that radionuclide and adding the ratios together. If the sum is equal to or exceeds 1, the quantity would be considered a category 2 quantity. Category 2 quantities of radioactive material do not include the radioactive material contained in any fuel assembly, subassembly, fuel rod, or fuel pellet.

Commission means the U.S. Nuclear Regulatory Commission or its duly authorized representatives.

Curie means that amount of radioactive material which disintegrates at the rate of 37 billion atoms per second.

Diversion means the unauthorized movement of radioactive material subject to this part to a location different from the material's authorized destination inside or outside of the site at which the material is used or stored.

Escorted access means accompaniment while in a security zone by an approved individual who maintains continuous direct visual surveillance at all times over an individual who is not approved for unescorted access.

Fingerprint orders means the orders issued by the U.S. Nuclear Regulatory Commission or the legally binding requirements issued by Agreement States that require fingerprints and criminal history records checks for individuals with unescorted access to category 1 and category 2 quantities of radioactive material or safeguards information-modified handling.

Government agency means any executive department, commission, independent establishment, corporation, wholly or partly owned by the United States of America which is an instrumentality of the United States, or any board, bureau, division, service, office, officer, authority, administration, or other establishment in the executive branch of the Government.

License, except where otherwise specified, means a license for byproduct material issued pursuant to the regulations in parts 30 through 36 and 39 of this chapter;

License issuing authority means the licensing agency that issued the license, *i.e.* the U.S. Nuclear Regulatory Commission or the appropriate agency of an Agreement State;

Local law enforcement agency (LLEA) means a public or private organization that has been approved by a federal, state, or local government to carry firearms and make arrests, and is authorized and has the capability to provide an armed response in the jurisdiction where the licensed category 1 or category 2 quantity of radioactive material is used, stored, or transported.

Lost or missing licensed material means licensed material whose location is unknown. It includes material that has been shipped but has not reached its destination and whose location cannot be readily traced in the transportation system.

Mobile device means a piece of equipment containing licensed radioactive material that is either mounted on wheels or casters, or otherwise equipped for moving without a need for disassembly or dismounting; or designed to be hand carried. Mobile devices do not include stationary equipment installed in a fixed location.

Movement control center means an operations center that is remote from transport activity and that maintains position information on the movement of radioactive material, receives reports of attempted attacks or thefts, provides a means for reporting these and other problems to appropriate agencies and can request and coordinate appropriate aid.

No-later-than arrival time means the date and time that the shipping licensee and receiving licensee have established as the time at which an investigation will be initiated if the shipment has not arrived at the receiving facility. The no-later-than-arrival time may not be more than 6 hours after the estimated arrival time for shipments of category 2 quantities of radioactive material.

Person means—

(1) Any individual, corporation, partnership, firm, association, trust, estate, public or private institution, group, Government agency other than the Commission or the DOE (except that the Department shall be considered a person within the meaning of the regulations in 10 CFR chapter I to the extent that its facilities and activities are subject to the licensing and related regulatory authority of the Commission under section 202 of the Energy Reorganization Act of 1974 (88 Stat. 1244), the Uranium Mill Tailings Radiation Control Act of 1978 (92 Stat. 3021), the Nuclear Waste Policy Act of 1982 (96 Stat. 2201), and section 3(b)(2) of the Low-Level Radioactive Waste Policy Amendments Act of 1985 (99 Stat. 1842), any State or any political subdivision of or any political entity within a State, any foreign government or nation or any political subdivision of any such government or nation, or other entity; and

(2) Any legal successor, representative, agent, or agency of the foregoing.

Reviewing official means the individual who shall make the trustworthiness and reliability determination of an individual to determine whether the individual may have, or continue to have, unescorted access to the category 1 or category 2 quantities of radioactive materials that are possessed by the licensee.

Sabotage means deliberate damage, with malevolent intent, to a category 1 or category 2 quantity of radioactive material, a device that contains a category 1 or category 2 quantity of radioactive material, or the components of the security system.

Safe haven means a readily recognizable and readily accessible site at which security is present or from which, in the event of an emergency, the transport crew can notify and wait for the local law enforcement authorities.

Security zone means any temporary or permanent area determined and established by the licensee for the physical protection of category 1 or category 2 quantities of radioactive material.

State means a State of the United States, the District of Columbia, the Commonwealth of Puerto Rico, the Virgin Islands, Guam, American Samoa, and the Commonwealth of the Northern Mariana Islands.

Telemetric position monitoring system means a data transfer system that captures information by instrumentation and/or measuring devices about the location and status of a transport vehicle or package between the departure and destination locations.

Trustworthiness and reliability are characteristics of an individual considered dependable in judgment, character, and performance, such that unescorted access to category 1 or category 2 quantities of radioactive material by that individual does not constitute an unreasonable risk to the public health and safety or security. A determination of trustworthiness and reliability for this purpose is based upon the results from a background investigation.

Unescorted access means solitary access to an aggregated category 1 or category 2 quantity of radioactive material or the devices that contain the material.

United States, when used in a geographical sense, includes Puerto Rico and all territories and possessions of the United States.

§ 37.7 Communications.

Except where otherwise specified or covered under the regional licensing program as provided in § 30.6(b) of this chapter, all communications and reports concerning the regulations in this part may be sent as follows:

(a) By mail addressed to: ATTN: Document Control Desk; Director, Office of Nuclear Reactor Regulation; Director, Office of New Reactors; Director, Office of Nuclear Material Safety and Safeguards; or Director, Division of Security Policy, Office of Nuclear Security and Incident Response, as appropriate, U.S. Nuclear Regulatory Commission, Washington, DC 20555–0001;

(b) By hand delivery to the NRC's offices at 11555 Rockville Pike, Rockville, Maryland 20852;

(c) Where practicable, by electronic submission, for example, Electronic Information Exchange, or CD–ROM. Electronic submissions must be made in a manner that enables the NRC to receive, read, authenticate, distribute, and archive the submission, and process and retrieve it a single page at a time. Detailed guidance on making electronic submissions can be obtained by visiting the NRC's Web site at *http://www.nrc.gov/site-help/e-submittals.html;* by email to *MSHD.Resource@nrc.gov;* or by writing the Office of the Chief Information Officer, U.S. Nuclear Regulatory Commission, Washington, DC 20555–0001. The guidance discusses, among other topics, the formats the NRC can accept, the use of electronic signatures, and the treatment of nonpublic information.

[78 FR 17007, Mar. 19, 2013, as amended at 79 FR 75740, Dec. 19, 2014; 80 FR 74979, Dec. 1, 2015]

§ 37.9 Interpretations.

Except as specifically authorized by the Commission in writing, no interpretations of the meaning of the regulations in this part by any officer or employee of the Commission other than a written interpretation by the General Counsel will be recognized as binding upon the Commission.

§ 37.11 Specific exemptions.

(a) The Commission may, upon application of any interested person or upon its own initiative, grant such exemptions from the requirements of the regulations in this part as it determines are authorized by law and will not endanger life or property or the common defense and security, and are otherwise in the public interest.

(b) Any licensee's NRC-licensed activities are exempt from the requirements of subparts B and C of this part to the extent that its activities are included in a security plan required by part 73 of this chapter.

(c) A licensee that possesses radioactive waste that contains category 1 or category 2 quantities of radioactive material is exempt from the requirements of subparts B, C, and D of this part. Except that any radioactive waste that contains discrete sources, ion-exchange resins, or activated material that weighs less than 2,000 kg (4,409 lbs) is not exempt from the requirements of this part. The licensee shall implement the following requirements to secure the radioactive waste:

(1) Use continuous physical barriers that allow access to the radioactive waste only through established access control points;

(2) Use a locked door or gate with monitored alarm at the access control point;

(3) Assess and respond to each actual or attempted unauthorized access to determine whether an actual or attempted theft, sabotage, or diversion occurred; and

(4) Immediately notify the LLEA and request an armed response from the LLEA upon determination that there was an actual or attempted theft, sabotage, or diversion of the radioactive waste that contains category 1 or category 2 quantities of radioactive material.

§ 37.13 Information collection requirements: OMB approval.

(a) The U.S. Nuclear Regulatory Commission has submitted the information collection requirements contained in this part to the Office of Management and Budget (OMB) for approval as required by the Paperwork Reduction Act (44 U.S.C. 3501 *et seq.*). The NRC may not conduct or sponsor, and a person is not required to respond to, a collection of information unless it displays a currently valid OMB control number. The OMB has approved the information collection requirements contained in this part under control number 3150–0214.

(b) The approved information collection requirements contained in this part appear in §§37.11, 37.21, 37.23, 37.25, 37.27, 37.29, 37.31, 37.33, 37.41, 37.43, 37.45, 37.49, 37.51, 37.55, 37.57, 37.71, 37.75, 37.77, 37.79, and 37.81.

Subpart B—Background Investigations and Access Authorization Program

§37.21 Personnel access authorization requirements for category 1 or category 2 quantities of radioactive material.

(a) *General.* (1) Each licensee that possesses an aggregated quantity of radioactive material at or above the category 2 threshold shall establish, implement, and maintain its access authorization program in accordance with the requirements of this subpart.

(2) An applicant for a new license and each licensee that would become newly subject to the requirements of this subpart upon application for modification of its license shall implement the requirements of this subpart, as appropriate, before taking possession of an aggregated category 1 or category 2 quantity of radioactive material.

(3) Any licensee that has not previously implemented the Security Orders or been subject to the provisions of this subpart B shall implement the provisions of this subpart B before aggregating radioactive material to a quantity that equals or exceeds the category 2 threshold.

(b) *General performance objective.* The licensee's access authorization program must ensure that the individuals specified in paragraph (c)(1) of this section are trustworthy and reliable.

(c) *Applicability.* (1) Licensees shall subject the following individuals to an access authorization program:

(i) Any individual whose assigned duties require unescorted access to category 1 or category 2 quantities of radioactive material or to any device that contains the radioactive material; and

(ii) Reviewing officials.

(2) Licensees need not subject the categories of individuals listed in §37.29(a)(1) through (13) to the investigation elements of the access authorization program.

(3) Licensees shall approve for unescorted access to category 1 or category 2 quantities of radioactive material only those individuals with job duties that require unescorted access to category 1 or category 2 quantities of radioactive material.

(4) Licensees may include individuals needing access to safeguards information-modified handling under part 73 of this chapter in the access authorization program under this subpart B.

§37.23 Access authorization program requirements.

(a) *Granting unescorted access authorization.* (1) Licensees shall implement the requirements of this subpart for granting initial or reinstated unescorted access authorization.

(2) Individuals who have been determined to be trustworthy and reliable shall also complete the security training required by §37.43(c) before being allowed unescorted access to category 1 or category 2 quantities of radioactive material.

(b) *Reviewing officials.* (1) Reviewing officials are the only individuals who may make trustworthiness and reliability determinations that allow individuals to have unescorted access to category 1 or category 2 quantities of radioactive materials possessed by the licensee.

(2) Each licensee shall name one or more individuals to be reviewing officials. After completing the background investigation on the reviewing official, the licensee shall provide under oath or affirmation, a certification that the reviewing official is deemed trustworthy and reliable by the licensee. The fingerprints of the named reviewing official must be taken by a law enforcement agency, Federal or State agencies that provide fingerprinting services to the public, or commercial fingerprinting services authorized by a State to take fingerprints. The licensee shall recertify that the reviewing official is deemed trustworthy and reliable every 10 years in accordance with §37.25(c).

(3) Reviewing officials must be permitted to have unescorted access to category 1 or category 2 quantities of radioactive materials or access to safeguards information or safeguards information-modified handling, if the licensee possesses safeguards information or safeguards information-modified handling.

(4) Reviewing officials cannot approve other individuals to act as reviewing officials.

(5) A reviewing official does not need to undergo a new background investigation before being named by the licensee as the reviewing official if:

(i) The individual has undergone a background investigation that included fingerprinting and an FBI criminal history records check and has been determined to be trustworthy and reliable by the licensee; or

(ii) The individual is subject to a category listed in § 37.29(a).

(c) *Informed consent.* (1) Licensees may not initiate a background investigation without the informed and signed consent of the subject individual. This consent must include authorization to share personal information with other individuals or organizations as necessary to complete the background investigation. Before a final adverse determination, the licensee shall provide the individual with an opportunity to correct any inaccurate or incomplete information that is developed during the background investigation. Licensees do not need to obtain signed consent from those individuals that meet the requirements of § 37.25(b). A signed consent must be obtained prior to any reinvestigation.

(2) The subject individual may withdraw his or her consent at any time. Licensees shall inform the individual that:

(i) If an individual withdraws his or her consent, the licensee may not initiate any elements of the background investigation that were not in progress at the time the individual withdrew his or her consent; and

(ii) The withdrawal of consent for the background investigation is sufficient cause for denial or termination of unescorted access authorization.

(d) *Personal history disclosure.* Any individual who is applying for unescorted access authorization shall disclose the personal history information that is required by the licensee's access authorization program for the reviewing official to make a determination of the individual's trustworthiness and reliability. Refusal to provide, or the falsification of, any personal history information required by this subpart is sufficient cause for denial or termination of unescorted access.

(e) *Determination basis.* (1) The reviewing official shall determine whether to permit, deny, unfavorably terminate, maintain, or administratively withdraw an individual's unescorted access authorization based on an evaluation of all of the information collected to meet the requirements of this subpart.

(2) The reviewing official may not permit any individual to have unescorted access until the reviewing official has evaluated all of the information collected to meet the requirements of this subpart and determined that the individual is trustworthy and reliable. The reviewing official may deny unescorted access to any individual based on information obtained at any time during the background investigation.

(3) The licensee shall document the basis for concluding whether or not there is reasonable assurance that an individual is trustworthy and reliable.

(4) The reviewing official may terminate or administratively withdraw an individual's unescorted access authorization based on information obtained after the background investigation has been completed and the individual granted unescorted access authorization.

(5) Licensees shall maintain a list of persons currently approved for unescorted access authorization. When a licensee determines that a person no longer requires unescorted access or meets the access authorization requirement, the licensee shall remove the person from the approved list as soon as possible, but no later than 7 working days, and take prompt measures to ensure that the individual is unable to have unescorted access to the material.

(f) *Procedures.* Licensees shall develop, implement, and maintain written procedures for implementing the access authorization program. The procedures must include provisions for the notification of individuals who are denied unescorted access. The procedures must include provisions for the review, at the request of the affected individual, of a denial or termination of unescorted access authorization. The procedures must contain a provision to ensure that the individual is informed of the grounds for the denial or termination of unescorted access authorization and allow the individual an opportunity to provide additional relevant information.

(g) *Right to correct and complete information.* (1) Prior to any final adverse determination, licensees shall provide each individual subject to this subpart with the right to complete, correct, and explain information obtained as a result of the licensee's background investigation. Confirmation of receipt by the individual of this notification must be maintained by the licensee for a period of 1 year from the date of the notification.

(2) If, after reviewing his or her criminal history record, an individual believes that it is incorrect or incomplete in any respect and wishes to change, correct, update, or explain anything in the record, the individual may initiate challenge procedures. These procedures include direct application by the individual challenging the record to the law enforcement agency that contributed the questioned information or a direct challenge as to the accuracy or completeness of any entry on the criminal history record to the Federal Bureau of Investigation, Criminal Justice Information Services (CJIS) Division, ATTN: SCU, Mod. D-2, 1000 Custer Hollow Road, Clarksburg, WV 26306 as set forth in 28 CFR 16.30 through 16.34. In the latter case, the Federal Bureau of Investigation (FBI) will forward the challenge to the agency that submitted the data, and will request that the agency verify or correct the challenged entry. Upon receipt of an official communication directly from the agency that contributed the original information, the FBI Identification Division makes any changes necessary in accordance with the information supplied by that agency. Licensees must provide at least 10 days for an individual to initiate action to challenge the results of an FBI criminal history records check after the record being made available for his or her review. The licensee may make a final adverse determination based upon the criminal history records only after receipt of the FBI's confirmation or correction of the record.

(h) *Records.* (1) The licensee shall retain documentation regarding the trustworthiness and reliability of individual employees for 3 years from the date the individual no longer requires unescorted access to category 1 or category 2 quantities of radioactive material.

(2) The licensee shall retain a copy of the current access authorization program procedures as a record for 3 years after the procedure is no longer needed. If any portion of the procedure is superseded, the licensee shall retain the superseded material for 3 years after the record is superseded.

(3) The licensee shall retain the list of persons approved for unescorted access authorization for 3 years after the list is superseded or replaced.

[78 FR 17007, Mar. 19, 2013, as amended at 80 FR 45843, Aug. 3, 2015]

§ 37.25 Background investigations.

(a) *Initial investigation.* Before allowing an individual unescorted access to category 1 or category 2 quantities of radioactive material or to the devices that contain the material, licensees shall complete a background investigation of the individual seeking unescorted access authorization. The scope of the investigation must encompass at least the 7 years preceding the date of the background investigation or since the individual's eighteenth birthday, whichever is shorter. The background investigation must include at a minimum:

(1) Fingerprinting and an FBI identification and criminal history records check in accordance with § 37.27;

(2) Verification of true identity. Licensees shall verify the true identity of the individual who is applying for unescorted access authorization to ensure that the applicant is who he or she

claims to be. A licensee shall review official identification documents (*e.g.*, driver's license; passport; government identification; certificate of birth issued by the state, province, or country of birth) and compare the documents to personal information data provided by the individual to identify any discrepancy in the information. Licensees shall document the type, expiration, and identification number of the identification document, or maintain a photocopy of identifying documents on file in accordance with § 37.31. Licensees shall certify in writing that the identification was properly reviewed, and shall maintain the certification and all related documents for review upon inspection;

(3) Employment history verification. Licensees shall complete an employment history verification, including military history. Licensees shall verify the individual's employment with each previous employer for the most recent 7 years before the date of application;

(4) Verification of education. Licensees shall verify that the individual participated in the education process during the claimed period;

(5) Character and reputation determination. Licensees shall complete reference checks to determine the character and reputation of the individual who has applied for unescorted access authorization. Unless other references are not available, reference checks may not be conducted with any person who is known to be a close member of the individual's family, including but not limited to the individual's spouse, parents, siblings, or children, or any individual who resides in the individual's permanent household. Reference checks under this subpart must be limited to whether the individual has been and continues to be trustworthy and reliable;

(6) The licensee shall also, to the extent possible, obtain independent information to corroborate that provided by the individual (*e.g.*, seek references not supplied by the individual); and

(7) If a previous employer, educational institution, or any other entity with which the individual claims to have been engaged fails to provide information or indicates an inability or unwillingness to provide information within a time frame deemed appropriate by the licensee but at least after 10 business days of the request or if the licensee is unable to reach the entity, the licensee shall document the refusal, unwillingness, or inability in the record of investigation; and attempt to obtain the information from an alternate source.

(b) *Grandfathering.* (1) Individuals who have been determined to be trustworthy and reliable for unescorted access to category 1 or category 2 quantities of radioactive material under the Fingerprint Orders may continue to have unescorted access to category 1 and category 2 quantities of radioactive material without further investigation. These individuals shall be subject to the reinvestigation requirement.

(2) Individuals who have been determined to be trustworthy and reliable under the provisions of part 73 of this chapter or the security orders for access to safeguards information, safeguards information-modified handling, or risk-significant material may have unescorted access to category 1 and category 2 quantities of radioactive material without further investigation. The licensee shall document that the individual was determined to be trustworthy and reliable under the provisions of part 73 of this chapter or a security order. Security order, in this context, refers to any order that was issued by the NRC that required fingerprints and an FBI criminal history records check for access to safeguards information, safeguards information-modified handling, or risk significant material such as special nuclear material or large quantities of uranium hexafluoride. These individuals shall be subject to the reinvestigation requirement.

(c) *Reinvestigations.* Licensees shall conduct a reinvestigation every 10 years for any individual with unescorted access to category 1 or category 2 quantities of radioactive material. The reinvestigation shall consist of fingerprinting and an FBI identification and criminal history records check in accordance with § 37.27. The reinvestigations must be completed within 10 years of the date on which these elements were last completed.

§37.27 Requirements for criminal history records checks of individuals granted unescorted access to category 1 or category 2 quantities of radioactive material.

(a) *General performance objective and requirements.* (1) Except for those individuals listed in §37.29 and those individuals grandfathered under §37.25(b), each licensee subject to the provisions of this subpart shall fingerprint each individual who is to be permitted unescorted access to category 1 or category 2 quantities of radioactive material. Licensees shall transmit all collected fingerprints to the Commission for transmission to the FBI. The licensee shall use the information received from the FBI as part of the required background investigation to determine whether to grant or deny further unescorted access to category 1 or category 2 quantities of radioactive materials for that individual.

(2) The licensee shall notify each affected individual that his or her fingerprints will be used to secure a review of his or her criminal history record, and shall inform him or her of the procedures for revising the record or adding explanations to the record.

(3) Fingerprinting is not required if a licensee is reinstating an individual's unescorted access authorization to category 1 or category 2 quantities of radioactive materials if:

(i) The individual returns to the same facility that granted unescorted access authorization within 365 days of the termination of his or her unescorted access authorization; and

(ii) The previous access was terminated under favorable conditions.

(4) Fingerprints do not need to be taken if an individual who is an employee of a licensee, contractor, manufacturer, or supplier has been granted unescorted access to category 1 or category 2 quantities of radioactive material, access to safeguards information, or safeguards information-modified handling by another licensee, based upon a background investigation conducted under this subpart, the Fingerprint Orders, or part 73 of this chapter. An existing criminal history records check file may be transferred to the licensee asked to grant unescorted access in accordance with the provisions of §37.31(c).

(5) Licensees shall use the information obtained as part of a criminal history records check solely for the purpose of determining an individual's suitability for unescorted access authorization to category 1 or category 2 quantities of radioactive materials, access to safeguards information, or safeguards information-modified handling.

(b) *Prohibitions.* (1) Licensees may not base a final determination to deny an individual unescorted access authorization to category 1 or category 2 quantities of radioactive material solely on the basis of information received from the FBI involving:

(i) An arrest more than 1 year old for which there is no information of the disposition of the case; or

(ii) An arrest that resulted in dismissal of the charge or an acquittal.

(2) Licensees may not use information received from a criminal history records check obtained under this subpart in a manner that would infringe upon the rights of any individual under the First Amendment to the Constitution of the United States, nor shall licensees use the information in any way that would discriminate among individuals on the basis of race, religion, national origin, gender, or age.

(c) *Procedures for processing of fingerprint checks.* (1) For the purpose of complying with this subpart, licensees shall use an appropriate method listed in §37.7 to submit to the U.S. Nuclear Regulatory Commission, Director, Division of Facilities and Security, 11545 Rockville Pike, ATTN: Criminal History Program/Mail Stop TWB–05 B32M, Rockville, Maryland 20852, one completed, legible standard fingerprint card (Form FD–258, ORIMDNRCOOOZ), electronic fingerprint scan or, where practicable, other fingerprint record for each individual requiring unescorted access to category 1 or category 2 quantities of radioactive material. Copies of these forms may be obtained by writing the Office of the Chief Information Officer, U.S. Nuclear Regulatory Commission, Washington, DC 20555–0001, by calling 1–630–829–9565, or by email to *FORMS.Resource@nrc.gov*. Guidance on submitting electronic fingerprints can be found at *http://www.nrc.gov/site-help/e-submittals.html.*

(2) Fees for the processing of fingerprint checks are due upon application. Licensees shall submit payment with the application for the processing of fingerprints through corporate check, certified check, cashier's check, money order, or electronic payment, made payable to "U.S. NRC." (For guidance on making electronic payments, contact the Security Branch, Division of Facilities and Security at 301–492–3531.) Combined payment for multiple applications is acceptable. The Commission publishes the amount of the fingerprint check application fee on the NRC's public Web site. (To find the current fee amount, go to the Electronic Submittals page at *http://www.nrc.gov/site-help/e-submittals.html* and see the link for the Criminal History Program under Electronic Submission Systems.)

(3) The Commission will forward to the submitting licensee all data received from the FBI as a result of the licensee's application(s) for criminal history records checks.

[78 FR 17007, Mar. 19, 2013, as amended at 80 FR 74979, Dec. 1, 2015]

§ 37.29 Relief from fingerprinting, identification, and criminal history records checks and other elements of background investigations for designated categories of individuals permitted unescorted access to certain radioactive materials.

(a) Fingerprinting, and the identification and criminal history records checks required by section 149 of the Atomic Energy Act of 1954, as amended, and other elements of the background investigation are not required for the following individuals prior to granting unescorted access to category 1 or category 2 quantities of radioactive materials:

(1) An employee of the Commission or of the Executive Branch of the U.S. Government who has undergone fingerprinting for a prior U.S. Government criminal history records check;

(2) A Member of Congress;

(3) An employee of a member of Congress or Congressional committee who has undergone fingerprinting for a prior U.S. Government criminal history records check;

(4) The Governor of a State or his or her designated State employee representative;

(5) Federal, State, or local law enforcement personnel;

(6) State Radiation Control Program Directors and State Homeland Security Advisors or their designated State employee representatives;

(7) Agreement State employees conducting security inspections on behalf of the NRC under an agreement executed under section 274.i. of the Atomic Energy Act;

(8) Representatives of the International Atomic Energy Agency (IAEA) engaged in activities associated with the U.S./IAEA Safeguards Agreement who have been certified by the NRC;

(9) Emergency response personnel who are responding to an emergency;

(10) Commercial vehicle drivers for road shipments of category 1 and category 2 quantities of radioactive material;

(11) Package handlers at transportation facilities such as freight terminals and railroad yards;

(12) Any individual who has an active Federal security clearance, provided that he or she makes available the appropriate documentation. Written confirmation from the agency/employer that granted the Federal security clearance or reviewed the criminal history records check must be provided to the licensee. The licensee shall retain this documentation for a period of 3 years from the date the individual no longer requires unescorted access to category 1 or category 2 quantities of radioactive material; and

(13) Any individual employed by a service provider licensee for which the service provider licensee has conducted the background investigation for the individual and approved the individual for unescorted access to category 1 or category 2 quantities of radioactive material. Written verification from the service provider must be provided to the licensee. The licensee shall retain the documentation for a period of 3 years from the date the individual no longer requires unescorted access to category 1 or category 2 quantities of radioactive material.

(b) Fingerprinting, and the identification and criminal history records checks required by section 149 of the Atomic Energy Act of 1954, as amended, are not required for an individual who has had a favorably adjudicated U.S. Government criminal history records check within the last 5 years, under a comparable U.S. Government program involving fingerprinting and an FBI identification and criminal history records check provided that he or she makes available the appropriate documentation. Written confirmation from the agency/employer that reviewed the criminal history records check must be provided to the licensee. The licensee shall retain this documentation for a period of 3 years from the date the individual no longer requires unescorted access to category 1 or category 2 quantities of radioactive material. These programs include, but are not limited to:

(1) National Agency Check;

(2) Transportation Worker Identification Credentials (TWIC) under 49 CFR part 1572;

(3) Bureau of Alcohol, Tobacco, Firearms, and Explosives background check and clearances under 27 CFR part 555;

(4) Health and Human Services security risk assessments for possession and use of select agents and toxins under 42 CFR part 73;

(5) Hazardous Material security threat assessment for hazardous material endorsement to commercial drivers license under 49 CFR part 1572; and

(6) Customs and Border Protection's Free and Secure Trade (FAST) Program.

[78 FR 17007, Mar. 19, 2013, as amended at 79 FR 58671, Sept. 30, 2014]

§37.31 Protection of information.

(a) Each licensee who obtains background information on an individual under this subpart shall establish and maintain a system of files and written procedures for protection of the record and the personal information from unauthorized disclosure.

(b) The licensee may not disclose the record or personal information collected and maintained to persons other than the subject individual, his or her representative, or to those who have a need to have access to the information in performing assigned duties in the process of granting or denying unescorted access to category 1 or category 2 quantities of radioactive material, safeguards information, or safeguards information-modified handling. No individual authorized to have access to the information may disseminate the information to any other individual who does not have a need to know.

(c) The personal information obtained on an individual from a background investigation may be provided to another licensee:

(1) Upon the individual's written request to the licensee holding the data to disseminate the information contained in his or her file; and

(2) The recipient licensee verifies information such as name, date of birth, social security number, gender, and other applicable physical characteristics.

(d) The licensee shall make background investigation records obtained under this subpart available for examination by an authorized representative of the NRC to determine compliance with the regulations and laws.

(e) The licensee shall retain all fingerprint and criminal history records (including data indicating no record) received from the FBI, or a copy of these records if the individual's file has been transferred, on an individual for 3 years from the date the individual no longer requires unescorted access to category 1 or category 2 quantities of radioactive material.

§37.33 Access authorization program review.

(a) Each licensee shall be responsible for the continuing effectiveness of the access authorization program. Each licensee shall ensure that access authorization programs are reviewed to confirm compliance with the requirements of this subpart and that comprehensive actions are taken to correct any noncompliance that is identified. The review program shall evaluate all program performance objectives and requirements. Each licensee shall periodically (at least annually) review the access program content and implementation.

(b) The results of the reviews, along with any recommendations, must be documented. Each review report must identify conditions that are adverse to the proper performance of the access authorization program, the cause of the condition(s), and, when appropriate, recommend corrective actions, and corrective actions taken. The licensee shall review the findings and take any additional corrective actions necessary to preclude repetition of the condition, including reassessment of the deficient areas where indicated.

(c) Review records must be maintained for 3 years.

Subpart C—Physical Protection Requirements During Use

§ 37.41 Security program.

(a) *Applicability.* (1) Each licensee that possesses an aggregated category 1 or category 2 quantity of radioactive material shall establish, implement, and maintain a security program in accordance with the requirements of this subpart.

(2) An applicant for a new license and each licensee that would become newly subject to the requirements of this subpart upon application for modification of its license shall implement the requirements of this subpart, as appropriate, before taking possession of an aggregated category 1 or category 2 quantity of radioactive material.

(3) Any licensee that has not previously implemented the Security Orders or been subject to the provisions of subpart C shall provide written notification to the NRC regional office specified in § 30.6 of this chapter at least 90 days before aggregating radioactive material to a quantity that equals or exceeds the category 2 threshold.

(b) *General performance objective.* Each licensee shall establish, implement, and maintain a security program that is designed to monitor and, without delay, detect, assess, and respond to an actual or attempted unauthorized access to category 1 or category 2 quantities of radioactive material.

(c) *Program features.* Each licensee's security program must include the program features, as appropriate, described in §§ 37.43, 37.45, 37.47, 37.49, 37.51, 37.53, and 37.55.

§ 37.43 General security program requirements.

(a) *Security plan.* (1) Each licensee identified in § 37.41(a) shall develop a written security plan specific to its facilities and operations. The purpose of the security plan is to establish the licensee's overall security strategy to ensure the integrated and effective functioning of the security program required by this subpart. The security plan must, at a minimum:

(i) Describe the measures and strategies used to implement the requirements of this subpart; and

(ii) Identify the security resources, equipment, and technology used to satisfy the requirements of this subpart.

(2) The security plan must be reviewed and approved by the individual with overall responsibility for the security program.

(3) A licensee shall revise its security plan as necessary to ensure the effective implementation of Commission requirements. The licensee shall ensure that:

(i) The revision has been reviewed and approved by the individual with overall responsibility for the security program; and

(ii) The affected individuals are instructed on the revised plan before the changes are implemented.

(4) The licensee shall retain a copy of the current security plan as a record for 3 years after the security plan is no longer required. If any portion of the plan is superseded, the licensee shall retain the superseded material for 3 years after the record is superseded.

(b) *Implementing procedures.* (1) The licensee shall develop and maintain written procedures that document how the requirements of this subpart and the security plan will be met.

(2) The implementing procedures and revisions to these procedures must be approved in writing by the individual with overall responsibility for the security program.

(3) The licensee shall retain a copy of the current procedure as a record for 3 years after the procedure is no longer

needed. Superseded portions of the procedure must be retained for 3 years after the record is superseded.

(c) *Training.* (1) Each licensee shall conduct training to ensure that those individuals implementing the security program possess and maintain the knowledge, skills, and abilities to carry out their assigned duties and responsibilities effectively. The training must include instruction in:

(i) The licensee's security program and procedures to secure category 1 or category 2 quantities of radioactive material, and in the purposes and functions of the security measures employed;

(ii) The responsibility to report promptly to the licensee any condition that causes or may cause a violation of Commission requirements;

(iii) The responsibility of the licensee to report promptly to the local law enforcement agency and licensee any actual or attempted theft, sabotage, or diversion of category 1 or category 2 quantities of radioactive material; and

(iv) The appropriate response to security alarms.

(2) In determining those individuals who shall be trained on the security program, the licensee shall consider each individual's assigned activities during authorized use and response to potential situations involving actual or attempted theft, diversion, or sabotage of category 1 or category 2 quantities of radioactive material. The extent of the training must be commensurate with the individual's potential involvement in the security of category 1 or category 2 quantities of radioactive material.

(3) Refresher training must be provided at a frequency not to exceed 12 months and when significant changes have been made to the security program. This training must include:

(i) Review of the training requirements of paragraph (c) of this section and any changes made to the security program since the last training;

(ii) Reports on any relevant security issues, problems, and lessons learned;

(iii) Relevant results of NRC inspections; and

(iv) Relevant results of the licensee's program review and testing and maintenance.

(4) The licensee shall maintain records of the initial and refresher training for 3 years from the date of the training. The training records must include dates of the training, topics covered, a list of licensee personnel in attendance, and related information.

(d) *Protection of information.* (1) Licensees authorized to possess category 1 or category 2 quantities of radioactive material shall limit access to and unauthorized disclosure of their security plan, implementing procedures, and the list of individuals that have been approved for unescorted access.

(2) Efforts to limit access shall include the development, implementation, and maintenance of written policies and procedures for controlling access to, and for proper handling and protection against unauthorized disclosure of, the security plan and implementing procedures.

(3) Before granting an individual access to the security plan or implementing procedures, licensees shall:

(i) Evaluate an individual's need to know the security plan or implementing procedures; and

(ii) If the individual has not been authorized for unescorted access to category 1 or category 2 quantities of radioactive material, safeguards information, or safeguards information-modified handling, the licensee must complete a background investigation to determine the individual's trustworthiness and reliability. A trustworthiness and reliability determination shall be conducted by the reviewing official and shall include the background investigation elements contained in § 37.25(a)(2) through (a)(7).

(4) Licensees need not subject the following individuals to the background investigation elements for protection of information:

(i) The categories of individuals listed in § 37.29(a)(1) through (13); or

(ii) Security service provider employees, provided written verification that the employee has been determined to be trustworthy and reliable, by the required background investigation in § 37.25(a)(2) through (a)(7), has been provided by the security service provider.

(5) The licensee shall document the basis for concluding that an individual is trustworthy and reliable and should

be granted access to the security plan or implementing procedures.

(6) Licensees shall maintain a list of persons currently approved for access to the security plan or implementing procedures. When a licensee determines that a person no longer needs access to the security plan or implementing procedures or no longer meets the access authorization requirements for access to the information, the licensee shall remove the person from the approved list as soon as possible, but no later than 7 working days, and take prompt measures to ensure that the individual is unable to obtain the security plan or implementing procedures.

(7) When not in use, the licensee shall store its security plan and implementing procedures in a manner to prevent unauthorized access. Information stored in nonremovable electronic form must be password protected.

(8) The licensee shall retain as a record for 3 years after the document is no longer needed:

(i) A copy of the information protection procedures; and

(ii) The list of individuals approved for access to the security plan or implementing procedures.

[78 FR 17007, Mar. 19, 2013, as amended at 79 FR 58671, Sept. 30, 2014]

§ 37.45 LLEA coordination.

(a) A licensee subject to this subpart shall coordinate, to the extent practicable, with an LLEA for responding to threats to the licensee's facility, including any necessary armed response. The information provided to the LLEA must include:

(1) A description of the facilities and the category 1 and category 2 quantities of radioactive materials along with a description of the licensee's security measures that have been implemented to comply with this subpart; and

(2) A notification that the licensee will request a timely armed response by the LLEA to any actual or attempted theft, sabotage, or diversion of category 1 or category 2 quantities of material.

(b) The licensee shall notify the appropriate NRC regional office listed in § 30.6(a)(2) of this chapter within 3 business days if:

(1) The LLEA has not responded to the request for coordination within 60 days of the coordination request; or

(2) The LLEA notifies the licensee that the LLEA does not plan to participate in coordination activities.

(c) The licensee shall document its efforts to coordinate with the LLEA. The documentation must be kept for 3 years.

(d) The licensee shall coordinate with the LLEA at least every 12 months, or when changes to the facility design or operation adversely affect the potential vulnerability of the licensee's material to theft, sabotage, or diversion.

§ 37.47 Security zones.

(a) Licensees shall ensure that all aggregated category 1 and category 2 quantities of radioactive material are used or stored within licensee-established security zones. Security zones may be permanent or temporary.

(b) Temporary security zones must be established as necessary to meet the licensee's transitory or intermittent business activities, such as periods of maintenance, source delivery, and source replacement.

(c) Security zones must, at a minimum, allow unescorted access only to approved individuals through:

(1) Isolation of category 1 and category 2 quantities of radioactive materials by the use of continuous physical barriers that allow access to the security zone only through established access control points. A physical barrier is a natural or man-made structure or formation sufficient for the isolation of the category 1 or category 2 quantities of radioactive material within a security zone; or

(2) Direct control of the security zone by approved individuals at all times; or

(3) A combination of continuous physical barriers and direct control.

(d) For category 1 quantities of radioactive material during periods of maintenance, source receipt, preparation for shipment, installation, or source removal or exchange, the licensee shall, at a minimum, provide sufficient individuals approved for unescorted access to maintain continuous surveillance of sources in temporary security zones and in any security zone in which physical barriers or intrusion detection systems have been disabled to allow such activities.

(e) Individuals not approved for unescorted access to category 1 or category 2 quantities of radioactive material must be escorted by an approved individual when in a security zone.

§37.49 Monitoring, detection, and assessment.

(a) *Monitoring and detection.* (1) Licensees shall establish and maintain the capability to continuously monitor and detect without delay all unauthorized entries into its security zones. Licensees shall provide the means to maintain continuous monitoring and detection capability in the event of a loss of the primary power source, or provide for an alarm and response in the event of a loss of this capability to continuously monitor and detect unauthorized entries.

(2) Monitoring and detection must be performed by:

(i) A monitored intrusion detection system that is linked to an onsite or offsite central monitoring facility; or

(ii) Electronic devices for intrusion detection alarms that will alert nearby facility personnel; or

(iii) A monitored video surveillance system; or

(iv) Direct visual surveillance by approved individuals located within the security zone; or

(v) Direct visual surveillance by a licensee designated individual located outside the security zone.

(3) A licensee subject to this subpart shall also have a means to detect unauthorized removal of the radioactive material from the security zone. This detection capability must provide:

(i) For category 1 quantities of radioactive material, immediate detection of any attempted unauthorized removal of the radioactive material from the security zone. Such immediate detection capability must be provided by:

(A) Electronic sensors linked to an alarm; or

(B) Continuous monitored video surveillance; or

(C) Direct visual surveillance.

(ii) For category 2 quantities of radioactive material, weekly verification through physical checks, tamper indicating devices, use, or other means to ensure that the radioactive material is present.

(b) *Assessment.* Licensees shall immediately assess each actual or attempted unauthorized entry into the security zone to determine whether the unauthorized access was an actual or attempted theft, sabotage, or diversion.

(c) *Personnel communications and data transmission.* For personnel and automated or electronic systems supporting the licensee's monitoring, detection, and assessment systems, licensees shall:

(1) Maintain continuous capability for personnel communication and electronic data transmission and processing among site security systems; and

(2) Provide an alternative communication capability for personnel, and an alternative data transmission and processing capability, in the event of a loss of the primary means of communication or data transmission and processing. Alternative communications and data transmission systems may not be subject to the same failure modes as the primary systems.

(d) *Response.* Licensees shall immediately respond to any actual or attempted unauthorized access to the security zones, or actual or attempted theft, sabotage, or diversion of category 1 or category 2 quantities of radioactive material at licensee facilities or temporary job sites. For any unauthorized access involving an actual or attempted theft, sabotage, or diversion of category 1 or category 2 quantities of radioactive material, the licensee's response shall include requesting, without delay, an armed response from the LLEA.

§37.51 Maintenance and testing.

(a) Each licensee subject to this subpart shall implement a maintenance and testing program to ensure that intrusion alarms, associated communication systems, and other physical components of the systems used to secure or detect unauthorized access to radioactive material are maintained in operable condition and are capable of performing their intended function when needed. The equipment relied on to meet the security requirements of this part must be inspected and tested for operability and performance at the manufacturer's suggested frequency. If there is no suggested manufacturer's suggested frequency, the testing must be performed at least annually, not to exceed 12 months.

(b) The licensee shall maintain records on the maintenance and testing activities for 3 years.

§ 37.53 Requirements for mobile devices.

Each licensee that possesses mobile devices containing category 1 or category 2 quantities of radioactive material must:

(a) Have two independent physical controls that form tangible barriers to secure the material from unauthorized removal when the device is not under direct control and constant surveillance by the licensee; and

(b) For devices in or on a vehicle or trailer, unless the health and safety requirements for a site prohibit the disabling of the vehicle, the licensee shall utilize a method to disable the vehicle or trailer when not under direct control and constant surveillance by the licensee. Licensees shall not rely on the removal of an ignition key to meet this requirement.

§ 37.55 Security program review.

(a) Each licensee shall be responsible for the continuing effectiveness of the security program. Each licensee shall ensure that the security program is reviewed to confirm compliance with the requirements of this subpart and that comprehensive actions are taken to correct any noncompliance that is identified. The review must include the radioactive material security program content and implementation. Each licensee shall periodically (at least annually) review the security program content and implementation.

(b) The results of the review, along with any recommendations, must be documented. Each review report must identify conditions that are adverse to the proper performance of the security program, the cause of the condition(s), and, when appropriate, recommend corrective actions, and corrective actions taken. The licensee shall review the findings and take any additional corrective actions necessary to preclude repetition of the condition, including reassessment of the deficient areas where indicated.

(c) The licensee shall maintain the review documentation for 3 years.

§ 37.57 Reporting of events.

(a) The licensee shall immediately notify the LLEA after determining that an unauthorized entry resulted in an actual or attempted theft, sabotage, or diversion of a category 1 or category 2 quantity of radioactive material. As soon as possible after initiating a response, but not at the expense of causing delay or interfering with the LLEA response to the event, the licensee shall notify the NRC's Operations Center (301–816–5100). In no case shall the notification to the NRC be later than 4 hours after the discovery of any attempted or actual theft, sabotage, or diversion.

(b) The licensee shall assess any suspicious activity related to possible theft, sabotage, or diversion of category 1 or category 2 quantities of radioactive material and notify the LLEA as appropriate. As soon as possible but not later than 4 hours after notifying the LLEA, the licensee shall notify the NRC's Operations Center (301–816–5100).

(c) The initial telephonic notification required by paragraph (a) of this section must be followed within a period of 30 days by a written report submitted to the NRC by an appropriate method listed in § 37.7. The report must include sufficient information for NRC analysis and evaluation, including identification of any necessary corrective actions to prevent future instances.

Subpart D—Physical Protection in Transit

§ 37.71 Additional requirements for transfer of category 1 and category 2 quantities of radioactive material.

A licensee transferring a category 1 or category 2 quantity of radioactive material to a licensee of the Commission or an Agreement State shall meet the license verification provisions listed below instead of those listed in § 30.41(d) of this chapter:

(a) Any licensee transferring category 1 quantities of radioactive material to a licensee of the Commission or an Agreement State, prior to conducting such transfer, shall verify with the NRC's license verification system or the license issuing authority that the transferee's license authorizes the receipt of the type, form, and quantity of radioactive material to be transferred and that the licensee is authorized to receive radioactive material at the location requested for delivery. If the verification is conducted by contacting the license issuing authority, the transferor shall document the verification. For transfers within the same organization, the licensee does not need to verify the transfer.

(b) Any licensee transferring category 2 quantities of radioactive material to a licensee of the Commission or an Agreement State, prior to conducting such transfer, shall verify with the NRC's license verification system or the license issuing authority that the transferee's license authorizes the receipt of the type, form, and quantity of radioactive material to be transferred. If the verification is conducted by contacting the license issuing authority, the transferor shall document the verification. For transfers within the same organization, the licensee does not need to verify the transfer.

(c) In an emergency where the licensee cannot reach the license issuing authority and the license verification system is nonfunctional, the licensee may accept a written certification by the transferee that it is authorized by license to receive the type, form, and quantity of radioactive material to be transferred. The certification must include the license number, current revision number, issuing agency, expiration date, and for a category 1 shipment the authorized address. The licensee shall keep a copy of the certification. The certification must be confirmed by use of the NRC's license verification system or by contacting the license issuing authority by the end of the next business day.

(d) The transferor shall keep a copy of the verification documentation as a record for 3 years.

§ 37.73 Applicability of physical protection of category 1 and category 2 quantities of radioactive material during transit.

(a) For shipments of category 1 quantities of radioactive material, each shipping licensee shall comply with the requirements for physical protection contained in §§ 37.75(a) and (e); 37.77; 37.79(a)(1), (b)(1), and (c); and 37.81(a), (c), (e), (g) and (h).

(b) For shipments of category 2 quantities of radioactive material, each shipping licensee shall comply with the requirements for physical protection contained in §§ 37.75(b) through (e); 37.79(a)(2), (a)(3), (b)(2), and (c); and 37.81(b), (d), (f), (g), and (h). For those shipments of category 2 quantities of radioactive material that meet the criteria of § 71.97(b) of this chapter, the shipping licensee shall also comply with the advance notification provisions of § 71.97 of this chapter.

(c) The shipping licensee shall be responsible for meeting the requirements of this subpart unless the receiving licensee has agreed in writing to arrange for the in-transit physical protection required under this subpart.

(d) Each licensee that imports or exports category 1 quantities of radioactive material shall comply with the requirements for physical protection during transit contained in §§ 37.75(a)(2) and (e); 37.77; 37.79(a)(1), (b)(1), and (c); and 37.81(a), (c), (e), (g), and (h) for the domestic portion of the shipment.

(e) Each licensee that imports or exports category 2 quantities of radioactive material shall comply with the requirements for physical protection during transit contained in §§ 37.79(a)(2), (a)(3), and (b)(2); and 37.81(b), (d), (f), (g), and (h) for the domestic portion of the shipment.

§ 37.75 Preplanning and coordination of shipment of category 1 or category 2 quantities of radioactive material.

(a) Each licensee that plans to transport, or deliver to a carrier for transport, licensed material that is a category 1 quantity of radioactive material outside the confines of the licensee's facility or other place of use or storage shall:

(1) Preplan and coordinate shipment arrival and departure times with the receiving licensee;

(2) Preplan and coordinate shipment information with the governor or the governor's designee of any State through which the shipment will pass to:

(i) Discuss the State's intention to provide law enforcement escorts; and

(ii) Identify safe havens; and

(3) Document the preplanning and coordination activities.

(b) Each licensee that plans to transport, or deliver to a carrier for transport, licensed material that is a category 2 quantity of radioactive material outside the confines of the licensee's facility or other place of use or storage shall coordinate the shipment no-later-than arrival time and the expected shipment arrival with the receiving licensee. The licensee shall document the coordination activities.

(c) Each licensee who receives a shipment of a category 2 quantity of radioactive material shall confirm receipt of the shipment with the originator. If the shipment has not arrived by the no-later-than arrival time, the receiving licensee shall notify the originator.

(d) Each licensee, who transports or plans to transport a shipment of a category 2 quantity of radioactive material, and determines that the shipment will arrive after the no-later-than arrival time provided pursuant to paragraph (b) of this section, shall promptly notify the receiving licensee of the new no-later-than arrival time.

(e) The licensee shall retain a copy of the documentation for preplanning and coordination and any revision thereof, as a record for 3 years.

§ 37.77 Advance notification of shipment of category 1 quantities of radioactive material.

As specified in paragraphs (a) and (b) of this section, each licensee shall provide advance notification to the NRC and the governor of a State, or the governor's designee, of the shipment of licensed material in a category 1 quantity, through or across the boundary of the State, before the transport, or delivery to a carrier for transport of the licensed material outside the confines of the licensee's facility or other place of use or storage.

(a) *Procedures for submitting advance notification.* (1) The notification must be made to the NRC and to the office of each appropriate governor or governor's designee. The contact information, including telephone and mailing addresses, of governors and governors' designees, is available on the NRC's Web site at *https://scp.nrc.gov/special/designee.pdf.* A list of the contact information is also available upon request from the Director, Division of Material Safety, State, Tribal, and Rulemaking Programs, Office of Nuclear Material Safety and Safeguards., U.S. Nuclear Regulatory Commission, Washington, DC 20555–0001. Notifications to the NRC must be to the NRC's Director, Division of Security Policy, Office of Nuclear Security and Incident Response, U.S. Nuclear Regulatory Commission, Washington, DC 20555–0001. The notification to the NRC may be made by email to *RAMQC_SHIPMENTS@nrc.gov* or by fax to 301–816–5151.

(2) A notification delivered by mail must be postmarked at least 7 days before transport of the shipment commences at the shipping facility.

(3) A notification delivered by any means other than mail must reach NRC at least 4 days before the transport of the shipment commences and must reach the office of the governor or the governor's designee at least 4 days before transport of a shipment within or through the State.

(b) *Information to be furnished in advance notification of shipment.* Each advance notification of shipment of category 1 quantities of radioactive material must contain the following information, if available at the time of notification:

(1) The name, address, and telephone number of the shipper, carrier, and receiver of the category 1 radioactive material;

(2) The license numbers of the shipper and receiver;

(3) A description of the radioactive material contained in the shipment, including the radionuclides and quantity;

(4) The point of origin of the shipment and the estimated time and date that shipment will commence;

(5) The estimated time and date that the shipment is expected to enter each State along the route;

(6) The estimated time and date of arrival of the shipment at the destination; and

(7) A point of contact, with a telephone number, for current shipment information.

(c) *Revision notice.* (1) The licensee shall provide any information not previously available at the time of the initial notification, as soon as the information becomes available but not later than commencement of the shipment, to the governor of the State or the governor's designee and to the NRC's Director of Nuclear Security, Office of Nuclear Security and Incident Response, U.S. Nuclear Regulatory Commission, Washington, DC 20555–0001.

(2) A licensee shall promptly notify the governor of the State or the governor's designee of any changes to the information provided in accordance with paragraphs (b) and (c)(1) of this section. The licensee shall also immediately notify the NRC's Director, Division of Security Policy, Office of Nuclear Security and Incident Response, U.S. Nuclear Regulatory Commission, Washington, DC 20555–0001 of any such changes.

(d) *Cancellation notice.* Each licensee who cancels a shipment for which advance notification has been sent shall send a cancellation notice to the governor of each State or to the governor's designee previously notified and to the NRC's Director, Division of Security Policy, Office of Nuclear Security and Incident Response, U.S. Nuclear Regulatory Commission, Washington, DC 20555–0001. The licensee shall send the cancellation notice before the shipment would have commenced or as soon thereafter as possible. The licensee shall state in the notice that it is a cancellation and identify the advance notification that is being cancelled.

(e) *Records.* The licensee shall retain a copy of the advance notification and any revision and cancellation notices as a record for 3 years.

(f) *Protection of information.* State officials, State employees, and other individuals, whether or not licensees of the Commission or an Agreement State, who receive schedule information of the kind specified in § 37.77(b) shall protect that information against unauthorized disclosure as specified in § 37.43(d) of this part.

[78 FR 17007, Mar. 19, 2013; 78 FR 31821, May 28, 2013; 79 FR 58671, Sept. 30, 2014; 80 FR 74979, Dec. 1, 2015]

§ 37.79 Requirements for physical protection of category 1 and category 2 quantities of radioactive material during shipment.

(a) *Shipments by road.* (1) Each licensee who transports, or delivers to a carrier for transport, in a single shipment, a category 1 quantity of radioactive material shall:

(i) Ensure that movement control centers are established that maintain position information from a remote location. These control centers must monitor shipments 24 hours a day, 7 days a week, and have the ability to communicate immediately, in an emergency, with the appropriate law enforcement agencies.

(ii) Ensure that redundant communications are established that allow the transport to contact the escort vehicle (when used) and movement control center at all times. Redundant communications may not be subject to the same interference factors as the primary communication.

(iii) Ensure that shipments are continuously and actively monitored by a telemetric position monitoring system or an alternative tracking system reporting to a movement control center. A movement control center must provide positive confirmation of the location, status, and control over the shipment. The movement control center must be prepared to promptly implement preplanned procedures in response to deviations from the authorized route or a notification of actual, attempted, or suspicious activities related to the theft, loss, or diversion of a shipment. These procedures will include, but not be limited to, the identification of and contact information for the appropriate LLEA along the shipment route.

(iv) Provide an individual to accompany the driver for those highway shipments with a driving time period greater than the maximum number of allowable hours of service in a 24-hour duty day as established by the Department of Transportation Federal Motor Carrier Safety Administration. The accompanying individual may be another driver.

(v) Develop written normal and contingency procedures to address:

(A) Notifications to the communication center and law enforcement agencies;

(B) Communication protocols. Communication protocols must include a strategy for the use of authentication codes and duress codes and provisions for refueling or other stops, detours, and locations where communication is expected to be temporarily lost;

(C) Loss of communications; and

(D) Responses to an actual or attempted theft or diversion of a shipment.

(vi) Each licensee who makes arrangements for the shipment of category 1 quantities of radioactive material shall ensure that drivers, accompanying personnel, and movement control center personnel have access to the normal and contingency procedures.

(2) Each licensee that transports category 2 quantities of radioactive material shall maintain constant control and/or surveillance during transit and have the capability for immediate communication to summon appropriate response or assistance.

(3) Each licensee who delivers to a carrier for transport, in a single shipment, a category 2 quantity of radioactive material shall:

(i) Use carriers that have established package tracking systems. An established package tracking system is a documented, proven, and reliable system routinely used to transport objects of value. In order for a package tracking system to maintain constant control and/or surveillance, the package tracking system must allow the shipper or transporter to identify when and where the package was last and when it should arrive at the next point of control.

(ii) Use carriers that maintain constant control and/or surveillance during transit and have the capability for immediate communication to summon appropriate response or assistance; and

(iii) Use carriers that have established tracking systems that require an authorized signature prior to releasing the package for delivery or return.

(b) *Shipments by rail.* (1) Each licensee who transports, or delivers to a carrier for transport, in a single shipment, a category 1 quantity of radioactive material shall:

(i) Ensure that rail shipments are monitored by a telemetric position monitoring system or an alternative tracking system reporting to the licensee, third-party, or railroad communications center. The communications center shall provide positive confirmation of the location of the shipment and its status. The communications center shall implement preplanned procedures in response to deviations from the authorized route or to a notification of actual, attempted, or suspicious activities related to the theft or diversion of a shipment. These procedures will include, but not be limited to, the identification of and contact information for the appropriate LLEA along the shipment route.

(ii) Ensure that periodic reports to the communications center are made at preset intervals.

(2) Each licensee who transports, or delivers to a carrier for transport, in a single shipment, a category 2 quantity of radioactive material shall:

(i) Use carriers that have established package tracking systems. An established package tracking system is a documented, proven, and reliable system routinely used to transport objects of value. In order for a package tracking system to maintain constant control and/or surveillance, the package tracking system must allow the shipper or transporter to identify when and where the package was last and when it should arrive at the next point of control.

(ii) Use carriers that maintain constant control and/or surveillance during transit and have the capability for immediate communication to summon appropriate response or assistance; and

(iii) Use carriers that have established tracking systems that require an authorized signature prior to releasing the package for delivery or return.

(c) *Investigations.* Each licensee who makes arrangements for the shipment of category 1 quantities of radioactive material shall immediately conduct an investigation upon the discovery that a category 1 shipment is lost or missing. Each licensee who makes arrangements for the shipment of category 2 quantities of radioactive material shall immediately conduct an investigation, in coordination with the receiving licensee, of any shipment that has not arrived by the designated no-later-than arrival time.

§37.81 Reporting of events.

(a) The shipping licensee shall notify the appropriate LLEA and the NRC's Operations Center (301–816–5100) within 1 hour of its determination that a shipment of category 1 quantities of radioactive material is lost or missing. The appropriate LLEA would be the law enforcement agency in the area of the shipment's last confirmed location. During the investigation required by §37.79(c), the shipping licensee will provide agreed upon updates to the NRC's Operations Center on the status of the investigation.

(b) The shipping licensee shall notify the NRC's Operations Center (301–816–5100) within 4 hours of its determination that a shipment of category 2 quantities of radioactive material is lost or missing. If, after 24 hours of its determination that the shipment is lost or missing, the radioactive material has not been located and secured, the licensee shall immediately notify the NRC's Operations Center.

(c) The shipping licensee shall notify the designated LLEA along the shipment route as soon as possible upon discovery of any actual or attempted theft or diversion of a shipment or suspicious activities related to the theft or diversion of a shipment of a category 1 quantity of radioactive material. As soon as possible after notifying the LLEA, the licensee shall notify the NRC's Operations Center (301–816–5100) upon discovery of any actual or attempted theft or diversion of a shipment, or any suspicious activity related to the shipment of category 1 radioactive material.

(d) The shipping licensee shall notify the NRC's Operations Center (301–816–5100) as soon as possible upon discovery of any actual or attempted theft or diversion of a shipment, or any suspicious activity related to the shipment, of a category 2 quantity of radioactive material.

(e) The shipping licensee shall notify the NRC's Operations Center (301–816–5100) and the LLEA as soon as possible upon recovery of any lost or missing category 1 quantities of radioactive material.

(f) The shipping licensee shall notify the NRC's Operations Center (301–816–5100) as soon as possible upon recovery of any lost or missing category 2 quantities of radioactive material.

(g) The initial telephonic notification required by paragraphs (a) through (d) of this section must be followed within a period of 30 days by a written report submitted to the NRC by an appropriate method listed in §37.7. A written report is not required for notifications on suspicious activities required by paragraphs (c) and (d) of this section. In addition, the licensee shall provide one copy of the written report addressed to the Director, Division of Security Policy, Office of Nuclear Security and Incident Response, U.S. Nuclear Regulatory Commission, Washington, DC 20555–0001. The report must set forth the following information:

(1) A description of the licensed material involved, including kind, quantity, and chemical and physical form;

(2) A description of the circumstances under which the loss or theft occurred;

(3) A statement of disposition, or probable disposition, of the licensed material involved;

(4) Actions that have been taken, or will be taken, to recover the material; and

(5) Procedures or measures that have been, or will be, adopted to ensure against a recurrence of the loss or theft of licensed material.

(h) Subsequent to filing the written report, the licensee shall also report any additional substantive information on the loss or theft within 30 days after the licensee learns of such information.

Subpart E [Reserved]

Subpart F—Records

§ 37.101 Form of records.

Each record required by this part must be legible throughout the retention period specified by each Commission regulation. The record may be the original or a reproduced copy or a microform, provided that the copy or microform is authenticated by authorized personnel and that the microform is capable of producing a clear copy throughout the required retention period. The record may also be stored in electronic media with the capability for producing legible, accurate, and complete records during the required retention period. Records such as letters, drawings, and specifications, must include all pertinent information such as stamps, initials, and signatures. The licensee shall maintain adequate safeguards against tampering with and loss of records.

§ 37.103 Record retention.

Licensees shall maintain the records that are required by the regulations in this part for the period specified by the appropriate regulation. If a retention period is not otherwise specified, these records must be retained until the Commission terminates the facility's license. All records related to this part may be destroyed upon Commission termination of the facility license.

Subpart G—Enforcement

§ 37.105 Inspections.

(a) Each licensee shall afford to the Commission at all reasonable times opportunity to inspect category 1 or category 2 quantities of radioactive material and the premises and facilities wherein the nuclear material is used, produced, or stored.

(b) Each licensee shall make available to the Commission for inspection, upon reasonable notice, records kept by the licensee pertaining to its receipt, possession, use, acquisition, import, export, or transfer of category 1 or category 2 quantities of radioactive material.

§ 37.107 Violations.

(a) The Commission may obtain an injunction or other court order to prevent a violation of the provisions of—

(1) The Atomic Energy Act of 1954, as amended;

(2) Title II of the Energy Reorganization Act of 1974, as amended; or

(3) A regulation or order issued pursuant to those Acts.

(b) The Commission may obtain a court order for the payment of a civil penalty imposed under section 234 of the Atomic Energy Act:

(1) For violations of—

(i) Sections 53, 57, 62, 63, 81, 82, 101, 103, 104, 107, or 109 of the Atomic Energy Act of 1954, as amended:

(ii) Section 206 of the Energy Reorganization Act;

(iii) Any rule, regulation, or order issued pursuant to the sections specified in paragraph (b)(1)(i) of this section;

(iv) Any term, condition, or limitation of any license issued under the sections specified in paragraph (b)(1)(i) of this section.

(2) For any violation for which a license may be revoked under Section 186 of the Atomic Energy Act of 1954, as amended.

§ 37.109 Criminal penalties.

(a) Section 223 of the Atomic Energy Act of 1954, as amended, provides for criminal sanctions for willful violation of, attempted violation of, or conspiracy to violate, any regulation issued under sections 161b, 161i, or 161o of the Act. For purposes of section 223, all the regulations in this part 37 are issued under one or more of sections 161b, 161i, or 161o, except for the sections listed in paragraph (b) of this section.

(b) The regulations in this part 37 that are not issued under sections 161b, 161i, or 161o for the purposes of section 223 are as follows: §§ 37.1, 37.3, 37.5, 37.7, 37.9, 37.11, 37.13, 37.107, and 37.109.

Appendix A to Part 37—Category 1 and Category 2 Radioactive Materials

Table 1—Category 1 and Category 2 Threshold

The terabecquerel (TBq) values are the regulatory standard. The curie (Ci) values specified are obtained by converting from the TBq value. The curie values are provided for practical usefulness only.

Radioactive material	Category 1 (TBq)	Category 1 (Ci)	Category 2 (TBq)	Category 2 (Ci)
Americium-241	60	1,620	0.6	16.2
Americium-241/Be	60	1,620	0.6	16.2
Californium-252	20	540	0.2	5.40
Cobalt-60	30	810	0.3	8.10
Curium-244	50	1,350	0.5	13.5
Cesium-137	100	2,700	1	27.0
Gadolinium-153	1,000	27,000	10	270
Iridium-192	80	2,160	0.8	21.6
Plutonium-238	60	1,620	0.6	16.2
Plutonium-239/Be	60	1,620	0.6	16.2
Promethium-147	40,000	1,080,000	400	10,800
Radium-226	40	1,080	0.4	10.8
Selenium-75	200	5,400	2	54.0
Strontium-90	1,000	27,000	10	270
Thulium-170	20,000	540,000	200	5,400
Ytterbium-169	300	8,100	3	81.0

NOTE: *Calculations Concerning Multiple Sources or Multiple Radionuclides*

The "sum of fractions" methodology for evaluating combinations of multiple sources or multiple radionuclides is to be used in determining whether a location meets or exceeds the threshold and is thus subject to the requirements of this part.

I. If multiple sources of the same radionuclide and/or multiple radionuclides are aggregated at a location, the sum of the ratios of the total activity of each of the radionuclides must be determined to verify whether the activity at the location is less than the category 1 or category 2 thresholds of Table 1, as appropriate. If the calculated sum of the ratios, using the equation below, is greater than or equal to 1.0, then the applicable requirements of this part apply.

II. First determine the total activity for each radionuclide from Table 1. This is done by adding the activity of each individual source, material in any device, and any loose or bulk material that contains the radionuclide. Then use the equation below to calculate the sum of the ratios by inserting the total activity of the applicable radionuclides from Table 1 in the numerator of the equation and the corresponding threshold activity from Table 1 in the denominator of the equation. Calculations must be performed in metric values (i.e., TBq) and the numerator and denominator values must be in the same units.

R_1 = total activity for radionuclide 1
R_2 = total activity for radionuclide 2
R_N = total activity for radionuclide n
AR_1 = activity threshold for radionuclide 1
AR_2 = activity threshold for radionuclide 2
AR_N = activity threshold for radionuclide n

$$\sum_{1}^{n}\left[\frac{R_1}{AR_1}+\frac{R_2}{AR_2}+\frac{R_n}{AR_n}\right]\geq 1.0$$

PART 39—LICENSES AND RADIATION SAFETY REQUIREMENTS FOR WELL LOGGING

AUTHORITY: Atomic Energy Act of 1954, secs. 53, 57, 62, 63, 65, 69, 81, 161, 181, 182, 183, 223, 234 (42 U.S.C. 2073, 2077, 2092, 2093, 2095, 2099, 2111, 2112, 2201, 2232, 2233, 2273, 2282); Energy Reorganization Act of 1974, secs. 201, 206 (42 U.S.C. 5841, 5846); 44 U.S.C. 3504 note.

SOURCE: 52 FR 8234, Mar. 17, 1987, unless otherwise noted.

Subpart A—General Provisions

§ 39.1 Purpose and scope.

(a) This part prescribes requirements for the issuance of a license authorizing the use of licensed materials including sealed sources, radioactive tracers, radioactive markers, and uranium sinker bars in well logging in a single well. This part also prescribes radiation safety requirements for persons using licensed materials in these operations. The provisions and requirements of this part are in addition to, and not in substitution for, other requirements of this chapter. In particular, the provisions of parts 19, 20, 21, 30, 37, 40, 70, 71, and 150 of this chapter apply to applicants and licensees subject to this part.

(b) The requirements set out in this part do not apply to the issuance of a license authorizing the use of licensed material in tracer studies involving multiple wells, such as field flooding studies, or to the use of sealed sources auxiliary to well logging but not lowered into wells.

[52 FR 8234, Mar. 17, 1987, as amended at 78 FR 17020, Mar. 19, 2013]

§ 39.2 Definitions.

Energy compensation source (ECS) means a small sealed source, with an activity not exceeding 3.7 MBq [100 microcuries], used within a logging tool, or other tool components, to provide a reference standard to maintain the tool's calibration when in use.

Field station means a facility where licensed material may be stored or used and from which equipment is dispatched to temporary jobsites.

Fresh water aquifer, for the purpose of this part, means a geologic formation that is capable of yielding fresh water to a well or spring.

Injection tool means a device used for controlled subsurface injection of radioactive tracer material.

Irretrievable well logging source means any sealed source containing licensed material that is pulled off or not connected to the wireline that suspends the source in the well and for which all reasonable effort at recovery has been expended.

Licensed material means byproduct, source, or special nuclear material received, processed, used, or transferred under a license issued by the Commission under the regulations in this chapter.

Logging assistant means any individual who, under the personal supervision of a logging supervisor, handles sealed sources or tracers that are not in logging tools or shipping containers or who performs surveys required by § 39.67.

Logging supervisor means an individual who uses licensed material or provides personal supervision in the use of licensed material at a temporary jobsite and who is responsible to the licensee for assuring compliance with the requirements of the Commission's regulations and the conditions of the license.

Logging tool means a device used subsurface to perform well logging.

Personal supervision means guidance and instruction by a logging supervisor, who is physically present at a temporary jobsite, who is in personal contact with logging assistants, and who can give immediate assistance.

Radioactive marker means licensed material used for depth determination or direction orientation. For purposes of this part, this term includes radioactive collar markers and radioactive iron nails.

Safety review means a periodic review provided by the licensee for its employees on radiation safety aspects of well logging. The review may include, as appropriate, the results of internal inspections, new procedures or equipment, accidents or errors that have been observed, and opportunities for employees to ask safety questions.

Sealed source means any licensed material that is encased in a capsule designed to prevent leakage or escape of the licensed material.

Source holder means a housing or assembly into which a sealed source is placed to facilitate the handling and use of the source in well logging.

Subsurface tracer study means the release of unsealed license material or a substance labeled with licensed material in a single well for the purpose of tracing the movement or position of the material or substance in the well or adjacent formation.

Surface casing for protecting fresh water aquifers means a pipe or tube used as a lining in a well to isolate fresh water aquifers from the well.

Temporary jobsite means a place where licensed materials are present for the purpose of performing well logging or subsurface tracer studies.

Tritium neutron generator target source means a tritium source used within a neutron generator tube to produce neutrons for use in well logging applications.

Uranium sinker bar means a weight containing depleted uranium used to pull a logging tool toward the bottom of a well.

Well means a drilled hole in which well logging may be performed. As used in this part, "well" includes drilled holes for the purpose of oil, gas, mineral, groundwater, or geological exploration.

Well logging means all operations involving the lowering and raising of measuring devices or tools which contain licensed material or are used to detect licensed materials in wells for the purpose of obtaining information about the well or adjacent formations which may be used in oil, gas, mineral, groundwater, or geological exploration.

[52 FR 8234, Mar. 17, 1987, as amended at 65 FR 20344, Apr. 17, 2000]

§ 39.5 Interpretations.

Except as specifically authorized by the Commission in writing, no interpretation of the meaning of the regulations in this part by any officer or employee of the Commission, other than a written interpretation by the General Counsel, will be recognized to be binding upon the Commission.

§ 39.8 Information collection requirements: OMB approval.

(a) The Nuclear Regulatory Commission has submitted the information collection requirements contained in this part to the Office of Management and Budget (OMB) for approval as required by the Paperwork Reduction Act (44 U.S. 3501 *et seq.*) The NRC may not conduct or sponsor, and a person is not required to respond to, a collection of information unless it displays a currently valid OMB control number. OMB has approved the information collection requirements contained in this part under control number 3150–0130.

(b) The approved information collection requirements contained in this part appear in §§ 39.11, 39.13, 39.15, 39.17, 39.31, 39.33, 39.35, 39.37, 39.39, 39.43, 39.51, 39.61, 39.63, 39.65, 39.67, 39.73, 39.75, 39.77, and 39.91.

(c) This part contains information collection requirements in addition to those approved under the control number specified in paragraph (a) of this section. These information collection requirements and the control numbers under which they are approved are as follows:

(1) In § 39.11, NRC Form 313 is approved under control 3150–0120.

(2) [Reserved]

[62 FR 52187, Oct. 6, 1997, as amended at 67 FR 67099, Nov. 4, 2002]

Subpart B—Specific Licensing Requirements

§ 39.11 Application for a specific license.

A person, as defined in § 30.4 of this chapter, shall file an application for a specific license authorizing the use of licensed material in well logging on Form NRC 313, "Application for Material License." Each application for a license, other than a license exempted from part 170 of this chapter, must be accompanied by the fee prescribed in § 170.31 of this chapter. The application must be sent to the appropriate NRC Regional Office listed in appendix D of part 20 of this chapter.

§ 39.13 Specific licenses for well logging.

The Commission will approve an application for a specific license for the use of licensed material in well logging if the applicant meets the following requirements:

(a) The applicant shall satisfy the general requirements specified in § 30.33 of this chapter for byproduct material, in § 40.32 of this chapter for source material, and in § 70.23 of this chapter for special nuclear material, as appropriate, and any special requirements contained in this part.

(b) The applicant shall develop a program for training logging supervisors and logging assistants and submit to the Commission a description of this program which specifies the—

(1) Initial training;

(2) On-the-job training;

(3) Annual safety reviews provided by the licensee;

(4) Means the applicant will use to demonstrate the logging supervisor's knowledge and understanding of and ability to comply with the Commission's regulations and licensing requirements and the applicant's operating and emergency procedures; and

(5) Means the applicant will use to demonstrate the logging assistant's knowledge and understanding of and ability to comply with the applicant's operating and emergency procedures.

(c) The applicant shall submit to the Commission written operating and emergency procedures as described in § 39.63 or an outline or summary of the procedures that includes the important radiation safety aspects of the procedures.

(d) The applicant shall establish and submit to the Commission its program for annual inspections of the job performance of each logging supervisor to ensure that the Commission's regulations, license requirements, and the applicant's operating and emergency procedures are followed. Inspection records must be retained for 3 years after each annual internal inspection.

(e) The applicant shall submit a description of its overall organizational structure as it applies to the radiation safety responsibilities in well logging, including specified delegations of authority and responsibility.

(f) If an applicant wants to perform leak testing of sealed sources, the applicant shall identify the manufacturers and the model numbers of the leak test kits to be used. If the applicant wants to analyze its own wipe samples, the applicant shall establish procedures to be followed and submit a description of these procedures to the Commission. The description must include the—

(1) Instruments to be used;

(2) Methods of performing the analysis; and

(3) Pertinent experience of the person who will analyze the wipe samples.

[52 FR 8234, Mar. 17, 1987, as amended at 76 FR 56963, Sept. 15, 2011]

§ 39.15 Agreement with well owner or operator.

(a) A licensee may perform well logging with a sealed source only after the licensee has a written agreement with the employing well owner or operator. This written agreement must identify who will meet the following requirements:

(1) If a sealed source becomes lodged in the well, a reasonable effort will be made to recover it.

(2) A person may not attempt to recover a sealed source in a manner which, in the licensee's opinion, could result in its rupture.

(3) The radiation monitoring required in § 39.69(a) will be performed.

(4) If the environment, any equipment, or personnel are contaminated with licensed material, they must be decontaminated before release from the site or release for unrestricted use; and

(5) If the sealed source is classified as irretrievable after reasonable efforts at recovery have been expended, the following requirements must be implemented within 30 days:

(i) Each irretrievable well logging source must be immobilized and sealed in place with a cement plug.

(ii) A means to prevent inadvertent intrusion on the source, unless the source is not accessible to any subsequent drilling operations; and

(iii) A permanent identification plaque, constructed of long lasting material such as stainless steel, brass, bronze, or monel, must be mounted at the surface of the well, unless the mounting of the plaque is not practical. The size of the plaque must be at least 17 cm [7 inches] square and 3 mm [1/8-inch] thick. The plaque must contain—

(A) The word "CAUTION";

(B) The radiation symbol (the color requirement in § 20.1901(a) need not be met);

(C) The date the source was abandoned;

(D) The name of the well owner or well operator, as appropriate;

(E) The well name and well identification number(s) or other designation;

(F) An identification of the sealed source(s) by radionuclide and quantity;

(G) The depth of the source and depth to the top of the plug; and

(H) An appropriate warning, such as, "DO NOT RE-ENTER THIS WELL."

(b) The licensee shall retain a copy of the written agreement for 3 years after the completion of the well logging operation.

(c) A licensee may apply, pursuant to § 39.91, for Commission approval, on a case-by-case basis, of proposed procedures to abandon an irretrievable well logging source in a manner not otherwise authorized in paragraph (a)(5) of this section.

(d) A written agreement between the licensee and the well owner or operator is not required if the licensee and the well owner or operator are part of the same corporate structure or otherwise similarly affiliated. However, the licensee shall still otherwise meet the requirements in paragraphs (a)(1) through (a)(5).

[52 FR 8234, Mar. 17, 1987, as amended at 56 FR 23472, May 21, 1991; 58 FR 67660, Dec. 22, 1993; 65 FR 20344, Apr. 17, 2000]

§ 39.17 Request for written statements.

Each license is issued with the condition that the licensee will, at any time before expiration of the license, upon the Commission's request, submit written statements, signed under oath or affirmation, to enable the Commission to determine whether or not the license should be modified, suspended, or revoked.

Subpart C—Equipment

§ 39.31 Labels, security, and transportation precautions.

(a) *Labels.* (1) The licensee may not use a source, source holder, or logging tool that contains licensed material unless the smallest component that is transported as a separate piece of equipment with the licensed material inside bears a durable, legible, and clearly visible marking or label. The marking or label must contain the radiation symbol specified in § 20.1901(a), without the conventional color requirements, and the wording "DANGER (or CAUTION) RADIOACTIVE MATERIAL."

(2) The licensee may not use a container to store licensed material unless the container has securely attached to it a durable, legible, and clearly visible label. The label must contain the radiation symbol specified in § 20.1901(a) of this chapter and the wording "CAUTION (or DANGER), RADIOACTIVE MATERIAL, NOTIFY CIVIL AUTHORITIES (or NAME OF COMPANY)."

(3) The licensee may not transport licensed material unless the material is packaged, labeled, marked, and accompanied with appropriate shipping papers in accordance with regulations set out in 10 CFR part 71.

(b) *Security precautions during storage and transportation.* (1) The licensee shall store each source containing licensed material in a storage container or transportation package. The container or package must be locked and physically secured to prevent tampering or removal of licensed material from storage by unauthorized personnel. The licensee shall store licensed material in a manner which will minimize danger from explosion or fire.

(2) The licensee shall lock and physically secure the transport package containing licensed material in the transporting vehicle to prevent accidental loss, tampering, or unauthorized removal of the licensed material from the vehicle.

[52 FR 8234, Mar. 17, 1987, as amended at 56 FR 23472, May 21, 1991; 58 FR 67660, Dec. 22, 1993]

§ 39.33 Radiation detection instruments.

(a) The licensee shall keep a calibrated and operable radiation survey instrument capable of detecting beta and gamma radiation at each field station and temporary jobsite to make the radiation surveys required by this part and by part 20 of this chapter. To satisfy this requirement, the radiation survey instrument must be capable of measuring 0.001 mSv (0.1 mrem) per hour through at least 0.5 mSv (50 mrem) per hour.

(b) The licensee shall have available additional calibrated and operable radiation detection instruments sensitive enough to detect the low radiation and contamination levels that could be encountered if a sealed source ruptured. The licensee may own the instruments or may have a procedure to obtain them quickly from a second party.

(c) The licensee shall have each radiation survey instrument required under paragraph (a) of this section calibrated—

(1) At intervals not to exceed 6 months and after instrument servicing;

(2) For linear scale instruments, at two points located approximately ⅓ and ⅔ of full-scale on each scale; for logarithmic scale instruments, at midrange of each decade, and at two points of at least one decade; and for digital instruments, at appropriate points; and

(3) So that an accuracy within plus or minus 20 percent of the calibration standard can be demonstrated on each scale.

(d) The licensee shall retain calibration records for a period of 3 years after the date of calibration for inspection by the Commission.

[52 FR 8234, Mar. 17, 1987, as amended at 63 FR 39483, July 23, 1998]

§ 39.35 Leak testing of sealed sources.

(a) *Testing and recordkeeping requirements.* Each licensee who uses a sealed source shall have the source tested for leakage periodically. The licensee shall keep a record of leak test results in units of microcuries and retain the record for inspection by the Commission for 3 years after the leak test is performed.

(b) *Method of testing*. The wipe of a sealed source must be performed using a leak test kit or method approved by the Commission or an Agreement State. The wipe sample must be taken from the nearest accessible point to the sealed source where contamination might accumulate. The wipe sample must be analyzed for radioactive contamination. The analysis must be capable of detecting the presence of 185 Bq [0.005 microcuries] of radioactive material on the test sample and must be performed by a person approved by the Commission or an Agreement State to perform the analysis.

(c) *Test frequency*. (1) Each sealed source (except an energy compensation source (ECS)) must be tested at intervals not to exceed 6 months. In the absence of a certificate from a transferor that a test has been made within the 6 months before the transfer, the sealed source may not be used until tested.

(2) Each ECS that is not exempt from testing in accordance with paragraph (e) of this section must be tested at intervals not to exceed 3 years. In the absence of a certificate from a transferor that a test has been made within the 3 years before the transfer, the ECS may not be used until tested.

(d) *Removal of leaking source from service*. (1) If the test conducted pursuant to paragraphs (a) and (b) of this section reveals the presence of 185 Bq [0.005 microcuries] or more of removable radioactive material, the licensee shall remove the sealed source from service immediately and have it decontaminated, repaired, or disposed of by an NRC or Agreement State licensee that is authorized to perform these functions. The licensee shall check the equipment associated with the leaking source for radioactive contamination and, if contaminated, have it decontaminated or disposed of by an NRC or Agreement State licensee that is authorized to perform these functions.

(2) The licensee shall submit a report to the appropriate NRC Regional Office listed in appendix D of part 20 of this chapter, within 5 days of receiving the test results. The report must describe the equipment involved in the leak, the test results, any contamination which resulted from the leaking source, and the corrective actions taken up to the time the report is made.

(e) *Exemptions from testing requirements*. The following sealed sources are exempt from the periodic leak test requirements set out in paragraphs (a) through (d) of this section:

(1) Hydrogen-3 (tritium) sources;

(2) Sources containing licensed material with a half-life of 30 days or less;

(3) Sealed sources containing licensed material in gaseous form;

(4) Sources of beta- or gamma-emitting radioactive material with an activity of 3.7 MBq [100 microcuries] or less; and

(5) Sources of alpha- or neutron-emitting radioactive material with an activity of 0.37 MBq [10 microcuries] or less.

[52 FR 8234, Mar. 17, 1987, as amended at 65 FR 20344, Apr. 17, 2000]

§39.37 Physical inventory.

Each licensee shall conduct a semi-annual physical inventory to account for all licensed material received and possessed under the license. The licensee shall retain records of the inventory for 3 years from the date of the inventory for inspection by the Commission. The inventory must indicate the quantity and kind of licensed material, the location of the licensed material, the date of the inventory, and the name of the individual conducting the inventory. Physical inventory records may be combined with leak test records.

§39.39 Records of material use.

(a) Each licensee shall maintain records for each use of licensed material showing—

(1) The make, model number, and a serial number or a description of each sealed source used;

(2) In the case of unsealed licensed material used for subsurface tracer studies, the radionuclide and quantity of activity used in a particular well and the disposition of any unused tracer materials;

(3) The identity of the logging supervisor who is responsible for the licensed material and the identity of logging assistants present; and

(4) The location and date of use of the licensed material.

(b) The licensee shall make the records required by paragraph (a) of this section available for inspection by the Commission. The licensee shall retain the records for 3 years from the date of the recorded event.

§ 39.41 Design and performance criteria for sources.

(a) A licensee may use a sealed source for use in well logging applications if—

(1) The sealed source is doubly encapsulated;

(2) The sealed source contains licensed material whose chemical and physical forms are as insoluble and nondispersible as practical; and

(3) Meets the requirements of paragraph (b), (c), or (d) of this section.

(b) For a sealed source manufactured on or before July 14, 1989, a licensee may use the sealed source, for use in well logging applications if it meets the requirements of USASI N5.10–1968, "Classification of Sealed Radioactive Sources," or the requirements in paragraph (c) or (d) of this section.

(c) For a sealed source manufactured after July 14, 1989, a licensee may use the sealed source, for use in well logging applications if it meets the oil-well logging requirements of ANSI/HPS N43.6–1997, "Sealed Radioactive Sources—Classification."

(d) For a sealed source manufactured after July 14, 1989, a licensee may use the sealed source, for use in well logging applications, if—

(1) The sealed source's prototype has been tested and found to maintain its integrity after each of the following tests:

(i) *Temperature.* The test source must be held at −40 °C for 20 minutes, 600 °C for 1 hour, and then be subject to a thermal shock test with a temperature drop from 600 °C to 20 °C within 15 seconds.

(ii) *Impact test.* A 5 kg steel hammer, 2.5 cm in diameter, must be dropped from a height of 1 m onto the test source.

(iii) *Vibration test.* The test source must be subject to a vibration from 25 Hz to 500 Hz at 5 g amplitude for 30 minutes.

(iv) *Puncture test.* A 1 gram hammer and pin, 0.3 cm pin diameter, must be dropped from a height of 1 m onto the test source.

(v) *Pressure test.* The test source must be subject to an external pressure of 1.695×10^7 pascals [24,600 pounds per square inch absolute].

(e) The requirements in paragraphs (a), (b), (c), and (d) of this section do not apply to sealed sources that contain licensed material in gaseous form.

(f) The requirements in paragraphs (a), (b), (c), and (d) of this section do not apply to energy compensation sources (ECS). ECSs must be registered with the Commission under § 32.210 of this chapter or with an Agreement State.

[65 FR 20345, Apr. 17, 2000]

§ 39.43 Inspection, maintenance, and opening of a source or source holder.

(a) Each licensee shall visually check source holders, logging tools, and source handling tools, for defects before each use to ensure that the equipment is in good working condition and that required labeling is present. If defects are found, the equipment must be removed from service until repaired, and a record must be made listing: the date of check, name of inspector, equipment involved, defects found, and repairs made. These records must be retained for 3 years after the defect is found.

(b) Each licensee shall have a program for semiannual visual inspection and routine maintenance of source holders, logging tools, injection tools, source handling tools, storage containers, transport containers, and uranium sinker bars to ensure that the required labeling is legible and that no physical damage is visible. If defects are found, the equipment must be removed from service until repaired, and a record must be made listing: date, equipment involved, inspection and maintenance operations performed, any defects found, and any actions taken to correct the defects. These records must be retained for 3 years after the defect is found.

(c) Removal of a sealed source from a source holder or logging tool, and maintenance on sealed sources or holders in which sealed sources are contained may not be performed by the licensee unless a written procedure developed pursuant to § 39.63 has been approved either by the Commission pursuant to § 39.13(c) or by an Agreement State.

(d) If a sealed source is stuck in the source holder, the licensee may not perform any operation, such as drilling, cutting, or chiseling, on the source holder unless the licensee is specifically approved by the Commission or an Agreement State to perform this operation.

(e) The opening, repair, or modification of any sealed source must be performed by persons specifically approved to do so by the Commission or an Agreement State.

§ 39.45 Subsurface tracer studies.

(a) The licensee shall require all personnel handling radioactive tracer material to use protective gloves and, if required by the license, other protective clothing and equipment. The licensee shall take precautions to avoid ingestion or inhalation of radioactive tracer material and to avoid contamination of field stations and temporary jobsites.

(b) A licensee may not knowingly inject licensed material into fresh water aquifers unless specifically authorized to do so by the Commission.

§ 39.47 Radioactive markers.

The licensee may use radioactive markers in wells only if the individual markers contain quantities of licensed material not exceeding the quantities specified in § 30.71 of this chapter. The use of markers is subject only to the requirements of § 39.37.

§ 39.49 Uranium sinker bars.

The licensee may use a uranium sinker bar in well logging applications only if it is legibly impressed with the words "CAUTION—RADIOACTIVE-DEPLETED URANIUM" and "NOTIFY CIVIL AUTHORITIES (or COMPANY NAME) IF FOUND."

[65 FR 20345, Apr. 17, 2000]

§ 39.51 Use of a sealed source in a well without a surface casing.

The licensee may use a sealed source in a well without a surface casing for protecting fresh water aquifers only if the licensee follows a procedure for reducing the probability of the source becoming lodged in the well. The procedure must be approved by the Commission pursuant to § 39.13(c) or by an Agreement State.

§ 39.53 Energy compensation source.

The licensee may use an energy compensation source (ECS) which is contained within a logging tool, or other tool components, only if the ECS contains quantities of licensed material not exceeding 3.7 MBq [100 microcuries].

(a) For well logging applications with a surface casing for protecting fresh water aquifers, use of the ECS is only subject to the requirements of §§ 39.35, 39.37 and 39.39.

(b) For well logging applications without a surface casing for protecting fresh water aquifers, use of the ECS is only subject to the requirements of §§ 39.15, 39.35, 39.37, 39.39, 39.51, and 39.77.

[65 FR 20345, Apr. 17, 2000]

§ 39.55 Tritium neutron generator target sources.

(a) Use of a tritium neutron generator target source, containing quantities not exceeding 1,110 GBg [30 curies] and in a well with a surface casing to protect fresh water aquifers, is subject to the requirements of this part except §§ 39.15, 39.41, and 39.77.

(b) Use of a tritium neutron generator target source, containing quantities exceeding 1,110 GBg [30 curies] or in a well without a surface casing to protect fresh water aquifers, is subject to the requirements of this part except § 39.41.

[68 FR 75390, Dec. 31, 2003]

Subpart D—Radiation Safety Requirements

§ 39.61 Training.

(a) The licensee may not permit an individual to act as a logging supervisor until that person—

(1) Has completed training in the subjects outlined in paragraph (e) of this section;

(2) Has received copies of, and instruction in—

(i) The NRC regulations contained in the applicable sections of parts 19, 20, and 39 of this chapter;

(ii) The NRC license under which the logging supervisor will perform well logging; and

(iii) The licensee's operating and emergency procedures required by § 39.63;

(3) Has completed on-the-job training and demonstrated competence in the use of licensed materials, remote handling tools, and radiation survey instruments by a field evaluation; and

(4) Has demonstrated understanding of the requirements in paragraphs (a) (1) and (2) of this section by successfully completing a written test.

(b) The licensee may not permit an individual to act as a logging assistant until that person—

(1) Has received instruction in applicable sections of parts 19 and 20 of this chapter;

(2) Has received copies of, and instruction in, the licensee's operating and emergency procedures required by § 39.63;

(3) Has demonstrated understanding of the materials listed in paragraphs (b) (1) and (2) of this section by successfully completing a written or oral test; and

(4) Has received instruction in the use of licensed materials, remote handling tools, and radiation survey instruments, as appropriate for the logging assistant's intended job responsibilities.

(c) The licensee shall provide safety reviews for logging supervisors and logging assistants at least once during each calendar year.

(d) The licensee shall maintain a record on each logging supervisor's and logging assistant's training and annual safety review. The training records must include copies of written tests and dates of oral tests given after July 14, 1987. The training records must be retained until 3 years following the termination of employment. Records of annual safety reviews must list the topics discussed and be retained for 3 years.

(e) The licensee shall include the following subjects in the training required in paragraph (a)(1) of this section:

(1) Fundamentals of radiation safety including—

(i) Characteristics of radiation;

(ii) Units of radiation dose and quantity of radioactivity;

(iii) Hazards of exposure to radiation;

(iv) Levels of radiation from licensed material;

(v) Methods of controlling radiation dose (time, distance, and shielding); and

(vi) Radiation safety practices, including prevention of contamination, and methods of decontamination.

(2) Radiation detection instruments including—

(i) Use, operation, calibration, and limitations of radiation survey instruments;

(ii) Survey techniques; and

(iii) Use of personnel monitoring equipment;

(3) Equipment to be used including—

(i) Operation of equipment, including source handling equipment and remote handling tools;

(ii) Storage, control, and disposal of licensed material; and

(iii) Maintenance of equipment.

(4) The requirements of pertinent Federal regulations. And

(5) Case histories of accidents in well logging.

§ 39.63 Operating and emergency procedures.

Each licensee shall develop and follow written operating and emergency procedures that cover—

(a) The handling and use of licensed materials including the use of sealed sources in wells without surface casing for protecting fresh water aquifers, if appropriate;

(b) The use of remote handling tools for handling sealed sources and radioactive tracer material except low-activity calibration sources;

(c) Methods and occasions for conducting radiation surveys, including surveys for detecting contamination, as required by § 39.67(c)–(e);

(d) Minimizing personnel exposure including exposures from inhalation and ingestion of licensed tracer materials;

(e) Methods and occasions for locking and securing stored licensed materials;

(f) Personnel monitoring and the use of personnel monitoring equipment;

(g) Transportation of licensed materials to field stations or temporary jobsites, packaging of licensed materials for transport in vehicles, placarding of vehicles when needed, and physically securing licensed materials in transport vehicles during transportation to prevent accidental loss, tampering, or unauthorized removal;

(h) Picking up, receiving, and opening packages containing licensed materials, in accordance with § 20.1906 of this chapter;

(i) For the use of tracers, decontamination of the environment, equipment, and personnel;

(j) Maintenance of records generated by logging personnel at temporary jobsites;

(k) The inspection and maintenance of sealed sources, source holders, logging tools, injection tools, source handling tools, storage containers, transport containers, and uranium sinker bars as required by § 39.43;

(l) Identifying and reporting to NRC defects and noncompliance as required by part 21 of this chapter;

(m) Actions to be taken if a sealed source is lodged in a well;

(n) Notifying proper persons in the event of an accident; and

(o) Actions to be taken if a sealed source is ruptured including actions to prevent the spread of contamination and minimize inhalation and ingestion of licensed materials and actions to obtain suitable radiation survey instruments as required by § 39.33(b).

[52 FR 8234, Mar. 17, 1987, as amended at 67 FR 77652, Dec. 19, 2002]

§ 39.65 Personnel monitoring.

(a) The licensee may not permit an individual to act as a logging supervisor or logging assistant unless that person wears, at all times during the handling of licensed radioactive materials, a personnel dosimeter that is processed and evaluated by an accredited National Voluntary Laboratory Accreditation Program (NVLAP) processor. Each personnel dosimeter must be assigned to and worn by only one individual. Film badges must be replaced at least monthly and other personnel dosimeters replaced at least quarterly. After replacement, each personnel dosimeter must be promptly processed.

(b) The licensee shall provide bioassay services to individuals using licensed materials in subsurface tracer studies if required by the license.

(c) The licensee shall retain records of personnel dosimeters required by paragraph (a) of this section and bioassay results for inspection until the Commission authorizes disposition of the records.

[52 FR 8234, Mar. 17, 1987, as amended at 65 FR 63752, Oct. 24, 2000]

§ 39.67 Radiation surveys.

(a) The licensee shall make radiation surveys, including but not limited to the surveys required under paragraphs (b) through (e) of this section, of each area where licensed materials are used and stored.

(b) Before transporting licensed materials, the licensee shall make a radiation survey of the position occupied by each individual in the vehicle and of the exterior of each vehicle used to transport the licensed materials.

(c) If the sealed source assembly is removed from the logging tool before departure from the temporary jobsite, the licensee shall confirm that the logging tool is free of contamination by energizing the logging tool detector or by using a survey meter.

(d) If the licensee has reason to believe that, as a result of any operation involving a sealed source, the encapsulation of the sealed source could be damaged by the operation, the licensee shall conduct a radiation survey, including a contamination survey, during and after the operation.

(e) The licensee shall make a radiation survey at the temporary jobsite before and after each subsurface tracer study to confirm the absence of contamination.

(f) The results of surveys required under paragraphs (a) through (e) of this section must be recorded and must include the date of the survey, the name of the individual making the survey, the identification of the survey, instrument used, and the location of the survey. The licensee shall retain records of surveys for inspection by the Commission for 3 years after they are made.

§ 39.69 Radioactive contamination control.

(a) If the licensee detects evidence that a sealed source has ruptured or licensed materials have caused contamination, the licensee shall initiate immediately the emergency procedures required by § 39.63.

(b) If contamination results from the use of licensed material in well logging, the licensee shall decontaminate all work areas, equipment, and unrestricted areas.

(c) During efforts to recover a sealed source lodged in the well, the licensee shall continuously monitor, with an appropriate radiation detection instrument or a logging tool with a radiation detector, the circulating fluids from the well, if any, to check for contamination resulting from damage to the sealed source.

Subpart E—Security, Records, Notifications

§ 39.71 Security.

(a) A logging supervisor must be physically present at a temporary jobsite whenever licensed materials are being handled or are not stored and locked in a vehicle or storage place. The logging supervisor may leave the jobsite in order to obtain assistance if a source becomes lodged in a well.

(b) During well logging, except when radiation sources are below ground or in shipping or storage containers, the logging supervisor or other individual designated by the logging supervisor shall maintain direct surveillance of the operation to prevent unauthorized entry into a restricted area, as defined in § 20.1003 of this chapter.

[52 FR 8234, Mar. 17, 1987, as amended at 63 FR 39483, July 23, 1998]

§ 39.73 Documents and records required at field stations.

Each licensee shall maintain the following documents and records at the field station:

(a) A copy of parts 19, 20, and 39 of NRC regulations;

(b) The license authorizing the use of licensed material;

(c) Operating and emergency procedures required by § 39.63;

(d) The record of radiation survey instrument calibrations required by § 39.33;

(e) The record of leak test results required by § 39.35;

(f) Physical inventory records required by § 39.37;

(g) Utilization records required by § 39.39;

(h) Records of inspection and maintenance required by § 39.43;

(i) Training records required by § 39.61(d); and

(j) Survey records required by § 39.67.

§ 39.75 Documents and records required at temporary jobsites.

Each licensee conducting operations at a temporary jobsite shall maintain the following documents and records at the temporary jobsite until the well logging operation is completed:

(a) Operating and emergency procedures required by § 39.63.

(b) Evidence of latest calibration of the radiation survey instruments in use at the site required by § 39.33.

(c) Latest survey records required by §§ 39.67 (b), (c), and (e).

(d) The shipping papers for the transportation of radioactive materials required by § 71.5 of this chapter; and

(e) When operating under reciprocity pursuant to § 150.20 of this chapter, a copy of the Agreement State license authorizing use of licensed materials.

§ 39.77 Notification of incidents and lost sources; abandonment procedures for irretrievable sources.

(a) The licensee shall immediately notify the appropriate NRC Regional Office by telephone and subsequently, within 30 days, by confirmation in writing, using an appropriate method listed in § 30.6(a) of this chapter, if the licensee knows or has reason to believe that a sealed source has been ruptured.

The written confirmation must designate the well or other location, describe the magnitude and extent of the escape of licensed materials, assess the consequences of the rupture, and explain efforts planned or being taken to mitigate these consequences.

(b) The licensee shall notify the Commission of the theft or loss of radioactive materials, radiation overexposures, excessive levels and concentrations of radiation, and certain other accidents as required by §§ 20.2201–20.2202, § 20.2203 and § 30.50 of this chapter.

(c) If a sealed source becomes lodged in a well, and when it becomes apparent that efforts to recover the sealed source will not be successful, the licensee shall—

(1) Notify the appropriate NRC Regional Office by telephone of the circumstances that resulted in the inability to retrieve the source and—

(i) Obtain NRC approval to implement abandonment procedures; or

(ii) That the licensee implemented abandonment before receiving NRC approval because the licensee believed there was an immediate threat to public health and safety; and

(2) Advise the well owner or operator, as appropriate, of the abandonment procedures under § 39.15 (a) or (c); and

(3) Either ensure that abandonment procedures are implemented within 30 days after the sealed source has been classified as irretrievable or request an extension of time if unable to complete the abandonment procedures.

(d) The licensee shall, within 30 days after a sealed source has been classified as irretrievable, make a report in writing to the appropriate NRC Regional Office. The licensee shall send a copy of the report to each appropriate State or Federal agency that issued permits or otherwise approved of the drilling operation. The report must contain the following information:

(1) Date of occurrence;

(2) A description of the irretrievable well logging source involved including the radionuclide and its quantity, chemical, and physical form;

(3) Surface location and identification of the well;

(4) Results of efforts to immobilize and seal the source in place;

(5) A brief description of the attempted recovery effort;

(6) Depth of the source;

(7) Depth of the top of the cement plug;

(8) Depth of the well;

(9) The immediate threat to public health and safety justification for implementing abandonment if prior NRC approval was not obtained in accordance with paragraph (c)(1)(ii) of this section;

(10) Any other information, such as a warning statement, contained on the permanent identification plaque; and

(11) State and Federal agencies receiving copy of this report.

[52 FR 8234, Mar. 17, 1987, as amended at 56 FR 64980, Dec. 13, 1991; 58 FR 67660, Dec. 22, 1993; 65 FR 20345, Apr. 17, 2000; 68 FR 58806, Oct. 10, 2003]

Subpart F—Exemptions

§ 39.91 Applications for exemptions.

The Commission may, upon application of any interested person or upon its own initiative, grant such exemptions from the requirements of the regulations in this part as it determines are authorized by law and will not endanger life or property or the common defense and security and are otherwise in the public interest.

Subpart G—Enforcement

§ 39.101 Violations.

(a) The Commission may obtain an injunction or other court order to prevent a violation of the provisions of—

(1) The Atomic Energy Act of 1954, as amended;

(2) Title II of the Energy Reorganization Act of 1974, as amended; or

(3) A regulation or order issued pursuant to those Acts.

(b) The Commission may obtain a court order for the payment of a civil penalty imposed under section 234 of the Atomic Energy Act:

(1) For violations of—

(i) Sections 53, 57, 62, 63, 81, 82, 101, 103, 104, 107, or 109 of the Atomic Energy Act of 1954, as amended;

(ii) Section 206 of the Energy Reorganization Act;

(iii) Any rule, regulation, or order issued pursuant to the sections specified in paragraph (b)(1)(i) of this section;

(iv) Any term, condition, or limitation of any license issued under the sections specified in paragraph (b)(1)(i) of this section.

(2) For any violation for which a license may be revoked under section 186 of the Atomic Energy Act of 1954, as amended.

[57 FR 55074, Nov. 24, 1992]

§ 39.103 Criminal penalties.

(a) Section 223 of the Atomic Energy Act of 1954, as amended, provides for criminal sanctions for willful violation of, attempted violation of, or conspiracy to violate, any regulation issued under sections 161b, 161i, or 161o of the Act. For purposes of section 223, all the regulations in part 39 are issued under one or more of sections 161b, 161i, or 161o, except for the sections listed in paragraph (b) of this section.

(b) The regulations in part 39 that are not issued under sections 161b, 161i, or 161o for the purposes of section 223 are as follows: §§ 39.1, 39.2, 39.5, 39.8, 39.13, 39.91, 39.101, and 39.103.

[57 FR 55074, Nov. 24, 1992]

PART 40—DOMESTIC LICENSING OF SOURCE MATERIAL

AUTHORITY: Atomic Energy Act of 1954, secs. 62, 63, 64, 65, 69, 81, 83, 84, 122, 161, 181, 182, 183, 184, 186, 187, 193, 223, 234, 274, 275 (42 U.S.C. 2092, 2093, 2094, 2095, 2099, 2111, 2113, 2114, 2152, 2201, 2231, 2232, 2233, 2234, 2236, 2237, 2243, 2273, 2282, 2021, 2022); Energy Reorganization Act of 1974, secs. 201, 202, 206, 211 (42 U.S.C. 5841, 5842, 5846, 5851); Uranium Mill Tailings Radiation Control Act of 1978, sec. 104 (42 U.S.C. 7914); 44 U.S.C. 3504 note.

SOURCE: 26 FR 284, Jan. 14, 1961, unless otherwise noted.

EDITORIAL NOTE: Nomenclature changes to part 40 appear at 79 FR 75740, Dec. 19, 2014.

GENERAL PROVISIONS

§ 40.1 Purpose.

(a) The regulations in this part establish procedures and criteria for the issuance of licenses to receive title to, receive, possess, use, transfer, or deliver source and byproduct materials, as defined in this part, and establish and provide for the terms and conditions upon which the Commission will issue such licenses. (Additional requirements applicable to natural and depleted uranium at enrichment facilities are set forth in § 70.22 of this chapter.) These regulations also provide for the disposal of byproduct material and for the long-term care and custody of byproduct material and residual radioactive material. The regulations in this part also establish certain requirements for the physical protection of import, export, and transient shipments of natural uranium. (Additional requirements applicable to the import and export of natural uranium are set forth in part 110 of this chapter.)

(b) The regulations contained in this part are issued under the Atomic Energy Act of 1954, as amended (68 Stat. 919), title II of the Energy Reorganization Act of 1974, as amended (88 Stat. 1242), and titles I and II of the Uranium Mill Tailings Radiation Control Act of 1978, as amended (42 U.S.C. 7901).

[55 FR 45597, Oct. 30, 1990, as amended at 56 FR 55997, Oct. 31, 1991]

§ 40.2 Scope.

Except as provided in §§ 40.11 to 40.14, inclusive, the regulations in this part apply to all persons in the United States. This part also gives notice to all persons who knowingly provide to any licensee, applicant, contractor, or subcontractor, components, equipment, materials, or other goods or services, that relate to a licensee's or applicant's activities subject to this part, that they may be individually subject to NRC enforcement action for violation of § 40.10.

[63 FR 1896, Jan. 13, 1998]

§ 40.2a Coverage of inactive tailings sites.

(a) Prior to the completion of the remedial action, the Commission will not require a license pursuant to 10 CFR chapter I for possession of residual radioactive materials as defined in this part that are located at a site where milling operations are no longer active, if the site is covered by the remedial action program of title I of the Uranium Mill Tailings Radiation Control Act of 1978, as amended. The Commission will exert its regulatory role in remedial actions primarily through concurrence and consultation in the execution of the remedial action pursuant to title I of the Uranium Mill Tailings Radiation Control Act of 1978, as amended. After remedial actions are completed, the Commission will license the long-term care of sites, where residual radioactive materials are disposed, under the requirements set out in § 40.27.

(b) The Commission will regulate byproduct material as defined in this part that is located at a site where milling operations are no longer active, if such site is not covered by the remedial action program of title I of the Uranium Mill Tailings Radiation Control Act of 1978. The criteria in appendix A of this part will be applied to such sites.

[45 FR 65531, Oct. 3, 1980, as amended at 55 FR 45598, Oct. 30, 1990]

§ 40.3 License requirements.

A person subject to the regulations in this part may not receive title to, own, receive, possess, use, transfer, provide for long-term care, deliver or dispose of byproduct material or residual radioactive material as defined in this part or any source material after removal from its place of deposit in nature, unless authorized in a specific or general license issued by the Commission under the regulations in this part.

[55 FR 45598, Oct. 30, 1990]

§ 40.4 Definitions.

Act means the Atomic Energy Act of 1954 (68 Stat. 919), including any amendments thereto;

Agreement State means any State with which the Atomic Energy Commission or the Nuclear Regulatory Commission has entered into an effective agreement under subsection 274b. of the Atomic Energy Act of 1954, as amended.

Alert means events may occur, are in progress, or have occurred that could lead to a release of radioactive material but that the release is not expected to require a response by offsite response organizations to protect persons offsite.

Byproduct Material means the tailings or wastes produced by the extraction or concentration of uranium or thorium from any ore processed primarily for its source material content, including discrete surface wastes resulting from uranium solution extraction processes. Underground ore bodies depleted by such solution extraction operations do not constitute "byproduct material" within this definition.

With the exception of "byproduct material" as defined in section 11e. of the Act, other terms defined in section 11 of the Act shall have the same meaning when used in the regulations in this part.

Commencement of construction means taking any action defined as "construction" or any other activity at the site of a facility subject to the regulations in this part that has a reasonable nexus to:

(1) Radiological health and safety; or

(2) Common defense and security.

Commission means the Nuclear Regulatory Commission or its duly authorized representatives.

Construction means the installation of wells associated with radiological operations (e.g., production, injection, or monitoring well networks associated with in-situ recovery or other facilities), the installation of foundations, or in-place assembly, erection, fabrication, or testing for any structure, system, or component of a facility or activity subject to the regulations in this part that are related to radiological safety or security. The term "construction" does not include:

(1) Changes for temporary use of the land for public recreational purposes;

(2) Site exploration, including necessary borings to determine foundation conditions or other preconstruction monitoring to establish background information related to the suitability of the site, the environmental impacts of construction or operation, or the protection of environmental values;

(3) Preparation of the site for construction of the facility, including clearing of the site, grading, installation of drainage, erosion and other environmental mitigation measures, and construction of temporary roads and borrow areas;

(4) Erection of fences and other access control measures that are not related to the safe use of, or security of, radiological materials subject to this part;

(5) Excavation;

(6) Erection of support buildings (e.g., construction equipment storage sheds, warehouse and shop facilities, utilities, concrete mixing plants, docking and unloading facilities, and office buildings) for use in connection with the construction of the facility;

(7) Building of service facilities (e.g., paved roads, parking lots, railroad spurs, exterior utility and lighting systems, potable water systems, sanitary sewerage treatment facilities, and transmission lines);

(8) Procurement or fabrication of components or portions of the proposed facility occurring at other than the final, in-place location at the facility; or

(9) Taking any other action that has no reasonable nexus to:

(i) Radiological health and safety, or

(ii) Common defense and security.

Corporation means the United States Enrichment Corporation (USEC), or its successor, a Corporation that is authorized by statute to lease the gaseous diffusion enrichment plants in Paducah, Kentucky, and Piketon, Ohio, from the Department of Energy, or any person authorized to operate one or both of the gaseous diffusion plants, or other facilities, pursuant to a plan for the privatization of USEC that is approved by the President.

Decommission means to remove a facility or site safely from service and reduce residual radioactivity to a level that permits—

(1) Release of the property for unrestricted use and termination of the license; or

(2) Release of the property under restricted conditions and termination of the license.

Department and *Department of Energy* means the Department of Energy established by the Department of Energy Organization Act (Pub. L. 95–91, 91 Stat. 565, 42 U.S.C. 7101 *et seq.*) to the extent that the Department, or its duly authorized representatives, exercises functions formerly vested in the U.S. Atomic Energy Commission, its Chairman, members, officers and components and transferred to the U.S. Energy Research and Development Administration and to the Administrator thereof pursuant to sections 104 (b), (c) and (d) of the Energy Reorganization Act of 1974 (Pub. L. 93–438, 88 Stat. 1233 at 1237, 42 U.S.C. 5814) and retransferred to the Secretary of Energy pursuant to section 301(a) of the Department of Energy Organization Act (Pub. L. 95–91, 91 Stat. 565 at 577–578, 42 U.S.C. 7151).

Depleted uranium means the source material uranium in which the isotope uranium-235 is less than 0.711 weight percent of the total uranium present. Depleted uranium does not include special nuclear material.

Effective kilogram means (1) for the source material uranium in which the uranium isotope uranium–235 is greater than 0.005 (0.5 weight percent) of the total uranium present: 10,000 kilograms, and (2) for any other source material: 20,000 kilograms.

Foreign obligations means the commitments entered into by the U.S. Government under Atomic Energy Act (AEA) section 123 agreements for cooperation in the peaceful uses of atomic energy. Imports and exports of material or equipment pursuant to such agreements are subject to these commitments, which in some cases involve an exchange of information on imports, exports, retransfers with foreign governments, peaceful end-use assurances, and other conditions placed on the transfer of the material or equipment. The U.S. Government informs the licensee of obligations attached to material.

Government agency means any executive department, commission, independent establishment, corporation, wholly or partly owned by the United States of America which is an instrumentality of the United States, or any board, bureau, division, service, office, officer, authority, administration, or other establishment in the executive branch of the Government.

License, except where otherwise specified, means a license issued pursuant to the regulations in this part.

Persons means: (1) Any individual, corporation, partnership, firm, association, trust, estate, public or private institution, group, Government agency other than the Commission or the Department of Energy except that the Department of Energy shall be considered a person within the meaning of the regulations in this part to the extent that its facilities and activities are subject to the licensing and related regulatory authority of the Commission pursuant to section 202 of the Energy Reorganization Act of 1974 (88 Stat. 1244) and the Uranium Mill Tailings Radiation Control Act of 1978 (92 Stat. 3021), any State or any political subdivision of, or any political entity within a State, any foreign government or nation or any subdivision of any such government or nation, or other entity; and (2) any legal successor, representative, agent or agency of the foregoing.

Pharmacist means an individual registered by a state or territory of the United States, the District of Columbia or the Commonwealth of Puerto Rico to compound and dispense drugs, prescriptions and poisons.

Physician means a medical doctor or doctor of osteopathy licensed by a State or Territory of the United States, the District of Columbia, or the Commonwealth of Puerto Rico to prescribe drugs in the practice of medicine.

Principal activities, as used in this part, means activities authorized by the license which are essential to achieving the purpose(s) for which the license was issued or amended. Storage during which no licensed material is accessed for use or disposal and activities incidental to decontamination or decommissioning are not principal activities.

Reconciliation means the process of evaluating and comparing licensee reports required under this part to the projected material balances generated by the Nuclear Materials Management and Safeguards System. This process is considered complete when the licensee resolves any differences between the reported and projected balances, including those listed for foreign obligated materials.

Residual radioactive material means: (1) Waste (which the Secretary of Energy determines to be radioactive) in the form of tailings resulting from the processing of ores for the extraction of uranium and other valuable constituents of the ores; and (2) other waste (which the Secretary of Energy determines to be radioactive) at a processing site which relates to such processing, including any residual stock of unprocessed ores or low-grade materials. This term is used only with respect to materials at sites subject to remediation under title I of the Uranium Mill Tailings Radiation Control Act of 1978, as amended.

Site area emergency means events may occur, are in progress, or have occurred that could lead to a significant release of radioactive material and that could require a response by offsite response organizations to protect persons offsite.

Source Material means: (1) Uranium or thorium, or any combination thereof, in any physical or chemical form or (2) ores which contain by weight one-twentieth of one percent (0.05%) or more of: (i) Uranium, (ii) thorium or (iii) any combination thereof. Source material does not include special nuclear material.

Special nuclear material means: (1) Plutonium, uranium 233, uranium enriched in the isotope 233 or in the isotope 235, and any other material which the Commission, pursuant to the provisions of section 51 of the Act, determines to be special nuclear material; or (2) any material artificially enriched by any of the foregoing.

Transient shipment means a shipment of nuclear material, originating and terminating in foreign countries, on a vessel or aircraft that stops at a United States port.

United States, when used in a geographical sense, includes Puerto Rico and all territories and possessions of the United States.

Unrefined and unprocessed ore means ore in its natural form prior to any processing, such as grinding, roasting or beneficiating, or refining. Processing does not include sieving or encapsulation of ore or preparation of samples for laboratory analysis.

Uranium enrichment facility means:

(1) Any facility used for separating the isotopes of uranium or enriching uranium in the isotope 235, except laboratory scale facilities designed or used for experimental or analytical purposes only; or

(2) Any equipment or device, or important component part especially designed for such equipment or device, capable of separating the isotopes of uranium or enriching uranium in the isotope 235.

Uranium Milling means any activity that results in the production of byproduct material as defined in this part.

[26 FR 284, Jan. 14, 1961]

EDITORIAL NOTE: For FEDERAL REGISTER citations affecting § 40.4, see the List of CFR Sections Affected, which appears in the Finding Aids section of the printed volume and at *www.fdsys.gov*.

§ 40.5 Communications.

(a) Unless otherwise specified or covered under the regional licensing program as provided in paragraph (b) of this section, any communication or report concerning the regulations in this part and any application filed under these regulations may be submitted to the Commission as follows:

(1) By mail addressed: ATTN: Document Control Desk, Director, Office of Nuclear Material Safety and Safeguards, or Director, Office of Nuclear Security, or Director, Office of Nuclear Security and Incident Response, as appropriate, U.S. Nuclear Regulatory Commission, Washington, DC 20555–0001.

(2) By hand delivery to the NRC's offices at 11555 Rockville Pike, Rockville, Maryland.

(3) Where practicable, by electronic submission, for example, via Electronic Information Exchange, or CD-ROM. Electronic submissions must be made in a manner that enables the NRC to receive, read, authenticate, distribute, and archive the submission, and process and retrieve it a single page at a time. Detailed guidance on making electronic submissions can be obtained by visiting the NRC's Web site at *http://www.nrc.gov/site-help/e-submittals.html;* by e-mail to *MSHD.Resource@nrc.gov*; or by writing the Office of the Chief Information Officer, U.S. Nuclear Regulatory Commission, Washington, DC 20555–0001. The guidance discusses, among other topics, the formats the NRC can accept, the use of electronic signatures, and the treatment of nonpublic information.

(b) The Commission has delegated to the four Regional Administrators licensing authority for selected parts of its decentralized licensing program for nuclear materials as described in paragraph (b)(1) of this section. Any communication, report, or application covered under this licensing program must be submitted to the appropriate Regional Administrator. The administrators' jurisdictions and mailing addresses are listed in paragraph (b)(2) of this section.

(1) The delegated licensing program includes authority to issue, renew, amend, cancel, modify, suspend, or revoke licenses for nuclear materials issued pursuant to 10 CFR parts 30 through 36, 39, 40, and 70 to all persons for academic, medical, and industrial uses, with the following exceptions:

(i) Activities in the fuel cycle and special nuclear material in quantities sufficient to constitute a critical mass in any room or area. This exception does not apply to license modifications relating to termination of special nuclear material licenses that authorize possession of larger quantities when the case is referred for action from NRC's Headquarters to the Regional Administrators.

(ii) Health and safety design review of sealed sources and devices and approval, for licensing purposes, of sealed sources and devices.

(iii) Processing of source material for extracting of metallic compounds (including Zirconium, Hafnium, Tantalum, Titanium, Niobium, etc.).

(iv) Distribution of products containing radioactive material under §§ 32.11 through 32.30 and 40.52 of this chapter to persons exempt from licensing requirements.

(v) New uses or techniques for use of byproduct, source, or special nuclear material.

(vi) Uranium enrichment facilities.

(2) *Submissions.*—(i) *Region I.* The regional licensing program involves all Federal facilities in the region and non-Federal licensees in the following Region I non-Agreement States and the District of Columbia: Connecticut, Delaware, and Vermont. All mailed or hand-delivered inquiries, communications, and applications for a new license or an amendment or renewal of an existing license specified in paragraph (b)(1) of this section must use the following address: U.S. Nuclear Regulatory Commission, Region I, Nuclear Material Section B, Region I, 2100 Renaissance Boulevard, Suite 100, King

of Prussia, PA 19406–2713; where email is appropriate it should be addressed to *RidsRgn1MailCenter.Resource@nrc.gov.*

(ii) *Region II.* The regional licensing program involves all Federal facilities in the region and non-Federal licensees in the following Region II non-Agreement States and territories: West Virginia, Puerto Rico, and the Virgin Islands. All mailed or hand-delivered inquiries, communications, and applications for a new license or an amendment or renewal of an existing license specified in paragraph (b)(1) of this section must use the following address: U.S. Nuclear Regulatory Commission, Region I, Nuclear Material Section B, Region I, 2100 Renaissance Boulevard, Suite 100, King of Prussia, PA 19406–2713; where email is appropriate it should be addressed to *RidsRgn1MailCenter.Resource@nrc.gov.*

(iii) *Region III.* (A) The regional licensing program for mining and milling involves all Federal facilities in the region, and non-Federal licensees in the Region III non-Agreement States of Indiana, Michigan, Missouri and Region III Agreement States of Minnesota, Wisconsin, and Iowa. All mailed or hand-delivered inquiries, communications, and applications for a new license or an amendment, renewal, or termination request of an existing license specified in paragraph (b)(1) of this section must use the following address: U.S. Nuclear Regulatory Commission, Region III, Material Licensing Section, 2443 Warrenville Road, Suite 210, Lisle, IL 60532–4352; where e-mail is appropriate it should be addressed to *RidsRgn3MailCenter.Resource@nrc.gov.*

(B) Otherwise, the regional licensing program involves all Federal facilities in the region and non-Federal licensees in the following Region III non-Agreement States: Indiana, Michigan, and Missouri. All mailed or hand-delivered inquiries, communications, and applications for a new license or an amendment, or renewal of an existing license specified in paragraph (b)(1) of this section must use the following address: U.S. Nuclear Regulatory Commission, Region III, Material Licensing Section, 2443 Warrenville Road, Suite 210, Lisle, IL 60532–4352; where e-mail is appropriate it should be addressed to *RidsRgn3MailCenter.Resource@nrc.gov.* Outside of this jurisdiction, concerning the licensing program involving mining and milling, the Agreement States of Illinois and Ohio should be contacted.

(iv) *Region IV.* (A) The regional licensing program for mining and milling involves all Federal facilities in the region, and non-Federal licensees in the Region IV non-Agreement States and territory of Alaska, Hawaii, Idaho, Montana, South Dakota, Wyoming and Guam and Region IV Agreement States of Oregon, California, Nevada, New Mexico, Louisiana, Mississippi, Arkansas, Oklahoma, Kansas, Nebraska, and North Dakota. All mailed or hand-delivered inquiries, communications, and applications for a new license or an amendment or renewal of an existing license specified in paragraph (b)(1) of this section must use the following address: U.S. Nuclear Regulatory Commission, Region IV, Division of Nuclear Materials Safety, 1600 E. Lamar Blvd., Arlington, TX 76011–4511; where email is appropriate, it should be addressed to *RidsRgn4MailCenter@nrc.gov.*

(B) Otherwise, the regional licensing program involves all Federal facilities in the region and non-Federal licensees in the following Region IV non-Agreement States and territory: Alaska, Hawaii, Idaho, Montana, South Dakota, Wyoming, and Guam. All mailed or hand-delivered inquiries, communications, and applications for a new license or an amendment or renewal of an existing license specified in paragraph (b)(1) of this section must use the following address: U.S. Nuclear Regulatory Commission, Region IV, Division of Nuclear Materials Safety, 1600 E. Lamar Blvd., Arlington, TX 76011–4511; where email is appropriate, it should be addressed to *RidsRgn4MailCenter@nrc.gov.*

[48 FR 16031, Apr. 14, 1983]

EDITORIAL NOTE: For FEDERAL REGISTER citations affecting § 40.5, see the List of CFR Sections Affected, which appears in the Finding Aids section of the printed volume and at *www.fdsys.gov.*

§40.6 Interpretations.

Except as specifically authorized by the Commission in writing, no interpretation of the meaning of the regulations in this part by any officer or employee of the Commission other than a written interpretation by the General Counsel will be recognized to be binding upon the Commission.

§40.7 Employee protection.

(a) Discrimination by a Commission licensee, an applicant for a Commission license, or a contractor or subcontractor of a Commission licensee or applicant against an employee for engaging in certain protected activities is prohibited. Discrimination includes discharge and other actions that relate to compensation, terms, conditions, or privileges of employment. The protected activities are established in section 211 of the Energy Reorganization Act of 1974, as amended, and in general are related to the administration or enforcement of a requirement imposed under the Atomic Energy Act or the Energy Reorganization Act.

(1) The protected activities include but are not limited to:

(i) Providing the Commission or his or her employer information about alleged violations of either of the statutes named in paragraph (a) introductory text of this section or possible violations of requirements imposed under either of those statutes;

(ii) Refusing to engage in any practice made unlawful under either of the statutes named in paragraph (a) introductory text or under these requirements if the employee has identified the alleged illegality to the employer;

(iii) Requesting the Commission to institute action against his or her employer for the administration or enforcement of these requirements;

(iv) Testifying in any Commission proceeding, or before Congress, or at any Federal or State proceeding regarding any provision (or proposed provision) of either of the statutes named in paragraph (a) introductory text.

(v) Assisting or participating in, or is about to assist or participate in, these activities.

(2) These activities are protected even if no formal proceeding is actually initiated as a result of the employee assistance or participation.

(3) This section has no application to any employee alleging discrimination prohibited by this section who, acting without direction from his or her employer (or the employer's agent), deliberately causes a violation of any requirement of the Energy Reorganization Act of 1974, as amended, or the Atomic Energy Act of 1954, as amended.

(b) Any employee who believes that he or she has been discharged or otherwise discriminated against by any person for engaging in protected activities specified in paragraph (a)(1) of this section may seek a remedy for the discharge or discrimination through an administrative proceeding in the Department of Labor. The administrative proceeding must be initiated within 180 days after an alleged violation occurs. The employee may do this by filing a complaint alleging the violation with the Department of Labor, Employment Standards Administration, Wage and Hour Division. The Department of Labor may order reinstatement, back pay, and compensatory damages.

(c) A violation of paragraphs (a), (e), or (f) of this section by a Commission licensee, an applicant for a Commission license, or a contractor or subcontractor of a Commission licensee or applicant may be grounds for—

(1) Denial, revocation, or suspension of the license.

(2) Imposition of a civil penalty on the licensee, applicant, or a contractor or subcontractor of the licensee or applicant.

(3) Other enforcement action.

(d) Actions taken by an employer, or others, which adversely affect an employee may be predicated upon nondiscriminatory grounds. The prohibition applies when the adverse action occurs because the employee has engaged in protected activities. An employee's engagement in protected activities does not automatically render him or her immune from discharge or discipline for legitimate reasons or from adverse action dictated by nonprohibited considerations.

(e)(1) Each specific licensee, each applicant for a specific license, and each general licensee subject to part 19 shall prominently post the revision of NRC Form 3, "Notice to Employees", referenced in 10 CFR 19.11(c).

(2) The posting of NRC Form 3 must be at locations sufficient to permit employees protected by this section to observe a copy on the way to or from their place of work. Premises must be posted not later than 30 days after an application is docketed and remain posted while the application is pending before the Commission, during the term of the license, and for 30 days following license termination.

(3) Copies of NRC Form 3 may be obtained by writing to the Regional Administrator of the appropriate U.S. Nuclear Regulatory Commission Regional Office listed in appendix D to part 20 of this chapter, via email to *Forms.Resource@nrc.gov*, or by visiting the NRC's online library at *http://www.nrc.gov/reading-rm/doc-collections/forms/*.

(f) No agreement affecting the compensation, terms, conditions, or privileges of employment, including an agreement to settle a complaint filed by an employee with the Department of Labor pursuant to section 211 of the Energy Reorganization Act of 1974, may contain any provision which would prohibit, restrict, or otherwise discourage an employee from participating in protected activity as defined in paragraph (a)(1) of this section including, but not limited to, providing information to the NRC or to his or her employer on potential violations or other matters within NRC's regulatory responsibilities.

[58 FR 52409, Oct. 8, 1993, as amended at 60 FR 24551, May 9, 1995; 61 FR 6765, Feb. 22, 1996; 68 FR 58806, Oct. 10, 2003; 72 FR 63973, Nov. 14, 2007; 73 FR 30458, May 28, 2008; 79 FR 66603, Nov. 10, 2014]

§ 40.8 Information collection requirements: OMB approval.

(a) The Nuclear Regulatory Commission has submitted the information collection requirements contained in this part to the Office of Management and Budget (OMB) for approval as required by the Paperwork Reduction Act (44 U.S.C. 3501 *et seq.*). The NRC may not conduct or sponsor, and a person is not required to respond to, a collection of information unless it displays a currently valid OMB control number. OMB has approved the information collection requirements contained in this part under control number 3150–0020.

(b) The approved information collection requirements contained in this part appear in §§ 40.9, 40.22, 40.23, 40.25, 40.26, 40.27, 40.31, 40.34, 40.35, 40.36, 40.41, 40.42, 40.43, 40.44, 40.51, 40.52, 40.53, 40.54, 40.55, 40.60, 40.61, 40.64, 40.65, 40.66, 40.67, and appendix A to this part.

(c) This part contains information collection requirements in addition to those approved under the control number specified in paragraph (a) of this section. These information collection requirements and the control numbers under which they are approved are as follows:

(1) In §§ 40.31, 40.43, 40.44, and appendix A, NRC Form 313 is approved under control number 3150–0120.

(2) In § 40.31, DOC/NRC Forms AP–1, AP–A, and associated forms are approved under control numbers 0694–0135.

(3) In § 40.31, Forms N–71 and associated forms are approved under control number 3150–0056.

(4) In § 40.42, NRC Form 314 is approved under control number 3150–0028.

(5) In § 40.64, DOE/NRC Form 741 is approved under control number 3150–0003.

(6) In §§ 40.25 and 40.35, NRC Form 244 is approved under control number 3150–0031.

[49 FR 19626, May 9, 1984, as amended at 56 FR 40768, Aug. 16, 1991; 58 FR 68731, Dec. 29, 1993; 62 FR 52187, Oct. 6, 1997; 73 FR 78604, Dec. 23, 2008; 77 FR 39906, July 6, 2012; 78 FR 32338, May 29, 2013]

§ 40.9 Completeness and accuracy of information.

(a) Information provided to the Commission by an applicant for a license or by a licensee or information required by statute or by the Commission's regulations, orders, or license conditions to be maintained by the applicant or the licensee shall be complete and accurate in all material respects.

(b) Each applicant or licensee shall notify the Commission of information identified by the applicant or licensee as having for the regulated activity a significant implication for public health and safety or common defense and security. An applicant or licensee violates this paragraph only if the applicant or licensee fails to notify the Commission of information that the applicant or licensee has identified as having a significant implication for public health and safety or common defense and security. Notification shall be provided to the Administrator of the appropriate Regional Office within two working days of identifying the information. This requirement is not applicable to information which is already required to be provided to the Commission by other reporting or undating requirements.

[52 FR 49371, Dec. 31, 1987]

§40.10 Deliberate misconduct.

(a) Any licensee, applicant for a license, employee of a licensee or applicant; or any contractor (including a supplier or consultant), subcontractor, employee of a contractor or subcontractor of any licensee or applicant for a license, who knowingly provides to any licensee, applicant, contractor, or subcontractor, any components, equipment, materials, or other goods or services that relate to a licensee's or applicant's activities in this part, may not:

(1) Engage in deliberate misconduct that causes or would have caused, if not detected, a licensee or applicant to be in violation of any rule, regulation, or order; or any term, condition, or limitation of any license issued by the Commission; or

(2) Deliberately submit to the NRC, a licensee, an applicant, or a licensee's or applicant's contractor or subcontractor, information that the person submitting the information knows to be incomplete or inaccurate in some respect material to the NRC.

(b) A person who violates paragraph (a)(1) or (a)(2) of this section may be subject to enforcement action in accordance with the procedures in 10 CFR part 2, subpart B.

(c) For the purposes of paragraph (a)(1) of this section, deliberate misconduct by a person means an intentional act or omission that the person knows:

(1) Would cause a licensee or applicant to be in violation of any rule, regulation, or order; or any term, condition, or limitation, of any license issued by the Commission; or

(2) Constitutes a violation of a requirement, procedure, instruction, contract, purchase order, or policy of a licensee, applicant, contractor, or subcontractor.

[63 FR 1896, Jan. 13, 1998]

EXEMPTIONS

§40.11 Persons using source material under certain Department of Energy and Nuclear Regulatory Commission contracts.

Except to the extent that Department facilities or activities of the types subject to licensing pursuant to section 202 of the Energy Reorganization Act of 1974 or the Uranium Mill Tailings Radiation Control Act of 1978 are involved, any prime contractor of the Department is exempt from the requirements for a license set forth in sections 62, 63, and 64 of the Act and from the regulations in this part to the extent that such contractor, under his prime contract with the Department, receives, possesses, uses, transfers or delivers source material for: (a) The performance of work for the Department at a United States Government-owned or controlled site, including the transportation of source material to or from such site and the performance of contract services during temporary interruptions of such transportation; (b) research in, or development, manufacture, storage, testing or transportation of, atomic weapons or components thereof; or (c) the use or operation of nuclear reactors or other nuclear devices in a United States Government-owned vehicle or vessel. In addition to the foregoing exemptions, and subject to the requirement for licensing of Department facilities and activities pursuant to section 202 of the Energy Reorganization Act of 1974 or the Uranium Mill Tailings Radiation Control Act of 1980, any prime contractor or subcontractor of the Department or the Commission is exempt from the requirements for a license set forth in sections 62, 63, and 64 of the Act and from the regulations in this part to the extent that such prime contractor or subcontractor receives, possesses, uses, transfers or delivers source material under his prime contract or subcontract when the Commission determines that the exemption of the prime contractor or subcontractor is authorized by law; and that, under the terms of the contract or subcontract, there is adequate assurance that the work thereunder can be accomplished without undue risk to the public health and safety.

[40 FR 8787, Mar. 3, 1975, as amended at 43 FR 6923, Feb. 17, 1978; 45 FR 65531, Oct. 3, 1980]

§ 40.12 Carriers.

(a) Except as specified in paragraph (b) of this section, common and contract carriers, freight forwarders, warehousemen, and the U.S. Postal Service are exempt from the regulations in this part and the requirements for a license set forth in section 62 of the Act to the extent that they transport or store source material in the regular course of the carriage for another or storage incident thereto.

(b) The exemption in paragraph (a) of this section does not apply to a person who possesses a transient shipment (as defined in § 40.4(r)), an import shipment, or an export shipment of natural uranium in an amount exceeding 500 kilograms, unless the shipment is in the form of ore or ore residue.

[52 FR 9651, Mar. 26, 1987]

§ 40.13 Unimportant quantities of source material.

(a) Any person is exempt from the regulations in this part and from the requirements for a license set forth in section 62 of the Act to the extent that such person receives, possesses, uses, transfers or delivers source material in any chemical mixture, compound, solution, or alloy in which the source material is by weight less than one-twentieth of 1 percent (0.05 percent) of the mixture, compound, solution or alloy. The exemption contained in this paragraph does not apply to Australian-obligated source material, nor does it include byproduct materials as defined in this part.

(b) Any person is exempt from the regulations in this part and from the requirements for a license set forth in section 62 of the act to the extent that such person receives, possesses, uses, or transfers unrefined and unprocessed ore containing source material; provided, that, except as authorized in a specific license, such person shall not refine or process such ore.

(c) Any person is exempt from the requirements for a license set forth in section 62 of the Act and from the regulations in this part and parts 19, 20, and 21 of this chapter to the extent that such person receives, possesses, uses, or transfers:

(1) Any quantities of thorium contained in (i) incandescent gas mantles, (ii) vacuum tubes, (iii) welding rods, (iv) electric lamps for illuminating purposes: *Provided*, That each lamp does not contain more than 50 milligrams of thorium, (v) germicidal lamps, sunlamps, and lamps for outdoor or industrial lighting: *Provided*, That each lamp does not contain more than 2 grams of thorium, (vi) rare earth metals and compounds, mixtures, and products containing not more than 0.25 percent by weight thorium, uranium, or any combination of these, or (vii) personnel neutron dosimeters: *Provided*, That each dosimeter does not contain more than 50 milligrams of thorium.

(2) Source material contained in the following products:

(i) Glazed ceramic tableware manufactured before August 27, 2013, provided that the glaze contains not more than 20 percent by weight source material;

(ii) Piezoelectric ceramic containing not more than 2 percent by weight source material;

(iii) Glassware containing not more than 2 percent by weight source material or, for glassware manufactured before August 27, 2013, 10 percent by weight source material; but not including commercially manufactured glass brick, pane glass, ceramic tile, or other glass or ceramic used in construction;

(iv) Glass enamel or glass enamel frit containing not more than 10 percent by weight source material imported or ordered for importation into the United States, or initially distributed by manufacturers in the United States, before July 25, 1983.[1]

[1] On July 25, 1983, the exemption of glass enamel or glass enamel frit was suspended.

(3) Photographic film, negatives, and prints containing uranium or thorium;

(4) Any finished product or part fabricated of, or containing tungsten or magnesium-thorium alloys, provided that the thorium content of the alloy does not exceed 4 percent by weight and that the exemption contained in this subparagraph shall not be deemed to authorize the chemical, physical or metallurgical treatment or processing of any such product or part; and

(5) Uranium contained in counterweights installed in aircraft, rockets, projectiles, and missiles, or stored or handled in connection with installation or removal of such counterweights: *Provided*, That:

(i) Each counterweight has been impressed with the following legend clearly legible through any plating or other covering: "Depleted Uranium";[2]

(ii) Each counterweight is durably and legibly labeled or marked with the identification of the manufacturer, and the statement: "Unauthorized Alterations Prohibited";[2] and

(iii) The exemption contained in this paragraph shall not be deemed to authorize the chemical, physical, or metallurgical treatment or processing of any such counterweights other than repair or restoration of any plating or other covering.

(iv) Consistent with §40.56, the counterweights are not manufactured for a military purpose using Australian-obligated source material.

(6) Natural or depleted uranium metal used as shielding constituting part of any shipping container: *Provided*, That:

(i) The shipping container is conspicuously and legibly impressed with the legend "CAUTION—RADIOACTIVE SHIELDING—URANIUM"; and

(ii) The uranium metal is encased in mild steel or equally fire resistant metal of minimum wall thickness of one-eighth inch (3.2 mm).

(7) Thorium or uranium contained in or on finished optical lenses and mirrors, provided that each lens or mirror does not contain more than 10 percent by weight thorium or uranium or, for lenses manufactured before August 27, 2013, 30 percent by weight of thorium; and that the exemption contained in this paragraph does not authorize either:

(i) The shaping, grinding or polishing of such lens or mirror or manufacturing processes other than the assembly of such lens or mirror into optical systems and devices without any alteration of the lens or mirror; or

(ii) The receipt, possession, use, or transfer of uranium or thorium contained in contact lenses, or in spectacles, or in eyepieces in binoculars or other optical instruments.

(8) Thorium contained in any finished aircraft engine part containing nickel-thoria alloy, *Provided*, That:

(i) The thorium is dispersed in the nickel-thoria alloy in the form of finely divided thoria (thorium dioxide); and

(ii) The thorium content in the nickel-thoria alloy does not exceed 4 percent by weight.

(9) The exemptions in this paragraph (c) do not authorize the manufacture of any of the products described.

(10) No person may initially transfer for sale or distribution a product containing source material to persons exempt under this paragraph (c), or equivalent regulations of an Agreement State, unless authorized by a license issued under §40.52 to initially transfer such products for sale or distribution.

(i) Persons initially distributing source material in products covered by the exemptions in this paragraph (c) before August 27, 2013, without specific authorization may continue such distribution for 1 year beyond this date. Initial distribution may also be continued until the Commission takes final action on a pending application for license or license amendment to specifically authorize distribution submitted no later than 1 year beyond this date.

The exemption was eliminated on September 11, 1984.

[2] The requirements specified in paragraphs (c)(5)(i) and (ii) of this section need not be met by counterweights manufactured prior to Dec. 31, 1969, provided that such counterweights were manufactured under a specific license issued by the Atomic Energy Commission and were impressed with the legend required by §40.13(c)(5)(ii) in effect on June 30, 1969.

(ii) Persons authorized to manufacture, process, or produce these materials or products containing source material by an Agreement State, and persons who import finished products or parts, for sale or distribution must be authorized by a license issued under § 40.52 for distribution only and are exempt from the requirements of parts 19 and 20 of this chapter, and § 40.32(b) and (c).

[26 FR 284, Jan. 14, 1961]

EDITORIAL NOTE: For FEDERAL REGISTER citations affecting § 40.13, see the List of CFR Sections Affected, which appears in the Finding Aids section of the printed volume and at *www.fdsys.gov.*

§ 40.14 Specific exemptions.

(a) The Commission may, upon application of any interested person or upon its own initiative, grant such exemptions from the requirements of the regulation in this part as it determines are authorized by law and will not endanger life or property or the common defense and security and are otherwise in the public interest.

(b) [Reserved]

(c) The Department of Energy is exempt from the requirements of this part to the extent that its activities are subject to the requirements of part 60 or 63 of this chapter.

(d) Except as specifically provided in part 61 of this chapter any licensee is exempt from the requirements of this part to the extent that its activities are subject to the requirements of part 61 of this chapter.

[37 FR 5747, Mar. 21, 1972, as amended at 39 FR 26279, July 18, 1974; 40 FR 8787, Mar. 3, 1975; 45 FR 65531, Oct. 3, 1980; 46 FR 13979, Feb. 25, 1981; 47 FR 57481, Dec. 27, 1982; 66 FR 55790, Nov. 2, 2001]

GENERAL LICENSES

§ 40.20 Types of licenses.

(a) Licenses for source material and byproduct material are of two types: general and specific. Licenses for long-term care and custody of residual radioactive material at disposal sites are general licenses. The general licenses provided in this part are effective without the filing of applications with the Commission or the issuance of licensing documents to particular persons. Specific licenses are issued to named persons upon applications filed pursuant to the regulations in this part.

(b) Section 40.27 contains a general license applicable for custody and long-term care of residual radioactive material at uranium mill tailings disposal sites remediated under title I of the Uranium Mill Tailings Radiation Control Act of 1978, as amended.

(c) Section 40.28 contains a general license applicable for custody and long-term care of byproduct material at uranium or thorium mill tailings disposal sites under title II of the Uranium Mill Tailings Radiation Control Act of 1978, as amended.

[55 FR 45598, Oct. 30, 1990]

§ 40.21 General license to receive title to source or byproduct material.

A general license is hereby issued authorizing the receipt of title to source or byproduct material, as defined in this part, without regard to quantity. This general license does not authorize any person to receive, possess, deliver, use, or transfer source or byproduct material.

[45 FR 65531, Oct. 3, 1980]

§ 40.22 Small quantities of source material.

(a) A general license is hereby issued authorizing commercial and industrial firms; research, educational, and medical institutions; and Federal, State, and local government agencies to receive, possess, use, and transfer uranium and thorium, in their natural isotopic concentrations and in the form of depleted uranium, for research, development, educational, commercial, or operational purposes in the following forms and quantities:

(1) No more than 1.5 kg (3.3 lb) of uranium and thorium in dispersible forms (e.g., gaseous, liquid, powder, etc.) at any one time. Any material processed by the general licensee that alters the chemical or physical form of the material containing source material must be accounted for as a dispersible form. A person authorized to possess, use, and transfer source material under this paragraph may not receive more than a total of 7 kg (15.4 lb) of uranium and

thorium in any one calendar year. Persons possessing source material in excess of these limits as of August 27, 2013, may continue to possess up to 7 kg (15.4 lb) of uranium and thorium at any one time for one year beyond this date, or until the Commission takes final action on a pending application submitted on or before August 27, 2014, for a specific license for such material; and receive up to 70 kg (154 lb) of uranium or thorium in any one calendar year until December 31, 2014, or until the Commission takes final action on a pending application submitted on or before August 27, 2014, for a specific license for such material; and

(2) No more than a total of 7 kg (15.4 lb) of uranium and thorium at any one time. A person authorized to possess, use, and transfer source material under this paragraph may not receive more than a total of 70 kg (154 lb) of uranium and thorium in any one calendar year. A person may not alter the chemical or physical form of the source material possessed under this paragraph unless it is accounted for under the limits of paragraph (a)(1) of this section; or

(3) No more than 7 kg (15.4 lb) of uranium, removed during the treatment of drinking water, at any one time. A person may not remove more than 70 kg (154 lb) of uranium from drinking water during a calendar year under this paragraph; or

(4) No more than 7 kg (15.4 lb) of uranium and thorium at laboratories for the purpose of determining the concentration of uranium and thorium contained within the material being analyzed at any one time. A person authorized to possess, use, and transfer source material under this paragraph may not receive more than a total of 70 kg (154 lb) of source material in any one calendar year.

(b) Any person who receives, possesses, uses, or transfers source material in accordance with the general license in paragraph (a) of this section:

(1) Is prohibited from administering source material, or the radiation therefrom, either externally or internally, to human beings except as may be authorized by the NRC in a specific license.

(2) Shall not abandon such source material. Source material may be disposed of as follows:

(i) A cumulative total of 0.5 kg (1.1 lb) of source material in a solid, non-dispersible form may be transferred each calendar year, by a person authorized to receive, possess, use, and transfer source material under this general license to persons receiving the material for permanent disposal. The recipient of source material transferred under the provisions of this paragraph is exempt from the requirements to obtain a license under this part to the extent the source material is permanently disposed. This provision does not apply to any person who is in possession of source material under a specific license issued under this chapter; or

(ii) In accordance with § 20.2001 of this chapter.

(3) Is subject to the provisions in §§ 40.1 through 40.10, 40.41(a) through (e), 40.46, 40.51, 40.56, 40.60 through 40.63, 40.71, and 40.81.

(4) Shall respond to written requests from the NRC to provide information relating to the general license within 30 calendar days of the date of the request, or other time specified in the request. If the person cannot provide the requested information within the allotted time, the person shall, within that same time period, request a longer period to supply the information by providing the Director of the Office of Nuclear Material Safety and Safeguards, using an appropriate method listed in § 40.5(a), a written justification for the request;

(5) Shall not export such source material except in accordance with part 110 of this chapter.

(c) Any person who receives, possesses, uses, or transfers source material in accordance with paragraph (a) of this section shall conduct activities so as to minimize contamination of the facility and the environment. When activities involving such source material are permanently ceased at any site, if evidence of significant contamination is identified, the general licensee shall notify the Director of the Office of Nuclear Material Safety and Safeguards by an appropriate method listed in § 40.5(a) about such contamination and may consult with the NRC as to the appropriateness of sampling and restoration activities to ensure that any contamination or residual source material remaining at the site where source material was used under this general license is not likely to result in exposures that exceed the limits in §20.1402 of this chapter.

(d) Any person who receives, possesses, uses, or transfers source material in accordance with the general license granted in paragraph (a) of this section is exempt from the provisions of parts 19, 20, and 21 of this chapter to the extent that such receipt, possession, use, and transfer are within the terms of this general license, except that such person shall comply with the provisions of §§20.1402 and 20.2001 of this chapter to the extent necessary to meet the provisions of paragraphs (b)(2) and (c) of this section. However, this exemption does not apply to any person who also holds a specific license issued under this chapter.

(e) No person may initially transfer or distribute source material to persons generally licensed under paragraph (a)(1) or (2) of this section, or equivalent regulations of an Agreement State, unless authorized by a specific license issued in accordance with §40.54 or equivalent provisions of an Agreement State. This prohibition does not apply to analytical laboratories returning processed samples to the client who initially provided the sample. Initial distribution of source material to persons generally licensed by paragraph (a) of this section before August 27, 2013, without specific authorization may continue for 1 year beyond this date. Distribution may also be continued until the Commission takes final action on a pending application for license or license amendment to specifically authorize distribution submitted on or before August 27, 2014.

[78 FR 32339, May 29, 2013]

§40.23 General license for carriers of transient shipments of natural uranium other than in the form of ore or ore residue.

(a) A general license is hereby issued to any person to possess a transient shipment of natural uranium, other than in the form of ore or ore residue, in amounts exceeding 500 kilograms.

(b)(1) Persons generally licensed under paragraph (a) of this section, who plan to carry a transient shipment with scheduled stops at a United States port, shall notify the Director, Division of Security Policy, Office of Nuclear Security and Incident Response, using an appropriate method listed in §40.5. The notification must be in writing and must be received at least 10 days before transport of the shipment commences at the shipping facility.

(2) The notification must include the following information:

(i) Location of all scheduled stops in United States territory;

(ii) Arrival and departure times for all scheduled stops in United States territory;

(iii) The type of transport vehicle;

(iv) A physical description of the shipment;

(v) The numbers and types of containers;

(vi) The name and telephone number of the carrier's representatives at each stopover location in the United States territory;

(vii) A listing of the modes of shipments, transfer points, and routes to be used;

(viii) The estimated date and time that shipment will commence and that each nation (other than the United States) along the route is scheduled to be entered;

(ix) For shipment between countries that are not party to the Convention on the Physical Protection of Nuclear Material (*i.e.*, not listed in appendix F to part 73 of this chapter), a certification that arrangements have been made to notify the Director, Division of Security Policy when the shipment is received at the destination facility.

(c) Persons generally licensed under this section making unscheduled stops at United States ports, immediately after the decision to make an unscheduled stop, shall provide to the Director, Division of Security Policy the information required under paragraph (b) of this section.

(d) A licensee who needs to amend a notification may do so by telephoning the Division of Security Policy at (301) 415–6828.

[52 FR 9651, Mar. 26, 1987, as amended at 53 FR 4110, Feb. 12, 1988; 60 FR 24551, May 9, 1995; 68 FR 58806, Oct. 10, 2003; 74 FR 62681, Dec. 1, 2009]

§ 40.24 [Reserved]

§ 40.25 General license for use of certain industrial products or devices.

(a) A general license is hereby issued to receive, acquire, possess, use, or transfer, in accordance with the provisions of paragraphs (b), (c), (d), and (e) of this section, depleted uranium contained in industrial products or devices for the purpose of providing a concentrated mass in a small volume of the product or device.

(b) The general license in paragraph (a) of this section applies only to industrial products or devices which have been manufactured or initially transferred in accordance with a specific license issued pursuant to § 40.34 (a) of this part or in accordance with a specific license issued by an Agreement State which authorizes manufacture of the products or devices for distribution to persons generally licensed by the Agreement State.

(c)(1) Persons who receive, acquire, possess, or use depleted uranium pursuant to the general license established by paragraph (a) of this section shall file NRC Form 244, "Registration Certificate—Use of Depleted Uranium Under General License," with the Director, Office of Nuclear Material Safety and Safeguards, by an appropriate method listed in § 40.5, with a copy to the appropriate NRC Regional Administrator. The form shall be submitted within 30 days after the first receipt or acquisition of such depleted uranium. The registrant shall furnish on NRC Form 244 the following information and such other information as may be required by that form:

(i) Name and address of the registrant;

(ii) A statement that the registrant has developed and will maintain procedures designed to establish physical control over the depleted uranium described in paragraph (a) of this section and designed to prevent transfer of such depleted uranium in any form, including metal scrap, to persons not authorized to receive the depleted uranium; and

(iii) Name and/or title, address, and telephone number of the individual duly authorized to act for and on behalf of the registrant in supervising the procedures identified in paragraph (c)(1)(ii) of this section.

(2) The registrant possessing or using depleted uranium under the general license established by paragraph (a) of this section shall report in writing to the Director, Office of Nuclear Material Safety and Safeguards, with a copy to the Regional Administrator of the appropriate U.S. Nuclear Regulatory Commission Regional Office listed in appendix D of part 20 of this chapter, any changes in information furnished by him in the NRC Form 244 "Registration Certificate—Use of Depleted Uranium Under General License." The report shall be submitted within 30 days after the effective date of such change.

(d) A person who receives, acquires, possesses, or uses depleted uranium pursuant to the general license established by paragraph (a) of this section:

(1) Shall not introduce such depleted uranium, in any form, into a chemical, physical, or metallurgical treatment or process, except a treatment or process for repair or restoration of any plating or other covering of the depleted uranium.

(2) Shall not abandon such depleted uranium.

(3) Shall transfer or dispose of such depleted uranium only by transfer in accordance with the provisions of § 40.51 of this part. In the case where the transferee receives the depleted uranium pursuant to the general license established by paragraph (a) of this section, the transferor shall furnish the transferee a copy of this section and a copy of Form NRC 244. In the case where the transferee receives the depleted uranium pursuant to a general license contained in an Agreement State's regulation equivalent to this section, the transferor shall furnish the transferee a copy of this section and a copy of Form NRC 244 accompanied by a note explaining that

use of the product or device is regulated by the Agreement State under requirements substantially the same as those in this section.

(4) Within 30 days of any transfer, shall report in writing to the Director, Office of Nuclear Material Safety and Safeguards, with a copy to the Regional Administrator of the appropriate U.S. Nuclear Regulatory Commission Regional Office listed in appendix D of part 20 of this chapter, the name and address of the person receiving the source material pursuant to such transfer.

(e) Any person receiving, acquiring, possessing, using, or transferring depleted uranium pursuant to the general license established by paragraph (a) of this section is exempt from the requirements of parts 19, 20 and 21 of this chapter with respect to the depleted uranium covered by that general license.

[41 FR 53331, Dec. 6, 1976, as amended at 42 FR 28896, June 6, 1977; 43 FR 6923, Feb. 17, 1978; 43 FR 52202, Nov. 9, 1978; 52 FR 31611, Aug. 21, 1987; 60 FR 24551, May 9, 1995; 68 FR 58807, Oct. 10, 2003; 73 FR 5720, Jan. 31, 2008]

§ 40.26 General license for possession and storage of byproduct material as defined in this part.

(a) A general license is hereby issued to receive title to, own, or possess byproduct material as defined in this part without regard to form or quantity.

(b) The general license in paragraph (a) of this section applies only: In the case of licensees of the Commission, where activities that result in the production of byproduct material are authorized under a specific license issued by the Commission pursuant to this part, to byproduct material possessed or stored at an authorized disposal containment area or transported incident to such authorized activity: *Provided*, That authority to receive title to, own, or possess byproduct material under this general license shall terminate when the specific license for source material expires, is renewed, or is amended to include a specific license for byproduct material as defined in this part.

(c) The general license in paragraph (a) of this section is subject to:

(1) The provisions of parts 19, 20, 21, and §§ 40.1, 40.2a, 40.3, 40.4, 40.5, 40.6, 40.41, 40.46, 40.60, 40.61, 40.62, 40.63, 40.65, 40.71, and 40.81 of part 40 of this chapter; and

(2) The documentation of daily inspections of tailings or waste retention systems and the immediate notification of the appropriate NRC regional office as indicated in appendix D to part 20 of this chapter, or the Director, Office of Nuclear Material Safety and Safeguards, U.S. Nuclear Regulatory Commission, Washington, DC 20555, of any failure in a tailings or waste retention system that results in a release of tailings or waste into unrestricted areas, or of any unusual conditions (conditions not contemplated in the design of the retention system) that if not corrected could lead to failure of the system and result in a release of tailings or waste into unrestricted areas; and any additional requirements the Commission may by order deem necessary. The licensee shall retain this documentation of each daily inspection as a record for three years after each inspection is documented.

(d) The general license in paragraph (a) of this section shall expire nine months from the effective date of this subparagraph unless an applicable licensee has submitted, pursuant to the provisions of § 40.31 of this part, an application for license renewal or amendment which includes a detailed program for meeting the technical and financial criteria contained in appendix A of this part.

[44 FR 50014, Aug. 24, 1979, as amended at 45 FR 12377, Feb. 26, 1980; 45 FR 65531, Oct. 3, 1980; 53 FR 19248, May 27, 1988; 56 FR 40768, Aug. 16, 1991; 73 FR 5720, Jan. 31, 2008]

§ 40.27 General license for custody and long-term care of residual radioactive material disposal sites.

(a) A general license is issued for the custody of and long-term care, including monitoring, maintenance, and emergency measures necessary to protect public health and safety and other actions necessary to comply with the standards promulgated under section 275(a) of the Atomic Energy Act of 1954, as amended, for disposal sites under title I of the Uranium Mill Tailings Radiation Control Act of 1978, as amended. The license is available only to the Department of Energy, or another Federal agency designated by the President to provide long-term care. The purpose of this general license is to ensure that uranium mill tailings disposal sites will be cared for in such a manner as to protect the public health, safety, and the environment after remedial action has been completed.

(b) The general license in paragraph (a) of this section becomes effective when the Commission accepts a site Long-Term Surveillance Plan (LTSP) that meets the requirements of this section, and when the Commission concurs with the Department of Energy's determination of completion of remedial action at each disposal site. There is no termination of this general license. The LTSP may incorporate by reference information contained in documents previously submitted to the Commission if the references to the individual incorporated documents are clear and specific. Each LTSP must include—

(1) A legal description of the disposal site to be licensed, including documentation on whether land and interests are owned by the United States or an Indian Tribe. If the site is on Indian land, then, as specified in the Uranium Mill Tailings Radiation Control Act of 1978, as amended, the Indian Tribe and any person holding any interest in the land shall execute a waiver releasing the United States of any liability or claim by the Tribe or person concerning or arising from the remedial action and holding the United States harmless against any claim arising out of the performance of the remedial action;

(2) A detailed description, which can be in the form of a reference, of the final disposal site conditions, including existing groundwater characterization and any necessary groundwater protection activities or strategies. This description must be detailed enough so that future inspectors will have a baseline to determine changes to the site and when these changes are serious enough to require maintenance or repairs. If the disposal site has continuing aquifer restoration requirements, then the licensing process will be completed in two steps. The first step includes all items other than groundwater restoration. Groundwater monitoring, which would be addressed in the LTSP, may still be required in this first step to assess performance of the tailings disposal units. When the Commission concurs with the completion of groundwater restoration, the licensee shall assess the need to modify the LTSP and report results to the Commission. If the proposed modifications meet the requirements of this section, the LTSP will be considered suitable to accommodate the second step.

(3) A description of the long-term surveillance program, including proposed inspection frequency and reporting to the Commission (as specified in appendix A, criterion 12 of this part), frequency and extent of groundwater monitoring if required, appropriate constituent concentration limits for groundwater, inspection personnel qualifications, inspection procedures, recordkeeping and quality assurance procedures;

(4) The criteria for follow-up inspections in response to observations from routine inspections or extreme natural events; and

(5) The criteria for instituting maintenance or emergency measures.

(c) The long-term care agency under the general license established by paragraph (a) of this section shall—

(1) Implement the LTSP as described in paragraph (b) of this section;

(2) Care for the disposal site in accordance with the provisions of the LTSP;

(3) Notify the Commission of any changes to the LTSP; the changes may not conflict with the requirements of this section;

(4) Guarantee permanent right-of-entry to Commission representatives for the purpose of periodic site inspections; and

(5) Notify the Commission prior to undertaking any significant construction, actions, or repairs related to the disposal site, even if the action is required by a State or another Federal agency.

(d) As specified in the Uranium Mill Tailings Radiation Control Act of 1978, as amended, the Secretary of the Interior, with the concurrence of the Secretary of Energy and the Commission, may sell or lease any subsurface mineral rights associated with land on which residual radioactive materials are disposed. In such cases, the Commission shall grant a license permitting use of the land if it finds that the use will not disturb the residual radioactive materials or that the residual radioactive materials will be restored to a safe and environmentally sound condition if they are disturbed by the use.

(e) The general license in paragraph (a) of this section is exempt from parts 19, 20, and 21 of this chapter, unless significant construction, actions, or repairs are required. If these types of actions are to be undertaken, the licensee shall explain to the Commission which requirements from these parts apply for the actions and comply with the appropriate requirements.

[55 FR 45598, Oct. 30, 1990, as amended at 81 FR 86909, Dec. 2, 2016]

§ 40.28 General license for custody and long-term care of uranium or thorium byproduct materials disposal sites.

(a) A general license is issued for the custody of and long-term care, including monitoring, maintenance, and emergency measures necessary to protect the public health and safety and other actions necessary to comply with the standards in this part for uranium or thorium mill tailings sites closed under title II of the Uranium Mill Tailings Radiation Control Act of 1978, as amended. The licensee will be the Department of Energy, another Federal agency designated by the President, or a State where the disposal site is located. The purpose of this general license is to ensure that uranium and thorium mill tailings disposal sites will be cared for in such a manner as to protect the public health, safety, and the environment after closure.

(b) The general license in paragraph (a) of this section becomes effective when the Commission terminates, or concurs in an Agreement State's termination of, the current specific license and a site Long-Term Surveillance Plan (LTSP) meeting the requirements of this section has been accepted by the Commission. There is no termination of this general license. If the LTSP has not been formally received by the NRC prior to termination of the current specific license, the Commission may issue a specific order to the intended custodial agency to ensure continued control and surveillance of the disposal site to protect the public health, safety, and the environment. The Commission will not unnecessarily delay the termination of the specific license solely on the basis that an acceptable LTSP has not been received. The LTSP may incorporate by reference information contained in documents previously submitted to the Commission if the references to the individual incorporated documents are clear and specific. Each LTSP must include—

(1) A legal description of the disposal site to be transferred (unless transfer is exempted under provisions of the Atomic Energy Act, § 83(b)(1)(A)) and licensed;

(2) A detailed description, which can be in the form of a reference of the final disposal site conditions, including existing groundwater characterization. This description must be detailed enough so that future inspectors will have a baseline to determine changes to the site and when these changes are serious enough to require maintenance or repairs;

(3) A description of the long-term surveillance program, including proposed inspection frequency and reporting to the Commission (as specified in appendix A, Criterion 12 of this part), frequency and extent of groundwater monitoring if required, appropriate constituent concentration limits for groundwater, inspection personnel qualifications, inspection procedures, recordkeeping and quality assurance procedures;

(4) The criteria for follow-up inspections in response to observations from routine inspections or extreme natural events; and

(5) The criteria for instituting maintenance or emergency measures.

(c) The long-term care agency who has a general license established by paragraph (a) of this section shall—

(1) Implement the LTSP as described in paragraph (b) of this section;

(2) Care for the disposal site in accordance with the provisions of the LTSP;

(3) Notify the Commission of any changes to the LTSP; the changes may not conflict with the requirements of this section;

(4) Guarantee permanent right-of-entry to Commission representatives for the purpose of periodic site inspections; and

(5) Notify the Commission prior to undertaking any significant construction, actions, or repairs related to the disposal site, even if the action is required by a State or another Federal agency.

(d) Upon application, the Commission may issue a specific license, as specified in the Uranium Mill Tailings Radiation Control Act of 1978, as amended, permitting the use of surface and/or subsurface estates transferred to the United States or a State. Although an application may be received from any person, if permission is granted, the person who transferred the land to DOE or the State shall receive the right of first refusal with respect to this use of the land. The application must demonstrate that—

(1) The proposed action does not endanger the public health, safety, welfare, or the environment;

(2) Whether the proposed action is of a temporary or permanent nature, the site would be maintained and/or restored to meet requirements in appendix A of this part for closed sites; and

(3) Adequate financial arrangements are in place to ensure that the byproduct materials will not be disturbed, or if disturbed that the applicant is able to restore the site to a safe and environmentally sound condition.

(e) The general license in paragraph (a) of this section is exempt from parts 19, 20, and 21 of this chapter, unless significant construction, actions, or repairs are required. If these types of actions are to be undertaken, the licensee shall explain to the Commission which requirements from these parts apply for the actions and comply with the appropriate requirements.

(f) In cases where the Commission determines that transfer of title of land used for disposal of any byproduct materials to the United States or any appropriate State is not necessary to protect the public health, safety or welfare or to minimize or eliminate danger to life or property (Atomic Energy Act, § 83(b)(1)(A)), the Commission will consider specific modifications of the custodial agency's LTSP provisions on a case-by-case basis.

[55 FR 45599, Oct. 30, 1990, as amended at 81 FR 86909, Dec. 2, 2016]

LICENSE APPLICATIONS

§ 40.31 Application for specific licenses.

(a) A person may file an application for specific license on NRC Form 313, "Application for Material License," in accordance with the instructions in § 40.5 of this chapter. Information contained in previous applications, statements or reports filed with the Commission may be incorporated by reference provided that the reference is clear and specific.

(b) The Commission may at any time after the filing of the original application, and before the expiration of the license, require further statements in order to enable the Commission to determine whether the application should be granted or denied or whether a license should be modified or revoked. All applications and statements shall be signed by the applicant or licensee or a person duly authorized to act for and on his behalf.

(c) Applications and documents submitted to the Commission in connection with applications will be made available for public inspection in accordance with the provisions of the regulations contained in parts 2 and 9 of this chapter.

(d) An application for a license filed pursuant to the regulations in this part will be considered also as an application for licenses authorizing other activities for which licenses are required by the Act: *Provided*, That the application specifies the additional activities for which licenses are requested and complies with regulations of the Commission as to applications for such licenses.

(e) Each application for a source material license, other than a license exempted from part 170 of this chapter, shall be accompanied by the fee prescribed in § 170.31 of this chapter. No fee will be required to accompany an application for renewal or amendment of a license, except as provided in § 170.31 of this chapter.

(f) An application for a license to possess and use source material for uranium milling, production of uranium hexafluoride, or for the conduct of any other activity which the Commission has determined pursuant to subpart A of part 51 of this chapter will significantly affect the quality of the environment shall be filed at least 9 months prior to commencement of construction of the plant or facility in which the activity will be conducted and shall be accompanied by any Environmental Report required pursuant to subpart A of part 51 of this chapter.

(g) An applicant for a license to possess and use source material, or the recipient of such a license shall report information to the Commission as follows:

(1) In response to a written request by the Commission, a uranium or thorium processing plant, and any other applicant for a license to possess and use source material, shall submit facility information described in § 75.10 of this chapter on Form N–71 and associated forms and site information on DOC/NRC Form AP–A, and associated forms;

(2) As required by the Additional Protocol, a uranium or thorium processing plant, and any other applicant for a license to possess and use source material, shall submit location information described in § 75.11 of this chapter on DOC/NRC Form AP–1 and associated forms; shall permit verification of this information by the International Atomic Energy Agency (IAEA); and shall take other actions as may be necessary to implement the US/IAEA Safeguards Agreement, as described in part 75 of this chapter; or

(3) As required by the Additional Protocol, an ore processing plant or a facility using or storing ore concentrates or other impure source materials shall submit the information described in § 75.11 of this chapter, as appropriate, on DOC/NRC Form AP–1 and associated forms; shall permit verification of this information by the International Atomic Energy Agency (IAEA); and shall take other actions as may be necessary to implement the US/IAEA Safeguards Agreement, as described in part 75 of this chapter.

(h) An application for a license to receive, possess, and use source material for uranium or thorium milling or byproduct material, as defined in this part, at sites formerly associated with such milling shall contain proposed written specifications relating to milling operations and the disposition of the byproduct material to achieve the requirements and objectives set forth in appendix A of this part. Each application must clearly demonstrate how the requirements and objectives set forth in appendix A of this part have been addressed. Failure to clearly demonstrate how the requirements and objectives in appendix A have been addressed shall be grounds for refusing to accept an application.

(i) As provided by § 40.36, certain applications for specific licenses filed under this part must contain a proposed decommissioning funding plan or a certification of financial assurance for decommissioning. In the case of renewal applications submitted before July 27, 1990, this submittal may follow the renewal application but must be submitted on or before July 27, 1990.

(j)(1) Each application to possess uranium hexafluoride in excess of 50 kilograms in a single container or 1000 kilograms total must contain either:

(i) An evaluation showing that the maximum intake of uranium by a member of the public due to a release would not exceed 2 milligrams; or

(ii) An emergency plan for responding to the radiological hazards of an accidental release of source material and to any associated chemical hazards directly incident thereto.

(2) One or more of the following factors may be used to support an evaluation submitted under paragraph (j)(1)(i) of this section:

(i) All or part of the radioactive material is not subject to release during an accident because of the way it is stored or packaged;

(ii) Facility design or engineered safety features in the facility would reduce the amount of the release; or

(iii) Other factors appropriate for the specific facility.

(3) An emergency plan submitted under paragraph (j)(1)(ii) of this section must include the following:

(i) *Facility description.* A brief description of the licensee's facility and area near the site.

(ii) *Types of accidents.* An identification of each type of accident for which protective actions may be needed.

(iii) *Classification of accidents.* A classification system for classifying accidents as alerts or site area emergencies.

(iv) *Detection of accidents.* Identification of the means of detecting each type of radioactive materials accident in a timely manner.

(v) *Mitigation of consequences.* A brief description of the means and equipment for mitigating the consequences of each type of accident, including those provided to protect workers onsite, and a description of the program for maintaining the equipment.

(vi) *Assessment of releases.* A brief description of the methods and equipment to assess releases of radioactive materials.

(vii) *Responsibilities.* A brief description of the responsibilities of licensee personnel should an accident occur, including identification of personnel responsible for promptly notifying offsite response organizations and the NRC; also responsibilities for developing, maintaining, and updating the plan.

(viii) *Notification and coordination.* A commitment to and a brief description of the means to promptly notify offsite response organizations and request offsite assistance, including medical assistance for the treatment of contaminated injured onsite workers when appropriate. A control point must be established. The notification and coordination must be planned so that unavailability of some personnel, parts of the facility, and some equipment will not prevent the notification and coordination. The licensee shall also commit to notify the NRC operations center immediately after notification of the offsite response organizations and not later than one hour after the licensee declares an emergency.[1]

(ix) *Information to be communicated.* A brief description of the types of information on facility status, radioactive releases, and recommended protective actions, if necessary, to be given to offsite response organizations and to the NRC.

(x) *Training.* A brief description of the frequency, performance objectives and plans for the training that the licensee will provide workers on how to respond to an emergency including any special instructions and orientation tours the licensee would offer to fire, police, medical and other emergency personnel. The training shall familiarize personnel with site-specific emergency procedures. Also, the training shall thoroughly prepare site personnel for their responsibilities in the event of accident scenarios postulated as most probable for the specific site, including the use of team training for such scenarios.

(xi) *Safe shutdown.* A brief description of the means of restoring the facility to a safe condition after an accident.

(xii) *Exercises.* Provisions for conducting quarterly communications checks with offsite response organizations and biennial onsite exercises to test response to simulated emergencies. Quarterly communications checks with offsite response organizations must include the check and update of all necessary telephone numbers. The licensee shall invite offsite response organizations to participate in the biennial exercises. Participation of offsite response organizations in biennial exercises although recommended is not required. Exercises must use accident scenarios postulated as most probable for the specific site and the scenarios shall not be known to most exercise participants. The licensee shall critique each exercise using individuals not having direct implementation responsibility for the plan. Critiques of exercises must evaluate the appropriateness of the plan,

[1] These reporting requirements do not supersede or release licensees of complying with the requirements under the Emergency Planning and Community Right-to-Know Act of 1986, Title III. Pub. L. 99–499 or other state or federal reporting requirements.

emergency procedures, facilities, equipment, training of personnel, and overall effectiveness of the response. Deficiencies found by the critiques must be corrected.

(xiii) *Hazardous chemicals.* A certification that the application has met its responsibilities under the Emergency Planning and Community Right-to-Know Act of 1986, title III, Pub. L. 99–499, if applicable to the applicant's activities at the proposed place of the use of the source material.

(4) The licensee shall allow the offsite response organizations expected to respond in case of an accident 60 days to comment on the licensee's emergency plan before submitting it to the NRC. The licensee shall provide any comments received within the 60 days to the NRC with the emergency plan.

(k) A license application for a uranium enrichment facility must be accompanied by an Environmental Report required under subpart A of part 51 of this chapter.

(l) A license application that involves the use of source material in a uranium enrichment facility must include the applicant's provisions for liability insurance.

(m) Each applicant for a license for the possession of source material at a facility for the production or conversion of uranium hexafluoride shall protect Safeguards Information against unauthorized disclosure in accordance with the requirements in §§ 73.21 and 73.22 of this chapter, as applicable. Each applicant for a license for source material shall protect Safeguards Information against unauthorized disclosure in accordance with the requirements in § 73.21 and the requirements of § 73.22 or § 73.23 of this chapter, as applicable.

[26 FR 284, Jan. 14, 1961, as amended at 31 FR 4669, Mar. 19, 1966; 34 FR 19546, Dec. 11, 1969; 36 FR 145, Jan. 6, 1971; 37 FR 5748, Mar. 21, 1972; 46 FR 13497, Feb. 23, 1981; 49 FR 9403, Mar. 12, 1984; 49 FR 19626, May 9, 1984; 49 FR 21699, May 23, 1984; 49 FR 27924, July 9, 1984; 53 FR 24047, June 27, 1988; 54 FR 14061, Apr. 7, 1989; 57 FR 18390, Apr. 30, 1992; 68 FR 58807, Oct. 10, 2003; 73 FR 63570, Oct. 24, 2008; 73 FR 78604, Dec. 23, 2008]

§ 40.32 General requirements for issuance of specific licenses.

An application for a specific license will be approved if:

(a) The application is for a purpose authorized by the Act; and

(b) The applicant is qualified by reason of training and experience to use the source material for the purpose requested in such manner as to protect health and minimize danger to life or property; and

(c) The applicant's proposed equipment, facilities and procedures are adequate to protect health and minimize danger to life or property; and

(d) The issuance of the license will not be inimical to the common defense and security or to the health and safety of the public; and

(e) In the case of an application for a license for a uranium enrichment facility, or for a license to possess and use source and byproduct material for uranium milling, production of uranium hexafluoride, or for the conduct of any other activity which the NRC determines will significantly affect the quality of the environment, the Director, Office of Nuclear Material Safety and Safeguardsor his/her designee, before commencement of construction, on the basis of information filed and evaluations made pursuant to subpart A of part 51 of this chapter, has concluded, after weighing the environmental, economic, technical and other benefits against environmental costs and considering available alternatives, that the action called for is the issuance of the proposed license, with any appropriate conditions to protect environmental values. Commencement of construction prior to this conclusion is grounds for denial of a license to possess and use source and byproduct material in the plant or facility. Commencement of construction as defined in § 40.4 may include non-construction activities if the activity has a reasonable nexus to radiological safety and security.

(f) The applicant satisfies any applicable special requirements contained in §§ 40.34, 40.52, and 40.54.

(g) If the proposed activity involves use of source material in a uranium enrichment facility, the applicant has satisfied the applicable provisions of part 140 of this chapter.

[26 FR 284, Jan. 14, 1961, as amended at 36 FR 12731, July 7, 1971; 40 FR 8787, Mar. 3, 1975; 41 FR 53332, Dec. 6, 1976; 43 FR 6924, Feb. 17, 1978; 49 FR 9403, Mar. 12, 1984; 57 FR 18390, Apr. 30, 1992; 73 FR 5721, Jan. 31, 2008; 76 FR 56964, Sept. 15, 2011; 78 FR 32340, May 29, 2013]

§40.33 Issuance of a license for a uranium enrichment facility.

(a) The Commission will hold a hearing pursuant to 10 CFR part 2, subparts A, G, and I, on each application with regard to the licensing of the construction and operation of a uranium enrichment facility. The Commission will publish public notice of the hearing in the FEDERAL REGISTER at least 30 days before the hearing.

(b) A license for a uranium enrichment facility may not be issued before the hearing is completed and a decision issued on the application.

[57 FR 18391, Apr. 30, 1992]

§40.34 Special requirements for issuance of specific licenses.

(a) An application for a specific license to manufacture industrial products and devices containing depleted uranium, or to initially transfer such products or devices, for use pursuant to §40.25 of this part or equivalent regulations of an Agreement State, will be approved if:

(1) The applicant satisfies the general requirements specified in §40.32,

(2) The applicant submits sufficient information relating to the design, manufacture, prototype testing, quality control procedures, labeling or marking, proposed uses, and potential hazards of the industrial product or device to provide reasonable assurance that possession, use, or transfer of the depleted uranium in the product or device is not likely to cause any individual to receive in 1 year a radiation dose in excess of 10 percent of the annual limits specified in §20.1201(a) of this chapter; and

(3) The applicant submits sufficient information regarding the industrial product or device and the presence of depleted uranium for a mass-volume application in the product or device to provide reasonable assurance that unique benefits will accrue to the public because of the usefulness of the product or device.

(b) In the case of an industrial product or device whose unique benefits are questionable, the Commission will approve an application for a specific license under this paragraph only if the product or device is found to combine a high degree of utility and low probability of uncontrolled disposal and dispersal of significant quantities of depleted uranium into the environment.

(c) The Commission may deny an applicant for a specific license under this paragraph if the end uses of the industrial product or device cannot be reasonably foreseen.

[41 FR 53332, Dec. 6, 1976, as amended at 43 FR 6924, Feb. 17, 1978; 58 FR 67661, Dec. 22, 1993; 59 FR 41643, Aug. 15, 1994]

§40.35 Conditions of specific licenses issued pursuant to §40.34.

Each person licensed pursuant to §40.34 shall:

(a) Maintain the level of quality control required by the license in the manufacture of the industrial product or device, and in the installation of the depleted uranium into the product or device;

(b) Label or mark each unit to: (1) Identify the manufacturer or initial transferor of the product or device and the number of the license under which the product or device was manufactured or initially transferred, the fact that the product or device contains depleted uranium, and the quantity of depleted uranium in each product or device; and (2) state that the receipt, possession, use, and transfer of the product or device are subject to a general license or the equivalent and the regulations of the U.S. NRC or of an Agreement State;

(c) Assure that the depleted uranium before being installed in each product or device has been impressed with the following legend clearly legible through any plating or other covering: "Depleted Uranium";

(d)(1) Furnish a copy of the general license contained in §40.25 and a copy of Form NRC 244 to each person to whom he transfers source material in a product or device for use pursuant to the general license contained in § 40.25; or

(2) Furnish a copy of the general license contained in the Agreement State's regulation equivalent to § 40.25 and a copy of the Agreement State's certificate, or alternately, furnish a copy of the general license contained in § 40.25 and a copy of Form NRC 244 to each person to whom he transfers source material in a product or device for use pursuant to the general license of an Agreement State. If a copy of the general license in § 40.25 and a copy of Form NRC 244 are furnished to such person, they shall be accompanied by a note explaining that use of the product or device is regulated by the Agreement State under requirements substantially the same as those in § 40.25; and

(e)(1) Report to the Director, Office of Nuclear Material Safety and Safeguards, by an appropriate method listed in § 40.5, all transfers of industrial products or devices to persons for use under the general license in § 40.25. Such report shall identify each general licensee by name and address, an individual by name and/or position who may constitute a point of contact between the Commission and the general licensee, the type and model number of device transferred, and the quantity of depleted uranium contained in the product or device. The report shall be submitted within 30 days after the end of each calendar quarter in which such a product or device is transferred to the generally licensed person. If no transfers have been made to persons generally licensed under § 40.25 during the reporting period, the report shall so indicate;

(2) Report to the responsible Agreement State Agency all transfers of industrial products or devices to persons for use under the general license in the Agreement State's regulation equivalent to § 40.25. Such report shall identify each general licensee by name and address, an individual by name and/or position who may constitute a point of contact between the Agency and the general licensee, the type and model number of device transferred, and the quantity of depleted uranium contained in the product or device. The report shall be submitted within 30 days after the end of each calendar quarter in which such product or device is transferred to the generally licensed person. If no transfers have been made to a particular Agreement State during the reporting period, this information shall be reported to the responsible Agreement State Agency;

(3) Keep records showing the name, address, and a point of contact for each general license to whom he or she transfers depleted uranium in industrial products or devices for use pursuant to the general license provided in § 40.25 or equivalent regulations of an Agreement State. The records must be retained for three years from the date of transfer and must show the date of each transfer, the quantity of depleted uranium in each product or device transferred, and compliance with the report requirements of this section.

(f) Licensees required to submit emergency plans by § 40.31(j)(1)–(4) shall follow the emergency plan approved by the Commission. The licensee may change the plan without Commission approval if the changes do not decrease the effectiveness of the plan. The licensee shall furnish the change to the Director, Office of Nuclear Material Safety and Safeguards, by an appropriate method listed in § 40.5, and to affected offsite response organizations, within six months after the change is made. Proposed changes that decrease the effectiveness of the approved emergency plan may not be implemented without application to and prior approval by the Commission.

[41 FR 53332, Dec. 6, 1976, as amended at 43 FR 6924, Feb. 17, 1978; 52 FR 31611, Aug. 21, 1987; 53 FR 19248, May 27, 1988; 54 FR 14062, Apr. 7, 1989; 68 FR 58807, Oct. 10, 2003; 73 FR 5721, Jan. 31, 2008; 82 FR 52825, Nov. 15, 2017]

§ 40.36 Financial assurance and recordkeeping for decommissioning.

Except for licenses authorizing the receipt, possession, and use of source material for uranium or thorium milling, or byproduct material at sites formerly associated with such milling, for which financial assurance requirements are set forth in appendix A of this part, criteria for providing financial assurance for decommissioning are as follows:

(a) Each applicant for a specific license authorizing the possession and use of more than 100 mCi of source material in a readily dispersible form shall submit a decommissioning funding plan as described in paragraph (d) of this section.

(b) Each applicant for a specific license authorizing possession and use of quantities of source material greater than 10 mCi but less than or equal to 100 mCi in a readily dispersible form shall either—

(1) Submit a decommissioning funding plan as described in paragraph (d) of this section; or

(2) Submit a certification that financial assurance for decommissioning has been provided in the amount of $225,000 by June 2, 2005 using one of the methods described in paragraph (e) of this section. For an applicant, this certification may state that the appropriate assurance will be obtained after the application has been approved and the license issued but before the receipt of licensed material. If the applicant defers execution of the financial instrument until after the license has been issued, a signed original of the financial instrument obtained to satisfy the requirements of paragraph (e) of this section must be submitted to NRC prior to receipt of licensed material. If the applicant does not defer execution of the financial instrument, the applicant shall submit to NRC, as part of the certification, a signed original of the financial instrument obtained to satisfy the requirements of paragraph (e) of this section.

(c)(1) Each holder of a specific license issued on or after July 27, 1990, which is covered by paragraph (a) or (b) of this section, shall provide financial assurance for decommissioning in accordance with the criteria set forth in this section.

(2) Each holder of a specific license issued before July 27, 1990, and of a type described in paragraph (a) of this section shall submit a decommissioning funding plan as described in paragraph (d) of this section or a certification of financial assurance for decommissioning in an amount at least equal to $1,125,000 in accordance with the criteria set forth in this section. If the licensee submits the certification of financial assurance rather than a decommissioning funding plan, the licensee shall include a decommissioning funding plan in any application for license renewal. Licensees required to submit the $1,125,000 amount must do so by December 2, 2004.

(3) Each holder of a specific license issued before July 27, 1990, and of a type described in paragraph (b) of this section shall submit, on or before July 27, 1990, a decommissioning funding plan, as described in paragraph (d) of this section, or a certification of financial assurance for decommissioning in accordance with the criteria set forth in this section.

(4) Any licensee who has submitted an application before July 27, 1990, for renewal of license in accordance with § 40.43 shall provide financial assurance for decommissioning in accordance with paragraphs (a) and (b) of this section. This assurance must be submitted when this rule becomes effective November 24, 1995.

(5) If, in surveys made under 10 CFR 20.1501(a), residual radioactivity in the facility and environment, including the subsurface, is detected at levels that would, if left uncorrected, prevent the site from meeting the 10 CFR 20.1402 criteria for unrestricted use, the licensee must submit a decommissioning funding plan within one year of when the survey is completed.

(d)(1) Each decommissioning funding plan must be submitted for review and approval and must contain—

(i) A detailed cost estimate for decommissioning, in an amount reflecting:

(A) The cost of an independent contractor to perform all decommissioning activities;

(B) The cost of meeting the 10 CFR 20.1402 criteria for unrestricted use, provided that, if the applicant or licensee can demonstrate its ability to meet the provisions of 10 CFR 20.1403, the cost estimate may be based on meeting the 10 CFR 20.1403 criteria;

(C) The volume of onsite subsurface material containing residual radioactivity that will require remediation; and

(D) An adequate contingency factor.

(ii) Identification of and justification for using the key assumptions contained in the DCE;

(iii) A description of the method of assuring funds for decommissioning from paragraph (e) of this section, including means for adjusting cost estimates and associated funding levels periodically over the life of the facility;

(iv) A certification by the licensee that financial assurance for decommissioning has been provided in the amount of the cost estimate for decommissioning; and

(v) A signed original, or if permitted, a copy, of the financial instrument obtained to satisfy the requirements of paragraph (e) of this section (unless a previously submitted and accepted financial instrument continues to cover the cost estimate for decommissioning).

(2) At the time of license renewal and at intervals not to exceed 3 years, the decommissioning funding plan must be resubmitted with adjustments as necessary to account for changes in costs and the extent of contamination. If the amount of financial assurance will be adjusted downward, this can not be done until the updated decommissioning funding plan is approved. The decommissioning funding plan must update the information submitted with the original or prior approved plan, and must specifically consider the effect of the following events on decommissioning costs:

(i) Spills of radioactive material producing additional residual radioactivity in onsite subsurface material;

(ii) Waste inventory increasing above the amount previously estimated;

(iii) Waste disposal costs increasing above the amount previously estimated;

(iv) Facility modifications;

(v) Changes in authorized possession limits;

(vi) Actual remediation costs that exceed the previous cost estimate;

(vii) Onsite disposal; and

(viii) Use of a settling pond.

(e) The financial instrument must include the licensee's name, license number, and docket number; and the name, address, and other contact information of the issuer, and, if a trust is used, the trustee. When any of the foregoing information changes, the licensee must, within 30 days, submit financial instruments reflecting such changes. The financial instrument submitted must be a signed original or signed original duplicate, except where a copy is specifically permitted. Financial assurance for decommissioning must be provided by one or more of the following methods:

(1) *Prepayment.* Prepayment is the deposit before the start of operation into an account segregated from licensee assets and outside the licensee's administrative control of cash or liquid assets such that the amount of funds would be sufficient to pay decommissioning costs. Prepayment must be made into a trust account, and the trustee and the trust must be acceptable to the Commission.

(2) *A surety method, insurance, or other guarantee method.* These methods guarantee that decommissioning costs will be paid. A surety method may be in the form of a surety bond, or letter of credit. A parent company guarantee of funds for decommissioning costs based on a financial test may be used if the guarantee and test are as contained in appendix A to part 30 of this chapter. For commercial corporations that issue bonds, a guarantee of funds by the applicant or licensee for decommissioning costs based on a financial test may be used if the guarantee and test are as contained in appendix C to part 30 of this chapter. For commercial companies that do not issue bonds, a guarantee of funds by the applicant or licensee for decommissioning costs may be used if the guarantee and test are as contained in appendix D to part 30 of this chapter. For nonprofit entities, such as colleges, universities, and nonprofit hospitals, a guarantee of funds by the applicant or licensee may be used if the guarantee and test are as contained in appendix E to part 30 of this chapter. Except for an external sinking fund, a parent company guarantee or guarantee by the applicant or licensee may not be used in combination with any other financial methods used to satisfy the requirements of this section. A guarantee by the applicant or licensee may not be used in any situation where the applicant or licensee has a parent company holding majority

control of the voting stock of the company. Any surety method or insurance used to provide financial assurance for decommissioning must contain the following conditions:

(i) The surety method or insurance must be open-ended or, if written for a specified term, such as five years, must be renewed automatically unless 90 days or more prior to the renewal date, the issuer notifies the Commission, the beneficiary, and the licensee of its intention not to renew. The surety method or insurance must also provide that the full face amount be paid to the beneficiary automatically prior to the expiration without proof of forfeiture if the licensee fails to provide a replacement acceptable to the Commission within 30 days after receipt of notification of cancellation.

(ii) The surety method or insurance must be payable to a trust established for decommissioning costs. The trustee and trust must be acceptable to the Commission. An acceptable trustee includes an appropriate State or Federal government agency or an entity which has the authority to act as a trustee and whose trust operations are regulated and examined by a Federal or State agency.

(iii) The surety method or insurance must remain in effect until the Commission has terminated the license.

(3) *An external sinking fund in which deposits are made at least annually, coupled with a surety method, insurance, or other guarantee method, the value of which may decrease by the amount being accumulated in the sinking fund.* An external sinking fund is a fund established and maintained by setting aside funds periodically in an account segregated from licensee assets and outside the licensee's administrative control in which the total amount of funds would be sufficient to pay decommissioning costs at the time termination of operation is expected. An external sinking fund must be in the form of a trust. If the other guarantee method is used, no surety or insurance may be combined with the external sinking fund. The surety, insurance, or other guarantee provisions must be as stated in paragraph (e)(2) of this section.

(4) In the case of Federal, State, or local government licensees, a statement of intent containing a cost estimate for decommissioning or an amount based on paragraph (b) of this section, and indicating that funds for decommissioning will be obtained when necessary.

(5) When a government entity is assuming custody and ownership of a site, an arrangement that is deemed acceptable by such government entity.

(f) Each person licensed under this part shall keep records of information important to the decommissioning of a facility in an identified location until the site is released for unrestricted use. Before licensed activities are transferred or assigned in accordance with § 40.41(b) licensees shall transfer all records described in this paragraph to the new licensee. In this case, the new licensee will be responsible for maintaining these records until the license is terminated. If records important to the decommissioning of a facility are kept for other purposes, reference to these records and their locations may be used. Information the Commission considers important to decommissioning consists of—

(1) Records of spills or other unusual occurrences involving the spread of contamination in and around the facility, equipment, or site. These records may be limited to instances when contamination remains after any cleanup procedures or when there is reasonable likelihood that contaminants may have spread to inaccessible areas as in the case of possible seepage into porous materials such as concrete. These records must include any known information on identification of involved nuclides, quantities, forms, and concentrations.

(2) As-built drawings and modifications of structures and equipment in restricted areas where radioactive materials are used and/or stored, and of locations of possible inaccessible contamination such as buried pipes which may be subject to contamination. If required drawings are referenced, each relevant document need not be indexed individually. If drawings are not available, the licensee shall substitute appropriate records of available information concerning these areas and locations.

(3) Except for areas containing depleted uranium used only for shielding or as penetrators in unused munitions, a list contained in a single document and updated every 2 years, of the following:

(i) All areas designated and formerly designated as restricted areas as defined under 10 CFR 20.1003;

(ii) All areas outside of restricted areas that require documentation under § 40.36(f)(1);

(iii) All areas outside of restricted areas where current and previous wastes have been buried as documented under 10 CFR 20.2108; and

(iv) All areas outside of restricted areas that contain material such that, if the license expired, the licensee would be required to either decontaminate the area to meet the criteria for decommissioning in 10 CFR part 20, subpart E, or apply for approval for disposal under 10 CFR 20.2002.

(4) Records of the cost estimate performed for the decommissioning funding plan or of the amount certified for decommissioning, and records of the funding method used for assuring funds if either a funding plan or certification is used.

(g) In providing financial assurance under this section, each licensee must use the financial assurance funds only for decommissioning activities and each licensee must monitor the balance of funds held to account for market variations. The licensee must replenish the funds, and report such actions to the NRC, as follows:

(1) If, at the end of a calendar quarter, the fund balance is below the amount necessary to cover the cost of decommissioning, but is not below 75 percent of the cost, the licensee must increase the balance to cover the cost, and must do so within 30 days after the end of the calendar quarter.

(2) If, at any time, the fund balance falls below 75 percent of the amount necessary to cover the cost of decommissioning, the licensee must increase the balance to cover the cost, and must do so within 30 days of the occurrence.

(3) Within 30 days of taking the actions required by paragraph (g)(1) or (g)(2) of this section, the licensee must provide a written report of such actions to the Director, Office of Nuclear Material Safety and Safeguards, and state the new balance of the fund.

[53 FR 24047, June 27, 1988, as amended at 58 FR 39633, July 26, 1993; 58 FR 67661, Dec. 22, 1993; 58 FR 68731, Dec. 29, 1993; 59 FR 1618, Jan. 12, 1994; 60 FR 38238, July 26, 1995; 61 FR 24674, May 16, 1996; 62 FR 39090, July 21, 1997; 63 FR 29543, June 1, 1998; 68 FR 57336, Oct. 3, 2003; 76 FR 35568, June 17, 2011; 78 FR 34247, June 7, 2013; 78 FR 75450, Dec. 12, 2013]

§ 40.38 Ineligibility of certain applicants.

A license may not be issued to the Corporation if the Commission determines that:

(a) The Corporation is owned, controlled, or dominated by an alien, a foreign corporation, or a foreign government; or

(b) The issuance of such a license would be inimical to—

(1) The common defense and security of the United States; or

(2) The maintenance of a reliable and economical domestic source of enrichment services.

[62 FR 6669, Feb. 12, 1997]

Licenses

§ 40.41 Terms and conditions of licenses.

(a) Each license issued pursuant to the regulations in this part shall be subject to all the provisions of the act, now or hereafter in effect, and to all rules, regulations and orders of the Commission.

(b) Neither the license nor any right under the license shall be assigned or otherwise transferred in violation of the provisions of the Act.

(c) Each person licensed by the Commission pursuant to the regulations in this part shall confine his possession and use of source or byproduct material to the locations and purposes authorized in the license. Except as otherwise provided in the license, a license issued pursuant to the regulations in this part shall carry with it the right to receive, possess, and use source or byproduct material. Preparation for shipment and transport of source or byproduct material shall be in accordance with the provisions of part 71 of this chapter.

(d) Each license issued pursuant to the regulations in this part shall be deemed to contain the provisions set forth in sections 183b.–d., of the Act, whether or not said provisions are expressly set forth in the license.

(e) The Commission may incorporate in any license at the time of issuance, or thereafter, by appropriate rule, regulation or order, such additional requirements and conditions with respect to the licensee's receipt, possession, use, and transfer of source or byproduct material as it deems appropriate or necessary in order to:

(1) Promote the common defense and security;

(2) Protect health or to minimize danger of life or property;

(3) Protect restricted data;

(4) Require such reports and the keeping of such records, and to provide for such inspections of activities under the license as may be necessary or appropriate to effectuate the purposes of the act and regulations thereunder.

(f)(1) Each licensee shall notify the appropriate NRC Regional Administrator, in writing, immediately following the filing of a voluntary or involuntary petition for bankruptcy under any chapter of title 11 (Bankruptcy) of the United States Code by or against:

(i) The licensee;

(ii) An entity (as that term is defined in 11 U.S.C. 101(14)) controlling the licensee or listing the license or licensee as property of the estate; or

(iii) An affiliate (as that term is defined in 11 U.S.C. 101(2)) of the licensee.

(2) This notification must indicate:

(i) The bankruptcy court in which the petition for bankruptcy was filed; and

(ii) The date of the filing of the petition.

(g) No person may commence operation of a uranium enrichment facility until the Commission verifies through inspection that the facility has been constructed in accordance with the requirements of the license. The Commission shall publish notice of the inspection results in the FEDERAL REGISTER.

(h) Each licensee shall ensure that Safeguards Information is protected against unauthorized disclosure in accordance with the requirements in § 73.21 and the requirements of § 73.22 or § 73.23 of this chapter, as applicable.

[26 FR 284, Jan. 14, 1961, as amended at 31 FR 15145, Dec. 2, 1966; 45 FR 65531, Oct. 3, 1980; 48 FR 32328, July 15, 1983; 52 FR 1295, Jan. 12, 1987; 57 FR 18391, Apr. 30, 1992; 73 FR 63571, Oct. 24, 2008]

§ 40.42 Expiration and termination of licenses and decommissioning of sites and separate buildings or outdoor areas.

(a) Each specific license expires at the end of the day on the expiration date stated in the license unless the licensee has filed an application for renewal under § 40.43 not less than 30 days before the expiration date stated in the existing license. If an application for renewal has been filed at least 30 days before the expiration date stated in the existing license, the existing license expires at the end of the day on which the Commission makes a final determination to deny the renewal application or, if the determination states an expiration date, the expiration date stated in the determination.

(b) Each specific license revoked by the Commission expires at the end of the day on the date of the Commission's final determination to revoke the license, or on the expiration date stated in the determination, or as otherwise provided by Commission Order.

(c) Each specific license continues in effect, beyond the expiration date if necessary, with respect to possession of source material until the Commission notifies the licensee in writing that the license is terminated. During this time, the licensee shall—

(1) Limit actions involving source material to those related to decommissioning; and

(2) Continue to control entry to restricted areas until they are suitable for release in accordance with NRC requirements;

(d) Within 60 days of the occurrence of any of the following, consistent with the administrative directions in § 40.5, each licensee shall provide notification to the NRC in writing and either begin decommissioning its site, or any separate building or outdoor area that contains residual radioactivity, so that the building or outdoor area is suitable for release in accordance with NRC requirements, or submit within 12 months of notification a decommissioning plan, if required by paragraph (g)(1) of this section, and begin decommissioning upon approval of that plan if—

(1) The license has expired pursuant to paragraph (a) or (b) of this section; or

(2) The licensee has decided to permanently cease principal activities, as defined in this part, at the entire site or in any separate building or outdoor area; or

(3) No principal activities under the license have been conducted for a period of 24 months; or

(4) No principal activities have been conducted for a period of 24 months in any separate building or outdoor area that contains residual radioactivity such that the building or outdoor area is unsuitable for release in accordance with NRC requirements.

(e) Coincident with the notification required by paragraph (d) of this section, the licensee shall maintain in effect all decommissioning financial assurances established by the licensee pursuant to § 40.36 in conjunction with a license issuance or renewal or as required by this section. The amount of the financial assurance must be increased, or may be decreased, as appropriate, to cover the detailed cost estimate for decommissioning established pursuant to paragraph (g)(4)(v) of this section.

(1) Any licensee who has not provided financial assurance to cover the detailed cost estimate submitted with the decommissioning plan shall do so when this rule becomes effective November 24, 1995.

(2) Following approval of the decommissioning plan, a licensee may reduce the amount of the financial assurance as decommissioning proceeds and radiological contamination is reduced at the site with the approval of the Commission.

(f) The Commission may grant a request to delay or postpone initiation of the decommissioning process if the Commission determines that such relief is not detrimental to the public health and safety and is otherwise in the public interest. The request must be submitted no later than 30 days before notification pursuant to paragraph (d) of this section. The schedule for decommissioning set forth in paragraph (d) of this section may not commence until the Commission has made a determination on the request.

(g)(1) A decommissioning plan must be submitted if required by license condition or if the procedures and activities necessary to carry out decommissioning of the site or separate building or outdoor area have not been previously approved by the Commission and these procedures could increase potential health and safety impacts to workers or to the public, such as in any of the following cases:

(i) Procedures would involve techniques not applied routinely during cleanup or maintenance operations;

(ii) Workers would be entering areas not normally occupied where surface contamination and radiation levels are significantly higher than routinely encountered during operation;

(iii) Procedures could result in significantly greater airborne concentrations of radioactive materials than are present during operation; or

(iv) Procedures could result in significantly greater releases of radioactive material to the environment than those associated with operation.

(2) The Commission may approve an alternate schedule for submittal of a decommissioning plan required pursuant to paragraph (d) of this section if the Commission determines that the alternative schedule is necessary to the effective conduct of decommissioning operations and presents no undue risk from radiation to the public health and safety and is otherwise in the public interest.

(3) The procedures listed in paragraph (g)(1) of this section may not be carried out prior to approval of the decommissioning plan.

(4) The proposed decommissioning plan for the site or separate building or outdoor area must include:

(i) A description of the conditions of the site or separate building or outdoor area sufficient to evaluate the acceptability of the plan;

(ii) A description of planned decommissioning activities;

(iii) A description of methods used to ensure protection of workers and the environment against radiation hazards during decommissioning;

(iv) A description of the planned final radiation survey; and

(v) An updated detailed cost estimate for decommissioning, comparison of that estimate with present funds set aside for decommissioning, and a plan for assuring the availability of adequate funds for completion of decommissioning.

(vi) For decommissioning plans calling for completion of decommissioning later than 24 months after plan approval, a justification for the delay based on the criteria in paragraph (i) of this section.

(5) The proposed decommissioning plan will be approved by the Commission if the information therein demonstrates that the decommissioning will be completed as soon as practicable and that the health and safety of workers and the public will be adequately protected.

(h)(1) Except as provided in paragraph (i) of this section, licensees shall complete decommissioning of the site or separate building or outdoor area as soon as practicable but no later than 24 months following the initiation of decommissioning.

(2) Except as provided in paragraph (i) of this section, when decommissioning involves the entire site, the licensee shall request license termination as soon as practicable but no later than 24 months following the initiation of decommissioning.

(i) The Commission may approve a request for an alternate schedule for completion of decommissioning of the site or separate building or outdoor area, and license termination if appropriate, if the Commission determines that the alternative is warranted by consideration of the following:

(1) Whether it is technically feasible to complete decommissioning within the allotted 24-month period;

(2) Whether sufficient waste disposal capacity is available to allow completion of decommissioning within the allotted 24-month period;

(3) Whether a significant volume reduction in wastes requiring disposal will be achieved by allowing short-lived radionuclides to decay;

(4) Whether a significant reduction in radiation exposure to workers can be achieved by allowing short-lived radionuclides to decay; and

(5) Other site-specific factors which the Commission may consider appropriate on a case-by-case basis, such as the regulatory requirements of other government agencies, lawsuits, groundwater treatment activities, monitored natural groundwater restoration, actions that could result in more environmental harm than deferred cleanup, and other factors beyond the control of the licensee.

(j) As the final step in decommissioning, the licensee shall—

(1) Certify the disposition of all licensed material, including accumulated wastes, by submitting a completed NRC Form 314 or equivalent information; and

(2) Conduct a radiation survey of the premises where the licensed activities were carried out and submit a report of the results of this survey, unless the licensee demonstrates in some other manner that the premises are suitable for release in accordance with the criteria for decommissioning in 10 CFR part 20, subpart E or, for uranium milling (uranium and thorium recovery) facilities, Criterion 6(6) of Appendix A to this part. The licensee shall, as appropriate—

(i) Report levels of gamma radiation in units of millisieverts (microroentgen) per hour at one meter from surfaces, and report levels of radioactivity, including alpha and beta, in units of megabecquerels (disintegrations per minute or microcuries) per 100 square centimeters removable and fixed for surfaces, megabecquerels (microcuries) per milliliter for water, and becquerels (picocuries) per gram for solids such as soils or concrete; and

(ii) Specify the survey instrument(s) used and certify that each instrument is properly calibrated and tested.

(k) Specific licenses, including expired licenses, will be terminated by written notice to the licensee when the Commission determines that:

(1) Source material has been properly disposed;

(2) Reasonable effort has been made to eliminate residual radioactive contamination, if present; and

(3)(i) A radiation survey has been performed which demonstrates that the premises are suitable for release in accordance with the criteria for decommissioning in 10 CFR part 20, subpart E or, for (uranium and thorium recovery) facilities, Criterion 6(6) of Appendix A to this part; or

(ii) Other information submitted by the licensee is sufficient to demonstrate that the premises are suitable for release in accordance with the criteria for decommissioning in 10 CFR part 20, subpart E or, for uranium milling (uranium and thorium recovery) facilities, Criterion 6(6) of Appendix A to this part.

(4) Records required by § 40.61 (d) and (f) have been received.

(l) Specific licenses for uranium and thorium milling are exempt from paragraphs (d)(4), (g) and (h) of this section with respect to reclamation of tailings impoundments and/or waste disposal areas.

[59 FR 36035, July 15, 1994, as amended at 60 FR 38239, July 26, 1995; 61 FR 1114, Jan. 16, 1996; 61 FR 24674, May 16, 1996; 61 FR 29637, June 12, 1996; 62 FR 39090, July 21, 1997; 66 FR 64738, Dec. 14, 2001; 68 FR 75390, Dec. 31, 2003; 73 FR 42674, July 23, 2008; 81 FR 86909, Dec. 2, 2016]

§ 40.43 Renewal of licenses.

Application for renewal of a specific license must be filed on NRC Form 313 and in accordance with § 40.31.

[75 FR 73943, Nov. 30, 2010]

§ 40.44 Amendment of licenses at request of licensee.

Applications for amendment of a license shall be filed on NRC Form 313 in accordance with § 40.31 and shall specify the respects in which the licensee desires the license to be amended and the grounds for such amendment.

[49 FR 19627, May 9, 1984, as amended at 56 FR 40768, Aug. 16, 1991]

§ 40.45 Commission action on applications to renew or amend.

In considering an application by a licensee to renew or amend his license the Commission will apply the applicable criteria set forth in § 40.32.

[26 FR 284, Jan. 14, 1961, as amended at 43 FR 6924, Feb. 17, 1978]

§ 40.46 Inalienability of licenses.

(a) No license issued or granted pursuant to the regulations in this part shall be transferred, assigned or in any manner disposed of, either voluntarily or involuntarily, directly or indirectly, through transfer of control of any license to any person, unless the Commission shall after securing full information, find that the transfer is in accordance with the provisions of this act, and shall give its consent in writing.

(b) An application for transfer of license must include:

(1) The identity, technical and financial qualifications of the proposed transferee; and

(2) Financial assurance for decommissioning information required by § 40.36 or Appendix A to this part, as applicable.

[26 FR 284, Jan. 14, 1961, as amended at 76 FR 35569, June 17, 2011]

Transfer of Source Material

§ 40.51 Transfer of source or byproduct material.

(a) No licensee shall transfer source or byproduct material except as authorized pursuant to this section.

(b) Except as otherwise provided in his license and subject to the provisions of paragraphs (c) and (d) of this section, any licensee may transfer source or byproduct material:

(1) To the Department of Energy;

(2) To the agency in any Agreement State which regulates radioactive materials pursuant to an agreement with the Commission or the Atomic Energy Commission under section 274 of the Act;

(3) To any person exempt from the licensing requirements of the Act and regulations in this part, to the extent permitted under such exemption;

(4) To any person in an Agreement State subject to the jurisdiction of that State who has been exempted from the licensing requirements and regulations of that State, to the extent permitted under such exemptions;

(5) To any person authorized to receive such source or byproduct material under terms of a specific license or a general license or their equivalents issued by the Commission or an Agreement State;

(6) To any person abroad pursuant to an export license issued under part 110 of this chapter; or

(7) As otherwise authorized by the commission in writing.

(c) Before transferring source or byproduct material to a specific licensee of the Commission or an Agreement State or to a general licensee who is required to register with the Commission or with an Agreement State prior to receipt of the source or byproduct material, the licensee transferring the material shall verify that the transferee's license authorizes receipt of the type, form, and quantity of source or byproduct material to be transferred.

(d) The following methods for the verification required by paragraph (c) of this section are acceptable:

(1) The transferor may have in his possession, and read, a current copy of the transferee's specific license or registration certificate;

(2) The transferor may have in his possession a written certification by the transferee that he is authorized by license or registration certificate to receive the type, form, and quantity of source or byproduct material to be transferred, specifying the license or registration certification number, issuing agency and expiration date;

(3) For emergency shipments the transferor may accept oral certification by the transferee that he is authorized by license or registration certificate to receive the type, form, and quantity of source or byproduct material to be transferred, specifying the license or registration certificate number, issuing agency and expiration date: *Provided*, That the oral certification is confirmed in writing within 10 days;

(4) The transferor may obtain other sources of information compiled by a reporting service from official records of the Commission or the licensing agency of an Agreement State as to the identity of licensees and the scope and expiration dates of licenses and registrations; or

(5) When none of the methods of verification described in paragraphs (d)(1) to (4) of this section are readily available or when a transferor desires to verify that information received by one of such methods is correct or up-to-date, the transferor may obtain and record confirmation from the Commission or the licensing agency of an Agreement State that the transferee is licensed to receive the source or byproduct material.

[45 FR 65532, Oct. 3, 1980]

§40.52 Certain items containing source material; requirements for license to apply or initially transfer.

An application for a specific license to apply source material to, incorporate source material into, manufacture, process, or produce the products specified in §40.13(c) or to initially transfer for sale or distribution any products containing source material for use under §40.13(c) or equivalent provisions of an Agreement State will be approved if:

(a) The applicant satisfies the general requirements specified in §40.32. However, the requirements of §40.32(b) and (c) do not apply to an application for a license to transfer products manufactured, processed, or produced in accordance with a license issued by an Agreement State or to the import of finished products or parts.

(b) The applicant submits sufficient information regarding the product pertinent to the evaluation of the potential radiation exposures, including:

(1) Chemical and physical form and maximum quantity of source material in each product;

(2) Details of construction and design of each product, if applicable. For coated lenses, this must include a description of manufacturing methods that will ensure that the coatings are unlikely to be removed under the conditions expected to be encountered during handling and use;

(3) For products with applicable quantity or concentration limits, quality control procedures to be followed in the fabrication of production lots of the product and the quality control standards the product will be required to meet;

(4) The proposed method of labeling or marking each unit, and/or its container with the identification of the manufacturer or initial transferor of the product and the source material in the product; and

(5) The means of providing radiation safety precautions and instructions relating to handling, use, and storage of products to be used under § 40.13(c)(1)(i) and (c)(1)(iii).

(c) Each product will contain no more than the quantity or the concentration of source material specified for that product in § 40.13(c).

[78 FR 32340, May 29, 2013]

§ 40.53 Conditions for licenses issued for initial transfer of certain items containing source material: Quality control, labeling, and records and reports.

(a) Each person licensed under § 40.52 shall ensure that the quantities or concentrations of source material do not exceed any applicable limit in § 40.13(c).

(b) Each person licensed under § 40.52 shall ensure that each product is labeled as provided in the specific exemption under § 40.13(c) and as required by their license. Those distributing products to be used under § 40.13(c)(1)(i) and (iii) or equivalent regulations of an Agreement State shall provide radiation safety precautions and instructions relating to handling, use, and storage of these products as specified in the license.

(c)(1) Each person licensed under § 40.52 shall file a report with the Director, Office of Nuclear Material Safety and Safeguards by an appropriate method listed in § 40.5(a), including in the address: ATTN: Document Control Desk/Exempt Distribution.

(2) The report must clearly identify the specific licensee submitting the report and include the license number of the specific licensee and indicate that the products are transferred for use under § 40.13(c), giving the specific paragraph designation, or equivalent regulations of an Agreement State.

(3) The report must include the following information on products transferred to other persons for use under § 40.13(c) or equivalent regulations of an Agreement State:

(i) A description or identification of the type of each product and the model number(s), if applicable;

(ii) For each type of source material in each type of product and each model number, if applicable, the total quantity of the source material; and

(iii) The number of units of each type of product transferred during the reporting period by model number, if applicable.

(4) The licensee shall file the report, covering the preceding calendar year, on or before January 31 of each year. Licensees who permanently discontinue activities authorized by the license issued under § 40.52 shall file a report for the current calendar year within 30 days after ceasing distribution.

(5) If no transfers of source material have been made to persons exempt under § 40.13(c) or the equivalent regulations of an Agreement State, during the reporting period, the report must so indicate.

(6) The licensee shall maintain all information concerning transfers that support the reports required by this section for 1 year after each transfer is included in a report to the Commission.

[78 FR 32340, May 29, 2013]

§ 40.54 Requirements for license to initially transfer source material for use under the 'small quantities of source material' general license.

An application for a specific license to initially transfer source material for use under § 40.22, or equivalent regulations of an Agreement State, will be approved if:

(a) The applicant satisfies the general requirements specified in § 40.32; and

(b) The applicant submits adequate information on, and the Commission approves the methods to be used for quality control, labeling, and providing safety instructions to recipients.

[78 FR 32340, May 29, 2013]

§ 40.55 Conditions of licenses to initially transfer source material for use under the 'small quantities of source material' general license: Quality control, labeling, safety instructions, and records and reports.

(a) Each person licensed under § 40.54 shall label the immediate container of each quantity of source material with the type of source material and quantity of material and the words, "radioactive material."

(b) Each person licensed under § 40.54 shall ensure that the quantities and concentrations of source material are as labeled and indicated in any transfer records.

(c) Each person licensed under § 40.54 shall provide the information specified in this paragraph to each person to whom source material is transferred for use under § 40.22 or equivalent provisions in Agreement State regulations. This information must be transferred before the source material is transferred for the first time in each calendar year to the particular recipient. The required information includes:

(1) A copy of §§ 40.22 and 40.51, or relevant equivalent regulations of the Agreement State.

(2) Appropriate radiation safety precautions and instructions relating to handling, use, storage, and disposal of the material.

(d) Each person licensed under § 40.54 shall report transfers as follows:

(1) File a report with the Director, Office of Nuclear Material Safety and Safeguards, U.S. Nuclear Regulatory Commission, Washington, DC 20555. The report shall include the following information:

(i) The name, address, and license number of the person who transferred the source material;

(ii) For each general licensee under § 40.22 or equivalent Agreement State provisions to whom greater than 50 grams (0.11 lb) of source material has been transferred in a single calendar quarter, the name and address of the general licensee to whom source material is distributed; a responsible agent, by name and/or position and phone number, of the general licensee to whom the material was sent; and the type, physical form, and quantity of source material transferred; and

(iii) The total quantity of each type and physical form of source material transferred in the reporting period to all such generally licensed recipients.

(2) File a report with each responsible Agreement State agency that identifies all persons, operating under provisions equivalent to § 40.22, to whom greater than 50 grams (0.11 lb) of source material has been transferred within a single calendar quarter. The report shall include the following information specific to those transfers made to the Agreement State being reported to:

(i) The name, address, and license number of the person who transferred the source material; and

(ii) The name and address of the general licensee to whom source material was distributed; a responsible agent, by name and/or position and phone number, of the general licensee to whom the material was sent; and the type, physical form, and quantity of source material transferred.

(iii) The total quantity of each type and physical form of source material transferred in the reporting period to all such generally licensed recipients within the Agreement State.

(3) Submit each report by January 31 of each year covering all transfers for the previous calendar year. If no transfers were made to persons generally licensed under § 40.22 or equivalent Agreement State provisions during the current period, a report shall be submitted to the Commission indicating so. If no transfers have been made to general licensees in a particular Agreement State during the reporting period, this information shall be reported to the responsible Agreement State agency upon request of the agency.

(e) Each person licensed under § 40.54 shall maintain all information that supports the reports required by this section concerning each transfer to a general licensee for a period of 1 year after the event is included in a report to the Commission or to an Agreement State agency.

[78 FR 32340, May 29, 2013]

§ 40.56 Restrictions on the use of Australian-obligated source material.

(a) In accordance with Article 8 of the Agreement between the Government of Australia and the Government of the United States of America Concerning Peaceful Uses of Nuclear Energy, dated 2010, Australian-obligated source material shall not be used for military purposes. As used in this section, "military purposes" includes, but is not limited to, the production of tritium for use in nuclear explosive devices; military nuclear propulsion; munitions, including depleted uranium munitions; and other direct military non-nuclear applications. "Military purposes" does not include the supply of electricity to a military base from any power network; the production of radioisotopes to be used for medical purposes in military hospitals; and such other similar purposes.

(b) Licensees are prohibited from receiving, processing, transferring, or otherwise using Australian-obligated source material for military purposes.

[76 FR 69122, Nov. 8, 2011. Redesignated at 76 FR 78805, Dec. 20, 2011]

RECORDS, REPORTS, AND INSPECTIONS

§ 40.60 Reporting requirements.

(a) *Immediate report.* Each licensee shall notify the NRC as soon as possible but not later than 4 hours after the discovery of an event that prevents immediate protective actions necessary to avoid exposures to radiation or radioactive materials that could exceed regulatory limits or releases of licensed material that could exceed regulatory limits (events may include fires, explosions, toxic gas releases, etc.).

(b) *Twenty-four hour report.* Each licensee shall notify the NRC within 24 hours after the discovery of any of the following events involving licensed material:

(1) An unplanned contamination event that:

(i) Requires access to the contaminated area, by workers or the public, to be restricted for more than 24 hours by imposing additional radiological controls or by prohibiting entry into the area;

(ii) Involves a quantity of material greater than five times the lowest annual limit on intake specified in appendix B of §§ 20.1001–20.2401 of 10 CFR part 20 for the material; and

(iii) Has access to the area restricted for a reason other than to allow isotopes with a half-life of less than 24 hours to decay prior to decontamination.

(2) An event in which equipment is disabled or fails to function as designed when:

(i) The equipment is required by regulation or license condition to prevent releases exceeding regulatory limits, to prevent exposures to radiation and radioactive materials exceeding regulatory limits, or to mitigate the consequences of an accident;

(ii) The equipment is required to be available and operable when it is disabled or fails to function; and

(iii) No redundant equipment is available and operable to perform the required safety function.

(3) An event that requires unplanned medical treatment at a medical facility of an individual with spreadable radioactive contamination on the individual's clothing or body.

(4) An unplanned fire or explosion damaging any licensed material or any device, container, or equipment containing licensed material when:

(i) The quantity of material involved is greater than five times the lowest annual limit on intake specified in appendix B of §§ 20.1001–20.2401 of 10 CFR part 20 for the material; and

(ii) The damage affects the integrity of the licensed material or its container.

(c) *Preparation and submission of reports.* Reports made by licensees in response to the requirements of this section must be made as follows:

(1) Licensees shall make reports required by paragraphs (a) and (b) of this section by telephone to the NRC Operations Center.[1] To the extent that the information is available at the time of notification, the information provided in these reports must include:

(i) The caller's name and call back telephone number;

[1] The commercial telephone number for the NRC Operations Center is (301) 816–5100.

(ii) A description of the event, including date and time;

(iii) The exact location of the event;

(iv) The isotopes, quantities, and chemical and physical form of the licensed material involved; and

(v) Any personnel radiation exposure data available.

(2) *Written report.* Each licensee who makes a report required by paragraph (a) or (b) of this section shall submit a written follow-up report within 30 days of the initial report. Written reports prepared pursuant to other regulations may be submitted to fulfill this requirement if the reports contain all of the necessary information and the appropriate distribution is made. These written reports must be sent to the NRC's Document Control Desk by an appropriate method listed in § 40.5, with a copy to the appropriate NRC regional office listed in appendix D to part 20 of this chapter. The reports must include the following:

(i) A description of the event, including the probable cause and the manufacturer and model number (if applicable) of any equipment that failed or malfunctioned;

(ii) The exact location of the event;

(iii) The isotopes, quantities, and chemical and physical form of the licensed material involved;

(iv) Date and time of the event;

(v) Corrective actions taken or planned and the results of any evaluations or assessments; and

(vi) The extent of exposure of individuals to radiation or to radioactive materials without identification of individuals by name.

(3) The provisions of § 40.60 do not apply to licensees subject to the notification requirements in § 50.72. They do apply to those part 50 licensees possessing material licensed under part 40 who are not subject to the notification requirements in § 50.72.

[56 FR 40768, Aug. 16, 1991, as amended at 59 FR 14086, Mar. 25, 1994; 68 FR 58807, Oct. 10, 2003]

§ 40.61 Records.

(a) Each person who receives source or byproduct material pursuant to a license issued pursuant to the regulations in this part shall keep records showing the receipt, transfer, and disposal of this source or byproduct material as follows:

(1) The licensee shall retain each record of receipt of source or byproduct material as long as the material is possessed and for three years following transfer or disposition of the source or byproduct material.

(2) The licensee who transferred the material shall retain each record of transfer of source or byproduct material until the Commission terminates each license that authorizes the activity that is subject to the recordkeeping requirement.

(3) The licensee shall retain each record of disposal of source or byproduct material until the Commission terminates each license that authorizes the activity that is subject to the recordkeeping requirement.

(4) If source or byproduct material is combined or mixed with other licensed material and subsequently treated in a manner that makes direct correlation of a receipt record with a transfer, export, or disposition record impossible, the licensee may use evaluative techniques (such as first-in-first-out), to make the records that are required by this part account for 100 percent of the material received.

(b) The licensee shall retain each record that is required by the regulations in this part or by license condition for the period specified by the appropriate regulation or license condition. If a retention period is not otherwise specified by regulation or license condition, each record must be maintained until the Commission terminates the license that authorizes the activity that is subject to the recordkeeping requirement.

(c)(1) Records which must be maintained pursuant to this part may be the original or reproduced copy or microform if the reproduced copy or microform is duly authenticated by authorized personnel and the microform is capable of producing a clear and legible copy after storage for the period specified by Commission regulations. The record may also be stored in electronic media with the capability for producing legible, accurate, and complete records during the required retention period. Records such as letters, drawings, specifications, must include all pertinent information such as stamps, initials, and signatures. The licensee shall maintain adequate safeguards against tampering with and loss of records.

(2) If there is a conflict between the Commission's regulations in this part, license condition, or other written Commission approval or authorization pertaining to the retention period for the same type of record, the retention period specified in the regulations in this part for such records shall apply unless the Commission, pursuant to § 40.14 of this part, has granted a specific exemption from the record retention requirements specified in the regulations in this part.

(d) Prior to license termination, each licensee authorized to possess source material, in an unsealed form, shall forward the following records to the appropriate NRC Regional Office:

(1) Records of disposal of licensed material made under § 20.2002 (including burials authorized before January 28, 1981[1]), 20.2003, 20.2004, 20.2005; and

(2) Records required by § 20.2103(b)(4).

(e) If licensed activities are transferred or assigned in accordance with § 40.41(b), each licensee authorized to possess source material, in an unsealed form, shall transfer the following records to the new licensee and the new licensee will be responsible for maintaining these records until the license is terminated:

(1) Records of disposal of licensed material made under § 20.2002 (including burials authorized before January 28, 1981[1]), 20.2003, 20.2004, 20.2005; and

(2) Records required by § 20.2103(b)(4).

(f) Prior to license termination, each licensee shall forward the records required by § 40.36(f) to the appropriate NRC Regional Office.

[45 FR 65532, Oct. 3, 1980, as amended at 53 FR 19248, May 27, 1988; 61 FR 24674, May 16, 1996; 80 FR 45843, Aug. 3, 2015]

[1] A previous § 20.304 permitted burial of small quantities of licensed materials in soil before January 28, 1981, without specific Commission authorization. See § 20.304 contained in the 10 CFR, parts 0 to 199, edition revised as of January 1, 1981.

§ 40.62 Inspections.

(a) Each licensee shall afford to the Commission at all reasonable times opportunity to inspect source or byproduct material and the premises and facilities wherein source or byproduct material is used or stored.

(b) Each licensee shall make available to the Commission for inspection, upon reasonable notice, records kept by him pursuant to the regulations in this chapter.

[45 FR 65532, Oct. 3, 1980]

§ 40.63 Tests.

Each licensee shall perform, or permit the Commission to perform, such tests as the Commission deems appropriate or necessary for the administration of the regulations in this part, including tests of:

(a) Source or byproduct material;

(b) Facilities wherein source or byproduct material is utilized or stored;

(c) Radiation detection and monitoring instruments; and

(d) Other equipment and devices used in connection with the utilization and storage of source or byproduct material.

[45 FR 65533, Oct. 3, 1980]

§ 40.64 Reports.

(a) Except as specified in paragraphs (d) and (e) of this section, each specific licensee who transfers, receives, or adjusts the inventory in any manner, of uranium or thorium source material with foreign obligations by one kilogram or more; or who imports or exports one kilogram or more of uranium or thorium source material; or who uses one kilogram or more of any uranium or thorium source material in enrichment services, downblending uranium that has an initial enrichment of the U^{235} isotope of 10 percent or more, or in the fabrication of mixed-oxide fuels, shall complete a Nuclear Material Transaction Report in computer-readable format as specified in the instructions in NUREG/BR–0006 and NMMSS Report D–24, "Personal Computer Data Input for NRC Licensees." Each licensee who exports one kilogram or more of uranium or thorium source material shall complete in the format listed above the licensee's portion of the Nuclear Material Transaction Report unless there is indication of loss, theft, or diversion as discussed under paragraph (d) of this section, in which case both the licensee's and the foreign facility's information must be reported. Licensees who import one kilogram or more of uranium or thorium source material shall complete the supplier's and the licensee's portion of the Nuclear Material Transaction Report. Copies of the instructions may be obtained either by writing the U.S. Nuclear Regulatory Commission, Division of Fuel Cycle Safety, Safeguards, and Environmental Review, Washington, DC 20555–0001, or by e-mail to *RidsNmssFcss@nrc.gov*. Each licensee who transfers the material shall submit a Nuclear Material Transaction Report in computer-readable format as specified in the instructions no later than the close of business the next working day. Each licensee who receives the material shall submit a Nuclear Material Transaction Report in computer-readable format in accordance with instructions within ten (10) days after the material is received. The Commission's copy of the report must be submitted to the address specified in the instructions. These prescribed computer-readable forms replace the DOE/NRC Form 741 previously submitted in paper form.

(b) Except as specified in paragraphs (d) and (e) of this section, each licensee who:

(1) Possesses, or had possessed in the previous reporting period, at any one time and location, one kilogram or more of uranium or thorium source material with foreign obligations as defined in this part, shall document holdings as of September 30 of each year and submit to the Commission within 30 days, a statement of its source material inventory with foreign obligations as defined in this part. Alternatively, this information may be submitted with the licensee's material status reports on special nuclear material filed under part 72 or 74 of this chapter, as a statement of its source material inventory with foreign obligations as defined in this part. This statement must be submitted to the address specified in the reporting instructions in NUREG/BR–0007, and include the Reporting Identification Symbol (RIS) assigned by the Commission to the licensee.

(2) Possesses, or had possessed in the previous reporting period, one kilogram or more of uranium or thorium source material pursuant to the operation of enrichment services, downblending uranium that has an initial enrichment of the U^{235} isotope of 10 percent or more, or in the fabrication of mixed-oxide fuels shall complete and submit, in computer-readable format, Material Balance and Physical Inventory Listing Reports concerning all source material that the licensee has received, produced, possessed, transferred, consumed, disposed of, or lost. Reports must be submitted for each Reporting Identification Symbol (RIS) account including all holding accounts. Each licensee shall prepare and submit these reports as specified in the instructions in NUREG/BR–0007 and NMMSS Report D–24, "Personal Computer Data Input for NRC Licensees." These reports must document holdings as of September 30 of each year and must be submitted to the Commission within 30 days. Alternatively, these reports may be submitted with the licensee's material status reports on special nuclear material filed under parts 72 or 74 of this chapter. Copies of the reporting instructions may be obtained either by writing to the U.S. Nuclear Regulatory Commission, Division of Fuel Cycle Safety, Safeguards, and Environmental Review, Washington, DC 20555–0001, or by e-mail to *RidsNmssFcss@nrc.gov*. Each licensee required to report material balance, inventory, and/or foreign obligation information, as detailed in this part, shall resolve any discrepancies identified during the report review and reconciliation process within 30 calendar days of notification of a discrepancy identified by the NRC.

(c)(1) Except as specified in paragraph (d) of this section, each licensee who is authorized to possess uranium or thorium pursuant to a specific license shall notify the NRC Headquarters Operations Center by telephone, at the numbers listed in appendix A of part 73 of this chapter, of any incident in which an attempt has been made or is believed to have been made to commit a theft or unlawful diversion of more than 6.8 kilograms (kg) [15 pounds] of such material at any one time or more than 68 kg [150 pounds] of such material in any one calendar year.

(2) The licensee shall notify the NRC as soon as possible, but within 4 hours, of discovery of any incident in which an attempt has been made or is believed to have been made to commit a theft or unlawful diversion of such material. A copy of the written followup notification should also be made to the Director, Division of Security Policy, Office of Nuclear Security and Incident Response, by an appropriate method listed in § 40.5.

(3) The initial notification shall be followed within a period of sixty (60) days by a written followup notification submitted in accordance with § 40.5. A copy of the written followup notification shall also be sent to: ATTN: Document Control Desk, Director, Division of Security Policy, Office of Nuclear Security and Incident Response, U.S. Nuclear Regulatory Commission, Washington, DC 20555–0001.

(4) Subsequent to the submission of the written followup notification required by this paragraph, the licensee shall promptly update the written followup notification, in accordance with this paragraph, with any substantive additional information, which becomes available to the licensee, concerning an attempted or apparent theft or unlawful diversion of source material.

(d) The reports described in paragraphs (a), (b), and (c) of this section are not required for:

(1) Processed ores containing less than five (5) percent of uranium or thorium, or any combination of uranium or thorium, by dry weight;

(2) Thorium contained in magnesium-thorium and tungsten-thorium alloys, if the thorium content in the alloys does not exceed 4 percent by weight;

(3) Chemical catalysts containing uranium depleted in the U-235 isotope to 0.4 percent or less, if the uranium content of the catalyst does not exceed 15 percent by weight; or

(4) Any source material contained in non-nuclear end use devices or components, including but not limited to permanently installed shielding, teletherapy, radiography, X-ray, accelerator devices, or munitions.

(e) Any licensee who is required to submit inventory change reports and material status reports pursuant to part 75 of this chapter (pertaining to implementation of the US/IAEA Safeguards Agreement) shall prepare and submit such reports only as provided in §§ 75.34 and 75.35 of this chapter (instead of as provided in paragraphs (a) and (b) of this section).

[35 FR 12195, July 30, 1970, as amended at 36 FR 10938, June 5, 1971; 38 FR 1272, Jan. 11, 1973; 38 FR 2330, Jan. 24, 1973; 40 FR 8787, Mar. 3, 1975; 41 FR 16446, Apr. 19, 1976; 45 FR 50710, July 31, 1980; 49 FR 24707, June 15, 1984; 51 FR 9766, Mar. 21, 1986; 52 FR 31611, Aug. 21, 1987; 59 FR 35620, July 13, 1994; 68 FR 10364, Mar. 5, 2003; 68 FR 58807, Oct. 10, 2003; 73 FR 32461, June 9, 2008; 74 FR 62681, Dec. 1, 2009]

§ 40.65 Effluent monitoring reporting requirements.

(a) Each licensee authorized to possess and use source material in uranium milling, in production of uranium hexafluoride, or in a uranium enrichment facility shall:

(1) Within 60 days after January 1, 1976 and July 1, 1976, and within 60 days after January 1 and July 1 of each year thereafter, submit a report to the Director, Office of Nuclear Material Safety and Safeguards, using an appropriate method listed in § 40.5, with a copy to the appropriate NRC Regional Office shown in appendix D to part 20 of this chapter; the report must specify the quantity of each of the principal radionuclides released to unrestricted areas in liquid and in gaseous effluents during the previous six months of operation, and such other information as the Commission may require to estimate maximum potential annual radiation doses to the public resulting from effluent releases. If quantities of radioactive materials released during the reporting period are significantly above the licensee's design objectives previously reviewed as part of the licensing action, the report shall cover this specifically. On the basis of such reports and any additional information the Commission may obtain from the licensee or others, the Commission

may from time to time require the licensee to take such action as the Commission deems appropriate.

(2) [Reserved]

(b) [Reserved]

[40 FR 53230, Nov. 17, 1975, as amended at 41 FR 21627, May 27, 1976; 42 FR 25721, May 19, 1977; 52 FR 31611, Aug. 21, 1987; 57 FR 18391, Apr. 30, 1992; 68 FR 58807, Oct. 10, 2003; 73 FR 5721, Jan. 31, 2008]

§40.66 Requirements for advance notice of export shipments of natural uranium.

(a) Each licensee authorized to export natural uranium, other than in the form of ore or ore residue, in amounts exceeding 500 kilograms, shall notify the Director, Division of Security Policy, Office of Nuclear Security and Incident Response, by an appropriate method listed in §40.5.

The notification must be in writing and must be received at least 10 days before transport of the shipment commences at the shipping facility.

(b) The notification must include the following information:

(1) The name(s), address(es), and telephone number(s) of the shipper, receiver, and carrier(s);

(2) A physical description of the shipment;

(3) A listing of the mode(s) of shipment, transfer points, and routes to be used;

(4) The estimated date and time that shipment will commence and that each nation (other than the United States) along the route is scheduled to be entered; and

(5) A certification that arrangements have been made to notify the Division of Security Policy, Office of Nuclear Security and Incident Response when the shipment is received at the receiving facility.

(c) A licensee who needs to amend a notification may do so by telephoning the Division of Security Policy, Office of Nuclear Security and Incident Response, at the numbers for the NRC Headquarters Operations Center listed in Appendix A to part 73 of this chapter.

[52 FR 9651, Mar. 26, 1987, as amended at 53 FR 4110, Feb. 12, 1988; 60 FR 24551, May 9, 1995; 68 FR 58808, Oct. 10, 2003; 69 FR 76600, Dec. 22, 2004; 74 FR 62681, Dec. 1, 2009]

§40.67 Requirement for advance notice for importation of natural uranium from countries that are not party to the Convention on the Physical Protection of Nuclear Material.

(a) Each licensee authorized to import natural uranium, other than in the form of ore or ore residue, in amounts exceeding 500 kilograms, from countries not party to the Convention on the Physical Protection of Nuclear Material (see appendix F to Part 73 of this chapter) shall notify the Director, Division of Security Policy, Office of Nuclear Security and Incident Response, using an appropriate method listed in §40.5. The notification must be in writing and must be received at least 10 days before transport of the shipment commences at the shipping facility.

(b) The notification must include the following information:

(1) The name(s), address(es), and telephone number(s) of the shipper, receiver, and carrier(s);

(2) A physical description of the shipment;

(3) A listing of the mode(s) of shipment, transfer points, and routes to be used;

(4) The estimated date and time that shipment will commence and that each nation along the route is scheduled to be entered.

(c) The licensee shall notify the Division of Security Policy by telephone at (301) 816–5100 when the shipment is received in the receiving facility.

(d) A licensee who needs to amend a notification may do so by telephoning the Division of Security Policy at (301) 816–5100.

[52 FR 9652, Mar. 26, 1987, as amended at 53 FR 4110, Feb. 12, 1988; 60 FR 24551, May 9, 1995; 68 FR 58808, Oct. 10, 2003; 69 FR 76600, Dec. 22, 2004; 74 FR 62681, Dec. 1, 2009]

MODIFICATION AND REVOCATION OF LICENSES

§40.71 Modification and revocation of licenses.

(a) The terms and conditions of each license shall be subject to amendment, revision, or modification by reason of amendments to the Act, or by reason of rules, regulations, or orders issued in accordance with the Act.

(b) Any license may be revoked, suspended, or modified, in whole or in part, for any material false statement in the application or any statement of fact required under section 182 of the Act, or because of conditions revealed by such application or statement of fact or any report, record, or inspection or other means which would warrant the Commission to refuse to grant a license on an original application, or for violation of, or failure to observe any of, the terms and conditions of the Act, or the license, or of any rule, regulation or order of the Commission.

(c) Except in cases of willfulness or those in which the public health, interest or safety requires otherwise, no license shall be modified, suspended, or revoked unless, prior to the institution of proceedings therefor, facts or conduct which may warrant such action shall have been called to the attention of the licensee in writing and the licensee shall have been accorded opportunity to demonstrate or achieve compliance with all lawful requirements.

[26 FR 284, Jan. 14, 1961, as amended at 35 FR 11460, July 17, 1970; 48 FR 32328, July 15, 1983]

ENFORCEMENT

§ 40.81 Violations.

(a) The Commission may obtain an injunction or other court order to prevent a violation of the provisions of—

(1) The Atomic Energy Act of 1954, as amended;

(2) Title II of the Energy Reorganization Act of 1974, as amended; or

(3) A regulation or order issued pursuant to those Acts.

(b) The Commission may obtain a court order for the payment of a civil penalty imposed under section 234 of the Atomic Energy Act:

(1) For violations of—

(i) Sections 53, 57, 62, 63, 81, 82, 101, 103, 104, 107, or 109 of the Atomic Energy Act of 1954, as amended;

(ii) Section 206 of the Energy Reorganization Act;

(iii) Any rule, regulation, or order issued pursuant to the sections specified in paragraph (b)(1)(i) of this section;

(iv) Any term, condition, or limitation of any license issued under the sections specified in paragraph (b)(1)(i) of this section.

(2) For any violation for which a license may be revoked under section 186 of the Atomic Energy Act of 1954, as amended.

[57 FR 55074, Nov. 24, 1992]

§ 40.82 Criminal penalties.

(a) Section 223 of the Atomic Energy Act of 1954, as amended, provides for criminal sanctions for willful violation of, attempted violation of, or conspiracy to violate, any regulation issued under sections 161b, 161i, or 161o of the Act. For purposes of section 223, all the regulations in part 40 are issued under one or more of sections 161b, 161i, or 161o, except for the sections listed in paragraph (b) of this section.

(b) The regulations in part 40 that are not issued under sections 161b, 161i, or 161o for the purposes of section 223 are as follows: §§ 40.1, 40.2, 40.2a, 40.4, 40.5, 40.6, 40.8, 40.11, 40.12, 40.13, 40.14, 40.20, 40.21, 40.31, 40.32, 40.34, 40.43, 40.44, 40.45, 40.52, 40.54, 40.71, 40.81, and 40.82.

[57 FR 55075, Nov. 24, 1992, as amended at 78 FR 32341, May 29, 2013]

APPENDIX A TO PART 40—CRITERIA RELATING TO THE OPERATION OF URANIUM MILLS AND THE DISPOSITION OF TAILINGS OR WASTES PRODUCED BY THE EXTRACTION OR CONCENTRATION OF SOURCE MATERIAL FROM ORES PROCESSED PRIMARILY FOR THEIR SOURCE MATERIAL CONTENT

Introduction. Every applicant for a license to possess and use source material in conjunction with uranium or thorium milling, or byproduct material at sites formerly associated with such milling, is required by the provisions of § 40.31(h) to include in a license application proposed specifications relating to milling operations and the disposition of tailings or wastes resulting from such milling activities. This appendix establishes technical, financial, ownership, and long-term site surveillance criteria relating to the siting, operation, decontamination, decommissioning, and reclamation of mills and tailings or waste systems and sites at which such mills and systems are located. As used in this appendix, the term "as low as is reasonably achievable" has the same meaning as in § 20.1003 of this chapter.

In many cases, flexibility is provided in the criteria to allow achieving an optimum tailings disposal program on a site-specific basis. However, in such cases the objectives, technical alternatives and concerns which must be taken into account in developing a tailings program are identified. As provided by the provisions of § 40.31(h) applications for licenses must clearly demonstrate how the criteria have been addressed.

The specifications must be developed considering the expected full capacity of tailings or waste systems and the lifetime of mill operations. Where later expansions of systems or operations may be likely (for example, where large quantities of ore now marginally uneconomical may be stockpiled), the amenability of the disposal system to accommodate increased capacities without degradation in long-term stability and other performance factors must be evaluated.

Licensees or applicants may propose alternatives to the specific requirements in this appendix. The alternative proposals may take into account local or regional conditions, including geology, topography, hydrology, and meterology. The Commission may find that the proposed alternatives meet the Commission's requirements if the alternatives will achieve a level of stabilization and containment of the sites concerned, and a level of protection for public health, safety, and the environment from radiological and nonradiological hazards associated with the sites, which is equivalent to, to the extent practicable, or more stringent than the level which would be achieved by the requirements of this appendix and the standards promulgated by the Environmental Protection Agency in 40 CFR part 192, subparts D and E.

All site specific licensing decisions based on the criteria in this appendix or alternatives proposed by licensees or applicants will take into account the risk to the public health and safety and the environment with due consideration to the economic costs involved and any other factors the Commission determines to be appropriate. In implementing this appendix, the Commission will consider "practicable" and "reasonably achievable" as equivalent terms. Decisions involved these terms will take into account the state of technology, and the economics of improvements in relation to benefits to the public health and safety, and other societal and socioeconomic considerations, and in relation to the utilization of atomic energy in the public interest.

The following definitions apply to the specified terms as used in this appendix:

Aquifer means a geologic formation, group of formations, or part of a formation capable of yielding a significant amount of groundwater to wells or springs. Any saturated zone created by uranium or thorium recovery operations would not be considered an aquifer unless the zone is or potentially is (1) hydraulically interconnected to a natural aquifer, (2) capable of discharge to surface water, or (3) reasonably accessible because of migration beyond the vertical projection of the boundary of the land transferred for long-term government ownership and care in accordance with Criterion 11 of this appendix.

As expeditiously as practicable considering technological feasibility, for the purposes of Criterion 6A, means as quickly as possible considering: the physical characteristics of the tailings and the site; the limits of *available technology*; the need for consistency with mandatory requirements of other regulatory programs; and *factors beyond the control of the licensee*. The phrase permits consideration of the cost of compliance only to the extent specifically provided for by use of the term *available technology*.

Available technology means technologies and methods for emplacing a final radon barrier on uranium mill tailings piles or impoundments. This term shall not be construed to include extraordinary measures or techniques that would impose costs that are grossly excessive as measured by practice within the industry (or one that is reasonably analogous), (such as, by way of illustration only, unreasonable overtime, staffing, or transportation requirements, etc., considering normal practice in the industry; laser fusion of soils, etc.), provided there is reasonable progress toward emplacement of the final radon barrier. To determine grossly excessive costs, the relevant baseline against which cost shall be compared is the cost estimate for tailings impoundment closure contained in the licensee's approved reclamation plan, but costs beyond these estimates shall not automatically be considered grossly excessive.

Closure means the activities following operations to decontaminate and decommission the buildings and site used to produce byproduct materials and reclaim the tailings and/or waste disposal area.

Closure plan means the Commission approved plan to accomplish closure.

Compliance period begins when the Commission sets secondary groundwater protection standards and ends when the owner or operator's license is terminated and the site is transferred to the State or Federal agency for long-term care.

Dike means an embankment or ridge of either natural or man-made materials used to prevent the movement of liquids, sludges, solids or other materials.

Disposal area means the area containing byproduct materials to which the requirements of Criterion 6 apply.

Existing portion means that land surface area of an existing surface impoundment on which significant quantities of uranium or thorium byproduct materials had been placed prior to September 30, 1983.

Factors beyond the control of the licensee means factors proximately causing delay in meeting the schedule in the applicable reclamation plan for the timely emplacement of the final radon barrier notwithstanding the good faith efforts of the licensee to complete the barrier in compliance with paragraph (1) of Criterion 6A. These factors may include, but are not limited to—

(1) Physical conditions at the site;

(2) Inclement weather or climatic conditions;

(3) An act of God;

(4) An act of war;

(5) A judicial or administrative order or decision, or change to the statutory, regulatory, or other legal requirements applicable to the licensee's facility that would preclude or delay the performance of activities required for compliance;

(6) Labor disturbances;

(7) Any modifications, cessation or delay ordered by State, Federal, or local agencies;

(8) Delays beyond the time reasonably required in obtaining necessary government permits, licenses, approvals, or consent for activities described in the reclamation plan proposed by the licensee that result from agency failure to take final action after the licensee has made a good faith, timely effort to submit legally sufficient applications, responses to requests (including relevant data requested by the agencies), or other information, including approval of the reclamation plan; and

(9) An act or omission of any third party over whom the licensee has no control.

Final radon barrier means the earthen cover (or approved alternative cover) over tailings or waste constructed to comply with Criterion 6 of this appendix (excluding erosion protection features).

Groundwater means water below the land surface in a zone of saturation. For purposes of this appendix, groundwater is the water contained within an aquifer as defined above.

Leachate means any liquid, including any suspended or dissolved components in the liquid, that has percolated through or drained from the byproduct material.

Licensed site means the area contained within the boundary of a location under the control of persons generating or storing byproduct materials under a Commission license.

Liner means a continuous layer of natural or man-made materials, beneath or on the sides of a surface impoundment which restricts the downward or lateral escape of byproduct material, hazardous constituents, or leachate.

Milestone means an action or event that is required to occur by an enforceable date.

Operation means that a uranium or thorium mill tailings pile or impoundment is being used for the continued placement of byproduct material or is in standby status for such placement. A pile or impoundment is in operation from the day that byproduct material is first placed in the pile or impoundment until the day final closure begins.

Point of compliance is the site specific location in the uppermost aquifer where the groundwater protection standard must be met.

Reclamation plan, for the purposes of Criterion 6A, means the plan detailing activities to accomplish reclamation of the tailings or waste disposal area in accordance with the technical criteria of this appendix. The reclamation plan must include a schedule for reclamation milestones that are key to the completion of the final radon barrier including as appropriate, but not limited to, wind blown tailings retrieval and placement on the pile, interim stabilization (including dewatering or the removal of freestanding liquids and recontouring), and final radon barrier construction. (Reclamation of tailings must also be addressed in the closure plan; the detailed reclamation plan may be incorporated into the closure plan.)

Surface impoundment means a natural topographic depression, man-made excavation, or diked area, which is designed to hold an accumulation of liquid wastes or wastes containing free liquids, and which is not an injection well.

Uppermost aquifer means the geologic formation nearest the natural ground surface that is an aquifer, as well as lower aquifers that are hydraulically interconnected with this aquifer within the facility's property boundary.

I. Technical Criteria

Criterion 1—The general goal or broad objective in siting and design decisions is permanent isolation of tailings and associated contaminants by minimizing disturbance and dispersion by natural forces, and to do so without ongoing maintenance. For practical reasons, specific siting decisions and design standards must involve finite times (e.g., the longevity design standard in Criterion 6). The following site features which will contribute to such a goal or objective must be considered in selecting among alternative tailings disposal sites or judging the adequacy of existing tailings sites:

Remoteness from populated areas;

Hydrologic and other natural conditions as they contribute to continued immobilization and isolation of contaminants from groundwater sources; and

Potential for minimizing erosion, disturbance, and dispersion by natural forces over the long term.

The site selection process must be an optimization to the maximum extent reasonably achievable in terms of these features.

In the selection of disposal sites, primary emphasis must be given to isolation of tailings or wastes, a matter having long-term impacts, as opposed to consideration only of short-term convenience or benefits, such as minimization of transportation or land acquisition costs. While isolation of tailings will be a function of both site and engineering design, overriding consideration must be given to siting features given the long-term nature of the tailings hazards.

Tailings should be disposed of in a manner that no active maintenance is required to preserve conditions of the site.

Criterion 2—To avoid proliferation of small waste disposal sites and thereby reduce perpetual surveillance obligations, byproduct material from in situ extraction operations, such as residues from solution evaporation or contaminated control processes, and wastes from small remote above ground extraction operations must be disposed of at existing large mill tailings disposal sites; unless, considering the nature of the wastes, such as their volume and specific activity, and the costs and environmental impacts of transporting the wastes to a large disposal site, such offsite disposal is demonstrated to be impracticable or the advantages of onsite burial clearly outweigh the benefits of reducing the perpetual surveillance obligations.

Criterion 3—The "prime option" for disposal of tailings is placement below grade, either in mines or specially excavated pits (that is, where the need for any specially constructed retention structure is eliminated). The evaluation of alternative sites and disposal methods performed by mill operators in support of their proposed tailings disposal program (provided in applicants' environmental reports) must reflect serious consideration of this disposal mode. In some instances, below grade disposal may not be the most environmentally sound approach, such as might be the case if a groundwater formation is relatively close to the surface or not very well isolated by overlying soils and rock. Also, geologic and topographic conditions might make full below grade burial impracticable: For example, bedrock may be sufficiently near the surface that blasting would be required to excavate a disposal pit at excessive cost, and more suitable alternative sites are not available. Where full below grade burial is not practicable, the size of retention structures, and size and steepness of slopes associated exposed embankments must be minimized by excavation to the maximum extent reasonably achievable or appropriate given the geologic and hydrologic conditions at a site. In these cases, it must be demonstrated that an above grade disposal program will provide reasonably equivalent isolation of the tailings from natural erosional forces.

Criterion 4—The following site and design criteria must be adhered to whether tailings or wastes are disposed of above or below grade.

(a) Upstream rainfall catchment areas must be minimized to decrease erosion potential and the size of the floods which could erode or wash out sections of the tailings disposal area.

(b) Topographic features should provide good wind protection.

(c) Embankment and cover slopes must be relatively flat after final stabilization to minimize erosion potential and to provide conservative factors of safety assuring long-term stability. The broad objective should be to contour final slopes to grades which are as close as possible to those which would be provided if tailings were disposed of below grade; this could, for example, lead to slopes of about 10 horizontal to 1 vertical (10h:1v) or less steep. In general, slopes should not be steeper than about 5h:1v. Where steeper slopes are proposed, reasons why a slope less steep than 5h:1v would be impracticable should be provided, and compensating factors and conditions which make such slopes acceptable should be identified.

(d) A full self-sustaining vegetative cover must be established or rock cover employed to reduce wind and water erosion to negligible levels.

Where a full vegetative cover is not likely to be self-sustaining due to climatic or other conditions, such as in semi-arid and arid regions, rock cover must be employed on slopes of the impoundment system. The NRC will consider relaxing this requirement for extremely gentle slopes such as those which may exist on the top of the pile.

The following factors must be considered in establishing the final rock cover design to avoid displacement of rock particles by human and animal traffic or by natural processes, and to preclude undercutting and piping:

Shape, size, composition, and gradation of rock particles (excepting bedding material average particles size must be at least cobble size or greater);

Rock cover thickness and zoning of particles by size; and

Steepness of underlying slopes.

Individual rock fragments must be dense, sound, and resistant to abrasion, and must be free from cracks, seams, and other defects that would tend to unduly increase their destruction by water and frost actions. Weak, friable, or laminated aggregate may not be used.

Rock covering of slopes may be unnecessary where top covers are very thick (on the order of 10 m or greater); impoundment slopes are very gentle (on the order of 10 h:1v or less); bulk cover materials have inherently favorable erosion resistance characteristics; and, there is negligible drainage catchment area upstream of the pile and good wind protection as described in points (a) and (b) of this Criterion.

Furthermore, all impoundment surfaces must be contoured to avoid areas of concentrated surface runoff or abrupt or sharp changes in slope gradient. In addition to rock cover on slopes, areas toward which surface runoff might be directed must be well protected with substantial rock cover (rip rap). In addition to providing for stability of the impoundment system itself, overall stability, erosion potential, and geomorphology of surrounding terrain must be evaluated to assure that there are not ongoing or potential processes, such as gully erosion, which would lead to impoundment instability.

(e) The impoundment may not be located near a capable fault that could cause a maximum credible earthquake larger than that which the impoundment could reasonably be expected to withstand. As used in this criterion, the term "capable fault" has the same meaning as defined in section III(g) of appendix A of 10 CFR part 100. The term "maximum credible earthquake" means that earthquake which would cause the maximum vibratory ground motion based upon an evaluation of earthquake potential considering the regional and local geology and seismology and specific characteristics of local subsurface material.

(f) The impoundment, where feasible, should be designed to incorporate features which will promote deposition. For example, design features which promote deposition of sediment suspended in any runoff which flows into the impoundment area might be utilized; the object of such a design feature would be to enhance the thickness of cover over time.

Criterion 5—Criteria 5A–5D and new Criterion 13 incorporate the basic groundwater protection standards imposed by the Environmental Protection Agency in 40 CFR part 192, subparts D and E (48 FR 45926; October 7, 1983) which apply during operations and prior to the end of closure. Groundwater monitoring to comply with these standards is required by Criterion 7A.

5A(1)—The primary groundwater protection standard is a design standard for surface impoundments used to manage uranium and thorium byproduct material. Unless exempted under paragraph 5A(3) of this criterion, surface impoundments (except for an existing portion) must have a liner that is designed, constructed, and installed to prevent any migration of wastes out of the impoundment to the adjacent subsurface soil, groundwater, or surface water at any time during the active life (including the closure period) of the impoundment. The liner may be constructed of materials that may allow wastes to migrate into the liner (but not into the adjacent subsurface soil, groundwater, or surface water) during the active life of the facility, provided that impoundment closure includes removal or decontamination of all waste residues, contaminated containment system components (liners, etc.), contaminated subsoils, and structures and equipment contaminated with waste and leachate. For impoundments that will be closed with the liner material left in place, the liner must be constructed of materials that can prevent wastes from migrating into the liner during the active life of the facility.

5A(2)—The liner required by paragraph 5A(1) above must be—

(a) Constructed of materials that have appropriate chemical properties and sufficient strength and thickness to prevent failure due to pressure gradients (including static head and external hydrogeologic forces), physical contact with the waste or leachate to which they are exposed, climatic conditions, the stress of installation, and the stress of daily operation;

(b) Placed upon a foundation or base capable of providing support to the liner and resistance to pressure gradients above and below the liner to prevent failure of the liner due to settlement, compression, or uplift; and

(c) Installed to cover all surrounding earth likely to be in contact with the wastes or leachate.

5A(3)—The applicant or licensee will be exempted from the requirements of paragraph 5A(1) of this criterion if the Commission finds, based on a demonstration by the applicant or licensee, that alternate design and operating practices, including the closure plan, together with site characteristics will prevent the migration of any hazardous constituents into groundwater or surface water at any future time. In deciding whether to grant an exemption, the Commission will consider—

(a) The nature and quantity of the wastes;

(b) The proposed alternate design and operation;

(c) The hydrogeologic setting of the facility, including the attenuative capacity and thickness of the liners and soils present between the impoundment and groundwater or surface water; and

(d) All other factors which would influence the quality and mobility of the leachate produced and the potential for it to migrate to groundwater or surface water.

5A(4)—A surface impoundment must be designed, constructed, maintained, and operated to prevent overtopping resulting from normal or abnormal operations, overfilling, wind and wave actions, rainfall, or run-on; from malfunctions of level controllers, alarms, and other equipment; and from human error.

5A(5)—When dikes are used to form the surface impoundment, the dikes must be designed, constructed, and maintained with sufficient structural integrity to prevent massive failure of the dikes. In ensuring structural integrity, it must not be presumed that the liner system will function without leakage during the active life of the impoundment.

5B(1)—Uranium and thorium byproduct materials must be managed to conform to the following secondary groundwater protection standard: Hazardous constituents entering the groundwater from a licensed site must not exceed the specified concentration limits in the uppermost aquifer beyond the point of compliance during the compliance period. Hazardous constituents are those constituents identified by the Commission pursuant to paragraph 5B(2) of this criterion. Specified concentration limits are those limits established by the Commission as indicated in paragraph 5B(5) of this criterion. The Commission will also establish the point of compliance and compliance period on a site specific basis through license conditions and orders. The objective in selecting the point of compliance is to provide the earliest practicable warning that the impoundment is releasing hazardous constituents to the groundwater. The point of compliance must be selected to provide prompt indication of groundwater contamination on the hydraulically downgradient edge of the disposal area. The Commission shall identify hazardous constituents, establish concentration limits, set the compliance period, and may adjust the point of compliance if needed to accord with developed data and site information as to the flow of groundwater or contaminants, when the detection monitoring established under Criterion 7A indicates leakage of hazardous constituents from the disposal area.

5B(2)—A constituent becomes a hazardous constituent subject to paragraph 5B(5) only when the constituent meets all three of the following tests:

(a) The constituent is reasonably expected to be in or derived from the byproduct material in the disposal area;

(b) The constituent has been detected in the groundwater in the uppermost aquifer; and

(c) The constituent is listed in Criterion 13 of this appendix.

5B(3)—Even when constituents meet all three tests in paragraph 5B(2) of this criterion, the Commission may exclude a detected constituent from the set of hazardous constituents on a site specific basis if it finds that the constituent is not capable of posing a substantial present or potential hazard to human health or the environment. In deciding whether to exclude constituents, the Commission will consider the following:

(a) Potential adverse effects on groundwater quality, considering—

(i) The physical and chemical characteristics of the waste in the licensed site, including its potential for migration;

(ii) The hydrogeological characteristics of the facility and surrounding land;

(iii) The quantity of groundwater and the direction of groundwater flow;

(iv) The proximity and withdrawal rates of groundwater users;

(v) The current and future uses of groundwater in the area;

(vi) The existing quality of groundwater, including other sources of contamination and their cumulative impact on the groundwater quality;

(vii) The potential for health risks caused by human exposure to waste constituents;

(viii) The potential damage to wildlife, crops, vegetation, and physical structures caused by exposure to waste constituents;

(ix) The persistence and permanence of the potential adverse effects.

(b) Potential adverse effects on hydraulically-connected surface water quality, considering—

(i) The volume and physical and chemical characteristics of the waste in the licensed site;

(ii) The hydrogeological characteristics of the facility and surrounding land;

(iii) The quantity and quality of groundwater, and the direction of groundwater flow;

(iv) The patterns of rainfall in the region;

(v) The proximity of the licensed site to surface waters;

(vi) The current and future uses of surface waters in the area and any water quality standards established for those surface waters;

(vii) The existing quality of surface water, including other sources of contamination and the cumulative impact on surface-water quality;

(viii) The potential for health risks caused by human exposure to waste constituents;

(ix) The potential damage to wildlife, crops, vegetation, and physical structures caused by exposure to waste constituents; and

(x) The persistence and permanence of the potential adverse effects.

5B(4)—In making any determinations under paragraphs 5B(3) and 5B(6) of this criterion about the use of groundwater in the area around the facility, the Commission will consider any identification of underground sources of drinking water and exempted aquifers made by the Environmental Protection Agency.

5B(5)—At the point of compliance, the concentration of a hazardous constituent must not exceed—

(a) The Commission approved background concentration of that constituent in the groundwater;

(b) The respective value given in the table in paragraph 5C if the constituent is listed in the table and if the background level of the constituent is below the value listed; or

(c) An alternate concentration limit established by the Commission.

5B(6)—Conceptually, background concentrations pose no incremental hazards and the drinking water limits in paragraph 5C state acceptable hazards but these two options may not be practically achievable at a specific site. Alternate concentration limits that present no significant hazard may be proposed by licensees for Commission consideration. Licensees must provide the basis for any proposed limits including consideration of practicable corrective actions, that limits are as low as reasonably achievable, and information on the factors the Commission must consider. The Commission will establish a site specific alternate concentration limit for a hazardous constituent as provided in paragraph 5B(5) of this criterion if it finds that the proposed limit is as low as reasonably achievable, after considering practicable corrective actions, and that the constituent will not pose a substantial present or potential hazard to human health or the environment as long as the alternate concentration limit is not exceeded. In making the present and potential hazard finding, the Commission will consider the following factors:

(a) Potential adverse effects on groundwater quality, considering—

(i) The physical and chemical characteristics of the waste in the licensed site including its potential for migration;

(ii) The hydrogeological characteristics of the facility and surrounding land;

(iii) The quantity of groundwater and the direction of groundwater flow;

(iv) The proximity and withdrawal rates of groundwater = users;

(v) The current and future uses of groundwater in the area;

(vi) The existing quality of groundwater, including other sources of contamination and their cumulative impact on the groundwater = quality;

(vii) The potential for health risks caused by human exposure to waste constituents;

(viii) The potential damage to wildlife, crops, vegetation, and physical structures caused by exposure to waste constituents;

(ix) The persistence and permanence of the potential adverse effects.

(b) Potential adverse effects on hydraulically-connected surface water quality, considering—

(i) The volume and physical and chemical characteristics of the waste in the licensed site;

(ii) The hydrogeological characteristics of the facility and surrounding land;

(iii) The quantity and quality of groundwater, and the direction of groundwater flow;

(iv) The patterns of rainfall in the region;

(v) The proximity of the licensed site to surface waters;

(vi) The current and future uses of surface waters in the area and any water quality standards established for those surface waters;

(vii) The existing quality of surface water including other sources of contamination and the cumulative impact on surface water quality;

(viii) The potential for health risks caused by human exposure to waste constituents;

(ix) The potential damage to wildlife, crops, vegetation, and physical structures caused by exposure to waste constituents; and

(x) The persistence and permanence of the potential adverse effects.

5C—MAXIMUM VALUES FOR GROUNDWATER PROTECTION

Constituent or property	Maximum concentration
Milligrams per liter:	
Arsenic	0.05
Barium	1.0
Cadmium	0.01
Chromium	0.05
Lead	0.05
Mercury	0.002
Selenium	0.01
Silver	0.05
Endrin (1,2,3,4,10,10-hexachloro-1,7 -expoxy-1,4,4a,5, 6,7,8,9a-octahydro-1, 4-endo, endo-5,8-dimethano naphthalene)	0.0002
Lindane (1,2,3,4,5,6-hexachlorocyclohexane, gamma isomer)	0.004
Methoxychlor (1,1,1-Trichloro-2,2-bis (p-methoxyphenylethane)	0.1
Toxaphene (C_{10} H_{10} $C1_6$, Technical chlorinated camphene, 67–69 percent chlorine)	0.005
2,4-D (2,4-Dichlorophenoxyacetic acid)	0.1
2,4,5-TP Silvex (2,4,5-Trichlorophenoxypropionic acid)	0.01
Picocuries per liter:	
Combined radium-226 and radium-228	5
Gross alpha—particle activity (excluding radon and uranium when producing uranium byproduct material or radon and thorium when producing thorium byproduct material)	15

5D—If the groundwater protection standards established under paragraph 5B(1) of this criterion are exceeded at a licensed site, a corrective action program must be put into operation as soon as is practicable, and in no event later than eighteen (18) months after the Commission finds that the standards have been exceeded. The licensee shall submit the proposed corrective action program and supporting rationale for Commission approval prior to putting the program into operation, unless otherwise directed by the Commission. The objective of the program is to return hazardous constituent concentration levels in groundwater to the concentration limits set as standards. The licensee's proposed program must address removing the hazardous constituents that have entered the groundwater at the point of compliance or treating them in place. The program must also address removing or treating in place any hazardous constituents that exceed concentration limits in groundwater between the point of compliance and the downgradient facility property boundary. The licensee shall continue corrective action measures to the extent necessary to achieve and maintain compliance with the groundwater protection standard. The Commission will determine when the licensee may terminate corrective action measures based on data from the groundwater monitoring program and other information that provide reasonable assurance that the groundwater protection standard will not be exceeded.

5E—In developing and conducting groundwater protection programs, applicants and licensees shall also consider the following:

(1) Installation of bottom liners (Where synthetic liners are used, a leakage detection system must be installed immediately below the liner to ensure major failures are detected if they occur. This is in addition to the groundwater monitoring program conducted as provided in Criterion 7. Where clay liners are proposed or relatively thin, in-situ clay soils are to be relied upon for seepage control, tests must be conducted with representative tailings solutions and clay materials to confirm that no significant deterioration of permeability or stability properties will occur with continuous exposure of clay to tailings solutions. Tests must be run for a sufficient period of time to reveal any effects if they are going to occur (in some cases deterioration has been observed to occur rather rapidly after about nine months of exposure)).

(2) Mill process designs which provide the maximum practicable recycle of solutions and conservation of water to reduce the net input of liquid to the tailings impoundment.

(3) Dewatering of tailings by process devices and/or in-situ drainage systems (At new sites, tailings must be dewatered by a drainage system installed at the bottom of the impoundment to lower the phreatic surface and reduce the driving head of seepage, unless tests show tailings are not amenable to such a system. Where in-situ dewatering is to be conducted, the impoundment bottom must be graded to assure that the drains are at a low point. The drains must be protected by suitable filter materials to assure that drains remain free running. The drainage system must also be adequately sized to assure good drainage).

(4) Neutralization to promote immobilization of hazardous constituents.

5F—Where groundwater impacts are occurring at an existing site due to seepage, action must be taken to alleviate conditions that lead to excessive seepage impacts and restore groundwater quality. The specific seepage control and groundwater protection method, or combination of methods, to be used must be worked out on a site-specific basis. Technical specifications must be prepared to control installation of seepage control systems. A quality assurance, testing, and inspection program, which includes supervision by a qualified engineer or scientist, must be established to assure the specifications are met.

5G—In support of a tailings disposal system proposal, the applicant/operator shall supply information concerning the following:

(1) The chemical and radioactive characteristics of the waste solutions.

(2) The characteristics of the underlying soil and geologic formations particularly as they will control transport of contaminants and solutions. This includes detailed information concerning extent, thickness, uniformity, shape, and orientation of underlying strata. Hydraulic gradients and conductivities of the various formations must be determined. This information must be gathered from borings and field survey methods taken within the proposed impoundment area and in surrounding areas where contaminants might migrate to groundwater. The information gathered on boreholes must include both geologic and geophysical logs in sufficient number and degree of sophistication to allow determining significant discontinuities, fractures, and channeled deposits of high hydraulic conductivity. If field survey methods are used, they should be in addition to and calibrated with borehole logging. Hydrologic parameters such as permeability may not be determined on the basis of laboratory analysis of samples alone; a sufficient amount of field testing (e.g., pump tests) must be conducted to assure actual field properties are adequately understood. Testing must be conducted to allow estimating chemi-sorption attenuation properties of underlying soil and rock.

(3) Location, extent, quality, capacity and current uses of any groundwater at and near the site.

5H—Steps must be taken during stockpiling of ore to minimize penetration of radionuclides into underlying soils; suitable methods include lining and/or compaction of ore storage areas.

Criterion 6—(1) In disposing of waste byproduct material, licensees shall place an earthen cover (or approved alternative) over tailings or wastes at the end of milling operations and shall close the waste disposal area in accordance with a design[1] which provides

[1] In the case of thorium byproduct materials, the standard applies only to design. Monitoring for radon emissions from thorium byproduct materials after installation
Continued

reasonable assurance of control of radiological hazards to (i) be effective for 1,000 years, to the extent reasonably achievable, and, in any case, for at least 200 years, and (ii) limit releases of radon-222 from uranium byproduct materials, and radon-220 from thorium byproduct materials, to the atmosphere so as not to exceed an average[2] release rate of 20 picocuries per square meter per second (pCi/m^2 s) to the extent practicable throughout the effective design life determined pursuant to (1)(i) of this Criterion. In computing required tailings cover thicknesses, moisture in soils in excess of amounts found normally in similar soils in similar circumstances may not be considered. Direct gamma exposure from the tailings or wastes should be reduced to background levels. The effects of any thin synthetic layer may not be taken into account in determining the calculated radon exhalation level. If non-soil materials are proposed as cover materials, it must be demonstrated that these materials will not crack or degrade by differential settlement, weathering, or other mechanism, over long-term intervals.

(2) As soon as reasonably achievable after emplacement of the final cover to limit releases of radon-222 from uranium byproduct material and prior to placement of erosion protection barriers or other features necessary for long-term control of the tailings, the licensee shall verify through appropriate testing and analysis that the design and construction of the final radon barrier is effective in limiting releases of radon-222 to a level not exceeding 20 pCi/m^2s averaged over the entire pile or impoundment using the procedures described in 40 CFR part 61, appendix B, Method 115, or another method of verification approved by the Commission as being at least as effective in demonstrating the effectiveness of the final radon barrier.

(3) When phased emplacement of the final radon barrier is included in the applicable reclamation plan, the verification of radon-222 release rates required in paragraph (2) of this criterion must be conducted for each portion of the pile or impoundment as the final radon barrier for that portion is emplaced.

(4) Within ninety days of the completion of all testing and analysis relevant to the required verification in paragraphs (2) and (3) of this criterion, the uranium mill licensee shall report to the Commission the results detailing the actions taken to verify that levels of release of radon-222 do not exceed 20 pCi/m^2s when averaged over the entire pile or impoundment. The licensee shall maintain records until termination of the license documenting the source of input parameters including the results of all measurements on which they are based, the calculations and/or analytical methods used to derive values for input parameters, and the procedure used to determine compliance. These records shall be kept in a form suitable for transfer to the custodial agency at the time of transfer of the site to DOE or a State for long-term care if requested.

(5) Near surface cover materials (*i.e.*, within the top three meters) may not include waste or rock that contains elevated levels of radium; soils used for near surface cover must be essentially the same, as far as radioactivity is concerned, as that of surrounding surface soils. This is to ensure that surface radon exhalation is not significantly above background because of the cover material itself.

(6) The design requirements in this criterion for longevity and control of radon releases apply to any portion of a licensed and/or disposal site unless such portion contains a concentration of radium in land, averaged over areas of 100 square meters, which, as a result of byproduct material, does not exceed the background level by more than: (i) 5 picocuries per gram (pCi/g) of radium-226, or, in the case of thorium byproduct material, radium-228, averaged over the first 15 centimeters (cm) below the surface, and (ii) 15 pCi/g of radium-226, or, in the case of thorium byproduct material, radium-228, averaged over 15-cm thick layers more than 15 cm below the surface.

Byproduct material containing concentrations of radionuclides other than radium in soil, and surface activity on remaining structures, must not result in a total effective dose equivalent (TEDE) exceeding the dose from cleanup of radium contaminated soil to the above standard (benchmark dose), and must be at levels which are as low as is reasonably achievable. If more than one residual radionuclide is present in the same 100-square-meter area, the sum of the ratios for each radionuclide of concentration present to the concentration limit will not exceed "1" (unity). A calculation of the potential peak annual TEDE within 1000 years to the average member of the critical group that would result from applying the radium standard (not including radon) on the site must be submitted for approval. The use of decommissioning plans with benchmark doses which exceed 100 mrem/yr, before application of ALARA, requires the approval of the Commission after consideration of the

---

of an appropriately designed cover is not required.

[2] This average applies to the entire surface of each disposal area over a period of a least one year, but a period short compared to 100 years. Radon will come from both byproduct materials and from covering materials. Radon emissions from covering materials should be estimated as part of developing a closure plan for each site. The standard, however, applies only to emissions from byproduct materials to the atmosphere.

recommendation of the NRC staff. This requirement for dose criteria does not apply to sites that have decommissioning plans for soil and structures approved before June 11, 1999.

(7) The licensee shall also address the nonradiological hazards associated with the wastes in planning and implementing closure. The licensee shall ensure that disposal areas are closed in a manner that minimizes the need for further maintenance. To the extent necessary to prevent threats to human health and the environment, the licensee shall control, minimize, or eliminate post-closure escape of nonradiological hazardous constituents, leachate, contaminated rainwater, or waste decomposition products to the ground or surface waters or to the atmosphere.

Criterion 6A—(1) For impoundments containing uranium byproduct materials, the final radon barrier must be completed *as expeditiously as practicable considering technological feasibility* after the pile or impoundment ceases operation in accordance with a written, Commission-approved reclamation plan. (The term *as expeditiously as practicable considering technological feasibility* as specifically defined in the Introduction of this appendix includes factors beyond the control of the licensee.) Deadlines for completion of the final radon barrier and, if applicable, the following interim milestones must be established as a condition of the individual license: windblown tailings retrieval and placement on the pile and interim stabilization (including dewatering or the removal of freestanding liquids and recontouring). The placement of erosion protection barriers or other features necessary for long-term control of the tailings must also be completed in a timely manner in accordance with a written, Commission-approved reclamation plan.

(2) The Commission may approve a licensee's request to extend the time for performance of milestones related to emplacement of the final radon barrier if, after providing an opportunity for public participation, the Commission finds that the licensee has adequately demonstrated in the manner required in paragraph (2) of Criterion 6 that releases of radon-222 do not exceed an average of 20 pCi/m²s. If the delay is approved on the basis that the radon releases do not exceed 20 pCi/m²s, a verification of radon levels, as required by paragraph (2) of Criterion 6, must be made annually during the period of delay. In addition, once the Commission has established the date in the reclamation plan for the milestone for completion of the final radon barrier, the Commission may extend that date based on cost if, after providing an opportunity for public participation, the Commission finds that the licensee is making good faith efforts to emplace the final radon barrier, the delay is consistent with the definition of *available technology*, and the radon releases caused by the delay will not result in a significant incremental risk to the public health.

(3) The Commission may authorize by license amendment, upon licensee request, a portion of the impoundment to accept uranium byproduct material or such materials that are similar in physical, chemical, and radiological characteristics to the uranium mill tailings and associated wastes already in the pile or impoundment, from other sources, during the closure process. No such authorization will be made if it results in a delay or impediment to emplacement of the final radon barrier over the remainder of the impoundment in a manner that will achieve levels of radon-222 releases not exceeding 20 pCi/m²s averaged over the entire impoundment. The verification required in paragraph (2) of Criterion 6 may be completed with a portion of the impoundment being used for further disposal if the Commission makes a final finding that the impoundment will continue to achieve a level of radon-222 releases not exceeding 20 pCi/m² s averaged over the entire impoundment. In this case, after the final radon barrier is complete except for the continuing disposal area, (a) only byproduct material will be authorized for disposal, (b) the disposal will be limited to the specified existing disposal area, and (c) this authorization will only be made after providing opportunity for public participation. Reclamation of the disposal area, as appropriate, must be completed in a timely manner after disposal operations cease in accordance with paragraph (1) of Criterion 6; however, these actions are not required to be complete as part of meeting the deadline for final radon barrier construction.

Criterion 7—At least one full year prior to any major site construction, a preoperational monitoring program must be conducted to provide complete baseline data on a milling site and its environs. Throughout the construction and operating phases of the mill, an operational monitoring program must be conducted to measure or evaluate compliance with applicable standards and regulations; to evaluate performance of control systems and procedures; to evaluate environmental impacts of operation; and to detect potential long-term effects.

7A—The licensee shall establish a detection monitoring program needed for the Commission to set the site-specific groundwater protection standards in paragraph 5B(1) of this appendix. For all monitoring under this paragraph the licensee or applicant will propose for Commission approval as license conditions which constituents are to be monitored on a site specific basis. A detection monitoring program has two purposes. The initial purpose of the program is to detect leakage of hazardous constituents from the disposal area so that the need to set groundwater protection standards is monitored. If leakage is detected, the second purpose of the program is to generate data and information needed for the Commission to establish the standards under Criterion 5B. The data and information must provide a sufficient basis to identify those hazardous constituents which require concentration limit standards and to enable the Commission to set the limits for those constituents and the compliance period. They may also need to provide the basis for adjustments to the point of compliance. For licenses in effect September 30, 1983, the detection monitoring programs must have been in place by October 1, 1984. For licenses issued after September 30, 1983, the detection monitoring programs must be in place when specified by the Commission in orders or license conditions. Once groundwater protection standards have been established pursuant to paragraph 5B(1), the licensee shall establish and implement a compliance monitoring program. The purpose of the compliance monitoring program is to determine that the hazardous constituent concentrations in groundwater continue to comply with the standards set by the Commission. In conjunction with a corrective action program, the licensee shall establish and implement a corrective action monitoring program. The purpose of the corrective action monitoring program is to demonstrate the effectiveness of the corrective actions. Any monitoring program required by this paragraph may be based on existing monitoring programs to the extent the existing programs can meet the stated objective for the program.

Criterion 8—Milling operations must be conducted so that all airborne effluent releases are reduced to levels as low as is reasonably achievable. The primary means of accomplishing this must be by means of emission controls. Institutional controls, such as extending the site boundary and exclusion area, may be employed to ensure that offsite exposure limits are met, but only after all practicable measures have been taken to control emissions at the source. Notwithstanding the existence of individual dose standards, strict control of emissions is necessary to assure that population exposures are reduced to the maximum extent reasonably achievable and to avoid site contamination. The greatest potential sources of offsite radiation exposure (aside from radon exposure) are dusting from dry surfaces of the tailings disposal area not covered by tailings solution and emissions from yellowcake drying and packaging operations. During operations and prior to closure, radiation doses from radon emissions from surface impoundments of uranium or thorium byproduct materials must be kept as low as is reasonably achievable.

Checks must be made and logged hourly of all parameters (e.g., differential pressures and scrubber water flow rates) that determine the efficiency of yellowcake stack emission control equipment operation. The licensee shall retain each log as a record for three years after the last entry in the log is made. It must be determined whether or not conditions are within a range prescribed to ensure that the equipment is operating consistently near peak efficiency; corrective action must be taken when performance is outside of prescribed ranges. Effluent control devices must be operative at all times during drying and packaging operations and whenever air is exhausting from the yellowcake stack. Drying and packaging operations must terminate when controls are inoperative. When checks indicate the equipment is not operating within the range prescribed for peak efficiency, actions must be taken to restore parameters to the prescribed range. When this cannot be done without shutdown and repairs, drying and packaging operations must cease as soon as practicable. Operations may not be restarted after cessation due to off-normal performance until needed corrective actions have been identified and implemented. All these cessations, corrective actions, and restarts must be reported to the appropriate NRC regional office as indicated in Criterion 8A, in writing, within ten days of the subsequent restart.

To control dusting from tailings, that portion not covered by standing liquids must be wetted or chemically stabilized to prevent or minimize blowing and dusting to the maximum extent reasonably achievable. This requirement may be relaxed if tailings are effectively sheltered from wind, such as may be the case where they are disposed of below grade and the tailings surface is not exposed to wind. Consideration must be given in planning tailings disposal programs to methods which would allow phased covering and reclamation of tailings impoundments because this will help in controlling particulate and radon emissions during operation. To control dusting from diffuse sources, such as tailings and ore pads where automatic controls do not apply, operators shall develop written operating procedures specifying the methods of control which will be utilized.

Milling operations producing or involving thorium byproduct material must be conducted in such a manner as to provide reasonable assurance that the annual dose equivalent does not exceed 25 millirems to the whole body, 75 millirems to the thyroid, and 25 millirems to any other organ of any member of the public as a result of exposures to the planned discharge of radioactive materials, radon-220 and its daughters excepted, to the general environment.

Uranium and thorium byproduct materials must be managed so as to conform to the applicable provisions of title 40 of the Code of Federal Regulations, part 440, "Ore Mining and Dressing Point Source Category: Effluent Limitations Guidelines and New Source Performance Standards, subpart C, Uranium, Radium, and Vanadium Ores Subcategory," as codified on January 1, 1983.

Criterion 8A—Daily inspections of tailings or waste retention systems must be conducted by a qualified engineer or scientist and documented. The licensee shall retain the documentation for each daily inspection as a record for three years after the documentation is made. The appropriate NRC regional office as indicated in appendix D to 10 CFR part 20 of this chapter, or the Director, Office of Nuclear Material Safety and Safeguards, U.S. Nuclear Regulatory Commission, Washington, DC 20555–0001, must be immediately notified of any failure in a tailings or waste retention system that results in a release of tailings or waste into unrestricted areas, or of any unusual conditions (conditions not contemplated in the design of the retention system) that if not corrected could indicate the potential or lead to failure of the system and result in a release of tailings or waste into unrestricted areas.

II. FINANCIAL CRITERIA

Criterion 9—(a) Financial surety arrangements must be established by each mill operator before the commencement of operations to assure that sufficient funds will be available to carry out the decontamination and decommissioning of the mill and site and for the reclamation of any tailings or waste disposal areas. The amount of funds to be ensured by such surety arrangements must be based on Commission-approved cost estimates in a Commission-approved plan, or a proposed revision to the plan submitted to the Commission for approval, if the proposed revision contains a higher cost estimate, for:

(1) Decontamination and decommissioning of mill buildings and the milling site to levels which allow unrestricted use of these areas upon decommissioning, and

(2) The reclamation of tailings and/or waste areas in accordance with technical criteria delineated in Section I of this appendix.

(b) Each cost estimate must contain—

(1) A detailed cost estimate for decontamination, decommissioning, and reclamation, in an amount reflecting:

(i) The cost of an independent contractor to perform the decontamination, decommissioning and reclamation activities; and

(ii) An adequate contingency factor;

(2) An estimate of the amount of radioactive contamination in onsite subsurface material;

(3) Identification of and justification for using the key assumptions contained in the DCE; and

(4) A description of the method of assuring funds for decontamination, decommissioning, and reclamation.

(c) The licensee shall submit this plan in conjunction with an environmental report that addresses the expected environmental impacts of the milling operation, decommissioning and tailings reclamation, and evaluates alternatives for mitigating these impacts. The plan must include a signed original of the financial instrument obtained to satisfy the surety arrangement requirements of this criterion (unless a previously submitted and approved financial instrument continues to cover the cost estimate for decommissioning). The surety arrangement must also cover the cost estimate and the payment of the charge for long-term surveillance and control required by Criterion 10 of this section.

(d) To avoid unnecessary duplication and expense, the Commission may accept financial sureties that have been consolidated with financial or surety arrangements established to meet requirements of other Federal or state agencies and/or local governing bodies for decommissioning, decontamination, reclamation, and long-term site surveillance and control, provided such arrangements are considered adequate to satisfy these requirements and that the portion of the surety which covers the decommissioning and reclamation of the mill, mill tailings site and associated areas, and the long-term funding charge is clearly identified and committed for use in accomplishing these activities.

(e) The licensee's surety mechanism will be reviewed annually by the Commission to assure, that sufficient funds would be available for completion of the reclamation plan if the work had to be performed by an independent contractor.

(f) The amount of surety liability should be adjusted to recognize any increases or decreases resulting from:

(1) Inflation;

(2) Changes in engineering plans;

(3) Activities performed;

(4) Spills, leakage or migration of radioactive material producing additional contamination in onsite subsurface material that must be remediated to meet applicable remediation criteria;

(5) Waste inventory increasing above the amount previously estimated;

(6) Waste disposal costs increasing above the amount previously estimated;

(7) Facility modifications;

(8) Changes in authorized possession limits;

(9) Actual remediation costs that exceed the previous cost estimate;

(10) Onsite disposal; and

(11) Any other conditions affecting costs.

(g) Regardless of whether reclamation is phased through the life of the operation or takes place at the end of operations, an appropriate portion of surety liability must be retained until final compliance with the reclamation plan is determined.

(h) The appropriate portion of surety liability retained until final compliance with the reclamation plan is determined will be at least sufficient at all times to cover the costs of decommissioning and reclamation of the areas that are expected to be disturbed before the next license renewal. The term of the surety mechanism must be open ended, unless it can be demonstrated that another arrangement would provide an equivalent level of assurance. This assurance would be provided with a surety instrument which is written for a specified time (e.g., 5 years) and which must be automatically renewed unless the surety notifies the beneficiary (the Commission or the State regulatory agency) and the principal (the licensee) with reasonable time (e.g., 90 days) before the renewal date of their intention not to renew. In such a situation the surety requirement still exists and the licensee would be required to submit an acceptable replacement surety within a brief time to allow at least 60 days for the regulatory agency to collect.

(i) Proof of forfeiture must not be necessary to collect the surety. In the event that the licensee can not provide an acceptable replacement surety within the required time, the surety shall be automatically collected before its expiration. The surety instrument must provide for collection of the full face amount immediately on demand without reduction for any reason, except for trustee fees and expenses provided for in a trust agreement, and that the surety will not refuse to make full payment. The conditions described previously would have to be clearly stated on any surety instrument which is not open-ended, and must be agreed to by all parties. Financial surety arrangements generally acceptable to the Commission are:

(1) Trust funds;

(2) Surety bonds;

(3) Irrevocable letters of credit; and

(4) Combinations of the financial surety arrangements or other types of arrangements as may be approved by the Commission. If a trust is not used, then a standby trust must be set up to receive funds in the event the Commission or State regulatory agency exercises its right to collect the surety. The surety arrangement and the surety or trustee, as applicable, must be acceptable to the Commission. Self insurance, or any arrangement which essentially constitutes self insurance (e.g., a contract with a State or Federal agency), will not satisfy the surety requirement because this provides no additional assurance other than that which already exists through license requirements.

Criterion 10—A minimum charge of $250,000 (1978 dollars) to cover the costs of long-term surveillance must be paid by each mill operator to the general treasury of the United States or to an appropriate State agency prior to the termination of a uranium or thorium mill license.

If site surveillance or control requirements at a particular site are determined, on the basis of a site-specific evaluation, to be significantly greater than those specified in Criterion 12 (e.g., if fencing is determined to be necessary), variance in funding requirements may be specified by the Commission. In any case, the total charge to cover the costs of long-term surveillance must be such that, with an assumed 1 percent annual real interest rate, the collected funds will yield interest in an amount sufficient to cover the annual costs of site surveillance. The total charge will be adjusted annually prior to actual payment to recognize inflation. The inflation rate to be used is that indicated by the change in the Consumer Price Index published by the U.S. Department of Labor, Bureau of Labor Statistics.

III. SITE AND BYPRODUCT MATERIAL OWNERSHIP

Criterion 11—A. These criteria relating to ownership of tailings and their disposal sites become effective on November 8, 1981, and apply to all licenses terminated, issued, or renewed after that date.

B. Any uranium or thorium milling license or tailings license must contain such terms and conditions as the Commission determines necessary to assure that prior to termination of the license, the licensee will comply with ownership requirements of this criterion for sites used for tailings disposal.

C. Title to the byproduct material licensed under this part and land, including any interests therein (other than land owned by the United States or by a State) which is used for the disposal of any such byproduct material, or is essential to ensure the long term stability of such disposal site, must be transferred to the United States or the State in which such land is located, at the option of such State. In view of the fact that physical isolation must be the primary means of long-term control, and Government land ownership is a desirable supplementary measure, ownership of certain severable subsurface interests (for example, mineral rights) may be determined to be unnecessary to protect the public health and safety and the environment. In any case, however, the applicant/operator must demonstrate a serious effort to obtain such subsurface rights, and must, in the event that certain rights cannot be obtained, provide notification in local public land records of the fact that the land is being used for the disposal of radioactive material and is subject to either an NRC general or specific license prohibiting the disruption and disturbance of the tailings. In some rare cases, such as may occur with deep burial where no ongoing site surveillance will be required, surface land ownership transfer requirements may be waived. For licenses issued before November

8, 1981, the Commission may take into account the status of the ownership of such land, and interests therein, and the ability of a licensee to transfer title and custody thereof to the United States or a State.

D. If the Commission subsequent to title transfer determines that use of the surface or subsurface estates, or both, of the land transferred to the United States or to a State will not endanger the public health, safety, welfare, or environment, the Commission may permit the use of the surface or subsurface estates, or both, of such land in a manner consistent with the provisions provided in these criteria. If the Commission permits such use of such land, it will provide the person who transferred such land with the right of first refusal with respect to such use of such land.

E. Material and land transferred to the United States or a State in accordance with this Criterion must be transferred without cost to the United States or a State other than administrative and legal costs incurred in carrying out such transfer.

F. The provisions of this part respecting transfer of title and custody to land and tailings and wastes do not apply in the case of lands held in trust by the United States for any Indian Tribe or lands owned by such Indian Tribe subject to a restriction against alienation imposed by the United States. In the case of such lands which are used for the disposal of byproduct material, as defined in this part, the licensee shall enter into arrangements with the Commission as may be appropriate to assure the long-term surveillance of such lands by the United States.

IV. Long-Term Site Surveillance

Criterion 12—The final disposition of tailings, residual radioactive material, or wastes at milling sites should be such that ongoing active maintenance is not necessary to preserve isolation. As a minimum, annual site inspections must be conducted by the government agency responsible for long-term care of the disposal site to confirm its integrity and to determine the need, if any, for maintenance and/or monitoring. Results of the inspections for all the sites under the licensee's jurisdiction will be reported to the Commission annually within 90 days of the last site inspection in that calendar year. Any site where unusual damage or disruption is discovered during the inspection, however, will require a preliminary site inspection report to be submitted within 60 days. On the basis of a site specific evaluation, the Commission may require more frequent site inspections if necessary due to the features of a particular disposal site. In this case, a preliminary inspection report is required to be submitted within 60 days following each inspection.

V. Hazardous Constituents

Criterion 13—Secondary groundwater protection standards required by Criterion 5 of this appendix are concentration limits for individual hazardous constituents. The following list of constituents identifies the constituents for which standards must be set and complied with if the specific constituent is reasonably expected to be in or derived from the byproduct material and has been detected in groundwater. For purposes of this appendix, the property of gross alpha activity will be treated as if it is a hazardous constituent. Thus, when setting standards under paragraph 5B(5) of Criterion 5, the Commission will also set a limit for gross alpha activity. The Commission does not consider the following list imposed by 40 CFR part 192 to be exhaustive and may determine other constituents to be hazardous on a case-by-case basis, independent of those specified by the U.S. Environmental Protection Agency in part 192.

Hazardous Constituents

Acetonitrile (Ethanenitrile)
Acetophenone (Ethanone, 1-phenyl)
3-(alpha-Acetonylbenzyl)-4-hydroxycoumarin and salts (Warfarin)
2-Acetylaminofluorene (Acetamide, N-(9H-fluoren-2-yl)-)
Acetyl chloride (Ethanoyl chloride)
1-Acetyl-2-thiourea (Acetamide, N-(aminothioxomethyl)-)
Acrolein (2-Propenal)
Acrylamide (2-Propenamide)
Acrylonitrile (2-Propenenitrile)
Aflatoxins
Aldrin (1,2,3,4,10,10-Hexachloro-1,4,4a,5,8,8a,8b-hexahydro-endo, exo-1,4:5,8-Dimethanonaphthalene)
Allyl alcohol (2-Propen-1-ol)
Aluminum phosphide
4-Aminobiphenyl ([1,1′-Biphenyl]-4-amine)
6-Amino-1,1a,2,8,8a,8b-hexahydro-8-(hydroxymethyl)-8a-methoxy-5 methyl-carbamate azirino[2′,3′:3,4]pyrrolo[1,2-a]indole-4,7-dione, (ester) (Mitomycin C) (Azirino[2′3′:3,4]pyrrolo(1,2-a)indole-4,7-dione, 6-amino-8-[((amino-cabonyl)oxy)methyl]-1,1a,2,8,8a,8b-hexahydro-8a methoxy-5-methy-)
5-(Aminomethyl)-3-isoxazolol (3(2H)-Isoxazolone, 5-(aminomethyl)-) 4-Aminopyridine (4-Pyridinamine)
Amitrole (1H-1,2,4-Triazol-3-amine)
Aniline (Benzenamine)
Antimony and compounds, N.O.S.[3]
Aramite (Sulfurous acid, 2-chloroethyl-, 2-[4-(1,1-dimethylethyl) phenoxy]-1-methylethyl ester)

[3]The abbreviation N.O.S. (not otherwise specified) signifies those members of the general class not specifically listed by name in this list.

Arsenic and compounds, N.O.S.[3]
Arsenic acid (Orthoarsenic acid)
Arsenic pentoxide (Arsenic (V) oxide)
Arsenic trioxide (Arsenic (III) oxide)
Auramine (Benzenamine, 4,4′-carbonimidoylbis[N,N-Dimethyl-, monohydrochloride)
Azaserine (L-Serine, diazoacetate (ester))
Barium and compounds, N.O.S.[3]
Barium cyanide
Benz[c]acridine (3,4-Benzacridine)
Benz[a]anthracene (1,2-Benzanthracene)
Benzene (Cyclohexatriene)
Benzenearsonic acid (Arsonic acid, phenyl-)
Benzene, dichloromethyl- (Benzal chloride)
Benzenethiol (Thiophenol)
Benzidine ([1,1′-Biphenyl]-4,4′ diamine)
Benzo[b]fluoranthene (2,3-Benzofluoranthene)
Benzo[j]fluoranthene (7,8-Benzofluoranthene)
Benzo[a]pyrene (3,4-Benzopyrene)
p-Benzoquinone (1,4-Cyclohexadienedione)
Benzotrichloride (Benzene, trichloromethyl)
Benzyl chloride (Benzene, (chloromethyl)-)
Beryllium and compounds, N.O.S.[3]
Bis(2-chloroethoxy)methane (Ethane, 1,1′-[methylenebis(oxy)]bis[2-chloro-])
Bis(2-chloroethyl) ether (Ethane, 1,1′-oxybis[2-chloro-])
N,N-Bis(2-chloroethyl)-2-naphthylamine (Chlornaphazine)
Bis(2-chloroisopropyl) ether (Propane, 2,2′-oxybis[2-chloro-])
Bis(chloromethyl) ether (Methane, oxybis[chloro-])
Bis(2-ethylhexyl) phthalate (1,2-Benzenedicarboxylic acid, bis(2-ethylhexyl) ester)
Bromoacetone (2-Propanone, 1-bromo-)
Bromomethane (Methyl bromide)
4-Bromophenyl phenyl ether (Benzene, 1-bromo-4-phenoxy-)
Brucine (Strychnidin-10-one, 2,3-dimethoxy-)
2-Butanone peroxide (Methyl ethyl ketone, peroxide)
Butyl benzyl phthalate (1,2-Benzenedicarboxylic acid, butyl phenylmethyl ester)
2-sec-Butyl-4,6-dinitrophenol (DNBP) (Phenol, 2,4-dinitro-6-(1-methylpropyl)-)
Cadmium and compounds, N.O.S.[3]
Calcium chromate (Chromic acid, calcium salt)
Calcium cyanide
Carbon disulfide (Carbon bisulfide)
Carbon oxyfluoride (Carbonyl fluoride)
Chloral (Acetaldehyde, trichloro-)
Chlorambucil (Butanoic acid, 4-[bis(2-chloroethyl)amino]benzene-)
Chlordane (alpha and gamma isomers) (4,7-Methanoindan, 1,2,4,5,6,7,8,8-octachloro-3,4,7,7a-tetrahydro-) (alpha and gamma isomers)
Chlorinated benzenes, N.O.S.[3]
Chlorinated ethane, N.O.S.[3]
Chlorinated fluorocarbons, N.O.S.[3]
Chlorinated naphthalene, N.O.S.[3]
Chlorinated phenol, N.O.S.[3]
Chloroacetaldehyde (Acetaldehyde, chloro-)
Chloroalkyl ethers, N.O.S.[3]
p-Chloroaniline (Benzenamine, 4-chloro-)
Chlorobenzene (Benzene, chloro-)
Chlorobenzilate (Benzeneacetic acid, 4-chloro-alpha-(4-chlorophenyl)-alpha-hydroxy-,ethyl ester)
p-Chloro-m-cresol (Phenol, 4-chloro-3-methyl)
1-Chloro-2,3-epoxypropane (Oxirane, 2-(chloromethyl)-)
2-Chloroethyl vinyl ether (Ethene, (2-chloroethoxy)-)
Chloroform (Methane, trichloro-)
Chloromethane (Methyl chloride)
Chloromethyl methyl ether (Methane, chloromethoxy-)
2-Chloronaphthalene (Naphthalene, betachloro-)
2-Chlorophenol (Phenol, o-chloro-)
1-(o-Chlorophenyl)thiourea (Thiourea, (2-chlorophenyl)-)
3-Chloropropionitrile (Propanenitrile, 3-chloro-)
Chromium and compounds, N.O.S.[3]
Chrysene (1,2-Benzphenanthrene)
Citrus red No. 2 (2-Naphthol, 1-[(2,5-dimethoxyphenyl)azo]-)
Coal tars
Copper cyanide
Creosote (Creosote, wood)
Cresols (Cresylic acid) (Phenol, methyl-)
Crotonaldehyde (2-Butenal)
Cyanides (soluble salts and complexes), N.O.S.[3]
Cyanogen (Ethanedinitrile)
Cyanogen bromide (Bromine cyanide)
Cyanogen chloride (Chlorine cyanide)
Cycasin (beta-D-Glucopyranoside, (methyl-ONN-azoxy)methyl-)
2-Cyclohexyl-4,6-dinitrophenol (Phenol, 2-cyclohexyl-4,6-dinitro-)
Cyclophosphamide (2H-1,3,2,-Oxazaphosphorine, [bis(2-chloroethyl) amino]-tetrahydro-,2-oxide)
Daunomycin (5,12-Naphthacenedione, (8S-cis)-8-acetyl-10-[(3-amino-2,3,6-trideoxy)-alpha-L-lyxo-hexopyranosyl)oxy]-7,8,9,10-tetrahydro-6,8,11-trihydroxy-1-methoxy-)
DDD (Dichlorodiphenyldichloroethane) (Ethane, 1,1-dichloro-2,2-bis(p-chlorophenyl)-)
DDE (Ethylene, 1,1-dichloro-2,2-bis(4-chlorophenyl)-)
DDT (Dichlorodiphenyltrichloroethane) (Ethane, 1,1,1-trichloro-2,2-bis (p-chlorophenyl)-)
Diallate (S-(2,3-dichloroallyl) diisopropylthiocarbamate)
Dibenz[a,h]acridine (1,2,5,6-Dibenzacridine)
Dibenz[a,j]acridine (1,2,7,8-Dibenzacridine)
Dibenz[a,h]anthracene (1,2,5,6-Dibenzanthracene)
7H-Dibenzo[c,g]carbazole (3,4,5,6-Dibenzcarbazole)
Dibenzo[a,e]pyrene (1,2,4,5-Dibenzpyrene)
Dibenzo[a,h]pyrene (1,2,5,6-Dibenzpyrene)

Dibenzo[a,i]pyrene (1,2,7,8-Dibenzpyrene)
1,2-Dibromo-3-chloropropane (Propane, 1,2-dibromo-3-chloro-)
1,2-Dibromoethane (Ethylene dibromide)
Dibromomethane (Methylene bromide)
Di-n-butyl phthalate (1,2-Benzenedicarboxylic acid, dibutyl ester)
o-Dichlorobenzene (Benzene, 1,2-dichloro-)
m-Dichlorobenzene (Benzene, 1,3-dichloro-)
p-Dichlorobenzene (Benzene, 1,4-dichlor-)
Dichlorobenzene, N.O.S.[3] (Benzene, dichloro-, N.O.S.[3])
3,3′-Dichlorobenzidine ([1,1′-Biphenyl]-4,4′-diamine, 3,3′-dichloro-)
1,4-Dichloro-2-butene (2-Butene, 1,4-dichloro-)
Dichlorodifluoromethane (Methane, dichlorodifluoro-)
1,1-Dichloroethane (Ethylidene dichloride)
1,2-Dichloroethane (Ethylene dichloride)
trans-1,2-Dichloroethene (1,2-Dichloroethylene)
Dichloroethylene, N.O.S.[3] (Ethene, dichloro-, N.O.S.[3])
1,1-Dichloroethylene (Ethene, 1,1-dichloro-)
Dichloromethane (Methylene chloride)
2,4-Dichlorophenol (Phenol, 2,4-dichloro-)
2,6-Dichlorophenol (Phenol, 2,6-dichloro-)
2,4-Dichlorophenoxyacetic acid (2,4-D), salts and esters (Acetic acid, 2,4-dichlorophenoxy-, salts and esters)
Dichlorophenylarsine (Phenyl dichloroarsine)
Dichloropropane, N.O.S.[3] (Propane, dichloro-, N.O.S.[3])
1,2-Dichloropropane (Propylene dichloride)
Dichloropropanol, N.O.S.[3] (Propanol, dichloro-, N.O.S.[3])
Dichloropropene, N.O.S.[3] (Propene, dichloro-, N.O.S.[3])
1,3-Dichloropropene (1-Propene, 1,3-dichloro-)
Dieldin (1,2,3,4,10,10-hexachloro-6,7-epoxy-1,4,4a,5,6,7,8,8a-octa-hydro-endo, exo-1,4:5,8-Dimethanonaphthalene)
1,2:3,4-Diepoxybutane (2,2′-Bioxirane)
Diethylarsine (Arsine, diethyl-)
N,N-Diethylhydrazine (Hydrazine, 1,2-diethyl)
O,O-Diethyl S-methyl ester of phosphorodithioic acid (Phosphorodithioic acid, O,O-diethyl S-methyl ester)
O,O-Diethylphosphoric acid, O-p-nitrophenyl ester (Phosphoric acid, diethyl p-nitrophenyl ester)
Diethyl phthalate (1,2-Benzenedicarboxylic acid, diethyl ester)
O,O-Diethyl O-2-pyrazinyl phosphorothioate (Phosphorothioic acid, O,O-diethyl O-pyrazinyl ester)
Diethylstilbesterol (4,4′-Stilbenediol,alpha,alpha-diethyl, bis(dihydrogen phosphate, (E)-)
Dihydrosafrole (Benzene, 1,2-methylenedioxy-4-propyl-)
3,4-Dihydroxy-alpha-(methylamino)methyl benzyl alcohol (1,2-Benzenediol, 4-[1-hydroxy-2-(methylamino)ethyl]-)
DiIsopropylfluorophosphate (DFP) (Phosphorofluoridic acid, bis(1-methylethyl) ester)
Dimethoate (Phosphorodithioic acid, O,O-dimethyl S-[2-(methylamino)-2-oxoethyl] ester)
3,3′-Dimethoxybenzidine ([1,1′-Biphenyl]- 4,4′-diamine, 3-3′-dimethoxy-)
p-Dimethylaminoazobenzene (Benzenamine, N,N-dimethyl-4-(phenylazo)-)
7,12-Dimethylbenz[a]anthracene (1,2-Benzanthracene, 7,12-dimethyl-)
3,3′-Dimethylbenzidine ([1,1′-Biphenyl]-4,4′-diamine, 3,3′-dimethyl-)
Dimethylcarbamoyl chloride (Carbamoyl chloride, dimethyl-)
1,1-Dimethylhydrazine (Hydrazine, 1,1-dimethyl-)
1,2-Dimethylhydrazine (Hydrazine, 1,2-dimethyl-)
3,3-Dimethyl-1-(methylthio)-2-butanone, O-[(methylamino) carbonyl] oxime (Thiofanox)
alpha,alpha-Dimethylphenethylamine (Ethanamine, 1,1-dimethyl-2-phenyl-)
2,4-Dimethylphenol (Phenol, 2,4-dimethyl-)
Dimethyl phthalate (1,2-Benzenedicarboxylic acid, dimethyl ester)
Dimethyl sulfate (Sulfuric acid, dimethyl ester)
Dinitrobenzene, N.O.S.[3] (Benzene, dinitro-, N.O.S.[3])
4,6-Dinitro-o-cresol and salts (Phenol, 2,4-dinitro-6-methyl-, and salts)
2,4-Dinitrophenol (Phenol, 2,4-dinitro-)
2,4-Dinitrotoluene (Benzene, 1-methyl-2,4-dinitro-)
2,6-Dinitrotoluene (Benzene, 1-methyl-2,6-dinitro-)
Di-n-octyl phthalate (1,2-Benzenedicarboxylic acid, dioctyl ester)
1,4-Dioxane (1,4-Diethylene oxide)
Diphenylamine (Benzenamine, N-phenyl-)
1,2-Diphenylhydrazine (Hydrazine, 1,2-diphenyl-)
Di-n-propylnitrosamine (N-Nitroso-di-n-propylamine)
Disulfoton (O,O-diethyl S-[2-(ethylthio)ethyl] phosphorodithioate)
2,4-Dithiobiuret (Thioimidodicarbonic diamide)
Endosulfan (5-Norbornene, 2,3-dimethanol, 1,4,5,6,7,7-hexachloro-, cyclic sulfite)
Endrin and metabolites (1,2,3,4,10,10-hexachloro-6,7-epoxy-1,4,4a,5,6,7,8,8a-octahydro-endo,endo-1,4:5,8-dimethanonaphthalene, and metabolites)
Ethyl carbamate (Urethan) (Carbamic acid, ethyl ester)
Ethyl cyanide (propanenitrile)
Ethylenebisdithiocarbamic acid, salts and esters (1,2-Ethanediyl-biscarbamodithioic acid, salts and esters)
Ethyleneimine (Aziridine)
Ethylene oxide (Oxirane)
Ethylenethiourea (2-Imidazolidinethione)

Ethyl methacrylate (2-Propenoic acid, 2-methyl-, ethyl ester)
Ethyl methanesulfonate (Methanesulfonic acid, ethyl ester)
Fluoranthene (Benzo[j,k]fluorene)
Fluorine
2-Fluoroacetamide (Acetamide, 2-fluoro-)
Fluoroacetic acid, sodium salt (Acetic acid, fluoro-, sodium salt)
Formaldehyde (Methylene oxide)
Formic acid (Methanoic acid)
Glycidylaldehyde (1-Propanol-2,3-epoxy)
Halomethane, N.O.S. [3]
Heptachlor (4,7-Methano-1H-indene, 1,4,5,6,7,8,8-heptachloro-3a,4,7,7a-tetrahydro-)
Heptachlor epoxide (alpha, beta, and gamma isomers) (4,7-Methano-1H-indene, 1,4,5,6,7,8,8-heptachloro-2,3-epoxy-3a,4,7,7-tetrahydro-, alpha, beta, and gamma isomers)
Hexachlorobenzene (Benzene, hexachloro-)
Hexachlorobutadiene (1,3-Butadiene, 1,1,2,3,4,4-hexachloro-)
Hexachlorocyclohexane (all isomers) (Lindane and isomers)
Hexachlorocyclopentadiene (1,3-Cyclopentadiene, 1,2,3,4,5,5-hexachloro-)
Hexachloroethane (Ethane, 1,1,1,2,2,2-hexachloro-)
1,2,3,4,10,10-Hexachloro-1,4,4a,5,8,8a-hexahydro-1,4:5,8-endo,endo-dimethanonaphthalene (Hexachlorohexahydro-endo,endo-dimethanonaphthalene)
Hexachlorophene (2,2′-Methylenebis(3,4,6-trichlorophenol)
Hexachloropropene (1-Propene, 1,1,2,3,3,3-hexachloro-)
Hexaethyl tetraphosphate (Tetraphosphoric acid, hexaethyl ester)
Hydrazine (Diamine)
Hydrocyanic acid (Hydrogen cyanide)
Hydrofluoric acid (Hydrogen fluoride)
Hydrogen sulfide (Sulfur hydride)
Hydroxydimethylarsine oxide (Cacodylic acid)
Indeno (1,2,3-cd)pyrene (1,10-(1,2-phenylene)pyrene)
Iodomethane (Methyl iodide)
Iron dextran (Ferric dextran)
Isocyanic acid, methyl ester (Methyl isocyanate)
Isobutyl alcohol (1-Propanol, 2-methyl-)
Isosafrole (Benzene, 1,2-methylenedioxy-4-allyl-)
Kepone (Decachlorooctahydro-1,3,4-Methano-2H-cyclobuta[cd]pentalen-2-one)
Lasiocarpine (2-Butenoic acid, 2-methyl-, 7-[(2,3-dihydroxy-2-(1-methoxyethyl)-3-methyl-1-oxobutoxy)methyl]-2,3,5,7a-tetrahydro-1H-pyrrolizin-1-yl ester)
Lead and compounds, N.O.S. [3]
Lead acetate (Acetic acid, lead salt)
Lead phosphate (Phosphoric acid, lead salt)
Lead subacetate (Lead, bis(acetato-0)tetrahydroxytri-)
Maleic anhydride (2,5-Furandione)
Maleic hydrazide (1,2-Dihydro-3,6-pyridazinedione)
Malononitrile (Propanedinitrile)
Melphalan (Alanine, 3-[p-bis(2-chloroethyl)amino]phenyl-,L-)
Mercury fulminate (Fulminic acid, mercury salt)
Mercury and compounds, N.O.S. [3]
Methacrylonitrile (2-Propenenitrile, 2-methyl-)
Methanethiol (Thiomethanol)
Methapyrilene (Pyridine. 2-[(2-dimethylamino)ethyl]-2-thenylamino-)
Metholmyl (Acetimidic acid, N-[(methylcarbamoyl)oxy]thio-, methyl ester)
Methoxychlor (Ethane, 1,1,1-trichloro-2,2′-bis(p-methoxyphenyl)-)
2-Methylaziridine (1,2-Propylenimine)
3-Methylcholanthrene (Benz[j]aceanthrylene, 1,2-dihydro-3-methyl-)
Methyl chlorocarbonate (Carbonochloridic acid, methyl ester)
4,4′-Methylenebis(2-chloroaniline) (Benzenamine, 4,4′-methylenebis- (2-chloro-)
Methyl ethyl ketone (MEK) (2-Butanone)
Methyl hydrazine (Hydrazine, methyl-)
2-Methyllactonitrile (Propanenitrile, 2-hydroxy-2-methyl-)
Methyl methacrylate (2-Propenoic acid, 2-methyl-, methyl ester)
Methyl methanesulfonate (Methanesulfonic acid, methyl ester)
2-Methyl-2-(methylthio)propionaldehyde-o-(methylcarbonyl) oxime (Propanal, 2-methyl-2-(methylthio)-, 0-[(methylamino)carbonyl]oxime)
N-Methyl-N′-nitro-N-nitrosoguanidine (Guanidine, N-nitroso-N-methyl-N′- nitro-)
Methyl parathion (0,0-dimethyl 0-(4-nitrophenyl) phosphorothioate)
Methylthiouracil (4-IH-Pyrimidinone, 2,3-dihydro-6-methyl-2-thioxo-)
Molybdenum and compounds, N.O.S. [3]
Mustard gas (Sulfide, bis(2-chloroethyl)-)
Naphthalene
1,4-Naphthoquinone (1,4-Naphthalenedione)
1-Naphthylamine (alpha-Naphthylamine)
2-Naphthylamine (beta-Naphthylamine)
1-Naphthyl-2-thiourea (Thiourea, 1-naphthalenyl-)
Nickel and compounds, N.O.S. [3]
Nickel carbonyl (Nickel tetracarbonyl)
Nickel cyanide (Nickel (II) cyanide)
Nicotine and salts (Pyridine, (S)-3-(1-methyl-2-pyrrolidinyl)-, and salts)
Nitric oxide (Nitrogen (II) oxide)
p-Nitroaniline (Benzenamine, 4-nitro-)
Nitrobenzine (Benzene, nitro-)
Nitrogen dioxide (Nitrogen (IV) oxide)
Nitrogen mustard and hydrochloride salt (Ethanamine, 2-chloro-, N-(2-chloroethyl)-N-methyl-, and hydrochloride salt)
Nitrogen mustard N-Oxide and hydrochloride salt (Ethanamine, 2-chloro-, N-(2-

chloroethyl)-N-methyl-, and hydrochloride salt)
Nitroglycerine (1,2,3-Propanetriol, trinitrate)
4-Nitrophenol (Phenol, 4-nitro-)
4-Nitroquinoline-1-oxide (Quinoline, 4-nitro-1-oxide-)
Nitrosamine, N.O.S.[3]
N-Nitrosodi-n-butylamine (1-Butanamine, N-butyl-N-nitroso-)
N-Nitrosodiethanolamine (Ethanol, 2,2′-(nitrosoimino)bis-)
N-Nitrosodiethylamine (Ethanamine, N-ethyl-N-nitroso-)
N-Nitrosodimethylamine (Dimethylnitrosamine)
N-Nitroso-N-ethylurea (Carbamide, N-ethyl-N-nitroso-)
N-Nitrosomethylethylamine (Ethanamine, N-methyl-N-nitroso-)
N-Nitroso-N-methylurea (Carbamide, N-methyl-N-nitroso-)
N-Nitroso-N-methylurethane (Carbamic acid, methylnitroso-, ethyl ester)
N-Nitrosomethylvinylamine (Ethenamine, N-methyl-N-nitroso-)
N-Nitrosomorpholine (Morpholine, N-nitroso-)
N-Nitrosonornicotine (Nornicotine, N-nitroso-)
N-Nitrosopiperidine (Pyridine, hexahydro-, N-nitroso-)
Nitrosopyrrolidine (Pyrrole, tetrahydro-, N-nitroso-)
N-Nitrososarcosine (Sarcosine, N-nitroso-)
5-Nitro-o-toluidine (Benzenamine, 2-methyl-5-nitro-)
Octamethylpyrophosphoramide (Diphosphoramide, octamethyl-)
Osmium tetroxide (Osmium (VIII) oxide)
7-Oxabicyclo[2.2.1]heptane-2,3-dicarboxylic acid (Endothal)
Paraldehyde (1,3,5-Trioxane, 2,4,6-trimethyl-)
Parathion (Phosphorothioic acid, O,O-diethyl O-(p-nitrophenyl)ester)
Pentachlorobenzene (Benzene, pentachloro-)
Pentachloroethane (Ethane, pentachloro-)
Pentachloronitrobenzene (PCNB) (Benzene, pentachloronitro-)
Pentachlorophenol (Phenol, pentachloro-)
Phenacetin (Acetamide, N-(4-ethoxyphenyl)-)
Phenol (Benzene, hydroxy-)
Phenylenediamine (Benzenediamine)
Phenylmercury acetate (Mercury, acetatophenyl-)
N-Phenylthiourea (Thiourea, phenyl-)
Phosgene (Carbonyl chloride)
Phosphine (Hydrogen phosphide)
Phosphorodithioic acid, O,O-diethyl S-[(ethylthio)methyl] ester (Phorate)
Phosphorothioic acid, O,O-dimethyl O-[p-((dimethylamino)sulfonyl)phenyl] ester (Famphur)
Phthalic acid esters, N.O.S.[3] (Benzene, 1,2-dicarboxylic acid, esters, N.O.S.[3])
Phthalic anhydride (1,2-Benzenedicarboxylic acid anhydride)
2-Picoline (Pyridine, 2-methyl-)
Polychlorinated biphenyl, N.O.S.[3]
Potassium cyanide
Potassium silver cyanide (Argentate(1-), dicyano-, potassium)
Pronamide (3,5-Dichloro-N-(1,1-dimethyl-2-propynyl)benzamide)
1,3-Propane sultone (1,2-Oxathiolane, 2,2-dioxide)
n-Propylamine (1-Propanamine)
Propylthiouracil (Undecamethylenediamine, N,N′-bis(2-chlorobenzyl-), dihydrochloride)
2-Propyn-1-ol (Propargyl alcohol)
Pyridine
Radium-226 and -228
Reserpine (Yohimban-16-carboxylic acid, 11,17-dimethoxy-18-[3,4,5-trimethoxybenzoyl)oxy]-, methyl ester)
Resorcinol (1,3-Benzenediol)
Saccharin and salts (1,2-Benzoisothiazolin-3-one, 1,1-dioxide, and salts)
Safrole (Benzene, 1,2-methylenedioxy-4-allyl-)
Selenious acid (Selenium dioxide)
Selenium and compounds, N.O.S.[3]
Selenium sulfide (Sulfur selenide)
Selenourea (Carbamimidoselenoic acid)
Silver and compounds, N.O.S.[3]
Silver cyanide
Sodium cyanide
Streptozotocin (D-Glucopyranose, 2-deoxy-2-(3-methyl-3-nitrosoureido)-)
Strontium sulfide
Strychnine and salts (Strychnidin-10-one, and salts)
1,2,4,5-Tetrachlorobenzene (Benzene, 1,2,4,5-tetrachloro-)
2,3,7,8-Tetrachlorodibenzo-p-dioxin (TCDD) (Dibenzo-p-dioxin, 2,3,7,8-tetrachloro-)
Tetrachloroethane, N.O.S.[3] (Ethane, tetrachloro-, N.O.S.[3])
1,1,1,2-Tetrachlorethane (Ethane, 1,1,1,2-tetrachloro-)
1,1,2,2-Tetrachlorethane (Ethane, 1,1,2,2-tetrachloro-)
Tetrachloroethane (Ethene, 1,1,2,2-tetrachloro-)
Tetrachloromethane (Carbon tetrachloride)
2,3,4,6,-Tetrachlorophenol (Phenol, 2,3,4,6-tetrachloro-)
Tetraethyldithiopyrophosphate (Dithiopyrophosphoric acid, tetraethyl-ester)
Tetraethyl lead (Plumbane, tetraethyl-)
Tetraethylpyrophosphate (Pyrophosphoric acide, tetraethyl ester)
Tetranitromethane (Methane, tetranitro-)
Thallium and compounds, N.O.S.[3]
Thallic oxide (Thallium (III) oxide)
Thallium (I) acetate (Acetic acid, thallium (I) salt)
Thallium (I) carbonate (Carbonic acid, dithallium (I) salt)
Thallium (I) chloride
Thallium (I) nitrate (Nitric acid, thallium (I) salt)
Thallium selenite

Thallium (I) sulfate (Sulfuric acid, thallium (I) salt)
Thioacetamide (Ethanethioamide)
Thiosemicarbazide (Hydrazinecarbothioamide)
Thiourea (Carbamide thio-)
Thiuram (Bis(dimethylthiocarbamoyl) disulfide)
Thorium and compounds, N.O.S.,[3] when producing thorium byproduct material
Toluene (Benzene, methyl-)
Toluenediamine (Diaminotoluene)
o-Toluidine hydrochloride (Benzenamine, 2-methyl-, hydrochloride)
Tolylene diisocyanate (Benzene, 1,3-diisocyanatomethyl-)
Toxaphene (Camphene, octachloro-)
Tribromomethane (Bromoform)
1,2,4-Trichlorobenzene (Benzene, 1,2,4-trichloro-)
1,1,1-Trichloroethane (Methyl chloroform)
1,1,2-Trichloroethane (Ethane, 1,1,2-trichloro-)
Trichloroethene (Trichloroethylene)
Trichloromethanethiol (Methanethiol, trichloro-)
Trichloromonofluoromethane (Methane, trichlorofluoro-)
2,4,5-Trichlorophenol (Phenol, 2,4,5-trichloro-)
2,4,6-Trichlorophenol (Phenol, 2,4,6-trichloro-)
2,4,5-Trichlorophenoxyacetic acid (2,4,5-T) (Acetic acid, 2,4,5-trichlorophenoxy-)
2,4,5-Trichlorophenoxypropionic acid (2,4,5-TP) (Silvex) (Propionoic acid, 2-(2,4,5-trichlorophenoxy)-)
Trichloropropane, N.O.S.[3] (Propane, trichloro-, N.O.S.[3])
1,2,3-Trichloropropane (Propane, 1,2,3-trichloro-)
O,O,O-Triethyl phosphorothioate (Phosphorothioic acid, O,O,O-triethyl ester)
sym-Trinitrobenzene (Benzene, 1,3,5-trinitro-)
Tris(1-azridinyl) phosphine sulfide (Phosphine sulfide, tris(1-aziridinyl-)
Tris(2,3-dibromopropyl) phosphate (1-Propanol, 2,3-dibromo-, phosphate)
Trypan blue (2,7-Naphthalenedisulfonic acid, 3,3′-[(3,3′-dimethyl (1,1′-biphenyl)- 4,4′-diyl)bis(azo)]bis(5-amino-4-hydroxy-, tetrasodium salt)
Uracil mustard (Uracil 5-[bis(2-chloroethyl)amino]-)
Uranium and compounds, N.O.S.[3]
Vanadic acid, ammonium salt (ammonium vanadate)
Vanadium pentoxide (Vanadium (V) oxide)
Vinyl chloride (Ethene, chloro-)
Zinc cyanide
Zinc phosphide

[50 FR 41862, Oct. 16, 1985, as amended at 52 FR 31611, Aug. 21, 1987; 52 FR 43562, Nov. 13, 1987; 53 FR 19248, May 27, 1988; 55 FR 45600, Oct. 30, 1990; 56 FR 23473, May 21, 1991; 58 FR 67661, Dec. 22, 1993; 59 FR 28229, June 1, 1994; 64 FR 17510, Apr. 12, 1999; 77 FR 35570, June 17, 2012; 81 FR 86909, Dec. 2, 2016]

PART 50—DOMESTIC LICENSING OF PRODUCTION AND UTILIZATION FACILITIES

STANDARDS FOR LICENSES, CERTIFICATIONS, AND REGULATORY APPROVALS

ISSUANCE, LIMITATIONS, AND CONDITIONS OF LICENSES AND CONSTRUCTION PERMITS

INSPECTIONS, RECORDS, REPORTS, NOTIFICATIONS

US/IAEA SAFEGUARDS AGREEMENT

TRANSFERS OF LICENSES—CREDITORS' RIGHTS—SURRENDER OF LICENSES

AMENDMENT OF LICENSE OR CONSTRUCTION PERMIT AT REQUEST OF HOLDER

REVOCATION, SUSPENSION, MODIFICATION, AMENDMENT OF LICENSES AND CONSTRUCTION PERMITS, EMERGENCY OPERATIONS BY THE COMMISSION

BACKFITTING

ENFORCEMENT

AUTHORITY: Atomic Energy Act of 1954, secs. 11, 101, 102, 103, 104, 105, 108, 122, 147, 149, 161, 181, 182, 183, 184, 185, 186, 187, 189, 223, 234 (42 U.S.C. 2014, 2131, 2132, 2133, 2134, 2135, 2138, 2152, 2167, 2169, 2201, 2231, 2232, 2233, 2234, 2235, 2236, 2237, 2239, 2273, 2282); Energy Reorganization Act of 1974, secs. 201, 202, 206, 211 (42 U.S.C. 5841, 5842, 5846, 5851); Nuclear Waste Policy Act of 1982, sec. 306 (42 U.S.C. 10226); National Environmental Policy Act of 1969 (42 U.S.C. 4332); 44 U.S.C. 3504 note; Sec. 109, Pub. L. 96–295, 94 Stat. 783.

SOURCE: 21 FR 355, Jan. 19, 1956, unless otherwise noted.

GENERAL PROVISIONS

§ 50.1 Basis, purpose, and procedures applicable.

The regulations in this part are promulgated by the Nuclear Regulatory Commission pursuant to the Atomic Energy Act of 1954, as amended (68 Stat. 919), and Title II of the Energy Reorganization Act of 1974 (88 Stat. 1242), to provide for the licensing of production and utilization facilities. This part also gives notice to all persons who knowingly provide to any licensee, applicant, contractor, or subcontractor, components, equipment, materials, or other goods or services, that relate to a licensee's or applicant's activities subject to this part, that they may be individually subject to NRC enforcement action for violation of § 50.5.

[63 FR 1897, Jan. 13, 1998]

§ 50.2 Definitions.

As used in this part,

Act means the Atomic Energy Act of 1954 (68 Stat. 919) including any amendments thereto.

Alternate ac source means an alternating current (ac) power source that is available to and located at or nearby a nuclear power plant and meets the following requirements:

(1) Is connectable to but not normally connected to the offsite or onsite emergency ac power systems;

(2) Has minimum potential for common mode failure with offsite power or the onsite emergency ac power sources;

(3) Is available in a timely manner after the onset of station blackout; and

(4) Has sufficient capacity and reliability for operation of all systems required for coping with station blackout and for the time required to bring and maintain the plant in safe shutdown (non-design basis accident).

Applicant means a person or an entity applying for a license, permit, or other form of Commission permission or approval under this part or part 52 of this chapter.

Atomic energy means all forms of energy released in the course of nuclear fission or nuclear transformation.

Atomic weapon means any device utilizing atomic energy, exclusive of the means for transporting or propelling the device (where such means is a separable and divisible part of the device), the prinicipal purpose of which is for use as, or for development of, a weapon, a weapon prototype, or a weapon test device.

Basic component means, for the purposes of § 50.55(e) of this chapter:

(1) When applied to nuclear power reactors, any plant structure, system, component, or part thereof necessary to assure

(i) The integrity of the reactor coolant pressure boundary,

(ii) The capability to shut down the reactor and maintain it in a safe shutdown condition, or

(iii) The capability to prevent or mitigate the consequences of accidents which could result in potential offsite exposures comparable to those referred to in § 50.34(a)(1), § 50.67(b)(2), or § 100.11 of this chapter, as applicable.

(2) When applied to other types of facilities or portions of such facilities for which construction permits are issued under § 50.23, a component, structure, system or part thereof that is directly procured by the construction permit holder for the facility subject to the regulations of this part and in which a defect or failure to comply with any applicable regulation in this chapter, order, or license issued by the Commission could create a substantial safety hazard.

(3) In all cases, *basic component* includes safety related design, analysis, inspection, testing, fabrication, replacement parts, or consulting services that are associated with the component hardware, whether these services are performed by the component supplier or other supplier.

Byproduct material means—

(1) Any radioactive material (except special nuclear material) yielded in, or made radioactive by, exposure to the radiation incident to the process of producing or using special nuclear material;

(2)(i) Any discrete source of radium-226 that is produced, extracted, or converted after extraction, before, on, or after August 8, 2005, for use for a commercial, medical, or research activity; or

(ii) Any material that—

(A) Has been made radioactive by use of a particle accelerator; and

(B) Is produced, extracted, or converted after extraction, before, on, or after August 8, 2005, for use for a commercial, medical, or research activity; and

(3) Any discrete source of naturally occurring radioactive material, other than source material, that—

(i) The Commission, in consultation with the Administrator of the Environmental Protection Agency, the Secretary of Energy, the Secretary of Homeland Security, and the head of any other appropriate Federal agency, determines would pose a threat similar to the threat posed by a discrete source of radium-226 to the public health and safety or the common defense and security; and

(ii) Before, on, or after August 8, 2005, is extracted or converted after extraction for use in a commercial, medical, or research activity.

Certified fuel handler means, for a nuclear power reactor facility, a non-licensed operator who has qualified in accordance with a fuel handler training program approved by the Commission.

Commission means the Nuclear Regulatory Commission or its duly authorized representatives.

Committed dose equivalent means the dose equivalent to organs or tissues of reference that will be received from an intake of radioactive material by an individual during the 50-year period following the intake.

Committed effective dose equivalent is the sum of the products of the weighting factors applicable to each of the body organs or tissues that are irradiated and the committed dose equivalent to these organs or tissues.

Common defense and security means the common defense and security of the United States.

Construction or *constructing* means, for the purposes of § 50.55(e), the analysis, design, manufacture, fabrication, quality assurance, placement, erection, installation, modification, inspection, or testing of a facility or activity which is subject to the regulations in this part and consulting services related to the facility or activity that are safety related.

Controls when used with respect to nuclear reactors means apparatus and mechanisms, the manipulation of which directly affects the reactivity or power level of the reactor.

Controls when used with respect to any other facility means apparatus and mechanisms, the manipulation of which could affect the chemical, physical, metallurgical, or nuclear process of the facility in such a manner as to affect the protection of health and safety against radiation.

Cost of service regulation means the traditional system of rate regulation, or similar regulation, including "price cap" or "incentive" regulation, in which a rate regulatory authority generally allows an electric utility to charge its customers the reasonable and prudent costs of providing electricity services, including capital, operations, maintenance, fuel, decommissioning, and other costs required to provide such services.

Decommission means to remove a facility or site safely from service and reduce residual radioactivity to a level that permits—

(1) Release of the property for unrestricted use and termination of the license; or

(2) Release of the property under restricted conditions and termination of the license.

Deep-dose equivalent, which applies to external whole-body exposure, is the dose equivalent at a tissue depth of 1 cm (1000mg/cm^2).

Defect means, for the purposes of § 50.55(e) of this chapter:

(1) A deviation in a basic component delivered to a purchaser for use in a facility or activity subject to a construction permit under this part, if on the basis of an evaluation, the deviation could create a substantial safety hazard; or

(2) The installation, use, or operation of a basic component containing, a defect as defined in paragraph (1) of this definition; or

(3) A deviation in a portion of a facility subject to the construction permit of this part provided the deviation could, on the basis of an evaluation, create a substantial safety hazard.

Department and *Department of Energy* means the Department of Energy established by the Department of Energy Organization Act (Pub. L. 95–91, 91 Stat. 565, 42 U.S.C. 7101 *et seq.*), to the extent that the department, or its duly authorized representatives, exercises functions formerly vested in the Atomic Energy Commission, its Chairman, members, officers and components and transferred to the U.S. Energy Research and Development Administration and to the Administrator thereof pursuant to sections 104 (b), (c) and (d) of the Energy Reorganization Act of 1974 (Pub. L. 93–438, 88 Stat. 1233 at 1237, 42 U.S.C. 5814) and retransferred to the Secretary of Energy pursuant to section 301(a) of the Department of Energy Organization Act (Pub. L. 95–91, 91 Stat. 565 at 577–578, 42 U.S.C. 7151).

Design bases means that information which identifies the specific functions to be performed by a structure, system, or component of a facility, and the specific values or ranges of values chosen for controlling parameters as reference bounds for design. These values may be (1) restraints derived from generally accepted "state of the art" practices for achieving functional goals, or (2) requirements derived from analysis (based on calculation and/or experiments) of the effects of a postulated accident for which a structure, system, or component must meet its functional goals.

Deviation means, for the purposes of § 50.55(e) of this chapter, a departure from the technical or quality assurance requirements defined in procurement documents, safety analysis report, construction permit, or other documents provided for basic components installed in a facility subject to the regulations of this part.

Director means, for the purposes of § 50.55(e) of this chapter, an individual, appointed or elected according to law, who is authorized to manage and direct the affairs of a corporation, partnership or other entity.

Discovery means, for the purposes of § 50.55(e) of this chapter, the completion of the documentation first identifying the existence of a deviation or failure to comply potentially associated with a substantial safety hazard within the evaluation procedures discussed in § 50.55(e)(1).

Electric utility means any entity that generates or distributes electricity and which recovers the cost of this electricity, either directly or indirectly, through rates established by the entity itself or by a separate regulatory authority. Investor-owned utilities, including generation or distribution subsidiaries, public utility districts, municipalities, rural electric cooperatives, and State and Federal agencies, including associations of any of the foregoing, are included within the meaning of "electric utility."

Evaluation means, for the purposes of § 50.55(e) of this chapter, the process of determining whether a particular deviation could create a substantial safety hazard or determining whether a failure to comply is associated with a substantial safety hazard.

Exclusion area means that area surrounding the reactor, in which the reactor licensee has the authority to determine all activities including exclusion or removal of personnel and property from the area. This area may be traversed by a highway, railroad, or waterway, provided these are not so close to the facility as to interfere with normal operations of the facility and provided appropriate and effective arrangements are made to control traffic on the highway, railroad, or waterway, in case of emergency, to protect the public health and safety. Residence within the exclusion area shall normally be prohibited. In any event, residents shall be subject to ready removal in case of necessity. Activities unrelated to operation of the reactor may be permitted in an exclusion area under appropriate limitations, provided that no significant hazards to the public health and safety will result.

Federal Government funding for conversion means funds appropriated to the Department of Energy or to any other Federal Agency to pay directly to or to reimburse non-power reactor licensees for costs attendant to conversion.

Federal licensee means any NRC licensee, the obligations of which are guaranteed by and supported by the full faith and credit of the United States Government.

Fuel acceptable to the Commission means that the fuel replacing the existing HEU fuel in a specific non-power reactor (1) meets the operating requirements of the existing license or, through appropriate NRC safety review and approval, can be used in a manner which protects public health and safety and promotes the common defense and security; and (2) meets the Commission's policy of limiting, to the maximum extent possible, the use of HEU fuel in that reactor.

Government agency means any executive department, commission, independent establishment, corporation, wholly or partly owned by the United States of America which is an instrumentality of the United States, or any board, bureau, division, service, office, officer, authority, administration, or other establishment in the executive branch of the Government.

Highly enriched uranium (HEU) fuel means fuel in which the weight percent of U–235 in the uranium is 20% or greater. Target material, special instrumentation, or experimental devices using HEU are not included.

Historical site assessment means the identification of potential, likely, or known sources of radioactive material and radioactive contamination based on existing or derived information for the purpose of classifying a facility or site, or parts thereof, as impacted or non-impacted.

Impacted areas mean the areas with some reasonable potential for residual radioactivity in excess of natural background or fallout levels.

Incentive regulation means the system of rate regulation in which a rate regulatory authority establishes rates that an electric generator may charge its customers that are based on specified performance factors, in addition to cost-of-service factors.

License means a license, including a construction permit or operating license under this part, an early site permit, combined license or manufacturing license under part 52 of this chapter, or a renewed license issued by the Commission under this part, part 52, or part 54 of this chapter.

Licensee means a person who is authorized to conduct activities under a license issued by the Commission.

Low enriched uranium (LEU) fuel means fuel in which the weight percent of U–235 in the uranium is less than 20%.

Low population zone means the area immediately surrounding the exclusion area which contains residents, the total number and density of which are such that there is a reasonable probability that appropriate protective measures could be taken in their behalf in the event of a serious accident. These guides do not specify a permissible population density or total population within this zone because the situation may vary from case to case. Whether a specific number of people can, for example, be evacuated from a specific area, or instructed to take shelter, on a timely basis will depend on many factors such as location, number and size of highways, scope and extent of advance planning, and actual distribution of residents within the area.

Major decommissioning activity means, for a nuclear power reactor facility, any activity that results in permanent removal of major radioactive components, permanently modifies the structure of the containment, or results in dismantling components for shipment containing greater than class C waste in accordance with § 61.55 of this chapter.

Major radioactive components means, for a nuclear power reactor facility, the reactor vessel and internals, steam generators, pressurizers, large bore reactor coolant system piping, and other large components that are radioactive to a comparable degree.

Non-bypassable charges mean those charges imposed over an established time period by a Government authority that affected persons or entities are required to pay to cover costs associated with the decommissioning of a nuclear power plant. Such charges include, but are not limited to, wire charges, stranded cost charges, transition charges, exit fees, other similar charges, or the securitized proceeds of a revenue stream.

Non-impacted areas mean the areas with no reasonable potential for residual radioactivity in excess of natural background or fallout levels.

Non-power reactor means a research or test reactor licensed under §§ 50.21(c) or 50.22 of this part for research and development.

Notification means the telephonic communication to the NRC Operations Center or written transmittal of information to the NRC Document Control Desk.

Nuclear reactor means an apparatus, other than an atomic weapon, designed or used to sustain nuclear fission in a self-supporting chain reaction.

Permanent cessation of operation(s) means, for a nuclear power reactor facility, a certification by a licensee to the NRC that it has permanently ceased or will permanently cease reactor operation(s), or a final legally effective order to permanently cease operation(s) has come into effect.

Permanent fuel removal means, for a nuclear power reactor facility, a certification by the licensee to the NRC that it has permanently removed all fuel assemblies from the reactor vessel.

Person means (1) any individual, corporation, partnership, firm, association, trust, estate, public or private institution, group, government agency other than the Commission or the Department, except that the Department shall be considered a person to the extent that its facilities are subject to the licensing and related regulatory authority of the Commission pursuant to section 202 of the Energy Reorganization Act of 1974, any State or any political subdivision of, or any political entity within a State, any foreign government or nation or any political subdivision of any such government or nation, or other entity; and (2) any legal successor, representative, agent, or agency of the foregoing.

Price-cap regulation means the system of rate regulation in which a rate regulatory authority establishes rates that an electric generator may charge its customers that are based on a specified maximum price of electricity.

Procurement document means, for the purposes of § 50.55(e) of this chapter, a contract that defines the requirements which facilities or basic components must meet in order to be considered acceptable by the purchaser.

Produce, when used in relation to special nuclear material, means (1) to manufacture, make, produce, or refine special nuclear material; (2) to separate special nuclear material from other substances in which such material may be contained; or (3) to make or to produce new special nuclear material.

Production facility means:

(1) Any nuclear reactor designed or used primarily for the formation of plutonium or uranium–233; or

(2) Any facility designed or used for the separation of the isotopes of plutonium, except laboratory scale facilities designed or used for experimental or analytical purposes only; or

(3) Any facility designed or used for the processing of irradiated materials containing special nuclear material, except (i) laboratory scale facilities designed or used for experimental or analytical purposes, (ii) facilities in which the only special nuclear materials contained in the irradiated material to be processed are uranium enriched in the isotope U–235 and plutonium produced by the irradiation, if the material processed contains not more than 10^{-6} grams of plutonium per gram of U–235 and has fission product activity not in excess of 0.25 millicuries of fission products per gram of U–235, and (iii) facilities in which processing is conducted pursuant to a license issued under parts 30 and 70 of this chapter, or equivalent regulations of an Agreement State, for the receipt, possession, use, and transfer of irradiated special nuclear material, which authorizes the processing of the irradiated material on a batch basis for the separation of selected fission products and limits the process batch to not more than 100 grams of uranium enriched in the isotope 235 and not more than 15 grams of any other special nuclear material.

Prototype plant means a nuclear reactor that is used to test design features, such as the testing required under § 50.43(e). The prototype plant is similar to a first-of-a-kind or standard plant design in all features and size, but may include additional safety features to protect the public and the plant staff from the possible consequences of accidents during the testing period.

Reactor coolant pressure boundary means all those pressure-containing components of boiling and pressurized water-cooled nuclear power reactors, such as pressure vessels, piping, pumps, and valves, which are:

(1) Part of the reactor coolant system, or

(2) Connected to the reactor coolant system, up to and including any and all of the following:

(i) The outermost containment isolation valve in system piping which penetrates primary reactor containment,

(ii) The second of two valves normally closed during normal reactor operation in system piping which does not penetrate primary reactor containment,

(iii) The reactor coolant system safety and relief valves.

For nuclear power reactors of the direct cycle boiling water type, the reactor coolant system extends to and includes the outermost containment isolation valve in the main steam and feedwater piping.

Research and development means (1) theoretical analysis, exploration, or experimentation; or (2) the extension of investigative findings and theories of a scientific or technical nature into practical application for experimental and demonstration purposes, including the experimental production and testing of models, devices, equipment, materials, and processes.

Responsible officer means, for the purposes of § 50.55(e) of this chapter, the president, vice-president, or other individual in the organization of a corporation, partnership, or other entity who is vested with executive authority over activities subject to this part.

Restricted Data means all data concerning (1) design, manufacture, or utilization of atomic weapons; (2) the production of special nuclear material; or (3) the use of special nuclear material in the production of energy, but shall not include data declassified or removed from the Restricted Data category pursuant to section 142 of the Act.

Safe shutdown (non-design basis accident (non-DBA)) for station blackout means bringing the plant to those shutdown conditions specified in plant technical specifications as Hot Standby or Hot Shutdown, as appropriate (plants have the option of maintaining the RCS at normal operating temperatures or at reduced temperatures).

Safety-related structures, systems and components means those structures, systems and components that are relied upon to remain functional during and following design basis events to assure:

(1) The integrity of the reactor coolant pressure boundary

(2) The capability to shut down the reactor and maintain it in a safe shutdown condition; or

(3) The capability to prevent or mitigate the consequences of accidents which could result in potential offsite exposures comparable to the applicable guideline exposures set forth in § 50.34(a)(1) or § 100.11 of this chapter, as applicable.

Source material means source material as defined in subsection 11z. of the Act and in the regulations contained in part 40 of this chapter.

Source term refers to the magnitude and mix of the radionuclides released from the fuel, expressed as fractions of the fission product inventory in the fuel, as well as their physical and chemical form, and the timing of their release.

Special nuclear material means (1) plutonium, uranium-233, uranium enriched in the isotope-233 or in the isotope-235, and any other material which the Commission, pursuant to the provisions of section 51 of the act, determines to be special nuclear material, but does not include source material; or (2) any material artificially enriched by any of the foregoing, but does not include source material.

Station blackout means the complete loss of alternating current (ac) electric power to the essential and nonessential switchgear buses in a nuclear power plant (*i.e.*, loss of offsite electric power system concurrent with turbine trip and unavailability of the onsite emergency ac power system). Station blackout does not include the loss of available ac power to buses fed by station batteries through inverters or by alternate ac sources as defined in this section, nor does it assume a concurrent single failure or design basis accident. At single unit sites, any emergency ac power source(s) in excess of the number required to meet minimum redundancy requirements (*i.e.*, single failure) for safe shutdown (non-DBA) is assumed to be available and may be designated as an alternate power source(s) provided the applicable requirements are met. At multi-unit sites, where the combination of emergency ac power sources exceeds the minimum redundancy requirements for safe shutdown (non-DBA) of all units, the remaining emergency ac power sources may be used as alternate ac power sources provided they meet the applicable requirements. If these criteria are not met, station blackout must be assumed on all the units.

Substantial safety hazard means, for the purposes of § 50.55(e) of this chapter, a loss of safety function to the extent that there is a major reduction in the degree of protection provided to public health and safety for any facility or activity authorized by the construction permit issued under this part.

Testing facility means a nuclear reactor which is of a type described in § 50.21(c) of this part and for which an application has been filed for a license authorizing operation at:

(1) A thermal power level in excess of 10 megawatts; or

(2) A thermal power level in excess of 1 megawatt, if the reactor is to contain:

(i) A circulating loop through the core in which the applicant proposes to conduct fuel experiments; or

(ii) A liquid fuel loading; or

(iii) An experimental facility in the core in excess of 16 square inches in cross-section.

Total Effective Dose Equivalent (TEDE) means the sum of the effective dose equivalent (for external exposures) and the committed effective dose equivalent (for internal exposures).

Unique purpose means a project, program, or commercial activity which cannot reasonably be accomplished without the use of HEU fuel, and may include: (1) A specific experiment, program, or commercial activity (typically long-term) that significantly serves the U.S. national interest and cannot be accomplished without the use of HEU fuel; (2) Reactor physics or reactor development based explicitly on the use of HEU fuel; (3) Research projects based on neutron flux levels or spectra attainable only with HEU fuel; or (4) A reactor core of special design that could not perform its intended function without using HEU fuel.

United States, when used in a geographical sense, includes Puerto Rico and all territories and possessions of the United States.

Utilization facility means:

(1) Any nuclear reactor other than one designed or used primarily for the formation of plutonium or U–233; or

(2) An accelerator-driven subcritical operating assembly used for the irradiation of materials containing special nuclear material and described in the application assigned docket number 50–608.

NOTE: Pursuant to subsections 11v. and 11cc., respectively, of the Act, the Commission may from time to time add to, or otherwise alter, the foregoing definitions of production and utilization facility. It may also include as a facility an important component part especially designed for a facility, but has not at this time included any component parts in the definitions.

[21 FR 355, Jan. 19, 1956]

EDITORIAL NOTE: For FEDERAL REGISTER citations affecting §50.2, see the List of CFR Sections Affected, which appears in the Finding Aids section of the printed volume and at *www.fdsys.gov*.

§50.3 Interpretations.

Except as specifically authorized by the Commission in writing, no interpretation of the meaning of the regulations in this part by any officer or employee of the Commission other than a written interpretation by the General Counsel will be recognized to be binding upon the Commission.

§50.4 Written communications.

(a) *General requirements.* All correspondence, reports, applications, and other written communications from the applicant or licensee to the Nuclear Regulatory Commission concerning the regulations in this part or individual license conditions must be sent either by mail addressed: ATTN: Document Control Desk, U.S. Nuclear Regulatory Commission, Washington, DC 20555–0001; by hand delivery to the NRC's offices at 11555 Rockville Pike, Rockville, Maryland, between the hours of 8:15 a.m. and 4 p.m. eastern time; or, where practicable, by electronic submission, for example, via Electronic Information Exchange, e-mail, or CD-ROM. Electronic submissions must be made in a manner that enables the NRC to receive, read, authenticate, distribute, and archive the submission, and process and retrieve it a single page at a time. Detailed guidance on making electronic submissions can be obtained by visiting the NRC's Web site at *http://www.nrc.gov/site-help/e-submittals.html;* by e-mail to *MSHD.Resource@nrc.gov;* or by writing the Office of the Chief Information Officer, U.S. Nuclear Regulatory Commission, Washington, DC 20555–0001. The guidance discusses, among other topics, the formats the NRC can accept, the use of electronic signatures, and the treatment of nonpublic information. If the communication is on paper, the signed original must be sent. If a submission due date falls on a Saturday, Sunday, or Federal holiday, the next Federal working day becomes the official due date.

(b) *Distribution requirements.* Copies of all correspondence, reports, and other written communications concerning the regulations in this part or individual license conditions must be submitted to the persons listed below (addresses for the NRC Regional Offices are listed in appendix D to part 20 of this chapter).

(1) *Applications for amendment of permits and licenses; reports; and other communications.* All written communications (including responses to: generic letters, bulletins, information notices, regulatory information summaries, inspection reports, and miscellaneous requests for additional information) that are required of holders of operating licenses or construction permits issued

pursuant to this part, must be submitted as follows, except as otherwise specified in paragraphs (b)(2) through (b)(7) of this section: to the NRC's Document Control Desk (if on paper, the signed original), with a copy to the appropriate Regional Office, and a copy to the appropriate NRC Resident Inspector, if one has been assigned to the site of the facility.

(2) *Applications for permits and licenses, and amendments to applications.* Applications for construction permits, applications for operating licenses and amendments to either type of application must be submitted as follows, except as otherwise specified in paragraphs (b)(3) through (b)(7) in this section.

(i) Applications for licenses for facilities described in § 50.21 (a) and (c) and amendments to these applications must be sent to the NRC's Document Control Desk, with a copy to the appropriate Regional Office. If the application or amendment is on paper, the submission to the Document Control Desk must be the signed original.

(ii) Applications for permits and licenses for facilities described in § 50.21(b) or § 50.22, and amendments to these applications must be sent to the NRC's Document Control Desk, with a copy to the appropriate Regional Office, and a copy to the appropriate NRC Resident Inspector, if one has been assigned to the site of the facility. If the application or amendment is on paper, the submission to the Document Control Desk must be the signed original.

(3) *Acceptance review application.* Written communications required for an application for determination of suitability for docketing under § 50.30(a)(6) must be submitted to the NRC's Document Control Desk, with a copy to the appropriate Regional Office. If the communication is on paper, the submission to the Document Control Desk must be the signed original.

(4) *Security plan and related submissions.* Written communications, as defined in paragraphs (b)(4)(i) through (iv) of this section, must be submitted to the NRC's Document Control Desk, with a copy to the appropriate Regional Office. If the communication is on paper, the submission to the Document Control Desk must be the signed original.

(i) Physical security plan under § 50.34;

(ii) Safeguards contingency plan under § 50.34;

(iii) Change to security plan, guard training and qualification plan, or safeguards contingency plan made without prior Commission approval under § 50.54(p);

(iv) Application for amendment of physical security plan, guard training and qualification plan, or safeguards contingency plan under § 50.90.

(5) *Emergency plan and related submissions.* Written communications as defined in paragraphs (b)(5)(i) through (iii) of this section must be submitted to the NRC's Document Control Desk, with a copy to the appropriate Regional Office, and a copy to the appropriate NRC Resident Inspector if one has been assigned to the site of the facility. If the communication is on paper, the submission to the Document Control Desk must be the signed original.

(i) Emergency plan under § 50.34;

(ii) Change to an emergency plan under § 50.54(q);

(iii) Emergency implementing procedures under appendix E.V of this part.

(6) *Updated FSAR.* An updated Final Safety Analysis Report (FSAR) or replacement pages, under § 50.71(e) must be submitted to the NRC's Document Control Desk, with a copy to the appropriate Regional Office, and a copy to the appropriate NRC Resident Inspector if one has been assigned to the site of the facility. Paper copy submissions may be made using replacement pages; however, if a licensee chooses to use electronic submission, all subsequent updates or submissions must be performed electronically on a total replacement basis. If the communication is on paper, the submission to the Document Control Desk must be the signed original. If the communications are submitted electronically, see Guidance for Electronic Submissions to the Commission.

(7) *Quality assurance related submissions.* (i) A change to the Safety Analysis Report quality assurance program description under § 50.54(a)(3) or § 50.55(f)(3), or a change to a licensee's

NRC-accepted quality assurance topical report under §50.54(a)(3) or §50.55(f)(3), must be submitted to the NRC's Document Control Desk, with a copy to the appropriate Regional Office, and a copy to the appropriate NRC Resident Inspector if one has been assigned to the site of the facility. If the communication is on paper, the submission to the Document Control Desk must be the signed original.

(ii) A change to an NRC-accepted quality assurance topical report from nonlicensees (*i.e.*, architect/engineers, NSSS suppliers, fuel suppliers, constructors, etc.) must be submitted to the NRC's Document Control Desk. If the communication is on paper, the signed original must be sent.

(8) *Certification of permanent cessation of operations.* The licensee's certification of permanent cessation of operations, under §50.82(a)(1), must state the date on which operations have ceased or will cease, and must be submitted to the NRC's Document Control Desk. This submission must be under oath or affirmation.

(9) *Certification of permanent fuel removal.* The licensee's certification of permanent fuel removal, under §50.82(a)(1), must state the date on which the fuel was removed from the reactor vessel and the disposition of the fuel, and must be submitted to the NRC's Document Control Desk. This submission must be under oath or affirmation.

(c) *Form of communications.* All paper copies submitted to meet the requirements set forth in paragraph (b) of this section must be typewritten, printed or otherwise reproduced in permanent form on unglazed paper. Exceptions to these requirements imposed on paper submissions may be granted for the submission of micrographic, photographic, or similar forms.

(d) *Regulation governing submission.* Licensees and applicants submitting correspondence, reports, and other written communications under the regulations of this part are requested but not required to cite whenever practical, in the upper right corner of the first page of the submission, the specific regulation or other basis requiring submission.

(e) *Conflicting requirements.* The communications requirements contained in this section and §§50.12, 50.30, 50.36, 50.36a. 50.44, 50.49, 50.54, 50.55, 50.55a, 50.59, 50.62, 50.71, 50.73, 50.82, 50.90, and 50.91 supersede and replace all existing requirements in any license conditions or technical specifications in effect on January 5, 1987. Exceptions to these requirements must be approved by the Office of the Chief Information Officer, Nuclear Regulatory Commission, Washington, DC 20555–0001, telephone (301) 415–7233, e-mail *INFOCOLLECTS@nrc.gov.*

[68 FR 58808, Oct. 10, 2003, as amended at 74 FR 62682, Dec. 1, 2009; 80 FR 74979, Dec. 1, 2015]

§50.5 Deliberate misconduct.

(a) Any licensee, applicant for a license, employee of a licensee or applicant; or any contractor (including a supplier or consultant), subcontractor, employee of a contractor or subcontractor of any licensee or applicant for a license, who knowingly provides to any licensee, applicant, contractor, or subcontractor, any components, equipment, materials, or other goods or services that relate to a licensee's or applicant's activities in this part, may not:

(1) Engage in deliberate misconduct that causes or would have caused, if not detected, a licensee or applicant to be in violation of any rule, regulation, or order; or any term, condition, or limitation of any license issued by the Commission; or

(2) Deliberately submit to the NRC, a licensee, an applicant, or a licensee's or applicant's contractor or subcontractor, information that the person submitting the information knows to be incomplete or inaccurate in some respect material to the NRC.

(b) A person who violates paragraph (a)(1) or (a)(2) of this section may be subject to enforcement action in accordance with the procedures in 10 CFR part 2, subpart B.

(c) For the purposes of paragraph (a)(1) of this section, deliberate misconduct by a person means an intentional act or omission that the person knows:

(1) Would cause a licensee or applicant to be in violation of any rule, regulation, or order; or any term, condition, or limitation, of any license issued by the Commission; or

(2) Constitutes a violation of a requirement, procedure, instruction, contract, purchase order, or policy of a licensee, applicant, contractor, or subcontractor.

[63 FR 1897, Jan. 13, 1998]

§ 50.7 Employee protection.

(a) Discrimination by a Commission licensee, an applicant for a Commission license, or a contractor or subcontractor of a Commission licensee or applicant against an employee for engaging in certain protected activities is prohibited. Discrimination includes discharge and other actions that relate to compensation, terms, conditions, or privileges of employment. The protected activities are established in section 211 of the Energy Reorganization Act of 1974, as amended, and in general are related to the administration or enforcement of a requirement imposed under the Atomic Energy Act or the Energy Reorganization Act.

(1) The protected activities include but are not limited to:

(i) Providing the Commission or his or her employer information about alleged violations of either of the statutes named in paragraph (a) introductory text of this section or possible violations of requirements imposed under either of those statutes;

(ii) Refusing to engage in any practice made unlawful under either of the statutes named in paragraph (a) introductory text or under these requirements if the employee has identified the alleged illegality to the employer;

(iii) Requesting the Commission to institute action against his or her employer for the administration or enforcement of these requirements;

(iv) Testifying in any Commission proceeding, or before Congress, or at any Federal or State proceeding regarding any provision (or proposed provision) of either of the statutes named in paragraph (a) introductory text.

(v) Assisting or participating in, or is about to assist or participate in, these activities.

(2) These activities are protected even if no formal proceeding is actually initiated as a result of the employee assistance or participation.

(3) This section has no application to any employee alleging discrimination prohibited by this section who, acting without direction from his or her employer (or the employer's agent), deliberately causes a violation of any requirement of the Energy Reorganization Act of 1974, as amended, or the Atomic Energy Act of 1954, as amended.

(b) Any employee who believes that he or she has been discharged or otherwise discriminated against by any person for engaging in protected activities specified in paragraph (a)(1) of this section may seek a remedy for the discharge or discrimination through an administrative proceeding in the Department of Labor. The administrative proceeding must be initiated within 180 days after an alleged violation occurs. The employee may do this by filing a complaint alleging the violation with the Department of Labor, Employment Standards Administration, Wage and Hour Division. The Department of Labor may order reinstatement, back pay, and compensatory damages.

(c) A violation of paragraph (a), (e), or (f) of this section by a Commission licensee, an applicant for a Commission license, or a contractor or subcontractor of a Commission licensee or applicant may be grounds for—

(1) Denial, revocation, or suspension of the license.

(2) Imposition of a civil penalty on the licensee, applicant, or a contractor or subcontractor of the licensee or applicant.

(3) Other enforcement action.

(d) Actions taken by an employer, or others, which adversely affect an employee may be predicated upon nondiscriminatory grounds. The prohibition applies when the adverse action occurs because the employee has engaged in protected activities. An employee's engagement in protected activities does not automatically render him or her immune from discharge or discipline for legitimate reasons or from adverse action dictated by nonprohibited considerations.

(e)(1) Each licensee and each applicant for a license shall prominently post the revision of NRC Form 3, "Notice to Employees," referenced in 10 CFR 19.11(c). This form must be posted at locations sufficient to permit employees protected by this section to observe a copy on the way to or from their place of work. Premises must be posted not later than 30 days after an application is docketed and remain posted while the application is pending before the Commission, during the term of the license, and for 30 days following license termination.

(2) Copies of NRC Form 3 may be obtained by writing to the Regional Administrator of the appropriate U.S. Nuclear Regulatory Commission Regional Office listed in appendix D to part 20 of this chapter, via email to *Forms.Resource@nrc.gov*, or by visiting the NRC's online library at *http://www.nrc.gov/reading-rm/doc-collections/forms/*.

(f) No agreement affecting the compensation, terms, conditions, or privileges of employment, including an agreement to settle a complaint filed by an employee with the Department of Labor pursuant to section 211 of the Energy Reorganization Act of 1974, as amended, may contain any provision which would prohibit, restrict, or otherwise discourage an employee from participating in protected activity as defined in paragraph (a)(1) of this section including, but not limited to, providing information to the NRC or to his or her employer on potential violations or other matters within NRC's regulatory responsibilities.

[58 FR 52410, Oct. 8, 1993, as amended at 60 FR 24551, May 9, 1995; 61 FR 6765, Feb. 22, 1996; 68 FR 58809, Oct. 10, 2003; 72 FR 63974, Nov. 14, 2007; 73 FR 30458, May 28, 2008; 79 FR 66603, Nov. 10, 2014]

§ 50.8 Information collection requirements: OMB approval.

(a) The Nuclear Regulatory Commission has submitted the information collection requirements contained in this part to the Office of Management and Budget (OMB) for approval as required by the Paperwork Reduction Act (44 U.S.C. 3501 *et seq.*). The NRC may not conduct or sponsor, and a person is not required to respond to, a collection of information unless it displays a currently valid OMB control number. OMB has approved the information collection requirements contained in this part under control number 3150–0011.

(b) The approved information collection requirements contained in this part appear in §§ 50.30, 50.33, 50.34, 50.34a, 50.35, 50.36, 50.36a, 50.36b, 50.44, 50.46, 50.47, 50.48, 50.49, 50.54, 50.55, 50.55a, 50.59, 50.60, 50.61, 50.61a, 50.62, 50.63, 50.64, 50.65, 50.66, 50.68, 50.69, 50.70, 50.71, 50.72, 50.74, 50.75, 50.80, 50.82, 50.90, 50.91, 50.120, 50.150, and appendices A, B, E, G, H, I, J, K, M, N,O, Q, R, and S to this part.

(c) This part contains information collection requirements in addition to those approved under the control number specified in paragraph (a) of this section. These information collection requirements and the control numbers under which they are approved are as follows:

(1) In § 50.73, NRC Form 366 is approved under control number 3150–0104.

(2) In § 50.78, Form N–71 and associated forms are approved under control number 3150–0056.

(3) In § 50.78, DOC/NRC Forms AP–1, AP–A, and associated forms are approved under control numbers 0694–0135.

[49 FR 19627, May 9, 1984, as amended at 58 FR 68731, Dec. 29, 1993; 60 FR 65468, Dec. 19, 1995; 61 FR 65172, Dec. 11, 1996; 62 FR 52187, Oct. 6, 1997; 67 FR 67099, Nov. 4, 2002; 68 FR 19727, Apr. 22, 2003; 69 FR 68046, Nov. 22, 2004; 70 FR 61887, Oct. 27, 2005; 73 FR 78605, Dec. 23, 2008; 74 FR 28145, June 12, 2009; 75 FR 22, Jan. 4, 2010; 77 FR 39907, July 6, 2012]

§ 50.9 Completeness and accuracy of information.

(a) Information provided to the Commission by an applicant for a license or by a licensee or information required by statute or by the Commission's regulations, orders, or license conditions to be maintained by the applicant or the licensee shall be complete and accurate in all material respects.

(b) Each applicant or licensee shall notify the Commission of information identified by the applicant or licensee as having for the regulated activity a significant implication for public health and safety or common defense and security. An applicant or licensee violates this paragraph only if the applicant or licensee fails to notify the Commission of information that the applicant or licensee has identified as having a significant implication for public health and safety or common defense and security. Notification shall be provided to the Administrator of the appropriate Regional Office within two working days of identifying the information. This requirement is not applicable to information which is already required to be provided to the Commission by other reporting or updating requirements.

[52 FR 49372, Dec. 31, 1987]

REQUIREMENT OF LICENSE, EXCEPTIONS

§ 50.10 License required; limited work authorization.

(a) *Definitions.* As used in this section, *construction* means the activities in paragraph (a)(1) of this section, and does not mean the activities in paragraph (a)(2) of this section.

(1) Activities constituting construction are the driving of piles, subsurface preparation, placement of backfill, concrete, or permanent retaining walls within an excavation, installation of foundations, or in-place assembly, erection, fabrication, or testing, which are for:

(i) Safety-related structures, systems, or components (SSCs) of a facility, as defined in 10 CFR 50.2;

(ii) SSCs relied upon to mitigate accidents or transients or used in plant emergency operating procedures;

(iii) SSCs whose failure could prevent safety-related SSCs from fulfilling their safety-related function;

(iv) SSCs whose failure could cause a reactor scram or actuation of a safety-related system;

(v) SSCs necessary to comply with 10 CFR part 73;

(vi) SSCs necessary to comply with 10 CFR 50.48 and criterion 3 of 10 CFR part 50, appendix A; and

(vii) Onsite emergency facilities, that is, technical support and operations support centers, necessary to comply with 10 CFR 50.47 and 10 CFR part 50, appendix E.

(2) Construction does not include:

(i) Changes for temporary use of the land for public recreational purposes;

(ii) Site exploration, including necessary borings to determine foundation conditions or other preconstruction monitoring to establish background information related to the suitability of the site, the environmental impacts of construction or operation, or the protection of environmental values;

(iii) Preparation of a site for construction of a facility, including clearing of the site, grading, installation of drainage, erosion and other environmental mitigation measures, and construction of temporary roads and borrow areas;

(iv) Erection of fences and other access control measures;

(v) Excavation;

(vi) Erection of support buildings (such as, construction equipment storage sheds, warehouse and shop facilities, utilities, concrete mixing plants, docking and unloading facilities, and office buildings) for use in connection with the construction of the facility;

(vii) Building of service facilities, such as paved roads, parking lots, railroad spurs, exterior utility and lighting systems, potable water systems, sanitary sewerage treatment facilities, and transmission lines;

(viii) Procurement or fabrication of components or portions of the proposed facility occurring at other than the final, in-place location at the facility;

(ix) Manufacture of a nuclear power reactor under a manufacturing license under subpart F of part 52 of this chapter to be installed at the proposed site and to be part of the proposed facility; or

(x) With respect to production or utilization facilities, other than testing facilities and nuclear power plants, required to be licensed under Section 104.a or Section 104.c of the Act, the erection of buildings which will be used for activities other than operation of a facility and which may also be used to house a facility (e.g., the construction of a college laboratory building with space for installation of a training reactor).

(b) *Requirement for license.* Except as provided in § 50.11 of this chapter, no person within the United States shall transfer or receive in interstate commerce, manufacture, produce, transfer, acquire, possess, or use any production or utilization facility except as authorized by a license issued by the Commission.

(c) *Requirement for construction permit, early site permit authorizing limited work authorization activities, combined license, or limited work authorization.* No person may begin the construction of a production or utilization facility on a site on which the facility is to be operated until that person has been issued either a construction permit under this part, a combined license under part 52 of this chapter, an early site permit authorizing the activities under paragraph (d) of this section, or a limited work authorization under paragraph (d) of this section.

(d) *Request for limited work authorization.* (1) Any person to whom the Commission may otherwise issue either a license or permit under Sections 103, 104.b, or 185 of the Act for a facility of the type specified in §§50.21(b)(2), (b)(3), or 50.22 of this chapter, or a testing facility, may request a limited work authorization allowing that person to perform the driving of piles, subsurface preparation, placement of backfill, concrete, or permanent retaining walls within an excavation, installation of the foundation, including placement of concrete, any of which are for an SSC of the facility for which either a construction permit or combined license is otherwise required under paragraph (c) of this section.

(2) An application for a limited work authorization may be submitted as part of a complete application for a construction permit or combined license in accordance with 10 CFR 2.101(a)(1) through (a)(5), or as a partial application in accordance with 10 CFR 2.101(a)(9). An application for a limited work authorization must be submitted by an applicant for or holder of an early site permit as a complete application in accordance with 10 CFR 2.101(a)(1) through (a)(4).

(3) The application must include:

(i) A safety analysis report required by 10 CFR 50.34, 10 CFR 52.17 or 10 CFR 52.79 of this chapter, as applicable, a description of the activities requested to be performed, and the design and construction information otherwise required by the Commission's rules and regulations to be submitted for a construction permit or combined license, but limited to those portions of the facility that are within the scope of the limited work authorization. The safety analysis report must demonstrate that activities conducted under the limited work authorization will be conducted in compliance with the technically-relevant Commission requirements in 10 CFR Chapter I applicable to the design of those portions of the facility within the scope of the limited work authorization;

(ii) An environmental report in accordance with §51.49 of this chapter; and

(iii) A plan for redress of activities performed under the limited work authorization, should limited work activities be terminated by the holder or the limited work authorization be revoked by the NRC, or upon effectiveness of the Commission's final decision denying the associated construction permit or combined license application, as applicable.

(e) *Issuance of limited work authorization.* (1) The Director of New Reactors or the Director of Nuclear Reactor Regulation may issue a limited work authorization only after:

(i) The NRC staff issues the final environmental impact statement for the limited work authorization in accordance with subpart A of part 51 of this chapter;

(ii) The presiding officer makes the finding in §51.105(c) or §51.107(d) of this chapter, as applicable;

(iii) The Director determines that the applicable standards and requirements of the Act, and the Commission's regulations applicable to the activities to be conducted under the limited work authorization, have been met. The applicant is technically qualified to engage in the activities authorized. Issuance of the limited work authorization will provide reasonable assurance of adequate protection to public health and safety and will not be inimical to the common defense and security; and

(iv) The presiding officer finds that there are no unresolved safety issues relating to the activities to be conducted under the limited work authorization that would constitute good cause for withholding the authorization.

(2) Each limited work authorization will specify the activities that the holder is authorized to perform.

(f) *Effect of limited work authorization.* Any activities undertaken under a limited work authorization are entirely at the risk of the applicant and, except as to the matters determined under paragraph (e)(1) of this section, the issuance of the limited work authorization has no bearing on the issuance of a construction permit or combined license with respect to the requirements of the Act, and rules, regulations, or orders issued under the Act. The environmental impact statement for a construction permit or combined license application for which a limited work authorization was previously issued will not address, and the presiding officer will not consider, the sunk costs of the holder of limited work authorization in determining the proposed action (*i.e.*, issuance of the construction permit or combined license).

(g) *Implementation of redress plan.* If construction is terminated by the holder, the underlying application is withdrawn by the applicant or denied by the NRC, or the limited work authorization is revoked by the NRC, then the holder must begin implementation of the redress plan in a reasonable time. The holder must also complete the redress of the site no later than 18 months after termination of construction, revocation of the limited work authorization, or upon effectiveness of the Commission's final decision denying the associated construction permit application or the underlying combined license application, as applicable.

[72 FR 57441, Oct. 9, 2007]

§ 50.11 Exceptions and exemptions from licensing requirements.

Nothing in this part shall be deemed to require a license for:

(a) The manufacture, production, or acquisition by the Department of Defense of any utilization facility authorized pursuant to section 91 of the Act, or the use of such facility by the Department of Defense or by a person under contract with and for the account of the Department of Defense;

(b) Except to the extent that Administration facilities of the types subject to licensing pursuant to section 202 of the Energy Reorganization Act of 1974 are involved;

(1)(i) The processing, fabrication or refining of special nuclear material or the separation of special nuclear material, or the separation of special nuclear material from other substances by a prime contractor of the Department under a prime contract for:

(A) The performance of work for the Department at a United States government-owned or controlled site;

(B) Research in, or development, manufacture, storage, testing or transportation of, atomic weapons or components thereof; or

(C) The use or operation of a production or utilization facility in a United States owned vehicle or vessel; or

(ii) By a prime contractor or subcontractor of the Commission or the Department under a prime contract or subcontract when the Commission determines that the exemption of the prime contractor or subcontractor is authorized by law; and that, under the terms of the contract or subcontract, there is adequate assurance that the work thereunder can be accomplished without undue risk to the public health and safety;

(2)(i) The construction or operation of a production or utilization facility for the Department at a United States government-owned or controlled site, including the transportation of the production or utilization facility to or from such site and the performance of contract services during temporary interruptions of such transportation; or the construction or operation of a production or utilization facility for the Department in the performance of research in, or development, manufacture, storage, testing, or transportation of, atomic weapons or components thereof; or the use or operation of a production or utilization facility for the Department in a United States government-owned vehicle or vessel: *Provided*, That such activities are conducted by a prime contractor of the Department under a prime contract with the Department.

(ii) The construction or operation of a production or utilization facility by a prime contractor or subcontractor of the Commission or the Department under his prime contract or subcontract when the Commission determines that the exemption of the prime contractor or subcontractor is authorized by law; and that, under the terms of the contract or subcontract, there is adequate assurance that the work thereunder can be accomplished without undue risk to the public health and safety.

(c) The transportation or possession of any production or utilization facility by a common or contract carrier or warehousemen in the regular course of carriage for another or storage incident thereto.

[40 FR 8788, Mar. 3, 1975, as amended at 65 FR 54950, Sept. 12, 2000]

§50.12 Specific exemptions.

(a) The Commission may, upon application by any interested person or upon its own initiative, grant exemptions from the requirements of the regulations of this part, which are—

(1) Authorized by law, will not present an undue risk to the public health and safety, and are consistent with the common defense and security.

(2) The Commission will not consider granting an exemption unless special circumstances are present. Special circumstances are present whenever—

(i) Application of the regulation in the particular circumstances conflicts with other rules or requirements of the Commission; or

(ii) Application of the regulation in the particular circumstances would not serve the underlying purpose of the rule or is not necessary to achieve the underlying purpose of the rule; or

(iii) Compliance would result in undue hardship or other costs that are significantly in excess of those contemplated when the regulation was adopted, or that are significantly in excess of those incurred by others similarly situated; or

(iv) The exemption would result in benefit to the public health and safety that compensates for any decrease in safety that may result from the grant of the exemption; or

(v) The exemption would provide only temporary relief from the applicable regulation and the licensee or applicant has made good faith efforts to comply with the regulation; or

(vi) There is present any other material circumstance not considered when the regulation was adopted for which it would be in the public interest to grant an exemption. If such condition is relied on exclusively for satisfying paragraph (a)(2) of this section, the exemption may not be granted until the Executive Director for Operations has consulted with the Commission.

(b) Any person may request an exemption permitting the conduct of activities prior to the issuance of a construction permit prohibited by §50.10. The Commission may grant such an exemption upon considering and balancing the following factors:

(1) Whether conduct of the proposed activities will give rise to a significant adverse impact on the environment and the nature and extent of such impact, if any;

(2) Whether redress of any adverse environment impact from conduct of the proposed activities can reasonably be effected should such redress be necessary;

(3) Whether conduct of the proposed activities would foreclose subsequent adoption of alternatives; and

(4) The effect of delay in conducting such activities on the public interest, including the power needs to be used by the proposed facility, the availability of alternative sources, if any, to meet those needs on a timely basis and delay costs to the applicant and to consumers.

Issuance of such an exemption shall not be deemed to constitute a commitment to issue a construction permit. During the period of any exemption granted pursuant to this paragraph (b), any activities conducted shall be carried out in such a manner as will minimize or reduce their environmental impact.

[37 FR 5748, Mar. 21, 1972, as amended at 40 FR 8789, Mar. 3, 1975; 50 FR 50777, Dec. 12, 1985]

§50.13 Attacks and destructive acts by enemies of the United States; and defense activities.

An applicant for a license to construct and operate a production or utilization facility, or for an amendment to such license, is not required to provide for design features or other measures for the specific purpose of protection against the effects of (a) attacks and destructive acts, including sabotage, directed against the facility by an enemy of the United States, whether a foreign government or other person, or (b) use or deployment of weapons incident to U.S. defense activities.

[32 FR 13445, Sept. 26, 1967]

CLASSIFICATION AND DESCRIPTION OF LICENSES

§ 50.20 Two classes of licenses.

Licenses will be issued to named persons applying to the Commission therefor, and will be either class 104 or class 103.

§ 50.21 Class 104 licenses; for medical therapy and research and development facilities.

A class 104 license will be issued, to an applicant who qualifies, for any one or more of the following: to transfer or receive in interstate commerce, manufacture, produce, transfer, acquire, possess, or use.

(a) A utilization facility for use in medical therapy; or

(b)(1) A production or utilization facility the construction or operation of which was licensed pursuant to subsection 104b of the Act prior to December 19, 1970;

(2) A production or utilization facility for industrial or commercial purposes constructed or operated under an arrangement with the Administration entered into under the Cooperative Power Reactor Demonstration Program, except as otherwise specifically required by applicable law; and

(3) A production or utilization facility for industrial or commercial purposes, when specifically authorized by law.

(c) A production or utilization facility, which is useful in the conduct of research and development activities of the types specified in section 31 of the Act, and which is not a facility of the type specified in paragraph (b) of this section or in § 50.22.

[21 FR 355, Jan. 19, 1956, as amended at 31 FR 15145, Dec. 2, 1966; 35 FR 19659, Dec. 29, 1970; 38 FR 11446, May 8, 1973; 43 FR 6924, Feb. 17, 1978]

§ 50.22 Class 103 licenses; for commercial and industrial facilities.

A class 103 license will be issued, to an applicant who qualifies, for any one or more of the following: To transfer or receive in interstate commerce, manufacture, produce, transfer, acquire, possess, or use a production or utilization facility for industrial or commercial purposes; *Provided, however,* That in the case of a production or utilization facility which is useful in the conduct of research and development activities of the types specified in section 31 of the Act, such facility is deemed to be for industrial or commercial purposes if the facility is to be used so that more than 50 percent of the annual cost of owning and operating the facility is devoted to the production of materials, products, or energy for sale or commercial distribution, or to the sale of services, other than research and development or education or training.

[38 FR 11446, May 8, 1973, as amended at 43 FR 6924, Feb. 17, 1978]

§ 50.23 Construction permits.

A construction permit for the construction of a production or utilization facility will be issued before the issuance of a license if the application is otherwise acceptable, and will be converted upon completion of the facility and Commission action, into a license as provided in § 50.56. However, if a combined license for a nuclear power reactor is issued under part 52 of this chapter, the construction permit and operating license are deemed to be combined in a single license. A construction permit for the alteration of a production or utilization facility will be issued before the issuance of an amendment of a license, if the application for amendment is otherwise acceptable, as provided in § 50.92.

[72 FR 49490, Aug. 28, 2007, as amended at 81 FR 86909, Dec. 2, 2016]

APPLICATIONS FOR LICENSES, CERTIFICATIONS, AND REGULATORY APPROVALS; FORM; CONTENTS; INELIGIBILITY OF CERTAIN APPLICANTS

§50.30 Filing of application; oath or affirmation.

(a) *Serving of applications.* (1) Each filing of an application for a standard design approval or license to construct and/or operate, or manufacture, a production or utilization facility (including an early site permit, combined license, and manufacturing license under part 52 of this chapter), and any amendments to the applications, must be submitted to the U.S. Nuclear Regulatory Commission in accordance with §50.4 or §52.3 of this chapter, as applicable.

(2) The applicant shall maintain the capability to generate additional copies of the general information and the safety analysis report, or part thereof or amendment thereto, for subsequent distribution in accordance with the written instructions of the Director, Office of Nuclear Reactor Regulation, Director, Office of New Reactors, or Director, Office of Nuclear Material Safety and Safeguards, as appropriate.

(3) Each applicant for a construction permit under this part, or an early site permit, combined license, or manufacturing license under part 52 of this chapter, shall, upon notification by the Atomic Safety and Licensing Board appointed to conduct the public hearing required by the Atomic Energy Act, update the application and serve the updated copies of the application or parts of it, eliminating all superseded information, together with an index of the updated application, as directed by the Atomic Safety and Licensing Board. Any subsequent amendment to the application must be served on those served copies of the application and must be submitted to the U.S. Nuclear Regulatory Commission as specified in §50.4 or §52.3 of this chapter, as applicable.

(4) The applicant must make a copy of the updated application available at the public hearing for the use of any other parties to the proceeding, and shall certify that the updated copies of the application contain the current contents of the application submitted in accordance with the requirements of this part.

(5) At the time of filing an application, the Commission will make available at the NRC Web site, *http://www.nrc.gov*, a copy of the application, subsequent amendments, and other records pertinent to the matter which is the subject of the application for public inspection and copying.

(6) The serving of copies required by this section must not occur until the application has been docketed under §2.101(a) of this chapter. Copies must be submitted to the Commission, as specified in §50.4 or §52.3 of this chapter, as applicable, to enable the Director, Office of New Reactors, or the Director, Office of Nuclear Reactor Regulation, or the Director, Office of Nuclear Material Safety and Safeguards, as appropriate, to determine whether the application is sufficiently complete to permit docketing.

(b) *Oath or affirmation.* Each application for a standard design approval or license, including, whenever appropriate, a construction permit or early site permit, or amendment of it, and each amendment of each application must be executed in a signed original by the applicant or duly authorized officer thereof under oath or affirmation.

(c) [Reserved]

(d) *Application for operating licenses.* The holder of a construction permit for a production or utilization facility shall, at the time of submission of the final safety analysis report, file an application for an operating license or an amendment to an application for a license to construct and operate a production or utilization facility for the issuance of an operating license, as appropriate. The application or amendment shall state the name of the applicant, the name, location and power level, if any, of the facility and the time when the facility is expected to be ready for operation, and may incorporate by reference any pertinent information submitted in accordance with §50.33 with the application for a construction permit.

(e) *Filing Fees.* Each application for a standard design approval or production or utilization facility license, including, whenever appropriate, a construction permit or early site permit, other than a license exempted from part 170 of this chapter, shall be accompanied by the fee prescribed in part 170 of this chapter. No fee will be required to accompany an application for renewal, amendment, or termination of a construction permit, operating license, combined license, or manufacturing license, except as provided in § 170.21 of this chapter.

(f) *Environmental report.* An application for a construction permit, operating license, early site permit, combined license, or manufacturing license for a nuclear power reactor, testing facility, fuel reprocessing plant, or other production or utilization facility whose construction or operation may be determined by the Commission to have a significant impact in the environment, shall be accompanied by an Environmental Report required under subpart A of part 51 of this chapter.

[23 FR 3115, May 10, 1958, as amended at 33 FR 10924, Aug. 1, 1968; 34 FR 6307, Apr. 3, 1969; 35 FR 19660, Dec. 29, 1970; 37 FR 5749, Mar. 21, 1972; 51 FR 40307, Nov. 6, 1986; 64 FR 48951, Sept. 9, 1999; 68 FR 58809, Oct. 10, 2003; 72 FR 49490, Aug. 28, 2007; 73 FR 5721, Jan. 31, 2008]

§ 50.31 Combining applications.

An applicant may combine in one his several applications for different kinds of licenses under the regulations in this chapter.

§ 50.32 Elimination of repetition.

In his application, the applicant may incorporate by reference information contained in previous applications, statements or reports filed with the Commission: *Provided,* That such references are clear and specific.

§ 50.33 Contents of applications; general information.

Each application shall state:

(a) Name of applicant;

(b) Address of applicant;

(c) Description of business or occupation of applicant;

(d)(1) If applicant is an individual, state citizenship.

(2) If applicant is a partnership, state name, citizenship and address of each partner and the principal location where the partnership does business.

(3) If applicant is a corporation or an unincorporated association, state:

(i) The state where it is incorporated or organized and the principal location where it does business;

(ii) The names, addresses and citizenship of its directors and of its principal officers;

(iii) Whether it is owned, controlled, or dominated by an alien, a foreign corporation, or foreign government, and if so, give details.

(4) If the applicant is acting as agent or representative of another person in filing the application, identify the principal and furnish information required under this paragraph with respect to such principal.

(e) The class of license applied for, the use to which the facility will be put, the period of time for which the license is sought, and a list of other licenses, except operator's licenses, issued or applied for in connection with the proposed facility.

(f) Except for an electric utility applicant for a license to operate a utilization facility of the type described in § 50.21(b) or § 50.22, information sufficient to demonstrate to the Commission the financial qualification of the applicant to carry out, in accordance with regulations in this chapter, the activities for which the permit or license is sought. As applicable, the following should be provided:

(1) If the application is for a construction permit, the applicant shall submit information that demonstrates that the applicant possesses or has reasonable assurance of obtaining the funds necessary to cover estimated construction costs and related fuel cycle costs. The applicant shall submit estimates of the total construction costs of the facility and related fuel cycle costs, and shall indicate the source(s) of funds to cover these costs.

(2) If the application is for an operating license, the applicant shall submit information that demonstrates the applicant possesses or has reasonable assurance of obtaining the funds necessary to cover estimated operation costs for the period of the license. The applicant shall submit estimates for total annual operating costs for each of the first five years of operation of the facility. The applicant shall also indicate the source(s) of funds to cover these costs. An applicant seeking to

renew or extend the term of an operating license for a power reactor need not submit the financial information that is required in an application for an initial license. Applicants to renew or extend the term of an operating license for a nonpower reactor shall include the financial information that is required in an application for an initial license.

(3) If the application is for a combined license under subpart C of part 52 of this chapter, the applicant shall submit the information described in paragraphs (f)(1) and (f)(2) of this section.

(4) Each application for a construction permit, operating license, or combined license submitted by a newly-formed entity organized for the primary purpose of constructing and/or operating a facility must also include information showing:

(i) The legal and financial relationships it has or proposes to have with its stockholders or owners;

(ii) The stockholders' or owners' financial ability to meet any contractual obligation to the entity which they have incurred or proposed to incur; and

(iii) Any other information considered necessary by the Commission to enable it to determine the applicant's financial qualification.

(5) The Commission may request an established entity or newly-formed entity to submit additional or more detailed information respecting its financial arrangements and status of funds if the Commission considers this information appropriate. This may include information regarding a licensee's ability to continue the conduct of the activities authorized by the license and to decommission the facility.

(g) If the application is for an operating license or combined license for a nuclear power reactor, or if the application is for an early site permit and contains plans for coping with emergencies under § 52.17(b)(2)(ii) of this chapter, the applicant shall submit radiological emergency response plans of State and local governmental entities in the United States that are wholly or partially within the plume exposure pathway emergency planning zone (EPZ),[4] as well as the plans of State governments wholly or partially within the ingestion pathway EPZ.[5] If the application is for an early site permit that, under 10 CFR 52.17(b)(2)(i), proposes major features of the emergency plans describing the EPZs, then the descriptions of the EPZs must meet the requirements of this paragraph. Generally, the plume exposure pathway EPZ for nuclear power reactors shall consist of an area about 10 miles (16 km) in radius and the ingestion pathway EPZ shall consist of an area about 50 miles (80 km) in radius. The exact size and configuration of the EPZs surrounding a particular nuclear power reactor shall be determined in relation to the local emergency response needs and capabilities as they are affected by such conditions as demography, topography, land characteristics, access routes, and jurisdictional boundaries. The size of the EPZs also may be determined on a case-by-case basis for gas-cooled reactors and for reactors with an authorized power level less than 250 MW thermal. The plans for the ingestion pathway shall focus on such actions as are appropriate to protect the food ingestion pathway.

(h) If the applicant, other than an applicant for a combined license, proposes to construct or alter a production or utilization facility, the application shall state the earliest and latest dates for completion of the construction or alteration.

(i) If the proposed activity is the generation and distribution of electric energy under a class 103 license, a list of the names and addresses of such regulatory agencies as may have jurisdiction over the rates and services incident to the proposed activity, and a list of trade and news publications which circulate in the area where the

---

[4] Emergency planning zones (EPZs) are discussed in NUREG–0396, EPA 520/1–78–016, "Planning Basis for the Development of State and Local Government Radiological Emergency Response Plans in Support of Light-Water Nuclear Power Plants," December 1978.

[5] If the State and local emergency response plans have been previously provided to the NRC for inclusion in the facility docket, the applicant need only provide the appropriate reference to meet this requirement.

proposed activity will be conducted and which are considered appropriate to give reasonable notice of the application to those municipalities, private utilities, public bodies, and cooperatives, which might have a potential interest in the facility.

(j) If the application contains Restricted Data or other defense information, it shall be prepared in such manner that all Restricted Data and other defense information are separated from the unclassified information.

(k)(1) For an application for an operating license or combined license for a production or utilization facility, information in the form of a report, as described in § 50.75, indicating how reasonable assurance will be provided that funds will be available to decommission the facility.

(2) On or before July 26, 1990, each holder of an operating license for a production or utilization facility in effect on July 27, 1990, shall submit information in the form of a report as described in § 50.75 of this part, indicating how reasonable assurance will be provided that funds will be available to decommission the facility.

[21 FR 355, Jan. 19, 1956, as amended at 35 FR 19660, Dec. 29, 1970; 38 FR 3956, Feb. 9, 1973; 45 FR 55408, Aug. 19, 1980; 49 FR 35752, Sept. 12, 1984; 53 FR 24049, June 27, 1988; 69 FR 4448, Jan. 30, 2004; 72 FR 49490, Aug. 28, 2007]

§ 50.34 Contents of applications; technical information.

(a) *Preliminary safety analysis report.* Each application for a construction permit shall include a preliminary safety analysis report. The minimum information[5] to be included shall consist of the following:

(1) Stationary power reactor applicants for a construction permit who apply on or after January 10, 1997, shall comply with paragraph (a)(1)(ii) of this section. All other applicants for a construction permit shall comply with paragraph (a)(1)(i) of this section.

(i) A description and safety assessment of the site on which the facility is to be located, with appropriate attention to features affecting facility design. Special attention should be directed to the site evaluation factors identified in part 100 of this chapter. The assessment must contain an analysis and evaluation of the major structures, systems and components of the facility which bear significantly on the acceptability of the site under the site evaluation factors identified in part 100 of this chapter, assuming that the facility will be operated at the ultimate power level which is contemplated by the applicant. With respect to operation at the projected initial power level, the applicant is required to submit information prescribed in paragraphs (a)(2) through (a)(8) of this section, as well as the information required by this paragraph, in support of the application for a construction permit, or a design approval.

(ii) A description and safety assessment of the site and a safety assessment of the facility. It is expected that reactors will reflect through their design, construction and operation an extremely low probability for accidents that could result in the release of significant quantities of radioactive fission products. The following power reactor design characteristics and proposed operation will be taken into consideration by the Commission:

(A) Intended use of the reactor including the proposed maximum power level and the nature and inventory of contained radioactive materials;

(B) The extent to which generally accepted engineering standards are applied to the design of the reactor;

(C) The extent to which the reactor incorporates unique, unusual or enhanced safety features having a significant bearing on the probability or consequences of accidental release of radioactive materials;

(D) The safety features that are to be engineered into the facility and those barriers that must be breached as a result of an accident before a release of radioactive material to the environment can occur. Special attention must be directed to plant design features intended to mitigate the radiological consequences of accidents. In

[5] The applicant may provide information required by this paragraph in the form of a discussion, with specific references, of similarities to and differences from, facilities of similar design for which applications have previously been filed with the Commission.

performing this assessment, an applicant shall assume a fission product release[6] from the core into the containment assuming that the facility is operated at the ultimate power level contemplated. The applicant shall perform an evaluation and analysis of the postulated fission product release, using the expected demonstrable containment leak rate and any fission product cleanup systems intended to mitigate the consequences of the accidents, together with applicable site characteristics, including site meteorology, to evaluate the offsite radiological consequences. Site characteristics must comply with part 100 of this chapter. The evaluation must determine that:

(*1*) An individual located at any point on the boundary of the exclusion area for any 2 hour period following the onset of the postulated fission product release, would not receive a radiation dose in excess of 25 rem[7] total effective dose equivalent (TEDE).

(*2*) An individual located at any point on the outer boundary of the low population zone, who is exposed to the radioactive cloud resulting from the postulated fission product release (during the entire period of its passage) would not receive a radiation dose in excess of 25 rem total effective dose equivalent (TEDE);

(E) With respect to operation at the projected initial power level, the applicant is required to submit information prescribed in paragraphs (a)(2) through (a)(8) of this section, as well as the information required by paragraph (a)(1)(i) of this section, in support of the application for a construction permit.

(2) A summary description and discussion of the facility, with special attention to design and operating characteristics, unusual or novel design features, and principal safety considerations.

(3) The preliminary design of the facility including:

(i) The principal design criteria for the facility.[8] Appendix A, General Design Criteria for Nuclear Power Plants, establishes minimum requirements for the principal design criteria for water-cooled nuclear power plants similar in design and location to plants for which construction permits have previously been issued by the Commission and provides guidance to applicants for construction permits in establishing principal design criteria for other types of nuclear power units;

(ii) The design bases and the relation of the design bases to the principal design criteria;

(iii) Information relative to materials of construction, general arrangement, and approximate dimensions, sufficient to provide reasonable assurance that the final design will conform to the design bases with adequate margin for safety.

(4) A preliminary analysis and evaluation of the design and performance of structures, systems, and components of the facility with the objective of assessing the risk to public health and safety resulting from operation of the facility and including determination of the margins of safety during normal operations and transient conditions anticipated during the life of the facility, and the adequacy of structures, systems, and components provided for the

[6] The fission product release assumed for this evaluation should be based upon a major accident, hypothesized for purposes of site analysis or postulated from considerations of possible accidental events. Such accidents have generally been assumed to result in substantial meltdown of the core with subsequent release into the containment of appreciable quantities of fission products.

[7] A whole body dose of 25 rem has been stated to correspond numerically to the once in a lifetime accidental or emergency dose for radiation workers which, according to NCRP recommendations at the time could be disregarded in the determination of their radiation exposure status (see NBS Handbook 69 dated June 5, 1959). However, its use is not intended to imply that this number constitutes an acceptable limit for an emergency dose to the public under accident conditions. Rather, this dose value has been set forth in this section as a reference value, which can be used in the evaluation of plant design features with respect to postulated reactor accidents, in order to assure that such designs provide assurance of low risk of public exposure to radiation, in the event of such accidents.

[8] General design criteria for chemical processing facilities are being developed.

[9] [Reserved]

prevention of accidents and the mitigation of the consequences of accidents. Analysis and evaluation of ECCS cooling performance and the need for high point vents following postulated loss-of-coolant accidents must be performed in accordance with the requirements of § 50.46 and § 50.46a of this part for facilities for which construction permits may be issued after December 28, 1974.

(5) An identification and justification for the selection of those variables, conditions, or other items which are determined as the result of preliminary safety analysis and evaluation to be probable subjects of technical specifications for the facility, with special attention given to those items which may significantly influence the final design: *Provided, however,* That this requirement is not applicable to an application for a construction permit filed prior to January 16, 1969.

(6) A preliminary plan for the applicant's organization, training of personnel, and conduct of operations.

(7) A description of the quality assurance program to be applied to the design, fabrication, construction, and testing of the structures, systems, and components of the facility. Appendix B, "Quality Assurance Criteria for Nuclear Power Plants and Fuel Reprocessing Plants," sets forth the requirements for quality assurance programs for nuclear power plants and fuel reprocessing plants. The description of the quality assurance program for a nuclear power plant or a fuel reprocessing plant shall include a discussion of how the applicable requirements of appendix B will be satisfied.

(8) An identification of those structures, systems, or components of the facility, if any, which require research and development to confirm the adequacy of their design; and identification and description of the research and development program which will be conducted to resolve any safety questions associated with such structures, systems or components; and a schedule of the research and development program showing that such safety questions will be resolved at or before the latest date stated in the application for completion of construction of the facility.

(9) The technical qualifications of the applicant to engage in the proposed activities in accordance with the regulations in this chapter.

(10) A discussion of the applicant's preliminary plans for coping with emergencies. Appendix E sets forth items which shall be included in these plans.

(11) On or after February 5, 1979, applicants who apply for construction permits for nuclear power plants to be built on multiunit sites shall identify potential hazards to the structures, systems and components important to safety of operating nuclear facilities from construction activities. A discussion shall also be included of any managerial and administrative controls that will be used during construction to assure the safety of the operating unit.

(12) On or after January 10, 1997, stationary power reactor applicants who apply for a construction permit, as partial conformance to General Design Criterion 2 of appendix A to this part, shall comply with the earthquake engineering criteria in appendix S to this part.

(13) On or after July 13, 2009, stationary power reactor applicants who apply for a construction permit shall submit the information required by 10 CFR 50.150(b) as a part of their preliminary safety analysis report.

(b) *Final safety analysis report.* Each application for an operating license shall include a final safety analysis report. The final safety analysis report shall include information that describes the facility, presents the design bases and the limits on its operation, and presents a safety analysis of the structures, systems, and components and of the facility as a whole, and shall include the following:

(1) All current information, such as the results of environmental and meteorological monitoring programs, which has been developed since issuance of the construction permit, relating to site evaluation factors identified in part 100 of this chapter.

(2) A description and analysis of the structures, systems, and components of the facility, with emphasis upon performance requirements, the bases, with technical justification therefor, upon

which such requirements have been established, and the evaluations required to show that safety functions will be accomplished. The description shall be sufficient to permit understanding of the system designs and their relationship to safety evaluations.

(i) For nuclear reactors, such items as the reactor core, reactor coolant system, instrumentation and control systems, electrical systems, containment system, other engineered safety features, auxiliary and emergency systems, power conversion systems, radioactive waste handling systems, and fuel handling systems shall be discussed insofar as they are pertinent.

(ii) For facilities other than nuclear reactors, such items as the chemical, physical, metallurgical, or nuclear process to be performed, instrumentation and control systems, ventilation and filter systems, electrical systems, auxiliary and emergency systems, and radioactive waste handling systems shall be discussed insofar as they are pertinent.

(3) The kinds and quantities of radioactive materials expected to be produced in the operation and the means for controlling and limiting radioactive effluents and radiation exposures within the limits set forth in part 20 of this chapter.

(4) A final analysis and evaluation of the design and performance of structures, systems, and components with the objective stated in paragraph (a)(4) of this section and taking into account any pertinent information developed since the submittal of the preliminary safety analysis report. Analysis and evaluation of ECCS cooling performance following postulated loss-of-coolant accidents shall be performed in accordance with the requirements of § 50.46 for facilities for which a license to operate may be issued after December 28, 1974.

(5) A description and evaluation of the results of the applicant's programs, including research and development, if any, to demonstrate that any safety questions identified at the construction permit stage have been resolved.

(6) The following information concerning facility operation:

(i) The applicant's organizational structure, allocations or responsibilities and authorities, and personnel qualifications requirements.

(ii) Managerial and administrative controls to be used to assure safe operation. Appendix B, "Quality Assurance Criteria for Nuclear Power Plants and Fuel Reprocessing Plants," sets forth the requirements for such controls for nuclear power plants and fuel reprocessing plants. The information on the controls to be used for a nuclear power plant or a fuel reprocessing plant shall include a discussion of how the applicable requirements of appendix B will be satisfied.

(iii) Plans for preoperational testing and initial operations.

(iv) Plans for conduct of normal operations, including maintenance, surveillance, and periodic testing of structures, systems, and components.

(v) Plans for coping with emergencies, which shall include the items specified in appendix E.

(vi) Proposed technical specifications prepared in accordance with the requirements of § 50.36.

(vii) On or after February 5, 1979, applicants who apply for operating licenses for nuclear power plants to be operated on multiunit sites shall include an evaluation of the potential hazards to the structures, systems, and components important to safety of operating units resulting from construction activities, as well as a description of the managerial and administrative controls to be used to provide assurance that the limiting conditions for operation are not exceeded as a result of construction activities at the multiunit sites.

(7) The technical qualifications of the applicant to engage in the proposed activities in accordance with the regulations in this chapter.

(8) A description and plans for implementation of an operator requalification program. The operator requalification program must as a minimum, meet the requirements for those programs contained in § 55.59 of part 55 of this chapter.

(9) A description of protection provided against pressurized thermal shock events, including projected values of the reference temperature for reactor vessel beltline materials as defined in § 50.61 (b)(1) and (b)(2).

(10) On or after January 10, 1997, stationary power reactor applicants who apply for an operating license, as partial conformance to General Design Criterion 2 of appendix A to this part, shall comply with the earthquake engineering criteria of appendix S to this part. However, for those operating license applicants and holders whose construction permit was issued before January 10, 1997, the earthquake engineering criteria in Section VI of appendix A to part 100 of this chapter continues to apply.

(11) On or after January 10, 1997, stationary power reactor applicants who apply for an operating license, shall provide a description and safety assessment of the site and of the facility as in § 50.34(a)(1)(ii). However, for either an operating license applicant or holder whose construction permit was issued before January 10, 1997, the reactor site criteria in part 100 of this chapter and the seismic and geologic siting criteria in appendix A to part 100 of this chapter continues to apply.

(12) On or after July 13, 2009, stationary power reactor applicants who apply for an operating license which is subject to 10 CFR 50.150(a) shall submit the information required by 10 CFR 50.150(b) as a part of their final safety analysis report.

(c) *Physical security plan.* (1) Each applicant for an operating license for a production or utilization facility that will be subject to §§ 73.50 and 73.60 of this chapter must include a physical security plan.

(2) Each applicant for an operating license for a utilization facility that will be subject to the requirements of § 73.55 of this chapter must include a physical security plan, a training and qualification plan in accordance with the criteria set forth in appendix B to part 73 of this chapter, and a cyber security plan in accordance with the criteria set forth in § 73.54 of this chapter.

(3) The physical security plan must describe how the applicant will meet the requirements of part 73 of this chapter (and part 11 of this chapter, if applicable, including the identification and description of jobs as required by § 11.11(a) of this chapter, at the proposed facility). Security plans must list tests, inspections, audits, and other means to be used to demonstrate compliance with the requirements of 10 CFR parts 11 and 73, if applicable.

(d) *Safeguards contingency plan.* (1) Each application for a license to operate a production or utilization facility that will be subject to §§ 73.50 and 73.60 of this chapter must include a licensee safeguards contingency plan in accordance with the criteria set forth in section I of appendix C to part 73 of this chapter. The "implementation procedures" required per section I of appendix C to part 73 of this chapter do not have to be submitted to the Commission for approval.

(2) Each application for a license to operate a utilization facility that will be subject to § 73.55 of this chapter must include a licensee safeguards contingency plan in accordance with the criteria set forth in section II of appendix C to part 73 of this chapter. The "implementing procedures" required in section II of appendix C to part 73 of this chapter do not have to be submitted to the Commission for approval.

(e) *Protection against unauthorized disclosure.* Each applicant for an operating license for a production or utilization facility, who prepares a physical security plan, a safeguards contingency plan, a training and qualification plan, or a cyber security plan, shall protect the plans and other related Safeguards Information against unauthorized disclosure in accordance with the requirements of § 73.21 of this chapter.

(f) *Additional TMI-related requirements.* In addition to the requirements of paragraph (a) of this section, each applicant for a light-water-reactor construction permit or manufacturing license whose application was pending as of February 16, 1982, shall meet the requirements in paragraphs (f)(1) through (3) of this section. This regulation applies to the pending applications by Duke Power Company (Perkins Nuclear Station, Units 1, 2, and 3), Houston Lighting & Power Company (Allens Creek Nuclear Generating Station, Unit 1), Portland General Electric Company (Pebble Springs Nuclear Plant, Units 1 and 2), Public Service Company of Oklahoma (Black Fox Station, Units 1 and 2), Puget Sound Power & Light Company (Skagit/Hanford Nuclear Power Project, Units 1 and 2), and Offshore Power Systems (License to Manufacture Floating Nuclear Plants). The number of units that will be specified in the manufacturing license above, if issued, will be that number whose start of manufacture, as defined in the license application, can practically begin within a 10-year period commencing on the date of issuance of the manufacturing license, but in no event will that number be in excess of ten. The manufacturing license will require the plant design to be updated no later than 5 years after its approval. Paragraphs (f)(1)(xii), (2)(ix), and (3)(v) of this section, pertaining to hydrogen control measures, must be met by all applicants covered by this regulation. However, the Commission may decide to impose additional requirements and the issue of whether compliance with these provisions, together with 10 CFR 50.44 and criterion 50 of appendix A to 10 CFR part 50, is sufficient for issuance of that manufacturing license which may be considered in the manufacturing license proceeding. In addition, each applicant for a design certification, design approval, combined license, or manufacturing license under part 52 of this chapter shall demonstrate compliance with the technically relevant portions of the requirements in paragraphs (f)(1) through (3) of this section, except for paragraphs (f)(1)(xii), (f)(2)(ix), and (f)(3)(v).

(1) To satisfy the following requirements, the application shall provide sufficient information to describe the nature of the studies, how they are to be conducted, estimated submittal dates, and a program to ensure that the results of these studies are factored into the final design of the facility. For licensees identified in the introduction to paragraph (f) of this section, all studies must be completed no later than 2 years following the issuance of the construction permit or manufacturing license.[10] For all other applicants, the studies must be submitted as part of the final safety analysis report.

(i) Perform a plant/site specific probabilistic risk assessment, the aim of which is to seek such improvements in the reliability of core and containment heat removal systems as are significant and practical and do not impact excessively on the plant. (II.B.8)

(ii) Perform an evaluation of the proposed auxiliary feedwater system (AFWS), to include (applicable to PWR's only) (II.E.1.1):

(A) A simplified AFWS reliability analysis using event-tree and fault-tree logic techniques.

(B) A design review of AFWS.

(C) An evaluation of AFWS flow design bases and criteria.

(iii) Perform an evaluation of the potential for and impact of reactor coolant pump seal damage following small-break LOCA with loss of offsite power. If damage cannot be precluded, provide an analysis of the limiting small-break loss-of-coolant accident with subsequent reactor coolant pump seal damage. (II.K.2.16 and II.K.3.25)

(iv) Perform an analysis of the probability of a small-break loss-of-coolant accident (LOCA) caused by a stuck-open power-operated relief valve (PORV). If this probability is a significant contributor to the probability of small-break LOCA's from all causes, provide a description and evaluation of the effect on small-break LOCA probability of an automatic PORV isolation system that would operate when the reactor coolant system pressure falls after the PORV has opened. (Applicable to PWR's only). (II.K.3.2)

(v) Perform an evaluation of the safety effectiveness of providing for separation of high pressure coolant injection (HPCI) and reactor core isolation cooling (RCIC) system initiation levels so that the RCIC system initiates at a higher water level than the HPCI system, and of providing that both systems restart on low water level. (For plants with high pressure core spray systems in lieu of high pressure coolant injection systems, substitute the words, "high pressure core spray" for "high pressure coolant injection" and "HPCS" for "HPCI") (Applicable to BWR's only). (II.K.3.13)

[10] Alphanumeric designations correspond to the related action plan items in NUREG 0718 and NUREG–0660, "NRC Action Plan Developed as a Result of the TMI–2 Accident." They are provided herein for information only.

(vi) Perform a study to identify practicable system modifications that would reduce challenges and failures of relief valves, without compromising the performance of the valves or other systems. (Applicable to BWR's only). (II.K.3.16)

(vii) Perform a feasibility and risk assessment study to determine the optimum automatic depressurization system (ADS) design modifications that would eliminate the need for manual activation to ensure adequate core cooling. (Applicable to BWR's only). (II.K.3.18)

(viii) Perform a study of the effect on all core-cooling modes under accident conditions of designing the core spray and low pressure coolant injection systems to ensure that the systems will automatically restart on loss of water level, after having been manually stopped, if an initiation signal is still present. (Applicable to BWR's only). (II.K.3.21)

(ix) Perform a study to determine the need for additional space cooling to ensure reliable long-term operation of the reactor core isolation cooling (RCIC) and high-pressure coolant injection (HPCI) systems, following a complete loss of offsite power to the plant for at least two (2) hours. (For plants with high pressure core spray systems in lieu of high pressure coolant injection systems, substitute the words, "high pressure core spray" for "high pressure coolant injection" and "HPCS" for "HPCI") (Applicable to BWR's only). (II.K.3.24)

(x) Perform a study to ensure that the Automatic Depressurization System, valves, accumulators, and associated equipment and instrumentation will be capable of performing their intended functions during and following an accident situation, taking no credit for non-safety related equipment or instrumentation, and accounting for normal expected air (or nitrogen) leakage through valves. (Applicable to BWR's only). (II.K.3.28)

(xi) Provide an evaluation of depressurization methods, other than by full actuation of the automatic depressurization system, that would reduce the possibility of exceeding vessel integrity limits during rapid cooldown. (Applicable to BWR's only) (II.K.3.45)

(xii) Perform an evaluation of alternative hydrogen control systems that would satisfy the requirements of paragraph (f)(2)(ix) of this section. As a minimum include consideration of a hydrogen ignition and post-accident inerting system. The evaluation shall include:

(A) A comparison of costs and benefits of the alternative systems considered.

(B) For the selected system, analyses and test data to verify compliance with the requirements of (f)(2)(ix) of this section.

(C) For the selected system, preliminary design descriptions of equipment, function, and layout.

(2) To satisfy the following requirements, the application shall provide sufficient information to demonstrate that the required actions will be satisfactorily completed by the operating license stage. This information is of the type customarily required to satisfy 10 CFR 50.35(a)(2) or to address unresolved generic safety issues.

(i) Provide simulator capability that correctly models the control room and includes the capability to simulate small-break LOCA's. (Applicable to construction permit applicants only) (I.A.4.2.)

(ii) Establish a program, to begin during construction and follow into operation, for integrating and expanding current efforts to improve plant procedures. The scope of the program shall include emergency procedures, reliability analyses, human factors engineering, crisis management, operator training, and coordination with INPO and other industry efforts. (Applicable to construction permit applicants only) (I.C.9)

(iii) Provide, for Commission review, a control room design that reflects state-of-the-art human factor principles prior to committing to fabrication or revision of fabricated control room panels and layouts. (I.D.1)

(iv) Provide a plant safety parameter display console that will display to operators a minimum set of parameters defining the safety status of the plant, capable of displaying a full range of important plant parameters and data trends on demand, and capable of indicating when process limits are being approached or exceeded. (I.D.2)

(v) Provide for automatic indication of the bypassed and operable status of safety systems. (I.D.3)

(vi) Provide the capability of high point venting of noncondensible gases from the reactor coolant system, and other systems that may be required to maintain adequate core cooling. Systems to achieve this capability shall be capable of being operated from the control room and their operation shall not lead to an unacceptable increase in the probability of loss-of-coolant accident or an unacceptable challenge to containment integrity. (II.B.1)

(vii) Perform radiation and shielding design reviews of spaces around systems that may, as a result of an accident, contain accident source term[11] radioactive materials, and design as necessary to permit adequate access to important areas and to protect safety equipment from the radiation environment. (II.B.2)

(viii) Provide a capability to promptly obtain and analyze samples from the reactor coolant system and containment that may contain accident source term[11] radioactive materials without radiation exposures to any individual exceeding 5 rems to the whole body or 50 rems to the extremities. Materials to be analyzed and quantified include certain radionuclides that are indicators of the degree of core damage (e.g., noble gases, radioiodines and cesiums, and nonvolatile isotopes), hydrogen in the containment atmosphere, dissolved gases, chloride, and boron concentrations. (II.B.3)

(ix) Provide a system for hydrogen control that can safely accommodate hydrogen generated by the equivalent of a 100% fuel-clad metal water reaction. Preliminary design information on the tentatively preferred system option of those being evaluated in paragraph (f)(1)(xii) of this section is sufficient at the construction permit stage. The hydrogen control system and associated systems shall provide, with reasonable assurance, that: (II.B.8)

(A) Uniformly distributed hydrogen concentrations in the containment do not exceed 10% during and following an accident that releases an equivalent amount of hydrogen as would be generated from a 100% fuel clad metal-water reaction, or that the post-accident atmosphere will not support hydrogen combustion.

(B) Combustible concentrations of hydrogen will not collect in areas where unintended combustion or detonation could cause loss of containment integrity or loss of appropriate mitigating features.

(C) Equipment necessary for achieving and maintaining safe shutdown of the plant and maintaining containment integrity will perform its safety function during and after being exposed to the environmental conditions attendant with the release of hydrogen generated by the equivalent of a 100% fuel-clad metal water reaction including the environmental conditions created by activation of the hydrogen control system.

(D) If the method chosen for hydrogen control is a post-accident inerting system, inadvertent actuation of the system can be safely accommodated during plant operation.

(x) Provide a test program and associated model development and conduct tests to qualify reactor coolant system relief and safety valves and, for PWR's, PORV block valves, for all fluid conditions expected under operating conditions, transients and accidents. Consideration of anticipated transients without scram (ATWS) conditions shall be included in the test program. Actual testing under ATWS conditions need not be carried out until subsequent phases of the test program are developed. (II.D.1)

(xi) Provide direct indication of relief and safety valve position (open or closed) in the control room. (II.D.3)

(xii) Provide automatic and manual auxiliary feedwater (AFW) system initiation, and provide auxiliary

[11] The fission product release assumed for these calculations should be based upon a major accident, hypothesized for purposes of site analysis or postulated from considerations of possible accidental events, that would result in potential hazards not exceeded by those from any accident considered credible. Such accidents have generally been assumed to result in substantial meltdown of the core with subsequent release of appreciable quantities of fission products.

feedwater system flow indication in the control room. (Applicable to PWR's only) (II.E.1.2)

(xiii) Provide pressurizer heater power supply and associated motive and control power interfaces sufficient to establish and maintain natural circulation in hot standby conditions with only onsite power available. (Applicable to PWR's only) (II.E.3.1)

(xiv) Provide containment isolation systems that: (II.E.4.2)

(A) Ensure all non-essential systems are isolated automatically by the containment isolation system,

(B) For each non-essential penetration (except instrument lines) have two isolation barriers in series,

(C) Do not result in reopening of the containment isolation valves on resetting of the isolation signal,

(D) Utilize a containment set point pressure for initiating containment isolation as low as is compatible with normal operation,

(E) Include automatic closing on a high radiation signal for all systems that provide a path to the environs.

(xv) Provide a capability for containment purging/venting designed to minimize the purging time consistent with ALARA principles for occupational exposure. Provide and demonstrate high assurance that the purge system will reliably isolate under accident conditions. (II.E.4.4)

(xvi) Establish a design criterion for the allowable number of actuation cycles of the emergency core cooling system and reactor protection system consistent with the expected occurrence rates of severe overcooling events (considering both anticipated transients and accidents). (Applicable to B&W designs only). (II.E.5.1)

(xvii) Provide instrumentation to measure, record and readout in the control room: (A) containment pressure, (B) containment water level, (C) containment hydrogen concentration, (D) containment radiation intensity (high level), and (E) noble gas effluents at all potential, accident release points. Provide for continuous sampling of radioactive iodines and particulates in gaseous effluents from all potential accident release points, and for onsite capability to analyze and measure these samples. (II.F.1)

(xviii) Provide instruments that provide in the control room an unambiguous indication of inadequate core cooling, such as primary coolant saturation meters in PWR's, and a suitable combination of signals from indicators of coolant level in the reactor vessel and in-core thermocouples in PWR's and BWR's. (II.F.2)

(xix) Provide instrumentation adequate for monitoring plant conditions following an accident that includes core damage. (II.F.3)

(xx) Provide power supplies for pressurizer relief valves, block valves, and level indicators such that: (A) Level indicators are powered from vital buses; (B) motive and control power connections to the emergency power sources are through devices qualified in accordance with requirements applicable to systems important to safety and (C) electric power is provided from emergency power sources. (Applicable to PWR's only). (II.G.1)

(xxi) Design auxiliary heat removal systems such that necessary automatic and manual actions can be taken to ensure proper functioning when the main feedwater system is not operable. (Applicable to BWR's only). (II.K.1.22)

(xxii) Perform a failure modes and effects analysis of the integrated control system (ICS) to include consideration of failures and effects of input and output signals to the ICS. (Applicable to B&W-designed plants only). (II.K.2.9)

(xxiii) Provide, as part of the reactor protection system, an anticipatory reactor trip that would be actuated on loss of main feedwater and on turbine trip. (Applicable to B&W-designed plants only). (II.K.2.10)

(xxiv) Provide the capability to record reactor vessel water level in one location on recorders that meet normal post-accident recording requirements. (Applicable to BWR's only). (II.K.3.23)

(xxv) Provide an onsite Technical Support Center, an onsite Operational Support Center, and, for construction permit applications only, a nearsite Emergency Operations Facility. (III.A.1.2).

(xxvi) Provide for leakage control and detection in the design of systems outside containment that contain (or might contain) accident source term[11] radioactive materials following an accident. Applicants shall submit a leakage control program, including an initial test program, a schedule for retesting these systems, and the actions to be taken for minimizing leakage from such systems. The goal is to minimize potential exposures to workers and public, and to provide reasonable assurance that excessive leakage will not prevent the use of systems needed in an emergency. (III.D.1.1)

(xxvii) Provide for monitoring of inplant radiation and airborne radioactivity as appropriate for a broad range of routine and accident conditions. (III.D.3.3)

(xxviii) Evaluate potential pathways for radioactivity and radiation that may lead to control room habitability problems under accident conditions resulting in an accident source term [11] release, and make necessary design provisions to preclude such problems. (III.D.3.4)

(3) To satisfy the following requirements, the application shall provide sufficient information to demonstrate that the requirement has been met. This information is of the type customarily required to satisfy paragraph (a)(1) of this section or to address the applicant's technical qualifications and management structure and competence.

(i) Provide administrative procedures for evaluating operating, design and construction experience and for ensuring that applicable important industry experiences will be provided in a timely manner to those designing and constructing the plant. (I.C.5)

(ii) Ensure that the quality assurance (QA) list required by Criterion II, app. B, 10 CFR part 50 includes all structures, systems, and components important to safety. (I.F.1)

(iii) Establish a quality assurance (QA) program based on consideration of: (A) Ensuring independence of the organization performing checking functions from the organization responsible for performing the functions; (B) performing quality assurance/quality control functions at construction sites to the maximum feasible extent; (C) including QA personnel in the documented review of and concurrence in quality related procedures associated with design, construction and installation; (D) establishing criteria for determining QA programmatic requirements; (E) establishing qualification requirements for QA and QC personnel; (F) sizing the QA staff commensurate with its duties and responsibilities; (G) establishing procedures for maintenance of "as-built" documentation; and (H) providing a QA role in design and analysis activities. (I.F.2)

(iv) Provide one or more dedicated containment penetrations, equivalent in size to a single 3-foot diameter opening, in order not to preclude future installation of systems to prevent containment failure, such as a filtered vented containment system. (II.B.8)

(v) Provide preliminary design information at a level of detail consistent with that normally required at the construction permit stage of review sufficient to demonstrate that: (II.B.8)

(A)(*1*) Containment integrity will be maintained (*i.e.*, for steel containments by meeting the requirements of the ASME Boiler and Pressure Vessel Code, Section III, Division 1, subarticle NE–3220, Service Level C Limits, except that evaluation of instability is not required, considering pressure and dead load alone. For concrete containments by meeting the requirements of the ASME Boiler Pressure Vessel Code, Section III, Division 2 subarticle CC–3720, Factored Load Category, considering pressure and dead load alone) during an accident that releases hydrogen generated from 100% fuel clad metal-water reaction accompanied by either hydrogen burning or the added pressure from post-accident inerting assuming carbon dioxide is the inerting agent. As a minimum, the specific code requirements set forth above appropriate for each type of containment will be met for a combination of dead load and an internal pressure of 45 psig. Modest deviations from these criteria will be considered by the staff, if good cause is shown by an applicant. Systems necessary to ensure containment integrity shall also be demonstrated to perform their function under these conditions.

(*2*) Subarticle NE–3220, Division 1, and subarticle CC–3720, Division 2, of section III of the July 1, 1980 ASME Boiler and Pressure Vessel Code, which are referenced in paragraphs (f)(3)(v)(A)(*1*) and (f)(3)(v)(B)(*1*) of this section, were approved for incorporation by reference by the Director of the Office of the Federal Register. A notice of any changes made to the material incorporated by reference will be published in the FEDERAL REGISTER. Copies of the ASME Boiler and Pressure Vessel Code may be purchased from the American Society of Mechanical Engineers, United Engineering Center, 345 East 47th St., New York, NY 10017. It is also available for inspection at the NRC Library, 11545 Rockville Pike, Rockville, Maryland 20852–2738.

(B)(*1*) Containment structure loadings produced by an inadvertent full actuation of a post-accident inerting hydrogen control system (assuming carbon dioxide), but not including seismic or design basis accident loadings will not produce stresses in steel containments in excess of the limits set forth in the ASME Boiler and Pressure Vessel Code, Section III, Division 1, subarticle NE–3220, Service Level A Limits, except that evaluation of instability is not required (for concrete containments the loadings specified above will not produce strains in the containment liner in excess of the limits set forth in the ASME Boiler and Pressure Vessel Code, Section III, Division 2, subarticle CC–3720, Service Load Category, (*2*) The containment has the capability to safely withstand pressure tests at 1.10 and 1.15 times (for steel and concrete containments, respectively) the pressure calculated to result from carbon dioxide inerting.

(vi) For plant designs with external hydrogen recombiners, provide redundant dedicated containment penetrations so that, assuming a single failure, the recombiner systems can be connected to the containment atmosphere. (II.E.4.1)

(vii) Provide a description of the management plan for design and construction activities, to include: (A) The organizational and management structure singularly responsible for direction of design and construction of the proposed plant; (B) technical resources director by the applicant; (C) details of the interaction of design and construction within the applicant's organization and the manner by which the applicant will ensure close integration of the architect engineer and the nuclear steam supply vendor; (D) proposed procedures for handling the transition to operation; (E) the degree of top level management oversight and technical control to be exercised by the applicant during design and construction, including the preparation and implementation of procedures necessary to guide the effort. (II.J.3.1)

(g) *Combustible gas control.* All applicants for a reactor construction permit or operating license whose application is submitted after October 16, 2003, shall include the analyses, and the descriptions of the equipment and systems required by § 50.44 as a part of their application.

(h) *Conformance with the Standard Review Plan (SRP).* (1)(i) Applications for light water cooled nuclear power plant operating licenses docketed after May 17, 1982 shall include an evaluation of the facility against the Standard Review Plan (SRP) in effect on May 17, 1982 or the SRP revision in effect six months prior to the docket date of the application, whichever is later.

(ii) Applications for light-water-cooled nuclear power plant construction permits docketed after May 17, 1982, shall include an evaluation of the facility against the SRP in effect on May 17, 1982, or the SRP revision in effect six months before the docket date of the application, whichever is later.

(2) The evaluation required by this section shall include an identification and description of all differences in design features, analytical techniques, and procedural measures proposed for a facility and those corresponding features, techniques, and measures given in the SRP acceptance criteria. Where such a difference exists, the evaluation shall discuss how the alternative proposed provides an acceptable method of complying with those rules or regulations of Commission, or portions thereof, that underlie the corresponding SRP acceptance criteria.

(3) The SRP was issued to establish criteria that the NRC staff intends to use in evaluating whether an applicant/licensee meets the Commission's regulations. The SRP is not a substitute for the regulations, and compliance is not

a requirement. Applicants shall identify differences from the SRP acceptance criteria and evaluate how the proposed alternatives to the SRP criteria provide an acceptable method of complying with the Commission's regulations.

(i) A description and plans for implementation of the guidance and strategies intended to maintain or restore core cooling, containment, and spent fuel pool cooling capabilities under the circumstances associated with the loss of large areas of the plant due to explosions or fire as required by § 50.54(hh)(2) of this chapter.

[33 FR 18612, Dec. 17, 1968, as amended at 81 FR 86909, Dec. 2, 2016]

EDITORIAL NOTE: For FEDERAL REGISTER citations affecting § 50.34, see the List of CFR Sections Affected, which appears in the Finding Aids section of the printed volume and at *www.fdsys.gov*.

§ 50.34a Design objectives for equipment to control releases of radioactive material in effluents—nuclear power reactors.

(a) An application for a construction permit shall include a description of the preliminary design of equipment to be installed to maintain control over radioactive materials in gaseous and liquid effluents produced during normal reactor operations, including expected operational occurrences. In the case of an application filed on or after January 2, 1971, the application shall also identify the design objectives, and the means to be employed, for keeping levels of radioactive material in effluents to unrestricted areas as low as is reasonably achievable. The term "as low as is reasonably achievable" as used in this part means as low as is reasonably achievable taking into account the state of technology, and the economics of improvements in relation to benefits to the public health and safety and other societal and socioeconomic considerations, and in relation to the use of atomic energy in the public interest. The guides set out in appendix I to this part provide numerical guidance on design objectives for light-water-cooled nuclear power reactors to meet the requirements that radioactive material in effluents released to unrestricted areas be kept as low as is reasonably achievable. These numerical guides for design objectives and limiting conditions for operation are not to be construed as radiation protection standards.

(b) Each application for a construction permit shall include:

(1) A description of the preliminary design of equipment to be installed under paragraph (a) of this section;

(2) An estimate of:

(i) The quantity of each of the principal radionuclides expected to be released annually to unrestricted areas in liquid effluents produced during normal reactor operations; and

(ii) The quantity of each of the principal radionuclides of the gases, halides, and particulates expected to be released annually to unrestricted areas in gaseous effluents produced during normal reactor operations.

(3) A general description of the provisions for packaging, storage, and shipment offsite of solid waste containing radioactive materials resulting from treatment of gaseous and liquid effluents and from other sources.

(c) Each application for an operating license shall include:

(1) A description of the equipment and procedures for the control of gaseous and liquid effluents and for the maintenance and use of equipment installed in radioactive waste systems, under paragraph (a) of this section; and

(2) A revised estimate of the information required in paragraph (b)(2) of this section if the expected releases and exposures differ significantly from the estimates submitted in the application for a construction permit.

(d) Each application for a combined license under part 52 of this chapter shall include:

(1) A description of the equipment and procedures for the control of gaseous and liquid effluents and for the maintenance and use of equipment installed in radioactive waste systems, under paragraph (a) of this section; and

(2) The information required in paragraph (b)(2) of this section.

(e) Each application for a design approval, a design certification, or a manufacturing license under part 52 of this chapter shall include:

(1) A description of the equipment for the control of gaseous and liquid

effluents and for the maintenance and use of equipment installed in radioactive waste systems, under paragraph (a) of this section; and

(2) The information required in paragraph (b)(2) of this section.

[72 FR 49492, Aug. 28, 2007]

§ 50.35 Issuance of construction permits.[1]

(a) When an applicant has not supplied initially all of the technical information required to complete the application and support the issuance of a construction permit which approves all proposed design features, the Commission may issue a construction permit if the Commission finds that (1) the applicant has described the proposed design of the facility, including, but not limited to, the principal architectural and engineering criteria for the design, and has identified the major features or components incorporated therein for the protection of the health and safety of the public; (2) such further technical or design information as may be required to complete the safety analysis, and which can reasonably be left for later consideration, will be supplied in the final safety analysis report; (3) safety features or components, if any, which require research and development have been described by the applicant and the applicant has identified, and there will be conducted, a research and development program reasonably designed to resolve any safety questions associated with such features or components; and that (4) on the basis of the foregoing, there is reasonable assurance that, (i) such safety questions will be satisfactorily resolved at or before the latest date stated in the application for completion of construction of the proposed facility, and (ii) taking into consideration the site criteria contained in part 100 of this chapter, the proposed facility can be constructed and operated at the proposed location without undue risk to the health and safety of the public.

NOTE: When an applicant has supplied initially all of the technical information required to complete the application, including the final design of the facility, the findings required above will be appropriately modified to reflect that fact.

(b) A construction permit will constitute an authorization to the applicant to proceed with construction but will not constitute Commission approval of the safety of any design feature or specification unless the applicant specifically requests such approval and such approval is incorporated in the permit. The applicant, at his option, may request such approvals in the construction permit or, from time to time, by amendment of his construction permit. The Commission may, in its discretion, incorporate in any construction permit provisions requiring the applicant to furnish periodic reports of the progress and results of research and development programs designed to resolve safety questions.

(c) Any construction permit will be subject to the limitation that a license authorizing operation of the facility will not be issued by the Commission until (1) the applicant has submitted to the Commission, by amendment to the application, the complete final safety analysis report, portions of which may be submitted and evaluated from time to time, and (2) the Commission has found that the final design provides reasonable assurance that the health and safety of the public will not be endangered by operation of the facility in accordance with the requirements of the license and the regulations in this chapter.

[27 FR 12915, Dec. 29, 1962, as amended at 31 FR 12780, Sept. 30, 1966; 35 FR 5318, Mar. 31, 1970; 35 FR 6644, Apr. 25, 1970; 35 FR 11461, July 7, 1970]

§ 50.36 Technical specifications.

(a)(1) Each applicant for a license authorizing operation of a production or utilization facility shall include in his application proposed technical specifications in accordance with the requirements of this section. A summary statement of the bases or reasons for such specifications, other than those covering administrative controls, shall also be included in the application, but

[1] The Commission may issue a provisional construction permit pursuant to the regulations in this part in effect on March 30, 1970, for any facility for which a notice of hearing on an application for a provisional construction permit has been published on or before that date.

shall not become part of the technical specifications.

(a)(2) Each applicant for a design certification or manufacturing license under part 52 of this chapter shall include in its application proposed generic technical specifications in accordance with the requirements of this section for the portion of the plant that is within the scope of the design certification or manufacturing license application.

(b) Each license authorizing operation of a production or utilization facility of a type described in §50.21 or §50.22 will include technical specifications. The technical specifications will be derived from the analyses and evaluation included in the safety analysis report, and amendments thereto, submitted pursuant to §50.34. The Commission may include such additional technical specifications as the Commission finds appropriate.

(c) Technical specifications will include items in the following categories:

(1) *Safety limits, limiting safety system settings, and limiting control settings.* (i)(A) Safety limits for nuclear reactors are limits upon important process variables that are found to be necessary to reasonably protect the integrity of certain of the physical barriers that guard against the uncontrolled release of radioactivity. If any safety limit is exceeded, the reactor must be shut down. The licensee shall notify the Commission, review the matter, and record the results of the review, including the cause of the condition and the basis for corrective action taken to preclude recurrence. Operation must not be resumed until authorized by the Commission. The licensee shall retain the record of the results of each review until the Commission terminates the license for the reactor, except for nuclear power reactors licensed under §50.21(b) or §50.22 of this part. For these reactors, the licensee shall notify the Commission as required by §50.72 and submit a Licensee Event Report to the Commission as required by §50.73. Licensees in these cases shall retain the records of the review for a period of three years following issuance of a Licensee Event Report.

(B) Safety limits for fuel reprocessing plants are those bounds within which the process variables must be maintained for adequate control of the operation and that must not be exceeded in order to protect the integrity of the physical system that is designed to guard against the uncontrolled release or radioactivity. If any safety limit for a fuel reprocessing plant is exceeded, corrective action must be taken as stated in the technical specification or the affected part of the process, or the entire process if required, must be shut down, unless this action would further reduce the margin of safety. The licensee shall notify the Commission, review the matter, and record the results of the review, including the cause of the condition and the basis for corrective action taken to preclude recurrence. If a portion of the process or the entire process has been shutdown, operation must not be resumed until authorized by the Commission. The licensee shall retain the record of the results of each review until the Commission terminates the license for the plant.

(ii)(A) Limiting safety system settings for nuclear reactors are settings for automatic protective devices related to those variables having significant safety functions. Where a limiting safety system setting is specified for a variable on which a safety limit has been placed, the setting must be so chosen that automatic protective action will correct the abnormal situation before a safety limit is exceeded. If, during operation, it is determined that the automatic safety system does not function as required, the licensee shall take appropriate action, which may include shutting down the reactor. The licensee shall notify the Commission, review the matter, and record the results of the review, including the cause of the condition and the basis for corrective action taken to preclude recurrence. The licensee shall retain the record of the results of each review until the Commission terminates the license for the reactor except for nuclear power reactors licensed under §50.21(b) or §50.22 of this part. For these reactors, the licensee shall notify the Commission as required by §50.72 and submit a Licensee Event Report to the Commission as required by §50.73. Licensees in these cases shall retain the records of the review for a period of three years following issuance of a Licensee Event Report.

(B) Limiting control settings for fuel reprocessing plants are settings for automatic alarm or protective devices related to those variables having significant safety functions. Where a limiting control setting is specified for a variable on which a safety limit has been placed, the setting must be so chosen that protective action, either automatic or manual, will correct the abnormal situation before a safety limit is exceeded. If, during operation, the automatic alarm or protective devices do not function as required, the licensee shall take appropriate action to maintain the variables within the limiting control-setting values and to repair promptly the automatic devices or to shut down the affected part of the process and, if required, to shut down the entire process for repair of automatic devices. The licensee shall notify the Commission, review the matter, and record the results of the review, including the cause of the condition and the basis for corrective action taken to preclude recurrence. The licensee shall retain the record of the results of each review until the Commission terminates the license for the plant.

(2) *Limiting conditions for operation.* (i) Limiting conditions for operation are the lowest functional capability or performance levels of equipment required for safe operation of the facility. When a limiting condition for operation of a nuclear reactor is not met, the licensee shall shut down the reactor or follow any remedial action permitted by the technical specifications until the condition can be met. When a limiting condition for operation of any process step in the system of a fuel reprocessing plant is not met, the licensee shall shut down that part of the operation or follow any remedial action permitted by the technical specifications until the condition can be met. In the case of a nuclear reactor not licensed under § 50.21(b) or § 50.22 of this part or fuel reprocessing plant, the licensee shall notify the Commission, review the matter, and record the results of the review, including the cause of the condition and the basis for corrective action taken to preclude recurrence. The licensee shall retain the record of the results of each review until the Commission terminates the license for the nuclear reactor or the fuel reprocessing plant. In the case of nuclear power reactors licensed under § 50.21(b) or § 50.22, the licensee shall notify the Commission if required by § 50.72 and shall submit a Licensee Event Report to the Commission as required by § 50.73. In this case, licensees shall retain records associated with preparation of a Licensee Event Report for a period of three years following issuance of the report. For events which do not require a Licensee Event Report, the licensee shall retain each record as required by the technical specifications.

(ii) A technical specification limiting condition for operation of a nuclear reactor must be established for each item meeting one or more of the following criteria:

(A) *Criterion 1.* Installed instrumentation that is used to detect, and indicate in the control room, a significant abnormal degradation of the reactor coolant pressure boundary.

(B) *Criterion 2.* A process variable, design feature, or operating restriction that is an initial condition of a design basis accident or transient analysis that either assumes the failure of or presents a challenge to the integrity of a fission product barrier.

(C) *Criterion 3.* A structure, system, or component that is part of the primary success path and which functions or actuates to mitigate a design basis accident or transient that either assumes the failure of or presents a challenge to the integrity of a fission product barrier.

(D) *Criterion 4.* A structure, system, or component which operating experience or probabilistic risk assessment has shown to be significant to public health and safety.

(iii) A licensee is not required to propose to modify technical specifications that are included in any license issued before August 18, 1995, to satisfy the criteria in paragraph (c)(2)(ii) of this section.

(3) *Surveillance requirements.* Surveillance requirements are requirements

relating to test, calibration, or inspection to assure that the necessary quality of systems and components is maintained, that facility operation will be within safety limits, and that the limiting conditions for operation will be met.

(4) *Design features.* Design features to be included are those features of the facility such as materials of construction and geometric arrangements, which, if altered or modified, would have a significant effect on safety and are not covered in categories described in paragraphs (c) (1), (2), and (3) of this section.

(5) *Administrative controls.* Administrative controls are the provisions relating to organization and management, procedures, recordkeeping, review and audit, and reporting necessary to assure operation of the facility in a safe manner. Each licensee shall submit any reports to the Commission pursuant to approved technical specifications as specified in § 50.4.

(6) *Decommissioning.* This paragraph applies only to nuclear power reactor facilities that have submitted the certifications required by § 50.82(a)(1) and to non-power reactor facilities which are not authorized to operate. Technical specifications involving safety limits, limiting safety system settings, and limiting control system settings; limiting conditions for operation; surveillance requirements; design features; and administrative controls will be developed on a case-by-case basis.

(7) *Initial notification.* Reports made to the Commission by licensees in response to the requirements of this section must be made as follows:

(i) Licensees that have an installed Emergency Notification System shall make the initial notification to the NRC Operations Center in accordance with § 50.72 of this part.

(ii) All other licensees shall make the initial notification by telephone to the Administrator of the appropriate NRC Regional Office listed in appendix D, part 20, of this chapter.

(8) *Written Reports.* Licensees for nuclear power reactors licensed under § 50.21(b) and § 50.22 of this part shall submit written reports to the Commission in accordance with § 50.73 of this part for events described in paragraphs (c)(1) and (c)(2) of this section. For all licensees, the Commission may require Special Reports as appropriate.

(d)(1) This section shall not be deemed to modify the technical specifications included in any license issued prior to January 16, 1969. A license in which technical specifications have not been designated shall be deemed to include the entire safety analysis report as technical specifications.

(2) An applicant for a license authorizing operation of a production or utilization facility to whom a construction permit has been issued prior to January 16, 1969, may submit technical specifications in accordance with this section, or in accordance with the requirements of this part in effect prior to January 16, 1969.

(3) At the initiative of the Commission or the licensee, any license may be amended to include technical specifications of the scope and content which would be required if a new license were being issued.

(e) The provisions of this section apply to each nuclear reactor licensee whose authority to operate the reactor has been removed by license amendment, order, or regulation.

[33 FR 18612, Dec. 17, 1968, as amended at 48 FR 33860, July 26, 1983; 51 FR 40308, Nov. 6, 1986; 53 FR 19249, May 27, 1988; 60 FR 36959, July 19, 1995; 61 FR 39299, July 29, 1996; 72 FR 49493, Aug. 28, 2007; 73 FR 54932, Sept. 24, 2008]

§ 50.36a Technical specifications on effluents from nuclear power reactors.

(a) To keep releases of radioactive materials to unrestricted areas during normal conditions, including expected occurrences, as low as is reasonably achievable, each licensee of a nuclear power reactor and each applicant for a design certification or a manufacturing license will include technical specifications that, in addition to requiring compliance with applicable provisions of § 20.1301 of this chapter, require that:

(1) Operating procedures developed pursuant to § 50.34a(c) for the control of effluents be established and followed and that the radioactive waste system, pursuant to § 50.34a, be maintained and used. The licensee shall retain the operating procedures in effect as a record until the Commission terminates the

license and shall retain each superseded revision of the procedures for 3 years from the date it was superseded.

(2) Each holder of an operating license, and each holder of a combined license after the Commission has made the finding under § 52.103(g) of this chapter, shall submit a report to the Commission annually that specifies the quantity of each of the principal radionuclides released to unrestricted areas in liquid and in gaseous effluents during the previous 12 months, including any other information as may be required by the Commission to estimate maximum potential annual radiation doses to the public resulting from effluent releases. The report must be submitted as specified in § 50.4, and the time between submission of the reports must be no longer than 12 months. If quantities of radioactive materials released during the reporting period are significantly above design objectives, the report must cover this specifically. On the basis of these reports and any additional information the Commission may obtain from the licensee or others, the Commission may require the licensee to take action as the Commission deems appropriate.

(b) In establishing and implementing the operating procedures described in paragraph (a) of this section, the licensee shall be guided by the following considerations: Experience with the design, construction, and operation of nuclear power reactors indicates that compliance with the technical specifications described in this section will keep average annual releases of radioactive material in effluents and their resultant committed effective dose equivalents at small percentages of the dose limits specified in § 20.1301 and in the license. At the same time, the licensee is permitted the flexibility of operation, compatible with considerations of health and safety, to assure that the public is provided a dependable source of power even under unusual conditions which may temporarily result in releases higher than such small percentages, but still within the limits specified in § 20.1301 of this chapter and in the license. It is expected that in using this flexibility under unusual conditions, the licensee will exert its best efforts to keep levels of radioactive material in effluents as low as is reasonably achievable. The guides set out in appendix I, provide numerical guidance on limiting conditions for operation for light-water cooled nuclear power reactors to meet the requirement that radioactive materials in effluents released to unrestricted areas be kept as low as is reasonably achievable.

[61 FR 39299, July 29, 1996, as amended at 72 FR 49493, Aug. 28, 2007]

§ 50.36b Environmental conditions.

(a) Each construction permit under this part, each early site permit under part 52 of this chapter, and each combined license under part 52 of this chapter may include conditions to protect the environment during construction. These conditions are to be set out in an attachment to the permit or license, which is incorporated in and made a part of the permit or license. These conditions will be derived from information contained in the environmental report submitted pursuant to § 51.50 of this chapter as analyzed and evaluated in the NRC record of decision, and will identify the obligations of the licensee in the environmental area, including, as appropriate, requirements for reporting and keeping records of environmental data, and any conditions and monitoring requirement for the protection of the nonaquatic environment.

(b) Each license authorizing operation of a production or utilization facility, including a combined license under part 52 of this chapter, and each license for a nuclear power reactor facility for which the certification of permanent cessation of operations required under § 50.82(a)(1) or § 52.110(a) of this chapter has been submitted, which is of a type described in § 50.21(b)(2) or (3) or § 50.22 or is a testing facility, may include conditions to protect the environment during operation and decommissioning. These conditions are to be set out in an attachment to the license which is incorporated in and made a part of the license. These conditions will be derived from information contained in the environmental report or the supplement to the environmental report submitted pursuant to §§ 51.50 and 51.53 of this chapter as analyzed and evaluated in the NRC record of decision, and will identify the obligations of the licensee in the environmental area, including, as appropriate, requirements for reporting and keeping records of environmental data, and any conditions and monitoring requirement for the protection of the nonaquatic environment.

[72 FR 49493, Aug. 28, 2007]

§50.37 Agreement limiting access to Classified Information.

As part of its application and in any event before the receipt of Restricted Data or classified National Security Information or the issuance of a license, construction permit, early site permit, or standard design approval, or before the Commission has adopted a final standard design certification rule under part 52 of this chapter, the applicant shall agree in writing that it will not permit any individual to have access to any facility to possess Restricted Data or classified National Security Information until the individual and/or facility has been approved for access under the provisions of 10 CFR parts 25 and/or 95. The agreement of the applicant becomes part of the license, or construction permit, or standard design approval.

[72 FR 49493, Aug. 28, 2007]

§50.38 Ineligibility of certain applicants.

Any person who is a citizen, national, or agent of a foreign country, or any corporation, or other entity which the Commission knows or has reason to believe is owned, controlled, or dominated by an alien, a foreign corporation, or a foreign government, shall be ineligible to apply for and obtain a license.

[21 FR 355, Jan. 16, 1956, as amended at 43 FR 6924, Feb. 17, 1978]

§50.39 Public inspection of applications.

Applications and documents submitted to the Commission in connection with applications may be made available for public inspection in accordance with the provisions of the regulations contained in part 2 of this chapter.

STANDARDS FOR LICENSES, CERTIFICATIONS, AND REGULATORY APPROVALS

§50.40 Common standards.

In determining that a construction permit or operating license in this part, or early site permit, combined license, or manufacturing license in part 52 of this chapter will be issued to an applicant, the Commission will be guided by the following considerations:

(a) Except for an early site permit or manufacturing license, the processes to be performed, the operating procedures, the facility and equipment, the use of the facility, and other technical specifications, or the proposals, in regard to any of the foregoing collectively provide reasonable assurance that the applicant will comply with the regulations in this chapter, including the regulations in part 20 of this chapter, and that the health and safety of the public will not be endangered.

(b) The applicant for a construction permit, operating license, combined license, or manufacturing license is technically and financially qualified to engage in the proposed activities in accordance with the regulations in this chapter. However, no consideration of financial qualification is necessary for an electric utility applicant for an operating license for a utilization facility of the type described in §50.21(b) or §50.22 or for an applicant for a manufacturing license.

(c) The issuance of a construction permit, operating license, early site permit, combined license, or manufacturing license to the applicant will not, in the opinion of the Commission, be inimical to the common defense and security or to the health and safety of the public.

(d) Any applicable requirements of subpart A of 10 CFR part 51 have been satisfied.

[72 FR 49493, Aug. 28, 2007]

§50.41 Additional standards for class 104 licenses.

In determining that a class 104 license will be issued to an applicant, the Commission will, in addition to applying the standards set forth in §50.40 be guided by the following considerations:

(a) The Commission will permit the widest amount of effective medical therapy possible with the amount of special nuclear material available for such purposes.

(b) The Commission will permit the conduct of widespread and diverse research and development.

(c) [Reserved]

[21 FR 355, Jan. 19, 1956, as amended at 35 FR 19660, Dec. 29, 1970; 73 FR 44620, July 31, 2008]

§ 50.42 Additional standard for class 103 licenses.

In determining whether a class 103 license will be issued to an applicant, the Commission will, in addition to applying the standards set forth in § 50.40, consider whether the proposed activities will serve a useful purpose proportionate to the quantities of special nuclear material or source material to be utilized.

[73 FR 44620, July 31, 2008]

§ 50.43 Additional standards and provisions affecting class 103 licenses and certifications for commercial power.

In addition to applying the standards set forth in §§ 50.40 and 50.42, paragraphs (a) through (e) of this section apply in the case of a class 103 license for a facility for the generation of commercial power. For a design certification under part 52 of this chapter, only paragraph (e) of this section applies.

(a) The NRC will:

(1) Give notice in writing of each application to the regulatory agency or State as may have jurisdiction over the rates and services incident to the proposed activity;

(2) Publish notice of the application in trade or news publications as it deems appropriate to give reasonable notice to municipalities, private utilities, public bodies, and cooperatives which might have a potential interest in the utilization or production facility; and

(3) Publish notice of the application once each week for 4 consecutive weeks in the FEDERAL REGISTER. No license will be issued by the NRC prior to the giving of these notices and until 4 weeks after the last notice is published in the FEDERAL REGISTER.

(b) If there are conflicting applications for a limited opportunity for such license, the Commission will give preferred consideration in the following order: First, to applications submitted by public or cooperative bodies for facilities to be located in high cost power areas in the United States; second, to applications submitted by others for facilities to be located in such areas; third, to applications submitted by public or cooperative bodies for facilities to be located in other than high cost power areas; and, fourth, to all other applicants.

(c) The licensee who transmits electric energy in interstate commerce, or sells it at wholesale in interstate commerce, shall be subject to the regulatory provisions of the Federal Power Act.

(d) Nothing shall preclude any government agency, now or hereafter authorized by law to engage in the production, marketing, or distribution of electric energy, if otherwise qualified, from obtaining a construction permit or operating license under this part, or a combined license under part 52 of this chapter for a utilization facility for the primary purpose of producing electric energy for disposition for ultimate public consumption.

(e) Applications for a design certification, combined license, manufacturing license, operating license or standard design approval that propose nuclear reactor designs which differ significantly from light-water reactor designs that were licensed before 1997. Or use simplified, inherent, passive, or other innovative means to accomplish their safety functions will be approved only if:

(1)(i) The performance of each safety feature of the design has been demonstrated through either analysis, appropriate test programs, experience, or a combination thereof;

(ii) Interdependent effects among the safety features of the design are acceptable, as demonstrated by analysis, appropriate test programs, experience, or a combination thereof; and

(iii) Sufficient data exist on the safety features of the design to assess the analytical tools used for safety analyses over a sufficient range of normal operating conditions, transient conditions, and specified accident sequences, including equilibrium core conditions; or

(2) There has been acceptable testing of a prototype plant over a sufficient range of normal operating conditions, transient conditions, and specified accident sequences, including equilibrium core conditions. If a prototype plant is used to comply with the testing requirements, then the NRC may impose additional requirements on siting, safety features, or operational conditions for the prototype plant to protect the public and the plant staff from the possible consequences of accidents during the testing period.

[21 FR 355, Jan. 19, 1956, as amended at 35 FR 19660, Dec. 29, 1970; 63 FR 50480, Sept. 22, 1998; 72 FR 49494, Aug. 28, 2007; 82 FR 52825, Nov. 15, 2017]

§50.44 Combustible gas control for nuclear power reactors.

(a) *Definitions*—(1) *Inerted atmosphere* means a containment atmosphere with less than 4 percent oxygen by volume.

(2) *Mixed atmosphere* means that the concentration of combustible gases in any part of the containment is below a level that supports combustion or detonation that could cause loss of containment integrity.

(b) *Requirements for currently-licensed reactors.* Each boiling or pressurized water nuclear power reactor with an operating license on October 16, 2003, except for those facilities for which the certifications required under §50.82(a)(1) have been submitted, must comply with the following requirements, as applicable:

(1) *Mixed atmosphere.* All containments must have a capability for ensuring a mixed atmosphere.

(2) *Combustible gas control.* (i) All boiling water reactors with Mark I or Mark II type containments must have an inerted atmosphere.

(ii) All boiling water reactors with Mark III type containments and all pressurized water reactors with ice condenser containments must have the capability for controlling combustible gas generated from a metal-water reaction involving 75 percent of the fuel cladding surrounding the active fuel region (excluding the cladding surrounding the plenum volume) so that there is no loss of containment structural integrity.

(3) *Equipment survivability.* All boiling water reactors with Mark III containments and all pressurized water reactors with ice condenser containments that do not rely upon an inerted atmosphere inside containment to control combustible gases must be able to establish and maintain safe shutdown and containment structural integrity with systems and components capable of performing their functions during and after exposure to the environmental conditions created by the burning of hydrogen. Environmental conditions caused by local detonations of hydrogen must also be included, unless such detonations can be shown unlikely to occur. The amount of hydrogen to be considered must be equivalent to that generated from a metal-water reaction involving 75 percent of the fuel cladding surrounding the active fuel region (excluding the cladding surrounding the plenum volume).

(4) *Monitoring.* (i) Equipment must be provided for monitoring oxygen in containments that use an inerted atmosphere for combustible gas control. Equipment for monitoring oxygen must be functional, reliable, and capable of continuously measuring the concentration of oxygen in the containment atmosphere following a significant beyond design-basis accident for combustible gas control and accident management, including emergency planning.

(ii) Equipment must be provided for monitoring hydrogen in the containment. Equipment for monitoring hydrogen must be functional, reliable, and capable of continuously measuring the concentration of hydrogen in the containment atmosphere following a significant beyond design-basis accident for accident management, including emergency planning.

(5) *Analyses.* Each holder of an operating license for a boiling water reactor with a Mark III type of containment or for a pressurized water reactor with an ice condenser type of containment, shall perform an analysis that:

(i) Provides an evaluation of the consequences of large amounts of hydrogen generated after the start of an accident (hydrogen resulting from the metal-water reaction of up to and including 75 percent of the fuel cladding surrounding the active fuel region, excluding the cladding surrounding the plenum volume) and include consideration of hydrogen control measures as appropriate;

(ii) Includes the period of recovery from the degraded condition;

(iii) Uses accident scenarios that are accepted by the NRC staff. These scenarios must be accompanied by sufficient supporting justification to show that they describe the behavior of the reactor system during and following an accident resulting in a degraded core.

(iv) Supports the design of the hydrogen control system selected to meet the requirements of this section; and,

(v) Demonstrates, for those reactors that do not rely upon an inerted atmosphere to comply with paragraph (b)(2)(ii) of this section, that:

(A) Containment structural integrity is maintained. Containment structural integrity must be demonstrated by use of an analytical technique that is accepted by the NRC staff in accordance with § 50.90. This demonstration must include sufficient supporting justification to show that the technique describes the containment response to the structural loads involved. This method could include the use of actual material properties with suitable margins to account for uncertainties in modeling, in material properties, in construction tolerances, and so on; and

(B) Systems and components necessary to establish and maintain safe shutdown and to maintain containment integrity will be capable of performing their functions during and after exposure to the environmental conditions created by the burning of hydrogen, including local detonations, unless such detonations can be shown unlikely to occur.

(c) *Requirements for future water-cooled reactor applicants and licensees.*[2] The requirements in this paragraph apply to all water-cooled reactor construction permits or operating licenses under this part, and to all water-cooled reactor design approvals, design certifications, combined licenses or manufacturing licenses under part 52 of this chapter, any of which are issued after October 16, 2003.

(1) *Mixed atmosphere.* All containments must have a capability for ensuring a mixed atmosphere during design-basis and significant beyond design-basis accidents.

(2) *Combustible gas control.* All containments must have an inerted atmosphere, or must limit hydrogen concentrations in containment during and following an accident that releases an equivalent amount of hydrogen as would be generated from a 100 percent fuel clad-coolant reaction, uniformly distributed, to less than 10 percent (by volume) and maintain containment structural integrity and appropriate accident mitigating features.

(3) *Equipment Survivability.* Containments that do not rely upon an inerted atmosphere to control combustible gases must be able to establish and maintain safe shutdown and containment structural integrity with systems and components capable of performing their functions during and after exposure to the environmental conditions created by the burning of hydrogen. Environmental conditions caused by local detonations of hydrogen must also be included, unless such detonations can be shown unlikely to occur. The amount of hydrogen to be considered must be equivalent to that generated from a fuel clad-coolant reaction involving 100 percent of the fuel cladding surrounding the active fuel region.

(4) *Monitoring.* (i) Equipment must be provided for monitoring oxygen in containments that use an inerted atmosphere for combustible gas control. Equipment for monitoring oxygen must be functional, reliable, and capable of continuously measuring the concentration of oxygen in the containment atmosphere following a significant beyond design-basis accident for

[2] The requirements of this paragraph apply only to water-cooled reactor designs with characteristics (e.g., type and quantity of cladding materials) such that the potential for production of combustible gases is comparable to light water reactor designs licensed as of October 16, 2003.

combustible gas control and accident management, including emergency planning.

(ii) Equipment must be provided for monitoring hydrogen in the containment. Equipment for monitoring hydrogen must be functional, reliable, and capable of continuously measuring the concentration of hydrogen in the containment atmosphere following a significant beyond design-basis accident for accident management, including emergency planning.

(5) *Structural analysis.* An applicant must perform an analysis that demonstrates containment structural integrity. This demonstration must use an analytical technique that is accepted by the NRC and include sufficient supporting justification to show that the technique describes the containment response to the structural loads involved. The analysis must address an accident that releases hydrogen generated from 100 percent fuel clad-coolant reaction accompanied by hydrogen burning. Systems necessary to ensure containment integrity must also be demonstrated to perform their function under these conditions.

(d) *Requirements for future non water-cooled reactor applicants and licensees and certain water-cooled reactor applicants and licensees.* The requirements in this paragraph apply to all construction permits and operating licenses under this part, and to all design approvals, design certifications, combined licenses, or manufacturing licenses under part 52 of this chapter, for non water-cooled reactors and water-cooled reactors that do not fall within the description in paragraph (c), footnote 1 of this section, any of which are issued after October 16, 2003. Applications subject to this paragraph must include:

(1) Information addressing whether accidents involving combustible gases are technically relevant for their design, and

(2) If accidents involving combustible gases are found to be technically relevant, information (including a design-specific probabilistic risk assessment) demonstrating that the safety impacts of combustible gases during design-basis and significant beyond design-basis accidents have been addressed to ensure adequate protection of public health and safety and common defense and security.

[68 FR 54141, Sept. 16, 2003]

§ 50.45 Standards for construction permits, operating licenses, and combined licenses.

(a) An applicant for an operating license or an amendment of an operating license who proposes to construct or alter a production or utilization facility will be initially granted a construction permit if the application is in conformity with and acceptable under the criteria of §§ 50.31 through 50.38, and the standards of §§ 50.40 through 50.43, as applicable.

(b) A holder of a combined license who proposes, after the Commission makes the finding under § 52.103(g) of this chapter, to alter the licensed facility will be initially granted a construction permit if the application is in conformity with and acceptable under the criteria of §§ 50.30 through 50.33, § 50.34(f), §§ 50.34a through 50.38, the standards of §§ 50.40 through 50.43, as applicable, and §§ 52.79 and 52.80 of this chapter.

[72 FR 49494, Aug. 28, 2007]

§ 50.46 Acceptance criteria for emergency core cooling systems for light-water nuclear power reactors.

(a)(1)(i) Each boiling or pressurized light-water nuclear power reactor fueled with uranium oxide pellets within cylindrical zircaloy or ZIRLO cladding must be provided with an emergency core cooling system (ECCS) that must be designed so that its calculated cooling performance following postulated loss-of-coolant accidents conforms to the criteria set forth in paragraph (b) of this section. ECCS cooling performance must be calculated in accordance with an acceptable evaluation model and must be calculated for a number of postulated loss-of-coolant accidents of different sizes, locations, and other properties sufficient to provide assurance that the most severe postulated loss-of-coolant accidents are calculated. Except as provided in paragraph (a)(1)(ii) of this section, the evaluation model must include sufficient supporting justification to show that the analytical technique realistically describes the behavior of the reactor system during a loss-of-coolant accident. Comparisons to applicable experimental data must be made and uncertainties in the analysis method and inputs must be identified and assessed so that the uncertainty in the calculated results can be estimated. This uncertainty must be accounted for, so that, when the calculated ECCS cooling performance is compared to the criteria set forth in paragraph (b) of this section, there is a high level of probability that the criteria would not be exceeded. Appendix K, Part II Required Documentation, sets forth the documentation requirements for each evaluation model. This section does not apply to a nuclear power reactor facility for which the certifications required under § 50.82(a)(1) have been submitted.

(ii) Alternatively, an ECCS evaluation model may be developed in conformance with the required and acceptable features of appendix K ECCS Evaluation Models.

(2) The Director of Nuclear Reactor Regulation may impose restrictions on reactor operation if it is found that the evaluations of ECCS cooling performance submitted are not consistent with paragraphs (a)(1) (i) and (ii) of this section.

(3)(i) Each applicant for or holder of an operating license or construction permit issued under this part, applicant for a standard design certification under part 52 of this chapter (including an applicant after the Commission has adopted a final design certification regulation), or an applicant for or holder of a standard design approval, a combined license or a manufacturing license issued under part 52 of this chapter, shall estimate the effect of any change to or error in an acceptable evaluation model or in the application of such a model to determine if the change or error is significant. For this purpose, a significant change or error is one which results in a calculated peak fuel cladding temperature different by more than 50 °F from the temperature calculated for the limiting transient using the last acceptable model, or is a cumulation of changes and errors such that the sum of the absolute magnitudes of the respective temperature changes is greater than 50 °F.

(ii) For each change to or error discovered in an acceptable evaluation model or in the application of such a model that affects the temperature calculation, the applicant or holder of a construction permit, operating license, combined license, or manufacturing license shall report the nature of the change or error and its estimated effect on the limiting ECCS analysis to the Commission at least annually as specified in § 50.4 or § 52.3 of this chapter, as applicable. If the change or error is significant, the applicant or licensee shall provide this report within 30 days and include with the report a proposed schedule for providing a reanalysis or taking other action as may be needed to show compliance with § 50.46 requirements. This schedule may be developed using an integrated scheduling system previously approved for the facility by the NRC. For those facilities not using an NRC approved integrated scheduling system, a schedule will be established by the NRC staff within 60 days of receipt of the proposed schedule. Any change or error correction that results in a calculated ECCS performance that does not conform to the criteria set forth in paragraph (b) of this section is a reportable event as described in §§ 50.55(e), 50.72, and 50.73. The affected applicant or licensee shall propose immediate steps to demonstrate compliance or bring plant design or operation into compliance with § 50.46 requirements.

(iii) For each change to or error discovered in an acceptable evaluation model or in the application of such a model that affects the temperature calculation, the applicant or holder of a standard design approval or the applicant for a standard design certification (including an applicant after the Commission has adopted a final design certification rule) shall report the nature of the change or error and its estimated effect on the limiting ECCS analysis to the Commission and to any applicant or licensee referencing the design approval or design certification at least annually as specified in § 52.3 of this chapter. If the change or error is significant, the applicant or holder of the design approval or the applicant for the design certification shall provide this report within 30 days and include with the report a proposed schedule for providing a reanalysis or taking other action as may be needed to show compliance with § 50.46 requirements. The affected applicant or holder shall propose immediate steps to demonstrate compliance or bring plant design into compliance with § 50.46 requirements.

(b)(1) *Peak cladding temperature.* The calculated maximum fuel element cladding temperature shall not exceed 2200 °F.

(2) *Maximum cladding oxidation.* The calculated total oxidation of the cladding shall nowhere exceed 0.17 times the total cladding thickness before oxidation. As used in this subparagraph total oxidation means the total thickness of cladding metal that would be locally converted to oxide if all the oxygen absorbed by and reacted with the cladding locally were converted to stoichiometric zirconium dioxide. If cladding rupture is calculated to occur, the inside surfaces of the cladding shall be included in the oxidation, beginning at the calculated time of rupture. Cladding thickness before oxidation means the radial distance from inside to outside the cladding, after any calculated rupture or swelling has occurred but before significant oxidation. Where the calculated conditions of transient pressure and temperature lead to a prediction of cladding swelling, with or without cladding rupture, the unoxidized cladding thickness shall be defined as the cladding cross-sectional area, taken at a horizontal plane at the elevation of the rupture, if it occurs, or at the elevation of the highest cladding temperature if no rupture is calculated to occur, divided by the average circumference at that elevation. For ruptured cladding the circumference does not include the rupture opening.

(3) *Maximum hydrogen generation.* The calculated total amount of hydrogen generated from the chemical reaction of the cladding with water or steam shall not exceed 0.01 times the hypothetical amount that would be generated if all of the metal in the cladding cylinders surrounding the fuel, excluding the cladding surrounding the plenum volume, were to react.

(4) *Coolable geometry.* Calculated changes in core geometry shall be such that the core remains amenable to cooling.

(5) *Long-term cooling.* After any calculated successful initial operation of the ECCS, the calculated core temperature shall be maintained at an acceptably low value and decay heat shall be removed for the extended period of time required by the long-lived radioactivity remaining in the core.

(c) As used in this section:

(1) Loss-of-coolant accidents (LOCA's) are hypothetical accidents that would result from the loss of reactor coolant, at a rate in excess of the capability of the reactor coolant makeup system, from breaks in pipes in the reactor coolant pressure boundary up to and including a break equivalent in size to the double-ended rupture of the largest pipe in the reactor coolant system.

(2) An evaluation model is the calculational framework for evaluating the behavior of the reactor system during a postulated loss-of-coolant accident (LOCA). It includes one or more computer programs and all other information necessary for application of the calculational framework to a specific LOCA, such as mathematical models used, assumptions included in the programs, procedure for treating the program input and output information, specification of those portions of analysis not included in computer programs, values of parameters, and all other information necessary to specify the calculational procedure.

(d) The requirements of this section are in addition to any other requirements applicable to ECCS set forth in this part. The criteria set forth in paragraph (b), with cooling performance calculated in accordance with an acceptable evaluation model, are in implementation of the general requirements with respect to ECCS cooling performance design set forth in this part, including in particular Criterion 35 of appendix A.

[39 FR 1002, Jan. 4, 1974, as amended at 53 FR 36004, Sept. 16, 1988; 57 FR 39358, Aug. 31, 1992; 61 FR 39299, July 29, 1996; 62 FR 59276, Nov. 3, 1997; 72 FR 49494, Aug. 28, 2007]

§ 50.46a Acceptance criteria for reactor coolant system venting systems.

Each nuclear power reactor must be provided with high point vents for the reactor coolant system, for the reactor vessel head, and for other systems required to maintain adequate core cooling if the accumulation of noncondensible gases would cause the loss of function of these systems. High point vents are not required for the tubes in U-tube steam generators. Acceptable venting systems must meet the following criteria:

(a) The high point vents must be remotely operated from the control room.

(b) The design of the vents and associated controls, instruments and power sources must conform to appendix A and appendix B of this part.

(c) The vent system must be designed to ensure that:

(1) The vents will perform their safety functions; and

(2) There would not be inadvertent or irreversible actuation of a vent.

[68 FR 54142, Sept. 16, 2003]

§ 50.47 Emergency plans.

(a)(1)(i) Except as provided in paragraph (d) of this section, no initial operating license for a nuclear power reactor will be issued unless a finding is made by the NRC that there is reasonable assurance that adequate protective measures can and will be taken in the event of a radiological emergency. No finding under this section is necessary for issuance of a renewed nuclear power reactor operating license.

(ii) No initial combined license under part 52 of this chapter will be issued unless a finding is made by the NRC that there is reasonable assurance that adequate protective measures can and will be taken in the event of a radiological emergency. No finding under this section is necessary for issuance of a renewed combined license.

(iii) If an application for an early site permit under subpart A of part 52 of this chapter includes complete and integrated emergency plans under 10 CFR 52.17(b)(2)(ii), no early site permit will be issued unless a finding is made by the NRC that the emergency plans provide reasonable assurance that adequate protective measures can and will be taken in the event of a radiological emergency.

(iv) If an application for an early site permit proposes major features of the emergency plans under 10 CFR 52.17(b)(2)(i), no early site permit will be issued unless a finding is made by the NRC that the major features are acceptable in accordance with the applicable standards of 10 CFR 50.47 and 10 CFR part 50, appendix E, within the scope of emergency preparedness matters addressed in the major features.

(2) The NRC will base its finding on a review of the Federal Emergency Management Agency (FEMA) findings and determinations as to whether State and local emergency plans are adequate and whether there is reasonable assurance that they can be implemented, and on the NRC assessment as to whether the applicant's onsite emergency plans are adequate and whether there is reasonable assurance that they can be implemented. A FEMA finding will primarily be based on a review of the plans. Any other information already available to FEMA may be considered in assessing whether there is reasonable assurance that the plans can be implemented. In any NRC licensing proceeding, a FEMA finding will constitute a rebuttable presumption on questions of adequacy and implementation capability.

(b) The onsite and, except as provided in paragraph (d) of this section, offsite emergency response plans for nuclear power reactors must meet the following standards:

(1) Primary responsibilities for emergency response by the nuclear facility licensee and by State and local organizations within the Emergency Planning Zones have been assigned, the emergency responsibilities of the various supporting organizations have been specifically established, and each principal response organization has staff to respond and to augment its initial response on a continuous basis.

(2) On-shift facility licensee responsibilities for emergency response are unambiguously defined, adequate staffing to provide initial facility accident response in key functional areas is maintained at all times, timely augmentation of response capabilities is

available and the interfaces among various onsite response activities and offsite support and response activities are specified.

(3) Arrangements for requesting and effectively using assistance resources have been made, arrangements to accommodate State and local staff at the licensee's Emergency Operations Facility have been made, and other organizations capable of augmenting the planned response have been identified.

(4) A standard emergency classification and action level scheme, the bases of which include facility system and effluent parameters, is in use by the nuclear facility licensee, and State and local response plans call for reliance on information provided by facility licensees for determinations of minimum initial offsite response measures.

(5) Procedures have been established for notification, by the licensee, of State and local response organizations and for notification of emergency personnel by all organizations; the content of initial and followup messages to response organizations and the public has been established; and means to provide early notification and clear instruction to the populace within the plume exposure pathway Emergency Planning Zone have been established.

(6) Provisions exist for prompt communications among principal response organizations to emergency personnel and to the public.

(7) Information is made available to the public on a periodic basis on how they will be notified and what their initial actions should be in an emergency (e.g., listening to a local broadcast station and remaining indoors), the principal points of contact with the news media for dissemination of information during an emergency (including the physical location or locations) are established in advance, and procedures for coordinated dissemination of information to the public are established.

(8) Adequate emergency facilities and equipment to support the emergency response are provided and maintained.

(9) Adequate methods, systems, and equipment for assessing and monitoring actual or potential offsite consequences of a radiological emergency condition are in use.

(10) A range of protective actions has been developed for the plume exposure pathway EPZ for emergency workers and the public. In developing this range of actions, consideration has been given to evacuation, sheltering, and, as a supplement to these, the prophylactic use of potassium iodide (KI), as appropriate. Evacuation time estimates have been developed by applicants and licensees. Licensees shall update the evacuation time estimates on a periodic basis. Guidelines for the choice of protective actions during an emergency, consistent with Federal guidance, are developed and in place, and protective actions for the ingestion exposure pathway EPZ appropriate to the locale have been developed.

(11) Means for controlling radiological exposures, in an emergency, are established for emergency workers. The means for controlling radiological exposures shall include exposure guidelines consistent with EPA Emergency Worker and Lifesaving Activity Protective Action Guides.

(12) Arrangements are made for medical services for contaminated injured individuals.

(13) General plans for recovery and reentry are developed.

(14) Periodic exercises are (will be) conducted to evaluate major portions of emergency response capabilities, periodic drills are (will be) conducted to develop and maintain key skills, and deficiencies identified as a result of exercises or drills are (will be) corrected.

(15) Radiological emergency response training is provided to those who may be called on to assist in an emergency.

(16) Responsibilities for plan development and review and for distribution of emergency plans are established, and planners are properly trained.

(c)(1) Failure to meet the applicable standards set forth in paragraph (b) of this section may result in the Commission declining to issue an operating license; however, the applicant will have an opportunity to demonstrate to the satisfaction of the Commission that deficiencies in the plans are not significant for the plant in question, that adequate interim compensating actions have been or will be taken promptly, or that there are other compelling reasons to permit plant operations. Where an applicant for an operating license asserts that its inability to demonstrate compliance with the requirements of paragraph (b) of this section results wholly or substantially from the decision of state and/or local governments not to participate further in emergency planning, an operating license may be issued if the applicant demonstrates to the Commission's satisfaction that:

(i) The applicant's inability to comply with the requirements of paragraph (b) of this section is wholly or substantially the result of the non-participation of state and/or local governments.

(ii) The applicant has made a sustained, good faith effort to secure and retain the participation of the pertinent state and/or local governmental authorities, including the furnishing of copies of its emergency plan.

(iii) The applicant's emergency plan provides reasonable assurance that public health and safety is not endangered by operation of the facility concerned. To make that finding, the applicant must demonstrate that, as outlined below, adequate protective measures can and will be taken in the event of an emergency. A utility plan will be evaluated against the same planning standards applicable to a state or local plan, as listed in paragraph (b) of this section, with due allowance made both for—

(A) Those elements for which state and/or local non-participation makes compliance infeasible and

(B) The utility's measures designed to compensate for any deficiencies resulting from state and/or local non-participation.

In making its determination on the adequacy of a utility plan, the NRC will recognize the reality that in an actual emergency, state and local government officials will exercise their best efforts to protect the health and safety of the public. The NRC will determine the adequacy of that expected response, in combination with the utility's compensating measures, on a case-by-case basis, subject to the following guidance. In addressing the circumstance where applicant's inability to comply with the requirements of paragraph (b) of this section is wholly or substantially the result of non-participation of state and/or local governments, it may be presumed that in the event of an actual radiological emergency state and local officials would generally follow the utility plan. However, this presumption may be rebutted by, for example, a good faith and timely proffer of an adequate and feasible state and/or local radiological emergency plan that would in fact be relied upon in a radiological emergency.

(2) Generally, the plume exposure pathway EPZ for nuclear power plants shall consist of an area about 10 miles (16 km) in radius and the ingestion pathway EPZ shall consist of an area about 50 miles (80 km) in radius. The exact size and configuration of the EPZs surrounding a particular nuclear power reactor shall be determined in relation to local emergency response needs and capabilities as they are affected by such conditions as demography, topography, land characteristics, access routes, and jurisdictional boundaries. The size of the EPZs also may be determined on a case-by-case basis for gas-cooled nuclear reactors and for reactors with an authorized power level less than 250 MW thermal. The plans for the ingestion pathway shall focus on such actions as are appropriate to protect the food ingestion pathway.

(d) Notwithstanding the requirements of paragraphs (a) and (b) of this section, and except as specified by this paragraph, no NRC or FEMA review, findings, or determinations concerning the state of offsite emergency preparedness or the adequacy of and capability to implement State and local or utility offsite emergency plans are required prior to issuance of an operating license authorizing only fuel loading or low power testing and training (up to 5 percent of the rated thermal power). Insofar as emergency planning and preparedness requirements are concerned, a license authorizing fuel loading and/or low power testing and training may be issued after a finding is made by the NRC that the state of onsite emergency preparedness provides reasonable assurance that adequate protective measures can and will be taken in the event of a radiological emergency. The NRC will base this finding on its assessment of the applicant's onsite emergency plans against the pertinent standards in paragraph (b) of this section and appendix E. Review of applicant's emergency plans will include the following standards with offsite aspects:

(1) Arrangements for requesting and effectively using offsite assistance on site have been made, arrangements to accommodate State and local staff at the licensee's Emergency Operations Facility have been made, and other organizations capable of augmenting the planned onsite response have been identified.

(2) Procedures have been established for licensee communications with State and local response organizations, including initial notification of the declaration of emergency and periodic provision of plant and response status reports.

(3) Provisions exist for prompt communications among principal response organizations to offsite emergency personnel who would be responding onsite.

(4) Adequate emergency facilities and equipment to support the emergency response onsite are provided and maintained.

(5) Adequate methods, systems, and equipment for assessing and monitoring actual or potential offsite consequences of a radiological emergency condition are in use onsite.

(6) Arrangements are made for medical services for contaminated and injured onsite individuals.

(7) Radiological emergency response training has been made available to those offsite who may be called to assist in an emergency onsite.

(e) Notwithstanding the requirements of paragraph (b) of this section and the provisions of § 52.103 of this chapter, a holder of a combined license under part 52 of this chapter may not load fuel or operate except as provided in accordance with appendix E to part 50 and § 50.54(gg).

[45 FR 55409, Aug. 8, 1980, as amended at 47 FR 30235, July 13, 1982; 47 FR 40537, Sept. 15, 1982; 49 FR 27736, July 6, 1984; 50 FR 19324, May 8, 1985; 52 FR 42085, Nov. 3, 1987; 53 FR 36959, Sept. 23, 1988; 56 FR 64976, Dec. 13, 1991; 61 FR 30132, June 14, 1996; 66 FR 5440, Jan. 19, 2001; 72 FR 49495, Aug. 28, 2007; 76 FR 72595, Nov. 23, 2011; 78 FR 34248, June 7, 2013]

§ 50.48 Fire protection.

(a)(1) Each holder of an operating license issued under this part or a combined license issued under part 52 of this chapter must have a fire protection plan that satisfies Criterion 3 of appendix A to this part. This fire protection plan must:

(i) Describe the overall fire protection program for the facility;

(ii) Identify the various positions within the licensee's organization that are responsible for the program;

(iii) State the authorities that are delegated to each of these positions to implement those responsibilities; and

(iv) Outline the plans for fire protection, fire detection and suppression capability, and limitation of fire damage.

(2) The plan must also describe specific features necessary to implement the program described in paragraph (a)(1) of this section such as—

(i) Administrative controls and personnel requirements for fire prevention and manual fire suppression activities;

(ii) Automatic and manually operated fire detection and suppression systems; and

(iii) The means to limit fire damage to structures, systems, or components important to safety so that the capability to shut down the plant safely is ensured.

(3) The licensee shall retain the fire protection plan and each change to the plan as a record until the Commission terminates the reactor license. The licensee shall retain each superseded revision of the procedures for 3 years from the date it was superseded.

(4) Each applicant for a design approval, design certification, or manufacturing license under part 52 of this chapter must have a description and analysis of the fire protection design features for the standard plant necessary to demonstrate compliance with Criterion 3 of appendix A to this part.

(b) Appendix R to this part establishes fire protection features required to satisfy Criterion 3 of appendix A to this part with respect to certain generic issues for nuclear power plants licensed to operate before January 1, 1979.

(1) Except for the requirements of Sections III.G, III.J, and III.O, the provisions of Appendix R to this part do

not apply to nuclear power plants licensed to operate before January 1, 1979, to the extent that—

(i) Fire protection features proposed or implemented by the licensee have been accepted by the NRC staff as satisfying the provisions of Appendix A to Branch Technical Position (BTP) APCSB 9.5–1 reflected in NRC fire protection safety evaluation reports issued before the effective date of February 19, 1981; or

(ii) Fire protection features were accepted by the NRC staff in comprehensive fire protection safety evaluation reports issued before Appendix A to Branch Technical Position (BTP) APCSB 9.5–1 was published in August 1976.

(2) With respect to all other fire protection features covered by Appendix R, all nuclear power plants licensed to operate before January 1, 1979, must satisfy the applicable requirements of Appendix R to this part, including specifically the requirements of Sections III.G, III.J, and III.O.

(c) *National Fire Protection Association Standard NFPA 805*—(1) *Approval of incorporation by reference.* National Fire Protection Association (NFPA) Standard 805, "Performance-Based Standard for Fire Protection for Light Water Reactor Electric Generating Plants, 2001 Edition" (NFPA 805), which is referenced in this section, was approved for incorporation by reference by the Director of the Federal Register pursuant to 5 U.S.C. 552(a) and 1 CFR part 51. Copies of NFPA 805 may be purchased from the NFPA Customer Service Department, 1 Batterymarch Park, P.O. Box 9101, Quincy, MA 02269–9101 and in PDF format through the NFPA Online Catalog (*www.nfpa.org*) or by calling 1–800–344–3555 or (617) 770–3000. Copies are also available for inspection at the NRC Library, Two White Flint North, 11545 Rockville Pike, Rockville, Maryland 20852–2738, and at the NRC Public Document Room, Building One White Flint North, Room O1-F15, 11555 Rockville Pike, Rockville, Maryland 20852–2738. Copies are also available at the National Archives and Records Administration (NARA). For information on the availability of this material at NARA, call (202) 741–6030, or go to: *http://www.archives.gov/federal_register/code_of_federal_regulations/ibr_locations.html.*

(2) *Exceptions, modifications, and supplementation of NFPA 805.* As used in this section, references to NFPA 805 are to the 2001 Edition, with the following exceptions, modifications, and supplementation:

(i) *Life Safety Goal, Objectives, and Criteria.* The Life Safety Goal, Objectives, and Criteria of Chapter 1 are not endorsed.

(ii) *Plant Damage/Business Interruption Goal, Objectives, and Criteria.* The Plant Damage/Business Interruption Goal, Objectives, and Criteria of Chapter 1 are not endorsed.

(iii) *Use of feed-and-bleed.* In demonstrating compliance with the performance criteria of Sections 1.5.1(b) and (c), a high-pressure charging/injection pump coupled with the pressurizer power-operated relief valves (PORVs) as the sole fire-protected safe shutdown path for maintaining reactor coolant inventory, pressure control, and decay heat removal capability (*i.e.*, feed-and-bleed) for pressurized-water reactors (PWRs) is not permitted.

(iv) *Uncertainty analysis.* An uncertainty analysis performed in accordance with

Section 2.7.3.5 is not required to support deterministic approach calculations.

(v) *Existing cables.* In lieu of installing cables meeting flame propagation tests as required by Section 3.3.5.3, a flame-retardant coating may be applied to the electric cables, or an automatic fixed fire suppression system may be installed to provide an equivalent level of protection. In addition, the italicized exception to Section 3.3.5.3 is not endorsed.

(vi) *Water supply and distribution.* The italicized exception to Section 3.6.4 is not endorsed. Licensees who wish to use the exception to Section 3.6.4 must submit a request for a license amendment in accordance with paragraph (c)(2)(vii) of this section.

(vii) *Performance-based methods.* Notwithstanding the prohibition in Section 3.1 against the use of performance-based methods, the fire protection program elements and minimum design requirements of Chapter 3 may be subject to the performance-based methods permitted elsewhere in the standard. Licensees who wish to use performance-based methods for these fire protection program elements and minimum design requirements shall submit a request in the form of an application for license amendment under §50.90. The Director of the Office of Nuclear Reactor Regulation, or a designee of the Director, may approve the application if the Director or designee determines that the performance-based approach;

(A) Satisfies the performance goals, performance objectives, and performance criteria specified in NFPA 805 related to nuclear safety and radiological release;

(B) Maintains safety margins; and

(C) Maintains fire protection defense-in-depth (fire prevention, fire detection, fire suppression, mitigation, and post-fire safe shutdown capability).

(3) *Compliance with NFPA 805.* (i) A licensee may maintain a fire protection program that complies with NFPA 805 as an alternative to complying with paragraph (b) of this section for plants licensed to operate before January 1, 1979, or the fire protection license conditions for plants licensed to operate after January 1, 1979. The licensee shall submit a request to comply with NFPA 805 in the form of an application for license amendment under §50.90. The application must identify any orders and license conditions that must be revised or superseded, and contain any necessary revisions to the plant's technical specifications and the bases thereof. The Director of the Office of Nuclear Reactor Regulation, or a designee of the Director, may approve the application if the Director or designee determines that the licensee has identified orders, license conditions, and the technical specifications that must be revised or superseded, and that any necessary revisions are adequate. Any approval by the Director or the designee must be in the form of a license amendment approving the use of NFPA 805 together with any necessary revisions to the technical specifications.

(ii) The licensee shall complete its implementation of the methodology in Chapter 2 of NFPA 805 (including all required evaluations and analyses) and, upon completion, modify the fire protection plan required by paragraph (a) of this section to reflect the licensee's decision to comply with NFPA 805, before changing its fire protection program or nuclear power plant as permitted by NFPA 805.

(4) *Risk-informed or performance-based alternatives to compliance with NFPA 805.* A licensee may submit a request to use risk-informed or performance-based alternatives to compliance with NFPA 805. The request must be in the form of an application for license amendment under §50.90 of this chapter. The Director of the Office of Nuclear Reactor Regulation, or designee of the Director, may approve the application if the Director or designee determines that the proposed alternatives:

(i) Satisfy the performance goals, performance objectives, and performance criteria specified in NFPA 805 related to nuclear safety and radiological release;

(ii) Maintain safety margins; and

(iii) Maintain fire protection defense-in-depth (fire prevention, fire detection, fire suppression, mitigation, and post-fire safe shutdown capability).

(d)–(e) [Reserved]

(f) Licensees that have submitted the certifications required under §50.82(a)(1) shall maintain a fire protection program to address the potential for fires that could cause the release or spread of radioactive materials (*i.e.*, that could result in a radiological hazard). A fire protection program that complies with NFPA 805 shall be deemed to be acceptable for complying with the requirements of this paragraph.

(1) The objectives of the fire protection program are to—

(i) Reasonably prevent these fires from occurring;

(ii) Rapidly detect, control, and extinguish those fires that do occur and that could result in a radiological hazard; and

(iii) Ensure that the risk of fire-induced radiological hazards to the public, environment and plant personnel is minimized.

(2) The licensee shall assess the fire protection program on a regular basis. The licensee shall revise the plan as appropriate throughout the various stages of facility decommissioning.

(3) The licensee may make changes to the fire protection program without NRC approval if these changes do not reduce the effectiveness of fire protection for facilities, systems, and equipment that could result in a radiological hazard, taking into account the decommissioning plant conditions and activities.

[65 FR 38190, June 20, 2000, as amended at 69 FR 33550, June 16, 2004; 72 FR 49495, Aug. 28, 2007]

§ 50.49 Environmental qualification of electric equipment important to safety for nuclear power plants.

(a) Each holder of or an applicant for an operating license issued under this part, or a combined license or manufacturing license issued under part 52 of this chapter, other than a nuclear power plant for which the certifications required under § 50.82(a)(1) or § 52.110(a)(1) of this chapter have been submitted, shall establish a program for qualifying the electric equipment defined in paragraph (b) of this section. For a manufacturing license, only electric equipment defined in paragraph (b) which is within the scope of the manufactured reactor must be included in the program.

(b) Electric equipment important to safety covered by this section is:

(1) Safety-related electric equipment.[3]

(i) This equipment is that relied upon to remain functional during and following design basis events to ensure—

(A) The integrity of the reactor coolant pressure boundary;

(B) The capability to shut down the reactor and maintain it in a safe shutdown condition; or

(C) The capability to prevent or mitigate the consequences of accidents that could result in potential offsite exposures comparable to the guidelines in § 50.34(a)(1), § 50.67(b)(2), or § 100.11 of this chapter, as applicable.

(ii) Design basis events are defined as conditions of normal operation, including anticipated operational occurrences, design basis accidents, external events, and natural phenomena for which the plant must be designed to ensure functions (b)(1)(i) (A) through (C) of this section.

(2) Nonsafety-related electric equipment whose failure under postulated environmental conditions could prevent satisfactory accomplishment of safety functions specified in subparagraphs (b)(1)(i)(A) through (C) of this section by the safety-related equipment.

(3) Certain post-accident monitoring equipment.[4]

(c) Requirements for (1) dynamic and seismic qualification of electric equipment important to safety, (2) protection of electric equipment important to safety against other natural phenomena and external events, and (3) environmental qualification of electric equipment important to safety located in a mild environment are not included within the scope of this section. A mild environment is an environment that would at no time be significantly more severe than the environment that would occur during normal plant operation, including anticipated operational occurrences.

(d) The applicant or licensee shall prepare a list of electric equipment important to safety covered by this section. In addition, the applicant or licensee shall include the information in paragraphs (d)(1), (2), and (3) of this section for this electric equipment important to safety in a qualification file. The applicant or licensee shall keep the list and information in the file current and retain the file in auditable form for the entire period during which the covered item is installed in the nuclear power plant or is stored for future use to permit verification that each

[3] Safety-related electric equipment is referred to as "Class 1E" equipment in IEEE 323–1974. Copies of this standard may be obtained from the Institute of Electrical and Electronics Engineers, Inc., 345 East 47th Street, New York, NY 10017.

[4] Specific guidance concerning the types of variables to be monitored is provided in Revision 2 of Regulatory Guide 1.97, "Instrumentation for Light-Water-Cooled Nuclear Power Plants to Assess Plant and Environs Conditions During and Following an Accident." Copies of the Regulatory Guide may be purchased through the U.S. Government Publishing Office by calling 202–512–1800 or by writing to the U.S. Government Publishing Office, P.O. Box 37082, Washington, DC 20013–7082.

item of electric equipment is important to safely meet the requirements of paragraph (j) of this section.

(1) The performance specifications under conditions existing during and following design basis accidents.

(2) The voltage, frequency, load, and other electrical characteristics for which the performance specified in accordance with paragraph (d)(1) of this section can be ensured.

(3) The environmental conditions, including temperature, pressure, humidity, radiation, chemicals, and submergence at the location where the equipment must perform as specified in accordance with paragraphs (d) (1) and (2) of this section.

(e) The electric equipment qualification program must include and be based on the following:

(1) *Temperature and pressure.* The time-dependent temperature and pressure at the location of the electric equipment important to safety must be established for the most severe design basis accident during or following which this equipment is required to remain functional.

(2) *Humidity.* Humidity during design basis accidents must be considered.

(3) *Chemical effects.* The composition of chemicals used must be at least as severe as that resulting from the most limiting mode of plant operation (e.g., containment spray, emergency core cooling, or recirculation from containment sump). If the composition of the chemical spray can be affected by equipment malfunctions, the most severe chemical spray environment that results from a single failure in the spray system must be assumed.

(4) *Radiation.* The radiation environment must be based on the type of radiation, the total dose expected during normal operation over the installed life of the equipment, and the radiation environment associated with the most severe design basis accident during or following which the equipment is required to remain functional, including the radiation resulting from recirculating fluids for equipment located near the recirculating lines and including dose-rate effects.

(5) *Aging.* Equipment qualified by test must be preconditioned by natural or artificial (accelerated) aging to its end-of-installed life condition. Consideration must be given to all significant types of degradation which can have an effect on the functional capability of the equipment. If preconditioning to an end-of-installed life condition is not practicable, the equipment may be preconditioned to a shorter designated life. The equipment must be replaced or refurbished at the end of this designated life unless ongoing qualification demonstrates that the item has additional life.

(6) *Submergence* (if subject to being submerged).

(7) *Synergistic effects.* Synergistic effects must be considered when these effects are believed to have a significant effect on equipment performance.

(8) *Margins.* Margins must be applied to account for unquantified uncertainty, such as the effects of production variations and inaccuracies in test instruments. These margins are in addition to any conservatisms applied during the derivation of local environmental conditions of the equipment unless these conservatisms can be quantified and shown to contain appropriate margins.

(f) Each item of electric equipment important to safety must be qualified by one of the following methods:

(1) Testing an identical item of equipment under identical conditions or under similar conditions with a supporting analysis to show that the equipment to be qualified is acceptable.

(2) Testing a similar item of equipment with a supporting analysis to show that the equipment to be qualified is acceptable.

(3) Experience with identical or similar equipment under similar conditions with a supporting analysis to show that the equipment to be qualified is acceptable.

(4) Analysis in combination with partial type test data that supports the analytical assumptions and conclusions.

(g) Each holder of an operating license issued prior to February 22, 1983, shall, by May 20, 1983, identify the electric equipment important to safety within the scope of this section already qualified and submit a schedule for either the qualification to the provisions of this section or for the replacement of the remaining electric equipment important to safety within the scope of this section. This schedule must establish a goal of final environmental qualification of the electric equipment within the scope of this section by the end of the second refueling outage after March 31, 1982 or by March 31, 1985, whichever is earlier. The Director of the Office of Nuclear Reactor Regulation may grant requests for extensions of this deadline to a date no later than November 30, 1985, for specific pieces of equipment if these requests are filed on a timely basis and demonstrate good cause for the extension, such as procurement lead time, test complications, and installation problems. In exceptional cases, the Commission itself may consider and grant extensions beyond November 30, 1985, for completion of environmental qualification.

The schedule in this paragraph supersedes the June 30, 1982, deadline, or any other previously imposed date, for environmental qualification of electric equipment contained in certain nuclear power operating licenses.

(h) Each license shall notify the Commission as specified in §50.4 of any significant equipment qualification problem that may require extension of the completion date provided in accordance with paragraph (g) of this section within 60 days of its discovery.

(i) Applicants for operating licenses granted after February 22, 1983, but prior to November 30, 1985, shall perform an analysis to ensure that the plant can be safely operated pending completion of equipment qualification required by this section. This analysis must be submitted, as specified in §50.4, for consideration prior to the granting of an operating license and must include, where appropriate, consideration of:

(1) Accomplishing the safety function by some designated alternative equipment if the principal equipment has not been demonstrated to be fully qualified.

(2) The validity of partial test data in support of the original qualification.

(3) Limited use of administrative controls over equipment that has not been demonstrated to be fully qualified.

(4) Completion of the safety function prior to exposure to the accident environment resulting from a design basis event and ensuring that the subsequent failure of the equipment does not degrade any safety function or mislead the operator.

(5) No significant degradation of any safety function or misleading information to the operator as a result of failure of equipment under the accident environment resulting from a design basis event.

(j) A record of the qualification, including documentation in paragraph (d) of this section, must be maintained in an auditable form for the entire period during which the covered item is installed in the nuclear power plant or is stored for future use to permit verification that each item of electric equipment important to safety covered by this section:

(1) Is qualified for its application; and

(2) Meets its specified performance requirements when it is subjected to the conditions predicted to be present when it must perform its safety function up to the end of its qualified life.

(k) Applicants for and holders of operating licenses are not required to requalify electric equipment important to safety in accordance with the provisions of this section if the Commission has previously required qualification of that equipment in accordance with "Guidelines for Evaluating Environmental Qualification of Class 1E Electrical Equipment in Operating Reactors," November 1979 (DOR Guidelines), or NUREG–0588 (For Comment version), "Interim Staff Position on Environmental Qualification of Safety-Related Electrical Equipment."

(l) Replacement equipment must be qualified in accordance with the provisions of this section unless there are sound reasons to the contrary.

[48 FR 2733, Jan. 21, 1983, as amended at 49 FR 45576, Nov. 19, 1984; 51 FR 40308, Nov. 6, 1986; 51 FR 43709, Dec. 3, 1986; 52 FR 31611, Aug. 21, 1987; 53 FR 19250, May 27, 1988; 61 FR 39300, July 29, 1996; 61 FR 65173, Dec. 11, 1996; 62 FR 47271, Sept. 8, 1997; 64 FR 72001, Dec. 23, 1999; 66 FR 64738, Dec. 14, 2001; 72 FR 49495, Aug. 28, 2007; 80 FR 45843, Aug. 3, 2015]

ISSUANCE, LIMITATIONS, AND CONDITIONS OF LICENSES AND CONSTRUCTION PERMITS

§50.50 Issuance of licenses and construction permits.

Upon determination that an application for a license meets the standards and requirements of the act and regulations, and that notifications, if any, to other agencies or bodies have been duly made, the Commission will issue a license, or if appropriate a construction permit, in such form and containing such conditions and limitations including technical specifications, as it deems appropriate and necessary.

§50.51 Continuation of license.

(a) Each license will be issued for a fixed period of time to be specified in the license but in no case to exceed 40 years from date of issuance. Where the operation of a facility is involved, the Commission will issue the license for the term requested by the applicant or for the estimated useful life of the facility if the Commission determines that the estimated useful life is less than the term requested. Where construction of a facility is involved, the Commission may specify in the construction permit the period for which the license will be issued if approved pursuant to §50.56. Licenses may be renewed by the Commission upon the expiration of the period. Renewal of operating licenses for nuclear power plants is governed by 10 CFR part 54. Application for termination of license is to be made pursuant to §50.82.

(b) Each license for a facility that has permanently ceased operations, continues in effect beyond the expiration date to authorize ownership and possession of the production or utilization facility, until the Commission notifies the licensee in writing that the license is terminated. During such period of continued effectiveness the licensee shall—

(1) Take actions necessary to decommission and decontaminate the facility and continue to maintain the facility, including, where applicable, the storage, control and maintenance of the spent fuel, in a safe condition, and

(2) Conduct activities in accordance with all other restrictions applicable to the facility in accordance with the NRC regulations and the provisions of the specific 10 CFR part 50 license for the facility.

[56 FR 64976, Dec. 13, 1991, as amended at 61 FR 39300, July 29, 1996]

§50.52 Combining licenses.

The Commission may combine in a single license the activities of an applicant which would otherwise be licensed severally.

§50.53 Jurisdictional limitations.

No license under this part shall be deemed to have been issued for activities which are not under or within the jurisdiction of the United States.

[21 FR 355, Jan. 19, 1956, as amended at 43 FR 6924, Feb. 17, 1978]

§50.54 Conditions of licenses.

The following paragraphs of this section, with the exception of paragraphs (r) and (gg), and the applicable requirements of 10 CFR 50.55a, are conditions in every nuclear power reactor operating license issued under this part. The following paragraphs with the exception of paragraph (r), (s), and (u) of this section are conditions in every combined license issued under part 52 of this chapter, provided, however, that paragraphs (i) introductory text, (i)(1), (j), (k), (l), (m), (n), (w), (x), (y), (z), and (hh) of this section are only applicable after the Commission makes the finding under §52.103(g) of this chapter.

(a)(1) Each nuclear power plant or fuel reprocessing plant licensee subject to the quality assurance criteria in appendix B of this part shall implement, under §50.34(b)(6)(ii) or §52.79 of this chapter, the quality assurance program described or referenced in the safety analysis report, including changes to that report. However, a holder of a combined license under part 52 of this chapter shall implement the quality assurance program described or referenced in the safety analysis report applicable to operation 30 days prior to the scheduled date for the initial loading of fuel.

(2) Each licensee described in paragraph (a)(1) of this section shall, by June 10, 1983, submit to the appropriate NRC Regional Office shown in appendix

D of part 20 of this chapter the current description of the quality assurance program it is implementing for inclusion in the Safety Analysis Report, unless there are no changes to the description previously accepted by NRC. This submittal must identify changes made to the quality assurance program description since the description was submitted to NRC. (Should a licensee need additional time beyond June 10, 1983 to submit its current quality assurance program description to NRC, it shall notify the appropriate NRC Regional Office in writing, explain why additional time is needed, and provide a schedule for NRC approval showing when its current quality assurance program description will be submitted.)

(3) Each licensee described in paragraph (a)(1) of this section may make a change to a previously accepted quality assurance program description included or referenced in the Safety Analysis Report without prior NRC approval, provided the change does not reduce the commitments in the program description as accepted by the NRC. Changes to the quality assurance program description that do not reduce the commitments must be submitted to the NRC in accordance with the requirements of § 50.71(e). In addition to quality assurance program changes involving administrative improvements and clarifications, spelling corrections, punctuation, or editorial items, the following changes are not considered to be reductions in commitment:

(i) The use of a QA standard approved by the NRC which is more recent than the QA standard in the licensee's current QA program at the time of the change;

(ii) The use of a quality assurance alternative or exception approved by an NRC safety evaluation, provided that the bases of the NRC approval are applicable to the licensee's facility;

(iii) The use of generic organizational position titles that clearly denote the position function, supplemented as necessary by descriptive text, rather than specific titles;

(iv) The use of generic organizational charts to indicate functional relationships, authorities, and responsibilities, or, alternately, the use of descriptive text;

(v) The elimination of quality assurance program information that duplicates language in quality assurance regulatory guides and quality assurance standards to which the licensee is committed; and

(vi) Organizational revisions that ensure that persons and organizations performing quality assurance functions continue to have the requisite authority and organizational freedom, including sufficient independence from cost and schedule when opposed to safety considerations.

(4) Changes to the quality assurance program description that do reduce the commitments must be submitted to the NRC and receive NRC approval prior to implementation, as follows:

(i) Changes made to the quality assurance program description as presented in the Safety Analysis Report or in a topical report must be submitted as specified in § 50.4.

(ii) The submittal of a change to the Safety Analysis Report quality assurance program description must include all pages affected by that change and must be accompanied by a forwarding letter identifying the change, the reason for the change, and the basis for concluding that the revised program incorporating the change continues to satisfy the criteria of appendix B of this part and the Safety Analysis Report quality assurance program description commitments previously accepted by the NRC (the letter need not provide the basis for changes that correct spelling, punctuation, or editorial items).

(iii) A copy of the forwarding letter identifying the change must be maintained as a facility record for three years.

(iv) Changes to the quality assurance program description included or referenced in the Safety Analysis Report shall be regarded as accepted by the Commission upon receipt of a letter to this effect from the appropriate reviewing office of the Commission or 60 days after submittal to the Commission, whichever occurs first.

(b) No right to the special nuclear material shall be conferred by the license except as may be defined by the license.

(c) Neither the license, nor any right thereunder, nor any right to utilize or produce special nuclear material shall be transferred, assigned, or disposed of in any manner, either voluntarily or involuntarily, directly or indirectly, through transfer of control of the license to any person, unless the Commission shall, after securing full information, find that the transfer is in accordance with the provisions of the act and give its consent in writing.

(d) The license shall be subject to suspension and to the rights of recapture of the material or control of the facility reserved to the Commission under section 108 of the act in a state of war or national emergency declared by Congress.

(e) The license shall be subject to revocation, suspension, modification, or amendment for cause as provided in the act and regulations, in accordance with the procedures provided by the act and regulations.

(f) The licensee shall at any time before expiration of the license, upon request of the Commission, submit, as specified in § 50.4, written statements, signed under oath or affirmation, to enable the Commission to determine whether or not the license should be modified, suspended, or revoked. Except for information sought to verify licensee compliance with the current licensing basis for that facility, the NRC must prepare the reason or reasons for each information request prior to issuance to ensure that the burden to be imposed on respondents is justified in view of the potential safety significance of the issue to be addressed in the requested information. Each such justification provided for an evaluation performed by the NRC staff must be approved by the Executive Director for Operations or his or her designee prior to issuance of the request.

(g) The issuance or existence of the license shall not be deemed to waive, or relieve the licensee from compliance with, the antitrust laws, as specified in subsection 105a of the Act. In the event that the licensee should be found by a court of competent jurisdiction to have violated any provision of such antitrust laws in the conduct of the licensed activity, the Commission may suspend or revoke the license or take such other action with respect to it as shall be deemed necessary.

(h) The license shall be subject to the provisions of the Act now or hereafter in effect and to all rules, regulations, and orders of the Commission. The terms and conditions of the license shall be subject to amendment, revision, or modification, by reason of amendments of the Act or by reason of rules, regulations, and orders issued in accordance with the terms of the act.

(i) Except as provided in § 55.13 of this chapter, the licensee may not permit the manipulation of the controls of any facility by anyone who is not a licensed operator or senior operator as provided in part 55 of this chapter.

(i–1) Within 3 months after either the issuance of an operating license or the date that the Commission makes the finding under § 52.103(g) of this chapter for a combined license, as applicable, the licensee shall have in effect an operator requalification program. The operator requalification program must, as a minimum, meet the requirements of § 55.59(c) of this chapter. Notwithstanding the provisions of § 50.59, the licensee may not, except as specifically authorized by the Commission decrease the scope of an approved operator requalification program.

(j) Apparatus and mechanisms other than controls, the operation of which may affect the reactivity or power level of a reactor shall be manipulated only with the knowledge and consent of an operator or senior operator licensed pursuant to part 55 of this chapter present at the controls.

(k) An operator or senior operator licensed pursuant to part 55 of this chapter shall be present at the controls at all times during the operation of the facility.

(l) The licensee shall designate individuals to be responsible for directing the licensed activities of licensed operators. These individuals shall be licensed as senior operators pursuant to part 55 of this chapter.

(m)(1) A senior operator licensed pursuant to part 55 of this chapter shall be present at the facility or readily available on call at all times during its operation, and shall be present at the facility during initial start-up and approach to power, recovery from an unplanned or unscheduled shut-down or significant reduction in power, and refueling, or as otherwise prescribed in the facility license.

(2) Notwithstanding any other provisions of this section, by January 1, 1984, licensees of nuclear power units shall meet the following requirements:

(i) Each licensee shall meet the minimum licensed operator staffing requirements in the following table:

MINIMUM REQUIREMENTS[1] PER SHIFT FOR ON-SITE STAFFING OF NUCLEAR POWER UNITS BY OPERATORS AND SENIOR OPERATORS LICENSED UNDER 10 CFR PART 55

Number of nuclear power units operating[2]	Position	One unit	Two units		Three units	
		One control room	One control room	Two control rooms	Two control rooms	Three control rooms
None	Senior Operator	1	1	1	1	1
	Operator	1	2	2	3	3
One	Senior Operator	2	2	2	2	2
	Operator	2	3	3	4	4
Two	Senior Operator	....	2	3	[3]3	3
	Operator	....	3	4	[3]5	5
Three	Senior Operator	....	....	....	3	4
	Operator	....	....	....	5	6

[1] Temporary deviations from the numbers required by this table shall be in accordance with criteria established in the unit's technical specifications.

[2] For the purpose of this table, a nuclear power unit is considered to be operating when it is in a mode other than cold shutdown or refueling as defined by the unit's technical specifications.

[3] The number of required licensed personnel when the operating nuclear power units are controlled from a common control room are two senior operators and four operators.

(ii) Each licensee shall have at its site a person holding a senior operator license for all fueled units at the site who is assigned responsibility for overall plant operation at all times there is fuel in any unit. If a single senior operator does not hold a senior operator license on all fueled units at the site, then the licensee must have at the site two or more senior operators, who in combination are licensed as senior operators on all fueled units.

(iii) When a nuclear power unit is in an operational mode other than cold shutdown or refueling, as defined by the unit's technical specifications, each licensee shall have a person holding a senior operator license for the nuclear power unit in the control room at all times. In addition to this senior operator, for each fueled nuclear power unit, a licensed operator or senior operator shall be present at the controls at all times.

(iv) Each licensee shall have present, during alteration of the core of a nuclear power unit (including fuel loading or transfer), a person holding a senior operator license or a senior operator license limited to fuel handling to directly supervise the activity and, during this time, the licensee shall not assign other duties to this person.

(3) Licensees who cannot meet the January 1, 1984 deadline must submit by October 1, 1983 a request for an extension to the Director of the Office of Nuclear Regulation and demonstrate good cause for the request.

(n) The licensee shall not, except as authorized pursuant to a construction permit, make any alteration in the facility constituting a change from the technical specifications previously incorporated in a license or construction permit pursuant to § 50.36 of this part.

(o) Primary reactor containments for water cooled power reactors, other than facilities for which the certifications required under §§ 50.82(a)(1) or 52.110(a)(1) of this chapter have been submitted, shall be subject to the requirements set forth in appendix J to this part.

(p)(1) The licensee shall prepare and maintain safeguards contingency plan procedures in accordance with appendix C of part 73 of this chapter for affecting the actions and decisions contained in the Responsibility Matrix of the safeguards contingency plan. The licensee may not make a change which would decrease the effectiveness of a physical security plan, or guard training and qualification plan, or cyber security plan prepared under § 50.34(c) or § 52.79(a), or part 73 of this chapter, or of the first four categories of information (Background, Generic Planning Base, Licensee Planning Base, Responsibility Matrix) contained in a licensee safeguards contingency plan prepared under § 50.34(d) or § 52.79(a), or part 73 of this chapter, as applicable, without prior approval of the Commission. A licensee desiring to make such a change shall submit an application for amendment to the licensee's license under § 50.90.

(2) The licensee may make changes to the plans referenced in paragraph (p)(1) of this section, without prior Commission approval if the changes do not decrease the safeguards effectiveness of the plan. The licensee shall maintain records of changes to the plans made without prior Commission approval for a period of 3 years from the date of the change, and shall submit, as specified in § 50.4 or § 52.3 of this chapter, a report containing a description of each change within 2 months after the change is made. Prior to the safeguards contingency plan being put into effect, the licensee shall have:

(i) All safeguards capabilities specified in the safeguards contingency plan available and functional,

(ii) Detailed procedures developed according to appendix C to part 73 of this chapter available at the licensee's site; and

(iii) All appropriate personnel trained to respond to safeguards incidents as outlined in the plan and specified in the detailed procedures.

(3) The licensee shall provide for the development, revision, implementation, and maintenance of its safeguards contingency plan. The licensee shall ensure that all program elements are reviewed by individuals independent of both security program management and personnel who have direct responsibility for implementation of the security program either:

(i) At intervals not to exceed 12 months; or

(ii) As necessary, based on an assessment by the licensee against performance indicators, and as soon as reasonably practicable after a change occurs in personnel, procedures, equipment, or facilities that potentially could adversely affect security, but no longer than 12 months after the change. In any case, all elements of the safeguards contingency plan must be reviewed at least once every 24 months.

(4) The review must include a review and audit of safeguards contingency procedures and practices, an audit of the security system testing and maintenance program, and a test of the safeguards systems along with commitments established for response by local law enforcement authorities. The results of the review and audit, along with recommendations for improvements, must be documented, reported to the licensee's corporate and plant management, and kept available at the plant for inspection for a period of 3 years.

(q) *Emergency plans*—(1) Definitions for the purpose of this section:

(i) *Change* means an action that results in modification or addition to, or removal from, the licensee's emergency plan. All such changes are subject to the provisions of this section except where the applicable regulations establish specific criteria for accomplishing a particular change.

(ii) *Emergency plan* means the document(s), prepared and maintained by the licensee, that identify and describe the licensee's methods for maintaining emergency preparedness and responding to emergencies. An emergency plan includes the plan as originally approved by the NRC and all subsequent changes made by the licensee with, and without, prior NRC review and approval under paragraph (q) of this section.

(iii) *Emergency planning function* means a capability or resource necessary to prepare for and respond to a radiological emergency, as set forth in the elements of section IV. of appendix E to this part and, for nuclear power reactor licensees, the planning standards of § 50.47(b).

(iv) *Reduction in effectiveness* means a change in an emergency plan that results in reducing the licensee's capability to perform an emergency planning function in the event of a radiological emergency.

(2) A holder of a license under this part, or a combined license under part 52 of this chapter after the Commission makes the finding under § 52.103(g) of this chapter, shall follow and maintain the effectiveness of an emergency plan that meets the requirements in appendix E to this part and, for nuclear power reactor licensees, the planning standards of § 50.47(b).

(3) The licensee may make changes to its emergency plan without NRC approval only if the licensee performs and retains an analysis demonstrating that the changes do not reduce the effectiveness of the plan and the plan, as changed, continues to meet the requirements in appendix E to this part and, for nuclear power reactor licensees, the planning standards of § 50.47(b).

(4) The changes to a licensee's emergency plan that reduce the effectiveness of the plan as defined in paragraph (q)(1)(iv) of this section may not be implemented without prior approval by the NRC. A licensee desiring to make such a change after February 21, 2012 shall submit an application for an amendment to its license. In addition to the filing requirements of §§ 50.90 and 50.91, the request must include all emergency plan pages affected by that change and must be accompanied by a forwarding letter identifying the change, the reason for the change, and the basis for concluding that the licensee's emergency plan, as revised, will continue to meet the requirements in appendix E to this part and, for nuclear power reactor licensees, the planning standards of § 50.47(b).

(5) The licensee shall retain a record of each change to the emergency plan made without prior NRC approval for a period of three years from the date of the change and shall submit, as specified in § 50.4, a report of each such change made after February 21, 2012, including a summary of its analysis, within 30 days after the change is put in effect.

(6) The nuclear power reactor licensee shall retain the emergency plan and each change for which prior NRC approval was obtained pursuant to paragraph (q)(4) of this section as a record until the Commission terminates the license for the nuclear power reactor.

(r) [Reserved]

(s)(1) [Reserved]

(2)(i) [Reserved]

(ii) If after April 1, 1981, the NRC finds that the state of emergency preparedness does not provide reasonable assurance that adequate protective measures can and will be taken in the event of a radiological emergency (*including findings based on requirements of appendix E, section IV.D.3*) and if the deficiencies (*including deficiencies based on requirements of appendix E, section IV.D.3*) are not corrected within four months of that finding, the Commission will determine whether the reactor shall be shut down until such deficiencies are remedied or whether other enforcement action is appropriate. In determining whether a shutdown or other enforcement action is appropriate, the Commission shall take into account, among other factors, whether the licensee can demonstrate to the Commission's satisfaction that the deficiencies in the plan are not significant for the plant in question, or that adequate interim compensating actions have been or will be taken promptly, or that there are other compelling reasons for continued operation.

(3) The NRC will base its finding on a review of the FEMA findings and determinations as to whether State and local emergency plans are adequate and capable of being implemented, and on the NRC assessment as to whether the licensee's emergency plans are adequate and capable of being implemented. Nothing in this paragraph shall be construed as limiting the authority of the Commission to take action under any other regulation or authority of the Commission or at any time other than that specified in this paragraph.

(t)(1) The licensee shall provide for the development, revision, implementation, and maintenance of its emergency preparedness program. The licensee shall ensure that all program elements are reviewed by persons who have no direct responsibility for the implementation of the emergency preparedness program either:

(i) At intervals not to exceed 12 months or,

(ii) As necessary, based on an assessment by the licensee against performance indicators, and as soon as reasonably practicable after a change occurs in personnel, procedures, equipment, or facilities that potentially could adversely affect emergency preparedness, but no longer than 12 months after the change. In any case, all elements of the emergency preparedness program must be reviewed at least once every 24 months.

(2) The review must include an evaluation for adequacy of interfaces with State and local governments and of licensee drills, exercises, capabilities, and procedures. The results of the review, along with recommendations for improvements, must be documented, reported to the licensee's corporate and plant management, and retained for a period of 5 years. The part of the review involving the evaluation for adequacy of interface with State and local governments must be available to the appropriate State and local governments.

(u) [Reserved]

(v) Each licensee subject to the requirements of Part 73 of this chapter shall ensure that Safeguards Information is protected against unauthorized disclosure in accordance with the requirements in §73.21 and the requirements in §73.22 or §73.23 of this chapter, as applicable.

(w) Each power reactor licensee under this part for a production or utilization facility of the type described in §50.21(b) or §50.22 shall take reasonable steps to obtain insurance available at reasonable costs and on reasonable terms from private sources or to demonstrate to the satisfaction of the NRC that it possesses an equivalent amount of protection covering the licensee's obligation, in the event of an accident at the licensee's reactor, to stabilize and decontaminate the reactor and the reactor station site at which the reactor experiencing the accident is located, provided that:

(1) The insurance required by paragraph (w) of this section must have a minimum coverage limit for each reactor station site of either $1.06 billion or whatever amount of insurance is generally available from private sources, whichever is less. The required insurance must clearly state that, as and to the extent provided in paragraph (w)(4) of this section, any proceeds must be payable first for stabilization of the reactor and next for decontamination of the reactor and the reactor station site. If a licensee's coverage falls below the required minimum, the licensee shall within 60 days take all reasonable steps to restore its coverage to the required minimum. The required insurance may, at the option of the licensee, be included within policies that also provide coverage for other risks, including, but not limited to, the risk of direct physical damage.

(2)(i) With respect to policies issued or annually renewed on or after April 2, 1991, the proceeds of such required insurance must be dedicated, as and to the extent provided in this paragraph, to reimbursement or payment on behalf of the insured of reasonable expenses incurred or estimated to be incurred by the licensee in taking action to fulfill the licensee's obligation, in the event of an accident at the licensee's reactor, to ensure that the reactor is in, or is returned to, and maintained in, a safe and stable condition and that radioactive contamination is removed or controlled such that personnel exposures are consistent with the occupational exposure limits in 10 CFR part 20. These actions must be consistent with any other obligation the licensee may have under this chapter and must be subject to paragraph (w)(4) of this section. As used in this section, an "accident" means an event that involves the release of radioactive material from its intended place of confinement within the reactor or on the reactor station site such that there is a present danger of release off site in amounts that would pose a threat to the public health and safety.

(ii) The stabilization and decontamination requirements set forth in paragraph (w)(4) of this section must apply uniformly to all insurance policies required under paragraph (w) of this section.

(3) The licensee shall report to the NRC on April 1 of each year the current levels of this insurance or financial security it maintains and the sources of this insurance or financial security.

(4)(i) In the event of an accident at the licensee's reactor, whenever the estimated costs of stabilizing the licensed reactor and of decontaminating the reactor and the reactor station site exceed $100 million, the proceeds of the insurance required by paragraph (w) of this section must be dedicated to and used, first, to ensure that the licensed reactor is in, or is returned to, and can be maintained in, a safe and stable condition so as to prevent any significant risk to the public health and safety and, second, to decontaminate the reactor and the reactor station site in accordance with the licensee's cleanup plan as approved by order of the Director of the Office of Nuclear Reactor Regulation. This priority on insurance proceeds must remain in effect for 60 days or, upon order of the Director, for such longer periods, in increments not to exceed 60 days except as provided for activities under the cleanup plan required in paragraphs (w)(4)(iii) and (w)(4)(iv) of this section, as the Director may find necessary to protect the public health and safety. Actions needed to bring the reactor to and maintain the reactor in a safe and stable condition may include one or more of the following, as appropriate:

(A) Shutdown of the reactor;

(B) Establishment and maintenance of long-term cooling with stable decay heat removal;

(C) Maintenance of sub-criticality;

(D) Control of radioactive releases; and

(E) Securing of structures, systems, or components to minimize radiation exposure to onsite personnel or to the offsite public or to facilitate later decontamination or both.

(ii) The licensee shall inform the Director of the Office of Nuclear Reactor Regulation in writing when the reactor is and can be maintained in a safe and stable condition so as to prevent any significant risk to the public health and safety. Within 30 days after the licensee informs the Director that the reactor is in this condition, or at such earlier time as the licensee may elect or the Director may for good cause direct, the licensee shall prepare and submit a cleanup plan for the Director's approval. The cleanup plan must identify and contain an estimate of the cost of each cleanup operation that will be required to decontaminate the reactor sufficiently to permit the licensee either to resume operation of the reactor or to apply to the Commission under § 50.82 for authority to decommission the reactor and to surrender the license voluntarily. Cleanup operations may include one or more of the following, as appropriate:

(A) Processing any contaminated water generated by the accident and by decontamination operations to remove radioactive materials;

(B) Decontamination of surfaces inside the auxiliary and fuel-handling buildings and the reactor building to levels consistent with the Commission's occupational exposure limits in 10 CFR part 20, and decontamination or disposal of equipment;

(C) Decontamination or removal and disposal of internal parts and damaged fuel from the reactor vessel; and

(D) Cleanup of the reactor coolant system.

(iii) Following review of the licensee's cleanup plan, the Director will order the licensee to complete all operations that the Director finds are necessary to decontaminate the reactor sufficiently to permit the licensee either to resume operation of the reactor or to apply to the Commission under § 50.82 for authority to decommission the reactor and to surrender the license voluntarily. The Director shall approve or disapprove, in whole or in part for stated reasons, the licensee's estimate of cleanup costs for such operations. Such order may not be effective for more than 1 year, at which time it may be renewed. Each subsequent renewal order, if imposed, may be effective for not more than 6 months.

(iv) Of the balance of the proceeds of the required insurance not already expended to place the reactor in a safe and stable condition pursuant to paragraph (w)(2)(i) of this section, an amount sufficient to cover the expenses of completion of those decontamination operations that are the subject of the Director's order shall be dedicated to such use, provided that, upon certification to the Director of the amounts expended previously and from time to time for stabilization and decontamination and upon further certification to the Director as to the sufficiency of the dedicated amount remaining, policies of insurance may provide for payment to the licensee or other loss payees of amounts not so dedicated, and the licensee may proceed to use in parallel (and not in preference thereto) any insurance proceeds not so dedicated for other purposes.

(x) A licensee may take reasonable action that departs from a license condition or a technical specification (contained in a license issued under this part) in an emergency when this action is immediately needed to protect the public health and safety and no action consistent with license conditions and technical specifications that can provide adequate or equivalent protection is immediately apparent.

(y) Licensee action permitted by paragraph (x) of this section shall be approved, as a minimum, by a licensed senior operator, or, at a nuclear power reactor facility for which the certifications required under § 50.82(a)(1) have been submitted, by either a licensed senior operator or a certified fuel handler, prior to taking the action.

(z) Each licensee with a utilization facility licensed pursuant to sections 103 or 104b. of the Act shall immediately notify the NRC Operations Center of the occurrence of any event specified in § 50.72 of this part.

(aa) The license shall be subject to all conditions deemed imposed as a matter of law by sections 401(a)(2) and 401(d) of the Federal Water Pollution Control Act, as amended (33 U.S.C.A. 1341 (a)(2) and (d).)

(bb) For nuclear power reactors licensed by the NRC, the licensee shall, within 2 years following permanent cessation of operation of the reactor or 5 years before expiration of the reactor operating license, whichever occurs first, submit written notification to the Commission for its review and preliminary approval of the program by which the licensee intends to manage and provide funding for the management of all irradiated fuel at the reactor following permanent cessation of operation of the reactor until title to the irradiated fuel and possession of the fuel is transferred to the Secretary of Energy for its ultimate disposal in a repository. Licensees of nuclear power reactors that have permanently ceased operation by April 4, 1994 are required to submit such written notification by April 4, 1996. Final Commission review will be undertaken as part of any proceeding for continued licensing under part 50 or part 72 of this chapter. The licensee must demonstrate to NRC that the elected actions will be consistent with NRC requirements for licensed possession of irradiated nuclear fuel and that the actions will be implemented on a timely basis. Where implementation of such actions requires NRC authorizations, the licensee shall verify in the notification that submittals for such actions have been or will be made to NRC and shall identify them. A copy of the notification shall be retained by the licensee as a record until expiration of the reactor operating license. The licensee shall notify the NRC of any significant changes in the proposed waste management program as described in the initial notification.

(cc)(1) Each licensee shall notify the appropriate NRC Regional Administrator, in writing, immediately following the filing of a voluntary or involuntary petition for bankruptcy under any chapter of title 11 (Bankruptcy) of the United States Code by or against:

(i) The licensee;

(ii) An entity (as that term is defined in 11 U.S.C. 101(14)) controlling the licensee or listing the license or licensee as property of the estate; or

(iii) An affiliate (as that term is defined in 11 U.S.C. 101(2)) of the licensee.

(2) This notification must indicate:

(i) The bankruptcy court in which the petition for bankruptcy was filed; and

(ii) The date of the filing of the petition.

(dd) A licensee may take reasonable action that departs from a license condition or a technical specification (contained in a license issued under this part) in a national security emergency:

(1) When this action is immediately needed to implement national security objectives as designated by the national command authority through the Commission, and

(2) No action consistent with license conditions and technical specifications that can meet national security objectives is immediately apparent.

A national security emergency is established by a law enacted by the Congress or by an order or directive issued by the President pursuant to statutes or the Constitution of the United States. The authority under this paragraph must be exercised in accordance with law, including section 57e of the Act, and is in addition to the authority granted under paragraph (x) of this section, which remains in effect unless otherwise directed by the Commission during a national security emergency.

(ee)(1) Each license issued under this part authorizing the possession of byproduct and special nuclear material produced in the operation of the licensed reactor includes, whether stated in the license or not, the authorization to receive back that same material, in the same or altered form or combined with byproduct or special nuclear material produced in the operation of another reactor of the same licensee located at that site, from a licensee of the Commission or an Agreement State, or from a non-licensed entity authorized to possess the material.

(2) The authorizations in this subsection are subject to the same limitations and requirements applicable to the original possession of the material.

(3) This paragraph does not authorize the receipt of any material recovered from the reprocessing of irradiated fuel.

(ff) For licensees of nuclear power plants that have implemented the earthquake engineering criteria in appendix S to this part, plant shutdown is required as provided in paragraph IV(a)(3) of appendix S to this part. Prior to resuming operations, the licensee shall demonstrate to the Commission that no functional damage has occurred to those features necessary for continued operation without undue risk to the health and safety of the public and the licensing basis is maintained.

(gg)(1) Notwithstanding 10 CFR 52.103, if, following the conduct of the exercise required by paragraph IV.f.2.a of appendix E to part 50 of this chapter, FEMA identifies one or more deficiencies in the state of offsite emergency preparedness, the holder of a combined license under 10 CFR part 52 may operate at up to 5 percent of rated thermal power only if the Commission finds that the state of onsite emergency preparedness provides reasonable assurance that adequate protective measures can and will be taken in the event of a radiological emergency. The NRC will base this finding on its assessment of the applicant's onsite emergency plans against the pertinent standards in § 50.47 and appendix E to this part. Review of the applicant's emergency plans will include the following standards with offsite aspects:

(i) Arrangements for requesting and effectively using offsite assistance onsite have been made, arrangements to accommodate State and local staff at the licensee's Emergency Operations Facility have been made, and other organizations capable of augmenting the planned onsite response have been identified.

(ii) Procedures have been established for licensee communications with State and local response organizations, including initial notification of the declaration of emergency and periodic provision of plant and response status reports.

(iii) Provisions exist for prompt communications among principal response organizations to offsite emergency personnel who would be responding onsite.

(iv) Adequate emergency facilities and equipment to support the emergency response onsite are provided and maintained.

(v) Adequate methods, systems, and equipment for assessing and monitoring actual or potential offsite consequences of a radiological emergency condition are in use onsite.

(vi) Arrangements are made for medical services for contaminated and injured onsite individuals.

(vii) Radiological emergency response training has been made available to those offsite who may be called to assist in an emergency onsite.

(2) The condition in this paragraph, regarding operation at up to 5 percent power, ceases to apply 30 days after FEMA informs the NRC that the offsite deficiencies have been corrected, unless the NRC notifies the combined license holder before the expiration of the 30-day period that the Commission finds under paragraphs (s)(2) and (3) of this section that the state of emergency preparedness does not provide reasonable assurance that adequate protective measures can and will be taken in the event of a radiological emergency.

(hh) (1) Each licensee shall develop, implement and maintain procedures that describe how the licensee will address the following areas if the licensee is notified of a potential aircraft threat:

(i) Verification of the authenticity of threat notifications;

(ii) Maintenance of continuous communication with threat notification sources;

(iii) Contacting all onsite personnel and applicable offsite response organizations;

(iv) Onsite actions necessary to enhance the capability of the facility to mitigate the consequences of an aircraft impact;

(v) Measures to reduce visual discrimination of the site relative to its surroundings or individual buildings within the protected area;

(vi) Dispersal of equipment and personnel, as well as rapid entry into site protected areas for essential onsite personnel and offsite responders who are necessary to mitigate the event; and

(vii) Recall of site personnel.

(2) Each licensee shall develop and implement guidance and strategies intended to maintain or restore core cooling, containment, and spent fuel pool cooling capabilities under the circumstances associated with loss of large areas of the plant due to explosions or fire, to include strategies in the following areas:

(i) Fire fighting;

(ii) Operations to mitigate fuel damage; and

(iii) Actions to minimize radiological release.

(3) This section does not apply to a nuclear power plant for which the certifications required under §50.82(a) or §52.110(a)(1) of this chapter have been submitted.

(ii) [Reserved]

(jj) Structures, systems, and components subject to the codes and standards in 10 CFR 50.55a must be designed, fabricated, erected, constructed, tested, and inspected to quality standards commensurate with the importance of the safety function to be performed.

[21 FR 355, Jan. 19, 1956]

EDITORIAL NOTE: For FEDERAL REGISTER citations affecting §50.54, see the List of CFR Sections Affected, which appears in the Finding Aids section of the printed volume and at *www.fdsys.gov*.

§50.55 Conditions of construction permits, early site permits, combined licenses, and manufacturing licenses.

Each construction permit for a utilization facility is subject to the following terms and conditions and the applicable requirements of §50.55a; each construction permit for a production facility is subject to the following terms and conditions with the exception of paragraph (i); each early site permit is subject to the terms and conditions in paragraph (f) of this section; each manufacturing license is subject to the terms and conditions in paragraphs (e), (f), and (i) of this section and the applicable requirements of §50.55a; and each combined license is subject to the terms and conditions in paragraphs (e), (f), and (i) of this section and the applicable requirements of §50.55a until the date that the Commission makes the finding under §52.103(g) of this chapter:

(a) The construction permit shall state the earliest and latest dates for completion of the construction or modification.

(b) If the proposed construction or modification of the facility is not completed by the latest completion date, the construction permit shall expire and all rights are forfeited. However, upon good cause shown, the Commission will extend the completion date for a reasonable period of time. The Commission will recognize, among other things, developmental problems attributable to the experimental nature of the facility or fire, flood, explosion, strike, sabotage, domestic violence, enemy action, an act of the elements, and other acts beyond the control of the permit holder, as a basis for extending the completion date.

(c) Except as modified by this section and § 50.55a, the construction permit shall be subject to the same conditions to which a license is subject.

(d) At or about the time of completion of the construction or modification of the facility, the applicant will file any additional information needed to bring the original application for license up to date, and will file an application for an operating license or an amendment to an application for a license to construct and operate the facility for the issuance of an operating license, as appropriate, as specified in § 50.30(d) of this part.

(e)(1) *Definitions.* For purposes of this paragraph, the definitions in § 21.3 of this chapter apply.

(2) *Posting requirements.* (i) Each individual, partnership, corporation, dedicating entity, or other entity subject to the regulations in this part shall post current copies of the regulations in this part; Section 206 of the Energy Reorganization Act of 1974 (ERA); and procedures adopted under the regulations in this part. These documents must be posted in a conspicuous position on any premises within the United States where the activities subject to this part are conducted.

(ii) If posting of the regulations in this part or the procedures adopted under the regulations in this part is not practicable, the licensee or firm subject to the regulations in this part may, in addition to posting Section 206 of the ERA, post a notice which describes the regulations/procedures, including the name of the individual to whom reports may be made, and states where the regulation, procedures, and reports may be examined.

(3) *Procedures.* Each individual, corporation, partnership, or other entity holding a facility construction permit subject to this part, combined license (until the Commission makes the finding under 10 CFR 52.103(g)), and manufacturing license under 10 CFR part 52 must adopt appropriate procedures to—

(i) Evaluate deviations and failures to comply to identify defects and failures to comply associated with substantial safety hazards as soon as practicable, and, except as provided in paragraph (e)(3)(ii) of this section, in all cases within 60 days of discovery, to identify a reportable defect or failure to comply that could create a substantial safety hazard, were it to remain uncorrected.

(ii) Ensure that if an evaluation of an identified deviation or failure to comply potentially associated with a substantial safety hazard cannot be completed within 60 days from discovery of the deviation or failure to comply, an interim report is prepared and submitted to the Commission through a director or responsible officer or designated person as discussed in paragraph (e)(4)(v) of this section. The interim report should describe the deviation or failure to comply that is being evaluated and should also state when the evaluation will be completed. This interim report must be submitted in writing within 60 days of discovery of the deviation or failure to comply.

(iii) Ensure that a director or responsible officer of the holder of a facility construction permit subject to this part, combined license (until the Commission makes the finding under 10 CFR 52.103(g)), and manufacturing license under 10 CFR part 52 is informed as soon as practicable, and, in all cases, within the 5 working days after completion of the evaluation described in paragraph (e)(3)(i) or (e)(3)(ii) of this section, if the construction or manufacture of a facility or activity, or a basic component supplied for such facility or activity—

(A) Fails to comply with the AEA, as amended, or any applicable regulation, order, or license of the Commission, relating to a substantial safety hazard;

(B) Contains a defect; or

(C) Undergoes any significant breakdown in any portion of the quality assurance program conducted under the requirements of appendix B to 10 CFR part 50 which could have produced a defect in a basic component. These breakdowns in the quality assurance program are reportable whether or not the breakdown actually resulted in a defect in a design approved and released for construction, installation, or manufacture.

(4) *Notification.* (i) The holder of a facility construction permit subject to this part, combined license (until the Commission makes the finding under 10 CFR 52.103(g)), and manufacturing license who obtains information reasonably indicating that the facility fails to comply with the AEA, as amended, or any applicable regulation, order, or license of the Commission relating to a substantial safety hazard must notify the Commission of the failure to comply through a director or responsible officer or designated person as discussed in paragraph (e)(4)(v) of this section.

(ii) The holder of a facility construction permit subject to this part, combined license, or manufacturing license, who obtains information reasonably indicating the existence of any defect found in the construction or manufacture, or any defect found in the final design of a facility as approved and released for construction or manufacture, must notify the Commission of the defect through a director or responsible officer or designated person as discussed in paragraph (e)(4)(v) of this section.

(iii) The holder of a facility construction permit subject to this part, combined license, or manufacturing license, who obtains information reasonably indicating that the quality assurance program has undergone any significant breakdown discussed in paragraph (e)(3)(iii)(C) of this section must notify the Commission of the breakdown in the quality assurance program through a director or responsible officer or designated person as discussed in paragraph (e)(4)(v) of this section.

(iv) A dedicating entity is responsible for identifying and evaluating deviations and reporting defects and failures to comply associated with substantial safety hazards for dedicated items; and maintaining auditable records for the dedication process.

(v) The notification requirements of this paragraph apply to all defects and failures to comply associated with a substantial safety hazard regardless of whether extensive evaluation, redesign, or repair is required to conform to the criteria and bases stated in the safety analysis report, construction permit, combined license, or manufacturing license. Evaluation of potential defects and failures to comply and reporting of defects and failures to comply under this section satisfies the construction permit holder's, combined license holder's, and manufacturing license holder's evaluation and notification obligations under part 21 of this chapter, and satisfies the responsibility of individual directors or responsible officers of holders of construction permits issued under § 50.23, holders of combined licenses (until the Commission makes the finding under § 52.103 of this chapter), and holders of manufacturing licenses to report defects, and failures to comply associated with substantial safety hazards under Section 206 of the ERA. The director or responsible officer may authorize an individual to provide the notification required by this section, provided that this must not relieve the director or responsible officer of his or her responsibility under this section.

(5) *Notification—timing and where sent.* The notification required by paragraph (e)(4) of this section must consist of—

(i) Initial notification by facsimile, which is the preferred method of notification, to the NRC Operations Center at (301) 816–5151 or by telephone at (301) 816–5100 within 2 days following receipt of information by the director or responsible corporate officer under paragraph (e)(3)(iii) of this section, on the identification of a defect or a failure to comply. Verification that the facsimile has been received should be made by calling the NRC Operations Center. This paragraph does not apply to interim reports described in paragraph (e)(3)(ii) of this section.

(ii) Written notification submitted to the Document Control Desk, U.S. Nuclear Regulatory Commission, by an appropriate method listed in § 50.4, with a copy to the appropriate Regional Administrator at the address specified in appendix D to part 20 of this chapter and a copy to the appropriate NRC resident inspector within 30 days following receipt of information by the director or responsible corporate officer under paragraph (e)(3)(iii) of this section, on the identification of a defect or failure to comply.

(6) *Content of notification.* The written notification required by paragraph (e)(5)(ii) of this section must clearly indicate that the written notification is being submitted under § 50.55(e) and include the following information, to the extent known.

(i) Name and address of the individual or individuals informing the Commission.

(ii) Identification of the facility, the activity, or the basic component supplied for the facility or the activity within the United States which contains a defect or fails to comply.

(iii) Identification of the firm constructing or manufacturing the facility or supplying the basic component which fails to comply or contains a defect.

(iv) Nature of the defect or failure to comply and the safety hazard which is created or could be created by the defect or failure to comply.

(v) The date on which the information of a defect or failure to comply was obtained.

(vi) In the case of a basic component which contains a defect or fails to comply, the number and location of all the basic components in use at the facility subject to the regulations in this part.

(vii) In the case of a completed reactor manufactured under part 52 of this chapter, the entities to which the reactor was supplied.

(viii) The corrective action which has been, is being, or will be taken; the name of the individual or organization responsible for the action; and the length of time that has been or will be taken to complete the action.

(ix) Any advice related to the defect or failure to comply about the facility, activity, or basic component that has been, is being, or will be given to other entities.

(7) *Procurement documents.* Each individual, corporation, partnership, dedicating entity, or other entity subject to the regulations in this part shall ensure that each procurement document for a facility, or a basic component specifies or is issued by the entity subject to the regulations, when applicable, that the provisions of 10 CFR part 21 or 10 CFR 50.55(e) applies, as applicable.

(8) *Coordination with 10 CFR part 21.* The requirements of § 50.55(e) are satisfied when the defect or failure to comply associated with a substantial safety hazard has been previously reported under part 21 of this chapter, under § 73.71 of this chapter, or under §§ 50.55(e) or 50.73. For holders of construction permits issued before October 29, 1991, evaluation, reporting and recordkeeping requirements of § 50.55(e) may be met by complying with the comparable requirements of part 21 of this chapter.

(9) *Records retention.* The holder of a construction permit, combined license, and manufacturing license must prepare and maintain records necessary to accomplish the purposes of this section, specifically—

(i) Retain procurement documents, which define the requirements that facilities or basic components must meet in order to be considered acceptable, for the lifetime of the facility or basic component.

(ii) Retain records of evaluations of all deviations and failures to comply under paragraph (e)(3)(i) of this section for the longest of:

(A) Ten (10) years from the date of the evaluation;

(B) Five (5) years from the date that an early site permit is referenced in an application for a combined license; or

(C) Five (5) years from the date of delivery of a manufactured reactor.

(iii) Retain records of all interim reports to the Commission made under paragraph (e)(3)(ii) of this section, or notifications to the Commission made under paragraph (e)(4) of this section for the minimum time periods stated in paragraph (e)(9)(ii) of this section;

(iv) Suppliers of basic components must retain records of:

(A) All notifications sent to affected licensees or purchasers under paragraph (e)(4)(iv) of this section for a minimum of ten (10) years following the date of the notification;

(B) The facilities or other purchasers to whom basic components or associated services were supplied for a minimum of fifteen (15) years from the delivery of the basic component or associated services.

(v) Maintaining records in accordance with this section satisfies the recordkeeping obligations under part 21 of this chapter of the entities, including directors or responsible officers thereof, subject to this section.

(f)(1) Each nuclear power plant or fuel reprocessing plant construction permit holder subject to the quality assurance criteria in appendix B of this part shall implement, pursuant to §50.34(a)(7) of this part, the quality assurance program described or referenced in the Safety Analysis Report, including changes to that report.

(2) Each construction permit holder described in paragraph (f)(1) of this section shall, by June 10, 1983, submit to the appropriate NRC Regional Office shown in appendix D of part 20 of this chapter the current description of the quality assurance program it is implementing for inclusion in the Safety Analysis Report, unless there are no changes to the description previously accepted by NRC. This submittal must identify changes made to the quality assurance program description since the description was submitted to NRC. (Should a permit holder need additional time beyond June 10, 1983 to submit its current quality assurance program description to NRC, it shall notify the appropriate NRC Regional Office in writing, explain why additional time is needed, and provide a schedule for NRC approval showing when its current quality assurance program description will be submitted.)

(3) After March 11, 1983, each construction permit holder described in paragraph (f)(1) of this section may make a change to a previously accepted quality assurance program description included or referenced in the Safety Analysis Report, provided the change does not reduce the commitments in the program description previously accepted by the NRC. Changes to the quality assurance program description that do not reduce the commitments must be submitted to NRC within 90 days. Changes to the quality assurance program description that do reduce the commitments must be submitted to NRC and receive NRC approval before implementation, as follows:

(i) Changes to the Safety Analysis Report must be submitted for review as specified in §50.4. Changes made to NRC-accepted quality assurance topical report descriptions must be submitted as specified in §50.4.

(ii) The submittal of a change to the Safety Analysis Report quality assurance program description must include all pages affected by that change and must be accompanied by a forwarding letter identifying the change, the reason for the change, and the basis for concluding that the revised program incorporating the change continues to satisfy the criteria of appendix B of this part and the Safety Analysis Report quality assurance program description commitments previously accepted by the NRC (the letter need not provide the basis for changes that correct spelling, punctuation, or editorial items).

(iii) A copy of the forwarding letter identifying the changes must be maintained as a facility record for three years.

(iv) Changes to the quality assurance program description included or referenced in the Safety Analysis Report shall be regarded as accepted by the Commission upon receipt of a letter to this effect from the appropriate reviewing office of the Commission or 60 days after submittal to the Commission, whichever occurs first.

(4) Each holder of an early site permit or a manufacturing license under part 52 of this chapter shall implement the quality assurance program described or referenced in the safety analysis report, including changes to that report. Each holder of a combined license shall implement the quality assurance program for design and construction described or referenced in the safety analysis report, including changes to that report, provided, however, that the holder of a combined license is not subject to the terms and conditions in this paragraph after the Commission makes the finding under §52.103(g) of this chapter.

(i) Each holder described in paragraph (f)(4) of this section may make a change to a previously accepted quality assurance program description included or referenced in the safety analysis report, if the change does not reduce the commitments in the program description previously accepted by the NRC. Changes to the quality assurance program description that do not reduce the commitments must be submitted to NRC within 90 days. Changes to the quality assurance program description that reduce the commitments must be submitted to NRC and receive NRC approval before implementation, as follows:

(A) Changes to the safety analysis report must be submitted for review as specified in § 50.4. Changes made to NRC-accepted quality assurance topical report descriptions must be submitted as specified in § 50.4.

(B) The submittal of a change to the safety analysis report quality assurance program description must include all pages affected by that change and must be accompanied by a forwarding letter identifying the change, the reason for the change, and the basis for concluding that the revised program incorporating the change continues to satisfy the criteria of appendix B of this part and the safety analysis report quality assurance program description commitments previously accepted by the NRC (the letter need not provide the basis for changes that correct spelling, punctuation, or editorial items).

(C) A copy of the forwarding letter identifying the changes must be maintained as a facility record for three (3) years.

(D) Changes to the quality assurance program description included or referenced in the safety analysis report shall be regarded as accepted by the Commission upon receipt of a letter to this effect from the appropriate reviewing office of the Commission or 60 days after submittal to the Commission, whichever occurs first.

(ii) [Reserved]

(g)–(h) [Reserved]

(i) Structures, systems, and components subject to the codes and standards in 10 CFR 50.55a must be designed, fabricated, erected, constructed, tested, and inspected to quality standards commensurate with the importance of the safety function to be performed.

[21 FR 355, Jan. 19, 1956, as amended at 32 FR 4055, Mar. 15, 1967; 35 FR 11461, July 17, 1970; 35 FR 19661, Dec. 29, 1970; 36 FR 11424, June 12, 1971; 37 FR 6460, Mar. 30, 1972; 38 FR 1272, Jan. 11, 1973; 41 FR 16446, Apr. 19, 1976; 42 FR 43385, Aug. 29, 1977; 48 FR 1029, Jan. 10, 1983; 51 FR 40309, Nov. 6, 1986; 56 FR 36091, July 31, 1991; 59 FR 14087, Mar. 25, 1994; 68 FR 58809, Oct. 10, 2003; 72 FR 49497, Aug. 28, 2007; 78 FR 34248, June 7, 2013; 79 FR 65798, Nov. 5, 2014]

§ 50.55a Codes and standards.

(a) *Documents approved for incorporation by reference.* The standards listed in this paragraph (a) have been approved for incorporation by reference by the Director of the Federal Register pursuant to 5 U.S.C. 552(a) and 1 CFR part 51. The standards are available for inspection, by appointment, at the NRC Technical Library, which is located at Two White Flint North, 11545 Rockville Pike, Rockville, Maryland 20852; telephone: 301–415–7000; email: *Library.Resource@nrc.gov;* or at the National Archives and Records Administration (NARA). For information on the availability of this material at NARA, call 202–741–6030 or go to *http://www.archives.gov/federal-register/cfr/ibr-locations.html.*

(1) *American Society of Mechanical Engineers (ASME),* Three Park Avenue, New York, NY 10016; telephone: 1–800–843–2763; *http://www.asme.org/Codes/.*

(i) *ASME Boiler and Pressure Vessel Code, Section III.* The editions and addenda for Section III of the ASME Boiler and Pressure Vessel Code (excluding Nonmandatory Appendices) (referred to herein as ASME BPV Code) are listed in this paragraph (a)(1)(i), but limited by those provisions identified in paragraph (b)(1) of this section.

(A) "Rules for Construction of Nuclear Vessels:"

(*1*) 1963 Edition,

(*2*) Summer 1964 Addenda,

(*3*) Winter 1964 Addenda,

(*4*) 1965 Edition,

(*5*) 1965 Summer Addenda,

(*6*) 1965 Winter Addenda,

(*7*) 1966 Summer Addenda,

(*8*) 1966 Winter Addenda,

(*9*) 1967 Summer Addenda,

(*10*) 1967 Winter Addenda,

(*11*) 1968 Edition,

(*12*) 1968 Summer Addenda,
(*13*)1968 Winter Addenda,
(*14*) 1969 Summer Addenda,
(*15*) 1969 Winter Addenda,
(*16*) 1970 Summer Addenda, and
(*17*) 1970 Winter Addenda.

(B) "Rules for Construction of Nuclear Power Plant Components:"
(*1*) 1971 Edition,
(*2*) 1971 Summer Addenda,
(*3*) 1971 Winter Addenda,
(*4*) 1972 Summer Addenda,
(*5*) 1972 Winter Addenda,
(*6*) 1973 Summer Addenda, and
(*7*) 1973 Winter Addenda.

(C) "Division 1 Rules for Construction of Nuclear Power Plant Components:"
(*1*) 1974 Edition,
(*2*) 1974 Summer Addenda,
(*3*) 1974 Winter Addenda,
(*4*) 1975 Summer Addenda,
(*5*) 1975 Winter Addenda,
(*6*) 1976 Summer Addenda, and
(*7*) 1976 Winter Addenda;

(D) "Rules for Construction of Nuclear Power Plant Components—Division 1";
(*1*) 1977 Edition,
(*2*) 1977 Summer Addenda,
(*3*) 1977 Winter Addenda,
(*4*) 1978 Summer Addenda,
(*5*) 1978 Winter Addenda,
(*6*) 1979 Summer Addenda,
(*7*) 1979 Winter Addenda,
(*8*) 1980 Edition,
(*9*) 1980 Summer Addenda,
(*10*) 1980 Winter Addenda,
(*11*) 1981 Summer Addenda,
(*12*) 1981 Winter Addenda,
(*13*) 1982 Summer Addenda,
(*14*) 1982 Winter Addenda,
(*15*) 1983 Edition,
(*16*) 1983 Summer Addenda,
(*17*) 1983 Winter Addenda,
(*18*) 1984 Summer Addenda,
(*19*) 1984 Winter Addenda,
(*20*) 1985 Summer Addenda,
(*21*) 1985 Winter Addenda,
(*22*) 1986 Edition,
(*23*) 1986 Addenda,
(*24*) 1987 Addenda,
(*25*) 1988 Addenda,
(*26*) 1989 Edition,
(*27*) 1989 Addenda,
(*28*) 1990 Addenda,
(*29*) 1991 Addenda,
(*30*) 1992 Edition,
(*31*) 1992 Addenda,
(*32*) 1993 Addenda,
(*33*) 1994 Addenda,
(*34*) 1995 Edition,
(*35*) 1995 Addenda,
(*36*) 1996 Addenda, and
(*37*) 1997 Addenda.

(E) "Rules for Construction of Nuclear Facility Components—Division 1:"
(*1*) 1998 Edition,
(*2*) 1998 Addenda,
(*3*) 1999 Addenda,
(*4*) 2000 Addenda,
(*5*) 2001 Edition,
(*6*) 2001 Addenda,
(*7*) 2002 Addenda,
(*8*) 2003 Addenda,
(*9*) 2004 Edition,
(*10*) 2005 Addenda,
(*11*) 2006 Addenda,
(*12*) 2007 Edition,
(*13*) 2008 Addenda,
(*14*) 2009b Addenda (including Subsection NCA; and Division 1 subsections NB through NH and Appendices),
(*15*) 2010 Edition (including Subsection NCA; and Division 1 subsections NB through NH and Appendices),
(*16*) 2011a Addenda (including Subsection NCA; and Division 1 subsections NB through NH and Appendices), and
(*17*) 2013 Edition (including Subsection NCA; and Division 1 subsections NB through NH and Appendices).

(ii) *ASME Boiler and Pressure Vessel Code, Section XI.* The editions and addenda for Section XI of the ASME BPV Code are listed in this paragraph (a)(1)(ii), but limited by those provisions identified in paragraph (b)(2) of this section.

(A) "Rules for Inservice Inspection of Nuclear Reactor Coolant Systems:"
(*1*) 1970 Edition,
(*2*) 1971 Edition,
(*3*) 1971 Summer Addenda,
(*4*) 1971 Winter Addenda,
(*5*) 1972 Summer Addenda,
(*6*) 1972 Winter Addenda,
(*7*) 1973 Summer Addenda, and
(*8*) 1973 Winter Addenda.

(B) "Rules for Inservice Inspection of Nuclear Power Plant Components:"
(*1*) 1974 Edition,
(*2*) 1974 Summer Addenda,

(*3*) 1974 Winter Addenda, and

(*4*) 1975 Summer Addenda.

(*5*) 1975 Winter Addenda,

(*6*) 1976 Summer Addenda, and

(*7*) 1976 Winter Addenda.

(C) "Rules for Inservice Inspection of Nuclear Power Plant Components—Division 1:"

(*1*) 1977 Edition,

(*2*) 1977 Summer Addenda,

(*3*) 1977 Winter Addenda,

(*4*) 1978 Summer Addenda,

(*5*) 1978 Winter Addenda,

(*6*) 1979 Summer Addenda,

(*7*) 1979 Winter Addenda,

(*8*) 1980 Edition,

(*9*) 1980 Winter Addenda,

(*10*) 1981 Summer Addenda,

(*11*) 1981 Winter Addenda,

(*12*) 1982 Summer Addenda,

(*13*) 1982 Winter Addenda,

(*14*) 1983 Edition,

(*15*) 1983 Summer Addenda,

(*16*) 1983 Winter Addenda,

(*17*) 1984 Summer Addenda,

(*18*) 1984 Winter Addenda,

(*19*) 1985 Summer Addenda,

(*20*) 1985 Winter Addenda,

(*21*) 1986 Edition,

(*22*) 1986 Addenda,

(*23*) 1987 Addenda,

(*24*) 1988 Addenda,

(*25*) 1989 Edition,

(*26*) 1989 Addenda,

(*27*) 1990 Addenda,

(*28*) 1991 Addenda,

(*29*) 1992 Edition,

(*30*) 1992 Addenda,

(*31*) 1993 Addenda,

(*32*) 1994 Addenda,

(*33*) 1995 Edition,

(*34*) 1995 Addenda,

(*35*) 1996 Addenda,

(*36*) 1997 Addenda,

(*37*) 1998 Edition,

(*38*) 1998 Addenda,

(*39*) 1999 Addenda,

(*40*) 2000 Addenda,

(*41*) 2001 Edition,

(*42*) 2001 Addenda,

(*43*) 2002 Addenda,

(*44*) 2003 Addenda,

(*45*) 2004 Edition,

(*46*) 2005 Addenda,

(*47*) 2006 Addenda,

(*48*) 2007 Edition,

(*49*) 2008 Addenda,

(*50*) 2009b Addenda,

(*51*) 2010 Edition,

(*52*) 2011a Addenda (Excluding Article IWB–2000: IWB–2500 "Examination and Inspection: Examination and Pressure Test Requirements," Table IWB–2500–1 "Examination Categories," Item numbers B5.11 and B5.71), and

(*53*) 2013 Edition (Excluding Article IWB–2000: IWB–2500 "Examination and Inspection: Examination and Pressure Test Requirements," Table IWB–2500–1 (B–F) "Examination Category B–F, Pressure Retaining Dissimilar Metal Welds in Vessel Nozzles," Item numbers B5.11 and B5.71; Article IWB–3000 "Acceptance Standards," IWB–3100 "Evaluation of Examination Results," IWB–3110 "Preservice Volumetric and Surface Examinations," IWB–3112 "Acceptance," paragraph (a)(3); and Article IWC–3000 "Acceptance Standards," IWC–3100 "Evaluation of Examination Results," IWC–3110 "Preservice Volumetric and Surface Examinations," IWC–3112 "Acceptance," paragraph (a)(3)).

(iii) *ASME Code Cases: Nuclear Components*—(A) *ASME BPV Code Case N–513–3 Mandatory Appendix I.* ASME BPV Code Case N–513–3, "Evaluation Criteria for Temporary Acceptance of Flaws in Moderate Energy Class 2 or 3 Piping Section XI, Division 1," Mandatory Appendix I, "Relations for F_m, F_b, and F for Through-Wall Flaws" (Approval Date: January 26, 2009). ASME BPV Code Case N–513–3 Mandatory Appendix I is referenced in paragraph (b)(2)(xxxiv)(B) of this section.

(B) *ASME BPV Code Case N–722–1.* ASME BPV Code Case N–722–1, "Additional Examinations for PWR Pressure Retaining Welds in Class 1 Components Fabricated with Alloy 600/82/182 Materials, Section XI, Division 1" (Approval Date: January 26, 2009), with the conditions in paragraph (g)(6)(ii)(E) of this section.

(C) *ASME BPV Code Case N–729–4.* ASME BPV Code Case N–729–4, "Alternative Examination Requirements for PWR Reactor Vessel Upper Heads With Nozzles Having Pressure-Retaining Partial-Penetration Welds Section XI, Division 1" (Approval Date: June 22, 2012), with the conditions in paragraph (g)(6)(ii)(D) of this section.

(D) *ASME BPV Code Case N–770–2.* ASME BPV Code Case N–770–2, "Alternative Examination Requirements and

Acceptance Standards for Class 1 PWR Piping and Vessel Nozzle Butt Welds Fabricated with UNS N06082 or UNS W86182 Weld Filler Material With or Without Application of Listed Mitigation Activities Section XI, Division 1" (Approval Date: June 9, 2011), with the conditions in paragraph (g)(6)(ii)(F) of this section.

(E) *ASME BPV Code Case N–824.* ASME BPV Code Case N–824, "Ultrasonic Examination of Cast Austenitic Piping Welds From the Outside Surface Section XI, Division 1" (Approval Date: October 16, 2012), with the conditions in paragraphs (b)(2)(xxxvii)(A) through (D) of this section.

(F) *ASME BPV Code Case N–852.* ASME BPV Code Case N–852, "Application of the ASME NPT Stamp, Section III, Division 1; Section III, Division 2; Section III, Division 3; Section III, Division 5" (Approval Date: February 9, 2015). ASME BPV Code Case N–852 is referenced in paragraph (b)(1)(ix) of this section.

(G) *ASME OM Code Case OMN–20.* ASME OM Code Case OMN–20, "Inservice Test Frequency," in the 2012 Edition of the ASME OM Code. OMN–20 is referenced in paragraph (b)(3)(x) of this section.

(iv) *ASME Operation and Maintenance Code.* The editions and addenda for the ASME Operation and Maintenance of Nuclear Power Plants (various edition titles referred to herein as ASME OM Code) are listed in this paragraph (a)(1)(iv), but limited by those provisions identified in paragraph (b)(3) of this section.

(A) "Code for Operation and Maintenance of Nuclear Power Plants:"

(*1*) 1995 Edition,

(*2*) 1996 Addenda,

(*3*) 1997 Addenda,

(*4*) 1998 Edition,

(*5*) 1999 Addenda,

(*6*) 2000 Addenda,

(*7*) 2001 Edition,

(*8*) 2002 Addenda,

(*9*) 2003 Addenda,

(*10*) 2004 Edition,

(*11*) 2005 Addenda, and

(*12*) 2006 Addenda.

(B) "Operation and Maintenance of Nuclear Power Plants, Division 1: Section IST Rules for Inservice Testing of Light-Water Reactor Power Plants:"

(*1*) 2009 Edition; and

(*2*) 2011 Addenda.

(C) "Operation and Maintenance of Nuclear Power Plants, Division 1: OM Code: Section IST:"

(*1*) 2012 Edition.

(*2*) [Reserved]

(v) *ASME Quality Assurance Requirements.* (A) ASME NQA–1, "Quality Assurance Program Requirements for Nuclear Facilities:"

(*1*) NQA–1—1983 Edition;

(*2*) NQA–1a—1983 Addenda;

(*3*) NQA–1b—1984 Addenda;

(*4*) NQA–1c—1985 Addenda;

(*5*) NQA–1—1986 Edition;

(*6*) NQA–1a—1986 Addenda;

(*7*) NQA–1b—1987 Addenda;

(*8*) NQA–1c—1988 Addenda;

(*9*) NQA–1—1989 Edition;

(*10*) NQA–1a—1989 Addenda;

(*11*) NQA–1b—1991 Addenda; and

(*12*) NQA–1c—1992 Addenda.

(B) ASME NQA–1, "Quality Assurance Requirements for Nuclear Facility Applications:"

(*1*) NQA–1—1994 Edition;

(*2*) NQA–1—2008 Edition; and

(*3*) NQA–1a—2009 Addenda.

(2) *Institute of Electrical and Electronics Engineers (IEEE) Service Center,* 445 Hoes Lane, Piscataway, NJ 08855; telephone: 1–800–678–4333; *http://ieeexplore.ieee.org.*

(i) *IEEE standard 279–1968.* (IEEE Std 279–1968), "Proposed IEEE Criteria for Nuclear Power Plant Protection Systems" (Approval Date: August 30, 1968), referenced in paragraph (h)(2) of this section. (Copies of this document may be purchased from IHS Global, 15 Inverness Way East, Englewood, CO 80112; *https://global.ihs.com.*)

(ii) *IEEE standard 279–1971.* (IEEE Std 279–1971), "Criteria for Protection Systems for Nuclear Power Generating Stations" (Approval Date: June 3, 1971), referenced in paragraph (h)(2) of this section.

(iii) *IEEE standard 603–1991.* (IEEE Std 603–1991), "Standard Criteria for Safety Systems for Nuclear Power Generating Stations" (Approval Date: June 27, 1991), referenced in paragraphs (h)(2) and (h)(3) of this section. All other standards that are referenced in IEEE Std 603–1991 are not approved for incorporation by reference.

(iv) *IEEE standard 603–1991, correction sheet.* (IEEE Std 603–1991 correction sheet), "Standard Criteria for Safety Systems for Nuclear Power Generating Stations, Correction Sheet, Issued January 30, 1995," referenced in paragraphs (h)(2) and (h)(3) of this section. (This correction sheet is available from IEEE at *http://standards.ieee.org/findstds/errata/*).

(3) *U.S. Nuclear Regulatory Commission (NRC) Public Document Room,* 11555 Rockville Pike, Rockville, Maryland 20852; telephone: 1–800–397–4209; email: *pdr.resource@nrc.gov; http://www.nrc.gov/reading-rm/doc-collections/reg-guides/.*

(i) *NRC Regulatory Guide 1.84, Revision 36.* NRC Regulatory Guide 1.84, Revision 36, "Design, Fabrication, and Materials Code Case Acceptability, ASME Section III," dated August 2014, with the requirements in paragraph (b)(4) of this section.

(ii) *NRC Regulatory Guide 1.147, Revision 17.* NRC Regulatory Guide 1.147, Revision 17, "Inservice Inspection Code Case Acceptability, ASME Section XI, Division 1," dated August 2014, which lists ASME Code Cases that the NRC has approved in accordance with the requirements in paragraph (b)(5) of this section.

(iii) *NRC Regulatory Guide 1.192, Revision 1.* NRC Regulatory Guide 1.192, Revision 1, "Operation and Maintenance Code Case Acceptability, ASME OM Code," dated August 2014, which lists ASME Code Cases that the NRC has approved in accordance with the requirements in paragraph (b)(6) of this section.

(b) *Use and conditions on the use of standards.* Systems and components of boiling and pressurized water-cooled nuclear power reactors must meet the requirements of the ASME BPV Code and the ASME OM Code as specified in this paragraph (b). Each combined license for a utilization facility is subject to the following conditions.

(1) *Conditions on ASME BPV Code Section III.* Each manufacturing license, standard design approval, and design certification under 10 CFR part 52 is subject to the following conditions. As used in this section, references to Section III refer to Section III of the ASME BPV Code and include the 1963 Edition through 1973 Winter Addenda and the 1974 Edition (Division 1) through the 2013 Edition (Division 1), subject to the following conditions:

(i) *Section III condition: Section III materials.* When applying the 1992 Edition of Section III, applicants or licensees must apply the 1992 Edition with the 1992 Addenda of Section II of the ASME Boiler and Pressure Vessel Code.

(ii) *Section III condition: Weld leg dimensions.* When applying the 1989 Addenda through the latest edition and addenda incorporated by reference in paragraph (a)(1) of this section, applicants and licensees may not apply the Section III provisions identified in Table I of this section for welds with leg size less than 1.09 t_n:

TABLE I—PROHIBITED CODE PROVISIONS

Editions and addenda	Code provision
1989 Addenda through 2013 Edition	Subparagraph NB–3683.4(c)(1); Subparagraph NB–3683.4(c)(2).
1989 Addenda through 2003 Addenda	Note 11 to Figure NC–3673.2(b)–1; Note 11 to Figure ND–3673.2(b)–1.
2004 Edition through 2010 Edition	Note 13 to Figure NC–3673.2(b)–1; Note 13 to Figure ND–3673.2(b)–1.
2011 Addenda through 2013 Edition	Note 11 to Table NC–3673.2(b)–1; Note 11 to Table ND–3673.2(b)–1.

(iii) *Section III condition: Seismic design of piping.* Applicants or licensees may use Subarticles NB–3200, NB–3600, NC–3600, and ND–3600 for seismic design of piping, up to and including the 1993 Addenda, subject to the condition specified in paragraph (b)(1)(ii) of this section. Applicants or licensees may not use these subarticles for seismic design of piping in the 1994 Addenda through the 2005 Addenda incorporated by reference in paragraph (a)(1) of this section, except that Subarticle NB–3200 in the 2004 Edition through the 2008 Addenda may be used by applicants and licensees, subject to the condition in paragraph (b)(1)(iii)(A) of this section. Applicants or licensees may use Subarticles NB–3600, NC–3600, and ND–3600 for the seismic design of piping in the 2006 Addenda through the 2008 Addenda, subject to the conditions of this paragraph corresponding to those subarticles.

(A) *Seismic design of piping: First provision.* When applying Note (1) of Figure NB–3222–1 for Level B service limits, the calculation of P_b stresses must include reversing dynamic loads (including inertia earthquake effects) if evaluation of these loads is required by NB–3223(b).

(B) *Seismic design of piping: Second provision.* For Class 1 piping, the material and D_o/t requirements of NB–3656(b) must be met for all Service Limits when the Service Limits include reversing dynamic loads, and the alternative rules for reversing dynamic loads are used.

(iv) *Section III condition: Quality assurance.* When applying editions and addenda later than the 1989 Edition of Section III, the requirements of NQA–1, "Quality Assurance Requirements for Nuclear Facility Applications," 1994 Edition, 2008 Edition, and the 2009–1a Addenda specified in either NCA–4000 or NCA–7000 of that edition and addenda of Section III may be used by an applicant or licensee, provided that the administrative, quality, and technical provisions contained in that edition and addenda of Section III are used in conjunction with the applicant's or licensee's appendix B to this part quality assurance program; and that the applicant's or licensee's Section III activities comply with those commitments contained in the applicant's or licensee's quality assurance program description. Where NQA–1 and Section III do not address the commitments contained in the applicant's or licensee's appendix B quality assurance program description, those licensee commitments must be applied to Section III activities.

(v) *Section III condition: Independence of inspection.* Applicants or licensees may not apply NCA–4134.10(a) of Section III, 1995 Edition through the latest edition and addenda incorporated by reference in paragraph (a)(1) of this section.

(vi) *Section III condition: Subsection NH.* The provisions in Subsection NH, "Class 1 Components in Elevated Temperature Service," 1995 Addenda through the latest edition and addenda incorporated by reference in paragraph (a)(1) of this section, may only be used for the design and construction of Type 316 stainless steel pressurizer heater sleeves where service conditions do not cause the components to reach temperatures exceeding 900 °F.

(vii) *Section III condition: Capacity certification and demonstration of function of incompressible-fluid pressure-relief valves.* When applying the 2006 Addenda through the 2013 Edition, applicants and licensees may use paragraph NB–7742, except that paragraph NB–7742(a)(2) may not be used. For a valve design of a single size to be certified over a range of set pressures, the demonstration of function tests under paragraph NB–7742 must be conducted as prescribed in NB–7732.2 on two valves covering the minimum set pressure for the design and the maximum set pressure that can be accommodated at the demonstration facility selected for the test.

(viii) *Section III condition: Use of ASME certification marks.* When applying editions and addenda earlier than the 2011 Addenda to the 2010 Edition, licensees may use either the ASME BPV Code Symbol Stamps or the ASME Certification Marks with the appropriate certification designators and class designators as specified in the 2013 Edition through the latest edition and addenda incorporated by reference in paragraph (a)(1) of this section.

(ix) *Section III Condition: NPT Code Symbol Stamps.* Licensees may use the NPT Code Symbol Stamp with the letters arranged horizontally as specified in ASME BPV Code Case N–852 for the service life of a component that had the NPT Code Symbol Stamp applied during the time period from January 1, 2005, through December 31, 2015.

(2) *Conditions on ASME BPV Code, Section XI.* As used in this section, references to Section XI refer to Section XI, Division 1, of the ASME BPV Code, and include the 1970 Edition through the 1976 Winter Addenda and the 1977 Edition through the 2013 Edition, subject to the following conditions:

(i) [Reserved]

(ii) *Section XI condition: Pressure-retaining welds in ASME Code Class 1 piping (applies to Table IWB–2500 and IWB–2500–1 and Category B–J).* If the facility's application for a construction permit was docketed prior to July 1, 1978, the extent of examination for Code Class 1 pipe welds may be determined by the requirements of Table IWB–2500 and Table IWB–2600 Category B–J of Section XI of the ASME BPV Code in the 1974 Edition and Addenda through the Summer 1975 Addenda or other requirements the NRC may adopt.

(iii)–(v) [Reserved]

(vi) *Section XI condition: Effective edition and addenda of Subsection IWE and Subsection IWL.* Licensees that implemented the expedited examination of containment, in accordance with Subsection IWE and Subsection IWL, during the period from September 9, 1996, to September 9, 2001, may use either the 1992 Edition with the 1992 Addenda or the 1995 Edition with the 1996 Addenda of Subsection IWE and Subsection IWL, as conditioned by the requirements in paragraphs (b)(2)(viii) and (ix) of this section, when implementing the initial 120-month inspection interval for the containment inservice inspection requirements of this section. Successive 120-month interval updates must be implemented in accordance with paragraph (g)(4)(ii) of this section.

(vii) *Section XI condition: Section XI references to OM Part 4, OM Part 6, and OM Part 10 (Table IWA–1600–1).* When using Table IWA–1600–1, "Referenced Standards and Specifications," in the Section XI, Division 1, 1987 Addenda, 1988 Addenda, or 1989 Edition, the specified "Revision Date or Indicator" for ASME/ANSI OM part 4, ASME/ANSI part 6, and ASME/ANSI part 10 must be the OMa–1988 Addenda to the OM–1987 Edition. These requirements have been incorporated into the OM Code, which is incorporated by reference in paragraph (a)(1)(iv) of this section.

(viii) *Section XI condition: Concrete containment examinations.* Applicants or licensees applying Subsection IWL, 1992 Edition with the 1992 Addenda, must apply paragraphs (b)(2)(viii)(A) through (E) of this section. Applicants or licensees applying Subsection IWL, 1995 Edition with the 1996 Addenda, must apply paragraphs (b)(2)(viii)(A), (b)(2)(viii)(D)(*3*), and (b)(2)(viii)(E) of this section. Applicants or licensees applying Subsection IWL, 1998 Edition through the 2000 Addenda, must apply paragraphs (b)(2)(viii)(E) and (F) of this section. Applicants or licensees applying Subsection IWL, 2001 Edition through the 2004 Edition, up to and including the 2006 Addenda, must apply paragraphs (b)(2)(viii)(E) through (G) of this section. Applicants or licensees applying Subsection IWL, 2007 Edition up to and including the 2008 Addenda must apply paragraph (b)(2)(viii)(E) of this section. Applicants or licensees applying Subsection IWL, 2007 Edition with the 2009 Addenda through the latest edition and addenda incorporated by reference in paragraph (a)(1)(ii) of this section, must apply paragraphs (b)(2)(viii)(H) and (I) of this section.

(A) *Concrete containment examinations: First provision.* Grease caps that are accessible must be visually examined to detect grease leakage or grease cap deformations. Grease caps must be removed for this examination when there is evidence of grease cap deformation that indicates deterioration of anchorage hardware.

(B) *Concrete containment examinations: Second provision.* When evaluation of consecutive surveillances of pre-stressing forces for the same tendon or tendons in a group indicates a trend of pre-stress loss such that the tendon force(s) would be less than the minimum design pre-stress requirements before the next inspection interval, an evaluation must be performed and reported in the Engineering Evaluation Report as prescribed in IWL–3300.

(C) *Concrete containment examinations: Third provision.* When the elongation corresponding to a specific load (adjusted for effective wires or strands) during re-tensioning of tendons differs by more than 10 percent from that recorded during the last measurement, an evaluation must be performed to determine whether the difference is related to wire failures or slip of wires in anchorage. A difference of more than 10 percent must be identified in the ISI Summary Report required by IWA–6000.

(D) *Concrete containment examinations: Fourth provision.* The applicant or licensee must report the following conditions, if they occur, in the ISI Summary Report required by IWA–6000:

(*1*) The sampled sheathing filler grease contains chemically combined water exceeding 10 percent by weight or the presence of free water;

(*2*) The absolute difference between the amount removed and the amount replaced exceeds 10 percent of the tendon net duct volume; and

(*3*) Grease leakage is detected during general visual examination of the containment surface.

(E) *Concrete containment examinations: Fifth provision.* For Class CC applications, the applicant or licensee must evaluate the acceptability of inaccessible areas when conditions exist in accessible areas that could indicate the presence of or the result in degradation to such inaccessible areas. For each inaccessible area identified, the applicant or licensee must provide the following in the ISI Summary Report required by IWA–6000:

(*1*) A description of the type and estimated extent of degradation, and the conditions that led to the degradation;

(*2*) An evaluation of each area, and the result of the evaluation; and

(*3*) A description of necessary corrective actions.

(F) *Concrete containment examinations: Sixth provision.* Personnel that examine containment concrete surfaces and tendon hardware, wires, or strands must meet the qualification provisions in IWA–2300. The "owner-defined" personnel qualification provisions in IWL–2310(d) are not approved for use.

(G) *Concrete containment examinations: Seventh provision.* Corrosion protection material must be restored following concrete containment post-tensioning system repair and replacement activities in accordance with the quality assurance program requirements specified in IWA–1400.

(H) *Concrete containment examinations: Eighth provision.* For each inaccessible area of concrete identified for evaluation under IWL–2512(a), or identified as susceptible to deterioration under IWL–2512(b), the licensee must provide the applicable information specified in paragraphs (b)(2)(viii)(E)(*1*), (*2*), and (*3*) of this section in the ISI Summary Report required by IWA–6000.

(I) *Concrete containment examinations: Ninth provision.* During the period of extended operation of a renewed license under part 54 of this chapter, the licensee must perform the technical evaluation under IWL–2512(b) of inaccessible below-grade concrete surfaces exposed to foundation soil, backfill, or groundwater at periodic intervals not to exceed 5 years. In addition, the licensee must examine representative samples of the exposed portions of the below-grade concrete, when such below-grade concrete is excavated for any reason.

(ix) *Section XI condition: Metal containment examinations.* Applicants or licensees applying Subsection IWE, 1992 Edition with the 1992 Addenda, or the 1995 Edition with the 1996 Addenda, must satisfy the requirements of paragraphs (b)(2)(ix)(A) through (E) of this section. Applicants or licensees applying Subsection IWE, 1998 Edition through the 2001 Edition with the 2003 Addenda, must satisfy the requirements of paragraphs (b)(2)(ix)(A) and (B) and (F) through (I) of this section. Applicants or licensees applying Subsection IWE, 2004 Edition, up to and including the 2005 Addenda, must satisfy the requirements of paragraphs (b)(2)(ix)(A) and (B) and (F) through (H) of this section. Applicants or licensees applying Subsection IWE, 2004 Edition with the 2006 Addenda, must satisfy the requirements of paragraphs (b)(2)(ix)(A)(*2*) and (b)(2)(ix)(B) of this section. Applicants or licensees applying Subsection IWE, 2007 Edition through the latest edition and addenda incorporated by reference in paragraph (a)(1)(ii) of this section, must satisfy the requirements of paragraphs (b)(2)(ix)(A)(*2*) and (b)(2)(ix)(B) and (J) of this section.

(A) *Metal containment examinations: First provision.* For Class MC applications, the following apply to inaccessible areas.

(*1*) The applicant or licensee must evaluate the acceptability of inaccessible areas when conditions exist in accessible areas that could indicate the presence of or could result in degradation to such inaccessible areas.

(*2*) For each inaccessible area identified for evaluation, the applicant or licensee must provide the following in the ISI Summary Report as required by IWA–6000:

(*i*) A description of the type and estimated extent of degradation, and the conditions that led to the degradation;

(*ii*) An evaluation of each area, and the result of the evaluation; and

(*iii*) A description of necessary corrective actions.

(B) *Metal containment examinations: Second provision.* When performing remotely the visual examinations required by Subsection IWE, the maximum direct examination distance specified in Table IWA–2210–1 (1992 Edition through 2004 Edition) or Table IWA–2211–1 (2005 Addenda through the latest edition and addenda incorporated by reference in paragraph (a)(1) of this section) may be extended and the minimum illumination requirements specified may be decreased provided that the conditions or indications for which the visual examination is performed can be detected at the chosen distance and illumination.

(C) *Metal containment examinations: Third provision.* The examinations specified in Examination Category E–B, Pressure Retaining Welds, and Examination Category E–F, Pressure Retaining Dissimilar Metal Welds, are optional.

(D) *Metal containment examinations: Fourth provision.* This paragraph (b)(2)(ix)(D) may be used as an alternative to the requirements of IWE–2430. If the examinations reveal flaws or areas of degradation exceeding the acceptance standards of Table IWE–3410–1, an evaluation must be performed to determine whether additional component examinations are required. For each flaw or area of degradation identified that exceeds acceptance standards, the applicant or licensee must provide the following in the ISI Summary Report required by IWA–6000:

(*1*) A description of each flaw or area, including the extent of degradation, and the conditions that led to the degradation;

(*2*) The acceptability of each flaw or area and the need for additional examinations to verify that similar degradation does not exist in similar components;

(*3*) A description of necessary corrective actions; and

(*4*) The number and type of additional examinations to ensure detection of similar degradation in similar components.

(E) *Metal containment examinations: Fifth provision.* A general visual examination as required by Subsection IWE must be performed once each period.

(F) *Metal containment examinations: Sixth provision.* VT–1 and VT–3 examinations must be conducted in accordance with IWA–2200. Personnel conducting examinations in accordance with the VT–1 or VT–3 examination method must be qualified in accordance with IWA–2300. The "owner-defined" personnel qualification provisions in IWE–2330(a) for personnel that conduct VT–1 and VT–3 examinations are not approved for use.

(G) *Metal containment examinations: Seventh provision.* The VT–3 examination method must be used to conduct the examinations in Items E1.12 and E1.20 of Table IWE–2500–1, and the VT–1 examination method must be used to conduct the examination in Item E4.11 of Table IWE–2500–1. An examination of the pressure-retaining bolted connections in Item E1.11 of Table IWE–2500–1 using the VT–3 examination method must be conducted once each interval. The "owner-defined" visual examination provisions in IWE–2310(a) are not approved for use for VT–1 and VT–3 examinations.

(H) *Metal containment examinations: Eighth provision.* Containment bolted connections that are disassembled during the scheduled performance of the examinations in Item E1.11 of Table IWE–2500–1 must be examined using the VT–3 examination method. Flaws or degradation identified during the performance of a VT–3 examination must be examined in accordance with the VT–1 examination method. The criteria in the material specification or IWB–3517.1 must be used to evaluate containment bolting flaws or degradation. As an alternative to performing VT–3 examinations of containment bolted connections that are disassembled during the scheduled performance of Item

E1.11, VT–3 examinations of containment bolted connections may be conducted whenever containment bolted connections are disassembled for any reason.

(I) *Metal containment examinations: Ninth provision.* The ultrasonic examination acceptance standard specified in IWE–3511.3 for Class MC pressure-retaining components must also be applied to metallic liners of Class CC pressure-retaining components.

(J) *Metal containment examinations: Tenth provision.* In general, a repair/replacement activity such as replacing a large containment penetration, cutting a large construction opening in the containment pressure boundary to replace steam generators, reactor vessel heads, pressurizers, or other major equipment; or other similar modification is considered a major containment modification. When applying IWE–5000 to Class MC pressure-retaining components, any major containment modification or repair/replacement must be followed by a Type A test to provide assurance of both containment structural integrity and leak-tight integrity prior to returning to service, in accordance with 10 CFR part 50, Appendix J, Option A or Option B on which the applicant's or licensee's Containment Leak-Rate Testing Program is based. When applying IWE–5000, if a Type A, B, or C Test is performed, the test pressure and acceptance standard for the test must be in accordance with 10 CFR part 50, Appendix J.

(x) *Section XI condition: Quality assurance.* When applying the editions and addenda later than the 1989 Edition of ASME BPV Code, Section XI, the edition and addenda of NQA–1, "Quality Assurance Requirements for Nuclear Facility Applications," 1994 Edition, the 2008 Edition, and the 2009–1a Addenda specified in either IWA–1400 or Table IWA 1600–1 of that edition and addenda of Section XI, may be used by a licensee provided that the licensee uses its appendix B to this part quality assurance program in conjunction with Section XI requirements and the commitments contained in the licensee's quality assurance program description. Where NQA–1 and Section XI do not address the commitments contained in the licensee's appendix B quality assurance program description, those licensee commitments must be applied to Section XI activities.

(xi) [Reserved]

(xii) *Section XI condition: Underwater welding.* The provisions in IWA–4660, "Underwater Welding," of Section XI, 1997 Addenda through the latest edition and addenda incorporated by reference in paragraph (a)(1)(ii) of this section, are approved for use on irradiated material with the following conditions:

(A) *Underwater welding: First provision.* Licensees must obtain NRC approval in accordance with paragraph (z) of this section regarding the welding technique to be used prior to performing welding on ferritic material exposed to fast neutron fluence greater than 1×10^{17} n/cm^2 (E > 1 MeV).

(B) *Underwater welding: Second provision.* Licensees must obtain NRC approval in accordance with paragraph (z) of this section regarding the welding technique to be used prior to performing welding on austenitic material other than P-No. 8 material exposed to thermal neutron fluence greater than 1×10^{17} n/cm^2 (E < 0.5 eV). Licensees must obtain NRC approval in accordance with paragraph (z) regarding the welding technique to be used prior to performing welding on P-No. 8 austenitic material exposed to thermal neutron fluence greater than 1×10^{17} n/cm^2 (E < 0.5 eV) and measured or calculated helium concentration of the material greater than 0.1 atomic parts per million.

(xiii) [Reserved]

(xiv) *Section XI condition: Appendix VIII personnel qualification.* All personnel qualified for performing ultrasonic examinations in accordance with Appendix VIII must receive 8 hours of annual hands-on training on specimens that contain cracks. Licensees applying the 1999 Addenda through the latest edition and addenda incorporated by reference in paragraph (a)(1)(ii) of this section may use the annual practice requirements in VII–4240 of Appendix VII of Section XI in place of the 8 hours of annual hands-on training provided that the supplemental practice is performed on material or welds that contain cracks, or by analyzing prerecorded data from material or welds that contain cracks. In either case, training must be completed no earlier than 6 months prior to performing ultrasonic examinations at a licensee's facility.

(xv) *Section XI condition: Appendix VIII specimen set and qualification requirements.* Licensees using Appendix VIII in the 1995 Edition through the 2001 Edition of the ASME Boiler and Pressure Vessel Code may elect to comply with all of the provisions in paragraphs (b)(2)(xv)(A) through (M) of this section, except for paragraph (b)(2)(xv)(F) of this section, which may be used at the licensee's option. Licensees using editions and addenda after 2001 Edition through the 2006 Addenda must use the 2001 Edition of Appendix VIII and may elect to comply with all of the provisions in paragraphs (b)(2)(xv)(A) through (M) of this section, except for paragraph (b)(2)(xv)(F) of this section, which may be used at the licensee's option.

(A) *Specimen set and qualification: First provision.* When applying Supplements 2, 3, and 10 to Appendix VIII, the following examination coverage criteria requirements must be used:

(*1*) Piping must be examined in two axial directions, and when examination in the circumferential direction is required, the circumferential examination must be performed in two directions, provided access is available. Dissimilar metal welds must be examined axially and circumferentially.

(*2*) Where examination from both sides is not possible, full coverage credit may be claimed from a single side for ferritic welds. Where examination from both sides is not possible on austenitic welds or dissimilar metal welds, full coverage credit from a single side may be claimed only after completing a successful single-sided Appendix VIII demonstration using flaws on the opposite side of the weld. Dissimilar metal weld qualifications must be demonstrated from the austenitic side of the weld, and the qualification may be expanded for austenitic welds with no austenitic sides using a separate add-on performance demonstration. Dissimilar metal welds may be examined from either side of the weld.

(B) *Specimen set and qualification: Second provision.* The following conditions must be used in addition to the requirements of Supplement 4 to Appendix VIII:

(*1*) Paragraph 3.1, Detection acceptance criteria—Personnel are qualified for detection if the results of the performance demonstration satisfy the detection requirements of ASME Section XI, Appendix VIII, Table VIII–S4–1, and no flaw greater than 0.25 inch through-wall dimension is missed.

(*2*) Paragraph 1.1(c), Detection test matrix—Flaws smaller than the 50 percent of allowable flaw size, as defined in IWB–3500, need not be included as detection flaws. For procedures applied from the inside surface, use the minimum thickness specified in the scope of the procedure to calculate a/t. For procedures applied from the outside surface, the actual thickness of the test specimen is to be used to calculate a/t.

(C) *Specimen set and qualification: Third provision.* When applying Supplement 4 to Appendix VIII, the following conditions must be used:

(*1*) A depth sizing requirement of 0.15 inch RMS must be used in lieu of the requirements in Subparagraphs 3.2(a) and 3.2(c), and a length sizing requirement of 0.75 inch RMS must be used in lieu of the requirement in Subparagraph 3.2(b).

(*2*) In lieu of the location acceptance criteria requirements of Subparagraph 2.1(b), a flaw will be considered detected when reported within 1.0 inch or 10 percent of the metal path to the flaw, whichever is greater, of its true location in the X and Y directions.

(*3*) In lieu of the flaw type requirements of Subparagraph 1.1(e)(1), a minimum of 70 percent of the flaws in the detection and sizing tests must be cracks. Notches, if used, must be limited by the following:

(*i*) Notches must be limited to the case where examinations are performed from the clad surface.

(*ii*) Notches must be semielliptical with a tip width of less than or equal to 0.010 inches.

(*iii*) Notches must be perpendicular to the surface within ±2 degrees.

(*4*) In lieu of the detection test matrix requirements in paragraphs 1.1(e)(2) and 1.1(e)(3), personnel demonstration test sets must contain a representative distribution of flaw orientations, sizes, and locations.

(D) *Specimen set and qualification: Fourth provision.* The following conditions must be used in addition to the requirements of Supplement 6 to Appendix VIII:

(*1*) Paragraph 3.1, Detection Acceptance Criteria—Personnel are qualified for detection if:

(*i*) No surface connected flaw greater than 0.25 inch through-wall has been missed.

(*ii*) No embedded flaw greater than 0.50 inch through-wall has been missed.

(*2*) Paragraph 3.1, Detection Acceptance Criteria—For procedure qualification, all flaws within the scope of the procedure are detected.

(*3*) Paragraph 1.1(b) for detection and sizing test flaws and locations—Flaws smaller than the 50 percent of allowable flaw size, as defined in IWB–3500, need not be included as detection flaws. Flaws that are less than the allowable flaw size, as defined in IWB–3500, may be used as detection and sizing flaws.

(*4*) Notches are not permitted.

(E) *Specimen set and qualification: Fifth provision.* When applying Supplement 6 to Appendix VIII, the following conditions must be used:

(*1*) A depth sizing requirement of 0.25 inch RMS must be used in lieu of the requirements of subparagraphs 3.2(a), 3.2(c)(2), and 3.2(c)(3).

(*2*) In lieu of the location acceptance criteria requirements in Subparagraph 2.1(b), a flaw will be considered detected when reported within 1.0 inch or 10 percent of the metal path to the flaw, whichever is greater, of its true location in the X and Y directions.

(*3*) In lieu of the length sizing criteria requirements of Subparagraph 3.2(b), a length sizing acceptance criteria of 0.75 inch RMS must be used.

(*4*) In lieu of the detection specimen requirements in Subparagraph 1.1(e)(1), a minimum of 55 percent of the flaws must be cracks. The remaining flaws may be cracks or fabrication type flaws, such as slag and lack of fusion. The use of notches is not allowed.

(*5*) In lieu of paragraphs 1.1(e)(2) and 1.1(e)(3) detection test matrix, personnel demonstration test sets must contain a representative distribution of flaw orientations, sizes, and locations.

(F) *Specimen set and qualification: Sixth provision.* The following conditions may be used for personnel qualification for combined Supplement 4 to Appendix VIII and Supplement 6 to Appendix VIII qualification. Licensees choosing to apply this combined qualification must apply all of the provisions of Supplements 4 and 6 including the following conditions:

(*1*) For detection and sizing, the total number of flaws must be at least 10. A minimum of 5 flaws must be from Supplement 4, and a minimum of 50 percent of the flaws must be from Supplement 6. At least 50 percent of the flaws in any sizing must be cracks. Notches are not acceptable for Supplement 6.

(*2*) Examination personnel are qualified for detection and length sizing when the results of any combined performance demonstration satisfy the acceptance criteria of Supplement 4 to Appendix VIII.

(*3*) Examination personnel are qualified for depth sizing when Supplement 4 to Appendix VIII and Supplement 6 to Appendix VIII flaws are sized within the respective acceptance criteria of those supplements.

(G) *Specimen set and qualification: Seventh provision.* When applying Supplement 4 to Appendix VIII, Supplement 6 to Appendix VIII, or combined Supplement 4 and Supplement 6 qualification, the following additional conditions must be used, and examination coverage must include:

(*1*) The clad-to-base-metal-interface, including a minimum of 15 percent T (measured from the clad-to-base-metal-interface), must be examined from four orthogonal directions using procedures and personnel qualified in accordance with Supplement 4 to Appendix VIII.

(*2*) If the clad-to-base-metal-interface procedure demonstrates detectability of flaws with a tilt angle relative to the weld centerline of at least 45 degrees, the remainder of the examination volume is considered fully examined if coverage is obtained in one parallel and one perpendicular direction. This must be accomplished using a procedure and personnel qualified for single-side examination in accordance with Supplement 6. Subsequent examinations of this volume may be performed using examination techniques qualified for a tilt angle of at least 10 degrees.

(*3*) The examination volume not addressed by paragraph (b)(2)(xv)(G)(*1*) of this section is considered fully examined if coverage is obtained in one parallel and one perpendicular direction, using a procedure and personnel qualified for single sided examination when the conditions in paragraph (b)(2)(xv)(G)(*2*) are met.

(H) *Specimen set and qualification: Eighth provision.* When applying Supplement 5 to Appendix VIII, at least 50 percent of the flaws in the demonstration test set must be cracks and the maximum misorientation must be demonstrated with cracks. Flaws in nozzles with bore diameters equal to or less than 4 inches may be notches.

(I) *Specimen set and qualification: Ninth provision.* When applying Supplement 5, Paragraph (a), to Appendix VIII, the number of false calls allowed must be D/10, with a maximum of 3, where D is the diameter of the nozzle.

(J) [Reserved]

(K) *Specimen set and qualification: Eleventh provision.* When performing nozzle-to-vessel weld examinations, the following conditions must be used when the requirements contained in Supplement 7 to Appendix VIII are applied for nozzle-to-vessel welds in conjunction with Supplement 4 to Appendix VIII, Supplement 6 to Appendix VIII, or combined Supplement 4 and Supplement 6 qualification.

(*1*) For examination of nozzle-to-vessel welds conducted from the bore, the following conditions are required to qualify the procedures, equipment, and personnel:

(*i*) For detection, a minimum of four flaws in one or more full-scale nozzle mock-ups must be added to the test set. The specimens must comply with Supplement 6, paragraph 1.1, to Appendix VIII, except for flaw locations specified in Table VIII S6–1. Flaws may be notches, fabrication flaws, or cracks. Seventy-five (75) percent of the flaws must be cracks or fabrication flaws. Flaw locations and orientations must be selected from the choices shown in paragraph (b)(2)(xv)(K)(*4*) of this section, Table VIII–S7–1—Modified, with the exception that flaws in the outer eighty-five (85) percent of the weld need not be perpendicular to the weld. There may be no more than two flaws from each category, and at least one subsurface flaw must be included.

(*ii*) For length sizing, a minimum of four flaws as in paragraph (b)(2)(xv)(K)(*1*)(*i*) of this section must be included in the test set. The length sizing results must be added to the results of combined Supplement 4 to Appendix VIII and Supplement 6 to Appendix VIII. The combined results must meet the acceptance standards contained in paragraph (b)(2)(xv)(E)(*3*) of this section.

(*iii*) For depth sizing, a minimum of four flaws as in paragraph (b)(2)(xv)(K)(*1*)(*i*) of this section must be included in the test set. Their depths must be distributed over the ranges of Supplement 4, Paragraph 1.1, to Appendix VIII, for the inner 15 percent of the wall thickness and Supplement 6, Paragraph 1.1, to Appendix VIII, for the remainder of the wall thickness. The depth sizing results must be combined with the sizing results from Supplement 4 to Appendix VIII for the inner 15 percent and to Supplement 6 to Appendix VIII for the remainder of the wall thickness. The combined results must meet the depth sizing acceptance criteria contained in paragraphs (b)(2)(xv)(C)(*1*), (b)(2)(xv)(E)(*1*), and (b)(2)(xv)(F)(*3*) of this section.

(*2*) For examination of reactor pressure vessel nozzle-to-vessel welds conducted from the inside of the vessel, the following conditions are required:

(*i*) The clad-to-base-metal-interface and the adjacent examination volume to a minimum depth of 15 percent T (measured from the clad-to-base-metal-interface) must be examined from four orthogonal directions using a procedure and personnel qualified in accordance with Supplement 4 to Appendix VIII as conditioned by paragraphs (b)(2)(xv)(B) and (C) of this section.

(*ii*) When the examination volume defined in paragraph (b)(2)(xv)(K)(*2*)(*i*) of this section cannot be effectively examined in all four directions, the examination must be augmented by examination from the nozzle bore using a procedure and personnel qualified in accordance with paragraph (b)(2)(xv)(K)(*1*) of this section.

(*iii*) The remainder of the examination volume not covered by paragraph (b)(2)(xv)(K)(*2*)(*ii*) of this section or a combination of paragraphs (b)(2)(xv)(K)(*2*)(*i*) and (*ii*) of this section, must be examined from the nozzle bore using a procedure and personnel qualified in accordance with paragraph (b)(2)(xv)(K)(*1*) of this section, or from the vessel shell using a procedure and personnel qualified for single sided examination in accordance with Supplement 6 to Appendix VIII, as conditioned by paragraphs (b)(2)(xv)(D) through (G) of this section.

(*3*) For examination of reactor pressure vessel nozzle-to-shell welds conducted from the outside of the vessel, the following conditions are required:

(*i*) The clad-to-base-metal-interface and the adjacent metal to a depth of 15 percent T (measured from the clad-to-base-metal-interface) must be examined from one radial and two opposing circumferential directions using a procedure and personnel qualified in accordance with Supplement 4 to Appendix VIII, as conditioned by paragraphs (b)(2)(xv)(B) and (C) of this section, for examinations performed in the radial direction, and Supplement 5 to Appendix VIII, as conditioned by paragraph (b)(2)(xv)(J) of this section, for examinations performed in the circumferential direction.

(*ii*) The examination volume not addressed by paragraph (b)(2)(xv)(K)(*3*)(*i*) of this section must be examined in a minimum of one radial direction using a procedure and personnel qualified for single sided examination in accordance with Supplement 6 to Appendix VIII, as conditioned by paragraphs (b)(2)(xv)(D) through (G) of this section.

(*4*) Table VIII–S7–1, "Flaw Locations and Orientations," Supplement 7 to Appendix VIII, is conditioned as follows:

TABLE VIII—S7–1—MODIFIED

[Flaw locations and orientations]

	Parallel to weld	Perpendicular to weld
Inner 15 percent	X	X
Outside Diameter Surface	X	
Subsurface	X	

(L) *Specimen set and qualification: Twelfth provision.* As a condition to the requirements of Supplement 8, Subparagraph 1.1(c), to Appendix VIII, notches may be located within one diameter of each end of the bolt or stud.

(M) *Specimen set and qualification: Thirteenth provision.* When implementing Supplement 12 to Appendix VIII, only the provisions related to the coordinated implementation of Supplement 3 to Supplement 2 performance demonstrations are to be applied.

(xvi) *Section XI condition: Appendix VIII single side ferritic vessel and piping and stainless steel piping examinations.* When applying editions and addenda prior to the 2007 Edition of Section XI, the following conditions apply.

(A) *Ferritic and stainless steel piping examinations: First provision.* Examinations performed from one side of a ferritic vessel weld must be conducted with equipment, procedures, and personnel that have demonstrated proficiency with single side examinations. To demonstrate equivalency to two sided examinations, the demonstration must be performed to the requirements of Appendix VIII, as conditioned by this paragraph and paragraphs (b)(2)(xv)(B) through (G) of this section, on specimens containing flaws with non-optimum sound energy reflecting characteristics or flaws similar to those in the vessel being examined.

(B) *Ferritic and stainless steel piping examinations: Second provision.* Examinations performed from one side of a ferritic or stainless steel pipe weld must be conducted with equipment, procedures, and personnel that have demonstrated proficiency with single side examinations. To demonstrate equivalency to two sided examinations, the demonstration must be performed to the requirements of Appendix VIII, as conditioned by this paragraph and paragraph (b)(2)(xv)(A) of this section.

(xvii) *Section XI condition: Reconciliation of quality requirements.* When purchasing replacement items, in addition to the reconciliation provisions of IWA–4200, 1995 Addenda through 1998 Edition, the replacement items must be purchased, to the extent necessary, in accordance with the licensee's quality assurance program description required by 10 CFR 50.34(b)(6)(ii).

(xviii) *Section XI condition: NDE personnel certification.* (A) *NDE personnel certification: First provision.* Level I and II nondestructive examination personnel must be recertified on a 3-year interval in lieu of the 5-year interval specified in the 1997 Addenda and 1998 Edition of IWA–2314, and IWA–2314(a) and IWA–2314(b) of the 1999 Addenda through the latest edition and addenda incorporated by reference in paragraph (a)(1)(ii) of this section.

(B) *NDE personnel certification: Second provision.* When applying editions and addenda prior to the 2007 Edition of Section XI, paragraph IWA–2316 may only be used to qualify personnel that observe leakage during system leakage and hydrostatic tests conducted in accordance with IWA 5211(a) and (b).

(C) *NDE personnel certification: Third provision.* When applying editions and addenda prior to the 2005 Addenda of Section XI, licensee's qualifying visual examination personnel for VT–3 visual examination under paragraph IWA–2317 of Section XI must demonstrate the proficiency of the training by administering an initial qualification examination and administering subsequent examinations on a 3-year interval.

(D) *NDE personnel certification: Fourth provision.* The use of Appendix VII and Subarticle VIII–2200 of the 2011 Addenda and 2013 Edition of Section XI of the ASME BPV Code is prohibited. When using ASME BPV Code, Section XI editions and addenda later than the 2010 Edition, licensees and applicants must use the prerequisites for ultrasonic examination personnel certifications in Table VII–4110–1 and Subarticle VIII–2200, Appendix VIII in the 2010 Edition.

(xix) *Section XI condition: Substitution of alternative methods.* The provisions for substituting alternative examination methods, a combination of methods, or newly developed techniques in the 1997 Addenda of IWA–2240 must be applied when using the 1998 Edition through the 2004 Edition of Section XI of the ASME BPV Code. The provisions in IWA–4520(c), 1997 Addenda through the 2004 Edition, allowing the substitution of alternative methods, a combination of methods, or newly developed techniques for the methods specified in the Construction Code, are not approved for use. The provisions in IWA–4520(b)(2) and IWA–4521 of the 2008 Addenda through the latest edition and addenda incorporated by reference in paragraph (a)(1)(ii) of this section, allowing the substitution of ultrasonic examination for radiographic examination specified in the Construction Code, are not approved for use.

(xx) *Section XI condition: System leakage tests*—(A) *System leakage tests: First provision.* When performing system leakage tests in accordance with IWA–5213(a), 1997 through 2002 Addenda, the licensee must maintain a 10-minute hold time after test pressure has been reached for Class 2 and Class 3 components that are not in use during normal operating conditions. No hold time is required for the remaining Class 2 and Class 3 components provided that the system has been in operation for at least 4 hours for insulated components or 10 minutes for uninsulated components.

(B) *System leakage tests: Second provision.* The NDE provision in IWA–4540(a)(2) of the 2002 Addenda of Section XI must be applied when performing system leakage tests after repair and replacement activities performed by welding or brazing on a pressure retaining boundary using the 2003 Addenda through the latest edition and addenda incorporated by reference in paragraph (a)(1)(ii) of this section.

(xxi) *Section XI condition: Table IWB–2500–1 examination requirements.* (A) *Table IWB–2500–1 examination requirements: First provision.* The provisions of Table IWB 2500–1, Examination Category B–D, Full Penetration Welded Nozzles in Vessels, Items B3.40 and B3.60 (Inspection Program A) and Items B3.120 and B3.140 (Inspection Program B) of the 1998 Edition must be applied when using the 1999 Addenda through the latest edition and addenda incorporated by reference in paragraph (a)(1)(ii) of this section. A visual examination with magnification that has a resolution sensitivity to resolve 0.044 inch (1.1 mm) lower case characters without an ascender or descender (*e.g.*, a, e, n, v), utilizing the allowable flaw length criteria in Table IWB–3512–1, 1997 Addenda through the latest edition and addenda incorporated by reference in paragraph (a)(1)(ii) of this section, with a limiting assumption on the flaw aspect ratio (*i.e.*, a/l = 0.5), may be performed instead of an ultrasonic examination.

(B) [Reserved]

(xxii) *Section XI condition: Surface examination.* The use of the provision in IWA–2220, "Surface Examination," of Section XI, 2001 Edition through the latest edition and addenda incorporated by reference in paragraph (a)(1)(ii) of this section, that allows use of an ultrasonic examination method is prohibited.

(xxiii) *Section XI condition: Evaluation of thermally cut surfaces.* The use of the provisions for eliminating mechanical processing of thermally cut surfaces in IWA–4461.4.2 of Section XI, 2001 Edition through the 2009 Addenda, is prohibited.

(xxiv) *Section XI condition: Incorporation of the performance demonstration initiative and addition of ultrasonic examination criteria.* The use of Appendix VIII and the supplements to Appendix VIII and Article I–3000 of Section XI of the ASME BPV Code, 2002 Addenda through the 2006 Addenda, is prohibited.

(xxv) *Section XI condition: Mitigation of defects by modification.* The use of the provisions in IWA–4340, "Mitigation of Defects by Modification," Section XI, 2001 Edition through the latest edition and addenda incorporated by reference in paragraph (a)(1)(ii) of this section are prohibited.

(xxvi) *Section XI condition: Pressure testing Class 1, 2 and 3 mechanical joints.* The repair and replacement activity provisions in IWA–4540(c) of the 1998 Edition of Section XI for pressure testing Class 1, 2, and 3 mechanical joints must be applied when using the 2001 Edition through the latest edition and addenda incorporated by reference in paragraph (a)(1)(ii) of this section.

(xxvii) *Section XI condition: Removal of insulation.* When performing visual examination in accordance with IWA–5242 of Section XI of the ASME BPV Code, 2003 Addenda through the 2006 Addenda, or IWA–5241 of the 2007 Edition through the latest edition and addenda incorporated by reference in paragraph (a)(1)(ii) of this section, insulation must be removed from 17–4 PH or 410 stainless steel studs or bolts aged at a temperature below 1100 °F or having a Rockwell Method C hardness value above 30, and from A–286 stainless steel studs or bolts preloaded to 100,000 pounds per square inch or higher.

(xxviii) *Section XI condition: Analysis of flaws.* Licensees using ASME BPV Code, Section XI, Appendix A, must use the following conditions when implementing Equation (2) in A–4300(b)(1):

For $R < 0$, ΔK_I depends on the crack depth (a), and the flow stress (σ_f). The flow stress is defined by $\sigma_f = 1/2(\sigma_{ys} + \sigma_{ult})$, where σ_{ys} is the yield strength and σ_{ult} is the ultimate tensilestrength in units ksi (MPa) and (a) is in units in. (mm). For $-2 \leq R \leq 0$ and $K_{max} - K_{min} \leq 0.8 \times 1.12\ \sigma_f\sqrt{(\pi a)}$, $S = 1$ and $\Delta K_I = K_{max}$. For $R < -2$ and $K_{max} - K_{min} \leq 0.8 \times 1.12\ \sigma_f\sqrt{(\pi a)}$, $S = 1$ and $\Delta K_I = (1 - R)\ K_{max}/3$. For $R < 0$ and $K_{max} - K_{min} > 0.8 \times 1.12\sigma_f\sqrt{(\pi a)}$, $S = 1$ and $\Delta K_I = K_{max} - K_{min}$.

(xxix) *Section XI condition: Nonmandatory Appendix R.* Nonmandatory Appendix R, "Risk-Informed Inspection Requirements for Piping," of Section XI, 2005 Addenda through the latest edition and addenda incorporated by reference in paragraph (a)(1)(ii) of this section, may not be implemented without prior NRC authorization of the proposed alternative in accordance with paragraph (z) of this section.

(xxx) [Reserved]

(xxxi) *Section XI condition: Mechanical clamping devices.* When installing a mechanical clamping device on an ASME BPV Code class piping system, Appendix W of Section XI shall be treated as a mandatory appendix and all of the provisions of Appendix W shall be met for the mechanical clamping device being installed. Additionally, use of IWA–4131.1(c) of the 2010 Edition of Section XI and IWA–4131.1(d) of the 2011 Addenda of the 2010 Edition and later versions of Section XI is prohibited on small item Class 1 piping and portions of a piping system that form the containment boundary.

(xxxii) *Section XI condition: Summary report submittal.* When using ASME BPV Code, Section XI, 2010 Edition through the latest edition and addenda incorporated by reference in paragraph (a)(1)(ii) of this section, Summary Reports described in IWA–6000 must be submitted to the NRC as described in IWA–6240(a) and IWA–6240(b). Preservice inspection summary reports shall be submitted prior to the date of placement of the unit into commercial service and inservice inspection summary reports shall be submitted within 90 calendar days of the completion of each refueling outage.

(xxxiii) *Section XI condition: Risk-Informed allowable pressure.* The use of Paragraph G–2216 in Appendix G in the 2011 Addenda and later editions and addenda of the ASME BPV Code, Section XI is prohibited.

(xxxiv) *Section XI condition: Nonmandatory Appendix U.* When using Nonmandatory Appendix U of the 2013 Edition of the ASME BPV Code, Section XI the following conditions apply:

(A) The repair or replacement activities temporarily deferred under the provisions of Nonmandatory Appendix U must be performed during the next scheduled refueling outage.

(B) In lieu of the appendix referenced in paragraph U–S1–4.2.1(c) of Appendix U the mandatory appendix in ASME BPV Code Case N–513–3 must be used.

(xxxv) *Section XI condition: Use of RT_{T0} in the K_{Ia} and K_{Ic} equations.* When using the 2013 Edition of the ASME BPV Code, Section XI, Appendix A, paragraph A–4200, if T_0 is available, then RT_{T0} may be used in place of RT_{NDT} for applications using the K_{Ic} equation and the associated K_{Ic} curve, but not for applications using the K_{Ia} equation and the associated K_{Ia} curve.

(xxxvi) *Section XI condition: Fracture toughness of irradiated materials.* When using the 2013 Edition of the ASME BPV Code, Section XI, Appendix A paragraph A–4400, the licensee shall obtain NRC approval under paragraph (z) of this section before using irradiated T_0 and the associated RT_{T0} in establishing fracture toughness of irradiated materials.

(xxxvii) *Section XI condition: ASME BPV Code Case N–824.* Licensees may use the provisions of ASME BPV Code Case N–824, "Ultrasonic Examination of Cast Austenitic Piping Welds From the Outside Surface Section XI, Division 1," subject to the following conditions.

(A) Ultrasonic examinations must be spatially encoded.

(B) Instead of Paragraph 1(c)(1)(–a), licensees shall use dual, transmit-receive, refracted longitudinal wave, multi-element phased array search units.

(C) Instead of Paragraph 1(c)(1)(–c)(–2), licensees shall use a phased array search unit with a center frequency of 500 kHz with a tolerance of ± 20 percent.

(D) Instead of Paragraph 1(c)(1)(–d), the phased array search unit must produce angles including, but not limited to, 30 to 55 degrees with a maximum increment of 5 degrees.

(3) *Conditions on ASME OM Code.* As used in this section, references to the ASME OM Code are to the ASME OM Code, Subsections ISTA, ISTB, ISTC, ISTD, ISTE, and ISTF; Mandatory Appendices I, II, III, and V; and Nonmandatory Appendices A through H and J through M, in the 1995 Edition through the 2012 Edition, as specified in paragraph (a)(1)(iv) of this section. Mandatory appendices must be used if required by the OM Code; nonmandatory appendices are approved for use by the NRC but need not be used. The following conditions are applicable when implementing the ASME OM Code:

(i) *OM condition: Quality assurance.* When applying editions and addenda of the ASME OM Code, the requirements of ASME Standard NQA–1, "Quality Assurance Requirements for Nuclear Facility Applications," 1994 Edition, 2008 Edition, and 2009–1a Addenda, are acceptable as permitted by either ISTA 1.4 of the 1995 Edition through 1997 Addenda or ISTA–1500 of the 1998 Edition through the latest edition and addenda of the ASME OM Code incorporated by reference in paragraph (a)(1)(iv) of this section, provided the licensee uses its appendix B to this part quality assurance program in conjunction with the ASME OM Code requirements and the commitments contained in the licensee's quality assurance program description. Where NQA–1 and the ASME OM Code do not address the commitments contained in the licensee's appendix B quality assurance program description, the commitments must be applied to ASME OM Code activities.

(ii) *OM condition: Motor-Operated Valve (MOV) testing.* Licensees must comply with the provisions for testing MOVs in ASME OM Code, ISTC 4.2, 1995 Edition with the 1996 and 1997 Addenda, or ISTC–3500, 1998 Edition through the latest edition and addenda incorporated by reference in paragraph (a)(1)(iv) of this section, and must establish a program to ensure that MOVs continue to be capable of performing their design basis safety functions. Licensees implementing ASME OM Code, Mandatory Appendix III, "Preservice and Inservice Testing of Active Electric Motor Operated Valve Assemblies in Light-Water Reactor Power Plants," of the 2009 Edition, 2011 Addenda, and 2012 Edition shall comply with the following conditions:

(A) *MOV diagnostic test interval.* Licensees shall evaluate the adequacy of the diagnostic test intervals established for MOVs within the scope of ASME OM Code, Appendix III, not later than 5 years or three refueling outages (whichever is longer) from initial implementation of ASME OM Code, Appendix III.

(B) *MOV testing impact on risk.* Licensees shall ensure that the potential increase in core damage frequency and large early release frequency associated with the extension is acceptably small when extending exercise test intervals for high risk MOVs beyond a quarterly frequency.

(C) *MOV risk categorization.* When applying Appendix III to the ASME OM Code, licensees shall categorize MOVs according to their safety significance using the methodology described in ASME OM Code Case OMN–3, "Requirements for Safety Significance Categorization of Components Using Risk Insights for Inservice Testing of LWR Power Plants," subject to the conditions applicable to OMN–3 which are set forth in Regulatory Guide 1.192, or using an MOV risk ranking methodology accepted by the NRC on a plant-specific or industry-wide basis in accordance with the conditions in the applicable safety evaluation.

(D) *MOV stroke time.* When applying Paragraph III–3600, "MOV Exercising Requirements," of Appendix III to the ASME OM Code, licensees shall verify that the stroke time of MOVs specified in plant technical specifications satisfies the assumptions in the plant's safety analyses.

(iii) *OM condition: New reactors.* In addition to complying with the provisions in the ASME OM Code with the conditions specified in paragraph (b)(3) of this section, holders of operating licenses for nuclear power reactors that received construction permits under this part on or after the date 12 months after August 17, 2017, and holders of combined licenses issued under 10 CFR part 52, whose initial fuel loading occurs on or after the date 12 months after August 17, 2017, shall also comply with the following conditions, as applicable:

(A) *Power-operated valves.* Licensees shall periodically verify the capability of power-operated valves to perform their design-basis safety functions.

(B) *Check valves.* Licensees must perform bi-directional testing of check valves within the IST program where practicable.

(C) *Flow-induced vibration.* Licensees shall monitor flow-induced vibration from hydrodynamic loads and acoustic resonance during preservice testing or inservice testing to identify potential adverse flow effects on components within the scope of the IST program.

(D) *High risk non-safety systems.* Licensees shall assess the operational readiness of pumps, valves, and dynamic restraints within the scope of the Regulatory Treatment of Non-Safety Systems for applicable reactor designs.

(iv) *OM condition: Check valves (Appendix II).* Licensees applying Appendix II, "Check Valve Condition Monitoring Program," of the ASME OM Code, 1995 Edition with the 1996 and 1997 Addenda, shall satisfy the requirements of paragraphs (b)(3)(iv)(A) through (C) of this section. Licensees applying Appendix II, 1998 Edition through the 2012 Edition, shall satisfy the requirements of paragraphs (b)(3)(iv)(A), (B), and (D) of this section. Appendix II of the ASME OM Code, 2003 Addenda through the 2012 Edition, is acceptable for use with the following requirements. Trending and evaluation shall support the determination that the valve or group of valves is capable of performing its intended function(s) over the entire interval. At least one of the Appendix II condition monitoring activities for a valve group shall be performed on each valve of the group at approximate equal intervals not to exceed the maximum interval shown in the following table:

TABLE II—MAXIMUM INTERVALS FOR USE WHEN APPLYING INTERVAL EXTENSIONS

Group size	Maximum interval between activities of member valves in the groups (years)	Maximum interval between activities of each valve in the group (years)
≥4	4.5	16
3	4.5	12
2	6	12
1	Not applicable	10

(A) *Check valves: First provision.* Valve opening and closing functions must be demonstrated when flow testing or examination methods (nonintrusive, or disassembly and inspection) are used;

(B) *Check valves: Second provision.* The initial interval for tests and associated examinations may not exceed two fuel cycles or 3 years, whichever is longer; any extension of this interval may not exceed one fuel cycle per extension with the maximum interval not to exceed 10 years. Trending and evaluation of existing data must be used to reduce or extend the time interval between tests.

(C) *Check valves: Third provision.* If the Appendix II condition monitoring program is discontinued, then the requirements of ISTC 4.5.1 through 4.5.4 must be implemented.

(D) *Check valves: Fourth provision.* The applicable provisions of subsection ISTC must be implemented if the Appendix II condition monitoring program is discontinued.

(v) *OM condition: Snubbers ISTD.* Article IWF–5000, "Inservice Inspection Requirements for Snubbers," of the ASME BPV Code, Section XI, must be used when performing inservice inspection examinations and tests of snubbers at nuclear power plants, except as conditioned in paragraphs (b)(3)(v)(A) and (B) of this section.

(A) *Snubbers: First provision.* Licensees may use Subsection ISTD, "Preservice and Inservice Examination and Testing of Dynamic Restraints (Snubbers) in Light-Water Reactor Power Plants," ASME OM Code, 1995 Edition through the latest edition and addenda incorporated by reference in paragraph (a)(1)(iv) of this section, in place of the requirements for snubbers in the editions and addenda up to the 2005 Addenda of the ASME BPV Code, Section XI, IWF–5200(a) and (b) and IWF–5300(a) and (b), by making appropriate changes to their technical specifications or licensee-controlled documents. Preservice and inservice examinations must be performed using the VT–3 visual examination method described in IWA–2213.

(B) *Snubbers: Second provision.* Licensees must comply with the provisions for examining and testing snubbers in Subsection ISTD of the ASME OM Code and make appropriate changes to their technical specifications or licensee-controlled documents when using the 2006 Addenda and later editions and addenda of Section XI of the ASME BPV Code.

(vi) *OM condition: Exercise interval for manual valves.* Manual valves must be exercised on a 2-year interval rather than the 5-year interval specified in paragraph ISTC–3540 of the 1999 through the 2005 Addenda of the ASME OM Code, provided that adverse conditions do not require more frequent testing.

* * * * *

(vii) *OM condition: Subsection ISTB.* Subsection ISTB, 2011 Addenda, is prohibited for use.

(viii) *OM condition: Subsection ISTE.* Licensees may not implement the risk-informed approach for inservice testing (IST) of pumps and valves specified in Subsection ISTE, "Risk-Informed Inservice Testing of Components in Light-Water Reactor Nuclear Power Plants," in the ASME OM Code, 2009 Edition, 2011 Addenda, or 2012 Edition, without first obtaining NRC authorization to use Subsection ISTE as an alternative to the applicable IST requirements in the ASME OM Code, pursuant to paragraph (z) of this section.

(ix) *OM condition: Subsection ISTF.* Licensees applying Subsection ISTF, 2012 Edition, shall satisfy the requirements of Mandatory Appendix V, "Pump Periodic Verification Test Program," of the ASME OM Code, 2012 Edition. Subsection ISTF, 2011 Addenda, is prohibited for use.

(x) *OM condition: ASME OM Code Case OMN-20.* Licensees may implement ASME OM Code Case OMN-20, "Inservice Test Frequency," which is incorporated by reference in paragraph (a)(1)(iii)(G) of this section, for editions and addenda of the ASME OM Code listed in paragraph (a)(1)(iv) of this section.

(xi) *OM condition: Valve Position Indication.* When implementing ASME OM Code, 2012 Edition, Subsection ISTC-3700, "Position Verification Testing," licensees shall verify that valve operation is accurately indicated by supplementing valve position indicating lights with other indications, such as flow meters or other suitable instrumentation, to provide assurance of proper obturator position.

(4) *Conditions on Design, Fabrication, and Materials Code Cases.* Each manufacturing license, standard design approval, and design certification application under part 52 of this chapter is subject to the following conditions. Licensees may apply the ASME BPV Code Cases listed in NRC Regulatory Guide 1.84, as incorporated by reference in paragraph (a)(3)(i) of this section, without prior NRC approval, subject to the following conditions:

(i) *Design, Fabrication, and Materials Code Case condition: Applying Code Cases.* When an applicant or licensee initially applies a listed Code Case, the applicant or licensee must apply the most recent version of that Code Case incorporated by reference in paragraph (a) of this section.

(ii) *Design, Fabrication, and Materials Code Case condition: Applying different revisions of Code Cases.* If an applicant or licensee has previously applied a Code Case and a later version of the Code Case is incorporated by reference in paragraph (a) of this section, the applicant or licensee may continue to apply the previous version of the Code Case as authorized or may apply the later version of the Code Case, including any NRC-specified conditions placed on its use, until it updates its Code of Record for the component being constructed.

(iii) *Design, Fabrication, and Materials Code Case condition: Applying annulled Code Cases.* Application of an annulled Code Case is prohibited unless an applicant or licensee applied the listed Code Case prior to it being listed as annulled in Regulatory Guide 1.84. If an applicant or licensee has applied a listed Code Case that is later listed as annulled in Regulatory Guide 1.84, the applicant or licensee may continue to apply the Code Case until it updates its Code of Record for the component being constructed.

(5) *Conditions on inservice inspection Code Cases.* Licensees may apply the ASME BPV Code Cases listed in NRC Regulatory Guide 1.147, as incorporated by reference in paragraph (a)(3)(ii) of this section, without prior NRC approval, subject to the following:

(i) *ISI Code Case condition: Applying Code Cases.* When a licensee initially applies a listed Code Case, the licensee must apply the most recent version of that Code Case incorporated by reference in paragraph (a) of this section.

(ii) *ISI Code Case condition: Applying different revisions of Code Cases.* If a licensee has previously applied a Code Case and a later version of the Code Case is incorporated by reference in paragraph (a) of this section, the licensee may continue to apply, to the end of the current 120-month interval, the previous version of the Code Case, as authorized, or may apply the later version of the Code Case, including any NRC-specified conditions placed on its use. Licensees who choose to continue use of the Code Case during subsequent 120-month ISI program intervals will be required to implement the latest version incorporated by reference into this section as listed in Tables 1 and 2 of NRC Regulatory Guide 1.147, as incorporated by reference in paragraph (a)(3)(ii) of this section.

(iii) *ISI Code Case condition: Applying annulled Code Cases.* Application of an annulled Code Case is prohibited unless a licensee previously applied the listed Code Case prior to it being listed as annulled in NRC Regulatory Guide 1.147. If a licensee has applied a listed Code Case that is later listed as annulled in NRC Regulatory Guide 1.147, the licensee may continue to apply the Code Case to the end of the current 120-month interval.

(6) *Conditions on ASME OM Code Cases.* Licensees may apply the ASME OM Code Cases listed in NRC Regulatory Guide 1.192, as incorporated by reference in paragraph (a)(3)(iii) of this section, without prior NRC approval, subject to the following:

(i) *OM Code Case condition: Applying Code Cases.* When a licensee initially applies a listed Code Case, the licensee must apply the most recent version of that Code Case incorporated by reference in paragraph (a) of this section.

(ii) *OM Code Case condition: Applying different revisions of Code Cases.* If a licensee has previously applied a Code Case and a later version of the Code Case is incorporated by reference in paragraph (a) of this section, the licensee may continue to apply, to the end of the current 120-month interval, the previous version of the Code Case, as authorized, or may apply the later version of the Code Case, including any NRC-specified conditions placed on its use. Licensees who choose to continue use of the Code Case during subsequent 120-month ISI program intervals will be required to implement the latest version incorporated by reference into this section as listed in Tables 1 and 2 of NRC Regulatory Guide 1.192, as incorporated by reference in paragraph (a)(3)(iii) of this section.

(iii) *OM Code Case condition: Applying annulled Code Cases.* Application of an annulled Code Case is prohibited unless a licensee previously applied the listed Code Case prior to it being listed as annulled in NRC Regulatory Guide 1.192. If a licensee has applied a listed Code Case that is later listed as annulled in NRC Regulatory Guide 1.192, the licensee may continue to apply the Code Case to the end of the current 120-month interval.

(c) *Reactor coolant pressure boundary.* Systems and components of boiling and pressurized water-cooled nuclear power reactors must meet the requirements of the ASME BPV Code as specified in this paragraph. Each manufacturing license, standard design approval, and design certification application under part 52 of this chapter and each combined license for a utilization facility is subject to the following conditions:

(1) *Standards requirement for reactor coolant pressure boundary components.* Components that are part of the reactor coolant pressure boundary must meet the requirements for Class 1 components in Section III[1,4] of the ASME BPV Code, except as provided in paragraphs (c)(2) through (4) of this section.

(2) *Exceptions to reactor coolant pressure boundary standards requirement.* Components that are connected to the reactor coolant system and are part of the reactor coolant pressure boundary as defined in § 50.2 need not meet the requirements of paragraph (c)(1) of this section, provided that:

(i) *Exceptions: Shutdown and cooling capability.* In the event of postulated failure of the component during normal reactor operation, the reactor can be shut down and cooled down in an orderly manner, assuming makeup is provided by the reactor coolant makeup system; or

(ii) *Exceptions: Isolation capability.* The component is or can be isolated from the reactor coolant system by two valves in series (both closed, both open, or one closed and the other open). Each open valve must be capable of automatic actuation and, assuming the other valve is open, its closure time must be such that, in the event of postulated failure of the component during normal reactor operation, each valve remains operable and the reactor can be shut down and cooled down in an orderly manner, assuming makeup is provided by the reactor coolant makeup system only.

(3) *Applicable Code and Code Cases and conditions on their use.* The Code edition, addenda, and optional ASME Code Cases to be applied to components of the reactor coolant pressure boundary must be determined by the provisions of paragraph NCA–1140, Subsection NCA of Section III of the ASME BPV Code, subject to the following conditions:

(i) *Reactor coolant pressure boundary condition: Code edition and addenda.* The edition and addenda applied to a component must be those that are incorporated by reference in paragraph (a)(1)(i) of this section;

(ii) *Reactor coolant pressure boundary condition: Earliest edition and addenda for pressure vessel.* The ASME Code provisions applied to the pressure vessel may be dated no earlier than the summer 1972 Addenda of the 1971 Edition;

(iii) *Reactor coolant pressure boundary condition: Earliest edition and addenda for piping, pumps, and valves.* The ASME Code provisions applied to piping, pumps, and valves may be dated no earlier than the Winter 1972 Addenda of the 1971 Edition; and

(iv) *Reactor coolant pressure boundary condition: Use of Code Cases.* The optional Code Cases applied to a component must be those listed in NRC Regulatory Guide 1.84 that is incorporated by reference in paragraph (a)(3)(i) of this section.

(4) *Standards requirement for components in older plants.* For a nuclear power plant whose construction permit was issued prior to May 14, 1984, the applicable Code edition and addenda for a component of the reactor coolant pressure boundary continue to be that Code edition and addenda that were required by Commission regulations for such a component at the time of issuance of the construction permit.

(d) *Quality Group B components.* Systems and components of boiling and pressurized water-cooled nuclear power reactors must meet the requirements of the ASME BPV Code as specified in this paragraph. Each manufacturing license, standard design approval, and design certification application under part 52 of this chapter, and each combined license for a utilization facility is subject to the following conditions:

(1) *Standards requirement for Quality Group B components.* For a nuclear power plant whose application for a construction permit under this part, or a combined license or manufacturing license under part 52 of this chapter, docketed after May 14, 1984, or for an application for a standard design approval or a standard design certification docketed after May 14, 1984, components classified Quality Group B[7] must meet the requirements for Class 2 Components in Section III of the ASME BPV Code.

(2) *Quality Group B: Applicable Code and Code Cases and conditions on their use.* The Code edition, addenda, and optional ASME Code Cases to be applied to the systems and components identified in paragraph (d)(1) of this section must be determined by the rules of paragraph NCA–1140, Subsection NCA of Section III of the ASME BPV Code, subject to the following conditions:

(i) *Quality Group B condition: Code edition and addenda.* The edition and addenda must be those that are incorporated by reference in paragraph (a)(1)(i) of this section;

(ii) *Quality Group B condition: Earliest edition and addenda for components.* The ASME Code provisions applied to the systems and components may be dated no earlier than the 1980 Edition; and

(iii) *Quality Group B condition: Use of Code Cases.* The optional Code Cases must be those listed in NRC Regulatory Guide 1.84 that is incorporated by reference in paragraph (a)(3)(i) of this section.

(e) *Quality Group C components.* Systems and components of boiling and pressurized water-cooled nuclear power reactors must meet the requirements of the ASME BPV Code as specified in this paragraph. Each manufacturing license, standard design approval, and design certification application under part 52 of this chapter and each combined license for a utilization facility is subject to the following conditions.

(1) *Standards requirement for Quality Group C components.* For a nuclear power plant whose application for a construction permit under this part, or a combined license or manufacturing license under part 52 of this chapter, docketed after May 14, 1984, or for an application for a standard design approval or a standard design certification docketed after May 14, 1984, components classified Quality Group C[7] must meet the requirements for Class 3 components in Section III of the ASME BPV Code.

(2) *Quality Group C applicable Code and Code Cases and conditions on their use.* The Code edition, addenda, and optional ASME Code Cases to be applied

to the systems and components identified in paragraph (e)(1) of this section must be determined by the rules of paragraph NCA–1140, subsection NCA of Section III of the ASME BPV Code, subject to the following conditions:

(i) *Quality Group C condition: Code edition and addenda.* The edition and addenda must be those incorporated by reference in paragraph (a)(1)(i) of this section;

(ii) *Quality Group C condition: Earliest edition and addenda for components.* The ASME Code provisions applied to the systems and components may be dated no earlier than the 1980 Edition; and

(iii) *Quality Group C condition: Use of Code Cases.* The optional Code Cases must be those listed in NRC Regulatory Guide 1.84 that is incorporated by reference in paragraph (a)(3)(i) of this section.

(f) *Preservice and inservice testing requirements.* Systems and components of boiling and pressurized water-cooled nuclear power reactors must meet the requirements for preservice and inservice testing (referred to in this paragraph (f) collectively as inservice testing) of the ASME BPV Code and ASME OM Code as specified in this paragraph (f). Each operating license for a boiling or pressurized water-cooled nuclear facility is subject to the following conditions. Each combined license for a boiling or pressurized water-cooled nuclear facility is subject to the following conditions, but the conditions in paragraphs (f)(4) through (6) of this section must be met only after the Commission makes the finding under § 52.103(g) of this chapter. Requirements for inservice inspection of Class 1, Class 2, Class 3, Class MC, and Class CC components (including their supports) are located in paragraph (g) of this section.

(1) *Inservice testing requirements for older plants (pre-1971 CPs).* For a boiling or pressurized water-cooled nuclear power facility whose construction permit was issued prior to January 1, 1971, pumps and valves must meet the test requirements of paragraphs (f)(4) and (5) of this section to the extent practical. Pumps and valves that are part of the reactor coolant pressure boundary must meet the requirements applicable to components that are classified as ASME Code Class 1. Other pumps and valves that perform a function to shut down the reactor or maintain the reactor in a safe shutdown condition, mitigate the consequences of an accident, or provide overpressure protection for safety-related systems (in meeting the requirements of the 1986 Edition, or later, of the BPV or OM Code) must meet the test requirements applicable to components that are classified as ASME Code Class 2 or Class 3.

(2) *Design and accessibility requirements for performing inservice testing in plants with CPs issued between 1971 and 1974.* For a boiling or pressurized water-cooled nuclear power facility whose construction permit was issued on or after January 1, 1971, but before July 1, 1974, pumps and valves that are classified as ASME BPV Code Class 1 and Class 2 must be designed and provided with access to enable the performance of inservice tests for operational readiness set forth in editions and addenda of Section XI of the ASME BPV Code incorporated by reference in paragraph (a)(1)(ii) of this section (or the optional ASME Code Cases listed in NRC Regulatory Guide 1.147 or NRC Regulatory Guide 1.192, as incorporated by reference in paragraphs (a)(3)(ii) and (iii) of this section, respectively) in effect 6 months before the date of issuance of the construction permit. The pumps and valves may meet the inservice test requirements set forth in subsequent editions of this Code and addenda that are incorporated by reference in paragraph (a)(1)(ii) of this section (or the optional ASME Code Cases listed in NRC Regulatory Guide 1.147 or NRC Regulatory Guide 1.192, as incorporated by reference in paragraphs (a)(3)(ii) and (iii) of this section, respectively), subject to the applicable conditions listed therein.

(3) *Design and accessibility requirements for performing inservice testing in plants with CPs issued after 1974.* For a boiling or pressurized water-cooled nuclear power facility whose construction permit under this part or design approval, design certification, combined license, or manufacturing license under part 52 of this chapter was issued on or after July 1, 1974:

(i)–(ii) [Reserved]

(iii) *IST design and accessibility requirements: Class 1 pumps and valves.* (A)

Class 1 pumps and valves: First provision. In facilities whose construction permit was issued before November 22, 1999, pumps and valves that are classified as ASME BPV Code Class 1 must be designed and provided with access to enable the performance of inservice testing of the pumps and valves for assessing operational readiness set forth in the editions and addenda of Section XI of the ASME BPV Code incorporated by reference in paragraph (a)(1)(ii) of this section (or the optional ASME Code Cases listed in NRC Regulatory Guide 1.147 or NRC Regulatory Guide 1.192, as incorporated by reference in paragraphs (a)(3)(ii) and (iii) of this section, respectively) applied to the construction of the particular pump or valve or the summer 1973 Addenda, whichever is later.

(B) *Class 1 pumps and valves: Second provision.* In facilities whose construction permit under this part, or design certification, design approval, combined license, or manufacturing license under part 52 of this chapter, issued on or after November 22, 1999, pumps and valves that are classified as ASME BPV Code Class 1 must be designed and provided with access to enable the performance of inservice testing of the pumps and valves for assessing operational readiness set forth in editions and addenda of the ASME OM Code (or the optional ASME OM Code Cases listed in NRC Regulatory Guide 1.192, as incorporated by reference in paragraph (a)(3)(iii) of this section), incorporated by reference in paragraph (a)(1)(iv) of this section at the time the construction permit, combined license, manufacturing license, design certification, or design approval is issued.

(iv) *IST design and accessibility requirements: Class 2 and 3 pumps and valves.*(A) *Class 2 and 3 pumps and valves: First provision.* In facilities whose construction permit was issued before November 22, 1999, pumps and valves that are classified as ASME BPV Code Class 2 and Class 3 must be designed and be provided with access to enable the performance of inservice testing of the pumps and valves for assessing operational readiness set forth in the editions and addenda of Section XI of the ASME BPV Code incorporated by reference in paragraph (a)(1)(ii) of this section (or the optional ASME BPV Code Cases listed in NRC Regulatory Guide 1.147, as incorporated by reference in paragraph (a)(3)(ii) of this section) applied to the construction of the particular pump or valve or the Summer 1973 Addenda, whichever is later.

(B) *Class 2 and 3 pumps and valves: Second provision.* In facilities whose construction permit under this part, or design certification, design approval, combined license, or manufacturing license under part 52 of this chapter, issued on or after November 22, 1999, pumps and valves that are classified as ASME BPV Code Class 2 and 3 must be designed and provided with access to enable the performance of inservice testing of the pumps and valves for assessing operational readiness set forth in editions and addenda of the ASME OM Code (or the optional ASME OM Code Cases listed in NRC Regulatory Guide 1.192, as incorporated by reference in paragraph (a)(3)(iii) of this section), incorporated by reference in paragraph (a)(1)(iv) of this section at the time the construction permit, combined license, or design certification is issued.

(v) *IST design and accessibility requirements: Meeting later IST requirements.* All pumps and valves may meet the test requirements set forth in subsequent editions of codes and addenda or portions thereof that are incorporated by reference in paragraph (a) of this section, subject to the conditions listed in paragraph (b) of this section.

(4) *Inservice testing standards requirement for operating plants.* Throughout the service life of a boiling or pressurized water-cooled nuclear power facility, pumps and valves that are within the scope of the ASME OM Code must meet the inservice test requirements (except design and access provisions) set forth in the ASME OM Code and addenda that become effective subsequent to editions and addenda specified in paragraphs (f)(2) and (3) of this section and that are incorporated by reference in paragraph (a)(1)(iv) of this section, to the extent practical within the limitations of design, geometry, and materials of construction of the components. The inservice test requirements for pumps and valves that are

within the scope of the ASME OM Code but are not classified as ASME BPV Code Class 1, Class 2, or Class 3 may be satisfied as an augmented IST program in accordance with paragraph (f)(6)(ii) of this section without requesting relief under paragraph (f)(5) of this section or alternatives under paragraph (z) of this section. This use of an augmented IST program may be acceptable provided the basis for deviations from the ASME OM Code, as incorporated by reference in this section, demonstrates an acceptable level of quality and safety, or that implementing the Code provisions would result in hardship or unusual difficulty without a compensating increase in the level of quality and safety, where documented and available for NRC review.

(i) *Applicable IST Code: Initial 120-month interval.* Inservice tests to verify operational readiness of pumps and valves, whose function is required for safety, conducted during the initial 120-month interval must comply with the requirements in the latest edition and addenda of the ASME OM Code incorporated by reference in paragraph (a)(1)(iv) of this section on the date 12 months before the date of issuance of the operating license under this part, or 12 months before the date scheduled for initial loading of fuel under a combined license under part 52 of this chapter (or the optional ASME OM Code Cases listed in NRC Regulatory Guide 1.192, as incorporated by reference in paragraph (a)(3)(iii) of this section, subject to the conditions listed in paragraph (b) of this section).

(ii) *Applicable IST Code: Successive 120-month intervals.* Inservice tests to verify operational readiness of pumps and valves, whose function is required for safety, conducted during successive 120-month intervals must comply with the requirements of the latest edition and addenda of the ASME OM Code incorporated by reference in paragraph (a)(1)(iv) of this section 12 months before the start of the 120-month interval (or the optional ASME Code Cases listed in NRC Regulatory Guide 1.147 or NRC Regulatory Guide 1.192 as incorporated by reference in paragraphs (a)(3)(ii) and (iii) of this section, respectively), subject to the conditions listed in paragraph (b) of this section.

(iii) [Reserved]

(iv) *Applicable IST Code: Use of later Code editions and addenda.* Inservice tests of pumps and valves may meet the requirements set forth in subsequent editions and addenda that are incorporated by reference in paragraph (a)(1)(iv) of this section, subject to the conditions listed in paragraph (b) of this section, and subject to NRC approval. Portions of editions or addenda may be used, provided that all related requirements of the respective editions or addenda are met.

(5) *Requirements for updating IST programs*—(i) *IST program update: Applicable IST Code editions and addenda.* The inservice test program for a boiling or pressurized water-cooled nuclear power facility must be revised by the licensee, as necessary, to meet the requirements of paragraph (f)(4) of this section.

(ii) *IST program update: Conflicting IST Code requirements with technical specifications.* If a revised inservice test program for a facility conflicts with the technical specifications for the facility, the licensee must apply to the Commission for amendment of the technical specifications to conform the technical specifications to the revised program. The licensee must submit this application, as specified in § 50.4, at least 6 months before the start of the period during which the provisions become applicable, as determined by paragraph (f)(4) of this section.

(iii) *IST program update: Notification of impractical IST Code requirements.* If the licensee has determined that conformance with certain Code requirements is impractical for its facility, the licensee must notify the Commission and submit, as specified in § 50.4, information to support the determination.

(iv) *IST program update: Schedule for completing impracticality determinations.* Where a pump or valve test requirement by the Code or addenda is determined to be impractical by the licensee and is not included in the revised inservice test program (as permitted by paragraph (f)(4) of this section), the basis for this determination must be submitted for NRC review and approval not later than 12 months after the expiration of the initial 120-month interval of operation from the start of facility commercial operation and each subsequent 120-month interval of operation during which the test is determined to be impractical.

(6) *Actions by the Commission for evaluating impractical and augmented IST Code requirements*—(i) *Impractical IST requirements: Granting of relief.* The Commission will evaluate determinations under paragraph (f)(5) of this section that code requirements are impractical. The Commission may grant relief and may impose such alternative requirements as it determines are authorized by law, will not endanger life or property or the common defense and security, and are otherwise in the public interest, giving due consideration to the burden upon the licensee that could result if the requirements were imposed on the facility.

(ii) *Augmented IST requirements.* The Commission may require the licensee to follow an augmented inservice test program for pumps and valves for which the Commission deems that added assurance of operational readiness is necessary.

(g) *Preservice and inservice inspection requirements.* Systems and components of boiling and pressurized water-cooled nuclear power reactors must meet the requirements of the ASME BPV Code as specified in this paragraph. Each operating license for a boiling or pressurized water-cooled nuclear facility is subject to the following conditions. Each combined license for a boiling or pressurized water-cooled nuclear facility is subject to the following conditions, but the conditions in paragraphs (g)(4) through (6) of this section must be met only after the Commission makes the finding under § 52.103(g) of this chapter. Requirements for inservice testing of Class 1, Class 2, and Class 3 pumps and valves are located in paragraph (f) of this section.

(1) *Inservice inspection requirements for older plants (pre-1971 CPs).* For a boiling or pressurized water-cooled nuclear power facility whose construction permit was issued before January 1, 1971, components (including supports) must meet the requirements of paragraphs (g)(4) and (g)(5) of this section to the extent practical. Components that are part of the reactor coolant pressure boundary and their supports must meet the requirements applicable to components that are classified as ASME Code Class 1. Other safety-related pressure vessels, piping, pumps and valves, and their supports must meet the requirements applicable to components that are classified as ASME Code Class 2 or Class 3.

(2) *Accessibility requirements*—(i) *Accessibility requirements for plants with CPs issued between 1971 and 1974.* For a boiling or pressurized water-cooled nuclear power facility whose construction permit was issued on or after January 1, 1971, but before July 1, 1974, components that are classified as ASME BPV Code Class 1 and Class 2 and supports for components that are classified as ASME BPV Code Class 1 and Class 2 must be designed and be provided with the access necessary to perform the required preservice and inservice examinations set forth in editions and addenda of Section III or Section XI of the ASME BPV Code incorporated by reference in paragraph (a)(1) of this section (or the optional ASME BPV Code Cases listed in NRC Regulatory Guide 1.147, as incorporated by reference in paragraph (a)(3)(ii) of this section) in effect 6 months before the date of issuance of the construction permit.

(ii) *Accessibility requirements for plants with CPs issued after 1974.* For a boiling or pressurized water-cooled nuclear power facility, whose construction permit under this part, or design certification, design approval, combined license, or manufacturing license under part 52 of this chapter, was issued on or after July 1, 1974, components that are classified as ASME BPV Code Class 1, Class 2, and Class 3 and supports for components that are classified as ASME BPV Code Class 1, Class 2, and Class 3 must be designed and provided with the access necessary to perform the required preservice and inservice examinations set forth in editions and addenda of Section III or Section XI of the ASME BPV Code incorporated by reference in paragraph (a)(1) of this section (or the optional ASME BPV Code Cases listed in NRC Regulatory Guide 1.147, as incorporated by reference in paragraph (a)(3)(ii) of this section) applied to the construction of the particular component.

(iii) *Accessibility requirements: Meeting later Code requirements.* All components (including supports) may meet the requirements set forth in subsequent editions of codes and addenda or portions thereof that are incorporated by reference in paragraph (a) of this section, subject to the conditions listed therein.

(3) *Preservice examination requirements*—(i) *Preservice examination requirements for plants with CPs issued between 1971 and 1974.* For a boiling or pressurized water-cooled nuclear power facility whose construction permit was issued on or after January 1, 1971, but before July 1, 1974, components that are classified as ASME BPV Code Class 1 and Class 2 and supports for components that are classified as ASME BPV Code Class 1 and Class 2 must meet the preservice examination requirements set forth in editions and addenda of Section III or Section XI of the ASME BPV Code incorporated by reference in paragraph (a)(1) of this section (or the optional ASME BPV Code Cases listed in NRC Regulatory Guide 1.147, as incorporated by reference in paragraph (a)(3)(ii) of this section) in effect 6 months before the date of issuance of the construction permit.

(ii) *Preservice examination requirements for plants with CPs issued after 1974.* For a boiling or pressurized water-cooled nuclear power facility, whose construction permit under this part, or design certification, design approval, combined license, or manufacturing license under part 52 of this chapter, was issued on or after July 1, 1974, components that are classified as ASME BPV Code Class 1, Class 2, and Class 3 and supports for components that are classified as ASME BPV Code Class 1, Class 2, and Class 3 must meet the preservice examination requirements set forth in the editions and addenda of Section III or Section XI of the ASME BPV Code incorporated by reference in paragraph (a)(1) of this section (or the optional ASME BPV Code Cases listed in NRC Regulatory Guide 1.147, as incorporated by reference in paragraph (a)(3)(ii) of this section) applied to the construction of the particular component.

(iii)–(iv) [Reserved]

(v) *Preservice examination requirements: Meeting later Code requirements.* All components (including supports) may meet the requirements set forth in subsequent editions of codes and addenda or portions thereof that are incorporated by reference in paragraph (a) of this section, subject to the conditions listed therein.

(4) *Inservice inspection standards requirement for operating plants.* Throughout the service life of a boiling or pressurized water-cooled nuclear power facility, components (including supports) that are classified as ASME Code Class 1, Class 2, and Class 3 must meet the requirements, except design and access provisions and preservice examination requirements, set forth in Section XI of editions and addenda of the ASME BPV Code (or ASME OM Code for snubber examination and testing) that become effective subsequent to editions specified in paragraphs (g)(2) and (3) of this section and that are incorporated by reference in paragraph (a)(1)(ii) or (iv) for snubber examination and testing of this section, to the extent practical within the limitations of design, geometry, and materials of construction of the components. Components that are classified as Class MC pressure retaining components and their integral attachments, and components that are classified as Class CC pressure retaining components and their integral attachments, must meet the requirements, except design and access provisions and preservice examination requirements, set forth in Section XI of the ASME BPV Code and addenda that are incorporated by reference in paragraph (a)(1)(ii) of this section, subject to the condition listed in paragraph (b)(2)(vi) of this section and the conditions listed in paragraphs (b)(2)(viii) and (ix) of this section, to the extent practical within the limitation of design, geometry, and materials of construction of the components.

(i) *Applicable ISI Code: Initial 120-month interval.* Inservice examination of components and system pressure tests conducted during the initial 120-month inspection interval must comply with the requirements in the latest edition and addenda of the ASME Code incorporated by reference in paragraph (a) of this section on the date 12 months before the date of issuance of the operating license under this part, or 12 months before the date scheduled for initial loading of fuel under a combined license under part 52 of this chapter (or the optional ASME Code Cases listed in NRC Regulatory Guide 1.147, when using ASME BPV Code, Section XI, or NRC Regulatory Guide 1.192, when using the ASME OM Code, as incorporated by reference in paragraphs (a)(3)(ii) and (iii) of this section, respectively), subject to the conditions listed in paragraph (b) of this section. Licensees may, at any time in their 120-month ISI interval, elect to use the Appendix VIII in the latest edition and addenda of the ASME BPV Code incorporated by reference in paragraph (a) of this section, subject to any applicable conditions listed in paragraph (b) of this section. Licensees using this option must also use the same edition and addenda of Appendix I as Appendix VIII, including any applicable conditions listed in paragraph (b) of this section.

(ii) *Applicable ISI Code: Successive 120-month intervals.* Inservice examination of components and system pressure tests conducted during successive 120-month inspection intervals must comply with the requirements of the latest edition and addenda of the ASME Code incorporated by reference in paragraph (a) of this section 12 months before the start of the 120-month inspection interval (or the optional ASME Code Cases listed in NRC Regulatory Guide 1.147, when using ASME BPV Code, Section XI, or NRC Regulatory Guide 1.192, when using the ASME OM Code, as incorporated by reference in paragraphs (a)(3)(ii) and (iii) of this section), subject to the conditions listed in paragraph (b) of this section. However, a licensee whose inservice inspection interval commences during the 12 through 18-month period after August 17, 2017, may delay the update of their Appendix VIII program by up to 18 months after August 17, 2017. Alternatively, licensees may, at any time in their 120-month ISI interval, elect to use the Appendix VIII in the latest edition and addenda of the ASME BPV Code incorporated by reference in paragraph (a) of this section, subject to any applicable conditions listed in paragraph (b) of this section. Licensees using this option must also use the same Edition and Addenda of Appendix I as Appendix VIII, including any applicable conditions listed in paragraph (b) of this section.

(iii) *Applicable ISI Code: Optional surface examination requirement.* When applying editions and addenda prior to the 2003 Addenda of Section XI of the ASME BPV Code, licensees may, but are not required to, perform the surface examinations of high-pressure safety injection systems specified in Table IWB–2500–1, Examination Category B–J, Item Numbers B9.20, B9.21, and B9.22.

(iv) *Applicable ISI Code: Use of subsequent Code editions and addenda.* Inservice examination of components and system pressure tests may meet the requirements set forth in subsequent editions and addenda that are incorporated by reference in paragraph (a) of this section, subject to the conditions listed in paragraph (b) of this section, and subject to Commission approval. Portions of editions or addenda may be used, provided that all related requirements of the respective editions or addenda are met.

(v) *Applicable ISI Code: Metal and concrete containments.* For a boiling or pressurized water-cooled nuclear power facility whose construction permit under this part or combined license under part 52 of this chapter was issued after January 1, 1956, the following are required:

(A) *Metal and concrete containments: First provision.* Metal containment pressure retaining components and their integral attachments must meet the inservice inspection, repair, and replacement requirements applicable to components that are classified as ASME Code Class MC;

(B) *Metal and concrete containments: Second provision.* Metallic shell and penetration liners that are pressure retaining components and their integral attachments in concrete containments must meet the inservice inspection, repair, and replacement requirements applicable to components that are classified as ASME Code Class MC; and

(C) *Metal and concrete containments: Third provision.* Concrete containment pressure retaining components and their integral attachments, and the post-tensioning systems of concrete containments, must meet the inservice inspections, repair, and replacement requirements applicable to components that are classified as ASME Code Class CC.

(5) *Requirements for updating ISI programs*—(i) *ISI program update: Applicable ISI Code editions and addenda.* The inservice inspection program for a boiling or pressurized water-cooled nuclear power facility must be revised by the licensee, as necessary, to meet the requirements of paragraph (g)(4) of this section.

(ii) *ISI program update: Conflicting ISI Code requirements with technical specifications.* If a revised inservice inspection program for a facility conflicts with the technical specifications for the facility, the licensee must apply to the Commission for amendment of the technical specifications to conform the technical specifications to the revised program. The licensee must submit this application, as specified in § 50.4, at least six months before the start of the period during which the provisions become applicable, as determined by paragraph (g)(4) of this section.

(iii) *ISI program update: Notification of impractical ISI Code requirements.* If the licensee has determined that conformance with a Code requirement is impractical for its facility the licensee must notify the NRC and submit, as specified in § 50.4, information to support the determinations. Determinations of impracticality in accordance with this section must be based on the demonstrated limitations experienced when attempting to comply with the Code requirements during the inservice inspection interval for which the request is being submitted. Requests for relief made in accordance with this section must be submitted to the NRC no later than 12 months after the expiration of the initial or subsequent 120-month inspection interval for which relief is sought.

(iv) *ISI program update: Schedule for completing impracticality determinations.* Where the licensee determines that an examination required by Code edition or addenda is impractical, the basis for this determination must be submitted for NRC review and approval not later than 12 months after the expiration of the initial or subsequent 120-month inspection interval for which relief is sought.

(6) *Actions by the Commission for evaluating impractical and augmented ISI Code requirements*—(i) *Impractical ISI requirements: Granting of relief.* The Commission will evaluate determinations under paragraph (g)(5) of this section that code requirements are impractical. The Commission may grant such relief and may impose such alternative requirements as it determines are authorized by law, will not endanger life or property or the common defense and security, and are otherwise in the public interest giving due consideration to the burden upon the licensee that could result if the requirements were imposed on the facility.

(ii) *Augmented ISI program.* The Commission may require the licensee to follow an augmented inservice inspection program for systems and components for which the Commission deems that added assurance of structural reliability is necessary.

(A) [Reserved]

(B) *Augmented ISI requirements: Submitting containment ISI programs.* Licensees do not have to submit to the NRC for approval of their containment inservice inspection programs that were developed to satisfy the requirements of Subsection IWE and Subsection IWL with specified conditions. The program elements and the required documentation must be maintained on site for audit.

(C) *Augmented ISI requirements: Implementation of Appendix VIII to Section XI.* (*1*) Appendix VIII and the supplements to Appendix VIII to Section XI, Division 1, 1995 Edition with the 1996 Addenda of the ASME BPV Code must be implemented in accordance with the following schedule: Appendix VIII and Supplements 1, 2, 3, and 8—May 22, 2000; Supplements 4 and 6—November 22, 2000; Supplement 11—November 22, 2001; and Supplements 5, 7, and 10—November 22, 2002.

(*2*) Licensees implementing the 1989 Edition and earlier editions and addenda of IWA–2232 of Section XI, Division 1, of the ASME BPV Code must implement the 1995 Edition with the 1996 Addenda of Appendix VIII and the supplements to Appendix VIII of Section XI, Division 1, of the ASME BPV Code.

(D) *Augmented ISI requirements: Reactor vessel head inspections—(1) Implementation.* Holders of operating licenses or combined licenses for pressurized-water reactors as of or after August 17, 2017 shall implement the requirements of ASME BPV Code Case N–729–4 instead of ASME BPV Code Case N–729–1, subject to the conditions specified in paragraphs (g)(6)(ii)(D)(*2*) through (*4*) of this section, by the first refueling outage starting after August 17, 2017.

(*2*) *Appendix I use.* Appendix I of ASME BPV Code Case N–729–4 shall not be implemented without prior NRC approval.

(*3*) *Bare metal visual frequency.* Instead of Note 4 of ASME BPV Code Case N–729–4, the following shall be implemented. If effective degradation years (EDY) < 8 and if no flaws are found that are attributed to primary water stress corrosion cracking:

(*i*) A bare metal visual examination is not required during refueling outages when a volumetric or surface examination is performed; and

(*ii*) If a wetted surface examination has been performed of all of the partial penetration welds during the previous non-visual examination, the reexamination frequency may be extended to every third refueling outage or 5 calendar years, whichever is less, provided an IWA–2212 VT–2 visual examination of the head is performed under the insulation through multiple access points in outages that the VE is not completed. This IWA–2212 VT–2 visual examination may be performed with the reactor vessel depressurized.

(*4*) *Surface exam acceptance criteria.* In addition to the requirements of Paragraph –3132.1(b) of ASME BPV Code Case N–729–4, a component whose surface examination detects rounded indications greater than allowed in Paragraph NB–5352 in size on the partial-penetration or associated fillet weld shall be classified as having an unacceptable indication and corrected in accordance with the provisions of paragraph–3132.2 of ASME BPV Code Case N–729–4.

(E) *Augmented ISI requirements: Reactor coolant pressure boundary visual inspections* [10]*—(1)* All licensees of pressurized water reactors must augment their inservice inspection program by implementing ASME Code Case N–722–1, subject to the conditions specified in paragraphs (g)(6)(ii)(E)(*2*) through (*4*) of this section. The inspection requirements of ASME Code Case N–722–1 do not apply to components with pressure retaining welds fabricated with Alloy 600/82/182 materials that have been mitigated by weld overlay or stress improvement.

(*2*) If a visual examination determines that leakage is occurring from a specific item listed in Table 1 of ASME Code Case N–722–1 that is not exempted by the ASME Code, Section XI, IWB–1220(b)(1), additional actions must be performed to characterize the location, orientation, and length of a crack or cracks in Alloy 600 nozzle wrought material and location, orientation, and length of a crack or cracks in Alloy 82/182 butt welds. Alternatively, licensees may replace the Alloy 600/82/182 materials in all the components under the item number of the leaking component.

(*3*) If the actions in paragraph (g)(6)(ii)(E)(*2*) of this section determine that a flaw is circumferentially oriented and potentially a result of primary water stress corrosion cracking, licensees must perform non-visual NDE inspections of components that fall under that ASME Code Case N–722–1 item number. The number of components inspected must equal or exceed the number of components found to be leaking under that item number. If circumferential cracking is identified in the sample, non-visual NDE must be performed in the remaining components under that item number.

(*4*) If ultrasonic examinations of butt welds are used to meet the NDE requirements in paragraphs (g)(6)(ii)(E)(*2*) or (*3*) of this section, they must be performed using the appropriate supplement of Section XI, Appendix VIII, of the ASME BPV Code.

(F) *Augmented ISI requirements: Examination requirements for Class 1 piping and nozzle dissimilar-metal butt welds—(1) Implementation.* Holders of operating licenses or combined licenses for pressurized-water reactors as of or after

August 17, 2017, shall implement the requirements of ASME BPV Code Case N–770–2 instead of ASME BPV Code Case N–770–1, subject to the conditions specified in paragraphs (g)(6)(ii)(F)(*2*) through (*13*) of this section, by the first refueling outage starting after August 17, 2017.

(*2*) *Categorization.* Full structural weld overlays, authorized by the NRC staff in accordance with the alternatives approval process of this section, may be categorized as Inspection Items C–1 or F–1, as appropriate. Welds that have been mitigated by the Mechanical Stress Improvement Process (MSIP™) may be categorized as Inspection Items D or E, as appropriate, provided the criteria in Appendix I of the code case have been met. For the purpose of determining ISI frequencies, all other butt welds that rely on Alloy 82/182 for structural integrity shall be categorized as Inspection Items A–1, A–2, or B until the NRC staff has reviewed the mitigation and authorized an alternative code case Inspection Item for the mitigated weld, or an alternative code case Inspection Item is used based on conformance with an ASME mitigation code case endorsed in NRC Regulatory Guide 1.147 with any applying conditions specified in NRC Regulatory Guide 1.147, as incorporated by reference in paragraph (a)(3)(ii) of this section. Paragraph –1100(e) of ASME BPV Code Case N–770–2 shall not be used to exempt welds that rely on Alloy 82/182 for structural integrity from any requirement of paragraph (g)(6)(ii)(F) of this section.

(*3*) *Baseline examinations.* Baseline examinations for welds in Table 1 of ASME BPV Code Case N–770–2, Inspection Items A–1, A–2, and B, if not previously performed or currently scheduled to be performed in an ongoing refueling outage as of August 17, 2017, in accordance with paragraph (g)(6)(ii)(F) of this section, shall be completed by the end of the next refueling outage. Previous examinations of these welds can be credited for baseline examinations only if they were performed within the re-inspection period for the weld item in Table 1 of ASME BPV Code Case N–770–2 and the examination of each weld meets the examination requirements of paragraphs –2500(a) or –2500(b) of ASME BPV Code Case N–770–2 as conditioned in this section. Other previous examinations that do not meet these requirements can be used to meet the baseline examination requirement, provided NRC approval in accordance with paragraph (z)(1) or (2) of this section, is granted prior to the end of the next refueling outage.

(*4*) *Examination coverage.* When implementing Paragraph –2500(a) of ASME BPV Code Case N–770–2, essentially 100 percent of the required volumetric examination coverage shall be obtained, including greater than 90 percent of the volumetric examination coverage for circumferential flaws. Licensees are prohibited from using Paragraphs –2500(c) and –2500(d) of ASME BPV Code Case N–770–2 to meet examination requirements.

(*5*) *Inlay/onlay inspection frequency.* All hot-leg operating temperature welds in Inspection Items G, H, J, and K shall be inspected each inspection interval. A 25 percent sample of Inspection Items G, H, J, and K cold-leg operating temperature welds shall be inspected whenever the core barrel is removed (unless it has already been inspected within the past 10 years) or within 20 years, whichever is less.

(*6*) *Reporting requirements.* For any mitigated weld whose volumetric examination detects growth of existing flaws in the required examination volume that exceed the previous IWB–3600 flaw evaluations or new flaws, a report summarizing the evaluation, along with inputs, methodologies, assumptions, and causes of the new flaw or flaw growth is to be provided to the NRC prior to the weld being placed in service other than modes 5 or 6.

(*7*) *Defining "t".* For Inspection Items G, H, J, and K, when applying the acceptance standards of ASME BPV Code, Section XI, IWB–3514, for planar flaws contained within the inlay or onlay, the thickness "t" in IWB–3514 is the thickness of the inlay or onlay. For planar flaws in the balance of the dissimilar metal weld examination volume, the thickness "t" in IWB–3514 is the combined thickness of the inlay or onlay and the dissimilar metal weld.

(*8*) *Optimized weld overlay examination.* Initial inservice examination of Inspection Item C–2 welds shall be performed between the third refueling outage and no later than 10 years after application of the overlay.

(*9*) *Deferral.* Note (11)(b)(1) in ASME BPV Code Case N–770–2 shall not be used to defer the initial inservice examination of optimized weld overlays (*i.e.*, Inspection Item C–2 of ASME BPV Code Case N–770–2).

(*10*) *Examination technique.* Note 14(b) of Table 1 and Note (b) of Figure 5(a) of ASME BPV Code Case N–770–2 may only be implemented if the requirements of Note 14(a) of Table 1 of ASME BPV Code Case N–770–2 cannot be met.

(*11*) *Cast stainless steel.* Examination of ASME BPV Code Class 1 piping and vessel nozzle butt welds involving cast stainless steel materials, shall be performed with Appendix VIII, Supplement 9 qualifications, or qualifications similar to Appendix VIII, Supplement 2 or 10 using cast stainless steel mockups no later than the next scheduled weld examination after January 1, 2022, in accordance with the requirements of Paragraph -2500(a).

(*12*) *Stress improvement inspection coverage.* Under Paragraph I.5.1, for cast stainless steel items, the required examination volume shall be examined by Appendix VIII procedures to the maximum extent practical including 100 percent of the susceptible material volume.

(*13*) *Encoded ultrasonic examination.* Ultrasonic examinations of non-mitigated or cracked mitigated dissimilar metal butt welds in the reactor coolant pressure boundary must be performed in accordance with the requirements of Table 1 for Inspection Item A–1, A–2, B, E, F–2, J, and K for 100 percent of the required inspection volume using an encoded method.

(h) *Protection and safety systems.* Protection systems of nuclear power reactors of all types must meet the requirements specified in this paragraph. Each combined license for a utilization facility is subject to the following conditions.

(1) [Reserved]

(2) *Protection systems.* For nuclear power plants with construction permits issued after January 1, 1971, but before May 13, 1999, protection systems must meet the requirements in IEEE Std 279–1968, "Proposed IEEE Criteria for Nuclear Power Plant Protection Systems," or the requirements in IEEE Std 279–1971, "Criteria for Protection Systems for Nuclear Power Generating Stations," or the requirements in IEEE Std 603–1991, "Criteria for Safety Systems for Nuclear Power Generating Stations," and the correction sheet dated January 30, 1995. For nuclear power plants with construction permits issued before January 1, 1971, protection systems must be consistent with their licensing basis or may meet the requirements of IEEE Std. 603–1991 and the correction sheet dated January 30, 1995.

(3) *Safety systems.* Applications filed on or after May 13, 1999, for construction permits and operating licenses under this part, and for design approvals, design certifications, and combined licenses under part 52 of this chapter, must meet the requirements for safety systems in IEEE Std. 603–1991 and the correction sheet dated January 30, 1995.

(i)–(y) [Reserved]

(z) *Alternatives to codes and standards requirements.* Alternatives to the requirements of paragraphs (b) through (h) of this section or portions thereof may be used when authorized by the Director, Office of Nuclear Reactor Regulation, or Director, Office of New Reactors, as appropriate. A proposed alternative must be submitted and authorized prior to implementation. The applicant or licensee must demonstrate that:

(1) *Acceptable level of quality and safety.* The proposed alternative would provide an acceptable level of quality and safety; or

(2) *Hardship without a compensating increase in quality and safety.* Compliance with the specified requirements of this section would result in hardship or unusual difficulty without a compensating increase in the level of quality and safety. Footnotes to § 50.55a:

[1] USAS and ASME Code addenda issued prior to the winter 1977 Addenda are considered to be "in effect" or "effective" 6 months after their date of issuance and after they are incorporated by reference in paragraph (a) of this section. Addenda to the ASME Code issued after the summer 1977 Addenda are considered to be "in effect" or "effective" after the date of publication of the addenda and after they are incorporated by reference in paragraph (a) of this section.

2–3 [Reserved].

4 For ASME Code editions and addenda issued prior to the winter 1977 Addenda, the Code edition and addenda applicable to the component is governed by the order or contract date for the component, not the contract date for the nuclear energy system. For the winter 1977 Addenda and subsequent editions and addenda the method for determining the applicable Code editions and addenda is contained in Paragraph NCA 1140 of Section III of the ASME Code.

5–6 [Reserved].

7 Guidance for quality group classifications of components that are to be included in the safety analysis reports pursuant to § 50.34(a) and § 50.34(b) may be found in Regulatory Guide 1.26, "Quality Group Classifications and Standards for Water-, Steam-, and Radiological-Waste-Containing Components of Nuclear Power Plants," and in Section 3.2.2 of NUREG–0800, "Standard Review Plan for Review of Safety Analysis Reports for Nuclear Power Plants."

8–9 [Reserved].

10 For inspections to be conducted once per interval, the inspections must be performed in accordance with the schedule in Section XI, paragraph IWB–2400, except for plants with inservice inspection programs based on a Section XI edition or addenda prior to the 1994 Addenda. For plants with inservice inspection programs based on a Section XI edition or addenda prior to the 1994 Addenda, the inspection must be performed in accordance with the schedule in Section XI, paragraph IWB–2400, of the 1994 Addenda.

[79 FR 65798, Nov. 5, 2014, as amended at 79 FR 66603, Nov. 10, 2014; 79 FR 73462, Dec. 11, 2014; 82 FR 52825, Dec. 15, 2017]

§ 50.56 Conversion of construction permit to license; or amendment of license.

Upon completion of the construction or alteration of a facility, in compliance with the terms and conditions of the construction permit and subject to any necessary testing of the facility for health or safety purposes, the Commission will, in the absence of good cause shown to the contrary, issue a license of the class for which the construction permit was issued or an appropriate amendment of the license, as the case may be.

[21 FR 355, Jan. 19, 1956, as amended at 35 FR 11461, July 17, 1970; 75 FR 73944, Nov. 30, 2010]

§ 50.57 Issuance of operating license.[1]

(a)Pursuant to § 50.56, an operating license may be issued by the Commission, up to the full term authorized by § 50.51, upon finding that:

(1) Construction of the facility has been substantially completed, in conformity with the construction permit and the application as amended, the provisions of the Act, and the rules and regulations of the Commission; and

(2) The facility will operate in conformity with the application as amended, the provisions of the Act, and the rules and regulations of the Commission; and

(3) There is reasonable assurance (i) that the activities authorized by the operating license can be conducted without endangering the health and safety of the public, and (ii) that such activities will be conducted in compliance with the regulations in this chapter; and

(4) The applicant is technically and financially qualified to engage in the activities authorized by the operating license in accordance with the regulations in this chapter. However, no finding of financial qualification is necessary for an electric utility applicant for an operating license for a utilization facility of the type described in § 50.21(b) or § 50.22.

(5) The applicable provisions of part 140 of this chapter have been satisfied; and

(6) The issuance of the license will not be inimical to the common defense and security or to the health and safety of the public.

(b) Each operating license will include appropriate provisions with respect to any uncompleted items of construction and such limitations or conditions as are required to assure that operation during the period of the completion of such items will not endanger public health and safety.

(c) An applicant may, in a case where a hearing is held in connection with a

1 The Commission may issue a provisional operating license pursuant to the regulations in this part in effect on March 30, 1970, for any facility for which a notice of hearing on an application for a provisional operating license or a notice of proposed issuance of a provisional operating license has been published on or before that date.

pending proceeding under this section make a motion in writing, under this paragraph (c), for an operating license authorizing low-power testing (operation at not more than 1 percent of full power for the purpose of testing the facility), and further operations short of full power operation. Action on such a motion by the presiding officer shall be taken with due regard to the rights of the parties to the proceedings, including the right of any party to be heard to the extent that his contentions are relevant to the activity to be authorized. Before taking any action on such a motion that any party opposes, the presiding officer shall make findings on the matters specified in paragraph (a) of this section as to which there is a controversy, in the form of an initial decision with respect to the contested activity sought to be authorized. The Director of Nuclear Reactor Regulation will make findings on all other matters specified in paragraph (a) of this section. If no party opposes the motion, the presiding officer will issue an order in accordance with § 2.319(p) authorizing the Director of Nuclear Reactor Regulation to make appropriate findings on the matters specified in paragraph (a) of this section and to issue a license for the requested operation.

[35 FR 5318, Mar. 31, 1970, as amended at 35 FR 6644, Apr. 25, 1970; 37 FR 11873, June 15, 1972; 37 FR 15142, July 28, 1972; 49 FR 35753, Sept. 12, 1984; 51 FR 7765, Mar. 6, 1986; 69 FR 2275, Jan. 14, 2004]

§ 50.58 Hearings and report of the Advisory Committee on Reactor Safeguards.

(a) Each application for a construction permit or an operating license for a facility which is of a type described in § 50.21(b) or § 50.22, or for a testing facility, shall be referred to the Advisory Committee on Reactor Safeguards for a review and report. An application for an amendment to such a construction permit or operating license may be referred to the Advisory Committee on Reactor Safeguards for review and report. Any report shall be made part of the record of the application and available to the public, except to the extent that security classification prevents disclosure.

(b)(1) The Commission will hold a hearing after at least 30-days' notice and publication once in the FEDERAL REGISTER on each application for a construction permit for a production or utilization facility which is of a type described in § 50.21(b) or § 50.22, or for a testing facility.

(2) When a construction permit has been issued for such a facility following the holding of a public hearing, and an application is made for an operating license or for an amendment to a construction permit or operating license, the Commission may hold a hearing after at least 30-days' notice and publication once in the FEDERAL REGISTER, or, in the absence of a request therefor by any person whose interest may be affected, may issue an operating license or an amendment to a construction permit or operating license without a hearing, upon 30-days' notice and publication once in the FEDERAL REGISTER of its intent to do so.

(3) If the Commission finds, in an emergency situation, as defined in § 50.91, that no significant hazards consideration is presented by an application for an amendment to an operating license, it may dispense with public notice and comment and may issue the amendment. If the Commission finds that exigent circumstances exist, as described in § 50.91, it may reduce the period provided for public notice and comment.

(4) Both in an emergency situation and in the case of exigent circumstances, the Commission will provide 30 days notice of opportunity for a hearing, though this notice may be published after issuance of the amendment if the Commission determines that no significant hazards consideration is involved.

(5) The Commission will use the standards in § 50.92 to determine whether a significant hazards consideration is presented by an amendment to an operating license for a facility of the type described in § 50.21(b) or § 50.22, or which is a testing facility, and may make the amendment immediately effective, notwithstanding the pendency before it of a request for a hearing from any person, in advance of the holding and completion of any required hearing, where it has determined that no

significant hazards consideration is involved.

(6) No petition or other request for review of or hearing on the staff's significant hazards consideration determination will be entertained by the Commission. The staff's determination is final, subject only to the Commission's discretion, on its own initiative, to review the determination.

[27 FR 12186, Dec. 8, 1962, as amended at 35 FR 11461, July 17, 1970; 39 FR 10555, Mar. 21, 1974; 51 FR 7765, Mar. 6, 1986]

§ 50.59 Changes, tests, and experiments.

(a) Definitions for the purposes of this section:

(1) *Change* means a modification or addition to, or removal from, the facility or procedures that affects a design function, method of performing or controlling the function, or an evaluation that demonstrates that intended functions will be accomplished.

(2) *Departure from a method of evaluation described in the FSAR (as updated) used in establishing the design bases or in the safety analyses* means:

(i) Changing any of the elements of the method described in the FSAR (as updated) unless the results of the analysis are conservative or essentially the same; or

(ii) Changing from a method described in the FSAR to another method unless that method has been approved by NRC for the intended application.

(3) *Facility as described in the final safety analysis report (as updated)* means:

(i) The structures, systems, and components (SSC) that are described in the final safety analysis report (FSAR) (as updated),

(ii) The design and performance requirements for such SSCs described in the FSAR (as updated), and

(iii) The evaluations or methods of evaluation included in the FSAR (as updated) for such SSCs which demonstrate that their intended function(s) will be accomplished.

(4) *Final Safety Analysis Report (as updated)* means the Final Safety Analysis Report (or Final Hazards Summary Report) submitted in accordance with § 50.34, as amended and supplemented, and as updated per the requirements of § 50.71(e) or § 50.71(f), as applicable.

(5) *Procedures as described in the final safety analysis report (as updated)* means those procedures that contain information described in the FSAR (as updated) such as how structures, systems, and components are operated and controlled (including assumed operator actions and response times).

(6) *Tests or experiments not described in the final safety analysis report (as updated)* means any activity where any structure, system, or component is utilized or controlled in a manner which is either:

(i) Outside the reference bounds of the design bases as described in the final safety analysis report (as updated) or

(ii) Inconsistent with the analyses or descriptions in the final safety analysis report (as updated).

(b) This section applies to each holder of an operating license issued under this part or a combined license issued under part 52 of this chapter, including the holder of a license authorizing operation of a nuclear power reactor that has submitted the certification of permanent cessation of operations required under § 50.82(a)(1) or § 50.110 or a reactor licensee whose license has been amended to allow possession of nuclear fuel but not operation of the facility.

(c)(1) A licensee may make changes in the facility as described in the final safety analysis report (as updated), make changes in the procedures as described in the final safety analysis report (as updated), and conduct tests or experiments not described in the final safety analysis report (as updated) without obtaining a license amendment pursuant to § 50.90 only if:

(i) A change to the technical specifications incorporated in the license is not required, and

(ii) The change, test, or experiment does not meet any of the criteria in paragraph (c)(2) of this section.

(2) A licensee shall obtain a license amendment pursuant to § 50.90 prior to implementing a proposed change, test, or experiment if the change, test, or experiment would:

(i) Result in more than a minimal increase in the frequency of occurrence of an accident previously evaluated in the final safety analysis report (as updated);

(ii) Result in more than a minimal increase in the likelihood of occurrence of a malfunction of a structure, system, or component (SSC) important to safety previously evaluated in the final safety analysis report (as updated);

(iii) Result in more than a minimal increase in the consequences of an accident previously evaluated in the final safety analysis report (as updated);

(iv) Result in more than a minimal increase in the consequences of a malfunction of an SSC important to safety previously evaluated in the final safety analysis report (as updated);

(v) Create a possibility for an accident of a different type than any previously evaluated in the final safety analysis report (as updated);

(vi) Create a possibility for a malfunction of an SSC important to safety with a different result than any previously evaluated in the final safety analysis report (as updated);

(vii) Result in a design basis limit for a fission product barrier as described in the FSAR (as updated) being exceeded or altered; or

(viii) Result in a departure from a method of evaluation described in the FSAR (as updated) used in establishing the design bases or in the safety analyses.

(3) In implementing this paragraph, the FSAR (as updated) is considered to include FSAR changes resulting from evaluations performed pursuant to this section and analyses performed pursuant to § 50.90 since submittal of the last update of the final safety analysis report pursuant to § 50.71 of this part.

(4) The provisions in this section do not apply to changes to the facility or procedures when the applicable regulations establish more specific criteria for accomplishing such changes.

(d)(1) The licensee shall maintain records of changes in the facility, of changes in procedures, and of tests and experiments made pursuant to paragraph (c) of this section. These records must include a written evaluation which provides the bases for the determination that the change, test, or experiment does not require a license amendment pursuant to paragraph (c)(2) of this section.

(2) The licensee shall submit, as specified in § 50.4 or § 52.3 of this chapter, as applicable, a report containing a brief description of any changes, tests, and experiments, including a summary of the evaluation of each. A report must be submitted at intervals not to exceed 24 months. For combined licenses, the report must be submitted at intervals not to exceed 6 months during the period from the date of application for a combined license to the date the Commission makes its findings under 10 CFR 52.103(g).

(3) The records of changes in the facility must be maintained until the termination of an operating license issued under this part, a combined license issued under part 52 of this chapter, or the termination of a license issued under 10 CFR part 54, whichever is later. Records of changes in procedures and records of tests and experiments must be maintained for a period of 5 years.

[64 FR 53613, Oct. 4, 1999, as amended at 66 FR 64738, Dec. 14, 2001; 72 FR 49500, Aug. 28, 2007]

§ 50.60 Acceptance criteria for fracture prevention measures for lightwater nuclear power reactors for normal operation.

(a) Except as provided in paragraph (b) of this section, all light-water nuclear power reactors, other than reactor facilities for which the certifications required under § 50.82(a)(1) have been submitted, must meet the fracture toughness and material surveillance program requirements for the reactor coolant pressure boundary set forth in appendices G and H to this part.

(b) Proposed alternatives to the described requirements in Appendices G and H of this part or portions thereof may be used when an exemption is granted by the Commission under § 50.12.

[48 FR 24009, May 27, 1983, as amended at 50 FR 50777, Dec. 12, 1985; 61 FR 39300, July 29, 1996]

§ 50.61 Fracture toughness requirements for protection against pressurized thermal shock events.

(a) *Definitions.* For the purposes of this section:

(1) *ASME Code* means the American Society of Mechanical Engineers Boiler and Pressure Vessel Code, Section III, Division I, "Rules for the Construction of Nuclear Power Plant Components," edition and addenda and any limitations and modifications thereof as specified in § 50.55a.

(2) *Pressurized Thermal Shock Event* means an event or transient in pressurized water reactors (PWRs) causing severe overcooling (thermal shock) concurrent with or followed by significant pressure in the reactor vessel.

(3) *Reactor Vessel Beltline* means the region of the reactor vessel (shell material including welds, heat affected zones and plates or forgings) that directly surrounds the effective height of the active core and adjacent regions of the reactor vessel that are predicted to experience sufficient neutron radiation damage to be considered in the selection of the most limiting material with regard to radiation damage.

(4) RT_{NDT} means the reference temperature for a reactor vessel material, under any conditions. For the reactor vessel beltline materials, RT_{NDT} must account for the effects of neutron radiation.

(5) $RT_{NDT(U)}$ means the reference temperature for a reactor vessel material in the pre-service or unirradiated condition, evaluated according to the procedures in the ASME Code, Paragraph NB–2331 or other methods approved by the Director, Office of Nuclear Reactor Regulation or Director, Office of New Reactors, as appropriate.

(6) *EOL Fluence* means the best-estimate neutron fluence projected for a specific vessel beltline material at the clad-base-metal interface on the inside surface of the vessel at the location where the material receives the highest fluence on the expiration date of the operating license.

(7) RT_{PTS} means the reference temperature, RT_{NDT}, evaluated for the EOL Fluence for each of the vessel beltline materials, using the procedures of paragraph (c) of this section.

(8) *PTS Screening Criterion* means the value of RT_{PTS} for the vessel beltline material above which the plant cannot continue to operate without justification.

(b) *Requirements.* (1) For each pressurized water nuclear power reactor for which an operating license has been issued under this part or a combined license issued under Part 52 of this chapter, other than a nuclear power reactor facility for which the certification required under § 50.82(a)(1) has been submitted, the licensee shall have projected values of RT_{PTS} or RT_{MAX-X}, accepted by the NRC, for each reactor vessel beltline material. For pressurized water nuclear power reactors for which a construction permit was issued under this part before February 3, 2010 and whose reactor vessel was designed and fabricated to the 1998 Edition or earlier of the ASME Code, the projected values must be in accordance with this section or § 50.61a. For pressurized water nuclear power reactors for which a construction permit is issued under this part after February 3, 2010 and whose reactor vessel is designed and fabricated to an ASME Code after the 1998 Edition, or for which a combined license is issued under Part 52, the projected values must be in accordance with this section. When determining compliance with this section, the assessment of RT_{PTS} must use the calculation procedures described in paragraph (c)(1) and perform the evaluations described in paragraphs (c)(2) and (c)(3) of this section. The assessment must specify the bases for the projected value of RT_{PTS} for each vessel beltline material, including the assumptions regarding core loading patterns, and must specify the copper and nickel contents and the fluence value used in the calculation for each beltline material. This assessment must be updated whenever there is a significant[2] change in projected values of RT_{PTS}, or upon request for a change in the expiration date for operation of the facility.

(2) The pressurized thermal shock (PTS) screening criterion is 270 °F for plates, forgings, and axial weld materials, and 300 °F for circumferential

[2] Changes to RT_{PTS} values are considered significant if either the previous value or the current value, or both values, exceed the screening criterion before the expiration of the operating license or the combined license under Part 52 of this chapter, including any renewed term, if applicable for the plant.

weld materials. For the purpose of comparison with this criterion, the value of RT_{PTS} for the reactor vessel must be evaluated according to the procedures of paragraph (c) of this section, for each weld and plate, or forging, in the reactor vessel beltline. RT_{PTS} must be determined for each vessel beltline material using the EOL fluence for that material.

(3) For each pressurized water nuclear power reactor for which the value of RT_{PTS} for any material in the beltline is projected to exceed the PTS screening criterion using the EOL fluence, the licensee shall implement those flux reduction programs that are reasonably practicable to avoid exceeding the PTS screening criterion set forth in paragraph (b)(2) of this section. The schedule for implementation of flux reduction measures may take into account the schedule for submittal and anticipated approval by the Director, Office of Nuclear Reactor Regulation, of detailed plant-specific analyses, submitted to demonstrate acceptable risk with RT_{PTS} above the screening limit due to plant modifications, new information or new analysis techniques.

(4) For each pressurized water nuclear power reactor for which the analysis required by paragraph (b)(3) of this section indicates that no reasonably practicable flux reduction program will prevent RT_{PTS} from exceeding the PTS screening criterion using the EOL fluence, the licensee shall submit a safety analysis to determine what, if any, modifications to equipment, systems, and operation are necessary to prevent potential failure of the reactor vessel as a result of postulated PTS events if continued operation beyond the screening criterion is allowed. In the analysis, the licensee may determine the properties of the reactor vessel materials based on available information, research results, and plant surveillance data, and may use probabilistic fracture mechanics techniques. This analysis must be submitted at least three years before RT_{PTS} is projected to exceed the PTS screening criterion.

(5) After consideration of the licensee's analyses, including effects of proposed corrective actions, if any, submitted in accordance with paragraphs (b)(3) and (b)(4) of this section, the Director, Office of Nuclear Reactor Regulation, may, on a case-by-case basis, approve operation of the facility with RT_{PTS} in excess of the PTS screening criterion. The Director, Office of Nuclear Reactor Regulation, will consider factors significantly affecting the potential for failure of the reactor vessel in reaching a decision.

(6) If the Director, Office of Nuclear Reactor Regulation, concludes, pursuant to paragraph (b)(5) of this section, that operation of the facility with RT_{PTS} in excess of the PTS screening criterion cannot be approved on the basis of the licensee's analyses submitted in accordance with paragraphs (b)(3) and (b)(4) of this section, the licensee shall request and receive approval by the Director, Office of Nuclear Reactor Regulation, prior to any operation beyond the criterion. The request must be based upon modifications to equipment, systems, and operation of the facility in addition to those previously proposed in the submitted analyses that would reduce the potential for failure of the reactor vessel due to PTS events, or upon further analyses based upon new information or improved methodology.

(7) If the limiting RT_{PTS} value of the plant is projected to exceed the screening criteria in paragraph (b)(2), or the criteria in paragraphs (b)(3) through (b)(6) of this section cannot be satisfied, the reactor vessel beltline may be given a thermal annealing treatment to recover the fracture toughness of the material, subject to the requirements of § 50.66. The reactor vessel may continue to be operated only for that service period within which the predicted fracture toughness of the vessel beltline materials satisfy the requirements of paragraphs (b)(2) through (b)(6) of this section, with RT_{PTS} accounting for the effects of annealing and subsequent irradiation.

(c) *Calculation of RT_{PTS}.* RT_{PTS} must be calculated for each vessel beltline material using a fluence value, f, which is the EOL fluence for the material. RT_{PTS} must be evaluated using the same procedures used to calculate RT_{NDT}, as indicated in paragraph (c)(1) of this section, and as provided in paragraphs (c)(2) and (c)(3) of this section.

(1) Equation 1 must be used to calculate values of RT_{NDT} for each weld and plate, or forging, in the reactor vessel beltline.

Equation 1: $RT_{NDT} = RT_{NDT(U)} + M + \Delta RT_{NDT}$

(i) If a measured value of $RT_{NDT(U)}$ is not available, a generic mean value for the class[3] of material may be used if there are sufficient test results to establish a mean and a standard deviation for the class.

(ii) For generic values of weld metal, the following generic mean values must be used unless justification for different values is provided: 0 °F for welds made with Linde 80 flux, and −56 °F for welds made with Linde 0091, 1092 and 124 and ARCOS B–5 weld fluxes.

(iii) *M* means the margin to be added to account for uncertainties in the values of $RT_{NDT(U)}$, copper and nickel contents, fluence and the calculational procedures. M is evaluated from Equation 2.

Equation 2: $$M = 2\sqrt{\sigma_U^2 + \sigma_\Delta^2}$$

(A) In Equation 2, σ_U is the standard deviation for $RT_{NDT(U)}$. If a measured value of $RT_{NDT(U)}$ is used, then σ_U is determined from the precision of the test method. If a measured value of $RT_{NDT(U)}$ is not available and a generic mean value for that class of materials is used, then σ_U is the standard deviation obtained from the set of data used to establish the mean. If a generic mean value given in paragraph (c)(1)(i)(B) of this section for welds is used, then σ_U is 17 °F.

(B) In Equation 2, σ_Δ is the standard deviation for ΔRT_{NDT}. The value of σ_Δ to be used is 28 °F for welds and 17 °F for base metal; the value of σ_Δ need not exceed one-half of ΔRT_{NDT}.

(iv) ΔRT_{NDT} is the mean value of the transition temperature shift, or change in RT_{NDT}, due to irradiation, and must be calculated using Equation 3.

Equation 3: $\Delta RT_{NDT} = (CF)f^{(0.28 - 0.10 \log f)}$

(A) *CF* (°F) is the chemistry factor, which is a function of copper and nickel content. CF is given in table 1 for welds and in table 2 for base metal (plates and forgings). Linear interpolation is permitted. In tables 1 and 2, "Wt − % copper" and "Wt − % nickel" are the best-estimate values for the material, which will normally be the mean of the measured values for a plate or forging. For a weld, the best estimate values will normally be the mean of the measured values for a weld deposit made using the same weld wire heat number as the critical vessel weld. If these values are not available, the upper limiting values given in the material specifications to which the vessel material was fabricated may be used. If not available, conservative estimates (mean plus one standard deviation) based on generic data[4] may be used if justification is provided. If none of these alternatives are available, 0.35% copper and 1.0% nickel must be assumed.

(B) *f* is the best estimate neutron fluence, in units of 10^{19} n/cm^2 (E greater than 1 MeV), at the clad-base-metal interface on the inside surface of the vessel at the location where the material in question receives the highest fluence for the period of service in question. As specified in this paragraph, the EOL fluence for the vessel beltline material is used in calculating KRT_{PTS}.

(v) Equation 4 must be used for determining RT_{PTS} using equation 3 with EOL fluence values for determining ΔRT_{PTS}.

Equation 4: $RT_{PTS} = RT_{NDT(U)} + M + \Delta RT_{PTS}$

(2) To verify that RT_{NDT} for each vessel beltline material is a bounding value for the specific reactor vessel, licensees shall consider plant-specific information that could affect the level of embrittlement. This information includes but is not limited to the reactor

[3] The class of material for estimating $RT_{NDT(U)}$ is generally determined for welds by the type of welding flux (Linde 80, or other), and for base metal by the material specification.

[4] Data from reactor vessels fabricated to the same material specification in the same shop as the vessel in question and in the same time period is an example of "generic data."

vessel operating temperature and any related surveillance program[5] results.

(i) Results from the plant-specific surveillance program must be integrated into the RT_{NDT} estimate if the plant-specific surveillance data has been deemed credible as judged by the following criteria:

(A) The materials in the surveillance capsules must be those which are the controlling materials with regard to radiation embrittlement.

(B) Scatter in the plots of Charpy energy versus temperature for the irradiated and unirradiated conditions must be small enough to permit the determination of the 30-foot-pound temperature unambiguously.

(C) Where there are two or more sets of surveillance data from one reactor, the scatter of ΔRT_{NDT} values must be less than 28 °F for welds and 17 °F for base metal. Even if the range in the capsule fluences is large (two or more orders of magnitude), the scatter may not exceed twice those values.

(D) The irradiation temperature of the Charpy specimens in the capsule must equal the vessel wall temperature at the cladding/base metal interface within ±25 °F.

(E) The surveillance data for the correlation monitor material in the capsule, if present, must fall within the scatter band of the data base for the material.

(ii)(A) Surveillance data deemed credible according to the criteria of paragraph (c)(2)(i) of this section must be used to determine a material-specific value of CF for use in Equation 3. A material-specific value of CF is determined from Equation 5.

$$\text{Equation 5:} \quad CF = \frac{\sum_{i=1}^{n}\left[A_i \times f_i^{(0.28-0.10\log f_i)}\right]}{\sum_{i=1}^{n}\left[f_i^{(0.56-0.20\log f_i)}\right]}$$

(B) In Equation 5, "n" is the number of surveillance data points, "A_i" is the measured value of ΔRT_{NDT} and "f_i" is the fluence for each surveillance data point. If there is clear evidence that the copper and nickel content of the surveillance weld differs from the vessel weld, *i.e.*, differs from the average for the weld wire heat number associated with the vessel weld and the surveillance weld, the measured values of ΔRT_{NDT} must be adjusted for differences in copper and nickel content by multiplying them by the ratio of the chemistry factor for the vessel material to that for the surveillance weld.

(iii) For cases in which the results from a credible plant-specific surveillance program are used, the value of σ_Δ to be used is 14 °F for welds and 8.5 °F for base metal; the value of σ_Δ need not exceed one-half of ΔRT_{NDT}.

(iv) The use of results from the plant-specific surveillance program may result in an RT_{NDT} that is higher or lower than those determined in paragraph (c)(1).

(3) Any information that is believed to improve the accuracy of the RT_{PTS} value significantly must be reported to the Director, Office of Nuclear Reactor Regulation or Director, Office of New Reactors, as appropriate. Any value of RT_{PTS} that has been modified using the procedures of paragraph (c)(2) of this section is subject to the approval of the Director, Office of Nuclear Reactor Regulation or Director, Office of New Reactors, as appropriate, when used as provided in this section.

[5] Surveillance program results means any data that demonstrates the embrittlement trends for the limiting beltline material, including but not limited to data from test reactors or from surveillance programs at other plants with or without surveillance program integrated per 10 CFR part 50, appendix H.

TABLE 1—CHEMISTRY FACTOR FOR WELD METALS, °F

Copper, wt-%	Nickel, wt-%						
	0	0.20	0.40	0.60	0.80	1.00	1.20
0	20	20	20	20	20	20	20
0.01	20	20	20	20	20	20	20
0.02	21	26	27	27	27	27	27
0.03	22	35	41	41	41	41	41
0.04	24	43	54	54	54	54	54
0.05	26	49	67	68	68	68	68
0.06	29	52	77	82	82	82	82
0.07	32	55	85	95	95	95	95
0.08	36	58	90	106	108	108	108
0.09	40	61	94	115	122	122	122
0.10	44	65	97	122	133	135	135
0.11	49	68	101	130	144	148	148
0.12	52	72	103	135	153	161	161
0.13	58	76	106	139	162	172	176
0.14	61	79	109	142	168	182	188
0.15	66	84	112	146	175	191	200
0.16	70	88	115	149	178	199	211
0.17	75	92	119	151	184	207	221
0.18	79	95	122	154	187	214	230
0.19	83	100	126	157	191	220	238
0.20	88	104	129	160	194	223	245
0.21	92	108	133	164	197	229	252
0.22	97	112	137	167	200	232	257
0.23	101	117	140	169	203	236	263
0.24	105	121	144	173	206	239	268
0.25	110	126	148	176	209	243	272
0.26	113	130	151	180	212	246	276
0.27	119	134	155	184	216	249	280
0.28	122	138	160	187	218	251	284
0.29	128	142	164	191	222	254	287
0.30	131	146	167	194	225	257	290
0.31	136	151	172	198	228	260	293
0.32	140	155	175	202	231	263	296
0.33	144	160	180	205	234	266	299
0.34	149	164	184	209	238	269	302
0.35	153	168	187	212	241	272	305
0.36	158	172	191	216	245	275	308
0.37	162	177	196	220	248	278	311
0.38	166	182	200	223	250	281	314
0.39	171	185	203	227	254	285	317
0.40	175	189	207	231	257	288	320

TABLE 2—CHEMISTRY FACTOR FOR BASE METALS, °F

Copper, wt-%	Nickel, wt-%						
	0	0.20	0.40	0.60	0.80	1.00	1.20
0	20	20	20	20	20	20	20
0.01	20	20	20	20	20	20	20
0.02	20	20	20	20	20	20	20
0.03	20	20	20	20	20	20	20
0.04	22	26	26	26	26	26	26
0.05	25	31	31	31	31	31	31
0.06	28	37	37	37	37	37	37
0.07	31	43	44	44	44	44	44
0.08	34	48	51	51	51	51	51
0.09	37	53	58	58	58	58	58
0.10	41	58	65	65	67	67	67
0.11	45	62	72	74	77	77	77
0.12	49	67	79	83	86	86	86
0.13	53	71	85	91	96	96	96
0.14	57	75	91	100	105	106	106
0.15	61	80	99	110	115	117	117
0.16	65	84	104	118	123	125	125
0.17	69	88	110	127	132	135	135
0.18	73	92	115	134	141	144	144
0.19	78	97	120	142	150	154	154
0.20	82	102	125	149	159	164	165
0.21	86	107	129	155	167	172	174
0.22	91	112	134	161	176	181	184
0.23	95	117	138	167	184	190	194
0.24	100	121	143	172	191	199	204
0.25	104	126	148	176	199	208	214
0.26	109	130	151	180	205	216	221
0.27	114	134	155	184	211	225	230
0.28	119	138	160	187	216	233	239
0.29	124	142	164	191	221	241	248
0.30	129	146	167	194	225	249	257
0.31	134	151	172	198	228	255	266
0.32	139	155	175	202	231	260	274
0.33	144	160	180	205	234	264	282
0.34	149	164	184	209	238	268	290
0.35	153	168	187	212	241	272	298
0.36	158	173	191	216	245	275	303
0.37	162	177	196	220	248	278	308
0.38	166	182	200	223	250	281	313
0.39	171	185	203	227	254	285	317
0.40	175	189	207	231	257	288	320

[60 FR 65468, Dec. 19, 1995, as amended at 61 FR 39300, July 29, 1996; 72 FR 49500, Aug. 28, 2007; 73 FR 5722, Jan. 31, 2008; 75 FR 23, Jan. 4, 2010]

§ 50.61a Alternate fracture toughness requirements for protection against pressurized thermal shock events.

(a) *Definitions*. Terms in this section have the same meaning as those presented in 10 CFR 50.61(a), with the exception of the term "ASME Code."

(1) *ASME Code* means the American Society of Mechanical Engineers Boiler and Pressure Vessel Code, Section III, Division I, "Rules for the Construction of Nuclear Power Plant Components," and Section XI, Division I, "Rules for Inservice Inspection of Nuclear Power Plant Components," edition and addenda and any limitations and modifications thereof as specified in § 50.55a.

(2) $RT_{MAX\text{-}AW}$ means the material property which characterizes the reactor vessel's resistance to fracture initiating from flaws found along axial weld fusion lines. $RT_{MAX\text{-}AW}$ is determined under the provisions of paragraph (f) of this section and has units of °F.

(3) $RT_{MAX\text{-}PL}$ means the material property which characterizes the reactor vessel's resistance to fracture initiating from flaws found in plates in regions that are not associated with

welds found in plates. RT_{MAX-PL} is determined under the provisions of paragraph (f) of this section and has units of °F.

(4) RT_{MAX-FO} means the material property which characterizes the reactor vessel's resistance to fracture initiating from flaws in forgings that are not associated with welds found in forgings. RT_{MAX-FO} is determined under the provisions of paragraph (f) of this section and has units of °F.

(5) RT_{MAX-CW} means the material property which characterizes the reactor vessel's resistance to fracture initiating from flaws found along the circumferential weld fusion lines. RT_{MAX-CW} is determined under the provisions of paragraph (f) of this section and has units of °F.

(6) RT_{MAX-X} means any or all of the material properties RT_{MAX-AW}, RT_{MAX-PL}, RT_{MAX-FO}, RT_{MAX-CW}, or sum of RT_{MAX-AW} and RT_{MAX-PL}, for a particular reactor vessel.

(7) φt means fast neutron fluence for neutrons with energies greater than 1.0 MeV. φt is utilized under the provisions of paragraph (g) of this section and has units of n/cm^2.

(8) φ means average neutron flux for neutrons with energies greater than 1.0 MeV. φ is utilized under the provisions of paragraph (g) of this section and has units of n/cm^2/sec.

(9) ΔT_{30} means the shift in the Charpy V-notch transition temperature at the 30 ft-lb energy level produced by irradiation. The ΔT_{30} value is utilized under the provisions of paragraph (g) of this section and has units of °F.

(10) *Surveillance data* means any data that demonstrates the embrittlement trends for the beltline materials, including, but not limited to, surveillance programs at other plants with or without a surveillance program integrated under 10 CFR part 50, appendix H.

(11) T_C means cold leg temperature under normal full power operating conditions, as a time-weighted average from the start of full power operation through the end of licensed operation. T_C has units of °F.

(12) *CRP* means the copper rich precipitate term in the embrittlement model from this section. The CRP term is defined in paragraph (g) of this section.

(13) *MD* means the matrix damage term in the embrittlement model for this section. The MD term is defined in paragraph (g) of this section.

(b) *Applicability.* The requirements of this section apply to each holder of an operating license for a pressurized water nuclear power reactor whose construction permit was issued before February 3, 2010 and whose reactor vessel was designed and fabricated to the ASME Boiler and Pressure Vessel Code, 1998 Edition or earlier. The requirements of this section may be implemented as an alternative to the requirements of 10 CFR 50.61.

(c) *Request for approval.* Before the implementation of this section, each licensee shall submit a request for approval in the form of an application for a license amendment in accordance with § 50.90 together with the documentation required by paragraphs (c)(1), (c)(2), and (c)(3) of this section for review and approval by the Director of the Office of Nuclear Reactor Regulation (Director). The application must be submitted for review and approval by the Director at least three years before the limiting RT_{PTS} value calculated under 10 CFR 50.61 is projected to exceed the PTS screening criteria in 10 CFR 50.61 for plants licensed under this part.

(1) Each licensee shall have projected values of RT_{MAX-X} for each reactor vessel beltline material for the EOL fluence of the material. The assessment of RT_{MAX-X} values must use the calculation procedures given in paragraphs (f) and (g) of this section. The assessment must specify the bases for the projected value of RT_{MAX-X} for each reactor vessel beltline material, including the assumptions regarding future plant operation (e.g., core loading patterns, projected capacity factors); the copper (Cu), phosphorus (P), manganese (Mn), and nickel (Ni) contents; the reactor cold leg temperature (T_C); and the neutron flux and fluence values used in the calculation for each beltline material. Assessments performed under paragraphs (f)(6) and (f)(7) of this section, shall be submitted by the licensee to the Director in its license

amendment application to utilize § 50.61a.

(2) Each licensee shall perform an examination and an assessment of flaws in the reactor vessel beltline as required by paragraph (e) of this section. The licensee shall verify that the requirements of paragraphs (e), (e)(1), (e)(2), and (e)(3) of this section have been met. The licensee must submit to the Director, in its application to use § 50.61a, the adjustments made to the volumetric test data to account for NDE-related uncertainties as described in paragraph (e)(1) of this section, all information required by paragraph (e)(1)(iii) of this section, and, if applicable, analyses performed under paragraphs (e)(4), (e)(5) and (e)(6) of this section.

(3) Each licensee shall compare the projected RT_{MAX-X} values for plates, forgings, axial welds, and circumferential welds to the PTS screening criteria in Table 1 of this section, for the purpose of evaluating a reactor vessel's susceptibility to fracture due to a PTS event. If any of the projected RT_{MAX-X} values are greater than the PTS screening criteria in Table 1 of this section, then the licensee may propose the compensatory actions or plant-specific analyses as required in paragraphs (d)(3) through (d)(7) of this section, as applicable, to justify operation beyond the PTS screening criteria in Table 1 of this section.

(d) *Subsequent requirements.* Licensees who have been approved to use 10 CFR 50.61a under the requirements of paragraph (c) of this section shall comply with the requirements of this paragraph.

(1) Whenever there is a significant change in projected values of RT_{MAX-X}, so that the previous value, the current value, or both values, exceed the screening criteria before the expiration of the plant operating license; or upon the licensee's request for a change in the expiration date for operation of the facility; a re-assessment of RT_{MAX-X} values documented consistent with the requirements of paragraph (c)(1) and (c)(3) of this section must be submitted in the form of a license amendment for review and approval by the Director. If the surveillance data used to perform the re-assessment of RT_{MAX-X} values meet the requirements of paragraph (f)(6)(v) of this section, the licensee shall submit the data and the results of the analysis of the data to the Director for review and approval within one year after the capsule is withdrawn from the vessel. If the surveillance data meet the requirements of paragraph (f)(6)(vi) of this section, the licensee shall submit the data, the results of the analysis of the data, and proposed ΔT_{30} and RT_{MAX-X} values considering the surveillance data in the form of a license amendment to the Director for review and approval within two years after the capsule is withdrawn from the vessel. If the Director does not approve the assessment of RT_{MAX-X} values, then the licensee shall perform the actions required in paragraphs (d)(3) through (d)(7) of this section, as necessary, before operation beyond the PTS screening criteria in Table 1 of this section.

(2) The licensee shall verify that the requirements of paragraphs (e), (e)(1), (e)(2), and (e)(3) of this section have been met. The licensee must submit, within 120 days after completing a volumetric examination of reactor vessel beltline materials as required by ASME Code, Section XI, the adjustments made to the volumetric test data to account for NDE-related uncertainties as described in paragraph (e)(1) of this section and all information required by paragraph (e)(1)(iii) of this section in the form of a license amendment for review and approval by the Director. If a licensee is required to implement paragraphs (e)(4), (e)(5), and (e)(6) of this section, the information required in these paragraphs must be submitted in the form of a license amendment for review and approval by the Director within one year after completing a volumetric examination of reactor vessel materials as required by ASME Code, Section XI.

(3) If the value of RT_{MAX-X} is projected to exceed the PTS screening criteria, then the licensee shall implement those flux reduction programs that are reasonably practicable to avoid exceeding the PTS screening criteria. The schedule for implementation of flux reduction measures may take into account the schedule for review

and anticipated approval by the Director of detailed plant-specific analyses which demonstrate acceptable risk with RT_{MAX-X} values above the PTS screening criteria due to plant modifications, new information, or new analysis techniques.

(4) If the analysis required by paragraph (d)(3) of this section indicates that no reasonably practicable flux reduction program will prevent the RT_{MAX-X} value for one or more reactor vessel beltline materials from exceeding the PTS screening criteria, then the licensee shall perform a safety analysis to determine what, if any, modifications to equipment, systems, and operation are necessary to prevent the potential for an unacceptably high probability of failure of the reactor vessel as a result of postulated PTS events. In the analysis, the licensee may determine the properties of the reactor vessel materials based on available information, research results and plant surveillance data, and may use probabilistic fracture mechanics techniques. This analysis and the description of the modifications must be submitted to the Director in the form of a license amendment at least three years before RT_{MAX-X} is projected to exceed the PTS screening criteria.

(5) After consideration of the licensee's analyses, including effects of proposed corrective actions, if any, submitted under paragraphs (d)(3) and (d)(4) of this section, the Director may, on a case-by-case basis, approve operation of the facility with RT_{MAX-X} values in excess of the PTS screening criteria. The Director will consider factors significantly affecting the potential for failure of the reactor vessel in reaching a decision. The Director shall impose the modifications to equipment, systems and operations described to meet paragraph (d)(4) of this section.

(6) If the Director concludes, under paragraph (d)(5) of this section, that operation of the facility with RT_{MAX-X} values in excess of the PTS screening criteria cannot be approved on the basis of the licensee's analyses submitted under paragraphs (d)(3) and (d)(4) of this section, then the licensee shall request a license amendment, and receive approval by the Director, before any operation beyond the PTS screening criteria. The request must be based on modifications to equipment, systems, and operation of the facility in addition to those previously proposed in the submitted analyses that would reduce the potential for failure of the reactor vessel due to PTS events, or on further analyses based on new information or improved methodology. The licensee must show that the proposed alternatives provide reasonable assurance of adequate protection of the public health and safety.

(7) If the limiting RT_{MAX-X} value of the facility is projected to exceed the PTS screening criteria and the requirements of paragraphs (d)(3) through (d)(6) of this section cannot be satisfied, the reactor vessel beltline may be given a thermal annealing treatment under the requirements of § 50.66 to recover the fracture toughness of the material. The reactor vessel may be used only for that service period within which the predicted fracture toughness of the reactor vessel beltline materials satisfy the requirements of paragraphs (d)(1) through (d)(6) of this section, with RT_{MAX-X} values accounting for the effects of annealing and subsequent irradiation.

(e) *Examination and flaw assessment requirements*. The volumetric examination results evaluated under paragraphs (e)(1), (e)(2), and (e)(3) of this section must be acquired using procedures, equipment and personnel that have been qualified under the ASME Code, Section XI, Appendix VIII, Supplement 4 and Supplement 6, as specified in 10 CFR 50.55a(b)(2)(xv).

(1) The licensee shall verify that the flaw density and size distributions within the volume described in ASME Code, Section XI,[1] Figures IWB–2500–1 and IWB–2500–2 and limited to a depth from the clad-to-base metal interface of 1-inch or 10 percent of the vessel thickness, whichever is greater, do not exceed the limits in Tables 2 and 3 of this section based on the test results from the volumetric examination. The

[1] For forgings susceptible to underclad cracking the determination of the flaw density for that forging from the licensee's inspection shall exclude those indications identified as underclad cracks.

values in Tables 2 and 3 represent actual flaw sizes. Test results from the volumetric examination may be adjusted to account for the effects of NDE-related uncertainties. The methodology to account for NDE-related uncertainties must be based on statistical data from the qualification tests and any other tests that measure the difference between the actual flaw size and the NDE detected flaw size. Licensees who adjust their test data to account for NDE-related uncertainties to verify conformance with the values in Tables 2 and 3 shall prepare and submit the methodology used to estimate the NDE uncertainty, the statistical data used to adjust the test data and an explanation of how the data was analyzed for review and approval by the Director in accordance with paragraphs (c)(2) and (d)(2) of this section. The verification of the flaw density and size distributions shall be performed line-by-line for Tables 2 and 3. If the flaw density and size distribution exceeds the limitations specified in Tables 2 and 3 of this section, the licensee shall perform the analyses required by paragraph (e)(4) of this section. If analyses are required in accordance with paragraph (e)(4) of this section, the licensee must address the effects on through-wall crack frequency (TWCF) in accordance with paragraph (e)(5) of this section and must prepare and submit a neutron fluence map in accordance with the requirements of paragraph (e)(6) of this section.

(i) The licensee shall determine the allowable number of weld flaws in the reactor vessel beltline by multiplying the values in Table 2 of this section by the total length of the reactor vessel beltline welds that were volumetrically inspected and dividing by 1000 inches of weld length.

(ii) The licensee shall determine the allowable number of plate or forging flaws in their reactor vessel beltline by multiplying the values in Table 3 of this section by the total surface area of the reactor vessel beltline plates or forgings that were volumetrically inspected and dividing by 1000 square inches.

(iii) For each flaw detected in the inspection volume described in paragraph (e)(1) with a through-wall extent equal to or greater than 0.075 inches, the licensee shall document the dimensions of the flaw, including through-wall extent and length, whether the flaw is axial or circumferential in orientation and its location within the reactor vessel, including its azimuthal and axial positions and its depth embedded from the clad-to-base metal interface.

(2) The licensee shall identify, as part of the examination required by paragraph (c)(2) of this section and any subsequent ASME Code, Section XI ultrasonic examination of the beltline welds, any flaws within the inspection volume described in paragraph (e)(1) of this section that are equal to or greater than 0.075 inches in through-wall depth, axially-oriented, and located at the clad-to-base metal interface. The licensee shall verify that these flaws do not open to the vessel inside surface using surface or visual examination technique capable of detecting and characterizing service induced cracking of the reactor vessel cladding.

(3) The licensee shall verify, as part of the examination required by paragraph (c)(2) of this section and any subsequent ASME Code, Section XI ultrasonic examination of the beltline welds, that all flaws between the clad-to-base metal interface and three-eighths of the reactor vessel thickness from the interior surface are within the allowable values in ASME Code, Section XI, Table IWB–3510–1.

(4) The licensee shall perform analyses to demonstrate that the reactor vessel will have a TWCF of less than 1×10^{-6} per reactor year if the ASME Code, Section XI volumetric examination required by paragraph (c)(2) or (d)(2) of this section indicates any of the following:

(i) The flaw density and size in the inspection volume described in paragraph (e)(1) exceed the limits in Tables 2 or 3 of this section;

(ii) There are axial flaws that penetrate through the clad into the low alloy steel reactor vessel shell, at a depth equal to or greater than 0.075 inches in through-wall extent from the clad-to-base metal interface; or

(iii) Any flaws between the clad-to-base metal interface and three-eighths[2] of the vessel thickness exceed the size allowable in ASME Code, Section XI, Table IWB–3510–1.

(5) The analyses required by paragraph (e)(4) of this section must address the effects on TWCF of the known sizes and locations of all flaws detected by the ASME Code, Section XI, Appendix VIII, Supplement 4 and Supplement 6 ultrasonic examination out to three-eights of the vessel thickness from the inner surface, and may also take into account other reactor vessel-specific information, including fracture toughness information.

(6) For all flaw assessments performed in accordance with paragraph (e)(4) of this section, the licensee shall prepare and submit a neutron fluence map, projected to the date of license expiration, for the reactor vessel beltline clad-to-base metal interface and indexed in a manner that allows the determination of the neutron fluence at the location of the detected flaws.

(f) *Calculation of RT_{MAX-X} values.* Each licensee shall calculate RT_{MAX-X} values for each reactor vessel beltline material using φt. The neutron flux (φ[t]), must be calculated using a methodology that has been benchmarked to experimental measurements and with quantified uncertainties and possible biases.[3]

(1) The values of RT_{MAX-AW}, RT_{MAX-PL}, RT_{MAX-FO}, and RT_{MAX-CW} must be determined using Equations 1 through 4 of this section. When calculating RT_{MAX-AW} using Equation 1, RT_{MAX-AW} is the maximum value of ($RT_{NDT(U)}$ + ΔT_{30}) for the weld and for the adjoining plates. When calculating RT_{MAX-CW} using Equation 4, RT_{MAX-CW} is the maximum value of ($RT_{NDT(U)}$ + ΔT_{30}) for the circumferential weld and for the adjoining plates or forgings.

(2) The values of ΔT_{30} must be determined using Equations 5, 6 and 7 of this section, unless the conditions specified in paragraph (f)(6)(v) of this section are not met, for each axial weld, plate, forging, and circumferential weld. The ΔT_{30} value for each axial weld calculated as specified by Equation 1 of this section must be calculated for the maximum fluence ($\varphi t_{AXIAL-WELD}$) occurring along a particular axial weld at the clad-to-base metal interface. The ΔT_{30} value for each plate calculated as specified by Equation 1 of this section must also be calculated using the same value of $\varphi t_{AXIAL-WELD}$ used for the axial weld. The ΔT_{30} values in Equation 1 shall be calculated for the weld itself and each adjoining plate. The ΔT_{30} value for each plate or forging calculated as specified by Equations 2 and 3 of this section must be calculated for the maximum fluence (φt_{MAX}) occurring at the clad-to-base metal interface over the entire area of each plate or forging. In Equation 4, the fluence ($\varphi t_{WELD-CIRC}$) value used for calculating the plate, forging, and circumferential weld ΔT_{30} value is the maximum fluence occurring for each material along the circumferential weld at the clad-to-base metal interface. The ΔT_{30} values in Equation 4 shall be calculated for the circumferential weld and for the adjoining plates or forgings. If the conditions specified in paragraph (f)(6)(v) of this section are not met, licensees must propose ΔT_{30} and RT_{MAX-X} values in accordance with paragraph (f)(6)(vi) of this section.

(3) The values of Cu, Mn, P, and Ni in Equations 6 and 7 of this section must represent the best estimate values for the material. For a plate or forging, the best estimate value is normally the mean of the measured values for that plate or forging. For a weld, the best estimate value is normally the mean of the measured values for a weld deposit made using the same weld wire heat number as the critical vessel weld. If these values are not available, either the upper limiting values given in the material specifications to which the vessel material was fabricated, or conservative estimates (*i.e.*, mean plus one standard deviation) based on generic data[4] as shown in Table 4 of this section for P and Mn, must be used.

[2] Because flaws greater than three-eights of the vessel wall thickness from the inside surface do not contribute to TWCF, flaws greater than three-eights of the vessel wall thickness from the inside surface need not be analyzed for their contribution to PTS.

[3] Regulatory Guide 1.190 dated March 2001, establishes acceptable methods for determining neutron flux.

[4] Data from reactor vessels fabricated to the same material specification in the same

Continued

(4) The values of $RT_{NDT(U)}$ must be evaluated according to the procedures in the ASME Code, Section III, paragraph NB–2331. If any other method is used for this evaluation, the licensee shall submit the proposed method for review and approval by the Director along with the calculation of RT_{MAX-X} values required in paragraph (c)(1) of this section.

(i) If a measured value of $RT_{NDT(U)}$ is not available, a generic mean value of $RT_{NDT(U)}$ for the class[5] of material must be used if there are sufficient test results to establish a mean.

(ii) The following generic mean values of $RT_{NDT(U)}$ must be used unless justification for different values is provided: 0 °F for welds made with Linde 80 weld flux; and −56 °F for welds made with Linde 0091, 1092, and 124 and ARCOS B–5 weld fluxes.

(5) The value of T_C in Equation 6 of this section must represent the time-weighted average of the reactor cold leg temperature under normal operating full power conditions from the beginning of full power operation through the end of licensed operation.

(6) The licensee shall verify that an appropriate RT_{MAX-X} value has been calculated for each reactor vessel beltline material by considering plant-specific information that could affect the use of the model (*i.e.*, Equations 5, 6 and 7) of this section for the determination of a material's ΔT_{30} value.

(i) The licensee shall evaluate the results from a plant-specific or integrated surveillance program if the surveillance data satisfy the criteria described in paragraphs (f)(6)(i)(A) and (f)(6)(i)(B) of this section:

(A) The surveillance material must be a heat-specific match for one or more of the materials for which RT_{MAX-X} is being calculated. The 30-foot-pound transition temperature must be determined as specified by the requirements of 10 CFR part 50, Appendix H.

(B) If three or more surveillance data points measured at three or more different neutron fluences exist for a specific material, the licensee shall determine if the surveillance data show a significantly different trend than the embrittlement model predicts. This must be achieved by evaluating the surveillance data for consistency with the embrittlement model by following the procedures specified by paragraphs (f)(6)(ii), (f)(6)(iii), and (f)(6)(iv) of this section. If fewer than three surveillance data points exist for a specific material, then the embrittlement model must be used without performing the consistency check.

(ii) The licensee shall estimate the mean deviation from the embrittlement model for the specific data set (*i.e.*, a group of surveillance data points representative of a given material). The mean deviation from the embrittlement model for a given data set must be calculated using Equations 8 and 9 of this section. The mean deviation for the data set must be compared to the maximum heat-average residual given in Table 5 or derived using Equation 10 of this section. The maximum heat-average residual is based on the material group into which the surveillance material falls and the number of surveillance data points. For surveillance data sets with greater than 8 data points, the maximum credible heat-average residual must be calculated using Equation 10 of this section. The value of σ used in Equation 10 of this section must be obtained from Table 5 of this section.

(iii) The licensee shall estimate the slope of the embrittlement model residuals (estimated using Equation 8) plotted as a function of the base 10 logarithm of neutron fluence for the specific data set. The licensee shall estimate the T-statistic for this slope (T_{SURV}) using Equation 11 and compare this value to the maximum permissible T-statistic (T_{MAX}) in Table 6. For surveillance data sets with greater than 15 data points, the T_{MAX} value must be calculated using Student's T distribution with a significance level (α) of 1 percent for a one-tailed test.

(iv) The licensee shall estimate the two largest positive deviations (*i.e.*, outliers) from the embrittlement model for the specific data set using Equations 8 and 12. The licensee shall

shop as the vessel in question and in the same time is an example of "generic data."

[5] The class of material for estimating $RT_{NDT(U)}$ must be determined by the type of welding flux (Linde 80, or other) for welds or by the material specification for base metal.

compare the largest normalized residual (r^*) to the appropriate allowable value from the third column in Table 7 and the second largest normalized residual to the appropriate allowable value from the second column in Table 7.

(v) The ΔT_{30} value must be determined using Equations 5, 6, and 7 of this section if all three of the following criteria are satisfied:

(A) The mean deviation from the embrittlement model for the data set is equal to or less than the value in Table 5 or the value derived using Equation 10 of this section;

(B) The T-statistic for the slope (T_{SURV}) estimated using Equation 11 is equal to or less than the Maximum permissible T-statistic (T_{MAX}) in Table 6; and

(C) The largest normalized residual value is equal to or less than the appropriate allowable value from the third column in Table 7 and the second largest normalized residual value is equal to or less than the appropriate allowable value from the second column in Table 7. If any of these criteria is not satisfied, the licensee must propose ΔT_{30} and RT_{MAX-X} values in accordance with paragraph (f)(6)(vi) of this section.

(vi) If any of the criteria described in paragraph (f)(6)(v) of this section are not satisfied, the licensee shall review the data base for that heat in detail, including all parameters used in Equations 5, 6, and 7 of this section and the data used to determine the baseline Charpy V-notch curve for the material in an unirradiated condition. The licensee shall submit an evaluation of the surveillance data to the NRC and shall propose ΔT_{30} and RT_{MAX-X} values, considering their plant-specific surveillance data, to be used for evaluation relative to the acceptance criteria of this rule. These evaluations must be submitted for review and approval by the Director in the form of a license amendment in accordance with the requirements of paragraphs (c)(1) and (d)(1) of this section.

(7) The licensee shall report any information that significantly influences the RT_{MAX-X} value to the Director in accordance with the requirements of paragraphs (c)(1) and (d)(1) of this section.

(g) *Equations and variables used in this section.*

$$\text{Equation 1: } RT_{MAX-AW} = MAX\left\{\left[RT_{NDT(U)-plate} + \Delta T_{30-plate}\right], \left[RT_{NDT(U)-axial\ weld} + \Delta T_{30-axial\ weld}\right]\right\}$$

$$\text{Equation 2: } RT_{MAX-PL} = RT_{NDT(U)-plate} + \Delta T_{30-plate}$$

$$\text{Equation 3: } RT_{MAX-FO} = RT_{NDT(U)-forging} + \Delta T_{30-forging}$$

$$\text{Equation 4: } RT_{MAX-CW} = MAX\left\{\left[RT_{NDT(U)-plate} + \Delta T_{30-plate}\right], \left[RT_{NDT(U)-circweld} + \Delta T_{30-circweld}\right], \left[RT_{NDT(U)-forging} + \Delta T_{30-forging}\right]\right\}$$

$$\text{Equation 5: } \Delta T_{30} = MD + CRP$$

$$\text{Equation 6: } MD = A \times (1 - 0.001718 \times T_C) \times (1 + 6.13 \times P \times Mn^{2.471}) \times \varphi t_e^{0.5}$$

$$\text{Equation 7: } CRP = B \times (1 + 3.77 \times Ni^{1.191}) \times f(Cu_e, P) \times g(Cu_e, Ni, \varphi t_e)$$

Where:

P [wt-&%] = phosphorus content
Mn [wt-%] = manganese content
Ni [wt-%] = nickel content
Cu [wt-%] = copper content
$A = 1.140 \times 10^{-7}$ for forgings
$A = 1.561 \times 10^{-7}$ for plates
$A = 1.417 \times 10^{-7}$ for welds
B = 102.3 for forgings
B = 102.5 for plates in non-Combustion Engineering manufactured vessels
B = 135.2 for plates in Combustion Engineering vessels
B = 155.0 for welds

$\varphi t_e = \varphi t$ for $\varphi \geq 4.39 \times 10^{10}$ n/cm²/sec
$\varphi t_e = \varphi t \times (4.39 \times 10^{10}/\varphi)^{0.2595}$ for $\varphi < 4.39 \times 10^{10}$ n/cm²/sec

Where:

φ [n/cm²/sec] = average neutron flux
t [sec] = time that the reactor has been in full power operation

φt [n/cm²] = $\varphi \times t$

$f(Cu_e,P) = 0$ for $Cu \leq 0.072$
$f(Cu_e,P) = [Cu_e - 0.072]^{0.668}$ for $Cu > 0.072$ and $P \leq 0.008$
$f(Cu_e,P) = [Cu_e - 0.072 + 1.359 \times (P - 0.008)]^{0.668}$ for $Cu > 0.072$ and $P > 0.008$

Where:

$Cu_e = 0$ for $Cu \leq 0.072$
Cu_e = MIN (Cu, maximum Cu_e) for $Cu > 0.072$
maximum Cu_e = 0.243 for Linde 80 welds
maximum Cu_e = 0.301 for all other materials

$g(Cu_e,Ni,\varphi t_e) = 0.5 + (0.5 \times \tanh\{[\log_{10}(\varphi t_e) + (1.1390 \times Cu_e) - (0.448 \times Ni) - 18.120]/0.629\}$

Equation 8: Residual (r) = measured ΔT_{30} − predicted ΔT_{30} (by Equations 5, 6 and 7)

$$\text{Equation 9: Mean deviation for a data set of n data points} = (1/n) \times \sum_{i=1}^{n} r_i$$

Equation 10: Maximum credible heat-average residual = $2.33\sigma/n^{0.5}$

Where:

n = number of surveillance data points (sample size) in the specific data set
σ = standard deviation of the residuals about the model for a relevant material group given in Table 5.

$$\text{Equation 11: } T_{SURV} = \frac{m}{se(m)}$$

Where:

m is the slope of a plot of all of the r values (estimated using Equation 8) versus the base 10 logarithm of the neutron fluence for each r value. The slope shall be estimated using the method of least squares.

se(m) is the least squares estimate of the standard-error associated with the estimated slope value *m*.

$$\text{Equation 12: } r^* = \frac{r}{\sigma}$$

Where:

r is defined using Equation 8 and σ is given in Table 5

TABLE 1—PTS SCREENING CRITERIA

Product form and RT_{MAX-X} values	RT_{MAX-X} limits [°F] for different vessel wall thicknesses[6] (T_{WALL})		
	$T_{WALL} \leq 9.5$ in.	9.5 in. $< T_{WALL} \leq 10.5$ in.	10.5 in. $< T_{WALL} \leq 11.5$ in.
Axial Weld—RT_{MAX-AW}	269	230	222
Plate—RT_{MAX-PL}	356	305	293
Forging without underclad cracks—RT_{MAX-FO}[7]	356	305	293
Axial Weld and Plate—$RT_{MAX-AW} + RT_{MAX-PL}$	538	476	445
Circumferential Weld—RT_{MAX-CW}[8]	312	277	269
Forging with underclad cracks—RT_{MAX-FO}[9]	246	241	239

[6] Wall thickness is the beltline wall thickness including the clad thickness.

[7] Forgings without underclad cracks apply to forgings for which no underclad cracks have been detected and that were fabricated in accordance with Regulatory Guide 1.43.

[8] RT_{PTS} limits contribute 1×10^{-8} per reactor year to the reactor vessel TWCF.

[9] Forgings with underclad cracks apply to forgings that have detected underclad cracking or were not fabricated in accordance with Regulatory Guide 1.43.

TABLE 2—ALLOWABLE NUMBER OF FLAWS IN WELDS

Through-wall extent, TWE [in.]		Maximum number of flaws per 1,000-inches of weld length in the inspection volume that are greater than or equal to TWE_{MIN} and less than TWE_{MAX}
TWE_{MIN}	TWE_{MAX}	
0	0.075	No Limit.
0.075	0.475	166.70.
0.125	0.175	90.80.
0.175	0.475	22.82.
0.225	0.475	8.66.
0.275	0.475	4.01.
0.325	0.475	3.01.
0.375	0.475	1.49.
0.425	0.475	1.00.
0.475	Infinite	0.00.

TABLE 3—ALLOWABLE NUMBER OF FLAWS IN PLATES AND FORGINGS

Through-wall extent, TWE [in.]		Maximum number of flaws per 1,000 square-inches of inside surface area in the inspection volume that are greater than or equal to TWE_{MIN} and less than TWE_{MAX}. This flaw density does not include underclad cracks in forgings
TWE_{MIN}	TWE_{MAX}	
0	0.075	No Limit.
0.075	0.375	8.05.
0.125	0.375	3.15.
0.175	0.375	0.85.
0.225	0.375	0.29.
0.275	0.375	0.08.
0.325	0.375	0.01.
0.375	Infinite	0.00.

TABLE 4—CONSERVATIVE ESTIMATES FOR CHEMICAL ELEMENT WEIGHT PERCENTAGES

Materials	P	Mn
Plates	0.014	1.45
Forgings	0.016	1.11
Welds	0.019	1.63

TABLE 5—MAXIMUM HEAT-AVERAGE RESIDUAL [°F] FOR RELEVANT MATERIAL GROUPS BY NUMBER OF AVAILABLE DATA POINTS (SIGNIFICANCE LEVEL = 1%)

Material group	σ [°F]	Number of available data points					
		3	4	5	6	7	8
Welds, for Cu >0.072	26.4	35.5	30.8	27.5	25.1	23.2	21.7
Plates, for Cu >0.072	21.2	28.5	24.7	22.1	20.2	18.7	17.5
Forgings, for Cu >0.072	19.6	26.4	22.8	20.4	18.6	17.3	16.1
Weld, Plate or Forging, for Cu ≤0.072	18.6	25.0	21.7	19.4	17.7	16.4	15.3

TABLE 6—T_{MAX} VALUES FOR THE SLOPE DEVIATION TEST (SIGNIFICANCE LEVEL = 1%)

Number of available data points (n)	T_{MAX}
3	31.82
4	6.96
5	4.54
6	3.75
7	3.36
8	3.14
9	3.00
10	2.90
11	2.82
12	2.76
13	2.72
14	2.68
15	2.65

TABLE 7—THRESHOLD VALUES FOR THE OUTLIER DEVIATION TEST (SIGNIFICANCE LEVEL = 1%)

Number of available data points (n)	Second largest allowable normalized residual value (r^*)	Largest allowable normalized residual value (r^*)
3	1.55	2.71
4	1.73	2.81
5	1.84	2.88
6	1.93	2.93
7	2.00	2.98
8	2.05	3.02
9	2.11	3.06
10	2.16	3.09
11	2.19	3.12
12	2.23	3.14
13	2.26	3.17
14	2.29	3.19
15	2.32	3.21

[75 FR 23, Jan. 4, 2010, as amended at 75 FR 5495, Feb. 3, 2010; 75 FR 10411, Mar. 8, 2010; 75 FR 72653, Nov. 26, 2010]

§ 50.62 Requirements for reduction of risk from anticipated transients without scram (ATWS) events for light-water-cooled nuclear power plants.

(a) *Applicability.* The requirements of this section apply to all commercial light-water-cooled nuclear power plants, other than nuclear power reactor facilities for which the certifications required under § 50.82(a)(1) have been submitted.

(b) *Definition.* For purposes of this section, *Anticipated Transient Without Scram* (ATWS) means an anticipated operational occurrence as defined in appendix A of this part followed by the failure of the reactor trip portion of the protection system specified in General Design Criterion 20 of appendix A of this part.

(c) *Requirements.* (1) Each pressurized water reactor must have equipment from sensor output to final actuation device, that is diverse from the reactor trip system, to automatically initiate the auxiliary (or emergency) feedwater system and initiate a turbine trip under conditions indicative of an ATWS. This equipment must be designed to perform its function in a reliable manner and be independent (from sensor output to the final actuation device) from the existing reactor trip system.

(2) Each pressurized water reactor manufactured by Combustion Engineering or by Babcock and Wilcox must have a diverse scram system from the sensor output to interruption of power to the control rods. This scram system must be designed to perform its function in a reliable manner and be independent from the existing reactor trip system (from sensor output to interruption of power to the control rods).

(3) Each boiling water reactor must have an alternate rod injection (ARI) system that is diverse (from the reactor trip system) from sensor output to the final actuation device. The ARI system must have redundant scram air header exhaust valves. The ARI must be designed to perform its function in a reliable manner and be independent (from the existing reactor trip system) from sensor output to the final actuation device.

(4) Each boiling water reactor must have a standby liquid control system (SLCS) with the capability of injecting into the reactor pressure vessel a borated water solution at such a flow rate, level of boron concentration and boron-10 isotope enrichment, and accounting for reactor pressure vessel volume, that the resulting reactivity control is at least equivalent to that resulting from injection of 86 gallons per minute of 13 weight percent sodium pentaborate decahydrate solution at the natural boron-10 isotope abundance into a 251-inch inside diameter reactor pressure vessel for a given core design. The SLCS and its injection location must be designed to perform its function in a reliable manner. The SLCS initiation must be automatic and must be designed to perform its function in a reliable manner for plants granted a construction permit after July 26, 1984, and for plants granted a construction permit prior to July 26, 1984, that have already been designed and built to include this feature.

(5) Each boiling water reactor must have equipment to trip the reactor coolant recirculating pumps automatically under conditions indicative of an ATWS. This equipment must be designed to perform its function in a reliable manner.

(6) Information sufficient to demonstrate to the Commission the adequacy of items in paragraphs (c)(1) through (c)(5) of this section shall be submitted to the Commission as specified in § 50.4.

(d) *Implementation.* For each light water-cooled nuclear power plant operating license issued before September 27, 2007, by 180 days after the issuance of the QA guidance for non-safety related components, each licensee shall develop and submit to the Commission, as specified in § 50.4, a proposed schedule for meeting the requirements of paragraphs (c)(1) through (c)(5) of this section. Each shall include an explanation of the schedule along with a justification if the schedule calls for final implementation later than the second refueling outage after July 26, 1984, or the date of issuance of a license authorizing operation above 5 percent of full power. A final schedule shall then be mutually agreed upon by the Commission and licensee. For each light-water-cooled nuclear power plant operating license application submitted after September 27, 2007, the applicant shall submit information in its final safety analysis report demonstrating how it will comply with paragraphs (c)(1) through (c)(5) of this section.

[49 FR 26044, June 26, 1984; 49 FR 27736, July 6, 1984, as amended at 51 FR 40310, Nov. 6, 1986; 54 FR 13362, Apr. 3, 1989; 61 FR 39301, July 29, 1996; 72 FR 49500, Aug. 28, 2007]

§ 50.63 Loss of all alternating current power.

(a) *Requirements.* (1) Each light-water-cooled nuclear power plant licensed to operate under this part, each light-water-cooled nuclear power plant licensed under subpart C of 10 CFR part 52 after the Commission makes the finding under § 52.103(g) of this chapter, and each design for a light-water-cooled nuclear power plant approved under a standard design approval, standard design certification, and manufacturing license under part 52 of this chapter must be able to withstand for a specified duration and recover from a station blackout as defined in § 50.2. The specified station blackout duration shall be based on the following factors:

(i) The redundancy of the onsite emergency ac power sources;

(ii) The reliability of the onsite emergency ac power sources;

(iii) The expected frequency of loss of offsite power; and

(iv) The probable time needed to restore offsite power.

(2) The reactor core and associated coolant, control, and protection systems, including station batteries and any other necessary support systems, must provide sufficient capacity and capability to ensure that the core is cooled and appropriate containment integrity is maintained in the event of a station blackout for the specified duration. The capability for coping with a station blackout of specified duration shall be determined by an appropriate coping analysis. Licensees are expected to have the baseline assumptions, analyses, and related information used in their coping evaluations available for NRC review.

(b) *Limitation of scope.* Paragraph (c) of this section does not apply to those plants licensed to operate prior to *July 21, 1988*, if the capability to withstand station blackout was specifically addressed in the operating license proceeding and was explicitly approved by the NRC.

(c) *Implementation*—(1) *Information Submittal.* For each light-water-cooled nuclear power plant licensed to operate on or before July 21, 1988, the licensee shall submit the information defined below to the Director of the Office of Nuclear Reactor Regulation by April 17, 1989. For each light-water-cooled nuclear power plant licensed to operate after July 21, 1988, but before September 27, 2007, the licensee shall submit the information defined in this section to the Director of the Office of Nuclear Reactor Regulation, by 270 days after the date of license issuance. For each light-water-cooled nuclear power plant operating license application submitted after September 27, 2007, the applicant shall submit the information defined below in its final safety analysis report.

(i) A proposed station blackout duration to be used in determining compliance with paragraph (a) of this section, including a justification for the selection based on the four factors identified in paragraph (a) of this section;

(ii) A description of the procedures that will be implemented for station blackout events for the duration determined in paragraph (c)(1)(i) of this section and for recovery therefrom; and

(iii) A list of modifications to equipment and associated procedures, if any, necessary to meet the requirements of paragraph (a) of this section, for the specified station blackout duration determined in paragraph (c)(1)(i) of this section, and a proposed schedule for implementing the stated modifications.

(2) *Alternate ac source:* The alternate ac power source(s), as defined in § 50.2, will constitute acceptable capability to withstand station blackout provided an analysis is performed which demonstrates that the plant has this capability from onset of the station blackout until the alternate ac source(s) and required shutdown equipment are started and lined up to operate. The

time required for startup and alignment of the alternate ac power source(s) and this equipment shall be demonstrated by test. Alternate ac source(s) serving a multiple unit site where onsite emergency ac sources are not shared between units must have, as a minimum, the capacity and capability for coping with a station blackout in any of the units. At sites where onsite emergency ac sources are shared between units, the alternate ac source(s) must have the capacity and capability as required to ensure that all units can be brought to and maintained in safe shutdown (non-DBA) as defined in § 50.2. If the alternate ac source(s) meets the above requirements and can be demonstrated by test to be available to power the shutdown buses within 10 minutes of the onset of station blackout, then no coping analysis is required.

(3) *Regulatory Assessment:* After consideration of the information submitted in accordance with paragraph (c)(1) of this section, the Director, Office of Nuclear Reactor Regulation, will notify the licensee of the Director's conclusions regarding the adequacy of the proposed specified station blackout duration, the proposed equipment modifications and procedures, and the proposed schedule for implementing the procedures and modifications for compliance with paragraph (a) this section.

(4) *Implementation Schedule:* For each light-water-cooled nuclear power plant licensed to operate on or before June 21, 1988, the licensee shall, within 30 days of the notification provided in accordance with paragraph (c)(3) of this section, submit to the Director of the Office of Nuclear Reactor Regulation a schedule commitment for implementing any equipment and associated procedure modifications necessary to meet the requirements of paragraph (a) of this section. This submittal must include an explanation of the schedule and a justification if the schedule does not provide for completion of the modifications within two years of the notification provided in accordance with paragraph (c)(3) of this section. A final schedule for implementing modifications necessary to comply with the requirements of paragraph (a) of this section will be established by the NRC staff in consultation and coordination with the affected licensee.

[53 FR 23215, June 21, 1988, as amended at 63 FR 50480, Sept. 22, 1998; 72 FR 49501, Aug. 28, 2007]

§ 50.64 Limitations on the use of highly enriched uranium (HEU) in domestic non-power reactors.

(a) *Applicability.* The requirements of this section apply to all non-power reactors.

(b) *Requirements.* (1) The Commission will not issue a construction permit after March 27, 1986 for a non-power reactor where the applicant proposes to use highly enriched uranium (HEU) fuel, unless the applicant demonstrates that the proposed reactor will have a unique purpose as defined in § 50.2.

(2) Unless the Commission has determined, based on a request submitted in accordance with paragraph (c)(1) of this section, that the non-power reactor has a unique purpose, each licensee authorized to possess and use HEU fuel in connection with the reactor's operation shall:

(i) Not initiate acquisition of additional HEU fuel, if low enriched uranium (LEU) fuel acceptable to the Commission for that reactor is available when it proposes that acquisition; and

(ii) Replace all HEU fuel in its possession with available LEU fuel acceptable to the Commission for that reactor, in accordance with a schedule determined pursuant to paragraph (c)(2) of this section.

(3) If not required by paragraphs (b)(1) and (2) of this section to use LEU fuel, the applicant or licensee must use HEU fuel of enrichment as close to 20% as is available and acceptable to the Commisson.

(c) *Implementation.* (1) Any request by a licensee for a determination that a non-power reactor has a unique purpose as defined in § 50.2 should be submitted with supporting documentation to the Director of the Office of Nuclear Reactor Regulation, U.S. Nuclear Regulatory Commission, Washington, DC 20555, by September 29, 1986.

(2) (i) By March 27, 1987 and at 12-month intervals thereafter, each licensee of a non-power reactor authorized to possess and use HEU fuel shall develop and submit to the Director of the Office of Nuclear Reactor Regulation a written proposal for meeting the requirements of paragraph (b) (2) or (3) of this section. The licensee shall include in the proposal a certification that Federal Government funding for conversion is available through the Department of Energy (DOE) or other appropriate Federal Agency. The licensee shall also include in the proposal a schedule for conversion, based upon availability of replacement fuel acceptable to the Commisson for that reactor and upon consideration of other factors such as the availability of shipping casks, implementation of arrangements for the available financial support, and reactor usage.

(ii) If Federal Government funding for conversion cannot be certified, the proposal's contents may be limited to a statement of this fact. If a statement of non-availability of Federal Government funding for conversion is submitted by a licensee, then it shall be required to resubmit a proposal for meeting the requirements of paragraph (b) (2) or (3) of this section at 12-month intervals.

(iii) The proposal shall include, to the extent required to effect the conversion, all necessary changes in the license, facility, or procedures. Supporting safety analyses should be provided so as to meet the schedule established for conversion. As long as Federal Government funding for conversion is not available, the resubmittal may be a reiteration of the original proposal. The Director of the Office of Nuclear Reactor Regulation shall review the proposal and confirm the status of Federal Government funding for conversion and, if a schedule for conversion has been submitted by the licensee, will then determine a final schedule.

(3) After review of the safety analysis required by paragraph (c)(2), the Director of the Office of Nuclear Reactor Regulation will issue an appropriate enforcement order directing both the conversion and, to the extent consistent with protection of the public health and safety, any necessary changes to the license, facility, or procedures.

[51 FR 6519, Feb. 25, 1986]

§ 50.65 Requirements for monitoring the effectiveness of maintenance at nuclear power plants.

The requirements of this section are applicable during all conditions of plant operation, including normal shutdown operations.

(a)(1) Each holder of an operating license for a nuclear power plant under this part and each holder of a combined license under part 52 of this chapter after the Commission makes the finding under § 52.103(g) of this chapter, shall monitor the performance or condition of structures, systems, or components, against licensee-established goals, in a manner sufficient to provide reasonable assurance that these structures, systems, and components, as defined in paragraph (b) of this section, are capable of fulfilling their intended functions. These goals shall be established commensurate with safety and, where practical, take into account industry-wide operating experience. When the performance or condition of a structure, system, or component does not meet established goals, appropriate corrective action shall be taken. For a nuclear power plant for which the licensee has submitted the certifications specified in § 50.82(a)(1) or 52.110(a)(1) of this chapter, as applicable, this section shall only apply to the extent that the licensee shall monitor the performance or condition of all structures, systems, or components associated with the storage, control, and maintenance of spent fuel in a safe condition, in a manner sufficient to provide reasonable assurance that these structures, systems, and components are capable of fulfilling their intended functions.

(2) Monitoring as specified in paragraph (a)(1) of this section is not required where it has been demonstrated that the performance or condition of a structure, system, or component is being effectively controlled through the performance of appropriate preventive maintenance, such that the structure, system, or component remains capable of performing its intended function.

(3) Performance and condition monitoring activities and associated goals and preventive maintenance activities shall be evaluated at least every refueling cycle provided the interval between evaluations does not exceed 24 months. The evaluations shall take into account, where practical, industry-wide operating experience. Adjustments shall be made where necessary to ensure that the objective of preventing failures of structures, systems, and components through maintenance is appropriately balanced against the objective of minimizing unavailability of structures, systems, and components due to monitoring or preventive maintenance.

(4) Before performing maintenance activities (including but not limited to surveillance, post-maintenance testing, and corrective and preventive maintenance), the licensee shall assess and manage the increase in risk that may result from the proposed maintenance activities. The scope of the assessment may be limited to structures, systems, and components that a risk-informed evaluation process has shown to be significant to public health and safety.

(b) The scope of the monitoring program specified in paragraph (a)(1) of this section shall include safety related and nonsafety related structures, systems, and components, as follows:

(1) Safety-related structures, systems and components that are relied upon to remain functional during and following design basis events to ensure the integrity of the reactor coolant pressure boundary, the capability to shut down the reactor and maintain it in a safe shutdown condition, or the capability to prevent or mitigate the consequences of accidents that could result in potential offsite exposure comparable to the guidelines in §50.34(a)(1), §50.67(b)(2), or §100.11 of this chapter, as applicable.

(2) Nonsafety related structures, systems, or components:

(i) That are relied upon to mitigate accidents or transients or are used in plant emergency operating procedures (EOPs); or

(ii) Whose failure could prevent safety-related structures, systems, and components from fulfilling their safety-related function; or

(iii) Whose failure could cause a reactor scram or actuation of a safety-related system.

(c) The requirements of this section shall be implemented by each licensee no later than July 10, 1996.

[56 FR 31324, July 10, 1991, as amended at 58 FR 33996, June 23, 1993; 61 FR 39301, July 29, 1996; 61 FR 65173, Dec. 11, 1996; 62 FR 47271, Sept. 8, 1997; 62 FR 59276, Nov. 3, 1997; 64 FR 38557, July 19, 1999; 64 FR 72001, Dec. 23, 1999; 72 FR 49501, Aug. 28, 2007]

EFFECTIVE DATE NOTE: See 64 FR 38551, July 19, 1999, for effectiveness of §50.65 (a)(3) and (a)(4).

§50.66 Requirements for thermal annealing of the reactor pressure vessel.

(a) For those light water nuclear power reactors where neutron radiation has reduced the fracture toughness of the reactor vessel materials, a thermal annealing may be applied to the reactor vessel to recover the fracture toughness of the material. The use of a thermal annealing treatment is subject to the requirements in this section. A report describing the licensee's plan for conducting the thermal annealing must be submitted in accordance with §50.4 at least three years prior to the date at which the limiting fracture toughness criteria in §50.61 or appendix G to part 50 would be exceeded. Within three years of the submittal of the Thermal Annealing Report and at least thirty days prior to the start of the thermal annealing, the NRC will review the Thermal Annealing Report and make available the results of its evaluation at the NRC Web site, *http://www.nrc.gov*. The licensee may begin the thermal anneal after:

(1) Submitting the Thermal Annealing Report required by paragraph (b) of this section;

(2) The NRC makes available the results of its evaluation of the Thermal Annealing Report at the NRC Web site, *http://www.nrc.gov;* and

(3) The requirements of paragraph (f)(1) of this section have been satisfied.

(b) *Thermal Annealing Report.* The Thermal Annealing Report must include: a Thermal Annealing Operating Plan; a Requalification Inspection and Test Program; a Fracture Toughness

Recovery and Reembrittlement Trend Assurance Program; and an Identification of Changes Requiring a License Amendment.

(1) *Thermal Annealing Operating Plan.* The thermal annealing operating plan must include:

(i) A detailed description of the pressure vessel and all structures and components that are expected to experience significant thermal or stress effects during the thermal annealing operation;

(ii) An evaluation of the effects of mechanical and thermal stresses and temperatures on the vessel, containment, biological shield, attached piping and appurtenances, and adjacent equipment and components to demonstrate that operability of the reactor will not be detrimentally affected. This evaluation must include:

(A) Detailed thermal and structural analyses to establish the time and temperature profile of the annealing operation. These analyses must include heatup and cooldown rates, and must demonstrate that localized temperatures, thermal stress gradients, and subsequent residual stresses will not result in unacceptable dimensional changes or distortions in the vessel, attached piping and appurtenances, and that the thermal annealing cycle will not result in unacceptable degradation of the fatigue life of these components.

(B) The effects of localized high temperatures on degradation of the concrete adjacent to the vessel and changes in thermal and mechanical properties, if any, of the reactor vessel insulation, and on detrimental effects, if any, on containment and the biological shield. If the design temperature limitations for the adjacent concrete structure are to be exceeded during the thermal annealing operation, an acceptable maximum temperature for the concrete must be established for the annealing operation using appropriate test data.

(iii) The methods, including heat source, instrumentation and procedures proposed for performing the thermal annealing. This shall include any special precautions necessary to minimize occupational exposure, in accordance with the As Low As Reasonably Achievable (ALARA) principle and the provisions of § 20.1206.

(iv) The proposed thermal annealing operating parameters, including bounding conditions for temperatures and times, and heatup and cooldown schedules.

(A) The thermal annealing time and temperature parameters selected must be based on projecting sufficient recovery of fracture toughness, using the procedures of paragraph (e) of this section, to satisfy the requirements of § 50.60 and § 50.61 for the proposed period of operation addressed in the application.

(B) The time and temperature parameters evaluated as part of the thermal annealing operating plan, and supported by the evaluation results of paragraph (b)(1)(ii) of this section, represent the bounding times and temperatures for the thermal annealing operation. If these bounding conditions for times and temperatures are violated during the thermal annealing operation, then the annealing operation is considered not in accordance with the Thermal Annealing Operating Plan, as required by paragraph (c)(1) of this section, and the licensee must comply with paragraph (c)(2) of this section.

(2) *Requalification Inspection and Test Program.* The inspection and test program to requalify the annealed reactor vessel must include the detailed monitoring, inspections, and tests proposed to demonstrate that the limitations on temperatures, times and temperature profiles, and stresses evaluated for the proposed thermal annealing conditions of paragraph (b)(1)(iv) of this section have not been exceeded, and to determine the thermal annealing time and temperature to be used in quantifying the fracture toughness recovery. The requalification inspection and test program must demonstrate that the thermal annealing operation has not degraded the reactor vessel, attached piping or appurtenances, or the adjacent concrete structures to a degree that could affect the safe operation of the reactor.

(3) *Fracture Toughness Recovery and Reembrittlement Trend Assurance Program.* The percent recovery of RT_{NDT} and Charpy upper-shelf energy due to

the thermal annealing treatment must be determined based on the time and temperature of the actual vessel thermal anneal. The recovery of RT_{NDT} and Charpy upper-shelf energy provide the basis for establishing the post-anneal RT_{NDT} and Charpy upper-shelf energy for each vessel material. Changes in the RT_{NDT} and Charpy upper-shelf energy with subsequent plant operation must be determined using the post-anneal values of these parameters in conjunction with the projected reembrittlement trend determined in accordance with paragraph (b)(3)(ii) of this section. Recovery and reembrittlement evaluations shall include:

(i) *Recovery Evaluations.* (A) The percent recovery of both RT_{NDT} and Charpy upper-shelf energy must be determined by one of the procedures described in paragraph (e) of this section, using the proposed lower bound thermal annealing time and temperature conditions described in the operating plan.

(B) If the percent recovery is determined from testing surveillance specimens or from testing materials removed from the reactor vessel, then it shall be demonstrated that the proposed thermal annealing parameters used in the test program are equal to or bounded by those used in the vessel annealing operation.

(C) If generic computational methods are used, appropriate justification must be submitted as a part of the application.

(ii) *Reembrittlement Evaluations.* (A) The projected post-anneal reembrittlement of RT_{NDT} must be calculated using the procedures in § 50.61(c), or must be determined using the same basis as that used for the pre-anneal operating period. The projected change due to post-anneal reembrittlement for Charpy upper-shelf energy must be determined using the same basis as that used for the pre-anneal operating period.

(B) The post-anneal reembrittlement trend of both RT_{NDT} and Charpy upper-shelf energy must be estimated, and must be monitored using a surveillance program defined in the Thermal Annealing Report and which conforms to the intent of appendix H of this part, "Reactor Vessel Material Surveillance Program Requirements."

(4) *Identification of Changes Requiring a License Amendment.* Any changes to the facility as described in the final safety analysis report (as updated) which requires a license amendment pursuant to § 50.59(c)(2) of this part, and any changes to the Technical Specifications, which are necessary to either conduct the thermal annealing or to operate the nuclear power reactor following the annealing must be identified. The section shall demonstrate that the Commission's requirements continue to be complied with, and that there is reasonable assurance of adequate protection to the public health and safety following the changes.

(c) *Completion or Termination of Thermal Annealing.* (1) If the thermal annealing was completed in accordance with the Thermal Annealing Operating Plan and the Requalification Inspection and Test Program, the licensee shall so confirm in writing to the Director, Office of Nuclear Reactor Regulation. The licensee may restart its reactor after the requirements of paragraph (f)(2) of this section have been met.

(2) If the thermal annealing was completed but the annealing was not performed in accordance with the Thermal Annealing Operating Plan and the Requalification Inspection and Test Program, the licensee shall submit a summary of lack of compliance with the Thermal Annealing Operating Plan and the Requalification Inspection and Test Program and a justification for subsequent operation to the Director, Office of Nuclear Reactor Regulation. Any changes to the facility as described in the final safety analysis report (as updated) which are attributable to the noncompliances and which require a license amendment pursuant to § 50.59(c)(2) and any changes to the Technical Specifications shall also be identified.

(i) If no changes requiring a license amendment pursuant to § 50.59(c)(2) or changes to Technical Specifications are identified, the licensee may restart its reactor after the requirements of paragraph (f)(2) of this section have been met.

(ii) If any changes requiring a license amendment pursuant to § 50.59(c)(2) or changes to the Technical Specifications are identified, the licensee may not restart its reactor until approval is obtained from the Director, Office of Nuclear Reactor Regulation and the requirements of paragraph (f)(2) of this section have been met.

(3) If the thermal annealing was terminated prior to completion, the licensee shall immediately notify the NRC of the premature termination of the thermal anneal.

(i) If the partial annealing was otherwise performed in accordance with the Thermal Annealing Operating Plan and relevant portions of the Requalification Inspection and Test Program, and the licensee does not elect to take credit for any recovery, the licensee need not submit the Thermal Annealing Results Report required by paragraph (d) of this section but instead shall confirm in writing to the Director, Office of Nuclear Reactor Regulation that the partial annealing was otherwise performed in accordance with the Thermal Annealing Operating Plan and relevant portions of the Requalification Inspection and Test Program. The licensee may restart its reactor after the requirements of paragraph (f)(2) of this section have been met.

(ii) If the partial annealing was otherwise performed in accordance with the Thermal Annealing Operating Plan and relevant portions of the Requalification Inspection and Test Program, and the licensee elects to take full or partial credit for the partial annealing, the licensee shall confirm in writing to the Director, Office of Nuclear Reactor Regulation that the partial annealing was otherwise performed in compliance with the Thermal Annealing Operating Plan and relevant portions of the Requalification Inspection and Test Program. The licensee may restart its reactor after the requirements of paragraph (f)(2) of this section have been met.

(iii) If the partial annealing was not performed in accordance with the Thermal Annealing Operating Plan and the Requalification Inspection and Test Program, the licensee shall submit a summary of lack of compliance with the Thermal Annealing Operating Plan and the Requalification Inspection and Test Program and a justification for subsequent operation to the Director, Office of Nuclear Reactor Regulation. Any changes to the facility as described in the final safety analysis report (as updated) which are attributable to the noncompliances and which require a license amendment pursuant to § 50.59(c)(2) and any changes to the technical specifications which are required as a result of the noncompliances, shall also be identified.

(A) If no changes requiring a license amendment pursuant to § 50.59(c)(2) or changes to Technical Specifications are identified, the licensee may restart its reactor after the requirements of paragraph (f)(2) of this section have been met.

(B) If any changes requiring a license amendment pursuant to § 50.59(c)(2) or changes to Technical Specifications are identified, the licensee may not restart its reactor until approval is obtained from the Director, Office of Nuclear Reactor Regulation and the requirements of paragraph (f)(2) of this section have been met.

(d) *Thermal Annealing Results Report.* Every licensee that either completes a thermal annealing, or that terminates an annealing but elects to take full or partial credit for the annealing, shall provide the following information within three months of completing the thermal anneal, unless an extension is authorized by the Director, Office of Nuclear Reactor Regulation:

(1) The time and temperature profiles of the actual thermal annealing;

(2) The post-anneal RT_{NDT} and Charpy upper-shelf energy values of the reactor vessel materials for use in subsequent reactor operation;

(3) The projected post-anneal re-embrittlement trends for both RT_{NDT} and Charpy upper-shelf energy; and

(4) The projected values of RT_{PTS} and Charpy upper-shelf energy at the end of the proposed period of operation addressed in the Thermal Annealing Report.

(e) *Procedures for Determining the Recovery of Fracture Toughness.* The procedures of this paragraph must be used to determine the percent recovery of

•RT_{NDT}, R_t, and percent recovery of Charpy upper-shelf energy, R_u. In all cases, R_t and R_u may not exceed 100.

(1) For those reactors with surveillance programs which have developed credible surveillance data as defined in §50.61, percent recovery due to thermal annealing (R_t and R_u) must be evaluated by testing surveillance specimens that have been withdrawn from the surveillance program and that have been annealed under the same time and temperature conditions as those given the beltline material.

(2) Alternatively, the percent recovery due to thermal annealing (R_t and R_u) may be determined from the results of a verification test program employing materials removed from the beltline region of the reactor vessel[6] and that have been annealed under the same time and temperature conditions as those given the beltline material.

(3) Generic computational methods may be used to determine recovery if adequate justification is provided.

(f) *Public information and participation.* (1) Upon receipt of a Thermal Annealing Report, and a minimum of 30 days before the licensee starts thermal annealing, the Commission shall:

(i) Notify and solicit comments from local and State governments in the vicinity of the site where the thermal annealing will take place and any Indian Nation or other indigenous people that have treaty or statutory rights that could be affected by the thermal annealing,

(ii) Publish a notice of a public meeting in the FEDERAL REGISTER and in a forum, such as local newspapers, which is readily accessible to individuals in the vicinity of the site, to solicit comments from the public, and

(iii) Hold a public meeting on the licensee's Thermal Annealing Report.

(2) Within 15 days after the NRC's receipt of the licensee submissions required by paragraphs (c)(1), (c)(2) and (c)(3)(i) through (iii) of this section, the NRC staff shall make available at the NRC Web site, *http://www.nrc.gov,* a summary of its inspection of the licensee's thermal annealing, and the Commission shall hold a public meeting:

(i) For the licensee to explain to NRC and the public the results of the reactor pressure vessel annealing,

(ii) for the NRC to discuss its inspection of the reactor vessel annealing, and

(iii) for the NRC to receive public comments on the annealing.

(3) Within 45 days of NRC's receipt of the licensee submissions required by paragraphs (c)(1), (c)(2) and (c)(3)(i) through (iii) of this section, the NRC staff shall complete full documentation of its inspection of the licensee's annealing process and make available this documentation at the NRC Web site, *http://www.nrc.gov.*

[60 FR 65472, Dec. 19, 1995, as amended at 64 FR 48952, Sept. 9, 1999; 64 FR 53613, Oct. 4, 1999]

EFFECTIVE DATE NOTE: See 64 FR 53582, Oct. 4, 1999, for effectiveness of §50.66 (b) introductory text, paragraphs (b)(4), (c)(2), and (c)(3)(iii).

§50.67 Accident source term.

(a) *Applicability.* The requirements of this section apply to all holders of operating licenses issued prior to January 10, 1997, and holders of renewed licenses under part 54 of this chapter whose initial operating license was issued prior to January 10, 1997, who seek to revise the current accident source term used in their design basis radiological analyses.

(b) *Requirements.* (1) A licensee who seeks to revise its current accident source term in design basis radiological consequence analyses shall apply for a license amendment under §50.90. The application shall contain an evaluation of the consequences of applicable design basis accidents[1] previously analyzed in the safety analysis report.

[6] For those cases where materials are removed from the beltline of the pressure vessel, the stress limits of the applicable portions of the ASME Code Section III must be satisfied, including consideration of fatigue and corrosion, regardless of the Code of record for the vessel design.

[1] The fission product release assumed for these calculations should be based upon a major accident, hypothesized for purposes of design analyses or postulated from considerations of possible accidental events, that would result in potential hazards not exceeded by those from any accident considered

Continued

(2) The NRC may issue the amendment only if the applicant's analysis demonstrates with reasonable assurance that:

(i) An individual located at any point on the boundary of the exclusion area for any 2-hour period following the onset of the postulated fission product release, would not receive a radiation dose in excess of 0.25 Sv (25 rem)[2] total effective dose equivalent (TEDE).

(ii) An individual located at any point on the outer boundary of the low population zone, who is exposed to the radioactive cloud resulting from the postulated fission product release (during the entire period of its passage), would not receive a radiation dose in excess of 0.25 Sv (25 rem) total effective dose equivalent (TEDE).

(iii) Adequate radiation protection is provided to permit access to and occupancy of the control room under accident conditions without personnel receiving radiation exposures in excess of 0.05 Sv (5 rem) total effective dose equivalent (TEDE) for the duration of the accident.

[64 FR 72001, Dec. 23, 1999]

§ 50.68 Criticality accident requirements.

(a) Each holder of a construction permit or operating license for a nuclear power reactor issued under this part or a combined license for a nuclear power reactor issued under part 52 of this chapter, shall comply with either 10 CFR 70.24 of this chapter or the requirements in paragraph (b) of this section.

(b) Each licensee shall comply with the following requirements in lieu of maintaining a monitoring system capable of detecting a criticality as described in 10 CFR 70.24:

(1) Plant procedures shall prohibit the handling and storage at any one time of more fuel assemblies than have been determined to be safely subcritical under the most adverse moderation conditions feasible by unborated water.

(2) The estimated ratio of neutron production to neutron absorption and leakage (k-effective) of the fresh fuel in the fresh fuel storage racks shall be calculated assuming the racks are loaded with fuel of the maximum fuel assembly reactivity and flooded with unborated water and must not exceed 0.95, at a 95 percent probability, 95 percent confidence level. This evaluation need not be performed if administrative controls and/or design features prevent such flooding or if fresh fuel storage racks are not used.

(3) If optimum moderation of fresh fuel in the fresh fuel storage racks occurs when the racks are assumed to be loaded with fuel of the maximum fuel assembly reactivity and filled with low-density hydrogenous fluid, the k-effective corresponding to this optimum moderation must not exceed 0.98, at a 95 percent probability, 95 percent confidence level. This evaluation need not be performed if administrative controls and/or design features prevent such moderation or if fresh fuel storage racks are not used.

(4) If no credit for soluble boron is taken, the k-effective of the spent fuel storage racks loaded with fuel of the maximum fuel assembly reactivity must not exceed 0.95, at a 95 percent probability, 95 percent confidence level, if flooded with unborated water. If credit is taken for soluble boron, the k-effective of the spent fuel storage racks loaded with fuel of the maximum fuel assembly reactivity must not exceed 0.95, at a 95 percent probability, 95 percent confidence level, if flooded with borated water, and the k-effective must remain below 1.0 (subcritical), at a 95 percent probability, 95 percent confidence level, if flooded with unborated water.

(5) The quantity of SNM, other than nuclear fuel stored onsite, is less than the quantity necessary for a critical mass.

credible. Such accidents have generally been assumed to result in substantial meltdown of the core with subsequent release of appreciable quantities of fission products.

[2] The use of 0.25 Sv (25 rem) TEDE is not intended to imply that this value constitutes an acceptable limit for emergency doses to the public under accident conditions. Rather, this 0.25 Sv (25 rem) TEDE value has been stated in this section as a reference value, which can be used in the evaluation of proposed design basis changes with respect to potential reactor accidents of exceedingly low probability of occurrence and low risk of public exposure to radiation.

(6) Radiation monitors are provided in storage and associated handling areas when fuel is present to detect excessive radiation levels and to initiate appropriate safety actions.

(7) The maximum nominal U–235 enrichment of the fresh fuel assemblies is limited to five (5.0) percent by weight.

(8) The FSAR is amended no later than the next update which §50.71(e) of this part requires, indicating that the licensee has chosen to comply with §50.68(b).

(c) While a spent fuel transportation package approved under Part 71 of this chapter or spent fuel storage cask approved under Part 72 of this chapter is in the spent fuel pool:

(1) The requirements in §50.68(b) do not apply to the fuel located within that package or cask; and

(2) The requirements in Part 71 or 72 of this chapter, as applicable, and the requirements of the Certificate of Compliance for that package or cask, apply to the fuel within that package or cask.

[63 FR 63130, Nov. 12, 1998, as amended at 71 FR 66652, Nov. 16, 2006]

§50.69 Risk-informed categorization and treatment of structures, systems and components for nuclear power reactors.

(a) *Definitions.*

Risk-Informed Safety Class (RISC)–1 structures, systems, and components (SSCs) means safety-related SSCs that perform safety significant functions.

Risk-Informed Safety Class (RISC)–2 structures, systems and components (SSCs) means nonsafety-related SSCs that perform safety significant functions.

Risk-Informed Safety Class (RISC)–3 structures, systems and components (SSCs) means safety-related SSCs that perform low safety significant functions.

Risk-Informed Safety Class (RISC)–4 structures, systems and components (SSCs) means nonsafety-related SSCs that perform low safety significant functions.

Safety significant function means a function whose degradation or loss could result in a significant adverse effect on defense-in-depth, safety margin, or risk.

(b) *Applicability and scope of risk-informed treatment of SSCs and submittal/approval process.* (1) A holder of a license to operate a light water reactor (LWR) nuclear power plant under this part; a holder of a renewed LWR license under part 54 of this chapter; an applicant for a construction permit or operating license under this part; or an applicant for a design approval, a combined license, or manufacturing license under part 52 of this chapter; may voluntarily comply with the requirements in this section as an alternative to compliance with the following requirements for RISC–3 and RISC–4 SSCs:

(i) 10 CFR part 21.

(ii) The portion of 10 CFR 50.46a(b) that imposes requirements to conform to Appendix B to 10 CFR part 50.

(iii) 10 CFR 50.49.

(iv) 10 CFR 50.55(e).

(v) The inservice testing requirements in 10 CFR 50.55a(f); the inservice inspection, and repair and replacement (with the exception of fracture toughness), requirements for ASME Class 2 and Class 3 SSCs in 10 CFR 50.55a(g); and the electrical component quality and qualification requirements in Section 4.3 and 4.4 of IEEE 279, and Sections 5.3 and 5.4 of IEEE 603–1991, as incorporated by reference in 10 CFR 50.55a(h).

(vi) 10 CFR 50.65, except for paragraph (a)(4).

(vii) 10 CFR 50.72.

(viii) 10 CFR 50.73.

(ix) Appendix B to 10 CFR part 50.

(x) The Type B and Type C leakage testing requirements in both Options A and B of Appendix J to 10 CFR part 50, for penetrations and valves meeting the following criteria:

(A) Containment penetrations that are either 1-inch nominal size or less, or continuously pressurized.

(B) Containment isolation valves that meet one or more of the following criteria:

(*1*) The valve is required to be open under accident conditions to prevent or mitigate core damage events;

(*2*) The valve is normally closed and in a physically closed, water-filled system;

(*3*) The valve is in a physically closed system whose piping pressure rating exceeds the containment design pressure rating and is not connected to the reactor coolant pressure boundary; or

(*4*) The valve is 1-inch nominal size or less.

(xi) Appendix A to part 100, Sections VI(a)(1) and VI(a)(2), to the extent that these regulations require qualification testing and specific engineering methods to demonstrate that SSCs are designed to withstand the Safe Shutdown Earthquake and Operating Basis Earthquake.

(2) A licensee voluntarily choosing to implement this section shall submit an application for license amendment under § 50.90 that contains the following information:

(i) A description of the process for categorization of RISC–1, RISC–2, RISC–3 and RISC–4 SSCs.

(ii) A description of the measures taken to assure that the quality and level of detail of the systematic processes that evaluate the plant for internal and external events during normal operation, low power, and shutdown (including the plant-specific probabilistic risk assessment (PRA), margins-type approaches, or other systematic evaluation techniques used to evaluate severe accident vulnerabilities) are adequate for the categorization of SSCs.

(iii) Results of the PRA review process conducted to meet § 50.69(c)(1)(i).

(iv) A description of, and basis for acceptability of, the evaluations to be conducted to satisfy § 50.69(c)(1)(iv). The evaluations must include the effects of common cause interaction susceptibility, and the potential impacts from known degradation mechanisms for both active and passive functions, and address internally and externally initiated events and plant operating modes (e.g., full power and shutdown conditions).

(3) The Commission will approve a licensee's implementation of this section if it determines that the process for categorization of RISC–1, RISC–2, RISC–3, and RISC–4 SSCs satisfies the requirements of § 50.69(c) by issuing a license amendment approving the licensee's use of this section.

(4) An applicant choosing to implement this section shall include the information in § 50.69(b)(2) as part of application. The Commission will approve an applicant's implementation of this section if it determines that the process for categorization of RISC–1, RISC–2, RISC–3, and RISC–4 SSCs satisfies the requirements of § 50.69(c).

(c) *SSC Categorization Process.* (1) SSCs must be categorized as RISC–1, RISC–2, RISC–3, or RISC–4 SSCs using a categorization process that determines if an SSC performs one or more safety significant functions and identifies those functions. The process must:

(i) Consider results and insights from the plant-specific PRA. This PRA must at a minimum model severe accident scenarios resulting from internal initiating events occurring at full power operation. The PRA must be of sufficient quality and level of detail to support the categorization process, and must be subjected to a peer review process assessed against a standard or set of acceptance criteria that is endorsed by the NRC.

(ii) Determine SSC functional importance using an integrated, systematic process for addressing initiating events (internal and external), SSCs, and plant operating modes, including those not modeled in the plant-specific PRA. The functions to be identified and considered include design bases functions and functions credited for mitigation and prevention of severe accidents. All aspects of the integrated, systematic process used to characterize SSC importance must reasonably reflect the current plant configuration and operating practices, and applicable plant and industry operational experience.

(iii) Maintain defense-in-depth.

(iv) Include evaluations that provide reasonable confidence that for SSCs categorized as RISC–3, sufficient safety margins are maintained and that any potential increases in core damage frequency (CDF) and large early release frequency (LERF) resulting from changes in treatment permitted by implementation of §§ 50.69(b)(1) and (d)(2) are small.

(v) Be performed for entire systems and structures, not for selected components within a system or structure.

(2) The SSCs must be categorized by an Integrated Decision-Making Panel

(IDP) staffed with expert, plant-knowledgeable members whose expertise includes, at a minimum, PRA, safety analysis, plant operation, design engineering, and system engineering.

(d) *Alternative treatment requirements*—(1) *RISC–1 and RISC 2 SSCs*. The licensee or applicant shall ensure that RISC–1 and RISC–2 SSCs perform their functions consistent with the categorization process assumptions by evaluating treatment being applied to these SSCs to ensure that it supports the key assumptions in the categorization process that relate to their assumed performance.

(2) *RISC–3 SSCs*. The licensee or applicant shall ensure, with reasonable confidence, that RISC–3 SSCs remain capable of performing their safety-related functions under design basis conditions, including seismic conditions and environmental conditions and effects throughout their service life. The treatment of RISC–3 SSCs must be consistent with the categorization process. Inspection and testing, and corrective action shall be provided for RISC–3 SSCs.

(i) Inspection and testing. Periodic inspection and testing activities must be conducted to determine that RISC–3 SSCs will remain capable of performing their safety-related functions under design basis conditions; and

(ii) Corrective action. Conditions that would prevent a RISC–3 SSC from performing its safety-related functions under design basis conditions must be corrected in a timely manner. For significant conditions adverse to quality, measures must be taken to provide reasonable confidence that the cause of the condition is determined and corrective action taken to preclude repetition.

(e) *Feedback and process adjustment*—(1) *RISC–1, RISC–2, RISC–3 and RISC–4 SSCs*. The licensee shall review changes to the plant, operational practices, applicable plant and industry operational experience, and, as appropriate, update the PRA and SSC categorization and treatment processes. The licensee shall perform this review in a timely manner but no longer than once every two refueling outages.

(2) *RISC–1 and RISC–2 SSCs*. The licensee shall monitor the performance of RISC–1 and RISC–2 SSCs. The licensee shall make adjustments as necessary to either the categorization or treatment processes so that the categorization process and results are maintained valid.

(3) *RISC–3 SSCs*. The licensee shall consider data collected in § 50.69(d)(2)(i) for RISC–3 SSCs to determine if there are any adverse changes in performance such that the SSC unreliability values approach or exceed the values used in the evaluations conducted to satisfy § 50.69(c)(1)(iv). The licensee shall make adjustments as necessary to the categorization or treatment processes so that the categorization process and results are maintained valid.

(f) *Program documentation, change control and records*. (1) The licensee or applicant shall document the basis for its categorization of any SSC under paragraph (c) of this section before removing any requirements under § 50.69(b)(1) for those SSCs.

(2) Following implementation of this section, licensees and applicants shall update their final safety analysis report (FSAR) to reflect which systems have been categorized, in accordance with § 50.71(e).

(3) When a licensee first implements this section for a SSC, changes to the FSAR for the implementation of the changes in accordance with § 50.69(d) need not include a supporting § 50.59 evaluation of the changes directly related to implementation. Thereafter, changes to the programs and procedures for implementation of § 50.69(d), as described in the FSAR, may be made if the requirements of this section and § 50.59 continue to be met.

(4) When a licensee first implements this section for a SSC, changes to the quality assurance plan for the implementation of the changes in accordance with § 50.69(d) need not include a supporting § 50.54(a) review of the changes directly related to implementation. Thereafter, changes to the programs and procedures for implementation of § 50.69(d), as described in the quality assurance plan may be made if the requirements of this section and § 50.54(a) continue to be met.

(g) *Reporting*. The licensee shall submit a licensee event report under

§ 50.73(b) for any event or condition that prevented, or would have prevented, a RISC–1 or RISC–2 SSC from performing a safety significant function.

[69 FR 68047, Nov. 22, 2004]

INSPECTIONS, RECORDS, REPORTS, NOTIFICATIONS

§ 50.70 Inspections.

(a) Each applicant for or holder of a license, including a construction permit or an early site permit, shall permit inspection, by duly authorized representatives of the Commission, of his records, premises, activities, and of licensed materials in possession or use, related to the license or construction permit or early site permit as may be necessary to effectuate the purposes of the Act, as amended, including Section 105 of the Act, and the Energy Reorganization Act of 1974, as amended.

(b)(1) Each licensee and each holder of a construction permit shall, upon request by the Director, Office of Nuclear Reactor Regulation or Director, Office of New Reactors, as appropriate, provide rent-free office space for the exclusive use of the Commission inspection personnel. Heat, air conditioning, light, electrical outlets, and janitorial services shall be furnished by each licensee and each holder of a construction permit. The office shall be convenient to and have full access to the facility and shall provide the inspector both visual and acoustic privacy.

(2) For a site with a single power reactor or fuel facility licensed under part 50 or part 52 of this chapter, or a facility issued a manufacturing license under part 52, the space provided shall be adequate to accommodate a full-time inspector, a part-time secretary and transient NRC personnel and will be generally commensurate with other office facilities at the site. A space of 250 square feet either within the site's office complex or in an office trailer or other onsite space is suggested as a guide. For sites containing multiple power reactor units or fuel facilities, additional space may be requested to accommodate additional full-time inspector(s). The office space that is provided shall be subject to the approval of the Director, Office of New Reactors, or the Director, Office of Nuclear Reactor Regulation. All furniture, supplies and communication equipment will be furnished by the Commission.

(3) The licensee or construction permit holder shall afford any NRC resident inspector assigned to that site, or other NRC inspectors identified by the Regional Administrator as likely to inspect the facility, immediate unfettered access, equivalent to access provided regular plant employees, following proper identification and compliance with applicable access control measures for security, radiological protection and personal safety.

(4) The licensee or construction permit holder (nuclear power reactor only) shall ensure that the arrival and presence of an NRC inspector, who has been properly authorized facility access as described in paragraph (b)(3) of this section, is not announced or otherwise communicated by its employees or contractors to other persons at the facility unless specifically requested by the NRC inspector.

[21 FR 355, Jan. 19, 1956; 44 FR 47919, Aug. 16, 1979, as amended at 52 FR 31612, Aug. 21, 1987; 53 FR 42942, Oct. 25, 1988; 72 FR 49501, Aug. 28, 2007; 73 FR 5722, Jan. 31, 2008; 75 FR 73944, Nov. 30, 2010]

§ 50.71 Maintenance of records, making of reports.

(a) Each licensee, including each holder of a construction permit or early site permit, shall maintain all records and make all reports, in connection with the activity, as may be required by the conditions of the license or permit or by the regulations, and orders of the Commission in effectuating the purposes of the Act, including Section 105 of the Act, and the Energy Reorganization Act of 1974, as amended. Reports must be submitted in accordance with § 50.4 or 10 CFR 52.3, as applicable.

(b) With respect to any production or utilization facility of a type described in § 50.21(b) or 50.22, or a testing facility, each licensee and each holder of a construction permit shall submit its annual financial report, including the certified financial statements, to the Commission, as specified in § 50.4, upon issuance of the report. However, licensees and holders of a construction permit who submit a Form 10-Q with the Securities and Exchange Commission or a Form 1 with the Federal Energy Regulatory Commission, need not submit the annual financial report or the certified financial statement under this paragraph.

(c) Records that are required by the regulations in this part or part 52 of this chapter, by license condition, or by technical specifications must be retained for the period specified by the appropriate regulation, license condition, or technical specification. If a retention period is not otherwise specified, these records must be retained until the Commission terminates the facility license or, in the case of an early site permit, until the permit expires.

(d)(1) Records which must be maintained under this part or part 52 of this chapter may be the original or a reproduced copy or microform if the reproduced copy or microform is duly authenticated by authorized personnel and the microform is capable of producing a clear and legible copy after storage for the period specified by Commission regulations. The record may also be stored in electronic media with the capability of producing legible, accurate, and complete records during the required retention period. Records such as letters, drawings, and specifications, must include all pertinent information such as stamps, initials, and signatures. The licensee shall maintain adequate safeguards against tampering with, and loss of records.

(2) If there is a conflict between the Commission's regulations in this part, license condition, or technical specification, or other written Commission approval or authorization pertaining to the retention period for the same type of record, the retention period specified in the regulations in this part for such records shall apply unless the Commission, pursuant to § 50.12 of this part, has granted a specific exemption from the record retention requirements specified in the regulations in this part.

(e) Each person licensed to operate a nuclear power reactor under the provisions of § 50.21 or § 50.22, and each applicant for a combined license under part 52 of this chapter, shall update periodically, as provided in paragraphs (e) (3) and (4) of this section, the final safety analysis report (FSAR) originally submitted as part of the application for the license, to assure that the information included in the report contains the latest information developed. This submittal shall contain all the changes necessary to reflect information and analyses submitted to the Commission by the applicant or licensee or prepared by the applicant or licensee pursuant to Commission requirement since the submittal of the original FSAR, or as appropriate, the last update to the FSAR under this section. The submittal shall include the effects[1] of all changes made in the facility or procedures as described in the FSAR; all safety analyses and evaluations performed by the applicant or licensee either in support of approved license amendments or in support of conclusions that changes did not require a license amendment in accordance with § 50.59(c)(2) or, in the case of a license that references a certified design, in accordance with § 52.98(c) of this chapter; and all analyses of new safety issues performed by or on behalf of the applicant or licensee at Commission request. The updated information shall be appropriately located within the update to the FSAR.

(1) The licensee shall submit revisions containing updated information to the Commission, as specified in § 50.4, on a replacement-page basis that is accompanied by a list which identifies the current pages of the FSAR following page replacement.

(2) The submittal shall include (i) a certification by a duly authorized officer of the licensee that either the information accurately presents changes made since the previous submittal, necessary to reflect information and analyses submitted to the Commission or prepared pursuant to Commission requirement, or that no such changes were made; and (ii) an identification of changes made under the provisions of

[1] Effects of changes includes appropriate revisions of descriptions in the FSAR such that the FSAR (as updated) is complete and accurate.

§ 50.59 but not previously submitted to the Commission.

(3)(i) A revision of the original FSAR containing those original pages that are still applicable plus new replacement pages shall be filed within 24 months of either July 22, 1980, or the date of issuance of the operating license, whichever is later, and shall bring the FSAR up to date as of a maximum of 6 months prior to the date of filing the revision.

(ii) Not less than 15 days before § 50.71(e) becomes effective, the Director of the Office of Nuclear Reactor Regulation shall notify by letter the licensees of those nuclear power plants initially subject to the NRC's systematic evaluation program that they need not comply with the provisions of this section while the program is being conducted at their plant. The Director of the Office of Nuclear Reactor Regulation will notify by letter the licensee of each nuclear power plant being evaluated when the systematic evaluation program has been completed. Within 24 months after receipt of this notification, the licensee shall file a complete FSAR which is up to date as of a maximum of 6 months prior to the date of filing the revision.

(iii) During the period from the docketing of an application for a combined license under subpart C of part 52 of this chapter until the Commission makes the finding under § 52.103(g) of this chapter, the update to the FSAR must be submitted annually.

(4) Subsequent revisions must be filed annually or 6 months after each refueling outage provided the interval between successive updates does not exceed 24 months. The revisions must reflect all changes up to a maximum of 6 months prior to the date of filling. For nuclear power reactor facilities that have submitted the certifications required by § 50.82(a)(1), subsequent revisions must be filed every 24 months.

(5) Each replacement page shall include both a change indicator for the area changed, e.g., a bold line vertically drawn in the margin adjacent to the portion actually changed, and a page change identification (date of change or change number or both).

(6) The updated FSAR shall be retained by the licensee until the Commission terminates their license.

(f) Each person licensed to manufacture a nuclear power reactor under subpart F of 10 CFR part 52 shall update the FSAR originally submitted as part of the application to reflect any modification to the design that is approved by the Commission under § 52.171 of this chapter, and any new analyses of the design performed by or on behalf of the licensee at the NRC's request. This submittal shall contain all the changes necessary to reflect information and analyses submitted to the Commission by the licensee or prepared by the licensee with respect to the modification approved under § 52.171 of this chapter or the analyses requested by the Commission under § 52.171 of this chapter. The updated information shall be appropriately located within the update to the FSAR.

(g) The provisions of this section apply to nuclear power reactor licensees that have submitted the certification of permanent cessation of operations required under §§ 50.82(a)(1)(i) or 52.110(a)(1) of this chapter. The provisions of paragraphs (a), (c), and (d) of this section also apply to non-power reactor licensees that are no longer authorized to operate.

(h)(1) No later than the scheduled date for initial loading of fuel, each holder of a combined license under subpart C of 10 CFR part 52 shall develop a level 1 and a level 2 probabilistic risk assessment (PRA). The PRA must cover those initiating events and modes for which NRC-endorsed consensus standards on PRA exist one year prior to the scheduled date for initial loading of fuel.

(2) Each holder of a combined license shall maintain and upgrade the PRA required by paragraph (h)(1) of this section. The upgraded PRA must cover initiating events and modes of operation contained in NRC-endorsed consensus standards on PRA in effect one year prior to each required upgrade. The PRA must be upgraded every four years until the permanent cessation of operations under § 52.110(a) of this chapter.

(3) Each holder of a combined license shall, no later than the date on which

the licensee submits an application for a renewed license, upgrade the PRA required by paragraph (h)(1) of this section to cover all modes and all initiating events.

[33 FR 9704, July 4, 1968, as amended at 41 FR 18303, May 3, 1976; 45 FR 30615, May 9, 1980; 51 FR 40310, Nov. 6, 1986; 53 FR 19250, May 27, 1988; 57 FR 39358, Aug. 31, 1992; 61 FR 39301, July 29, 1996; 64 FR 53614, Oct. 4, 1999; 71 FR 29246, May 22, 2006; 72 FR 49501, Aug. 28, 2007]

EFFECTIVE DATE NOTE: See 64 FR 53582, Oct. 4, 1999, for effectiveness of §50.71(e) introductory text.

§50.72 Immediate notification requirements for operating nuclear power reactors.

(a) *General requirements.*[1] (1) Each nuclear power reactor licensee licensed under §§50.21(b) or 50.22 holding an operating license under this part or a combined license under part 52 of this chapter after the Commission makes the finding under §52.103(g), shall notify the NRC Operations Center via the Emergency Notification System of:

(i) The declaration of any of the Emergency Classes specified in the licensee's approved Emergency Plan;[2] or

(ii) Those non-emergency events specified in paragraph (b) of this section that occurred within three years of the date of discovery.

(2) If the Emergency Notification System is inoperative, the licensee shall make the required notifications via commercial telephone service, other dedicated telephone system, or any other method which will ensure that a report is made as soon as practical to the NRC Operations Center.[3]

(3) The licensee shall notify the NRC immediately after notification of the appropriate State or local agencies and not later than one hour after the time the licensee declares one of the Emergency Classes.

(4) The licensee shall activate the Emergency Response Data System (ERDS)[4] as soon as possible but not later than one hour after declaring an Emergency Class of alert, site area emergency, or general emergency. The ERDS may also be activated by the licensee during emergency drills or exercises if the licensee's computer system has the capability to transmit the exercise data.

(5) When making a report under paragraph (a)(1) of this section, the licensee shall identify:

(i) The Emergency Class declared; or

(ii) Paragraph (b)(1), "One-hour reports," paragraph (b)(2), "Four-hour reports," or paragraph (b)(3), "Eight-hour reports," as the paragraph of this section requiring notification of the non-emergency event.

(b) *Non-emergency events*—(1) *One-hour reports.* If not reported as a declaration of an Emergency Class under paragraph (a) of this section, the licensee shall notify the NRC as soon as practical and in all cases within one hour of the occurrence of any deviation from the plant's Technical Specifications authorized pursuant to §50.54(x) of this part.

(2) *Four-hour reports.* If not reported under paragraphs (a) or (b)(1) of this section, the licensee shall notify the NRC as soon as practical and in all cases, within four hours of the occurrence of any of the following:

(i) The initiation of any nuclear plant shutdown required by the plant's Technical Specifications.

(ii)–(iii) [Reserved]

(iv)(A) Any event that results or should have resulted in emergency core cooling system (ECCS) discharge into the reactor coolant system as a result of a valid signal except when the actuation results from and is part of a preplanned sequence during testing or reactor operation.

(B) Any event or condition that results in actuation of the reactor protection system (RPS) when the reactor is critical except when the actuation results from and is part of a preplanned sequence during testing or reactor operation.

(v)–(x) [Reserved]

[1] Other requirements for immediate notification of the NRC by licensed operating nuclear power reactors are contained elsewhere in this chapter, in particular §§20.1906, 20.2202, 50.36, 72.216, and 73.71.

[2] These Emergency Classes are addressed in Appendix E of this part.

[3] Commercial telephone number of the NRC Operations Center is (301) 816–5100.

[4] Requirements for ERDS are addressed in Appendix E, Section VI.

(xi) Any event or situation, related to the health and safety of the public or onsite personnel, or protection of the environment, for which a news release is planned or notification to other government agencies has been or will be made. Such an event may include an onsite fatality or inadvertent release of radioactively contaminated materials.

(3) *Eight-hour reports.* If not reported under paragraphs (a), (b)(1) or (b)(2) of this section, the licensee shall notify the NRC as soon as practical and in all cases within eight hours of the occurrence of any of the following:

(i) [Reserved]

(ii) Any event or condition that results in:

(A) The condition of the nuclear power plant, including its principal safety barriers, being seriously degraded; or

(B) The nuclear power plant being in an unanalyzed condition that significantly degrades plant safety.

(iii) [Reserved]

(iv)(A) Any event or condition that results in valid actuation of any of the systems listed in paragraph (b)(3)(iv)(B) of this section, except when the actuation results from and is part of a pre-planned sequence during testing or reactor operation.

(B) The systems to which the requirements of paragraph (b)(3)(iv)(A) of this section apply are:

(*1*) Reactor protection system (RPS) including: Reactor scram and reactor trip.[5]

(*2*) General containment isolation signals affecting containment isolation valves in more than one system or multiple main steam isolation valves (MSIVs).

(*3*) Emergency core cooling systems (ECCS) for pressurized water reactors (PWRs) including: High-head, intermediate-head, and low-head injection systems and the low pressure injection function of residual (decay) heat removal systems.

(*4*) ECCS for boiling water reactors (BWRs) including: High-pressure and low-pressure core spray systems; high-pressure coolant injection system; low pressure injection function of the residual heat removal system.

(*5*) BWR reactor core isolation cooling system; isolation condenser system; and feedwater coolant injection system.

(*6*) PWR auxiliary or emergency feedwater system.

(*7*) Containment heat removal and depressurization systems, including containment spray and fan cooler systems.

(*8*) Emergency ac electrical power systems, including: Emergency diesel generators (EDGs); hydroelectric facilities used in lieu of EDGs at the Oconee Station; and BWR dedicated Division 3 EDGs.

(v) Any event or condition that at the time of discovery could have prevented the fulfillment of the safety function of structures or systems that are needed to:

(A) Shut down the reactor and maintain it in a safe shutdown condition;

(B) Remove residual heat;

(C) Control the release of radioactive material; or

(D) Mitigate the consequences of an accident.

(vi) Events covered in paragraph (b)(3)(v) of this section may include one or more procedural errors, equipment failures, and/or discovery of design, analysis, fabrication, construction, and/or procedural inadequacies. However, individual component failures need not be reported pursuant to paragraph (b)(3)(v) of this section if redundant equipment in the same system was operable and available to perform the required safety function.

(vii)–(xi) [Reserved]

(xii) Any event requiring the transport of a radioactively contaminated person to an offsite medical facility for treatment.

(xiii) Any event that results in a major loss of emergency assessment capability, offsite response capability, or offsite communications capability (e.g., significant portion of control room indication, Emergency Notification System, or offsite notification system).

(c) *Followup notification.* With respect to the telephone notifications made

[5] Actuation of the RPS when the reactor is critical is reportable under paragraph (b)(2)(iv)(B) of this section.

under paragraphs (a) and (b) of this section, in addition to making the required initial notification, each licensee, shall during the course of the event:

(1) *Immediately report* (i) any further degradation in the level of safety of the plant or other worsening plant conditions, including those that require the declaration of any of the Emergency Classes, if such a declaration has not been previously made, or (ii) any change from one Emergency Class to another, or (iii) a termination of the Emergency Class.

(2) *Immediately report* (i) the results of ensuing evaluations or assessments of plant conditions, (ii) the effectiveness of response or protective measures taken, and (iii) information related to plant behavior that is not understood.

(3) Maintain an open, continuous communication channel with the NRC Operations Center upon request by the NRC.

[48 FR 39046, Aug. 29, 1983; 48 FR 40882, Sept. 12, 1983; 55 FR 29194, July 18, 1990, as amended at 56 FR 944, Jan. 10, 1991; 56 FR 23473, May 21, 1991; 56 FR 40184, Aug. 13, 1991; 57 FR 41381, Sept. 10, 1992; 58 FR 67661, Dec. 22, 1993; 59 FR 14087, Mar. 25, 1994; 65 FR 63786, Oct. 25, 2000; 72 FR 49502, Aug. 28, 2007]

§ 50.73 Licensee event report system.

(a) *Reportable events.* (1) The holder of an operating license under this part or a combined license under part 52 of this chapter (after the Commission has made the finding under § 52.103(g) of this chapter) for a nuclear power plant (licensee) shall submit a Licensee Event Report (LER) for any event of the type described in this paragraph within 60 days after the discovery of the event. In the case of an invalid actuation reported under § 50.73(a)(2)(iv), other than actuation of the reactor protection system (RPS) when the reactor is critical, the licensee may, at its option, provide a telephone notification to the NRC Operations Center within 60 days after discovery of the event instead of submitting a written LER. Unless otherwise specified in this section, the licensee shall report an event if it occurred within 3 years of the date of discovery regardless of the plant mode or power level, and regardless of the significance of the structure, system, or component that initiated the event.

(2) The licensee shall report:

(i)(A) The completion of any nuclear plant shutdown required by the plant's Technical Specifications.

(B) Any operation or condition which was prohibited by the plant's Technical Specifications except when:

(*1*) The Technical Specification is administrative in nature;

(*2*) The event consisted solely of a case of a late surveillance test where the oversight was corrected, the test was performed, and the equipment was found to be capable of performing its specified safety functions; or

(*3*) The Technical Specification was revised prior to discovery of the event such that the operation or condition was no longer prohibited at the time of discovery of the event.

(C) Any deviation from the plant's Technical Specifications authorized pursuant to § 50.54(x) of this part.

(ii) Any event or condition that resulted in:

(A) The condition of the nuclear power plant, including its principal safety barriers, being seriously degraded; or

(B) The nuclear power plant being in an unanalyzed condition that significantly degraded plant safety.

(iii) Any natural phenomenon or other external condition that posed an actual threat to the safety of the nuclear power plant or significantly hampered site personnel in the performance of duties necessary for the safe operation of the nuclear power plant.

(iv)(A) Any event or condition that resulted in manual or automatic actuation of any of the systems listed in paragraph (a)(2)(iv)(B) of this section, except when:

(*1*) The actuation resulted from and was part of a pre-planned sequence during testing or reactor operation; or

(*2*) The actuation was invalid and;

(*i*) Occurred while the system was properly removed from service; or

(*ii*) Occurred after the safety function had been already completed.

(B) The systems to which the requirements of paragraph (a)(2)(iv)(A) of this section apply are:

(*1*) Reactor protection system (RPS) including: reactor scram or reactor trip.

(*2*) General containment isolation signals affecting containment isolation valves in more than one system or multiple main steam isolation valves (MSIVs).

(*3*) Emergency core cooling systems (ECCS) for pressurized water reactors (PWRs) including: high-head, intermediate-head, and low-head injection systems and the low pressure injection function of residual (decay) heat removal systems.

(*4*) ECCS for boiling water reactors (BWRs) including: high-pressure and low-pressure core spray systems; high-pressure coolant injection system; low pressure injection function of the residual heat removal system.

(*5*) BWR reactor core isolation cooling system; isolation condenser system; and feedwater coolant injection system.

(*6*) PWR auxiliary or emergency feedwater system.

(*7*) Containment heat removal and depressurization systems, including containment spray and fan cooler systems.

(*8*) Emergency ac electrical power systems, including: emergency diesel generators (EDGs); hydroelectric facilities used in lieu of EDGs at the Oconee Station; and BWR dedicated Division 3 EDGs.

(*9*) Emergency service water systems that do not normally run and that serve as ultimate heat sinks.

(v) Any event or condition that could have prevented the fulfillment of the safety function of structures or systems that are needed to:

(A) Shut down the reactor and maintain it in a safe shutdown condition;

(B) Remove residual heat;

(C) Control the release of radioactive material; or

(D) Mitigate the consequences of an accident.

(vi) Events covered in paragraph (a)(2)(v) of this section may include one or more procedural errors, equipment failures, and/or discovery of design, analysis, fabrication, construction, and/or procedural inadequacies. However, individual component failures need not be reported pursuant to paragraph (a)(2)(v) of this section if redundant equipment in the same system was operable and available to perform the required safety function.

(vii) Any event where a single cause or condition caused at least one independent train or channel to become inoperable in multiple systems or two independent trains or channels to become inoperable in a single system designed to:

(A) Shut down the reactor and maintain it in a safe shutdown condition;

(B) Remove residual heat;

(C) Control the release of radioactive material; or

(D) Mitigate the consequences of an accident.

(viii)(A) Any airborne radioactive release that, when averaged over a time period of 1 hour, resulted in airborne radionuclide concentrations in an unrestricted area that exceeded 20 times the applicable concentration limits specified in appendix B to part 20, table 2, column 1.

(B) Any liquid effluent release that, when averaged over a time period of 1 hour, exceeds 20 times the applicable concentrations specified in appendix B to part 20, table 2, column 2, at the point of entry into the receiving waters (*i.e.*, unrestricted area) for all radionuclides except tritium and dissolved noble gases.

(ix)(A) Any event or condition that as a result of a single cause could have prevented the fulfillment of a safety function for two or more trains or channels in different systems that are needed to:

(*1*) Shut down the reactor and maintain it in a safe shutdown condition;

(*2*) Remove residual heat;

(*3*) Control the release of radioactive material; or

(*4*) Mitigate the consequences of an accident.

(B) Events covered in paragraph (a)(2)(ix)(A) of this section may include cases of procedural error, equipment failure, and/or discovery of a design, analysis, fabrication, construction, and/or procedural inadequacy. However, licensees are not required to report an event pursuant to paragraph (a)(2)(ix)(A) of this section if the event results from:

(*1*) A shared dependency among trains or channels that is a natural or expected consequence of the approved plant design; or

(*2*) Normal and expected wear or degradation.

(x) Any event that posed an actual threat to the safety of the nuclear power plant or significantly hampered site personnel in the performance of duties necessary for the safe operation of the nuclear power plant including fires, toxic gas releases, or radioactive releases.

(b) *Contents.* The Licensee Event Report shall contain:

(1) A brief abstract describing the major occurrences during the event, including all component or system failures that contributed to the event and significant corrective action taken or planned to prevent recurrence.

(2)(i) A clear, specific, narrative description of what occurred so that knowledgeable readers conversant with the design of commercial nuclear power plants, but not familiar with the details of a particular plant, can understand the complete event.

(ii) The narrative description must include the following specific information as appropriate for the particular event:

(A) Plant operating conditions before the event.

(B) Status of structures, components, or systems that were inoperable at the start of the event and that contributed to the event.

(C) Dates and approximate times of occurrences.

(D) The cause of each component or system failure or personnel error, if known.

(E) The failure mode, mechanism, and effect of each failed component, if known.

(F) The Energy Industry Identification System component function identifier and system name of each component or system referred to in the LER.

(*1*) The Energy Industry Identification System is defined in: IEEE Std 803–1983 (May 16, 1983) Recommended Practice for Unique Identification in Power Plants and Related Facilities—Principles and Definitions.

(*2*) IEEE Std 803–1983 has been approved for incorporation by reference by the Director of the Federal Register in accordance with 5 U.S.C. 552(a) and 1 CFR part 51.

(*3*) A notice of any changes made to the material incorporated by reference will be published in the FEDERAL REGISTER. Copies may be obtained from the Institute of Electrical and Electronics Engineers, 445 Hoes Lane, P.O. Box 1331, Piscataway, NJ 08855–1331. IEEE Std 803–1983 is available for inspection at the NRC's Technical Library, which is located in the Two White Flint North Building, 11545 Rockville Pike, Rockville, Maryland 20852–2738; or at the National Archives and Records Administration (NARA). For information on the availability of this material at NARA, call 202–741–6030, or go to: *http://www.archives.gov/federal_register/code_of_federal_regulations/ibr_locations.html.*

(G) For failures of components with multiple functions, include a list of systems or secondary functions that were also affected.

(H) For failure that rendered a train of a safety system inoperable, an estimate of the elapsed time from the discovery of the failure until the train was returned to service.

(I) The method of discovery of each component or system failure or procedural error.

(J) For each human performance related root cause, the licensee shall discuss the cause(s) and circumstances.

(K) Automatically and manually initiated safety system responses.

(L) The manufacturer and model number (or other identification) of each component that failed during the event.

(3) An assessment of the safety consequences and implications of the event. This assessment must include:

(i) The availability of systems or components that could have performed the same function as the components and systems that failed during the event, and

(ii) For events that occurred when the reactor was shutdown, the availability of systems or components that are needed to shutdown the reactor and maintain safe shutdown conditions, remove residual heat, control the release of radioactive material, or mitigate the consequences of an accident.

(4) A description of any corrective actions planned as a result of the event, including those to reduce the probability of similar events occurring in the future.

(5) Reference to any previous similar events at the same plant that are known to the licensee.

(6) The name and telephone number of a person within the licensee's organization who is knowledgeable about the event and can provide additional information concerning the event and the plant's characteristics.

(c) *Supplemental information.* The Commission may require the licensee to submit specific additional information beyond that required by paragraph (b) of this section if the Commission finds that supplemental material is necessary for complete understanding of an unusually complex or significant event. These requests for supplemental information will be made in writing and the licensee shall submit, as specified in § 50.4, the requested information as a supplement to the initial LER.

(d) *Submission of reports.* Licensee Event Reports must be prepared on Form NRC 366 and submitted to the U.S. Nuclear Regulatory Commission, as specified in § 50.4.

(e) *Report legibility.* The reports and copies that licensees are required to submit to the Commission under the provisions of this section must be of sufficient quality to permit legible reproduction and micrographic processing.

(f) [Reserved]

(g) *Reportable occurrences.* The requirements contained in this section replace all existing requirements for licensees to report "Reportable Occurrences" as defined in individual plant Technical Specifications.

[48 FR 33858, July 26, 1983, as amended at 49 FR 47824, Dec. 7, 1984; 51 FR 40310, Nov. 6, 1986; 56 FR 23473, May 21, 1991; 56 FR 61352, Dec. 3, 1991; 57 FR 41381, Sept. 10, 1992; 58 FR 67661, Dec. 22, 1993; 59 FR 50689, Oct. 5, 1994; 63 FR 50480, Sept. 22, 1998; 65 FR 63787, Oct. 25, 2000; 69 FR 18803, Apr. 9, 2004; 72 FR 49502, Aug. 28, 2007]

§ 50.74 Notification of change in operator or senior operator status.

Each licensee shall notify the appropriate Regional Administrator as listed in appendix D to part 20 of this chapter within 30 days of the following in regard to a licensed operator or senior operator:

(a) Permanent reassignment from the position for which the licensee has certified the need for a licensed operator or senior operator under § 55.31(a)(3) of this chapter;

(b) Termination of any operator or senior operator;

(c) Permanent disability or illness as described in § 55.25 of this chapter.

[52 FR 9469, Mar. 25, 1987, as amended at 60 FR 13616, Mar. 14, 1995; 68 FR 58809, Oct. 10, 2003]

§ 50.75 Reporting and recordkeeping for decommissioning planning.

(a) This section establishes requirements for indicating to NRC how a licensee will provide reasonable assurance that funds will be available for the decommissioning process. For power reactor licensees (except a holder of a manufacturing license under part 52 of this chapter), reasonable assurance consists of a series of steps as provided in paragraphs (b), (c), (e), and (f) of this section. Funding for the decommissioning of power reactors may also be subject to the regulation of Federal or State Government agencies (e.g., Federal Energy Regulatory Commission (FERC) and State Public Utility Commissions) that have jurisdiction over rate regulation. The requirements of this section, in particular paragraph (c) of this section, are in addition to, and not substitution for, other requirements, and are not intended to be used by themselves or by other agencies to establish rates.

(b) Each power reactor applicant for or holder of an operating license, and each applicant for a combined license under subpart C of 10 CFR part 52 for a production or utilization facility of the type and power level specified in paragraph (c) of this section shall submit a decommissioning report, as required by § 50.33(k).

(1) For an applicant for or holder of an operating license under part 50, the report must contain a certification that financial assurance for decommissioning will be (for a license applicant), or has been (for a license holder), provided in an amount which may be more, but not less, than the amount

stated in the table in paragraph (c)(1) of this section adjusted using a rate at least equal to that stated in paragraph (c)(2) of this section. For an applicant for a combined license under subpart C of 10 CFR part 52, the report must contain a certification that financial assurance for decommissioning will be provided no later than 30 days after the Commission publishes notice in the FEDERAL REGISTER under §52.103(a) in an amount which may be more, but not less, than the amount stated in the table in paragraph (c)(1) of this section, adjusted using a rate at least equal to that stated in paragraph (c)(2) of this section.

(2) The amount to be provided must be adjusted annually using a rate at least equal to that stated in paragraph (c)(2) of this section.

(3) The amount must be covered by one or more of the methods described in paragraph (e) of this section as acceptable to the NRC.

(4) The amount stated in the applicant's or licensee's certification may be based on a cost estimate for decommissioning the facility. As part of the certification, a copy of the financial instrument obtained to satisfy the requirements of paragraph (e) of this section must be submitted to NRC; *provided, however*, that an applicant for or holder of a combined license need not obtain such financial instrument or submit a copy to the Commission except as provided in paragraph (e)(3) of this section.

(c) Table of minimum amounts (January 1986 dollars) required to demonstrate reasonable assurance of funds for decommissioning by reactor type and power level, P (in MWt); adjustment factor.[1]

	Millions
(1)(i) For a PWR:	
greater than or equal to 3400 MWt	$105
between 1200 MWt and 3400 MWt (For a PWR of less than 1200 MWt, use P = 1200 MWt)	$(75 + 0.0088P)
(ii) For a BWR:	
greater than or equal to 3400 MWt	$135
between 1200 MWt and 3400 MWt (For a BWR of less than 1200 MWt, use P = 1200 MWt)	$(104 + 0.009P)

[1]Amounts are based on activities related to the definition of "Decommission" in §50.2 of this part and do not include the cost of removal and disposal of spent fuel or of nonradioactive structures and materials beyond that necessary to terminate the license.

(2) An adjustment factor at least equal to 0.65 L + 0.13 E + 0.22 B is to be used where L and E are escalation factors for labor and energy, respectively, and are to be taken from regional data of U.S. Department of Labor Bureau of Labor Statistics and B is an escalation factor for waste burial and is to be taken from NRC report NUREG–1307, "Report on Waste Burial Charges."

(d)(1) Each non-power reactor applicant for or holder of an operating license for a production or utilization facility shall submit a decommissioning report as required by §50.33(k) of this part.

(2) The report must:

(i) Contain a cost estimate for decommissioning the facility;

(ii) Indicate which method or methods described in paragraph (e) of this section as acceptable to the NRC will be used to provide funds for decommissioning; and

(iii) Provide a description of the means of adjusting the cost estimate and associated funding level periodically over the life of the facility.

(e)(1) Financial assurance is to be provided by the following methods.

(i) *Prepayment*. Prepayment is the deposit made preceding the start of operation or the transfer of a license under §50.80 into an account segregated from licensee assets and outside the administrative control of the licensee and its subsidiaries or affiliates of cash or liquid assets such that the amount of funds would be sufficient to pay decommissioning costs at the time permanent termination of operations is expected. Prepayment may be in the form of a trust, escrow account, or Government fund with payment by, certificate of deposit, deposit of government or other securities or other method acceptable to the NRC. This trust, escrow account, Government fund, or other type of agreement shall be established in writing and maintained at all times in the United States with an entity that is an appropriate State or Federal government agency, or an entity whose operations in which the prepayment deposit is managed are regulated and examined by a Federal or State agency. A licensee that has prepaid funds based on a site-specific estimate under § 50.75(b)(1) of this section may take credit for projected earnings on the prepaid decommissioning trust funds, using up to a 2 percent annual real rate of return from the time of future funds' collection through the projected decommissioning period, provided that the site-specific estimate is based on a period of safe storage that is specifically described in the estimate. This includes the periods of safe storage, final dismantlement, and license termination. A licensee that has prepaid funds based on the formulas in § 50.75(c) of this section may take credit for projected earnings on the prepaid decommissioning funds using up to a 2 percent annual real rate of return up to the time of permanent termination of operations. A licensee may use a credit of greater than 2 percent if the licensee's rate-setting authority has specifically authorized a higher rate. However, licensees certifying only to the formula amounts (*i.e.*, not a site-specific estimate) can take a pro-rata credit during the immediate dismantlement period (*i.e.*, recognizing both cash expenditures and earnings the first 7 years after shutdown). Actual earnings on existing funds may be used to calculate future fund needs.

(ii) External sinking fund. An external sinking fund is a fund established and maintained by setting funds aside periodically in an account segregated from licensee assets and outside the administrative control of the licensee and its subsidiaries or affiliates in which the total amount of funds would be sufficient to pay decommissioning costs at the time permanent termination of operations is expected. An external sinking fund may be in the form of a trust, escrow account, or Government fund, with payment by certificate of deposit, deposit of Government or other securities, or other method acceptable to the NRC. This trust, escrow account, Government fund, or other type of agreement shall be established in writing and maintained at all times in the United States with an entity that is an appropriate State or Federal government agency, or an entity whose operations in which the external linking fund is managed are regulated and examined by a Federal or State agency. A licensee that has collected funds based on a site-specific estimate under § 50.75(b)(1) of this section may take credit for projected earnings on the external sinking funds using up to a 2 percent annual real rate of return from the time of future funds' collection through the decommissioning period, provided that the site-specific estimate is based on a period of safe storage that is specifically described in the estimate. This includes the periods of safe storage, final dismantlement, and license termination. A licensee that has collected funds based on the formulas in § 50.75(c) of this section may take credit for collected earnings on the decommissioning funds using up to a 2 percent annual real rate of return up to the time of permanent termination of operations. A licensee may use a credit of greater than 2 percent if the licensee's rate-setting authority has specifically authorized a higher rate. However, licensees certifying only to the formula amounts (*i.e.*, not a site-specific estimate) can take a pro-rata credit during the dismantlement period (*i.e.*, recognizing both cash expenditures and earnings the first 7 years after shutdown). Actual earnings on existing funds may be used to calculate future fund needs. A licensee, whose rates for decommissioning costs cover only a portion of these costs, may make use of this method only for the portion of these costs that are collected in one of the manners described in this paragraph, (e)(1)(ii). This method may be used as the exclusive mechanism relied upon for providing financial assurance for decommissioning in the following circumstances:

(A) By a licensee that recovers, either directly or indirectly, the estimated total cost of decommissioning through rates established by "cost of service" or similar ratemaking regulation. Public utility districts, municipalities, rural electric cooperatives, and State and Federal agencies, including associations of any of the foregoing, that establish their own rates and are able to recover their cost of service allocable to decommissioning, are assumed to meet this condition.

(B) By a licensee whose source of revenues for its external sinking fund is a "non-bypassable charge," the total amount of which will provide funds estimated to be needed for decommissioning pursuant to §§ 50.75(c), 50.75(f), or 50.82 of this part.

(iii) A surety method, insurance, or other guarantee method:

(A) These methods guarantee that decommissioning costs will be paid. A surety method may be in the form of a surety bond, or letter of credit. Any surety method or insurance used to provide financial assurance for decommissioning must contain the following conditions:

(*1*) The surety method or insurance must be open-ended, or, if written for a specified term, such as 5 years, must be renewed automatically, unless 90 days or more prior to the renewal day the issuer notifies the NRC, the beneficiary, and the licensee of its intention not to renew. The surety or insurance must also provide that the full face amount be paid to the beneficiary automatically prior to the expiration without proof of forfeiture if the licensee fails to provide a replacement acceptable to the NRC within 30 days after receipt of notification of cancellation.

(*2*) The surety or insurance must be payable to a trust established for decommissioning costs. The trustee and trust must be acceptable to the NRC. An acceptable trustee includes an appropriate State or Federal government agency or an entity that has the authority to act as a trustee and whose trust operations are regulated and examined by a Federal or State agency.

(B) A parent company guarantee of funds for decommissioning costs based on a financial test may be used if the guarantee and test are as contained in appendix A to 10 CFR part 30.

(C) For commercial companies that issue bonds, a guarantee of funds by the applicant or licensee for decommissioning costs based on a financial test may be used if the guarantee and test are as contained in appendix C to 10 CFR part 30. For commercial companies that do not issue bonds, a guarantee of funds by the applicant or licensee for decommissioning costs may be used if the guarantee and test are as contained in appendix D to 10 CFR part 30. For non-profit entities, such as colleges, universities, and non-profit hospitals, a guarantee of funds by the applicant or licensee may be used if the guarantee and test are as contained in appendix E to 10 CFR part 30. A guarantee by the applicant or licensee may not be used in any situation in which the applicant or licensee has a parent company holding majority control of voting stock of the company.

(iv) For a power reactor licensee that is a Federal licensee, or for a non-power reactor licensee that is a Federal, State, or local government licensee, a statement of intent containing a cost estimate for decommissioning, and indicating that funds for decommissioning will be obtained when necessary.

(v) Contractual obligation(s) on the part of a licensee's customer(s), the total amount of which over the duration of the contract(s) will provide the licensee's total share of uncollected funds estimated to be needed for decommissioning pursuant to §§ 50.75(c), 50.75(f), or § 50.82. To be acceptable to the NRC as a method of decommissioning funding assurance, the terms of the contract(s) shall include provisions that the electricity buyer(s) will pay for the decommissioning obligations specified in the contract(s), notwithstanding the operational status either of the licensed power reactor to which the contract(s) pertains or force majeure provisions. All proceeds from the contract(s) for decommissioning funding will be deposited to the external sinking fund. The NRC reserves the right to evaluate the terms of any contract(s) and the financial qualifications of the contracting entity(ies) offered as assurance for decommissioning funding.

(vi) Any other mechanism, or combination of mechanisms, that provides, as determined by the NRC upon its evaluation of the specific circumstances of each licensee submittal, assurance of decommissioning funding equivalent to that provided by the mechanisms specified in paragraphs (e)(1)(i) through (v) of this section. Licensees who do not have sources of funding described in paragraph (e)(1)(ii) of this section may use an external sinking fund in combination with a guarantee mechanism, as specified in paragraph (e)(1)(iii) of this section, provided that the total amount of funds estimated to be necessary for decommissioning is assured.

(2) The NRC reserves the right to take the following steps in order to ensure a licensee's adequate accumulation of decommissioning funds: review, as needed, the rate of accumulation of decommissioning funds; and, either independently or in cooperation with the FERC and the licensee's State PUC, take additional actions as appropriate on a case-by-case basis, including modification of a licensee's schedule for the accumulation of decommissioning funds.

(3) Each holder of a combined license under subpart C of 10 CFR part 52 shall, 2 years before and 1 year before the scheduled date for initial loading of fuel, consistent with the schedule required by § 52.99(a), submit a report to the NRC containing a certification updating the information described under paragraph (b)(1) of this section, including a copy of the financial instrument to be used. No later than 30 days after the Commission publishes notice in the FEDERAL REGISTER under 10 CFR 52.103(a), the licensee shall submit a report containing a certification that financial assurance for decommissioning is being provided in an amount specified in the licensee's most recent updated certification, including a copy of the financial instrument obtained to satisfy the requirements of paragraph (e) of this section.

(f)(1) Each power reactor licensee shall report, on a calendar-year basis, to the NRC by March 31, 1999, and at least once every 2 years thereafter on the status of its decommissioning funding for each reactor or part of a reactor that it owns. However, each holder of a combined license under part 52 of this chapter need not begin reporting until the date that the Commission has made the finding under § 52.103(g) of this chapter. The information in this report must include, at a minimum, the amount of decommissioning funds estimated to be required pursuant to 10 CFR 50.75(b) and (c); the amount of decommissioning funds accumulated to the end of the calendar year preceding the date of the report; a schedule of the annual amounts remaining to be collected; the assumptions used regarding rates of escalation in decommissioning costs, rates of earnings on decommissioning funds, and rates of other factors used in funding projections; any contracts upon which the licensee is relying pursuant to paragraph (e)(1)(v) of this section; any modifications occurring to a licensee's current method of providing financial assurance since the last submitted report; and any material changes to trust agreements. If any of the preceding items is not applicable, the licensee should so state in its report. Any licensee for a plant that is within 5 years of the projected end of its operation, or where conditions have changed such that it will close within 5 years (before the end of its licensed life), or that has already closed (before the end of its licensed life), or that is involved in a merger or an acquisition shall submit this report annually.

(2) Each power reactor licensee shall report, on a calendar-year basis, to the NRC by March 31, 1999, and at least once every 2 years thereafter on the status of its decommissioning funding for each reactor or part of a reactor that it owns. The information in this report must include, at a minimum, the amount of decommissioning funds estimated to be required pursuant to 10 CFR 50.75(b) and (c); the amount of decommissioning funds accumulated to the end of the calendar year preceding the date of the report; a schedule of the annual amounts remaining to be collected; the assumptions used regarding rates of escalation in decommissioning costs, rates of earnings on decommissioning funds, and rates of other factors used in funding projections; any contracts upon which the licensee is relying pursuant to paragraph (e)(1)(v) of this section; any modifications occurring to a licensee's current method of providing financial assurance since the

last submitted report; and any material changes to trust agreements. If any of the preceding items is not applicable, the licensee should so state in its report. Any licensee for a plant that is within 5 years of the projected end of its operation, or where conditions have changed such that it will close within 5 years (before the end of its licensed life), or that has already closed (before the end of its licensed life), or that is involved in a merger or an acquisition shall submit this report annually.

(3) Each power reactor licensee shall at or about 5 years prior to the projected end of operations submit a preliminary decommissioning cost estimate which includes an up-to-date assessment of the major factors that could affect the cost to decommission.

(4) Each non-power reactor licensee shall at or about 2 years prior to the projected end of operations submit a preliminary decommissioning plan containing a cost estimate for decommissioning and an up-to-date assessment of the major factors that could affect planning for decommissioning. Factors to be considered in submitting this preliminary plan information include—

(i) The decommissioning alternative anticipated to be used. The requirements of §50.82(b)(4)(i) must be considered at this time;

(ii) Major technical actions necessary to carry out decommissioning safely;

(iii) The current situation with regard to disposal of high-level and low-level radioactive waste;

(iv) Residual radioactivity criteria;

(v) Other site specific factors which could affect decommissioning planning and cost.

(5) If necessary, the cost estimate, for power and non-power reactors, shall also include plans for adjusting levels of funds assured for decommissioning to demonstrate that a reasonable level of assurance will be provided that funds will be available when needed to cover the cost of decommissioning.

(g) Each licensee shall keep records of information important to the safe and effective decommissioning of the facility in an identified location until the license is terminated by the Commission. If records of relevant information are kept for other purposes, reference to these records and their locations may be used. Information the Commission considers important to decommissioning consists of—

(1) Records of spills or other unusual occurrences involving the spread of contamination in and around the facility, equipment, or site. These records may be limited to instances when significant contamination remains after any cleanup procedures or when there is reasonable likelihood that contaminants may have spread to inaccessible areas as in the case of possible seepage into porous materials such as concrete. These records must include any known information on identification of involved nuclides, quantities, forms, and concentrations.

(2) As-built drawings and modifications of structures and equipment in restricted areas where radioactive materials are used and/or stored and of locations of possible inaccessible contamination such as buried pipes which may be subject to contamination. If required drawings are referenced, each relevant document need not be indexed individually. If drawings are not available, the licensee shall substitute appropriate records of available information concerning these areas and locations.

(3) Records of the cost estimate performed for the decommissioning funding plan or of the amount certified for decommissioning, and records of the funding method used for assuring funds if either a funding plan or certification is used.

(4) Records of:

(i) The licensed site area, as originally licensed, which must include a site map and any acquisition or use of property outside the originally licensed site area for the purpose of receiving, possessing, or using licensed materials;

(ii) The licensed activities carried out on the acquired or used property; and

(iii) The release and final disposition of any property recorded in paragraph (g)(4)(i) of this section, the historical site assessment performed for the release, radiation surveys performed to support release of the property, submittals to the NRC made in accordance with §50.83, and the methods employed to ensure that the property met the radiological criteria of 10 CFR Part 20, Subpart E, at the time the property was released.

(h)(1) Licensees that are not "electric utilities" as defined in § 50.2 that use prepayment or an external sinking fund to provide financial assurance shall provide in the terms of the arrangements governing the trust, escrow account, or Government fund, used to segregate and manage the funds that—

(i) The trustee, manager, investment advisor, or other person directing investment of the funds:

(A) Is prohibited from investing the funds in securities or other obligations of the licensee or any other owner or operator of any nuclear power reactor or their affiliates, subsidiaries, successors or assigns, or in a mutual fund in which at least 50 percent of the fund is invested in the securities of a licensee or parent company whose subsidiary is an owner or operator of a foreign or domestic nuclear power plant. However, the funds may be invested in securities tied to market indices or other non-nuclear sector collective, commingled, or mutual funds, provided that this subsection shall not operate in such a way as to require the sale or transfer either in whole or in part, or other disposition of any such prohibited investment that was made before the publication date of this rule, and provided further that no more than 10 percent of trust assets may be indirectly invested in securities of any entity owning or operating one or more nuclear power plants.

(B) Is obligated at all times to adhere to a standard of care set forth in the trust, which either shall be the standard of care, whether in investing or otherwise, required by State or Federal law or one or more State or Federal regulatory agencies with jurisdiction over the trust funds, or, in the absence of any such standard of care, whether in investing or otherwise, that a prudent investor would use in the same circumstances. The term "prudent investor," shall have the same meaning as set forth in the Federal Energy Regulatory Commission's "Regulations Governing Nuclear Plant Decommissioning Trust Funds" at 18 CFR 35.32(a)(3), or any successor regulation.

(ii) The licensee, its affiliates, and its subsidiaries are prohibited from being engaged as investment manager for the funds or from giving day-to-day management direction of the funds' investments or direction on individual investments by the funds, except in the case of passive fund management of trust funds where management is limited to investments tracking market indices.

(iii) The trust, escrow account, Government fund, or other account used to segregate and manage the funds may not be amended in any material respect without written notification to the Director, Office of Nuclear Reactor Regulation, Director, Office of New Reactors, or Director, Office of Nuclear Material Safety and Safeguards, as applicable, at least 30 working days before the proposed effective date of the amendment. The licensee shall provide the text of the proposed amendment and a statement of the reason for the proposed amendment. The trust, escrow account, Government fund, or other account may not be amended if the person responsible for managing the trust, escrow account, Government fund, or other account receives written notice of objection from the Director, Office of Nuclear Reactor Regulation, Director, Office of New Reactors, or Director, Office of Nuclear Material Safety and Safeguards, as applicable, within the notice period; and

(iv) Except for withdrawals being made under § 50.82(a)(8) or for payments of ordinary administrative costs (including taxes) and other incidental expenses of the fund (including legal, accounting, actuarial, and trustee expenses) in connection with the operation of the fund, no disbursement or payment may be made from the trust, escrow account, Government fund, or other account used to segregate and manage the funds until written notice of the intention to make a disbursement or payment has been given to the Director, Office of Nuclear Reactor Regulation, Director, Office of New Reactors, or Director, Office of Nuclear Material Safety and Safeguards, as applicable, at least 30 working days before the date of the intended disbursement or payment. The disbursement or payment from the trust, escrow account, Government fund or other account may be made following the 30-working day notice period if the person responsible for managing the trust, escrow account, Government fund, or other account does not receive written notice of objection from the Director, Office of Nuclear Reactor Regulation, Director, Office of New Reactors, or Director, Office of Nuclear Material Safety and Safeguards, as applicable, within the notice period. Disbursements or payments from the trust, escrow account, Government fund, or other account used to segregate and manage the funds, other than for payment of ordinary administrative costs (including taxes) and other incidental expenses of the fund (including legal, accounting, actuarial, and trustee expenses) in connection with the operation of the fund, are restricted to decommissioning expenses or transfer to another financial assurance method acceptable under paragraph (e) of this section until final decommissioning has been completed. After decommissioning has begun and withdrawals from the decommissioning fund are made under §50.82(a)(8), no further notification need be made to the NRC.

(2) Licensees that are "electric utilities" under §50.2 that use prepayment or an external sinking fund to provide financial assurance shall include a provision in the terms of the trust, escrow account, Government fund, or other account used to segregate and manage funds that except for withdrawals being made under §50.82(a)(8) or for payments of ordinary administrative costs (including taxes) and other incidental expenses of the fund (including legal, accounting, actuarial, and trustee expenses) in connection with the operation of the fund, no disbursement or payment may be made from the trust, escrow account, Government fund, or other account used to segregate and manage the funds until written notice of the intention to make a disbursement or payment has been given the Director, Office of Nuclear Reactor Regulation, Director, Office of New Reactors, or Director, Office of Nuclear Material Safety and Safeguards, as applicable, at least 30 working days before the date of the intended disbursement or payment. The disbursement or payment from the trust, escrow account, Government fund or other account may be made following the 30-working day notice period if the person responsible for managing the trust, escrow account, Government fund, or other account does not receive written notice of objection from the Director, Office of Nuclear Reactor Regulation, Director, Office of New Reactors, or Director, Office of Nuclear Material Safety and Safeguards, as applicable, within the notice period. Disbursements or payments from the trust, escrow account, Government fund, or other account used to segregate and manage the funds, other than for payment of ordinary administrative costs (including taxes) and other incidental expenses of the fund (including legal, accounting, actuarial, and trustee expenses) in connection with the operation of the fund, are restricted to decommissioning expenses or transfer to another financial assurance method acceptable under paragraph (e) of this section until final decommissioning has been completed. After decommissioning has begun and withdrawals from the decommissioning fund are made under §50.82(a)(8), no further notification need be made to the NRC.

(3) A licensee that is not an "electric utility" under §50.2 and using a surety method, insurance, or other guarantee method to provide financial assurance shall provide that the trust established for decommissioning costs to which the surety or insurance is payable contains in its terms the requirements in paragraphs (h)(1)(i), (ii), (iii), and (iv) of this section.

(4) Unless otherwise determined by the Commission with regard to a specific application, the Commission has determined that any amendment to the license of a utilization facility that does no more than delete specific license conditions relating to the terms and conditions of decommissioning trust agreements involves "no significant hazards consideration."

(5) The provisions of paragraphs (h)(1) through (h)(3) of this section do not apply to any licensee that as of December 24, 2003, has existing license conditions relating to decommissioning

trust agreements, so long as the licensee does not elect to amend those license conditions. If a licensee with existing license conditions relating to decommissioning trust agreements elects to amend those conditions, the license amendment shall be in accordance with the provisions of paragraph (h) of this section.

[53 FR 24049, June 27, 1988, as amended at 58 FR 68731, Dec. 29, 1993; 59 FR 1618, Jan. 12, 1994; 61 FR 39301, July 29, 1996; 63 FR 50480, Sept. 22, 1998; 63 FR 57236, Oct. 27, 1998; 68 FR 19727, Apr. 22, 2003; 67 FR 78350, Dec. 24, 2002; 68 FR 12571, Mar. 17, 2003; 68 FR 65388, Nov. 20, 2003; 72 FR 49502, Aug. 28, 2007; 73 FR 5722, Jan. 31, 2008; 77 FR 35571, June 17, 2012]

§ 50.76 Licensee's change of status; financial qualifications.

An electric utility licensee holding an operating license (including a renewed license) for a nuclear power reactor, no later than seventy-five (75) days prior to ceasing to be an electric utility in any manner not involving a license transfer under § 50.80, shall provide the NRC with the financial qualifications information that would be required for obtaining an initial operating license as specified in § 50.33(f)(2). The financial qualifications information must address the first full five years of operation after the date the licensee ceases to be an electric utility.

[69 FR 4448, Jan. 30, 2004]

US/IAEA Safeguards Agreement

§ 50.78 Facility information and verification.

(a) In response to a written request by the Commission, each applicant for a construction permit or license and each recipient of a construction permit or a license shall submit facility information, as described in § 75.10 of this chapter, on Form N–71, and associated forms and site information on DOC/NRC Form AP–A and associated forms;

(b) As required by the Additional Protocol, shall submit location information described in § 75.11 of this chapter on DOC/NRC Form AP–1 and associated forms; and

(c) Shall permit verification thereof by the International Atomic Energy Agency (IAEA) and take other action as necessary to implement the US/IAEA Safeguards Agreement, as described in part 75 of this chapter.

[73 FR 78605, Dec. 23, 2008]

Transfers of Licenses—Creditors' Rights—Surrender of Licenses

§ 50.80 Transfer of licenses.

(a) No license for a production or utilization facility (including, but not limited to, permits under this part and part 52 of this chapter, and licenses under parts 50 and 52 of this chapter), or any right thereunder, shall be transferred, assigned, or in any manner disposed of, either voluntarily or involuntarily, directly or indirectly, through transfer of control of the license to any person, unless the Commission gives its consent in writing.

(b)(1) An application for transfer of a license shall include:

(i) For a construction permit or operating license under this part, as much of the information described in §§ 50.33 and 50.34 of this part with respect to the identity and technical and financial qualifications of the proposed transferee as would be required by those sections if the application were for an initial license. The Commission may require additional information such as data respecting proposed safeguards against hazards from radioactive materials and the applicant's qualifications to protect against such hazards.

(ii) For an early site permit under part 52 of this chapter, as much of the information described in §§ 52.16 and 52.17 of this chapter with respect to the identity and technical qualifications of the proposed transferee as would be required by those sections if the application were for an initial license.

(iii) For a combined license under part 52 of this chapter, as much of the information described in §§ 52.77 and 52.79 of this chapter with respect to the identity and technical and financial qualifications of the proposed transferee as would be required by those sections if the application were for an initial license. The Commission may require additional information such as data respecting proposed safeguards against hazards from radioactive materials and the applicant's qualifications to protect against such hazards.

(iv) For a manufacturing license under part 52 of this chapter, as much of the information described in §§ 52.156 and 52.157 of this chapter with respect to the identity and technical qualifications of the proposed transferee as would be required by those sections if the application were for an initial license.

(2) The application shall include also a statement of the purposes for which the transfer of the license is requested, the nature of the transaction necessitating or making desirable the transfer of the license, and an agreement to limit access to Restricted Data pursuant to § 50.37. The Commission may require any person who submits an application for license pursuant to the provisions of this section to file a written consent from the existing licensee or a certified copy of an order or judgment of a court of competent jurisdiction attesting to the person's right (subject to the licensing requirements of the Act and these regulations) to possession of the facility or site involved.

(c) After appropriate notice to interested persons, including the existing licensee, and observance of such procedures as may be required by the Act or regulations or orders of the Commission, the Commission will approve an application for the transfer of a license, if the Commission determines:

(1) That the proposed transferee is qualified to be the holder of the license; and

(2) That transfer of the license is otherwise consistent with applicable provisions of law, regulations, and orders issued by the Commission pursuant thereto.

[26 FR 9546, Oct. 10, 1961, as amended at 35 FR 19661, Dec. 29, 1970; 38 FR 3956, Feb. 9, 1973; 65 FR 44660, July 19, 2000; 70 FR 61888, Oct. 27, 2005; 72 FR 49503, Aug. 28, 2007]

§ 50.81 Creditor regulations.

(a) Pursuant to section 184 of the Act, the Commission consents, without individual application, to the creation of any mortgage, pledge, or other lien upon any production or utilization facility not owned by the United States which is the subject of a license or upon any leasehold or other interest in such facility: *Provided:*

(1) That the rights of any creditor so secured may be exercised only in compliance with and subject to the same requirements and restrictions as would apply to the licensee pursuant to the provisions of the license, the Atomic Energy Act of 1954, as amended, and regulations issued by the Commission pursuant to said Act; and

(2) That no creditor so secured may take possession of the facility pursuant to the provisions of this section prior to either the issuance of a license from the Commission authorizing such possession or the transfer of the license.

(b) Any creditor so secured may apply for transfer of the license covering such facility by filing an application for transfer of the license pursuant to § 50.80(b). The Commission will act upon such application pursuant to § 50.80 (c).

(c) Nothing contained in this regulation shall be deemed to affect the means of acquiring, or the priority of, any tax lien or other lien provided by law.

(d) As used in this section:

(1) *License* includes any license under this chapter, any construction permit under this part, and any early site permit under part 52 of this chapter, which may be issued by the Commission with regard to a facility;

(2) "Creditor" includes, without implied limitation, the trustee under any mortgage, pledge or lien on a facility made to secure any creditor, any trustee or receiver of the facility appointed by a court of competent jurisdiction in any action brought for the benefit of any creditor secured by such mortgage, pledge or lien, any purchaser of such facility at the sale thereof upon foreclosure of such mortgage, pledge, or lien or upon exercise of any power of sale contained therein, or any assignee of any such purchaser.

(3) *Facility* includes but is not limited to, a site which is the subject of an early site permit under subpart A of part 52 of this chapter, and a reactor manufactured under a manufacturing license under subpart F of part 52 of this chapter.

[26 FR 9546, Oct. 10, 1961, as amended at 32 FR 2562, Feb. 7, 1967; 72 FR 49504, Aug. 28, 2007]

§ 50.82 Termination of license.

For power reactor licensees who, before the effective date of this rule, either submitted a decommissioning plan for approval or possess an approved decommissioning plan, the plan is considered to be the PSDAR submittal required under paragraph (a)(4) of this section and the provisions of this section apply accordingly. For power reactor licensees whose decommissioning plan approval activities have been relegated to notice of opportunity for a hearing under subpart G of 10 CFR part 2, the public meeting convened and 90-day delay of major decommissioning activities required in paragraphs (a)(4)(ii) and (a)(5) of this section shall not apply, and any orders arising from proceedings under subpart G of 10 CFR part 2 shall continue and remain in effect absent any orders from the Commission.

(a) For power reactor licensees—

(1)(i) When a licensee has determined to permanently cease operations the licensee shall, within 30 days, submit a written certification to the NRC, consistent with the requirements of § 50.4(b)(8);

(ii) Once fuel has been permanently removed from the reactor vessel, the licensee shall submit a written certification to the NRC that meets the requirements of § 50.4(b)(9) and;

(iii) For licensees whose licenses have been permanently modified to allow possession but not operation of the facility, before the effective date of this rule, the certifications required in paragraphs (a)(1) (i)–(ii) of this section shall be deemed to have been submitted.

(2) Upon docketing of the certifications for permanent cessation of operations and permanent removal of fuel from the reactor vessel, or when a final legally effective order to permanently cease operations has come into effect, the 10 CFR part 50 license no longer authorizes operation of the reactor or emplacement or retention of fuel into the reactor vessel.

(3) Decommissioning will be completed within 60 years of permanent cessation of operations. Completion of decommissioning beyond 60 years will be approved by the Commission only when necessary to protect public health and safety. Factors that will be considered by the Commission in evaluating an alternative that provides for completion of decommissioning beyond 60 years of permanent cessation of operations include unavailability of waste disposal capacity and other site-specific factors affecting the licensee's capability to carry out decommissioning, including presence of other nuclear facilities at the site.

(4)(i) Prior to or within 2 years following permanent cessation of operations, the licensee shall submit a post-shutdown decommissioning activities report (PSDAR) to the NRC, and a copy to the affected State(s). The PSDAR must contain a description of the planned decommissioning activities along with a schedule for their accomplishment, a discussion that provides the reasons for concluding that the environmental impacts associated with site-specific decommissioning activities will be bounded by appropriate previously issued environmental impact statements, and a site-specific DCE, including the projected cost of managing irradiated fuel.

(ii) The NRC shall notice receipt of the PSDAR and make the PSDAR available for public comment. The NRC shall also schedule a public meeting in the vicinity of the licensee's facility upon receipt of the PSDAR. The NRC shall publish a notice in the FEDERAL REGISTER and in a forum, such as local newspapers, that is readily accessible to individuals in the vicinity of the site, announcing the date, time and location of the meeting, along with a brief description of the purpose of the meeting.

(5) Licensees shall not perform any major decommissioning activities, as defined in § 50.2, until 90 days after the NRC has received the licensee's PSDAR submittal and until certifications of permanent cessation of operations and permanent removal of fuel from the reactor vessel, as required under § 50.82(a)(1), have been submitted.

(6) Licensees shall not perform any decommissioning activities, as defined in § 50.2, that—

(i) Foreclose release of the site for possible unrestricted use;

(ii) Result in significant environmental impacts not previously reviewed; or

(iii) Result in there no longer being reasonable assurance that adequate funds will be available for decommissioning.

(7) In taking actions permitted under § 50.59 following submittal of the PSDAR, the licensee shall notify the NRC, in writing and send a copy to the affected State(s), before performing any decommissioning activity inconsistent with, or making any significant schedule change from, those actions and schedules described in the PSDAR, including changes that significantly increase the decommissioning cost.

(8)(i) Decommissioning trust funds may be used by licensees if—

(A) The withdrawals are for expenses for legitimate decommissioning activities consistent with the definition of decommissioning in § 50.2;

(B) The expenditure would not reduce the value of the decommissioning trust below an amount necessary to place and maintain the reactor in a safe storage condition if unforeseen conditions or expenses arise and;

(C) The withdrawals would not inhibit the ability of the licensee to complete funding of any shortfalls in the decommissioning trust needed to ensure the availability of funds to ultimately release the site and terminate the license.

(ii) Initially, 3 percent of the generic amount specified in § 50.75 may be used for decommissioning planning. For licensees that have submitted the certifications required under § 50.82(a)(1) and commencing 90 days after the NRC has received the PSDAR, an additional 20 percent may be used. A site-specific decommissioning cost estimate must be submitted to the NRC prior to the licensee using any funding in excess of these amounts.

(iii) Within 2 years following permanent cessation of operations, if not already submitted, the licensee shall submit a site-specific decommissioning cost estimate.

(iv) For decommissioning activities that delay completion of decommissioning by including a period of storage or surveillance, the licensee shall provide a means of adjusting cost estimates and associated funding levels over the storage or surveillance period.

(v) After submitting its site-specific DCE required by paragraph (a)(4)(i) of this section, and until the licensee has completed its final radiation survey and demonstrated that residual radioactivity has been reduced to a level that permits termination of its license, the licensee must annually submit to the NRC, by March 31, a financial assurance status report. The report must include the following information, current through the end of the previous calendar year:

(A) The amount spent on decommissioning, both cumulative and over the previous calendar year, the remaining balance of any decommissioning funds, and the amount provided by other financial assurance methods being relied upon;

(B) An estimate of the costs to complete decommissioning, reflecting any difference between actual and estimated costs for work performed during the year, and the decommissioning criteria upon which the estimate is based;

(C) Any modifications occurring to a licensee's current method of providing financial assurance since the last submitted report; and

(D) Any material changes to trust agreements or financial assurance contracts.

(vi) If the sum of the balance of any remaining decommissioning funds, plus earnings on such funds calculated at not greater than a 2 percent real rate of return, together with the amount provided by other financial assurance methods being relied upon, does not cover the estimated cost to complete the decommissioning, the financial assurance status report must include additional financial assurance to cover the estimated cost of completion.

(vii) After submitting its site-specific DCE required by paragraph (a)(4)(i) of this section, the licensee must annually submit to the NRC, by March 31, a report on the status of its funding for managing irradiated fuel. The report must include the following information, current through the end of the previous calendar year:

(A) The amount of funds accumulated to cover the cost of managing the irradiated fuel;

(B) The projected cost of managing irradiated fuel until title to the fuel and possession of the fuel is transferred to the Secretary of Energy; and

(C) If the funds accumulated do not cover the projected cost, a plan to obtain additional funds to cover the cost.

(9) All power reactor licensees must submit an application for termination of license. The application for termination of license must be accompanied or preceded by a license termination plan to be submitted for NRC approval.

(i) The license termination plan must be a supplement to the FSAR or equivalent and must be submitted at least 2 years before termination of the license date.

(ii) The license termination plan must include—

(A) A site characterization;

(B) Identification of remaining dismantlement activities;

(C) Plans for site remediation;

(D) Detailed plans for the final radiation survey;

(E) A description of the end use of the site, if restricted;

(F) An updated site-specific estimate of remaining decommissioning costs; and

(G) A supplement to the environmental report, pursuant to § 51.53, describing any new information or significant environmental change associated with the licensee's proposed termination activities.

(H) Identification of parts, if any, of the facility or site that were released for use before approval of the license termination plan.

(iii) The NRC shall notice receipt of the license termination plan and make the license termination plan available for public comment. The NRC shall also schedule a public meeting in the vicinity of the licensee's facility upon receipt of the license termination plan. The NRC shall publish a notice in the FEDERAL REGISTER and in a forum, such as local newspapers, which is readily accessible to individuals in the vicinity of the site, announcing the date, time and location of the meeting, along with a brief description of the purpose of the meeting.

(10) If the license termination plan demonstrates that the remainder of decommissioning activities will be performed in accordance with the regulations in this chapter, will not be inimical to the common defense and security or to the health and safety of the public, and will not have a significant effect on the quality of the environment and after notice to interested persons, the Commission shall approve the plan, by license amendment, subject to such conditions and limitations as it deems appropriate and necessary and authorize implementation of the license termination plan.

(11) The Commission shall terminate the license if it determines that—

(i) The remaining dismantlement has been performed in accordance with the approved license termination plan, and

(ii) The final radiation survey and associated documentation, including an assessment of dose contributions associated with parts released for use before approval of the license termination plan, demonstrate that the facility and site have met the criteria for decommissioning in 10 CFR part 20, subpart E.

(b) For non-power reactor licensees—

(1) A licensee that permanently ceases operations must make application for license termination within 2 years following permanent cessation of operations, and in no case later than 1 year prior to expiration of the operating license. Each application for termination of a license must be accompanied or preceded by a proposed decommissioning plan. The contents of the decommissioning plan are specified in paragraph (b)(4) of this section.

(2) For decommissioning plans in which the major dismantlement activities are delayed by first placing the facility in storage, planning for these delayed activities may be less detailed. Updated detailed plans must be submitted and approved prior to the start of these activities.

(3) For decommissioning plans that delay completion of decommissioning by including a period of storage or surveillance, the licensee shall provide that—

(i) Funds needed to complete decommissioning be placed into an account segregated from the licensee's assets and outside the licensee's administrative control during the storage or surveillance period, or a surety method or fund statement of intent be maintained in accordance with the criteria of § 50.75(e); and

(ii) Means be included for adjusting cost estimates and associated funding levels over the storage or surveillance period.

(4) The proposed decommissioning plan must include—

(i) The choice of the alternative for decommissioning with a description of activities involved. An alternative is acceptable if it provides for completion of decommissioning without significant delay. Consideration will be given to an alternative which provides for delayed completion of decommissioning only when necessary to protect the public health and safety. Factors to be considered in evaluating an alternative which provides for delayed completion of decommissioning include unavailability of waste disposal capacity and other site-specific factors affecting the licensee's capability to carry out decommissioning, including the presence of other nuclear facilities at the site.

(ii) A description of the controls and limits on procedures and equipment to protect occupational and public health and safety;

(iii) A description of the planned final radiation survey;

(iv) An updated cost estimate for the chosen alternative for decommissioning, comparison of that estimate with present funds set aside for decommissioning, and plan for assuring the availability of adequate funds for completion of decommissioning; and

(v) A description of technical specifications, quality assurance provisions and physical security plan provisions in place during decommissioning.

(5) If the decommissioning plan demonstrates that the decommissioning will be performed in accordance with the regulations in this chapter and will not be inimical to the common defense and security or to the health and safety of the public, and after notice to interested persons, the Commission will approve, by amendment, the plan subject to such conditions and limitations as it deems appropriate and necessary. The approved decommissioning plan will be a supplement to the Safety Analysis report or equivalent.

(6) The Commission will terminate the license if it determines that—

(i) The decommissioning has been performed in accordance with the approved decommissioning plan, and

(ii) The terminal radiation survey and associated documentation demonstrate that the facility and site are suitable for release in accordance with the criteria for decommissioning in 10 CFR part 20, subpart E.

(c) For a facility that has permanently ceased operation before the expiration of its license, the collection period for any shortfall of funds will be determined, upon application by the licensee, on a case-by-case basis taking into account the specific financial situation of each licensee.

[61 FR 39301, July 29, 1996, as amended at 62 FR 39091, July 21, 1997; 68 FR 19727, Apr. 22, 2003; 76 FR 35571, June 17, 2011; 79 FR 66603, Nov. 10, 2014]

§ 50.83 Release of part of a power reactor facility or site for unrestricted use.

(a) Prior written NRC approval is required to release part of a facility or site for unrestricted use at any time before receiving approval of a license termination plan. Section 50.75 specifies recordkeeping requirements associated with partial release. Nuclear power reactor licensees seeking NRC approval shall—

(1) Evaluate the effect of releasing the property to ensure that—

(i) The dose to individual members of the public does not exceed the limits and standards of 10 CFR Part 20, Subpart D;

(ii) There is no reduction in the effectiveness of emergency planning or physical security;

(iii) Effluent releases remain within license conditions;

(iv) The environmental monitoring program and offsite dose calculation manual are revised to account for the changes;

(v) The siting criteria of 10 CFR Part 100 continue to be met; and

(vi) All other applicable statutory and regulatory requirements continue to be met.

(2) Perform a historical site assessment of the part of the facility or site to be released; and

(3) Perform surveys adequate to demonstrate compliance with the radiological criteria for unrestricted use specified in 10 CFR 20.1402 for impacted areas.

(b) For release of non-impacted areas, the licensee may submit a written request for NRC approval of the release if a license amendment is not otherwise required. The request submittal must include—

(1) The results of the evaluations performed in accordance with paragraphs (a)(1) and (a)(2) of this section;

(2) A description of the part of the facility or site to be released;

(3) The schedule for release of the property;

(4) The results of the evaluations performed in accordance with § 50.59; and

(5) A discussion that provides the reasons for concluding that the environmental impacts associated with the licensee's proposed release of the property will be bounded by appropriate previously issued environmental impact statements.

(c) After receiving an approval request from the licensee for the release of a non-impacted area, the NRC shall—

(1) Determine whether the licensee has adequately evaluated the effect of releasing the property as required by paragraph (a)(1) of this section;

(2) Determine whether the licensee's classification of any release areas as non-impacted is adequately justified; and

(3) Upon determining that the licensee's submittal is adequate, inform the licensee in writing that the release is approved.

(d) For release of impacted areas, the licensee shall submit an application for amendment of its license for the release of the property. The application must include—

(1) The information specified in paragraphs (b)(1) through (b)(3) of this section;

(2) The methods used for and results obtained from the radiation surveys required to demonstrate compliance with the radiological criteria for unrestricted use specified in 10 CFR 20.1402; and

(3) A supplement to the environmental report, under § 51.53, describing any new information or significant environmental change associated with the licensee's proposed release of the property.

(e) After receiving a license amendment application from the licensee for the release of an impacted area, the NRC shall—

(1) Determine whether the licensee has adequately evaluated the effect of releasing the property as required by paragraph (a)(1) of this section;

(2) Determine whether the licensee's classification of any release areas as non-impacted is adequately justified;

(3) Determine whether the licensee's radiation survey for an impacted area is adequate; and

(4) Upon determining that the licensee's submittal is adequate, approve the licensee's amendment application.

(f) The NRC shall notice receipt of the release approval request or license amendment application and make the approval request or license amendment application available for public comment. Before acting on an approval request or license amendment application submitted in accordance with this section, the NRC shall conduct a public meeting in the vicinity of the licensee's facility for the purpose of obtaining public comments on the proposed release of part of the facility or site. The NRC shall publish a document in the FEDERAL REGISTER and in a forum, such as local newspapers, which is readily accessible to individuals in the vicinity of the site, announcing the date, time, and location of the meeting, along with a brief description of the purpose of the meeting.

[68 FR 19727, Apr. 22, 2003]

AMENDMENT OF LICENSE OR CONSTRUCTION PERMIT AT REQUEST OF HOLDER

§ 50.90 Application for amendment of license, construction permit, or early site permit.

Whenever a holder of a license, including a construction permit and operating license under this part, and an early site permit, combined license, and manufacturing license under part 52 of this chapter, desires to amend the license or permit, application for an amendment must be filed with the Commission, as specified in §§ 50.4 or

52.3 of this chapter, as applicable, fully describing the changes desired, and following as far as applicable, the form prescribed for original applications.

[72 FR 49504, Aug. 28, 2007]

§50.91 Notice for public comment; State consultation.

The Commission will use the following procedures for an application requesting an amendment to an operating license under this part or a combined license under part 52 of this chapter for a facility licensed under §§50.21(b) or 50.22, or for a testing facility, except for amendments subject to hearings governed by 10 CFR part 2, subpart L. For amendments subject to 10 CFR part 2, subpart L, the following procedures will apply only to the extent specifically referenced in §2.309(b) of this chapter, except that notice of opportunity for hearing must be published in the FEDERAL REGISTER at least 30 days before the requested amendment is issued by the Commission:

(a) *Notice for public comment.* (1) At the time a licensee requests an amendment, it must provide to the Commission, in accordance with the distribution requirements specified in §50.4, its analysis about the issue of no significant hazards consideration using the standards in §50.92.

(2)(i) The Commission may publish in the FEDERAL REGISTER under §2.105 an individual notice of proposed action for an amendment for which it makes a proposed determination that no significant hazards consideration is involved, or, at least once every 30 days, publish a periodic FEDERAL REGISTER notice of proposed actions which identifies each amendment issued and each amendment proposed to be issued since the last such periodic notice, or it may publish both such notices.

(ii) For each amendment proposed to be issued, the notice will (A) contain the staff's proposed determination, under the standards in §50.92, (B) provide a brief description of the amendment and of the facility involved, (C) solicit public comments on the proposed determination, and (D) provide for a 30-day comment period.

(iii) The comment period will begin on the day after the date of the publication of the first notice, and, normally, the amendment will not be granted until after this comment period expires.

(3) The Commission may inform the public about the final disposition of an amendment request for which it has made a proposed determination of no significant hazards consideration either by issuing an individual notice of issuance under §2.106 of this chapter or by publishing such a notice in its periodic system of FEDERAL REGISTER notices. In either event, it will not make and will not publish a final determination on no significant hazards consideration, unless it receives a request for a hearing on that amendment request.

(4) Where the Commission makes a final determination that no significant hazards consideration is involved and that the amendment should be issued, the amendment will be effective on issuance, even if adverse public comments have been received and even if an interested person meeting the provisions for intervention called for in §2.309 of this chapter has filed a request for a hearing. The Commission need hold any required hearing only after it issues an amendment, unless it determines that a significant hazards consideration is involved, in which case the Commission will provide an opportunity for a prior hearing.

(5) Where the Commission finds that an emergency situation exists, in that failure to act in a timely way would result in derating or shutdown of a nuclear power plant, or in prevention of either resumption of operation or of increase in power output up to the plant's licensed power level, it may issue a license amendment involving no significant hazards consideration without prior notice and opportunity for a hearing or for public comment. In such a situation, the Commission will not publish a notice of proposed determination on no significant hazards consideration, but will publish a notice of issuance under §2.106 of this chapter, providing for opportunity for a hearing and for public comment after issuance. The Commission expects its licensees to apply for license amendments in timely fashion. It will decline to dispense with notice and comment on the determination of no significant hazards

consideration if it determines that the licensee has abused the emergency provision by failing to make timely application for the amendment and thus itself creating the emergency. Whenever an emergency situation exists, a licensee requesting an amendment must explain why this emergency situation occurred and why it could not avoid this situation, and the Commission will assess the licensee's reasons for failing to file an application sufficiently in advance of that event.

(6) Where the Commission finds that exigent circumstances exist, in that a licensee and the Commission must act quickly and that time does not permit the Commission to publish a FEDERAL REGISTER notice allowing 30 days for prior public comment, and it also determines that the amendment involves no significant hazards considerations, it:

(i)(A) Will either issue a FEDERAL REGISTER notice providing notice of an opportunity for hearing and allowing at least two weeks from the date of the notice for prior public comment; or

(B) Will use local media to provide reasonable notice to the public in the area surrounding a licensee's facility of the licensee's amendment and of its proposed determination as described in paragraph (a)(2) of this section, consulting with the licensee on the proposed media release and on the geographical area of its coverage;

(ii) Will provide for a reasonable opportunity for the public to comment, using its best efforts to make available to the public whatever means of communication it can for the public to respond quickly, and, in the case of telephone comments, have these comments recorded or transcribed, as necessary and appropriate;

(iii) When it has issued a local media release, may inform the licensee of the public's comments, as necessary and appropriate;

(iv) Will publish a notice of issuance under § 2.106;

(v) Will provide a hearing after issuance, if one has been requested by a person who satisfies the provisions for intervention specified in § 2.309 of this chapter;

(vi) Will require the licensee to explain the exigency and why the licensee cannot avoid it, and use its normal public notice and comment procedures in paragraph (a)(2) of this section if it determines that the licensee has failed to use its best efforts to make a timely application for the amendment in order to create the exigency and to take advantage of this procedure.

(7) Where the Commission finds that significant hazards considerations are involved, it will issue a FEDERAL REGISTER notice providing an opportunity for a prior hearing even in an emergency situation, unless it finds an imminent danger to the health or safety of the public, in which case it will issue an appropriate order or rule under 10 CFR part 2.

(b) *State consultation.* (1) At the time a licensee requests an amendment, it must notify the State in which its facility is located of its request by providing that State with a copy of its application and its reasoned analysis about no significant hazards considerations and indicate on the application that it has done so. (The Commission will make available to the licensee the name of the appropriate State official designated to receive such amendments.)

(2) The Commission will advise the State of its proposed determination about no significant hazards consideration normally by sending it a copy of the FEDERAL REGISTER notice.

(3) The Commission will make available to the State official designated to consult with it about its proposed determination the names of the Project Manager or other NRC personnel it designated to consult with the State. The Commission will consider any comments of that State official. If it does not hear from the State in a timely manner, it will consider that the State has no interest in its determination; nonetheless, to ensure that the State is aware of the application, before it issues the amendment, it will make a good faith effort to telephone that official. (Inability to consult with a responsible State official following good faith attempts will not prevent the Commission from making effective a license amendment involving no significant hazards consideration.)

(4) The Commission will make a good faith attempt to consult with the State

before it issues a license amendment involving no significant hazards consideration. If, however, it does not have time to use its normal consultation procedures because of an emergency situation, it will attempt to telephone the appropriate State official. (Inability to consult with a responsible State official following good faith attempts will not prevent the Commission from making effective a license amendment involving no significant hazards consideration, if the Commission deems it necessary in an emergency situation.)

(5) After the Commission issues the requested amendment, it will send a copy of its determination to the State.

(c) *Caveats about State consultation.* (1) The State consultation procedures in paragraph (b) of this section do not give the State a right:

(i) To veto the Commission's proposed or final determination;

(ii) To a hearing on the determination before the amendment becomes effective; or

(iii) To insist upon a postponement of the determination or upon issuance of the amendment.

(2) These procedures do not alter present provisions of law that reserve to the Commission exclusive responsibility for setting and enforcing radiological health and safety requirements for nuclear power plants.

[51 FR 7765, Mar. 6, 1986, as amended at 51 FR 40310, Nov. 6, 1986; 61 FR 39303, July 29, 1996; 69 FR 2276, Jan. 14, 2004; 72 FR 49504, Aug. 28, 2007]

§50.92 Issuance of amendment.

(a) In determining whether an amendment to a license, construction permit, or early site permit will be issued to the applicant, the Commission will be guided by the considerations which govern the issuance of initial licenses, construction permits, or early site permits to the extent applicable and appropriate. If the application involves the material alteration of a licensed facility, a construction permit will be issued before the issuance of the amendment to the license, provided however, that if the application involves a material alteration to a nuclear power reactor manufactured under part 52 of this chapter before its installation at a site, or a combined license before the date that the Commission makes the finding under §52.103(g) of this chapter, no application for a construction permit is required. If the amendment involves a significant hazards consideration, the Commission will give notice of its proposed action:

(1) Under §2.105 of this chapter before acting thereon; and

(2) As soon as practicable after the application has been docketed.

(b) The Commission will be particularly sensitive to a license amendment request that involves irreversible consequences (such as one that permits a significant increase in the amount of effluents or radiation emitted by a nuclear power plant).

(c) The Commission may make a final determination, under the procedures in §50.91, that a proposed amendment to an operating license or a combined license for a facility or reactor licensed under §§50.21(b) or 50.22, or for a testing facility involves no significant hazards consideration, if operation of the facility in accordance with the proposed amendment would not:

(1) Involve a significant increase in the probability or consequences of an accident previously evaluated; or

(2) Create the possibility of a new or different kind of accident from any accident previously evaluated; or

(3) Involve a significant reduction in a margin of safety.

[51 FR 7767, Mar. 6, 1986, as amended at 72 FR 49504, Aug. 28, 2007]

Revocation, Suspension, Modification, Amendment of Licenses and Construction Permits, Emergency Operations by the Commission

§50.100 Revocation, suspension, modification of licenses, permits, and approvals for cause.

A license, permit, or standard design approval under parts 50 or 52 of this chapter may be revoked, suspended, or modified, in whole or in part, for any material false statement in the application or in the supplemental or other statement of fact required of the applicant; or because of conditions revealed by the application or statement of fact of any report, record, inspection, or other means which would warrant the

Commission to refuse to grant a license, permit, or approval on an original application (other than those relating to §§ 50.51, 50.42(a), and 50.43(b)); or for failure to manufacture a reactor, or construct or operate a facility in accordance with the terms of the permit or license, provided, however, that failure to make timely completion of the proposed construction or alteration of a facility under a construction permit under part 50 of this chapter or a combined license under part 52 of this chapter shall be governed by the provisions of § 50.55(b); or for violation of, or failure to observe, any of the terms and provisions of the act, regulations, license, permit, approval, or order of the Commission.

[72 FR 49504, Aug. 28, 2007]

§ 50.101 Retaking possession of special nuclear material.

Upon revocation of a license, the Commission may immediately cause the retaking of possession of all special nuclear material held by the licensee.

[21 FR 355, Jan. 19, 1956, as amended at 40 FR 8790, Mar. 3, 1975]

§ 50.102 Commission order for operation after revocation.

Whenever the Commission finds that the public convenience and necessity, or the Department finds that the production program of the Department requires continued operation of a production or utilization facility, the license for which has been revoked, the Commission may, after consultation with the appropriate federal or state regulatory agency having jurisdiction, order that possession be taken of such facility and that it be operated for a period of time as, in the judgment of the Commission, the public convenience and necessity or the production program of the Department may require, or until a license for operation of the facility shall become effective. Just compensation shall be paid for the use of the facility.

[40 FR 8790, Mar. 3, 1975]

§ 50.103 Suspension and operation in war or national emergency.

(a) Whenever Congress declares that a state of war or national emergency exists, the Commission, if it finds it necessary to the common defense and security, may,

(1) Suspend any license it has issued.

(2) Cause the recapture of special nuclear material.

(3) Order the operation of any licensed facility.

(4) Order entry into any plant or facility in order to recapture special nuclear material or to operate the facility.

(b) Just compensation shall be paid for any damages caused by recapture of special nuclear material or by operation of any facility, pursuant to this section.

[21 FR 355, Jan. 19, 1956, as amended at 35 FR 11416, July 17, 1970; 40 FR 8790, Mar. 3, 1975]

BACKFITTING

§ 50.109 Backfitting.

(a)(1) Backfitting is defined as the modification of or addition to systems, structures, components, or design of a facility; or the design approval or manufacturing license for a facility; or the procedures or organization required to design, construct or operate a facility; any of which may result from a new or amended provision in the Commission's regulations or the imposition of a regulatory staff position interpreting the Commission's regulations that is either new or different from a previously applicable staff position after:

(i) The date of issuance of the construction permit for the facility for facilities having construction permits issued after October 21, 1985;

(ii) Six (6) months before the date of docketing of the operating license application for the facility for facilities having construction permits issued before October 21, 1985;

(iii) The date of issuance of the operating license for the facility for facilities having operating licenses;

(iv) The date of issuance of the design approval under subpart E of part 52 of this chapter;

(v) The date of issuance of a manufacturing license under subpart F of part 52 of this chapter;

(vi) The date of issuance of the first construction permit issued for a duplicate design under appendix N of this part; or

(vii) The date of issuance of a combined license under subpart C of part 52 of this chapter, provided that if the combined license references an early site permit, the provisions in § 52.39 of this chapter apply with respect to the site characteristics, design parameters, and terms and conditions specified in the early site permit. If the combined license references a standard design certification rule under subpart B of 10 CFR part 52, the provisions in § 52.63 of this chapter apply with respect to the design matters resolved in the standard design certification rule, provided however, that if any specific backfitting limitations are included in a referenced design certification rule, those limitations shall govern. If the combined license references a standard design approval under subpart E of 10 CFR part 52, the provisions in § 52.145 of this chapter apply with respect to the design matters resolved in the standard design approval. If the combined license uses a reactor manufactured under a manufacturing license under subpart F of 10 CFR part 52, the provisions of § 52.171 of this chapter apply with respect to matters resolved in the manufacturing license proceeding.

(2) Except as provided in paragraph (a)(4) of this section, the Commission shall require a systematic and documented analysis pursuant to paragraph (c) of this section for backfits which it seeks to impose.

(3) Except as provided in paragraph (a)(4) of this section, the Commission shall require the backfitting of a facility only when it determines, based on the analysis described in paragraph (c) of this section, that there is a substantial increase in the overall protection of the public health and safety or the common defense and security to be derived from the backfit and that the direct and indirect costs of implementation for that facility are justified in view of this increased protection.

(4) The provisions of paragraphs (a)(2) and (a)(3) of this section are inapplicable and, therefore, backfit analysis is not required and the standards in paragraph (a)(3) of this section do not apply where the Commission or staff, as appropriate, finds and declares, with appropriated documented evaluation for its finding, either:

(i) That a modification is necessary to bring a facility into compliance with a license or the rules or orders of the Commission, or into conformance with written commitments by the licensee; or

(ii) That regulatory action is necessary to ensure that the facility provides adequate protection to the health and safety of the public and is in accord with the common defense and security; or

(iii) That the regulatory action involves defining or redefining what level of protection to the public health and safety or common defense and security should be regarded as adequate.

(5) The Commission shall always require the backfitting of a facility if it determines that such regulatory action is necessary to ensure that the facility provides adequate protection to the health and safety of the public and is in accord with the common defense and security.

(6) The documented evaluation required by paragraph (a)(4) of this section shall include a statement of the objectives of and reasons for the modification and the basis for invoking the exception. If immediately effective regulatory action is required, then the documented evaluation may follow rather than precede the regulatory action.

(7) If there are two or more ways to achieve compliance with a license or the rules or orders of the Commission, or with written licensee commitments, or there are two or more ways to reach a level of protection which is adequate, then ordinarily the applicant or licensee is free to choose the way which best suits its purposes. However, should it be necessary or appropriate for the Commission to prescribe a specific way to comply with its requirements or to achieve adequate protection, then cost may be a factor in selecting the way, provided that the objective of compliance or adequate protection is met.

(b) Paragraph (a)(3) of this section shall not apply to backfits imposed prior to October 21, 1985.

(c) In reaching the determination required by paragraph (a)(3) of this section, the Commission will consider how the backfit should be scheduled in light of other ongoing regulatory activities at the facility and, in addition, will consider information available concerning any of the following factors as may be appropriate and any other information relevant and material to the proposed backfit:

(1) Statement of the specific objectives that the proposed backfit is designed to achieve;

(2) General description of the activity that would be required by the licensee or applicant in order to complete the backfit;

(3) Potential change in the risk to the public from the accidental off-site release of radioactive material;

(4) Potential impact on radiological exposure of facility employees;

(5) Installation and continuing costs associated with the backfit, including the cost of facility downtime or the cost of construction delay;

(6) The potential safety impact of changes in plant or operational complexity, including the relationship to proposed and existing regulatory requirements;

(7) The estimated resource burden on the NRC associated with the proposed backfit and the availability of such resources;

(8) The potential impact of differences in facility type, design or age on the relevancy and practicality of the proposed backfit;

(9) Whether the proposed backfit is interim or final and, if interim, the justification for imposing the proposed backfit on an interim basis.

(d) No licensing action will be withheld during the pendency of backfit analyses required by the Commission's rules.

(e) The Executive Director for Operations shall be responsible for implementation of this section, and all analyses required by this section shall be approved by the Executive Director for Operations or his designee.

[53 FR 20610, June 6, 1988, as amended at 54 FR 15398, Apr. 18, 1989; 72 FR 49504, Aug. 28, 2007]

ENFORCEMENT

§ 50.110 Violations.

(a) The Commission may obtain an injunction or other court order to prevent a violation of the provisions of—

(1) The Atomic Energy Act of 1954, as amended;

(2) Title II of the Energy Reorganization Act of 1974, as amended; or

(3) A regulation or order issued pursuant to those Acts.

(b) The Commission may obtain a court order for the payment of a civil penalty imposed under Section 234 of the Atomic Energy Act:

(1) For violations of—

(i) Sections 53, 57, 62, 63, 81, 82, 101, 103, 104, 107, or 109 of the Atomic Energy Act of 1954, as amended;

(ii) Section 206 of the Energy Reorganization Act;

(iii) Any rule, regulation, or order issued pursuant to the sections specified in paragraph (b)(1)(i) of this section;

(iv) Any term, condition, or limitation of any license issued under the sections specified in paragraph (b)(1)(i) of this section.

(2) For any violation for which a license may be revoked under section 186 of the Atomic Energy Act of 1954, as amended.

[57 FR 55075, Nov. 24, 1992]

§ 50.111 Criminal penalties.

(a) Section 223 of the Atomic Energy Act of 1954, as amended, provides for criminal sanctions for willful violation of, attempted violation of, or conspiracy to violate, any regulation issued under sections 161b, 161i, or 161o of the Act. For purposes of section 223, all the regulations in part 50 are issued under one or more of sections 161b, 161i, or 161o, except for the sections listed in paragraph (b) of this section.

(b) The regulations in 10 CFR part 50 that are not issued under sections 161b, 161i, or 161o for the purposes of section 223 are as follows: §§ 50.1, 50.2, 50.3, 50.4, 50.8, 50.11, 50.12, 50.13, 50.20, 50.21, 50.22, 50.23, 50.30, 50.31, 50.32, 50.33, 50.34a, 50.35, 50.36b, 50.37, 50.38, 50.39, 50.40, 50.41, 50.42, 50.43, 50.45, 50.50, 50.51, 50.52, 50.53, 50.56, 50.57, 50.58, 50.81, 50.90, 50.91,

50.92, 50.100, 50.101, 50.102, 50.103, 50.109, 50.110, 50.111.

[57 FR 55075, Nov. 24, 1992, as amended at 61 FR 39303, July 29, 1996]

ADDITIONAL STANDARDS FOR LICENSES, CERTIFICATIONS, AND REGULATORY APPROVALS

§50.120 Training and qualification of nuclear power plant personnel.

(a) *Applicability.* The requirements of this section apply to each applicant for and each holder of an operating license issued under this part and each holder of a combined license issued under part 52 of this chapter for a nuclear power plant of the type specified in §50.21(b) or §50.22.

(b) *Requirements.* (1)(i) Each nuclear power plant operating license applicant, by 18 months prior to fuel load, and each holder of an operating license shall establish, implement, and maintain a training program that meets the requirements of paragraphs (b)(2) and (b)(3) of this section.

(ii) Each holder of a combined license shall establish, implement, and maintain the training program that meets the requirements of paragraphs (b)(2) and (b)(3) of this section, as described in the final safety analysis report no later than 18 months before the scheduled date for initial loading of fuel.

(2) The training program must be derived from a systems approach to training as defined in 10 CFR 55.4, and must provide for the training and qualification of the following categories of nuclear power plant personnel:

(i) Non-licensed operator.

(ii) Shift supervisor.

(iii) Shift technical advisor.

(iv) Instrument and control technician.

(v) Electrical maintenance personnel.

(vi) Mechanical maintenance personnel.

(vii) Radiological protection technician.

(viii) Chemistry technician.

(ix) Engineering support personnel.

(3) The training program must incorporate the instructional requirements necessary to provide qualified personnel to operate and maintain the facility in a safe manner in all modes of operation. The training program must be developed to be in compliance with the facility license, including all technical specifications and applicable regulations. The training program must be periodically evaluated and revised as appropriate to reflect industry experience as well as changes to the facility, procedures, regulations, and quality assurance requirements. The training program must be periodically reviewed by licensee management for effectiveness. Sufficient records must be maintained by the licensee to maintain program integrity and kept available for NRC inspection to verify the adequacy of the program.

[72 FR 49505, Aug. 28, 2007]

§50.150 Aircraft impact assessment.

(a) *Assessment requirements.* (1) *Assessment.* Each applicant listed in paragraph (a)(3) shall perform a design-specific assessment of the effects on the facility of the impact of a large, commercial aircraft. Using realistic analyses, the applicant shall identify and incorporate into the design those design features and functional capabilities to show that, with reduced use of operator actions:

(i) The reactor core remains cooled, or the containment remains intact; and

(ii) spent fuel cooling or spent fuel pool integrity is maintained.

(2) *Aircraft impact characteristics.*[1] The assessment must be based on the beyond-design-basis impact of a large, commercial aircraft used for long distance flights in the United States, with aviation fuel loading typically used in such flights, and an impact speed and angle of impact considering the ability of both experienced and inexperienced pilots to control large, commercial aircraft at the low altitude representative of a nuclear power plant's low profile.

(3) *Applicability.* The requirements of paragraphs (a)(1) and (a)(2) of this section apply to applicants for:

(i) Construction permits for nuclear power reactors issued under this part after July 13, 2009;

(ii) Operating licenses for nuclear power reactors issued under this part

[1] Changes to the detailed parameters on aircraft impact characteristics set forth in guidance shall be approved by the Commission.

for which a construction permit was issued after July 13, 2009;

(iii)(A) Standard design certifications issued under part 52 of this chapter after July 13, 2009;

(B) Renewal of standard design certifications in effect on July 13, 2009 which have not been amended to comply with the requirements of this section by the time of application for renewal;

(iv) Standard design approvals issued under part 52 of this chapter after July 13, 2009;

(v) Combined licenses issued under part 52 of this chapter that:

(A) Do not reference a standard design certification, standard design approval, or manufactured reactor; or

(B) Reference a standard design certification issued before July 13, 2009 which has not been amended to address the requirements of this section; and

(vi) Manufacturing licenses issued under part 52 of this chapter that:

(A) Do not reference a standard design certification or standard design approval; or

(B) Reference a standard design certification issued before July 13, 2009 which has not been amended to address the requirements of this section.

(b) *Content of application.* For applicants identified in paragraph (a)(3) of this section, the preliminary or final safety analysis report, as applicable, must include a description of:

(1) The design features and functional capabilities identified in paragraph (a)(1) of this section; and

(2) How the design features and functional capabilities identified in paragraph (a)(1) of this section meet the assessment requirements in paragraph (a)(1) of this section.

(c) *Control of changes.* (1) For construction permits which are subject to paragraph (a) of this section, if the permit holder changes the information required by 10 CFR 50.34(a)(13) to be included in the preliminary safety analysis report, then the permit holder shall consider the effect of the changed feature or capability on the original assessment required by 10 CFR 50.150(a) and amend the information required by 10 CFR 50.34(a)(13) to be included in the preliminary safety analysis report to describe how the modified design features and functional capabilities continue to meet the assessment requirements in paragraph (a)(1) of this section.

(2) For operating licenses which are subject to paragraph (a) of this section, if the licensee changes the information required by 10 CFR 50.34(b)(12) to be included in the final safety analysis report, then the licensee shall consider the effect of the changed feature or capability on the original assessment required by 10 CFR 50.150(a) and amend the information required by 10 CFR 50.34(b)(12) to be included in the final safety analysis report to describe how the modified design features and functional capabilities continue to meet the assessment requirements in paragraph (a)(1) of this section.

(3) For standard design certifications which are subject to paragraph (a) of this section, generic changes to the information required by 10 CFR 52.47(a)(28) to be included in the final safety analysis report are governed by the applicable requirements of 10 CFR 52.63.

(4)(i) For combined licenses which are subject to paragraph (a) of this section, if the licensee changes the information required by 10 CFR 52.79(a)(47) to be included in the final safety analysis report, then the licensee shall consider the effect of the changed feature or capability on the original assessment required by 10 CFR 50.150(a) and amend the information required by 10 CFR 52.79(a)(47) to be included in the final safety analysis report to describe how the modified design features and functional capabilities continue to meet the assessment requirements in paragraph (a)(1) of this section.

(ii) For combined licenses which are not subject to paragraph (a) of this section but reference a standard design certification which is subject to paragraph (a) of this section, proposed departures from the information required by 10 CFR 52.47(a)(28) to be included in the final safety analysis report for the referenced standard design certification are governed by the change control requirements in the applicable design certification rule.

(iii) For combined licenses which are not subject to paragraph (a) of this section but reference a manufactured reactor which is subject to paragraph (a) of this section, proposed departures from the information required by 10 CFR 52.157(f)(32) to be included in the final safety analysis report for the manufacturing license are governed by the applicable requirements in 10 CFR 52.171(b)(2).

(5)(i) For manufacturing licenses which are subject to paragraph (a) of this section, generic changes to the information required by 10 CFR 52.157(f)(32) to be included in the final safety analysis report are governed by the applicable requirements of 10 CFR 52.171.

(ii) For manufacturing licenses which are not subject to paragraph (a) of this section but reference a standard design certification which is subject to paragraph (a) of this section, proposed departures from the information required by 10 CFR 52.47(a)(28) to be included in the final safety analysis report for the referenced standard design certification are governed by the change control requirements in the applicable design certification rule.

[74 FR 28146, June 12, 2009]

APPENDIX A TO PART 50—GENERAL DESIGN CRITERIA FOR NUCLEAR POWER PLANTS

Table of Contents

CRITERIA—Continued

	Number
Prevention of Criticality in Fuel Storage and Handling	62
Monitoring Fuel and Waste Storage	63
Monitoring Radioactivity Releases	64

INTRODUCTION

Under the provisions of §50.34, an application for a construction permit must include the principal design criteria for a proposed facility. Under the provisions of 10 CFR 52.47, 52.79, 52.137, and 52.157, an application for a design certification, combined license, design approval, or manufacturing license, respectively, must include the principal design criteria for a proposed facility. The principal design criteria establish the necessary design, fabrication, construction, testing, and performance requirements for structures, systems, and components important to safety; that is, structures, systems, and components that provide reasonable assurance that the facility can be operated without undue risk to the health and safety of the public.

These General Design Criteria establish minimum requirements for the principal design criteria for water-cooled nuclear power plants similar in design and location to plants for which construction permits have been issued by the Commission. The General Design Criteria are also considered to be generally applicable to other types of nuclear power units and are intended to provide guidance in establishing the principal design criteria for such other units.

The development of these General Design Criteria is not yet complete. For example, some of the definitions need further amplification. Also, some of the specific design requirements for structures, systems, and components important to safety have not as yet been suitably defined. Their omission does not relieve any applicant from considering these matters in the design of a specific facility and satisfying the necessary safety requirements. These matters include:

(1) Consideration of the need to design against single failures of passive components in fluid systems important to safety. (See Definition of Single Failure.)

(2) Consideration of redundancy and diversity requirements for fluid systems important to safety. A "system" could consist of a number of subsystems each of which is separately capable of performing the specified system safety function. The minimum acceptable redundancy and diversity of subsystems and components within a subsystem, and the required interconnection and independence of the subsystems have not yet been developed or defined. (See Criteria 34, 35, 38, 41, and 44.)

(3) Consideration of the type, size, and orientation of possible breaks in components of the reactor coolant pressure boundary in determining design requirements to suitably protect against postulated loss-of-coolant accidents. (See Definition of Loss of Coolant Accidents.)

(4) Consideration of the possibility of systematic, nonrandom, concurrent failures of redundant elements in the design of protection systems and reactivity control systems. (See Criteria 22, 24, 26, and 29.)

It is expected that the criteria will be augmented and changed from time to time as important new requirements for these and other features are developed.

There will be some water-cooled nuclear power plants for which the General Design Criteria are not sufficient and for which additional criteria must be identified and satisfied in the interest of public safety. In particular, it is expected that additional or different criteria will be needed to take into account unusual sites and environmental conditions, and for water-cooled nuclear power units of advanced design. Also, there may be water-cooled nuclear power units for which fulfillment of some of the General Design Criteria may not be necessary or appropriate. For plants such as these, departures from the General Design Criteria must be identified and justified.

DEFINITIONS AND EXPLANATIONS

Nuclear power unit. A nuclear power unit means a nuclear power reactor and associated equipment necessary for electric power generation and includes those structures, systems, and components required to provide reasonable assurance the facility can be operated without undue risk to the health and safety of the public.

Loss of coolant accidents. Loss of coolant accidents mean those postulated accidents that result from the loss of reactor coolant at a rate in excess of the capability of the reactor coolant makeup system from breaks in the reactor coolant pressure boundary, up to and including a break equivalent in size to the double-ended rupture of the largest pipe of the reactor coolant system.[1]

Single failure. A single failure means an occurrence which results in the loss of capability of a component to perform its intended safety functions. Multiple failures resulting from a single occurrence are considered to be a single failure. Fluid and electric systems are considered to be designed against an assumed single failure if neither (1) a single failure of any active component (assuming passive components function properly) nor (2) a single failure of a passive component

[1] Further details relating to the type, size, and orientation of postulated breaks in specific components of the reactor coolant pressure boundary are under development.

(assuming active components function properly), results in a loss of the capability of the system to perform its safety functions.[2]

Anticipated operational occurrences. Anticipated operational occurrences mean those conditions of normal operation which are expected to occur one or more times during the life of the nuclear power unit and include but are not limited to loss of power to all recirculation pumps, tripping of the turbine generator set, isolation of the main condenser, and loss of all offsite power.

CRITERIA

I. Overall Requirements

Criterion 1—Quality standards and records. Structures, systems, and components important to safety shall be designed, fabricated, erected, and tested to quality standards commensurate with the importance of the safety functions to be performed. Where generally recognized codes and standards are used, they shall be identified and evaluated to determine their applicability, adequacy, and sufficiency and shall be supplemented or modified as necessary to assure a quality product in keeping with the required safety function. A quality assurance program shall be established and implemented in order to provide adequate assurance that these structures, systems, and components will satisfactorily perform their safety functions. Appropriate records of the design, fabrication, erection, and testing of structures, systems, and components important to safety shall be maintained by or under the control of the nuclear power unit licensee throughout the life of the unit.

Criterion 2—Design bases for protection against natural phenomena. Structures, systems, and components important to safety shall be designed to withstand the effects of natural phenomena such as earthquakes, tornadoes, hurricanes, floods, tsunami, and seiches without loss of capability to perform their safety functions. The design bases for these structures, systems, and components shall reflect: (1) Appropriate consideration of the most severe of the natural phenomena that have been historically reported for the site and surrounding area, with sufficient margin for the limited accuracy, quantity, and period of time in which the historical data have been accumulated, (2) appropriate combinations of the effects of normal and accident conditions with the effects of the natural phenomena and (3) the importance of the safety functions to be performed.

Criterion 3—Fire protection. Structures, systems, and components important to safety shall be designed and located to minimize, consistent with other safety requirements, the probability and effect of fires and explosions. Noncombustible and heat resistant materials shall be used wherever practical throughout the unit, particularly in locations such as the containment and control room. Fire detection and fighting systems of appropriate capacity and capability shall be provided and designed to minimize the adverse effects of fires on structures, systems, and components important to safety. Firefighting systems shall be designed to assure that their rupture or inadvertent operation does not significantly impair the safety capability of these structures, systems, and components.

Criterion 4—Environmental and dynamic effects design bases. Structures, systems, and components important to safety shall be designed to accommodate the effects of and to be compatible with the environmental conditions associated with normal operation, maintenance, testing, and postulated accidents, including loss-of-coolant accidents. These structures, systems, and components shall be appropriately protected against dynamic effects, including the effects of missiles, pipe whipping, and discharging fluids, that may result from equipment failures and from events and conditions outside the nuclear power unit. However, dynamic effects associated with postulated pipe ruptures in nuclear power units may be excluded from the design basis when analyses reviewed and approved by the Commission demonstrate that the probability of fluid system piping rupture is extremely low under conditions consistent with the design basis for the piping.

Criterion 5—Sharing of structures, systems, and components. Structures, systems, and components important to safety shall not be shared among nuclear power units unless it can be shown that such sharing will not significantly impair their ability to perform their safety functions, including, in the event of an accident in one unit, an orderly shutdown and cooldown of the remaining units.

II. Protection by Multiple Fission Product Barriers

Criterion 10—Reactor design. The reactor core and associated coolant, control, and protection systems shall be designed with appropriate margin to assure that specified acceptable fuel design limits are not exceeded during any condition of normal operation, including the effects of anticipated operational occurrences.

[2] Single failures of passive components in electric systems should be assumed in designing against a single failure. The conditions under which a single failure of a passive component in a fluid system should be considered in designing the system against a single failure are under development.

Criterion 11—Reactor inherent protection. The reactor core and associated coolant systems shall be designed so that in the power operating range the net effect of the prompt inherent nuclear feedback characteristics tends to compensate for a rapid increase in reactivity.

Criterion 12—Suppression of reactor power oscillations. The reactor core and associated coolant, control, and protection systems shall be designed to assure that power oscillations which can result in conditions exceeding specified acceptable fuel design limits are not possible or can be reliably and readily detected and suppressed.

Criterion 13—Instrumentation and control. Instrumentation shall be provided to monitor variables and systems over their anticipated ranges for normal operation, for anticipated operational occurrences, and for accident conditions as appropriate to assure adequate safety, including those variables and systems that can affect the fission process, the integrity of the reactor core, the reactor coolant pressure boundary, and the containment and its associated systems. Appropriate controls shall be provided to maintain these variables and systems within prescribed operating ranges.

Criterion 14—Reactor coolant pressure boundary. The reactor coolant pressure boundary shall be designed, fabricated, erected, and tested so as to have an extremely low probability of abnormal leakage, of rapidly propagating failure, and of gross rupture.

Criterion 15—Reactor coolant system design. The reactor coolant system and associated auxiliary, control, and protection systems shall be designed with sufficient margin to assure that the design conditions of the reactor coolant pressure boundary are not exceeded during any condition of normal operation, including anticipated operational occurrences.

Criterion 16—Containment design. Reactor containment and associated systems shall be provided to establish an essentially leak-tight barrier against the uncontrolled release of radioactivity to the environment and to assure that the containment design conditions important to safety are not exceeded for as long as postulated accident conditions require.

Criterion 17—Electric power systems. An onsite electric power system and an offsite electric power system shall be provided to permit functioning of structures, systems, and components important to safety. The safety function for each system (assuming the other system is not functioning) shall be to provide sufficient capacity and capability to assure that (1) specified acceptable fuel design limits and design conditions of the reactor coolant pressure boundary are not exceeded as a result of anticipated operational occurrences and (2) the core is cooled and containment integrity and other vital functions are maintained in the event of postulated accidents.

The onsite electric power supplies, including the batteries, and the onsite electric distribution system, shall have sufficient independence, redundancy, and testability to perform their safety functions assuming a single failure.

Electric power from the transmission network to the onsite electric distribution system shall be supplied by two physically independent circuits (not necessarily on separate rights of way) designed and located so as to minimize to the extent practical the likelihood of their simultaneous failure under operating and postulated accident and environmental conditions. A switchyard common to both circuits is acceptable. Each of these circuits shall be designed to be available in sufficient time following a loss of all onsite alternating current power supplies and the other offsite electric power circuit, to assure that specified acceptable fuel design limits and design conditions of the reactor coolant pressure boundary are not exceeded. One of these circuits shall be designed to be available within a few seconds following a loss-of-coolant accident to assure that core cooling, containment integrity, and other vital safety functions are maintained.

Provisions shall be included to minimize the probability of losing electric power from any of the remaining supplies as a result of, or coincident with, the loss of power generated by the nuclear power unit, the loss of power from the transmission network, or the loss of power from the onsite electric power supplies.

Criterion 18—Inspection and testing of electric power systems. Electric power systems important to safety shall be designed to permit appropriate periodic inspection and testing of important areas and features, such as wiring, insulation, connections, and switchboards, to assess the continuity of the systems and the condition of their components. The systems shall be designed with a capability to test periodically (1) the operability and functional performance of the components of the systems, such as onsite power sources, relays, switches, and buses, and (2) the operability of the systems as a whole and, under conditions as close to design as practical, the full operation sequence that brings the systems into operation, including operation of applicable portions of the protection system, and the transfer of power among the nuclear power unit, the offsite power system, and the onsite power system.

Criterion 19—Control room. A control room shall be provided from which actions can be taken to operate the nuclear power unit safely under normal conditions and to maintain it in a safe condition under accident conditions, including loss-of-coolant accidents. Adequate radiation protection shall be provided to permit access and occupancy of the control room under accident conditions without personnel receiving radiation exposures in excess of 5 rem whole body, or its equivalent to any part of the body, for the duration of the accident. Equipment at appropriate locations outside the control room shall be provided (1) with a design capability for prompt hot shutdown of the reactor, including necessary instrumentation and controls to maintain the unit in a safe condition during hot shutdown, and (2) with a potential capability for subsequent cold shutdown of the reactor through the use of suitable procedures.

Applicants for and holders of construction permits and operating licenses under this part who apply on or after January 10, 1997, applicants for design approvals or certifications under part 52 of this chapter who apply on or after January 10, 1997, applicants for and holders of combined licenses or manufacturing licenses under part 52 of this chapter who do not reference a standard design approval or certification, or holders of operating licenses using an alternative source term under § 50.67, shall meet the requirements of this criterion, except that with regard to control room access and occupancy, adequate radiation protection shall be provided to ensure that radiation exposures shall not exceed 0.05 Sv (5 rem) total effective dose equivalent (TEDE) as defined in § 50.2 for the duration of the accident.

III. Protection and Reactivity Control Systems

Criterion 20—Protection system functions. The protection system shall be designed (1) to initiate automatically the operation of appropriate systems including the reactivity control systems, to assure that specified acceptable fuel design limits are not exceeded as a result of anticipated operational occurrences and (2) to sense accident conditions and to initiate the operation of systems and components important to safety.

Criterion 21—Protection system reliability and testability. The protection system shall be designed for high functional reliability and inservice testability commensurate with the safety functions to be performed. Redundancy and independence designed into the protection system shall be sufficient to assure that (1) no single failure results in loss of the protection function and (2) removal from service of any component or channel does not result in loss of the required minimum redundancy unless the acceptable reliability of operation of the protection system can be otherwise demonstrated. The protection system shall be designed to permit periodic testing of its functioning when the reactor is in operation, including a capability to test channels independently to determine failures and losses of redundancy that may have occurred.

Criterion 22—Protection system independence. The protection system shall be designed to assure that the effects of natural phenomena, and of normal operating, maintenance, testing, and postulated accident conditions on redundant channels do not result in loss of the protection function, or shall be demonstrated to be acceptable on some other defined basis. Design techniques, such as functional diversity or diversity in component design and principles of operation, shall be used to the extent practical to prevent loss of the protection function.

Criterion 23—Protection system failure modes. The protection system shall be designed to fail into a safe state or into a state demonstrated to be acceptable on some other defined basis if conditions such as disconnection of the system, loss of energy (e.g., electric power, instrument air), or postulated adverse environments (e.g., extreme heat or cold, fire, pressure, steam, water, and radiation) are experienced.

Criterion 24—Separation of protection and control systems. The protection system shall be separated from control systems to the extent that failure of any single control system component or channel, or failure or removal from service of any single protection system component or channel which is common to the control and protection systems leaves intact a system satisfying all reliability, redundancy, and independence requirements of the protection system. Interconnection of the protection and control systems shall be limited so as to assure that safety is not significantly impaired.

Criterion 25—Protection system requirements for reactivity control malfunctions. The protection system shall be designed to assure that specified acceptable fuel design limits are not exceeded for any single malfunction of the reactivity control systems, such as accidental withdrawal (not ejection or dropout) of control rods.

Criterion 26—Reactivity control system redundancy and capability. Two independent reactivity control systems of different design principles shall be provided. One of the systems shall use control rods, preferably including a positive means for inserting the rods, and shall be capable of reliably controlling reactivity changes to assure that under conditions of normal operation, including anticipated operational occurrences, and with appropriate margin for malfunctions such as stuck rods, specified acceptable fuel design limits are not exceeded. The second reactivity control system shall be capable of reliably controlling the rate of reactivity changes resulting from planned, normal power changes (including xenon burnout) to assure acceptable fuel design limits are not exceeded. One of the systems shall be capable of holding the reactor core subcritical under cold conditions.

Criterion 27—Combined reactivity control systems capability. The reactivity control systems shall be designed to have a combined capability, in conjunction with poison addition by the emergency core cooling system, of reliably controlling reactivity changes to assure that under postulated accident conditions and with appropriate margin for stuck rods the capability to cool the core is maintained.

Criterion 28—Reactivity limits. The reactivity control systems shall be designed with appropriate limits on the potential amount and rate of reactivity increase to assure that the effects of postulated reactivity accidents can neither (1) result in damage to the reactor coolant pressure boundary greater than limited local yielding nor (2) sufficiently disturb the core, its support structures or other reactor pressure vessel internals to impair significantly the capability to cool the core. These postulated reactivity accidents shall include consideration of rod ejection (unless prevented by positive means), rod dropout, steam line rupture, changes in reactor coolant temperature and pressure, and cold water addition.

Criterion 29—Protection against anticipated operational occurrences. The protection and reactivity control systems shall be designed to assure an extremely high probability of accomplishing their safety functions in the event of anticipated operational occurrences.

IV. Fluid Systems

Criterion 30—Quality of reactor coolant pressure boundary. Components which are part of the reactor coolant pressure boundary shall be designed, fabricated, erected, and tested to the highest quality standards practical. Means shall be provided for detecting and, to the extent practical, identifying the location of the source of reactor coolant leakage.

Criterion 31—Fracture prevention of reactor coolant pressure boundary. The reactor coolant pressure boundary shall be designed with sufficient margin to assure that when stressed under operating, maintenance, testing, and postulated accident conditions (1) the boundary behaves in a nonbrittle manner and (2) the probability of rapidly propagating fracture is minimized. The design shall reflect consideration of service temperatures and other conditions of the boundary material under operating, maintenance, testing, and postulated accident conditions and the uncertainties in determining (1) material properties, (2) the effects of irradiation on material properties, (3) residual, steady state and transient stresses, and (4) size of flaws.

Criterion 32—Inspection of reactor coolant pressure boundary. Components which are part of the reactor coolant pressure boundary shall be designed to permit (1) periodic inspection and testing of important areas and features to assess their structural and leaktight integrity, and (2) an appropriate material surveillance program for the reactor pressure vessel.

Criterion 33—Reactor coolant makeup. A system to supply reactor coolant makeup for protection against small breaks in the reactor coolant pressure boundary shall be provided. The system safety function shall be to assure that specified acceptable fuel design limits are not exceeded as a result of reactor coolant loss due to leakage from the reactor coolant pressure boundary and rupture of small piping or other small components which are part of the boundary. The system shall be designed to assure that for onsite electric power system operation (assuming offsite power is not available) and for offsite electric power system operation (assuming onsite power is not available) the system safety function can be accomplished using the piping, pumps, and valves used to maintain coolant inventory during normal reactor operation.

Criterion 34—Residual heat removal. A system to remove residual heat shall be provided. The system safety function shall be to transfer fission product decay heat and other residual heat from the reactor core at a rate such that specified acceptable fuel design limits and the design conditions of the reactor coolant pressure boundary are not exceeded.

Suitable redundancy in components and features, and suitable interconnections, leak detection, and isolation capabilities shall be provided to assure that for onsite electric power system operation (assuming offsite power is not available) and for offsite electric power system operation (assuming onsite power is not available) the system safety function can be accomplished, assuming a single failure.

Criterion 35—Emergency core cooling. A system to provide abundant emergency core cooling shall be provided. The system safety function shall be to transfer heat from the reactor core following any loss of reactor coolant at a rate such that (1) fuel and clad damage that could interfere with continued effective core cooling is prevented and (2) clad metal-water reaction is limited to negligible amounts.

Suitable redundancy in components and features, and suitable interconnections, leak detection, isolation, and containment capabilities shall be provided to assure that for onsite electric power system operation (assuming offsite power is not available) and for offsite electric power system operation (assuming onsite power is not available) the system safety function can be accomplished, assuming a single failure.

Criterion 36—Inspection of emergency core cooling system. The emergency core cooling system shall be designed to permit appropriate periodic inspection of important components, such as spray rings in the reactor pressure vessel, water injection nozzles, and piping, to assure the integrity and capability of the system.

Criterion 37—Testing of emergency core cooling system. The emergency core cooling system shall be designed to permit appropriate periodic pressure and functional testing to assure (1) the structural and leaktight integrity of its components, (2) the operability and performance of the active components of the system, and (3) the operability of the system as a whole and, under conditions as close to design as practical, the performance of the full operational sequence that brings the system into operation, including operation of applicable portions of the protection system, the transfer between normal and emergency power sources, and the operation of the associated cooling water system.

Criterion 38—Containment heat removal. A system to remove heat from the reactor containment shall be provided. The system safety function shall be to reduce rapidly, consistent with the functioning of other associated systems, the containment pressure and temperature following any loss-of-coolant accident and maintain them at acceptably low levels.

Suitable redundancy in components and features, and suitable interconnections, leak detection, isolation, and containment capabilities shall be provided to assure that for onsite electric power system operation (assuming offsite power is not available) and for offsite electric power system operation (assuming onsite power is not available) the system safety function can be accomplished, assuming a single failure.

Criterion 39—Inspection of containment heat removal system. The containment heat removal system shall be designed to permit appropriate periodic inspection of important components, such as the torus, sumps, spray nozzles, and piping to assure the integrity and capability of the system.

Criterion 40—Testing of containment heat removal system. The containment heat removal system shall be designed to permit appropriate periodic pressure and functional testing to assure (1) the structural and leaktight integrity of its components, (2) the operability and performance of the active components of the system, and (3) the operability of the system as a whole, and under conditions as close to the design as practical the performance of the full operational sequence that brings the system into operation, including operation of applicable portions of the protection system, the transfer between normal and emergency power sources, and the operation of the associated cooling water system.

Criterion 41—Containment atmosphere cleanup. Systems to control fission products, hydrogen, oxygen, and other substances which may be released into the reactor containment shall be provided as necessary to reduce, consistent with the functioning of other associated systems, the concentration and quality of fission products released to the environment following postulated accidents, and to control the concentration of hydrogen or oxygen and other substances in the containment atmosphere following postulated accidents to assure that containment integrity is maintained.

Each system shall have suitable redundancy in components and features, and suitable interconnections, leak detection, isolation, and containment capabilities to assure that for onsite electric power system operation (assuming offsite power is not available) and for offsite electric power system operation (assuming onsite power is not available) its safety function can be accomplished, assuming a single failure.

Criterion 42—Inspection of containment atmosphere cleanup systems. The containment atmosphere cleanup systems shall be designed to permit appropriate periodic inspection of important components, such as filter frames, ducts, and piping to assure the integrity and capability of the systems.

Criterion 43—Testing of containment atmosphere cleanup systems. The containment atmosphere cleanup systems shall be designed to permit appropriate periodic pressure and functional testing to assure (1) the structural and leaktight integrity of its components, (2) the operability and performance of the active components of the systems such as fans, filters, dampers, pumps, and valves and (3) the operability of the systems as a whole and, under conditions as close to design as practical, the performance of the full operational sequence that brings the systems into operation, including operation of applicable portions of the protection system, the transfer between normal and emergency power sources, and the operation of associated systems.

Criterion 44—Cooling water. A system to transfer heat from structures, systems, and components important to safety, to an ultimate heat sink shall be provided. The system safety function shall be to transfer the combined heat load of these structures, systems, and components under normal operating and accident conditions.

Suitable redundancy in components and features, and suitable interconnections, leak detection, and isolation capabilities shall be provided to assure that for onsite electric power system operation (assuming offsite power is not available) and for offsite electric power system operation (assuming onsite power is not available) the system safety function can be accomplished, assuming a single failure.

Criterion 45—Inspection of cooling water system. The cooling water system shall be designed to permit appropriate periodic inspection of important components, such as heat exchangers and piping, to assure the integrity and capability of the system.

Criterion 46—Testing of cooling water system. The cooling water system shall be designed to permit appropriate periodic pressure and functional testing to assure (1) the structural and leaktight integrity of its components, (2) the operability and the performance of the active components of the system, and (3) the operability of the system as a whole and, under conditions as close to design as practical, the performance of the full operational sequence that brings the system into operation for reactor shutdown and for loss-of-coolant accidents, including operation of applicable portions of the protection system and the transfer between normal and emergency power sources.

V. Reactor Containment

Criterion 50—Containment design basis. The reactor containment structure, including access openings, penetrations, and the containment heat removal system shall be designed so that the containment structure and its internal compartments can accommodate, without exceeding the design leakage rate and with sufficient margin, the calculated pressure and temperature conditions resulting from any loss-of-coolant accident. This margin shall reflect consideration of (1) the effects of potential energy sources which have not been included in the determination of the peak conditions, such as energy in steam generators and as required by § 50.44 energy from metal-water and other chemical reactions that may result from degradation but not total failure of emergency core cooling functioning, (2) the limited experience and experimental data available for defining accident phenomena and containment responses, and (3) the conservatism of the calculational model and input parameters.

Criterion 51—Fracture prevention of containment pressure boundary. The reactor containment boundary shall be designed with sufficient margin to assure that under operating, maintenance, testing, and postulated accident conditions (1) its ferritic materials behave in a nonbrittle manner and (2) the probability of rapidly propagating fracture is minimized. The design shall reflect consideration of service temperatures and other conditions of the containment boundary material during operation, maintenance, testing, and postulated accident conditions, and the uncertainties in determining (1) material properties, (2) residual, steady state, and transient stresses, and (3) size of flaws.

Criterion 52—Capability for containment leakage rate testing. The reactor containment and other equipment which may be subjected to containment test conditions shall be designed so that periodic integrated leakage rate testing can be conducted at containment design pressure.

Criterion 53—Provisions for containment testing and inspection. The reactor containment shall be designed to permit (1) appropriate periodic inspection of all important areas, such as penetrations, (2) an appropriate surveillance program, and (3) periodic testing at containment design pressure of the leaktightness of penetrations which have resilient seals and expansion bellows.

Criterion 54—Piping systems penetrating containment. Piping systems penetrating primary reactor containment shall be provided with leak detection, isolation, and containment capabilities having redundancy, reliability, and performance capabilities which reflect the importance to safety of isolating these piping systems. Such piping systems shall be designed with a capability to test periodically the operability of the isolation valves and associated apparatus and to determine if valve leakage is within acceptable limits.

Criterion 55—Reactor coolant pressure boundary penetrating containment. Each line that is part of the reactor coolant pressure boundary and that penetrates primary reactor containment shall be provided with containment isolation valves as follows, unless it can be demonstrated that the containment isolation provisions for a specific class of lines, such as instrument lines, are acceptable on some other defined basis:

(1) One locked closed isolation valve inside and one locked closed isolation valve outside containment; or

(2) One automatic isolation valve inside and one locked closed isolation valve outside containment; or

(3) One locked closed isolation valve inside and one automatic isolation valve outside containment. A simple check valve may not be used as the automatic isolation valve outside containment; or

(4) One automatic isolation valve inside and one automatic isolation valve outside containment. A simple check valve may not be used as the automatic isolation valve outside containment.

Isolation valves outside containment shall be located as close to containment as practical and upon loss of actuating power, automatic isolation valves shall be designed to take the position that provides greater safety.

Other appropriate requirements to minimize the probability or consequences of an accidental rupture of these lines or of lines connected to them shall be provided as necessary to assure adequate safety. Determination of the appropriateness of these requirements, such as higher quality in design, fabrication, and testing, additional provisions for inservice inspection, protection against more severe natural phenomena, and additional isolation valves and containment, shall include consideration of the population density, use characteristics, and physical characteristics of the site environs.

Criterion 56—Primary containment isolation. Each line that connects directly to the containment atmosphere and penetrates primary reactor containment shall be provided with containment isolation valves as follows, unless it can be demonstrated that the containment isolation provisions for a specific class of lines, such as instrument lines, are acceptable on some other defined basis:

(1) One locked closed isolation valve inside and one locked closed isolation valve outside containment; or

(2) One automatic isolation valve inside and one locked closed isolation valve outside containment; or

(3) One locked closed isolation valve inside and one automatic isolation valve outside containment. A simple check valve may not be used as the automatic isolation valve outside containment; or

(4) One automatic isolation valve inside and one automatic isolation valve outside containment. A simple check valve may not be used as the automatic isolation valve outside containment.

Isolation valves outside containment shall be located as close to the containment as practical and upon loss of actuating power, automatic isolation valves shall be designed to take the position that provides greater safety.

Criterion 57—Closed system isolation valves. Each line that penetrates primary reactor containment and is neither part of the reactor coolant pressure boundary nor connected directly to the containment atmosphere shall have at least one containment isolation valve which shall be either automatic, or locked closed, or capable of remote manual operation. This valve shall be outside containment and located as close to the containment as practical. A simple check valve may not be used as the automatic isolation valve.

VI. Fuel and Radioactivity Control

Criterion 60—Control of releases of radioactive materials to the environment. The nuclear power unit design shall include means to control suitably the release of radioactive materials in gaseous and liquid effluents and to handle radioactive solid wastes produced during normal reactor operation, including anticipated operational occurrences. Sufficient holdup capacity shall be provided for retention of gaseous and liquid effluents containing radioactive materials, particularly where unfavorable site environmental conditions can be expected to impose unusual operational limitations upon the release of such effluents to the environment.

Criterion 61—Fuel storage and handling and radioactivity control. The fuel storage and handling, radioactive waste, and other systems which may contain radioactivity shall be designed to assure adequate safety under normal and postulated accident conditions. These systems shall be designed (1) with a capability to permit appropriate periodic inspection and testing of components important to safety, (2) with suitable shielding for radiation protection, (3) with appropriate containment, confinement, and filtering systems, (4) with a residual heat removal capability having reliability and testability that reflects the importance to safety of decay heat and other residual heat removal, and (5) to prevent significant reduction in fuel storage coolant inventory under accident conditions.

Criterion 62—Prevention of criticality in fuel storage and handling. Criticality in the fuel storage and handling system shall be prevented by physical systems or processes, preferably by use of geometrically safe configurations.

Criterion 63—Monitoring fuel and waste storage. Appropriate systems shall be provided in fuel storage and radioactive waste systems and associated handling areas (1) to detect conditions that may result in loss of residual heat removal capability and excessive radiation levels and (2) to initiate appropriate safety actions.

Criterion 64—Monitoring radioactivity releases. Means shall be provided for monitoring the reactor containment atmosphere, spaces containing components for recirculation of loss-of-coolant accident fluids, effluent discharge paths, and the plant environs for radioactivity that may be released from normal operations, including anticipated operational occurrences, and from postulated accidents.

[36 FR 3256, Feb. 20, 1971, as amended at 36 FR 12733, July 7, 1971; 41 FR 6258, Feb. 12, 1976; 43 FR 50163, Oct. 27, 1978; 51 FR 12505, Apr. 11, 1986; 52 FR 41294, Oct. 27, 1987; 64 FR 72002, Dec. 23, 1999; 72 FR 49505, Aug. 28, 2007]

Appendix B to Part 50—Quality Assurance Criteria for Nuclear Power Plants and Fuel Reprocessing Plants

Introduction. Every applicant for a construction permit is required by the provisions of §50.34 to include in its preliminary safety analysis report a description of the quality assurance program to be applied to the design, fabrication, construction, and testing of the structures, systems, and components of the facility. Every applicant for an operating license is required to include, in its final safety analysis report, information pertaining to the managerial and administrative controls to be used to assure safe operation. Every applicant for a combined license under part 52 of this chapter is required by the provisions of §52.79 of this chapter to include in its final safety analysis report a description of the quality assurance applied to the design, and to be applied to the fabrication, construction, and testing of the structures, systems, and components of the facility and to the managerial and administrative controls to be used to assure safe operation. For applications submitted after September 27, 2007, every applicant for an early site permit under part 52 of this chapter is required by the provisions of § 52.17 of this chapter to include in its site safety analysis report a description of the quality assurance program applied to site activities related to the design, fabrication, construction, and testing of the structures, systems, and components of a facility or facilities that may be constructed on the site. Every applicant for a design approval or design certification under part 52 of this chapter is required by the provisions of 10 CFR 52.137 and 52.47, respectively, to include in its final safety analysis report a description of the quality assurance program applied to the design of the structures, systems, and components of the facility. Every applicant for a manufacturing license under part 52 of this chapter is required by the provisions of 10 CFR 52.157 to include in its final safety analysis report a description of the quality assurance program applied to the design, and to be applied to the manufacture of, the structures, systems, and components of the reactor. Nuclear power plants and fuel reprocessing plants include structures, systems, and components that prevent or mitigate the consequences of postulated accidents that could cause undue risk to the health and safety of the public. This appendix establishes quality assurance requirements for the design, manufacture, construction, and operation of those structures, systems, and components. The pertinent requirements of this appendix apply to all activities affecting the safety-related functions of those structures, systems, and components; these activities include designing, purchasing, fabricating, handling, shipping, storing, cleaning, erecting, installing, inspecting, testing, operating, maintaining, repairing, refueling, and modifying.

As used in this appendix, "quality assurance" comprises all those planned and systematic actions necessary to provide adequate confidence that a structure, system, or component will perform satisfactorily in service. Quality assurance includes quality control, which comprises those quality assurance actions related to the physical characteristics of a material, structure, component, or system which provide a means to control the quality of the material, structure, component, or system to predetermined requirements.

I. ORGANIZATION

The applicant[1] shall be responsible for the establishment and execution of the quality assurance program. The applicant may delegate to others, such as contractors, agents, or consultants, the work of establishing and executing the quality assurance program, or any part thereof, but shall retain responsibility for the quality assurance program. The authority and duties of persons and organizations performing activities affecting the safety-related functions of structures, systems, and components shall be clearly established and delineated in writing. These activities include both the performing functions of attaining quality objectives and the quality assurance functions. The quality assurance functions are those of (1) assuring that an appropriate quality assurance program is established and effectively executed; and (2) verifying, such as by checking, auditing, and inspecting, that activities affecting the safety-related functions have been correctly performed. The persons and organizations performing quality assurance functions shall have sufficient authority and organizational freedom to identify quality problems; to initiate, recommend, or provide solutions; and to verify implementation of solutions. There persons and organizations performing quality assurance functions shall report to a management level so that the required authority and organizational freedom, including sufficient independence from cost and schedule when opposed to safety considerations, are provided. Because of the many variables involved, such as the number of personnel, the type of activity being performed, and the location or locations where activities are performed, the organizational structure for executing the quality assurance program may take various forms, provided that the persons and organizations assigned the quality assurance functions have the required authority and organizational freedom. Irrespective of the organizational structure, the individual(s) assigned the responsibility for assuring effective execution of any portion of the quality assurance program at any location where activities subject to this appendix are being performed, shall have direct access to the levels of management necessary to perform this function.

II. QUALITY ASSURANCE PROGRAM

The applicant shall establish at the earliest practicable time, consistent with the schedule for accomplishing the activities, a

[1] While the term "applicant" is used in these criteria, the requirements are, of course, applicable after such a person has received a license to construct and operate a nuclear power plant or a fuel reprocessing plant or has received an early site permit, design approval, design certification, or manufacturing license, as applicable. These criteria will also be used for guidance in evaluating the adequacy of quality assurance programs in use by holders of construction permits, operating licenses, early site permits, design approvals, combined licenses, and manufacturing licenses.

quality assurance program which complies with the requirements of this appendix. This program shall be documented by written policies, procedures, or instructions and shall be carried out throughout plant life in accordance with those policies, procedures, or instructions. The applicant shall identify the structures, systems, and components to be covered by the quality assurance program and the major organizations participating in the program, together with the designated functions of these organizations. The quality assurance program shall provide control over activities affecting the quality of the identified structures, systems, and components, to an extent consistent with their importance to safety. Activities affecting quality shall be accomplished under suitably controlled conditions. Controlled conditions include the use of appropriate equipment; suitable environmental conditions for accomplishing the activity, such as adequate cleanness; and assurance that all prerequisites for the given activity have been satisfied. The program shall take into account the need for special controls, processes, test equipment, tools, and skills to attain the required quality, and the need for verification of quality by inspection and test. The program shall provide for indoctrination and training of personnel performing activities affecting quality as necessary to assure that suitable proficiency is achieved and maintained. The applicant shall regularly review the status and adequacy of the quality assurance program. Management of other organizations participating in the quality assurance program shall regularly review the status and adequacy of that part of the quality assurance program which they are executing.

III. DESIGN CONTROL

Measures shall be established to assure that applicable regulatory requirements and the design basis, as defined in §50.2 and as specified in the license application, for those structures, systems, and components to which this appendix applies are correctly translated into specifications, drawings, procedures, and instructions. These measures shall include provisions to assure that appropriate quality standards are specified and included in design documents and that deviations from such standards are controlled. Measures shall also be established for the selection and review for suitability of application of materials, parts, equipment, and processes that are essential to the safety-related functions of the structures, systems and components.

Measures shall be established for the identification and control of design interfaces and for coordination among participating design organizations. These measures shall include the establishment of procedures among participating design organizations for the review, approval, release, distribution, and revision of documents involving design interfaces.

The design control measures shall provide for verifying or checking the adequacy of design, such as by the performance of design reviews, by the use of alternate or simplified calculational methods, or by the performance of a suitable testing program. The verifying or checking process shall be performed by individuals or groups other than those who performed the original design, but who may be from the same organization. Where a test program is used to verify the adequacy of a specific design feature in lieu of other verifying or checking processes, it shall include suitable qualifications testing of a prototype unit under the most adverse design conditions. Design control measures shall be applied to items such as the following: reactor physics, stress, thermal, hydraulic, and accident analyses; compatibility of materials; accessibility for inservice inspection, maintenance, and repair; and delineation of acceptance criteria for inspections and tests.

Design changes, including field changes, shall be subject to design control measures commensurate with those applied to the original design and be approved by the organization that performed the original design unless the applicant designates another responsible organization.

IV. PROCUREMENT DOCUMENT CONTROL

Measures shall be established to assure that applicable regulatory requirements, design bases, and other requirements which are necessary to assure adequate quality are suitably included or referenced in the documents for procurement of material, equipment, and services, whether purchased by the applicant or by its contractors or subcontractors. To the extent necessary, procurement documents shall require contractors or subcontractors to provide a quality assurance program consistent with the pertinent provisions of this appendix.

V. INSTRUCTIONS, PROCEDURES, AND DRAWINGS

Activities affecting quality shall be prescribed by documented instructions, procedures, or drawings, of a type appropriate to the circumstances and shall be accomplished in accordance with these instructions, procedures, or drawings. Instructions, procedures, or drawings shall include appropriate quantitative or qualitative acceptance criteria for determining that important activities have been satisfactorily accomplished.

VI. DOCUMENT CONTROL

Measures shall be established to control the issuance of documents, such as instructions, procedures, and drawings, including changes thereto, which prescribe all activities affecting quality. These measures shall assure that documents, including changes, are reviewed for adequacy and approved for release by authorized personnel and are distributed to and used at the location where the prescribed activity is performed. Changes to documents shall be reviewed and approved by the same organizations that performed the original review and approval unless the applicant designates another responsible organization.

VII. CONTROL OF PURCHASED MATERIAL, EQUIPMENT, AND SERVICES

Measures shall be established to assure that purchased material, equipment, and services, whether purchased directly or through contractors and subcontractors, conform to the procurement documents. These measures shall include provisions, as appropriate, for source evaluation and selection, objective evidence of quality furnished by the contractor or subcontractor, inspection at the contractor or subcontractor source, and examination of products upon delivery. Documentary evidence that material and equipment conform to the procurement requirements shall be available at the nuclear power plant or fuel reprocessing plant site prior to installation or use of such material and equipment. This documentary evidence shall be retained at the nuclear power plant or fuel reprocessing plant site and shall be sufficient to identify the specific requirements, such as codes, standards, or specifications, met by the purchased material and equipment. The effectiveness of the control of quality by contractors and subcontractors shall be assessed by the applicant or designee at intervals consistent with the importance, complexity, and quantity of the product or services.

VIII. IDENTIFICATION AND CONTROL OF MATERIALS, PARTS, AND COMPONENTS

Measures shall be established for the identification and control of materials, parts, and components, including partially fabricated assemblies. These measures shall assure that identification of the item is maintained by heat number, part number, serial number, or other appropriate means, either on the item or on records traceable to the item, as required throughout fabrication, erection, installation, and use of the item. These identification and control measures shall be designed to prevent the use of incorrect or defective material, parts, and components.

IX. CONTROL OF SPECIAL PROCESSES

Measures shall be established to assure that special processes, including welding, heat treating, and nondestructive testing, are controlled and accomplished by qualified personnel using qualified procedures in accordance with applicable codes, standards, specifications, criteria, and other special requirements.

X. INSPECTION

A program for inspection of activities affecting quality shall be established and executed by or for the organization performing the activity to verify conformance with the documented instructions, procedures, and drawings for accomplishing the activity. Such inspection shall be performed by individuals other than those who performed the activity being inspected. Examinations, measurements, or tests of material or products processed shall be performed for each work operation where necessary to assure quality. If inspection of processed material or products is impossible or disadvantageous, indirect control by monitoring processing methods, equipment, and personnel shall be provided. Both inspection and process monitoring shall be provided when control is inadequate without both. If mandatory inspection hold points, which require witnessing or inspecting by the applicant's designated representative and beyond which work shall not proceed without the consent of its designated representative are required, the specific hold points shall be indicated in appropriate documents.

XI. TEST CONTROL

A test program shall be established to assure that all testing required to demonstrate that structures, systems, and components will perform satisfactorily in service is identified and performed in accordance with written test procedures which incorporate the requirements and acceptance limits contained in applicable design documents. The test program shall include, as appropriate, proof tests prior to installation, preoperational tests, and operational tests during nuclear power plant or fuel reprocessing plant operation, of structures, systems, and components. Test procedures shall include provisions for assuring that all prerequisites for the given test have been met, that adequate test instrumentation is available and used, and that the test is performed under suitable environmental conditions. Test results shall be documented and evaluated to assure that test requirements have been satisfied.

XII. CONTROL OF MEASURING AND TEST EQUIPMENT

Measures shall be established to assure that tools, gages, instruments, and other measuring and testing devices used in activities affecting quality are properly controlled, calibrated, and adjusted at specified periods to maintain accuracy within necessary limits.

XIII. HANDLING, STORAGE AND SHIPPING

Measures shall be established to control the handling, storage, shipping, cleaning and preservation of material and equipment in accordance with work and inspection instructions to prevent damage or deterioration. When necessary for particular products, special protective environments, such as inert gas atmosphere, specific moisture content levels, and temperature levels, shall be specified and provided.

XIV. INSPECTION, TEST, AND OPERATING STATUS

Measures shall be established to indicate, by the use of markings such as stamps, tags, labels, routing cards, or other suitable means, the status of inspections and tests performed upon individual items of the nuclear power plant or fuel reprocessing plant. These measures shall provide for the identification of items which have satisfactorily passed required inspections and tests, where necessary to preclude inadvertent bypassing of such inspections and tests. Measures shall also be established for indicating the operating status of structures, systems, and components of the nuclear power plant or fuel reprocessing plant, such as by tagging valves and switches, to prevent inadvertent operation.

XV. NONCONFORMING MATERIALS, PARTS, OR COMPONENTS

Measures shall be established to control materials, parts, or components which do not conform to requirements in order to prevent their inadvertent use or installation. These measures shall include, as appropriate, procedures for identification, documentation, segregation, disposition, and notification to affected organizations. Nonconforming items shall be reviewed and accepted, rejected, repaired or reworked in accordance with documented procedures.

XVI. CORRECTIVE ACTION

Measures shall be established to assure that conditions adverse to quality, such as failures, malfunctions, deficiencies, deviations, defective material and equipment, and nonconformances are promptly identified and corrected. In the case of significant conditions adverse to quality, the measures shall assure that the cause of the condition is determined and corrective action taken to preclude repetition. The identification of the significant condition adverse to quality, the cause of the condition, and the corrective action taken shall be documented and reported to appropriate levels of management.

XVII. QUALITY ASSURANCE RECORDS

Sufficient records shall be maintained to furnish evidence of activities affecting quality. The records shall include at least the following: Operating logs and the results of reviews, inspections, tests, audits, monitoring of work performance, and materials analyses. The records shall also include closely-related data such as qualifications of personnel, procedures, and equipment. Inspection and test records shall, as a minimum, identify the inspector or data recorder, the type of observation, the results, the acceptability, and the action taken in connection with any deficiencies noted. Records shall be identifiable and retrievable. Consistent with applicable regulatory requirements, the applicant shall establish requirements concerning record retention, such as duration, location, and assigned responsibility.

XVIII. AUDITS

A comprehensive system of planned and periodic audits shall be carried out to verify compliance with all aspects of the quality assurance program and to determine the effectiveness of the program. The audits shall be performed in accordance with the written procedures or check lists by appropriately trained personnel not having direct responsibilities in the areas being audited. Audit results shall be documented and reviewed by management having responsibility in the area audited. Followup action, including reaudit of deficient areas, shall be taken where indicated.

[35 FR 10499, June 27, 1970, as amended at 36 FR 18301, Sept. 11, 1971; 40 FR 3210, Jan. 20, 1975; 72 FR 49505, Aug. 28, 2007]

APPENDIX C TO PART 50—A GUIDE FOR THE FINANCIAL DATA AND RELATED INFORMATION REQUIRED TO ESTABLISH FINANCIAL QUALIFICATIONS FOR CONSTRUCTION PERMITS AND COMBINED LICENSES

GENERAL INFORMATION

This appendix is intended to appraise applicants for construction permits and combined licenses for production or utilization facilities of the types described in §50.21(b) or §50.22, or testing facilities, of the general kinds of financial data and other related information that will demonstrate the financial qualification of the applicant to carry out the activities for which the permit or license is sought. The kind and depth of information described in this guide is not intended to be a rigid and absolute requirement. In some instances, additional pertinent material may be needed. In any case, the applicant should include information other than that specified, if the information is pertinent to establishing the applicant's financial ability to carry out the activities for which the permit or license is sought.

It is important to observe also that both §50.33(f) and this appendix distinguish between applicants which are established organizations and those which are newly-formed entities organized primarily for the purpose of engaging in the activity for which the permit is sought. Those in the former category will normally have a history of operating experience and be able to submit financial statements reflecting the financial results of past operations. With respect, however, to the applicant which is a newly formed company established primarily for the purpose of carrying out the licensed activity, with little or no prior operating history, somewhat more detailed data and supporting documentation will generally be necessary. For this reason, the appendix describes separately the scope of information to be included in applications by each of these two classes of applicants.

In determining an applicant's financial qualification, the Commission will require the minimum amount of information necessary for that purpose. No special forms are prescribed for submitting the information. In many cases, the financial information usually contained in current annual financial reports, including summary data of prior years, will be sufficient for the Commission's needs. The Commission reserves the right, however, to require additional financial information at the construction permit stage, particularly in cases in which the proposed power generating facility will be commonly owned by two or more existing companies or in which financing depends upon long-term arrangements for sharing of the power from the facility by two or more electrical generating companies.

Applicants are encouraged to consult with the Commission with respect to any questions they may have relating to the requirements of the Commission's regulations or the information set forth in this appendix.

I. Applicants Which Are Established Organizations

A. Applications for Construction Permits or Combined Licenses

1. *Estimate of construction costs.* For electric utilities, each applicant's estimate of the total cost of the proposed facility should be broken down as follows and be accompanied by a statement describing the bases from which the estimate is derived:

(a) Total nuclear production plant costs	$.........
(b) Transmission, distribution, and general plant costs	$.........
(c) Nuclear fuel inventory cost for first core[1]	$.........
Total estimated cost	$.........

[1] Section 2.790 of 10 CFR part 2 and §9.5 of 10 CFR part 9 indicate the circumstances under which information submitted by applicants may be withheld from public disclosure.

If the fuel is to be acquired by lease or other arrangement than purchase, the application should so state. The items to be included in these categories should be the same as those defined in the applicable electric plant and nuclear fuel inventory accounts prescribed by the Federal Energy Regulatory Commission or an explanation given as to any departure therefrom.

Since the composition of construction cost estimates for production and utilization facilities other than nuclear power reactors will vary according to the type of facility, no particular format is suggested for submitting such estimates. The estimate should, however, be itemized by categories of cost in sufficient detail to permit an evaluation of its reasonableness.

2. *Source of construction funds.* The application should include a brief statement of the applicant's general financial plan for financing the cost of the facility, identifying the source or sources upon which the applicant relies for the necessary construction funds, e.g., internal sources such as undistributed earnings and depreciation accruals, or external sources such as borrowings.

3. *Applicant's financial statements.* The application should also include the applicant's latest published annual financial report, together with any current interim financial statements that are pertinent. If an annual financial report is not published, the balance sheet and operating statement covering the latest complete accounting year together with all pertinent notes thereto and certification by a public accountant should be furnished.

II. Applicants Which Are Newly Formed Entities

A. Applications for Construction Permits or Combined Licenses

1. *Estimate of construction costs.* The information that will normally be required of applicants which are newly formed entities will not differ in scope from that required of established organizations. Accordingly, applicants should submit estimates as described above for established organizations.

2. *Source of construction funds.* The application should specifically identify the source or sources upon which the applicant relies for the funds necessary to pay the cost of constructing the facility, and the amount to be obtained from each. With respect to each source, the application should describe in detail the applicant's legal and financial relationships with its stockholders, corporate affiliates, or others (such as financial institutions) upon which the applicant is relying for financial assistance. If the sources of funds relied upon include parent companies or other corporate affiliates, information to support the financial capability of each such

company or affiliate to meet its commitments to the applicant should be set forth in the application. This information should be of the same kind and scope as would be required if the parent companies or affiliates were in fact the applicant. Ordinarily, it will be necessary that copies of agreements or contracts among the companies be submitted.

As noted earlier in this appendix, an applicant which is a newly formed entity will normally not be in a position to submit the usual types of balance sheets and income statements reflecting the results of prior operations. The applicant should, however, include in its application a statement of its assets, liabilities, and capital structure as of the date of the application.

III. ANNUAL FINANCIAL STATEMENT

Each holder of a construction permit for a production or utilization facility of a type described in § 50.21(b) or § 50.22 or a testing facility, and each holder of a combined license issued under part 52 of this chapter, is required by § 50.71(b) to file its annual financial report with the Commission at the time of issuance. This requirement does not apply to licensees or holders of construction permits for medical and research reactors.

IV. ADDITIONAL INFORMATION

The Commission may, from time to time, request the applicant, whether an established organization or newly formed entity, to submit additional or more detailed information respecting its financial arrangements and status of funds if such information is deemed necessary to enable the Commission to determine an applicant's financial qualifications for the license.

[49 FR 35753, Sept. 12, 1984, as amended at 50 FR 18853, May 3, 1985; 72 FR 49506, Aug. 28, 2007; 81 FR 86909, Dec. 2, 2016]

APPENDIX D TO PART 50 [RESERVED]

APPENDIX E TO PART 50—EMERGENCY PLANNING AND PREPAREDNESS FOR PRODUCTION AND UTILIZATION FACILITIES

Table of Contents

I. INTRODUCTION

1. Each applicant for a construction permit is required by § 50.34(a) to include in the preliminary safety analysis report a discussion of preliminary plans for coping with emergencies. Each applicant for an operating license is required by § 50.34(b) to include in the final safety analysis report plans for coping with emergencies. Each applicant for a combined license under subpart C of part 52 of this chapter is required by § 52.79 of this chapter to include in the application plans for coping with emergencies. Each applicant for an early site permit under subpart A of part 52 of this chapter may submit plans for coping with emergencies under § 52.17 of this chapter.

2. This appendix establishes minimum requirements for emergency plans for use in attaining an acceptable state of emergency preparedness. These plans shall be described generally in the preliminary safety analysis report for a construction permit and submitted as part of the final safety analysis report for an operating license. These plans, or major features thereof, may be submitted as part of the site safety analysis report for an early site permit.

3. The potential radiological hazards to the public associated with the operation of research and test reactors and fuel facilities licensed under 10 CFR parts 50 and 70 involve considerations different than those associated with nuclear power reactors. Consequently, the size of Emergency Planning Zones[1] (EPZs) for facilities other than power reactors and the degree to which compliance with the requirements of this section and sections II, III, IV, and V of this appendix as necessary will be determined on a case-by-case basis.[2]

---

[1] EPZs for power reactors are discussed in NUREG–0396; EPA 520/1–78–016, "Planning Basis for the Development of State and Local Government Radiological Emergency Response Plans in Support of Light Water Nuclear Power Plants," December 1978. The size of the EPZs for a nuclear power plant shall be determined in relation to local emergency response needs and capabilities as they are affected by such conditions as demography, topography, land characteristics, access routes, and jurisdictional boundaries. The size of the EPZs also may be determined on a case-by-case basis for gas-cooled nuclear reactors and for reactors with an authorized power level less than 250 MW thermal. Generally, the plume exposure pathway EPZ for nuclear power plants with an authorized power level greater than 250 MW thermal shall consist of an area about 10 miles (16 km) in radius and the ingestion pathway EPZ shall consist of an area about 50 miles (80 km) in radius.

[2] Regulatory Guide 2.6 will be used as guidance for the acceptability of research and test reactor emergency response plans.

4. Notwithstanding the above paragraphs, in the case of an operating license authorizing only fuel loading and/or low power operations up to 5 percent of rated power, no NRC or FEMA review, findings, or determinations concerning the state of offsite emergency preparedness or the adequacy of and the capability to implement State and local offsite emergency plans, as defined in this Appendix, are required prior to the issuance of such a license.

5. Each applicant for a combined license or early site permit under part 52 of this chapter whose application is docketed before December 23, 2011 may defer compliance with any change to emergency preparedness regulations under the final rule issued November 23, 2011. If that applicant chooses to defer compliance, it shall subsequently request to amend the combined license or early site permit to comply with those changes no later than December 31, 2013. An applicant that does not receive a combined license or early site permit before December 31, 2013, shall revise its combined license or early site permit application to comply with those changes no later than December 31, 2013. Notwithstanding any Commission finding under 10 CFR 52.103(g) regarding the combined license holder's facility, the combined license holder may not operate the facility until the NRC has approved the license amendment demonstrating compliance with the final rule.

6. The Tennessee Valley Authority Watts Bar Nuclear Plant, Unit 2, holding a construction permit under the provisions of part 50 of this chapter, shall meet the requirements of the final rule issued November 23, 2011 as applicable to operating nuclear power reactor licensees.

II. The Preliminary Safety Analysis Report

The Preliminary Safety Analysis Report shall contain sufficient information to ensure the compatibility of proposed emergency plans for both onsite areas and the EPZs, with facility design features, site layout, and site location with respect to such considerations as access routes, surrounding population distributions, land use, and local jurisdictional boundaries for the EPZs in the case of nuclear power reactors as well as the means by which the standards of § 50.47(b) will be met.

As a minimum, the following items shall be described:

A. Onsite and offsite organizations for coping with emergencies and the means for notification, in the event of an emergency, of persons assigned to the emergency organizations.

B. Contacts and arrangements made and documented with local, State, and Federal governmental agencies with responsibility for coping with emergencies, including identification of the principal agencies.

C. Protective measures to be taken within the site boundary and within each EPZ to protect health and safety in the event of an accident; procedures by which these measures are to be carried out (e.g., in the case of an evacuation, who authorizes the evacuation, how the public is to be notified and instructed, how the evacuation is to be carried out); and the expected response of offsite agencies in the event of an emergency.

D. Features of the facility to be provided for onsite emergency first aid and decontamination and for emergency transportation of onsite individuals to offsite treatment facilities.

E. Provisions to be made for emergency treatment at offsite facilities of individuals injured as a result of licensed activities.

F. Provisions for a training program for employees of the licensee, including those who are assigned specific authority and responsibility in the event of an emergency, and for other persons who are not employees of the licensee but whose assistance may be needed in the event of a radiological emergency.

G. A preliminary analysis that projects the time and means to be employed in the notification of State and local governments and the public in the event of an emergency. A nuclear power plant applicant shall perform a preliminary analysis of the time required to evacuate various sectors and distances within the plume exposure pathway EPZ for transient and permanent populations, noting major impediments to the evacuation or taking of protective actions.

H. A preliminary analysis reflecting the need to include facilities, systems, and methods for identifying the degree of seriousness and potential scope of radiological consequences of emergency situations within and outside the site boundary, including capabilities for dose projection using real-time meteorological information and for dispatch of radiological monitoring teams within the EPZs; and a preliminary analysis reflecting the role of the onsite technical support center and the emergency operations facility in assessing information, recommending protective action, and disseminating information to the public.

III. The Final Safety Analysis Report; Site Safety Analysis Report

The final safety analysis report or the site safety analysis report for an early site permit that includes complete and integrated emergency plans under § 52.17(b)(2)(ii) of this chapter shall contain the plans for coping with emergencies. The plans shall be an expression of the overall concept of operation; they shall describe the essential elements of advance planning that have been considered and the provisions that have been made to cope with emergency situations. The plans shall incorporate information about the emergency response roles of supporting organizations and offsite agencies. That information shall be sufficient to provide assurance of coordination among the supporting groups and with the licensee. The site safety analysis report for an early site permit which proposes major features must address the relevant provisions of 10 CFR 50.47 and 10 CFR part 50, appendix E, within the scope of emergency preparedness matters addressed in the major features.

The plans submitted must include a description of the elements set out in Section IV for the emergency planning zones (EPZs) to an extent sufficient to demonstrate that the plans provide reasonable assurance that adequate protective measures can and will be taken in the event of an emergency.

IV. CONTENT OF EMERGENCY PLANS

1. The applicant's emergency plans shall contain, but not necessarily be limited to, information needed to demonstrate compliance with the elements set forth below, *i.e.*, organization for coping with radiological emergencies, assessment actions, activation of emergency organization, notification procedures, emergency facilities and equipment, training, maintaining emergency preparedness, recovery, and onsite protective actions during hostile action. In addition, the emergency response plans submitted by an applicant for a nuclear power reactor operating license under this part, or for an early site permit (as applicable) or combined license under 10 CFR part 52, shall contain information needed to demonstrate compliance with the standards described in § 50.47(b), and they will be evaluated against those standards.

2. This nuclear power reactor license applicant shall also provide an analysis of the time required to evacuate various sectors and distances within the plume exposure pathway EPZ for transient and permanent populations, using the most recent U.S. Census Bureau data as of the date the applicant submits its application to the NRC.

3. Nuclear power reactor licensees shall use NRC approved evacuation time estimates (ETEs) and updates to the ETEs in the formulation of protective action recommendations and shall provide the ETEs and ETE updates to State and local governmental authorities for use in developing offsite protective action strategies.

4. Within 365 days of the later of the date of the availability of the most recent decennial census data from the U.S. Census Bureau or December 23, 2011, nuclear power reactor licensees shall develop an ETE analysis using this decennial data and submit it under § 50.4 to the NRC. These licensees shall submit this ETE analysis to the NRC at least 180 days before using it to form protective action recommendations and providing it to State and local governmental authorities for use in developing offsite protective action strategies.

5. During the years between decennial censuses, nuclear power reactor licensees shall estimate EPZ permanent resident population changes once a year, but no later than 365 days from the date of the previous estimate, using the most recent U.S. Census Bureau annual resident population estimate and State/local government population data, if available. These licensees shall maintain these estimates so that they are available for NRC inspection during the period between decennial censuses and shall submit these estimates to the NRC with any updated ETE analysis.

6. If at any time during the decennial period, the EPZ permanent resident population increases such that it causes the longest ETE value for the 2-mile zone or 5-mile zone, including all affected Emergency Response Planning Areas, or for the entire 10-mile EPZ to increase by 25 percent or 30 minutes, whichever is less, from the nuclear power reactor licensee's currently NRC approved or updated ETE, the licensee shall update the ETE analysis to reflect the impact of that population increase. The licensee shall submit the updated ETE analysis to the NRC under § 50.4 no later than 365 days after the licensee's determination that the criteria for updating the ETE have been met and at least 180 days before using it to form protective action recommendations and providing it to State and local governmental authorities for use in developing offsite protective action strategies.

7. After an applicant for a combined license under part 52 of this chapter receives its license, the licensee shall conduct at least one review of any changes in the population of its EPZ at least 365 days prior to its scheduled fuel load. The licensee shall estimate EPZ permanent resident population changes using the most recent U.S. Census Bureau annual resident population estimate and State/local government population data, if available. If the EPZ permanent resident population increases such that it causes the longest ETE value for the 2-mile zone or 5-mile zone, including all affected Emergency Response Planning Areas, or for the entire 10-mile EPZ, to increase by 25 percent or 30 minutes, whichever is less, from the licensee's currently approved ETE, the licensee shall update the ETE analysis to reflect the impact of that population increase. The licensee shall submit the updated ETE analysis to the NRC for review under § 50.4 of this chapter no later than 365 days before the licensee's scheduled fuel load.

A. Organization

The organization for coping with radiological emergencies shall be described, including definition of authorities, responsibilities, and duties of individuals assigned to the licensee's emergency organization and the means for notification of such individuals in the event of an emergency. Specifically, the following shall be included:

1. A description of the normal plant operating organization.

2. A description of the onsite emergency response organization (ERO) with a detailed discussion of:

a. Authorities, responsibilities, and duties of the individual(s) who will take charge during an emergency;

b. Plant staff emergency assignments;

c. Authorities, responsibilities, and duties of an onsite emergency coordinator who shall be in charge of the exchange of information with offsite authorities responsible for coordinating and implementing offsite emergency measures.

3. A description, by position and function to be performed, of the licensee's headquarters personnel who will be sent to the plant site to augment the onsite emergency organization.

4. Identification, by position and function to be performed, of persons within the licensee organization who will be responsible for making offsite dose projections, and a description of how these projections will be made and the results transmitted to State and local authorities, NRC, and other appropriate governmental entities.

5. Identification, by position and function to be performed, of other employees of the licensee with special qualifications for coping with emergency conditions that may arise. Other persons with special qualifications, such as consultants, who are not employees of the licensee and who may be called upon for assistance for emergencies shall also be identified. The special qualifications of these persons shall be described.

6. A description of the local offsite services to be provided in support of the licensee's emergency organization.

7. By June 23, 2014, identification of, and a description of the assistance expected from, appropriate State, local, and Federal agencies with responsibilities for coping with emergencies, including hostile action at the site. For purposes of this appendix, "hostile action" is defined as an act directed toward a nuclear power plant or its personnel that includes the use of violent force to destroy equipment, take hostages, and/or intimidate the licensee to achieve an end. This includes attack by air, land, or water using guns, explosives, projectiles, vehicles, or other devices used to deliver destructive force.

8. Identification of the State and/or local officials responsible for planning for, ordering, and controlling appropriate protective actions, including evacuations when necessary.

9. By December 24, 2012, for nuclear power reactor licensees, a detailed analysis demonstrating that on-shift personnel assigned emergency plan implementation functions are not assigned responsibilities that would prevent the timely performance of their assigned functions as specified in the emergency plan.

B. Assessment Actions

1. The means to be used for determining the magnitude of, and for continually assessing the impact of, the release of radioactive materials shall be described, including emergency action levels that are to be used as criteria for determining the need for notification and participation of local and State agencies, the Commission, and other Federal agencies, and the emergency action levels that are to be used for determining when and what type of protective measures should be considered within and outside the site boundary to protect health and safety. The emergency action levels shall be based on in-plant conditions and instrumentation in addition to onsite and offsite monitoring. By June 20, 2012, for nuclear power reactor licensees, these action levels must include hostile action that may adversely affect the nuclear power plant. The initial emergency action levels shall be discussed and agreed on by the applicant or licensee and state and local governmental authorities, and approved by the NRC. Thereafter, emergency action levels shall be reviewed with the State and local governmental authorities on an annual basis.

2. A licensee desiring to change its entire emergency action level scheme shall submit an application for an amendment to its license and receive NRC approval before implementing the change. Licensees shall follow the change process in § 50.54(q) for all other emergency action level changes.

C. Activation of Emergency Organization

1. The entire spectrum of emergency conditions that involve the alerting or activating of progressively larger segments of the total emergency organization shall be described. The communication steps to be taken to alert or activate emergency personnel under each class of emergency shall be described. Emergency action levels (based not only on onsite and offsite radiation monitoring information but also on readings from a number of sensors that indicate a potential emergency, such as the pressure in containment and the response of the Emergency Core Cooling System) for notification of offsite agencies shall be described. The existence, but not the details, of a message authentication scheme shall be noted for such agencies.

The emergency classes defined shall include: (1) Notification of unusual events, (2) alert, (3) site area emergency, and (4) general emergency. These classes are further discussed in NUREG–0654/FEMA–REP–1.

2. By June 20, 2012, nuclear power reactor licensees shall establish and maintain the capability to assess, classify, and declare an emergency condition within 15 minutes after the availability of indications to plant operators that an emergency action level has been exceeded and shall promptly declare the emergency condition as soon as possible following identification of the appropriate emergency classification level. Licensees shall not construe these criteria as a grace period to attempt to restore plant conditions to avoid declaring an emergency action due to an emergency action level that has been exceeded. Licensees shall not construe these criteria as preventing implementation of response actions deemed by the licensee to be necessary to protect public health and safety provided that any delay in declaration does not deny the State and local authorities the opportunity to implement measures necessary to protect the public health and safety.

D. Notification Procedures

1. Administrative and physical means for notifying local, State, and Federal officials and agencies and agreements reached with these officials and agencies for the prompt notification of the public and for public evacuation or other protective measures, should they become necessary, shall be described. This description shall include identification of the appropriate officials, by title and agency, of the State and local government agencies within the EPZs.

2. Provisions shall be described for yearly dissemination to the public within the plume exposure pathway EPZ of basic emergency planning information, such as the methods and times required for public notification and the protective actions planned if an accident occurs, general information as to the nature and effects of radiation, and a listing of local broadcast stations that will be used for dissemination of information during an emergency. Signs or other measures shall also be used to disseminate to any transient population within the plume exposure pathway EPZ appropriate information that would be helpful if an accident occurs.

3. A licensee shall have the capability to notify responsible State and local governmental agencies within 15 minutes after declaring an emergency. The licensee shall demonstrate that the appropriate governmental authorities have the capability to make a public alerting and notification decision promptly on being informed by the licensee of an emergency condition. Prior to initial operation greater than 5 percent of rated thermal power of the first reactor at a site, each nuclear power reactor licensee shall demonstrate that administrative and physical means have been established for alerting and providing prompt instructions to the public within the plume exposure pathway EPZ. The design objective of the prompt public alert and notification system shall be to have the capability to essentially complete the initial alerting and initiate notification of the public within the plume exposure pathway EPZ within about 15 minutes. The use of this alerting and notification capability will range from immediate alerting and notification of the public (within 15 minutes of the time that State and local officials are notified that a situation exists requiring urgent action) to the more likely events where there is substantial time available for the appropriate governmental authorities to make a judgment whether or not to activate the public alert and notification system. The alerting and notification capability shall additionally include administrative and physical means for a backup method of public alerting and notification capable of being used in the event the primary method of alerting and notification is unavailable during an emergency to alert or notify all or portions of the plume exposure pathway EPZ population. The backup method shall have the capability to alert and notify the public within the plume exposure pathway EPZ, but does not need to meet the 15-minute design objective for the primary prompt public alert and notification system. When there is a decision to activate the alert and notification system, the appropriate governmental authorities will determine whether to activate the entire alert and notification system simultaneously or in a graduated or staged manner. The responsibility for activating such a public alert and notification system shall remain with the appropriate governmental authorities.

4. If FEMA has approved a nuclear power reactor site's alert and notification design report, including the backup alert and notification capability, as of December 23, 2011, then the backup alert and notification capability requirements in Section IV.D.3 must be implemented by December 24, 2012. If the alert and notification design report does not include a backup alert and notification capability or needs revision to ensure adequate backup alert and notification capability, then a revision of the alert and notification design report must be submitted to FEMA for review by June 24, 2013, and the FEMA-approved backup alert and notification means must be implemented within 365 days after FEMA approval. However, the total time period to implement a FEMA-approved backup alert and notification means must not exceed June 22, 2015.

E. Emergency Facilities and Equipment

Adequate provisions shall be made and described for emergency facilities and equipment, including:

1. Equipment at the site for personnel monitoring;

2. Equipment for determining the magnitude of and for continuously assessing the impact of the release of radioactive materials to the environment;

3. Facilities and supplies at the site for decontamination of onsite individuals;

4. Facilities and medical supplies at the site for appropriate emergency first aid treatment;

5. Arrangements for medical service providers qualified to handle radiological emergencies onsite;

6. Arrangements for transportation of contaminated injured individuals from the site to specifically identified treatment facilities outside the site boundary;

7. Arrangements for treatment of individuals injured in support of licensed activities on the site at treatment facilities outside the site boundary;

8.a. (i) A licensee onsite technical support center and an emergency operations facility from which effective direction can be given and effective control can be exercised during an emergency;

(ii) For nuclear power reactor licensees, a licensee onsite operational support center;

b. For a nuclear power reactor licensee's emergency operations facility required by paragraph 8.a of this section, either a facility located between 10 miles and 25 miles of the nuclear power reactor site(s), or a primary facility located less than 10 miles from the nuclear power reactor site(s) and a backup facility located between 10 miles and 25 miles of the nuclear power reactor site(s). An emergency operations facility may serve more than one nuclear power reactor site. A licensee desiring to locate an emergency operations facility more than 25 miles from a nuclear power reactor site shall request prior Commission approval by submitting an application for an amendment to its license. For an emergency operations facility located more than 25 miles from a nuclear power reactor site, provisions must be made for locating NRC and offsite responders closer to the nuclear power reactor site so that NRC and offsite responders can interact face-to-face with emergency response personnel entering and leaving the nuclear power reactor site. Provisions for locating NRC and offsite responders closer to a nuclear power reactor site that is more than 25 miles from the emergency operations facility must include the following:

(1) Space for members of an NRC site team and Federal, State, and local responders;

(2) Additional space for conducting briefings with emergency response personnel;

(3) Communication with other licensee and offsite emergency response facilities;

(4) Access to plant data and radiological information; and

(5) Access to copying equipment and office supplies;

c. By June 20, 2012, for a nuclear power reactor licensee's emergency operations facility required by paragraph 8.a of this section, a facility having the following capabilities:

(1) The capability for obtaining and displaying plant data and radiological information for each reactor at a nuclear power reactor site and for each nuclear power reactor site that the facility serves;

(2) The capability to analyze plant technical information and provide technical briefings on event conditions and prognosis to licensee and offsite response organizations for each reactor at a nuclear power reactor site and for each nuclear power reactor site that the facility serves; and

(3) The capability to support response to events occurring simultaneously at more than one nuclear power reactor site if the emergency operations facility serves more than one site; and

d. For nuclear power reactor licensees, an alternative facility (or facilities) that would be accessible even if the site is under threat of or experiencing hostile action, to function as a staging area for augmentation of emergency response staff and collectively having the following characteristics: the capability for communication with the emergency operations facility, control room, and plant security; the capability to perform offsite notifications; and the capability for engineering assessment activities, including damage control team planning and preparation, for use when onsite emergency facilities cannot be safely accessed during hostile action. The requirements in this paragraph 8.d must be implemented no later than December 23, 2014, with the exception of the capability for staging emergency response organization personnel at the alternative facility (or facilities) and the capability for communications with the emergency operations facility, control room, and plant security, which must be implemented no later than June 20, 2012.

e. A licensee shall not be subject to the requirements of paragraph 8.b of this section for an existing emergency operations facility approved as of December 23, 2011;

9. At least one onsite and one offsite communications system; each system shall have a backup power source. All communication plans shall have arrangements for emergencies, including titles and alternates for those in charge at both ends of the communication links and the primary and backup means of communication. Where consistent with the function of the governmental agency, these arrangements will include:

a. Provision for communications with contiguous State/local governments within the plume exposure pathway EPZ. Such communications shall be tested monthly.

b. Provision for communications with Federal emergency response organizations. Such communications systems shall be tested annually.

c. Provision for communications among the nuclear power reactor control room, the onsite technical support center, and the emergency operations facility; and among the nuclear facility, the principal State and local emergency operations centers, and the field assessment teams. Such communications systems shall be tested annually.

d. Provisions for communications by the licensee with NRC Headquarters and the appropriate NRC Regional Office Operations Center from the nuclear power reactor control room, the onsite technical support center, and the emergency operations facility. Such communications shall be tested monthly.

F. Training

1. The program to provide for: (a) The training of employees and exercising, by periodic drills, of emergency plans to ensure that employees of the licensee are familiar with their specific emergency response duties, and (b) The participation in the training and drills by other persons whose assistance may be needed in the event of a radiological emergency shall be described. This shall include a description of specialized initial training and periodic retraining programs to be provided to each of the following categories of emergency personnel:

i. Directors and/or coordinators of the plant emergency organization;

ii. Personnel responsible for accident assessment, including control room shift personnel;

iii. Radiological monitoring teams;

iv. Fire control teams (fire brigades);

v. Repair and damage control teams;

vi. First aid and rescue teams;

vii. Medical support personnel;

viii. Licensee's headquarters support personnel;

ix. Security personnel.

In addition, a radiological orientation training program shall be made available to local services personnel; e.g., local emergency services/Civil Defense, local law enforcement personnel, local news media persons.

2. The plan shall describe provisions for the conduct of emergency preparedness exercises as follows: Exercises shall test the adequacy of timing and content of implementing procedures and methods, test emergency equipment and communications networks, test the public alert and notification system, and ensure that emergency organization personnel are familiar with their duties.[3]

a. A full participation[4] exercise which tests as much of the licensee, State, and local emergency plans as is reasonably achievable without mandatory public participation shall be conducted for each site at which a power reactor is located. Nuclear power reactor licensees shall submit exercise scenarios under § 50.4 at least 60 days before use in a full participation exercise required by this paragraph 2.a.

(i) For an operating license issued under this part, this exercise must be conducted within 2 years before the issuance of the first operating license for full power (one authorizing operation above 5 percent of rated thermal power) of the first reactor and shall include participation by each State and local government within the plume exposure pathway EPZ and each state within the ingestion exposure pathway EPZ. If the full participation exercise is conducted more than 1 year prior to issuance of an operating licensee for full power, an exercise which tests the licensee's onsite emergency plans must be conducted within one year before issuance of an operating license for full power. This exercise need not have State or local government participation.

(ii) For a combined license issued under part 52 of this chapter, this exercise must be conducted within two years of the scheduled date for initial loading of fuel. If the first full participation exercise is conducted more than one year before the scheduled date for initial loading of fuel, an exercise which tests the licensee's onsite emergency plans must be conducted within one year before the scheduled date for initial loading of fuel. This exercise need not have State or local government participation. If FEMA identifies one or more deficiencies in the state of offsite emergency preparedness as the result of the first full participation exercise, or if the Commission finds that the state of emergency preparedness does not provide reasonable assurance that adequate protective measures can and will be taken in the event

[3] Use of site specific simulators or computers is acceptable for any exercise.

[4] Full participation when used in conjunction with emergency preparedness exercises for a particular site means appropriate offsite local and State authorities and licensee personnel physically and actively take part in testing their integrated capability to adequately assess and respond to an accident at a commercial nuclear power plant. Full participation includes testing major observable portions of the onsite and offsite emergency plans and mobilization of State, local and licensee personnel and other resources in sufficient numbers to verify the capability to respond to the accident scenario.

of a radiological emergency, the provisions of § 50.54(gg) apply.

(iii) For a combined license issued under part 52 of this chapter, if the applicant currently has an operating reactor at the site, an exercise, either full or partial participation,[5] shall be conducted for each subsequent reactor constructed on the site. This exercise may be incorporated in the exercise requirements of Sections IV.F.2.b. and c. in this appendix. If FEMA identifies one or more deficiencies in the state of offsite emergency preparedness as the result of this exercise for the new reactor, or if the Commission finds that the state of emergency preparedness does not provide reasonable assurance that adequate protective measures can and will be taken in the event of a radiological emergency, the provisions of § 50.54(gg) apply.

b. Each licensee at each site shall conduct a subsequent exercise of its onsite emergency plan every 2 years. Nuclear power reactor licensees shall submit exercise scenarios under § 50.4 at least 60 days before use in an exercise required by this paragraph 2.b. The exercise may be included in the full participation biennial exercise required by paragraph 2.c. of this section. In addition, the licensee shall take actions necessary to ensure that adequate emergency response capabilities are maintained during the interval between biennial exercises by conducting drills, including at least one drill involving a combination of some of the principal functional areas of the licensee's onsite emergency response capabilities. The principal functional areas of emergency response include activities such as management and coordination of emergency response, accident assessment, event classification, notification of offsite authorities, assessment of the onsite and offsite impact of radiological releases, protective action recommendation development, protective action decision making, plant system repair and mitigative action implementation. During these drills, activation of all of the licensee's emergency response facilities (Technical Support Center (TSC), Operations Support Center (OSC), and the Emergency Operations Facility (EOF)) would not be necessary, licensees would have the opportunity to consider accident management strategies, supervised instruction would be permitted, operating staff in all participating facilities would have the opportunity to resolve problems (success paths) rather than have controllers intervene, and the drills may focus on the onsite exercise training objectives.

c. Offsite plans for each site shall be exercised biennially with full participation by each offsite authority having a role under the radiological response plan. Where the offsite authority has a role under a radiological response plan for more than one site, it shall fully participate in one exercise every two years and shall, at least, partially participate in other offsite plan exercises in this period. If two different licensees each have licensed facilities located either on the same site or on adjacent, contiguous sites, and share most of the elements defining co-located licensees,[6] then each licensee shall:

(1) Conduct an exercise biennially of its onsite emergency plan;

(2) Participate quadrennially in an offsite biennial full or partial participation exercise;

(3) Conduct emergency preparedness activities and interactions in the years between its participation in the offsite full or partial participation exercise with offsite authorities, to test and maintain interface among the affected State and local authorities and the licensee. Co-located licensees shall also participate in emergency preparedness activities and interaction with offsite authorities for the period between exercises;

(4) Conduct a hostile action exercise of its onsite emergency plan in each exercise cycle; and

(5) Participate in an offsite biennial full or partial participation hostile action exercise in alternating exercise cycles.

d. Each State with responsibility for nuclear power reactor emergency preparedness should fully participate in the ingestion pathway portion of exercises at least once every exercise cycle. In States with more than one nuclear power reactor plume exposure pathway EPZ, the State should rotate this participation from site to site. Each State with responsibility for nuclear power reactor emergency preparedness should fully participate in a hostile action exercise at least once every cycle and should fully participate in one hostile action exercise by December 31, 2015. States with more than one

[5] Partial participation when used in conjunction with emergency preparedness exercises for a particular site means appropriate offsite authorities shall actively take part in the exercise sufficient to test direction and control functions; *i.e.*, (a) protective action decision making related to emergency action levels, and (b) communication capabilities among affected State and local authorities and the licensee.

[6] Co-located licensees are two different licensees whose licensed facilities are located either on the same site or on adjacent, contiguous sites, and that share most of the following emergency planning and siting elements:

a. Plume exposure and ingestion emergency planning zones;

b. Offsite governmental authorities;

c. Offsite emergency response organizations;

d. Public notification system; and/or

e. Emergency facilities.

nuclear power reactor plume exposure pathway EPZ should rotate this participation from site to site.

e. Licensees shall enable any State or local government located within the plume exposure pathway EPZ to participate in the licensee's drills when requested by such State or local government.

f. Remedial exercises will be required if the emergency plan is not satisfactorily tested during the biennial exercise, such that NRC, in consultation with FEMA, cannot (1) find reasonable assurance that adequate protective measures can and will be taken in the event of a radiological emergency or (2) determine that the Emergency Response Organization (ERO) has maintained key skills specific to emergency response. The extent of State and local participation in remedial exercises must be sufficient to show that appropriate corrective measures have been taken regarding the elements of the plan not properly tested in the previous exercises.

g. All exercises, drills, and training that provide performance opportunities to develop, maintain, or demonstrate key skills must provide for formal critiques in order to identify weak or deficient areas that need correction. Any weaknesses or deficiencies that are identified in a critique of exercises, drills, or training must be corrected.

h. The participation of State and local governments in an emergency exercise is not required to the extent that the applicant has identified those governments as refusing to participate further in emergency planning activities, pursuant to §50.47(c)(1). In such cases, an exercise shall be held with the applicant or licensee and such governmental entities as elect to participate in the emergency planning process.

i. Licensees shall use drill and exercise scenarios that provide reasonable assurance that anticipatory responses will not result from preconditioning of participants. Such scenarios for nuclear power reactor licensees must include a wide spectrum of radiological releases and events, including hostile action. Exercise and drill scenarios as appropriate must emphasize coordination among onsite and offsite response organizations.

j. The exercises conducted under paragraph 2 of this section by nuclear power reactor licensees must provide the opportunity for the ERO to demonstrate proficiency in the key skills necessary to implement the principal functional areas of emergency response identified in paragraph 2.b of this section. Each exercise must provide the opportunity for the ERO to demonstrate key skills specific to emergency response duties in the control room, TSC, OSC, EOF, and joint information center. Additionally, in each eight calendar year exercise cycle, nuclear power reactor licensees shall vary the content of scenarios during exercises conducted under paragraph 2 of this section to provide the opportunity for the ERO to demonstrate proficiency in the key skills necessary to respond to the following scenario elements: hostile action directed at the plant site, no radiological release or an unplanned minimal radiological release that does not require public protective actions, an initial classification of or rapid escalation to a Site Area Emergency or General Emergency, implementation of strategies, procedures, and guidance developed under §50.54(hh)(2), and integration of offsite resources with onsite response. The licensee shall maintain a record of exercises conducted during each eight year exercise cycle that documents the content of scenarios used to comply with the requirements of this paragraph. Each licensee shall conduct a hostile action exercise for each of its sites no later than December 31, 2015. The first eight-year exercise cycle for a site will begin in the calendar year in which the first hostile action exercise is conducted. For a site licensed under Part 52, the first eight-year exercise cycle begins in the calendar year of the initial exercise required by Section IV.F.2.a.

G. Maintaining Emergency Preparedness

Provisions to be employed to ensure that the emergency plan, its implementing procedures, and emergency equipment and supplies are maintained up to date shall be described.

H. Recovery

Criteria to be used to determine when, following an accident, reentry of the facility would be appropriate or when operation could be resumed shall be described.

I. Onsite Protective Actions During Hostile Action

By June 20, 2012, for nuclear power reactor licensees, a range of protective actions to protect onsite personnel during hostile action must be developed to ensure the continued ability of the licensee to safely shut down the reactor and perform the functions of the licensee's emergency plan.

V. IMPLEMENTING PROCEDURES

No less than 180 days before the scheduled issuance of an operating license for a nuclear power reactor or a license to possess nuclear material, or the scheduled date for initial loading of fuel for a combined license under part 52 of this chapter, the applicant's or licensee's detailed implementing procedures for its emergency plan shall be submitted to the Commission as specified in §50.4.

VI. EMERGENCY RESPONSE DATA SYSTEM

1. The Emergency Response Data System (ERDS) is a direct near real-time electronic data link between the licensee's onsite computer system and the NRC Operations Center

that provides for the automated transmission of a limited data set of selected parameters. The ERDS supplements the existing voice transmission over the Emergency Notification System (ENS) by providing the NRC Operations Center with timely and accurate updates of a limited set of parameters from the licensee's installed onsite computer system in the event of an emergency. When selected plant data are not available on the licensee's onsite computer system, retrofitting of data points is not required. The licensee shall test the ERDS periodically to verify system availability and operability. The frequency of ERDS testing will be quarterly unless otherwise set by NRC based on demonstrated system performance.

2. Except for Big Rock Point and all nuclear power facilities that are shut down permanently or indefinitely, onsite hardware shall be provided at each unit by the licensee to interface with the NRC receiving system. Software, which will be made available by the NRC, will assemble the data to be transmitted and transmit data from each unit via an output port on the appropriate data system. The hardware and software must have the following characteristics:

a. Data points, if resident in the in-plant computer systems, must be transmitted for four selected types of plant conditions: Reactor core and coolant system conditions; reactor containment conditions; radioactivity release rates; and plant meteorological tower data. A separate data feed is required for each reactor unit. While it is recognized that ERDS is not a safety system, it is conceivable that a licensee's ERDS interface could communicate with a safety system. In this case, appropriate isolation devices would be required at these interfaces.[7] The data points, identified in the following parameters will be transmitted:

(i) For pressurized water reactors (PWRs), the selected plant parameters are: (1) Primary coolant system: pressure, temperatures (hot leg, cold leg, and core exit thermocouples), subcooling margin, pressurizer level, reactor coolant charging/makeup flow, reactor vessel level, reactor coolant flow, and reactor power; (2) Secondary coolant system: Steam generator levels and pressures, main feedwater flows, and auxiliary and emergency feedwater flows; (3) Safety injection: High- and low-pressure safety injection flows, safety injection flows (Westinghouse), and borated water storage tank level; (4) Containment: pressure, temperatures, hydrogen concentration, and sump levels; (5) Radiation monitoring system: Reactor coolant radioactivity, containment radiation level, condenser air removal radiation level, effluent radiation monitors, and process radiation monitor levels; and (6) Meteorological data: wind speed, wind direction, and atmospheric stability.

(ii) For boiling water reactors (BWRs), the selected parameters are: (1) Reactor coolant system: Reactor pressure, reactor vessel level, feedwater flow, and reactor power; (2) Safety injection: Reactor core isolation cooling flow, high-pressure coolant injection/high-pressure core spray flow, core spray flow, low-pressure coolant injection flow, and condensate storage tank level; (3) Containment: drywell pressure, drywell temperatures, drywell sump levels, hydrogen and oxygen concentrations, suppression pool temperature, and suppression pool level; (4) Radiation monitoring system: Reactor coolant radioactivity level, primary containment radiation level, condenser off-gas radiation level, effluent radiation monitor, and process radiation levels; and (5) Meteorological data: Wind speed, wind direction, and atmospheric stability.

b. The system must be capable of transmitting all available ERDS parameters at time intervals of not less than 15 seconds or more than 60 seconds. Exceptions to this requirement will be considered on a case by case basis.

c. All link control and data transmission must be established in a format compatible with the NRC receiving system[8] as configured at the time of licensee implementation.

3. Maintaining Emergency Response Data System:

a. Any hardware and software changes that affect the transmitted data points identified in the ERDS Data Point Library[9] (site specific data base residing on the ERDS computer) must be submitted to the NRC within 30 days after the changes are completed.

b. Hardware and software changes, with the exception of data point modifications, that could affect the transmission format and computer communication protocol to the ERDS must be provided to the NRC as soon as practicable and at least 30 days prior to the modification.

c. In the event of a failure of the NRC supplied onsite modem, a replacement unit will be furnished by the NRC for licensee installation.

4. Implementing the Emergency Response Data System Program:

a. Each licensee shall develop and submit an ERDS implementation program plan to the NRC by October 28, 1991. To ensure compatibility with the guidance provided for the ERDS, the ERDS implementation program plan,[10] must include, but not be limited to,

[7] See 10 CFR 50.55a(h) Protection Systems.

[8] Guidance is provided in NUREG–1394, Revision 1.

[9] See NUREG–1394, Revision 1, appendix C, Data Point Library.

[10] See NUREG–1394, Revision 1, section 3.

information on the licensee's computer system configuration (*i.e.*, hardware and software), interface, and procedures.

b. Licensees must comply with appendix E to part 50, section V.

c. Licensees that have submitted the required information under the voluntary ERDS implementation program will not be required to resubmit this information. The licensee shall meet the implementation schedule of appendix E to part 50, section VI.4d.

d. Each licensee shall complete implementation of the ERDS by February 13, 1993, or before initial escalation to full power, whichever comes later. Licensees with currently operational ERDS interfaces approved under the voluntary ERDS implementation program[11] will not be required to submit another implementation plan and will be considered to have met the requirements for ERDS under appendix E to part 50, section VI.1 and 2 of this part.

[45 FR 55410, Aug. 19, 1980; 46 FR 28839, May 29, 1981, as amended at 46 FR 63032, Dec. 30, 1981; 47 FR 30236, July 13, 1982; 47 FR 57671, Dec. 28, 1982; 49 FR 27736, July 6, 1984; 51 FR 40310, Nov. 6, 1986; 52 FR 16829, May 6, 1987; 52 FR 42086, Nov. 3, 1987; 56 FR 40185, Aug. 13, 1991; 59 FR 14090, Mar. 25, 1994; 61 FR 30132, June 14, 1996; 72 FR 49506, Aug. 28, 2007; 73 FR 42674, July 23, 2008; 76 FR 72596, Nov. 23, 2011; 78 FR 34248, June 7, 2013; 80 FR 74980, Dec. 1, 2015]

EDITORIAL NOTE: At 72 FR 49506, Aug. 28, 2007, Appendix E to part 50 was amended by redesignating footnotes 6, 7, 8, 9, 10, 11 as 7, 8, 9, 10, 11, 12; however, the amendment could not be incorporated due to inaccurate amendatory instruction.

APPENDIX F TO PART 50—POLICY RELATING TO THE SITING OF FUEL REPROCESSING PLANTS AND RELATED WASTE MANAGEMENT FACILITIES

1. Public health and safety considerations relating to licensed fuel reprocessing plants do not require that such facilities be located on land owned and controlled by the Federal Government. Such plants, including the facilities for the temporary storage of high-level radioactive wastes, may be located on privately owned property.

2. A fuel reprocessing plant's inventory of high-level liquid radioactive wastes will be limited to that produced in the prior 5 years. (For the purpose of this statement of policy, "high-level liquid radioactive wastes" means those aqueous wastes resulting from the operation of the first cycle solvent extraction system, or equivalent, and the concentrated wastes from subsequent extraction cycles, or equivalent, in a facility for reprocessing irradiated reactor fuels.) High-level liquid radioactive wastes shall be converted to a dry solid as required to comply with this inventory limitation, and placed in a sealed container prior to transfer to a Federal repository in a shipping cask meeting the requirements of 10 CFR part 71. The dry solid shall be chemically, thermally, and radiolytically stable to the extent that the equilibrium pressure in the sealed container will not exceed the safe operating pressure for that container during the period from canning through a minimum of 90 days after receipt (transfer of physical custody) at the Federal repository. All of these high-level radioactive wastes shall be transferred to a Federal repository no later than 10 years following separation of fission products from the irradiated fuel. Upon receipt, the Federal repository will assume permanent custody of these radioactive waste materials although industry will pay the Federal Government a charge which together with interest on unexpended balances will be designed to defray all costs of disposal and perpetual surveillance. The Department of Energy will take title to the radioactive waste material upon transfer to a Federal repository. Before retirement of the reprocessing plant from operational status and before termination of licensing pursuant to § 50.82, transfer of all such wastes to a Federal repository shall be completed. Federal repositories, which will be limited in number, will be designated later by the Commission.

3. Disposal of high-level radioactive fission product waste material will not be permitted on any land other than that owned and controlled by the Federal Government.

4. A design objective for fuel reprocessing plants shall be to facilitate decontamination and removal of all significant radioactive wastes at the time the facility is permanently decommissioned. Criteria for the extent of decontamination to be required upon decommissioning and license termination will be developed in consultation with competent groups. Opportunity will be afforded for public comment before such criteria are made effective.

5. Applicants proposing to operate fuel reprocessing plants, in submitting information concerning financial qualifications as required by § 50.33(f), shall include information enabling the Commission to determine whether the applicant is financially qualified, among other things, to provide for the removal and disposal of radioactive wastes, during operation and upon decommissioning of the facility, in accordance with the Commission's regulations, including the requirements set out in this appendix.

6. With respect to fuel reprocessing plants already licensed, the licenses will be appropriately conditioned to carry out the purposes of the policy stated above with respect

[11] See NUREG–1394, Revision 1.

to high-level radioactive fission product wastes generated after installation of new equipment for interim storage of liquid wastes, or after installation of equipment required for solidification without interim liquid storage. In either case, such equipment shall be installed at the earliest practicable date, taking into account the time required for design, procurement and installation thereof. With respect to such plants, the application of the policy stated in this appendix to existing wastes and to wastes generated prior to the installation of such equipment, will be the subject of a further rulemaking proceeding.

[35 FR 17533, Nov. 14, 1970, as amended at 36 FR 5411, Mar. 23, 1971; 42 FR 20139, Apr. 18, 1977; 45 FR 14201, Mar. 5, 1980; 70 FR 3599, Jan. 26, 2005]

APPENDIX G TO PART 50—FRACTURE TOUGHNESS REQUIREMENTS

I. Introduction and scope.
II. Definitions.
III. Fracture toughness tests.
IV. Fracture toughness requirements.

I. INTRODUCTION AND SCOPE

This appendix specifies fracture toughness requirements for ferritic materials of pressure-retaining components of the reactor coolant pressure boundary of light water nuclear power reactors to provide adequate margins of safety during any condition of normal operation, including anticipated operational occurrences and system hydrostatic tests, to which the pressure boundary may be subjected over its service lifetime.

The ASME Code forms the basis for the requirements of this appendix. "ASME Code" means the American Society of Mechanical Engineers Boiler and Pressure Vessel Code. If no section is specified, the reference is to Section III, Division 1, "Rules for Construction of Nuclear Power Plant Components." "Section XI" means Section XI, Division 1, "Rules for Inservice Inspection of Nuclear Power Plant Components." If no edition or addenda are specified, the ASME Code edition and addenda and any limitations and modifications thereof, which are specified in § 50.55a, are applicable.

The sections, editions and addenda of the ASME Boiler and Pressure Vessel Code specified in § 50.55a have been approved for incorporation by reference by the Director of the Federal Register. A notice of any changes made to the material incorporated by reference will be published in the FEDERAL REGISTER. Copies of the ASME Boiler and Pressure Vessel Code may be purchased from the American Society of Mechanical Engineers, United Engineering Center, 345 East 47th Street, New York, NY 10017, and are available for inspection at the NRC Library, 11545 Rockville Pike, Two White Flint North, Rockville, MD 20852–2738.

The requirements of this appendix apply to the following materials:

A. Carbon and low-alloy ferritic steel plate, forgings, castings, and pipe with specified minimum yield strengths not over 50,000 psi (345 MPa), and to those with specified minimum yield strengths greater than 50,000 psi (345 MPa) but not over 90,000 psi (621 MPa) if qualified by using methods equivalent to those described in paragraph G–2110 of appendix G of section XI of the latest edition and addenda of the ASME Code incorporated by reference into § 50.55a(b)(2).

B. Welds and weld heat-affected zones in the materials specified in paragraph I.A. of this appendix.

C. Materials for bolting and other types of fasteners with specified minimum yield strengths not over 130,000 psi (896 MPa).

NOTE: The adequacy of the fracture toughness of other ferritic materials not covered in this section must be demonstrated to the Director, Office of Nuclear Reactor Regulation or the Director, Office of New Reactors, as appropriate, on an individual case basis.

II. DEFINITIONS

A. *Ferritic material* means carbon and low-alloy steels, higher alloy steels including all stainless alloys of the 4xx series, and maraging and precipitation hardening steels with a predominantly body-centered cubic crystal structure.

B. *System hydrostatic tests* means all preoperational system leakage and hydrostatic pressure tests and all system leakage and hydrostatic pressure tests performed during the service life of the pressure boundary in compliance with the ASME Code, Section XI.

C. *Specified minimum yield strength* means the minimum yield strength (in the unirradiated condition) of a material specified in the construction code under which the component is built under § 50.55a.

D. RT_{NDT} means the reference temperature of the material, for all conditions.

(i) For the pre-service or unirradiated condition, RT_{NDT} is evaluated according to the procedures in the ASME Code, Paragraph NB–2331.

(ii) For the reactor vessel beltline materials, RT_{NDT} must account for the effects of neutron radiation.

E. ΔRT_{NDT} means the transition temperature shift, or change in RT_{NDT}, due to neutron radiation effects, which is evaluated as the difference in the 30 ft-lb (41 J) index temperatures from the average Charpy curves measured before and after irradiation.

F. *Beltline* or *Beltline region of reactor vessel* means the region of the reactor vessel (shell material including welds, heat affected zones, and plates or forgings) that directly surrounds the effective height of the active core and adjacent regions of the reactor vessel that are predicted to experience sufficient neutron radiation damage to be considered in the selection of the most limiting material with regard to radiation damage.

III. FRACTURE TOUGHNESS TESTS

A. To demonstrate compliance with the fracture toughness requirements of section IV of this appendix, ferritic materials must be tested in accordance with the ASME Code and, for the beltline materials, the test requirements of appendix H of this part. For a reactor vessel that was constructed to an ASME code earlier than the Summer 1972 Addenda of the 1971 Edition (under § 50.55a), the fracture toughness data and data analysis must be supplemented in a manner approved by the Director, Office of Nuclear Reactor Regulation or Director, Office of New Reactors, as appropriate, to demonstrate equivalence with the fracture toughness requirements of this appendix.

B. Test methods for supplemental fracture toughness tests described in paragraph IV.A.1.b of this appendix must be submitted to and approved by the Director, Office of Nuclear Reactor Regulation or Director, Office of New Reactors, as appropriate, prior to testing.

C. All fracture toughness test programs conducted in accordance with paragraphs III.A and III.B must comply with ASME Code requirements for calibration of test equipment, qualification of test personnel, and retention of records of these functions and of the test data.

IV. FRACTURE TOUGHNESS REQUIREMENTS

A. The pressure-retaining components of the reactor coolant pressure boundary that are made of ferritic materials must meet the requirements of the ASME Code, supplemented by the additional requirements set forth below, for fracture toughness during system hydrostatic tests and any condition of normal operation, including anticipated operational occurrences. Reactor vessels may continue to be operated only for that service period within which the requirements of this section are satisfied. For the reactor vessel beltline materials, including welds, plates and forgings, the values of RT_{NDT} and Charpy upper-shelf energy must account for the effects of neutron radiation, including the results of the surveillance program of appendix H of this part. The effects of neutron radiation must consider the radiation conditions (*i.e.*, the fluence) at the deepest point on the crack front of the flaw assumed in the analysis.

1. Reactor Vessel Charpy Upper-Shelf Energy Requirements

a. Reactor vessel beltline materials must have Charpy upper-shelf energy[1] in the transverse direction for base material and along the weld for weld material according to the ASME Code, of no less than 75 ft-lb (102 J) initially and must maintain Charpy upper-shelf energy throughout the life of the vessel of no less than 50 ft-lb (68 J), unless it is demonstrated in a manner approved by the Director, Office of Nuclear Reactor Regulation or Director, Office of New Reactors, as appropriate, that lower values of Charpy upper-shelf energy will provide margins of safety against fracture equivalent to those required by Appendix G of Section XI of the ASME Code. This analysis must use the latest edition and addenda of the ASME Code incorporated by reference into § 50.55a(b)(2) at the time the analysis is submitted.

b. Additional evidence of the fracture toughness of the beltline materials after exposure to neutron irradiation may be obtained from results of supplemental fracture toughness tests for use in the analysis specified in section IV.A.1.a.

c. The analysis for satisfying the requirements of section IV.A.1 of this appendix must be submitted, as specified in § 50.4, for review and approval on an individual case basis at least three years prior to the date when the predicted Charpy upper-shelf energy will no longer satisfy the requirements of section IV.A.1 of this appendix, or on a schedule approved by the Director, Office of Nuclear Reactor Regulation or Director, Office of New Reactors, as appropriate.

2. Pressure-Temperature Limits and Minimum Temperature Requirements

a. Pressure-temperature limits and minimum temperature requirements for the reactor vessel are given in table 1, and are defined by the operating condition (i.e., hydrostatic pressure and leak tests, or normal operation including anticipated operational occurrences), the vessel pressure, whether or not fuel is in the vessel, and whether the core is critical. In table 1, the vessel pressure is defined as a percentage of the preservice system hydrostatic test pressure. The appropriate requirements on both the pressure-temperature limits and the minimum permissible temperature must be met for all conditions.

b. The pressure-temperature limits identified as "ASME Appendix G limits" in table 1 require that the limits must be at least as conservative as limits obtained by following the methods of analysis and the margins of

[1] Defined in ASTME 185–79 and –82 which are incorporated by reference in appendix H to part 50.

safety of Appendix G of Section XI of the ASME Code.

c. The minimum temperature requirements given in table 1 pertain to the controlling material, which is either the material in the closure flange or the material in the beltline region with the highest reference temperature. As specified in table 1, the minimum temperature requirements and the controlling material depend on the operating condition (i.e., hydrostatic pressure and leak tests, or normal operation including anticipated operational occurrences), the vessel pressure, whether fuel is in the vessel, and whether the core is critical. The metal temperature of the controlling material, in the region of the controlling material which has the least favorable combination of stress and temperature must exceed the appropriate minimum temperature requirement for the condition and pressure of the vessel specified in table 1.

d. Pressure tests and leak tests of the reactor vessel that are required by Section XI of the ASME Code must be completed before the core is critical.

B. If the procedures of section IV.A. of this appendix do not indicate the existence of an equivalent safety margin, the reactor vessel beltline may be given a thermal annealing treatment to recover the fracture toughness of the material, subject to the requirements of § 50.66. The reactor vessel may continue to be operated only for that service period within which the predicted fracture toughness of the beltline region materials satisfies the requirements of section IV.A. of this appendix using the values of RT_{NDT} and Charpy upper-shelf energy that include the effects of annealing and subsequent irradiation.

TABLE 1—PRESSURE AND TEMPERATURE REQUIREMENTS FOR THE REACTOR PRESSURE VESSEL

Operating condition	Vessel pressure [1]	Requirements for pressure-temperature limits	Minimum temperature requirements
1. Hydrostatic pressure and leak tests (core is not critical):			
1.a Fuel in the vessel	≤20%	ASME Appendix G Limits	(2)
1.b Fuel in the vessel	>20%	ASME Appendix G Limits	(2) + 90 °F (6)
1.c No fuel in the vessel (Preservice Hydrotest Only).	ALL	(Not Applicable)	(3) + 60 °F
2. Normal operation (incl. heat-up and cool-down), including anticipated operational occurrences:			
2.a Core not critical	≤20%	ASME Appendix G Limits	(2)
2.b Core not critical	>20%	ASME Appendix G Limits	(2) + 120 °F (6)
2.c Core critical	≤20%	ASME Appendix G Limits + 40 °F	Larger of [(4)] or [(2) + 40 °F]
2.d Core critical	>20%	ASME Appendix G Limits + 40 °F	Larger of [(4)] or [(2) + 160 °F]
2.e Core critical for BWR (5)	≤20%	ASME Appendix G Limits + 40 °F	(2) + 60 °F

[1] Percent of the preservice system hydrostatic test pressure.
[2] The highest reference temperature of the material in the closure flange region that is highly stressed by the bolt preload.
[3] The highest reference temperature of the vessel.
[4] The minimum permissible temperature for the inservice system hydrostatic pressure test.
[5] For boiling water reactors (BWR) with water level within the normal range for power operation.
[6] Lower temperatures are permissible if they can be justified by showing that the margins of safety of the controlling region are equivalent to those required for the beltline when it is controlling.

[60 FR 65474, Dec. 19, 1995, as amended at 73 FR 5723, Jan. 31, 2008; 78 FR 34248, June 7, 2013; 78 FR 75450, Dec. 12, 2013]

APPENDIX H TO PART 50—REACTOR VESSEL MATERIAL SURVEILLANCE PROGRAM REQUIREMENTS

I. Introduction
II. Definitions
III. Surveillance Program Criteria
IV. Report of Test Results

I. INTRODUCTION

The purpose of the material surveillance program required by this appendix is to monitor changes in the fracture toughness properties of ferritic materials in the reactor vessel beltline region of light water nuclear power reactors which result from exposure of these materials to neutron irradiation and the thermal environment. Under the program, fracture toughness test data are obtained from material specimens exposed in surveillance capsules, which are withdrawn periodically from the reactor vessel. These data will be used as described in section IV of appendix G to part 50.

ASTM E 185–73, "Standard Recommended Practice for Surveillance Tests for Nuclear Reactor Vessels"; ASTM E 185–79, "Standard Practice for Conducting Surveillance Tests for Light-Water Cooled Nuclear Power Reactor Vessels"; and ASTM E 185–82, "Standard Practice for Conducting Surveillance Tests for Light-Water Cooled Nuclear Power Reactor Vessels"; which are referenced in the following paragraphs, have been approved for incorporation by reference by the Director of the Federal Register. Copies of ASTM E 185–73, –79, and –82, may be purchased from the American Society for Testing and Materials, 1916 Race Street, Philadelphia, PA 19103 and are available for inspection at the NRC Library, 11545 Rockville Pike, Two White Flint North, Rockville, MD 20852–2738.

II. DEFINITIONS

All terms used in this appendix have the same meaning as in appendix G.

III. SURVEILLANCE PROGRAM CRITERIA

A. No material surveillance program is required for reactor vessels for which it can be conservatively demonstrated by analytical methods applied to experimental data and tests performed on comparable vessels, making appropriate allowances for all uncertainties in the measurements, that the peak neutron fluence at the end of the design life of the vessel will not exceed 10^{17} n/cm^2 (E >1 MeV).

B. Reactor vessels that do not meet the conditions of paragraph III.A of this appendix must have their beltline materials monitored by a surveillance program complying with ASTM E 185, as modified by this appendix.

1. The design of the surveillance program and the withdrawal schedule must meet the requirements of the edition of ASTM E 185 that is current on the issue date of the ASME Code to which the reactor vessel was purchased. Later editions of ASTM E 185 may be used, but including only those editions through 1982. For each capsule withdrawal, the test procedures and reporting requirements must meet the requirements of ASTM E 185–82 to the extent practicable for the configuration of the specimens in the capsule.

2. Surveillance specimen capsules must be located near the inside vessel wall in the beltline region so that the specimen irradiation history duplicates, to the extent practicable within the physical constraints of the system, the neutron spectrum, temperature history, and maximum neutron fluence experienced by the reactor vessel inner surface. If the capsule holders are attached to the vessel wall or to the vessel cladding, construction and inservice inspection of the attachments and attachment welds must be done according to the requirements for permanent structural attachments to reactor vessels given in Sections III and XI of the American Society of Mechanical Engineers Boiler and Pressure Vessel Code (ASME Code). The design and location of the capsule holders must permit insertion of replacement capsules. Accelerated irradiation capsules may be used in addition to the required number of surveillance capsules.

3. A proposed withdrawal schedule must be submitted with a technical justification as specified in § 50.4. The proposed schedule must be approved prior to implementation.

C. Requirements for an Integrated Surveillance Program.

1. In an integrated surveillance program, the representative materials chosen for surveillance for a reactor are irradiated in one or more other reactors that have similar design and operating features. Integrated surveillance programs must be approved by the Director, Office of Nuclear Reactor Regulation or the Director, Office of New Reactors, as appropriate, on a case-by-case basis. Criteria for approval include the following:

a. The reactor in which the materials will be irradiated and the reactor for which the materials are being irradiated must have sufficiently similar design and operating features to permit accurate comparisons of the predicted amount of radiation damage.

b. Each reactor must have an adequate dosimetry program.

c. There must be adequate arrangement for data sharing between plants.

d. There must be a contingency plan to assure that the surveillance program for each reactor will not be jeopardized by operation at reduced power level or by an extended outage of another reactor from which data are expected.

e. There must be substantial advantages to be gained, such as reduced power outages or reduced personnel exposure to radiation, as a direct result of not requiring surveillance capsules in all reactors in the set.

2. No reduction in the requirements for number of materials to be irradiated, specimen types, or number of specimens per reactor is permitted.

3. After (the effective date of this section), no reduction in the amount of testing is permitted unless previously authorized by the Director, Office of Nuclear Reactor Regulation or the Director, Office of New Reactors, as appropriate.

IV. REPORT OF TEST RESULTS

A. Each capsule withdrawal and the test results must be the subject of a summary technical report to be submitted, as specified in § 50.4, within one year of the date of capsule withdrawal, unless an extension is granted by the Director, Office of Nuclear Reactor Regulation.

B. The report must include the data required by ASTM E 185, as specified in paragraph III.B.1 of this appendix, and the results of all fracture toughness tests conducted on the beltline materials in the irradiated and unirradiated conditions.

C. If a change in the Technical Specifications is required, either in the pressure-temperature limits or in the operating procedures required to meet the limits, the expected date for submittal of the revised Technical Specifications must be provided with the report.

[60 FR 65476, Dec. 19, 1995, as amended at 68 FR 75390, Dec. 31, 2003; 73 FR 5723, Jan. 31, 2008]

APPENDIX I TO PART 50—NUMERICAL GUIDES FOR DESIGN OBJECTIVES AND LIMITING CONDITIONS FOR OPERATION TO MEET THE CRITERION "AS LOW AS IS REASONABLY ACHIEVABLE" FOR RADIOACTIVE MATERIAL IN LIGHT-WATER-COOLED NUCLEAR POWER REACTOR EFFLUENTS

SECTION I. *Introduction*. Section 50.34a provides that an application for a construction permit shall include a description of the preliminary design of equipment to be installed to maintain control over radioactive materials in gaseous and liquid effluents produced during normal conditions, including expected occurrences. In the case of an application filed on or after January 2, 1971, the application must also identify the design objectives, and the means to be employed, for keeping levels of radioactive material in effluents to unrestricted areas as low as practicable. Sections 52.47, 52.79, 52.137, and 52.157 of this chapter provide that applications for design certification, combined license, design approval, or manufacturing license, respectively, shall include a description of the equipment and procedures for the control of gaseous and liquid effluents and for the maintenance and use of equipment installed in radioactive waste systems.

Section 50.36a contains provisions designed to assure that releases of radioactive material from nuclear power reactors to unrestricted areas during normal conditions, including expected occurrences, are kept as low as practicable.

SECTION II. *Guides on design objectives for light-water-cooled nuclear power reactors licensed under 10 CFR part 50 or part 52 of this chapter*. The guides on design objectives set forth in this section may be used by an applicant for a construction permit as guidance in meeting the requirements of § 50.34a(a), or by an applicant for a combined license under part 52 of this chapter as guidance in meeting the requirements of § 50.34a(d), or by an applicant for a design approval, a design certification, or a manufacturing license as guidance in meeting the requirements of § 50.34a(e). The applicant shall provide reasonable assurance that the following design objectives will be met.

A. The calculated annual total quantity of all radioactive material above background[1] to be released from each light-water-cooled nuclear power reactor to unrestricted areas will not result in an estimated annual dose or dose commitment from liquid effluents for any individual in an unrestricted area from all pathways of exposure in excess of 3 millirems to the total body or 10 millirems to any organ.

B.1. The calculated annual total quantity of all radioactive material above background to be released from each light-water-cooled nuclear power reactor to the atmosphere will not result in an estimated annual air dose from gaseous effluents at any location near ground level which could be occupied by individuals in unrestricted areas in excess of 10 millirads for gamma radiation or 20 millirads for beta radiation.

2. Notwithstanding the guidance of paragraph B.1:

(a) The Commission may specify, as guidance on design objectives, a lower quantity of radioactive material above background to be released to the atmosphere if it appears that the use of the design objectives in paragraph B.1 is likely to result in an estimated annual external dose from gaseous effluents to any individual in an unrestricted area in excess of 5 millirems to the total body; and

(b) Design objectives based upon a higher quantity of radioactive material above background to be released to the atmosphere than the quantity specified in paragraph B.1 will be deemed to meet the requirements for keeping levels of radioactive material in gaseous effluents as low as is reasonably achievable if the applicant provides reasonable assurance that the proposed higher quantity will not result in an estimated annual external dose from gaseous effluents to any individual in unrestricted areas in excess of 5 millirems to the total body or 15 millirems to the skin.

C. The calculated annual total quantity of all radioactive iodine and radioactive material in particulate form above background to be released from each light-water-cooled nuclear power reactor in effluents to the atmosphere will not result in an estimated annual dose or dose commitment from such radioactive iodine and radioactive material in particulate form for any individual in an unrestricted area from all pathways of exposure in excess of 15 millirems to any organ.

D. In addition to the provisions of paragraphs A, B, and C above, the applicant shall

[1] Here and elsewhere in this appendix background means radioactive materials in the environment and in the effluents from light-water-cooled power reactors not generated in, or attributable to, the reactors of which specific account is required in determining design objectives.

include in the radwaste system all items of reasonably demonstrated technology that, when added to the system sequentially and in order of diminishing cost-benefit return, can for a favorable cost-benefit ratio effect reductions in dose to the population reasonably expected to be within 50 miles of the reactor. As an interim measure and until establishment and adoption of better values (or other appropriate criteria), the values $1000 per total body man-rem and $1000 per man-thyroid-rem (or such lesser values as may be demonstrated to be suitable in a particular case) shall be used in this cost-benefit analysis. The requirements of this paragraph D need not be complied with by persons who have filed applications for construction permits which were docketed on or after January 2, 1971, and prior to June 4, 1976, if the radwaste systems and equipment described in the preliminary or final safety analysis report and amendments thereto satisfy the Guides on Design Objectives for Light-Water-Cooled Nuclear Power Reactors proposed in the Concluding Statement of Position of the Regulatory Staff in Docket-RM-50-2 dated February 20, 1974, pp. 25–30, reproduced in the annex to this appendix I.

SECTION III. *Implementation.* A.1. Conformity with the guides on design objectives of Section II shall be demonstrated by calculational procedures based upon models and data such that the actual exposure of an individual through appropriate pathways is unlikely to be substantially underestimated, all uncertainties being considered together. Account shall be taken of the cumulative effect of all sources and pathways within the plant contributing to the particular type of effluent being considered. For determination of design objectives in accordance with the guides of Section II, the estimations of exposure shall be made with respect to such potential land and water usage and food pathways as could actually exist during the term of plant operation: *Provided,* That, if the requirements of paragraph B of Section III are fulfilled, the applicant shall be deemed to have complied with the requirements of paragraph C of Section II with respect to radioactive iodine if estimations of exposure are made on the basis of such food pathways and individual receptors as actually exist at the time the plant is licensed.

2. The characteristics attributed to a hypothetical receptor for the purpose of estimating internal dose commitment shall take into account reasonable deviations of individual habits from the average. The applicant may take account of any real phenomenon or factors actually affecting the estimate of radiation exposure, including the characteristics of the plant, modes of discharge of radioactive materials, physical processes tending to attenuate the quantity of radioactive material to which an individual would be exposed, and the effects of averaging exposures over times during which determining factors may fluctuate.

B. If the applicant determines design objectives with respect to radioactive iodine on the basis of existing conditions and if potential changes in land and water usage and food pathways could result in exposures in excess of the guideline values of paragraph C of Section II, the applicant shall provide reasonable assurance that a monitoring and surveillance program will be performed to determine:

1. The quantities of radioactive iodine actually released to the atmosphere and deposited relative to those estimated in the determination of design objectives;

2. Whether changes in land and water usage and food pathways which would result in individual exposures greater than originally estimated have occurred; and

3. The content of radioactive iodine and foods involved in the changes, if and when they occur.

SECTION IV. *Guides on technical specifications for limiting conditions for operation for light-water-cooled nuclear power reactors licensed under 10 CFR part 50 or part 52 of this chapter.* The guides on limiting conditions for operation for light-water-cooled nuclear power reactors set forth below may be used by an applicant for an operating license under this part or a design certification or combined license under part 52 of this chapter, or a licensee who has submitted a certification of permanent cessation of operations under §50.82(a)(1) or §52.110 of this chapter as guidance in developing technical specifications under §50.36a(a) to keep levels of radioactive materials in effluents to unrestricted areas as low as is reasonably achievable.

Section 50.36a(b) provides that licensees shall be guided by certain considerations in establishing and implementing operating procedures specified in technical specifications that take into account the need for operating flexibility and at the same time assure that the licensee will exert his best effort to keep levels of radioactive material in effluents as low as is reasonably achievable. The guidance set forth below provides additional and more specific guidance to licensees in this respect.

Through the use of the guides set forth in this section it is expected that the annual release of radioactive material in effluents from light-water-cooled nuclear power reactors can generally be maintained within the levels set forth as numerical guides for design objectives in Section II.

At the same time, the licensee is permitted the flexibility of operations, compatible with considerations of health and safety, to assure that the public is provided a dependable source of power even under unusual conditions which may temporarily result in releases higher than numerical guides for design objectives but still within levels that assure that the average population exposure is equivalent to small fractions of doses from natural background radiation. It is expected that in using this operational flexibility under unusual conditions, the licensee will exert his best efforts to keep levels of radioactive material in effluents within the numerical guides for design objectives.

A. If the quantity of radioactive material actually released in effluents to unrestricted areas from a light-water-cooled nuclear power reactor during any calendar quarter is such that the resulting radiation exposure, calculated on the same basis as the respective design objective exposure, would exceed one-half the design objective annual exposure derived pursuant to Sections II and III, the licensee shall:[2]

1. Make an investigation to identify the causes for such release rates;

2. Define and initiate a program of corrective action; and

3. Report these actions as specified in § 50.4, within 30 days from the end of the quarter during which the release occurred.

B. The licensee shall establish an appropriate surveillance and monitoring program to:

1. Provide data on quantities of radioactive material released in liquid and gaseous effluents to assure that the provisions of paragraph A of this section are met;

2. Provide data on measurable levels of radiation and radioactive materials in the environment to evaluate the relationship between quantities of radioactive material released in effluents and resultant radiation doses to individuals from principal pathways of exposure; and

3. Identify changes in the use of unrestricted areas (e.g., for agricultural purposes) to permit modifications in monitoring programs for evaluating doses to individuals from principal pathways of exposure.

C. If the data developed in the surveillance and monitoring program described in paragraph B of Section III or from other monitoring programs show that the relationship between the quantities of radioactive material released in liquid and gaseous effluents and the dose to individuals in unrestricted areas is significantly different from that assumed in the calculations used to determine design objectives pursuant to Sections II and III, the Commission may modify the quantities in the technical specifications defining the limiting conditions in a license to operate a light-water-cooled nuclear power reactor or a license whose holder has submitted a certification of permanent cessation of operations under § 50.82(a)(1).

SECTION V. *Effective dates.* A. The guides for limiting conditions for operation set forth in this appendix shall be applicable in any case in which an application was filed on or after January 2, 1971, for a construction permit for a light-water-cooled nuclear power reactor under this part, or a design certification, a combined license, or a manufacturing license for a light-water-cooled nuclear power reactor under part 52 of this chapter.

B. For each light-water-cooled nuclear power reactor constructed pursuant to a permit for which application was filed prior to January 2, 1971, the holder of the permit or a license, authorizing operation of the reactor shall, within a period of twelve months from June 4, 1975, file with the Commission:

1. Such information as is necessary to evaluate the means employed for keeping levels of radioactivity in effluents to unrestricted areas as low as is reasonably achievable, including all such information as is required by § 50.34a (b) and (c) not already contained in his application; and

2. Plans and proposed technical specifications developed for the purpose of keeping releases of radioactive materials to unrestricted areas during normal reactor operations, including expected operational occurrences, as low as is reasonably achievable.

CONCLUDING STATEMENT OF POSITION OF THE REGULATORY STAFF (DOCKET-RM-50-2)

GUIDES ON DESIGN OBJECTIVES FOR LIGHT-WATER-COOLED NUCLEAR POWER REACTORS

A. For radioactive material above background[1] in liquid effluents to be released to unrestricted areas:

1. The calculated annual total quantity of all radioactive material from all light-water-cooled nuclear power reactors at a site should not result in an annual dose or dose commitment to the total body or to any organ of an individual in an unrestricted area from all pathways of exposure in excess of 5 millirems; and

[2] Section 50.36a(a)(2) requires the licensee to submit certain reports to the Commission with regard to the quantities of the principal radionuclides released to unrestricted areas. It also provides that, on the basis of such reports and any additional information the Commission may obtain from the licensee and others, the Commission may from time to time require the license to take such action as the Commission deems appropriate.

[1] "Background," means the quantity of radioactive material in the effluent from light-water-cooled nuclear power reactors at a site that did not originate in the reactors.

2. The calculated annual total quantity of radioactive material, except tritium and dissolved gases, should not exceed 5 curies for each light-water-cooled reactor at a site.

3. Notwithstanding the guidance in paragraph A.2, for a particular site, if an applicant for a permit to construct a light-water-cooled nuclear power reactor has proposed baseline in-plant control measures[2] to reduce the possible sources of radioactive material in liquid effluent releases and the calculated quantity exceeds the quantity set forth in paragraph A.2, the requirements for design objectives for radioactive material in liquid effluents may be deemed to have been met provided:

a. The applicant submits, as specified in § 50.4, an evaluation of the potential for effects from long-term buildup on the environment in the vicinity of the site of radioactive material, with a radioactive half-life greater than one year, to be released; and

b. The provisions of paragraph A.1 are met.

B. For radioactive material above background in gaseous effluents the annual total quantity of radioactive material to be released to the atmosphere by all light-water-cooled nuclear power reactors at a site:

1. The calculated annual air dose due to gamma radiation at any location near ground level which could be occupied by individuals at or beyond the boundary of the site should not exceed 10 millirads; and

2. The calculated annual air dose due to beta radiation at any location near ground level which could be occupied by individuals at or beyond the boundary of the site should not exceed 20 millirads.

3. Notwithstanding the guidance in paragraphs B.1 and B.2, for a particular site:

a. The Commission may specify, as guidance on design objectives, a lower quantity of radioactive material above background in gaseous effluents to be released to the atmosphere if it appears that the use of the design objectives described in paragraphs B.1 and B.2 is likely to result in an annual dose to an individual in an unrestricted area in excess of 5 millirems to the total body or 15 millirems to the skin; or

b. Design objectives based on a higher quantity of radioactive material above background in gaseous effluents to be released to the atmosphere than the quantity specified in paragraphs B.1 and B.2 may be deemed to meet the requirements for keeping levels of radioactive material in gaseous effluents as low as practicable if the applicant provides reasonable assurance that the proposed higher quantity will not result in annual doses to an individual in an unrestricted area in excess of 5 millirems to the total body or 15 millirems to the skin.

C. For radioactive iodine and radioactive material in particulate form above background released to the atmosphere:

1. The calculated annual total quantity of all radioactive iodine and radioactive material in particulate form from all light-water-cooled nuclear power reactors at a site should not result in an annual dose or dose commitment to any organ of an individual in an unrestricted area from all pathways of exposure in excess of 15 millirems. In determining the dose or dose commitment the portion thereof due to intake of radioactive material via the food pathways may be evaluated at the locations where the food pathways actually exist; and

2. The calculated annual total quantity of iodine-131 in gaseous effluents should not exceed 1 curie for each light-water-cooled nuclear power reactor at a site.

3. Notwithstanding the guidance in paragraphs C.1 and C.2 for a particular site, if an applicant for a permit to construct a light-water-cooled nuclear power reactor has proposed baseline in-plant control measures[3] to reduce the possible sources of radioactive iodine releases, and the calculated annual quantities taking into account such control measures exceed the design objective quantities set forth in paragraphs C.1 and C.2, the requirements for design objectives for radioactive iodine and radioactive material in particulate form in gaseous effluents may be deemed to have been met provided the calculated annual total quantity of all radioactive iodine and radioactive material in particulate form that may be released in gaseous effluents does not exceed four times the quantity calculated pursuant to paragraph C.1.

[40 FR 19442, May 5, 1975, as amended at 40 FR 40818, Sept. 4, 1975; 40 FR 58847, Dec. 19, 1975; 41 FR 16447, Apr. 19, 1976; 42 FR 20139, Apr. 18, 1977; 51 FR 40311, Nov. 6, 1986; 61 FR 39303, July 29, 1996; 72 FR 49507, Aug. 28, 2007]

[2] Such measures may include treatment of clear liquid waste streams (normally tritiated, nonaerated, low conductivity equipment drains and pump seal leakoff), dirty liquid waste streams (normally nontritiated, aerated, high conductivity building sumps, floor and sample station drains), steam generator blowdown streams, chemical waste streams, low purity and high purity liquid streams (resin regenerate and laboratory wastes), as appropriate for the type of reactor.

[3] Such in-plant control measures may include treatment of steam generator blowdown tank exhaust, clean steam supplies for turbine gland seals, condenser vacuum systems, containment purging exhaust and ventilation exhaust systems and special design features to reduce contaminated steam and liquid leakage from valves and other sources such as sumps and tanks, as appropriate for the type of reactor.

APPENDIX J TO PART 50—PRIMARY REACTOR CONTAINMENT LEAKAGE TESTING FOR WATER-COOLED POWER REACTORS

This appendix includes two options, A and B, either of which can be chosen for meeting the requirements of this appendix.

OPTION A—PRESCRIPTIVE REQUIREMENTS

Table of Contents

I. INTRODUCTION

One of the conditions of all operating licenses under this part and combined licenses under part 52 of this chapter for water-cooled power reactors as specified in §50.54(o) is that primary reactor containments shall meet the containment leakage test requirements set forth in this appendix. These test requirements provide for preoperational and periodic verification by tests of the leak-tight integrity of the primary reactor containment, and systems and components which penetrate containment of water-cooled power reactors, and establish the acceptance criteria for these tests. The purposes of the tests are to assure that (a) leakage through the primary reactor containment and systems and components penetrating primary containment shall not exceed allowable leakage rate values as specified in the technical specifications or associated bases; and (b) periodic surveillance of reactor containment penetrations and isolation valves is performed so that proper maintenance and repairs are made during the service life of the containment, and systems and components penetrating primary containment. These test requirements may also be used for guidance in establishing appropriate containment leakage test requirements in technical specifications or associated bases for other types of nuclear power reactors.

II. EXPLANATION OF TERMS

A. "Primary reactor containment" means the structure or vessel that encloses the components of the reactor coolant pressure boundary, as defined in §50.2, and serves as an essentially leak-tight barrier against the uncontrolled release of radioactivity to the environment.

B. "Containment isolation valve" means any valve which is relied upon to perform a containment isolation function.

C. "Reactor containment leakage test program" includes the performance of Type A, Type B, and Type C tests, described in II.F, II.G, and II.H, respectively.

D. "Leakage rate" for test purposes is that leakage which occurs in a unit of time, stated as a percentage of weight of the original content of containment air at the leakage rate test pressure that escapes to the outside atmosphere during a 24-hour test period.

E. "Overall integrated leakage rate" means that leakage rate which obtains from a summation of leakage through all potential leakage paths including containment welds, valves, fittings, and components which penetrate containment.

F. "Type A Tests" means tests intended to measure the primary reactor containment overall integrated leakage rate (1) after the containment has been completed and is ready for operation, and (2) at periodic intervals thereafter.

G. "Type B Tests" means tests intended to detect local leaks and to measure leakage across each pressure-containing or leakage-limiting boundary for the following primary reactor containment penetrations:

1. Containment penetrations whose design incorporates resilient seals, gaskets, or sealant componds, piping penetrations fitted with expansion bellows, and electrical penetrations fitted with flexible metal seal assemblies.

2. Air lock door seals, including door operating mechanism penetrations which are part of the containment pressure boundary.

3. Doors with resilient seals or gaskets except for seal-welded doors.

4. Components other than those listed in II.G.1, II.G.2, or II.G.3 which must meet the acceptance criteria in III.B.3.

H. "Type C Tests" means tests intended to measure containment isolation valve leakage rates. The containment isolation valves included are those that:

1. Provide a direct connection between the inside and outside atmospheres of the primary reactor containment under normal operation, such as purge and ventilation, vacuum relief, and instrument valves;

2. Are required to close automatically upon receipt of a containment isolation signal in response to controls intended to effect containment isolation;

3. Are required to operate intermittently under postaccident conditions; and

4. Are in main steam and feedwater piping and other systems which penetrate containment of direct-cycle boiling water power reactors.

I. Pa (p.s.i.g.) means the calculated peak containment internal pressure related to the design basis accident and specified either in the technical specification or associated bases.

J. Pt (p.s.i.g.) means the containment vessel reduced test pressure selected to measure the integrated leakage rate during periodic Type A tests.

K. La (percent/24 hours) means the maximum allowable leakage rate at pressure Pa as specified for preoperational tests in the technical specifications or associated bases, and as specified for periodic tests in the operating license or combined license, including the technical specifications in any referenced design certification or manufactured reactor used at the facility.

L. Ld (percent/24 hours) means the design leakage rate at pressure, Pa, as specified in the technical specifications or associated bases.

M. Lt (percent/24 hours) means the maximum allowable leakage rate at pressure Pt derived from the preoperational test data as specified in III.A.4.(a)(iii).

N. Lam, Ltm (percent/24 hours) means the total measured containment leakage rates at pressure Pa and Pt, respectively, obtained from testing the containment with components and systems in the state as close as practical to that which would exist under design basis accident conditions (e.g., vented, drained, flooded or pressurized).

O. "Acceptance criteria" means the standard against which test results are to be compared for establishing the functional acceptability of the containment as a leakage limiting boundary.

III. LEAKAGE TESTING REQUIREMENTS

A program consisting of a schedule for conducting Type A, B, and C tests shall be developed for leak testing the primary reactor containment and related systems and components penetrating primary containment pressure boundary.

Upon completion of construction of the primary reactor containment, including installation of all portions of mechanical, fluid, electrical, and instrumentation systems penetrating the primary reactor containment pressure boundary, and prior to any reactor operating period, preoperational and periodic leakage rate tests, as applicable, shall be conducted in accordance with the following:

A. *Type A test*—1. *Pretest requirements.* (a) Containment inspection in accordance with V. A. shall be performed as a prerequisite to the performance of Type A tests. During the period between the initiation of the containment inspection and the performance of the Type A test, no repairs or adjustments shall be made so that the containment can be tested in as close to the "as is" condition as practical. During the period between the completion of one Type A test and the initiation of the containment inspection for the subsequent Type A test, repairs or adjustments shall be made to components whose leakage exceeds that specified in the technical specification as soon as practical after identification. If during a Type A test, including the supplemental test specified in III.A.3.(b), potentially excessive leakage paths are identified which will interfere with satisfactory completion of the test, or which result in the Type A test not meeting the acceptance criteria III.A.4.(b) or III.A.5.(b), the Type A test shall be terminated and the leakage through such paths shall be measured using local leakage testing methods. Repairs and/or adjustments to equipment shall be made and Type A test performed. The corrective action taken and the change in leakage rate determined from the tests and overall integrated leakage determined from local leak and Type A tests shall be included in the summary report required by V.B.

(b) Closure of containment isolation valves for the Type A test shall be accomplished by normal operation and without any preliminary exercising or adjustments (e.g., no tightening of valve after closure by valve motor). Repairs of maloperating or leaking valves shall be made as necessary. Information on any valve closure malfunction or valve leakage that require corrective action before the test, shall be included in the summary report required by V.B.

(c) The containment test conditions shall stabilize for a period of about 4 hours prior to the start of a leakage rate test.

(d) Those portions of the fluid systems that are part of the reactor coolant pressure boundary and are open directly to the containment atmosphere under post-accident conditions and become an extension of the boundary of the containment shall be opened or vented to the containment atmosphere prior to and during the test. Portions of closed systems inside containment that penetrate containment and rupture as a result of a loss of coolant accident shall be vented to the containment atmosphere. All vented systems shall be drained of water or other fluids to the extent necessary to assure exposure of the system containment isolation valves to containment air test pressure and to assure they will be subjected to the post accident differential pressure. Systems that are required to maintain the plant in a safe condition during the test shall be operable in their normal mode, and need not be vented. Systems that are normally filled with water and operating under post-accident conditions, such as the containment heat removal system, need not be vented. However, the containment isolation valves in the systems defined in III.A.1.(d) shall be tested in accordance with III.C. The measured leakage rate from these tests shall be included in the summary report required by V.B.

2. *Conduct of tests.* Preoperational leakage rate tests at either reduced or at peak pressure, shall be conducted at the intervals specified in III.D.

3. *Test Methods.* (a) All Type A tests shall be conducted in accordance with the provisions of the American National Standards N45.4–1972, "Leakage Rate Testing of Containment Structures for Nuclear Reactors," March 16, 1972. In addition to the Total time and Point-to-Point methods described in that standard, the Mass Point Method, when used with a test duration of at least 24 hours, is an acceptable method to use to calculate leakage rates. A typical description of the Mass Point method can be found in the American National Standard ANSI/ANS 56.8–1987, "Containment System Leakage Testing Requirements," January 20, 1987. Incorporation of ANSI N45.4–1972 by reference was approved by the Director of the Federal Register. Copies of this standard, as well as ANSI/ANS–56.8–1987, "Containment System Leakage Testing Requirements" (dated January 20, 1987) may be obtained from the American Nuclear Society, 555 North Kensington Avenue, La Grange Park, IL 60525. A copy of each of these standards is available for inspection at the NRC Library, 11545 Rockville Pike, Rockville, Maryland 20852–2738.

(b) The accuracy of any Type A test shall be verified by a supplemental test. An acceptable method is described in Appendix C of ANSI N45.4–1972. The supplemental test method selected shall be conducted for sufficient duration to establish accurately the change in leakage rate between the Type A and supplemental test. Results from this supplemental test are acceptable provided the difference between the supplemental test data and the Type A test data is within 0.25 La (or 0.25 Lt). If results are not within 0.25 La (or 0.25 Lt), the reason shall be determined, corrective action taken, and a successful supplemental test performed.

(c) Test leakage rates shall be calculated using absolute values corrected for instrument error.

4. *Preoperational leakage rate tests.* (a) *Test pressure*—(1) *Reduced pressure tests.* (i) An initial test shall be performed at a pressure Pt, not less than 0.50 Pa to measure a leakage rate Ltm.

(ii) A second test shall be performed at pressure Pa to measure a leakage rate Lam.

(iii) The leakage characteristics yielded by measurements Ltm and Lam shall establish the maximum allowable test leakage rate Lt of not more than La (Ltm/Lam). In the event Ltm/Lam is greater than 0.7, Lt shall be specified as equal to La (Pt/Pa).[1]

(2) *Peak pressure tests.* A test shall be performed at pressure Pa to measure the leakage rate Lam.

(b) *Acceptance criteria*—(1) *Reduced pressure tests.* The leakage rate Ltm shall be less than 0.75 Lt.

(2) *Peak pressure tests.* The leakage rate Lam shall be less than 0.75 La and not greater than Ld.

5. *Periodic leakage rate tests*—(a) *Test pressure.* (1) Reduced pressure tests shall be conducted at Pt;

(2) Peak pressure tests shall be conducted at Pa.

(b) *Acceptance criteria*—(1) *Reduced pressure tests.* The leakage rate Ltm shall be less than 0.75 Lt. If local leakage measurements are taken to effect repairs in order to meet the acceptance criteria, these measurements shall be taken at a test pressure Pt.

(2) *Peak pressure tests.* The leakage rate Lam shall be less than 0.75 La. If local leakage measurements are taken to effect repairs in order to meet the acceptance criteria, these measurements shall be taken at a test pressure Pa.

6. *Additional requirements.* (a) If any periodic Type A test fails to meet the applicable acceptance criteria in III.A.5.(b), the test schedule applicable to subsequent Type A tests will be reviewed and approved by the Commission.

(b) If two consecutive periodic Type A tests fail to meet the applicable acceptance criteria in III.A.5(b), notwithstanding the periodic retest schedule of III.D., a Type A test shall be performed at each plant shutdown for refueling or approximately every 18 months, whichever occurs first, until two consecutive Type A tests meet the acceptance criteria in III.A.5(b), after which time the retest schedule specified in III.D. may be resumed.

B. *Type B tests*—1. *Test methods.* Acceptable means of performing preoperation and periodic Type B tests include:

(a) Examination by halide leak-detection method (or by other equivalent test methods such as mass spectrometer) of a test chamber, pressurized with air, nitrogen, or pneumatic fluid specified in the technical specifications or associated bases and constructed as part of individual containment penetrations.

(b) Measurement of the rate of pressure loss of the test chamber of the containment penetration pressurized with air, nitrogen, or pneumatic fluid specified in the technical specifications or associated bases.

(c) Leakage surveillance by means of a permanently installed system with provisions for continuous or intermittent pressurization of individual or groups of containment penetrations and measurement of rate of pressure loss of air, nitrogen, or pneumatic fluid specified in the technical specification or associated bases through the leak paths.

---

[1] Such inservice inspections are required by §50.55a.

2. *Test pressure.* All preoperational and periodic Type B tests shall be performed by local pneumatic pressurization of the containment penetrations, either individually or in groups, at a pressure not less than Pa.

3. *Acceptance criteria.* (See also Type C tests.) (a) The combined leakage rate of all penetrations and valves subject to Type B and C tests shall be less than 0.60 La, with the exception of the valves specified in III.C.3.

(b) Leakage measurements obtained through component leakage surveillance systems (e.g., continuous pressurization of individual containment components) that maintains a pressure not less than Pa at individual test chambers of containment penetrations during normal reactor operation, are acceptable in lieu of Type B tests.

C. *Type C tests*—1. *Test method.* Type C tests shall be performed by local pressurization. The pressure shall be applied in the same direction as that when the value would be required to perform its safety function, unless it can be determined that the results from the tests for a pressure applied in a different direction will provide equivalent or more conservative results. The test methods in III.B.1 may be substituted where appropriate. Each valve to be tested shall be closed by normal operation and without any preliminary exercising or adjustments (e.g., no tightening of valve after closure by valve motor).

2. *Test pressure.* (a) Valves, unless pressurized with fluid (e.g., water, nitrogen) from a seal system, shall be pressurized with air or nitrogen at a pressure of Pa.

(b) Valves, which are sealed with fluid from a seal system shall be pressurized with that fluid to a pressure not less than 1.10 Pa.

3. *Acceptance criterion.* The combined leakage rate for all penetrations and valves subject to Type B and C tests shall be less than 0.60 La. Leakage from containment isolation valves that are sealed with fluid from a seal system may be excluded when determining the combined leakage rate: *Provided,* That;

(a) Such valves have been demonstrated to have fluid leakage rates that do not exceed those specified in the technical specifications or associated bases, and

(b) The installed isolation valve seal-water system fluid inventory is sufficient to assure the sealing function for at least 30 days at a pressure of 1.10 Pa.

D. *Periodic retest schedule*—1. *Type A test.* (a) After the preoperational leakage rate tests, a set of three Type A tests shall be performed, at approximately equal intervals during each 10-year service period. The third test of each set shall be conducted when the plant is shutdown for the 10-year plant inservice inspections.[2]

(b) Permissible periods for testing. The performance of Type A tests shall be limited to periods when the plant facility is nonoperational and secured in the shutdown condition under the administrative control and in accordance with the safety procedures defined in the license.

2. *Type B tests.* (a) Type B tests, except tests for air locks, shall be performed during reactor shutdown for refueling, or other convenient intervals, but in no case at intervals greater than 2 years. If opened following a Type A or B test, containment penetrations subject to Type B testing shall be Type B tested prior to returning the reactor to an operating mode requiring containment integrity. For primary reactor containment penetrations employing a continuous leakage monitoring system, Type B tests, except for tests of air locks, may, notwithstanding the test schedule specified under III.D.1., be performed every other reactor shutdown for refueling but in no case at intervals greater than 3 years.

(b)(i) Air locks shall be tested prior to initial fuel loading and at 6-month intervals thereafter at an internal pressure not less than P_a.

(ii) Air locks opened during periods when containment integrity is not required by the plant's Technical Specifications shall be tested at the end of such periods at not less than P_a.

(iii) Air locks opened during periods when containment integrity is required by the plant's Technical Specifications shall be tested within 3 days after being opened. For air lock doors opened more frequently than once every 3 days, the air lock shall be tested at least once every 3 days during the period of frequent openings. For air lock doors having testable seals, testing the seals fulfills the 3-day test requirements. In the event that the testing for this 3-day interval cannot be at P_a, the test pressure shall be as stated in the Technical Specifications. Air lock door seal testing shall not be substituted for the 6-month test of the entire air lock at not less than P_a.

(iv) The acceptance criteria for air lock testing shall be stated in the Technical Specifications.

3. *Type C tests.* Type C tests shall be performed during each reactor shutdown for refueling but in no case at intervals greater than 2 years.

IV. Special Testing Requirements

A. *Containment modification.* Any major modification, replacement of a component

[2] Such inservice inspections are required by §50.55a.

which is part of the primary reactor containment boundary, or resealing a seal-welded door, performed after the preoperational leakage rate test shall be followed by either a Type A, Type B, or Type C test, as applicable for the area affected by the modification. The measured leakage from this test shall be included in the summary report required by V.B. The acceptance criteria of III.A.5.(b), III.B.3., or III.C.3., as appropriate, shall be met. Minor modifications, replacements, or resealing of seal-welded doors, performed directly prior to the conduct of a scheduled Type A test do not require a separate test.

B. *Multiple leakage barrier or subatmospheric containments.* The primary reactor containment barrier of a multiple barrier or subatmospheric containment shall be subjected to Type A tests to verify that its leakage rate meets the requirements of this appendix. Other structures of multiple barrier or subatmospheric containments (e.g., secondary containments for boiling water reactors and shield buildings for pressurized water reactors that enclose the entire primary reactor containment or portions thereof) shall be subject to individual tests in accordance with the procedures specified in the technical specifications, or associated bases.

V. INSPECTION AND REPORTING OF TESTS

A. *Containment inspection.* A general inspection of the accessible interior and exterior surfaces of the containment structures and components shall be performed prior to any Type A test to uncover any evidence of structural deterioration which may affect either the containment structural integrity or leak-tightness. If there is evidence of structural deterioration, Type A tests shall not be performed until corrective action is taken in accordance with repair procedures, non destructive examinations, and tests as specified in the applicable code specified in §50.55a at the commencement of repair work. Such structural deterioration and corrective actions taken shall be included in the summary report required by V.B.

B. *Recordkeeping of test results.* 1. The preoperational and periodic tests must be documented in a readily available summary report that will be made available for inspection, upon request, at the nuclear power plant. The summary report shall include a schematic arrangement of the leakage rate measurement system, the instrumentation used, the supplemental test method, and the test program selected as applicable to the preoperational test, and all the subsequent periodic tests. The report shall contain an analysis and interpretation of the leakage rate test data for the Type A test results to the extent necessary to demonstrate the acceptability of the containment's leakage rate in meeting acceptance criteria.

2. For each periodic test, leakage test results from Type A, B, and C tests shall be included in the summary report. The summary report shall contain an analysis and interpretation of the Type A test results and a summary analysis of periodic Type B and Type C tests that were performed since the last type A test. Leakage test results from type A, B, and C tests that failed to meet the acceptance criteria of III.A.5(b), III.B.3, and III.C.3, respectively, shall be included in a separate accompanying summary report that includes an analysis and interpretation of the test data, the least squares fit analysis of the test data, the instrumentation error analysis, and the structural conditions of the containment or components, if any, which contributed to the failure in meeting the acceptance criteria. Results and analyses of the supplemental verification test employed to demonstrate the validity of the leakage rate test measurements shall also be included.

OPTION B—PERFORMANCE-BASED REQUIREMENTS

Table of Contents

I. INTRODUCTION

One of the conditions required of all operating licenses and combined licenses for light-water-cooled power reactors as specified in §50.54(o) is that primary reactor containments meet the leakage-rate test requirements in either Option A or B of this appendix. These test requirements ensure that (a) leakage through these containments or systems and components penetrating these containments does not exceed allowable leakage rates specified in the technical specifications; and (b) integrity of the containment structure is maintained during its service life. Option B of this appendix identifies the performance-based requirements and criteria for preoperational and subsequent periodic leakage-rate testing.[3]

II. DEFINITIONS

Performance criteria means the performance standards against which test results are to

[3] Specific guidance concerning a performance-based leakage-test program, acceptable leakage-rate test methods, procedures, and analyses that may be used to implement these requirements and criteria are provided in Regulatory Guide 1.163, "Performance-Based Containment Leak-Test Program."

be compared for establishing the acceptability of the containment system as a leakage-limiting boundary.

Containment system means the principal barrier, after the reactor coolant pressure boundary, to prevent the release of quantities of radioactive material that would have a significant radiological effect on the health of the public.

Overall integrated leakage rate means the total leakage rate through all tested leakage paths, including containment welds, valves, fittings, and components that penetrate the containment system.

La (percent/24 hours) means the maximum allowable leakage rate at pressure Pa as specified in the Technical Specifications.

Pa (p.s.i.g) means the calculated peak containment internal pressure related to the design basis loss-of-coolant accident as specified in the Technical Specifications.

III. PERFORMANCE-BASED LEAKAGE-TEST REQUIREMENTS

A. Type A Test

Type A tests to measure the containment system overall integrated leakage rate must be conducted under conditions representing design basis loss-of-coolant accident containment peak pressure. A Type A test must be conducted (1) after the containment system has been completed and is ready for operation and (2) at a periodic interval based on the historical performance of the overall containment system as a barrier to fission product releases to reduce the risk from reactor accidents. A general visual inspection of the accessible interior and exterior surfaces of the containment system for structural deterioration which may affect the containment leak-tight integrity must be conducted prior to each test, and at a periodic interval between tests based on the performance of the containment system. The leakage rate must not exceed the allowable leakage rate (La) with margin, as specified in the Technical Specifications. The test results must be compared with previous results to examine the performance history of the overall containment system to limit leakage.

B. Type B and C Tests

Type B pneumatic tests to detect and measure local leakage rates across pressure retaining, leakage-limiting boundaries, and Type C pneumatic tests to measure containment isolation valve leakage rates, must be conducted (1) prior to initial criticality, and (2) periodically thereafter at intervals based on the safety significance and historical performance of each boundary and isolation valve to ensure the integrity of the overall containment system as a barrier to fission product release to reduce the risk from reactor accidents. The performance-based testing program must contain a performance criterion for Type B and C tests, consideration of leakage-rate limits and factors that are indicative of or affect performance, when establishing test intervals, evaluations of performance of containment system components, and comparison to previous test results to examine the performance history of the overall containment system to limit leakage. The tests must demonstrate that the sum of the leakage rates at accident pressure of Type B tests, and pathway leakage rates from Type C tests, is less than the performance criterion (La) with margin, as specified in the Technical Specification.

IV. RECORDKEEPING

The results of the preoperational and periodic Type A, B, and C tests must be documented to show that performance criteria for leakage have been met. The comparison to previous results of the performance of the overall containment system and of individual components within it must be documented to show that the test intervals established for the containment system and components within it are adequate. These records must be available for inspection at plant sites.

If the test results exceed the performance criteria (La) as defined in the plant Technical Specifications, those exceedances must be assessed for Emergency Notification System reporting under §§50.72 (b)(1)(ii) and §50.72 (b)(2)(i), and for a Licensee Event Report under §50.73 (a)(2)(ii).

V. APPLICATION

A. Applicability

The requirements in either or both Option B, III.A for Type A tests, and Option B, III.B for Type B and C tests, may be adopted on a voluntary basis by an operating nuclear power reactor licensee as specified in §50.54 in substitution of the requirements for those tests contained in Option A of this appendix. If the requirements for tests in Option B, III.A or Option B, III.B are implemented, the recordkeeping requirements in Option B, IV for these tests must be substituted for the reporting requirements of these tests contained in Option A of this appendix.

B. Implementation

1. Specific exemptions to Option A of this appendix that have been formally approved by the AEC or NRC, according to 10 CFR 50.12, are still applicable to Option B of this appendix if necessary, unless specifically revoked by the NRC.

2. A licensee or applicant for an operating license under this part or a combined license under part 52 of this chapter may adopt Option B, or parts thereof, as specified in Section V.A of this appendix, by submitting its

implementation plan and request for revision to technical specifications (see paragraph B.3 of this section) to the Director, Office of Nuclear Reactor Regulation or Director, Office of New Reactors, as appropriate.

3. The regulatory guide or other implementation document used by a licensee or applicant for an operating license under this part or a combined license under part 52 of this chapter to develop a performance-based leakage-testing program must be included, by general reference, in the plant technical specifications. The submittal for technical specification revisions must contain justification, including supporting analyses, if the licensee chooses to deviate from methods approved by the Commission and endorsed in a regulatory guide.

4. The detailed licensee programs for conducting testing under Option B must be available at the plant site for NRC inspection.

[38 FR 4386, Feb. 14, 1973; 38 FR 5997, Mar. 6, 1973, as amended at 41 FR 16447, Apr. 19, 1976; 45 FR 62789, Sept. 22, 1980; 51 FR 40311, Nov. 6, 1986; 53 FR 45891, Nov. 15, 1988; 57 FR 61786, Dec. 29, 1992; 59 FR 50689, Oct. 5, 1994; 60 FR 13616, Mar. 14, 1995; 60 FR 49504, Sept. 26, 1995; 72 FR 49508, Aug. 28, 2007; 73 FR 5723, Jan. 31, 2008]

APPENDIX K TO PART 50—ECCS EVALUATION MODELS

I. Required and Acceptable Features of Evaluation Models.

II. Required Documentation.

I. REQUIRED AND ACCEPTABLE FEATURES OF THE EVALUATION MODELS

A. *Sources of heat during the LOCA.* For the heat sources listed in paragraphs I.A.1 to 4 of this appendix it must be assumed that the reactor has been operating continuously at a power level at least 1.02 times the licensed power level (to allow for instrumentation error), with the maximum peaking factor allowed by the technical specifications. An assumed power level lower than the level specified in this paragraph (but not less than the licensed power level) may be used provided the proposed alternative value has been demonstrated to account for uncertainties due to power level instrumentation error. A range of power distribution shapes and peaking factors representing power distributions that may occur over the core lifetime must be studied. The selected combination of power distribution shape and peaking factor should be the one that results in the most severe calculated consequences for the spectrum of postulated breaks and single failures that are analyzed.

1. *The Initial Stored Energy in the Fuel.* The steady-state temperature distribution and stored energy in the fuel before the hypothetical accident shall be calculated for the burn-up that yields the highest calculated cladding temperature (or, optionally, the highest calculated stored energy.) To accomplish this, the thermal conductivity of the UO_2 shall be evaluated as a function of burn-up and temperature, taking into consideration differences in initial density, and the thermal conductance of the gap between the UO_2 and the cladding shall be evaluated as a function of the burn-up, taking into consideration fuel densification and expansion, the composition and pressure of the gases within the fuel rod, the initial cold gap dimension with its tolerances, and cladding creep.

2. *Fission Heat.* Fission heat shall be calculated using reactivity and reactor kinetics. Shutdown reactivities resulting from temperatures and voids shall be given their minimum plausible values, including allowance for uncertainties, for the range of power distribution shapes and peaking factors indicated to be studied above. Rod trip and insertion may be assumed if they are calculated to occur.

3. *Decay of Actinides.* The heat from the radioactive decay of actinides, including neptunium and plutonium generated during operation, as well as isotopes of uranium, shall be calculated in accordance with fuel cycle calculations and known radioactive properties. The actinide decay heat chosen shall be that appropriate for the time in the fuel cycle that yields the highest calculated fuel temperature during the LOCA.

4. *Fission Product Decay.* The heat generation rates from radioactive decay of fission products shall be assumed to be equal to 1.2 times the values for infinite operating time in the ANS Standard (Proposed American Nuclear Society Standards—"Decay Energy Release Rates Following Shutdown of Uranium-Fueled Thermal Reactors." Approved by Subcommittee ANS–5, ANS Standards Committee, October 1971). This standard has been approved for incorporation by reference by the Director of the Federal Register. A copy of the standard is available for inspection at the NRC Library, 11545 Rockville Pike, Rockville, Maryland 20852–2738. The fraction of the locally generated gamma energy that is deposited in the fuel (including the cladding) may be different from 1.0; the value used shall be justified by a suitable calculation.

5. *Metal—Water Reaction Rate.* The rate of energy release, hydrogen generation, and cladding oxidation from the metal/water reaction shall be calculated using the Baker-Just equation (Baker, L., Just, L.C., "Studies of Metal Water Reactions at High Temperatures, III. Experimental and Theoretical Studies of the Zirconium-Water Reaction," ANL–6548, page 7, May 1962). This publication has been approved for incorporation by reference by the Director of the Federal Register. A copy of the publication is available

for inspection at the NRC Library, 11545 Rockville Pike, Two White Flint North, Rockville, Maryland 20852–2738. The reaction shall be assumed not to be steam limited. For rods whose cladding is calculated to rupture during the LOCA, the inside of the cladding shall be assumed to react after the rupture. The calculation of the reaction rate on the inside of the cladding shall also follow the Baker-Just equation, starting at the time when the cladding is calculated to rupture, and extending around the cladding inner circumference and axially no less that 1.5 inches each way from the location of the rupture, with the reaction assumed not to be steam limited.

6. *Reactor Internals Heat Transfer.* Heat transfer from piping, vessel walls, and non-fuel internal hardware shall be taken into account.

7. *Pressurized Water Reactor Primary-to-Secondary Heat Transfer.* Heat transferred between primary and secondary systems through heat exchangers (steam generators) shall be taken into account. (Not applicable to Boiling Water Reactors.)

B. Swelling and Rupture of the Cladding and Fuel Rod Thermal Parameters

Each evaluation model shall include a provision for predicting cladding swelling and rupture from consideration of the axial temperature distribution of the cladding and from the difference in pressure between the inside and outside of the cladding, both as functions of time. To be acceptable the swelling and rupture calculations shall be based on applicable data in such a way that the degree of swelling and incidence of rupture are not underestimated. The degree of swelling and rupture shall be taken into account in calculations of gap conductance, cladding oxidation and embrittlement, and hydrogen generation.

The calculations of fuel and cladding temperatures as a function of time shall use values for gap conductance and other thermal parameters as functions of temperature and other applicable time-dependent variables. The gap conductance shall be varied in accordance with changes in gap dimensions and any other applicable variables.

C. Blowdown Phenomena

1. *Break Characteristics and Flow.* a. In analyses of hypothetical loss-of-coolant accidents, a spectrum of possible pipe breaks shall be considered. This spectrum shall include instantaneous double-ended breaks ranging in cross-sectional area up to and including that of the largest pipe in the primary coolant system. The analysis shall also include the effects of longitudinal splits in the largest pipes, with the split area equal to the cross-sectional area of the pipe.

b. *Discharge Model.* For all times after the discharging fluid has been calculated to be two-phase in composition, the discharge rate shall be calculated by use of the Moody model (F.J. Moody, "Maximum Flow Rate of a Single Component, Two-Phase Mixture," Journal of Heat Transfer, Trans American Society of Mechanical Engineers, 87, No. 1, February, 1965). This publication has been approved for incorporation by reference by the Director of the Federal Register. A copy of this publication is available for inspection at the NRC Library, 11545 Rockville Pike, Rockville, Maryland 20852–2738. The calculation shall be conducted with at least three values of a discharge coefficient applied to the postulated break area, these values spanning the range from 0.6 to 1.0. If the results indicate that the maximum clad temperature for the hypothetical accident is to be found at an even lower value of the discharge coefficient, the range of discharge coefficients shall be extended until the maximum clad temperatures calculated by this variation has been achieved.

c. *End of Blowdown.* (Applies Only to Pressurized Water Reactors.) For postulated cold leg breaks, all emergency cooling water injected into the inlet lines or the reactor vessel during the bypass period shall in the calculations be subtracted from the reactor vessel calculated inventory. This may be executed in the calculation during the bypass period, or as an alternative the amount of emergency core cooling water calculated to be injected during the bypass period may be subtracted later in the calculation from the water remaining in the inlet lines, downcomer, and reactor vessel lower plenum after the bypass period. This bypassing shall end in the calculation at a time designated as the "end of bypass," after which the expulsion or entrainment mechanisms responsible for the bypassing are calculated not to be effective. The end-of-bypass definition used in the calculation shall be justified by a suitable combination of analysis and experimental data. Acceptable methods for defining "end of bypass" include, but are not limited to, the following: (1) Prediction of the blowdown calculation of downward flow in the downcomer for the remainder of the blowdown period; (2) Prediction of a threshold for droplet entrainment in the upward velocity, using local fluid conditions and a conservative critical Weber number.

d. *Noding Near the Break and the ECCS Injection Points.* The noding in the vicinity of and including the broken or split sections of pipe and the points of ECCS injection shall be chosen to permit a reliable analysis of the thermodynamic history in these regions during blowdown.

2. *Frictional Pressure Drops.* The frictional losses in pipes and other components including the reactor core shall be calculated using models that include realistic variation of

friction factor with Reynolds number, and realistic two-phase friction multipliers that have been adequately verified by comparison with experimental data, or models that prove at least equally conservative with respect to maximum clad temperature calculated during the hypothetical accident. The modified Baroczy correlation (Baroczy, C. J., "A Systematic Correlation for Two-Phase Pressure Drop," *Chem. Enging. Prog. Symp. Series*, No. 64, Vol. 62, 1965) or a combination of the Thom correlation (Thom, J.R.S., "Prediction of Pressure Drop During Forced Circulation Boiling of Water," *Int. J. of Heat & Mass Transfer*, 7, 709–724, 1964) for pressures equal to or greater than 250 psia and the Martinelli-Nelson correlation (Martinelli, R. C. Nelson, D.B., "Prediction of Pressure Drop During Forced Circulation Boiling of Water," *Transactions of ASME*, 695–702, 1948) for pressures lower than 250 psia is acceptable as a basis for calculating realistic two-phase friction multipliers.

3. *Momentum Equation.* The following effects shall be taken into account in the conservation of momentum equation: (1) temporal change of momentum, (2) momentum convection, (3) area change momentum flux, (4) momentum change due to compressibility, (5) pressure loss resulting from wall friction, (6) pressure loss resulting from area change, and (7) gravitational acceleration. Any omission of one or more of these terms under stated circumstances shall be justified by comparative analyses or by experimental data.

4. *Critical Heat Flux.* a. Correlations developed from appropriate steady-state and transient-state experimental data are acceptable for use in predicting the critical heat flux (CHF) during LOCA transients. The computer programs in which these correlations are used shall contain suitable checks to assure that the physical parameters are within the range of parameters specified for use of the correlations by their respective authors.

b. Steady-state CHF correlations acceptable for use in LOCA transients include, but are not limited to, the following:

(1) *W 3.* L. S. Tong, "Prediction of Departure from Nucleate Boiling for an Axially Non-uniform Heat Flux Distribution," *Journal of Nuclear Energy*, Vol. 21, 241–248, 1967.

(2) *B&W-2.* J. S. Gellerstedt, R. A. Lee, W. J. Oberjohn, R. H. Wilson, L. J. Stanek, "Correlation of Critical Heat Flux in a Bundle Cooled by Pressurized Water," *Two-Phase Flow and Heat Transfer in Rod Bundles*, ASME, New York, 1969.

(3) *Hench-Levy.* J. M. Healzer, J. E. Hench, E. Janssen, S. Levy, "Design Basis for Critical Heat Flux Condition in Boiling Water Reactors," APED–5186, GE Company Private report, July 1966.

(4) *Macbeth.* R. V. Macbeth, "An Appraisal of Forced Convection Burnout Data," *Proceedings of the Institute of Mechanical Engineers*, 1965–1966.

(5) *Barnett.* P. G. Barnett, "A Correlation of Burnout Data for Uniformly Heated Annuli and Its Uses for Predicting Burnout in Uniformly Heated Rod Bundles," AEEW-R 463, 1966.

(6) *Hughes.* E. D. Hughes, "A Correlation of Rod Bundle Critical Heat Flux for Water in the Pressure Range 150 to 725 psia," IN–1412, Idaho Nuclear Corporation, July 1970.

c. Correlations of appropriate transient CHF data may be accepted for use in LOCA transient analyses if comparisons between the data and the correlations are provided to demonstrate that the correlations predict values of CHF which allow for uncertainty in the experimental data throughout the range of parameters for which the correlations are to be used. Where appropriate, the comparisons shall use statistical uncertainty analysis of the data to demonstrate the conservatism of the transient correlation.

d. Transient CHF correlations acceptable for use in LOCA transients include, but are not limited to, the following:

(1) *GE transient CHF.* B. C. Slifer, J. E. Hench, "Loss-of-Coolant Accident and Emergency Core Cooling Models for General Electric Boiling Water Reactors," NEDO–10329, General Electric Company, Equation C–32, April 1971.

e. After CHF is first predicted at an axial fuel rod location during blowdown, the calculation shall not use nucleate boiling heat transfer correlations at that location subsequently during the blowdown even if the calculated local fluid and surface conditions would apparently justify the reestablishment of nucleate boiling. Heat transfer assumptions characteristic of return to nucleate boiling (rewetting) shall be permitted when justified by the calculated local fluid and surface conditions during the reflood portion of a LOCA.

5. *Post-CHF Heat Transfer Correlations.* a. Correlations of heat transfer from the fuel cladding to the surrounding fluid in the post-CHF regimes of transition and film boiling shall be compared to applicable steady-state and transient-state data using statistical correlation and uncertainty analyses. Such comparison shall demonstrate that the correlations predict values of heat transfer coefficient equal to or less than the mean value of the applicable experimental heat transfer data throughout the range of parameters for which the correlations are to be used. The comparisons shall quantify the relation of the correlations to the statistical uncertainty of the applicable data.

b. The Groeneveld flow film boiling correlation (equation 5.7 of D.C. Groeneveld, "An Investigation of Heat Transfer in the Liquid Deficient Regime," AECL–3281, revised December 1969) and the Westinghouse correlation of steady-state transition boiling

("Proprietary Redirect/Rebuttal Testimony of Westinghouse Electric Corporation," USNRC Docket RM–50–1, page 25–1, October 26, 1972) are acceptable for use in the post-CHF boiling regimes. In addition, the transition boiling correlation of McDonough, Milich, and King (J.B. McDonough, W. Milich, E.C. King, "An Experimental Study of Partial Film Boiling Region with Water at Elevated Pressures in a Round Vertical Tube," Chemical Engineering Progress Symposium Series, Vol. 57, No. 32, pages 197–208, (1961) is suitable for use between nucleate and film boiling. Use of all these correlations is restricted as follows:

(1) The Groeneveld correlation shall not be used in the region near its low-pressure singularity,

(2) The first term (nucleate) of the Westinghouse correlation and the entire McDonough, Milich, and King correlation shall not be used during the blowdown after the temperature difference between the clad and the saturated fluid first exceeds 300 °F,

(3) Transition boiling heat transfer shall not be reapplied for the remainder of the LOCA blowdown, even if the clad superheat returns below 300 °F, except for the reflood portion of the LOCA when justified by the calculated local fluid and surface conditions.

c. Evaluation models approved after October 17, 1988, which make use of the Dougall-Rohsenow flow film boiling correlation (R.S. Dougall and W.M. Rohsenow, "Film Boiling on the Inside of Vertical Tubes with Upward Flow of Fluid at Low Qualities," MIT Report Number 9079 26, Cambridge, Massachusetts, September 1963) may not use this correlation under conditions where nonconservative predictions of heat transfer result. Evaluation models that make use of the Dougall-Rohsenow correlation and were approved prior to October 17, 1988, continue to be acceptable until a change is made to, or an error is corrected in, the evaluation model that results in a significant reduction in the overall conservatism in the evaluation model. At that time continued use of the Dougall-Rohsenow correlation under conditions where nonconservative predictions of heat transfer result will no longer be acceptable. For this purpose, a significant reduction in the overall conservatism in the evaluation model would be a reduction in the calculated peak fuel cladding temperature of at least 50 °F from that which would have been calculated on October 17, 1988, due either to individual changes or error corrections or the net effect of an accumulation of changes or error corrections.

6. *Pump Modeling.* The characteristics of rotating primary system pumps (axial flow, turbine, or centrifugal) shall be derived from a dynamic model that includes momentum transfer between the fluid and the rotating member, with variable pump speed as a function of time. The pump model resistance used for analysis should be justified. The pump model for the two-phase region shall be verified by applicable two-phase pump performance data. For BWR's after saturation is calculated at the pump suction, the pump head may be assumed to vary linearly with quality, going to zero for one percent quality at the pump suction, so long as the analysis shows that core flow stops before the quality at pump suction reaches one percent.

7. *Core Flow Distribution During Blowdown.* (Applies only to pressurized water reactors.)

a. The flow rate through the hot region of the core during blowdown shall be calculated as a function of time. For the purpose of these calculations the hot region chosen shall not be greater than the size of one fuel assembly. Calculations of average flow and flow in the hot region shall take into account cross flow between regions and any flow blockage calculated to occur during blowdown as a result of cladding swelling or rupture. The calculated flow shall be smoothed to eliminate any calculated rapid oscillations (period less than 0.1 seconds).

b. A method shall be specified for determining the enthalpy to be used as input data to the hot channel heatup analysis from quantities calculated in the blowdown analysis, consistent with the flow distribution calculations.

D. Post-Blowdown Phenomena; Heat Removal by the ECCS

1. *Single Failure Criterion.* An analysis of possible failure modes of ECCS equipment and of their effects on ECCS performance must be made. In carrying out the accident evaluation the combination of ECCS subsystems assumed to be operative shall be those available after the most damaging single failure of ECCS equipment has taken place.

2. *Containment Pressure.* The containment pressure used for evaluating cooling effectiveness during reflood and spray cooling shall not exceed a pressure calculated conservatively for this purpose. The calculation shall include the effects of operation of all installed pressure-reducing systems and processes.

3. *Calculation of Reflood Rate for Pressurized Water Reactors.* The refilling of the reactor vessel and the time and rate of reflooding of the core shall be calculated by an acceptable model that takes into consideration the thermal and hydraulic characteristics of the core and of the reactor system. The primary system coolant pumps shall be assumed to have locked impellers if this assumption leads to the maximum calculated cladding temperature; otherwise the pump rotor shall be assumed to be running free. The ratio of the total fluid flow at the core exit plane to the total liquid flow at the core inlet plane

(carryover fraction) shall be used to determine the core exit flow and shall be determined in accordance with applicable experimental data (for example, "PWR FLECHT (Full Length Emergency Cooling Heat Transfer) Final Report," Westinghouse Report WCAP–7665, April 1971; "PWR Full Length Emergency Cooling Heat Transfer (FLECHT) Group I Test Report," Westinghouse Report WCAP–7435, January 1970; "PWR FLECHT (Full Length Emergency Cooling Heat Transfer) Group II Test Report," Westinghouse Report WCAP–7544, September 1970; "PWR FLECHT Final Report Supplement," Westinghouse Report WCAP–7931, October 1972).

The effects on reflooding rate of the compressed gas in the accumulator which is discharged following accumulator water discharge shall also be taken into account.

4. *Steam Interaction with Emergency Core Cooling Water in Pressurized Water Reactors.* The thermal-hydraulic interaction between steam and all emergency core cooling water shall be taken into account in calculating the core reflooding rate. During refill and reflood, the calculated steam flow in unbroken reactor coolant pipes shall be taken to be zero during the time that accumulators are discharging water into those pipes unless experimental evidence is available regarding the realistic thermal-hydraulic interaction between the steam and the liquid. In this case, the experimental data may be used to support an alternate assumption.

5. *Refill and Reflood Heat Transfer for Pressurized Water Reactors.* a. For reflood rates of one inch per second or higher, reflood heat transfer coefficients shall be based on applicable experimental data for unblocked cores including FLECHT results ("PWR FLECHT (Full Length Emergency Cooling Heat Transfer) Final Report," Westinghouse Report WCAP–7665, April 1971). The use of a correlation derived from FLECHT data shall be demonstrated to be conservative for the transient to which it is applied; presently available FLECHT heat transfer correlations ("PWR Full Length Emergency Cooling Heat Transfer (FLECHT) Group I Test Report," Westinghouse Report WCAP–7544, September 1970; "PWR FLECHT Final Report Supplement," Westinghouse Report WCAP–7931, October 1972) are not acceptable. Westinghouse Report WCAP–7665 has been approved for incorporation by reference by the Director of the Federal Register. A copy of this report is available for inspection at the NRC Library, 11545 Rockville Pike, Rockville, Maryland 20852–2738. New correlations or modifications to the FLECHT heat transfer correlations are acceptable only after they are demonstrated to be conservative, by comparison with FLECHT data, for a range of parameters consistent with the transient to which they are applied.

b. During refill and during reflood when reflood rates are less than one inch per second, heat transfer calculations shall be based on the assumption that cooling is only by steam, and shall take into account any flow blockage calculated to occur as a result of cladding swelling or rupture as such blockage might affect both local steam flow and heat transfer.

6. *Convective Heat Transfer Coefficients for Boiling Water Reactor Fuel Rods Under Spray Cooling.* Following the blowdown period, convective heat transfer shall be calculated using coefficients based on appropriate experimental data. For reactors with jet pumps and having fuel rods in a 7 × 7 fuel assembly array, the following convective coefficients are acceptable:

a. During the period following lower plenum flashing but prior to the core spray reaching rated flow, a convective heat transfer coefficient of zero shall be applied to all fuel rods.

b. During the period after core spray reaches rated flow but prior to reflooding, convective heat transfer coefficients of 3.0, 3.5, 1.5, and 1.5 Btu-hr^{-1}-ft^{-2} °F^{-1} shall be applied to the fuel rods in the outer corners, outer row, next to outer row, and to those remaining in the interior, respectively, of the assembly.

c. After the two-phase reflooding fluid reaches the level under consideration, a convective heat transfer coefficient of 25 Btu-hr^{-1}-ft^{-2} °F^{-1} shall be applied to all fuel rods.

7. *The Boiling Water Reactor Channel Box Under Spray Cooling.* Following the blowdown period, heat transfer from, and wetting of, the channel box shall be based on appropriate experimental data. For reactors with jet pumps and fuel rods in a 7 × 7 fuel assembly array, the following heat transfer coefficients and wetting time correlation are acceptable.

a. During the period after lower plenum flashing, but prior to core spray reaching rated flow, a convective coefficient of zero shall be applied to the fuel assembly channel box.

b. During the period after core spray reaches rated flow, but prior to wetting of the channel, a convective heat transfer coefficient of 5 Btu-hr^{-1}-ft^{-2}- °F^{-1} shall be applied to both sides of the channel box.

c. Wetting of the channel box shall be assumed to occur 60 seconds after the time determined using the correlation based on the Yamanouchi analysis ("Loss-of-Coolant Accident and Emergency Core Cooling Models for General Electric Boiling Water Reactors," General Electric Company Report NEDO–10329, April 1971). This report was approved for incorporation by reference by the Director of the Federal Register. A copy of the report is available for inspection at the NRC Library, 11545 Rockville Pike, Rockville, Maryland 20852–2738.

II. REQUIRED DOCUMENTATION

1. a. A description of each evaluation model shall be furnished. The description shall be sufficiently complete to permit technical review of the analytical approach including the equations used, their approximations in difference form, the assumptions made, and the values of all parameters or the procedure for their selection, as for example, in accordance with a specified physical law or empirical correlation.

b. A complete listing of each computer program, in the same form as used in the evaluation model, must be furnished to the Nuclear Regulatory Commission upon request.

2. For each computer program, solution convergence shall be demonstrated by studies of system modeling or noding and calculational time steps.

3. Appropriate sensitivity studies shall be performed for each evaluation model, to evaluate the effect on the calculated results of variations in noding, phenomena assumed in the calculation to predominate, including pump operation or locking, and values of parameters over their applicable ranges. For items to which results are shown to be sensitive, the choices made shall be justified.

4. To the extent practicable, predictions of the evaluation model, or portions thereof, shall be compared with applicable experimental information.

5. General Standards for Acceptability—Elements of evaluation models reviewed will include technical adequacy of the calculational methods, including: For models covered by § 50.46(a)(1)(ii), compliance with required features of section I of this appendix K; and, for models covered by § 50.46(a)(1)(i), assurance of a high level of probability that the performance criteria of § 50.46(b) would not be exceeded.

[39 FR 1003, Jan. 4, 1974, as amended at 51 FR 40311, Nov. 6, 1986; 53 FR 36005, Sept. 16, 1988; 57 FR 61786, Dec. 29, 1992; 59 FR 50689, Oct. 5, 1994; 60 FR 24552, May 9, 1995; 65 FR 34921, June 1, 2000]

APPENDIXES L–M TO PART 50 [RESERVED]

APPENDIX N TO PART 50—STANDARDIZATION OF NUCLEAR POWER PLANT DESIGNS: PERMITS TO CONSTRUCT AND LICENSES TO OPERATE NUCLEAR POWER REACTORS OF IDENTICAL DESIGN AT MULTIPLE SITES

Section 101 of the Atomic Energy Act of 1954, as amended, and § 50.10 of this part require a Commission license to transfer or receive in interstate commerce, manufacture, produce, transfer, acquire, possess, use, import or export any production or utilization facility. The regulations in this part require the issuance of a construction permit by the Commission before commencement of construction of a production or utilization facility, except as provided in § 50.10(e), and the issuance of an operating license before operation of the facility.

The Commission's regulations in part 2 of this chapter specifically provide for the holding of hearings on particular issues separately from other issues involved in hearings in licensing proceedings (§ 2.761a, appendix A, section I(c)), and for the consolidation of adjudicatory proceedings and of the presentations of parties in adjudicatory proceedings such as licensing proceedings (§§ 2.715a, 2.716).

This appendix sets out the particular requirements and provisions applicable to situations in which applications are filed by one or more applicants for licenses to construct and operate nuclear power reactors of essentially the same design to be located at different sites.[1]

1. Except as otherwise specified in this appendix or as the context otherwise indicates, the provisions of this part applicable to construction permits and operating licenses, including the requirement in § 50.58 for review of the application by the Advisory Committee on Reactor Safeguards and the holding of public hearings, apply to construction permits and operating licenses subject to this appendix N.

2. Applications for construction permits submitted pursuant to this appendix must include the information required by §§ 50.33, 50.34(a) and 50.34a(a) and (b) and be submitted as specified in § 50.4. The applicant shall also submit the information required by § 51.50 of this chapter.

3. Applications for operating licenses submitted pursuant to this appendix N shall include the information required by §§ 50.33, 50.34(b) and (c), and 50.34a(c). The applicant shall also submit the information required by § 51.53 of this chapter. For the technical information required by §§ 50.34(b)(2) through (5) and 50.34a(c), reference may be made to a single final safety analysis of the design.

[40 FR 2977, Jan. 17, 1975, as amended at 49 FR 9405, Mar. 12, 1984; 51 FR 40311, Nov. 6, 1986; 70 FR 61888, Oct. 27, 2005]

[1] If the design for the power reactor(s) proposed in a particular application is not identical to the others, that application may not be processed under this appendix and subpart D of part 2 of this chapter.

APPENDIXES O–P TO PART 50 [RESERVED]

APPENDIX Q TO PART 50—PRE-APPLICATION EARLY REVIEW OF SITE SUITABILITY ISSUES

This appendix sets out procedures for the filing, Staff review, and referral to the Advisory Committee on Reactor Safeguards of requests for early review of one or more site suitability issues relating to the construction and operation of certain utilization facilities separately from and prior to the submittal of applications for construction permits for the facilities. The appendix also sets out procedures for the preparation and issuance of Staff Site Reports and for their incorporation by reference in applications for the construction and operation of certain utilization facilities. The utilization facilities are those which are subject to §51.20(b) of this chapter and are of the type specified in §50.21(b) (2) or (3) or §50.22 or are testing facilities. This appendix does not apply to proceedings conducted pursuant to subpart F of part 2 of this chapter.

1. Any person may submit information regarding one or more site suitability issues to the Commission's Staff for its review separately from and prior to an application for a construction permit for a facility. Such a submittal shall be accompanied by any fee required by part 170 of this chapter and shall consist of the portion of the information required of applicants for construction permits by §§50.33(a)–(c) and (e), and, insofar as it relates to the issue(s) of site suitability for which early review is sought, by §§50.34(a)(1) and 50.30(f), except that information with respect to operation of the facility at the projected initial power level need not be supplied.

2. The submittal for early review of site suitability issue(s) must be made in the same manner and in the same number of copies as provided in §§50.4 and 50.30 for license applications. The submittal must include sufficient information concerning a range of postulated facility design and operation parameters to enable the Staff to perform the requested review of site suitability issues. The submittal must contain suggested conclusions on the issues of site suitability submitted for review and must be accompanied by a statement of the bases or the reasons for those conclusions. The submittal must also list, to the extent possible, any long-range objectives for ultimate development of the site, state whether any site selection process was used in preparing the submittal, describe any site selection process used, and explain what consideration, if any, was given to alternative sites.

3. The Staff shall publish a notice of docketing of the submittal in the FEDERAL REGISTER, and shall send a copy of the notice of docketing to the Governor or other appropriate official of the State in which the site is located. This notice shall identify the location of the site, briefly describe the site suitability issue(s) under review, and invite comments from Federal, State, and local agencies and interested persons within 120 days of publication or such other time as may be specified, for consideration by the staff in connection with the initiation or outcome of the review and, if appropriate by the ACRS, in connection with the outcome of their review. The person requesting review shall serve a copy of the submittal on the Governor or other appropriate official of the State in which the site is located, and on the chief executive of the municipality in which the site is located or, if the site is not located in a municipality, on the chief executive of the county. The portion of the submittal containing information required of applicants for construction permits by §§50.33(a)–(c) and (e) and 50.34(a)(1) will be referred to the Advisory Committee on Reactor Safeguards (ACRS) for a review and report. There will be no referral to the ACRS unless early review of the site safety issues under §50.34(a)(1) is requested.

4. Upon completion of review by the NRC staff and, if appropriate by the ACRS, of a submittal under this appendix, the NRC staff shall prepare a Staff Site Report which shall identify the location of the site, state the site suitability issues reviewed, explain the nature and scope of the review, state the conclusions of the staff regarding the issues reviewed and state the reasons for those conclusions. Upon issuance of an NRC Staff Site Report, the NRC staff shall publish a notice of the availability of the report in the FEDERAL REGISTER and shall make the report available at the NRC Web site, *http://www.nrc.gov*. The NRC staff shall also send a copy of the report to the Governor or other appropriate official of the State in which the site is located, and to the chief executive of the municipality in which the site is located or, if the site is not located in a municipality, to the chief executive of the county.

5. Any Staff Site Report prepared and issued in accordance with this appendix may be incorporated by reference, as appropriate, in an application for a construction permit for a utilization facility which is subject to §51.20(b) of this chapter and is of the type specified in §50.21(b) (2) or (3) or §50.22 of this chapter or is a testing facility. The conclusions of the Staff Site Report will be reexamined by the staff where five years or more have elapsed between the issuance of the Staff Site Report and its incorporation by reference in a construction permit application.

6. Issuance of a Staff Site Report shall not constitute a commitment to issue a permit or license, to permit on-site work under

§50.10(e), or in any way affect the authority of the Commission, Atomic Safety and Licensing Appeal Panel, Atomic Safety and Licensing Board, and other presiding officers in any proceeding under subpart F and/or G of part 2 of this chapter.

7. The staff will not conduct more than one review of site suitability issues with regard to a particular site prior to the full construction permit review required by subpart A of part 51 of this chapter. The staff may decline to prepare and issue a Staff Site Report in response to a submittal under this appendix where it appears that, (a) in cases where no review of the relative merits of the submitted site and alternative sites under subpart A of part 51 of this chapter is requested, there is a reasonable likelihood that further Staff review would identify one or more preferable alternative sites and the Staff review of one or more site suitability issues would lead to an irreversible and irretrievable commitment of resources prior to the submittal of the analysis of alternative sites in the Environmental Report that would prejudice the later review and decision on alternative sites under subpart F and/or G of part 2 and subpart A of part 51 of this chapter; or (b) in cases where, in the judgment of the Staff, early review of any site suitability issue or issues would not be in the public interest, considering (1) the degree of likelihood that any early findings on those issues would retain their validity in later reviews, (2) the objections, if any, of cognizant state or local government agencies to the conduct of an early review on those issues, and (3) the possible effect on the public interest of having an early, if not necessarily conclusive, resolution of those issues.

[42 FR 22887, May 5, 1977, as amended at 49 FR 9405, Mar. 12, 1984; 51 FR 40311, Nov. 6, 1986; 53 FR 43420, Oct. 27, 1988; 64 FR 48952, Sept. 9, 1999]

APPENDIX R TO PART 50—FIRE PROTECTION PROGRAM FOR NUCLEAR POWER FACILITIES OPERATING PRIOR TO JANUARY 1, 1979

I. INTRODUCTION AND SCOPE

This appendix applies to licensed nuclear power electric generating stations that were operating prior to January 1, 1979, except to the extent set forth in §50.48(b) of this part. With respect to certain generic issues for such facilities it sets forth fire protection features required to satisfy Criterion 3 of appendix A to this part.

Criterion 3 of appendix A to this part specifies that "Structures, systems, and components important to safety shall be designed and located to minimize, consistent with other safety requirements, the probability and effect of fires and explosions."

When considering the effects of fire, those systems associated with achieving and maintaining safe shutdown conditions assume major importance to safety because damage to them can lead to core damage resulting from loss of coolant through boiloff.

The phrases "important to safety," or "safety-related," will be used throughout this appendix R as applying to all safety functions. The phrase "safe shutdown" will be used throughout this appendix as applying to both hot and cold shutdown functions.

Because fire may affect safe shutdown systems and because the loss of function of systems used to mitigate the consequences of design basis accidents under postfire conditions does not per se impact public safety, the need to limit fire damage to systems required to achieve and maintain safe shutdown conditions is greater than the need to limit fire damage to those systems required to mitigate the consequences of design basis accidents. Three levels of fire damage limits are established according to the safety functions of the structure, system, or component:

Safety function	Fire damage limits
Hot Shutdown	One train of equipment necessary to achieve hot shutdown from either the control room or emergency control station(s) must be maintained free of fire damage by a single fire, including an exposure fire.[1]
Cold Shutdown	Both trains of equipment necessary to achieve cold shutdown may be damaged by a single fire, including an exposure fire, but damage must be limited so that at least one train can be repaired or made operable within 72 hours using onsite capability.
Design Basis Accidents.	Both trains of equipment necessary for mitigation of consequences following design basis accidents may be damaged by a single exposure fire.

[1] *Exposure Fire.* An exposure fire is a fire in a given area that involves either in situ or transient combustibles and is external to any structures, systems, or components located in or adjacent to that same area. The effects of such fire (e.g., smoke, heat, or ignition) can adversely affect those structures, systems, or components important to safety. Thus, a fire involving one train of safe shutdown equipment may constitute an exposure fire for the redundant train located in the same area, and a fire involving combustibles other than either redundant train may constitute an exposure fire to both redundant trains located in the same area.

The most stringent fire damage limit shall apply for those systems that fall into more than one category. Redundant systems used to mitigate the consequences of other design basis accidents but not necessary for safe shutdown may be lost to a single exposure fire. However, protection shall be provided so that a fire within only one such system will not damage the redundant system.

II. GENERAL REQUIREMENTS

A. *Fire protection program.* A fire protection program shall be established at each nuclear power plant. The program shall establish the fire protection policy for the protection of structures, systems, and components important to safety at each plant and the procedures, equipment, and personnel required to implement the program at the plant site.

The fire protection program shall be under the direction of an individual who has been delegated authority commensurate with the responsibilities of the position and who has available staff personnel knowledgeable in both fire protection and nuclear safety.

The fire protection program shall extend the concept of defense-in-depth to fire protection in fire areas important to safety, with the following objectives:

- To prevent fires from starting;
- To detect rapidly, control, and extinguish promptly those fires that do occur;
- To provide protection for structures, systems, and components important to safety so that a fire that is not promptly extinguished by the fire suppression activities will not prevent the safe shutdown of the plant.

B. *Fire hazards analysis.* A fire hazards analysis shall be performed by qualified fire protection and reactor systems engineers to (1) consider potential in situ and transient fire hazards; (2) determine the consequences of fire in any location in the plant on the ability to safely shut down the reactor or on the ability to minimize and control the release of radioactivity to the environment; and (3) specify measures for fire prevention, fire detection, fire suppression, and fire containment and alternative shutdown capability as required for each fire area containing structures, systems, and components important to safety in accordance with NRC guidelines and regulations.

C. *Fire prevention features.* Fire protection features shall meet the following general requirements for all fire areas that contain or present a fire hazard to structures, systems, or components important to safety.

1. In situ fire hazards shall be identified and suitable protection provided.

2. Transient fire hazards associated with normal operation, maintenance, repair, or modification activities shall be identified and eliminated where possible. Those transient fire hazards that can not be eliminated shall be controlled and suitable protection provided.

3. Fire detection systems, portable extinguishers, and standpipe and hose stations shall be installed.

4. Fire barriers or automatic suppression systems or both shall be installed as necessary to protect redundant systems or components necessary for safe shutdown.

5. A site fire brigade shall be established, trained, and equipped and shall be on site at all times.

6. Fire detection and suppression systems shall be designed, installed, maintained, and tested by personnel properly qualified by experience and training in fire protection systems.

7. Surveillance procedures shall be established to ensure that fire barriers are in place and that fire suppression systems and components are operable.

D. *Alternative or dedicated shutdown capability.* In areas where the fire protection features cannot ensure safe shutdown capability in the event of a fire in that area, alternative or dedicated safe shutdown capability shall be provided.

III. Specific Requirements

A. *Water supplies for fire suppression systems.* Two separate water supplies shall be provided to furnish necessary water volume and pressure to the fire main loop.

Each supply shall consist of a storage tank, pump, piping, and appropriate isolation and control valves. Two separate redundant suctions in one or more intake structures from a large body of water (river, lake, etc.) will satisfy the requirement for two separated water storage tanks. These supplies shall be separated so that a failure of one supply will not result in a failure of the other supply.

Each supply of the fire water distribution system shall be capable of providing for a period of 2 hours the maximum expected water demands as determined by the fire hazards analysis for safety-related areas or other areas that present a fire exposure hazard to safety-related areas.

When storage tanks are used for combined service-water/fire-water uses the minimum volume for fire uses shall be ensured by means of dedicated tanks or by some physical means such as a vertical standpipe for other water service. Administrative controls, including locks for tank outlet valves, are unacceptable as the only means to ensure minimum water volume.

Other water systems used as one of the two fire water supplies shall be permanently connected to the fire main system and shall be capable of automatic alignment to the fire main system. Pumps, controls, and power supplies in these systems shall satisfy the requirements for the main fire pumps. The use of other water systems for fire protection shall not be incompatible with their functions required for safe plant shutdown. Failure of the other system shall not degrade the fire main system.

B. *Sectional isolation valves.* Sectional isolation valves such as post indicator valves or key operated valves shall be installed in the fire main loop to permit isolation of portions of the fire main loop for maintenance or repair without interrupting the entire water supply.

C. *Hydrant isolation valves.* Valves shall be installed to permit isolation of outside hydrants from the fire main for maintenance or repair without interrupting the water supply to automatic or manual fire suppression systems in any area containing or presenting a fire hazard to safety-related or safe shutdown equipment.

D. *Manual fire suppression.* Standpipe and hose systems shall be installed so that at least one effective hose stream will be able to reach any location that contains or presents an exposure fire hazard to structures, systems, or components important to safety.

Access to permit effective functioning of the fire brigade shall be provided to all areas that contain or present an exposure fire hazard to structures, systems, or components important to safety.

Standpipe and hose stations shall be inside PWR containments and BWR containments that are not inerted. Standpipe and hose stations inside containment may be connected to a high quality water supply of sufficient quantity and pressure other than the fire main loop if plant-specific features prevent extending the fire main supply inside containment. For BWR drywells, standpipe and hose stations shall be placed outside the dry well with adequate lengths of hose to reach any location inside the dry well with an effective hose stream.

E. *Hydrostatic hose tests.* Fire hose shall be hydrostatically tested at a pressure of 150 psi or 50 psi above maximum fire main operating pressure, whichever is greater. Hose stored in outside hose houses shall be tested annually. Interior standpipe hose shall be tested every three years.

F. *Automatic fire detection.* Automatic fire detection systems shall be installed in all areas of the plant that contain or present an exposure fire hazard to safe shutdown or safety-related systems or components. These fire detection systems shall be capable of operating with or without offsite power.

G. *Fire protection of safe shutdown capability.* 1. Fire protection features shall be provided for structures, systems, and components important to safe shutdown. These features shall be capable of limiting fire damage so that:

a. One train of systems necessary to achieve and maintain hot shutdown conditions from either the control room or emergency control station(s) is free of fire damage; and

b. Systems necessary to achieve and maintain cold shutdown from either the control room or emergency control station(s) can be repaired within 72 hours.

2. Except as provided for in paragraph G.3 of this section, where cables or equipment, including associated non-safety circuits that could prevent operation or cause maloperation due to hot shorts, open circuits, or shorts to ground, of redundant trains of systems necessary to achieve and maintain hot shutdown conditions are located within the same fire area outside of primary containment, one of the following means of ensuring that one of the redundant trains is free of fire damage shall be provided:

a. Separation of cables and equipment and associated non-safety circuits of redundant trains by a fire barrier having a 3-hour rating. Structural steel forming a part of or supporting such fire barriers shall be protected to provide fire resistance equivalent to that required of the barrier;

b. Separation of cables and equipment and associated non-safety circuits of redundant trains by a horizontal distance of more than 20 feet with no intervening combustible or fire hazards. In addition, fire detectors and an automatic fire suppression system shall be installed in the fire area; or

c. Enclosure of cable and equipment and associated non-safety circuits of one redundant train in a fire barrier having a 1-hour rating, In addition, fire detectors and an automatic fire suppression system shall be installed in the fire area;

Inside noninerted containments one of the fire protection means specified above or one of the following fire protection means shall be provided:

d. Separation of cables and equipment and associated non-safety circuits of redundant trains by a horizontal distance of more than 20 feet with no intervening combustibles or fire hazards;

e. Installation of fire detectors and an automatic fire suppression system in the fire area; or

f. Separation of cables and equipment and associated non-safety circuits of redundant trains by a noncombustible radiant energy shield.

3. Alternative or dedicated shutdown capability and its associated circuits,[1] independent of cables, systems or components in the area, room, zone under consideration should be provided:

a. Where the protection of systems whose function is required for hot shutdown does not satisfy the requirement of paragraph G.2 of this section; or

b. Where redundant trains of systems required for hot shutdown located in the same fire area may be subject to damage from fire suppression activities or from the rupture or inadvertent operation of fire suppression systems.

In addition, fire detection and a fixed fire suppression system shall be installed in the area, room, or zone under consideration.

[1] Alternative shutdown capability is provided by rerouting, relocating, or modifying existing systems; dedicated shutdown capability is provided by installing new structures and systems for the function of post-fire shutdown.

H. *Fire brigade.* A site fire brigade trained and equipped for fire fighting shall be established to ensure adequate manual fire fighting capability for all areas of the plant containing structures, systems, or components important to safety. The fire brigade shall be at least five members on each shift. The brigade leader and at least two brigade members shall have sufficient training in or knowledge of plant safety-related systems to understand the effects of fire and fire suppressants on safe shutdown capability. The qualification of fire brigade members shall include an annual physical examination to determine their ability to perform strenuous fire fighting activities. The shift supervisor shall not be a member of the fire brigade. The brigade leader shall be competent to assess the potential safety consequences of a fire and advise control room personnel. Such competence by the brigade leader may be evidenced by possession of an operator's license or equivalent knowledge of plant safety-related systems.

The minimum equipment provided for the brigade shall consist of personal protective equipment such as turnout coats, boots, gloves, hard hats, emergency communications equipment, portable lights, portable ventilation equipment, and portable extinguishers. Self-contained breathing apparatus using full-face positive-pressure masks approved by NIOSH (National Institute for Occupational Safety and Health—approval formerly given by the U.S. Bureau of Mines) shall be provided for fire brigade, damage control, and control room personnel. At least 10 masks shall be available for fire brigade personnel. Control room personnel may be furnished breathing air by a manifold system piped from a storage reservoir if practical. Service or rated operating life shall be a minimum of one-half hour for the self-contained units.

At least a 1-hour supply of breathing air in extra bottles shall be located on the plant site for each unit of self-contained breathing appratus. In addition, an onsite 6-hour supply of reserve air shall be provided and arranged to permit quick and complete replenishment of exhausted air supply bottles as they are returned. If compressors are used as a source of breathing air, only units approved for breathing air shall be used and the compressors shall be operable assuming a loss of offsite power. Special care must be taken to locate the compressor in areas free of dust and contaminants.

I. *Fire brigade training.* The fire brigade training program shall ensure that the capability to fight potential fires is established and maintained. The program shall consist of an initial classroom instruction program followed by periodic classroom instruction, fire fighting practice, and fire drills:

1. *Instruction*

a. The initial classroom instruction shall include:

(1) Indoctrination of the plant fire fighting plan with specific identification of each individual's responsibilities.

(2) Identification of the type and location of fire hazards and associated types of fires that could occur in the plant.

(3) The toxic and corrosive characteristics of expected products of combustion.

(4) Identification of the location of fire fighting equipment for each fire area and familiarization with the layout of the plant, including access and egress routes to each area.

(5) The proper use of available fire fighting equipment and the correct method of fighting each type of fire. The types of fires covered should include fires in energized electrical equipment, fires in cables and cable trays, hydrogen fires, fires involving flammable and combustible liquids or hazardous process chemicals, fires resulting from construction or modifications (welding), and record file fires.

(6) The proper use of communication, lighting, ventilation, and emergency breathing equipment.

(7) The proper method for fighting fires inside buildings and confined spaces.

(8) The direction and coordination of the fire fighting activities (fire brigade leaders only).

(9) Detailed review of fire fighting strategies and procedures.

(10) Review of the latest plant modifications and corresponding changes in fire fighting plans.

NOTE: Items (9) and (10) may be deleted from the training of no more than two of the non-operations personnel who may be assigned to the fire brigade.

b. The instruction shall be provided by qualified individuals who are knowledgeable, experienced, and suitably trained in fighting the types of fires that could occur in the plant and in using the types of equipment available in the nuclear power plant.

c. Instruction shall be provided to all fire brigade members and fire brigade leaders.

d. Regular planned meetings shall be held at least every 3 months for all brigade members to review changes in the fire protection program and other subjects as necessary.

e. Periodic refresher training sessions shall be held to repeat the classroom instruction program for all brigade members over a two-year period. These sessions may be concurrent with the regular planned meetings.

2. *Practice*

Practice sessions shall be held for each shift fire brigade on the proper method of fighting the various types of fires that could occur in a nuclear power plant. These sessions shall provide brigade members with experience in actual fire extinguishment and the use of emergency breathing apparatus under strenuous conditions encountered in fire fighting. These practice sessions shall be provided at least once per year for each fire brigade member.

3. *Drills*

a. Fire brigade drills shall be performed in the plant so that the fire brigade can practice as a team.

b. Drills shall be performed at regular intervals not to exceed 3 months for each shift fire brigade. Each fire brigade member should participate in each drill, but must participate in at least two drills per year.

A sufficient number of these drills, but not less than one for each shift fire brigade per year, shall be unannounced to determine the fire fighting readiness of the plant fire brigade, brigade leader, and fire protection systems and equipment. Persons planning and authorizing an unannounced drill shall ensure that the responding shift fire brigade members are not aware that a drill is being planned until it is begun. Unannounced drills shall not be scheduled closer than four weeks.

At least one drill per year shall be performed on a "back shift" for each shift fire brigade.

c. The drills shall be preplanned to establish the training objectives of the drill and shall be critiqued to determine how well the training objectives have been met. Unannounced drills shall be planned and critiqued by members of the management staff responsible for plant safety and fire protection. Performance deficiencies of a fire brigade or of individual fire brigade members shall be remedied by scheduling additional training for the brigade or members. Unsatisfactory drill performance shall be followed by a repeat drill within 30 days.

d. At 3-year intervals, a randomly selected unannounced drill must be critiqued by qualified individuals independent of the licensee's staff. A copy of the written report from these individuals must be available for NRC review and shall be retained as a record as specified in section III.I.4 of this appendix.

e. Drills shall as a minimum include the following:

(1) Assessment of fire alarm effectiveness, time required to notify and assemble fire brigade, and selection, placement and use of equipment, and fire fighting strategies.

(2) Assessment of each brigade member's knowledge of his or her role in the fire fighting strategy for the area assumed to contain the fire. Assessment of the brigade member's conformance with established plant fire fighting procedures and use of fire fighting equipment, including self-contained emergency breathing apparatus, communication equipment, and ventilation equipment, to the extent practicable.

(3) The simulated use of fire fighting equipment required to cope with the situation and type of fire selected for the drill. The area and type of fire chosen for the drill should differ from those used in the previous drill so that brigade members are trained in fighting fires in various plant areas. The situation selected should simulate the size and arrangement of a fire that could reasonably occur in the area selected, allowing for fire development due to the time required to respond, to obtain equipment, and organize for the fire, assuming loss of automatic suppression capability.

(4) Assessment of brigade leader's direction of the fire fighting effort as to thoroughness, accuracy, and effectiveness.

4. *Records*

Individual records of training provided to each fire brigade member, including drill critiques, shall be maintained for at least 3 years to ensure that each member receives training in all parts of the training program. These records of training shall be available for NRC review. Retraining or broadened training for fire fighting within buildings shall be scheduled for all those brigade members whose performance records show deficiencies.

J. *Emergency lighting*. Emergency lighting units with at least an 8-hour battery power supply shall be provided in all areas needed for operation of safe shutdown equipment and in access and egress routes thereto.

K. *Administrative controls*. Administrative controls shall be established to minimize fire hazards in areas containing structures, systems, and components important to safety. These controls shall establish procedures to:

1. Govern the handling and limitation of the use of ordinary combustible materials, combustible and flammable gases and liquids, high efficiency particulate air and charcoal filters, dry ion exchange resins, or other combustible supplies in safety-related areas.

2. Prohibit the storage of combustibles in safety-related areas or establish designated storage areas with appropriate fire protection.

3. Govern the handling of and limit transient fire loads such as combustible and flammable liquids, wood and plastic products, or other combustible materials in buildings containing safety-related systems or equipment during all phases of operating, and especially during maintenance, modification, or refueling operations.

4. Designate the onsite staff member responsible for the inplant fire protection review of proposed work activities to identify potential transient fire hazards and specify required additional fire protection in the work activity procedure.

5. Govern the use of ignition sources by use of a flame permit system to control welding, flame cutting, brazing, or soldering operations. A separate permit shall be issued for each area where work is to be done. If work

continues over more than one shift, the permit shall be valid for not more than 24 hours when the plant is operating or for the duration of a particular job during plant shutdown.

6. Control the removal from the area of all waste, debris, scrap, oil spills, or other combustibles resulting from the work activity immediately following completion of the activity, or at the end of each work shift, whichever comes first.

7. Maintain the periodic housekeeping inspections to ensure continued compliance with these administrative controls.

8. Control the use of specific combustibles in safety-related areas. All wood used in safety-related areas during maintenance, modification, or refueling operations (such as lay-down blocks or scaffolding) shall be treated with a flame retardant. Equipment or supplies (such as new fuel) shipped in untreated combustible packing containers may be unpacked in safety-related areas if required for valid operating reasons. However, all combustible materials shall be removed from the area immediately following the unpacking. Such transient combustible material, unless stored in approved containers, shall not be left unattended during lunch breaks, shift changes, or other similar periods. Loose combustible packing material such as wood or paper excelsior, or polyethylene sheeting shall be placed in metal containers with tight-fitting self-closing metal covers.

9. Control actions to be taken by an individual discovering a fire, for example, notification of control room, attempt to extinguish fire, and actuation of local fire suppression systems.

10. Control actions to be taken by the control room operator to determine the need for brigade assistance upon report of a fire or receipt of alarm on control room annunciator panel, for example, announcing location of fire over PA system, sounding fire alarms, and notifying the shift supervisor and the fire brigade leader of the type, size, and location of the fire.

11. Control actions to be taken by the fire brigade after notification by the control room operator of a fire, for example, assembling in a designated location, receiving directions from the fire brigade leader, and discharging specific fire fighting responsibilities including selection and transportation of fire fighting equipment to fire location, selection of protective equipment, operating instructions for use of fire suppression systems, and use of preplanned strategies for fighting fires in specific areas.

12. Define the strategies for fighting fires in all safety-related areas and areas presenting a hazard to safety-related equipment. These strategies shall designate:

a. Fire hazards in each area covered by the specific prefire plans.

b. Fire extinguishants best suited for controlling the fires associated with the fire hazards in that area and the nearest location of these extinguishants.

c. Most favorable direction from which to attack a fire in each area in view of the ventilation direction, access hallways, stairs, and doors that are most likely to be free of fire, and the best station or elevation for fighting the fire. All access and egress routes that involve locked doors should be specifically identified in the procedure with the appropriate precautions and methods for access specified.

d. Plant systems that should be managed to reduce the damage potential during a local fire and the location of local and remote controls for such management (e.g., any hydraulic or electrical systems in the zone covered by the specific fire fighting procedure that could increase the hazards in the area because of overpressurization or electrical hazards).

e. Vital heat-sensitive system components that need to be kept cool while fighting a local fire. Particularly hazardous combustibles that need cooling should be designated.

f. Organization of fire fighting brigades and the assignment of special duties according to job title so that all fire fighting functions are covered by any complete shift personnel complement. These duties include command control of the brigade, transporting fire suppression and support equipment to the fire scenes, applying the extinguishant to the fire, communication with the control room, and coordination with outside fire departments.

g. Potential radiological and toxic hazards in fire zones.

h. Ventilation system operation that ensures desired plant air distribution when the ventilation flow is modified for fire containment or smoke clearing operations.

i. Operations requiring control room and shift engineer coordination or authorization.

j. Instructions for plant operators and general plant personnel during fire.

L. *Alternative and dedicated shutdown capability*. 1. Alternative or dedicated shutdown capability provided for a specific fire area shall be able to (a) achieve and maintain subcritical reactivity conditions in the reactor; (b) maintain reactor coolant inventory; (c) achieve and maintain hot standby[2] conditions for a PWR (hot shutdown[2] for a BWR); (d) achieve cold shutdown conditions within 72 hours; and (e) maintain cold shutdown conditions thereafter. During the postfire shutdown, the reactor coolant system process variables shall be maintained within those predicted for a loss of normal a.c.

[2] As defined in the Standard Technical Specifications.

power, and the fission product boundary integrity shall not be affected; i.e., there shall be no fuel clad damage, rupture of any primary coolant boundary, of rupture of the containment boundary.

2. The performance goals for the shutdown functions shall be:

a. The reactivity control function shall be capable of achieving and maintaining cold shutdown reactivity conditions.

b. The reactor coolant makeup function shall be capable of maintaining the reactor coolant level above the top of the core for BWRs and be within the level indication in the pressurizer for PWRs.

c. The reactor heat removal function shall be capable of achieving and maintaining decay heat removal.

d. The process monitoring function shall be capable of providing direct readings of the process variables necessary to perform and control the above functions.

e. The supporting functions shall be capable of providing the process cooling, lubrication, etc., necessary to permit the operation of the equipment used for safe shutdown functions.

3. The shutdown capability for specific fire areas may be unique for each such area, or it may be one unique combination of systems for all such areas. In either case, the alternative shutdown capability shall be independent of the specific fire area(s) and shall accommodate postfire conditions where offsite power is available and where offsite power is not available for 72 hours. Procedures shall be in effect to implement this capability.

4. If the capability to achieve and maintain cold shutdown will not be available because of fire damage, the equipment and systems comprising the means to achieve and maintain the hot standby or hot shutdown condition shall be capable of maintaining such conditions until cold shutdown can be achieved. If such equipment and systems will not be capable of being powered by both onsite and offsite electric power systems because of fire damage, an independent onsite power system shall be provided. The number of operating shift personnel, exclusive of fire brigade members, required to operate such equipment and systems shall be on site at all times.

5. Equipment and systems comprising the means to achieve and maintain cold shutdown conditions shall not be damaged by fire; or the fire damage to such equipment and systems shall be limited so that the systems can be made operable and cold shutdown can be achieved within 72 hours. Materials for such repairs shall be readily available on site and procedures shall be in effect to implement such repairs. If such equipment and systems used prior to 72 hours after the fire will not be capable of being powered by both onsite and offsite electric power systems because of fire damage, an independent onsite power system shall be provided. Equipment and systems used after 72 hours may be powered by offsite power only.

6. Shutdown systems installed to ensure postfire shutdown capability need not be designed to meet seismic Category I criteria, single failure criteria, or other design basis accident criteria, except where required for other reasons, e.g., because of interface with or impact on existing safety systems, or because of adverse valve actions due to fire damage.

7. The safe shutdown equipment and systems for each fire area shall be known to be isolated from associated non-safety circuits in the fire area so that hot shorts, open circuits, or shorts to ground in the associated circuits will not prevent operation of the safe shutdown equipment. The separation and barriers between trays and conduits containing associated circuits of one safe shutdown division and trays and conduits containing associated circuits or safe shutdown cables from the redundant division, or the isolation of these associated circuits from the safe shutdown equipment, shall be such that a postulated fire involving associated circuits will not prevent safe shutdown.[3]

M. *Fire barrier cable penetration seal qualification.* Penetration seal designs must be qualified by tests that are comparable to tests used to rate fire barriers. The acceptance criteria for the test must include the following:

1. The cable fire barrier penetration seal has withstood the fire endurance test without passage of flame or ignition of cables on the unexposed side for a period of time equivalent to the fire resistance rating required of the barrier;

2. The temperature levels recorded for the unexposed side are analyzed and demonstrate that the maximum temperature is sufficiently below the cable insulation ignition temperature; and

3. The fire barrier penetration seal remains intact and does not allow projection of water beyond the unexposed surface during the hose stream test.

N. *Fire doors.* Fire doors shall be self-closing or provided with closing mechanisms and shall be inspected semiannually to verify that automatic hold-open, release, and closing mechanisms and latches are operable.

---

[3] An acceptable method of complying with this alternative would be to meet Regulatory Guide 1.75 position 4 related to associated circuits and IEEE Std 384–1974 (Section 4.5) where trays from redundant safety divisions are so protected that postulated fires affect trays from only one safety division.

One of the following measures shall be provided to ensure they will protect the opening as required in case of fire:

1. Fire doors shall be kept closed and electrically supervised at a continuously manned location;

2. Fire doors shall be locked closed and inspected weekly to verify that the doors are in the closed position;

3. Fire doors shall be provided with automatic hold-open and release mechanisms and inspected daily to verify that doorways are free of obstructions; or

4. Fire doors shall be kept closed and inspected daily to verify that they are in the closed position.

The fire brigade leader shall have ready access to keys for any locked fire doors.

Areas protected by automatic total flooding gas suppression systems shall have electrically supervised self-closing fire doors or shall satisfy option 1 above.

O. *Oil collection system for reactor coolant pump.* The reactor coolant pump shall be equipped with an oil collection system if the containment is not inerted during normal operation. The oil collection system shall be so designed, engineered, and installed that failure will not lead to fire during normal or design basis accident conditions and that there is reasonable assurance that the system will withstand the Safe Shutdown Earthquake.[4]

Such collection systems shall be capable of collecting lube oil from all potential pressurized and unpressurized leakage sites in the reactor coolant pump lube oil systems. Leakage shall be collected and drained to a vented closed container that can hold the entire lube oil system inventory. A flame arrester is required in the vent if the flash point characteristics of the oil present the hazard of fire flashback. Leakage points to be protected shall include lift pump and piping, overflow lines, lube oil cooler, oil fill and drain lines and plugs, flanged connections on oil lines, and lube oil reservoirs where such features exist on the reactor coolant pumps. The drain line shall be large enough to accommodate the largest potential oil leak.

[45 FR 76611, Nov. 19, 1980; 46 FR 44735, Sept. 8, 1981, as amended at 53 FR 19251, May 27, 1988; 65 FR 38191, June 20, 2000; 77 FR 39907, July 6, 2012]

Appendix S to Part 50—Earthquake Engineering Criteria for Nuclear Power Plants

General Information

This appendix applies to applicants for a construction permit or operating license under part 50, or a design certification, combined license, design approval, or manufacturing license under part 52 of this chapter, on or after January 10, 1997. However, for either an operating license applicant or holder whose construction permit was issued before January 10, 1997, the earthquake engineering criteria in Section VI of appendix A to 10 CFR part 100 continue to apply. Paragraphs IV.a.1.i, IV.a.1.ii, IV.4.b, and IV.4.c of this appendix apply to applicants for an early site permit under part 52.

I. Introduction

(a) Each applicant for a construction permit, operating license, design certification, combined license, design approval, or manufacturing license is required by §§ 50.34(a)(12), 50.34(b)(10), or 10 CFR 52.47, 52.79, 52.137, or 52.157, and General Design Criterion 2 of appendix A to this part, to design nuclear power plant structures, systems, and components important to safety to withstand the effects of natural phenomena, such as earthquakes, without loss of capability to perform their safety functions. Also, as specified in § 50.54(ff), nuclear power plants that have implemented the earthquake engineering criteria described herein must shut down if the criteria in paragraph IV(a)(3) of this appendix are exceeded.

(b) These criteria implement General Design Criterion 2 insofar as it requires structures, systems, and components important to safety to withstand the effects of earthquakes.

II. Scope

The evaluations described in this appendix are within the scope of investigations permitted by § 50.10(c)(1).

III. Definitions

As used in these criteria:

Combined license means a combined construction permit and operating license with conditions for a nuclear power facility issued under subpart C of part 52 of this chapter.

Design Approval means an NRC staff approval, issued under subpart E of part 52 of this chapter, of a final standard design for a nuclear power reactor of the type described in 10 CFR 50.22.

Design Certification means a Commission approval, issued under subpart B of part 52 of this chapter, of a standard design for a nuclear power facility.

Manufacturing license means a license, issued under subpart F of part 52 of this chapter, authorizing the manufacture of nuclear power reactors but not their installation into facilities located at the sites on which the facilities are to be operated.

Operating basis earthquake ground motion (OBE) is the vibratory ground motion for which those features of the nuclear power

[4] See Regulatory Guide 1.29—"Seismic Design Classification" paragraph C.2.

plant necessary for continued operation without undue risk to the health and safety of the public will remain functional. The operating basis earthquake ground motion is only associated with plant shutdown and inspection unless specifically selected by the applicant as a design input.

Response spectrum is a plot of the maximum responses (acceleration, velocity, or displacement) of idealized single-degree-of-freedom oscillators as a function of the natural frequencies of the oscillators for a given damping value. The response spectrum is calculated for a specified vibratory motion input at the oscillators' supports.

Safe-shutdown earthquake ground motion (SSE) is the vibratory ground motion for which certain structures, systems, and components must be designed to remain functional.

Structures, systems, and components required to withstand the effects of the safe-shutdown earthquake ground motion or surface deformation are those necessary to assure:

(1) The integrity of the reactor coolant pressure boundary;

(2) The capability to shut down the reactor and maintain it in a safe-shutdown condition; or

(3) The capability to prevent or mitigate the consequences of accidents that could result in potential offsite exposures comparable to the guideline exposures of § 50.34(a)(1).

Surface deformation is distortion of geologic strata at or near the ground surface by the processes of folding or faulting as a result of various earth forces. Tectonic surface deformation is associated with earthquake processes.

IV. APPLICATION TO ENGINEERING DESIGN

The following are pursuant to the seismic and geologic design basis requirements of § 100.23 of this chapter:

(a) *Vibratory Ground Motion.* (1) *Safe Shutdown Earthquake Ground Motion.* (i) The Safe Shutdown Earthquake Ground Motion must be characterized by free-field ground motion response spectra at the free ground surface. In view of the limited data available on vibratory ground motions of strong earthquakes, it usually will be appropriate that the design response spectra be smoothed spectra. The horizontal component of the Safe Shutdown Earthquake Ground Motion in the free-field at the foundation level of the structures must be an appropriate response spectrum with a peak ground acceleration of at least 0.1g.

(ii) The nuclear power plant must be designed so that, if the Safe Shutdown Earthquake Ground Motion occurs, certain structures, systems, and components will remain functional and within applicable stress, strain, and deformation limits. In addition to seismic loads, applicable concurrent normal operating, functional, and accident-induced loads must be taken into account in the design of these safety-related structures, systems, and components. The design of the nuclear power plant must also take into account the possible effects of the Safe Shutdown Earthquake Ground Motion on the facility foundations by ground disruption, such as fissuring, lateral spreads, differential settlement, liquefaction, and landsliding, as required in § 100.23 of this chapter.

(iii) The required safety functions of structures, systems, and components must be assured during and after the vibratory ground motion associated with the Safe Shutdown Earthquake Ground Motion through design, testing, or qualification methods.

(iv) The evaluation must take into account soil-structure interaction effects and the expected duration of vibratory motion. It is permissible to design for strain limits in excess of yield strain in some of these safety-related structures, systems, and components during the Safe Shutdown Earthquake Ground Motion and under the postulated concurrent loads, provided the necessary safety functions are maintained.

(2) *Operating Basis Earthquake Ground Motion.* (i) The Operating Basis Earthquake Ground Motion must be characterized by response spectra. The value of the Operating Basis Earthquake Ground Motion must be set to one of the following choices:

(A) One-third or less of the Safe Shutdown Earthquake Ground Motion design response spectra. The requirements associated with this Operating Basis Earthquake Ground Motion in Paragraph (a)(2)(i)(B)(*1*) can be satisfied without the applicant performing explicit response or design analyses, or

(B) A value greater than one-third of the Safe Shutdown Earthquake Ground Motion design response spectra. Analysis and design must be performed to demonstrate that the requirements associated with this Operating Basis Earthquake Ground Motion in Paragraph (a)(2)(i)(B)(*1*) are satisfied. The design must take into account soil-structure interaction effects and the duration of vibratory ground motion.

(*1*) When subjected to the effects of the Operating Basis Earthquake Ground Motion in combination with normal operating loads, all structures, systems, and components of the nuclear power plant necessary for continued operation without undue risk to the health and safety of the public must remain functional and within applicable stress, strain, and deformation limits.

(3) *Required Plant Shutdown.* If vibratory ground motion exceeding that of the Operating Basis Earthquake Ground Motion or if significant plant damage occurs, the licensee must shut down the nuclear power plant. If systems, structures, or components necessary for the safe shutdown of the nuclear

power plant are not available after the occurrence of the Operating Basis Earthquake Ground Motion, the licensee must consult with the Commission and must propose a plan for the timely, safe shutdown of the nuclear power plant. Prior to resuming operations, the licensee must demonstrate to the Commission that no functional damage has occurred to those features necessary for continued operation without undue risk to the health and safety of the public and the licensing basis is maintained.

(4) *Required Seismic Instrumentation.* Suitable instrumentation must be provided so that the seismic response of nuclear power plant features important to safety can be evaluated promptly after an earthquake.

(b) *Surface Deformation.* The potential for surface deformation must be taken into account in the design of the nuclear power plant by providing reasonable assurance that in the event of deformation, certain structures, systems, and components will remain functional. In addition to surface deformation induced loads, the design of safety features must take into account seismic loads and applicable concurrent functional and accident-induced loads. The design provisions for surface deformation must be based on its postulated occurrence in any direction and azimuth and under any part of the nuclear power plant, unless evidence indicates this assumption is not appropriate, and must take into account the estimated rate at which the surface deformation may occur.

(c) *Seismically Induced Floods and Water Waves and Other Design Conditions.* Seismically induced floods and water waves from either locally or distantly generated seismic activity and other design conditions determined pursuant to § 100.23 of this chapter must be taken into account in the design of the nuclear power plant so as to prevent undue risk to the health and safety of the public.

[61 FR 65173, Dec. 11, 1996, as amended at 72 FR 49508, Aug. 28, 2007]

FINDING AIDS

A list of CFR titles, subtitles, chapters, subchapters and parts and an alphabetical list of agencies publishing in the CFR are included in the CFR Index and Finding Aids volume to the Code of Federal Regulations which is published separately and revised annually.

Table of CFR Titles and Chapters

(Revised as of January 1, 2018)

Title 1—General Provisions

I Administrative Committee of the Federal Register (Parts 1—49)
II Office of the Federal Register (Parts 50—299)
III Administrative Conference of the United States (Parts 300—399)
IV Miscellaneous Agencies (Parts 400—599)
VI National Capital Planning Commission (Parts 600—699)

Title 2—Grants and Agreements

SUBTITLE A—OFFICE OF MANAGEMENT AND BUDGET GUIDANCE FOR GRANTS AND AGREEMENTS

I Office of Management and Budget Governmentwide Guidance for Grants and Agreements (Parts 2—199)
II Office of Management and Budget Guidance (Parts 200—299)

SUBTITLE B—FEDERAL AGENCY REGULATIONS FOR GRANTS AND AGREEMENTS

III Department of Health and Human Services (Parts 300—399)
IV Department of Agriculture (Parts 400—499)
VI Department of State (Parts 600—699)
VII Agency for International Development (Parts 700—799)
VIII Department of Veterans Affairs (Parts 800—899)
IX Department of Energy (Parts 900—999)
X Department of the Treasury (Parts 1000—1099)
XI Department of Defense (Parts 1100—1199)
XII Department of Transportation (Parts 1200—1299)
XIII Department of Commerce (Parts 1300—1399)
XIV Department of the Interior (Parts 1400—1499)
XV Environmental Protection Agency (Parts 1500—1599)
XVIII National Aeronautics and Space Administration (Parts 1800—1899)
XX United States Nuclear Regulatory Commission (Parts 2000—2099)
XXII Corporation for National and Community Service (Parts 2200—2299)
XXIII Social Security Administration (Parts 2300—2399)
XXIV Housing and Urban Development (Parts 2400—2499)
XXV National Science Foundation (Parts 2500—2599)
XXVI National Archives and Records Administration (Parts 2600—2699)

Title 2—Grants and Agreements—Continued

Chap.	
XXVII	Small Business Administration (Parts 2700—2799)
XXVIII	Department of Justice (Parts 2800—2899)
XXIX	Department of Labor (Parts 2900—2999)
XXX	Department of Homeland Security (Parts 3000—3099)
XXXI	Institute of Museum and Library Services (Parts 3100—3199)
XXXII	National Endowment for the Arts (Parts 3200—3299)
XXXIII	National Endowment for the Humanities (Parts 3300—3399)
XXXIV	Department of Education (Parts 3400—3499)
XXXV	Export-Import Bank of the United States (Parts 3500—3599)
XXXVI	Office of National Drug Control Policy, Executive Office of the President (Parts 3600—3699)
XXXVII	Peace Corps (Parts 3700—3799)
LVIII	Election Assistance Commission (Parts 5800—5899)
LIX	Gulf Coast Ecosystem Restoration Council (Parts 5900—5999)

Title 3—The President

I	Executive Office of the President (Parts 100—199)

Title 4—Accounts

I	Government Accountability Office (Parts 1—199)

Title 5—Administrative Personnel

I	Office of Personnel Management (Parts 1—1199)
II	Merit Systems Protection Board (Parts 1200—1299)
III	Office of Management and Budget (Parts 1300—1399)
IV	Office of Personnel Management and Office of the Director of National Intelligence (Parts 1400—1499)
V	The International Organizations Employees Loyalty Board (Parts 1500—1599)
VI	Federal Retirement Thrift Investment Board (Parts 1600—1699)
VIII	Office of Special Counsel (Parts 1800—1899)
IX	Appalachian Regional Commission (Parts 1900—1999)
XI	Armed Forces Retirement Home (Parts 2100—2199)
XIV	Federal Labor Relations Authority, General Counsel of the Federal Labor Relations Authority and Federal Service Impasses Panel (Parts 2400—2499)
XVI	Office of Government Ethics (Parts 2600—2699)
XXI	Department of the Treasury (Parts 3100—3199)
XXII	Federal Deposit Insurance Corporation (Parts 3200—3299)
XXIII	Department of Energy (Parts 3300—3399)
XXIV	Federal Energy Regulatory Commission (Parts 3400—3499)
XXV	Department of the Interior (Parts 3500—3599)
XXVI	Department of Defense (Parts 3600—3699)

Chap.	
XXVIII	Department of Justice (Parts 3800—3899)
XXIX	Federal Communications Commission (Parts 3900—3999)
XXX	Farm Credit System Insurance Corporation (Parts 4000—4099)
XXXI	Farm Credit Administration (Parts 4100—4199)
XXXIII	Overseas Private Investment Corporation (Parts 4300—4399)
XXXIV	Securities and Exchange Commission (Parts 4400—4499)
XXXV	Office of Personnel Management (Parts 4500—4599)
XXXVI	Department of Homeland Security (Parts 4600—4699)
XXXVII	Federal Election Commission (Parts 4700—4799)
XL	Interstate Commerce Commission (Parts 5000—5099)
XLI	Commodity Futures Trading Commission (Parts 5100—5199)
XLII	Department of Labor (Parts 5200—5299)
XLIII	National Science Foundation (Parts 5300—5399)
XLV	Department of Health and Human Services (Parts 5500—5599)
XLVI	Postal Rate Commission (Parts 5600—5699)
XLVII	Federal Trade Commission (Parts 5700—5799)
XLVIII	Nuclear Regulatory Commission (Parts 5800—5899)
XLIX	Federal Labor Relations Authority (Parts 5900—5999)
L	Department of Transportation (Parts 6000—6099)
LII	Export-Import Bank of the United States (Parts 6200—6299)
LIII	Department of Education (Parts 6300—6399)
LIV	Environmental Protection Agency (Parts 6400—6499)
LV	National Endowment for the Arts (Parts 6500—6599)
LVI	National Endowment for the Humanities (Parts 6600—6699)
LVII	General Services Administration (Parts 6700—6799)
LVIII	Board of Governors of the Federal Reserve System (Parts 6800—6899)
LIX	National Aeronautics and Space Administration (Parts 6900—6999)
LX	United States Postal Service (Parts 7000—7099)
LXI	National Labor Relations Board (Parts 7100—7199)
LXII	Equal Employment Opportunity Commission (Parts 7200—7299)
LXIII	Inter-American Foundation (Parts 7300—7399)
LXIV	Merit Systems Protection Board (Parts 7400—7499)
LXV	Department of Housing and Urban Development (Parts 7500—7599)
LXVI	National Archives and Records Administration (Parts 7600—7699)
LXVII	Institute of Museum and Library Services (Parts 7700—7799)
LXVIII	Commission on Civil Rights (Parts 7800—7899)
LXIX	Tennessee Valley Authority (Parts 7900—7999)
LXX	Court Services and Offender Supervision Agency for the District of Columbia (Parts 8000—8099)
LXXI	Consumer Product Safety Commission (Parts 8100—8199)
LXXIII	Department of Agriculture (Parts 8300—8399)

Title 5—Administrative Personnel—Continued

Chap.	
LXXIV	Federal Mine Safety and Health Review Commission (Parts 8400—8499)
LXXVI	Federal Retirement Thrift Investment Board (Parts 8600—8699)
LXXVII	Office of Management and Budget (Parts 8700—8799)
LXXX	Federal Housing Finance Agency (Parts 9000—9099)
LXXXIII	Special Inspector General for Afghanistan Reconstruction (Parts 9300—9399)
LXXXIV	Bureau of Consumer Financial Protection (Parts 9400—9499)
LXXXVI	National Credit Union Administration (Parts 9600—9699)
XCVII	Department of Homeland Security Human Resources Management System (Department of Homeland Security—Office of Personnel Management) (Parts 9700—9799)
XCVIII	Council of the Inspectors General on Integrity and Efficiency (Parts 9800—9899)
XCIX	Military Compensation and Retirement Modernization Commission (Parts 9900—9999)
C	National Council on Disability (Parts 10000—10049)

Title 6—Domestic Security

I	Department of Homeland Security, Office of the Secretary (Parts 1—199)
X	Privacy and Civil Liberties Oversight Board (Parts 1000—1099)

Title 7—Agriculture

	SUBTITLE A—OFFICE OF THE SECRETARY OF AGRICULTURE (PARTS 0—26)
	SUBTITLE B—REGULATIONS OF THE DEPARTMENT OF AGRICULTURE
I	Agricultural Marketing Service (Standards, Inspections, Marketing Practices), Department of Agriculture (Parts 27—209)
II	Food and Nutrition Service, Department of Agriculture (Parts 210—299)
III	Animal and Plant Health Inspection Service, Department of Agriculture (Parts 300—399)
IV	Federal Crop Insurance Corporation, Department of Agriculture (Parts 400—499)
V	Agricultural Research Service, Department of Agriculture (Parts 500—599)
VI	Natural Resources Conservation Service, Department of Agriculture (Parts 600—699)
VII	Farm Service Agency, Department of Agriculture (Parts 700—799)
VIII	Grain Inspection, Packers and Stockyards Administration (Federal Grain Inspection Service), Department of Agriculture (Parts 800—899)
IX	Agricultural Marketing Service (Marketing Agreements and Orders; Fruits, Vegetables, Nuts), Department of Agriculture (Parts 900—999)

Chap.	
X	Agricultural Marketing Service (Marketing Agreements and Orders; Milk), Department of Agriculture (Parts 1000—1199)
XI	Agricultural Marketing Service (Marketing Agreements and Orders; Miscellaneous Commodities), Department of Agriculture (Parts 1200—1299)
XIV	Commodity Credit Corporation, Department of Agriculture (Parts 1400—1499)
XV	Foreign Agricultural Service, Department of Agriculture (Parts 1500—1599)
XVI	Rural Telephone Bank, Department of Agriculture (Parts 1600—1699)
XVII	Rural Utilities Service, Department of Agriculture (Parts 1700—1799)
XVIII	Rural Housing Service, Rural Business-Cooperative Service, Rural Utilities Service, and Farm Service Agency, Department of Agriculture (Parts 1800—2099)
XX	Local Television Loan Guarantee Board (Parts 2200—2299)
XXV	Office of Advocacy and Outreach, Department of Agriculture (Parts 2500—2599)
XXVI	Office of Inspector General, Department of Agriculture (Parts 2600—2699)
XXVII	Office of Information Resources Management, Department of Agriculture (Parts 2700—2799)
XXVIII	Office of Operations, Department of Agriculture (Parts 2800—2899)
XXIX	Office of Energy Policy and New Uses, Department of Agriculture (Parts 2900—2999)
XXX	Office of the Chief Financial Officer, Department of Agriculture (Parts 3000—3099)
XXXI	Office of Environmental Quality, Department of Agriculture (Parts 3100—3199)
XXXII	Office of Procurement and Property Management, Department of Agriculture (Parts 3200—3299)
XXXIII	Office of Transportation, Department of Agriculture (Parts 3300—3399)
XXXIV	National Institute of Food and Agriculture (Parts 3400—3499)
XXXV	Rural Housing Service, Department of Agriculture (Parts 3500—3599)
XXXVI	National Agricultural Statistics Service, Department of Agriculture (Parts 3600—3699)
XXXVII	Economic Research Service, Department of Agriculture (Parts 3700—3799)
XXXVIII	World Agricultural Outlook Board, Department of Agriculture (Parts 3800—3899)
XLI	[Reserved]
XLII	Rural Business-Cooperative Service and Rural Utilities Service, Department of Agriculture (Parts 4200—4299)

Title 8—Aliens and Nationality

Chap.

I Department of Homeland Security (Immigration and Naturalization) (Parts 1—499)

V Executive Office for Immigration Review, Department of Justice (Parts 1000—1399)

Title 9—Animals and Animal Products

I Animal and Plant Health Inspection Service, Department of Agriculture (Parts 1—199)

II Grain Inspection, Packers and Stockyards Administration (Packers and Stockyards Programs), Department of Agriculture (Parts 200—299)

III Food Safety and Inspection Service, Department of Agriculture (Parts 300—599)

Title 10—Energy

I Nuclear Regulatory Commission (Parts 0—199)

II Department of Energy (Parts 200—699)

III Department of Energy (Parts 700—999)

X Department of Energy (General Provisions) (Parts 1000—1099)

XIII Nuclear Waste Technical Review Board (Parts 1300—1399)

XVII Defense Nuclear Facilities Safety Board (Parts 1700—1799)

XVIII Northeast Interstate Low-Level Radioactive Waste Commission (Parts 1800—1899)

Title 11—Federal Elections

I Federal Election Commission (Parts 1—9099)

II Election Assistance Commission (Parts 9400—9499)

Title 12—Banks and Banking

I Comptroller of the Currency, Department of the Treasury (Parts 1—199)

II Federal Reserve System (Parts 200—299)

III Federal Deposit Insurance Corporation (Parts 300—399)

IV Export-Import Bank of the United States (Parts 400—499)

V Office of Thrift Supervision, Department of the Treasury (Parts 500—599)

VI Farm Credit Administration (Parts 600—699)

VII National Credit Union Administration (Parts 700—799)

VIII Federal Financing Bank (Parts 800—899)

IX Federal Housing Finance Board (Parts 900—999)

X Bureau of Consumer Financial Protection (Parts 1000—1099)

XI Federal Financial Institutions Examination Council (Parts 1100—1199)

XII Federal Housing Finance Agency (Parts 1200—1299)

Title 12—Banks and Banking—Continued

Title 13—Business Credit and Assistance

Title 14—Aeronautics and Space

Title 15—Commerce and Foreign Trade

Title 15—Commerce and Foreign Trade—Continued

Chap.

XI National Technical Information Service, Department of Commerce (Parts 1100—1199)

XIII East-West Foreign Trade Board (Parts 1300—1399)

XIV Minority Business Development Agency (Parts 1400—1499)

SUBTITLE C—REGULATIONS RELATING TO FOREIGN TRADE AGREEMENTS

XX Office of the United States Trade Representative (Parts 2000—2099)

SUBTITLE D—REGULATIONS RELATING TO TELECOMMUNICATIONS AND INFORMATION

XXIII National Telecommunications and Information Administration, Department of Commerce (Parts 2300—2399) [Reserved]

Title 16—Commercial Practices

I Federal Trade Commission (Parts 0—999)

II Consumer Product Safety Commission (Parts 1000—1799)

Title 17—Commodity and Securities Exchanges

I Commodity Futures Trading Commission (Parts 1—199)

II Securities and Exchange Commission (Parts 200—399)

IV Department of the Treasury (Parts 400—499)

Title 18—Conservation of Power and Water Resources

I Federal Energy Regulatory Commission, Department of Energy (Parts 1—399)

III Delaware River Basin Commission (Parts 400—499)

VI Water Resources Council (Parts 700—799)

VIII Susquehanna River Basin Commission (Parts 800—899)

XIII Tennessee Valley Authority (Parts 1300—1399)

Title 19—Customs Duties

I U.S. Customs and Border Protection, Department of Homeland Security; Department of the Treasury (Parts 0—199)

II United States International Trade Commission (Parts 200—299)

III International Trade Administration, Department of Commerce (Parts 300—399)

IV U.S. Immigration and Customs Enforcement, Department of Homeland Security (Parts 400—599) [Reserved]

Title 20—Employees' Benefits

I Office of Workers' Compensation Programs, Department of Labor (Parts 1—199)

II Railroad Retirement Board (Parts 200—399)

Title 20—Employees' Benefits—Continued

Title 21—Food and Drugs

Title 22—Foreign Relations

Title 23—Highways

Title 23—Highways—Continued

Title 24—Housing and Urban Development

Title 24—Housing and Urban Development—Continued

Chap.

XXIV Board of Directors of the HOPE for Homeowners Program (Parts 4000—4099) [Reserved]

XXV Neighborhood Reinvestment Corporation (Parts 4100—4199)

Title 25—Indians

I Bureau of Indian Affairs, Department of the Interior (Parts 1—299)

II Indian Arts and Crafts Board, Department of the Interior (Parts 300—399)

III National Indian Gaming Commission, Department of the Interior (Parts 500—599)

IV Office of Navajo and Hopi Indian Relocation (Parts 700—899)

V Bureau of Indian Affairs, Department of the Interior, and Indian Health Service, Department of Health and Human Services (Part 900)

VI Office of the Assistant Secretary, Indian Affairs, Department of the Interior (Parts 1000—1199)

VII Office of the Special Trustee for American Indians, Department of the Interior (Parts 1200—1299)

Title 26—Internal Revenue

I Internal Revenue Service, Department of the Treasury (Parts 1—End)

Title 27—Alcohol, Tobacco Products and Firearms

I Alcohol and Tobacco Tax and Trade Bureau, Department of the Treasury (Parts 1—399)

II Bureau of Alcohol, Tobacco, Firearms, and Explosives, Department of Justice (Parts 400—699)

Title 28—Judicial Administration

I Department of Justice (Parts 0—299)

III Federal Prison Industries, Inc., Department of Justice (Parts 300—399)

V Bureau of Prisons, Department of Justice (Parts 500—599)

VI Offices of Independent Counsel, Department of Justice (Parts 600—699)

VII Office of Independent Counsel (Parts 700—799)

VIII Court Services and Offender Supervision Agency for the District of Columbia (Parts 800—899)

IX National Crime Prevention and Privacy Compact Council (Parts 900—999)

XI Department of Justice and Department of State (Parts 1100—1199)

Title 29—Labor

Chap.

SUBTITLE A—OFFICE OF THE SECRETARY OF LABOR (PARTS 0—99)

SUBTITLE B—REGULATIONS RELATING TO LABOR

I National Labor Relations Board (Parts 100—199)

II Office of Labor-Management Standards, Department of Labor (Parts 200—299)

III National Railroad Adjustment Board (Parts 300—399)

IV Office of Labor-Management Standards, Department of Labor (Parts 400—499)

V Wage and Hour Division, Department of Labor (Parts 500—899)

IX Construction Industry Collective Bargaining Commission (Parts 900—999)

X National Mediation Board (Parts 1200—1299)

XII Federal Mediation and Conciliation Service (Parts 1400—1499)

XIV Equal Employment Opportunity Commission (Parts 1600—1699)

XVII Occupational Safety and Health Administration, Department of Labor (Parts 1900—1999)

XX Occupational Safety and Health Review Commission (Parts 2200—2499)

XXV Employee Benefits Security Administration, Department of Labor (Parts 2500—2599)

XXVII Federal Mine Safety and Health Review Commission (Parts 2700—2799)

XL Pension Benefit Guaranty Corporation (Parts 4000—4999)

Title 30—Mineral Resources

I Mine Safety and Health Administration, Department of Labor (Parts 1—199)

II Bureau of Safety and Environmental Enforcement, Department of the Interior (Parts 200—299)

IV Geological Survey, Department of the Interior (Parts 400—499)

V Bureau of Ocean Energy Management, Department of the Interior (Parts 500—599)

VII Office of Surface Mining Reclamation and Enforcement, Department of the Interior (Parts 700—999)

XII Office of Natural Resources Revenue, Department of the Interior (Parts 1200—1299)

Title 31—Money and Finance: Treasury

SUBTITLE A—OFFICE OF THE SECRETARY OF THE TREASURY (PARTS 0—50)

SUBTITLE B—REGULATIONS RELATING TO MONEY AND FINANCE

I Monetary Offices, Department of the Treasury (Parts 51—199)

II Fiscal Service, Department of the Treasury (Parts 200—399)

IV Secret Service, Department of the Treasury (Parts 400—499)

V Office of Foreign Assets Control, Department of the Treasury (Parts 500—599)

Title 31—Money and Finance: Treasury—Continued

Chap.

VI Bureau of Engraving and Printing, Department of the Treasury (Parts 600—699)

VII Federal Law Enforcement Training Center, Department of the Treasury (Parts 700—799)

VIII Office of Investment Security, Department of the Treasury (Parts 800—899)

IX Federal Claims Collection Standards (Department of the Treasury—Department of Justice) (Parts 900—999)

X Financial Crimes Enforcement Network, Department of the Treasury (Parts 1000—1099)

Title 32—National Defense

SUBTITLE A—DEPARTMENT OF DEFENSE

I Office of the Secretary of Defense (Parts 1—399)

V Department of the Army (Parts 400—699)

VI Department of the Navy (Parts 700—799)

VII Department of the Air Force (Parts 800—1099)

SUBTITLE B—OTHER REGULATIONS RELATING TO NATIONAL DEFENSE

XII Defense Logistics Agency (Parts 1200—1299)

XVI Selective Service System (Parts 1600—1699)

XVII Office of the Director of National Intelligence (Parts 1700—1799)

XVIII National Counterintelligence Center (Parts 1800—1899)

XIX Central Intelligence Agency (Parts 1900—1999)

XX Information Security Oversight Office, National Archives and Records Administration (Parts 2000—2099)

XXI National Security Council (Parts 2100—2199)

XXIV Office of Science and Technology Policy (Parts 2400—2499)

XXVII Office for Micronesian Status Negotiations (Parts 2700—2799)

XXVIII Office of the Vice President of the United States (Parts 2800—2899)

Title 33—Navigation and Navigable Waters

I Coast Guard, Department of Homeland Security (Parts 1—199)

II Corps of Engineers, Department of the Army, Department of Defense (Parts 200—399)

IV Saint Lawrence Seaway Development Corporation, Department of Transportation (Parts 400—499)

Title 34—Education

SUBTITLE A—OFFICE OF THE SECRETARY, DEPARTMENT OF EDUCATION (PARTS 1—99)

SUBTITLE B—REGULATIONS OF THE OFFICES OF THE DEPARTMENT OF EDUCATION

I Office for Civil Rights, Department of Education (Parts 100—199)

Title 34—Education—Continued

Chap.

II Office of Elementary and Secondary Education, Department of Education (Parts 200—299)

III Office of Special Education and Rehabilitative Services, Department of Education (Parts 300—399)

IV Office of Career, Technical and Adult Education, Department of Education (Parts 400—499)

V Office of Bilingual Education and Minority Languages Affairs, Department of Education (Parts 500—599) [Reserved]

VI Office of Postsecondary Education, Department of Education (Parts 600—699)

VII Office of Educational Research and Improvement, Department of Education (Parts 700—799) [Reserved]

SUBTITLE C—REGULATIONS RELATING TO EDUCATION

XI (Parts 1100—1199) [Reserved]

XII National Council on Disability (Parts 1200—1299)

Title 35 [Reserved]

Title 36—Parks, Forests, and Public Property

I National Park Service, Department of the Interior (Parts 1—199)

II Forest Service, Department of Agriculture (Parts 200—299)

III Corps of Engineers, Department of the Army (Parts 300—399)

IV American Battle Monuments Commission (Parts 400—499)

V Smithsonian Institution (Parts 500—599)

VI [Reserved]

VII Library of Congress (Parts 700—799)

VIII Advisory Council on Historic Preservation (Parts 800—899)

IX Pennsylvania Avenue Development Corporation (Parts 900—999)

X Presidio Trust (Parts 1000—1099)

XI Architectural and Transportation Barriers Compliance Board (Parts 1100—1199)

XII National Archives and Records Administration (Parts 1200—1299)

XV Oklahoma City National Memorial Trust (Parts 1500—1599)

XVI Morris K. Udall Scholarship and Excellence in National Environmental Policy Foundation (Parts 1600—1699)

Title 37—Patents, Trademarks, and Copyrights

I United States Patent and Trademark Office, Department of Commerce (Parts 1—199)

II U.S. Copyright Office, Library of Congress (Parts 200—299)

III Copyright Royalty Board, Library of Congress (Parts 300—399)

IV National Institute of Standards and Technology, Department of Commerce (Parts 400—599)

Title 38—Pensions, Bonuses, and Veterans' Relief

Title 39—Postal Service

Title 40—Protection of Environment

Title 41—Public Contracts and Property Management

Title 41—Public Contracts and Property Management—Continued

Chap.

SUBTITLE E—FEDERAL INFORMATION RESOURCES MANAGEMENT REGULATIONS SYSTEM [RESERVED]

SUBTITLE F—FEDERAL TRAVEL REGULATION SYSTEM

300 General (Parts 300–1—300–99)

301 Temporary Duty (TDY) Travel Allowances (Parts 301–1—301–99)

302 Relocation Allowances (Parts 302–1—302–99)

303 Payment of Expenses Connected with the Death of Certain Employees (Part 303–1—303–99)

304 Payment of Travel Expenses from a Non-Federal Source (Parts 304–1—304–99)

Title 42—Public Health

I Public Health Service, Department of Health and Human Services (Parts 1—199)

ii—III [Reserved]

IV Centers for Medicare & Medicaid Services, Department of Health and Human Services (Parts 400—699)

V Office of Inspector General-Health Care, Department of Health and Human Services (Parts 1000—1099)

Title 43—Public Lands: Interior

SUBTITLE A—OFFICE OF THE SECRETARY OF THE INTERIOR (PARTS 1—199)

SUBTITLE B—REGULATIONS RELATING TO PUBLIC LANDS

I Bureau of Reclamation, Department of the Interior (Parts 400—999)

II Bureau of Land Management, Department of the Interior (Parts 1000—9999)

III Utah Reclamation Mitigation and Conservation Commission (Parts 10000—10099)

Title 44—Emergency Management and Assistance

I Federal Emergency Management Agency, Department of Homeland Security (Parts 0—399)

IV Department of Commerce and Department of Transportation (Parts 400—499)

Title 45—Public Welfare

SUBTITLE A—DEPARTMENT OF HEALTH AND HUMAN SERVICES (PARTS 1—199)

SUBTITLE B—REGULATIONS RELATING TO PUBLIC WELFARE

II Office of Family Assistance (Assistance Programs), Administration for Children and Families, Department of Health and Human Services (Parts 200—299)

Title 45—Public Welfare—Continued

Title 46—Shipping

Title 47—Telecommunication

Title 47—Telecommunication—Continued

Chap.

IV National Telecommunications and Information Administration, Department of Commerce, and National Highway Traffic Safety Administration, Department of Transportation (Parts 400—499)

V The First Responder Network Authority (Parts 500—599)

Title 48—Federal Acquisition Regulations System

1 Federal Acquisition Regulation (Parts 1—99)

2 Defense Acquisition Regulations System, Department of Defense (Parts 200—299)

3 Health and Human Services (Parts 300—399)

4 Department of Agriculture (Parts 400—499)

5 General Services Administration (Parts 500—599)

6 Department of State (Parts 600—699)

7 Agency for International Development (Parts 700—799)

8 Department of Veterans Affairs (Parts 800—899)

9 Department of Energy (Parts 900—999)

10 Department of the Treasury (Parts 1000—1099)

12 Department of Transportation (Parts 1200—1299)

13 Department of Commerce (Parts 1300—1399)

14 Department of the Interior (Parts 1400—1499)

15 Environmental Protection Agency (Parts 1500—1599)

16 Office of Personnel Management, Federal Employees Health Benefits Acquisition Regulation (Parts 1600—1699)

17 Office of Personnel Management (Parts 1700—1799)

18 National Aeronautics and Space Administration (Parts 1800—1899)

19 Broadcasting Board of Governors (Parts 1900—1999)

20 Nuclear Regulatory Commission (Parts 2000—2099)

21 Office of Personnel Management, Federal Employees Group Life Insurance Federal Acquisition Regulation (Parts 2100—2199)

23 Social Security Administration (Parts 2300—2399)

24 Department of Housing and Urban Development (Parts 2400—2499)

25 National Science Foundation (Parts 2500—2599)

28 Department of Justice (Parts 2800—2899)

29 Department of Labor (Parts 2900—2999)

30 Department of Homeland Security, Homeland Security Acquisition Regulation (HSAR) (Parts 3000—3099)

34 Department of Education Acquisition Regulation (Parts 3400—3499)

51 Department of the Army Acquisition Regulations (Parts 5100—5199)

52 Department of the Navy Acquisition Regulations (Parts 5200—5299)

53 Department of the Air Force Federal Acquisition Regulation Supplement (Parts 5300—5399) [Reserved]

Chap.

54 Defense Logistics Agency, Department of Defense (Parts 5400—5499)

57 African Development Foundation (Parts 5700—5799)

61 Civilian Board of Contract Appeals, General Services Administration (Parts 6100—6199)

99 Cost Accounting Standards Board, Office of Federal Procurement Policy, Office of Management and Budget (Parts 9900—9999)

Title 49—Transportation

SUBTITLE A—OFFICE OF THE SECRETARY OF TRANSPORTATION (PARTS 1—99)

SUBTITLE B—OTHER REGULATIONS RELATING TO TRANSPORTATION

I Pipeline and Hazardous Materials Safety Administration, Department of Transportation (Parts 100—199)

II Federal Railroad Administration, Department of Transportation (Parts 200—299)

III Federal Motor Carrier Safety Administration, Department of Transportation (Parts 300—399)

IV Coast Guard, Department of Homeland Security (Parts 400—499)

V National Highway Traffic Safety Administration, Department of Transportation (Parts 500—599)

VI Federal Transit Administration, Department of Transportation (Parts 600—699)

VII National Railroad Passenger Corporation (AMTRAK) (Parts 700—799)

VIII National Transportation Safety Board (Parts 800—999)

X Surface Transportation Board (Parts 1000—1399)

XI Research and Innovative Technology Administration, Department of Transportation (Parts 1400—1499) [Reserved]

XII Transportation Security Administration, Department of Homeland Security (Parts 1500—1699)

Title 50—Wildlife and Fisheries

I United States Fish and Wildlife Service, Department of the Interior (Parts 1—199)

II National Marine Fisheries Service, National Oceanic and Atmospheric Administration, Department of Commerce (Parts 200—299)

III International Fishing and Related Activities (Parts 300—399)

IV Joint Regulations (United States Fish and Wildlife Service, Department of the Interior and National Marine Fisheries Service, National Oceanic and Atmospheric Administration, Department of Commerce); Endangered Species Committee Regulations (Parts 400—499)

V Marine Mammal Commission (Parts 500—599)

Title 50—Wildlife and Fisheries—Continued

Alphabetical List of Agencies Appearing in the CFR

(Revised as of January 1, 2018)

Agency	CFR Title, Subtitle or Chapter
Administrative Committee of the Federal Register	1, I
Administrative Conference of the United States	1, III
Advisory Council on Historic Preservation	36, VIII
Advocacy and Outreach, Office of	7, XXV
Afghanistan Reconstruction, Special Inspector General for	5, LXXXIII
African Development Foundation	22, XV
Federal Acquisition Regulation	48, 57
Agency for International Development	2, VII; 22, II
Federal Acquisition Regulation	48, 7
Agricultural Marketing Service	7, I, IX, X, XI
Agricultural Research Service	7, V
Agriculture Department	2, IV; 5, LXXIII
Advocacy and Outreach, Office of	7, XXV
Agricultural Marketing Service	7, I, IX, X, XI
Agricultural Research Service	7, V
Animal and Plant Health Inspection Service	7, III; 9, I
Chief Financial Officer, Office of	7, XXX
Commodity Credit Corporation	7, XIV
Economic Research Service	7, XXXVII
Energy Policy and New Uses, Office of	2, IX; 7, XXIX
Environmental Quality, Office of	7, XXXI
Farm Service Agency	7, VII, XVIII
Federal Acquisition Regulation	48, 4
Federal Crop Insurance Corporation	7, IV
Food and Nutrition Service	7, II
Food Safety and Inspection Service	9, III
Foreign Agricultural Service	7, XV
Forest Service	36, II
Grain Inspection, Packers and Stockyards Administration	7, VIII; 9, II
Information Resources Management, Office of	7, XXVII
Inspector General, Office of	7, XXVI
National Agricultural Library	7, XLI
National Agricultural Statistics Service	7, XXXVI
National Institute of Food and Agriculture	7, XXXIV
Natural Resources Conservation Service	7, VI
Operations, Office of	7, XXVIII
Procurement and Property Management, Office of	7, XXXII
Rural Business-Cooperative Service	7, XVIII, XLII
Rural Development Administration	7, XLII
Rural Housing Service	7, XVIII, XXXV
Rural Telephone Bank	7, XVI
Rural Utilities Service	7, XVII, XVIII, XLII
Secretary of Agriculture, Office of	7, Subtitle A
Transportation, Office of	7, XXXIII
World Agricultural Outlook Board	7, XXXVIII
Air Force Department	32, VII
Federal Acquisition Regulation Supplement	48, 53
Air Transportation Stabilization Board	14, VI
Alcohol and Tobacco Tax and Trade Bureau	27, I
Alcohol, Tobacco, Firearms, and Explosives, Bureau of	27, II
AMTRAK	49, VII
American Battle Monuments Commission	36, IV
American Indians, Office of the Special Trustee	25, VII

Agency	CFR Title, Subtitle or Chapter
Animal and Plant Health Inspection Service	7, III; 9, I
Appalachian Regional Commission	5, IX
Architectural and Transportation Barriers Compliance Board	36, XI
Arctic Research Commission	45, XXIII
Armed Forces Retirement Home	5, XI
Army Department	32, V
Engineers, Corps of	33, II; 36, III
Federal Acquisition Regulation	48, 51
Bilingual Education and Minority Languages Affairs, Office of	34, V
Blind or Severely Disabled, Committee for Purchase from People Who Are	41, 51
Broadcasting Board of Governors	22, V
Federal Acquisition Regulation	48, 19
Career, Technical and Adult Education, Office of	34, IV
Census Bureau	15, I
Centers for Medicare & Medicaid Services	42, IV
Central Intelligence Agency	32, XIX
Chemical Safety and Hazardous Investigation Board	40, VI
Chief Financial Officer, Office of	7, XXX
Child Support Enforcement, Office of	45, III
Children and Families, Administration for	45, II, III, IV, X, XIII
Civil Rights, Commission on	5, LXVIII; 45, VII
Civil Rights, Office for	34, I
Council of the Inspectors General on Integrity and Efficiency	5, XCVIII
Court Services and Offender Supervision Agency for the District of Columbia	5, LXX
Coast Guard	33, I; 46, I; 49, IV
Coast Guard (Great Lakes Pilotage)	46, III
Commerce Department	2, XIII; 44, IV; 50, VI
Census Bureau	15, I
Economic Analysis, Bureau of	15, VIII
Economic Development Administration	13, III
Emergency Management and Assistance	44, IV
Federal Acquisition Regulation	48, 13
Foreign-Trade Zones Board	15, IV
Industry and Security, Bureau of	15, VII
International Trade Administration	15, III; 19, III
National Institute of Standards and Technology	15, II; 37, IV
National Marine Fisheries Service	50, II, IV
National Oceanic and Atmospheric Administration	15, IX; 50, II, III, IV, VI
National Technical Information Service	15, XI
National Telecommunications and Information Administration	15, XXIII; 47, III, IV
National Weather Service	15, IX
Patent and Trademark Office, United States	37, I
Secretary of Commerce, Office of	15, Subtitle A
Commercial Space Transportation	14, III
Commodity Credit Corporation	7, XIV
Commodity Futures Trading Commission	5, XLI; 17, I
Community Planning and Development, Office of Assistant Secretary for	24, V, VI
Community Services, Office of	45, X
Comptroller of the Currency	12, I
Construction Industry Collective Bargaining Commission	29, IX
Consumer Financial Protection Bureau	5, LXXXIV; 12, X
Consumer Product Safety Commission	5, LXXI; 16, II
Copyright Royalty Board	37, III
Corporation for National and Community Service	2, XXII; 45, XII, XXV
Cost Accounting Standards Board	48, 99
Council on Environmental Quality	40, V
Court Services and Offender Supervision Agency for the District of Columbia	5, LXX; 28, VIII
Customs and Border Protection	19, I
Defense Contract Audit Agency	32, I
Defense Department	2, XI; 5, XXVI; 32, Subtitle A; 40, VII
Advanced Research Projects Agency	32, I

Agency	CFR Title, Subtitle or Chapter
Air Force Department	32, VII
Army Department	32, V; 33, II; 36, III; 48, 51
Defense Acquisition Regulations System	48, 2
Defense Intelligence Agency	32, I
Defense Logistics Agency	32, I, XII; 48, 54
Engineers, Corps of	33, II; 36, III
National Imagery and Mapping Agency	32, I
Navy Department	32, VI; 48, 52
Secretary of Defense, Office of	2, XI; 32, I
Defense Contract Audit Agency	32, I
Defense Intelligence Agency	32, I
Defense Logistics Agency	32, XII; 48, 54
Defense Nuclear Facilities Safety Board	10, XVII
Delaware River Basin Commission	18, III
Denali Commission	45, IX
District of Columbia, Court Services and Offender Supervision Agency for the	5, LXX; 28, VIII
Drug Enforcement Administration	21, II
East-West Foreign Trade Board	15, XIII
Economic Analysis, Bureau of	15, VIII
Economic Development Administration	13, III
Economic Research Service	7, XXXVII
Education, Department of	2, XXXIV; 5, LIII
Bilingual Education and Minority Languages Affairs, Office of	34, V
Career, Technical and Adult Education, Office of	34, IV
Civil Rights, Office for	34, I
Educational Research and Improvement, Office of	34, VII
Elementary and Secondary Education, Office of	34, II
Federal Acquisition Regulation	48, 34
Postsecondary Education, Office of	34, VI
Secretary of Education, Office of	34, Subtitle A
Special Education and Rehabilitative Services, Office of	34, III
Career, Technical, and Adult Education, Office of	34, IV
Educational Research and Improvement, Office of	34, VII
Election Assistance Commission	2, LVIII; 11, II
Elementary and Secondary Education, Office of	34, II
Emergency Oil and Gas Guaranteed Loan Board	13, V
Emergency Steel Guarantee Loan Board	13, IV
Employee Benefits Security Administration	29, XXV
Employees' Compensation Appeals Board	20, IV
Employees Loyalty Board	5, V
Employment and Training Administration	20, V
Employment Standards Administration	20, VI
Endangered Species Committee	50, IV
Energy, Department of	2, IX; 5, XXIII; 10, II, III, X
Federal Acquisition Regulation	48, 9
Federal Energy Regulatory Commission	5, XXIV; 18, I
Property Management Regulations	41, 109
Energy, Office of	7, XXIX
Engineers, Corps of	33, II; 36, III
Engraving and Printing, Bureau of	31, VI
Environmental Protection Agency	2, XV; 5, LIV; 40, I, IV, VII
Federal Acquisition Regulation	48, 15
Property Management Regulations	41, 115
Environmental Quality, Office of	7, XXXI
Equal Employment Opportunity Commission	5, LXII; 29, XIV
Equal Opportunity, Office of Assistant Secretary for	24, I
Executive Office of the President	3, I
Environmental Quality, Council on	40, V
Management and Budget, Office of	2, Subtitle A; 5, III, LXXVII; 14, VI; 48, 99
National Drug Control Policy, Office of	2, XXXVI; 21, III
National Security Council	32, XXI; 47, 2

Agency	CFR Title, Subtitle or Chapter
Presidential Documents	3
Science and Technology Policy, Office of	32, XXIV; 47, II
Trade Representative, Office of the United States	15, XX
Export-Import Bank of the United States	2, XXXV; 5, LII; 12, IV
Family Assistance, Office of	45, II
Farm Credit Administration	5, XXXI; 12, VI
Farm Credit System Insurance Corporation	5, XXX; 12, XIV
Farm Service Agency	7, VII, XVIII
Federal Acquisition Regulation	48, 1
Federal Aviation Administration	14, I
Commercial Space Transportation	14, III
Federal Claims Collection Standards	31, IX
Federal Communications Commission	5, XXIX; 47, I
Federal Contract Compliance Programs, Office of	41, 60
Federal Crop Insurance Corporation	7, IV
Federal Deposit Insurance Corporation	5, XXII; 12, III
Federal Election Commission	5, XXXVII; 11, I
Federal Emergency Management Agency	44, I
Federal Employees Group Life Insurance Federal Acquisition Regulation	48, 21
Federal Employees Health Benefits Acquisition Regulation	48, 16
Federal Energy Regulatory Commission	5, XXIV; 18, I
Federal Financial Institutions Examination Council	12, XI
Federal Financing Bank	12, VIII
Federal Highway Administration	23, I, II
Federal Home Loan Mortgage Corporation	1, IV
Federal Housing Enterprise Oversight Office	12, XVII
Federal Housing Finance Agency	5, LXXX; 12, XII
Federal Housing Finance Board	12, IX
Federal Labor Relations Authority	5, XIV, XLIX; 22, XIV
Federal Law Enforcement Training Center	31, VII
Federal Management Regulation	41, 102
Federal Maritime Commission	46, IV
Federal Mediation and Conciliation Service	29, XII
Federal Mine Safety and Health Review Commission	5, LXXIV; 29, XXVII
Federal Motor Carrier Safety Administration	49, III
Federal Prison Industries, Inc.	28, III
Federal Procurement Policy Office	48, 99
Federal Property Management Regulations	41, 101
Federal Railroad Administration	49, II
Federal Register, Administrative Committee of	1, I
Federal Register, Office of	1, II
Federal Reserve System	12, II
Board of Governors	5, LVIII
Federal Retirement Thrift Investment Board	5, VI, LXXVI
Federal Service Impasses Panel	5, XIV
Federal Trade Commission	5, XLVII; 16, I
Federal Transit Administration	49, VI
Federal Travel Regulation System	41, Subtitle F
Financial Crimes Enforcement Network	31, X
Financial Research Office	12, XVI
Financial Stability Oversight Council	12, XIII
Fine Arts, Commission of	45, XXI
Fiscal Service	31, II
Fish and Wildlife Service, United States	50, I, IV
Food and Drug Administration	21, I
Food and Nutrition Service	7, II
Food Safety and Inspection Service	9, III
Foreign Agricultural Service	7, XV
Foreign Assets Control, Office of	31, V
Foreign Claims Settlement Commission of the United States	45, V
Foreign Service Grievance Board	22, IX
Foreign Service Impasse Disputes Panel	22, XIV
Foreign Service Labor Relations Board	22, XIV
Foreign-Trade Zones Board	15, IV
Forest Service	36, II
General Services Administration	5, LVII; 41, 105

Agency	CFR Title, Subtitle or Chapter
Contract Appeals, Board of	48, 61
Federal Acquisition Regulation	48, 5
Federal Management Regulation	41, 102
Federal Property Management Regulations	41, 101
Federal Travel Regulation System	41, Subtitle F
General	41, 300
Payment From a Non-Federal Source for Travel Expenses	41, 304
Payment of Expenses Connected With the Death of Certain Employees	41, 303
Relocation Allowances	41, 302
Temporary Duty (TDY) Travel Allowances	41, 301
Geological Survey	30, IV
Government Accountability Office	4, I
Government Ethics, Office of	5, XVI
Government National Mortgage Association	24, III
Grain Inspection, Packers and Stockyards Administration	7, VIII; 9, II
Gulf Coast Ecosystem Restoration Council	2, LIX; 40, VIII
Harry S. Truman Scholarship Foundation	45, XVIII
Health and Human Services, Department of	2, III; 5, XLV; 45, Subtitle A
Centers for Medicare & Medicaid Services	42, IV
Child Support Enforcement, Office of	45, III
Children and Families, Administration for	45, II, III, IV, X, XIII
Community Services, Office of	45, X
Family Assistance, Office of	45, II
Federal Acquisition Regulation	48, 3
Food and Drug Administration	21, I
Indian Health Service	25, V
Inspector General (Health Care), Office of	42, V
Public Health Service	42, I
Refugee Resettlement, Office of	45, IV
Homeland Security, Department of	2, XXX; 5, XXXVI; 6, I; 8, I
Coast Guard	33, I; 46, I; 49, IV
Coast Guard (Great Lakes Pilotage)	46, III
Customs and Border Protection	19, I
Federal Emergency Management Agency	44, I
Human Resources Management and Labor Relations Systems	5, XCVII
Immigration and Customs Enforcement Bureau	19, IV
Transportation Security Administration	49, XII
HOPE for Homeowners Program, Board of Directors of	24, XXIV
Housing and Urban Development, Department of	2, XXIV; 5, LXV; 24, Subtitle B
Community Planning and Development, Office of Assistant Secretary for	24, V, VI
Equal Opportunity, Office of Assistant Secretary for	24, I
Federal Acquisition Regulation	48, 24
Federal Housing Enterprise Oversight, Office of	12, XVII
Government National Mortgage Association	24, III
Housing—Federal Housing Commissioner, Office of Assistant Secretary for	24, II, VIII, X, XX
Housing, Office of, and Multifamily Housing Assistance Restructuring, Office of	24, IV
Inspector General, Office of	24, XII
Public and Indian Housing, Office of Assistant Secretary for	24, IX
Secretary, Office of	24, Subtitle A, VII
Housing—Federal Housing Commissioner, Office of Assistant Secretary for	24, II, VIII, X, XX
Housing, Office of, and Multifamily Housing Assistance Restructuring, Office of	24, IV
Immigration and Customs Enforcement Bureau	19, IV
Immigration Review, Executive Office for	8, V
Independent Counsel, Office of	28, VII
Independent Counsel, Offices of	28, VI
Indian Affairs, Bureau of	25, I, V
Indian Affairs, Office of the Assistant Secretary	25, VI

Agency	CFR Title, Subtitle or Chapter
Federal Procurement Regulations System	41, 50
Labor-Management Standards, Office of	29, II, IV
Mine Safety and Health Administration	30, I
Occupational Safety and Health Administration	29, XVII
Public Contracts	41, 50
Secretary of Labor, Office of	29, Subtitle A
Veterans' Employment and Training Service, Office of the Assistant Secretary for	41, 61; 20, IX
Wage and Hour Division	29, V
Workers' Compensation Programs, Office of	20, I, VII
Labor-Management Standards, Office of	29, II, IV
Land Management, Bureau of	43, II
Legal Services Corporation	45, XVI
Library of Congress	36, VII
Copyright Royalty Board	37, III
U.S. Copyright Office	37, II
Local Television Loan Guarantee Board	7, XX
Management and Budget, Office of	5, III, LXXVII; 14, VI; 48, 99
Marine Mammal Commission	50, V
Maritime Administration	46, II
Merit Systems Protection Board	5, II, LXIV
Micronesian Status Negotiations, Office for	32, XXVII
Military Compensation and Retirement Modernization Commission	5, XCIX
Millennium Challenge Corporation	22, XIII
Mine Safety and Health Administration	30, I
Minority Business Development Agency	15, XIV
Miscellaneous Agencies	1, IV
Monetary Offices	31, I
Morris K. Udall Scholarship and Excellence in National Environmental Policy Foundation	36, XVI
Museum and Library Services, Institute of	2, XXXI
National Aeronautics and Space Administration	2, XVIII; 5, LIX; 14, V
Federal Acquisition Regulation	48, 18
National Agricultural Library	7, XLI
National Agricultural Statistics Service	7, XXXVI
National and Community Service, Corporation for	2, XXII; 45, XII, XXV
National Archives and Records Administration	2, XXVI; 5, LXVI; 36, XII
Information Security Oversight Office	32, XX
National Capital Planning Commission	1, IV, VI
National Commission for Employment Policy	1, IV
National Commission on Libraries and Information Science	45, XVII
National Council on Disability	5, C; 34, XII
National Counterintelligence Center	32, XVIII
National Credit Union Administration	5, LXXXVI; 12, VII
National Crime Prevention and Privacy Compact Council	28, IX
National Drug Control Policy, Office of	2, XXXVI; 21, III
National Endowment for the Arts	2, XXXII
National Endowment for the Humanities	2, XXXIII
National Foundation on the Arts and the Humanities	45, XI
National Geospatial-Intelligence Agency	32, I
National Highway Traffic Safety Administration	23, II, III; 47, VI; 49, V
National Imagery and Mapping Agency	32, I
National Indian Gaming Commission	25, III
National Institute of Food and Agriculture	7, XXXIV
National Institute of Standards and Technology	15, II; 37, IV
National Intelligence, Office of Director of	5, IV; 32, XVII
National Labor Relations Board	5, LXI; 29, I
National Marine Fisheries Service	50, II, IV
National Mediation Board	29, X
National Oceanic and Atmospheric Administration	15, IX; 50, II, III, IV, VI
National Park Service	36, I
National Railroad Adjustment Board	29, III
National Railroad Passenger Corporation (AMTRAK)	49, VII
National Science Foundation	2, XXV; 5, XLIII; 45, VI

Agency	CFR Title, Subtitle or Chapter
Securities and Exchange Commission	5, XXXIV; 17, II
Selective Service System	32, XVI
Small Business Administration	2, XXVII; 13, I
Smithsonian Institution	36, V
Social Security Administration	2, XXIII; 20, III; 48, 23
Soldiers' and Airmen's Home, United States	5, XI
Special Counsel, Office of	5, VIII
Special Education and Rehabilitative Services, Office of	34, III
State Department	2, VI; 22, I; 28, XI
Federal Acquisition Regulation	48, 6
Surface Mining Reclamation and Enforcement, Office of	30, VII
Surface Transportation Board	49, X
Susquehanna River Basin Commission	18, VIII
Tennessee Valley Authority	5, LXIX; 18, XIII
Thrift Supervision Office, Department of the Treasury	12, V
Trade Representative, United States, Office of	15, XX
Transportation, Department of	2, XII; 5, L
Commercial Space Transportation	14, III
Emergency Management and Assistance	44, IV
Federal Acquisition Regulation	48, 12
Federal Aviation Administration	14, I
Federal Highway Administration	23, I, II
Federal Motor Carrier Safety Administration	49, III
Federal Railroad Administration	49, II
Federal Transit Administration	49, VI
Maritime Administration	46, II
National Highway Traffic Safety Administration	23, II, III; 47, IV; 49, V
Pipeline and Hazardous Materials Safety Administration	49, I
Saint Lawrence Seaway Development Corporation	33, IV
Secretary of Transportation, Office of	14, II; 49, Subtitle A
Transportation Statistics Bureau	49, XI
Transportation, Office of	7, XXXIII
Transportation Security Administration	49, XII
Transportation Statistics Bureau	49, XI
Travel Allowances, Temporary Duty (TDY)	41, 301
Treasury Department	2, X;5, XXI; 12, XV; 17, IV; 31, IX
Alcohol and Tobacco Tax and Trade Bureau	27, I
Community Development Financial Institutions Fund	12, XVIII
Comptroller of the Currency	12, I
Customs and Border Protection	19, I
Engraving and Printing, Bureau of	31, VI
Federal Acquisition Regulation	48, 10
Federal Claims Collection Standards	31, IX
Federal Law Enforcement Training Center	31, VII
Financial Crimes Enforcement Network	31, X
Fiscal Service	31, II
Foreign Assets Control, Office of	31, V
Internal Revenue Service	26, I
Investment Security, Office of	31, VIII
Monetary Offices	31, I
Secret Service	31, IV
Secretary of the Treasury, Office of	31, Subtitle A
Thrift Supervision, Office of	12, V
Truman, Harry S. Scholarship Foundation	45, XVIII
United States and Canada, International Joint Commission	22, IV
United States and Mexico, International Boundary and Water Commission, United States Section	22, XI
U.S. Copyright Office	37, II
Utah Reclamation Mitigation and Conservation Commission	43, III
Veterans Affairs Department	2, VIII; 38, I
Federal Acquisition Regulation	48, 8
Veterans' Employment and Training Service, Office of the Assistant Secretary for	41, 61; 20, IX
Vice President of the United States, Office of	32, XXVIII
Wage and Hour Division	29, V
Water Resources Council	18, VI

List of CFR Sections Affected

All changes in this volume of the Code of Federal Regulations (CFR) that were made by documents published in the FEDERAL REGISTER since January 1, 2013 are enumerated in the following list. Entries indicate the nature of the changes effected. Page numbers refer to FEDERAL REGISTER pages. The user should consult the entries for chapters, parts and subparts as well as sections for revisions.

For changes to this volume of the CFR prior to this listing, consult the annual edition of the monthly List of CFR Sections Affected (LSA). The LSA is available at *www.fdsys.gov*. For changes to this volume of the CFR prior to 2001, see the "List of CFR Sections Affected, 1949–1963, 1964–1972, 1973–1985, and 1986–2000" published in 11 separate volumes. The "List of CFR Sections Affected 1986–2000" is available at *www.fdsys.gov*.

2013

10 CFR

78 FR Page

Chapter I

1 Nomenclature change 34247
2.311 (b) revised..............................34247
2.346 (e) revised..............................34247
20 Policy statement..........................663
20.2201 (c) revised..........................17006
30 Policy statement..........................663
Policy statement; interim 33691
30.6 (a) introductory text revised..17006
(b)(1)(iv) revised...........................32338
30.13 Revised 17006
30.33 (a)(4) revised..........................17006
32.1 (b) revised 17006
33.1 Revised....................................17006
34.1 Revised....................................17006
35.1 Revised....................................17006
36.1 (a) revised 17007
37 Added..17007
37.77 (a) correctly amended...........31821
39.1 (a) revised 17020
40 Policy statement..........................663
Policy statement; interim 33691
40.4 Amended...................................32338
40.5 (b)(1)(iv) revised......................32338
40.8 (b) revised 32338
40.13 (c) introductory text, (2)(i), (iii), (7) and footnote 2 revised; (c)(5)(i) and (d) removed; (c)(10) added; (c)(5)(ii) through (v) redesignated as new (c)(5)(i) through (iv) 32338
40.22 Revised 32339

10 CFR—Continued

78 FR Page

Chapter I—Continued

40.32 (f) revised 32340
40.36 (e)(2) introductory text revised..34247
(e)(2) introductory text correctly amended 75450
40.52 Added......................................32340
40.53 Added......................................32340
40.54 Added......................................32340
40.55 Added......................................32340
40.82 (b) revised..............................32341
50 Policy statement..........................663
50.47 (d) introductory text amended..34248
50.54 Introductory text amended 34248
50.55 (e)(4)(i), (iii) and (6) introductory text revised 34248
50 Appendices E and G amended 34248
Appendix G correctly amended 75450

2014

10 CFR

79 FR Page

Chapter I

Chapter I Regulatory review plan 9981
1.3 (a) revised.................................75737
1.5 (a)(3) revised; (a)(4) removed 75737
1.18 Removed.................................75737

10 CFR—Continued

79 FR Page

Chapter I—Continued

1.19 (b) and (c) removed; (d) redesignated as new (b)....................75737
1.32 (b) amended....................75737
1.38 Added....................75737
1.41 Removed....................75737
1.42 Revised....................75737
2 Nomenclature changes....................75739
2.101 (a)(1) amended....................75739
2.103 (a) amended....................75739
2.106 (d) amended....................75739
2.340 (e)(2) and (k) amended....................75739
2.810 (e) revised....................66601
2.1023 (a) introductory text revised....................66601
2.1210 (a) introductory text revised....................66601
2.1406 (c) revised....................66602
15.20 (d) and (e) amended....................66602
15.33 (b)(1) amended....................66602
19.11 (e)(2) revised....................66602
20 Appendix D amended....................66602
26.135 (c) revised....................66602
26.159 (i) revised....................66602
26.717 (g) revised....................66603
30 Nomenclature change....................75739
30.4 Amended; eff. 1-28-15....................58671
30.7 (e)(3) revised....................66603
30.32 (k) removed; eff. 1-28-15....................58671
30.34 (l) removed; eff. 1-28-15....................58671
31 Nomenclature change....................75739
32 Nomenclature change....................75739
34 Nomenclature change....................75739
35 Nomenclature change....................75739
37 Nomenclature change....................75739
37.7 Amended....................75740
37.29 (a)(10) revised; eff. 1-28-15....................58671
37.43 (d)(1) revised; (d)(9) removed; eff. 1-28-15....................58671
37.77 (f) revised; eff. 1-28-15....................58671
40 Nomenclature changes....................75740
40.7 (e)(3) revised....................66603
50 Authority citation revised....................62334, 65798
Technical correction....................65541
50.2 Amended....................62335
50.7 (e)(2) revised....................66603
50.54 Introductory text revised; (jj) added....................65798
50.55 Introductory text revised; (i) added....................65798
50.55a Revised....................65798
(b)(2)(viii)(B), (C) and (ix)(J) amended....................66603
(a)(1)(ii)(B)(*5*), (*6*) and (*7*) added; (e)(1) amended....................73462
50.82 (a)(4)(i) revised....................66603

2015

10 CFR

80 FR Page

Chapter I

1 Authority citation revised....................54232
1.3 (c) amended....................45842, 74977
1.32 (b) amended....................74978
1.35 Heading and introductory text revised; (f) and (g) amended; (h) through (l) added....................74978
1.38 Removed....................74978
1.42 (b)(3) amended....................74978
2 Authority citation revised....................54232
Nomenclature changes....................74978
2.202 (c)(2) revised....................63419
2.802 Revised....................60526
2.803 Revised....................60526
2.811 (e) revised....................60527
4 Authority citation revised....................54232
4.5 Amended....................74978
7 Authority citation revised....................54232
7.2 Amended....................74978
7.22 (b) amended....................74978
9 Authority citation revised....................54233
Nomenclature change....................74978
10 Authority citation revised....................54233
11 Authority citation revised....................54233
11.15 (a)(1) amended....................74978
12 Authority citation revised....................54233
13 Authority citation revised....................54233
14 Authority citation revised....................54233
15 Authority citation revised....................54233
15.3 Amended....................74978
16 Authority citation revised....................54233
19 Authority citation revised....................54233
19.17 (a) amended....................74978
20 Authority citation revised....................54233
Authority citation correctly revised....................58574
Nomenclature change....................74979
21 Authority citation revised....................54233
21.5 Amended....................74979
25 Authority citation revised....................54233
25.9 Amended....................74979
26 Authority citation revised....................54233
26.11 Amended....................74979
30 Technical correction....................3865
Authority citation revised....................54233
30.4 Regulation at 79 FR 58671 eff. date confirmed....................3865
30.6 (a)(3) amended....................74979
30.32 Regulation at 79 FR 58671 eff. date confirmed....................3865
30.34 Regulation at 79 FR 58671 eff. date confirmed....................3865
31 Authority citation revised....................54233
32 Actions on petitions....................45413
Authority citation revised....................54234

10 CFR—Continued

80 FR Page

Chapter I—Continued

Authority citation correctly revised 58574
32.1 (c)(1) amended 74979
33 Authority citation revised 54234
34 Authority citation revised 54234
35 Authority citation revised 54234
36 Authority citation revised 54234
37 Technical correction 3865
Authority citation revised 54234
Nomenclature change 74979
37.23 (b)(2) amended 45843
37.29 Regulation at 79 FR 58671 eff. date confirmed 3865
37.43 Regulation at 79 FR 58671 eff. date confirmed 3865
37.77 Regulation at 79 FR 58671 eff. date confirmed 3865
(a)(1) amended 74979
39 Authority citation revised 54234
40 Authority citation revised 54234
Nomenclature change 74979
40.5 (a)(3) amended 74979
40.61 (a)(2) revised 45843
50 Authority citation revised 54234
50.4 (a) and (e) amended 74979
50.34 (f)(3)(v)(A)(*1*) and (B)(*1*) amended 74980
50.49 Footnote 4 revised 45843
50.54 Introductory text amended 45843
50.55a (a)(2)(i), (ii), (iii) and (h)(2) revised; (a)(2)(iv) added 45843
50 Appendix E amended 74980

2016

10 CFR

81 FR Page

Chapter I

Policy statement 47689
2 Authority citation revised 43021
2.205 (j) revised; interim 43021
2.305 (g)(1) amended 86909
2.327 (d) revised 47006
2.390 (a)(5) revised; eff. 1-30-17 96346
9.17 (a)(5) revised; (c) redesignated as (d); new (c) added; eff. 1-30-17 96346
9.19 (b)(1) amended; eff. 1 30-17 96346
9.21 (c) introductory text and (5) revised; eff. 1-30-17 96346
9.25 (c) revised; (f) amended; eff. 1-30-17 96346
9.27 (a) and (b)(5) amended; (b)(6) and (7) added; eff. 1-30-17 96346
9.29 (a) amended; eff. 1-30-17 96346
9.30 Added; eff. 1-30-17 96346

10 CFR—Continued

81 FR Page

Chapter I—Continued

9.39 (f) added; eff. 1-30-17 96346
9.43 (d) amended; eff. 1-30-17 96347
9.45 Revised; eff. 1-30-17 96347
9.201 Revised 41185
10 Nomenclature change 86909
13 Authority citation revised 43021
13.3 (a)(1)(iv) and (b)(1)(ii) revised; interim 43021
20 Policy statement 49863, 52974, 95410
26 Policy statement 49863
Nomenclature change 86909
30 Nomenclature change 86909
32 Policy statement 49863
37 Regulation at 78 FR 17007 request for comment 13263
40 Policy statement 49863
Nomenclature change 86909
50 Actions on petitions 29761
Policy statement 49863, 88615, 95410
50.23 Amended 86909
50.34 (a)(3)(i) amended 86909
50 Appendices C and J amended 86909

2017

10 CFR

82 FR Page

Chapter I

2.205 (j) revised 8135
2.1200 Amended 52825
9 Amended 52825
13.3 (a)(1)(iv) and (b)(1)(ii) revised 8135
20 Policy statement 46666
40.35 (f) amended 52825
50.43 (e) introductory text revised 52825

10 CFR—Continued

82 FR Page

Chapter I—Continued

50.55a (a) introductory text, (1)(i) introductory text, (E)(*12*), (*13*), (ii) introductory text, (C)(*48*), (*49*), (iii)(A), (B), (C), (1)(iv) introductory text, (b) introductory text, (1) introductory text, (ii), (iv), (vii), (2) introductory text, (vi), (viii) introductory text, (ix) introductory text, (D), (x), (xii), (xxi)(A), (xxiii), (3) introductory text, (i), (ii), (iv) introductory text, (4) introductory text, (5), (6), (f) heading, introductory text, (2), (3)(iii)(A), (B), (iv)(A), (B), (4) introductory text, (i), (ii), (g) heading and introductory text, (2), (3) heading, (i), (ii), (v), (4)(i), (ii), (6)(ii)(D)(*1*) through (*4*), and (F)(*1*) through (*10*) revised; (a)(1)(i)(E)(*14*) through (*17*), (ii)(C)(*50*) through (*53*), (iii)(D) through (G), (iv)(B), (C), (v), (b)(1)(viii), (ix), (2)(viii)(H), (I),(xviii)(D), (xxx), (xxxi) through (xxxvii), (3)(iii), (3)(vii) through (xi), (g)(6)(ii)(F)(*11*), (*12*), (*13*) added; (g)(3) introductory text, (6)(ii)(D)(*5*) and (*6*) removed....... 32977

10 CFR—Continued

82 FR Page

Chapter I—Continued

(b)(2)(ix)(B) revised 52825

www.ingramcontent.com/pod-product-compliance
Lightning Source LLC
LaVergne TN
LVHW052201200926
848481LV00001B/5